D1219495

Thru the Bible
with J. Vernon McGee

By J. Vernon McGee

Thru the Bible
with J. Vernon McGee

By J. Vernon McGee

VOLUME V
1 Corinthians—Revelation

Thomas Nelson Publishers
Nashville

Copyright © 1983 by J. Vernon McGee.

Compiled from previous publications by J. Vernon McGee.

All rights reserved. Written permission must be secured from the publisher to use or reproduce any part of this book, except for brief quotations in critical reviews or articles.

Published in Nashville, Tennessee, by Thomas Nelson, Inc., Publishers and distributed in Canada by Lawson Falle, Ltd., Cambridge, Ontario.

From *Systematic Theology* by Lewis Sperry Chafer. Copyright 1947. Dallas Seminary. All rights reserved. Used by permission.

From *Word Studies in the New Testament* by Marvin R. Vincent. Copyright 1957. William B. Eerdmans Publishing Company. Used by permission.

From *Word Studies in the Greek New Testament* (Jude) by Kenneth S. Wuest. William B. Eerdmans Publishing Company. Used by permission.

From *International Standard Bible Encyclopedia* edited by James Orr. William B. Eerdmans Publishing Company. Used by permission.

From *The Amplified New Testament*. The Lockman Foundation. Copyright © 1954, 1958. Used by permission.

From a poem by Frances Ridley Havergal in *Opened Treasures*. Loizeaux Brothers, Inc., Neptune, New Jersey. Used by permission.

From *Studies in the Epistle to the Hebrews* by E. Schuyler English. Loizeaux Brothers, Inc., Neptune, New Jersey. Used by permission.

From *Epistles of John* by H. A. Ironside. Loizeaux Brothers, Inc., Neptune, New Jersey. Used by permission.

From *The Revelation of Jesus Christ* by John Walvoord. Copyright © 1966. Moody Press, Moody Bible Institute of Chicago. Used by permission.

From *The Scofield Reference Bible*. Copyright 1909, 1917; renewed 1937, 1945 by Oxford University Press, Inc. Reprinted by permission.

From *The Salt Cellars* (2 vols.) by Charles Haddon Spurgeon. Pilgrim Publications, Pasadena, Texas. Used by permission.

From "Turn Your Eyes Upon Jesus" by Helen Lemmel. Copyright © 1922. Renewal 1950 by Helen Lemmel. Assigned to Singspiration, Inc. Used by Permission.

From *Be Confident* by Warren W. Wiersbe. Victor Books. Used by permission.

Unless otherwise indicated, all Scripture quotations are from the Thru the Bible Radio Special Edition of The King James Version, copyright © 1976 by Thomas Nelson Publishers.

Library of Congress Cataloging in Publication Data

McGee, J. Vernon (John Vernon), 1904-
    Thru the Bible with J. Vernon McGee.

    Based on the Thru the Bible radio program.
    Includes bibliographies.
    Contents: v. 1. Genesis—Deuteronomy—
v. 5 1 Corinthians—Revelation
    1. Bible—Commentaries.   I.   Thru the Bible
(Radio program)   II.   Title.
BS491.2.M37   220.7'7   81-3930
ISBN 0-8407-4973-2 (Nelson) v. 1
ISBN 0-8407-4978-3 (Royal) v. 1
ISBN 0-8407-4977-5 (Nelson)v. 5
ISBN 0-8407-4982-1 (Royal) v. 5

Printed in the United States of America

15 16 17 18 19 20 - 97

TABLE OF CONTENTS

PREFACE

The radio broadcasts of the Thru the Bible Radio five-year program were transcribed, edited, and published first in single-volume paperbacks to accommodate the radio audience. From the beginning there was a demand that they be published in a more permanent form and in fewer volumes. This new hardback edition is an attempt to meet that need.

There has been a minimal amount of further editing for this publication. Therefore, these messages are not the word-for-word recording of the taped messages which went out over the air. The changes were necessary to accommodate a reading audience rather than a listening audience.

These are popular messages, prepared originally for a radio audience. They should not be considered a commentary on the entire Bible in any sense of that term. These messages are devoid of any attempt to present a theological or technical commentary on the Bible. Behind these messages is a great deal of research and study in order to interpret the Bible from a popular rather than from a scholarly (and too-often boring) viewpoint.

We have definitely and deliberately attempted "to put the cookies on the bottom shelf so that the kiddies could get them."

The fact that these messages have been translated into many languages for radio broadcasting and have been received with enthusiasm reveals the need for a simple teaching of the whole Bible for the masses of the world.

I am indebted to many people and to many sources for bringing this volume into existence. I should express my especial thanks to my secretary, Gertrude Cutler, who supervised the editorial work; to Dr. Elliott R. Cole, my associate, who handled all the detailed work with the publishers; and finally, to my wife Ruth for tenaciously encouraging me from the beginning to put my notes and messages into printed form.

Solomon wrote, ". . . of making many books there is no end; and much study is a weariness of the flesh" (Eccl. 12:12). On a sea of books that flood the marketplace, we launch this series of THRU THE BIBLE with the hope that it might draw many to the one Book, *The Bible*.

J. VERNON MCGEE

The First Epistle
to the
CORINTHIANS
INTRODUCTION

Paul addressed this epistle to the church which was in the city of Corinth. He wrote it from Ephesus around A.D. 55–57 (more likely 57). Carnal Corinth was the sin center of the Roman Empire in Paul's day. It was labeled "Vanity Fair." Its location was about forty miles west of Athens on a narrow isthmus between Peloponnesus and the mainland. It was the great commercial center of the Roman Empire with three harbors, of which two were important: Lechaeum, about one and one half miles to the west, and Cenchrea, about eight and one half miles to the east. Since the time of Paul, a canal has been put through the isthmus, and Corinth is no longer an important city.

Even the ruins of Corinth were lost to history for many years. A fishing village had been built over them. In 1928 an earthquake uncovered them, and now much of the city has been excavated.

During that time in history when Greece was independent, Corinth was the head of the Achaean League. Later, in 196 B.C., Rome declared it a free city. In 146 B.C. Corinth rebelled and was totally destroyed by Mummius, the Roman general. Its art treasures were taken to Rome and for a century it lay desolate. One hundred years later, in 46 B.C., Julius Caesar rebuilt the city in great elegance, restoring it to its former prominence and returning its former splendor.

In Paul's day there were about four hundred thousand inhabitants in Corinth. It was located on this important isthmus, as we previously mentioned, and the commerce of the world flowed through the two harbors connected with the city of Corinth. The population consisted of Greeks, Jews, Italians, and a mixed multitude. Sailors, merchants, adventurers, and refugees from all corners of the Roman Empire filled its streets. A perpetual "Vanity Fair" was held here. The vices of the East and of the West met and clasped hands in the work of human degradation.

Religion itself was put to ignoble uses. A magnificent temple was built for the Greek goddess Aphrodite, or Venus as we know her by the Roman name. In it were a thousand priestesses who ministered to a base worship.

Those thousand so-called priestesses were actually nothing in the world but prostitutes. Sex was a religion there. I believe that Corinth could teach this generation about sex. However, I think this generation already knows enough about that subject. We are overwhelmed with it *ad nauseam* today.

Not only was their religion debased, but the Greek philosophy was in its decay also. The city was given over to licentiousness and pleasure. The Isthmian games were conducted here. The people went on in endless discussions. It was into this kind of setting that Paul came, and later he said, "For I determined not to know any thing among you, save Jesus Christ, and him crucified" (1 Cor. 2:2). This was a people given over to pleasure, debauchery, and drunkenness. In fact, they coined a word in the Roman Empire which was to "corinthianize." Believe me, when you would "corinthianize," it meant that you went to the very limit in sin.

Against this corrupt background Paul preached the gospel in Corinth. He founded a church there and later wrote two epistles to them. Paul came to Corinth on his second missionary journey, and it was the terminus of his third missionary journey. Acts 18:1–18 gives us the account of eighteen months spent in Corinth. It was in Corinth that he met Aquila and Priscilla. They had been driven out of Rome by an edict of Emperor Claudius. Suetonius writes that this edict was issued because of tumults raised by the Jews who were persecuting their Christian brethren.

When Paul first came to Corinth, he preached in the synagogue. As usual, a riot was the result. Paul usually had a riot, revolution, and revival wherever he went. Corinth was no exception.

On Paul's third journey he spent a long period of time in Ephesus. It was in Ephesus that he did some of his outstanding work as a missionary. Probably that area was more thoroughly evangelized than any other. However, this caused the Corinthians to become disturbed. They were baby Christians, and they were urging Paul to come to them. Apparently Paul wrote them a letter to correct some of the errors that had come into that church. They, in turn, wrote to Paul asking questions that they wanted answered about political issues, religion, domestic problems, heathenism, and morality. Paul answered them and responded to more reports which were brought to him. We do not have that first letter which Paul wrote to them. The letter that followed the reports brought to him is the letter we know today as 1 Corinthians. That is the epistle we are about to study. Later on Paul wrote the letter we now call 2 Corinthians.

The keynote of this epistle is the supremacy of Christ, the Lordship of Jesus. That is so important for us to note, because that is the solution to the problems. You will find here that *He* is the solution to correct moral, social, and ecclesiastical disorders.

In this epistle we will also find the true doctrine of the Resurrection set forth. That makes this epistle tremendously significant.

A broad outline of this book divides it into three major divisions:

1. Salutation and thanksgiving, 1:1–9

2. Carnalities, 1:10–11:34
   (Conditions in the Corinthian church)
3. Spiritualities, 12–16
   (Spiritual gifts)

The spiritualities are far more important than the carnalities. I think we need to realize that over nineteen hundred years ago the church in Corinth was beset with problems. They had lost sight of the main objective, and they had gotten away from the person of Christ. As a consequence, they were overwhelmed with these problems.

Our contemporary church is likewise beset with problems. It is almost shocking to discover that the problems of the church today are the same as they were in Corinth over nineteen hundred years ago. I believe that the real problem today is that we have lost sight of the centrality of Christ crucified. We have lost sight of the Lordship of Jesus Christ. That was the problem then, and it is still the problem now. Our study of this epistle should be a relevant and pertinent study for us.

OUTLINE

CHAPTER 1

THEME: Centrality of Christ crucified; correction of divisions

SALUTATION AND THANKSGIVING

Paul, called to be an apostle of Jesus Christ through the will of God, and Sosthenes our brother [1 Cor. 1:1].

Will you notice in your Bible that the little verb "to be" is in italics, which means it is not in the original. It should read, "Paul, called an apostle." This declares what kind of an apostle he is. He is a called apostle. God called him; the Lord Jesus Christ waylaid him on the Damascus road. Then the Spirit of God taught him yonder in the desert of Arabia. He is a *called* apostle.

He is an apostle of Jesus Christ "through the will of God." It is the will of God that made him an apostle. This is so important.

It is wonderful today to be able to say, "I am where I am and I am doing what I am doing because of the will of God." Is that your situation? If you can say that, then I do not need to add that you are a very happy, joyful Christian. You are not only a happy, joyful Christian, but you are one who is well-oriented into life. You have no frustrations. Of course you may have disturbing experiences occasionally, but down deep underneath there is that tremendous satisfaction. Paul had that when he could say that he was an apostle of Jesus Christ through the will of God.

"Sosthenes our brother"—apparently Sosthenes had brought the message from the church at Corinth, and now he is going to carry this epistle back to them. He is the one who is joining Paul in these greetings.

Unto the church of God which is at Corinth, to them that are sanctified in Christ Jesus, called to be saints, with all that in every place call upon the name of Jesus Christ our Lord, both theirs and ours [1 Cor. 1:2].

Notice it is "unto the church of God which is at Corinth." It is called the church of God because He is the One who is the Architect of the church. The letter is directed to the "sanctified in Christ Jesus."

The church is *at* Corinth, but it is *in* Christ Jesus. The address of the church is not important, but the person of Christ is all-important. What does it mean to be a Christian? It means to be in Christ! Whether you are at Corinth or at Los Angeles, at Ephesus or at New York City is incidental. The important question is: Are you in Christ Jesus?

Paul calls them "sanctified in Christ Jesus." The term *sanctification* is used in several different ways, as we have already seen in Romans. Here it is *positional* sanctification, which is the position we have in Christ. When sanctification is joined to God the Father or God the Son, the Lord Jesus Christ, then it is generally positional. When sanctification is connected with the Holy Spirit, then that is practical sanctification. We will learn in verse 30 that Christ has been made unto us sanctification—along with wisdom and righteousness and redemption. *He* is our sanctification.

You see, friend, you are not going to heaven until you are perfect—I am not either. And I am not perfect, not even near it. The fact of the matter is that if you knew me like I know myself, you wouldn't listen to me. But wait a minute! Don't tune me out because, if I knew you like you know yourself, I wouldn't speak to you. So let's just stay connected here, if you don't mind.

Sanctification is a position we have in Christ. If you have trusted Him, He has been made over to you your sanctification. You are as saved right now as you will be a million years from now, because you are saved in Christ. You cannot add anything to that.

There is also a *practical* sanctification, which is something that varies. These Corinthians don't sound like sanctified saints. The work of the Holy Spirit was not very much in evidence in their lives. But they were *positionally* sanctified in Christ Jesus.

They were "called to be saints"—again, note that "to be" is in italics, which means it is not in the original. Just as Paul was a *called* apostle, they were *called* saints. We are also called saints. We do not become saints by what we do; we become saints because of our position in Christ. The word *saint* actually means "set aside to God." Every Christian should be set aside to God. For example, the pans and vessels that were used in the tabernacle and later in the temple were called holy vessels. Holy? Yes, because they were for the use of God. On what basis is a child of God a saint or holy? On the basis that he is for the use of God. This is the position that we have. I repeat again, one is not a saint on the basis of what one does. All of mankind is divided between the "saints" and the "ain'ts." If you "ain't" in Christ, then you are an "ain't." If you are in Christ, then you are a "saint."

The Corinthians are called saints together "with all that in every place call upon the name of Jesus Christ our Lord, both theirs and ours." Possibly it would be more correct to say, "with all that in every place, both theirs and ours, who call upon the name of Jesus Christ our Lord." This also indicates that the teaching of this epistle is addressed to the church at large, which is composed of all who call upon the Lord Jesus, whether it be in Corinth or elsewhere.

Now Paul uses his usual introduction: "grace and peace."

Grace be unto you, and peace, from God our Father, and from the Lord Jesus Christ [1 Cor. 1:3].

Grace and *peace* are always in that sequence. Grace (*charis*) was the word of greeting in the Greek world. Peace is the Hebrew *shalom*, a form of greeting in the religious world. Paul combined these two words and lifted them to the highest level. You and I are saved by the grace of God; it is love in action. When we have been saved by the grace of God, then we can have the peace of God in our hearts. Have you received Christ as your Savior? Are your sins on Christ? If they are, you will have peace in your heart because He bore your sins. "Therefore being justified by faith, we have peace with God through our Lord Jesus Christ" (Rom. 5:1). *Grace* and *peace* are two great words.

I thank my God always on your behalf, for the grace of God which is given you by Jesus Christ [1 Cor. 1:4].

"By Jesus Christ" would be better translated "*in* Jesus Christ," because it is in Christ that we have all of these blessings. We are blessed with all spiritual blessings in heavenly places in Christ (see Eph. 1:3). This is the place of blessing.

"Jesus Christ" should be Christ Jesus— *Christ* is His title, while *Jesus* is His human name. *Christ* is literally *anointed*, which is the official appellation of the long-promised Savior. Is it important to say Christ Jesus instead of Jesus Christ? It was to Paul. Paul tells us that he never knew Him after the flesh. That is, he didn't know the Jesus who walked this earth in the days of His flesh. He may have seen Him; I think he was present at the Crucifixion. But his first personal contact was with the resurrected Christ, and to Paul He was always the Lord of glory. In most of Paul's

epistles it should read Christ Jesus rather than Jesus Christ.

That in every thing ye are enriched by him, in all utterance, and in all knowledge [1 Cor. 1:5].

This is what Paul is talking about in Colossians 3:16 when he says: "Let the word of Christ dwell in you richly in all wisdom; teaching and admonishing one another in psalms and hymns and spiritual songs, singing with grace in your hearts to the Lord." Since I can't sing it, I can say it; that is, I can talk about the Word of God. In some churches the Psalms are sung. I think the whole Bible could be put to music. But I couldn't sing it. The important thing is to have the Word of Christ in our hearts. That does not necessarily mean to memorize it. It means to obey it. If Christ is in your heart, you are obeying Him, and you are thinking upon Him. He occupies your mind and your heart. Some of the meanest little brats that I have ever met have memorized over a hundred verses of Scripture. That doesn't mean no one should memorize Scripture just because some mean brats have memorized it. It does mean that simply memorizing Scripture is not what is meant by hiding it in your heart. You hide it in your heart, my friend, when you obey Him, think about Him, are occupied with Him. "In every thing ye are enriched in [not *by*] him." When He becomes the Lord in your life, it will solve many of your problems. That is what Paul is going to talk about in this epistle.

Even as the testimony of Christ was confirmed in you:

So that ye come behind in no gift; waiting for the coming of our Lord Jesus Christ [1 Cor. 1:6–7].

Here he intimates one of the problems that this church was having. They were carnal. They were occupied with only one gift. Paul says at the very beginning that he doesn't want them to come behind in any gift. There are many gifts. Paul wants all these gifts to be manifested in the church.

"Waiting for the coming of our Lord Jesus Christ" means that they are to be occupied with Him.

Who shall also confirm you unto the end, that ye may be blameless in the day of our Lord Jesus Christ [1 Cor. 1:8].

He says "blameless"; he does not say they will be faultless. There will always be someone who will find fault with you. But you are not to be worthy of blame. "That ye may be blameless in the day of our Lord Jesus Christ." And the "day of our Lord Jesus Christ" is not only referring to the present day, but to the day He will come and take His church out of the world. Paul will talk about that in this epistle also.

Now we come to the last verse of Paul's introduction, the salutation and thanksgiving. This verse could easily be passed over with the feeling that you hadn't missed very much. Yet I feel that verse 9 is probably the key to the epistle. It emphasizes that the Lord Jesus Christ is the solution to the problems that they had in the church and also to the personal problems that were present among the believers in Corinth. It is startling to note the similarities between the problems in the Corinthian church and the problems today. The solution is the same now as it was then.

God is faithful, by whom ye were called unto the fellowship of his Son Jesus Christ our Lord [1 Cor. 1:9].

Have you noticed that the Lord Jesus Christ is mentioned in this section in practically every verse? Actually, it isn't practically every verse; it is *every* verse. This is the ninth reference to Him in nine verses. It is obvious that Paul is putting an emphasis upon the person of the Lord Jesus Christ.

There is an extended name given to our Lord here—"called unto the fellowship of his Son Jesus Christ our Lord." This gives four points of identification for Him. So there is no way of misunderstanding.

He makes two tremendous statements: God is faithful, and we are called unto the fellowship of His Son.

"God is faithful." Men are not always faithful. Even believers are not always faithful. But God is faithful.

"By whom ye were called" is the high calling of God in Christ Jesus.

We are called "unto the fellowship of his Son Jesus Christ our Lord." The word that is important here in connection with the Lord Jesus Christ is *fellowship*. The word is the Greek *koinonia*, and it is used by Paul again and again. Actually, the word can have several different meanings. It can mean fellowship as we understand it today. It can be used to mean a contribution. In Romans 15:26 he says they made a certain *koinonia* for the poor saints which were at Jerusalem, and there it means a contribution. In 1 Corinthians 10:16 the word *koinonia* is used in connection with Commu-

nion. He is speaking of the Lord's Supper and writes: "The cup of blessing which we bless, is it not the [*koinonia*] communion of the blood of Christ? The bread which we break, is it not the [*koinonia*] communion of the body of Christ?"

Koinonia can also mean a partnership, and I believe that is the way it is used here in this ninth verse. "God is faithful, by whom ye were called unto the [partnership] fellowship of his Son Jesus Christ our Lord." Now this is without doubt one of the greatest privileges that is given to us. If you are in Christ, if you have come to Him and accepted Him as your Savior, then you are in partnership with Christ. He is willing to be our partner. Therefore this means an intimate relationship to Christ.

There are different kinds of partnerships. There can be a partnership in business. I know two men who are in partnership. These fellows were friends in the military service, and when they came out of the service years ago, they formed a partnership in business. One of them was converted to Christ; the other was not. It has been an unhappy partnership ever since then. They have a big business with a lot of investments and the partnership cannot be broken. It is a partnership, but it is not a happy one.

Then there is marriage with a partnership in a love relationship. This should be a very close, intimate relationship. There is a passage in the Old Testament that makes me smile because I know God had man and wife in mind when He wrote it. He said among other things that they were not to hitch an ox and an ass together for plowing. They were not to plow together. Well, in marriage I have seen many an ox and an ass hitched up together! That ought not to be, because marriage is a partnership.

What does it mean, then, to be in partnership with the Lord Jesus? For one thing, it means that in business you own things together with Him. Everything that I own belongs to Jesus Christ. It belongs to Him as much as it does to me. Therefore, He is interested in what I own. Now I must confess that there was a time when I owned a few things that I don't think He cared about. There was a time when I very selfishly thought only of myself in connection with what I owned. But now, although I don't own too much—when He is in partnership with me, He is not in what you would call big business—what I have is His. I have a nice Chevrolet car because a wonderful dealer helped me get it. When I drove out with it, it was mine, but I told the Lord Jesus that it was His, too. He has taken many a ride in it with me, by the way. Whatever I have is His also. I thank Him for my house, and I thank Him for taking care of it because it is His, too, you see. Whatever I have is His.

The marriage partnership means different things. It means having mutual interests. I'm in that kind of partnership with the Lord Jesus, too. That means that Christ is interested in me and I am interested in Him. That carries it to a pretty high plane, you see. Also, we have a mutual devotion. His resources are mine, and mine are His. He doesn't get very much, but He owns me. I have presented my body to Him. Now that answers quite a few questions for me about where I can go and what I can do. For example, I used to smoke quite a bit. Now I have metastatic cancer in the lungs, and it would be pretty foolish for me to smoke now. However, long ago when I made the discovery, not just that my body is the temple of the Holy Spirit, but also that Christ belongs to me and I belong to Christ, I wanted to give Him the best body that I could. That is when I gave up smoking. That decided the question for me. Do you see that our decisions are made on a higher plane than simply "Dare I do this?" or "Ought I do that?" We belong to Jesus Christ and Jesus Christ belongs to us.

Also in the love partnership there is a mutual service. God accommodates Himself to our weakness. I need His gentleness, and I accept His power. A verse of Scripture which deals with this is a verse that I believe has been mistranslated. This was called to my attention by G. Campbell Morgan. The verse is Isaiah 63:9: "In all their affliction he was afflicted, and the angel of his presence saved them: in his love and in his pity he redeemed them; and he bare them, and carried them all the days of old." It sounds as if in our weakness He becomes weak. The better translation puts it in the negative: "In all affliction he was *not* afflicted." That is a lot more meaningful to me. It means that when I stumble and fall, He does not stumble and fall. He accommodates Himself to my stumbling, my blindness, my ignorance, my weakness. Although He accommodates Himself to that, He does not become weak at all. I heard a preacher make the statement that if you get into trouble ignorantly without realizing it, or you are caught by circumstances, He will help you out of it. But if you go into sin deliberately and foolishly, He will let you alone rather than help you work it out. I am here to say that this has *not* been my

experience. I have made many blunders, and I have stumbled and I have fallen. Many times I have done it deliberately. Yet my Lord never let me down. He was always there. He accommodated Himself to my weakness. How wonderful that is, friend! The partnership of Jesus Christ is the solution to the problems of life.

Verse 9 concludes Paul's salutation. Actually, all the rest of the epistle is a big parenthesis until we come to 1 Corinthians 15:58: "Therefore, my beloved brethren, be ye stedfast, unmoveable, always abounding in the work of the Lord, forasmuch as ye know that your labour is not in vain in the Lord." "Therefore" gathers up all this marvelous epistle and goes way back here to verse 9. I can depend on the faithfulness of God "by whom ye were called unto the fellowship of his Son Jesus Christ our Lord."

It has taken me a long time to learn this. In fact, I have had to retire to learn this. I am just going ahead with Him as my partner. I face all of today's problems with Him as my partner. I can count on Him. I can look to Him. He is part and parcel of all of it. This is the solution to the problems and the frustrations of life, my beloved.

This concludes the introduction, which is a salutation and thanksgiving. The body of the epistle concerns conditions in the Corinthian church, and there were real problems, as we shall see.

DIVISIONS AND PARTY SPIRIT

Verse 10 begins a new section in Paul's first epistle to the Corinthian believers. He is addressing himself now to the primary problem in the Corinthian church. It is surprising to see that their problems have a very familiar ring. I don't know of a church today that does not have problems, and many of them are the same as those that the Corinthian believers faced.

CENTRALITY OF CHRIST CRUCIFIED CORRECTS DIVISIONS

Now I beseech you, brethren, by the name of our Lord Jesus Christ, that ye all speak the same thing, and that there be no divisions among you; but that ye be perfectly joined together in the same mind and in the same judgment [1 Cor. 1:10].

Notice that the Lord Jesus Christ is again mentioned in this verse. This epistle emphasizes the lordship of Christ. We hear a great deal about His lordship, but we see very little of it today. For this reason the church and individual Christians have serious problems. It is not enough to talk about the lordship of Christ. Is He *your* Lord? Have *you* made Him your Lord and your Master?

"That ye all speak the same thing" doesn't mean that everyone must say the identical words. It means believers shouldn't be clawing one another to death, fighting with each other, hating each other.

The word for "divisions" is *schisma*. It means there should be no open break, no fracturing of the church, which is done by fighting, by gossip, criticism, hatred, or bitterness. Believe me, friend, I see that in many contemporary churches. These things cannot be in your life if Jesus Christ is your partner.

Let "there be no divisions among you; but that ye be perfectly joined together in the same mind and in the same judgment." What is "the same mind"? Well, it is the mind of Christ (see Phil. 2:5–8).

For it hath been declared unto me of you, my brethren, by them which are of the house of Chloe, that there are contentions among you [1 Cor. 1:11].

The word for "contentions" here is *eris*. Now Eris was the goddess of strife and wrangling. There was strife, quarreling, schisms, and wranglings in the church at Corinth. Paul got his information firsthand—he named his source—he said he got his information from Chloe. My friend, if you are going to make a charge, back it up with your name like Chloe did. When I first became pastor in downtown Los Angeles, a man came to me and said, "I want to tell you about a certain situation." He told me about a certain man and, believe me, it wasn't very nice. He wanted me to do something about it. He said, "You ought to bring this up before the board, and if they can't handle it, then it should be brought before the church." I answered, "Fine, that is the way it should be done. What night can you come?" "Oh!" he said, "I don't intend to come. You're the pastor, you are the one to handle it." I answered, "You are right. I am the one to handle it. I am the pastor now. However, you will need to be present to make the charge." "Oh," he said, "I won't do that." So I told him, "If you are not willing to sign your name to the charge, we will forget it." And we forgot it, because he refused to back up the charge with his name. One must admire Chloe there in Corinth. Chloe told it as it was, brought it out into the open, and said, "There is trouble in

our church, bad trouble, and it needs to be dealt with."

My friend, when there is sin in the church, it is like a cancer. It needs to be dealt with. When I had cancer, I went to my doctor for help. Imagine him saying, "Now we don't want to get excited; we don't want to get disturbed; we don't want to become emotional; we don't want to cause any trouble. We want you to have a nice, peaceful mind; so I will sprinkle a little talcum powder on this place and everything will be all right." Well, friend, I would have smelled good, but I would have died of the cancer. You've got to deal with a cancer, and you've got to deal with trouble in the church. Woe to the man who exposes it, but if that is not done, the church is going to suffer. Of course it will!

The trouble with the church in Corinth was that they had a bunch of baby Christians. Babies generally do a lot of howling, you know. When I was a pastor in Pasadena, we had a nursery room for babies, and we called it The Bawl Room. I have learned that in some churches the entire church is a bawl room, because of the bawling baby Christians.

Now this I say, that every one of you saith, I am of Paul; and I of Apollos; and I of Cephas; and I of Christ [1 Cor. 1:12].

Divisions were being caused by believers following different leaders of the church. They formed cliques around certain men. In one group were the proud pupils of Paul; in another the adoring admirers of Apollos, and there were some who liked Simon Peter, or Cephas, and they formed the chummy cult of Cephas.

We know quite a lot about Paul. He was intellectual, he was brilliant, and he was courageous—but apparently not attractive physically. Simon Peter was fiery. He had been weak at first, but he became a rugged preacher of the gospel. He had a great heart and was very emotional. Apollos was one of the great preachers of the apostolic church. He was not an apostle and has not been given much recognition, but he was a great preacher. I think he was the Billy Graham of that day. All three of these men had strong personalities, but they did not cause the divisions. They all contended together for the faith. They maintained the unity of the Spirit, and they all exalted Jesus Christ. It was the members of the church in Corinth who were guilty of making the divisions.

One little group said, "Oh, we love brother

Paul because he's so spiritual." Another group said, "We like Simon Peter because he pounds the pulpit and is so evangelistic." Another said, "we love this man Apollos. He soars to the heights, and he reaches the multitudes." They were not taking into account the fact that all three of them were God's men. Paul is going to write to them about this. He is going to show them that the centrality of Christ is the answer to the factions and fractures in the church. My friend, there will be no solution until men and women are willing to come to the person of Christ.

In addition to the three groups, a fourth group was saying, "We are of Christ." They were not actually putting Christ first, but they were the super-duper spiritual group. It is my private opinion that this was the worst group of all. They made a little cult of Christ. They had their little clique in the church and they excluded other believers. They were the spiritual snobs.

Do you realize that you and I are living in a day when the church has been destroyed from the inside? The problems are not on the outside today. Innumerable churches have long since been destroyed by liberals in the pulpit. Go around on Sunday night or at midweek service and see what the attendance is. Many churches are destroyed by the man in the pulpit. If the man in the pulpit is sound in the faith, you'll find troublemakers in the pew. That is where strife is stirred up. This does more damage to the cause of Christ than alcohol or atheism or worldliness. In many churches they are doing what they did in the mountains of Kentucky and Tennessee; they're feudin' and fussin' like the Martins and the Coys.

Oh, the Martins and the Coys,
    They was reckless mountain boys,
And they took up fam'ly feudin' when
    they'd meet.
    They would shoot each other quicker
    Than it took your eye to flicker.
They could knock a squirrel's eye at
    ninety feet.

Oh, the Martins and the Coys,
    They was reckless mountain boys,
But old Abel Martin was the next to go.
    Though he saw the Coys a-comin'
    He had hardly started runnin'
'Fore a volley shook the hills and laid him
    low.

After that they started out to fight in
    earnest

And they scarred the mountains up
    with shot and shell.
There was uncles, brothers, cousins,
They say they bumped them off by doz-
    ens,
Just how many bit the dust is hard to tell.

Oh, the Martins and the Coys,
    They was reckless mountain boys,
At the art of killin' they became quite
    deft.
    They all knowed they shouldn't do it,
    But before they hardly knew it,
On each side they only had one person
    left.

"The Martins and the Coys"
—Ted Weems and Al Cameron

This may sound corny and very silly, but unfortunately feudin' and fussin' go on inside churches. This is what they were doing in the Corinthian church. Now Paul tackles this problem. He asks,

Is Christ divided? was Paul crucified for you? or were ye baptized in the name of Paul? [1 Cor. 1:13].

The answer is obvious. Of course, Christ is not divided. Anything that breaks up the unity in Christ has something wrong with it—regardless of what it is. The crucifixion of Christ is the bedrock of Christian unity, and it is absurd to contemplate establishing a unity on any other basis.

"Were ye baptized in the name of Paul?" In this instance I do not believe Paul is referring to water baptism, which was always in the name of the Father, Son, and Holy Spirit. Rather, he is referring to the baptism of the Holy Spirit. His question is: "Were ye baptized in the name of Paul?" They would have to say, "Of course not! We weren't baptized in your name. The baptism that placed us in the body of Christ was the baptism of the Holy Spirit. No man could do that for us." You see, Paul is attempting to direct their thinking away from man and back to Christ. They needed to be occupied with the person of Christ. Very candidly, I have always been able to fellowship with any man, regardless of his label, if he can meet with me around the person of Christ.

I thank God that I baptized none of you, but Crispus and Gaius;

Lest any should say that I had baptized in mine own name [1 Cor. 1:14–15].

Here he is talking about water baptism. He is saying that he didn't specialize even in that because of the danger of folk thinking that he was baptizing in his own name. You see, he is focusing on the centrality of Christ. There are folk even in our day who think that water baptism saves them or that it actually has some mystical power that cannot be gotten otherwise.

And I baptized also the household of Stephanas: besides, I know not whether I baptized any other [1 Cor. 1:16].

Paul attached so little importance to baptism that he couldn't really remember whether he had baptized anyone else or not.

For Christ sent me not to baptize, but to preach the gospel: not with wisdom of words, lest the cross of Christ should be made of none effect [1 Cor. 1:17].

It is important for us to see today that there are a great many people who are dividing and separating over many secondary issues. This causes schisms and strife in the church. The church in Corinth was fractured by that kind of party spirit. Three men, Apollos, Paul, and Cephas, had brought to Corinth a *message* that had a unifying quality and power. The gospel they preached emphasized fusion and not faction. However, because these people were baby Christians, they began to put the emphasis on individuals. Now Paul is drawing their attention away from their factions and their party spirit and turning them to the centrality of Christ.

In the city of Corinth, as well as in many other cities of that day, the emphasis was on philosophy. We shall see this as we move into the chapter.

For the preaching of the cross is to them that perish foolishness; but unto us which are saved it is the power of God [1 Cor. 1:18].

The cross divides men. The cross divides the saved from the unsaved, but it doesn't divide the saved people. It should unite them, you see. A Dutch artist painted a picture called "The Last Judgment." It depicts the throne of God, and away from that throne the lost are falling into space. And as they fall, they *cling together*. This is an accurate picture of the one world that men are working for today. The lost want to come together in one great unity, and they are going to accomplish a great union in the last days. But cutting across the grain of the ecumenical environment and the contem-

porary thought is the gospel of Christ. The Lord Jesus called Himself a divider of men, and the dividing line is His cross. The preaching of the Cross is to them that perish foolishness; but unto the saved person it is the power of God.

Paul makes it very clear that his method was not in the wisdom of the words of the world, not in the method of dialectics of divisions or differences or opinions or theories, but he just presented the cross of Christ. That brought about a unity of those who were saved. To those who perish, the cross of Christ is foolishness; but to the saved man it becomes the power of God. The cross of Christ divides the world, but it does not divide the church.

For it is written, I will destroy the wisdom of the wise, and will bring to nothing the understanding of the prudent.

Where is the wise? where is the scribe? where is the disputer of this world? hath not God made foolish the wisdom of this world?

For after that in the wisdom of God the world by wisdom knew not God, it pleased God by the foolishness of preaching to save them that believe [1 Cor. 1:19–21].

Notice that it is not foolish preaching but the foolishness of preaching.

For the Jews require a sign, and the Greeks seek after wisdom:

But we preach Christ crucified, unto the Jews a stumblingblock, and unto the Greeks foolishness [1 Cor. 1:22–23].

Notice that Paul divides mankind into two great ethnic groups: the Jews and the Greeks (meaning Gentiles). He recognizes this twofold division. The Jew represented religion. He had a God-given religion. The Jews felt that they had the truth, and they did—as far as the Old Testament was concerned. The problem was that it had become just a ritual to them. They had departed from the Scriptures and followed tradition, which was their interpretation of the Scriptures. The power was gone. Therefore, when Christ appeared, they asked for a sign. Rather than turning to their Scriptures, they asked for a sign. "Then certain of the scribes and of the Pharisees answered, saying, Master, we would see a sign from thee. But he answered and said unto them, An evil and adulterous generation seeketh after a sign; and there shall no sign be given to it, but the sign of the prophet Jonas: For as Jonas was three days and three nights in the whale's belly; so shall the Son of man be three days and three nights in the heart of the earth" (Matt. 12:38–40). The Lord Jesus gave to them the sign of resurrection.

The Greeks were the Gentiles. They represented philosophy. They were the lovers of wisdom. They said they were seeking the truth; they were searching and scanning the universe for truth. They were the rationalists. While the Jews ended up in ritual, the Gentiles ended up as rationalists and had to conform to a pattern of reason.

About four hundred years before Christ came, the Greek nation constructed on the horizon of history a brilliance of mind and artistic accomplishment of such dimensions that it still dazzles and startles mankind. It continued for about three centuries. By the time of Christ, the glory of Greece was gone. It just fizzled out. There were men like Pericles, Anaxagoras, Thales, Socrates, Plato, and Aristotle who left certain schools such as the Epicurean school, the Stoic school of philosophy, and the Peripatetic school. Then they all disappeared.

There followed two thousand years of philosophical sterility and stagnation in the world. Then there appeared men like Bacon, Hobbes, and Descartes, and there was a rebirth of great thinkers for a brief period of brilliance. This was again followed by decadence, and we are still in it today—even though some of our boys think they are very smart.

"What is truth?" asked the fatalistic Pilate. Bacon asked the same question, and philosophy is still asking that question. Philosophy still has no answers to the problems of life. "Where is the wise? where is the scribe? where is the disputer of this world? hath not God made foolish the wisdom of this world?"

Someone has defined philosophy as a blind man in a dark room looking for a black cat that isn't there. The Greeks sought after wisdom. Today man is still searching for some theory or formula, and he thinks that it is through science that he will get the answers to some of the questions of life. Do you think that man today has the answers to the questions of life? I was interested in a statement which I found in a periodical: "The truth is that modern man is overimpressed by his own achievements. To put a rocket into an orbit that is more than a hundred miles from the surface of the earth takes a great deal of joint thought and effort, but we tend to overstate the case. Though men who ride a few miles above the earth are called

astronauts, this is clearly a misnomer. Men will not be astronauts until they ride among the stars, and it is important to remember that most of the stars are thousands of light-years away. The Russians are even more unrestrained in their overstatements, calling their men cosmonauts. Someone needs to say, 'Little man, don't take yourself quite so seriously.'"

Man today thinks he has a few answers. Where are the wise today? It is a good question to ask. You see, God has made foolish the wisdom of this world.

"For after that in the wisdom of God the world by wisdom knew not God, it pleased God by the foolishness of preaching to save them that believe." This is a tremendous statement.

"But we preach Christ crucified, unto the Jews a stumbling block, and unto the Greeks foolishness." The Jews found the Cross to be a stumblingblock, a *skandalon*. They wanted a sign. They wanted someone to show the way. They wanted a pointer, a highway marker. They would have accepted a deliverer on a white charger who was putting down the power of Rome. But a crucified Christ was an insult to them. That meant *defeat*—not victory. They didn't want to accept that at all. "As it is written, Behold, I lay in Sion a stumblingstone and rock of offence: and whosoever believeth on him shall not be ashamed" (Rom. 9:33). And Peter wrote this: "Unto you therefore which believe he is precious: but unto them which be disobedient, the stone which the builders disallowed, the same is made the head of the corner, And a stone of stumbling, and a rock of offence, even to them which stumble at the word, being disobedient: whereunto also they were appointed" (1 Pet. 2:7–8). A crucified Christ was a stumblingblock to the Jew.

To the Greeks (or Gentiles) the cross was foolishness, an absurdity. They considered it utterly preposterous and ridiculous and contrary to any rational, worldly system. In Rome there has been found a caricature of Christianity, a figure on the cross with an ass' head. Also in our day our Savior is being ridiculed.

Now Paul bears down on philosophy. While he was in the city of Corinth, he was preaching Christ. "And when they opposed themselves, and blasphemed, he shook his raiment, and said unto them, Your blood be upon your own heads; I am clean: from henceforth I will go unto the Gentiles" (Acts 18:6). Can philosophy lift man out of the cesspool of this life? It never has. Notice that men will be saved, not by foolish preaching, but by the preaching of "foolishness," that is, by the preaching of the Cross. It is not the method but the message that the natural man considers foolish. Men still reject it. Today the wisdom of the world is to have an antipoverty program or some other kind of program. Or the wisdom of the world is to save man from his problems by education. May I say that what man needs today is the *gospel*. The wisdom of the world has never considered that.

Now Paul introduces another class of mankind. "Unto them which are called, both Jews and Greeks"—these are the called, the elect. They have not only heard the invitation, they have responded to it. And they have found in the cross of Christ the wisdom and power of God which has transformed their lives, made them new men. The Lord Jesus molded eleven men, then called Saul of Tarsus, and sent them out. They took the gospel to Corinth with its sin, to Ephesus with its religion. For over nineteen hundred years the gospel has been going around the world, and it is the only help and the only hope of mankind.

But unto them which are called, both Jews and Greeks, Christ the power of God, and the wisdom of God.

Because the foolishness of God is wiser than men; and the weakness of God is stronger than men.

For ye see your calling, brethren, how that not many wise men after the flesh, not many mighty, not many noble, are called [1 Cor. 1:24–26].

Some folk like to give emphasis to the prominent folk who have accepted Christ—the entertainment greats, the leaders in industry, and the prominent in government. But God majors in average people. He is calling simple folk like you and me.

But God hath chosen the foolish things of the world to confound the wise; and God hath chosen the weak things of the world to confound the things which are mighty [1 Cor. 1:27].

This does not mean these men are foolish. It means they seem foolish to the world. They are not weak; they are weak in the estimation of the world. This is God's method. He even chooses the base.

And base things of the world, and things which are despised, hath God chosen, yea, and things which are not, to bring to nought things that are:

That no flesh should glory in his presence [1 Cor. 1:28–29].

We do not have a thing to glory about.

But of him are ye in Christ Jesus, who of God is made unto us wisdom, and righteousness, and sanctification, and redemption [1 Cor. 1:30].

Oh, my friend, He is everything that we need. I wish I could get that over to you. He has been made to us wisdom. He is our righteousness. He is our sanctification and our redemption. Whatever it is that you need today, you will find it in Him.

That, according as it is written, He that glorieth, let him glory in the Lord [1 Cor. 1:31].

Our glory should be in the Lord. We should glory in the Lord Jesus Christ today. Let me ask you, what do you glory in? What are you boasting of today? Are you boasting of your degrees? Of your wisdom? Of your wealth? Of your power? Are you boasting today of your position and your character? My friend, you don't have a thing of which you can boast—and I know I haven't. But we can boast of Christ. *He* is everything. He is everything that we need.

CHAPTER 2

THEME: The clarity of the Holy Spirit corrects human wisdom

And I, brethren, when I came to you, came not with excellency of speech or of wisdom, declaring unto you the testimony of God [1 Cor. 2:1].

First, I would like to call your attention to the fact that Paul did not use the philosophic method of preaching. He was not a textual or a topical preacher; he was an expositor of the Word of God. I personally believe that is God's method. It was the method our Lord used, by the way. Neither did Paul use flowery nor oratorical language.

Secondly, Paul did not come in the wisdom of the world, declaring the testimony or the *mystery* of God. What does he mean by a mystery? We will be confronted with this word again in the epistle. A mystery simply means "that which had not been revealed before." The mystery of God which Paul preached was that Jesus Christ had been crucified. That had not been preached before but now had been revealed. In the Old Testament the crucifixion of Christ was revealed in type and in prophecy only. The actual event was something new, something not previously revealed.

For I determined not to know any thing among you, save Jesus Christ, and him crucified [1 Cor. 2:2].

Paul did not enter into philosophical discussions that gender strife. He simply stayed right with the preaching of the cross of Christ. He preached a crucified Savior, One who had died for the sins of the world. That is the type of ministry which is so desperately needed today.

And I was with you in weakness, and in fear, and in much trembling [1 Cor. 2:3].

Paul opens his heart and lets us see his inmost thoughts. He makes it very clear that while he was among them he was greatly disturbed. He was "in weakness, and in fear, and in much trembling." Little wonder that he could say that God had chosen the weak things of this world. Paul had no exalted conception of himself; yet he was a great intellect and a great man in many ways. Obviously, he never thought of himself as great.

And my speech and my preaching was not with enticing words of man's wis-dom, but in demonstration of the Spirit and of power [1 Cor. 2:4].

In our day we have a great many words of man's wisdom. There is a great deal of preaching, but very little of it is done "in demonstration of the Spirit and of power." The feeling is that we only need the right method or the right topic or the right style. Oh, how we need the power of the Holy Spirit in our preaching!

That your faith should not stand in the wisdom of men, but in the power of God [1 Cor. 2:5].

In other words, if human wisdom is used to win a man, then his faith stands on human wisdom. If a man is brought to faith through the power of God, then his faith rests upon that. This is the reason I sincerely question a great deal of this apologetic preaching today—such as trying to prove that the Bible is God's Word or that the first chapter of Genesis is scientific or that the Flood really happened. Don't misunderstand me, there is a place for that, and I thank God for men who have specialized in those areas. But we need to understand that salvation does not rest upon whether we can actually prove the inspiration of Scripture, although I certainly believe we can prove it. The question is: What does your faith rest upon? Apologetic preaching will call our attention to the Word of God, but our faith must rest on the power of God.

Howbeit we speak wisdom among them that are perfect: yet not the wisdom of this world, nor of the princes of this world, that come to nought [1 Cor. 2:6].

Paul says, "I do not use the worldly methods at all."

But we speak the wisdom of God in a mystery, even the hidden wisdom, which God ordained before the world unto our glory [1 Cor. 2:7].

Again here is this word *mystery*. Let's be clear on this word. It has no reference to what we commonly think of as an enigma or with a "who-done-it"—that is, a story dealing with the solution of a mysterious crime. It is not something of a secretive quality or character. The word *mystery*, as used in the Scriptures, refers to something which was not known in the past but is now revealed. This word occurs about twenty-seven times in the New Testament. Our Lord used it when He said "Because it is given unto you to know the mysteries of the kingdom of heaven. . ." (Matt. 13:11). The parables that follow in Matthew 13 are the "mystery parables." Why are they called the mystery parables? It is because in them Jesus explains the direction that the kingdom is going to take in the interval between the rejection of the King and the time when He comes to set up His kingdom. That segment of history was actually not revealed in the Old Testament at all. God had not yet revealed that to men. When Jesus spoke the mystery parables in Matthew 13, He was revealing this for the first time. What had been previously hidden, Jesus revealed.

Now here in the Epistle to the Corinthians, Paul says, "God's wisdom in a mystery." This is quite interesting because it is a word that came out of Greek schools of philosophy, of the occult, and of science. Paul fastens on this Greek word, and he says, "We speak God's wisdom in a mystery," but he gives it an entirely new meaning. *Mystery* comes from the word meaning "mouth," and it means to shut the mouth—it is something secretive. However, Paul never used it in that way. Rather, that which had been silent has now become vocal. That which had not been known and *could* not be known by human investigation now is known. "Mystery" in the New Testament always means something undiscoverable by the activity of the human intellect but is revealed so that human intellect can apprehend it.

"We speak the wisdom of God"—Paul says, "We have a philosophy." It is not of this age, not of this world, but it is *God's* wisdom, and it pertains to the cross of Christ. "We speak the wisdom of God in a mystery, even the hidden wisdom, which God ordained before the world unto our glory."

Which none of the princes of this world knew: for had they known it, they would not have crucified the Lord of glory [1 Cor. 2:8].

You see, they did not know.

But as it is written, Eye hath not seen, nor ear heard, neither have entered into the heart of man, the things which God hath prepared for them that love him [1 Cor. 2:9].

This verse surely has been misunderstood. It has gone to a funeral too many times. This is a verse that should never go to a funeral. It has been wrongly used so many times to imply: Here lies dear Mr. So-and-So. His remains are here before us. In this life he didn't understand too well, but now he is in glory and he understands all things. This is not what Paul intended this verse to convey! Paul is saying that right here and now there are certain things that the eye has not seen. We get a great deal of information through the eye-gate. We learn more through our eye-gate than we do in any other way. Another way we gain human wisdom is through the ear-gate. We certainly learn by hearing. Paul says there are certain things we simply cannot learn by hearing. Then he says, "neither have entered into the heart of man," that is, by cogitation, thinking, or reasoning. There are certain things which cannot be attained by human means. You cannot discover God by searching for Him. The things which God has prepared for them who love Him are not gotten through the eye-gate, the ear-gate, or by reasoning. Then how are you going to get them?

But God hath revealed them unto us by his Spirit: for the Spirit searcheth all things, yea, the deep things of God [1 Cor. 2:10].

What we cannot get through the eye-gate or the ear-gate, the Spirit of God can teach us. There are many things we can learn by studying the Bible—such as the history of it, the poetry of it—but we cannot get spiritual truths that way. Why? Because "God hath revealed them unto us by his Spirit." There are certain things that only the Spirit of God can reveal to us.

For what man knoweth the things of a man, save the spirit of man which is in him? even so the things of God knoweth no man, but the Spirit of God [1 Cor. 2:11].

You and I can understand each other because we have human spirits. For instance, I know how you feel when you fall down. It's embarrassing, isn't it? One snowy morning in Nashville I watched an elder of my church come out of his house with two scuttles full of ashes that he was taking out to the alleyway to dump into his garbage can. He slipped and fell, but he held onto the scuttles. He didn't spill an ash, but he really fell hard. He got up and looked all over the landscape to see if anybody had watched him. Why did he do that? He was embarrassed. I knew exactly how he felt, because it sure did look funny and I couldn't help but laugh. Because I have the spirit of man and he has the spirit of man, I knew exactly how he felt. However, I do not know how God feels. If I am to understand anything about God, He will have to reveal it to me.

Now we have received, not the spirit of the world, but the spirit which is of God; that we might know the things that are freely given to us of God [1 Cor. 2:12].

There are certain things that we can understand only if the Spirit of God reveals them to us, and He does this freely. He *wants* to be our Teacher!

Which things also we speak, not in the words which man's wisdom teacheth, but which the Holy Ghost teacheth; comparing spiritual things with spiritual [1 Cor. 2:13].

Now Paul will make a very profound statement, and it is one of the axioms of Scripture.

But the natural man receiveth not the things of the Spirit of God: for they are foolishness unto him: neither can he know them, because they are spiritually discerned [1 Cor. 2:14].

The natural man cannot receive the things of God. Why not? Because they are foolishness to him. If you are not a Christian, my friend, what I am saying seems foolish to you. If it doesn't, there is something wrong with you or there is something wrong with me—one of us is wrong. God says the natural man finds the preaching of the cross of Christ for salvation foolish. It simply does not make sense to him. "Neither can he know them." When I was a student in college, I had the high-minded notion that anything that any man wrote I could understand. Well, I have found that isn't true. Certainly I cannot understand the Word of God until the Spirit of God opens my heart and mind to understand. It is spiritually discerned. Only the Spirit of God can take the things of Christ and show them unto us. The Lord Jesus said that: "Howbeit when he, the Spirit of truth, is come, he will guide you into all truth: for he shall not speak of himself; but whatsoever he shall hear, that shall he speak: and he will shew you things to come. He shall glorify me: for he shall receive of mine, and shall shew it unto you" (John 16:13–14). My friend, unless the Spirit of God shows you the things of Christ, this Epistle to the Corinthians will mean very little to you.

But he that is spiritual judgeth all things, yet he himself is judged of no man.

For who hath known the mind of the Lord, that he may instruct him? But we have the mind of Christ [1 Cor. 2:15–16].

"He that is spiritual" is the one who has the Holy Spirit within him; he is a child of God.

He "judgeth all things" means that he understands these things. "Yet he himself is judged of no man" means that he is not understood. The spiritual man is in contrast to the natural man. He understands divine truth, but he is misunderstood by the natural man.

"Who hath known the mind of the Lord, that he may instruct him?" Who can instruct God? Who understands the mind of the Lord? We cannot tell God anything, but God can reveal a great deal to us. However, the Spirit of God cannot reveal spiritual things to us until we have the mind of Christ. If you are not a saved person, don't you really think that the preaching of the Cross is foolishness? Don't you think that a man dying on a cross is totally defeated? Doesn't that impress you more as a bit of foolishness rather than the actual way of salvation? Yet God says that His method and His wisdom was to give His Son to die on the cross for us in order that we might be saved and that we must put our trust in Him. If you are being honest, I believe you must admit that it does sound foolish.

The other day I read a letter from a man who is a comedian. He says he is a comedian in a nightclub. He listens to me teach the Bible by radio, and he thinks I am an oddball. In fact, he thinks I am funnier than he is! Well, that is the way he *should* feel. Why? Because he is a natural man and cannot discern spiritual things.

You will remember that we labeled this chapter *The clarity of the Holy Spirit corrects human wisdom.* Paul has presented two classes of mankind: the natural man and the spiritual man.

The natural man is the man who is the son of Adam, born into the world with a sinful nature, a propensity to do evil. In fact, that is all the natural man can do. Even when we "do good," we act from mixed motives. (After we become believers, we ought always to search our hearts to see if we are acting from mixed motives, even when we are trying to do the Lord's work.) Paul says that the natural man will not receive the things of the Spirit of God; they are foolishness to him.

Yesterday in the mail I received a letter

from a politician, a representative from this area to Washington, D.C. Reading this letter would lead one to think he is going to bring in Utopia and the Millennium altogether. My, he has happy solutions for all the problems of the world! Of course, the opposite party doesn't have the benefit of his vast wisdom and knowledge. When I had read his letter through, I had the feeling of keen disappointment. First of all, I know he cannot do what he is saying he will do. Secondly, I realize that he is a natural man. He has no understanding of that which is spiritual. He is not interested in any spiritual solutions to the problems. He thinks he knows how to solve the drug problem, but not in a spiritual way. He promises to solve lawlessness, but not in a spiritual way. He knows no more about spiritual matters than a goat grazing upon grass on the hillside. Years ago it was Gladstone who said that the mark of a great statesman is that he knows the direction God is going to take for the next fifty years. This politician would certainly not qualify by that definition. Actually, we cannot expect too much of the natural man. He will tell you, "I do the very best I can," which is probably an accurate statement.

Then there is the other man, the spiritual man. Paul says that the spiritual man "judgeth all things," meaning he understands, he has a spiritual discernment. His spiritual discernment causes him to be misunderstood by the world because the natural man simply cannot understand why he does the things he does. That is the difference between the spiritual man and the natural man.

You will note that they are the kind of men they are because of their relationship to the Book, the Word of God. To the natural man it is foolishness. The spiritual man discerns the Word of God and recognizes its importance.

CHAPTER 3

THEME: *Correct conception of God clarifies Christian service*

As we have seen in chapter 2, Paul has presented two classes of mankind: the natural man and the spiritual man. Now he makes a further division, and it is among believers: carnal Christians and spiritual Christians. Their status as carnal or as spiritual will manifest itself in their lives and in their Christian service.

And I, brethren, could not speak unto you as unto spiritual, but as unto carnal, even as unto babes in Christ [1 Cor. 3:1].

So here we have the third class. He is the unnatural Christian or the unnatural man. We learned about the natural man, also we learned about the spiritual man—whom we can call the supernatural man. Here we have the unnatural man. He is unnatural because he is a Christian but is still carnal. He is still a babe in Christ.

In the entire first part of this epistle Paul is speaking about carnalities. In the last part of the epistle he speaks of spiritualities. I think Paul got very tired of talking about carnalities because, when he reached chapter 12, you can almost hear him heave a sigh of relief. And he begins to talk to them about something else:

"Now concerning spiritual gifts, brethren, I would not have you ignorant" (1 Cor. 12:1).

The carnal Christian is the one who hasn't grown up spiritually, and it is evident that he lacks spiritual discernment—not because he doesn't have the Holy Spirit dwelling within him, but because he is not growing in grace and in the knowledge of Christ. Again this is a consequence of his relationship to the Word of God. That is so important to see. This unnatural man, this carnal Christian, is a babe in Christ. He has an ability but no desire. A baby has the potential to become a learned man, but he has to start out by drinking milk. Paul carries this figure of speech over to the spiritual level.

I have fed you with milk, and not with meat: for hitherto ye were not able to bear it, neither yet now are ye able [1 Cor. 3:2].

Paul cannot talk to such folk about spiritualities. They are not yet ready for it. First he must talk to them about their carnalities. Unfortunately, it is on this level that most church members are living today.

How can we identify the carnal Christian? It is the Christian who is using the weak arm of the flesh. He uses carnal methods to obtain spiritual goals. An obvious example is the kind of Christian who says, "Let's have a banquet or let's put on a musical and introduce some of this modern music." This is carnality.

The Greek word for *carnal* is *sarkikos*, which means "fleshly." In Latin and French the word *carna* means "sensual." We get our word *carnival* from two words, *carne vale*, which mean "farewell flesh." You see, carnival was something they had before the season of Lent. During Lent they would practice farewell to the flesh with certain denials of pleasure to the flesh; so just before Lent they would gorge and gourmandize the flesh, get drunk, satisfy and satiate the flesh in every possible way. Then they would be able to do without such things during Lent! An example of this is the Mardi Gras in New Orleans. That literally means "fat Tuesday" and refers to the Tuesday before Lent begins.

Paul described folk like this when he used the expression, ". . .whose God is their belly. . ." (Phil. 3:19). You say, "Oh, that's crude." I agree with you; it is crude. But the thing it speaks about is even more crude. This would be an apt description of a lot of folk. Their motto is: Do what comes naturally. Let the flesh have its way.

Perhaps you are saying, "Well, I'm not a carnal Christian. I don't believe in carnivals—I even get sick on a Ferris wheel. I am a separated Christian." What is the mark of carnality? Paul will tell us here.

For ye are yet carnal: for whereas there is among you envying, and strife, and divisions, are ye not carnal, and walk as men? [1 Cor. 3:3].

You see, the carnal Christian is not necessarily one who rides on roller coasters. It does not mean one who promotes carnivals in his church. What is a carnal Christian? Where do you see him in evidence? Wherever there is strife and division, there is actually a "carnival" going on. In many of the fundamental churches one can see divisions and gossip and strife and bitterness and hatred. When that is going on, we know that the flesh is on display. Sometimes Christians can lose their tempers and cover it over by saying, "Well, I am just being frank." No, they are just being mean, that's all. My friend, you can turn a Sunday school class into a carnival, a missionary society into a carnival, or a prayer meeting into a carnival when you gossip or stir up strife and envy and division.

My friend, you may not do "worldly things"

and still you may be a carnal Christian. Listen to Paul:

For while one saith, I am of Paul; and another, I am of Apollos; are ye not carnal?

Who then is Paul, and who is Apollos, but ministers by whom ye believed, even as the Lord gave to every man?

I have planted, Apollos watered; but God gave the increase [1 Cor. 3:4–6].

Paul says, "Both of us are workmen for God." Paul was the one who was the missionary—he had opened up new territory. Apollos came along and held meetings and preached and built up the saints. They were both servants of God.

So then neither is he that planteth any thing, neither he that watereth; but God that giveth the increase [1 Cor. 3:7].

The important thing is not who the preacher is; the important thing is whether God is using him. If God is using him, then God should have the credit for the results. Give God the praise and the glory.

Now he that planteth and he that watereth are one: and every man shall receive his own reward according to his own labour [1 Cor. 3:8].

We need to recognize that God uses many workmen. They may each be doing things a little bit differently. That is why we should not go into a tirade against any individual whom the Lord is using. There are many men who use different methods. Many men do things in a different way from the way I would do them. Yet God uses these men. We are all workmen together with God.

For we are labourers together with God: ye are God's husbandry, ye are God's building.

According to the grace of God which is given unto me, as a wise masterbuilder, I have laid the foundation, and another buildeth thereon. But let every man take heed how he buildeth thereupon [1 Cor. 3:9–10].

The foundation was put down over nineteen hundred years ago. You and I cannot put it down. All we can do is to point to that foundation which is Jesus Christ. We can build on that foundation. The important thing is to get out the Word of God and to preach the gospel which alone can save men.

For other foundation can no man lay than that is laid, which is Jesus Christ [1 Cor. 3:11].

Are you building on Him? That is the important question for the believer. When you came to Christ, you came with no works. You came bringing nothing to receive everything! You were put on that Rock which is Christ. Now you can build on that. This is where good works come in.

Now if any man build upon this foundation gold, silver, precious stones, wood, hay, stubble;

Every man's work shall be made manifest: for the day shall declare it, because it shall be revealed by fire; and the fire shall try every man's work of what sort it is [1 Cor. 3:12–13].

Paul says that you can build on the foundation that has already been laid with six different kinds of material: gold, silver, precious stones, wood, hay, stubble. Fire won't hurt the first three on the list. Actually, the fire purifies gold and silver and precious stones. But fire certainly gets rid of the last three on the list. Wood, hay, and stubble will all disappear into smoke. The believer is at liberty to build on the foundation with any of these materials: gold, silver, precious stones, wood, hay, stubble.

This teaches that the believer can work for a reward. If any man's work abides, work that he has built on the foundation that has already been laid, he shall receive a reward.

If any man's work abide which he hath built thereupon, he shall receive a reward [1 Cor. 3:14].

That is, he shall receive a reward if he is building with gold, silver, or precious stones.

I am of the opinion that we have many wonderful saints of God about us today. I have been able to meet some of these folk—some of them personally and some by letter—whom God is using in a marvelous way. They are building in gold.

As you well know, a little piece of gold isn't as visible as a hay stack. Possibly God is the only One who knows that it is gold. Now a haystack is another thing—I have traveled across flat farmland, and it seemed to me I could see haystacks that were twenty miles away. There are a lot of folk building

haystacks, and everybody hears about what they are doing. The haystacks are going to be tested someday, and then there won't be one haystack left, because the testing is going to be by fire. The same thing will be true of works of wood or stubble.

If any man's work shall be burned, he shall suffer loss: but he himself shall be saved; yet so as by fire [1 Cor. 3:15].

You see the contrast: "If any man's work abide" which he built on the foundation, he shall receive a reward; if any man's work goes up in smoke, he will suffer a terrible loss, but he himself will be saved. He does not lose his salvation if he is on the foundation, which is trust in Christ, even though he receives no reward.

Friend, what are you building today? What kind of material are you using? If you are building with gold, it may not be very impressive now. If you are building an old haystack, it will really stand out on the horizon, but it will go up in smoke. I like to put it like this: there are going to be some people in heaven who will be there because their foundation is Christ but who will smell as if they had been bought at a fire sale! Everything they ever did will have gone up in smoke. They will not receive a reward for their works.

Now if you are a carnal Christian, you cannot expect a reward because you have not been rightly related to God through the Word of God. The carnal Christian is the one who does not know the Word of God. You see, one can identify the three categories which Paul mentions by their relation to the Word of God. The natural man says it is foolishness. The spiritual man discerns the Word, and it gives him spiritual insight. The carnal Christian says, "Let's have a banquet and not a Bible study." Or he says, "Let's listen to music rather than to the teaching of the Word of God." That is the way you can identify the carnal Christian.

Know ye not that ye are the temple of God, and that the Spirit of God dwelleth in you?

If any man defile the temple of God, him shall God destroy; for the temple of God is holy, which temple ye are [1 Cor. 3:16–17].

The child of God is the temple of the Holy Spirit. Paul will bring this matter to our attention again. Our very bodies belong to Him!

THE BELIEVER POSSESSES ALL THINGS IN CHRIST

Let no man deceive himself. If any man among you seemeth to be wise in this world, let him become a fool, that he may be wise [1 Cor. 3:18].

Unfortunately, most of our seminaries today are trying to train "intellectual" preachers. I have listened to some of them, and very few of them are really intellectual. May I say again that the important thing is to know and preach the Word of God. Oh, if only I could get that across to some of these smart-aleck young fellows in seminary! I have the privilege of speaking in many seminaries today, and I have met so many boys in the seminaries who want to be "intellectual."

For the wisdom of this world is foolishness with God. For it is written, He taketh the wise in their own craftiness.

And again, The Lord knoweth the thoughts of the wise, that they are vain.

Therefore let no man glory in men. For all things are yours;

Whether Paul, or Apollos, or Cephas, or the world, or life, or death, or things present, or things to come; all are yours;

And ye are Christ's; and Christ is God's [1 Cor. 3:19–23].

Oh, how wonderful it is that we do not have to be confined to one narrow group or one particular denomination. Instead of feeling that we belong to so-and-so and can be taught by only one particular teacher or preacher, we can know that all the men of God belong to us. How wonderful! The reason I get along with the Pentecostal brethren is because I know they belong to God. Oh, my friend, those folk belong to me, too. And I belong to them. How glorious it is to meet around the person of Christ with other believers who are on the foundation which is Jesus Christ!

CHAPTER 4

THEME: *Conditions of Christ's servants constrain Christian conduct*

This is the final chapter in which Paul is dealing with the divisions and the party spirit which was in the church in Corinth. In this chapter, he speaks of the conditions of Christ's servants—and that is what should constrain Christian conduct.

Let a man so account of us, as of the ministers of Christ, and stewards of the mysteries of God [1 Cor. 4:1].

Let us pause to look at this wonderful verse. We are all "the ministers of Christ." Every believer is a minister of Christ. Sometimes a member of a congregation will say, "There is my minister." Well, I hope he is rather a minister of Christ, because he is responsible to Him. And you, as a minister of Christ, are responsible to Him.

We are all ministers. You are a preacher, whether you like it or not. Now don't get angry with me for saying that. There was a man living near our church in Pasadena, when I was pastor there, who was an alcoholic, a

real sot. He lived with his mother who was a wonderful Christian lady, and she asked me to talk with him. One day when I saw him staggering down the street, I just sort of detoured him into my study. He sat down and I told him what a sorry fellow he was. He agreed with every bit of it. Then I said to him, "Do you know that you are a preacher?" Well, he stood up and said, "Don't you call me that—I'll hit you!" He didn't mind being called a drunkard or an alcoholic, but he surely didn't want to be called a preacher! Well, we are all preachers. As I told him, "We preach some message by our lives. You are saying something to the world and to those around you by your life. You can't help it. I live my life unto you and you live your life unto me. It's just that way. We have that kind of influence." My friend, if you are a believer, you are a minister of Christ. What kind of message are you giving?

Notice that a minister of Christ is a "steward of the mysteries of God." In Paul's day, a steward was the person who managed the household for the owner. He had charge of the house, the food, the clothing, and that sort of thing. He would give out things to the household as they needed them. Just so, a minister of Christ should dispense the Word of God to the members of the household.

Here we have that word *mystery* again. Remember that mysteries are those things which had not been revealed before but are now made known. The mysteries cannot be understood by the natural man. It is only the Spirit of God who can take the things of Christ and show them to us. The "mystery" here is actually the gospel, the Word of God. Since we are stewards of the "mysteries of God," we are to dispense those mysteries.

After concluding His "mystery parables" in Matthew 13, "Jesus saith unto them, Have ye understood all these things? They say unto him, Yea, Lord" (Matt. 13:51). I'm inclined to think that they didn't really understand at that time; Jesus doesn't say whether or not they understood Him. But He does go on to say to them, ". . . Therefore every scribe which is instructed unto the kingdom of heaven is like unto a man that is an householder, which bringeth forth out of his treasure things new and old" (Matt. 13:52). That is what a steward of the mysteries of God should be doing—bringing forth out of the Word of God things new and things old. Folk sometimes say to me after a Bible study or after a sermon, "That's old. I've heard that before." I answer, "Well, I am a steward to bring forth things both new and old. Today I brought forth a little of the old. It is my business to bring forth the old as well as the new." That is the calling of a steward of the mysteries of God, and I can't think of any calling higher than that.

Moreover it is required in stewards, that a man be found faithful [1 Cor. 4:2].

Notice that it is not required of a steward to be eloquent or to have many gifts, only that he be found faithful. There are so many who will be rewarded someday, not because they did some great thing or had some great gift, but because they were faithful in what they did and how they did it. I learned over the years as a pastor of a church that there were always the faithful few. I could depend on them. And I knew where they stood.

But with me it is a very small thing that I should be judged of you, or of man's judgment: yea, I judge not mine own self.

For I know nothing by myself; yet am I not hereby justified: but he that judgeth me is the Lord [1 Cor. 4:3–4].

These two verses actually present the three courts before which we all must appear. They may seem to be rather difficult verses, but actually they are not. They tell us that you have no right to sit in judgment on me, and I have no right to sit in judgment on you, because we both are going to stand before a higher court.

1. The first court is the lower court. It is the court of the opinion of others. He says, "But with me it is a very small thing that I should be judged of you, or of man's judgment." Phillips, in his paraphrase, gives an excellent interpretation of this. "But, as a matter of fact, it matters very little to me what you, or any man, thinks of me . . ." (1 Cor. 4:3, PHILLIPS). That is not a literal translation, but it is a good interpretation.

This is a striking statement, and it may sound as if Paul were antisocial. However, Paul was not callous or contemptuous of the opinion of others. He was not immune to the expression and the estimation of those about him. He defended his apostleship with great feeling when he was challenged by his critics. He was always hurt by false rumors. Right here in this very chapter he made mention of it: "Even unto this present hour we both hunger, and thirst, and are naked, and are buffeted, and have no certain dwellingplace; And labour, working with our own hands: being reviled, we bless; being persecuted, we suffer it: Being defamed, we entreat: we are made as the filth of the world, and are the offscouring of all things unto this day" (vv. 11–13). You can see that Paul was very sensitive to the opinions of others; yet his life was not directed by them. They were not at the steering wheel of his life.

Whether we like it or not, we all stand before the judgment seat of others. It is something that we cannot avoid. Abraham Lincoln said, "Public opinion in this country is everything." Unfortunately, it is true. There is a danger to defer to the opinion of others, to yield to the criticism of our enemies and surrender to them. Many of our courts favor the popularity of the crowd instead of justice—certainly the politicians favor the crowd. Some will surrender principles and honor and reputation. John Milton said, "The last infirmity of a noble mind is the love of fame." Unfortunately, that is what many go out to seek today. Horace Greeley of the *New York Tribune* said, "Fame is a vapor, popularity an accident, riches take wings, those who cheer today will curse tomorrow, only one thing endures—character." Someone else has said, "The trouble with most of us is that we would rather be ruined by praise than saved by criticism." I'm afraid that is true, also.

Although Paul was sensitive to the opinion of others, that opinion did not become the guiding principle of his life. "With me it is a very small thing that I should be judged of you, or of man's judgment."

2. The second court is a higher court. It is the court of one's own conscience. "Yea, I judge not mine own self."

Is conscience a safe guide? Paul says that it is not an accurate guide. We are to be led of the *Spirit*. We have already studied about the age of conscience in the Book of Genesis, and there we saw that it ended in the judgment of the Flood. Christians should have an enlightened conscience. When it rebukes us and tells us that we are wrong, we should obey it. However, our conscience can also approve our easygoing ways and can appeal to our vanity and can flatter us. Then we should beware of it. We all stand or fall before this court.

It was Longfellow who put it like this: "Not in the clamor of the crowded street, Not in the shouts and plaudits of the throng, But in ourselves, are triumph and defeat." An honest man will not be guided by the opinion of others, but he will do what he thinks is right. It is a brave formula. It is a noble rule. Yet Paul said that *he* didn't follow it: ". . . I don't even value my opinion of myself . . . but that doesn't justify me before God" (1 Cor. 4:4, PHILLIPS). It wasn't that Paul knew some bit of evidence against himself. On the contrary, he says he knew nothing against himself, but that still didn't clear him before God. It is characteristic of our human nature to be harsh on others and very lenient with ourselves.

That was David's problem. He could see the evil in someone else, but he couldn't see it in himself. How about us? When others hold tenaciously to some opinion, we call them contentious, but when we do it, we are showing the courage of our convictions. Others cause divisions and make trouble, but we are standing for the right. Others are backslidden when they forsake God's house, but we have a good reason. You know we are not very apt to be severe upon ourselves. We always like to cast ourselves in a leading role, and generally we distort it.

No, we do not stand or fall before ourselves.

God may reverse the decision of this second court, the court of our own conscience.

3. There is a third court before which we must stand—"he that judgeth me is the Lord." The supreme court is of the one and only Master; it is the *bēma* or the judgment seat of Christ. Paul says that he is going to stand someday before the judgment seat of Christ. Each one of us will appear before that judgment seat. (He will say more about this in chapter 5 of his Second Epistle to the Corinthians.)

What is going to be judged there? We know that we shall not be judged for our sins, because a believer's sins have been removed as far as the east is from the west (see Ps. 103:12). Our sins are under the blood of Jesus Christ and God remembers them no more. The believer will be judged for his stewardship. All our physical possessions—our bodies, our material resources, our giving—these are the things that will be brought up for judgment. So you can see that being a faithful steward is very important.

After all, we own nothing. We have learned before that all things are Christ's and that we belong to him. We are in partnership with Him. We saw at the close of chapter 3 that all things are ours. Paul is ours and Apollos is ours. Calvin is ours and John Wesley is ours and Martin Luther is ours. This world we live in is ours—we can enjoy the beauty of its scenery, the mountains, the trees, the ocean, and life itself. (I wouldn't want to be dead today, would you?) But even death is ours! Dr. Parker says, "Death is yours. It belongs to you. Death is not to master you, you are going to master it." Death is yours. How wonderful that is. When we belong to Christ, all things are ours—present and future. And we are stewards of all He has entrusted to us.

Therefore judge nothing before the time, until the Lord come, who both will bring to light the hidden things of darkness, and will make manifest the counsels of the hearts: and then shall every man have praise of God [1 Cor. 4:5].

He is the One who will judge. If we sit in judgment on someone else, we are taking the Lord's place. This is why we need not react to insult or criticism by fighting back. God will judge us fairly, and He knows all the facts. (Anyway, we probably know worse things about ourselves than does the person who is criticizing us!) The hidden works of darkness are going to be brought out into the light in the presence of Jesus Christ. He will make manifest the counsels of the hearts. This is why we should be very careful how we live today.

Then there is this remarkable statement: "then shall every man have praise of God." I believe that He is going to find something for which He can *praise* every saint of God.

In the Book of Revelation Christ has a word of commendation for each of the seven churches of Asia Minor—with the exception of Laodicea, which probably was not really His church anyway. He had words of commendation for the churches in spite of their faults. And I think He will be equally gracious to each individual saint.

A dear little lady in a church years ago always had something good to say about everybody, especially the preacher. One day they had a visiting preacher who delivered the most miserable sermon they had ever heard. The people wondered what in the world the dear little lady would say about such a sermon, and they gathered round as she went out. She smiled and shook hands with the preacher, then she said, "Oh, pastor, you had a wonderful *text* today!" And, my friend, I think our Lord is going to find something praiseworthy in each of us!

THE APPLICATION

And these things, brethren, I have in a figure transferred to myself and to Apollos for your sakes; that ye might learn in us not to think of men above that which is written, that no one of you be puffed up for one against another [1 Cor. 4:6].

Remember that one of the problems in the Corinthian church was divisions. So now Paul says that he is using this for an illustration for them. Paul and Apollos were friends; they both belonged to Christ, and Christ belonged to both of them. Both men were exercising their gifts.

For who maketh thee to differ from another? and what hast thou that thou didst not receive? now if thou didst receive it, why dost thou glory, as if thou hadst not received it? [1 Cor. 4:7].

Do you have a gift? You may have a very outstanding gift, but you have nothing to boast about, because God gave it to you. You are not the originator of your gift. We ought to thank God for our gifts.

Now ye are full, now ye are rich, ye have reigned as kings without us: and I would to God ye did reign, that we also might reign with you.

For I think that God hath set forth us the apostles last, as it were appointed to death: for we are made a spectacle unto the world, and to angels, and to men [1 Cor. 4:8–9].

The apostles in that great martyr period of the church have been set before the world as a spectacle. Not only are they a spectacle to the world but also to angels and to men—and I think that refers to us today. Other men have labored, my friend, and we have entered into their labors.

Now Paul will tell us what he had gone through in order that we might have this epistle and be enjoying the study of it right now.

We are fools for Christ's sake, but ye are wise in Christ; we are weak, but ye are strong; ye are honourable, but we are despised.

Even unto this present hour we both hunger, and thirst, and are naked, and are buffeted, and have no certain dwellingplace;

And labour, working with our own hands: being reviled, we bless; being persecuted, we suffer it:

Being defamed, we entreat: we are made as the filth of the world, and are the offscouring of all things unto this day [1 Cor. 4:10–13].

You and I can't imagine how the apostle Paul suffered in order to get out the gospel of Jesus Christ. He *evangelized* Asia Minor. We are told that in the province of Asia everyone, both Jew and Gentile, heard the Word of God!

I write not these things to shame you, but as my beloved sons I warn you.

For though ye have ten thousand instructors in Christ, yet have ye not many fathers: for in Christ Jesus I have begotten you through the gospel [1 Cor. 4:14–15].

Paul was the missionary who led them to Christ. It is a wonderful thing to be the spiritual father of someone whom you have led to Christ.

For this cause have I sent unto you Timotheus, who is my beloved son, and

faithful in the Lord, who shall bring
you into remembrance of my ways
which be in Christ, as I teach every
where in every church [1 Cor. 4:17].

We see here the personal esteem Paul had for
Timothy.

**Now some are puffed up, as though I
would not come to you.**

**But I will come to you shortly, if the
Lord will, and will know, not the speech
of them which are puffed up, but the
power.**

**For the kingdom of God is not in word,
but in power [1 Cor. 4:18–20].**

Paul says that he is not so much interested in
their talk, but he wants to know whether or
not there is power in their lives.

**What will ye? shall I come unto you
with a rod, or in love, and in the spirit
of meekness? [1 Cor. 4:21].**

Their attitude and action will determine how
Paul shall come to them. Will he need to come
with a "rod" of correction, or can he come in
love and in a spirit of meekness?

CHAPTERS 5–6

THEME: *Scandals in the Corinthian church*

IMPURITY

**It is reported commonly that there is
fornication among you, and such fornication as is not so much as named
among the Gentiles, that one should
have his father's wife [1 Cor. 5:1].**

This was a case that was up before the
church. This was not gossip. It could be
translated: "It is reported actually and fac-
tually." This was not just a rumor that was
going around. This case was common knowledge. It was such fornication that was not
even mentioned among the Gentiles. It was
the sordid story of a man who took his father's
wife, his own stepmother.

**And ye are puffed up, and have not
rather mourned, that he that hath done
this deed might be taken away from
among you [1 Cor. 5:2].**

The apostle is using strong language here. He
is dealing with a very grievous sin. The congregation in Corinth was compromising with
this evil.

We need to recognize that flagrant sin in the
church must be dealt with. The Lord Jesus
had given detailed instructions in Matthew 18:
"Moreover if thy brother shall trespass
against thee, go and tell him his fault between
thee and him alone: if he shall hear thee, thou
hast gained thy brother. But if he will not hear
thee, then take with thee one or two more,
that in the mouth of two or three witnesses
every word may be established. And if he shall

neglect to hear them, tell it unto the church:
but if he neglect to hear the church, let him be
unto thee as an heathen man and a publican"
(Matt. 18:15–17).

They did not carry out this procedure in
Corinth. This was a case of compromise with
evil. John Morley has said that compromise is
the most immoral word in the English
language. I think I would agree to that. The
church in Corinth was compromising itself by
compromising with this evil.

There are certain things about this case that
we need to note. This case was an acknowledged situation which had no need of proof.
This was not a matter of gossip or of hearsay.
Paul would never have brought up something
like this if it had simply been a rumor.

Also we need to note that it was not a questionable sin. It was a glaring sin, and it was
actually recognized by the world outside as
being sin. It was incest. This is in contrast to
questionable activities, which should not be
brought out in the open and dealt with by the
church. Let me give an illustration of what I
mean.

A lady was converted in the church where I
served as pastor. She called me one day about
three months after her conversion, and she
was very disturbed. She said, "I'm very disappointed and very discouraged. I have been a
chain smoker and have wanted to give up cigarettes. I have tried for three months and I
have failed. I have come to the place where I
hate them and I hate myself for not being able
to give them up. What should I do?" I gave her

several suggestions. I said, "Look, it is a questionable sin, and it is one that you hate and want to give up. I don't blame you; your testimony is involved. First of all, continue to pray, and ask your personal friends to continue to pray for you, as you say they are doing. Also I will pray for you. I know God will give you the victory, because you want it. Secondly, don't be discouraged. And the third thing is: please do not tell it to the dear saints in the church. If you do, they will absolutely skin you alive, because they consider it the worst sin in the world." After about three months I saw her coming into the church, and I could tell by her face something had happened. After the service she could hardly wait to talk to me. She said, "I have wonderful news for you. From the day I talked to you down to the present, I haven't smoked once. God has given me deliverance!"

Now, smoking is one of the things I classify as a questionable sin. It is not mentioned in the Word of God; nor does it have any question of immorality connected with it. Therefore, it is to be handled differently. It is not to be brought before the church for judgment. By contrast, this case of immorality in the Corinthian church was a flaunting of God's law. Therefore, this needed to be handled with church discipline. There was no doubt about this being a sin. It is not a questionable matter. It was such a horrible sin that it was not even practiced by the Gentiles outside the church.

I would like to say something to our present generation. Living together without being married is sin in God's sight. It makes no difference what public opinion says about it or how many people are practicing it. The Word of God calls this sin, and there is no other way one can look at it. It is not a questionable sin as far as the Word of God is concerned.

The church in Corinth did not need to establish the fact that the man was living in sin. Their error was that they tolerated it. They condoned the sin by doing nothing about it. They compromised, and that is the worst thing they could have done. You can put this down as an axiom: A pure church is a powerful church; an impure church is a paralyzed church. You can look around you at churches today and see whether or not that is true.

For I verily, as absent in body, but present in spirit, have judged already, as though I were present, concerning him that hath so done this deed,

In the name of our Lord Jesus Christ, when ye are gathered together, and my spirit, with the power of our Lord Jesus Christ,

To deliver such an one unto Satan for the destruction of the flesh, that the spirit may be saved in the day of the Lord Jesus [1 Cor. 5:3–5].

Paul is telling them to meet together, and if this brother will not forsake his sin, they are to deliver him over to Satan. That is a tremendous statement. Does he really mean that? He said it; apparently he meant it.

This is something that the Word of God teaches. Do you remember that Job was delivered over to Satan? Satan came to the Lord and complained that He wouldn't let him touch Job. He told God in effect, "You tell me how good a man Job is, but if You will just let me get to him, I will show You whether or not Job really is true to You. He will curse You to Your face!" So the Lord gave Satan permission to test Job—with the limitation that he could not take Job's life. There is a great comfort in this for us: Satan cannot touch a child of God unless he has the permission of God Himself. And if God does permit it, then it is for a reason.

You will also remember that the Lord Jesus told Peter that Satan desired to have him to sift him as wheat. The Lord Jesus permitted Satan to do this to Peter. Peter was turned over to Satan, and that night he denied his Lord. What he did was just as dastardly as the crime of Judas Iscariot. However, Peter hated himself and he hated what he had done, but it taught him how weak he was. God used this experience to produce the kind of man who would get up and preach the sermon that Peter preached on the Day of Pentecost.

Then there is the example in 1 Timothy 1:20 where Paul writes: "Of whom is Hymenaeus and Alexander; whom I have delivered unto Satan, that they may learn not to blaspheme." These two men were professing Christians, but they were blaspheming. Paul says he delivered them over to Satan.

Now I realize there is danger of our feelings and our emotions getting involved, and there is a danger of fanaticism to which some people are inclined; but in our churches today we do have certain men and women who are hurting the cause of Christ. I believe we have the right to ask God to deliver them into the hands of Satan, to be dealt with, so that they won't hurt and harm the body of Christ. I pray that God will deliver certain men over to Satan to let him give them a good workout. It will either bring them to God (if they are true believers) or it will reveal the fact that they are not genuine believers at all. If they are Christians, then they will come out clear-cut and come out clean for God and for the Lord Jesus Christ. I think we have a right to pray that prayer.

This is strong medicine! And for these carnal Corinthians it was strong medicine. Paul is writing that, although he can't be with them in his body, he is with them in his spirit. He tells them the way he is voting. And his prayer is to deliver this man into the hands of Satan.

Your glorying is not good. Know ye not that a little leaven leaveneth the whole lump? [1 Cor. 5:6].

Do you know what the church in Corinth was doing? At the same time that they were shutting their eyes to the sin that was in their own congregation, they were bragging about their other activities. They were glorying—boasting. Probably they bragged about the missionaries they sent out and about being true to the Scriptures and about winning souls for Christ. What hypocrisy! Yet there are many folk who feel that being busy in Christian work covers a multitude of sins. Paul says that their glorying was not good. Didn't they know that a little leaven leavens the whole lump? Leaven is never a symbol of the gospel; it is always a principle of evil, and it represents evil in this instance.

Purge out therefore the old leaven, that ye may be a new lump, as ye are unleavened. For even Christ our passover is sacrificed for us [1 Cor. 5:7].

What does leaven do to the bread? Well, you put it in the dough, set it in a warm place, and the bread begins to puff up. When it gets to a certain height, the bread is put into the hot oven. Why? To stop the leavening process. If the bread did not get into the oven, that leavening process would go on and the bread would rise higher and higher. Finally the whole loaf would be corrupt and rotten. Now that is exactly what happens with evil in the church if it is not dealt with. Finally the whole thing will blow up and will destroy the effectiveness of the church. A little leaven will leaven the whole lump; so it must be purged out.

In the Old Testament, after the Feast of the Passover there followed immediately the Feast of Unleavened Bread. Paul says that Christ, the true Passover Lamb, has now been sacrificed for us. This should be followed by lives that are free from leaven. Instead, this Corinthian congregation was allowing leaven—that is, evil—to come right into their church. These were the very ones who were talking about the death of Christ and the crucifixion of Christ, and yet they permitted leaven to enter into the church.

Therefore let us keep the feast, not with old leaven, neither with the leaven of malice and wickedness; but with the unleavened bread of sincerity and truth [1 Cor. 5:8].

Paul is not talking about how a person is saved. He is talking about the walk of the believer after he has been saved. Sincerity never saved anyone. But if you are a child of God, you will be sincere. The world today needs to see sincerity among believers and needs truth among believers. Paul says, "Let's have sincerity and truth in the church there in Corinth." You see, the church there was really insincere. They had gross immorality in their midst. They thought they could get by with this, and they pretended that everything was all right. They were pretending that they were telling the truth and living the truth when actually they were not.

I wrote unto you in an epistle not to company with fornicators:

Yet not altogether with the fornicators of this world, or with the covetous, or extortioners, or with idolaters; for then must ye needs go out of the world.

But now I have written unto you not to keep company, if any man that is called a brother be a fornicator, or covetous, or an idolater, or a railer, or a drunkard, or an extortioner; with such an one no not to eat [1 Cor. 5:9–11].

Paul had previously written to them and had condemned these sins. Corinth was a city given over to immorality. There were a thousand priestesses at the temple of Venus or Aphrodite who were nothing in the world but harlots. They were prostitutes, and the whole city was given over to this immorality in the name of religion. Now here they are permitting this immoral man to come into their fellowship and to eat with them. They patted him on the back and accepted him as one of their own when they knew he was living in sin. The church in Corinth thought they could drop down to the level of the world.

Does the church today think it can drop

down to the immorality of the world and get away with it? My friend, the church today has lost its power. I am speaking of the church in general. Thank God there are still wonderful churches left, churches that stand out like beacon lights across this land, Bible churches that stand for the Word of God. The other day I heard of a young preacher who took a stand when they tried to introduce hard rock music into his church. It meant that he lost several hundred of his members who walked out. I thank God for a preacher like that, one with intestinal fortitude. Most men today are compromising and shutting their eyes and letting the world come in. The church has lost its power. An impure church is a paralyzed church, and a pure church is a powerful church. That is true for the individual also.

Now Paul says this does not apply to fornication only. He also applies it to covetousness. How about a deacon in the church who has sticky fingers? How about the man in the church who has his hand on a lot of money? Paul also includes idolaters, those who are fooling around with other religions. I heard about a leading officer of a church who walked out and joined a cult. I am telling you that the Word of God teaches that a little infection in the church must be dealt with or else it is going to corrupt and wreck the church. A little leaven will leaven the whole lump.

For what have I to do to judge them also that are without? do not ye judge them that are within?

But them that are without God judgeth. Therefore put away from among yourselves that wicked person [1 Cor. 5:12–13].

Paul says that he is not judging the people on the outside. That is not his business. He is to judge those inside the church. God will judge those who are on the outside. It is the business of the church to judge evil which is in the church.

We are interested to know how things worked out in Corinth. To find the answer we need to turn to 2 Corinthians 2:4–8: "For out of much affliction and anguish of heart I wrote unto you with many tears; not that ye should be grieved, but that ye might know the love which I have more abundantly unto you. But if any have caused grief, he hath not grieved me, but in part: that I may not overcharge you all. Sufficient to such a man is this punishment, which was inflicted of many. So that contrariwise ye ought rather to forgive him, and comfort him, lest perhaps such a one should be swallowed up with overmuch sorrow. Wherefore I beseech you that ye would confirm your love toward him."

This immoral man had come in deep repentance after Paul put it down on the line in his previous epistle. Today we need a great deal of courage—not compromise—in the church to point out these things and say, "This is sin." I think that when this is done, the believer who is in sin will confess, like this man in Corinth and like David did, and will repent and change his ways. The Corinthian church handled this very nicely. Why? Because Paul had the courage to write this kind of letter. In 2 Corinthians Paul explains why he had done it: "Wherefore, though I wrote unto you, I did it not for his cause that had done the wrong, nor for his cause that suffered wrong, but that our care for you in the sight of God might appear unto you" (2 Cor. 7:12).

Paul says that he wrote as he did for the welfare of the church of the Lord Jesus Christ. Today we hear this flimsy, hypocritical attitude: "Well, we don't want to air this thing. We don't want to cause trouble. We'll just sweep it under the rug." My friend, God cannot bless a church or an individual that does this. If God did bless, God would be a liar. And you know that God is no liar. He will judge inaction in a case like this.

This chapter has a tremendous lesson for us. And it is very practical, is it not?

LAWSUITS AMONG MEMBERS

Chapter 6 will deal with the subject of the Christian and his relation to the state. The Christian is told that he has a dual citizenship. I think that is often misconstrued by outsiders as well as by believers. Philippians 3:20 states: "For our conversation is in heaven; from whence also we look for the Saviour, the Lord Jesus Christ." The Greek word for "conversation" is *politeuma*, which literally means "Our politics is in heaven; from whence also we look for the Saviour, the Lord Jesus Christ."

His citizenship in heaven does not relieve the Christian of his responsibility to the state. The Christian has a responsibility to each, that is, to God and to the state. Our Lord expressed this when the Herodians pressed on Him the subject of taxation. The Herodians asked, "Tell us therefore, What thinkest thou? Is it lawful to give tribute unto Caesar, or not?" (Matt. 22:17). Jesus answered, ". . . Render therefore unto Caesar the things which are Caesar's; and unto God the things that are

God's" (Matt. 22:21). The Christian has a responsibility to the state, and he also has a responsibility to God. The Christian has both secular and spiritual responsibilities.

The apostle Paul defines some very specific responsibilities of Christians to the state. There are certain guidelines which cannot be misunderstood. Paul writes in 1 Timothy 2:1–4: "I exhort therefore, that, first of all, supplications, prayers, intercessions, and giving of thanks, be made for all men; For kings, and for all that are in authority; that we may lead a quiet and peaceable life in all godliness and honesty. For this is good and acceptable in the sight of God our Saviour; Who will have all men to be saved, and to come unto the knowledge of the truth." Our obligation to the state is to attempt to have a peaceful, law-abiding society with recognition of authority. Why is this so important for the Christian? It is in order that we might get out the message of the gospel.

Paul discusses the same subject in Romans 13:1–4: "Let every soul be subject unto the higher powers. For there is no power but of God: the powers that be are ordained of God. Whosoever therefore resisteth the power, resisteth the ordinance of God: and they that resist shall receive to themselves damnation. For rulers are not a terror to good works, but to the evil. Wilt thou then not be afraid of the power? do that which is good, and thou shalt have praise of the same: For he is the minister of God to thee for good. . . ."

This was written at a time when the Roman government was tyrannical. The emperors of that era were dictators, and many of them were persecutors of the church. If anyone tried to oppose the Roman government, he was in real trouble, because there was no place to which one could flee where the government could not find him and arrest him. Even in that government, however, there was a freedom to preach the Word of God. That is the thing that Christians should keep in mind.

Back in Genesis we are shown that it was God Himself who ordained the state. As far as I can tell, that has never been changed. God put down this principle: "Whoso sheddeth man's blood, by man shall his blood be shed: for in the image of God made he man" (Gen. 9:6). To maintain the dignity and a respect for humanity, capital punishment must be used.

I have a letter from a very sweet lady who is very softhearted and feels that I am terrible because I believe in capital punishment. She says that Jesus wouldn't do that. She wants to know whether I would be willing to pull the switch at the electric chair. Very candidly, I wouldn't like to do it—that is not my job; I have been called to do something else. But I do want to say this: If this sweet lady wants to be safe in her home, there had better be somebody who is willing to pull that electric switch. We are living in a time of lawlessness. The reason is that we have softhearted judges, and I'm afraid some have been softheaded as well.

The church and the state were to be kept separate. The church was not to dominate the state, not to dictate to it. The state was not to control the church nor to take the place of God. In a secular society, secularism always takes the place of God. That is modern idolatry today. A great many people are putting secularism in the place of God. Someone sent me a modern-day parody on Psalm 23 which begins, "Science is my shepherd, I shall not want." We find the church getting involved in secularism. I have a quotation from a liberal which reads: "To rebel against human law in the name of a higher law can be creative, saving the world from stagnation, but to disobey the law can also be anarchic and destructive, for too easily can men convince themselves that their opinions are those of God." Too many of our statesmen today think they stand in the place of God and that they speak in the place of God.

With that kind of background I think we are prepared to look at chapter 6 of 1 Corinthians. We are still in that division of the epistle which deals with scandals in the Corinthian church. The first was concerned with impurity, and this chapter is concerned with lawsuits among members.

Dare any of you, having a matter against another, go to law before the unjust, and not before the saints? [1 Cor. 6:1].

This may sound to you like a very strange statement, and it may need some explanation. He does not say that Christians are not to go to law. If Christians did not use the benefit of the law, they would suffer great loss at the hands of the unsaved. He is saying that Christians should not go to law against each other— Christian against Christian. The differences between believers are not to be taken to a secular court. They should be settled by believers. This is something which churches and believers in general ignore today.

After I had come to Southern California as a pastor, I was rather amazed one day when a man came in quite excitedly and wanted to bring a charge against an officer of the church.

He claimed this man had beat him out of a sum of money in a business deal. He said, "Now I want you to bring him up before the board and to make him settle with me." I told him, "I think you are approaching this the right way. When can you appear before the board and make your charges?" "Oh," he said, "I've told you about it. That is all that is necessary." I pointed out to him that I had no way to verify the charge. It would be necessary for both men to appear before the board. Then I asked him, "Would you be willing to accept the verdict of the board?" "Well," he said, "it all depends on how they decided it. If they decided in my favor, I would accept it." So then I asked him if he would accept the verdict if it were against him, and he assured me that he would not. Of course, I told him that we might as well forget the whole matter. I said, "You are not really willing to turn this issue over to other believers for a verdict."

Church fights should not be aired in state courts before unbelievers. Individual differences among Christians should be adjudicated by believers. It is bad enough when two Christians are divorced, but it is an extremely serious matter when Christians go before a secular court and air their differences before unbelievers. When a Christian couple come to me and tell me they simply cannot get along, and I see there is no way of working out a reconciliation, I advise a legal separation, not a court trial.

Why should a believer let other believers be the judges rather than take his case to the unsaved world for their judgment? Again, this does not forbid a Christian from going to court with an unbeliever. Why should two believers bring their differences to be settled by other believers? Paul gives a threefold reason regarding the capabilities of believers to judge.

THE CAPABILITY OF THE BELIEVERS

Do ye not know that the saints shall judge the world? and if the world shall be judged by you, are ye unworthy to judge the smallest matters? [1 Cor. 6:2].

My friend, if you are a believer in Christ, you will have a part with the Lord Jesus in ruling the earth someday. This is not talking about the judgment at the Great White Throne, which will be the judgment when the lost appear before Christ. No, this has to do with the adjudication of the affairs of the universe down through eternity.

1. Saints will judge the world.

The saints shall judge the world. I believe this has to do with what Paul wrote to Timothy, "If we suffer, we shall also reign with him: if we deny him, he also will deny us" (2 Tim. 2:12). I believe this means that we shall pass judgment on the affairs in this world.

Know ye not that we shall judge angels? how much more things that pertain to this life? [1 Cor. 6:3].

2. Saints will judge angels.

Paul is using a series of "know ye nots." When Paul said, "Know ye not," you can be sure that the brethren did not know. This was a polite way of saying they were ignorant of these things.

This certainly opens up a whole new vista of truth. I do not understand what this means; it is beyond my comprehension. All I know is that man was made a little lower than the angels, and through redemption man was lifted into a place of fellowship with God, a position above the angels. Also, God permitted man to fall. He never would have permitted that if it would not work out for good. It will result in bringing man into a higher position. The old bromide is not true that says that the bird with the broken wing never flies so high again. Man flies higher. We are going to be above the angels. We are going to judge them and have charge of them. May I say again, this is beyond my comprehension, but I believe it.

To pick up the third "know ye not," we skip down to verse 9:

Know ye not that the unrighteous shall not inherit the kingdom of God? Be not deceived: neither fornicators, nor idolaters, nor adulterers, nor effeminate, nor abusers of themselves with mankind,

Nor thieves, nor covetous, nor drunkards, nor revilers, nor extortioners, shall inherit the kingdom of God [1 Cor. 6:9–10].

3. Unrighteousness is not in the kingdom.

Listen very carefully because this is important. No secular judge or jury is equipped to make spiritual decisions, because they do not comprehend spiritual principles. That is why court cases that pertain to churches and Christians go haywire the minute they hit the legal mills. A secular judge may know the material in the law books, but he knows nothing about spiritual decisions. He has no spiritual discernment.

To be very candid with you, it would be with fear and trembling that I would go into court and have a secular judge handle me or my property. I don't think a secular judge is capable of doing that, and I don't think a secular jury can either. Following a trial here in Southern California I looked at the jury shown on television and said to my wife, "I thank God my life is not in the hands of the twelve people I see there." After the trial was over, some of the jurors made statements for the television program which revealed that they were not capable of judging the case. Yet Christians will trust that crowd rather than take their cases to other believers who do have spiritual discernment.

I speak to your shame. Is it so, that there is not a wise man among you? no, not one that shall be able to judge between his brethren?

But brother goeth to law with brother, and that before the unbelievers [1 Cor. 6:5–6].

Of course, not every Christian is a capable judge, but Paul is saying, "I speak to your shame, isn't there a wise man among you?" When you go to a secular court, you are saying that *none* of the saints are capable of judging. Well, I know some dear brethren in the Lord with whom I would be willing to risk my life. I am confident they would render a just verdict.

Now why does a Christian have a capability to judge? Paul will give us three reasons:

And such were some of you: but ye are washed, but ye are sanctified, but ye are justified in the name of the Lord Jesus, and by the Spirit of our God [1 Cor. 6:11].

"Ye are washed." It is "not by works of righteousness which we have done, but according to his mercy he saved us, by the washing of regeneration . . ." (Titus 3:5). We have been born again, washed. Because the mercy of God has reached down and touched us, we ought to know how to extend mercy. We can be merciful because we have experienced mercy. We should recognize that there are many wonderful believers today who have been washed. We should trust ourselves to them rather than to the unsaved.

"Ye are sanctified." Sanctification in the Corinthian epistles is of two kinds, but I think here it means positional sanctification, that is, being *in* Christ. This means that Christ is on our side and all believers are brothers in

Christ. If another Christian judges me, it means that one of my *brothers* is judging me. I would be willing to trust myself to the judgment of a brother. A little girl was carrying a heavy baby down the street. A man saw her and asked, "Little girl, isn't that baby too heavy for you?" "Oh, no," she said, "he's my *brother.*" The relationship makes a lot of difference. A brother is not too heavy. I am in Christ and my brother is in Christ; so I should be willing to trust my brother.

"Ye are justified." The third reason my brother is capable of being a judge is that his sins are already forgiven, as mine are. He has been declared righteous before the throne of God, as I have been. "Who shall lay any thing to the charge of God's elect? It is God that justifieth" (Rom. 8:33). "But to him that worketh not, but believeth on him that justifieth the ungodly, his faith is counted for righteousness" (Rom. 4:5). A fellow Christian knows this, and I feel that he could handle my case better than anyone else.

THE BELIEVER'S BODY IS THE TEMPLE OF THE HOLY SPIRIT

All things are lawful unto me, but all things are not expedient: all things are lawful for me, but I will not be brought under the power of any [1 Cor. 6:12].

There are a lot of things which a believer can do, but they are not expedient to do. I could mention many things; Paul mentions one here:

Meats for the belly, and the belly for meats: but God shall destroy both it and them. Now the body is not for fornication, but for the Lord; and the Lord for the body [1 Cor. 6:13].

Meats shall be destroyed someday. Our stomachs shall be destroyed someday. There is Christian liberty in what we eat.

In contrast, our bodies are not to be used for fornication. Our bodies belong to the Lord.

And God hath both raised up the Lord, and will also raise up us by his own power.

Know ye not that your bodies are the members of Christ? shall I then take the members of Christ, and make them the members of an harlot? God forbid [1 Cor. 6:14–15].

Young folks today think that they can live together without being married. One such couple came to me wanting to talk about going into Christian service. They weren't married, but they were living together! I told them, "You get married." They asked, "Why?" I said, "Because God commands it. That is the way *God* wants it to be. Until you are willing to do that, you cannot serve Him."

What? know ye not that he which is joined to an harlot is one body? for two, saith he, shall be one flesh.

But he that is joined unto the Lord is one spirit.

Flee fornication. Every sin that a man doeth is without the body; but he that committeth fornication sinneth against his own body [1 Cor. 6:16–18].

My friend, you cannot live in immorality and serve Christ. Unfortunately, we find that public opinion generally accepts immoral persons; but *God* does not accept them.

What? know ye not that your body is the temple of the Holy Ghost which is in you, which ye have of God, and ye are not your own?

For ye are bought with a price: therefore glorify God in your body, and in your spirit, which are God's [1 Cor. 6:19–20].

Here is a remarkable truth which many believers have not received. Our bodies are the temple of the Holy Spirit. Because our bodies belong to God, we are not to share our bodies in fornication. This leads to a discussion of marriage, which will be the subject of the next chapter.

CHAPTER 7

THEME: *Marriage*

This chapter concerns marriage; so we shall be discussing the subject of sex. I think we will probably handle it in a more dignified manner than is usual today because we are going to follow Paul.

In the previous chapter Paul had given them the spiritual truths that, by application to the problem of marriage, can solve matters that relate to sex in marriage. You will remember that he emphasized that our bodies belong to God and that our bodies are the temple of the Holy Ghost. Our bodies are to be used for the glory of God.

Now concerning the things whereof ye wrote unto me: It is good for a man not to touch a woman [1 Cor. 7:1].

It is obvious that the Corinthian believers had written a letter to Paul concerning this problem. We do not have the question, but we do have Paul's answer. Paul has taken a long time to get to this. He first dealt with the divisions and the scandals in their midst. However, he has no reluctance in dealing with the subject of marriage, and he writes boldly and very frankly. Before we get into the text itself, I wish to deal with two introductory matters.

First there is the question: Was Paul ever married? If Paul was never married, then in his explanation he is simply theorizing. He is not speaking from experience. However, Paul did not do that. Paul always spoke from experience. It was not the method of the Spirit of God to choose a man who knew nothing about the subject on which the Spirit of God wanted him to write.

It has always been assumed that Paul was not married on the basis of the seventh verse: "For I would that all men were even as I myself. But every man hath his proper gift of God, one after this manner, and another after that." If we are going to assume that Paul was not married, we need to pay attention to the verse that follows: "I say therefore to the unmarried and widows, It is good for them if they abide even as I." Someone will say, "He still says that he is unmarried." Granted. We know he was not married. But notice that he mentions two classes here: the unmarried and the widows (or widowers). He could have been unmarried or a widower.

It is difficult to believe that Paul had always been unmarried because of his background and because of who he was. Paul was a member of the Sanhedrin. In Acts 26:10 Paul says, "Which thing I also did in Jerusalem: and many of the saints did I shut up in prison, having received authority from the chief priests; and when they were put to death, I gave my voice against them." How could he give his *voice* against them? It was by his vote in the Sanhedrin, which means he was a member of the Sanhedrin. Since Paul was a member of the Sanhedrin, he must have been a married man because that was one of the conditions of membership.

There was an insistence upon Jewish young men to marry. The Mishna said this should be at the age of eighteen. In the *Yebhamoth,* in the commentary on Genesis 5:2 it states: "A Jew who has no wife is not a man." I believe it is an inescapable conclusion that Paul at one time was a married man. He undoubtedly was a widower who had never remarried. In chapter 9 we read, "Have we not power to lead about a sister, a wife, as well as other apostles, and as the brethren of the Lord, and Cephas?" (1 Cor. 9:5). I think Paul is saying, "I could marry again if I wanted to; I would be permitted to do that. But I'm not going to for the simple reason that I would not ask a woman to follow me around in the type of ministry God has given to me."

It is my conviction that in the past Paul had loved some good woman who had reciprocated his love, because he spoke so tenderly of the marriage relationship. "Husbands, love your wives, even as Christ also loved the church, and gave himself for it" (Eph. 5:25).

I would like to give you a quotation from F. W. Farrar who writes in his *Life and Work of St. Paul:* "The other question which arises is, Was Saul married? Had he the support of some loving heart during the fiery struggles of his youth? Amid the to-and-fro contentions of spirit which resulted from an imperfect and unsatisfying creed, was there in the troubled sea of his life one little island home where he could find refuge from incessant thoughts? Little as we know of his domestic relations, little as he cared to mingle mere private interests with the great spiritual truths which occupy his soul, it seems to me that we must answer this question in the affirmative."

The position of many expositors is that Paul had been married and that his wife had died. Paul never made reference to her, but he spoke so tenderly of the marriage relationship I believe he had been married.

The second introductory matter is not a question but a statement. We need to understand the Corinth of that day. If we do not, we are going to fall into the trap of saying that Paul is commending the single state above the married state. One must understand the local

situation of Corinth to know what he is talking about. Notice the first two verses again.

Now concerning the things whereof ye wrote unto me: It is good for a man not to touch a woman.

Nevertheless, to avoid fornication, let every man have his own wife, and let every woman have her own husband [1 Cor. 7:1–2].

We need to understand Corinth. I have been to the ruins of ancient Corinth. Towering above those ruins is the mountain which was the acropolis, called Acro-Corinthus. The city was dominated by the Acro-Corinthus, and on top of it was the temple of Aphrodite. It towered over the city like a dark cloud. Today the ruins of a Crusader fort are there. When the Crusaders came, they used the stones from the temple of Aphrodite to build their fortress.

This temple was like most heathen temples. Sex was a religion. There were one thousand so-called vestal virgins there. In that temple you could get food, drink, and sex. Those vestal virgins were nothing in the world but one thousand prostitutes. Sex was carried on in the name of religion. That was the philosophy of Plato, by the way.

People tend to forget the immorality of that culture. A man once said to me, "Socrates wrote in a very lofty language." Yes, sometimes he did. He also told prostitutes how they ought to conduct themselves. The whole thought was to get rid of the desires of the body by satisfying them. That is heathenism. That came out in two basic philosophies of the Greeks. Stoicism said the basic desires were to be denied; Epicureanism said they were to be fulfilled all the way.

The wife in the Roman world was a chattel. She was a workhorse. A man generally had several wives. One had charge of the kitchen, another had charge of the living area, another was in charge of the clothes. Sex was secondary because the man went up to the temple where the good-looking girls were kept. There they celebrated the seasons of fertility, and believe me, friend, that is what was carried on.

You will still find the same thing among the Bedouins in Palestine today. They have several wives, and it is a practical thing for them. One takes care of the sheep, another goes with the man as he wanders around, another stays back at the home base where they have a tent and probably a few fruit trees. He thinks he needs at least three wives.

Now Paul lifts marriage up to the heights, out of this degradation, and says to the Corinthians they are not to live like that. Every man is to have one wife, and every woman is to have her own husband. Paul lifted woman from the place of slavery in the pagan world, the Roman Empire, and made her a companion of man. He restored her to her rightful position. He was in Ephesus when he wrote to the Corinthians, and in Ephesus there was much the same thing in the awful temple of Diana. It was to the Ephesians that Paul wrote, "Husbands, love your wives, even as Christ also loved the church, and gave himself for it" (Eph. 5:25).

Now I know somebody is going to say that he also told wives to obey their husbands. I would like to know where he said that. He did write, "Wives, submit yourselves unto your own husbands, as unto the Lord" (Eph. 5:22). Have you ever looked up the word *submit* to see what it means? To submit means to respond. Wives are to respond to their own husbands. The wife is to react to the man. Man is the aggressor. He initiates the expression of love, and the woman is the receiver. This is not a matter of sex alone; it involves a couple mentally, spiritually, psychologically, and physically. Man is the aggressor; woman is the receiver.

God created man and woman that way in the beginning. He created woman as the "helpmeet," a helper suitable for him or corresponding to him. She is the other part of man. When a husband says, "I love you," she answers, "I love you." When a man admits that he has a cold wife, he is really saying that he is a failure as a husband and that he is to blame for the condition.

Paul lifts woman from the slave state to that of a partner of man. Listen to the next verse:

Let the husband render unto the wife due benevolence: and likewise also the wife unto the husband [1 Cor. 7:3].

She is to respond to him. He is to tell her that he loves her.

The wife hath not power of her own body, but the husband: and likewise also the husband hath not power of his own body, but the wife [1 Cor. 7:4].

The man is not to run up to that temple of Aphrodite. That is sin. Love and sex are to take place at home. That is exactly what he is saying here. The only motive for marriage is love—not sex, but love. I am convinced that Paul had known the love of a good and great woman.

So many of the great men in Scripture knew the love of a woman. There are Adam and Eve, Jacob and Rachel, Boaz and Ruth, David and Abigail—it was Abigail who told David, ". . .the soul of my lord shall be bound in the bundle of life with the LORD thy God . . ." (1 Sam. 25:29).

It is said of John Wesley that when he came to America he was not a saved man. He wrote, "I came to this country to convert Indians, but who is going to convert John Wesley?" The story goes that the crown had sent to America an insipid nobleman. Due to the terrible custom of that day, the nobility was entitled to marry the finest, and he had married a woman of striking beauty and strong personality, who also was an outstanding Christian. Then there came into their colony this fiery young missionary. And these two fell in love. But she said, "No, John, God has called you to go back to England to do some great service for Him." It was she who sent John Wesley back to England—to marry the Methodist church. Back in England Wesley was converted, and she was his inspiration. Behind every great man is a great woman.

Now Paul continues his guidelines for conduct in marriage.

Defraud ye not one the other, except it be with consent for a time, that ye may give yourselves to fasting and prayer; and come together again, that Satan tempt you not for your incontinency.

But I speak this by permission, and not of commandment [1 Cor. 7:5–6].

He says this is not a commandment, but it is a guideline to follow so that Satan will not have an opportunity to tempt either member of the marriage relationship.

For I would that all men were even as I myself. But every man hath his proper gift of God, one after this manner, and another after that [1 Cor. 7:7].

At this time Paul did not have a wife. He did not remarry. He was not taking a wife along with him on his travels.

There are people in the Lord's work who have not married. They have made that kind of sacrifice—some for several years, some for their whole lifetime. You remember that the Lord Jesus said, "For there are some eunuchs, which were so born from their mother's womb:

and there are some eunuchs, which were made eunuchs of men: and there be eunuchs, which have made themselves eunuchs for the kingdom of heaven's sake . . ." (Matt. 19:12).

When I began in the ministry, I attempted to imitate a man who was a bachelor. I thought that was the happiest state, but I soon learned that it wasn't for me. I wanted a wife. Paul says that is all right—"every man hath his proper gift of God."

I say therefore to the unmarried and widows, It is good for them if they abide even as I.

But if they cannot contain, let them marry: for it is better to marry than to burn [1 Cor. 7:8–9].

It is better to marry than to burn with passion.

COMMAND TO THE MARRIED

And unto the married I command, yet not I, but the Lord, Let not the wife depart from her husband:

But and if she depart, let her remain unmarried, or be reconciled to her husband: and let not the husband put away his wife [1 Cor. 7:10–11].

Here is a commandment. Paul is putting it on the line. The wife is not to leave her husband, and the husband is not to leave his wife. If one or the other is going to leave, then they are to remain unmarried.

Now there was a new problem which presented itself in Corinth. After Paul had come and had preached the gospel to them, a husband in a family would accept Christ but the wife would not. In another family it might be that the wife would accept Christ and the husband would not. What were the believers to do under such circumstances?

But to the rest speak I, not the Lord: If any brother hath a wife that believeth not, and she be pleased to dwell with him, let him not put her away.

And the woman which hath an husband that believeth not, and if he be pleased to dwell with her, let her not leave him.

For the unbelieving husband is sanctified by the wife, and the unbelieving wife is sanctified by the husband: else were your children unclean; but now are they holy [1 Cor. 7:12–14].

If one was married to an unsaved man or to an unsaved woman and there were children in the family, Paul said they should try to see it through. Paul says, "Stay right where you are if you can."

But if the unbelieving depart, let him depart. A brother or a sister is not under bondage in such cases: but God hath called us to peace [1 Cor. 7:15].

If the unbeliever walks out of the marriage, that is another story. Then the believer is free. Now the question which is asked is whether that one is free to marry again. I believe that under certain circumstances Paul would have given permission for that. I do not think one can put down a categorical rule either way for today. I think that each case stands or falls on its own merits. I'm afraid this can easily be abused, even by Christians. I am afraid sometimes a husband or a wife tries to get rid of the other and forces them to leave in order that they might have a "scriptural ground" for divorce.

For what knowest thou, O wife, whether thou shalt save thy husband? or how knowest thou, O man, whether thou shalt save thy wife? [1 Cor. 7:16].

This should be the goal of the wife. I know several women who were married to unsaved men and tried to win them for Christ. This also should be the goal of the husband who is married to an unsaved woman. Winning them for Christ should be uppermost in their consideration.

But as God hath distributed to every man, as the Lord hath called every one, so let him walk. And so ordain I in all churches [1 Cor. 7:17].

Paul is advising people to stay in the situation in which they are. They are not to walk out of their marriage after they have heard and accepted the gospel. They are to stay married if the unbelieving partner will allow it.

This ought to answer the question for today. Unfortunately, there are some ministers and evangelists who have advised people who have had a divorce and have remarried to go back to their first mate after they had come to Christ. May I say, I can't think of anything more tragic than that kind of advice. I know one woman who finally ended up in a mental institution because she followed the advice of some evangelist who told her to leave her second husband and her lovely Christian home and go back to a drunken husband whom she had previously divorced. How foolish can one be? We need to understand what Paul is saying here.

Is any man called being circumcised? let him not become uncircumcised. Is any called in uncircumcision? let him not be circumcised.

Circumcision is nothing, and uncircumcision is nothing, but the keeping of the commandments of God.

Let every man abide in the same calling wherein he was called [1 Cor. 7:18–20].

Paul now expands the application of this principle. It applies to other relationships in life. For instance, if when you are converted you belong to the circumcised, that is, if you are an Israelite, don't try to become a Gentile. If you are a Gentile, don't try to become an Israelite. Circumcision or uncircumcision is no longer important. Obedience to Christ is the issue now. The Israelite and the Gentile are one in Christ.

The whole point here is that in whatever state you find yourself when you accept Christ, stay right there. I have known many businessmen who get into some Christian organization after their conversion, and the next thing I know they come to me and say that they are thinking of giving up the business and going into full-time Christian work. My friend, if you are a successful businessman, God may have given you a gift to minister in that particular area. He may not intend for you to change and go into full-time Christian work. Let's go on and listen to what Paul says.

Art thou called being a servant? care not for it: but if thou mayest be made free, use it rather.

For he that is called in the Lord, being a servant, is the Lord's freeman: likewise also he that is called, being free, is Christ's servant [1 Cor. 7:21–22].

In that day there were slaves and freemen. If a person were a slave or a servant of a man, he was not to try to get loosed from that, thinking that God wanted him to be freed from his master.

I find today that there are many housewives who get the notion that they are to become great Bible teachers. They get so involved in it that they neglect their families.

I shall never forget the story I heard about the late Gypsy Smith. A woman came to him in Dallas, Texas, and said, "Gypsy Smith, I feel called to go into the ministry." He asked her a very pertinent question (he had a way of doing that), "Are you married?" She said that she was. "How many children do you have?" She answered that she had five. He said, "That's wonderful. God has called you into the ministry, and He has already given you your congregation!"

Ye are bought with a price; be not ye the servants of men [1 Cor. 7:23].

You have been redeemed by the blood of Jesus Christ. Now don't be a slave to someone. Does this sound like a contradiction? Let me explain by an example. A cocktail waitress was converted by hearing the gospel on our radio broadcast. Everything about the Bible was brand new to her. She asked me a question about whether she should give up being a cocktail waitress because she just didn't feel right about it. I answered her that it was up to her. I said, "That is a decision that you must make. If you have a conviction about it, then give it up. If you want to know what I think about it personally, I think you ought to give it up. However don't give it up because I say so, but give it up if that becomes your conviction." She did give it up and found another job within a couple of weeks. She had been bought with a price; she was not to be a servant of man.

Brethren, let every man, wherein he is called, therein abide with God [1 Cor. 7:24].

This is the important consideration. When a person is converted, whatever he is doing, wherever he is, he is to remain in that position as long as he is free in his relationship to God. God must be first. "Therein abide with God." If his situation will not permit God to be first, then he should change the situation, as the cocktail waitress did.

CONCERNING MARRIAGEABLE DAUGHTERS

The discussion for the remainder of this chapter is an answer to the second question which the Corinthians had asked Paul and is related to the first question. Remember that all this must be interpreted in the light of what Corinth was in Paul's day, and then it can be applied to the day in which we live. Corinth was such a corrupt place, and manhood was corrupted there. When womanhood is corrupted, manhood will descend to a low level—

that has always been the story. So there was this question among Christian parents in Corinth: What should they do about their marriageable daughters? Before they were converted, their friends were drunken sots who went up to the temple of Aphrodite to the prostitutes there. What should the single Christian girls do now? Paul will deal with this question.

Now concerning virgins I have no commandment of the Lord: yet I give my judgment, as one that hath obtained mercy of the Lord to be faithful [1 Cor. 7:25].

"Now concerning virgins"—several of the translations have it: "Now concerning virgin *daughters*," which I think clarifies it. That is really what he is talking about here.

This reveals that Paul knew the commandments of the Lord Jesus Christ and what He taught. However, he specifically says here that concerning virgins he has no commandment of the Lord. "But," he says, "I give my own judgment." He is giving his opinion as a capable judge because he had obtained the mercy of God and he wanted to be faithful to God. In other words, he possessed the qualifications a judge should have, as he had told them in chapter 6.

I suppose therefore that this is good for the present distress, I say, that it is good for a man so to be.

Art thou bound unto a wife? seek not to be loosed. Art thou loosed from a wife? seek not a wife [1 Cor. 7:26–27].

"The present distress" was that awful situation in Corinth which Paul knew was not going to continue. Someone asked me, "Do you think this excessive immorality and this lawlessness in our nation will continue?" If it does continue, my friend, it will bring down our houses and destroy our nation—then it will be ended for sure.

Now what does he say? In the present distress, since you have come to Christ at such a difficult time, if you are bound to a wife, stay with her. If she is unsaved, stay with her as long as you can. If you are not married, then, because of the present distress with the tremendous immorality that is here, it would be best for you to remain single. Paul says this is his judgment.

But and if thou marry, thou hast not sinned; and if a virgin marry, she hath

not sinned. Nevertheless such shall have trouble in the flesh: but I spare you [1 Cor. 7:28].

Of course it is not sinful to marry. But the sea of matrimony is rough under the most favorable circumstances. He is trying to save them from much trouble. That reminds me of the country boy who was being married. The preacher said to him, "Wilt thou have this woman to be thy lawfully wedded wife?" The young fellow answered, "I wilt." And I guess he did! In our day we are seeing the shipwreck of a growing number of marriages—even among Christians. The divorces in Southern California are now about equal in number to the marriages. That reveals we also have a "present distress."

Now Paul goes on to discuss other things with them, all in the light of the present distress, the shortness of time, the urgency and immediacy of the hour. He mentions five things which are necessary, which are inevitable, and which are the common experience of mankind in this world. He discusses marriage, sorrow, joy, commerce, and then relation to the world in general.

Marriage is the first one he discusses. "Sure," Paul says in effect, "it is all right to go ahead and marry, but remember that you will have trouble." And they will. In counseling I have tried to tell young people that the romantic period will pass. When the first month's rent comes due and there is not much money in the treasury, believe me, romance flies out the window.

But this I say, brethren, the time is short: it remaineth, that both they that have wives be as though they had none [1 Cor. 7:29].

Paul is saying that in spite of the stress of the times, they are to put God first. If you are married, can you act as if you are not married in that you put God first?

And they that weep, as though they wept not; and they that rejoice, as though they rejoiced not; and they that buy, as though they possessed not [1 Cor. 7:30].

"And they that weep, as though they wept not." Are you going to let some sorrow, some tragedy in your life keep you from serving God?

"And they that rejoice, as though they rejoiced not." Are you going to let pleasure take the place of your relationship to God, as many do?

"And they that buy, as though they possessed not." Will you let your business take the place of God? Many a man has made business his god.

And they that use this world, as not abusing it: for the fashion of this world passeth away [1 Cor. 7:31].

You and I are *in* the world, not *of* the world; but this doesn't mean that we are to walk around with an attitude of touch not, taste not, handle not. We are to use this world. This past summer I made a trip up into the Northwest, and I stopped many times to look upon those glorious forests that they have up there. I used them—they blessed my heart. I enjoyed them. But I didn't fall down and worship any one of those trees! We are to use the things of this world but not abuse them. We are not to substitute them for the Creator.

"The fashion of this world passeth away." Do the things of this life control your life, or does Christ control your life? This is what Paul is talking about.

Now he goes back to a discussion of marriage.

But I would have you without carefulness. He that is unmarried careth for the things that belong to the Lord, how he may please the Lord [1 Cor. 7:32].

Paul now gives some practical observations. The unmarried person doesn't have to worry about changing the baby's diapers or going out to buy food for the family. He or she can give his or her time to the things of God.

But he that is married careth for the things that are of the world, how he may please his wife [1 Cor. 7:33].

The married man tries to please his wife. This is normal and natural, and Paul is not saying it is wrong.

There is difference also between a wife and a virgin. The unmarried woman

careth for the things of the Lord, that she may be holy both in body and in spirit: but she that is married careth for the things of the world, how she may please her husband.

And this I speak for your own profit; not that I may cast a snare upon you, but for that which is comely, and that ye may attend upon the Lord without distraction [1 Cor. 7:34–35].

Paul is making it very clear that the important thing is to put God first. That should be the determining factor for every person in a marriage relationship. I don't care who you are or how spiritual you think you may be, if you are not putting God first in your marriage, then your marriage, my friend, is not the ideal Christian marriage.

He comes back to his judgment that the single person can attend upon the Lord without distraction.

The wife is bound by the law as long as her husband liveth; but if her husband be dead, she is at liberty to be married to whom she will; only in the Lord [1 Cor. 7:39].

That is, she is to marry another Christian, of course.

But she is happier if she so abide, after my judgment: and I think also that I have the Spirit of God [1 Cor. 7:40].

Paul makes it clear again that this is his judgment, his advice. The important thing is to serve God, to put God first in your life. If a person is married, God should still be first in his life. Unfortunately, there are many Christian couples who are compatible—they are not going to the divorce court—but God does not have first place in their marriage.

In deciding your marital status, the most important consideration is not what your Christian friends will say or how society in general will regard you. The question you need to ask yourself is: In what way can I put God first in my life?

CHAPTER 8

THEME: *Christian liberty regarding eating meat*

We are in the section of the epistle dealing with Christian liberty, which extends from chapter 8 to the first verse of chapter 11. It touches on several aspects of Christian liberty. Chapter 8 deals with the problem of whether or not we should eat meat and the liberty that a child of God should have in this particular area.

We need to recognize as we go through this section of the epistle that Paul is writing to the Corinthians and that he has called them carnal, babes in Christ. He deals first with carnalities, and later he will deal with spiritualities. Since it is in the level of carnalities that the contemporary church lives and moves and has its being, this section is pertinent for you and me.

The subject of diet is just as controversial as marriage and divorce. Diet is a fad with many people. (Right at the moment diet is more than a fad with me, because my doctor has put me on a very strict diet.)

Diet generally is an essential part of the ritual of many of the cults and "isms." Many of them have stringent rules about diet. It is interesting that God in the Old Testament gave Israel certain restrictions about eating meat. An edible animal had a parted hoof and chewed the cud. That eliminated the pig whose hoof is parted but does not chew the cud. There were also certain fowl and fish which were designated by name as unfit for food. You can find these listed in the Book of Leviticus and also in Deuteronomy, chapter 14.

A friend of mine, who belonged to a cult that would not eat pork, was discussing this with me one day. So I asked him, "Have you ever eaten ossifrage?" "A what?" "An ossifrage." "Well," he said, "I don't even know what it is." So I told him, "You'd better find out what it is because you may come to my house someday and I might serve you roast ossifrage, which for you would be as wrong to eat as pork." It is amazing that the cults that place such importance on the Old Testament dietary regulations are so ignorant of the actual details.

Why did God give a special diet to Israel? He makes it very clear: "Ye are the children of the LORD your God: ye shall not cut yourselves, nor make any baldness between your eyes for the dead. For thou art an holy people unto the LORD thy God, and the LORD hath

chosen thee to be a peculiar people unto himself, above all the nations that are upon the earth. Thou shalt not eat any abominable thing" (Deut. 14:1–3). Also, I do believe that diet is important for health. God gave Israel foods that were good for them. Even doctors today prescribe diets which exclude certain foods.

The Bible puts up a red light and is very specific on many things which are wrong for us to do. For example, God condemns drunkenness. There can be no argument nor question about that. However, there is a gray area, questionable practices, doubtful things about which the Bible is silent. These are things which are neither black nor white, and the Bible doesn't give us specific instructions. For example: Should a Christian smoke? In the South they think that mixed bathing is wrong and smoking is all right. On the West Coast boys and girls, men and women swim together without compunction, but they condemn smoking. There are different rules which have been put down by certain groups of Christians. They may be good rules or they may be bad rules—I'm not going to argue about that. What I want you to see is the great principle which Paul is laying down here.

There is another preliminary consideration which is an understanding of Corinth in Paul's day. If you do not understand the background, you will miss the whole point of the chapter. It is this: the best place to eat in Corinth was not at the swankiest restaurant; the best place to get good meat was in the meat shop that was run by the temple.

In Corinth the people brought sacrifices of animals to offer to the idols. They would bring the best animals they had. The meat was offered to the idol, but it didn't stay there long because they believed that the spirit of the idol ate the spirit of the animal—and that finished the meal for the idol. Then they took the meat to the shambles or stalls around the temple, which was the meat market where the meat was sold. If you wanted to buy fillet or the best steaks or the best prime rib roast in Corinth, you had to go to one of those shops at the temple to get meat which had been offered to idols.

Some of the Christians in Corinth were offended by this practice and were asking Paul about it. They would be invited out to dinner with another Christian family and would be served a lovely fillet mignon. During the course of the conversation they would say, "My, this is wonderful meat. Where did you get it?" The lady would answer that she got it at the temple meat market. This would offend the couple who felt that it was wrong to eat anything that had been offered to idols. This is the question which Paul discusses in this chapter. Should a Christian eat meat that had been offered to idols? This was a real problem to the people in Corinth, because many of them had come out of that background of idolatry, and they thought it was a compromise with idolatry. Others in the church felt that it made no difference. Let's listen to Paul as he discusses this problem in the city of Corinth.

CHRISTIAN LIBERTY CONCERNING MEAT

Now as touching things offered unto idols, we know that we all have knowledge. Knowledge puffeth up, but charity edifieth.

And if any man think that he knoweth any thing, he knoweth nothing yet as he ought to know [1 Cor. 8:1–2].

Knowlege blows up like a balloon or like an automobile tire. Love doesn't blow up, but it fills up. Love for God and love for others should determine our conduct. Knowledge alone puffs up and tends to make us harsh in our dealings with others. This is a danger with a great many folk who feel that they have a lot of knowledge and yet in reality know very little.

Let me give an illustration. We had just concluded a service at a Bible conference in which six young men had received Christ. A man came to me and insisted that I break away from everyone else and discuss with him the subject of election (he erroneously felt that I had alluded to it in my message). I took a few moments to talk with him until I discovered that he didn't want to discuss it; *he* wanted to tell me what he thought about election. I discovered that he had been reading on that subject recently and that he thought he knew everything about it. As I listened to him, I could picture myself as a young seminary student going into the office of a theological professor to tell him what I thought about election. I thought I was telling him something he didn't know! Well, I don't care what stage of spiritual development you are in today, you don't know everything about any subject—and I don't either. All of us are in the

learning process. Paul could say of himself, "That I may know him, and the power of his resurrection, and the fellowship of his sufferings . . ." (Phil. 3:10). It is the knowledge of Christ which we need above everything else. If the man who wanted to argue about election had been governed by love, he would have been rejoicing over the conversion of these young men and would not have taken me away from folk who needed encouragement and counsel.

Paul is saying that we have a certain knowledge and, because of that certain knowledge, our behavior is governed by it.

But if any man love God, the same is known of him [1 Cor. 8:3].

We ought to be governed by love rather than knowledge.

As concerning therefore the eating of those things that are offered in sacrifice unto idols, we know that an idol is nothing in the world, and that there is none other God but one [1 Cor. 8:4].

After you have come to Christ, after you have the Word of God, you know that an idol is nothing. That is the way Paul spoke of the idols—they are nothing. There is but one God. So he says that the meat that was offered to the idol was not affected. Nothing happened to it. It was not contaminated. In fact, it was prime meat. So the instructed Christian could go there to get his meat and eat it with no problem.

For though there be that are called gods, whether in heaven or in earth, (as there be gods many, and lords many,)

But to us there is but one God, the Father, of whom are all things, and we in him; and one Lord Jesus Christ, by whom are all things, and we by him [1 Cor. 8:5–6].

These idols were merely called gods. As I stood in the ruins of the temple of Apollo in Corinth, I thought of this passage of Scripture. I thought of all the sacrifices that had been offered to that image of Apollo there. It was nothing. The meat was brought in to the idol, put there for a little while, and then it was taken to the meat shop. It didn't make any difference in the meat—the idol was nothing. The instructed Christian knew that. He knew there is but one God, the Father, and that there is but one Lord Jesus Christ. He made all things, and all things belong to Him.

Howbeit there is not in every man that knowledge: for some with conscience of the idol unto this hour eat it as a thing offered unto an idol; and their conscience being weak is defiled [1 Cor. 8:7].

The weak ones, the babes in Christ, the carnal Christians, these were the ones who were offended by the meat offered to idols. They did not have the knowledge. Their consciences bothered them. So they criticized the others who felt at liberty to eat the meat.

May I say that we still find the same thing today. We have people who call themselves separated Christians. They think they are being very spiritual when, actually, they are revealing that they don't have the knowledge. They are the ones who say you can't do this and that. They are the ones who are offended at Christians who use their Christian liberty. They are like the Christians at Corinth who were offended when they were served meat offered to idols and said, "Oh, no, we are separated. We won't touch that meat." That kind of separation is not due to spirituality; it is due to ignorance.

Now Paul lays down a great principle:

But meat commendeth us not to God: for neither, if we eat, are we the better; neither, if we eat not, are we the worse [1 Cor. 8:8].

Meat has nothing to do with our relationship to God.

You will remember that Simon Peter had trouble with this. He had been brought up to consider certain things unclean according to the Mosaic Law. When the sheet came down from heaven in his vision and the Lord told Peter to arise and eat, Peter refused. He said, ". . . Not so, Lord; for I have never eaten any thing that is common or unclean" (Acts 10:14). (He calls Him Lord at the same time that he is failing to obey Him.) Then the Lord said, ". . . What God hath cleansed, that call not thou common" (Acts 10:15). In other words, God is no longer making the distinction between the clean and the unclean animals. That is passed. Now we can eat any animal that we wish to eat.

Down in San Antonio, Texas, they can rattlesnake meat. Now if you are going to have rattlesnake for dinner, please don't invite me to come over. This has nothing to do with religious scruples, but it has a lot to do with a weak stomach.

Paul has stated a great principle here. Meat does not commend you to God. You may do as you please in such matters. This is the liberty that a believer has.

But take heed lest by any means this liberty of yours become a stumblingblock to them that are weak [1 Cor. 8:9].

Now it is not a question of its being right or wrong to eat meat. It is a concern for others. You have the liberty to eat the meat if you want to. But what about your concern for others? You have the knowledge, but what about your love? Do you have love for your weak brother? Are you concerned how this will affect him?

For if any man see thee which hast knowledge sit at meat in the idol's temple, shall not the conscience of him which is weak be emboldened to eat those things which are offered to idols [1 Cor. 8:10].

The reason many of us who are in Christian service do not do certain things is so that we may not offend others. Let me give an illustration. There was a time when I loved to dance. In fact, I was chairman of the dance committee of an organization before I accepted Christ. After I started studying for the ministry, I gave up dancing.

In college the president of the ministerial students was also president of the student body, and he was active in promoting dancing. Knowing I had been chairman of a dance committee, he tried to get me to help him. I told him, "No. I can't do that." I am not going to argue if it was right or wrong, because it is not a question of knowledge. There are many things I am at liberty to do which I do not do. Why? Well, my decision is on the basis of love. I do not want to hurt my weak brother. Because of my example, he might be out there on the floor dancing the fandango—or whatever they dance today—and I don't want to be responsible for drawing him away from the Lord. He is a weak brother.

And through thy knowledge shall the weak brother perish, for whom Christ died? [1 Cor. 8:11].

You see, we operate on a different principle. It is not a question of an activity being right or wrong. It is a question of its effect on that weak brother or upon your neighbor. You see, knowledge, after all is a very dangerous thing.

But when ye sin so against the brethren, and wound their weak conscience, ye sin against Christ [1 Cor. 8:12].

When we are responsible for a believer falling away from Christ, we are affecting Christ Himself.

Wherefore, if meat make my brother to offend, I will eat no flesh while the world standeth, lest I make my brother to offend [1 Cor. 8:13].

Here is the motivation for action on these things. Paul will go over this same principle again in chapter 10, "All things are lawful for me, but all things are not expedient: all things are lawful for me, but all things edify not" (1 Cor. 10:23).

There is no point in arguing about whether something is right or wrong. It is a question of the effect upon the weak brother. It is not a question of knowledge. All things are lawful for me. The liberty of the Christian is not pinned down by legality. He is not circumscribed by rules of conduct. His liberty is limited by love. His motivation should be not to offend the brother but to be a blessing to him. That is how to determine Christian conduct. That is the motivation for Christian conduct. My knowledge can tell me that it is perfectly all right for me to do something, but my love for the weak brother will keep me from doing it.

CHAPTER 9

THEME: *Christian liberty regarding service for Christ*

In chapter 8 Paul dealt with the matter of Christian liberty in regard to eating meat which had been offered to idols. The principle he laid down was that in doubtful matters the motive for Christian conduct was regard for fellow believers. We won't do anything which causes a weak brother to stumble.

This shows us that there is a limitation on our Christian liberty. This can be stated in a graphic way. You have a perfect right to swing your fist any way you want to, but where my nose begins your liberty ends.

Paul lays down this principle several times in the Epistle to the Corinthians. "All things are lawful unto me, but all things are not expedient: all things are lawful for me, but I will not be brought under the power of any" (1 Cor. 6:12). "But meat commendeth us not to God: for neither, if we eat, are we the better; neither, if we eat not, are we the worse" (1 Cor. 8:8). "All things are lawful for me, but all things are not expedient: all things are lawful for me, but all things edify not" (1 Cor. 10:23). He goes on to say that no man should seek his own, but every man should seek the good of his neighbor. Christian liberty has its limitations for this reason.

Now Paul is going to illustrate this matter of Christian liberty in another field. He will discuss his own right as an apostle, his official right. Then he will discuss his right to be supported by the church. He had the right to expect the church to care for him and all his needs as a preacher of the gospel. He uses these personal matters to illustrate Christian liberty.

Paul first defends his official right as an apostle. Paul was in the habit of defending his apostleship because it was challenged in many places.

Am I not an apostle? am I not free? have I not seen Jesus Christ our Lord? are not ye my work in the Lord? [1 Cor. 9:1].

"Am I not an apostle?" Of course the answer is, "Yes, Paul, you are an apostle." The way this question is couched in the Greek demands a positive answer.

"Am I not free?" The answer is, "Yes, Paul, you are free."

"Have I not seen Jesus Christ our Lord?" One qualification of an apostle was that he had personally seen Jesus Christ. Paul had satisfied that requirement.

"Are not ye my work in the Lord?" The Corinthian believers were the evidence of his apostleship.

If I be not an apostle unto others, yet doubtless I am to you: for the seal of mine apostleship are ye in the Lord [1 Cor. 9:2].

"If I be not an apostle unto others"—but he was an apostle to others. The "if" is the *if* of condition.

"Yet doubtless I am to you: for the seal of mine apostleship are ye in the Lord."

As far as the Corinthian church was concerned, he didn't have to defend his apostleship. It was evident to the Christians there that he was an apostle.

Mine answer to them that do examine me is this,

Have we not power to eat and to drink? [1 Cor. 9:3–4].

The word for "answer" in the Greek really means *defense*. It is as if Paul were in court and were being charged concerning his apostleship. He is giving his defense to those who examine him. What is his defense?

"Have we not power to eat and to drink?" As an apostle of the Lord Jesus Christ, Paul had a right to eat and to drink. As an apostle he had that liberty. However, that liberty is curbed and curtailed by others. He had made the bold declaration, "Wherefore, if meat make my brother to offend, I will eat no flesh while the world standeth, lest I make my brother to offend" (1 Cor. 8:13). He had the right to eat meat, but he was not going to eat meat. Now that is an exercise of free will, isn't it? It is free will to be able to do something and then choose not to do it. In a sense, that is a higher liberty, perhaps the highest liberty that there is. If you cannot do something, you do not do it; there is no exercise of free will in that. But if you are able to do something and then choose not to do it, that is a revelation of your free will.

Have we not power to lead about a sister, a wife, as well as other apostles, and as the brethren of the Lord, and Cephas? [1 Cor. 9:5].

Evidently "the brethren of the Lord" refers to the half brothers of Jesus, James and Jude, who were apparently married. And Peter was married. They took their wives with them when they went out on their missionary journeys. Paul says that he has the same freedom, but he chose not to have a wife because he felt his ministry would be curtailed and hindered.

Today in Bible conference work if you take your wife, they wonder whether you can't go anywhere without her. If you don't take your wife, they wonder what is wrong. A preacher is in a bad way. When my daughter was growing up, my wife stayed at home to take care of her, and I would go alone to the Bible conferences. I would be quizzed by some of the curious saints and I would have to go into detail to explain why Mrs. McGee wasn't with me. Now my daughter is grown and married, so my wife goes everywhere with me. Every now and then one of the saints asks, "Does your wife go with you *all* the time?" as if to say, "Can't you ever get away from her?" In the ministry you will be questioned regardless of what you do.

Paul faced this same sort of thing. Paul says that he has the right to take a wife with him— he has that liberty—but he has made his decision to remain single. After all, he was a pioneer missionary, and his was a very rugged life.

Or I only and Barnabas, have not we power to forbear working? [1 Cor. 9:6].

He is saying that he and Barnabas could stay home if they wished. In other words, "We don't have to go as missionaries—our salvation wouldn't be affected if we stayed home."

Now he is going to get around to this matter of paying the preacher.

Who goeth a warfare any time at his own charges? who planteth a vineyard, and eateth not of the fruit thereof? or who feedeth a flock, and eateth not of the milk of the flock?

Say I these things as a man? or saith not the law the same also?

For it is written in the law of Moses, Thou shalt not muzzle the mouth of the ox that treadeth out the corn. Doth God take care for oxen? [1 Cor. 9:7–9].

In those days an ox was used to tread out the corn. They hitched the ox to a horizontal wheel, and he walked around in a circle over the grain. This separated the grain from the chaff. Then the chaff was pitched up into the air so the wind would blow it away, and the good grain would fall down onto the threshing floor. God said they were not to muzzle the ox that was treading out the grain. Why? He was working and was to be permitted to eat the grain as he worked. That was the way God took care of the ox—He made that a law. The application is that the preacher is not to be muzzled. He is to be fed for his work.

I heard a story about a preacher in Kentucky who drove a very fine, beautiful horse, but the preacher himself was a very skinny fellow. One day one of his church officers asked him the question (which had been a matter of discussion), "How is it, preacher, that your horse is so fine looking and you are such a skinny fellow?" The preacher answered, "I will tell you. I feed my horse, and you are the ones who feed me."

God says not to muzzle the ox that is working for you, and Paul applies that principle to pastors and teachers. God not only cares for oxen, He cares for preachers. Paul is saying that he, as an apostle who has fed others, has a right to be fed.

Or saith he it altogether for our sakes? For our sakes, no doubt, this is written: that he that ploweth should plow in hope; and that he that thresheth in hope should be partaker of his hope.

If we have sown unto you spiritual things, is it a great thing if we shall reap your carnal things? [1 Cor. 9:10–11].

Paul mentions this again in the Epistle to the Galatians. If folk have given you spiritual blessings, spiritual riches, then you should share your carnal blessings with them. I heard Torrey Johnson down in Bibletown in Florida say several times—and I think it is a good principle—that you ought to support the place where you get your blessing. Suppose you go down to eat at a certain restaurant. You don't walk down the street and around the corner into another restaurant to pay your bill; you pay the restaurant that fed you. Yet many people do that sort of thing with their spiritual food. They get their spiritual blessings in one place, and they give their offerings in another place.

If others be partakers of this power over you, are not we rather? Nevertheless we have not used this power; but suffer all things, lest we should hinder the gospel of Christ [1 Cor. 9:12].

Paul has a right to be supported for his work. Yet, he doesn't want to do anything that would hinder the gospel of Christ. Therefore he doesn't receive any remuneration; he supports himself by plying his trade, which is tentmaking.

In our day there are many religious rackets. To say there are not is to be as blind as a bat. Unfortunately, there are men who make merchandise of the gospel of Christ—there is no doubt about it. However, it is God's method that those who have a spiritual ministry are to be supported by those who benefit.

Do ye not know that they which minister about holy things live of the things of the temple? and they which wait at the altar are partakers with the altar? [1 Cor. 9:13].

That is God's method.

Even so hath the Lord ordained that they which preach the gospel should live of the gospel [1 Cor. 9:14].

It is not wrong for the minister who has been a blessing to his people to be supported by the people. I have discovered that, when people receive a blessing, for the most part they will support the place where they get their blessing.

But I have used none of these things: neither have I written these things, that it should be so done unto me: for it were better for me to die, than that any man should make my glorying void [1 Cor. 9:15].

You see, Paul did not take a salary. He was able to say that the church in Corinth was not supporting him; he didn't receive anything from them. Paul supported himself by tentmaking.

For though I preach the gospel, I have nothing to glory of: for necessity is laid upon me; yea, woe is unto me, if I preach not the gospel! [1 Cor. 9:16].

I understand Paul's feeling. To be frank with you, necessity is laid on me also. I dare not stop giving out the Word of God. Of course, I would not lose my salvation if I stopped, but I continue because I feel an inner compulsion, and also I love to teach and preach the gospel.

For if I do this thing willingly, I have a reward: but if against my will, a dispensation of the gospel is committed unto me.

What is my reward then? Verily that, when I preach the gospel, I may make the gospel of Christ without charge, that I abuse not my power in the gospel [1 Cor. 9:17–18].

Paul did not preach the gospel for an ulterior motive and neither do I. Yet God has promised a reward. I know we will not be disappointed.

For though I be free from all men, yet have I made myself servant unto all, that I might gain the more [1 Cor. 9:19].

He had the freedom to make himself a servant!

Now he gives this very familiar testimony of his own ministry.

And unto the Jews I became as a Jew, that I might gain the Jews; to them that are under the law, as under the law, that I might gain them that are under the law;

To them that are without law, as without law, (being not without law to God, but under the law to Christ,) that I might gain them that are without law.

To the weak became I as weak, that I might gain the weak: I am made all things to all men, that I might by all means save some.

And this I do for the gospel's sake, that I might be partaker thereof with you [1 Cor. 9:20–23].

Paul says, "I'm doing all of this because I am out on the racetrack. I am like an athlete out there running." Running for what? A prize.

Know ye not that they which run in a race run all, but one receiveth the prize? So run, that ye may obtain [1 Cor. 9:24].

In an athletic event, only one can come in first. But in the spiritual race all of us can win the prize if we are getting out the Word of God.

And every man that striveth for the mastery is temperate in all things. Now

they do it to obtain a corruptible crown; but we an incorruptible [1 Cor. 9:25].

The awards that God gives won't swell your bank account down here and remain here when you leave; they will be for your eternal enrichment.

I therefore so run, not as uncertainly; so fight I, not as one that beateth the air [1 Cor. 9:26].

Paul says that he is not just shadowboxing. He is not just playing at this thing. He is not playing church. This is real.

But I keep under my body, and bring it into subjection: lest that by any means, when I have preached to others, I myself should be a castaway [1 Cor. 9:27].

The translation "castaway" is unfortunate. The Greek word is *adokimos*, which means "not approved." Paul is thinking of the judgment seat of Christ where the rewards are given. In his Second Epistle to the Corinthians he will talk about the fact that we shall all appear before the judgment seat of Christ where awards are given. Paul says that he is out on that racetrack trying to run so that he will get a reward. That is the reason he preaches the gospel as he does. Paul has liberty. This is the choice that he has made.

I think every Christian ought to work for a reward. We do not work for salvation; that is a gift given by the grace of God. My friend, if you are going to get a reward, you will have to work for it. If you are going to get a reward, then you had better get out on the racetrack and start moving.

CHAPTER 10

THEME: *Liberty is not license*

We are still in the section concerning Christian liberty, which extends through this chapter and into the first verse of chapter 11. We are going to see another area of liberty illustrated through the nation Israel.

Moreover, brethren, I would not that ye should be ignorant, how that all our fathers were under the cloud, and all passed through the sea [1 Cor. 10:1].

"Moreover, brethren" ties into the last verse of chapter 9. Paul had just been saying that he did not want to be disapproved at the judgment seat of Christ, but he wanted to receive a reward.

"I would not that ye should be ignorant." When Paul writes that, you can be sure that the brethren were ignorant or unaware of something he is going to explain to them.

The church in Corinth was a mixed church;

that is, it was made up of both Jews and Gentiles. Today a Jewish Christian is somewhat unusual, but in that day a Gentile Christian was more unusual, since the first Christians were Jews.

When Paul says, "All our fathers," he is speaking to the Jewish part of the congregation. They, along with Paul, were Israelites and shared the same history.

"Our fathers were under the cloud, and all passed through the sea" refers, of course, to the time when the people of Israel were escaping from Egyptian bondage and crossed the Red Sea.

And were all baptized unto Moses in the cloud and in the sea;

And did all eat the same spiritual meat;

And did all drink the same spiritual drink: for they drank of that spiritual Rock that followed them: and that Rock was Christ.

But with many of them God was not well pleased: for they were overthrown in the wilderness [1 Cor. 10:2–5].

"Many of them" is in the Greek "*most* of them."

This shows how far a person can go and still not be a believer. It reveals the wonderful liberty the Israelites had when they crossed the Red Sea. The Mosaic Law had not been given at that time; so they were not under law. They had great liberty, but they abused that liberty. Privilege is no insurance against ultimate failure. Many a rich man's son has had to learn that. It has also been learned by many men who had certain privileges granted them in the political realm or in the business world or in the social world.

They "were under the cloud"—that is, they had guidance. They all passed safely through the sea.

They "were all baptized unto Moses." Here we come again to that word *baptized*. *Baptized* can mean many things. I have a classical Greek lexicon which gives twenty meanings for the Greek word *baptizō*. Our translators never did translate the word; they merely transliterated it. They simply took the word out of the Greek and gave it an English spelling. Therefore, to try to say exactly what the writer had in mind is difficult, because the translators did not attempt to do that. They just spelled the word out. A great many folk have dogmatically narrowed down the word to one meaning.

Now *baptizō* means to "identify." In fact, water baptism has that meaning, as it speaks of our identification with Christ. We are buried with Him by baptism—by the baptism of the Holy Spirit—that is what the baptism of the Holy Spirit is. He identifies us with the body of Christ—He puts us into the body as a member. "For by one Spirit are we all baptized into one body" (1 Cor. 12:13). Paul will deal with this in chapter 12.

But here we have the statement that they were "baptized unto Moses." How were they baptized unto Moses? Don't try to tell me that Moses had a baptismal service at the Red Sea and baptized them, because, actually, they did not get wet at all! The record in Exodus tells us that they went through the sea on dry ground. When God dried up the Red Sea for them, He dried it up—they didn't get wet at all. They went over on dry land. The folk who really got wet were the Egyptians. They were soaked through and through. So obviously when it says they were baptized unto Moses, he is not talking about water. Neither is it the baptism of the Holy Spirit, because it says they were baptized unto *Moses*. Well, it simply means that they were *identified* with Moses. Hebrews 11:29 says, "By faith they passed through the Red sea as by dry land: which the Egyptians assaying to do were drowned." The children of Israel were identified with Moses. By faith they passed through the Red Sea. Whose faith was it? It wasn't their faith. They had none. Read the story in Exodus—they wanted to go back to Egypt, and they were blaming Moses for bringing them out into that awful wilderness. It was *Moses* who had the faith. It was *Moses* who went down to the water and smote the Red Sea as God had commanded. It was *Moses* who led them across on dry ground. When they got to the other side, they sang the song of Moses (see Exod. 15). What a song it was! The people of Israel were identified with Moses.

All of this is a picture of our salvation. Christ went through the waters of death. And we are brought through by His death, identified with Him, and now identified with a living Savior, baptized into Christ. That is the way baptism saves us. When we trust Christ, the baptism of the Holy Spirit puts us in Christ.

Water baptism illustrates this and is very important, but it is merely ritual baptism. *Real* baptism is the work of the Holy Spirit.

Now the people of Israel were baptized unto Moses, and they were able to cross the Red

Sea. "And did all eat the same spiritual meat"—the manna. "And did all drink the same spiritual drink: for they drank of that spiritual Rock that followed them: and that Rock was Christ"—that is, it sets forth Christ.

"But with most of them God was not well pleased: for they were overthrown in the wilderness."

Why was all of this recorded for us? Paul tells us the reason:

Now these things were our examples, to the intent we should not lust after evil things, as they also lusted [1 Cor. 10:6].

The first five verses give us the illustration of the liberty that these people enjoyed as a nation. Now in this very searching section we learn that these people abused their liberty. He makes an application of that for us. It happened to them for examples unto us. This was written for you and for me, and so we ought to pay close attention to it. The Israelites had this wonderful liberty, and what did they do with it?

It says that they lusted after evil things. What were those things? Well, we can turn back and see: "And the mixed multitude that was among them fell a-lusting: and the children of Israel also wept again, and said, Who shall give us flesh to eat? We remember the fish, which we did eat in Egypt freely; the cucumbers, and the melons, and the leeks, and the onions, and the garlick: But now our soul is dried away: there is nothing at all, beside this manna, before our eyes" (Num. 11:4–6). They lusted, we are told, after *evil* things. What was wrong with leeks, onions, and garlic? Well, if they ate those things they wouldn't be very desirable companions, but the point is that they lusted for that which was outside the will of God for them. This was the beginning of their defection.

Have you noticed how many times it is desire that leads to sin? It started back in the Garden of Eden. "And when the woman saw that the tree was good for food, and that it was pleasant to the eyes, and a tree to be desired to make one wise, she took of the fruit thereof, and did eat, and gave also unto her husband with her; and he did eat" (Gen. 3:6). It was the desire for something outside the will of God. What is desire, after all? Psychologists talk about inhibitions and prohibitions, and they speak of desire as the supreme thing in life. What is desire? In these instances it was to want that which was outside of the will of God.

It wasn't God's will for them to have those things at that particular time.

Neither be ye idolaters, as were some of them; as it is written, The people sat down to eat and drink, and rose up to play [1 Cor. 10:7].

An idol is anything in your life that you put in the place of God.

Neither let us commit fornication, as some of them committed, and fell in one day three and twenty thousand.

Neither let us tempt Christ, as some of them also tempted, and were destroyed of serpents.

Neither murmur ye, as some of them also murmured, and were destroyed of the destroyer [1 Cor. 10:8–10].

Paul lists some of the sins of the people. These people had continually murmured and complained against God. This is an illustration of those who want those things that are outside the will of God. God always has something good for His people. That was true then, and it is still true now. But they constantly wanted something that was beyond God's will for them.

Now all these things happened unto them for ensamples: and they are written for our admonition, upon whom the ends of the world are come [1 Cor. 10:11].

We are to learn a lesson from all this. We do have Christian liberty, but our desires are to be according to the will of God. That is so important for us to see.

Wherefore let him that thinketh he standeth take heed lest he fall [1 Cor. 10:12].

It makes no difference who you are, you could fall today. It would be very easy for any one of us to blunder and stumble and fall. One can be a mature Christian, a real saint, and still fall. Therefore, you and I need to be very careful that we stay in the realm of the will of God where we are not quenching the Spirit of God in our lives.

There hath no temptation taken you but such as is common to man: but God is faithful, who will not suffer you to be tempted above that ye are able; but will with the temptation also make a way to

escape, that ye may be able to bear it [1 Cor. 10:13].

A great many people feel that nobody has ever been tempted as they are tempted. My friend, no matter what temptation you experience, there have been others who have had the same kind of temptation. The encouraging thing is that God will make a way of escape for you. God is faithful; He will not let you be tempted beyond what you can endure.

Dr. Hutton used to say it like this: "God always makes a way of escape and sometimes the way of escape is the king's highway and a good pair of heels." In other words, let the Devil see your heels—run as hard as you can to get away from the temptation. One of the reasons we yield to temptation is that we are like the little boy in the pantry. His mother heard a noise because he had taken down the cookie jar. She said, "Willie, where are you?" He answered that he was in the pantry. "What are you doing there?" He said, "I'm fighting temptation." My friend, that is not the place to fight temptation! That is the place to start running.

Wherefore, my dearly beloved, flee from idolatry.

I speak as to wise men; judge ye what I say [1 Cor. 10:14–15].

Idolatry was a temptation in Corinth. Idolatry may not be a temptation to you, but the Bible tells us that covetousness is idolatry. There is a lot of that around today.

Paul is going on to teach that fellowship at the Lord's Table requires separation.

The cup of blessing which we bless, is it not the communion of the blood of Christ? The bread which we break, is it not the communion of the body of Christ?

For we being many are one bread, and one body: for we are all partakers of that one bread.

Behold Israel after the flesh: are not they which eat of the sacrifices partakers of the altar?

What say I then? that the idol is any thing, or that which is offered in sacrifice to idols is any thing? [1 Cor. 10:16–19].

Paul's argument here is quite logical. He says that an idol is nothing. So if you offer meat to an idol, it is nothing—the meat is not affected at all.

But I say, that the things which the Gentiles sacrifice, they sacrifice to devils, and not to God: and I would not that ye should have fellowship with devils [1 Cor. 10:20].

Paul is still talking about Christian liberty. Although the idol is nothing, behind the idol is demonism—Paul recognizes this.

Ye cannot drink the cup of the Lord, and the cup of devils: ye cannot be partakers of the Lord's table, and of the table of devils [1 Cor. 10:21].

That is, for some people to eat meat which had been sacrificed to idols *would* be idolatry. A believer would have to examine his heart very carefully.

Do we provoke the Lord to jealousy? are we stronger than he? [1 Cor. 10:22].

Paul now comes back to what he said at the very beginning of this section on Christian liberty.

All things are lawful for me, but all things are not expedient: all things are lawful for me, but all things edify not [1 Cor. 10:23].

Paul says that he has the freedom to do these questionable things, things on which the Bible is silent as to their being right or wrong. For example, I think Paul would say, "If I felt that I should go to the games, I would go." I think Paul must have attended the great Olympic events which took place in his day, because many of his illustrations are taken from athletic events that were carried on in the great Colosseum and stadiums of that day. Paul says all such things are lawful for him, but all things are not expedient because of the fact that the thing he could do might hurt a weak believer. He says, "All things are lawful for me, but all things edify not." That is, they don't "build *me* up in the faith."

A young preacher once asked me, "Do you think a preacher ought to go to ball games?" He knew I didn't go. I said this to him, "Although I always enjoyed participating in all athletic events, I've never been much of a spectator at any of them. I don't have much interest in watching somebody else play football or baseball, especially when they are being paid for it. I always played for fun and enjoyed it. However, when I was in school, I read a very helpful book which pointed out that a preacher should confine his life to that which he can use in his ministry—what he sees, where he goes, what he experiences—because his total life is his ministry. Everything should be grist for his mill. In other words, a minister should take into the pulpit his entire life (he is not to have a hidden part) and be able to use all of it." So I said to him regarding baseball, "If you can use the baseball game—and you can—there would be nothing wrong in your going. You could draw many good illustrations from a baseball game. However, it might not be expedient for you to go because it might have a bad influence on someone else."

So Paul lays down this guideline:

Let no man seek his own, but every man another's wealth [1 Cor. 10:24].

The Christian has a tremendous liberty in Christ. However, we are to seek the welfare of the other man. So a Christian's life should not be primarily directed and dictated by liberty. Liberty is limited by love. A Christian is not pinned down by legality; he is not circumscribed by strict rules. He is limited by love. He should be concerned about his influence and effect on others. That is the thought which Paul has here.

Whatsoever is sold in the shambles, that eat, asking no question for conscience sake:

For the earth is the Lord's, and the fulness thereof [1 Cor. 10:25–26].

The Christian can enjoy all the things of God's creation—the beauties of it and the produce of it. The Lord has provided it.

Now Paul is going to give a very practical suggestion. He says that when you go out to eat, don't say to your host, "This is a very lovely steak that you have here today. Where did you get it? My butcher doesn't have meat like this to sell to the public." Then your friend may tell you that he went to the temple to buy the meat. The best thing to do is not to ask where the meat came from.

Now Paul gives a very practical illustration:

If any of them that believe not bid you to a feast, and ye be disposed to go; whatsoever is set before you, eat, asking no question for conscience sake [1 Cor. 10:27].

If you are invited to the home of an unbeliever, go and eat whatever is put before you. Don't ask any questions.

But if any man say unto you, This is offered in sacrifice unto idols, eat not

for his sake that shewed it, and for conscience sake: for the earth is the Lord's, and the fulness thereof [1 Cor. 10:28].

Now there is another principle involved, and this is an entirely new matter. Paul has advised to eat everything and ask no questions. But suppose there is someone else at the table who sees you eat the meat and says, "This meat has been offered to idols." In that case you should not eat the meat—not because eating it is wrong, but because it is obvious it may harm the person who pointed it out to you. It is not because of your conscience but because of *his* conscience that you should not eat the meat. There is no rule that you should not eat the meat. But out of your love, out of your desire to help that brother whose conscience is bothered, you should not eat the meat. That is the whole point.

Let me illustrate this. Down in Georgia they have a berry that is called a scuppernong. It is similar to a grape, but it grows singly on a vine. They make wine out of it. A friend of mine told me that he went to preach in a certain church and was invited out to dinner by one of the church officers. He was handed a glass of scuppernong. He didn't know what it was, but he tasted of it. He realized that it had an alcoholic content—he is not a super pious individual, but he put the glass down. His host said to him, "What's the matter? Don't you like it?" He said, "I think it is delicious, but I noticed that it is wine, and I feel that I as a Christian should not drink it." Well, that created a tense moment, but he got his point across. I feel that he did the right thing.

The question would arise: did that minister have as much right to drink it as the elder did? He did—there's no question about that. But he also had a testimony, which is the reason he did not drink it. So many Christians are harsh in their dealing with others because their motive is legality—"I don't do this, and you shouldn't do it." However, if their motive were love, the approach would be altogether different. Love for the other believer should be the motive in the Christian's conduct.

Conscience, I say, not thine own, but of the other: for why is my liberty judged of another man's conscience? [1 Cor. 10:29].

Why should I be restricted by some of these weak brethren?

For if I by grace be a partaker, why am I evil spoken of for that for which I give thanks? [1 Cor. 10:30].

Paul asks, "Isn't it unfair to judge me because of another man's conscience?" He answers by stating a great principle:

Whether therefore ye eat, or drink, or whatsoever ye do, do all to the glory of God [1 Cor. 10:31].

Paul has stated certain great principles that relate to Christian liberty. One of those principles is: "All things are lawful for me, but all things are not expedient." Also, "all things are lawful for me, but all things edify not." Now here is another one: "Whether therefore ye eat, or drink, or whatsoever ye do, do all to the glory of God." This is the test every believer should apply to his life. Not "should I do this, or should I do that," but "can I do it for the glory of God?" Unfortunately, there are Christians who don't even go to church for the glory of God. They go for some other reason—maybe to criticize or to gossip. With a motive like that it is better to stay at home. Whatever a believer does should be done for the glory of God. That is very important.

Give none offence, neither to the Jews, nor to the Gentiles, nor to the church of God [1 Cor. 10:32].

Here Paul divides the whole world into three groups: Jews, Gentiles, and church of God. Some of these folks have differing beliefs. An example would be the Jewish abhorrence of pork. It would certainly give offense to invite a Jewish friend for dinner and serve him ham. A believer should love other people enough so that his actions will not offend them. There are a lot of Gentiles who have peculiar notions, too. It would be impossible to please all of them, but we should try not to offend those with whom we have contact. Neither should we offend those who are of the church of God. Some young people who were rebelling against "the establishment" came to me and said they had attended a certain church and were rebuked because of the way they dressed. They asked me if I thought the members of that church were all wrong. I told them I thought that both groups were wrong. Neither acted in love. The members of the church were wrong in criticizing them before others. On the other hand, these young folk knew

their clothes and hair would be an offense to the members of the church. So none of them showed love toward the other. We are told that we are not to offend either the Jews, the Gentiles, or the church of God. This includes the entire human family. These are the three divisions of the human family today, but one of these days the church of God is going to leave this earth. Then there will be only the Jews and Gentiles in the world, and God has a tremendous program which will take place at that time.

Even as I please all men in all things, not seeking mine own profit, but the profit of many, that they may be saved [1 Cor. 10:33].

Now primarily what we do we are to do for the glory of God—"Whether therefore ye eat, or drink, or whatsoever ye do, do all to the glory of God." A Christian woman can wash dishes and sweep the floor to the glory of God. A Christian man can mow the lawn and dig a ditch for the glory of God. Regardless of what you are doing, if you cannot do it for the glory of God, you should not be doing it. As we live like this we are a testimony to the world—that those who are lost might be saved.

Friend, it is more important for us to make tracks in the world than to give out tracts. A zealous man in Memphis, Tennessee, was handing out tracts to everyone. He handed a tract to a man, but he would not accept it. He asked, "What is that?" "A tract," was the answer. "I can't read," said the man, "but I'll tell you what I'll do, I'll just watch your tracks." That is much more impressive. People read our tracks in life better than they read tracts that we hand out. It is a good thing to give out tracts, but along with them we must also make the right kind of tracks.

Now the first verse of chapter 11 belongs in this division:

Be ye followers of me, even as I also am of Christ [1 Cor. 11:1].

This is something that very few of us can say. Well, I shouldn't include *you*, but it is something that I dare not say. I want you to be a follower of Christ and a follower of Paul—but don't follow me in everything. What a tremendous testimony Paul gives in that statement!

CHAPTER 11

THEME: Women's dress; the Lord's Table

We have concluded the section concerning Christian liberty, which extended from chapter 8 to the first verse of this chapter. Now Paul is dealing with other matters about which the Corinthian church had written him.

Someone is probably saying, "Do you mean to say that God is giving instructions regarding trivialities like a woman's dress? Certainly God cannot be concerned with what a woman wears or whether a man gets a hair cut!" Well, the Bible makes it clear that God is interested in what we are wearing and how we fix our hair. God says, "But the very hairs of your head are all numbered" (Matt. 10:30). This idea that only your hairdresser knows is not true; God knows, my friend. He has a great deal to say about these and related subjects. The most intimate details of our lives are under His inspection. There is probably no single item that takes up more space in newspapers, magazines, radio time, and television time than what men and women wear. The Word of God has some things to say about that, too.

WOMEN'S DRESS

Now I praise you, brethren, that ye remember me in all things, and keep the ordinances, as I delivered them to you [1 Cor. 11:2].

Up to this point he had said, "I praise you not," but here Paul has an item of praise for them. He praises them because they have remembered him in prayer and in their giving, and they were practicing the ordinances he had taught them.

But I would have you know, that the head of every man is Christ; and the head of the woman is the man; and the head of Christ is God [1 Cor. 11:3].

I realize full well that there are people today who like to emphasize the middle statement: "the head of the woman is the man." But, my friend, when you put all these statements together, you don't come up with a lopsided viewpoint. Paul is putting down another great principle here: This is authority for the sake of order, to eliminate confusion.

This principle is important in the church as well as in the home. Several years ago a pastor was having trouble in his church, and I asked him what the problem was. He said it was that he had too many chiefs and not enough In-dians—everyone wanted to be a leader. Today we find churches which have courses in leadership training. I'd like to know where you find that in the Bible. There are organizations which exist solely for the purpose of training young people to be public speakers. Paul says we are to "study to be quiet" (1 Thess. 4:11). I wish we could put the emphasis where the Bible puts it. We don't need all this leadership training. We need folk who will act and live like Christians. That is the important thing.

The important word here is *head.* "The head of every man is Christ; and the head of the woman is the man; and the head of Christ is God." The head is that portion of the body that gives the direction.

This verse does not say that the head of every *Christian* man is Christ. The word *man* is generic—it is a general item. It says the head of *every* man is Christ. It is the normal and correct order for Christ to be the head of every man. Until a man is mastered by Christ, he is not a normal man. Some men are mastered by drink; some are mastered by passion; most are mastered by the flesh. Every man should be mastered by *Christ.* Augustine said, "The heart of man is restless until it finds its rest in thee" (*Confessions,* Bk. 1, sec. 1). The heart of man is restless until he makes Christ the head. Men who have accomplished great things for God have done this. I think of Martin Luther and Wilberforce and Augustine who were profligate until they were mastered by Christ. I hear it said of a man today, "He is a Christian man." Is he mastered by Christ? That is the important thing, and that is what Paul is saying.

"The head of the woman is man"—there is no article in the Greek, it is not *the* man. Notice it is not *every* woman; it is not an absolute. It refers to marriage where the woman is to respond to the man. It is normal for the woman to be subject to the man in marriage. If a woman cannot look up to a man and respect him, she ought not to follow him and surely ought not to marry him. But a real woman responds with every fiber of her being to the man she loves. He, in turn, must be the man who is willing to *die* for her—"Husbands, love your wives, even as Christ also loved the church, and gave himself for it" (Eph. 5:25).

Dr. G. Campbell Morgan told about a friend of his and his wife's who was a very brilliant woman. She had a strong personality, was an outstanding person, and was not married. He asked her one day the pointed question, "Why have you never married?" Her answer was, "I have never found a man who could master me." So she never married. May I say that until a woman finds that man, she would make a mistake to get married. If she marries a Mr. Milquetoast, she will be in trouble from that day on.

"The head of Christ is God." There is a great mystery here. Jesus said, "I and my Father are one" (John 10:30), but He also said, ". . . for my Father is greater than I" (John 14:28). In the work of redemption, He voluntarily took a lower place and was made lower than the angels. He walked a lowly path down here. We are admonished, "Let this mind be in you, which was also in Christ Jesus: Who, being in the form of God, thought it not robbery to be equal with God: But made himself of no reputation, and took upon him the form of a servant, and was made in the likeness of men" (Phil. 2:5–7).

Now Paul is going to apply this principle of headship to the situation in Corinth. An unveiled woman in Corinth was a prostitute. The situation in your church or in your community may be different than it was in Corinth, but there is a principle here and it still applies today.

Every man praying or prophesying, having his head covered, dishonoureth his head [1 Cor. 11:4].

The rabbis of that day taught that a man was to cover his head. Paul says that they actually misinterpreted Moses and the reason for the veil. "And not as Moses, which put a veil over his face, that the children of Israel could not stedfastly look to the end of that which is abolished" (2 Cor. 3:13). This refers to an experience Moses had when he came down from the mount where he had communed with God. When he first came down, the skin of his face shone, but after awhile that glory began to disappear. Therefore, he covered his face so they wouldn't discover the glory was disappearing (see Exod. 34:33–35).

Paul is saying to the men that they ought *not* to cover their heads. A man created in the image of God, who is in Christ by redemption, is to have his head uncovered as a symbol of dignity and of liberty. He is not to be covered when he prays or when he prophesies. When he is praying, he is speaking for man to God, making intercession. When he is prophesying, he is speaking for God to man. Whenever he is standing in these two sacred, holy positions, he is to have his head uncovered.

But every woman that prayeth or prophesieth with her head uncovered dishonoureth her head: for that is even all one as if she were shaven [1 Cor. 11:5].

They had a women's liberation movement going in Corinth centuries ago, and it was going in the wrong direction. Paul says that the man should have his head uncovered but that the woman should have her head covered.

I want you to note that it says "every woman that prayeth or prophesieth," which means that a woman can pray in public and it means she can speak in public. Folk who maintain that the Bible says a woman cannot do these things are entirely wrong. The woman has the right to do these things if God has given her that gift. Some women have the gift.

I know several women today who are outstanding Bible teachers. They can out-teach any man. One preacher told me this very candidly, "My wife is a much better Bible teacher than I am." An officer of the church said they would much rather hear her speak than hear him speak. She had the gift of teaching.

For if the woman be not covered, let her also be shorn: but if it be a shame for a woman to be shorn or shaven, let her be covered [1 Cor. 11:6].

This had a peculiar and particular application to Corinth. The unveiled woman in Corinth was a prostitute. Many of them had their heads shaved. The vestal virgins in the temple of Aphrodite who were really prostitutes had their heads shaved. The women who had their heads uncovered were the prostitutes. Apparently some of the women in the church at Corinth were saying, "All things are lawful for me, therefore, I won't cover my head." Paul says this should not be done because the veil is a mark of subjection, not to man, but to God. Now this had a local application; it was given to the women in Corinth. Does it apply to our day and society? Well, I have heard that a new hat is a morale builder for women. A wife said to her husband, "Every time I get down in the dumps, I go and buy a new hat." His response was, "I have been wondering where you got those hats!" Seriously, regulations for a woman's dress are in regard to her ministry. If she is to lead, she ought to have her head covered. Other passages will give us more information about this. "I will therefore that men pray every where, lifting up holy hands, without wrath and doubting. In like manner also, that women adorn themselves in modest apparel, with shamefacedness and sobriety; not with broided hair, or gold, or pearls, or costly array; But (which becometh women professing godliness) with good works" (1 Tim. 2:8–10). This states that if the woman is to lift up holy hands in the service in leading, she is not to adorn herself to draw attention to herself. Very candidly, it means that the woman is not to use sex appeal in the service of God. That is exactly what it means, my friend. She is not to use sex appeal at all—it will not win her husband to Christ either.

The Bible has more to say on this subject. "Likewise, ye wives, be in subjection to your own husbands; that, if any obey not the word, they also may without the word be won by the conversation of the wives . . . . Whose adorning let it not be that outward adorning of plaiting the hair, and of wearing of gold, or of putting on of apparel; But let it be the hidden man of the heart, in that which is not corruptible, even the ornament of a meek and quiet spirit, which is in the sight of God of great price" (1 Pet. 3:1, 3–4). God is saying that a wife cannot win her husband to Christ by sex appeal. This does not mean that she is not to be appealing to her husband, but it does mean that a woman never wins her husband to Christ by sex appeal. There are women in the Bible who had sex appeal: Jezebel, Esther, Salome. Then there are some who stand out in Scripture as being wonderful, marvelous, godly women whom God used: Sarah, Deborah, Hannah, Abigail, and Mary the mother of Jesus. Then there is also something said to the husbands. "Likewise, ye husbands, dwell with them according to knowledge, giving honour unto the wife, as unto the weaker vessel, and as being heirs together of the grace of life; that your prayers be not hindered" (1 Pet. 3:7). Many a family today have their prayers hindered because the husband and wife are not getting along as they should.

Now Paul goes back to the principle he laid down for men in verse 4.

For a man indeed ought not to cover his head, forasmuch as he is the image and glory of God: but the woman is the glory of the man.

For the man is not of the woman; but the woman of the man.

Neither was the man created for the woman; but the woman for the man [1 Cor. 11:7–9].

The woman's place is to be a helpmeet to the man. She is to be the other part of him. No man is complete without a woman except where God has given special grace to a man for a special work. Listen to the next verse.

For this cause ought the woman to have power on her head because of the angels [1 Cor. 11:10].

Now here is a reference to angels that I don't understand. I am of the opinion that we are being observed by God's created intelligences. We are on a stage in this little world, and all God's created intelligences are watching us. They are finding out about the love of God, because they know we are not worthy of the love of God. They probably think God would have done well to have gotten rid of us because we are rebellious creatures in His universe. But He didn't! He loves us! That display of His love is in His grace to save us. The angels probably marvel at His grace and patience with little man.

Nevertheless neither is the man without the woman, neither the woman without the man, in the Lord [1 Cor. 11:11].

The power of the woman is to hold her man because she is a woman. The man holds his woman because he is a man. This is the marriage relationship as God ordained it. When that relationship doesn't exist, then God's ideal is lost.

For as the woman is of the man, even so is the man also by the woman; but all things of God [1 Cor. 11:12].

They are inseparable. Man is not a sphere but a hemisphere; woman is not a sphere but a hemisphere. It is nonsense for either man or women to talk about liberation. The man needs the woman, and the woman needs the man. This is true liberty in the glorious relationship of marriage.

Judge in yourselves: is it comely that a woman pray unto God uncovered? [1 Cor. 11:13].

A woman ought not to call attention to herself when she is speaking for the Lord or teaching a Bible class or praying. There should be no sex appeal. Also, she needs to remember that her sex appeal is a tremendous thing which has the power to either lift a man up or drag him down.

Doth not even nature itself teach you, that, if a man have long hair, it is a shame unto him? [1 Cor. 11:14].

As I write this, long hair is a fad among men. Men who let their hair grow so long that you can hardly recognize them seem to me to be expressing a lack of purpose in life. I wonder if it is a movement toward the animal world. Notice that Paul asks, "Doth not even nature itself teach you, that, if a man have long hair, it is a shame unto him?" We have an example of this in the Old Testament. The Nazarite vow was an act of consecrating oneself to God. It was symbolized by long, uncut hair. This meant that a Nazarite was willing to bear shame for God's name. Even at that time men's long hair was considered shameful.

But if a woman have long hair, it is a glory to her: for her hair is given her for a covering [1 Cor. 11:15].

Now it is true that today we have liberty in Christ. The length of the hair is really not so much the issue as the motive behind it. Many men wear long hair as a sign of rebellion, and many women cut their hair as a sign of rebellion. Our moral values get turned upside down, and there is a danger of being an extremist in either direction.

Extremism leads to strange behavior like the lady who went to the psychiatrist because her family had urged her to go. The psychiatrist asked her, "What really seems to be your trouble?" She said, "They think it is strange that I like pancakes." He answered, "There is nothing wrong in liking pancakes. I like pancakes myself." So she said, "You do? Well, come over sometime; I have trunks filled with them!" You see, my friend, you can be an extremist in that which is a normal thing.

Now Paul says that it is not really the haircut or the style of the dress that is of utmost importance.

But if any man seem to be contentious, we have no such custom, neither the churches of God [1 Cor. 11:16].

Paul concludes by saying that the church ought not to make rules in connection with the matter of women's dress or men's hair. The really important issue is the inner man. It is the old nature which needs a haircut and the robe of righteousness. My friend, if we are clothed with the robe of Christ's righteousness and if our old nature is under the control of the Holy Spirit, that will take care of the outer man. The haircut and the style of clothes won't make much difference. Paul is saying that he is not giving a rule to the churches. He just states what is best in his opinion. We should remember that in all our Christian liberty we are to think of others and of our testimony to others. We should be guided by the principles he has laid down: to glorify God, and not to offend others.

THE LORD'S SUPPER

Now we move to a new topic, and it seems we go from one extreme to the other—from hair and dress to the Lord's Supper. This is probably the most sacred part of our relationship to God. I am confident that the Lord's Supper is something that is greatly misunderstood in our churches. As a result, it is almost blasphemy the way it is observed in some places. Paul is going to say here that God judges us in the way that we observe the Lord's Supper. Actually, among the Corinthians some were sick and some had died because of the way they observed it. They did not discern the body of Christ. I wonder whether we discern the body of Christ today. Most of us observe the method that is used. We note every detail of the ritual, but do we really discern the body of Christ in the Lord's Supper?

The Lord's Supper is the highest expression and the holiest exercise of Christian worship. In Corinth it had dropped to such a low secular level that they were practically blaspheming it. I would have included this section in the "spiritual" division of this epistle except for the fact that Paul is dealing with a very bad situation in Corinth. Therefore, I place it in the "carnal" division of the epistle.

Three of the four Gospels record the institution of the Lord's Supper, and it is repeated in this epistle. It is interesting that nowhere are we commanded to remember the Lord's birthday, but we are requested and commanded that those who are His own should remember His deathday.

Paul attached the utmost importance to the Lord's Supper. In verse 23 he says, "For I have received of the Lord that which also I delivered unto you, That the Lord Jesus the same night in which he was betrayed took bread." Paul received this by direct revelation: "For I delivered unto you first of all that which I also received, how that Christ died for our sins according to the scriptures" (1 Cor. 15:3). Paul received a direct revelation of the gospel and a direct revelation of the Lord's Supper. The Lord gave him special instructions concerning it—remember that Paul was not in the Upper Room at the institution of the Lord's Supper.

I admit that it is rather difficult to see the connection of what Paul says to the Corinthian church with our celebration of the Lord's Supper. There is no exact parallel, because the situations are not similar. In that day the Lord's Supper was preceded by a social meal. It was probably celebrated in the homes and celebrated daily. Acts tells us, "And they, continuing daily with one accord in the temple, and breaking bread from house to house, did eat their meat with gladness and singleness of heart, Praising God, and having favour with all the people. And the Lord added to the church daily such as should be saved" (Acts 2:46–47).

Aristides, an Athenian philosopher who lived in the early part of the second century, describes the way the Christians of his day lived: "Every morning and all hours and on the account of the goodness of God towards them they praise and laud Him. . . . And if any righteous person of their number passes away from the world they rejoice and give thanks to God. . . . If a child chance to die in its infancy they praise God mightily, as for one who has passed through this world without sin." That is the statement from one who was not a member of the church but observed it from the outside in the second century.

The church in Corinth followed the procedure of having a meal in connection with the Lord's Supper. After all, the Passover was that kind of celebration in the Upper Room. After our Lord had celebrated the Passover supper, He took bread and broke it. On the dying embers of a fading feast, He did something new. Out of the ashes of that dead feast, He erected a new monument, not of marble or bronze, but of simple elements of food.

Today we have a custom among churches, clubs, fraternities, banks, and insurance companies of getting together and having a meal and a time of fellowship together. A great many folk criticize church banquets, and I have too, when they center only on the physical man. In the early church they had these dinners for fellowship, and they were called an *agape* or "love feast." This was a part of the fellowship of the church, the *koinonia*. In that day the social gathering led right into the Lord's Supper. It was kept separate, but the *agape* always preceded the Eucharist. Later on these feasts were separated, and they are not practiced like that today. We do not have a "love feast" or dinner which precedes the Lord's Supper.

Because of the separation, we do not duplicate the bad situation that prevailed in the Corinthian church. However, there are certain lessons here for us.

Now in this that I declare unto you I praise you not, that ye come together not for the better, but for the worse [1 Cor. 11:17].

The word *declare* is actually a command, and *unto you* in the Authorized Version is in italics, which means it is not in the original text. It should be "Now in this I command, I praise you not, that ye come together not for the better, but for the worse." In other words, they should have come together for a great spiritual blessing, but it didn't amount to that.

For first of all, when ye come together in the church, I hear that there be divisions among you; and I partly believe it [1 Cor. 11:18].

He is not talking about an edifice, a building. He is talking about when the believers come together—that is the true church. Today when we speak of a church, we always identify a building as the church. We think of the Baptist church, the Methodist church, the Presbyterian church, or the independent church down on the corner. The chances are that those buildings are closed and nobody is there. The building is not the church—it is just a building. The church is the people. It is difficult for us to think in a context like that.

When the Corinthian believers came together, the divisive or party spirit that we saw in chapter 1 was carried over into the Lord's Supper. That division was there.

For there must be also heresies among you, that they which are approved may be made manifest among you [1 Cor. 11:19].

This helps to explain the cults and "isms" such as we have in Southern California. Why does God permit them? Let me give you an illustration. Have you ever noticed when a woman is cooking something and there is an accumulation on the top that she skims it off? Well, that is what God does. To tell the truth, I think the churches are filled with unbelievers today. A large percentage of the people in the churches are not saved at all. They are just members of a church. The Lord skims them off. How does He do that? Well, they go off into the cults and the "isms." That is what Paul is saying here: "There must be also heresies among you, that they which are approved may be made manifest among you." Heresy comes along in these cults or "isms," and a lot of people go out of the churches and flock to them. The Lord is skimming them off so that those who are genuine may be revealed.

When ye come together therefore into one place, this is not to eat the Lord's supper [1 Cor. 11:20].

The "this," which is in italics in the Authorized Version, is not in the original. He is saying, "When ye come together into one place, it is not possible to eat the Lord's Supper." It is impossible for them to celebrate the Lord's Supper because of the way that they conducted the feast which preceded it. Under such circumstances they couldn't celebrate the Lord's Supper.

For in eating every one taketh before other his own supper: and one is hungry, and another is drunken [1 Cor. 11:21].

What a comment that is! Some poor fellow would come to the dinner, and he couldn't even bring a covered dish of scalloped potatoes. He was that poor. And he was hungry. Next to him would sit a rich fellow who had fried chicken and ice cream, and he wouldn't pass one bit of food to the poor fellow who was hungry. The fellowship was broken. There could not be fellowship when there was a situation like that.

And then there was something else.

What? have ye not houses to eat and to drink in? or despise ye the church of God, and shame them that have not? What shall I say to you? shall I praise you in this? I praise you not [1 Cor. 11:22].

If they were not going to share in true fellowship, they should have eaten at home. What they were doing was fracturing and rupturing the church. And some were actually getting drunk during this agape love feast. They were in no condition to remember the death of Christ at all. It would all be fuzzy and hazy to them. Paul says again, "Shall I praise you in this? I praise you not."

THE REVELATION TO PAUL

For I have received of the Lord that which also I delivered unto you, That the Lord Jesus the same night in which he was betrayed took bread [1 Cor. 11:23].

Sometimes people say they want to celebrate the Lord's Supper exactly as the Lord did—then they have it at an eleven o'clock morning service. If you want to have it at the time the Lord had it, it must be at night. They went in at night to eat the Pass-over supper, and it was at that supper that the Lord instituted the Lord's Supper.

It was the very same night in which He was betrayed. At that supper He took bread.

And when he had given thanks, he brake it, and said, Take, eat: this is my body, which is broken for you: this do in remembrance of me [1 Cor. 11:24].

Paul wasn't present in the Upper Room. He got this as a direct revelation from the Lord. It was the night when the forces of hell met to destroy our Savior. I think the simplicity and the sublimity and the sanity of this supper is tremendous.

Notice that it says, "when he had given thanks." He gave thanks that night while the shadow of the cross hung over the Upper Room. Sin was knocking at the door of the Upper Room, demanding its pound of flesh. And He gave thanks. He gave thanks to God.

Then, "he brake it." There has always been a difference of opinion among believers on that. Do you break the bread, or do you serve it as it is? The Roman Catholics break it, the Lutherans do not, and most Protestant churches do not.

In several churches in which I served I instituted an evening communion, because the Lord instituted the Lord's Supper at night. I also tried something else. I asked the one who served the bread to the congregation to take a piece and break it before them. That spoke of the broken body of our Lord.

The breaking of the bread also indicates that this is something that is to be shared. Bengal made this statement: "The very mention of the breaking involves distribution, and rebukes the Corinthian plan of every man his own."

After the same manner also he took the cup, when he had supped, saying, This cup is the new testament in my blood: this do ye, as oft as ye drink it, in remembrance of me [1 Cor. 11:25].

The bread speaks of His broken body; the cup speaks of the New Covenant. Have you noticed that it is called the *cup*? (It is also called the fruit of the vine in some instances, but it is never called *wine*). Have I heard that argued! "Should we have fermented or unfermented wine for the Lord's Supper?" That is baby talk to ask questions like that. My friend, we can know it was unfermented. This is Passover, the time of the Feast of Unleavened Bread. Do you think that they had unleavened bread and leavened grape juice (wine is leavened grape juice)? The whole business was unleavened—it had to be at the Passover feast. But the interesting thing is that here Jesus calls it the cup. His body was the cup that held the blood. He was born to die and to shed that blood. Again and again the apostles remind us that we have forgiveness of sins because of the blood, that He has extended mercy to us because of the blood. He did not open the back door of heaven and slip us in under cover of darkness. He brings us in the front door as *sons* because the penalty of sin was paid when the demands of a holy God were met. Let's not forget that, my beloved, in this day when the notion is that God can shut His eyes to sin and do nothing about it. He has *done* something about it. This is the cup; it holds the blood of the New Covenant.

For as often as ye eat this bread, and drink this cup, ye do shew the Lord's death till he come [1 Cor. 11:26].

Paul here adds something new. In 1 Corinthians he is always opening up a door or raising a shade, letting us see something new. Here it is "till he come." When we observe the Lord's Supper, that table looks in three different directions. (1) It is a commemoration. He repeats, "This do . . . in remembrance of me." This table looks back over nineteen hundred years to His death upon the cross. He says, "Don't forget that. It is important." That is to the past. (2) This table is a communion (sometimes we call it a communion service). It speaks of the present, of the fact that today there is a *living* Christ, my beloved. (3) It is a commitment. It looks to the future—that He is coming again. This table won't last forever; it is temporary. After the service it is removed, and we may not celebrate it again because we just do it until He comes. It speaks of an absent Lord who is coming back. It looks to the future.

The Lord Jesus Christ took these frail elements—bread and grape juice, which will spoil in a few days, the weakest things in the world—and He raised a monument. It's not of marble, bronze, silver, or gold; it is *bread* and *juice*—that's all. But it speaks of Him, and it tells me that I am responsible for His death.

Wherefore whosoever shall eat this bread, and drink this cup of the Lord, unworthily, shall be guilty of the body and blood of the Lord.

But let a man examine himself, and so let him eat of that bread, and drink of that cup.

For he that eateth and drinketh unworthily, eateth and drinketh damnation to himself, not discerning the Lord's body [1 Cor. 11:27–29].

What does he mean to "discern" the Lord's body? Looking back in church history you will find that the churches had a great problem in determining the meaning of this. What *does* it mean to discern the Lord's body? The answer of the Roman Catholic church is that transubstantiation takes place, that when the priest officiates at the altar, the bread actually becomes the body of Christ, also that the juice actually becomes the blood of Christ. If this were true, to eat it would be cannibalism. (Thank the Lord, it does not change; it is still bread and juice). But they were wrestling with the problem. How do you discern the Lord's body in this? In the Lutheran church (Martin Luther didn't want to come too far, as he had been a Roman Catholic priest), it is consubstantiation. That is, it is *in, by, with, through,* and *under* the bread that you get the body of Christ. It is not the body, but it *is* the body. You can figure that one out—I can't. Then Zwingli, the Swiss Reformation leader, came all the way. He said it was just a symbol. And the average Protestant today thinks that is all it is, a symbol. I disagree with that explanation as much as I do with the other two. It is more than a symbol.

Follow me now to the Emmaus road, and I think we shall find there recorded in Luke's gospel, chapter 24, what it means to discern Christ's body and His death.

Two of Jesus' disciples, two believers, are walking home after having witnessed the terrible Crucifixion in Jerusalem and the events that followed it. Are they down in the dumps! As they walk along discussing these things, our resurrected Lord joins them and asks what they are talking about that makes them so sad. Thinking Him to be a stranger, they tell Him about Jesus' being condemned to death and crucified and about the report of the women who went to the tomb. "And certain of them which were with us went to the sepulchre, and found it even so as the women had said: but him they saw not. Then he [Christ] said unto them, O fools, and slow of heart to believe all that the prophets have spoken: Ought not Christ to have suffered these things, and to enter into his glory? And beginning at Moses and all the prophets, he expounded unto them in all the Scriptures the things concerning himself. And they drew nigh unto the village, whither they went: and he made as though he would have gone further." He acted as if He were going through the town without stopping. "But they constrained him, saying, Abide with us: for it is toward evening, and the day is far spent." It was dangerous to walk those highways at night.

"And he went in to tarry with them. And it came to pass, as he sat at meat with them . . . ." A few days before He had eaten the Passover with His own, now these are two other disciples, and here is the first time after His resurrection He is observing the Lord's Supper. "And it came to pass, as he sat at meat with them, he took bread, and blessed it, and brake, and gave to them." Wasn't that wonderful to have Him present for the meal! In the meal He takes the bread, He breaks it, He blesses it, He gives it to them. "And their eyes were opened, and they knew him; and he vanished out of their sight. And they said one to another, Did not our heart burn within us . . ." (Luke 24:24–32). He had a meal with them. Then what did He do? He *revealed* Himself. That was the Lord's Supper.

Oh, friend, when you observe the Lord's Supper, He is present. Yes, He is! This is not just a symbol. It means you must discern the body of Christ. You have bread in your mouth, but you have Christ in your heart. May God help us to so come to the table that Jesus Christ will be a *reality* to us. God forgive us for making it a dead, formal ritual!

For this cause many are weak and

sickly among you, and many sleep [1 Cor. 11:30].

They suffered sickness and death. Why? Because they had participated in the Lord's Supper unworthily—that is, in an unworthy manner.

For if we would judge ourselves, we should not be judged.

But when we are judged, we are chastened of the Lord, that we should not be condemned with the world [1 Cor. 11:31–32].

This is talking about believers. We can judge ourselves when we are wrong. If we don't, He will judge us. When we are judged of the Lord, we are chastened so that we shall not be condemned with the world. He is going to judge the world in the future. Therefore He has to deal with His own now.

Wherefore, my brethren, when ye come together to eat, tarry one for another.

And if any man hunger, let him eat at home; that ye come not together unto condemnation. And the rest will I set in order when I come [1 Cor. 11:33–34].

There were other things wrong in the Corinthian church, but Paul is not going to write about them now. He says that he will straighten out those things when he gets there.

CHAPTER 12

THEME: Endowment of gifts

The first section of 1 Corinthians had to do with carnalities, as we have seen. Chapter 12 begins a new section which deals with spiritualities. And the first three chapters concern spiritual gifts: chapter 12, the *endowment* of gifts; chapter 13, the *energy* of gifts; chapter 14, the *exercise* of gifts.

GIFTS ARE GIVEN TO MAINTAIN UNITY IN DIVERSITY

Now concerning spiritual gifts, brethren, I would not have you ignorant [1 Cor. 12:1].

Notice that in the text of your Bible the word *gifts* is in italics, which means that that word is not in the original. It was added for the sake of clarity; but, very frankly, I don't think adding the word clarified anything. Actually, it has added confusion. In *The Revised Standard Version* it is spiritual gifts; in *The New English Bible* it is gifts of the Spirit; in *The Berkeley Translation* it is spiritual endowments. *The Scofield Reference Bible* has a good footnote about this.

The Greek word is *pneumatika*, which literally means "spiritualities." It is in contrast to carnalities. One does not need to add the word "gifts." Back in the third chapter Paul was discussing the divisions among the Corinthian believers, and he wrote, "And I, brethren, could not speak unto you as unto spiritual, but as unto carnal, even as unto babes in Christ" (1 Cor. 3:1). That first section is about carnalities, because their questions were about carnalities and the things that carnal Christians would be interested in. The carnalities had to do with their divisions, their wrangling about different leaders, about adultery, about going to court against a brother, the sex problem, women's dress and men's haircuts, the love feast, gluttony and drunkenness at the Lord's Supper. That is all carnality, and we can find the same things in the church today. The section on carnalities was corrective.

Now we come to the section on spiritualities, and this is constructive. Paul was glad to change the subject; I think he heaved a sigh of relief when he got here to chapter 12. He was willing to discuss the other problems with them, but he really wanted to talk to them about the spiritualities.

The modern church needs to change the same old subjects which are discussed. In a very sophisticated manner Christian educators say that we should tell our young people about sex. Friend, we had better tell them about spiritual things. There are so many programs in the churches that the young people never get anywhere near the Bible. They have conferences on whatever carnality is the popular issue or the fad for the moment. All of that is a sign of carnality.

In this section Paul will touch on three subjects: the unifying Spirit, the law of love, and the triumph the believer has in the Resurrection. The gifts of the Spirit just happen to be one of the spiritualities, by the way.

Ye know that ye were Gentiles, carried away unto these dumb idols, even as ye were led [1 Cor. 12:2].

The idols were voiceless, dumb idols. Remember that previously Paul said the idols are "nothings." That is why the meat offered to the idols was not contaminated. The idols were nothing. Unfortunately, everyone doesn't quite understand that. Back in Psalm 115:5 the psalmist says, "They have mouths, but they speak not: eyes have they, but they see not." This is what Habakkuk wrote: "What profiteth the graven image that the maker thereof hath graven it; the molten image, and a teacher of lies, that the maker of his work

trusteth therein, to make dumb idols?" (Hab. 2:18).

The very interesting thing is that he is going to talk about the gifts that the living God gives to believers. So first he reminds them how they formerly were carried away unto these dumb idols.

Wherefore I give you to understand, that no man speaking by the Spirit of God calleth Jesus accursed: and that no man can say that Jesus is the Lord, but by the Holy Ghost [1 Cor. 12:3].

Here is a great truth, an absolute verity of the Christian life: the lordship of Jesus Christ. "No man speaking by the Spirit of God calleth Jesus accursed." You cannot belittle Jesus Christ by the Spirit of God. It won't work. Also, "no man can say that Jesus is the Lord, but by the Holy [Spirit] Ghost." Oh, of course we can pronounce the word *Lord*. But remember what the Lord Jesus said: "Not every one that saith unto me, Lord, Lord, shall enter into the kingdom of heaven; but he that doeth the will of my Father which is in heaven. Many will say to me in that day, Lord, Lord, have we not prophesied in thy name? and in thy name have cast out devils? and in thy name done many wonderful works? And then will I profess unto them, I never knew you: depart from me, ye that work iniquity" (Matt. 7:21–23). Why will that be? Because their profession is on the surface. The Lord Jesus was not their Lord.

Making Jesus Lord is a conviction of the soul. What is the central truth of the Christian faith? There are those who say it is the cross of Christ, but I rather disagree with that. Although we come to the Cross to be saved, we do not stay at the Cross. We become united to the living Christ. That is the thing which is all important.

Listen to the way Simon Peter concluded his message on the Day of Pentecost: "Therefore let all the house of Israel know assuredly, that God hath made that same Jesus, whom ye have crucified, both Lord and Christ" (Acts 2:36). He is the Lord. He is sovereign. His sovereignty is the important thing in the Christian life.

The Holy Spirit commands the soul's obedience and allegiance to Jesus. The true church is made up of those who have gathered around that truth as interpreted by the Holy Spirit. The Holy Spirit interprets the lordship of Jesus to my life. Remember the great question which Jesus asked, ". . . whom say ye that I am?" (Matt. 16:15). Jesus is still asking that same question. You may be of any occupation, any color, any status in life—whoever you are, wherever you are, however you are—Jesus asks you, "Whom say *ye* that I am?" He asked His disciples that question, and Simon Peter spoke for the group. He said, ". . . Thou art the Christ, the Son of the living God" (Matt. 16:16). He is the Anointed One. He is the King. He is the Lord. No man is fit to serve Christ's church unless he has been mastered by Jesus Christ. We have seen that earlier in this epistle. Now Paul emphasizes that again.

The *unifying* work of the Holy Spirit today is to reveal the lordship of Jesus to all believers. Within this unity there is *diversity* of gifts.

Now there are diversities of gifts, but the same Spirit [1 Cor. 12:4].

There is a distribution of gifts. In order to have the unity, He gives different gifts to different individuals. The Greek word for "gifts" is *charisma*. Some people try to make this word apply to tongues, and they speak of the charismatic movement. This reveals their ignorance, as the word refers to *all* the gifts which the Holy Spirit gives to the believers in the church.

And there are differences of administrations, but the same Lord [1 Cor. 12:5].

That is, there are diversities of ministrations, but the same Lord—the Lord Jesus Christ. It doesn't make any difference which gift you may have. It is the Lord Jesus who is using that gift, and He is using it for His glory.

And there are diversities of operations, but it is the same God which worketh all in all [1 Cor. 12:6].

There are diversities of operations—that is, of the energy. But it is the same God who works in all, and He is the One who works in the believer.

This reminds us that there is but one God—but He is a Trinity. The Trinity works together; there is a unity. But there is a diversity in unity. Notice this: The Holy Spirit bestows the gifts; the Lord Jesus Christ administers the gifts—they are under His direction; the Father God supplies the power, and He energizes the gifts. All of this is for the one purpose of exalting and glorifying the lordship of Jesus Christ.

But the manifestation of the Spirit is given to every man to profit withal [1 Cor. 12:7].

First of all, let's define a *gift*. What is a gift of the Spirit? It is a capacity for service. It is a function. This is Dr. Lewis Sperry Chafer's definition: "A gift in the spiritual sense means the Holy Spirit doing a particular service through the believer and using the believer to do it." To this I would like to add that it must be done in the power of the Spirit of God. To make this personal: I am nothing, I have nothing, I am of no use to God or man. That is not a pious platitude; it is a fact. But He gave me a gift, and I'm to exercise that gift. That is, I believe, the only way the Spirit of God will manifest Himself in my life.

"The manifestation of the Spirit is given to every man to profit withal." "Manifestation of the Spirit"—that is what a gift is. A gift is the manifestation of the Spirit.

This does not necessarily mean the exercise of a natural gift. For example, a woman has a gift of singing. She has a marvelous voice. But if she does not sing in the power of the Holy Spirit, God can't use it—and He *doesn't* use it. This is the reason that music in the average contemporary church has sunk to such a low level. Musicians think that all they need is talent and training. They think if they have that, they have it made, and the Lord can't get along without them. The fact of the matter is that He can get along *better* without them. I have been in many, many places across the country and have ministered in many pulpits. I have learned much through the years, and I can tell when a musician is adding to the service or detracting from it. I have had the experience of hearing a solo sung immediately before the message that absolutely ruined the message before I even stood to my feet. I have felt like getting up, pronouncing the benediction, and going home. Now let me make it very clear that I believe the Holy Spirit can use the natural ability of a believer if the believer will let Him do it. But natural talent alone is nothing unless it is under the control of the Holy Spirit.

There are those who have no particular natural talent. They say that since they can't sing in the choir or teach in the Sunday school, there is nothing for them to do but to sit in the pew. That is one of the most tragic mistakes made in the church.

This verse tells us that every believer has a gift. *Every* believer! "But the manifestation of the Spirit is given to every man to profit withal."

The word for "man" in the Greek is *anthropos*, which is a generic term and actually means man or woman, boy or girl. It doesn't make any difference who you are. If you are a child of God, you have a gift. You have been put into the body of believers as a member of the body, and you are to function as a member of the body of Christ.

"The manifestation of the Spirit is given to every man to profit withal." What is the purpose of the gift? It is to build up the church, the body of believers. It is not to be exercised selfishly, but is to give spiritual help to other believers.

For to one is given by the Spirit the word of wisdom; to another the word of knowledge by the same Spirit [1 Cor. 12:8].

"Wisdom" means insight into truth. I do not think everyone can come to an understanding of the Bible, which is the reason we need teachers, and the Spirit of God has given us teachers. "Wisdom" is insight into the truth of the Word of God. "Knowledge" means to investigate or to dig into the truth. Many people simply do not have the time to dig into the Word of God, to dig out the nuggets. One man who supports our radio program very generously says, "I'm just paying for the nuggets that you deliver to me." As a businessman and executive he does not have hours and hours to study. I don't think God is asking him to do that. He supports the program, and I do the digging for him. I think that is my gift. So he and I are working together as partners, each exercising his own gift. This is very practical.

To another faith by the same Spirit; to another the gifts of healing by the same Spirit [1 Cor. 12:9].

Faith, we are told in the Scriptures, is the substance of things hoped for. That is a gift. Some people have the gift of faith.

I have a combination of Scottish and German blood in me. When you get that combination, it's bad. I have pessimist blood in me, and I look at everything from that point of view. In every church in which I served, God gave me several people who had the gift of faith. Many a time an officer has come and put his arm around my shoulder and said, "Look, preacher, this thing is going to come through just right." And you know, it did. He had the faith; I didn't. Faith is a gift of the Spirit.

"To another the gifts of healing by the same Spirit." That means that the sick were healed by the laying on of hands. I believe this was a gift given to the apostles and to men in the early church. I don't think that gift is needed today. We should take our case directly to the

Great Physician. We don't need to go through a man or woman down here and ask them to pray for us or lay their hands on us. Take your case directly to Him.

Remember that the centurion came to Jesus and asked Him to heal his servant. He didn't ask Jesus to lay hands on his servant. He simply asked Jesus to say the word and his servant would be healed. He had faith, such faith that Jesus marveled at him and said, ". . . I say unto you, I have not found so great faith, no, not in Israel" (Luke 7:9). So take your case directly to the Great Physician. It reveals a lack of faith in Him to go to a so-called healer.

I believe that the Holy Spirit gives certain gifts that are peculiar for specific ages. No one today has the same gift that Martin Luther had in his day. I think the Spirit of God gives gifts to the body of Christ so that it might function in the age in which it finds itself in order that the whole body might profit from it.

To another the working of miracles; to another prophecy; to another discerning of spirits; to another divers kinds of tongues; to another the interpretation of tongues [1 Cor. 12:10].

"The working of miracles" is to do supernatural things. There were miracles in the apostolic age, but today we are seeing greater things. When Jesus was here and *He* spoke a word to a person—like the woman at the well or to Nicodemus—and that person was converted, I don't marvel at that. But when *I* speak the Word or *you* speak the Word and somebody is saved, that is a greater work.

To "prophesy" means to declare the will of Christ. That is, to prophesy is to preach the Word of God. We need people today who are willing to do that. We need people who will speak the Word of God and then trust God to use that Word through His Spirit.

The "discerning of spirits" means the ability to distinguish between the false and the true. I am convinced that I do not have that gift at all. I have been deceived probably more than any preacher ever has been deceived. I have trusted men—certain preachers and certain church officers—and thought they were genuine; yet they have let me down horribly. I have been deceived by liars and dishonest folk whom I thought to be wonderful people. On the other hand, you find some people who have discerning of spirits. My wife has been a great help to me in this connection. She tells me, "Now you be careful there, watch out for that individual," or, "I think this one is a very wonderful person." She is generally right, and I am generally wrong. She has the discerning of spirits.

Another gift is "kinds of tongues" (the word *divers* is not in the original). Are these unknown tongues? No, you do not find unknown tongues in Scripture. These are known languages. There are still many, many languages into which the Bible has not been translated. Instead of wasting time trying to invent an unknown language, let's get the gospel translated into these known languages that don't have it yet. Some folk have the gift of translating.

But all these worketh that one and the selfsame Spirit, dividing to every man severally as he will [1 Cor. 12:11].

The Holy Spirit is sovereign in all this. However, we do have the right to pray for the best gifts, which is what Paul is going to tell these Corinthians. They were carnal Christians, living on a very low spiritual level. They were fascinated by the tongues movement. That is why Paul is discussing it in this epistle. He was trying to correct the things that were wrong in the Corinthian church, and there were many things wrong. He is showing them that there are many gifts and that the Holy Spirit distributes to each one individually as *He* wills.

MEMBERS OF THE HUMAN BODY COMPARED TO GIFTS OF THE HOLY SPIRIT

For as the body is one, and hath many members, and all the members of that one body, being many, are one body: so also is Christ [1 Cor. 12:12].

In the consideration of this passage let us drop down to include two other verses: "But now are they many members, yet but one body" (v. 20) and "Now ye are the body of Christ, and members in particular" (v. 27). Paul is using a comparison to the human body. As one body has many members performing different functions, so the members of the church need to perform different functions. The human body has many members, hundreds, even thousands of members. In the church, the body of Christ, there are many gifts, hundreds, probably thousands of gifts.

On a hunting trip I stepped off a cliff and hurt my foot. When I went to the doctor, I asked him how many bones were in the foot. He told me there were twenty-seven. I said, "I think I hurt all twenty-seven of them!" "No,"

he said, "you hurt only one." Now I tell you, I may have hurt only one of them, but my whole foot was painful. When one member suffers, they all suffer.

The body is composed of many members. There are the bones and muscles, the glands and the organs, the nerves and the blood vessels. On one occasion, after I had spoken at a baccalaureate service in a prep school in Atlanta, Georgia, I went to a doctor's home for dinner. He asked me if I knew which was the most important part of my body while I had been speaking. I guessed it was my tongue. "No," he said, "the most important part of your body today was a member that no one was conscious of. It was your big toe. If you didn't have a couple of big toes, you wouldn't have been able to stand up there at all."

I have thought a great deal about that. Suppose when I would go somewhere to preach, my big toe would rebel and say, "Look here, I refuse to go. I've been going with you for years and you have never called attention to me. People see your lips and tongue and your face, but they don't ever see me. Why don't you ever take off your shoe and sock and let them get a look at me sometime?" Well, now, I don't think folk would be interested in seeing my big toe—it is not very attractive. In fact, it is unattractive, yet it is an important part of my body.

There are many members in the body of Christ. Some of them we don't ever see. Some of the most important members in churches where I have served have been men and women whom the church knew nothing about. They weren't the officers or the Sunday school teachers or the soloist or the preacher. They were quiet, unobtrusive folk who prayed and who exercised their gift of faith.

Now how does a person get into this body of believers?

For by one Spirit are we all baptized into one body, whether we be Jews or Gentiles, whether we be bond or free; and have been all made to drink into one Spirit [1 Cor. 12:13].

This is the baptism of the Holy Spirit. It is the Holy Spirit who puts us into the body of believers and who gives a gift to each particular member. We are to function in that body, and we are to use that gift. It may be that we are the "big toes" with an unseen but important ministry. We each have a gift, and we are each to function.

For the body is not one member, but many.

If the foot shall say, Because I am not the hand, I am not of the body; is it therefore not of the body?

And if the ear shall say, Because I am not the eye, I am not of the body; is it therefore not of the body?

If the whole body were an eye, where were the hearing? If the whole were hearing, where were the smelling? [1 Cor. 12:14–17].

Suppose there would be a return of the gift of tongues such as there was in the apostolic times. It still would be true that not everyone would speak in tongues. The analogy is to our bodies. Our bodies are not all tongue. (I have met a few people who seemed to be all tongue, but they are exceptions!) The Holy Spirit is not going to give the same gift to every person. Like the human body, there need to be eyes and ears and feet and hands. Different people are given different gifts by the Spirit of God so that the body of Christ can function in all its necessary capacities.

But now hath God set the members every one of them in the body, as it hath pleased him [1 Cor. 12:18].

God is the One who sovereignly gives the gifts, and He gives them as it pleases Him. He is the One to be pleased, you see. These gifts are in the body so that the body can function.

A man in one of my congregations had an unusual gift. He was not an usher, but he would stand in the back of the church and if there was any kind of disruption or commotion in the service, he would take care of it. If a baby was crying in the church, one of the ushers might ask the mother to leave and antagonize her by doing so. But this man had a gift. He would go to the mother and play with the baby a few minutes and then say, "By the way, we have a nursery here. Would you like me to take the baby down there or show you where the nursery is?" The mothers always responded. He just had a way of handling people. As I told him, he had a rare gift and one that is needed in the church.

You may be surprised that something like that is a gift. Of course, it is a gift, and so is cooking or baking or sewing.

We can get some idea about gifts from incidents in the Bible. Ananias and Sapphira had gifts, but they had not submitted to the lordship of Jesus Christ, and their gifts were not functioning for the Lord. So they fell down dead before Simon Peter. They couldn't exist in the early church. They had gifts, but they were not exercising them as they should.

There was a woman by the name of Dorcas who had a gift of sewing, and she used that gift under the lordship of Christ. She exercised it in the will of God. When she died, Simon Peter went to Joppa and the widows had a regular fashion show as they showed Peter the dresses that Dorcas had made. The reason they wore them was that these were all that those poor women had to wear. Dorcas and her gift were important in the early church, so much so that Peter raised her from the dead. She had a gift that was still needed.

Simon Peter had a gift. He was the great preacher on the Day of Pentecost. God used him mightily. When God no longer needed his gift, he died—he was not raised from the dead.

My friend, the Spirit of God is sovereign in all this. He is the One who determines what is important and what is not important. If God has called you to bake a cake or to sew a dress, then do it. That is a gift. The Holy Spirit wants us to use our gifts and to bring them under the lordship of Jesus Christ.

And if they were all one member, where were the body?

But now are they many members, yet but one body.

And the eye cannot say unto the hand, I have no need of thee: nor again the head to the feet, I have no need of you.

Nay, much more those members of the body, which seem to be more feeble, are necessary [1 Cor. 12:19–22].

You and I need each other, and the Lord wants to use all of us.

And those members of the body, which we think to be less honourable, upon these we bestow more abundant honour; and our uncomely parts have more abundant comeliness.

For our comely parts have no need: but God hath tempered the body together, having given more abundant honour to that part which lacked:

That there should be no schism in the body; but that the members should have the same care one for another [1 Cor. 12:23–25].

You have seen some little, underdeveloped boy taking exercises and lifting weights. He is trying to develop some muscles and trying to develop some strength. Just so, God pays attention to the body of believers so that the small gifts are developed. I think there are many gifts in the church which need to be developed today.

Perhaps you feel that you are not doing anything for the Lord. One of the most thrilling things in the world, especially if you are a young person, is to find out what God wants you to do and where He wants you to go. What a thrill, what an experience, what an adventure to find out what gift God has given you!

Paul goes on to say that this should all be done so that there is no schism in the body. The members should all have the same care one for another.

And whether one member suffer, all the members suffer with it; or one member be honoured, all the members rejoice with it [1 Cor. 12:26].

My friend, there is no place for jealousy in the church—we all are members of the same body. If one is honored, we all receive that honor. And when one member is suffering, we all suffer with him.

Now ye are the body of Christ, and members in particular.

And God hath set some in the church, first apostles, secondarily prophets, thirdly teachers, after that miracles, then gifts of healings, helps, governments, diversities of tongues [1 Cor. 12:27–28].

What about the gift of "helps"? Oh, what a wonderful gift that is! If you have it, I hope you are exercising it.

Are all apostles? are all prophets? are all teachers? are all workers of miracles?

Have all the gifts of healing? do all speak with tongues? do all interpret? [1 Cor. 12:29–30].

Some of these gifts have disappeared. They are not in the church because they are not needed in the church today. There are no longer apostles in the church, nor are there prophets—in the sense of being able to foretell future events.

Paul also makes it very clear that all people do not have all the gifts. Are all apostles? The obvious answer is, "No." Do all work miracles, or do all have the gift of healing, or do all speak with tongues? The answer is, "No, they do not."

But covet earnestly the best gifts: and yet shew I unto you a more excellent way [1 Cor. 12:31].

Although the Holy Spirit is sovereign in bestowing gifts, we have the right to ask God for the gift we want. He says we are to "covet earnestly the best gifts."

Not having been brought up in a Christian home, I had no Christian training at all. When I went away to seminary, I didn't even know the books of the Bible. I had graduated from a college where the emphasis was placed on the intellectual and the philosophical, and I was trying to be that kind of preacher. Then I heard Dr. Harry Ironside speak. He explained Scripture in a simple manner. And I heard him make the statement, "Put the cookies on the bottom shelf so the kiddies can get them." And I remembered that my Lord had said, "Feed my sheep" (see John 21:16). He hadn't said, "Feed my giraffes." So I went to God and prayed, "Lord, I want to be *that* kind of preacher."

Later, I substituted for Dr. Ironside at Dallas Theological Seminary, and when he passed on, the seminary's president, Dr. Lewis Sperry Chafer, called me on the phone. He asked, "Would you take Dr. Ironside's lectures here at the seminary?" I could hardly answer him clearly, and I almost rudely hung up the phone. I dropped to my knees, and I confess that I wept as I thanked God. I said, "Lord I prayed that You would let me teach like Dr. Ironside, and You have answered my prayer!" I coveted earnestly the best gift, and He answered my prayer. Although I am no Dr. Ironside, how I thrill today at the experience and the privilege of teaching the Word of God!

My friend, you have the right to ask God for the *best* gift. Several folk have written this to me: "I certainly hope you receive the baptism of the Holy Spirit." Well, for your information, I have received it, not as an experience or something I received after I was saved, but the Holy Spirit has put me into this body of believers, which is the *baptism* of the Holy Spirit. Also these folk say, "We hope that you will speak in tongues." Well, my prayer is that I can speak in the English language a little better. Why? For the simple reason that the gift God gives us is for the profit—the wealth—of the church. Regardless of the gift God gives to you, the purpose of it is to be helpful to other believers, other members of the body.

CHAPTER 13

THEME: Love—the energy of the gifts

This chapter is properly called the *love* chapter of the Bible. Many men have attempted to give an exposition of it. Frankly, I have preached on it only once or twice in my ministry. Although I have taught it whenever I have come to it in a program of going through the Bible on radio or at any of the churches I have served, candidly, it is a passage that passes beyond my comprehension and capability. In 1884 Henry Drummond wrote a very brilliant essay entitled, *The Greatest Thing in the World*. It was put into my hands very early in my Christian life. It is a great little book on this thirteenth chapter.

The word *charity*, which is used throughout this chapter, should be *love*. The Vulgate, which is the Latin translation, and Wycliffe's English translation used the word *charity*, and this word was carried over into the King James Version. The Greek word is *agape*, which is properly translated *love*.

You will not find a definition of love in this chapter. Sometimes definitions are destructive. To try to define love would actually be a very serious violation of this chapter. When you try to define a rose, you can read the description of a rose that botany gives you, but that definition doesn't picture a rose like I know a rose to be. Or have you ever had anyone describe a sunset for you? I remember one evening at the Island of Saint Thomas in the Virgin Islands standing on the deck of a little boat and seeing the moon come up. It was such a thrill that it made the goose pimples come up all over me. I wish I could picture it for you, but I cannot. This chapter gives to us a *display* of love, not a definition.

There are three words in the Greek which are all translated by our one word *love*. There is the word *eros*. That is the word for passion, the word used for lust. It is used of Aphrodite and Eros, or Venus and Cupid as we more commonly know them. *Sex* would be our word for it today. This word does not occur in the New Testament at all.

Then there is the word *phileō*, which means "affection." We find that root in our words *Philadelphia* and *philanthropist*. It means a love of man, a love of a brother. It means human love at its highest, a noble love.

The word *agapaō* is the highest word for love in the New Testament and means "divine love." It is more than love in the emotion; it is love in the will. It is love that chooses its object. It is a definition of God, for God is love.

Now I am going to give you an outline of the chapter. Again, this seems like a violation of the chapter, but the mechanics will help us understand it.

The preeminence of love—its value (vv. 1–3)

The prerogative of love—its virtue (vv. 4–7)

The permanence of love—its victory (vv. 8–13)

Remember how this chapter follows the thought in chapter 12, which was the *endowment* of gifts. Chapter 13 tells of the *energy* of the gifts. All gifts of the Spirit are to be exercised in love.

PREEMINENCE OF LOVE—ITS VALUE

Though I speak with the tongues of men and of angels, and have not charity, I am become as sounding brass, or a tinkling cymbal [1 Cor. 13:1].

I am sure the tongues of angels means eloquence. I have never heard an angel speak, but I think Paul had heard them.

The most marvelous eloquence without love is nothing in the world but a noisy bell. Dr. Scroggie says it like this: "Language without love is noise without melody." McGee says it like this: "Chatter without charity is sound without soul." You can sing like a seraph, but without love it is nothing but the hiss of hell. Love gives meaning and depth and reality, and it makes eloquence meaningful.

And though I have the gift of prophecy, and understand all mysteries, and all knowledge; and though I have all faith, so that I could remove mountains, and have not charity, I am nothing [1 Cor. 13:2].

The first verse was speaking of love as it comes from the heart. This is from the mind, love as an act of the intellect. Knowledge alone is not sufficient. Love must be added to that knowledge. Understanding alone is not enough. Love must be added to that understanding. I feel this is the sad plight of Bible-believing churches in our day. There is a knowledge of the Bible and an understanding of the truths of the Bible but a lack of love. How terrible to find churches filled with gossip, bitterness, and hatred! Along with knowledge there must be love.

And though I bestow all my goods to feed the poor, and though I give my body to be burned, and have not charity, it profiteth me nothing [1 Cor. 13:3].

This love is an act of the will. Love involves the heart (v. 1), the mind (v. 2), and the will (v. 3). Love is a fruit of the Holy Spirit. Although we are to covet earnestly the best gifts, they are to be exercised in love—and only the Spirit of God can do that.

Look at it this way: Write down a string of zeros—eloquence alone is zero, prophecy alone is zero, knowledge alone is zero, faith alone is zero, sacrifice alone is zero, martyrdom alone is zero. Six zeros still add up to nothing. But you put the numeral 1 to the left of that string of zeros, and every zero amounts to something. And, friend, love is the thing that needs to be added to every gift of the Spirit. Without love your gift is worthless.

PREROGATIVE OF LOVE—ITS VIRTUE

Charity suffereth long, and is kind; charity envieth not; charity vaunteth not itself, is not puffed up [1 Cor. 13:4].

"Love suffers long," which means it is patient and kind. Love is impossible without kindness. Love without kindness is like springtime without flowers, like fire without heat. Remember how Paul admonished, "And be ye kind one to another, tenderhearted, forgiving one another, even as God for Christ's sake hath forgiven you" (Eph. 4:32). This is the positive side. Now notice the negative side.

"Love envieth not." Love does not envy, which means that love is content with its lot. We all know that life is filled with inequality. Some men are rich, and I hear Christians ask, "Why did God bless that man with so much wealth and not give me some?" Love recognizes that there are inequalities, and love is satisfied with its lot. Remember that the very first murder, when Cain slew Abel, was prompted by envy.

We do well to ponder the example of John the Baptist who showed no envy when the ministry of Jesus was growing in popularity with the people. John said, "He must increase, but I must decrease" (John 3:30). When we consider that we each have a different lot in life and each have a different ministry for the Lord, we should consider the words of our Lord Himself when He talked to Peter: ". . . If I will that he tarry till I come, what is that to thee? follow thou me" (John 21:22). Bacon said that envy "is a vile affection and it's most depraved of any thing."

An example of a man who loved another man without envy is Jonathan. Although he was the crown prince, he did not envy David even though he knew that David would occupy the throne in his stead.

"Love vaunteth not itself." Moffitt translates this "makes no parade." It is not boastful or ostentatious. You know, there is a vulgarity about boasting.

A young preacher stood up in a conference in Tennessee and said, "I want you to know that I'm not a trained minister. I am an ignorant minister, and I'm proud of it." The bishop answered him, "I can see you have a lot to be proud of, and, young man, it is dangerous to boast even about ignorance."

Love is "not puffed up." That means it does not travel on air—it is not inflated. You know what it is like to be traveling on a tire filled with air, then suddenly have a flat tire. There is many a flat tire even among Christians because there are so many who are puffed up. When the air is gone, there is nothing there!

Doth not behave itself unseemly, seeketh not her own, is not easily provoked, thinketh no evil [1 Cor. 13:5].

Love does not behave itself unseemly; that is, it doesn't act peculiar. It is true that in 1 Peter the believers are called a peculiar people, but they shouldn't act peculiar. It literally means a people for His possession. We are to exercise courtesy. We are not to be rude. We are not to act like strange people. We ought to be polite. Unfortunately, there is so much today that can be called unlovely religion. But love does not behave itself unseemly.

Love "seeketh not her own." Love inquires into the motives for action; that is, it asks, *Why* am I doing this?" Since I have been retired, I have examined my own heart as I never did before. I have searched out my own motives. Am I doing it out of love for Christ? That is so important. Love is the secret of service.

Love "is not easily provoked." It doesn't have a bad temper. Being provoked is the vice of the virtuous. I'm afraid it is the vice of many of us.

Love "thinketh no evil." How sad it is to see people thrive on gossip. There are Christians who ladle up dirt. They are suggestive in what they have to say.

Rejoiceth not in iniquity, but rejoiceth in the truth [1 Cor. 13:6].

Love does not rejoice in iniquity, but love rejoices in the truth. What brings joy to your heart? Bad or good? Which is it? If you hear something bad about someone who is your enemy or whom you do not like, do you rejoice? Or does it make you sad to see your enemy suffer?

Beareth all things, believeth all things, hopeth all things, endureth all things [1 Cor. 13:7].

Love bears all things. "Bears" has the thought of protection. Love puts up an umbrella for others.

Love "believeth all things." That does not mean that love is foolishly credulous. It does mean that love does not regard people with suspicion.

Love "hopeth all things." Oh, the optimism of love!

It "endureth all things." Love remains strong through testing.

We learn from all this that love is an abstract noun, but it is not to remain abstract. It is to be translated into life and action. It is to express itself in action through patience, through kindness, without envy, without boastfulness.

PERMANENCE OF LOVE—ITS VICTORY

Charity never faileth: but whether there be prophecies, they shall fail; whether there be tongues, they shall cease; whether there be knowledge, it shall vanish away [1 Cor. 13:8].

Love never fails. That is why at the end of the chapter it says, "Now abideth faith, hope, charity, these three; but the greatest of these is charity. Love abides. It is permanent.

Elizabeth Barrett Browning wrote a poem entitled "I Loved Once," in which she writes, "They never loved who dreamed that they loved once," and "Love looks beyond the bounds of time and space, Love takes eternity in its embrace." Love is deathless. It is never defeated, never disillusioned, never disappointed. Love that is a passion burns like a straw stack and is soon consumed. That is the reason there are so many divorces today. It was not the kind of love that holds two hearts together. Love is eternal. It is permanent. God's love is that kind of love. How wonderful that is! His love looks beyond the bounds of time and space and takes eternity in its embrace. Christ never ceased loving. You can't do anything to keep Him from loving. No sinner has committed an unpardonable sin. You may be in the state of unbelief, but He still loves you. You may have committed ever so great a sin, but He still loves you. You cannot keep Him from loving you. You can put up an umbrella to keep yourself out of the rain, but you cannot stop the rain from falling. Neither can you stop God from loving you—regardless of the umbrella of sin or unbelief that you are under.

It is so wrong to tell children that God won't love them. I used to be in a Sunday school class of little fellows. They were a bunch of mean brats—I was the only good boy in the class! The teacher would say to us, "God won't love you boys if you keep acting that way." I used to think, *God surely can't love me very much.* But He *did* in spite of my meanness. How wonderful it is to know that God loves us!

Prophecies shall fail—that is, they will be fulfilled. They will then be history, not prophecy. Tongues are going to stop. Knowledge will vanish away. For example, the science that I learned in college is already out of date. The science of today will be replaced by the science of tomorrow. Knowledge is progressive. It vanishes away.

For we know in part, and we prophesy in part.

But when that which is perfect is come, then that which is in part shall be done away [1 Cor. 13:9–10].

Paul says this:

When I was a child, I spake as a child, I understood as a child, I thought as a child: but when I became a man, I put away childish things.

For now we see through a glass, darkly; but then face to face: now I know in part; but then shall I know even as also I am known [1 Cor. 13:11–12].

A great many people ask, "Will I know my loved ones in heaven?" You surely will. What is the scriptural proof? "Now we see through a glass, darkly." You have never seen me. It is possible you may think you have seen me, but what you saw was a suit of clothes with a head and two hands sticking out of it. You didn't really see me. And I have never really seen you, because we just see through a glass, darkly, but then face to face. Now I know only in part, but then I shall know even as also I am known. Someone asked G. Campbell Morgan,

"Do you think we will know our loved ones in heaven?" Dr. Morgan in his truly British manner answered, "I do not expect to be a bigger fool in heaven than I am here, and I know my loved ones here."

And now abideth faith, hope, charity, these three; but the greatest of these is charity [1 Cor. 13:13].

The object of our faith will be fulfilled. All our hopes will be realized. There will be nothing left to hope for; so hope will disappear. There will be no need for faith. However, love is going to abide. The greatest of these is love. Faith, hope, and love are the high words of the Christian vocabulary.

In this chapter Paul is not describing an abstract term—love. He is writing a biography of Jesus Christ. Of Him it was written, ". . . having loved his own which were in the world, he loved them unto the end" (John 13:1). The love of Jesus is an eternal love. My friend, Jesus Christ will never cease loving you.

CHAPTER 14

THEME: *Exercise of gifts*

We are in the section of the epistle concerning spiritual gifts. In chapter 12 we saw the endowment of gifts. Gifts were given to maintain the unity of the church in a diversity. Each member has a separate gift; yet all are to function together as the body functions with its many members. The eye cannot do what the ear does, and the ear cannot do what the eye does. Each must function in its own way.

We are put into the body of Christ by the Holy Spirit, and we are placed there to exercise a gift. Paul tells us at the end of chapter 12 that we should covet earnestly the best gifts, and yet he will show us a more excellent way. That way is by love. The entire chapter 13 is on the subject of love. He concludes by saying that the greatest of these is love, and he continues by saying that we are to follow after love.

GIFT OF PROPHECY IS SUPERIOR TO GIFT OF TONGUES

Paul now follows right on and says that we should follow after love, but we should desire spiritualities.

Follow after charity, and desire spiritual gifts, but rather that ye may prophesy [1 Cor. 14:1].

We should desire spiritual gifts—I think it would be unusual if a Christian didn't want that—"but rather that ye may prophesy." To prophesy is to give out the Word of God, to speak it simply and to speak it intelligently.

He makes a distinction between the gifts which the Spirit gives and the fruit of the Spirit. The fruit of the Spirit is love, joy, peace, etc., which are more important than the gifts of the Spirit. Some very sincere people say to me, "Dr. McGee, I am going to pray that you receive the gift of the Spirit." I tell them I appreciate their interest, but I would rather they would pray that I may have the fruit of the Spirit. I wish I could see more fruit of the Spirit in the lives of the believers and in myself. I would like to see more love. That is the essential thing, and that is the fruit of the Holy Spirit. Only the Spirit of God can produce fruit in our lives.

"But rather that ye may prophesy." Actually, Paul was trying to get the Corinthians off this preoccupation with tongues. In effect he is saying to them in this whole section, "Cool it, brethren, don't go off into fanaticism or an emotional binge. Hold all things in their right proportion." In the previous chapter he said that tongues will cease. They will stop. That is the same word that we see posted on the highway. A traffic officer once told me that s-t-o-p means stop! I am afraid a great many folk do not understand what Paul is saying here: "Whether there be tongues, they shall stop." It was Dr. A. T. Robertson who made this statement: "Tongues seem to have ceased first of all the gifts." Chrysostom, one of the early church fathers, writing in the third or fourth century, stated: "This whole passage is very obscure; but the obscurity arises from our ignorance of the facts described, which, though familiar to those to whom the apostle wrote, have ceased to occur."

It is interesting to note that Jesus never spoke in tongues. There is no record of the apostles speaking in tongues after Pentecost. We do not have an historical record of Paul speaking in tongues or any sermon delivered in a tongue—although we know from verse 18 that Paul did speak in tongues because he said, "I thank my God, I speak with tongues more than ye all." I did not realize the import of this statement until I was in Turkey. I visited the ruins of the seven churches there, and obviously Paul had preached in all of them; then going way out into the interior, into Anatolia, I realized that Paul had walked across that section—all the way from Tarsus, his hometown. It is a distance of hundreds of miles, and in that section there was tribe after tribe speaking different languages. I have often wondered how Paul was able to speak to them. Well, he spoke as the apostles did on the Day of Pentecost. Every man heard him speak in his own tongue. He probably said to the Corinthians, "If you want tongues, go out on the mission field and start speaking in the languages of those people."

Today God has raised up certain organizations like the Wycliffe Bible Translators who are attempting to translate the Bible into all the known tongues of the world. That, my friend, is the greatest tongues movement that I know anything about!

We know that at one time Paul was caught up to the third heaven. He tells us that he heard *unspeakable* words. I don't think those were *unknown* words or unknown tongues; they were words that he was not permitted to speak. Tongues are not a rapturous, ecstatic, mysterious language. They are not a mixed-up medley of rhapsody. Tongues were foreign languages. On the Day of Pentecost the apostles spoke in foreign languages so that every man there heard the gospel in his own language.

Now notice that chapter 14 is an extension of the love chapter. It begins: "Follow after charity [love], and desire spiritual gifts, but rather that ye may prophesy."

For he that speaketh in an unknown tongue speaketh not unto men, but unto God: for no man understandeth him; howbeit in the spirit he speaketh mysteries [1 Cor. 14:2].

Note that the word *unknown* is in italics in your Bible, and that means it is not in the original Greek. Nowhere in the Bible does it speak of unknown tongues. It should read: "For he that speaketh in a tongue speaketh not unto men, but unto God: for no man understandeth him; howbeit in the spirit he speaketh mysteries." Because nobody will understand him, he is not to speak in a language that is unknown to the group—unless somebody there can interpret.

We will see in this chapter that there are three gifts which Paul emphasizes: prophecy, tongues, and the interpretation of tongues. Have you ever noticed that there is very little reference to tongues in the Bible except in these three chapters? There are references to it in Mark 16:17 and Acts 2:3–4,11; 10:46; 19:6. Cornelius and his household spoke in tongues. The disciples of John in Ephesus spoke in tongues after Paul had preached the gospel to them. We find, therefore, that tongues were used at the institution of the dispensation of grace. Every time tongues were used, they were used in that connection. There was speaking in tongues on the Day of Pentecost when the gospel went to the nation of Israel. There was speaking in tongues at the home of Cornelius when the gospel was opened to the Gentiles. There was speaking in tongues in Ephesus when the gospel moved out into the uttermost parts of the earth. Those are the three instances.

"For he that speaketh in a tongue speaketh not unto men, but unto God: for no man understandeth him; howbeit in the spirit he speaketh mysteries." That is, he doesn't understand it.

But he that prophesieth speaketh unto men to edification, and exhortation, and comfort [1 Cor. 14:3].

Paul is emphasizing the gift of prophecy. He asks them not to go into the tongues which were delighting them, but to speak the Word of God which is for edification, for comfort, and for exhortation.

He that speaketh in an unknown tongue edifieth himself; but he that prophesieth edifieth the church [1 Cor. 14:4].

The tongue, when it is exercised by the individual, is a selfish sort of gift, but prophesying, or teaching, is for the edification of the church.

I would that ye all spake with tongues, but rather that ye prophesied: for greater is he that prophesieth than he that speaketh with tongues, except he

interpret, that the church may receive edifying [1 Cor. 14:5].

To prophesy is to give forth the Word of God. The important thing is not a tongues meeting but a Bible study. "He that prophesieth" is one that teaches. No one is to speak in tongues unless there is someone there to interpret so learning can take place.

Now, brethren, if I come unto you speaking with tongues, what shall I profit you, except I shall speak to you either by revelation, or by knowledge, or by prophesying, or by doctrine? [1 Cor. 14:6].

Paul is saying, "If I don't make any sense when I come to talk to you, what is the use of my coming?"

And even things without life giving sound, whether pipe or harp, except they give a distinction in the sounds, how shall it be known what is piped or harped?

For if the trumpet give an uncertain sound, who shall prepare himself to the battle? [1 Cor. 14:7–8].

I have often thought that I could be a musician if I could do with a musical instrument what the "unknown tongues" folk do with sounds. Although I cannot read music and have no ear for it, I could just toot away on a horn. But of course it would just be a meaningless noise. Even a lifeless instrument like that is to have meaning in this world.

"If the trumpet give an uncertain sound, who shall prepare himself to the battle?" The trumpet was used to alert the troops for battle. And, my friend, today we need a clear-cut presentation of the gospel.

So likewise ye, except ye utter by the tongue words easy to be understood, how shall it be known what is spoken? for ye shall speak into the air [1 Cor. 14:9].

Paul says in effect, "Let's get off this kick. Let's start making sense, if you don't mind."

There are, it may be, so many kinds of voices in the world, and none of them is without signification.

Therefore if I know not the meaning of the voice, I shall be unto him that speaketh a barbarian, and he that speaketh shall be a barbarian unto me.

Even so ye, forasmuch as ye are zealous of spiritual gifts, seek that ye may excel to the edifying of the church [1 Cor. 14:10–12].

There are many languages in the world. However, there cannot be communication between people who do not speak the same language. If you speak in a language that no one in the church can understand, how can this edify the people in the church? That is the important issue. Does it edify the church? Does it build up the believers?

Wherefore let him that speaketh in an unknown tongue pray that he may interpret [1 Cor. 14:13].

Anything that is said in a tongue should be interpreted. Otherwise it does not make any sense to anyone. If the speaker cannot interpret, then there must be someone else there who has the gift of interpretation.

For if I pray in an unknown tongue, my spirit prayeth, but my understanding is unfruitful [1 Cor. 14:14].

That, my friend, is the answer to those who say that they speak in tongues for their private devotions. If the "understanding is unfruitful," you don't get a spiritual lift out of it; that is, the Holy Spirit is not ministering to you. If you get a lift, it is merely psychological. Paul says your understanding is unfruitful.

What is it then? I will pray with the spirit, and I will pray with the understanding also: I will sing with the spirit, and I will sing with the understanding also.

Else when thou shalt bless with the spirit, how shall he that occupieth the room of the unlearned say Amen at thy giving of thanks, seeing he understandeth not what thou sayest? [1 Cor. 14:15–16].

In other words, say something profitable so a brother can say "amen" to it.

For thou verily givest thanks well, but the other is not edified.

I thank my God, I speak with tongues more than ye all:

Yet in the church I had rather speak five words with my understanding, that by my voice I might teach others also,

than ten thousand words in an unknown tongue [1 Cor. 14:17-19].

Now I think Paul means that, as a missionary,
he had spoken in at least a dozen different
tongues—and probably that could be multiplied by four or five. When he was out on the
mission field with a foreign tribe, they
couldn't understand his language and he
couldn't understand theirs. Then he spoke to
them in their tongue. He made sense to them,
but it didn't make sense to Paul himself. But
when he is in the church where there are
believers who speak the same language as he
does, he will speak in a tongue that everyone
can understand.

**Brethren, be not children in under-
standing: howbeit in malice be ye children, but in understanding be men
[1 Cor. 14:20].**

He is chiding the Corinthians again. He has
called them carnal—babes in Christ. Now he
tells them not to act like children.

**In the law it is written, With men of
other tongues and other lips will I
speak unto this people; and yet for all
that will they not hear me, saith the
Lord [1 Cor. 14:21].**

You see, he *does* mean a language that is understood. He says, "I am going to speak to
another people in *their* tongue."

**Wherefore tongues are for a sign, not to
them that believe, but to them that believe not: but prophesying serveth not
for them that believe not, but for them
which believe [1 Cor. 14:22].**

This is what he is saying: "When I went out to
the mission field [let's say Antioch in Pisidia],
they were speaking a different language, so I
spoke to them in their own tongue. And when
I presented the gospel to them in their own
language, they believed. Now when I meet
with these folk in the land of Israel, I speak in
the language they know and I know. Therefore
I am prophesying. That is, I am teaching the
Word of God to them."

ORDER IN LOCAL CHURCH
FOR EXERCISE OF ANY GIFT

**If therefore the whole church be come
together into one place, and all speak
with tongues, and there come in those
that are unlearned, or unbelievers, will
they not say that ye are mad? [1 Cor.
14:23].**

We do not want a stranger to step into the
church and think he has entered into a
group of people who have gone mad. If there is
one thing we need today, it is the logical,
meaningful presentation of the Word of God.
People in this world are intelligent, they are
scientific, they are sophisticated. They want a
logical message which can be understood. The
Word of God needs to be presented so it can be
understood.

**But if all prophesy, and there come in
one that believeth not, or one unlearned, he is convinced of all, he is
judged of all:**

**And thus are the secrets of his heart
made manifest; and so falling down on
his face, he will worship God, and report that God is in you of a truth [1 Cor.
14:24-25].**

In other words, if you are preaching the Word
of God and an unbeliever comes in, he will
come under conviction and be converted.

**How is it then, brethren? when ye come
together, every one of you hath a psalm,
hath a doctrine, hath a tongue, hath a
revelation, hath an interpretation. Let
all things be done unto edifying [1 Cor.
14:26].**

If there is going to be any speaking in a
tongue, there must be an interpreter there,
and the message must be edifying. A former
student of mine, who had been a Roman Catholic, went into a tongues meeting and recited
part of a mass in Latin. When he sat down,
another man rose up to interpret. He went on
to say this, that, and the other thing. Then
this friend of mine got up and said, "I just
want you to know that *that* is not what I said. I
gave you the Latin mass." And as he started
to tell them what he had really said, the
ushers hustled him out of the meeting and told
him not to come back. I don't blame them for
that, and I do not think it was proper for my
friend to do that. I simply tell this to emphasize the fact that speaking in a tongue may be
the least edifying and may even be a hoax.

**If any man speak in an unknown
tongue, let it be by two, or at the most
by three, and that by course; and let one
interpret.**

**But if there be no interpreter, let him
keep silence in the church; and let him
speak to himself, and to God [1 Cor.
14:27-28].**

Not only must there be edification, but there must be order. If someone is going to speak in a tongue, there must be an interpreter, and the message must make sense in conformity with the Word of God. If it is otherwise, the Spirit of God is not in it—you may be sure of that. If no interpreter is there, or if two or three have already spoken, the one wanting to speak in a tongue is to be silent. He can go off somewhere and speak by himself.

Let the prophets speak two or three, and let the other judge.

If any thing be revealed to another that sitteth by, let the first hold his peace [1 Cor. 14:29–30].

There were prophets in the church of that day, and they could speak prophetically. We know that the daughters of Philip prophesied (see Acts 21:9). In the same chapter we are told that Agabus also prophesied. We don't have that gift of foretelling the future anymore. Even the weatherman doesn't do very well in the area of prediction!

For ye may all prophesy one by one, that all may learn, and all may be comforted [1 Cor. 14:31].

They may all prophesy one by one. Everyone can have something to say about the Word of God. I have been greatly blessed by statements that some folk have made in testimony meetings.

And the spirits of the prophets are subject to the prophets.

For God is not the author of confusion, but of peace, as in all churches of the saints [1 Cor. 14:32–33].

A church service is to be orderly.

Let your women keep silence in the churches: for it is not permitted unto them to speak; but they are commanded to be under obedience, as also saith the law [1 Cor. 14:34].

Now what is he talking about here? Tongues. He is not saying that a woman is not to speak in church; he is saying that she is not to speak in tongues in the church. My friend, if you take the women out of the tongues movement, it would die overnight. You may say, "That's not a nice thing to say." I know it's not nice, but it is true.

And if they will learn any thing, let them ask their husbands at home: for it is a shame for women to speak in the church.

What? came the word of God out from you? or came it unto you only? [1 Cor. 14:35–36].

The Word of God came *to* them, of course.

If any man think himself to be a prophet, or spiritual, let him acknowledge that the things that I write unto you are the commandments of the Lord.

But if any man be ignorant, let him be ignorant [1 Cor. 14:37–38].

This is the real test. If a man today says that he is a prophet or that he is spiritual—because he can speak in tongues—let him acknowledge that what Paul is saying here is a commandment of the Lord.

Wherefore, brethren, covet to prophesy, and forbid not to speak with tongues.

Let all things be done decently and in order [1 Cor. 14:39–40].

Here again we are encouraged to covet the best gift. Evidently teaching the Word of God is the best one, and I thank God for that.

"Let all things be done decently and in order." This is a great principle. When I attended a tongues meeting in the South, I must confess that I could see neither rhyme nor reason in the entire service. It was all in confusion—not even an organized confusion, but *hopeless* confusion. Paul says that this is not the way things of God should be carried on.

This brings us to the conclusion of this section. If you have disagreed with me, I trust you will not fall out with me, but that you will search this Scripture. If I am wrong, pray for me.

CHAPTER 15

THEME: *Resurrection*

We have come to a chapter that can be classified as one of the most important and crucial chapters of the Bible. If you would select ten of the greatest chapters of the Bible—which men have done from the beginning of the Christian era—you will find that 1 Corinthians 15 will be on your list and has been on practically all the lists ever made. It is that important. It is so important that it actually answers the first heresy of the church, which was the denial of the bodily resurrection of the Lord Jesus Christ.

In this chapter Paul is coming to the third great spirituality. You will recall that first he dealt with carnalities. He dealt with those things which seemed so important to the Corinthians and still seem so important to us today. Then Paul turned from the carnalities to the spiritualities. How wonderful it is to know that every believer has a *gift* from the Holy Spirit. I can't think of anything more thrilling than to know that God has given you and me a gift to function in this world and that we are to be partners with Jesus Christ in the tremendous enterprise of making Him known!

Then Paul goes on to the great love chapter. All gifts are to be exercised in love, and love is a fruit of the Holy Spirit. It isn't something that we can work up. It is given to us. Above everything else we need to see love, this fruit of the Spirit, in the life of a believer.

Now we come to the third great spirituality, which is the fact of the resurrection of Jesus Christ and our own resurrection. The glory of the Chrisitan faith is that it never views life as ending with death. This life is not all there is. The Christian faith always looks beyond the sunset to the sunrise. It looks out yonder into eternity—and what a hope it offers! This is another factor which gives meaning and purpose to life. I expect to live an eternity. I am not in a hurry to get there, and I want to stay in this life as long as I can because I think that this is the place of service. I think this is the place of preparation. I think that rewards are determined by what we do down here, and I want to get a few good works on my side of the ledger. That is why I would like to stay here and serve Him as long as He will allow me to stay. We used to sing a song, "Will there be any stars in my crown?" I don't hear that sung anymore. Why not? Well, it is because people are trying to be the star down here. Oh, my friend, that we might get the tremendous

view which the resurrection of Jesus Christ should give to the believer. We have lost sight of the Ascension, and we have our minds on the incidentals. This adds up to one tragedy after another in the lives of professing Christians.

This great resurrection chapter actually deals with the gospel. It shows that the most important part of the gospel is the resurrection of Christ. Frankly, without that, everything else—even the death of Christ—is meaningless. He was delivered for our offenses and was raised again for our justification according to Romans 4:25. In His death He subtracted our sins, but in His resurrection He gave to us a sure, abundant entrance into heaven. We stand in His righteousness. He was delivered for our offenses, but He was raised again for our justification (our righteousness).

Before we get into this chapter, it would be well to define and delineate very sharply the meaning of the Resurrection. The Resurrection is not spiritual, but it is physical. The word is *anastasis nekrōn*, which means the "standing up of a corpse." These bodies of ours are to be raised; the Resurrection in Scripture always refers to the body. *Anastasis* means "to stand up." *Histemi* means "to cause to stand." *Ana* means the standing up of the body. It cannot refer to a spiritual resurrection.

C. S. Lewis, the brilliant Oxford don, ridiculed the liberals in England in his day. They would talk about the Resurrection being spiritual, so Lewis would ask, "What position does a spirit take when it stands up?" That is a question for the liberal to kick around for a while. Scripture teaches that the Resurrection means to stand up.

In Paul's day, in Corinth and in the Roman world, there were three philosophies concerning death and life after death. There was Stoicism, which taught that the soul merged into deity at death. There was, therefore, a destruction of the personality. Such a concept makes the Resurrection a nonentity. Then there was the Epicurean philosophy, which was materialistic. It taught that there was no existence beyond death. Death was the end of existence. The third was Platonism which taught the immortality of the soul, believing in a process like a transmigration. You still find that teaching in Platonism today in the religions of India and in the cults of America. It denies the bodily resurrection. Because of these philosophies, when Paul mentioned the Resurrection while he was in Athens, they thought he was talking about a new god.

We need to understand very clearly that Paul is not talking about a *spiritual* resurrection. The soul does not die. The minute a body dies, the person goes somewhere. If the person is a child of God, to be absent from the body means to be present with the Lord (see 2 Cor. 5:6–8). If a person is not a child of God, then he goes to the place of torment—our Lord labeled it that.

The divisions of this chapter are as follows:
1. The prominence of the Resurrection in the gospel—verses 1–4
2. The proofs of the Resurrection—verses 5–19
3. The parade of the Resurrection—verses 20–28
4. The program and pattern of the Resurrection—verses 29–50
5. The power of the Resurrection—verses 51–58

PROMINENCE OF RESURRECTION IN THE GOSPEL

Paul states that the Resurrection is part of the gospel; in fact, there is no gospel without the Resurrection. Dr. Machen says that Christianity does not rest on a set of ideas or creeds, but on facts. The gospel is not the Ten Commandments or the Sermon on the Mount. The gospel is a series of facts concerning a Person and that Person is Jesus Christ.

Now listen to the way Paul states it:

Moreover, brethren, I declare unto you the gospel which I preached unto you, which also ye have received, and wherein ye stand;

By which also ye are saved, if ye keep in memory what I preached unto you, unless ye have believed in vain.

For I delivered unto you first of all that which I also received, how that Christ died for our sins according to the scriptures;

And that he was buried, and that he rose again the third day according to the scriptures [1 Cor. 15:1–4].

The question sometimes arises whether the gospel originated with Paul. He says, "I delivered unto you . . . that which I received." From whom did he receive it and where? He received it out yonder in that Arabian desert where the Lord took him and taught him. When Paul was confronted by the Lord on the Damascus road, he did not know that Jesus was back from the dead. He asked, ". . . Who art thou, Lord? . . ." (Acts 9:5). He didn't dream that "the Lord" was Jesus. Paul himself had to be convinced of the resurrection of Jesus Christ. He didn't think it up. He received it.

Paul says that he declares the gospel to them. What is the gospel? "Christ died for our sins according to the scriptures; And that he was buried, and that he rose again the third day according to the scriptures." That is the gospel. These are the facts. My friend, there is no gospel apart from those three facts. That is what the gospel is. Jesus Christ died for you and for me. He was buried and He rose again. That is gospel—it's good news.

Now suppose that you come to me today and say, "Teacher, I have good news for you—I would like to see you become a millionaire." I would say, "Well, that would be nice." Then you would tell me your plan. You would say, "You get a job, and in a thousand years you will be worth a million dollars." I would say, "Well, I sure would like to have a million dollars; I could use it to get the gospel out, but if you think by my working I can make a million dollars, you are wrong. That's not good news. In fact, it is bad news!" However, suppose you come to me and say, "I have discovered someone who was interested in you. In fact, he loved you so much that when he died he left you a million dollars!" That, my friend, would be good news!

The gospel does not tell us something that we must do. The gospel tells us what Jesus Christ has already done for us. He died for our sins according to the Scriptures, He was buried, He rose again the third day.

He died. That is an historical fact. Very few would deny that. He was buried—that needs to be added. Why is that so important? It proves that He didn't just disappear. It means that they actually, literally had His body. Nicodemus and Joseph of Arimathaea and the others who saw Him crucified knew who He was. They knew it was Jesus. They buried Jesus. That is very important. It confirms His death.

He rose again the third day according to the Scriptures. The Resurrection is a part of the gospel. The tomb was empty. That is the proof. The gospel is that Jesus died, was buried, and rose again. This is the first proof.

There is another proof of the Resurrection,

and that is the experience of the Corinthians. Let's listen to it again. "Moreover, brethren, I declare unto you the gospel which I preached unto you, which also ye have received, and wherein ye stand; By which also ye are saved, if ye keep in memory what I preached unto you, unless ye have believed in vain" (vv. 1–2). "Unless ye have believed in vain"—that is, unless it was an empty faith.

There is a faith that is an empty faith, of course. But he says, "By which also ye are *saved*." The church is the proof of the Resurrection.

There were eleven discouraged men in Jerusalem or its environs. They were ready to go back to fishing. They had just gone through enough trouble. If Jesus was dead, they didn't want the body out of the grave. They wanted it to stay there. They wouldn't go break a Roman seal and face a Roman guard to steal a body which could only bring them more trouble. Then what happened? Word came to them that Jesus Christ had risen from the dead! That fact transformed these men. That revolutionary fact brought the church into existence. Through nineteen centuries there have been millions of people who have said that Jesus Christ is alive. You simply cannot explain the church apart from the Resurrection. I am saved by the death and resurrection of Jesus. Without His resurrection I would have no gospel, no living Christ, no Savior. The existence of the body of believers is the second great proof of the Resurrection.

There is another proof. Notice that it says He died for our sins "according to the scriptures" and that He was buried and rose again the third day "according to the scriptures." What Scriptures? The Old Testament Scriptures. I would love to have been with Paul the apostle when he arrived in Europe and went to Philippi, Thessalonica, then down to Athens, and over to Corinth. I think he had with him a parchment which was the Old Testament. I imagine that when he went into a synagogue and mentioned the death of the Lord Jesus, the Jews said, "But this is not in our Scriptures." Then he would turn to the Book of Genesis and say, "I'd like to remind you about the offering of Isaac and how Abraham received him back from the 'dead'—he was ready to kill the boy. Now God spared not His own Son, but delivered Him up freely for us all." Then he would turn to the Mosaic system of sacrifice, to the five offerings in Leviticus, and show them how they pictured Christ, then to the great Day of Atonement and the two goats which pictured Christ's death

and resurrection. Also he would cite Aaron's rod that budded and the Book of Jonah, which typifies resurrection. Then he would turn to Psalm 22 and Psalm 16. He would show them Isaiah 25 and in Isaiah 53 he would point out that He was wounded for our transgressions and He was bruised for our iniquities. All we like sheep have gone astray, we have turned everyone to his own way, and the Lord hath laid on Him the iniquity of all of us. So he could show them from the Old Testament Scriptures that Jesus Christ was to die and to rise again. The expectation of the Old Testament was not for this life only but also for the life that is to come.

There are some folk who say they do not believe in a "hereafter religion"; they want a here-and-now religion. May I say to you that I have both—a here-and-now religion and a hereafter religion.

PROOFS OF RESURRECTION—
WITNESSES

Now as another proof of the Resurrection Paul lists a number of witnesses. You just can't get around witnesses. Any lawyer today would love to have as many witnesses for his position as Paul lists here as proofs of the Resurrection.

And that he was seen of Cephas, then of the twelve [1 Cor. 15:5].

He mentions Cephas first. This is, of course, Simon Peter, to whom Jesus appeared privately. You may ask, "What took place?" It is none of my business, and I guess it is none of yours. It is not recorded for us. Jesus appeared to Peter. After all, he had denied Him. Peter had to get things straightened out with the Lord. You see, our Lord is still in the footwashing business.

Then He was seen "of the twelve." Who are the Twelve? He appeared to Cephas privately, then He appeared to the ten (Judas was dead at this time). "The Twelve" was used as a collective term for the body of disciples. It does not necessarily imply that twelve disciples were present. However, when you put them all together and Paul joins them, you have twelve men.

After that, he was seen of above five hundred brethren at once; of whom the greater part remain unto this present, but some are fallen asleep [1 Cor. 15:6].

Jesus was seen of five hundred people at one time. I think this was up yonder around the Sea of Galilee. Remember that He had told them He would meet with them in Galilee. So I believe that His true followers went up to Galilee to meet Him there. As they traveled northward, I'm sure folk would ask them, "Now that Jesus is dead, are you going back to fishing?" They would answer, "No, Jesus is back from the dead and we're going up there to meet Him." There were five hundred of His followers who met Him there.

After that, he was seen of James; then of all the apostles.

And last of all he was seen of me also, as of one born out of due time [1 Cor. 15:7–8].

"He was seen of James"—this was probably a private interview. He was seen again by all the apostles. Lastly, He was seen by Paul. My friend, it is very difficult to argue with a man who has seen Him.

For I am the least of the apostles, that am not meet to be called an apostle, because I persecuted the church of God.

But by the grace of God I am what I am: and his grace which was bestowed upon me was not in vain; but I laboured more abundantly than they all: yet not I, but the grace of God which was with me [1 Cor. 15:9–10].

Paul calls himself the least of the apostles. He is being very modest here. Inspiration guarantees that this is a statement which came from his heart. My heart says, "Paul, you're great. I can't consider you the least of the apostles." But Paul says he isn't worthy to be called an apostle because he persecuted the church of God. He considered himself to be the chief of sinners. Yet he was the hardest worker of any of the apostles. But, very candidly, he tells us that it was the grace of God that enabled him to accomplish what he did.

Therefore whether it were I or they, so we preach, and so ye believed [1 Cor. 15:11].

I am tired of men talking about being Christians and denying the facts of the gospel. You are not a Christian if you deny the death, burial, and resurrection of Christ. You have a perfect right to deny these things if you wish, but you have no right then to call yourself a Christian. It says here that when these Corinthians heard the gospel, they believed, and that is when they became Christians.

This is so crucial and so critical that we are going to review it to emphasize it. What is the gospel? It is the good news that Christ died, was buried, and rose again on the third day. He didn't vanish or disappear. He rose again. The tomb is empty. Jesus Christ is alive today. These are the historical facts. The gospel is not a theory, not an idea, not a religion. The gospel consists of objective facts. This is the gospel which Paul preached. It is not simply a subjective experience which Paul had; it is fact.

It tells us in verse 1 that the Corinthians received it and in verse 11 that they believed it. What does it mean to receive Christ? John 1:11–13 tells us, "He came unto his own, and his own received him not. But as many as received him, to them gave he power to become the sons of God, even to them that believe on his name: Which were born, not of blood, nor of the will of the flesh, nor of the will of man, but of God." To receive Christ means to believe on His name. Our first verse says of the gospel relative to the Corinthians, "which also ye have received, and wherein ye stand." That was their current state. They stood in a living faith in relationship with a living Lord Jesus Christ. Where do you stand today?

The second verse says, "By which also ye are saved." The gospel does not save if it is just a head knowledge. It is not just a nodding assent to the facts. It is the *One* of whom the gospel speaks who does the saving—Christ saves. When you accept the facts of the gospel, when you put your faith in Christ absolutely, then you are saved. As Spurgeon put it, "It is not thy joy in Christ that saves thee. It is not thy hope in Christ that saves thee. It is Christ. It is not even thy faith in Christ, though that be the instrument." It is Christ's blood and merit that saves.

This gospel was preached to the Corinthians. Paul said, "You received it, you stand in it, and you are saved." Then he adds, "Unless ye have believed in vain." If their faith does not rest upon the facts, then it is a vain faith, of no effect, and theirs is not a genuine conversion. Faith itself has no merit. The important thing is the object of your faith—in *whom* you believe. Have you trusted a Savior who died, who was buried, and who rose again from the dead?

We spoke of the significance of the testimony of the Old Testament Scriptures as an evidence of the Resurrection. Then there were the witnesses who were alive at the time Paul was writing: Cephas, the twelve, the five hundred, James, all the apostles, and finally he himself, all of whom saw the resurrected

Christ. Of himself he says, "as of one born out of due time." That is, his was not a late birth but an abortion, a premature birth. He is a picture of that remnant which is to be saved after the church is removed from this earth.

Now if Christ be preached that he rose from the dead, how say some among you that there is no resurrection of the dead? [1 Cor. 15:12].

Some of these people with backgrounds of Stoicism, Epicureanism, and Platonism were denying the Resurrection. It wasn't that they were specifically denying the resurrection of Jesus Christ, but they did not believe in any resurrection at all.

Now Paul begins a series of "ifs"—"if Christ be not risen." Paul faced the fact. My Christian friend, don't hide your head like an ostrich under the sand and say, "Well, we can't be sure about the Resurrection, so let's not say too much about it. Let's walk as if we were walking on eggshells." My friend, I am on a foundation; that foundation is the Rock, and the Rock is Christ. He came back from the dead. Paul is not afraid that Christ might not have risen from the dead. He puts down these "ifs" as a demonstration of the importance of the resurrection of Jesus Christ.

But if there be no resurrection of the dead, then is Christ not risen [1 Cor. 15:13].

If there is no resurrection from the dead, then Christ is not risen. They are linked together. And it is on the basis of the resurrection of Christ—Paul is going to say later on—that Jesus Christ is the firstfruits. That means there will be more to follow. He is the firstfruits, and later at His coming there will be the resurrection of those who are His.

And if Christ be not risen, then is our preaching vain, and your faith is also vain [1 Cor. 15:14].

Perhaps you belong to a church which denies that Christ arose from the dead. If Christ is not bodily risen from the dead, then our preaching is vain. Not only that, but our faith is vain also. You might just as well drop your church membership. It's no good. There is no reason to go to church or to hear a sermon if Christ is not raised from the dead.

Yea, and we are found false witnesses of God; because we have testified of God that he raised up Christ: whom he raised not up, if so be that the dead rise not [1 Cor. 15:15].

All the apostles were liars if Christ had not risen. Every one of these men was a false witness if Christ is still in the grave. Have you ever noticed that men do not die for that which they know to be a lie? Men *do* die for a lie, but they think it is the truth. For instance, millions of men died for Hitler because they believed in him. The apostles testified that they saw the risen Christ, and they were willing to die for that declaration. I'll let you decide if they were right or wrong. But men do *not* die for what they *know* is a lie.

For if the dead rise not, then is not Christ raised:

And if Christ be not raised, your faith is vain; ye are yet in your sins [1 Cor. 15:16–17].

If Christ is not raised, then, my friend, you are a lost, hell-doomed sinner, and that is all you can ever be. If Christ be not raised, every one of us is still in our sins.

Then they also which are fallen asleep in Christ are perished [1 Cor. 15:18].

There have been millions upon millions of believers who have died trusting Christ as their Savior. If Christ is not risen, then every one of them has perished.

If in this life only we have hope in Christ, we are of all men most miserable [1 Cor. 15:19].

May I say to you that I think Christianity is a here-and-now religion. Paul makes that clear in the sixth chapter of Romans. But Christianity is also a hereafter religion. If Christ be not raised, we have been deluded and we are about the most miserable people in this world today. But we're not! We are rejoicing!

That is the end of Paul's "*ifs.*" Will you face up to the possibilities which he presents? Go through the "*ifs*" logically and you will see that the human family is lost and hopeless if Christ had not been raised from the dead.

PARADE OF THE RESURRECTION

So I want to join Paul as he declares the Resurrection—

But now is Christ risen from the dead, and become the firstfruits of them that slept [1 Cor. 15:20].

Christ is the firstfruits. In the Old Testament they had the festival of firstfruits when they would bring the first sheaf of grain to the Lord. This meant that there would be more to come, otherwise it couldn't be the firstfruits. The fulfillment of that is in the resurrection of Jesus Christ. He came back from the dead in a glorified body. And He is the only one who has come back from the dead in a glorified body.

For since by man came death, by man came also the resurrection of the dead.

For as in Adam all die, even so in Christ shall all be made alive [1 Cor. 15:21–22].

After the festival of the firstfruits came Pentecost, which was fifty days later. That found its fulfillment in Pentecost in the New Testament when the church began. But it will find its ultimate fulfillment when Christ comes for His own and they shall all rise to meet Him in the air. That will be the real Pentecost. A Pentecostal brother of mine said, "You know, Brother McGee, I'm expecting a Pentecost." I shocked him when I said, "I'm looking for Pentecost too." He said, "Oh, you don't mean it!" I said, "I don't mean it like *you* mean it— you think you are going to repeat the Day of Pentecost down here. The Pentecost I am waiting for is when the Lord Jesus comes to take His church out of his world." Christ is the firstfruits.

But every man in his own order: Christ the firstfruits; afterward they that are Christ's at his coming [1 Cor. 15:23].

How wonderful that is! "Christ is risen from the dead, and become the firstfruits of them that slept"—meaning the sleep of death. "For since by man came death [that man is Adam], by man came also the resurrection of the dead." "In Adam all die"—the proof that you are in the family of Adam is that you are going to die unless the Lord comes to take you in the Rapture. "Even so in Christ shall all be made alive." Jesus is the Resurrection and the Life.

"But every man in his own order." There is not a general resurrection day. It is interesting that the Reformers recovered a great deal of the truth of the Bible, but they didn't recover all of it. We are living in a day when there is much Bible study in the field of eschatology; that is, the doctrine of the last things—prophecy. It is a study of prophecy. In times when great truths are being recovered one also finds a lot of heresy and just plain "nutty" ideas. There is a lot of false teaching about prophecy, largely because of ignorance of the whole scope of Scripture. I firmly believe that the Book of Revelation should not be taught unless one has studied the other books of the Bible first. Prophecy is important, but it is not everything. The great Reformers recovered much Bible truth, but they missed this teaching of the Bible that every man will be raised in his own order, that there is not a general resurrection day.

Christ is the firstfruits, and then "afterward they that are Christ's at his coming." What is He coming for? He is coming for His church, my friend.

Then cometh the end, when he shall have delivered up the kingdom to God, even the Father; when he shall have put down all rule and all authority and power [1 Cor. 15:24].

"Then cometh the end"—the end of what? The end of the age. How will the age end? There will come the Great Tribulation, and then there is going to be the millennial kingdom here on the earth. Satan will be released again for a little while, then he will be cast forever into the lake of fire, and the Lord Jesus Christ will establish His kingdom forever. That will be the eternal kingdom. Actually, the eternal kingdom is a further projection of the millennial kingdom, only the millennial kingdom will be a time of trial. "Then cometh the end, when he shall have delivered up the kingdom to God." When will this take place? At the end of the millennial kingdom, Christ will put down all rule and all authority and power.

For he must reign, till he hath put all enemies under his feet [1 Cor. 15:25].

That is Satan.

The last enemy that shall be destroyed is death [1 Cor. 15:26].

I'll be glad when we get rid of that fellow!

For he hath put all things under his feet. But when he saith all things are put under him, it is manifest that he is excepted, which did put all things under him [1 Cor. 15:27].

So Christ is not subject to God—but wait a minute, notice what the next verse says.

And when all things shall be subdued unto him, then shall the Son also himself be subject unto him that put all things under him, that God may be all in all [1 Cor. 15:28].

This means that when Christ has completed His millennial reign here upon this earth and has established His eternal reign (I believe that He will turn over to David His throne on the earth), then He will return back to His place in the Godhead where He was in the beginning, so that "God may be all in all."

PROGRAM AND PATTERN OF THE RESURRECTION

Else what shall they do which are baptized for the dead, if the dead rise not at all? why are they then baptized for the dead? [1 Cor. 15:29].

"What shall they do"—that is, what shall they accomplish?

We have already learned that the word *baptize* means identification with someone or something. In this case Paul is speaking of identification as a dead person. He asks, "What shall they accomplish which are baptized for the dead, if the dead rise not at all?" Why are they then identified as the dead? This does not imply that the Corinthian believers were being baptized for their dead relatives or friends. It means that they were baptized or identified with Christ Jesus—who had died for them and He was now risen from the dead. They were dead to the world but were alive to Christ.

And why stand we in jeopardy every hour?

I protest by your rejoicing which I have in Christ Jesus our Lord, I die daily [1 Cor. 15:30–31].

Paul is saying that if Christ be not raised from the dead, then they are foolish to put their lives in danger. However, since Christ *is* raised from the dead, believers are identified with Him. As Paul said to the believers at Rome, "Know ye not, that so many of us as were baptized into Jesus Christ were baptized into his death? Therefore we are buried with him by baptism into death: that like as Christ was raised up from the dead by the glory of the Father, even so we also should walk in newness of life" (Rom. 6:3–4). We are joined to a resurrected, living Christ. "Now if Christ was not resurrected, then," Paul says, "I am foolish to make the sacrifices I have made down here—my life stands in jeopardy every hour. I am constantly in danger of death."

If after the manner of men I have fought with beasts at Ephesus, what advantageth it me, if the dead rise not? let us eat and drink; for to-morrow we die [1 Cor. 15:32].

Paul asks, "Why should I be put in a lions' cage for my faith in Christ if Christ did not rise

from the dead? I am identified—I am baptized—into His death. I am identified as a dead man because I am joined to a living Christ." Being identified with Christ in His death and resurrection is a tremendous fact! Let's not reduce it to some little water baptismal service that would be meaningless.

If Christ is not risen and if the dead will not be resurrected, then we might as well adopt the hedonistic philosophy of the Epicureans who say, "Let us eat and drink; for to-morrow we die."

Be not deceived: evil communications corrupt good manners.

Awake to righteousness, and sin not; for some have not the knowledge of God: I speak this to your shame [1 Cor. 15:33–34].

The Corinthian believers were being deceived by those who questioned the Resurrection. They were listening to those who had plenty to say but no knowledge of God. Paul is saying that if they get the wrong information, they will act wrong. He admonishes them to stop sinning—because there *will* be a resurrection.

But some man will say, How are the dead raised up? and with what body do they come? [1 Cor. 15:35].

Paul will answer two questions: the *how* and the *what*. Men fail to distinguish the difference between the resurrection of the body and the immortality of the soul. Plato and Cicero argued for the immortality of the soul. Paul is arguing for the resurrection of the body. The Sadducees denied any resurrection, any life after death. And Christ Himself had answered them: "But as touching the resurrection of the dead, have ye not read that which was spoken unto you by God, saying, I am the God of Abraham, and the God of Isaac, and the God of Jacob? God is not the God of the dead, but of the living" (Matt. 22:31–32).

Paul has answered those who denied the resurrection of the body by the resurrection of Christ whose body was raised up.

Now the question is, "How can a body that dies be raised up again and be the same?" Paul says that we learn from nature that the bodies are not identical—they are the same but not identical.

Thou fool, that which thou sowest is not quickened, except it die [1 Cor. 15:36].

The answer to the first question: the *how*. He says in effect, "If you only had sense enough to see it, you would see that in a seed which is planted, there is dissolution and continuity—a seed that is planted will produce seeds which are essentially the same as that seed. But the seed itself has died and disintegrated, so that the seed it produces is not the very seed that died. It is like that seed, but it is not the same seed. In the seed that is planted there is a disintegration and yet there is a continuity. It is a mystery, but it is not an impossibility."

What is death? Death is a separation. It is not the ending of the spirit or of the personality. These do not die. The real "you" goes on to be with the Lord if you are a child of God. It is the body that disintegrates. Death is a separation of the body from the individual, from the person. The body disintegrates, decays, decomposes. Dust to dust and ashes to ashes applies only to the body.

Paul now answers the second question: *What* body is raised up?

> **And that which thou sowest, thou sowest not that body that shall be, but bare grain, it may chance of wheat, or of some other grain [1 Cor. 15:37].**

The sowing of grain is the illustration. Christ is the firstfruits, then we'll be coming along later. We are waiting for the rapture of the church when Christ takes the believers out of the world. If at the time of the Rapture we are already dead, we will be raised up. If we are still alive at the time of the Rapture, we'll be caught up and changed. The seed, you see, does not provide itself with a new body, neither does the sower, but God provides it:

> **But God giveth it a body as it hath pleased him, and to every seed his own body [1 Cor. 15:38].**

Then Paul moves into another area. All of this is the mystery of life. Actually the mystery of life is greater than the mystery of death. When you sow wheat, wheat comes up—not barley or corn. That little grain that forms on the stalk is like the one you sowed—not identical, but certainly very similar.

Now he moves from the area of botany to zoology.

> **All flesh is not the same flesh: but there is one kind of flesh of men, another flesh of beasts, another of fishes, and another of birds [1 Cor. 15:39].**

The difference between a dead body and the resurrection body is greater than the difference between men and beasts, fish and birds. Paul says that all flesh is not the same flesh.

> **There are also celestial bodies, and bodies terrestrial: but the glory of the celestial is one, and the glory of the terrestrial is another.**

> **There is one glory of the sun, and another glory of the moon, and another glory of the stars: for one star differeth from another star in glory [1 Cor. 15:40–41].**

Now he has moved into the realm of astronomy and says that all the bodies of the solar system are not the same. The sun is not the same material as the moon, neither is it the same as the stars. The stars differ from each other. There is a solar system, a stellar system, planets, and suns.

> **So also is the resurrection of the dead. It is sown in corruption; it is raised in incorruption [1 Cor. 15:42].**

You see, the body that was given Adam was always subject to death. Although he would not have died if he had not sinned, his body would have been subject to death. However, by resurrection we get a body that is incorruptible.

> **It is sown in dishonour; it is raised in glory: it is sown in weakness; it is raised in power [1 Cor. 15:43].**

We will get glory and color and beauty and power—all of these things—with the new body.

> **It is sown a natural body; it is raised a spiritual body. There is a natural body, and there is a spiritual body [1 Cor. 15:44].**

Many years ago in the city of New York (in fact, it was way back in the day when liberalism was called modernism, back in the 1920s) they had an argument about whether resurrection was spiritual. The liberal even today claims it's spiritual. He doesn't believe in bodily resurrection at all. A very famous Greek scholar from the University of Chicago read a paper on the passage from this verse. His paper put the emphasis on the word *spiritual*. He concluded by saying, "Now, brethren, you can see that resurrection is spiritual because it says it's spiritual." The liberals all applauded, and somebody made a motion that they print that manuscript and circulate it. Well, a very fine Greek scholar was there, and he stood up. And when he stood up all the liberals were a little uneasy. He could ask very embarrassing questions. He said, "I'd like to ask the author of the paper a question." Very reluctantly, the good doctor stood up. "Now, doctor, which is stronger, a noun or an adjective? A very simple question, but I'd like for you to answer it." He could see the direction he was going and didn't want to answer it, but he had to. "Well," he said, "a noun is stronger, of course." "Now doctor, I'm amazed that you presented the paper that you did today. You put the emphasis upon an adjective, and the strong word is the noun. Now let's look at that again. 'It is sown a natural body; it is raised a spiritual body.'" He said, "The only thing that is carried over in resurrection is the body. It's one kind of body when it dies, a natural body. It's raised a body, but a spiritual body, dominated now by the spirit—but it's still a body." And, you know, they never did publish that paper. They decided it would be better not to publish it. May I say to you, just a simple little exercise in grammar answered this great professor's whole manuscript and his entire argument which he presented at that time.

And so it is written, The first man Adam was made a living soul; the last Adam was made a quickening spirit [1 Cor. 15:45].

You see, the first man, Adam, was psychical—*psuchen* and *zosan* in the Greek. That means he was physical and psychological. The last Adam (Christ) is spiritual—*pneuma* or pneumatical, if you want the English equivalent.

Howbeit that was not first which is spiritual, but that which is natural; and afterward that which is spiritual.

The first man is of the earth, earthy: the second man is the Lord from heaven [1 Cor. 15:46–47].

The first man is of the earth and is earthy—*choikos*, meaning "clay," rubbish if you please. There is so much talk of ecology today. Who messed up this earth anyway? Man. Because man is earthy. Everything that is the refuse of man is rubbish. He is that kind of creature. He fills the garbage cans. But the Second Man is the Lord from heaven.

As is the earthy, such are they also that are earthy: and as is the heavenly, such are they also that are heavenly.

And as we have borne the image of the earthy, we shall also bear the image of the heavenly.

Now this I say, brethren, that flesh and blood cannot inherit the kingdom of God; neither doth corruption inherit incorruption [1 Cor. 15:48–50].

We are all earthy. We are from Adam and that is our condition. But we are also in Christ. We are joined to Him, and therefore we have a hope, the hope of the resurrection in an eternal body which will forever be with Christ. Today we bear the image of the earthy, but we look forward to the day when we will bear the image of the heavenly.

Flesh and blood cannot inherit the kingdom of God. Our old bodies are not going to heaven—I'm glad of that. I would like to trade mine in. God is not going to send these bodies into a repair shop. Corruption cannot inherit incorruption. This body must be put into the ground, like a seed. It will come up a new body, a new tabernacle for us to live in. It will not be identical to the old body and yet it will be like the old body.

Out here on the west coast there are many atheists who have their ashes scattered out over the Pacific Ocean after they die. In other words, they challenge God to try to put all of those atoms together again. Our bodies are made up of a few chemicals. Most of the body's composition is water, hydrogen, and oxygen, with other atoms thrown in with it. Do you think that God cannot bring those atoms together? Or maybe He wants to use other atoms. After all, hydrogen atoms are all very much alike. It wouldn't make any difference to me if He used other atoms to make my new body. What nonsense to discount the Resurrection because of this! Yet one of the foremost arguments against the possibility of resurrection is that God would not be able to regather all those atoms! My friend, since He made the body to begin with, He certainly can make another like it. He is God, isn't He? God will get your body together again whether it comes out of the grave or its ashes are scattered out there in the ocean.

The first heresy in the church was the denial of the bodily resurrection. We see how Paul has shown the truth of the Resurrection. He has spoken against the three major philosophies of his day. Stoicism said the soul merged into Deity at death and there was a destruction of personality. Paul says our bodies shall rise. Epicureanism said there was no existence beyond death. Paul says Jesus Christ was raised from the dead and our bodies, too, shall rise. Platonism believed in the immortality of the soul but denied the bodily resurrection. Paul says that our physical bodies shall be made alive as spiritual bodies.

POWER OF THE RESURRECTION

Behold, I shew you a mystery; We shall not all sleep, but we shall all be changed [1 Cor. 15:51].

What is a mystery? We have already discussed it several times. A mystery is something which had not been revealed in the Old Testament but is now revealed in the New Testament. It is something which you cannot learn by the eye-gate or the ear-gate. Nor has it entered into the heart of man—that is, it is not something man would have thought of. It is a fact which must be revealed by God.

"Behold, I shew you a mystery; We shall not all sleep"—we are not all going down through the doorway of death. "But we shall all be changed." Whether you die or don't die, you must still be changed, friend. Sometimes we hear people say, "I hope I am alive at the coming of Christ; so I will just go into His presence." Well, before any of us can go into His presence, we'll have to be changed.

In a moment, in the twinkling of an eye, at the last trump: for the trumpet shall sound, and the dead shall be raised incorruptible, and we shall be changed [1 Cor. 15:52].

"In a moment," in the smallest particle of time. The word is *en atomo* from which we get our word "atom." Scientists made a big mistake when they called that little fellow an atom. They thought they had found the smallest particle of matter, and now they can cut up the little atom like a railroad restaurant pie. It would have been better if we had named it a *stoicheion*, which means "a building block." Actually, Simon Peter uses this word in his second epistle when he says that the elements *(stoicheion)* shall melt with a fervent heat. And he wasn't even a scientist; he was a fisherman. But the Spirit of God knew a little about science!

We shall all be changed "in the twinkling of an eye." How long is that? Is a twinkle when the lid goes down or when it comes up, or is it both of them? Well, it simply means in a moment, in a fraction of a second. There won't even be time to say, "Here He comes" or "He is here!"

"At the last trump." What is that? That is His last call. The trumpet is His voice. John tells us in the Book of Revelation, "I was in the

Spirit on the Lord's day, and heard behind me a great voice, as of a trumpet," and when he turned to see who was speaking, he saw Christ (see Rev. 1:10–13). So "at the last trump" is the voice of the Lord Jesus. On His last call to mankind, He will call the dead back to life. He said, ". . . Lazarus, come forth" (John 11:43). Someday He will say to me, "Vernon, come forth." And He will also call you by name.

"And the dead shall be raised incorruptible, and we shall be changed."

For this corruptible must put on incorruption, and this mortal must put on immortality [1 Cor. 15:53].

Notice the word *must*—it is emphatic. We cannot go to heaven as we are now. We cannot go to heaven with the old bodies we have. We wouldn't be able to see what is really up there, nor could we hear the music. Our bodies are quite limited. We are almost deaf and blind as far as heaven is concerned. Even here on earth there is so little of the spectrum that we actually see and so little of the sounds that we actually hear. If we went to heaven in these old bodies, we would miss half of what was taking place. And, my friend, when I go up there, I don't want to miss a thing! Therefore I'm going to need a new body. "This corruptible must put on incorruption, and this mortal must put on immortality."

So when this corruptible shall have put on incorruption, and this mortal shall have put on immortality, then shall be brought to pass the saying that is written, Death is swallowed up in victory [1 Cor. 15:54].

This is the victory of the Resurrection.

O death, where is thy sting? O grave, where is thy victory?

The sting of death is sin; and the strength of sin is the law.

But thanks be to God, which giveth us the victory through our Lord Jesus Christ [1 Cor. 15:55–57].

I heard a Bible teacher say that since God has taken the sting out of death, it is like a bee that has his stinger removed. Well, I can't tell when a bee's stinger has been removed. I can't stop every bee and ask, "Say, do you have a stinger?" Therefore, I am afraid of every bee.

Death has lost its sting, because we are to look way out beyond death. It is a doorway that opens up the vast regions of eternity. It starts us down the hallway, not of time, but of eternity. But I don't like going through that door.

"O grave, where is thy victory?" It looks as if the grave wins. Many a man has been a successful businessman, but death finally won over him. Many a politician gets elected to high office, even to the presidency, and then dies in office. They reach the heights, but death walks in on them and claims a victory. Death is an awful monster. However, Christ has been down through that way. Just as the ark went down into the Jordan River and over to the other side, so Christ has gone down through the waters of death for me, and He tells me, "I'm your Shepherd. Remember, I not only lead you through this life, but I'll lead you through the deep waters of death, and I will bring you into eternity." So like a little child I'm afraid, but I'll put my hand in His nail-pierced hand, and He will lead me to the other side. "O grave, where is thy victory?"

"The sting of death is sin." It is sin that has the real stinger.

"The strength of sin is the law." The law is the mirror that shows us we are sinners.

"But thanks be to God, which giveth us the victory." How? Because we are smart and clever and are overcomers? No, the victory is through our Lord Jesus Christ. Speaking of the tribulation saints, Revelation 12:11 says that they overcame Satan by the blood of the Lamb. That is the only way any of us will overcome.

Therefore, my beloved brethren, be ye stedfast, unmoveable, always abounding in the work of the Lord, forasmuch as ye know that your labour is not in vain in the Lord [1 Cor. 15:58].

I think this verse goes all the way back to chapter 1:9. "God is faithful [Oh, how faithful He is], by whom ye were called unto the fellowship of his Son Jesus Christ our Lord." I have been called into the fellowship of His Son. Paul has already told us in this epistle that all things are ours. He said that Paul and Apollos and Cephas and the world and life and death and things present and things to come are all ours, and we are Christ's. Life is ours, and I want to enjoy life. Death is ours, for we have the One who got the victory over death. Things present (the things of time) and things out yonder in the future are all ours. We are more than conquerors through Him who loved us!

CHAPTER 16

THEME: *Final exhortations*

In this chapter we will find a potpourri, that is, a collection of things. First Paul discusses the collection for the poor saints in Jerusalem, but then he goes on to discuss other things. He will talk about opportunities and opposition, about watching and praying, about the conduct of the church, about the acid test of doctrine, and about that which is ecclesiastical. The total church is in view here. Verses 1–4 concern the collection; verses 5–9 are personal—Paul discusses his personal plans; verses 10–24 deal with personalities, folk who walked down the streets of corrupt Corinth and lived for Christ.

THE COLLECTION

Now concerning the collection for the saints, as I have given order to the churches of Galatia, even so do ye [1 Cor. 16:1].

Paul begins this chapter by talking about taking up an offering! You would think that after Paul had discussed the Resurrection, that most glorious doctrine of the Christian faith, he would say, "Brethren, we are up in the heavenlies, so let's just stay up in the clouds." Instead, all of a sudden it seems like he has pulled out the plug. We find that we have just gone down to the very bottom. He is talking about a collection of money for the poor saints in Jerusalem.

Some pious folk say, "You shouldn't talk about a collection—that is a material matter. You should talk only of spiritual things." Generally those people don't want it talked about because the subject is a little bit embarrassing for them. Paul is going to lay out a method for Christian giving.

Now I hope you have your Bible open and that you will watch very carefully because I am not going to read it correctly. "On the Sabbath day let every one of you give tithes and offerings so that there will not be an offering when I come. It may be that when I get there we will have a special offering or probably a retiring offering." Somebody will say, "You surely didn't read it like it is." No, I didn't. But I read it the way it is often practiced today.

Now let us read it the way Paul wrote it.

Upon the first day of the week let every one of you lay by him in store, as God hath prospered him, that there be no gatherings when I come [1 Cor. 16:2].

"Upon the first day of the week." If you don't meet on the first day of the week to worship God, then you will want to meet on that day to make your offering, which is a part of worship. That is ridiculous, of course. When he says to bring your offering on the first day of the week, this was the day on which the church came together to remember the Lord Jesus in His death and in His resurrection. He rose on the first day of the week, which is Sunday, not the sabbath day.

"Let every one of you lay by him in store, as God hath prospered him." He says nothing about tithes and offerings. They were to put aside their offerings as God had prospered them.

When I was pastoring a church in Texas, one of my officers owned several Coca-Cola plants, and one of them was in our town. He was a man of means, and he owned a ranch where we used to go to hunt and fish. Often he would ask me why I didn't preach on tithing. One day I said, "Why should I preach on tithing?" He said, "Because it is the Bible way of giving." I agreed, "Yes, it was the Old Testament way of giving, but under grace I don't believe tithing is the way it should be done." So he asked me, "How do you think it ought to be done?" I took him to this verse: "As God hath prospered him." Now this was during the depression. If you are as old as I am, you will remember that the depression in the 1930s was a very serious time. So I said to him, "For some strange reason, Coca-Cola is selling, and you are doing very well. However, there are some members in our church who couldn't give a tithe right now. I don't believe God is asking them to give a tenth. There are a few people who are doing well, and they are to give as they have been prospered—and they are not to stop with a tenth. Probably they ought to give a half." Do you know that this man never again suggested that I preach on

tithing! The reason was that he was tithing, but he didn't want to give as God had prospered him.

"That there be no gatherings when I come." Paul didn't want his meeting with them to be spoiled by high pressure methods of taking up an offering. In my day I sometimes had to give as much attention to the offering as to dealing with new converts. Paul tells us how an offering should be collected.

And when I come, whomsoever ye shall approve by your letters, them will I send to bring your liberality unto Jerusalem.

And if it be meet that I go also, they shall go with me [1 Cor. 16:3–4].

Paul asks them to pick a committee to take the collection to Jerusalem with him. It is well for more than one man to be responsible for the offering. It is dangerous to turn the offering over to a single individual and let one man handle it. Is it that there is a doubt about a man's honesty if he is a Christian? Well, there may be. Even if a man is honest, there is a certain temptation involved. Paul gives us the best way to handle a collection. He uses very businesslike methods.

Paul talks here of their "liberality." It is interesting to study the words used for Christian giving. In our passage here he calls it a *logia* or "a collection." Then he speaks of their *charis* or "liberality"—that is the word for "grace." In Romans 15:26 a "contribution" is called a *koinōnia*, a fellowship. In 2 Corinthians 9:5 it is called a *eulogia*, which means "a bounty" or "a blessing." Second Corinthians 9:12 calls it a *diakonia*, which is "an administration" or "ministry." Acts 24:17 speaks of *alms—eleēmosunē*, which is "a kind act." All of these words refer to giving to the Lord, and each of these words can be used.

The interesting word here is "liberality," which should be *grace giving*. How has God blessed you? Could your giving to the Lord be considered liberality? In the Book of Leviticus instructions are given about tithing by God's people in the Old Testament. In the beginning the nation of Israel was a theocracy, and the tithes that the Israelites were to give supported both the government and the temple. They added up to about 30 percent of their total income. This gives us an indication of what the Israelite gave in the Old Testament under the economy of the Law. What do you think would be liberality under grace?

PERSONAL COMMENTS

Now I will come unto you, when I shall pass through Macedonia: for I do pass through Macedonia.

And it may be that I will abide, yea, and winter with you, that ye may bring me on my journey whithersoever I go [1 Cor. 16:5–6].

"Whithersoever I go" means that Paul doesn't know where he is going. Do you mean to tell me that the great Apostle of the Gentiles didn't have a blueprint or a road map from the Lord telling him everywhere he was to go? No, he says that the Lord just leads him along. Paul is in the wonderful position of being gloriously unsettled. He is not sure what he is to do. This is a great satisfaction to me, because I don't know about the future either. There are folk in Christian service who tell me where they are going and what they will be doing five years from now. This worries me, because I have never received directions like that from the Lord, and I hate to think they have a private line to the Lord that I don't have! Then when I read about Paul's not knowing what was ahead for him, it is a great comfort. To Paul and me the Lord doesn't give a road map; He just leads us from day to day. We are gloriously unsettled.

For I will not see you now by the way; but I trust to tarry a while with you, if the Lord permit [1 Cor. 16:7].

Paul is saying here that he does plan to go to Corinth, but only if the Lord permits it. Shouldn't we have plans? By all means we should make plans, but those plans always should be amenable to the will of God. We should be willing to change them. We should be willing to shuffle things around. When Paul went out, he did not have a rigid schedule for his missionary journeys. He went as the Lord led him. We see in the Book of Acts how the Lord just practically detoured him on the second missionary journey. Paul was going down into Asia; the Spirit of God sent him over to Europe. He didn't know he was going to Europe—he didn't have a visa for Europe—but in that day he didn't need a visa. He went where the Holy Spirit led him.

But I will tarry at Ephesus until Pentecost [1 Cor. 16:8].

That was his plan.

For a great door and effectual is opened unto me, and there are many adversaries [1 Cor. 16:9].

This is a wonderful verse that I have put with Revelation 3:8, (which is Christ's message to the church in Philadelphia): ". . . behold, I have set before thee an open door. . . ." And Paul says, "A great door and effectual is opened unto me." These two verses I have found to be true in the ministry God has given to me. Also it is true today that there are many adversaries. Any man who will stand for the Word of God has many enemies. That was the experience of Paul, and it has been my experience also. However, the Lord opens the door and no man can shut it. Thank God for that!

So we see Paul, gloriously happy, rejoicing in the will of God. If the Lord wants him to go to Corinth, he will go.

PERSONALITIES

Now we come to the personalities. These were the folk who walked down the streets of Corinth. Corinth was a most corrupt city, a sensual city given over to immorality. They knew more about illicit sex than this generation knows today. Yet here were folk, walking the streets of Corinth, who knew the Lord Jesus and who lived for Him. They kept themselves unspotted from the world.

Now if Timotheus come, see that he may be with you without fear: for he worketh the work of the Lord, as I also do.

Let no man therefore despise him: but conduct him forth in peace, that he may come unto me: for I look for him with the brethren [1 Cor. 16:10–11].

Why would they despise Timothy? Paul wrote in 1 Timothy 4:12, "Let no man despise thy youth. . . ." So he is telling the church in Corinth to accept Timothy although he is a young man. He is a preacher of the Word of God.

As touching our brother Apollos, I greatly desired him to come unto you with the brethren: but his will was not at all to come at this time; but he will come when he shall have convenient time [1 Cor. 16:12].

Remember that the Corinthian church had divisions over Paul and Apollos and Peter. But Paul loved Apollos, and he makes it clear that they are serving the Lord together. He assures them that Apollos will come to visit them at a later time.

Watch ye, stand fast in the faith, quit you like men, be strong.

Let all your things be done with charity [1 Cor. 16:13–14].

What words these are for us today!

I beseech you, brethren, (ye know the house of Stephanas, that it is the first-fruits of Achaia, and that they have addicted themselves to the ministry of the saints,)

That ye submit yourselves unto such, and to every one that helpeth with us, and laboureth [1 Cor. 16:15–16].

When we read that word *addicted*, we immediately think of drug addiction. But these people were addicted to the ministry of the saints. That was a great ministry!

He urges the Corinthians to submit to those who come to serve them.

I am glad of the coming of Stephanas and Fortunatus and Achaicus: for that which was lacking on your part they have supplied [1 Cor. 16:17].

They apparently made up the delegation that brought the letter from the Corinthian church over to Paul. Paul tells the folk in Corinth that these three Christian fellows were so wonderful that they made up for the whole church.

For they have refreshed my spirit and yours: therefore acknowledge ye them that are such [1 Cor. 16:18].

Paul is saying, "Give them a vote of thanks when they get back."

The churches of Asia salute you. Aquila and Priscilla salute you much in the Lord, with the church that is in their house [1 Cor. 16:19].

That is where many of these people came to know about Christ.

All the brethren greet you. Greet ye one another with an holy kiss [1 Cor. 16:20].

Is this a permit for kissing? It certainly is—if it is a holy kiss. Most kisses are not!

The salutation of me Paul with mine own hand [1 Cor. 16:21].

Paul dictated this epistle and then signed it.

If any man love not the Lord Jesus Christ, let him be Anathema Maranatha [1 Cor. 16:22].

The Lord Jesus asked Simon Peter, "Do you love Me?" (see John 21:17). He didn't ask Peter if he would deny Him again. He just asked, "Do you love Me?" That is the acid test today. Do you love Him?

Anathema means "accursed." Paul is saying, "If any one does not love the Lord, let him be accursed." *Maranatha* means "our Lord cometh."

The grace of our Lord Jesus Christ be with you.

My love be with you all in Christ Jesus. Amen [1 Cor. 16:23–24].

If you love the Lord Jesus, you will love the saints. The epistle closes on the high note of love.

(For Bibliography to 1 Corinthians, see Bibliography at the end of 2 Corinthians.)

The Second Epistle to the
CORINTHIANS
INTRODUCTION

The author of the epistle is Paul. Paul had written 1 Corinthians from Ephesus where he had been engaged in a great ministry. He had written, "For a great door and effectual is opened unto me, and there are many adversaries" (1 Cor. 16:9). I believe that Paul had his greatest ministry in Asia Minor—Ephesus being the springboard and the sounding board for the gospel. I believe that the gospel covered that area in a manner that was probably more effective than it has ever been in any other place at any other time. That is what Paul meant—"For a great door and effectual is opened unto me."

Because of that ministry, Paul just couldn't leave and go over to Corinth. In Corinth was that baby church which he had started. That church was filled with carnal Christians. They acted like babies. They wanted Paul to come, because they wanted attention. They wanted food and they wanted a change of garments—I guess you could say they were all wet. They were crying as babies cry. Paul couldn't come, and they were a little miffed and a little hurt by it. So Paul had written his first letter and had told them that he would be coming later.

Paul remained in Ephesus approximately three years. He didn't get to Corinth, and the Corinthians were still disturbed. He had sent Titus to Corinth because he could not personally go there at that time. Timothy had been with Paul in Ephesus, and these two left Ephesus and proceeded to Troas to wait for Titus to bring word from Corinth (see 2 Cor. 2:12–13). When Titus did not come, Paul and Timothy went on to Philippi. It was there that Titus met them and brought Paul word about the Corinthians. He brought good news from Corinth—that the Corinthians were obeying the things that Paul had told them to do in his first answer to their questions; that is, in 1 Corinthians.

At Philippi Paul sat down to write this second epistle. The Corinthians still wanted the great apostle to come and be with them. However, any breach between Paul and the Corinthian church was healed. In this epistle Paul opens his heart in a very wonderful way. To tell the truth, Paul lets us come to know him better personally in this epistle than in any other letter.

Second Corinthians deals with conditions of the *ministry* within the church. (First Corinthians dealt with conditions and *corrections* in the church.)

OUTLINE

This epistle is difficult to outline, as it is less organized than any of Paul's other letters, but it contains more personal details. In each chapter there is always a minor theme developed, which sometimes seems to take the place of the major theme and is generally expressed in some striking verse. This may explain the seeming difficulty in outlining and organizing this epistle. We will note this as we consider each chapter.

I. **Comfort of God, Chapters 1–7**
   Christian Living
   A. Introduction, Chapter 1:1–2
   B. God's Comfort for Life's Plans, Chapter 1:3–24
   C. God's Comfort in Restoring a Sinning Saint, Chapter 2
   D. God's Comfort in the Glorious Ministry of Christ, Chapter 3
   E. God's Comfort in the Ministry of Suffering for Christ, Chapter 4
   F. God's Comfort in the Ministry of Martyrdom for Christ, Chapter 5
   G. God's Comfort in All Circumstances of the Ministry of Christ, Chapter 6
   H. God's Comfort in the Heart of Paul, Chapter 7

II. **Collection for the Poor Saints at Jerusalem, Chapters 8–9**
   Christian Giving
   A. Example of Christian Giving, Chapter 8:1–6
   B. Exhortation to Christian Giving, Chapter 8:7–15
   C. Explanation of Christian Giving, Chapter 8:16–9:5
   D. Encouragement to Christian Giving, Chapter 9:6–15

III. **Calling of the Apostle Paul, Chapters 10–13**
   Christian Guarding
   A. Authentication of Paul's Apostleship, Chapter 10
   B. Vindication of Paul's Apostleship, Chapter 11
   C. Revelation of Paul's Apostleship, Chapter 12
   D. Execution of Paul's Apostleship, Chapter 13:1–10
   E. Conclusion of Paul's Apostleship, Chapter 13:11–14

CHAPTER 1

THEME: God's comfort for life's plans

The first two verses are an introduction to the epistle. Then the rest of chapter 1 is about God's comfort for life's plans. Paul really begins this epistle on a high note.

INTRODUCTION

Paul, an apostle of Jesus Christ by the will of God, and Timothy our brother, unto the church of God which is at Corinth, with all the saints which are in all Achaia [2 Cor. 1:1].

Paul is writing in the *authority* of "an apostle." I feel that any minister today should speak with authority. There is no use trying to give out God's Word unless the speaker is convinced of the truth of it himself. If he isn't speaking the Word with authority, then he ought to start selling insurance, or work in a filling station, or do something else. He should not be in the ministry. We already have too many men who are unsure that the Bible actually is the Word of God—that is the weakness of the contemporary church.

In the early church, when persecution began, the believers said, "O Lord, Thou art God." My friend, if you are not sure that He is God, you are not sure of anything. And they were sure of the Word of God. They rested upon it at all times. And Paul writes with this authority.

Paul was an apostle "by the will of God." You can't go any higher than that. That is authority. If your life is in the will of God, there is no question in your mind. If you are in the will of God, it makes no difference *where* you are or *how* you are or *what* your circumstances may be, you are in a wonderful, glorious place. You may even be lying in a hospital bed. If that is the will of God, that is the proper place for you. I have a friend who is a music director, and he generally begins a song service on some humorous note. I heard him say one time, "Wouldn't you rather be here than in the best hospital in town?" I have always laughed about that, but I have also thought about it a great deal. If it is God's will for you to be in the best hospital in town, then that is the greatest place for you to be.

"And Timothy our brother." I love that. He is a Christian brother to Paul and to the church at Corinth. In another place Paul calls Timothy his *son* in the faith. However, when Paul is writing to the church, he puts Timothy right on a par with himself. I love the way Paul has of putting others on the same plane with himself.

"Unto the church of God"—this is *God's* church we are talking about. I hear people say, "*My* church," and sometimes they act as if it were *their* church. They forget that it is God's church, that it is the church of the Lord Jesus Christ which He purchased with His blood. In view of the fact that He paid such a price for the church, you and I better not be cheap Christians, expressing our little will in the church. Let's remember it is His church.

"Which is at Corinth, with all the saints which are in all Achaia." Paul didn't confine this to Corinth alone. Paul extended it to all Achaia because, everywhere the gospel went in that day, these people were witnesses. They carried the gospel out to others.

I have gone through that land of Achaia. It is beautiful country. They have the most beautiful grape vineyards I have ever seen anywhere. And beautiful flowers! I can visualize those early Christians, steeped in sin in the city of Corinth. Then when Paul came with the gospel, the scales fell from their eyes. The light broke upon their darkened souls. They turned from their sins to the living Christ. Then they went all over Achaia witnessing for Christ. Many were won for Christ. Paul was also talking to all of them—to "all the saints which are in all Achaia." How wonderful that is.

Now friend, the church of God which Paul happens to be addressing is this church in Corinth. The church in your hometown, the church in your neighborhood, is also God's church. Don't forget that.

Grace be to you and peace from God our Father, and from the Lord Jesus Christ [2 Cor. 1:2].

Paul uses this salutation frequently. Grace and peace are those great gifts from God to the believer.

GOD'S COMFORT IN LIFE'S PLANS

Blessed be God, even the Father of our Lord Jesus Christ, the Father of mercies, and the God of all comfort [2 Cor. 1:3].

The word for "blessed" is actually *praise*—Praise be to God. I wonder how much we really praise Him. I find that I am doing a better job of praising Him since I have retired than I did when I was a pastor.

David put it like this: "I will bless the LORD at all times: his praise shall continually be in my mouth" (Ps. 34:1). That ought to get rid of the complaining of the saints. We are to *praise* the Lord. "Whoso offereth praise glorifieth me . . ." (Ps. 50:23).

"Blessed be God, even the Father of our Lord Jesus Christ." God is the Father. That is His position in the Trinity. God so loved the world that He gave His only begotten Son. Jesus Christ wasn't begotten in the sense of being born. He is the only begotten One in the sense that He occupies a position that is totally unique. He is the eternal Son, and God is the everlasting Father. If you have a Father and a Son like that, then there never was a time when there was any begetting in the sense of being born, of having a beginning. Rather, it expresses the positions in the Trinity. They are both eternal.

Now Paul calls Him "the Father of mercies, and the God of all comfort." I want to stop here and spend a little time on three words: *love, mercy, grace*.

So much is being said today about love. It is sloppy theology to say that God saves us by His love. Now it is true that God loves us. Oh, how He loves us! We just don't know how much He loves us. It would break our hearts if we could comprehend how much God loves us. But God does not save us by His love. The Scriptures teach that we are saved by God's *grace*.

Now what is grace? We call it unmerited favor, which means that God saves us on a different basis than merit. God loves us, but He does not save us by His love. He saves us by His grace. Why? Because He is also the God of all mercies—the father of mercies. Mercy means that God so loved us that He provided a Savior for us because He couldn't save us any other way. Anything that we have today is a mercy from God. He is the Father of mercy. In fact, He is said to be rich in grace and rich in mercy.

Do you need any mercy today? If you need money, you go to a bank to get it. If you need mercy, go to the One who is the Father of mercies. If you need any help, go to Him. After all, anything and everything that you have today is a mercy from God. You don't *deserve* it. I don't deserve anything that I have. I don't have much, but what I have is a mercy of God.

God was merciful to put me into the ministry. You don't know me like I know myself. If you knew me as I know myself, you wouldn't listen to me. Wait a minute—don't cut me off. If I knew you like you know yourself, I wouldn't be talking to you. I would quit right now. You see, you and I have been extended mercy, and I am in the ministry because of the mercy of God.

Now I must say something that is difficult for me to say: I have had cancer, probably still have it in my body, by the mercy of God. I hate to say it, but it is true. Everything that we have is a mercy. Not only is He the Father of mercies, He is also the God of all comfort. You can test that in the crucible of life. Suffering is the acid test. He is the God of all comfort. He will comfort you in the hospital. He will comfort you at the funeral home when you have a loved one there. He can comfort you in any place at any time. He is the God of all comfort.

There is an authentic comfort, and there is a counterfeit one. I don't like to hear people sigh and say, "God has permitted this to come to me and I accept it," when they *don't* accept it but rebel against it. Be honest with God. Tell Him how you feel. Tell Him you don't like what is happening to you. He knows all about it anyway. He wants you to talk frankly with Him. Comfort can be genuine or fake.

There is a popular notion that comfort is some sort of saccharin sweet sentimentality with a note of weakness. I can remember that when I was a little fellow I was always falling down and skinning my knees. I always wondered why my mother didn't put me in long pants, but she never did. When I'd skin my knee, she would kiss it and say, "It's all well now." She kidded me into thinking it was well and I would quit crying. Now that is sentiment; it's sweet and lovely. But there came a day when I went away to school and I got discouraged because I didn't have any money. Then she sat down and talked to me. It was pretty strong medicine. She said, "Now you must be a man, my son." That was comfort also.

People turn to all sorts of things for comfort. There is a whiskey called "Southern Comfort." Well, I'm a Southerner, but that is not a comfort, my friend. That will ruin a home. Others turn to drugs for comfort, but there is no comfort there.

The Greek word for "comfort" is *parakaleo*, which means "to call alongside of." The Holy Spirit is called the Paraclete. He is called to our side. When the Lord Jesus promised to send the Holy Spirit, He said, "I will not leave you comfortless . . ." (John 14:18). The word

He used there is *orphanos*—"I will not leave you orphans. I will send the Comforter to you, the Paraclete." He said to His own men, ". . . It is expedient for you that I go away: for if I go not away, the Comforter will not come unto you; but if I depart, I will send him unto you" (John 16:7).

What is the Comforter then? He is not someone who simply kisses a bruise. He is a helper, a strengthener, an advocate. He is One who is called to help me and to strengthen me, to relieve the loneliness and assuage the grief and calm the fears. He means help in time of terrifying trouble. "Hear, O LORD, and have mercy upon me: LORD, be thou my helper" (Ps. 30:10). That is the cry of the soul that needs the Comforter. God is the God of all comfort.

Who comforteth us in all our tribulation, that we may be able to comfort them which are in any trouble, by the comfort wherewith we ourselves are comforted of God [2 Cor. 1:4].

It is a very wonderful thing that we have a God who can comfort us in all our troubles. It is one thing to have comfort when the sun is shining and with someone patting us on the back. But, my friend, what we really need is comfort in the time of trouble.

We will see that Paul experienced that kind of comfort in his time of trouble. You see, we need the assurance of the presence of God in all the circumstances of life—in the area of our greatest need, in our loneliness, in the desperate hour of life.

Christianity is just a theory to many people. It is merely a profession; it is like a garment to be put on for special occasions and then wear lightly. It is a stagnant ritual and an empty vocabulary. My friend, may I say to you that the proof of Christianity is how it walks in shoe leather. It wasn't just a theory to the apostle Paul.

For as the sufferings of Christ abound in us, so our consolation also aboundeth by Christ.

And whether we be afflicted, it is for your consolation and salvation, which is effectual in the enduring of the same sufferings which we also suffer: or whether we be comforted, it is for your consolation and salvation [2 Cor. 1:5–6].

We will find that Paul is going to talk a great deal about the trouble he had and was pres-ently having and of God's comfort through it all.

And our hope of you is stedfast, knowing, that as ye are partakers of the sufferings, so shall ye be also of the consolation.

For we would not, brethren, have you ignorant of our trouble which came to us in Asia, that we were pressed out of measure, above strength, insomuch that we despaired even of life:

But we had the sentence of death in ourselves, that we should not trust in ourselves, but in God which raiseth the dead:

Who delivered us from so great a death, and doth deliver: in whom we trust that he will yet deliver us [2 Cor. 1:7–10].

This is wonderful. This explains why God permits us to have trouble or to be sick. Paul here says that he was sick nigh unto death. In fact, he had "the sentence of death" in him. He was so ill that I think the doctor told him he would die. There are others who think he is referring to the time the mob tried to attack him in Ephesus. They would have torn Paul to pieces, and he would have been made a martyr. He could have been referring to either experience; both would have carried the sentence of death. But Paul says that God who raises the dead "delivered us from so great a death, and doth deliver: in whom we trust that he will yet deliver us." That is quite wonderful, and it ought to be practical for us today.

Let me say that God permits Christians to suffer. He has a good reason, a very wonderful purpose in it all. He intends for it to work out for the good of these believers. He intends for it to serve a good purpose so they can comfort someone else.

Everything that you and I have we have because of the mercy of God. And we have it for the benefit of others. Regardless of what you have, God has given it to you so that you can share it with others. He has given it to you as a mercy. If you have health, wealth, youth, talent, or a gift, He wants you to use it to share with others. Each issues from the mercy of God. And wait a minute—suffering also. If you are suffering for Christ, He permits that to happen to you.

Dr. Harry Ironside used to tell the story of a friend of his who was in Vienna, Austria, on a sightseeing bus trip. As they were traveling, some sheep got in the way of the bus and they were held up. The man sitting next to his friend was annoyed by it all because there were only two sheep dogs that were herding those sheep. So this friend, a Christian, said to this annoyed man sitting next to him, "Do you know the names of those two sheep dogs?" And he said, "Why, no, I don't know the names. Do you know the names?" "Yes, I think I do." "What are they?" His friend said, "One of them is named 'Goodness' and the other is named 'Mercy.'" He said, "How in the world do you know that?" "Well, he said, I'll tell you how. David said, 'Surely goodness and mercy shall follow us all the days of our lives.'"

You might not think it was goodness and mercy to have a couple of dogs yapping at you to keep you from going to the left or to the right, but it is God's mercy that keeps us in the straight and narrow way, and He uses trial and difficulty for that very purpose. He is "the Father of mercies."

Now I am going to be personal. I had several recurrences of cancer and, I'll be frank with you, my doctor didn't offer me much hope. But God has been delivering me—it is amazing. That monster can turn on me at any moment; yet I trust that God will deliver. I received a letter from a man who to me seems arrogant. He wrote, "God has told me that you are going to get well; so you don't need to worry about it any more." I wonder, since I was the fellow who had the cancer, why didn't God tell me that? Well, I'm just waiting on the Lord. I can say with Paul that I trust He will deliver me. We cannot be arrogant with God; we need to walk softly.

Paul is walking softly, but he can say with great assurance, "He *has* delivered me from death." And he can say, "Right at the present, *He is* delivering me." And then, without any boasting, he says, "We trust that *He will* yet deliver us." Paul didn't know that He would, but he believed that He would. Therefore, on the basis of that, Paul could rejoice in the fact that God was permitting him to give out the gospel in that day.

Paul appeals to these Corinthian believers for prayer.

Ye also helping together by prayer for us, that for the gift bestowed upon us by the means of many persons thanks may be given by many on our behalf [2 Cor. 1:11].

God wants us to do this. And I have appealed for prayer. Thank God, folk have been praying for me down through the years.

Yet I think God allows us to have trouble that we might comfort others. Our suffering is for the benefit of others—"that we may be able to comfort them which are in any trouble." It is amazing how my experience with cancer has been a comfort to others. God permits us to have trouble so that we may be able to comfort others.

Listen to Paul again, "For we would not, brethren, have you ignorant of our trouble which came to us in Asia, that we were pressed out of measure, above strength, insomuch that we despaired even of life" (v. 8).

If you are as old as I am, you may remember the fable we used to have in our readers in school. The sun and the wind were having a contest to see who was the stronger. There was a man walking down the street with his coat on and the wind said, "I can make him take his coat off." So the wind began to blow. I tell you, it almost blew the man away. The harder the wind blew, the tighter the man wrapped his coat around him. The sun said, "Now it's my turn to try." The sun shone down so warm and nice that the man took his coat off. The sun accomplished what the wind could not do.

Now, generally, the wind of adversity won't take us away from God. When the wind begins to blow, when it gets rough and tough, we turn to our Father who can comfort us. However, we are in a dangerous place when things are going too well for us. When the sun is shining, Christians have it too easy. They remove that robe of practical righteousness, and they begin to compromise with the world. This is exactly what many have done in our day.

For our rejoicing is this, the testimony of our conscience, that in simplicity and godly sincerity, not with fleshly wisdom, but by the grace of God, we have had our conversation in the world, and more abundantly to you-ward [2 Cor. 1:12].

"Our conversation" means our manner of life in the world. Paul says that he can rejoice because of the testimony of his life. He makes it clear that it was not by "fleshly wisdom." And, my friend, it is not by *our* wisdom that our lives are a testimony to those around us. If we have been a testimony for God, it is because we have lived our lives in "simplicity and godly sincerity." Paul is saying that by God's grace suffering has produced this in his life. You see, suffering is a mercy of God, and it produces qualities in our lives that are to be shared.

When I was in the hospital for my initial cancer surgery, someone sent me this little poem:

I NEEDED THE QUIET

I needed the quiet so He drew me aside,
Into the shadows where we could confide.

Away from the bustle where all the day long
I hurried and worried when active and strong.

I needed the quiet though at first I rebelled.
But gently, so gently, my cross He upheld,

And whispered so sweetly of spiritual things.
Though weakened in body, my spirit took wings

To heights never dreamed of when active and gay.
He loved me so greatly He drew me away.

I needed the quiet. No prison my bed,
But a beautiful valley of blessings instead—

A place to grow richer in Jesus to hide.
I needed the quiet so He drew me aside.

—Alice Hansche Mortenson

My friend, if today you are on a bed of pain, and you are in the will of God, that bed can become a greater pulpit than the one preachers stand behind.

For we write none other things unto you, than what ye read or acknowledge; and I trust ye shall acknowledge even to the end;

As also ye have acknowledged us in part, that we are your rejoicing, even as ye also are ours in the day of the Lord Jesus.

And in this confidence I was minded to come unto you before, that ye might have a second benefit [2 Cor. 1:13–15].

Paul is saying, "Wasn't I a blessing to you the first time? Now I am coming a second time, and I want to be a blessing to you."

And to pass by you into Macedonia, and to come again out of Macedonia unto you, and of you to be brought on my way toward Judaea.

When I therefore was thus minded, did I use lightness? or the things that I purpose, do I purpose according to the flesh, that with me there should be yea yea, and nay nay? [2 Cor. 1:16–17].

Paul had hoped that he would be able to come to Corinth, but he hadn't come there yet. Some of his enemies in Corinth were saying that he didn't mean what he said. They accused him of being insincere. Now Paul is telling them that he certainly was sincere. He says that when he says yes, he means yes, and when he says no, he means no.

Believers today ought to be that kind of folk. They should not use lightness in making appointments and arrangements in the business world and in their daily appointments. We need Christian men and women who will stand by the things that they have said.

But as God is true, our word toward you was not yea and nay [2 Cor. 1:18].

Paul didn't say, "I will come," then, "I won't come"—as though he was being fickle. Why? Because *God* had led him. He was in the will of *God*.

For the Son of God, Jesus Christ, who was preached among you by us, even by me and Silvanus and Timotheus, was not yea and nay, but in him was yea [2 Cor. 1:19].

The gospel that he had preached was a glorious, positive gospel, and it was "yea." The gospel is something God has done for us—it is good news. We have not only the faithful God, but the sure Lord Jesus Christ.

For all the promises of God in him are yea, and in him Amen, unto the glory of God by us [2 Cor. 1:20].

Everything is positive in Christ. You see, God means well by you, Christian friend.

Now he which stablisheth us with you in Christ, and hath anointed us, is God;

Who hath also sealed us, and given the earnest of the Spirit in our hearts [2 Cor. 1:21–22].

Now you have here not only the faithful God, the true God, and the sure Lord Jesus, but you have the indwelling Holy Spirit. And I believe, very candidly, that you have here in this statement the total ministry of the Holy Spirit today.

"He which stablisheth us." Now how do you become established? When Paul had written his first letter to these Corinthians—and they had been so fickle—he concluded by saying, ". . . be ye stedfast, unmoveable, always abounding in the work of the Lord, forasmuch as ye know that your labour is not in vain in the Lord" (1 Cor. 15:58). What does it mean to be established? We believe that is the work of the Holy Spirit. First of all, the Holy Spirit convicts. The Lord Jesus said that when the Holy Spirit came into the world, He would convict the world of sin, righteousness, and judgment. And the second thing that He would do (if, having been convicted, we confessed our sin and accepted Christ as our Savior) would be to regenerate us, you see. And He not only would regenerate us, He would indwell us. And not only would He indwell us, but He would baptize us.

And by the way, this expression here is quite interesting: "Now he which stablisheth us with you in [into] Christ, and hath anointed us, is *God*." God who? God the Holy Spirit, if you please.

Sometimes, especially at funerals, we hear the song, "Safe in the Arms of Jesus." Well, the word here is not safe *in* the arms of Jesus. When you are put into Christ by the baptism of the Holy Spirit, you are a part of His body. Rather than being safe *in* His arms, you are as safe *as* an arm of Jesus Christ. You are as safe as a member of His body. What a wonderful security that is!

In speaking of the work of the Holy Spirit, Paul uses the present tense. This is what He is doing for you today, my friend: He convicts you, He regenerates you, He indwells you, and He baptizes you.

"Now he which . . . hath anointed us, is God." The anointing of the Holy Spirit is a neglected truth in our day. In 1 John 2:20 we are told, "But ye have an unction [that is, an *anointing*] from the Holy One, and ye know all things." That anointing is the Holy Spirit. It takes the Holy Spirit to lead and guide us into all truth. "But the anointing which ye have received of him abideth in you, and ye need not that any man teach you: but as the same anointing teacheth you of all things, and is truth, and is no lie, and even as it hath taught you, ye shall abide in him" (1 John 2:27). This ministry of the Holy Spirit is very important. He doesn't give you a mail-order degree, nor does this knowledge come in a gift-wrapped box. You have the Holy Spirit to teach you, Christian friend, and He alone can open the Word of God to you. That is the reason this is a miracle Book. The Lord Jesus said to His own men, "I have yet many things to say unto you,

but ye cannot bear them now. Howbeit when he, the Spirit of truth, is come, he will guide you into all truth . . ." (John 16:12–13). He *wants* to guide you into all truth.

"Who hath also sealed us"—that is a marvelous ministry of the Spirit. "And grieve not the holy Spirit of God, whereby ye are sealed unto the day of redemption" (Eph. 4:30). Is it possible to grieve Him away? No, He has sealed us and is going to deliver us someday. This is somewhat like taking a letter down to the post office. Occasionally some of the mail is lost and never does get delivered. If we want to be very sure that a certain piece of mail arrives, we have that letter registered and a seal put on it. The postal service guarantees that they will get that letter to the person to whom it is addressed. Also, all legal documents bear a seal—"In witness thereof I set my seal" is the phraseology that has come down to us from old English. It is also a brand, a mark of ownership. In the early days of the West, when there were no fences, the cattlemen would brand their cattle. The brand was a mark of ownership.

The Holy Spirit puts a brand on you to show that you belong to God. My friend, if you are a little sheep of His, you are not going to get lost. Oh, you may stray away, but He will come to find you. The Holy Spirit is pictured in Luke's parable as the woman sweeping the floor, looking for the lost coin until she *found* it (see Luke 15:8).

"And given the earnest of the Spirit in our hearts" would be better translated: you are "given the earnest, which is the Holy Spirit in our hearts." You know that "earnest money" indicates there will be more to follow. When you put down earnest money on a piece of property, it is a pledge that you are going to pay more money on that property. In such a way, God has given us the Holy Spirit, which indicates there is more to follow. This is a wonderful thing.

When people buy on the installment plan, there is a possibility that the buyer may later defect, even though he has put a down payment on the merchandise. But there is no defection in this Buyer. He has purchased us with His blood. He has put down a purchase price, which guarantees that the saved soul will be delivered safely to the Father. It means that the saved soul is in escrow today.

God has put His Holy Spirit into every believer. He is the earnest. He has come into the life of the believer to bring the fullness of God to bear in our experiences. What is it that you need today? You know that He is rich in mercy—He is the Father of mercies. What do you need? Why don't you go to Him and ask Him for it? Do you need power? Do you need joy? Do you need wisdom? Do you need help? These are comforts—He is the God of all comfort. Paul knew this; he had experienced it. Also, the writer knows it; he has *experienced* it.

Moreover I call God for a record upon my soul, that to spare you I came not as yet unto Corinth [2 Cor. 1:23].

Paul says that if he had come earlier, he would have done what he did in his first epistle. You have seen that 1 Corinthians is filled with correction. Paul was really stern in that epistle. In effect, he is saying, "If I had come, I would have been stern with you. But I wanted to spare you that; I wanted to see if you would work this thing out yourselves."

Not for that we have dominion over your faith, but are helpers of your joy: for by faith ye stand [2 Cor. 1:24].

Paul is saying, "I am not the bishop of your souls. I am not trying to lord it over you. You have complete freedom in Christ. I just want to be a helper of your joy; 'for by faith ye stand.'" You and I too must stand in our own faith, my friend. Paul stayed away so that their faith might be strengthened and that they might grow in the Lord. And this is one of the reasons God permits many of us to undergo certain hardships and certain difficulties in our lives.

CHAPTER 2

THEME: God's comfort in restoring a sinning saint

This epistle is teaching us wonderful truths about God's comfort. In the first chapter we saw God's comfort for life's plans. Now we see God's comfort in restoring a sinning saint. Before the apostle gets into this subject, he continues with the subject of chapter 1. He is explaining his motives for not coming for an earlier visit. Then he discusses the sinning saint in the congregation in Corinth. Finally, he shows that God causes us to triumph in Christ.

PAUL'S EXPLANATION CONTINUES

But I determined this with myself, that I would not come again to you in heaviness [2 Cor. 2:1].

Paul admits that he was discouraged with them. If he had come to visit them, it would have been in sorrow.

For if I make you sorry, who is he then that maketh me glad, but the same which is made sorry by me? [2 Cor. 2:2].

Paul didn't want to come in his sorrow, with tears in his eyes. He would have had them weeping, too. Then who would make Paul glad? They would all have been boo-hooing into their handkerchiefs.

And I wrote this same unto you, lest, when I came, I should have sorrow from them of whom I ought to rejoice; having confidence in you all, that my joy is the joy of you all [2 Cor. 2:3].

Paul wanted to come to them in joy. He had been hoping to get word from them telling him that they had corrected those things about which he had written them.

Now Paul opens his heart to them.

For out of much affliction and anguish of heart I wrote unto you with many tears; not that ye should be grieved, but that ye might know the love which I have more abundantly unto you [2 Cor. 2:4].

A great many people today fall out with the preacher when he preaches a message that is rather severe. Sometimes correction from the Word of God will really bear down on the congregation. Some people think that a pastor should not do that. May I say to you, my friend, that a faithful pastor *must* do that. The command is: "I charge thee therefore before God, and the Lord Jesus Christ, who shall judge the quick and the dead at his appearing and his kingdom; Preach the word; be instant in season, out of season; reprove, rebuke, exhort with all longsuffering and doctrine" (2 Tim. 4:1–2). Any man who stands in the pulpit today has a tremendous responsibility to *rebuke* what is wrong. Many of the saints don't like this. Paul tells them here that his rebuke was not because he was opposed to them, but because he loved them. A faithful pastor shows his love by preaching the Word of God as it is rather than "buttering up" the congregation.

RESTORING A SINNING SAINT

Let me remind you that in Paul's first letter to the Corinthian church, he rebuked them because they were permitting gross immorality in the congregation. In fact, they had a case of incest in their congregation, and they were shutting their eyes to it. (Yet they were acting as if they were very spiritual!) This kind of gross immorality was something that was even shocking to the heathen; yet the congregation was ignoring it. Paul had written them to get this matter straightened out. He read the riot act to them. He told them, ". . . put away from among yourselves that wicked person" (1 Cor. 5:13).

The congregation did listen to Paul. They excommunicated the man.

But if any have caused grief, he hath not grieved me, but in part: that I may not overcharge you all.

Sufficient to such a man is this punishment, which was inflicted of many [2 Cor. 2:5–6].

They had obeyed Paul. They had excommunicated the man, which was the right thing for them to do.

Then the man acknowledged his sin and came under great conviction. Now what ought they to do? They should forgive him.

So that contrariwise ye ought rather to forgive him, and comfort him, lest perhaps such a one should be swallowed up with overmuch sorrow.

Wherefore I beseech you that ye would confirm your love toward him [2 Cor. 2:7–8].

"He will be overwhelmed, not only because of his sin, but because you won't receive him. So now put your arm about him, and restore him to your fellowship." To the Galatian believers Paul wrote: "Brethren, if a man be overtaken in a fault, ye which are spiritual, restore such an one in the spirit of meekness; considering thyself, lest thou also be tempted" (Gal. 6:1).

For to this end also did I write, that I might know the proof of you, whether ye be obedient in all things.

To whom ye forgive any thing, I forgive also: for if I forgave any thing, to whom I forgave it, for your sakes forgave I it in the person of Christ;

Lest Satan should get an advantage of us: for we are not ignorant of his devices [2 Cor. 2:9–11].

You see, the Devil tries to push us one way or another. Sometimes the Devil gets us to shut our eyes to gross immorality. There are many instances of that in our churches today. I know one preacher who has had trouble with women in three different churches. Each church he went to serve knew his past record, and still they accepted him as pastor! In shutting their eyes to gross immorality, they were hurting the cause of Christ Jesus.

Now suppose he had repented and had really turned from his sin (which he did not), then they should have forgiven him. Unfortunately, many of our stiff-backed brethren will not forgive anything. That can be the work of the Devil as well as shutting one's eyes to immorality. Satan gets the advantage of a great many Christians because they are unforgiving. There are two things that we don't hear very often even in our conservative churches: we don't hear folk admitting their sins and asking for forgiveness nor do we hear folk forgiving those who confess. There is an unforgiving spirit in many of our churches.

We need to remember that we are all capable of any sin. Whatever the other man has done, we are also capable of doing. When such a man repents from his sin, he is to be restored in the spirit of meekness. He is to be brought back into fellowship. This is part of the ministry. It is a glorious ministry, isn't it?

Furthermore, when I came to Troas to preach Christ's gospel, and a door was opened unto me of the Lord [2 Cor. 2:12].

He came to Troas, and there he found an open door. It was the will of God for him to stay there and to preach the gospel rather than proceed on to Corinth at that time. Paul was not being fickle. He was being faithful. He was faithful to the opportunity which God gave him.

I had no rest in my spirit, because I found not Titus my brother: but taking my leave of them, I went from thence into Macedonia [2 Cor. 2:13].

Even while he was preaching the gospel in Troas, he was grieved at heart because Titus hadn't come to bring him word concerning the congregation in Corinth. He waited for Titus to come, but Titus didn't come. Then Paul went over to Philippi in Macedonia. It was there that Titus came and brought word that the Corinthians had dealt with this sin in their congregation and that the man had now repented and had turned from his sin.

THE TRIUMPHANT MINISTRY

Now we come to what some have called the power of the ministry. It is part of the greatness of the ministry, and I rejoice today to be able to preach the kind of gospel and the kind of Word of God that we have to give. We are dealing here with a grand and glorious picture.

Now thanks be unto God, which always causeth us to triumph in Christ, and maketh manifest the savour of his knowledge by us in every place [2 Cor. 2:14].

In this dramatic picture, Paul is saying that preaching the gospel is like leading a triumphal entry. The background is a Roman triumphal entry. One of the great Roman generals would go out to the frontier—to Europe where my ancestors were at that time, or down into Africa—where he would have victory after victory, for Rome was victorious in most campaigns. The conqueror would then return to Rome, and there would be a big, triumphal entry into the city. It is said that sometimes the triumphal entry would begin in the morning and go on far into the night. The Roman conqueror would be bringing in animals and other booty which he had captured. In the front of the procession would be the people who were going to be released. They had been captured but would be freed and would become Roman citizens. In the back of the procession would be the captive people who were to be executed.

In these triumphal entries there was always the burning of incense. They would be burning the incense to their gods to whom they gave credit for the victory. All the way through the procession would be clouds of smoke from the incense, sometimes even obscuring the procession as it passed by.

With this as a background, Paul is saying,

"Thanks be unto God,which always causeth us to triumph in Christ." This is wonderful, friend. You can't lose when you are in Christ. You cannot lose! Paul says that God *always* causeth us to triumph. Wait a minute, Paul. Always? In every place? We know you had wonderful success in Ephesus, but you didn't do so well in Athens. Do you feel that you triumphed in both places? "Yes," Paul says, "He always causes us to triumph in Christ!"

"And maketh manifest the savour [the sweet incense] of his knowledge by us in every place." Are you having a victory when no one turns to Christ? "Oh, yes," Paul says.

For we are unto God a sweet savour of Christ, in them that are saved, and in them that perish [2 Cor. 2:15].

In that triumphal entry were those who were going to be set free and those who were going to be executed—but all of them were in the triumphal entry.

To the one we are the savour of death unto death; and to the other the savour of life unto life. And who is sufficient for these things? [2 Cor. 2:16].

Paul is overwhelmed by this—"who is sufficient for these things?" My friend, the greatest privilege in the world is to give out the Word of God. There is nothing like it. I would never want to run for the presidency of the United States. It is difficult to understand why anyone would want to be president in this day of unsolvable problems. But it is glorious to give out the Word of God! Do you know why? Because He always causes us to triumph!

While I was a pastor in Los Angeles, we very seldom had a Sunday when someone didn't turn to Christ, and many times there were a great many folk.

When the gospel is preached and the multitudes accept Christ, that is wonderful. We can see the triumph there. We are a "savour of life" unto those who are saved. But now wait a minute—what about the crowd which rejects Christ? We are a "savour of death" to them. I often say to the congregation after I have preached a message, "If you go out of here after rejecting Christ, I am probably the worst enemy you will ever have, because now you cannot go into the presence of God and say that you never heard the gospel." However, all people are now in the triumphal entry. Many will not be set free; they will be judged. But regardless of our destiny, we are in the great triumphal entry of Jesus Christ, because He is going to *win*, my friend! Every knee must bow to him, and every tongue shall confess that Jesus Christ is Lord. Every individual will have to bow to Him someday—regardless of whether He is the person's Savior or Judge. No wonder Paul exclaims, "Who is sufficient for these things?"

"To the one we are the savour of death unto death; and to the other the savour of life unto life." Today the incense is ascending; the Word is going out. And we are a savor of life to some and a savor of death to others.

For we are not as many, which corrupt the word of God: but as of sincerity, but as of God, in the sight of God speak we in Christ [2 Cor. 2:17].

This is the entire plan of the Christian ministry. We are not to corrupt the Word of God or distort it or make merchandise of it, but to give it out in sincerity as the Spirit of God reveals its truth to us.

CHAPTER 3

THEME: God's comfort in the glorious ministry of Christ

Paul has spoken of the triumph of the ministry. Now he deals with the accreditation of the ministry. He will reach the heights in this chapter.

Do we begin again to commend ourselves? or need we, as some others, epistles of commendation to you, or letters of commendation from you? [2 Cor. 3:1].

Paul is asking, "Do I need a letter of recommendation from my employer? Do I need a letter from God testifying that I am His minister?" Paul says, "No, I don't need to have that"—for this reason:

Ye are our epistle written in our hearts, known and read of all men:

Forasmuch as ye are manifestly declared to be the epistle of Christ ministered by us, written not with ink, but with the Spirit of the living God; not in tables of stone, but in fleshy tables of the heart [2 Cor. 3:2–3].

The proof of the effectiveness of any ministry is whether or not it has a recommendation from God. He is not giving out letters of recommendation; the proof lies in the epistles that are written in the fleshly tables of the heart. I read many letters from folk who have turned to Christ because of my radio ministry. Several years ago a wonderful family came up to me in Houston, Texas. If no one else turned to Christ through my radio program there, I still would consider it worthwhile. They lis-

tened to the radio program for three months before they made a decision for Christ, and then the entire family, a handsome family, all received Christ. They are some of the epistles I have down in Texas. I have such epistles in practically every state of these United States and on many foreign shores. They are my letters of commendation.

Paul says to the Corinthian believers, "*You are our epistles written in our hearts, known and read of all men.*"

And such trust have we through Christ to God-ward [2 Cor. 3:4].

This gives me confidence. I know the Bible is the Word of God. When I was in seminary, I believed it was the Word of God. I think that intellectually it can be determined that it is the Word of God. But today I don't even need the intellectual demonstrations anymore. I've passed that. To me it is very simple—the proof of the Word of God is what it does. They say that the proof of the pudding is in the eating. God put it like this: "O taste and see that the LORD is good . . ." (Ps. 34:8). This is His challenge to you.

Not that we are sufficient of ourselves to think any thing as of ourselves; but our sufficiency is of God [2 Cor. 3:5].

I am sure that you have already sensed the weakness of the apostle Paul in this epistle of 2 Corinthians. But Paul could say, "For when I am weak, then am I strong" (2 Cor. 12:10). God is not looking for some big something or some big somebody. If He had wanted that, He couldn't use me and He couldn't use you. God chooses the weak things of this world, little things, insignificant things to accomplish His purposes. Our sufficiency is of God.

CONTRASTS BETWEEN THE OLD AND NEW COVENANTS

Who also hath made us able ministers of the new testament; not of the letter, but of the spirit: for the letter killeth, but the spirit giveth life [2 Cor. 3:6].

We are ministers "of the new testament" would be better translated, ministers of the New *Covenant*. We will see a contrast between the old covenant (the Old Testament) and the New Covenant (the New Testament). There is a contrast here in several different ways.

"Not of the letter, but of the spirit." In the Old Testament, and specifically in the Law, the letter kills; the letter of the Law actually condemns us. The Law says that you and I are guilty sinners. Those letters which were written on the tablets of stone condemned man. The Mosaic Law never gave life. That is the contrast he is making here. The letter kills. "For the letter killeth, but the spirit giveth life."

I have often challenged congregations to name somebody who was saved by the Law. Did you know that even Moses, the law-giver, could not be saved by the Law? Do you know why not? He was a murderer! Also David broke the Law even though he was a man after God's own heart. Friend, you can't be saved by keeping the Law. The Law kills you; the Law condemns you.

But if the ministration of death, written and engraven in stones, was glorious, so that the children of Israel could not stedfastly behold the face of Moses for the glory of his countenance; which glory was to be done away [2 Cor. 3:7].

The old covenant, the Law, was a ministration of death. When it says that it was written and engraved on stones, we know he is talking about the Ten Commandments.

It "was glorious." It is the will of God, and it is good, even though it condemns me. There is nothing wrong with the Law. The problem is with me. It shows me that I am a sinner. "So that the children of Israel could not stedfastly behold the face of Moses for the glory of his countenance; which glory was to be done

away." That glory on Moses' face slowly disappeared.

How shall not the ministration of the spirit be rather glorious? [2 Cor. 3:8].

If the Old Testament was glorious, how much more the New Testament!

For if the ministration of condemnation be glory, much more doth the ministration of righteousness exceed in glory [2 Cor. 3:9].

"The ministration of righteousness" is the righteousness which we have in Christ Jesus.

For even that which was made glorious had no glory in this respect, by reason of the glory that excelleth.

For if that which is done away was glorious, much more that which remaineth is glorious [2 Cor. 3:10–11].

"That which is done away" is the Law. Notice that it *is* "done away." Then how much more glorious is that which remains, that New Covenant. He is making a contrast between the giving of the Mosaic Law and the day of grace in which we live.

Seeing then that we have such hope, we use great plainness of speech:

And not as Moses, which put a veil over his face, that the children of Israel could not stedfastly look to the end of that which is abolished [2 Cor. 3:12–13].

To what is he having reference?

We need to recognize that there was a first giving and a second giving of the Law. When Moses went to the top of Mount Sinai, *God* gave him the tablets of stone, and *God* Himself wrote the Law on them. That was the Law that the children of Israel were to live by and actually be saved by (if they could keep it—which no one could). And they were going to be judged by it. While Moses was up on the mountain with God, the children of Israel were already breaking the first two commandments: "Thou shalt have no other gods before me" (Exod. 20:3) and "Thou shalt not make unto thee any graven image . . ." (Exod. 20:4). The Mosaic Law was a very strict, rigid law. Even Moses said, ". . . I exceedingly fear and quake:" (Heb. 12:21). It demanded an eye for an eye, a tooth for a tooth, burning for burning, and cutting for cutting. It was absolute, intrinsic righteousness and holiness. Whatever a man deserved according to the Law that was what he was to receive. In Exodus 32 the people were already breaking the Law. What is going to happen? God told Moses to go down to the people. When Moses went down the mountain, he could see from a distance that the children of Israel were breaking the first two commandments, and he didn't dare bring the tables of the Law into the camp. Why not? If he had, the entire nation of Israel would have been blotted out at that very moment. They would have been judged immediately because the breaking of those laws meant instant death. So Moses smashed those tablets of stone; then he went into the camp.

Now when Moses goes back to the top of Mount Sinai into the presence of God, we see that something happens. Moses recognizes that all Israel should be destroyed because of their sin, but he asks God for mercy. And God gives them a second chance as He gives Moses the second tables of the Law. Moses now understands that God is tempering the Law with mercy and grace. At the very heart of the Mosaic system is to be a tabernacle and a sacrificial system that will be the basis of approach to God, which is ". . . without shedding of blood [there] is no remission" of sin (Heb. 9:22). But "without holiness, no man is going to see God" (see Heb. 12:14). How in the world are we going to get into His presence? Well, God will have to make a way for us, and God did make a way. What a glorious, wonderful revelation this is. No wonder Moses' face shone!

When Moses came down from the mount, he had the second tables of the Law, which was a ministration of condemnation and a ministration of death, demanding a righteousness of man which he was unable to produce of himself; but also there was the sacrificial system that manifested the grace of God. It was the grace of God, fulfilled in the death and resurrection of Christ, that Paul the apostle found—Paul, who had been a man under the Law, a Pharisee of the Pharisees—and that brought him to the place where he could say, "And be found in him [Jesus], not having mine own righteousness, which is of the law, but that which is through the faith of Christ, the righteousness which is of God by faith" (Phil. 3:9). Now here is a ministration of glory indeed, and this is the glorious *gospel*.

The Law was glorious. It offered man a way of salvation, but man was too feeble to fulfill its demands. It was a glorious way of life that was pleasing to God, but for man it became a ministration of death because of his lost condition.

However, the glory of the grace of God fulfilled in Christ is a ministration of glory indeed! In another passage it is called "the glorious gospel of the blessed God." The word *blessed* means "happy"—the happy God. What is it that makes God happy? The thing that makes God happy is that He is a lover of men and He delights in mercy. He wants to save man. We are told in Micah 7:18: "Who is a God like unto thee, that pardoneth iniquity, and passeth by the transgression of the remnant of his heritage? he retaineth not his anger for ever, because he delighteth in mercy." It is not God's will that any of the human family should be lost. To the prophet Ezekiel God said, "Say unto them, As I live, saith the Lord GOD, I have no pleasure in the death of the wicked; but that the wicked turn from his way and live: turn ye, turn ye from your evil ways; for why will ye die, O house of Israel?" (Ezek. 33:11). God wants to save—saving man is the thing that makes Him happy. We have a happy God. What a glorious picture this gives us.

When Moses came down from the mountain the second time, there was *joy* in his heart and his face *shone*. Now there was a way for the children of Israel to come into the presence of God through the sacrificial system.

Now let's make this very clear again that the veil Moses put on his face was not because his face was shining with a glory so that they couldn't look at him. It was because that glory was beginning to fade away. The fact that Moses' face shone was a glorious thing, but the glory began to fade.

But their minds were blinded: for until this day remaineth the same veil untaken away in the reading of the old testament; which veil is done away in Christ [2 Cor. 3:14].

Their minds are blinded until this very day.

The veil that Moses wore on his face is now a veil on the minds of God's ancient people. It is still there because of the fact that these people actually do not see that Christ is the end of the Law for righteousness. They do not see that *He* is the fulfillment of the whole law. The blindness is still there.

When we get into the next chapter, we will find that the "god of this world" has blinded the minds of those who do not believe, and we will see why this is true.

But even unto this day, when Moses is read, the veil is upon their heart [2 Cor. 3:15].

When they read the Law, they actually think that they are able to keep it. But in reading the Old Testament we do not find the confidence that you would expect in the hearts and minds of God's people. Even David raised some questions. Job was in absolute bewilderment. Hezekiah turned his face to the wall and wept when he faced death. However, in this day of grace in which you and I live, even the weakest saint who trusts Jesus has absolute assurance of his perfect acceptance with God.

Nevertheless when it shall turn to the Lord, the veil shall be taken away [2 Cor. 3:16].

"It" refers to the heart. When the heart turns to the Lord Jesus Christ, the veil is taken away. Man's trouble is heart trouble. He is blinded because of the sin in his life. When he is willing to turn from his sin and receive the Lord Jesus as his Savior, "the veil shall be taken away."

Now the Lord is that Spirit: and where the Spirit of the Lord is, there is liberty [2 Cor. 3:17].

Only the Spirit of God can lift the veil and help us to see that Christ is the Savior. He alone can do that. He is the One and the *only* One.

You notice that Paul here is saying the very same thing which Simon Peter had said: "To him give all the prophets witness, that through his name whosoever believeth in him shall receive remission of sins" (Acts 10:43). My friend, if you do not see the Lord Jesus Christ in the Old Testament, the Spirit of God is not your Teacher because the Spirit of God takes the things of Christ and shows them unto us. The Spirit of God brings you into the place of liberty. He doesn't put you under law. He delivers you from law and brings you to Christ. When He does—

But we all, with open face beholding as in a glass the glory of the Lord, are changed into the same image from glory to glory, even as by the Spirit of the Lord [2 Cor. 3:18].

This is a very wonderful passage of Scripture. Paul has been talking about the veil being on the heart; then when we turn to Christ, that veil is taken away. Now as believers we are looking upon the Lord Jesus Christ—but even as believers our eyes are veiled when there is sin in our lives. But when that sin is confessed, and we are in fellowship with Him, we look to Him. Then we, with "open face" or unveiled face, beholding (not *reflecting* as another version translates it) as in a mirror the glory of the Lord—the idea is not of reflecting in order to transform, but rather that of beholding *until* transformed. Then we can reflect His image. I feel that a more accurate translation is: we "beholding as in a mirror the glory of the Lord, are *transformed* into the same image from glory to glory, even as from the Lord, the Spirit."

Frances E. Siewert, who lived here in Southern California in Sierra Madre, worked on The Amplified Bible. When she was still alive, she and I used to carry on a friendly battle. She would hear me on the radio and sometimes when I referred to her amplified version, I would question some things. She was a brilliant woman, and I want to be very frank and say that I lost most of the battles. However, I won a friendly battle over this verse. Let me quote this verse to you from her earliest amplified version. "And all of us, as with unveiled face, [because we] continue to behold [in the Word of God] as in a mirror the glory of the Lord, are constantly being transfigured into His *very own* image in ever increasing splendor *and* from one degree of glory to another; [for this comes] from the Lord [Who is] the Spirit." This is an excellent translation except for the word *transfigured*. Only the Lord Jesus was transfigured—I've never seen a saint yet that I thought had been transfigured. It is true that the Word of God is the mirror that we are to look at, and we are beholding Him—just looking at Christ. That is the reason we need to stay in the Word of God and behold the Lord Jesus. As you behold Him, you are transformed. In other words, the Word of God does more than regenerate you (we are regenerated by the Spirit of God using the Word of God). "Being born again, not of corruptible seed, but of incorruptible, by the word of God, which liveth and abideth for ever" (1 Pet. 1:23). Also the Word of God transforms us. Oh, this is so important! I wish I had spent more time looking in the mirror, beholding Him more. My friend, in the Word of God we see Him. He is not a super star; He is not just a man. In the Word of God we see the unveiled *Christ*. Oh, how wonderful He is!

Dr. H.A. Ironside told the story about an old Scot who lay suffering and, actually, dying. The physician told him he didn't have very long to live. A friend came to spend a little time with him and said to him, "They tell me you'll not be with us long." That's a nice thing to say to a man who is dying. Then he continued, "I hope you get a wee glimpse of the Savior's blessed face as you are going through the valley of the shadow." The dying man looked up when he gathered a little strength and answered, "Away with the glimpse, mon; it's a full view of His blessed face I've had these forty years, and I'll not be satisfied with any of your wee glimpses now." How wonderful to behold Him today.

Perhaps some of you remember Nathaniel Hawthorne's story about the great stone face. A little lad lived in a village where there was a mountain with a rock formation which they called the great stone face. The people had a legend that someday someone would come to the village who would look like the great stone face. He would do wonderful things for the village and be a means of great blessing. That story really took hold of the lad. During his lifetime he would gaze at the great stone face at every opportunity that he had, and he would dream of the time someone looking like the great stone face would come to the village. Years passed and as time went by, he became a young man, then an old man. He was tottering down the street one day when someone looked up and saw him coming and shouted, "He has come. The one who looks like the great stone face is here." This man had looked at the great stone face for so long that now he bore its image.

Listen to me. Do you want to be Christlike? Then spend time looking at Jesus. I recall that Dr. Lewis Sperry Chafer at the Dallas Theological Seminary used to stop us when we would sing the song, "Take time to be holy, speak oft with thy Lord" by William D. Longstaff. He would say, "Change that first line. Let us sing 'Take time to *behold* Him.'" Do you want to be holy? Then behold Him.

Turn your eyes upon Jesus;
Look full in His wonderful face;
And the things of earth will grow
    strangely dim
In the light of His glory and grace.

I need this. I hope you, too, sense a need of seeing Jesus Christ on the pages of the Word of God so that you might grow more like Him.

CHAPTER 4

THEME: *God's comfort in the ministry of suffering for Christ*

Here we have another facet of God's comfort. We have seen God's comfort for life's plans in chapter 1. Then in chapter 2 it was God's comfort in restoring sinning saints. Chapter 3 showed God's comfort in the glorious ministry of Christ—wasn't that third chapter wonderful? Now we are not going to come down from the mountain, but we are going to stay right up there as we see God's comfort in the ministry of suffering for Christ. We may even have to climb a little higher, and I'm not sure but what we may get into an atmosphere where I really have difficulty in breathing. Paul says, "Come up higher," and that's what we want to do.

Therefore seeing we have this ministry, as we have received mercy, we faint not [2 Cor. 4:1].

This is a glorious ministry. God has given to us a message which no man could have conceived. It would be impossible for a man to work out such a plan as the gospel presents. I don't know why God allowed me to be a minister of the glorious gospel other than because of His mercy. We have seen before that God is *rich* in mercy. God did not exhaust His mercy before He got to me, because He saw that I would need a whole lot of it. He has been rich in mercy to me. By mercy He has permitted me to have a Bible-teaching radio program. Since it is by His mercy, we faint not. We rejoice in it!

What is so wonderful about this ministry? I'll tell you what is wonderful about it. When I was in seminary, I studied religions. In fact, they so fascinated me that in the first few years of my ministry I almost decided to specialize in the field of comparative religions. Although I didn't do that, I am acquainted with quite a few religions of the world. I want you to know the difference between Christianity—the gospel of the grace of God—and the religions of the world. It is very simply expressed by one word. All the religions of the world say, "Do, do, do." The gospel says, "Done." The gospel tells me that God has done something for me; I am to believe it; I am to trust Him. The only way I can come to Him is by faith. That is my approach to Him. "But without faith it is impossible to please him . . ." (Heb. 11:6). In contrast to this, the religions of this world all say, "Do." It is almost amusing to see what the cults in this country say one must do to be right with God. One cult declares there are four things, one of them says there are seven things you must do, another has ten things you must do—the Ten Commandments.

Some of these cults say you must have faith. However, by "faith" they do not mean a trust in Jesus Christ, but rather an acknowledgment as historical fact that Jesus lived and that He died over nineteen hundred years ago. May I say to you, it will not save you simply to believe that Jesus died. My friend, Jesus Christ died *for* our *sins* and rose again, according to the Scriptures. That is the important distinction. In His finished work we must put our trust. It is done.

At one time Paul had been under the Law. He knew what it was to be under a system of "do, do, do." He says he was "an Hebrew of the Hebrews; as touching the law, a Pharisee . . . touching the righteousness which is in the law, blameless" (Phil. 3:5–6). He was really under the Law, and he hoped that he would be able to work out his salvation. Then one day he met the Lord Jesus Christ on the Damascus road. After he came to know Him as Lord and Savior, he wrote, "That I may . . . be found in him, not having mine own righteousness, which is of the law, but that which is through the faith of Christ, the righteousness which is of God by faith" (Phil. 3:8–9). You see, after Paul had stood in the presence of Jesus Christ, he saw that he could never make it on his own. Any righteousness he might have by the Law would not be enough. He would need to have the righteousness of Christ. Paul says that was a new day for him.

It is a new day for each of us when we recognize this fact. Today we need mercy. God has been merciful; God loved us. God in His mercy provided a Savior for us, and now He saves us by His grace. How wonderful He is!

But have renounced the hidden things of dishonesty, not walking in craftiness, nor handling the word of God deceitfully; but by manifestation of the truth commending ourselves to every man's conscience in the sight of God [2 Cor. 4:2].

We are saved by the grace of God through faith in Christ Jesus. However, after we have been saved, that gospel must live in us. We have renounced the hidden things of dishonesty. Coming to Christ and trusting Him is more than an intellectual assent to the fact that Christ died on the cross. It is placing our *trust* in Him and experiencing His regeneration. When Christ has saved us, we ought to be an example of the gospel. In other words, the man who preaches the gospel should be a holy man. Paul says that we have "renounced the hidden things of dishonesty."

The translation of this verse from *The Amplified Bible* is very good, and it brings out all the facets of these words which Paul uses in this verse. Compare your Bible with this version: "We have renounced disgraceful ways— secret thoughts, feelings, desires and underhandedness, methods and arts that men hid through shame; we refuse to deal craftily (to practice trickery and cunning) or to adulterate or handle dishonestly the Word of God; but we state the truth openly—clearly and candidly. And so we commend ourselves in the sight and presence of God to every man's conscience."

We are not to walk in hypocrisy. We should not be unreal. Our behavior should not contradict that which we are preaching. It ought to be a conduct which meets the approval of the Lord Jesus Christ. We are not perfect, but we are to walk in a way that is well pleasing to Him.

We are not to handle "the word of God deceitfully." Someone has translated that "huckstering." We are not to be huckstering the Word of God. This gets right down to where we live. Mr. Preacher, why do you preach? Are you preaching for money? You say that you preach for the love of souls, but is it really the love of souls? Or is it for money? I need to examine my own heart on this score. Paul wrote, ". . . woe is unto me, if I preach not the gospel!" (1 Cor. 9:16).

A person can preach the gospel and say things that are absolutely true, but at the same time his life can be speaking another message. I pray a great deal about this in my own life. I pray, "O God, don't let me preach unless I can have a clear conscience, and unless I am preaching in the power of the Spirit of God." I don't want to preach unless there are those two things. It is a glorious thing to preach the gospel, but it is an awful thing to preach it if down underneath there is a lack of sincerity, a lack of being committed to Him and having a conviction about Him.

Actually, this is directed to the Christian layman. Do you want to be a witness for

Christ? You are a witness either for or against Him. When Paul speaks of the ministry here, he is not referring to the clergy or the man in the pulpit; he is speaking of the man in the pew. The man in the pulpit is to train people for the work of the ministry. Our business is to help equip them for that work.

I heard a tremendous analogy the other day: Sheep produce sheep. The shepherd cannot produce sheep. He watches over the sheep. It is the sheep today who are going to win sheep, because sheep produce sheep. My business is to equip the layman to witness.

By the way, are you doing something to get out the Word of God? That is witnessing. God may have given you the gift of making money. Do you use it to send out the Word of God? Perhaps you are a man or woman of prayer, interceding for those who preach and teach the Word of God. You have contact with some person whom no one else could reach. Many people will not listen to me. They tune me in and then they tune me out. Maybe you can reach a person who will not listen to anyone else. God has called you to be a witness, my friend. This is tremendous!

But if our gospel be hid, it is hid to them that are lost:

In whom the god of this world hath blinded the minds of them which believe not, lest the light of the glorious gospel of Christ, who is the image of God, should shine unto them [2 Cor. 4:3–4].

"The god of this world" should be translated "the god of this *age*." I don't like to hear Satan called the god of this *world*. One fall Mrs. McGee and I had the privilege of driving through eastern Ohio, West Virginia, Pennsylvania, and Maryland, around Virginia and across into Indiana, Illinois, Missouri, and Arkansas. How beautiful it was! May I say to you that it was God's world that we were looking at. Although sin has marred it, it is still God's world.

Satan *is* the god of this age. He is running it. He runs the United Nations; he runs all the amusements; he is running the whole show as far as I can tell. He is the god of this age.

He has "blinded the minds of them which believe not." Have you ever heard someone say, "I don't understand the gospel. I have heard it all my life, but it doesn't mean anything to me." I have heard people say that again and again. What has happened? The Devil has blinded them. The light is shining, but the Devil has blinded their eyes so they cannot see. This always reminds me of a group of miners who were trapped in a mine in West Virginia after an explosion. Finally rescuers got food over to them, and then they got an electric light over to the place where they were trapped. A young miner there was looking right into the light and said, "Why don't they turn on the lights?" All of the men looked at him, startled. He had been blinded by the explosion. Satan blinds many folk. They say, "Why don't you turn on the light? I don't see the gospel at all." That is the blindness that comes from Satan.

There are other folk who say, "There are things in the Bible that I cannot believe. I don't know why, but I just can't believe them." I had a letter the other day from a man who accused me of preaching a gospel that is not true and of knowing that the Bible is not true. Oh, what arrogance! I wrote to him that I had never read a letter in which I had seen such a display of arrogance and ignorance. But do you know what was really his problem? It was not that there are things in the Bible which he couldn't believe. The problem was that there was *sin* in his life, sin that the Bible condemns. He didn't *want* to believe. That is the condition of a lot of folk today. The problem is not with the Bible; the problem is with their lives. My friend, if you choose to go on indulging your sins, then you can go on doing that. It is your loss. But you *can* turn to Christ. Don't tell me you cannot. You can turn to Christ if you will. The moment a man comes to the place where he sees himself as a sinner and says, "I am ready to renounce my sin; I'm ready to receive Christ as my Savior," he will be saved. The Word of God is light. Instead of saying you cannot see the light and instead of trying to blame the Bible, why don't you face your sins before God? Then there will be no difficulty about your believing.

I would like to give you a quotation from Sir Isaac Newton. Certainly no one could say that he was not an intellectual or that he was not a man of remarkable ability. One day someone said this to him: "Sir Isaac, I do not understand. You seem to be able to believe the Bible like a little child. I have tried but I cannot. So many of its statements mean nothing to me. I cannot believe; I cannot understand." This was the reply of Sir Isaac Newton: "Sometimes I come into my study and in my absent-mindedness I attempt to light my candle when the extinguisher is over it, and I fumble about trying to light it and cannot; but when I remove the extinguisher then I am able to light the candle. I am afraid the extinguisher in your case is the love of your sins; it is deliberate unbelief that is in you. Turn to God in repentance; be prepared to let the Spirit of God reveal His truth to you, and it will be His joy to show the glory of the grace of God shining in the face of Jesus Christ." Sir Isaac Newton was not only a great scientist but also a great preacher. Why don't people believe? Because Satan has blinded their eyes "lest the light of the glorious gospel of Christ, who is the image of God, should shine unto them." It is a glorious gospel, but it is glorious because it reveals the glory of Christ. Apparently that is what men do not want to see.

For we preach not ourselves, but Christ Jesus the Lord; and ourselves your servants for Jesus' sake [2 Cor. 4:5].

We preach Christ Jesus the Lord. Believe me, my friend, you and I are helpless when we give out the Word of God. There is an enemy opposed to us, and he blinds the minds of people.

For God, who commanded the light to shine out of darkness, hath shined in our hearts, to give the light of the knowledge of the glory of God in the face of Jesus Christ [2 Cor. 4:6].

Paul goes back to the time of creation when God created light. I don't know when creation took place. A great many folk believe that in order to be a fundamentalist one must believe that God created this universe in 4,004 B.C. I do not know any of my fundamental brethren who hold that asinine viewpoint. Way back yonder in the beginning God created it. He did not give us the date. Our God is a God of eternity. He wasn't just sitting around twiddling His thumbs waiting for man to appear on the scene. Man is a Johnny-come-lately, of course, but God has been here a long, long, long time. I hold the position that this universe has been here for a long time and that something happened to it. It bears evidence of some titanic convulsion that took place. Something must have happened to a perfect creation. We are told in Genesis 1 that God moved in. The Spirit of God moved, or the actual word is *brooded*, upon the face of the waters. Then God said, "Let there be light," and there was light!

Now Paul tells us that God, "who commanded the light to shine out of darkness [in Genesis 1], hath shined in our hearts, to give the light of the knowledge of the glory of God in the face of Jesus Christ." Just as the Spirit of God brooded over the waters, so the Spirit of God broods over a soul. He moves in to bring conviction to our hearts. Then He regenerates us. And the light of the glorious gospel of Christ, who is the image of God, shines in. Here we are back looking at Him. As someone has said, "The look saves, but the gaze sanctifies." We need to spend a lot of time looking at Him. But even doing this, we are weak vessels.

But we have this treasure in earthen vessels, that the excellency of the power may be of God, and not of us [2 Cor. 4:7].

We are just an "earthen vessel." The picture here is a vivid one. The Greek word for "earthen" is *ostrakinos*—this is what archaeologists are digging up today. Actually, many of their diggings are in the old city dumps where all the broken pottery (clay vessels) was thrown. When I was in Lebanon, I went down to Tyre and walked along an excavation. It goes across the place where Alexander the Great filled in between the mainland and the island to form a peninsula there. I walked out on that to see the excavation going on. There was so much broken pottery there that I could have filled bushel baskets. That is how we are pictured here—weak clay vessels, pottery that can be broken.

"But we have this treasure." What is the treasure? That is the glorious gospel. We carry this glorious gospel in our little, old earthen vessels. That is why Paul says, "For we preach not ourselves, but Christ Jesus the Lord; and ourselves your servants for Jesus' sake." Sometimes we get the idea we want to be a great preacher or even a great Christian. That is one reason that I am not sure we ought to be having all these testimonies that we hear today. It is pretty easy for a man to begin to brag in his testimony. If Jesus Christ is not glorified in a testimony, there is no point in it whatsoever. After all, we are just servants. That is the best that can be said of us.

The simile of earthen vessels takes us back to the incident at the time of Gideon. In Judges 7 we read that Gideon took only three hundred men with him to free their land of innumerable Midianite invaders. Each man had a trumpet and a torch and a pitcher or an earthen vessel. They carried their torches in the earthen vessels so that the light couldn't be seen from a distance. Then when they got among the Midianites, they broke the earthen vessels. It wasn't until the earthen vessel was broken that the light could shine out.

My friend, that is the thing which we need

today. We need the vessel to be broken. The apostle Paul was a man who knew what it was to suffer for Jesus' sake. That vessel had to be broken. The trouble today is that we don't have very many who are willing to do that. I remember that Dr. George Gill used to tell us this in class: "When someone is born, someone has to travail. The reason that more people are not being born again is that there are not enough who are willing to travail." We hear a great deal about witnessing today, but, my friend, what kind of a price are you willing to pay? It is not enough to just knock on a door and visit someone. I'm not minimizing that, and I'm not saying it isn't important, but I am saying that the earthen vessel must be broken. We cannot have our way *and* His way in our lives. We need to make up our minds whether we are going to follow Him or not.

We are troubled on every side, yet not distressed; we are perplexed, but not in despair [2 Cor. 4:8].

Paul is making a comparison here. He says, "We are troubled." That is a comparative degree. But he says, "Yet not distressed." That is a superlative. He was pressed for room, as it were, but he still had room to preach the gospel. There was hand-to-hand combat in the corner, but he still could turn to God.

"We are perplexed"—he was unable to find a way out—"but not in despair." He did get out—the Spirit of God led him.

Persecuted, but not forsaken; cast down, but not destroyed [2 Cor. 4:9].

He was "persecuted," pursued by enemies, but he was "not forsaken"—he was not overtaken by the enemies. When he was in prison, he could write to the Philippians, "But I would ye should understand, brethren, that the things which happened unto me have fallen out rather unto the furtherance of the gospel; So that my bonds in Christ are manifest in all the palace, and in all other places" (Phil. 1:12–13). Even when he was in prison he could always say that the Lord stood by him.

"Cast down, but not destroyed." This is tremendous—he was smitten down; the enemy got him down, but the enemy did not destroy or kill him. Actually, in all these phrases Paul is making a play on words which is lost in the translation into English. If I could paraphrase it in English, it would be something like this: "I am struck down, but I'm not struck out." Even at the end of his life Paul could say, ". . . I have *finished* my course . . ." (2 Tim. 4:7, italics mine). Paul seems to be fighting a losing

battle. Can't you sense that this man is very weak? And yet, in his weakness, he is *strong*. If we could have seen this little crippled, weak, sick Jew up against the mighty juggernaut of Roman power, we would have concluded that he was *nothing*. But, my friend, the fact is he brought a message that *withered* the Roman Empire. Even the historian Gibbon said that the Roman Empire could not stand up against the preaching of the gospel of Christ. (May I say that the gospel still continues to topple thrones.) Paul seemed to be so weak, and yet God delivered him again and again. He used miraculous means and He also used natural means. God will never forsake His servants.

You and I live in a day of compromise, a day of expediency, a day when we seem to measure a man by how popular he is or by how many friends he has. The late Dr. Bob Shuler, pastor in downtown Los Angeles, used to say, "I measure a man by the enemies he has." It is important to make the right kind of enemies. Jesus said that if we would love Him and follow Him, the world would hate us. Paul had the right kind of enemies. I am confident that I have the right kind of enemies also.

Always bearing about in the body the dying of the Lord Jesus, that the life also of Jesus might be made manifest in our body [2 Cor. 4:10].

Remember that in 1 Corinthians 15:31 Paul could say that he died daily. In Romans 8:36 he wrote, "As it is written, For thy sake we are killed all the day long; we are accounted as sheep for the slaughter." In 1 Corinthians 4:9 he wrote: "For I think that God hath set forth us the apostles last, as it were appointed to death: for we are made a spectacle unto the world, and to angels, and to men." Christian, do not be afraid to suffer. Jesus said the world would hate us if we were following Him. It is wonderful to take our place with the Lord Jesus Christ in these days.

For we which live are alway delivered unto death for Jesus' sake, that the life also of Jesus might be made manifest in our mortal flesh [2 Cor. 4:11].

We may actually be the strongest at the moment we feel the weakest.

So then death worketh in us, but life in you.

We having the same spirit of faith, according as it is written, I believed, and

therefore have I spoken; we also believe, and therefore speak;

Knowing that he which raised up the Lord Jesus shall raise up us also by Jesus, and shall present us with you [2 Cor. 4:12–14].

It is interesting to note here, and this is very important to see, that Paul did not consider death to be the end. He is looking on beyond. Death is merely one of the experiences which he will have. In the next chapter he will speak of the comfort in the ministry of martyrdom for Christ. There is a comfort in laying down your life for Jesus' sake. He is saying here that he is joined to a living Christ. He is dead to the things of the world because he is joined to a living Christ. "He which raised up the Lord Jesus shall raise up us also by Jesus."

For all things are for your sakes, that the abundant grace might through the thanksgiving of many redound to the glory of God.

For which cause we faint not; but though our outward man perish, yet the inward man is renewed day by day [2 Cor. 4:15–16].

This is a wonderful verse. As we grow older, we sort of begin to die out as far as the body is concerned. However, we grow in grace and in the knowledge of Christ. I said to my wife no later than yesterday, "I wish that I were thirty-five years old and knew what I know now." This old body that I have is dying. I can tell it all over. I'm ready to trade it in on a new model. It is beginning to waste away, but the inward man is renewed day by day. I feel closer to the Lord today than I did the day I entered the ministry. I was young then and I had a lot of enthusiasm, but I didn't know very much. What a stumbler I was and how often I failed. I was a real ignoramus then. Now I know a little more; I have grown a little down through the years.

For our light affliction, which is but for a moment, worketh for us a far more exceeding and eternal weight of glory;

While we look not at the things which are seen, but at the things which are not seen: for the things which are seen are temporal; but the things which are not seen are eternal [2 Cor. 4:17–18].

Again he makes a contrast. Down here we seem to have a lot of trouble and, my, it does seem to last a long time, doesn't it? It seems so hard. But when we begin to measure it by the weight of glory that is coming someday, it is a *light* affliction compared to that *weight* of glory. Someone has said, "At eventide it shall be light." ". . . we spend our years as a tale that is told" (Ps. 90:9). Our years pass as ". . . a watch in the night" (Ps. 90:4). "For our light affliction, which is but for a moment, worketh for us a far more exceeding and eternal weight of glory." We are not to fix our gaze on the things which are seen. These things that we see around us are all passing away. The things which are not seen are eternal.

I think of the changes that have taken place right here in Southern California. There were a number of very wonderful Christians whom I knew when I came here in 1940. Many of them are gone today. The cities have changed—everything is different. The things which are seen are passing away. The things which are not seen, those are the things of eternal value, and they are beginning to loom larger and larger. "For the things which are seen are temporal; but the things which are not seen are eternal."

My friend, I am looking for that city whose builder and maker is God. I love Pasadena; I love Southern California, but I can truthfully say that I am now looking for another city.

CHAPTER 5

THEME: God's comfort in the ministry of martyrdom for Christ

In this section on the comfort of God, we have seen God's comfort in the glorious ministry of Christ (ch. 3). How wonderful that He is an unveiled Christ whom we declare today! Also we have seen God's comfort in the ministry of suffering for Christ (ch. 4), and now we shall see the comfort of God in the ministry of martyrdom for Christ.

For we know that if our earthly house of this tabernacle were dissolved, we have a building of God, an house not made with hands, eternal in the heavens [2 Cor. 5:1].

I want you especially to notice what Paul is saying here. He says, "For we know [not we *hope* or we *expect* or even that we *believe*] that if our earthly house of this tabernacle were dissolved, we have a building of God, an house not made with hands, eternal in the heavens." This is a positive "know." He knows because of the fact that the Spirit of God has made it real to him.

The word for "tabernacle" is *skēnē*, which means "tent." That is the same word that was used for the wilderness tabernacle of the Old Testament in the Septuagint, a translation of the Old Testament into the Greek. The Old Testament tabernacle, the Mosaic tabernacle, was a *skēnē*, a tent. It was a flimsy sort of thing.

This verse has always been a big question mark to me. I have never been too dogmatic about the interpretation of it. But I have now come to the conviction that what he is talking about here is *not* a temporary body. For many years I thought that God would have sort of a temporary body for us when we got to heaven. It would be like taking your car to the garage for repair work and having a loaner to drive until it is fixed. I thought that the Lord would give us a temporary body until our new body was given to us. I never liked that idea, but it seemed to be what Paul was saying. Now I don't believe he is referring to a temporary body, because he says it is "eternal in the heavens." He is talking about that new body that we are going to get.

We need to realize that there is an outward man and an inward man. Paul talked about that in the preceding chapter. The outward man perishes, but the inward man is renewed day by day. A great many people misunderstand that. I had a letter from a man who said the Bible is filled with contradictions, and he said, "I can prove there are contradictions. You talk about So-and-so having gone to be with the Lord, and then you talk about the body that is going to be raised and say that the person is going to be raised from the dead down here. Now that is a contradiction." This man has missed the entire point. The body is put in the grave, but the individual, the real person, has gone to be with Christ—if that individual is a believer.

The things that are seen are temporal. Maybe you have seen me and maybe you haven't. When I go to other areas for speaking engagements, some folk drive long distances because they have heard me on the radio and they want to see me. A family in Ohio drove fifty miles just to see how I looked. But actually they didn't see me, they just saw the house, this old tent, I live in. I'll be very frank with you, this old tent is becoming very weak, and it is flapping around. Solomon described old age in Ecclesiastes: "In the day when the keepers of the house shall tremble, and the strong men shall bow themselves, and the grinders cease because they are few, and those that look out of the windows be darkened, And the doors shall be shut in the streets, when the sound of the grinding is low, and he shall rise up at the voice of the bird, and all the daughters of music shall be brought low" (Eccl. 12:3–4). The "keepers of the house" are the legs, and my old knees are beginning to tremble. "The strong men," which are my shoulders, are bowed. My wife tells me to stand up straight, and I tell her I can't stand straight. "Those that look out of the windows" are my eyes—I am wearing trifocals now. "The sound of the grinding is low"—I don't hear as well as I used to hear. This is old age taking place in the outward man. The things that are seen are temporal.

Also, there is an inward man, and the inward man is spiritual. It is difficult for us to understand that. God is a person, but God is not a physical, a material Being. God is a Spirit. "God is a Spirit: and they that worship him must worship him in spirit and in truth," Jesus told the woman at the well in John 4:24.

I hear people say they don't like getting old. My friend, I am enjoying it. I am really enjoying my retirement from a church because I am doing now what I want to do, and it is wonderful to be able to do that. My doctor has told me, "I want you to do what you want to do." When my wife tells me to do something, I say to her, "Look, my doctor tells me to do what I *want* to do, and I don't *want* to do this thing that you want me to do." Sometimes I can get by with that, but not always!

Seriously, it is wonderful to know that every passing year brings me closer to Him. I am going to see Him someday; I am going to see the face of the Lord Jesus, the One who loved me and gave Himself for me. I rejoice in that prospect. To be very frank with you, I don't have as much conflict with the world, the flesh, and the Devil as I used to have. I think they've given up on me. This old house is getting old.

Someone asked President Adams how he felt after he had become an old man. He answered, "I feel fine. This old house that I live in is really getting feeble. The shingles are coming off the top and the foundation seems to be coming out from underneath, but Mr. Adams is just fine, thank you."

My friend, we have a house eternal in the heavens. This body of ours will be sown a natural body, but it will be raised a spiritual body. He is going to give us a new body up yonder.

For in this we groan, earnestly desiring to be clothed upon with our house which is from heaven [2 Cor. 5:2].

I'm groaning in this body. One just can't help but groan. Several years ago I built a study up over my garage, which is right next to the house. I couldn't study in my office at the church; so I transferred my study to this room above the garage. Sometimes, when I start down the steps in the morning, I notice that it isn't as easy as it was some years ago. I used to come bounding down those steps in the morning, but now I groan with every step. My wife tells me, "You ought not to groan like that." I remind her, "It's scriptural to groan. Paul says we groan in this house, and I'm going to groan while I am in this old house of mine."

If so be that being clothed we shall not be found naked [2 Cor. 5:3].

This is interesting. One of these days Jesus is going to call His own out of the world. We will be caught up to meet our Lord in the air, and we are going to stand before Him. What will it be like for us? We will be clothed in His righteousness. We will not be found naked.

Not everyone will be clothed in His righteousness when they are raised from the dead.

Christ ". . . was delivered for our offences, and was raised again for our justification" (Rom. 4:25)—that is, our righteousness. But some folk have not accepted His righteousness. They have rejected Christ. Therefore, there is a resurrection of the just and of the unjust. Paul mentions this in Acts 24:15, ". . . that there shall be a resurrection of the dead, both of the just and unjust." Jesus said the same thing in John 5:29. "And shall come forth; they that have done good, unto the resurrection of life; and they that have done evil, unto the resurrection of damnation." My friend, you are going to stand in His presence someday. Will you be clothed in the righteousness of Christ? Are you accepted in the Beloved?

This is a good time to mention that the Bible does not teach only one judgment day, but many judgments. (1) There was the judgment which Jesus Christ bore on the cross. It is because Jesus bore this judgment for us that He could say, "Verily, verily, I say unto you, He that heareth my word, and believeth on him that sent me, hath everlasting life, and shall not come into condemnation [judgment]; but is passed from death unto life" (John 5:24). (2) There is self judgment. We are told in 1 Corinthians 11:31, "For if we would judge ourselves, we should not be judged." (3) Also there is the chastisement of God for the believer. The Lord takes us to His woodshed. "For whom the Lord loveth he chasteneth, and scourgeth every son whom he receiveth" (Heb. 12:6). (4) The works of the believer are to be judged, as we will see later in this chapter. (5) The nation Israel is to be judged. (6) The gentile nations are to be judged. (7) Fallen angels are to be judged. (8) Finally, there is the judgment of the Great White Throne. All the lost ones are brought there. They will appear naked. They will not be clothed in His righteousness. They will be judged according to their works, which is the way they wanted it to be.

For we that are in this tabernacle do groan, being burdened: not for that we would be unclothed, but clothed upon, that mortality might be swallowed up of life [2 Cor. 5:4].

If you feel like groaning, you just groan, my friend. It's scriptural. We are burdened. Yes, we are. That is why we groan in these bodies. It is not that we are worried about being unclothed; we know that we shall be clothed with the righteousness of Christ. If He is our Savior, He is our only hope.

Now he that hath wrought us for the selfsame thing is God, who also hath given unto us the earnest of the Spirit [2 Cor. 5:5].

The earnest of the Spirit implies there is more to follow. He has given us the Holy Spirit down here in these weak bodies with all our feebleness, all our frailty. The Holy Spirit is just the earnest. Earnest money is the down payment. Christ has purchased us, and the Holy Spirit indwelling the believer is the down payment. One of these days we will move out of this old house and we will meet the Lord in the air. How wonderfully this opens up such a vista for us.

Therefore we are always confident, knowing that, whilst we are at home in the body, we are absent from the Lord [2 Cor. 5:6].

We are at home in the body. I like this body of mine. I still have a scar on the side of my temple where I fell against the bed when I was learning to walk. Down through the years I have gotten used to this body of mine, and I feel at home in it. However, as long as I am at home in this body, I am absent from the Lord.

(For we walk by faith, not by sight:) [2 Cor. 5:7].

How could Paul be so sure that when we leave this body we will be present with the Lord? Paul says that we walk by faith. We take God at His Word. I would rather take His Word than anyone else's word. Faith is taking God at His Word. We are living in these bodies, and we are absent from the Lord.

We are confident, I say, and willing rather to be absent from the body, and to be present with the Lord [2 Cor. 5:8].

A better translation would be "at home with the Lord." It contrasts being at home in the body or being at home with the Lord. Remember that the soul does not die. The soul never dies; the soul goes to be with Christ. It is the body that is put to sleep. It is the body that must be changed. Remember that there will be a generation that will not go through death, but their bodies will still need to be changed. "Behold, I shew you a mystery; We shall not all sleep, but we shall all be changed. . . . For this corruptible must put on incorruption, and this mortal must put on immortality" (1 Cor. 15:51, 53). It is the body that goes to sleep and it is the body that is raised. Resurrection does not refer to the soul or the spirit. The English word *resurrection* is the Greek word *anastasis*, which means "a standing up." It is the *body* which will stand up. Knowing these things, we walk by faith.

Wherefore we labour, that, whether present or absent, we may be accepted of him [2 Cor. 5:9].

The Greek word *philotim* that is translated "labour" literally means "to esteem as an honor"—to be ambitious. It is the same Greek word which is translated "study" in 1 Thessalonians 4:11: "And that ye study to be quiet, and to do your own business, and to work with your own hands. . . ." Be ambitious to mind your own business! In the verse before us it is translated "labour"—we should be ambitious, we should labor, in such a way that we will be accepted of Him. This is not ambition to become a great somebody.

We are accepted *in* the Beloved. Paul makes this clear in Ephesians, "Having predestinated us unto the adoption of children by Jesus Christ to himself, according to the good pleasure of his will, To the praise of the glory of his grace, wherein he hath made us accepted in the beloved" (Eph. 1:5–6). Being accepted in Christ is my standing before God. God sees me in Christ, and He is made unto me all that I need: wisdom and righteousness and sanctification and redemption (see 1 Cor. 1:30). He is my perfection. God sees me *in* Christ, and I am complete in Him. You cannot add anything to completeness. When a person has 100 percent, that person has *all* of it. We who are believers have Christ, and we are accepted *in* the Beloved. Accepted in Christ is the *standing* that all believers have before God.

To be accepted *of* Him is a different thing. This has to do with our *state* and refers to the way we live our lives. Do we live for Christ? Are we ambitious to be accepted of Him? To be ambitious to be accepted of Christ certainly does not mean that we are to crawl over everybody and step on them in order to get to the top. I am afraid we have people in Christian work who are like that because they want to make a name for themselves.

Dr. G. Campbell Morgan tells how he wrestled with this problem. He was a school teacher when he was called as a minister. It was a very solemn moment for him. He felt that the Lord was saying to him, "You have been set apart definitely for the ministry of the Word. Now do you want to be a great preacher, or do you want to be My servant?" The first thought that Dr. Morgan had was, *I want to be a great preacher.* That ought to be a wonderful ambition, but after a while the Lord began to press it in upon him, "Do you want to be a great preacher, or do you want to be My servant?" Finally Dr. Morgan came to it. He saw that he had to make a choice. Finally he said, "O blessed Lord, I would rather be Thy servant than anything else." He was willing to be an obscure preacher. May I say that in my opinion God made G. Campbell Morgan not only His servant but also made him a great preacher. Sometimes we think that our ambition ought to be to do something great for God. God says that He wants us to be His servants. That's all. You and I need to come to the place where we can say, "Lord, just take me and make me and break me and do with me what You will." God gave this word through Jeremiah: "And seekest thou great things for thyself? seek them not . . ." (Jer. 45:5). That's putting it plain enough, isn't it? My friend, are you trying to get great things for yourself? Oh, there are a lot of ambitious preachers and a lot of ambitious laymen and a lot of ambitious Christian workers and a lot of ambitious Christians—but with selfish ambition. Do you really want to be God's servant? If you do, then you can accomplish something for which He will be able to reward you. To be honest with you, I'm beginning to become just a little worried about this. I want to make sure that I am His *servant.*

1. I am going to have to stand before Him someday and give an account of my service—and so are you. This should motivate us to serve Him acceptably.

For we must all appear before the judgment seat of Christ; that every one may receive the things done in his body, according to that he hath done, whether it be good or bad [2 Cor. 5:10].

This is the judgment seat, literally, the *bēma.* There is still a *bēma* in Corinth, and when we were there on tour, we took pictures of the ruins of it. This was the place where the judges of the city would meet the citizens and would judge them for certain things—there was no question of life or death. At the judgment seat of Christ only believers will appear. It is not a judgment of the believer's sins, which Christ fully atoned for on the cross. The judgment is to see whether you are going to receive a reward or not.

When Paul says, "*We* must all appear," remember that he is writing to believers. All we believers will be judged, that we may receive the things done in the body. We will be judged on the way we lived the Christian life, how we have lived in these bodies down here. When we go into His presence, we will be finished with these old bodies. The question He will ask is how we *used* these bodies. How did we live down here?

Paul faces this question when he writes to the Philippians. He says in Philippians 1:21, "For to me to live is Christ, and to die is gain." Then he talks of his desire to go to be with Christ but also of his desire to live longer so that he can minister to the Philippians. He wants to stay so that he can preach the gospel of Christ a little longer. I had the same reaction the first time I had surgery for cancer and there was not too much hope for me.

You see, I felt like the little boy years ago in my southland. The preacher asked one night, "How many want to go to heaven?" Everybody put up his hand except that one boy. The preacher looked down at him and said, "Don't you want to go to heaven?" The boy answered, "Sure, I want to go to heaven, but I thought you was gettin' up a load for tonight." Like that boy, I didn't want to go right away when I had the cancer. Paul didn't want to go. He said he wanted to stay in his body and preach a little longer. He wanted Christ to be magnified in his body that he might be accepted of Him and that he might receive a reward.

This is the way I feel. I want to stay in this body and do as much for the Lord as I possibly can. Here is the first motivation for believers: We are all going to appear before the judgment seat of Christ, and we will answer to the Lord for our lives. We are going to give a report to Him. Let me make it very clear that this is not the Great White Throne Judgment of Revelation 20:11–15 where only the unsaved will stand. If you are a believer, your name is written in the Book of Life, and you have eternal life. However, you will stand before the *bēma,* the judgment seat of Christ, to be judged for rewards. You and I will stand before Him. This should motivate us to serve Him acceptably. Then when we come into His presence, He will be able to say, "Well done, thou good and faithful servant."

2. The fear of the Lord urges us to persuade men.

Knowing therefore the terror of the Lord, we persuade men; but we are made manifest unto God; and I trust also are made manifest in your consciences [2 Cor. 5:11].

I think the word *terror* could better be translated "fear." There is a great deal said in the

Bible about the fear of the Lord. We are told that the fear of the Lord is the beginning of wisdom (see Prov. 9:10).

One of the tenets of liberalism is that we don't need to be afraid of God. They characterize God as a sweet, indulgent old man whom you can treat most any way. Liberalism teaches the universal fatherhood of God and the universal brotherhood of man, which is one of the most damnable doctrines abroad today. Do you know that the Word of God says: "It is a fearful thing to fall into the hands of the living God" (Heb. 10:31)? Let us not give ersatz bread to the people. Let us not preach a watered-down, sunshiny gospel. Our God is a holy God, a righteous God. It is this holy God who loves you. It is this holy God who wants to save you. But, my friend, if you don't come to God *His* way, you will have to come before Him in judgment. "Knowing therefore the terror [fear] of the Lord, we persuade men." There is many a pulpit from which is never preached a sermon on hell. There are few sermons on punishment, few sermons on judgment. As a result, God's judgment is almost a lost note in Protestantism today. The Lord Jesus said that He had come to seek and to save that which was *lost.* My friend, it is a fearful thing to fall into the hands of the living God. We need to fear the judgment of God. We need to recognize that we are going to be held accountable to Him.

For we commend not ourselves again unto you, but give you occasion to glory on our behalf, that ye may have somewhat to answer them which glory in appearance, and not in heart [2 Cor. 5:12].

In other words, if you are declaring the full counsel of God, you can do it in a loving manner. You don't have to bring down thunder and lightning. However, we need to recognize and we need to state very clearly that men are lost. If we do say that, we are not commending ourselves; that is, we are not trying to become popular. I am always afraid of the soft-soap type of thing we hear today. There is so much today that goes the way of psychology, how to become a well-adjusted human being. May I say to you that if you are without Christ, it is not a psychological adjustment that you need. You are a hell-doomed sinner, and you are on the way to hell. What you need is Christ!

It may not make me popular to say this to you, but it is the Word of God. We don't commend ourselves to you. We don't want you to glory in us. The important thing for us to do is to declare the whole counsel of God. Our motivation to get out the Word of God is a recognition of God's judgment. That is the thing that would arouse many a sleepy church member today.

Missionaries come and tell about the needs out yonder. May I say that there is a real need in this land of ours. The United States is one of the greatest mission fields today. People in our land are on the way to hell. You rub shoulders with them every day.

For whether we be beside ourselves, it is to God: or whether we be sober, it is for your cause [2 Cor. 5:13].

Paul says that the people may think he is crazy. That is all right. He is doing this for God. Or some people may think he is sober—well, it is for their sakes that he is sober.

3. The love of Christ constrains us.

For the love of Christ constraineth us; because we thus judge, that if one died for all, then were all dead:

And that he died for all, that they which live should not henceforth live unto themselves, but unto him which died for them, and rose again [2 Cor. 5:14–15].

"Constraineth us" is a phrase that has been misunderstood. The thought has been that the love of Christ restricts us or straps us down. That is not the meaning of the word that Paul is using here. He says it is the love of Christ that is pushing us out. It is the love of Christ that is motivating us. It is the love of Christ that causes us to give out the Word of God. The love of Christ constrains us.

"Because we thus judge, that if one died for all, then were all dead." It was this that sent Paul out to the ends of the earth with the message of the gospel.

"Because we thus judge, that if one died for all, then were all dead." Mankind is under the sentence of death. When Adam was yonder in the Garden of Eden, he was our federal head; he was the head of that old creation. That old creation was on trial in Adam. God told him, ". . . Of every tree of the garden thou mayest freely eat: But of the tree of the knowledge of good and evil, thou shalt not eat of it: for in the day that thou eatest thereof thou shalt surely die" (Gen. 2:16–17). Adam deliberately disobeyed God. He came under the sentence of death, and when he did that, he took the entire human race down with him, for all were represented in him. You and I have been born into a family of death. All mankind now is under the sentence of death.

Someone has said, "The very moment that gives you life begins to take it away from you." When David wrote, "Yea though I walk through the valley of the shadow of death . . ." (Ps. 23:4), he was not referring to the end of life; he was saying that all of life is like walking down through the great canyon of death, which gets darker and narrower until, finally, we must go through that doorway of death.

Dr. Ironside used to illustrate this in an unusual way, and I'll give you my version of his very wonderful illustration. Behind my home is a lovely range of mountains called the Sierra Madre. Mount Wilson is in this range, and on top of Mount Wilson is the Hale observatory. Now let's think of Mount Wilson as representing Paradise, the place where God put man when He first created him. Adam had everything that was good for him, but there was one thing that God told him he was not to do. Adam was a sinless man and he faced a choice. God had asked him not to do one thing, and that was the very thing which Adam did. He fell. We call it the fall of Adam. He came tumbling down off that high mountain and landed way down in the valley where we are today. After he had fallen down into the valley, he began to bring into this world a race of people. They don't come into this world way up yonder where Adam had been on the mountaintop, on the plane where he had been when he was innocent, but down in the valley, the place to which Adam fell.

The Lord Jesus Christ came to this world all the way from heaven. He was the absolutely sinless One. He was holy, harmless, undefiled, separate from sinners. He came down here to save sinners. He came down from heaven, but He didn't go to the mountaintop. There are no people there—He couldn't find any man on that plane of holiness. They are all in the valley. They are all dead in trespasses and sins. So what did He do? He came down into the valley. He came down into the place of death where all men are. "And that he died for all." Because men were dead, He went down into death, and now He brings believers up with Him in resurrection life. Does He take them back up to the mountaintop where Adam had been? No, He takes them with Him into the heavenlies. We who believe in the Lord Jesus Christ are now seated in the heavenlies. He has ". . . raised us up together, and made us sit together in heavenly places in Christ Jesus" (Eph. 2:6).

"If one died for all, then were all dead." He took our place. And those who believe on Him are risen with Him. They are not risen so they can be put back on the mountaintop and come tumbling down again. No, He takes them all the way up to the heavenlies. Christ took our place. And if we are going to live, it is going to be by faith in Him—that those through faith "should not henceforth live unto themselves, but unto him which died for them, and rose again." Christ died, not only that we should be delivered from death and judgment, but also that we should be brought up from our state of death into newness of life. Now our lives should be devoted to Him that we should live henceforth to the glory of God.

For the child of God this puts a whole new interpretation on the human family.

Wherefore henceforth know we no man after the flesh: yea, though we have known Christ after the flesh, yet now henceforth know we him no more [2 Cor. 5:16].

Now we do not know men "after the flesh." Now we see men through different eyes from those we used when we belonged to the world. Out in the world there are only lost men. I know a Ph.D. who teaches at Cal Tech in Pasadena. He is a brilliant fellow, but he is a lost man because he is not in Christ. I know a man from the gutter; he is also a lost man because he is not in Christ. "Henceforth know we no man after the flesh." That is to say, we do not evaluate men according to their racial background or their social background or their color. We know that according to the old nature they are all lost in sin. But Christ died for all of them. Christ died for the Ph.D. and He died for the man in the gutter. He died for all.

James writes about this in the second chapter of his epistle. He says it is wrong to give the honored place to a rich man who comes into your midst with a ring on his finger and with fine clothing on his back while you give the poor fellow a place to stand in the back. Why is that wrong? Because as the children of God we are to look upon the whole human family as sinners for whom Christ died. Even the line between Jew and Gentile has been erased. All in the human family are sinners before God. The only solution for all is the gospel of Jesus Christ. We do not recognize any man after the flesh. All are on the same level.

"Though we have known Christ after the flesh, yet now henceforth know we him no more." I believe that Paul did know Christ after the flesh. I think that he was present at the crucifixion of Christ. I can't imagine that brilliant young Pharisee not being present at the Crucifixion in Jerusalem.

Jesus Christ walked on this earth over nineteen hundred years ago. He was born in Bethlehem, raised in Nazareth, walked in Galilee, began His ministry in Cana of Galilee, went to Jerusalem, died on a cross there, was buried outside the city in Joseph's tomb, rose again the third day, appeared to those who were His own, and ascended back into heaven. We don't know Him anymore as the Man of Galilee, friend. There is no Man of Galilee today.

At Christmastime there are a great many people who make a trek to Bethlehem. The place is crowded. What are they looking for? Are they looking for the Babe? He isn't there! Jerusalem is crowded with tourists at Eastertime. Our risen Lord isn't there. You see, we don't know Him after the flesh anymore.

Right now, at this very moment, He is up yonder at God's right hand. He is the glorified Christ. "Though we have known Christ after the flesh," now we don't know Him that way anymore. We are not identified with the One who walked on this earth over nineteen hundred years ago; we are identified with Him who is in glory. That is why it says that we have died with Him and have risen with Him and are now in Christ Jesus in the heavenlies.

Therefore if any man be in Christ, he is a new creature: old things are passed away; behold, all things are become new [2 Cor. 5:17].

Here we have a tremendous statement. Allow me to change the word *creature* to the word *creation*. "If any man be in Christ, he is a new creation." We hear this verse often at testimony meetings. People will quote this verse and tell about their conversion. They say they no longer indulge in certain bad habits that they had before their conversion, and they consider this change in their habits to be a fulfillment of this verse.

If you and I are a new creation in Christ Jesus, what are the old things that have passed away? Remember that we have talked about all mankind living at the bottom of the hill where all of us are sinners. Now that we have trusted Christ, those old relationships have passed away. We are no longer identified with Adam. We are no longer identified with the world system. We are now identified with Christ. We have been baptized into the body of believers and we belong to Him. The old things have passed away, and the new thing is this new relationship to the Lord Jesus

Christ. We are now in a relationship with the glorified Christ.

Let's be very practical about this. You may ask, "I know that is a wonderful verse, but how may I know absolutely that I am a new creation in Christ?" Listen to what the Lord Jesus said: "Verily, verily, I say unto you, He that heareth my word, and believeth on him that sent me, hath everlasting life, and shall not come into condemnation; but is passed from death unto life" (John 5:24). Have you believed in the Lord Jesus Christ? Do you trust Him? If you do, He assures you that you have eternal life and will not come into judgment; you have passed from death unto life. This makes you a new creation, no longer subject to judgment and death. You have passed into life.

Do not try to base your confidence on experience. You are a new creation because Jesus says so. The basis is the Word of God. You no longer belong to the old creation that fell in Adam. The new creation stands in Christ Jesus, and you are *in Him* if you are putting your trust in Him. You and I stand in the place of danger and temptation; we may fail in many, many ways, but the wonderful truth is that the Lord Jesus Christ has redeemed us and we are a new creation in Him.

Now Paul is going on to talk about that.

And all things are of God, who hath reconciled us to himself by Jesus Christ, and hath given to us the ministry of reconciliation [2 Cor. 5:18].

The ministry of reconciliation is actually God's call to lost men everywhere to come to Him with all their sins, all their burdens, all their problems, all their difficulties, and to be reconciled to God. I want to spend some time here to look at this matter of reconciliation. The word is used twice in this verse, twice in the next verse, and once in the following verse. Verse 21 doesn't have the word in it, but it sums it all up. This is a most important subject, and we are in a very important section here.

First let me state that reconciliation is not the same as salvation. Reconciliation goes a step further. It is more than having our sins forgiven and divine justice being satisfied. Reconciliation involves a changed relationship—completely changed. It means to change something inside out and upside down and right side up. "If any man be in Christ, he is a new creation."

Notice that there is the Godward side of reconciliation. He is the One who did the reconciling. "God, who hath reconciled us to himself by Jesus Christ." It is repeated in the next verse.

To wit, that God was in Christ, reconciling the world unto himself, not imputing their trespasses unto them; and hath committed unto us the word of reconciliation [2 Cor. 5:19].

Reconciliation is the ministry of changing completely. But who is changing completely? God is never changing—He is the same yesterday, today, and forever. It says that God has reconciled *us* to Himself. "God was in Christ, reconciling the *world* unto himself." It is the world that has been reconciled. God has reconciled the world. As we look at the world, we can see that it is going on its sinful way. "We have turned everyone to his own way" (see Isa. 53:6). But it is through Christ that the world is reconciled to God, through the *death* of Christ. This marvelous ministry of reconciliation is the work that Christ has done.

Let me call in another passage of Scripture concerning this. "And, having made peace through the blood of his cross, by him to reconcile all things unto himself; by him, I say, whether they be things in earth, or things in heaven. And you, that were sometime alienated and enemies in your mind by wicked works, yet now hath he reconciled In the body of his flesh through death, to present you holy and unblameable and unreproveable in his sight" (Col. 1:20–22). Compare this with Philippians 2:10 in which it says that at the name of Jesus every knee will bow, of things in heaven, and things in earth, and things under the earth—"*under* the earth" refers to hell. I want you to notice in the passage in Colossians, when it is speaking of reconciliation, only *heaven* and *earth* are mentioned. Hell is not reconciled to God. Although every being in hell will bow to Him, only those in heaven and earth are reconciled. In what way are they reconciled? "And you, that were sometime alienated and enemies in your mind by wicked works, yet now hath he reconciled In the body of his flesh through death, to present you holy and unblameable and unreproveable in his sight" (Col. 1:21–22). The death of Christ is what reconciled the world to God.

Notice that *God* is not reconciled—He has not changed. But the world has been put in a different position. Why? Because Christ died. You see, when Adam sinned back there in the Garden of Eden, a holy God couldn't reach down and save him. God had to do something about his sin. God had to judge man. "The soul that sinneth, it shall die . . ." (Ezek. 18:20). God had told Adam, ". . . for in the day that thou eatest thereof thou shalt surely die" (Gen. 2:17). Adam did die spiritually on that very day, and nine hundred years later he also died physically. When he died spiritually, he became alienated and separated from God; and he had no capacity for God. That is the condition of the world, and God had to judge that.

Now that Christ has died, the position of the world has been changed. Today God has His arms outstretched to a lost world. He says to a lost world, "You can come to Me." The worst sinner in the world can come to Him. Today it doesn't make any difference who you are, you can come to Him. Because Christ died, a holy God no longer deals with us in judgment, but now He reaches down to save all those who will come to Him. Jesus Christ bore all that judgment on Himself so that now the world is reconciled to God. You don't have to do anything to win God over. God is not waiting around the corner to hit you over the head with a billy club. God is not angry with you. God does not hate you. God *loves* you. Christ did not come to charge man's sins against him but to pay man's debt.

The woman taken in adultery is an illustration of this (see John 8:1–11). The Lord Jesus said to that crowd of hypocritical religious leaders, ". . . He that is without sin among you, let him first cast a stone at her." Then Jesus wrote something in the sand, wrote something on the earth. It is interesting that in Jeremiah 17:13 it says, ". . . they that depart from me shall be written in the earth, because they have forsaken the LORD, the fountain of living waters."

It tells us that they left—beginning with the old Pharisees and then down to the younger ones. The older ones had more sense than the young fellows who hung around a little longer. I think probably one of the old fellows had had an affair with a woman over in Corinth. He thought nobody knew about it, but of course the Lord knew all about it. Perhaps Jesus just wrote down the name of that girl, and when the old Pharisee looked down and saw that name written on the ground, he said, "I just remembered I have another engagement," and he tore out of there in a hurry. Before long they were all gone except one—only Jesus Christ was left. The only One who could have thrown a stone at her did not throw a stone. He asked, "Woman where are those thine accusers? hath no man condemned thee? She said, No man, Lord. And Jesus said unto her,

Neither do I condemn thee: go, and sin no more" (John 8:10–11). "God was in Christ, reconciling the world unto himself, not imputing their trespasses unto them." Jesus was not shutting His eyes to her sin, but for all that sin He was going to the cross. The condemnation was to fall on Him, and because she trusted Him, He could send her away uncondemned.

Now then we are ambassadors for Christ, as though God did beseech you by us: we pray you in Christ's stead, be ye reconciled to God [2 Cor. 5:20].

Who is an ambassador? Webster says an ambassador is a minister of the highest rank accredited to a foreign government or sovereign as the official representative of his own government or sovereign. "Now then we are ambassadors for Christ." We are in a foreign land—Peter says that we are pilgrims and strangers down here. Paul says, "For our conversation [citizenship] is in heaven; from whence also we look for the Saviour, the Lord Jesus Christ" (Phil. 3:20). Since our citizenship is in heaven, we are ambassadors down here.

When one government sends an ambassador to another government, it means they are on friendly relations. God is still friendly with this world. He has sent us as His ambassadors. One day He will call His ambassadors home. Then judgment will begin.

When man sinned, God in His holiness had to turn away from the world. But God loved man, so He sent His own Son to die on the cross. Now God can hold out His arms to the world and say, "You can come." We are His ambassadors. As His ambassadors, we are to tell folk, "God will save you!" All God is asking any man to do is to come to Him. God will not try to get even with you. He doesn't want to punish you. He doesn't want to lay a hand on

you. He invites all people everywhere to come to Him.

This is a great day. We have the privilege of saying to you, "Be ye reconciled to God." All He asks you to do is to turn to Him. How can He do this? It is because Christ bore it all for us.

On Him almighty vengeance fell
That would have sunk a world to hell,
He bore it for a chosen race,
And thus becomes our hiding place.

God is reconciled. You don't need to do one thing to win Him over. You don't have to shed tears to soften the heart of God. He loves you. He wants to save you. Why?

For he hath made him to be sin for us, who knew no sin; that we might be made the righteousness of God in him [2 Cor. 5:21].

Jesus Christ took my place down here. He, who knew no sin, came that we might be made the righteousness of God in Him. He has given me His place, clothed in His righteousness. He took my hell down here so that I might have His heaven up yonder. He did that for me.

Christian friend, have you been able to get out this wonderful Word to anyone else? Whoever you are, wherever you are, however you are, what are you doing today to get this Word of reconciliation out to a lost world? God is reconciled. He is the same yesterday, today, and forever. He feels toward you just as He did the day Christ died on the cross for you and for all mankind. This is what the world needs to hear from you. The world is reconciled to Him, but they will have to turn around and by faith come to Him. Let's get this word out, my friend.

CHAPTER 6

THEME: God's comfort in all circumstances of the ministry of Christ

We find set before us here the requirements of a good minister of Jesus Christ. None of us can read this without saying again, "Who is sufficient for these things?" None of us could meet these high standards. But I want you to notice that we are still in the section of God's comfort. Here we see God's comfort in all circumstances of the ministry of Christ.

TRYING EXPERIENCES OF THE MINISTRY

We then, as workers together with him, beseech you also that ye receive not the grace of God in vain [2 Cor. 6:1].

You will notice in your Bible that "with him" is in italics, which means that these two words have been supplied by the translators. It should be "We then, as workers together."

There is a line that needs to be rubbed out, and that is the line between the clergy and laity. There are certain ones who have been given the gift of teaching. If I have any gift, it would have to be that one, because if I can't claim that one, I don't have any at all. There are those who are gifted to teach, those who are gifted to be pastors, and those who are gifted to be missionaries. We would term them the clergy. But God gives a gift to each member of the body of Christ. There ought not to be the distinction between the pulpit and the pew that we make today. We are all workers together. If you are one who sits in the pew, may I say that you are as responsible to get out the Word of God as I am. I have been given the gift of teaching. You may be a bank president or the president of a large corporation, a truck driver, a housewife, but you are responsible today to get out the Word of God. God has given to the church certain men who will teach, certain men who will act as pastors, certain men who have gifts that are used for the work of the ministry, which is the equipping of the believers to serve.

Again let me repeat the comment of Dr. Earl Radmacher, who is currently president of the Western Conservative Baptist Seminary: "Shepherds do not produce sheep. Sheep produce sheep." You see, a great many people think it is the business of the evangelist and the preacher to win people for Christ. May I

say to you that it is *your* business. God has given teachers and preachers and evangelists and missionaries to fill out and prepare the body of believers so that those who are sitting in the pews might be equipped for their ministry of going out to witness for Christ. The shepherd doesn't produce the sheep. He feeds the sheep and he watches over the sheep. He shepherds the sheep, but he doesn't produce sheep. He can't. The sheep produce sheep.

Today the whole work of the church is bogged down because the sheep are not out witnessing. I want to raise the question again, and I know I am being very personal about it, what are *you* doing today to get the Word of God out to others? You can do something that I cannot do and that no preacher in the country can do. There are some people who have confidence in you. They will listen to you but they won't listen to a preacher—unless you encourage them to listen. I know a very fine businessman who has a speech impediment and doesn't feel he can speak very well to people. He takes tapes from our program and circulates them everywhere. He knocks on the door of one of his workers or associates, takes along a tape and a tape recorder, and invites them to listen to the tape with him. There is an example of witnessing. We are workers together.

Then Paul says, "We . . . beseech you also that ye receive not the grace of God in vain." How can one receive the grace of God in vain? God has been showering His goodness and mercy on us. To receive His great goodness and to rejoice in the salvation of the grace of God and yet to live carnal, worldly lives is what it means to receive the grace of God in vain. Let me ask you this question: What response are we making today to the love of God's heart?

(For he saith, I have heard thee in a time accepted, and in the day of salvation have I succoured thee: behold, now is the accepted time; behold, now is the day of salvation.) [2 Cor. 6:2].

"Have I succoured thee" means I have helped you.

A great many people say, "Well, I won't accept Christ now. I will do it some other time." They postpone it. Some people want to wait until a certain evangelist comes to town or until they can attend a great meeting. Now I don't know who you are or where you are right now, but if you are not saved, "now is the accepted time." Look at your clock. Whatever time it is right *now* is the time for you. Somebody will ask, "Can't I accept Him tomorrow?" Probably, but you have no promise of a tomorrow. The important thing is that God says the time is right now.

Giving no offence in any thing, that the ministry be not blamed [2 Cor. 6:3].

We need to be very careful about personal behavior. We are to give no offense in anything. An offense here doesn't mean hurting people's feelings. I don't think anyone can serve in the church today without hurting the feelings of someone. Some folk are there for no other purpose than to get their feelings hurt. You have heard the old saying about carrying your feelings on your sleeve. Well, a lot of the saints do just that. Dr. Harry Ironside put it something like this: If you don't shake hands with them, they feel you intended to slight them. If you do shake hands with them, you hurt their arthritis. If you stop to speak with them, you are interrupting them. But if you do not, you are a little snooty. If you write them a letter, they know you are after their money. If you do not write, then you are neglecting them. If you stop to visit them, you hinder them from their work and bother them, but if you do not visit them, it shows you have no interest in them.

My wife and I got up early one morning and drove two hundred miles before breakfast. We were really hungry and we stopped in a dumpy little place where they served a good Texas breakfast with grits and hot biscuits. When I went to pay the bill, I noticed a sign up by the cash register. "We can't please everybody but we try." That may be a familiar sign to you, but it was new to me that morning and it made my day.

"Giving no offence" means that you are so to live that no one can point to you and say, "Because of that man's life I have no confidence in the salvation he professes."

Now Paul lists things that should characterize the ministry. They are quite interesting.

But in all things approving ourselves as the ministers of God, in much patience, in afflictions, in necessities, in distresses [2 Cor. 6:4].

"In much patience." That is number one on the list. Believe me, I am bowled over by this very first one. I'll be very frank to admit to you that patience is something I have always lacked. My wife and my best friends say this to me: "Vernon McGee, if you ever preach a sermon on patience and I am there, I'm going to walk out because I don't think you are the fellow to speak on patience." So do you know what? I'm not going to speak about patience now. I just want you to notice it is number one on the list.

"In afflictions." This is something that a great many men in the ministry today must still bear.

"In necessities." Folk who came through the depression or who were born in a poor home understand this. When I was a boy, I saw the time that there was not a one dollar bill in my home. We would have gone hungry had it not been for the fact that the grocer would sell us groceries on credit. There was many a time I had nothing in the world for supper, the evening meal, but just a glass of sweet milk with crumbled, cold biscuits in it. And do you want to know something? I still think that is delicious. It is better than a lot of French pastry I have eaten.

Dr. Harry Ironside tells about the time he as a young preacher preached in a place for three days and didn't have a thing to eat during those three days. He was preaching to a group of people who thought he was living by faith, and they surely did let him do it. No money was given him for food. On the fourth morning he was debating whether to stay in bed for breakfast or to get up and tighten up his belt another notch when he noticed a letter being slipped under the door. He got up and opened it and all it said was, "Enclosed is an expression of Christian fellowship," and there was a ten dollar bill in it. That morning he went out and had the best breakfast he had ever had in his life.

"In afflictions, in necessities, in distresses." There are a great many folk living today who know what these are. The younger generation doesn't know. That is what has made the generation gap. I try to tell my daughter about the depression. She answers me, "Dad, I don't even know what you are talking about." And she doesn't know.

In stripes, in imprisonments, in tumults, in labours, in watchings, in fastings [2 Cor. 6:5].

"In stripes." I have a notion that very few of us know what physical stripes are such as Paul experienced. "Stripes" consisted of forty blows with a rod. However, we have been cut across the face many times by some insulting remark made by some pious saint in a very pious voice. There used to be a dear lady in my congregation who had a very sharp tongue. She would go out of the evening service and would say to me, "Pastor, you had a wonderful sermon this *morning*"—implying that I could preach a good sermon in the morning but that the evening sermon was not good. That is a way some folk hit a minister across the face.

Paul lists other things that he experienced in his ministry (which few men in my day have had to pass through): Imprisonments, tumults, labors, watchings, fastings—all were familiar to Paul.

Now he goes on to give another set of identifications of the ministry.

By pureness, by knowledge, by longsuffering, by kindness, by the Holy Ghost, by love unfeigned,

By the word of truth, by the power of God, by the armour of righteousness on the right hand and on the left [2 Cor. 6:6–7].

"By pureness." Believe me, it is important that a minister be pure in his life. Lack of pureness is one thing that hits and hurts the ministry today. It is always tragic when a minister turns up as a bad egg and is found guilty of immorality and impurity. Pureness is important—and it is important to God. "By knowledge." I do not think that knowledge refers only to a knowledge of the Word of God. A minister of the Word should know a great many things, and he should keep himself abreast of the times in which he lives. "By longsuffering." Here that comes up again. Longsuffering is patience in a different suit of clothes. "By kindness." Oh, how folk long to have a pastor who has tender, kindly interest in them! "By the Holy Ghost." God have mercy on any preacher who tries to preach without the Spirit of God leading and guiding. I am more concerned about that than any other thing. I was pastor in downtown Los Angeles for twenty-one years, and I had followed many great men. I often thought about Dr. R. A. Torrey, the great evangelist of the past, who had been the first pastor of that church. When I would go out to preach, the last thing I would say was, "O Lord, help me to preach in the power of the Holy Spirit!" Vernon McGee in himself is not very much in comparison to those men who went before him. An effective ministry can only be by the Holy Ghost. "By love unfeigned." Genuine love is so desperately needed today. We do not

need pious pretenders quoting pious platitudes. We do not need phony professors of faith who tell you how much they love you and then put a knife in your back. We need real, genuine love. We need the love that the Spirit of God puts into hearts. "By the word of truth." The "word of truth" means that a preacher should know his Bible. He should preach "by the power of God," which is possible only as a pastor spends time alone with God before he steps into the pulpit. "By the armour of righteousness on the right hand and on the left" is right living in all areas.

Next Paul gives us a set of nine paradoxes which should characterize a man of God.

By honour and dishonour, by evil report and good report: as deceivers, and yet true;

As unknown, and yet well known; as dying, and, behold, we live; as chastened, and not killed;

As sorrowful, yet alway rejoicing; as poor, yet making many rich; as having nothing, and yet possessing all things [2 Cor. 6:8–10].

"By honour and dishonour." Some may approve and some may disapprove. This gives a well-balanced ministry. "By evil report and good report." Although some folk will say ugly things about us, we continue to serve the Lord. Shakespeare has one of his characters say, "They praise me and make an ass of me; now my foes tell me plainly I am an ass: so that by my foes, sir, I profit in the knowledge of myself, and by my friends I am abused." Flattery harms us more than criticism! "As deceivers, and yet true"—we are called deceivers, yet we are giving out the true Word of God. "As unknown, and yet well known." A minister of God may not be well known to the world, but he is known to God. "As dying, and, behold, we live"—Paul had taken the place of death, yet he had had new life in Christ. "Chastened, and not killed." He often experienced persecution, beatings, whippings, stonings, and yet he lived on. "Sorrowful, yet alway rejoicing." Sorrow was for the sins of the people and their rejection of the gospel, yet he was rejoicing in Christ. "As poor, yet making many rich." Whenever you find a minister who is rich, watch out. Folk are not supposed to get rich in the ministry. "Having nothing, and yet possessing all things." You recall that Paul had said in his first letter to the Corinthians that all things were theirs. This includes things in the world, life, death, present or future. ". . . All are yours; And ye are Christ's; and Christ is God's" (1 Cor. 3:22–23)—oh, how rich we are! And yet we are poor.

Paul has given us three sets of things which characterize the ministry. You will notice that the first set pertains to things which are physical, the second to things which are mental, and the third to things which are spiritual. All are important.

PERSONAL APPEAL OF PAUL

Paul just seems to cry out here. Oh, how he yearned for those converts of his in Corinth. They were little baby Christians, babes in Christ, carnal Christians, but his heart went out to them. It seems his heart almost breaks in this chapter and the next one.

O ye Corinthians, our mouth is open unto you, our heart is enlarged.

Ye are not straitened in us, but ye are straitened in your own bowels.

Now for a recompence in the same, (I speak as unto my children,) be ye also enlarged [2 Cor. 6:11–13].

Paul is opening up his great heart of love, and he stirs up the hearts of those who love him. The interesting thing is that he apparently also stirred up the hearts of those who hated God and His Word and who tried to work injury upon those who loved Him and loved the Scripture. We find that was true in the early history of the church, and it is true today. If you stand for God, you will find that it will really cost you something.

We come now to an important passage of Scripture. It is a section which has been often abused and misinterpreted. Some folk try to make it hard as nails, unyielding and unloving. Yet what Paul is saying here is coming from the tender heart of a man whose heart was almost breaking because of his great concern for the Corinthian believers.

Be ye not unequally yoked together with unbelievers: for what fellowship hath righteousness with unrighteousness? and what communion hath light with darkness? [2 Cor. 6:14].

Paul here makes an appeal to the Corinthian believers to make a clean break with idolatry. They are to make a break from the sins of the flesh. They are to be separated from the worldliness that is in the world. Today we use the term "separated believers." There are many folk who consider themselves to be "sep-arated believers" who are actually as worldly as can be.

Back in the Old Testament under the Mosaic Law God gave a law to His people who were largely engaged in agriculture. He said that they were not to yoke together an ox and an ass. That would be yoking together unequal animals.

One was a clean animal and the other was an unclean animal. Here God is speaking to believers, and He says that the believer should not be yoked together with an unbeliever. How are people yoked together? Well, they are yoked together in any form of real union such as a business enterprise, a partnership, a marriage, a long-term enterprise.

Certainly marriage is the yoking together of two people. An unbeliever and a believer should not marry. A clean animal and an unclean animal should not be yoked together to plow. A child of God and a child of the Devil cannot be yoked together and pull together in their life goals.

Another example of such a relationship is identification with an institution. If a man is a professor in a seminary and he is conservative and holds the great truths of the Bible, but the seminary has gone liberal, such a man should get out of that seminary, because he is drawing a salary there and he is identified with their work and their organization. He is associated with it in a very tangible, real way. He is unequally yoked with unbelievers.

Suppose, however, that an evangelist comes to town and holds services for one or two weeks. Although he uses certain methods that you would not condone, he is preaching Christ and God is blessing his ministry, are you to join with him?

When I was a pastor in Nashville, Tennessee, an evangelist came to town and, without saying a word to any of us who were conservative men, put his tent right across from my church and the Baptist church in that end of the city. Then he came over to solicit our help. I was somewhat reluctant because of the ethics of the man. He was really a sort of screwball in many ways. He would conduct the most informal services. He would stop in the middle of his sermon because he had forgotten to make an announcement or had forgotten to take up an offering. The Baptist pastor and I were good friends and both conservative, so we talked it over. We didn't like all the methods of the evangelist, but we decided that we would support him. He was there for a couple of weeks and people were saved through his ministry. I would never have joined with him in any sort of permanent commitment because of his methods, but I gave him my support for the time he was there. We were by no means yoked together.

Notice how Paul did it. Paul would first go to the synagogue when he entered into a new city. Can you imagine a place where there would be more opposition to Jesus Christ than in the synagogue? Yet that is where Paul began. I am not condemning him for it because God led him to do it that way. Now if Paul had *joined* himself to one of those synagogues and had become the rabbi in one of them and had stayed there, then that could have been considered a yoke.

You see, Paul is talking about being yoked together in a permanent arrangement like marriage or a business partnership or a professorship in a school or membership in a church. This verse has no reference to my support of an evangelistic crusade. There are many men who do not carry on their ministries the way I do mine—and some of them are so much more successful than I am, that maybe they are right and I am wrong. Of course, I feel that I am right and I intend to go along as I am now. But this won't keep me from having fellowship with men who do things a little differently as long as they are preaching the same gospel that I preach and they believe the Bible is the Word of God. Paul is talking about yoking ourselves with *unbelievers*, as he makes clear in the next verse.

And what concord hath Christ with Belial? or what part hath he that believeth with an infidel? [2 Cor. 6:15].

Well, I certainly don't have any part with them. I am not joining with them permanently in anything, and I trust you are not. Let's not confuse this with our relationship with other believers who do things in a different way from what we do them.

And what agreement hath the temple of God with idols? for ye are the temple of the living God; as God hath said, I will dwell in them, and walk in them; and I will be their God, and they shall be my people [2 Cor. 6:16].

Now Paul specifically mentions idolatry. The temple of God has no agreement with idols. Where is the temple of God? Today the temple of God is the human body of each and every believer. We are the temples of the Holy Spirit. The one in whom God dwells cannot be in agreement with idols.

Wherefore come out from among them, and be ye separate, saith the Lord, and touch not the unclean thing; and I will receive you,

And will be a Father unto you, and ye shall be my sons and daughters, saith the Lord Almighty [2 Cor. 6:17-18].

Paul is appealing to the Christian for separation and for cleansing. He is not to be in agreement with idolatry. He is to be separate from worldliness and from the spirit of worldliness which can creep even into the churches and into the lives of believers. The believer should not even touch the unclean thing.

Back in the Book of Joshua we learned how Joshua and the Israelites took the fortified city of Jericho by faith. However, Achan took the "accursed thing." Israel had touched what God had declared to be unclean. Then they went up to the little city of Ai with great confidence because they were sure of an easy victory, but Joshua and Israel were overcome and defeated at Ai. God asks for a separation from worldliness and from the unclean thing.

There are a great many Christians who consider themselves separated. They wouldn't think of doing this or of doing that. Yet they gossip and have the meanest tongues, never realizing that that very thing is worldly and unclean. Or they go in for the latest in dress or for gluttony and yet consider themselves to be separate from worldliness. I don't mean to sit in judgment—and we ought not to sit in judgment on each other—yet I feel I must point out these things because we need to be very, very careful. It is very easy to talk about the things of God, to claim the Lord Jesus Christ as Savior, to say we love Him, to consider ourselves separated unto Him, and still not in reality be separate from the world and separated unto Him.

When I made my decision to enter the ministry, the vice-president of the bank where I worked called me into his office. He was a godless man—he could swear as I've never heard anyone swear. I think it rather moved him when I announced that I was giving up my job to study for the ministry. He called me over to his desk and said, "Vernon, I want to tell you a story." This is what he told me: During World War I he was working in another bank and with him worked a man as godless and worldly as could be. However, this man was the soloist in a church. One day the man who was now the vice-president went to church, and there he heard his co-worker sing a solo, "Jesus Satisfies." A dear lady said to him afterwards, "Wasn't that a marvelous solo? It sounded like it came out of heaven!" Since he knew this man at work, he knew that Jesus did not satisfy him. One day this same woman came into the bank to do some business, and the teller who had been the soloist was attempting to get a balance sheet balanced, but it was off, and he began to rip out oaths and curses. The lady was really shocked at this and asked my friend, "Who is that man?" He answered, "That is the voice you heard the other Sunday and thought it came right out of heaven." The vice-president of the bank was a skeptic and a rascal because he had seen a professing Christian singing, "Jesus Satisfies," when he knew Jesus did not satisfy that man. He knew that man was immoral, a drinker, and a man of vile language. He knew a Christian should not be like that, and it made him a cynical individual. He reached over and touched me on the knee and said to me, "Vernon, don't be a preacher unless you mean it." I have never forgotten that.

God says, "Come out from among them, and be ye separate, . . . and touch not the unclean thing." Don't be a Christian unless you mean it. Don't say that Jesus satisfies you if He is not really satisfying you. This is what Paul is talking about.

Then there is this glorious promise: "And I will receive you, And will be a Father unto you, and ye shall be my sons and daughters, saith the Lord Almighty." You will be the kind of son or daughter who brings honor to the Father.

A man told me about his boy going away to college. The boy had become alienated from his dad. He was still the man's son, but the father said to me, "I can't deal with him as I would like to as a father. I simply can't talk to him the way I'd like to as a father." This is what God is saying here.

If you are a believer in Jesus Christ, God is always your Father. Don't forget that. What God is saying here is that He would like to act like a Father to you. He would like to treat you as a son. If you are going off into worldliness, if you don't mean what you say, if you are hypocritical in your life, then you can be sure of one thing: God the Father will take you to His woodshed. My friend, God does not want to be everlastingly taking you to the woodshed. That is why He asks you to come out from among them, to be separate, not to touch the unclean thing. Then God can have an intimate relationship with you as a Father with a son.

CHAPTER 7

THEME: *God's comfort in the heart of Paul*

This is the last chapter in the section on the comfort of God. This is God's comfort in the very heart of Paul, a very personal and a very wonderful chapter.

As a background for this chapter we need to remember that there had been a man in the church in Corinth who had been guilty of gross immorality. He had had an incestuous and adulterous relationship with his own father's wife, his stepmother. The church hadn't dealt with that situation, and Paul had reprimanded them in his first epistle and had said they must deal with it. Now as Paul is writing his second letter to them, they had dealt with this man with the result that he repented and confessed his sin. The church had been accurate in dealing with him. Paul's letter had had the right kind of effect. Titus came to Paul with the report that this man had been weeping

over his sin and that he felt utterly unworthy of further recognition by the church. It is to this matter that Paul is referring.

Having therefore these promises, dearly beloved, let us cleanse ourselves from all filthiness of the flesh and spirit, perfecting holiness in the fear of God [2 Cor. 7:1].

What promises is he talking about? He is referring to those at the end of chapter 6. God has said that if we will obey Him, He will be a real Father to us, we will be real sons and daughters to Him, and He can deal with us in that relationship. This does not say that if we don't come out and be separate, we will lose our salvation. It does mean that if we do not lead a clean life, God can't treat us as a Father would want to treat His child. I gave the illustration of the father of a wayward son who said, "I'd like to treat him like my son but I cannot. He is alienated from me and he is in trouble and difficulty. He resents me and I can't be a father to him." He *was* the father of the boy, but he couldn't *act* like a father. God wants to treat us as a Father. A great many of us do not know by *experience* what a wonderful Father we have. We don't give Him a chance to be a real Father to us. What can we do to change that? Paul tells us, "Having therefore these promises, dearly beloved, let us cleanse ourselves." How can we cleanse ourselves? We cannot cleanse our own conscience from the guilt of sin. I am unable to wash out the stain of a guilty conscience, but God has done that through the death of Christ and the shedding of His blood. After we have been cleansed from our sins by the blood of Christ, our hearts still need a daily cleansing from the contamination of each day. When I receive the Word in faith and I act upon that Word, I am cleansed from all the filthiness of the flesh and spirit. This is what the Lord Jesus meant when He said, "Sanctify them through thy truth: thy word is truth" (John 17:17). The best bar of soap in the world is the Word of God. It will really clean us up. The Holy Spirit enables us to deal with the sin in our lives.

Paul says we are to cleanse ourselves from all filthiness of the flesh and of the spirit. All sin is filthiness in the sight of God. Then what is the difference between the sins of the flesh and the sins of the spirit?

The filthiness of the flesh are those sins which we commit in the body. This has to do with unholy lusts, unbridled appetites, drunkenness, gluttony, licentiousness, inordinate affection. These are the sins of the flesh. These are the dirty things. You and I need to be aware of the fact that we are living in a world today that is giving a respectability to the sins of the flesh.

An illustration of this is the attitude of the world toward liquor. Most people today say that alcohol is all right. It is well advertised in the media. The other day I heard an advertisement which said, "The mark of a mature, sensible, and successful man today is one who is able to drink cocktails." What propaganda! What brainwashing of the people! No political dictator has done a more thorough job. The liquor interests do a fantastic amount of brainwashing. But wait a minute! The ad which I was quoting was not for Southern Comfort or Old Crow or some other brand of whiskey. It was an advertisement from an organization which deals with alcoholics. They added, "There are some people who just don't know how to handle their liquor." I'll say there are! There are a whole lot of them—several million of them—and we, the taxpayers, are paying the hospital bills that the liquor interests create. This is an example of the sins of the flesh.

What does the Bible say about this? Listen to Habakkuk 2:15: "Woe unto him that giveth his neighbour drink, that puttest thy bottle to him, and makest him drunken also, that thou mayest look on their nakedness!" God have mercy on you if you serve cocktails in your home and tempt your neighbor to drunkenness. The Word of God rebukes that.

Another illustration of the filthiness of the flesh is the bookstands filled with the vilest pornographic literature that is imaginable which glorifies the human body and sex. In this permissive society God's Word still condemns the sins of the flesh. If you as a Christian are going to indulge in them, my friend, then God cannot act toward you as your Father. Although you may actually be His son, He cannot treat you as a Father would like to treat His son.

Now Paul mentions the filthiness of the spirit. What are some of those sins? Well, how about gossip, my friend? How about vicious slander against some Christian brother? There are a great many people who would never take a gun and pull the trigger to shoot a man down, but they will take the dagger of gossip and put it in his back when he is not listening. Some of the dear saints in the church engage in that kind of practice.

There are the secret sins of the spirit such as vanity and pride. Conceit, haughtiness, unbelief, and covetousness are the dirty sins of the spirit. There are a lot of saints in the church who live by a series of "don'ts"—don't drink, don't smoke, don't play cards. Not one of them would have a cigarette on the end of his tongue, but the words on the end of his tongue burn more deeply than a cigarette could burn. These are some of the sins of the spirit.

Now Paul says that we should "cleanse ourselves from all filthiness of the flesh and spirit, perfecting holiness in the fear of God." The writer to the Hebrews puts it this way: "And make straight paths for your feet, lest that which is lame be turned out of the way; but let it rather be healed. Follow peace with all men, and holiness, without which no man shall see the Lord" (Heb. 12:13–14). Christ is my righteousness. Christ is my holiness. The problem is that my life and His perfection are really far apart. God says we are not to have such a big holiness gap. He wants us to be holy in our lives.

Receive us; we have wronged no man, we have corrupted no man, we have defrauded no man [2 Cor. 7:2].

Paul assures them that he has corrupted no man. He has defrauded no man. He didn't come to them to take up offerings for all sorts of projects. I wish a great many Christians could say the same thing. I feel that sometimes things are not done correctly by the deacon boards in our churches. I think that if a person makes a donation for a specific purpose, it is the duty of the deacon board to make sure the money is used for that specific purpose. They do not have the liberty to say, "Oh, we'll just put this in the general fund," or, "We think it would be more important to use this to retire our debt on a building." Paul could assure them that he had wronged no man, corrupted no man, defrauded no man.

I speak not this to condemn you: for I have said before, that ye are in our hearts to die and live with you [2 Cor. 7:3].

Paul loved these Christians. They were constantly on his heart.

Great is my boldness of speech toward you, great is my glorying of you: I am filled with comfort, I am exceeding joyful in all our tribulation [2 Cor. 7:4].

Now he tells them that he is comforted and is filled with joy. He goes on to give the reason for this.

For, when we were come into Macedonia, our flesh had no rest, but we were troubled on every side; without were fightings, within were fears.

Nevertheless God, that comforteth those that are cast down, comforted us by the coming of Titus;

And not by his coming only, but by the consolation wherewith he was comforted in you, when he told us your earnest desire, your mourning, your fervent mind toward me; so that I rejoiced the more.

For though I made you sorry with a letter, I do not repent, though I did repent: for I perceive that the same epis- **tle hath made you sorry, though it were but for a season.**

Now I rejoice, not that ye were made sorry, but that ye sorrowed to repentance: for ye were made sorry after a godly manner, that ye might receive damage by us in nothing [2 Cor. 7:5–9].

Now this is quite lovely, and the background will help us appreciate what he is saying. Remember that in Paul's first epistle to them he wrote a very sharp letter. He called them "babes" and "carnal." He pointed out the gross immorality among them, and he commanded them to deal with it and put it away. And they did deal with it as Paul had instructed them. When Titus arrived in Philippi to join Paul, he brought the news that the church in Corinth had dealt with the situation and that the guilty man had repented of his gross immorality. So Paul wrote in the second chapter of this second epistle that now they should forgive him and comfort him so that he wouldn't be swallowed up in sorrow. He is to be taken back into the fellowship.

After he had left Ephesus, he had gone to Troas, and there he waited, but Titus didn't come. Then he began to rebuke himself. He thought, *Maybe I shouldn't have written such a sharp letter to them after all. Or maybe I should have gone to them directly.* He went on to Philippi, and it was there that Titus met him and brought him word from Corinth.

Someone is going to say to me, "I thought that the Scripture is verbally inspired and that Paul was writing by inspiration of the Holy Spirit when he wrote to the Corinthians." That is correct. This is the inspired Word of God. I believe that with all my heart. How is it then that Paul was rebuking himself? It was because Paul was human. God had him write like that to let you and me know how human he really was. Also it shows us how tender and sweet and loving he was and that you and I ought to be the same way. What a lesson in this for us! Once Paul had received the news he could write, "I am filled with comfort, I am exceeding joyful in all our tribulation."

It is possible that someone reading this page should sit down and write a letter to an individual whom he hurt years ago. If that someone is you, tell him that you are sorry and want to make things right. Do you know what you would do for him? You would make him exceedingly joyful. We all need to do more of that.

Paul gets very personal when he says, "When we were come into Macedonia, our flesh had no rest, but we were troubled on every side; without were fightings, within were fears." This is so personal I almost feel that we shouldn't read it. But God used a man to comfort Paul: "Nevertheless God, that comforteth those that are cast down, comforted us by the coming of Titus."

You could help some dear saint of God and be a comfort to him. My friend, when was the last time you went to your preacher and put your arm on his shoulder and said, "Brother, I've been praying for you. I see that you are working hard and standing for the things of God, and I just want you to know I am standing with you." He would appreciate that.

Paul continues: "And not by his [Titus'] coming only, but by the consolation wherewith he was comforted in you, when he told us your earnest desire, your mourning, your fervent mind toward me; so that I rejoiced the more." In other words, "You comforted Titus and Titus comforted me."

The other day I was in a church service and a man came to me and said, "My brother who lives back East wrote me. He says that he has been listening by radio to that fellow McGee from California and that, if ever I should meet him, I should tell him that my brother accepted Christ as his Savior." Now I don't know why that man's brother didn't write to me and tell me that, but he didn't. He wrote to his brother and his brother told me. I want to say to you that I was *comforted* by that. It made me know that my radio program is something that I should continue.

The Corinthians had said nice things about Paul. Friend, don't be so hesitant to say something nice about someone else. Really, your tongue won't fall out if you say some nice things.

"For though I made you sorry with a letter, I do not repent, though I did repent: for I perceive that the same epistle hath made you sorry, though it were but for a season. Now I rejoice, not that ye were made sorry, but that ye sorrowed to repentance." You see, repentance and the shedding of tears are not the same. "For ye were made sorry after a *godly* manner, that ye might receive damage by us in nothing."

For godly sorrow worketh repentance to salvation not to be repented of: but the sorrow of the world worketh death [2 Cor. 7:10].

Here we find God's definition of repentance— real repentance. Repentance is a change of mind. As far as I can tell, the only repentance

God asks of the lost is in the word *believe*. Believe on the Lord Jesus Christ! What happens when one believes? There is a change of mind. There is a turning from something to Someone. Listen to what Paul wrote to the Thessalonians: ". . . how ye turned to God from idols . . ." (1 Thess. 1:9)—that was a change of mind. How did it come about? They first turned to Christ. When Paul had come to them, he hadn't preached against idolatry, he had preached Christ to them. And they turned to Christ. But they were idolaters. So when they turned to Christ in faith, what else happened? They turned *from* the idols, and that turning from idols was repentance. That is the repentance of the unsaved; it is the repentance to salvation. I don't know if God wants us to emphasize repentance to the unsaved; He does want us to emphasize *Christ*. When they respond to Christ, there will be a turning from their old unbelief to Christ.

However, God does emphasize repentance for the believer if he is going in the wrong direction, walking in sin. For him there is to be a turning, a repentance. A lot of people simply shed tears, which may not indicate true repentance. That kind of sorrow is the sorrow of the world and works death. True repentance is godly sorrow, which "worketh repentance to salvation not to be repented of"—that is, repentance without regret.

My dad used to tell about a boat on the Mississippi River that had a little bitty boiler and a great big whistle. When it would blow its whistle while going upstream, the boat would start to drift downstream because the boiler was so small it couldn't propel the boat and blow the whistle at the same time. There are a lot of folk who have a great big whistle and a little bitty boiler. They shed a lot of tears and make a big display, but there is no real repentance. They shed tears, but they keep on going in the same direction.

But with these Corinthian believers their repentance was real.

For behold this selfsame thing, that ye sorrowed after a godly sort, what carefulness it wrought in you, yea, what clearing of yourselves, yea, what indignation, yea, what fear, yea, what vehement desire, yea, what zeal, yea, what revenge! In all things ye have approved yourselves to be clear in this matter.

Wherefore, though I wrote unto you, I did it not for his cause that had done the wrong, nor for his cause that suffered

wrong, but that our care for you in the sight of God might appear unto you.

Therefore we were comforted in your comfort: yea, and exceedingly the more joyed we for the joy of Titus, because his spirit was refreshed by you all [2 Cor. 7:11–13].

He commends them for the fact that they really repented.

For if I have boasted any thing to him of you, I am not ashamed; but as we spake all things to you in truth, even so our

boasting, which I made before Titus, is found a truth.

And his inward affection is more abundant toward you, whilst he remembereth the obedience of you all, how with fear and trembling ye received him.

I rejoice therefore that I have confidence in you in all things [2 Cor. 7:14–16].

Paul has opened his heart and has shown his inmost feelings. He is full of joy and rejoicing. He has been comforted. This has been God's comfort in the heart of Paul.

CHAPTER 8

THEME: *Example of Christian giving*

The subject now changes. For the previous seven chapters Paul has talked of the comfort of God. I trust it has brought comfort and strength to you to know that you have a Helper in your Christian life. Our natural reaction is to say, "Paul, go on—tell us more about comfort." However, he changes the subject abruptly. He now talks about the collection for the poor saints of Jerusalem. He brings us back to earth with a thump! The subject changes from Christian *living* to Christian *giving*, which is as vital a part as living.

This section, which includes chapters 8 and 9, divides this way:

1. *Example* of Christian Giving, chapter 8:1–6
2. *Exhortation* to Christian Giving, chapter 8:7–15
3. *Explanation* of Christian Giving, chapters 8:16–9:5
4. *Encouragement* to Christian Giving, chapter 9:6–15

During my twenty-one years as a pastor in downtown Los Angeles I do not think that I preached more than three messages on giving, yet we saw the giving double and triple several times during that period. This confirms my belief that God's people will support a ministry that teaches and preaches the Word of God. I resent the high-pressure promotion and money-raising schemes which are being

used in Christian work. I do not think they are scriptural by any means.

These two chapters give us the most extended and complete section on Christian giving that we have in the Scriptures. Actually, all we need to know is here. There are no rules, but there are certain clear-cut principles for giving. That may strike you as being unusual. Someone may say, "I thought we were to give a tithe." No, that is not the rule for today. It might be a principle that you would like to follow, but it is not a rule for anyone today.

The word that is important in this section is the word *grace*. In this chapter the word *grace* occurs seven times, and it occurs three times in chapter 9—ten times in these two chapters. The subject is the grace of giving.

EXAMPLE OF CHRISTIAN GIVING

Moreover, brethren, we do you to wit of the grace of God bestowed on the churches of Macedonia [2 Cor. 8:1].

I want to spend a little time here on that word *grace*. We find it here in the first verse. We find it again in the fourth verse: "Praying us with much entreaty that we would receive the gift, and take upon us the fellowship of the ministering to the saints." The word *gift* in our translation is actually "grace." Another way of translation would be, "Praying us with much entreaty that we would give effect to the grace and fellowship of the service to the saints." The word appears again in the sixth verse. "Insomuch that we desired Titus, that as he had begun, so he would also finish in you the same grace also."

He is calling giving a grace. It is a grace of God. It is a disposition created by the Spirit of God. He is writing to the Corinthians and is telling them that the Macedonians had that kind of grace, and he is hoping that the Corinthians will have that same grace.

The theologian defines grace as the unmerited favor of God. I agree with that, and yet it does not adequately describe this word. It may cause you to miss the rich flavor of it. I studied classical Greek before I studied Koiné, the Greek of the Scriptures, and I found that the Greek word *charis* means an outward grace like beauty or loveliness or charm or kindness or goodwill or gratitude or delight or pleasure. The Greeks had three graces: good, fine, noble. The Greeks were missionary-minded about their culture, and they wanted to impart this to others.

The Holy Spirit chose this word, gave it a new luster and a new glory, and the Christian writers adopted it. Paul uses it again and again. Now notice carefully this definition: The grace of God is the passion of God to share all His goodness with others. Grace means that God wants to bestow upon you good things, goodnesses. He wants to make you fine and noble, and He wants to bring you into the likeness of His Son. This is the grace of which Paul writes in Ephesians: "For by grace are ye saved through faith; and that not of yourselves: it is the gift of God: Not of works, lest any man should boast" (Eph. 2:8–9). We were lost sinners; we had nothing to offer God for our salvation; so He saved us by grace. He had a passion for wanting to save us. He loved us, but He could not arbitrarily forgive us because He is a holy God. He had to provide a way, and that way was that He sent His Son to die for us. We are told that "God so loved the world that he gave his only begotten Son" (see John 3:16). God is in the business of giving, not receiving. We need to make that very clear.

I think sometimes we give the impression that God is poor and that He needs our gifts. He doesn't. God is not poor. He says, "For every beast of the forest is mine, and the cattle upon a thousand hills. I know all the fowls of the mountains: and the wild beasts of the field are mine. If I were hungry, I would not tell thee: for the world is mine, and the fulness thereof" (Ps. 50:10–12). God doesn't get hungry. Even if He did, He would not tell us! God is not in need of anything.

The early church considered giving to be a grace. It was a passion, an overwhelming desire to share the things of God with others.

Paul is writing specifically of a local situation, and we need to recognize that. The Jerusalem church had been the first to give out the gospel—the gospel had begun there. Jesus had told the disciples they should be witnesses unto Him beginning in Jerusalem. The apostles loved Jerusalem, and they locked their arms around their beloved city until persecution drove them from it, scattered them abroad, sent them down the highways into Judea and Samaria and finally to the uttermost parts of the earth. The church in Jerusalem was weakened because of persecution. In fact, there was famine going on, and the church was poverty-stricken.

Now as Paul went about on his third missionary journey, he collected an offering for the church in Jerusalem. That is rather revolutionary. Here the mission churches are sending an offering to help the mother church. Today it is just the opposite. The home church sends out missionaries and supports them out in the foreign field. But in Paul's day the foreign field was supporting the home church.

Paul was not yet able to come to Corinth; so in this letter he sends instructions to them about how to give. Because he intends to come to Corinth, he tells them that he doesn't want any kind of promotion for giving—he doesn't want to be taking up a collection while he is there. He doesn't want to spend time talking about money after he gets there. This collection was to be done beforehand and then, when he arrived, he could spend his time teaching them the Word of God.

What a contrast that is to the usual method today. The usual invitation that I receive is to come over and hold a meeting and while I am there a love offering will be taken for me. If it were done as Paul suggested, a love offering would be taken before an evangelist or a Bible teacher came to speak.

Now I have given to you the color of the local situation and the background of the instructions in this epistle. The *facts* of the local situation have now passed into history, but the *principles* which Paul lays down abide. I believe they are as sharp and fresh today as they were when Paul first gave them.

In the first verse Paul cited the Macedonian believers as examples in Christian giving— this referred to the church at Philippi. In verse 2 he lists their motives and methods of giving.

How that in a great trial of affliction the abundance of their joy and their deep poverty abounded unto the riches of their liberality [2 Cor. 8:2].

Notice that the Macedonians gave out of their "deep poverty." They didn't have riches. They didn't give of their surplus or of their abundance; they gave out of their poverty. I'm afraid we don't know much about that kind of giving today.

For to their power, I bear record, yea, and beyond their power they were willing of themselves;

Praying us with much entreaty that we would receive the gift, and take upon us the fellowship of the ministering to the saints [2 Cor. 8:3–4].

It would be more accurate to translate this: "Praying us with much entreaty that we would receive the *grace*"—that gift they had taken up was a grace, and it was fellowship, which means it was a sharing of the things of Christ.

You and I cannot realize the love that they had one for another. We talk about social action in the church today; I must confess that we have almost lost sight of it in our fundamental churches. It is a wonderful thing to give to the missions, but must we neglect folks in our own congregations who are in need? Many of them don't even want their needs to be known in the local congregation because they know it would become a subject of gossip in the church. They don't want to accept help because they feel it would be more or less a disgrace. I've discovered this in my own ministry. Sometimes I could not reveal the name of the person in need to a committee or a group that wanted to know to whom the help was going, because the committee would not keep it in confidence, and by the time it got to their wives, it would be throughout the church. We have lost today this wonderful grace of giving.

Now notice what the believers in Macedonia had done—this is unusual.

And this they did, not as we hoped, but first gave their own selves to the Lord, and unto us by the will of God [2 Cor. 8:5].

Paul says this was not something that he had expected. First of all, they had given themselves to the Lord. That is basic. Secondly, they had given themselves, apparently, to some local work of Christ and they were sold out to it. They gave themselves to Paul by the will of God, which means they helped him to get out the gospel. You see, they were sold out to God.

Back in Paul's first letter to the Corinthians he wrote about the Resurrection and heaven (see ch. 15), and they were about to say, "Brother Paul, tell us more about heaven." Then Paul shook them right down to their shoestrings by saying, "Now concerning the collection for the saints, as I have given order to the churches of Galatia, even so do ye" (1 Cor. 16:1). He wanted to talk to them about something very practical. And he tells them here in his second letter that they are not to give grudgingly. The Macedonian believers gave out of "the abundance of their joy and their deep poverty." What a picture! God loves a cheerful giver, and we see it in shoeleather here—it was a fellowship. They shared what they had.

They owed the home church in Jerusalem for all their spiritual blessings. They had received the gospel from them. Now they were returning material gifts to the home church which was in such a sad situation. Paul writes in Galatians 6:6: "Let him that is taught in the word communicate unto him that teacheth in all good things." That literally means, "Pay the preacher." It means, my friend, that you ought to support the work from which you derive a spiritual blessing.

A man, living out of fellowship with the Lord, heard our radio messages and the Word of God brought him back to the Lord. We have a building which belongs to "Thru the Bible" because he gave that building to us. He gave it hilariously. He gave it joyously. That is the way it should be given. It should be out of the abundance of joy. We are never to give reluctantly or because we think we ought to give. We should have a passion to give so that the Word of God can reach others.

You remember that the Lord Jesus stood aside and watched the people give in the temple—I think He still does that. The rich came in and gave large gifts, but the poor little widow came and put in her two mites. The Lord said she had cast in more than they all (see Mark 12:41–44). She gave of her poverty and she gave all that she had. If you measured the value of those little coppers against the riches of that temple, they didn't amount to anything. But the Lord Jesus gives God's evaluation: "And he said, Of a truth I say unto you, that this poor widow hath cast in more than they all: For all these have of their abundance cast in unto the offerings of God: but she of her penury hath cast in all the living that she had" (Luke 21:3–4).

It has been said, "When it comes to giving, some people stop at nothing." That is where a great many folk stop.

The story is told of a Scottish church that was attempting to raise money for a new building. One member of the church was a rich Scot who was known to be worth fifty thousand pounds. He was a typical Scot and was pretty stingy, like most of us are. A deacon came to see him and asked, "Brother, how much are you going to give for the new church?" The Scot replied, "Oh, I guess I'll be able to put in the widow's mite." The deacon called out in the next meeting, "Brethren, we have all the money we need. This brother is going to give fifty thousand pounds." The man was amazed. "I didn't say I would give fifty thousand pounds; I said I would give the widow's mite." The deacon replied, "Well, she gave her all, and I thought that is what you meant to give!" It is interesting that God notes what you give but also what you keep for yourself.

In another church they were taking up an offering for a building program. The man calling on one of the members said to him, "How much are you going to give, brother?" "Well," he said, "I guess I could give ten dollars and not feel it." The man replied, "Then why don't you make it twenty dollars and *feel* it?" You see, the blessing only comes when you feel it, my friend. This is the meaning of "It is more blessed to give than to receive."

The Macedonian believers gave themselves to God. And, my friend, if God doesn't have you, He doesn't want anything from you. If God doesn't have the hand, He doesn't want the gift that is in the hand.

Insomuch that we desired Titus, that as he had begun, so he would also finish in you the same grace also [2 Cor. 8:6].

Paul says that the grace which motivated the Macedonians should be the same grace that would motivate the Corinthians. The real test of any person lies in what he gives. Someone has said there are three books that are essential for a worship service: the first book is the Bible, the second is the hymn book, and the third is the pocketbook. Giving is a part of our worship to God. If we do not have the grace of giving, we should pray to God and ask Him to give us a generous, sharing spirit.

EXHORTATION TO CHRISTIAN GIVING

Therefore, as ye abound in every thing, in faith, and utterance, and knowledge, and in all diligence, and in your love to us, see that ye abound in this grace also [2 Cor. 8:7].

Paul is commending them. They abound in faith; they were able to witness; they had knowledge and diligence; and they had love for Paul and for the other apostles. Now he asks them to abound in this grace also. What does he refer to? He means the grace of giving.

I speak not by commandment, but by occasion of the forwardness of others, and to prove the sincerity of your love [2 Cor. 8:8].

Paul is saying here that giving today is not by law, by rote, or by ritual. I know that there are good Bible expositors who say we are to give the tithe. Obviously, the tithe was basic back in the Old Testament. However, if you examine it very carefully, you will find that the people gave *three* tithes. One was actually for the support of the government, which would be what we call taxes today. So the "tithe" is not the basis on which Christians are to give. Paul says, "I speak not by commandment." He is not asking the Corinthians to give because it is a commandment.

Paul gives two reasons why he is asking them to give. The first is "by occasion of the forwardness of others"—which would be the example which the Macedonians had given. The second reason is to "prove the sincerity of your love." It is still true today that the pocketbook is really the test of a man's love. It is the most sensitive area of a Christian.

For ye know the grace of our Lord Jesus Christ, that, though he was rich, yet for your sakes he became poor, that ye through his poverty might be rich [2 Cor. 8:9].

If you are looking for a standard for giving, here it is: the Lord Jesus Christ Himself. He was rich but He became poor. He came down here and took a place of poverty. Imagine leaving heaven and coming down to this earth to be born in Bethlehem, to live in Nazareth, to die on a cross outside the walls of Jerusalem, and to be put into the darkness of a tomb! He was rich but He became poor for you and me.

And herein I give my advice: for this is expedient for you, who have begun before, not only to do, but also to be forward a year ago [2 Cor. 8:10].

This indicates that the Corinthians had made a pledge or a promise and had begun to give for this collection a year earlier. This raises the issue of making a pledge to give a certain amount of money. Some people say they don't think a Christian should make a pledge. I think we need to recognize that we sign pledges for everything else, and I think that people ought to be willing to make a pledge to God's work. We promise to pay our rent; we sign notes when we buy an automobile or a refrigerator. I say that we can sign on the dotted line for God's work, too.

Now therefore perform the doing of it; that as there was a readiness to will, so there may be a performance also out of that which ye have [2 Cor. 8:11].

Paul is saying they should carry through with their pledge. They should put their money where their mouth is. However, remember that this is not a commandment. We are not commanded to make a pledge. However, this verse does tell us that if we do make a pledge, then we are to carry it through and perform it.

For if there be first a willing mind, it is accepted according to that a man hath, and not according to that he hath not [2 Cor. 8:12].

Here is something very important to note. Each should give according to "that a man hath," and he is to do it with a willing mind. No one is to give according to what he does not have.

In the section on 1 Corinthians, I gave an illustration which I will repeat because it is a very fine example of this principle.

When I was pastoring a church in Texas, one of my officers owned several Coca-Cola plants, and one of them was in our town. He was a man of means, and he owned a ranch where we used to go out to hunt and fish. Often he would ask me why I didn't preach on tithing. One day I said, "Why should I preach on tithing?" He said, "Because it is the Bible way of giving." I agreed, "Yes, it was the Old Testament way of giving, but under grace I don't believe tithing is the way it should be done." So he asked me, "How do you think it ought to be done?" I took him to this verse: "As God has prospered him." Now this was during the depression. If you are as old as I am, you will remember that the depression in the 1930s was a very serious time. So I said to him, "For some strange reason, Coca-Cola is selling, and you are doing very well. However, there are some members in our church who

couldn't give a tithe right now. I don't believe God is asking them to give a tenth. There are a few people who are doing well, and they are to give as they have been prospered—and they are not to stop with a tenth. Probably they ought to give a half." Do you know that this man never again suggested that I preach on tithing! The reason was that he found out that a man is to give according to what he hath, not according to what he hath not.

The tithes were a basic measurement in the Old Testament, and I cannot believe that any Christian today who has a good income should give less than one tenth. In this time of great abundance Christians should be giving more than a tenth.

For I mean not that other men be eased, and ye burdened [2 Cor. 8:13].

Paul is saying that a burden should not be placed on anyone.

But by an equality, that now at this time your abundance may be a supply for their want, that their abundance also may be a supply for your want: that there may be equality [2 Cor. 8:14].

Perhaps you have been blessed with a good automobile, a lovely home, nice furniture, and all the appliances that are considered necessary in our contemporary culture. May I say to you that God expects you to share in the Lord's work. You may be like my rancher friend who would like to settle for the tithe. He wanted me to preach on the tithe so he would feel comfortable in his giving. After I had talked with him, I don't think he ever felt comfortable about his tithe-giving. Those who are able to give should give, and we should not burden those who are unable to give.

As it is written, He that had gathered much had nothing over; and he that had gathered little had no lack [2 Cor. 8:15].

Paul gives the example of the gathering of the manna in the wilderness. Each was to gather enough for one day. Some man might go out with several baskets and say, "Let's just fill them up. I'll gather bushel baskets of manna while I can." He would go out and greedily gather up much more than he needed. What would happen? After he had eaten what he needed for that day, he would find that all the rest had spoiled by the next morning. It was God's plan that each one should have just enough and no more.

We will learn in chapter 9, verse 6, that ". . . He which soweth sparingly shall reap also sparingly; and he which soweth bountifully shall reap also bountifully." I think that God will begin to deal with you as you have been dealing with Him. I think that God keeps books. He does not put us under law because He wants our giving to be a grace, a passion, a desire to share. It should be a joyful experience. You ought to be able to say to other folk, "You ought to listen to Dr. McGee. He's talking about the most wonderful privilege in the world. He is telling us how we can be happy by giving." That may sound crazy to you, but that is exactly what Paul is saying here.

EXPLANATION OF CHRISTIAN GIVING

But thanks be to God, which put the same earnest care into the heart of Titus for you [2 Cor. 8:16].

"Thanks" is the same Greek word *charis*, which has been translated "grace." Although "thanks" is a good translation, it would be equally correct to translate it "grace be to God."

Paul is saying that he sent Titus to get their offering, but it was already a grace in his heart. Titus wanted as much as Paul did to take up an offering for the poor saints in Jerusalem.

For indeed he accepted the exhortation; but being more forward, of his own accord he went unto you.

And we have sent with him the brother, whose praise is in the gospel throughout all the churches;

And not that only, but who was also chosen of the churches to travel with us with this grace, which is administered by us to the glory of the same Lord, and declaration of your ready mind [2 Cor. 8:17–19].

You see, Titus and his companion had this grace in their hearts. The giving was to be for the glory of God. Whatever we give, my friend, should be for the glory of God.

Avoiding this, that no man should blame us in this abundance which is administered by us [2 Cor. 8:20].

Paul is saying, "We are going to be honest in the use of the money we collect from you and in the way we handle it."

Providing for honest things, not only in the sight of the Lord, but also in the sight of men [2 Cor. 8:21].

This is one of the more sensitive areas in the Lord's work. Many Christian organizations and churches major in heavy promotion to encourage giving to a certain work. No effort—or at best, *little* effort—is made to tell how the money is used. There should be the presentation of tangible evidence that the money is used to give out the Word of God and that there are results that can be documented—not just isolated cases. There should be confidence in the organization to which we give—that it is honest and is operated on the highest level of integrity. We should not support an organization about which we have doubts. We must remember that this is a big, bad world and that there are religious racketeers in it. We need to beware.

Even Paul, this great apostle, says, "Providing for honest things, not only in the sight of the Lord, but also in the sight of men." It should be obvious that the money is being used for the purpose for which it is given.

And we have sent with them our brother, whom we have oftentimes proved diligent in many things, but now much more diligent, upon the great confidence which I have in you.

Whether any do inquire of Titus, he is my partner and fellow-helper concerning you: or our brethren be inquired of, they are the messengers of the churches, and the glory of Christ [2 Cor. 8:22–23].

They can trust Titus. He will make a good report. They can trust Paul who will also report to them. The money will not be delivered by just one person.

Wherefore shew ye to them, and before the churches, the proof of your love, and of our boasting on your behalf [2 Cor. 8:24].

Paul is asking for proof of their love. You see, friend, if you really mean business, there will be more than verbiage. Giving will be a tangible expression of your love.

I'm afraid there are a great many Christians who are like the young fellow who wrote to his girl: "I would cross the widest ocean for you. I'd swim the deepest river for you. I would scale the highest mountain for you. I'd crawl across the burning sands of the desert for you." Then he concluded with a P.S.: "If it doesn't rain Wednesday night, I'll be over to see you." A great many of us like to talk about how we love Jesus, but we are not willing to sacrifice much for Him.

Paul is urging the Corinthians to show the *proof* of their love.

CHAPTER 9

THEME: Collection for the poor saints at Jerusalem

This chapter continues directly with the same subject which we had in chapter 8. There it was the *grace* of giving; now we have before us what Christian giving *is*.

EXPLANATION OF CHRISTIAN GIVING
(Continued)

For as touching the ministering to the saints, it is superfluous for me to write to you:

For I know the forwardness of your mind, for which I boast of you to them of Macedonia, that Achaia was ready a year ago; and your zeal hath provoked very many.

Yet have I sent the brethren, lest our boasting of you should be in vain in this behalf; that, as I said, ye may be ready:

Lest haply if they of Macedonia come with me, and find you unprepared, we (that we say not, ye) should be ashamed in this same confident boasting [2 Cor. 9:1–4].

Paul says that he would be very embarrassed if he came over there, having boasted of them to other folk, and then found out they hadn't given anything. Liberal giving is a real test of any church. I go to some churches that have real spiritual vigor; they are great churches, and I have found out that they are generous in their giving. I have also been to some churches that are really dead spiritually. And I have discovered that they don't give much either. They are dead in their giving, too. The size of the offering is a pretty good barometer.

Now you see that these Corinthian Christians had made a pledge that they would give something toward the relief of believers in Jerusalem. May I say here that any pledge that a Christian makes is between that person and the Lord. It is a pledge to the *Lord* that you will do something or that you will give something.

I know a wealthy man who was asked, "How in the world did you become so rich when you give so much away?" "Well," he answered, "The Lord shovels it in and I shovel it out and God has the bigger shovel." My friend, we can never outgive God.

Therefore I thought it necessary to exhort the brethren, that they would go before unto you, and make up beforehand your bounty, whereof ye had notice before, that the same might be ready, as a matter of bounty, and not as of covetousness [2 Cor. 9:5].

You will notice that the gift is called a bounty. That indicates that it would be a generous gift, which is the evidence of the grace of God working in the heart.

ENCOURAGEMENT TO CHRISTIAN GIVING

But this I say, He which soweth sparingly shall reap also sparingly; and he which soweth bountifully shall reap also bountifully [2 Cor. 9:6].

When Paul was talking to the Ephesian elders, he reminded them of this same thing. "I have shewed you all things, how that so labouring ye ought to support the weak, and to remember the words of the Lord Jesus, how he said, It is more blessed to give than to receive" (Acts 20:35). Apparently, "it is more blessed to give than to receive" was an expression which the Lord Jesus used constantly. I know that this has become a very trite bromide today. It is quoted a great deal and practiced very little.

The word *blessed* actually means "happy." It will make you more happy to give than to receive. How does it affect you when you give?

Here is an acid test for you and for me today. Do we sow sparingly? Do we give in that way? Suppose a farmer would sow a bushel of grain on a particular plot of ground and reap an abundant harvest. Suppose he would say the next year, "There is no use wasting a bushel of grain on this ground this year; I will save *half* a bushel for myself and sow only half a bushel." Any farmer knows that he would get a very small yield. The principle is that whoever sows sparingly will reap sparingly, and he who sows bountifully will reap bountifully.

When I was speaking at Siloam Springs, Arkansas, some folk came from Oklahoma City. The lady is about my age and she was raised in a little place called Tishomingo, Oklahoma. My father was killed in a cotton gin there and is buried there. In that day it was the custom when there was a death in a family for the neighbors and friends to send food to the bereaved family. I shall never forget the wonderful food that was sent to us at that time. This lady told me that she could recall as a girl that her mother cooked up a great deal of food and sent it over to our house. She said, "I never knew that years later I would be listening to you. We gave you physical food, and now you supply spiritual food for us." They didn't sow sparingly, and I hope they are reaping abundantly. I believe this is a true principle in every area of life. One of the reasons some of us are so poor today is that we are so tightfisted when we are dealing with the Lord.

Every man according as he purposeth in his heart, so let him give; not grudgingly, or of necessity: for God loveth a cheerful giver [2 Cor. 9:7].

What you feel right down in your heart you *ought* to give, *that* is what you should give. But here is the test: "not grudgingly." God does not want any grudging giving. What does that mean? God does not want one penny from you if you would rather keep it for yourself.

Perhaps you say, "Well, I am an officer in the church and it is my responsibility to give." Or, "I am a member of that church and I feel responsible." It is true that the church may say that to you. As a pastor, I've told people, "This is your church and you ought to support it." But *God* does not say that. He says that if you are going to give grudgingly, He doesn't want it. Not only does God not want it, but I believe that God doesn't use it either.

Not only does it say God does not want you to give if you give grudgingly, neither does He want you to give "of necessity." He doesn't want you to give at all unless you are giving willingly and gladly.

Some folk say, "Well, I had better give because everybody else is giving, and it would look bad if I didn't give something." That is giving of necessity. God does not want that kind of giving.

"God loveth a cheerful giver." That should be the happiest part of the service. I have been in many churches where they take up an offering and then the congregation stands and sings, "Praise God from whom all blessings flow." I think that is wonderful. The only thing that would be better would be if they would sing it *first*. This would put them in the attitude of giving and of giving joyfully. Also they would be able to reach for their wallets as they stood up! God loves a cheerful giver. If you can't give cheerfully, God doesn't want you to give.

And God is able to make all grace abound toward you; that ye, always having all sufficiency in all things, may abound to every good work [2 Cor. 9:8].

I have never known anyone who has gone broke giving to the Lord's work. There may be some who have, but I have never met them in my ministry. I believe that God will bless you. I don't think the blessings He gives to you will always be material blessings. A great many folk think they can hold God to a promise of material blessings. I don't think you can. He does promise to bless us with all spiritual blessings.

(As it is written, He hath dispersed abroad; he hath given to the poor: his righteousness remaineth for ever.

Now he that ministereth seed to the sower both minister bread for your food, and multiply your seed sown, and increase the fruits of your righteousness;) [2 Cor. 9:9–10].

This is a quotation from Psalm 112. It calls the man blessed who fears the Lord and who gives to the poor. We are to share with those who do not have as much. I believe that in the church we ought to take care of our own. There are so many opportunities to share with folk. Many Christians have the *gift* of hospitality—and that is a gift. They have a way of opening their homes and making people feel at home. Often they take folk to church first so they hear the gospel and then have them in their home for dinner afterward. That is a marvelous way of witnessing. It is a way to reach the lonely and those who lack fellowship.

Paul gives the illustration of the farmer who doesn't mind going out to scatter bushel after bushel of seed, because he believes that he will get an abundant harvest. It is God who multiplies the seed of the farmer. It is God who will multiply everything that you do for Him. So don't be afraid to give to the Lord's work.

I had an experience once when I had to encourage a young man *not* to give. He had been recently saved, and he was actually giving so much that he was not keeping enough for his own family. The Bible says that we are worse than the heathen if we do not take care of our own family (see 1 Tim. 5:8). I pointed this out to him and told him that he also needed to care for the necessities of his family, and after that he should give generously to the Lord.

God does not want us to be extremists even in this matter of giving. We need to be balanced. We need good, sound, common sense and good, consecrated judgment.

Being enriched in every thing to all bountifulness, which causeth through us thanksgiving to God.

For the administration of this service not only supplieth the want of the saints, but is abundant also by many thanksgivings unto God [2 Cor. 9:11–12].

You see, when you give, it will cause people to thank God for you. It is God who will get the praise and the glory.

Whiles by the experiment of this ministration they glorify God for your professed subjection unto the gospel of Christ, and for your liberal distribution unto them, and unto all men [2 Cor. 9:13].

While I was visiting the mission field in Venezuela a certain missionary there told me about a family that I knew back in Los Angeles. The missionary said, "How generous they have been to me! I thank God for them." That is the way Paul said it would be. Missionaries in Venezuela were thanking God for a family in Los Angeles. Is anyone anywhere thanking God for your generosity?

And by their prayer for you, which long after you for the exceeding grace of God in you [2 Cor. 9:14].

Giving is a grace. We are not commanded to give a tithe. It is not to be something done under law. It is a grace. God asks us to give as a grace according to our circumstances. Some Christians should be giving much more than a tithe. Other Christians are not able to give at all. We are to give as we "are able." Now Paul caps the whole subject of giving by saying:

Thanks be unto God for his unspeakable gift [2 Cor. 9:15].

Regardless of how much you are giving, you cannot give like God gives. He has given an unspeakable gift. No man can approach the gift that God gave in giving His own Son to die. Think of this for a moment. We are back to what was said in chapter 8, verse 9. Though He was rich, He left heaven, left all the glory, came down as a missionary to this world. He came not only to live but to give His life in death for you. He came to die on a cross. He came to be brutally killed in order that you and I might have eternal life. He made His soul a sacrifice for sin for you and for me.

We are told in Hebrews that He did this "for the joy that was set before him" (Heb. 12:3). Oh, my friend, He is the wonderful, glorious Savior! Don't ever bring Him down to a low level. He is the Bright and Morning Star. He is the Son of God who has redeemed us. He is the unspeakable gift to you and me. That is the very apex of giving. No one can go beyond that kind of giving.

CHAPTER 10

THEME: *Authentication of Paul's apostleship*

Now we come to the last great division of this epistle, which is the calling of the apostle Paul. The first division I have called Christian *living*, the second one I called Christian *giving*, and this one I call Christian *guarding*. It was a radical change when we saw Paul begin to write about Christian giving. Now we come to an altogether new section, and it marks such a radical change in tone and style that many critics have supposed that this is the beginning of a third epistle.

Candidly, I cannot accept that theory. The change in tone can be explained easily on another basis.

As we have seen, the church in Corinth was a divided church. Paul said when he first wrote to them, "For it hath been declared unto me of you, my brethren, by them which are of the house of Chloe, that there are contentions among you" (1 Cor. 1:11). The majority of the church respected the authority of Paul. There was a minority who opposed Paul and rejected his authority. It would seem that in the first nine chapters he is addressing the majority. In chapters 10, 11, and 12 he is addressing the minority. It is like changing from daylight to darkness.

In this section we will find the apostle opening his great heart of love—his heart as a missionary and as a human being. We will meet him as we have never met him before because in this section he actually defends his apostleship.

Now I Paul myself beseech you by the meekness and gentleness of Christ, who in presence am base among you, but being absent am bold toward you [2 Cor. 10:1].

You remember that Paul had written a strong letter of correction. The minority criticized him severely, and they were saying, "Paul writes big, but when he is among us he is a nobody."

Paul beseeches them by "the meekness and gentleness of Christ." Paul came to Corinth as a tentmaker. He wasn't chargeable to anyone, and he didn't want to be. He would work in the marketplace all day. He would perspire and his hands would get dirty. He was working there, and he was talking to the multitude as they passed by. Now the Corinthians would say of him, "He's not an apostle. Look at him. He's a tentmaker. He is just an ordinary man." Well, friend, he was an ordinary man, but he happened also to be an apostle. Paul looked just like anyone else. In fact, some people would have looked down on him because he labored with his hands. So when he says, "I Paul myself beseech you by the meekness and gentleness of Christ," he is saying that he is like the Lord when He was here on earth. He says, "Who in presence am base among you." He was not something special to see. He wasn't a somebody. He was just an ordinary fellow making tents. So the Corinthians would be apt to say, "When he is among us, he is base. But when he writes to us, he is bold and writes with authority. Who does he think he is?"

Paul writes in the meekness and the gentleness of Christ. Our Lord didn't lift up His voice to defend Himself. Our Lord was not striking in personal appearance, and He did not look as different as the artists would have us believe. He didn't walk around with a halo around His head. He was meek and lowly, and that is to be the badge of His followers. That is the fraternity pin of believers.

So Paul writes to them and says, "Don't let looks fool you." Paul had the authority of an apostle. Paul had a divine mission. He spoke with authority. He was conscious of supernatural power, and he exercised supernatural power. Paul urges them not to force him to exercise his authority. He would like to come again in meekness and gentleness. He urges them not to think of him simply in the flesh.

I don't think a minister of the gospel today needs to wear a robe or needs to button his collar in the back to prove he is a minister of the Lord Jesus Christ. I believe he can prove it by his life and in the fact that he preaches the Word of God. We still find the same tendency among some people as was present in Corinth. They want to degrade the man who teaches the Word of God. The Devil is very clever in this matter. Right now the Devil does not seem to be attacking the Word of God. There is a real interest in the Word of God among multitudes of people. So what does the Devil do? He attacks the reputation of the man of God who is preaching the Word of God. This is the way he gets in. He tries to discredit the man. That is exactly what happened to Paul.

I know of a church where the pastor taught the Word of God. There were some members there who didn't like him at all, and when he left the church they attempted to crucify the man. Yet they would tell you they believed the Word of God, and they all carried big Bibles under their arms. They don't really believe the Word of God—in fact, they don't even know what is in it. If a pastor preaches the Word of God and does not cater to such a group, believe me, he is in trouble. That is the Devil's method.

But I beseech you, that I may not be bold when I am present with that confidence, wherewith I think to be bold against some, which think of us as if we walked according to the flesh [2 Cor. 10:2].

Paul is saying to them that they should not think of him as walking according to the flesh because he made tents and his hands got dirty and he was sweaty as he worked. This is the way they had evaluated him.

For though we walk in the flesh, we do not war after the flesh [2 Cor. 10:3].

The Greek word for flesh is *sarx*, and it can be used in three different ways. It can speak of the body, the physical body that we have, the meat that is on the bones. It can speak of weakness, meaning that which is psychological. It can also mean that corrupt nature which you and I have, that fallen nature. That is the spiritual meaning. So this word can be used in a physical sense, in a psychological sense, and in a spiritual sense.

Paul uses the word *flesh* in all three senses but more frequently in the sense of the old Adamic, fallen nature. "For I know that in me (that is, in my flesh,) dwelleth no good thing . . ." (Rom. 7:18). He is referring to the corrupt nature—he is using *flesh* in the spiritual sense.

When he says, "For though we walk in the flesh, we do not war after the flesh," he is using *flesh* in the psychological sense. Paul says that he walked in the flesh—weakness. I do not think that Paul came to Corinth in the energy of the flesh. The warfare was spiritual warfare. In his letter to the Ephesians he wrote, "For we wrestle not against flesh and blood, but against principalities, against powers, against the rulers of the darkness of this world, against spiritual wickedness in high places" (Eph. 6:12).

Paul did not come as an ordinary man who was dependent upon the principles of the natural. Paul didn't come to Corinth to put on a Madison Avenue campaign. He didn't use the methods of advertising and organization in human effort and energy. This does not mean that there is no time for us to use these. I am just saying that Paul didn't use them. He was not one of the "personality boys" who use cleverness with many quotations and clichés and who soar to heights of beautiful language. He didn't come on an anti-Nero or an anti-Caesar campaign. He didn't come to Corinth to clean up the city. He didn't come at the invitation of the Christians to put on a campaign.

Paul had written in 1 Corinthians 2:2, "For I determined not to know any thing among you, save Jesus Christ, and him crucified." Paul had a grand perspective of an entire battlefield. There was a heaven to gain, and there was a hell to shun. He was in a warfare that was spiritual and that required spiritual weapons.

(For the weapons of our warfare are not carnal, but mighty through God to the pulling down of strong holds;) [2 Cor. 10:4].

This is a parenthesis, and in this verse Paul does not even list the weapons. Spiritual warfare means that we have a spiritual enemy, and a spiritual enemy requires spiritual weapons. We are told that we have some weapons and they are mighty. They are effective. Are you able to identify those spiritual weapons which we need today?

Our first weapon is the *Word of God*. We need to have confidence in the Word of God. It is the sword of the Spirit. Paul could come to Corinth, that citadel of philosophy and religion, with the weapon of the Word of God. That is exactly the weapon that he used. Paul writes in Ephesians, "And take the helmet of salvation, and the sword of the Spirit, which is the word of God" (Eph. 6:17). Paul drew his trusty sword, and he depended upon the naked blade of it. He wrote, "For I am not ashamed of the gospel of Christ: for it is the power of God unto salvation to every one that believeth; to the Jew first, and also to the Greek" (Rom. 1:16).

We, too, need to have confidence in the Word of God. We need to have a firm confidence in the verbal inspiration of the Scriptures. This must be more than just a creed. I listened to a preacher who said he believed in the verbal inspiration of the Bible. He quoted poetry and some cute clichés and some pert epigrams. He had every form of philosophical argument but no exposition of the Word of God. May I say to you, *that* is not confidence in the Word of God, nor is it using the Word as a weapon.

I am conservative in my theology. I believe in the inspiration of the Word of God, which includes the Book of Genesis and especially the account of creation. I believe in hell. In fact, I believe the Bible from the beginning to the end. It is the sword of the Spirit, my friend. It is one of our weapons.

The second weapon is the presence of the *Holy Spirit*. Paul recognized his own human weakness. He knew that he was sealed by the Holy Spirit and empowered by the Holy Spirit.

Another weapon of our warfare is *prayer*. Now it is true that there is very little about prayer in either of the Corinthian epistles. However, Paul certainly believed in prayer. In the Book of Ephesians he lists this as one of the offensive weapons. ". . . and the sword of the Spirit, which is the word of God: Praying always with all prayer and supplication in the Spirit, and watching thereunto with all perseverance and supplication for all saints" (Eph. 6:17–18).

Casting down imaginations, and every high thing that exalteth itself against the knowledge of God, and bringing into captivity every thought to the obedience of Christ [2 Cor. 10:5].

In this spiritual battle the warriors are successful. When I say this, I do not mean they are victorious. God gets the victory. When we are successful, the glory all goes to Him. "Now thanks be unto God, which always causeth us to triumph"—how? "in Christ, and maketh manifest the savour of his knowledge by us in every place" (2 Cor. 2:14). We won't win everyone to Christ, but we can get the Word of God out. Thank God for the open door of witnessing in our day. We are not victorious, but we sure can be successful.

And having in a readiness to revenge all disobedience, when your obedience is fulfilled.

Do ye look on things after the outward appearance? If any man trust to himself that he is Christ's, let him of himself think this again, that, as he is Christ's, even so are we Christ's [2 Cor. 10:6–7].

Speaking to the opposition, Paul says, "We belong to Christ as much as anyone."

For though I should boast somewhat more of our authority, which the Lord hath given us for edification, and not for your destruction, I should not be ashamed [2 Cor. 10:8].

Paul has the authority of an apostle. It is not to destroy them, but for their edification—that is, to build them up in the faith.

That I may not seem as if I would terrify you by letters.

For his letters, say they, are weighty and powerful; but his bodily presence is weak, and his speech contemptible [2 Cor. 10:9–10].

Paul does not want his letters to be bold and terrifying and then he himself to be weak among them. I believe this indicates to us that Paul was not what one would call an attractive man. When people heard Paul, it was obvious to them that he was not preaching to them under his own physical strength or by his eloquence or by his personal magnetism. I think he must have been a weak-looking vessel. Perhaps, as with Samson in the time of the judges, it was obvious that his strength was not within himself but came from the Spirit of God.

Let such an one think this, that, such as we are in word by letters when we are absent, such will we be also in deed when we are present.

For we dare not make ourselves of the number, or compare ourselves with some that commend themselves: but they measuring themselves by themselves, and comparing themselves among themselves, are not wise [2 Cor. 10:11–12].

Paul is injecting a little note of humor. A great many folk compare themselves among themselves, which is the reason that many people in our churches think they have arrived. They feel they are really fine, outstanding, spiritual Christians because they compare themselves with other Christians in their group. That is not the yardstick we are to use, my friend. This is one of the tragedies of the hour. A person can be in a cold church and grow cold himself and yet not be conscious of it because he compares himself with the cold Christians around him. We all need to be around other Christians who challenge us. There are too many Christians who are in some little clique or group or church, and they feel smug and satisfied because they are all in the same boat.

But we will not boast of things without our measure, but according to the measure of the rule which God hath distributed to us, a measure to reach even unto you [2 Cor. 10:13].

The complaint of the Corinthian believers was that Paul would not come to see them. They said he would spend time with others but would not come to Corinth to see them.

How many Christians criticize their pastor because he doesn't spend time visiting with them! They want more and more of his time. My friend, when a pastor spends his time petting and pampering people, he is wasting the Lord's time. He needs to spend his time with those who are desperately in need of help. He also needs to spend time in the Word of God.

For we stretch not ourselves beyond our measure, as though we reached not unto you: for we are come as far as to you also in preaching the gospel of Christ:

Not boasting of things without our measure, that is, of other men's labours; but having hope, when your faith is increased, that we shall be enlarged by you according to our rule abundantly,

To preach the gospel in the regions beyond you, and not to boast in another

man's line of things made ready to our hand [2 Cor. 10:14–16].

Paul tells them they must remember that he came to them first. He was the first one to bring the gospel to them, and he had traveled a long way from home to do that. He tells them that his method is not to come and be a pastor of a church. He had been called to be a missionary. After he would begin a work, he would travel on. He was always moving out to the frontier. He never built on another man's foundation.

But he that glorieth, let him glory in the Lord.

For not he that commendeth himself is approved, but whom the Lord commendeth [2 Cor. 10:17–18].

We stand before the Lord for His commending. This is actually a word of warning to us. Don't criticize someone before you find out what his calling from the Lord is. One man may be gifted in personal visitation, another man may be gifted in the pulpit. If you have a man who is gifted in the pulpit, don't criticize him, but give him the necessary time to prepare his messages. If he is doing that, then he cannot be spending his time running around to visit you. Another man may not be a brilliant preacher but may be an excellent organizer. Then that is his gift. Find out what the person's gift is and help that person to exercise his gift. Don't sit in judgment on him if he is not doing everything *you* think he should do.

Paul is telling the Corinthian believers that he is doing what God had called him to do. He was called to be a missionary, and that is what he is doing.

CHAPTER 11

THEME: *Vindication of Paul's apostleship*

Paul writes very intimately and very personally in this chapter. Paul reminds these folk that they are joined to the living Christ, and he expresses his deep concern for them. I can certainly say that the message of this epistle has been beneficial to me. I have spent a great deal of time studying it, and I have found it has had a real message to my own heart.

This final section of the Epistle to the Corinthians concerns the calling of the apostle Paul. In chapter 10 we found the authentication of Paul's apostleship. Now we come to a very personal section which is the vindication of Paul's apostleship.

Would to God ye could bear with me a little in my folly: and indeed bear with me.

For I am jealous over you with godly jealousy: for I have espoused you to one husband, that I may present you as a chaste virgin to Christ [2 Cor. 11:1–2].

Paul came to Corinth. He preached the gospel. A church came into existence because Paul had espoused these people, these believers, to Christ.

But I fear, lest by any means, as the serpent beguiled Eve through his subtilty, so your minds should be corrupted from the simplicity that is in Christ [2 Cor. 11:3].

I cannot overemphasize the need of more simplicity in getting out the Word of God. So many of our young preachers are the products of seminaries which are trying to train intellectuals. I was listening to one of these men the other day, and I couldn't tell what he was talking about. After about fifteen minutes, I was convinced that *he* didn't know what he was talking about. They try to be so intellectual that they end up saying nothing. What he needed to do was give out the Word of God. Oh, the simplicity that is in Christ Jesus!

Paul is still making an appeal to that minority group which had stirred up trouble against him and was trying to discredit his ministry. He has already explained the reason he didn't come to spend more time with them. He had not been called to be a pastor. He was an "evangelist"—literally a missionary who did not want to build on another man's foundation. He traveled onward and he moved out to the frontier. That was his service, his ministry.

Now he wants them to know that he is an *accredited* apostle. He writes, "I am jealous over you with godly jealousy." Why was Paul willing to actually make himself a fool, as it were, for them? Although he would rather speak to them about Christ than to spend the time defending himself, now it was necessary to defend himself—"So I am speaking foolishly."

He mentions this several times in this chapter. "Would to God ye could bear with me a little in my folly: and indeed bear with me," in verse 1. "I say again, Let no man think me a fool; if otherwise, yet as a fool receive me, that I may boast myself a little," in verse 16. He says it is going to be necessary for him to defend himself, to speak foolishly. The Greek word which is translated "foolish" or "fool" can mean stupid or ignorant or egotistic. Literally it would be "mindlessness," with no purpose. Paul is saying that spending time in his defense is mindless because it is not getting out the gospel. It doesn't serve the purpose of his ministry, and yet he feels he must do it because of the opposition of this critical group in Corinth. This is why he asks them to bear with his folly, to suffer him to be foolish so that he can defend his apostleship.

We see the working of Satan in all this. At the very beginning of the early church the Devil used the method of persecution, but he found that he wasn't stopping the spread of Christianity. The fact of the matter is that the church has never grown as it did those first one hundred years after Christ lived. It swept across the Roman Empire, and by A. D. 315 it had gone into every nook and corner of the Roman Empire. That was during a period of persecution.

When the Devil saw that persecution would not stop the church, he changed to a different tactic. He joined the church. He began to hurt the church from the inside. He still does that today. He attacks the validity of the Word of God, and he tries to discredit the gospel. If that doesn't work, he tries to discredit the man who preaches the gospel. So he tried to discredit Paul.

Paul makes it very clear that he would rather be preaching the gospel than be spending time defending himself. He takes the time to defend himself because he is jealous over the Corinthians. He loves them. He is afraid they will be beguiled by Satan just as Eve was beguiled by his subtlety. Paul knows that Satan works "so your minds should be corrupted from the simplicity that is in Christ."

For if he that cometh preacheth another Jesus, whom we have not preached, or if ye receive another spirit, which ye have not received, or another gospel, which ye have not accepted, ye might well bear with him [2 Cor. 11:4].

We still face the problem today of the preaching of another Jesus, another spirit, another gospel. Some time ago there was a musical production called "Jesus Christ, Superstar," which denies His deity and presents a "Jesus" who never lived. It is the "Jesus" of liberalism dressed in a new wardrobe. And the Jesus of liberalism never existed. If they deny the virgin birth of Jesus, they are talking about some other Jesus, not the Jesus Christ of the Bible. If they do not believe that He performed miracles, they have a different Jesus in mind, because the Jesus in the Gospels is the One who performed miracles. He is the One who died for the sins of the world, which they deny. They deny that He was raised from the dead bodily. They deny that He is the God-Man. Yet one of the oldest creeds declares that He is very God of very God and very man of very man. If that is denied, then a different Jesus is being presented.

For I suppose I was not a whit behind the very chiefest apostles [2 Cor. 11:5].

I would rate Paul as the number one apostle; he says he is not the *least* of the apostles. He wants these Corinthians to know that he is just as much an apostle as any of the others. Just because he came to them as a tentmaker and because he walked in the meekness and gentleness of Christ does not mean that he is not an apostle. You see how Paul is forced to defend himself.

But though I be rude in speech, yet not in knowledge; but we have been throughly made manifest among you in all things [2 Cor. 11:6].

Paul was a brilliant man, but he used simple language. There are two men who have had a great influence on my life. One was a scholarly man in Memphis, Tennessee, who taught in simplicity. The other was Dr. Harry A. Ironside who was known as a simple preacher. He was a brilliant man, but he preached with simplicity. He put the cookies on the lower shelf where the kiddies could get them. Simplicity was the method of Paul.

Paul says that he was rude in speech. I think that he actually adopted the language that the Corinthians would understand, and I am of the opinion that it may have been a rather rude approach. However, Paul was a brilliant man. From his writings I would judge that he had the highest I.Q. of any man who has walked this earth.

> Have I committed an offence in abasing myself that ye might be exalted, because I have preached to you the gospel of God freely?
>
> I robbed other churches, taking wages of them, to do you service.
>
> And when I was present with you, and wanted, I was chargeable to no man: for that which was lacking to me the brethren which came from Macedonia supplied: and in all things I have kept myself from being burdensome unto you, and so will I keep myself [2 Cor. 11:7–9].

Paul would not allow the Corinthians to contribute to his support at all. He had to work hard at making tents. Some others sent him some support to enable him to spend some time preaching the gospel, but the Corinthians did not help him. That his hands were calloused did not indicate that he was not an outstanding apostle.

> As the truth of Christ is in me, no man shall stop me of this boasting in the regions of Achaia.
>
> Wherefore? because I love you not? God knoweth.
>
> But what I do, that I will do, that I may cut off occasion from them which desire occasion; that wherein they glory, they may be found even as we [2 Cor. 11:10–12].

Paul says that he is boasting because it is the truth and because he is jealous over them and fearful for them. Other men, such as Apollos, may have been more eloquent and polished than Paul and did not stoop to do manual labor. Comparison with others is not the issue. Paul worked as a tentmaker. He did not take remuneration from the Corinthians. This does not detract from his apostleship.

> For such are false apostles, deceitful workers, transforming themselves into the apostles of Christ.
>
> And no marvel; for Satan himself is transformed into an angel of light [2 Cor. 11:13–14].

Evidently there were deceitful workers who attempted to make themselves apostles of Christ when they were not. They were actually servants of Satan.

People have the idea that Satan has cloven feet and horns. This kind of erroneous idea comes from the great god Pan of Greek mythology, who was portrayed as half animal and was worshiped as Dionysus. Likening Satan to Pan certainly is not the scriptural point of view. Satan himself is an angel of *light*. If he would make himself visible to you, you would see a being of breathtaking beauty. Paul draws from that this conclusion:

> Therefore it is no great thing if his ministers also be transformed as the ministers of righteousness; whose end shall be according to their works [2 Cor. 11:15].

The frightening statement here is that Satan has ministers. It makes your hair stand on end. As Satan is transformed into an angel of light, so his ministers are transformed as the ministers of righteousness. They are very attractive.

I remember as a boy in my teens I went to hear a lecturer from a certain cult. I was not brought up in a Christian family, and I didn't know how to differentiate truth from untruth. This man read questions from the audience. I am of the opinion that no one really asked this question but that he made it up himself so that he would be able to make a point. He said someone asked whether he could explain the halo of light that was around his head. Well, I took a good, hard look and I couldn't see any halo of light around his head. But don't you see what he was doing? He was making himself to be a minister of light. He was glorifying himself. All Satan's ministers glorify themselves. This is one way you can tell whether a man is preaching the simplicity of the Word of God or whether he is preaching some other Jesus and some other gospel.

> I say again, Let no man think me a fool; if otherwise, yet as a fool receive me, that I may boast myself a little.
>
> That which I speak, I speak it not after the Lord, but as it were foolishly, in this confidence of boasting [2 Cor. 11:16–17].

Paul says he must go on in this *mindlessness*, and they should indulge him in this.

> Seeing that many glory after the flesh, I will glory also.

For ye suffer fools gladly, seeing ye yourselves are wise [2 Cor. 11:18–19].

He adds a bit of holy sarcasm.

For ye suffer, if a man bring you into bondage, if a man devour you, if a man take of you, if a man exalt himself, if a man smite you on the face [2 Cor. 11:20].

He gives them strong reproof here. He says someone can come in to them, put them back under the bondage of the Law, he can live off them, exalt himself, smite them, and they will put up with that. They will take that kind of treatment from a false teacher.

Now we come to a section where Paul describes his own life as a minister of the gospel. I must confess that I have been in the ministry for many years but when I read what this man Paul went through, I recognize that I have just been playing at it. I have not been a real servant of Christ as this man had been.

I speak as concerning reproach, as though we had been weak. Howbeit whereinsoever any is bold, (I speak foolishly,) I am bold also.

Are they Hebrews? so am I. Are they Israelites? so am I. Are they the seed of Abraham? so am I [2 Cor. 11:21–22].

Paul says, "I can prove my genealogy." There was no question who he was.

Are they ministers of Christ? (I speak as a fool) I am more; in labours more abundant, in stripes above measure, in prisons more frequent, in deaths oft.

Of the Jews five times received I forty stripes save one [2 Cor. 11:23–24].

The Jews had a method in those days of delivering thirty-nine stripes, and to prevent killing the person, they would apply thirteen stripes on one side, thirteen stripes on the other side, and thirteen stripes on the back. Paul had had this kind of torture five times.

Thrice was I beaten with rods, once was I stoned, thrice I suffered shipwreck, a night and a day I have been in the deep;

In journeyings often, in perils of waters, in perils of robbers, in perils by mine own countrymen, in perils by the heathen, in perils in the city, in perils in the wilderness, in perils in the sea, in perils among false brethren;

In weariness and painfulness, in watchings often, in hunger and thirst, in fastings often, in cold and nakedness [2 Cor. 11:25–27].

How many of us today could say that we have been through even the smallest part of anything like that? We sit in the lap of luxury. We live in an affluent society. We know practically nothing of hardship for the sake of Jesus Christ.

Beside those things that are without, that which cometh upon me daily, the care of all the churches [2 Cor. 11:28].

Those of us who are pastors have experienced the burden of a church. Paul had the burden of "all" the churches. We know a little of what that entailed.

Who is weak, and I am not weak? who is offended, and I burn not?

If I must needs glory, I will glory of the things which concern mine infirmities.

The God and Father of our Lord Jesus Christ, which is blessed for evermore, knoweth that I lie not [2 Cor. 11:29–31].

Paul says, "Here is my report as a minister of Jesus Christ."

In Damascus the governor under Aretas the king kept the city of the Damascenes with a garrison, desirous to apprehend me:

And through a window in a basket was I let down by the wall, and escaped his hands [2 Cor. 11:32–33].

How embarrassing it must have been to have been let down in a basket! When I (and I'm sure other pastors have the same experience) go to a city to hold a meeting or a Bible conference, they always put me in a comfortable motel and are very hospitable to me. I am received with dignity. Imagine Paul having to be let down by the wall in a basket to escape those who were lying in wait to kill him. How embarrassing! Paul did all this for Jesus' sake.

My friend, don't brag about what you suffer for Christ. Read this over again. We must all bow our heads in shame and say, "Oh, Lord Jesus, help me to be true to You. Help me to be faithful to You."

CHAPTER 12

THEME: Revelation of Paul's apostleship

We hear a great deal in our day about space travel. This has been a big subject through the decades of the 60s and 70s. Men have been to the moon. Actually, that isn't really very far when one considers space travel. It is a long distance to the moon, and yet it is small compared to the distances to Mars and other planets. Then when one measures the distance to our neighboring constellation of Andromeda that is way out there in space, we must say that man hasn't been very far yet.

The very interesting thing is that the Bible has the record of three men who journeyed into outer space and then returned—none of whom are in the Old Testament. I know someone will say, "What about Enoch and Elijah?" I do not think they were caught up to heaven. The Lord Jesus said, "And no man hath ascended up to heaven, but he that came down from heaven, even the Son of man which is in heaven" (John 3:13). Someone will say, "I thought Elijah was caught up to heaven." Yes, but after all there are three heavens. There is the first heaven where there are the birds of heaven. There is the second heaven where there are the stars of heaven. There is the third heaven which is the abode of God. Elijah had been caught up into the air spaces. Up to the time that the Lord Jesus made that statement possibly there had been no one else who had been in outer space. He said that the Son of Man came down from heaven. Then we know of two other men who have been to heaven and returned. The apostle John on the Island of Patmos was caught up into heaven. He writes about what he saw and heard in the Book of the Revelation. He was in the third heaven where the throne of God is. "After this I looked, and, behold, a door was opened in heaven: and the first voice which I heard was as it were of a trumpet talking with me; which said, Come up hither, and I will shew thee things which must be hereafter. And immediately I was in the spirit; and, behold, a throne was set in heaven, and one sat on the throne" (Rev. 4:1–2). Paul was the other man who was taken up into heaven. The record of this is in the chapter before us.

Therefore there are three men who have been able to report from heaven. The Lord Jesus, who is God manifest in the flesh, said more about heaven than anyone else did, and yet He really said very little about it. John doesn't have too much to say about it. Paul doesn't have anything to say about it.

Paul tells us something here that he would not have mentioned at all if he had not been forced to defend his apostleship. He tells about his trip into outer space.

PAUL'S EXPERIENCE

It is not expedient for me doubtless to glory. I will come to visions and revelations of the Lord [2 Cor. 12:1].

Paul had just listed many incidents showing how he had suffered for Christ's sake. There wasn't much glory in that. I think that the Spirit of God had him write down all his experiences so that no man would ever be able to say, "I endured more than Paul the apostle."

Actually, we should be very careful about the songs we sing. I think of the one:

"Jesus, I my cross have taken
All to leave and follow Thee;
Naked, poor, despised, forsaken,
Thou from hence my all shall be."
—Henry F. Lyte

I heard a so-called converted Hollywood star sing that song! I don't believe that person had given up very much. It would be hypocritical for most of us to sing it. It would be better if we all sang a song like this:

"Alas, and did my Saviour bleed
And did my Sovereign die!
Would He devote that sacred head
For such a worm as I?"
—Isaac Watts

It is the Lord Jesus who needs to be glorified. Today we hear testimonies from men and women about their conversions. Generally the testimony is a remarkable conversion. We don't often hear about the "ordinary" conversions. The thing which I note in a testimony is the place the Lord Jesus occupies. Too often the story goes on and on about the person and what he did and how he lived in sin and how remarkably he changed, while very little is said about the Lord Jesus. Sometimes one wonders whether the Lord Jesus was really needed or not. He gets very little praise and very little glory in most testimonies I hear.

I just received a letter from a man who said,

"I turned from a religious system to Christ." Then Jesus became the center of his life and his sole occupation. He wants to grow in the knowledge of the Lord Jesus Christ. That is the thing that is important.

Having told us how much he had suffered for Christ's sake, now Paul will come to visions and revelations from the Lord. We already know that the Lord had appeared to Paul on the Damascus road. Have you ever noticed that Paul has very little to say about those personal appearances? Now here is another such incident.

I knew a man in Christ above fourteen years ago, (whether in the body, I cannot tell; or whether out of the body, I cannot tell: God knoweth;) such an one caught up to the third heaven [2 Cor. 12:2].

It was the Lord Jesus who spoke of the birds of heaven, which fly up in the air spaces. They don't go up very high. Out beyond that is the space that contains the stars of heaven. That still is not the same as the third heaven where the throne of God is to be found. How ridiculous it was for the cosmonauts in the Russian sputnik to say they didn't see God when they went to the moon. They didn't go far enough, friend. They must go to the third heaven to find the throne of God.

Paul speaks of his experience of being taken up into the third heaven. He dates it for us. He says it happened fourteen years before he wrote this epistle. That would be approximately the time when he had made his first missionary journey. We are told about his experience at Lystra on that first journey. "And there came thither certain Jews from Antioch and Iconium, who persuaded the people, and, having stoned Paul, drew him out of the city, supposing he had been dead. Howbeit, as the disciples stood round about him, he rose up, and came into the city: and the next day he departed with Barnabas to Derbe" (Acts 14:19–20).

Was he dead? I don't think they would have left him there unless they were pretty sure he was dead. It is my personal opinion that God raised him from the dead. Paul was rather uncertain whether this was a vision or whether he had been caught up in reality at that time. It is quite evident that he is describing his own experience here.

And I knew such a man, (whether in the body, or out of the body, I cannot tell: God knoweth;) [2 Cor. 12:3].

Was he actually dead and caught up into heaven? Or had he been knocked unconscious and had a vision? Paul is not dogmatic about it, and we should not be dogmatic about it either. As I have said, I believe he was dead and that God raised him from the dead, but the result was the same either way. He saw the third heaven.

Notice his report:

How that he was caught up into paradise, and heard unspeakable words, which it is not lawful for a man to utter [2 Cor. 12:4].

Most men would have written several volumes of ponderous tomes on such an experience. And they would have given a whole series of messages about it. But this is all that Paul says. This is his report. He says so much and yet he says so little. There is no description, no Chamber of Commerce advertisement, no promotion, no sales talk, no display, no hero worship of man.

Of such an one will I glory: yet of myself I will not glory, but in mine infirmities.

For though I would desire to glory, I shall not be a fool; for I will say the truth: but now I forbear, lest any man should think of me above that which he seeth me to be, or that he heareth of me [2 Cor. 12:5–6].

There is no self-glory here. The man who was taken up into the third heaven and heard unspeakable words is the same man who was let over the wall in a basket.

PAUL'S THORN IN THE FLESH

And lest I should be exalted above measure through the abundance of the revelations, there was given to me a thorn in the flesh, the messenger of Satan to buffet me, lest I should be exalted above measure [2 Cor. 12:7].

Paul says he will tell us about his infirmities, but he will not tell us about third heaven. Why? Because he was told not to talk about it.

I think many times Satan tries to remove God's witnesses from the earthly scene. He wants to get rid of them. He uses sickness, disease, a thorn in the flesh.

What was Paul's thorn in the flesh? I want to let you in on something, give you a little secret information which I hope you won't divulge to anyone: I don't know. I don't know what Paul saw and heard in the third heaven, and I don't know what was his thorn in the flesh. I don't know because he didn't tell us.

An old Scotch commentator said Paul's thorn in the flesh was his wife. Well, I'll imagine that old Scot was having trouble at home, and I think he was wrong. I believe that Paul had been married but was a widower. He wrote lovingly of womanhood, and I think he had once had a wonderful wife. He would not remarry because he didn't want to subject any woman to the hardships which he had to endure.

It is interesting that God put a zipper on the mouth of Paul and silenced him. He simply does not reveal these things to us.

Someone has said that the reason a dog has so many friends is because he wags his tail instead of his tongue! I suppose most of us would have wagged our tongues a great deal if we had been caught up into the third heaven. Now why did God give Paul a thorn in the flesh? It was to keep him humble, to keep him from exalting himself above measure, having had such a vision.

For this thing I besought the Lord thrice, that it might depart from me.

And he said unto me, My grace is sufficient for thee: for my strength is made perfect in weakness. Most gladly therefore will I rather glory in my infirmities, that the power of Christ may rest upon me [2 Cor. 12:8–9].

Now I have a notion that Paul's problem was very poor vision. When we get to his Epistle to the Galatians, we will find that he mentions that he had to write in large letters, which would indicate that he did not see well. We will discuss that later. Whatever the thorn was, Paul asked the Lord three times to remove it, and the Lord refused. The Lord heard him the first time and the second time and the third time. It was not that the Lord did not hear his prayers; it was that the answer of the Lord was no.

Sometimes you and I keep asking the Lord for something to which He has already answered no. If He doesn't give us what we ask for, we think He has not answered our prayer. More often than not His answer to my prayers is no. And eventually I discover that His no was the best possible answer He could have given me.

He said to Paul, "My grace is sufficient for thee." He said He would not remove the thorn but that He would give Paul the grace to bear

the thorn. That is the wonderful thing about it all. "My strength is made perfect in weakness." In other words, it was obvious in Paul's ministry that he was so physically weak that the Spirit of God was empowering him. "Most gladly therefore will I rather glory in my infirmities, that the power of Christ may rest upon me." This was Paul's response to the Lord's answer. Paul would glory in his infirmities and not in the fact that he had had a vision. That is something you might turn over in your mind the next time you hear someone tell about a vision they have had of the Lord. It probably would be better if that person had a zipper on his mouth. The chances are that he had no vision at all but had eaten something he should not have eaten the night before.

Therefore I take pleasure in infirmities, in reproaches, in necessities, in persecutions, in distresses for Christ's sake: for when I am weak, then am I strong [2 Cor. 12:10].

What a contrast this man is to Samson in the Old Testament. The Spirit of God came upon Samson and he became strong. People marveled at his physical strength, but there came a day when he was very weak. The strong are made weak, and the weak are made strong. God can use the weak man.

I am become a fool in glorying; ye have compelled me: for I ought to have been commended of you: for in nothing am I behind the very chiefest apostles, though I be nothing [2 Cor. 12:11].

Notice how he elaborates on this. He is apologizing again even as he has done many times earlier. Paul considered himself the least of the apostles, yet he says, "In nothing am I behind the very chiefest apostles, though I be nothing." Someone should have defended him but, apparently, no one did.

Truly the signs of an apostle were wrought among you in all patience, in signs, and wonders, and mighty deeds [2 Cor. 12:12].

There were certain sign gifts which were given to the apostles to authenticate their message. They had the gift of healing. They could raise the dead and speak in tongues, which does not mean *unknown* tongues but languages and dialects. Paul had gone through the Galatian country, and there must have been fifty dialects and languages in that area. Paul could speak them all. Had he studied them? No. In that early day it was necessary to get the Word of God out into the Roman Empire in a hurry, and so these apostles were equipped with these gifts. Today missionaries and translators must spend years learning the languages they will use. "Signs of an apostle were wrought among you." They could identify him as an apostle because he had the gifts of an apostle.

We have just come through a wonderful section of Scripture. Someone has said that one of the reasons Paul was not to tell us about heaven was because there would be a mass exodus up out of this world to get there. I don't know about that, but it is true that we could spend our time contemplating heaven and lose sight of a lost world that needs to hear of the Savior. Heaven is a wonderful place, but very little is said about it in the Word of God. Probably it is so wonderful that human language cannot describe it. It is our business to try to reach folk with the gospel so that they will be in heaven someday.

Although I cannot tell you much about heaven, I can tell you about the One who is in heaven. We can talk about Him, the Lord Jesus Christ, and we are to fix our eyes on Him. My, how this epistle has emphasized that! Beholding Him, we will become like Him in many ways. The pilgrim journey through this world will be a great deal easier if we will keep our eyes fixed on Him. The sun won't be so hot, the burden of the day won't be so heavy, the storms of life won't be so fierce if we keep our attention fixed upon the Lord Jesus Christ.

PAUL PLANS TO REVISIT CORINTH

For what is it wherein ye were inferior to other churches, except it be that I myself was not burdensome to you? forgive me this wrong.

Behold, the third time I am ready to come to you; and I will not be burdensome to you: for I seek not yours, but you: for the children ought not to lay up for the parents, but the parents for the children [2 Cor. 12:13–14].

Paul, you see, was their spiritual father. He had led them to Christ and had founded the church in Corinth.

And I will very gladly spend and be spent for you; though the more abundantly I love you, the less I be loved [2 Cor. 12:15].

Paul says, "The more I love you, the less I am loved in return." It sounds like a complaint, doesn't it? But the Spirit of God insisted that he not tell about what he had seen in heaven but that he tell about his sufferings and disappointments down here.

But be it so, I did not burden you: nevertheless, being crafty, I caught you with guile [2 Cor. 12:16].

Oh, notice this man. He says, "I wasn't after what you have, I was after *you*; I wanted to win *you* for Christ." Isn't that what the Lord Jesus had told His apostles? He said to them, "Follow me, and I will make you fishers of men" (Matt. 4:19)—and He didn't say that every fish they caught would have a gold piece in its mouth! He made them fishers of *men*—that is the emphasis.

Did I make a gain of you by any of them whom I sent unto you?

I desired Titus, and with him I sent a brother. Did Titus make a gain of you? walked we not in the same spirit? walked we not in the same steps? [2 Cor. 12:17–18].

Paul didn't use clever methods; he preached the Word of God in simplicity. He didn't send other men along after him to make a gain out of the Corinthians.

Again, think ye that we excuse ourselves unto you? we speak before God in Christ: but we do all things, dearly beloved, for your edifying.

For I fear, lest, when I come, I shall not find you such as I would, and that I shall be found unto you such as ye would not: lest there be debates, envyings, wraths, strifes, backbitings, whisperings, swellings, tumults [2 Cor. 12:19–20].

These are the things Paul expected to find in the church when he would get there. They expected a great deal of Paul. Paul expected a great deal of them. But what would he find? There would be debates and arguing.

I have been in the ministry for many years, and I am now to the place where I am in no mood for debate. Occasionally I get long letters from folk who listen to my radio program and want to debate a doctrine or a statement I've made on the radio. Friend, go on with your viewpoint and pray for me so that, if I am wrong, I will be led to the truth by the Spirit of God. You will not convince me with a long letter, because, frankly, I don't have the patience to read it. Someone may say that I am very bigoted and narrow-minded. Well, maybe I am, but I just don't believe that arguing and debating accomplish anything. Our business is to get out the Word of God, and I am not attempting to debate anything. I teach the Word as I come to it as I teach through the Bible.

The contemporary church is filled with the things Paul mentions here—debates, envyings, wraths, strifes, and backbitings.

"Have you heard about So-and-so?"

"No, I haven't heard."

"Well, I want to tell you."

Then they say some pretty mean things about a certain individual. And there are the whisperings. Someone has said that some people will believe anything if it is whispered to them.

Then there is that word *swellings*. I have often wondered what Paul meant. Probably the best explanation is the one I heard Dr. H. A. Ironside give. He said this reminded him of a frog sitting on the bank of a creek or a pond all swelled up. He looks twice as big as he would ordinarily be. Then what happens? You throw a rock at him and, believe me, he becomes little again and goes right down into the water. Probably the best word that we have to describe "swellings" would be our word *pompous*. There are some pompous Christians.

"Tumults" are troubles in the church. Little cliques get together and they cause trouble. They circulate petitions to be signed and that sort of thing. That causes a tumult.

And lest, when I come again, my God will humble me among you, and that I shall bewail many which have sinned already, and have not repented of the uncleanness and fornication and lasciviousness which they have committed [2 Cor. 12:21].

Corinth was a vile city. It was known as a sin center throughout the Roman Empire. It was the Las Vegas and Reno and any other sinful city that you want to put with it all rolled into one. It was the place people went to sin. It is true that where sin abounded there grace did much more abound. Yet it caused the people of Corinth to look lightly upon these sinful things.

This does not present an attractive picture of the church, does it? I'm sure that as we have gone through this epistle you have thought, *The local church in Corinth certainly was not a very good church*. That is true. Not only was it true of that church, but it is also true of many of our churches today.

Let's stop to look at this for a moment. Suppose the Lord took the church out of the world right now. What would happen if He removed all true believers who are in the world? We believe that the Great Tribulation would then begin. A part of the contribution to the Great Tribulation will be the absence of the church. The church today is the salt of the earth, the light of the world, and the Holy Spirit indwells the church today.

Is the world getting better or worse? Some people say that the church hasn't improved the world because the world is worse now than it was nineteen hundred years ago. I disagree with that. I know it says in 2 Timothy 13:13, "But evil men and seducers shall wax worse and worse, deceiving, and being deceived," but that doesn't say the *world* is getting worse; it says that evil *men*, will wax worse and worse. I think this means they will get worse in their lifetime and then another generation will come on.

The world is a little better today than it was over nineteen hundred years ago because at that time the world committed a sin which would have been an unpardonable sin had not the Lord Jesus said, ". . . Father, forgive them; for they know not what they do . . ." (Luke 23:34). They crucified the Son of God. I recognize that the world today by its rejection of Jesus Christ is crucifying Him afresh. The greatest sin in all the world is the rejection of Christ. The world of each generation has been guilty of that. The Lord Jesus said that when the Holy Spirit would come, He would convict the world of sin, "Of sin, because they believe not on me" (John 16:9). There are many sins which are bad, but the worst sin of all is the rejection of Jesus Christ. The greatest crime that was ever committed on this earth was the murder of the Son of God over nineteen hundred years ago. The world today is still just as corrupt, just as vile, just as mean, and just as wicked as it was then.

I will say that the world today is a better place to have a home than it was nineteen hundred years ago. We can live more comfortably. There are a great many things which make life easier and better than it was nineteen hundred years ago. However, we need to understand very clearly that it was never the purpose of the church to plant flowers in the world any more than it was Israel's business to plant flowers in the wilderness. They were pilgrims passing through it and they had a message and a witness. This also has been the purpose of the church down through the ages.

The church is a group of people who ought to be holy unto God, ought to be living for God. I wish I could point to the church and say it is doing that and how wonderful it is. Its failure in this area is one of the reasons the present interest in the Word of God has in most instances bypassed the local church. It is too busy with its internal problems. Yet that does not destroy the fact that the church is that group which is loved by the Lord Jesus Christ. He gave Himself for it that He might wash it, that He might cleanse it, and that He might make each believer acceptable to God. Although we are far from what we should be, we should be moving in that direction.

So here in Paul's Corinthian epistles we have an insight into a church which was in the worst city of the Roman Empire, and how bad it was! I don't like to hear it said that the church does not in any way affect the world around it. It may look as if it has very little effect, and yet, then as now, if that group of godly people were to be removed from this world, the world would be much worse.

CHAPTER 13

THEME: The execution and conclusion of Paul's apostleship

EXECUTION OF PAUL'S APOSTLESHIP

This is the third time I am coming to you. In the mouth of two or three witnesses shall every word be established [2 Cor. 13:1].

Paul is repeating what he has said earlier. He is going to Corinth for the third time to exercise his office as an apostle. Everything is to be authenticated when he gets there. Everything is going to be brought right out in the open. Paul is going to exercise his office as an apostle, and he is going to show proof of his apostleship by the power of Christ working through Paul's weakness.

I told you before, and foretell you, as if I were present, the second time; and being absent now I write to them which heretofore have sinned, and to all other, that, if I come again, I will not spare:

Since ye seek a proof of Christ speaking in me, which to you-ward is not weak, but is mighty in you [2 Cor. 13:2–3].

Paul had come to them in weakness, but the Word of God was mighty and had transformed them in that sin-sick city.

For though he was crucified through weakness, yet he liveth by the power of God. For we also are weak in him, but we shall live with him by the power of God toward you [2 Cor. 13:4].

Paul says, "For though he was crucified through weakness." It sounds strange to hear about the weakness of God. What is this weakness? When He went to the cross, my friend, that was the weakness of God. "Yet he liveth by the power of God."

Now Paul goes on to something that is very important. There is an inventory which every Christian should make regularly.

Examine yourselves, whether ye be in the faith; prove your own selves. Know ye not your own selves, how that Jesus Christ is in you, except ye be reprobates? [2 Cor. 13:5].

This has nothing to do with free will or election or the security of the believer. Paul says we should examine ourselves to see whether we are in the faith or not. We should be willing to face up to this issue. I think two or three times a year we should do this.

When my daughter was just a little thing, she made a confession of her faith to her mother when they were back visiting her grandmother in Texas. She came in one day and said out of a clear sky that she wanted to accept Jesus as her Savior. My wife took her into the bedroom, she got down on her knees and accepted Christ. Regularly after that I would ask her about her relation to Christ. When she got into her teens, she asked, "Daddy, why do you keep asking me whether I am a Christian or not or whether I really trust in Jesus?" I told her, "I just want to make sure. After all, you are my offspring and I want to be sure." Now not only did I do that for her, I did it for myself also. I think every believer ought to do that.

But I trust that ye shall know that we are not reprobates [2 Cor. 13:6].

Paul has made an inventory of himself, and he wants them to know that he is in the faith.

Now I pray to God that ye do no evil; not that we should appear approved, but that ye should do that which is honest, though we be as reprobates [2 Cor. 13:7].

Paul is saying that he just wants them to be the type of believers they should be.

For we can do nothing against the truth, but for the truth [2 Cor. 13:8].

Here is another great truth we should mark well. My friend, you can't do anything against the truth. That is why I don't worry about folk who are disagreeing about the Word of God. They cannot do anything against the truth. We should declare the Word of God and not spend our time defending it. God doesn't ask us to defend it. He asks us to declare it, to give it out.

For we are glad, when we are weak, and ye are strong: and this also we wish, even your perfection [2 Cor. 13:9].

"Even your perfection" does not mean perfect as we usually think of perfection, but it means maturity. He wishes them to be mature Christians. He wants them to grow in grace and in the knowledge of Christ Jesus. We still hear that expression today—"Why don't you grow up?" That is what Paul is saying to them. Grow up in Christ!

Therefore I write these things being absent, lest being present I should use sharpness, according to the power which the Lord hath given me to edification, and not to destruction [2 Cor. 13:10].

Paul is glad he can write to them at this time. He is writing for the purpose of building them up and not tearing them down.

CONCLUSION OF PAUL'S APOSTLESHIP

Finally, brethren, farewell. Be perfect, be of good comfort, be of one mind, live in peace; and the God of love and peace shall be with you [2 Cor. 13:11].

Again he says, "Be perfect"—grow up. Stop being baby Christians. That is something which could be said to many believers today.

"Be of good comfort." He goes back to the word he used when he began this letter—the comfort of God. Remember that it means *help*. It means God is the One who is called to our side to help us, to strengthen us, to encourage us. God wants to do that for you today, my friend. No matter who you are, where you are, or how you are, God wants to help you. He can help you through His Word by means of the ministering of the Holy Spirit.

What great verses these are. God is with us to comfort us. We are to grow and mature. We can do nothing against the truth, but for the truth. Certainly we ought to go forward for God with such encouragement.

"Be of one mind" means to have the mind of Christ.

"Live in peace." We cannot make peace, but we can live in peace.

"And the God of love and peace shall be with you." This is the peace of God which passeth all understanding. It is the peace that God made through the blood of the cross. We are to live in that peace today. We are to rejoice in our salvation.

The God of love and peace shall be "with you." Don't miss that. You are not alone—God is *with* you today. How wonderful that is.

Greet one another with an holy kiss [2 Cor. 13:12].

I hope you won't mind my telling you a story about the late Dr. Walter Wilson. A friend came to see him and his lovely wife. The friend greeted Dr. Wilson with a kiss because he was such a wonderful saint of God. Then he kissed his wife. He said to Dr. Wilson, "Now when I greet you, it is a holy kiss, but when I kiss your wife—wow!" May I say to you, my friend, if you are going to kiss, make sure it is a holy kiss. I would suggest that we confine our kissing to those of the same sex if we intend for it to be a *holy* kiss!

All the saints salute you.

The grace of the Lord Jesus Christ, and the love of God, and the communion of the Holy Ghost, be with you all. Amen [2 Cor. 13:13–14].

I have jokingly said that the apostle Paul was a Southerner because he uses the expression "you all." You know that I am from the South and so you will forgive me if I, too, say, "you all."

When he says that the blessing of the Trinity should be with "you all," he includes us with the folk in the church in Corinth. We ought to revel in all that we have in Christ Jesus: the *grace* of the Lord Jesus Christ, and the *love* of God, and the *communion* of the Holy Ghost. How we ought to bear witness not only to the world but also to our own churches.

BIBLIOGRAPHY

(Recommended for Further Study)

Boyer, James L. *For a World Like Ours: Studies in I Corinthians.* Grand Rapids, Michigan: Baker Book House, 1971. (Excellent for individual or group study.)

DeHaan, M. R. *Studies in First Corinthians.* Grand Rapids, Michigan: Zondervan Publishing House, 1956.

Gromacki, Robert G. *Called to Be Saints* (I Corinthians). Grand Rapids, Michigan: Baker Book House, n.d.

Gromacki, Robert G. *Stand Firm in the Faith* (II Corinthians). Grand Rapids, Michigan: Baker Book House, 1978.

Hodge, Charles. *An Exposition of First and Second Corinthians.* Carlisle, Pennsylvania: The Banner of Truth Trust, 1869. (For advanced students.)

Hughes, Philip E. *Paul's Second Epistle to the Corinthians.* Grand Rapids, Michigan: Wm. B. Eerdmans Publishing Co., 1962. (A comprehensive study.)

Ironside, H. A. *Addresses on First Corinthians.* Neptune, New Jersey: Loizeaux Brothers, 1938. (A fine survey.)

Kelly, William. *Notes on the First Epistle to the Corinthians.* Addison, Illinois: Bible Truth Publishers, 1878.

Kelly, William. *Notes on the Second Epistle to the Corinthians.* Addison, Illinois: Bible Truth Publishers, 1882.

Kent, Homer A., Jr. *A Heart Opened Wide: Studies in II Corinthians.* Grand Rapids, Michigan: Baker Book House, 1982. (Excellent.)

Luck, G. Coleman. *First Corinthians.* Chicago, Illinois: Moody Press, 1958. (A good survey.)

Luck, G. Coleman. *Second Corinthians.* Chicago, Illinois: Moody Press, 1960. (A good survey.)

Morgan, G. Campbell. *The Corinthian Letters of Paul.* Westwood, New Jersey: Fleming H. Revell Co., 1946.

Morris, Leon. *The First Epistle to the Corinthians.* Grand Rapids, Michigan: Wm. B. Eerdmans Publishing Co., 1958.

Moule, Handley C. G. *The Epistle of Second Corinthians.* Fort Washington, Pennsylvania: Christian Literature Crusade, n.d.

Robertson, A. T. *The Glory of the Ministry.* Grand Rapids, Michigan: Baker Book House, 1911. (Deals with II Corinthians 2:12–6:10, and should be read by every Christian worker.)

Tasker, R. V. G. *The Second Epistle of Paul to the Corinthians.* Grand Rapids, Michigan: Wm. B. Eerdmans Publishing Co., 1958.

Vine, W. E. *First Corinthians.* Grand Rapids, Michigan: Zondervan Publishing House, 1951.

The Epistle to the
GALATIANS
INTRODUCTION

This epistle was probably written by Paul (Gal. 1:1) about A.D. 57, on the third missionary journey from Ephesus during his two years of residence there. There is substantial basis, however, for the claim that it was written from Corinth, shortly before Paul wrote the Epistle to the Romans. Dr. Lenski advances the theory that it was written from Corinth on the second missionary journey about April, A.D. 53. After Paul visited the Galatians, he discovered that the Judaizers had followed him and the churches were listening to them. Paul wrote this letter to counteract their message and to state clearly the gospel.

Paul visited the Galatian churches on each of his three missionary journeys. There is no mention in the epistle of another visit to the churches. This epistle was evidently Paul's last word to these churches, written after he had visited them on his third missionary journey.

In the case of the Epistle to the Galatians, the *people* to whom it was sent are important, which is not always true with other epistles. Also, the destination of this book has given rise to what is known as the North Galatian and the South Galatian theories. It seems more reasonable to suppose that it was sent to the churches in the area Paul visited on his first missionary journey, but this does not preclude the possibility that it had a wider circulation, even as far north as Pessinus, Ancyra, and Tavium. I believe that Paul was writing to *all* the churches of Galatia. This area was large and prominent and many churches had been established there.

The word *Galatians* could be used either in an ethnographic sense, which would refer to the nationality of the people, or it could be used in a geographic sense, which would refer to the Roman province by that name. Regardless of the position which is taken, there was a common blood strain which identified people in that area where there was a mixture of population. The people for whom the province was named were Gauls, a Celtic tribe from the same stock which inhabited France. In the fourth century B.C. they invaded the Roman Empire and sacked Rome. Later they crossed into Greece and captured Delphi in 280 B.C. They were warlike people and on the move. At the invitation of Nikomedes I, king of Bithynia, they crossed over into Asia Minor to help him in a civil war. They soon established themselves in Asia Minor. They liked it there. The climate was delightful, and the country was beautiful. When I visited Turkey, I was pleasantly surprised to find how lovely it is along the Aegean and inland, also along the Mediterranean.

In 189 B.C. these Celtic tribes were made subjects of the Roman Empire and became a province. Their boundaries varied, and for many years they retained their customs and own language. They actually were blond Orientals. The churches Paul established on his first missionary journey were included at one time in the territory of Galatia, and this is the name which Paul would normally give to these churches.

These Gallic Celts had much of the same temperament and characteristics of the American population, that is, of those who came out of Europe or England. It is interesting to see what was said concerning my ancestors (and maybe yours). Many of these Germanic tribes were wild and fierce. Caesar said of them: "The infirmity of the Gauls is that they are fickle in their resolves, fond of change, and not to be trusted." This description fits the majority of Americans in our day. We are fickle in our resolves. We are fond of change—we want a new car every year. We like to get the magazine that is dated next week. Another described them as "frank, impetuous, impressible, eminently intelligent, fond of show, but extremely inconstant, the fruit of excessive vanity." That is a picture of the American population today. A man runs for office and we vote for him. Then in four years we forget him. Do you remember who was president ten years ago? Or twenty years ago? We are fickle people, not very constant. I'm very happy that it was said we are eminently intelligent, because that's what we think also. And the reason for our high estimation of ourselves is the fruit of excessive vanity.

In the Book of Acts we read that the Galatians wanted to make Paul a god one day, and the next day they stoned him. What do we do? We elect a man to the presidency and then we try to kill him in office. I think it is quite interesting that our system of government has survived as long as it has.

Therefore the Epistle to the Galatians has a particular message for us because it was written to people who were like us in many ways. They had a like temper, and they were beset on every hand by cults and "isms" innumerable—which take us, likewise, from our moorings in the gospel of grace.

1. It is a stern, severe, and solemn message (see Gal. 1:6–9; 3:1–5). It does not correct conduct as the Corinthian letters do, but it is corrective. The Galatian believers were in grave peril because the foundations of their faith were being attacked—everything was threatened.

The epistle, therefore, contains no word of commendation, praise, or thanksgiving. There is no request for prayer, and there is no mention of their standing in Christ. No one with him is mentioned by name. If you compare this epistle with the other Pauline epistles, you will see that it is different.

2. In this epistle the heart of Paul the apostle is laid bare, and there is deep emotion and strong feeling. This is his *fighting epistle*—he has on his war paint. He has no toleration for legalism. Someone has said that the Epistle to the Romans comes from the head of Paul while the Epistle to the Galatians comes from the heart of Paul. A theologian has said, "Galatians takes up controversially what Romans puts systematically."

3. This epistle is a *declaration of emancipation* from legalism of any type. It is interesting to note that legalists do not spend much time with Galatians. It is a rebuke to them. This was Martin Luther's favorite epistle. He said, "This is *my* epistle. I am wedded to it." It was on the masthead of the Reformation. It has been called the Magna Carta of the early church. It is the manifesto of Christian liberty, the impregnable citadel, and a veritable Gibraltar against any attack on the heart of the gospel. As someone put it, "Immortal victory is set upon its brow."

This is the epistle that moved John Wesley. He came to America as a missionary to the Indians. But he made a startling discovery. He said, "I came to America to convert Indians, but who is going to convert John Wesley?" He went back to London, England, and was converted. When I was in London I had a guide take us to Aldersgate and we saw the marker that designates the place where John Wesley was converted. (His was called an "evangelical conversion," which is the only kind of conversion the Bible speaks of.) John Wesley went out to begin a revival—preaching from this Epistle to the Galatians—that saved England from revolution and brought multitudes to a saving knowledge of Christ. Wilberforce, one of his converts, had a great deal to do with the matter of child labor and the Industrial Revolution that brought about changes for the working man.

In a sense I believe this epistle has been the backbone and background for every great spiritual movement and revival that has taken place in the past nineteen hundred years. And, my friend, it will be the background for other revivals. I would like to see the Spirit of God move in our land today. I would like to hear the Epistle to the Galatians declared to America. I believe it would revolutionize lives.

4. Galatians is the strongest declaration and defense of the doctrine of *justification by faith* in or out of Scripture. It is God's polemic on behalf of the most vital truth of the Christian faith against any attack. Not only is a sinner saved by grace through faith plus nothing, but the saved sinner lives by grace. Grace is a way *to* life and a way *of* life. These two go together, by the way.

OUTLINE

I. Introduction, Chapter 1:1–10
A. Salutation—Cool Greeting, Chapter 1:1–5
B. Subject Stated—Warm Declamation, Chapter 1:6–10

II. Personal—Authority of the Apostle and Glory of the Gospel, Chapters 1:11–2:14
A. Experience of Paul in Arabia, Chapter 1:11–24
B. Experience of Paul with the Apostles in Jerusalem, Chapter 2:1–10
C. Experience of Paul in Antioch with Peter, Chapter 2:11–14

III. Doctrinal—Justification by Faith, Chapters 2:15–4:31
Faith vs. Works, Liberty vs. Bondage
A. Justification by Faith—Doctrine Stated, Chapter 2:15–21
B. Justification by Faith—Experience of Galatians, Chapter 3:1–5
C. Justification by Faith—Illustration of Abraham, Chapters 3:6–4:18
D. Justification by Faith—Allegory of Hagar and Sarai, Chapter 4:19–31

IV. Practical—Sanctification by the Spirit, Chapters 5:1–6:10
Spirit vs. Flesh, Liberty vs. Bondage
A. Saved by Faith and Living by Law Perpetrates Falling from Grace, Chapter 5:1–15
B. Saved by Faith and Walking in the Spirit Produces Fruit of the Spirit, Chapter 5:16–26
C. Saved by Faith and Fruit of the Spirit Presents Christian Character, Chapter 6:1–10

V. Autographed Conclusion, Chapter 6:11–18
A. Paul's Own Handwriting, Chapter 6:11
B. Paul's Own Testimony, Chapter 6:12–18
   1. Cross of Christ vs. Circumcision, Chapter 6:12–15
   2. Christ's Handwriting on Paul's Body, Chapter 6:16–18
      The New Circumcision of the New Creation

CHAPTER 1

THEME: *Salutation—cool greeting; subject stated—warm declamation; Paul's experience in Arabia*

Galatians is God's polemic against legalism of every and any description. The Mosaic Law is neither discredited, despised, nor disregarded. Its majesty, perfection, demands, fullness, and purpose are maintained. Yet these very qualities make it utterly impossible for man to come this route to God. Another way is opened for man to be justified before God, a way which entirely bypasses the Mosaic Law. The new route is by faith. Justification by faith is the theme, with the emphasis upon *faith*.

Three epistles in the New Testament quote Habakkuk 2:4, "The just shall live by his faith." Romans 1:17 emphasizes *the just*. Hebrews 10:38 emphasizes *shall live*. Galatians 3:11 emphasizes *by faith*.

In Romans the emphasis is upon the fact that man apart from the Mosaic Law is justified before God by faith. In Galatians Paul is defending the gospel from those who would add law to justification by faith. Faith plus law was the thrust of Judaism. Faith plus nothing was the answer of Paul.

The Judaizers questioned Paul's authority as an apostle and his teaching that simple faith was adequate for salvation. Paul defends his apostleship and demonstrates the sufficiency of the gospel of grace to save.

SALUTATION—COOL GREETING

Paul, an apostle, (not of men, neither by man, but by Jesus Christ, and God the Father, who raised him from the dead;) [Gal. 1:1].

Actually there is no parenthesis necessary in this verse. Paul is simply stating that he is an apostle. The word *apostle* is used in a twofold sense:

1. One of the Twelve (Acts 1:21–26)
   (a) With Jesus during His three year ministry (v. 21);
   (b) Witness of His postresurrection ministry (v. 22);
   (c) Chosen by Christ (v. 22; Acts 9:15; 26:16–17).
2. One sent forth. This is the wider sense as used in Acts 11:22.

Paul, in my judgment, took the place of Judas. After the resurrection of Jesus, Matthias was chosen by the disciples to fill the place of Judas, but no information is given about Matthias except the account given in Acts 1:15–26. Matthias is never mentioned again. If the Holy Spirit had chosen him, certainly somewhere along the way He would have set His seal upon this man. Paul, however, proved he was an apostle, and Matthias did not. The election of Matthias as an apostle was held *before* Pentecost, which was before the Holy Spirit came into the church. For that reason I do not think that the Holy Spirit had anything to do with the selection of Matthias. There are also many elections in our churches today that are obviously not ordered by the Holy Spirit. I believe that Paul is the man whom the Spirit of God chose to take Judas' place.

In this verse Paul also says that he is not "of men." The preposition *apo* conveys the meaning of "not from men," that is, it is not legalistic. He is not an apostle by appointment or commission after having attended a school or having taken a prescribed course.

Paul also declares that his apostleship is not "by man." The preposition *dia* indicates that it was not through man, that is, not ritualistic by means of laying on of hands, as by a bishop or church court. Paul did not have the other apostles lay their hands on his head and say, "Hocus pocus, you are an apostle."

Paul was an apostle. How? He was an apostle by Jesus Christ, and God the Father, who raised Him from the dead. Jesus laid His hand upon Paul, called him, and set him apart for the office (see Acts 9:15–16).

Now I am an ordained minister from men and through men. I was told that I had to finish seminary and obtain certain degrees before I could be ordained. I did that. That was from men. That was the legalistic side. Next I went before a church body that examined me. Their decision was that I should be an ordained minister. In the Second Presbyterian Church in Nashville, Tennessee, I knelt, and a group of men put their hands on me and said, "You are now an ordained minister." That is the kind of minister I am. Paul said, "I am *not* that kind of an apostle. Men had nothing to do with it. I am an apostle directly by Jesus Christ and God the Father who raised Him from the dead."

And all the brethren which are with me, unto the churches of Galatia [Gal. 1:2].

You will notice that Paul's greeting is cool, brief, formal, and terse. No one is personally mentioned. He is not writing just to one church. He is writing to several churches— "churches of Galatia."

The word *church* is used in two ways in the New Testament. One meaning of church includes the entire body of believers, of all different groups, who have trusted Christ as Savior. The other meaning of church refers to local assemblies, which is how Paul uses the word here. There were churches, or local assemblies, in many parts of Galatia. There was a church in Antioch of Pisidia, in Derbe, in Lystra, and in other places he had visited. Paul was writing to *all* the churches, to all of the local assemblies; hence the local church— not the corporate body of believers—is in view here. In the Epistle to the Ephesians we look at the church as a corporate body of believers—the invisible church. But the invisible body is to make itself visible today in a corporate body. Believers should be identified with a local body of believers.

Grace be to you and peace from God the Father, and from our Lord Jesus Christ [Gal. 1:3].

This is Paul's formal greeting that he uses in most of his epistles. The word *grace (charis)* in this verse was the gentile form of greeting in that day, while *peace (shalom)* was the religious greeting of the Jews. Now the grace of God must be experienced before the peace that is from God the Father can be experienced.

Who gave himself for our sins, that he might deliver us from this present evil world, according to the will of God and our Father [Gal. 1:4].

This is another marvelous verse—I can't rise to the level of it; I will simply say some things about it.

Jesus Christ "gave himself for our sins." There is nothing that we can add to the value of His sacrifice. Nothing! He gave Himself. What do you have to give, friend? Anything? Can you add anything to His sacrifice? He gave Himself. How wonderful and glorious that is! I am speechless when I read a verse like this. He gave Himself! When you give yourself, you have given everything—who you are, what you have, your time, your talent— everything. He gave Himself. He couldn't give

any more. Paul just couldn't wait to say it. Having mentioned Him, he says, "Who gave himself for our sins." This is the germ of Paul's subject.

Paul calls Him, "*our* Lord Jesus Christ." He is *my* Savior. Can you say, "The Lord is *my* Shepherd?" It is one thing to say He is a Shepherd; it is another thing to make it possessive. The Lord is *my* Shepherd. The Lord is *my* Savior. Can you say that He is yours?

Paul goes on to say, "that he might deliver us from this present evil world." Notice that the Lord delivers us from this present evil age. There is, therefore, a present value of the gospel which proves its power and genuineness. The gospel can deliver you. I have received letters from thousands of folks who have turned to Christ and have been delivered. They have been delivered from drugs, from alcohol, and from sex sins. Christ alone can deliver in cases like that. This proves the genuineness of the gospel. Christ gave Himself for our sins. He took your place and my place on that cross. He died for us and rose from the dead "that he might deliver us from this present evil world."

All we have seen so far does not exhaust the richness of this verse.

Notice that His deliverance is "according to the will of God and our Father." He *can* deliver us—and it will not be according to law. But it must be according to the *will* of God, my friend. The will of God is that, after He has saved us, we are not to live in sin. How wonderful this is! He *can* deliver us. He *wants* to deliver us. He *will* deliver us, and He will do it according to the will of God. It is God's will that you be delivered.

This verse still is not exhausted. Christ gave Himself that He might deliver us according to the will of God. God can deliver us, but it will not be according to the Law. It must be according to the will of God, my friend. The will of God is that when He saves you, you are not to live in sin. He can deliver us and He wants to deliver us. It is His will that you be delivered. My friend, this is a verse that makes you feel like throwing your hat in the air, does it not?

To whom be glory for ever and ever. Amen [Gal. 1:5].

This is a moment wherein Paul stops to render praise to God. I am convinced that we should praise God more than we do. Let us get right down to the nitty-gritty, right down where the rubber meets the road. Did you praise the Lord's name this morning when you got up?

Did you thank Him for a new day? You say, "It was raining." But did you thank Him for it? Did you praise His name that He brought you to a new day?

I had to have a bout with cancer before I came to the place where I thank Him as I should. Now the first thing I do every morning—whether the sun is shining or it's pouring down rain—is to say, "Lord, thank you for bringing me to a new day." How wonderful He is! We need to praise Him more. I want glory to go to the name of my God and my Savior. I don't want to stand on the sidelines and compromise by endorsing these contemporary dramatic productions and songs that are belittling the Lord Jesus Christ. I am speaking out against them, because He is God manifest in the flesh. He gave Himself for me. I want to praise His name! "To whom be glory for ever and ever."

"For ever and ever" begins right now and is going on right into eternity.

This concludes Paul's salutation. Although it contains some glorious truths, I think you will have to admit that it is a cool, impersonal greeting from the apostle Paul.

SUBJECT STATED—WARM DECLAMATION

Paul now states his subject. He goes from cold to hot. In fact, he is hot under the collar. Why? Because there are those who are mutilating the gospel. Paul would give his life for the gospel.

I marvel that ye are so soon removed from him that called you into the grace of Christ unto another gospel [Gal. 1:6].

There are two aspects of the gospel, and it can be used in two senses: (1) the facts of the gospel, and (2) the interpretation of the facts. The facts of the gospel are the death, burial, and bodily resurrection of Christ. Paul said to the Corinthians, "For I delivered unto you first of all that which I also received [Paul didn't originate the gospel; he *received* it], how that Christ died for our sins according to the scriptures; And that he was buried, and that he rose again the third day according to the scriptures" (1 Cor. 15:3–4). These are the historical facts of the gospel which cannot be changed. You have never preached the gospel unless you have stated these facts. The second aspect of the gospel is the interpretation of the facts. They are to be received by faith plus nothing.

Now the subject of Paul's letter to the Galatian believers concerns the interpretation of the facts of the gospel. The Judaizers had followed Paul into the Galatian country. They did not challenge the facts of the gospel. After all, five hundred people at once saw the Lord Jesus after His resurrection. When you have that many people around as witnesses, you don't run around denying the facts of the gospel. The heresy they were promoting concerned the interpretation of those facts. They were very sly and subtle and said something like this, "Did Brother Paul come here among you?" The folk would say, "Yes, he came and preached the gospel and we accepted it. We are converted. We know Christ as our Savior, and we are in the body of believers." The Judaizers would respond, "Oh, that's wonderful. Brother Paul is accurate as far as he goes, but he doesn't go far enough. Did he tell you that you should keep the Mosaic Law? Oh, he didn't? Well, he should have told you that. Yes, you are to trust Christ, but you must also follow the Mosaic Law or you won't be saved."

This is one of the oldest heresies known, and it is still with us today. It is adding something to the gospel of grace; it is *doing* something rather than simply believing something. It is faith plus something rather than faith plus nothing. Every cult and "ism" has something for you to *do* in order to be saved.

It is interesting that Paul said to the Philippian jailer, ". . . Believe on the Lord Jesus Christ, and thou shalt be saved . . ." (Acts 16:31). Simon Peter said to the Sanhedrin, "Neither is there salvation in any other; for there is none other name under heaven given among men, whereby we must be saved" (Acts 4:12). Christ told the apostles to preach the gospel of salvation by grace. They were not to do anything to gain their salvation, but they were to trust what Christ already had done for them. The gospel shuts out all works.

Now Paul is writing to the Galatian believers and saying, "I marvel that ye are so soon removed from him that called you into the grace of Christ unto another gospel"—

Which is not another; but there be some that trouble you, and would pervert the gospel of Christ [Gal. 1:7].

The word *pervert* is the Greek word *metastrephō*. It is a strong word, used by Dr. Luke in speaking of the sun *turned* to darkness (see Acts 2:20), and by James, speaking of laughter *turned* to mourning (see James 4:9). To attempt to change the gospel has the effect of making it the very opposite of what it really is. This is important to see.

But though we, or an angel from heaven, preach any other gospel unto you than that which we have preached unto you, let him be accursed [Gal. 1:8].

This verse is as strong as anything could possibly be. Paul says that if an angel dared to declare any other message than the gospel, he would be dismissed with a strong invective.

If an angel should appear to me right now and say, "You are right as far as you go, but you also have to *do* something to be saved"; or if an angel should appear to you as you read this and say, "McGee is correct as far as he goes, but you have to *do* something else," both you and I should say, "Get out of here; I'm not listening to you although you are an angel from heaven."

My friend, in our day we hear many speakers who are trying to give us another "gospel." They may look like angels to you—after all, Satan himself is transformed into an angel of light, and his ministers are transformed as the ministers of righteousness (see 2 Cor. 11:14–15). Now hear Paul—

As we said before, so say I now again, If any man preach any other gospel unto you than that ye have received, let him be accursed [Gal. 1:9].

In strong language Paul says, "If any man preach any other gospel unto you than that ye have received, let him be accursed," which literally means let him be damned. Friend, I cannot make that statement any stronger.

The gospel shuts out all works. Romans 4:5 says, "But to him that worketh not, but believeth on him that justifieth the ungodly, his faith is counted for righteousness." I find a great many folk who think they have to become good enough to be saved. The other day a man said to me, "McGee, I want to become a Christian. I am going to try to be a little better, and if I improve, I am going to become a Christian." I said to him, "If you improve, you will never become a Christian. The only class that God is saving is the ungodly. The Lord Jesus said He didn't come to call the righteous; He came to call sinners. The reason He said that was because there is none righteous, no, not one. Even the righteousness of man is as filthy rags in God's sight. Law condemns us, and it must make us speechless before grace can save us."

Romans 3:19 tells us that, "Now we know that what things soever the law saith, it saith to them who are under the law: that every mouth may be stopped, and all the world may become guilty before God." The real difficulty is not that people should be "good enough" to be saved, but that they are not "bad enough" to be saved. Humanity refuses to recognize its lost condition before God. This is the human predicament.

The Judaizers did not deny the facts of the gospel—that Jesus died and rose again. What they denied was that this was adequate. They insisted that you have to keep the Law plus trusting Christ. Paul is saying that whoever tries to mingle law and grace—let him be damned! Why? Because they pervert the gospel. They do not deny the fact of the gospel, but they misinterpret those facts. They pervert the gospel.

For do I now persuade men, or God? or do I seek to please men? for if I yet pleased men, I should not be the servant of Christ [Gal. 1:10].

The word *persuade* means "to make a friend of." The *Scofield Reference Bible* translates it "seek the favor of." In 1 Thessalonians 2:4 and 4:1 it is "please God" in contrast to self or others. The preaching of the gospel is not pleasing to lost man. No man can please both God and man.

If you preach the gospel of grace today, you may get into trouble because it is the gospel of the grace of God that the sinner hates. Many unsaved church members do not want to hear the message of grace. They want to hear a message that appeals to the flesh. The gospel of grace puts us in the dust and makes us beggars before God.

By nature man responds to legalism. He thinks he doesn't need a Savior. All he needs is a helper. Oh, my friend, we are sinking for the third time! We need somebody to *save* us. Those who preach law are popular. Not long ago I listened to a local Southern California preacher on television. From a technical and professional standpoint he has one of the finest programs. In his message he talked about Jesus coming into the world. He spoke of Christ's death and resurrection. But he failed to mention that the people to whom he was speaking were sinners and needed a Savior. He neglected to inform his audience that Jesus died for them and they needed to trust Him to be saved. Rather, he talked about commitment. He invited folk to commit their lives to Christ. Let us be honest, friend. Christ does not want your old life and He does not want mine. We have nothing to commit to Him. He wants to do something through us today. Oh, if only we could learn that!

God is not even asking you to live the Christian life. In fact, you cannot live it. God is asking that He might live the Christian life through you. The Epistle to the Galatians teaches this. But first of all we must come to Christ as sinners and be saved. Our churches are filled today with people who are not saved. Do you know why? They have never come to Christ and received Him as Savior. They feel like they have something to commit to Him. You have *nothing* to commit to Him, my friend. He wants to commit something to you. He is the One who died, and He is on the giving end. "For the wages of sin is death; but the gift of God is eternal life through Jesus Christ our Lord" (Rom. 6:23). It is just as simple as that. Have you accepted Jesus Christ as your Savior? This is the important thing.

Man's conscience witnesses to the law, and legal conviction will lead to works. Man tries to compensate for the fact that he is not doing enough. He tries to balance his good works against his sins and have enough on the plus side to be saved. The apostle Paul, you recall, tried to do this. And he had a whole lot on the plus side. But one day he came to Christ. Then he said, "What was gain for me became loss, and what was loss became gain" (see Phil. 3:7–8).

The Holy Spirit witnesses to grace today. This is gospel conviction that leads to faith. Actually the law denies the fall of man—this was the position of Cain. Grace acknowledges the fall of man, as Abel did when he brought his offering to God.

We come now to a new section that deals with the apostle Paul personally—his experience in Arabia, his experience with the apostles in Jerusalem, and his experience in Antioch with Peter. This will take us through the first half of chapter 2.

PERSONAL—PAUL'S EXPERIENCE IN ARABIA

But I certify you, brethren, that the gospel which was preached of me is not after man [Gal. 1:11].

Paul is stating once again, as he did in verse 1, that he is a God-appointed apostle. When he says, "I certify you," he means, "I remind you." "After man" should be "according to man." Paul did not get the gospel he preached from man. The Judaizers not only questioned Paul's message, they also questioned his apostleship. He was not one of the original Twelve, but a Johnny-come-lately.

They cast a shadow upon the validity of Paul's authority as an apostle. Paul is going to take up this matter with them and show that his apostleship rests upon the fact that he was called directly by the revelation of Jesus Christ.

For I neither received it of man, neither was I taught it, but by the revelation of Jesus Christ [Gal. 1:12].

Paul did not receive his apostleship by going to school. Neither did he receive it by being ordained or by hands being laid on his head. Paul's apostleship and gospel came directly by a revelation *(apokalupsis)* of Jesus Christ. The Book of Revelation, sometimes called the Apocalypse, is from the same word. The gospel is a revelation as much as is the Book of Revelation. The gospel was unveiled to the apostle Paul. He did not become an apostle through Peter, James, or John. He was an apostle by the direct call of Jesus Christ.

For ye have heard of my conversation in time past in the Jews' religion, how that beyond measure I persecuted the church of God, and wasted it:

And profited in the Jews' religion above many my equals in mine own nation, being more exceedingly zealous of the traditions of my fathers [Gal. 1:13–14].

Paul says, "For ye have heard of my conversation," that is, you have heard of my manner of life. Paul now calls the religion in which he was brought up the "Jews' religion." Paul was saved, not *in* Judaism, not *by* Judaism, but *from* Judaism.

Now notice this tremendous statement:

But when it pleased God, who separated me from my mother's womb, and called me by his grace,

To reveal his Son in me, that I might preach him among the heathen; immediately I conferred not with flesh and blood:

Neither went I up to Jerusalem to them which were apostles before me; but I went into Arabia, and returned again unto Damascus [Gal. 1:15–17].

The phrase "but when it pleased God," in verse 15, means that Paul was called according to the will of God. The word *heathen* in verse 16 refers to Gentiles. Paul conferred not with flesh and blood—he didn't get it from any man. Paul received the gospel directly from Jesus Christ.

Many years ago a so-called modernist, who taught old heresy, wrote a book about Paul. He also gave lectures, which I heard. He gave the apostle Paul credit for being a great brain. (I personally believe Paul had the greatest mind of any man who has ever lived. Many scholars, who are better acquainted with Paul than I am, also make this statement.) He pointed out that Paul was a brilliant student of the Mosaic system of Judaism and was a brilliant student of Greek philosophy, and then declared that Paul combined the two and came up with Christianity. Now Paul says here in Galatians that he didn't get the gospel that way. He received the gospel by direct revelation from Jesus Christ.

Then after three years I went up to Jerusalem to see Peter, and abode with him fifteen days [Gal. 1:18].

I suppose that this verse is the same record that is given in Acts 9:26–29 which says, "And when Saul was come to Jerusalem, he assayed to join himself to the disciples: but they were all afraid of him, and believed not that he was a disciple. But Barnabas took him, and brought him to the apostles, and declared unto them how he had seen the Lord in the way, and that he had spoken to him, and how he had preached boldly at Damascus in the name of Jesus. And he was with them coming in and going out at Jerusalem. And he spake boldly in the name of the Lord Jesus, and disputed against the Grecians: but they went about to slay him."

When all of this is added up, it means that Paul spent less than three years in the desert. It is interesting how God has trained His men. He trained Moses in the desert. He put Abraham in a rather unique place to train him, and Elijah had that same type of experience. It has been God's method to put His man out on the desert to train him. David was trained outdoors in the caves of the earth while he was running away from King Saul. Remember that he cried out to God that he was hunted like a partridge—it was open season on him all the time. The Lord used the same method with Paul. God sent him into the desert for less than three years. Then he went to Jerusalem, saw Peter, and stayed with him for fifteen days.

But other of the apostles saw I none, save James the Lord's brother [Gal. 1:19].

Paul had no contact with the apostles except Peter and James, the Lord's brother. That is all the contact he had with them, and he received nothing from them, as we shall see.

Now the things which I write unto you, behold, before God, I lie not [Gal. 1:20].

The modernist or liberal, to whom I referred, said that Paul got his gospel by making an homogenized stew out of Greek philosophy and the Mosaic system. Paul says here that he didn't get the gospel from anyone else. Paul also says he does not lie. Someone is lying. I am too polite to call that modernist a liar, but in effect Paul does.

Afterwards I came into the regions of Syria and Cilicia;

And was unknown by face unto the churches of Judaea which were in Christ:

But they had heard only, That he which persecuted us in times past now preacheth the faith which once he destroyed.

And they glorified God in me [Gal. 1:21–24].

The believers in Jerusalem were rather reluctant to accept the apostle Paul. Without the help of Barnabas, Paul would probably have waited a long time before the church in Jerusalem would have received him. These men were hesitant to receive Paul because he had persecuted the church, but they knew what it was to be converted. They knew what it was to have an absolutely earth-shaking experience that would transform a man. Yet they could not believe that Saul of Tarsus could be converted. It seemed not only improbable but impossible.

In verses 21–24 Paul outlines his first years after his conversion. I don't think, friend, that they were the happiest years of his life. Apparently he tells us something about the failure in his own personal life in the seventh chapter of Romans. There were three periods in the life of the apostle Paul. Notice briefly the first two periods.

1. Paul was a proud Pharisee. He had a marvelous mind and was an expert in the Mosaic Law. As many of his biographers have said, the world would have heard of Paul even if he had not been an apostle and even if he had not been converted. I don't think there is any question about that. He was an outstanding man. But he was a proud young Pharisee who thought he knew it all. He hated Christ. He hated the church and attempted to elimi-

nate it. He was ruthless in his persecution of the church.

2. The second period began on the Damascus road when he was knocked down into the dust. This brilliant Pharisee found out that he did not know Jesus Christ, whom to know is life. He had thought Jesus was dead. And he asked, "Who art thou, Lord?" Jesus replied, "I am Jesus whom you persecute. When you persecute My church, you persecute Me" (see Acts 9:5). When Paul became acquainted with his Lord, he immediately asked, "Lord, what wilt thou have me to do?" After Paul met Christ, he spent some time in Arabia. During those first years he attempted to minister and found that what he wanted to do he could not do. Finally he cried out, "O wretched man that I am! who shall deliver me from the body of this death?" (Rom. 7:24). It was not an unsaved man who said that; it was Paul the apostle in the first stages of his conversion.

3. Then came that glorious period when he walked in the Spirit. That was the time he could live for God. That is the place where many of us need to be today. There are so many unhappy Christians. They are saved, I think, but as Dwight L. Moody put it in his quaint way, "Some people have just enough religion to make them miserable."

I wish we had more information on Paul's experience with the apostles in Jerusalem. I am sure a question has already come to your mind. If Paul received the gospel apart from the other apostles—who were with the Lord for three years and saw the resurrected Christ—is Paul preaching the same gospel? This is an important matter at this point because if Paul is not preaching the same gospel, something is radically wrong. In the next chapter we shall see that the apostles in Jerusalem approved Paul's gospel and that it was the same Good News.

CHAPTER 2

THEME: Experience of Paul with the apostles in Jerusalem; experience of Paul in Antioch with Peter; justification by faith stated

Now we come to the second division of this personal section in Galatians. We have seen that the Lord Jesus Christ communicated the gospel directly to Paul. Was it the same gospel that the other apostles had received from the lips of the Lord? We will see the oneness of the gospel and Paul's experience with the apostles in Jerusalem. We will see the communication of the gospel and see that the church in Jerusalem approved Paul's gospel.

EXPERIENCE OF PAUL
WITH THE APOSTLES IN JERUSALEM

Then fourteen years after I went up again to Jerusalem with Barnabas, and took Titus with me also [Gal. 2:1].

It was a master stroke of Paul to take Titus with him. Titus was a young preacher and a Gentile. This, I believe, was the first great council in Jerusalem as recorded in Acts 15. The question to be settled was whether men are saved by the grace of God or whether they should come in under the Mosaic Law. Paul had Titus there as exhibit number one. Titus

had not been circumcised. Will he be forced to become circumcised? This was to become a very important matter.

You see, the Judaizers were going about saying that the church in Jerusalem held that all believers in Christ should be under the Mosaic Law. All of the men there at the Jerusalem church, which was an all-Jewish church, had certainly been under it. Many of them still went to the temple to worship. In fact, that must have been the Christian's meeting place. Paul and Barnabas came there to get the official word regarding law and grace.

And I went up by revelation, and communicated unto them that gospel which I preach among the Gentiles, but privately to them which were of reputation, lest by any means I should run, or had run, in vain [Gal. 2:2].

Paul recognized that if he were preaching a different gospel from what the other apostles were preaching, there was something radically wrong. Paul was willing to admit, "If I were preaching a different gospel, I would be wrong. I have run in vain. I have certainly been disillusioned and misinformed." So he goes to Jerusalem and communicates that gospel to the apostles there.

But neither Titus, who was with me, being a Greek, was compelled to be circumcised:

And that because of false brethren unawares brought in, who came in privily to spy out our liberty which we have in Christ Jesus, that they might bring us into bondage [Gal. 2:3–4].

Out where Paul was preaching some folk had come into the church under false colors. Apparently they were not believers. They just came in to spy out the liberty which believers had in Christ. They found out that this young preacher, Titus, was a Greek and Paul had not compelled him to be circumcised. So what will the church at Jerusalem decide about him? Paul says, "Well, they didn't compel him to be circumcised. They didn't listen to the false brethren. If they had, we would be put right back under the bondage of the Mosaic Law rather than enjoying the freedom by the Spirit of God and the freedom in Christ."

To whom we gave place by subjection, no, not for an hour; that the truth of the gospel might continue with you [Gal. 2:5].

Paul stood by his guns. These false brethren said, "This man Titus who is here meeting with the church (and it was practically all Jewish then) has not even been circumcised!" Paul says, "No, and he's not going to be circumcised. He is as much a believer as any of you. He has been saved by faith apart from the Law. He is not about to follow any part of the Law for salvation." This is a tremendous stand that Paul is taking.

But of these who seemed to be somewhat, (whatsoever they were, it maketh no matter to me: God accepteth no man's person:) for they who seemed to be somewhat in conference added nothing to me [Gal. 2:6].

Paul says, "We sat down with the apostles [at least *he* did, and I suppose Barnabas and Titus were there also] and communicated the gospel." They said, "Now, Brother Paul, we've been hearing these reports. Tell us what you preach." And Paul told them. Paul finds out that these apostles didn't have anything to add to what he was preaching. He was preaching

the grace of God; they were preaching the grace of God. They find they are in full agreement. They all are preaching the same gospel. This is tremendous!

But contrariwise, when they saw that the gospel of the uncircumcision was committed unto me, as the gospel of the circumcision was unto Peter [Gal. 2:7].

Let's understand that there were not two gospels in the sense of Peter's gospel and Paul's gospel. These men were in complete agreement. The gospel of the circumcision and the gospel of the uncircumcision refer to the groups the gospel was going to. The Gentiles were the group that Paul was speaking to. He was called to go to the Gentiles, the uncircumcised. Peter was called to go to his own Jewish brethren who were the circumcised.

(For he that wrought effectually in Peter to the apostleship of the circumcision, the same was mighty in me toward the Gentiles:) [Gal. 2:8].

The proof of the pudding, of course, is always in the eating. What results were they getting? When Peter preached the gospel, quite a few people were saved. When Paul preached the gospel, quite a few people were saved. They were both preaching the same gospel.

Now bringing this principle down to where we live, the real test of any Christian work is not promotion. The real test is the results it gets. God's people should be very sure that they are supporting a ministry that gets results. If it is not producing results, why in the world do you support it?

And when James, Cephas, and John, who seemed to be pillars, perceived the grace that was given unto me, they gave to me and Barnabas the right hands of fellowship; that we should go unto the heathen, and they unto the circumcision [Gal. 2:9].

The apostles accepted Paul's apostleship. "The right hands of fellowship"—fellowship is the Greek *koinonia*, one of the great words of the gospel and the highest expression of a personal relationship. It means sharing the things of Christ.

Only they would that we should remember the poor; the same which I also was forward to do [Gal. 2:10].

Paul came back later with an offering for the poor saints in Jerusalem because that church had been persecuted and was in a sad condition. Because Paul himself before his conversion had led the persecution, he wanted to bring the gift for the Jerusalem church with his own hands.

This was social service. A thing that we fundamentalists are guilty of is a lack of real service in this area. James, in his very practical epistle, says, "If a brother or sister be naked, and destitute of daily food, And one of you say unto them, Depart in peace, be ye warmed and filled; notwithstanding ye give them not those things which are needful to the body; what doth it profit? Even so faith, if it hath not works, is dead, being alone" (James 2:15–17). And the apostles there in Jerusalem said, "Now, Brother Paul, don't forget to help the poor folk." And Paul said, "That was the very thing I was eager to do."

EXPERIENCE OF PAUL IN ANTIOCH WITH PETER

In this personal section of Paul's life we have seen his experience in Arabia with the Lord Jesus Christ, and his experience with the apostles in Jerusalem. Now we see Paul's experience in Antioch with Simon Peter—I love this section.

The church in Antioch was largely a gentile church, although it was a mixture of Jew and Gentile. We will not understand what happened there unless we consider how the early church operated. They had a love feast which was held in connection with the Lord's Supper. Paul has a great deal to say about this subject in 1 Corinthians. The early believers came together for a meal, a love feast, before they celebrated the Lord's Supper. When Gentiles were saved, a problem was raised. In the congregation were Jews who had never eaten anything which had been sacrificed to idols. The Gentiles had been idolaters, and they were accustomed to eating meat that had first been offered to idols. They also ate pork and other animals designated as unclean in the law of Moses. It made no difference to them because they had been reared that way.

What was going to be done to keep from offending the Jewish Christians? Well, in Antioch two tables were established. One was the kosher table; the other was the gentile table. Paul ate at the gentile table. Although he was a Jew, he ate with the Gentiles because he taught that whether you eat meat or you don't eat meat makes no difference—meat will not commend you to God.

When Simon Peter came up to visit Paul in Antioch, it was a new experience for him because, although converted, he had never eaten anything unclean. Remember what Peter told the Lord on the roof in Joppa before he went to the home of Cornelius. He had a vision of heaven opening and a sheet being lowered in which were all kinds of unclean animals. "And there came a voice to him, Rise, Peter; kill, and eat. But Peter said, Not so, Lord; for I have never eaten any thing that is common or unclean. And the voice spake unto him again the second time, What God hath cleansed, that call not thou common" (Acts 10:13–15).

Peter had been a believer for some time when he came to visit Paul in Antioch, but he had still followed the Jewish eating pattern. When Peter came to the church, he found there a gentile table and a kosher table. Now notice Peter's reaction:

But when Peter was come to Antioch, I withstood him to the face, because he was to be blamed.

For before that certain came from James, he did eat with the Gentiles: but when they were come, he withdrew and separated himself, fearing them which were of the circumcision [Gal. 2:11–12].

Now this is probably what happened. When the time came to eat, Simon Peter went over to the kosher table, while Paul went over to the gentile table. Peter noticed that there was pork roast on the gentile table. After dinner Peter joined Paul and they went outside for a little walk. Peter said, "I noticed that you ate at the gentile table." "Yes," Paul said. "And I noticed that you ate pork tonight. Is it good? I never have tasted it." "Yes," Paul said, "it's delicious." Then Peter asked, "Do you think it would be all right if I ate over there?" And Paul said, "Well, it is my understanding that we are going to have some nice pork chops in the morning for breakfast. Why don't you try it?" So in the morning when he came to breakfast, he went over to the gentile table, sat down gingerly and rather reluctantly took a pork chop. After he had tasted it, he said to Paul, "It is delicious, isn't it!" Paul said, "Yes. After all, under grace you can either eat it or not eat it. It makes no difference. Meat won't commend you to God." So Simon Peter said, "I'll be here tonight and I understand you are having ham tonight. I want to try that." So at dinner time he starts rushing for the gentile table when he looks over and sees some of the elders from the Jerusalem church who had come to visit also. So Simon Peter went all the way around that gentile table, went over to the kosher table, and sat down like a little whipped puppy. Paul saw him do that, and this is what happened:

> And the other Jews dissembled likewise with him; insomuch that Barnabas also was carried away with their dissimulation.
>
> But when I saw that they walked not uprightly according to the truth of the gospel, I said unto Peter before them all, If thou, being a Jew, livest after the manner of Gentiles, and not as do the Jews, why compellest thou the Gentiles to live as do the Jews? [Gal. 2:13–14].

It was all right for Peter to eat at either table, kosher or Gentile. But after he had been eating at the gentile table and for fear of the brethren from Jerusalem goes back to the kosher table, he is saying by his action that the gentile table is wrong and the kosher table is right.

Now these brethren from Jerusalem were austere legalists. And under grace that was their privilege. I have no objection to folk today who feel that they should not eat certain meats. But they are also to give me the liberty of eating what I choose to eat. Frankly, I do not eat much pork myself for health reasons. But it is not a religious matter at all. Simon Peter turned from the liberty he had in Christ back to Judaism again.

The nature of Paul's rebuke shows, first of all, the inconsistency of lawkeeping. If it was right for Simon Peter to live as the gentile believers lived, why should he desire the Gentiles to live as the Jews? That is what he was saying when he left the gentile table for the kosher table. If gentile living under grace apart from the Law was good enough for Peter, was it bad for the Gentiles themselves? If Simon Peter was free to live outside the Law, was it not lawful for the Gentiles to do the same?

DOCTRINAL—JUSTIFICATION BY FAITH

This brings us to the doctrinal section of this marvelous epistle, which deals with justification by faith. In this section Paul takes his position as a Jew.

> We who are Jews by nature, and not sinners of the Gentiles [Gal. 2:15].

The Jew in that day looked upon the Gentile as a sinner. In fact, Gentile and sinner were synonymous terms. Therefore, the rebuke that Paul gave shows the folly of lawkeeping—how really foolish it is.

> Knowing that a man is not justified by the works of the law, but by the faith of Jesus Christ, even we have believed in Jesus Christ, that we might be justified by the faith of Christ, and not by the works of the law: for by the works of the law shall no flesh be justified [Gal. 2:16].

This is a clear-cut and simple statement of justification by faith. Believe me, the legalist has trouble with this verse. I once heard a legalist preach on it, and it was certainly a travesty of interpretation. This verse will upset every legal system there is today. To say that you have to add *anything* to faith in Christ absolutely mutilates the gospel.

Notice what Paul says here. If a Jew had to leave the Law behind—that is, forsake it—in order to be justified by faith, Paul's question is, "Why should the Gentile be brought under the Law?" That was the great argument at the council of Jerusalem in Acts 15: "Should the Gentile be brought under the Law?" Thank God, the answer, guided by the Spirit of God, was that the Gentile was not under the Law for salvation—not for his daily living, as he was called to a much higher plane.

Could the Gentile find justification under the Law when the Jew had already proven that it was impossible? The Jews had had the Law for almost fifteen hundred years and had not been able to keep the Law at all. Why force the Gentile under that which had not saved even one Israelite? Gentile believers were already justified by grace. It would be folly for the Gentiles to turn from grace to the Law which had been unable to justify the Jew.

"Knowing that a man." Now let's pick this verse apart. This is something you can *know*—you can know whether you are saved or not. What kind of "man" is this verse speaking about? *Anthrōpos* is the Greek word, a generic term meaning "mankind." It speaks of the solidarity of the race, the common humanity that we all have. This breaks the social barrier of color. It breaks the barrier of race. It breaks the social barrier. All men are on one level before the Cross, and that level happens to be "sinner." You are a sinner. I am a sinner. I don't care who you are, you are a sinner in God's sight.

"Knowing that a man is not justified by the works of the law"—the word *the* is not in the original; so it should read "not justified by works of law." This includes the Mosaic system, and it includes any legal system. This is what I mean: if you say that you have to join a certain church or that you have to have a certain experience, or that you have to be baptized to be saved, you are contradicting this verse. "Knowing that a man is not justified by works of law"—any law. Paul embraces the whole legal system that is found in every religion. This makes Christianity different from every religion on topside of the earth. Every religion that I know anything about—and I have studied many of the cults and religions of this world—instruct us to *do* something. Christianity is different. It tells us that we are justified by faith; that is, faith is an accomplished act and fact for you. Every other religion says *do*. Christianity says *done*. The great transaction is *done*, and we are asked to believe it.

Let me call your attention to an important verse in 1 Corinthians: "Wherefore I give you to understand, that no man speaking by the Spirit of God calleth Jesus accursed: and that no man can say that Jesus is the Lord, but by the Holy Ghost" (1 Cor. 12:3). Now the question for you and me is: how can we call Jesus accursed? If you say to me, "McGee, when you came to Christ and accepted Him as your Savior, you didn't get all that was coming to you. The Holy Spirit can give you something that you didn't get in Christ, and you ought to seek that today." My friend, to do that depreciates the work of the Lord Jesus on the cross when He came to this earth to die for you and work out a salvation so perfect that when He went back to heaven He sat down at the right hand of God (see Heb. 1:3). He sat down because there was nothing else to be done. If there had been anything else, He would have done it before He sat down. When you say that He didn't do it all for me, you are saying that Jesus is accursed. And you can't say that by the Holy Spirit of God. That is, you are not giving me the word of the Holy Spirit. Jesus said, "Howbeit when he, the Spirit of truth, is come, he will guide you into all truth: for he shall not speak of himself; but whatsoever he shall hear, that shall he speak: and he will shew you things to come. He shall glorify me: for he shall receive of mine, and shall shew it unto you" (John 16:13–14). My friend, when you came to Christ, He gave you everything you will need in this life. Christ is the One who administers all the gifts. The Holy Spirit is the One who gives them, but He is working down here under the supervision of the second Person of the Godhead. The Lord Jesus Christ is the Head of the church. My friend, we have everything in Him. He is the Alpha and the Omega. He is the Amen—and when you say

"amen," you are through, my friend. Christ did it all.

This verse is so clear it is impossible to misunderstand it. "Knowing that a man [any human being—man or woman, black or white, rich or poor, Roman, American, Chinese] is not justified by the works of the law, but by the faith of Jesus Christ." It is not faith plus something; it is faith plus *nothing*.

The verse continues: "even we have believed in Jesus Christ, that we might be justified by the faith of Christ." Who does Paul mean by "we"? He includes himself, meaning we Israelites. He is saying that he and his fellow Jews had to leave the Law, come to Christ, and trust Him in order to be justified by the faith of Christ rather than by the works of law.

The conclusion of this verse is so clear I feel that anybody can understand it: "for by the works of the law shall *no flesh be justified*." Let's not depreciate the work of the Lord Jesus by saying that we didn't get everything from Him. I was a hell-doomed sinner. I trusted Him as my Savior, and I received a perfect salvation from Him.

Now the next verse, I am frank to say, is a little more difficult to understand.

But if, while we seek to be justified by Christ, we ourselves also are found sinners, is therefore Christ the minister of sin? God forbid [Gal. 2:17].

The word *justified* is the Greek *dikaioō*, which means "to declare a person right," or "to make him right." We are declared to be right by our faith in Jesus Christ. It means that a sinner who is guilty before God, who is under condemnation and judgment, is declared to be right with God on the basis of his faith in the redemption which we have in Christ. It is not only forgiveness of sins, which is subtraction; it is the addition of the righteousness of Christ. He is declared righteous. The righteousness I have is not my own righteousness, because *my* righteousness is not acceptable; but I have a perfect righteousness which is Christ.

The sense of this verse seems to be this: Since the Jew had to forsake the Law in order to be justified by Christ and therefore take his place as a sinner, is Christ the One who makes him a sinner? Paul's answer is, "Of course not." The Jew, like the Gentile, was a sinner by nature. He could not be justified by the Law, as he demonstrated. This same thought was given by Peter in his address before the great council at Jerusalem: "Now therefore why tempt ye God, to put a yoke upon the neck of the disciples, which neither our fathers nor we were able to bear? But we believe that through the grace of the Lord Jesus Christ we shall be saved, even as they" (Acts 15:10–11). You see, Peter and Paul were in agreement on the doctrine of justification by faith.

For if I build again the things which I destroyed, I make myself a transgressor [Gal. 2:18].

In other words, Paul is saying, "If I go back under law, I make myself a transgressor."

However, he is free from the Law. How did he become free from the Law?

For I through the law am dead to the law, that I might live unto God [Gal. 2:19].

Paul is saying, "When Christ died, He died for me. He died in my stead because the Law had condemned me." You see, the Law was a ministration of condemnation; a ministration of death is what Paul calls it in 2 Corinthians 3:7. It condemns me. Even under the legal system, God would have had to destroy the nation Israel. But He gave the sacrificial system—five sacrifices—all of them pointing to Christ. God, by His marvelous grace, was able to save. Therefore the mercy seat was a throne of grace where a nation could find forgiveness of sins. The Law, therefore, condemned me. The Law has accused man. We stand guilty before the Law. So the Law actually is responsible for Jesus' dying for us. The Law condemned us—said we had to die. All right now, if I am dead to the Law, then I am no longer responsible to the Law. The Law has already killed me. It has executed me, and I am dead—dead to the Law. Therefore, the Law could not do for me what Christ has done for me. He not only took my place and died for me, but He also did something else. He was able to give me life. He came back from the dead. You see, the Law arrested, condemned, sentenced, and slew us—that is all the Law could do for us. If you want to come by the Law route, you'll get death. Only Christ can give you life. And, after all, life is what we need today.

I am crucified with Christ: nevertheless I live; yet not I, but Christ liveth in me: and the life which I now live in the flesh I live by the faith of the Son of God, who loved me, and gave himself for me [Gal. 2:20].

This verse states a fact which is true of every believer. We are not to *seek* to be crucified with Christ. I have been to many young peo-

ple's conferences, and I do not think I am exaggerating when I say that I have seen thousands of young people accept Christ. I have also heard many of those young people at testimony meetings quote verse 20 as they put a faggot on the fire. They did not know any more about what this verse means than does a goat grazing on a hillside.

There are many people today who talk about wanting to live the "crucified" life. That is not what Paul is talking about in this verse. We are not to seek to be crucified with Christ. We have already been crucified with Him. The principle of living is not by the Law which has slain us because it found us guilty. Now we are to live by faith. Faith in what? Faith in the Son of God. You see, friend, the death of Christ upon the cross was not only penal (that is, paying the penalty for our sins), but it was substitutionary also. He was not only the *sacrifice* for sin; He was the *substitute* for all who believe.

Paul declares, therefore, that under the Law he was tried, found guilty, was condemned, and in the person of his Substitute he was slain. When did that take place? It took place when Christ was crucified. Paul was crucified with Christ. But "nevertheless I live." How do I live? In Christ. He is alive today at God's right hand. We are told that we have been put in Christ. You cannot improve on that. That ought to get rid of the foolish notion that we can crucify ourselves.

When I was a pastor in Los Angeles, a young man came to me after a service and asked, "Dr. McGee, are you living the crucified life?" I think I rather startled the boy when I replied, "No, I am not." Then I asked him, "Are you?" He hesitated for a moment and then said, "Well, I am trying to." Then I told him, "That is not the question you asked me. You wanted to know if I am living the crucified life. I told you no. Now you tell me yes or no about your life. Are you living the crucified life?" Once again he replied, "I am trying to." I said to him, "You are either living it, or you are not living it. The fact of the matter is you cannot live it." "Oh," he said, "why can't I?" So I pointed out to him that there is something interesting to note about crucifixion. You can commit suicide in many different ways. You can hang yourself, shoot yourself, take poison, jump off of a high building, or jump in front of a truck. There are many ways to end your life, but you cannot crucify yourself. When you nail one hand to the cross, who is going to nail your other hand to the cross? You cannot do it yourself. You must understand what Paul is talking about when he says, "I am crucified with Christ." Paul was crucified with Christ when Christ died. Christ died a substitutionary death. He died for Paul. He died for you. He died for me.

In Romans 6 we are told that we have been buried with Christ by baptism, by identification. We have been raised with Him in newness of life, and now we are joined to the living Christ. Paul says that we do not know Him any more after the flesh. He is not the Man of Galilee walking around the Sea of Galilee. I walked about in that area some time ago and did not see Him; He is not there today. He is at God's right hand. He is the glorified Christ.

Paul is saying, "I am crucified with Christ: nevertheless I live." You see, the Law executed us. The Law could not give us life. Who gave us life? "I am crucified with Christ: nevertheless *I live*." How do you live? "Yet not I, but *Christ liveth in me*." My friend, that is the important thing. He died for me down here that I might live in Him up yonder and that He might live in me down here. "And the life," Paul says, "which I now live in the flesh I live by the faith of the Son of God." What kind of life is this? It is a life of faith—saved by faith, live by faith, walk by faith. This is what it means to walk in the Spirit.

"I live by the faith of the Son of God"—how tender this is—"who *loved* me, and gave himself for me." Christ loved me, but He could not *love* me into heaven. He had to *give* Himself for me. The gift of God is eternal life in Christ Jesus. You can only receive a gift by faith. This applies to any gift, for that matter. You have to believe that the giver who holds out the gift to you is sincere. You must believe that he is telling the truth when he holds it out to you and says, "It is yours." You have to reach out in faith and take it before it belongs to you. God offers you the gift of eternal life in Christ Jesus.

The content of this verse leads me to believe that Paul was present at the crucifixion of Christ. Paul was a Pharisee, and they were the ones who led in the Crucifixion. Paul was a leader in the persecution of the church. He was also one who hated the Lord Jesus Christ. He probably was attending school in Jerusalem, in the school of Gamaliel, at the time of the Crucifixion. I cannot believe this zealous young man would stay home on the day Jesus was crucified. The Scriptures tell us that the Pharisees ridiculed Jesus. They told Him to come down from the cross. Then they sat down and watched Him die—you cannot sink any lower than that. I believe Paul was there that day.

Now after Paul came to know the glorified Christ, the One who died down here, the One who rose again and is at God's right hand, Paul could remember that day and say, "While I was there ridiculing Him, shooting out the lip at Him, expressing my hatred for Him, He loved me and He gave Himself for me!" He gave Himself—the supreme sacrifice. Paul called himself the chief of sinners, which was not hyperbole or an oratorical gesture. It was an actual fact; he was the chief of sinners.

My friend, you can tread underfoot the precious blood of Christ by ignoring Him, turning away from Him, or turning against Him as Paul did. But it was for that crowd that Jesus prayed, ". . . Father, forgive them; for they know not what they do . . ." (Luke 23:34). Even if you hate Him, He was loving you and giving Himself for you.

I do not frustrate the grace of God: for if righteousness come by the law, then Christ is dead in vain [Gal. 2:21].

The main thought in this verse is simply that if there had been any other way to save sinners, then God would have used that method. If a law or a religion could have been given that would save sinners, God would have given it. The only way that an infinite God could save you and me was to send His Son to die. He was willing to make the supreme sacrifice.

CHAPTER 3

THEME: *Justification by faith; experience of the Galatians; illustration of Abraham*

EXPERIENCE OF THE GALATIANS

Paul now goes back to the experience of the Galatians. How were they saved? Were they saved by law or were they saved by faith in Jesus Christ? I personally believe in experience. I had a Methodist background as a boy. I went down to a penitent altar underneath a brush arbor in back of an unpainted Methodist church in southern Oklahoma. I was just a little fellow and I knelt there with an open heart. I believe in experience and when we come to chapter 4, we will deal further with the subject of experience.

> **O foolish Galatians, who hath bewitched you, that ye should not obey the truth, before whose eyes Jesus Christ hath been evidently set forth, crucified among you? [Gal. 3:1].**

"O foolish Galatians"—senseless Galatians. The Greek word is *anoetoi* from the root word *nous*, meaning "mind." He is saying, "You're not using your mind—you're not using your *nous*."

"Who hath bewitched you?" Let me translate that in good old Americano: What's gotten into you? "Before whose eyes Jesus Christ hath been evidently set forth"—"set forth" is literally *placarded* or *painted*. I am not sure that Paul actually drew pictures for the Galatians, but I am sure that he painted word pictures for them. I used to show a great many slides when I was a pastor. It is a marvelous way of teaching the Word of God. For example, I would not attempt to teach the tabernacle without using slides. Now that is the way you "set forth" a teaching, and that is the word Paul uses. "Set forth, crucified among you"— it was His death on the cross that made possible your salvation!

> **This only would I learn of you, Received ye the Spirit by the works of the law, or by the hearing of faith? [Gal. 3:2].**

Now we need to be very careful here. The gospel is true irrespective of experience. What experience does is corroborate the gospel. There are many people today who reason from experience to truth. I personally believe that the Word of God reasons from truth to experience. Experience is not to be discounted, but it must be tested by truth.

Everyone has different experiences. I heard one of the founders of a cult tell about her experience. Then I heard another woman tell about her experience—and they are entirely different. Which person am I going to follow? To tell the truth, I am not going to follow either one of them.

One time a man got up in a meeting and read a passage of Scripture. He said, "Because there is a difference of opinion concerning the interpretation of this passage, and we don't want any controversy, let me tell you about my experience." Well, his experience was as far removed from what that Scripture said as anything could possibly be. He was basing truth on his experience. You simply cannot do that. Experience must corroborate the gospel.

"Received ye the Spirit by the works of the law, or by the hearing of faith?" What does Paul mean by the *hearing* of faith? Does he mean the ear, the organ of hearing, or the receiving of the message, or the message itself? I think he means the whole process. You have to hear something before you can be saved, because the gospel is something God has done for you, and you need to know about it.

In this section Paul is raising several questions. He tells these folk to look back on what had happened to them and asks six questions that have to do with their experience.

This is his first question: "Received ye the Spirit by the works of the law, or by the hearing of faith?" Nowhere—not even in the Old Testament—did anyone ever receive the Holy Spirit by the works of the Law. He is received by the hearing of faith. The Galatians never received the Spirit by the Law. The Holy Spirit is evidence of conversion. Scripture tells us, "But ye are not in the flesh, but in the Spirit, if so be that the Spirit of God dwell in you. Now if any man have not the Spirit of Christ, he is none of his" (Rom. 8:9). "In whom ye also trusted, after that ye heard the word of truth, the gospel of your salvation: in whom also after that ye believed, ye were sealed with that holy Spirit of promise" (Eph. 1:13).

Now here is the second question:

> **Are ye so foolish? having begun in the Spirit, are ye now made perfect by the flesh? [Gal. 3:3].**

What Paul is asking is this: "If the Holy Spirit is the One who converted you, brought you to

Christ, and now you are indwelt by the Spirit of God, are you going to turn back to the Law (which was given to control the flesh) and think you are going to live on a high plane?"

Have ye suffered so many things in vain? if it be yet in vain [Gal. 3:4].

Paul asked the Galatians, "Are you going to let all of the things you have suffered come to naught?" He reminded them that they had paid a price for receiving the gospel. Was it all going to be in vain, without a purpose?

Now he raises this question:

He therefore that ministereth to you the Spirit, and worketh miracles among you, doeth he it by the works of the law, or by the hearing of faith? [Gal. 3:5].

Paul refers to the ministry that he has had among them. You will recall that his apostleship was attacked by the Judaizers. They said that he was a Johnny-come-lately apostle—not one of the original Twelve. He was not with Christ during His ministry but came along later. Paul reminded the Galatians that he was the one who had come into their country, preached the Word of God to them, and performed miracles among them. He did not do it by the works of the Law—Paul would be very careful to say that. He preached the Lord Jesus Christ as the One who died for them, was raised again, and in whom they placed their trust. When they did that, a miraculous thing took place. They were regenerated. Paul had the evidence that he was an apostle. In that day signs were given to the apostles. As I understand it, the apostles had practically all the gifts mentioned in Scripture; they certainly had all the *sign* gifts. Paul could perform miracles. He could heal the sick. He could raise the dead. Simon Peter, one of the original Twelve, could do that also. To do this was the mark of an apostle in that day.

Now the apostles have given us the Word of God. We have a faith that is built upon Jesus Christ as the chief cornerstone, and a faith built upon the foundation which was laid by the apostles and prophets. That which gave credence to the truth of their message was their ability to perform miracles. They had the sign gifts. (After they had given us the Word of God, the sign gifts disappeared. In fact, I think they disappeared with the apostles.) The important thing for us to note here is that Paul came to the Galatians not as a Pharisee preaching the Law, but as an apostle preaching Jesus Christ. That was something these

people had experienced, and Paul rested upon that.

In summary, we have seen that justification by faith was the experience of the Galatians. That is why he asked them, "What has gotten into you?" He mentions the Holy Spirit three times in this section. He reminds them that they did not receive the Spirit by the Law. The Holy Spirit is evidence of conversion. It is important to see that the gospel is true irrespective of the experience of the Galatians or anyone else. The gospel is objective; it deals with what the Lord Jesus Christ did for us. Experience will corroborate the gospel, and that is what Paul is demonstrating in this section. The gospel is sufficient—experience confirms this.

ILLUSTRATION OF ABRAHAM

This section of justification by faith using Abraham as an illustration looms large in this epistle. Then follows an allegory of Hagar and Sarai, which takes us through the rest of chapter 4. So now we come to the heart of this book, the high water mark, where Abraham will be the illustration.

Even as Abraham believed God, and it was accounted to him for righteousness [Gal. 3:6].

This verse is a quote from Genesis 15:6 concerning Abraham, "And he believed in the LORD; and he counted it to him for righteousness." This verse is also quoted in Romans 4:3. The illustration comes from the early part of the life of Abraham, his life of faith. Abraham is the great illustration of justification by faith. Paul uses him as an example in both the Roman and Galatian epistles. It cannot be said that Abraham was justified by the Law because the Mosaic Law was not given until four hundred years after Abraham. Neither can it be said that he was justified by circumcision because he was justified *before* God gave him the commandment of circumcision. Circumcision was the badge and evidence of Abraham's faith, just as baptism is the badge and evidence of a believer's faith today. Neither circumcision nor baptism can save. In fact, they make no contribution to salvation. They are simply outward evidences of an inward work.

The incident referred to is in Genesis 15. After Abraham encountered the kings of the East in his rescue of his nephew Lot, he refused to accept any booty from the kings of Sodom and Gomorrah. God appeared to Abraham to assure him that he had done right in turning down the booty, saying, "I am your shield, and your exceeding great reward." Abraham was a practical sort of individual, and he began talking to the Lord rather straight—and I feel that the Lord wants us to do that, friend. He said, "I don't have a son, and You told me I would." The Lord said, "I'm glad you brought that up, Abraham, I've been wanting to tell you something." God had already told him that his seed would be as numberless as the sand on the seashore. Now God takes him by the hand and tells him to look toward the heavens. It must have been night time. I am told that in that section of the world one can see about five thousand stars with the naked eye. With a sixteen inch telescope you would see fifty thousand stars, and I don't know what you would see with a hundred inch or two hundred inch telescope. Be that as it may, I don't think any telescope could give you the exact number of stars which could be seen at that time. In effect, God said to Abraham, "You can't count the stars, and neither can you count your offspring." Do you know what Abraham's response was? "And he believed in the LORD; and he counted it to him for righteousness" (Gen. 15:6). In the original it is very expressive. Literally it means that Abraham said "amen" to the Lord. God said, "I'm going to do it." And Abraham said, "Amen."

Does this have an application for your life and mine? It certainly does. God says to you and me, "I gave My Son to die for you. If you believe on Him you won't perish. You will have everlasting life." Will you say "amen" to that? Will you believe God? Will you accept His Son? If you do, you are justified by faith. This is what Abraham did. He believed God, and at that moment God declared him righteous. Because of his works? No! His works were imperfect. He didn't have perfection to offer to God. (Paul will develop this thought a little later on.) Although Abraham did not have perfection at that time, afterwards he did because his faith was counted for righteousness. That is the doctrine of justification. Abraham stands justified before God.

Next Abraham said to the Lord, "Would you mind putting what you have told me in writing?" Perhaps you are saying, "I have read the Book of Genesis, and I don't remember anything like that." Well, it's here in Genesis 15. Now notice: "And he said unto him, I am the LORD that brought thee out of Ur of the Chaldees, to give thee this land to inherit it" (Gen. 15:7). Listen to Abraham's response. He is talking back to the Lord—he's not one of these superpious saints. "And he said, Lord GOD, whereby shall I know that I shall inherit it?" (Gen. 15:8). In other words, put it in writing. God said to Abraham, "Meet me down at the courthouse and I will put it in writing." Now somebody says, "Wait a minute. It doesn't say that." But it does, friend. "And he said unto him, Take me an heifer of three years old, and a she goat of three years old, and a ram of three years old, and a turtledove, and a young pigeon" (Gen. 15:9). That is the way they made contracts in that day. (Jeremiah also tells about making a contract in this way in Jeremiah 34:18.) You see, when a contract was made in that day, one man agreed to do something, and the other man agreed to do something in turn. They cut a sacrifice into two parts and put half on one side and half on the other side, then they would join hands and walk between the two halves. That sealed the contract. It was the same as going before a notary at the courthouse.

So Abraham prepared the sacrifices and waited—he waited all day. Fowls came down upon the carcasses and Abraham drove them away. God was late meeting Abraham; He did not get there until sundown. "And when the sun was going down, a deep sleep fell upon Abram; and, lo, an horror of great darkness fell upon him" (Gen. 15:12). Just as he is about to sign the contract, God puts Abraham into a deep sleep. The reason for this is that Abraham is not to walk with God through the two halves—Abraham is not to promise anything. God is doing the promising. "And it came to pass, that, when the sun went down, and it was dark, behold a smoking furnace, and a burning lamp that passed between those pieces" (Gen. 15:17). You see, God passed through between those two halves alone because God made the covenant. And Abraham's part was only to believe God. If the covenant depended on Abraham's faithfulness—perhaps on his saying his prayers every night—he might miss one night, and then the promise would be no good. So God was the One who did all the promising, and the covenant depended on God's faithfulness.

Friend, over nineteen hundred years ago Jesus Christ went to the cross to pay for your sins and mine. God is not asking you to say your prayers or be a nice little Sunday school boy to be saved. He is asking you to trust His Son who died for you. *He* makes the contract. He is the One who makes the promise, the covenant, and He will save you. That is the new contract, friend. The old covenant He made with Abraham. Abraham believed God. He said, "amen," to God. Abraham believed, and it was accounted to him for righteousness.

God is still asking us to believe Him. Put your trust in Christ and you will be saved. What a glorious picture we have here.

Know ye therefore that they which are of faith, the same are the children of Abraham [Gal. 3:7].

God did this for Abraham before the Law was ever given. God did not make the covenant with him because of Abraham's good works. He told Abraham, "I'll do this for you if you believe Me." Abraham said, "I believe You."

God wants your faith to rest on a solid foundation. But, my friend, if you come to God, you must come to Him by faith. He has come to the door of your heart. He cannot come any farther. He will not break down the door. He will knock and say, "Behold, I stand at the door, and knock: if any man hear my voice, and open the door, I will come in to him, and will sup with him, and he with me" (Rev. 3:20). Only you can open the door by faith, my friend. When you and I trust Christ as Savior, we are saved the same way that Abraham was saved—by faith.

And the scripture, foreseeing that God would justify the heathen through faith, preached before the gospel unto Abraham, saying, In thee shall all nations be blessed [Gal. 3:8].

"And the scripture, foreseeing that God would justify the heathen through faith, preached before the gospel unto Abraham." If faith without works was sufficient for Abraham, why should we desire something different? And as the blessing was not for Abraham's law-works, but for his faith, why should we turn from faith to law-works?

"God . . . preached . . . the gospel unto Abraham." When did He do that? Well, the first illustration Paul gave us was at the beginning of Abraham's life of faith. Now Paul refers to an incident near the end of Abraham's life of faith recorded in Genesis 22. It was after Abraham had offered Isaac upon the altar. I say he offered him because he was just within a hair's breadth of offering him when God stopped him. God considered that Abraham had actually done it. He demonstrated that he had faith in God, believing that God could raise Isaac from the dead (see Heb. 11:19). Now notice God's response to Abraham's act of faith: "And the angel of the LORD called unto Abraham out of heaven the second time, And said, By myself have I sworn, saith the LORD, for because thou hast done this thing, and hast not withheld thy son, thine only son: That in

blessing I will bless thee, and in multiplying I will multiply thy seed as the stars of the heaven, and as the sand which is upon the sea shore; and thy seed shall possess the gate of his enemies; And in thy seed shall all the nations of the earth be blessed; because thou hast obeyed my voice" (Gen. 22:15–18). Apparently at this time God preached the gospel to Abraham, because the offering of Isaac is one of the finest pictures of the offering of Christ. Although God spared Abraham's son, God did not spare His own Son but delivered Him up for us all.

The important thing that Paul wants us to see in Abraham's life is that he obeyed the voice of God. Abraham was willing to offer his son when God commanded it, and when God said stop, he stopped. He obeyed the voice of God. He demonstrated by his action that he had faith in God. Again he believed God and He counted it to him for righteousness.

Some people are troubled because they feel that there is a contradiction in Scripture between what Paul says about Abraham and what James says about him. Paul says that Abraham was justified by faith. James says, "But wilt thou know, O vain man, that faith without works is dead? Was not Abraham our father justifed by works, when he had offered Isaac his son upon the altar?" (James 2:20–21). However, James goes on to say, "Seest thou how faith wrought with his works, and by works was faith made perfect?" (James 2:22). John Calvin said it like this: "Faith alone saves, but the faith that saves is not alone." In other words, saving faith is a dynamic, vital faith that leads to works. I hope you understand that James is not talking about the works of law. James is talking about the works of faith. Faith produces works. This idea of saying that works will save you is putting the cart before the horse—in fact, some men put the horse *in* the cart!

It is important to see that faith leads to works, as it did in the life of Abraham. God sees our hearts. He knows whether or not we have trusted Christ as Savior. He knows whether or not we are genuine. Church member, why not be genuine? You can fool the people in the church, and you can fool your neighbors, and you can put up a pious front. But why not be *real* and have a lot of fun at the same time? You don't have to pretend. You can be real and trust Christ as your Savior. And a living, dynamic faith will produce works.

A careful reading of the passage in James 2 reveals that James used the history of Abraham to show that faith without works is dead—it is the last of Abraham's history because this is the last time God appeared to him. It is not that portion of Scripture to which Paul refers in Galatians where he says that Abraham was justified by faith. Paul says that faith alone is sufficient and proves his point from Abraham's history as recorded in the fifteenth chapter of Genesis. James says that faith without works is dead and *proves* it by referring to Abraham's history as found in the twenty-second chapter of Genesis. If Abraham had welshed in Genesis 22 and had said to God, "Wait a minute, I really do not believe what You say. I have been putting on an act all of these years," then it would have been obvious that Abraham's faith was a pseudofaith. But God knew back in Genesis 15 that Abraham had a genuine faith.

The works that James speaks about are not works of law at all. The Law had not been given during Abraham's day. We need to recognize that. James 2:23 says, "And the scripture was fulfilled which saith, Abraham believed God, and it was imputed unto him for righteousness: and he was called the Friend of God." James, at the beginning of this verse, is going back to the reference that Paul gives at first concerning the beginning of Abraham's life of faith. Then Paul says that the gospel was preached to Abraham at the end of his life when God made this promise to him.

There is no contradiction when you examine passages like the ones written by Paul and James. They are saying the same thing. One is looking at faith at the beginning. The other is looking at faith at the end. One is looking at the *root* of faith. The other is looking at the *fruit* of faith. The root of faith is "faith alone saves you," but that saving faith will produce works.

So then they which be of faith are blessed with faithful Abraham [Gal. 3:9].

The word *faithful* in this verse is "believing"—believing Abraham. God saves the sinner today on the same basis that He saved Abraham. God asks *faith* of the sinner. God asked Abraham to believe that He would do certain things for him. God asks you and me to believe that He already has done certain things for us in giving His Son, Jesus Christ, to die for us. Faith is the modus operandi by which man is saved today.

For as many as are of the works of the law are under the curse: for it is written, Cursed is every one that continueth not in all things which are written in the book of the law to do them [Gal. 3:10].

The important word here is "continueth." I am willing to grant that maybe there was a day in your life when you felt very good, when you were on top of the world and singing, "Everything's coming up daisies." On that day you walked with the Lord and did not stub your toe. Then you say, "Well, because I did that, God saved me." But notice what this verse says, "Cursed is every one that *continueth* not in all things which are written in the book of the law." How about that? Do you keep the law day and night, twenty-four hours every day, seven days a week, fifty-two weeks out of the year in thought, word, and deed? If you are a human being, somewhere along the line you let down. You are not walking on top of the world all of the time. My friend, when you let down, the law can only condemn you.

I know a fine preacher who is always going around saying, "Hallelujah, praise the Lord." Someone asked his wife if he was like that all the time. She said, "No, he has his bad days." We all have bad days, don't we?

If you are going to put yourself under the law, my friend, and you have a good day, you are not going to be rewarded for it. Suppose I had kept all of the laws of Pasadena, which is my home city, for twenty years. Then I wait at my house for the officials of Pasadena to come and present me with a medal for keeping those laws. Let me tell you, they do not give medals for keeping the law in Pasadena. If I had kept every law for twenty years and then stole something or broke a speeding law, I would be arrested. You see, the law does not reward you. It does not give you life. The law penalizes you.

Faith, my friend, *gives* you something. It gives you life.

But that no man is justified by the law in the sight of God, it is evident: for, The just shall live by faith [Gal. 3:11].

Even the Old Testament taught that man was saved by faith. It does not say that anyone was saved by keeping the law. If you find that somebody living back under the law was saved by keeping the law, let me know. I have never read of anyone who was saved by keeping the Mosaic Law. As you know, the heart of the Mosaic system was the sacrificial system. Moses rejoiced that God could extend mercy and grace to people even under the law—that is the reason his face shone as it did. In

Habakkuk 2:4 it says that ". . . the just shall live by his faith."

And the law is not of faith: but, The man that doeth them shall live in them [Gal. 3:12].

This also is an important verse. Faith and law are contrary principles for salvation and also for living. One cancels out the other. They are diametrically opposed to each other. If you are going to live by the Law, then you cannot be saved by faith. You cannot combine them. They are contrary.

Let me illustrate this. Our daughter came to visit us while we were in Florida, and we wanted to return to California by train. That was the time when passenger trains were being phased out. We tried to get a train route to California without going through Chicago—both of us wanted to avoid Chicago. Well, it seemed as though we would have to go half-way around the world to go from Florida to California; so we had to come back by plane. When we got the tickets, I said, "Wouldn't it be nice if we could go by train and plane at the same time—sit in the plane and put our feet down in the train!" (I would feel much safer with my feet in the train, I assure you.) But that's absurd. If we go by plane, we go by plane; if we go by train, we go by train. They have made no arrangements for passengers to sit in a plane and put their feet down in a train. My friend, neither has God any arrangement for you to be saved by faith and by law. You have to choose one or the other. If you want to go by law, then you can try it—but I'll warn you that God has already said you won't make it. "The law is not of faith: but, The man that doeth them shall live in them."

Christ hath redeemed us from the curse of the law, being made a curse for us: for it is written, Cursed is every one that hangeth on a tree [Gal. 3:13].

"Christ hath redeemed us from the curse of the law"—the Mosaic Law *condemned* us. It is like the illustration I gave regarding keeping the civil laws in my hometown. I am not rewarded for keeping those laws, and if I break one I am condemned. Christ has redeemed us from the penalty of the Mosaic Law. How did He do it? By "being made a curse for us." Christ bore that penalty.

"For it is written, Cursed is every one that hangeth on a tree." This is a quotation from the Old Testament, as we shall see, and is a remarkable passage of Scripture for several reasons. One reason is that the children of

Israel did not use hanging on a tree as a method of public execution. Instead they used stoning. When my wife went with me to the land of Israel, she noticed something that I had not thought of. She said, "I have often wondered why they used stoning as a means of execution. Now I know. Anywhere you turn in this land there are plenty of stones." Capital punishment in Israel was by stoning, not hanging. However, when a reprehensible crime had been committed, this was the procedure: "And if a man have committed a sin worthy of death, and he be to be put to death, and thou hang him on a tree: His body shall not remain all night upon the tree, but thou shalt in any wise bury him that day; (for he that is hanged is accursed of God;) that thy land be not defiled, which the LORD thy God giveth thee for an inheritance" (Deut. 21:22 –23). That is, if he had committed an awful crime and had been stoned to death, his body could be strung up on a tree that it might be a spectacle. But it was not to be left there overnight. The reason He gives is this: he is accursed of God—"that thy land be not defiled, which the LORD thy God giveth thee for an inheritance."

Christ was "made a curse for us." The question is: When did Christ become a curse? Did He become a curse in His incarnation? Oh, no. When He was born He was called ". . . that holy thing . . ." (Luke 1:35). Did He become a curse during those silent years of which we have so little record? No, it says that He advanced ". . . in favour with God and man" (Luke 2:52). Did He become a curse during his ministry? Oh, no. It was during His ministry that the Father said, ". . . This is my beloved Son, in whom I am well pleased" (Matt. 3:17). Then He must have become a curse while He was on the cross. Yes, but not during the first three hours on the cross, because when He offered up Himself, He was without blemish. It was during those last three hours on the cross that He was made a curse for us. It was then that it pleased the Lord to bruise Him and put Him to grief. He made His soul an offering for sin (see Isa. 53:10).

"Cursed is everyone that hangeth on a tree." The Greek word for "tree" is *xulon*, meaning "wood, timber, or tree." Christ was hanged on a tree. What a contrast we have here. He went to that cross, which was to Him a tree of death, in order that He might make it for you and me a tree of life!

That the blessing of Abraham might come on the Gentiles through Jesus

Christ; **that we might receive the promise of the Spirit through faith** [Gal. 3:14].

Israel had the Law for fifteen hundred years and failed to live by it. At the council of Jerusalem, in Acts 15, Peter said in effect, "We and our fathers were not able to keep the law. Why do we want to put the Gentiles under it? If we could not keep it, they won't be able to keep it either." Christ took our place that we might receive what the Law could never do. The Spirit is the peculiar gift in this age of grace.

Brethren, I speak after the manner of men; Though it be but a man's covenant, yet if it be confirmed, no man disannulleth, or addeth thereto [Gal. 3:15].

Suppose you make a contract with a man to pay him one hundred dollars. Then about a year later you decide you will pay him only fifty dollars. You go to him and say, "Here is the fifty dollars I owe you." The man says, "Wait a minute, you agreed to pay me one hundred dollars." You say, "Well, I've changed that." He says, "Oh, no, you don't! You can't change your contract after it has been made."

Now to Abraham and his seed were the promises made. He saith not, And to seeds, as of many; but as of one, And to thy seed, which is Christ [Gal. 3:16].

God called Abraham and promised to make him a blessing to the world. He made him a blessing to the world through Jesus Christ, a descendant of Abraham. Christ is the One who brought salvation to the world.

The word *seed* refers specifically to Christ (see Gen. 22:18). Christ said, "Your father Abraham rejoiced to see my day: and he saw it, and was glad" (John 8:56).

And this I say, that the covenant, that was confirmed before of God in Christ, the law, which was four hundred and thirty years after, cannot disannul, that it should make the promise of none effect [Gal. 3:17].

God made a promise, a covenant, with Abraham. When the Law came along "four hundred and thirty years" later, it didn't change anything as far as the promises made to Abraham were concerned. Actually, God never goes back on His promises. God promised Abraham, "I am going to give you this land. I am going to give you a son and a people that will be as numberless as the sand on the seashore." God fulfilled that promise and brought from Abraham the nation of Israel—and several other nations—but the promises were given through Isaac whose line led to the Lord Jesus Christ, the "Seed" of verse 16. God also promised Abraham that He would make him a blessing to all people. The only blessing, my friend, in this world today is in Christ. You may not get a very good deal from your neighbor or from your business or from your church. I don't think the world is prepared to give you a good deal. But the Lord Jesus Christ has been given to you—that is a good deal! In fact it is the supreme gift which God has made. It is a fulfillment of God's promise that He would save those who would trust Christ.

For if the inheritance be of the law, it is no more of promise: but God gave it to Abraham by promise [Gal. 3:18].

The promise concerning Christ was made before the Mosaic Law was given, and that promise holds as good as though there had been no law given, my friend. The promise was made irrespective of the Law.

The question arises: Why was the Law given, of what value is it? Now don't think that Paul is playing down the Law. Rather, he is trying to help the people understand the *purpose* of the Law. He shows the Law in all of its majesty, in its fullness, and in its perfection. But he shows that this very perfection the Law reveals is the reason it creates a hurdle which you and I cannot get over in order to be accepted of God.

Now listen to Paul as he talks about the purpose of the Law.

Wherefore then serveth the law? It was added because of transgressions, till the seed should come to whom the promise was made; and it was ordained by angels in the hand of a mediator [Gal. 3:19].

The question is: Wherefore then serveth the Law? He is giving a purpose sentence—what was the purpose of the Law? Paul says it was something that was added. It was added because—or better still—for the sake of transgressions.

"Till the seed should come"—that little word *till* is an important time word. It means the Law was temporary. The Law was given for the interval between the time of Moses until the time of Christ. "For the law was given by Moses, but grace and truth came by Jesus Christ" (John 1:17). It is very important to see that the Law was temporary "until the seed should come"—and that Seed is Christ.

The Law was added "because of [for the sake of] transgressions. It was given to *reveal* not *remove* sin. It was not given to keep man from sin because sin had already come. It was to show man himself as being a natural, ugly, crude sinner before God. Any man who is honest will look at himself in the light of the Law and see himself guilty. It was not given to prove that all men were sinners, nor was it given (as many liberals are saying today) as a standard by which man becomes holy. Oh, my friend, you would never become holy this way, because, first of all, you can't keep the Law in your own strength.

Many folk think that man becomes a sinner when he commits a sinful act, that he is all right until he breaks over and commits sin. This is not true. It is because he is already a sinner that a man commits an act of sin. A man steals because he is a thief. A man lies because he is a liar. I find myself guilty of lying— although I blame it on other folk. I leave my house in the morning and the first person I meet says, "My, what a beautiful day!" And I say, "Yes, it is"—when truthfully it is a smoggy day here in pleasant California. I lie about it. Then he asks, "How are you feeling today?" Well, to be honest, I don't feel well, but I say, "Oh, I'm feeling fine." Right there in the first few minutes I have lied twice! It's just natural for us to be that way, my friend. Some of us commit more serious lying than that. Why do we do it? We have that fallen nature. And the Law was given to show that we are sinners, and that you and I need a mediator— One to stand between us and God, One to help us out.

Is the law then against the promises of God? God forbid: for if there had been a law given which could have given life, verily righteousness should have been by the law [Gal. 3:21].

"Is the law then against the promises of God?" The expression "God forbid" means certainly not. Why? If there had been another way of saving sinners, God would have used that way. If He could have given a law by which sinners could be saved, He would have done so.

But the scripture hath concluded all under sin, that the promise by faith of Jesus Christ might be given to them that believe [Gal. 3:22].

We have seen that the Law brought death— "The soul that sinneth, it shall die . . ." (Ezek. 18:20). The Scripture has "concluded all under sin;" therefore all died. What is needed, therefore, is life. We have seen that the Law brings death, which is all that it can do. It is not actually the degree of sin but the mere fact of sin that brings death. Hence, all are equally dead and equally in need. You may not have committed as great a sin as Stalin committed, but you and I have the same kind of nature that he had. In fact, it was Goethe, the great German writer, who made this statement: "I have never seen a crime committed but what I too might have committed that crime." He recognized he had that kind of a nature. It is not the degree of sin, but the very *fact* that we are sinners that brings death.

Let me illustrate this fact of sin and not the degree. Picture a building about twenty-four stories high. There are three men on top of the building, and the superintendent goes up to see them and warns, "Now be very careful, don't step off of this building or you will be killed. It will mean death for you." One of the fellows says, "This crazy superintendent is always trying to frighten people. I don't believe that if I step off this building I will die." So he deliberately walks to the edge of the building and steps off into the air. Suppose that when he passes the tenth floor, somebody looks out the window and asked him, "Well, how is it going?" And he says, "So far, so good." But, my friend, he hasn't arrived yet. There is death at the bottom. The superintendent was right. The man is killed. Now suppose another fellow becomes frightened at what the superintendent said. He runs for the elevator, or the steps, and accidentally slips. He skids right off the edge of the building and falls to the street below. He, too, is killed. The third fellow, we'll say, is thrown off the building by some gangsters because he is their enemy. He is killed. Now the man who was thrown off of the building is just as dead as the man who deliberately stepped off and the man who accidentally slipped off the building. All of these men broke the law of gravitation, and death was inevitable for all of them. It is the fact, you see, and not the degree. It is the fact that they went over the edge—they all broke the law of gravitation.

The question is, "Can the law of gravitation which took them down to death give them life?" It cannot. The Mosaic Law cannot give you life any more than a natural law can give you life after you have broken it and died. You cannot reverse the situation and come back from the street below to the top of the building and live, as it is done in running a movie in reverse. Death follows wherever sin comes.

The law of sin knows nothing of extenuating circumstances. It knows nothing about mercy. It has no elasticity. It is inflexible, inexorable, and immutable. God's Word says, "The soul that sinneth, it shall die . . ." (Ezek. 18:20). To Adam and Eve in the Garden of Eden God said, "But of the tree of the knowledge of good and evil, thou shalt not eat of it: for in the day that thou eatest thereof thou shalt surely die" (Gen. 2:17). And in Exodus 34:7, He says that He ". . . will by no means clear the guilty. . . ." Therefore, all have sinned and by the Law we are all dead. The Law slew us. It is called by Paul a ". . . ministration of death . . ." (2 Cor. 3:7). It is a ministration of condemnation. The Law condemns all of us.

Can the Law bring life? My friend, the Law can no more bring life than a fall from a high roof can bring life to one who died by that fall. The purpose of the Law was never to give life. It was given to show us that we are guilty sinners before God.

"The scripture hath concluded all under sin, that the promise by faith of Jesus Christ might be given to them that believe" is a tremendous statement.

But before faith came, we were kept under the law, shut up unto the faith which should afterwards be revealed [Gal. 3:23].

"Before faith came" means, of course, faith in Jesus Christ who died for us.

Until the Lord Jesus Christ came, the Law had in it *mercy* because it had a mercy seat. It had an altar where sacrifices for sin could be brought and forgiveness could be obtained. Mercy could be found there. All the sacrifices for sin pointed to Christ. Before faith came, Paul says, we were kept under the Law—"shut up unto the faith which should afterwards be revealed."

Wherefore the law was our schoolmaster to bring us unto Christ, that we might be justified by faith [Gal. 3:24].

This is a remarkable section. Paul is making it very clear here that the Mosaic Law could not save. Romans 4:5 tells us, "But to him that worketh not, but believeth on him that justifieth the ungodly, his faith is counted for righteousness." God refuses to accept the works of man for salvation. God says that all of our righteousnesses are as filthy rags (Isa. 64:6). God refuses to accept law-keeping. The Law cannot save; it can only condemn. It was not given to save sinners but to let them know that they were sinners. The Law does not remove sin; it reveals sin. It will not keep you from sin, because sin has already come. The Law shows that man is not the way Hollywood portrays him—a sophisticated, refined, trained sinner. Man is actually an ugly sinner in the raw.

I want to use a homely illustration that I think might be helpful. I am going to take you to the bathroom. I hope you are not shocked—television does it everyday, showing someone taking a bath or a shower. I am confident that almost everyone has a bathroom, and in that bathroom is a washbasin with a mirror above it. That washbasin serves a purpose and so does the mirror. When you get dirt on your face, you go to the bathroom to remove it. Now you don't use the mirror to remove the dirt, do you? If you see a smudged spot on your face, and you lean over and rub your face against the mirror, and one of your loved ones sees you, he will call a psychiatrist and make an appointment to find out what is wrong with you. But, my friend, that won't happen because none of us is silly enough to try to remove dirt with a mirror.

Today, however, multitudes of people in our churches are rubbing up against the mirror of the law thinking they are going to remove their sin. The Word of God is a mirror which shows us who we are and what we are—that we are sinners and that we have come short of the glory of God. That is what the Law reveals. But, thank God, beneath the mirror there is a basin. As the hymn writer puts it,

There is a fountain filled with blood
Drawn from Immanuel's veins;
And sinners plunged beneath that flood,
Lose all their guilty stains.
—William Cowper

That is where you remove the spot. It is the blood of the Lord Jesus Christ that cleanses. The Law proves man a sinner; it never makes him a saint. The Law was given, as Paul says in Romans, that every mouth might be stopped and the whole world become guilty before God (see Rom. 3:19).

"Wherefore the law was our schoolmaster," Paul says. Now he will go on to tell us what he means by this.

But after that faith is come, we are no longer under a schoolmaster [Gal. 3:25].

"Schoolmaster" is the Greek *paidagōgos*, and it doesn't mean school teacher. *Schoolmaster* is a good word, but it meant something quite different back in the days of Paul. It meant a servant or a slave who was part of a Roman household. Half of the Roman Empire was slave. Of the 120 million, 60 million were slaves. In the home of a patrician, a member of the Praetorian Guard, or the rich in the Roman Empire, were slaves that cared for the children. When a child was born into such a home, he was put in the custody of a servant or a slave who actually raised him. He put clean clothes on him, bathed him, blew his nose when it was necessary, and paddled him when he needed it. When the little one grew to a certain age and was to start to school, this servant was the one who got him up in the morning, dressed him, and took him to school. (That is where he got the name of *paidagōgos*. *Paid* has to do with the feet—and we get our word *pedal* from it; *agogos* means "to lead.") It means that he takes the little one by the hand, leads him to school, and turns him over to the school teacher. This servant, the slave, was not capable of teaching him beyond a certain age, so he took him to school.

Now what Paul is saying here is that the Law is our *paidagōgos*. The Law said, "Little fellow, I can't do any more for you. I now want to take you by the hand and bring you to the cross of Christ. You are lost. You need a Savior." The purpose of the Law is to bring men to Christ—not to give them an expanded chest so they can walk around claiming they keep the Law. You *know* you don't keep the Law; all you have to do is examine your own heart to know that.

For ye are all the children of God by faith in Christ Jesus [Gal. 3:26].

Paul is going to show in the remainder of this chapter, and in the first part of chapter 4, some of the benefits that come to us by trusting Christ that we could never receive under law. The Law never could give a believer the *nature* of a son of God. Christ can do that. Only faith in Christ can make us sons of God.

In this verse the word *children* is from the Greek *huios*, meaning "sons." Only faith in Christ can make us legitimate sons of God. I use the word *legitimate* for emphasis, because the only sons God has are legitimate sons. You are made a true son of God by faith in Christ, and that is *all* it takes. Not faith plus something equals salvation, but faith plus nothing makes you a son of God. Nothing else can make you a son of God. "For ye are all sons of God." How? "By faith in Christ Jesus."

An individual Israelite under the Law in the Old Testament was never a son, only a servant. God called the nation "Israel my son" (see Exod. 4:22), but the individual in that corporate nation was never called a son. He was called a servant of Jehovah. For example, Moses was on very intimate terms with God; yet God said of him, "Moses my servant is dead" (see Josh. 1:2). That was his epitaph. Also, although David was a man after God's own heart, God calls him "David my servant" (see 1 Kings 11:38).

My friend, even if you kept the Law, which you could not do, your righteousness would still be inferior to the righteousness of God. Sonship requires *His* righteousness, you see. The New Testament definitely tells us, "But as many as received him, to them gave he power to become the sons of God, even to them that believe on his name" (John 1:12). We are given the power (Greek *exousian*, meaning "the authority, the right") to become the sons of God by doing no more nor less than simply trusting Him. A Pharisee by the name of Nicodemus, religious to his fingertips (he had a God-given religion although it had gone to seed), followed the Law meticulously, yet he was not a son of God. Jesus said to him, "Ye must be born again" (John 3:7). I want to be dogmatic and very plain—neither your prayers, your fundamental separation, your gifts, nor your baptism will ever make you a son of God. Only faith in Christ can make you a son of God.

The most damnable heresy today is the "universal Fatherhood of God and the universal brotherhood of man." It is this teaching of liberalism that has caused this nation to give away billions of dollars throughout the world, and because of it we are hated everywhere. All people are the children of God, they say, and so we have sat at council tables and have engaged in diplomatic squabbles with some of the biggest rascals the world has ever seen. We talk about being honest and honorable, that we are all the children of God, and we must act like sons of God. Well, the Lord Jesus Christ never said anything like that. He once looked at a group of religious rulers and said to them, "Ye are of your father the devil, and the lusts of your father ye will do . . ." (John 8:44). Now *I* did not say that; gentle Jesus said that. Evidently there were some people in His day who were not sons of God. My friend, I think the Devil still has a lot of children running around in this world today. They are not all the sons of God! The only way you can become a son of God is through faith in Jesus Christ.

For as many of you as have been baptized into Christ have put on Christ [Gal. 3:27].

I hope you realize that this verse is not a reference to water baptism. Water baptism is ritual baptism, and I feel that it is for every believer. Also I believe that the mode of water baptism should be by immersion (in spite of the fact that I am an ordained Presbyterian preacher), because immersion more clearly pictures real baptism, which is the baptism of the Holy Spirit. The baptism of the Holy Spirit places you in the body of believers. Paul says, "For by one Spirit are we all baptized into one body, whether we be Jews or Gentiles, whether we be bond or free; and have been all made to drink into one Spirit" (1 Cor. 12:13). This means that we are identified, we are put in reality and truth into the body of believers, the church. "For as many of you as have been baptized into Christ have put on Christ." God sees you in Christ. Therefore He sees you as perfect!

There is neither Jew nor Greek, there is neither bond nor free, there is neither male nor female: for ye are all one in Christ Jesus [Gal. 3:28].

In this body of believers "there is neither Jew nor Greek." In Christ are no racial lines. Any man in Christ is my brother, and I don't care about the color of his skin. It is the color of his heart that interests me. There are a lot of white people walking around with black hearts, my friend, and they are not my brothers. It is only in Christ Jesus that we are made

one. Thank God, I receive letters from folk of every race. They call me brother and I call them brother—because we *are* brothers. We are one in Christ, and we will be together throughout eternity.

"There is neither bond nor free." In our day, capital and labor are at odds with one another. The only thing that could bring them together is Christ, of course.

"There is neither male nor female." Christ does what "women's lib" can never do. He can make us one in Christ. How wonderful it is!

And if ye be Christ's, then are ye Abraham's seed, and heirs according to the promise [Gal. 3:29].

How can we be Abraham's descendants? Because of the fact that Abraham was saved by *faith*, and we are saved by *faith*. Abraham brought a little animal to sacrifice, which looked forward to the coming of the Son of God, the supreme sacrifice. In my day, Christ has already come, and I can look back in history and say, "Nineteen hundred years ago the Son of God came and died on the cross for me that I might have life, and I trust Him." Some time ago I had the privilege of speaking to a group of wonderful Jewish folk, and I started by saying, "Well, it is always a privilege for me to speak to the sons of Abraham." And they all smiled. Then I added, "Because I am a son of Abraham, too." They didn't all smile at that. In fact, some of them had a question mark on their faces, and rightly so. If I am in Christ and you are in Christ, then we belong to Abraham's seed, and we are heirs according to the promise. How wonderful this is!

CHAPTER 4

THEME: *Justification by faith; allegory of Hagar and Sarai*

Chapter 4 continues the section of justification by faith. Here we see that there is something else that comes through faith in Christ that we could never get by the works of the Law: it gives us the *position* of sons of God. It brings us to the place of full-grown sons. When we start out in the Christian life, we are babes and we are to grow to maturation. However, God gives us the position of a full-grown son to furnish us with a *capacity* that we would not otherwise have.

Now I say, That the heir, as long as he is a child, differeth nothing from a servant, though he be lord of all [Gal. 4:1].

The word *child* in this verse is not the same as *child* in Galatians 3:26 where it is from the Greek word *huios*, meaning "son." Here it is *nepios*, meaning a little child without full power of speech. "The heir, as long as he is a child (a little one in the family), differeth nothing from a servant."

Again we will have to go back to the Roman customs to see Paul's illustration in action. In a Roman home servants had charge of different possessions of the master. Some had charge of the chattels, others of the livestock, others kept books for him, and others had charge of his children. When a little one was born into the home, the servants cared for him and dressed him in playclothes so that he didn't look any different from the children of the servants with whom he was playing. And he had to obey the servants just like the other children did.

But is under tutors and governors until the time appointed of the father [Gal. 4:2].

"Until the time appointed of the father." What time was that? It was the time when the father recognized that his son was capable of making decisions of his own, and he brought him into the position of a full-grown son. Notice that it is the father who determined when his son reached the age of maturity. It wasn't an arbitrary law as we have in our society. It used to be that a young person became of age at twenty-one; now it's eighteen. I think that some folk are as mature at eighteen as they are at twenty-one. Also there are other folk who haven't reached maturity at sixty-five. But in Paul's day, it was the father who decided when the age of maturity was reached. Then they held a ceremony, known as the *toga virilis*, which gave him the position of a full-grown son in the family.

In a Roman home it must have worked something like this. Suppose the father is a centurion in Caesar's army. Caesar carries on a campaign way up in Gaul, and the man is up there several years—because that is where *our* ancestors were, and believe me, they were heathen! So he has trouble with them. He has to put them down, and it takes several years to do it. Because the army is pushing back the frontier of the Roman Empire, the father of the home is away for several years. Finally he returns home. He goes in to shave, and all of a sudden you hear him yell out, "Who's been using my razor?" Well, I tell you, all the servants come running, because he is the head of the house. They say to him, "Your son." He says, "You mean to tell me that my boy is old enough to use a razor!" The boy has grown to be a great big fellow. And the father says, "Bring him here." So they bring him in—he's a fine strapping boy—and the father says, "Well, now we must have the *toga virilis*, and we'll send out invitations to the grandmas, the

grandpas, the aunts, and the uncles." So they all come in for the ceremony of the *toga virilis*, and that day the father puts around the boy a toga, a robe. That is what our Lord meant in His parable of the Prodigal Son. When the boy came home the father didn't receive him as just an ordinary son, he received him as a full-grown son, put the robe around him, and put a ring on his finger. The ring had on it the signet of his father, which was equivalent to his signature and gave him the father's authority. You could see that boy walking down the street now with that robe on. The servant better not say anything to correct him now, and he'd better not try to paddle him now. In fact, he'll be paddling the servant from here on because he has now reached the age of a full-grown son. That is what Paul meant when he went on to say:

Even so we, when we were children, were in bondage under the elements of the world [Gal. 4:3].

"Under the elements of the world" means under the Law. Paul is saying that it was the childhood of the nation Israel when they were under rules and regulations.

But when the fulness of the time was come, God sent forth his Son, made of a woman, made under the law [Gal. 4:4].

At the time determined by God, God the Father sent forth God the Son, born of a woman, born under the Law. Mary was a Jewish woman. Out here on the West Coast there is a woman who is saying that Jesus did not belong to any race. How absolutely puerile and senseless! It is an attempt to take a saccharine sweet position which has no meaning whatsoever. The woman at the well (as recorded in the fourth chapter of John's gospel) knew more than the woman out here knows today. She said, "How is it that thou, being a *Jew*, askest drink of me, which am a woman of Samaria? . . ." (John 4:9, italics mine). She thought He was a Jew, and our Lord didn't correct her; so I conclude that she was accurate. If you don't mind, I'll follow her rather than some of my contemporaries who try to play down the fact that Jesus, according to the flesh, was a Jew. He had a perfect humanity. He also was *God* manifest in the flesh. In my day that is being questioned. However, the only *historical* Jesus that we have is the One who is described in one of the oldest creeds of the church as "very man of very man and very God of very God." I agree with that creed because it is exactly what the Word of God teaches.

Now what was God's purpose in sending forth His Son?

To redeem them that were under the law, that we might receive the adoption of sons [Gal. 4:5].

God had a twofold purpose: (1) To redeem those under the Law. They were children under the Law. You see, the Law never made anyone a son of God. (2) That they might receive the adoption of sons.

Adoption has a meaning different from that of our contemporary society. We think of it in relationship with a couple that may not have children of their own. They go to a home where there are children for adoption and see a precious little baby there. Their hearts go out to him, and they adopt him in their family by going through legal action. When the little one becomes their child we call that adoption. However, the Roman custom in Paul's day was to adopt one's own son. That, you recall, was what was done in the *toga virilis* ceremony. *Adoption* (the Greek word is *huiothesia*) means "to place as a son." A believer is placed in the family of God as a full grown son, capable of understanding divine truth.

In 1 Corinthians 2:9–10 we read, "But as it is written, Eye hath not seen, nor ear heard, neither have entered into the heart of man, the things which God hath prepared for them that love him. But God hath revealed them unto us by his Spirit: for the Spirit searcheth all things, yea, the deep things of God." This simply means that the truth in the Word of God can only be interpreted by the Spirit of God, and until He interprets it, man cannot understand it. The Holy Spirit alone can interpret the Word of God for us. That is what makes the difference today in certain men. A man can bring to the Word of God a brilliant mind. He can learn something about history, archaeology, and language. He can become an expert in Hebrew and Greek but can still miss the meaning. Why? Because the Spirit of God is the teacher. Even Isaiah the prophet said that: "For since the beginning of the world men have not heard, nor perceived by the ear, neither hath the eye seen, O God, beside thee, what he hath prepared for him that waiteth for him" (Isa. 64:4). If you want to know about Christ, only the Spirit of God can reveal Him to you. Even a mature Christian who has been in the Word for years is as helpless in studying the Bible as a newborn babe in Christ, because the Spirit of God will have to teach each of them.

I hope you will pardon my using a personal illustration. The only way I know a lot of these things is by pouring them through my own hopper—experiencing these truths myself. When I first started my training for the ministry, I was the youngest one in my class. When my father died, I had to quit school for three or four years in order to go to work. At that time I was the youngest one in my class. When I started my training for the ministry, I had those years of high school to make up, and when I went back to school, I was the oldest one in my class. When I entered seminary, I found that I was very ignorant of the Bible. I had never seen a Bible in my home. I had never heard a prayer in my home. I did not know the books of the Bible. I was ignorant, friend. No one could have been more ignorant of the Word of God than I was, and I felt it. I had to spend a lot of time memorizing the books of the Bible and many other basic things that I did not know when I first started studying. I developed an inferiority complex. When I preached as a young man, and I saw people with gray hair in the congregation, I would say to myself, *What I am going to say will be baby stuff for those folks because they really know the Bible.* However, I really had my eyes opened. I found out that there are still many people with gray hair who are babes in Christ. They have never grown up. The great truth which was given to me at this time was that the Spirit of God could teach me as a young believer as much as He could teach a mature Christian. We both could understand it if the Spirit of God was our teacher. This was a brand new truth for me, and it was a great encouragement as I was starting out in the ministry.

My friend, if you are a new believer, the same Spirit of God who is teaching me can teach you. If you are God's child, He has brought you into the position of a full-grown son, into the adoption. And, my friend, there is nothing quite as wonderful as that! That gave me confidence when I was a young believer and it gives me confidence to this good day. My friend, the Spirit of God will lead you and guide you into all truth if you *want* to know it, if you are willing for Him to be your teacher.

This brings us to the third thing that faith in Christ does for us that the Law could never do for us, which is the *experience* of sons of God.

And because ye are sons, God hath sent forth the Spirit of his Son into your hearts, crying, Abba, Father [Gal. 4:6].

"And because ye are sons" is a very strong statement.

Romans 8:16 says it this way, "The Spirit itself beareth witness with our spirit, that we are the children [the sons] of God." Paul continues to say in Romans, "But if the Spirit of him that raised up Jesus from the dead dwell in you, he that raised up Christ from the dead shall also quicken your mortal bodies by his Spirit that dwelleth in you. Therefore, brethren, we are debtors, not to the flesh, to live after the flesh. For if ye live after the flesh, ye shall die: but if ye through the Spirit do mortify the deeds of the body, ye shall live [as sons]. For as many as are led by the Spirit of God, they are the sons of God" (Rom. 8:11–14). If you are a child of God, you will want to be led by the Spirit of God. The flesh may get a victory in your life, but it will never make you happy. You will never be satisfied with it, because ". . . ye have not received the spirit of bondage again to fear." You don't need to say, "My, I'm not living as I should live, and I wonder if I'm a child of God." My friend, "ye have received the Spirit of adoption, whereby we cry, Abba, Father. The Spirit itself beareth witness with our spirit, that we are the children of God" (Rom. 8:15–16). This passage in the Epistle to the Romans is the unabridged edition of the parallel passage in Galatians. I wanted you to see all of it.

The word *Abba* was not translated, I am told, because the translators of the King James Version had a great reverence for the Word of God. When they came to the word *Abba*, they didn't dare translate it into English because it was such an intimate word. It could be translated "my daddy." God is my wonderful heavenly Father, but I would hesitate to call Him "daddy."

Wherefore thou art no more a servant, but a son; and if a son, then an heir of God through Christ [Gal. 4:7].

The Spirit, therefore, gives us an experience of being a son of God, whereby we can cry out—not just saying the word or putting on a false "piosity"—and call God our *Father*, because the Spirit is bearing witness with our spirit. This gives us the experience of being a son of God.

There are many folk who believe that the only way you can have an experience is either by reaching a high degree of sanctification—you've got to become holy—or you have to seek the baptism of the Holy Spirit, as they call it. They insist that if you don't get up to that level, you will never have an experience.

My friend, let me assure you, if you are a new believer or a weak believer, that you can have an experience as a son of God without reaching those levels, because sonship comes to you through faith in Jesus Christ. When folk have reached a high level of spirituality, they tend to think they are superior to the rest of us. However, we are always God's foolish little children. We are always filled with ignorance and stubbornness and sin and fears and weaknesses. *We* are never wonderful; *He* is wonderful. The Lord Jesus is wonderful, and faith in Him will give us an experience. I believe in experience, and I feel that a great many folk today need an experience with God.

Paul Rader, who was one of the greatest preachers this country has ever produced, used some very striking expressions. One day on the platform he said, "The old nature that you and I have is just like an old dead cat. What you need to do is reach down and get that old dead cat by the tail and throw it as far away as you can." I can say "amen" to that. I wish I could get rid of my old nature. One day Dr. Chafer heard him use this illustration, and he said to him afterward, "Paul, you forget that the old dead cat has nine lives. When you throw him away, he is going to be right back tomorrow." We will never become perfect saints of God, but we can experience being sons of God by faith in Jesus Christ. "And because ye are sons, God hath sent forth the Spirit of his Son into your hearts, crying, Abba, Father. Wherefore thou art no more a servant, but a son; and if a son, then an heir of God through Christ." Many times you and I plod along in our Christian lives, and we don't have an experience with God. Sometimes life becomes very drab and a little monotonous. But there are other times, especially when God puts us on trial and really tests us, that we have a wonderful experience with our Heavenly Father.

I recall when I was taken to the hospital to be operated on for cancer. No one was ever as frightened as I was because I am a coward, and I don't like hospitals. (I thank God for them, but I still don't like them.) I put on that funny looking nightgown they give you that is open in the back instead of the front, and I was trying to get up into the bed. I just couldn't make it. A nurse came in and said, "What's the matter? Are you sick?" I said, "No, I'm scared to death!" Then, when she came to get me ready for the operation, I said, "Just let me have a few moments alone." I had visited in that hospital many times as a pastor—in fact, several hundred times. Now I turned my face to the wall just like Hezekiah did and I said, "Lord, I want you to know that I have been here many times, and I have patted people on the hand and told them that You would be with them. As their pastor I prayed for them and then walked out. But I am not walking out today. I am going to have to stay and be operated on myself. I don't know what the outcome will be." I had some things I wanted to tell God. I wanted to tell Him how He ought to work it out. But I just welled up inside, and said, "My Father, I'm in Your hands. Whatever You want done, You do it. You're my Father." He was so wonderful to me. That is when He becomes a reality, my beloved. We need to experience Him as our Abba, Father. "The Spirit itself beareth witness with our spirit, that we are the children [sons] of God" (Rom. 8:16). Now, I don't wish you any trouble, but I think it is generally in times of trouble that God makes Himself real to us. I hope that someday you will have such an experience with our wonderful heavenly Father.

There is one more illustration I want to use before I move on. John G. Paton was a pioneer missionary in the New Hebrides. He went to the mission field as a young man with a young bride. When their first child was born, the child died and the wife died. He buried them with his own hands. Because he was among cannibals, he sat over the grave for many days and nights to prevent them from digging up the bodies and eating them. His testimony was that if the Lord Jesus Christ had not made Himself real to him during that time, he would have gone mad.

God makes Himself real during times of distress. When Paul was in prison, he could say, "At my first answer no man stood with me, but all men forsook me: I pray God that it may not be laid to their charge. Notwithstanding the Lord stood with me, and strengthened me . . ." (2 Tim. 4:16–17). The Lord stood by Paul. He stood by John Paton. He stood by me. He will stand by you. How reassuring it is to have a Father like that! At such a time He says, ". . . I will never leave thee, nor forsake thee" (Heb. 13:5). I trust you are His son.

Howbeit then, when ye knew not God, ye did service unto them which by nature are no gods [Gal. 4:8].

Paul is speaking of the fact that the Galatians had been idolaters. When I visited that Galatian country in Asia Minor, where the seven churches were located, I saw how completely the population then was given over to the worship of idols. Paul describes idols as vanities— "nothings." In 1 Corinthians 12:2 Paul called them "dumb idols." They were nothing and could say nothing. He is telling the Galatians that idols are not real and cannot make themselves real to those who worship them.

But now, after that ye have known God, or rather are known of God, how turn ye again to the weak and beggarly elements, whereunto ye desire again to be in bondage? [Gal. 4:9].

"Known of God" actually means *approved* of God or to be *acknowledged* of God. They had come to Christ through faith and God accepts that. Most of the believers in the Galatian churches were Gentiles. Now that they were Christians, they were turning to the Mosaic Law, which is, as Paul says, like going back into the idolatry they came out of.

Ye observe days, and months, and times, and years [Gal. 4:10].

"Ye observe days," meaning the sabbath days. Paul said to the Colossians, "Let no man therefore judge you in meat, or in drink, or in respect of an holyday, or of the new moon, or of the sabbath days" (Col. 2:16).

"Months" probably refers to the observance of the "new moon" practiced by the people of Israel in the time of the kings. The prophets warned them against it.

"Times" should be translated *seasons*, meaning feasts. God had given Israel seven feasts, but they all had pointed to the Lord Jesus Christ.

"Years" of course would refer to the sabbatic years. The observance of all these things would put these gentile believers completely back under the Mosaic Law.

Today I hear legalists claim they are keeping the Mosaic Law, yet they are keeping only the sabbath day. My friend, all the law comes in one package, including the sabbatic year and the Year of Jubilee. James in his epistle said, "For whosoever shall keep the whole law, and yet offend in one point, he is guilty of all" (James 2:10). That is, he is guilty of being a lawbreaker.

I am afraid of you, lest I have bestowed upon you labour in vain [Gal. 4:11].

Paul is saying, in a nice way, that he thinks he has wasted his time among them. Since they have been saved by grace, their returning to the Law is the same as returning to their former idolatry. He reminded them that they had not known God by means of the Mosaic Law but by faith in Jesus Christ.

We have come now to a personal section (vv. 12–18). It is a polite word that Paul is injecting in this epistle.

Brethren, I beseech you, be as I am; for I am as ye are: ye have not injured me at all [Gal. 4:12].

"Be as I am" is better translated *become* as I am. The Galatians had been listening to false teachers, and they were looking upon Paul as an enemy because he told them the truth. Paul is saying, "We are all on the same plane. We are all believers, all in the body of Christ. In view of this we ought to be very polite to one another."

Ye know how through infirmity of the flesh I preached the gospel unto you at the first [Gal. 4:13].

Now Paul makes an appeal to them on the basis of his thorn in the flesh. What was that thorn? Let's read on.

And my temptation which was in my flesh ye despised not, nor rejected; but received me as an angel of God, even as Christ Jesus [Gal. 4:14].

"And my temptation which was in my flesh" means the *trial*, which elsewhere he calls his thorn in the flesh.

Where is then the blessedness ye spake of? for I bear you record, that, if it had been possible, ye would have plucked out your own eyes, and have given them to me [Gal. 4:15].

Probably Paul's thorn in the flesh was some sort of eye trouble, and it evidently made him very unattractive. I cannot conceive of them wanting to pluck out their eyes and give them to Paul if what he really needed was another leg. Apparently Paul had an eye disease which is common in that land and is characterized by excessive pus that runs out of the eyes. You can well understand how unattractive that would be to look at while he was ministering to them. Paul says, "You just ignored it, and received me so wonderfully when I preached the gospel to you."

Am I therefore become your enemy, because I tell you the truth? [Gal. 4:16].

I had always wanted to place on the pulpit, facing the preacher, the words, "Sir, we would see Jesus." A very fine officer of the church I served in downtown Los Angeles did this for me after he heard me express this desire. There is another verse I wanted to place on the audience side of the pulpit, but I never had the nerve to do it. It is these words of Paul: "Am I therefore become your enemy, because I tell you the truth?" As you know, many folk today really don't want the preacher to tell the truth from the pulpit. They would much rather he would say something complimentary that would smooth their feathers and make them feel good. We all like to have our backs rubbed, and there is a lot of back-rubbing from the contemporary pulpit rather than the declaration of the truth.

They zealously affect you, but not well; yea, they would exclude you, that ye might affect them.

But it is good to be zealously affected always in a good thing, and not only when I am present with you [Gal. 4:17–18].

These verses are more easily understood in the American Standard Version which says, "They zealously seek you in no good way; nay, they desire to shut you out, that ye may seek them. But it is good to be zealously sought in a good matter at all times, and not only when I am present with you." Paul is saying that it is good to seek that which is the very best, but these Judaizers are after you in order to scalp you. They want to put your scalp on their belt and be able to say, "We were over at Galatia, and we had so many converts"—which, of course, would not be actually true. Paul had somewhat the same thing to say to the Corinthian believers: "Truly the signs of an apostle were wrought among you in all patience, in signs, and wonders, and mighty deeds. For what is it wherein ye were inferior to other churches, except it be that I myself was not burdensome to you? forgive me this wrong. Behold, the third time I am ready to come to you; and I will not be burdensome to you: for I seek not yours, but you: for the children ought not to lay up for the parents, but the parents for the children. And I will very gladly spend and be spent for you; though the more abundantly I love you, the less I be loved" (2 Cor. 12:12–15).

You see, this same crowd of Judaizers had gone to Corinth. The Corinthian believers had loved Paul also, and Paul had to warn them of these men. False teachers are often very attractive. I am amazed at the very fine presentation the cults make. I have watched them on television programs that are done to perfection. That is the subtle part of it. Everything is beautiful to look at, and those taking part are attractive individuals. Also they present a certain amount of truth. For example, I listened to a man who is a liberal give the Christmas story during the Christmas season. No one could have told it better than he did. It was an excellent presentation. But when he began to interpret it, I realized that he didn't even believe in the virgin birth of Christ. You see, the warning of Paul both to the Galatian and Corinthian believers is very timely for our generation also.

ALLEGORY OF HAGAR AND SARAI

This chapter concludes with an allegory of Hagar and Sarai. All is contrast in this section between these two women. Hagar, and every reference to her under other figures of speech, represents the Law. Sarai, and every reference to her under other figures of speech, represents faith in Christ.

My little children, of whom I travail in birth again until Christ be formed in you [Gal. 4:19].

Paul addresses his allegory to the Galatian believers by using this tender expression, "My little children"—*children* is the Greek word *teknia*, meaning "born ones." Paul has a very tender heart, and he likens himself to a mother.

I desire to be present with you now, and to change my voice; for I stand in doubt of you [Gal. 4:20].

Paul wanted to be present so that he could speak differently. He was deeply concerned about these people. He had been using strong language in his letter, but you can see his tender heart.

Tell me, ye that desire to be under the law, do ye not hear the law? [Gal. 4:21].

There are people who talk about the Ten Commandments or some legal system, but they don't talk about the *penalty* imposed by the Law. They don't present the Law in the full orb of its ministry of condemnation. Notice what happened when God called Moses to the mountain to give the Law: "And it came to pass on the third day in the morning, that there were thunders and lightnings, and a thick cloud upon the mount, and the voice of the trumpet exceeding loud; so that all the people that was in the camp trembled. And Moses brought forth the people out of the camp to meet with God; and they stood at the nether part of the mount. And mount Sinai was altogether on a smoke, because the LORD descended upon it in fire: and the smoke thereof ascended as the smoke of a furnace, and the whole mount quaked greatly. And when the voice of the trumpet sounded long, and waxed louder and louder, Moses spake, and God answered him by a voice. And the LORD came down upon mount Sinai, on the top of the mount: and the LORD called Moses up to the top of the mount; and Moses went up. And the LORD said unto Moses, Go down, charge the people, lest they break through unto the LORD to gaze, and many of them perish" (Exod. 19:16–21).

God told the people to stand back, actually to stand afar off, when He gave Moses the Law. Exodus 20:18–19 says, "And all the people saw the thunderings, and the lightnings, and the noise of the trumpet, and the mountain smoking: and when the people saw it, they removed, and stood afar off. And they said unto Moses, Speak thou with us, and we will hear: but let not God speak with us, lest we die."

We cannot conceive of how holy God is. You and I are renegades in God's universe. We are in the position of being lost sinners in God's universe with no capacity to follow or obey Him. Romans 8:6 says, "For to be carnally minded is death; but to be spiritually minded is life and peace." The carnal mind is enmity against God. My friend, the world is against God; it is not for God. The world is not getting better. It is becoming more evil each day, and it has been bad since the day God put Adam and Eve out of the Garden of Eden. Romans 8:7 goes on to say, "Because the carnal mind is enmity against God: for it is not subject to the law of God, neither indeed can be." No wonder the children of Israel trembled and moved away from the mountain and said, "We will die."

Now, my friend, God is high and holy and lifted up, and He dwells in *glory*. You and I are down here making mud pies in the world because physically we are made out of mud. We creatures walk about here on earth and have the audacity to walk contrary to the will of God! The carnal mind is enmity against God. That is man's position in the world.

Paul says, "Listen to the Law. You haven't even heard it yet." It was true. The Galatians had not actually heard the Law. The giving of the Law was not beautiful and cozy, but terrifying. The Galatians seemed to want to be under law so Paul was going to let them hear it.

For it is written, that Abraham had two sons, the one by a bondmaid, the other by a freewoman [Gal. 4:22].

Using an illustration from the life of Abraham (Gen. 16; 17; 18; 20; 21), Paul is going to make a contrast between these two boys that were born, one to Hagar and one to Sarai. One was the son of a bondwoman; the other was the son of a freewoman. The freewoman represents grace, and the bondwoman represents the Mosaic Law. He is going to point out the contrast between them in what he calls an allegory.

Paul is not saying that the story of Abraham is an allegory—some have interpreted this statement as meaning that—but Paul is saying that the incident of the two women who bore Abraham sons *contains* an allegory. It has a message for us today.

But he who was of the bondwoman was born after the flesh; but he of the freewoman was by promise [Gal. 4:23].

"He who was of the bondwoman was born after the flesh." The Code of Hammurabi, which governed the culture in Abraham's day, stated that the son of a slave woman was a slave. So even though Ishmael was Abraham's son, he was a slave.

"He of the freewoman was by promise." Isaac was a miracle child, that is, his birth was miraculous. Abraham was too old to father a child, and Paul says that the womb of Sarai was dead. She had passed the age of childbearing. The womb of Sarai was like a tomb, and out of death God brought life.

Which things are an allegory: for these are the two covenants; the one from the mount Sinai, which gendereth to bondage, which is Agar [Gal. 4:24].

"Which things are an allegory," meaning that these events in Abraham's life *contain* an allegory. Paul is going to draw a lesson from it.

"For these are the two covenants"—the first is the covenant of the Law which Moses received from God on Mount Sinai.

"Which is Agar" (*Agar* is the Greek form of the name *Hagar*). Paul compares Hagar to Mount Sinai which is synonymous with the Mosaic Law.

For this Agar is mount Sinai in Arabia, and answereth to Jerusalem which now is, and is in bondage with her children [Gal. 4:25].

In Paul's allegory Hagar is Mount Sinai which corresponds to Jerusalem (the earthly Jerusa-

lem of Paul's day), because she was still in slavery with her children. In other words, Jerusalem (representing the nation of Israel) was still under the bondage of the Law.

But Jerusalem which is above is free, which is the mother of us all [Gal. 4:26].

"Jerusalem which is above" is the New Jerusalem which is presented to us in the twentieth chapter of Revelation as it comes down from God out of heaven. As old Jerusalem is the mother city of those under the law, so the New Jerusalem is the mother city of the believer under grace. The believer neither here nor hereafter has any connection with legalism.

For it is written, Rejoice, thou barren that bearest not; break forth and cry, thou that travailest not: for the desolate hath many more children than she which hath an husband [Gal. 4:27].

From Sarai (who was barren until the birth of Isaac) there came more descendants than ever came from Hagar. Today the Arabs are fewer than the children of Israel. In this allegory, Paul is saying that God is saving under grace more members of the human family than He ever saved under the Mosaic Law by the sacrificial system.

Now we, brethren, as Isaac was, are the children of promise [Gal. 4:28].

Believers today are also children of promise. Our birth is a *new* birth, which comes about by our believing God's promise: "For God so loved the world, that he gave his only begotten Son, that whosoever believeth in him should not perish, but have everlasting life" (John 3:16). God has said that if we trust Him, we'll be born again. "Being born again, not of corruptible seed, but of incorruptible, by the word of God, which liveth and abideth for ever" (1 Pet. 1:23).

But as then he that was born after the flesh persecuted him that was born after the Spirit, even so it is now [Gal. 4:29].

My friend, the legalist hates the gospel of the free grace of God. When I was first ordained to the ministry, I preached a sermon on prophecy and made the comment that preaching on prophecy would get me into trouble. After the service, an elder came to me and said, "Vernon, you are mistaken. Preaching on prophecy will never get you into trouble. In fact, you'll generally get a good crowd. People like to hear prophecy. But if you preach the grace of

God, you're going to get into trouble." This is the reason that the gospel is trimmed down as it is today. I hear very little gospel, that is, the pure grace of God, preached these days. And I know why—if you preach that, you get a barrage of criticism. Folk insist that I have to also *do* something or *seek* something from another source—from the Holy Spirit, for instance, or go through some ceremony in order to receive something that I did not get when I trusted Jesus Christ. My friend, to say that is calling Christ a curse. If you have to add anything to what He did for you, then His death on the cross was in vain. Christ was made a curse for us; but if you don't accept what He did for you, you are saying that you are not guilty, but that He is guilty. These words of Paul are as relevant in our day as they were in his day: "But as then he that was born after the flesh persecuted him that was born after the Spirit, even so it is now." The natural man hates the gospel of the grace of God. My friend, it is *in* us to hate it, because it doesn't require any *doing* on our part. Rather, it glorifies Christ and turns our eyes to Him.

Nevertheless what saith the scripture? Cast out the bondwoman and her son: for the son of the bondwoman shall not be heir with the son of the freewoman [Gal. 4:30].

God commanded the expulsion of the bondwoman and her son (see Gen. 21:10). Today God is saying to you and to me, "Get rid of your legalism. Put all of the emphasis on Jesus Christ."

So then, brethren, we are not children of the bondwoman, but of the free [Gal. 4:31].

Abraham could not have both the son of Hagar and the son of Sarai. He had to make a choice. Paul is saying that you can't be saved by law and grace. You have to make a choice. If you try to be saved by Christ and also by law, you are not saved.

Let me ask you, have you really trusted Christ, or are you carrying a spare tire on your little omnibus; that is, do you feel that you are *doing* something or *being* something or trying to *attain* to something which adds to what Jesus Christ did for you on the cross? If you do, forget it and look to Christ alone; receive everything from Him. He is our Savior. He is our Lord. He is to receive all praise and glory.

CHAPTER 5

THEME: Sanctification by the Spirit; saved by faith and living by law perpetrates falling from grace; saved by faith and walking in the Spirit produces fruit of the Spirit

SANCTIFICATION BY THE SPIRIT

This brings us to the third major division in Galatians after the Introduction. The first section was *personal*, and it was important for us to know the personal experience Paul had had. Following this was the *doctrinal* section of justification by faith in which Paul insisted that our salvation must rest upon *God's* salvation and that there is only one gospel.

We come now to the practical side, which is sanctification by the Spirit. Justification is by faith; sanctification is by the Spirit of God. Scripture tells us, however, that the Lord Jesus Christ has been made unto us sanctification—that is, God sees us complete in Him. Regardless of how good you become, you will never meet His standard. You will never be like Christ in this life. Christ is the only One about whom God said, ". . . This is my beloved Son, in whom I am well pleased" (Matt. 3:17). But the body of believers, the church, has been put *in* Christ. He is the Head of the body; those of us who are believers are His body in the world today—and we should represent Him, by the way.

The method of sanctification is by the Spirit. In this section we see the Spirit versus the flesh. Either it is a do-it-yourself Christian life or somebody else will have to do it *through* you. His method is doing it through you.

In this section we see liberty versus bondage. Any legal system puts you under bondage, and you have to follow it meticulously. Let me illustrate this from my own experience with civil law with which all of us are familiar.

As I was driving my car early one Sunday morning, I came to a corner where there was a stop sign. It was so early, no one else was out; I looked up and down the street, but I didn't stop—I just crawled through. A traffic officer appeared behind me; he came up to me and asked, "Did you see that stop sign?" I said, "Yes, I saw the sign; I just didn't see *you!*" Then he asked, "Do you know what that sign means?" And he proceeded to give me a primary lesson in law. He said, "Stop means *stop.*" Well, I already knew that; I just wasn't doing it. Believe me, the law puts you in bondage. And if you are going to drive a car, you had better be under law, because a lot of folk drive through stop signs and cause accidents. Stop means stop. I agreed with him on everything except one: I didn't think I deserved a ticket. I argued with him about that. And he was a very nice fellow; he saw my point. He said, "Well, I grant you that there is nobody out this morning, but hereafter you stop. Will you?" I assured him that I would stop. Ever since then, even if it is early Sunday morning, I stop at that sign—and wherever I see a stop sign. Now that is legalism. It is an example of legalism that we all understand.

SAVED BY FAITH AND LIVING BY LAW PERPETRATES FALLING FROM GRACE

Paul begins on the note of liberty which we have in Christ. His subject in these first fifteen verses is "Saved by faith and living by law perpetrates falling from grace." This is what it means to fall from grace: you are saved by faith, then you drop down to a *law* level to live. We will see this illustrated as we move into this section.

Stand fast therefore in the liberty wherewith Christ hath made us free, and be not entangled again with the yoke of bondage [Gal. 5:1].

He is saying here that not only are we saved by faith rather than by law, but law is not to be the rule of life for the believer. We are not to live by law at all. The law principle is not the rule for Christian living. Paul is saying that since we have been saved by grace we are to continue on in this way of living. Grace supplies the indwelling and filling of the Spirit to enable us to live on a higher plane than law demanded. This all is our portion when we trust Christ as Savior. It is in Christ that we receive everything—salvation and sanctifica-

tion. Don't tell me I need to seek a second blessing. When I came to Christ, I got everything I needed. Paul tells me that I have been blessed with all spiritual blessings in Christ Jesus. Let's believe Him and start trusting. Let's stop trying some legal system or rote of rules.

We have a liberty in Christ. He does not put us under some little legal system. We do not use the Ten Commandments as a law of life. I don't mean we are to break the Ten Commandments—I think we all understand that breaking most of them (i.e., thou shalt not kill; thou shalt not steal, etc.) would lead to our arrest by local authorities. Certainly Christians do not break the Commandments, but we are called to a higher level to live. That level is where there is liberty in Christ. I have a liberty in Jesus Christ, and that liberty is not a rule, but a principle. It is that I am to please Him. My conduct should be to please Jesus Christ—not to please you, not to please any organization, but only to please Him. That is the liberty that we have in the Lord Jesus Christ. "Stand fast therefore in the liberty wherewith Christ hath made us free, and be not entangled again with the yoke of bondage."

Behold, I Paul say unto you, that if ye be circumcised, Christ shall profit you nothing [Gal. 5:2].

Circumcision was the badge of the Law. A badge indicates to what organization or lodge you belong. Perhaps Christians should wear a badge because that is about the only way you could tell that some people are Christians. But Paul says that if you so much as put on the badge of the Law, which is circumcision, then Christ does not profit you anything.

Let me use a homely illustration to prove the point. Years ago a tonic called Hadacol was advertised. I don't think it is sold any more. I am not sure of the details, but they found it was about seventy-five percent alcohol. A lot of people were using it. The company that made it was giving out glowing testimonials about its product. Now suppose a testimonial read something like this: "I took 513 bottles of your medicine. Before I began using Hadacol, I could not walk. Now I am able to run, and I am actually able to fly! I really have improved. But I think you ought to know that during that time I also concocted a bottle of my own medicine and used it also." Now, my friend, that final sentence certainly muddied the water. There is no way to tell if it was the 513 bottles of Hadacol that cured him or his own concoction. The minute you put something else into the formula, you are not sure.

Now notice carefully what Paul is saying. If you trust Christ plus something else you are not saved. If you go so far as to be circumcised, which is only the badge of the Law, or if you go through some other experience and rest your salvation on that, "Christ shall profit you nothing." How can He profit you anything when you have made up a bottle of your own concoction rather than trusting Him alone for your salvation?

The way Dr. Lewis Sperry Chafer put it always impressed me. It was something like this: "I want to so trust Christ that when I come into His presence and He asks me, 'Why are you here?' I can say, 'I am here because I trusted You as my Savior.' If He asked me, 'Well, that is commendable, but what have you done? I happen to know that you were president of a seminary, and that you were baptized. You were also a member of a church. You did many fine things during your ministry,' then I would reply, 'It is all true, but I never trusted in any of it for salvation. I trusted only You, my Lord.'" My friend, is that the way you are trusting Christ? Paul makes it very strong when he says, "if ye be circumcised, Christ shall profit you nothing." If you trust anything other than Christ, you are not a Christian.

For I testify again to every man that is circumcised, that he is a debtor to do the whole law [Gal. 5:3].

You cannot draw out of the Law just those things that you like. You cannot leave out the penalties and a great deal of the detail. You must take the whole Law or nothing. I am delighted that I am not under the Law. I have liberty in Christ! I must confess that I have a problem of always pleasing Him, but He is the One I am trying to please. I am not following some legal system. "For I testify again to every man that is circumcised, that he is a debtor to do the whole law."

Christ is become of no effect unto you, whosoever of you are justified by the law; ye are fallen from grace [Gal. 5:4].

If you have been saved by trusting Christ, then go down to the low level of living by the Law, you have fallen from grace. This is what "falling from grace" actually means. I can remember as a student in a denominational seminary hearing one theologian say, "Falling from grace is the doctrine which the Method-

ists believe and the Presbyterians practice." However, falling from grace does not mean falling into some open sin or careless conduct, and by so doing forfeiting your salvation so that you have to be saved all over again. It has no reference to that at all. "Falling from grace" is the opposite of "once saved always saved," although both expressions are unfortunate terminology. Paul deals with this matter of falling from grace in the remainder of this chapter. He also deals with it in his Epistle to the Romans. In Romans he begins with man in the place of total bankruptcy—without righteousness, completely depraved, as unprofitable as rotten fruit. Man is a sinner before God. Then at the conclusion of Romans you see man in the service of God and being admonished to perform certain things. Not only is he admonished to perform certain things, he is completely separated to God, and he must be obedient to God.

There are two mighty works of God which stand between the man in his fallen condition and man in service to God. These are: salvation and sanctification. As we have seen, salvation is justification by faith. That is all-important. Sanctification means that after you are saved you are to come up to a new plane of living. I think the greatest fallacy is to believe that service is essential in the Christian life, that you must get busy immediately. The early church was more concerned with its manner of life, and that life was a witness to the world. Today the outside world is looking at the church and passing it by because we are busy, as busy as termites, but we do not have lives to back up our witness. Rather than concentrating on trying to do good, we ought to live "good." If we are pleasing Christ, we will be doing good also. I think there is more about sanctification in the Epistles to the Romans and to the Galatians than anything else.

Now how does God make a saved sinner good? Well, He gives him a new nature. Then he is to keep the Law? Oh, no. Emphatically no. This doesn't mean he is to break the Law, but he is called to live on a higher plane. There is no good in the old nature. Paul found that out, and he also found out from experience that there is no power in the new nature. As to salvation, he said, "For I know that in me (that is, in my flesh,) dwelleth no good thing," and he also found out, ". . . to *will* is present with me; but how to perform that which is good I find not" (Rom. 7:18, italics mine). And he cries out as a saved man, "O wretched man that I am! who shall deliver me from the body of this death?" (Rom. 7:24). He is not afraid that he is going to lose his salvation, but he is a defeated Christian. God gives a new principle. We will find in this chapter that the new principle is the fruit of the Spirit.

Living the Christian life by this method for some Christians is as farfetched as living on the moon! They never expect to live there. Perhaps they have never even heard about the possibility. My friend, this is the life He wants us to live—by *faith*. We are saved by grace; we are to live by grace.

For we through the Spirit wait for the hope of righteousness by faith [Gal. 5:5].

"The hope of righteousness" is the only prophetic reference in the entire epistle. This is quite remarkable, because in all Paul's epistles he has something to say about the rapture of the church or about Christ's coming to earth to establish His kingdom. But here in Galatians he says only this: "the hope of righteousness by faith," and the hope of righteousness is the Lord Jesus Christ. The only hope is the blessed hope, and Christ is made unto us righteousness.

As I have pointed out, the Epistle to the Galatians was very important to Martin Luther and to the other reformers. This is one of the reasons, I am confident, that they spent so little time on prophecy.

All the schools of prophecy—the premillennialists, the amillennialists, and the postmillennialists have quoted Martin Luther and the other reformers on this matter of prophecy. But I do not think that there was any development of prophecy beyond what the early church wrote until the twentieth century. In this twentieth century there has been tremendous development in prophecy. The Bible institutes were probably the beginning of this movement, then two or three of our seminaries that have emphasized the premillennial position have forced the others to study prophecy. Actually, amillennialists are just a group of the postmillennialists who were forced into the study of prophecy and came up with the theory of amillennialism. Of course, they have been great at quoting the fathers of the postapostolic period. They say, Augustine said thus and so, and he did say it. He was attempting to build the kingdom here, that is, the church was going to bring in the kingdom. This led to postmillennialism, which was, of course, a false position. I don't feel that we should criticize Augustine for that since he was living in a day when the study of prophecy was not developed. The person of Christ was

the great subject during his time, as salvation was the great subject later on.

Therefore the fact that Paul has only this brief reference to prophecy in his Epistle to the Galatians is understandable, since his emphasis is on the gospel and the Christian life. It is important to note the priorities in any book of the Bible and also the priorities that were in existence in any given period. Failing to do this leads to misinterpretation and misunderstanding which is the case in quoting church fathers on the matter of prophecy. After all, the authorities on prophecy are Paul, Peter, James, Matthew, Mark, and Luke. We need to note what they have written on the subject of prophecy. But to the Galatians Paul writes simply, "For we through the Spirit wait for the hope of righteousness by faith." I think Paul's reason for saying this here is that believers are not going to reach perfection in this life. And the greatest imperfection I know of today is to *think* you have reached perfection. Folk who think they are perfect are imperfect like the rest of us—but they don't know it.

For in Jesus Christ neither circumcision availeth any thing, nor uncircumcision; but faith which worketh by love [Gal. 5:6].

No legal apparatus will produce a Christian life. The formula is simple: "faith which worketh by love." As we advance in Galatians, Paul will give us the modus operandi, but let us remember that it is a simple formula: "Faith which worketh by love." That is the way to live the Christian life. Faith will work by love. Love will be the fruit of the Holy Spirit.

Ye did run well; who did hinder you that ye should not obey the truth? [Gal. 5:7].

Paul chides the Galatians. He is giving them a gentle rebuke. They were doing excellently until the Judaizers came along. "The truth" is the gospel, of course, and the Lord Jesus Christ in person.

This persuasion cometh not of him that calleth you [Gal. 5:8].

It didn't come from Christ but from a different source.

A little leaven leaveneth the whole lump [Gal. 5:9].

In Scripture, both Old and New Testaments, leaven is always used as a principle of evil. In Matthew 13:33, when the woman hid leaven in three measures of meal, the leaven was not the gospel. It may be the kind of a "gospel" that is passing around today as legal tender, but it is still evil. In fact, Paul says that it is no gospel at all. The Lord Jesus warned His disciples of the leaven of the Pharisees (see Matt. 16:6). I think we need to be warned today of the leaven of legalism. It is an awful thing. Legalism says that when Christ died on the cross for you and me over nineteen hundred years ago, He did not give us a full package of salvation, but that I have to go through a ritual of baptism or seek something else from the Holy Spirit to get the rest of it. My friend, I received it *all* when I accepted Christ. Now I may have experiences after I am saved, but that does not add to my salvation. Christ is the One who wrought out our salvation. The Lord Jesus said that the woman would take the leaven and hide it in three measures of meal, symbolic of the gospel. In other words, leaven has been hidden in the gospel—and that makes it palatable to the natural man.

I was brought up in the South, and I never knew there was any kind of biscuits but *hot* biscuits. My mother used to bake them every day. Even yet I can see those biscuits in the dough stage, rising on the back of the stove. When they reached a certain height, she stuck them in the oven. They had leaven in them. When the biscuits were done, I would put butter and honey on them. There was nothing better! That is still my favorite dessert. There is a lot of leaven being put in the gospel today to make it more palatable. Natural man likes the leavened bread. It tastes good. However, we are warned not to do that.

I have confidence in you through the Lord, that ye will be none otherwise minded: but he that troubleth you shall bear his judgment, whosoever he be [Gal. 5:10].

Paul believed that the Galatians would ultimately reject the teaching of the Judaizers. He says, "I have confidence in you" that when you get your feet back on the ground, and your heads out of the clouds, you will return to the gospel that was preached to you, and you will see that the teaching of the Judaizers was an intrusion, that it was leaven.

And I, brethren, if I yet preach circumcision, why do I yet suffer persecution? then is the offence of the cross ceased [Gal. 5:11].

This verse is important to note. Paul asks, "If I preach circumcision, why am I persecuted?" Adding something to the gospel makes it ac-ceptable. The gospel, by itself, is not acceptable to the natural man. Preaching the gospel does antagonize some folk. Paul asks, "If I am including something else in the gospel, why am I being persecuted?"

"Then is the offence of the cross ceased." Actually, the cross of Christ is an offense to all that man prides himself in. It is an offense to his morality because it tells him his work cannot justify him. It is an offense to his philosophy because its appeal is to faith and not to reason. It is an offense to the culture of man because its truths are revealed to babes. It is an offense to his sense of caste because God chooses the poor and humble. It is an offense to his will because it calls for an unconditional surrender. It is an offense to his pride because it shows the exceeding sinfulness of the human heart. And it is an offense to himself because it tells him he must be born again. You know, that was almost insulting to the Pharisee Nicodemus that night when Jesus told him, religious as he was, that he must be born again. For the same reason, a lot of ministers who are preaching the New Birth get in trouble with their congregations. Some members don't want to be born again—they feel like they're good enough as they are. It's an insult to them. The Cross is an offense, but we need to guard against magnifying it.

One of my professors in seminary said a very wise thing. He said, "Young gentlemen, do not tone down the gospel, do not change it, because there is the offense of the Cross. You need to recognize it, but don't *magnify* the offense." Sometimes we become offensive in the way we give the gospel—may the Lord forgive us for doing that. When I was a pastor, a man on my staff antagonized a family and caused them to leave the church. I said to him, "Now look, you and I are not to antagonize people. If anything antagonizes them, let it be the *gospel* I preach—not you or me, but the gospel."

I would they were even cut off which trouble you [Gal. 5:12].

I wish these Judaizers were removed from you.

For, brethren, ye have been called unto liberty; only use not liberty for an occasion to the flesh, but by love serve one another [Gal. 5:13].

There are three methods of trying to live the Christian life—two of them will not work. One is a life of legalism, which Paul has been discussing. The other is the life of license, which

Paul discussed in Romans 6: After we are saved by grace, can we live in sin? Paul's answer is, "God forbid." You can't live in sin and be a Christian. Now you may fall into sin, but you will get out of it. The Prodigal Son can get in the pig pen, but he won't settle down there—the pig pen won't be his forwarding address. He will leave it. The Christian life is neither the life of legalism nor the life of license.

The third method of living the Christian life is the life of liberty, and in the remainder of this chapter he will give us the modus operandi for living by liberty. The life of legalism includes not only the Ten Commandments, but a set of regulations that Bible believers follow today. They tell you where you can't go, and what you can't do. I remember a wonderful woman who was a Bible teacher in Texas. She did an outstanding job of teaching the Bible. One day a dear little saint came up to me and asked, "Do you think she is really a Christian? She uses makeup!" Who in the world ever said that makeup was a test of whether or not a person is a Christian? I told this dear saint that the Bible teacher was living under liberty. She might have been using too much makeup, but at her age she probably needed to spread it on a little thicker. Candidly, I do not think it helps her too much, but she has liberty in Christ. Whether you eat meat or do not eat meat won't commend you to God. Whether you use makeup or don't use makeup won't commend you to God. Paul is saying that you can keep every commandment and still not live the Christian life. You can not only keep all Ten Commandments, you can follow every commandment others put down for you to live by, and you still would not be living the Christian life. Also there are the antinomians who think they can do as they please and be living the Christian life. These folk are as extreme as the legalists. The Christian life is not either one; it is liberty *in* Christ.

"Only use not liberty for an occasion to the flesh." What does the gospel of grace do for the believer? It is grace, not law, that frees us from doing wrong and allows us to do right. Grace does not set us free *to* sin, but it sets us free *from* sin. You see, the believer should desire to please God, not because he must please Him like a slave, but because he is a son and he *wills* to please his Father. He does what *God* wants, not because he fears to do otherwise like an enemy, but because he wants to do it, for God is his friend. God is the One who loves him. He serves God, not because of pressure from without such as the Law, but because of a great principle within— even the life of Christ that is within him.

We serve God because we *love* Him. The Lord Jesus said to His disciples, "If you love Me, keep My commandments" (see John 14:15). I have often wondered if a disciple had said, "I don't love You," would our Lord have said, "Then forget about My commandments"? The whole basis of obedience is a love relationship to Him. The Law never could bring us to that place. It was negative to begin with. It produced a negative goodness—which is the kind of goodness a great many people have today. Oh, if I could only get this truth through to a great many of the saints! Your negative goodness is a *legal* goodness. You can say, "I don't do this and I don't do that." But what *do* you do? My friend, all legal systems produce only negative goodness. They never rise to the sphere of positive goodness where one does things to please God for the very love of pleasing Him. He wants us to serve Him on that kind of basis.

Now Paul is going to reduce it to a simple statement, then he will amplify what he means.

For all the law is fulfilled in one word, even in this; Thou shalt love thy neighbour as thyself [Gal. 5:14].

Here the Law is reduced to the lowest common denominator. This is the acid test for those who think they are living by the Law. "Thou shalt love thy neighbour as thyself." The "one word" is *love*.

But if ye bite and devour one another, take heed that ye be not consumed one of another [Gal. 5:15].

I have always wanted to preach a sermon on this text, and I would entitle it "Christian Cannibals." Did you know that in many churches today the Christians bite, eat, and devour one another? And the bite is as bad as that of a mad dog. There is nothing you can take that will cure the wound. All you can do is suffer. There are a lot of mad dogs running around today. They will bite and devour you. Unfortunately, the world has passed by the church in our day, and I'm sorry it has because there are many fine people in our churches and many wonderful preachers throughout this country. But the lives of some Christians are keeping the world away from certain churches. I personally know examples of this. I know churches in which the Christians have no love for each other, but they bite and devour one another. It is a terrible thing!

SAVED BY FAITH AND WALKING IN THE SPIRIT PRODUCES FRUIT OF THE SPIRIT

Now Paul is going to contrast what it is to live in the desires of the flesh with the walk in the Spirit. This whole section gives the modus operandi.

As we enter this important section, I want to make a recapitulation and tie it in with what we have had. In this section the theme is sanctification by the Spirit. Paul has told us that we are to "stand fast in the liberty wherewith Christ hath made us free" (v. 1). From what has Christ set us free? Paul has already mentioned several things in this epistle. In chapter 1, verse 4, he tells us that Christ has set us free from this present evil world. That is, we don't have to serve it. Then in chapter 2, verse 20, he says, "I live; yet not I." You and I cannot live the Christian life, but Christ can live it in us. What wonderful liberty! In chapter 3, verse 13, he tells us that we have been delivered from the curse of the Law. We have been delivered from the judgment and the condemnation of the Law. In fact, we have been delivered from the very Law itself: "But when the fulness of the time was come, God sent forth his Son, made of a woman, made under the law, To redeem them that were under the law, that we might receive the adoption of sons" (Gal. 4:4–5).

Now Paul is going to contrast what it is to live in the desires of the flesh with the life of walking in the Spirit. Here is his injunction.

This I say then, Walk in the Spirit, and ye shall not fulfil the lust of the flesh [Gal. 5:16].

This verse states the great principle of Christian living—*walk by means of the Spirit*. The word for *walk* is *peripateō*, which means just "to walk up and down." This Greek word was used for a school of philosophy in Athens, Greece, in which the founder walked up and down as he taught. The principle for us is walking in the Spirit. If we do, we will not "fulfil the lust of the flesh."

The word *lust* in our usage today has an evil connotation, which the Greek word does not have. *Lust* of the flesh refers to the desires of the flesh, many of which are not immoral, but are of the flesh (music, art, and works of do-gooders, etc.). There are many things which in themselves are not evil, but they can take the place of spiritual things. Some Christians can get wrapped up in a hobby which takes them away from the Word of God. Many Christians spend a lot of time worshiping before that little idiot box we call TV. Now don't misunderstand—I watch TV. I am not under any law that says I can't watch TV. There are a few programs one can enjoy. But watching TV is a desire of the flesh. If it takes you away from that which is spiritual, then it is wrong.

For the flesh lusteth against the Spirit, and the Spirit against the flesh: and these are contrary the one to the other: so that ye cannot do the things that ye would [Gal. 5:17].

A transliteration of this verse will help convey the meaning: "For the flesh *warreth* against the Spirit, and the Spirit *warreth* against the flesh: and these are contrary the one to the other: so that ye cannot do the things that ye would" that is, the things that the old nature wanted to do. This is very important to see— the flesh wars against the Spirit, and the Spirit wars against the flesh.

A believer has a new nature. This is what our Lord said to Nicodemus when He said, "That which is born of the flesh is flesh; and that which is born of the Spirit is spirit" (John 3:6). The believer still has that old nature of the flesh, and he won't get rid of it in this life. The idea that we can get rid of that old nature is a tragic mistake. John said, "If we say that we have no sin, we deceive ourselves, and the truth is not in us" (1 John 1:8). My friend, if the *truth* is not in you, then you must be a liar. That puts the "perfect" individual in the position of being a liar.

We have two natures—the old and the new. That is what Paul describes in the last part of Romans. He himself experienced the turmoil of two natures, and this has also been the experience of many believers. The flesh wars against the Spirit, and the Spirit wars against the flesh. Therefore, we cannot do the things that we would like to do. The new nature rebels against the old nature. They are contrary; they are at war with each other. Have you experienced this in your own life?

There is a song we sing entitled "Come Thou Fount" by Robert Robinson.

Come, Thou Fount of every blessing,
Tune my heart to sing Thy grace;
Streams of mercy, never ceasing,
Call for songs of loudest praise.

It is a wonderful hymn. In the last stanza are these words:

Prone to wander, Lord, I feel it,
Prone to leave the God I love;

After this song was written, someone looked at it and said, "That is not my experience—I'll change that." So in some hymnbooks we find these words:

Prone to worship, Lord, I feel it,
Prone to love the God I serve.

Which is true? Well, both are true. I have a nature that is prone to wander, prone to leave the God I love. There are times when this old nature of mine wants to wander away from the Lord! Have you had this experience? Also I have a new nature that is prone to worship the Lord. There are times when I am riding along alone in my car, and I just cry out to Him, "Oh, Lord, how wonderful You are! I love You and worship You." That is the expression of my new nature; my old nature never gets around to praising Him or loving Him. Every believer has an old and a new nature.

There are folk who say, "Well, I can't tell whether I am walking in the Spirit or not." Don't kid yourself about this. You *can* know. Paul has spelled it out here so that you cannot miss it.

But if ye be led of the Spirit, ye are not under the law [Gal. 5:18].

The Holy Spirit of God brings us to a higher plane.

Now Paul makes clear what the works of the flesh are:

Now the works of the flesh are manifest, which are these; Adultery, fornication, uncleanness, lasciviousness,

Idolatry, witchcraft, hatred, variance, emulations, wrath, strife, seditions, heresies,

Envyings, murders, drunkenness, revellings, and such like: of the which I tell you before, as I have also told you in time past, that they which do such things shall not inherit the kingdom of God [Gal. 5:19–21].

This is an ugly brood of sensual sins, religious sins, social sins, and personal sins.

| Sensual Sins | Adultery—omitted from the best manuscripts, included in fornication
Fornication—prostitution
Uncleanness—*(akatharsia)* impurity, sexual sins including pornography
Lasciviousness—brutality, sadism (we see this abounding in our day) |
|---|---|
| Religious Sins | Idolatry—worship of idols (this includes money and everything that takes the place of God)
Witchcraft—*(pharmakeia)* drugs (drugs are used in all heathen religions)
Hatred—enmity
Variances—*eris* (The Greek Eris was the goddess of strife) contentions, quarrels |
| Social Sins | Emulations—*(zelos)* rivalry, jealousy
Wrath—*(thumos)* a hot temper
Strife—factions, cliques (little cliques in a church hurt the cause of Christ)
Seditions—divisions
Heresies—parties, sects
Envyings—*(phthonos)*
Murders—omitted from the best manuscripts probably because it is included in other sins mentioned here. The Lord said if you hate you are guilty of murder |
| Personal Sins | Drunkenness
Revelings, wantonness |

Notice that Paul concludes this list of the works of the flesh by "and such like," which means there are many others he could have mentioned.

"They which do such things shall not inherit the kingdom of God." "Which do" indicates continuous action. Our Lord gave the illustration of the Prodigal Son who got down in the pig pen but didn't stay there. The only ones that stay in a pig pen are pigs. If a son gets there, he will be very unhappy until he gets out. If you can continue to live in sin, you are in a dangerous position. It means you are not a child of God.

Now, having listed the works of the flesh, Paul will list the fruit of the Spirit. Notice the contrast: *works* of the flesh and *fruit* of the Spirit. The works of the flesh are what you *do*. The Ten Commandments were given to control the flesh. But now the Christian life is to produce the fruit of the Spirit.

But the fruit of the Spirit is love, joy, peace, longsuffering, gentleness, goodness, faith,

Meekness, temperance: against such there is no law [Gal. 5:22–23].

The Lord Jesus Christ talked about the fruit of the Spirit in John 15. He said that without Him we could do nothing. And fruit is what He wants in our lives. He wants fruit, *more* fruit, and *much* fruit. In His parable of the sower, He spoke of seed bringing forth thirtyfold, sixtyfold, and an hundredfold (see Matt. 13). He wants us to bear *much* fruit. Now the fruit is produced by the Lord Jesus using the Spirit of God in our lives. He wants to live His life through us. That is the reason I keep saying that you are never asked to live the Christian life. You are asked to let Him live through you. No believer can live the Christian life himself. The old nature cannot produce the fruit of the Spirit.

Paul makes it clear in Romans 7:18 that the new nature has no *power* to produce the fruit of the Spirit. He said, ". . . to will is present with me; but how to perform that which is good I find not." That is the problem with many of us. How do you do it? This is not a do-it-yourself operation. But how are we going to let the Spirit of God produce the fruit of the Spirit in our lives?

The subject of fruit bearing is an interesting one. When speaking about it, I like to use the illustration of my ranch. I have a ranch in Pasadena. It is not what you would call a big ranch. It is 72 feet wide and goes back about 123 feet. My house is right in the middle of it. I have a nice nectarine tree out in front, which really produces fruit. I have three orange trees, four avocado trees, a lemon tree, and a few other trees. There is never a period during the year in California that I do not have some fruit on some tree. I have observed that fruit is produced by the tree, not by self-effort. As far as I can tell, the branches never get together and say, "Let's all work hard and see what we can do for this fellow, McGee, because he likes fruit." I do enjoy fruit but, as far as I can tell, these branches that bear fruit just open up themselves to the sunshine and to the rain. Bloom appears, then the little green fruit forms, grows, and then ripens.

Another thing that I have noticed is that the limbs never leave the trunk of the tree—they don't get down and run around. Our Lord said, ". . . As the branch cannot bear fruit of itself, except it abide in the vine; no more can ye, except ye abide in me" (John 15:4). Our problem is that we offer ourselves to God as a living sacrifice, but when the altar gets hot, we crawl off. We are to *abide* in Christ if we are to produce fruit.

Paul is stating the principle of fruit-bearing so that we can understand it. The fruit is produced by *yielding*—by yielding to the sweet influences that are about us. I am not talking about the world and neither is Paul. We are to *yield* to the Holy Spirit who indwells us. The Holy Spirit wants to produce fruit—it is called the fruit of the Spirit.

"The fruit of the Spirit *is* love, joy, peace." Notice it is singular: is, not *are*. You can argue about the grammar used here, but it happens to be singular in the Greek. This indicates that love is the fruit, and from it stems all other fruits. Love is primary.

Paul says that without love we ". . . become as sounding brass, or a tinkling cymbal" (1 Cor. 13:1). First Corinthians 13 was never intended to be removed from the Bible, beautifully framed, and hung on the wall. It belongs to the *gifts* of the Spirit, and the gifts are not to be exercised except by the fruit of the Spirit, which is love. You cannot exercise a gift without doing it by the fruit of the Spirit. Love is all-important. Paul continues to say in 1 Corinthians 13 that if you give your body to be burned and give everything that you have, but don't have love, you are a nothing. We need to recognize the importance of what Paul is saying.

Another thing that Paul says in 1 Corinthians 13 is that "love never seeks its own." Love is always doing something for others. A gift is always to be exercised in the church. It is a manifestation of the Spirit to all believers. All believers have a gift, and it is to be exercised for the profit of the body of believers. My eyes operate for the benefit of the rest of my body. They guide my body in the right direction. They are important. I cannot imagine my eyes walking out on the rest of my body and saying, "We like looking around, and your feet get tired, so we are going to leave you for awhile." They never do that. We need to recognize that no gift apart from the fruit of the Spirit is to be exercised—and that fruit is love. This is the kind of fruit the Lord Jesus was talking about in John 15. The fruit is the fruit of the Spirit.

"But the fruit of the Spirit is love, joy, peace, longsuffering, gentleness, goodness, faith, meekness, temperance: against such there is no law" (vv. 22–23).

There is "no law" against them, and no law which will produce them. You cannot produce any of these by your own effort. Have you ever tried being meek, for instance? If you tried being meek, and accomplished it, you would be proud that you became meek, and then you would lose your meekness and humility.

For a moment let us look at the fruit of the Spirit. It should characterize the lives of believers. I used to hear the late Dr. Jim McGinley say, "I am not to judge you, but I am a fruit inspector, and I have a right to look at the fruit you are producing." The question is, are you producing any fruit in your life?

Now love ought to be in your heart and life if you are a believer. But, friend, if there are sensual sins in your life, you will never know what real love is. There are many young people today who know a great deal about sex, but they know nothing about love. Love is a fruit of the Spirit, and God will give this love to a husband for his wife, and to the wife for her husband. I don't think anyone can love like two Christians can love. My, how they can love each other!

I shall never forget the night I proposed to my wife. She did not accept me that night, but when she did, we had prayer and dedicated our lives to the Lord. I told her, "I am a preacher who speaks out plainly. I may get into trouble some day. We may find ourselves out on the street." I shall never forget what she said to me: "Well, I'll just beat the drum for you if you have to get out on the street!" That is love on a higher plane.

When we lost our first little girl, I did not want the doctor to tell my wife—*I* wanted to tell her. When I gave her the news, we wept together and then we prayed. Love like that is the fruit of the Holy Spirit.

Joy is a fruit that the Lord Jesus wants you to have in your life. He came that we might have joy—that we might have fun. I wish we had more fun times in our churches today. The world has what they call the "happy hour" in cocktail parlors all across our land. People don't look too happy when they go in, and they sure don't look happy when they come out! They are a bunch of sots, if you please. That's not joy. John says, "And these things write we unto you, that your joy may be full" (1 John 1:4). These things were written that you might really enjoy life. Are you really living it up today, friend? I hope you are as a believer.

The third fruit is peace, the peace of God. Religion can never give this to you. Only Christ can give you deep-down peace—". . . being justified by faith, we have peace with God through our Lord Jesus Christ" (Rom. 5:1).

There are some other fruits. Are you long-suffering—that is, patient and long tempered? This is an area where I need some help, and only the Spirit of God can do it. I found out that *I* cannot do it.

Then there is the fruit of gentleness, which means kindness; there is goodness, which means kind but firm.

Faith, in this list, means faithfulness. If you are a child of God, you will be faithful. If you are married, you will be faithful to your husband or wife. If you are an employee, you are going to be faithful to your job and to your boss. If you are a church member, you are going to be faithful to your church. You are going to be faithful wherever you are and in whatever you do.

Next comes meekness, and that does not mean mildness. Two men who were truly meek were Moses and the Lord Jesus Christ. Perhaps you don't think Moses was meek when he came down from the Mount, found the people were worshiping a golden calf, and administered disciplinary judgment (see Exod. 32). But he was meek. Was Jesus meek when He ran the money-changers out of the temple? Meekness is not mildness and it is not weakness. Meekness means that you will do God's will, that you are willing to yield your will to the will of God. Finally, there is temperance, which is self-control—Christian poise is so needed today.

And they that are Christ's have crucified the flesh with the affections and lusts [Gal. 5:24].

When was the flesh crucified? When they reckon that when Christ died, they died, they will yield themselves on that basis. In Romans 6:13 Paul says, "Neither yield ye your members as instruments of unrighteousness unto sin: but yield yourselves unto God, as those that are alive from the dead, and your members as instruments of righteousness unto God."

"For ye are dead, and your life is hid with Christ in God" (Col. 3:3). "I am crucified with Christ: nevertheless I live; yet not I, but Christ liveth in me: and the life which I now live in the flesh I live by the faith of the Son of God, who loved me, and gave himself for me" (Gal. 2:20). In all of these passages the thought is that when Christ was crucified, the believer was crucified at the same time. The believer is now joined to the living Christ, and the victory is not by struggling but by surrendering to Christ. The scriptural word is *yield;* it is an act of the will.

This is the key to it all:

If we live in the Spirit, let us also walk in the Spirit [Gal. 5:25].

A professor in a theological seminary called my attention to the word *walk* in this verse several years ago, and it has meant a great deal to me. As you recall, back in verse 16 a *"walk* in the Spirit" is *parapateō*, but here "walk" is a different Greek word. It is *stoichomen*, which is basic and elemental, meaning "to proceed or step in order." In verse 16 we were given the principle of walk; here in verse 25 it means to learn to walk. Just as we learned to walk physically by the trial and error method, so are we to begin to walk by the Spirit—it is a learning process.

Let me illustrate this principle with a ridiculous illustration. What is walking? Walking is putting one foot in front of the other. You may have heard about the knock-kneed girl. One knee said to the other, "If you let me by this time, I will let you by next time." That is walking, putting one foot in front of the other. This means to learn to walk. How did you learn to walk? Were you given a lecture on the subject? Did you go to a school and take a course in learning to walk? One summer my grandson, who was about twelve months old at the time, stayed with us for a time. He was just standing and wobbling along. I did not put him in his high chair and tell him about the physical mechanism of the foot. I did not give him a lecture on the psychology of walking or the sociological implications of walking. If I had explained all of these things to my grandson, could he have lifted the tray of his high chair and walked off? No, my friend, that is not the way you learn to walk. You learn to walk by trial and error. One time my grandson fell down hard, and he had a big knot on his forehead. He fell many times, but before long he was walking and running and climbing as surefooted as a mountain goat. He learned to do it by just *doing* it, by trial and error.

This is the way we are to learn to walk in the Spirit—by trial and error. I know people who have attended Keswick conferences, spiritual life conferences, and Bible conferences; they have their notebooks filled with notes on how to live the Christian life. Still they are not living it. What is the problem?

You have to *learn* to walk in the Spirit, which means you are to start out. Why not start now? Say, "I am going to walk in the Spirit. I am going to depend upon the Holy Spirit to produce the fruits in my life." Perhaps you are thinking that you might fall down. I have news for you—you are going to fall. It will hurt. You say, "How many times will I fall?" I don't know. I am still falling. But that is the way you are going to walk in the Spirit, and that's the only way. My friend, you need to step out today and begin leaning upon the Spirit of God. Yield yourself to Him; it is an act of the will.

Every day I start my day by saying, "Lord, I can't live today in a way that pleases You, and I want You to do it through me." I find there are times when I don't get but a few blocks from home when something happens. One morning a woman in a Volkswagen cut in front of me. I had been so nice and sweet up to then, but I drove up beside her car and I told her what she had done. And she told me a thing or two right back. When she drove off, I thought, *My, I sure fell on my face!* When I do that, I just get up and start over again.

Let us not be desirous of vain glory, provoking one another, envying one another [Gal. 5:26].

"Let us not be desirous of vain glory"—you and I are *never* going to be wonderful saints of God. *He* is wonderful. Oh, how wonderful He is! He is worthy of our worship. Let's start walking, depending on Him like little children. That's what He wants us to do.

"Provoking one another" is challenging one another. We are not to challenge and envy one another. We are to get down from our high chairs and start walking in the Spirit. The Christian life is not a balloon ascension with some great overpowering experience of soaring to the heights. Rather it is a daily walk; it is a matter of putting one foot ahead of the other, in dependence upon the Holy Spirit.

CHAPTER 6

THEME: *Saved by faith and fruit of the Spirit presents Christian character; autographed conclusion; Paul's testimony*

This final chapter of Galatians brings us to the third step in this practical section of sanctification by the Spirit. We have seen that being saved by faith and living by law perpetrates falling from grace. Also we have seen that being saved by faith and walking in the Spirit produces fruit of the Spirit. In other words, we have seen what it means to walk in the Spirit. It is something we are to begin, and though we fail, we are to keep at it. Now we will see how the fruit of the Spirit will work out in our lives. Here is where we see it put in shoe leather where it can hit the pavement of our hometown.

SAVED BY FAITH AND FRUIT OF THE SPIRIT PRESENTS CHRISTIAN CHARACTER

Brethren, if a man be overtaken in a fault, ye which are spiritual, restore such an one in the spirit of meekness; considering thyself, lest thou also be tempted [Gal. 6:1].

Who is the "man" mentioned in this verse? It is a generic term and refers to any man or woman who is a Christian. The word *fault*, taken from the Greek *paraptōma*, means "a falling aside or mishap." It means "to stumble." It may not refer to a great sin but to an awful blunder.

Now what is to be done to a person who is overtaken in a fault? Well, the "spiritual" folk, and many think they are spiritual, interpret this as meaning they are to beat him on the head with a baseball bat because he has done something wrong. There is a danger of not really wanting to restore him. We would much rather criticize and condemn him. However, the believer does not lose his salvation when he sins. If a Christian is overtaken in a fault, a spiritual Christian is to restore that one in the spirit of meekness. Meekness is one of the fruits of the Spirit.

The word used for "fault" in this verse is the same word used to describe the Lord Jesus Christ in the Garden of Gethsemane when He fell on His face and prayed (see Matt. 26:39). It means "to stumble." If a man be overtaken in a fault, he stumbles. He may commit a small sin or an awful blunder.

One of the wonderful things said about the Lord Jesus in prophecy is found in Isaiah 63:9,

"In all their affliction he was afflicted, and the angel of his presence saved them: in his love and in his pity he redeemed them; and he bare them, and carried them all the days of old." Now the better manuscripts say, "In all their affliction He was *not* afflicted." I like that much better. The Lord Jesus goes along with me through life, and when I stumble and fall down, He does not fall. He is not afflicted. He is there beside me and He picks me up, brushes me off, and tells me to start out again. It is a comforting thing to know that I have One near me who is not afflicted in my affliction.

The word used for "restore" in this verse is a verb which means "to set a broken bone." If a fellow falls down and breaks his leg, what are you going to do? Are you going to walk off and leave him in pain? God says, "You who are spiritual set the broken bone. Get him back on his feet again." It is to be done in the spirit of meekness.

One of the great preachers of the South was marvelously converted when he was a drunkard. His ministry was quite demanding and after a great deal of pressure and temptation he got drunk one night. He was so ashamed that the very next day he called in his board of deacons and turned in his resignation. He told them, "I want to resign." They were amazed. They asked why. He frankly told them, "I got drunk last night. A preacher should not get drunk, and I want to resign." It was obvious that he was ashamed, and do you know what those wonderful deacons did? They put their arms around him and said, "Let's all pray." They would not accept his resignation. A man who was present in the congregation that next Sunday said, "I never heard a greater sermon in my life than that man preached." Those deacons were real surgeons—they set a broken bone; they restored him. There are some people who would have put him out of the ministry, but these deacons put that preacher back on his feet, and God marvelously used him after that.

"Ye which are spiritual, restore such an one in the spirit of meekness." Notice that you are to restore him in the spirit of *meekness*. A spiritual man will have the fruit of the Spirit in his life: love, joy, peace, longsuffering, gentleness, goodness, faithfulness, and *meekness*. You are to restore him in meekness.

"Considering thyself, lest thou also be tempted." Don't think that you are immune to what you are pointing your finger and blaming another brother for doing. You could do the same thing. So restore him in the spirit of meekness.

Bear ye one another's burdens, and so fulfil the law of Christ [Gal. 6:2].

This is a verse that caused me as a boy to wonder about the accuracy of the Bible.

Most little towns of a bygone day had a character known as the town atheist, a free-thinker, generally a ne'er-do-well, although sometimes he was one of the leading citizens of the community. The little town in which I lived as a boy lacked many things. It didn't have street lights. In fact, we didn't have electric lights in our home, and I can remember using the lamp to study by in those days. Our little town didn't have sidewalks; it didn't have paved streets. It didn't have running water—except what you ran out to the well to get; and we didn't have inside plumbing. There were many things our little town lacked, but we did have a town atheist. He called himself a social-ist. Each Sunday morning, weather permit-ting, he was down at the street corner on the town square, speaking. Generally he had about a dozen listeners, who were also loafers. On my way to Sunday school—I killed as much time as possible—I always stopped to listen to him. The thing that impressed me about this atheist was that his mouth was cut on a bias, and as he chewed tobacco an amazing thing took place. He not only defied the Word of God, he also defied the law of gravitation. You would think, according to the law of gravita-tion, that the tobacco juice would run out of the lower corner of his mouth. But it didn't. It ran out of the upper corner. I used to stand there as a boy and wonder how he did it.

This man, I remember, always ridiculed the Bible, and he pointed out supposed contradic-tions. His favorites were these two verses in the sixth chapter of Galatians: "Bear ye one another's burdens, and so fulfil the law of Christ" (v. 2). Then he would read, "For every man shall bear his own burden" (v. 5). He would read both verses, then lift his head and leer at the crowd and say, "You see, there is a contradiction in the Bible. One place it says that you're to bear one another's burdens, and then it says you are to bear your own bur-dens." None of us in the little town knew how to answer him, so we just stood there with our mouths open and listened to him. Actually, the answer was very simple, but we didn't know it in those days.

There are in the Scriptures eleven different words that are translated by our one English word *burden*. This means there are different kinds of burdens. There are some burdens that you can share; there are burdens that you must bear and you cannot share them with anyone. That is a very simple but a very satis-factory answer.

Now burdens are those things that we all have in common. All of us have burdens. Not all of us have wealth, but we have burdens. Not all of us have health, but we have burdens. Not all of us have talents, but we have bur-dens. Some of us lack even physical mem-bers—not all of us can see, not all of us can hear, not all of us have arms and legs, and certainly not all of us have good looks. We say that we all have the same blood, but it is not the same; it comes in different types. We do not have very much in common, but we all have burdens.

There is a Spanish proverb that goes some-thing like this: "No home is there anywhere that does not sooner or later have its hush." Also the French have a proverb: "Everyone thinks his own burden is heaviest." A woman in Southern California who has done a great deal of work with children said, "Even chil-dren have burdens." Burdens are common to the human family. We all have burdens.

However, not all of us have the same bur-dens. We have many different burdens. What Paul is doing in this sixth chapter of Galatians is dividing burdens into two classes: burdens which we can share, and burdens which we must bear, and cannot share. Those of us in our little town didn't know there were two different words used in the Greek. In verse 2 you could translate it like this: "The burdens of each other, keep bearing." The Greek word for burden is *baros*, meaning "something heavy." Our Lord used it when He spoke about the *burden* and the heat of the day (see Matt. 20:12). And for the early church, when it met in its first council in Jerusalem, made this decision: "For it seemed good to the Holy Spirit and to us, to lay upon you no greater *burden* than these necessary things" (Acts 15:28, italics mine), speaking of a burden they were to share with the church in Jerusalem. Someone has said that a load is only half a load when two are carrying it. There are burdens today that we can share.

A woman boarded a bus with a very heavy basket. She sat down beside a man and put the basket on her lap. After noticing her discomfort he said, "Lady, if you would put that heavy basket down on the floor you would find that the bus would carry both you and your load!" May I say to you, there are burdens that you can let someone else bear with you.

Now *burden (baros)* means "fault"—"If a man be overtaken in a fault." That's his burden. You could help him bear it. It also means infirmity, a weakness, an ignorance, a pressure, a tension, a grief.

I think everybody has a fault. A man speaking to a group asked the question, "Is there anyone here who does not have a fault or do you know someone who does not have a fault?" No one raised his hand. After he had repeated the question several times, a little fellow in the back, a Mr. Milquetoast type, raised his hand. The speaker asked him to stand. "Are you the one who has no faults?" "Oh, no," he said, "I'm not the one." "Then do you know someone who does not have any faults?" "Well," he said, "I don't exactly know him, but I have heard of him." The man who was lecturing said, "Tell me, who is he?" The little fellow said, "He's my wife's first husband." And I have a notion that he had heard of him quite a few times, by the way.

All of us have faults, and that's a burden. Many times we fall down, and many times we see a brother fall down. "Ye which are spiritual, restore such an one."

Then there is another burden that you and I can share: tensions. Now you can take a tranquilizer, but, my friend, that really won't solve your problems. We are living today in a time of tension such as the human family has never before experienced. I don't know about you, but I live in "Tension Town." Many of us in these great metropolitan areas are under pressure and tension today. This is certainly a burden we need to bear with one another.

Let me illustrate. A very dear man, in one of the churches I pastored, came to me and said, "Do you have something against me?" "No," I said, "why do you say that?" "Well, I met you down on the street and you didn't even speak to me." I was amazed. "I didn't?" "No. You just passed me right by. You looked right at me." I said, "I didn't see you." "You must have—you looked right at me." So I asked him what day that was, and realized it was the day the airlines got my tickets mixed up, and I was going down there to straighten them out. My friend, we are under tension at a time like that. And my friend was also under tension for assuming I had snubbed him. Well, I never shall forget, he put his arm around me and said, "I'm glad to know that." You see, he

was helping me bear the burden of tension. That's something we can share with each other.

Now I come to the third burden you and I can share. That is the burden known as grief. The burden of tragedy, the burden of sorrow, the burden of disappointment is inevitable in the human family. If it hasn't come to you, it will come. And when it comes we need somebody, a friend, to stand with us. The three friends of Job—we criticize them because they began a talking marathon, but actually they first spent seven days sitting with Job and sorrowing with him.

In a book of natural history there is a statement that reads: "Man is the only one that knows nothing, and that can learn nothing without being taught. He can neither speak, nor walk, nor eat. In short, he can do nothing at the prompting of nature but weep." All that you and I know to do when we come into this world is weep. We come into this world with a cry, and we need comfort. From the very beginning and all through life we need comfort because of the fact that we have been born into this world of woe.

Ruth could say to Boaz, "Thou hast comforted me" (see Ruth 2:13). She was a stranger, an outcast, who had come from a foreign country and expected to be kept on the outside, but into her life came someone who showed an interest in her and extended to her certain courtesies. With appreciation she said, "Thou hast comforted me."

Mary broke an alabaster box of ointment upon our Lord. She did this shortly before His crucifixion because she knew what was going to take place. No one else seemed to realize what was happening, but she knew. Jesus said, "Let her alone; for the day of my burial hath she kept this" (see Matt. 26:12). She alone entered into His sufferings. And He said, "Verily I say unto you, Wheresoever this gospel shall be preached in the whole world, there shall also this, that this woman hath done, be told for a memorial of her" (Matt. 26:13). And the fragrance of that ointment has filled the world. Grief is a burden that you can share. There will be those who will come to you in your sorrow.

Our faults, our tensions, our griefs are some of the burdens that you and I can share.

Is thy cruse of comfort failing?
    Raise and share it with a friend,
And thro' all the years of famine
    It shall serve thee to the end.

Love Divine will fill thy storehouse,
  Or thy handful still renew;
Scanty fare for one will often
  Make a royal feast for two.

Lost and weary on the mountains,
  Wouldst thou sleep amidst the snow?
Chafe that frozen form beside thee,
  And together both shall glow.

Art thou wounded in life's battle?
  Many stricken round thee moan;
Give to them thy precious ointment,
  And that balm shall heal thine own.
                    —Author unknown

There are burdens that we can share.

Now let's look at the other verse that tells us there are burdens which we cannot share.

But let every man prove his own work, and then shall he have rejoicing in himself alone, and not in another [Gal. 6:4].

I think he means that we are not to run around getting everybody to carry our burdens.

For every man shall bear his own burden [Gal. 6:5].

The word *burden* here is the Greek *phortion*, meaning "a load to be borne." This word is used to speak of a ship's cargo. Actually, it is used to speak of a child in the womb—only the mother could bear it, you see. This is a load that is impossible to share. While I never recommend J. B. Phillips' *New Testament in Modern English* as a translation (it should not be called a translation), it is a most excellent explanation. Many times it throws light on a passage of Scripture. He gives this paraphrase of Galatians 6:5: "For every man must 'shoulder his own pack.'" That's it. Each man must shoulder his own pack. There is an old bromide: "To every man his work." And another, a rather crude one, "Every tub must sit on its own bottom." In other words, there are burdens today that you and I cannot share.

Every life, in one sense, is separated, it is isolated, it is segregated, it is quarantined from every other life. Dr. Funk, of the Funk and Wagnalls Dictionary, has compiled a list of words in which the saddest word in the English language is *alone*. There are certain burdens that you and I will have to bear alone. I will mention just a few of them here—you will think of others.

The first one I want to mention is suffering. You will have to suffer alone. No one can suffer for you. You are born into this world alone—and it's a world of woe; you will suffer alone. You will have to face certain problems alone. There will be physical suffering that will come to you. You will get sick, and no one can take your place.

When my daughter was a very little thing, we were coming back from Texas, and she started running a high fever. We took her to the hospital at Globe, Arizona. A doctor gave her certain medication and told us, "You give her this and the fever will go down. It is getting late in the afternoon so keep driving to California and get out of this heat." So we started out. In Phoenix we stopped for gasoline, and my wife took her temperature. It registered 104°—her temperature hadn't gone down. We were frightened. We went to a motel, called a doctor, and told him the situation. He said to continue the medication and to bring her to the hospital in the morning. Never shall I forget my feelings as I carried her to the hospital and laid her down. Never in my life had I had that experience. I would have gladly taken that fever in my own body—*gladly* would I have done it. But, my friend, I could not do it. We have to suffer alone. You cannot get someone to substitute for you. Suffering is one thing that we cannot share. Mental anguish is another type of suffering that you cannot share. Oh, the number of folk who are disappointed. They are even bitter today because of some great disappointment. Suffering is a burden that we have to bear alone.

There is another burden that you and I cannot share with anyone else. It is death. We cannot share this with another. There will come a time when each of us will go down through the valley of the shadow of death, and we will go alone. Thomas Hobbes, an agnostic all of his life, a very brilliant man, said when he came to his death, "I am taking a fearful leap into the dark!" And then he cried out, "Oh, God, it is lonely!" Yes, it is. Death is a burden you cannot share. John Haye, at one time Secretary of State, was quite a writer. He wrote a poem portraying death entitled "The Stirrup Cup," having in mind the cavalrymen who used to drink when they mounted their steeds. This is the way he began:

My short and happy day is done,
The long and lonely night comes on:
And at my door the pale horse stands
To bear me forth to unknown lands.

And, my friend, when death comes, you and I will be riding alone. Death is a burden that you will have to bear alone.

We come now to the third and last burden that I shall mention. It bears an unusual name, by the way. It is the *Bēma*. The *Bēma* is the judgment seat of Christ. It is not for the unsaved; it is for Christians. Oh, yes, there is a judgment for the unbeliever, the Great White Throne Judgment described in the twentieth chapter of Revelation. But the *Bēma Seat* is for the Christian. "For we must all appear before the judgment seat of Christ; that every one may receive the things done in his body, according to that he hath done, whether it be good or bad" (2 Cor. 5:10). Everything that we have done in the flesh as a Christian is to be judged to see whether or not we receive a reward. Salvation is not in question—that was settled for the believer at the cross of Christ. It is the works of the believer that are to be judged at the *Bēma Seat*. "So then every one of us shall give account of himself to God" (Rom. 14:12).

Then Paul puts down a principle which is applicable to every avenue of life but is specifically given to believers: "Be not deceived; God is not mocked: for whatsoever a man soweth, that shall he also reap" (v. 7). This principle is true in the realm of nature. You sow cotton; you reap cotton. You sow wheat; you reap wheat. And as a Christian you will reap what you sow. We like to sing "The Old Account Was Settled Long Ago." In a believer's life this is true—but what about the new account? What about the account since you were saved? What has your life been since you accepted Christ? Do you have sin in your life? Have you confessed it? We are all to appear before the judgment seat of Christ. "But if we walk in the light, as he is in the light, we have fellowship one with another, and the blood of Jesus Christ his Son cleanseth us from all sin" (1 John 1:7).

Somebody will say, "I'm a Christian. I don't have any sin." You don't? Then you are not in the light. If you will get in the light you will see the sin that is in your life. The light—which is the Word of God—reveals what is there. Try this one on for size: "Therefore to him that knoweth to do good, and doeth it not, to him it is sin" (James 4:17). Does that fit you today? I think it will fit all of us. He that knows to do good, and does it not, sins. Your life as a child of God is a burden that you carry, and you will have to bring it before Him some day.

Now there is another type of burden which you can neither bear nor share. It is a burden the Scriptures speak of: the burden of sin. Paul speaks of it in the first part of Romans.

David in the Psalms says: "For mine iniquities are gone over mine head: as an heavy burden they are too heavy for me" (Ps. 38:4). Sin is a burden you cannot share with anyone else. And sin is a burden you cannot bear, my friend. "My iniquities," David says, "are gone over my head: as an heavy burden they are too heavy for me." Also from the Psalms comes this longing: "And I said, Oh that I had wings like a dove! for then would I fly away, and be at rest" (Ps. 55:6). Have you ever felt like that? Sometimes the doctor recommends that we get away from it all. The psalmist says, "If I could only run away from it." But you and I cannot run away from it because we have a guilt complex. A psychologist out here at the University of Southern California tells me that the guilt complex is as much a part of us as our right arm. The psychologists have tried to get rid of it. They have not succeeded. Everyone has it. Sir Arthur Conan Doyle, the writer of detective stories, and creator of Sherlock Holmes, liked to play practical jokes. At one time he sent a telegram to twelve famous people in London whom he knew. The telegram read, "Flee at once. All is discovered." All twelve of them left the country—yet all of them were upright citizens. May I say to you, my beloved, we all have a guilt complex. Sin is that burden which we can neither share nor bear. It is too heavy for us.

There is only one place you can get rid of it, and that is at the cross of Christ. "Cast thy burden upon the LORD, and he shall sustain thee: he shall never suffer the righteous to be moved" (Ps. 55:22). The Lord Jesus said: "Come unto me, all ye that labour and are heavy laden, and I will give you rest" (Matt. 11:28). He alone can lift the heavy burden of sin today, and it is because He paid the penalty for it. He alone can lift it; He alone can take it from you.

There are two famous pieces of sculpture that depict this. One is the "Dying Gaul" and the other is "The Laocoön," which is in Rome at the Vatican. "The Dying Gaul" depicts a man who has been brought down as a captive and slave to Rome, then put into the arena as a gladiator and mortally wounded. He is lying there, his life blood flowing from him, and he is looking up for help. He is in a strange land, and there is nobody, nobody there to help him. A dying gladiator. May I say to you that this is a picture of any man today without Christ. Christ alone can help us, for that is the reason He came into the world. He said: "For the Son of man is come to seek and to save that which was lost" (Luke 19:10). He also said: ". . . the

Son of man came not to be ministered unto, but to minister, and to give his life a ransom for many" (Mark 10:45). Christ paid the penalty for your sin and my sin. Like the dying gladiator, we can look to Him and be saved.

The other piece of sculpture is "The Laocoön." A priest of Troy looked out and saw two sea serpents come and coil themselves about his two sons. He went to their aid, but he could not help them because the sea serpents also enmeshed him in their coils. There they are—all three of them going down to death. To me this illustrates the fact that personal sin is a burden that we cannot cope with. It will take us down to death—eternal death.

What do you do with your burdens?

There are some burdens that you can share. There are others that you must bear alone. But the burden of personal sin is a burden too heavy for you; it is the burden you cannot bear. Over nineteen hundred years ago Christ took the burden of your sin, and He bore it on the cross. Today your burden is either on you, or by faith you have received Christ as your Savior and it is on Him. It cannot be both places—your sin is either on you or it is on Christ. And Christ does not *share* it—He bore it all.

Let him that is taught in the word communicate unto him that teacheth in all good things [Gal. 6:6].

This is probably the bluntest verse in the Bible. Paul is really putting it on the line. The Greek word *koinōneō*, translated "communicate," means sharing, taking part—sharing the things of Christ together. Paul is bluntly saying this: "Pay your preacher. If someone ministers to your spiritual benefits, minister to him with material benefits." If God has blessed you materially and you are being blessed by someone spiritually, then you ought to minister to that person with material benefits. This is put on a grace basis of sharing, but believe me, friend, if you go into a grocery store and buy bread and meat and go by the checkout stand without paying for it, you are in trouble. There are many people who are ministered to spiritually, but when they go by the checkout counter, they don't share. No one thinks anything about it. The Word of God says that you are to share with those who minister to you.

Be not deceived; God is not mocked: for whatsoever a man soweth, that shall he also reap [Gal. 6:7].

This is one of those remarkable verses in Scripture. This is an immutable law that operates in every sphere of life. In agriculture and horticulture if you sow corn, you get corn; if you sow cotton, you reap cotton. In the moral sphere you also reap what you sow. In the Book of Matthew, chapter 13, the Lord Jesus Christ told about a sower that went forth to sow. He also told us about a reaper that went forth to reap.

One day a visitor in a penitentiary passed by a cell where a man was patching his prison garb with needle and thread. The visitor, wanting to begin a conversation with the prisoner, said, "What are you doing? Sewing?" The prisoner looked up and replied, "No, *reaping!*" That is the point of this verse. The principle stated here is immutable, invariable, unalterable, and cannot be revoked. It cannot be changed one iota, and it is applicable to every sphere and field of life. When you sow wheat, you will get wheat. You will never pick a squash off of a walnut tree. Sometimes a watermelon vine extends out twenty feet in one direction, but it has never been known to make the mistake of putting a pumpkin on the end of it. It always puts a watermelon out there. There is wheat being found in tombs in Egypt that was put there five thousand years ago. They planted it and it came up wheat. In five thousand years the seed did not forget that it was wheat. What *you* sow you will reap and that will never change.

There are many men in the Bible who illustrate this principle. One of them is Jacob, whose story is told in Genesis 27–29. Jacob deceived his father, Isaac. He put on a goatskin and pretended to be his brother Esau, who was a hairy outdoorsman, in order to receive the blessing given to the oldest son. After deceiving his father, Jacob ran away and lived with his Uncle Laban for several years. He thought he had gotten away with deceiving his father. But remember, God says that what you sow you will reap. You won't reap something similar; you will reap the identical thing that you sow. What happened to Jacob? He fell in love with Rachel, Laban's youngest daughter. He served seven years for her. They had the wedding, and when he lifted the veil, what did he have? He did not have Rachel, the younger daughter; he had Leah, the older daughter. I have a notion that Jacob learned a real lesson on his honeymoon. He had deceived his father by pretending to be the older son when he was actually the younger son. Now his uncle gave him the older daughter when he thought he was getting the younger daughter. Believe me, chickens do come home to roost!

In 1 Kings 21 we find the story of Ahab and Jezebel and their murderous plot to take Naboth's vineyard. Ahab coveted Naboth's vineyard, but Naboth did not want to sell his land. But since Ahab and Jezebel were king and queen, they usually took what they wanted. Jezebel had Naboth killed and Ahab took possession of the vineyard. They thought they would get away with their evil deed, but God sent Elijah to them with a message: ". . . Thus saith the Lord, In the place where dogs licked the blood of Naboth shall dogs lick thy blood, even thine" (1 Kings 21:19). Later Ahab was wounded in battle. He told his chariot driver to take him out of the battle, and the blood from his wound ran out into his chariot. After the battle, he was brought back to Samaria, and there in the pool of Samaria they washed the chariot, and the dogs licked up the blood.

Another example is the apostle Paul. He was a leader in the stoning of Stephen, and after his conversion, when he was over in the Galatian country, he was stoned. You may think that, because he was converted and his sins were forgiven, he would not reap what he had sowed. But it is a law of God that "whatsoever a man soweth, that shall he also reap."

I remember well hearing Mel Trotter, the evangelist who was a drunkard before his conversion. I had invited him to Nashville, Tennessee, to hold evangelistic meetings. One night after a meeting we went to a place called Candyland and everybody ordered a great big sloppy banana split, or a milkshake, or a malt. All Mel Trotter ordered was a little bitty glass of carbonated water. Everyone began to rib him about it, and asked him for the reason. I shall never forget his answer, "When the Lord gave me a new heart at my conversion, He did not give me a new stomach. I am paying for the years I spent drinking." May I say again, "Whatsoever a man soweth, that shall he also reap." Don't be deceived. God is not mocked. You won't get by with it.

I wish young people would realize the truth of this principle. Many of them are taking drugs. Many are trying to satisfy themselves by indulging in easy sex, free love. Some of them are already beginning to reap the results of what they have sown. Venereal disease has reached epidemic proportions in many states in America, and there is an alarming rise in mental disorders. Why? God says that you will not get by with sin—regardless of how many pills you take. God says you will reap what you sow. God will not be mocked. When you sow

corn, you reap corn. When you sow sin, that is what you will reap. Someone may say, "I got converted." That is wonderful, but you are still going to have a payday someday. You will still reap what you have sown.

For he that soweth to his flesh shall of the flesh reap corruption; but he that soweth to the Spirit shall of the Spirit reap life everlasting [Gal. 6:8].

Reaping "life everlasting" includes the fruit of the Spirit in this life and the glorious prospect of the future.

I think many Christians really ought to be fearful of the return of Christ for His own, because it is then that we shall go before the judgment seat of Christ to give an account of the things done in the flesh. My friend, you may be saved, but it may still be very embarrassing for you in that day when you give an account of your life to Him. John mentions the fact that it is possible to be ashamed at His appearing (see 1 John 2:28). If you are going to live in the flesh, you will produce the things of the flesh. That does not, however, mean that you will lose your salvation, but it does mean that you will lose your reward, which will make it a day of shame and regret when you stand before Him.

God has put up a red light; now He puts up a green light. Here are words for your comfort and encouragement.

And let us not be weary in well-doing: for in due season we shall reap, if we faint not [Gal. 6:9].

A father said to me some time ago, "I'm concerned about my boys." He is a doctor, and he said, "The tide is against me. The schools are against me. Other parents seem to be against me, and even some friends are against me. But I want to raise my boys right." If that is your concern, my friend, let me encourage you to sow the right seed. Be patient, and you will reap what you have sown. In Kansas you can't go out and cut grain in January. You have to wait until the time of reaping comes. So just keep sowing. You may have problems and difficulties today, but just keep sowing the Word of God. The Lord has promised: "For as the rain cometh down, and the snow from heaven, and returneth not thither, but watereth the earth, and maketh it bring forth and bud, that it may give seed to the sower, and bread to the eater: So shall my word be that goeth forth out of my mouth: it shall not return unto me void, but it shall accomplish that which I please, and it shall prosper in the thing whereto I sent it" (Isa. 55:10–11).

Remember that Abraham believed God and walked with Him in the land of Canaan. At that time the Canaanite—wicked and idolatrous—was in the land. A son, Isaac, was born to Abraham. When Isaac became a young man, Abraham took him to the top of Mount Moriah. In obedience to God's command, Abraham prepared to offer his son as a sacrifice. God, however, did not let him go through with it. Abraham sowed to the Spirit and he reaped life everlasting.

Jochebed was the mother of Moses. Because of the terrible times in which they lived, she devised a plan to save his life, and he was adopted by Pharaoh's daughter. By God's wonderful arrangement, Jochebed was able to be his nursemaid while he was young. Undoubtedly she taught Moses about God and His call to Abraham and about His purpose for Israel. Then she saw her boy grow up like an Egyptian. All Egypt was against her—the culture of Egypt, the pleasures of Egypt, the philosophy of Egypt, and the religion of Egypt. But there came a day when Moses forsook the pleasures and sins of Egypt and went out to take his place with God's people. Jochebed reaped what she had sown.

We also have an illustration of this principle in the life of David. His sin was glaring, and many folk think of him as being a cruel, sinful man. But sin did not characterize David's life. It is interesting that a drop of black ink on a white tablecloth can be seen from a long distance, but a drop of black ink on a black suit would never be noticed. Other kings during that period of time were so bad that, when they committed a sin such as David did, it would not be noticed. But in David's life it stands out like a horrible blot. David had a heart for God. Even in his confession, he reveals his hunger and thirst for God. But David sowed sin and reaped a terrible harvest in the lives of his own children.

We reap what we sow, my friend. "And let us not be weary in well-doing: for in due season we shall reap, if we faint not."

As we have therefore opportunity, let us do good unto all men, especially unto them who are of the household of faith [Gal. 6:10].

Now Paul moves on. He says that we ought to be do-gooders. Now I recognize that the entire religion of liberalism is one of "doing good." I believe in doing good, but you have to have the right foundation under the good

deeds. The right foundation is the gospel of the grace of God and walking in the Spirit of God. When you walk in the Spirit, the fruit of the Spirit is produced. Then, my friend, you are going to do good. You will do good for all men, especially for other believers.

AUTOGRAPHED CONCLUSION

This brings us to the last major division of the epistle to the Galatians. Three handwritings are mentioned in this final section. The first is Paul's own handwriting.

Ye see how large a letter I have written unto you with mine own hand [Gal. 6:11].

"How large a letter" doesn't mean a long letter. This Epistle to the Galatians is only six chapters, while his Epistle to the Romans (which deals with practically the same subject) is sixteen chapters. This could not be called a long letter. But Paul is saying that he has written with large letters, which is characteristic with folk who have poor vision. This, I believe, bears out the theory that Paul's "thorn in the flesh" was eye trouble (see 2 Cor. 12:7). As you recall, he had said to them earlier, ". . . I bear you record, that, if it had been possible, ye would have plucked out your own eyes, and have given them to me" (Gal. 4:15). I am sure that Paul had a serious visual problem.

When Paul wrote his Epistle to the Romans, he dictated it to a secretary. And at the conclusion of the letter, Paul said to the secretary, "Now if you want to put in your greetings, go ahead and do it." So in Romans 16:22 we have the secretary's salutation: "I Tertius, who wrote this epistle, salute you in the Lord."

However, when Paul wrote to the Galatians, he was angry. He had heard that they were mixing the gospel with law—and when that is done, the gospel of the grace of God is absolutely destroyed. He couldn't wait for a secretary to arrive—he just sat down and wrote to them himself. Because he didn't see clearly, he wrote with large letters.

I studied Shakespeare under a very skillful scholar who was partially blind. During class he would put the book right up to his nose and move it back and forth as he read. When he graded our papers, he would write his comments in large letters in the margin. His comments were brief because the words he wrote were so large. Apparently, Paul's writing was like that.

PAUL'S TESTIMONY

As many as desire to make a fair shew in the flesh, they constrain you to be circumcised; only lest they should suffer persecution for the cross of Christ [Gal. 6:12].

By exerting pressure and stressing circumcision among the Gentiles, the Judaizers hoped to escape the anger and wrath of Jews who were not believers. The Judaizers were the legalists of the day. Actually, you never get in trouble preaching legalism. It appeals to the natural man because law is given to curb him. A great many of us certainly feel that the old nature of the other man should be curbed.

I was talking to a man in a public place the other day when a boy drove about seventy-five miles an hour right through a dangerous intersection. This man wanted that boy arrested and put in jail. He wanted the boy to be forced to obey the law. This man rejects the grace of God—he is an unsaved man—but he certainly is for legalism. Every man wants the other man to obey the law.

Frankly, we also like a law we can obey. When I was a boy in school, I did some high jumping. In those days we started off with a three and one-half foot jump. When I jumped four feet, I had some difficulty. So when I practiced jumping, I always kept the bar at the four foot level. That is the way most people are about legalism. They want to be able to clear the hurdle, but they don't want it to be too high for them. Legalism is popular. The grace of God is unpopular. The human heart finds it repulsive. It is the offense of the Cross.

For neither they themselves who are circumcised keep the law; but desire to have you circumcised, that they may glory in your flesh [Gal. 6:13].

By forcing the Gentiles to be circumcised the Judaizers would gain the credit for bringing them under the Law.

It is interesting that those who claim they live under the Law are not actually living by the Law. Many people who say that they live by the Sermon on the Mount are hypocrites. I know that to be true because of the experiences I have had in my ministry.

Let me cite an experience I had many years ago at a luncheon at the Chamber of Commerce in Nashville, Tennessee. When I was a pastor in that city, one of the elders in my church, who was a banker, was president of

the Chamber of Commerce that year and invited me to speak to the group. I was a young pastor then—in fact, I was not yet married; it was my first pastorate. I arrived early and one of the officials was already at the speaker's table. He began talking with me, and I have never heard a man swear more than he did—and I've heard some who are experts at it. I didn't rebuke him, I just let him talk. Finally, in our conversation he asked me, "By the way, what's your racket?" I told him I was a preacher. He looked at me in amazement and asked, "Are you the speaker today?" When I said I was, he immediately began to tread water fast! He said, "Well, we're glad to have you, and I want you to know that *I'm* a Christian." That was certainly news, because I would never have suspected it by the way he was talking. Then he enlarged upon it. He told me he was an officer of a very fashionable church in Nashville. He told me about all the wonderful things that he did, then he concluded by saying, "The Sermon on the Mount is *my* religion." I said, "Fine. That's great!" I shook hands with him, then asked, "How are you coming with it?" He looked rather puzzled and asked, "What do you mean 'how am I coming with it?'" So I explained, "Well, you say the Sermon on the Mount is your religion, and I'd just like to know if you are living by it." He said he tried to. "But that is not what the Sermon on the Mount is all about. It puts down a pretty severe standard and it hasn't anything in there about *trying*. You either do it or you don't do it. Now you say it's your religion so I assume you do it." He told me that he certainly tried. Then I began to push him a little, "Do you keep it?" He said, "I guess I do." "Well, let's see if you do. The Lord Jesus said that if you are angry with your brother you are guilty of murder. How do you make out on that one?" He hesitated, "Well, I might have a little trouble there, but I think I get by." "All right, let's try another commandment that the Lord Jesus lifted to the nth degree. He said if you so much as look upon a woman to lust after her, you're guilty of adultery. How about that one?" "Oh," he said, "that one would get me." I thought it would. I said, "Look, you're not keeping the Sermon on the Mount. If I were you I'd change my religion and get one I could keep." Do you see what he was? That man was a hypocrite. He went around telling others that he was living by the Sermon on the Mount and he was breaking it at every turn. He needed the grace of God. And there are multitudes of people just like him in many churches today. Paul mentions that with this tremendous statement:

But God forbid that I should glory, save in the cross of our Lord Jesus Christ, by whom the world is crucified unto me, and I unto the world [Gal. 6:14].

Between Paul and the world there was a cross. That should be the position of every believer today. That will have more to do with shaping your conduct than anything else. You will not boast about the fact that you are keeping the Sermon on the Mount, or that you belong to a certain church, or that you are a church officer, or a preacher, or a Sunday school teacher. You will not be able to *boast* of anything. You will just *glory* in the Cross and the One who died there.

For in Christ Jesus neither circumcision availeth any thing, nor uncircumcision, but a new creature [Gal. 6:15].

This brings us to the second kind of handwriting mentioned in these final verses.

Circumcision was the handwriting of religion and the Law. It was sort of a handwriting on the body. It served as a badge signifying that you belonged under the Abrahamic covenant. It never availed anything. Wearing a button or a pin, signifying that you belong to a lodge or a fraternity can become almost meaningless. "In Christ Jesus neither circumcision availeth any thing, nor uncircumcision"—uncircumcision is of no value either. These things carry no value whatsoever. There are folk today who like to boast of what great sinners they were before their conversion. Well, whether or not you have been circumcised—whatever was your state—is of no importance. The essential thing is: Has the Spirit of God come into your life and made you a new creature in Christ Jesus? This can come about *only* through faith in Christ.

You see, Paul would never have had any difficulty with the legalism of his day if he had presented the gospel as only a competitor in the field. Let me illustrate what I mean. We have an abundance of soaps on the market. Those who promote them tell us they will make you smell good or make you feel good or are kind to your skin. So let's you and me get out a new brand of soap, and we'll call it *Clean*, since getting you clean is the purpose of soap, and that seems to be the one thing the advertisers have forgotten. We'll start advertising it by claiming that it is the only soap that will make you clean. Our slogan will be "Buy Clean and get clean." Now that will get us in trouble

immediately when we claim that it is the *only* soap that will get you clean. Manufacturers of other soaps will really begin to howl. But this is what Paul was claiming for the gospel. If he had said, "Judaism is good but Christianity is better," he wouldn't have been in trouble, because that's what advertisers say today—our product is better than other soaps on the market. That's competition. No one would dare say that their soap is the *only* soap that would do the job. Notice that Paul is not claiming that his soap is only a little better than the soap of Judaism; he is saying that Judaism is *nothing*, that circumcision is *nothing*, that whether you are circumcised or not circumcised is *nothing*. He is saying that only the writing of the Holy Spirit in your life, giving you a new nature, is essential. My friend, that is putting it on the line!

Now we come to the third and final handwriting presented to us in this section.

And as many as walk according to this rule, peace be on them, and mercy, and upon the Israel of God.

From henceforth let no man trouble me: for I bear in my body the marks of the Lord Jesus [Gal. 6:16–17].

Notice the word *marks*. Paul is saying, "I bear in my body the 'marks'"—the Greek word is *stigmata*—meaning 'scar marks.' If you want to see the handwriting of Jesus, look upon Paul's body. In 2 Corinthians 11:23–27 he tells us, "Are they ministers of Christ? (I speak as a fool) I am more; in labours more abundant, in stripes above measure, in prisons more frequent, in deaths oft. Of the Jews five times received I forty stripes save one. Thrice was I beaten with rods, once was I stoned, thrice I suffered shipwreck, a night and a day I have been in the deep; In journeyings often, in perils of waters, in perils of robbers, in perils by mine own countrymen, in perils by the heathen, in perils in the city, in perils in the wilderness, in perils in the sea, in perils among false brethren; In weariness and painfulness, in watchings often, in hunger and thirst, in fastings often, in cold and nakedness." The *stigmata* were the sufferings of Paul which he endured for the sake of the Lord Jesus.

In Paul's day *stigmata* was used in three ways. When a runaway slave was found and brought back to his master, he was branded on the forehead. Also soldiers who belonged to famous companies had the names of their commanders tatooed on their foreheads. Then, too, devotees of a pagan goddess (and there was much of this in Asia Minor and throughout the Roman Empire in Paul's day) had her name branded on their foreheads. Paul says, "I have on my body the *stigmata* of the Lord Jesus." He is saying this in effect, "I have written to you out of deep emotion and with great conviction. If you want to know if I truly believe what I have written and if these things are real in my own life, read my body—look at my scars."

I lived as a boy in west Texas before there were many fences, and we used to identify cattle by the brand of their owner. My friend, circumcision costs you nothing. It is only an outward sign. Paul says it is *nothing*, although

he himself had been circumcised. But he bore the brand marks of the Lord Jesus upon his body and upon his life. I believe that in our day the Lord Jesus still stoops to write, not upon the shifting sands of the temple floor, but he writes upon the lives of those who are His own. His branding iron is on our hearts for eternity. Do we proudly wear His *stigmata*, willing to bear reproach for Jesus' sake?

Brethren, the grace of our Lord Jesus Christ be with your spirit. Amen [Gal. 6:18].

Paul concludes this marvelous epistle by commending the brethren to the grace of God.

BIBLIOGRAPHY

(Recommended for Further Study)

Cole, R. Alan. *The Epistle of Paul to the Galatians.* Grand Rapids, Michigan: Wm. B. Eerdmans Publishing Co., 1965.

DeHaan, M. R. *Galatians.* Grand Rapids, Michigan: Radio Bible Class, 1960.

Gromacki, Robert G. *Galatians: Stand Fast in Liberty.* Grand Rapids, Michigan: Baker Book House, 1979.

Hendriksen, William. *Exposition of Galatians.* Grand Rapids, Michigan: Baker Book House, 1968. (Comprehensive.)

Hogg, C. F. and Vine, W. E. *The Epistle to the Galatians.* Grand Rapids, Michigan: Kregel Publications, 1922. (Excellent.)

Ironside, H. A. *Expository Messages on the Epistle to the Galatians.* Neptune, New Jersey: Loizeaux Brothers, 1940. (All of his books are especially fine for young Christians.)

Kelly, William. *Lectures on the Epistle to the Galatians.* Addison, Illinois: Bible Truth Publishers, n.d.

Kent, Homer A., Jr. *The Freedom of God's Sons: Studies in Galatians.* Grand Rapids, Michigan: Baker Book House, 1976. (Excellent for personal or group study.)

Luther, Martin. *Commentary on Galatians.* 1525. Reprint. Grand Rapids, Michigan: Kregel Publications, n.d. (Abridged.)

Ridderbos, Herman N. *The Epistle of Paul to the Galatians.* Grand Rapids, Michigan: Wm. B. Eerdmans Publishing Co., 1953.

Strauss, Lehman. *Devotional Studies in Galatians and Ephesians.* Neptune, New Jersey: Loizeaux Brothers, 1957.

Tenney, Merrill C. *Galatians: The Charter of Christian Liberty.* Grand Rapids, Michigan: Wm. B. Eerdmans Publishing Co., 1954. (Excellent illustration of ten methods of Bible study.)

Vaughan, Curtis. *Galatians: A Study Guide Commentary.* Grand Rapids, Michigan: Zondervan Publishing House, 1972.

Vos, Howard F. *Galatians—A Call to Christian Liberty.* Chicago, Illinois: Moody Press, 1971. (An excellent, inexpensive survey.)

Wiersbe, Warren W. *Be Free (Galatians).* Wheaton, Illinois: Scripture Press (Victor Books), n.d.

Wuest, Kenneth S. *Galatians in the Greek New Testament for English Readers.* Grand Rapids, Michigan: Wm. B. Eerdmans Publishing Co., 1944.

The Epistle to the
EPHESIANS
INTRODUCTION

A quartet of men left Rome in the year A.D. 62 bound for the province of Asia which was located in what was designated as Asia Minor and is currently called Turkey. These men had on their persons four of the most sublime compositions of the Christian faith. These precious documents would be invaluable if they were in existence today. Rome did not comprehend the significance of the writings of an unknown prisoner. If she had, these men would have been apprehended and the documents seized.

When these men bade farewell to the apostle Paul, each was given an epistle to bear to his particular constituency. These four letters are in the Word of God, and they are designated the "Prison Epistles of Paul," since he wrote them while he was imprisoned in Rome. He was awaiting a hearing before Nero who was the Caesar at that time. Paul as a Roman citizen had appealed his case to the emperor, and he was waiting to be heard.

This quartet of men and their respective places of abode can be identified:

(1) Epaphroditus was from Philippi, and he had the Epistle to the Philippians (see Phil. 4:18); (2) Tychicus was from Ephesus, and he had the Epistle to the Ephesians (see Eph. 6:21); (3) Epaphras was from Colosse, and he had the Epistle to the Colossians (see Col. 4:12); and (4) Onesimus was a runaway slave from Colosse, and he had the Epistle to Philemon who was his master (see Philem. 10).

These epistles present a composite picture of Christ, the church, the Christian life, and the interrelationship and functioning of them all. These different facets present the Christian life on the highest plane.

Ephesians presents the church which is Christ's body. This is the invisible church of which Christ is the Head.

Colossians presents Christ as the Head of the body, the church. The emphasis is upon Christ rather than on the church. In Ephesians the emphasis is on the body, and in Colossians the emphasis is on the Head.

Philippians presents Christian living with Christ as the dynamic. "I can do all things through Christ which strengtheneth me" (Phil. 4:13).

Philemon presents Christian living in action in a pagan society. Paul wrote to Philemon, who was the master of Onesimus and a Christian: "If thou count me therefore a partner, receive him as myself. If he hath wronged thee, or oweth thee aught, put that on mine account" (Philem. 17–18).

The gospel walked in shoe leather in the first century, and it worked. This is the thing that we are going to see in this Epistle to the Ephesians.

Ephesians reveals the church as God's masterpiece, a mystery not revealed in the Old Testament (see Eph. 2:10). It is more wonderful than any temple made with hands, constructed of living stones, indwelt by the Holy Spirit. It is the body of Christ in the world to walk as He would walk and to wrestle against the wiles of the Devil. Someday the church will leave the world and be presented to Christ as a bride.

Dr. Arthur T. Pierson called Ephesians, "Paul's third-heaven epistle." Another has called it "the Alps of the New Testament." It is the Mount Whitney of the High Sierras of all Scripture. This is the *church epistle.* Many expositors consider this the highest peak of scriptural truth, the very apex of Bible revelation. That may well be true. Some have even suggested that Ephesians is so profound that none but the very elect (in other words, the chosen few) can understand it. I have always noticed that the folk who say this include themselves in that inner circle. To be candid with you, I do not even pretend to be able to probe or plumb the depths of this epistle nor to ascend to its heights. This epistle is lofty and it is heady. It is difficult to breathe the rarefied air of this epistle—you will find this to be true when we get into it. We will do the very best we can, with the aid of the Holy Spirit who is our guide, to understand it.

On several occasions I have had the privilege of visiting Turkey, and I have visited the sites of all seven churches of Asia Minor. Ephesus is where I spent the most time. I reveled in the opportunity of visiting Ephesus which was the leading church of the seven churches and was in a great city.

The Holy Spirit would not permit Paul on his second missionary journey to enter the province of Asia where Ephesus was the prominent center: "Now when they had gone throughout Phrygia and the region of Galatia, and were forbidden of the Holy Ghost to preach the word in Asia" (Acts 16:6). The Holy Spirit put up a roadblock and said to Paul, "You can't go down there now." We are not told the reason, but we know God's timing is perfect. He would send him there later. So Paul traveled west into Macedonia—to Philippi, down to Berea, down to Athens, over to Corinth, and then, on the way back, he came by Ephesus. Oh, what a tremendous opportunity he saw there! "And he came to Ephesus, and left them there: but he himself entered into the synagogue, and reasoned with the Jews" (Acts 18:19).

Paul was so favorably impressed by the opportunities for missionary work that he promised to return, which he did on his third missionary journey. He discovered that another missionary by the name of Apollos had been there in the interval between his second and third missionary journeys. Apollos had preached only the baptism of John and not the gospel of grace of our Lord Jesus Christ. At that time Apollos didn't know about the Lord Jesus, but later on he himself became a great preacher of the gospel.

Paul began a far-reaching ministry in Ephesus. For two years he spoke in the school of Tyrannus, and the gospel penetrated into every center of the province of Asia. Evidently it was at this time that the churches addressed in the second and third chapters of Revelation were founded by this ministry of Paul.

It is my firm conviction, after having visited Turkey and seen that area and having read a great deal on the excavations that have been made there, that the greatest ministry the gospel has ever had was in what is today modern Turkey. In that day there were millions of people living there. It was the very heart of the Roman Empire. The culture of Greece was no longer in Greece; it was along this coast, the western coast of Turkey, where Ephesus was the leading city. It was a great cultural center and a great religious center. The climate was pleasing, and it was a wonderful place to visit. The Roman emperors came to this area for a vacation. This is where the gospel had its greatest entrance.

Ephesus was the principal city of Asia Minor and probably of the entire eastern section of the Roman Empire. It was second only to Rome. The city had been founded around 2000 B.C. by the Hittites. It was what we call an oriental city, an Asian city, until about 1000 B.C. when the Greeks entered. There one

would find a mixture of east and west. Kipling was wrong as far as Ephesus was concerned. He said, "East is east and West is west and ne'er the twain shall meet," but they did meet in Ephesus.

Over this long period of about twenty-five hundred years, Ephesus was one of the great cities of the world. It was on a harbor that is now all filled up, silted in. It is not a harbor anymore; in fact, it is about six miles from the ocean today. At the time Paul went there, he sailed right up to that beautiful white marble freeway. It was a very wide street, and the marble for it was supplied from the quarries of Mount Prion.

The Temple of Diana in Ephesus was one of the seven wonders of the ancient world. It was the largest Greek temple ever constructed, 418 by 239 feet, four times larger than the Parthenon but very similar to it. It was built over a marsh on an artificial foundation of skins and charcoal so that it was not affected by earthquakes. The art and wealth of the Ephesian citizens contributed to its adornment. It had 127 graceful columns, some of them richly carved and colored. It contained works of art, such as the picture painted by Apelles of Alexander the Great hurling the thunderbolt.

Inside this beautiful temple was the idol of Diana. This was not the beautiful Diana of Greek mythology. It was the oriental, actually the Anatolian, conception of the goddess of fertility. It was not the goddess of the moon, but the goddess of fertility, a vulgar, many-breasted idol of wood. All sorts of gross immorality took place in the shadow of this temple.

A flourishing trade was carried on in the manufacture of silver shrines or models of the temple. These are often referred to by ancient writers. Few strangers seem to have left Ephesus without such a memorial of their visit, and this artistic business brought no small gain to the craftsmen.

It was to such a city that Paul came. He went first to the synagogue and spoke boldly for the space of three months. Then he went into the school of Tyrannus and continued there for two years ". . . so that all they which dwelt in Asia heard the word of the Lord Jesus, both Jews and Greeks" (Acts 19:10). This was probably the high water mark in the missionary labors of Paul. He considered Ephesus his great opportunity and stayed there longer than in any other place. The people of Ephesus heard more Bible teaching from Paul than did any other people, which is the reason he could write to them the deep truths contained in this epistle.

Paul wrote to the Corinthians, "But I will tarry at Ephesus until Pentecost. For a great door and effectual is opened unto me, and there are many adversaries" (1 Cor. 16:8–9). Because Paul's preaching was putting the silversmiths out of business, there was great opposition, and as a result there was a riot in the city. Paul was preaching the gospel of the living God and life through Jesus Christ. God marvelously preserved him, which encouraged him to continue (see Acts 19:23–41). Paul loved this church in Ephesus. His last meeting with the Ephesian elders was a tender farewell (see Acts 20:17–38).

A great company of believers turned to Christ. I think the gospel was more effective in this area than in any place and at any time in the history of the world. I believe the Ephesian church was the highest church spiritually. It is an amazing thing to me that there were people living in that pagan city who understood this epistle—Paul wouldn't have written it to them if they couldn't have understood it. Furthermore, in the Book of Revelation we find that Ephesus is the first one of the seven churches of Asia mentioned in a series of churches that gives the entire history of the church. Ephesus was the church at its best, the church at the highest spiritual level.

You and I today cannot conceive the high spiritual level that the Spirit of God had produced in these Ephesian believers. They loved the person of the Lord Jesus and were drawn to Him. I have been a pastor for many years and I love to minister in our churches today. I must confess, however, that we are far from the person of Christ today. We are so enamored with programs, with church work, with an office in the church, that we get farther and farther from the person of Christ. The essential question is how much we love Him. Paul wrote to the Ephesians that Christ loved the church and gave Himself for it. Do we return that love? Do we respond to Him? Can we say, "I love Him because He first loved me"? This letter to the Ephesians ought to bring us very close to Christ.

Two books of the Bible which the critic says cannot be understood are Ephesians and Revelation. Liberalism says that Revelation is just a conglomerate of symbols that no one can decipher. Liberalism also says that Ephesians is so high it is beyond us.

Let me say that the two books of the Bible which can be arranged mathematically and logically are Ephesians and Revelation. There are no books more logical than they are. Years ago I got tired of hearing folk say, "I believe the Bible from cover to cover," when they didn't even know what was between the covers. They were just making a pious statement. If one really believes it is God's Word, he will try to find out what it says. We need to get off this gimmick of methods and how to communicate to the younger generation and how to better organize the church and instead really learn what is in the Book. To help folk learn what the Bible is all about, I wrote a book called *Briefing the Bible* in which I attempted to give a helpful outline of every book in the Bible. As I was doing this, I found that Ephesians and Revelation were the two easiest books in the Bible to outline. Do you know why? Because they are logical. I don't pretend to understand everything that is in these books, but I do say that they are logical and they are easily outlined.

Paul is logical in Ephesians and John is logical in Revelation. John was told to write of the things he had seen, of things that are, and of things that will be. There is a clear threefold division. And the book is arranged according to sevens. You couldn't find anything better than that. The Epistle to the Ephesians is very logical. Of the six chapters, the first three are about the heavenly calling of the church and are doctrinal. The last three are about the earthly conduct of the church which is very practical. You see, the church has a Head. The Head of the church is Christ, and He is in heaven. We are identified with Him. But the feet of the church are down here on the earth. Paul won't leave us sitting up there in the heavenlies; he says, "Walk worthy of the vocation wherewith ye are called" (Eph. 4:1). In other words, Christian, it's nice to sit up there in the heavenlies and boast of your position in Christ, but, for goodness' sake, get down out of your high chair and start walking. We need to remember that in Paul's day believers were walking in a pagan society in the Roman world. The first half is doctrinal and the last half is practical, which makes a very logical division in the book. We need both. We are not to live in the first three chapters only. They are wonderful, but the message must get down here where we live, down where the rubber meets the road.

The doctrinal section is also very logical. In chapter 1 the church is a body. In chapter 2 the church is a temple. In chapter 3 the church is a mystery.

When we get to the practical section, we

find in chapter 4 that the church is a new man. The church is to exhibit something new in the world: walking through the world as a new man. In chapter 5 the church will be a bride. Don't get the idea that the church is a bride now; the church is not a bride today. Paul wrote in 2 Corinthians 11:2, ". . . for I have espoused you to one husband, that I may present you as a chaste virgin to Christ." In effect he says, "I'm getting you engaged to Christ today, and someday the church will be His bride." In chapter 6 the church is a soldier. A wag who heard me give this outline said to me, "That's interesting. The church will be a bride, you say, and the church is a soldier. In a lot of marriages down here, they get married and then the fighting starts." Well, that is not the way Paul meant it. He was being very practical. The church is a soldier, and there is an enemy to be fought. There is a battle going on in this world. The bugle has sounded. We need to stand for God today.

OUTLINE

CHAPTER 1

THEME: The church is a body; Introduction; God the Father planned the church; God the Son paid the price for the church; God the Holy Spirit protects the church; prayer of Paul for knowledge and power for the Ephesians

Ephesians begins with the doctrinal section concerning the heavenly calling of the church, the vocalization.

INTRODUCTION

Paul, an apostle of Jesus Christ by the will of God, to the saints which are at Ephesus, and to the faithful in Christ Jesus:

Grace be to you, and peace, from God our Father, and from the Lord Jesus Christ [Eph. 1:1–2].

This is the briefest of all the introductions to Paul's epistles. It's brief because, very frankly, this epistle was sent to the church in Ephesus but was intended to be for all the churches. In some of the better manuscripts *en Epheso* is left out—it's not there. Ephesians was apparently the epistle that Paul referred to when he said in Colossians to read the epistle to the Laodiceans. In other words, this was a circular letter for the churches in that day. He's not writing here to the local church as much as he is to the church in general, that is, the invisible body of believers.

"Paul, an apostle of Jesus Christ" should be changed to Paul, an apostle of Christ Jesus. I hope you'll not think I'm splitting hairs here, but all the way through this epistle and in many other places it should be Christ Jesus. The word *Christ* is His title. That's who He is: ". . . Thou art the Christ, the Son of the living God" (Matt. 16:16). *Jesus* was His human name. Paul could say that "We know Him no longer after the flesh" (see 2 Cor. 5:16). Paul didn't know Him as the Jesus of the three-years' ministry but rather as the glorified Christ he met on the Damascus road. Paul always emphasized the name of *Christ* first—Christ Jesus.

Paul states that he is "an apostle." What is an apostle? It is the highest office the church has ever had. No one today is an apostle in the church for the simple reason that they cannot meet the requirements of an apostle. Here are the requirements: (1) The apostles received their commission directly from the living lips of Jesus. Paul made that claim for himself. He wrote, "Paul, an apostle, (not of men, neither by man, but by Jesus Christ, and God the Father, who raised him from the dead;)" (Gal. 1:1). This is the reason I believe Paul took the place of Judas. The disciples had selected Matthias, but I don't find anywhere that Jesus Christ made him an apostle. Apparently all the apostles received their commission directly from the Lord Jesus. (2) The apostles saw the Savior after His resurrection. Paul could meet that requirement. (3) The apostles exercised a special inspiration. They expounded and wrote Scripture (see John 14:26; 16:13; Gal. 1:11–12). Certainly Paul measures up to that more than any other apostle. (4) They exercised supreme authority (see John 20:22–23; 2 Cor. 10:8). (5) The badge of their authority was the power to work miracles (see Mark 6:13; Luke 9:1–2; Acts 2:43). I do not believe such power is invested in men today. That was the badge of an apostle. John wrote at the end of the first century, "If there come any unto you, and bring not this doctrine, receive him not into your house, neither bid him God speed" (2 John 10). The badge was no longer the ability to work miracles but having the right doctrine. (6) They were given a universal commission to found churches (see 2 Cor. 11:28). Paul expressly met these six requirements for apostleship.

"Paul, an apostle of Christ Jesus by the will of God." Paul rested his apostleship upon the will of God rather than any personal ambition or will of man or request of a church. He wrote to the Galatians: "But when it pleased *God*, who separated me from my mother's womb, and called me by his grace, To reveal his Son in me, that I might preach him among the heathen . . ." (Gal. 1:15–16, italics mine). Paul said to Timothy: "And I thank Christ Jesus our Lord, who hath enabled me, for that he counted me faithful, putting me into the ministry; Who was before a blasphemer, and a persecutor, and injurious: but I obtained mercy, because I did it ignorantly in unbelief" (1 Tim. 1:12–13). Paul made constant reference to the will of God as the foundation of his apostleship. You can check 1 Corinthians 1:1; 2 Corinthians 1:1; Colossians 1:1; 2 Timothy 1:1. He says it in all these places.

"To the saints . . . at Ephesus." The word for saint is *hagios* which means "holy" or "separated." The primary intent of the word is "set aside for the sole use of God, that which belongs to God." The pots and pans in the tabernacle were called holy vessels. Why? Because they were especially holy and very fine and nice? No. I think they were all beat up and battered after that long wilderness journey. They were holy because they were for the use of God. A saint, my friend, is one who has trusted Christ and is set aside for the sole use of God. There are only two kinds of people today: the saints and the ain'ts. If you are a saint, then you are not an ain't. If you ain't an ain't, then you are a saint. Now there are some saints who are not being used of God. That is their fault. They are set aside for the use of God and for His service. Saints should act saintly, it's true. But they're not saints because of the way they act. They are saints because of their position in Christ. They belong to Him to be used of Him.

"At Ephesus." We have already referred to that. You can put in the name of your town here. For me it could be "at Pasadena."

"And to the faithful in Christ Jesus." These are the believers. The believers and the saints are the same, you see. A saint should be saintly and a believer should be faithful. A believer is one who has trusted Christ and a saint is the same one. The term *saint* is the Godward aspect of the Christian. The term *believer* is the manward aspect of the Christian.

"In Christ Jesus." This is the most wonderful thing of all. This epistle is going to amplify that so much, that I will be dwelling on that in more detail later on. To me the most important word in the New Testament is the little preposition *in*. Theologians have come up with some "lulus" trying to tell us what it means to be saved. How do you define our salvation? There are words like redemption, atonement, justification, reconciliation, propitiation, and the vicarious, substitutionary sacrifice of Christ. All of these words are good; they are wonderful, but each one of them merely gives one aspect of our salvation. What does it really mean to be saved? It means to be *in Christ*. We are irrevocably and organically joined to Christ by the baptism of the Holy Spirit (see 1 Cor. 12:12–13). We are put into the body of believers. We are told, ". . . he that is joined unto the Lord is one spirit" (1 Cor. 6:17). We belong to Him, and there's nothing as wonderful as that. "There is therefore now no condemnation to them which are in Christ Jesus . . ." (Rom. 8:1). Can you improve on that? Being in Christ Jesus is the great accomplishment of salvation. Dr. Lewis Sperry Chafer found that the word *in* occurred one hundred and thirty times in the New Testament. The Lord Jesus said, "Ye *in* me and I *in* you" (see John 15:4). How wonderful! We are *in* Christ. I can't explain it; it's so profound. Analogies may help us here:

The bird is in the air; the air is in the bird.
The fish is in the water; the water is in the fish.
The iron is in the fire; the fire is in the iron.

The believer is in Christ and Christ is in the believer. We are joined to Him. The head is in the body and the body is in the head. My body can't move without the head directing it. The church, which is "the body of Christ" is *in* Christ, the Head. All the truths of Ephesians revolve around this fact.

Take time to look carefully at this epistle. I feel very keenly that along with Romans, 1 and 2 Corinthians, and Galatians, Ephesians should be given top priority among the epistles. I feel that these epistles have a throbbing, personal, living message for you and me today, probably as no other portion of Scripture does. They are the great doctrinal epistles. When God said to Joshua, ". . . arise, go over this Jordan" (Josh 1:2), I know He's not talking to me; but He is giving instructions to Joshua. Yet, to me it has an application. The Epistle to the Ephesians is the Book of Joshua of the New Testament, and it speaks directly to me in a personal way.

"Grace be to you." *Grace* was the form of greeting of the Gentile world in Paul's day. The Greek word was *charis*. Two men met on the street and one would say to the other, "Charis." I walked down the streets of Athens with a Greek friend of mine who is a missionary. He spoke to several people as we went by, and I said to him, "It sounds to me like you greet them with the word *charis*." He laughed and said, "Well, it's similar to it." Apparently it's still a form of greeting today.

"And peace." The greeting in the religious world was, "Peace." That is the word you hear in Jerusalem: "Shalom!"

Paul takes these two words which were the common greeting of the day and gives both of them a wonderful meaning and lifts them to the heights. The grace of God is the means by which He saves us. You must know the grace of God before you can experience the peace of God. Paul always puts them in that order— grace before peace. You must have grace before you can experience peace. "Therefore being justified by faith, we have peace with God through our Lord Jesus Christ" (Rom. 5:1).

You see the word *peace* everywhere today. Generally it refers to peace in some section of the world, or world peace. But the world can never know peace until it knows the grace of God. The interesting thing is, you don't see the word *grace* around very much. You see the word *love* and the word *peace*. They are very familiar words, and they are supposed to be taken from the Bible, but often they don't mean what they mean in the Word of God. *Peace* is peace with God because our sins are forgiven. Our sins can never be forgiven until we know something of the grace of God.

"From God our Father, and from the Lord Jesus Christ." The grace and peace are from God our Father. In fact, He becomes our Father when we experience the grace of God and are regenerated by the Spirit of God. Grace and peace also come from the Lord Jesus Christ. Why didn't Paul say they also came from the Holy Spirit? Doesn't Paul believe in the Trinity? Oh, yes, but the Holy Spirit was already in Ephesus indwelling believers. The Lord Jesus was seated at God's right hand in the heavens. We need to keep our geography straight when we study the Bible. A great many people get their theology warped because they don't have their geography right; and when we get that straightened out, it even helps our theology.

GOD THE FATHER PLANNED THE CHURCH

We come now to the second major division of the first chapter. It begins with a most marvelous verse.

Blessed be the God and Father of our Lord Jesus Christ, who hath blessed us with all spiritual blessings in heavenly places in Christ [Eph. 1:3].

We notice something that is very important here. He has blessed us. We praise Him with our lips because He first made us blessed. Our blessing is a declaration. His blessings are deeds. We *pronounce* Him blessed. He *makes* us blessed. The word *blessed* has in it the thought of happiness and joy. God is rejoicing today. He is happy because He has a way of saving you and He can bless you. It says He hath blessed us. I can't think of anything more wonderful than this. He is not speaking here of something that may be ours when we get to heaven but of something that is ours right

now. Somebody says to me, "Have you had the second blessing?" Second blessing! My friend, I'm working way up in the hundreds—in fact, up in the thousands. I've not only had a second blessing; I've had a thousand blessings. He's blessed us, and He's done it in Christ.

"In heavenly places in Christ." You will notice that "places" is in italics in the text. It literally states, "in the heavenlies in Christ." Here we are, blessed with all spiritual blessings, and it is in the heavenlies. I don't know exactly where the heavenlies are, but I do know where the Lord Jesus is. He is at God's right hand, and we are told here that these blessings are *in* Christ. May I say to you that we need to be careful with this. It does not say here that these blessings are with Christ (there are those who read it like that). Right now you and I are seated *in* Christ. When somebody asks, "Are you going to heaven some day?" the answer generally given is, "Well, I hope so." Let me say this to you: if you're going to heaven, you're already there in Christ. He has blessed you in the heavenlies in Christ, and you are there regardless of what your position is down here. Your practice down here may not be good, but if you are a child of God, you are already in Christ. Some people even misunderstand it in another way. I was teaching Ephesians at a conference once, and they called on a brother at the end of the service to lead the prayer. He started by saying, "Lord, we just thank you that this morning we've been sitting in the heavenly places in Christ." Well, he missed the point. We don't have to come to a Bible study (as important as that is) and have our hearts thrilled with these great spiritual truths to be sitting in the heavenlies. The fact of the matter is, you are in the heavenlies in Christ even when you are down in the dumps. Everyone who is in Christ is seated in the heavenlies in Him. That is the position which He has given to us.

"Blessed be the God and Father of our Lord Jesus Christ." We praise Him. Why? Because He has blessed us. He has blessed us with all spiritual blessings. The parallel here is Joshua in the Old Testament. We saw in the study of that book that Canaan was given to the children of Israel by God. Canaan is not a picture of heaven. Canaan is a picture of where we live today. It could never be heaven because there were enemies to be fought and battles to be won. Down here is where the battle is being fought. When we get to heaven, there will be no more battles. The interesting point here is that God *gave* them Canaan. All they had to do was lay hold of their possession. God told Joshua, "Every place that the sole of your foot shall tread upon, that have I given unto you, as I said unto Moses" (Josh. 1:3). Joshua could say, "Well, Lord, you've already given it to us. You let us walk in and take it."

My friend, God has blessed us with all spiritual blessings. We are in Christ. Have you ever stopped to think of what we have in Christ? Christ has been made unto us justification and sanctification. When I started out in church as a boy, I was working for my salvation. I didn't do very well with that. Then I learned that Christ is my justification. I tried to work to be good after I was saved, and I didn't do very well at that either. Then I learned that Christ has been made unto me sanctification. You see, I have everything in Christ; I have been blessed with all spiritual blessings. You can't improve on that, can you? When you come to Christ, you have everything in Him. Don't come and tell me today that I have to wait until later on, that I have to tarry for the Holy Spirit to give me something special—for example, a baptism. I have it all in Christ. When you tell me that I did not get everything in Christ, you are denying what Christ did for me. I got *everything* when I came to Him.

Now there are two ways to treat these blessings, which are actually your spiritual possessions: either to lay hold of them or not to lay hold of them. Two stories illustrate what I mean, and both of them are true. When I was in Chicago many years ago, I picked up the evening paper during the week and read a little article and clipped it out. It was way down at the bottom of the front page and wasn't apt to be noticed. It read "The flophouses and saloons of Chicago's Skid Row were searched today for one Stanley William McKenna Walker, 50, an Oxford graduate and heir to half of an $8,000,000 English estate. The missing persons detail hoped that somewhere among the down-and-outers who line the curbs and sleep off wine binges in the cheap hotels they would find Walker, son of a wealthy British shipbuilder." I thought how tragic it was. Imagine being an heir to half of $8,000,000 and being a wino who's sleeping in two-bit hotels. I felt like sitting down and weeping for that poor fellow. Then I began thinking of the children of God today who are living in cheap hotels, living off the little "wine" of this world. I don't mean that literally, but that they engage in cheap entertainment down here. They are wealthy beyond the dreams of Croesus and are blessed with all

spiritual blessings, but they live like paupers down here. There are a lot of folk in our churches who live like that today, and it's tragic. I was telling this story when I was a pastor in Los Angeles, and a lady who was visiting from Chicago came up afterward and asked, "Dr. McGee, do you know the end of that story?" I said, "No, I never heard." She said, "Well, they found him." "Oh," I replied, "that was wonderful." "No," she said, "they found him dead in a doorway on a cold night later on that fall." How tragic to die like that man died. Many Christians live and die like that, and yet they are blessed with all spiritual blessings in the heavenlies in Christ.

The second true story happened out West here, years ago. An heir to a British nobleman was living in poverty and barely eking out an existence. After the nobleman died, they began to look for his heir and when they found him, they told him about his inheritance. A great deal of publicity was made of it. Do you know what that fellow did? He immediately went down to the clothing store and ordered their best suit and then bought a first class ticket to return to England in style. Do you know why? He believed the inheritance was his, and he acted upon it. My friend, you can go either route. You can travel your Christian life in first class or in steerage. You can go second, third, or fourth class, and there are a lot of Christians doing that today. God wants you to know that you've been blessed with *all* spiritual blessings. He hasn't promised us physical blessings, but He has promised spiritual ones, and these are in the heavenlies in Christ. My friend, you're not going to have any spiritual blessing in this life that doesn't come to you through Jesus Christ. That's just how important He is. He not only has saved us, but He is also the One who blesses us. How we need to lay hold of Him today and to start living as a child of God should live!

We come now to a very important section. We are in that division of the outline which states that God the Father planned the church. You would not build a house today without a blueprint. What is God's blueprint? What did God do in planning for the church? We find in this section that He did three things: (1) He chose us in Christ; (2) He predestinated us to the place of sonship; and (3) He made us accepted in the Beloved.

Now I know that we have come to a passage of Scripture that is difficult. You'll have to gird up the loins of your mind because this is a very strong passage in the Word of God. We are going to talk about election and about predestination. These are two words that are frightening. Many people run for cover when they hear these words mentioned. But they are Bible words, and they have a meaning which is important for us to see.

According as he hath chosen us in him before the foundation of the world, that we should be holy and without blame before him in love [Eph. 1:4].

This verse and the verses that follow are essentially the most difficult verses in Scripture to grasp. They are repulsive to the natural man, and the average believer finds them difficult to accept at face value. Although the statements are clear, the truth they contain is hard to receive. These verses are like a walnut—hard to crack but with a lot of goodies on the inside.

"According as" is a connective which modifies the preceding statement in verse three. The spiritual blessings which you and I are given are in accord with the divine will. All is done in perfect unison with God's purpose. This world and this universe *will* operate according to the plan and purpose of Almighty God. "According as" looks back to the three-in-one blessing of the last verse. There are actually and ought to be three *in*s in verse three. There is, first of all, "*in* all spiritual blessings," which are then wrapped "*in* the heavenlies," and finally put in the larger package of "*in* Christ." The whole thought is: Open your gift and see what God has done for you, and then move out in faith and lay hold of it and live today on the high plane to which God has brought you. He's made you a son and blessed you with all spiritual blessings. We need to live like that in the world today.

Now all this was according to His plan. God the Father planned the church, God the Son paid for the church, and God the Holy Spirit protects the church. The source of all our blessings is the God and Father of our Lord Jesus Christ. He carries our mind back to eternity past to make us realize that salvation is altogether of God and not at all of ourselves. You and I are not the originators or the promoters or the consummators of our salvation. God did it all. An old hymn puts it like this:

'Tis not that I did choose Thee
For, Lord, that could not be.
This heart would still refuse Thee
But Thou hast chosen me.

A favorite hymn of today says:

Jesus sought me when a stranger
Wandering from the fold of God.
He, to rescue me from danger,
Interposed His precious blood.

"According as he hath chosen us in him before the foundation of the world." God planned our salvation way back yonder in eternity before you and I were even in this world at all. The Lord Jesus Christ is the One who came down in time, and He wrought out our salvation upon the cross when the fullness of time had come. God the Holy Spirit is the One who convicts us today. He brings us to the place of faith in Christ and to a saving knowledge of the grace of God that is revealed in the Lord Jesus Christ.

I heard this story many years ago. A black boy in Memphis, Tennessee, wanted to join a conservative, fundamental church, and the deacons were examining him. They asked him, "How did you get saved?" He answered, "I did my part, and God did His part." The deacons thought they had him, so they asked him what was his part and what was God's part. He said, "My part was the sinning. I ran from God as fast as these rebellious legs would take me and my sinful heart would lead me. I ran from Him. But you know, He done took out after me 'til He done run me down." My friend, there is nothing in a theology book that tells it as well as that. God is the One who did the saving. Our part was the sinning.

The late Dr. Harry A. Ironside told this story. A little boy was asked, "Have you found Jesus?" The little fellow answered, "Sir, I didn't know He was lost. But I was lost and He found me." My friend, you don't find Jesus. *He* finds you. He is the One who went out after the lost sheep, and He is the One who found that sheep.

God chose believers in Christ before the foundation of the world, way back in eternity past. That means that you and I didn't do the choosing. He did not choose us because we were good or because we would do some good, but He did choose us so that we *could* do some good. The entire choice is thrown back upon the sovereignty of the wisdom and goodness of God alone. It was Charles Spurgeon who once said, "God chose me before I came into the world, because if He'd waited until I got here, He never would have chosen me." It is God who has chosen us—we have not chosen Him. The Lord Jesus said to His own in the Upper Room, "Ye have not chosen me, but I have chosen you . . ." (John 15:16). Dr. G. Campbell Morgan commented, "That puts the responsibility on Him. If He did the choosing, then He's responsible." That makes it quite wonderful!

Israel furnishes us an example of this divine choosing. "Hear this word that the LORD hath spoken against you, O children of Israel, against the whole family which I brought up from the land of Egypt, saying, You only have I known of all the families of the earth: therefore I will punish you for all your iniquities" (Amos 3:1–2). God chose Israel in time; He chose the church in eternity. Since God made the choice in eternity, there has not arisen anything unforeseen to Him which has caused Him to revamp His program or change His mind. He knew the end from the beginning (see Acts 15:18).

God did all this for a purpose: "that we should be holy and without blame before him in love." God chose us in order to sanctify us. He saves us and He sanctifies us that we might be holy. That's the positive side of His purpose. It has to do with the inner life of the believer. A holy life is demanded by God's election. Now don't tell me that you can say, "Well, I'm one of the elected. I have been saved by grace, and now I can do as I please." Paul answered that kind of reasoning. "What shall we say then? Shall we continue in sin, that grace may abound? God forbid. How shall we, that are dead to sin, live any longer therein?" (Rom. 6:1–2). You can't use grace as a license to sin, my friend. If you go on living in sin, it is because you are a sinner who hasn't been saved. A sinner who has been saved will show a change in his way of living.

Not only did God elect us in order that we should be holy but also that we should be "without blame." Now this is the negative side. The believer in Christ is seen before God as without blame. Again we see an example of this in Israel. God would not permit Balaam to curse Israel or to find fault with His people. "He hath not beheld iniquity in Jacob, neither hath he seen perverseness in Israel: the LORD his God is with him, and the shout of a king is among them" (Num. 23:21). Yes, but if you had gone down there into the camp of Israel, you would have found that God did find fault with them and He judged them—He was sanctifying and purifying that camp.

God has chosen you in order that He might make you holy and in order that He might make you without blame. It means that your life has been changed. If there is no evidence of change, then you are not one of the elect. God wants his children to live lives which are not marked or spotted with sin. He has made every provision to absolve them from all blame. "My little children, these things write I unto you, that ye sin not. And if any man sin, we have an advocate with the Father, Jesus Christ the righteous: And he is the propitiation for our sins: and not for ours only, but also for the sins of the whole world" (1 John 2:1–2).

By the way, that answers once and for all the question of a limited atonement, that is, that Christ died only for the elect. This verse in 1 John makes it clear that He died for the world. I don't care who you are, there is a legitimate offer that has been sent out to you today from God, and that offer is that Jesus Christ has died for you. You can't hide and say, "I am not one of the elect." You are of the elect if you hear His voice. You also have free will not to hear His voice. It is a glorious and wonderful thing that the God of heaven would elect some of us down here and save us. I don't propose to understand all that—I just believe it.

The Lord gave us a picture of a great big, wide highway and off that highway is a little, narrow entrance. Over the entrance it says, ". . . I am the way, the truth, and the life: no man cometh unto the Father, but by me" (John 14:6), and "I am the door . . ." (John 10:9). Now the interesting thing is that the broad highway on which most of the people are traveling leads down and gets narrower and narrower until finally it leads to destruction. You can keep on that broad highway if you wish, but you can also turn off if you want to. You can turn off at the invitation, ". . . him that cometh to me I will in no wise cast out" (John 6:37). You can enter in at that narrow way, and the interesting thing is that the entrance is narrow, but then the road widens out. ". . . I am come that they might have life, and that they might have it more abundantly" (John 10:10). You talk about the broad way! The broad way comes after you get through the narrow gate. But, you see, *you* must make the choice. Whosoever will may come—that includes you. It is a legitimate invitation.

D. L. Moody put it in his quaint way. He said, "The whosoeverwills are the elect and the whosoeverwon'ts are the nonelect." It is up to you. The Lord has extended the invitation. Whosoever will may come. Don't try to say that you are left out. God so loved the *world. Whosoever* believeth in Him shall not perish. That "whosoever" means J. Vernon McGee. It means you—you can put your name right in there. Just because there are the elect, it does not mean we know who they are. You have no right to say that you are of the nonelect. If you will open your heart, you can come. That is all you have to do. I don't believe in the idea today that you can have "mental reservations." The problem is that you have sin in your life, and the Bible condemns it. If you come to Christ, it means you'll have to turn from that sin, and some folk just don't want to turn from their sin.

"Chosen us in him." Again and again the Word of God emphasizes God's sovereign choice. Paul states, "But we are bound to give thanks alway to God for you, brethren beloved of the Lord, because God hath from the beginning chosen you to salvation through sanctification of the Spirit and belief of the truth: Whereunto he called you by our gospel, to the obtaining of the glory of our Lord Jesus Christ" (2 Thess. 2:13–14). Peter writes in 1 Peter 1:2, "Elect according to the foreknowledge of God the Father, through sanctification of the Spirit, unto obedience and sprinkling of the blood of Jesus Christ. . . ." The interesting thing is that election and sanctification seem to go together and they are both in the Lord Jesus Christ. If God has saved you, He hasn't saved you because you are good but because you are not good. Paul puts it in such a marvelous way: "What shall we say then? Is there unrighteousness with God? God forbid. For he saith to Moses, I will have mercy on whom I will have mercy, and I will have compassion on whom I will have compassion. So then it is not of him that willeth, nor of him that runneth, but of God that sheweth mercy" (Rom. 9:14–16). Moses had gone to God in prayer, and God had answered, "Moses, I am going to hear and answer your prayer, but it is not because you are Moses and the deliverer. It is because I will show mercy on whom I will and I'll show compassion on whom I will. It is not to him that wills nor to him that works but it is I who shows compassion." Now, do you want to experience the compassion of God? Then you will have to turn to Him.

I think the best illustration of this is over in Acts 27. You remember that Paul was in a ship and there was a terrific storm so that the ship was listing and about ready to go down. They had already cast some of the cargo overboard to lighten the ship. Then Paul went to the captain and said, "And now I exhort you to be of good cheer: for there shall be no loss of any man's life among you, but of the ship. For there stood by me this night the angel of God, whose I am, and whom I serve, Saying, Fear not, Paul; thou must be brought before Caesar: and, lo, God hath given thee all them that sail with thee" (Acts 27:22–24). Now that was

God's foreknowledge. That is election. God had elected that nobody on that ship would be lost. Just a little later, Paul found a group of the sailors about to let down a lifeboat into the sea. They intended to go overboard, hoping to get to land in that way. Then Paul said to the captain, ". . . Except these abide in the ship, ye cannot be saved" (Acts 27:31). The captain could have said, "Wait a minute. You already told me that none would perish," and he would have been right. That is what Paul had said. That was God's side of it—none would perish. But the condition was, "Except these abide in the ship, ye cannot be saved." That was man's side of it—they had to stay in the ship.

Now God knows who the elect are. I don't. Someone came to Spurgeon one time and said, "Mr. Spurgeon, if I believed as you do, I would not preach like you do. You say you believe that there are the elect, and yet you preach as if everybody can be saved." Spurgeon's answer was, "They can all be saved. If God had put a yellow streak up and down the backs of the elect, I'd go up and down the streets lifting up shirt tails to find out who had the yellow streak up and down his back. Then I'd give that person the gospel. But God didn't do that. He told me to preach the gospel to every creature and that whosoever will may come." That is our marching order, and as far as I am concerned, until God gives me the roll call of the elect, I am going to preach the "whosoever will" gospel. That is the gospel we are to preach today.

Someone else has put it like this. On the door to heaven, from our side, it says, "Whosoever will may enter. I am the door: by Me if any man. . . ." Any man—that means you. You can come in and find pasture and find life. When you get on the other side of the door someday in heaven, you're going to look back, and on that door you will find written, "Chosen in Him before the foundation of the world." I haven't seen that side of the door yet; therefore, I give God (since He is God) the right to plan His church.

A friend of mine down in Florida once showed me the blueprint of a home he was going to build. He had planned it and had it all marked out in the blueprint. They had only laid the foundation, but he and his wife showed me where everything was going to be. Later on when we were in that home to visit them, it was just like they planned it. They didn't have supernatural knowledge, but as far as I know, no one has questioned whether they had the right to do that or not. They did have the right, and they did it according to their plan. God has planned the church. After all, this is His universe, and the church is His church. What is His plan? "According as he hath chosen us in him before the foundation of the world, that we should be holy and without blame before him in love."

Now the words *in love* are not connected with verse four, but actually with verse five. "In love,"

Having predestinated us unto the adoption of children by Jesus Christ to himself, according to the good pleasure of his will [Eph. 1:5].

Somebody says, "Oooh, there's that word *predestination*, and that's another frightful term!" Friend, that's one of the most *wonderful* words we have in Scripture, and this a glorious section. It is something we don't hear too much about today. If I were not going through the Bible, I would have probably avoided this and would have chosen something else. I would have talked about the comfort there is for the saints, which is the big theme of even most fundamental preachers today. We're all talking about comfort, but what we have here is strong medicine. Some folk won't be able to take the medicine; but if you take it, it'll do you good. We need something pretty strong in this flabby age in which we live. We need to *know* that we've been chosen in Him in order to stand for God today. It will make a world of difference in your life.

We are treading on the mountain tops in Ephesians. We're in eternity past when God planned the church. I wasn't back there to give Him any suggestions or tell Him how I wanted it done, but He's telling me how He did it. In essence, God says to you and me, "You either take it or leave it. This is the way I did it. Maybe you don't like it, but this is the way I did it, and I'm the One who is running this universe, you see." God hasn't turned it over to any political party yet. Thank God for that! He hasn't turned it over to any individual either. We can thank Him for that. He certainly hasn't turned it over to me, and I tell you, all of us can shout a hearty "Amen" to that and thank Him He didn't do it that way. God has done three things for us, however, in planning the church. First of all, we've seen that *He* chose us—and that's a pretty hard pill for us to swallow. Secondly, the Father predestinated us to the place of sonship. Thirdly, the Father made us accepted in the Beloved.

I cannot repeat often enough that election is God's choosing us in Christ. I emphasize again that men are not lost because they have not been elected. They are lost because they are sinners and that is the way they want it and that is the way they have chosen. The free will of man is never violated because of the election of God. The lost man makes his own choice. Augustine expressed it like this: "If there be not free will grace in God, how can He save the world? And if there be not free will in man, how can the world by God be judged?" Here again is Paul's strong statement, "What shall we say then? Is there unrighteousness with God? God forbid" (Rom. 9:14). Now if you think that there is some unrighteousness with God, you had better change your mind.

I get the impression in some of the evangelistic campaigns today that people are asked to come forward and even that coming forward is doing something. May I say to you that God says He is not saving any of us because we came forward, or because we are nice little boys or nice little girls, or because we have joined a church, or even because we have an inclination to turn to Him. God says that it is because He extends mercy. He had to say that even to Moses. Moses could have gone to the Lord and said, "Look, I'm Moses. I'm leading the children of Israel out of Egypt. I'm really up there at the top. You'd have a problem getting along without me. Therefore, I want You to hear my prayer." If you read his prayers, Moses never prayed like that. It was God who said, "I will have mercy on whom I will have mercy and compassion on whom I will have compassion." He told Moses that He was going to hear and answer his prayer, but not because he was Moses, but because ". . . it is not of him that willeth, nor of him that runneth, but of God that sheweth mercy" (Rom. 9:16).

My friend, I'm going to be in heaven someday, and I'm not going to be there because Vernon McGee is a nice little boy. He's not. You don't know me like I know myself. If you knew me, you would tune me out right now. But wait a minute—don't tune me out, because if I knew you like you know yourself, I wouldn't even speak to you. So let's stay together, shall we? We are both in the same boat—we are all lost sinners. I will not be in heaven because I am a preacher or because I joined a church. It will not be because I was baptized. I have been sprinkled *and* immersed. My wife belonged to a Southern Baptist church and she has always prided herself on being immersed. I tease her and say it sure will be funny if we get to heaven and find out the Lord really meant sprinkling after all. I tell her that that would leave her out, but I'm safe because I've been baptized both ways. You see, that is ridiculous—none of those things will put a person into heaven. The only reason I am going to be in heaven is because of the mercy of God. I am a lost sinner. Until you and I are willing to come to God as a nobody and then let Him make us a somebody, you and I will never be saved.

> Your best resolutions must totally be waived,
> Your highest ambitions be crossed.
> You need never think that you will ever be saved,
> Until first you have learned that you're lost.

It is to the lost sinner that God is prepared to extend His mercy.

Don't tell me you have "intellectual problems"—hurdles to get over. The problem with you and the problem with me was not that we had trouble with Jonah, or with Noah and the ark. Our problem today is that the Bible condemns the sin in our lives. God will save you when your heart is willing to turn to Him. He's planned it like this in order that He might bring you and me into heaven someday; and when we get there, we are going to find out that He's the One who did it.

Now in verse five we come to the next thing God did for us. "In love having predestinated us." Some are going to say that they never knew you could get predestination and love together even in the same county, let alone in the same verse. But here they are. God's love is involved in this word which has been frightful to a great many people. The word *predestination* comes from the Greek *proorisos*, and it literally means "to define, to mark out, to set apart." It means "to horizon." If you go outside and look around (especially if you're in flat country), you only can see to the horizon. You're "horizoned"; you're put in that area. When it refers to God, predestination has to do with God's purpose with those He chooses.

Predestination is never used in reference to unsaved people. God has never predestinated anybody to be lost. If you are lost, it is because you have rejected God's remedy. It is like a dying man to whom the doctor offers curing medicine. "If you take this, it'll heal you." The man looks at the doctor in amazement and says, "I don't believe you." Now the man dies and the doctor's report says he died of a certain disease, and that's accurate. But may I say to you, there was a remedy, and he actually died because he didn't take the rem-edy. God has provided a remedy. Let me repeat, God has never predestined anybody to be lost. That's where your free will comes in, and you have to determine for yourself what your choice will be.

Predestination refers only to those who are saved. What it actually means is that when God starts out with one hundred sheep, He is going to come through with one hundred sheep. "And we know that all things work together for good to them that love God, to them who are the called according to his purpose. For whom he did foreknow, he also did predestinate to be conformed to the image of his Son, that he might be the firstborn among many brethren" (Rom. 8:28–29). Dr. R. A. Torrey used to say that this is a wonderful pillow for a tired heart. Those who are called according to His purpose are predestinated to be conformed to the image of His Son. We're talking now about saved people. Romans goes on to explain how this is done. "Moreover whom he did predestinate, them he also called: and whom he called, them he also justified: and whom he justified, them he also glorified" (Rom. 8:30). When God starts out with one hundred sheep, He will come through with one hundred sheep. You must admit that that is a good percentage.

Years ago I was told by a sheep rancher in San Angelo, Texas, that he would appreciate coming out with 65 percent. He said, "We can make money if we get to market 65 percent of the sheep that we start out with." That makes you feel that it wouldn't hurt too much if one little sheep got lost.

The Lord Jesus told a parable about a man who had one hundred sheep, and one little sheep got lost. You know, most of us get lost even after we have been saved. That doesn't mean we lose our salvation, but we surely get out of fellowship with Him. Some people can get lost so far that they actually fear they have lost their salvation. But the little lost sheep is still a sheep even though he is way out yonder and lost. "All we like sheep have gone astray . . ." (Isa. 53:6). That's our propensity; that's our tendency; that's the direction we go. We don't go toward God, but we go away from Him. So what does the Shepherd do? He goes out to look for that one lost sheep! I'm confident that the man who raised sheep in Texas wouldn't get up and go out into a cold, blustery, stormy night to get one little sheep. I think he would say, "Let him go." Thank God, we have a Shepherd who never says that! He says, "I started out with one hundred sheep and I'm going to come through with that one hundred sheep." Now, suppose the day comes when He is counting His sheep up in heaven, way out there somewhere in the future. He starts out, "One, two, three four, five . . . ninety-six, ninety-seven, ninety-eight, ninety-nine, ninety-nine, ninety-nine—what in the world happened to Vernon McGee? Well, We've just lost one, so We'll let it go at that. A lot of folk didn't think Vernon McGee was going to make it anyway." Thank God, He will not do it that way. If I am not there when He counts in His sheep, He is going to go out and look for me, and He is going to bring me in. That is what predestination means. I *love* that word. It is God's guarantee. "My sheep hear my voice, and I know them, and they follow me: And I give unto them eternal life; and they shall never perish, neither shall any man pluck them out of my hand" (John 10:27–28). Always remember that if sheep are saved, it is not because they were smart little sheep. They are stupid little fellows. If they are safe, it is because they have a wonderful Shepherd. That is the glorious truth.

We are predestinated "unto the adoption of children by Jesus Christ to himself." Adoption means that we are brought into the place of full-grown sons. We have dealt with that in the Epistle to the Galatians. It implies two very important things. Adoption into sonship means regeneration. We have been regenerated by the Spirit of God. The child of God has been born again ". . . not of corruptible seed, but of incorruptible, by the word of God, which liveth and abideth for ever" (1 Pet. 1:23). He is born again into a new relationship. That is what the Lord Jesus meant when He told Nicodemus that he must be born again. Adoption also means a place of position and privilege. When we are saved, we are born into the family of God as a babe in Christ; but, in addition, we are given the position of an adult son. We are in a position where we can understand the Word of the Father because He has given us the Holy Spirit as our Teacher.

When my little grandson was almost two years old, he talked constantly, but I could understand only a few words that he said. Yet I could pretty well tell what he wanted and needed. He was just a little, bitty fellow and he couldn't understand why I didn't know what he was saying. He didn't always understand me either, by the way. The wonderful thing is that I have a Heavenly Father today— and I've been a babe a long time—and He's told me that He's put me in a position where I can understand Him. How wonderful it's going to be as my grandson grows up and we can really understand one another. God, however, communicates to us now. Paul tells us how: "Now we have received, not the spirit of the world, but the spirit which is of God; that we might know the things that are freely given to us of God" (1 Cor. 2:12). All of this is done in Christ Jesus. "For there is one God, and one mediator between God and men, the man Christ Jesus" (1 Tim. 2:5).

To the praise of the glory of his grace, wherein he hath made us accepted in the beloved [Eph. 1:6].

Since all is for the glory of God, Paul sings this glorious doxology, this wonderful psalm of praise. All is done on the basis of His grace and the end is the glory of God. The inception is grace; the concepton is adoption; the reception is for His glory.

"Wherein he hath made us accepted in the beloved." Who is the Beloved? It is the Lord Jesus Christ. It is the Lord Jesus who said, "Father, I will that they also, whom thou hast given me, be with me where I am; that they may behold my glory, which thou hast given me: for thou lovedst me before the foundation of the world" (John 17:24). God sees the believer in Christ and He accepts the believer just as He receives His own Son. That is wonderful. That is the only basis on which I will be in heaven. I cannot stand there on the merit of Vernon McGee. I am accepted only in the Beloved. God loves me just as He loves Christ, because I am *in* Christ. Jesus said, "I in them, and thou in me, that they may be made perfect in one; and that the world may know that thou hast sent me, and hast loved them, as thou hast loved me" (John 17:23).

There has been, therefore, a threefold work performed by God the Father. He chose us in Christ. He predestinated us to the place of sonship. He has made us accepted in the Beloved. It is all to the praise of the glory of His grace. He is the One who gets the praise. He is the One who did it all.

All of this is for your good and my good. I just like to revel in this, I like to rejoice in this, and I talk about this because it is worth talking about. It is so much more valuable than a lot of the chitchat that I hear today that goes under the name of religion. How we need to see the grace of God as it is revealed in Christ!

GOD THE SON PAID THE PRICE FOR THE CHURCH

In whom we have redemption through his blood, the forgiveness of sins, ac-

cording to the riches of his grace [Eph. 1:7].

Back in eternity past God chose us, predestinated us, and made us accepted in the Beloved. Now we move out of eternity into time, where the plans of God the Father are placed into the hands of Christ, who moves into space and time to construct the church.

It is an historical fact that Jesus was born into this world over nineteen hundred years ago. God intruded into humanity and after being on this earth for thirty-three years, He died upon a cross, was buried, rose again bodily, and ascended into heaven. Those are the historical facts that the Word of God gives us. While He was here, He redeemed us, and that redemption is through His blood. This is something which is not popular today. Most people want a beautiful religion, one that appeals to their esthetic nature. The cross of Christ does not appeal to the esthetic part of man; it doesn't appeal to the pride of man. Unfortunately, the liberal churches and even a few so-called Bible churches make an appeal to the old nature of man and, therefore, there is no emphasis on the blood of Christ—it is considered repulsive.

Years ago a lady came up to the late Dr. G. Campbell Morgan. She was one of these dowagers who had a lorgnette (a lorgnette is a sneer on the end of a stick). She looked at him through her lorgnette and said, "Dr. Morgan, I don't like to hear about the blood. It is repulsive to me and offends my esthetic nature." Dr. Morgan replied, "I agree with you that it is repulsive, but the only thing repulsive about it is your sin and mine." *Sin* is the thing that is repulsive about the blood redemption, my friend.

A new pastor came to a great church in Washington, D.C., and a couple came to him and said, "We trust that you will not put too much emphasis on the blood. The former pastor we had talked a great deal about the blood, and we hope that you will not emphasize it too much." He answered, "You can be assured that I won't emphasize it too much." They looked pleased and thanked him for it. He said, "Wait a minute. It is not possible to emphasize it too much." And he continued to stress the blood. It is repulsive to man, but it is through His blood that we have redemption.

After God the Father had drawn the blueprint, the Son came to this earth to form the church with nail-pierced hands. The entire context of the Old Testament sets forth the expiation of sins by the blood of an animal sacrifice. Yet this could not take away sins—only Christ could execute that. The writer to the Hebrews says it this way: "In burnt offerings and sacrifices for sin thou hast had no pleasure. Then said I, Lo, I come (in the volume of the book it is written of me,) to do thy will, O God. Above when he said, Sacrifice and offering and burnt offerings and offering for sin thou wouldest not, neither hadst pleasure therein; which are offered by the law; Then said he, Lo, I come to do thy will, O God. He taketh away the first, that he may establish the second. By the which will we are sanctified through the offering of the body of Jesus Christ once for all. And every priest standeth daily ministering and offering oftentimes the same sacrifices, which can never take away sins: But this man, after he had offered one sacrifice for sins for ever, sat down on the right hand of God; From henceforth expecting till his enemies be made his footstool" (Heb. 10:6–13).

"In whom we have redemption." "In whom" refers to the Beloved, who is Christ. We are accepted in the Beloved, in Christ. Redemption is the primary work of Christ. The literal here is "In whom we have *the* redemption." The word *the* gives it prominence, and the fact that it is named first gives it top priority. This is the reason Christ came to earth. "Even as the Son of man came not to be ministered unto, but to minister, and to give his life a ransom for many" (Matt. 20:28). He came to pay a price for your redemption and mine. We were slaves in sin, and He came to deliver us and give us liberty by paying a price for us.

There are three Greek words in the New Testament which are translated by the one English word *redemption*. The Greek word *agorazo* means "to buy at the marketplace." Here is the picture of a housewife out in the morning shopping for the day. She sees some vegetables and a roast and puts down cash on the barrelhead. She pays the price and now they belong to her, of course. The only thought in this word *agorazo*, then, is to buy and take out. This is the word Paul used in 1 Corinthians 6:20: "For ye are bought with a price: therefore glorify God in your body, and in your spirit, which are God's."

The Greek word *exagorazo* means "to buy out of the market," and it has the thought of buying something for one's own use. You see, somebody could go into the marketplace and buy that roast and those vegetables and go down to the next town, where they are short of those items, and put them up for sale at a profit. *Exagorazo* means, however, to take goods out of the market place and never to sell them again, but rather to keep them for one's own use. This is the word which is used in Galatians 3:13: "Christ hath redeemed us from the curse of the law, being made a curse for us: for it is written, Cursed is every one that hangeth on a tree." This means that Christ redeemed us so that we would not be exposed for sale again. He has paid the price, and He has taken us off the market. We belong to Him.

The third Greek word for redemption is *apolutrosis* which is the word used here in verse seven. It means "to liberate by the paying of a ransom in order to set a person free." It carries this same meaning in Luke 21:28: "And when these things begin to come to pass, then look up, and lift up your heads; for your redemption draweth nigh." *Redemption* is a marvelous word. It means not only to go into the marketplace and put cash on the barrelhead; it means not only to take it out of the market for your own private use, never to sell it to anyone else; but it also means to set free or to liberate after paying the price. The last applies to buying a slave out of slavery in order to set him free, and this is the word for redemption we have here in this verse. Man has been sold under sin and is in the bondage of sin. All one needs to do is look around to see that this is true. Man is a rotten, corrupt sinner and he cannot do anything else but sin—he is a slave to sin. Christ came to pay the price of man's freedom. That is what the Lord Jesus meant when He said, "If the Son therefore shall make you free, ye shall be free indeed" (John 8:36).

This redemption is "through his blood"— that was the price which He paid. "Forasmuch as ye know that ye were not redeemed with corruptible things, as silver and gold, from your vain conversation received by tradition from your fathers; But with the precious blood of Christ, as of a lamb without blemish and without spot" (1 Pet. 1:18–19). The blood of Christ is more valuable than silver and gold. For one thing, there is not much of it. A limited supply increases the value of a substance, but that really is not the reason for its value. One drop of the blood of the holy Son of God can save every sinner on topside of this earth, if that sinner will put his trust in the Savior. We have redemption through His blood, and the reason He saves us in that way is because ". . . without shedding of blood is no remission" (Heb. 9:22). This is an Old Testament principle which is applicable to the entire human race from Adam down to the last man.

We have been redeemed now, not with the blood of bulls and goats—that can't redeem you—but with the precious blood of Christ.

"The forgiveness of sins." Forgiveness is not the act of an indulgent deity who is moved by sentiment to the exclusion of justice, righteousness, and holiness. Forgiveness depends on the shedding of blood: it demands and depends on the payment of the penalty for sin. Christ's death and the shedding of His blood is the foundation for forgiveness and, without that, there could be no forgiveness.

I think here we need to learn the distinction between human forgiveness and divine forgiveness—they are not the same. Human forgiveness is always based on the fact that a penalty is deserved and that the penalty is not imposed. It simply means that one wipes out the account. God is holy and righteous. Therefore divine forgiveness is always based on the fact that there has been the execution of the penalty and the price has been paid. Human forgiveness comes before the penalty is executed. Divine forgiveness depends upon the penalty being executed. It is really too bad that this is something which has bogged down our entire legal system today. That is why we are living in a lawless nation where it is not even safe to be on the streets of our cities at night. There has been a confusion between human forgiveness and the righteousness of the law. We are in trouble because of the leniency on the part of certain judges throughout our land. They sit on the bench and think they are being bighearted by letting the criminal go free. My friend, the righteousness of the law demands that a penalty must be paid. I once heard a judge say, "If God can forgive, then I can forgive." But God paid the penalty and *then* He forgave. Is the judge on the bench willing to go and pay the penalty? I don't think you have any right to take men out of death row unless you are willing to take their place, because a penalty must be executed.

A righteous God forgives on the basis that a penalty has been executed. When was it executed? When Jesus Christ shed His blood over nineteen hundred years ago. Sure, that's not esthetic. It doesn't appeal to the refined nature of civilized man today. Of course it doesn't—man thinks his sin doesn't really seem so bad. He tries to be sophisticated; he thinks he is suave and very clever. Friend, we are lost, hell-doomed sinners, and God cannot forgive us until the penalty has been executed. The good news is that the penalty has been executed. That is the reason that in the Word of God you will find forgiveness back to back with the blood of Jesus Christ. Forgiveness depends on the blood of Christ. That is how valuable His blood is. I have said it before, and I will say it again: you come to God as a nobody and let Him make you a somebody. He can forgive you your sins because He paid the penalty for your sins. This is the only way that you and I can have forgiveness for our sins.

The Lord Jesus said to His disciples, ". . . Thus it is written, and thus it behoved Christ to suffer, and to rise from the dead the third day: And that repentance and remission of sins should be preached in his name among all nations, beginning at Jerusalem" (Luke 24:46–47). Paul says the same thing in Colossians 1:14: "In whom we have redemption through his blood, even the forgiveness of sins." When Jesus met Paul on the Damascus road, He told him to go to the Gentiles, "to open their eyes, and to turn them from darkness to light, and from the power of Satan unto God, that they may receive forgiveness of sins, and inheritance among them which are sanctified by faith that is in me" (Acts 26:18). The shedding of the blood of Christ and His death on the cross is the foundation for forgiveness—*sine qua non* or without this there is nothing. God cannot forgive until the penalty has been paid.

The word for *sins* is *paraptoma* which means "an offense or a falling aside." Paul describes the first sin of man as an offense in Romans 5:15. He uses the same word in Romans 4:25, "Who was delivered for our offences, and was raised again for our justification." "Sins" includes the entire list of sins which is chargeable to man. Augustine stated it succinctly: "Christ bought the church foul that He might make it fair." He bought it with His own blood and paid the penalty for our sin.

"According to the riches of his grace." That is an interesting expression. It doesn't say *out of* the riches of His grace but *according to* the riches of His grace. Let me illustrate the difference. I read many years ago that when the late John D. Rockefeller played golf in Florida he always gave the caddy a dime. I always felt that that must have almost broke the man to pay out such a handsome sum. You see, he didn't give according to his riches—he gave out of his riches. I think he could have done a little better than that, and if he had paid according to his riches, the caddy would have been rich. God has redeemed us according to the riches of His grace. God is rich in grace, and He is willing to give according to His riches of grace. He has had to bestow so much

on me, but He has enough left for you who are reading this way up in Alaska. It may be cold up there, but God's grace is rich up there. Some of you across the Pacific may read this, and He has grace for you. God can save you, and He can keep you, and it is due to His grace.

We are dealing with the work of God the Son on behalf of the church. That work is threefold: (1) Christ redeemed us through His blood; (2) He has revealed the mystery of His will; and (3) He rewards us with an inheritance.

We looked at the Greek words for redemption and saw that it involved the paying of a price which was the blood of Christ: we can have forgiveness because He paid the price. We know that God went into the marketplace where we were sold on the slave block of sin and He bought us, all of us. He is going to use us for Himself—He establishes a personal relationship. We saw also that He bought us in order to set us free. Now somebody will ask, "Doesn't that upset the hymn that says, 'I gave, I gave My life for thee. What hast thou done for Me?'?" My friend, it surely does. The very word for *redemption* in verse seven, *apolutrosis*, means that God never asks you what you have done for Him. That is the glorious thing about grace: when God saves you by grace, it doesn't put you in debt to Him. He bought you in order to set you free.

Someone else will ask, "But aren't we supposed to serve Him?" Certainly. But it is on another basis, a new relationship—the relationship now is love. The Lord Jesus said, "If ye love me, keep my commandments" (John 14:15). He didn't say, "Because I'm dying for you, you are to keep My commandments." He said, "If you love Me." Today, if you love Him, He wants your service. If you don't love Him, then forget about this business of service. One hears so much today about commitment to Christ. Friend, you and I have very little to commit to Him. We are to respond in love to Him, and that is a different basis altogether. We love Him because He first loved us.

I heard this story many years ago, and it's the kind of story that you are not supposed to tell today, but I still tell it. I guess I'm still a square. It illustrates a great truth. In the South—and I hate to say, in the days of slavery—there was a beautiful girl who was put on the slave block to be sold. There was a very cruel slave owner, a brutal fellow, who began to bid for her. Every time he would bid, the girl would cringe and a look of fear would come over her face. A plantation owner who was kind to his slaves was there, and he began to bid for the girl. He outbid the other fellow and purchased her. He put down the price and started to walk away. The girl followed him, but he turned to her and said, "You misunderstand. I didn't buy you because I needed a slave. I bought you to set you free." She simply stood there, stunned for just a moment. Then she suddenly fell to her knees. "Why," she said, "I will serve you forever!" Now that illustrates the basis on which the Lord Jesus wants us to serve Him. He loved you. He paid a price for you. He gave Himself and shed His blood so that you could have forgiveness of sins. This is all yours if you are willing to come to Him and accept Him as your Savior.

Now what if someone says, "But I don't love Him." Then He is not asking you to serve Him. But if you do love Him, then He wants you to serve Him. That is what it is all about. Never forget, your redemption and your forgiveness are "according to the riches of his grace."

Now we are ready for the second work of God the Son on behalf of the church: Christ revealed the mystery of His will.

Wherein he hath abounded toward us in all wisdom and prudence;

Having made known unto us the mystery of his will, according to his good pleasure which he hath purposed in himself:

That in the dispensation of the fulness of times he might gather together in one all things in Christ, both which are in heaven, and which are on earth; even in him [Eph. 1:8–10].

What is a mystery in Scripture? It is not a whodunit or a mystery story, and it is not something you wonder about, like, *Was it the butler who committed the crime?* It is not something Agatha Christie wrote or a Sherlock Holmes story, by any means. A mystery in Scripture means that God is revealing something that, up to that time, He had not revealed. There are two elements which always enter into a New Testament mystery: (1) It cannot be discovered by human agencies, for it is always a revelation from God; and (2) it is revealed at the proper time and not concealed, and enough is revealed to establish the fact without all the details being disclosed.

The Scofield Reference Bible (p. 1014) lists eleven mysteries in the New Testament:

The greater mysteries are: (1) the mysteries of the kingdom of heaven (Mt. 13:3–50); (2) the mystery of Israel's blindness during this age (Rom. 11:25, with context); (3) the mystery of the translation of living saints at the end of this age (1 Cor. 15:51–52; 1 Th. 4:13–17); (4) the mystery of the N.T. Church as one body composed of Jews and Gentiles (Eph. 3:1–12; Rom. 16:25; Eph. 6:19; Col. 4:3); (5) the mystery of the Church as the bride of Christ (Eph. 5:23–32); (6) the mystery of the in-living Christ (Gal. 2:20; Col. 1:26–27); (7) the "mystery of God even Christ," i.e., Christ as the incarnate fullness of the Godhead embodied, in whom all the divine wisdom for man subsists (1 Cor. 2:7; Col. 2:2,9); (8) the mystery of the processes by which godlikeness is restored to man (1 Tim. 3:16); (9) the mystery of iniquity (2 Th. 2:7; cp. Mt. 13:33); (10) the mystery of the seven stars (Rev. 1:20); and (11) the mystery of Babylon (Rev. 17:5,7).

Yet, even with all these, did you know that God hasn't told us everything? There are a lot of things God hasn't told us. There are many questions that I would like to ask God myself. A great many people send us questions, and we attempt to answer them. I have questions, too, but I don't know who to ask because nobody down here knows the answers. Someday He will reveal them to us.

A mystery then is something God hasn't previously revealed but now reveals to us. Now in these verses is a wonderful mystery that was not revealed in the Old Testament. First let me restate verses eight and nine to amplify their meaning somewhat: "Which He caused (made) to abound toward us: having made known [aorist tense] unto us in all wisdom and prudence the mystery of His will, according to His good pleasure which He purposed in Him (Christ)." Notice that "in all wisdom and prudence" properly belongs with verse nine. What is the mystery of His will? First of all, it is something which is revealed according to wisdom and prudence. It is not some simple little "a-b-c" something. I very frankly rejoice that there are so many agencies and individuals who try to get out what they call the "simple gospel." I thank the Lord that people write and tell us that we are making the gospel simple and they can understand it. I appreciate that because that is what we must do. Dr. H. A. Ironside used to say, "Put the cookies on the bottom shelf where the kiddies can get to them." There is a "simple gospel" but, may I say to you, there are the depths and the wisdom of God that you and I can't easily probe—sometimes not at all. We need to use all the mental acumen that we have in order to try to understand something of the great purposes of God, the plan of God. God wants us to know these things because now this mystery has been revealed.

"That in the dispensation of the fulness of times he might gather together in one all things in Christ." *Dispensation* is another word like *mystery*. It is often misunderstood, and a great many people today think it is a dirty word. It is a great word! Some Bible teachers won't even use the word because it is a word that is hated. There are a lot of words in the Bible that are hated—words like *blood*, and *redemption*, and *the cross*. Paul says the Cross is an offense, but that cannot keep us from preaching about it. The Bible teaches dispensations, and so we will not avoid the subject at all.

Let me say first of all that a dispensation is not a period of time. That is where *dispensation* differs from the word *age*. We hear of the "age of grace"—that is a period of time. *Dispensation* is an altogether different word that is translated in several different ways. It can mean "a stewardship," "an order," or "an administration." An English transliteration of the Greek word would be "economy." It is an order or a system that is put into effect; it is the way of doing things.

For example, girls in school take a course called home economics or domestic economy. They learn how to run a household. When a woman has her own home, she may decide to have baked beans one night and a roast the next night. She sets up the order of meals and that is the way she organizes her schedule. Down the street the mother in another family decides they won't have a roast that night, but they will have fish. That is the way she runs her house, and she has a right to run it like that. There is also a political economy—a subject that is taught in our colleges today. A lot of young men go into that field, and they learn how to run the government, the way to run a nation. England runs her government differently from the way we do in the United States. Each has a right to its own system and I wouldn't say that either place has the right system. Russia has an entirely different system; we certainly wouldn't better ours by taking theirs. Countries even have different systems of running traffic. In England they drive down the left side of the street. I en-

joyed kidding our driver when we were in England, "Look out, there comes a car on the wrong side of the street!" "That's all right," he would say, "I'm going on the wrong side myself." In England, the right side is the left side. Now that is confusing to a poor American visiting over there.

A dispensation *may* fit into a certain period of time, but it actually means the way God runs something at a particular time: it is the way God does things. It is evident that God had Adam on a different arrangement than He has for you and me. I think even the most ardent antidispensationalist can understand that the Garden of Eden was different from Southern California today. And God dealt with Adam in a different way than He deals with us. (Now, I will admit that when people first moved out to Southern California, they thought it was the Garden of Eden. I thought so, too, when I first came here, but now it is filled with smog and traffic!)

Now God has never had but one method of saving folk; everything rests upon one method of salvation. The approach and the man under the system have been different, however. For example, Abel offered a lamb to God, and so did Abraham. The Old Testament priests offered lambs to God. God had said that was the right way. But I hope you didn't bring a lamb to church last Sunday! That is not the way God tells us to approach Him today. We are under a different economy.

"Of the fulness of times." What is the "fulness of times"? I can't go into all phases of that, but God is moving everything forward to the time when Christ will rule over all things in heaven and earth. This is the fullness, the *pleroma*, when everything is going to be brought under the rulership of Jesus Christ. The *pleroma* is like a vast receptacle into which centuries and millenniums have been falling. All that is past, present, and future is moving toward the time when every knee must bow and every tongue must confess that Jesus is Lord. This is the mystery that is revealed to us, "That in the dispensation of the fulness of times he might gather together in one all things in Christ, both which are in heaven, and which are on earth; even in him." We learn this about Christ, that God ". . . hast put all things in subjection under his feet. For in that he put all in subjection under him, he left nothing that is not put under him. But now we see not yet all things put under him" (Heb. 2:8). This states very clearly that we have not yet come to that time. We are under a different dispensation today; we live under a different economy. But God has revealed this to us that is to come to pass, something that had not been revealed in the past.

Heaven and earth are not in tune today—we are playing our own little tune. We have our rock music going down here, while the only Rock up there is the Lord Jesus. He is *the* Rock: He is that precious Stone that is the foundation upon which the church rests today. And the day will come when heaven and earth will be in tune and all things will be gathered together in Christ.

Now we come to the third work of God the Son on behalf of the church: Christ rewards us with an inheritance.

In whom also we have obtained an inheritance, being predestinated according to the purpose of him who worketh all things after the counsel of his own will:

That we should be to the praise of his glory, who first trusted in Christ [Eph. 1:11–12].

Here is another marvelous truth. He gives us an inheritance—He rewards us for something we have not done. It is the overall purpose and plan of God that believers should have a part in Christ's inheritance. They are going to inherit with Christ because they are *in* Christ. Paul writes, "And if children, then heirs; heirs of God, and joint-heirs with Christ; if so be that we suffer with him, that we may be also glorified together" (Rom. 8:17). "Therefore let no man glory in men. For all things are yours; Whether Paul, or Apollos, or Cephas, or the world, or life, or death, or things present, or things to come; all are yours; And ye are Christ's; and Christ is God's" (1 Cor. 3:21–23). I really don't grasp at all this tremendous statement God makes to us, but it causes me to be lifted from the seat in which I'm sitting and carries me right into the sky. Everything is mine! Christ belongs to me. Paul belongs to me. Even death may belong to me. *All* is mine. It is mine because He has given it to me. Christ is mine. God is mine. What an experience for us!

I feel like shouting because this is so wonderful. God has predestinated this; He has determined it. This refers to the saved—remember that God never predestinated anybody to be lost. He predestinated us to receive an inheritance. If He hadn't predestinated it to me, I would never get one. It is something I do not deserve. It is a reward out of His grace and not out of my merit. This is God's will, and that is the only basis on which it is done. It is good, and it is right, and it is the best. Why? Because God has purposed it. You just can't have it any better than that.

Oh, these are the three marvelous things Christ has done for us: He's redeemed us with His blood; He's revealed the mystery of His will; and He rewards us with an inheritance. How wonderful it is—I can't lose! He paid for the church, and I belong to Him because He paid a price.

May I say that the church is very important to Him today. The little plans of men down here—they're not important. We think they are. Men are running around with a blueprint for the world today, but they won't even be around here in the next one hundred years—that crowd will all be gone. But God's great plans *will* be carried out. Thank God for that!

Verse twelve is one of those glorious doxologies that we find throughout the epistles. You will notice that Paul stops and "sings" the doxology after he tells what each person of the Godhead has done. He has just finished telling us about the work of the Son. Then he writes, "That we should be to the praise of his glory, who first trusted in Christ." God does not exist to satisfy the whim and wish of the believer. The believer exists for the glory of God. When the believer is in the center of the will of God, he is living a life of fullness and of satisfaction and of joy. That will deliver you from the hands of psychologists, friend. But when you are not in the will of God, there is trouble brewing for you. Living in God's will adds purpose and meaning to life: we are going to be for the praise of His glory. God will be able throughout the endless ages of eternity future to point to you and me and say, "Look there, they weren't worth saving but I loved them and I saved them." That is the thing which gives worth and standing and dignity and purpose and joy and glory to life. We exist today to the praise of His glory and that is enough.

This doxology looks forward, of course, to the coming of Christ. The third doxology, we shall see, concerns the work of the Holy Spirit.

GOD THE HOLY SPIRIT PROTECTS THE CHURCH

When we look at the work of the Holy Spirit, we see that (1) He regenerates us, (2) He is a refuge for us, and (3) He gives reality to our lives. We come first to regeneration.

In whom ye also trusted, after that ye heard the word of truth, the gospel of

your salvation: in whom also after that ye believed, ye were sealed with that holy Spirit of promise [Eph. 1:13].

This section, I believe, is one of the most wonderful in Scripture. "Well," somebody says, "he doesn't mention regeneration here." Actually he does, and in a marvelous way, because now we're passing from God's work *for us* to the work of the Holy Spirit *in us*. The work of God in planning the church and the work of the Lord Jesus in redeeming the church and paying for it were objective. The work of the Holy Spirit in protecting the church is different because it is subjective; it is *in us*.

In this work of regeneration and renewing, the Holy Spirit causes a sinner to hear and believe in his heart, and that makes him a child of God. The Lord Jesus said, ". . . Ye must be born again" (John 3:7). How are we to be born again? John explains, "But as many as received him, to them gave he power to become the sons of God, even to them that believe on his name" (John 1:12). We need simply to believe on His name.

"In whom ye also trusted, after that ye heard the word of truth." Hearing means to hear not just the sound of words but to hear with understanding. Paul wrote, "But we preach Christ crucified, unto the Jews a stumblingblock, and unto the Greeks foolishness; But unto them which are called, both Jews and Greeks, Christ the power of God, and the wisdom of God" (1 Cor. 1:23–24). Who are the called? Are they the ones that just heard the sound of words? No, it means those who heard with understanding. God called them. It was not just a call of hearing words, but a call where the Holy Spirit made those words real. Faith comes by hearing, and hearing by the Word of God, according to Romans 10:17. Those who are called hear the Word of God and they respond to it. Then what happens? Peter puts it this way: "Being born again, not of corruptible seed, but of incorruptible, by the word of God, which liveth and abideth for ever" (1 Pet. 1:23). The word of God goes out as it is going out even through this printed page. We are saying that the Son of God died for you and if you trust Him, you will be saved. "Well," someone may say, "I read these words, but they mean nothing to me." Someone else, however, will read or hear this message, and the Spirit of God will apply it to his heart so that he believes—he trusts—and the moment he trusts in Christ, he is regenerated. Believing is the logical step after hearing. It may not be the next chronological step, but it is the logical step. "In whom ye also trusted, after that ye heard the word of truth." This is the best explanation of what it means to be born again that I know of in the Word of God. You hear the word of truth—the gospel of your salvation, the good news of your deliverance—and you put your trust in Christ.

"In whom also after that ye believed, ye were sealed with that holy Spirit of promise." I would like to remove the word *after* from this verse because these are not time clauses. They are what is known in the Greek as genitive absolutes, and they are all the same tense as the main verb. It means that when you heard and you believed, you were also sealed: it all took place at the same time. A truer translation would be, "In whom also you, upon hearing [aorist tense] the word of truth, the good news of your salvation, in whom also on believing [aorist tense] you were sealed with the Holy Spirit of promise." This is, by the way, when the baptism of the Holy Spirit occurs. You are baptized the moment that you trust Christ. You are also sealed the moment that you trust Christ. The Holy Spirit first opens the ear to hear, and then He implants faith. His next logical step, you see, is to seal the believer.

There are people today who argue whether God the Father or God the Son seals with the Holy Spirit, or whether the Holy Spirit Himself does the sealing. That type of argument wearies me. They tried to split hairs in that way in the Middle Ages and would argue how many angels could dance on the point of a needle. You toss that around for a little while, and it will get you nowhere. I understand this verse to mean that the Holy Spirit is the seal. God the Father gave the Son to die on the cross, but the Son offered up Himself willingly. So both the Father and the Son gave. God the Father and God the Son both sent the Holy Spirit to perform a definite work, but it is the Spirit who does the work. He regenerates the sinner and He seals the sinner at the same time, and I think that the Spirit Himself is that seal.

There is a twofold purpose in the sealing work of the Holy Spirit. He implants the image of God upon the heart to give reality to the believer. You know that a seal is put down on a document and that seal has an image on it. I think that is exactly what the Spirit of God does to the believer. "He that hath received his testimony hath set to his seal that God is true" (John 3:33). Apparently, this is the thought here—God has put His implant upon the believer.

The second purpose of the sealing is to denote rightful ownership. "Nevertheless the foundation of God standeth sure, having this seal, The Lord knoweth them that are his. And, Let every one that nameth the name of Christ depart from iniquity" (2 Tim. 2:19). The fact that He makes you secure does not mean that you can live in sin. If you name the name of Christ, you are going to depart from iniquity. If there is not this evidence, then you were not regenerated or sealed.

The Holy Spirit is the seal, and that guarantees that God is going to deliver us. We are sealed until the day of redemption. The day will come when the Holy Spirit will deliver us to Christ. It's nice to be sealed like that—we are just like a letter that is insured. In the old days they would put a seal on it. Today they just stamp it with a special stamp, but it still means that the post office guarantees to deliver that letter.

Now we come to the third and final work of the Holy Spirit in protecting the church.

Which is the earnest of our inheritance until the redemption of the purchased possession, unto the praise of his glory [Eph. 1:14].

Earnest money is the money that is put forth as a down payment and pledge on a piece of property. It means you want them to hold the property for you. It also means that you promise there is more money to follow. The Holy Spirit is our earnest money. He has been given as a pledge and token that there is more to follow in the way of spiritual blessings. We have already seen that we have an inheritance—there is more to follow. The Holy Spirit is that earnest, that guarantee.

All of this is to "the praise of his glory." This is now the third doxology in this chapter. As we have seen, Paul gives a doxology after he considers the work of each member of the Trinity. Here it is to the praise of the glory of God that the Holy Spirit regenerates us, becomes our refuge and seal, and gives us reality. All these glorious truths now move Paul to prayer.

PRAYER OF PAUL FOR KNOWLEDGE AND POWER FOR THE EPHESIANS

Wherefore I also, after I heard of your faith in the Lord Jesus, and love unto all the saints,

Cease not to give thanks for you, making mention of you in my prayers [Eph. 1:15–16].

The Ephesian church was noted for its faith and love. Love wasn't just a motto, not just a bumper sticker, for these people. There was real love expressed by the saints. It was based on their faith in the Lord Jesus. This was the church at its highest. In the Book of Revelation the Ephesian church represents the early church at its very best. Because of their faith and love, Paul thanks God for the Ephesians.

It seems that the circumstances that motivate us to pray are trouble, sickness, distress, or a crisis. People asked me to pray for a church recently because it was in trouble: there was no love for the brethren, it was filled with gossip, and Bible study no longer held the highest priority. I love this church and I do pray for them, but it is sad that there are so many negative things that always seem to motivate us to pray. Paul was often motivated by the good things. When you hear something good about a child of God, are you motivated to say, "Oh God, I thank You for this brother and the way You are using him"? When you hear of a wonderful Bible church where God is blessing the preacher, and the Word of God is going out, do you get down on your knees and thank God for it? My friend, isn't it true that too often we turn in a kind of grocery list to God? "I want this, I want that, I want the other thing." "Lord, will You do this, will You do that?" God is not a messenger boy. Why don't we thank Him sometimes? We need more thanksgiving services. I think He would appreciate all of us having a time of thanksgiving regularly—not just once a year.

A preacher friend of mine told me that their prayer meeting got so stale and so dull and so small that they tried something new. They decided that at the prayer meeting they would do nothing but praise God and thank Him. He declared, "We sure had some brief prayers, but we had a good prayer meeting that night. Nobody asked God for anything. They just thanked Him for what He had done."

Paul says, when he heard the good news and wonderful reports about the Ephesian church, "I. . . . cease not to give thanks for you." It's interesting that we don't too often think of Paul as an oustanding man of prayer. We would put him at the top of the list as a great missionary of the cross. We can't think of any greater example of apostleship than Paul. If you were to make a list of ten of the greatest preachers of the church, you would certainly put Paul as number one. He was also one of the greatest teachers. The Lord Jesus was, of course, the greatest of all—". . . Never man spake like this man" (John 7:46)—and Paul certainly followed in that tradition. He is also an example of a good pastor. According to Dr. Luke, Paul wept with the believers at Ephesus when he took leave of them. He loved them, and they loved him.

I always judge the spiritual life of a church by the way they love their pastor, providing he stands for the Word of God. One can pretty well judge the attitude of the people by the way they love their pastor. Today we need to judge folk by their attitude toward the Word of God rather than how big a Bible they carry under their arms. The Ephesians not only loved Paul, but they loved God's Word.

When you think of anyone excelling in any field of service in the early church, Paul the apostle must be up toward the top. How about being representative of a great man of prayer—would you put Paul in that list? We think of Moses as the great intercessor on the top of the mountain. We think of David with his psalms and his confession of his awful sin. We think of Elijah who stood alone before an altar drenched with water at Mount Carmel. Then there was Daniel who opened his window toward Jerusalem and prayed even though he lived in a hostile land under a hostile power. The Lord Jesus was the Man of prayer, so much so that one of His disciples asked Him, ". . . Lord, teach us to pray . . ." (Luke 11:1). Did you know that Paul was also a great man of prayer? When I was teaching in the Bible Institute of Los Angeles, I would ask the students during their study of the epistles of Paul to make a list of all the prayers of the apostle Paul. They were to put down every time he said he was praying for someone. Lo and behold, student after student would come to me and say, "I had no idea that Paul had such a prayer list. I didn't know he prayed for so many people!" Paul was a great man of prayer.

There are two of the prayers of Paul in this epistle. We are looking at the first one. Having set before us the church as the body of Christ, Paul falls to his knees and begins to pray. The other prayer is at the end of the third chapter. These two prayers in this epistle indicate Paul's concern as a child of God for other believers. One of the ways one can judge whether or not a person is a child of God is by his prayer life. How much does he feel a dependence on God? If he has a need, he will go to God in prayer for himself. He will also go to God in intercession for others. Many people who have written from all over this country, and from other countries as well, have told me when I've met them, "I remember you in

prayer." Well, that to me is an indication of their faith. Remember that Ananias in the city of Damascus was disturbed when the angel told him to go to Saul of Tarsus. He objected because Saul was the man who was persecuting the church, but the angel said to him, ". . . behold, he prayeth" (Acts 9:11). That was an indication to Ananias that something had happened to Saul of Tarsus.

"Cease not to give thanks for you." Paul first of all gives thanks to God for the Ephesians. They were on his prayer list, and I guess all the churches were.

"Making mention of you in my prayers." That means he called them all by name. I was with a great preacher one time, and some folk came up and spoke to him and shook hands with us. One man said to him, "I'm praying for you." I shall never forget what the preacher asked him, "Thank you very much, but do you mention me by name? I don't want the Lord to get me mixed up with somebody else." Call people by name when you pray for them.

We have seen that the motive for Paul's prayer was good news. Now we will see that he does not pray for material things but for spiritual blessings. These are the blessings that are all-important.

That the God of our Lord Jesus Christ, the Father of glory, may give unto you the spirit of wisdom and revelation in the knowledge of him [Eph. 1:17].

Paul, having written that the church is the body of Christ, and that God the Father planned it, God the Son paid for it, and God the Holy Spirit protects it, recognized that the Ephesians wouldn't be able to understand all this unless the Spirit of God was their teacher and opened the Word of God to them. Only the Holy Spirit of God could reveal the knowledge of God.

When Dr. H. A. Ironside lived in Southern California as a young man and was preaching in this area, he would sometimes visit a wonderful man of God who had come from Northern Ireland because of his health. This man had what was called in those days "galloping consumption," and he was living his last days in a little tent out back of the home of Dr. Ironside's parents. He had been greatly used of God in teaching the Word. While Dr. Ironside would sit with him, he would open up the Scriptures in such an amazing way that Dr. Ironside one day asked him, "Where did you learn that?" "Well," this man said, "I didn't get it by going to seminary because I never went to seminary. I never learned it by going to college. No one particularly taught me. Rather I learned these things on my knees on the mud floor of a little sod cottage in the north of Ireland. There with my open Bible before me, I used to kneel for hours at a time and ask the Spirit of God to reveal Christ to my soul, and open the Word to my heart. He taught me more on my knees on that mud floor than I could have learned in all the seminaries and colleges of the world."

Having known Dr. Ironside personally, I can say that he too practiced a dependence on the Holy Spirit in his own ministry. I remember when he was teaching us the Song of Solomon, he said that he was never satisfied with what he found in the commentaries, and he just got down on his knees and asked God to reveal to him the message of that book. Well, he wrote a commentary on the Song of Solomon and, very frankly, his interpretation of it is the only one that has ever satisfied my own heart.

What a wonderful, glorious thing it is to have the Spirit of God be the One to teach us. "That the God of our Lord Jesus Christ . . . may give unto you the spirit of wisdom and revelation in the knowledge of him." How will that take place? It will take place by the Spirit of God—the only One who can open our eyes—teaching us God's Word.

The eyes of your understanding being enlightened; that ye may know what is the hope of his calling, and what the riches of the glory of his inheritance in the saints [Eph. 1:18].

More literally it reads, "the eyes of your heart being enlightened." It is not the eyes of your mind but the eyes of your heart that must understand. One can be very brilliant intellectually, but that is no guarantee that there will be an understanding of spiritual truth. Scripture puts more emphasis on the understanding of the heart than of the head. Paul writes, "That if thou shalt confess with thy mouth the Lord Jesus, and shalt believe in thine heart that God hath raised him from the dead, thou shalt be saved. For with the heart man believeth unto righteousness; and with the mouth confession is made unto salvation" (Rom. 10:9–10).

I have no understanding of music whatsoever. I can't sing and I can't carry a tune. I recognize very few tunes, and I do not know what a pitch is. It is all a foreign field to me. One time a music director made the statement publicly that he could teach anybody to sing. I stood up immediately and said, "Brother, you have a pupil. Nobody has ever been able to teach me to sing." The congregation laughed, and we made an engagement. I met with him every Thursday afternoon for a month, and at the end of the month he gave up. He said, "I believe you are right. You'll never be able to learn music." I asked, "How could I ever learn?" He said, "The only way in the world would be for you to be born again." He didn't mean spiritually; he meant born another person. My friend, as far as spiritual knowledge is concerned, no person can understand it apart from the Spirit of God. This is what we are told in 1 Corinthians 2:9–10: "But as it is written, Eye hath not seen, nor ear heard, neither have entered into the heart of man, the things which God hath prepared for them that love him. But God hath revealed them unto us by his Spirit: for the Spirit searcheth all things, yea, the deep things of God."

I knew a dear lady in Sherman, Texas. We all called her "Grandma," and she was a wonderful lady, but she could neither read nor write. I was just a first-year seminary student and I thought I had the answer to everything, so I went to visit her. I started out by trying to explain John 14 to her. I thought I'd make it simple for Grandma. She listened about five minutes and then said, "Young man, have you ever noticed this in that chapter?"—and then she went on to point out something from that Scripture. Well, to be honest, I hadn't noticed it. I couldn't understand how she could have such insight when she couldn't read or write. She knew things I couldn't find in the commentaries. How did she know? The eyes of her heart were opened by the Spirit of God.

The Spirit of God wants to teach us today. One of the reasons that God's people are not in the Word of God is because they are not willing for the Spirit of God to teach them. They depend on a poor preacher like me or on a home Bible class. These all have their place but, Christian friend, why don't you let the Spirit of God teach you? Spend time in the Scriptures. When you come to a particular passage of Scripture, you may think it to be a barren place. If you don't understand it and you read it many times and don't seem to see much of anything in it, then get down on your knees before the Lord and say to the Lord, "I missed the point and You will have to teach me." This is what I do. He teaches me, and I know He will teach you.

"That ye may know what is the hope of his calling, and what the riches of the glory of his inheritance in the saints." We have learned that we have an inheritance in the Lord. We are also to know that He has an inheritance in us. I think an illustration of this would be the land of Canaan. The land belonged to God, but He gave it to the children of Israel as their possession. The children of Israel are tied into that land; yet the day will come when God will take possession of this entire universe and will reclaim Israel as well as the land as His own. Today you and I, as believers, are His church and God operates through us, but the time is coming when we shall rule and reign with Him. He will claim us as *His* inheritance. I have wondered about that—this is an area that is just too deep for me to apprehend. I need the Spirit of God to make this real to me.

Paul continues his petition:

And what is the exceeding greatness of his power to us-ward who believe, according to the working of his mighty power [Eph. 1:19].

Let me amplify this: What is the exceeding (intense) greatness of His power (*dunameos*—dynamite power) to usward who believe, according to the working (*energeian*—the energizing) of the strength of His might.

How great is that dynamite power, that energizing strength?

Which he wrought in Christ, when he raised him from the dead, and set him at his own right hand in the heavenly places [Eph. 1:20].

It is power enough to raise Christ from the dead—a tremendous power. Not only is it resurrection power, but it is the power that set Christ at God's right hand, and that is ascension power. We don't make much of the Ascension in our Bible churches today; we emphasize Christmas and Easter, but we seem to forget the events after that. Have you ever stopped to think of the power that took Him back to the right hand of God? That, my friend, is power. We are beginning to see a little of it. Think of the power it takes to lift a missile off its base and take it out into space, and the power it took to take men to the moon and bring them back. That is power in the physical realm. The power that took Christ to the right hand of God is the same power that is available to believers today. That is why Paul prays that believers may know the greatness of that power. He writes, "That I may know

him, and the power of his resurrection . . ." (Phil. 3:10).

Far above all principality, and power, and might, and dominion, and every name that is named, not only in this world, but also in that which is to come:

And hath put all things under his feet, and gave him to be the head over all things to the church,

Which is his body, the fulness of him that filleth all in all [Eph. 1:21–23].

Paul concludes on a tremendously high note. The church is the body of Christ, and Christ is the head of the church. Someday everything is going to be under Him. The writer to the Hebrews makes it clear, "Thou hast put all things in subjection under his feet. For in that he put all in subjection under him, he left nothing that is not put under him. But now we see not yet all things put under him" (Heb. 2:8).

At the present time the only thing that is under Him is the church. By this I mean the true church, the real believers. There are many organized groups who call themselves churches who are not listening to the Lord Jesus. These churches are paralyzed. You see, the most tragic sight is a child of God lying on a bed, helpless, as if his brain is detached from his body. I've been in many churches that have been like that, and there are many individual Christians today who act as if they are detached from Christ, the head of the body. He says, "If ye love me, keep my commandments" (John 14:15). In other words, I can wiggle my little finger because my head is in charge of it; and when He wants you to "wiggle"—that is, exercise whatever gift He has given you—down here, you do it because of love, or else you're not attached to Him. How important this is today! Paul pictures the church and our relationship to it in this way: "For as the body is one, and hath many members, and all the members of that one body, being many, are one body: so also is Christ. For by one Spirit are we all baptized into one body, whether we be Jews or Gentiles, whether we be bond or free; and have been all made to drink into one Spirit" (1 Cor. 12:12–13). The thing we need to see is that Christ is the head of the body, His church, and we are under Him.

CHAPTER 2

THEME: *The church is a temple; the material for temple construction; the method of construction; the meaning of the construction*

This chapter begins with the little conjunction *and;* so it is actually a continuation of the thought of the first chapter. Paul has been talking about that tremendous power that raised Jesus from the dead. We shall see that this power is the same power that makes us, when we were dead in trespasses and sins, alive in Christ. That takes power! It takes *resurrection* power. It is this power that so many of God's children want to experience. Frances Ridley Havergal expresses it in as lovely and fine a way as it could be, and I'm sure it is a prayer in the hearts of many Christians today.

Oh, let me know
The power of the resurrection;
Oh, let me show
Thy risen life in calm and clear reflection;
Oh, let me give
Out of the gifts thou freely gavest;
Oh, let me live
With life abundantly because thou livest.

—Frances Ridley Havergal

Now it seems that God is rather reluctant about letting man have power. I think we can see why. God let centuries go by with man knowing nothing of atomic power. Then man discovered atomic power, and it changed the world. What did it do to the world? Did it make it a wonderful place in which to live? You know that it made the world a frightful place in which to live because it gave man the power to destroy the world. Man is dangerous today. We live like an ostrich with our head in the sand if we think to ourselves that no nation dares to release that atomic power. There are men in positions of power today who would turn it loose tomorrow, or even today, if they thought they could get by with it. Man is dangerous with the use of physical power. I think God is reluctant to give man power.

However, the power of God which the epistle speaks of is the power that God will release in the life of one who will turn to Jesus Christ. He will lift that person out of spiritual death into spiritual life. This power will be exhibited by the church because the church is the body of Christ in the world. The Lord Jesus expresses Himself in the world today through His church.

In many ways the church as a temple corresponds to the temple of the Old Testament which was, in turn, preceded by the tabernacle of the wilderness. The comparison is self-evident. The contrasts are sharp and striking. The tabernacle and the temple, for instance, were made of living trees of acacia wood that were hewn into dead boards. In order to form the church, God takes dead material and makes it into a living temple. The temple and tabernacle were dwelling places for the glory of God. The church is a dwelling place for the person of the Holy Spirit. The tabernacle and temple were for the performance of a ritual and the repetition of a sacrifice for sin. The church is built upon the one sacrifice of Christ in the historical past, a sacrifice which is not repeated. "Nor yet that he should offer himself often, as the high priest entereth into the holy place every year with blood of others; For then must he often have suffered since the foundation of the world: but now once in the end of the world hath he appeared to put away sin by the sacrifice of himself" (Heb. 9:25–26). Nor does the church have a ritual. It is a functional organism in which the Holy Spirit moves through the living stones.

Let me emphasize here that God has not given a ritual to the church as there was a ritual in the temple. Some folk think that they have had a church service by opening with the doxology, saying a prayer, singing hymns, and then sitting down to listen to the Scripture being expounded. Yet to them it was only a meaningless ritual—and the church has not been given a ritual. Someone may ask, "Then we're not to do that?" Well, the point is that just going through the exercise of mouthing words has become a meaningless ritual to a lot of folk today. These things should have *meaning.* They are proper, of course, when meaning is expressed.

Now the church is not only minus a temple ritual; it is also not a temple "made with hands." The impressive fact of the church age is that God is indwelling individual believers. Notice the following verses: "God that made the world and all things therein, seeing that he is Lord of heaven and earth, dwelleth not in temples made with hands; Neither is worshipped with men's hands, as though he needed any thing, seeing he giveth to all life, and breath, and all things" (Acts 17:24–25). "What? know ye not that your body is the temple of the Holy Ghost which is in you, which ye have of God, and ye are not your own? For ye are bought with a price: therefore glorify God in your body, and in your spirit, which are God's" (1 Cor. 6:19–20).

I want to emphasize here that Israel never did believe that God was confined to the temple. When Solomon was dedicating the temple, he prayed, "But will God indeed dwell on the earth? behold, the heaven and heaven of heavens cannot contain thee; how much less this house that I have builded?" (1 Kings 8:27). Every instructed Israelite understood that God did not live in a temple—a little box. The liberals try to give the impression that they had such a conception. I heard a Vanderbilt University professor say that the Israelites had a primitive viewpoint of God; they thought He could dwell in a little box. I'd like to say that the professor had a primitive view of the Bible. If he had just read his Old Testament, he would have known that Israel did not believe that. God had told them that the temple was the place where He would meet with them. That is why they came to the temple with a sacrifice and a ritual. The church has none of that today.

Another sharp contrast to the Old Testament temple is the position of Gentiles. You will recall that the Gentiles had to come as proselytes and were confined to the court of the Gentiles. In Jerusalem today at the Holy City Hotel is a replica of the city of Jerusalem as it looked in the days of Herod, which were, or course, the days of Christ. The court of the Gentiles was way off to the left as you look into the temple. The Gentiles didn't get very close. That is why Paul says in this chapter, "But now in Christ Jesus ye who sometimes were far off are made nigh by the blood of Christ" (v. 13). You see, we who are Gentiles have been brought in pretty close. In fact, we are seated in the heavenlies in Christ! You just can't improve on that.

THE MATERIAL FOR
TEMPLE CONSTRUCTION

And you hath he quickened, who were dead in trespasses and sins;

Wherein in time past ye walked according to the course of this world, according to the prince of the power of the air, the spirit that now worketh in the children of disobedience [Eph. 2:1–2].

Now let me quote my own translation of these verses. (My translation is published only in my book, *Exploring Through Ephesians*. I have made no attempt to produce a polished translation. I simply pull the original Greek words over into English so that you might be able to get a little different viewpoint. I have done this for years—in Southern California it is known as *The McGee-icus Ad Absurdum Translation*.) Now here is a literal translation of the verse: And you being dead in your trespasses and sins, in which you once walked according to the age (spirit of the age, secularism, course, principle) of this world (cosmos, society, civilization), according to the prince of the power (authority) of the air (haze, smog), of the spirit that now worketh (energizes) in the sons (children) of disobedience.

"And you being dead in your trespasses and sins." Perhaps you notice that I left out "hath he quickened," which in your Bible is printed in italics. This means it was not in the original text but was inserted to smooth out the translation. I am perfectly willing to admit that something belongs there to give explanation, and "hath he quickened" is all right, but I am trying to pull out the original and give you the meaning without smoothing out the translation.

"You being dead in your trespasses and sins in which you once walked according to the age"—the spirit of the age. That is, according to secularism, according to the way of the world, or according to the principle of this world. The "world" does not mean the physical universe. It means the cosmos, society, civilization, life-pattern, or life-style of the world today.

"According to the prince of the power [authority] of the air, the spirit that now worketh (that is, energizes) in the children [sons] of disobedience." The Devil takes this dead material (we are dead in trespasses and sins) and he energizes us. That is the reason the cults are as busy as termites, and with the same results. False religionists put us to shame in their zeal. Satan is energizing them. People ask me whether I am aware that miracles are being performed in the cults. I won't argue that. Maybe they are. I know some things are exaggerated in our day, but maybe some of them are true. Then who is doing the miracles? Satan is able to duplicate a great many of the miracles that are scriptural miracles. After all, weren't the magicians of Egypt able to duplicate the first miracles performed by Moses? Of course the later miracles they could not duplicate. When man gets into the realm of the New Birth and closeness to God, Satan is powerless against him, but he is potent today to delude and to deceive and to lead people astray. He is potent today in the cults and false "isms" of the world.

> **Among whom also we all had our conversation in times past in the lusts of our flesh, fulfilling the desires of the flesh and of the mind; and were by nature the children of wrath, even as others [Eph. 2:3].**

To better understand verses 1–7, we need to recognize that they comprise a single periodic sentence in the Greek language. Classical Greek is filled with periodic sentences, all kinds of genitive absolutes, phrases, and tenses—it is difficult to read. Koine Greek is generally easy to read, but here is a periodic sentence which reveals that Paul was capable of writing better Greek than the Koine of his day. The Authorized Version, by the way, breaks this into a sentence that ends at verse three. That is permissible and entirely right because verse four is a contrasting statement joined by the conjunction *but.*

We have already noted that the chapter begins with *and*, which connects it to the preceding chapter. In chapter 1 Paul had been talking about salvation and picked up the theme of the mighty greatness of His power in verse 19. This is the power that quickens dead sinners. Now here in chapter 2, verse 1, he says that we were dead in trespasses and sins. That speaks of the death of Adam which is imputed to us. "Wherefore, as by one man sin entered into the world, and death by sin; and so death passed upon all men, for that all have sinned" (Rom. 5:12). Adam's sin made us the sons of a fallen man, and we all have the same nature that Adam had. It is a fallen nature with no capacity or inclination to God.

When I look back upon my own conversion, I really think it was a miracle. How in the world could God save a boy who had been brought up as I had been? My father had high moral principles and was known as an honest man, but he was not a Christian and was antagonistic to the church. He never darkened the door of a church, but he made me go to Sunday school as a boy—and I always protested about going. Then my dad died when I was fourteen, and I found myself adrift in the world. I ran all the way to Detroit, Michigan, to get away from every authority. I turned down work for Ford Motor Company and took a job with Cadillac. There I got into awful sin.

I associated with a group of men, particularly a man from Hungary who thought I looked like his son who had died. He took me under his wing. But he was a sinful man and took me places where a sixteen-year-old boy ought not to go. I got homesick and went back home, and when I think back to it now, I realize that it was God who made me homesick. If I hadn't gone back home, the Devil would have won the day. I was dead to God and to the things of God. Then a man told me I could have peace with God through Jesus Christ. How wonderful that was! I say it was a miracle. I wasn't looking for God. I was running from Him as fast as I could because I was dead in trespasses and sins.

Adam died spiritually the day he disbelieved and disobeyed God. He ran away from God and tried to hide. He wasn't looking for God. That is the position of natural man today. This idea that men have a little spark of the divine and are looking for God is as false as can be. On the day Adam disobeyed, he died to God and to the things of God, although he didn't die physically until nine hundred years after he had eaten the fruit. But he had lost his capacity and longing for God. He was separated from God. After all, death is separation. All death is a separation. Physical death is separation of the spirit and the soul from the body. When someone dies, we don't see the separation of the spirit and the soul; we see only the dead body. Spiritual death is a separation from God. After man sinned, he could go on living physically and mentally, but he was spiritually dead, separated from God. He passed that same dead nature on to all his offspring. It is only the convicting work of the Holy Spirit that can prick the conscience of any man in this world today. You can't do it and I can't do it. Only the Spirit of God can do it.

I had the privilege of being pastor of a great church in downtown Los Angeles. I followed great preachers including the first pastor of that church, Dr. R. A. Torrey. I wanted to do a creditable job, and I wanted to bring glory to God. I would always pray as I left the radio room to go to the pulpit platform to preach, "Lord God, I recognize that I am helpless and hopeless. I will be speaking into a graveyard—many sitting out there are dead in trespasses and sins. Oh God, I can be powerful if the Spirit of God will move." Only the Spirit of God can speak so that dead men will hear. Thank God, the Spirit of God did move and continues to move so that dead men are able to hear! The Lord Jesus told His disciples that

He would send the Comforter to them, "And when he is come, he will reprove [convict] the world of sin, and of righteousness, and of judgment" (John 16:8). Do you know that you and I who live in this world are living in a cemetery? Men are dead.

A famous judge traveled around this country years ago giving a lecture entitled: "Millions Now Living Will Never Die." A great preacher followed him on his speaking circuit with this message. "Millions Now Living Are Already Dead." He was more accurate than the judge had been. Millions, actually billions, are dead in trespasses and sins.

An old Irishman was asked to define a cemetery. He said, "A cemetery is a place where the dead live." That describes our world.

A trespass is what Adam did. He stepped over God's bounds. Sin means to miss the mark. We just don't come up to God's standard at all. That is our condition: dead in trespasses and sins and energized by Satan. That is the description of us before we were saved, and every unsaved man is walking around in this world like a spiritual zombie.

The description of our past is not very pretty. We walked according to the spirit of the age. We conformed to the society and the civilization and the life-style of the world. We were walking according to the prince of the power of the air, the spirit that energizes the sons of disobedience. That is Satan and he takes folks and leads them around.

Today, when Christians talk about being separated from the world, they think of that which is fleshly or carnal or godless. The characteristic sins of the lost world are the mental and spiritual sins; and these are, actually, I think, in God's sight, worse than the physical sins.

Listen to James 4:1–4: "From whence come wars and fightings among you? come they not hence, even of your lusts that war in your members? Ye lust, and have not: ye kill, and desire to have, and cannot obtain: ye fight and war, yet ye have not, because ye ask not. Ye ask, and receive not, because ye ask amiss, that ye may consume it upon your lusts. Ye adulterers and adulteresses, know ye not that the friendship of the world is enmity with God? whosoever therefore will be a friend of the world is the enemy of God."

A great many folk come to church on Sunday, pious as a church mouse (however pious that may be), and think they are separated from the world. On Monday morning they start out in this rough, workaday world just as mean and hard and after the almighty dollar as everyone else. They want it to consume it on their own selves, for their own selfish desires. That is what James is talking about. The believer has been saved from that.

John puts it in these words: "Love not the world, neither the things that are in the world. If any man love the world, the love of the Father is not in him. For all that is in the world, the lust of the flesh, and the lust of the eyes, and the pride of life, is not of the Father, but is of the world. And the world passeth away, and the lust thereof: but he that doeth the will of God abideth for ever" (1 John 2:15–17).

There are a great many people today who say they do not live in gross sin. They say, "No, I would not commit these sins. I wouldn't live and act like certain people do." Dr. G. Campbell Morgan used to ask the question, "Would you *like* to live as they do?" Do you like to watch people sinning on the TV screen because that way you do those same things vicariously? I've always felt that the reason the story of the Prodigal Son is so popular with some is because of the way it is sometimes preached. You notice that the Lord Jesus never mentioned any of the sins that boy committed when he was in the far country, but I've heard sermons in which you were taken along with him from one night club to another, from one barroom to another, from one brothel to another. Some saints really enjoyed those sermons because they could enjoy the sin vicariously. That's what John is talking about when he says love not the world. Do you really love it? How do you feel about it?

I remember when Mrs. McGee and I first came to California. We were just fresh out of Texas. In fact, I had never seen a body of water that I couldn't throw a stone across. We were amazed at the ocean. We drove from San Diego to San Francisco. At that time Treasure Island was there with bright lights and colored walls and soft music. It was beautiful. We had a wonderful day. When my wife and I left that night, we boarded the ferry and we went up to the top deck. We were country—we wanted to see the whole thing. As we watched, Treasure Island began to fade away into the fog, and the music died out. I said to my wife, "I have had one of the most pleasant days of my life. I enjoyed every bit of it. But if right now Treasure Island disappeared and went down under into the bay, I wouldn't shed a tear because I don't love anything that is over there." Then I added, "I hope I can always have that kind of an attitude toward the world."

Christian friend, do you really long for the coming of the Lord for the rapture of the church? It is a wonderful thing to talk about, but I would like to ask you some questions: Will you weep when you leave this world because you are so wrapped up in it? Are you all wrapped up in a job or in a business, in a home or in some club, or in a worldly church? Would you be reluctant to go because everything will be changed? This is the way Simon Peter described the lost world: "Which have forsaken the right way, and are gone astray, following the way of Balaam the son of Bosor, who loved the wages of unrighteousness; But was rebuked for his iniquity: the dumb ass speaking with man's voice forbad the madness of the prophet" (2 Pet. 2:15–16). This is a picture of the lost world. Do you as a child of God fit into this picture?

Before we knew Christ we walked "according to the prince of the power of the air," who is Satan. He was the energizer. We cannot serve both God and mammon. The one to whom we yield is our master. Even the Christian must choose whom he will serve. Some folk think that serving God means that you refrain from worldly dress and amusements and refuse associations with people who are liberal in their theology. That's not separation, yet that's what I hear today. It's absurd to talk like that when your own life is filled with bitterness and hatred and selfishness, which are the gross sins, by the way.

"Among whom also we all had our conversation in times past in the lusts of our flesh." Notice Paul now says "we." He includes himself; it is the first person, plural pronoun that he adopts. He puts himself right with this crowd, and you and I need to do this also. This verse could be amplified to read: "Among whom also we all had our conversation (our activities, our life-style) in times past in the desires of the flesh (that is, our old nature), doing the desires of the flesh and of the thoughts (our old nature and our mind), and we were by nature children of wrath even as others." Unfortunately, there are Christians who live for that old carnal nature. They live just like the man of the world is living today. Their life-style is prompted and motivated by a godless philosophy and is controlled by satanic principles.

I visited the home of a man who is supposed to be an outstanding Christian businessman. He showed me his lovely home and told me about his children. Then he told me about his business and about the honors that had been conferred upon him. He never once referred to his relationship with Jesus Christ. You see, there is something wrong with a life-style that includes everything in the world but leaves Christ out of it.

In this section of the second chapter of Ephesians Paul is giving a description of the past, present, and future of the church and of all believers. It is a common experience to see a sign up by a house that reads, "Your Future Told." Generally they have it figured out that soon you will come into a great fortune. The thing that always amuses me is that those places are usually in the poor section of town. They are not able to make a good living for themselves; yet they tell others that they will have a fortune coming to them. The Christian does not need to turn to such persons. God has already revealed to us our future as well as our past and present.

But God, who is rich in mercy, for his great love wherewith he loved us,

Even when we were dead in sins, hath quickened us together with Christ, (by grace ye are saved;)

And hath raised us up together, and made us sit together in heavenly places in Christ Jesus [Eph. 2:4–6].

This little conjunction *but* is so important. But God, being rich in mercy, on account of His great love with which He loved us made us alive together with Christ. God is *rich* in mercy. He had mercy on me. He has had mercy on you. This is such a radical change from the first three verses, which are as black and hopeless as anything can be. Man is a complete failure. He is incapable of saving himself. God comes on this scene of death with His mercy. He does not have too little, too late. He has a surplus, for He is an infinite God who is rich in infinite mercy. He has what man needs. He has what you need. The only requirement is that you believe Him.

A poor woman from the slums of London was invited to go with a group of people for a holiday at the ocean. She had never seen the ocean before, and when she saw it, she burst into tears. Those around her thought it was strange that she should cry when such a lovely holiday had been given her. They asked her, "Why in the world are you crying?" Pointing to the ocean she answered, "This is the only thing I have ever seen that there was enough of." My friend, God has *oceans* of mercy. There is enough of it. He saves us by His grace.

What does it mean to be saved by the grace of God? We were dead in trespasses and sins and completely incapable of saving ourselves. God comes on the scene and by grace He reaches down to us. Why does He do it? He does not find the reason in us; He finds it in Himself. When God came down to deliver Israel, it wasn't because they were good and beautiful and were serving Him. They were not. They were a stiff-necked people. And they were idolaters—they worshiped a golden calf out there in the wilderness. But God says that He heard their cry. Why did that appeal to Him? Because He loved them. He loves you and He loves me. However, He doesn't save us by His love. He saves us by His grace.

For years I had a Bible class in San Diego County. During that period Christian groups of young folk had worked on the beaches down there and had led quite a few of those young people to Christ. Some of them belonged to what we called the hippie group, but I want to say that I found many of them to be genuine believers. I have come to the place that I do not judge a man by his dress any more than I would judge a book by its cover. They had listened to our radio program and to our tapes and had used our books—but I didn't know that at that time. When I went down there for my first class one year, sitting on the first two rows were a bunch of these young people. I want to tell you, some of them were dressed in a very unusual manner! They had long hair and all that was associated with that culture. Very frankly, they shocked me at first, but I found out that they had their Bibles and notebooks, and some *spiritual* life, which you don't always find in our churches today. These young people were actually showing real life.

One young fellow who had been attending came up to me. He had on a funny hat with "Love, love, love" written all over it. He had on a funny coat with "Love, love, love" written all over it. He had "Love, love" on his trousers and even on his shoes. I asked, "Why in the world do you have 'love' written all over you?" "Man," he said, "God is love." "Well," I said, "I agree with you. Nothing could be truer than that." Then he added, "God saves us by His love." I answered, "I don't agree with that. God doesn't save us by His love. Can you give me a verse that says He does?" He scratched his head and thought a while and then admitted he couldn't think of one. "Well," he said, "if God doesn't save us by love, then how does He save us?" I answered, "Very frankly, I'm glad you asked me that question because the Bible says, 'By grace are ye saved through faith; and

that not of yourselves: it is the gift of God: Not of works, lest any man should boast.' God saves us by His grace." Then the boy wanted to know the difference. This is how I explained it to him: "God does love you. Don't lose sight of that. God loves all of us. But God cannot, on the basis of His love, open the back door of heaven and slip us in under cover of darkness. He can't let down the bars of heaven at the front door and bring us in because of His love. God is also light. God is the moral ruler of this universe. God is righteous. He is holy and He is good. That adds up to one thing: God cannot do things that are wrong—that is, wrong according to His own standard. So God couldn't save us by love. Love had God strapped—we could say it put Him in a bind. He could love without being able to save. I thought you would quote John 3:16 to me. Let's look at what that verse says: 'For God so loved the world, that he gave his only begotten Son, that whosoever believeth in him should not perish, but have everlasting life.' Does it say God so loved the world that He saved the world? No, that's exactly what it doesn't say. God so loved this world that He gave His only begotten Son. You see, God couldn't save the world by love because He goes on to say, 'that whosoever believeth in him should not perish.' You and I are going to perish. We're lost sinners, and God still loves us, but the love of God can't bring us into heaven. God had to provide a salvation, and He paid the penalty for our sins. Now a God of love can reach out His hands to a lost world and say, 'If you will believe in My Son, because He died for you—if you will come on that basis—I can save you.' God doesn't save us by His love. God saves us by His grace."

Frankly, it is more wonderful this way. When I was a boy, I would get out of favor with my parents because of something I did wrong. But I can never get out of the favor of God. I can lose my fellowship with Him, because sin breaks fellowship, but I can never get out of His favor. I can grieve the Spirit of God, but I can always come back to Him. "If we confess our sins, he is faithful and just to forgive us our sins, and to cleanse us from all unrighteousness" (1 John 1:9). If we walk in darkness and say that we have fellowship with Him, we are lying. "But if we walk in the light, as he is in the light, we have fellowship one with another, and the blood of Jesus Christ his Son cleanseth us from all sin" (1 John 1:7). If I walk in the light of the Word of God and I see that I have come short, the blood of Jesus Christ, God's Son, just keeps on cleansing me from all sin. Why? God does it by His grace. He is rich in mercy and grace.

God has His arms outstretched to a lost world and He says, "You may come if you will come My way." Let me remind you that this is God's universe, and He is doing things His way. You may think you have a better way, but you don't have a universe to rule. He makes the rules in His universe and you're going to have to come His way. He loves you; you can't keep Him from loving you. Neither can you keep the sun from shining, but you can get out of the sunshine. Sin, being out of the will of God, turning your back on Him, all these will keep you from experiencing the love of God. If you will come to Him through Christ, He will save you and you will experience His love. God is rich in mercy.

God has lifted us out of a spiritual graveyard. Our present position is that He has "raised us up together, and made us sit together in heavenly places in Christ Jesus." What is our future?

That in the ages to come he might shew the exceeding riches of his grace in his kindness toward us through Christ Jesus [Eph. 2:7].

I translate it this way: "In order that He might show forth in the ages which are coming the exceeding (overflowing, intense) riches of His grace in kindness toward us in Christ." Someday I am going to be on exhibit. Angels will go by and say, "See that fellow McGee. He was lost and wasn't worth saving, but he's here in heaven today. It is only through the grace and kindness of God that he was saved and brought here." That is going to be for the praise of God throughout eternity. I am not going to get any credit at all, but I'm going to be there, and that's good enough for me. I'm going to join that angelic host in singing praises to God because He saved me. This is the most wonderful expectation that we have—as far as I know. It is through grace. It is the "amazing grace," as the hymn writer John Newton put it, "that saved a wretch like me."

For by grace are ye saved through faith; and that not of yourselves: it is the gift of God:

Not of works, lest any man should boast [Eph. 2:8–9].

These are the great verses that consummate this section on the believer's past, present, and future. We were dead in trespasses and sin, God saved us by His grace, raising us now to heavenly places in Christ Jesus, and we will someday be in heaven displaying the grace of God. None of this depends on our own works or merit, "for by grace ye have been saved." Notice I have changed it to the literal phrase "*the* grace." The article points out that it is something special. The great emphasis is upon the grace of God. It is favor bestowed on the unworthy and undeserving.

Now don't come along and say, "I hope to be saved." If you have put your trust in Christ, you can say, "I *am* saved." Someone may say, "Oh, I wouldn't dare make a statement like that because I don't know what the future holds." Friend, your salvation rests upon the *grace* of God—not upon your faithfulness. You can be confident of this very thing, ". . . that he which hath begun a good work in you will perform it until the day of Jesus Christ" (Phil. 1:6). If you are a child of God, you may wander from Him, but He will always make a way back for you because it is by His grace and that alone that you are saved. You have a finished salvation. On the basis of what Christ has done for you and on the fact that the Holy Spirit has inclined you toward Christ and you have believed the Word of God and have trusted Him, you can say, "I am saved." It's not an "I hope so" salvation or an "I'll try" salvation. It is a salvation that is by the grace of God, by means of faith, and it is not of yourself. It is a gift of God.

The grace of God has been defined theologically as "unmerited favor." I like to speak of it as "love in action." Dr. Lewis Sperry Chafer, the man who taught me theology, made this important statement about God's grace and God's love in his book, *The Ephesian Letter Doctrinally Considered.*

A sharp distinction is properly drawn between the compassionate love of God for sinners, and His grace which is now offered to them in Jesus Christ. Divine love and divine grace are not one and the same. God might love sinners with an unutterable compassion and yet, because of the demands of outraged divine justice and holiness, be unable to rescue them from a righteous doom. However, as has been before stated, if love shall graciously provide for the sinner all that outraged justice and holiness could ever demand, the love of God would then be free to act without restraint in behalf of those for whom the perfect substitutionary sacrifice was made. This is Christ's achievement on the cross. On the other hand, divine grace in salvation is the unrestrained compassion of God acting toward the sinner on the basis of that freedom already secured through the righteous judgment against sin—secured by Christ in His sacrificial death. Divine love might desire to save, yet be unable righteously to do so; but divine grace is free to act since Christ has died. It is to be observed, then, that the eternal purpose of God is not the manifestation of His *love* alone, though His love and His mercy are, like His grace, mentioned in this context and expressed in Christ's death; but it is rather the manifestation of His grace.

Out of God's infinite treasure chest He lavishes His grace upon sinners without restraint or hindrance.

Now faith is the instrumental cause of salvation. It is the only element that the sinner brings to the great transaction of salvation. Yet it too is the gift of God. I know someone will say to me, "Since faith is the gift of God and God hasn't given it to me, then I guess I'm not to blame if I don't believe." The answer is this: God has made it very clear that faith comes by hearing and hearing by the Word of God. If you want to trust Christ, you will have to listen to the Word of God. God will give faith to all who give heed to the message of the gospel.

We find this taught in 2 Corinthians. Moses had a veil over his face, not because he was blinding everybody like a headlight, but so that the people could not view the glory that was fading away. It was the glory that belonged to the Mosaic system and that belonged to the Law. "But their minds were blinded: for until this day remaineth the same veil untaken away in the reading of the old testament; which veil is done away in Christ" (2 Cor. 3:14). There is no need for a veil today because He is the unveiled Christ; the gospel is freely declared. But we are told, "But even unto this day, when Moses is read, the veil is upon their heart. Nevertheless when it shall turn to the Lord, the veil shall be taken away" (2 Cor. 3:15–16). What is "it"? It is the heart. When the heart shall turn to the Lord, the veil shall be taken away. Anytime that you are ready to turn to Christ, you can turn to Christ.

Someone else objects, "Maybe I'm not given the gift of faith." That's not your problem. Your problem is that you don't want to give up your sins which the Bible condemns. Whenever you get sick of your sins, when you want

to turn from yourself, from the things of the world, from religion, from everything the Bible condemns, and turn to Christ, then you will be given faith. You can trust Him.

I am weary of hearing folk say they don't believe because they have intellectual problems. Actually they have moral rather than intellectual problems if only they would face up to them. Sin is the real problem in the hearts of a great many folk today. Even many of the saints don't enjoy their salvation for that very reason. Psychologists at Duke University made a study and found that the second most frequent reason people are emotionally disturbed and mentally unstable is because they live in the past. They are preoccupied with past mistakes and failures, and they look to themselves instead of looking to Christ and trusting Him.

Faith is that instrument of salvation. Spurgeon says, "It is not thy joy in Christ that saves thee; it is Christ. It is not thy hope in Christ that saves thee; it is Christ. It is not even thy faith in Christ, though that be the instrument; it is Christ's blood and merit." That is where the power is, and that is where the salvation is.

Paul is not talking about *faith* when he says, "And that not of yourselves." He is talking about *salvation*. Salvation is a gift that eliminates boasting. It is all of God and not of us. It is God's *gift*.

For we are his workmanship, created in Christ Jesus unto good works, which God hath before ordained that we should walk in them [Eph. 2:10].

"We are his workmanship." The Greek word is *poiema* from which we get our word *poem*. The church is His poem and His new creation. Paul is not talking about the local church here, but rather about that body of believers from the day of Pentecost to the Rapture, the *real* believers (and most of them are members of local churches). That body of believers is His workmanship and His new creation in Christ Jesus.

For what are we created? For good works. When we get to the last part of this epistle, we will be told how we are to walk in a way that is creditable and acceptable to God. While we are seated in the heavenlies in Christ Jesus, we are to walk down here in a way that will bring glory to His name.

THE METHOD OF CONSTRUCTION

Now we come to the method of the construction of the church as a temple of God.

Wherefore remember, that ye being in time past Gentiles in the flesh, who are called Uncircumcision by that which is called the Circumcision in the flesh made by hands;

That at that time ye were without Christ, being aliens from the commonwealth of Israel, and strangers from the covenants of promise, having no hope, and without God in the world [Eph. 2:11–12].

The church in Ephesus was made up largely of Gentiles. There was just a small colony of Jews there. Gentiles are further identified as the "Uncircumcision." This label was put on them by the so-called "Circumcision," the Jews.

God made a real distinction between Jew and Gentile, beginning with Abraham and advancing to the advent of the Holy Spirit at Pentecost. Israel occupied a unique position among the nations. A Gentile could come in only as a proselyte. In time, this valid distinction caused friction because Israel became proud of her position. Israelites came to look down on Gentiles, and hatred crept into the hearts of both groups.

In these verses there is a description of the sad lot and hopeless plight of the Gentile. It is also an accurate picture of any lost man. This is what it means to be lost:

1. "Without Christ." That is the best definition of a lost man. It is the opposite of being *in* Christ.

2. "Aliens from the commonwealth of Israel" or, alienated from the citizenship of Israel. That is the accurate definition of a Gentile. The Gentile had no God-given religion as had Israel. They had no right to go back in the Old Testament and take the promises which God made to Israel and then appropriate them for themselves. We don't have that right either. God didn't make those promises to us.

3. "Strangers from the covenants of promise." God had made certain promises to the nation Israel. The covenants which God made with Israel are still valid, but no Gentile has any right to appropriate them. God has promised the children of Israel the land of Israel— all of it. They will get it someday, but it will be on God's terms, not their terms.

When I was in Israel, I didn't attempt to homestead or stake out a claim on the basis that God had promised it in the Old Testament. I understood that He was talking to Israel and not to me. The promise He has given to me is, ". . . I go to prepare a place for you. And if I go and prepare a place for you, I will come again, and receive you unto myself; that where I am, there ye may be also" (John 14:2–3).

4. "Having no hope." Look at the religions of the world. They have no hope. They cannot promise resurrection and are pretty hazy about what happens after death. The cults offer no hope at all. They put up a hurdle that no honest human being could get over. Having no hope was the tragic plight of the Gentiles. To the lost man the present life is all-important, and if he misses out on the fun here, then he is doubly hopeless.

When Paul wrote this, my ancestors from one side of the family were walking through the forests of Germany, as heathen and pagan as they could be. The others were over in Scotland, and I am told their paganism and heathenism were even worse. That was our condition.

5. "And without God in the world." This does not mean that God has removed Himself from man, but rather that man has removed himself from God. A man is godless because of choice. He is in the darkness, wandering about with the rest of lost humanity. Frankly, if I were in the position of the lost man today, I would crawl up on a bar stool and try to drink and forget it all. What else would a person do? I would have no hope. The only hope I could have here in this world would be to squeeze this life like an orange and get all the juice out of it that I could. There would be nothing to look forward to over there. That is what it would be like to be without hope and without God.

This is a terrible, awful condition that Paul describes. But now notice that something has happened.

But now in Christ Jesus ye who sometimes were far off are made nigh by the blood of Christ [Eph. 2:13].

In the temple was the court of the Gentiles way off to the side. Gentiles were permitted to come, but they were away far off. But now— for the Gentiles who are in Christ—all has changed. They were without Christ; now they are in Christ. The distance and barriers which separated them from God have been removed. They have been made nigh, not by their efforts or merits, but by the blood of Christ.

For he is our peace, who hath made both one, and hath broken down the middle wall of partition between us;

Having abolished in his flesh the enmity, even the law of commandments contained in ordinances; for to make in himself of twain one new man, so making peace;

And that he might reconcile both unto God in one body by the cross, having slain the enmity thereby:

And came and preached peace to you which were afar off, and to them that were nigh [Eph. 2:14–17].

When you come to Jesus Christ, you are not only brought into a body, but you are also brought into a place where you stand before God on a par with anybody. I stand with you and you stand with me on equal footing. So today there should never be a point of separation for believers on any basis at all. We have been made one in Christ. If you are a believer in Christ—it makes no difference who you are—you and I are going to be together throughout eternity. It wouldn't be a bad idea for us to speak to each other every now and then down here, would it?

The contrast in the passage is really between the Jew and Gentile. The Lord Jesus Christ is the peace that has been made between them. The middle wall, the fence, or partition, the enmity between the two, has been broken down. He has made a new man. We have been put together in Christ, and He has made peace. It means that we now have peace with God, and we should also have peace with each other.

God's reconciliation is already complete. He is ready to receive you if you are ready to come. Therefore, the message that goes out is ". . . be ye reconciled to God" (2 Cor. 5:20). If you will be reconciled, you will be brought into a new body, a body of believers, and it doesn't make any difference whether you are Jew or Gentile. The color of your skin makes no difference. White, brown, red, black—all are one in Christ. We have been made one new man, and we should have peace.

The emphasis in this passage is upon the glorious person of Christ. He not only made peace by the Cross, but those who trust Him are placed in Him and become new men. God had made a difference originally by separating the Jew from the nations. The Jew eventually developed a spiritual pride, and this led to the ultimate hatred between Jew and Gentile. When a Jew and a Gentile are placed in Christ, there is peace. There is peace not only because of the new position, but also because

something new has come into existence. Paul identifies this as a new man. That is why Paul wrote to the Corinthians, "Give none offence, neither to the Jews, nor to the Gentiles, nor to the church of God" (1 Cor. 10:32). That "church" is the new man.

It is not that the Gentile has been elevated to the status of the Jew. God has elevated both to a higher plane. Chrysostom has stated it this way: "He does not mean that He has elevated us to that high dignity of theirs, but He has raised both us and them to one still higher. . . . I will give you an illustration. Let us imagine that there are two statues, one of silver and the other of lead, and then that both shall be melted down, and the two shall come out gold. So thus He has made the two one." This is a marvelous illustration of how we have been brought together in Christ.

I do not believe in the universal brotherhood of man and the universal Fatherhood of God. To me that is a damnable heresy. I believe a true brotherhood is composed of those who are in Christ. A man may have skin as white as the driven snow, but if he is not a child of God, he is not my brother. A man may have skin as black as midnight, and if he is a child of God, he is my brother. We are something new. We are in Christ—a new man. This is the building, the temple, God is building today.

Rather than say the Gentile was elevated to the status of the Jew, one might say the Jew was brought down to the level of the Gentile because both Jew and Gentile are in the same state of sin. Actually we are all brothers as sinners, all sons of Adam. "What then? are we better than they? No, in no wise: for we have before proved both Jews and Gentiles, that they are all under sin" (Rom. 3:9). That is the state we were all in. The peace referred to is between the Jew and the Gentile. When the Jew and Gentile come to the Cross as sinners, they are made into a new creation. They become a new man, the body of Christ, the temple of the Holy Spirit.

The Old Testament temple which succeeded the Mosaic tabernacle was marked by partitions. There were three entrances into the three departments: the outer court, the Holy Place, and the Holy of Holies. Then there were sections partitioned off for priests, Israel, women, and Gentiles. Christ, by His death, took out the veil, and He became the Way (the outer court), the Truth (the Holy Place), and the Life (the Holy of Holies). Now we come through Christ directly into the presence of God the Father. Those who come to

Him are removed from their little departments and are placed in Christ, the new Temple where there are no departments. The Cross dissolves the fences, and the gospel is preached to the Gentiles, those who were afar off, and to the Jews, those who were near. What a picture we have here!

For through him we both have access by one Spirit unto the Father [Eph. 2:18].

I wonder whether you have noticed that this little verse is a big verse? It is like a little atom. It has in it the Trinity. "For through Him [Christ] we both have access in one Spirit [the Holy Spirit] unto the Father [God the Father]." Jew and Gentile are on the same footing as sinners at the foot of the cross. In addition, through Christ they both have equal access to God, which is a glorious privilege for any human being. Paul makes it clear in Romans 5 that justification by faith is a benefit available to all. We have access to God through Jesus Christ, and that is wonderful.

Now I don't think this means we can brazenly rush into the presence of God, but it does give us the real privilege to have access to the Father through the Lord Jesus Christ. Any one believer has as much access to God as any other believer. People ask me why I didn't have a select few pray for me when I had my bout with cancer. Why did I ask everybody to pray? I did it because I believe in the priesthood of believers, that is, all believers have access to Him.

THE MEANING OF THE CONSTRUCTION

Now therefore ye are no more strangers and foreigners, but fellow-citizens with the saints, and of the household of God;

And are built upon the foundation of the apostles and prophets, Jesus Christ himself being the chief corner stone [Eph. 2:19–20].

Paul reminds the gentile believers that though they were strangers and alienated from God, their present position is infinitely bettered. They are no more strangers and sojourners (foreigners). They are now fellow citizens with the saints.

"Saints" is not a reference to Old Testament saints. Gentile believers are fellow citizens with the New Testament Jewish saints, the other members of the body of Christ. They belong to a household, not as servants, but as relatives, as members of the family of God.

They are His dear children. "I write unto you, little children, because your sins are forgiven you for his name's sake" (1 John 2:12). We are little children. This is a new relationship, a relationship foreign to the Old Testament. Even David, the man after God's own heart, is called "my servant David" in 2 Samuel 7:8; and God's term for Moses was also "my servant" in Numbers 12:7.

Now this citizenship is not in Israel and the earthly Jerusalem, but it is in heaven. "For our conversation [citizenship] is in heaven; from whence also we look for the Saviour, the Lord Jesus Christ" (Phil. 3:20). We are now fellow citizens. We belong to heaven at the present time. The word *conversation* should rightly be changed to *citizenship* and is translated that way in the *American Standard Version*. Another has well translated it, "Our city home is in heaven."

We are "built upon the foundation of the apostles and prophets." This is important. It does not mean that the apostles and prophets were the foundation but that they personally laid the foundation. The early church built its doctrine upon that of the apostles. "And they continued stedfastly in the apostles' doctrine and fellowship, and in breaking of bread, and in prayers" (Acts 2:42).

Much has been written about the identity of the prophets in verse twenty. Are they Old Testament prophets or New Testament prophets? The fact that the prophets are in the same classification as apostles without the article *the* would seem to designate them as New Testament prophets. I think you will find this confirmed when we get into the third chapter.

"Jesus Christ himself being the chief corner stone" reveals that Christ is the Rock on which the church is built. Paul makes this very clear: "For other foundation can no man lay than that is laid, which is Jesus Christ" (1 Cor. 3:11). Peter states it like this: "Wherefore also it is contained in the scripture, Behold, I lay in Sion a chief corner stone, elect, precious: and he that believeth on him shall not be confounded. Unto you therefore which believe he is precious: but unto them which be disobedient, the stone which the builders disallowed, the same is made the head of the corner, And a stone of stumbling, and a rock of offence, even to them which stumble at the word, being disobedient: whereunto also they were appointed" (1 Pet. 2:6–8). The important thing to note here is that Peter says that the Lord Jesus is that chief cornerstone. Therefore Peter understood what the Lord meant when He said, "And I say also unto thee, That thou art

Peter, and upon this rock I will build my church; and the gates of hell shall not prevail against it" (Matt. 16:18). Jesus is talking about Himself. He is the Rock on which the church is built. The apostles and prophets put down the foundation, and Christ is the chief cornerstone, the Rock.

In whom all the building fitly framed together groweth unto an holy temple in the Lord:

In whom ye also are builded together for an habitation of God through the Spirit [Eph. 2:21–22].

The analogy to the temple of the Old Testament is obvious; yet there is a contrast revealed in the analogy. There were several buildings in the temple at Jerusalem. However, I don't think Paul is referring to the different buildings. He means each individual believer is fitted into the total structure. Peter expressed it in the same way when he wrote that we are stones fitted in and built into a spiritual house (see 1 Pet. 2:5).

Paul speaks of the church as a temple which is currently under construction. That is quite interesting because in Paul's day Herod's temple was unfinished. It had been forty years in the building already in our Lord's day, and it was destroyed in A.D. 70. Even when it was destroyed, it had not yet been completely built. The church is under construction today, and it will be finished.

"Groweth unto an holy temple"—it is growing unto an holy temple in the Lord. This confirms the fact that it is still unfinished. The structure is also different. It is not one stone put on top of another in a cold way. This temple is growing. God is taking dead material, dead in trespasses and sins, and is giving it

life. The living, born again, stones are growing into a living temple.

As Solomon's temple was built without the sound of hammer, so the Holy Spirit silently places each dead sinner into the living temple through regeneration and baptism. "For by one Spirit are we all baptized into one body, whether we be Jews or Gentiles, whether we be bond or free; and have been all made to drink into one Spirit" (1 Cor. 12:13).

It is called "an holy temple" or holy sanctuary. It is holy because the Holy Spirit indwells it. By the baptism of the Holy Spirit the saved sinner is placed "in the Lord." The Holy Spirit indwells each believer. "But ye are not in the flesh, but in the Spirit, if so be that the Spirit of God dwell in you. Now if any man have not the Spirit of Christ, he is none of his" (Rom. 8:9).

The church, the body of Christ, is "an habitation," a permanent temple, of God in the Spirit. When believers come together in a building to worship, the Holy Spirit is present. In that sense God is in that building. But when every believer has left the building, God has left it also. God is not in any church building anymore than He is in any barroom. Today God indwells believers, not buildings. We have previously stated that God has never dwelt in any building made with hands, and it is a pagan philosophy which places God in a human-made structure.

The purpose of the church as a temple is to reveal the presence and the glory of God on earth. When believers assemble together in a church, the impression should be made upon the world, even in this age, that God is in His holy temple. The world should feel that God can be found in a church service. My question is: Can He? Perhaps more people would be attracted to the church if they were sure that God was present.

CHAPTER 3

THEME: The church is a mystery; the explanation of the mystery; the definition of the mystery; prayer for power and knowledge

This is the final chapter in the doctrinal section of this epistle. We have learned that the church is a body and the church is a temple. Now we learn that the church is a mystery.

Let me give a preliminary word about what it means when we say the church is a mystery. There has been gross misunderstanding concerning the church as a mystery. The word for *mystery* bears no resemblance to the modern connotation of "whodunit?" In this sense, a mystery is something that had not previously been revealed but is currently made manifest. In this case it is the church which was not revealed in the Old Testament but is solely revealed in the New Testament. Moffatt translates the word *mystery* as "divine secret," and Weymouth uses the word "truth." I like the expression "divine secret." A divine secret was something that God had not revealed up to a certain point. Now He is ready to reveal it. It has nothing to do with mystery such as those written by Agatha Christie or Conan Doyle, as I mentioned earlier when we discussed *mystery* in the first chapter.

There are two extreme viewpoints taken in our day concerning the mystery of the church, and I must say that these viewpoints are a mystery to me. One extreme group ignores the clear-cut statement of Paul that the church is *not* a revelation of the Old Testament. They treat the church as a continuation of Israel. This is known as covenant theology. They appropriate all the promises that God made to Israel and apply them to the church.

Years ago Dr. Harry Ironside showed me a Bible used by the group holding the covenant theology viewpoint. In the books of the Old Testament prophets, they had headed some of the chapters: "Blessings for the Church." Other chapters were headed: "Curses for Israel." It's quite interesting that the church took the blessings but left the curses for Israel! The truth is that both the blessings and the curses apply to Israel.

The other group places undue emphasis on Paul's statements: "he made known unto me the mystery," and "my knowledge in the mystery of Christ," and they treat the mystery as the peculiar revelation to Paul. This is known as hyperdispensationalism. As a result there has been the pernicious practice of shifting the beginning of the church to some date after Pentecost. On this sliding scale several dates have been suggested, and when one becomes untenable, another is adopted. This claim to superior knowledge has ministered to spiritual pride. May I say that the church was not revealed in the Old Testament. When it was revealed, the revelation was not confined to the apostle Paul. One professor I had in a denominational seminary tried to trace the church back to the Garden of Eden! But the church is not in the Old Testament. On the other hand, one must admit something happened on the Day of Pentecost. On that day the Holy Spirit began forming the body of believers. That will continue until He takes the church out of the world. We are sealed by the Holy Spirit of God until the day of redemption, the day we are taken out of the world and presented to Christ. I don't believe you can wash back and forth over the Day of Pentecost like the tide washing over the beach. Something *did* happen on that day—that was the birthday of the church.

THE EXPLANATION OF THE MYSTERY

For this cause I Paul, the prisoner of Jesus Christ for you Gentiles,

If ye have heard of the dispensation of the grace of God which is given me to you-ward [Eph. 3:1–2].

Let me give you my literal translation: "For this cause I Paul, the prisoner of (the) Christ Jesus on behalf of you Gentiles, if so be (upon the supposition) that ye heard of the economy (dispensation) of the grace of God which is given me to you."

Paul speaks of his present condition as a prisoner. He became a prisoner because he took the gospel to the Gentiles. Now the Gentiles are accorded new privileges, which he has enumerated in the preceding chapter. Those who were afar off, strangers, without hope, and without God, are now brought in through Christ. Because of all that, Paul is going to pray for them. But before he gets to his prayer, he digresses to speak of the mystery. Then he picks up his thread of thought again in verse 14. Notice the connection: "For this cause I Paul, the prisoner of Jesus Christ for you Gentiles. . . . bow my knees unto the

Father of our Lord Jesus Christ." Everything between verses 1 and 14 is a parenthesis, a digression. Before he comes to his prayer, he is going to talk about the mystery.

"If so be" marks the beginning of the parenthesis. It is on the supposition that "ye have heard of the economy (or dispensation) of the grace of God which is given me to you." Paul is speaking of the divine plan and arrangement by which God had called and sent him to the Gentiles. As compared to the other apostles, Paul's ministry was different and special. "But contrariwise, when they saw that the gospel of the uncircumcision was committed unto me, as the gospel of the circumcision was unto Peter" (Gal. 2:7). The message was not different, but the ones to whom the message was to be given were different folk in a different category. Paul went to the Gentiles and told them, "You have been afar off, and now you can be brought in through Christ." Peter went to his own people (Israel) and said, ". . . there is none other name under heaven given among men, whereby we must be saved" (Acts 4:12). Paul said to the Gentile, Philippian jailor, ". . . Believe on the Lord Jesus Christ, and thou shalt be saved, and thou house" (Acts 16:31). Both Peter and Paul had the same message, although it was to two different groups of people.

There is now a brand new thing taking place. It is a different economy or a different dispensation from what they had back in the Old Testament. When Paul had been a Pharisee and lived by the Law, he never went out to preach to the Gentiles—he was under a different economy. Now Paul is under a new economy, and he is a missionary to the Gentiles. This doesn't mean that God's method of salvation had changed. No man was saved by keeping the Law, but by bringing a bloody sacrifice when he saw that he had come short of the glory of God. That sacrifice pointed to Christ.

Now Paul is going to talk about this new economy.

How that by revelation he made known unto me the mystery; (as I wrote afore in a few words,

Whereby, when ye read, ye may understand my knowledge in the mystery of Christ) [Eph. 3:3–4].

"By revelation." The hyperdispensationalists hold that because Paul said the mystery had been made known to him, he was the only one who knew it. However, in verse 5 Paul makes

it clear that all the apostles knew it. That "revelation" began with Paul's conversion when Christ informed him that when he persecuted the church he was actually persecuting Christ. The church is the body of Christ. Paul learned that God was doing something new. A church had come into existence on the Day of Pentecost.

I repeat that "the mystery," the divine secret, was something not revealed in the Old Testament and therefore unknown to man. Now it is revealed in the New Testament. The word is used twenty-seven times in the New Testament, and it refers to about eleven different mysteries. Paul seems to be making a contrast with the mystery religions of the Graeco-Roman world. In my book *Exploring Through Ephesians* I include a thesis on those mystery religions that I wrote when I was in seminary. There were many in that day. These were secret lodges in which sadistic rites were performed. The initiate was warned not to reveal the secrets of the mystery religion. To the Greek, a mystery was a secret imparted to the initiate. To them it meant something disclosed or revealed to a candidate for admission, not something hidden or impossible to understand. To the man on the street who was not a member, these secrets would be a mystery in our sense of the word. In contrast to this, Paul says, "Woe is me if I preach not the gospel." And we today are "stewards of the mysteries of God." We are to give out the message. The gospel is not something to be kept in a secret lodge; it is the good news that is to be shouted from the housetops.

Paul uses the word *mystery* earlier in this epistle. In Ephesians 1:9 he says, "Having made known unto us the mystery of his will." In Ephesians 2:14–15 he explains what the mystery is. The mystery is that Christ is risen and is the Head of a new body made up of Jews and Gentiles and of all tribes and peoples of the earth. This was not revealed in the Old Testament. Paul put it like this: "Now to him that is of power to stablish you according to my gospel, and the preaching of Jesus Christ, according to the revelation of the mystery, which was kept secret since the world began" (Rom. 16:25). Paul says it again in Colossians 1:26, "Even the mystery which hath been hid from ages and from generations, but now is made manifest to his saints."

I would say that those who insist that the church is back in the Old Testament are more or less usurping the place of the Lord. They are telling something the Lord Himself didn't tell. They act as if they know something God didn't know. Mystery means that it was not revealed in the Old Testament. And since He didn't reveal it, it isn't there.

THE DEFINITION OF THE MYSTERY

Which in other ages was not made known unto the sons of men, as it is now revealed unto his holy apostles and prophets by the Spirit;

That the Gentiles should be fellow-heirs, and of the same body and partakers of his promise in Christ by the gospel [Eph. 3:5–6].

Paul certainly makes it clear here that this was not revealed to him alone.

Now he clarifies what he means by the mystery. There is a sharp contrast between the sons of men in past generations and the apostles and prophets of the church. No one in the Old Testament had a glimmer of light relative to the church. It is now revealed to His holy apostles. They are "holy" because they have been set aside for this office by God. The "prophets" are definitely New Testament prophets.

The "Spirit," the Holy Spirit, is the teacher of this mystery. This is what the Lord Jesus promised when He told His disciples of the coming of the Holy Spirit. "All things that the Father hath are mine: therefore said I, that he shall take of mine, and shall shew it unto you" (John 16:15).

What precisely is the mystery? It is *not* the fact that Gentiles would be saved. The Old Testament clearly taught that Gentiles would be saved. Let me cite several passages: "And in that day there shall be a root of Jesse, which shall stand for an ensign of the people; to it shall the Gentiles seek: and his rest shall be glorious" (Isa. 11:10). Another: "And the Gentiles shall come to thy light, and kings to the brightness of thy rising" (Isa. 60:3). Isaiah also wrote: "I the LORD have called thee in righteousness, and will hold thine hand, and will keep thee, and give thee for a covenant of the people, for a light of the Gentiles" (Isa. 42:6). Zechariah also mentions it: "And many nations shall be joined to the LORD in that day, and shall be my people: and I will dwell in the midst of thee, and thou shalt know that the LORD of hosts hath sent me unto thee" (Zech. 2:11). And Malachi: "For from the rising of the sun even unto the going down of the same my name shall be great among the Gentiles; and in every place incense shall be offered unto my name, and a pure offering: for my name shall be great among the heathen, saith the LORD of hosts" (Mal. 1:11).

If the mystery is not that the Gentiles would be saved, what is the mystery? Mark it carefully. The mystery was that the Gentiles and Israel were placed *on the same basis*. By faith in Christ they were both brought into a new body which is the church. Christ is the Head of that new body.

Therefore, now there is a threefold division in the human race:

All people were Gentiles from Adam to Abraham—2000 years (plus)

All people were either Jews or Gentiles from Abraham to Christ—2000 years

The threefold division is Jews, Gentiles, and the church from the Day of Pentecost to the Rapture—2000 years (plus)

Paul referred to this threefold division when he said, "Give none offence, neither to the Jews, nor to the Gentiles, nor to the church of God" (1 Cor. 10:32). Paul included the whole human family when he said that.

The church is not in the Old Testament *de facto*, although there are types of it in the Old Testament. Christ said, ". . . upon this rock I *will* build my church . . ." (Matt. 16:18, italics mine), and when He spoke that, it was still future. The church began on the Day of Pentecost, after Christ had returned to heaven. To say that the church began beyond the Day of Pentecost makes the church a pair of Siamese twins—a Jewish church and a gentile church coexisting. It is true that the church was all Jewish when it began, but there was a period of transition when Gentiles were brought into it. The church is one body, made up of both Jew and Gentile, and Christ is the Head of that body.

Whereof I was made a minister, according to the gift of the grace of God given unto me by the effectual working of his power [Eph. 3:7].

Paul assumed no place of superiority in the knowledge of the mystery by virtue of the fact that he was the Apostle to the Gentiles. He takes only the title of *diakonos* which is translated "minister" and means a worker or helper or deacon.

It was the gift of God's grace which had transformed him from Saul, the proud Pharisee who persecuted the church, to Paul, the apostle who was now a prisoner for Jesus Christ. He had been taken out of one group and put into another. He is now a member of the body of Christ. All that had been accomplished was through the working of the power of the Holy Spirit. Paul had both the gift and the power of an apostle.

Unto me, who am less than the least of all saints, is this grace given, that I should preach among the Gentiles the unsearchable riches of Christ;

And to make all men see what is the fellowship of the mystery, which from the beginning of the world hath been hid in God, who created all things by Jesus Christ [Eph. 3:8–9].

We are living today in the economy, or the dispensation, or the mystery of the church (the gospel of grace), which from the ages past has been hid in God who created all things. My friend, there are a lot of things God has not told us yet, which is one of the reasons I am anticipating heaven. If you think I don't know very much now, you are right. When I get to heaven, I am really going to start learning things. Really, God hasn't told us very much. It's amazing to think how little He has told us. For example, He never told anybody about that little atom. Nor did He tell anybody that there were diamonds deep in the earth. He has kept a lot of things to Himself. He allows man to make discoveries, but there are some things man can never find out except by revelation. The church was a mystery in that sense.

In verse 8 Paul calls himself "less than the least of all saints"—it is a comparative superlative. Paul always took the place of humility as an apostle. "For I am the least of the apostles, that am not meet to be called an apostle, because I persecuted the church of God" (1 Cor. 15:9). "And I thank Christ Jesus our Lord, who hath enabled me, for that he counted me faithful, putting me into the ministry; Who was before a blasphemer, and a persecutor, and injurious: but I obtained mercy, because I did it ignorantly in unbelief" (1 Tim. 1:12–13).

A mighty revolution took place in the life of Paul. He was chosen to preach among the Gentiles the unsearchable riches of Christ. How wonderful!

"And to make all men see"—the mystery is not to be argued or debated but is to be preached. And Paul was to make all men see the economy (the dispensation) of the mystery.

To the intent that now unto the principalities and powers in heavenly places might be known by the church the manifold wisdom of God,

According to the eternal purpose which he purposed in Christ Jesus our Lord [Eph. 3:10–11].

Another purpose of the mystery is revealed here. God's created intelligences are learning something of the wisdom of God through the church. They not only see the love of God displayed and lavished upon us, but the wisdom of God is revealed to His angels.

In whom we have boldness and access with confidence by the faith of him [Eph. 3:12].

We, the Gentiles, and Paul, the persecutor, have freedom of speech before God and an access or introduction to Him. This all is made possible in Christ.

Wherefore I desire that ye faint not at my tribulations for you, which is your glory [Eph. 3:13].

He says, "I entreat you that you not lose heart in my troubles for you, which is your glory." Because of the great goals of the mystery which Paul has enumerated, he is willing to suffer imprisonment as the Apostle to the Gentiles. He didn't want the Ephesians to be discouraged, because the imprisonment of Paul was working for his good and their glory. "Who now rejoice in my sufferings for you, and fill up that which is behind of the afflictions of Christ in my flesh for his body's sake, which is the church" (Col. 1:24).

PRAYER FOR POWER AND KNOWLEDGE

For this cause I bow my knees unto the Father of our Lord Jesus Christ [Eph. 3:14].

What was the cause? It was because of his deep interest in these Ephesians. He wanted them to enter into the great truth of this dispensation, this new economy in which we live, and to experience all the riches of His grace in Christ Jesus. That was the background. That is why he inserted the parenthesis between verses 1 and 14.

We have already called attention to the fact that Paul was a man of prayer. This is the second great prayer of Paul in this epistle. As he viewed the church as the poem of God, the temple of the Holy Spirit, the mystery of the ages, he went to God in prayer that these great truths might become realities in the lives of believers.

In this verse we have another characteristic of the prayers of Paul. It reveals his posture in prayer. I do not want to be splitting hairs, but here it is: "I bow my knees unto the Father of our Lord Jesus Christ." I don't insist that we all get down on our knees in our public prayer meetings today. However, I rather wish that we did.

During my first pastorate in Nashville, Tennessee, I conducted a meeting in Stone's River Church near Murfreesboro, Tennessee. It was one of the best meetings I have ever had. It was a little country church, and when I began, I said, "Let's bow our heads in prayer." I shut my eyes and heard a rumbling. It sounded as if everyone was walking out; so I ventured a look. I didn't see a soul and thought they had really walked out on me. Since I was praying to the Lord, I just continued to pray. When I said, "Amen," I opened my eyes and these people came up between those pews just like corn coming up out of the ground! They had all been down on their knees. We had a wonderful meeting. Now don't misunderstand me—I'm not saying we had a great meeting just because they were down on their knees, but I do want to say that I think it helped a great deal.

In the formality and ritual of our new churches with plush seats and carpeted floors we are missing something in our relationship to the Lord. My feeling is that there ought to be more easy familiarity with each other in our churches but more worship and reverence for God, especially at the time of prayer.

As creatures we ought to assume our proper place before our Creator and go down on all fours before Him. Paul prayed that way and I have always felt that was the proper posture. I must confess that since I have arthritis I don't do it like I used to when I would get down right on my face in my study and pray there. It is amazing how such a posture helps a person to pray. I think it is something that is good for man. I don't insist on this; I merely call your attention to it. This is the way Paul did it, and I think he is a very good example for us today. Aren't we told that our Lord went into the Garden of Gethsemane and fell on His face? I think it would be proper for us if we would get down on our faces before God.

There is another point which I think is rather important to note. We have here that Paul prayed to God the Father in the name of the Lord Jesus Christ. You will also notice that back in chapter 1, verse 17, he prayed to the "God of our Lord Jesus Christ." We find that this was his formula, and I think it is a rather tight formula to address all prayers to God the Father in the name of our Lord Jesus Christ. Someone may say, "Aren't you splitting hairs?" Listen to the Lord Jesus: "And in that day ye shall ask me nothing. Verily, verily, I say unto you, Whatsoever ye shall ask the *Father* in *my* name, he will give it you" (John 16:23, italics mine).

The disciples had been with our Lord for three years. I think they were like a group of children in many ways. I think it was, "Gimme, gimme" a great deal of the time. Then our Lord told them that He would be leaving them. After that they would not ask Jesus for anything. They were to direct their requests to the Father in the name of Jesus. What does Jesus mean by that? He means simply that if you and I were to pray to the Lord Jesus directly, we would rob ourselves of an intercessor. Jesus Christ is our great Intercessor. To pray in Jesus' name means we go to God the Father with a prayer that the Lord Jesus Himself can lift to the Father for you and me.

We need to be very careful in our prayer life. Now that I am retired, I notice things I never noticed before. I was in a service not long ago in which they called on a visiting brother to pray for the meetings at this conference. The conference had gotten off to a marvelous start. The music had been excellent, the pastor had presided well, then they called on this brother to pray. He prayed for a great many things, and I counted three times that he prayed for me. When he prayed for me the second time, my reaction was, *Well, you don't need to tell the Lord that again!* Then when he said it the third time, I thought, *He will turn the Lord off—He'll get tired of hearing that repetitious prayer.* Perhaps after this brother had looked me over he decided I really needed praying for three times! Nevertheless, it was vain repetition as the heathen use. The Lord heard him the first time. We need to be very careful in our prayer life.

Have you noticed that Paul's prayers are brief? Both prayers here in Ephesians and his prayer in Philippians are brief. In fact, all the prayers of Scripture are quite brief. The Lord Jesus said that we are not to use vain repetition as the heathen do—they think they will be heard for their much speaking. Moses' great prayer for Israel is recorded in only three verses. Elijah, on top of Mount Carmel as he stood alone for God against the prophets of Baal, prayed a great prayer which is only one verse long. Nehemiah's great prayer is recorded in only seven verses. The prayer of our Lord in John 17 takes only three minutes to read. But the briefest prayer is that of Simon Peter, ". . . Lord, save me" (Matt. 14:30). He cried out this prayer when he was beginning to sink beneath the waves of the Sea of Galilee. Some people think that was not a prayer because it was so short. My friend, that was a prayer, and it was answered immediately. If Simon Peter had prayed like some of us preachers pray on Sunday morning, "Lord, Thou who art the omnipotent, the omniscient, the omnipresent One. . . ." he would have been twenty feet under water before he got to his request. I tell you, he got down to business. Prayer should be brief and to the point.

Of whom the whole family in heaven and earth is named [Eph. 3:15].

God has a wonderful family. A great many folk think that it is only me and mine—we four and no more. But it's a little wider than that. Some folk feel that their little clique in the church is the only group the Lord is listening to. Some people think their local church constitutes the saints. Then there are others who think their denomination is the whole family of God. Then there are some who think it is just the church—that is, those saved from the Day of Pentecost to the Rapture. My friend, God saved people long before the church came into existence, and He is going to be saving people after the church leaves. Also God has other members of His family. The angels belong to His family. He has created intelligences which the apostle John saw and said cannot be numbered. All of those are the family of God.

That he would grant you, according to the riches of his glory, to be strengthened with might by his Spirit in the inner man;

That Christ may dwell in your hearts by faith; that ye, being rooted and grounded in love,

May be able to comprehend with all saints what is the breadth, and length, and depth, and height;

And to know the love of Christ, which passeth knowledge, that ye might be filled with all the fulness of God [Eph. 3:16–19].

Notice again that he prays *according to* the riches of His glory, not *out of* the riches of His glory. If He would take it out of His riches, He would be like Mr. Rockefeller who used to give his caddy a dime.

There are four definite petitions here which Paul makes on behalf of the Ephesian believers.

1. The petition is that the believers might "be strengthened with might [power] by his Spirit in the inner man." The spiritual nature of the believer needs prayer as well as does the physical. How often the spiritual is neglected while all the attention is given to the physical side. Paul prays for the inner man because he realizes that the outward man is passing away. Power is needed to live the Christian life, to grow in grace, and to develop into full maturity—which is the work of the Holy Spirit.

We tend to pray a great deal for the outward man. It is a marvelous way to pray, praying for the physical needs of folk. Paul did, and he prayed for himself. Three times he asked God to remove the thorn in his flesh. It is wonderful to know that God does hear and does answer prayer, but we need to remember that the spiritual nature of the believer needs prayer as well as the physical. Only the Holy Spirit can supply power, living, and growth for the full maturity of the believer.

2. In the second petition Paul prays that "Christ may dwell in your hearts by faith." This is to think the Lord's thoughts after Him. "Ye in me and I in you." Paul could exclaim, ". . . Christ liveth in me . . ." (Gal. 2:20). *In Christ* is the high word of this epistle. The wonderful counterpart of it is that Christ is in us. In Christ—that is our position. Christ in us—that is our possession. That is the practical side of it. "Examine yourselves, whether ye be in the faith; prove your own selves. Know ye not your own selves, how that Jesus Christ is in you, except ye be reprobates?" (2 Cor. 13:5).

Christ has not come as a temporary visitor. He has come as a permanent tenant by means of the Spirit to live in our lives. "I am the vine, ye are the branches: He that abideth in me, and I in him, the same bringeth forth much fruit: for without me ye can do nothing" (John 15:5).

3. The third petition is a request that the believers may know the dimensions of the knowledge-surpassing love of Christ. He prays that they may be "rooted and grounded in love." "Rooted" refers to botany, to life. "Grounded" refers to architecture, to stability. This is for all the saints.

Paul wants them to "know the love of Christ, which passeth knowledge." The vast expanse of the love of Christ is the love of God Himself. From this launching pad we can begin to measure that which is immeasurable and to know that which passes knowledge. This is one of the many paradoxes of the believer's life.

The *breadth*. The arms of Christ reach around the world. "I am the door: by me if any man enter in, he shall be saved . . ." (John 10:9). ". . . him that cometh to me I will in no wise cast out" (John 6:37).

The *length*. The length of it begins with the Lamb slain before the foundation of the world and proceeds unto the endless ages of eternity.

The *depth*. The depth goes all the way to Christ's death on the cross. "And being found in fashion as a man, he humbled himself, and became obedient unto death, even the death of the cross" (Phil. 2:8).

The *height*. The height reaches to the throne of God. "Who, being in the form of God, thought it not robbery to be equal with God" (Phil. 2:6).

Only the Holy Spirit can lead a believer into this vast experience of the love of Christ. Since it is infinite, it is beyond human comprehension.

4. The fourth petition is a final outburst of an all-consuming fervor that believers "might

be filled up to all the fulness of God." Christ was thus filled. In proportion to our comprehension of the love of Christ, we shall be filled with all the fullness of God.

Now unto him that is able to do exceeding abundantly above all that we ask or think, according to the power that worketh in us,

Unto him be glory in the church by Christ Jesus throughout all ages, world without end. Amen [Eph. 3:20–21].

This is both a doxology and a benediction which concludes the prayer of Paul. It also concludes the first main division of this epistle. This is a mighty outburst of spiritual praise, which any comment would only tarnish. We are not able to so much as touch the hem of the garment of the spiritual gifts that God is prepared to give to His own. How wonderful this is! He wants to give to us superabundantly. How good He is, and how small we are. We cannot even contain all of His blessings.

CHAPTER 4

THEME: *The church is a new man; the exhibition of the new man; the inhibition of the new man; the prohibition of the new man*

We have now come to a new section of the Epistle to the Ephesians. The subjects of these last three chapters are the *conduct of the church* and the *vocation of the believer*. We have learned of the heavenly calling of the believer, and now we come to the believer's manner of life, his earthly walk. This is not a worldly walk, but it is an earthly walk. The true believers, which collectively we call the *church*, are seated in the heavenlies in Christ. Christ is the Head of the body and He is seated at God's right hand. But the church is to live down here on this earth.

In chapters 1–3 we have considered the *calling, construction*, and the *constitution* of the church. In this last section of the epistle we shall consider the *conduct* of the church, the *confession* of the church, and the *conflict* of the church. The church is a new man; in the future the church will be a bride; and the church is also a good soldier of Jesus Christ.

In the first three chapters we have been on the mountain peak of the Transfiguration, probably the highest spiritual point in the New Testament. That is the reason we spent so much time in those chapters. In this last division we descend to the plane of living where we confront a demon-possessed world and a skeptical mob. It is right down where the rubber meets the road. Are we able to translate the truths of the mountain top into shoe leather? Are we able to stand and walk through the world in a way that is pleasing to God? Our Lord said that we are *in* the world but not *of* the world.

It has been stated that Ephesians occupies the same position theologically as the Book of Joshua does in the Old Testament. Now we come to the position where this truth is manifest. Joshua entered the Land of Promise on the basis of the promise made to Abraham, Isaac, Jacob, and Moses. It was his by right of promise, and he led the children of Israel over the Jordan into the land. Passing over Jordan is symbolic of the death, burial, and resurrection of Christ. We as believers have been brought into the Promised Land. That is where you and I live—at least we *should* be living in resurrection territory today.

Joshua had to appropriate the land by taking possession of it for the enjoyment of it and for blessing in the land. *Possession* is the great word in the Book of Joshua. Although enemies and other obstacles stood in his way, Joshua had to overcome and occupy.

Position was a key word in the first half of Ephesians—God has blessed us "with all spiritual blessings" (Eph. 1:3). God has given them over to us, but are we walking down here in *possession* of them? The children of Israel had been promised their land, but it remained a "never-never" land to them until they entered it. "Every place that the sole of your foot shall tread upon, that have I given unto you, as I said unto Moses" (Josh. 1:3). God says, "Joshua, all of it is yours, but you will enjoy only that which you lay hold of."

Now the believer is privileged to move in and occupy "all spiritual blessings in the heavenlies." However, the unsearchable riches in Christ must be searched out with the spiritual Geiger counter, which is the Word of God. Up until now the epistle has been glorious declarations, but now there will be commands. Those who have been called to such an exalted place are now commanded to a way of life which is commensurate with the calling.

Some people dwell on the first part of the epistle and become rather super-duper saints, very spiritual. I remember a family like this when I first came to Southern California. They attended the church which I pastored but were not members. They were lovely, active people. I asked them one day why they didn't join the church. They looked up to the ceiling and said, "We're members of the *invisible* church," and fluttered their eyelids. I have learned that a lot of these folk who are members of the "invisible" church are *really* invisible—invisible on Sunday night and invisible on Wednesday night. In fact, they are invisible when you need help from them. Now, my friend, let's be practical about this: the invisible church is to make itself visible down here in a local assembly.

We have come to the practical side of Ephesians, the earthly conduct of the church; and in this chapter the church is portrayed as a new man. The new man is to exhibit himself down here. The members of the invisible church are to make themselves visible. They are to be extroverts, if you please, and they are to get out the Word of God.

What follows here is restricted to those who are in Christ. The Spirit of God is talking to saved people. If you are not a Christian, God is not asking you to do the commands in this epistle. First you must become a child of His through faith in Christ; you must become a member of His body. What follows in this epistle is for those who have been redeemed and have heard the Word of truth. Dead men cannot walk no matter how insistently they are urged to walk. The dead man must first be made alive. Paul has told us that we were dead in trespasses and sins. That is the condition of all who are lost. The top sergeant doesn't go out to the cemetery and yell, "Attention! Forward march!" If he did, there certainly wouldn't be any marching. Nobody would move. They must first have life. It is interesting that the religions are saying to a dying world, "Do something and you will be somebody." God says just the opposite: "Be somebody and then you can do something." If you are not a Christian, you just stay on the sidelines and listen. You will learn what God would ask of you if you are going to become a believer; and when you look around you, you will know whether or not the saints are living as God wants them to live.

THE EXHIBITION OF THE NEW MAN

I therefore, the prisoner of the Lord, beseech you that ye walk worthy of the vocation wherewith ye are called [Eph. 4:1].

"**T**herefore" is a connective, a transitional word. It is in view of all that God has done for the believer, which we have seen in the first three chapters of this epistle.

Paul is a "prisoner of the Lord." He is a prisoner because of his position in Christ. Isn't it interesting that Paul can be seated in the heavenlies in Christ and can also be seated in a prison because he was a witness for Christ to the Gentiles?

I "beseech [or beg] you that ye walk worthy of the vocation wherewith ye are called." This word for beseech or beg is the same word that we find in Romans 12:1. It is not the command of Sinai with fire and thunder; it is the gentle wooing of love: "I beseech you therefore, brethren, by the mercies of God . . ." (Rom. 12:1).

We are to "walk worthy" of our calling. It is a call to walk on a plane commensurate with the position we have in Christ. "Only let your conversation [that is, your manner of life or your life-style] be as it becometh the gospel of Christ: that whether I come and see you, or else be absent, I may hear of your affairs, that ye stand fast in one spirit, with one mind striving together for the faith of the gospel" (Phil 1:27). Again Paul writes, "That ye might walk worthy of the Lord unto all pleasing, being fruitful in every good work, and increasing in the knowledge of God" (Col. 1:10). Paul points to his own life as an example of the Christian's walk: "Ye are witnesses, and God also, how holily and justly and unblameably we behaved ourselves among you that believe" (1 Thess. 2:10).

Paul begs us to walk worthy of the gospel. People may not be telling you this, but they are evaluating whether you are a real child of God through faith in Christ. The only way they can tell is by your walk. It's not so much *how* you walk as it is *where* you walk. "But if we walk in the light, as he is in the light, we have fellowship one with another, and the blood of Jesus Christ his Son cleanseth us from all sin" (1 John 1:7). Walking in "the light" is in the light of the Word of God. How much time do you really spend in the Word of God? Your children know how much time you spend in the Bible. Also your neighbors know, and the people in the church know. If we wish to walk in fellowship with God, we must walk in the light of the Word of God.

We have previously told the incident of a man handing out tracts, a ministry, by the way, that takes much prayer and intelligence. A black man who could neither read nor write was handed a tract. He asked, "What is this?" When he was told it was a tract, he said, "Well I can't read it; so I'll watch your tracks." That was the greatest short sermon this Christian could ever have had preached to him. Someone was watching his tracks.

Paul does his beseeching on the basis of their calling. He has just explained to the Ephesians that they live in the economy of the grace of God. They live under that dispensation.

With all lowliness and meekness, with longsuffering, forbearing one another in love;

Endeavouring to keep the unity of the Spirit in the bond of peace [Eph. 4:2–3].

"Lowliness" means a mind brought low. Paul practiced what he preached. Lowliness means the opposite of pride. I wish our seminaries today would stop trying to make intellectual preachers and teach the young men to walk in lowliness of mind.

Years ago I heard the story of a very fashionable church in Edinburgh that wanted a pulpit-supply; so the seminary sent out to them a very fine young man who was brilliant in the classroom at the school. He had never had any experience, and he was filled with pride at ministering in this great church. When he got up before that group of people, he was struck with stage fright. He forgot everything he ever knew. He had memorized his sermon, but he forgot it. He stumbled through it and left the pulpit in humiliation, because he knew how miserably he had failed. A dear little Scottish lady went up to him and said, "Young man, I was watching you this morning, and I'd like to say to you that if you had gone up into that pulpit like you came down out of that pulpit, then you would have come down out of that pulpit like you went up into that pulpit." He had gone up with pride, but he had come down with lowliness and meekness.

Lowliness is the flagship of all Christian virtues. "Let nothing be done through strife or vainglory; but in lowliness of mind let each esteem other better than themselves" (Phil. 2:3). Lowliness characterized our Lord. He said, "Take my yoke upon you, and learn of me; for I am meek and lowly in heart . . ." (Matt. 11:29). There are too many Christians today who have a pride of race, a pride of place, a pride of face, and even a pride of grace—they are even proud that they have been saved by grace! Oh, how we need to walk in lowliness of mind!

The story is told of a group of people who went in to see Beethoven's home in Germany. After the tour guide had showed them Beethoven's piano and had finished his lecture, he asked if any of them would like to come up and sit at the piano for a moment and play a chord or two. There was a sudden rush to the piano by all the people except a gray-haired gentleman with long, flowing hair. The guide finally asked him, "Wouldn't you like to sit down at the piano and play a few notes?" He answered, "No, I don't feel worthy." That man was Paderewski, the only man who was really worthy to play the piano of Beethoven.

How often the saints rush in and do things when they have no gift for doing them. We say we have difficulty in finding folk who will do the work of the church, but there is another extreme—folk who attempt to do things for which they have no gift. We need to walk in lowliness of mind.

"With all lowliness and meekness." Meekness means mildness but it does not mean weakness. To be meek does not mean to be a Mr. Milquetoast. There are two men in Scripture who are noted for being meek. In the Old Testament it was Moses, and in the New Testament it was the Lord Jesus. When you see Moses come down from the mount and break the Ten Commandments written on the stone tablets and when you hear what he said to his brother Aaron and to the children of Israel, would you call that meekness? God called it that. When the Lord Jesus went in and drove the money changers out of the temple, was that meekness? It certainly was. The world has a definition of meekness and that makes it synonymous with weakness. The Bible calls meekness a willingness to stand and do the will of God regardless of the cost. Meekness is bowing yourself to the will of God.

"With longsuffering." Longsuffering means a long temper. This is a fruit of the Spirit (see Gal. 5:22). In other words, we should not have a short fuse. That is longsuffering.

"Forbearing one another in love" means to hold one's self back in the spirit of love. "Forbearing one another, and forgiving one another, if any man have a quarrel against any: even as Christ forgave you, so also do ye" (Col. 3:13).

"Endeavouring to keep the unity of the Spirit." The Lord Jesus prayed that we might be one: "That they all may be one; as thou, Father, art in me, and I in thee, that they also may be one in us: that the world may believe that thou hast sent me" (John 17:21). The Spirit of God has baptized us into one body. "For by one Spirit are we all baptized into one body, whether we be Jews or Gentiles, whether we be bond or free; and have been all made to drink into one Spirit" (1 Cor. 12:13). Now believers are to keep the unity which the Holy Spirit has made. We cannot *make* that unity. We cannot join into an ecumenical movement to force a kind of unity. Only the Holy Spirit makes the unity, but we are to maintain it. All true believers in Christ Jesus belong to one body, and we should realize that we are one in Christ.

Now he goes on to list seven of those unities:

There is one body, and one Spirit, even as ye are called in one hope of your calling;

One Lord, one faith, one baptism,

One God and Father of all, who is above all, and through all, and in you all [Eph. 4:4–6].

1. "One body" refers to the total number of believers from Pentecost to the Rapture. This one body is also called the invisible church, but this is not wholly accurate. All true believers should also be visible.

2. "One Spirit" refers to the Holy Spirit who baptizes each believer into the body of Christ. The work of the Holy Spirit is to unify believers in Christ. This is the unity that the believer is instructed to keep.

3. "One hope of your calling" refers to the goal set before all believers. They will be taken out of this world into the presence of Christ. This is the blessed hope (see Titus 2:13).

4. "One Lord" refers to the Lord Jesus Christ. His lordship over believers brings into existence the unity of the church.

5. "One faith" refers to the body of truth called the apostles' doctrine (see Acts 2:42). When this is denied, there are divisions. There must be substance to form an adhesion of believers. This substance is correct doctrine.

6. "One baptism" has reference to the baptism of the Holy Spirit, which is real baptism. Ritual baptism is by water. Water baptism is a symbol of the real baptism of the Holy Spirit by which believers are actually made one.

7. "One God and Father of all" refers to God's fatherhood of believers. Since there is only one Father, He is not the Father of unbelievers. Sonship can come only through Christ. The unity of believers produces a sharp distinction between believers and unbelievers. He is Father of all who are His by regeneration.

Paul has been talking about the church, the body of Christ, joined to Him who is in heaven at the right hand of the Father. The church is a new man. It is a mystery. This is all true because it is in Christ. Now some people can be so involved in these truths who are—as the saying goes—so heavenly-minded that they are no earthly good. Paul is trying to show that we still walk down here in a very evil, very sinful world.

In his discussion of this walk of the believer, Paul speaks first to the individual. The individual is to walk in lowliness and meekness. Then he widens out to the entire church, which is one body and one spirit. Finally, he brings this passage to a great, tremendous crescendo, which pictures the eminence and transcendence of God.

God is "above all, and through all, and in you all." This means that God is transcendent. He is above His creation. He is not dependent upon His creation. He doesn't depend upon oxygen to breathe. He doesn't have to bring up some supplies from the rear or go Saturday shopping in order to have food for the weekend. He is transcendent. He is not only transcendent, He is also eminent. He is not only above all, but He is through all and in you all. That means He is in this universe in which you and I live. He is motivating it and He is moving it according to His plan and purpose. That is what adds meaning to life. That is what makes life worthwhile.

Life gets a little humdrum now and then, doesn't it? There is a monotony to it. Although I love taping broadcasts for my radio program, sometimes when I'm in my study every day for a couple of weeks, it gets monotonous, and I get weary. But then I come to this great thought: all of this is in the plan and purpose of God. Then I feel like singing the doxology or the Hallelujah chorus, and when I do, everybody moves out of earshot. But I can sing unto the Lord with a song that comes from my heart. The Bible says, ". . . making melody in your heart to the Lord" (Eph. 5:19), and that is where mine certainly comes from—not from my mouth, but from my heart.

This chapter reminds me of a great symphony orchestra. When I first went to Nashville as pastor, some friends asked me to go to the symphony with them. They thought they were doing me a favor, but there are other things I would rather do than go to a symphony concert. Although I'm not musically educated, and I don't understand music at all, I got a message at that concert. We had arrived early and I noticed all the instruments. It looked like over a hundred men came out from all the different wings and each went to his own instrument. My friends told me that they were "tuning up." Each one played his own little tune and, I give you my word, there was no melody in it. It was terrible! They quit after a few moments, for which I was thankful. Then they disappeared into the wings. Soon they all appeared again. This time they were in full dress with white shirts and bow ties. Each man came to his instrument, but no man dared play it. Then the spotlight went to the side of the stage and caught the conductor as he walked out. He bowed several times and there was thunderous applause. Then he picked up a little stick and turned his back to the audience. When he lifted that baton, you could have heard a pin drop in that auditorium, then when he lowered it—oh, what music came out of that great orchestra! I had never heard anything that was more thrilling. It made goose pimples come over me and made my hair stand on end.

After that first tremendous number, I got a little bored; I began comparing it with life on this earth. Out in the world every person is playing his own little tune. Everyone is trying to be heard above the clamor of voices or carrying his own little placard of protest. Everyone seems to be out of tune, out of harmony, with everyone else. It doesn't look very hopeful in the world today, and we look to the future with pessimism. Like Simon Peter walking on the lake, we see huge threatening waves. But one of these days there is going to step out from the wings of this universe, from God's right hand, the Conductor. He is called the King of Kings and the Lord of Lords. He will lift that baton, that scepter, with nail-pierced hands. When He does that, the whole world will be in tune. He is eminent and He is transcendent. He is "above all, through all, and in you all." So don't give up—the Conductor is coming. He will get us all in tune.

The church is to walk as a new man in this world. There is to be an exhibition. The church is to be an extrovert, to witness, to manifest life.

THE INHIBITION OF THE NEW MAN

Now we find that the church also has inhibitions and these are also important.

A little child doesn't have inhibitions. I think of a time when I visited some people who were church members. They put on quite a performance of how pious and how religious they were. When we sat down at the table, they called on me to return thanks for the meal. Their little three-year-old was sitting in his high chair at the table with us. When I finished, he turned to his mother and said, "What did that man do?" Obviously, they didn't very often give thanks for their meal. The little fellow was completely uninhibited in what he said.

Now a child may be uninhibited, but the church is not to manifest itself as a baby all the time. It is to grow up and develop some inhibitions. There are certain things an adult doesn't say that a little child may say. The church is not to remain in babyhood but is to mature, and God has given to each child of His grace in which to grow.

But unto every one of us is given grace according to the measure of the gift of Christ [Eph. 4:7].

God has given gifts to believers, as we see in Romans 12 and again in 1 Corinthians, chapters 12–14. Although believers are to give diligence to maintain the unity of the Spirit, this does not mean that each is a carbon copy of the other. Each believer is given a gift so that he may function in the body of believers in a particular way. Paul writes, "But the manifestation of the Spirit is given to every man to profit withal" (1 Cor. 12:7). This means that a gift is the Spirit of God doing something through the believer for the purpose of building up the body of believers. It is for the profit of the whole body of believers. No gift is given to you to develop you spiritually. A gift is given to you in order that you might function in the body of believers to benefit and bless the church.

Many folks say, "Dr. McGee, we do not speak in tongues in the church. We do it for our private devotions." I can say to them categorically from the Word of God that they are wrong. Gifts are given to profit the church. No gift is to be used selfishly for personal profit. In fact, it is not a gift if it is being used that way. A gift is given to every member of the body to enable him to function for a very definite reason in his position in the body.

Suppose my eyes would tell me that they are sleepy and will not get up with me. Suppose my legs say they won't carry me downstairs to my study. I need both my eyes and my legs, and I hope my brain cooperates too. In fact, all the members of my body need to work together, each member doing the job it's supposed to do.

Each believer is given a gift so that he may function in the body of believers in a particular way. When he does this, the body functions. That is where we find the unity of the Spirit. Along with the gift it says every one of us is given grace to exercise that gift in the power and fullness of the Spirit of God. When each believer functions in his peculiar gift, it produces a harmony, as does each member of the human body. However, when one member of the body suffers, the whole body suffers. This means, my friend, that if you do not exercise your gift in the body, you throw us all out of tune.

Wherefore he saith, When he ascended up on high, he led captivity captive, and gave gifts unto men [Eph. 4:8].

You will notice that this is a quotation from Psalm 68:18: "Thou hast ascended on high, thou hast led captivity captive: thou hast received gifts for men; yea, for the rebellious also, that the LORD God might dwell among them." Someone may point out that apparently there is a discrepancy here. Ephesians says, "He gave gifts unto men" and the psalm says, "He received gifts for men." Is this a misquote from the Old Testament?

Please note that an author has a right to change his own writings, but nobody else has that right. I was misquoted in an article and the publisher had to apologize for misquoting me. However, I have a right to misquote my own writing if I want to do so, and if it serves my purpose.

In the verse before us the Holy Spirit changes the words, and He does it for a purpose. Back in the Book of Psalms we are told that the Lord Jesus had received gifts for men. He had all the gifts ready. Then He came to earth. Now that He has been here and has gone back to the Father, He is distributing the gifts among men. He is giving them to us through the Holy Spirit. Actually this passage shows again how very accurate the Bible is and that this is not a misquote.

"When he ascended up on high" refers to the ascension of Christ. At that time He did two things: (1) He led captivity captive, which refers, I believe, to the redeemed of the Old Testament who went to paradise when they died. Christ took these believers with Him out of paradise into the very presence of God when He ascended. Today when a believer dies, we are not told that he goes to paradise, but rather he is absent from the body and present with the Lord (see 2 Cor. 5:8; Phil. 1:23). (2) When Christ ascended He also gave gifts to men. This means that He conferred gifts upon living believers in the church so that they might witness to the world. In His ascension, Christ not only brought the Old Testament saints into God's presence, but He also, through the Holy Spirit, bestowed His gifts. At the Day of Pentecost the Holy Spirit baptized believers into the body of Christ and then endowed them with certain gifts, enabling them to function as members of the body. The Holy Spirit put each of them in a certain place in the body, and He has been doing the same with each new believer ever since.

(Now that he ascended, what is it but that he also descended first into the lower parts of the earth?

He that descended is the same also that ascended up far above all heavens, that he might fill all things.) [Eph. 4:9–10].

The logical explanation of these verses is that since Christ ascended, He must have of necessity descended at some previous period. Some see only the Incarnation in this. The early church fathers saw in it the work of Christ in bringing the Old Testament saints out of paradise up to the throne of God. We are told that He descended into hell. It is not necessary, however, to assume that He entered into some form of suffering after His death. His incarnation and death were His humiliation and descent, and they were adequate to bring the redeemed of the Old Testament into the presence of God. That would explain His fullness here. "He that descended is the same also that ascended up far above all heavens, that he might fill all things." I recognize, however, that there are other interpretations.

And he gave some, apostles; and some, prophets; and some, evangelists; and some, pastors and teachers;

For the perfecting of the saints, for the work of the ministry, for the edifying of the body of Christ:

Till we all come in the unity of the faith, and of the knowledge of the Son of God, unto a perfect man, unto the measure of the stature of the fulness of Christ [Eph. 4:11–13].

I translate it this way: "He Himself gave some [as] apostles, and some [as] prophets and some [as] evangelists, and some [as] pastors and teachers." This verse does not refer to the gifts He has given to men, although it is true that it is He who has given the gifts. What Paul is saying here is that Christ takes certain men who have been given certain gifts and He gives *them* to the church.

Now notice the purpose for which these men are given to the church: "For the perfecting of the saints, for the work of the ministry, for the edifying of the body of Christ." These gifted men are given to the church that it might be brought to full maturity.

"Till we all attain unto the unity of the faith, and of the full knowledge of the Son of God, unto a full grown man, unto the measure of the stature of the fulness of Christ." This may sound selfish, but I trust it is understood. What is the purpose of the church in the world? It is to complete itself that it might grow up.

"He Himself"—this is very emphatic—it is the Lord Jesus Himself who gives gifted men to perfect the church. The Lord Jesus is the One who has the authority and is the One who bestows gifts.

He gave "some, apostles" to the church. An apostle was a man who had not only seen the resurrected Christ but had also been directly and personally commissioned by Him to be an apostle. He enjoyed a special inspiration. This is why Paul could state: "Paul, an apostle, (not of men, neither by man, but by Jesus Christ, and God the Father, who raised him from the dead;). . . . For I neither received it of man, neither was I taught it, but by the revelation of Jesus Christ" (Gal. 1:1, 12). This office, by virtue of its very nature, has long since disappeared from the church.

He gave "some, prophets." Here, as in other epistles, this has reference to New Testament prophets. They were men who were given, as were the apostles, particular insight into the doctrines of the faith (see Eph. 3:5). They were under the immediate influence and inspiration of the Holy Spirit, which distinguishes them from teachers (see 1 Cor. 12:10). There is no one around today with the office of apostle or prophet in that sense. They themselves passed off the scene long ago, but they are still members of His church. His church exists not only on earth; part of the church is up in heaven with Him. They are part of that host which is in the presence of God. In another sense they are still with us today. Aren't we studying the Epistle to the Ephesians right now? And who wrote it? The apostle Paul, and he is still with us even though he is up in heaven with Christ. He is absent from the body but present with Christ. Yet he is still a member of the church and he is still an apostle to us.

"Some, evangelists." The evangelists were traveling missionaries. Paul was an evangelist. They were not evangelists as we think of them today. There was no committee or organization to set up a campaign. They went into new territory, and they did it all alone with the Spirit of God who went before them.

He also gave "some, pastors." These men were the shepherds of the flock.

He gave some, "teachers," the men who were to instruct the flock. This is the gift which is mentioned in Romans 12:7; 1 Corinthians 12:28–29; and 1 Timothy 3:2.

God has given all these men to the church so that the church might be brought to full maturation where there will be inhibitions. You see, the church is not to make a "nut" of herself before the world; she is not to appear ignorant before the world. All these men are to prepare the church so that the believers might do the work of ministering and building up the body of Christ.

We call the pastor of a church a minister, but if you are a Christian, you are as much a minister as he is. You don't have to be ordained to be a minister. The pastor has a special gift, a gift of teaching the Word of God so that his members, those who are under him, might do the work of the *ministry*—they are the ones to go out and do the visitation and the witnessing. I am afraid we have the church in reverse today.

At one time Dr. Lewis Sperry Chafer led his own singing and also did the preaching when he started out as an evangelist. A dear lady came to him one night and said, "Dr. Chafer, you're doing too much. You ought not to lead the singing and do the preaching both. Why don't you get someone else to do the preaching?" Well, he was a musician, but he was primarily a great teacher. Teaching was his great gift, and he used it to equip others for the ministry.

At this point let me say that probably no man in the church has all the gifts; so do not expect your pastor or your minister to be all things. Don't take the viewpoint that he has many gifts. His business is to build the members of the church for the work of the ministry.

Here is a little article that appeared in the bulletin of a small church in the East:

For centuries the principal responsibility for evangelism has been borne by the clergy. The laity were neither called to evangelistic activity nor believed it to be their responsibility. One of the most significant developments in the church (possibly the single most important development in recent centuries) is the revival of lay activity and the growing recognition that the layman is called to a ministry no less important than that of the minister. Elton Trueblood has said, "The Reformation has opened up the *Bible* to the common man; a new Reformation will open up the *ministry* to the common man."

I agree with this article wholeheartedly, and I rejoice that today we are seeing laymen becoming more involved. So many young people today, young Christians, are getting involved in doing the witnessing. Now they need teaching. I think the only reason in the world that they listen to me is because they feel that I can teach them. Believers need teaching so that they can do the work of the ministry.

Sometimes folk get excited when they hear another using my materials. I had a call from a lady in Ohio. Apparently a preacher there was doing a pretty good job of imitating me. He was teaching from my book on Ruth and was even using my illustrations. She said, "I think it is terrible, and you ought to stop him." I asked her if he was doing a good job, and she said he was. So I said, "Praise the Lord. I always felt someone would come along who would do it much better than I do it." You see, my business is to try to prepare others to do the work of the ministry.

One minister wrote and said that he wanted to preach a sermon of mine and asked if he could have permission to do that. I replied, "There is only one thing I ask of you. Do it better than I did, brother." Use the material. We are to build up the body of Christ.

I am going to talk to you very frankly. Don't expect your pastor to do it all. He is there to train you that you might do the work of the ministry and that the church might become mature. We are not to act like a bunch of nitwits today. We are to give a good, clear-cut, intelligent witness to the world. I think the greatest sin in the local church today is the ignorance of the man sitting in the pew; he doesn't know the Word of God, and that is a tragedy. I would hate to get into an airplane if the pilot didn't know any more about flying than the average church member knows about Christianity and the Word of God. The plane wouldn't make it—I think it would crash before it got ten feet into the air. That is the condition of the church today. All believers need to be trained in the Word of God so they can do the work of the ministry.

That we henceforth be no more children, tossed to and fro, and carried about with every wind of doctrine, by the sleight of men, and cunning craftiness, whereby they lie in wait to deceive [Eph. 4:14].

"That we henceforth be no more children." We are to have inhibitions. We are not to run around like a bunch of crying babies. You remember that Paul told the church in Corinth that they were carnal and that they were babies in Christ and a disgrace.

We are not (to use my translation) to be "tossed up and down and driven about with every wind of doctrine (teaching)." Notice that Paul does some mixing of metaphors here. He is trying to bring out vividly the danger of a believer continuing as a babe. You wouldn't, for example, put a baby in a plane to pilot it. My little grandson is a smart boy, but he is not that smart. I wouldn't allow him up there; he would crash. If children were in command of a ship, they would be tossed up and down, driven here and there without direction over the vast expanse of sea. They would become discouraged and seasick. They would lose their way. This is a frightful picture of the possible fate of a child of God.

The figure of speech changes again. "By the sleight of men, and cunning craftiness, whereby they lie in wait to deceive." If you sent babes into the gambling den, the sharpies would take them in with their system of error. I wouldn't think of sending my grandson to Las Vegas to play the slot machines! In fact, I wouldn't want him there even if he lived to be a hundred years old.

Christ's purpose in giving men with different gifts to the church is to develop believers from babyhood to full maturity. Teachers are to be pediatricians. I sometimes use the expression that I am primarily a pediatrician, not an obstetrician. The obstetrician brings the baby into the world. I know he has to get up sometimes at one o'clock in the morning to deliver a baby and that he spends many nights at his work, but he is through with the little angel after he is born. He turns him over to the pediatrician, who makes sure he has everything he needs for normal growth. I have been a pediatrician in my ministry and, only secondly, an obstetrician. I feel that I am called to be the pediatrician—that is, to give the saints the Word of God so they can grow.

But speaking the truth in love, may grow up into him in all things, which is the head, even Christ:

From whom the whole body fitly joined together and compacted by that which every joint supplieth, according to the effectual working in the measure of every part, maketh increase of the body unto the edifying of itself in love [Eph. 4:15–16].

Believers are not to remain children, but rather that in "speaking the truth in love, [they] may grow up into him in all things." The believer is to follow the truth in love; that is, he is to love truth, live it, and speak it. Christ is the truth and the believer must sail his little bark of life with everything pointed toward Christ. Christ is his compass and his magnetic pole.

"Which is the head, even Christ: From whom the whole body fitly joined together and compacted." The body of believers is compared to the physical body and is called the body of Christ.

The body not only receives orders from the Head, who is Christ, but also spiritual nutriment. This produces a harmony where each member is functioning in his place as he receives spiritual supplies from the Head. Also the body has an inward dynamic whereby it renews itself. Likewise the spiritual body is to renew itself in love.

THE PROHIBITION OF THE NEW MAN

This I say therefore, and testify in the Lord, that ye henceforth walk not as other Gentiles walk, in the vanity of their mind,

Having the understanding darkened, being alienated from the life of God through the ignorance that is in them, because of the blindness of their heart:

Who being past feeling have given themselves over unto lasciviousness, to work all uncleanness with greediness [Eph. 4:17–19].

We have seen the *exhibition* of the new man and the *inhibition* of the new man. Now we come to the *prohibition* of the new man. There is the negative side of the believer's life, which I think is important for us to see. There is not enough emphasis on it. We talk about "new morality" which is nothing in the world but old sin. There is a liberty in Christ, but it is not a license to sin.

Scriptural prohibitions for the new man are different from some of the prohibitions that people set up. I can't find, for example, where it says that women should not wear makeup. I know a group who for years judged the spirituality of women by the amount of makeup they wore. I've also seen young girls who thought they were spiritual because they had disheveled hair and no makeup on, and actually they looked like walking zombies. Christians should do the best they can with what they have. That doesn't mean, of course, that they should be painted up like a barber pole. However, some Christians insist upon a number of these man-made prohibitions which are not found in Scripture.

God's prohibitions for the new man are the negatives of His Word. We have had too much on the power of positive thinking today. We need a little of the power of negative thinking.

Have you ever thought that in the Garden of Eden the primary command was a negative command? "But of the tree of the knowledge of good and evil, thou shalt not eat of it: for in the day that thou eatest thereof thou shalt surely die" (Gen. 2:17). Then you come to the Ten Commandments. They are very negative but also very good. Now here in Ephesians we see some negative thinking, some prohibitions for the child of God. We are not to walk "as other Gentiles walk." This is the negative side.

Paul returns at this juncture to the practical aspect of the believer's walk. He had introduced it in verses 1–3, but he was detoured by the introduction of the subject of the unity of the church. Now he gives a picture of the lives of Gentiles and the lives of the Ephesians before their conversion. Remember in chapter 2, verses 11–12, he told how they had been far off, strangers without hope and without God, living in sin. That was their picture.

This is still a graphic picture of the lost man today. Paul gives four aspects of the walk of the Gentiles which illustrate the absolute futility and insane purpose of the life of the lost man.

"In the vanity of their mind" means the empty illusion of the life that thinks there is satisfaction in sin. Oh, how many people walk that way! I feel so sorry for these young people who have been taken in by the promoters of immorality as a life style. A girl told me that she had had two abortions—murdered two babies, and was not married—what a life! That is not the life of happiness that God has planned for His children, my friend. It is the walk of a lost person, walking in the vanity of the mind. It is an empty illusion of life.

Drinking cocktails is another illusion. Alcoholism takes its toll. An alcoholic woman has started listening to our Bible teaching program and is now fighting a battle to be delivered from alcohol. She says, "Oh, it seemed so smart, so sophisticated to drink cocktails!" How tragic.

"Having the understanding darkened" means that the lost man has lost his perception of moral values. That is exactly what is being promoted in our day—a loss of perception of moral values.

"Being alienated from the life of God through the ignorance that is in them" is a picture of all mankind without Christ. It is the rebellion of Adam which is inherited by all his children. What a picture it is of a man today. He thinks he is living. One man told me he spent a week's wages for one evening in a nightclub. What for? To try to have a good time. That's an expensive way to try to have fun. He was alienated from the life of God; he had no communication with God: he was dead in trespasses and sin. Such a man is ignorant of the inestimable advantage of a relationship with God. The result is a hardening of the heart.

"Who being past feeling have given themselves over unto lasciviousness [which is uncleanness], to work all uncleanness with greediness [or covetousness]." Their continuance in this state of moral ineptitude brings them down to the level where they have no feeling of wrongdoing. There are a lot of folk like that today. They are apathetic. The resultant condition is to plunge further into immorality and lasciviousness. This vicious cycle leads to a desire to go even deeper into sin. If you paint the town red tonight, you have to have a bigger bucket and a bigger brush for tomorrow night. The meaning here is to covet the very depths of immorality. Men in sin are never satisfied with sin. They become abandoned to sin. This is what it means in chapter 1 of Romans that God gave them up to all uncleanness through their own lusts. You can reach the place, my friend, where you are an abandoned sinner.

But ye have not so learned Christ;

If so be that ye have heard him, and have been taught by him, as the truth is in Jesus [Eph. 4:20–21].

Here is the contrast with the life of the Gentiles. If anyone is not listening to Jesus, then Jesus must not be his Savior. The Lord Jesus is the Shepherd and His *sheep* hear His voice. If you haven't heard His voice, then you are not one of His sheep.

What will change the Gentiles from their old nature? What are they to do? They are to listen to Christ. They are to hear Him. They are to be taught by Him. Those who are not His sheep will not hear Him.

When an unsaved man writes to me and says that he disagrees with me, I am not upset. I think, *Fine. I hope you don't agree with me.* Something would be wrong if he did agree. The saved person looks to the Lord Jesus as his Shepherd. He listens to the Shepherd and he follows Him. The unsaved person goes his own way.

"The truth is in Jesus." Although His life on earth cannot be imitated by anyone, the very life of Jesus is an example to the believer. Jesus is the One who has been the pioneer; He is the example of life here on earth. He is the

One who also went through the doorway of death for us. There is no reason for any believer to be in the dark today or to be ignorant or to be blind.

That ye put off concerning the former conversation the old man, which is corrupt according to the deceitful lusts;

And be renewed in the spirit of your mind;

And that ye put on the new man, which after God is created in righteousness and true holiness [Eph. 4:22–24].

"That ye put off concerning . . . the old man . . . and that ye put on the new man." We are to put off the old man and put on the new man in the same manner that we change our clothes. It is like putting off an old and unclean garment and then putting on a garment that is new and clean. The putting off the old man and putting on the new man cannot be done by self-effort, nor can it be done by striving to imitate Christ's conduct. It has been done *for* the believing sinner by the death of Christ. We are like babes who cannot dress themselves. I have learned with my little grandson that a child doesn't do very well when he tries to dress himself. As Christians we never reach the place where we can do that, and we don't need to try. It already has been done for us. We are told in the Epistle to the Romans that the old man has already been crucified in the death of Christ. "Knowing this, that our old man is crucified with him, that the body of sin might be destroyed, that henceforth we should not serve sin" (Rom. 6:6). In view of the truth that the old man has already been crucified with Christ, we are to put it off in the power of the Holy Spirit. This does not mean that the flesh, the old nature, is ever eliminated in this life. We do not get rid of the old nature, but we are not to live in it; that is, we are not to allow it to control our lives.

On the other hand, we do have a new nature. This is the result of regeneration by the Holy Spirit. Any man in Christ is a new creature. We are to live in that new nature, that new man. This is a repetition of the great message of Romans.

"Which after God is created in righteousness and true holiness." This shows that this is the imputed righteousness of Christ, and that all is to be done consistent with the holy character of God. Since we have been declared righteous and we are in Christ seated in the heavenlies, our walk down here should be commensurate with our position.

Wherefore putting away lying, speak every man truth with his neighbour: for we are members one of another.

Be ye angry, and sin not: let not the sun go down upon your wrath:

Neither give place to the devil [Eph. 4:25–27].

Paul returns to the prohibitions which he began in verse 17. The believer is told to walk no longer as the Gentiles walk. These injunctions continue through the remainder of the epistle.

"Speak every man truth" is the injunction that leads all the rest. When the old man was put off in the crucifixion of Christ, the lying tongue and deceitful heart were put on the cross. One of the reasons Jesus had to die for us was because you and I are liars. We ought always speak the truth. David said, "I said in my haste, All men are liars" (Ps. 116:11). I remember hearing Dr. W. I. Carroll quote this years ago. He pointed out that David said he thought this "in his haste." Dr. Carroll remarked, "I've had a long time to think it over, and I still agree with David."

Speaking the truth would resolve most of the problems in the average church. Long ago I gave up the idea of trying to straighten out all of the lies that I hear in Christian circles. I found out that I could spend all my time doing that. Since believers are members of one body, speaking the truth is imperative.

Chrysostom drew this ridiculous analogy but it does illustrate the truth:

Let not the eye lie to the foot, nor the foot to the eye. If there be a deep pit and its mouth covered with reeds shall present to the eye the appearance of solid ground, will not the eye use the foot to ascertain whether it is hollow underneath, or whether it is firm and resists? Will the foot tell a lie, and not the truth as it is? And what, again, if the eye were to spy a serpent or a wild beast, will it lie to the foot?

The feet wouldn't deceive the eyes because they are members of the same body. Neither would the eye deceive the feet. So in the church there ought to be honesty and truth among the members.

"Be ye angry, and sin not." The believer is commanded to be angered with certain conditions and with certain people. There seems to be an idea today that a Christian is one who is a "blah," that he is sweet under all circumstances and conditions. Will you hear me carefully? No believer can be neutral in the battle of truth. He should hate the lying and gossiping tongue, especially of another Christian. However, we should not hate or loathe the person with an innate hatred or malice, as Peter calls it. Malice is something that should not be in the life of the believer. "Wherefore laying aside all malice . . ." (1 Pet. 2:1). Malice has been described as congealed anger. When the wrong is corrected, there should be no animosity. Forgive and forget is the principle. Harboring hatred and sinful feelings gives the Devil an advantage in our lives. Many people have certain hang-ups. They hate certain people—they can't get over it and can't forgive. My friend, we should forgive and forget if the person is willing to give up his lying.

The Lord Jesus showed anger. He went into the synagogue, and there was a man with a withered hand. What angered Him was that the Pharisees had planted that man there just to see what He would do. "And when he had looked round about on them with anger, being grieved for the hardness of their hearts, he saith unto the man, Stretch forth thine hand. And he stretched it out: and his hand was restored whole as the other" (Mark 3:5). Our Lord was *angry* at the Pharisees for doing such a thing. Also we are told that God is angry all day long with the wicked, but that the minute they give up their wickedness and turn to Him, He will save them. That should be the attitude of the believer.

I heard of a custodian who had remained in a church which had had lots of problems. There was trouble, bitterness, hatred, and little cliques in the church. They had had one pastor after another, but the custodian remained through the years. A visitor who knew about the church asked him how he had been able to stay so long under such circumstances. He replied, "I just get into neutral and let them push me around." A great many people think that that is being a Christian. May I say to you that no Christian can be neutral. We are in a great battle, as we shall see later in this epistle.

Let him that stole steal no more: but rather let him labour, working with his hands the thing which is good, that he may have to give to him that needeth.

Let no corrupt communication proceed out of your mouth, but that which is good to the use of edifying, that it may minister grace unto the hearers [Eph. 4:28–29].

"Let him that stole steal no more." Man by his sinful nature is a thief as well as a liar. When I was a boy, I ran around with a mean gang of boys—I was the only good boy in the crowd, of course. During watermelon season, we stole watermelons. The farmer might have given us one out of his patch, but they tasted better if we swiped them. We also stole peaches and apples from the orchards. And in the wintertime we would steal eggs and take them down to Old Buzzard Creek and roast them. There wasn't anything that was safe from us.

After I was converted, I still had this impulse. In fact, once I was going to visit a man who had a marvelous watermelon patch by the side of a country road. I was so tempted to take one of his watermelons that I actually stopped and got out of the car. Then I thought, "Wait a minute. I am going to see the man in a few minutes. He'll give me one. There's no reason for me to do this." I got back in the car and drove off. When I told him my experience, he laughed. "You know," he said, "I might have shot you if you had gone into that watermelon patch. I've had a lot of thieves in there stealing my watermelons, and they are pretty valuable today." Stealing is in our hearts. We are just naturally that way. Paul says here that we are to steal no more, even when it may look as if it is all right.

"But rather let him labour, working with his hands the thing which is good, that he may have to give to him that needeth." The believer is not to get rich for his own selfish ends. Rather, he is to help others with whatever he has that is surplus. Today there are many fine Christian ministries that lag and wilt for lack of funds. Why? Because many believers are accumulating riches for themselves and are not giving as they should give.

"Corrupt communication" means filthy speech—that which is rotten or putrid. An uncontrolled tongue in the mouth of a believer is the index of a corrupt life. Believers who use the shady or questionable story reveal a heart of wickedness. What is in the well of the heart will come up through the bucket of the mouth. The speech of the believer should be on the high plane of instructing and communicating encouragement to other believers. You can have fun and enjoy life—humor has its place—but our humor should not be dirty or filthy.

And grieve not the holy Spirit of God, whereby ye are sealed unto the day of redemption [Eph. 4:30].

"Grieve not the holy Spirit of God." The Holy Spirit is a person who can be grieved. What is it that grieves Him? It is the offenses that have been listed. When a Christian lies, it grieves the Holy Spirit. When a Christian has dirty thoughts, it grieves the Holy Spirit. What happens when any person is grieved? It breaks the fellowship. The Holy Spirit cannot work in your life when you have grieved Him, when fellowship with Him has been broken.

"Whereby ye are sealed"—this tells us that we can grieve the Holy Spirit, but we cannot grieve Him *away*, because we are sealed in Him. How wonderful this is! You were sealed in the Holy Spirit at the moment of regeneration.

"Unto the day of redemption"—He seals you until the day when He will present you to the Lord Jesus Christ. A believer cannot unseal His work which continues to the day of redemption, but the believer may grieve Him. What is the great difference between Christians today? The real difference is that some Christians live with a grieved Holy Spirit and some live with an ungrieved Holy Spirit.

Let all bitterness, and wrath, and anger, and clamour, and evil speaking, be put away from you, with all malice:

And be ye kind one to another, tenderhearted, forgiving one another, even as God for Christ's sake hath forgiven you [Eph. 4:31–32].

These last two verses are in sharp contrast one with the other. There is an additional listing of that which grieves the Holy Spirit in verse 31—these are sins of the emotional nature. Instead, the emotional responses, which God wants us to have, are given in verse 32.

"Bitterness" is an irritable state of mind which produces harsh and hard opinions of others. Someone once came up to me and told me what he thought of another Christian. A third Christian who was present later said, "Don't put too much stress on what he said, Dr. McGee, because he is bitter." A great many people are speaking out of bitterness, and when they do, it hurts. This grieves the Holy Spirit.

"Wrath, and anger" are outbursts of passion. Bishop Moule makes this distinction between them, "Wrath denotes rather the *acute* passion, and the other the *chronic*."

"Clamour" means the bold assertion of supposed rights and grievances. There are people in the church who feel that the pastor isn't paying attention to them if he doesn't shake their hand. Sometimes they even become bitter and clamorous over a supposed slight. Who can say that the pastor must run around and shake hands with everyone simply to keep people happy? It is this kind of attitude that grieves the Holy Spirit.

"Evil speaking" is blasphemy, but it also means all kinds of slander; and "malice," as we have noted before, is congealed hatred.

"Be put away from you." All these sins are to be put away or, literally, taken away. In the Greek it is an aorist imperative, requiring a one-time decisive act if the Holy Spirit is not to be grieved. We must make a decision to put these sins away.

Now comes a marked contrast. "Be (become) ye" denotes the radical change that should take place in the believer so that there will be no vacuum in his life.

"Kind one to another" means Christian courtesy. "Tenderhearted" is a more intense word than kind. It means to be full of deep and mellow affection. Some believers are like that—they are wonderful friends. When they see you, they put their arms around you. I went to college and then to seminary with a fellow and then helped him in meetings for years. He is retired now. When we saw each other in Florida some time back, we just flung our arms around each other. We were tenderhearted toward one another—we love each other in the Lord.

"Forgiving one another" is a reflexive form of phrase. It is literally, "forgiving one another yourselves." It means to give and take in relation to the faults of one another. We are to forgive rather than magnify the faults of others.

"Even as God for Christ's sake hath forgiven you." All of this is to be done on a twofold basis. First, this conduct will not grieve the Holy Spirit. Second, the basis of forgiveness is not legal, but gracious. This is not a command under law but is on the basis of the grace of God exhibited in our forgiveness because Christ died for us. We are to forgive because we have been forgiven. It is not that we forgive in order to get forgiveness. Note the contrast: Christ was stating the *legal* grounds for forgiveness in the Sermon on the Mount when He said, "For if ye forgive men their trespasses, your heavenly Father will also forgive you: But if ye forgive not men their trespasses, neither will your Father forgive your trespasses" (Matt. 6:14–15). Here in Ephesians we are told to forgive on the basis of the *grace* of God which He exhibited in our forgiveness for Christ's sake, because Christ died for us. This is quite wonderful!

CHAPTER 5

THEME: The church will be a bride; the engagement of the church; the experience of the church; the expectation of the church

There is really a mixing of metaphors here. In chapter 4 the church is called a new man, and now the church is to be a bride. The emphasis of this chapter is on the future—the church *will be* a bride. The church is not a bride today. The church is a new man walking in the world, and the church is espoused (engaged) to Christ but is not yet wedded to Him. The wedding hasn't taken place yet. The church will be a bride with Christ after the Rapture. "And I John saw the holy city, new Jerusalem, coming down from God out of heaven, prepared as a bride adorned for her husband. . . . And there came unto me one of the seven angels which had the seven vials full of the seven last plagues, and talked with me, saying, Come hither, I will shew thee the bride, the Lamb's wife" (Rev. 21:2, 9).

On this earth we are to walk as a future bride. We are engaged now. This is what Paul wrote to the Corinthians: ". . . for I have espoused you to one husband, that I may present you as a chaste virgin to Christ" (2 Cor. 11:2). When a girl is engaged and preparing for her wedding, she doesn't have time for her old boyfriends. She won't be going out with Tom tonight and with Dick tomorrow night and with Harry the following night. She is engaged, and she has no interest in them anymore. How can we who are engaged to Christ live as the world lives? We are going to be presented to Christ someday. We are going to live with Him throughout eternity, and He is going to be our Lord and our Master.

THE ENGAGEMENT OF THE CHURCH

Be ye therefore followers of God, as dear children;

And walk in love, as Christ also hath loved us, and hath given himself for us an offering and a sacrifice to God for a sweet-smelling savour [Eph. 5:1–2].

"Therefore" connects this section with the preceding where the walk of the believer is under consideration and continues the injunctions for Christian conduct. These injunctions have a definite bearing upon the church which will be presented to Christ without spot or blemish. Such a high and lofty goal, which is entirely the work of Christ, is a compelling dynamic for chaste conduct here and now.

We have learned that the Holy Spirit indwells every believer and seals every believer, but that we can grieve the Holy Spirit. If we engage in those things mentioned in chapter 4, verse 31, it means we will grieve the Holy Spirit—but it does not mean that we are no longer children of God. It does mean that the unsaved world won't believe that we are the children of God. We are, however, sealed by the Spirit of God until the day of redemption, the day when the Spirit of God will present the church to the Lord Jesus. This goal should lead us to chaste conduct.

The believer is to be an imitator of God, especially in the matter of forgiveness. However, this applies to all aspects of the Christian walk. The Gentiles who formerly walked on a very low plane are now lifted to the high level of love. They are now called "dear children" or beloved children. The plane of love to which they are lifted is the love which Christ exhibited when He loved us enough to give Himself as an offering and a sacrifice for us.

"And hath given himself for us an offering and a sacrifice to God for a sweet-smelling savour" is a clear-cut reference to the cross. It makes the death of Christ more than the public execution of a criminal. The cross was the brazen altar where the Lamb of God was offered as the burnt sacrifice. That sacrifice takes away the sin of the world. It identifies Christ with every sacrifice that was offered in the Old Testament by God's command. They all pointed to Him.

It is in view of the substitutionary, vicarious death of Christ upon the cross that the believer is to attain to such an exalted plane of love. The believer cannot walk with a grieved Holy Spirit, for only the Spirit can bring forth this fruit in the life. Remember that love is first on the list of the fruit of the Spirit in Galatians 5:22.

But fornication, and all uncleanness, or covetousness, let it not be once named among you, as becometh saints;

Neither filthiness, nor foolish talking, nor jesting, which are not convenient: but rather giving of thanks [Eph. 5:3–4].

The sins described here are those which are prevalent among unbelievers. These are the common sins in the world today. All of them have to do with low forms of immorality. Paul is saying that the child of God cannot habitually engage in these. Even a slight indulgence brings about a revulsion and agony of soul. I have made this statement many times, and I repeat it again: If you can get into sin and not be troubled or bothered by it, you are not a child of God. I do not think there is any other alternative. But if there is conviction in your heart, you can rise and go to your Father as the Prodigal Son did. You are a son of the Father, and only sons want to go to the Father's house. I have never heard of a pig that wanted to go there. The sins listed here are low sins which characterize the ungodly person.

When you as a believer go to God to confess your sins, you don't just bundle them up and hand the bundle to God. It is not a wholesale affair. Rather, you spell out each sin to Him. For example, if you have a biting tongue and are a gossip who hurts people, tell Him *that* is your sin. When you go to God in confession and name the specific sin, it restores fellowship with Him. These sins are sins that believers drop into sometimes. When they do, they are to confess them to God. Fénelon puts it like this:

Tell God all that is in your heart, as one unloads one's heart, its pleasures and its pains, to a dear friend. Tell Him your troubles, that He may comfort you; tell Him your joys, that He may sober them; tell Him your longings, that He may purify them; tell Him your dislikes, that He may help you to conquer them; talk to Him of your temptations, that He may shield you from them; show Him the wounds of your heart, that He may heal them; lay bare your indifference to good, your depraved tastes for evil, your instability. Tell Him how self-love makes you unjust to others, how vanity tempts you to be insincere, how pride disguises you to yourself as to others.

If you thus pour out all your weaknesses, needs, troubles, there will be no lack of what to say. You will never exhaust the subject. It is continually being renewed. People who have no secrets from each other never want subjects of conversation. They do not weigh their words, for there is nothing to be held back; neither do they seek for something to say. They talk out of the abundance of the heart, without consideration, just what they think. Blessed are they who attain to such familiar, unreserved intercourse with God.

The great need of all believers is to go to God and tell Him what is really in our hearts. Someone may say, "It is just unbelievable that Christians would even commit such sins as are listed here." Friend, if you had been a pastor as long as I have, you would know that they do fall into these sins. Many Christian people feel that they have committed an unpardonable sin, but they have not. There *is* a way back to God!

"Fornication" is accepted by the world as a norm of conduct. It is a sin that is looked upon as not being very bad. When the gross immorality of the hour started creeping in, it was called the *new* morality. Some time ago many of us were shocked when we heard that in the college dormitories the boys and girls were in the same building but on different floors. Now it has changed so that boys and girls are roommates. When I went to college, the boys could visit in the living room of the girls' dormitory. And I still think that is the best way to do it. I'll stick with the Bible. Fornication is a sin. Regardless of where you are or who you are, if you are living in fornication today, you cannot be a child of God. Someone may say, "Wait a minute. You said a child of God could confess a sin and come back into fellowship with God." That is right, but a child of God cannot confess a sin and then persist in *living in* that sin. That is a dead giveaway that such a person is not a child of God.

"All uncleanness" includes all forms of immorality.

"Covetousness" is a grasping desire—and not just for money or material wealth. It may be a desire to be mentally superior to someone else. It could be coveting a home or a position. Some people love to be president of something. Of course, it also includes the covetousness for money. It has been said that the miser thinks dollars are flat so he can stack them, and the prodigal thinks they are round so he can roll them. Whether one stacks them or spends them, covetousness means gaining everything for your own selfish ends.

Some people try to garner together all the honors of this world. I know ministers who would never be guilty of trying to get rich, but they surely are after position. They want a position in their denomination or in their community. Covetousness is a rotten sin that is in our old natures.

"Let it not be once named among you." This

means they are not to be spoken of with approval or desire. Obviously, I am naming these sins with neither approval nor desire.

"Filthiness" speaks of the utmost in depravity. These are the low-down, dirty things one hears today.

"Foolish talking" means to gloat or brag about sinning. Have you ever heard men or even women boast about how much they drank at a party? Have you heard them boast of their conquests in the realm of sex? That is foolish talking.

"Jesting" does not mean good, clean humor—I'd be guilty of jesting if it meant that. Jesting means to make light of sensuality and immorality. It means telling dirty stories.

"But rather giving of thanks" is to be the context of Christian conversation. I would often play golf with a very wonderful Christian layman whom I loved in the Lord. Sometimes an unsaved man would join us. He would make a few bad shots, and then he would lose his temper. He would ask God to damn the golf course, the sand traps, his golf clubs, and anything else he could think of. My friend would always say, "Praise the Lord, bless the Lord." The unbeliever would ask, "Why do you say that?" The Christian would ask, "Why do you take God's name in vain?" The reply would be, "It's a habit." "It's also a habit with me," my friend would say. "Every time I hear a man ask God to damn something, I praise and thank Him for something. I sort of want to balance the budget down here." On several occasions that stopped the cussing. And it is good for us as Christians to make a habit of giving thanks.

For this ye know, that no whoremonger, nor unclean person, nor covetous man, who is an idolater, hath any inheritance in the kingdom of Christ and of God [Eph. 5:5].

It is clearly understood that the unregenerate man who practices these sins has no portion in the kingdom of Christ and God. If a professing Christian practices these sins, he immediately classifies himself. No matter what his testimony may be on Sunday or what position he may have in the church, such a person is saying to the lost world that he is not a child of God. To *live* in the corruption of the flesh is to place one's self beyond the pale of a child of God.

Let no man deceive you with vain words: for because of these things cometh the wrath of God upon the children of disobedience.

Be not ye therefore partakers with them [Eph. 5:6–7].

In view of the fact that the wrath of God will be poured out on the unregenerate because of these sins, it follows that the child of God cannot participate in them without incurring the displeasure and judgment of God. If such a person is really a child of God, God will judge him. He judged David, you may recall. When David slipped into sin, God put the lash on his back and never took it off. "For if we would judge ourselves, we should not be judged. But when we are judged, we are chastened of the Lord, that we should not be condemned with the world" (1 Cor. 11:31–32).

If you can sin and get by with it, you are not a child of God. Do you know why? Because God would have to condemn you with the world, which would mean that you are not saved. If you are a child of God and do these things, God will chasten you—He will take you to the woodshed right here and now. If God doesn't chasten you, you are in a frightful condition. It means you are not His child, because God does not spank the Devil's children.

For ye were sometimes darkness, but now are ye light in the Lord: walk as children of light:

(For the fruit of the Spirit is in all goodness and righteousness and truth;)

Proving what is acceptable unto the Lord [Eph. 5:8–10].

Paul reminds the believers of their former state prior to conversion. They were not just *in* darkness, they *were* darkness. We speak of the unregenerate as being in darkness, but it is worse than that. When I went alone to play golf on one occasion, I was teamed up with a man who was unsaved—in fact, he was a bartender. As he talked, I realized that he was not only *in* darkness, he *was* darkness. My, what a life that man had!

"Now are ye light in the Lord," which means we are to reflect Him who is the Light of the world. Paul identifies the fruit of light. He marks out those characteristics which always accompany light: "In all goodness," which means kindness; "righteousness," meaning moral rectitude; and "truth," referring primarily to sincerity and genuineness. The believer is to prove or test his life in this manner to see if he is in the will of God and therefore well-pleasing to Him.

You will remember that 1 John 1:7 speaks of walking in the light as He is in the light.

Someone asked me what it means to walk in the light of God. Here we have a description of it from the Word of God: walk in kindness, in goodness, in righteousness (moral rectitude), and in truth, which is sincerity and genuineness. And this is to be our walk seven days a week—not only on Sunday. And it means twenty-four hours of those seven days and sixty minutes of every hour.

And have no fellowship with the unfruitful works of darkness, but rather reprove them.

For it is a shame even to speak of those things which are done of them in secret.

But all things that are reproved are made manifest by the light: for whatsoever doth make manifest is light [Eph. 5:11–13].

We are to "have no fellowship with the unfruitful works of darkness." A child of God simply cannot go along with the "works of darkness" as light and darkness cannot mingle in the physical world. For the things done in secret by them are even shameful to speak of. We are not even to talk about them.

Rather, we are to "reprove" or convict them. This does not mean that the believer is to become a reformer. It does mean that by the light of his life he is a rebuke to the works of darkness. Light reveals what the darkness conceals. Darkness is not driven away by preaching at it; darkness is dissipated by the presence of light.

There are too many Christians who take the critical method or the preaching method. They try to correct an unsaved person by saying, "You shouldn't be doing that." My friend, that is not the way to approach the darkness. You are to be light. You cannot preach to people about these things. You cannot tell them what to do and not do. I constantly get letters from people who are telling me that I should preach against certain sins. No, my business is to turn on the light of the Word of God—that which God calls right. You see, you are not able to win a person to Christ by lecturing to him and telling him what is wrong. You are not to try to get the unsaved man to change his conduct; he *cannot* change his conduct. He needs to be born again in order to change. You are not to shake your finger under his nose and say, "Don't do that. Don't be a bad boy." You are to be light, and light will always affect darkness.

I remember a very dear lady in my congregation when I was a pastor in downtown Los Angeles. She was a dominant character, however. She came to me and told me that her husband was unsaved and asked me to remember him in prayer. I did so faithfully. Then she came to me and told me that he was coming to church but would never accept the invitation to receive Christ as his Savior. Then she told me this: "At breakfast I talk to him with tears about receiving Christ. Again at dinner I talk to him and cry." I got to thinking what it would be like to have two meals a day with a crying woman. So I told her absolutely never to mention the subject to him again. She should fix him the nicest meals possible and be the sweetest person she knew how to be. "Oh," she said, "that wouldn't work. We are supposed to witness." You see, she didn't really understand what it meant to be a witness. Anyway, she did try the plan. She quit blubbering in his presence, and she stopped lecturing to him. In less than six months that man made a decision for Christ. He had been listening to the wrong preacher before that. She had been preaching to him when she should have been a light. Remember that darkness is not dissipated by lecturing or by preaching. Darkness is dissipated by light.

Wherefore he saith, Awake thou that sleepest, and arise from the dead, and Christ shall give thee light [Eph. 5:14].

Here is a command which is humanly impossible to obey. How can a person awake from the dead? How can a person awake out of spiritual death? Only God can awaken us. I think what Paul means here is that the believers who have fallen into a spiritual stupor are to wake up.

See then that ye walk circumspectly, not as fools, but as wise,

Redeeming the time, because the days are evil.

Wherefore be ye not unwise, but understanding what the will of the Lord is [Eph. 5:15–17].

My own translation is: "Look carefully how ye walk, not as unwise, but be as wise men, buying up the time, because the days are evil. On this account become not senseless (foolish) but understanding (being prudent) what the will of the Lord is." This is another injunction regarding the walk of the believer. He is to walk wisely. His walk is to reveal the urgency of the hour and the importance of living for God. The entire objective in his walk is to stay in the will of God. He walks in the will of God as a train runs on the track. His walk in this world demonstrates that he belongs to Christ.

When you walk into a place of business, you will find the salesman in there on his toes: he is dynamic. If a man is a child of God, how does he act when he is not in his place of business trying to make a dollar? Is he on his toes? Is he dynamic? Is he living for God? The believer is to walk in this world as though he belonged to Christ.

There is a saying that you never ask a Texan if he is a Texan. If he is a Texan, he'll let you know it without your asking. If he is not a Texan, you wouldn't want to embarrass him! My friend, a Christian ought to walk in such a way that you know he is a child of God without asking him. We all need to look carefully how we walk.

THE EXPERIENCE OF THE CHURCH

Each real believer should have an experience—I believe in experience. Now notice what is to be his experience:

And be not drunk with wine, wherein is excess; but be filled with the Spirit;

Speaking to yourselves in psalms and hymns and spiritual songs, singing and making melody in your heart to the Lord [Eph. 5:18–19].

My translation puts it like this: "Be not made drunk with wine in which is riot (dissoluteness), but be filled with the Spirit; speaking one to another in psalms and hymns and spiritual songs, singing and making melody in your heart to the Lord." This is not just a dry discourse against the evils of drunkenness, even though drunkenness was the besetting sin of the ancient world—and is still the besetting sin of the hour. It may actually be the sin that will destroy America. But this is not a lecture on drunkenness. Actually, Paul is making a comparison. Don't be drunk with wine. Why not? because it will stimulate temporarily: it will energize the flesh, but then it will let you down and lead you in the direction of profligacy and dissoluteness and will finally eventuate in desperation and despair and delirium tremens. That is not what you need. Now it is true that people today feel a need for something, which I think explains the cocktail hour and the barroom. They turn to hard liquor to fill that need. If they are not children of God, they have no other resource or recourse. However, the child of God is to be filled with the Holy Spirit. This is to be the *experience* of the believer.

What does it mean to be filled with the Holy Spirit? We can find the analogy in the man who is drinking, which is the reason Paul uses it here. The man who is drinking is possessed by the wine. You can tell that a man is drunk. In contrast, it is the Holy Spirit who should be the One to possess the believer. It is a divine intoxication that is to fill that need. This is not an excessive emotionalism but that which furnishes the dynamic for living and for accomplishing something for God. When we are filled by the Holy Spirit, it means that we are *controlled* by the Holy Spirit.

The walk of the believer and his being filled with the Spirit are closely related. Paul says a believer is to walk carefully and "circumspectly" and "be filled with the Spirit." These are commands which are given to the believer. This filling is a constant renewal of the believer's life for strength and action, which is indicated here by the use of the present tense. The Spirit-filled believer not only walks wisely, but his Christian character is evidenced by the fruit of the Spirit (see Gal. 5:22–23).

A believer is never commanded to be baptized with the Holy Spirit, but we *are* told that we are baptized into one body . . ." (1 Cor. 12:13). Did we do that by some effort on our part? No, it was by our faith in Jesus Christ. The Holy Spirit regenerates and indwells us. The Holy Spirit seals us, and the Holy Spirit baptizes us and puts us into the body of believers.

However, the believer needs the filling of the Spirit to serve Christ. The disciples were gathered on the Day of Pentecost. They needed to go out into the world for Christ, and they were filled with the Spirit. They had that experience which enabled them to witness on that day.

To be filled with the Spirit is, I think, as simple as driving to a filling station and saying, "Fill it up." As I start out in the morning with the Lord I say, "Lord, I want to walk today in the Spirit. I cannot do it myself. I need Your power. I need Your help." We as believers need to start the day by asking for an infilling of the Holy Spirit. This is something which is desperately needed by believers.

You may have been filled with the Spirit yesterday or last week, but that won't suffice for today. I buy gasoline from a friend of mine who runs the station. I got my tank filled up one morning, and the next morning I was back again and said, "Fill 'er up." He asked, "Where in the world have you been?" So I told him that I had been down to Yucca Valley, where I had spoken at a sunrise service and then a church service. You see, friend, when you are filled with the Spirit, you will do something for God; you will be walking in the Spirit. But that doesn't mean you will have enough for tomorrow. You need another infilling for tomorrow. The old gas tank needs another fill up.

This is the reason some people can be so mightily used of God one day and feel so empty the next. I have had that feeling, and I'm sure you have. We need a fresh infilling of the Holy Spirit. This will enable us to walk in the Spirit. We may stumble and fall at times. My little grandson is learning to walk and right now he has a bruised spot on his forehead and on his nose. But he gets up and tries again and someday he will be a good walker. God wants you and me to learn to walk in the Spirit. He wants us to be filled with the Spirit.

Now what is one of the evidences of being filled with the Holy Spirit? It is "speaking to yourselves in psalms and hymns and spiritual songs, singing and making melody in your heart to the Lord." It is a good thing that the Spirit of God said it was *speaking* one to another. If He had said *singing*, it would have left me out. I think "psalms" refers to the Book of Psalms, as probably all of them had been set to music. "Hymns" were composed by men to glorify God. They were on a very high plane. The "spiritual songs" were less formal than either psalms or hymns. Probably some of them were composed as the person was singing. This is the manifestation of the infilling of the Spirit because He brings joy into the life of the believer.

I'd like to mention one more thing about the comparison of being drunk with wine and being filled with the Spirit. I notice in motels and hotels where we stay as we go across the country that they have what they call the "happy hour" or the "attitude adjustment hour" or something else. Around five o'clock people go in, sit on a bar stool and drink so they will be sociable by six or seven and fit to live with for awhile. I have watched people go into those places, and they didn't look happy when they went in, but neither did they look happy when they came out.

Now, believers need an attitude adjustment, but they don't need the spirits that come from a bottle; they need to be filled with the Holy Spirit so that they might radiate the joy of the Lord. The apostle John says that one of the reasons he wrote his epistle was so that "your joy may be full" (see John 15:11). This fullness of joy is to be through our fellowship with the Father and with Jesus Christ (see 1 John 1:3–4). We ought to have a good time and we ought to have fun in the church—I don't mean a period of silliness—but the joy of the Lord should be there. That kind of joy comes through the filling of the Holy Spirit.

Giving thanks always for all things unto God and the Father in the name of our Lord Jesus Christ [Eph. 5:20].

Another evidence of being filled with the Spirit is an attitude of thankfulness. We note in the Book of Psalms a great amount of thanksgiving and praise to God. And it is on a high level. We don't have enough of that among believers today. We should all say, "Praise the Lord, and thanks be to God for His unspeakable gift." Can you say that from the heart? It is no good unless it comes from the heart. The filling of the Spirit produces a life of thankfulness so that we can honestly thank God for *all* things.

As I write this, there is a great deal of nonsense being promoted which I call sloppy agape. I heard recently, "Just say to everybody, 'I love you.'" My friend, if you don't love them, don't say it. If you do love them, *show* it.

Dr. Howard Kelly was a great surgeon and a great obstetrician. He wrote in the field of obstetrics, and his works were classic among doctors for a long time. He was also a great Christian, a wonderful man of God. The story is told of his taking a walk in the country outside the city of Baltimore in one of those lovely rural areas. He became thirsty and stopped at a farmhouse to ask for a drink of water. A little girl answered the door. She said that her parents had gone to town and there was no water in the house but there was cold milk down at the spring. Would he like a glass of milk? He said "I surely would." So he sat on the porch while she got a glass of milk and brought it to him. My, it was delicious! She asked, "Would you like another glass?" He said, "I surely would." So she brought him another glass. He thanked her, then went on his way down the road, thinking what a lovely little girl she was. Not many days later the little girl became sick. She had a pain in her side and was taken to the Johns Hopkins Hospital. Who do you suppose was the doctor who came in and examined her? It was Dr. Kelly, and he recognized her as the little girl who had given him the glasses of milk. He performed the necessary surgery and took special care of her. When it was time for her to go home, her parents came for her and waited anxiously for the bill because they didn't have the money to pay for the operation and the hospital costs. When the bill was presented to them, they opened it with trembling hands. Under the total balance was written, "Paid in full with two glasses of milk," signed "Dr. Howard Kelly." This was love in action, and the love he expressed was the fruit of the Spirit, because Dr. Kelly was a wonderful Christian.

My friend, you don't have to run around telling everyone you love them—*show* them that you love them. Be filled with the Spirit so there will be love and joy and thanksgiving in your life. This is very practical. This is down where the rubber meets the road.

Why don't you "drive into the filling station" and ask God to fill you up? The old gas tank is empty. You and I don't have anything worthwhile in ourselves. We need to go to Him and tell Him that we are empty and that we need the filling of the Holy Spirit so we can live for Him. We need to see that it is an impossibility by ourselves but that He can do it through us.

Let me repeat this because it is so important: we are told to be filled with the Holy Spirit—this is the only command given to the believer relative to the Holy Spirit. The other ministries of the Holy Spirit are accomplished in us when we receive Christ. Every believer is *regenerated* by the Holy Spirit. "But as many as received him, to them gave he power to become the sons of God . . ." (John 1:12). The believer is also *indwelt* by the Spirit. ". . . Now if any man have not the Spirit of Christ, he is none of his" (Rom. 8:9). And the believer is *sealed* by the Holy Spirit ". . . in whom also after that ye believed, ye were sealed with that holy Spirit of promise" (Eph. 1:13). Also the believer is *baptized* by the Holy Spirit. "For by one Spirit are we all baptized into one body . . ." (1 Cor. 12:13). These four ministries of the Holy Spirit take place the moment the believer puts his trust in Christ. It is all accomplished for us. The only thing which is left up to us is to obey His command to be *filled* with the Holy Spirit (see v. 18).

Submitting yourselves one to another in the fear of God [Eph. 5:21].

"Submit" is a very interesting word. It does not mean obey. Paul is not saying that the child of God is a buck private in the rear rank taking orders from somebody in the church who thinks he is a sergeant or a captain. We do take orders, but they are from the Captain of our salvation.

Joshua thought he was a general of the chil-

dren of Israel. He saw a Man with His sword drawn standing at the edge of the camp. He asked, ". . . Art thou for us, or for our adversaries?" If I may put it in good old Americana, he said, "Who told you to draw a sword? I'm the general here!" It was actually a rebuke. Then that One (who was the preincarnate Christ) turned and said, ". . . Nay; but as captain of the host of the LORD am I now come . . ." (Josh. 5:13–14). Joshua went down on his face and even took off his shoes because he was on holy ground. He learned that he had a Captain.

You and I are under a Captain, but the relationship is not military but on the basis of love. Our Lord said, "If ye love me, keep my commandments" (John 14:15). I think there is an alternative there: "If you don't love me, forget the commandments."

Now we see here that you and I are to submit ourselves "one to another in the fear of God." That doesn't mean we are to salute and fall down before some human being who outranks us. It does mean that in the fear of Christ we are to walk with one another in lowliness of mind.

If you will turn back to chapter 4, verses 1–2, you will see that Paul begins this section by saying that our walk should be in lowliness and meekness. That is the same thing that we have here. But notice in chapter 4 it begins with "I . . . beseech you." This is not a command. It is the language of love. The fires of Sinai have died down, and now it is based on what has been done by Christ at Calvary. It is based on the grace of God. "I therefore, the prisoner of the Lord, beseech you that ye walk worthy of the vocation wherewith ye are called, With all lowliness and meekness. . . ."

"Submitting yourselves one to another in the fear of God." This means that you do not try to run the church. Pastors, officers in the church, members of the church, all of us are to submit ourselves one to another in the fear of Christ. It cannot be a "my way" proposition. No one can say, "I want you to know that I'll do as I please. If I want to do it this way, I will do it this way." Such an attitude is not a mark of a Spirit-filled believer. Submitting ourselves one to another in the fear of God is another mark of being Spirit-filled.

Wives, submit yourselves unto your own husbands, as unto the Lord.

For the husband is the head of the wife, even as Christ is the head of the church: and he is the saviour of the body.

Therefore as the church is subject unto Christ, so let the wives be to their own husbands in every thing [Eph. 5:22–24].

I have been doing some research on that word *submit*, and I have some rather startling things to tell you. The word *submit* relative to wives needs to be understood a little differently from the way it has been so often interpreted in the past. It is not, "Wives, *obey* your husbands. *Submit* is a very mild word. It is a loving word. It means to respond to your own husband as unto the Lord. The way we respond to the Lord is that we love Him because He first loved us. And notice that it says "unto your own husbands." A very personal, loving relationship is the ground for submission. Paul is definitely speaking to believers about Christian marriage.

In this relationship of husband and wife, the man is the aggressor. He is the aggressor physically. He is the one who makes love. He is the aggressor in the home. He should be the breadwinner, the one who goes out with the lunch pail each day. And that doesn't give him the authority to be a top sergeant in the home either, by the way. The wife is to respond to him as the believer is to respond to Christ—in a love relationship.

A rough old boy came to my office one day with a request. He said, "Dr. McGee, I want you to talk to my wife. She's very cold, and she's not acting as a wife should." He didn't know it, but that was a dead giveaway—he was admitting failure as a husband. He showed what kind of a husband he was to draw that kind of response. I asked him, "Have you told her lately that you love her?" He said, "No. She knows I love her. I don't need to tell her that." I said to him, "I think you do. She does not need to tell you that she loves you until you say it first."

Woman is the responder, and man is the aggressor. The man is to say, "I love you," and he is the one who does the proposing. She is the one to say, "Yes." No woman is asked to say "I love you" to a man until he has said "I love you." When a man says he has a cold wife, it is because she has a cold husband. He is not being the husband that he should be. It is not her business to be the aggressor. Her role is the sweet submission of love.

"The husband is the head of the wife, even as Christ is the head of the church." In what way? It is a love relationship, and the husband is to be the head for the sake of order. You will find in this section of Ephesians that there are four different areas in which there is headship

for the sake of order. Wives are to be subject to their husbands. Husbands are to be subject to Christ. Children are to be subject to parents. Servants are to be subject to masters. It is to be a sweet subjection, a willing subjection to someone who loves you. It is to be that kind of relationship. If there is no love in it, the idea of submission isn't worth a snap of the finger.

I have done a great deal of marriage counseling in my day, and I would say that 75 percent of the fault in marriages is on the side of the men. It is the man who is to keep the lovelight burning. In the beautiful Song of Solomon, the bridegroom says to the bride, "Behold, thou art fair, my love; behold, thou art fair . . ." (Song 1:15), and she responds, "My beloved is mine, and I am his . . ." (Song 2:16). He expresses his love first, and then she responds.

I know someone will say I am very idealistic and romantic about all this. Well, back in the Garden of Eden God made them that way. God started off with a romantic pair, Adam and Eve. Probably He didn't give that woman to Adam until Adam realized that he needed someone. She was given as a *helpmeet*. A helpmeet is just the other half of man. Man is half a man without a wife. God joined them together and called them Adam—not the Adams.

Some young man will say, "Preacher, I'm not that kind of person. I'm no hero." May I say to you that God never said that every girl would fall in love with you. Ninety-nine women may pass you by and see in you only the uninteresting boy next door. But one day there will come a woman who will see in you the knight in shining armor. It is God who gives that highly charged chemistry between a certain man and a certain woman.

My wife told me she thought I was the knight in shining armor. I want to tell you how it ended. Perhaps you have seen the television commercial of a knight in armor riding across the screen holding a can of cleanser. Do you know where he ended up? In that kitchen! Now that I am retired, that is where I have ended up. A friend of mine told me, "Now that you are retired, do things with your wife. When she washes the dishes, you wash the dishes with her. When she mops the floor, you mop the floor with her!" Well, I'm not about to do that, but I surely do wash dishes more than I ever did before.

Now let me say a word to you if you are a young woman. Perhaps you are not beautiful of face or figure. God never said you would attract every male—only animals do that. Ninety-nine men will pass you by and see no more in you than what Kipling described as a rag, a bone, and a hank of hair. But one day there will come by a man who will love you if you are the right kind of person. You will become his inspiration. You may inspire him to greatness—perhaps to write a book or to compose a masterpiece. If you are his inspiration, do not ignore him, do not run from him. God may have put you together for that very purpose.

You may be saying, "Preacher, you're in the realm of theory. What you are talking about is idealistic. It sounds good in a storybook, but it doesn't happen in real life." You are wrong. It does happen.

Matthew Henry wrote the driest commentary I have ever read in my life, but, I want to tell you, he had a wonderful, romantic life as a young preacher. You would never think in reading his commentary that he was ever a romantic, but he was. In London he met a girl who belonged to the nobility. He was just a poor boy, but he fell in love with her and she loved him. Finally she went to her father to tell him about it, and her father tried to discourage her. He said, "That young man has no background. You don't even know where he came from." She answered, "You are right. I don't know where he came from, but I know where he is going, and I want to go with him!" And she did.

Nathaniel Hawthorne was a clerk. He worked in a government customs office in New York City, and he was fired for inefficiency. He came home and sat down discouraged and defeated. His wife came up and put her arm around him and said, "Now, Nathaniel, you can do what you always wanted to do: you can *write.*" He wrote *The House of the Seven Gables, The Scarlet Letter,* "The Great Stone Face", and other great works. So, you see, it does work out in life. It has worked out in the lives of multitudes of folk.

Paul's instructions regarding the home teach that the Christian home is to be a mirror of the relation between Christ and the church. Christ's relationship to the church is different from the relationship of husband and wife in that "Christ is the head of the church: and he is the saviour of the body." The husband is not the savior of the wife. But in the realm of submission the wife should be subject to the husband and to the Lord Jesus Christ.

THE EXPECTATION OF THE CHURCH

Husbands, love your wives, even as Christ also loved the church, and gave himself for it [Eph. 5:25].

God never asked a woman to submit to any man who doesn't love her and love her like this. Oh, this is Christian love on a high plane. Today young people are finding out about sex, and there are innumerable books on the subject of marriage. I may sound to you like an antiquated preacher when I say that they are nonsense. Only the Christian can know what is real love in marriage, because it is carried to the high plane of the relationship between Christ and the church. There is nothing else like that, my friend.

That he might sanctify and cleanse it with the washing of water by the word [Eph. 5:26].

"Christ also loved the church, and gave himself for it"—that is in the *past.* In the *present* He is sanctifying the church with the water of the Word of God. The cleanser, which is the Bible, is better than any cleanser advertised on radio or television. The Word of God will not only take out the soiled spots, it will keep you from getting further spots in your life.

That he might present it to himself a glorious church, not having spot, or wrinkle, or any such thing; but that it should be holy and without blemish [Eph. 5:27].

In the *future* He will present it to Himself a glorious church, without a spot or wrinkle but holy and without blemish. We will see the church presented to Christ as a bride adorned for her husband when we study the Book of Revelation. May I say that every woman is beautiful on her wedding day. I have officiated at many weddings during my lifetime, and I have never seen an ugly bride. I have seen them before and after their wedding day, and I can't honestly say that all of them are beautiful. But on the day of their marriage they are beautiful.

No young man engaged to a young lady thinks that she ought to be put through the fires of persecution or the Great Tribulation before he marries her. That is unheard of. So imagine anyone saying that the church must go through the Great Tribulation! She is engaged to *Him,* and He is cleansing the church by the washing of the Word of God. Keep in mind that when we use the word *church* we are not talking about an organization with a steeple, a pulpit, and an organ. We are talking about the body of true believers. This verse means that He is washing each believer, preparing each one for that great event. I believe that is something which is really taking place in our day.

So we have seen the past, present, and future. Christ loved the church and gave Himself for it. He is sanctifying the church with the washing of water by the Word. In the future the church will be presented to Him as a radiant bride with all sin removed. Then the church will be holy and unblamable.

So ought men to love their wives as their own bodies. He that loveth his wife loveth himself.

For no man ever yet hated his own flesh; but nourisheth and cherisheth it, even as the Lord the church:

For we are members of his body, of his flesh, and of his bones.

For this cause shall a man leave his father and mother, and shall be joined unto his wife, and they two shall be one flesh.

This is a great mystery: but I speak concerning Christ and the church [Eph. 5:28–32].

I have quoted this entire passage so you can see how Paul draws on these two themes and goes back and forth, husband and wife, Christ and the church. After talking about Christ and the church, the subject goes back to husband and wife: "So ought men to love their wives as their own bodies."

The thing a couple needs for their marriage ceremony is not a champagne supper. They both need to be filled with the Holy Spirit. They will have the greatest honeymoon that any couple ever had. Those sophisticated boys and girls who talk about sex and extramarital relationships today don't even know what real love is. They know a lot about sex, but they do not know anything at all about the beauty and the ecstasy and the sweetness of a real Christian marriage.

The husband is to love his wife because the marriage relationship makes the wife a part of his own body. It is like the church is the body of Christ and Christ is the head of that body. On this basis the husband is the head of the wife. It is unnatural for a man to hate his own flesh, so the husband is to love his wife because she is his own flesh.

Christ, knowing the weakness of the church, nourishes and cherishes her. Husbands are to do the same.

Verse 31 is a quotation from Genesis 2:24. Paul here refers to the relationship that existed in the Garden of Eden between Adam and Eve. That first couple is a figure of the future union of Christ and the church as Bridegroom and bride. Eve was created to be a helpmeet for Adam. She was taken from his side, not molded from the ground as were the animals. Adam was incomplete until they were together. God fashioned her, and I think she was the loveliest thing in creation when God brought her to Adam. One wag has said that she had to be better looking than man because God had practiced on man but He had experience when He made woman. She was a helpmeet for Adam. She compensated for what he lacked. She was made for him and they became one. In the Hebrew the word for "man" is *ish* and for "woman" it is *isha*. The word is almost the same—she was taken out of man.

I have two illustrations, taken from history, of this wonderful relationship between man and woman. That kind of thing is often lost today. The "new" morality and sexual freedom are putting a lot of young people in slavery. It simply will not work. God meant for Christians to have this relationship on a much higher plane.

The first illustration is the story of Abelard and Heloïse. When John Lord wrote his *Great Women*, he used Heloïse as the example of love, marital love. The story concerns a young ecclesiastic by the name of Abelard. He was a brilliant young teacher and preacher in what became the University of Paris. The canon had a niece by the name of Heloïse whom he sent to be under Abelard's instruction. She was a remarkable person; he was a remarkable man. You know the story—they fell madly in love. But according to the awful practice of that day the marriage of a priest was deemed a lasting disgrace. When John Lord wrote their story, he gave this introduction which I would like to share with you. It is almost too beautiful to read in this day. It is like a dew-drenched breeze blowing from a flower-strewn mountain meadow over the slop bucket and pigsty of our contemporary literature. Here is what he wrote:

When Adam and Eve were expelled from Paradise, they yet found one flower, wherever they wandered, blooming in perpetual beauty. This flower represents a great certitude, without which few would be happy,—subtle, mysterious, inexplicable,—a great boon recognized alike by poets and moralists, Pagan and Christian; yea, identified not only with happiness, but human existence, and pertaining to the soul in its highest aspirations. Allied with the transient and the mortal, even with the weak and corrupt, it is yet immortal in its nature and lofty in its aims,—at once a passion, a sentiment, and an inspiration.

To attempt to describe woman without this element of our complex nature, which constitutes her peculiar fascination, is like trying to act the tragedy of Hamlet without Hamlet himself,—an absurdity; a picture without a central figure, a novel without a heroine, a religion without a sacrifice. My subject is not without its difficulties. The passion or sentiment is degrading when perverted, it is exalting when pure. Yet it is not vice I would paint, but virtue; not weakness, but strength; not the transient, but the permanent; not the mortal, but the immortal,—all that is ennobling in the aspiring soul.

Abelard and Heloïse, having fallen in love, were not permitted by the church to marry. Therefore they were married secretly by a friend of Abelard. He continued to teach. But the secret came out when a servant betrayed them, and she was forced into a nunnery. Abelard was probably the boldest thinker whom the Middle Ages produced. At the beginning of the twelfth century he began to preach and teach that the Word of God was man's authority, not the church. This man, a great man, became bitter and sarcastic in his teaching because of what had been denied him. When he was on his deathbed, for he died a great while before Heloïse, being twenty years her senior, he asked that she be permitted to come to see him. The church did the cruelest thing of all—they would not allow her to come. Therefore he penned her a letter. To me it is the most pathetic thing I have ever read. He concludes it with this prayer: "When it pleased Thee, O Lord, and as it pleased Thee, Thou didst join us, and Thou didst separate us. Now, what Thou hast so mercifully begun, mercifully complete; and after separating us in this world, join us together eternally in heaven." And I believe in God's heaven they are together.

John Wesley's story is not told in England; it is told in this country, in Georgia. When John Wesley came as a young missionary to Georgia, the crown had already sent a nobleman out there—I think they wanted to get rid of him at court because he was an insipid fellow, devoid of personality and masculinity. Yet due to the terrible custom of that day, the nobility was entitled to marry the finest, and he had married a woman not only of striking beauty and strong personality, but one who was an outstanding Christian. Then there came into their colony this fiery young missionary. Again you know the story—they fell in love. And that happens to be John Wesley's love story. He begged her to flee with him and go live among the Indians. She said, "No, John, God has called you to go back to England, and He has called you to do some great service for Him." It was she who sent John Wesley back to England. The night came for his ship to sail; they had to wait for the tide and the wind, and she came down to bid him good-bye. Oh, yes, she held him that night and he held her, but even the worst critics of Wesley say that nothing took place that was wrong. He still begged her to go with him among the Indians and live. The biographer of Wesley says that he came down that gangplank twice, but she sent him back, back to England—to marry the Methodist church. He returned to England a brokenhearted man; yet she had become his inspiration.

It is God who gives this kind of love to believers who are filled with the Holy Spirit. May I say to the young people today: Don't accept anything that is second-rate. Don't take anything but the very best that God has to offer you.

Nevertheless let every one of you in particular so love his wife even as himself; and the wife see that she reverence her husband [Eph. 5:33].

"Nevertheless" brings us down to earth with a jolt. This is the practical part about marriage. Oh, how sin has marred this glorious relationship—as it has marred everything else—but this relationship can be yours if you want it to be the best.

Paul brings the reader back to the ordinary routine of Christian living in the home. "Let each love his wife as himself." This shows the kind of husband to whom the wife is to be in subjection. The husband and the wife in the home are to set forth in simplicity the mystery of the coming glory. This is a very practical application of that which is highly idealistic. He brings the romantic into the realm of reality.

CHAPTER 6

THEME: *The church is a soldier; the soldier's relationships; the soldier's enemy; the soldier's protection; the soldier's example—Paul was a good soldier of Christ; benediction*

In the preceding chapter the church was designated as the *bride* of Christ. Now in this chapter it is to be a good soldier of Jesus Christ. I have told you that my humorous friend says this sequence is to be expected—after a couple gets married, the war begins. Therefore, the church should be a good soldier. He was being facetious, of course. In the *future* the church is to be presented as the bride of Christ. This is the expectation of the church. Today is the period of the engagement and exhibition of the church before the world.

Now the chapter before us presents another side of the life of a believer. In the world today the church is to be a good soldier of Jesus Christ. In Ephesus there stood the great temple of Diana, one of the seven wonders of the ancient world. It stood for all that was pagan and heathen; it was grossly immoral. It was time for the believers in Ephesus to recognize that they had an enemy. Not only did the Christians in Ephesus have an enemy, but we have an enemy today. Our enemy is not the worship at the temple of Diana. I think we have something infinitely worse than that. We are seeing immorality and heathenism not only in the name of religion but actually in the name of *Christianity*—when it is not Christian at all!

The first part of the chapter opens with instructions to children, parents, servants, and masters. This may seem foreign to the life of a soldier. However, a soldier's training does not start in boot camp; it begins when he is a child in the home.

In World War II they had a saying in the navy that in the early days of our nation we had wooden ships and iron men, but now we have iron ships and paper-doll men. That is probably not entirely accurate, but a report from the Great Lakes Naval Training Station tells us that a shocking percentage of all young men in the United States attaining the age of navy enlistment years must be rejected because of previous criminal records and because of personality, psychological, or health problems; also an alarming number of all enlistees fail to measure up to recruit training. Severe problems are faced in the training of young men who must be trained in the simple things that should have been learned at home. At

seventeen a young man ought to be ready to launch into the training program. The navy finds that they can easily put a uniform on the man. It is putting a man into the uniform that is causing such problems.

This same type of breakdown is attested to by foreign mission boards. A survey reveals that a very small percentage of students graduating from Christian Bible schools and colleges go into foreign missions, and a startling number return after the first term as casualties. Training is essential if the soldier is to fight properly and be victorious over the enemy.

The preparation of a soldier must begin in the home when he is a child—not in the church or in the Sunday school but in the home. Every child who doesn't get that first lesson is handicapped. One of the great problems of our young people today, and some older ones too, is that they were not properly trained in the home. Proper training means discipline.

THE SOLDIER'S RELATIONSHIPS

Children, obey your parents in the Lord: for this is right [Eph. 6:1].

It is right because it is according to the will of God. It is actually more than right; it is just. It is a righteous thing to do because it is God's way.

The first lesson that a soldier must learn is obedience to those in authority. He must follow orders. This basic training is learned in the home. After the soldier has learned to obey, then he is in a position to be promoted to the rank of an officer where he gives commands to others. To know how to give orders depends largely on how the soldier learned to obey. This basic training is found in the home with the parent-child relationship, and then with the master-servant relationship. The victories of the Christian life are won in the home and in the place of business.

You will remember that it is said of the Lord Jesus that as a boy He went down to Nazareth, and He was subject to Joseph and Mary.

There are two essential factors which must be taken into account in this verse and in this section:

1. It is assumed that Paul is talking about a Christian home, a home such as he had been

discussing in chapter 5 regarding the marriage relationship. Obedience of children to parents is confined to the circumference of "in the Lord." Christian parents have the privilege of claiming their children for the Lord. I think we all should do that. Even where only one parent is a believer, he may claim his children for God. "For the unbelieving husband is sanctified by the wife, and the unbelieving wife is sanctified by the husband: else were your children unclean; but now are they holy" (1 Cor. 7:14). This, of course, does not mean that the child is a believer just because he has a Christian parent. It does mean that the parent has a right to claim that child.

Notice that it says, "Obey your parents in the Lord." I have great sympathy for a boy who accepts the Lord and has an unsaved father or mother. There may be times when such a child must obey God rather than men.

2. The word for "obey" here is different from the word found in verse 22 of chapter 5. The wife is to submit. The wife occupies a place of equality with the husband, and submission is merely a question of headship. Here the child is to obey as the servant is to obey—the same word is used in verse 5.

Disobedience to parents is the last and lowest form of lawlessness to occur on this earth. "This know also, that in the last days perilous times shall come. For men shall be lovers of their own selves, covetous, boasters, proud, blasphemers, disobedient to parents, unthankful, unholy" (2 Tim. 3:1–2). Disobedience to parents is one of the characteristics of the last days. Today we hear of many cases of children rejecting parental authority and even killing their parents! This is indicative of the times in which we live.

Of course there will come a time in a boy's life when he begins to rebel against his parents because it is time for him to move out and get married and start a home of his own. God has given him a nature that rebels against being a mama's boy, tied to his mama's apron strings for the rest of his life. God wants him to stand on his own two feet. This kind of rebellion, this struggle for independence, is different from disobedience.

When I was a pastor, I remember visiting in a home in which the father and I couldn't even carry on a conversation because his little boy occupied the center ring of the circus. He was a little circus himself, and if you ask me, the dear little fellow was a brat. The father said, "I just can't make that child obey me." The father weighed about two hundred pounds, and the boy weighed about thirty pounds. Yet the father said, "I just can't make him obey me." Well, I think he *could* have, and I think he *should* have. God intended for the father to make him obey at that age.

Honour thy father and mother; which is the first commandment with promise;

That it may be well with thee, and thou mayest live long on the earth [Eph. 6:2–3].

We have learned that the Ten Commandments are not the norm for Christian living—but that doesn't mean you can *break* them. A youngster in the home is to honor father and mother, and as we grow older we are to continue to honor them by the life that we live. (It is interesting that all the Ten Commandments are repeated in the New Testament with the exception of the commandment concerning the Sabbath day.) Honoring your father and mother carries with it a promise of long life to those who keep it (see Exod. 20:12), and that promise is repeated here. It is the first commandment with promise. The other commandments promised something if they were *not* kept, but they didn't promise anything if they were kept.

Samson and Absalom are two examples in Scripture of boys who did not follow this commandment, and their lives were short. Samson, a judge, died when he was a young man. Absalom rebelled against his father David, and he was killed when he was a young man.

And, ye fathers, provoke not your children to wrath: but bring them up in the nurture and admonition of the Lord [Eph. 6:4].

"Nurture" means discipline, and "admonition" means instruction. Bring them up in the discipline and instruction of the Lord. No such commandment was given to parents under the Law. Under grace there are always mutual responsiblities and interactive duties. The parent is not to vent a bad disposition on a child or punish him in a fit of rage. It is the parents' duty to teach the child the truths of the Scriptures and then to live them before the child. Don't provoke your children to wrath. As a believer, you are to live at home like a believer.

"Fathers" includes the mothers also. However, the emphasis, I think, is on the father because the disciplining and training of the child is actually his responsibility, but it does include the mother also.

Children are not to be provoked to anger.

This doesn't mean that they are to be treated as if they were a cross between an orchid and a piece of Dresden china. I think that the board of education should be applied to the seat of learning whenever it is needed. The writer of Proverbs had a great deal to say about this: "He that spareth his rod hateth his son: but he that loveth him chasteneth him betimes" (Prov. 13:24). "Chasten thy son while there is hope, and let not thy soul spare for his crying" (Prov. 19:18). "Foolishness is bound in the heart of a child; but the rod of correction shall drive it far from him" (Prov. 22:15). "Withhold not correction from the child: for if thou beatest him with the rod, he shall not die. Thou shalt beat him with the rod, and shalt deliver his soul from hell" (Prov. 23:13–14). "The rod and reproof give wisdom: but a child left to himself bringeth his mother to shame. . . . Correct thy son, and he shall give thee rest; yea, he shall give delight unto thy soul" (Prov. 29:15, 17).

There is the story of the father whipping the little boy and saying, "Son, this hurts me more than it hurts you." The boy replied, "Yeah, but not in the same place!"

These little ones who simply will not obey need to be spanked. They need a trip to the woodshed. A child should never be whipped while the parent is angry; this is stated very clearly. We are never to provoke our children to wrath, which will happen if they see that we are simply venting a mean disposition on them. They should be disciplined.

In Proverbs 23 we are told that when we spank our children they won't die. I can remember that my mother whipped me a great deal more than my father did. She was the one at home with us, so she would get a switch and she could make it hurt. I was such a good boy I don't know why it was that I got such a number of switchings! I did learn that if I would yell at the top of my voice, "You're killing me, you're killing me," she would always let up because she didn't want the neighbors to hear and say, "My, that poor boy's mother is killing him!" I found out it sort of softened the punishment. Of course, she wasn't trying to kill me. She was giving me the punishment I needed.

"Correct thy son, and he shall give thee rest . . . [and] delight unto thy soul"—a child in a Christian home should be given Christian instruction so that he might come to a vital relationship with Christ and be fortified when he comes in contact with the world. Every parent ought to have the privilege of leading his child to a saving knowledge of Christ.

My wife was never my assistant pastor—I insisted on that. I never let her become president of the missionary society or hold any office in any women's organization in any church that I served. When I accepted a pastorate, I told my board, "My wife is my *wife*. She is not the assistant pastor. Her business is to take care of the home and the child." I think that is important. My wife had the privilege that I'm afraid very few parents have today. I was out on a trip and my wife was visiting with her mother. Our daughter was about seven or eight years old at the time. She came in and said, "Mama, I want to accept Jesus." My wife took her into the bedroom and got down on her knees with her and had the privilege of leading her own little girl to the Lord. I always felt that this was much more important than to try to be a personal worker in the church. I know a great number of personal workers in the church who have lost their own children. My friend, your first responsibility is to your own child. You had better concentrate on that child—do that instead of tending to everyone else's business and trying to raise everyone else's children. I realize it won't make me popular to make such a statement, but God's Word makes it clear that He gives us the responsibility for our own children.

"Bring them up in the nurture [discipline] . . . of the Lord." Notice again that the discipline is to be *of the Lord*. The discipline and instruction are to be administered in the name of the Lord. That is important. Paul has taken the subject of submission first into the home with the husband and wife relationship, then with the parent-child relationship. Now he moves out of the home into the street, the workshop, the marts of trade. It is a different situation here, for there are no bonds of love such as are found in a home; yet children of God who are filled with the Holy Spirit will be submissive one to another.

Servants, be obedient to them that are your masters according to the flesh, with fear and trembling, in singleness of your heart, as unto Christ;

Not with eye-service, as men-pleasers; but as the servants of Christ, doing the will of God from the heart;

With good will doing service, as to the Lord, and not to men:

Knowing that whatsoever good thing any man doeth, the same shall he receive of the Lord, whether he be bond or free [Eph. 6:5–8].

Servants (lit., slaves) are to be obedient to masters according to the flesh, meaning the masters down here on earth. Servants are not to serve with eyeservice—with one eye on the clock or working only when the boss is looking. They are not to serve as "men-pleasers." In other words, they are not to butter up the boss. Service is to be done as the servants of Christ, doing the will of God from the soul.

There is a responsibility put upon a believer who is a laborer and also a responsibility put upon one who is a capitalist or an employer. This is the employer-employee relationship. In Paul's day it was an even sharper division than it is now—it was really master and slave. Remember that this entire section began in chapter 5, verse 21, which says, "Submitting yourselves one to another in the fear of God." That sounds all right for Sunday, for the church service, but what about Monday morning when we go to work? Christian workers working for Christian owners of the factory will not need a labor boss to go to the capitalist and tell him what to do. I know of several businesses run by dedicated Christians. They have chapel service on company time, and they pay their workers while they are attending chapel. They are prosperous—God has blessed them. They don't need a union. An employee in one of these companies told me, "If we were under a union, we wouldn't be making what we are making right here." We are talking about Christians, Christian workers and Christian owners. There are both sides to the coin. This gets right down to the nitty-gritty.

It is estimated that half of the 120 millions of people living in the Roman Empire were slaves. Christianity never attacked the evil of slavery. Rather it reached down to the slave in his degradation and lifted him up, assuring him of his liberty in Christ. The very nature of the gospel condemned slavery. It eventually broke the shackles of slavery from the bodies of men and cut the fetters from their minds and souls. Multitudes of slaves came to Christ, as we learn in Romans 16—many of those named there were slaves or members of the Praetorian guard.

In the United States of America the South had to lose the Civil War. I am a southerner, but I recognize the South had to lose because slavery was *wrong*. That doesn't mean that the North was right in the method used, but it does mean that the principle of slavery was wrong.

"Servants, be obedient to them that are your masters." Notice the Word of God says to "be *obedient*." This reveals that Christianity did not instigate revolution against the evil practice of slavery. It preached a gospel which was more revolutionary than revolution has ever been. Revolution has always had bad side effects, leaving bitterness and hatred which has lasted through the centuries. The gospel of Christ will break down the middle wall of partition—which in our day is prejudice and discrimination of one race against another—and will replace it with real brotherly love.

If the Word of God were preached as it was in the early days of these United States, and if those who profess to be Christian were obedient and loyal to those to whom they owe obedience and loyalty, it would change the entire complexion of American life today. A man is not a Christian just because he has made a profession of Christianity and calls himself a child of God on Sunday. Whether or not he is a genuine Christian is revealed by his loyalty to his employer, to his family, to his home, to his church, and to his pastor. When a professing Christian is disloyal in these areas of his life, the chances are he will also be disloyal to Christ. He certainly has no effective witness for Christ.

"Servants, be obedient to . . . your masters according to the flesh" makes it clear that slavery applied only to the bodies of men and not to their souls. This obedience was to be with "fear and trembling." This does not mean abject and base cringing before a master, but it does mean treating him with respect and dignity.

"In singleness of your heart" means there should not be any taint of duplicity. There should be no two-facedness. There should not be the licking of the boots of the employer when he is around and then stabbing him in the back when he is away. Such action should never be in the life of a Christian.

The servant's obedience is to be done "as unto Christ." This shows that the slave has been lifted from the base position of degradation where he sullenly worked as little as possible and only when his master was watching. Now he is the slave of Christ, and Christ has made him free. He is to look above the earthly master in his attempt to please his Master in heaven. An earthly master could control only the bodies of the slaves. The slaves of Christ have yielded their souls to Him, even their total personalities. Remember that Paul called himself the bondslave of Jesus Christ.

"With good will doing service" shows that their attitudes should reflect their Christian service. When a child of God—whether a slave or a master, employer or employee—gets to the place where the motive of his life is to please Christ, then the hurdles posed by capital and labor are easily passed over.

In our day there is a new kind of slavery, and it is sweeping over the nations of the world. In our own land there is a slavery that is not only of the body but of the mind. Such slavery is far more pernicious and deadly than that of the Roman Empire. Multiplied thousands are willing to make any sacrifice today to foreign ideology, and you can call it any name you choose.

I had the privilege of speaking to a group of university students from Berkeley, California. These young men, who are majoring in political economy, have turned to the Lord. There was a time when they were slaves to a particular system of political economy, but now they are delivered from that. One young man told me, "One time I thought we could manipulate the economy and that we could make everyone prosperous and happy. I see now that only Christ will be able to bring in that kind of a society. That doesn't mean we are not going to work for it, but it does mean that we know our goal is limited and only Christ can do it."

What can break a man's shackles? Only the power of the gospel of Christ. He will make you free. "If the Son therefore shall make you free, ye shall be free indeed" (John 8:36). It is Christ who offers freedom. Think of the thousands today who are trapped by drugs and by alcohol. There is slavery on every side of us.

We should be slaves to Christ and to no one or nothing else. Saul of Tarsus was a slave to an ideology. He was a Pharisee. When he came to Christ, he was made free. However, immediately he yielded to a new Master and said, ". . . Lord, what wilt thou have me to do? . . ." (Acts 9:6). He had become a bond-slave to Jesus Christ.

The Lord has lifted the employee to a high position; He has dignified labor. It doesn't make any difference whether a man is working at a bench or digging a ditch or working in an office or mining down in the bowels of the earth or farming the land on the top of the earth. If he is a child of God, he can say, "I serve the Lord Christ."

William Carey was a shoemaker who applied to go as a foreign missionary. Someone asked him, "What is your business?" meaning to humiliate him, because he was not an ordained minister. Carey answered, "My business is serving the Lord, and I make shoes to pay expenses." He was a servant of Christ. Oh, that men were that kind of workers to-day—it would change the whole labor scene.

And, ye masters, do the same things unto them, forbearing threatening: knowing that your Master also is in heaven; neither is there respect of persons with him [Eph. 6:9].

Something is also said to the masters. If you are an employer, before Christ you are just another man. God is no respecter of persons. What He has said to labor also applies to you. You come under the same category since you also have a Master, and your Master is Christ. This is the Christian relationship of capital and labor. The responsibilities are mutual. Masters are not to take advantage of their position as master. They are not to abuse their power. They are not to threaten. In the presence of Christ, the master and the servant stand on the same footing. They are brothers in Christ.

We find a very practical demonstration of this in the Epistle to Philemon. Philemon was a master who had a slave named Onesimus. Onesimus ran away from his master, and according to the law of that day, his master could have put him to death. However, after Onesimus trusted Christ, Paul sent him back to his master with the letter to Philemon. This is what Paul wrote: "For perhaps he therefore departed for a season, that thou shouldest receive him for ever; Not now as a servant, but above a servant, a brother beloved, specially to me, but how much more unto thee, both in the flesh, and in the Lord?" (Philem. 15–16). When both capital and labor are believers, they are brothers.

Don't tell me Christianity is not practical. It *is* practical, and it will work. A great Chinese Christian, who had attended college here in the United States and knew America pretty well, said, "It is not that in America Christianity has been tried and found wanting. The problem over there is it never has been tried." That is still the problem today—we have kept it behind stained glass windows. My friend, if Christianity cannot move out of the sanctuary and get down into the secular, there is something radically wrong. It will *work* if it is tried. It will work in this capital-labor relationship.

THE SOLDIER'S ENEMY

Now we come to the theme of this chapter, which is "the church is a good soldier of Jesus Christ." We have seen the Christian in his relationships: God begins with him in the home. Then God has something to say to him as he moves out into the world where he is either an employee or an employer—he has to be one or the other, and as a child of God he has to contribute to the welfare of contemporary society. He needs to be a producer one way or the other.

Now we learn of the soldier's enemy. There is a battle to be fought. One of the things that is commonly misunderstood today is that the child of God is in a battle, and the battle is being fought along *spiritual* lines.

If the duties which relate to the commonplace are not faithfully followed, there can be no great spiritual victories in the high realm of Christian attainments. It is pretty well known that I represent the fundamental position. I am premillennial, pretribulational, and a dispensationalist in my belief. I get a little weary and a little bored with folk who so insistently hold these same views, yet whose lives are lived in a very careless manner, not commensurate with this exalted, high position that we have. We are seated in the heavenlies! How wonderful. My friend, we are walking right down here on this earth, and our theology has to walk in shoeleather. If you are not living a life that pleases Christ, you are wasting your time attending Keswick conferences and Bible classes. Often in Christian circles we see a display of bitterness, vitriol, and hatred, which hurts the cause of Christ a great deal. Why is it that we can have so much exalted teaching and such low living? There are too many who are fundamental in their heads but liberal in their feet. There is a great danger in thinking that all we need is a head knowledge and a vocabulary so that we can spout out our position lucidly and fluently but can lead careless Christian lives. To do this is to misunderstand where the battle is being fought.

I do not think the Devil is concentrating in the nightclubs or on skid row or in the underworld or in the Mafia. I think he is concentrating on the church on Sunday morning. He is working on the spiritual front, and too many sleepy Christians seem to be totally unaware of that. Too many Christians are concerned about closing up the cocktail parlors when they need to be closing their mouths from gossiping and criticizing. The Devil is working in an area where we least expect to find him. He is not out on the town on Saturday night. He has gone to bed early so he can get up and go to church on Sunday morning. The spiritual battle is being fought wherever a man is giving out the Word of God, where a church is standing for the Word of God. That is the place the Devil wants to destroy, and that is the place of the spiritual battle.

Sometimes the most dangerous place you can be is in church on Sunday morning. Where was the most dangerous place in Jerusalem the night Jesus was arrested? Was it with the Pharisees? Was it with the cutthroats of the underworld? No. The most dangerous place was in the Upper Room with Jesus. Do you know why? That is where the Devil was that night. It is said that he entered into Judas Iscariot to betray Him. The Devil was *there*. I believe both Judas Iscariot and Simon Peter would testify to the fact that that was the most dangerous place to have been that night in Jerusalem. We need to recognize where the battle is being fought.

You may remember that at the beginning of our study in this Epistle to the Ephesians I compared it to the Book of Joshua. What Joshua is to the Old Testament, Ephesians is to the New Testament. Joshua led the children of Israel across the Jordan River into the land of Canaan, and there were enemies in the land. There were battles to be fought, and there were victories to be won.

The Jordan River is not a picture of our death, and the Promised Land is not a picture of heaven. If you want to sing "On Jordan's stormy banks I stand and cast a wistful eye," you may, but that does not speak of *our* death. It actually speaks of the death and resurrection of Jesus Christ, and you and I cross over—through the death and resurrection of Christ—*out* of the wilderness of this world *into* Canaan. The child of God should be living today in Canaan. Remember that Canaan does not represent heaven—it could not because there were enemies in Canaan and battles to be fought. You and I as believers are in the place of soldier service. The soldier's enemy is identified, and the battle is before us.

When Joshua entered the Promised Land, there were three enemies that confronted him. First there was the city of Jericho, standing right in the way. Jericho represents the world today. What Jericho was to Joshua, the world is to the Christian. Joshua was told to march around the city—not fight it. We cannot overcome the world by fighting the world. It is a mistake if we try that method. "For whatsoever is born of God overcometh the world: and this is the victory that overcometh the world, even our faith. Who is he that overcometh the world, but he that believeth that Jesus is the Son of God?" (1 John 5:4–5). The only way we can overcome the world is by our faith and trust in God. "Love not the world, neither the things that are in the world. If any man love the world, the love of the Father is not in him" (1 John 2:15). The things of the world are passing away, and the child of God is not to love them. Our experience here is to be a Canaan experience.

The second enemy confronted by Joshua was the little town of Ai. Ai represents the flesh. Joshua thought it would be easy to overcome Ai, so he sent up a small detachment, and they were really whipped. When they came back, Joshua got down on his face and began to whimper and cry before God. God told him, ". . . Get thee up; wherefore liest thou thus upon thy face? Israel hath sinned . . ." (Josh. 7:10–11). And that sin had to be confessed and put away before God would give Israel the victory. And this is what you and I must do if we are to overcome the flesh.

Many Christians have a victory over the world; they are marching around Jericho, tooting a horn as the children of Israel blew their trumpets, saying, "I don't do this and I don't do that." But they are being defeated by the flesh. They are overcome by temper. They are overcome by gossiping. One Christian man came to me and said, "Why in the world is it that I just continue to lie about everything?" Well, that's what the flesh will do. The flesh is getting the victory over many of us, my friend. Ai represents the flesh.

Then thirdly, Joshua had to contend with the Gibeonites. They were clever, sly rascals. They lived just over the hill, but they took old, moldy bread and wore worn-out shoes and made everything look as if they had come on a long journey. They came into the camp where Joshua was and said, "Brother, we have heard about you. My, we've heard how God delivered you from Egypt and gave you victories over Sihon and Og, and we want to make a treaty with you. We want to be your friends" (see Josh. 9:4–11). That is the way the Devil approaches *us*. He is the deceiver, and he makes his ministers seem like angels of light.

Someone described a leader of a cult by saying, "I listen to that man. He is so attractive, so personable. He is really wonderful, and what he says thrills me." Now listen to this and remember it: ". . . for Satan himself is transformed into an angel of light. Therefore it is no great thing if his ministers also be transformed as the ministers of righteousness; whose end shall be according to their works" (2 Cor. 11:14–15). Do you think that the Devil is going to knock at your door and say, "Look, I'm the Devil; I'm here to take you in; I'm here to fool you"? Obviously, that is not the way

the Devil will approach you. He will use every possible way to deceive you. He may send someone to knock at your door and offer you literature that will "explain" the Bible. Or, he may approach you this way if you are in a church that is going liberal: "Remember, grandpa had a pew in the church and that window over there is named for grandma. You can't afford to leave this church because you have so much invested here." The Word of God says, "Wherefore come out from among them, and be ye separate, saith the Lord . . ." (2 Cor. 6:17). And the Devil says, "But we really need you here, so why don't you just stick around?" You see, he is subtle.

The Gibeonites represent the Devil. They fooled Joshua, and he made a treaty with them. They were the ones who got him into trouble. At Ai the sin had to be confessed and dealt with severely before God would give them the victory, and that is the way we overcome the flesh. But what about the Gibeonites? Joshua made an alliance with them, and they gave him trouble. If we line up with Satan, we will find ourselves defeated. What can we do? Listen: We *cannot* overcome him ourselves. You and I are no match for the Devil. We are not even told to fight the Devil. We are told that God will fight for us.

Finally, my brethren, be strong in the Lord, and in the power of his might [Eph. 6:10].

Allow me to again use my translation: "Finally (in conclusion) be strengthened in the Lord, and in the power of His might. Put on the armor *(panoplian)* of God in order that ye may be able to stand against the strategems *(methodias)* of the Devil. For our wrestling is not against blood and flesh, but against the principalities, against powers, against the world rulers of this darkness, against the spiritual hosts of evil in the heavenly (places and things)."

Put on the whole armour of God, that ye may be able to stand against the wiles of the devil [Eph. 6:11].

What in the world is Paul talking about? He is talking about spiritual wickedness, about that which is satanic. Notice that he is coming to the end of the epistle and says, "In conclusion be strengthened in the Lord, and in the power of His might." You cannot overcome the Devil in your own strength and your own power. Paul is definitely making a play upon two Greek words: The *panoplian* of God is needed and available to meet the *methodias* of the

Devil. "Be strengthened in the Lord"—that is the only place you and I get power.

For we wrestle not against flesh and blood, but against principalities, against powers, against the rulers of the darkness of this world, against spiritual wickedness in high places [Eph. 6:12].

The enemy whom the Christian is to fight is *not* flesh and blood. The enemy is spiritual, and the warfare is spiritual. That is why we need spiritual power. It is well to note that the flesh of the believer is not the enemy to be fought. The believer is to reckon the flesh dead and to *yield* to God. The way of victory over the flesh is outlined in Romans 6. Fighting the old nature will lead to defeat, and Paul records such an experience in Romans 7.

It is only God's armor which can withstand the strategy and onslaught of Satan who has all kinds of weapons (spiritual missiles). We need an antimissile system if we are going to overcome him. That is why it is so important for the Christian soldier to recognize that he does not fight an enemy who is flesh and blood. We are not to fight other men. The enemy is spiritual, and the warfare is spiritual. The Devil is the enemy of every believer and the one here whom we are told we fight. The way to victory over the Devil is to obey the commands to "put on the whole armour of God" and "to stand" (v. 11).

We are in a spiritual battle. The Devil has in battle array his minions arranged by ranks. It says that we wrestle against them. This speaks of the hand-to-hand encounter with the spiritual forces of wickedness. The translation of verse twelve is not as strong as it should be. It should actually read, "For our wrestling is not against blood and flesh, but against the principalities, against powers, against the world rulers of this darkness [and these are all spiritual], against the spiritual hosts of evil in the heavenly places." This is our warfare, and it's in progress now.

There is a demonic world around us and it is manifesting itself at the present hour. If I had said this when I was a young preacher, many would not have believed it. Or they would have said as did one dear lady, "Dr. McGee, you sound positively spooky." Today, however, demonism is a popular subject and is plainly exhibited. We have the Church of Satan in many of our cities. There are strange things happening to certain of these weird, way-out groups. A man said to me recently, "Dr. McGee, this thing is real today." Who said it wasn't real? If you are an unbeliever in this area, open your eyes and

see what is happening about us. People are being ensnared and led into all kinds of demonism. There are spiritual forces working in the world, evil forces working against the church. They are working against the believer, against God, against Christ. Don't try to pooh-pooh these things. It is happening, and you and I alone are no match for it.

The fact that there is a spiritual enemy to overcome is well illustrated in the tenth chapter of the Book of Daniel. Daniel had been praying, and he didn't get any answer. He had been praying for three weeks. "In those days I Daniel was mourning three full weeks. I ate no pleasant bread, neither came flesh nor wine in my mouth, neither did I anoint myself at all, till three whole weeks were fulfilled" (Dan. 10:2–3). Finally, an angel came and touched him and said, ". . . O Daniel, a man greatly beloved, understand the words that I speak unto thee, and stand upright: for unto thee am I now sent. And when he had spoken this word unto me, I stood trembling. Then said he unto me, Fear not, Daniel: for from the first day that thou didst set thine heart to understand, and to chasten thyself before thy God, thy words were heard, and I am come for thy words" (Dan. 10:11–12). If that was true, then Daniel had every right to ask, "Then where in the world have you been for three weeks?" Listen to the angel continue, "But the prince of the kingdom of Persia withstood me one and twenty days: but, lo, Michael, one of the chief princes, came to help me; and I remained there with the kings of Persia" (Dan. 10:13). He was in conflict with a demon, and he had to go back for reinforcement. This was a spiritual battle that was going on, and we likewise have one today.

We have said that these powers are organized. *Principalities* are the demons who have the oversight of nations. They would correspond to the rank of generals. *Powers* are the privates who are the demons wanting to possess human beings. The *rulers of* the *darkness of this world* are those demons who have charge of Satan's worldly business. *Spiritual wickedness in high places* are the demons in the heavenlies who have charge of religion.

Satan has a well-organized group, and his organization is manipulating in this world right now. The heartbreak, the heartache, the suffering, the tragedies of life are the work of Satan in the background. He is the cause of the great problems that are in the world today.

We have the enemy located and identified. That enemy is spiritual. It is Satan who heads up his demonic forces. Now we need to recognize where the battle is. I think the church has largely lost sight of the spiritual battle. We feel that if we have a lovely church building and are attracting crowds and if the finances are coming in, everything is going nicely. The financial condition of a church, however, is not where the battle is. I will grant that, if a church which has been supporting itself begins to get into debt, it is an indication that something is wrong: actually, it means the battle is being lost in the spiritual realm. There should be questions such as: Are the members of the church being built up in Christ? Is the Word of God being taught? Is there a spirit of love and cooperation among the members? Is gossip reduced to a minimum? There must not be an exercise in legalism but an exercise in right relationships among those who are the brethren in Christ. Where there is a spirit of criticism and of bitterness and of hatred, the Spirit of God cannot work.

Churches like to talk about the numbers who come to Christ. They like to talk about how many decisions they have had. Yet when the facts are really boiled down and examined and you look for the so-called converts two years later, you often find that they have disappeared. We don't seem to realize that there is a spiritual warfare being carried on today and that people need to be grounded in the Word of God. It is a manifestation of demonic power that people are being blinded and carried away into all kinds of cults and religions and "isms" with false beliefs. As a result of all this, the Word of God sinks into insignificance in such churches and organizations. This is the work of the enemy, Satan and his demonic hosts.

THE SOLDIER'S PROTECTION

Wherefore take unto you the whole armour of God, that ye may be able to withstand in the evil day, and having done all, to stand [Eph. 6:13].

We have identified the enemy. Now Paul begins to identify the arsenal which is available for defense. Nowhere is the believer urged to attack and advance. The key to this entire section is the phrase *to stand*.

The Bible speaks of believers as pilgrims. As pilgrims we are to walk through the world. The Bible speaks of us as witnesses, and we are to go to the ends of the earth. As athletes we are to run. We are to run with our eyes fixed upon the Lord Jesus Christ: ". . . and let us run with patience the race that is set before us, Looking unto Jesus the author and finisher of our faith . . ." (Heb. 12:1–2). However, when the Bible speaks of us as fighters, it says we are to stand. Very frankly, I would rather do a great deal of old-fashioned standing than fighting.

Many years ago Billy Sunday, the evangelist, attracted a great deal of attention by saying that up on the speaker's platform he was fighting the Devil. I think that there was a great element of truth in that, because it was a spiritual battle. The battle is carried on wherever the Word of God is preached and the gospel is given out. That's the battle line today. That is where the enemy is working. The enemy is not working down on skid row or partying it up on Saturday night.

Years ago when I was active in Youth for Christ as a young preacher, I was out every Saturday night. We used to say at that time that Saturday night was the Devil's night and we were making it the Lord's night. Well, now that I have had many more years to observe the situation, I think the Devil was at home in bed. I think he was resting up so he could come to church the next morning. Why should he want to fight his own crowd? They belong to him. I'm not sure he's proud of them. In fact, I think he's ashamed of a lot of these alcoholics and these down-and-outers and these up-and-outers. He could take no pride in them. He would rather be out fighting where the spiritual battle is.

Personally, I never felt that I should carry on that battle. That is, I never felt I should make the attack. The command is to stand. It is the Devil who will make the attack. Our command is, "Having done all, to stand."

I have never been enthusiastic about a group of defeated Christians singing, "Onward, Christian soldiers, marching as to war." I think it is more scriptural for the believer to sing, "Stand up, stand up for Jesus, ye soldiers of the cross." Just to be able to stand in an evil day is a victory for the believer.

This is an hour when my heart is sad as I look at a great many churches. I love the local church and the local pastors. There are a great number of wonderful pastors fighting the battle. They are the men who are really on the battlefront today. I go to so many Bible conferences as a speaker because I want to help them. I have been a pastor long enough to know how wonderful it felt and how I always appreciated it when others came to me and stood shoulder to shoulder with me. My heart is sick when I see the attendance way down and the interest gone in churches that at one time were great churches. The members were blind to the fact that a battle was being fought there, a spiritual battle.

Do you pray for your pastor on Saturday night? Don't criticize him, but rather *pray* for him. He needs your prayers. The Devil gives him enough opposition. You don't need to join the crowd that crucifies the man who is preaching the Word of God. You ought to uphold his hands as Aaron and Hur upheld the hands of Moses on behalf of Israel. My heart goes out to pastors who are in need of congregations who will stand with them.

Stand therefore, having your loins girt about with truth, and having on the breastplate of righteousness;

And your feet shod with the preparation of the gospel of peace [Eph. 6:14–15].

"Stand therefore." This is the fourth time he gives this exhortation to the believer. This is the only place that I find Paul laying it on the line and speaking like a sergeant. Earlier he said, "I beseech you," but now he gives the command to stand. Not only are we to be in a standing position, but we are also to have on certain armor to protect ourselves. We are not to be outwitted by the wiles of the Devil; we are to be ready for his attacks.

"Having your loins girt about with truth." In the ancient garment of that day, the girdle about the loins held in place every other part of the uniform of the soldier. It was essential. To tell you the truth, if the girdle was lost, you lost everything. The garments would fly open and the pants would fall down. We see this routine in comedies, and the people laugh to see a man trying to run or fight with his trousers drooping down. It looks funny in a comedy routine, but it is not funny in a battle. A great battle in the past, we are told, was won by a clever general who told his men to cut the belts of their enemy while they were sleeping. The next morning the enemy troops were so busy holding up their trousers that they weren't able to shoot their guns and, therefore, they lost the battle. We are told to be girded with truth in the face of the enemy. Truth is that which holds everything together. What is that truth? It is the Word of God.

We need people to give out the Word of God and to give it out just as it is written. Today we have many people giving testimonies. We have football players, baseball players, movie stars, television stars, all giving testimonies. Many of them do not know any more Bible than does a goat grazing grass on a hillside.

We need people whose loins are girt about with truth. They need to *know* the Word of God. (I could give you the names of a dozen personalities who have gone off on all sorts of tangents, into cults and "isms.") I admit that some testimonies are thrilling to hear, but they are coming from folk who are standing there about to lose all their spiritual garments! They are not girded about with truth, which is the Word of God.

Every piece of this armor really speaks of Christ. We are in Christ in the heavenlies, and we should put on Christ down here in our earthly walk. Paul has already told us to put on Christ. He is the One who is the truth, and we should put Him on in our lives.

Any testimony that does not glorify Jesus Christ should not be given. There are too many testimonies that glorify the individual, such as, "I was a great athlete," or, "I was a great performer, and now I am turning over my wonderful talent to Jesus." The implication is: *Believe me, He is lucky to have me in His crowd!* Friend, you are lucky if you have *Him.* He didn't get very much when He got you, and He didn't get very much when He got me. This is a day when the little fellow really doesn't have very much to say. We get the impression that we need to be someone great in the eyes of the world. No, what we need is to have our loins girt about with truth so that we can give a testimony that glorifies Christ. Christ is the truth. Truth alone can meet error.

"Having on the breastplate of righteousness." Christ is the righteousness of the believer. I do think, however, that it includes the practical righteousness of the believer. Let's be clear that the filthy rags of self-righteousness are useless as a breastplate, but I do think that underneath there should be a heart and a conscience that is right with God. Only the righteousness of Christ can enable the believer to stand before men and before God, but the heart that is to be protected should be a heart that is not condemning the believer. It is an awful condition to have sin in the life while we are trying to carry on the battle. We can never win it that way.

"Your feet shod with the preparation of the gospel of peace." Shoes are necessary for standing. They speak of the foundation. We need a good, solid foundation, and preparation is foundational. I remember in hand-to-hand combat we were taught to make sure our feet were anchored. Are your feet anchored on the Rock? Christ is your foundation in this world. No other foundation can any man lay but the one that is laid, Jesus Christ (see 1 Cor. 3:11). We are to put on Christ. Oh, how we need Him today as we face a gainsaying world and also spiritual wickedness in the darkness of this world!

Above all, taking the shield of faith, wherewith ye shall be able to quench all the fiery darts of the wicked.

And take the helmet of salvation, and the sword of the Spirit, which is the word of God:

Praying always with all prayer and supplication in the Spirit, and watching thereunto with all perseverance and supplication for all saints [Eph. 6:16–18].

The armor of the believer is a spiritual armor because we fight against a spiritual enemy. We are to stand in that armor, and that armor is Christ, the living Christ. Satan himself, in the Book of Job, describes how God protects His own. He said, "Hast not thou made an hedge about him, and about his house, and about all that he hath on every side? . . ." (Job 1:10). God has provided protection for us today in the armor He supplies.

"Above all, taking the shield of faith." The shield covered all of the armor. The shield referred to is a large shield the size of a door. It was the shield of the heavy infantry. A soldier stood behind it and was fully protected. Christ is both the door to salvation and the door that protects the believer from the enemy without. This is the picture in John, chapter 10. Christ is both salvation and security.

"Faith" enables us to enter the door: "I am the door: by me if any man enter in, he shall be saved, and shall go in and out, and find pasture" (John 10:9). That is salvation. What about security? Faith places us securely in His hands: "My sheep hear my voice, and I know them, and they follow me: And I give unto them eternal life; and they shall never perish, neither shall any man pluck them out of my hand" (John 10:27–28). Faith enables us to lay hold of the Lord Jesus Christ. Faith also enables us to stand behind that shield which will quench all the fiery darts of the wicked one.

"The fiery darts of the wicked." He is shooting them fast and furiously. I remember that when I was in college, I had a brilliant philosophy professor who had studied in Germany. I respected his intellect, although I didn't realize at the time that he was intellectually dishonest. I looked up to him but, very frankly,

he was taking my feet out from under me. I would try to answer him in class when I probably should have kept my mouth shut. But we became friends, and we used to walk together across the campus after class and discuss the questions I had raised. I came to the place where I went to the Lord in prayer and said, "Lord, if I can't believe Your Word, I don't want to go into the ministry." Then the Lord in a very miraculous way sent me to hear a man who was the most brilliant man, I think, whom I have ever heard. He gave me the answer to my questions. Then I began to learn that when a fiery dart comes my way and I don't have the answer, I am to put up the shield of faith. And this is what I have been doing ever since. I have found that the shield of faith has batted down the fiery darts of the wicked one.

I remember that I was upset about questions concerning the Genesis record of creation. I was ready to get out of the ministry because I couldn't accept certain things. The problem was not with my pygmy intellect, although I thought it was at the time; I just didn't know enough. So I put up the shield of faith.

Someone was walking with me in Israel as we were observing some excavations. He asked me, "Suppose they dig up something down there that looks like it disproves the Bible. What position would you take?" I answered, "I would put up the shield of faith, and that would bat down the fiery darts of the wicked one. I have learned that when a fiery dart is batted down, I will get the correct answer later on." I remember a time when the authorship of John was being questioned—was the Gospel of John written by John? Today it is pretty well established that John was the writer, but at one time I had questions about it.

The fiery darts of the wicked one come fast and furiously, and they are going to continue to come. The only thing that will bat them down is this shield of faith. It is like a big door. The hoplites, the heavily armed soldiers in the Greek infantry, could move with those tremendous shields, put them out in front of them, and stand protected shoulder to shoulder, while the enemy shot everything they had at them. When the enemy was out of ammunition, they would move in, certain of victory. That is the way to stand against the fiery darts of the evil one.

"And take the helmet of salvation." The helmet protects the head, and God does appeal to the mind of man. I recognize that He appeals to the heart, but God also appeals to the intellect. Throughout the Scriptures God uses reason with man. "Come now, and let us reason together, saith the LORD: though your sins be as scarlet, they shall be as white as snow; though they be red like crimson, they shall be as wool" (Isa. 1:18). "And as he reasoned of righteousness, temperance, and judgment to come, Felix trembled, and answered, Go thy way for this time; when I have a convenient season, I will call for thee" (Acts 24:25). Paul reasoned with Felix; he appealed to the mind of the man as well as to his heart. "So then faith cometh by hearing, and hearing by the word of God" (Rom. 10:17).

A theology professor who was a liberal said many years ago when I was a student, "Faith is a leap in the dark." That is not true. God does not ask you to take a leap into the dark. In fact, God says if it is a leap in the dark, don't take it. God wants you to leap into the light. God has a solid foundation for you, and how wonderful it is!

Christ is the salvation of the sinner. He is the One to receive the glory in it all. That plume on the top of the helmet is Christ. He has been made unto us salvation. "And she shall bring forth a son, and thou shalt call his name JESUS: for he shall save his people from their sins" (Matt. 1:21). Even before His birth in Bethlehem He was marked out as the Savior.

Paul mentions this helmet in connection with salvation again in another epistle. "But let us, who are of the day, be sober, putting on the breastplate of faith and love; and for an helmet, the hope of salvation" (1 Thess. 5:8).

All the parts of the armor mentioned so far have been for defense. Have you noticed that? Everything is for the front of the individual. There is no protection for his back; nothing is provided for retreat. Believe me, a retreating Christian is certainly open season for the enemy; the enemy can get through to him.

Now we have two weapons for offense. The first one is the Word of God, called the sword of the Spirit. "For the word of God is quick, and powerful, and sharper than any two-edged sword, piercing even to the dividing asunder of soul and spirit, and of the joints and marrow, and is a discerner of the thoughts and intents of the heart" (Heb. 4:12). Christ is the living Word of God. He used the Word of God to meet Satan in the hour of His temptation. Out of His mouth goeth a sharp two-edged sword in the battle of Armageddon (see Rev. 1:16; 19:21). He gains the victory with that sword. What is it? It is the Word of God.

We need that sharp sword going out of our mouths today. The Word of God is a powerful weapon of offense. You and I are to use it.

Our second weapon of offense is prayer—"praying always with all prayer and supplication in the Spirit." Praying in the Holy Spirit is not turning in a grocery list to God. It means that you and I recognize our enemy and that we lay hold of God for spiritual resources. We lay hold of God for that which is spiritual that we might be filled with all the fullness of God. Paul here distinguishes between prayer and supplication. Prayer is general; supplication is specific. All effective prayer must be in the Spirit.

THE SOLDIER'S EXAMPLE—PAUL WAS A GOOD SOLDIER OF JESUS CHRIST

Here is Paul's example for us from his own experience:

And for me, that utterance may be given unto me, that I may open my mouth boldly, to make known the mystery of the gospel,

For which I am an ambassador in bonds: that therein I may speak boldly, as I ought to speak [Eph. 6:19–20].

"And for me." Paul now asks for prayer on behalf of himself. As he comes to the conclusion of this epistle, he moves into the area of the personal. He was a prisoner in Rome, and he suffered from a thorn in the flesh. Yet he does not ask for prayer that these physical handicaps be removed, but that he might proclaim courageously the mystery of the gospel.

"To make known the mystery of the gospel." The gospel is a mystery that was not revealed in the Old Testament as it is now. The New Testament reveals that Christ died for all sins, was buried, rose again on the third day. This is the gospel and the message Paul was preaching.

"I am an ambassador in bonds." Paul had just written about the spiritual warfare, and now we see that he was experiencing the onslaught of the enemy at the very moment he was writing.

"That therein I may speak boldly." Paul asks for prayer that he may speak the gospel with boldness. We need that same prayer. We need a boldness to declare the Word of God.

But that ye also may know my affairs, and how I do, Tychicus, a beloved brother and faithful minister in the

Lord, shall make known to you all things:

Whom I have sent unto you for the same purpose, that ye might know our affairs, and that he might comfort your hearts [Eph. 6:21–22].

Tychicus not only carried the epistle to the Ephesian believers, but he also gave a personal account of the conditions of and the prospects for the apostle Paul. Tychicus, the pastor of the Ephesian church, is an example of the many faithful servants of Christ in the early church. The apostle Paul had great confidence in him.

"That he might comfort your hearts." Tychicus would allay any fears that the Ephesians might have about the condition of the apostle Paul. The brotherly love exhibited in the early church is the undertone of all of Paul's epistles. Paul had a real concern for the brethren.

BENEDICTION

General Douglas MacArthur said that old soldiers do not die; they just fade away. Listen to Paul's farewell.

Peace be to the brethren, and love with faith, from God the Father and the Lord Jesus Christ.

Grace be with all them that love our Lord Jesus Christ in sincerity. Amen [Eph. 6:23–24].

Paul's own swan song is found in 2 Timothy 4:6–8: "For I am now ready to be offered, and the time of my departure is at hand. I have fought a good fight, I have finished my course, I have kept the faith: Henceforth there is laid up for me a crown of righteousness, which the Lord, the righteous judge, shall give me at that day: and not to me only, but unto all them also that love his appearing." Paul reflected what a good soldier of Christ should be and what rewards awaited him.

He closes with a twofold benediction. Most of the great words of the gospel are contained in it: peace, love, faith, grace. Hope is absent, for the believer is in the heavenly places where all is realized.

"Peace" was the form of greeting of the Jewish world. A sinner must know the grace of God before he can experience the peace of God. This is the peace of God which passes all understanding.

"Love" in verse 23 means love for the other believers. This is a fruit of the Holy Spirit.

In verse 24 the "love" is of the believer for the Lord Jesus Christ, and this love is *in incorruptness* (a better translation than "in sincerity").

"Faith" means faith in Christ which produces active love. These flow from God the Father and the Lord Jesus Christ.

"Grace" is the key word of the epistle. It opened the epistle (Eph. 1:2) and is the subject of the epistle (Eph. 2:7–8). It now concludes the epistle. It is a fitting word because it is God's grace which saved us and which sustains us today.

BIBLIOGRAPHY

(Recommended for Further Study)

Bruce, F. F. *The Epistle to the Ephesians.* Westwood, New Jersey: Fleming H. Revell Co., 1961.

Foulkes, Francis. *The Epistle of Paul to the Ephesians.* Grand Rapids, Michigan: Wm. B. Eerdmans Publishing Co., 1963.

Hendriksen, William. *Exposition of Ephesians.* Grand Rapids, Michigan: Baker Book House, 1967.

Hodge, Charles. *An Exposition of Ephesians.* Grand Rapids, Michigan: Wm. B. Eerdmans Publishing Co., 1856.

Ironside, H. A. *In the Heavenlies.* Neptune, New Jersey: Loizeaux Brothers, 1937. (Especially good for young Christians.)

Kelly, William. *Lectures on Ephesians.* Oak Park, Illinois: Bible Truth Publishers, n.d.

Kent, Homer A., Jr. *Ephesians: The Glory of the Church.* Chicago, Illinois: Moody Press, 1971. (An excellent, inexpensive survey.)

McGee, J. Vernon. *Exploring Through Ephesians.* Pasadena, California: Thru the Bible Books, 1961.

Meyer, F. B. *Ephesians—Key Words of the Inner Life*. Fort Washington, Pennsylvania: Christian Literature Crusade, n.d. (Devotional.)

Moule, Handley C. G. *Studies in Ephesians*. Grand Rapids, Michigan: Kregel Publications, 1893. (Excellent. Romans, Philippians, Colossians, and Philemon in the same series; 2 Timothy apart from this series.)

Paxson, Ruth. *Wealth, Walk, and Warfare of the Christian*. Westwood, New Jersey: Fleming H. Revell Co., 1939. (Excellent devotional emphasis.)

Strauss, Lehman. *Devotional Studies in Galatians and Ephesians*. Neptune, New Jersey: Loizeaux Brothers, 1957.

Vaughan, W. Curtis. *Ephesians: A Study Guide Commentary*. Grand Rapids, Michigan: Zondervan Publishing House, n.d.

Wiersbe, Warren W. *Be Rich*. Wheaton, Illinois: Victor Books, n.d.

Wuest, Kenneth S. *Ephesians and Colossians in the Greek New Testament*. Grand Rapids, Michigan: Wm. B. Eerdmans Publishing Co., 1953.

The Epistle to the
PHILIPPIANS
INTRODUCTION

The Epistle of Paul to the Philippians is one of the Prison Epistles. Paul wrote four epistles when he was in prison, and we have labeled them Prison Epistles. They are Ephesians, Philippians, Colossians, and the little Epistle to Philemon.

The Epistle of Paul to the Philippians was written to the believers in Europe in the city of Philippi. This letter came out of a wonderful relationship that Paul had with the Philippian church. It seems that this church was closer to Paul than was any other church. Their love for him and his love for them are mirrored in this epistle. This epistle deals with Christian experience at the level on which all believers should be living. It is not a level on which all of us are, but it is where God wants us to be.

Paul visited Philippi on his second missionary journey. You will recall that he and Barnabas went on their first missionary journey to the Galatian country, where they had a wonderful ministry and founded many churches in spite of the persecution they encountered. Paul wanted to visit these churches on his second missionary journey. He wanted to take Barnabas with him again, but Barnabas insisted on taking his nephew, John Mark, who had been with them at the beginning of the first missionary journey. This young fellow, John Mark, you may remember, turned chicken and ran home to mama when they had landed on the coast of Asia Minor. Therefore, Paul did not want to take him the second time. So this split the team of Paul and Barnabas. Barnabas took John Mark and went in another direction. Paul, with Silas for a companion, retraced his steps into the Galatian country, visiting the churches which they had established on the first missionary journey.

It would seem that Paul intended to widen his circle of missionary activity in that area, because a great population was there, and it was highly civilized. Actually, Greek culture and Greek learning were centered there at this particular time. Dr. Luke in recording it says that Paul attempted to go south into Asia, meaning the province of Asia, of which Ephesus was the leading city. But when he attempted to go south, the Spirit of God put up a roadblock. Since he wasn't to go south, Paul thought he would go north (where Tur-

key is today), but when ". . . they assayed to go into Bithynia . . . the Spirit suffered them not" (Acts. 16:7).

Now he can't go south, he can't go north, he has come from the east, there is but one direction to go. So Paul went west as far as Troas. That was the end of the line. To go west of Troas he would have to go by boat. So Paul was waiting for instructions from God.

Sometimes we feel that God must lead us immediately, but God can let us wait. I think He lets us cool our heels many times, waiting for Him to lead us. If you are one who is fretting today, "Oh, what shall I do? Which way shall I turn?" Wait, just wait. If you are really walking with the Lord, He will lead you in His own good time.

So Paul continued to wait in the city of Troas (we know it as Troy) for orders, and he got them finally. He was given the vision of the man of Macedonia, recorded in Acts 16:9–10.

Paul and his companions boarded a ship that took them to the continent of Europe. To me this is the greatest crossing that ever has taken place because it took the gospel to Europe. I am thankful for that because at this particular time my ancestors were in Europe. One family was in the forests of Germany. I am told that they were as pagan and heathen as they possibly could have been. Another branch of the family was over in Scotland. And they, I am told, were the filthiest savages that ever have been on topside of this earth. Now don't you look askance at me, because your ancestors were probably in the cave right next to my ancestors and they were just as dirty as mine were. I thank God today that the gospel went in that direction, because somewhere down the line some of these ancestors heard the Word of God, responded to it, and handed down to us a high type of civilization.

So Paul crossed over into Europe, and his first stop was Philippi. "And on the sabbath we went out of the city by a river side, where prayer was wont to be made; and we sat down, and spake unto the women which resorted thither. And a certain woman named Lydia, a seller of purple, of the city of Thyatira, which worshipped God, heard us: whose heart the Lord opened, that she attended unto the things which were spoken of Paul. And when she was baptized, and her household, she besought us, saying, If ye have judged me to be faithful to the Lord, come into my house, and abide there. And she constrained us" (Acts 16:13–15).

Paul, you see, found out that the man of Macedonia was a woman by the name of Lydia, holding a prayer meeting down by the river. That prayer meeting probably had a lot to do with bringing Paul to Europe. I'm of the opinion there were many people in Philippi who saw that group of women down there by the river praying and thought it wasn't very important. But it just happened to be responsible for the greatest crossing that ever took place! And Lydia was the first convert in Europe.

Now Lydia was a member of the Philippian church to which Paul wrote this epistle. We know something about some of the other members of this church also. There was a girl who was delivered from demon possession. "And it came to pass, as we went to prayer, a certain damsel possessed with a spirit of divination met us, which brought her masters much gain by soothsaying: The same followed Paul and us, and cried, saying, These men are the servants of the most high God, which shew unto us the way of salvation. And this did she many days. But Paul, being grieved, turned and said to the spirit, I command thee in the name of Jesus Christ to come out of her. And he came out the same hour" (Acts 16:16–18).

Also the Philippian jailer and his family were members of this church. You recall that Paul and Silas were thrown into jail at the instigation of the masters of the demon-possessed girl who had been deprived of their income. God intervened for Paul and Silas in such a miraculous way that their jailer came to know Christ. "And [the jailer] brought them out, and said, Sirs, what must I do to be saved? And they said, Believe on the Lord Jesus Christ, and thou shalt be saved, and thy house. . . . And when he had brought them into his house, he set meat before them, and rejoiced, believing in God with all his house" (Acts 16:30–31, 34).

There were, of course, other members of this Philippian church whose stories we do not know. They were a people very close to the apostle Paul. They followed him in his journeys and ministered to him time and time again. But when Paul was arrested in Jerusalem, they lost sight of him for two years. They did not know where he was. Finally they heard that he was in Rome in prison. The hearts of these people went out to him, and immediately they dispatched their pastor, Epaphroditus, with a gift that would minister to Paul's needs.

So Paul wrote this epistle to thank the church and to express his love for them. He had no doctrine to correct as he did in his Epistle to the Galatians. Neither did he have to correct their conduct, as he did in his Epistle to the Corinthians. There was only one small ripple in the fellowship of the church between two women, Euodias and Syntyche, and Paul gave them a word of admonishment near the end of his letter. He didn't seem to treat the matter as being serious.

His letter to the Philippian believers is the great epistle of Christian experience. This is Paul's subject in his epistle to the Philippians.

OUTLINE

III. Prize for Christian Living, Chapter 3
A. Paul Changed His Bookkeeping System of the Past, Chapter 3:1–9
B. Paul Changed His Purpose for the Present, Chapter 3:10–19
C. Paul Changed His Hope for the Future, Chapter 3:20–21

IV. Power for Christian Living, Chapter 4
A. Joy—the Source of Power, Chapter 4:1–4
B. Prayer—the Secret of Power, Chapter 4:5–7
C. Contemplation of Christ—the Sanctuary of Power, Chapter 4:8–9
D. In Christ—the Satisfaction of Power, Chapter 4:10–23

CHAPTER 1

THEME: *Philosophy of Christian living—Introduction; Paul's tender feeling for the Philippians; bonds and afflictions further the gospel; in life or death—Christ*

Paul's letter to the Philippians is practical. It gets right down where we live. As we study this epistle, we won't be seated in the heavenlies as we were in his letter to the Ephesians, but we will be right down where the rubber meets the road. It is a wonderful little epistle, and we will be enriched by the sweetness of it.

INTRODUCTION

Paul and Timotheus, the servants of Jesus Christ, to all the saints in Christ Jesus which are at Philippi, with the bishops and deacons [Phil. 1:1].

"Paul and Timotheus"—Paul associates Timothy with himself. Paul brings this young preacher and puts him right beside himself, encouraging him. Paul loved this young man Timothy. He was Paul's son in the Lord, that is, he had won him to Christ; and Paul was very interested in him. Paul is constantly identifying certain young preachers with himself.

Now that I am getting old, I receive letters from former students and from many folk who in my ministry over the years have come to a knowledge of Christ. I feel that all of these are my children. I have a lot of children scattered around over this world, and I love them in the Lord. I understand how Paul felt about Timothy. Paul's name has come down through the centuries, and everywhere you hear about Paul, you will hear about Timothy—Paul was responsible for that. How wonderful!

"The servants of Jesus Christ." Paul identifies himself and Timothy as the servants of Jesus Christ. The word *servants* actually means "bondslaves." This is in contrast to his epistle to the Galatians where he was defending his apostleship. He began with, "Paul, an *apostle.*" He did the same thing to the Corinthians. He had to declare and defend his apostleship and wanted them to know he was apostle not *of* men, neither *by* man. He didn't need to defend himself with these Philippians. They loved him, and they accepted his apostleship. They had all been led to the Lord by him. So Paul takes a humble place, his rightful position: "Paul and Timotheus, we both are servants of the Lord Jesus Christ."

"To all the saints in Christ Jesus which are at Philippi." Paul is not writing to one little clique in the Philippian church; he is writing to all the saints, and every believer is a saint. The human family is divided into two groups: the saints and the ain'ts. Saints are believers in Christ. They are saints, not because of their conduct, but because of their position in Christ. *Saint* means "holy," set apart for God. Anything that is holy is separated for the use of God. Even the old pots and pans in the tabernacle were called "holy vessels," and they were probably beaten and battered after forty years in the wilderness. They may not have looked holy, but they were. Why? Because they had been set aside for the use of God. Now that should be the position of every child of God. We are set aside for the use of God. Now, friend, if you ain't a saint, then you are an ain't.

The saints are "in Christ Jesus." What does it mean to be saved? It means to be *in* Christ Jesus. When you put your trust in the Lord Jesus, the Spirit of God comes to dwell in you. The Holy Spirit baptizes you into the body of Christ. You are put in Christ by the Spirit of God.

Now these saints were *in* Christ, but they were *at* Philippi. You see, it doesn't make any difference where you are *at*—that may not be grammatically correct, but it is a true statement. You may be at Los Angeles or Duluth or Moscow or Philippi. It won't make any difference where you are *at*; the important matter is being *in* Christ Jesus.

I believe the little phrase *in Christ* comprises the most important words that we have in the New Testament. What does it mean to be saved? I asked a theology professor that question, and he gave me quite a lecture on the subject. I was a little dizzy when he finished. He explained words like *propitiation* and *reconciliation* and *redemption.* These are all marvelous words, and they are all Bible words, but not one of them covers the entire spectrum of salvation. The Spirit of God chose just one little word, the preposition *in,* to explain what salvation is. It is to be *in Christ.* How do you get in Christ? You get *in Christ* when you accept Him as your Savior.

"With the bishops and deacons." Notice he is addressing a local church with officers. "Bishop" means overseer or shepherd. The word *bishop* actually refers to the office, while the word *elder* refers to the individual who is in that office, and they should be men who are mature spiritually. "Deacons" refers to spiritual men who are performing a secular service (see Acts 6).

Grace be unto you, and peace, from God our Father, and from the Lord Jesus Christ [Phil. 1:2].

"Grace be unto you, and peace." You will find this form of address in all of Paul's epistles, and grace and peace will always be in that sequence. Grace and peace were both commonplace words of Paul's day.

Grace was the word of greeting in the Greek world. In the Greek language it is *charis*. If you had walked down the street in that day, you would have heard folk greeting each other with, "Charis." In fact, this greeting is still used in modern Greece. It means grace. They say it as we say, "Have a good day." And God is saying to you, "Have a good eternity." When folk say to me, "Have a good day," they don't contribute anything to make it a good day other than just saying that. But God has made the arrangement whereby you can have a good eternity, and it is by the grace of God.

"Peace" always follows grace; it never precedes it. While *charis* comes out of the Greek world, "peace" *(shalom)* comes out of the religious world; it is the Hebrew form of greeting. Actually, the name *Jerusalem* means "the city of peace." Jeru-shalom—city of peace. It has never been that; it has been a city of war. Right now it is a thorn in the flesh of the world. No one knows what to do with it. There will never be peace in Jerusalem or in the world until the Prince of Peace comes to rule.

There is, however, a peace that comes to the believer through the grace of God. "Therefore being justified by faith, we have peace with God through our Lord Jesus Christ" (Rom. 5:1). This is the peace that a sinner can have with a holy God because Christ died for us, paid our penalty, and now God in His grace can save us. It is not that we bring God something for our salvation. Very frankly, we have nothing to bring to Him. I have never brought anything to Him—except sin. Christ paid the penalty for that sin so that a holy God can receive me. And He can receive you. In a world of turmoil, a world of tension, a world of trial, a world that is filled with things that are wrong, we can know the peace of God in our hearts. This is the peace of God that He gives to those who trust Jesus Christ as their own personal Savior. We must know the grace of

God before we can experience the peace of God.

This grace and peace is "from God our Father, and from the Lord Jesus Christ." Let me ask this theological question: Isn't Paul a trinitarian? Doesn't he believe in the Trinity? Then why doesn't he include the Holy Spirit with the Father and the Son? The reason is that the Holy Spirit is already over there in Philippi, indwelling the believers. Certainly Paul believed in the Trinity: Father, Son, and Holy Spirit; and he is being very accurate here.

PAUL'S TENDER FEELING FOR THE PHILIPPIANS

I thank my God upon every remembrance of you [Phil. 1:3].

He begins the body of his letter in this very lovely manner, which reveals the sweet relationship between Paul and the Philippian believers. That is the way it ought to be today among believers, especially between pastor and congregation. The literal translation would be, "All my remembrance of you causes me to thank God." Every time anybody would mention Philippi, Paul would just thank God for the believers there. That is something really quite wonderful.

Every now and then I get a letter from some organization that wants me to do something for them. That is perfectly legitimate for them to make such a request, but they begin the letter with, "I thank my God upon every remembrance of you." Sometimes I'm not so sure they really feel that way about me, but they are preparing me for the request that is coming. But how wonderful it would be to have a church like the Philippian church. And how wonderful to be the kind of person about which it can be said, "All my remembrance of you causes me to thank God." If Paul hadn't said anything else about his relationship to this church, this would have been enough to reveal how special it was. You can check the other epistles—he didn't say this to the other churches, certainly not about the Galatians or the Corinthians.

Always in every prayer of mine for you all making request with joy [Phil. 1:4].

"Always"—not just sometimes. Always in every prayer Paul remembered the Philippian believers.

The phrase "for you all" makes it very clear that Paul was speaking to all the saints that were in that church, the corporate body in the local church. When we reach the final chapter of this epistle, we will find that there was a little ripple of discord between two women in the Philippian church: Syntyche and Euodias. So Paul at the very beginning was careful to include all the saints in order that one group couldn't say to the other, "He is writing to us and not to you."

"Making request with joy." Bengel said that the sum of this epistle is: "I rejoice; rejoice ye." We realize what a remarkable expression this is when we consider where Paul was when he wrote. He was over in Rome in prison! He probably was not in the Mamertine prison at this time, but he was in a place equally as disagreeable.

Although the word *joy* appears nineteen times in this epistle, I have never felt that it should be called the "joy epistle." If we are going to pick out the word that occurs more than any other word, we must take the name of Jesus Christ. His name appears over forty times in this epistle. He is the center of the epistle. He is the One who is the very source of joy. Therefore, the emphasis should be put upon Him rather than upon the joy. As we shall see, the *philosophy* of Christian living has to do with Him; the *pattern* has to do with Him. The *price* of Christian living has to do with Him, and the *power* has to do with Him. Actually, it is a personal relationship with Christ that brings joy to a believer's life.

We try to produce joy in the church by external means. We have a program and tell folks, "Come and you will enjoy it." We have a banquet—people enjoy a banquet—so we have joy, we say. Actually, joy does not depend upon outward circumstances. Real joy depends upon the inward condition of the individual. It depends on the proper attitude toward life. If you are complaining and whining about your lot in life, certainly you will not be experiencing joy. You may be able to go to a church banquet and have a little fun, but that will not be joy. When you and I get to the place where we find ourselves in the center of the will of God and know we are in His will regardless of our circumstances, then there will be joy in our lives.

Paul said, "Always in every prayer of mine for you all making request with joy." The time of prayer was not an ordeal for Paul. He didn't say *Oh, I've got to go through the ordeal of praying for those folk again!* No. He said, "As I am here in jail, it is a lot of fun to pray for you Philippians; it brings joy to my heart."

Now, having told them he thanked God for them, he gives a reason.

For your fellowship in the gospel from the first day until now [Phil. 1:5].

"For your fellowship in the gospel." Now we have come to a very important word in this epistle. We do not want to pass over this word *fellowship*. This word is used widely in the church and outside the church. I don't think that most people really know what the word means, and therefore they don't use it properly.

Years ago I was invited down to Huntington Beach about once a year to give a message at a Rotary Club luncheon. A Christian doctor was chairman of the program committee down there, and he would invite me to come at Christmastime or Eastertime and give them the gospel—both barrels, which is what I always tried to do.

Over the speaker's table they had a slogan: "Food, Fun, Fellowship." Those three things belonged to the early church, and I didn't feel that the Rotary Club should have bragged about having any one of the three. For food there would be embalmed chicken with peas as hard as bullets. For fun they had corny jokes. The fellowship consisted of patting someone on the back and saying, "Hello, Bill. How's business?"

Now that is not fellowship in the biblical sense of the word. The Greek word is *koinōnia*, and it means that which believers can share of the things of Christ. There are three elements that must enter into it: spiritual communication, sympathetic cooperation, and sweet communion. (1) Spiritual communication is sharing the things of Christ. This would be sharing the great truths concerning Christ. (2) Sympathetic cooperation means working together for Christ. That is why, when Paul used the word *fellowship*, he could be talking about Bible reading or Bible study together or prayer or celebrating the Lord's Supper or taking up an offering. Paul called all of these *koinōnia*—fellowship. The result would be (3) sweet communion. It makes us partners with Christ. This is true *koinōnia*.

Paul wrote that this church was having fellowship with him. He had communicated to them the gospel. They had shared with Paul in a sympathetic cooperation. They had sent a gift to him and had ministered to his physical needs again and again. Then when they were together, they had sweet communion.

"From the first day until now"—Paul had enjoyed wonderful fellowship with them from the first day, that day he had met Lydia and her group praying by the riverside.

Being confident of this very thing, that he which hath begun a good work in you will perform it until the day of Jesus Christ [Phil. 1:6].

Because this is my life verse and therefore very meaningful to me, I hope you won't mind if I tell you about it. I was a very poor boy when I went away to college. My dad had been killed in an accident in a cotton gin when I was fourteen years old. My mother took my sister and me to Nashville, Tennessee. I had to get a permit that allowed a boy of fourteen to go to work, and I worked for a wholesale hardware concern. I had to be up by five o'clock in the morning to pick up the mail and have it sorted and on the desks of all the officials in each department. I should have been in school, and I wanted to go to school. Later I had the privilege of going back to school because a wonderful friend acted as a father to me. He had a son who was a drunkard. He had wanted his son to get a college education, but he didn't; so the man helped me get a job, and I was able to go to college. Every year I thought it would be my last year. I never thought God would see me through—I had very little faith. The last year I was in college was during the depression; 1928 and 1929 were bad years. I couldn't get a job and had no money.

On graduation day, after receiving my degree, I returned to my room in the dormitory, still in my cap and gown, and sat dejectedly on the edge of my bed. My roommate came and asked, "What in the world—did somebody die?" I said, "Just as well to. I thought God had called me to the ministry. I'm through college, the depression has hit, and I don't even have a job for this summer. I haven't a dime to go to seminary next year." While we were still talking, the phone rang. It was for me. On the other end of the line was a dear little lady who asked me to stop by her home where she lived with her sister. They were both widows, and they looked as if they had come out of the antebellum days. They attended the church where I taught a class of intermediate boys, and I herded the boys into the church service every Sunday morning. The sisters sat in the pew behind us, and I always thought they disapproved. But in their home that day each handed me an envelope in memory of her husband. I left as soon as it was polite to go, hurried around the corner, and opened the envelopes. The first contained a check for $250; I hurriedly opened the other envelope and found another check for $250. Do you know what $500 was like during the depression? I felt like a millionaire!

That night the Sunday school had a banquet for me, a farewell banquet, and they gave me a check for $100. So now I had $600! That is the money with which I went to seminary the next year. That night at the banquet someone gave me this verse: "Being confident of this very thing, that he which hath begun a good work in you will perform it until the day of Jesus Christ." That has been my life verse ever since that night.

Now let's consider this verse for a moment.

"Being confident" is causative and could be translated, "*Since* I am confident of this very thing"—Paul knew what he was talking about.

"He which hath begun . . . will perform." The word for "perform" means to carry through. He will consummate what He began.

"Until the day of Jesus Christ." You and I today are not living in the Day of the Lord; we are not living in the day of the Old Testament; we are not living in the day of the Millennium; we are not living in the day of eternity; we are living in the day of Jesus Christ. That day will be consummated when He comes to take His own out of this world. And the Holy Spirit has sealed you and me until the day of redemption. Paul wrote to the Ephesian believers, "And grieve not the Holy Spirit of God, whereby ye are sealed unto the day of redemption" (Eph. 4:30). And until then, you can count upon God to consummate whatever He intends for you. He is going to see it through. How wonderful!

Now, my friend, let me ask you this: Is this practical for you and me? I don't know what your circumstances are, but if you are a child of God, I am sure you can testify that God has brought you up to the present moment, hasn't He? Can't you look back over your life and see how He has led you and provided for you? Then why should you be concerned about tomorrow? Do you think He is going to let you down now? I confess that this was my thinking when I finished college.

You see, I went through college, but I didn't enjoy it as I should have. I never had joy because I always was afraid I couldn't go on. I just didn't believe God would see me through. So many times we Christians act like unbelievers. In fact, we live and act like practical atheists. The graduation was a happy experience for my classmates. I could see those rich kids being hugged by their parents. No one was there to throw their arms around me, but it wouldn't have made any difference if there had been a whole delegation of well-wishers, because I thought I was through. I felt called to the ministry, but there was no possible way for me to go on to seminary. However, I had a wonderful heavenly Father who, through Philippians 1:6, put His arms around me and said, "I'll see you through."

And I want to testify today that He is still keeping His promise. It has been a comfort to me since I have had several bouts with cancer to know that my heavenly Father said, "Being confident of this very thing, that he which hath begun a good work in you will perform it until the day of Jesus Christ." He is a good Doctor also; in fact, He is the Great Physician, and He has said, "Whatever I have in store for you, I'm going to see you through until the day of Jesus Christ." So I am in His hands.

This is a great verse of Scripture. Oh, I have held onto this during many a dark night when the storm outside was beating against my little bark. My, how wonderful to have a heavenly Father like this!

Even as it is meet for me to think this of you all, because I have you in my heart; inasmuch as both in my bonds, and in the defence and confirmation of the gospel, ye all are partakers of my grace [Phil. 1:7].

"Even as it is meet"—*meet* is an old Elizabethan word that means "right." Even as it is right for me to think this of you all.

"Because I have you in my heart." Isn't that a wonderful place to carry your Christian friends?

"Partakers of my grace" brings us back to the word *fellowship*. It is *koinōnia* with a preposition that intensifies it: *suqkoinōnous*, meaning "being all wrapped up together." You may remember that lovely Abigail used these words when she talked to David: ". . . but the soul of my lord shall be bound in the bundle of life with the Lord thy God . . ." (1 Sam. 25:29). Paul is saying that he and the Philippians are all wrapped up together as partners in the gospel.

This is what I mean when I say that there were tender feelings of the apostle Paul for this church at Philippi. He was closer to them than to any other church. It is so wonderful to have Christian friends like this who are sharing in the great enterprise of getting out the Word of God. There is that sympathetic cooperation, besides the spiritual communication, and it always produces sweet communion.

For God is my record, how greatly I long after you all in the bowels of Jesus Christ [Phil. 1:8].

That word *bowels* is offensive to some folk. One sweet little lady, who I'm sure had never used a bad word in her life, came to me and said, "Dr. McGee, don't read it like that. That's crude." I answered, "That's the way it is in the Bible, and that's the way I think it should be read—just as it is." *Bowels* really means tender feelings. This is really a marvelous statement. Paul says that he longs for all of them in the tender feelings of Jesus Christ. Actually, it is quite accurate to use the word *bowels* for tender feelings.

I was teaching this one night at Bible study, and at that time a psychologist from the University of Southern California attended the classes. I was teaching that bowels meant tender feelings. He said, "The ancients were right. They were accurate when they talked about our feelings being in the region of the bowels." He said, "The average person thinks that everything he does is because he has thought it over and that he is very smart." Then he touched me on the head and said, "Very little really takes place up here." I really felt that he knew *me* when he said that.

He went on to explain that the brain is really a very marvelous telephone exchange. A message comes up through the sensory nervous system, up through the synaptical connections from the hand to the brain. Immediately there is a transfer made over to a motor neuron, and the message goes down over a different set of synaptical connections. For example, when you touch a hot stove, immediately the message goes up to the brain, and the brain returns the message, "Take your finger off that—you'll get burned." You react instantly. You do it without thinking, but there was a connection made up in the brain. By the way, many people drive an automobile like that—without thinking, which is quite obvious. Then he asked me, "How did you feel the first time you saw your wife? Where did that take place? Was it in the brain?" The psychologist pointed to my tummy and said, "There is where you live and move and have your being." So Paul is expressing his most tender feelings, "I long after you." It is not because they have given him something. His reaction is not mental but emotional. This is a wonderful expression.

And this I pray, that your love may abound yet more and more in knowledge and in all judgment [Phil. 1:9].

There is a lot of silly thinking about this word *love*. I often get letters such as this one: "You gave me the surprise of my life when you said that there are certain preachers who spread damnable heresies. Doesn't Jesus say in His Holy Word that we are to love our enemies and do good to those who hate you?" Of course He said that, but we need to notice to whom He said it. The Lord Jesus had some very harsh things to say about the religious rulers of His day. He said "Ye are of your father the devil, and the lusts of your father ye will do . . ." (John 8:44). Also He said, "Ye serpents, ye generation of vipers, how can ye escape the damnation of hell?" (Matt. 23:33). He called the Devil their father and a snake their mother! I don't think any person could be more extreme.

Paul prays that your "love may abound yet more and more in knowledge and in all judgment [or *discernment*]." We are to love all believers in Christ. Some of the believers are a little difficult to love. Some of our friends are even difficult to love. We are to love the unlovely, but we are to love with knowledge and with discernment. That does not mean we just let our love slop over on every side. It is to abound with discernment. Let me give you an illustration out of my own experience.

When I first went to downtown Los Angeles as a pastor, I soon found that there are certain groups that move through that downtown area and prey on church people and new preachers especially. One Sunday morning one of the personal workers came to me and said, "There's a man here who has come forward and wants to talk to you about his salvation." Well, I felt complimented. This man wants to talk to *me*; he won't talk to anybody else. So I went over to talk to him, and by that time practically everybody had left the church. I began to explain the plan of salvation. I never saw a fellow so interested. He took my Bible and read the verses I indicated. Oh, he had it down to a system! Finally I asked him if he wanted to accept Christ. Tears came to his eyes and ran down his face. He said yes, he did. We got down on our knees, and he prayed. When we stood up, I made a mistake. I asked him how he was getting along. And he told me, "I hate to tell you this, but my suitcase is down here in a certain hotel. They won't let me have it because I owe them seven dollars." Well, what would you do? You had just led a man to the Lord, supposedly; you're a Christian; you're a preacher; you ought to love the brother. Well, I gave him the seven dollars, and I felt expansive. I told my wife about it and felt very good inside that I had been so generous. About six weeks after that I was going through the daily paper, and there was a

picture of this man. I thought, *How in t[he] world did he get into the paper?* And I re[ad] that he'd been arrested. He had spent t[he] previous six months in Los Angeles living [off] the preachers, and his comment was, "Th[ey] are the biggest saps in the world." And I w[as] one of them! I called up the late Dr. B[ob] Schuler, who was pastoring in downtown L[os] Angeles at Trinity Methodist Church, an[d] asked, "Did this fellow come down to you[?]" "Yes," he said. "Did you let him have seve[n] dollars?" He said, "No. That's what he wante[d] but I've been down here a long time, Verno[n]. After you've been down here awhile, you find there are some you can't love."

Paul says to let your love abound more a[nd] more, but let it abound in judgment, let [it] abound in being able to discern. Over th[e] years when I would drive to my study in L[os] Angeles, I used to say to the Lord, "I'm goin[g] to meet new people today, and I don't kno[w] them. Some of them I'll be able to help. Othe[rs] of them will put a knife in my back. Lord, he[lp] me to be able to distinguish between the tw[o]. Show me which I should help." Actually th[is] verse rescues a Christian from being nai[ve] and gullible. His love is to abound in knowl[edge] and discernment.

That ye may approve things that are excellent; that ye may be sincere and without offence till the day of Christ [Phil. 1:10].

Here is another important verse that need[s] some explanation. When Paul says, "That y[ou] may approve things that are excellent," h[e] means that you need to *try* the things th[at] differ. This has to do, I believe, with the Lord[s] will for your life. There are times when w[e] must come to a decision when there are two o[r] more routes that we could go. What one sha[ll] we take? Frankly, there are times when w[e] don't know. The Lord will not send an angel t[o] tell us, nor will He turn on red or green light[s] to give us signals. He expects us to use a littl[e] consecrated and concentrated gumptio[n]. Therefore we need to try the things that di[f]fer.

A man was telling me about his busines[s]. He had two routes open to him, and he praye[d] about his decision. He tried one of them, an[d] it didn't work. He told me that when he saw i[t] wouldn't work, he came back to the crossroad[s] and tried the other route. He said, "Then [I] was sure of the Lord's will. The one rout[e] didn't work, so there was only one other wa[y] open for me. I followed that one, and it wa[s] the right one." God says we are to try th[e] things that differ. Actually, that is the way He leads us.

"That ye may be sincere"—"sincere" is an interesting word which comes from the Latin *sincerus*, which means without wax. When the Romans became a world power, they were a very strong and rather brutal people. They destroyed a great many of the art treasures of Greece in many places. In the cities of Asia Minor, we can still see evidence of that. I was interested in looking at several of the temples over there; the temple of Diana must have been a beautiful thing from the architectural standpoint. But many of the art troves of Greece were broken up. When the Romans reached the point of development in their culture that they appreciated these things, they began to gather them up. Many of them were broken. When there was a crack in a statue or a vase, a dishonest dealer would fill it in with wax so that one couldn't tell that it had been broken. Then he would sell it as a genuine, perfect piece. An unsuspecting man would buy it, take it to his villa, and display it in his garden. The next hot day he would walk out and, lo and behold, the wax would be running out of a crack in that lovely art treasure! Finally the reputable art dealers began to put on their material the word *sincerus*, meaning without wax. In other words, they guaranteed it was a perfect piece.

Paul is saying, "Don't be a phony. Be real, be genuine, be sincere." Applying this to the previous verse, don't go around patting everyone on the back with a "Praise the Lord, Hallelujah" and telling them how much you love them, if you are going to stick a knife in their backs the minute they leave your presence. That is what he is saying here. Be sincere.

"Without offence" means *blameless*, which would be a better translation, because we cannot live the Christian life or preach the Word of God without offense to somebody. Remember that people were offended at Paul and his preaching. That is the reason believers should pray for their pastor if he is preaching the Bible. If he is really giving out the Word of God, there will be offense. He needs your support, your defense of him, your prayers for him.

I officiated at a funeral service for a movie star several years ago. I preached the Word of God, and the crowd attending the service didn't appreciate what I said. They were antagonistic. I even got some telephone calls from some of the people. One of the television newscasters gave the report of the funeral and

said, "Hollywood heard something today that they have never heard before"—I understand he was a Christian. But my message was an offense to most of that crowd. So you see, the Christian life and the preaching of the Word of God will not be without offense to someone, but Paul is saying that believers should be *blameless*.

When I first became pastor in downtown Los Angeles, I met Dr. Jim McGinnis who was in Chicago at that time. He asked me how I liked being a pastor in downtown Los Angeles. I said, "Well, I certainly am enjoying it. It is a marvelous opportunity, and the crowds are coming to church, but I find I can't defend myself. I hear reports about me that are terrible." He answered, "That's all right. Just be sure that none of them is true." We can be blameless, but we cannot be without offense.

"Till the day of Christ" has reference to His coming for His own. This is the second time the Rapture is mentioned in this epistle. A child of God should walk in the light of the imminent return of Christ all the time.

Being filled with the fruits of righteousness, which are by Jesus Christ, unto the glory and praise of God [Phil. 1:11].

The "fruits of righteousness" are the fruits of the Holy Spirit. The Holy Spirit is producing fruit in the lives of the believers. ". . . The fruit of the Spirit is love, joy, peace, longsuffering, gentleness, goodness, faith, meekness, temperance . . ." (Gal. 5:22–23).

BONDS AND AFFLICTIONS FURTHER THE GOSPEL

But I would ye should understand, brethren, that the things which happened unto me have fallen out rather unto the furtherance of the gospel [Phil. 1:12].

Paul is speaking very emphatically to them. When the believers in Philippi heard that Paul was in prison, they sent a message to him by their pastor, Epaphroditus, and it probably went something like this: "Oh, poor brother Paul, we feel so sorry for you. Now your great missionary journeys are curtailed; you are in prison, and the gospel is not going out!" Paul said, "Look, I want you to know that the gospel *is* going out, and the things that have happened to me have not curtailed but have actually furthered the gospel."

Now he will make clear what he means by this.

So that my bonds in Christ are manifest in all the palace, and in all other places [Phil. 1:13].

The palace was actually Caesar's court. Acts 28:16 tells us, "And when we came to Rome, the centurion delivered the prisoners to the captain of the guard: but Paul was suffered to dwell by himself with a soldier that kept him." Paul was chained to a member of the Praetorian Guard, and these men were the Roman patricians, members of Caesar's household.

When Paul was converted, the Lord Jesus said that Paul would ". . . bear my name before the Gentiles, and kings, and the children of Israel" (Acts 9:15). Well, up to this time Paul had taken the gospel largely to the common, vegetable variety of citizens in the Roman Empire. But now he has members of the royalty chained to him! Every four hours, at the change of the guard, one guard would leave and be replaced by a new guard who would be chained to Paul. What do you think Paul talked about during those four hours? Can you imagine having your congregation chained to you? My guess is that some of them were happy to see their relief guard come. They would say, "Boy, am I glad to see you! This man Paul is trying to make a Christian out of me." Many of them did come to know Christ. The gospel penetrated Caesar's household. Later Tertullian wrote that the Roman government became disturbed when it was discovered that Christians were in positions of authority. Many of these men later died for their faith in the Lord Jesus Christ.

This is the first evidence Paul gave that his imprisonment had not hindered the furtherance of the gospel but that it had enabled him to bring the gospel right into Caesar's household.

Not only did Paul's imprisonment enable him to reach into Caesar's household with the gospel, but it also accomplished something else:

And many of the brethren in the Lord, waxing confident by my bonds, are much more bold to speak the word without fear [Phil. 1:14].

In the early church there were many men who were willing to go out as witnesses for Christ, but after hearing Paul speak, they would say something like this, "Man, I'd like to witness for the Lord, but I can't tell it like Paul tells it." So long as Paul was out preaching the gospel, others would feel unworthy, not competent or sufficiently trained. They considered Paul so much more effective than they could be. But then one day the word went down the Roman roads to all those centers where churches had been established that Paul was in prison in Rome. In many of those churches men would say, "Look, Paul's in prison. He can't go out anymore. I'll go." As a result many men started to preach the gospel. I am confident that hundreds and maybe even thousands of men hit the Roman roads and moved out from door to door to tell people about Christ. So Paul says, "Many of the brethren in the Lord, waxing confident by my bonds, are much more bold to speak the word without fear."

Now I believe there is a third effect of Paul's imprisonment which he does not mention. We can only get this from the perspective of history. Paul may not have realized the importance of his writing, but if he had not been put into prison, we would not have the Prison Epistles: Ephesians, Philippians, Colossians, Philemon. They are all marvelous epistles, and we would not have them today if Paul had not been in prison. I'm sure the Lord could have gotten this teaching to us some other way, but this was the way He chose. So Paul could say about his imprisonment that it had "fallen out rather unto the furtherance of the gospel."

There was, however, a tragic difficulty in Paul's day. We have the same thing happening in this day, and it is still tragic.

Some indeed preach Christ even of envy and strife; and some also of good will [Phil. 1:15].

When I first began to study the Bible, it was unbelievable to me that the preaching of the gospel of Christ could be done in envy and strife. But now that I've been in the ministry for a long time—I was ordained in 1933—I know that one of the things that hurts the preaching of the gospel probably more than any other single thing is the envy and the strife. Paul will mention envy and strife several times in this epistle. There must have been quite a few who were preaching the gospel in that way, envious of the apostle Paul, jealous because they didn't have the results that Paul had.

One of the solutions to this problem of envy is for every Christian to recognize that he has a gift. We do not all have the same gift. The body could not function if we did. The problem is that some men who have one gift are envious of a man who has a different gift. You will remember that Paul told the Corinthians that the gifts are to be exercised in love. Every gift is to be exercised in love. My friend, if you will exercise your gift in love, you will not envy someone else. ". . . Love envieth not; love vaunteth not itself, is not puffed up" (1 Cor. 13:4). Envy says, "I don't think much of you," and pride says, "What do you think of me?" That is the difference between envy and pride, and the believer is warned against both of them. Paul put it very bluntly when he wrote, "For who maketh thee to differ from another? and what hast thou that thou didst not receive? now if thou didst receive it, why dost thou glory, as if thou hadst not received it?" (1 Cor. 4:7).

Strife is an interesting word. It is the Greek word *eris*, which means "to stir up"—referring to demons, the spirits, that stir up strife. Envy and strife! Those two still hurt the church. Alcohol and drugs on the outside of the church cannot hurt it nearly as much as the envy and strife on the inside of the church.

Notice, however, that there were some who preached Christ of good will.

The one preach Christ of contention, not sincerely, supposing to add affliction to my bonds [Phil. 1:16].

Those motivated by envy and strife preached Christ, but not sincerely. They actually did it to try to belittle Paul. They were envious of the apostle Paul, but they had not been able to say anything against him. Now that he was in prison and unable to defend himself, these men would go out and preach the gospel, but they also would have a few little things to say against Paul.

But the other of love, knowing that I am set for the defence of the gospel [Phil. 1:17].

These are the two groups. What is Paul's attitude toward them?

What then? notwithstanding, every way, whether in pretence, or in truth, Christ is preached; and I therein do rejoice, yea, and will rejoice [Phil. 1:18].

The important thing to Paul was that Christ be preached, no matter whether it was done in pretense or by true motives. It is tragic that at times Christ is preached in envy and strife. He is still preached in that way today, but we can always rejoice whenever Christ is preached.

I am a little rough on female preachers because I believe they are unscriptural, but, as I have said on several occasions, some women are preaching Christ better than the average male preacher. What is my position? I *rejoice* and thank God that Christ is being preached.

Dr. Ironside told the story of walking through a park in Oakland, California. A woman was preaching there, and his friend said to him, "Isn't it a shame that this woman is here preaching?" Dr. Ironside said, "It's a shame that there is not some man to take her place." That is the problem. Thank God, Christ is being preached. That is the important thing. We can rejoice today whenever the Word of God is given out.

At the time I am writing, a great many folk are getting concerned about home Bible classes. I am *rejoicing* over them. I know sometimes they go off on a tangent, but not any more than some churches go off on tangents. We can rejoice that the Word of God is being taught.

It is interesting and also comforting to know that Christ can be preached insincerely, and yet people can still be saved. God honors His *Word*, not the man or the organization. We need to recognize that today. The Spirit of God is the *only* One who can bring blessings, and He can bless *only* when the Word of God is given out.

For I know that this shall turn to my salvation through your prayer, and the supply of the Spirit of Jesus Christ [Phil. 1:19].

By the word *salvation* Paul means his deliverance from prison.

"Through your prayer." People have asked me why I asked everyone to pray for me when I had cancer. They said, "Didn't you know that God would heal you if *you* go to Him in prayer?" May I say that the Bible makes it clear that God hears and answers the prayers of His people. We need to ask God's people to pray for us. Paul says that through their prayers he hopes to be set free.

"Through . . . the supply of the Spirit of Jesus Christ." The only way you and I can get that supply that we need is through prayer.

According to my earnest expectation and my hope, that in nothing I shall be ashamed, but that with all boldness, as always, so now also Christ shall be magnified in my body, whether it be by life, or by death [Phil. 1:20].

Paul said he did not want to be ashamed of his witness while in this life, and he did not want to be ashamed when he came into the presence of the Lord Jesus Christ. The apostle

John mentions the fact that when Christ comes to take His church with Him, it is possible for believers to be ashamed at His appearing (see 1 John 2:28). We need to bear that in mind. All Christians ought to be concerned about that.

Years ago I began a prophetic congress in downtown Los Angeles which has spread over this entire area and has given a tremendous emphasis to prophecy. This has been carried out across our country today. I probably have spoken in more prophetic congresses than any one individual. So I want to say this: there are too many people who are talking about the coming of the Lord but are not *ready* for the coming of the Lord. You may ask, "Aren't they saved?" Yes, they are saved. But I'm afraid they will be ashamed at His appearing. Their lives do not commend the gospel. Paul says that he doesn't want to be ashamed before Christ at His coming.

You will recall that this chapter gives the philosophy of Christian living. You will find that Paul will sum up the theme of each of these four chapters in one verse, and sometimes in one sentence. The next verse puts this chapter in a nutshell.

IN LIFE OR DEATH—CHRIST

For to me to live is Christ, and to die is gain [Phil. 1:21].

Notice in your Bible that the verb *is* is in italics. That means it is not in the original but had been added to make the meaning clearer. The verse is actually, "For to me to live Christ, and to die gain."

This is the philosophy of Christian living: To live Christ; to die gain. Dr. William L. Pettingill used to say that *gain* is always more of the same thing. If to live is Christ, then to die would be more of Christ. It means to go and be with Him.

Although it has taken me a long time to arrive at this conclusion, I am convinced that the most important thing in my life as a Christian is to have the reality of Jesus Christ in my life. This is not too popular today. People would rather talk about being dedicated, wanting to serve Him, or doing this and that. But the most important thing is to have fellowship with Him so that your joy might be full. Then we will have a powerful witness. The problem is that most people want the end but forget all about the means. The means, in this case, is fellowship with the Lord Jesus Christ. Everything else is the fruitage of this fellowship. For to me to live Christ; to die is to be with Him.

Now we know why Paul was undisturbed by the criticism being leveled at him. You can't hurt a man who is in fellowship with Jesus Christ. What could anyone do to such a man? "For to me to live Christ, and to die gain" is a high plane on which to live. I wish I could say I have reached that plane. I'm on my way, and I haven't arrived, but that is my *goal*. What a glorious one it is!

But if I live in the flesh, this is the fruit of my labour: yet what I shall choose I wot not [Phil. 1:22].

Paul didn't know about his future, just as you and I don't know about our future. We don't know what any single day will bring forth.

For I am in a strait betwixt two, having a desire to depart, and to be with Christ; which is far better:

Nevertheless to abide in the flesh is more needful for you [Phil. 1:23–24].

Paul says he was torn between wanting to go to be with the Lord, which is the better of the two, or to stay with the Philippian believers because they needed him.

The first time I had cancer surgery, a letter came from a lady that said, "I know that everybody is praying that you will get well, but I am praying that the Lord will take you home because to be with Christ is far better." I wrote back and said, "Would you mind letting the Lord decide about this? I want to stay." I want to stay a while longer to give out the Word of God. I've just now gotten to the best part of my ministry, and I don't want to leave it. I'm asking God to let me stay with it. I think that is a normal feeling for a child of God.

It reminds me of a story of an incident that took place in my southland in a black church. The preacher asked one night, "How many of you want to go to heaven?" Everyone put up his hand except one little boy. The preacher asked him, "Don't you want to go to heaven?" He answered, "I sure do, but I thought you were getting up a load for tonight."

We all want to go to heaven, but not *right now*!

And having this confidence, I know that I shall abide and continue with you all for your furtherance and joy of faith;

That your rejoicing may be more abundant in Jesus Christ for me by my coming to you again [Phil. 1:25–26].

Paul is practical. He still has work to do. These folk need his ministry. He wanted to get out of prison and go to be with them again.

People who are always saying, "Oh, if the Lord would only come," should get busy. This is the only place where we can do any work that is going to count for a reward for Him. This is the stage on which you and I play our part. I want to stay as long as possible, and I have promised the Lord I will teach the Word as long as He lets me stay.

Only let your conversation be as it becometh the gospel of Christ: that whether I come and see you, or else be absent, I may hear of your affairs, that ye stand fast in one spirit, with one mind striving together for the faith of the gospel [Phil. 1:27].

The word *conversation* means your way of life. Not only our speech but our entire way of life should be a credit to the gospel of Christ.

"Stand fast in one spirit, with one mind striving together for the faith of the gospel"— oh, how God's people need to stand together for the furtherance of the gospel! If the church were what it should be in the world today, the world would listen to the message it proclaims.

Here Paul uses the word *strive* which is so different from the word *strife* about which he wrote earlier in the chapter. In the word *strive* is the thought of agonizing. We are to agonize together for the faith of the gospel.

And in nothing terrified by your adversaries: which is to them an evident token of perdition, but to you of salvation, and that of God.

For unto you it is given in the behalf of Christ, not only to believe on him, but also to suffer for his sake [Phil. 1:28–29].

When you get to the place where He lets you suffer for Him, you have arrived—that is the high calling of Christ Jesus.

Having the same conflict which ye saw in me, and now hear to be in me [Phil. 1:30].

Paul certainly knew what it was to suffer for Christ. Suffering for Christ is a token of blessing, not a sign that God has turned His face away.

This concludes chapter 1 in which we have seen the philosophy of Christian living. The chapter is summed up in one verse: "For to me to live Christ, and to die gain."

CHAPTER 2

THEME: Pattern for Christian living—others; mind of Christ— humble; mind of God—exaltation of Christ; mind of Paul—things of Christ; mind of Timothy—like-minded with Paul; mind of Epaphroditus—the work of Christ

In the first chapter we saw the *philosophy* of Christian living summed up in one verse: "For to me to live is Christ, and to die is gain." Christ was the very center of Paul's life. Now in this chapter we come to the *pattern* for Christian living, which is the mind of Christ, as we shall see.

It cannot be by imitation. I hear people talking today about following Jesus. I sometimes would like to ask these folk what they mean by that—especially when their lives do not conform to what they are saying. Are they trying to imitate Jesus? When Paul says here that Christ is the pattern for Christian living, he is not talking about imitation. He is talking about *impartation*. That is, the mind of Christ should be *in* us, and it can be there only by the power of the Spirit of God.

I learned a long time ago that when Vernon McGee does things, they are not only not done well, they are done wrong—always. I am accused of being rather strong-willed, and I have a tendency to move ahead on my own volition. But when I do that, I stub my toe. Then I say,

"Lord, I'm ready now for You to take over." It has been wonderful to see how the Lord does take over.

We need to learn to sit back and watch the Spirit of God move. That doesn't mean that we simply sit and twiddle our thumbs. Of course we carry on the program that God has given us to carry on, but the power and the dynamic come from the Spirit of God.

In this chapter is one of the greatest theological statements made in Scripture concerning the person of Christ. Down through the centuries one of the most controversial issues has come out of that theological statement. In fact, it is the thing that probably divided Europe—it had more to do with it than anything else. The theory promoted was the *kenosis* theory, which is that at Christ's incarnation He emptied Himself of His deity. This chapter will make it clear that He did *not* empty Himself of His deity.

THE PATTERN FOR CHRISTIAN LIVING—OTHERS

Before we get into the controversial issue, let's notice the practical side—this is a practical epistle.

If there be therefore any consolation in Christ, if any comfort of love, if any fellowship of the Spirit, if any bowels and mercies [Phil. 2:1].

The "if" which begins this verse is not the *if* of condition—this is not a conditional clause. You will find that many times Paul uses *if* as an argument rather than a condition. Paul is a logical thinker. It has been said that if you do not find Paul logical, you are not reading him aright. It would be more accurate to translate it: "*Since* there is consolation in Christ, and *since* there is comfort of love, and *since* there is the fellowship of the Spirit, and *since* there are bowels [tenderness] and mercy."

Now in view of all this, Paul says:

Fulfil ye my joy, that ye be like-minded, having the same love, being of one accord, of one mind [Phil. 2:2].

Even though he is in prison, he is rejoicing in the Lord, but he says that he would rejoice even more if he knew the gospel was working in the lives of the Philippian believers.

"That ye be like-minded, having the same love, being of one accord, of one mind." You see, there had been a little difficulty, as we noted before, in the Philippian church—not much, but a little. Paul wants them to be of one mind.

He is not asking them to be carbon copies of each other. In most churches there are two groups of people: one group *for* the pastor and one group *against* the pastor. The folk that comprise these groups are not thinking for themselves but are carbon copies of the group leaders.

To be of one mind is to let the mind of Christ be in you. That permits differences of expressions, differences in gifts, differences in methods of service, even differences in minor doctrines. We won't be beating each other on the head because we disagree on these things. If we have the mind of Christ, we will agree on the major tenets of the faith.

Let nothing be done through strife or vainglory; but in lowliness of mind let each esteem other better than themselves [Phil. 2:3].

You remember that Paul has mentioned this before. He said that there were some people who were preaching Christ out of envy and strife. Now he says, "Let nothing be done through strife or vainglory." I would say most of the difficulties in the church today are not due to doctrinal differences. They are due to strife and envy. Some people just naturally cause trouble. If we could follow this injunction, "Let nothing be done through strife or vainglory," I think it would solve 90 percent or maybe even 100 percent of the problems in churches today.

If you are doing something through strife in the church, you had better not do it at all. The same is true if you do things because you expect to be recognized. One of the reasons I don't like to go to organizational meetings is that I get tired of people having to thank Mrs. So-and-so because she brought a bouquet of petunias or Mr. So-and-so because he brought in an extra chair—and you don't dare leave out anyone because if you do, you will be in trouble. Do Christians need to be recognized and complimented and commended for things they do? "Let nothing be done through strife or vainglory"—trying to make a name for yourself.

"But in lowliness of mind let each esteem other better than themselves." Perhaps this was the problem between Euodias and Syntyche. It may be that each felt she was being put down by the other.

If this verse were obeyed, I believe it would solve the problems in most of the music departments in our churches. It would eliminate this attitude: "Why don't they call on me to sing? I have a much better voice than So-and-so." The same could be said for problems on boards and on committees. It would eliminate the "power struggle" that goes on in some churches among the church officers.

Look not every man on his own things, but every man also on the things of others [Phil. 2:4].

Others! That is an important word.

I was absolutely overwhelmed to get a letter from another broadcaster with a gift for our broadcast enclosed. It came from a man whose broadcast is carried on one of the same stations as our broadcast in the state of Florida. He wrote, "What a blessing your broadcast is." I don't know anything about this man's broadcast, but I can tell you something about his person. He was exhibiting the mind of Christ. He was carrying out the admonition of this verse: "Look not every man on his own things, but every man also on the things of others." His letter was a very humbling experience for me.

"Others" is the key to this passage. It is the Christian faith which first made that word *others* important. Why did Christ come from heaven's glory to this earth? It was for others. Why should we carry the gospel? For others. To think of others rather than ourselves is having the mind of Christ.

MIND OF CHRIST—HUMBLE

Now Paul is going to tell us about the mind of Christ.

Let this mind be in you, which was also in Christ Jesus [Phil. 2:5].

The mind of Christ—what is the one thing that characterized it? Humility. You may recall that in Ephesians 4 we were told, ". . . walk worthy of the vocation wherewith ye are called." Then it goes on to describe this, "With all lowliness and meekness, with longsuffering, forbearing one another in love" (Eph. 4:1–2). That is the mind of Christ.

You and I can't be humble. We can't be meek. We are not made that way. We want to stand on our own two feet and have our little say. All of us are like that. Don't say you are not, because you really are. None of us wants to be offended. None of us wants to be ignored. We develop hang-ups if we are brought up in such a way that we have been trampled on.

I heard about the son of a very fine minister who had become a vagrant. Why? It was because he had an older brother who was a brilliant fellow. This boy was always hearing about the brilliant things his older brother was doing. So he just went in the opposite direction, rebelling against it. That is the natural reaction of the natural man. It wouldn't even help matters to go to the boy and say, "Now listen, son, you just ignore all that." He is not going to ignore it. A man who is not born again is not even in the territory of being willing to take a humble place.

We come now to one of the great theological statements in the Scripture. Some consider it the greatest doctrinal statement in the New Testament relative to the person of Christ, and it is known as the *kenosis*, the "emptying." This passage will make it clear that He did not empty Himself of His deity. It will give us the seven steps of humiliation which Christ took. I wish I were capable of sketching for you the magnitude of what is being said in these next few verses. I wish we could grasp how high He was and how low He came. The billions of light years across known space are nothing compared to the distance He came.

We find here seven steps downward. Then we have listed for us seven steps upward, the exaltation of Christ. First, then, in humiliation, we see the mind of Christ. Then we will see the mind of God. It is in the mind of God the Father to exalt the Lord Jesus Christ. If you want to know what you can do that will put you in the will of God—I don't know where you are to *go* or what you *do*—but I can tell you this: Since it is the purpose of God the Father to exalt Jesus Christ, I believe that is the will of God for every one of us. We are to exalt Jesus Christ, wherever we are and in whatever we do. We are to be one with the Father in this ultimate purpose of the exaltation of Jesus Christ.

The *first* step downward was when He left heaven's glory. He came down and down and down to this earth, all the way to where we are. You and I cannot even conceive of what a big step it was from heaven's glory all the way down to this earth. Absolutely, it is beyond human comprehension to understand what our Lord really did for us.

Who, being in the form of God, thought it not robbery to be equal with God [Phil. 2:6].

This is, I confess, a rather stilted translation. When Christ was at the right hand of God the Father, He wasn't hanging on to His position. There was no danger of His losing His place in the Godhead because of any lack on His part or because of the ability and ambition of a contender. He hadn't gone to school to learn to become God; He had not advanced from another position. He *was* God. It wasn't as if the Lord Jesus had to say to God the Father, "Now You be sure to keep My position for Me while I'm gone for thirty-three years. Keep a sharp eye out for Gabriel—I think he would like to have My place." I am not being irreverent; I am trying to show you that this was not something that He had to hold on to. The position belonged to Him. He was God.

Nor did He leave heaven reluctantly. At no time did He say, "Oh, I just hate to leave heaven. I don't want to go down on that trip." He came joyfully. ". . . for the *joy* that was set before him . . ." (Heb. 12:2, italics mine) He endured the cross. He said, ". . . Lo, I come (in the volume of the book it is written of me,) to do thy will, O God" (Heb. 10:7). He came to this earth with joy. He was not releasing something that He wanted to hold on to when He came to this earth.

Now we see the *second* step down.

But made himself of no reputation, and took upon him the form of a servant, and was made in the likeness of men [Phil. 2:7].

"Made himself of no reputation" means *to empty*—the Greek word is *kenoō*. The kenosis theory derives its name from the word *kenoō*. Christ emptied Himself. The question is: Of what did He empty Himself? There are those who say He emptied Himself of His deity. All of the Gnostics in the early church propounded the first heresy that He emptied Himself of His deity, that the deity entered into Him at the time of His baptism and left Him at the cross. Well, this theory is not substantiated anywhere in the Word of God. He emptied Himself of something, but it was not of His deity. He was 100 percent God when He was a baby reclining helplessly on the bosom of Mary. Even at that time He could have spoken this universe out of existence because He was God. There was never a moment when He was not God. The apostle John writes, "In the beginning was the Word, and the Word was with God, and the Word was God. The same was in the beginning with God. All things were made by him; and without him was not any thing made that was made. . . . And the Word was made flesh, and dwelt among us . . ." (John 1:1–3,14).

Well, then, of what did the Lord Jesus empty Himself when He came to this earth? I believe that He emptied Himself of the *prerogatives* of deity. He lived on this earth with certain limitations, but they were self-limitations. There was never a moment when He wasn't God. And He was not less God because He was man, yet He emptied Himself of His prerogatives of deity.

The few shepherds and wise men, and even the multitude of angels, were a sorry turnout for the Son of God when He came to this earth. Not only should that crowd have been there, but the whole universe should have been there. All of God's created intelligences should have been there. The hierarchy of Rome should have been there. There should not have been just a few wise men from the East. They should have come from the West, and the North, and the South. And the temple in Jerusalem should have been empty that day—they should all have gone down to Bethlehem. But they didn't.

Why didn't He force them to come? Because He had laid aside His prerogatives of deity. He was willing to be born in a dirty, filthy place—not the pretty, clean stable of Christmas pageants and Christmas cards. He was willing to grow to manhood in a miserable town named Nazareth. He was willing to be an unknown carpenter. He could have had the *shekinah* glory with Him all the time, but He didn't. He didn't have a halo around His head as we see in so many paintings of Him. Judas had to kiss Him the night He was betrayed so that the crowd would know which was the man they were to capture. He didn't stand out from other men by some kind of inner light or glory around Him. He was a human being, but He was *God* manifest in the flesh. He laid aside the prerogatives of His deity.

Can we be sure of that? I think we can. After He had finished His ministry, He gathered His own about Him on His last night on earth, and He prayed a very wonderful prayer to His heavenly Father. One thing He said in that prayer was this: "And now, O Father, glorify thou me with thine own self with the glory which I had with thee before the world was" (John 17:5). Notice this carefully: He prayed to have His *glory* restored. He did not pray to have His *deity* restored, because He had never given up His deity. But now that He is returning to heaven, He is asking that His glory, the glory light, a prerogative of deity, be restored. Obviously He had laid that aside. "Who, being in the form of God, thought it not robbery to be equal with God: But made himself of no reputation."

The *third* step downward in the humiliation of Christ is this: "And took upon him the form of a servant."

Jesus came to this earth as a servant. He

worked as a carpenter. I suppose if you had lived in Nazareth in that day, you could have gone by the shop where Jesus worked and told Him you needed some repair work done at your house—"I have a door that is coming off the hinges; I wonder if You would come and fix it?" I think He would have said, "I'll be right over." You see, He took upon Himself the form of a servant. He could have been born in Caesar's palace. He was a king, but He never made that claim during those early years—in fact, He didn't make it until He rode into Jerusalem in the so-called Triumphal Entry.

He came into this world as a working man, a humble man, a little man. Not only did He humiliate Himself to become a human being, but He came among the majority where most of us are today. He was one of the little people.

The prophet Isaiah wrote that Christ would come as a "root of Jesse" (see Isa. 11:10). As a young preacher I often wondered why Isaiah didn't call Him a root out of David. Well, I have discovered the reason. When Jesus was born, Mary, who was in the line of David (and Joseph, who was also in the Davidic line by another route), was a peasant. They were working folk living in that little, miserable, gentile town called Nazareth. Then wasn't Jesus in the line of David? Oh, yes. David was anointed king, but his father Jesse was a farmer in Bethlehem, and his line had dropped back to the place of a peasant. Our Lord was born into a peasant family.

"He took upon him the form of a servant."

The *fourth* step in His humiliation is this: "And was made in the likeness of men."

For years this did not impress me at all, because I am a man and I like being a man. I couldn't see that being a man was a humiliation. I think there is a dignity about being a human being that is quite wonderful. How can it be humbling?

Let me give you a very homely illustration that I trust might be as helpful to you as it is to me. I confess it is rather ridiculous, but it will illustrate the humiliation of Christ in His incarnation.

When we first came to California in 1940, we had the experience of living in a place where the bugs and the ants are not killed off in the wintertime. We got here the first of November and had not been here long until I found in the kitchen one morning a freeway of ants coming into the sink. They were coming down one side and going back on the other side. Also I found they had discovered the sugar bowl, and they had a freeway in and out of it. I don't know about you, but I don't want ants in the sink and I don't want ants in the sugar bowl. So I began to investigate and learned that the thing we had to do was to kill them. Now I'm just not sadistic; I'm not brutal; I don't like to kill things. But I began to kill ants. I got ant poison, and we got rid of ants. Then when we moved over to our own home, here were ants. They had found out where we'd moved. I have a wonderful Christian friend who is in the bug-killing business. He comes to my place twice a year, sprays everything—under the house, under the eaves, the trees—everything, and you can't find an ant on my place.

Now I do not know this to be a fact, but I have a notion that the ants had a protest meeting around my lot. Maybe they carried banners that read, "Down with McGee. He hates ants!" But, frankly, I don't hate ants. That's not my hang-up at all. If I had some way of communicating with those ants and getting a message to them, I'd say, "Look here. I don't hate you. Just stay out of the sugar bowl, and stay out of the sink. I'll put sugar and water outside for you—I'd be glad to do that if you'd just stay outside." But I do not know how to get that message over to the ants—except by becoming an ant. Now suppose that I had the power to become an ant. (If I *could* do it, I would *not* do it because I know some folk who would step on me if I were an ant!) But listen, if I could become an ant—from where I am now down to the position of an ant—that would be humiliation, wouldn't it? I'd *hate* to become an ant. But, my friend, that is nothing compared to what my Lord did when He left heaven's glory and became a man, when He took upon Himself our humanity, when He was made in the likeness of men.

And being found in fashion as a man, he humbled himself, and became obedient unto death, even the death of the cross [Phil. 2:8].

The *fifth* step in our Lord's humiliation is that He humbled Himself. "And being found in fashion as a man, he humbled himself." You and I have been humbled by someone doing or saying something which has been humiliating to us. But notice that Christ "humbled himself." This is a most difficult thing to do.

One of the finest things I ever heard about John Wesley was concerning an incident when he was about to cross a brook over which was a very narrow bridge, just wide enough for one person. As he was starting over, he met a liberal preacher of that day. This preacher swelled up and said, "I never give way to a fool." John Wesley looked at him for a moment, smiled, and began to back off, saying, "I always do." My friend, it is difficult to take that humble place, but it has made me think a great deal more of John Wesley. We find it difficult to humble ourselves, but our Lord humbled Himself.

Many of us have had humbling experiences. I am reminded of a summer conference at which I was speaking years ago. One of the speakers at this conference was a most dignified Englishman. He was a gifted speaker and very dignified. He was shocked when I wore a sport shirt even on the platform. To him that was the unpardonable sin. He wore a white shirt, collar, and tie; in fact, he wore a frock coat for the evening services! Well, one afternoon it rained, and in the auditorium a window glass had been broken out so that it had rained in on the platform. In those early days all the speakers in any week would march onto the platform every night, regardless of who was bringing the message. On that particular night I walked behind this dignified, formally dressed Englishman, and when he hit that wet spot on the platform, his feet went out from under him. Oh, how he sprawled! And, you know, everybody laughed. I laughed so hard I had to leave the platform. After I went back and sat down on the platform, I thought I never could quit laughing. The next night we started in as usual, and he was right ahead of me again. I reached over and said, "Say, it'd be nice to have a repeat performance tonight." "Oh," he said, "wasn't that humbling!" Yes, he was humbled, but he did not humble himself. Many times we are humbled, are we not? But we do not humble ourselves.

The Lord Jesus humbled Himself, and that is altogether different.

We come now to the *sixth* step in His humiliation: "and [He] became obedient unto death." Death is a very humiliating sort of thing. It is not natural. Sometimes at funerals I hear people say, "Doesn't he look natural?" It is generally said by some well-meaning friend who wants to comfort the loved ones. I don't know why it would be a source of comfort to think that Grandpa looks natural in death. I bite my lip to keep from saying, "No, he doesn't look natural." Death is not natural. God didn't create man to die. Man dies because of sin, because of his transgression. Death came by the transgression of one man, and that man was Adam, and death has passed down to all men. Death is not natural. God did not create man to die.

Now when the Lord Jesus came to this earth, He was a little different from the rest of us. You and I came to live. I honestly don't want to die; I want to live. I have come to the most fruitful part of my ministry, and I want to live as long as the Lord will let me. But the Lord Jesus was born to die. He came to this earth to die. He didn't have to die, but He "became obedient unto death" and gave Himself up willingly. I have to die, but I don't want to. He didn't have to die, but He wanted to. Why? In order that He might save you and me if we will put our trust in Him. This is what He said, "As the Father knoweth me, even so know I the Father: and I lay down my life for the sheep. . . . Therefore doth my Father love me, because I lay down my life, that I might take it again. No man taketh it from me, but I lay it down of myself. I have power to lay it down, and I have power to take it again . . ." (John 10:15, 17–18).

The *seventh* and last step in the humiliation of Christ is "even the death of the cross." Not only did He become obedient unto death, but to the death of the *cross*. This would make a greater impact on our consciousness if we said that Christ died in the electric chair or the gas chamber or by the hangman's noose. It was that kind of disgraceful death. He came from the highest glory to the lowest place of humiliation. Why did He do it? Let's go back to the word *others*. "Look not every man on his own things, but every man also on the things of others." He left all the glory of heaven and came down to this earth, became a man, and suffered the death of a criminal for others—for you and me. Thank God for that! This is the mind of Christ.

MIND OF GOD—
EXALTATION OF CHRIST

Now the mind of God the Father is to glorify Christ. We have seen the seven steps downward; now we will see the seven steps upward. The mind of God is the exaltation of Christ.

Wherefore God also hath highly exalted him, and given him a name which is above every name [Phil. 2:9].

Here is the *first* step up: "God also hath highly exalted him." The supreme purpose of God the Father in this universe today is that Jesus Christ be glorified in the universe which He created and that He be glorified on the earth where man dwells, where man rebelled against God.

The thing that makes this little earth significant and important is the death of Christ down here—nothing else. Astronomers tell us that we are a little speck in space, and if our little world were to be blotted out, it wouldn't make any difference to the universe. And that is absolutely true. Someone else has said that man is a "disease on the epidermis of a minor planet." That is what we are! The thing that has lent dignity to man and has caused him to look up into the heavens and sing the doxology is the fact that Jesus Christ came to this earth and died on the cross for him. "Wherefore God also hath highly exalted him."

Now the *second* step: "and given him a name which is above every name." The next time you take His name in vain, think of this. God intends to exalt that name that you use as a curse word and drag in the mud. The other day a pilot who stepped off a plane on which a bomb had exploded—and it was almost a miracle that he was able to land the plane—just stood over at the side of the crowd and said, "Jesus Christ, Jesus Christ!" I don't know if he was saying it as profanity—God have mercy on him if he did it that way. I hope that it was a prayer. The name of Jesus Christ will be exalted above the names of all the great men of this world and above the names of all the angels in glory.

That at the name of Jesus every knee should bow, of things in heaven, and things in earth, and things under the earth [Phil. 2:10].

In this verse we find the next three steps of Christ's exaltation.

The *third* step: "That at the name of Jesus"—*Jesus* means "Savior." Before His birth in Bethlehem, the angel said, ". . . thou shalt call his name JESUS: for he shall save his people from their sins" (Matt. 1:21). Now notice the reference to prophecy: "Now all this was done, that it might be fulfilled which was spoken of the Lord by the prophet, saying, Behold, a virgin shall be with child, and shall bring forth a son, and they shall call his name Emmanuel, which being interpreted is, God with us" (Matt. 1:22–23).

Can you show me anyplace in the Bible where He was called Emmanuel? When I entered the ministry, I had no problem with "Behold a virgin shall conceive." Since He is God, how else could He get into the human family except by a miraculous birth? But the thing that did cause a problem in this verse was, "He shall be called Emmanuel" because I couldn't find any place where they called Him

Emmanuel. "Well, then," you may say, "that prophecy was not fulfilled."

Oh, my friend, this is one of the most wonderful fulfillments of prophecy you can imagine. The angel said, "Call Him Jesus because He'll save His people from their sins." Now think through this. You couldn't call me *Jesus*—I can't even save myself. Neither would it be accurate to call you *Jesus* because you can't save yourself. You see, all of us are in the same ship today. The human family is on a sinking ship, and it's going down. If there is to be a Savior, He's got to come from the outside. There are those who want to throw out a lifeline. But to do that is like being on a ship that is sinking, and somebody on the top deck says to those down in the steerage, "Let me throw you a lifeline." But the top deck is going down too! You see, the rope has to come from some other place than the human ship. No human being can be a Savior. "You shall call His name *Jesus* because He is going to save His people from their sins." How can He save His people from their sins? Because He will be Emmanuel, God with us. That little Baby who came yonder to Bethlehem is God with us. He took upon Himself, not the likeness of angels, but our humanity. He is Emmanuel, God with us. And because He is that, He can be called Jesus. And friend, nobody else can properly be called *Jesus*.

Now God says, "I'm going to exalt the name which was given to Him when He came to earth above every other name."

Now notice the *fourth* step of His exaltation: "Of things in heaven."

And the *fifth* step: "And things in earth."

And the *sixth* step: "And things under the earth." This verse is used by the Restitutionalists to support their theory that ultimately everybody will be saved. We had a spokesman of this cult in Los Angeles for many years. He made the statement that Judas Iscariot and the Devil would be walking down the streets of heaven together because ultimately all would be saved. Of course it was unfortunate that he used this verse because when you compare it with Colossians 1:20, you see its true meaning. The subject in the Philippians passage is the lordship of Jesus. God has highly exalted Him, that at the name of Jesus every knee must bow, in heaven, in earth, and under the earth. That is, even hell will have to bow to Him because He is the Lord. He is God. But merely bowing does not imply salvation. Colossians 1:20 is not talking about lordship, but about Christ's reconciling work, His redemptive work. And what was reconciled? What was redeemed? Was hell included? No. The things *under the earth* are not mentioned here. Why? Because this verse is talking about redemption, and there is no redemption in hell. By putting these two verses together it is clear that those in hell who bow to Jesus are merely acknowledging His lordship. "That at the name of Jesus every knee should bow, of things in heaven, and things in earth, and things under the earth."

Here now is the *seventh* and final step of Christ's exaltation:

And that every tongue should confess that Jesus Christ is Lord, to the glory of God the Father [Phil. 2:11].

Every tongue shall "confess that Jesus Christ is Lord." That doesn't mean that every tongue will confess Him as Savior. It is interesting that even in hell they must recognize the lordship of Jesus, which will, I think, increase their anguish.

I want to give a word of caution here. Be very careful about calling Jesus your Lord if He is not your Lord. He made the statement that many would call Him Lord, Lord, and even perform miracles in His name, yet He will say, "I never knew you" (see Matt. 7:21–23). My friend, you had better know Him as your Savior before you say He is your Lord. If He is your Savior, then you can become obedient to Him as your Lord.

I don't even like to hear people sing, "What a Friend we have in Jesus." We have a friend in Him all right, but listen to the words of Jesus: "Ye are my friends, *if* ye do whatsoever I command you" (John 15:14, italics mine). We can call Him our friend if we do what He commands us to do. He is not our Lord unless we obey Him.

MIND OF PAUL—THINGS OF CHRIST

We have been learning about the mind of Christ. We have seen it is not something which can be imitated. "Let this mind be in you which was also in Christ Jesus" can only happen by *impartation*. It is the work of the Spirit of God within us which will produce the fruit of meekness or humility in our lives.

Now we are going to see the mind of Christ as it walked down the Roman roads. We will see it lived in Roman homes and in a Roman jail. We will see three examples given to us: the mind of Paul, the mind of Timothy, and the mind of Epaphroditus (pastor of the church at Philippi). In this heathen empire there were these three men who exhibited the mind of Christ and there may have been three million

more, but these are the ones who are presented to us in this epistle.

Wherefore, my beloved, as ye have always obeyed, not as in my presence only, but now much more in my absence, work out your own salvation with fear and trembling [Phil. 2:12].

"Salvation" in this verse is used, I believe, in a general sense. Paul is talking about working out their problems which they had in the church and working out the problems in their own Christian lives. He is not there to help them and is not sure that he ever will be there again because he is in a Roman prison. So he tells them to work out their "own salvation with fear and trembling."

A preacher was reading this verse of Scripture in the morning service. A little girl whispered to her mother, "Mother, you can't work *out* salvation unless it has first been worked *in*, can you?" Now that is a very good question. The next verse answers it.

For it is God which worketh in you both to will and to do of his good pleasure [Phil. 2:13].

So God works out that which He had worked in. If God has saved you, He has saved you by faith—plus nothing. God is not accepting any kind of good works for salvation. But *after* you are saved, God talks to you about your works. The salvation that He worked in by faith is a salvation He will work out also.

Calvin expressed it this way: "Faith alone saves, but the faith that saves is not alone." James states it like this: "Even so faith, if it hath not works, is dead, being alone. Yea, a man may say, Thou hast faith, and I have works: shew me thy faith without thy works, and I will shew thee my faith by my works" (James 2:17–18). Only God can see the heart; He knows our true condition. He knows if I have saving faith; He knows if you have saving faith. But your neighbor can't see your faith. The only thing he can see is the works of faith. True faith will work itself out so that the people around us will be able to tell that we are different, that we are Christians. We don't need to wear a placard or some sort of symbol to identify ourselves as Christians.

Paul will talk about that faith which will work itself out in the lives of the Philippian believers.

Do all things without murmurings and disputings [Phil. 2:14].

Don't accept an office in the church or in the Sunday school if you have to grumble about doing it. That absolutely wrecks more Christian work than anything else. Do *all* things without grumbling or disputing.

That ye may be blameless and harmless, the sons of God, without rebuke, in the midst of a crooked and perverse nation, among whom ye shine as lights in the world [Phil. 2:15].

Be like a light. When we go out at night we see the stars up there. When God looks down on this dark world, He sees those who are His own as little lights down here. The children sing "This Little Light of Mine." Well, my friend, that's exactly what it is. Paul says, "Among whom ye shine as lights in the world." As the stars are up there, we are down here.

Holding forth the word of life; that I may rejoice in the day of Christ, that I have not run in vain, neither laboured in vain [Phil. 2:16].

Life and light are related. When we hold forth the Word of Life, we are lights in the world. Paul rejoices when he hears that the Philippian believers are manifesting their faith in good works. These believers were very close to the heart of Paul because they were his converts.

Yea, and if I be offered upon the sacrifice and service of your faith, I joy, and rejoice with you all [Phil. 2:17].

Here is one of the most wonderful verses in the entire Word of God. It pictures what the Christian life really should be. He is referring to one of the earliest offerings in the Old Testament. When we go back to Genesis 35:14, we find that Jacob set up a pillar at Beth-el, "and he poured a drink offering thereon, and he poured oil thereon." Then in the books of Leviticus and Numbers the sacrifices are described. We learn that there was a drink offering which was to be added to the burnt offering and the meal offering. It was never added to the sin offering or the trespass offering. It was a most unusual offering in that it had nothing to do with redemption; it had nothing to do with the person of Christ. They would bring in a skin of wine and just pour it on the sacrifice which was being consumed by fire. What happened to it? It would go up in steam and disappear.

Paul is saying, "I want my life to be poured out like a drink offering on the offering of Christ." Paul knows that the Lord Jesus

Christ made the supreme sacrifice. He wanted his life to be a drink offering—just poured out to go up in steam. He wanted to be so consumed and obscured that all that is seen is just Jesus Christ. He wanted Christ to receive all the honor and the glory. This was the mind of Paul. I can think of no higher wish for the Christian life.

For the same cause also do ye joy, and rejoice with me [Phil. 2:18].

In other words, "If your life commends the gospel, my life is just poured out as a drink offering. Together we'll rejoice over this." It is a walk in humility. Only a person with the mind of Christ could be so poured out as a drink offering. How gloriously wonderful that is.

Paul ends on a note of joy and rejoicing. Today we often rejoice over the wrong things. We need to rejoice over the fact that Jesus *died* for us and that we can *serve* Him. When we hear of someone whom God is using or hear of a wonderful church where people are being saved and built up in the faith, we ought to rejoice. If we are walking in humility, we will rejoice at the success of others. We have too much strife and vainglory. That was hurting the cause of Christ in Paul's day, and it still hurts the cause of Christ. The mind of Christ in the believer will bring joy and will bring glory to God.

MIND OF TIMOTHY— LIKE-MINDED WITH PAUL

But I trust in the Lord Jesus to send Timotheus shortly unto you, that I also may be of good comfort, when I know your state [Phil. 2:19].

Timothy was Paul's spiritual son. Paul had great confidence in him. He could trust Timothy to care for the state of the Philippian believers.

For I have no man likeminded, who will naturally care for your state [Phil. 2:20].

Here we have described the mind of Timothy, and we find that he is like-minded with Paul. Since he was like-minded with Paul, it means that he had the mind of Christ, and he was characterized by humility. We don't need a National Council or World Council of Churches to bring men together. In fact, we don't need any organization to bring them together. If they both have the mind of Christ, they *are* together.

Timothy had been faithful to Paul. Sometimes a convert later turns against the person who led him to the Lord. This is like a child turning against a parent. Paul had had that happen to him, but Timothy was faithful to him. Paul was sending him to the Philippian believers because he could trust him. It is wonderful to have men like-minded with Christ so they can work together.

For all seek their own, not the things which are Jesus Christ's [Phil. 2:21].

There were many others who were seeking their own glory. They wanted to make a name for themselves. Because they were seeking their own glory, they were willing to belittle Paul.

How do *you* respect others who are standing for the Word of God today? When I hear a man of God being criticized, I recognize that somewhere there is strife and vainglory. The mind of Christ will not allow you to criticize another man who stands for Christ. Paul says, "I can't trust these other men."

But ye know the proof of him, that, as a son with the father, he hath served with me in the gospel [Phil. 2:22].

People speak a lot about togetherness in our day. There can be no more togetherness than for two people to have the mind of Christ. They are together even though they may be miles apart. That is why there is such a bond between fellow Christians who have the mind of Christ.

When a Christian young man and a Christian young lady fall in love, there is a togetherness that you cannot have in just a sexual marriage. A relationship that is simply physical can be bought on any street corner. But when a husband and wife have the mind of Christ, they are really together. There is no human ceremony that can bring two people together in that way. It is a glorious, wonderful relationship.

Him therefore I hope to send presently, so soon as I shall see how it will go with me.

But I trust in the Lord that I also myself shall come shortly [Phil. 2:23–24].

Paul wanted Timothy to be the one who would bring them the message about what was going to happen to him there in the prison. Paul had hopes that he would be released from prison. Tradition says that he was released from prison and had quite an itinerant ministry

after this, although this is not recorded in Scripture. When the Christians were persecuted under Nero, naturally Paul, the leader, was brought back and executed.

MIND OF EPAPHRODITUS— THE WORK OF CHRIST

Epaphroditus was another who had the mind of Christ. He and Paul and Timothy were all together, brethren in the Lord, serving the Lord. Remember that he is the pastor of the church in Philippi.

Yet I supposed it necessary to send to you Epaphroditus, my brother, and companion in labour, and fellowsoldier, but your messenger, and he that ministered to my wants [Phil. 2:25].

Paul had founded the church at Philippi, but Epaphroditus was not jealous of Paul. Paul loved Epaphroditus because he had the mind of Christ and Paul could trust him. He calls him "my brother, and my companion in labour, and my fellowsoldier." Paul says, "He is my fellowsoldier—he fights with me. He doesn't stick a knife in my back when I'm away. He doesn't side with my enemies. He stands shoulder to shoulder with me for the faith."

"But your messenger, and he that ministered to my wants." He was of practical help to Paul who is confined there in chains.

For he longed after you all, and was full of heaviness, because that ye had heard that he had been sick [Phil. 2:26].

This is almost humorous here. Epaphroditus got sick, and word was sent back to the church at Philippi that their own pastor was sick. He longed for them—he probably was a little homesick also. Then when he heard that the church back there was mourning for him because he was sick, he had a relapse because it hurt him that they were hurt because he was sick! There was sort of a vicious circle set in motion here. But it was good because it revealed the marvelous relationship between the church at Philippi and their pastor.

In my conference ministry I speak in many churches, and I have learned that I can judge a church by its attitude toward a pastor who preaches and teaches the Word of God. When a deacon takes me aside and says, "Dr. McGee, we have a fine young pastor, and he is preaching the Word of God," this rejoices my heart. But sometimes a deacon takes me aside and says, "Say, how do we get rid of a pastor like we have? He is too opinionated, too dogmatic, and he wants to run things." I ask him,

"Is he teaching and preaching the Word?" When the deacon's answer is, "Oh, yes, but we have had that all along," I can see that the Word has had no effect upon that man. If his feeling is shared by the church in general, that church is doomed. The rejection of a Bible-teaching preacher is the death knell of many churches across this land of ours. You see, the Devil has been very clever. He has shifted his attack from the Word of God itself to the man who teaches the Word of God. I find this is true across the length and breadth of our nation. The real test of a church is its attitude toward its pastor.

Epaphroditus was greatly loved by his church, and that speaks well for the church in Philippi.

For indeed he was sick nigh unto death: but God had mercy on him; and not on him only, but on me also, lest I should have sorrow upon sorrow [Phil. 2:27].

Let me point out something here that you may not notice. Many sincere believers today hold the theory that Christians should not be sick, that they should trust God to heal them. Let me ask a question: Why didn't Paul heal Epaphroditus? He was so sick he almost died! You see, Paul and the other apostles had "sign gifts" because they did not have what we have today, a New Testament. When Paul started out with the gospel message, nothing of the New Testament had been written. Paul himself wrote 1 Thessalonians, the second book of the New Testament to be penned. When he went into a new territory with his message, what was his authority? He had no authority except sign gifts, which included the gift of healing. But now Paul is nearing the conclusion of his ministry. You will remember that Paul had a thorn in the flesh which the Lord Jesus would not remove. Instead, He gave Paul the grace to bear it. Then you remember that Timothy had stomach trouble. If Paul had been a faith healer, why hadn't he healed Timothy? Actually, he told him to take a little wine for his stomach's sake. And in 2 Timothy 4:20 he said that he had left Trophimus in Miletum *sick*. Why hadn't he healed him? And now Paul says he has this young preacher, Epaphroditus, with him, and he was so sick he almost died. Paul didn't heal him. Rather, he gives all the credit to God; he says that God had mercy on him. His healing came about in a natural sort of way. Paul made it a matter of prayer, and God heard and answered prayer. Why hadn't Paul used his gift of healing? Because at this late stage, even before the apos-

tles disappeared from the scene, the emphasis was moving back to the Great Physician.

You see, this epistle is emphasizing the mind of Christ, a humble mind. If I were a faith healer, I would be in the limelight; I would be somebody very great and very famous. But I'm not. The Lord Jesus is the Great Physician. When it was first discovered that I had cancer, I received a great number of letters advising me to go to this healer and that healer. No, I didn't go to anyone, my friend, except a very fine cancer specialist and the Great Physician. I had an appointment with Him and I told Him I wanted to live. I turned over my case to Him. And He gets the credit for what happened to me.

So here is Paul the apostle toward the end of his ministry putting no emphasis on healing whatsoever. He has a sick preacher with him, but he does not exercise the gift of healing that he had. Why? Because Paul is shifting the emphasis where it should be, upon the person of the Lord Jesus Christ.

Now Paul is sending Epaphroditus back to them.

I sent him therefore the more carefully, that, when ye see him again, ye may rejoice, and that I may be the less sorrowful [Phil. 2:28].

Paul wants them to rejoice, not sorrow. "And that I may be the less sorrowful"—he was disturbed about the church in Philippi because it had been mourning instead of rejoicing.

Receive him therefore in the Lord with all gladness; and hold such in reputation [Phil. 2:29].

How gracious Paul was with this preacher from Philippi! A man like Epaphroditus should be respected and loved.

And, my friend, we should respect the one who is teaching the Word of God. If he has a gift of teaching which God is using, both the gift and the individual should be respected. Our attention should be focused upon the Word of God. I just don't participate anymore in conventions and seminars that focus attention on problems—the drug problem, the alcohol problem, the sex problem, the youth problems, and the senior citizen problems—and offer psychological solutions for them. My friend, the *problem* is that we don't get back to the Word of God. It is the Word of God that reveals Christ and the mind of Christ.

Because for the work of Christ he was nigh unto death, not regarding his life,

to supply your lack of service toward me [Phil. 2:30].

Epaphroditus was doing the work of Christ. He had to have the mind of Christ to do that.

It sends chills up and down my spine to read about these men. This is in the first century, at the time of the Roman Empire. The empire of Caesar Augustus moved out and took over the world. The law of Rome became supreme everywhere. There was no mercy shown to anyone, but there was law and order everywhere. There was not a power in that day that could protest against Rome. Then there went out this little man, Paul the apostle, and those who were like-minded with him, and they preached a gospel that there is a God of the universe who, through a redemption that He had wrought on a Roman cross, had provided mercy for mankind. Multitudes turned to the Lord Jesus in that day.

Now I see this little man, Paul the apostle, chained to a Roman soldier. What is he doing? Well, he is witnessing for Christ, and he is rejoicing in the Lord. He has the mind of Christ. Also I see a fine young man, Timothy, walking in that pagan city. You say you cannot live for Christ in a godless society? Look at Timothy. He did pretty well. He had the mind of Christ. And then I take a look at Ephaphroditus, a faithful pastor way up yonder in the city of Philippi—it was a Roman colony, but it was a pagan, heathen city. Epaphroditus had the mind of Christ.

Then I look at Vernon McGee, and I say to him, *Stop offering excuses in this day in which you are living*! If these men could have the mind of Christ in the first century, today in the twentieth century right where we are now, you and I can have the mind of Christ. Not by imitation, but by yielding to Him the Spirit of God can produce in our own lives the mind of Christ. Oh, how desperately this is needed in our day!

CHAPTER 3

THEME: Prize for Christian living; Paul changed his bookkeeping system of the past; Paul changed his purpose for the present; Paul changed his hope for the future

We have seen the *philosophy* of Christian living: "For to me to live is Christ, and to die is gain" (Phil. 1:21). We have seen the *pattern* for Christian living: "Let this mind be in you, which was also in Christ Jesus" (Phil. 2:5). Now we come to the *prize* for Christian living which is summarized in Paul's personal testimony: "I press toward the mark for the prize of the high calling of God in Christ Jesus" (v. 14).

We will see in this chapter that Paul changed his bookkeeping system of the *past*, he changed his purpose for the *present*, and he changed his hope for the *future*. Paul believed that God was going to establish a kingdom on this earth; he never changed his view on that. But he did see that there is a marvelous, wonderful hope for believers in Christ—both Jew and Gentile—the day when Christ will take His own out of the world.

PAUL CHANGED HIS BOOKKEEPING SYSTEM OF THE PAST

Finally, my brethren, rejoice in the Lord. To write the same things to you, to me indeed is not grievous, but for you it is safe [Phil. 3:1].

"Finally, my brethren" gives us the impression that Paul is coming to the conclusion of this epistle. He must have intended this to be a very brief thank-you note to the Philippian believers. But we are just midway in the epistle; so obviously the Spirit of God prompted him to go on.

My wife reminded me in a conference some time ago that when I was speaking I said, "Let me say this to you in the final analysis, and then I'll be through"—then I went on talking for another fifteen minutes. She said, "You weren't through at all." So I told her I was just being scriptural, that I was doing it the way Paul did it.

His final message was going to be, "Rejoice in the Lord." I think that would still be his final message if he were here today. He has shown how three men, himself, Timothy, and Epaphroditus, all had the mind of Christ. They were able to rejoice even in sickness and imprisonment. The early church could rejoice amid the fires of persecution.

Besides, Paul is saying that it has been no burden to him to write this letter. He has no burden on his heart such as there had been when he wrote to the Galatians and the Corinthians. The Philippians have been a great joy to him. Now he wants them to rejoice, too. Notice that it is actually a command: "Rejoice in the Lord."

"To write the same things to you, to me indeed is not grievous, but for you it is safe." It is safe for him to write to the Philippians. They were spiritually mature. They loved Paul, and he loved them. He felt close to them. So he says it is not grievous, or irksome, to write to them. It is safe for him to write to them because he knows they will understand.

Beware of dogs, beware of evil workers, beware of the concision [Phil. 3:2].

"Beware of dogs." This is not a word of warning to the mailmen. I once had a dog that hated mailmen, and I don't know why. We changed mailmen several times during the period we had him, and he had the same attitude toward each of them. But Paul is not referring to animals in this verse. We will get some insight into his thinking by turning back to the prophecy of Isaiah who warned against the false prophets of his day: "His watchmen are blind: they are all ignorant, they are all dumb dogs, they cannot bark; sleeping, lying down, loving to slumber" (Isa. 56:10). Isaiah was warning the people against the false prophets who were attempting to comfort the people and were telling them that everything was fine instead of warning them of coming disaster. The northern kingdom had already gone into captivity because the false prophets had given them a false sense of security. God was warning the southern kingdom not to do the same thing. He was calling the false prophets "dumb dogs." They won't speak out. They won't tell it as it is. Dogs are those who are not declaring the full counsel of God.

We have the same grave danger in our affluent society. Comfort is the word of the day. We look for comfortable places to stay when we are traveling. We enjoy all the creature comforts that we can afford. The desire for comfort has carried over into the church. There is a danger of just comforting the people of the congregation because that is what they would like to have coming from the pulpit.

A prominent member of a congregation which I served left the church because he said I never gave him any comforting messages. I found out later that in his business he was not always ethical. In fact, some considered him very unethical. Frankly, he didn't need messages of comfort. He needed messages of warning. I think that was what he didn't like. It may be that he thought I knew something of his business dealings, which I absolutely did not know at the time. In fact, I have never preached a sermon at any individual in my life. I have tried to preach what the Word of God says. Often that is not a comforting message.

When I went to see my doctor, I tried my best to be evasive with him. I told him that I knew someone who had the same trouble I did and he was given medicine and recovered. As he examined me, he said, "Dr. McGee, if you need medication, I will give it to you, but I don't think you need medication. You are in trouble." Well, that was not a comforting message! He told me candidly, "I'm going to tell you the truth, because if I don't, you will not have confidence in me. You have cancer." I have thanked him for that ever since. I wanted to hear the truth. Don't you want to hear the truth?

In Isaiah's day there were a great many false prophets who were comforting the people when they should have been warning them. Isaiah likens the false prophets to dumb dogs. You see, a good sheep dog is constantly alert to danger. If a lion or a bear makes a foray into the flock, that dog will bark like mad and run it away if he can. He gives warning of the approach of any kind of danger. But the false prophets gave no warning at all. Therefore the southern kingdom had been lulled to sleep and resented Isaiah's effort to arouse them.

America today is in the same position. We are going to sleep, my friend, under the comfortable blanket of affluence. We like the idea of comfort, of getting something for nothing, of taking it easy, of having a good day. My feeling is that somebody ought to do a little barking.

So Paul warned, "Beware of dogs"—beware of men who are constantly comforting you and are not giving you the Word of God.

"Beware of evil workers." This is another group that would actually abuse and use believers. They are not honest.

"Beware of the concision"—he slurred the word *circumcision* and said *concision*. He is saying that they are no longer of the true circumcision, referring to the legalizers, those who were attempting to force Christians to keep the law of Moses for salvation and sanctification.

For we are the circumcision, which worship God in the spirit, and rejoice in Christ Jesus, and have no confidence in the flesh [Phil. 3:3].

"We are the circumcision." What does Paul mean by that? He makes it very clear at the end of the Epistle to the Galatians: "For in Christ Jesus neither circumcision availeth any thing, nor uncircumcision, but a new creature" (Gal. 6:15). The old circumcision is out. God is not looking for a mere external observance. True circumcision is of the heart. It is the new birth, a new heart attitude toward God. True circumcision is being *in* Christ.

"And have no confidence in the flesh." We do not have confidence in our old nature. We trust Christ alone. We do not look to ourselves for salvation, nor can we live the Christian life in our old nature. It must be Christ in us.

These legalizers would follow Paul in his missionary journeys. After he was gone, they would meet with the believers and say something like this: "Well, we know that brother Paul says we are to have no confidence in the flesh, that we are not to trust the rituals nor the sacrifices, and that the Law won't save us. He does well to say that, because he doesn't have very much to rest upon. He doesn't have the background in Judaism that we do. He says that because of his ignorance and the failure of his life to measure up to the requirements of the Law. So of course he has no confidence in the flesh."

Now Paul is going to answer that.

Though I might also have confidence in the flesh. If any other man thinketh that he hath whereof he might trust in the flesh, I more [Phil. 3:4].

Paul says, "If there is any person who could have confidence in the flesh, then I could have even more confidence." He is willing to stack his religious life against that of any man, and he knows that he could measure up to him and surpass him—"I more."

Now he is going to list seven things in which he trusted at one time. This is religion. If anyone could have been saved by religion, Saul of Tarsus would have been the man.

Circumcised the eighth day, of the stock of Israel, of the tribe of Benjamin, an Hebrew of the Hebrews; as touching the law, a Pharisee;

Concerning zeal, persecuting the church; touching the righteousness which is in the law, blameless [Phil. 3:5–6].

These are still things that people boast about today, but none of them can save you.

1. "Circumcised the eighth day." This is a basic rite of the Mosaic system. Well, of course he didn't get up out of the crib on the eighth day and go down to the temple or synagogue to have circumcision performed. It means that his parents took him on his eighth day to be circumcised. He is making it clear that he had godly parents. They reared him according to the Mosaic Law. You will remember that the Lord Jesus also had godly parents who brought Him to the temple to be circumcised.

One of the things that hurt me and held me back in my early ministry was the fact that I had not been brought up in a Christian home. My dad was a heavy drinker who would not darken the door of a church. He was very bitter and very prejudiced. He did make me go to Sunday school, and I thank God for that. But I never saw a Bible or heard a prayer in my home. When I went away to seminary, I did not know even the books of the Bible. I would meet other fellows who had been brought up in Christian homes. They seemed to know so much. I always felt deprived, felt that I had missed something. Well, Paul did not have this handicap. He could say, "I was circumcised on the eighth day," which means he had godly parents.

2. "Of the stock of Israel." Probably many of the Judaizers were half-breeds; Paul was not. He was of the stock of Israel. I think you could have checked Paul's genealogy in the temple in that day. Paul had a genealogy, a background, and he knew he belonged.

3. "Of the tribe of Benjamin." This is like saying that he belonged to the best family. Benjamin had been the favorite son of old Jacob. Rachel had given birth to Benjamin when she died, and she had called him "son of my sorrow," but Jacob had named him "son of my right hand." Rachel had been the bright spot in his life before Peniel, and when he had looked in the crib at little Benjamin, he had seen him as Rachel's son. Benjamin became his right hand, his walking stick, the one on whom he leaned. Also the first king of Israel came from the tribe of Benjamin. His name was Saul, and I have a notion that Saul of Tarsus was named after him. So Paul could say with pride that he came from the tribe of Benjamin.

It is an advantage to be able to say, "My father was a minister of the Word of God," or, "My father was a layman who stood for the Word of God." On the other hand, sometimes it can work for a hindrance. I find people who say, "Dr. McGee, I was brought up in such-and-such a church; my grandfather was a founder of the church. There is even a window in the church dedicated to him. So I'll never leave that church." That can be a hindrance if the church has become liberal and the Word of God is no longer preached there. But for Paul, being of the tribe of Benjamin was a definite asset.

4. "An Hebrew of the Hebrews." This means he was a leader. He was in the highest stratum of the religious circle. He was up at the top.

5. "As touching the law, a Pharisee." The Pharisees represented the very best in Israel. They were a religious-political party, and their aim was to establish the kingdom. They had arisen sometime after or during the Captivity. They were fundamental. They believed in the integrity of the Scriptures; they believed in angels; they believed in the resurrection and in miracles. They were also extremely nationalistic in their politics.

I think the reason they sent Nicodemus to see Jesus was because they thought, *Here is a prophet come out of Galilee. If he will just let us hitch our wagon to his star, we'll go places because we know how to manipulate Rome.* The Pharisees thought they could bring the kingdom by political manipulation. They wanted to establish the kingdom of God here upon this earth. Paul could say that *he* was a Pharisee.

6. "Concerning zeal, persecuting the church." Paul thought he was doing God's will when he persecuted the church. The other Pharisees were willing to relax when they had run the Christians out of Jerusalem, but Paul was determined to ferret them out all over the world. That was his purpose on his way to Damascus at the time of his conversion.

7. "Touching the righteousness which is in the law, blameless." Notice that he does not say he was sinless or perfect; he says he was blameless. In Romans 7:7 Paul tells us his story: ". . . I had not known sin, but by the law: for I had not known lust, except the law had said, Thou shalt not covet." Paul does not claim sinless perfection. This commandment showed him his sin.

Now if you break the commandment, Thou shalt not steal, you'll have the evidence or you may leave your fingerprints back at the scene of the crime. The same thing could be said about murder—you would have a *corpus delicti* on your hands. It is impossible to commit adultery without somebody else knowing about it. But you can covet and nobody would

be the wiser. If Paul had kept quiet, we might think he had reached the place of sinless perfection, but he very frankly said he had not. He says that the Law "slew him."

What he means by "touching the righteousness which is in the law, blameless" is that he had brought the proper sacrifice for his sin to make things right before God. Paul was sincere. Regarding the Law, Paul was a supersaint. He had every right to say, "If any other man thinketh that he hath whereof he might trust in the flesh, I more."

These were the things that Paul had on the credit side of the ledger. It was such a big total that he felt all of these things commended him to God. He thought they were all credits to him.

On the debit side of his ledger was a Person he hated. That was Jesus Christ. Out of his hatred Paul was trying to eliminate the followers of Jesus Christ.

Then one day the Lord Jesus met Paul on the road to Damascus, and Paul changed his whole bookkeeping system. What had been a debit became a credit, and what he had considered a credit became a debit. It was a complete revolution.

But what things were gain to me, those I counted loss for Christ [Phil. 3:7].

On the credit side of the ledger Paul had been adding up his background and his character and his religion. It seemed like an impressive list—and it *was*, on the human plane. Suddenly it all became a debit—he no longer trusted in those things because he met Jesus Christ. He had hated Him before and was on the way to Damascus to persecute His followers, but now the One on the debit side was moved to the credit side. He put his entire trust in the Lord Jesus Christ.

Now, my friend, if the bookkeeping system of this country were transformed like that, it would upset the economy of the world. It would be a revolution. Actually, any conversion is a revolution because what things are gain become a loss, and loss becomes gain. It turns you upside down and right side up. It gets you in an altogether different position. That is what conversion is.

Now there is a time lapse between verses 7 and 8. I don't know the length of time, but I think it extends all the way through Paul's life from his conversion to the time he was writing this epistle. He had gone on his missionary journeys, and now he was in a prison in Rome.

Yea doubtless, and I count all things but loss for the excellency of the knowl-

edge of Christ Jesus my Lord: for whom I have suffered the loss of all things, and do count them but dung, that I may win Christ [Phil. 3:8].

Paul's conversion was not just an experience of a moment. Conversion is not a balloon ascension. A great many people think that you can go down to some altar and have an experience, see a vision, and be carried to the heights—and that's it. Oh, my friend, conversion is something that stays with you. It is not for just a moment. Although it happens in a moment of time, it continues for a lifetime. And sanctification is not a great emotional experience; it is a daily walk in dependence upon God.

Paul says that since that moment of his conversion he lives for Christ. He has suffered the loss of all things. Jesus Christ is uppermost in his thinking. The things that he used to consider most precious he now considers to be *dung*—that is strong language! He says he flushes his religion down the drain. He flushes away all the things he used to trust. Now he trusts the Lord Jesus and Him *only* for his salvation.

I remember hearing Dr. Carroll say, "When I was converted, I lost my religion." A great many people need to lose their religion and find Jesus Christ as Paul did. He was so revolutionized that what had been his prized possession is now relegated to the garbage can!

Paul goes on with a theological statement of what happened to him.

And be found in him, not having mine own righteousness, which is of the law, but that which is through the faith of Christ, the righteousness which is of God by faith [Phil. 3:9].

This is the verse that came to John Bunyan as he walked through the cornfields one night, wondering how he could stand before God. He said that suddenly he saw himself—not just as a sinner, but as sin from the crown of his head to the soles of his feet. He realized that he had nothing, and that Christ had everything.

"Not having mine own righteousness"—his own righteousness, as he has made clear, is of the Law; that is, it is law-keeping. For example, he could boast of the fact that he kept the Sabbath day. But Paul now says to let no man judge you in respect of the Sabbath days (see Col. 2:16). My friend, I could boast of the fact that I preach so many times during the year and that I have a daily radio program, but these things count *nothing* for salvation. "Mine own righteousness" is a legal righteous-

ness, and God has already declared that all our righteousnesses are as filthy rags in His sight (see Isa. 64:6), and God is just not taking in dirty laundry. However, He will take in dirty sinners, and He is the One who will clean them up.

Paul had given up his claim to all of his own righteousness.

When speaking at the Hollywood Christian group years ago, I recall a young couple who had been converted. They were talented kids and were really beautiful people. On the human side they had everything. They were called on to give a testimony before my message. They said that now that they had been converted they were going to use their wonderful talent for the Lord. So after I had finished teaching that night, I met with them over a cup of coffee. I said, "I have a question I would like to ask you that sort of bothers me. You made the statement that you have a wonderful talent to use for Jesus. I would like to know what it is. You danced in nightclubs, you sang in nightclubs, and you told stories in nightclubs. Do you think Jesus could use that?" Well, they said they hadn't thought of it like that. I said, "Look, when you come to Christ, you come as bankrupt sinners. You don't offer Him anything. You come with *nothing*. You are beggars. You have nothing; He has *everything*, and He offers it to you."

Oh, my friend, let's get this verse into our thinking! "Be found in him, not having mine own righteousness, which is of the law, but that which is through the faith of Christ, the righteousness which is of God by faith."

"By faith" is the important word. That is the only way in the world you can get it. You can't work for it; you can't buy it; you can't steal it. You just trust Him.

"The righteousness which is of God" came about because, when Christ died on the cross, He subtracted your sins, and He rose again from the dead for your justification, your *righteousness*. My friend, God can't even *stand* us in our unregenerate state. We are not attractive to Him! The very fact that He loved us and gave His Son for us is the most amazing statement ever made. We are accepted in the Beloved.

PAUL CHANGED HIS PURPOSE FOR THE PRESENT

Paul is no longer going to try to build up legal righteousness. He isn't going to see how religious and pious he can be or how much he can persecute the church. Since he has changed his bookkkeeping system of the past, he is also going to change his purpose for the present. Listen to what he is going to do:

That I may know him, and the power of his resurrection, and the fellowship of his sufferings, being made conformable unto his death;

If by any means I might attain unto the resurrection of the dead [Phil. 3:10–11].

Some people get the impression that being saved by faith means there is no motivation for conduct and works. They think that if a person is saved by grace it must mean he just sits around and twiddles his thumbs. Nothing could be farther from the truth. Saving faith is a faith that *moves* you. James said (and he is not talking about law-works but faith-works), ". . . shew me thy faith without thy works, and I will shew thee my faith by my works" (James 2:18). My friend, if you have been saved, I want to see your works. If you don't have works, you are not saved! That is exactly what Paul is saying. If you have been saved by faith you have a new motivation, a new life purpose, a new life-style. If your faith in Christ hasn't changed you, you haven't been saved. You are still the same old man producing the same old life. Paul dissipates any notion that being saved by faith means you can sit in a rocking chair and rock yourself all the way to heaven.

Paul exhibits an effort and an energy that is derived from the Holy Spirit, which is far greater than any legal effort. Under the Law, this man was willing to go to Damascus to stamp out the followers of Christ. Under the grace-faith system, he will go to the end of the earth to make followers of Christ and to witness for Him. Faith produces something. Let us be perfectly clear about this. Your works have nothing to do with your salvation. You are shut up to a cross for salvation. God has only one question for the lost sinner to answer: "What will you do with Jesus who died for you?" If you will accept Him as your Savior, you are saved by faith. That is the righteousness that comes only by faith. Even your life after salvation doesn't build up a righteousness that has anything to do with your salvation. Your faith in Christ is a motivation for you to live for God. That is the reason Paul went on to live as he did.

I just do not understand people who are doing nothing for God. Some people say that they can't do anything. Well, to be very candid with you, you can help me or other Bible teachers get out the Word of God. I'm an old man, but I am not going to quit. I'm going to press toward the mark for the prize of the high calling of God. I have told God that if He would let me live, I'd get out His Word as long as I live. Oh, my friend, our faith in Christ gives a real motivation to work for Him!

"That I may know him"—Paul at the end of his life still had the ambition to know Christ. Today some saints give me the impression that they have complete knowledge and they only need to polish their halo every morning and are ready to take off at any moment. Yet Paul, the greatest missionary the world has ever seen, said at the end of his life, "My ambition is still to know Christ—His person and the power of His resurrection."

The greatest comfort in my life is the reality of Christ. I need the reality of Christ in my life—now don't point an accusing finger at me, because that's what you need also.

"And the fellowship of his sufferings"—oh, how we need to know the fellowship of His sufferings! I was moved to tears by a letter from someone who, after reading our message on Psalm 22, wrote, "Oh, I never knew how much Christ suffered for me!" My friend, I want to know the fellowship of His sufferings, I want to enter into them. To know Christ and His work of redemption will engage our attention for eternity. We are going to spend all eternity praising Him for that. If you are bored with it now, if you don't enjoy praising Christ now, I don't know why you should want to go to heaven.

"If by any means I might attain unto the resurrection of the dead." When Paul uses the word *if* he is not expressing a doubt about his participation in the Rapture. Rather, he is affirming that he will have part in it with great *joy.* Paul did not expect to attain perfection in this life; therefore, he wanted to have full participation in the coming Rapture. When someone tells me that he does not believe in the Rapture, I wonder about his relationship to the person of Christ. Paul is saying, "My ambition, the thing I'm moving toward, is not only that I might know Him but that I might have a meaningful, joyous part in the 'out-resurrection,' which is the rapture of the church." The Old Testament saints are not to be raised until the end of the Great Tribulation Period (see Dan. 12:1–3). The rest of the dead will not be raised until the end of the Millennium.

Have you ever stopped to think what the coming of Christ really means? Most of us think, "Boy, it will get us out of this old world." Paul says, "It will get me into His presence."

Not as though I had already attained, either were already perfect: but I follow after, if that I may apprehend that for which also I am apprehended of Christ Jesus [Phil. 3:12].

The knowledge that he will not attain perfection does not deter Paul from moving in that direction. Perfection means complete maturity. Paul knew he had not arrived. He certainly agreed with Peter that we should ". . . grow in grace, and in the knowledge of our Lord and Saviour Jesus Christ . . ." (2 Pet. 3:18).

Now the next verse will give us the *modus operandi* of the life of Paul:

Brethren, I count not myself to have apprehended: but this one thing I do, forgetting those things which are behind, and reaching forth unto those things which are before [Phil. 3:13].

"I count not myself to have apprehended"— Paul is saying that he hadn't arrived. Oh, so many saints feel comfortable in their ignorance. They think they know it all.

"This one thing I do." Talk about the simple life—if we could get the Christian life down to where we should have it, it would really be an uncomplicated life. Paul had whittled his life down to one point.

"Forgetting those things which are behind." He is leaving the past behind with all his mistakes, not letting it handicap him for the future. The future—he lives in the present in the anticipation of the future when he will grow and develop. (Someone has well said that today is the tomorrow you worried about yesterday.)

I press toward the mark for the prize of the high calling of God in Christ Jesus [Phil. 3:14].

"I press toward the mark for the prize." Paul likens himself to a track star, running for a prize. We must remember that Paul had witnessed the Olympic Games—at least, he had every opportunity to do so. There was a great amphitheater in Ephesus which seated one hundred thousand people, and the Olympic Games were held there at times. Paul was living in Ephesus for three years, and it is difficult for me to believe that he hadn't seen the games, especially since he used so many figures of speech that were taken from those athletic events.

"The prize of the high calling of God in Christ Jesus"—the prize is not some earthly reward but is to be caught up and be in the presence of Christ. "The high calling of God" is sometimes translated "the upward call of God." We are going to be in His presence. We are going to be like Him. These are things that Paul says are out yonder in the future for him.

Now let's be clear on one thing: we don't run for salvation. Salvation is not the prize. Either we have Christ or we don't have Him. We either trust Him or we don't trust Him. The only way we can have salvation is through faith in Christ. It is a *gift*. A gift is different from a prize. The wonderful folk on our radio staff presented me with a birthday gift. Somebody said, "We have a gift for you, Dr. McGee," and handed a box to me. I believed them and I took it. I didn't put my hands behind my back and say, "Well, I'm not sure you really mean business. I am not sure that you intend to do this for me." I just accepted it and thanked them for it. I didn't have to run a race to win it; I didn't have to work for it. It was a gift. "For by grace are ye saved through faith; and that not of yourselves: it is the gift of God; Not of works, lest any man should boast" (Eph. 2:8–9). Salvation is not won at a race. Salvation is a gift which is accepted.

Now Paul, after receiving eternal life, is out running for a prize. Christ became everything to him, and he is running a race that he might win Christ. In what way? Well, someday he is going to appear in His presence. His whole thought is: "When I come into His presence, I don't want to be ashamed." John said that it is possible to be ashamed at His appearing: "And now, little children, abide in him; that, when he shall appear, we may have confidence, and not be ashamed before him at his coming" (1 John 2:28). There are a great many Christians today talking about wishing Christ would come, who, if they really knew what it will mean to them, would probably like to postpone it for awhile. If you think that you can live a careless Christian life and not have to answer for it, you are entirely wrong. One of these days you will have to stand before the judgment seat of Christ to give an account of the way you lived your life. I suggest that you get down on the racecourse and start living for Him.

Let us therefore, as many as be perfect, be thus minded: and if in any thing ye be otherwise minded, God shall reveal even this unto you [Phil. 3:15].

"As many as be perfect"—what does he mean by that? I think I can illustrate this by my orange trees. My three orange trees are loaded with fruit this year. Some of the oranges are still green, but for this particular time of year, they are perfect. They are perfect oranges. But if you come and see me in a month, they will not be perfect oranges if they stay just like they are now. You see, when Paul says "perfect," he means arriving where one should be in maturation. Another illustration would be that of a baby. Suppose we have a baby here seventeen months old. My, what a wonderful baby he is—he wins a blue ribbon. But if you see him seventeen years later and he is still saying, "Da-da," there is something radically wrong. Maturation is the thought Paul has in mind. He is saying this: "Let us, therefore, as many as are complete in Christ, who are growing normally in Christ, let us be thus minded." In other words, have the same mind as Paul. Get out on the racetrack with Paul and press on toward the same goal.

"And if in any thing ye be otherwise minded, God shall reveal even this unto you." Maybe you have some other idea, and maybe God does have something else for you to do. If you are willing to do it, He will show it to you. God is able to lead a *willing* believer. You may remember that the psalmist told us not to be like the horse and the mule that must have a bridle in his mouth in order to be led. If God must lead you around like that, it will hurt. Why not let Him lead you by His eye? That is the way He would like to do it. This is what Paul is talking about—"God shall reveal even this unto you." God will reveal His will to you if you want to be led. I hear Christians say, "If only I knew the will of God." It's a matter of being in touch with the Lord Jesus Christ. It is a matter of drawing close to Him. It is a willingness to do His will when He shows it to you. There is no little formula for discovering the will of God. One cannot live a careless life and expect a vision or an angel or some green light to appear to show the way to go in a crisis. Knowing the will of God comes through a day-by-day walk with Him and a willingness to be led by Him. This will keep you on the right route through life, and it will be a great joy to your heart.

Nevertheless, whereto we have already attained, let us walk by the same rule, let us mind the same thing [Phil. 3:16].

Paul is encouraging the Philippian believers to get out on the racetrack. He wants them to press on for the prize—the high calling of God in Christ Jesus.

Then he goes on to give himself as an example.

Brethren, be followers together of me, and mark them which walk so as ye have us for an ensample [Phil. 3:17].

I wish I could say that. I can't, but Paul could. He says, "If you want to know how to do it, watch me." This is not to be an imitation. What he means is that you learn to share the power of Christ in the body of Christ, the church.

I believe it is proper for a believer to function within a Christian organization, a church. It doesn't have to be a building with a tall steeple on it. Many folk think they must go to a certain type of building. That is not necessary. You can function within a Christian organization. My feeling is that if there is a good Bible church in your community where the Word of God is given out, you are out of the will of God if you are not identified with it. If there is a good Christian organization in your town through which God is working, and you are not supporting it, I think you are out of the will of God. This, I believe, is what Paul means here and what he says elsewhere.

Now Paul discusses the negative side.

(For many walk, of whom I have told you often, and now tell you even weeping, that they are the enemies of the cross of Christ:

Whose end is destruction, whose God is their belly, and whose glory is in their shame, who mind earthly things.) [Phil. 3:18–19].

This is as severe a condemnation as you can find of those who profess to be Christians. They claim to be Christian, yet they contradict their profession by their lives. Their God is their *belly*—that's an awful thing! This means that they are led by their appetites. Some professing Christians have an appetite for money. They will do most anything for the almighty dollar. Others have such an appetite for sex that it becomes actually their god. Others covet—that is the cause of much of the strife and vainglory. The basic cause of it is that they have their hearts and minds on earthly things. They live for self and self only, and they actually glory in this. They are proud of what they should be ashamed.

Paul is saying that if you have trusted Christ, if you have had that kind of revolution that happened to him on the Damascus road, if Christ is the all-absorbing thinking of your mind and your time and your talent and your possessions, then this will tell in your life. James put it like this: "Even so faith, if it hath not works, is dead, being alone. Yea, a man may say, Thou hast faith, and I have works: shew me thy faith without thy works, and I will shew thee my faith by my works" (James 2:17–18). In other words, my friend, if you haven't any works you are not going to convince your neighbor. He will judge your faith by your works. As Calvin said, "Faith alone saves, but the faith that saves is not alone." Some folk feel that the statement "whose God is their belly" is crude. Well, the statement is not crude, but the condition it speaks of is certainly crude. How tragic it is to see Christians who are given over to the passing things of this world, who "mind earthly things."

PAUL CHANGED HIS HOPE
FOR THE FUTURE

For our conversation is in heaven; from whence also we look for the Saviour, the Lord Jesus Christ [Phil. 3:20].

A better translation for "conversation" is *citizenship*. It means the total way of life; it means a new life-style. An even better translation is that made by Mrs. Montgomery: "For our city home is in heaven." Probably that is closer to what Paul is saying. The Greek word for "conversation" is *politeuō*, meaning "to act as a citizen." The city of Philippi was a Roman colony. In Philippi the laws of Rome were enforced. The people wore the same kind of styles that were worn in Rome. They spoke Latin. Everything in Philippi was like Rome because it was a colonial city.

Today, believers, collectively called the church, should be a colony of heaven, and they ought to act like they act in heaven and speak the language of heaven. Unfortunately, this is not always the case, but it should be our goal. Paul is saying that we are ambassadors of Christ here on this earth; we are to represent heaven and heaven's message here upon earth today, because "our citizenship is in heaven."

"From whence also we look for the Saviour, the Lord Jesus Christ." Paul expresses the hope of the believer on the high plane of praise to God. It is the joyful anticipation of His return.

The hope of the believer in the New Testament is never the Great Tribulation Period. After he says our citizenship is in heaven, he says that from there "we look for the Saviour, the Lord Jesus Christ." He doesn't say anything about going through the Great Tribulation Period, which will be a time of *judgment*, and the church is delivered from judgment. Believers will not go through the Great Tribulation any more than Enoch went through the Flood. Many folk maintain that the Lord can preserve the church through the Great Tribulation. Yes, He can; God kept Noah in a boat through the Flood, but He took Enoch out of the world. There will be two groups of people who will be His during the Great Tribulation Period. One will be taken out, as He says to the church in Philadelphia: "Because thou hast kept the word of my patience, I also will keep thee from the hour of temptation, which shall come upon all the world, to try them that dwell upon the earth" (Rev. 3:10). The other group will be going through the Great Tribulation. There will be a great company of Gentiles and there will be 144,000 of Israel who will go through the Great Tribulation Period because they are to be sealed by God.

Let me digress to say that the teaching that the church is to go through the Great Tribulation is becoming increasingly absurd to me. The advocates of this theory maintain that there is not a verse in Scripture that says the church will *not* go through the Great Tribulation. While it is true that it doesn't say it in those words, neither is there a verse in Scripture that has anything to say about the church *not* doing other things. For instance, I am confident that we are all going to have a position, a job to do, throughout eternity, but Scripture does not go into detail on that sort of thing. However, Scripture is very clear on the fact that the church has a glorious, wonderful hope for the future. It seems to many of us that it is tissue-thin between where we are now and the Rapture of the church. However, Scripture does not tell us *when* Christ will come. Apparently Paul felt that during his lifetime the Lord could come, and there is no record of Paul's expecting to first go through the Great Tribulation. He experienced a lot of trouble during his life, but he never interpreted *that* as the Great Tribulation. With a note of glad expectancy Paul says, "For our conversation [citizenship] is in heaven; from whence also we look for the Saviour, the Lord Jesus Christ"—*after* we go through the real Tribulation? It doesn't say that in my Bible. Nowhere does it say the church is going through the Great Tribulation, my friend. Paul's joyful expectancy makes it very clear that he was looking for Christ's return, *not* for the Great Tribulation.

Who shall change our vile body, that it may be fashioned like unto his glorious body, according to the working whereby he is able even to subdue all things unto himself [Phil. 3:21].

"Our vile body" might be better translated "body of humiliation" or "body of corruption." It means that He shall change our earthly body. This body that we have is an earthly body, subject to all kinds of limitations. It is adapted to this earth. We are not naturally equipped to go up into space. Our bodies are earthly bodies.

"That it may be fashioned like unto his glorious body." These bodies are corruptible bodies. One of these days you and I will move out of these bodies. We will leave them because they are corruptible. They are going to be changed—I'd like to trade mine in right now—"fashioned like unto his glorious body." It will be a body like the one the Lord Jesus had after His resurrection. It will be a glorified body. Paul speaks of it in his letter to the Corinthians: "Behold, I shew you a mystery; We shall not all sleep, but we shall all be changed, In a moment, in the twinkling of an eye, at the last trump . . ." (1 Cor. 15:51–52). The point is that it will be sudden—when the trumpet shall sound.

While I am dealing with misinterpretations of this passage, let me say that some folk assume that one of the angels spoken of in the Book of Revelation is to blow this trumpet. However, the one blowing the trumpet is not indicated here. The Book of Revelation deals with Israel. In the Old Testament we read that Israel was moved on the wilderness march by the blowing of two silver trumpets. Israel is accustomed to trumpets; we are not. Perhaps you are remembering that the "last trump" is mentioned in connection with the Rapture in 1 Thessalonians: "For the Lord himself shall descend from heaven with a shout, with the voice of the archangel, and with the trump of God . . ." (1 Thess. 4:16). Notice it is the trump of *God*. Whoever turned it over to Gabriel and said Gabriel will blow his horn? I question if Gabriel even owns a horn. It is the *Lord* who will descend with the voice of an archangel and the trump of God. Both speak of the dignity and the majesty of that shout of His. His voice will be penetrating and awe-inspiring. Listen to the way John describes the voice of the glorified Christ: "I was in the Spirit on the Lord's day, and heard behind me a great voice, as of a trumpet" (Rev. 1:10). And when he turned to see who was speaking, he saw the glorified Christ. It was His voice that John heard. There are no trumpets connected with the church.

Today Christ's word to us is this: "Behold, I stand at the door, and knock: if any man hear my voice, and open the door, I will come in to him, and will sup with him, and he with me" (Rev. 3:20). It is His invitation to the evening meal—the last call for dinner. It is an invitation to come to Him before the night of the Great Tribulation falls. When the door is opened, there will go from this earth a group of people who have been put on the launching pad of faith—and they won't go through the Great Tribulation Period. May I say to you that those who expect the church to go through the Tribulation have, in my judgment, the flimsiest theory that is abroad, yet there are many intelligent men who hold this view. However, I find that these men spend more time with philosophy and psychology and history and related subjects than they do with the study of the Word of God.

"Who shall change our vile body, that it may be fashioned like unto his glorious body." This is exactly the same thought that John had: "Beloved, now are we the sons of God, and it doth not yet appear what we shall be: but we know that, when he shall appear, we shall be like him; for we shall see him as he is" (1 John 3:2). Christ hasn't appeared yet, but when He appears, we shall be like Him. Notice the high hope, the expectancy and excitement, the great anticipation of Christ's return. (There is not the slightest suggestion that either Paul or John expected to first go through the Great Tribulation Period.)

Paul had a hope for the future. What is your hope for the future? The Great Tribulation Period? My friend, if that is your prospect, you are about as hopeless as the man who has no hope!

Taking a trip recently to the Hawaiian Islands, instead of flying the direct route, we came in from the north. The reason the pilot gave us was that there was a storm front on the southern route, and he skirted it, although it made us about thirty minutes late. I appreciated the fact that he went around the storm. It used to be that a pilot would say, "There is a storm front ahead of us, and we are going to have turbulence for the next thirty minutes." I didn't look forward to that—it was no blessed hope for me! But it surely is nice to have him say we are taking another route so we will miss the storm. And the Lord says to the church, "We're going to miss the storm, the Great Tribulation." My friend, you can twist it around to suit your own theory, but that is what He says. "For our conversation is in heaven; from whence also we look for the Saviour, the Lord Jesus Christ." That was Paul's hope for the future, and it is our hope.

CHAPTER 4

THEME: Power for Christian living; joy—the source of power; prayer—the secret of power; contemplation of Christ—the sanctuary of power; in Christ—the satisfaction of power

We have seen the *philosophy* of Christian living, the *pattern* for Christian living, the *prize* for Christian living, and now we shall see the *power* for Christian living. All the others would be meaningless and useless if there were no power for them. A philosophy of life is no good unless there is power to carry it out. A pattern is no good unless there is power supplied to have that pattern in our own lives. A prize is no good if we cannot achieve the goal. Therefore, power is all important.

I would think one of the reasons that the Spirit of God did not let Paul end this epistle when he wrote in 3:1, "Finally, my brethren," was because He wanted to let us know today that there is *power* for Christian living. We need to know that we can do all things through Christ who strengthens us.

We will find in this chapter that joy is the *source* of power; prayer is the *secret* of power; and contemplation of Christ is the *sanctuary* of power.

JOY—THE SOURCE OF POWER

Therefore, my brethren dearly beloved and longed for, my joy and crown, so stand fast in the Lord, my dearly beloved [Phil. 4:1].

"My joy and crown"—you see, they were going to be in the presence of Christ someday, and Paul expected to receive a *crown* for winning these folk to the Lord. Also they were his *joy* down here. Oh, how he loved these believers in Philippi!

"So stand fast in the Lord, my dearly beloved." And, as Paul said to the Ephesian believers, ". . . take unto you the whole armour of God, that ye may be able to withstand in the evil day, and having done all, to stand" (Eph. 6:13). The Christian faith will produce stability of life.

I beseech Euodias, and beseech Syntyche, that they be of the same mind in the Lord [Phil. 4:2].

Now he comes to the only problem in the Philippian church. There was a ripple on the surface, but it was not serious. Paul doesn't even mention it until near the end of his letter. Apparently these two ladies were not speaking to each other. We have already seen this when he admonished the Philippian believers to be of the same mind in the Lord. He did not mean they must be carbon copies of each other. They may have differences of opinion about many different things, but that will not separate two people who have the mind of Christ. It is one of the glorious truths about the body of Christ that each member can be different and yet all are one in Christ.

And I entreat thee also, true yokefellow, help those women which laboured with me in the gospel, with Clement also, and with other my fellow-labourers, whose names are in the book of life [Phil. 4:3].

It is apparent that women occupied a prominent place in the early church, and for a woman to be prominent was unusual in that day.

Now that I am no longer a pastor I can say this (I always said it reluctantly or very carefully before): I believe that the reason women become preachers is because women have not been given their proper place in the church. The office of deaconess, even if it exists in the church, is treated very lightly. I believe that is an important office and should be recognized as such. The more I study the Word of God, the more I am convinced of this. Paul plainly said that "those women . . . laboured with me in the gospel."

"With Clement also"—here is a believer over in Philippi whom we haven't met before.

"With other my fellow-labourers"—apparently there was a great company of believers in Philippi "whose names are in the book of life." That was the important thing: their names are in the Book of Life.

Rejoice in the Lord alway: and again I say, Rejoice [Phil. 4:4].

This is a commandment to a Christian, a believer. Rejoice in the Lord always. That means regardless of the day, whether it is dark or bright, whether it is difficult or easy, whether it brings problems and temptations or clear sailing on cloud nine. We are commanded to rejoice. He repeats it, in case we missed it the first time: "again I say, Rejoice." Joy is something we cannot produce ourselves; it is a fruit of the Holy Spirit.

There is no power in a Christian's life if he has no joy. One who does not experience the joy of the Lord has no power at all.

After Nehemiah had finished building the wall of Jerusalem, they set up a pulpit at the Water Gate, and there Ezra read from the Scriptures from morning until midday. These people had come out of captivity in Babylon. Most of them had never in their lives heard the Word of God. It overwhelmed them. They began to mourn and to weep. So Nehemiah said, "Wait a minute—you're not to weep! This is a great day. You are to share in the blessings, the physical blessings, that God has given to you, and God wants you to enjoy them." God has given to us richly all things to enjoy, and to enjoy means to rejoice. That's your strength, that's your power. You can't be a Christian with power without joy—that's what gets up the steam. Joy is the source of power.

Let me illustrate this because it is something that the world has taken over. In fact, the commercial world has made it rather hypocritical. A successful salesman is a very happy fellow. You have never gone into a store to buy something and had the salesperson weep on your shoulder when you asked about a certain product! Of course not. He begins to smile and say how wonderful the item is. How far would the Fuller brush man get if he were a sad little fellow who went around weeping at every door? Believe me, he doesn't use that approach.

The Fuller brush man calls at our house on Saturdays. He is not a sorrowful fellow by any means. I don't know whether he is having trouble at home or not, but he sure radiates joy. One Saturday morning my wife had gone to the market, and from my study window I saw him coming. I thought, *I'll ignore him because I'm busy, and I'm not going to fool with brushes today.* So he came and pushed the doorbell. I let him push it. He pushed it two or three times. I thought, *He'll leave now.* But he didn't leave. He knew somebody was in the house, so he just put his thumb down on the doorbell and held it. Finally in self-defense I had to go to the door. When I opened the door, I expected him to be a little irritated because I had made him wait. But no, he was happy about it. Everything pleased him. He greeted me joyfully, "Dr. McGee, I didn't expect to see you today!" With a scowl I said, "My wife has gone to the market. She'll see you the next time you are around." But that wasn't enough for him. I do not know how he did it, but in the next ten seconds he was in the living room and I was holding a little brush in my hand. Then I couldn't order him out— he'd given me a little brush. And so I stood there listening to his sales pitch. When he had finished, I said, "Now look, I don't buy brushes and I don't need one. My wife generally buys from you, and she'll probably buy next time, but I haven't time to look at them. I'm busy this morning." So he thanked me and started down the walkway *whistling!* You would have thought I had bought every brush he had! I met a man who trains Fuller brush salesmen, and I told him about this experience. He said that they were so instructed; they are trained to radiate joy.

Now I do not know if that Fuller brush man was happy or not, but a child of God ought to have *real* joy, the joy of the Lord, in his life.

The world spends a great deal of money trying to produce joy, which they call happiness. Comedians are millionaires because they tell a few funny stories. People shell out the money to hear them. Why? Because they want to laugh. They are trying to find a little happiness as they go through life. The child of God who goes through life with a sour look and a jaundiced approach to this world, will never have any power in his life. "Rejoice in the Lord alway: and again I say, Rejoice."

The world tries to work up joy in another way. They call it the *happy hour* or *attitude adjustment hour.* They spend a couple of hours drinking and hope it will help them overcome the problems of life and give them a little happiness. I have watched the folk who go in there, and none of them look happy when they go in. In an hour or two when they come out, I can't see that there has been any improvement. But they have had a "happy hour." A great many people are trying to compensate for the inadequacies in their own lives in that manner.

I have thought it would be nice if churches could have an *attitude adjustment hour.* Here comes Mrs. Brown. She has just heard some choice gossip during the week, and she can hardly wait to spread it around in the church. Wouldn't it be wonderful to take her into an attractive room and have a cup of coffee with her and get her into a sweet mood and rejoicing in the Lord so she would not go around spreading her gossip? Here comes Deacon Jones, breathing fire like a dragon because something doesn't suit him. It would be nice to take him to that room and help him recover his cool so he could go in and enjoy the sermon. We need an attitude adjustment hour, a happy hour, in the church. Frankly, the Devil has gotten in his licks—he has made folk believe they can't have fun going to church, and I think they can. I think it ought to be a joyful place and a place of power.

Sometimes prayer meetings are called the hour of power. Well, that is nice, but we need to get back to the *source* of the power which is joy. In our prayer meetings, before we ask God for something else, let's pray that He'll give us joy in our lives. There was a little song we used to sing at summer Bible schools (which I used to conduct as a young preacher) with these words:

Down in the dumps I'll never go;
That's where the Devil keeps me low.

That song has a sound theological message, because this is exactly what the Devil tries to do. He attempts to take away our joy because it is the source of power.

PRAYER—THE SECRET OF POWER

Let your moderation be known unto all men. The Lord is at hand [Phil. 4:5].

Matthew Arnold, in one of his delightful essays, interprets it this way: "Let your sweet reasonableness be known unto all men." I like that. We need to be reasonable believers, not bigots in our faith. Of course we ought to have deep convictions, but we should not be given to bigotry or riding a hobbyhorse—always emphasizing some little point. What we need to do is emphasize the *big* point—we *do* have one—the big point is the person of Christ. If we are going to ride a hobbyhorse, let Him be the hobbyhorse. "Let your sweet reasonableness be known unto all men."

"The Lord is at hand." Paul believed that the Lord Jesus would come at any moment. He was not expecting to enter the Great Tribulation; he says, "The *Lord* is at *hand*." That's quite wonderful!

Be careful for nothing; but in every thing by prayer and supplication with thanksgiving let your requests be made known unto God [Phil. 4:6].

"Be careful for nothing" is sometimes translated: Be anxious for nothing, or not overly anxious. The fact of the matter is that Paul seems to be making a play upon two indefinite pronouns: *nothing* and *everything*. Let me give you my translation, which I call the McGee-icus Ad Absurdum. It goes like this: "Worry about nothing; pray about everything." Prayer is the secret of power.

"Worry about nothing." In verse 4 we were given one of the new commandments God has given us: Rejoice. Now here is another commandment: Worry about nothing; pray about everything.

Nothing is a very interesting word. If you have *something*, it's not *nothing*—that is not correct grammar, but it is an accurate statement. Nothing is nothing, and you are to worry about nothing. Does this mean we are to look at life through rose-colored glasses, that we are not to face reality? Are we to believe that sin is not real, that sickness is not real, that problems are not real? Are we to ignore these things? No. Paul says that we are to worry about nothing because we are to pray about everything. *Nothing* is the most exclusive word in the English language. It leaves out everything. "Worry about *nothing*." I confess that this is a commandment I sometimes break—I worry.

But the reason we are to worry about nothing is because we are to pray about everything. This means that we are to talk to the Lord about everything in our lives. Nothing should be left out. Some years ago, I am told, a dowager in Philadelphia came to Dr. G. Campbell Morgan with this question, "Dr. Morgan, do you think we should pray about the *little* things in our lives?" Dr. Morgan in his characteristically British manner said, "Madam, can you mention anything in your life that is *big* to God?" When we say that we take our big problems to God, what do we mean? They are all little stuff to Him. And what we call little He wants us to bring to Him also. As believers we need to get in the habit of bringing everything to Him in prayer—nothing excluded. When I go on a trip in my car and it involves several hours of driving, I invite the Lord Jesus to go along with me. I talk to Him and tell Him everything about Vernon McGee, things I wouldn't tell you or anyone else. I tell Him everything. I think we ought to learn to do that. We ought to pray about everything.

Let me share with you an admonition by Fenelon, one of the mystics of the Middle Ages, which seems to encompass what Paul meant when he said, "Pray about everything."

Tell God all that is in your heart, as one unloads one's heart, its pleasures and its pains, to a dear friend. Tell Him your troubles, that He may comfort you; tell Him your joys, that He may sober them; tell Him your longings, that He may purify them; tell Him your dislikes, that He may help you to conquer them; talk to Him of your temptations, that He may shield you from them; show Him the wounds of your heart, that He may heal them; lay bare your indifference to good, your depraved tastes for evil, your instability. Tell Him how self-love makes you unjust to others, how vanity tempts you to be insincere, how pride disguises you to yourself as to others.

If you thus pour out all your weaknesses, needs, troubles, there will be no lack of what to say. You will never exhaust the subject. It is continually being renewed. People who have no secrets from each other never want subjects of conversation. They do not weigh their words, for there is nothing to be held back; neither do they seek for something to say. They talk out of the abundance of the heart, without consideration, just what they think. Blessed are they who attain to such familiar, unreserved intercourse with God.

For many years I have carried this quotation in my Bible, and every now and then I take it out and read it.

Maybe you think it sounds very pious when I am willing to testify that I take my burdens to the Lord in prayer. I must confess that after I spread everything out before Him, when I finish praying, I pick it all right back up, put the problems back on my shoulders, and start out with the burden again. That is my problem. The Lord wants us to trust Him so that we worry about nothing, pray about everything. I wish I could say to you that I'm as free as the bird in the trees, free as the bees gathering honey. That's the way He wants us to be.

We have a mockingbird in our yard. He gets my fruit, but I feel it is right for me to pay him something for the song he sings for me in the night. Now, actually, he isn't singing for me. I don't think he cares much whether I hear him or not. But he has a mate sitting on some eggs, and it would be a pretty boring job to sit on a bunch of eggs. So this mockingbird sings to his wife all during the night. The other morning I awakened around two o'clock, and, my, how he was singing to her! How lovely. While sitting outside on my patio I noticed this mockingbird. He looked at me with disdain, flew right over to my apricot tree and started to eat apricots. He never asked me for permission to eat. He is free. He doesn't worry about finding something to eat. He knows those apricots will be there for him. My friend, do we really trust God like that? Worry about nothing and pray about everything.

"With thanksgiving let your requests be made known unto God." Paul never lets prayer become a leap in the dark. It rests on a foundation. "So then faith cometh by hearing, and hearing by the Word of God" (Rom. 10:17). Prayer rests on faith, and faith rests on the Word of God. Now he says that when you go to God with a request, thank Him. Thank Him right then and there.

I know some commentators who interpret this to mean that when you get your answer to your prayer, you are to go back and thank God. Well, that's not what Paul said. Paul was able to express himself in the most versatile language which has ever been in the world, the Greek language, and he was able to say what he wanted to say. What he says is that when you make your requests, right there and then you are to thank God for hearing and answering your prayer.

Now perhaps you are thinking, *But maybe God won't answer my prayer. I have many unanswered prayers.* My Christian friend, I do not believe that you have unanswered prayers, and I think you ought to be ashamed of yourself for saying that you have a heavenly Father who won't hear and answer your prayers. You may have prayed for a certain thing and didn't get it, but you did get an answer to your prayer.

Let me illustrate this with a very homely illustration. My dad was not a Christian, but he was a good dad. He ran a cotton gin, and the machine would always be running. I would go in there when I was a little fellow and ask for a nickel for candy. He would reach down in his pocket and give me a nickel. One time I asked him for a bicycle. He said he couldn't afford it, and the answer was "No." I can tell you today that I never made a request of him that he didn't hear and answer. Most of the time the answer was no. Actually, my dad's *no* was more positive than his *yes*. His *no* ended the discussion. In fact, I have never understood young folk today who keep on arguing with their parents after the parents have handed down a decision. When my dad said, "No," that was the end of the discussion. I have learned now that the wise reply to most of my requests was no, although I did not think so at the time. But the fact is that he gave an answer to my every request.

God has a lot of spoiled children. When He says no to them, they pout and say, "I have unanswered prayers." You don't have unanswered prayers. God always hears and answers your prayers.

You can take anything to God in prayer, the big things and the little things. How can you sort them out? They are all little things to God. Let me give you another homely illustration. At the time of the building of the Panama Canal, after two or three failures, when the successful project was under way they wanted to go right through with it, and so the crew had no vacations. To compensate for it, the workers' families were sent down to be with them. So a certain young engineer, his wife and little son were sent down. Because of the danger of malaria, they were put out on a houseboat. Every afternoon that young engineer could be seen rowing himself out to the houseboat. One evening he had those long blueprints all spread out while his little son with his toy wagon was playing at his feet. Suddenly the child began to cry. A wheel had come off his wagon. The little fellow had worked with it and tried his best to put it back, but it was a hopeless project for him. Now would you think that the dad would shush him and put him out of the room—maybe tell the mother to come and get him because he was disturbing his work? No. He just laid aside the blueprints of that great canal, picked up his little boy and asked him what was the matter. The youngster held up his wagon in one hand and the wheel in the other. The father took the wheel and put it on the wagon with just one twist of the wrist. He kissed away the little fellow's fears and put him back on the floor where he played happily. He was a good father.

Now, my friend, it is *God* who put that father instinct deep down in the human heart of man because *He* is a compassionate Father. When a wheel comes off your wagon, it may look like an impossible problem to you, but He will hear and answer your cry. If He says no, it is because that is the *best* answer you could have. After I lost my human father, I lived several years before I turned to God and found that I had a heavenly Father. I learned that I can go to Him with my requests, and He answers me, as my human father used to do. And many times His answers are no.

When I was a young pastor in Texas, just married, I went to a certain city to candidate in a church. It was considered a strategic, outstanding church. After I'd preached twice that Sunday, I was given a call by the church. Then later they had to come back and tell me that the denomination would not permit them

to call me. As I said, it was a strategic church and they needed a church politician there—which I was not. I didn't go into the ministry for that purpose. But I felt that the Lord had made a great mistake by not letting me go to that church as pastor. Several years ago Mrs. McGee and I went by that church just to see it. It had gone into liberalism. Things have happened there that I'll not mention. I said to her, "Do you remember years ago when I thought I should have had the call for that church?" She said, "Yes." Then I said, "I thank God that He heard and answered my prayer the *right* way—not the way I prayed it." I can look back and remember how I had cried to the Lord. I told Him how He had failed me and caused me to miss the greatest opportunity I ever had. Oh, I blamed Him, and I found fault with Him, and I actually scolded Him because He didn't seem to know what was the best for me! He had shut that door so tight that the resounding slam was in my ears for several years after that. My friend, my heavenly Father had answered my prayer, and I am ashamed of the fact that I did not thank Him at the time. My advice to you is this: Instead of saying that God has not answered your prayers, say, "My heavenly Father heard my prayer, but He told me no, which was the right answer." We are to let our "requests be made known unto God *with thanksgiving.*"

And the peace of God, which passeth all understanding, shall keep your hearts and minds through Christ Jesus [Phil. 4:7].

The Scripture speaks of other kinds of peace which we can understand. There is *world peace*. We have the assurance that someday peace will cover the earth as the waters cover the sea. It will come through the person of Christ, the Prince of Peace. Also there is the peace that comes when *sins are forgiven*. "Therefore being justified by faith, we have peace with God through our Lord Jesus Christ" (Rom. 5:1). Then there is the peace that is *tranquility*. The Lord Jesus said, "Peace I leave with you, my peace I give unto you . . ." (John 14:27). That is a marvelous peace, but it is not "the peace . . . which passeth all understanding." I do not know how to tell you this, but I do know it is a peace in which we do not live at all times. I think it is a peace that sweeps over our souls at certain times. I stood on the big island of Hawaii and looked out at a sunset with Mauna Kea, that great snowcapped mountain out there in the tropics, in the foreground. As I looked at the majesty of God's creation, what a peace came to me. I can't tell you what it was—it "passeth all understanding." And that same peace came when my heavenly Father let me have cancer. I went to the hospital frightened to death, and then the night I committed it all to him and told Him I wanted to know *He* was real, He made Himself real and that peace that "passeth all understanding" flooded my soul. I don't know how to tell you what it is; I can only say that it is wonderful.

This peace "shall keep your hearts and minds through Christ Jesus." There are those who say that prayer changes things. I can't argue with that; prayer *does* change things. But that is not the primary purpose of prayer.

Notice that we entered this passage in anxiety, with worry, and we come out of the passage with peace. Between the two was prayer. Have things changed? Not really. The storm may still be raging, the waves still rolling high, the thunder still resounding. Although the storm has not abated, something has happened in the individual. Something has happened to the human soul and the human mind. In our anxiety we want God to change everything around us. "Give us this." "Don't let this happen." "Open up this door." We should be praying, "Oh, God, change *me*." Prayer is the secret of power. We enter with worry, we can come out in peace.

Joy is the *source* of power; prayer is the *secret* of power.

CONTEMPLATION OF CHRIST— THE SANCTUARY OF POWER

Finally, brethren, whatsoever things are true, whatsoever things are honest, whatsoever things are just, whatsoever things are pure, whatsoever things are lovely, whatsoever things are of good report; if there be any virtue, and if there be any praise, think on these things [Phil. 4:8].

"**F**inally, brethren"—remember that he said, "Finally, my brethren" at the beginning of chapter 3, when he was just halfway through? Well, now he is nearly through and is giving his last admonitions.

This has been called the briefest biography of Christ. He is the One who is "true." He is the Way, the Truth, and the Life. "Whatsoever things are honest"—He is honest. "Whatsoever things are just"—He is called the Just One. "Pure"—the only pure individual who ever walked this earth was the Lord Jesus. He asked the question, "Which of you convicteth me of sin?" No one did. He also said, ". . . the prince of this world cometh, and hath nothing in me" (John 14:30). Satan always finds something he can hook onto in me. How about you? But there was nothing in the Lord Jesus. He was ". . . holy, harmless, undefiled, separate from sinners . . ." (Heb. 7:26). He was *lovely* which means "gracious." *Virtue* has to do with strength and courage. He was the One of courage, a real man. He took upon Himself our humanity. "If . . . any praise"—He is the One you can praise and worship today.

You and I live in a dirty world. You cannot walk on the streets of any city without getting dirty. Your mind gets dirty; your eyes get dirty. Do you ever get tired of the filth of it?

Hollywood ran out of ideas years ago, which is the reason Hollywood has dried up. Television is boring; it cannot help but repeat the same old thing. So what have they done? They have substituted filth for genius. Someone has called it the great wasteland. It is like looking at an arid desert, and yet millions keep their eyes glued to it. Their minds are filled with dirt and filth and violence.

If a Christian is going to spend his time with the dirt and filth and questionable things of this world, there will not be power in his life. The reason we have so many weak Christians is that they spend their time with the things of the world, filling their minds and hearts and tummies with the things of this world. Then they wonder why there is no power in their lives.

We need a sanctuary. We need something to think upon that will clean up our minds. Here are some questions to think about: How much time do you spend with the Word of God? How much time do you spend contemplating Christ? "But we all, with open face beholding as in a glass the glory of the Lord, are changed into the same image from glory to glory, even as by the spirit of the Lord" (2 Cor. 3:18). The Word of God is a mirror, and in it we behold the glory of the Lord. The only way you can behold the living Christ is in the Word of God. As you behold Him, there is a liberty, a freedom, and a growth that He gives you. You cannot come by it in any other way.

Oh, how puerile, how inconsequential is the impact of believers' lives! I am amazed at how easily Christians are taken in by every wind of doctrine that comes along. They are not able to discern truth and error. The one explanation, as I have pondered it in my mind, is ignorance of the Word of God. To have power in our lives we must contemplate the person of

Jesus Christ, contemplating Him in the Word of God.

Too often people come to the church to be entertained. Someone has said that people come to church to eye the clothes or to close the eyes. Many seem to sit in a daze for an hour just to feel religious or pious. My friend, only the Word of God can bring strength to you. You need physical food when you are weak; you need bread and meat to give you strength. The Word of God is your spiritual bread and meat. The only way to grow spiritually is to spend time in the Word of God. It is the Word that reveals Jesus Christ. I believe He is on every page of Scripture if only we have eyes to see Him. We *need* to see Him. We need to have the reality of Christ in our lives. This is made possible as we, with an open face, behold the glory of the Lord.

I think one of the things that will cause believers to be ashamed at the appearing of Christ will be their ignorance of the Scriptures when they stand in His presence. I'm of the opinion He will say to many of us, "I gave you all the information you needed in the Scriptures. You didn't listen to Me; you didn't hear Me." We say that one of the problems with our children is that they don't listen to their parents. The problem with the children of God is that they don't listen to their heavenly Father. Contemplation of Christ—that is the sanctuary of power. Many of us need to leave the busyness and dirtiness of this world and go aside with the Word of God where we can contemplate Him, worship Him, and praise Him.

Those things, which ye have both learned, and received, and heard, and seen in me, do: and the God peace shall be with you [Phil. 4:9].

A better word for "do" is *practice*. Paul could say something that would be audacious if you or I said it: "Do what *I* do." I don't want my little grandson to follow down the pathway that I went. I don't want him to have his grandpa for an example. But Paul could make his life an example to other believers. Paul lived in that sanctuary of power because He had made Christ the very center and periphery of his life.

IN CHRIST—THE SATISFACTION OF POWER

But I rejoiced in the Lord greatly, that now at the last your care of me hath flourished again; wherein ye were also careful, but ye lacked opportunity [Phil. 4:10].

At the beginning I said that the Epistle to the Philippians is primarily a thank-you note. Before Paul got down to the thank-you part, he dealt with Christian experience. He has been talking about Christian experience throughout the epistle. Now he is thanking them for their gift.

For two years the church in Philippi had lost touch with Paul. They did not know where he was after he had been arrested in Jerusalem and then put in prison for two years. The next time they heard about him, he had been transferred to a prison in Rome. They apologized to him for not having contact with him and for not communicating their gifts to him during those years. Paul is excusing them in a most gracious manner. He says, "I rejoiced in the Lord greatly, that now at the last your care of me hath flourished again; wherein ye were also careful, but ye lacked opportunity." In other words, "You had lost contact with me so that you didn't have the opportunity to be helpful to me." How gracious Paul was!

Not that I speak in respect of want: for I have learned, in whatsoever state I am, therewith to be content [Phil. 4:11].

Paul said that he never made an appeal to them. He never sent out an SOS for help. Paul had learned to be content in whatsoever state he was. It didn't matter whether he was in prison or out of prison. Many of us think that if things are going right and if we are in the right place, then we will be contented. That means that we depend on the circumstances of life for our contentment. I have asked the Lord to give me contentment. I have prayed for Him to make me just as content tape-recording in my office as I am out in Hawaii enjoying the beautiful scenery. Our circumstances have a great deal to do with our contentment, don't they? But Paul had learned to be content regardless of his state.

I know both how to be abased, and I know how to abound: every where and in all things I am instructed both to be full and to be hungry, both to abound and to suffer need [Phil. 4:12].

Paul says, "Though I appreciate your sympathy, I know how to live on the lowest plane economically, and I know how to live on the highest plane. I have done both." There were times when he had nothing, and he was content. There were times when God had given him an abundance, and he had learned how to abound.

When I retired from the pastorate, I told my wife that there would be a terrible letdown in income and in our standard of living. I knew it would be hard for us. Paul knew how to abound and how to be abased, but we're not very good at that. I guess the Lord knew all about it, because due to the generosity of some very wonderful folk our standard hasn't come down. We have been able to live just like we did before. We were prepared to come down, but the Lord didn't bring us down, and we do thank Him and praise His name for it.

It was the custom of Dr. Harry Ironside to go every year to Grand Rapids for a Bible conference at Mel Trotter's mission. Mel Trotter had been an alcoholic, and after he had come to Christ, he opened a mission to reach other men who were in his former condition. The owner of a hotel which had just been built in Grand Rapids had been an alcoholic and had been led to Christ by Mel Trotter. He told Mel, "When you have a speaker or visitor come to your mission, you send him over to the hotel. We will keep him here free of charge." When Dr. Ironside arrived at that hotel, the man ushered him up to the presidential suite. He had the best apartment in the hotel. Dr. Ironside had never been in a place like that before. He called Mel on the phone and said, "Listen, Mel, you don't have to put me up like this. I don't need all this luxury. All I want is a room with a comfortable bed, and a desk and a lamp where I can study." Mel assured him that the room was not costing him or the mission anything; it was being provided free of charge. He said, "Harry, Paul said he knew how to abound and he knew how to be abased. Now you learn to abound this week, will you?"

Now we come to a verse that is often quoted, but I think there are only certain circumstances in which it should be quoted. This verse is geared to life. It gets down where the rubber meets the road. This verse needs to be worked out in life.

I can do all things through Christ which strengtheneth me [Phil. 4:13].

This really should be translated the way Paul wrote it: "I can do all things *in* Christ which strengtheneth me."

When Paul says *all things*, does he literally mean all things? Does it mean you can go outside and jump over your house? Of course not. Paul says, "I can do all things in Christ"— that is, in the context of the will of Christ for your life. Whatever Christ has for you to do, He will supply the power. Whatever gift He gives you, He will give the power to exercise

that gift. A gift is a manifestation of the Spirit of God in the life of the believer. As long as you function in Christ, you will have power.

Let me give you an illustration. My favorite mode of travel is by train. I fly only because I must. The train has lots more romance connected with it, and it is much more enjoyable. It gets you there later, but it gets you there. The Santa Fe Railroad used to have a train called the Super Chief which ran between Los Angeles and Chicago. That was a wonderful train, and I enjoyed traveling on it. It traveled with tremendous power. That Super Chief could say, "I can do all things a Super Chief is supposed to do on the tracks between Chicago and Los Angeles. I can pull up the Cajon Pass, the highest pass for any railroad in this country. I slow down a little bit, but I do not hesitate. I go right up to the top and down the other side. I can do all things!"

Now suppose the Super Chief had said, "For years I have been taking people back and forth from Chicago to Los Angeles, Los Angeles to Chicago, and it gets a little monotonous. I noticed a little group of people got off at Williams, Arizona, to go to the Grand Canyon. I've been coming by here for years, and I've never seen the Grand Canyon. I think I'll just take off across the desert here and look at the canyon for myself." Now I don't *know* that the train actually ever said that, but I do know that it left the tracks one day over on the side toward the Grand Canyon. I'm here to tell you that it never did make it to the Grand Canyon. The minute it left the tracks, it was a wreck. The train was helpless and hopeless the moment it left the tracks. As long as the Super Chief was on the tracks, as long as it was doing the thing it was supposed to do, it could do all things a Super Chief should do. It could go up and down over those mountains, back and forth from Chicago to Los Angeles. But it was absolutely helpless when it left the tracks.

This is what Paul is saying about himself— "I can do all things *in Christ*." Now, friend, if you are a member of Christ's body, He is the Head, and you are to function in the context of His will for your life. His will is the track on which you are to run.

Now Paul is not saying that we can do all things. I can't jump like a grasshopper can jump. When I was in school I was the high jumper, but I can't jump anymore. You see, I can't do *all* things, but I can do all things which God has for me to do from the time He saved me to the time He will take me out of this world.

"Through Christ which strengtheneth me." Christ is the One who will strengthen you and enable you to do all that is in His will for you. He certainly does not mean that He is putting into your hands unlimited power to do anything you want to do. Rather, He will give you the enablement to do all things in the context of His will for you. When you and I are in Christ, and we are moving in Christ on those tracks, we are irresistible. There is no stopping us. But the minute you and I step out of that glorious position, step out of God's will either by sinning, by our own willfulness, or by lack of fellowship, we are as much a wreck as that Santa Fe Super Chief was, and we are not going anywhere. But if we stay on that track, we can do all things in Christ. "If ye abide in me, and my words abide in you, ye shall ask what ye will, and it shall be done unto you" (John 15:7). We had better make sure where we are before we start asking. It is essential to be in His will.

My friend, let me emphasize this: It is essential to be in God's will, and His will is determined by a knowledge of His Bible. So many folk feel that if they can take a little course, it will solve all their problems. Well, it won't solve them. I asked a fellow who paid out quite a sum of money to take a certain course, and he told me how it had helped him and his family—he said it had revolutionized them. Several months later I asked, "How is it going for you now?" He said, "We're just about back where we were before we took the course." Apparently it was not the problem-solver he thought it was. Then I asked him a direct question, "How much time do you really spend in the Word of God?" My friend, the Word of God is the answer; and it's so simple I'm not able to charge for it! Why not forget the little courses that are being offered and get down to a serious study of the Word of God? Don't stop with the Gospel of John, wonderful as it is. There are sixty-five other books in the Bible. If you get the total Word of God, you will get the total will of God for this life, and you will have a basis on which you can operate. There is joy, there is satisfaction and sheer delight in being in the will of God and doing what God wants you to do.

Notwithstanding ye have well done, that ye did communicate with my affliction [Phil. 4:14].

Paul wants them to know that he appreciates their gift—"Ye have done well, that ye did communicate with my affliction." This is his personal thank-you.

Now ye Philippians know also, that in the beginning of the gospel, when I departed from Macedonia, no church communicated with me as concerning giving and receiving, but ye only [Phil. 4:15].

This church was a jewel. There are churches like it across this country today. They have a wonderful fellowship and a heart for the things of God. God is blessing them in marvelous, wonderful ways. The Philippian church was close to the apostle Paul. They were the ones who sent support to him—Paul was their missionary. Wouldn't you have loved to have had Paul as your missionary and to have had a part in his support?

For even in Thessalonica ye sent once and again unto my necessity [Phil. 4:16].

We know from the account in Acts 16 and 17 that Paul had to leave Philippi by the request of the authorities. He went on to Thessalonica where those who opposed the gospel he was preaching set the city in an uproar. No one was helping Paul but the Philippian believers—"For even in Thessalonica ye sent once and again unto my necessity."

Not because I desire a gift: but I desire fruit that may abound to your account [Phil. 4:17].

That church in Philippi has been getting dividends on their contribution right down to the present time. Paul wrote them this epistle to thank them. We are studying the epistle today, and we are profiting from this study. This is a part of the dividends of their contribution. They have stock in the apostle Paul, if you please. They still have a part in getting out the Word of God!

But I have all, and abound: I am full, having received of Epaphroditus the things which were sent from you, an odour of a sweet smell, a sacrifice acceptable, well-pleasing to God [Phil. 4:18].

The priest in the Old Testament went into the holy place to put incense on the altar, and it ascended with a sweet smell. A Christian in his giving is like a priest making an offering to God. When it is made in the right spirit, it is, as Paul is saying to the Philippian believers, more than just making a donation or taking up a collection. It is an offering, an odor of a sweet smell to God. And that is what your gift is when it is given in the right spirit.

But my God shall supply all your need according to his riches in glory by Christ Jesus [Phil. 4:19].

Thinking of their sacrifice to supply his need, Paul assures them that God would supply all their needs. He doesn't say all their *wants*—he doesn't include luxury items—but all their *needs*. However, He does supply luxury items many times. When He does, it is surplus. He does it out of His loving-kindness.

Now unto God and our Father be glory for ever and ever. Amen [Phil. 4:20].

God gets all the glory. He will not share His glory with another.

Salute every saint in Christ Jesus. The brethren which are with me greet you.

All the saints salute you, chiefly they that are of Caesar's household [Phil. 4:21–22].

He greets each believer personally. The believers who are with Paul also send their greetings. Again we are told that some were patricians, nobility, members of the household of Caesar. They now belong to Christ, and they want to be remembered to the Christians in Philippi.

The grace of our Lord Jesus Christ be with you all. Amen [Phil. 4:23].

Paul closes with a benediction, and I will close with a benediction. The grace of our Lord Jesus Christ be with you all. Amen.

BIBLIOGRAPHY

(Recommended for Further Study)

Boice, James Montgomery. *Philippians, an Expository Commentary.* Grand Rapids, Michigan: Zondervan Publishing House, 1971.

Getz, Gene A. *A Profile of Christian Maturity: A Study of Philippians.* Grand Rapids, Michigan: Zondervan Publishing House, 1976.

Gromacki, Robert G. *Stand United in Joy: An Exposition of Philippians.* Grand Rapids, Michigan: Baker Book House, 1980.

Hendriksen, William. *A Commentary on Philippians.* Grand Rapids, Michigan: Baker Book House, 1963.

Ironside, H. A. *Notes on Philippians.* Neptune, New Jersey: Loizeaux Brothers, n.d.

Johnstone, Robert. *Lectures on Philippians.* Grand Rapids, Michigan: Baker Book House, 1875. (An excellent, comprehensive treatment.)

Kelly, William. *Lectures on Philippians and Colossians.* Addison, Illinois: Bible Truth Publishers, n.d.

King, Guy H. *The Joy Way.* Fort Washington, Pennsylvania: Christian Literature Crusade, 1952. (A splendid devotional study in Philippians.)

McGee, J. Vernon. *Probing Through Philippians.* Pasadena, California: Thru the Bible Books, 1971.

Meyer, F. B. *The Epistle to the Philippians.* Grand Rapids, Michigan: Kregel Publications. (Devotional.)

Moule, Handley C. G. *Studies in Philippians.* Grand Rapids, Michigan: Kregel Publications, 1893. (This is a reprint from *The Cambridge University Bible for Schools and Colleges* and covers Romans, Ephesians, Philippians, and Colossians. Very helpful.)

Muller, Jac. J. *The Epistle of Paul to the Philippians and to Philemon.* Grand Rapids, Michigan: Wm. B. Eerdmans Publishing Co., 1955.

Pentecost, J. Dwight. *The Joy of Living.* Grand Rapids, Michigan: Zondervan Publishing House, 1973. (A practical study of Philippians.)

Robertson, A. T. *Epochs in the Life of Paul.* Grand Rapids, Michigan: Baker Book House, 1909.

Robertson, A. T. *Paul's Joy in Christ: Studies in Philippians*. Grand Rapids, Michigan: Baker Book House, 1917. (Excellent.)

Strauss, Lehman. *Devotional Studies in Philippians*. Neptune, New Jersey: Loizeaux Brothers, 1959.

Vine, W. E. *Philippians and Colossians*. London: Oliphants, 1955. (Excellent treatment by a Greek scholar.)

Vos, Howard. *Philippians—A Study Guide*. Grand Rapids, Michigan: Zondervan Publishing House, 1975. (Excellent for individual or group study.)

Walvoord, John F. *Philippians: Triumph in Christ*. Chicago, Illinois: Moody Press, 1971. (Excellent, inexpensive survey.)

Wiersbe, Warren W. *Be Joyful*. Wheaton, Illinois: Victor Books, n.d.

Wuest, Kenneth S. *Philippians in the Greek New Testament*. Grand Rapids, Michigan: Wm. B. Eerdmans Publishing Co., 1942.

The Epistle to the
COLOSSIANS
INTRODUCTION

The author of this epistle is the apostle Paul as stated in Colossians 1:1.

The Epistle to the Colossians is one of the Prison Epistles which are so called because they were written by Paul while he was in prison in Rome. The Prison Epistles include Ephesians, Philippians, Colossians, and the very personal Epistle to Philemon.

The year was about A.D. 62. Four messengers left Rome unobserved, but they each carried a very valuable document. Tychicus was carrying the Epistle to the Ephesians over to Ephesus where he was the pastor or the leader of that church. Epaphroditus was carrying the Epistle to the Philippians as he was the pastor in Philippi. Epaphras was carrying the Epistle to the Colossians; apparently he was the leader of the church in Colosse. Onesimus was carrying the Epistle to Philemon. Philemon was his master, and Onesimus, who had run away, was returning to him.

These four are companion epistles and together have been called the anatomy of Christianity, or the anatomy of the church. We can see that the subjects of these epistles cover all aspects of the Christian faith:

Ephesians is about the body of believers called the church, of which Christ is the head.

Colossians directs our attention to the head of the body who is Christ. The body itself is secondary. Christ is the theme. He is the center of the circle around which all Christian living revolves. Colossians emphasizes the *plērōma*; Christ is the fullness of God.

Philippians shows the church walking here on earth. Christian living is the theme; it is the periphery of the circle of which Christ is the center. Philippians emphasizes the *kenōsis*, Christ becoming a servant.

Philemon gives us Christianity in action. We would say it is where the rubber meets the road, or in that day it was where the sandals touched the Roman road. It demonstrates Christianity worked out in a pagan society.

We can see why these four documents have been called the anatomy of the church—they belong together to make a whole.

I don't think any armored car ever carried four more valuable documents. Do you realize that if today you possessed those four original documents as they came from the hand of Paul, you could probably get any price you wanted for them—you would have the wealth of a king! Well, we measure it in terms other than the dollar sign; their spiritual value cannot be estimated in human terms at all.

I have never been to Colosse although I have been in sight of it—I have seen it from a distance. The ruins of it stand there in the gates of Phrygia. It is over in the same area where Laodicea and Hierapolis are. There are some ruins of the city; there are no ruins of any church. The church at Colosse met in the home of Philemon. I doubt that there ever was a church building there.

A great civilization and a great population were in that area. It was more or less a door to the Orient, to the East; it was called the gates of Phrygia. Here the East and the West met. Here is where the Roman Empire attempted to tame the East and to bring it under Roman subjugation.

Colosse was a great fortress city as were Laodicea, Philadelphia, Sardis, Thyatira, and Pergamum. All of these had been great cities of defense against invasion from the East. But by the time of Paul the apostle the danger had been relieved because the Roman Empire was pretty much in charge of the world by then. As a result, the people had lapsed into paganism and gross immorality at the time of Paul. And Colosse was typical of the great cities of that day.

As far as the record is concerned, Paul never visited the city of Colosse. After I visited the Bible lands I could understand many things in Scripture that I had not understood before. Why didn't Paul visit Colosse? It seems that he did not come in through the gates of Phrygia, but instead he came in to the north of Colosse over at Sardis. Apparently he took that Roman road to Ephesus and bypassed Colosse.

Even though Paul was never in the city of Colosse, he was the founder of the church there. Epaphras was the leader of the church, and he may have been the *direct* founder, but Paul founded the church at Colosse. He was the founder in very much the same way as he was the founder of the church at Rome: he touched multitudes of people in the Roman Empire who later gravitated to Rome and formed the church there. Paul may have visited Laodicea (although I doubt that very seriously), and believers may have come from there to Colosse. But converts from Paul's ministry in Ephesus very definitely could have come to Colosse to form the nucleus of that church. Colosse is located just seventy-five to one hundred miles east of Ephesus.

Paul spent three years of ministry in Ephesus, two of them teaching in the school of Tyrannus. There was a tremendous civilization in that area—the culture of the Roman Empire was centered there. It was no longer centered in Greece which had pretty much deteriorated along with her philosophy and culture. But the Greek culture was virile in Asia Minor, the area known as Turkey today. It was in this area that Paul did his greatest work along with his co-workers. There were with him John Mark, Barnabas, Silas, Timothy, and apparently some of the other apostles. We know that the apostle John became the pastor at Ephesus later on.

Asia Minor was a great cultural center, but it was also a center for heathenism, paganism, and the mystery religions. There was already abroad that which is known as Gnosticism, the first heresy of the church. There were many forms of Gnosticism, and in Colosse there were the Essenes. There are three points of identification for this group:

1. They had an *exclusive spirit*. They were the aristocrats in wisdom. They felt that they were *the* people—they had knowledge in a jug and held the stopper in their hands. They felt they had the monopoly of it all. As a result, they considered themselves super-duper in knowledge and thought they knew more than any of the apostles. Paul will issue them a warning in the first chapter: "Whom we preach, warning every man, and teaching every man in all wisdom; that we may present every man perfect in Christ Jesus" (Col. 1:28). Perfection is not to be found in any cult or any heresy, but in Christ Jesus. All wisdom is found in Him.

2. They held *speculative tenets on creation*. They taught that God did not create the universe directly, but created a creature who in turn created another creature, until one finally created the physical universe. Christ was considered a creature in this long series of creations. This was known in pantheistic Greek philosophy as the *demiurge*. Paul refutes this in Colossians 1:15–19 and 2:18.

3. Another identifying mark of this group was their ethical practice of *asceticism and unrestrained licentiousness*. They got the asceticism from the influence of Greek Stoicism and the unrestrained licentiousness from the influence of Greek Epicureanism. Paul refutes this in Colossians 2:16,23 and 3:5–9.

Colossians is the chart and compass which enables the believer to sail between the ever present Scylla and Charybdis. On the one hand there is always the danger of Christianity freezing into a form, into a ritual. It has done that in many areas and in many churches so that Christianity involves nothing more than going through a routine. On the other hand is the danger that Christianity will evaporate into a philosophy. I had an example of that when a man who was liberal in his theology asked me, "What theory of inspiration do you hold?" I answered him, "I don't hold a *theory* of inspiration. I believe that the Word of God is the revelation of God as it says it is. That is not a theory." We find people talking about theories of inspiration and theories of atonement—that is the evaporation of Christianity into a philosophy.

So there are two dangers. One is to freeze into form and become nothing but a ritualistic church; the other is to evaporate into steam and be lost in liberalism and false philosophy. You will remember that the Lord Jesus said that He was the Water of Life. He didn't say, "I am the ice of life"; neither did he say, "I am the steam of life." He is the *Water* of Life— water at the temperature of life, neither freezing nor boiling.

The Water of Life is "Christ in you, the hope of glory" (Col. 1:27). Christ is to live in you. He is to walk down the street where you live. Christianity is Christ down where we live, Christ in the nitty-gritty of life, down where the rubber meets the road.

There has always been the danger of adding something to or subtracting something from Christ—the oldest heresy is also the newest heresy, by the way. Christianity is not a mathematical problem of adding or subtracting: Christianity is Christ. This is what Paul teaches in this epistle: "For in him dwelleth all the fulness of the Godhead bodily" (Col. 2:9)— in Him dwelleth all the *plērōma*. All you need is to be found in Christ Jesus.

Here is a quotation from William Sanday: "In the Ephesian Epistle the church is the primary object, and the thought passes upward to Christ as the head of the church. In the Colossian Epistle Christ is the primary object, and the thought passes downward to the church as the body of Christ."

The dominating thought in this epistle is: Christ is all. He is all I need; He is everything. Charles Wesley put it like this in his lovely hymn, "Thou, O Christ, art all I want; more than all in Thee I find."

Charles Spurgeon said, "Look on thine own nothingness; be humble, but look at Jesus, thy great representative, and be glad. It will save thee many pangs if thou will learn to think of thyself as being *in Him*"—accepted in the Beloved, finding Him our all in all.

I received a letter from a dear lady here in Pasadena. She is eighty years old and doesn't expect to live much longer, but she is resting in Christ's loving forgiveness. My friend, you cannot find a better place to rest.

If you are resting in Him, you will find that you don't need to go through a ritual. You won't need to do a lot of gyrations and genuflections. You won't be discussing the theories of inspiration. You either believe that the Bible is the Word of God, or you don't believe it is the Word of God.

Let us stop this so-called intellectual approach that we find in our churches today. It's no good. When I started out as a pastor, I tried to be intellectual. An elder in the church in which I served came to me and talked to me about it, and he said, "We would rather have a genuine Vernon McGee than an imitation of anybody else." You see, I was trying to imitate intellectual men whom I admired. We don't need to do that kind of thing—we need to be ourselves. We need to get down off our high horses. Remember that the Lord Jesus is feeding sheep, not giraffes.

The practical section of this epistle shows us Christ, the fullness of God, poured out in the lives of the believers. The alabaster box of ointment needs to be broken today. The world not only needs to see something, but it needs to smell something. The pollution of this world is giving a very bad odor in these days. We need something of the fragrance and loveliness of Jesus Christ, and only the church is permitted to break that alabaster box of ointment and let out the fragrance.

OUTLINE

I. **Doctrinal: Christ, the Fullness *(plērōma)* of God; in Christ We Are Made Full, Chapters 1–2**

   A. Introduction, Chapter 1:1–8

   B. Paul's Prayer, Chapter 1:9–14

   C. Person of Christ, Chapter 1:15–19

   D. Objective Work of Christ for Sinners, Chapter 1:20–23

   E. Subjective Work of Christ for Saints, Chapter 1:24–29

   F. Christ, the Answer to Philosophy (For the Head), Chapter 2:1–15

   G. Christ, the Answer to Ritual (For the Heart), Chapter 2:16–23

II. **Practical: Christ, the Fullness of God, Poured out in Life through Believers, Chapters 3–4**

   A. Thoughts and Affections of Believers Are Heavenly, Chapter 3:1–4

   B. Living of Believers Is Holy, Chapters 3:5–4:6

   C. Fellowship of Believers Is Hearty, Chapter 4:7–18

CHAPTER 1

THEME: Christ, the fullness of God—in Christ we are made full; Introduction; Paul's prayer; person of Christ; objective work of Christ for sinners; subjective work of Christ for saints

INTRODUCTION

The four Prison Epistles of Paul which include the Epistle to the Colossians have been called the anatomy of the Church because their subjects cover all aspects of the Christian faith. In Colossians our attention is directed to the head of the body who is Christ. The body, the church, is secondary. Instead, Christ is the theme, and Christian living is centered in Him.

Paul, an apostle of Jesus Christ by the will of God, and Timotheus our brother,

To the saints and faithful brethren in Christ which are at Colosse: Grace be unto you, and peace, from God our Father and the Lord Jesus Christ [Col. 1:1–2].

Paul calls himself "an apostle of Jesus Christ," and he always says it is "by the will of God." Paul was in the will of God when he was an apostle. *God* made him an apostle.

Are you in the will of God today? Are you serving Christ? Are you sure you are in the proper place? Are you sure you are doing the proper thing? I believe that every believer is called to *function* in the body of believers, but it is important to be functioning in the right way. There are too many people who are active, doing something that they are not supposed to be doing. Too often we try to imitate other people. We think, "I'll get busy doing what brother so-and-so is doing." We need to remember that our gifts are different, and we are each going to function a little differently. But we ought to be *functioning*. God made Paul an apostle. Did God put you where you are? When you know you are in the will of God, there is a deep satisfaction in life, by the way.

"To the saints and faithful brethren in Christ which are at Colosse." He is not talking about two groups of people. The saints and the believing brethren are the same. Faithful brethren are believing brethren, and they are saints. We are not saints because of what we do. We are saints by our position. The Greek word for *saints* means "to be set apart for God." Those who are set apart for God and the believing brethren are the same group of people.

Notice that they are "in Christ" but they are "at Colosse." The most important question is not, Where are you *at*? but Who are you *in*? That may not be good grammar, but it sure is good Bible. The saints are *at Colosse*—it is important that we have an address down here. But we ought to have an address up yonder also: *in Christ.*

"Grace be unto you, and peace, from God our Father and the Lord Jesus Christ." We must know the grace of God in order to experience the peace of God.

In the better manuscripts "and the Lord Jesus Christ" is not added. It says simply, "Grace be unto you, and peace, from God our Father." It is important to remember that Paul is writing to counteract Gnosticism which was the first heresy in the church. This was the Essene branch of Gnosticism. They relegated God to a place far removed from man and taught that one had to go through emanations to get to God. Have you ever noticed that all heathen religions and cults have some sort of an "open sesame" before you can get in to God? Paul makes it very clear here that grace and peace come directly "from God our Father." We can come directly to Him through Christ.

We give thanks to God and the Father of our Lord Jesus Christ, praying always for you [Col. 1:3].

We can go *directly* to God. We do not need to go through any form of emanation at all. Anyone who is in Christ Jesus has access to God the Father. One of the benefits of being justified by faith is access to God through our Lord Jesus Christ.

"Praying always for you." You would find it very challenging to compile a list of the folk Paul said he was praying for, and add the Colossian believers to the list. He always prayed for them; they were on his prayer list.

Since we heard of your faith in Christ Jesus, and of the love which ye have to all the saints,

For the hope which is laid up for you in heaven, whereof ye heard before in the word of the truth of the gospel [Col. 1:4–5].

Here Paul links the trinity of graces for believers: (1) faith—past; (2) love—present; and (3) hope—future.

Paul is going to talk about the good points of these believers. They had *faith* toward God. Faith rests upon historical facts; it is based on the past. It was based on what they had heard before "in the word of the truth of the gospel." This refers to the content of the gospel, the great truths that pertain to the gospel of the grace of God. God has us shut up to a cross, and He asks us to believe Him. You haven't really heard the gospel until you have heard something to believe. The gospel is not something for us to do. It tells what *He* did for you and for me over nineteen hundred years ago. "So then faith cometh by hearing, and hearing by the word of God" (Rom. 10:17). Faith is not a leap in the dark. It rests upon historical facts; it is believing God.

"And of the love which ye have to all the saints"—faith is based upon the past, but *love* is for the present.

It is nonsense today to boast of the fundamentalism of our doctrine and then to spend our time crucifying our brethren and attempting to find fault with them. There are too many "wonderful saints" looking down on their fellow believers who have not measured up to their high standard and who are not separated like they are separated. My friend, the world is not interested in that kind of approach. The world is looking to see whether Christians love each other or not. It is hypocrisy to consider oneself a Christian and then not to demonstrate love for the brethren. If we have disagreements with our brethren, we are to bear with them, we are to pray for them, and we are to love them. Remember that a Christian is a sinner saved by grace. None of us will ever be perfect in this life.

A man came to me to criticize a certain Christian leader—and I don't agree with everything that leader does either—but the Spirit of God is using that man in a mighty way. So I asked the man who was complaining, "Do you ever pray for him?" He answered, "No, I don't." I replied, "I think that you ought to pray for him. You may not agree with him on every point, but the Spirit of God is using him."

These Colossian believers had their good points. They were sound in the faith toward God. They were fundamental in their belief, and they also had love for the brethren. And Paul says that they had *hope* for the future— "For the hope which is laid up for you in heaven."

In 1 Corinthians also Paul lists these three graces, but he lists them a little differently: "And now abideth faith, hope, charity, these three; but the greatest of these is charity" (1 Cor. 13:13). He puts hope in second position and love is listed last. Why? Because love is the only thing that is going to abide. Love is for the present, it is true, but it is also going to make it into eternity. It is very important that we begin to exhibit love down here upon this earth, don't you agree?

That "hope which is laid up for you in heaven" is the blessed hope. We are to look for the coming of Christ; we are to love His appearing.

"Whereof ye heard before in the word of the truth [content] of the gospel." The gospel is a simple message which God simply asks you to believe. You are asked to believe on the basis of certain facts: Jesus Christ was virgin born. He performed miracles. He is the God-man. He died on a cross, was buried, and rose again. He ascended back into heaven. He sent the Holy Spirit into the world on the Day of Pentecost to form the church. And He is sitting at God's right hand today; His position there indicates that our redemption is complete. We are asked to enter into the rest which He offers to those who will come to Him. He has a present ministry of intercession for us. I think He has other ministries, too. And finally, He is going to return to this earth again. These are all part of the glorious gospel. This is the "content" of the gospel, as Paul expresses it here.

Which is come unto you, as it is in all the world; and bringeth forth fruit, as it doth also in you, since the day ye heard of it, and knew the grace of God in truth [Col. 1:6].

Paul says the gospel has come to the Colossians as it has come to "all the world." Dr. Marvin R. Vincent, a great expositor of the Epistle to the Colossians, as well as other expositors, believes this is hyperbole. I'll be honest with you, I also had difficulty accepting this statement. Is Paul trying to say that at this particular time when he was in prison in Rome the gospel had reached the world? That is what he says. I have come to the position that I believe he meant what he said *literally*; it is not hyperbole. When I visited Asia Minor, I stood in Turkey at the city of Sardis and saw part of a Roman road that had been uncovered by excavation. That is the road that Paul traveled when he came down out of the Galatian country on the way to Ephesus. For three years he preached the gospel in Ephesus to people who were there from all over the Roman Empire. As a result, the gospel had gone ahead to Rome long before Paul was taken there as a prisoner.

The word for "world" here is *kosmos*, and it simply means the Roman Empire of that day. The gospel at that time had penetrated into the farthest reaches of the Roman Empire. It may have even crossed over to Great Britain. Every part of the Roman world had heard the gospel. I tell you, my friend, those early apostles were on the move! I am reluctant to criticize anything they did. Paul says here that the gospel had gone into all the Roman world.

"And bringeth forth fruit." Wherever the gospel is preached it will bring forth fruit. Paul says that, and it is true.

I must confess my faith was weak when we began our radio program. I determined to give out the Word of God, but I'll be honest with you, I expected to fall on my face and see great failure. The biggest surprise of my life was that God blessed His Word. Was I surprised! I thought He would let me down, but He didn't. He said He would bless His Word, and we can count on Him to do that. It "bringeth forth fruit, as it doth also in you, since the day ye heard of it, and knew the grace of God in truth." I am overwhelmed today by the letters and by the people I meet who say they were brought to Christ through our radio ministry. It started out so weakly. It was just a Mickey Mouse operation if there ever was one. But God blesses His Word. I don't only believe that; I know it. I won't even argue with anybody about that. Some fellow comes to me and says, "Dr. McGee, I don't believe the Bible is the Word of God." And I say, "You don't?" He says, "No. Aren't you going to argue with me to persuade me?" I say, "Well, no." And he asks "Why not?" I have to say, "Because I know it is the Word of God. I don't only believe it; I *know* it."

It would be just as if someone came to me and said, "Dr. McGee, I want to argue with you about whether you love your wife or not. I can give you several philosophical arguments that will show that you don't love your wife." Do you know, that fellow might out-argue me and whip me down intellectually. He might show me by logic and all types of argument that I don't love my wife. Do you know what I would say? I'd say, "Brother, I don't know about those arguments, but I want you to know one thing: I love my wife." You see, that is something I know. I know I love her. I don't need all those cogent, sophisticated, astute,

esoteric arguments. There are some things we simply know.

And we should not let what we don't know upset what we do know. That is important for us to see. Paul says that the gospel *will* bring forth fruit. That is the wonderful confidence that we can have.

As ye also learned of Epaphras our dear fellow-servant, who is for you a faithful minister of Christ [Col. 1:7].

Apparently Epaphras was the leader or the pastor of the church in Colosse. (*Epaphras* sounds like the name of a medicine to me, but nevertheless, that was the name of the fellow.) Paul calls him "our dear fellow-servant." Have you noticed how graciously Paul could talk about other servants of God? Paul had something good to say about those who were preaching the Word of God. But when he found a rascal, he was just like our Lord in that he would really reprimand evil when he saw it.

The Lord Jesus was so merciful to sinners. The woman taken in adultery should have been stoned to death, but notice how gracious our Lord was to her (see John 8:1–11). Then there was that arrogant Pharisee, Nicodemus, who came to the Lord Jesus and attempted to pay Him a compliment: ". . . Rabbi, we know that thou art a teacher come from God" (John 3:2). In effect, "We Pharisees know. And, brother, when we know something, that's it!" The Lord Jesus so gently and so graciously pulled him down off his high horse. When the Lord got through with him, he was just plain, little old Nicky. Little old Nicodemus was trying to be somebody, but he was nothing in the world but a religious robot going through rituals. The Lord Jesus brought him down to the place where he could humbly ask, "How can these things be?" Then the Lord Jesus led him to see the Cross. How gracious He was in dealing with folk like that!

Who also declared unto us your love in the Spirit [Col. 1:8].

We will not find a great emphasis on the Holy Spirit in this epistle, but Paul does make it clear to the Colossian believers that they would not have been able to exhibit this love unless it were by the Holy Spirit. It was to the Galatians that Paul wrote that the fruit of the Spirit is love. In this epistle he will not dwell on that aspect. He is going to dwell on the person of Christ. As he does that, the Spirit of God will take the things of Christ and will show them unto us. That is the important work of the Holy Spirit.

PAUL'S PRAYER

In this next section we have Paul's prayer for the Colossians. This is one of the most wonderful prayers in Scripture. It is a prayer that I think touches all the bases, and it will be very helpful for us to notice what Paul prays for.

It is very interesting that today we find people who are praying *for* these things. Paul makes it clear that we already *have* these things. Dr. H. A. Ironside speaks of the prayers that we hear people say which go something like this: "We pray Thee, forgive us our sins and wash us in the blood of Jesus. Receive us into Thy kingdom. Give us of Thy Holy Spirit, and save us at last for Christ's sake. Amen." Did you know that God has already answered every one of those petitions? God has forgiven us all our trespasses. We are cleansed by the blood of Christ. He has already translated us out of the kingdom of darkness into the kingdom of the Son of His love. He has sealed us with His Holy Spirit. ". . . if any man have not the Spirit of Christ, he is none of his" (Rom. 8:9). He has saved us eternally from the very moment we first believed the gospel. Therefore it would be more fitting to thank and praise Him for all these things than to be petitioning Him for what we already have. Instead of praying, "We ask this of Thee," the prayer should be, "We thank Thee for all that You have already done."

Now we come to this wonderful prayer that Paul prayed. First he will make several petitions, and then he will thank the Lord for the things He has already done for us.

For this cause we also, since the day we heard it, do not cease to pray for you, and to desire that ye might be filled with the knowledge of his will in all wisdom and spiritual understanding [Col. 1:9].

The first thing for which Paul prayed was that they might be filled with knowledge. The Greek word is *epignōsis* which means "a super knowledge." The Gnostics, the heretics there in Colosse, boasted that they had a super knowledge. Paul says here, "I pray that you might be filled with knowledge, that you might have a super knowledge." But Paul confines this knowledge to knowledge of the will of God—this knowledge must be "in all wisdom and spiritual understanding."

Let me merely call attention to the fact that the word *wisdom* occurs six times in this short epistle.

That ye might walk worthy of the Lord unto all pleasing, being fruitful in every good work, and increasing in the knowledge of God [Col. 1:10].

His second petition is that they might be pleasing to God. That means that these Christians will not be bowing down to men or attempting to please them.

His third request is that they might be "fruitful in every good work." The Christian is a fruit-bearing branch. Christ is the vine, and we should bring forth fruit.

"Increasing in the knowledge of God." A Christian should not be static but alive and growing in the Word of God. So their increase in the knowledge of God is Paul's fourth request.

Strengthened with all might, according to his glorious power, unto all patience and longsuffering with joyfulness [Col. 1:11].

Here is his fifth request. Strength and power can come only from God; they are produced by the Holy Spirit. These believers are to be strengthened with all might "unto all patience and longsuffering." And this patience and longsuffering is to be "with joyfulness."

Giving thanks unto the Father, which hath made us meet to be partakers of the inheritance of the saints in light [Col. 1:12].

Here is the beginning of the list of things for which Paul is thankful. All our prayers should be filled with thanksgiving. Paul is thankful that God by His grace has given us an inheritance with the saints in light. We ought to lay hold of that today. We should believe God and believe that His promise is true.

Who hath delivered us from the power of darkness, and hath translated us into the kingdom of his dear Son [Col. 1:13].

Paul is thankful that we have been delivered from the kingdom of Satan. We were dead in trespasses and sins, going the way of the world. Now we have been translated into the kingdom of the Son of His love. This is the present aspect of the kingdom of God here on earth today. You can't build the kingdom of God. The only way you can be a part of it is to open your heart and receive Christ as your Savior. That translates you into the kingdom of His dear Son.

In whom we have redemption through his blood, even the forgiveness of sins [Col. 1:14].

Not only have we been translated into His kingdom, but we also have forgiveness of sins in Him. This is always associated with the blood of Christ. God does not arbitrarily and sentimentally forgive sins. We have redemption through His blood—"redemption" is *apolutrōsis* which means "to set free an enslaved people." He paid a price to deliver us out of slavery.

Paul has given thanks for five wonderful truths. If we are trusting Christ, God has made us meet to be partakers of the inheritance of the saints in light. He has delivered us from the power of darkness and has translated us into the kingdom of His dear Son. God has redeemed us through Christ and has forgiven us our sins through His blood. Yet there are a great many Christian people today who pray for all five of these things. My believing friend, they are yours. Why don't you thank Him for them?

PERSON OF CHRIST

We spoke of the person of Jesus Christ in our study of the Song of Solomon. In Colossians we come in close on the subject and learn the theology of it. This is a very lofty, very exalted, and very grand section of this epistle. The subject here is the person of Jesus Christ. We cannot say too much about Him, and we will never in this life be able to comprehend Him in all of His wonder and in all of His glory.

This section provides an answer to those who would deny the deity of Jesus Christ. To understand these verses is to realize how wonderful He really is. Paul is specifically attempting to answer one of the oldest heresies in the church, Gnosticism. Another of the first heresies was Arianism. Arius of Alexandria said that the Lord Jesus Christ was a creature, a created being. The Council of Nicaea in A.D. 325 answered this heresy saying, "The Son is very Man of very man, and very God of very God." Later on in the history of the church, Socinus propagated the heresy that Jesus was not God and that mankind did not need a Savior from sin. He taught that we were not totally depraved. Today this is the basis of Unitarianism and some of the cults, including Jehovah's Witnesses.

There are given here nine marks of identification of Christ which make Him different from and superior to any other person who has ever lived.

Who is the image of the invisible God, the firstborn of every creature [Col. 1:15].

1. He is the "image of the invisible God." "Image" is *eikōn*. How could He be the image of the invisible God? You cannot take a photograph or an image of that which is invisible. How could He be that? John makes this clear in the prologue to his gospel: "In the beginning was the Word." That is a beginning that has no beginning—Christ has no beginning. "In the beginning was the Word, and the Word was with God, and the Word was God." (John 1:1). And then John says, "And the Word was made [born] flesh . . ." (John 1:14). If you want the Christmas story in John's gospel, that is it: He was *born flesh*. This is the way that He became the image of the invisible God. How could He be that? Because He *is* God. If He were not God, He could not have been the image of the invisible God.

2. He is "the first born of every creature." This reveals His relationship to the Father and His position in the Trinity. God is the everlasting Father; the Son is the everlasting Son. His position in the Trinity is that of Son.

"Firstborn" indicates His priority before all creation. His headship of all creation does not mean that He was born first. We need to understand what the Scriptures mean by "firstborn."

Nowhere does Scripture teach that Jesus Christ had His beginning at Bethlehem. We are told in the great prophecy of Micah 5:2 that He would be born in Bethlehem, but that He came forth from *everlasting*. Isaiah 9:6 tells us, "For unto us a child is born, unto us a son is given. . . ." The child is *born*, but the Son is *given*. He came out of eternity and took upon Himself our humanity.

Paul is dealing with one of the philosophies of that day, one of the mystery religions. It is called the *demiurge*, and it held that God created a creature just beneath Him; then that creature created a creature beneath him; then that creature created a creature beneath him. You can just keep on going down that ladder until finally you come to a creature that created this universe. These were emanations from God. Gnosticism taught that Jesus was one of these creatures, an emanation from God. Now Paul is answering that. He says that Jesus Christ is the Firstborn of all creation, He is back of all creation. The Greek word is *prōtotokos* meaning "before all creation." He was not born in creation. He is the One who came down over nineteen hundred years ago and became flesh. He existed before any creation: "In the beginning was the Word, and the Word was with God, and the Word was God. The same was in the beginning with God. All things were made by him; and without him was not any thing made that was made" (John 1:1–3). God the Father is the everlasting Father. God the Son is the everlasting Son. There never was a time when Christ was begotten.

There are several places in Scripture where the Lord Jesus is called the Firstborn. He is called the Firstborn of all creation; He is called the Firstborn from the dead; and He is called the only begotten.

He is called the Firstborn from the dead later in this first chapter, verse 18. This is what the psalmist spoke of: "I will declare the decree: the LORD hath said unto me, Thou art my Son; this day have I begotten thee" (Ps. 2:7). Paul explained this idea further in that great sermon that he preached at Antioch of Pisidia in the Galatian country. Paul said there that the psalmist meant that Christ was begotten from the *dead:* "And we declare unto you glad tidings, how that the promise which was made unto the fathers, God hath fulfilled the same unto us their children, in that he hath raised up Jesus again; as it is also written in the second psalm, Thou art my Son, this day have I begotten thee" (Acts 13:32–33).

When Jesus Christ is called the Firstborn of all creation, it is not referring to His birth at Bethlehem. This is no Christmas verse. It means that He has top priority of position. It has nothing to do with His origin at all. The psalmist wrote, "Also I will make him my firstborn, higher than the kings of the earth" (Ps. 89:27). This makes it very clear that Christ as the eternal Son holds the position of top priority to all creation. In other words, He is the Creator. There is no *demiurge,* no series of creatures being created one after another. He Himself created all things.

Let me mention some other verses of Scripture that speak of the person of Christ. In Hebrews 1:3 we read: "Who being the brightness of his glory, and the express image of his person, and upholding all things by the word of his power, when he had by himself purged our sins, sat down on the right hand of the Majesty on high." That doesn't sound very much like He is a mere creature, does it? He is the Second Person of the Godhead. "And of the angels he saith, Who maketh his angels spirits, and his ministers a flame of fire." Now

the Lord Jesus is *not* one of these creatures: "But unto the Son he saith, Thy throne, O God, is for ever and ever: a sceptre of righteousness is the sceptre of thy kingdom" (Heb. 1:7–8).

So, my friend, what we are talking about here is not that the Lord Jesus was born a creature; we are talking about the fact that He is God. When He came into the world, a child was born but *the Son was given* and He had come out of eternity. The angel's announcement to Mary was ". . . that holy thing which shall be born of thee shall be called the Son of God" (Luke 1:35). Why? Because that is who He is. He was the Son of God before He came into this world. ". . . Thou art the Christ, the Son of the living God" (Matt. 16:16).

Now we come to the next two great statements concerning the Lord Jesus:

For by him were all things created, that are in heaven, and that are in earth, visible and invisible, whether they be thrones, or dominions, or principalities, or powers: all things were created by him, and for him [Col. 1:16].

3. "By him were all things created." If all things were created by Him, that clears up the question of His being a creature or the Creator. The statement that He is the Firstborn of all creation does not mean that He was created, but rather He is the One who did the creating.

There are two kinds of creation, the "visible and invisible." It is very interesting here to note that he mentions different gradations of rank in spiritual intelligences: thrones, dominions, principalities, powers. There are gradations in the angelic hosts. Other verses in Scripture tell us that there are seraphim and cherubim, and also the archangels. And then there are just the common, everyday, vegetable variety of angels.

In Ephesians we note the fact that our enemy is a spiritual enemy. Satan has a spiritual host that rebelled with him. So there are different gradations of rank among our spiritual enemies, too.

4. It is wonderful to know that all things were created by Him. But there is another truth given to us here: All things were created "for him."

If you were to go out tonight and look up at the heavens, you would see a number of stars. Have you ever wondered why each star is in its own special position? Why is that star in that part of the heavens? It is in that part of the heavens because that is where Jesus wanted it. Not only did He create all things, but they were created *for* Him.

One of the most wonderful truths in this connection is that we are told that we are heirs of God and joint-heirs with the Lord Jesus Christ. We have a big hunk of real estate coming to us someday. Maybe He will turn over a whole star to us. I don't know; I have often wondered. I think we will be very busy in eternity. We will not be earthlings then, but we will be given a new body which is free from gravitation. We will be living in a city called the New Jerusalem. We will be able to travel through God's vast universe. I don't know how much of that universe He is going to turn over to us. He made it all, created it out of nothing, and He is going to run it to suit Himself. This is *His* universe. If you have wondered why a certain tree has a certain kind of leaf, it is because that is the way He wanted it. It was made *by* Him, and it was made *for* Him. We are going to enter into that someday: there is an inheritance prepared for us. I have never dwelt upon that very much because I feel that it is rather speculative. But I am sure that all of us wonder what it will be like when we are with Him in eternity. We do know it will be wonderful.

You and I are living down here in tents. Paul calls these bodies of ours just that—tents. He says, "For we know that if our earthly house of this tabernacle were dissolved . . ." (2 Cor. 5:1). A tabernacle is a tent. This tent will go right back to the ground because the body is to be put into the ground at death. We will have moved out of our tent. He says, ". . . willing rather to be absent from the body, and to be present with the Lord" (2 Cor. 5:8). When we are absent from these old bodies down here, we will be present with the Lord. We will be at home with Him.

You may be living in a home that cost $500,000. I have news for you: you are actually living in a flabby, old, frail tent—all of us are. But one of these days we will have our glorified bodies, and then we will receive our inheritance! You can have your $500,000 house—you won't be in it long, anyway. Our new body is for eternity, and we will be at home with Him forever. This is the prospect ahead for the child of God. I'm rather looking forward to it. "All things were created by him, and for him."

And he is before all things, and by him all things consist [Col. 1:17].

5. "He is before all things." All fullness dwells in the preincarnate Christ, and all fullness dwells in the incarnate Christ. "For in him dwelleth all the fulness of the Godhead bodily" (Col. 2:9). We are made complete in Him. He was before all things. He is the preincarnate Christ.

6. "By him all things consist." He holds everything together. He maintains creation. He directs it. "Consist" is *sunistēmi* which means to hold together. He is the super glue of the universe.

A few years ago in our lifetime, man did a very daring, and I think now, a very dastardly deed: he untied the atom. The Lord Jesus tied each one of those little fellows together when He created the atom. Man did what he called splitting the atom. Believe me, did he release power! Have you ever stopped to think of the tremendous power that there is in the atoms of this universe? If one bomb that we can hold in our hand can blow a whole area to smithereens, then how much power is tied up on this vast physical universe? Who is holding all that together? We are told that Christ not only created it but that He holds it together. I would say that holding it all together is a pretty big job. The Lord Jesus Christ is the One who is able to do that.

We have this same truth repeated for us in Hebrews: "Who being the brightness of his glory, and the express image of his person, and upholding all things by the word of his power, when he had by himself purged our sins, sat down on the right hand of the Majesty on high" (Heb. 1:3). He's a wonderful person, isn't He? He's a glorious person!

And he is the head of the body, the church: who is the beginning, the first-born from the dead; that in all things he might have the preeminence [Col. 1:18].

7. "He is the head of the body, the church." I believe this is the key to the Epistle to the Colossians, which is really a companion epistle to the Epistles to the Ephesians and the Philippians. In Ephesians we had the emphasis on the fact that the church is the body of Christ down here in the world. The emphasis was upon the body. In Colossians the emphasis is upon the head of the body, the person of the Lord Jesus Christ. In Ephesians we read, "And hath put all things under his feet, and gave him to be the head over all things to the church" (Eph. 1:22). And finally, in Philippians we see the church with feet, walking through the world—we see the experience of the church, the experience of the believer. These are companion epistles.

"The firstborn from the dead." Did you

know that there is only one Man who has been raised in a glorified body today? He is the firstfruits of them that sleep. When a loved one who is in Christ dies and you put that body into the grave, you are just putting it into a motel. It is like putting it into a hotel for a few days, because there is a bright morning coming. The body is put to sleep, but the individual has gone to be with the Lord. When Christ comes to take His church out of this world, then that body is going to be raised on the basis of His resurrection. It is sown in corruption, but it will be raised in incorruption (see 1 Cor. 15:42). We shall be just as He is. "Beloved, now are we the sons of God, and it doth not yet appear what we shall be: but we know that, when he shall appear, we shall be like him; for we shall see him as he is" (1 John 3:2).

8. "That in all things he might have the preeminence." You cannot think of anything more wonderful than this. The will of Christ *must* prevail throughout all of God's creation. That is God's intention. Even in spite of the rebellion of man down here on earth, God says, "Yet have I set my king upon my holy hill of Zion" (Ps. 2:6). God is moving forward today undeviatingly, unhesitatingly, uncompromisingly toward one goal. That goal is to put Jesus on the throne of this world which today is in rebellion against God. That is the objective of God.

For it pleased the Father that in him should all fulness dwell [Col. 1:19].

9. "It pleased the Father that in him should all fulness dwell." The fullness is the *plērōma*. That is one of the most important words in this epistle. Over in Philippians it was the *kenōsis*. That is, it emphasized that Christ emptied Himself and became a servant; He emptied Himself of the glory that He had with the Father. He didn't empty Himself of His deity—He was God when He came to this earth. The *plērōma*, the full fullness of God, dwells in Him.

When He was down here on this earth, the *plērōma* was at home in Jesus. He was 100 percent God—not 99.44 percent, but 100 percent. That little baby that was lying on the bosom of Mary over nineteen hundred years ago seemed so helpless, but He could have spoken this universe out of existence. He is Man of very man; He is God of very God. That is who He is.

We can outline these verses from another perspective. I would like to do this for you in

order to add to our understanding of this portion of Scripture.

1. Christ's relationship to the Father— verse 15
2. Christ's relationship to creation— verses 16–17
3. Christ's relationship to the church— verses 18–19
4. Christ's relationship to the cross— verse 20

OBJECTIVE WORK OF CHRIST FOR SINNERS

We are going to see here the things Christ has done for us.

And, having made peace through the blood of his cross, by him to reconcile all things unto himself; by him, I say, whether they be things in earth, or things in heaven [Col. 1:20].

"Having made peace through the blood of his cross" means that by His paying the penalty on the cross for your sin and my sin, peace has been made between God and the sinner. God does not approach man today and say to him, "Look here, fellow, I'm against you. You have been rebelling against Me. You are a sinner, and I am forced to punish you for that." No, God is saying something entirely different to the lost sinner today. He says to you and to me, "I have already borne the punishment, I have already paid the penalty for all your sin. I want you to know that you can come to Me. Peace has already been made in Christ Jesus, if you will just turn and come to Me."

This is what Paul meant when he wrote, "Therefore being justified by faith, we have peace with God through our Lord Jesus Christ" (Rom. 5:1). Peace has been made through the *blood* of His cross. Paul puts forgiveness of sin right along with the blood of the cross. God can forgive because the penalty has already been paid. Jesus paid that penalty through the blood of His cross; therefore a righteous God can forgive you. God is not a disagreeable neighbor who is waiting around the corner to pounce on the sinner and to find fault with him. God has His arms outstretched and is saying, "Come, and I will give you redemption rest."

"By him to reconcile all things unto himself." Reconciliation is toward man; redemption is toward God. God is saying to all men today, "I am reconciled to you. Now will you be reconciled to Me?" That is the decision a man must make.

Paul explains this very clearly in his letter

to the Corinthians. "And all things are of God, who hath reconciled us to himself by Jesus Christ, and hath given to us the ministry of reconciliation; To wit, that God was in Christ, reconciling the world unto himself, not imputing their trespasses unto them; and hath committed unto us the word of reconciliation. Now then we are ambassadors for Christ, as though God did beseech you by us: we pray you in Christ's stead, be ye reconciled to God" (2 Cor. 5:18–20).

A great many people have the idea that a man must do something to win God over to him. My friend, God is trying to win *you* over—the shoe is on the other foot. God *is* reconciled. He is asking man to be reconciled to Him.

"Reconcile all things"—some people take this statement and get the foolish notion that everybody is going to be saved. To understand this we need to pay a little attention to the grammar that is here. What are the "all things"? We will see that it is limited to all things that are to be reconciled, those which are appointed for reconciliation.

Maybe it would help us if we look at Philippians 3:8 where Paul says, "Yea doubtless, and I count all things but loss for the excellency of the knowledge of Christ Jesus my Lord. . . ." What are the "all things" here? Does Paul include everything in the whole world? No, it refers to all the things that Paul had to lose. In the verses just previous Paul had enumerated all the religious pluses which he had had in his life. It is all these things which Paul counted for loss. Paul couldn't lose something that he didn't have.

"Whether they be things in earth, or things in heaven." You will notice that Paul limits the "all things" that are appointed to reconciliation—he doesn't mention things *under* the earth. In Ephesians 1:22 it says, "And hath put all things under his feet, and gave him to be the head over all things to the church." What are the "all things" that are going to be put under His feet? Well, in Philippians Paul wrote, "That at the name of Jesus every knee should bow, of things in heaven, and things in earth, and things under the earth" (Phil. 2:10). Notice that all things are going to acknowledge the lordship of Jesus Christ—all things in heaven, in earth, and under the earth. That doesn't mean that they are all reconciled. Paul makes no mention of things under the earth being reconciled to God.

My friend, don't listen to the deception, the siren song, that all is going to work out well. Don't think you can depend on God being nice and sweet and pleasant like a little old lady. Things in heaven and in earth are reconciled to God, but not the things under the earth. The things under the earth will have to bow to Him, but they are not reconciled to Him at all. *This* is the place and this is the life in which we need to be reconciled to God.

"Things in heaven"—not only must we be made ready for heaven, but heaven must be made ready to receive us. The Lord Jesus said, ". . . I go to prepare a place for you" (John 14:2). By the Incarnation God came down to man; by the blood of Jesus man is brought up to God. This blood also purifies things in heaven according to Hebrews 9:23–24. Heaven must also be reconciled.

And you, that were sometime alienated and enemies in your mind by wicked works, yet now hath he reconciled [Col. 1:21].

God did not wait until we promised to scrub our faces, put on our Sunday clothes, and go to Sunday school before He agreed to do this work of reconciliation. It was while you and I were in rebellion against Him, while we were doing wicked works, that He reconciled us to Himself. No man can say, "I'm lost because God has not made adequate provision for me." A man is lost because he wants to be lost, because he is in rebellion against God.

"That were sometime alienated and enemies in your mind." This reminds us that there is a *mental* alienation from God as well as a moral alienation. A great many people think that men are lost because they have committed some terrible sin. The reason people are lost is that their minds are alienated from God. I think this explains the fierce antagonism toward God on the part of the so-called intellectuals of our day. There is an open hatred and hostility toward God.

Some time ago I had the funeral of a certain movie star out here in California. The Hollywood crowd came to the funeral. One of the television newscasters commented on the funeral, and I appreciated what he had to say about it. He said, "Today Hollywood heard something that it had never heard before." But I also saw something there at that funeral that I had never seen before. I had never seen so much hatred in the eyes of men and women as I saw when I attempted to present Jesus Christ and to explain how wonderful He is and how He wants to save people. There is an alienation in the mind and heart of man.

In the body of his flesh through death, to present you holy and unblameable

and unreproveable in his sight [Col. 1:22].

"The body of his flesh"—here is an explicit declaration that Christ suffered—not just in appearance—but He suffered in a real body. This directly countered one of the heresies of Gnosticism in Paul's day.

"To present you holy and unblameable and unreproveable in his sight." *Unblameable* means "without blemish." That was the requirement of the sacrificial animal in the Old Testament. You and I cannot present perfection to God, and God cannot accept anything short of perfection. That is the reason we cannot be saved by our works or by our character. We simply cannot meet the demands of a righteous God. But He is able to present us unblameable. Why? Because He took our place. "For he hath made him to be sin for us, who knew no sin; that we might be made the righteousness of God in him" (2 Cor. 5:21).

Unreproveable means "unaccusable or unchargeable." God is the One who justified us. If God declares us to be justified, who can bring any kind of a charge against us? He is the One who has cleared us of all guilt.

If ye continue in the faith grounded and settled, and be not moved away from the hope of the gospel, which ye have heard, and which was preached to every creature which is under heaven; whereof I Paul am made a minister [Col. 1:23].

This is not a conditional clause that is based on the future. The *if* that Paul uses here is the *if* of argument. It does not mean that something *shall be* if something else is true; rather it means that something *was* if something else is true. We would say, "*Since* ye continue in the faith grounded and settled." Paul's point is that we have been reconciled—it is an accomplished fact. So if you are a child of God today, you will continue in the faith grounded and settled. You will not be moved away from the hope of the gospel which you have heard.

"Whereof I Paul am made a minister." Paul loved to look back and rest in his glorious privilege of being a minister of Jesus Christ. I consider that the greatest honor that can come to any person. I thank God every day for the privilege that He has given me of declaring His Word—there is nothing quite like that.

SUBJECTIVE WORK OF CHRIST FOR SAINTS

Who now rejoice in my sufferings for you, and fill up that which is behind of the afflictions of Christ in my flesh for his body's sake, which is the church [Col. 1:24].

Let me give you a free translation of this verse. "Now I, Paul, rejoice in the midst of my sufferings for you, and I am filling up in my flesh that which is lacking of the afflictions of Christ for His body's sake, which is the church." Paul is saying here that it was necessary for him to fill up in suffering that which was lacking in the suffering of Christ. Isn't that a startling statement? Someone will say, "Doesn't that contradict what you have been teaching all along? You say Christ suffered for us and paid the penalty and there is nothing we can do for salvation." That is very true, and this verse does not contradict that at all.

Paul was suffering in his body for the sake of Christ's body. The implication seems to be that there was something lacking in the sufferings of Christ. A second implication could be that it was necessary for Paul, and I think in turn for all believers, to make up that which is lacking. In other words, when Paul suffers for them, it completes the suffering of Christ.

All of this is rather startling because we have just called attention to the fact that this epistle teaches the fullness of Christ. "For in him dwelleth all the fulness of the Godhead bodily" (Col. 2:9). Everything is centered in Him. He is to have the preeminence in all things. Yet here it would seem that there is still something to be done.

Paul is writing this epistle from prison, and he says he has fulfilled all his sufferings. You may remember that the Lord Jesus revealed to Ananias the reason He had saved Paul and how He was going to use him. "But the Lord said unto him [Ananias], Go thy way: for he [Paul] is a chosen vessel unto me, to bear my name before the Gentiles, and kings, and the children of Israel: For I will shew him how great things he must suffer for my name's sake" (Acts 9:15–16). Now Paul writes from prison and says that he has fulfilled that.

In our discussion of this verse I want to make one thing very, very clear, The sufferings of Paul were *not redemptive*. There was no merit in his suffering for others or even for himself as concerning redemption. Paul is very careful in his selection of words here. When Paul speaks of the redemption of Christ, he does not speak of suffering but of a cross, a death, and His blood.

There are two kinds of suffering. There is *ministerial* suffering and there is *mediatorial* suffering. Christ's suffering for us was mediatorial. Actually, we can consider the sufferings of Christ and divide them into two further classifications. There is a sharp distinction between them. We will do that to clarify this passage of Scripture.

1. There are the sufferings of Christ which He endured and in which we cannot share.

He suffered as a man. He endured *human suffering*. He bore the suffering that is common to humanity when He was born in Bethlehem at His incarnation over nineteen hundred years ago. When He was born, did He cry like other little babies that come into the world? I have wondered about that, and I rather think that He did. He was clad in the garment of that frail flesh that you and I have. He could get hungry. He could become thirsty. He experienced loneliness. He suffered anguish and pain and sorrow. He could go to sleep in the boat because He was weary and tired. Those are human sufferings. We all have those.

Paul wrote, "For every man shall bear his own burden" (Gal. 6:5). There are certain burdens we must each bear alone. We are born alone. So was our Lord. We feel pain alone. There are certain problems in life that each of us must face, and we face them alone. There is a sorrow that comes that no one can share with us. We become sick, and no one can take our place.

When my daughter was just a little girl I remember crossing the desert of Arizona coming back from the East. It was the hot summertime, and she had been sick. My wife took her temperature, and it was up to 104 degrees. We took her to the hospital in Phoenix. As she was lying there with that high temperature, I would have given anything in the world at that moment if I could have taken her place. I would gladly have taken that fever for her, but I couldn't do it. We can't share such things.

There will come a time when you and I will go down through the valley of the shadow of death. Humanly speaking, we will each die alone. That is the reason it is so wonderful to be a Christian and to know that Jesus is with us at that time when no one else can go through death with us.

Jesus Christ suffered human suffering. That is a suffering which cannot be shared.

The second suffering which He could not share was His *suffering as the Son of God*. He is God, yet He identified Himself with mankind. No mortal has ever had to endure what He went through. He was made like unto His brethren, and He Himself suffered; but He suffered as the Son of God.

We see this suffering in Psalm 69. It tells us in verses 11 and 12 that He was the song of the drunkards in that little town of Nazareth. And He said that He made sackcloth His garment. Oh, what He suffered because He was the Son of God! He was arrested. The soldiers of the high priest mocked Him. They put a robe on Him and a crown of thorns. They played a Roman game known as "Hot Hand" in which they blindfolded Him and then all the soldiers would hit Him with their fists. One of the soldiers would not hit Him, and when they removed the blindfold He was supposed to say which one had not. Even if He named the right one, they would never have admitted that He was right. Then they would put the blindfold on and play the game again. They all pounded Him until the Lord Jesus Christ was marred more than any man. They had beaten His face to a pulp before they ever put Him on the cross. He suffered in a way that no other man has suffered, because He suffered as the Son of God.

And then He *suffered as the sacrifice for the sin of the world*. He is the Lamb of God who takes away the sin of the world, and none of us can enter into that suffering at all. We can appropriate His death for us, we can recognize the fact that He took our place, but we cannot enter into it. He alone went to the cross. He was forsaken of God and forsaken by men. His was not the blood of martyrdom; His was the blood of sacrifice.

In His first three hours on the cross, man did his worst. It was light from nine o'clock until noon; man was there at his evil worst. In the second three hours, from noon until three o'clock, it was dark; that was when God was doing His best. At that time the cross became an altar on which the Lamb of God was slain to take away the sin of the world. "For Christ also hath once suffered for sins, the just for the unjust . . ." (1 Pet. 3:18). That's a suffering that you and I cannot bear; He could not share that with anyone else.

2. On the other hand, there are the sufferings Christ endured which we can share. These are the sufferings which Paul refers to in verse 24.

There is the *suffering for righteousness' sake*. In the synagogue in Nazareth, His own hometown, Jesus said, "But now ye seek to kill me, a man that hath told you the truth . . ." (John 8:40). He suffered for righteousness' sake, and we are told very definitely that we will do the same: "But and if ye suffer for righteousness' sake, happy are ye . . ." (1 Pet. 3:14). Paul wrote to young Timothy: "Yea, and all that will live godly in Christ Jesus shall suffer persecution" (2 Tim. 3:12).

May I say to you that if you are going to live for God, if you are going to take a stand for the right, you will find that you will be passed by. God's men are passed by today in the distribution of earthly honors. The world will damn the man of God with faint praise, and they will praise him with faint damns. That is the way the world treats God's men today. Athletes are lauded, people in the entertainment world are praised, politicians are praised, and professors are honored; but the man of God is not praised. If you stand for the things that are right in this world, you will suffer for righteousness' sake. Paul understood this, and he wrote, "As it is written, For thy sake we are killed all the day long; we are accounted as sheep for the slaughter" (Rom. 8:36). That will be the lot of anyone who stands for God.

Then there is the *suffering in the measure we identify ourselves with Christ for the proclamation of the gospel.* John wrote, ". . . because as he is, so are we in this world" (1 John 4:17). The Lord Jesus made it very clear, "If the world hate you, ye know that it hated me before it hated you. If ye were of the world, the world would love his own: but because ye are not of the world, but I have chosen you out of the world, therefore the world hateth you" (John 15:18–19). If you are not of the world, the world *will* hate you.

The popularity of the Christian with the world is in inverse ratio with his popularity with Christ. If you are popular with the world as a Christian, then you are not popular with Christ. If you are going to be popular with Christ, you are not going to be popular in this world. The child of God is to take his rightful place and identify himself with Christ. When we suffer for Christ, the Lord Jesus is also suffering through us, through His church.

You remember when the Lord Jesus appeared to Saul on the road to Damascus, He said, ". . . Saul, Saul, why persecutest thou me?" (Acts 9:4). That young Pharisee was startled and puzzled. Saul of Tarsus thought that he was persecuting Christians. He was shocked to learn that he was actually persecuting the Lord Jesus Christ.

This is what Peter wrote about our suffering: "Beloved, think it not strange concerning the fiery trial which is to try you, as though some strange thing happened unto you: But rejoice, inasmuch as ye are partakers of Christ's sufferings; that, when his glory shall be revealed, ye may be glad also with exceeding joy" (1 Pet. 4:12–13).

There is one thing for certain: If the gospel is to go forward today, someone must suffer. The late Dr. George Gill said that when a child is born into this world, some woman must travail in pain; and the reason there are not more people being born again is because there are not enough believers who are willing to travail. Suffering is not popular—but that is what Paul is talking about in this verse.

All of us would like to see revival. We talk glibly about witnesssing and about living for God and all that sort of thing. My friend, may I say to you that if the gospel is going to go forward today and if people are going to be saved, someone is going to have to pay a price. How much are you paying to get out the Word of God? What is it really costing you? Are you willing to suffer for the sake of the gospel?

Whereof I am made a minister, according to the dispensation of God which is given to me for you, to fulfil the word of God [Col. 1:25].

The word *dispensation* means economy—even by transliteration; it is a stewardship. We talk of political economy, domestic economy, business economy. God deals with the world on the basis of different economies or stewardships, but they have always been based on the redemption which is in Christ Jesus. Before Jesus was born into this world, men brought a little lamb as a sacrifice, and they looked forward to the coming of Christ. They were not saved by that little lamb; but they brought the lamb in faith, and they were saved by the Christ who would some day die for them. That was the economy or the stewardship which God had set for the Jews in the Old Testament. We don't bring a little lamb for a sacrifice today because it is now an historical fact that Christ has already come. All we have to do today is trust Him.

"The dispensation of God which is given to me for you," Paul writes to the gentile people in Colosse. They are a part of this new dispensation. The Gentiles are to be included in the church.

"To fulfil the word of God." This was something that had been hidden in the Old Testament, but now God has declared that the gospel must go to the Gentiles.

Even the mystery which hath been hid from ages and from generations, but now is made manifest to his saints [Col. 1:26].

A "mystery" is something that had not been revealed in the Old Testament but is now revealed. We learn in Ephesians that the mystery was not the fact that Gentiles would be saved—that was known in the Old Testament. The mystery, the new thing, was that God would now put Israel on the same basis as the Gentiles. All men are lost; all men have sinned; all men have come short of the glory of God. Now God is taking both Jews and Gentiles, men out of all races, and He is putting them into a new body which is called the church. That was never revealed in the Old Testament, but it is now being revealed.

"Now is made manifest to his saints"—Paul wasn't the only one who understood this mystery. God was making it known to His saints in that day.

> **To whom God would make known what is the riches of the glory of this mystery among the Gentiles; which is Christ in you, the hope of glory [Col. 1:27].**

"Christ in you, the hope of glory"—we are *in Christ*. The moment you put your trust in Christ Jesus, the Holy Spirit baptizes you and puts you in the body of believers. You and I have been brought into something new, the church, and the church has a glorious prospect ahead of it.

> **Whom we preach, warning every man, and teaching every man in all wisdom; that we may present every man perfect in Christ Jesus [Col. 1:28].**

"Whom we preach." The gospel is not *what* we preach, but it is *whom* we preach. No man has ever preached the gospel who hasn't preached Christ. Jesus Christ is the gospel. He is eternal life. John wrote that he was going to show us eternal life, that he had seen eternal life (see 1 John 1:1–2). Whom had John seen? He'd seen Christ. And, my friend, today you either

have Him or you don't have Him. The gospel is Christ—what He has done for us in His death and resurrection and what He is going to do in the future.

"Warning every man, and teaching every man in all wisdom." I believe there are two commands here for ministers today—these are two things we should be doing. We are to preach the gospel in order to win sinners to Christ and to save them from the wrath that is to come, and we are to teach every man in all wisdom. In other words, we are to seek to build up men and women so that they may grow in grace and be faithful members of the body of Christ; they are to be encouraged to serve Christ in the local assembly.

I am told that my teaching of the Bible helps the local churches, and that is the reason I have the support of so many pastors across this country. If I am not doing that, then I would have to say I am not fulfilling my ministry.

"That we may present every man perfect in Christ Jesus." *Perfect* actually means "complete or mature." This is the goal of the teaching of the Word of God.

> **Whereunto I also labour, striving according to his working, which worketh in me mightily [Col. 1:29].**

Striving means "to agonize." Paul is giving us his very personal testimony: "This is what I'm laboring, striving to do."

"According to his working, which worketh in me mightily." Oh, this should be the desire of everyone today who is working for Christ—that He would work in us mightily to do two things: to get out the gospel that men might be saved and then to build them up in the faith. These are the two things the church should be doing today.

CHAPTER 2

THEME: *Christ, the answer to philosophy; Christ, the answer to ritual*

In the first fifteen verses of this chapter we will see that Christ is the answer to philosophy. The remainder of the chapter will show that He is the answer to ritual. The answer to philosophy is for the head; the answer to ritual is for the heart.

Christianity has always been in the danger of sailing between Scylla and Charybdis. On one extreme Christianity is in danger of evaporating into a philosophy—then it becomes nothing but steam. The opposite danger is that it will freeze into a form and become nothing more than a ritual. There is a real peril on either side. But the Lord Jesus called Himself the *Water* of Life. He is neither steam nor ice—neither can sustain life. That is why we need to guard against following the line of philosophy or following the line of ritual. Christianity is Christ!

There were five errors that endangered the Colossian church which Paul will deal with in this chapter. They were:

1. Enticing words—verses 4–7
2. Philosophy—verses 8–13
3. Legality—verses 14–17
4. Mysticism—verses 18–19
5. Asceticism—verses 20–23

These are still dangers today. I think that most of us could sit down with this chapter and go through it to make an inventory of our spiritual lives. It would show us the direction in which we are going. A great many even so-called Bible believers have slipped into one or more of these errors.

CHRIST, THE ANSWER TO PHILOSOPHY
(For the Head)

For I would that ye knew what great conflict I have for you, and for them at Laodicea, and for as many as have not seen my face in the flesh [Col. 2:1].

Laodicea was near to Colosse. I have been to Laodicea but not to Colosse. Yet I stood on the high point of Laodicea and looked across the Lycos valley. There alongside the mountains at the gates of Phrygia, which lead into the Orient, were the ruins of Colosse. It was a great city, but it was not nearly as great as Laodicea. In Laodicea was one of the seven churches of the Book of Revelation; it was the church that is described as being lukewarm.

"Conflict" is our word *agony*. MacPhail calls this a prayer of agony. Paul saw that there was a grave danger in Colosse and in Laodicea, and it caused great conflict in the heart of the apostle. They were in danger of going off in one of two directions. There is still such danger, and we need a lot of agonizing prayer for the church today. This explains why we find the Laodiceans' lukewarm condition in the Book of Revelation: they had lost sight of the person of Christ. Christ is the answer to man's head; He is also the answer to man's heart.

"For as many as have not seen my face in the flesh." Colosse is located about 100 miles inland from ancient Ephesus. When Paul came through that area (which he did twice), he did not come down to Colosse and Laodicea. Even when he attempted to go down into Asia on his second missionary journey, the Spirit of God forbade him; so he turned and took the northern route. Then when he came on his third missionary journey, walking over the land, he again took the northern route, perhaps because he was already familiar with it. It is clear that he had not been to these cities because he writes, "and for as many as have not seen my face in the flesh." This might be interpreted to mean that many new believers had come into the church since he had been there and that they had not seen his face. That meaning is highly unlikely; I think it means that Paul had never been there.

That their hearts might be comforted, being knit together in love, and unto all riches of the full assurance of understanding, to the acknowledgement of the mystery of God, and of the Father, and of Christ [Col. 2:2].

"That their hearts might be comforted." *Heart* indicates the entire inner man. That means the whole propulsive nature of man. He is praying that their hearts, their humanity, their whole persons might be comforted.

"Being knit together in love" means compacted in love. Love will draw them together. After all, a church is not united by gifts or even by what we term today as spirituality. The bond that unites believers is love. It is the cement that holds us together—it is the Elmer's glue of the church.

"Unto all riches of the full assurance of understanding." *Full assurance* is an interesting expression; it literally means "to be under full sail." It means that believers should be moving along spiritually—they should be moving along for God.

"To the acknowledgement of the mystery of God, and of the Father, and of Christ." I grant that is a rather awkward expression, and a better translation would be: "the mystery of God, even of the Father, and of Christ." Better and easier yet might be, "the mystery of God, even Christ." I think that is the correct meaning of it.

What is "the mystery of God, even Christ"? The church is the mystery, for it had not been revealed in the Old Testament. God was going to save Gentiles—that had been made clear in the Old Testament, and He did save them. But on the Day of Pentecost God started a *new* thing. He began to call out a group of people into the body of believers, baptized by the Spirit of God into this body. This is what Paul is explaining in 1 Corinthians 12:12: "For as the body is one, and hath many members, and all the members of that one body, being many, are one body: so also is Christ." You see, Christ had a physical body while He was here on this earth, and He has a spiritual body down here today. That body is the body of believers that have trusted Him, and the body is called Christ. That is why the Lord said to Saul of Tarsus, "Why are you persecuting me?" (see Acts 9:4). Saul was persecuting Him *personally*. The church is Christ—it belongs to Him. "The mystery of God, even Christ."

In 1 Corinthians 12:13, Paul goes on to say of the church: "For by one Spirit are we all baptized into one body, whether we be Jews or Gentiles, whether we be bond or free; and have been all made to drink into one Spirit." We have all been baptized into Christ. We have all been made to drink into one Spirit. That is what brings the unity into the church. We are never commanded to make a unity of the church. It is impossible to join some organization and to expect that organization to bring about church unity. The Holy Spirit has already made that unity. He puts all believers into one body, and we are told to *keep* the unity of the Spirit. Our problem today is that we are not keeping the unity of the Spirit.

In whom are hid all the treasures of wisdom and knowledge [Col. 2:3].

All that we need is in Christ. If only we could learn that! He is the reservoir of all knowledge.

In the science building where I went to college there was a motto on the bulletin board. It hung there the whole time that I was in college, and it made a great impression on me. I'm afraid I remember it better than I do the sciences that I studied there. It said, "Next to knowing is knowing where to find out." I love that. I willingly admit that I don't know everything—I'm sure you have found that out by now. But I know where to find out, because I know Somebody who does know. Christ has been made unto us wisdom. We need to rest in that. All the treasures of wisdom and knowledge are in Him—how wonderful this is!

1. Now Paul will discuss the error of *enticing words*.

And this I say, lest any man should beguile you with enticing words [Col. 2:4].

He is going to deal with the matter of philosophy and enticing words. Philosophy and psychology have been substituted for the Bible, and this is the thing that is enticing to so many young preachers in our seminaries today. I am amazed to find that some of these men with a Ph.D. degree from a seminary know so little about the Bible! They know all about Bultmann and Kant and Plato, but they don't seem to know very much about the Word of God. That is the great problem of our day.

There was that same danger in Colosse and also in Laodicea. I think that is what actually killed the church in Colosse, and it made the church in Laodicea the weakest of the seven churches in Asia Minor. It was in the worst spiritual condition, and yet the people thought that they were well off. These cities were wealthy. They boasted of their wealth and affluence and also of their knowledge, but they were blind to their true spiritual condition.

Paul says, "Don't let any man beguile you with enticing words." *Beguile* means "to victimize." *Enticing words* are a lot of oratory or sweet-talk.

I heard of a theologian who uses big words and tries to be very deep in his thinking. He was talking to a group of men for about half an hour. Another man walked up to the group and asked one of the men on the outside of the circle, "What's he talking about?" The fellow answered, "He hasn't said yet." That is the problem—he never would say. All he did was talk with enticing words.

I know a dear lady who attends a certain church because, as she says "I just love to go there because the preacher uses such flowery language and he makes me feel so good all over." That is the danger today. A great many people love this pretense toward intellectuality among preachers rather than the simple Word of God.

I started preaching before I went to college, and then in college I was exposed to liberalism because I went to a liberal college. That was all I knew at that time; I was not grounded in the Word of God at all, even though I had had a wonderful pastor. I thought I wanted to be an intellectual preacher—I thought that would be great. I thank God that that was knocked out of me in my second year of college. I became concerned with teaching the Word of God

Paul warns us to beware that they will beguile us with enticing words and will victimize us. Their words cause many people to follow a certain individual instead of the Word of God. Like the Pied Piper of Hamlin, he starts playing, and the unwary start following.

For though I be absent in the flesh, yet am I with you in the spirit, joying and beholding your order, and the stedfastness of your faith in Christ [Col. 2:5].

At this time the word that was coming back to Paul was that this church *was* standing.

"Beholding your order." *Order* is a military term, and it means "to stand shoulder to shoulder." That is what believers ought to be doing—standing shoulder to shoulder. Instead, many today are trying to undermine or take advantage of another believer. Oh that we could stand shoulder to shoulder with one another!

Stedfastness means "to have a solid front, to be immovable." The literal translation would be "stereotype," or the opposite of movable type. Paul writes this same thought to the Corinthians: "Therefore, my beloved brethren, be ye stedfast, unmoveable, always abounding in the work of the Lord, forasmuch as ye know that your labour is not in vain in the Lord" (1 Cor. 15:58). The Colossian church had a reputation for steadfastness, and Paul wanted them to continue like that and not be led away by the oratory of some.

As ye have therefore received Christ Jesus the Lord, so walk ye in him [Col. 2:6].

What does it mean to be saved, to be a Christian? Well, I have a letter from a man who tells me that I am not saved because I have frankly admitted that I am not perfect, that I do not keep all the Ten Commandments. He says that I am not saved until I do. My friend, salvation is to receive a person, and that person is Jesus Christ—"As ye have therefore received Christ Jesus the Lord."

"So walk ye in him." Now that you have received Him, *walk* in Him, walk in the Spirit. Walking is not a balloon ascension. A great many people think the Christian life is some great, overwhelming experience and you take off like a rocket going out into space. That's not where you live the Christian life. Rather, it is in your home, in your office, in the schoolroom, on the street. The way you get around in this life is to *walk*. You are to walk in Christ. God grant that you and I might be joined to Him in our daily walk.

Rooted and built up in him, and stablished in the faith, as ye have been taught, abounding therein with thanksgiving [Col. 2:7].

"Rooted" means rooted like a tree, and a tree is a living thing. And we are to be "built up" as a house. A house is not a living thing, but it requires a tremendous foundation. Paul tells us in Ephesians that the foundation is Jesus Christ. Having received Christ, we are to walk in Him. Doing what? Being rooted, drawing our life from Him as a tree, and built up in Him, your faith resting upon Him.

That is why he adds, "and stablished in the faith." A better translation would be "by your faith." Faith is the means by which you and I lay hold of Christ.

2. Now Paul moves on to discuss the danger of *philosophy*.

Beware lest any man spoil you through philosophy and vain deceit, after the tradition of men, after the rudiments of the world, and not after Christ [Col. 2:8].

"Beware"—Look out! Stop, look, and listen!

"Lest any man spoil you through philosophy and vain deceit." If you were to follow the history of philosophy beginning with Plato, including many of the church fathers, and coming down to more recent times (including Kant, Locke, and Bultmann, who seems to be the craze with some theologians right now), you would find that none of them have a high view of the inspiration of the Word of God. They are looking for answers to the problems of life, but they will not be found in philosophy.

A true philosopher is a seeker after truth, but truth is not found in human wisdom. Christ is the answer, the answer to philosophy. Paul wrote, "But of him are ye in Christ Jesus, *who of God is made unto us wisdom*

. . ." (1 Cor. 1:30, italics mine). But false philosophy is like a blind man looking in a dark room for a black cat that isn't there—there is no hope for its search for truth. Paul warns the Colossians to beware of this.

"After the tradition of men." You may remember that the Lord Jesus condemned the religious rulers in His day because they taught the tradition of men rather than the Word of God. Very frankly, this is one of the reasons I have turned to the teaching of the total Word of God. It is so easy to lift out some peculiar interpretation of some particular passage and then ride that like a hobby horse. I believe in prophecy, but there is more in the Word of God than just prophecy. Some preachers dwell on the Christian life. That certainly is in the Bible, but there is more than just that. This is why I think it is so important for us to study the *total* Word of God.

"After the rudiments of the world, and not after Christ." The Greek word for "rudiments" is *stoicheion*, which means "that which is basic," the ABC's. Some people try to build their Christian living on some worldly system that seems so simple. Our base is not philosophy or a worldly system; our base is Christ.

Now Paul will speak of Christ:

For in him dwelleth all the fulness of the Godhead bodily [Col. 2:9].

In Him dwelleth all the *plerōma*—this is a clear-cut statement of the deity of Christ. It could not be stated any stronger than it is here. In Him dwells *all* the fullness of the Godhead—not just 99.44 percent but 100 percent.

And ye are complete in him, which is the head of all principality and power [Col. 2:10].

You "are complete in him." "Complete" is a nautical term, and it could be translated in this very vivid way: You are ready for the voyage of life in Him. Isn't that a wonderful way of saying it? You are ready for the voyage of life in Christ, and whatever you need for the voyage of life you will find in Him. This is where we say that Christ is the answer. What is your question? What is it you need today? Are you carried away by human philosophy? Then turn to Christ. Are you carried away by enticing words? Are you carried away by the systems and traditions of men? Turn to Christ.

In whom also ye are circumcised with the circumcision made without hands, in putting off the body of the sins of the flesh by the circumcision of Christ [Col. 2:11].

Paul is telling them to get rid of that which is outward. The real circumcision is the New Birth. He explained this to the Galatians: "For in Christ Jesus neither circumcision availeth any thing, nor uncircumcision, but a new creature" (Gal. 6:15). You and I become new creatures when we come to Christ and trust Him as our Savior. We rest in Him; we are identified with Him.

Buried with him in baptism, wherein also ye are risen with him through the faith of the operation of God, who hath raised him from the dead [Col. 2:12].

Lord Lyndhurst was the Lord Chancellor of Great Britain and possessed a sharp legal mind. He made this statement: "I know pretty well what evidence is; and I tell you, such evidence as that for the Resurrection has never broken down yet." The death and resurrection of Christ is an historical fact. When Christ died you and I died with Him; He took our place. And when He was raised, we were raised in Him, and we are now joined to a living Christ. It is so important for us to see that we are joined to a *living* Savior.

It is so important to keep in mind that no outward ceremony brings us to Christ. The issue is whether or not we are born again, whether we really know Christ as Savior. If we do know Him, we are identified with Him. Identification with Christ is "putting off the body of the sins of the flesh by the circumcision of Christ," which is a spiritual circumcision.

When you put your trust in the Lord Jesus Christ, the Holy Spirit baptizes you into the body of Christ. It is by this baptism that we are identified with Christ, and we are also "risen with him"—joined to the living Christ.

"Through the faith of the operation of God who hath raised him from the dead"—salvation is accomplished by the resurrection power of God. It's not some philosophy; it's not some gimmick; it's not some little system; it's not the taking of some course that will enable you to live for God.

And you, being dead in your sins and the uncircumcision of your flesh, hath he quickened together with him, having forgiven you all trespasses [Col. 2:13].

Salvation is not the improvement of the old nature; it is the impartation of a new nature.

Remember that Paul had to deal with two systems of Greek philosophy which were very popular in his day. They were diametrically opposed to each other, but they both came out at the same end of the horn. One philosophy was Stoicism, and the other was Epicureanism.

The Stoic taught that man was to live nobly and that death could not matter. The idea was to hold the appetites in check and to become indifferent to changing conditions. In effect they said, "Be not uplifted by good fortune nor cast down by adversity." They believed that man is more than circumstances and that the soul is greater than the universe. It was a brave philosophy, you see. But the problem was how to live it. It was like the people who say that they are living by the Sermon on the Mount when actually they are many miles from it.

The Epicurean taught that all is uncertain. "We know not whence we came; we know not whither we go. We only know that after a brief life we disappear from this scene, and it is vain to deny ourselves any present joy in view of the possible future ill. Let us eat and drink, for tomorrow we die."

The interesting thing to observe is that both these systems attempted to deal with the flesh—that is, the old nature that you and I have—not the meat on our bones. The old nature works through our old habits, old desires, old testings and temptations. How are we going to bring that under control?

There are all kinds of gimmicks and systems that are set before us today to enable us to live the Christian life. I know people who have been to Bible conferences where the Christian life is taught, and at home they have a drawer filled with notebooks. But they are not doing so well in living the Christian life. Why not? Because we need to recognize this one important thing that Paul is saying here: we are joined to the living Christ. Now, if you are joined to Him, my friend, you are going to live as if you are. How close are you to Him? Do you walk with Him? Do you turn to Him in all the emergencies of this life? Is He the One who is the very center of your life?

3. As Paul turns now to the error of *legality*, we will again find that the answer is to come to the Word of God and through it to come into a personal relationship with Jesus Christ.

> A glory gilds the sacred page,
> Majestic like the sun.
> It sheds a light on every age;
> It gives but borrows none.

Blotting out the handwriting of ordinances that was against us, which was contrary to us, and took it out of the way, nailing it to his cross [Col. 2:14].

"Blotting out the handwriting of ordinances that was against us." This old flesh of ours has been condemned. When Christ died, He died for you and me; He paid the penalty for our sin.

When the Lord Jesus died, Pilate wrote a title and put it on the cross: "This is Jesus of Nazareth the King of the Jews" (see John 19:19). He was being publicly executed on the grounds that He had led in a rebellion. This was, of course, not true, but that was the charge against Him. When the people standing there read that sign they understood that He had been disloyal to Caesar in that He had made Himself to be a king. To them that was the reason He was dying on a cross.

But when God looked upon that cross, He saw an altar on which the Lamb of God who takes away the sin of the world was offered. God saw another inscription there high above the inscription that man had written. "Blotting out the handwriting of ordinances that was against us, which was contrary to us, and took it out of the way, *nailing it to his cross.*" What did God write on that cross? He wrote the ordinances—He wrote the Ten Commandments. He wrote a law which I cannot keep, ordinances of which I am guilty of breaking. When Christ died there, He did not die because He broke them; He was sinless. But it was because I broke them, because I am a sinner, and because you are. "For all have sinned, and come short of the glory of God" (Rom. 3:23).

Therefore, my friend, if God has saved you and raised you from the dead and joined you to a living Christ, why should you go back to a law that you couldn't keep in the first place? You can't even keep the law today in your own power and in your own strength. You see, the law was given to discipline the old nature. But now the believer is given a new nature, and the law has been removed as a way of life.

Let me give you an illustration. A man once came to me and said, "I'll give you $100 if you will show me where the Sabbath day has been changed." I answered, "I don't think it has been changed. Saturday is Saturday, it is the seventh day of the week, and it is the Sabbath day. I realize our calendar has been adjusted and can be off a few days, but we won't even consider that point. The seventh day is still Saturday and is still the Sabbath day." He got a gleam in his eye and said, "Then why don't you keep the Sabbath day if it hasn't been changed?" I answered, "The *day* hasn't changed, but *I* have been changed. I've been given a new creation. We celebrate the first day because that is the day He rose from the grave." That is what it means when he says that the ordinances which were against us have been nailed to His cross.

And having spoiled principalities and powers, he made a shew of them openly, triumphing over them in it [Col. 2:15].

The spiritual victory that Christ won for the believer is of inestimable value.

CHRIST, THE ANSWER TO RITUAL
(For the Heart)

Let no man therefore judge you in meat, or in drink, or in respect of an holyday, or of the new moon, or of the sabbath days:

Which are a shadow of things to come; but the body is of Christ [Col. 2:16–17].

A believer is not to observe ordinances that are only ritual and liturgical; they have no present value. God did give certain rituals for the people in the Old Testament. So what has changed? Paul explains that they were merely "a shadow of things to come." We get our word *photograph* from the Greek word used here for "shadow." All the rituals of the Law in the Old Testament were like a negative or a picture—they were just pictures of Christ. Now that Christ has come, we have the reality. Why should we go back and look at a picture?

I remember that, during the days of World War II, I performed the wedding ceremony of two wonderful young people here in Pasadena. (We knew a number of young men who went to war, and some of them gave their lives.) This young fellow was sent overseas, and while he was gone, his young bride carried the biggest purse I have ever seen (and I have seen some big ones). In that purse she carried a huge photograph of him. Most people carry a little bitty picture with them, but not this girl; she carried a photograph that you could have hung on the wall. She was everlastingly drawing it out and showing it to people. She'd say, "Isn't he handsome?" (Between you and me, he wasn't what I would call a handsome boy. He was a wonderful boy, but he was not handsome.) Then the day came when the war was over, and he was coming home. She went all the way to Seattle, Washington, to meet him. Now what do you think she did when she saw him coming down the gangplank? She hadn't

seen him in a couple of years. Do you think she took out that picture and looked at it? Do you think she looked at the picture and said, "Isn't he wonderful?" I don't think she even had that picture with her! She saw *him* and when she saw him, she didn't need a picture—she threw her arms around *him*.

Many of us need to get off the merry-go-round of attending seminars, adapting gimmicks, jumping through everybody's little hoop, and taking a shortcut to the abundant life. Have we really arrived? Some think they have. Let's stop carrying around a faded photograph when we have the reality—"Christ in you, the hope of glory."

4. We come now to the warning against *mysticism*.

Let no man beguile you of your reward in a voluntary humility and worshipping of angels, intruding into those things which he hath not seen, vainly puffed up by his fleshly mind,

And not holding the Head, from which all the body by joints and bands having nourishment ministered, and knit together, increaseth with the increase of God [Col. 2:18–19].

This is another point at which people get off the track. Paul is here condemning the Gnostics who made a pretense of wisdom. And we have today in our church circles a great many folk who assume a pious superiority—they are what I call "spiritual snobs." It has been my experience that these people generally are very ignorant of the Bible. "Intruding into those things which he hath not seen"—that's a pretense, putting on, acting like you have something that you don't really have.

"And not holding the Head" means that such people have a loose relationship with Christ. In other words, *their* head is not screwed on as it should be, by the way.

5. The final warning is against the error of *asceticism*.

Wherefore if ye be dead with Christ from the rudiments of the world, why, as though living in the world, are ye subject to ordinances,

(Touch not; taste not; handle not;

Which all are to perish with the using;) after the commandments and doctrines of men?

Which things have indeed a shew of wisdom in will-worship, and humility, and

neglecting of the body; not in any honour to the satisfying of the flesh [Col. 2:20–23].

Here again, when Paul says "if ye be dead with Christ," the translation would be better as, "since ye be dead with Christ." In other words, since you have died when Christ died, do not return to pre-cross living.

I think, very candidly, that this is a terrible problem. There are people who follow some passing fad in the church. A few years ago the fad was that women couldn't use lipstick (and some of them sure looked pale). I remember when I was teaching in a school that wouldn't permit the girls to wear lipstick, a girl came to me and asked, "Do you think it is all right to use lipstick?" I answered her, "There are a lot of these folk around here who would look better if they used a little lipstick. God wants us to look the best that we can. Even when we have little to work with, we ought to do the best we can with it."

What we are dealing with here is "the pride that apes humility" that Juvenal speaks of. It is the pride that says, "I deny myself, and I don't do these things. Just look at me. I'm really sprouting wings, and I shine my halo every morning."

"Not in any honour" means it is not of any value. My friend, that is asceticism that is no good. God wants you to rejoice in Him; Christ wants you to be close to Him. And if you're going to walk with Him, my friend, you are going to have a good time!

CHAPTER 3

THEME: *Christ, the fullness of God, poured out in life through believers; thoughts and affections of believers are heavenly; living of believers is holy*

We come now to the line of division in this little epistle, which conforms to Paul's regular way of dividing his epistles. He always gives the doctrinal section and then the practical section. Chapters 3 and 4 comprise the practical section of Colossians.

We have seen the preeminence of Christ in chapters 1–2. We have seen Him as He is, a member of the Trinity. He is very man of very man, but He is very God of very God. He is preeminent in creation because He is the Creator. He is preeminent in redemption for He is the Redeemer. He is preeminent in the church because He is the One who gave Himself for the church.

Now we have come to the place where Paul will insist that He must be made preeminent in our lives. Today we hear a great deal of talk about dedication. Well, what is dedication? A very brief definition is: Dedication is Christ preeminent in our lives.

You cannot just say, "I am a dedicated Christian," and then live your life as you please as a great many people are trying to do today. No, if Christ is preeminent in your life, then you are going to live out His life down here on earth. Paul has already made this clear in the doctrinal section: "For in him [in Christ] dwelleth all the fulness [*plerōma*] of the Godhead bodily. And ye are complete in him . . ." (Col. 2:9–10). You are made full in Him. You are ready for the voyage of life in Him. In other words, Christ is really the solution to all the problems of life.

Paul has discussed the different things that lead people away from the person of Christ. He has warned against enticing words which carry people away by great oratory. He has warned against philosophy, legality, mysticism, and asceticism. All these lead people away from the person of Christ.

The Christian life is to live out the life of Christ. You and I will find in Christ Jesus all that we need. In this practical section of the epistle, Paul will show us Christ, the fullness of God, poured out in life *through believers*— that is the only way He can be poured out.

THOUGHTS AND AFFECTIONS OF BELIEVERS ARE HEAVENLY

If ye then be risen with Christ, seek those things which are above, where Christ sitteth on the right hand of God [Col. 3:1].

Again, this is not the *if* of condition; it is really the *if* of argument. We saw this same thing back in Colossians 1:23 where we read: "*If* ye continue in the faith grounded and settled. . . ." There was no question about their continuing in the faith grounded and settled. The lives of these Colossian Christians evidenced their salvation. What was the evidence? It was faith, hope, and love—the fruit of the Spirit was in their lives. "Since we heard of your faith in Christ Jesus"—the word had gotten around that they had a living faith in Christ Jesus; "and of the love which ye have to all the saints"—they loved the believers (Col. 1:4). Love among the believers is so important, and I do not mean this sentimental stuff that you hear so much about today. For instance, if you are a minister, you evidence your love for your congregation if you give them the Word of God, and you show your love for your pastor as a member of the church if you support his Bible-teaching ministry. My friend, love is very practical—it gets right down where the rubber meets the road. If it doesn't, it's no good at all. Love is that which manifests itself in reality. The Colossians had faith, and they had love. They also had hope: "For the hope which is laid up for you in heaven . . ." (Col. 1:5). That hope is the coming of the Lord Jesus Christ for His church. These three—faith, hope, and love—were the manifestation of the Holy Spirit in the lives of the believers in Colosse. Therefore, when Paul says "if," it is the *if* of argument. Verse 1 here in chapter 3 would be better translated, "*Since* you are risen with Christ."

"Seek those things which are above, where Christ sitteth on the right hand of God." Where is Christ today? He's sitting at the right hand of God.

What are we to do today? We are to "seek those things which are above." *Seek* is an interesting word. It actually means "having an urgency and a desire and an ambition." There should be an excitement that goes with seeking spiritual things.

When we watch the Olympic games, we see folk who are running or performing some athletic feat to win a gold medal. Believe me, those folk are *seeking*. I don't see many saints looking for gold medals today, but we are to be seeking Christ with that kind of urgency.

"Those things which are above"—these are the things of Christ. I want you to note that Paul is not saying that we should seek such courses as are offered today that are a mixture of pseudopsychology with a smattering of Bible. This kind of teaching is handed out in a few night classes, and then some poor crippled Christians think they have the answers to the problems of life—all the way from a neurotic mother-in-law to a boss who is a dirty old man. They think some little course will teach them how to treat everybody and every problem. They consider it a do-it-yourself kit, a kind of an open sesame to a new life. Now I say to you, and I say it very carefully, you will only experience the new life as you "seek those things which are above, where Christ sitteth on the right hand of God."

I will get even more personal in my illustration. You cannot find the answers in anything I have produced—either a book or a tape-recorded message. Now I am stepping on some toes, including my own toes. A couple came to me this past summer at a conference and said, "Dr. McGee, we have a certain tape of yours, and we play it at least once a week and listen to it." My reaction was that they had better burn that tape. I had the feeling they were beginning to worship that tape and that tape wasn't getting them through to Christ.

And now I'm *really* going to step on toes: Paul doesn't say here to seek out and listen to any preacher or teacher! May I say this to you very kindly and very frankly: Don't make Dr. McGee or any man your idol. If you do, you have an idol who has feet of clay. You would be looking to a man who is just like you are. I make a lot of mistakes. I'm not near the man I'd like to be, nor the husband I'd like to be, nor the father or grandfather I'd like to be. Don't make anything man produces a god for yourself.

The purpose of this poor preacher is to get out the Word of God to you so that you can see the living Christ and get through to Him. If the Holy Spirit doesn't use my ministry to get you through to the living Christ, then I have failed—then I have fallen flat on my face, and I am willing to quit. I believe with all my heart that the Bible is the one Book which reveals the living Christ, and that is my purpose in teaching it.

I would like to give you an illustration of this. I went to school with a fellow who was a Canadian, and he told me about his first trip to Niagara Falls. (By the way, Mrs. McGee and I saw it for the first time this past summer. When we were looking over the falls, I said to her, "Honey, I promised you we would go to Niagara Falls on our honeymoon. I think we are still on our honeymoon, and here we are.") Well, my classmate told me that as a boy he got on a train on the Canadian side of the falls, which is the prettiest side. He said, "When I got off the train, I could hear the roar of the falls, but I couldn't see them. I began to move toward the sound, and I came to a big building. I went into that building, which was like a Union Station in the United States: there was the popcorn vendor, the soda pop machine, the gift shop, and candy papers, chewing gum wrappers and even chewing gum on the floor. People were sitting all around. I was really disappointed, but I could still hear the roar of the falls. Then I looked down to the end of the building, and there I saw the biggest picture I had ever seen in my life. The frame of the picture took in most of the end of that building. It was a picture of Niagara Falls. I couldn't believe that right there at the falls they would have a picture of them. I began to walk down toward that picture, and as I drew closer to it, I began to realize that through a frame I was looking at the real, living, running Niagara Falls!"

My friend, when you read the Bible, you are not looking at a dead person. You are looking at the real, living Christ. He is the One at God's right hand. We are to seek those things which are above—we are to seek *Him*. That is why I have a ministry of teaching through the Bible. There is no shortcut. Some have suggested that I cut it down to a one-year program, but that certainly is not adequate. And, really, five years is not adequate. Some have suggested that I lengthen it to ten years, but that is not feasible for me. Even if we took ten, or even twenty years, we would not know it all. At the end of his life Paul could still say: "That I may know him, and the power of his resurrection, and the fellowship of his sufferings, being made conformable unto his death" (Phil. 3:10).

Real study of the Word of God will get you through to the living Christ. Let me illustrate this with a letter from a listener to our radio program:

When we were studying Romans and Corinthians, I began to realize just how much of a carnal Christian I really was. I began to desire much more than that. So I began to pray that I might truly know Christ as God would want me to. Nothing happened for a while, but I kept praying. And then God did answer my prayer. One day you said that God sees us *in Christ*, and it was as though some dark, hidden thing had been brought out into the light. I had read Ephesians many times before, but that day your message really struck home. It is a wonderful thing to know that Paul's prayer is still being answered today. I realized that day that God no

longer looked down upon me as a poor sinner struggling upon this earth, but *in Christ* and that I belong to Him as a child. . . .

May I say to you from my heart, *get through to Christ*. "Seek those things which are above, where Christ sitteth at the right hand of God."

Set your affection on things above, not on things on the earth [Col. 3:2].

Actually the word for "affection" is *mind*. Think about the things that are above. In Philippians Paul said that whatever things are true and honest and just and lovely, think on these things—the things of Christ. Life is full of its smaller problems (like whether or not you can get along with your mother-in-law), and they are very real to us, but by far the greatest need is for us to get through to Christ. That should come before everything else. "Set your affection on things above."

For ye are dead, and your life is hid with Christ in God [Col. 3:3].

"For ye are dead" might better be translated "for ye have died." If you have died, *when* did you die? Paul wrote to the Galatians, "I am crucified with Christ . . ." (Gal. 2:20). You died more than nineteen hundred years ago when Christ died. He took my place; He took your place. We died in Him.

"Your life is hid with Christ in God." I have been taken out of the old Adam by baptism; that is, by the baptism of the Holy Spirit. I have been taken out of Adam and placed in Christ. I am now *in* Christ. Now that I am in Christ, I should live out His life and let His fullness be lived out through me.

When Christ, who is our life, shall appear, then shall ye also appear with him in glory [Col. 3:4].

If you have any life, it is Christ's life. John wrote in his first epistle that it was his intent to "shew unto you that eternal life." How could he show eternal life? He was going to show us Christ; Christ is eternal life. And one of these days those who belong to Him are going to "appear with him in glory."

LIVING OF BELIEVERS IS HOLY

If we are truly risen with Christ this will be evident in two areas of our lives: (1) our personal holiness, and (2) our fellowship with others who are about us.

It seems that Christians are frightened of this matter of holiness. When I was a young preacher, I heard the late Bishop Moore of the old Southern Methodist church make this statement: "If Methodists were as afraid of sin as they are of holiness, it would be a wonderful thing." This isn't true of Methodists alone; it is true of most Christians. Somehow we don't like this term *holiness*. It is a very good word, and that is Paul's subject here—*personal holiness*.

Christ was born as a little Babe in Bethlehem, but He is no longer in that inn. He is up yonder at God's right hand at this very moment. He's on a throne—not in a cradle and not in an inn but in heaven itself. And He's there for you and me today. Now, if you are in Christ, if you have accepted Him as your Savior, then that is going to show in your life down here. Friend, if it doesn't tell in your life down here, then maybe you are not in Him up yonder!

Mortify therefore your members which are upon the earth; fornication, uncleanness, inordinate affection, evil concupiscence, and covetousness, which is idolatry [Col. 3:5].

Mortify means "to put to death, or put in the place of death."

Fornication means "sexual immorality." Is that your sin today? Let's not kid ourselves—there are a great many folk who are covering up this sin, and yet they still talk about being dedicated Christians! Paul brings this right out into the open and tells us that we are to put our physical members in the place of death. Do your eyes cause you trouble? Do you look with the eye of covetousness, or the eye of lust? Put those eyes in the place of death, and now use them as the eyes of Christ to look upon Him. My friend, that will change things, will it not?

Uncleanness includes thoughts, words, looks, gestures, and the jokes we tell.

Inordinate affection means "uncontrolled passion or lust." Every now and then someone will confess to me a sin in his life, and he will say, "Well, I couldn't help myself." My friend, you ought not to get in that spot in the first place. It's like the little boy whose mama called to him one night when she heard him in the kitchen, "Where are you?" He said, "I'm in the pantry." He had the cookie jar open. She called, "What are you doing?" He answered, "I'm fighting temptation!" My friend, that is the wrong place to fight temptation. Don't fight it there at the cookie jar, if you're not to have the cookies. The same thing applies to inordinate affection.

Evil concupiscence—that means "evil desires." Put them to death, my friend.

"Covetousness, which is idolatry" means when we always must have more. Is the almighty dollar your god today? Are you more interested in the dollar than you are in the living Christ? These questions can begin to hurt! Our bodies are the tabernacle of the Holy Spirit, and they are to be used for God.

When I drove to my office this morning there were a great many people on their way to work. Many of them were professional men and business executives. One man went by me in a Cadillac. He didn't see me or anyone else because he was in such a hurry. I don't know why he was hurrying, but I can guess. We see pictures of people in other lands going to heathen temples and worshiping there, and we feel sorry for them in the darkness of their idolatry. But I suspect that the fellow in the Cadillac was also in darkness, that he was on his way to worship his idol and to bow before it. His idol was the almighty dollar, and he was rushing to work to see how many he could make. A great many folk are overcome by this matter of covetousness. They covet the material things of this world—they want more money.

I would venture to say that covetousness is the root of most of the problems in our country today. ". . . the love of money is the root of all evil . . ." (1 Tim. 6:10). Money is not the problem—it can even be used for the glory of God. But there are many men, even Christians, who are working on that second million, and they don't need it. It is because they worship an idol. If you are in Christ, He will come first and you will seek those things which are above.

For which things' sake the wrath of God cometh on the children of disobedience [Col. 3:6].

"For which things' sake"—Paul means the things he has just been speaking of, the things which the world does.

"The wrath of God cometh on the children of disobedience." Men are not lost simply because they do these things, neither are they lost because they haven't heard of Christ. Men are lost because they are sinners, sinners in their hearts. And, because they are sinners, they do these things.

In the which ye also walked some time, when ye lived in them [Col. 3:7].

Those of us who now know the Lord practiced these sins in our lives at one time. I hope that we are not still doing them.

I met a young millionaire in Florida quite a few years ago. He very frankly admitted that before he was saved he worshiped the almighty dollar. He was always after the next dollar and then the next one. When he came to Christ, he decided to retire. He had already made a million dollars and any more that he made he wanted to put into the Lord's work. He wanted to spend his time seeking the things of Christ.

Oh, my friend, do we put Him first? Or are we engaged in the very things that the world is engaged in and for which God intends to judge them? Well, how then can we expect that we shall escape the judgment of God? If you are in Christ, seek those things which are above, and you will not find yourself involved in the things of the world.

But now ye also put off all these; anger, wrath, malice, blasphemy, filthy communication out of your mouth [Col. 3:8].

These are the habits that we are to put off as we would put off a garment. We call a garment a habit, do we not? Many folk have a riding habit or a golfing habit. I have an old pair of slacks that I play golf in—that's my golfing habit. (I don't look very good, but that is what I wear.) Different people have different habits that they wear. Paul says that we are to put off these old practices as you'd put off a dirty, filthy garment. You don't send it to the laundry—you throw it away! You put it in the garbage can. You "put off all these."

The first is "anger." There is a place for anger that is justified. You remember that the Lord Jesus was angry at the Pharisees because of the hardness of their hearts. That is not a sinful anger. The problem is that we become angry over the wrong things.

Anger becomes "wrath" when we develop an unforgiving spirit.

Someone has said that "malice" is congealed anger. It is an anger that has been nursed along. It is an anger that tries to take revenge and get even. Paul says that a Christian is to put that off like an old, dirty, filthy garment. That kind of behavior does not represent Christ.

"Blasphemy" can be of two kinds. There is a blasphemy against God and a blasphemy against man. The first type of blasphemy is to defame the name of God. It is not just taking His name in vain, but it is to misrepresent Him, to hate Him. I received a letter from a lady that tells about the death of her little three-year-old child and how she *hated* God

because of that. Somebody gave her our little booklet, *The Death of a Little Child,* and she was brought to the Lord. She realized that she had been only a church member before and had not really been born again. You see that hating God for something that has happened is really blasphemy.

Did you know that you can also blaspheme another Christian when you make a statement about him that is not true? I remember years ago a statement that was made by a man about a preacher who was Arminian in his theology. The man who made the statement was a Calvinist, and he said that the preacher was "of Satan." Well, my friend, when you say things like that, untrue things about a child of God, you are guilty of blasphemy.

"Filthy communication out of your mouth" means *foul* communication and includes both that which is abusive and that which is filthy. I can't believe that Christians would want to indulge in that, but I am told that there are certain little groups which meet together and share dirty jokes. Some Christians use swear words. In fact, I have heard of Christian leaders doing that. I do not believe that you can be a child of God, friend, and live like that. These are things that are to be put off.

Lie not one to another, seeing that ye have put off the old man with his deeds [Col. 3:9].

To whom is Paul speaking? He is writing this to believers, because he says, "seeing that ye have put off the old man with his deeds." Is it possible for a Christian to lie? It certainly is. That doesn't mean that you have lost your salvation when you do—otherwise many of us would have lost ours a long time ago. It does reveal that you don't reach a place of perfection, my friend, nor do you get rid of the old nature, when you become a child of God.

I believe one of the first sins a little child commits is to lie. I heard the story about the little boy who came running into the house and said, "Mama, Mama, a lion just ran across our front lawn." The mother said, "Willie, you *know* that was not a lion. That was a big dog that ran across the lawn. You go upstairs and confess to the Lord that you lied about that." Little Willie went upstairs and after a while he came down again. His mother asked, "Did you confess your lie to the Lord?" He answered, "Yes, I did. But the Lord said when He first saw him, He thought he was a lion, too!" Lying is something that is deep-rooted in the human heart, and many Christians still indulge in it.

And have put on the new man, which is renewed in knowledge after the image of him that created him [Col. 3:10].

"Put on the new man." If you take off the old garment, the old man, you put on the new garment, the new man. Nature abhors a vacuum. Putting off is not enough, we must live in the new man by the power of the Holy Spirit.

You and I have an old nature which has controlled us for so long that we have set up certain habits. That is why *garment* is such an effective term here—it's a habit. We have developed certain patterns in the way we say and do things. We also have within us a complex nervous system that is conditioned to respond in a set fashion. If I put my hand down on a red hot stove, a message travels through the nervous system to the brain. The message gets switched over to a motor nerve which goes back down to the hand and says, "Say, you crazy fool, take your hand off that red hot stove. You're getting burned!" And you jerk your hand off the stove. Of course, it all happens more quickly than I can tell it. It is a reflex reaction that occurs very quickly. In the same way, our habit patterns are formed.

It is psychologically true that we are able to put off old habits and form new ones. But it is especially true for the believer because he has the power of the Holy Spirit within him. We are to "put on the new man."

"Renewed in knowledge after the image of him that created him." You are to put on the new man, and that new Man is Christ. In that way the church is able to represent Him on this earth.

Where there is neither Greek nor Jew, circumcision nor uncircumcision, Barbarian, Scythian, bond nor free: but Christ is all, and in all [Col. 3:11].

"Neither Greek nor Jew"—in the church, the body of believers, there is neither Greek nor Jew. This was a religious division or distinction that was made in Paul's day.

"Circumcision nor uncircumcision." This was also a religious division.

"Barbarian, Scythian." Barbarians were those who were not Greeks, those whom we would call heathen today. The Scythian was the worst kind of barbarian. Scythia was north of the Black Sea and the Caspian Sea. The people who lived there were probably the most barbaric the world has known. You talk about pagan, heathen, brutal, and mean! They would take their enemies and scalp them; then they would use the skull as a cup and drink the blood of their victims out of the skull! I cannot

think of anything more heathen than that! Did you know that the ancestors of many of us who have white skin came from that territory? We are called Caucasians after the area where these barbarians lived.

Even in Paul's day, some of these people were being led to Christ. The gospel had reached out and done a tremendous work, and some of them were in the church at Colosse. Missionaries had gone north beyond the Black and Caspian Seas—Scythians had been won for Jesus Christ. Even though they were barbarians, they were brought into that one body which is the church.

"But Christ is all, and in all." You just can't have it any more wonderful than that, my friend. This is something that is beyond description. Christ is the catalyst who brings together individuals and groups who are separate and makes them one in Him. A catalyst is a substance that is placed with elements that are opposed to each other and brings them together into a new compound. This is exactly what Christ does. We have all been made one in Him!

Remember that we are in the practical section of Colossians. In the doctrinal section we saw Christ who is the fullness of God and the head of the church. Believers have been made full, made complete in Him. We will find all that we need in Christ, not in any man-made legal or philosophical system.

Since we have risen with Christ, we are to seek those things that are above where Christ is at the right hand of God. We have seen that this will lead to personal holiness. Beginning now with verse 12 we will find that it will also lead to *holiness in our relationship to others;* then verses 18–21 will deal with holiness in the home; and verses 22–25 with holiness on the job. The Christian life is living out the fullness of Christ in our walk in the home, on the job, and in our social relationships.

Paul has clearly labeled the things of the old man that are to be put off. Now he will label the specifics that are to make up the wardrobe of the new man. We are going to see the latest in fashions for Christians, by the way. In fact, I have written a message on this passage of Scripture, and I have called it, "What the Well-Dressed Christian Will Wear This Year."

Put on therefore, as the elect of God, holy and beloved, bowels of mercies, kindness, humbleness of mind, meekness, longsuffering [Col. 3:12].

"The elect of God." There is a great deal of discussion about this matter of election. The fact of the matter is that if you have trusted Christ, you have on this new garment, and you are one of the elect. If these things that Paul is going to list are in your life, you're of the elect. I couldn't begin to tell you otherwise, nor argue any further about that—you're of the elect. The elect of God are clothed in the righteousness of Jesus Christ.

You will notice that the garments Paul is mentioning here are actually the fruit of the Holy Spirit. You and I cannot produce them in our lives. The minute you and I think about the wonderful position that we have in Christ and the high calling we have in Him, we have to recognize as we look at ourselves that we are impotent. We are weak and powerless, unable to "put on" these fruits. We are in the same position as the bride in the Song of Solomon. She had been kissed with the kiss of peace. Peace has been made with God. He has kissed us, my friend, and told us that our sins are forgiven us in Christ. How wonderful that is! But as the children of God we still sin. Then we need to remember the boy who got away from his father and his home, who lived in sin and wasted his fortune in riotous living. When he came back home, his father saw him afar off and ran and fell on his neck. What did he do? He kissed his son. That is the kiss of pardon, the kiss of forgiveness which God gives to His children.

We are in the position of the bride who says in the Song of Solomon, "Draw me, draw me" (see Song. 1:4). I am not able to attain to this wonderful position that I have in Christ. I can't do it myself. So you and I find ourselves cast upon Him. This is where the Spirit of God moves in and enables us to walk in the Spirit.

Bowels of mercies means "heart of compassion." How heartless this world is today. How indifferent and mechanical it has become! I find that much of the time I am simply a number. In the few business transactions that I have, a computer—a machine—does business with me. I can't tell that machine how I feel. I can't tell that machine when it has made a mistake. I can't tell that machine when I have made a mistake. I just do business with that machine. It sends me a bill and I pay it—that's all. I also do business with a bank. It has as much heart as the computer. In fact, the computer *is* the heart of the bank. Since I have had cancer I must also do business with my doctor. I have a very wonderful doctor who takes care of me, but when I had to be taken to the emergency room and had a strange doctor, I found that he considered me just a boy with a stomachache. I wasn't a person to

him at all. He just talked in big medical terms—that's all I was to him.

Paul is saying that as believers we should have a heart of compassion in our relationships with those around us.

Kindness is a word that Paul uses that carries with it the thought of being "profitable." It means to be helpful to others. There is another Greek word for kindness that has an element of sternness in it. You can be kind and still be stern, as when I tell my grandson, "Don't you do that." When I say that, I mean to be stern with him. But there is the kindness that means *gentleness*, and that is the word that Paul uses here.

Humbleness is "meekness." As I say so often, meekness does not mean weakness. Notice that here Paul's emphasis is "humbleness *of mind.*"

Meekness. Here the emphasis is meekness *of spirit.*

Longsuffering is the Greek word *makrothumia*, which means "long-burning"—it burns a long time. We shouldn't have a short fuse with our friends and Christian brethren. We shouldn't make snap judgments.

Forbearing one another, and forgiving one another, if any man have a quarrel against any: even as Christ forgave you, so also do ye [Col. 3:13].

Quarrel actually is "complaint." Paul is including situations where there is blame involved and the complaint is justified.

What are we to do in such circumstances? "Even as Christ forgave you, so also do ye." This does not mean that you become a doormat. But it does mean that when we have a complaint, we're to go to the individual and try to work out the matter.

There are always going to be some people with whom you cannot work out things—we must realize that. When our Lord denounced the Pharisees, there was no mention of forgiveness—He just denounced them. They did not seek His forgiveness, of course.

Paul's thought here is that Christ has forgiven us so much that it won't hurt us to forgive somebody who has stepped on our toes. We are to forgive others in the same way that Christ has forgiven us.

And above all these things put on charity, which is the bond of perfectness.

And let the peace of God rule in your hearts, to the which also ye are called in one body; and be ye thankful [Col. 3:14–15].

Charity is "love." Put on love. We have here in these verses two fruits of the Spirit: love and peace.

Rule means "to umpire." The peace of God should govern our hearts.

Let the word of Christ dwell in you richly in all wisdom; teaching and admonishing one another in psalms and hymns and spiritual songs, singing with grace in your hearts to the Lord [Col. 3:16].

There are many people who are great on doctrine and want to be fundamental in the faith. That is all-important, and I don't think anyone emphasizes it any more than I do. These people can often be heard praising Bible study, yet they do not attend Bible study, and they know so little about the Word of God.

"The word of Christ." The Lord Jesus said, "Now ye are clean through the word which I have spoken unto you" (John 15:3). The best Saturday night bath that you can take is to study the Word of God.

Dwell means "to be at home, to be given the run of the house." We should be familiar with the Word of God. The Bible should not be a strange book to you as it is to so many people today.

"Let the peace of God rule in your hearts"— let it be an umpire. And then "let the word of Christ *dwell* in you richly in all wisdom"—let it be at home. Know Him. Be familiar with the Word of Christ; study it and know what He's saying to you. That is where He is going to speak to you today, my friend—in His Word.

"Teaching and admonishing one another"— in what? "In psalms and hymns and spiritual songs."

"Singing with grace in your hearts to the Lord." I can't sing—so my singing never does get beyond that which is in the heart. The point is that we are to let the Word of God have this marvelous influence in our lives that Paul has described here.

And whatsoever ye do in word or deed, do all in the name of the Lord Jesus, giving thanks to God and the Father by him [Col. 3:17].

Do you want a norm for Christian conduct? Do you want a standard to go by? Do you want a principle rather than a lot of little rules? Paul gives us such a principle here. He does not say what we should or should not do. He simply says, "Do all in the name of the Lord Jesus, giving thanks to God and the Father by him." My friend, whatever you do—at your place of employment, in your home, and in all relationships with others—can you say, "I'm doing this in the name of the Lord Jesus"? If you can say that, if you are doing it in His name, then go ahead and do it. This is a marvelous standard, a yardstick that we can put down on our lives.

Now Paul comes to the subject of *holiness in the home.* You will notice that he is dealing with the same things that he dealt with in the Epistle to the Ephesians. There he told them to be filled with the Holy Spirit, and then he gave them these same instructions. Here in Colossians he writes, "Let the word of Christ dwell in you richly in all wisdom," and then he goes on to give instructions for living.

What does it mean to be filled with the Holy Spirit? It means that you will have to be filled with the Word of Christ also. The Word of God is inspired by the Spirit of God. If the Word of God dwells in you richly, then you are filled with the Spirit of God. I do not believe that you can be filled with the Holy Spirit or that you can serve Christ until you are filled with the knowledge of His Word. "Let the word of Christ dwell in you richly."

Now, if the Word of Christ dwells in you richly, it will work itself out in your life, and it will have an effect on your home.

Wives, submit yourselves unto your own husbands, as it is fit in the Lord [Col. 3:18].

This is for the purpose of order in the home. This is not for the purpose of producing a browbeating husband. I do not believe that God intends for a wife to submit to an unsaved husband who beats her or orders her to do things contrary to her walk with the Lord.

A woman wrote to me and said that her husband was an unsaved man. When he would get drunk, he would beat her. She felt as a Christian she ought to stay with him. I advised her to leave him. I do not believe that God ever asks any woman to stay with a drunken husband. She loses her own personality; she loses her own dignity, and she will find herself being brought down to his level if she submits to that. She is to submit "as it is fit in the Lord."

Husbands, love your wives, and be not bitter against them [Col. 3:19].

The husband who loves his wife is the one to whom the wife is to submit. She is not to be the one to take the lead in the family, but she is to urge him to take the lead. I think we have had this thing all wrong for a long time. In my entire ministry I have removed the word *obey* from the marriage ceremony. I don't think it belongs in there at all.

Children, obey your parents in all things: for this is well pleasing unto the Lord [Col. 3:20].

Children are to obey their parents. They are to honor their parents all their lives, but when they are children they are to obey them.

However, the child also needs to grow up. I don't think this verse means that a twenty-four-year-old boy must stay tied to his mama's apron strings. Whether he is married or single, when he has reached maturity, he is ready to get away from his parents. We see so many teenagers rebelling against their parents in our day. I believe that God may have put into the hearts of teenagers the necessity to get away. There is a period in their lives that is a weaning time, and they need to learn to be independent. I have seen some literature that tells young married couples that they are still to go to their parents and obey them. I think that is nonsense and entirely unscriptural (see Gen. 2:24). "Children, obey your parents in all things" is a verse for children, for minors.

Fathers, provoke not your children to anger, lest they be discouraged [Col. 3:21].

Let me refer you to my book on Ephesians and my comment on Ephesians 6:4. The remarkable feature of this verse, as given both in Ephesians and Colossians, is that under the Mosaic Law, the commandment referred only to the children. There was no reference to parents. Had the Law developed in the parents a dictatorship rather than a directorship? No. The Book of Proverbs reveals that the responsibility to find God's will for the child had been given to the parents: "Train up a child in the way he should go: and when he is old, he will not depart from it" (Prov. 22:6).

Now the apostle moves on to the subject of *holiness on the job*, at the place of employment. He will discuss the relationships that exist on the job, the relationship of capital to labor.

Servants, obey in all things your masters according to the flesh; not with eye-service, as men-pleasers; but in singleness of heart, fearing God [Col. 3:22].

Eye-service is a word peculiar in the New Testament to the writings of Paul. He means, "Don't keep your eye on the clock. Keep your eye on Christ. He is the One whom you are serving." That is the way you ought to do your job.

Sometimes Christians talk about being dedicated to the Lord and wanting to serve the Lord, but they are lazy. We had one boy working here at our radio headquarters who was like that. He stood around with his hands in his pockets all the while his mouth was going, but he thought he was dedicated! May I say something very frankly? If you are lazy on the job, you are *not* dedicated to Jesus Christ.

Paul had reduced the Christian life to its lowest common denominator. He had one simple goal: ". . . forgetting those things which are behind, and reaching forth unto those things which are before, I press toward the mark for the prize of the high calling of God in Christ Jesus" (Phil. 3:13–14). He had his eye, his mind, his heart, and his total affections fixed upon Jesus Christ.

"In singleness of heart, fearing God." The idea here is not to fear the boss, but to fear God.

And whatsoever ye do, do it heartily, as to the Lord, and not unto men [Col. 3:23].

When Paul says to work "heartily," he means work from your soul. We have heard a lot about a "soul brother," but we ought to have a little more "soul work." If you can't do something with enthusiasm unto the Lord, regardless of what it is, it is wrong for you. Some people write in and ask me, "Is it right for me to do this?" or "Is it right for me to go to this place?" Here is your standard: "Whatsoever ye do, do it heartily, as to the Lord." That applies to everything. Even if you cannot go to a church with enthusiasm, I would recommend you quit going to that church.

"As to the Lord, and not unto men." Whatever we do should be done to the Lord, not to men. We are not to be men pleasers.

Knowing that of the Lord ye shall receive the reward of the inheritance: for ye serve the Lord Christ [Col. 3:24].

Maybe you're not going to have to report to your boss; or when his back is turned he doesn't see that you are loafing on the job, not really giving him a full day's work. But the Lord Jesus sees, and you are going to answer to Him. You are in Him, and you belong to Him. Therefore, you have to give an account of your life to Him.

Since we represent the Lord Jesus down here upon this earth, He is going to ask that

His representatives be found faithful. There are a great many folk who are humble, little-known people that you and I know nothing about who have been *faithful* on the job. They have been faithful to their employer, faithful to their church, faithful to their homes, faithful to their pastor. Very few people know about them. The Lord knows. They will receive a reward. I think you and I are going to be surprised by the reward some people will get.

"For ye serve the Lord Christ." This puts a different complexion upon Christian service down here. There are many people who are lazy in God's work. I would say that laziness is one of the curses of the ministry. It is found in the church staff. It is so easy to loaf on the job because nobody is looking, nobody is watching. We need to remember that we serve the Lord Jesus, and we are going to give an account to Him.

But he that doeth wrong shall receive for the wrong which he hath done: and

there is no respect of persons [Col. 3:25].

He is going to straighten out everything in your life and in my life that we don't straighten out down here. This is exactly what this means.

It is a privilege to be in God's service. It is a privilege to teach a Sunday school class. But don't ever think that this makes you something special. When the Lord judges you, He will judge you on *faithfulness*. All will be judged alike. God is no respecter of persons.

My friend, we are joined to a living Christ. How wonderful it is! I cannot attain to it in my own strength. But He says He is going to help me. Only the Holy Spirit working in me can attain this high and holy calling. He wants me to mirror Him in every relationship I have down here. What a glorious calling you and I have! Doesn't that give you enthusiasm today? Don't look to the Babe in Bethlehem. Go to the living Christ who is at God's right hand.

CHAPTER 4

THEME: *Fellowship of believers is hearty*

We are in the section of this epistle which is dealing with holiness on the job, at the place of employment. Chapter 3 concluded with exhortations to servants or to employees. Chapter 4 will continue with exhortations to masters or to employers.

Masters, give unto your servants that which is just and equal; knowing that ye also have a Master in heaven [Col. 4:1].

"Masters"—Paul has something to say not only to the servant but also to the masters, to the bosses.

"Equal" means not to level down but to level up. The master is to do right by his servant.

"Knowing that ye also have a Master in heaven." The master will stand before Christ someday. Every Christian employer, as well as employee, will stand before God. This does put the gospel in shoe leather, does it not? It gets right down where the rubber meets the road. Or, in this case, it gets right down where your foot is walking in the factory or in the office. Whatever you're doing, you are to do it

unto the Lord, because you are going to answer to Him if you are His child.

Now the next few verses present three more areas of Christian conduct which are important. They are prayer, our public walk, and speech.

Continue in prayer, and watch in the same with thanksgiving [Col. 4:2].

These two words go together: Pray and watch. They are very important. They remind us of the experience of Nehemiah. When the enemy tried to stop him from rebuilding the walls of Jerusalem, he didn't just throw in the towel and cry out that he couldn't do the job. Nor did he simply say, "Well, we'll make it a matter of prayer," and then go on as he had been. No, this is what Nehemiah said: "Nevertheless we made our prayer unto our God, and set a watch against them day and night, because of them" (Neh. 4:9). This is what Paul tells us here: Watch and pray.

An old pastor in Georgia used to make this statement: "When a farmer prays for a corn crop, God expects him to say 'Amen' with a hoe." If you are praying about a certain matter, get busy with it.

I'm afraid we hear a lot of pious nonsense about prayer. I received a letter from a preacher who has cancer. He said, "I've been to Mayo Clinic. They found that I have cancer, and they recommend an operation. But I have come home and decided that I would do like you did: I will just trust the Lord." I sat down and wrote him a letter in a hurry. I said, "Brother, I did trust the Lord but that wasn't all that I did. I went to whom I think is the finest cancer specialist out here on the West Coast. My case was brought up before the UCLA Medical Clinic and was discussed there. They recommended the best thing that medical science knew to do. I have had two operations for cancer. My Christian brother, if you want to be an intelligent Christian (and I think you are), then you go back to Mayo Clinic as quickly as you can and tell them to operate if that is what they think is best. Then you trust the Lord, and He will bring you through it. *That* is what I did." Watch and pray. Be on the job. This is so practical.

"With thanksgiving." Be sure and thank God always because He is going to hear and answer your prayer. Maybe it won't be the answer you wanted, but He will answer. This is like breathing: inhale by prayer, exhale by thanksgiving.

Withal praying also for us, that God would open unto us a door of utterance, to speak the mystery of Christ, for which I am also in bonds:

That I may make it manifest, as I ought to speak [Col. 4:3–4].

"Withal praying also for us"—Paul says, "Don't forget to pray for us." My friend, you can't help Paul any longer by praying for him, but you can help your pastor and other Christian ministries.

"That God would open unto us a door of utterance, to speak the mystery of Christ, for which I am also in bonds." Paul was in prison when he wrote this. He wanted to be released and go out through an open door that he might preach the gospel.

I consider every aspect of my ministry to be a door, and I ask God to keep the doors open. He has promised that He would. This is the verse that I have chosen for my ministry: ". . . behold, I have set before thee an open door, and no man can shut it: for thou hast a little strength, and hast kept my word, and hast not denied my name" (Rev. 3:8). He has set a lot of open doors before me, and I ask Him to open even more doors.

Walk in wisdom toward them that are without, redeeming the time [Col. 4:5].

"Walk in wisdom." The child of God has a responsibility before the world today. Don't be foolish as a child of God.

We hear so much pious nonsense in our day. There are those who said the Lord would return by 1980. I don't know where they got such information. There were probably a lot of embarrassed folk with red faces in 1980. Christians have no right to make such statements before an unsaved world. Nor should we say we are trusting the Lord when our actions show that we really are not trusting Him. We should not do foolish things before the world.

A woman in Southern California wrote me a letter and rebuked me for going to the doctor for treatment of my cancer. She said that that was not trusting the Lord. She wrote, "I have cancer and I am trusting the Lord. I don't go to the doctor." They buried her not long ago; she died of her cancer. I'm afraid at times we are guilty of causing our neighbors to smile and say, "This Christianity is a foolish sort of thing." We need to learn to "walk in wisdom toward them that are without."

"Redeeming the time." Buy up your opportunities. When you see an opportunity, pray that the Lord will lead you. Don't force yourself on people. Just pray and ask the Lord to open the door, and He will open it. I wish I had space to tell you how many times this has happened in my life and in the lives of others. Let Him open the door—before you make the mistake of putting your foot in your mouth. I knocked on many doors when I was a pastor, and I often stepped in and put my foot in my mouth the very first thing. Since then I have learned to do a lot more praying before I walk in.

Let your speech be alway with grace, seasoned with salt, that ye may know how ye ought to answer every man [Col. 4:6].

Some people think this verse says, "Let your speech be salt," and they really sting you with their little sarcastic remarks! But what it says is, "alway with grace, seasoned with salt." A child of God should have a conversation that *deters* evil. It should withhold evil rather than promote it. I think it also means that a Christian should not be boring. We should be enthusiastic—"That ye may know how ye ought to answer every man."

FELLOWSHIP OF BELIEVERS IS HEARTY

We come now to a remarkable list of names of people whom Paul knew. They are men and women who lived back there in the first century. They walked down the Roman roads, lived in Roman cities, and were under Roman rule. They were in the midst of paganism, but they were God's children.

Many of these people lived in Ephesus. When I was in Ephesus, I climbed up in the theater there and from that height I could look down that great marble boulevard—I would call it Harbor Boulevard, because it leads right down to where the harbor was in that day. I thought, *This is where one could have seen Paul come walking up the boulevard. There would be Tychicus coming up the way; and there's Onesimus and Aristarchus and Epaphras—all those fellows.* They were all Christians. They were God's men back yonder in the first century.

The interesting thing is that Paul had never been to Rome nor had he been to Colosse, yet he gives a list of people that he knew, and many of them are from those two cities. This reveals that Paul had led many people to Christ who returned home to cities that he never was able to reach directly or personally. His ministry was a tremendous, far-reaching ministry.

All my state shall Tychicus declare unto you, who is a beloved brother, and a faithful minister and fellow-servant in the Lord:

Whom I have sent unto you for the same purpose, that he might know your estate, and comfort your hearts [Col. 4:7–8].

"Tychicus" was the pastor of the church in Ephesus. He is mentioned in Ephesians 6:21, Acts 20:4, and 2 Timothy 4:12. He was a wonderful brother in the Lord.

With Onesimus, a faithful and beloved brother, who is one of you. They shall make known unto you all things which are done here [Col. 4:9].

"Onesimus" was a slave of Philemon in Colosse. He had run away from his master, had been led to the Lord through the ministry of Paul, and was now being sent back to his master by him. Paul wrote a letter to Philemon when he sent Onesimus back, and he tells Philemon that Onesimus is his "beloved brother." You can see from this that there is a new relationship in Christ. Master and slave are now brothers in Christ Jesus.

Aristarchus my fellow-prisoner saluteth you, and Marcus, sister's son to Barnabas, (touching whom ye received commandments: if he come unto you, receive him;) [Col. 4:10].

"Aristarchus" was a fellow prisoner with Paul, and he was his friend.

"Marcus" is John Mark, the nephew of Barnabas—the son of his sister. He is the writer of the Gospel of Mark. You will remember that Mark left Paul and Barnabas on their first missionary journey, and because of this Paul didn't want to take him along on the second missionary journey. Paul was wrong in his judgment of John Mark. The boy made good, and Paul acknowledges that here. Paul gives the Colossians instructions, "Don't reject him like I did. You folks receive him." Paul mentions John Mark again in his second letter to Timothy: ". . .Take Mark, and bring him with thee: for he is profitable to me for the ministry" (2 Tim. 4:11).

And Jesus, which is called Justus, who are of the circumcision. These only are my fellow-workers unto the kingdom of God, which have been a comfort unto me [Col. 4:11].

"Jesus, which is called Justus" would be the name *Joshua* in the Hebrew language. Being "of the circumcision" indicates he was Jewish. This shows us that there were a few Israelites in the church in Colosse. However, there were not many; the Colossian church was mostly Gentile. These men were wonderful brethren, helpers of Paul, and great missionaries themselves.

Epaphras, who is one of you, a servant of Christ, saluteth you, always labouring fervently for you in prayers, that ye may stand perfect and complete in all the will of God [Col. 4:12].

"Epaphras" was the pastor in Colosse. Now he is in prison, so he has a new ministry, the ministry of prayer. I received a letter from a young preacher who is paralyzed and cannot preach any more. He wrote a most discouraged letter. I answered him like this: "I have a job for you: Pray for me." Prayer is a ministry, too. If God takes you out of active service, pray for God's servants. It simply means God has given you a new ministry; He has something different for you to do.

For I bear him record, that he hath a great zeal for you, and them that are in Laodicea, and them in Hierapolis [Col. 4:13].

These three cities were very close together. Hierapolis and Laodicea were about six to ten miles apart; they were both near Colosse. There were churches in all three places.

Luke, the beloved physician, and Demas, greet you [Col. 4:14].

"Luke, the beloved physician." Isn't that a wonderful designation for him?

When Paul first mentioned Demas, he called him a fellow worker. Here he simply says, "and Demas"; I think this may indicate that Paul isn't really sure about him at this time. Later on Demas will forsake Paul. How tragic that is.

Salute the brethren which are in Laodicea, and Nymphas, and the church which is in his house [Col. 4:15].

These cities had great heathen temples, but the Christians met in homes. I used to hold the viewpoint and I still do—although I don't emphasize it today as I did at one time—that as the church started in the home, it is going to come back to the home.

And when this epistle is read among you, cause that it be read also in the church of the Laodiceans; and that ye likewise read the epistle from Laodicea [Col. 4:16].

"The epistle from Laodicea." Paul does not say that he had written an epistle to the Laodiceans. Apparently the letters of Paul were circulated around, and the Laodiceans had read one of them. A great many of the scholars believe that this might be a reference to the Epistle to the Ephesians. Paul is telling the Colossians to read that epistle also and to share theirs with the Laodiceans.

And say to Archippus, Take heed to the ministry which thou hast received in the Lord, that thou fulfil it [Col. 4:17].

"Archippus" is another man on Paul's list in this letter. We do not know anything more about him than is mentioned here. He is a man who had a gift, and Paul is urging him to use that gift.

The salutation by the hand of me Paul. Remember my bonds. Grace be with you. Amen [Col. 4:18].

Paul dictated most of his letters. (The letter to the Galatians was written in his own hand.) Here he gives his signature to the letter which he has dictated.

This is the second time that Paul says, "Remember my bonds"—or, "Pray for me."

"Grace be with you. Amen." Isn't this a wonderful letter that we have read? Paul wrote to a church that he had never visited, but he knew many of the people and had led them to the knowledge of the Lord Jesus Christ.

BIBLIOGRAPHY

(Recommended for Further Study)

Gromacki, Robert G. *Stand Perfect in Wisdom: An Exposition of Colossians and Philemon.* Grand Rapids, Michigan: Baker Book House, 1981.

Harrison, Everett F. *Colossians: Christ-All-Sufficient.* Chicago, Illinois: Moody Press, 1971.

Hendriksen, William, *Exposition of Colossians and Philemon.* Grand Rapids, Michigan: Baker Book House, 1965.

Ironside, H. A. *Lectures on the Epistle to the Colossians.* Neptune, New Jersey: Loizeaux Brothers, 1929.

Kelly, William. *Lectures on the Epistles to the Philippians and Colossians.* Oak Park, Illinois: Bible Truth Publishers, n.d.

Kent, Homer A., Jr. *Treasures of Wisdom: Studies in Colossians and Philemon.* Grand Rapids, Michigan: Baker Book House, 1978. (Excellent.)

King, Guy H. *Crossing the Border.* Fort Washington, Pennsylvania: Christian Literature Crusade, 1957. (Devotional.)

Moule, Handley C. G. *Colossians and Philemon.* Grand Rapids, Michigan: Kregel Publications, 1893. (This is a reprint from *The Cambridge University Bible for Schools and Colleges.* This helpful series also covers Romans, Ephesians, and Philippians.)

Nicholson, William. *Oneness with Christ.* Grand Rapids, Michigan: Kregel Publications, 1903. (Devotional.)

Robertson, A. T. *Paul and the Intellectuals.* Grand Rapids, Michigan: Baker Book House, 1928.

Thomas, W. H. Griffith. *Studies in Colossians and Philemon.* Grand Rapids, Michigan: Baker Book House, 1973. (Excellent.)

Vaughan, Curtis. *Colossians and Philemon: A Study Guide.* Grand Rapids, Michigan: Zondervan Publishing House, 1980.

Vine, W. E. *Philippians and Colossians.* London: Oliphants, 1955. (This is an excellent treatment.)

Wiersbe, Warren W. *Be Complete.* Wheaton, Illinois: Victor Books, 1981.

Wuest, Kenneth S. *Ephesians and Colossians in the Greek New Testament.* Grand Rapids, Michigan: Wm. B. Eerdmans Publishing Co., 1953.

The First Epistle to the
THESSALONIANS
INTRODUCTION

This wonderful epistle is almost at the end of Paul's epistles as far as their arrangement in the New Testament is concerned. However, it was actually the first epistle that Paul wrote. It was written by Paul in A.D. 52 or 53.

Thessalonica was a Roman colony. Rome had a somewhat different policy with their captured people from what many other nations have had. For example, it seems that we try to Americanize all the people throughout the world, as if that would be the ideal. Rome was much wiser than that. She did not attempt to directly change the culture, the habits, the customs, or the language of the people whom she conquered. Instead, she would set up colonies which were arranged geographically in strategic spots throughout the empire. A city which was a Roman colony would gradually adopt Roman laws and customs and ways. In the local department stores you would see the latest things they were wearing in Rome itself. Thus these colonies were very much like a little Rome. Thessalonica was such a Roman colony, and it was an important city in the life of the Roman Empire.

Thessalonica was located fifty miles west of Philippi and about one hundred miles north of Athens. It was Cicero who said, "Thessalonica is in the bosom of the empire." It was right in the center or the heart of the empire and was the chief city of Macedonia.

The city was first named Therma because of the hot springs in that area. In 316 B. C. Cassander, who was one of the four generals who divided up the empire of Alexander the Great, took Macedonia and made Thessalonica his home base. He renamed the city in memory of his wife, Thessalonike, who was a half sister of Alexander. The city is still in existence and is now known as Salonika.

The church in Thessalonica, established on Paul's second missionary journey, was a model church. Paul mentions this in the first chapter; "So that ye were ensamples to all that believe in Macedonia and Achaia" (1 Thess. 1:7). This church was a testimony to the whole area that we would call Greece today. Paul also speaks of this church as being an example to the Corinthians in 2 Corinthians 8:1–5.

You will recall that Paul and Barnabas separated prior to the second missionary journey. Paul took Silas with him, and along the route he picked up Timothy and Dr. Luke. He revisited the churches in Galatia and then attempted to make a wider circle in the densely populated area of Asia Minor, known as Turkey today. I think he intended to carry on his missionary work there, because in his third missionary journey he did make Ephesus his headquarters and did what was probably his greatest missionary work. But on his second missionary journey, the Spirit of God put up a roadblock and would not let him go south. He attempted to go up into Bithynia, but again the Spirit of God prevented him. He couldn't go north, and he couldn't go south. So he moved to the west and came to Troas to await orders. He had the vision of the man of Macedonia, so he crossed over to Philippi. He found that the man of Macedonia was instead a woman by the name of Lydia, a seller of purple—she probably ran a department store there. Paul led her to the Lord along with others of the city. Thus, a church was established at Philippi.

Then Paul went to Thessalonica, and we are told in chapter 17 of Acts that he was there for three Sabbaths. So Paul was there a little less than a month, but in that period of time he did a herculean task of mission work. Paul was an effective missionary—he led multitudes to Christ there. And in that brief time he not only organized a local church, but he also taught them the great doctrines of the Christian faith.

Now Paul had to leave Thessalonica posthaste due to great opposition to the gospel. He was run out of town and went down to Berea. The enemy pursued him to Berea, and again Paul was forced to leave. Paul left Silas and Timothy at Berea, but he went on to Athens. After some time at Athens, he went on to Corinth. Apparently it was at Corinth that Timothy and Silas came to him and brought him word concerning the Thessalonians (see 1 Thess. 3:6). Timothy also brought some questions to Paul, problems troubling the believers in Thessalonica. Paul wrote this first epistle in response to their questions, to instruct them further and give them needed comfort.

Although Paul had been in Thessalonica less than a month, he had touched on many of the great doctrines of the church, including the second coming of Christ. It is interesting that

Paul did not consider this subject to be above the heads of the new converts. Yet there are churches today that have been in existence for more than one hundred years whose members have but a vague understanding of the rapture of the church and the coming of Christ to establish His kingdom here on earth. The Thessalonian church was not even a month old, and Paul was teaching them these great doctrines!

The apostle obviously had emphasized the second coming of Christ for believers and had taught that the return of Christ was imminent; for during the period of time since Paul had left, some of the saints who had come to know and believe in Christ Jesus had died, and this had naturally raised the question in the minds of the Thessalonians as to whether these saints would be in the Rapture or not. Paul presents the second coming of Christ in relationship to believers as a *comfort*, and this forms the theme of the epistle. This emphasis is in sharp contrast to Christ's catastrophic and cataclysmic coming in glory to establish His kingdom by putting down all unrighteousness, as seen in Revelation 19:11–16.

The epistle has a threefold purpose: (1) To *confirm* young converts in the elementary truth of the gospel; (2) to *condition* them to go on unto holy living; and (3) to *comfort* them regarding the return of Christ. Paul's message offered a marked contrast to the paganism and heathenism which were present in Thessalonica. A heathen inscription in Thessalonica read: "After death no reviving, after the grave no meeting again."

In 1 Thessalonians the emphasis is upon the rapture of believers, the coming of Christ to take His church out of the world. The fact that the coming of Christ is a purifying hope should lead to sanctification in our lives. There are a lot of people today who want to argue prophecy, and there is a great deal of curiosity about it. But John tells us, "And every man that hath this hope in him purifieth himself, even as he is pure" (1 John 3:3). This hope should have a purifying effect in our lives. I am not interested in how enthusiastic and excited you get over the truth of the rapture of the church; I want to know how you are living. Does this hope get right down to where you are living, and does it change your life?

In 2 Thessalonians the emphasis shifts to the coming of Christ to the earth to establish His kingdom. There is a great deal of difference in our being caught *up* to meet the Lord in the air and His coming *down* to the earth to establish His kingdom. I think there is a lot of upside down theology today. We need to make a distinction between our being caught *up* and His coming *down*.

OUTLINE

For this book we are suggesting two outlines. Each one gives a needed emphasis that is not in the other.

II. Coming of Christ Is a Working Hope, Chapter 2

A. Motive and Method of a True Witness for Christ, Chapter 2:1–6

B. Mother Side of the Apostle's Ministry (Comfort), Chapter 2:7–9

C. Father Side of the Apostle's Ministry (Charge), Chapter 2:10–13

D. Brother Side of the Apostle's Ministry (Challenge), Chapter 2:14–16

E. Reward of a True Witness for Christ, Chapter 2:17-20

III. Coming of Christ Is a Purifying Hope, Chapters 3:1–4:12

Sanctification

A. Timothy Brings Good Report of Thessalonians, Chapter 3:1–8

B. Paul Urges Thessalonians to Continue to Grow in Faith, Chapter 3:9–13

C. How Believers Are to Walk, Chapter 4:1–12

IV. Coming of Christ Is a Comforting Hope, Chapter 4:13–18

What death means to a Christian; what the Rapture means to the church

V. Coming of Christ Is a Rousing Hope, Chapter 5

Leads to action; dead believers are asleep in Jesus; living believers are awake for Jesus

A. Call to Be Awake and Alert in View of Christ's Coming, Chapter 5:1–10

B. Commandments for Christians, Chapter 5:11–28

CHAPTER 1

THEME: The coming of Christ is an inspiring hope

INTRODUCTION

Paul, and Silvanus, and Timotheus, unto the church of the Thessalonians which is in God the Father and in the Lord Jesus Christ: Grace be unto you, and peace, from God our Father, and the Lord Jesus Christ [1 Thess. 1:1].

This introduction is typical of Paul's other epistles, but there are some differences to which we need to call attention. Paul joins Silas and Timothy with himself in his greeting. Remember that Silas and Timothy had just returned to Paul with their report from Thessalonica. By joining their names with his, the Thessalonians would know they are all in agreement concerning this letter.

Also, Paul reveals his humility when he joins these men with himself. Silas and Timothy would have been unknown had not Paul associated himself with them. This is a very noble gesture on the part of Paul. He is always identifying himself with the brethren. He was not aloof, separated, and segregated above all the others who were working for the Lord Jesus.

This is something we need to remember today in regard to the ministry. Don't put your preacher on a pedestal; let him be right down among you. Those of us who are ministers are largely responsible for trying to make a difference between the clergy and laity. When I entered the ministry, I bought a Prince Albert coat with a long coattail. I wore a wing collar and a very white shirtfront and either a white or a black necktie. When I stood up in the pulpit, I looked like one of those little mules looking over a whitewashed fence, and I felt like one when I wore that garb! One day it came to me how ridiculous it was for me to dress differently from the officers and members of my church. None of them wore a robe or a Prince Albert coat, and I was no different from any of them. I don't think that God is asking me to live any differently either. However, when I am teaching the Word of God, I am to be very conscious of the fact that I'm giving out His Word and actually acting in His behalf, and He expects that of everyone who gives out His Word. But as far as living is concerned, God expects all of us to live on a very high plane; the life of the teacher or minister is to be no different from the life of every believer in Christ Jesus.

I wish we could eliminate this distinction between the clergy and the laity. According to the Word of God, it is a false distinction. God has a very high standard of living for all of us. I am frank to say that a paid ministry has been the curse of the church, although I don't think it could have been done otherwise in this day of specialization. However, we need to recognize that the heresies of the church have come in through a paid ministry.

There are two situations in the church which are dangerous. One is a minister who tries to exalt himself. The other is a layman who tries to be an authority on the Bible and has not really studied the Bible but has gone off on a tangent. The greatest discipline for me has been to teach the total Word of God. If a person will teach the *total* Word of God, he will deal with every subject in the Bible—he will be forced to play every key on the organ and to pull out every stop. It isn't possible to ride one hobbyhorse and emphasize one theme to the exclusion of all others if one teaches the entire Bible. I wish we had that kind of discipline in our churches today. I wish every church would go through the entire Bible.

"Unto the church of the Thessalonians which is in God the Father and in the Lord Jesus Christ." They may have a little different life-style and have different problems from the church in Philippi, but, just like the church in Philippi, it is *in* God the Father and *in* the Lord Jesus Christ. We don't read that in his other epistles because this is the first epistle Paul has written. He says it only once, and this will be enough. He won't go over this again. When the Lord Jesus prayed to the Father, He asked, "That they all may be one; as thou, Father, art in me, and I in thee, that they also may be one in us: that the world may believe that thou hast sent me. And the glory which thou gavest me I have given them; that they may be one, even as we are one: I in them, and thou in me, that they may be made perfect in one . . ." (John 17:21–23). Any believer who is in Christ Jesus is also in God the Father. That is a very safe place to be, safer than any safety deposit box!

"Grace be unto you, and peace, from God our Father, and the Lord Jesus Christ" is a formal introduction which Paul uses in all of his epistles. Grace comes first, followed by the peace of God. Both the grace and the peace come from God the Father and from the Lord Jesus Christ.

We give thanks to God always for you all, making mention of you in our prayers [1 Thess. 1:2].

Paul prayed for all of the churches that he had founded. Paul had a tremendous prayer list, and it would make an interesting study for you to find all the people who were on that list. You would be surprised how many different churches, individuals, and groups of people Paul prayed for.

"We give thanks to God always for you all." Paul gives thanks for this church because of many things, and one of the most important was because they were an example; it was a model church.

The next verse is one of the most remarkable in the Bible, and it follows a pattern of the apostle Paul which we find in his writing. He emphasized the number three.

Remembering without ceasing your work of faith, and labour of love, and patience of hope in our Lord Jesus Christ, in the sight of God and our Father [1 Thess. 1:3].

"Remembering without ceasing [1] your work of faith, [2] and labour of love, [3] and patience of hope in our Lord Jesus Christ."

This is a very important verse of Scripture and contains a wealth of meaning. Paul associates the three Christian graces: faith and love and hope. In 1 Corinthians he also brought those three graces together. "And now abideth faith, hope, love, these three; but the greatest of these is love" (1 Cor. 13:13).

In New Jersey several years ago I had lunch with the scientist who had designed the heat shield that was on the space capsules to protect them when they go out into space and then reenter our atmosphere. He remarked to me, "Have you ever noticed that the universe is divided into a trinity?"

"No, what do you mean by that?"

"You and I live in a physical universe that is divided into time, space, and matter. Can you think of a fourth?"

I couldn't think of any, so he continued, "Time is divided into three parts: past, present, and future. Can you think of a fourth?"

Again I couldn't, so he went on. "Space is divided into length and breadth and height. They speak of a 'fourth dimension,' but it doesn't happen to be in this material universe."

You can see that this universe in which you and I live bears the mark of the Trinity. The interesting thing is that the Word of God does the same thing. Paul speaks of man as a trinity. We will discuss this specifically when we get into the fifth chapter, verse 23: ". . . and I pray God your whole spirit and soul and body be preserved blameless unto the coming of our Lord Jesus Christ." This tells us that man is a trinity.

There are some other interesting examples of the significance of the number three. For example, have you noticed that in Genesis only three sons of Adam are named? I am sure that Adam and Eve had more than three sons; they probably had one hundred or more—they started the human race—but only three of the sons are named: Cain, Abel, and Seth.

In this verse Paul actually gives three graces of the Christian life. The past is the work of faith. The present is a labor of love. The future is the patience of hope. That is the biography of the Christian and the abiding, permanent, and eternal features of the Christian life.

Faith, hope, and love are abstract nouns. They seem to be way up yonder, but we are way down here. How can we get them out of space and theory into the reality of life down here? How can we make them concrete instead of abstract qualities?

This is like the story of the contractor who loved children. He put down a sidewalk one day—finished it in the afternoon. He came back the next morning to find that some children had walked on the concrete and had left their footmarks in it. He was very angry and was talking very loudly. A man who was standing by said, "I thought you loved children." The contractor said, "I love them in the abstract but not in the concrete!"

So the question here is how we are going to get these words down into something concrete. Paul takes these three words from the "beautiful isle of somewhere" and puts them into shoe leather. He gets them down to where the shoe leather meets the sidewalks of our hometown. He fleshes up these abstract qualities by taking them out of the morgue of never-never land.

Notice how he does it. From the "work of faith," the "labour of love," and the "patience of hope," he cites the three steps in the lives of the Thessalonian believers: "How ye turned to God from idols"—that's the work of faith; "to serve the living and true God," a labor of love;

"to wait for his Son from heaven" is the patience of hope.

Now the "work of faith" is a strange expression because we are told that ". . . by grace are ye saved through faith; and that not of yourselves: it is the gift of God: Not of works, lest any man should boast" (Eph. 2:8–9). Yet here it is called the work of faith. I think that Paul is making it very clear that he and James do not contradict each other. James writes, "Yea, a man may say, Thou hast faith, and I have works: shew me thy faith without thy works, and I will shew thee my faith by my works" (James 2:18). That is the work of faith. It is the way faith is demonstrated to others. (The writings of James and the writings of Paul certainly do not contradict each other—as some have suggested—because they are both writing about the same thing.)

Faith is the response of the soul of man to the Word of God. When a man responds to the Word of God, then he walks by faith. Paul says this in 2 Corinthians 5:7: "For we walk by faith, not by sight." The Lord Jesus said the same thing: "Then said they unto him, What shall we do, that we might work the works of God? Jesus answered and said unto them, This is the work of God, that ye believe on him whom he hath sent" (John 6:28–29). He didn't say that you can come to God with your works, but that you must come to God by *faith*. Then a faith that is living will make itself manifest; it will reveal itself in the life that is lived.

There is a good illustration of this in the life of the disciples, as recorded in Luke 5:4–5. The Lord Jesus said to Simon Peter, ". . . Launch out into the deep, and let down your nets for a draught. And Simon answering said unto him, Master, we have toiled all the night, and have taken nothing." That is a statement of fact, a declaration of naked truth: "We fished all night, and we caught nothing. We know this sea, and there is no use going back out there." But notice what Simon Peter adds, "Nevertheless at thy word I will let down the net." He says he will go back and fish again. My friend, that is the work of faith. As believers we need to realize that the work of faith is acting upon the Word of God. What is the work of God? It is to believe on Jesus Christ— that is how the Lord Jesus defined it: ". . . This is the work of God, that ye believe on him whom he hath sent" (John 6:29). When you act on what the Word of God says, your faith will be evident to the world. That is the work of faith.

We have the same thing illustrated in the life of Cain and Abel. What was the problem with Cain? He was a sinner by nature, but he was also a sinner by choice and act. We are told, "By faith Abel offered unto God a more excellent sacrifice than Cain, by which he obtained witness that he was righteous . . ." (Heb. 11:4). How? By being a nice little Sunday school boy? No. Although he was a sinner as Cain was a sinner, Abel responded to the Word of God, and he believed God. When he believed God, he was saved. He manifested that faith by bringing the proper sacrifice. Faith is the connection between the believer and God. It communicates His Word to your heart and you respond. And that is what conversion is. Conversion is to believe God.

These Thessalonians turned to God from idols. Paul didn't go into Thessalonica and say, "I don't think it is proper for you people to worship idols. That's a terrible thing to do." He never said anything like that. When he went there he preached Christ! Idolatry wasn't repulsive to these people, but when they heard Paul present Christ, they believed God and they turned to God. When they turned to God, they automatically turned from idols.

People often say to me, "You converted me." I haven't converted anyone—I can't do that! One man said to me, "You saved me many years ago, and I'll never forget you." I answered him, "I appreciate your not forgetting me, but I didn't save you. All I did was to present the Word of God. You believed the Word of God, and the Spirit of God did a work in your heart." That is really quite wonderful, my friend.

Paul remembered without ceasing not only the work of faith of the Thessalonian believers but also their "labour of love." Now, what is the labor of love? God does not save by love; He saves by grace, which is love in action. Labor and love don't seem to fit together. But, you see, love will labor. And when it does, it just doesn't seem to be labor. Let me repeat the illustration of a little girl carrying a heavy baby. A man passing by said to her, "Isn't that baby too heavy for you?" She answered, "Oh no, he's my brother." Love makes all the difference in the world. Labor isn't labor when it is a labor of love.

The Lord Jesus really put it right on the line when He said, "If ye love me, keep my commandments" (John 14:15). If you don't love Him, you will find it nothing but tedium and labor to try to keep His commandments. I don't think it is worthwhile trying.

Several years ago my daughter and I were riding into Los Angeles to the church which I was pastoring. She was helping us with some work at the church. We were stuck in the traffic on the freeway, and I remarked to her, "Look at all these people going to work this morning. Notice that nobody looks happy. Everyone has a tense look on his face. They are anxious and uptight. Ninety-nine out of a hundred are going to a job they hate doing." I say it is wonderful to do what you love to do. Then it is a labor of love.

If working for the Lord is a great burden to you today, I believe the Lord Jesus would say to you, "Give it up, brother. Don't bother with it." He doesn't want it to be like that. We are to love Him. Then whatever we do for Him will be a labor of love. That should characterize the life of the believer.

One time when Dwight L. Moody came home, his family said to him, "Cancel your next meeting. You look so weary and we know you are tired." He gave this tremendous response, "I am weary *in* the work, but I am not weary *of* the work." I tell you, it is wonderful to get weary in the work of God but not to get weary of the work of God.

Love to God is expressed in obedience. I get tired of all this talk about being a dedicated Christian. If you want to make that claim, then prove it, brother. Prove it by your love, and love manifests itself in obedience.

Now the third thing for which Paul commends the Thessalonian believers is their "patience of hope." After they had turned to God from idols to serve the living and true God, they also waited for His Son from heaven. That is the patience of hope.

Every man lives with some hope for the future. And that hope, whatever it is, will sustain him. Down through the centuries man has expressed this. Martin Luther said, "Everything that is done in the world is done by hope." Long before him Sophocles, the pagan, had written: "It is hope which maintains most of mankind." A modern man, O. S. Marden, says, "There is no medicine like hope, no incentive so great, and no tonic so powerful as expectation of something better tomorrow." The poet, Alexander Pope, wrote: "Hope springs eternal in the human breast." A statesman, Thomas Jefferson, said, "I steer my bark with hope in the head, leaving fear astern." And Carlyle, the Scottish philosopher, commented, "Man is, properly speaking, based upon hope, he has no other possession but hope; this world of his is emphatically the place of hope."

What a glorious, wonderful life it is to serve the living and true God and to wait for His Son from heaven. That is the "blessed hope." Multitudes today place their hope in man, thinking that man can resolve all his problems and bring peace and prosperity to the world. Man cannot do that. If your hope is in this world, you are chasing a will-o'-the-wisp of happiness that will shatter like a bubble when you get it in your hands. You are following a Pied Piper who is playing, "I'm forever blowing bubbles." God put man out of Paradise because man was a sinner, and man has been trying to build a paradise outside ever since. The church for years thought it was building the kingdom of heaven, and it was not. God wouldn't even let man live forever in sin, and we can thank Him for that. Every age comes to a time of cosmic crisis and says, "Somehow we'll work our way out." Frederick the Great, the great emperor of Germany, said, "The time I live in is a time of turmoil. My hope is in God." What is your hope today? Is your hope in some political party or in some man-made organization? God have mercy on anyone whose hope rests upon some little, frail bark that man is paddling! I don't think that any man or any party or any group down here can work out the problems of this world. The sceptre of this universe is in nail-pierced hands, and He will move at the right time. This one thing I know: all things do work together for good to them who love God, to them who are the called according to His eternal and holy purpose (see Rom. 8:28).

So here Paul has brought together faith and love and hope, the three tenses of the Christian life: the work of faith, which looks back to the Cross and produces good works in the life; the labor of love, which is the present basis and motivation on which a child of God is to serve Christ; and the patience of hope, which looks into the future.

What a wonderful trinity of Christian graces! It should be the biography of every believer. It was the biography of the church in Thessalonica, and I hope it is the biography of your church, too.

Now Paul takes up another great truth—

Knowing, brethren beloved, your election of God [1 Thess. 1:4].

Here we come again to that word *election*. I dealt with this when I taught Ephesians: "According as he hath chosen us in him before the foundation of the world, that we should be holy and without blame before him in love" (Eph. 1:4). Afterward I received some letters criticizing me for being weak in emphasizing election, claiming that I had soft-pedaled it; others wrote that I was rather extreme and had gone too far in talking about it. Since I got both reactions, I came to the conclusion it must have been about right. I knew it couldn't have been both extremes; so it must have been somewhere in the middle, which must be close to accurate.

Paul doesn't mind writing about election in this epistle to the Thessalonian believers. And he presents it from God's side of the ledger. You and I do not see His side, and we have never seen it. But there are certain great axioms of truth that we must put down. When I studied plane geometry, certain axioms were stated without being proven, such as the shortest distance between two points is a straight line. I have never had an occasion to dispute it, but nobody has ever attempted to prove it to me, although there is a proposition in geometry that will prove it. Nevertheless, there are certain things that we accept as fact without proof. And one of the things is the fact that there are certain things which *cannot* be proven to be true. Likewise Paul doesn't attempt to argue election or to prove election; he simply states it as a fact. "Knowing, brethren beloved, your election of God." That is God's side of the picture.

The Creator has His sovereign right. Dr. Albert Hyma, of the University of Michigan, said that for the past fifty years America has been under the control of men who do not know the origin and the beginning of our nation. They do not realize that the Puritans had a tremendous impact upon this nation. One of the great truths that the Puritans stood for, and which was basic to their entire life-style, was the sovereignty of God. Behind election and all of life is the sovereignty of God. The Creator has His sovereign right.

We need to recognize that God created the universe. I'm not concerned with *how* He did it, nor am I concerned with the account in Genesis. I simply want to emphasize the fact that in the beginning *God* created the heaven and the earth.

Now there are those who are willing to say He created, but they deny Him the right to *direct* the universe. They deny Him the right to give a *purpose* to it. May I say to you that we live in a universe that was created by God and exists for His glory. Even in the Sermon on the Mount the Lord Jesus Christ said, "Let your light so shine before men, that they may see your good works, and glorify your Father which is in heaven" (Matt. 5:16). He didn't say your good works were to glorify *yourself.* Oh, no! They are to glorify the Father in heaven. May I say especially to you, my Christian friend, that God is the Creator, and this universe exists for His glory. He is God, and beside Him there is none other. He doesn't look to anybody for advice. He is running this universe for His own purpose. He is directing it for His own glory. You and I live in a universe which is theocentric, that is, God-centered. It is not anthropocentric, man-centered; nor is it geocentric, earth-centered; but it is uranocentric, heaven-centered. This is God's universe, and He is running it His way.

Something else needs to be said: God is no tyrant. God is righteous. God is just. God is holy. Everything that God does is right. You may not always think so, but I have news for you. If you do not think God is right in what He is doing, and if you think that God is not following the best plan, the news I have for you is that you are *wrong.* God is not wrong. *You* are wrong. You are the person who needs to get his thinking corrected, because if you don't, you are out of step with the universe. This universe exists for God, for His glory, and for His purpose. There is nothing going to happen that will not work out to His glory. He is in charge, and He is running this universe today.

With this in mind, let's consider something else. Have you ever stopped to consider the fact that you were *born*? You could have been nonexistent. I could have been nonexistent. God did not come to me and ask, "Vernon McGee, do you want to come into existence?" I wasn't even in existence so that He could ask me! *He* is the One who thought of it. He is the One who is responsible for my existence. And He did not ask me whether I wanted to be male or female. He didn't ask me whether I wanted to be born in this day and age. He didn't ask me to choose my parents. He didn't ask me to decide whether my parents would be godly or whether they would be wealthy— and they were neither one. God today is running this universe because it is His. You may not like it, but that just happens to be the way it is.

Now God is no tyrant—no one is chosen against his will, and no one is rejected against his will. God is right in all that He does. Paul asks, "What shall we say then? Is there unrighteousness with God?" And he answers his own question with a strong negative, "God forbid" (Rom. 9:14). God is *right* in all that He does.

We need to get back to that place where we recognize that we are mere creatures. Not only creatures, but we are totally depraved creatures. I know it's not popular to say this in our day. We like to scratch each other's backs and tell each other how wonderful we are. That's the reason they hand out loving cups, and these knife-and-fork clubs are always recognizing somebody as the outstanding something or other. The human race must do that in order to bolster us up and make us think that we are great down here. The fact is that we are in rebellion against God.

The fact that God even considers us as a nation is due to the early Puritans who founded this country. They are being downgraded in our day, but we have this great country because of them. Other men have labored, and we have entered into their labors. And one of the things that they emphasized was the liberty of each individual for private judgment. Even we as sinners have that right. Why? Because no other sinner has any right to make a decision for you and me. Today you and I enjoy the freedom that we have because of our Puritan forefathers. The present generation of politicians doesn't even know what it's all about, which is the reason democracy isn't working. There is no way democracy can work unless the people understand the sovereignty of God, recognize they are His creatures, and fall down before Him.

Now let me repeat what Paul has said to the Thessalonian believers (v. 4): "Knowing, brethren beloved, your election of God." Maybe you don't like this verse, but this is the way it happened. And God is running this universe. Instead of joining a protest march against Him, I suggest that you fall down on your face before Him and thank Him that He has brought you into existence, and that He has given you the opportunity as a free moral agent to make a decision for Him. His invitation still stands, ". . . If any man thirst, let him come unto me, and drink" (John 7:37). Are you thirsty? Then come to Christ. He stands ready to receive you. You say you are not thirsty? Then forget it. God offers a full and free salvation to this lost world today. He says to men and women, "Take it or leave it." That is where our freedom comes in. We can either choose Him or reject Him. There is no middle ground. Each person has the freedom to do one or the other.

GOSPEL RECEIVED IN MUCH ASSURANCE AND MUCH AFFLICTION

Now here is another tremendous verse for us to study—

For our gospel came not unto you in word only, but also in power, and in the Holy Ghost, and in much assurance; as ye know what manner of men we were among you for your sake [1 Thess. 1:5].

Paul is saying, "You knew that when we came among you, we were just human beings—just weak human beings with lips and tongues of clay. All we could do was say words, but we gave out the Word of God. And the Word of God came to you, not in word only, but in power and in the Holy Spirit." My friend, this fact makes my job the most wonderful job in the world. I love it. I love to teach the Word of God. Do you know why? Because when I give out the Word of God—although they are just words as far as Vernon McGee is concerned—when the Spirit of God takes those words and uses them, they are *powerful*! I suppose I have about five hundred letters on my desk right now that bear this out. For example, a wife has written that the first time she turned on my radio program, her husband spent thirty minutes cussing this preacher. But she continued to tune in the program, and one day he argued back at me. Then one day she forgot to dial in the program and he reminded her of it, and he listened. Finally the day came when he knelt by the radio and received Christ as his Savior! My friend, if you think that happened because I am a super-duper salesman, you are wrong. I'm not even a salesman—I couldn't even *give away* five-dollar bills, because folk would think they were phony! But the thing that is so tremendous is that the Spirit of God will use the Word of God. That is our confidence.

Now hear me carefully: I believe that the Bible is the inerrant Word of God. And please don't write to me and explain to me all the introductions and all the problems about text. I've been through seminary, and I have even taught introductory courses so that I do know a little about them. But I accept the Word of God as the inerrant Word of God, that it is God speaking to us. And I go further than that. I believe that the Spirit of God can cause the Word of God to penetrate into your heart and life and my heart and life so that we are transformed people. People are not born again by the weakness of the human flesh, not by saying a few words by radio or by the printed page. But they are ". . . born again, not of corruptible seed, but of incorruptible, by the word of God, which liveth and abideth for ever" (1 Pet. 1:23). I believe the Spirit of God can take the Word of God and make it *real* to you. I believe the Word of God is that kind of thing. I don't think the Spirit of God could do much with the telephone directory or the Sears and Roebuck catalog or with popular magazines that are published today. But I do believe that the Spirit of God can and will take the Word of God and perform the greatest miracle possible—changing an unbelieving, lost sinner into a child of God!

The Word of God went into Thessalonica, that Roman colony which was pagan and heathen and was controlled by one of the greatest political and military powers this world has known, and there it reached the hearts and lives of people and transformed them. That is what happened in Thessalonica, and it can still do the same today.

Let me repeat verse 5 because it is such an important verse: "For our gospel came not unto you in word only, but also in power, and in the Holy Ghost, and in much assurance; as ye know what manner of men we were among you for your sake."

The first thing necessary is for a person to *hear* the Word of God. That is the factual basis. People must hear the gospel. "So then faith cometh by hearing, and hearing by the word of God" (Rom. 10:17). That is the natural part of the process. But that doesn't end it, because the Word of God is a supernatural book. Without the Holy Spirit the gospel is merely words. With the Holy Spirit it is the power of God unto salvation to everyone that believes. This is exactly what the Lord Jesus said the Holy Spirit would do: "Nevertheless I tell you the truth; It is expedient for you that I go away: for if I go not away, the Comforter will not come unto you; but if I depart, I will send him unto you. And when he is come, he will reprove the world of sin, and of righteousness, and of judgment: Of sin, because they believe not on me; Of righteousness, because I go to my Father, and ye see me no more; Of judgment, because the prince of this world is judged" (John 16:7–11).

And ye became followers of us, and of the Lord, having received the word in much affliction, with joy of the Holy Ghost [1 Thess. 1:6].

Paul could cite Silas and Timothy and himself as examples. Personally, I would hesitate to give myself as an example; I don't think I am a very good one. But Paul the apostle, going from place to place throughout the Roman Empire, offered himself as an example to these believers.

"Having received the word in much affliction, with joy of the Holy Ghost." *Affliction* (or suffering) and *joy* are two words that are actually antipodes apart—they are as far apart as the east is from the west. They don't belong together. They are as extreme as night is from daylight, as cold is from heat. They are not things that we would associate together. If a person is suffering and in affliction, he cannot have any joy, according to our natural way of looking at it. And if he's having joy in his life, then surely he isn't suffering!

Yet there have been wonderful saints of God who have endured affliction and at the same time have had the joy of the Lord in their hearts. That is real triumph. We hear a lot about healing today, and I thank God that He has healed me. How wonderful it is! But I know some saints of God who are a lot more wonderful than I ever hope to be. These people are lying right now on beds of pain, beds of affliction, and they have the joy of the Lord in their hearts.

There is not a person today who is enjoying the world's entertainment and is suffering at the same time. The world cannot put these two together. Paul says that the Word was received "in much affliction"—there was suffering, persecution, and heartache. But there was the joy of the Holy Spirit also. That is the bittersweet of life; that is like the Chinese dish they call "sweet-and-sour." For the Christian there can be that which is sour and bitter in life, while at the same time there is sweetness in the heart and life.

A woman who was a rather famous poetess here in Southern California was a member of my church. I had the privilege of baptizing her. We baptized her in a bathtub because we couldn't take her anywhere else. The minute I touched her she screamed, because she was in pain all the time. She gave me a copy of one of her last books of poetry. It was titled, *Heart Held High.* In the midst of extreme human suffering she had the joy of the Lord in her life. I always left her with the distinct feeling that I was the one who had been ministered to. I never felt that I did much ministering to her. It is wonderful to see a Christian who is suffering like that and can still rejoice in the Lord.

So that ye were ensamples to all that believe in Macedonia and Achaia [1 Thess. 1:7].

"In Macedonia and Achaia"—this refers to the European section of the Greco-Macedonia empire of Alexander the Great. The church at Thessalonica, a Roman colony, was an example—after just a few months—to all the other churches. What a glorious, wonderful testimony they had.

Today we often hear of individual Christians who are examples to others. However, there are actually very few churches which are known far and near as being examples of the Christian faith. I think it is strange that we do not have more local churches which are examples to all believers. It has been my privilege to travel around the country and speak in many churches across America. There are a few, but only a few, that I would name as examples.

GOSPEL RESULTS

For from you sounded out the word of the Lord not only in Macedonia and Achaia, but also in every place your faith to God-ward is spread abroad; so that we need not to speak any thing [1 Thess. 1:8].

Paul found that wherever he traveled the reputation of this church had already gone ahead of him. The believers were already talking about the church in Thessalonica; so it wasn't necessary for Paul to tell them anything about it. This reveals something of the great reputation this church had in that day.

For they themselves shew of us what manner of entering in we had unto you, and how ye turned to God from idols to serve the living and true God;

And to wait for his Son from heaven, whom he raised from the dead, even Jesus, which delivered us from the wrath to come [1 Thess. 1:9–10].

We have already looked at these two verses in connection with verse 3. Their response gave witness to the kind of "entering in" Paul and Silas and Timothy had had with them. Paul tells what that response was: (1) Your work of faith—how ye turned to God from idols; (2) your labor of love—to serve the living and true God; and (3) your patience of hope—to wait for His Son from heaven.

Now I would like to look at these verses from a little different point of view. When Paul arrived in Thessalonica, he did not announce that he would give a series of messages denouncing idolatry or telling about the errors that were involved in the worship of Apollo, Venus, or any of the other gods and goddesses of the Roman Empire. But when Paul arrived in Thessalonica, he preached Christ. When he preached Christ, they turned to God from idols. Notice that he doesn't say they turned

from idols to God. Someone will say, "You're splitting hairs." I surely am. These are hairs that need to be split. We need to do some straight thinking about this.

"How ye turned to God from idols." We hear today that repentance is essential to salvation. Repentance and believing are presented as two steps in a process. Actually, they are both wrapped up in the same package, and you have them both right here. When Paul preached Christ, they turned *to* God *from* idols. I want you to see something that is very important. When they turned *to* God, that is the work of faith; that is what faith did. The Lord Jesus said, ". . . This is the work of God, that ye *believe* on him whom he hath sent" (John 6:29, italics mine). These people turned to God from idols; they turned *from* idols, too. That's right—and that is repentance. The repentance followed the turning to God. It didn't precede it. When they turned to God, they automatically turned from idols.

Take your hand and hold it so the palm of your hand is facing toward you. Now turn your hand around. When you turned your hand around, the back side of your hand now faces you, and the palm of your hand automatically turned away from you. Just so, you cannot turn to Christ Jesus without turning from something, my friend. That turning from something is repentance.

We need to hold up Jesus Christ as the Savior from sin. A man needs to know that he is a lost sinner. He can sit and weep about his sins until Judgment Day, and it won't do him one bit of good. I know an alcoholic man who died an alcoholic. He could sit in my study and cry about the fact that he was an alcoholic and how terrible he was to be a drunkard. He could shed great tears and repent, but nothing changed because he never did turn to Christ!

My dad used to tell about a little boat that went up and down the Mississippi River. It had a little bitty boiler and a great big whistle. When that boat was carrying a load and was going upstream, it was in trouble when the whistle would blow, because the boat would begin to drift downstream. There are a lot of people who have a little boiler and a great big whistle. They can repent and shed tears all over the place, but that doesn't do any good. It is only when a person turns to Christ that he will turn from something. He will turn from his sin. If a man doesn't turn from his sin, it is because he hasn't turned to Christ.

I am sure that when the Thessalonian believers turned from their idols, they wept over the time they had wasted in idol worship.

After they had turned to God, there was a real repentance over the misspent years. The turning to God came first, then they realized that turning to God meant turning from idols.

Now I want to point out that Jesus Christ the Savior of the world is to be preached to a world of lost sinners, but the message of repentance is preached to the church. Read the messages to the seven churches of Asia as recorded in Revelation, chapters 2 and 3. The message of the Lord Jesus to the churches is to repent. Today it seems that the church is telling everyone outside the church to repent. The Bible teaches that it is the people *in* the church who need to repent. We need to get down on our faces before God and repent. That is not the message for us to give to the unsaved man down the street. He needs to know that he has a Savior.

"To serve the living and true God." The Thessalonians were now serving God; it was the labor of love. You cannot serve Christ unless you love Him. The Lord Jesus said, "If ye love me, keep my commandments" (John 14:15). Suppose you don't love Him? Then there are none of His commandments for you. You think you want to go out to preach the gospel, but you don't love Him? Then stay home. To go into all the world and preach the gospel to every creature is a command, and it is for those who love Him. If you don't love Him, don't do it.

When the Lord Jesus talked to Simon Peter (as recorded in John 21), He didn't ask, "Peter, why in the world did you deny Me?" He didn't say, "Peter, do you promise Me you will do better if I let you preach the sermon on the Day of Pentecost?" He never said anything like that. He asked, "Peter, do you love Me?" If Peter had said, "No," I think the Lord would have told him to forget about service. Does that sound harsh to you? I didn't say it; Jesus did: "If ye love me, keep my commandments."

"And to wait for his Son from heaven." That doesn't mean to wait sitting down. It means you are busy. If you love Him, you will serve Him. You are busy for Him while you wait for Him.

When I first went to Cleburne, Texas, all the downtown churches had outdoor evening services on the lawn of the First Baptist Church. Since I was the new preacher in town, I was asked to preach the first night I was there. An officer of one of the churches had heard that I was a fundamentalist and a premillennialist. The next day he said to me, "I heard your sermon last night. You didn't sound to me like one of those fellows who has his nose pressed against the window waiting for the Lord to come." I told him that people who are waiting for the Lord to come don't have their noses against the window. They are out, busy, working for the Lord. This was during the depression, but I told him that while his and other denominations were calling their missionaries back from the field, the China Inland Mission, which was fundamental and premillennial, was asking for one hundred more missionaries to go to China. Who was really waiting for the Lord to come?

"To wait for his Son from heaven" does not mean to sit down. It means to be busy for the Lord. That is the patience of hope. It means to keep on serving the Lord, giving out the Word of God while you wait. The coming of Christ to take His church out of the world is not an escape mechanism. Rather, it is an incentive to serve Him and to give out the Word of God. ". . . Even so, come, Lord Jesus" (Rev. 22:20).

CHAPTER 2

THEME: The coming of Christ is a working hope

The coming of Christ for His church is called the rapture of the church. It is not a doctrine to argue about; it is a doctrine to *live*. Unfortunately, there are many who believe Christ is coming after the Great Tribulation. There are those who believe He is coming before, and some believe He is coming during that period of time. Then there are others who don't believe that He is coming at all, and yet they say that they trust Him as their Savior. For all the groups there is one important question: How does your interpretation affect your life? Does it do anything for you? If your view has no effect on your life, then you should reconsider what you believe. The expectation of the return of the Lord should be a motivating factor in the life of the believer.

MOTIVE AND METHOD
OF A TRUE WITNESS FOR CHRIST

For yourselves, brethren, know our entrance in unto you, that it was not in vain [1 Thess. 2:1].

"In vain" means empty, without results. Paul says, "When we came to you, it was not just some theoretical proposition that we presented to you. We didn't come to declare to you something that was new and novel and which had no effect on you at all. We didn't just entertain you for a few days and then leave you." Paul's work was not in vain; it was not empty. When he came to Thessalonica, it rocked a great many folk, bringing many to a saving knowledge of Christ. And it brought a church into existence. Paul was not simply talking about a theory or a philosophy, but about something that *worked* in Thessalonica. The gospel walked down the streets of that city, and it got into the hearts and homes and lives of men and women.

But even after that we had suffered before, and were shamefully entreated, as ye know, at Philippi, we were bold in our God to speak unto you the gospel of God with much contention [1 Thess. 2:2].

The Greek word for "contention" is *agoni*, which means "conflict" or "agony." There was a great deal of conflict and much inward agony when Paul came to them.

Paul says that he had been shamefully treated in Philippi. We know about that from the account in Acts 16. But when he came to Thessalonica, he came in boldness. In other words, he didn't slow down because of his previous experience. He didn't play down the gospel. After his terrifying experience, Paul didn't say, "Now I'm going to change my approach. I'm going to be more tactful and less outspoken about the gospel." No, Paul was not a secret believer. He spoke right out, just as he had done at Philippi.

You see, it would have been so easy for Paul to rationalize. He could have decided that he had better be more careful to win friends and influence people. Excessive tact and the soft sell were not Paul's method. He boldly declared the gospel, and his experiences did not affect his approach.

Now when he entered in among them, he presented the Word of God. If you were asked to choose, what would you select as the greatest sermon of the apostle Paul? If we took a poll, I'm sure we would get many different answers. Rightly so. There was the great sermon at Damascus after his conversion. There was the sermon before Sergius Paulus on the island of Cyprus when he began his missionary work. Then there was a sermon in the synagogue at Antioch of Pisidia on his first missionary journey—I consider that one of the greatest of his sermons. Then there were sermons in Athens on Mars Hill, in Ephesus at the school of Tyrannus, and his defense in Corinth. I think all of these are great. Someone might choose the message he gave in Jerusalem when he was arrested, or when he was brought before Felix and Festus and Agrippa. The one given before Agrippa is a masterpiece. Then there is his farewell speech on the beach to the elders of Ephesus. In every message he always presented Christ, His death and His resurrection.

If I were to pick the greatest sermon of Paul, I would actually pick none of these. I would choose instead *his life* in Thessalonica. His greatest sermon was not in writing or speaking, but in walking. It was not in exposition, but in experience; not in his profession, but in his practice. He took his text from James 2:26, ". . . faith without works is dead. . . ." and he made his points on the pavement of the streets of Thessalonica.

Every believer is a preacher. Maybe you don't like me to call you a preacher, but you are one nonetheless. You can't escape it—you are saying something to somebody by the life you live. Perhaps your life is speaking to the child in your home. I think that is one of the reasons we have so many of our young people out on the highways and byways, the streets and alleys of this world. They watched mom and dad at home, and they didn't like what they saw; so they took to the highways. The greatest sermon you will ever preach is by the life that you live.

Paul is going to tell us about the sermon he preached at Thessalonica (vv. 3–6), and he then will describe the relationship he had with the Thessalonians. He was like a *mother* to them in that he comforted them (see v. 7); he was like a *father* to them in that he charged them (v. 11); and he was like a *brother* to the Thessalonians in that he challenged them (v. 14).

For our exhortation was not of deceit, nor of uncleanness, nor in guile [1 Thess. 2:3].

Deceit means "error." The content of Paul's exhortation was not adulterated. Paul did not water down the gospel. He never changed it to suit different groups.

One of the things that disturbs me about some ministers is that they give a good, clear-cut gospel message in one place, but then they show up in another place where they need to be equally clear in giving out the gospel, and they are fuzzy! This was not true of the apostle Paul—his "exhortation was not of deceit."

Uncleanness means "sensuality." Paul was not motivated by greed. He didn't come to Thessalonica for the offering he would get or for the notoriety he would gain. He wasn't seeking to be ministered to personally, but he came with pure motives. There was no uncleanness in that sense.

"Nor in guile"—he did not use wrong methods with them. He did not lower his standards to accommodate the prejudices and passions of the old nature. He did not use an appeal to the sinful flesh.

Many of us can learn a lesson from the apostle Paul at this point. I once knew a minister who had been a great preacher. But I lost much respect for this man because he went back to a church which he had formerly pastored, knowing that there was criticism of the present pastor. He played upon that criticism and encouraged it. Paul would never have done a thing like that. He didn't bring the gospel to people in any form of guile at all.

Everyone who teaches the Word of God needs to ask himself whether he is doing it with any deceit or uncleanness or guile. We need to be honest with ourselves; we need to check our own motives. Do we teach in order to win friends and influence people? Or are we honestly trying to give out the Word of God? My friend, I must confess that I have made many mistakes. I have failed the Lord so many times that it is amazing that He doesn't throw me overboard. If I were God, I would have been disgusted with Vernon McGee long ago. But I promised the Lord when I entered the ministry that I wouldn't pull any punches. Honestly, I expected to get into real trouble, but the Lord has been good to me. I think He knew that I would start running if there were an occasion for it. I am grateful that I can look up to the Lord right now and say, "Lord, I've made a lot of mistakes and I have failed You, but I have given out Your Word the best I know how. If I could give it better, I would, but I'm doing the best that I possibly can by Your grace."

I love this passage. Paul could tell the Thessalonians, "When I came to you, I want you to know that I had no ulterior motives. I didn't come for your offering. I didn't come in order to shear your sheep. I came to give you the gospel and then to build you up in the faith. That was my motive." With that kind of motive a person is really sailing on a marvelous sea. There may be storms, but the Lord will bring His servant through.

But as we were allowed of God to be put in trust with the gospel, even so we speak; not as pleasing men, but God, which trieth our hearts [1 Thess. 2:4].

The word *allowed* means "to be tested or approved." Paul was saying that he was no novice. He was not a manpleaser, nor had he ever sought popularity. He wasn't trying to make a name for himself. When Paul preached, he was not preaching to find out what men would think of him, but what God would think of him. Paul used the blue litmus paper of God to put down in his life, and it stood the test. He never used any low or tricky methods.

For neither at any time used we flattering words, as ye know, nor a cloak of covetousness; God is witness [1 Thess. 2:5].

Paul is speaking pretty frankly. He says that he never came into their midst to flatter anyone. He never played up to the rich people in the congregation. He didn't try to butter up anyone.

Flattery disarms us—we really never know

what to say. When people criticize me, I know what to say, but I never know what to say when someone flatters me. It disarms a person. In *Twelfth-Night* Shakespeare has his clown say, "Marry, sir, they praise me and make an ass of me; now my foes tell me plainly I am an ass: so that by my foes, sir, I profit in the knowledge of myself, and by my friends I am abused." Our friends are probably more dangerous at times than our enemies!

Paul never used flattery. There is a group of wealthy laymen across this country who are literally owned by the people who flatter them. If a Christian work or program doesn't butter them up, they are not the least bit interested in helping that program financially. God pity the church or the work that must depend on men who require flattery and compliments before they will give their support to the work. I think this is one of the curses in the Christian church today.

Paul did not use a "cloak of covetousness." I really don't think that money is the sin of the ministry. I have never felt that money was a great temptation for the men whom I know in the ministry. But the cloak of covetousness is a cloak of many colors. There are men who covet honor and fame and position. We need to search our hearts in order to uncover any covetousness there.

Many colleges have attempted to buy men by giving them honorary doctoral degrees. They have been given out by the score. The college then hopes for a donation or some other type of support. That is one reason it would be well if all doctoral degrees had to be earned.

Nor of men sought we glory, neither of you, nor yet of others, when we might have been burdensome, as the apostles of Christ [1 Thess. 2:6].

Paul never sought position or honors. He never received any honorary degrees. He had pure motives.

THE MOTHER SIDE OF THE APOSTLE'S MINISTRY (COMFORT)

But we were gentle among you, even as a nurse cherisheth her children [1 Thess. 2:7].

The word *nurse* here means "a nursing mother," like a mother bird. This is Paul's positive expression of his relationship to the Thessalonians: "I've been a nursing mother, a mother bird to you." Oh, the gentleness of Paul! He was as tender as a woman in his dealings with the church at Thessalonica.

The Lord Jesus said of Jerusalem: "O Jerusalem, Jerusalem, thou that killest the prophets, and stonest them which are sent unto thee, how often would I have gathered thy children together, even as a hen gathereth her chickens under her wings, and ye would not!" (Matt. 23:37). Jesus identifies Himself in many ways in Scripture. He calls Himself the Good Shepherd who gave His life for the sheep. He protects His sheep, and someday He is going to gather them all into a fold where they will be safe with Him. Then He also uses this idea of the mother hen with her little chicks.

I was raised in the country, and I remember that in the spring of the year we would put an old setting hen on some eggs. Soon she had a little flock of chicks. She would go all around the yard clucking. We didn't have a special chicken yard because we lived on a great big place by a cotton gin, and these chickens would roam over an area about a quarter mile square. When the rain would come, the mother hen would cluck, cluck, cluck, calling her chicks to the hen house. Sometimes they wouldn't quite make it; so the mother hen would get all those little chicks under her, and she would cover them with her feathers. The rain would be running down off her, but all the little ones were safe under her wings. How many times the Lord Jesus says to us, "Just come in under My wings."

Paul was that kind of minister. He loved the Thessalonians with a mother's love. They were dear to him. There are still ministers like that today. Maybe they aren't all great expositors, but they believe the Word of God and preach it. Such godly and experienced pastors are able to counsel people who are in need of help. You don't need to be afraid to sit down and open your heart to such a man and let him help you.

So being affectionately desirous of you, we were willing to have imparted unto you, not the gospel of God only, but also our own souls, because ye were dear unto us [1 Thess. 2:8].

Dear is "beloved." Paul had a genuine love for the Thessalonian believers, and he was willing literally to give his life for them.

For ye remember, brethren, our labour and travail: for labouring night and day, because we would not be chargeable unto any of you, we preached unto you the gospel of God [1 Thess. 2:9].

"Travail . . . labouring night and day"—that's a mother's work. We are familiar with the expression: "Man's work is from sun to sun, but a woman's work [or a mother's work] is never done." A mother is not a paid nurse. Paul is saying that he wasn't a paid nurse who worked by the hour. He wasn't a hired baby-sitter. He did not belong to a union.

Have you ever heard of a mothers' union which insisted a mother would work only for eight hours of the day? Have you known any mothers who punch the clock and then turn away from their crying babies because they refuse to work anymore? Maybe some mothers will work out some kind of union agreement like that, but I don't think *real* mothers would want it. Mothers work a little differently—night and day.

In New England there were two girls who worked together in the cotton mills. One of them quit working, and they didn't see each other for several years. They met on the street one day, and the girl from the mill said, "What are you doing now? Are you still working?" The other one replied, "No, I'm not working—I'm married. I not only have a husband, but I also have a little boy. I get up at three in the morning to feed the baby. Then I get up early to fix breakfast and make a lunch for my husband. I take care of the baby through the day, and then I prepare dinner for my husband." The first girl exclaimed, "I remember when you worked at the mill how you used to watch the clock. When that five o'clock whistle blew, you were out of there!" The young mother explained: "I don't watch the clock anymore. I'm working longer hours, but it isn't really work." This girl was motivated by love, and it didn't seem like work anymore.

That is what Paul is saying here. He loved these people. He labored over them night and day because he loved them.

A member of my church once asked me to go visit someone. He said, "You're *paid* to do that." Do you know what I told him? I said, "*You* go to see him—because you are not paid to do it, and you will probably do a better job than I could do. We are not to do the Lord's work on the basis of *pay!*" I'm afraid that put him in an awkward position. He had to make that call, and I can assure you, he never asked that of me again. We are to care for one another with the tender care of a mother. That was what Paul did.

THE FATHER SIDE OF THE APOSTLE'S MINISTRY (CHARGE)

Ye are witnesses, and God also, how holily and justly and unblameably we behaved ourselves among you that believe [1 Thess. 2:10].

"Ye are witnesses"—Paul is speaking of something which they know to be true. Notice the way Paul conducted himself among them.

"Holily"—he carefully discharged his duty to God. That is what holy living is. "Justly"—he also carefully discharged his duty to man. Paul had a duty to God and a duty to man; he discharged both of them.

I hear so many people talk about being "dedicated Christians." If you hope to be a dedicated Christian, you must live a holy life before God. Watch God, and don't watch the clock. Don't work only when the boss is around. You should work all the time, because God is always around. Going down front in a church service, shedding a few tears, and having someone pray over you will not produce a dedicated life. What does your *boss* think of you? Or if you are a student, what does your teacher think of you? If you are lazy, then you are not dedicated. A dedicated life is a holy life, lived always in the presence of God.

"Unblameably." This means that no charge could be maintained against the apostle and his companions. This doesn't mean that his enemies didn't accuse him—because they did—but the charges didn't stick.

People will say ugly things about you, but the important thing is to make sure the criticisms are not true. Paul and his companions maintained a holy life. A holy life does count. It has nothing to do with obtaining your salvation, but it has everything to do with the salvation of folk around you, because they are watching you.

As ye know how we exhorted and comforted and charged every one of you, as a father doth his children [1 Thess. 2:11].

"Exhorted." The Greek word is *parakaleo*, which means that Paul came to the side of them to help, to entreat, and to convict them. It is the same word which is used for the Holy Spirit. You remember that the Lord Jesus said He would send the Holy Spirit who would convict the world of sin, of righteousness, and of judgment (see John 16:7–11).

I have always felt that the gospel is not presented in the power of the Holy Spirit unless it is presented as something that the Holy Spirit can use to convict a man. That means that He convinces a man of sin, of righteousness, and of judgment. Those three elements are always in the gospel message.

Comforted is not used here in the sense we use the word today. We saw that meaning on the mother side of the apostle's ministry. Rather, the word here means "to persuade." There was an urgency in Paul's message to the Thessalonians. He often said, "I beseech you"—I *beg* you. That is the way the gospel should be presented even today.

Paul "charged" them. This has a note of severity in it—it involves discipline. It is a virile word, a robust, firm, masculine word. I'm afraid that we find a lot of sissy preaching in our pulpits today. The popular thing is to have a little sermonette given by a preacherette to Christianettes. There is so little urgency. Someone has defined the average church service in a liberal church as when a mild-mannered man gets up before a group of mild-mannered people and urges them to be more mild-mannered. Oh, that is sickening, my friend!

My wife says that I indulge my flesh at Eastertime because I just have to laugh when I look through the paper and see what the liberal preachers are going to preach for the Resurrection. They have a problem with that. And I enjoy their discomfort! One preacher's subject was given as "Easter Is a Time of Flowers." Oh boy, don't you imagine that was a virile, robust sermon? No wonder there are so many sick saints when they are being fed such watered down soup. A great Methodist evangelist in the South once said, "Some sermons don't have enough gospel in them to make soup for a sick grasshopper." In contrast, what a glorious thing the ministry of the apostle Paul was!

That ye would walk worthy of God, who hath called you unto his kingdom and glory [1 Thess. 2:12].

"Walk worthy." This is what Paul also wrote to the Ephesians: "I therefore, the prisoner of the Lord, beseech you that ye walk worthy of the vocation wherewith ye are called" (Eph. 4:1).

God has called the saints unto "his kingdom," which refers to the millennial kingdom, and unto "glory," which refers to the eternal kingdom. In other words, get a perspective of God's great plan and purpose. Live in the light of eternity.

For this cause also thank we God without ceasing, because, when ye received the word of God which ye heard of us, ye received it not as the word of men, but as it is in truth, the word of God, which effectually worketh also in you that believe [1 Thess. 2:13].

Now here is the other side of the giving of the gospel. Paul has already said, "For our gospel came not unto you in word only, but also in power, and in the Holy Ghost . . ." (1 Thess. 1:5). That is the way the gospel should be *given out*. But I hear a great many people criticize preachers, and I want to say this: If a man is presenting the gospel and it is going out in power, it should also be *received* as the Word of God.

How do you receive the Word of God? Do you receive it as the Word of *God*? Or do you get angry? Does the hair stand up on the back of your neck? Twice in all my years of ministry I was approached by a man after a sermon and asked if I had him in mind when I preached the sermon that morning. My friend, I didn't even know those men were there! They were giving themselves an added sense of importance that wasn't justified. But the real issue is that they weren't receiving the Word of God as the Word of *God*.

The Word should go out as the Word of God, and it should be received as the Word of God. And, my friend, if you will receive it that way, then it will be able to work in you, and there's blessing there for you. Otherwise, you are wasting your time in church.

We have seen how Paul has been giving out the Word of God. It irritated some people because God's Word is salt, and salt stings when it gets into a fresh wound of sin in the life of an individual. The Word of God is also a light, but there are a lot of people who love darkness because their deeds are evil.

Paul is teaching in this chapter that the church of God should mirror the family of God down here on earth. He talks about a mother relationship to believers, a father relationship, and now a brother relationship. Sometimes people say, "Our church is a family church." What they mean is that there is a nursery for the little baby, a junior church for all the little children of junior age, a teenage group, a couples' group for dad and mom, and finally a senior citizens' group for grandma and grandpa. That is what folk call a "family church." I am not sure Paul would ever have divided up the church like that, and this is not what we mean when we say the church should mirror the family of God.

The church should be a *revelation* of *God* to the community just as a family should be. The relationships of husband, wife, and child in the home should reveal the threefold aspect of the love of God and Christ for the world. Paul has already spoken of the *mother* side of the local church. He was willing to work day and night to nurture them as a little bird is nurtured by its mother. He didn't work an eight-hour day, but he was on the job for them all the time.

Then Paul says he was like a *father* to that church. A child in a home needs to experience both mother-love and father-love. It is a tragedy for children in our day when the parents are separated or divorced. The child very often fails to receive the love of the father. That father-love is expressed in discipline. Paul says he was like a father to the Thessalonian church.

There are some very fine Bible teachers who never preach anything but comfort. They are always comforting the saints. People love it, because everyone likes to be comforted. I like to have my back rubbed and my head also. That is physically comforting, and it is a joy. But we are not to have comfort alone; we also need discipline. I'm afraid that the father-side, the discipline-side, is woefully lacking, not only in our homes and in the state, but also in the church.

THE BROTHER SIDE
OF THE APOSTLE'S MINISTRY
(CHALLENGE)

Now the *brother*-side of the ministry within the church is represented by the child in the family.

For ye, brethren, became followers of the churches of God which in Judaea are in Christ Jesus: for ye also have suffered like things of your own countrymen, even as they have of the Jews [1 Thess. 2:14].

"Brethren"—that is, brothers. What is it that makes men brothers? There are two things that make brothers. Regardless of race or color, it is true that we have all sinned and come short of the glory of God. No one escapes that category. This is the brotherhood of sinners. Since it is a brotherhood of sinners, it is not a loving brotherhood. You had better watch your brother; you can't always trust him.

Now what is it that Paul says drew the Thessalonians together as brothers? "For ye also have suffered like things of your own countrymen." The Thessalonian church was largely a gentile church, and they were already experiencing persecution, although this was not yet the time of the great persecutions under the emperors. They were suffering in Thessalonica. Paul could say to them, "Before

you began suffering, the brethren over in Jerusalem were already suffering at the hands of *their* racial brothers. This suffering draws you together and holds you together." They were brothers in suffering; suffering is a cement that holds believers together.

The church is coming "unglued" in some areas of the world, and the reason for this is the same thing that was said of Israel in Deuteronomy 32:15: "Jeshurun waxed fat, and kicked." That is, they entered a period of affluence, and they became critical. The church in America lives in affluence. But, frankly, I think that persecution may be just around the corner.

There are many in the church who are praying for revival. I know of a number of prayer groups which meet regularly to pray for revival. I have never heard of them praying that they might all suffer or be persecuted in order to bring in revival. I do not think that revival will come to this country under the present state of conditions. Right now there is a renewed interest in the Word of God, and some call it revival. However, I don't call this revival. I believe that if revival came to the church, we would all know it. No one would need to ask, "Do you think this is revival?"

But I do believe that if suffering came to the church, it would draw believers together. We would cut out all this nonsense of picking at the other fellow. We would recognize that every child of God is our brother. There may be some disagreement on various points, but every believer in the Lord Jesus Christ is my brother. We are in the family of God, and we should mirror this before the world. When the church *really* mirrors this before the world, then revival will come.

We try to make a detour and a shortcut to revival by praying for it. Why don't we pray for the *conditions* that produce revival? It was man's *extremity* that brought revival at times in the past. The great Wesleyan movement came out of the dark days in England when they were on the verge of a revolution. It seems it takes such conditions for revival to occur. Maybe we are not far from that in our country today.

Who both killed the Lord Jesus, and their own prophets, and have persecuted us; and they please not God, and are contrary to all men:

Forbidding us to speak to the Gentiles that they might be saved, to fill up their sins alway: for the wrath is come upon

them to the uttermost [1 Thess. 2:15–16].

This I consider to be a remarkable passage of Scripture. It reveals a great principle: God permits sin to run its full course. The figure of speech which the prophets used was that the cup of iniquity must be filled up. God is permitting the cup to be filled. God won't check it so that Satan will never be able to say, "See, I never was given a chance because God wouldn't permit me to go all the way." I think the time of the Great Tribulation is the time when God will allow Satan full rein.

REWARD OF A TRUE WITNESS FOR CHRIST

But we, brethren, being taken from you for a short time in presence, not in heart, endeavoured the more abundantly to see your face with great desire [1 Thess. 2:17].

"**B**rethren"—again, this is the real brotherhood. This is the real ecumenical movement. When a person is in Christ Jesus, he is a brother to all others who are in Christ. Outside of Christ there is only the brotherhood of sinners.

"Being taken from you for a short time in presence, not in heart." Isn't this lovely of the apostle Paul? He was actually run out of Thessalonica, but his heart was still there. He hated to leave these Christians and wanted to be able to see them again. By the way, he did.

Wherefore we would have come unto you, even I Paul, once and again; but Satan hindered us [1 Thess. 2:18].

Paul had spiritual discernment to see that it was Satan's strategy that kept him from going to Thessalonica. The word *Satan* actually means "adversary."

I believe that today Satan seeks to hinder any program of getting out the Word of God. We have seen several instances of this. Many times my Bible teaching program has been on a radio station by which we were reaching an entire area, and things were going so nicely. Then a godless man would buy the station, and he would take all religious programs off the air. That is the work of the enemy, the adversary. He doesn't want the Word of God to be given out.

For what is our hope, or joy, or crown of rejoicing? Are not even ye in the presence of our Lord Jesus Christ at his coming?

For ye are our glory and joy [1 Thess. 2:19–20].

Paul says that one of the great things he anticipates when Christ comes to take His church will be the opportunity to see these people whom he has led to the Lord. The Thessalonian believers whom he had won to Christ were a joy for him here and would be hereafter.

By the way, is anyone going to be in heaven who will come up to you and thank you for having a part in giving out the Word of God? Have you given your support to missions? If you have, someone you have never known, someone from the other side of the earth, may come up to you and thank you for your support of missions. He will thank you for being interested in getting out the Word of God because the Word reached him and enabled him to be saved. That, my friend, is going to be part of the reward that we will get in heaven. We need to recognize that. It is a wonderful hope to look forward to the time when Christ Jesus takes the church out of this world. It is even more joyous to know that someone who trusted Christ because of your witness will go along with you to meet the Lord!

CHAPTER 3

THEME: The coming of Christ is a purifying hope

The great theme of 1 Thessalonians is the rapture of the church. The great theme of 2 Thessalonians is the revelation of Christ; that is, His coming to the earth to establish His kingdom. The thing that impresses me is the practicality of these doctrines which Paul taught to the Thessalonians. Today the schools of eschatology, or prophecy, have gotten this teaching way out into left field where it becomes sort of an extraneous thing. It becomes something that is nice to talk about and even to argue about, but it is not too meaningful to life. They do not teach it as something that must be geared into life and that can walk in shoe leather down here. Paul's teaching is entirely different.

The theme of this chapter is that the coming of Christ is a purifying hope. It will change your life, affect your life-style, if you hold to the hope of the rapture of the church; that is, the imminent coming of Christ for His own. If that doesn't affect your life, you don't really believe it. It is just sort of a theory or a philosophy with you. This theme becomes the very heart of the epistle, and we will be dealing with it from chapter 3 through verse 12 of chapter 4.

TIMOTHY BRINGS A GOOD REPORT OF THE THESSALONIANS

Wherefore when we could no longer forbear, we thought it good to be left at Athens alone [1 Thess. 3:1].

Paul longs to return to the Thessalonians but remains back at Athens alone so that he could send Timothy, and perhaps Silas, Dr. Luke, and others to Thessalonica.

Wherefore—this important word ties this chapter back in with what Paul had talked about in the previous chapter: the family relationship that exists in the church. He had been a mother to the church, a father to them, and a brother. He had led them to the Lord, and he loved them. He said that they would be his glory and his joy at the coming *(parousia)* of Christ, at the appearance of the Lord Jesus when all believers will receive their rewards.

Now because Paul had a real affection for them, he was frustrated in not being able to return to them. He had been hindered by Satan. Paul had to leave Thessalonica so quickly that there were many unfinished teachings and doctrines that he had not been able to develop fully. He not only longed to return,

but he wondered about the future of the believers there. Paul desired to comfort them. In other words, he was demonstrating the thing he mentioned at the beginning of the letter—a labor of love.

Love is not affection or just a nice, comfortable, warm feeling around your heart. Love seeks the welfare of another. That is the way love is expressed for anyone. If you love someone, you seek his welfare and you actually would jeopardize your own life for the person whom you love.

And sent Timotheus, our brother, and minister of God, and our fellow-labourer in the gospel of Christ, to establish you, and to comfort you concerning your faith [1 Thess. 3:2].

Because of his concern, Paul sent Timothy back to the Thessalonians. He calls Timothy "our brother, and minister of God." The word for "minister" is the Greek *diakonos* from which we get our English word *deacon*; it literally means "servant."

"Our fellow-labourer in the gospel of Christ." The gospel of Christ is the sphere of service. Paul was not just a do-gooder. Sometimes fundamentalists are criticized because our main objective is to get out the Word of God. We make that primary. We are criticized for not emphasizing the social aspect of the gospel enough. May I say that there has never been any great social movement that was not anchored in the preaching of the gospel. The child labor laws came out of the great Wesley meetings. The labor movement today owes a great deal to John Wesley even though they have moved so far from the source that they don't recognize it. Hospitals have followed the preaching of the Word of God. If people will respond to the message of the gospel of Christ, their lives will be transformed, and then these good works will flow out of that change.

We are moving more and more into a welfare program in our country. This has become one of the most corrupt things that has ever taken place in our government. I don't think any of us can grasp the corruption that is connected with this vast program. Why does that happen? Because it is not anchored in the gospel of Christ.

The liberals who do the criticizing of us act as if they are the do-gooders. Have you ever known a do-gooder who really did something good? What *are* they doing? They actually encourage immorality and license. They haven't lifted up mankind. They are not able to release the kids from drugs. In fact, when I was in Portland, Oregon, one of the liberal churches there was using the church as a place to dispense birth control pills to the girls who wanted them!

Paul says that Timothy was a servant and that his sphere of service was the gospel of Christ. That is to be our sphere also. And when the gospel of Christ is given out, my friend, there will be a whole lot of doing good that will take place. The only criticism I've ever had of the do-gooders is that their doing good is merely temporary assistance. They are not helping folk permanently by bringing them into a right relationship with God. Only the gospel of Christ can do that.

"To *establish* you . . . concerning your faith." This same wonderful word was used back in the Book of Exodus when Moses went up to the mountain to hold up his hands in prayer to assure Israel's victory: "But Moses' hands were heavy; and they took a stone, and put it under him, and he sat thereon; and Aaron and Hur *stayed up* his hands, the one on the one side, and the other on the other side; and his hands were steady until the going down of the sun" (Exod. 17:12, italics mine). "Stayed up" is the same word as "establish." Paul sent Timothy over to them to stay them up, to hold them up, to establish them. People still need the same thing today. They need to be established in the faith.

"To comfort you concerning your faith." *Comfort* means "to encourage." He sent Timothy to hold the Thessalonians up and to encourage them in the faith.

That no man should be moved by these afflictions: for yourselves know that we are appointed thereunto [1 Thess. 3:3].

Here is a statement that is a little hard for any of us to swallow. He says that "no man should be moved," which means he should not be disturbed, "by these afflictions." *Afflictions* here means "pressures, tensions."

Then Paul makes the amazing statement that "we are appointed thereunto." We know that we are going to go through storms. They will be temporary storms, but we cannot escape them. We are going to have trouble down here. The Word of God makes that very clear. Paul wants the Thessalonians to stand for the Lord in the midst of afflictions.

There are other passages of Scripture which teach this same truth. The Lord Jesus said, "These things I have spoken unto you, that in me ye might have peace. In the world ye shall have tribulation: but be of good cheer; I have overcome the world" (John 16:33). *Tribulation* is the trouble that all of us are going to have. There is no way around it. Yet the Lord Himself tells us to be of good cheer even in the midst of trouble.

If you are a believer, you are not going to escape trouble. To accept Christ does not mean to take out an insurance policy against suffering. The fact of the matter is that you *will* have trouble after you become a child of God, even if you haven't had any trouble before. He has never promised that we would miss the storm, but we will go through all the storms of life. What He does say very definitely and dogmatically is that He will go with us through the storms and that we will reach the harbor. Any boat which He is in will not go to the bottom of the Sea of Galilee but will reach the other side. You and I are in the process of going to the other side.

Paul reinforces this: "Yea, and all that will live godly in Christ Jesus *shall suffer persecution*" (2 Tim. 3:12, italics mine). There are no "ifs," "ands," or "buts" about it (see 1 Pet. 4:12–19).

The time to be concerned is when there is no cloud in the sky, no ripple on the sea, and everything is smooth and nice. Then you might question your salvation. But if you are experiencing trouble down here, if the pressures and tensions of life are on you, then that is a sign that you are a child of God. This is the way God teaches us to rely on Him.

For verily, when we were with you, we told you before that we should suffer tribulation; even as it came to pass, and ye know [1 Thess. 3:4].

I remember hearing about a black congregation in Memphis, Tennessee, where the pastor asked for some favorite verses of Scripture. One man got up and said his favorite verse was, "And it came to pass." He sat down, and everyone looked puzzled. The pastor asked him how in the world that could be his favorite passage. He answered, "When I get in trouble, I turn to where it says, 'It came to pass,' and I know my troubles came to *pass*. They didn't come to stay." God will bring us through the storms. We will finally be rid of all our troubles. How wonderful that is. Our brother may have misapplied the verse, but his theology was absolutely accurate and agrees with what Paul is saying here.

Tribulation is the same word as *affliction*. This does not refer to the Great Tribulation. It refers to the "little tribulations." We are all going to have a little trouble down here. Such troubles are for the purpose of bringing us closer to God. They promote sanctification in the life of the believer.

For this cause, when I could no longer forbear, I sent to know your faith, lest by some means the tempter have tempted you, and our labour be in vain [1 Thess. 3:5].

"The tempter" is none other than Satan. In chapter 2 Paul said, "Satan hindered us." In other words, Paul is saying to the Thessalonians, "Satan is giving me a bad time, and I fear he may be giving you a bad time also."

Another purpose of afflictions is to test the genuineness of our belief. *Trouble* is the acid that tests the genuineness of the coin of belief. There are true believers and there are a lot of counterfeit ones. One thing that will really reveal the genuineness of faith is the ability to endure trouble through faith in God. Afflictions reveal the genuine believer, and this is the occasion of Paul's rejoicing.

But now when Timotheus came from you unto us, and brought us good tidings of your faith and charity, and that ye have good remembrance of us always, desiring greatly to see us, as we also to see you [1 Thess. 3:6].

It was wonderful when Paul got word from them, and that word was a good report. They were enduring their afflictions.

Therefore, brethren, we were comforted over you in all our affliction and distress by your faith [1 Thess. 3:7].

"In all our affliction"—Paul tells them that he has also had afflictions. The good report from them is a comfort to him.

For now we live, if ye stand fast in the Lord [1 Thess. 3:8].

"We live" means that as believers we enjoy life. *If* should really be translated "since"— "since ye stand fast in the Lord." Even in trouble you can enjoy it—that's not always easy to do, my friend. This is what Peter writes: "Beloved, think it not strange concerning the fiery trial which is to try you, as though some strange thing happened unto you: But rejoice, inasmuch as ye are partakers of Christ's sufferings; that, when his glory shall be revealed, ye may be glad also with

exceeding joy" (1 Pet. 4:12–13). You cannot lose as a Christian. Even if you have trouble, it is going to work out for your good—you can always be sure of that.

PAUL URGES CONTINUING GROWTH

For what thanks can we render to God again for you, for all the joy wherewith we joy for your sakes before our God [1 Thess. 3:9].

Joy is associated with life, and sorrow is associated with death. However, sorrow increases the capacity of the heart for joy. Paul wants the Thessalonians to know how to rejoice. Being a Christian is a wonderful thing!

Night and day praying exceedingly that we might see your face, and might perfect that which is lacking in your faith? [1 Thess. 3:10].

Paul's labor in Thessalonica was very rudely interrupted—he was run out of town—and he wanted to return to continue his teaching ministry. Paul *wanted* to teach the Word of God.

Now God himself and our Father, and our Lord Jesus Christ, direct our way unto you [1 Thess. 3:11].

Oh, how Paul prayed for the opportunity to return to them!

And the Lord make you to increase and abound in love one toward another, and toward all men, even as we do toward you:

To the end he may stablish your hearts unblameable in holiness before God, even our Father, at the coming of our Lord Jesus Christ with all his saints [1 Thess. 3:12–13].

"Abound in love." *Abound* means "exceed," and *love* is the Greek *agape*. In this epistle, love is seen only in action—"labor of love." It is not affection, but an active seeking of the welfare of another.

"To the end"—love has a purpose; it is not an end in itself.

"He may stablish your hearts unblameable in holiness"—the desired end of their love for one another is that they would develop a character of holiness. If you were tried in court for being a Christian, would there be enough evidence to convict you? We are going to appear before Him someday, and He is going to judge our works. This may terrify you, but He also is going to judge our character as believers and determine the reward we will receive. My

Christian friend, what kind of a life are you living today?

"At the coming of our Lord Jesus Christ with all his saints." Most schools of thought would agree that this verse indicates that the saints are going to come with Christ when He comes to the earth to establish His kingdom. But this verse also seems to indicate that He doesn't reward them until that time when He comes to the earth to establish His kingdom. Yet many of us believe that believers will come before the judgment seat of Christ *before* that; that is, we believe that when He takes the church out of the world, the world enters the Great Tribulation Period, and then He comes to establish His kingdom at the end of the Great Tribulation Period. So the question naturally arises: When is He going to present us "unblameable in holiness before God"? Is it when He takes the church out of the world? Or, will it be at the time He comes to the earth to establish His kingdom? The answer depends upon our understanding of this phrase, "at the coming of our Lord Jesus Christ with all his saints."

There are different Greek words for "coming" or "appearing." The first of these words is *epiphaneia*; we get our word *epiphany* from it. The first coming of Christ was an epiphany. It has the idea of a shining through. The King James translation uses the word *appeared*: "For the grace of God that bringeth salvation hath appeared to all men" (Titus 2:11). The Lord Jesus came in person as a little Babe in Bethlehem more than nineteen hundred years ago. It was a breaking through, a shining through of the Lord. It was His epiphany. This word can be used of His first coming or His coming to take the church out of the world or His coming to set up His kingdom. All three have the idea of a breaking through, a shining through, and the actual presence of the Lord Jesus.

A second Greek word is *apokalupsis*, which means a "revelation" or an "unveiling." That is actually the name of the Book of Revelation.

One could hardly call His first coming an unveiling, because actually His glory was veiled in human flesh when He was born in Bethlehem. It was like the *shekinah* glory in the tabernacle of the Old Testament which was back in the Holy of Holies where only the high priest was allowed to enter. There was a veil which separated the Holy of Holies from the rest of the tabernacle. When the Lord Jesus was here the first time, His glory did not show forth; it was veiled in human flesh. When He comes again, His glory will shine forth. So this is a word that refers to His second coming.

The third Greek word is *parousia*. It literally means "presence" or "being alongside." It is commonly translated "coming," but it actually means "presence." We use *coming* in that same way today. I have been introduced to an audience with the words, "We are thankful for the coming of Dr. McGee." I wasn't coming at that time: I was already there. It means that I was present, sitting on the platform, and they were happy that I had come. Sometimes in the King James translation, *parousia* is translated as "presence" and sometimes as "coming." "Wherefore, my beloved, as ye have always obeyed, not as in my presence only . . ." (Phil. 2:12). In 1 Thessalonians 2:19 as well as in the verse we are considering, *parousia* is translated "coming."

Therefore, "at the coming of our Lord Jesus" refers to the fact that believers are going to be *present* with the Lord Jesus at the very moment that we are caught up to meet the Lord in the air. He will take us home to glory, to the place that He has prepared for us. So that this "coming" does not refer to the return of the Lord with His saints to establish His kingdom, but to our coming to heaven into the presence of the Father. We have the same thought in 1 Thessalonians 2:19: "For what is our hope, or joy, or crown of rejoicing? Are not even ye in the presence of our Lord Jesus Christ at his coming?" We will come into the presence of the Lord Jesus and at that time will be presented "unblameable in holiness before God."

THEME: The coming of Christ is a purifying hope; the coming of Christ is a comforting hope

HOW BELIEVERS ARE TO WALK

Furthermore then we beseech you, brethren, and exhort you by the Lord Jesus, that as ye have received of us how ye ought to walk and to please God, so ye would abound more and more [1 Thess. 4:1].

This section teaches how the believers are to walk down here in light of the coming of Christ. It is bound up in that little word *walk*, which we find in this verse and again in the twelfth verse. This is the practical aspect of the hope of the coming of the Lord. We like to look forward to the day when we shall be caught up to meet the Lord in the air. But, my friend, in the meantime our feet are down here on the ground and we need to do some walking. We are to walk in a way that will please God.

"As ye have received of us how ye ought to walk and to please God, so ye would abound more and more." We should keep improving. We should *grow* in grace and in the knowledge of Him. The walk of the believer is very important. It is emphasized in many portions of Scripture, and it is the emphasis here. A believer cannot do as he pleases; he does as Christ pleases.

For ye know what commandments we gave you by the Lord Jesus [1 Thess. 4:2].

In regard to their walk, we will find Paul giving some commandments to the Thessalonians. You will remember that the Lord Jesus also gave commandments. Some of these commandments are new commandments.

Let me say this very carefully: The Ten Commandments have no part in a sinner's salvation, nor are they standard for Christian conduct. The purpose of the Ten Commandments is to take us by the hand, as a pedagogue would take a little child by the hand, to bring us to the Cross and say to us, "Little fellow, you need a Savior!" The Ten Commandments are like a mirror which lets us see that we are sinners. The Ten Commandments were not given to save us; they were given to show us that we are sinners and that we need a Savior. That is their purpose.

However, there are commandments for believers, and the standard for Christian conduct which they set is on a much higher plane than the Ten Commandments. In chapter 5 we will find twenty-two commandments for believers given.

Now the question naturally arises: If man could not keep the Ten Commandments, how can he keep higher commandments? The Bible makes it very clear that man was not able to keep the Ten Commandments. The nation Israel transgressed these commandments as Simon Peter confessed: "And when there had been much disputing, Peter rose up, and said unto them, Men and brethren, ye know how that a good while ago God made choice among us, that the Gentiles by my mouth should hear the word of the gospel, and believe. . . . Now therefore why tempt ye God, to put a yoke upon the neck of the disciples, which neither our fathers nor we were able to bear? But we believe that through the grace of the Lord Jesus Christ we shall be saved, even as they" (Acts 15:7, 10–11).

Now if we can't keep the Ten Commandments, how are we to keep any higher commandments of Christian conduct? Man cannot do it himself. This can be attained only by the power of the Holy Spirit who dwells within the believer (see v. 8).

"For ye know what commandments we gave you by the Lord Jesus." Paul has some commandments for believers. We are not lawless. We should be disciplined, and we should be in obedience to Christ. It should be a love relationship—we should be motivated by love—the Lord Jesus said, "If ye love me, keep my commandments" (John 14:15).

For this is the will of God, even your sanctification, that ye should abstain from fornication [1 Thess. 4:3].

Sanctification is a very wonderful word, but I am afraid that it is greatly misunderstood. If you go through the Scriptures, you will find that sanctification has several different meanings. When it is used in reference to Christ, as it is here, it means that He has been made over to us sanctification—and you cannot improve on that! Therefore, it does not simply refer to a sinless state, but rather that we have been set apart for God. For example, Simon Peter speaks of the fact that ". . . holy men of God spake as they were moved by the Holy Ghost" (2 Pet. 1:21). Now some of those holy men have life stories that don't make them sound very holy! Moses, for instance, was a murderer. David, who wrote so many wonderful psalms, was also a murderer. But they were sanctified, holy, because they had been set aside for God.

Sanctification of the believer is a work of the Spirit of God. We need to review the threefold aspect of it, because this is so very important:

Positional sanctification means that Christ has been made unto us sanctification. We are accepted in the Beloved, and we will never be more saved than at the moment we put our trust in Christ. We are never accepted because of who we are, but because of what Christ has done. This positional sanctification is perfection in Christ.

Practical sanctification is the Holy Spirit working in our lives to produce a holiness in our walk. This practical sanctification will never be perfect so long as we are in these bodies with our old sinful flesh.

Total sanctification will occur in the future when we are conformed to the image of Christ Jesus. Then both the position *and* the practice of sanctification will be perfect.

The literal meaning of the word *sanctification* is to be "set apart for God." The moment a lost sinner comes to Christ and accepts Christ as Savior, that person is set aside for God's use. This is clearly taught in the Old Testament in the tabernacle. God taught the Old Testament believers great doctrinal truths through very simple, practical lessons. In the tabernacle there were vessels and instruments which were used in the sacrifices. After they had gone through the wilderness for forty years, those pots and pans and forks and spoons were pretty well beaten and battered. I don't think they were very attractive. I think that any good housewife would have said, "Let's trade them in on a new set. Let's throw these away." However, God called them *holy* vessels. They were holy because they were set aside for the use of God. That is what made them holy.

In the same way this applies to a person. When he comes to Christ, he is saved. He is redeemed; he belongs to Christ. Paul says, "This is the will of God, even your sanctification." You have been set aside for a holy purpose, for God's use. Every child of God—not just preachers or missionaries or Christian workers, but every believer—is set aside for the use of God.

"That ye should abstain from fornication." Don't think it was only the Thessalonians who needed this admonition from Paul. Don't think

they were the only ones who engaged in sins, especially the sins of the flesh. Don't think it was only in Roman times that idolatry involved sins of sex. Today we are seeing the rise of the worship of Satan and the practice of the occult. There are all kinds of amulets and rituals connected with such worship. Also there is astrology which seeks to tell people about themselves. And there is always sex involved in all of it.

The great tragedy today is to hear of some Christian worker who has become involved in sexual sin. And, unfortunately, there are even churches that will defend a minister who has been guilty of such. We are people who are supposed to be set aside for the use of God! Paul says that you cannot be involved in sexual sin and at the same time be used of God. One cannot live in sin and be a preacher or singer or Sunday school teacher or an officer in the church. I don't care who you are, if you do, you will wreck the work of God.

Now, should a Christian strive for holiness? I think so. But you and I need to recognize that it is only in Christ that we can be acceptable to God. Paul says that we have been sanctified, brought to this high state, set apart for the use of God. Now what?—

That every one of you should know how to possess his vessel in sanctification and honour;

Not in the lust of concupiscence, even as the Gentiles which know not God [1 Thess. 4:4–5].

All around these Thessalonian believers were the pagans who combined sex and religion. Sex was a religion among the Greeks. You could go to Corinth and find that out, but you didn't have to go to Corinth—you could find it out right in Thessalonica.

Paul says that we are to live a life that commends the gospel. The loose living that we find among some believers today brings the gospel into disrepute. Such people are not living for God or serving God. You cannot serve God and live in sin. He doesn't accept that.

"That every one of you should know how to possess his vessel in sanctification and honour." The immorality that exists in our day is absolutely astounding. A very fine Christian leader who holds Bible classes on the campus of a college here in California told me that the boys' dormitory is Sodom and the girls' dormitory is Gomorrah. These poor kids know all about sex, but they don't know about love. God says that the body should be saved for the marriage relationship, and this applies to men and women. There are all sorts of reasons given for the fact that there is so much unhappiness in marriage. The problem is that the marriage partners are not people who have been set apart for the use of God and who are faithful to each other in a love relationship. When a person saves his body for marriage and is faithful to his partner, he is possessing his vessel "in sanctification and honour." Such should be the practice of every child of God. Believe me, Paul puts it on the line.

That no man go beyond and defraud his brother in any matter: because that the Lord is the avenger of all such, as we also have forewarned you and testified [1 Thess. 4:6].

"That no man go beyond and defraud his brother in any matter." You have to be honest if you are going to be a child of God.

"Because that the Lord is the avenger of all such." I've lived long enough as a Christian and as a pastor to see this principle worked out in the lives of many believers. I've observed certain believers who have been dishonest in their dealings with others, and God *is* an avenger—He moves in and judges them.

For God hath not called us unto uncleanness, but unto holiness [1 Thess. 4:7].

A child of God cannot continue in sin. The Prodigal Son may get in the pigpen for a time, but he won't *live* in the pigpen.

He therefore that despiseth, despiseth not man, but God, who hath also given unto us his holy Spirit [1 Thess. 4:8].

A child of God is indwelt by the Holy Spirit. He cannot continue to live in sin because the Holy Spirit is the *Holy* Spirit. The time will come when the child of God will long for holiness in his own life.

The Holy Spirit is the only means by which we can live for God. We see in Paul's Galatian epistle that the child of God is not to indulge in the sins of the flesh. Instead, there should be the manifestation of the fruit of the Spirit in the life. In Romans 8:3, Paul makes it very clear: "For what the law could not do. ... ." Why? Is the Law wrong? No, the Law is not wrong; the Ten Commandments are not wrong. The problem is with man, not with the Law. Man cannot attain to the level of the Ten Commandments, nor can he live by the commandments in the New Testament. It is the Holy Spirit within the believer who has been given to him to enable him to live a life for God.

God has given the Holy Spirit to *every* believer. He is not something to be sought after a person is saved. The moment a sinner trusts Christ, that person is indwelt by the Spirit of God. In Acts 19 we find that when Paul arrived in Ephesus, he found people who were professing to be Christians, but he saw that they were not indwelt by the Spirit of God. He asked them whether they had received the Holy Spirit when they were saved. They told him they had never even heard about such things; they had heard only of the baptism of John. So Paul preached the gospel to them, and then they were saved and received the Holy Spirit. You receive the Holy Spirit only when you are converted and come to Christ. At that point the believer receives and is baptized with the Holy Spirit and is placed into the body of believers to function in it. A person may have many infillings of the Spirit after that, and I think we need a constant infilling of the Holy Spirit. It is only the indwelling Holy Spirit that enables us to lead holy lives.

But as touching brotherly love ye need not that I write unto you: for ye yourselves are taught of God to love one another [1 Thess. 4:9].

Love is the subject, and the statement he makes is rather amazing. A believer must have love for the brethren. It is a supernatural love that is taught of God: "The fruit of the Spirit is love." It is not a theoretical kind of love, not just an abstract term. We have mentioned before that it cannot be just love in the abstract, but it must be love in the concrete. Such love can only be produced in the hearts of believers by the Holy Spirit. Notice that after Paul speaks of the Holy Spirit, brotherly love is the first thing that he mentions.

He writes, "As touching brotherly love ye need not that I write unto you: for ye yourselves are taught of God to love one another." I believe that love is the identifying mark of a child of God.

My roommate in college and I could wrestle, fight, argue, try to get dates with the same girl, and all that sort of thing. One day we really had had a knock-down-drag-out fight. We had literally torn up the room. He proceeded to tell me what he thought of me, and it was not very complimentary. Then I proceeded to tell him what I thought of him and that wasn't very complimentary either. All of a sudden it occurred to me, "Look, you are the greatest proof that I am a child of God! One of the evidences that a person is a child of God is that he loves his brother. John emphasizes it and it is in 1 Thessalonians that we are taught of God to love our brother. In spite of the fact that you are the most contemptible person I have ever met, the most unlovely person I have ever met, I love you!" He looked startled and began to laugh. "You know, I love you, and you're lots worse than I am!"

This man is now a retired preacher, just as I am. Once in awhile we have an opportunity to see one another. He is still a very ornery individual, but I love him because he is a child of God. And I think he loves me. That is the proof that we are the children of God.

And indeed ye do it toward all the brethren which are in all Macedonia: but we beseech you, brethren, that ye increase more and more [1 Thess. 4:10].

Love for the brethren is an area for growth and development. Very candidly, some of the saints are not very lovely. Someone has put that fact into this little jingle:

> To dwell above with saints in love
> Oh, that will be glory.
> But to stay below with the saints
>   I know—
> Well, that's another story.

These Thessalonians did love the brethren, but evidently their love had not reached the *summum bonum* of life. They weren't perfect in their love, and there was still room for improvement.

There are going to be some personality conflicts among the saints. It may be better for such people not to be together too much nor to put arms around each other and walk together. That doesn't mean we should hate them. We can still love them as the children of God. For example, I know a minister whose methods I absolutely despise, but I can truthfully say that I love him. I know of no one who gets up and presents Jesus Christ as wonderfully as this man does, and I love him for it.

The real test is our love for the brethren. If you want to put the blue litmus paper down in your life to test it and find out whether or not you are a genuine believer, this is the place to put it down: Do you love the brethren?

And that ye study to be quiet, and to do your own business, and to work with your own hands, as we commanded you [1 Thess. 4:11].

"That ye study to be quiet." That is an interesting commandment for Christians. We have all kinds of schools today to teach people to speak. Every seminary has a public speaking class. Perhaps they should also have a class that would teach their students to be quiet. A lot of saints need such a course!

A lady went to a "tongues meeting," and the leader thought she was interested in speaking in tongues. He asked her, "Madam, would you like to speak in tongues?" She answered, "No, I would like to lose about forty feet off the one I have now!" We need to study to be quiet. That is a commandment.

"And to do your own business"—that is another good commandment. It means to mind your own business. "Tend to your own knitting" is the way I used to hear it as a boy. Keep your nose out of the affairs of other people. This is good advice for Christians.

"And to work with your own hands, as we commanded you." I believe that every Christian should have some type of activity whereby he is doing something that is tangible for God. That would be a wonderful thing.

That ye may walk honestly toward them that are without, and that ye may have lack of nothing [1 Thess. 4:12].

"Walk honestly"—this is also something that the saints of God need to do today. It will gain the respect and the confidence of mankind. Our walk should be honest before God and man.

I have letters from several organizations which use methods to raise money that seem very questionable to me. Certain organizations have men out contacting people who have become senile, attempting to get them to make their wills over to their organizations. That is one reason you ought to make your will *before* you become senile. There are unscrupulous people who are out to get your money—there is no question about that. A child of God cannot do such questionable things because we are to "walk honestly toward them that are without." That means that all dealings with unbelievers are to be scrupulously honest. God will judge us if we do not walk honestly.

THE COMING OF CHRIST IS A COMFORTING HOPE

We come now to the next section of this epistle, a section which has been labeled one of the most important prophetic passages in the Scriptures. It teaches the *imminent* and *impending* coming of Christ for His church. That does not mean the immediate or soon coming of Christ. Paul never uses an expression like that. He did not want people to assume it would be in their own lifetime or shortly afterward. It has been more than nineteen hundred years now. But when we say that the coming of Christ is imminent, we mean that it is approaching or that it is the next event on the agenda of God's program.

Let me illustrate my point. One time when Mrs. McGee and I flew to Florida on a new DC-10 from the Los Angeles International Airport, we had a friendly captain who began to talk to us soon after our flight had begun: "The weather is lovely here in Southern California as you can see. The weather in Miami, Florida, is also very good, and we expect it to be nice when we arrive there. We fly over Texas, and of course nobody knows what the weather will be there, but we should have a good flight today. Our next stop is Miami." Now there was not a single passenger who jumped up, grabbed his luggage, and rushed for the door because the captain had said, "Our next stop is Miami." That stop was imminent. In other words, we would not make any other stop before that one. It would be five hours before we would arrive at Miami, but we were prepared for that stop because it was imminent—it was the next stop.

The difference between waiting for the stop at Miami and waiting for the coming of Christ for His church is that we knew that Miami was five hours away. We don't know how far away the coming of Christ is. It could be five hours or five days or five weeks or five months or five years or five hundred years. We simply do not know. Still, it is imminent; it is *the next event*.

Paul makes it very clear that he believed in the imminent return of Christ. In verse 15 of this chapter he says, "We which are alive and remain unto the coming of the Lord." Paul believed that the Lord Jesus Christ *could* come in his lifetime. He did not say or believe that He *would* come in his lifetime, but he said that He could come. This was the attitude he expressed as he wrote to Titus: "Looking for that blessed hope, and the glorious appearing of the great God and our Saviour Jesus Christ" (Titus 2:13).

There are those who accuse Paul of changing his position on the imminent coming of Christ as he himself grew older. Remember that this epistle to the Thessalonians was his earliest letter. Did Paul change his theology? When he wrote to the Philippians he was an old man, a prisoner in Rome, and he said: "For our conversation [citizenship] is in heaven; from whence also we look for the Saviour, the Lord Jesus Christ" (Phil. 3:20). Paul, at the end of his life, was still looking for Him. In other words, Christ's coming was imminent.

Paul labeled this coming of Christ for His church, when we are to be caught up to meet the Lord in the air, the *rapture* of the church. There are those today who hold a different viewpoint. They say the Bible does not teach the Rapture and that one cannot find that word in the New Testament. I insist that it is there. It is found in this chapter in verse 17: "Then we which are alive and remain shall be caught up together with them in the clouds, to meet the Lord in the air: and so shall we ever be with the Lord." The Greek word translated as "caught up" is *harpazō*. It means "to catch up or grasp hastily, to snatch up, to lift, to transport, or to rapture." *Rapture* is just as good a word as *caught up*. It is a matter of semantics, whichever word you choose to use. The fact is that the Bible teaches that believers in Christ are to be caught up in the clouds to meet the Lord in the air. Paul taught the rapture of the church. Now if you would like, you could just say you believe in the *harpazō*—that's the original Greek word, and it means "rapture" and it means "caught up." Nonetheless, the point is that the rapture of the church can take place at any moment; it is the next happening in the program of God.

Now I want to make a very startling statement about this passage of Scripture. Actually, the primary consideration here is not the Rapture. The precise question Paul is answering is: What about believers who have died before the Rapture has taken place?

We need to review the background of this epistle in order to understand why this question was so important to the Thessalonian believers. Paul went to Thessalonica on his second missionary journey. ". . . three sabbath days [he] reasoned with them out of the scriptures" (Acts 17:2). That means that Paul was there less than a month. In that month's time, he performed a herculean task. He did the work of a missionary. He preached the gospel, converts were made, and he established a church. Then he taught these new believers the great truths of the Christian faith. It is interesting that he even taught them of the rapture of the church.

When I was a young preacher in a denomination, they didn't have much to say about prophecy. Very candidly, I don't think the ministers knew very much about it. They would give an excuse, saying, "You shouldn't preach on that. That is deep truth and should be given to mature saints. It shouldn't be given to new believers." Well, it's too bad that Paul didn't know that, because he hadn't been with the Thessalonians for a complete month and yet he was teaching them prophecy. In fact, when we get to the second epistle we will find that he taught them about the Great Tribulation and the Man of Sin, the Antichrist who is to come. Paul ran the whole gamut of prophecy for these Thessalonians. It is nonsense to say this is not to be given to new believers. It is to be taught to them, and Paul is the demonstration of that.

It is clear that Paul taught the Thessalonians that the rapture of the church might occur at any moment, that it was imminent. Then Paul left Thessalonica; he went to Berea, established a church and was there for some time. Then he took a ship and went over to Athens. We don't know how long he was there either. He was waiting for Timothy and Silas to bring word from Thessalonica. They didn't come, and he went on down to Corinth. After he was there for awhile, Timothy and Silas came. They came with questions from the Thessalonians to ask of Paul. So Paul wrote 1 Thessalonians to encourage them and to answer their specific questions with regard to the rapture of the church. During this unknown interval of time after Paul had left them, some of the saints in Thessalonica had died. A question arose in the minds of the believers. *Had they missed the Rapture?*

Obviously Paul had taught them the imminent coming of Christ, or this question would not be pertinent at all. Paul had told them that the Lord Jesus might come at any moment. These saints had died, and the Lord hadn't come—had they missed the Rapture? What would happen to them? Paul gives the answer to this question in this epistle.

To us the question the Thessalonians had is not meaningful in the same way as it was to them. That is because you and I live nineteen hundred years this side of 1 Thessalonians, and literally millions of believers have already gone down through the doorway of death. Therefore, most of the church has already gone ahead, and a small minority remains in the world.

Paul had taught the Thessalonians that the coming of Christ was imminent, and this is still what we believe today. Between where we are right this moment and the coming of Christ for the church it is tissue-thin, which means it could happen any moment—even before you finish reading this page—or the coming of Christ could be way down yonder in the future.

There is a grave danger today in setting dates for the coming of the Lord. Some are doing that, and it is dangerous because they do not know when He will return. The Lord said that we do not know the hour He will come. They might pick the year correctly, but they surely won't pick the hour—I don't think they will even hit the year. When they set dates, they are robbing believers of the opportunity of looking for Him to come.

Now the Thessalonians were concerned about the saints who had died before the Rapture had taken place. We need to keep that in mind as we go through the rest of this chapter.

But I would not have you to be ignorant, brethren, concerning them which are asleep, that ye sorrow not, even as others which have no hope [1 Thess. 4:13].

"I would not have you to be ignorant." I love the way Paul says that. We have seen it before in the Corinthian epistles. When Paul says, "I would not have you ignorant, brethren," you can pretty well put it down that the brethren are ignorant. Paul just didn't come out and say so in a flat-footed and crude way. He is more polite and diplomatic. I would say that he did it in a very Christian way.

"Concerning them which are asleep." Paul is referring to the death of the body. This never refers to the soul or the spirit of man, because the spirit of man does not die. We shall note that as we move through this section, but first I want to mention several reasons that the death of the body is spoken of as being "asleep."

1. There is a similarity between sleep and death. A dead body and a sleeping body are actually very similar. I'm sure you have been to a funeral where someone has remarked that So-and-so looks just as if he were asleep. Well, in a way it is true—the body of a believer is asleep. A sleeper does not cease to exist, and the inference is that the dead do not cease to exist just because the body is asleep. Sleep is temporary; death is also temporary. Sleep has its waking; death has its resurrection. It is not that life is existence and death is non-existence, you see.

2. The word which is translated "asleep" has its root in the Greek word *keimai*, which means "to lie down." And the very interesting thing is that the word for "resurrection" is a word that refers only to the body. It is *anastasis*, and it comes from two Greek words: *histemi* which means "to stand," and *ana*, the

preposition, "up." It is only the body which can stand up in resurrection.

C. S. Lewis in his *Screwtape Letters* uses a little sarcasm to ridicule the liberals who believe that the resurrection is a resurrection of the spirit and not of the body. He asks what position the soul or the spirit takes when it lies down in death, or what position the spirit takes when it stands up in resurrection! If you want to believe in soul sleep, you must explain how a soul can lie down and then stand up. Obviously "asleep" refers to the body.

The same Greek word for "sleep" is used here as is used when referring to a natural sleep when the body lies down in bed. Let me give you two illustrations of this. "And when he rose up from prayer, and was come to his disciples, he found them *sleeping* for sorrow" (Luke 22:45, italics mine). Imagine that Peter, James, and John went to sleep at this time of crisis! The word is the same word that is used here in 1 Thessalonians. Again, in Acts 12:6, "And when Herod would have brought him forth, the same night Peter was *sleeping* between two soldiers, bound with two chains: and the keepers before the door kept the prison" (italics mine). One thing we know for sure about Simon Peter is that he didn't have insomnia! Even at times of great crisis, he was able to sleep. Again, the same word for "sleep" is used, and it is the natural sleep of the body.

3. The Bible teaches that the body returns to the dust from which it was created, but the spirit returns to God who gave it. Even the Old Testament teaches this. In Ecclesiastes 12:7 we read: "Then shall the dust return to the earth as it was: and the spirit shall return unto God who gave it." "The dust"—that is our body. God told Adam, ". . . for dust thou art, and unto dust shalt thou return" (Gen. 3:19). It was the body that was taken from the dust, and then God breathed into man the breath of life, or the spirit, you see. It is the body that will go to sleep until the resurrection— only the body. The spirit of a believer will return to God.

The spirit or the soul does not die, and therefore the spirit or the soul is not raised. Only the body can lie down in death, and only the body can stand up in resurrection. This is quite obvious when Paul says that to be absent from the body is to be present with the Lord (see 2 Cor. 5:8).

The body is merely a frail tent that is laid aside temporarily in death. "For we know that if our earthly house of this tabernacle were dissolved, we have a building of God, an house not made with hands, eternal in the heavens"

(2 Cor. 5:1). The Greek word for "tabernacle" here is *skenos,* which means "a tent." The bodies we live in are tents. I have news for you: You may live in a home that cost $250,000, but the place where you really live is in a little tent. God put every single one of us into a tent. It is not a matter of some living in a hovel and some in a mansion—we have all been given the same kind of tent. You could reduce the body to its component chemicals, and I am told the whole amount would sell for about $4.00, although inflated prices may push it a little higher. Every one of us lives in a tent that is worth about $4.00! It can be blown down at any moment. If you don't believe that, step in front of a car and you will find that your tent will fold up and silently slip away. Our bodies are actually very frail.

"For in this we groan, earnestly desiring to be clothed upon with our house which is from heaven" (2 Cor. 5:2). "For we that are in this tabernacle do groan . . ." (2 Cor. 5:4). We groan within our tents. Have you discovered that?

I met an old man at the corner bus stop many years ago. He must have been pretty close to eighty. He was swearing like a sailor. I said to him, "Brother, you won't be here very long, and you are going to have to answer to God."

"How do you know I won't be here very long?" he asked.

"God is telling you so. He has put gray in your hair, a totter in your step, a stoop in your shoulder, and a shortness of breath when you walk. He is trying to tell you that you won't be here much longer. You are living in a little tent down here, and you are going to be slipping away soon."

I am told that when President Adams was an old man, a friend inquired about his health. He answered that he was fine, but the house he lived in was getting rickety and was not in good repair. That is the kind of body each of us is living in, my friend.

When I was a young man, I could bound up and down the steps to my study. Today it is different. I come down the steps one at a time, and there is no more bounding. My knees hurt, and I groan. My wife tells me I groan too much, but I tell her it is scriptural to groan. Paul said that we groan in these bodies.

These old bodies are going to be put into the grave, and there they are going to sleep. The spirit goes to be with the Lord.

Paul wrote, "Therefore we are always confident, knowing that, whilst we are at home in the body, we are absent from the Lord: (For we walk by faith, not by sight:)" (2 Cor. 5:6–7). Now we are at home in this body; this is where we live. People don't really get to see *us*, you know—we are hidden in our bodies. Sometimes people who come to rallies or services when I speak, tell me they have heard me on the radio and they have come just to see how I look. I always feel like saying, "You really haven't seen me. All you have seen is a head and two hands sticking out of a suit of clothes. You don't see me—I live within this body." This house I live in isn't in such good repair, but that's where I will live as long as I walk on this earth.

Paul goes on to say, "We are confident, I say, and willing rather to be absent from the body, and to be present with the Lord" (2 Cor. 5:8). I can't think of anything lovelier than that. If you should attend my funeral, I wouldn't want you to come by and say that I look so natural. Friend, I won't even be there. You will just be looking at my tent that I have left behind. It's my old house, that has been put to sleep. I will be gone to be with the Lord. At the resurrection our bodies will be raised up.

Many years ago in the city of New York (in fact, it was way back in the day when liberalism was called modernism, back in the 1920s) they had an argument about whether resurrection was spiritual. The liberal even today claims it's spiritual. He doesn't believe in bodily resurrection at all. A very famous Greek scholar from the University of Chicago read a paper on the passage from 1 Corinthians 15: "It is sown a natural body; it is raised a spiritual body. There is a natural body, and there is a spiritual body" (1 Cor. 15:44). His paper put the emphasis on the word *spiritual*. He concluded by saying, "Now, brethren, you can see that resurrection is spiritual because it says it's spiritual." The liberals all applauded, and somebody made a motion that they print that manuscript and circulate it.

Well, a very fine conservative Greek scholar was there, and he stood up. When he stood, all the liberals were a little uneasy because he could ask very embarrassing questions. He said, "I'd like to ask the author of the paper a question." Very reluctantly, the good doctor stood up. "Now, doctor, which is stronger, a noun or an adjective? A very simple question, but I'd like for you to answer it." He could see the direction he was going and didn't want to answer it, but he had to say that a noun is stronger, of course. "Now doctor, I'm amazed that you presented the paper that you did today. You put the emphasis upon an adjective, and the strong word is the noun. Now,

let's look at that again. 'It is sown a natural body; it is raised a spiritual *body.*'" He said, "The only thing that is carried over in resurrection is the body. It's one kind of body when it dies, a natural body. It's raised a body, but a spiritual body, dominated now by the spirit—but it's still a body." And they never did publish that paper. They decided it would be better not to publish it. May I say to you, just a simple little exercise in grammar would have answered this great professor's whole manuscript and his entire argument which he presented at that time.

Daniel is another writer who spoke of the death of the body as "sleep." "And many of them that sleep in the dust of the earth shall awake, some to everlasting life, and some to shame and everlasting contempt" (Dan. 12:2). Dust will go back to dust—that's the body; but the spirit goes to God who sent it.

4. The early Christians adopted a very wonderful word for the burying places of their loved ones—the Greek word *koimeterion*, which means "a rest house for strangers, a sleeping place." It is the same word from which we get our English word *cemetery*. The same word was used in that day for inns, or what we would call a hotel or motel. A Hilton Hotel, a Ramada Inn or a Holiday Inn—they are the places where you spend the night to sleep. You expect to get up the next day and continue your journey. This is the picture of the place where you bury your believing loved ones. You don't weep when you have a friend who goes and spends a weekend in a Hilton Hotel, do you? No, you rejoice with him. The body of the believer has just been put into a motel until the resurrection. One day the Lord is coming and that body is going to be raised up.

Now let us return to our consideration of the actual text of verse 13: "That ye sorrow not, even as others [the rest] which have no hope." The pagan world had no hope; so for them death was a frightful thing. In Thessalonica they have found an inscription that says: "After death no reviving, after the grave no meeting again." The Greek poet Theocritus wrote, "Hopes are among the living; the dead are without hope." That was the belief of the ancient world. It is pretty pessimistic and doleful.

Believers are not to sorrow as the pagans. I have officiated at many funeral services during the years of my ministry, and I can always tell if the family is Christian. I can tell by the way the people weep whether they have hope or not. Christians weep, of course—there is nothing wrong with that. Paul never says that believers are not to weep. What he does say is that we are not to sorrow as the others which have no hope. A Christian has a sorrow at the death of a loved one, but he also has hope.

For if we believe that Jesus died and rose again, even so them also which sleep in Jesus will God bring with him [1 Thess. 4:14].

I want you to notice that Paul says that "Jesus *died* and rose again." It doesn't say Jesus slept—He *died*. How accurate this is!

There are three kinds of death in Scripture. There is *physical death*, which is the separation of the spirit from the body. That is what we ordinarily call death. Adam didn't actually die physically until 930 years after the Fall.

Then there is *spiritual death*. Paul says that to be carnally minded is death, which is separation from God. This is what happened to man in the Garden of Eden when God said that man would die in the day he ate of the fruit. Man became separated from God. Adam hid from God; he ran from God when God came into the garden—there was now a separation between them. Adam *did* die the day he ate the fruit—a spiritual death. Paul describes this spiritual death in Ephesians 2:1: "And you hath he quickened, who were dead in trespasses and sins."

A famous judge toured around this country some years ago giving a lecture entitled "Millions Now Living Will Never Die." There followed him a famous Baptist preacher whose lecture was "Millions Now Living Are Already Dead." And they *were* dead—spiritually dead.

The third death is *eternal death*. That is eternal separation from God. This is the second death described in Revelation 20:14.

For this we say unto you by the word of the Lord, that we which are alive and remain unto the coming of the Lord shall not prevent them which are asleep [1 Thess. 4:15].

"By the word of the Lord" is Paul's assurance that he is giving God's answer to their question. Paul knows that they had been worrying about those who had died before the Rapture and wants them to know that the dead in Christ will have part in the Rapture.

"We which are alive and remain unto the coming of the Lord shall not prevent them which are asleep." The word *prevent* is an old English word meaning "precede." Those who are alive at the time of the Rapture will not be going ahead of them—in fact, the dead in Christ will be going first.

For the Lord himself shall descend from heaven with a shout, with the voice of the archangel, and with the trump of God: and the dead in Christ shall rise first [1 Thess. 4:16].

"The Lord himself shall descend from heaven." I love that—He won't be sending angels. When He comes to the earth to establish His kingdom, He will send His angels to the four corners of the earth to gather the elect, who will be both Israelites and Gentiles who enter the kingdom. However, there is no angel ministry connected with the rapture of the church. Angels announced the birth of Christ, but how was He announced? As the Son of David, the newborn King. He was announced as a *King*. The wise men wanted to know where they could find Him who was born King of the Jews. In contrast to this, at the establishment of the church on the Day of Pentecost, there were no angels. The Holy Spirit Himself came down. When the Lord takes His church out of the world, the Lord Himself shall descend from heaven. There will be no angels. Angels are connected with Israel but not with the church at all.

He will descend from heaven "with a shout." That is the voice of command. It is the same voice which He used when He stood at the tomb of Lazarus and said, "Lazarus, come forth" (see John 11:43).

"The voice of the archangel." Now wait, isn't that an angel connected with the Rapture? No, it is *His* voice that will be like the voice of an archangel. It is the quality of His voice, the majesty and the authority of it.

"The trump of God." Will there be trumpets there? No, it is *His* voice that will be like a trumpet. Can we be sure of this? In Revelation 1:10, John, who was exiled to the Isle of Patmos, wrote, "I was in the Spirit on the Lord's day, and heard behind me a great voice, as of a trumpet." He turned to see who it was, and he saw the glorified Christ. It is the voice of the glorified Christ that is like the sound of a trumpet.

That ought to get rid of all this foolishness about Gabriel blowing his horn or blowing a trumpet. I don't think Gabriel even owns a trumpet, but if he has one, he won't need to blow it. The Lord Jesus is not going to need the help of Gabriel. Do you think the Lord Jesus needed Gabriel to come and help Him raise Lazarus from the dead? Can you imagine the Lord Jesus at the tomb of Lazarus saying,

"Gabriel, won't you come over here and help Me get this man out of the grave?" How absolutely foolish! The Lord Jesus will not need anyone to help Him. When He calls His church, their bodies will come up out of the graves.

Then we which are alive and remain shall be caught up together with them in the clouds, to meet the Lord in the air: and so shall we ever be with the Lord [1 Thess. 4:17].

Again, "caught up" is the Greek *harpazō*, meaning "to grasp hastily, snatch up, to lift, transport, or rapture."

It is going to be a very orderly procedure. The dead will rise first. Here comes Stephen out of the grave. It may be that he will lead the procession since he was the first martyr. Then there will be the apostles and all those millions who have laid down their lives for Jesus. They will just keep coming from right down through the centuries. Finally, if we are alive at that time, we will bring up the rear of the parade. We will be way down at the tail end of it. Most of the church has already gone in through the doorway of death.

Wherefore comfort one another with these words [1 Thess. 4:18].

Does he say, "Wherefore terrify one another with these words"? Of course not. My Bible says, "Wherefore *comfort* one another." It not only means to comfort in the usual sense of the word, but also to instruct and to exhort one another and to *talk* about these things. My friend, Jesus is going to take His own out of this world someday! What a glorious, wonderful comfort this is! The bodies of the dead will be lifted out. Then whoever is alive at that time will be caught up together with them to meet the Lord in the air. So shall we ever be with the Lord. In fact, we shall come back with Him to the earth to reign with Him at the time He sets up His kingdom.

CHAPTER 5

THEME: The coming of Christ is a rousing hope

In this final chapter of 1 Thessalonians we see the Christian's *actions* in view of the return of Christ. In chapter 1, you will recall, we considered the Christian's *attitude* toward the return of Christ. Now, if the attitude does not lead to action, something is radically wrong. The coming of Christ is a rousing hope which leads to action!

CALL TO BE AWAKE AND ALERT IN VIEW OF CHRIST'S COMING

The believer in Christ is to be awake and alert in view of Christ's coming, because the believer will not enter into that awful night of the Great Tribulation Period, which is labeled the *Day* of the Lord. That Day of the Lord begins with night because that is God's way of marking time. He begins that way in Genesis where it says that the evening and the morning were the first day. God begins in night but moves to light. So the Great Tribulation leads into the glorious millennial reign of Christ when the Sun of Righteousness will arise with healing in His wings.

The *Day of the Lord* is an expression we need to examine.

But of the times and the seasons, brethren, ye have no need that I write unto you [1 Thess. 5:1].

"Times and seasons" are not the property of the church; they belong to this earth and to an earthly people—both Israel and the Gentiles who will be saved in that day. The church is looking for a Person, not for times and seasons. The word for "time" is the Greek *chronos*, from which we get our English word *chronology*. The times and seasons or the chronology is not for the church.

For yourselves know perfectly that the day of the Lord so cometh as a thief in the night [1 Thess. 5:2].

The Lord Jesus does not come to the church like a thief in the night. The church is looking for and waiting for the Lord to come. You don't wait for a thief and look for him and leave a note for him on the back door when you leave your house—"I left the back door open for you, Mr. Thief, and you'll find the family silver in the third drawer to the right in the dining room." I don't imagine you have ever left such a note. The chances are that you check everything before you leave the house, making sure that your home is doubly locked. You want to keep the thief out. So the Lord Jesus does not come as a thief to the church. However, the Lord Jesus does come like a thief to the world *after* the church has been raptured. As I have said, the Day of the Lord will come suddenly to the earth, and it will begin with the night of the Great Tribulation Period; then finally Christ will come personally to this earth.

The Day of the Lord will come *suddenly*—

For when they shall say, Peace and safety; then sudden destruction cometh upon them, as travail upon a woman with child; and they shall not escape [1 Thess. 5:3].

Do you notice the change of pronouns here? In the first two verses Paul is addressing the "brethren," and he says that it is not necessary for him to write to them about the times and seasons, because they will have nothing to do with it—believers will be gone at that time. But here in verse 3 the pronoun changes to "they"—"when *they* shall say, Peace and safety."

Again let me repeat that the Day of the Lord is a period of time which begins with the Great Tribulation and goes through the millennial reign of Christ here upon the earth. There are many passages of Scripture which speak of this. For example, in Isaiah, chapters 12–13, you can read how God moves down in judgment on society and government, on the military and commerce and art and pomp and pride and religion. "Behold, the day of the LORD cometh, cruel both with wrath and fierce anger, to lay the land desolate: and he shall destroy the sinners thereof out of it" (Isa. 13:9). It starts out as a day of wrath: "For the stars of heaven and the constellations thereof shall not give their light: the sun shall be darkened in his going forth, and the moon shall not cause her light to shine" (Isa. 13:10). In the prophecy of Joel we are told: "Alas for the day! for the day of the LORD is at hand, and as a destruction from the Almighty shall it come" (Joel 1:15). Joel goes on in chapter 2 to describe it as "a day of darkness and of gloominess, a day of clouds and of thick darkness . . ." (Joel 2:2). That is the picture given to us in the Old Testament. The Day of the Lord is a period which begins with the Great Tribulation and goes through the millennial reign of Christ. That is a theme in the Old Testament.

Now the event described in chapter 4—the coming of Christ to take the church out of the world—is not even mentioned in the Old Testament. It is there by type, of course, such as the experiences of Enoch and Elijah, both of whom were taken up alive to be with the Lord. But it is not taught in the Old Testament that the Lord Jesus is going to take a company of people out of this earth to be with Himself. This is a glorious, wonderful truth which was revealed first in the Upper Room when the Lord Jesus said, ". . . I go to prepare a place for you. And if I go and prepare a place for you, I will come again, and receive you unto myself; that where I am, there ye may be also" (John 14:2–3). As far as I know, that is the first time this truth is revealed in the Bible. And Paul developed it in 1 Thessalonians 4.

However, in the fifth chapter he is speaking of something which was well known in the Old Testament.

"When they shall say, Peace and safety; then sudden destruction cometh upon them." It is going to be a big surprise to the world. They are not going to expect it. I believe that the "big lie," which we will see in the second chapter of 2 Thessalonians, is the promise of peace and safety. The Lord Jesus warned of that: "Take heed that no man deceive you." The world expects to enter a great era of peace, the Millennium, but they will find themselves plunged into the Great Tribulation, which will include the greatest war the world has ever seen. It will come upon them suddenly like a thief in the night.

But ye, brethren, are not in darkness, that that day should overtake you as a thief.

Ye are all the children of light, and the children of the day: we are not of the night, nor of darkness [1 Thess. 5:4–5].

The rapture of the church actually does two things: (1) It ends this day of grace in which we are today, this calling out a people for His name and bringing many sons home to glory. This is what God is doing in our day. The Rapture not only ends that, but (2) it begins the Day of the Lord. The Great Tribulation will get under way when the church leaves the earth. The one event of the Rapture will end the day of grace and begin the Day of the Lord. It closes one day and opens another.

"But ye, brethren, are not in darkness, that that day should overtake you as a thief." Why won't it? Well, because we won't be here. We found in chapter 4 that "the Lord himself shall descend from heaven with a shout" and take His church out of the world.

"Ye are all the children of light." In other words, you don't belong to that dispensation which is coming in the future. You belong to the dispensation of grace in which we are today.

Friend, if you do not learn these distinctions which are made in the Scripture, you will be hopelessly confused. I know of no one so hopelessly confused as some theologians in seminaries today. I've talked to them. One man told me that he had simply given up on the study of prophecy and would have nothing to do with it. Why? Because he was not willing to sit down and study the entire Scriptures.

When the Day of the Lord comes, we are going to be with the Lord. We are not in darkness. That day will not overtake us as a thief in the night. He doesn't come as a thief to take His church. The church is *looking* for that blessed hope and the glorious appearing of our great God and Savior.

Now Paul gives the admonition to the believers—

Therefore let us not sleep, as do others; but let us watch and be sober [1 Thess. 5:6].

You see, the rapture of the church, that blessed hope, could take place at any time. Because of this, we should not be sleeping Christians.

I heard a song leader down in Georgia, who, in his very quaint way, uttered a great many wise sayings. He was right on target with his remarks. He said, "We are now going to sing 'Standing on the Promises.' There are a lot of folk today who are singing 'Standing on the Promises,' but they are just *sitting* on the *premises*!" And some of them are actually sleeping pillars in the church today.

Now Paul is saying that, in view of the fact that the Lord Jesus is going to take His church out of the world before that awful period of tribulation, "let us not sleep, as do others; but let us watch and be sober."

The word *sober* has several meanings. It can mean "to stay sober" in the sense of not using an alcoholic stimulant, but there are also other kinds of drunkenness besides that caused by alcohol or drugs. A lot of people get drunk on power or on the making of money or on the pleasures of this world. The child of God is to stay sober and is to watch. Why? Because these tremendous events are to take place in the future.

I believe we are close to the time of the return of the Lord. I don't *know*, of course, but I think we are. And I *know* I can say with

Paul: ". . . for now is our salvation nearer than when we believed" (Rom. 13:11).

For they that sleep sleep in the night; and they that be drunken are drunken in the night.

But let us, who are of the day, be sober, putting on the breastplate of faith and love; and for an helmet, the hope of salvation [1 Thess. 5:7–8].

Again he mentions the word *sober*. Let's understand that we have a duty to perform.

"Putting on the breastplate of faith and love; and for an helmet, the hope of salvation." This speaks of a soldier's duty and is a call to that kind of duty. The breastplate of faith and love is to cover the heart, the vital part of the body. The helmet is the hope of salvation. As I write this, it isn't the style for men or women to wear hats—most people today go bareheaded—but it should be the style for every Christian to wear the helmet of the hope of salvation.

"Faith . . . love . . . hope"—this is now the third time these key words have appeared in this epistle: the labor of love, the work of faith, the patience of hope. Faith is a saving faith, and a saving faith produces works. Calvin said, "Faith alone saves, but the faith that saves is not alone." "Faith" looks to the past when we accepted the Lord Jesus Christ. "Love" is for the present, which is the relationship the believer should have with those around him. The "hope of salvation" is that blessed hope of the future. We are not looking for the Great Tribulation Period. I don't see how there could be any rejoicing in that! We are looking for that blessed hope, which is the consummation of our salvation.

John writes, "Beloved, now are we the sons of God, and it doth not yet appear what we shall be: but we know that, when he shall appear, we shall be like him; for we shall see him as he is" (1 John 3:2). God is not through with me, so don't you be impatient with me. A little lady down in West Texas in a testimony meeting said, "Most Christians ought to have written on their backs, 'This is not the best that the grace of God can do.'" I know that I ought to have that written on my back. Since He is not through with me yet, don't be impatient with me, and I won't be impatient with you—because I don't think He is through with you either. Today we have "the hope of salvation," which is that He will consummate that which He has begun in us. "Being confident of this very thing, that he which hath begun a good work in you will perform it until the day of Jesus Christ" (Phil. 1:6).

For God hath not appointed us to wrath, but to obtain salvation by our Lord Jesus Christ [1 Thess. 5:9].

"God hath not appointed us to wrath"—that ought to be clear even to amillennialists, but for some reason they miss the point. God hasn't appointed us to the day of wrath, the Great Tribulation. It is a time of judgment, and the church is not going through it because Christ bore our judgment.

Perhaps you are saying, "McGee, do you think you are good enough to be taken out in the Rapture?" No, I'm not even good enough to be saved. But God saved me by His grace, and when He comes to take His church out of the world, I'm going along with all the super-duper saints—because of the grace of God.

"But to obtain salvation by our Lord Jesus Christ." God has not destined us for wrath, for the Great Tribulation, but for salvation through our Lord Jesus Christ.

Who died for us, that, whether we wake or sleep, we should live together with him [1 Thess. 5:10].

Whether we die first or whether we live until His coming, we shall live together with Him. Most of the church has already gone through the doorway of death. What a parade that will be someday—beginning with Stephen and the apostles, the martyrs, all those who have fallen asleep in Jesus down through the years, and then those who are still alive at His coming, and if you and I are still alive, we will bring up the rear. Thank God, we shall be there by the grace of God!

Now what will these wonderful truths do for you? The next verse tells us: "Wherefore comfort yourselves together." What a comfort all of this is to us as believers!

COMMANDMENTS FOR CHRISTIANS

We come now to a series of twenty-two commandments for Christians. These are the commandments for believers—not just ten of them but twenty-two of them! Up to the time we are saved, God has us shut up to a cross. That is, God is not asking anything of us except this question: "What will you do with My Son who died for you?" After we have accepted Jesus Christ as our Savior, *then* God talks to us about our lives. The child of God is not under the Ten Commandments as the way of life—he is way above it. He is to live on a much higher plane, as we can see by the com-

mandments in this section. These commandments are practical—right down where the rubber meets the road. It is a wonderful, glorious thing to keep looking for the coming of Christ, but it is also very important that we keep walking down here on the sidewalks of life—at home, in the office, in the schoolroom, wherever we are called to walk.

The Lord Jesus said, "If ye love me, keep my commandments" (John 14:15). There are some Christians who have never listened to His commandments. Well, here are twenty-two of them. They are given like military orders, brief and terse. They are barked out like a second lieutenant would give them to you. We were just told to be sober and to put on the uniform of warfare (see v. 8). Now the orders are given, and they seem to be categorized—that is, certain ones are related to each other.

Wherefore comfort yourselves together, and edify one another, even as also ye do [1 Thess. 5:11].

The first commandment is to "comfort yourselves together," which means to encourage one another in the faith.

The second commandment is to "edify one another." The Thessalonian believers were already doing that, Paul says. *Edify* means "to build up one another." You and I should be a team working together, edifying each other with the Word of God.

And we beseech you, brethren, to know them which labour among you, and are over you in the Lord, and admonish you;

And to esteem them very highly in love for their work's sake. And be at peace among yourselves [1 Thess. 5:12–13].

Here are three commandments that seem to belong together. "Know" or understand those who teach the Word of God. It means we should *recognize* them. When Paul wrote this, he was speaking to the local situation in Thessalonica. He had been with them less than a month. He had won them to Christ and had taught them. A church had been started, we would say, "from scratch." There wasn't a believer there before Paul had arrived and presented the gospel to them (see Acts 17:2–3). So all the Thessalonian believers had come to know Christ at about the same time. Now among them certain ones would have been given the gift of teaching. Some would have the gift of preaching and some of helping. Every believer receives a gift when he is saved, and that gift is to be exercised in the body of believers to build up the body of believers. But I have a notion that among the believers in Thessalonica there could have been this attitude: *So-and-so and I were saved at the same time. I knew him before he was a believer. Where did he get the idea that he could teach me?* So Paul is telling them that certain men and women had been given certain gifts of leadership, and they should respect them. They should look to them for admonition.

We still have the problem today that very few people in the church pay any attention to the teachers God has given them. People say they believe the Bible is the Word of God and they believe every word of it. Then why don't they obey it? Why don't they listen when it is being taught? One man said to me very candidly, "I believe the Bible from cover to cover, and I am ignorant of what is between the covers." Now that is an untenable position to hold. I think if people knew what was between the covers, they *would* believe it. But it is a hypocritical position to say you believe it and then be ignorant of what it says. Anyone who says he believes the Bible is the Word of God is obligated to know what it says. Therefore, those who are preaching and teaching the Word of God should have the attention of the believers.

Now the fourth commandment is "to esteem them very highly in love for their work's sake." I have always appreciated people who love the Word of God because I have found that they become my friends. One of the things I have so appreciated about my radio ministry is the number of friends that God has raised up for me across this country. Many of them have written to say their home is open to me (of course, I can't accept all those invitations), but when I am in their town, they do nice things for me. They reveal their love. When they reveal that love to me—and I'm *hard* to love—it reveals that they honor the Word of God since I teach the Word of God.

Then the fifth commandment: "And be at peace among yourselves." These all come together in one package. You can't have everybody running the church. You can't have everybody running any kind of organization. There must be a certain one with authority.

I think one of the great problems in many churches today is a case of the old bromide, "too many cooks spoil the broth." There needs to be one who is the leader and who is followed. With that arrangement you can have peace. But when everybody is trying to play

his own tune, you have anything but harmony and peace!

Now here are the sixth through the ninth commandments—

Now we exhort you, brethren, warn them that are unruly, comfort the feebleminded, support the weak, be patient toward all men [1 Thess. 5:14].

"Warn them that are unruly." This would naturally follow the fifth commandment: "Be at peace among yourselves." The "unruly" are those who are out of step. My feeling is that they are loners, and they like to do their own little thing rather than support the work which God is doing. They are to be warned.

"Comfort the feebleminded." What does he mean by "feebleminded"? Well, a better word would be *fainthearted*. He is not referring to folk with mental problems. But here are folk who are fearful to move out for God, and they need encouraging. There is many a saint today who needs someone to put his arm around him and say, "Brother, you're going to make it. I'm *for* you and I am praying for you." My, what comfort and encouragement that would be to the fearful, the fainthearted—and sometimes all of us get discouraged and become fainthearted!

"Support the weak" is the eighth commandment. There are folk who are weak in the faith. They *cannot* get in step because they are little babies. They are not able to march with the rest; so *help* them. Lift them up, and carry them along.

"Be patient toward all men." That means: Don't lose your temper. That is so difficult! In business or in our other relationships with people, we meet ungodly, unholy, cantankerous, unsaved people who are definitely trying to trip us or to abuse us in some way, and it becomes very difficult to be patient and not to lose our tempers. But God commands us to be patient with everybody.

See that none render evil for evil unto any man; but ever follow that which is good, both among yourselves, and to all men [1 Thess. 5:15].

Now here is the tenth commandment: "See that none render evil for evil unto any man." In other words, don't fight one another.

The eleventh—"but ever follow that which is good, both among yourselves, and to all men." There are three philosophies of life or three standards of conduct. The pagan world operates on a philosophy which does evil in spite of good. In other words, you get the other fellow before he gets you. Use any kind of method. He may have treated you well, but if you can get the advantage over him, do that. That is pagan and heathen philosophy.

Then there is the standard of the so-called refined, cultured, and educated world. That is, do good to those who do good to you. The political parties in our country operate on that principle. If one person helps a man to get into political office, the politician reciprocates by offering the man a job or office. You take care of your own. That is the philosophy of the so-called civilized world. Jesus said, "And if ye do good to them which do good to you, what thank have ye? for sinners also do even the same" (Luke 6:33).

The Christian is to live under a different standard. We are to do good to those who do evil to us. That is contrary to the natural man. The minute someone hits us, we just naturally want to hit him back. This is the philosophy that Paul is talking about—"See that none render evil for evil unto any man; but ever follow that which is good"—even to those who do evil to you.

Now the twelfth commandment—

Rejoice evermore [1 Thess. 5:16].

I think these next three commandments go together. "Rejoice" does not mean to be happy. This is not the happy hour that he is talking about—*happy* is not a New Testament word. This is a *joy* in the Lord as Paul wrote to the Philippians, "Rejoice in the Lord alway: and again I say, Rejoice" (Phil. 4:4). My, what a commandment! You won't find that in the Ten Commandments! The child of God has no right to go around with a sour puss. The child of God has no right to be a cantankerous individual. If you are a child of God, you are to *rejoice* evermore! That, incidentally, is a fruit of the Holy Spirit—love, *joy*, peace. If you cannot rejoice, then begin reading the Word of God and calling on God to put joy in your heart. He will do it.

Pray without ceasing [1 Thess. 5:17].

This has to do with an attitude of prayer. I don't think this means that one is to stay on his knees all the time. But it means to pray regularly and to be constantly in the attitude of prayer.

Associated with that is this fourteenth commandment—

In every thing give thanks: for this is the will of God in Christ Jesus concerning you [1 Thess. 5:18].

This tells us to "give thanks" in all circumstances, not just once a year, but all the time.

This "is the will of God in Christ Jesus concerning you." If you come to me and ask what is the will of God for you, I can tell you three specific things that are the will of God for you: Rejoice always, pray without ceasing, and give thanks in everything. That is the will of God for you.

Now the fifteenth—

Quench not the Spirit [1 Thess. 5:19].

One of the figures that is used for the Holy Spirit is fire. How do you quench a fire? You dampen it down and don't let it burn. To quench the Spirit means that you refuse to do the will of God; that is, you are not listening to the Holy Spirit. You refuse to let the Holy Spirit be your Guide to lead you. You and I quench the Holy Spirit when we take matters into our own hands.

This is the same teaching that Paul gave to the Ephesian believers: "And grieve not the holy Spirit of God, whereby ye are sealed unto the day of redemption" (Eph. 4:30). You cannot grieve a *thing*; you grieve a *Person*. The Holy Spirit is a Person, and He is grieved by sin in our lives. Also, He is quenched when we step out of the will of God.

Despise not prophesyings [1 Thess. 5:20].

Do not look down upon Bible study as something that is beneath you. Do not be indifferent to the Word of God. We have a lot of folk who are in Christian service, but they are ignorant of the Bible and they look down on Bible study. Occasionally I hear such a person saying, "You just spend all your time in Bible study and you don't *do* anything. What you need to do is get out and get busy." Well, what is needed is to get busy studying the Word of God, and after you do that you will see how to get busy and really be *effective*.

We had a Bible study downtown in Los Angeles, averaging fifteen hundred people every Thursday night over a period of twenty-one years—what a thrill that was! What a privilege that was! But sometimes folks would make a remark like, "You need to get out and do something, not just go to sit and listen to the Bible." The interesting thing is that those people who came to sit and listen to the Bible *did* go out and do something. There are several hundred of those people who are out on the mission field; there are several hundred who are witnessing for God; and there are several hundred in the ministry. I notice that the boys who do not study the Word of God run down like an eight-day clock. Their ministries don't last too long. The sixteenth commandment which Paul gives the Thessalonians is "despise not prophesyings," that is, the teaching of the Word of God.

Prove all things; hold fast that which is good [1 Thess. 5:21].

"Prove all things." Don't be taken in. To put it crudely, don't be a sucker. Don't be misled into supporting a project just because somebody sends you a picture of pathetic looking orphans. Don't contribute to things you know nothing about. Don't fall for some promotion job. Investigate. Investigate anything to which you give your support. Christians ought not to be gullible. We are to prove all things. This also means that we are not to be taken in by flattery. There are many deceivers in the world.

"Hold fast that which is good." Hold to that which is true and genuine.

Abstain from all appearance of evil [1 Thess. 5:22].

This nineteenth commandment is the answer for questionable pastimes and amusements. If there is any question in your mind whether something is right or wrong, then it is wrong for you. Abstain from all *appearance* of evil.

Now notice that man is a triune being—

And the very God of peace sanctify you wholly; and I pray God your whole spirit and soul and body be preserved blameless unto the coming of our Lord Jesus Christ [1 Thess. 5:23].

Man is a triune being; body, soul (mind), and spirit. "Sanctify you wholly"—not perfectly, but we are to reach a place of maturation. We should not continue to be babes in Christ; we should be growing to maturity.

Faithful is he that calleth you, who also will do it [1 Thess. 5:24].

You can depend upon God.

Brethren, pray for us [1 Thess. 5:25].

This twentieth command is to pray for those who give out the gospel. You can't pray for Paul today, but you can pray for me, and I would appreciate it. You can pray for your pastor and your missionaries. I know they would appreciate it also.

Greet all the brethren with an holy kiss [1 Thess. 5:26].

This is a commandment, too. Just make sure it is a *holy* kiss! In our culture and with our customs, a warm handshake will do.

I charge you by the Lord that this epistle be read unto all the holy brethren [1 Thess. 5:27].

That is the twenty-second commandment, and I have obeyed it by quoting this entire epistle to you!

The grace of our Lord Jesus Christ be with you. Amen [1 Thess. 5:28].

And I pray that the grace of our Lord Jesus Christ may be with *you* my beloved.

(For Bibliography to 1 Thessalonians, see Bibliography at the end of 2 Thessalonians.)

The Second Epistle to The
THESSALONIANS
INTRODUCTION

The second epistle followed shortly after the first epistle in A.D. 52 or 53.

The Christians in Thessalonica were still baby Christians when Paul wrote 2 Thessalonians. His first letter to them had given rise to further questions, and Paul is attempting to answer them in his second letter. There was circulating in the Thessalonian church a letter or report, purported to have come from Paul, which was inclined to disturb the Christians. This false report claimed that Christ had already come and had already gathered out the church to Himself, and that the world was then living in the judgments of the "day of the Lord." These people were being persecuted, as we saw in the first epistle. They were suffering for the gospel's sake, and it was easy for them to believe that they had entered the Great Tribulation Period, and that all of the believers (not only the dead) had missed the Rapture. Paul attempts to allay their fears by writing this epistle and stating definitely that "our gathering together unto him" is yet future (2 Thess. 2:1), and that "the day of the Lord" has certain forerunners which must first come: the apostasy and the "man of sin" must come first. Therefore they could reasonably believe they were not in the Great Tribulation.

Paul says that the outward organization of the professing church is going to go into total apostasy. In Luke 18:8 the Lord asked, ". . . when the Son of man cometh, shall he find faith on the earth?" The way the question is couched in the Greek it demands a negative answer. He will *not* find the faith on the earth when He comes again. The organized church will be in total apostasy. This is confirmed in the Book of Revelation. In the fourth chapter the church has been removed from the earth, and nothing is left but an empty shell of an organization that has a form of godliness but denies the power of it. That same organization is the great harlot in chapter 17 of Revelation, which is about as frightful a picture as you will find in the Word of God.

The Thessalonian believers thought they had entered the Great Tribulation Period, and ever since that time folk who have gone through persecutions and tribulations have believed that they were in the Great Tribulation Period. For example, during World War II at the time of the blitz in Britain, some of the British ministers who were conservative in their faith came to the conclusion that they had entered the Great Tribulation and that the church was going to go through it.

A good friend of mine, a preacher from England, believes that the church will go through the Tribulation. In fact, he believes the church is in it right now. Well, he is living in California now, and one day we were having lunch together with a mutual friend who was a layman, who had bought us big T-bone steaks. The subject of the church and the Tribulation came up, and he insisted that the church was in the Great Tribulation. To confirm his argument he said, "McGee, if you had been in Great Britain during the blitz, and night after night had gone down into the subways with your people, the members of your church, and practically every night one person would have a nervous breakdown because of the strain, and would have to be taken the next day to the country, you would share my belief." I said to him, "If I had been in Great Britain, and in the blitz as you were, I am convinced that I would have thought as you did, *Boy, this is the Great Tribulation!* But after the war was over if I had come to the United States and was having lunch with a couple of friends and was eating a T-bone steak, I think I would pinch myself and ask myself, *Is this really the Great Tribulation Period?* If this is the Tribulation, let's have more of it since it will mean more T-bone steaks." He looked at me and said in that British disdainful voice, "McGee, you are being ridiculous!" So I told him that I didn't think I was being ridiculous; I thought *he* was being ridiculous.

The description of the Tribulation in the Bible is much worse than anything that happened during World War II. This period has been so clearly identified by Christ that there is no reason for getting panicky and for being stampeded into an unwarranted position. Christ said that there is coming a small interval which will be blocked off by ". . . such as was not since the beginning of the world to this time, no, nor ever shall be" (Matt. 24:21). Nothing like it has taken place before, and nothing like it will ever take place afterward.

While 1 Thessalonians emphasized the return of Christ for His church in what we call the "Rapture," 2 Thessalonians emphasizes the return of Christ to the earth the second time, when He returns in judgment and sets up His kingdom here upon this earth. This is called the *revelation*. You see, at the Rapture, the emphasis is not upon His coming to earth, because He doesn't come to the *earth*. He makes it clear that "we shall be caught up to meet the Lord in the *air*" (see 1 Thess. 4:17). "Caught up" is the Greek word *harpazō*, meaning "to snatch away." We shall be snatched away or raptured to meet Christ in the air. However, the revelation of Christ is when He returns to the earth to set up His kingdom. In the time gap between these two events will be the Great Tribulation Period.

As we saw in 1 Thessalonians, the Rapture is not a subject of the Old Testament; that teaching does not appear in the Old Testament. The hope of the Old Testament saints was an earthly hope. They were looking for their Messiah to come and establish a kingdom here upon this earth—which would be heaven upon earth. The expression "kingdom of heaven" means the reign of the heavens over the earth. That is putting it as simply as I know how. Some of the theologians really have made it complicated—so complicated that I wonder if they are trying to establish some kind of a theory. But the kingdom of heaven which Jesus talked about is the reign of the heavens over the earth, because this earth is going to become a heaven when He is here.

OUTLINE

I. **Persecution of Believers Now; Judgment of Unbelievers Hereafter (at Christ's Coming), Chapter 1:1–12**
   A. Introduction, Chapter 1:1–2
   B. Persecution of Believers and Fruits of It, Chapter 1:3–7
   C. Judgment of Wicked at Christ's Coming, Chapter 1:8–12

II. **Program for World in Connection with Christ's Coming, Chapter 2:1–12**
   A. Rapture Occurs First, Chapter 2:1
   B. Day of Lord Follows; Introduced by Total Apostasy and Appearance of Man of Sin, Chapter 2:2–5
   C. Mystery of Lawlessness Working Today; Lawless One Restrained by Holy Spirit, Chapter 2:6–8
   D. Lawless One to Appear in Great Tribulation Period, Chapter 2:9–12

III. **Practicality of Christ's Coming, Chapters 2:13–3:18**
   A. Believers Should Be Established in Word, Chapter 2:13–17
   B. Believers Should Be Established in Walk, Chapter 3:1–7
   C. Believers Should Be Established in Work, Chapter 3:8–18

CHAPTER 1

THEME: *Persecution of believers now and judgment of unbelievers hereafter (at Christ's coming)*

INTRODUCTION

Paul, and Silvanus, and Timotheus, unto the church of the Thessalonians in God our Father and the Lord Jesus Christ [2 Thess. 1:1].

Paul's greeting is his usual friendly greeting to a church which is theologically and spiritually sound. Paul includes the greetings of Silas (a contraction of the name Silvanus) and Timothy (Timotheus is the Greek form). These three men had endured a great deal for the sake of the gospel. Paul and Silas were in the prison at Philippi. Paul, Silas, and Timothy had gone to Thessalonica together, and later Paul had to leave them. He waited for them in Athens and, when they did not come, he went on to Corinth where they finally met. It was at that time Paul wrote his first epistle to the Thessalonians to answer some of the questions that had come up since he had been there.

When Paul writes his second epistle, he identifies his two co-workers who are brethren with him. He would identify himself with men who, for us today, would be totally unknown had not Paul included them in these epistles. This reveals something of the character of Paul. A man who had been a proud young Pharisee has become a humble follower of the Lord Jesus Christ and a servant of His and an apostle of His.

"Unto the church of the Thessalonians." That was the local church in Thessalonica. Paul believed in the local church, and that church in Thessalonica was "in God our Father and the Lord Jesus Christ." He probably did not mention the Holy Spirit because the Spirit was in the church in Thessalonica indwelling the believers. The indwelling Spirit enabled them to manifest the life of Christ and to walk worthy of the high calling of God. Their position, however, was in God the Father and in the Lord Jesus Christ. This means, my friend, that Paul taught the deity of Christ. There was no doubt in Paul's mind that Jesus Christ was God the Son.

In John 10:27–29 the Lord Jesus said, "My sheep hear my voice, and I know them, and they follow me: And I give unto them eternal life; and they shall never perish, neither shall any man pluck them out of my hand. My Father, which gave them me, is greater than all; and no man is able to pluck them out of my Father's hand." In this first verse you have the two hands of deity which belong to the Lord Jesus and God the Father. That is where the church is positionally—the Thessalonian church was there, and I hope your church is there. The important thing is not the name of your church. The important thing is that you and other true believers are in Christ Jesus, and that makes the local church very important. The Holy Spirit indwells true believers, and by His power they can manifest Christ in the local neighborhood, in the community, in the town, in the state, and in the world, showing forth the life of God. That is what Paul is saying to these believers in his introduction.

Grace unto you, and peace, from God our Father and the Lord Jesus Christ [2 Thess. 1:2].

Grace and *peace* are two important words in the gospel. Grace comes first. If you have experienced the grace of God, that means you have been saved. "For by grace are ye saved through faith; and that not of yourselves: it is the gift of God: Not of works, lest any man should boast" (Eph. 2:8–9). When you come to God as a lost sinner, bringing nothing, and receiving everything from Him, then you have experienced the grace of God. He offers you salvation—the gift of God is eternal life. You cannot work for a gift, and if you do, it ceases to be a gift and it becomes something you have earned. It becomes a payment. God is not patting you on the back because you are a nice Sunday school boy. Salvation is God offering you, a lost, hell-doomed sinner, eternal life if you trust Christ. That is grace.

"Peace"—if you have experienced God's grace, then you know something about His peace. Peace is the world's softest pillow that you can sleep on at night. It is the peace that comes when you know that your sins are forgiven. Peace comes, not from some psychological gyrations you go through, or through the counsel of a psychiatrist, but it comes from a supernatural source—from "God our Father and the Lord Jesus Christ"; it is supernatural. If you don't have it, you *can* have it, because it is the gift of God which is given to sinners who turn to Christ.

PERSECUTION OF BELIEVERS AND FRUITS OF IT

We are bound to thank God always for you, brethren, as it is meet, because that your faith groweth exceedingly, and the charity of every one of you all toward each other aboundeth [2 Thess. 1:3].

The word *charity* in this verse is "love." In verse 4 Paul speaks of patience and faith. In verses 3 and 4 we have that little trinity that Paul uses: faith, love, and patience. These three words are abstract terms, but we must bring them out of the abstract into the concrete. Get them walking on the sidewalks today. This again is the "work of faith" which Paul mentioned in 1 Thessalonians 1:3. Saving faith produces works. A saving faith will produce a love in the heart for God's children. My friend, if you are a child of God, you will have to love me whether or not you want to, and I'm going to have to love you. It is a wonderful arrangement!

In the next verse Paul picks up the third word, which he uses with "love" and "faith." It is "patience." This is not the patience of waiting in a traffic jam or waiting for a light to turn green. It is the patience that is willing to live for God and accept whatever He sends your way, knowing that all things do work together for good. It is the patience that has as its goal coming into God's presence someday. This enables you to get over the rough places that come into your life. The life of a Christian reminds me of traveling over a highway. Many years ago I used to cross the country by automobile from Texas to California. There would be many places where a detour sign would put us on a rough old road. But along the way we would see a sign that read "5 miles to the double highway," and the rough road became a little bit smoother by knowing that we would hit the asphalt or the concrete in a little while. And many of us are on a detour in this life. The road is rough, and we are called upon to suffer. Well, if you have a good view of the future, it will give you the patience of hope—a hope that looks way down yonder to the good smooth road coming up. And it may be closer than you think.

"We are bound to thank God always for you, brethren, as it is meet." The word *meet* means "proper"—it is right and fitting for us to thank God for you.

"Because that your faith groweth exceedingly, and the charity [love] of every one of you all toward each other aboundeth." You cannot grow toward God without growing outward toward your brother. When you grow toward God in grace and knowledge and faith, you grow toward your brother in love.

And God must send us a little trouble because that is the discipline which produces patience in our lives. It enables us to look down into the future with hope.

So that we ourselves glory in you in the churches of God for your patience and faith in all your persecutions and tribulations that ye endure [2 Thess. 1:4].

"Tribulations" are afflictions. The church will not go through the Great Tribulaton, but we will go through the little tribulation. We all will have trouble down here. If you are not having any troubles, then there must be something wrong with you, because the Lord disciplines His children.

Patience is an interesting word. The Greek word translated by the English word *patience* has the literal meaning of "standing under." It means to be placed under. A great many people try to get out from *under* the problems and difficulties. The person who is patient is able to stay under, and he keeps on carrying the load. He doesn't throw it off; he doesn't try to get rid of his responsibility.

These Thessalonian Christians had a real testimony in the Roman world of that day. (Thessalonica was a Roman colony, and people were going to and fro from that colony, so the word got out everywhere.) The patience and faith of these Christians were unshaken as they were enduring a great deal of trouble, persecutions, and afflictions.

Trouble is not something strange. The Word of God makes it clear that we are going to have trouble in this life. Peter expressed it like this: "Beloved, think it not strange concerning the fiery trial which is to try you, as though some strange thing happened unto you" (1 Pet. 4:12). Sometimes we hear Christians say, "I don't know why God let this happen to me. Nobody else has ever had to go through this." It is safe to say that such a statement is not true. Whatever you are going through, you have company. It is not a strange thing for suffering to come to us. Peter goes on to say, "But rejoice, inasmuch as ye are partakers of Christ's sufferings; that, when his glory shall be revealed, ye may be glad also with exceeding joy" (1 Pet. 4:13). Peter warns that Christians sometimes get *themselves* into trouble. "But let none of you suffer as a murderer, or as a thief, or as an evildoer, or as a busybody in other men's matters" (1 Pet. 4:15). A Christian can get himself in hot water because he talks too much—talking about others. Or he can suffer persecution because he is dishonest. There is no advantage to that kind of suffering. That is not the discipline in life which will develop patience. That is simply getting what you have coming to you. Peter goes on, "Yet if any man suffer as a Christian, let him not be ashamed; but let him glorify God on this behalf" (1 Pet. 4:16). There is a difference between being disciplined to learn patience and the punishment of the wicked. God disciplines His children for their development, for their growth, that they might have patience and a hope for the future. We don't need to get too comfortable down here. When we do, we no longer have the hope before us of the Lord's return.

Which is a manifest token of the righteous judgment of God, that ye may be counted worthy of the kingdom of God, for which ye also suffer [2 Thess. 1:5].

Our suffering has nothing to do with salvation, but it sure prepares us for our eternal state. When you and I look back to this life on earth, maybe some of us will wish that we had had a little bit more discipline than we got!

While the judgment of the wicked begins with verse 8, this is certainly the introduction to it.

Seeing it is a righteous thing with God to recompense tribulation to them that trouble you [2 Thess. 1:6].

When God judges, God is righteous in it. Paul asks the question: "Is there unrighteousness with God?" The answer is, Let it not be—"God forbid" (see Rom. 9:14). Whatever God does is absolutely right. He can do no wrong. Sometimes we complain about the things that happen to us because we are ignorant; we do not understand God's ways. But God has a very definite purpose for all that He does. And God is righteous in sending the Great Tribulation. It is a judgment of sinners.

And to you who are troubled rest with us, when the Lord Jesus shall be revealed from heaven with his mighty angels [2 Thess. 1:7].

The Lord Jesus is coming in judgment.

JUDGMENT OF WICKED AT CHRIST'S COMING

In flaming fire taking vengeance on them that know not God, and that obey not the gospel of our Lord Jesus Christ:

Who shall be punished with everlasting destruction from the presence of the Lord, and from the glory of his power [2 Thess. 1:8–9].

The Word of God actually says very little about heaven. One of the reasons is that it is so wonderful we could not comprehend it. And the Lord does not want us to get so heavenly minded that we are no earthly good. He wants us to keep our eyes on our pathway down here, and I think He wants us to keep our noses to the grindstone much of the time. In other words, He has a purpose for our lives on earth, and He wants us to fulfill that purpose.

Scripture not only says very little about heaven, it says *less* about the condition of the lost. It is so awful that the Holy Spirit has drawn a veil over it. There is nothing given to satisfy the morbid curiosity or the lust for revenge. When *God* judges, He does not do it in a vindictive manner. He does it in order to vindicate His righteousness and His holiness. There is nothing in the Scriptures to satisfy our curiosity about hell, but there is enough said to give us a warning. It does not mean that it is less real because so little is said. Actually, Christ Himself said more about hell than did anyone else. Hell is an awful reality. I am not going to speculate about it; I'm just quoting what is said right here: He is coming "in flaming fire taking vengeance on them that know not God, and that obey not the gospel of our Lord Jesus Christ: who shall be punished with everlasting destruction from the presence of the Lord, and from the glory of his power."

Hell is ridiculed today, but that does not mean it doesn't exist. Our beliefs are sometimes only wishful thinking. For example, it was the popular notion that Hitler would not plunge Europe into a war and turn Europe into a holocaust of flaming fire. But he did. Chamberlain, the man with the umbrella, went over to meet with Hitler and Mussolini, and he came back saying that we would have peace in our time. Well, we didn't have peace, and we don't have peace in the world today. Also, many people thought that Japan would never attack America. Our government did not believe she would, and the liberal churches at that time were teaching pacifism. Well, whether they believed it or not, there was a vicious attack at Pearl Harbor.

Friend, we might as well face the fact that there is a hell. Christ is returning to this earth some day. First He will take His own out of the earth, and then His coming will be a terror to the wicked; it will be a judgment upon those who "know not God, and that obey not the gospel of our Lord Jesus Christ." "And this is life eternal, that they might know thee the only true God, and Jesus Christ, whom thou hast sent" (John 17:3). Do you want to work for your salvation? Jesus said, ". . . This is the work of God, that ye believe on him whom he hath sent" (John 6:29). That is what the Word of God teaches.

I know that it is not popular to talk about hell and judgment. Even the Christian testimonies that we hear and read are filled with I, I, I—"I became successful in business. I saved my marriage. My personality changed." Nothing very much is said about the Lord Jesus. How many testimonies have you heard in which it is said, "I was a hell-doomed sinner going straight to hell, I was lost, and He saved me"? The important thing to say in a testimony is not what He has given you but from what He has delivered you. That was the whole purpose for the coming of our Savior. He came to redeem us! He didn't come to give us new personalities or to make us successful. He came to *deliver* us from *hell!* That's not popular to say. Folk don't like to hear it.

There are too few people today who are willing to confront folk with the fact that they are lost. Suppose you were asleep in a burning building, and a man rushed into that building to rescue you. He awakened you, picked you up, and carried you bodily out of that burning building. He liked you; so he made you his son. He brought you into his lovely home and gave you many wonderful gifts. Now if you had the opportunity to stand before a group of people and tell about this man and express your appreciation in his presence, what would you thank him for? Would you thank him for making you his son? I hope you would. But wouldn't you really thank him most for the fact that he risked his life to save you out of a burning building? Nothing else would have mattered if he had not rescued you from a flaming death.

Now, my friend, the judgment of the lost is coming. If you want to stay in that class, you shall be judged. Somebody needs to tell you the facts, and I am telling them to you right now.

Again, who are the lost? They are those who (1) "know not God" and who (2) "obey not the gospel of our Lord Jesus Christ." Let me repeat verse 9: "Who shall be punished with everlasting destruction from the presence of the Lord, and from the glory of his power."

When he shall come to be glorified in his saints, and to be admired in all them that believe (because our testimony among you was believed) in that day [2 Thess. 1:10].

The coming of Christ to the earth in judgment will justify the believers who have put their trust in Him, and it will glorify the Savior.

Wherefore also we pray always for you, that our God would count you worthy of this calling, and fulfil all the good pleasure of his goodness, and the work of faith with power:

That the name of our Lord Jesus Christ may be glorified in you, and ye in him, according to the grace of our God and the Lord Jesus Christ [2 Thess. 1:11–12].

"That the name of our Lord Jesus Christ may be glorified in you." If God has prospered you, made you a financial success, and you can glorify Christ, that's fine. But somehow I am more impressed by a little woman who has been flat on her back in a hospital most of her life—yet has a radiant testimony for Christ. Certainly Christ is being glorified in her.

CHAPTER 2

THEME: *The program for the world in connection with Christ's coming*

Back in 1 Thessalonians, beginning at verse 13 of chapter 4, we called attention to the rapture of the church; we also spoke of the Day of the Lord, the Great Tribulation, and the coming of Christ in glory to this earth. In this epistle the emphasis is going to be on the Great Tribulation Period, but we are also going to find one of the finest passages on the rapture of the church.

THE RAPTURE OCCURS FIRST

Now we beseech you, brethren, by the coming of our Lord Jesus Christ, and by our gathering together unto him [2 Thess. 2:1].

"Our gathering together unto him" is the rapture of the church. The first aspect of Christ's coming is in view in this verse. There is no judgment at this time.

THE DAY OF THE LORD FOLLOWS THE RAPTURE

That ye be not soon shaken in mind, or be troubled, neither by spirit, nor by word, nor by letter as from us, as that the day of Christ is at hand [2 Thess. 2:2].

In many good Bibles with notes you will find the note in the margin—if it has not already been changed in the text—that this should read "the day of the Lord is at hand" rather than "the day of Christ is at hand." The Day of the Lord has no reference to the church. After the Rapture, the day of Christ, or the age of grace, comes to an end and the Day of the Lord begins. The Day of the Lord is a subject which is often mentioned in the Old Testament, whereas the Rapture is not. The Day of the Lord begins with night. Joel tells us it is darkness and not light. It is a time of judgment. It opens with night just like every Hebrew day opens: ". . . the *evening* and the morning were the first day" (Gen. 1:5, italics mine).

"Nor by word, nor by letter"—apparently someone had been circulating a letter or an oral word among the Thessalonians that the Day of the Lord had come. It is interesting that there is always a group of super-duper saints who seem to think they get direct information from the Lord. They don't think they

need to study the Word of God; they imagine they get their information directly through dreams or visions or special revelations. Now, friend, I admit that it is much easier to pick up all your information in a telephone conversation than it is to go to school or take up the Bible and study it, but it won't be coming straight from God. So there was circulating in Thessalonica a word that had come to them, and it was a special "revelation," something that Brother Paul had not told them.

"Nor by letter" would indicate that a spurious letter had been circulating. Or perhaps someone simply said they had seen such a letter.

"Nor by letter as from us" would mean that they said the letter supposedly came from Paul, Timothy, and Silas.

The word they circulated was that "the day of the Lord is at hand." This had caused a problem with the Thessalonian believers, and we can see why. They were enduring persecution. Because they were having trouble, it was very easy for someone to say, "Well, this is the Great Tribulation that we are in. The Day of the Lord has come, and we are already in it."

The Day of the Lord is a technical phrase that speaks of the period beginning with the Great Tribulation and continuing through the Millennium. It is a day that begins with judgment. Joel describes the Day of the Lord in some detail in chapter 2 of his prophecy, and Peter quoted him on the Day of Pentecost. His listeners knew that there was a day coming when the Spirit of God would be poured out—but it was the coming Day of the Lord of which they knew. In Acts 2:20 Peter says, "The sun shall be turned into darkness, and the moon into blood, before that great and notable day of the Lord come." Certainly that had not happened at Pentecost. At the crucifixion of Christ there had been an earthquake and darkness, but on the Day of Pentecost there was nothing like that at all. There was a rushing sound like a mighty wind, and it had the appearance of tongues of fire as it rested upon each of those present. There was no wind, but it sounded like a hurricane when it hit the town, and it caused everybody to rush up to the temple area to see what had happened. Peter is saying that the Day of Pentecost was *similar* to the day Joel described: "You think these men are drunk? They are not; they are filled with the Holy Spirit." Because of Joel's prophecy, the orthodox Jews in that day believed there was a day coming when God would pour out His Spirit on *all* flesh—but on the Day of Pentecost it was not poured out on all flesh. The Day of the Lord is yet future.

Peter refers to the Day of the Lord again in his epistle: "But the day of the Lord will come as a thief in the night." We have already seen that for the church He will *not* come as a thief in the night (1 Thess. 5). The church is to be awake and waiting for Him. It is to the sleepy world that He will come as a thief in the night. Peter goes on to say, ". . . in the which the heavens shall pass away with a great noise, and the elements shall melt with fervent heat, the earth also and the works that are therein shall be burned up" (2 Pet. 3:10). Again, this did not happen on the Day of Pentecost.

Another Scripture which shows that the Day of the Lord has no reference to the church is Revelation 6:17: "For the great day of his wrath is come; and who shall be able to stand?" That is not for the church. The church is to look for *Him*—a Person—to come, because we are identified with Him.

Let no man deceive you by any means: for that day shall not come, except there come a falling away first, and that man of sin be revealed, the son of perdition [2 Thess. 2:3].

"Let no man deceive you by any means." If we are not to be deceived, then let's listen to Paul.

"For that day shall not come." Which day? The Day of the Lord—not the Rapture. The Day of the Lord shall not come except there be the fulfilling of two conditions: (1) "There come a falling away first" and (2) "that man of sin be revealed, the son of perdition." Both of these things must take place before the Day of the Lord can begin, and neither one of them has taken place as yet.

There must be "a falling away first." Many have interpreted this to mean the apostasy, and I agree that it does refer to that. But I think it means more than that, as a careful examination of the word will reveal. The Greek word that is here translated as "falling away" is *apostasia*. The root word actually means "departure or removal from."

Paul says that before the Day of the Lord begins there must first come a removing. There are two kinds of removing that are going to take place. First, the organized church will depart from the faith—that is what we call apostasy. But there will be *total* apostasy when the Lord comes, and that cannot take place until the true church is removed. The Lord asked, ". . . when the Son of man cometh [to the earth], shall he find [the] faith . . . ?" (Luke 18:8). When He says "the faith," He means that body of truth which He left here. The answer to His question is no, He will not find the faith here when He returns. There will be total apostasy because of two things: (1) the organization of the church has departed from the faith—it has apostatized and (2) there has been another departure, the departure of the true church from the earth. The departure of the true church leads into the total apostatizing of the organized church. The Day of the Lord cannot begin—nor the Great Tribulation Period—until the departure of the true church has taken place.

Paul is not going into detail about the rapture of the church because he has already written about that in his first epistle: "For the Lord himself shall descend from heaven with a shout, with the voice of the archangel, and with the trump of God: and the dead in Christ shall rise first: Then we which are alive and remain shall be caught up together with them in the clouds, to meet the Lord in the air: and so shall we ever be with the Lord" (1 Thess. 4:16–17). That is the departure, the removal, of the church.

The organized church which is left down here will totally depart from the faith. We see it pictured as the great harlot in Revelation 17. The Laodicean church, which is the seventh and last church described in the Book of Revelation, is in sad condition. I think that is the period we are in right now. When the true believers are gone, it will get even worse. It will finally end in total apostasy.

From the viewpoint of the earth the removal of believers is a departure. From the viewpoint of heaven, it is a rapture, a snatching or catching up. I think the world is going to say at that time, "Oh, boy, they are gone!" They think that fellow McGee and other Bible teachers are a nuisance, and they will be glad when they are gone. The world will rejoice. They do not realize that it will be a sad day for them. They think they will be entering into the blessing of the Millennium, not realizing they are actually entering into the Great Tribulation Period, which will be a time of trouble such as the world has never before seen.

Sometime ago Mrs. McGee and I were at the Los Angeles airport to take a morning flight to Florida. We always go early to have breakfast at the airport. While we were waiting, a big 747 was getting ready to go to the Hawaiian Islands. There was a fine-looking

Marine Corps fellow there with his pretty wife and a precious little baby. But they looked so sad. A few minutes later when it came time to board the plane, they stood up. The father put his arms around them both, and they just wept. Then he picked up his bag and disappeared through the gate. It was a departure. It was an *apostasia*, a removal. The young wife picked up the baby and slowly walked back to the escalator, tears running down her face. My heart went out to her. Life would be hard for her now.

I couldn't help but think that that is the way it will be for the world. When the church departs, many people will be glad to see us go. The liberals will be glad to get rid of us. There will be rejoicing. But they do not realize how hard it will be for them. They are going to enter the Great Tribulation Period.

The second thing which must happen is that the "man of sin be revealed, the son of perdition." When he is revealed the Great Tribulation Period has already begun. Here he is called "the man of sin." John calls him "the antichrist." John is the only one who uses that term, by the way. The Antichrist has about thirty different titles in the Bible. He is a subject of the Old Testament. He is going to be Satan's man. This is the man who will put the Roman Empire back together again, and he will finally become a world dictator. He is going to deceive the world. He could be in our midst today, but he won't be able to appear in power or reveal who he is until after the Great Tribulation Period begins.

Paul tells us more about him—

Who opposeth and exalteth himself above all that is called God, or that is worshipped; so that he as God sitteth in the temple of God, shewing himself that he is God [2 Thess. 2:4].

One of his claims will be that he is God. In Revelation 13 we find that the beast out of the sea (the Antichrist) brings together western Europe, and he will put it back together again. When he does this, he will show himself as God. The world will think that he is Christ. That is the big lie.

Remember ye not, that, when I was yet with you, I told you these things? [2 Thess. 2:5].

Paul hadn't hesitated to talk about these things. Some say that a preacher shouldn't dwell on these topics. Well, Paul did. Paul says, "When I was with you, I told you about him."

MYSTERY OF LAWLESSNESS WORKING TODAY, RESTRAINED BY THE HOLY SPIRIT

And now ye know what withholdeth that he might be revealed in his time [2 Thess. 2:6].

What *can* withhold evil in the world? The only One I know who can do that is the Holy Spirit. Governments can't do it—they are not doing it. The Roman Empire couldn't do it; it was an evil force itself.

For the mystery of iniquity doth already work: only he who now letteth will let, until he be taken out of the way [2 Thess. 2:7].

Let me give you a clearer translation of this verse: "For the mystery of lawlessness doth already work: only he who now hinders will hinder, until he be taken out of the way."

"The mystery of lawlessness" had begun to work already in Paul's day, and it continues to work. The Lord Jesus gave a parable in Matthew 13 which reveals the condition of the world today. These are the mysteries of the kingdom of heaven, and they explain the condition of the world and of the church in the world today. The Word of God is being sown out in the field of the world, but an enemy has come in and has sown tares. The tares and the wheat are growing together—the Word of God and lawlessness grow together today. The world is getting worse, and in a sense, the world is getting better, because I think the Word of God is going out more than it ever has in the history of the world. The doors are open—the Word is growing, the wheat is growing. But the tares are growing also.

Lawlessness will continue to get worse and worse, but the Holy Spirit will not let Satan go all the way in this age. When the Holy Spirit will be removed, it will be like taking the stopper out of the bottle—the liquid of lawlessness will pour out all over the world in that day.

When will the Holy Spirit be taken out? He will be taken out with the church. Won't the Holy Spirit be in the world during the Great Tribulation? Yes. Wasn't He in the world before Pentecost? He surely was. He was present in the days of the Old Testament, but He was on a different mission. And He will be on a different mission after the church is removed. Now the Spirit of God is sealing us until the day of redemption when He will present us and deliver us to the Lord Jesus. If He didn't do that, we would never make it.

After He does that, I believe He will come back to the earth to resume His former mission down here. But He will not hinder evil—He will let the Devil have his day for a while. Believe me, I don't want to be on the earth when the Devil has it! It looks bad enough to me as it is today; so I don't want to be here when it is turned over to him.

And then shall that Wicked be revealed, whom the Lord shall consume with the spirit of his mouth, and shall destroy with the brightness of his coming [2 Thess. 2:8].

"That Wicked"—the Antichrist, the Man of Sin—will be a world dictator. Nobody can stop him. No power on earth—only the coming of Christ will stop him. As God's people in Egypt were helpless and hopeless until God delivered them, so the believers during the Tribulation will be helpless under the power of the Antichrist until the Lord Jesus comes to the earth to establish His kingdom. "The Lord shall consume with the spirit of his mouth," that is, the Word of God which is the two-edged sword that proceeds from His mouth shall consume the Antichrist. It was the Word of God that created this universe. All God had to do was to speak. God said, "Let there be light: and there was light" (Gen. 1:3). The Lord Jesus Christ is the living Word of God. Today we have the Bible, which is the written Word of God. The written Word is about the living Word, and it is alive and potent. When the Lord Jesus returns, He comes as the living Word of God.

"And shall destroy with the brightness of his coming." "Brightness" is the Greek word *epiphaneia* or "epiphany" in English, and it refers to the shining forth of His coming. When the Lord Jesus came to Bethlehem, it was His first epiphany. Titus 2:11 uses that word *epiphaneia* when it says, "For the grace of God that bringeth salvation hath *appeared* to all men" (italics mine). That was the gracious appearing of His coming.

As George Macdonald put it:

> "Thou cam'st, a little baby thing,
> That made a woman cry."

When He comes again it will be another epiphany. He will take His church out of the world, and then He is coming to the earth to establish His kingdom. His first coming had two episodes of coming, if you want to look at it that way. He came to Bethlehem as a little baby, and then later He began His ministry at the age of thirty years when He walked into the temple and cleansed it. His second coming also has two phases. He calls for His church to meet Him in the air, and then He comes down to the earth to establish His kingdom. At that time the Antichrist shall be consumed and destroyed with the brightness of His coming.

LAWLESS ONE TO APPEAR IN GREAT TRIBULATION

Even him, whose coming is after the working of Satan with all power and signs and lying wonders [2 Thess. 2:9].

This is the Antichrist, Satan's man, the Man of Sin, the lawless one. He will come "after the working of Satan with all power and signs and lying wonders."

"Power" here is *dunamis* in the Greek. It means a physical power whose source is supernatural. He will be quite a healer and a miracle worker. I think he will be able to walk on water. I think he might be able to control the wind. Remember that Satan at one time let a wind destroy the sons and daughters of Job. I am always afraid when anyone tells me of someone who is performing miracles today, because the next miracle worker predicted by the Bible is the one whose coming is after the working of Satan. I am always afraid that miracle workers have not come from heaven. The Devil will send this man with power and signs and lying wonders. That is the reason it is so important for us to get our eyes off men and to get them on Christ, to walk by faith in Him.

"Signs" means tokens. They have the purpose of appealing to the understanding. This man will have signs which will appeal to the scientific world of that day as well as to politicians and the religious world. I am amazed how even today people are taken in by the phoniest kinds of things. Someone has asked me, "Why do you think that happens?" I believe the answer can be expressed like this, "Those who do not stand for something will fall for anything." People who are not rooted and grounded in the Word of God will fall for all kinds of signs.

"Lying wonders" will produce an effect upon observers. In that day, people all over the world will be talking about the Man of Sin, saying, "My, this world ruler we have is a great fellow. Look at what he can do!"

Who is it that will fall for his lying wonders? Those who would not believe the gospel—

And with all deceivableness of unrighteousness in them that perish; because they received not the love of the truth, that they might be saved [2 Thess. 2:10].

He will do this "with all deceivableness of unrighteousness in them that perish." Why?— "because they received not the love of the truth, that they might be saved." I *do* believe that the gospel is going to go out to the ends of the earth. It may even be the church that accomplishes this. I think it is penetrating pretty well today by radio into areas where individuals cannot go. But there will be those who hear and refuse to receive the truth.

And for this cause God shall send them strong delusion, that they should believe a lie [2 Thess. 2:11].

God will let the world believe a lie. Why does He do that? Isn't that a little unfair? No, it is just like it was when God hardened Pharaoh's heart. Pharaoh wasn't weeping for the children of Israel, longing to let them go free, being held back from his good intentions by God! If you think that, you are entirely wrong. Pharaoh did not want to let them go, and what God did was to force him to make a stand and come to a decision. God forced him into a situation which revealed what was already in his heart. We see a lot of people pussy-footing around today. They won't take a stand for God. They won't listen to the gospel. They are closed to it. God graciously gives them His Word, but they don't want it. After they have heard the Word of God but have refused to accept it, God will send them "strong delusion." Why? Because they would not receive the truth. Then they are open to believe the lie.

People who have stopped going to churches where they heard the gospel are wide open to the cults and the "isms" of our day. That is why so many of the cultists go around on Sunday morning, knocking at doors. They know that the weak people will not be in church on Sunday morning. They are not interested enough in the Word of God to be in church. The cults know that they can get those people, because if they will not receive the truth, they are open for anything else that comes along.

I have been simply amazed at some intelligent people who have sat in church, heard the gospel, rejected it, and then turned to the wildest cult imaginable. They will follow some individual who is absolutely a phony—not giving out the Word of God at all. Why? Because God says that is the way it is: When people reject the truth, they will believe the lie.

God is separating the sheep from the goats. God uses the best way in the world to do it. If people will not receive the love of the truth, then God sends them a "strong delusion, that

they should believe a lie." What is the "lie"? The lie of Antichrist is that Jesus Christ is not the Lord, that He is not who He says He is. He will tell people that they are really smart in not becoming religious nuts who believe in Jesus. He'll have some good explanation for the departure of the saints from the earth at the Rapture and will congratulate the people on having waited to build a kingdom on earth with him. The people will believe him and will believe that Antichrist will bring them the Millennium. They will not realize that they are entering into the Great Tribulation. That is the lie, and people will believe it because they believed not the truth.

That they all might be damned who believed not the truth, but had pleasure in unrighteousness [2 Thess. 2:12].

God is going to judge those who have rejected the truth. I have said this many times, and I am going to say it again: If you can sit and read the Word of God in this book and continue to reject Jesus Christ, then you are wide open for anything that comes along to delude and deceive you. You will never be able to go into the presence of God and say, "I never heard the gospel." If you turn your back on the Lord Jesus Christ, then you are wide open for delusion and you are a subject for judgment. As a believer giving out the gospel, I am a savor of life to those that are saved and a savor of death to those that perish (see 2 Cor. 2:15–16). I have really put you out on a limb, because you cannot say you have never heard the gospel. You have heard it, and you have probably heard it in several different places. If you reject Jesus Christ, then I am the savor of death to you. If you accept Jesus Christ as your own Lord and Savior, then I am the savor of life to you.

PRACTICALITY OF CHRIST'S COMING

Now Paul moves into the practical side of this epistle. In the light of the knowledge of future events, the believer should live a life that demonstrates that he believes in the coming of Christ. Believing in the coming of Christ doesn't mean to run out and look up into the sky and say, "Oh, I wish Jesus would come!" That is just pious nonsense. It will be manifest in three different ways if a person believes in the coming of Christ: it will affect his attitude toward the Word, his walk, and his work.

BELIEVERS SHOULD BE
ESTABLISHED IN THE WORD

But we are bound to give thanks alway to God for you, brethren beloved of the

Lord, because God hath from the beginning chosen you to salvation through sanctification of the Spirit and belief of the truth:

Whereunto he called you by our gospel, to the obtaining of the glory of our Lord Jesus Christ [2 Thess. 2:13–14].

I believe these two verses give the total spectrum of salvation. In other words, they give you salvation "from Dan to Beer-sheba"—all the way from the past, the present, and down into the future.

1. "Chosen you to salvation." This is so clearly taught in Romans 8: "And we know that all things work together for good to them that love God, to them who are the called according to his purpose. [Dr. R. A. Torrey used to say that this verse was a soft pillow for a tired heart. It surely is that.] For whom he did foreknow, he also did predestinate to be conformed to the image of his Son, that he might be the firstborn among many brethren. Moreover whom he did predestinate, them he also called: and whom he called, them he also justified: and whom he justified, them he also glorified. What shall we then say to these things? If God be for us, who can be against us?" (Rom. 8:28–31).

That is exactly what Paul is writing here in 2 Thessalonians: "God hath from the beginning chosen you to salvation." That looks back to the past. All I know is what it says, and I believe it. Do you mean to tell me that God chose us before we even got here? Spurgeon used to put it something like this: "I am glad God chose me before I got here, because if He had waited until I got here He never would have chosen me." It simply means that you do not surprise God when you trust Christ. But there is another side of the coin: "Whosoever will may come." The "whosoever wills" are the chosen ones, and the "whosoever won'ts" are the nonelect. Jesus said, ". . . If any man thirst, let him come unto me, and drink" (John 7:37). That is a legitimate offer of salvation—a sincere, definite offer with no complications attached. If you don't come, the reason is *not* because you are not elected. Not at all. The reason you don't come is that you're not thirsty; that is, you don't think you need a Savior. If you are thirsty, then come to Christ.

2. "Through sanctification of the Spirit." "Chosen you to salvation" looked back to the past, and now sanctification by the Spirit looks to the present. You are sanctified both as to position and as to practice. When you accept Jesus Christ as your own Savior, you

are *in Christ*—that is positional sanctification; that is the past tense of salvation. Then there is also the practical side of sanctification which concerns your life. Through the Spirit of God you are to grow in grace.

3. "Belief of the truth." That means that a believer is going to study the Word of God. That is the way he is going to grow and develop.

4. "To the obtaining of the glory of our Lord Jesus Christ." This is future. This refers to the Rapture. "Beloved, now are we the sons of God, and it doth not yet appear what we shall be: but we know that, when he shall appear, we shall be like him; for we shall see him as he is" (1 John 3:2). Then there is the statement in Colossians 1:27, "To whom God would make known what is the riches of the glory of this mystery among the Gentiles; which is Christ in you, the hope of glory." That looks forward to the future. What a glorious, wonderful prospect we have before us!

We see that these two verses have given us the full spectrum of salvation: we *have been* saved, we *are being* saved, we *shall be* saved. It is all the work of God.

Therefore, brethren, stand fast, and hold the traditions which ye have been taught, whether by word, or our epistle [2 Thess. 2:15].

Paul is referring to what he had taught them when he was with them. It is the Word which enables the believer to stand and be stable.

Now our Lord Jesus Christ himself, and God, even our Father, which hath loved us, and hath given us everlasting consolation and good hope through grace,

Comfort your hearts, and stablish you in every good word and work [2 Thess. 2:16–17].

The Lord Jesus Christ brings comfort and consolation to our hearts. He does this through His Word. That will establish us in every good word and work. The study of the Word of God will lead to the work of the Lord.

Not only will the Word of God "comfort" us, but it will also edify us. "Stablish you" means we are to be rooted and grounded in the Word of God so that we are not carried away by every wind of doctrine. Our minds and hearts will be centered on Him. That will keep us from going out after every fad of the day and reading every new book that comes off the press. Nor will we be running to little study courses here and there to be built up for the moment. We need to be *established* in the faith.

It is the Word of God then that will lead you to do the work of God. In chapter 3 we will see that believers should also be established in their walk and in their work down here. You see, it is rather deceitful (to yourself and others) to talk about how much you love the coming of the Lord if you do not study His Word. Then your belief does not manifest itself in your life and it doesn't make you work. If you really believe Christ is coming, you're going to be busy working for Him. You are going to give account to Him someday. If He is going to be here tomorrow, we want to be busy today. We shouldn't have our noses pressed against the window looking for Him to come, or to be always looking up into heaven for Him. Instead, we should be looking around doing the work of the Lord down here. That is the greatest proof that we believe in His coming.

CHAPTER 3

THEME: *The practicality of Christ's coming*

Chapter 2 concluded with the fact that believers should be established in the Word—the Word of God. Paul spoke about God comforting our hearts and establishing us in every good word and work. This has to do with loyalty to the person of the Lord Jesus Christ. Also Paul spoke in chapter 2, verses 13–14, of the marvelous position we have in Christ. We are *chosen*—"God hath from the beginning chosen you to salvation through sanctification of the Spirit." And we are called of God "to the obtaining of the glory of our Lord Jesus Christ." This is heady stuff! It is exciting and thrilling.

Now here in chapter 3 Paul says that there are certain responsibilities that we have as believers. As Paul put it to the Ephesian believers, ". . . walk worthy of the vocation wherewith ye are called" (Eph. 4:1). Now Paul is saying the same thing to the Thessalonian believers.

BELIEVERS SHOULD BE ESTABLISHED IN THEIR WALK

Finally, brethren, pray for us, that the word of the Lord may have free course, and be glorified, even as it is with you:

And that we may be delivered from unreasonable and wicked men: for all men have not faith [2 Thess. 3:1–2].

He is saying here that the Word of God enables the believer to walk before the wicked world. The Word establishes a believer in his walk.

"Finally, brethren"—he is coming to the conclusion of his letter.

"Pray for us." Prayer is something that every believer can engage in. I do not think prayer is a gift of the Spirit. Prayer is something that all believers should do. Every work must have prayer behind it if it is to succeed. Every successful evangelist and preacher of the Word, every teacher of the Word who is being used of God, has people who are praying for him. Paul is asking the Thessalonians for prayer so that "the word of the Lord may have free course." Paul had a very unique ministry. He was a missionary. He was an evangelist as we think of evangelists today. Actually that word *evangelist* in the New Testament means "missionary." Also, he was a pastor and a teacher of the Word. He fulfilled all those offices, and he had fulfilled them all to the Thessalonians. He had led them to the Lord and taught them; now he is acting as their pastor in his letters. He is not only instructing them in the Word, but he is attempting to comfort them and to counsel them. One of the things he enjoins them to do is *pray*. "Pray for us, that the word of the Lord may have free course, and be glorified, even as it is with you."

You cannot pray for Paul today, but you can pray for Vernon. I would appreciate your prayers that the Word of the Lord as I give it out may have free course and be glorified. The Word of God needs to be exalted today. Pray that people will exalt the Word of God in their own lives. It troubles me and it worries me to see that even those who claim to believe the Word of God give so little attention to it. Pray that if people profess to believe the Word of God, they will get into it and find out what it says.

My friend, let me urge you to pray for your

pastor. Let me say something very carefully. I know what it is to be a pastor, and I know what it is to be a Bible teacher holding conferences. I want to say to you that it is a lot easier to go around and hold conferences than it is to be a pastor. A pastor has a great responsibility because, very frankly, he deals with a great many folk who are unreasonable. Paul asks prayer that he "may be delivered from unreasonable and wicked men." Did you know that there are wicked persons in the church? A pastor needs to be delivered from such folk.

The work of an evangelist is like the work of an obstetrician. He delivers the little baby into the world, and that is quite an undertaking, of course. But then he turns over the little one to the pediatrician. He is the one who sees to it that his diet is right, that he is burped properly, that he gets his shots, and so forth. The pastor, you see, is the pediatrician. He is the one who must deal with cantankerous saints and baby Christians. That is quite a job. My heart goes out to the pastor.

When I go out to speak at conferences, I meet some wonderful pastors. The only churches I want to go to are the ones where the pastor is preaching and teaching the Word of God and stands for the things of God. On the other side of the coin, that is the only kind of man who will have me in his pulpit! Recently, as we left such a church, I said to my wife: "We have had a wonderful ministry here at this church for the week. I've been here just long enough—I think these people are wonderful, and they think I am wonderful! I left before they got acquainted with me and I got acquainted with them. Also I think I helped the pastor; he tells me that I did. But he is the one who is carrying the burden and the load there. He is the one who has the problems. I can simply walk away from them." I think the work of an evangelist or of an itinerant Bible teacher, as some of us are, is easy compared to the work of the man who is the pastor.

Paul asked for prayer that he might be delivered from "unreasonable and wicked men." I find that the spreading of the gospel is hindered more by people in the church than by anything else. No liquor industry, no barroom, no gangster ring has ever attacked me—at least I have never known about it. But I have had so-called saints in the churches attack me. As you know, in our churches we have the saints and the "ain'ts," and there are a lot of "ain'ts." They can give a pastor a rough time. It's too bad that we can't all settle down and give out the Word of God.

Now when he says, "For all men have not faith," that is really "*the* faith." All men do not have *the* faith. That is, they do not hold to the doctrines as the apostles taught them. The foundation of the church rests upon the doctrine which the apostles have given to the church. That is what we should teach and preach.

It is one thing to hold the truth of the coming of Christ, to love His appearing; but it is another thing to walk worthy of that great truth. This is what Paul is writing about to the Thessalonians. If we really love His appearing, we will prove it by our relationship to the Word of God and by our walk through this life.

But the Lord is faithful, who shall stablish you, and keep you from evil [2 Thess. 3:3].

That is so wonderful! I have let Him down on several occasions, but He has never let me down. He is faithful. He is always faithful. Christians should hold tenaciously to this little verse. The Lord is faithful, and He will establish you.

Christians need to be established. Right now the home is in disarray, the church is in disarray, and the lives of believers are in disarray. We need to be *established.* How can you as a believer be established? By coming to the Word of God and letting it have its influence in your life. The Lord operates through His Word. The Word of God will keep you from evil. Someone has said, "The Bible will keep you from sin, and sin will keep you from the Bible."

And we have confidence in the Lord touching you, that ye both do and will do the things which we command you [2 Thess. 3:4].

Christians are commanded to do certain things, and there are specific commandments for Christians. We saw that in Paul's first epistle to the Thessalonians where he records twenty-two commandments in the fifth chapter. There are not only ten but twenty-two commandments which the believers are to do. The Lord Jesus said, "If you love Me, keep My commandments" (see John 14:15) and these are His commandments.

Paul had "confidence in the Lord touching" them. He committed them to the Lord with the confidence that they were doing and would continue doing the things which he commanded. He believed that this Thessalonian church which had a wonderful testimony would continue to maintain that testimony.

And the Lord direct your hearts into the love of God, and into the patient waiting for Christ [2 Thess. 3:5].

The believer is to walk in "the love of God." My friend, if you are walking today in the sunshine of His love, the love of God is shed abroad in your heart and you know He loves you. And you can manifest that love by the power of the Spirit, because only the Spirit of God can make God's love real to us. Love is a fruit of the Spirit. You can't naturally love every Tom, Dick, and Harry—and I'm of the opinion God does not expect that of us. Paul wrote to the Philippian Christians that our love is to be in *judgment*, which implies that we should be careful about loving those around us. There are folk who will hurt us if we open our arms to them.

"Into the patient waiting for Christ." This does not mean that you are to argue about being premillennial or pretribulational or posttribulational or amillennial, but that you are to be patiently waiting for the coming of Christ. Oh, what wonderful verses these are!

Now we command you, brethren, in the name of our Lord Jesus Christ, that ye withdraw yourselves from every brother that walketh disorderly, and not after the tradition which he received of us [2 Thess. 3:6].

"Now we command you, brethren"—Paul doesn't beat around the bush!

The believer is not to walk with the "disorderly." I know men who insist that we should go into the barrooms, sit down with the drunkard and have a beer with him as we witness to him. Unfortunately, I know of a young lady who became an alcoholic by following that procedure. God says that we are to "withdraw" ourselves from the disorderly. Certainly we are to witness to them, but we are not to fraternize on their level.

God makes it very clear whom we are to follow—

For yourselves know how ye ought to follow us: for we behaved not ourselves disorderly among you [2 Thess. 3:7].

Birds of a feather flock together. You will be like the crowd you run around with. Believers need to be very careful about the company they keep and the people with whom they associate.

BELIEVERS SHOULD BE ESTABLISHED IN THEIR WORK

The Thessalonians were walking in a right relationship to the Lord Jesus, and they were being persecuted for it. Paul comforted them, instructed, and encouraged them. Now he lets them know that he also is undergoing persecution and difficulty. And, friend, if *you* stand for the Lord, it will cost you something.

We have seen that the believer is to be established in the *Word* of God. Then we have noted how important the *walk* of the believer is, and how his walk should be grounded in the Word. Now we come to the *work* of the believer, which is also very practical. This involves things in which we need to be engaged—that the Word of God may have its way in our hearts and lives.

Neither did we eat any man's bread for nought; but wrought with labour and travail night and day, that we might not be chargeable to any of you [2 Thess. 3:8].

"Neither did we eat any man's bread for nought"—that is, for nothing; he paid for what he ate.

"But wrought with labour and travail night and day, that we might not be chargeable to any of you." His practice was that he would not let anyone pay him for his missionary work among them. I think this applied especially to his first missionary journey. When he arrived in town as a missionary, there was no reservation for him at the local motel. There was no stipend given to him, no love offering taken for him the first time he was there. He was very careful about paying his own way. He mentions that to the Thessalonians and also to the Corinthians. When he was establishing churches he supported himself by tentmaking.

However, after the churches were established and Paul had come back to visit them a second and a third time, he did receive an offering from them. He makes it clear to the Galatians that they should give. He thanks the Philippians for their gift. He himself took an offering on his third missionary journey to be given to the poor saints in Jerusalem. Obviously, the great truth of the coming of Christ had not caused Paul to become some sort of a fanatic or to take some unreasonable position in relation to money matters.

In every age there are fanatical people. In the last century there were those who expected the return of Christ; so they sold their homes and property, wrapped themselves in white sheets and got on the top of the roof to wait for the Lord to come! There were several actions which identified them as fanatics. For example, why get on the roof? Couldn't the Lord draw a person into the air from the ground as easily as from a roof? If one needed to get up on a roof, then wouldn't a mountain-top be better? And then, why in the world would one need a white sheet? I think the Lord is going to furnish us with suitable cover-ings when we come into His presence. And why would they sell their property and turn it into money? Did they think they could take the money with them? You see, people can do some very peculiar, senseless things because they say they believe in the soon coming of Christ. The fact is that there is no other doc-trine in the Bible that will make you work harder or more sensibly for Christ. If you believe that He is coming, you will work for Him. You will be busy for the Lord in some phase of His work. You will be putting out a few seeds of the Word of God in the field of the world so that they might bring forth a harvest.

Not because we have not power, but to make ourselves an ensample unto you to follow us [2 Thess. 3:9].

Paul is saying that as an apostle who had led them to the Lord and established a church among them, he had the right, the authority, to claim an offering. However, he did not do this because he wanted to be an example to the believers in Thessalonica that they might not be led to some fanatical position.

A young couple who had been in my classes when I taught at a Bible institute were in-clined toward fanaticism. They thought they were super-duper saints, way out ahead of everyone else. But their exam papers were graded Cs or Ds, because they didn't really know the Word, although they affected to be very spiritual. (Incidentally, I don't think a person can be truly spiritual and be ignorant of the Word of God.) They came to me after I had become a pastor in that city and said they wanted to go to the mission field. They at-tended the church I served although they were not members. I asked them if they had their financial support. They said no. I asked, "Do you mean that you are going to the mis-sion field without support?" "Oh," they said, "we're going to trust the Lord." Well, I said, "It's nice to trust the Lord, but can't you trust Him to raise your support here? Must you wait until you get into the mission field to trust Him for support? Why don't you get under a reputable mission board and work

with them? If the Lord has called you to go to the mission field, He will raise up support for you—the Lord will lay your needs on the hearts of certain folk who will pray for you and support you financially." No, they didn't want to do it that way, they were just going to trust the Lord. Well, this young couple went out to the mission field, and there they became casu-alties. They had to be brought home with money that some friends raised to pay their passage. Since that time they have separated and are divorced. She is married again. I have heard that he has lost his faith altogether, although I doubt that he ever really had faith. Their behavior was foolish and fanatical.

Paul was making missionary work very practical. He supported himself by working with his hands, and he did it to be an example to the Thessalonian believers. He is going to make a point of this in the next verse.

For even when we were with you, this we commanded you, that if any would not work, neither should he eat [2 Thess. 3:10].

A believer who is looking for the Lord to re-turn is not a dreamer; he is a worker. No work—no food. That is the rule laid down by the apostle. "If any would not work, neither should he eat."

It is amazing how fanatical people can get about these things. The dean of men at Moody Bible Institute told about an incident that hap-pened about fifty years ago. Two young men roomed together who were other examples of those super-duper saints who thought they were completely sanctified. One day they didn't appear in the dining room for breakfast or for lunch or for dinner; so the dean went up to see what the problem was. They were just sitting there, looking out into space. He asked them if they were sick. No, they weren't sick. "Then why haven't you come down for meals?" They said, "We're just trusting the Lord. We are waiting for Him to tell us whether we should go down to eat." "Are you hungry?" They admitted that they were hungry. "Don't you think that is one of the ways the Lord has of letting you know that you ought to go down to eat?" They said, "No, we are waiting for special revelation from Him, and we are not going to move until then." So the dean said to them, "I have news for you. You *are* going to move, but not down to the dining room. You are going to move out of school. You cannot stay here." There is no place for that kind of fanaticism.

Today we are seeing a kind of fanaticism in

the area of prophecy. It is quite interesting that in this epistle which deals largely in prophecy, almost half of it is given over to that which is practical. He puts the emphasis on the practical side of the great truth of the coming of Christ for His church. It is one thing to get fanatical about prophecy; it is quite another thing to believe the prophetic truth and then have it meshed and geared into our living down here so that it becomes practical and working.

We are to work while we wait. A gardener for a large estate in northern Italy was conducting a visitor through the castle and the beautiful, well-groomed grounds. As the visitor had lunch with the gardener and his wife, he commended them for the beautiful way they were keeping the gardens. He asked, "By the way, when was the last time the owner was here?" "It was about ten years ago," the gardener said. The visitor asked, "Then why do you keep up the gardens in such an immaculate, lovely manner?" The gardener answered, "Because I'm expecting him to return." He persisted, "Is he coming next week?" The gardener replied, "I don't know when he is coming, but I am expecting him today." Although he didn't come that day, he was living in the light of the owner's imminent return. The gardener wasn't hanging over the gate, watching down the road to see whether his master was coming. He was in the garden, trimming, cutting, mowing, planting. He was busy. That is what Paul is talking about when he says we should be established in the work of the Lord in view of the fact that He is returning.

"If any would not work, neither should he eat." You see, the Thessalonians had a few fanatics who simply withdrew themselves and decided that they were going to spend all their time looking for the Lord's return. Paul writes, "Don't feed them. They have to go to work."

For we hear that there are some which walk among you disorderly, working not at all, but are busybodies [2 Thess. 3:11].

Here we are told the situation. There were some who were not working at anything constructive. They were not interested in getting out the Word of God, but they were busy—they were busybodies. They were really making a nuisance of themselves, and they were causing trouble in the church in Thessalonica. It takes just one bad apple to spoil the barrel; it takes just one little fly to spoil the ointment;

and one fanatic in the church can affect the spiritual life of a great many people. That is the reason Paul had said before that they were to withdraw themselves from the ones who walk disorderly, and I'm sure he had the busybodies in mind. They were busy as termites and just as effective as termites in the church at Thessalonica.

Now them that are such we command and exhort by our Lord Jesus Christ, that with quietness they work, and eat their own bread [2 Thess. 3:12].

This doesn't sound very spiritual, does it? It doesn't sound very theological. But it certainly is practical. It would solve a great many problems in the average church if the busybodies, the troublemakers, would work with quietness and do something constructive. It is interesting that the man who was the biggest troublemaker in any church that I served was the smallest contributor—and I found that out by accident. The treasurer of the church was talking to me about the trouble this fellow had been, and I said, "Well, he is a man of means, and I suppose a very generous giver, and he naturally is interested in how his money is being spent." The treasurer looked at me and laughed. He said, "That man gives ten dollars a year for the Lord's work!" Believe me, he certainly gave us more than ten dollars worth of trouble! There must have been people like that in Thessalonica. Paul says that they were to quietly go to work and mind their own business.

But ye, brethren, be not weary in well-doing [2 Thess. 3:13].

How wonderful this is! A believer who holds the blessed hope should not grow weary of working for the Lord. As Moody put it, "I get weary *in* the work, but not weary *of* the work."

And if any man obey not our word by this epistle, note that man, and have no company with him, that he may be ashamed [2 Thess. 3:14].

People in the church ought to withdraw from troublemakers in the church. However, many people more or less court their favor, because they don't want those people to talk about them, knowing they have vicious tongues. But withdrawing from the gossips would be the best thing that could happen in many churches.

Yet count him not as an enemy, but admonish him as a brother [2 Thess. 3:15].

An attempt should be made to win the wayward member.

Now the Lord of peace himself give you peace always by all means. The Lord be with you all [2 Thess. 3:16].

Isn't this lovely!

The salutation of Paul with mine own hand, which is the token in every epistle: so I write [2 Thess. 3:17].

This is an epistle from Paul signed with his own hand.

The grace of our Lord Jesus Christ be with you all. Amen [2 Thess. 3:18].

His letter ends with a benediction. It is the conclusion of a wonderful epistle which teaches that the knowledge of prophecy, rather than leading to fanaticism or laziness, brings peace to the heart.

BIBLIOGRAPHY

(Recommended for Further Study)

Hiebert, D. Edmond. *The Thessalonian Epistles, A Call to Readiness*. Chicago, Illinois: Moody Press, 1971. (An excellent, comprehensive treatment.)

Hogg, C. F. and Vine, W. E. *The Epistles of Paul to the Thessalonians*. Grand Rapids, Michigan: Kregel Publications, 1914. (An excellent, comprehensive treatment.)

Ironside, H. A. *Addresses on I and II Thessalonians*. Neptune, New Jersey: Loizeaux Brothers, n.d.

Kelly, William. *The Epistles to the Thessalonians*. Oak Park, Illinois: Bible Truth Publishers, 1893.

MacDonald, William. *Letters to the Thessalonians*. Kansas City, Missouri: Walterick Publishers, 1969.

Ryrie, Charles C. *First and Second Thessalonians*. Chicago, Illinois: Moody Press, 1959. (Fine, inexpensive survey.)

Walvoord, John F. *The Thessalonian Epistles*. Grand Rapids, Michigan: Zondervan Publishing House, 1955.

The First Epistle to

TIMOTHY

INTRODUCTION

The First Epistle to Timothy introduces us to a new set of epistles which were written by Paul. There are three of them that belong together (1 and 2 Timothy and Titus), and they are called "The Pastoral Epistles," because they have to do with local churches. You will find that these pastoral epistles are in contrast, for instance, to the Epistle to the Ephesians. There Paul speaks of the church as the body of believers who are in Christ and the glorious, wonderful position that the church has. The church which is invisible, made up of *all* believers who are in the body of Christ, *manifests* itself down here upon the earth in local assemblies, in the local churches.

Now, just to put a steeple on a building and a bell in the steeple and a pulpit down front and a choir in the loft singing the doxology doesn't mean it is a local church in the New Testament sense of the word. There must be certain identifying features. I have written a booklet called *The Spiritual Fingerprints of the Visible Church*, in which I point out that a local church must manifest itself in a certain way in order to meet the requirements of a church of the Lord Jesus.

These three epistles were written to two young preachers who worked with Paul: Timothy and Titus. They were a part of his fruit; that is, they were led to Christ through the ministry of Paul. He had these men with him as helpers, and he instructed them about the local church.

In all three epistles Paul is dealing with two things: the *creed* of the church and the *conduct* of the church. For the church within, the worship must be right. For the church outside, good works must be manifested. Worship is inside; works are outside. That's the way the church is to manifest itself.

Paul deals with these two topics in each of the three epistles. For instance, in 1 Timothy, chapter 1, is faith, the *faith* of the church—its doctrine. Chapter 2 is the *order* of the church. Chapter 3 concerns the *officers* of the church. Chapter 4 describes the *apostasy* that was coming, and chapters 5 and 6 tell of the *duties* of the officers.

In 2 Timothy, Paul deals with the *afflictions* of the church in chapter 1 and the *activity* of the church in chapter 2. Then the *apostasy* of the church and the *allegiance* of the church follow in chapters 3 and 4.

Titus has the same theme. Chapter 1 tells of the *order* of the church, chapter 2 is about the *doctrine* of the church, and chapter 3 is the *good works* of the church.

So there is *creed* on the inside of the church and *conduct* on the outside. Within is worship and without are good works.

The church today manifests itself in a local assembly. It first puts up a building. In Paul's day, they didn't have a building. That's one thing they didn't need because they were not building churches. They generally met in homes and probably in public buildings. We know in Ephesus that Paul used—probably rented—the school of Tyrannus. I suppose Paul used the auditorium during the siesta time each day. People came in from everywhere to hear him preach. That could be characterized as a local assembly, and it became a local church in Ephesus.

In order to be a local assembly, the church must have certain things to characterize it. It must have a creed, and its doctrine must be accurate. There are two verses that summarize Paul's message in these epistles: "As I besought thee to abide still at Ephesus, when I went into Macedonia, that thou mightest charge some that they teach no other [different] doctrine" (1 Tim. 1:3). It is important that a church have *correct* doctrine. That's what I mean when I say that a steeple on a building doesn't make it a local church by any means. Then again Paul said to this young preacher: "But if I tarry long, that thou mayest know how thou oughtest to behave thyself in the house of God, which is the church of the living God, the pillar and ground of the truth" (1 Tim. 3:15). The local church is made up of believers who are members of the body of Christ. In order for them to function, they need leadership. Somebody has to be appointed to sweep the place out and somebody to build a fire in the stove—if they have one.

In the first little church that I served, I swept the church out sometimes, and on Sunday morning, because it was a little country church, the first one who got there built a fire in the stove. I always tried to be a little late, but I'd say that half the time I built the fire. Those things are essential. Also it's nice to have a choir and a song leader. In addition to this, Paul is going to say that officers are essential for a church to be orderly. There must be officers, and they must meet certain requirements. The church should function in an orderly manner and manifest itself in the community by its good works. Unfortunately today that is idealistic in most places because the local church doesn't always manifest what it should.

From these Pastoral Epistles have come three different types of church government which have been used by the great denominations of the church. The churches never disagreed on doctrine in the old days as much as they disagreed on this matter of church government, that is, how the local church is to function. I marvel that they could get three different forms of government out of these three Pastoral Epistles, but they did.

1. There is the *episcopal* form of government where there is one man, or maybe several men, who are in charge at the top. The Roman Catholic church calls that man a pope. In other churches he is called the archbishop; if there are several leaders, they are called bishops. The Church of England and other churches follow the episcopal form of government. They are controlled by men at the top who are outside the local church.

2. Another form of church government is known as the *presbyterian* or representative form of government. The local church elects certain men from its membership, called elders and deacons, to be officers, and the government of the local church is in their hands. Unfortunately, the churches were bound together by an organization above the level of the local church, and that organization could control the local church.

3. The third type of church government is the opposite extreme from the episcopal form, called the *congregational* form of government. You see it, of course, in the Congregational and Baptist churches. The *people* are the ones who make the decisions and who are actually in control. The entire church votes on taking in members and on everything else that concerns the local church.

Perhaps you are wondering how they could get three forms of church government from the same words in the Pastoral Epistles. Well, of course, certain words were interpreted differently. I'll try to call attention to these various interpretations as we go through the Pastoral Epistles.

The very interesting thing is that in the early days all three forms of church government functioned and seemed to work well. But in recent years all three forms of government have fallen on evil days; they don't seem to

work as they once did. Men who are members of all three forms of government tell me that there is internal strife and disorder and dissension. What is wrong? Immediately somebody says, "Well, the *system* is wrong."

This is an interesting question since we have a representative form of civil government in this country. It was patterned after the church government. You see, the early colonists didn't want a king. That was the only form of government they had known, and they had had enough of a king. They did not want an autocratic form of government, and they were rather reluctant to let the people rule. That may seem strange to you when you listen to local politicians today who talk about "everybody having a vote." In colonial times women didn't vote; men who were not landowners did not vote. Only those who had property and belonged to a certain elite class voted.

The reason the colonists did not want a king to rule over them was because they couldn't trust human nature, which means they couldn't trust each other. We think of those men as being wonderful, political, patriotic saints. Well, they were human beings and filled with foibles. They knew they couldn't trust each other, so they would not put power in the hands of one man. They were also afraid to put power in the people's hands because they had no confidence in the people either.

That contradicts the concept that the politician purports when he says that the majority can't be wrong—or "The voice of the people is the voice of God." Frankly, that's just not true.

Why is it, then, that our forms of church government are not working as they should? Well, I want to say—and I hope I'm not misunderstood, because I recognize my inability to express it in the way I'd like to express it to you—that I believe Paul is saying in this epistle that the form of government, important as it is, is not as important as the caliber and character of the men who are holding office.

These epistles outline certain requirements for officers, such as being sober, having one wife, etc. These requirements are essential and are the subjects of debate in the local churches. But here is something more important that I have never heard argued in my forty long years as a pastor, and that is the most *basic* requirement for officers. Paul is trying to convey to us that the men who are officers must be *spiritual*, because no system will function unless the men who are in the place and position of authority are right. If they are wrong, no system—whether it is congregational or episcopal or presbyterian—will *work*.

That, my friend, is the problem. It is the problem today in politics, and it is the problem today in the church. When we elect a man, he must be successful in his vocation and he should have leadership ability. I think those are good requirements, but we need to determine if he is a *spiritual* man.

Paul is going to emphasize two aspects of the spiritual officer: he must be a man of *faith*, and he must be motivated by *love*. Unless those two characteristics are operating in his life, the officer can't function in the church no matter how much ability he has.

What this simply means is that the authority the officers have is actually no authority at all. Paul says that when you've been made an elder or a bishop or a deacon in the church, you have an office and you may feel very pompous and authoritative, but Paul says you really have no authority. Well, what does he mean? He means that *Christ* is the Head of the church, and the *Holy Spirit* is the One to give the leading and the guiding and the direction. The officer is never to assert *his* will in anything; he is to find out what the will of God is. That means he will have to be a man of faith.

He also will have to be motivated by love. Now that doesn't mean that he is to go around soft-soaping everybody and scratching their backs, trying to be a man-pleaser, but he is to carry through the *will of Christ* in that church. It is his job to make sure that Christ is the Head of the church. Oh, how I've spent weary hours in board meetings talking about some little thing that had absolutely nothing to do with the spiritual welfare of the church, but had a lot to do with the will of some hardheaded, stubborn officer who thought he was a spiritual man. Such a man had no idea that he was to carry through the will of Christ because, to begin with, he had never sought the will of Christ. All he was attempting to do was to serve his own will because he thought his will was right.

Oh, my friend, Christ is the Head of the local church today. We see this in the very first verse where Paul calls Him "the Lord Jesus Christ." He is the *Lord*, and, remember, that means He is Number One. The Lord Jesus said in His day, "And why call ye me, Lord, Lord, and do not the things which I say?" (Luke 6:46). A lot of people call Him "Lord" today in the church, and they're not following Him at all. To be an officer in the church means that you're to carry through the will of Christ, His commandments, and His desires. He is the Head of the local church. That is what is needed today, is it not?

Therefore, I am not prepared to argue with anybody about the form of government in his church. If you think yours is the best form, fine! You go along with it. But it will work only if you have the right men. It won't work—no matter what the form is—if you have the wrong men. The unspiritual officer is the monkey wrench in the machinery of the church today. Although it is the business of the church to get Him through to the world, that is the reason we don't see much evidence of Christ.

In 1 Timothy, then, we deal with the nitty-gritty of the local church, with the emphasis that it is the character and caliber of her leaders that will determine whether the church is really a church of the Lord Jesus Christ.

OUTLINE

I. The Faith of the Church, Chapter 1
  A. Introduction, Chapter 1:1–2
  B. Warning against Unsound Doctrine, Chapter 1:3–10
  C. Personal Testimony of Paul, Chapter 1:11–17
  D. Charge to Timothy, Chapter 1:18–20

II. Public Prayer and Woman's Place in the Churches, Chapter 2
  A. Public Prayer for the Public and Public Officials, Chapter 2:1–7
  B. How Men Are to Pray, Chapter 2:8
  C. How Women Are to Pray, Chapter 2:9–15

III. Officers in the Churches, Chapter 3
  A. Requirements for Elders, Chapter 3:1–7
  B. Requirements for Deacons, Chapter 3:8–13
  C. Report of Paul to Timothy, Chapter 3:14–16

IV. Apostasy in the Churches, Chapter 4
  A. How to Recognize the Apostates, Chapter 4:1–5
  B. What the "Good Minister" Can Do in Times of Apostasy, Chapter 4:6–16

V. Duties of Officers of the Churches, Chapters 5–6
  A. Relationship of Ministers to Different Groups in the Local Church, Chapter 5
  B. Relationship of Believers to Others, Chapter 6

CHAPTER 1

THEME: The faith of the church

Paul's emphasis here will not be a doctrinal statement of the Christian church, but a warning against false teachers in the local church. He will stress that the gospel of the grace of God is central in doctrine and concerns the person of Christ.

INTRODUCTION

The introduction to 1 Timothy is unlike any other in Paul's epistles. Perhaps you had come to the conclusion that they were all the same, but the introductions to the Pastoral Epistles are a little different. Dr. Marvin R. Vincent has said that the salutation on 1 Timothy as a whole has no parallel in Paul.

Paul, an apostle of Jesus Christ by the commandment of God our Saviour, and Lord Jesus Christ, which is our hope;

Unto Timothy, my own son in the faith: Grace, mercy, and peace, from God our Father and Jesus Christ our Lord [1 Tim. 1:1–2].

"Paul, an apostle of Jesus Christ by the commandment of God." Paul asserts his apostleship to Timothy, and he has certainly done so before. In Ephesians he says, "Paul, an apostle of Jesus Christ by the *will* of God . . ." (Eph. 1:1, italics mine). Now what is the difference between the *commandment* and the *will* of God? The will of God and the commandment of God are the same, but yet they are not exactly synonymous. All the commandments which you find in the Bible reveal the will of God. This would include much more than the Ten Commandments. For example, we are told that it is the will of God that we pray: "Pray without ceasing. In every thing give thanks: for this is the will of God in Christ Jesus concerning you" (1 Thess. 5:17–18). There are many things which are the will of God, and they are expressed in His commandments. However, I do not think that we have revealed to us all of the will of God, even in the sum total of the commandments in Scripture. The will of God is therefore a much broader term than the commandment of God.

Remember, however, that we have revealed to us enough of the will of God to know that man is *not* saved by obedience to the commandments of God. This is important to reiterate as there are so many today who say the Law is essential to our salvation.

In verse 8 of this chapter, Paul writes, "But we know that the law is good, if a man use it lawfully." How are we to use the Law? First, we need to see that the Law *is* good: "Wherefore the law is holy, and the commandment holy, and just, and good" (Rom. 7:12). It is the very fact that the Law is good and demands absolute goodness from man (in whom there is no good thing) that the sinner cannot obey it. Paul says, "For I know that in me (that is, in my flesh,) dwelleth no good thing . . ." (Rom. 7:18). The Law or the commandments of God were given to *reveal the will of God* and to show that in order for a sinner to be saved it is necessary to find a way other than obedience to a perfect law; to understand this is to use the law "lawfully."

The glory of the gospel is that God found a way that He might be just *and* the justifier of him that believeth in Jesus. In Acts Paul preached: "Be it known unto you therefore, men and brethren, that through this man [that is, the Lord Jesus] is preached unto you the forgiveness of sins: And by him all that believe are justified from all things, from which ye could not be justified by the law of Moses" (Acts 13:38–39). Why could they not be justified by the law of Moses? Because it was a ministration of death: the Law condemned them. The Law wasn't given to save us, but to reveal that God is holy and that you and I are not holy. The way that God found to save us is the way of the Cross, the way of the Lord Jesus. "I am the way," He says, "the truth, and the life" (John 14:6). The Law is not the way to God; *Christ* is the way.

When Paul wrote to the Ephesians that he was an apostle by the will of God, that was true. But when he wrote to this young preacher Timothy, he said, "I am an apostle by the commandment of God. He made me an apostle. It is not just because I am in the will of God today that I am an apostle. There was a time when He *commanded* me to be an apostle." I think Paul might have been rather reluctant to become an apostle. I'm sure he could have offered excuses to the Lord as Moses did. He hadn't been with the Lord as the other eleven apostles had been. He never knew Him in the days of His flesh; he knew Him only as the glorified Christ. He said he was unworthy to be an apostle. But the Lord Jesus had said, "I *command* you," and that is the reason Paul could walk into a synagogue or go before a gainsaying audience in Athens, or a group of rotten, corrupt sinners in Corinth, and boldly declare the gospel. He was a soldier under orders, an apostle by commandment—not by commission, but by commandment. No one laid hands on Paul to make him an apostle, but the Lord Jesus personally gave him the authority.

Jeremiah had this same kind of authority. He was a shrinking violet, a retiring sort of person, the man with a broken heart. Yet he stepped out and gave some of the strongest statements that ever came from God. Why could he do that? He was a soldier under orders—under orders from God.

Any man who is going to speak for God today needs to do it with authority or he ought to keep quiet. A man who gets up in the pulpit and says, "If you believe *in a fashion*, I expect that *maybe* you'd be saved if you believe *in a way* on Jesus." Such a wishy-washy man has nothing to say for God at all. Paul was an apostle who spoke with the authority of God.

"God our Saviour"—is God our *Savior*? He certainly is: ". . . God so loved the world, that he gave his only begotten Son . . ." (John 3:16). God provided the sacrifice, and the Lord Jesus is the One who came to this earth and executed it.

"And the Lord Jesus Christ, which is our hope." To say that Christ is our *hope* may seem strange to you, as it is not found often in Scripture. Actually, the only other time you will find it is in Colossians 1:27: ". . . Christ in you, the hope of glory." The Lord Jesus died to save you. He lives to keep you saved. He is going to come someday to take you to be with Himself and to consummate that salvation. He is our faith when we look backwards; He is love when we look around us today; and He is our hope as we look ahead. But it is hope, actually, all the way through our lives, and that hope is anchored in the person of the Lord Jesus Christ.

"Timothy"—sometimes he is called Timothy and sometimes Timotheus. Timotheus is made up of two Greek words which mean "that which is dear to God." Timothy was dear to God, he was dear to the apostle Paul, and he was dear to the local churches.

We read of Timothy in the books of Acts, Ephesians, and Philippians. His father was a Greek. His grandmother, Lois, and his mother, Eunice, became Christians before him. He lived in Lystra where Paul was stoned. I feel that Paul was actually raised from the dead at that time, and this may have had a lot to do with the conversion of Timothy.

As a young man he probably was rather skeptical, and this event may have helped convince him and bring him to conversion. After his conversion he became an avowed follower of Paul.

Timothy was a man who had a good reputation. We read of him in Acts 16:2–5: "Which was well reported of by the brethren that were at Lystra and Iconium. Him would Paul have to go forth with him; and took and circumcised him because of the Jews which were in those quarters: for they knew all that his father was a Greek. And as they went through the cities, they delivered them the decrees for to keep, that were ordained of the apostles and elders which were at Jerusalem. And so were the churches established in the faith, and increased in number daily." As Timothy worked with Paul he became one in whom Paul had the utmost confidence, while others in the churches proved to be false brethren who deceived him.

It is the joy of every pastor to have wonderful friends in his church. I have lived and ministered in Pasadena, California, since 1940. I meet people everywhere, some who came to know the Lord as early as 1940 or 1941, who are still following in the Lord's steps, and they are loyal, faithful friends of mine. That is why we keep our ministry's headquarters here, for we have a host of wonderful, trusted friends in this area.

Paul had those whom he couldn't trust, but Timothy was one he could trust. He wrote in Philippians: "But I trust in the Lord Jesus to send Timotheus shortly unto you, that I also may be of good comfort, when I know your state. For I have no man likeminded, who will naturally care for your state. For all seek their own, not the things which are Jesus Christ's. But ye know the proof of him, that, as a son with the father, he hath served with me in the gospel. Him therefore I hope to send presently, so soon as I shall see how it will go with me" (Phil. 2:19–23).

"Timothy, my own son in the faith" could be translated as "my true son in the faith" or "my genuine son in the faith." Paul had led Timothy to the Lord, and they were very close.

"Grace, mercy, and peace, from God our Father and Jesus Christ our Lord." At first this may appear to be the same as the introductions to Paul's other epistles. Yes, Paul has used *grace* and *peace* before, but we have another word here, and that is *mercy*. *Mercy* is a word that was used in the Old Testament and was equivalent to the word *grace*. It was the Old Testament sacrifice that made the holy and righteous and just throne of God into a *mercy* seat.

When you and I come to God, we don't want justice, for we would be condemned. What we want and need from God is mercy. And God has provided mercy for all His creatures. He has all the mercy that you need. Yet His mercy is just like money in the bank which will do you no good unless you write a check, and the check you need to write is the check of faith. God is rich in mercy, but when He saves you, He saves you by His grace. God is merciful to you, and He is merciful to all sinners in the world, even those who blaspheme Him and repudiate Him and turn their back on Him. He sends rain on the just and the unjust—He doesn't play favorites, even with His own people. Sinners today get rich and they prosper. They often seem to do better than God's own people. He is merciful to sinners. But when you come to God, you must come by *faith*— write the check of faith—and then God will save you by His *grace*.

These three words—love, mercy, and grace—are a little trinity. *Love* is that in God which existed before He could care to exercise mercy or grace. God is love; it is His nature, His attribute. *Mercy* is that in God which provided for the need of sinful man. *Grace* then is that in Him which acts freely to save because all the demands of His holiness have been satisfied. Therefore, because God is merciful, you can come to Him, and by His grace He'll save you. You don't have to bring anything, you cannot bring anything, because it would only be filthy rags to God.

A do-gooder is one who thinks he does not need the mercy of God, that his own good works will save him. I knew a man who, although he was on his deathbed, said to me, "Preacher, you don't need to tell me that I need Christ as a Savior and that I need the mercy and the grace of God. I don't need it: I'm willing to stand before Him just like I am." Then he went on to tell me all that he had done in his life. He had been deeply involved with the Community Chest and with an orphans' home and on and on. Oh, he was a do-gooder, and he was going to stand before God on that! My friend, a do-good salvation will not do you any good when you really need it. The salvation God provides will enable you to do good, the kind of good which is acceptable to Him. The righteousness of man is filthy rags in His sight.

So we have found that Paul uses here (and throughout all of the Pastoral Epistles) expressions that we will not see elsewhere in his writings. He obviously spoke to these young preachers in an intimate and more personal way than he did in his public speaking or writing. Wouldn't you love to have been Timothy, to have traveled with Paul and have the great apostle open his mind and heart to you? Well, my friend, the Spirit of God is here and He is talking to us through this epistle which Paul wrote to Timothy.

Although 1 Timothy is intimate and personal, it has to do with the affairs of the local church, the body of believers as it manifests itself in the community. And I want to say here—perhaps it reveals the pastor in me— that every believer should be identified with some local church.

"God our Father"—God is Paul's Father, He is Timothy's Father, and He is your Father if you have received Christ. He is my Father because I have received Christ and been brought into the family of God. What a privilege that is! Paul had been a Pharisee, and in Judaism he had never had the privilege of calling God his Father.

"Jesus Christ our Lord." Anything that is done in the local church needs to be done in the name of Christ and at His command. He is the Head of the church; He is the Lord. The Lord Jesus said, "You call Me Lord, Lord, and yet you don't do the things I say; you don't obey Me." Could He say the same thing to many of us today? He warned that there are going to be many at the judgment who will say, "Lord, Lord, didn't we do this and that, and the other thing? We were as busy as termites for You!" And He will have to say to them, "I don't even know you. I didn't know you were doing that in My name, for you certainly didn't seek My will. You didn't seek to obey Me." We need not only to *call* Him Lord but also *obey* Him as Lord.

WARNING AGAINST UNSOUND DOCTRINE

We have said that this epistle deals with the creed and the conduct of the local church. Your creed must be right before your conduct can be right. It is almost an impossibility to think wrong and act right. One time a man complained to me: "When a woman driver puts her hand out the window at an intersection it means nothing but that the window is open! You never know what she is going to do, because sometimes she signals left and turns right, and sometimes signals right and turns left!" It is sad that man often tries to act right even though his thinking is very wrong.

It is impossible to keep that up for very long, my friend.

As I besought thee to abide still at Ephesus, when I went into Macedonia, that thou mightest charge some that they teach no other doctrine [1 Tim. 1:3].

"That thou mightest charge some that they teach no other doctrine"—in other words, that they teach no *different* doctrine. Paul wrote to the Galatians that there was no other gospel. The Judaizers there were preaching another gospel, but Paul said there was none other. There is only one gospel, and there is only one doctrine.

"Doctrine" refers to the teaching of the church. What should be the teaching of the local church? It should be what it was from the very beginning. Following the Day of Pentecost it is recorded that "they continued in the apostles' doctrine." This was one of the four things which characterized that church: (1) The apostles' doctrine; (2) fellowship; (3) prayers; and (4) the breaking of bread, or the Lord's Supper. These are the four "fingerprints" of the visible church. A church is not a true church of Christ if its doctrine is not the apostles' doctrine.

I recognize that our varying interpretations of the Scriptures lead us to disagree on some points of doctrine. I had lunch one time with a very fine, outstanding Pentecostal preacher here in Southern California. We talked over what we agreed on and what we disagreed on, and it was not as severe a difference as some might think. As we concluded he said to me, "Dr. McGee, we agree on so much, and we agree on what is basic, therefore we ought not to fall out on the things that actually are not essential things." I was glad he felt that way. I am sorry everybody doesn't believe like I do, but there are some who don't.

However, we must hold to the apostles' doctrine, the basic truths of the faith. The apostles taught the plenary, verbal inspiration of the Scriptures, the integrity and inerrancy of the Word of God. And they taught the deity of Christ. We will see in this very epistle that Paul had an exalted view of the Lord Jesus Christ. There are those who say he did not teach the deity of Christ. Well, of all things, that is one thing on which Paul is as clear as the noonday sun. He clearly taught the deity of Christ. Even here in this chapter when he says, "God our Father and Jesus Christ our Lord," he places Christ right beside God, making it clear that He is God.

"I besought thee to abide still at Ephesus."

Paul had left Timothy in Ephesus while he himself was in Macedonia. Ephesus was a very important city, and Paul had spent more time there than anywhere else and had his greatest ministry there. Timothy was to remind the Ephesians to teach no other doctrine. If the teaching of the church is not right, it is not a church. It does not matter how many deacons, elders, pastors, song leaders, choirs, or Sunday schools it might have. If the doctrine is not there, it is not a church. The doctrine must be that of the apostles.

Neither give heed to fables and endless genealogies, which minister questions, rather than godly edifying which is in faith: so do [1 Tim. 1:4].

"Neither give heed to fables," or do not give heed to *myths*. Ephesus was the heartland of the mystery religions of that day. In that great center there was the temple to Hadrian, the temple to Trajan, and the great temple of Diana. All of that centered in Ephesus. These were all based on the mythology of the Greeks, and the Ephesian believers were to shun them.

Paul's reference to "fables" or myths could possibly mean the philosophy of Philo. Philo was an outstanding and brilliant Israelite who took the Old Testament and spiritualized it. In other words, he attempted to introduce the myth viewpoint. We have some of this same teaching in our old-line denominational seminaries today. They teach, for example, that the Book of Genesis is a myth, that the stories there are myths and the men didn't actually live. There is such an accumulation of evidence to support the Book of Genesis from the recent findings of archaeology that the liberals seem to have backed down from this teaching somewhat.

"Endless genealogies." This could refer to the false teaching that the church is just a continuation of Judaism, that it is just one genealogy following another and not a matter of God dealing with man in different dispensations. Such teaching leads to great confusion as to the positions of Israel and the church in God's program.

Also the Greeks were teaching at that time what was known as the *demiurge*, and this teaching became a part of the first heresy within the church, which was Gnosticism. They taught that there were emanations from a divine center. The original created a being, and that being created another being below him, and he created another, and then another, and so on down the line. They wanted to fit Jesus in somewhere along that line as one of the created beings.

"Which minister questions, rather than godly edifying which is in faith." In other words, Paul tells Timothy that all these types of false teaching won't build you up in the faith. I think we can observe today in the liberal churches the fruit of their many years of unbelief. It has produced a hard core of almost heartless individuals who absolutely lack faith. They have rejected the Word of God, and the results we see in their churches are unbelievable.

Now the end of the commandment is charity out of a pure heart, and of a good conscience, and of faith unfeigned [1 Tim. 1:5].

"Charity [love] out of a pure heart." Paul again is using intimate expressions in writing to this young preacher that you will not find in his epistles to the churches. He tells Timothy that what is taught in the church should produce love out of a pure heart. A "pure heart" is in contrast to our old nature. It means a person who has been made righteous in Christ and can now manifest the fruit of the Spirit, which includes love.

There are three things that should be manifest in the church. The first is faith—faith in God and in His Word. The second is love. Love is not something you simply mouth all the time. Love is an active concern for others, which means you won't gossip about them or in any way bring harm to them.

I know of one church that has done everything it can to wreck the ministry of its pastor. The one thing they aren't justified in saying is that he didn't teach the Word of God—he did teach it. Yet they had accused him of not having taught it. And at the same time they talk about love. What hypocrisy! Love is not something you just talk about; it is something that must be made manifest.

Faith should be lived out in the life of a church, and love should be lived out. You do need an organization and church officers, but whether you have an episcopal or congregational or presbyterian form of government does not make much difference. If faith and love are lacking, you have nothing more than a lodge, a religious club of some sort. But if faith and love are manifest, the form of government is not too important.

The third thing that should be manifest in the life of a church is "a good conscience." I do not believe that conscience is a good guide even for a believer; yet a believer ought to have a good conscience. When you lie down at night, do you feel bad about something you've said or done during the day? Many sensitive Christians are like that. I had a call one time from a person who was weeping and said, "I said something about you that I should not have, and I hope you'll forgive me." I hadn't known anything about it, by the way, but apparently he hadn't been able to sleep that night because of it. It is good to have a sensitive conscience. Many have consciences that have been seared with a hot iron; that is, they are insensitive to right or wrong.

These three wonderful graces—love, a good conscience, and faith—are the things Paul says should be manifested by believers in a local church.

From which some having swerved have turned aside unto vain jangling [1 Tim. 1:6].

"Vain jangling" means empty chatter, beautiful words, flowery language. There are people who will butter you up and pat you on the back, but it means nothing. It's all just talk.

Desiring to be teachers of the law; understanding neither what they say, nor whereof they affirm [1 Tim. 1:7].

Paul is really laying it on the line. He makes it clear there are those who teach error, and they do it with assurance. They reject the Word of God and actually do not understand what they are talking about.

But we know that the law is good, if a man use it lawfully [1 Tim. 1:8].

In this section where Paul is warning believers against unsound doctrine, he has mentioned the mystery religions and the idolatry that abounded in Ephesus where young Timothy was. He has also warned against the false teaching that sought to make the Old Testament merely a mythology. Now Paul warns against legalists, those who taught that the law is a means of salvation and a means of sanctification after salvation.

The Law served a purpose, but God did not give it as a means of salvation. The Law condemns us; it reveals to man that he is a sinner in need of a Savior. Under the Law the best man in the world is absolutely condemned, but under the gospel the worst man can be justified if he will believe in Christ.

The sinner cannot be saved by good works for he is unable to perform any good works. Paul wrote in Romans, "So then they that are in the flesh cannot please God" (Rom. 8:8).

This idea that in and of yourself you can please God absolutely contradicts the Word of God. It is impossible to please Him—you *cannot* meet His standard.

Good works cannot produce salvation, but salvation can produce good works. We are not saved *by* good works, but we are saved *unto* good works. Paul makes this very clear in Ephesians 2:8–10 where we read: "For by grace are ye saved through faith; and that not of yourselves: it is the gift of God: Not of works, lest any man should boast. For we are his workmanship, created in Christ Jesus unto good works, which God hath before ordained that we should walk in them."

"We know that the law is good, if a man use it lawfully." The Law reveals the will of God—it is morally excellent. It is good for moral conduct but not for obtaining salvation. It cannot save a sinner, but it can correct him or reveal that he is a sinner. *That* is its purpose.

Knowing this, that the law is not made for a righteous man, but for the lawless and disobedient, for the ungodly and for sinners, for unholy and profane, for murderers of fathers and murderers of mothers, for manslayers,

For whoremongers, for them that defile themselves with mankind, for menstealers, for liars, for perjured persons, and if there be any other thing that is contrary to sound doctrine [1 Tim. 1:9–10].

The Law was not given to the righteous man, the one who has been made righteous because of his faith in Christ. That man has been called to a much higher plane before God. The Law was given for the lawless. "Thou shalt not kill" is not given to the child of God who has no thought of murdering anyone, who does not want to hurt but wants to help. That commandment was given to the man who is a murderer at heart. It is given to control the natural man. The Law is "for whoremongers, for them that defile themselves with mankind, for menstealers, for liars, for perjured persons." Those who have come to Christ were not saved by the Law, but by the grace of God. They have been brought into the family of God and have been brought to a plane of living higher even than that given in the Law.

Let me give two illustrations of this that I trust will be helpful. Imagine a judge on a bench who has a lawbreaker brought before him. He is guilty, and he should pay a heavy fine and go to prison. However, the judge says, "I have a son who loves this prisoner although he has broken the law and I must condemn him. My son is a wealthy man and has agreed to pay his fine. He's also agreed to go to prison on behalf of this man. Therefore, his penalty has been fully paid. I am going to take this criminal into my home, and I am going to treat him as a son of mine." When the judge takes the criminal into his home, he no longer says things like, "Thou shalt not kill" or "Thou shalt not steal" (Exod. 20:13,15). The man is now his son. The judge will talk to him about loving the other members of his family, how he is to conduct himself at the table, treat his wife with respect, and take part in the family chores. You see, this man is treated on an altogether different basis from what he was before. That is what God has done for the believing sinner. We are above and beyond the law. The law is for that fellow out yonder who is a lawbreaker. It is given to control the old nature, the flesh.

The other illustration is one that Dr. Harry Ironside told me years ago. After teaching at an Indian conference in Flagstaff, Arizona, Dr. Ironside took one of the Christian Indians with him to Oakland, California. Among other things, this Indian was asked to speak at a young people's group that was mixed up on the ideas of law and grace. They were confused about the place of the law in the Christian life. The Indian told the group, "I came here from Flagstaff on the train, and we stopped over for several hours in Barstow. There in the station's waiting room I noticed signs on the walls which said, 'Do Not Spit on the Floor.' That was the rule there. I looked down on the floor, and observed that nobody had paid any attention to the law. But when we got here to Oakland I was invited to stay in a lovely, Christian home. As I sat in the living room I looked around and noticed pretty pictures on the walls, but no signs which said 'Do Not Spit on the Floor.' I got down on my hands and knees and felt the rug and, you know, nobody had spit on the floor. In Barstow it was law, but in the home in which I'm staying it is grace."

Under law man never kept it, he couldn't measure up to it, and he broke it continually. Under grace a man is brought into the family of God, and he is not going to murder or lie. If he does, he is surely out of fellowship with God.

"Any other thing that is contrary to sound doctrine." Paul adds this in case he had left out something. It covers any and all sin he may have omitted in his list.

PERSONAL TESTIMONY OF PAUL

According to the glorious gospel of the blessed God, which was committed to my trust [1 Tim. 1:11].

Again this is one of those unique statements that Paul uses in writing to this young preacher which you will not find in his epistles to the churches. It might be translated: "According to the gospel of glory of the blessed God, which was committed to my trust." Isn't that a wonderful way to speak of it!

And I thank Christ Jesus our Lord, who hath enabled me, for that he counted me faithful, putting me into the ministry [1 Tim. 1:12].

"I thank Christ Jesus our Lord" —Paul emphasizes the Lordship of Christ.

"He counted me faithful, putting me into the ministry." The idea of *ministry* is greatly misunderstood in our day. All believers are in the ministry; not one of us is out of the ministry if he is a child of God. The word Paul uses here for ministry is the same as the word for deacon, and every believer is a minister of the Lord Jesus Christ.

Paul even calls rulers ministers—"ministers of God." We say that we have voted for a certain man or that the people put a man into his office, but I think that sometimes God overrules who is to be put into office. Rulers are supposed to function as ministers of God.

Paul is grateful to God that He has put him into His service as a missionary. Every believer has some service to perform for the Lord.

Who was before a blasphemer, and a persecutor, and injurious: but I obtained mercy, because I did it ignorantly in unbelief [1 Tim. 1:13].

"Who was before a blasphemer"—Paul uses this awful word and says that he was a blasphemer. He had blasphemed the Lord Jesus, and he had hated Him. I think he was present at the Crucifixion and ridiculed the Lord Jesus. Paul says that he had been a blasphemer, a persecutor, and that he had injured the church.

"But I obtained mercy." When Paul speaks of his salvation he says he was saved by the *grace* of God. It was the *mercy* of God that put him into the ministry.

I have never really figured out why the Lord has used me in this ministry of giving out the Word of God. If you had said to me

when I was a young, smart-alecky bank clerk that I was someday going to be in the ministry, I would have said it was absurd. I didn't want it, and I didn't have anything that would commend me to it. But God by His mercy, my friend, has put me into His service, His ministry. He is rich in mercy, and I have used quite a bit of it in my lifetime!

"Because I did it ignorantly in unbelief." This was Paul's condition, and it was the condition of all of us before we came to Christ.

And the grace of our Lord was exceeding abundant with faith and love which is in Christ Jesus [1 Tim. 1:14].

Paul was saved by the grace of God who brought him to the place of faith and love "which is in Christ Jesus." Again, these are the things that will be manifest in the life of a believer.

This is a faithful saying, and worthy of all acceptation, that Christ Jesus came into the world to save sinners; of whom I am chief [1 Tim. 1:15].

This is a very important verse of Scripture because it affirms that "Christ Jesus came into the world to save sinners." He didn't come to be the greatest teacher the world has ever known, although He was that. He didn't come to set a moral example, but He did do that. He came into the world to save sinners.

When you give your testimony make sure that you don't tell people how wonderful *you* are or all *you* have accomplished. Tell them you were a *sinner* and that *Christ* saved you. That is what is important.

"Of whom I am chief." When Paul says he was the chiefest of sinners, he is not using hyperbole. He is not using high-flung oratory. He is speaking the truth. He was the chief of sinners; he blasphemed the Lord Jesus and shot out his lip at Him.

"But," Paul says, "I've been saved." The Lord Jesus came to save sinners, and if you say, "I don't think Christ can save me—I'm the worst," you are wrong. Paul is the chief of sinners, and the chief of sinners has already been saved. So *you* will be able to be saved if you want to be. The decision rests with you. All you need do is turn to Christ, and He'll do the rest. He is faithful—Paul says, "This is a *faithful* saying."

Howbeit for this cause I obtained mercy, that in me first Jesus Christ might shew forth all longsuffering, for a pattern to them which should hereaf-

ter believe on him to life everlasting [1 Tim. 1:16].

"Howbeit for this cause I obtained mercy"— you see, he needed mercy in order to become a minister, to be a missionary.

"That in me first Jesus Christ might shew forth all long-suffering, for a pattern to them which should hereafter believe on him to life everlasting."

Paul said that he was not only a preacher of, but also an example of, the gospel.

Now unto the King eternal, immortal, invisible, the only wise God, be honour and glory for ever and ever. Amen [1 Tim. 1:17].

Paul simply couldn't go any further without sounding out this tremendous doxology. Who is "the King eternal"? He is the Lord Jesus Christ. And who is the Lord Jesus? He is "the only wise God." Don't tell me that Paul did not teach that the Lord Jesus was God. Paul considered Him to be God manifest in the flesh, and here he gives this wonderful testimony to that.

CHARGE TO TIMOTHY

This charge I commit unto thee, son Timothy, according to the prophecies which went before on thee, that thou by them mightest war a good warfare [1 Tim. 1:18].

"This charge I commit unto thee, son Timothy." Although his letter to Timothy is very practical and has to do with the local church and Timothy's responsibilities in it, it also reveals something of the wonderful personal relationship that must have existed between the apostle Paul and Timothy. This is Paul's personal charge to Timothy as a young man in the ministry.

"Son Timothy"—he was Paul's spiritual son; Paul had led him to Christ.

"According to the prophecies which went before on thee." Paul had real spiritual discernment, and evidently God had directed him to take this young man along with him and allow him to have the position which he held in the early church.

"That thou by them mightest war a good warfare." You ought never to fight a war unless your heart is in it, unless you are fighting for a real cause and intend to get the victory. As a Christian, Timothy had a real enemy. He was involved in a spiritual warfare. Paul wanted him to fight a good fight and not to make shipwreck of the faith—as others were doing.

Holding faith, and a good conscience; which some having put away concerning faith have made shipwreck [1 Tim. 1:19].

Living the Christian life is not as simple as some would like us to believe. It is more complex than walking when the light is green and not walking when the light turns red. We have intricate personalities, and Paul is saying there is real danger for us in our human inconsistencies and failures. I assume you are not living in some ivory tower somewhere. Some Christians feel they are, that they are above the landscape and the smog and are way up yonder. But for those of us today who are walking on the sidewalks of our cities and rubbing shoulders with rough humanity and the problems of the world, we find that there are inconsistencies and failures in our lives. The danger we face is that of accommodating our faith to our failure.

A man I knew came home from the mission field and got a job doing something rather ordinary. He said, "The *Lord* led me to do this." He had trained about nine years to be a missionary, and now he said the Lord had led him back home to take a job that just wasn't very important. I asked him if he really felt that that was the way the Lord leads, and he insisted it was. He repeats this so frequently that I am afraid what actually happened was that he accommodated his faith to his human failure on the mission field. That is a grave danger for all of us. My friend, when you and I fail—when there is inconsistency in our lives—we ought to go to Him and tell Him that we have fallen short, that we haven't measured up. As we will read shortly in 1 Timothy, the Lord Jesus is a wonderful mediator between God and man. We need not be afraid to go to Him.

Of whom is Hymenaeus and Alexander; whom I have delivered unto Satan, that they may learn not to blaspheme [1 Tim. 1:20].

"Of whom is Hymenaeus and Alexander"— Paul cites two examples of apostates in his day. He mentions them elsewhere in Scripture, and he doesn't have much good to say about either one of them. In 2 Timothy he writes, "Alexander the coppersmith did me much evil . . ." (2 Tim. 4:14).

"Whom I have delivered unto Satan." These men had failed, they were apostates, and Paul exercised a ministry which I feel only an apostle can exercise. He says, "I have delivered [them] unto Satan." This is not something we could put under the name of ecclesiastical discipline or excommunication today. It is Paul exercising what was his prerogative and position as an apostle; he hands over these men to Satan.

We have another occasion of this mentioned in 1 Corinthians where Paul writes: "For I verily, as absent in body, but present in spirit, have judged already, as though I were present, concerning him that hath so done this deed, In the name of our Lord Jesus Christ, when ye are gathered together, and my spirit, with the power of our Lord Jesus Christ, To deliver such an one unto Satan for the destruction of the flesh, that the spirit may be saved in the day of the Lord Jesus" (1 Cor. 5:3–5). This is an authority the apostles had which we do not have today. We have no right to deliver any man over to Satan, but the apostles did. Peter exercised it also: I imagine that if we could talk to Ananias and Sapphira they would be able to tell us something of his authority as an apostle (see Acts 5:1–11).

CHAPTER 2

THEME: *Public prayer and woman's place in the churches*

PUBLIC PRAYER

Public prayer is prayer for the public and for public officials.

I exhort therefore, that, first of all, supplications, prayers, intercessions, and giving of thanks, be made for all men;

For kings, and for all that are in authority; that we may lead a quiet and peaceable life in all godliness and honesty [1 Tim. 2:1–2].

Paul says that Christians are to pray for public officials, and I take it that he meant that the prayers were to be made in the church. To bring this up-to-date, he is saying the Democrats ought to pray for the Republicans, and the Republicans ought to pray for the Democrats. Many years ago a famous chaplain of the Senate was asked by a visitor, "Do you pray for the senators?" He replied, "No, I look at the senators, and then I pray for the country!" That is exactly what Paul says we need to do. We need to pray for our country, and we need to pray for those who have authority over us. If you are a Republican and a Democrat is in office, pray for him. If you are a Democrat and a Republican is in office, pray for him.

"For kings." Paul says we are to pray for the kings who rule. You may ask, "Yes, but are we to pray when the government is a corrupt one?" Paul is saying we are to pray even if it's a corrupt government. We are to pray for whoever is in power. Remember that the man who was in power in Rome when Paul wrote was bloody Nero, yet he says we are to pray for kings, whoever they are.

"That we may lead a quiet and peaceable life in all godliness and honesty." Any government is better than no government. Some people may question that, but an evil, corrupt government, if it really governs, is better than anarchy. I agree with those who argue that politics is crooked—man has certainly corrupted and misused political power—but there does remain a semblance of law and order. Civil government is a gift from God, and we ought to give thanks for it and pray for it. Many of us fall short of praying for our government in order that we might continue to live quietly and peaceably.

For this is good and acceptable in the sight of God our Saviour;

Who will have all men to be saved, and to come unto the knowledge of the truth [1 Tim. 2:3–4].

A second reason we should pray for government is in order that the gospel might continue to go out to the lost. I believe that we are actually going to see the persecution of Christians in this country in the future. I do not mean the persecution of church members—the liberal church is so compromised today that they will go along with whatever comes along. I am saying that genuine believers in Christ may encounter persecution. Paul was beginning to experience persecution himself, and he said the believers were to pray for the leaders who were responsible for it. It was "good and acceptable in the sight of God" to pray for these men. Why? Because it is God's will that all men might be saved.

It is not important for you and me to get a certain man elected to office. I have never in my ministry recommended a candidate for office. I am not called to do that, and I don't believe any minister is. I am to pray for our leaders regardless of who they are in order that the gospel can go out. I want a man in office who is going to make it possible for the Word of God to continue to be given to the lost. This should be our concern and our prayer.

For there is one God, and one mediator between God and men, the man Christ Jesus [1 Tim. 2:5].

"For there is one God." The Romans worshiped many gods, and today people worship many gods in a different sort of way. People are giving themselves to many things—some to pleasure, some to entertainment, and so on. The entertainment world, for example, has become a religion of sorts for many people. There are women who would sacrifice their virtue in a moment and men who would sacrifice their honor in order to become a movie or television star. People have many different gods today. But there is only *one God*, and He is the Creator.

"And one mediator between God and men, the man Christ Jesus." In Old Testament times the Israelite went to the temple where there were many priests. He could go to God through them. Paul is saying that now there is only one Mediator to whom we are to go. We are not to go to any human being down here; it is not necessary to go through a minister. There is a Mediator between God and man.

We need a mediator, we need a priest, and we have one, the Great High Priest. Job's heart cry even in his day was, "Neither is there any daysman betwixt us, that might lay his hand upon us both" (Job 9:33). In effect, Job was crying out, "Oh, if there were somebody who could take hold of God's hand and then take hold of my hand and bring us together that there might be communication and understanding between us!"

Well, my friend, today we have a Mediator—the Lord Jesus Christ has come. He has one hand in the hand of Deity because He is *God*. He is able to save to the uttermost because He is God, and He has paid the price for our salvation. He is a Mediator because He has also become *man*. He can hold my hand; He understands me. He understands you; you can go to Him, and He is not going to be upset with you. He will not lose His temper or strike you or hurt you in any way. You may say, "Well, I've failed. I've done such-and-such, and I've come short of the glory of God." My friend, He knows that, and He still loves you and wants to put His arm around you.

Isaiah wrote of the Lord: "In all their affliction he was afflicted . . ." (Isa. 63:9). Some scholars say that this should read, "In all their affliction he was *not* afflicted." Either way you read it, it is wonderful. I think maybe God wants us to see it both ways, but I like it, "In all their affliction he was *not* afflicted." God went through the wilderness with the children of Israel. When they failed and disobeyed at Kadesh-Barnea, He didn't say, "Well, good-bye—I'm through with you, you've failed." No, He went with them for forty years. But He also went on ahead: He gave Moses their instructions for living for the time when they would enter the Promised Land. But He waited for them and dealt patiently with them in their time of affliction in the wilderness. He wasn't afflicted; He didn't break down and fail but just stayed there with them.

He has dealt with me in the same way, and it is wonderful to have such a Mediator through whom we can go to God. And you should go through Him, because there is really no use coming and telling me your troubles. I may not be sympathetic with you; I might not really understand your case. He does. He's human. He is a daysman, a Mediator. He has put His hand in mine. I don't put my hand in His; He puts *His* hand in mine. That is the wonder of it all! He has come down and put His hand in mine and taken hold of me, but He also holds on to God because He is God, and He has brought us together.

This Mediator is the One the world needs to know because there is but *one* way to salvation. Peter said to the religious leaders of his day: "Neither is there salvation in any other: for there is none other name under heaven given among men, whereby we must be saved" (Acts 4:12). Christ is the only way, but the tremendous thing is that He *will* bring you right through to God if you will turn to Him.

One time while in Canada I was told that I needed to get onto a certain freeway to get to Detroit, Michigan, but if I missed that freeway I was in real trouble. It took a great deal of manipulating around, but once I managed to find that freeway it brought me right into Detroit. I was thankful for the man who had said, "There is only one way." I am also thankful that I have been told there is one way to God, one Mediator. He is the only One who can bring us together: He can bring us to God because He is God and He is also a man, "the man Christ Jesus."

Who gave himself a ransom for all, to be testified in due time [1 Tim. 2:6].

"Ransom" is *antilutron* in the Greek, and it means a "redemption price." Christ paid a price for our redemption. We needed to be redeemed—you and I were lost sinners, and He was the ransom.

Whereunto I am ordained a preacher, and an apostle, (I speak the truth in Christ, and lie not;) a teacher of the Gentiles in faith and verity [1 Tim. 2:7].

"I am ordained" might be better translated "I am appointed." Paul says that he was appointed a preacher and an apostle.

"Preacher" comes from the Greek word *kerux*, which means "a herald or a trumpet," referring to one who gives out the gospel. He has been appointed one to declare the gospel.

"(I speak the truth in Christ, and lie not;)." It might seem strange to you that Paul would say this to a young preacher who is his personal friend. I think he is saying it to encourage him—Timothy knows it is true.

"A teacher of the Gentiles in faith and verity [truth]." Again this is something that he did not write to the churches. He has always said that he is an apostle of the Gentiles; here he says that he is not only the apostle to give the gospel, but he is also the one to *teach* the Gentiles.

HOW MEN ARE TO PRAY

I will therefore that men pray every where, lifting up holy hands, without wrath and doubting [1 Tim. 2:8].

"I will"—Paul is not making this a matter of his will, but is saying, "I desire."

"That men pray every where"—that is, in every place where believers meet. Paul is talking about *public* prayer, prayer in the public service.

"Lifting up holy hands." This was a custom practiced in the early church. It revealed the dedication in the lives of those praying.

Now there are those who lift up their hands in services today, and they are sometimes criticized for it. There is nothing wrong with lifting up your hands if it is something you feel you want to do. Personally, I have always hesitated to do it because I'm not too sure about

my hands, whether they are clean or not, clean physically or otherwise. Notice that Paul says, "holy hands." This would mean that they are hands dedicated to God's service. My friend, you ought not to poke up your hands in a meeting if those hands are not used for the service of Christ.

"Without wrath"—all sins have been confessed. You don't come in prayer with anger in your heart, or a bitter spirit, but with all your sins confessed.

"Without . . . doubting." In Hebrews 11:6 we read: "But without faith it is impossible to please him; for he that cometh to God must believe that he is, and that he is a rewarder of them that diligently seek him." When we come to God in prayer, we are to come in faith. One of the reasons I feel that our prayer meetings are not better attended today is that people lack faith. They do not believe that God is going to hear and answer prayer.

I do not mean to be irreverent, but I sometimes think that the Lord must yawn during our prayer meetings because they are so boresome. Prayer should be made in our public services by those who have their sins confessed, who come without bitterness in their hearts, and who come in faith, believing that God will hear and answer. It is this kind of prayer that will make a prayer meeting what it ought to be.

HOW WOMEN ARE TO PRAY

Paul has given the way that men ought to pray, and now he will say how women are to pray. This passage will also touch on the matter of women's dress and their place in the local church.

We live in a day when there are two extreme positions relative to the place women should occupy in the local and visible church. Both positions use this passage of Scripture to support their stand.

One position permits women to occupy a place of prominence and leadership in all public services. They have women preachers, choir directors, and officers. No position is withheld from them and, as a result, the women are not only prominent but we find that they become dominant in the church.

When I was a pastor in Nashville, Tennessee, a tent was put up across the street from my church. The Baptist preacher in town was a good friend of mine and together we went over to meet the husband and wife team who were going to hold meetings. The wife did the preaching, and the husband did all the leg work. We watched him putting up the tent and setting out the benches and all that sort of thing. He also led the singing. That's all right if you like it that way, but I don't. However, the Baptist preacher and I gave the meetings all the support we could, because they had good meetings and she *did* preach the gospel. This is an example of the fact that God has used some of these groups who have women preachers in a definite way; but I think, frankly, that He has used them in spite of, not because of, the position of women among them.

The other extreme position on this issue is taken by those who do not allow women any place at all in their public services. You never hear the voice of a woman in public in their meetings, not even in singing. I have had opportunity for good ministry among some of these folk, but believe me, they push their women to the background. I fear that they lose a great deal of talent and that the women could make a marvelous contribution if they were permitted to do so.

To illustrate this, allow me to tell you a story, and I hope you understand that I do so in a facetious manner. There is a little town in the Midwest where there lived a very prominent maiden lady. Everyone agreed that she would have made some man a wonderful wife, but she had never been asked and she died an old maid. The society editor for the local newspaper who normally would cover such a story was out of town, and the sports editor was asked to write up a little notice of this lady's death. He concluded the article with these words:

Here lie the bones of Nancy Jones:
For her, life held no terrors.
She lived an old maid, she died an old maid:
No hits, no runs, no errors.

Churches miss something when they will not use the talent of their women. God can and will use them in His work.

The confusion that exists about this rather practical issue has been brought about by a misunderstanding of this passage of Scripture and also by an unfamiliarity with the Roman world of Paul's day.

Let's establish first that God *has* used women. In the Word of God we see Deborah, Queen Esther, Ruth, and others. In church history, we find women like Mary Fletcher and Priscilla Gurney. There are multitudes of others whom God has used in a wonderful way.

However, in the Roman world the female principle was a part of all the heathen religions, and women occupied a prominent place. The worship of Aphrodite at Corinth was probably one of the most immoral in which prostitution was actually made into a religion. The thousand vestal virgins who were in the temple of Aphrodite on top of the Acropolis there in Corinth were nothing in the world but prostitutes. They were characterized by very disheveled hair. The reason God said that a woman should have her head covered was so she would not be associated at all with religions like this. Also, in Ephesus where Timothy was at this time, women occupied a very prominent position in the worship at the temple of Diana. In all the mystery religions there were priestesses. It is because of these heathen practices that Paul is emphasizing in this passage that this matter of sex is not to enter into the public prayer in the services of the Christian churches. We need to approach this passage with these factors in mind.

In like manner also, that women adorn themselves in modest apparel, with shamefacedness and sobriety; not with broided hair, or gold, or pearls, or costly array;

But (which becometh women professing godliness) with good works [1 Tim. 2:9–10].

"In like manner also"—Paul has said how men are to pray in public, and now he will say how women are to pray. Note that he is saying women *are* to pray. That is not the issue, but he is telling them the *way* in which they are to pray in public. His emphasis will be upon inner adornment rather than outward adornment. Women are to pray in public, but they should not dress up from the viewpoint of appealing to God in a sexual or physical way.

I want to make it very clear that I feel that a woman should dress as nicely as she possibly can. There is nothing wrong with a woman dressing in a way that is appealing to her husband (or, if she is single, to a man). I have made this statement before, and one lady wrote me in reaction to it:

I never thought I'd see the day when I would feel a need to take you to task over anything. Usually I agree with you on everything that you say. But on Friday morning in your last study in Proverbs, I guess you hit a raw nerve. You were admonishing young men on choosing a wife, and you said, "First of all, make sure she's a Christian." I agree with that. Then you said, "And if possible, choose a pretty one." Really, Dr. McGee, do you think that's quite fair? After all, there are far more plain, ordinary-looking girls and women than really pretty ones, and pray tell, where would they be if men chose only pretty ones? I happen to be one of those plain, ordinary-looking women, and I'm so glad my husband didn't choose one of the pretty ones, or I'd have missed out on twenty-five years of happy married life. I'm not really angry with you. How could I be when you've taught me so much of the deep truths of God's Word? I just wanted you to know that I think you ought to say a little something for us women whom the Lord did not choose to bless with physical beauty.

I want to say something to that woman and to others: Have you ever stopped to realize that when your husband fell in love with you he thought you were beautiful? Yes, he did. I shall never forget the night that I met my wife. It was a summer night in Texas, and we were invited to the home of mutual friends for dinner. Frankly, these friends were trying to bring us together. I didn't want to go because I had an engagement in Fort Worth that night. My wife didn't want to go because she was going with another fellow! But that night when I saw her—I never shall forget her dark hair, her brown eyes—there in the candlelight I looked at her, and I fell in love with her. I proposed to her on our second date, and the reason I didn't propose on that first date was that I didn't want her to think I was in a hurry! She'd never won a beauty contest, but she was beautiful. How wonderful it was!

I have a notion your husband thought you were beautiful also, and there is nothing wrong in dressing in a way to be attractive to him. But when you go to God in prayer, you don't need that outward adornment. You need that inward adornment. When a woman is going to sing in church, to speak or to have any part in a church service, she ought to keep in mind that her appeal should in no way be on the basis of sex. She should seek to please God, and there is no way in which she can appeal to Him on the basis of sex at all. Such appeal characterized the pagan religions in the Roman world, and Paul is stressing that it should not be a part of the public services of the Christian churches.

Let the woman learn in silence with all subjection.

But I suffer not a woman to teach, nor to usurp authority over the man, but to be in silence [1 Tim. 2:11–12].

These verses have to do with the learning and teaching of doctrine. Keep in mind that the women led in the mystery religions of Paul's day, and they were sex orgies. Paul is cautioning women not to speak publicly with the idea of making an appeal on the basis of sex. Paul strictly forbade women to speak in tongues in 1 Corinthians 14:34.

For Adam was first formed, then Eve.

And Adam was not deceived, but the woman being deceived was in the transgression.

Notwithstanding she shall be saved in childbearing, if they continue in faith and charity and holiness with sobriety [1 Tim. 2:13–15].

It was the sin of Eve that brought sin into the world. Now every time a woman bears a child, she brings a *sinner* into the world—that is all she can bring into the world. But Mary brought the Lord Jesus, the Savior into the world. So how are women saved? By childbearing—because Mary brought the Savior into the world. Don't ever say that woman brought sin into the world, unless you are prepared to add that woman also brought the Savior into the world. My friend, no *man* provided a Savior: a *woman* did. However, each individual woman is saved by faith, the same as each man is saved by faith. She is to grow in love and holiness just as a man is.

CHAPTER 3

THEME: *Officers in the churches*

REQUIREMENTS OF ELDERS

This is a true saying, If a man desire the office of a bishop, he desireth a good work [1 Tim. 3:1].

"This is a *true* saying" could be translated, "This is a *faithful* saying." In other words, this is a saying that stands the test of time; it is one you can depend upon.

"If a man *desire* the office of a bishop" means if a man *seeks* the office of a bishop. This has in it the thought that there will be the active seeking of the office. I believe that a man who has the qualifications ought to seek the office. He ought to want a place where he can use the gift that the Spirit of God has given him. If the Spirit of God has not given him the gift and is not leading him, then it would be a tragedy indeed if a man sought the office of bishop. This also suggests that there was not just one bishop in the church, but there were several.

"The office of a bishop." *Bishop* is a word that has been misinterpreted and interpreted differently by different groups. Those who practice the episcopal form of church government put great emphasis upon this word and its interpretation.

Bishop actually means "an overseer, a superintendent." In the early church the pastor was called by several different titles: (1) he was called a presbyter, or elder; (2) he was called a pastor, or shepherd; (3) he was called a bishop, or an overseer; and (4) he was called a minister. The pastor was never called "reverend," and I don't think any preacher should be so called. *Reverend* means "terrible, that which incites terror." It is a name which applies only to God.

I take the position that the terms *elder* and *bishop* refer to the same person. Those who hold to the episcopal form of church government will, of course, disagree with me altogether. I believe that the use of "elder" (*presbuteros* in the Greek) refers to the *person* who holds the office, and it suggests that he must be a mature Christian. On the other hand, the use of "bishop" (*episkopos* in the Greek) refers to the *office* that is held. Therefore, these two words apply to the same individual or office.

A bishop in the early church never had authority over other bishops or elders. He did not have authority over churches. You do not find such a practice presented in the Word of God. Even Paul, who founded a number of churches, never spoke of himself as the bishop of a church, or as the one who was ruling a church in any way whatsoever. Therefore, the minister is one who is to serve the church, not rule over it.

"He desireth a good work"—he is seeking a place where he can serve in the church.

A bishop then must be blameless, the husband of one wife, vigilant, sober, of good behaviour, given to hospitality, apt to teach [1 Tim. 3:2].

We have given here the positive requirements of an elder—the things he *ought* to be.

"Blameless." The thing that must be understood is that you *will* be blamed for things if you hold an office, any office, in the church. What is important is that the accusation must not be true. An elder must be blameless in the sense that he will not be found guilty of anything that he might be accused of.

Shortly after I had been called to a pastorate in downtown Los Angeles, I met Dr. James McGinley in Chicago. He asked me, "How do you like being pastor in that great church?" "Well," I said, "it's a marvelous opportunity, but I find myself in a very unique place: I am accused of many things, and I can't defend myself. You cannot spend all your time answering everybody, so I've determined to just preach the Word of God and not try to answer them." Dr. McGinley said, "Just rejoice that the things you are accused of are not true." It is nice to be in that position, and that should be the position of a bishop—blameless: accused but not guilty.

"The husband of one wife." This can be interpreted two ways. It could mean that he ought to be married. I feel that Paul had this in mind. You may say, "Well, Paul was not married." I take the position that Paul had been married and his wife had died. He could not have been a member of the Sanhedrin without being married. He simply had not married again, perhaps because of his travels as an apostle.

When I first became a pastor I was not married and I was frequently kidded by a friend who said I had no right to be a pastor if I wasn't married. Using this verse, he would say, "You should be the husband of one wife." However, I think that the primary meaning here is that the bishop or elder should not have *two* wives. Polygamy was common in Paul's day, and bigamy was certainly prevalent. The officer in the church should be the husband of one wife.

"Vigilant" means temperate. The elder should be calm and not credulous. He should be a man who knows how to keep his cool.

"Sober" means sober-minded or serious. He means business. This does not mean an elder cannot have a sense of humor, but he should be serious about the office which he holds.

"Of good behaviour." An elder should be orderly in his conduct. He doesn't do questionable things. I knew a minister who got himself into a great deal of difficulty because of his careless actions. The rumors were that he had had an affair with a woman in his congregation. I'm confident from all the information that came to me from several sources that he was not guilty, but he certainly had been careless in his conduct. He was a young minister, and often at church social gatherings, he would kiddingly say that he was going to take another man's wife home. He would take her, leave her off at her door, and then go on to his home. All this was done with a great deal of kidding, but it caused some people to raise their eyebrows and start talking. My feeling is that the conduct of an officer or a minister should be absolutely above reproach. Kidding is fine, but it should not lead to questionable activity.

"Given to hospitality" means that an elder is to be a hospitable individual. He is the type of fellow who invites his preacher or others out to lunch. I've always liked fellows like that and have had the privilege in recent years of meeting many wonderful and hospitable laymen in my travels all over the country. One will come and put his arm around me and say, "Now can I help you in some way? Is there anything I can do?" They do things like having a bowl of fruit or a bouquet of flowers sent to my hotel room where I happen to be staying. One time in San Diego I broke off a capped tooth, and a doctor friend recommended a dentist there. That dentist is such a wonderful man I still go all the way to San Diego for my dental care. Such hospitable men can be found all across our country.

"Apt to teach." This is something I emphasize, because I do not feel any man ought to be an elder in a church unless he can teach the Word of God. I used to say to my church officers that I wished it was possible to give a theological exam to each one of them to determine if he was qualified to be an officer. I never actually did that, but I always thought it would be a good idea.

> **Not given to wine, no striker, not greedy of filthy lucre; but patient, not a brawler, not covetous [1 Tim. 3:3].**

Now we come to the negative qualifications—the things an elder should *not* be.

"Not given to wine"—he should not be a drunkard.

"No striker"—not violent or pugnacious.

"Not greedy of filthy lucre." He shouldn't have a love of money. The love of money is a root of all evil we are told in Scripture (1 Tim. 6:10). The way a church officer handles his money can lead him into a great deal of trouble—either his own money or the church's money.

"Patient" means reasonable. He should be a reasonable man, someone you can talk to or reason with.

"Not a brawler." He should not be a contentious person. Men who are constantly stirring up trouble in a church should never be selected as church officers.

"Not covetous" again refers to the love of money, but it also suggests an idolatry, actually the worship of money. He should not be a man who puts the pursuit of wealth above everything else.

> **One that ruleth well his own house, having his children in subjection with all gravity [1 Tim. 3:4].**

An elder should have the authority in his own home—without being a dictator.

> **(For if a man know not how to rule his own house, how shall he take care of the church of God?) [1 Tim. 3:5].**

A man does not know how to rule the house of God if he cannot rule his own home.

> **Not a novice, lest being lifted up with pride he fall into the condemnation of the devil [1 Tim. 3:6].**

"Not a novice" means not a recent convert, not someone who has recently been saved. Sometimes a man is converted one week, and the next week he is made a church officer or asked to give his testimony. He is not ready for it. This is a caution that needs to be heeded today.

I had the privilege for several years of teaching a Bible study group of Christians in Hollywood. It was natural for them to want to push to the front some prominent personality who had recently made a decision for Christ.

However, the cause of Christ is hurt when those who are young in the faith attempt to speak on matters of doctrine about which they are not knowledgeable.

"Lest being lifted up with pride he fall into the condemnation of the devil." Pride was the Devil's great sin. Also it is often the sin of officers in the church and of preachers. It is a danger for all of us, but it is reprehensible when it is in the church.

Moreover he must have a good report of them which are without; lest he fall into reproach and the snare of the devil [1 Tim. 3:7].

"Them which are without" means those who are outside the church. In other words, if a man has a bad reputation on the outside—if he doesn't pay his bills, is untrustworthy, or is a liar—he immediately is *not* a candidate to be an officer in the church. If he is such a man he is really a candidate of the Devil—he would better represent the Devil than he would represent the cause of Christ.

REQUIREMENTS OF DEACONS

Likewise must the deacons be grave, not double-tongued, not given to much wine, not greedy of filthy lucre [1 Tim. 3:8].

The word that is translated "deacon" here is the same word that is sometimes translated as "minister." Paul and Apollos are called deacons. The Lord Jesus is called a minister in Matthew 20:28. In Romans 13:4 government officials are called ministers, and in 2 Corinthians 11:15 ministers of Satan have the word applied to them. *Deacon* or *minister*, therefore, is a general term for a servant or a worker.

We think of the account in Acts 6 as giving the occasion when the office of deacon began in the early church. However, the Greek word for *deacon* is not even used there. But I'm confident we have scriptural grounds to say that those men were being appointed as deacons in the church.

A deacon, although he deals with the material matters of the church, should be a *spiritual* man. We have a problem today when we appoint a man as a deacon on the basis of physical rather than spiritual qualifications. We think that because a man is a successful businessman he will make a good deacon. There are too many men who are appointed to office on that basis.

I have attempted to emphasize in 1 Timothy that the local church is an organization that needs to make itself manifest in the community, and in doing so it gets right down where the rubber meets the road. It must deal with the problems of a building, supplying heat and light, and a lot of material issues that don't seem very romantic. However, the important matter is still that a church is to have a *spiritual* ministry in the community. We often put the material qualifications first, but the men who are in office must have the spiritual qualifications for their office. Someone has put it like this: "When a church ceases to be in touch with another world, she is no longer in touch with this one." I agree with that 100 percent. Until the spiritual aspects are emphasized, a church cannot accomplish the material and practical functions down here. The deacons, therefore, are to have certain spiritual qualifications.

"Grave"—he should be a man of dignity.

"Not double-tongued." A deacon should not be two-faced. A man's word should amount to something. It can be dangerous when a man tries to please everybody or doesn't have the courage to stand on his own two feet. There is a fine balance between being a Mr. Milquetoast and being a dictator. An officer in the church needs to be somewhere between those two.

"Not given to much wine." I take this just as it is: the Bible teaches temperance, and that is important to see. I do not think the Bible teaches total abstinence because there weren't many medicines in those days and wine was used as a medicine. In 1 Timothy 5:23 Paul encourages Timothy to use a little wine for his stomach's sake. Even today many of the medicines we take contain a high percentage of alcohol.

The problem we encounter with alcohol in our day is the way it is used as a beverage, and I feel that the church should teach total abstinence because the abuse of alcohol is so prevalent. I do not believe that a Christian should use alcohol as a refreshment or a drink.

"Not greedy of filthy lucre." This means that a deacon should not have an insatiable love of money. He should be a man of integrity and should handle the money of the church in an honest way. There is nothing that can hurt a church more than the accusation that the deacons are juggling the finances. Money given to a church for a specific cause needs to be carefully allotted to the intended cause.

I have discovered in my experience in the ministry that most of the churches I know are run by men of high integrity, but it is that small minority of dishonest men who are muddying the waters and causing difficulty. If there is one thing a church ought to be able to present to the world it is the fact that it is honest and holds a place of high integrity in financial matters.

Holding the mystery of the faith in a pure conscience [1 Tim. 3:9].

"The mystery of the faith" means the revelation of the gospel of Christ. When Paul says "*the* faith" he is not speaking of the abstract quality of faith, but of the doctrines of the faith. He speaks of it as a "mystery" because these doctrines were not revealed in the Old Testament but are now revealed in the New Testament. We are told in Acts that the early church "continued in the apostles' doctrine." The apostles' doctrine was "the faith" of the early church. It should be the faith of the church today, and the church needs to represent that faith before the world.

There are a great many people who think the faith is outmoded and needs to be changed. An editorial in one of our national magazines a number of years ago supported this idea by suggesting an updated list of the "seven deadly sins." Their new list included selfishness, intolerance, indifference, cruelty, violence, and destructiveness. The list replaced lust, of course, with prudery. Lust was replaced, they said, because it had become as commonplace as the neighborhood newsstand or cinema. Gluttony was not included because it was considered a cholesterol problem but not a theological one. Words like *covetousness* and *sloth* were deemed antiquated. The article noted that different segments of society have different concepts of what constitutes sin. For example, young people would have placed irrelevance and hypocrisy high on their list of sins, but destructiveness would not have been included unless it meant only destructiveness of the environment. Similarly, elderly people would want noise, hair, and incivility included on their list. Some would argue that the new list simply contained old sins under new names. For example, selfishness had merely replaced covetousness. The article contended that the old names were obsolescent and needed changing if sin was to retain any contemporary, moral force at all. It concluded by affirming that sin is a concept well worth saving!

I would emphatically agree that sin is a concept worth saving, but I must insist also that sin has in no way changed. What the Bible calls sin is still sin. Human nature is still

human nature. The spiritual qualifications which the Bible lays down for church officers must still hold good today if the church is to represent the Lord Jesus Christ here on this earth. The church and its officers must hold to New Testament doctrine, calling sin the sins which are clearly labeled as such in the Word of God.

"In a pure conscience"—not with the conscience that has been seared with a hot iron (see 1 Tim. 4:2).

And let these also first be proved; then let them use the office of a deacon, being found blameless [1 Tim. 3:10].

A man should not be shoved into office a month after he joins a church and before he has proved that he is the type of man that Scripture has described here.

Now Paul has a word about the wives of deacons. They must measure up to certain standards also.

Even so must their wives be grave, not slanderers, sober, faithful in all things [1 Tim. 3:11].

"Grave"—they should be serious, able to be calm and cool.

"Not slanderers" means they are not to be gossips. A gossipy deacon's wife can cause much trouble in the church.

"Sober," again, is sober-minded.

"Faithful in all things." She should be faithful to her husband, to Christ Himself, and to His cause.

Let the deacons be the husbands of one wife, ruling their children and their own houses well [1 Tim. 3:12].

The deacons are to meet the same personal and family requirements that were given for the elders.

For they that have used the office of a deacon well purchase to themselves a good degree, and great boldness in the faith which is in Christ Jesus [1 Tim. 3:13].

"Good degree" could be read "good standing." In other words, a deacon who serves well will become known as a man who is to be trusted.

"Boldness" means confidence and courage in witnessing. Remember that a deacon primarily has a *spiritual* office. I remember the case of one man who was a deacon and was asked to take the office of an elder. Well, he didn't think he was spiritual enough or knew the Bible well enough to be an elder. If that was true, then he should not have been a deacon either, but he had been selected a deacon because he was a successful businessman. The spiritual requirements should be met by both elders and deacons before they are allowed to represent the church of Christ.

REPORT OF PAUL TO TIMOTHY

These things write I unto thee, hoping to come unto thee shortly [1 Tim. 3:14].

Paul was in Macedonia, and Timothy was in Ephesus. Paul was hoping to be able to join Timothy shortly.

But if I tarry long, that thou mayest know how thou oughtest to behave thyself in the house of God, which is the church of the living God, the pillar and ground of the truth [1 Tim. 3:15].

I have selected this as the key verse of this epistle because 1 Timothy is a book about church order. While he is away Paul writes, "I've written this to you so you will know how to act in the house of God."

"The church of the living God"—Paul is speaking to the church that *is* the church.

"The pillar and ground of the truth." "Pillar" means the stay, the prop, or that which is foundational. What Paul is saying is that the church is the pillar, the bedrock—it is the prop and support of the truth. If the officers do not represent the truth, the church has no foundation, no prop, and it cannot hold up the truth of God.

Some men purport to represent the truth, but they actually do not represent the truth in the way they lead their lives. I knew a deacon once who carried the biggest Bible I have ever seen. Every time you saw him he was weighed down on one side carrying that Bible. But he was a man you couldn't depend upon—there was a question about his integrity. He hurt the church he served and brought it into disrepute. Paul is writing to tell the church how it should act so that it can represent and proclaim the truth of God to the world on the outside.

And without controversy great is the mystery of godliness: God was manifest in the flesh, justified in the Spirit, seen of angels, preached unto the Gentiles, believed on in the world, received up into glory [1 Tim. 3:16].

This verse probably constitutes one of the earliest creeds of the church. Some think that it was one of the songs of the early church.

"Without controversy"—means confessedly, or obviously.

"Great is the mystery of godliness." The mystery of godliness is that God in the person of Jesus Christ entered this world in which we live, paid the penalty of sin, and is making men and women godly—that is, with God-likeness.

"God was manifest in the flesh." Certainly Paul is teaching the virgin birth of Christ, but he is also speaking of Christ's existence before His incarnation. That existence was spiritual: He was ". . . in the form of God . . ." (Phil. 2:6). Hebrews speaks of Christ as ". . . being the brightness [effulgence] of his [God's] glory, and the express image of his person . . ." (Heb. 1:3). The Lord Jesus Himself said, "God is a Spirit . . ." (John 4:24).

Now from this condition as God—not seen with human eyes—Christ came into manifestation—into sight—in the flesh. He became a man and entered into human conditions. And under these human conditions the attributes of His essential spiritual personality were veiled. This is the thought John gives in his gospel: ". . . The Word was made [became] flesh." He was *born* flesh "and dwelt [pitched His tent here] among us . . ." (see John 1:14). Just as God was not visible in the tabernacle in the wilderness, so Jesus Christ was veiled when He tabernacled among us in human flesh. He did not appear to men what He really was; man did not recognize who He was. The One who in the beginning was God, was with God, and who made all things, became a little, helpless baby. He was the image of the invisible God and had all power in heaven and in earth, but down here He took upon Himself human flesh. Because He was not recognized by man, He was treated as an imposter, a usurper, and a blasphemer. He was hated, persecuted, and murdered. God manifest in the flesh was poor, was tempted and tried, and actually shed tears.

"Justified in the Spirit." Yet in all that, He was not justified in the flesh, but in the Spirit. He was manifest in the *flesh*—that is how the world saw Him; but He was justified or vindicated in the *Spirit* in His resurrection. There were times when His glory broke out down here; there were revelations and expressions and witnesses of who He really was. There were angels at His virgin birth. His glory was seen at His baptism, at His transfiguration, and at the time of His arrest. The things that occurred at the time of His crucifixion caused the watching centurion to say, "Truly this was the Son of God" (see Matt. 27:54). But it was when He came back from the dead that we see Him now justified. He was manifest in the flesh, but justified in the Spirit: "sown a natural body; raised a spiritual body" (see 1 Cor. 15:44). No enemy laid a hand upon Him after He was raised from the dead. He will never be dishonored again.

However, because He came down here and has now returned to the right hand of God, *we* can be justified. Down here He was delivered up for our offenses—He took our place as a sinner, and now He gives us His place up yonder and we are justified. How wonderful this is!

"Seen of angels"—it doesn't say that He saw angels; rather, they saw Him. He has gone back to heaven, and now all the created intelligences of heaven worship Him because He wrought redemption for mankind. Little man down here hasn't caught on yet, but the song that will be sung throughout eternity is the song of redemption.

"Preached unto the Gentiles [the nations]"—this is still happening today.

"Believed on in the world." Many today are trusting Him as their Savior.

"Received up into glory." Today Christ is at God's right hand. At this very moment, my friend, He is there. Have you talked to Him today? Have you told Him that you love Him, and have you thanked Him for all He has done? How wonderful He is!

CHAPTER 4

THEME: *Apostasy in the churches*

HOW TO RECOGNIZE THE APOSTATES

Now the Spirit speaketh expressly, that in the latter times some shall depart from the faith, giving heed to seducing spirits, and doctrines of devils [1 Tim. 4:1].

"**N**ow" would be better translated "but." This would set in sharp contrast the early doctrinal creed given in the final verse of the preceding chapter and the apostasy within the church that Paul is now going to discuss.

"That in the latter times." Elsewhere in my writings on 1 Timothy I have said that this expression refers to the last days of the church on the earth, but I want to change my mind on that. I now feel that this refers to the days of the church beginning immediately after the life of Paul. The apostasy of the church had begun even at that time. You remember that when Paul was in Ephesus he warned them that there would come wolves in sheep's clothing who would deceive the believers. John said, "Already there are many antichrists"— already error had entered the church. The first great church was the Coptic church in Africa; it was way ahead of the others. North Africa produced some of the greatest saints in the early church, including Augustine, Tertullian, and Athanasius, but that church went off into heresy and departed from the faith.

When Paul says here, "in the latter times," he does not have the second coming of Christ in view at all. However, in 2 Timothy 3:1 where he says, "This know also, that *in the last days* perilous times shall come" (italics mine), he is using a technical expression that always refers to the last days of the church on the earth before the Lord Jesus takes it out. The "latter times" mentioned here refers to our times today—Paul was speaking of what lay just ahead for the church in his day.

"Some shall depart from the faith." Paul is warning that there will be heretical teachers who will mislead a great company of people. There will be a departure from the faith. Paul wrote also in 2 Thessalonians 2 of the apostasy to come. Actually this matter of apostasy has been in the church a long time, and it will not be new at the end of the age by any means.

It has grown and will continue to grow, however. When the church of Christ is raptured, there will be left behind a totally apostate organized church.

"Depart" is *aphistemi* in the Greek, and it means "to stand away from." A departure suggests not only that you have a point to which you are going, but also a point from which you have come. Those who apostatize are ones who have professed at one time to hold to the faith, but now they have departed from it. There cannot be an apostasy in paganism because they have never professed the faith. They never professed to trust Christ as Savior. They have never heard about Him, and there can be no apostasy among them. The apostasy comes within the organized church among those who profess to the faith and then depart from it.

"Giving heed to seducing spirits." Now when they depart from the faith, what is responsible for it? What has caused them to depart? Is it because they have become better educated, more intellectual? Is it because of scientific developments and increased knowledge which reveals that the faith can no longer be held? No, Paul says, "Some shall depart from the faith, *giving heed to seducing spirits.*"

"Seducing" actually means wandering, roving, and it comes from the word *vagabond* or *deceiver* or *seducer.* In fact, Satan is all those things. They shall give heed to satanic spirits.

"Doctrines of devils [demons]." People will give heed to doctrines of demons. It is alarming to a great many people that even in our very materialistic age there is a return to the things of the spirit world and a great emphasis upon it.

Christians are told to ". . . try the spirits whether they are of God . . . ," because there have gone out into the world these seducing spirits (1 John 4:1). The test that we should apply is the creed that was given in 1 Timothy 3:16: ". . . God was manifest in the flesh, justified in the Spirit . . . ." The only way of salvation is through the death of Christ, and it is by this truth we can test the doctrines of demons today.

There is a small segment of those who claim to be believers who are placing a great emphasis on demonism. They are very interested in this subject and are reading everything they can find about it. I think that we are seeing a real manifestation of the spirit world today, but the best thing you and I can do regarding the Devil is to show him a clean pair of heels. We should not be a bunch of heels, sticking around and getting ourselves involved in all of this. Paul warns us against being seduced by the doctrines of demons. We should stay clear of them, testing each spirit by its acknowledgment of the deity of Christ and by its acknowledgment that God was manifest in the flesh and that we are justified through the redemption He wrought for us on the cross.

Speaking lies in hypocrisy; having their conscience seared with a hot iron [1 Tim. 4:2].

"Speaking lies in hypocrisy." The apostate will pretend to be very pious and very religious. I have come to be suspicious of this pious posi-

tion taken by super-duper saints who claim to have something special. My friend, if you do have the truth it will make you humble, because the first thing you will find out is how little you know. I realize that I have much more to learn about the Bible. There are those today, however, who know very little about the Word of God, but they speak as if they were authorities. "Speaking lies in hypocrisy," they pretend to be something they are not.

"Having their conscience seared with a hot iron." In 1 Timothy 1:5 we read that the things which should characterize the visible church are faith, love, and a good conscience. We should be tenderhearted people.

There is far too much talk about sex in the church today. I have heard of things happening in some churches that make my hair curl. Things are being said and done which I do not think could be done unless your conscience has been seared with a hot iron and you have gotten away from the Word of God. It is important in the plan and purpose of God that the church have a tender conscience and not stoop to such low levels.

Forbidding to marry, and commanding to abstain from meats, which God hath created to be received with thanksgiving of them which believe and know the truth [1 Tim. 4:3].

Even in Christ's day there were folk who went off from Judaism into cults and "isms." This is not something new in our day; it has been going on for a long time.

"Forbidding to marry." In Christ's day there was a group down by the Dead Sea known as the Essenes. It was from among them that the Dead Sea Scrolls were found. When Christianity came along, many probably joined the Palestinian church and helped to produce most of its characteristic heresies, including the regulation of not marrying.

"Commanding to abstain from meats." There are those who make certain rules and regulations about diet that are not in the Word of God. They go off on this as if food could commend them to God. It is true that if you eat the wrong kind of food you will get a tummy ache, but it has nothing to do with your spiritual life, my friend.

For every creature of God is good, and nothing to be refused, if it be received with thanksgiving:

For it is sanctified by the word of God and prayer [1 Tim. 4:4–5].

The Word of God does not condemn food; it commends it. If you can return thanks for the food, that sanctifies it for your body. "If it be received with thanksgiving"—there are some foods I cannot be thankful for. There are certain foods that would really put me down physically if I ate them, and I cannot be thankful for them. Also, I am told that there is a place in San Antonio, Texas, that cans rattlesnake meat! It is a delicacy, they say. Well, if you served me rattlesnake meat for dinner and asked me to return thanks for it, I'm not sure that I could. But if you can receive it with thanksgiving, my friend, then go ahead and eat it, whatever it might be—it's perfectly all right.

WHAT THE "GOOD MINISTER" CAN DO IN TIMES OF APOSTASY

If thou put the brethren in remembrance of these things, thou shalt be a good minister of Jesus Christ, nourished up in the words of faith and of good doctrine, whereunto thou hast attained [1 Tim. 4:6].

"If thou put the brethren in remembrance of these things." Paul has warned Timothy of the apostasy and false teachings that were to come into the church. There will be men who profess to the faith and then come to the place where they deny it. In turn, Timothy is to warn the believers about these things.

"Thou shalt be a good minister of Jesus Christ." Every believer is a minister, but here Paul has in mind Timothy as a *teacher* of the Word of God. That is a gift that some men have and some don't. But all believers are ministers.

"Nourished up in the words of faith and of good doctrine"—this is how the believer is to grow in the Word of God. We are not to go off on tangents about diet or some other aesthetic program as if it would commend us to God. Instead our diet is to be "nourished up in the words of faith and of good doctrine."

"Whereunto thou hast attained." Some interpreters think that there was a danger in Ephesus in the midst of so much false religion and work of Satan that Timothy would go off into it all, but Paul said that Timothy had attained unto the things he has mentioned and commends him for it.

Paul has warned Timothy about apostasy and false teachings, but he will mention more things that Timothy should avoid:

But refuse profane and old wives' fables, and exercise thyself rather unto godliness [1 Tim. 4:7].

"But refuse profane and old wives' fables." As a young boy I remember there were a lot of sayings that the older people would quote to us children. I remember one dear Christian woman who had some peculiar ideas. One was that everybody should take sulphur and tartar mixed with a little honey or molasses. I was fed that because my mother listened to her. I took enough sulphur and tartar to make a small mountain! I have no idea whether it did me any good or not, but she thought it was the *only* thing I needed as a boy. Similarly, when it was discovered that I had cancer I was given over a hundred books on diet to help rid me of the cancer. I couldn't have followed one of these books without contradicting another! One said to eat plenty of grapes, the other said not to eat grapes. One would say to take honey, another to keep away from it. I decided to listen to the Great Physician and to leave my case in His hands.

"And exercise thyself rather unto godliness"—Timothy is to practice godliness in his life. Too many people emphasize the don'ts more than they do the exercise of godliness.

For bodily exercise profiteth little: but godliness is profitable unto all things, having promise of the life that now is, and of that which is to come [1 Tim. 4:8].

"For bodily exercise profiteth little." There are those who believe that Paul is downgrading physical exercise. I don't understand it that way at all. Paul spent about three years in Ephesus where there was a great coliseum in which the Olympic Games were held at times. The coliseum seated 100,000 people, and foot races were often held there. Paul uses the figure of the race and makes a correspondence to the Christian life and walk in 1 Corinthians 9:24–27. I believe Paul knew something about exercise. I stood in the city of Sardis one time and observed the Roman road that was being excavated to the east and the west of that city. Paul walked that road nineteen hundred years ago, preaching the gospel of Christ. He didn't travel in a bus or in an automobile. He didn't ride a horse or even a donkey. Paul *walked* there, and it took a rugged individual to cover the ground that he covered throughout the Roman Empire. He may not have done much jogging, but he did a great deal of walking.

Paul's emphasis on godliness rather than on physical exercise is because the Ephesians were a people given over to games and athletics. We are also that kind of a nation. Many of our cities have coliseums where great spectacles are conducted, and many believers put more emphasis on athletics than they do on the things of God. There are church officers who spend more time during the summer in the ball park than they spend in prayer meetings. Paul is not saying bodily exercise is wrong. He is saying, "Let's hold things in correct perspective."

"But godliness is profitable unto all things, having promise of the life that now is, and of that which is to come." Bodily exercise will help you only in this life, because when you get a new body it won't make any difference whether you've exercised this one or not. "But godliness is profitable unto all things." Those who argue that a Christian can fall into sin and can always come back to God on easy terms, are right. But, my friend, a godly life pays off not only down here, it will pay off in eternity. The Prodigal Son lost a great deal by going to the far country, and any Christian who lives a careless life rather than a godly life will find that even in eternity he will pay for it. Are you as anxious about godliness as you are about physical exercise, about athletic events? The physical ends at the end of this life, but godliness is carried over into the next.

This is a faithful saying and worthy of all acceptation [1 Tim. 4:9].

Paul is emphasizing the point he has just made. In other words, he says, "Here's something you can count on." You could count on it in the first century in Ephesus, and you can count on it in Los Angeles in the twentieth century. And we can count on it in the twenty-first century, if we make it that far.

For therefore we both labour and suffer reproach, because we trust in the living God, who is the Saviour of all men, specially of those that believe [1 Tim. 4:10].

"For therefore we both labour and suffer reproach." If you stand for Jesus Christ today it will cost you something. There is no question about that.

"Who is the Saviour of all men." We hear a great deal of discussion about what color of eyes Christ had. Was He blond or brunette? How tall was He? I talked to one man who was disturbed to see a picture of Christ painted as a black man. "Why not," I said, "He's the Savior of *all* men." The color of His skin or of His hair is not the important thing. Scripture never gives us that kind of information about Him. Even the FBI doesn't know. What Scripture does say is that He is the Savior of all men. Whoever you are, He's your Savior and He's the only Savior.

"Specially of those that believe." He is the Savior of all men, but you can turn Him down if you want to. Let me illustrate this for you. They say that a plane leaves the Los Angeles International Airport every minute, and I could get on any one of them (if I had the courage!). All I need to do is get a ticket and get on the plane. It's a plane for everybody, you see, but not everybody will take it. Christ is the Savior of all men, but only those who believe will be saved (see John 3:16; 1 John 2:2).

These things command and teach.

Let no man despise thy youth; but be thou an example of the believers, in word, in conversation, in charity, in spirit, in faith, in purity [1 Tim. 4:11–12].

"Let no man despise thy youth." Paul knew that there would be those in the church who would say of Timothy, "Well, he's just a young fellow—he doesn't know yet." Maybe there were some things he didn't know, but he was not to let anyone despise his youth.

"But be thou an example of the believers." How could Timothy keep people from despising his youth? By not acting like a young fool. When I began as a young minister, even before I was ordained, I told an old, retired minister that I felt a little embarrassed and even frightened when someone with gray hair would come into the church to hear this young preacher who was still a student. He advised me, "Don't ever worry about that. Don't let anyone despise your youth, but make dead sure you are an example of the believers." The important thing is not your age, but whether you are an example.

Paul tells Timothy in what ways he is to be an example: "in word, in conversation, in charity, in spirit, in faith, in purity." There is nothing new about the "new morality" today, but, believe me, the morality of the Bible *is* brand new to some folk! This is God's standard—six ways in which we should be an example.

Till I come, give attendance to reading, to exhortation, to doctrine [1 Tim. 4:13].

The minister is to read the Scripture publicly. For what purpose? To comfort and to teach.

The Word of God needs to be read, and until the church is getting people into the Word of God, it is missing its main function.

This was applicable to Timothy personally also. The minister can grow personally only by reading the Word for his exhortation and instruction. A growing minister will make a growing church. One of the greatest things ever said concerning Dwight L. Moody was said by a neighbor: "Every time Mr. Moody comes home, you can just tell how much he's grown spiritually." Are *you* further along spiritually today than you were this time last year? Are you growing in grace and the knowledge of Christ? The only way to do so is by reading the great truths of the Word of God.

Neglect not the gift that is in thee, which was given thee by prophecy, with the laying on of the hands of the presbytery [1 Tim. 4:14].

"Neglect not the gift that is in thee." The Spirit of God gives to every believer a gift, and Timothy had a gift that he was to use.

"Which was given thee by prophecy"—evidently Paul had predicted what this young man would do.

"With the laying on of the hands of the presbytery"—the laying on of the hands of the officers of the church. The laying on of hands never communicates anything, my friend. There are those who believe that something will be transferred to the person by the laying on of hands, but the only thing that will be transferred is disease germs—that's all! Laying on of hands indicates partnership in the ministry. I always insisted that my church officers lay their hands on every missionary we commissioned. Every minister who is ordained should have hands put on him by those who are partners with him. That is what it means, and it is quite meaningful.

Meditate upon these things; give thyself wholly to them; that thy profiting may appear to all [1 Tim. 4:15].

"Meditate upon these things"—be diligent in your study. There is no excuse for a minister not to study the Word of God, and there is no excuse for any Christian not to study the Word of God.

"Give thyself wholly to them." I will not accept a daily devotional time as a substitute for reading and studying the Word of God. It will not work to open your Bible to read a chapter at night when you have one eye closed and both feet already in bed. Nor will it work in the morning when you are half awake, or at the breakfast table when you are about to take off for work. My friend, you couldn't study geometry, higher mathematics, or science like that. The Word of God is worthy of all that you and I can give to it, and we can never give as much as it should have.

"That thy profiting may appear to all." The greatest compliment you could give your preacher would be to be able to say, "You are really improving in your preaching." That's the best thing you could say.

Take heed unto thyself, and unto the doctrine; continue in them: for in doing this thou shalt both save thyself, and them that hear thee [1 Tim. 4:16].

May I say this kindly, but I must say it: God have mercy on the minister who is not giving out the Word of God! That is a frightful sin. It would be better to be a gangster than to be a man who is supposed to give out the Word of God and fails to do so.

CHAPTER 5

THEME: Duties of officers in the churches

Both chapters 5 and 6 will deal with this very practical matter of the duties of officers in the church. This gets right down to the nitty-gritty of church life today. There is nothing romantic in this, but it is very realistic and meaningful for us.

RELATIONSHIP OF MINISTERS TO DIFFERENT GROUPS IN THE LOCAL CHURCH

Rebuke not an elder, but entreat him as a father; and the younger men as brethren [1 Tim. 5:1].

"An elder"—the first relationship discussed is Timothy's relationship to elders. There has been some difference of opinion as to whether Paul is referring to the office of elder or to an elder person, someone who was older than Timothy. In the early church the "elder" was an office, but the word used here refers to the individual. I think Paul had both aspects in mind: he is speaking of a mature child of God, and a man who occupied a certain office. Paul means both for the simple fact that an elder was an elder—an older man.

"Rebuke not an elder, but entreat [exhort] him as a father." Timothy was not to rebuke an elder publicly, but he was to entreat him privately. Timothy was a young man, and he needed to be very tactful in his relationship with these older men in the church. In other words, he was not to take the position of a know-it-all or of a dictator over these older men. He was to encourage them and have a word privately with them if he thought it was necessary.

"And the younger men as brethren." A sweet relationship should exist between Timothy and the older men and also with those of his own age.

The elder women as mothers; the younger as sisters, with all purity [1 Tim. 5:2].

"With all purity." A minister of a church should be very careful in his relationships with the opposite sex. Nothing hurts a church more or has more frequently wrecked the ministry of a church than sin in this area. When a minister must leave a church because of such a problem, the spiritual deadness in the church is very noticeable. Nothing can destroy the spiritual life of a church more than this kind of an experience. The "new morality" cannot and will not work in the church.

Paul has discussed Timothy's relationship with the men in the church—older and younger, and then the women—older and younger. He comes now to his relationship with a third group—

Honour widows that are widows indeed [1 Tim. 5:3].

"Honour" is a very interesting word, and in the Greek it is the same word from which we get our English word *honorarium*. It has in it the thought of value being attached to something. Sometimes when I speak at a church on a Sunday or for a week of special services I receive a check that says on it, "Honorarium." In other words, they have attached value to what I have done.

The early church took care of their widows, and they were very careful about it. The care of widows was the problem that arose in Acts 6. The Greeks (who were Jews from outside of Israel) felt that their widows were being neglected in favor of the others. The apostles had men appointed to handle the care of the widows so that they themselves could continue to concentrate on the preaching of the Word. Paul is giving instruction here as to how the care of the widows is to be carried out.

"Honour widows that are widows indeed." The instruction given in the Word of God is very practical. It uses a whole lot of common sense and is not moved by sentimentality. Christians are known to be tenderhearted, and there are a lot of people today who have their hands out to us. We need to be very careful. The early church took care of widows, but they didn't do it in some haphazard, sentimental way. The deacons were to make an investigation to see who were truly widows, where the need was, and how much need there was.

There are not many liberal or even conservative churches who are taking care of the widows in their midst. This is a much neglected area today.

Paul is going to go into this in very specific detail:

But if any widow have children or nephews, let them learn first to shew piety at home, and to requite their parents: for that is good and acceptable before God [1 Tim. 5:4].

"Nephews" here are grandchildren. The investigation should determine whether the widow in question has children. Why aren't they supporting her? Does she have grandchildren? They have a responsibility toward her. This was God's method, and I think it still is God's method.

Now she that is a widow indeed, and desolate, trusteth in God, and continueth in supplications and prayers night and day [1 Tim. 5:5].

Now this widow is "a widow indeed"—a real widow. She is "desolate," that is, she is in need. She is a godly woman, and she prays. She not only prays for the church and the pastor, but she prays for herself and for her need. She has a right to do that. And I want to say that God uses us to help answer such prayers. He makes it clear that when we find a widow like this we are to help her. It is quite lovely when we do things God's way.

But she that liveth in pleasure is dead while she liveth [1 Tim. 5:6].

But if you go over to a widow's house and find that she is having a cocktail party, I would say that she is not the widow to help. It does not matter how prominent her son, or her sister, or her brother might be in the church, she is not to be helped.

And these things give in charge, that they may be blameless [1 Tim. 5:7].

Paul is saying, "Timothy, you make this very clear to the church in order that they might act in an honorable way in these matters."

But if any provide not for his own, and specially for those of his own house, he hath denied the faith, and is worse than an infidel [1 Tim. 5:8].

My friend, I don't know how I could make this any stronger than it's made right here: the widow is to be taken care of by her own flesh and blood. It does not matter what type of testimony a man may give at a businessmen's meeting, or what kind of a testimony a woman may give to the missionary society, if they are not taking care of their own, they have no testimony for God. They are worse than infidels. Scripture is very clear here—you might miss some things in Scripture, but you cannot miss this.

Let not a widow be taken into the number under threescore years old, having been the wife of one man [1 Tim. 5:9].

"Into the number" refers to the group of widows which were to be helped. Why did they have this age limit? Because if she was under that age she could still work and take care of herself.

Well reported of for good works; if she have brought up children, if she have lodged strangers, if she have washed the saints' feet, if she have relieved the afflicted, if she have diligently followed every good work [1 Tim. 5:10].

"Well reported of for good works." Paul is saying that it is good to consider what kind of person the widow has been in the past. Check back in her life. Don't help everyone who comes along. But if she is the kind of person he has described and she is in need, you are to help her.

I wish that the church could get back to these very basic and simple principles and get away from the sentimental and emotional appeals that we hear instead. We respond to sentimental pleas from unworthy causes which are appealing to our soft hearts and neglect those in our very midst who have real need. We overlook the wonderful widow in our own church who is lonely and seldom visited. Her children have moved away or have died, and she may have physical need. Too often the church ignores such need. But if a church took care of its widows, its testimony would not go unnoticed by the world.

I believe that these widows who are helped by the church ought to be deaconesses in the church—they should render some service to the church. For example, several years ago I called a widow in my church and asked her to visit a lady whose husband's funeral service I had just conducted. The death had left the lady without family or friends, and I asked the widow to visit her because she would understand the woman's need—she had been through it herself. They became warm friends and grew in their relationship to God because of it. A widow can and should serve in some way in the church.

But the younger widows refuse: for when they have begun to wax wanton against Christ, they will marry;

Having damnation, because they have cast off their first faith [1 Tim. 5:11–12].

The younger widow is likely to want to remarry—and that's all right, as I see it. But notice that there is the danger of remarrying for the wrong reasons. There is the danger that she will forget all about her faith. The church is to be very careful and test the young widows also.

And withal they learn to be idle, wandering about from house to house; and not only idle, but tattlers also and busybodies, speaking things which they ought not [1 Tim. 5:13].

In other words, they carry garbage from one place to another, and the garbage is gossip. They go about, "speaking things which they ought not." There is the danger for the young widow, who has been relieved of the responsibility of being a wife and homemaker (perhaps having no children), that she will become a regular gadabout.

I will therefore that the younger women marry, bear children, guide the house, give none occasion to the adversary to speak reproachfully [1 Tim. 5:14].

The woman is the homemaker.

In this whole section Paul is giving instructions about the behavior of men and women who are in the church. He is stressing that these relationships should be on the highest level as a testimony before the world—that they "give none occasion to the adversary to speak reproachfully."

For some are already turned aside after Satan [1 Tim. 5:15].

They were not genuine believers, of course.

If any man or woman that believeth have widows, let them relieve them, and let not the church be charged; that it may relieve them that are widows indeed [1 Tim. 5:16].

Each family should support its own widows, so that the church can concentrate on the widows who are without family and are in real need.

Let the elders that rule well be counted worthy of double honour, especially they who labour in the word and doctrine [1 Tim. 5:17].

The early church paid their teachers, and a good teacher, I think, was paid a little bit more.

For the scripture saith, Thou shalt not muzzle the ox that treadeth out the corn. And, The labourer is worthy of his reward [1 Tim. 5:18].

Paul is quoting here from Deuteronomy 25:4 and Luke 10:7. I have known very few preachers who I thought were money-lovers; most men are in the ministry for a different motive than that. You are not going to hurt the preacher if you give him a generous offering. Be generous also to a visiting Bible teacher if his ministry is a blessing to you.

Against an elder receive not an accusation, but before two or three witnesses [1 Tim. 5:19].

If this procedure were observed it would cut down a great deal on the gossip and misunderstanding and the strife that goes on in our churches today. Paul says that the pastor and every member of the church should refuse to let anyone whisper into his ear any gossip about the pastor or a church officer. People should be able to *prove* their accusations before witnesses. The important thing is that you should have the facts before you talk. And if you have the facts, rather than scatter the scandal abroad, you should seek to correct the problem by going to the proper authorities. Any accusation should be given before more than one witness.

Them that sin rebuke before all, that others also may fear [1 Tim. 5:20].

If the facts are known that a church leader *has* sinned, he is to be rebuked. The question arises, Is this to be done publicly? I believe that when a member of a church sins and it does not concern the congregation it should never be brought out into the open, nor should it be confessed publicly. However, when a leader of the church, an officer in the church, sins, and it has hurt the church, then I think it is time to call names. It may also be time to drop his name from the roll of membership. Great harm can be done to a church by sin in the life of its leaders, and this is the way Paul says it should be dealt with.

I charge thee before God, and the Lord Jesus Christ, and the elect angels, that thou observe these things without preferring one before another, doing nothing by partiality [1 Tim. 5:21].

Timothy is to treat everyone in the church alike. There may be an officer in the church who is a wealthy man and who has been good to the pastor. Perhaps he has bought the pastor a suit of clothes or helped him buy a new car. A pastor will often brag that such a man is a member of his church, and he may not feel inclined to bring any charges against him even though it is evident the man is guilty. Paul says that we are *not* to show partiality in the church. James said the same thing in James 2.

Lay hands suddenly on no man, neither be partaker of other men's sins: keep thyself pure [1 Tim. 5:22].

We read earlier that the officers were to be installed by the laying on of hands (see 1 Tim. 4:14). We saw that the laying on of hands indicates partnership in the ministry. The thought here is that this is not to be done "suddenly," not to a neophyte, someone who has been recently converted.

If we exalt a young Christian to the position of a teacher before he is thoroughly grounded in the Word, the theology he teaches is apt to be weird theology. The church ought to be a place of instruction where the Word of God is taught and men and women are built up in the faith. Instead, today we often develop what I call Alka-Seltzer Christians and Alka-Seltzer churches—it's all fizz, foam, and froth, a lot of emotion, and a lot of talk about love, love, love. It is important that love be displayed in a church, but it needs to be anchored in the Word of God. Our mistake is that we often interpret some sort of experience as being the test of spiritual maturity. We've got the cart before the horse. The Word of God is the test, and experience can prove the truth of it. We can be certain that an experience which contradicts the clear teaching of the Bible is not from God at all.

There were many young converts in the Ephesus area, and they needed teaching. It was a serious business for young Timothy to select the teachers and appoint them to teach the Word of God.

"Neither be partaker of other men's sins: keep thyself pure." In other words, "Don't compromise, Timothy. Don't let someone talk you into letting a young convert teach. You will be a partner in sin if you do. Make sure the teachers are anchored in the Word of God."

Drink no longer water, but use a little wine for thy stomach's sake and thine often infirmities [1 Tim. 5:23].

I have to smile when I read this verse. It has certainly been abused in its many interpreta-

tions. Obviously the wine is not being used as a beverage but as a medicine.

Some men's sins are open beforehand, going before to judgment; and some men they follow after [1 Tim. 5:24].

Sometimes God will judge a Christian's sin right here and now, but if He doesn't judge him immediately it does not mean that He is not going to judge. I have observed this over many years and have seen that eventually God will move in judgment.

Paul wrote about this to the Corinthians where there were some who were not commemorating the Lord's Supper in the proper manner. He said, "For this cause many are weak and sickly among you, and many sleep" (1 Cor. 11:30). Paul said that some were already being judged by God. Some were actually sick; others had died as a judgment of God.

Paul went on in 1 Corinthians to say, "For if we would judge ourselves, we should not be judged" (1 Cor. 11:31). When a Christian sins, he can judge himself. That doesn't mean he is just to feel sorry for his sin. He is to deal with it: that is, if it has hurt somebody, he's to make it right; *and* he is to turn from that sin. If he doesn't do these things, he has not judged himself.

First Corinthians continues: "But when we are judged, we are chastened of the Lord, that we should not be condemned with the world" (1 Cor. 11:32). The world commits these sins, and God judges. Neither is a Christian going to get by with them: either you will judge yourself, or God will judge you. If you judge yourself, the matter is settled. If not, He will judge. Sometimes that judgment will occur here and now. If not, it will be dealt with when you appear before the judgment seat of Christ.

Likewise also the good works of some are manifest beforehand; and they that are otherwise cannot be hid [1 Tim. 5:25].

The same principle applies to good works. Sometimes God blesses a believer down here for something he's done for which God can reward him. Others are going to have to wait until they are in His presence to receive their reward, which will be the case of a great many Christians.

CHAPTER 6

THEME: Duties of officers in the churches (concluded)

RELATIONSHIPS OF BELIEVERS TO OTHERS

Let as many servants as are under the yoke count their own masters worthy of all honour, that the name of God and his doctrine be not blasphemed.

And they that have believing masters, let them not despise them, because they are brethren; but rather do them service, because they are faithful and beloved, partakers of the benefit. These things teach and exhort [1 Tim. 6:1–2].

"Servants"—Paul is going to deal with the relationship of capital and labor. The Christian should render a full day's work for whomever he is working. If he agrees to work until five o'clock, he should work until five o'clock. Then sometimes workers leave with their pickaxe hanging in the air—they don't finish up. The Christian is to turn in a full day's work for a full day's pay.

Now suppose a Christian has a Christian boss. That puts their relationship on a different basis; it brings it to a level above any kind of contract. I know of a manufacturing plant in Dallas, Texas, where the owners are Christians and many seminary students are employed. I have had the privilege of speaking to them in a forty-five minute chapel service they have and for which time the workers are paid. The spirit is marvelous there, and one time I commended the management for it. They replied, "Don't commend *us*! We find that these Christian men are better workers than anybody else. It's a two-way street. They are such wonderful employees that we don't feel that we are giving them anything. They give so much to us." What a wonderful relationship!

You see, Christianity gets out into the workshop. It gets its hands greasy. It gets its feet down in the mud sometimes—not the mud of sin, but the mud of hard work.

If any man teach otherwise, and consent not to wholesome words, even the words of our Lord Jesus Christ, and to the doctrine which is according to godliness;

He is proud, knowing nothing, but doting about questions and strifes of words, whereof cometh envy, strife, railings, evil surmisings,

Perverse disputings of men of corrupt minds, and destitute of the truth, supposing that gain is godliness: from such withdraw thyself [1 Tim. 6:3–5].

There are some proud men in the ministry, and they do cause trouble. Pride will always cause trouble, and it is unbecoming in a child of God. We ought to recognize that we are *sinners* saved by the grace of God. Pride is a constant danger—pride of place, pride of race, pride of face, and pride of grace. Some people are even proud that they've been saved by the grace of God! But, my friend, we Christians have plenty to be humble about. We have a very sorry and sordid background. We are sinners saved by the grace of God.

But godliness with contentment is great gain [1 Tim. 6:6].

It is important that the child of God find satisfaction with his position in life.

For we brought nothing into this world, and it is certain we can carry nothing out [1 Tim. 6:7].

This is a true axiom. As one of our American millionaires was dying, his heirs waited outside his room. When the doctor and lawyer finally came out, they eagerly asked, "How much did he leave?" And the lawyer said, "He left everything. He didn't take anything with him." We come into the world empty-handed, and that is the way we leave it. This is the reason a child of God ought to be using his money for the work of God. I believe that making a will is fine, but it is often much abused. As someone has rhymed it,

> Do your givin'
> While you're livin'.
>
> Then you're knowin'
> Where it's goin'.

A child of God should make sure that he is supporting the work of God in some way.

And having food and raiment let us be therewith content.

But they that will be rich fall into temptation and a snare, and into many foolish and hurtful lusts, which drown men in destruction and perdition [1 Tim. 6:8–9].

Riches will not bring satisfaction.

For the love of money is the root of all evil: which while some coveted after, they have erred from the faith, and pierced themselves through with many sorrows [1 Tim. 6:10].

Money is not evil in itself—it is amoral. Notice it is the *love* of money that is *a* (rather than *the*) root of all evil.

But thou, O man of God, flee these things; and follow after righteousness, godliness, faith, love, patience, meekness [1 Tim. 6:11].

These are the virtues that a man of God should pursue.

Fight the good fight of faith, lay hold on eternal life, whereunto thou art also called, and hast professed a good profession before many witnesses [1 Tim. 6:12].

"Fight the good fight of faith." This fight may be outward or inward, physical or spiritual.

"Lay hold on eternal life." Let me ask you a question: If you were arrested for being a Christian and were brought into court, would there be enough evidence to convict you? This is what Paul is talking about. "Lay hold on eternal life"—make it clear by your life that you are a child of God.

I give thee charge in the sight of God, who quickeneth all things, and before Christ Jesus, who before Pontius Pilate witnessed a good confession;

That thou keep this commandment without spot, unrebukeable, until the appearing of our Lord Jesus Christ [1 Tim. 6:13–14].

"God, who quickeneth all things" means God who *gives life* to all things.

"Keep this commandment without spot, unrebukeable" means to keep the commandments Paul had given him without stain and reproach. My friend, if you are following Christ, you will act like a child of God.

Which in his times he shall shew, who is the blessed and only Potentate, the King of kings, and Lord of lords;

Who only hath immortality, dwelling in the light which no man can approach unto; whom no man hath seen, nor can see: to whom be honour and power everlasting. Amen [1 Tim. 6:15–16].

"Who only hath immortality." Jesus Christ is the only One who has been raised from the dead in a glorified body.

Charge them that are rich in this world, that they be not highminded, nor trust in uncertain riches, but in the living God, who giveth us richly all things to enjoy;

That they do good, that they be rich in good works, ready to distribute, willing to communicate;

Laying up in store for themselves a good foundation against the time to come, that they may lay hold on eternal life [1 Tim. 6:17–19].

"Charge them that are rich." These verses are a warning to those who are rich.

"Ready to distribute" means ready to sympathize, ready to share.

"Lay hold on eternal life" means the life which is life indeed.

O Timothy, keep that which is committed to thy trust, avoiding profane and vain babblings, and oppositions of science falsely so called:

Which some professing have erred concerning the faith. Grace be with thee. Amen [1 Tim. 6:20–21].

In other words, don't try to be an intellectual preacher or teacher or Christian.

"Science falsely so called" should be translated *the falsely named knowledge.* Paul is speaking of the Gnostic heresy, but this can certainly be applied to all human philosophies.

(For Bibliography to 1 Timothy, see Bibliography at the end of 2 Timothy.)

The Second Epistle to
TIMOTHY
INTRODUCTION

The following is an approximate calendar of events which will orient us to the position that the Second Epistle to Timothy occupied in the ministry of the apostle Paul. Paul wrote this epistle around A.D. 67.

[c. A.D. 58]—Paul was apparently arrested in Jerusalem.

[c. A.D. 61]—This is the approximate time that Paul arrived in Rome. He had spent these three years in prison, going from one trial to another before different Roman rulers.

[c. A.D. 61–63]—Paul underwent his first Roman imprisonment. We do not have this recorded in the Book of Acts, which breaks off at the very beginning of Paul's first Roman imprisonment.

[c. A.D. 64–67]—Paul was released from prison, and during this period he covered a great deal of territory. It was during this time that he wrote 1 Timothy and Titus from Macedonia.

[c. A.D. 67]—Paul was arrested again.

[c. A.D. 68]—Paul was beheaded in Rome. Before his death he wrote 2 Timothy.

The two verses that state the theme and sound the tone of this second epistle are these: "Study to shew thyself approved unto God, a workman that needeth not to be ashamed, rightly dividing the word of truth" (2 Tim. 2:15). "Preach the word; be instant in season, out of season; reprove, rebuke, exhort with all longsuffering and doctrine" (2 Tim. 4:2).

You can, I think, emphasize one word in this epistle above other words. That word is *loyalty*: (1) loyalty in suffering (ch. 1); (2) loyalty in service (ch. 2); (3) loyalty in apostasy (ch. 3–4:5); and (4) Lord loyal to His servants in desertion (ch. 4:6–22).

The deathbed statement of any individual has an importance which is not attached to other remarks. This is what lends significance to 2 Timothy. It is the final communication of Paul. It has a note of sadness which is not detected in his other epistles. Nevertheless, there is the overtone of triumph: "I have fought a good fight, I have finished my course, I have kept the faith," written by Paul as his own epitaph (2 Tim. 4:7). Also, because this was his last letter, Paul was very personal. In these short four chapters, there are approximately twenty-five references to individuals.

In this little book of 2 Timothy an ominous dark cloud is seen on the horizon. It is the coming apostasy. Today apostasy has broken like a storm, like a Texas tornado, on the world and in the church. What do we mean by *apostasy*? Webster defines apostasy as "total desertion of the principles of faith." So apostasy is not due to ignorance; it is a heresy. Apostasy is *deliberate* error. It is intentional departure from the faith. An apostate is one who knows the truth of the gospel and the doctrines of the faith, but he has repudiated them.

Paul here in 2 Timothy speaks of the ultimate outcome of gospel preaching. The final fruition will not be the total conversion of mankind, nor will it usher in the Millennium. On the contrary, there will come about an apostasy which will well-nigh blot out *the* faith from the earth. In fact, there are two departures that will occur at the end of the age: One is the departure of the church, which we call the Rapture, translated from the Greek *harpazō*, meaning "caught up." "For the Lord himself shall descend from heaven with a shout, with the voice of the archangel, and with the trump of God: and the dead in Christ shall rise first: Then we which are alive and remain shall be caught up [or *raptured*] together with them in the clouds, to meet the Lord in the air . . ." (1 Thess. 4:16–17). When the believers are gone, the organization, the old shell of the church that's left down here, will totally depart from the faith. That is the second departure, the departure from the faith. The Lord Jesus Himself gave this startling statement concerning it: ". . . when the Son of man cometh, shall he find faith on the earth?" (Luke 18:8). As couched in the Greek language, it demands a negative answer. So the answer must be, "No, He will not find *the* faith on the earth when He returns."

This view is not in keeping with the social gospel today, which expects to transform the world by tinkering with the social system. Such vain optimists have no patience with the doleful words of 2 Timothy, and they classify me as an *intellectual obscurantist*! But, in spite of that, the cold and hard facts of history and the events of the present hour demonstrate the accuracy of Paul. We are now in the midst of an apostasy which is cut to the pattern of Paul's words in remarkable detail.

The visible church has entered the orbit of an awful apostasy. The invisible church—that is, the real body of believers—is not affected. The invisible church today is still here; and, although I wish it were a little more visible than it is, it's on its way to the epiphany of glory. It is moving toward the Rapture. That is a very comforting thought in these days in which we live.

Because of the threat of apostasy, Paul emphasizes the Word of God here more than he does in any other epistle. In fact, both Paul and Peter agree. Each of them in his "swan song" (2 Tim. and 2 Pet.) emphasizes the Word of God and the gospel.

My friend, the gospel rests upon a tremendous fact, and that fact is the total depravity of man. In other words, man is a lost sinner. A contemporary educator has put it something like this:

Where education assumes that the moral nature of man is capable of improvement, traditional Christianity assumes that the moral nature of man is corrupt and absolutely bad. Where it is assumed in education that an outside human agent may be instrumental in the moral improvement of men, in traditional Christianity it is assumed that the agent is God, and even so, the moral nature of man is not improved but exchanged for a new one.

Man is in such a state that he cannot be saved by perfect obedience—because he cannot render it. Neither can he be saved by imperfect obedience—because God will not accept it.

Therefore, the only solution is the gospel of the grace of God which reaches down and saves the sinner on the basis of the death and resurrection of Christ. Faith in Christ transforms human life. We have a showcase today all over this globe of men and women who have been transformed by the gospel of the grace of God.

Liberal preaching, instead of presenting the grace of God to sinful man, goes out in three different directions. From some liberal pulpits we hear what is really popular psychology. It majors in topics such as this: "How to Overcome" or "How to Think Creatively" or "How to Think Affirmatively or Positively." It says that we're on the way upward and onward forever! That is popular psychology, and it doesn't seem to be getting us anywhere.

A second type of liberal preaching involves ethics. It preaches a nice little sweet gospel—a sermonette preached by a preacherette to Christianettes. The message goes something like this: "Good is better than evil because it's *nicer* and gets you into less trouble." The picture of the average liberal church is that of a mild-mannered man standing before a group of mild-mannered people, urging them to be more mild-mannered! There's nothing quite as insipid as that. No wonder the Lord Jesus said to the church of Laodicea: "I know thy works, that thou art neither cold nor hot: I would thou wert cold or hot. So then because thou art lukewarm, and neither cold nor hot, I will spue thee out of my mouth" (Rev. 3:15–16). That would make anybody sick to his tummy. That's another reason I call these people Alka-Seltzer Christians. They're not only fizz, foam, and froth, but they cause you to need an Alka-Seltzer.

Then there's a third type of liberal preaching which is called the social gospel. They preach better race relations, pacifism, social justice, and the Christian social order. It is Christian socialism pure and simple.

In contrast, when the true gospel is preached and men come to Christ, they all become brothers. We don't need all this talk about better race relations. You cannot create better relationships by forcing people together. Only the gospel of the grace of God will make a man into a brother of mine. When that happens the color of a man's skin makes no difference at all.

The solution of man's problems can come only through preaching the *grace* of God. We need to recognize (as Martin Luther put it) that God creates out of nothing. Until a man is nothing, God can make nothing out of him. The grace of God through Jesus Christ is the way to transform and save mankind. That is what this epistle teaches, and that is why it is important for us to study 2 Timothy.

OUTLINE

I. **Afflictions of the Gospel, Chapter 1**
   A. Introduction, Chapter 1:1–7
   B. Not Ashamed, but a Partaker of Affliction, Chapter 1:8–11
   C. Not Ashamed, but Assured, Chapter 1:12–18

II. **Active in Service, Chapter 2**
   A. A Son, Chapter 2:1–2
   B. A Good Soldier, Chapter 2:3–4
   C. An Athlete, Chapter 2:5
   D. A Farmer, Chapter 2:6–14
   E. A Workman, Chapter 2:15–19
   F. A Vessel, Chapter 2:20–23
   G. A Servant, Chapter 2:24–26

III. **Apostasy Coming; Authority of the Scriptures, Chapters 3:1–4:5**
   A. Conditions in the Last Days, Chapter 3:1–9
   B. Authority of Scriptures in the Last Days, Chapter 3:10–17
   C. Instructions for the Last Days, Chapter 4:1–5

IV. **Allegiance to the Lord and of the Lord, Chapter 4:6–22**
   A. Deathbed Testimony of Paul, Chapter 4:6–8
   B. Last Words, Chapter 4:9–22
   "The Lord stood with me."

CHAPTER 1

THEME: *Afflictions of the gospel*

INTRODUCTION

Paul, an apostle of Jesus Christ by the will of God, according to the promise of life which is in Christ Jesus [2 Tim. 1:1].

"**P**aul, an apostle of Jesus Christ by the will of God." You recall that in Paul's first epistle to Timothy he said, "by the *commandment* of God" (1 Tim. 1:1), and we saw that the commandments of God revealed the will of God, but that they were not the *total* will of God. Here he says "by the will of God, according to the *promise* of life which is in Christ Jesus." How do you accept a promise? You do it by faith. That is the only way you can obtain eternal life. He offers it to you as a gift. You accept a gift because you believe the giver. You receive eternal life by believing in the Giver. The Lord Jesus gives you eternal life when you trust Him as Savior because He paid the penalty of your sin. He today can offer you heaven on the basis of your faith and trust in Him. When you believe Him and come His way, you honor Him. Therefore "the promise of life which is *in Christ Jesus*" makes it clear that through Christ is the only way you can get eternal life, my friend.

To Timothy, my dearly beloved son: Grace, mercy, and peace, from God the Father and Christ Jesus our Lord [2 Tim. 1:2].

Paul greets Timothy as his "dearly beloved son" because Timothy was a great joy to the apostle Paul. Then he goes on to say, "Grace, mercy, and peace." As we mentioned in studying 1 Timothy, the salutation includes the word *mercy* (which is not found in the greetings of Paul's other letters). God is merciful when He does not give us what we deserve; that is, judgment and condemnation. Paul needed a great deal of mercy, and we do too. Fortunately, God is rich in mercy toward us.

"From God the Father and Christ Jesus our Lord." The emphasis here is upon the lordship of Jesus Christ.

I thank God, whom I serve from my forefathers with pure conscience, that without ceasing I have remembrance of thee in my prayers night and day [2 Tim. 1:3].

Timothy was on the apostle Paul's prayer list. When I taught at a Bible institute, I always had the students find out who was on the apostle Paul's prayer list. They made the list by going through the letters of Paul and noting every time Paul said he prayed for somebody. By the way, how many preachers do you have on your prayer list? I hope you have your pastor.

Greatly desiring to see thee, being mindful of thy tears, that I may be filled with joy [2 Tim. 1:4].

It is quite obvious that Paul loved Timothy, and this verse tells us that Timothy also loved Paul. The fact that Paul has been arrested, is back in prison, and even faces death really affects Timothy. Paul says, "I am mindful of your tears. And if I could only see you, that would bring joy to my heart."

When I call to remembrance the unfeigned faith that is in thee, which dwelt first in thy grandmother Lois, and thy mother Eunice; and I am persuaded that in thee also [2 Tim. 1:5].

Paul came out of Judaism, but this boy Timothy, apparently, was brought up in a Christian home. Both his grandmother and his mother were Christians. I'm sure that had a lot to do with this young man turning to Christ. Timothy's father was a Greek, and it is not known whether he was in the faith.

Wherefore I put thee in remembrance that thou stir up the gift of God, which is in thee by the putting on of my hands [2 Tim. 1:6].

When Paul put his hands on Timothy, that meant that Timothy was a partner with Paul; he shared with him the gift of teaching the Word of God. I am of the opinion that Paul intended for his mantle to fall upon Timothy. This young man was close to Paul, and when Paul was in prison in Rome, he said of Timothy, ". . . I have no man likeminded . . ." (Phil. 2:20). Here was a man who could carry on the teaching and preaching of Paul, and therefore Paul made him his partner. They were together in the ministry.

Now notice that Paul admonishes Timothy to "stir up the gift of God, which is in thee." This man had a gift, and Paul urges him to stir it up. What would that indicate to you? I wonder if Paul was concerned about Timothy there in Ephesus. Ephesus housed the temple of Diana and was one of the great "sin spots" in the Roman world. Paul had spent three years in Ephesus himself, and he knew that there were many allurements and enticements in the city. I wonder if he was afraid that Timothy might be reluctant and hold back from teaching the whole counsel of God. We can see Paul's concern for this young man whom he called "my dearly beloved son."

For God hath not given us the spirit of fear; but of power, and of love, and of a sound mind [2 Tim. 1:7].

The word *fear* is better translated "cowardice." I think that many of us have misinterpreted this—I know I have in the past. I remember that when I first began to travel by air, I didn't want to, but I was forced to use that mode of travel to meet my engagements. I certainly didn't enjoy it. At first, this disturbed me a great deal. I would make a flight, and then I would rebuke myself because of my fear. I tried to fight my fear.

Well, fear is a natural thing, and it is a good thing. For example, I am afraid of a lion. If there were one loose in the street, I would find a good place to hide. It is normal and good to have a sense of fear. But many of us, for some reason, have a fear of height, which makes us fear flying. I prayed about it and wondered why God didn't remove that from me, because I read in this verse that "God hath not given us the spirit of fear."

However, Paul is speaking not of a good kind of fear, but of cowardice. Paul is saying, "God hath not given us the spirit of cowardice; but of power, and of love, and of a sound mind."

"A sound mind" means discipline. In other words, God does not intend that defeat should be the norm of Christian living. We should be disciplined Christians rather than slaves to our emotions. We are all moved by our emotions. That is why people will send money to organizations that advertise with the picture of a poor, hungry, little orphan. But Christians are not to be motivated by their emotions. Our emotions are not to master us. We are to be disciplined.

How does this apply to the question of fear? Is it wrong for me to have a fear of flying? No. It would be wrong for me to stay at home. You see, if I am a disciplined Christian, I am going to grit my teeth, go down and get that ticket, and take that trip because God has called me to an itinerant teaching ministry. Overcoming emotions means not letting your emotions stop you from doing something you should be doing. When you have a fear of flying, you discipline yourself to fly anyway. But you still live with your emotions. If you do like I do, you sit there on the plane, gritting your teeth and wondering how many more hours it will be, with every hour seeming like an eternity. If the plane starts bouncing around, I have a tendency to grab the seat in front of me. I know that the seat in front of me is not any safer than the seat I'm sitting in, but somehow I feel better when I have hold of it! Paul's admonition to Timothy is a wonderful help to me. God is telling me that I am not to be a defeated Christian; I should not let my emotions control my life.

On a tour to Bible lands I didn't want to go with the tour to Egypt, because on a previous trip I'd had a bad experience there, and I was very emotional about it. I didn't like Cairo, and I didn't want to go there. But the Lord forced me to overcome my feelings. I had planned to go ahead to Jerusalem, rest there a couple of days, and wait for the tour to reach me. But every hotel was filled, and we couldn't get a reservation. Then I thought of another way. I could stay in Athens and then just fly into Jerusalem at the same time the tour group did. But do you know what? There wasn't any hotel space in Athens, either. The only place I could go was to Cairo! The Lord made me overcome my emotions, and I'm thankful He did, because I had a delightful visit, and I learned a great deal.

NOT ASHAMED, BUT A PARTAKER OF AFFLICTION

Be not thou therefore ashamed of the testimony of our Lord, nor of me his prisoner: but be thou partaker of the afflictions of the gospel according to the power of God [2 Tim. 1:8].

I have labeled this chapter, "Afflictions of the gospel" because there is a feeling today that the Christian life is a life that ought to be very easy, nice and sweet, bright and breezy. A great many of us think that we have an indulgent heavenly Father who is just going to put us on a bed of roses, remove every stone out of our pathway, and not let anything serious happen to us. A retired lawyer sent me this statement which he found in a will. It read: "To my son I leave the pleasure of earning a living. For twenty-five years he thought the pleasure was mine. He was mistaken." And a great many Christians expect their heavenly Father to make things easy for them.

The Lord Jesus made it clear that we would have trouble. He said, ". . . In the world ye shall have tribulation [trouble]" (John 16:33). Christians will not go through the Great Tribulation, but you and I are certainly going through our own little tribulations. Samuel Rutherford made this statement: "If you were not strangers here, the hounds of the world would not bark at you." The Lord Jesus warned us that the world would not like Christians. He told His disciples, "If the world hate you, ye know that it hated me before it hated you" (John 15:18). There is something wrong if you become too popular as a Christian. I am afraid that many Christians are thinking like a little boy in Sunday school whose teacher asked, "Johnny, which of the parables do you like best?" The little fellow answered, "The one where everybody loafs and fishes." No, my friend, the Christian life is not a bed of roses. We are to be "partakers of the afflictions of the gospel according to the power of God."

Who hath saved us, and called us with an holy calling, not according to our works, but according to his own purpose and grace, which was given us in Christ Jesus before the world began [2 Tim. 1:9].

"Who hath saved us, and called us with an holy calling"—not because of who we are or what we have done—"not according to our works." But—

"According to his own purpose and grace." God's wonderful purpose in the gospel was hidden in ages past but is now revealed through Paul. It had been a mystery in the Old Testament, an unrevealed secret, but is now revealed in the New Testament.

"Which was given us in Christ Jesus before the world began"—all along God had this plan for us.

But is now made manifest by the appearing of our Saviour Jesus Christ, who hath abolished death, and hath brought life and immortality to light through the gospel [2 Tim. 1:10].

Now this is a verse that deserves great emphasis.

"Who hath abolished death" is literally *since He has made of none effect death*. Death means something altogether different to the child of God—Christ made it of no effect. Now, God did not eliminate death. Remember that Paul is writing this letter from prison where

the sentence of death is upon him. But Paul is not talking about physical death. He means spiritual death, eternal death, which is separation from God. Christ has indeed abolished spiritual death so that no sinner need go to a place where he'll be eternally separated from God. Christ is our Mediator, the one Mediator between God and man. God is satisfied with what Christ has done for us. The question is: Are *you* satisfied? Or are you trying to save yourself by your own good works? Let me repeat what I have said before: Man cannot be saved by perfect obedience, because he is incapable of rendering it. He cannot be saved by imperfect obedience, because God will not accept it. There is only one solution to the dilemma, and that is the One who said, ". . .I am the way, the truth, and the life: no man cometh unto the Father, but by me" (John 14:6).

Whereunto I am appointed a preacher, and an apostle, and a teacher of the Gentiles [2 Tim. 1:11].

Paul says he's a "preacher," a herald of the Word of God. He also says that he's "an apostle, and a teacher." As an apostle he had several gifts. I personally doubt whether any man since the apostles has more than one gift. I've met preachers who thought they could sing, but my experience has been that either they couldn't sing or they couldn't preach—it was one or the other. I don't believe He will give us two or more gifts, because it is difficult enough to exercise one.

NOT ASHAMED, BUT ASSURED

For the which cause I also suffer these things: nevertheless I am not ashamed: for I know whom I have believed, and am persuaded that he is able to keep that which I have committed unto him against that day [2 Tim. 1:12].

"I am not ashamed." Although he was in prison and the sentence of death was upon him, he was not ashamed of the gospel. Paul had written to the Romans in 1:16: "For I am not ashamed of the gospel of Christ: for it is the power of God unto salvation to every one that believeth. . . ." And back in verse 8 of the first chapter of 2 Timothy, Paul urges Timothy not to be ashamed either. Sometimes Christians are very reluctant to witness. We are all tongue-tied at times, but we ought not to be.

"He is able to keep that which I have committed [entrusted] unto him." Literally, the *deposit*. This means that Paul deposited his faith in Christ until the day of judgment. Or it can mean that "God made a deposit with me." God's deposit of gifts in Paul's life made him a debtor to the entire world.

My friend, you and I are debtors. Perhaps you are saying, "I want you to know that I pay my honest debts." Well, you and I have not paid our honest debts until every person on topside of this earth has heard the gospel.

"He is able to keep that which I have committed." It is a great comfort to know that all we are and all we have is in His hands.

Hold fast the form of sound words, which thou hast heard of me, in faith and love which is in Christ Jesus [2 Tim. 1:13].

"Sound words"—the words of Scripture are inspired. I believe in the verbal plenary inspiration of the Word of God and do not think that any other viewpoint is satisfactory, and certainly it does not satisfy the demands of Scripture.

That good thing which was committed unto thee keep by the Holy Ghost which dwelleth in us [2 Tim. 1:14].

It is important to see that the Christian life can be lived only in the power of the Holy Spirit. Paul talked about power, love, and a sound mind back in verse 7, all of which are fruit of the Holy Spirit. Paul wrote that ". . . the fruit of the Spirit is love, joy, peace, longsuffering, gentleness, goodness, faith, meekness, temperance . . ." (Gal. 5:22–23).

This thou knowest, that all they which are in Asia be turned away from me; of whom are Phygellus and Hermogenes [2 Tim. 1:15].

Paul gives the actual names of those who have been unfaithful to him. Back in the first chapter of 1 Timothy Paul noted that *some* had fallen away, here it is *all*—that is, all who are now in Asia who had formerly been with him in Rome. I call your attention to this because it seems to me that apostasy is not the thing that characterizes only the last days of the church. It has occurred throughout the entire history of the church. I had a church history professor who said that the history of the church is the history of apostasy or, as he put it, the history of heresies. How true that has been.

The Lord give mercy unto the house of Onesiphorus; for he oft refreshed me, and was not ashamed of my chain:

But, when he was in Rome, he sought me out very diligently, and found me.

The Lord grant unto him that he may find mercy of the Lord in that day: and in how many things he ministered unto me at Ephesus, thou knowest very well [2 Tim. 1:16–18].

Here is a wonderful saint of God. I'd have loved to have been Onesiphorus (and I would have hated to have been Hermogenes). Onesiphorus, apparently from Ephesus, was in Rome on business. He was a busy man, but he had time to look up Paul who was in prison. How lovely! Probably Paul had led him to the Lord, and you can't despise a man who has led you to Christ.

CHAPTER 2

THEME: Active in service

The second chapter of 2 Timothy is delightful. In these verses there are seven figures of speech that are used to describe the duty and the activity of a believer, which need to be impressed upon us more and more as we approach the end time.

A SON

Thou therefore, my son, be strong in the grace that is in Christ Jesus [2 Tim. 2:1].

Paul begins with the first figure of speech, "Thou therefore, my son." Timothy was not the son of Paul in a physical way. He was his spiritual son in the sense that it was under Paul's ministry that this young man had turned to Christ. A child of God is born into God's family by means of his faith in Christ. "Being born again, not of corruptible seed, but of incorruptible, by the word of God, which liveth and abideth for ever" (1 Pet. 1:23). Timothy is in the family of God, and he is a child of God. Because of this very reason, Paul says these words to Timothy:

"Be strong in the grace that is in Christ Jesus." I love this—"be strong in grace." My friend, if you think that you can grit your teeth and go out and live the Christian life on your own, you're in for a great disappointment. If you feel that you can follow a few little rules or some clever gimmicks to make you a mature Christian, then you have fallen into a subtle trap of legalism. Paul gives no rules, and the Word of God has no rules to tell the child of God how to live the Christian life. We are saved by grace, and now we are to live by the grace of God and be *strong* in that grace.

Let me give you an example from my boyhood. My dad traveled a great deal in his work, and he always put down a few rules for me to follow while he was away. Some of them I obeyed. I had to cut the wood, and I didn't mind that. One time we had a place with a lot of trees on it, and I really enjoyed the exercise of cutting the trees into firewood. But my father had some other rules that I frankly didn't go for. I hate to admit this, but one of those rules was that I should attend Sunday school. The interesting thing is that he never went himself, but he always made me go. Anyway, when he was away from home, I didn't go. One time I was fishing, and he came home suddenly and found me. I had just pulled out a fish, turned around, and there stood my dad. He said, "Son, are you having any luck?" Well, my luck ran out right at that moment! I appealed to him and admitted that I had done wrong, and by grace he was good to me. He said, "I brought home a sack of candy for you and your sister to divide. I wasn't going to let you have it, but I think I will now." I really took advantage of his good nature and the fact that I was his son.

My father died when I was fourteen, but now I have a heavenly Father, and I sure do appeal to His grace. When things go wrong down here, I go to Him and appeal to Him. When I fail, I don't run from Him like I used to. I have found that when I am away from Him, the whipping He gives me hurts lots worse. I don't want to get out at the end of that switch where it really stings. I come in close to Him, and the closer I am the less it hurts. I am a *son* of my heavenly Father. What a marvelous figure of speech!

When I hear Christians say, "I don't do this, and I don't do that, and I am following a set of rules," I immediately recognize that they know very little about the grace of God. They are trying to live the Christian life in their own strength. Paul says, "Be strong in the *grace* that is in *Christ Jesus*."

And the things that thou hast heard of me among many witnesses, the same commit thou to faithful men, who shall be able to teach others also [2 Tim. 2:2].

Paul was greatly concerned about the future. He wondered, just as we do when we approach the end of our ministry, if other men will come along who will preach and teach the Word of God. Sometimes we develop an Elijah complex. At times when I was a pastor in Los Angeles, I cried like Elijah, "Oh, Lord, I'm the only one left!" But I found out that was not true. All over the country I've seen the Lord raise up fine young preachers who are standing for the things of God. It is a real concern to us older men that there be young men who will be faithful in teaching God's Word. So Paul was admonishing Timothy to pass along the things he had been teaching him to "faithful men, who shall be able to teach others also." And God will raise up men with gifts of teaching—this is the way He moves even today.

As sons of God we ought to be concerned about our Father's business. The Lord Jesus in His humanity as a boy said, "I must be about my Father's business." Well, I have become a son of God—not like the Lord Jesus, but I've become a son of God through faith in Christ. "But as many as received him, to them gave he power [the authority] to become the sons of God, even to them that [do no more nor less than] believe on his name" (John 1:12). Now that I am a son of God I am interested in my Father's business. By the way, are you interested in your Father's business? And the main business is getting out the Word of God. But we need to recognize that we need the grace of God to do the business of God—as well as in every facet of our lives as His children.

Perhaps you are thinking that you are disappointed with yourself. If you are, that means you must have believed in yourself. You should not have. You are to walk by the grace of God—"We walk by faith and not by sight." Or perhaps you are discouraged. If you are, that means you do not believe God's Word and way of blessing. You really thought you could do it your way, and now you are discouraged. Or you may be saying, "I hope I can do better in the future." Then you do expect to get some good out of the old nature! Oh, my friend, be strong in the grace of God.

A GOOD SOLDIER

Thou therefore endure hardness, as a good soldier of Jesus Christ.

No man that warreth entangleth himself with the affairs of this life; that he may please him who hath chosen him to be a soldier [2 Tim. 2:3–4].

The Christian is a soldier. How is the child of God a soldier? The last chapter of Ephesians tells us that the believer is fighting a spiritual battle and that he needs to put on the armor of God. Paul said to the Ephesians: "For we wrestle not against flesh and blood, but against principalities, against powers, against the rulers of the darkness of this world, against spiritual wickedness in high places. Wherefore take unto you the whole armour of God, that ye may be able to withstand in the evil day, and having done all, to stand" (Eph. 6:12–13).

"No man that warreth entangleth himself with the affairs of this life." Imagine a soldier in the midst of battle going to his sergeant or his lieutenant and saying, "Sir, I'm sorry to have to leave, but I have to go over into the city to see about some business; and then I have a date with a local girl, and I just won't be able to be here for the battle tonight!" A great many Christians are trying to fight like that today!

"That he may please him who hath chosen him to be a soldier." The believer is to establish his priorities. Here he is to endure hardness, which means to suffer hardness, as Paul was suffering. There are those who interpret this verse to mean that a Christian is not to get married. Well, he is not talking about celibacy, but he is talking about being so entangled in worldliness that he is not able to live the Christian life.

Let me give you an example. A lady called me one morning while I was a pastor in Los Angeles. She said, "I was at church yesterday when you asked for those who wanted to accept Christ. Well, I did accept Christ, but I made no move to come forward for a particular reason that I want to tell you about. My husband died recently and left to me the operation of our liquor store. I am calling you now because I don't think I can continue operating it. If you say to get a hammer and break every bottle, I'll do it. But tell me what I should do." What would you have said? I'll tell you what I told her, "Don't go in there and break bottles. You won't stop the liquor business by breaking up a few bottles. If you could, I'd be in

favor of it. But that has been your only income. I would say that you should sell the store and go out of the business."

In that way we are not to entangle ourselves in the things of this life. The child of God is to recognize that he is a soldier. And we are to recognize that the Christian life is not a playground; it is a battlefield. It is a battlefield where battles are being won, and where battles are being lost also. There is a real spiritual battle going on.

AN ATHLETE

And if a man also strive for masteries, yet is he not crowned, except he strive lawfully [2 Tim. 2:5].

Here Paul is comparing the Christian to an athlete. "Strive" refers to contending in the game. He wants to win, and he is doing everything he can to be the winner. Someone has said in a very succinct manner, "The only exercise some Christians get is jumping to conclusions, running down their friends, sidestepping responsibility, and pushing their luck." That is not the kind of exercise Paul is talking about. He spoke of the Christian life as being a racecourse, and he said, "I press toward the mark for the prize of the high calling of God in Christ Jesus" (Phil. 3:14). Paul also said that he wanted to keep his body under control (see 1 Cor. 9:24–27). Paul's goal was to run the Christian race in such a way that the One who is at the end of the race—the Lord Jesus—would be able to reward him and be able to say, "Well done, thou good and faithful servant" (Matt. 25:21). A child of God is to "strive"; God intends that he *win* the race. Every child of God needs to recognize this.

He is to "strive lawfully." That is, he has to play by the rules. There is no shortcut toward living the Christian life. Forget the gimmickry today that condenses Christianity into a little course or a few rules and regulations. God gave us sixty-six books, and each one of them is very important. It takes the composite picture to give us the mind and the Word of God. We are to study the whole Bible. An athlete can't cut the corner of a racetrack. Neither can a baseball player run by second base without touching it; he has to touch all the bases to score. A child of God has to do that, too. If you're going to win, you can't take any shortcuts.

A FARMER

The husbandman that laboureth must be first partaker of the fruits [2 Tim. 2:6].

The fourth description of a believer is a husbandman or farmer, the one who tills the field and sows the seed of the Word of God. We hear a great deal today about "laying sheaves at the feet of Jesus." I certainly hope that we will be able to put a few there, but also there has to be the sowing and laboring in the field. After the farmer has done that, there will be a harvest. This is the reason I don't cooperate with the great movements abroad that are going to convert the world by evangelism. My feeling is that the Word of God has to be sown, and I take the position that the *total* Word has to be sown before there can be a harvest.

Consider what I say; and the Lord give thee understanding in all things.

Remember that Jesus Christ of the seed of David was raised from the dead according to my gospel [2 Tim. 2:7–8].

"Remember that Jesus Christ"—the word *that* is not in the original but was supplied by the translators. Paul just stops to say, "Remember Jesus Christ." Isn't that lovely! What about Him? He's of the seed of David. That means He's going to sit on David's throne down here. Also, He was raised from the dead, "according to my gospel." It is Paul's gospel because he's the one who preached this gospel.

Wherein I suffer trouble, as an evildoer, even unto bonds; but the word of God is not bound.

Therefore I endure all things for the elect's sakes, that they may also obtain the salvation which is in Christ Jesus with eternal glory [2 Tim. 2:9–10].

"Wherein I suffer trouble." You may get in a little trouble if you stand for the Word of God. Paul got into trouble "as an evil doer, even unto bonds." He was in prison for teaching the Word of God.

"But the word of God is not bound." Although Paul was in chains, he discovered that the Word of God was still going out in the Roman world. Even with a mad caesar on the throne, a dictator of dictators, who had imprisoned Paul to silence him, the Word of God was not bound. Thank God, it still is going out to the world in our day.

It is a faithful saying: For if we be dead with him, we shall also live with him [2 Tim. 2:11].

"It is a faithful saying" or better: "Faithful is the saying, for if we be dead with him, we shall also live with him."

"If we be dead with him" should be "if we *have died* with him." When did we die with Him? When He died over nineteen hundred years ago. When we come to Christ and receive Him as our Savior, His death becomes our death. We are identified with Him and are raised with Him in newness of life. This means that this very day He wants to live His life out through us by the power of the Holy Spirit.

If we suffer, we shall also reign with him: if we deny him, he also will deny us [2 Tim. 2:12].

"If we suffer, we shall also reign with him." I personally believe that not all believers are going to reign with Him. I believe that this verse narrows it down to those who have suffered for Him. I'd be embarrassed if I were put on the same par with the apostle Paul in heaven, because I haven't suffered as he did. I would be apologizing to him constantly for being placed beside him. I believe this verse is referring to a definite group of Christians who have really suffered for Christ. In the Roman world of Paul's day there were many Christians who were martyred—five million of them, according to Fox—because they refused to deny Christ.

"If we deny him, he also will deny us." This is very strong language. It reveals, however, that Paul believes that faith without works is dead (see James 2:17). You see, Paul and James never contradict each other. James is talking about the works of faith, and Paul is saying that genuine faith will produce works. Calvin put it like this: "Faith alone saves, but the faith that saves is not alone."

If we believe not, yet he abideth faithful: he cannot deny himself [2 Tim. 2:13].

God "cannot deny himself." He cannot accept as true one who is false. That's the reason He gave such a scathing denunciation of the religious rulers of His day. He called them *hypocrites* because they were pretending to be something they were not. If Christ accepted someone who is not genuine, He actually would be denying Himself because He is true. Therefore, we should be genuine, my friend.

Of these things put them in remembrance, charging them before the Lord that they strive not about words to no profit, but to the subverting of the hearers [2 Tim. 2:14].

"Strive not about words" means *disputes* of words. God's people need to stick to essentials. We don't need to argue about empty words or philosophies or our little differences. The pastor of an Assembly of God church wrote to me saying that he appreciated our ministry and that he recommends our notes and outlines to his church, although we don't agree on everything. And we don't—I can't see his point of view on some matters and he can't see mine. Perhaps when we get to heaven, we will find it true that there are three sides to every question: your side, my side, and the right side. Maybe the Lord will have to straighten out both of us. But the important thing is that he and I ought not to argue since we agree on the essentials. And that is the way we both want it. I think we waste a lot of time in a negative approach and trying to correct other believers. Instead of doing that, let's try to stay on the positive side and enjoy each other's fellowship in the gospel.

A WORKMAN, A TEACHER

Study to shew thyself approved unto God, a workman that needeth not to be ashamed, rightly dividing the word of truth [2 Tim. 2:15].

"Study to shew thyself approved unto God." You are to study, eager to do your utmost, to present yourself approved unto God. The workman here is evidently a teacher, which means he is to be a diligent student of the Word of God.

"Rightly dividing the word of truth" means to handle rightly the Word of God. To rightly divide the Word the Christian is to be a skilled workman like an artisan. The student of the Word must understand that the Word of God is one great bundle of truth and that it has certain right divisions. The Bible is built according to a certain law and structure, which must be observed and obeyed as you go through the Word of God. You can't just lift out a verse here and a verse there and choose to ignore a passage here and a passage there. It is so easy to do this, but the Bible is not that kind of Book. This is the reason I maintain that the Bible is to be taught in its entirety.

Here is a quotation that reveals the ignorance of a man who failed to recognize that the Word of God is one great unity that needs to be rightly divided to be understood. I'm quoting from an article: "In short, one way to describe the Bible, written by many different hands over a period of three thousand years and more, would be to say that it is a disorderly collection of sixty-odd books which are often tedious, barbaric, obscure, and teeming with contradictions and inconsistencies. It is a swarming compost of a book, an Irish stew of poetry and propaganda, law and legalism, myth and murk, history and hysteria." That man really spoke a mouthful. His verbiage is quite verbose and reveals a woeful ignorance of the Bible. And he reveals the result of not rightly dividing the Word of God.

Now what is meant by rightly dividing the Word of truth? Well, there are certain dispensations in the Word of God, different methods whereby God dealt with man. The basis of salvation always remains the same. Man is saved only by believing in the atoning death of Christ. But man expresses his faith in God in different ways. For example, Abel and Abraham brought little lambs to sacrifice to the Lord. But I hope you don't take a lamb to church next Sunday morning, because you would be entirely out of order. It's all right for Mary to have a little lamb that follows her to school, but your little lamb should not follow you to church. The reason is that the Lamb of God that taketh away the sin of the world has already come. That Lamb is Jesus (see John 1:29). You see, Abel and Abraham looked forward to the Lamb of God, and we look back to His death. That is an illustration of rightly dividing the Word of truth. I wish that the man who wrote the article I quoted knew a little bit about the Bible. In his article he says that the Bible is the Book nobody reads, and obviously he belongs in that class. Before any person can speak authoritatively on any subject he has to know the subject. I would certainly recommend that this man study the Word of God before he attempts to write about it!

A child of God needs to *study* the Word of God. When I began my study for the ministry, I attended a denominational school, and I confess that the Bible was utter confusion to me. At that point I would have agreed with the author of this article. Then there was placed in my hands a *Scofield Reference Bible*, and I sat under the teaching of a wonderful pastor who led me to listen to men like Dr. Harry Ironside, Dr. Lewis Sperry Chafer, and Dr. Arthur I. Brown. Those men blessed my soul, and the Bible became a new Book to me. It started making sense because it was being rightly divided, according to dispensations which exhibit the progressive order of God's dealings with humanity. For instance, to recognize the distinction between law and grace is basic to the understanding of the Scriptures. And Paul is telling Timothy to *study*, to be diligent in his study of the Word, so that he may be a teacher who rightly divides the Word of truth.

But shun profane and vain babblings: for they will increase unto more ungodliness [2 Tim. 2:16].

Avoid empty chatter that has no value whatsoever.

And their word will eat as doth a canker: of whom is Hymenaeus and Philetus [2 Tim. 2:17].

I don't know much about these two men Paul mentions here, but they apparently were apostates.

Who concerning the truth have erred, saying that the resurrection is past already; and overthrow the faith of some [2 Tim. 2:18].

In that day, there were some who were teaching that the resurrection had already taken place, which meant that those still living had missed it!

Nevertheless the foundation of God standeth sure, having this seal, The Lord knoweth them that are his. And, Let every one that nameth the name of Christ depart from iniquity [2 Tim. 2:19].

"Having this seal." The seal was a mark of authentication and ownership. "The Lord knoweth them that are his." Back in Deuteronomy 6:8–9 God told His people to take His commandments, "And thou shalt bind them for a sign upon thine hand, and they shall be as frontlets between thine eyes. And thou shalt write them upon the posts of thy house, and on thy gates." The Israelite was to use his house as a billboard for the Word of God. That identified him as a worshiper of God.

Now how about the believer today? How does he advertise the fact that he is a child of God? "Let every one that nameth the name of Christ depart from iniquity." That is how the people are going to know who belongs to God. This is what separation is: separation from evil and separation unto Christ. If you name the name of Christ, be sure you're not living in sin. Unfortunately, there are some who assert fundamental doctrines and faith, and then it turns up that they have had an affair with a woman or have been proven dishonest. The Lord knows those who are His because He can discern the heart, but all that the world can look at is the outward life. My friend, the world certainly makes sin look attractive by clever advertisements on billboards. How do we as believers compare? Are our lives an attractive advertisement for Christ?

A VESSEL

But in a great house there are not only vessels of gold and of silver, but also of wood and of earth; and some to honour, and some to dishonour.

If a man therefore purge himself from these, he shall be a vessel unto honour, sanctified, and meet for the master's use, and prepared unto every good work [2 Tim. 2:20–21].

In these verses a believer is pictured as a vessel. If a vessel is to be usable, it must be clean. For example, imagine you are walking across a desert, and you come to an oasis. You are parched and almost dying of thirst. You find two cups there. One is made of gold and highly ornamented, but it's dirty. The other is an old crock cup. It will just barely hold water because it is cracked, but it is clean. Which one would you use? Now give God credit for having as much intelligence as you have. He too uses clean vessels; He does not use dirty vessels. Remember in the second chapter of John's gospel we read of the Lord Jesus making wine at a wedding. He had the servants drag out the old beat-up crocks (which the Jews used for purification) and had them filled with water. He took those old unattractive crocks and used them for His glory. And today God is looking for clean vessels to use—not beautiful, but *clean.*

Flee also youthful lusts: but follow righteousness, faith, charity, peace, with them that call on the Lord out of a pure heart [2 Tim. 2:22].

Oh, how many times He has placed together "faith, love, and peace," and they do sum up the Christian life. These things should not be just mouthed from the pulpit but should be lived out through the lives of those in the pew.

But foolish and unlearned questions avoid, knowing that they do gender strifes [2 Tim. 2:23].

Some folk are continually wanting to argue with me about nonessentials. I don't have time for that. We are living in a world that is on fire! Let's get the Word of God to it before it is too late.

A SERVANT

And the servant of the Lord must not strive; but be gentle unto all men, apt to teach, patient,

In meekness instructing those that oppose themselves; if God peradventure will give them repentance to the acknowledging of the truth [2 Tim. 2:24–25].

Finally, a believer is like a servant, and he is to be gentle to all men. It may seem like we have a contradiction here. The soldier was to fight, but the servant is not to fight. Is this a contradiction? No, it is a paradox. When you are standing for the truth, you are to be definite and let people know where you stand. Don't be a coward! Someone has put it this way, It is said that silence is golden, but sometimes it is just yellow! My friend, *stand* for the truth. However—

"In meekness instructing those that oppose themselves." If you are trying to win a person to Christ, don't argue with him. If he disagrees with you, let him disagree with you. Just keep on giving him the Word of God.

And that they may recover themselves out of the snare of the devil, who are taken captive by him at his will [2 Tim. 2:26].

CHAPTER 3

THEME: *The coming apostasy and the authority of Scripture*

In this chapter Paul warns of the apostasy that will come in the last days. He also gives us the antidote for that apostasy, which is the Word of God. That is why this chapter is so important and meaningful for us today.

APOSTASY IN THE LAST DAYS

This know also, that in the last days perilous times shall come [2 Tim. 3:1].

"This know also." Paul is telling Timothy something very important that he wants him to know. He is telling him what to expect and what is to be the future of the church—it is not a very bright future for the organized church.

"The last days" is a technical term used in several places in the New Testament; it speaks of the last days of the church, immediately preceding the rapture of the church. The last days of the church are not the same as the last days of the nation Israel, which is mentioned repeatedly in the Old Testament. In the Old Testament the last days are called the "end of the age" or "the time of the end," which is the Great Tribulation Period. That is quite different from the last days of the church, which precede the rapture of the church.

The apostasy that began in the church in Paul's day will continue. Paul warned the church at Ephesus that false leaders would enter the church after his decease. He told them in Acts 20:29–30: "For I know this, that after my departing shall grievous wolves enter in among you, not sparing the flock. Also of your own selves shall men arise, speaking perverse things, to draw away disciples after them." They won't give out the Word of God but will fleece the congregations. Believe me, false teachers shear the sheep pretty close!

"Perilous times shall come," which means grievous or desperate times are coming. That doesn't look like the conversion of the world, does it? It doesn't appear that the church is going to bring in the Millennium or is going to convert the world. The Bible doesn't teach that it will. That is the pipe dream of a great many idealists and a great many folk who have lived with their heads ostrich-like in the sand and have never faced reality.

Instead, notice what will be coming in the last days. We have nineteen different descriptions given in the next few verses. It is an ugly brood, but we want to look at them because they present the best scriptural picture of what is happening today. We are, I believe, moving into the last days of the church. My reason for saying this is that the things mentioned in these verses have appeared today. If you look back in the history of the church, you could certainly find some of these things in evidence, but I don't think you could ever find a period in which all of them are so manifested as they are today. I believe we are now in these "perilous" days which are described in this section. I don't know how much longer it will last, but I'm sure it's going to get worse, not better.

For men shall be lovers of their own selves, covetous, boasters, proud, blasphemers, disobedient to parents, unthankful, unholy,

Without natural affection, trucebreakers, false accusers, incontinent, fierce, despisers of those that are good,

Traitors, heady, highminded, lovers of pleasures more than lovers of God [2 Tim. 3:2–4].

There are nineteen words or phrases used to describe the last days.

1. "Lovers of their own selves"—self-lovers. This is very much in evidence in our culture today. An article by a newspaper correspondent who had covered Washington, D.C., for many years, noted that the one thing which has characterized Washington for the past twenty years is that those who are in position want the reporters to praise them. In fact, they insist upon it. That is not confined to Washington. Hollywood is probably one of the greatest places for scratching each other's backs. One actor will publicly say something nice about another, then the other one will return the favor. You find this in every walk of life. Even schools have self-love. If a man boosts a school, then the school boosts him by giving him an honorary degree. Also, you can find this in the churches. Paul goes on to say, in chapter 4, verse 3, that congregations will follow teachers "having itching ears." These teachers want their ears scratched—they want to be complimented. To be complimented, you have to compliment. So the teachers compliment their congregations and their boards of officers. They don't tell the people that they are sinners and need a Savior; they tell them how wonderful they are. It is interesting that the love of self characterizes our contemporary society. Probably there has never been a time when it has been so common.

2. "Covetous" means lovers of money. This follows self-love, because lovers of self become lovers of money. This old nature likes to have a lot of money spent on it. Remember that Paul said in 1 Timothy 6:10, ". . . the love of money is the root of all evil. . . ." Money itself is not bad. The problems come in our attitude toward our money. Covetousness reveals itself not only in the acquisition of wealth but also in the use of it.

3. "Boasters." That word has in it the idea of swaggerers. You can sometimes tell a proud man by the way he walks. He walks like a peacock; he swaggers.

4. "Proud" means haughty.

5. "Blasphemers" is better translated *railers*. I remember the story of a fellow whose wife said to him, "Everyone in town is talking about the Smiths' quarrel. Some of them are taking her part and some are taking his part." He chimed in, "Well, I suppose a few eccentric individuals are minding their own business." Well, railers include those who are always poking their noses into somebody else's business.

6. "Disobedient to parents." Certainly this is self-evident. Oh, the thousands of boys and girls and teenagers who are in complete rebellion against their parents!

7. "Unthankful." Many people receive kindnesses from others without even thinking of thanking them. And they accept *everything* from God without ever returning thanks to Him.

8. "Unholy" is profane. They are actually against God in their conversation and in their manner of life.

9. "Without natural affection" means having abnormal relationships. We are living in a day when homosexuality is being accepted as normal conduct. Yet in Romans 1:24 Paul clearly states, "Wherefore God also gave them up to uncleanness through the lusts of their own hearts, to dishonour their own bodies between themselves." Humanity sinks to its lowest level when it accepts homosexuality.

10. "Trucebreakers" are people who are impossible to get along with. They are irreconcilable—they won't let you get along with them. I recall seeing a little sign in a restaurant out in West Texas which read, "We can't please everybody, but we try." Well, you can't please everybody; there are folk who are impossible to please.

11. "False accusers" certainly abound today!

12. "Incontinent" means without self-control. That, again, characterizes a large segment of our contemporary society.

13. "Fierce" means savage. In our day the city streets have become asphalt jungles. Many of them are unsafe even in the daytime.

14. "Despisers of those that are good" is better translated *haters* of the good. We see evidence of that abroad!

15. "Traitors" are betrayers. There are some folk whom you don't dare trust.

16. "Heady" means reckless.

17. "Highminded" means blinded by pride or drunk with pride.

18. "Lovers of pleasures more than lovers of God." This actually characterizes mankind in our day. Never has there been a time when so much money has been spent in order to provide pleasure. Look at the athletic and entertainment events today. These are the things that are attracting millions of people. That is exactly the route Rome took when it went down. The mob was provided with grain and circuses, and then Rome fell. That same thing is happening today. I have always loved to participate in athletics, but I could never understand this type of athletics that just sits and beholds. I never thought that it was very exciting to go out to the coliseum and sit with 85,000 people to watch twenty-two men working for $25,000 (or more) apiece. Of course I would like to be out there myself, but I am not interested in watching them as much as I would be in watching a ditchdigger because he is not as money hungry. I don't blame any man for making as much money as he can, but the point is that billions of dollars are being spent for entertainment because men are lovers of pleasure more than lovers of God.

Having a form of godliness, but denying the power thereof: from such turn away [2 Tim. 3:5].

19. "Having a form of godliness, but denying the power thereof." They go through the rituals of religion but lack life and reality.

"From such turn away" means that the believer is to avoid them. Let me ask you a question: If you are in a dead, cold, liberal church, and you are a true believer, what are you doing there when the Word of God says to avoid those things? All across this country there are wonderful pastors who are faithfully preaching the Word of God. Why aren't you supporting and standing with these fine men?

For of this sort are they which creep into houses, and lead captive silly women laden with sins, led away with divers lusts,

Ever learning, and never able to come to the knowledge of the truth [2 Tim. 3:6–7].

"Silly women" means silly women of both sexes. There are some people who have attended Bible conferences for years, but they don't know any more about the Word of God now than they did when they began. They have never matured. Their lives are not changed. Friend, if you find yourself in that category today, get down on your knees and ask God to forgive you!

Now as Jannes and Jambres withstood Moses, so do these also resist the truth: men of corrupt minds, reprobate concerning the faith [2 Tim. 3:8].

"Jannes and Jambres" apparently were the names of the two magicians called in by Pharaoh when Moses began the miracles and the plagues came upon Egypt. We would never have known the names of these magicians if Paul hadn't given them to us. Of course, that opens a great reservoir of speculation as to where Paul got those names. The simple answer is that the names were revealed to him by the Spirit of God. I don't think that the specific names add much information to the account, but it does reveal that Paul *knew* their names and that the magicians were real individuals who did withstand Moses. You can read about them in the seventh chapter of Exodus.

The account in Exodus reveals that Satan has power, supernatural power, and also that he is a great little imitator—he imitates the things that God does. Jannes and Jambres were able to perform miracles by the power of Satan. Moses did them by the power of God. This is, I believe, the reason reference is made to them here. We need to understand in our day that Satan can imitate the power of God. John warns us in 1 John 4:1, "Beloved, believe not every spirit, but try the spirits whether they are of God: because many false prophets are gone out into the world." Satan can imitate the power of God. In our day I'm afraid that in many places a manifestation of power is misunderstood as coming from God when it really comes from Satan.

"Men of corrupt minds, reprobate concerning the faith." Paul is saying that men on the contemporary scene, like Jannes and Jambres, have corrupt or depraved minds. "Reprobate concerning the faith" means that they have discarded the faith—rejected it totally. We have had a classic example of this within the past few years. There was a bishop of the Episcopal church out here on the West Coast, a man apparently of tremendous ability, but he and his family were delving into that which was spiritualistic, bordering on the supernatural. As nearly as I can tell, this man rejected the great truths of Scripture, and he made a trip to Palestine in an attempt to disprove some of the great truths of the Word of God. Well, rather than disproving any of them, he certainly proved some of them—and this is one of them. A very strange thing happened out there in a wilderness area for the man to die as he did. I don't propose to offer any explanation, other than he is a noteworthy example of one who once professed to believe the Word of God but became, as the Scripture says, a reprobate, a castaway. He discarded the faith.

But they shall proceed no further: for their folly shall be manifest unto all men, as theirs also was [2 Tim. 3:9].

The experience of that Episcopal bishop should be a tremendous warning to Christians. You can dabble in spiritism if you want to, but you are toying with something that is dangerous. There is a manifestation of satanic power about us in our day. It is an anomaly that our crassly materialistic age, which had rejected the supernatural altogether, is discovering the reality of the supernatural, although much of it is satanic, of course.

AUTHORITY OF SCRIPTURES IN THE LAST DAYS

But thou hast fully known my doctrine, manner of life, purpose, faith, long-suffering, charity, patience [2 Tim. 3:10].

Timothy knew Paul, knew him well. Paul's life was an open book, as every Christian's life ought to be.

Persecutions, afflictions, which came unto me at Antioch, at Iconium, at Lystra; what persecutions I endured: but out of them all the Lord delivered me [2 Tim. 3:11].

Timothy knew well Paul's suffering which he had endured in his journeys. Antioch of Pisidia, Iconium, and Lystra were all places in the Galatian country where Paul had gone on his first, second, and third missionary journeys. When Paul was at Lystra, he was stoned and left for dead—I think he *was* dead and God raised him up from the dead. Paul said that God intervened in his behalf: "But out of them all the Lord delivered me." Timothy knew of these things because he and his family were from that area.

Yea, and all that will live godly in Christ Jesus shall suffer persecution [2 Tim. 3:12].

I believe that we are beginning to move into a time in this country when it will cost you something to be a Christian. Melvin Laird, long before he was Secretary of Defense, made a statement in San Francisco at a Republican convention. I do not know the circumstances which prompted the statement, but he said, "In this world it is becoming more and more unpopular to be a Christian. Soon it may become dangerous." We are seeing the accuracy of this statement. Real Christianity and real Christians are becoming very unpopular.

I am not really moved today when the press cries that there is no freedom of the press. The bleeding-heart press has played that theme for all it's worth, but have they said anything about the fact that real Christianity is stifled by the press? When was the last time you read a sympathetic article of the biblical position? The media stifles news that presents real Christianity. If a fundamental preacher gets any publicity, it will be distorted and misrepresented. Of course, if a preacher gets on the wrong side of the law he will make the front page; but if he saves a group of people from going to hell he is ignored. Friend, we are moving into an orbit when Christians may have to pay a price to stand for the faith.

But evil men and seducers shall wax worse and worse, deceiving, and being deceived [2 Tim. 3:13].

"Seducers" are sorcerers or imposters—either one. "Deceiving, and being deceived"—leading astray, then in turn led astray themselves.

Such is the picture of the last days before the rapture of the church. Now what can a child of God do in days like these?

ANTIDOTE FOR APOSTASY

But continue thou in the things which thou hast learned and hast been assured of, knowing of whom thou hast learned them;

And that from a child thou hast known the holy scriptures, which are able to make thee wise unto salvation through faith which is in Christ Jesus [2 Tim. 3:14–15].

The only antidote against a world of apostasy is the Word of God. The only resource and recourse for the child of God is the Word of God.

Paul tells Timothy to continue in the things he had learned. He had learned the Holy

Scriptures because his grandmother and mother were Jewish women and had seen to it that Timothy grew up on the Word of God.

"Which are able to make thee wise unto salvation." What kind of salvation is he talking about? After all, Timothy was already saved. Well, salvation occurs in three tenses. There is the past tense: I *have been* saved from sin. The present tense is: I *am being* saved from sin. The third tense is future: I *shall be* saved from sin. Let me elaborate. In the past tense, we have been saved. Christ bore a judgment death for us. When we believe on Him, we pass from death to life, and we are no longer under condemnation—"There is therefore now no condemnation to them which are in Christ Jesus . . ." (Rom. 8:1). We are also *being saved*. He is working out a salvation in us, and we won't even have that perfected in this life. But as we look into the future we know a day is coming when ". . . it doth not yet appear what we shall be: but we know that, when he shall appear, we shall be like him. . ." (1 John 3:2). Paul is saying that the Scriptures not only give us the *modus operandi* of being saved (that is, passing from death to life and having eternal life and becoming a child of God), but it saves us in this present evil world—enables us to grow and gives us deliverance down here. It is my contention that the constant study of the Word of God is the only help that any of us has. It is able to make us "wise unto salvation through faith which is in Christ Jesus." And I think it makes us wise in knowing how to live down here.

All scripture is given by inspiration of God, and is profitable for doctrine, for reproof, for correction, for instruction in righteousness [2 Tim. 3:16].

When Paul says "all scripture," he means *all* of it, from Genesis to Revelation. Somebody will say, "But don't you know that Revelation hadn't been written at the time 2 Timothy was written?" Yes, I know that. But the important thing to know is that Revelation became Scripture, so it is covered by this word *all*.

The word *inspiration* means "God-breathed." The writers of Scripture were not just pens that the Lord picked up and wrote with. The marvel is that God used these men's personalities, expressed things in their own thought patterns, yet got through exactly what He wanted to say. Through these men God has given us His Word. He has nothing more to say to us today. If He spoke out of heaven today, He wouldn't add anything to what He has already said.

"Is profitable for doctrine." Scripture is good "for doctrine," that is, for teaching. That's why we teach it.

It is good "for reproof," which means conviction. Studying the Bible should bring conviction to us. In fact, that is the way you can test whether the Word of God is moving in your life. If you read this Book like any other book, then the Spirit of God is not moving in your life. But if it convicts you, then you know the Holy Spirit is at work within you.

It is "for correction," that is, setting things right in your life—correction of error.

It is "for instruction," which means discipline, thinking and acting in accordance with God's will.

That the man of God may be perfect, throughly furnished unto all good works [2 Tim. 3:17].

"Perfect" doesn't mean that you and I will reach the kind of perfection where absolutely everything we do is right. Rather, it means we will attain full maturation. (There are a lot of baby Christians around today.) We'll be complete, full-grown people.

"Throughly furnished" is *thoroughly* furnished. That is, the Word of God can fit you out for life for every good work. My friend, I am against these little programs and systems that purport to bring you to Christian maturity in a few easy lessons. *All* Scripture is given by inspiration of God, and all of it is to be used in order to meet your needs.

As we come to the conclusion of chapter 3, let me remind you that Paul has talked to Timothy in a very personal way. Timothy had been *taught* the Word of God, and now he is to *declare* the Word of God. Paul has emphasized that in the days of apostasy our resource, our recourse, is to the Word of God, and it will adequately meet our need.

This is exactly what the Word of God is doing in the lives of multitudes of folk who write to me in response to my Bible-teaching radio program. We have seen that all Scripture is given by inspiration of God—it is God-breathed. It says what God wants said, and it has said *everything* He wants to say. For this reason it meets the needs of the human heart. Let me share one letter with you that bears testimony to this fact. It came from Nashville, Tennessee:

I do not intend to make this lengthy. In my mind I have composed page after page to tell you what your teaching of the Word has meant to me and my husband. We were in the same boat, floating along without a navigator. Some day I hope to be able to tell you how *joy* has been brought into our lives at a time of many family problems and unanswerable questions, how in our middle years we know more love and hope and zest for living than in our younger years, how our Father used sorrow and you and the "Thru the Bible" ministry to be a great part in bringing this about. I want to point out three things that neither of us (reared by believing parents, and ourselves lifelong church-goers) knew until two years ago when we started tuning you in. We don't know why we didn't see for ourselves. We had teachers who tried to tell us, and we read the Bible. I think the Lord was preparing us. I'm able to see His providence now. But we knew nothing of our sin nature or of the Holy Spirit except as mentioned in the Apostles' Creed. We knew the Holy Spirit came upon Mary, and we believed this. But we didn't know that the Holy Spirit was within us. Nor did we know of the resurrected life. We were fighting the losing battle of trying to be good and had just about given up on it when we started listening to "Thru the Bible." We then realized that indeed we did have to give up and that God would start us in the right direction through His grace manifested by Jesus Christ and the gift of the Holy Spirit.

The reason I have quoted this letter is to show you that the proof of the pudding is in the eating. God says that His Word is profitable, and this couple in Nashville has certainly proven that it is. When it gets into your life it does something that no other Book can do because it *is* the very Word of God.

CHAPTER 4

THEME: *Instructions for the last days*

It is with a note of sadness that we come to the final chapter of 2 Timothy. Paul will be giving Timothy instructions for the last days. Then we will have Paul's deathbed testimony, which probably are his last written words. We will detect his feeling of loneliness. He is in Rome, alone and incarcerated in that horrible Mamertine prison. He is cold and asks Timothy to bring his cloak. I have been down in that prison—I'd hate to be imprisoned there! He is lonely and the hours are long. He asks Timothy to bring his books, especially the parchments.

But with the sadness and loneliness we will also hear a note of victory as Paul gives his final charge to his son in the faith. As we hear him, we will be hearing from God the thing He wants us to hear. This is His final word to you and me. If you are not prepared to accept this, I don't think that He has anything more to say to you.

PAUL'S CHARGE TO TIMOTHY

I charge thee therefore before God, and the Lord Jesus Christ, who shall judge the quick and the dead at his appearing and his kingdom [2 Tim. 4:1].

This is a very solemn charge or command in the presence of God and the Lord Jesus Christ.

"Who shall judge the quick and the dead," the *living* and the dead.

"At his appearing and his kingdom." Christ's appearing and His kingdom are not the same thing. His appearing is the epiphany, the rapture of the church. His kingdom refers to the revelation of Christ when He returns to earth to establish His kingdom. Twice He will do some judging. He will judge His own when He takes them out of the world. Also, He will judge those who turn to God in the Great Tribulation. All of us who are believers will come before Him for judgment at one time or another. Our lives are going to be tested to see if we are to receive a reward or not.

Paul is saying, "In view of the fact that you, Timothy, are going to stand before Him to have your life judged, this is what you are to do." These instructions to Timothy are just as pertinent in our day as at the time they were given by the mouth of Paul. This is what God is saying to you and me right now.

Preach the word; be instant in season, out of season; reprove, rebuke, exhort with all longsuffering and doctrine [2 Tim. 4:2].

"Preach the word" means to proclaim the Word, to give it out, to herald it. This phrase is sort of a rallying cry, a motto that people respond to. You remember that we had such a thing during World War II: "Remember Pearl Harbor." Back in the Spanish-American War, it was "Remember the Maine." This is our rallying cry today: "Preach the Word."

"Be instant [diligent] in season, out of season." In other words, he means we should preach at any time. If someone wakes you up at two o'clock in the morning you ought to be able to give out the Word of God.

Notice that He does not say to preach *about* the Bible. A wiseacre student in my class at seminary often came up with some good comments. One day he said to the professor, "You could graduate from this seminary and never own a Bible." Why did he say that? He said that because we studied *about* the Bible; we did very little studying *of* the Bible itself. Paul tells us to preach the Word, not just talk about it.

Here is another subtle point: Paul does not say to preach *from* the Word. He does not say to lift a verse from the Bible and then weave a sermon around it. Someone has well said that a text is a pretext that's taken out of its context. We are not to preach *about* the Word of God or *from* the Word of God, but preach the Word of God itself!

"Be instant in season, out of season." The word *instant* means "diligent," or even better "urgent." There is a compulsion upon us. We should be chafing at the bit, ready to give out the Word of God. "In season, out of season" means any time of the day or night, any time of the year, under any and all circumstances.

"Reprove"—it should be given with conviction.

"Rebuke" actually means to threaten! It reminds me of a black minister, a wonderful man of God, whose pulpit I have often shared. I heard him really threaten his people. He said he didn't want any deacons who were not going to "deac." If they didn't intend to "deac" he didn't want them on the board. Not many preachers have the courage to say that!

"Exhort" means comfort. There are times when believers really need comfort.

"With all longsuffering" means that all of us who give out the Word of God need to exercise a great deal of patience.

"Doctrine" means, as we have said previously, teaching. Every minister should have a teaching ministry.

All of this is included in preaching the Word of God.

For the time will come when they will not endure sound doctrine; but after their own lusts shall they heap to themselves teachers, having itching ears [2 Tim. 4:3].

"The time will come when they will not endure sound doctrine." I wonder if our contemporary society has come to this place. Although we are startled, amazed, and overwhelmed by the number of people today who are listening to the teaching of the Word, compared to the total population, that group is a very small percentage indeed. There are very few church members who will endure sound doctrine. They don't want to hear it. What do they want?

"After their own lusts shall they heap to themselves teachers, having itching ears." Dr. Marvin R. Vincent discusses the meaning of this sentence in his *Word Studies in the New Testament*, Volume IV, pages 320–321:

> [They] shall invite teachers *en masse*. In periods of unsettled faith, skepticism, and mere curious speculation in matters of religion, teachers of all kinds swarm like the flies in Egypt. The demand creates the supply. The hearers invite and shape their own preachers. If the people desire a calf to worship, a ministerial calf-maker is readily found.

That certainly is true today. Someone has said that the modern pulpit is a sounding board that is merely saying back to the people what they want to hear.

"Having itching ears." Again I quote Dr. Vincent, page 321:

> Clement of Alexandria describes certain teachers as "scratching and tickling, in no human way, the ears of those who eagerly desire to be scratched. . . ." Seneca says: "Some come to *hear*, not to *learn*, just as we go to the theatre, for pleasure, to delight our ears with the speaking or the voice or the plays."

What a picture of our day! As someone has said, some people go to church to close their eyes and others to eye the clothes! In other words, they don't go to church to hear sound (lit., *healthy*) doctrine! They don't want to hear the Word of God; they want a substitute. Dr. Warren Wiersbe, former pastor of Moody Church in Chicago, has said:

> They want religious entertainment from Christian performers who will tickle their ears. We have a love for novelty in the churches today: emotional movies, pageants, foot-tapping music, colored lights, etc. The man who simply opens the Bible is rejected while the shallow religious entertainer becomes a celebrity. And verse 4 indicates that itching ears soon will become deaf ears as people turn away from the truth and believe man-made fables.

That is a very excellent statement, and now let us read verse 4—

And they shall turn away their ears from the truth, and shall be turned unto fables [2 Tim. 4:4].

They want something novel, something that will entertain them.

When I first came to California, the late Dr. Arno C. Gaebelein, a great man of God who had been a very outstanding teacher, wintered out here in Pasadena, and I went to visit him. He asked me how I liked California, and I replied, "I love it here, but it's very interesting that if I teach the Book of Revelation, I can fill the church (even during midweek service), but if I begin teaching the Epistle to the Romans, I can practically empty the church. I find there are people who will run all the way across this area to find out from a speaker just how many hairs are in the horse's tail in Revelation." He then made a statement to me that I shall never forget, "Dr. McGee, you're going to find out in your own ministry that there are a great many people more interested in Antichrist than they are in Christ."

There are a lot of folk with itching ears. They like to hear about these strange, weird, unusual things. They want to be entertained, but they don't want to be given the Word of God. Many people have told me that, when they started listening to me on the radio, they not only didn't like my accent, they didn't like what I said. They accused me of stepping on their toes. But I didn't even know them—I didn't step on their toes; the Word of God did. I was just preaching the Scriptures. Then as they continued to listen, they found out that the Word of God was good for them. I'm sure there are many folk from whom I have never heard who tuned me in, then tuned me out—

because they didn't want to hear the Word of God; they preferred to be entertained.

But watch thou in all things, endure afflictions, do the work of an evangelist, make full proof of thy ministry [2 Tim. 4:5].

The work of an evangelist didn't mean what it does today. In Paul's day an evangelist was a traveling teacher, a missionary. Paul was an evangelist in that sense. Now he says to Timothy, "You are to do the work of an evangelist," which is what he did do when he was with the apostle Paul.

"Endure afflictions"—he warned that Timothy would suffer hardships for preaching the Word of God in the last days.

PAUL'S DEATHBED TESTIMONY

Now we come to a great passage of Scripture. Paul has written here his own epitaph.

For I am now ready to be offered, and the time of my departure is at hand.

I have fought a good fight, I have finished my course, I have kept the faith:

Henceforth there is laid up for me a crown of righteousness, which the Lord, the righteous judge, shall give me at that day: and not to me only, but unto all them also that love his appearing [2 Tim. 4:6–8].

"I am now ready to be offered." If you had gone into that execution room in Rome, you would have seen a bloody spectacle. Very candidly, it would have been sickening to see him put his head on the chopping block, to watch the big, burly, brutal Roman soldier lift that tremendous blade above his head, then with one fell swoop sever the head from the body and see the head drop into a basket on one side and the body fall limp and trembling on the other side. But Paul says if that's all you saw, you really didn't see very much. That happened to be an altar, and his life was being poured out as a libation, a drink offering. Paul used that figure of speech before in his letter to the Philippians, when he was arrested for the first time and thought death was before him. He wrote in Philippians 2:17, "Yea, and if I be offered [poured out as a drink offering] upon the sacrifice and service of your faith, I joy, and rejoice with you all." He wanted his life to be poured out. Now he could say at the end of his life that his life had been poured out like a drink offering.

What was the drink offering? There were no specific instructions given by God to the Israelites concerning the drink offering. However, it is mentioned again and again in Exodus and Leviticus. The wine was taken and poured over the sacrifice, which, of course, was really hot because it was on a brazen altar with fire underneath it. You know exactly what would happen. The drink offering would go up in steam. It would just evaporate and disappear. That is exactly what Paul is saying here. "I have just poured out my life as a drink offering on the sacrifice of Christ. It has been nothing for me but everything for Him." Paul's life would soon disappear, and all that could be seen was Christ. This is one of the most wonderful figures of speech he has used. So many Christians try to be remembered by having their names chiseled in stone or by having a building named in their memory. Paul was not interested in that type of thing. He says, "My life is a drink offering poured out; Christ—not Paul—is the One who is to be exalted." This is a very rich passage of Scripture. Paul's epitaph is divided into two sections. The first is retrospect, in which Paul looks back upon his earthly life—this is right before he is executed. Then the second part of the epitaph is the prospect. He looks forward to eternal life. The earthly life and the eternal life are separated by what we call death down here.

Paul sums up his life in three different ways: "I have fought a good fight." He has been a soldier, a good soldier. There had been a battle to be fought and a victory to be won. Here at the end of his life he says, "I have been a soldier of my Savior." My friend, all believers should take that position. There is a battle to be fought, and every Christian should be a defender of the Word of God and stand for the great truths of the Bible.

"I have finished my course." Life is not only a battle, life is a race. Paul was a disciplined athlete who was striving to win the prize. During the race Paul was keeping his body under subjection. He was attempting to live the Christian life in such a way that he would not be disapproved. He wrote in 1 Corinthians 9:27, "But I keep under my body, and bring it into subjection. . . ." Paul also wrote in Hebrews 12:1–2 (I consider him the author of that book): ". . . let us run with patience the race that is set before us, Looking unto Jesus the author and finisher of our faith. . . ." Now at the end of his life he could say, "I have finished my course"—he had touched all the bases; he had completed all that God had planned for Him.

"I have kept the faith." Life had been a trust from God, and he had been a good steward. He had kept the faith. He had never veered from the great truths and doctrines in the Word of God.

What tremendous statements these are!

Now let's return to his statement in verse 6: "my departure is at hand." *Departure* is from a different Greek word than the one used in 1 Thessalonians for the departure of the church at the Rapture from this earth. Paul himself was going through a different doorway. Believers who are living when the Rapture takes place will not go through the doorway of death. ". . . We shall not all sleep, but we shall all be changed, In a moment, in the twinkling of an eye. . ." (1 Cor. 15:51–52). The Greek word which Paul uses in speaking of his departure is *analusis*, an entirely different word. It is made up of two words, one of which is *luo*, which means "to untie or unloose." *Analusis* could be used to refer to untying anything, but basically it was a nautical term used for a ship which was tied up at the harbor, ready to put out to sea.

Paul had an altogether different conception than that which is popular today. I've heard this so often at funeral services: "Dear Brother So-and-so. He's come into the harbor at last. He's been out yonder on a pretty wild sea, but the voyage is over now, and he's come into the harbor." Paul is really saying just the opposite of this. He's saying, "I've been tied down to the harbor." And that is what life is—we haven't been anywhere yet; we've just been tied down to this little earth.

I know of only one writer from the past who has caught this meaning of Paul's. Tennyson wrote as the first verse of his poem, "Crossing the Bar":

> Sunset and evening star,
> And one clear call for me!
> And may there be no moaning of the bar,
> When I put out to sea.

That's what death is for the child of God. It is a release for us.

Paul says, "Don't look at my execution and let blood make you sick. I'm like a ship that has been tied up at the harbor. When death comes, I'm really taking off to go and be with Christ, which will be far better."

"Henceforth there is laid up for me a crown of righteousness, which the Lord, the righteous judge, shall give me at that day." This brings us to the positive side. Paul is looking forward to the future. He is expecting a crown of righteousness. A crown is a reward, and he will receive his reward someday. I don't think it has been given to him yet, but the Lord has it for him when He starts passing them out.

There are several such crowns mentioned in the New Testament. For example, 1 Corinthians 9:24–25 reads: "Know ye not that they which run in a race run all, but one receiveth the prize? So run, that ye may obtain. And every man that striveth for the mastery is temperate in all things. Now they do it to obtain a corruptible crown; but we an incorruptible." That is the athlete's crown for being a winner on the racetrack of life. Also there is the soulwinner's crown, mentioned in Philippians 4:1: ". . . my brethren dearly beloved and longed for, my joy and crown. . . ." A crown is given for having a part in leading folk to the Lord. Paul will have many crowns—there is no doubt about that.

"A crown of righteousness" is, I believe, the reward for a righteous life, and Paul will receive that.

"Unto all them also that love his appearing" does not refer to the doctrine you hold regarding His appearing. You may be a premillennialist, a postmillennialist, or an amillennialist. I have news for you: there's no reward for holding any one of those views. The question is: Do you *love* His appearing? To love His appearing means that you will have to love *Him*. Oh, my friend, do you have a close relationship with Him? Have you ever told Him that you love Him? (I have a notion that Paul told the Lord every day that he loved Him, because he had hated and persecuted Him before.) There is a crown for those who love His appearing. I would like to have that crown. I believe it will shine brighter than all the others.

PAUL'S LAST WORDS

We have heard a triumphant note in the preceding verses, but now it's not so triumphant. Paul faces the reality of his situation.

Do thy diligence to come shortly unto me [2 Tim. 4:9].

Why does he say this? He is lonesome. When I visited that Mamertine prison, I thought of these words.

For Demas hath forsaken me, having loved this present world, and is de-parted unto Thessalonica; Crescens to Galatia, Titus unto Dalmatia [2 Tim. 4:10].

Demas took off—he couldn't stand the heat. So he left Paul and went to Thessalonica, which was quite a distance.

"Titus unto Dalmatia." I don't know if these other brethren had a legitimate excuse for leaving Paul, but I think Titus did. Paul probably sent him to Dalmatia to perform a ministry in his behalf. I don't know enough about Crescens to defend him.

Only Luke is with me. Take Mark, and bring him with thee: for he is profitable to me for the ministry [2 Tim. 4:11].

"Only Luke is with me"—good old Dr. Luke stood by Paul clear to the end.

"Take Mark, and bring him with thee." Remember that Paul wouldn't take John Mark with him on his second missionary journey. But Paul had been wrong about Mark, and now he was able to say that Mark was profitable to him in his ministry—and I am glad he said that here as one of his last words.

And Tychicus have I sent to Ephesus [2 Tim. 4:12].

Paul sent him back to Ephesus because he was the pastor of the church there. He couldn't stick around Rome indefinitely since he was pastoring a church.

Now notice something that is quite revealing—

The cloak that I left at Troas with Carpus, when thou comest, bring with thee, and the books, but especially the parchments [2 Tim. 4:13].

Paul asks for his cloak or coat which he had left at Troas. This reveals a little of Paul's suffering. I have been in that prison in May and June, and it was cold in there. This is a request for his physical need.

"And the books, but especially the parchments"—he needed something to read, something for his mind.

Alexander the coppersmith did me much evil: the Lord reward him according to his works [2 Tim. 4:14].

His "reward" won't be what Alexander would consider a reward! I am sure God will judge him for what he did to Paul.

Of whom be thou ware also; for he hath greatly withstood our words [2 Tim. 4:15].

Paul warns Timothy to be on guard against him. He is one of those laymen who will soft-soap you, then put a knife in you when you turn your back. Watch out for him.

At my first answer no man stood with me, but all men forsook me: I pray God that it may not be laid to their charge [2 Tim. 4:16].

"At my first answer" was either the preliminary hearing which opened Paul's final trial, or it was his first trial in Rome three years earlier. Paul was alone at that time.

Notwithstanding the Lord stood with me, and strengthened me; that by me the preaching might be fully known, and that all the Gentiles might hear: and I was delivered out of the mouth of the lion [2 Tim. 4:17].

Paul had asked Timothy for his cloak—something for his body—and his books and parchments—something for his mind; now here is something for his spirit: "The Lord stood with me." All of us, whether in or out of prison, have needs in these three areas. It is wonderful to be able to say, "The Lord is with me."

"I was delivered out of the mouth of the lion"—he was spared execution at that time.

And the Lord shall deliver me from every evil work, and will preserve me unto his heavenly kingdom: to whom be glory for ever and ever. Amen [2 Tim. 4:18].

Paul knew he was going to be translated to heaven.

Paul concludes this personal letter to Timothy with references to these mutual friends—

Salute Prisca and Aquila, and the household of Onesiphorus.

Erastus abode at Corinth: but Trophimus have I left at Miletum sick.

Do thy diligence to come before winter. Eubulus greeteth thee, and Pudens, and Linus, and Claudia, and all the brethren.

The Lord Jesus Christ be with thy spirit. Grace be with you. Amen [2 Tim. 4:19–22].

Notice that he again urges Timothy to come, and to come before winter. This concludes the tremendous swan song of the apostle Paul.

BIBLIOGRAPHY

(Recommended for Further Study)

Berry, Harold J. *Studies in II Timothy*. Lincoln, Nebraska: Back to the Bible Broadcast, 1975.

Garrod, G. W. *The Epistles of St. Paul to Timothy*. Ripon, England: William Harrison, 1898. (An analysis.)

Guthrie, Donald. *Pastoral Epistles*. Grand Rapids, Michigan: Wm. B. Eerdmans Publishing Company, 1957.

Hendriksen, William. *Exposition of the Pastoral Epistles*. Grand Rapids, Michigan: Baker Book House, 1957. (Comprehensive.)

Hiebert, D. Edmond. *First Timothy*. Chicago, Illinois: Moody Press, 1957. (Fine, inexpensive survey.)

Hiebert, D. Edmond. *Second Timothy*. Chicago, Illinois: Moody Press, 1958. (Fine, inexpensive survey.)

Ironside, H. A. *Timothy, Titus, and Philemon*. Neptune, New Jersey: Loizeaux Brothers, n.d.

Kelly, William. *An Exposition of the Epistle to Timothy*. London: C. A. Hammond, 1889.

Kent, Homer A., Jr. *The Pastoral Epistles*. Chicago, Illinois: Moody Press, 1958. (Excellent.)

King, Guy H. *A Leader Led*. Fort Washington, Pennsylvania: Christian Literature Crusade, 1951. (Excellent devotional treatment of 1 Timothy.)

King, Guy H. *To My Son.* Fort Washington, Pennsylvania: Christian Literature Crusade, 1944. (Excellent devotional treatment of 2 Timothy.)

Moule, Handley C. G. The *Second Epistle of Timothy.* London: Religious Tract Society, 1906. (Devotional.)

Stock, Eugene. *Plain Talks on the Pastoral Epistles.* London: Robert Scott, 1914.

Stott, John R. W. *Guard the Gospel.* Downers Grove, Illinois: InterVarsity Press, 1973. (2 Timothy.)

Vine, W. E. *The Epistles to Timothy and Titus.* Grand Rapids, Michigan: Zondervan Publishing House, 1965. (Excellent.)

Wuest, Kenneth S. *The Pastoral Epistles in the Greek New Testament.* Grand Rapids, Michigan: Wm. B. Eerdmans Publishing Company, 1952.

The Epistle to

TITUS

INTRODUCTION

Apparently Paul and Titus had been together in a ministry on the island of Crete (see Titus 1:5). I do not know how long they had been there. As we go through the epistle we will learn something about the people who lived on this island—Paul didn't think too much of them, by the way. Paul evidently left to go to another place and then wrote this epistle to Titus, giving him instructions about what he was to do as a young preacher while remaining in Crete. The date he wrote it was around A.D. 64–67.

The fact that Paul's and Titus' ministry on Crete is not mentioned in Acts reveals that the Book of Acts does not contain all the record of the early church. Actually, it is a very small record, and only the ministries of two of the apostles are emphasized: Peter in the first part of the book and Paul in the second part. We do not have a complete record of even these two men's ministries.

In the two epistles to the Thessalonians Paul's great emphasis is on the coming of Christ—it is a bright and beautiful hope for him. Critics of Paul will point out that this was his position early in his ministry but that later on he did not emphasize it. However, Titus was written about the same time as 1 Timothy, right at the end of the ministry of the apostle Paul. In Titus 2:13 Paul writes: "Looking for that blessed hope, and the glorious appearing of the great God and our Saviour Jesus Christ." My friend, Paul had not lost the blessed hope of the church. I think it was shining bright and will shine even brighter ". . . until the day dawn, and the day star arise in your hearts" (2 Pet. 1:19).

Timothy and Titus were two young preachers whom Paul had the privilege of leading to the Lord. Paul calls both of them his sons, his genuine sons; that is, he led both of them to a saving knowledge of Christ.

Paul wrote letters to both of these brethren; we have two epistles to Timothy and one epistle to Titus. These letters are called *Pastoral Epistles* because in them Paul gives instruction to these young preachers concerning the local church. These letters also prove very profitable to us today. We have so much other instruction relative to the local church—I suppose we could fill a whole library with the books that have been written on how to run the local church. In Scripture we have only these three epistles, and they are very brief; yet they do give us the essential *modus operandi* for the church. What they do impress upon us is that if there is a lack or a need in a church, it isn't a problem with the organization or with the system that is being used. Rather, if there is a need in a church, it is a *spiritual* need.

Frankly, we know very little about either of these young preachers, Timothy and Titus. Titus, however, seems to have been a stronger man, both physically and spiritually. Paul expressed less concern for Titus' welfare than he did for Timothy's. Titus was probably more mature, and he possessed a virile personality.

Timothy was a Jew who was circumcised by Paul, but Titus was a Gentile, and Paul refused to circumcise him. We read in Galatians that Paul took Titus with him to Jerusalem, and since he was a Gentile, Paul would not permit him to be circumcised (see Gal. 2:1–3). But when he took Timothy with him, Paul had him circumcised (see Acts 16:1–3). Paul circumcised one young preacher and refused to circumcise the other. If you must draw a rule from that, it can only be this: "For in Christ Jesus neither circumcision availeth any thing, nor uncircumcision, but a new creature" (Gal. 6:15).

Paul said that he wanted to be all things to all men that he might win some to Christ—to the Jew he wanted to be a Jew, and to the Gentile he wanted to be as a Gentile. He had Timothy circumcised because they were going to go into the synagogues. But in that great council of the church in Jerusalem, the gospel was at stake, and Paul would not permit one bit of legalism to slip in (see Acts 15); therefore he refused to let Titus be circumcised.

It is a dangerous thing to put down a series of little rules that are nothing in the world but a ritual whereby you attempt to live the Christian life. My friend, unless you have a personal relationship with Jesus Christ all else comes absolutely to nought.

In this epistle to Titus we have a fine picture of the New Testament church in its full-orbed realization in the community as an organization. I hear many folk today who say they are members of "a New Testament church." I would like to ask them if they have had anybody drop dead in their church recently. I am sure that they would exclaim that they had not had that experience! Well, in the early church, the New Testament church, we read of Ananias and Sapphira who dropped dead in the church because they had lied to the Holy Spirit (see Acts 5). I think that if this principle were operating in our churches today, the average church would need to be turned into a hospital or even a mortuary!

The ideal church, according to this epistle, (1) has an orderly organization, (2) is sound in doctrine, and (3) is pure in life, ready to every good work. This is the picture of the New Testament church that this epistle to Titus presents to us. In Timothy the emphasis was upon the need for *sound teaching* in the church. In Titus the emphasis is put upon the importance of *God's order* for the conduct of the churches. In fact, Titus 1:5 is the key to the entire epistle: "For this cause left I thee in Crete, that thou shouldest set in order the things that are wanting, and ordain elders in every city, as I had appointed thee." Titus was to set things in order in the churches in Crete.

In chapter 1 Paul says that the church is to be an orderly organization (see Titus 1:5). In chapter 2 he emphasizes that the church is to teach and preach the Word of God: "But speak thou the things which become sound doctrine" (Titus 2:1). He says that the church must be doctrinally sound in the faith. And then in chapter 3 we see that the church is to perform good works: "Put them in mind to be subject to principalities and powers, to obey magistrates, to be ready to every good work" (Titus 3:1). In other words, the church is saved by *grace*, is to live by *grace*, and is to demonstrate her faith to the world by her *good works*.

I would say that it would be very difficult today to find a church that is using all three of these prongs, that is stressing all three of these tremendous emphases. Some will emphasize one, while others emphasize another. Let's look at each one a little more closely:

First of all, the church is to be an orderly church. Everything, Paul wrote to the Corinthians, should be done decently and in order (see 1 Cor. 14:40). Sometimes you don't find much order in a church, and often the reason is that there are a few officers who are trying to run the whole thing. Such a church is in real trouble and is a heartbreak to its pastor. The church is to be an orderly church, not run by a couple of deacons.

Secondly, in many churches you will find that there is no emphasis at all upon sound doctrine. Because of this, I always stress to young pastors that they should not focus on building a church or building an empire of any kind. I tell them just to teach and give out the Word of God. Rather than build an organization—that is, a lot of buildings—they should build into the lives of men and women. Whatever organization they have built in a church may be wrecked by others later on after they have left. That will be a real heartbreak to a pastor unless he has before him the goal of building into the lives of men and women. That should be the emphasis in any church.

Finally, a church should be ready for every good work. Sometimes we fundamentalists put such a great emphasis on doctrine (although I don't think we overemphasize it) that we *do* underemphasize good works. A church should be engaged in good works. Many Christian organizations are so concerned with getting in the finances to carry on their program that they become more interested in getting people to give than in helping those people. A lot of folk need help—not just spiritual help but also physical help. We need to *do* things for people, to help them with their physical needs.

I am happy that I can say there are many churches which are carrying on a work of helping people. I know of one church which has people who go out and visit shut-ins; they read to them, sew for them, and do many other helpful chores. That's a lovely thing to do. Our government is able to provide some care for the poor and needy, and that is wonderful, but *we* can go and sit down and talk with lonely people like this, which is a much-needed ministry today.

This is only a brief resumé of this epistle to Titus. Liberalism has attempted to emphasize the third chapter which deals with good works, forgetting the two chapters on order and doctrine which precede it. Until a church has all three of these aspects that Paul has outlined, it has no claim to be called "a New Testament church."

OUTLINE

CHAPTER 1

***THEME:** The church is an organization*

INTRODUCTION

The introduction to Titus is characteristic of those in the Pastoral Epistles, but it is not characteristic of Paul's other epistles.

Paul, a servant of God, and an apostle of Jesus Christ, according to the faith of God's elect, and the acknowledging of the truth which is after godliness [Titus 1:1].

"A servant of God"—the word *servant* here actually means "bond slave." Paul says that he is a bond slave of God. We know from the Old Testament that a bond slave was one who chose to remain a slave of his master for life.

"An apostle of Jesus Christ." Paul is defending his apostleship. The reason that he asserts his apostleship here is that he is going to give instructions to the organized church. These instructions come from an apostle, the appointed writer of the Lord Jesus who was now communicating with His church through His apostles. The Epistle to Titus is a communication from the Lord Jesus to us also.

"According to the faith of God's elect." Paul does not say *"for* the faith," but *"according to* the faith"—in other words, according to the norm or standard of faith which is set for God's elect today. Whether you are saved or not *does* rest on what you believe. Tell me what you think of Jesus Christ; tell me what you believe about His death on the cross and what it means to you; tell me what you believe about His resurrection and what it means to you; tell me whether you believe the Bible to be the Word of God. With this information I think I can deduce whether you are a child of God or not. This is the norm, you see: "according to the faith of God's elect."

"God's elect"—this is the way Paul speaks of saved people. He is not discussing the doctrine of election at all.

"And the acknowledging of the truth which is after godliness." This could be better translated "the *knowledge* of the truth which is *according to* godliness." The Greek preposition is *kata,* meaning "according to." My friend, if the truth that you have does not lead to a godly life, there is something radically wrong with your faith.

I was told once of a preacher who drinks, cusses, and runs with the country club crowd. On Sunday he preaches the gospel, and people come forward every week. Another pastor in that community asked me, "Dr. McGee, how is it that that man is prospering?" I told him I honestly did not think the man was prospering. Maybe he is bringing a lot of numbers into the church, but he is not building the church of the Lord Jesus Christ. Truth will lead to godliness, and if it doesn't lead to godliness, it is not truth, my friend.

Paul will dwell on this theme that when the gospel is believed it will lead to godliness because the people on the island of Crete were abusing the grace of God. They said that if they had been saved by grace they were free to live in sin if they wanted to. Paul answers that right here in this first verse by saying that when the truth of God is believed it will lead to godliness. Grace saves us, but it also lays down certain disciplines for our lives and calls us to live on a high plane. You cannot use the doctrine of the grace of God to excuse sin. If you think that you can be saved by grace and live in sin—may I say this kindly, but I must say it—you are not saved by grace; you are not saved at all. Salvation by grace leads to a godly life.

In hope of eternal life, which God, that cannot lie, promised before the world began [Titus 1:2].

"In hope of eternal life." The idea here is *resting* upon the hope of eternal life. In Titus we will see that Paul speaks of grace in three time zones. In Titus 2:11–13 we see all three: "For the grace of God that bringeth salvation"— that is *past;* "teaching us"—that is *present;* and "looking for that blessed hope"—that is *future.* This is the hope that Paul is speaking of, and he says we are to rest upon that hope.

"Which God, that cannot lie." This hope was promised by a God who cannot lie. In Romans 3:4 Paul wrote: "God forbid: yea, let God be true, but every man a liar. . . ."

Sometimes we believers almost make God out a liar by the lives we live. We say we believe something, but we don't really believe, and we *act* as if we don't believe. Paul says God cannot lie.

I have often wanted to preach a sermon on things that God cannot do. This is one: God cannot lie. Do you also know that you see something every day that God has never seen? You have seen your equal; God has never seen His equal. Why cannot God lie when we can? Well, you can do something God cannot do.

You see, God *must* be true to Himself. He is holy and He is righteous—that is His nature, and there are certain things He cannot do because of His nature. It is not because it is impossible for Him to do it; but because God is true to His nature, He cannot do it. He is righteous, He is just, and He never deceives. He is One you can depend upon.

"Promised before the world began"—this promise was made back in eternity.

But hath in due times manifested his word through preaching, which is committed unto me according to the commandment of God our Saviour [Titus 1:3].

"In due times" means in His own seasons. God moves in a very orderly manner in what He does. God has made the peach tree to bud in the spring—it will not stick out those beautiful buds when the first snow falls; it waits until spring.

"Hath in due times manifested his word through preaching." The word that is translated here as "preaching" comes from the Greek word *kerux*, which means "a herald" or "trumpet." A trumpet was used in that day to make a proclamation. If a ruler had a proclamation to make, a trumpeter came out and blew a trumpet, and then the proclamation was made. That is the idea here. Paul is saying that God has in the correct seasons manifested His Word through a proclamation. He then adds that it has been committed to him to proclaim the Word "according to the commandment of God our Saviour."

To Titus, mine own son after the common faith: Grace, mercy, and peace, from God the Father and the Lord Jesus Christ our Saviour [Titus 1:4].

"To Titus, mine own son" or my *genuine* son. Paul had led Titus to a saving knowledge of the Lord Jesus Christ. Titus was Paul's spiritual son.

"After the common faith"—the common faith is the faith that is shared by all, the faith that all believers must have. It is a living faith in the Lord Jesus Christ.

"Grace, mercy, and peace, from God the Father and the Lord Jesus Christ our Saviour." The grace of God has appeared, and, therefore, God extends mercy to us today. I don't know about you, but I use up a whole lot of the mercy of God. I am grateful that He is good to me and does not deal with me according to my orneriness and disobedience. He has simply been good to me. Grace, mercy, and

peace—peace is the present possession of the believer, but there is a peace coming when the Prince of Peace comes also. All these are "from God the Father and the Lord Jesus Christ our Saviour."

AN ORDERLY CHURCH MUST HAVE ORDAINED ELDERS WHO MEET THE PRESCRIBED REQUIREMENTS

That is a pretty long title, but it belongs to a very important section of Scripture.

For this cause left I thee in Crete, that thou shouldest set in order the things that are wanting, and ordain elders in every city, as I had appointed thee [Titus 1:5].

Paul had left Titus in Crete to organize local churches with elders as spiritual leaders. The island of Crete is one of the largest islands in the Mediterranean Sea. There was a great deal of mythology and tradition connected with this island as there generally was with all of the Greek islands. According to their tradition, Minos was the one who first gave laws to the Cretans. He conquered the Aegean pirates who were there, and he established a navy. After the Trojan War, the principal cities of the island formed themselves into several republics, mostly independent. Crete was annexed to the Roman Empire about 67 B.C. These chief cities were Knossos, Cydonia, and Gortyna, and apparently there were churches now in all these places. Paul seems to have done a very effective missionary work on the island, but we have no record of it in Scripture whatsoever. There is actually no absolute proof that before his voyage to Rome he ever went to the island of Crete. But from the information we are given in this little epistle, we are led to believe that he was there and left Titus to organize the churches which were founded by him and Titus.

Crete was evidently a pretty bad place, and the people were not very good people. Paul himself says that they were liars, and that is certainly the thing for which they were noted in that day. There was a Greek word, *kretizein*, which means to speak like a Cretan and was synonymous with being a liar. One of their own poets wrote, "Crete, which a hundred cities doth maintain, cannot deny this, though to lying given."

Although they were known as liars, and Paul will have other uncomplimentary things to say about them, many of them turned to the Lord, and Paul writes to Titus to organize their churches.

"Set in order the things that are wanting, and ordain elders in every city." The gift of an elder is a gift of men to the church. Putting your hand on the head of some men and going through a little ritual will not make them elders. But I believe it is important to do that with men who do have the gift of elders. I think the churches in Crete had elders, but they had never been ordained, or set aside. They were men who had a gift of supervision of the churches and were exercising that gift without an authority. Titus is to "ordain elders"—appoint them, set them aside—"in every city."

"As I had appointed thee." Paul says, "I have appointed you, Titus, and you are to appoint elders in these cities."

A man who holds the office of elder should have the gift of an elder. There are certain men who are made officers in the church who have no gift for it at all. That is half of our problem in many churches today, and the other half is that there are good men who have the gift and are not made officers in the church. As a result, some of our churches get into the hands of the wrong folk, and all sorts of problems arise.

Now here are the requirements for the men who are to hold this office:

If any be blameless, the husband of one wife, having faithful children not accused of riot or unruly [Titus 1:6].

"If any be blameless"—that does not mean he must be perfect, without sin. It does mean that any accusation that is brought against him must not be found to be true. His life must be above reproach.

When someone can point a finger at an officer of the church and accurately accuse him of dishonesty, then the cause of Christ is hurt. It does not matter how naturally gifted a man may be, if someone can say that his speech does not reflect a dedication to Christ, then the cause of Christ is hurt, and that man should not be an officer of the church.

"The husband of one wife, having faithful children." The idea here of "faithful children" means *believing* children. If a man cannot lead his own children to the Lord, he ought not to be an officer in the church. Please do not misunderstand me. I recognize that today in many wonderful Christian homes there is a son or daughter who is away from the Lord and who gives no evidence of godly upbringing. A man may be a fine, godly man who has a wonderful Christian home, and he may not be guilty of anything that caused that boy or girl to turn from Christ, but he should not be an officer in the church. As an officer in the church, he might be called upon to make a judgment about someone else. That person in turn could point his finger and say, "What about you? What about your son, your daughter? What right have you to talk to me?" For the cause of Christ and for the sake of the office, an officer in the church must have believing, obedient children.

"Not accused of riot or unruly." "Of riot" could be translated *of profligacy*. They are not to be out in a protest movement carrying placards, but instead they should be concerned with living a life glorifying to the Lord Jesus and with getting out His Word.

For a bishop must be blameless, as the steward of God; not selfwilled, not soon angry, not given to wine, no striker, not given to filthy lucre [Titus 1:7].

This is so practical! A bishop (or elder) must not be "selfwilled" for he is a steward of God as well as a representative of the people. He is in the church to find and do God's will.

"Not soon angry" means not touchy.

"Not given to filthy lucre," that is, not covetous.

These are to be characteristic of "a bishop." As we have said before, elder and bishop are synonymous terms. The word *elder (presbuteros)* refers to the individual, and he was to be a mature person both physically and spiritually. A *bishop (episkopos)* was an overseer; he ruled the church. Therefore, this word has reference to the office. But never was a church to have only one man made bishop or presbyter. There were always several.

There has been some disagreement as to whether there were elders already in the churches in Crete and Titus was to ordain them, or whether there were none and Titus was to now appoint some. If the latter was the case (which I do not think it was), then I feel that the churches would have had to agree upon the men Titus appointed. However, that is not the main issue, and it should not be the issue in churches today. Paul's emphasis is upon a man's personal requirements to hold such a position in a church.

But a lover of hospitality, a lover of good men, sober, just, holy, temperate [Titus 1:8].

These are the requirements of the elder, and their meaning is familiar to us.

Holding fast the faithful word as he hath been taught, that he may be able

by sound doctrine both to exhort and to convince the gainsayers [Titus 1:9].

A better rendering of this verse would be: "Holding fast the trustworthy word according to the teaching, that he may be able to exhort in the sound teaching and to convict the gainsayers (heretics)."

There were two things that an officer should do: (1) He should be able to exhort, that is, to teach the Word of God; and (2) he must be able to confute or refute the heretics. I feel that men who hold office in a church should be Bible-trained men. During World War II we had what was called "ninety-day wonders." The army needed more officers and so they put them through a short course in a hurry, and they came up with some rather peculiar second lieutenants in those days. Remember that Paul told Timothy to "lay hands suddenly on no man . . ." (1 Tim. 5:22). You are not to have a man converted one night, ask him to give his testimony the next night, make him an officer in the church on the third night, an evangelist on the fourth, and the pastor of the church on the fifth night! We sometimes do things like that today, and it is very unfortunate for the church. A church officer should be able to stand on the Word of God and to give it out.

THE BAD REPUTATION OF THE CRETANS

Paul is now going to talk about the bad reputation of the Cretans. We must remember that all men are sinners; we are all brothers in the sense that we are all sinners. All men are not in the brotherhood of God, because that comes only through the New Birth by becoming a son of God through faith in Christ. But surely we are all sons of Adam, and "in Adam all die," because all have sinned (see 1 Cor. 15:22). However, these Cretans had a particularly bad reputation:

For there are many unruly and vain talkers and deceivers, specially they of the circumcision [Titus 1:10].

"Vain talkers" means empty chatterers. There are certain Christians (perhaps you know some) who are rather frothy at the mouth; they just talk a blue streak. I rode once with a man for two hundred miles, and from the moment I got in his car until I got out, the only thing I had to do was grunt and he would keep on talking! If you had added up all he had to say, it was just a great big bag of nothing, a whole lot of hot air. There are many empty talkers. It is all right to have fun and be light-

hearted, but what Paul is condemning is constant chattering with nothing but empty words.

"Deceivers, specially they of the circumcision." Paul is referring to those who were seeking to contradict his teaching.

Whose mouths must be stopped, who subvert whole houses, teaching things which they ought not, for filthy lucre's sake [Titus 1:11].

"Who subvert whole houses" means to overthrow whole families. This was very serious. Wherever the Word of God is sown, the Devil gets in—he's the enemy and he always sows tares among the wheat. I have found this to be true in my own experience. I was back East one time in an area in which our radio program is heard. We are reaching multitudes there, and many have come to Christ. But while I was there I learned that our broadcast is immediately followed by the broadcast of one of the cults. The speaker on that program attempts to "correct" my teaching of the Bible—the Devil always gets in. Similarly, a great work of Christ had been done in Crete, but the enemy was right there to sow his own seed.

One of themselves, even a prophet of their own, said, The Cretians are alway liars, evil beasts, slow bellies [Titus 1:12].

"Evil beasts" means the Cretans were rude and cruel. "Slow bellies" means lazy gluttons. Paul is not being very complimentary here, is he? But this is the reputation they had in the Roman world of Paul's day. Paul is quoting a Cretan poet, Epimenides, who was born in Crete several centuries earlier. Another poet wrote, "Crete, which a hundred cities doth maintain, cannot deny this, though to lying given." Paul said, "Cretians are alway liars." This does not mean that everybody who lived in Crete was a liar anymore than when you say that all Scottish people are tightfisted—some are very generous. But the Cretans had the general reputation of being liars.

It is marvelous what the grace of God can do and did do among the people of Crete. They were liars, beastly, lazy people, who were big eaters. Many of them turned to Christ, and their lives were changed.

This witness is true. Wherefore rebuke them sharply, that they may be sound in the faith [Titus 1:13].

Paul tells Titus that he is going to have to be a little more strict with the Cretans than he would with others because of their background and their very nature.

Not giving heed to Jewish fables, and commandments of men, that turn from the truth [Titus 1:14].

"Not giving heed to Jewish fables." Paul's reference here is not just to legalism. There grew up around the Mosaic Law a great deal of writing, which includes the Talmud and much more. I have not read very much in these Jewish writings because they never really interested me. But I have read some, and there are some pretty wild tales in them.

"Commandments of men, that turn from the truth." The Lord Jesus rebuked the religious rulers for adding traditions to God's law, and that is what Paul is talking about here. The teaching of legalism is in two phases—one is that you are *saved* by the Law, and the other is that you are to *live* by the Law. Both of these teachings are very dangerous. We are saved by the grace of God and are actually called to live on a higher plane than that of the Ten Commandments. God gave the Ten Commandments to a *nation*, and I feel that they should be the law of the world today. When God says, "Thou shalt not kill," that is for everyone, Christian and non-Christian—that is for the whole world. However, those who are saved by the grace of God are given instructions for living that is on an even higher plane than that.

Unto the pure all things are pure: but unto them that are defiled and unbelieving is nothing pure; but even their mind and conscience is defiled [Titus 1:15].

This is the verse that is used by the folk who say that if we are saved by grace, it doesn't make any difference how we live; that is, if we are saved, we are pure and can live in any way we like. Certain cults have developed this teaching, saying they can live in sin (they don't call it sin—it's not sin for them) because "unto the pure all things are pure."

What Paul is talking about has nothing to do with *moral* issues at all. He is speaking to this issue of legalism and the eating of meats. The teaching of many legalistic cults often includes a very unusual diet. But Paul says, "Unto the pure all things are pure." In other words, whether you eat meat or don't eat meat makes no difference at all. All food is clean. If you want to eat rattlesnake meat, that is your business; it's my business to keep away from it if I can! You can eat anything you want—"unto the pure all things are pure."

If you are an unbeliever, any special diet you might concoct will make no difference in your relationship to God—it will not save you. You can eat all the vegetables you want, but if you are not right with God, they will not make you pure. The Lord Jesus said that it is not the thing that goes into a man that defiles him, but what comes out of him (see Matt. 15:18–20).

They profess that they know God; but in works they deny him, being abominable, and disobedient, and unto every good work reprobate [Titus 1:16].

"They profess that they know God; but in works they deny him." Many believers today can deny and do deny God by the lives that they live. And they deny the Word of God. I knew a man who was an officer in the church, and he carried the biggest Bible I have ever seen. When he put it under his arm, he leaned to that side! Everybody believed him to be very pious, but outside the church he had the reputation of not really being honest. He carried a big Bible, but he didn't really believe it. You see, you can deny the Bible by the life you live, and you can deny God by the life you live.

"Being abominable, and disobedient, and unto every good work reprobate." Ceremonies and rituals cannot change the evil heart of man. Only the Word of God can change the human heart. When the heart is changed, the life will reveal the change. Paul and James were never in disagreement—they both said that faith without works is dead. Saving faith produces a godly life. As Calvin said, "Faith alone saves, but the faith that saves is not alone."

CHAPTER 2

THEME: The church is to teach and preach the Word of God

THE CHURCH MUST TEACH SOUND DOCTRINE

The church must teach sound doctrine or it is not a church. I have written a little book entitled *The Spiritual Fingerprints of the Visible Church* in which I go back to the Day of Pentecost where we are told that those who were added to the church on that day ". . . continued stedfastly in the apostles' doctrine and fellowship, and in breaking of bread, and in prayers" (Acts 2:42). These were the identification marks of the early church: the apostles' doctrine, fellowship, breaking of bread, and prayer. It really doesn't matter how high the steeple may be or how beautifully the chimes may play, it is the message that is going out from the pulpit which will tell you whether the church is really a church, organized as Paul understood it and as the Word of God declares it.

In the first chapter we found that the elders whom Titus was to ordain were to be able to do two things: to exhort and to refute or confute the heretics. It is important not to spend your entire ministry refuting everybody. There are some men who have what I would call a negative ministry—all they do is attack the enemies of the gospel. That is important, but I believe we all need a balanced ministry. An elder should be able to exhort from the Word of God as well as be able to answer a heretic. In this second chapter Paul's emphasis will be upon the teaching of the Word of God.

But speak thou the things which become sound doctrine [Titus 2:1].

"Sound doctrine" means the apostles' doctrine. The number one thing of importance to the early church was the apostles' doctrine. What we read in these epistles is also a part of the apostles' doctrine, by the way.

First of all, Paul has a message for the senior citizen—for the senior citizen who is male and for the senior citizen who is female.

That the aged men be sober, grave, temperate, sound in faith, in charity, in patience [Titus 2:2].

They are to be sound in their love and in patience. They are to be "sober," that is, very vigilant, very serious. They should be men who are respected and self-controlled.

The aged women likewise, that they be in behaviour as becometh holiness, not false accusers, not given to much wine, teachers of good things [Titus 2:3].

"In behaviour as becometh holiness"—the aged women are to be reverent in their behavior.

"Not false accusers," that is, not gossips, and "not given to much wine," or not drunkards.

"Teachers of good things." The older women are to teach the younger women:

That they may teach the young women to be sober, to love their husbands, to love their children,

To be discreet, chaste, keepers at home, good, obedient to their own husbands, that the word of God be not blasphemed [Titus 2:4–5].

"Keepers at home" means they are to be workers at home. I may get in trouble here, but I must say this: A wife's first responsibility is in her home. The home is not a playpen; it is a serious responsibility to be a wife and to care for children in the home. It is not something to be taken lightly.

I am confident that Paul would never have approved of the women's lib movement. I will stick my neck out even further and say that I am opposed to it—I think it's wrong. I believe that a woman wants to be treated like a woman and not like a man. I was in a large business establishment recently where there were fifty stenographers, and from what I heard they were really promoting women's lib in that office. I agree that women should be promoted according to their ability and paid according to their ability, but I noticed when we came to get on the elevator the ladies felt like they should get on first. I let them do that because I was taught to do so. If these women really want equality in every way, they should not be working just in offices, but they should also take work as ditchdiggers. However, I am convinced that that is not really what they want. My friend, the biggest and most important business in the world is the making of a home.

"Good" means kindly.

"Obedient to their own husbands." The idea of obedience here is that the women should *respond* to their husbands. Paul uses the same Greek word in Romans 8:7 where it is translated "subject." He says there, "Because the carnal mind is enmity against God: for it is not *subject* to the law of God, neither indeed can be" (italics mine). Paul's thought is that the natural man *cannot* respond to God; he cannot obey God; he has no way to respond to God. Now the wife is to respond to her husband; he is the aggressor, and she is to respond to him.

A great, big, brawny fellow once came to see me in my office, and he said, "I want you to talk to my wife and tell her to obey me!" I told him I would do nothing of the kind, and he asked me why. I said, "When's the last time you told your wife that you loved her?" He couldn't remember and said, "What has that got to do with it?" I told him, "That has everything in the world to do with it! Until you tell her that you love her, I don't see why she should respond to you. Didn't you tell her you loved her when you were courting? Well, just keep that up. The thing to do is to just keep up the courtship. You keep telling her that you love her, and she will respond to you a great deal better than she has been." The wife is to respond to the love of her husband.

Young men likewise exhort to be sober minded [Titus 2:6].

Now Paul turns his attention to the young men, and he probably means that Titus is the one who is to teach the young men.

In all things shewing thyself a pattern of good works: in doctrine shewing uncorruptness, gravity, sincerity [Titus 2:7].

Paul says to this young preacher Titus, "You be a pattern, an example, for the other young men."

"In doctrine shewing uncorruptness." "Uncorruptness" has the idea of incorruptness—that is, in his teaching he is to show his complete faith in the Word of God and appreciate the seriousness of the matters he is dealing with.

Sound speech, that cannot be condemned; that he that is of the contrary part may be ashamed, having no evil thing to say of you [Titus 2:8].

In other words, your conversation should reveal the fact that you are a child of God.

Exhort servants to be obedient unto their own masters, and to please them well in all things; not answering again [Titus 2:9].

"Exhort servants"—now Paul turns his attention to another group. In the early church there were many slaves. In fact, 90 percent of the names on the walls of the catacombs are those of slaves or ex-slaves. The gospel met a great need for this class of people in that day.

"To be obedient unto their own masters, and to please them well in all things." Again, the idea behind obedience is that they should respond to their masters, be interested in them and in their work. Anyone, especially those in Christian work, should put their heart into their job or else get out of it. If you work for a Christian organization, you do it because you *want* to work for it. I hope you get a good living out of it, but that is not the point. Christian work is to be done with the heart as well as with the head and hands.

"Not answering again," that is, not talking back to your employer.

Not purloining, but shewing all good fidelity; that they may adorn the doctrine of God our Saviour in all things [Titus 2:10].

"Not purloining" means not stealing. Businesses lose many millions of dollars each year because employees steal from them. "Not purloining" means you should not be a thief.

"But shewing all good fidelity"—showing faithfulness.

"That they may adorn the doctrine of God our Saviour in all things." The Greek word for "adorn" is the same word from which we get our English word *cosmetics*. I am often asked whether I feel Christian women should wear makeup. I would say yes, the kind Paul is speaking of here, and plenty of it. "Adorn the doctrine of God"—in other words, if you are sound in the faith, you should be wearing the appropriate cosmetics. I would like to see more of the lipstick of a kind tongue. Speaking kindly is a mighty fine lipstick. And then the face powder of sincerity and reality. My, there are all kinds of cosmetics that you should use today as a Christian.

THE CHURCH MUST PREACH THE GRACE OF GOD

Now Paul interrupts these admonitions to put a doctrinal foundation under the lives of these people. He states the gospel, and he states it in three time zones—the past, the present, and the future.

I grew up in the horse-and-buggy days, and I never cease to wonder at the speed of jet travel. Beside the actual speed of the planes, the crossing of time zones makes it possible to arrive at the end of a three- or four-hour flight and see that it is only an hour later than it was when you started. I understand they are working now on a plane that will travel three times the speed of sound. That means you could leave Dallas, Texas, and arrive in Los Angeles two hours before you left Dallas! That would be a wonderful thing.

However, I think the most wonderful thing in the world is that the grace of God is in three time zones. We see that in the next three verses: "For the grace of God that bringeth salvation hath appeared" (v. 11)—that's the past time zone; "teaching us" (v. 12)—that's the present time zone of grace; and "looking for that blessed hope" (v. 13)—that is the future time zone. These, then, are the three time zones of grace. Let us look at them a little more closely:

For the grace of God that bringeth salvation hath appeared to all men [Titus 2:11].

Paul says to the Cretans, "I want to put under you the doctrine of the grace of God because you need a solid foundation." The grace of God is the way God saves us. Years ago I heard a great preacher, Dr. Dodd, in Shreveport, Louisiana, say, "My pulpit is a place for good news; my study is the place for good advice." The gospel is not good advice—it is good *news*. It is even more than that; it is the power of God unto salvation.

Paul is enjoining Titus to demand of the Cretans that they live lives that adorn the gospel, for it is the *power* of God. There is absolutely no excuse for any Christian to live a life of defeat and failure—"for the grace of God that bringeth salvation hath appeared to all men."

"Hath appeared" means it shines forth—it is the epiphany. What the Lord Jesus did for us when He came more than nineteen hundred years ago is the gospel, the good news. He died for us, and He rose again. God doesn't save us by His love, and He doesn't save us by His mercy. Ephesians tells us: "For by *grace* are ye saved through faith; and that not of yourselves: it is the gift of God" (Eph. 2:8, italics mine). *Mercy* is the compassion of God that prompted Him to send a Savior to mankind. If one man could be saved by the mercy of God, all mankind would be saved. It wouldn't have been necessary for Christ to die; the cross would have been circumvented.

God loved men, but He didn't save us by His love. *Love* is the divine motive, but God is not only love, He is righteous and holy and just. The holy demands of God, His just claims, and His righteous standard had to be met. The love of God may long to save us, but the immutable law of justice makes love powerless to do so. Therefore, Christ, by dying for our sins, met the holy demands of God's justice, and He can now save us by *grace*. How wonderful it is to be saved by the grace of God! When we were guilty, Christ paid the penalty. Grace is not complicated or implicated with human effort. God doesn't ask your cooperation; He doesn't ask for your conduct or your character in order to save you. God only asks men to believe Him, to trust Him, and to accept Christ. God's way is the best way, and it is the *only* way.

Teaching us that, denying ungodliness and worldly lusts, we should live soberly, righteously, and godly, in this present world [Titus 2:12].

God is not trying to reform this world; He is redeeming men who accept Christ. The gospel does not appeal to Christ-rejecting men to do better. When a person says, "I am going to try to do better," I think he is a liar. If you have rejected Jesus Christ, you might as well try to get all you can out of this life, because this life is all that you are going to get. Today our government is trying to get people to stop smoking; they're trying to educate people to the dangers of cigarettes. However, God is not asking you to do such things. You might as well eat, drink, and be merry, for tomorrow you'll die. God doesn't want to reform you; He wants to redeem you.

"Teaching us"—*teaching* means child-training. God *is* calling those who are His own, who are redeemed, to live for Him and to avoid "worldly lusts."

Looking for that blessed hope, and the glorious appearing of the great God and our Saviour Jesus Christ [Titus 2:13].

"Looking for that blessed hope"—this is the next happening in the program of God: Christ is coming to take His church out of this world.

"The glorious appearing of the great God and our Saviour Jesus Christ." This reveals that Paul taught the deity of Christ; he speaks of the great God who is our Savior, and who is He? He is Jesus Christ. And what did He do?—

Who gave himself for us, that he might redeem us from all iniquity, and purify unto himself a peculiar people, zealous of good works [Titus 2:14].

He gave Himself for us that He might redeem us. He paid a price for us that He might redeem us "from all iniquity."

"And purify unto himself a peculiar people, zealous of good works." "A peculiar people" would be better translated "a people for His possession." It is true that God wants you to live for Him and wants you to do good works,

but He will have to redeem you first, my friend.

These things speak, and exhort, and rebuke with all authority. Let no man despise thee [Titus 2:15].

Paul says to Titus, "You are a young man. Don't let them despise you because of the life you live." Titus should be able to teach all these things with authority.

This has been a wonderful epistle. Every young preacher ought to study carefully the Book of Titus.

CHAPTER 3

THEME: *The church is to perform good works*

This epistle gives us the picture which covers the entire spectrum of what God wants for the church. We saw in the first chapter that God wants the church to be an orderly organization. Then we saw in the next chapter that the church is to be sound in doctrine. Now we shall learn that, to be all that God wants for the church, the church is to perform good works.

GOOD WORKS ARE AN EVIDENCE OF SALVATION

Put them in mind to be subject to principalities and powers, to obey magistrates, to be ready to every good work [Titus 3:1].

The very first thing he mentions here is the fact that the church must have members who are law abiding. A believer should obey the laws of the land in which he lives unless those laws conflict or contradict his duty and relationship to God.

I always felt embarrassed when I taught evening Bible classes in downtown Los Angeles and would be requested to announce that someone had parked in a *no parking* place. Or sometimes I had to announce that a car was blocking a driveway so that the people who owned the driveway couldn't get out. That kind of parking was breaking the law on the part of someone in my class who apparently didn't pay very much attention to the fact that a Christian is to be subject to principalities and powers.

Now that brings up the question of what a

believer should do when the laws of the land conflict with his duty and relationship to God. For example, should a young man who is drafted into military service go out to war when his real Christian conviction tells him otherwise? Fortunately in our country such a young man with real convictions against war can be a conscientious objector. He need not go into the armed forces to carry a gun, but he can spend the same amount of time as the other young men in the army but be assigned noncombat duties. I think any young man should be commended for that, because I believe it takes courage and conviction for a young man under those circumstances to stand on his two feet and say, "Yes, I'll serve; I'll wear the uniform, but I cannot conscientiously carry a gun." I think that sympathy and understanding should be granted to such a young man.

On the other hand, there have been many young men in this country who have run away to escape the draft. They did not run away because of religious conviction. I can't think of any other explanation than that they were disloyal to their country. They were not obedient to this nation. These young men wanted to enjoy all the blessings and benefits of our nation but did not want to meet its responsibilities. They have broken the law and should pay the penalty.

We are to be subject to the principalities and powers over us. A church should teach this; part of the message that should be given to church members is that they should be obedient to the powers that be. That obedience is not to the *man* but to the *office* that he represents. Perhaps you resent the manner in which a police officer gives you a citation for a traffic violation, but you should respect the uniform he wears. He represents the segment of our society that protects our persons and our property. Without them we would be in a bad way today.

This verse also raises the question of whether a Christian should go into politics or not. I believe that the individual Christian is free to go into politics, but I do not believe that the church should go into politics. If we would have a real moving of the Spirit of God, many of the men from our churches would go into these different offices in government today.

A good example of this is the Wesleyan movement in England. Wesley never tried to straighten out the king of England or even the Church of England. He just went out and preached the Word of God. Men were converted, among whom were men like William Wilberforce, the great philanthropist and abolitionist. They were men who had been gamblers and drunkards, with no concern for the poor, until they came to know Christ. These men started the great labor movement associated with the Wesleyan revival in England, which was the beginning of the movement against child labor and the protection of workmen on the job. We need individuals who will enter into government and take social action, but the church as an organization is not called upon to go into politics.

"To be ready to every good work." The church is to instruct individuals to be eager, to be anxious, and to learn to perform good works. We'll note this as we go along.

Now there is also a negative side to the exhortation:

To speak evil of no man, to be no brawlers, but gentle, shewing all meekness unto all men [Titus 3:2].

"Speak evil of no man" means we are to malign no one, and we are not to repeat gossip. It has been said that you can't *believe* everything you hear today, but you can *repeat* it! That is what he is talking about here—we are *not* to repeat what we hear. Many evil reports are passed from person to person without even a shred of evidence that the report is true. Another old saying is that some people will believe anything if it is *whispered* to them!

However, if the church has solid evidence that a member is doing something evil, that member should be named. You may remember

that Paul named certain men who were evil men: Phygellus and Hermogenes, Hymenaeus and Philetus, and Alexander the coppersmith. Then he also said that Demas had forsaken him, having loved this present world.

For we ourselves also were sometimes foolish, disobedient, deceived, serving divers lusts and pleasures, living in malice and envy, hateful, and hating one another [Titus 3:3].

This is a picture of the unsaved today, and a picture of you and me before we knew Christ. We were foolish, disobedient, deceived, enslaved to lusts and pleasures, living selfishly, and hating others. That is a picture of the lost world.

You can go to visit in non-Christian homes, and you will find these things. Go into any business, any office, any factory, and you will see these things present. Unfortunately, you can see some of these same things in our churches. There can be a pretense of loving, but under it there is envying and hating and gossiping. You can find churches divided into little cliques and groups; yet they boast about how sound they are in the faith. That is a disgrace to the cause of Christ. This is a picture of the unsaved given to us here. It ought never to be a picture of you or me as believers.

But after that the kindness and love of God our Saviour toward man appeared,

Not by works of righteousness which we have done, but according to his mercy he saved us, by the washing of regeneration, and renewing of the Holy Ghost [Titus 3:4–5].

"Not by works of righteousness which we have done." Verse 3 gave us a picture of how we were before we came to know Christ. It is important to understand that becoming a Christian doesn't mean just turning over a new leaf—you will find yourself writing on the new leaf the same things that you wrote on the old leaf. Making New Year's resolutions and promising to do better doesn't make you a Christian. Nor are you saved on the basis of works of righteousness, good deeds, which you have done.

"But according to his mercy he saved us." Because Christ died for us and paid the penalty for our sins, God is prepared to extend mercy to us; it is according to His *mercy* that He saved us. And He is *rich* in mercy, which means He has plenty of it. Whoever you are, He can save you today because Christ died for you. He paid the penalty and makes over to you His righteousness!

"By the washing of regeneration." "Washing" means *laver*—it is the laver of regeneration. In the Old Testament the laver, which stood in the court of the tabernacle and later the temple, represented this.

This washing of regeneration is what the Lord was speaking about in the third chapter of John: ". . .Except a man be born of water and of the Spirit, he cannot enter into the kingdom of God" (John 3:5). The water represents the Word of God—the Bible will *wash* you. It has a sanctifying power, a cleansing power. We are cleansed by the Word of God. The Holy Spirit uses the Word of God—"born of water and of the Spirit." That is the way we are born again.

"And renewing of the Holy Ghost"—He regenerates us.

Which he shed on us abundantly through Jesus Christ our Saviour [Titus 3:6].

Have you noticed that in everything God does there is a surplus? He is able to do exceeding abundantly above all that we ask or think.

That being justified by his grace, we should be made heirs according to the hope of eternal life [Titus 3:7].

"The hope of eternal life" is again pointing to the great hope of the believer, the coming of Christ for His church.

GOOD WORKS ARE PROFITABLE FOR THE PRESENT AND FUTURE

This is a faithful saying, and these things I will that thou affirm constantly, that they which have believed in God might be careful to maintain good works. These things are good and profitable unto men [Titus 3:8].

The fact that the believer is saved by the grace of God does not excuse him from performing good works. The fact of the matter is, he is to "be careful to maintain good works." Paul says that Titus should just keep affirming this constantly.

My friend, after you have been saved, God is going to talk to you about good works. Until that time, God is not even interested in your "good works" because what you call a good work, God calls dirty laundry. The righteousness of man is filthy rags in His sight (see Isa. 64:6). He doesn't want any of that. He wants to *save* you. If you do come to Him just as you

are, He will save you, because He has *done* something for you. He is not asking you to do something—what could you do for God? After you are saved, after you are a child of God, then He wants to talk to you about producing good works. He wants you to get involved in getting out the Word of God to others.

"Be *careful* to maintain good works." These are things that you should think about and consider; ponder, be anxious to be producing works for God.

But avoid foolish questions, and genealogies, and contentions, and strivings about the law; for they are unprofitable and vain [Titus 3:9].

We are to defend the faith, Paul says, but we are not to do it by argument or debate. That does no good; that never led anyone to the Lord. You may whip a man down intellectually by your arguments, but that does not touch his heart and win him for Christ. Stay away from foolish questions and genealogies and contentions.

That is the reason I do not develop certain subjects that are sensational. For example, during this period of time in which I am writing, demonism seems to be the topic of the hour. I have had any number of letters saying, "Dr. McGee, give a series on demonism. Write a book about it." Let's not get involved in that kind of thing. I would much rather tell you about the Holy Spirit who can indwell you. If He is in you, no demon could ever possess you! ". . . greater is he that is in you, than he that is in the world" (1 John 4:4). That is what we need to know. It is so easy to get sidetracked.

A man that is an heretic after the first and second admonition reject [Titus 3:10].

We have been asked to join in certain projects in which there are some heretics. I am not interested in being joined with anyone who has views that are in opposition to the Word of God. God tells us here to be separate from heretics. Just let them alone; reject them.

Knowing that he that is such is subverted, and sinneth, being condemned of himself [Titus 3:11].

The heretic is one who has turned aside from the truth.

When I shall send Artemas unto thee, or Tychicus, be diligent to come unto me to Nicopolis: for I have determined there to winter.

Bring Zenas the lawyer and Apollos on their journey diligently, that nothing be wanting unto them.

And let ours also learn to maintain good works for necessary uses, that they be not unfruitful [Titus 3:12–14].

Paul gives a final admonition about good works. We must "learn" to maintain good works. It's something that must be worked at. A great many people think it is easy; we need to know what God considers good works, and we need to *learn* how to do them.

Paul concludes this practical letter to Titus with a benediction.

All that are with me salute thee. Greet them that love us in the faith. Grace be with you all. Amen [Titus 3:15].

(For Bibliography to Titus, see Bibliography at the end of 2 Timothy.)

The Epistle to
PHILEMON
INTRODUCTION

This is one of the most remarkable epistles in the Scripture. It is only one chapter; so you may have trouble finding it. If you can find Titus, just keep on going; if you find Hebrews, you have gone too far.

The Epistles (letters) in the New Testament were a new form of revelation. Before them, God had used law, history, poetry, prophecy, and the gospel records. When God used the Epistles, He adopted a more personal and direct method. And there are different kinds of epistles. Some were directed to churches; some were directed to individuals and are rather intimate.

Frankly, I believe that Paul had no idea his letter to Philemon would be included in the canon of Scripture, and I think he would be a little embarrassed. Reading this epistle is like looking over the shoulder of Philemon and reading his personal mail. Paul wrote this letter to him personally. That does not detract from the inspiration and value of this epistle. The Holy Spirit has included it in the Scriptures for a very definite reason.

Behind this epistle there is a story, of course. Philemon lived in a place called Colossae. It was way up in the Phrygian country in the Anatolian section of what is Turkey today. No city is there today—just ruins. But it was a great city in Paul's day. One of Paul's epistles was written to the Colossian believers. There is no record that Paul ever visited Colossae, but since there are many things we do not know, I suspect that Paul did visit that city.

The story of this epistle was enacted on the black background of slavery. There were approximately sixty million slaves in the Roman Empire where the total population did not exceed one hundred twenty million. A slave was a chattel. He was treated worse than an enemy. He was subject to the whim of his master.

In Colossae was this very rich man who had come to a saving faith in Christ. He apparently had come down to Ephesus, as Paul was there for two years speaking in the school of Tyrannus every day, and people were coming in from all over that area to hear him. There were millions of people in Asia Minor, and Philemon was just one of the men who came to know the Lord Jesus.

Now Philemon owned slaves, and he had a slave named Onesimus. Onesimus took a chance one day, as any slave would have done, and made a run for it. He did what most runaway slaves apparently did—he moved into a great metropolis. This slave made it all the way to Rome. In that great population, he could be buried, as it were, and never be recognized.

One day, this man Onesimus, who had been a slave, found out that there was a slavery in freedom and there was a freedom in slavery. When he was a slave, he didn't worry about where he was going to sleep or what he was going to eat. His master had to take care of that. Now he has a real problem in Rome. I think he's homesick and maybe hungry. I can imagine him going down the street one day and seeing a group of people gathered around listening to a man. Onesimus wormed his way into the crowd, got up front, and saw that the man was in chains. Onesimus had run away from chains, and he thought he was free, but when he listened to that man—by the way, his name was Paul—he thought, *That man's free, and I'm still a slave—a slave to appetite, a slave to the economy. I'm still a slave, but that man, although he is chained, is free.*

Onesimus waited until the others had drifted away and then went up to Paul. He wanted to know more about what Paul was preaching, and Paul led him to Christ; that is, he presented the gospel to him, told him how Jesus had died for him and how He had been buried but rose again on the third day. He asked Onesimus to put his trust in Christ, and he did. Onesimus became a new creation in Christ Jesus.

Then Onesimus did what any man does who has been converted; he thought back on his past life and the things which were wrong that he wanted to make right. He said to Paul, "Paul, there is something I must confess to you. I'm a runaway slave." Paul asked him where he had come from, and Onesimus told Paul it was from Asia Minor, from the city of Colossae. Paul said, "There's a church over there. Who was your master?"

"My master was Philemon."

"You mean Philemon who lives on Main Street?"

"Yes."

"Why, he is one of my converts also. He owes me a great deal."

"Well, Paul, do you think I should go back to him?"

"Yes, you should. Onesimus, you must go back, but you are going to go back to a different situation. I will send a letter with you."

And we have his letter before us—the Epistle of Paul to Philemon.

In the human heart there has always been a great desire to be free. But right now there are millions of Americans who are slaves to alcohol. They are not free. They are alcoholics. Then there are those who are slaves to drugs. There are those who are slaves to the economy. There are slaves to the almighty dollar. We are living in a day when people pride themselves on being free. They think they are free, but the Lord Jesus said, "If the Son makes you free, then are you free indeed" (see John 8:36). You will not get arguments for or against slavery from this epistle. What you do learn is the freedom that is above all the slavery of this world. It is the freedom that every one of us wants to have.

OUTLINE

The *primary* purpose of this epistle is to reveal Christ's love for us in what He did for us in pleading our case before God. This is one of the finest illustrations of substitution. "If he hath wronged thee, or oweth thee aught, put that on mine account" (v. 18). We can hear Christ agreeing to take our place and to have all our sin imputed to Him. He took our place in death, but He gives us His place in life. "If thou count me therefore a partner, receive him as myself" (v. 17). We have the standing of Christ before God, or we have no standing at all. Onesimus, the unprofitable runaway slave, was to be received as Paul, the great apostle, would have been received in the home of Philemon.

The *practical* purpose is to teach brotherly love. Paul spoke of the new relationship between master and servant in the other Prison Epistles. Here he demonstrates how it should work. These men, belonging to two different classes in the Roman Empire, hating each other and hurting each other, are now brothers in Christ, and they are to act like it. This is the only solution to the problem of capital and labor.

GENIAL GREETING TO PHILEMON AND HIS FAMILY

Paul, a prisoner of Jesus Christ, and Timothy our brother, unto Philemon our dearly beloved, and fellow-labourer [Philem. 1].

Paul does not mention the fact that he is an apostle. When he was writing to the churches, he gave his official title: an apostle of Jesus Christ. But this is a personal letter to a personal friend. He doesn't need to defend his apostleship. He intended for this to be very personal, and I think he would really be surprised to know it can be read by the whole world.

"Paul, a prisoner of Jesus Christ." I have noticed that several of the commentaries try to change this and explain it away by teaching that Paul really meant that he was a prisoner because he was preaching the gospel of Jesus Christ. But that is not what Paul said, and Paul had the ability of saying exactly what he had in mind. He was using the Greek language, which is a very flexible, versatile language. He said he was a prisoner of Jesus Christ.

If we had been there we might have had a conversation with Paul like this:

"Poor Paul, it's too bad these Romans put you in jail."

"They didn't put me in jail."

"Oh, we know what you mean. Those hateful religious rulers brought a charge against you."

"They didn't put me in jail either."

"Who put you in jail, then?"

"Jesus Christ. I'm *His* prisoner."

"You mean to tell me that you would serve Someone who would put you in prison?"

"Yes, when it's His will for me to be in prison, I'm in prison. When it's His will for me to be out of prison, I'll be out of prison. When it's His will for me to be sick, I'm going to be sick. I belong to Him. Since I belong to Him, I have learned to be content in whatsoever state I am in. Everything is all right. Don't worry about me."

Obviously, the letter to Philemon is one of the Prison Epistles. It goes along with Ephesians, Philippians, and Colossians.

"And Timothy our brother" is really "and Timothy *the* brother." That means he is not only Philemon's brother and Paul's brother, but he is *your* brother if you are a Christian. We all are brothers in Christ.

"Unto Philemon our dearly beloved." Does that sound as if Paul is really buttering him up? I think so. But he loved this man, and he is going to make a request of him.

And to our beloved Apphia, and Archippus our fellow-soldier, and to the church in thy house [Philem. 2].

"And to our beloved Apphia." She apparently was the wife of Philemon. While *Philemon* is a Greek name, and he was a citizen of Colossae, *Apphia* is a Phrygian name. That would suggest to me that a young businessman by the name of Philemon went into new territory. He didn't go west as a young man; he went east—way up on the frontier. He got into business in Colossae and became a wealthy man there. He met and married a Phrygian girl named Apphia. They both now have become Christians. Isn't that lovely?

"And Archippus our fellow-soldier." I would assume this is their son. He is not a soldier of the Roman army, but a soldier in the army of Jesus Christ. Paul had written elsewhere that we all are to be good soldiers of Jesus Christ.

"And to the church in thy house." Not only had they been converted, but they had a church in their house. Let's think about this for a moment. The church building has become so all-important to people today that it is all out of relationship to the real purpose of the local church. The local church in Paul's day wasn't down on the corner in a separate building—they didn't have any building. There were the great temples to the pagan gods, but the early church didn't have buildings; they met in homes. It is estimated that for two hundred years the church met in homes.

The great cathedrals of the past were actually never meant for public meetings. Westminster Abbey in England, for example, was never intended for public services. It was built in the shape of a cross as a monument to Jesus Christ. Although I think they had the wrong idea—instead of spending all that money on a cathedral, they should have used it to send out missionaries—that was their way of expressing their devotion. The idea of putting the emphasis on a building and on a building program is a little out of line with the example of the early church.

> **Grace to you, and peace, from God our Father and the Lord Jesus Christ [Philem. 3].**

This is the usual greeting of Paul to every person and every church to which he wrote.

GOOD REPUTATION OF PHILEMON

> **I thank my God, making mention of thee always in my prayers [Philem. 4].**

Here is a man for whom Paul prayed. If you are writing out a prayer list of the apostle Paul, be sure to put Philemon on that list. The thought here is that every time Philemon's name was mentioned, Paul prayed for him. This would indicate that Philemon was a rather prominent person.

> **Hearing of thy love and faith, which thou hast toward the Lord Jesus, and toward all saints [Philem. 5].**

The life of Philemon was a testimony. Paul describes it in a lovely way. He showed love toward the Lord Jesus and toward other believers. His faith was toward the Lord Jesus, and he was faithful to other believers. That is interesting.

> **That the communication of thy faith may become effectual by the acknowledging of every good thing which is in you in Christ Jesus [Philem. 6].**

His faith was shared. The life of Philemon was a testimony. "Every good thing" was the re-

sult of the fact that ". . . it is God which worketh in you both to will and to do of his good pleasure" (Phil. 2:13).

> **For we have great joy and consolation in thy love, because the bowels of the saints are refreshed by thee, brother [Philem. 7].**

Paul had great joy and consolation in the love of Philemon for other believers and for him.

"Bowels" or *heart* implies the entire psychological nature. It is the inner life of the believers that had great satisfaction through him.

There are many wonderful Christians across this land whom I have had the privilege of meeting, of being in their homes, and of having fellowship with them. That has been one of the greatest joys of my ministry. Philemon was the kind of person who would have entertained evangelists and conference speakers in his home. He was a marvelous individual.

GRACIOUS PLEA FOR ONESIMUS

> **Wherefore, though I might be much bold in Christ to enjoin thee that which is convenient,**

> **Yet for love's sake I rather beseech thee, being such an one as Paul the aged, and now also a prisoner of Jesus Christ [Philem. 8–9].**

Paul is making a gracious plea for Onesimus. He is coming to the purpose of his letter. He approaches his subject diplomatically and cautiously and lovingly. He is going to make his request to Onesimus on a threefold basis:

"For love's sake." This is the love of Paul and Philemon for each other as believers in Christ Jesus.

"Being such an one as Paul the aged." Paul was only in his sixties, but he was an old man. He had suffered and had been persecuted as a missionary for Christ. This had aged him. Paul says to Philemon, "You know that I am an old man now."

"A prisoner of Jesus Christ." It is evident that he could not come to Philemon in person.

> **I beseech thee for my son Onesimus, whom I have begotten in my bonds [Philem. 10].**

Paul is pleading on behalf of his son. Paul was not married, but he had many sons. He calls Timothy and Titus his sons, and now Onesimus. These are his spiritual sons. He had led Onesimus to the Lord even though he himself was a prisoner at the time.

Which in time past was to thee unprofitable, but now profitable to thee and to me [Philem. 11].

The name *Onesimus* means "profitable." Paul really has a play on words here that is tremendous. He is good at that, by the way. Since his name literally means profitable, Paul is saying, "When you had Profitable, you didn't have Profitable. Now that you don't have Profitable, you do have Profitable." You see, as a slave Onesimus wasn't very useful. He didn't work because he wanted to work. His heart wasn't in it, and I guess I can't blame him for that. But now Paul is sending him back to Philemon as a believer, and he says, "He is going to be profitable to you now. However, I don't want him to be received as a slave."

Whom I have sent again: thou therefore receive him, that is, mine own bowels:

Whom I would have retained with me, that in thy stead he might have ministered unto me in the bonds of the gospel [Philem. 12–13].

Paul is asking Philemon to receive Onesimus just as if he were receiving Paul. Now Paul admits that he would have liked to have kept Onesimus. I'm sure Paul would say, "My first thought was that this man knows how to serve, and I need somebody. I am here in prison, old and sick and cold. This fellow could help me. My first thought was to keep him here and just let you know that I have him here with me." But Paul couldn't do that. He says—

But without thy mind would I do nothing; that thy benefit should not be as it were of necessity, but willingly [Philem. 14].

Paul is saying, "I wouldn't keep Onesimus because that wouldn't be right—although I thought of it. If you willingly want to send him back to me, that will be all right." Did Philemon send Onesimus back to Paul? Again, that is something we do not know. I think he did. I would imagine that on the next boat going to Rome, there was Onesimus with a lot of things to add to Paul's comfort.

For perhaps he therefore departed for a season, that thou shouldest receive him for ever;

Not now as a servant, but above a servant, a brother beloved, specially to me, but how much more unto thee, both in the flesh, and in the Lord? [Philem. 15–16].

Since Onesimus has become a believer, his status and relationship to Philemon are different. He is still a slave according to the Roman law, but he is more than that to Philemon. He is now a beloved brother.

GUILTLESS SUBSTITUTES FOR GUILTY

This verse, together with the next verse, gives us one of the grandest illustrations of full substitution and imputation. Behind Paul's plea is Christ's plea to the Father on behalf of the sinner who trusts Christ as the Savior. That sinner is received on the same standing that Christ is received. In other words, the saved sinner has as much right in heaven as Christ has, for he has *His* right to be there. We are accepted in the beloved (see Eph. 1:6).

If thou count me therefore a partner, receive him as myself [Philem. 17].

"Since you count me as a partner, I want you to receive him just like you would receive me. You always put me up in that guest room. Don't send him out in the cold; put him up in the guest room."

GLORIOUS ILLUSTRATION OF IMPUTATION

If he hath wronged thee, or oweth thee aught, put that on mine account [Philem. 18].

We think that the credit card is something new in our day. We can buy almost anything with a credit card—from a gallon of gas to a chain of motels. Credit cards are used so much that one restaurant posted the sign: "We take money too."

Paul also had a credit card. He had a credit card because he was a believer in Christ. Paul says, "Look, if Onesimus stole something from you or did something wrong, just put it on my account. Put it on my credit card."

All of this is a glorious picture. When I come to God the Father for salvation, I can hear the Lord Jesus Christ say, "If Vernon McGee has wronged Thee or oweth Thee anything, put that on My account." Christ on the cross paid the penalty for my sins. But that isn't all. I am sure that God the Father would say, "That fellow Vernon McGee is not fit for heaven."

Then the Lord Jesus would say, "If Thou count Me therefore a partner, receive Vernon McGee as Myself." That is what it means to be in Christ—accepted in the Beloved. Oh, what a picture this is of the way God the Father and the Lord Jesus Christ accept you and accept me. That makes this a very precious epistle.

GENERAL AND PERSONAL ITEMS AND REQUESTS

I Paul have written it with mine own hand, I will repay it: albeit I do not say to thee how thou owest unto me even thine own self besides [Philem. 19].

"I Paul have written it with mine own hand, I will repay it." The Lord Jesus Christ gave His life and shed His blood to pay our entire debt of sin.

"Albeit I do not say to thee how thou owest unto me even thine own self besides." Paul had led Philemon to the Lord. How could he ever repay Paul for that?

Yea, brother, let me have joy of thee in the Lord: refresh my bowels in the Lord [Philem. 20].

Paul is pleading for Onesimus.

Having confidence in thy obedience I wrote unto thee, knowing that thou wilt also do more than I say [Philem. 21].

As you can see, this is a personal letter, and in a sense we are reading it over the shoulder of Philemon. Paul expresses his confidence in him and actually feels that Philemon will do more than he requests.

It is characteristic of real believers to do more than is requested. Jesus asks us to go the second mile. Maybe the reason that some of us are so poor today is that we have been stingy with the Lord. The Lord is a generous Lord. We should be generous people.

But withal prepare me also a lodging: for I trust that through your prayers I shall be given unto you [Philem. 22].

Paul expects to be released from prison. He requests prayers for that purpose. Since this letter was probably written during Paul's first confinement in Rome, he was released and probably visited Philemon personally.

There salute thee Epaphras, my fellow-prisoner in Christ Jesus;

Marcus, Aristarchus, Demas, Lucas, my fellow-labourers.

The grace of our Lord Jesus Christ be with your spirit. Amen [Philem. 23–25].

This beautiful little letter concludes with personal greetings to mutual friends.

(For Bibliography to Philemon, see Bibliography at the end of 2 Timothy.)

The Epistle to the
HEBREWS
INTRODUCTION

The Epistle to the Hebrews is of such importance that I rank it beside the Epistle to the Romans (which is excelled by no other book). I have wondered how to give this magnificent Epistle to the Hebrews the introduction it deserves. Before me are excellent expository works that other men have written, and I have decided to let four of them introduce this epistle to the Hebrews to you, since each of them makes statements that are all-important. They have said what I would like to say. First I will quote from G. Campbell Morgan's book, *God's Last Word to Man:*

The letter to the Hebrews has an especial value today because there is abroad a very widespread conception of Christ which is lower than that of the New Testament. To illustrate what I mean by this, a recent writer has said:

"One of the best things we can say about human nature is this, that whenever a situation occurs which can only be solved by an individual 'laying down his life for his friends,' some heroic person is certain to come forth, sooner or later, and offer himself as the victim—a Curtius to leap into the gulf, a Socrates to drink the hemlock, a Christ to get himself crucified on Calvary."

I am not proposing to discuss that at any length, but at once say that to place Christ in that connection is to me little short of blasphemy. We may properly speak of "a Curtius," "a Socrates," but when we speak of "a Christ," our reference to Him is not only out of harmony with the New Testament presentation, but implicitly a contradiction of what it declares concerning the uniqueness of His Person.

This is a tremendous beginning for the Epistle to the Hebrews.

Dr. William Pettingill, in his book *Into the Holiest: Simple Studies in Hebrews*, has a different emphasis in his opening statement:

From Adam to Moses, through 2500 years, and from Moses to Malachi, through 1100 years, the prophets were speaking for God to man. But at the end of the 3600 years their revelation of God was only partial. Then after a silence of 400 years, when the fulness of the time was come, God sent forth His Son, and in that Son the revelation of God is perfect.

That is another tremendous statement.

Now I'm going to give a third introduction to the Epistle to the Hebrews. It comes from the excellent book by E. Schuyler English, *Studies in The Epistle to the Hebrews:*

The Epistle to the Hebrews, one of the most important books of the New Testament in that it contains some of the chief doctrines of the Christian faith, is, as well, a book of infinite logic and great beauty. To read it is to breathe the atmosphere of heaven itself. To study it is to partake of strong spiritual meat. To abide in its teachings is to be led from immaturity to maturity in the knowledge of Christian truth and of Christ Himself. It is to "go on unto perfection."

And here is a further statement:

The theme of the Epistle to the Hebrews, the only book of the New Testament in which our Lord is presented in His high priestly office, is the supreme glory of Christ, the Son of God and Son of man.

This is tremendous!

Now I turn to the fourth author, Sir Robert Anderson, and quote from his book, *The Hebrews Epistle in the Light of the Types*. As we go through this epistle I trust I shall be able to emphasize this which he emphasizes so well, and I also trust that this introduction will clarify the thought:

That the professing Church on earth is "the true vine"—this is the daring and impious lie of the apostasy. That it is "the olive tree" is a delusion shared by the mass of Christians in the churches of the Reformation. But the teaching of Scripture is explicit, that Christ Himself is the vine, and Israel the olive. For "God hath NOT cast away His people whom He foreknew."

This Epistle to the Hebrews was not accepted by the Western church for a long time, and the reason is found at this particular juncture: the church wanted to usurp the place of Israel. They adopted all the promises God had made to Israel and spiritualized them, applying them to themselves and rejecting God's purposes in the nation Israel. As a result, you'll find that the church in those early days became actually anti-Semitic and persecuted the Jew! Therefore, to say that God is through with the nation Israel is a sad blunder, and I trust that this epistle may be helpful in our understanding the great truth that a Hebrew is a Hebrew, and when he becomes a Christian, he is still a Hebrew. When any person becomes a child of God, it does not change his nationality at all, but it brings him into a new body of believers called the church. Today God is calling out of both Jews and Gentiles a people for His name. When that is consummated, God will take His church out of the world, and He will pursue His purpose with the nation Israel, fulfilling all of His promises to them and through them to the gentile world in that day. I am indebted to these four wonderful expositors of the Word of God for helping us to get on the springboard so that we can plunge into the water of the Word.

The human author of the Epistle to the Hebrews has always been a moot question. Although the Authorized Version has the heading, "Epistle of Paul the Apostle to the Hebrews," there is still a question as to authorship. The Revised Version and other later versions correct this and simply entitle it the Epistle (or letter) to the Hebrews. If you are acquainted with the literature of the Scriptures, you recognize that there is no unanimity of thought and no agreement as to who is the author of this epistle. When I was a seminary student, I wrote a thesis on the authorship of Hebrews, and I attempted to sustain the position that the apostle Paul is the author.

When I wrote my thesis I thought I had solved the problem and that the world would be in agreement that Paul wrote Hebrews! But I find that there is just as much disagreement today about the authorship as there was before I wrote my thesis! Neither John Calvin nor Martin Luther accepted Paul's authorship, and neither did many others of the past. On the other hand, many do accept Paul as the author. However, the human author is not the important thing, but the fact that the Epistle to the Hebrews is part of God's inspired Word is important.

In spite of the fact that the Pauline authorship cannot be stated in a dogmatic fashion, there is abundant evidence that Paul was the author. Both internal and external evidence support the authorship of Paul. The writer had been in bonds (see Heb. 10:34). He wrote from Italy (see Heb. 13:24). His companion was Timothy (see Heb. 13:23). The writing is Pauline. Also, in my opinion, Peter identifies Paul as the writer (see 2 Pet. 3:15–16). I believe that there is good and sufficient reason for Paul's changing his style and for not giving his name in the epistle. I'll call attention to these things as we go along. (See the Appendix for a full treatment of the subject of authorship.)

The date of writing is particularly important in the case of the Epistle to the Hebrews because of the authorship question. Many scholars, even sound scholars, have taken the position that it was written after A.D. 70. Some give the date of A.D. 85, A.D. 96, and others up in the 90s. However, as you read this epistle, you are forced to the conclusion that the temple at Jerusalem was still standing at the time it was written. This means it had to have been written before A.D. 70, since Titus the Roman destroyed the temple in A.D. 70 and Paul had already gone to be with the Lord. I believe that it was written by the apostle Paul and it was written before A.D. 70.

Coleridge said that Romans revealed the *necessity* of the Christian faith but that Hebrews revealed the *superiority* of the Christian faith. This thought, running all the way through, is expressed in the use of the comparative word *better*, which occurs thirteen times. The Epistle to the Hebrews tells us that the Law was good, but that grace, under Christ, is better and that the glory that is coming is going to be the best. The Epistle to the Hebrews presents that which is better. The word *perfect* occurs fifteen times (with cognate words). It is an epistle that challenges us. *Let us* occurs thirteen times, and *let* occurs five times.

Two verses especially convey to us this "better" way: "Wherefore, holy brethren, partakers of the heavenly calling, consider the Apostle and High Priest of our profession, Christ Jesus" (Heb. 3:1). We are to *consider* Him. Then in Hebrews 12:3 we read the challenge: "For consider him that endured such contradiction of sinners against himself, lest ye be wearied and faint in your minds." That is exactly what we are going to do as we study the Epistle to the Hebrews. We are going to *consider* Him, the Lord Jesus Christ. I am convinced that that is the most important thing which any Christian can do.

OUTLINE

CHAPTER 1

THEME: Christ is superior to the prophets; Christ is superior to angels

The first section in this epistle is *doctrinal*. The first ten chapters reveal that Christ is better than the Old Testament economy. The second and last section of this epistle is *practical*, showing that Christ brings better benefits and duties. By the way, this is a pattern that the apostle Paul follows in his other epistles; that is, the doctrinal side and then the practical side. In my opinion, there is an abundance of evidence that Paul did write this epistle to the Hebrews.

Although I cannot be dogmatic about the authorship of Hebrews, I can say very dogmatically that we are dealing with the Word of God—that which the Spirit of God has given to us. Because the Holy Spirit is unquestionably the author of this epistle, the human writer and the dating are secondary. The Epistle to the Hebrews is one of the greatest epistles we have in the Word of God. It is not pious cant when I say that I do not feel worthy or competent to deal with this great epistle. This is the reason I let four outstanding expositors introduce the epistle for me. From four different viewpoints each one came to this one point of emphasizing the person of Jesus Christ. Therefore I claim the promise of the Lord Jesus when He said that when the Spirit of God would come He would take the things of Christ and show them unto us (see John 16:12–15.)

We need to keep in mind that this epistle is directed to Hebrew believers who stood at the juncture of two great dispensations. The dispensation of law had come to an end. The sacrifices in the temple that had once been so meaningful were now meaningless. What God had before required was now actually *sin* for a believer to practice, as this epistle will make very clear. The Epistle to the Hebrews is addressed to Hebrew believers, although its teachings are for believers of every race in every age. It is very meaningful to you and to me today. However, we do need to keep in mind that it was written to and for Hebrew believers. For example, to say that Christ is superior to the prophets would be especially meaningful to a Hebrew.

CHRIST IS SUPERIOR TO THE PROPHETS

God, who at sundry times and in divers [diverse] manners spake in time past unto the fathers by the prophets [Heb. 1:1].

You will notice that this verse and this book begin with the word *God*. There are certain premises upon which this book rests. When you study geometry, there are certain axioms with which you must begin, and if you don't, you won't begin at all. If two plus two does not equal four, then you are at sea as far as mathematics is concerned. A straight line is the shortest distance between two points; that is a proven fact, and it is accepted. When that fact is established, you can move on and prove something else. In the Book of Hebrews, as in the Book of Genesis, no attempt is made to prove God's existence. Both books *assume* that there is a God. The Bible makes no effort to try to prove the existence of God. There are courses in seminaries today that try to build up some philosophic system by which the existence of God can be proven. I have been through courses like that, and I know what I'm talking about when I say it is a great waste of time. There is something wrong with you if you can't walk out and look up at the mountains, or go down to the seashore and look at the sea, or look up into the heavens, and recognize that there is a Creator. "The heavens declare the glory of God; and the firmament sheweth his handiwork" (Ps. 19:1). My friend, if the created universe is not saying something to you about a Creator, there is something radically wrong with your thinking. As a young fellow said to me about an atheist, "Dr. McGee, he isn't dealing with a full deck!" It is the fool who has said in his heart that there is no God (see Ps. 14:1).

The second assumption we find in Hebrews 1:1 is that God has spoken. Realizing that God is an intelligent Person and that He has given mankind a certain degree of intelligence, if we didn't already have a revelation from Him, I would suggest that we wait for it. It is only logical that the Creator would get a message through to us. Well, my friend, He *has* communicated with us. And the revelation that we have is the inspired Word of God. The first verse of Hebrews assumes that the Scriptures we have are divinely inspired. The revelation to which he refers is the revelation of the Old Testament as we have it today.

There are those who feel that Paul did not write the Book of Hebrews because it was written in such magnificent Greek. It was written by one who was a master of the Greek language. There is a smoothness and beauty in it that we miss in the English translation. Right at the beginning of this book there is a play upon two words. The word for "sundry times" in the Greek is *polumerōs*, and the word for "divers manners" is *polutropōs*. Notice the beauty of that—*polumerōs* and *polutropōs*. It is almost poetic—it sounds like Homer. But there is more than beauty; it is a tremendous statement.

"Sundry times" does not speak of time as we think of it. The emphasis is that God spoke through Moses, but before that He spoke to Abraham. He apparently spoke to Abraham through dreams and by sending the angel of the Lord to him, but when He spoke to Abraham He did not tell him what He told Moses. God didn't say anything at all to Abraham about the Law. He did not give him the Ten Commandments, but later God did give the Ten Commandments to Moses. Even later on He told David that a king would be coming in his line who would be a Savior. And when David was an old man, he said that there was a king coming in his line who would be *his* Savior. God did not give that information to Moses, and He did not give it to Abraham. In fact, God gave Moses a law that Israel was not to have an earthly king because God would be their king. God, however, knew the human heart, and in time Israel wanted to be like the other nations round about them and have a human king. It was marvelous how God moved in a time like that. He granted their request, although He sent leanness to their souls. He used that as the method of getting the Messiah, the Savior, into the world. This first verse is telling us that God did not give all of His truth to Abraham, but added to it as He dealt with different men through the years. And in the fullness of time God sent forth His Son. There is a development of the truth in the Bible.

"Divers [diverse] manners" means that God used different ways of communicating. He appeared in dreams to Abraham, but He gave Moses the Law. Later on He made certain promises to Joshua. He spoke through dreams, He spoke through the Law, He spoke through the types, He spoke through ritual, He spoke through history, He spoke through poetry, and He spoke through prophecy. He used all these different ways over a long period of time, using about forty-five writers and communicating His Word over a period of about fifteen hundred years. The writer to the Hebrews is saying something quite wonderful to us at this point.

Have you ever stopped to think that the multiplicity of writers in and of itself makes the Bible a remarkable book? Shakespeare's writing was great on the human plane, but Shakespeare was the only author of his works. He didn't wait for a modern Hollywood writer to write any of his plays. (In fact, the Hollywood writers wreck Shakespeare's plays!) On the other hand, God used many human writers to write the Bible. He used men with different backgrounds and different abilities. One of them, Simon Peter, did not do so well with the Greek language, but I am not going to criticize him because I had nine years of Greek and I do much worse with it than Simon Peter did. But God used Peter, nevertheless. The writer of the Epistle to the Hebrews (and I believe it was Paul) was a master of the Greek language. When Paul wrote to the Galatians and to the Corinthians, he got right down where the rubber meets the road. He used the language that they used down on the waterfront, and Paul had been down on the waterfront because He traveled a great deal by boat. But his letter to the Hebrews is a work of art.

Oh, this epistle opens on a grand scale: "God!" There is nothing before it to try to prove He exists. If you deny the existence of God, the problem is with you, not with God. So many little men who carry a Ph.D. degree deny that God exists. My thought is, *Who are they*? Put one of those puny, little minds down by the side of God and it becomes obvious why God did not waste His time proving who He is. If any person is going to come to God, that person must first believe that God is.

"Spake in time past unto the fathers." Who are the fathers mentioned in this verse? They are Abraham, Isaac, Jacob, Joshua, Moses, David, Isaiah, etc. These are *the* fathers, but they are not *my* fathers—and they may not be your fathers either. Obviously this is being written to people who could call Abraham, Isaac, and Jacob their fathers, which is the reason it is called the Epistle to the *Hebrews*. Nevertheless, He is God of the Gentiles also, and we can be thankful for that!

"Spake in time past unto the fathers by the prophets." A prophet is one who speaks for God, and in the order of speaking for God he could speak of things that were in the future. God spoke through many men who were prophets, and they were tremendous men with tremendous messages. It took all of them put together to give us the Old Testament, but the best that could be said is that they gave merely a partial revelation.

But now we will see that God has spoken finally, completely, adequately, and assuredly in His Son—

Hath in these last days spoken unto us by his Son, whom he hath appointed heir of all things, by whom also he made the worlds [Heb. 1:2].

Now God has spoken finally through His Son—literally, "spoke to us *in* Son." Or, as Dr. Westcott put it, "God spoke to us in one who has the character that He is a Son." God has spoken through His Son. If He spoke out of heaven at this moment, He would repeat something which He has already said, because, my friend, we have the last word from God to this world in Jesus Christ.

"Hath in these last days spoken unto us." The word *us* is very important, referring to the same ones to whom He spoke through the prophets in Old Testament times—Hebrew believers. You remember that the Father spoke out of heaven saying, ". . . This is my beloved Son, in whom I am well pleased; hear ye him" (Matt. 17:5). Since the Father has given His final word in the Lord Jesus Christ, it is the final word for you and me also. The Son is the One who is before us.

"Spoken unto us by his Son." Therefore Christ is superior to all of the Old Testament writers, because the revelation is filled up in Him. He fulfills all of the Old Testament, and He Himself gives God's final word to man. As Christ Jesus said when He was here over nineteen hundred years ago, ". . . he [the Holy Spirit] shall take of mine, and shall shew it unto you" (John 16:15), so that the Spirit of God, speaking through John and James and Dr. Luke and Paul and Peter and the other writers of the New Testament, has given us the full revelation from God.

Now we are shown the superiority of the Son in seven matchless statements. None of us, I am sure, feel that we can comprehend any one of them completely.

"Whom he hath appointed heir of all things." The Lord Jesus Christ is heir of all things. Now this raises a question. In John 1:3 we read, "All things were made by him; and without him was not any thing made that was made." Creation is His, for He created it, we are told. It belongs to Him already, so how can He be the *heir* of all things? Well, He came to earth and took upon Himself our humanity. The first man in the human race was given dominion over this creation. We do not empha-

size this enough, because in Genesis tremendous statements are made in just a few words. Once, when we took a group to Israel, we had an Israeli Christian speak to us. When he came to the end of his message, he wanted to give an illustration, and he said, "I want to say this to you in little words." What he meant was *a few* words; he intended to make it brief. That is the way Moses wrote the first eleven chapters of Genesis—with "little words." He made it brief. When God says He gave man dominion over all the earth (see Gen. 1:26), He did not make him sort of a first class gardener to set out rose bushes and prune the plum trees. That is not what Adam did. Adam had *dominion*. Dominion has to do with rulership. All creation was under him. I believe that when Adam wanted more moisture over on the west forty, he needed only to call for it. When he wanted the heat turned on, he could turn it on. I think he controlled this earth; but when he sinned, he lost that control.

When the Lord Jesus came to this earth, He became a man. He performed miracles in every realm. He had control of the human body. He had control of nature—He could still storms, and He could feed five thousand people. He recovered what Adam had lost. The Lord Jesus is going to be *heir* of all things, and we are told in Scripture that we are heirs of God. Romans 8:16–17 tells us, "The Spirit itself beareth witness with our spirit, that we are the children of God: And if children, then heirs; heirs of God, and joint-heirs with Christ. . . ." *Joint-heirs* is an interesting word. It does not mean *equal* heirs. Let me illustrate that. Some folk have been very interested in our radio program and have given us wonderful support. They will mention us in their will. Sometimes we are mentioned as a joint-heir in the will, and sometimes we are mentioned as an equal heir. For example, a will might read, "I want so much to go to such and such a cause and so much to go to the Thru the Bible Radio Network." That makes us an equal heir with someone else. When an inheritance is left to us like this, we are free to do whatever we want to with it. But when we are a joint-heir in a will, it means that somebody else has the control of the inheritance, and they allocate just so much out to each one at the proper time; they manage the estate. Well, the Lord Jesus Christ is the heir, and we are just the joint-heirs. He will be in control, and He may put you or me in charge of a little something in the universe. In that way we are joint-heirs with Christ—we have an inheritance that is incorruptible, undefiled, unfading, and it is reserved in heaven for us. We have this inheritance because of the many wonderful things the Lord has done for us. He recovered what Adam lost, and even more than that, He has made us joint-heirs with Himself. Christ is the One who is going to inherit everything. As far as we know, no prophet in the Old Testament was ever promised anything like that. You see, the writer of this epistle is showing us that Christ is superior to the prophets.

"By whom also he made the worlds." Many people believe this refers to the creative act— "In the beginning God created the heaven and the earth" (Gen. 1:1). Actually, it does not refer to that at all. The Greek word here for "worlds" is *aiōn*. It means "ages"—"by whom He made the ages." This goes beyond His being the Creator. This lends purpose to everything. He is the heir who gives the program for the future. He made the ages, giving purpose for everything. Not only did He create everything, He did it for a purpose.

The Bible makes sense. God had a reason for the things He did, and He has a reason today for the things He continues to do.

For example, God created man and put him in a garden. He put down one condition for living there: Man was not to eat the fruit from a certain tree. There was nothing wrong with the fruit; it was God's test to that man to see if he would obey Him. (The problem was not the fruit on the tree; it was the pair on the ground!) Man absolutely and completely failed God's test at that time.

God has a program and purpose in everything. There came other periods when God tested man. The time came when He gave man the Mosaic Law. It, again, was a test of man's obedience. Today you and I live under grace. We are saved by grace; we could never be saved by the Law. Firstly, it wasn't given to us in this age, and, secondly, we couldn't keep it. We cannot measure up to the righteous standard that God has set. It ought to be quite obvious to every person that God cannot save us by works. He cannot save us by perfect works because we cannot produce perfection; neither can He save us by imperfect works because His standard is higher than that. Therefore God had to have another way, and today it is by grace that we are saved.

The Lord Jesus Christ is the Creator of this universe, and there is purpose to it. Abroad today is the idiotic notion that the universe is running at breakneck speed through time and space like a car that has lost the driver. The interesting thing is that when a car loses the driver there is a wreck, but this universe, even according to the scientists, has been running millions of years, and it has been doing pretty well, by the way. The sun comes up at a certain time every morning; it is very precise. The moon stays in a predictable orbit. As one of the men who works on the moon modules says, all they have to do is aim, and the moon will be there when the module gets there. You can always depend upon the moon. It is not running wild. The moon doesn't head in another direction when it sees a module coming toward it. The movement of the moon is absolutely predictable. This is not a mad universe in which you and I live. It has purpose, and the Lord Jesus is the One who gives it purpose.

Who being the brightness of his glory, and the express image of his person, and upholding all things by the word of his power, when he had by himself purged our sins, sat down on the right hand of the Majesty on high [Heb. 1:3].

What tremendous statements we have here!

"Who being the brightness of his glory." *Brightness* means "the outshining"; it means "the effulgence." The material sun out in space gives us a good illustration of this. We could never know the glory of the sun by looking at it because we can't look at it directly—it would blind us if we tried. But from the rays of the sun we get light and we get heat, and probably we get healing from it. That is the way we know about the sun. Now in somewhat the same way we would know very little about God apart from the revelation that God has given in His Son. The Lord Jesus Christ is the brightness we see. No one has seen God, but we know about Him now through Jesus Christ. Just as the rays of the sun with their warmth and light tell me about the physical sun, so the Lord Jesus reveals God to us today.

"The express image of his person." That word "express image" is the Greek *charaktēr*, the impressed character, like a steel engraving. We get our English word *character* from this. We say that the Lord Jesus Christ is the revelation of God because He *is* God. He is not just the printed material; He is the steel engraving of God because He is the exact copy, the image of God. Paul said in Colossians 2:9, ". . . in him dwelleth all the fulness of the Godhead bodily." How wonderful He is!

"Upholding all things by the word of his power." That little baby Jesus lying helplessly on the bosom of Mary in Bethlehem could have spoken this universe out of existence. He upholds all things by the word of His power. He not only created all things by His word, but He holds everything together.

Have you ever stopped to think about the amount of power that is required to hold it together? Man has learned very little about that power, but he has learned something. For instance, man has discovered the atom, a little bitty fellow. And when man untied the atom (they call it splitting the atom), he sure did release a lot of power. Who put all that power in the atom? Who holds all the little atoms together? The Lord Jesus Christ. He furnishes the program and the purpose; He is the person of God, and He is the preserver of all things. He not only created the universe by His word, but He holds everything together. If He let go today—well, since you and I are held on this earth by His glue, His stick'em, which we call gravitation—we would go flying out into space. He holds everything together. This universe would come unglued without His constant supervision and power. He is not like an Atlas holding up the earth passively, He is actively engaged in maintaining all of creation. As far as I can see, that is greater than creating it in the beginning. He keeps the thing running, keeps it functioning. This is one of the tremendous things He is doing today.

"When he had by himself purged our sins." The Lord Jesus Christ provided the cleansing for our sins. This, by the way, is the only purgatory mentioned in the Bible. He went through it for you and me; there is no purgatory for anyone who trusts Christ because He purged our sins. He has paid the penalty for them. How wonderful He is! The purging was accomplished by what He did on Calvary for you and for me. And today we are accepted in the Beloved. The one who comes to Christ receives a full redemption and complete forgiveness of sins.

"Sat down on the right hand of the Majesty on high." This actually is the message of Hebrews. The Lord Jesus received a glory and a majesty when He went back to the Father's throne that He never had before. There is something in heaven today that was not there twenty-five hundred years ago or in eternity past, because in the glory now is the man with nail-pierced hands and the prints of nails in His feet and a spear wound in His side. Even in His glorified body they are there, and when we see Him, we shall know Him by the prints of the nails in His hands. Twenty-five hundred years ago He was God, but today He is the God-man.

"Sat down" does not indicate that He is resting because He is tired—or that He is doing nothing. It means that when He finished our redemption, He sat down because it was complete. This is exactly what the seventh day meant in creation—God rested on the seventh day. Was He tired? No. As John Wesley said, when He created the universe He didn't half try. He rested because it was complete; there was nothing more that He needed to do.

Never, since I have been a pastor, have I been able to close my desk and go home with the satisfaction that everything has been done. There is always something incomplete—you should see my desk right now! My work is never complete, but Christ sat down because His work of redemption was complete. Friend, you cannot lift your little finger today to add to the redemption He wrought for us on the cross. He has completed our redemption, and we are complete in Christ. In Colossians 2:9–10 we are told, "For in him dwelleth all the fulness of the Godhead bodily. And ye are complete in him, which is the head of all principality and power." We are made complete in Him, made full in Him, and we are accepted in the Beloved.

The present ministry of Christ is another aspect of this. This, I think, was in the mind of the writer who said, "There is a man in the glory, but the church has lost sight of Him." His present ministry can be expressed like this: He died down here to save us; He lives up there to keep us saved. He has a ministry of intercession, a ministry of shepherding, a ministry of disciplining His own. Although He is at God's right hand now, He is still vitally interested in those who are His own, and He is available to us.

My friend, what do you need? Do you need mercy? Do you need help? Do you need wisdom? Whatever you need, why don't you go to Him for it? If you ask Him to intervene in your behalf, He will work it out according to His will (not yours). Prayer is not to persuade God to do something that He didn't intend to do; prayer is to get you and me in line with the program of God. And Christ is at the right hand of the Father, ever living to make intercession for us. We can obtain mercy and find grace to help in time of need. This is the present ministry of Christ, and it makes these verses in Hebrews pretty real to you and to me. My friend, Buddha can't help you; Mohammed can't help you; no founder of the modern religions can help you. A friend told me of how he was healed by a so-called faith healer who is now dead. I asked him, "Can she help you now?" He retorted, "No, of course not, she is dead!" "Well," I said, "*Jesus* is alive. Our Great High Priest is alive today."

When we were at the Garden Tomb in Jerusalem I heard a thrilling story about a group of young people in Moscow who unfurled a banner at Lenin's tomb on Easter Sunday morning. The banner read, "Lenin is dead—Jesus is alive." Then they sang some resurrection songs. I don't know that anyone was won to the Lord through this, but it certainly was a brave effort on the part of youth, and their message is the message of the Book of Hebrews. "Lenin is dead—Jesus is alive." He is the One who can help us. He is the One to whom we can turn. This is the great message of the Epistle to the Hebrews. When He "sat down on the right hand of the Majesty on high," He took with Him a glory that even God did not have, which was the body in which He had wrought out your redemption and mine upon this earth. He gave *Himself;* He shed His precious blood that you and I might have life.

CHRIST IS SUPERIOR TO ANGELS

Being made so much better than the angels, as he hath by inheritance obtained a more excellent name than they [Heb. 1:4].

Christ is superior to the angels. Angels were prominent in their ministry to Israel in the Old Testament. The law was given by the agency of angels (Ps. 68:17; Acts 7:53; Gal. 3:19). Cherubim were woven into the veil of the tabernacle, and cherubim were fashioned of gold for the mercy seat. We find that Isaiah had a vision of the seraphim. And in the Book of Revelation we find that after the church is removed, there is an angel ministry of judgment that is going to take place.

Now I say this rather carefully: angel ministry is not connected with the church. I know someone is going to say, "Brother McGee, after all, we have a guardian angel." Where did that idea come from? I don't think we have guardian angels. Some people say, "Oh, but we need to have a guardian angel." Let me ask you a question: "Are you a child of God?" If you are, you are indwelt by the Holy Spirit of God, who is the third Person of the Godhead. What could a guardian angel do for you that He couldn't do for you? Do you want to think that over for a while? My feeling is that the angel ministry is not connected with the church at all. This subject is becoming exceedingly difficult and dangerous today because there is a

manifestation of demonism, and several writers are saying that demons are directing them—but they call them angels. My friend, an angel ministry is not for our day.

The idea of an active angelic ministry in the church came about because some of the early church members who were marvelous artists liked to paint angels. I doubt whether any of them ever saw an angel, but they painted angels. If you have ever been in the Sistine Chapel in Rome and looked up at the ceiling, you get the feeling that angels are hovering over you. They are as thick as pigeons up there! They are everywhere. They are connected with everybody and everything. Michelangelo certainly did like to paint angels. Although I am glad that I've seen the Sistine Chapel, I wouldn't give five cents to see it again. I know that statement will be a heartbreak for some art lovers, but I don't care to see it again because it teaches the fact that there are angels connected with our lives today. My friend, *we* have to do with a *living Savior*! Let's just push the angels aside because we don't have to go to God through angels. We have the Holy Spirit, and we have Christ, our great intercessor. Let us get our minds off of angels and center them upon the person of Christ. He is superior to angels.

"Being made so much better than the angels." The word *angel* simply means "messenger," and it doesn't mean anything else other than that. Angels worship the Lord Jesus. They are created creatures. Christ is *better* than the angels, and that statement is made definitely and dogmatically for us in Hebrews. In the Old Testament it is believed by many that the Lord Jesus Christ is referred to as "the angel of the Lord." But in the New Testament He becomes a man, and having assumed human form, He does not appear as the angel of the Lord any longer. He is the *man*, Christ Jesus. He is the Son of Man today. That is the emphasis of this Hebrew epistle.

Beginning with Hebrews 1:5 there is a series of quotations from the Old Testament; in fact, there are seven quotations, and six of them are from the Book of Psalms. The Psalms have more to say about Christ than they have to say about any other person. It is a H-I-M book—it was the hymn book of the temple, but it is all about Him; it is praise to Him. You have a more complete picture of Christ in the Psalms than you have in the Gospels. These quotations in Hebrews are very important. The writer of Hebrews quotes from the Old Testament to enforce his point, which is superiority of the Son over the angels.

For unto which of the angels said he at any time, Thou art my Son, this day have I begotten thee? And again, I will be to him a Father, and he shall be to me a Son? [Heb. 1:5].

"Thou art my Son, this day have I begotten thee" is a quotation from Psalm 2:7. In Acts 13 we have recorded Paul's great sermon at Antioch in Pisidia in which he quoted Psalm 2:7. Paul said that it had no reference to Bethlehem, but it referred to the *Resurrection* of Christ—when He was brought back from the dead. Therefore, Christ is the only One who could die for the sins of the world. No angel could save us, my friend. Only Christ could become a man and pay the penalty, which was death. "The wages of sin is death." He had to shed His blood, for without the shedding of blood there is no remission of sins. Therefore, He made that redemption for you and for me. Then He was brought back from the dead. Why? Because He is the Son. He was *begotten* from the dead.

"I will be to him a Father, and he shall be to me a Son" is a quotation from 2 Samuel. This is God's promise to David when He made His covenant with him: "And when thy days be fulfilled, and thou shalt sleep with thy fathers, I will set up thy seed after thee, which shall proceed out of thy bowels, and I will establish his kingdom. He shall build an house for my name, and I will stablish the throne of his kingdom for ever. I will be his father, and he shall be my son . . ." (2 Sam. 7:12–14). Now, there are those who say that this one in David's line was only Solomon. Well, Hebrews 1:5 makes it very clear that when God gave that promise to David it had reference to the Lord Jesus Christ. I have heard arguments pro and con on this, but arguments are pointless when we have the clear scriptural confirmation that this refers to Christ. He alone fulfilled it.

And again, when he bringeth in the first begotten into the world, he saith, And let all the angels of God worship him [Heb. 1:6].

Now let me rearrange this a little: "And again he bringeth in the first begotten into the world. He saith, And let all the angels of God worship him."

This verse is a quotation from Psalm 97:7 and Deuteronomy 32:43 in the Septuagint Version (though not in the Hebrew of the Old Testament). The angels of God are wonderful, but they are inferior to the Son. They are *His* angels, they are *His* ministers, and they are *His* worshipers. They worship Him. He does not worship them.

And of the angels he saith, Who maketh his angels spirits, and his ministers a flame of fire [Heb. 1:7].

This is a quotation from Psalm 104:4. The angels belong to the Lord. They are His ministers and worshipers. This is very important to see. The writer of Hebrews, who I believe is Paul, is showing that Christ is superior to the angels, and He is using the Old Testament Scriptures to prove it. Can you see how absolutely important the first two chapters of Hebrews are? They put down a foundation for the rest of the book which deals with the present ministry of Christ for believers today. Oh, that we might be conscious of the fact that there is a living Christ at God's right hand at this very moment! He is more real than I am, because when you read these words, there is no telling where I will be. We just don't know what a day will bring forth. But Christ is going to be right up yonder at God's right hand for you and for me. He is the real, living Christ today.

It is easy to understand that angels were very important to the Hebrews because most of them were well acquainted with the Old Testament. They thought of angels as next to the very throne of God. They had read of the appearance of angels to many of God's servants and to many of the prophets. Angels were very important beings to them.

As I have already mentioned, I do not believe there is an angel ministry to the church in our day. I do not believe that angels appear to men. If you think you have seen an angel, you should check with your doctor or with a psychologist because you saw something besides an angel.

This reminds me of the two black fellows who met after not having seen each other for a long time. One of them said, "Are you married?" The other one replied, "Yes, I'm married." His friend then asked, "What kind of a girl did you marry?" "Well," replied the other fellow, "I married an angel." The other one said, "You sure are lucky. Mine is still alive!"

Well, human beings never become angels. God has made this universe so that there are things visible and invisible. In Colossians 1:16 we read that Christ created things visible and invisible. For example, you cannot see an atom, but it is material, and it becomes energy. God created intelligences that are above man. You and I live in a universe about which the Lord has said, "In my Father's house are many *monē*, meaning "abiding places" (see John 14:2). Created intelligences live in these abiding places, and God has created a great deal more in this universe than you and I could ever dream of today. Man did not come from animals. There is a material kingdom. There is the animal kingdom, the human kingdom, and a spirit kingdom. There are creatures below man and creatures that are above man. We did not come from animals, and we will never become angels.

You may remember the song, "I want to be an angel and with the angels sing." When I was a little boy in Sunday school, the teacher would line up the little brats (I was the only good boy in the class) and have us sing, "I want to be an angel and with the angels sing." The last thing I wanted to be was an angel! And I still feel that way. I am very happy that the Scripture makes it clear that I am not going to be an angel.

The word *angel* (Gr.: *aggelos*) means "messenger" and may be applied to a human or divine messenger. There is an order of creatures that is supernatural, and we see that in the Scriptures. I think it would really surprise us if we had any conception of the number of angels in the universe. They are called the "host of heaven," and that means there are a whole lot of them. Their numbers apparently are not diminished or added to in any way, but we have no idea how many angels there are. They have an important part in God's plan, but Christ is superior to the angels.

But unto the Son he saith, Thy throne, O God, is for ever and ever: a sceptre of righteousness is the sceptre of thy kingdom.

Thou hast loved righteousness, and hated iniquity; therefore God, even thy God, hath anointed thee with the oil of gladness above thy fellows [Heb. 1:8–9].

These verses are a quotation from Psalm 45:6–7 which reveals that it is one of the great messianic psalms. Psalm 45 tells us that there is One coming in the line of David who will rule in righteousness. David is so thrilled about this prospect that he says, ". . . My tongue is the pen of a ready writer" (Ps. 45:1). David is saying, "I could *tell* you about this much better than I could write about it." This One who is coming, according to the writer to the Hebrews, is the Lord Jesus Christ. He is the One who will rule in righteousness. God

has not given the right to rule the earth to any angel.

"Thou hast loved righteousness, and hated iniquity" is a tremendous statement. Imagine this old earth being ruled by One who loves righteousness and hates iniquity!

"Thy throne, O God." This is God the Father calling God the Son *God*! Do you want to deny that Christ is God manifest in the flesh? If you do, then may I say that you are contradicting God Himself. God called the Lord Jesus *God*. What are you going to call Him? I don't know about you, but I am also going to call Him *God*. He is God manifest in the flesh. He is superior to angels because He is going to rule over the universe. He is the Messiah. He is the King of Kings and Lord of Lords who is going to rule over the earth some day.

And, Thou, Lord, in the beginning hast laid the foundation of the earth; and the heavens are the works of thine hands:

They shall perish; but thou remainest; and they all shall wax old as doth a garment;

And as a vesture shalt thou fold them up, and they shall be changed: but thou art the same, and thy years shall not fail [Heb. 1:10–12].

These verses are quoted from Psalm 102:25–27. This is a tremendous statement telling us that the Lord Jesus is the Creator. These are tremendous contrasts given to us in this section: Angels are the creatures; the Lord is the Creator.

But to which of the angels said he at any time, Sit on my right hand, until I make thine enemies thy footstool? [Heb. 1:13].

This verse is a quote from Psalm 110:1, a psalm that is quoted more than any other psalm in the New Testament. The Psalms teach the deity of Christ. There is a more complete picture of Christ in the Psalms than in the Gospels.

Are they not all ministering spirits, sent forth to minister for them who shall be heirs of salvation? [Heb. 1:14].

Right away somebody is going to say, "Doesn't it say here that the angels are going to minister to the heirs of salvation?" Let's read the verse like it is. The angels are going to minister to those "who *shall* be heirs of salvation." This verse is looking forward to the time when God turns again to the nation Israel, and to the gentile world—*after* the church is removed from earth. Notice that it does not say that the angels are ministering to those who are *right now* the heirs of salvation. You see, God is moving according to His program and He has a purpose for everything He does.

Christ is the Son; angels are servants. Christ is King; angels are subjects. Christ is the Creator; angels are creatures. Christ at this moment is waiting until His enemies will be made His footstool. The Father never gave such a promise to an angel, but He says that some day His Son shall rule. This tremendous section sets before us the deity of the Lord Jesus Christ and the exaltation of the Lord Jesus Christ. He is higher than the angels.

CHAPTER 2

THEME: *Humanity of Christ*

After seeing the exaltation of the Lord Jesus Christ in chapter 1, we come to the *humiliation* of Christ in chapter 2. He became a man, and when He did, He became *lower* than the angels. He was created a man in the womb of the Virgin Mary and took upon Himself our humanity. Therefore, Christ is the revealer of God, and He is the representative of man. We are going to find out two things about Christ in the Book of Hebrews: (1) He reveals God to man; and (2) He represents man before God.

I have a representative in heaven; I have someone there who represents *me*. I don't know about you, but I get the feeling that in my state capital and in my national capital those who are elected to represent me are not representing me at all. They are all out for themselves and their own little pet programs, and it doesn't make much difference to them what happens to the public. The only time they are interested in me is when I vote, and then I become the darling of the politicians. Then you and I are the intelligent public who cannot go wrong, provided we vote for them!

It is wonderful to have a representative before God, one who *does* represent us. It is good to know that we have somebody there for us, because Scripture tells us that Satan, the accuser of the brethren, has access to God and accuses us before God day and night (see Rev. 12:10). Satan could tell God some pretty bad things about us, and so I am thankful I have a representative in heaven.

First we saw Christ higher than the angels, because He is God. Now we see Him become lower than the angels. He was made in the likeness of man, and we see here His humanity.

There are *six* danger signals in the Book of Hebrews. They are warnings to the people of Israel that they fail not to enter into the full blessings which God has provided through Christ. These six danger signals can be likened to highway markers to warn the reader. These danger signals are as follows:

Peril of drifting, 2:1–4
Peril of doubting, 3:7–4:2
Peril of dull hearing, 5:11–14
Peril of departing, 6:1–20
Peril of despising, 10:26–39
Peril of denying, 12:15–29

There are two places in which a believer can live. He can live in the desert and have a wilderness experience, or he can enter into the blessings of God by spiritually crossing the Jordan River. We find the example of this in Israel. God warned them at Kadesh-Barnea that they would miss His full blessings if they failed to enter into the land.

Now I have literally crossed the Jordan River, and it wasn't pleasant at all. I was on a bus that stopped five times, and by the time we got to the Allenby Bridge I was so disgusted I didn't know whether I even wanted to cross the Jordan River. As we drove over it, I looked at that little muddy stream and thanked God that I had crossed the spiritual Jordan in Jesus Christ through His death and resurrection. That is, I had been buried with Him in baptism and raised with Him in newness of life. That is what is meant by a Christian crossing the Jordan. Joshua *literally* led the children of Israel across the Jordan. Christ *spiritually* leads the ones who believe in Him across the Jordan into a newness of life.

THE FIRST DANGER SIGNAL: PERIL OF DRIFTING

Let's realize that this is a warning for every child of God in our day also, a warning that there is a danger of drifting.

Therefore we ought to give the more earnest heed to the things which we have heard, lest at any time we should let them slip [Heb. 2:1].

Because this last revelation was superior to the Old Testament dispensation and came from One who is superior to angels, we are to pay particular attention to the warning. The responsibility is now greater.

"Let them slip" is *drift past them*. It indicates neglect, that is all. Neglect in any area of life is tragic, but in the spiritual realm, hearing the gospel message and doing nothing about it is infinitely more tragic. What must I do to be lost? Nothing!

The story is told of the man who went to sleep in his boat one night on the Niagara River. Before long his boat drifted down to the rapids and he was caught. It was too late for him to do anything. He went over the falls and was killed. Someone asks the question, "What must I do to be lost?" We are given the answer for "What must I do to be saved?" in Acts 16:31: ". . . Believe on the Lord Jesus Christ, and thou shalt be saved. . . ." But what is the answer for "What must I do to be lost?" Well, the answer is *nothing*. You and I belong to a lost human family. We are not on trial. I get a little weary of hearing that God has us on trial. He doesn't have us on trial; we are lost. Today He is saving some—those who will turn to Christ. The rest are already lost. You don't do *anything* to be lost, because that is your natural condition.

There is great danger in neglect in every area of life. Many years ago I had a wonderful secretary who developed cancer of the hip. The doctor told her that she must have an operation, but she kept postponing it. Finally the day came when it was too late to do anything. She had been warned, but she just drifted, just neglected taking any action until it was too late.

When you move neglect to a higher realm, hearing the gospel message and doing nothing about it is infinitely more tragic. A great many folk hear the gospel and give mental assent to it, but do nothing about it.

Some time ago a man said to me, "McGee, some day I am going to take up your offer and accept Christ." Right now, however, this man is drifting. I don't know how far along he is, but the day will come when he will be in the rapids, and then it will be too late—he will go over the falls. He may have a heart attack or be in an accident, and his chance to receive Christ will be gone. I would like to get all the folk that hear the gospel into the "now" generation. "Now" is the accepted time. "Now" is the day of salvation. There is a real danger of drifting, and Hebrews warns us about it.

For if the word spoken by angels was stedfast, and every transgression and disobedience received a just recompence of reward [Heb. 2:2].

For example, when the two angels came to Sodom with the announcement that Sodom was to be destroyed, Sodom *was* destroyed exactly as they said. In fact, whenever an angel brought a message, you could depend on its being carried out just as it was stated.

Now notice the question—

How shall we escape, if we neglect so great salvation; which at the first began to be spoken by the Lord, and was confirmed unto us by them that heard him [Heb. 2:3].

A great Welsh preacher began his sermon by saying, "I have a question to ask. I cannot answer it. You cannot answer it. Even God cannot answer it." Then he gave this as his text: "How shall we escape, if we neglect so great salvation?" And I have a sermon entitled, "A Question that God Cannot Answer." I do not mean to be irreverent, but God makes it clear that He cannot answer the question, "How shall we escape, if we neglect so great salvation?" Do you know a way of escape? The only way is Christ. He said so in John 14:6: "Jesus saith unto him, I am the way, the truth, and the life: no man cometh unto the Father, but by me." In the Scriptures we also read, "There is a way that seemeth right unto a man, but the end thereof are the ways of death" (Prov. 16:25). There are many *ways* that seem right to men. In California you can hear about as many ways as you want to hear. If you are looking for a religion, you will find one in California. If you don't find one that you like, you can start one, and I will guarantee that you will find some followers who will go along with you. There is a way that seems right to a man, but the end are the ways of death. How shall we escape, if we neglect so great a salvation? What do you do to be lost? Nothing. You can be lost by neglect.

"Which at the first began to be spoken by the Lord" is, of course, the Lord Jesus when

He was here. He said, "Come unto me, all ye that labour and are heavy laden . . ." (Matt. 11:28) and "For the Son of man is come to seek and to save that which was lost" (Luke 19:10).

"And was confirmed unto us by them that heard him," refers to His disciples and others who heard Him and witnessed His death and resurrection—then went everywhere preaching the gospel.

God also bearing them witness, both with signs and wonders, and with divers miracles, and gifts of the Holy Ghost, according to his own will? [Heb. 2:4].

I think the writer of Hebrews has definite reference here to the Day of Pentecost when the gifts of the Holy Spirit were exercised. The gifts, of course, confirmed the message. To whom? To the nation Israel.

What tremendous truths we have here in this first danger warning. It is a warning sign, not about speeding up but about drifting—just drifting *by* these great truths which we may have been taking for granted.

SUPERIORITY OF CHRIST TO ANGELS IN HIS HUMANITY

The humanity of Christ needs to be emphasized as well as His deity. You see, He brought deity down to this earth, and He took humanity back to heaven.

For unto the angels hath he not put in subjection the world to come, whereof we speak [Heb. 2:5].

To begin with, let us understand what *world* the author is talking about. A great many folk think immediately that the "world to come" is heaven. However, the word for "world" in this verse means "inhabited earth" in the Greek. This verse is talking about the people of this earth. It is used in Matthew 24:14 which says, "And this gospel of the kingdom shall be preached in all the world [inhabited earth] for a witness unto all nations; and then shall the end come." It is also used in Romans 10:18, "But I say, Have they not heard? Yes verily, their sound went into all the [inhabited] earth, and their words unto the ends of the world." The word *world* could not refer to heaven or to eternity. It does not refer to this dispensation of grace in which we live today. It speaks of the messianic kingdom, the kingdom that is coming on the earth. Hebrew believers, schooled in the Old Testament, knew that the theme song of that book was the coming kingdom over which one in David's line would rule.

The messianic kingdom became the theme song of every one of the prophets.

"Unto the angels hath he not put in subjection the world to come"—the millennial kingdom that is coming upon the earth. Not only have angels not ruled in the past, they will not rule in the future. They have been servants and messengers in the past, and they will continue to be servants in the future. This is the thought expressed here.

Now he turns to Psalm 8 and gives us an interpretation of that marvelous psalm which has to do with creation.

But one in a certain place testified, saying, What is man, that thou art mindful of him? or the son of man, that thou visitest him? [Heb. 2:6].

Verses 6–8 are a quote from Psalm 8:4–6. Let us pause here for just a moment. Who is man anyway? Man is just a small creature on one of the minor planets. Someone put it like this, "Man is a rash on the epidermis of a minor planet." That really puts man in his place, but I suppose it is more or less accurate. We are very small in God's universe. Someone else has said, "When you pick up the minutest piece of creation, the parts of an atom, and then you reach out to the largest, man is probably halfway between." Man stands about halfway in the physical creation, but the important thing is that the Lord of Glory, the second person of the Godhead, became Jesus, a *man*.

"What is man, that thou art mindful of him?" The answer to that is, "Jesus became a man. He left heaven's glory, came down to this earth, and He didn't become an angel." That is what the writer of the Epistle to the Hebrews is going to tell us. "What is man, that thou art mindful of him? or the son of man, that thou visitest him?" What is man?

Of himself, man is nothing. Physically, if you break down the elements of his body into chemical components and put them on the market, at one time he would only have been worth about ninety-eight cents. Today due to inflation man's worth is a little more than that. But it is not of much value, especially when you think of how much a dollar is worth. So, physically, man is not very valuable. Mentally, man thinks he is something, but he knows very little. What does man actually know about this vast universe in which we live? We have spent billions of dollars to send a man to the moon to see if we could find out how it all began. Since our nation doesn't believe the first chapter of Genesis, we are exploring the moon! Genesis 1:1 certainly sounds a lot better than any of man's theories. Man today isn't very much physically or mentally. He can't lift very much, and he can't do very much. Man is quite limited. When you take a good look at man, you see that he is a lost sinner. He is in terrible condition. What is man that God was mindful of him?

"Or the son of man, that thou visitest him?" Well, He visited us because He wanted to communicate with us, and He wanted to save us because He saw our lost condition.

Thou madest him a little lower than the angels; thou crownedst him with glory and honour, and didst set him over the works of thy hands [Heb. 2:7].

God made man lower than the angels at the time of creation. Psalm 8 makes it abundantly clear that man was made lower than the angels. The One who was superior, higher than the angels, was willing to come down below angels. He became not an angel but a man!

Many of us believe that the One called the "angel of the Lord" in the Old Testament is Christ. I went across the brook Jabbok not long ago (Jabbok is in the kingdom of Jordan) and remembered that somewhere along that little creek (and that is all I would call it) the angel of the Lord wrestled with Jacob. That Angel of the Lord we believe is Christ.

We read in the New Testament that when Christ came to earth He became lower than the angels. Apparently angels are the measuring rod; they are the standard of the bureau of standards. Christ was above the angels, but when He became a man, He became lower than the angels. Why did the Lord do it? He did it so that He could reveal God. Also He is the representative of man before God. He brought God to earth and took man back to heaven. If you and I get to heaven it will be because we are in Christ.

This is God's original purpose with man—"Thou crownedst him with glory and honour, and didst set him over the works of thy hands." Man is going to do something that angels have never been able to do. Angels do not rule God's universe. They are God's messengers. There was an angel who attempted to rebel against God. He tried to set up his own kingdom. He attempted to become a ruler. His name was Lucifer, son of the morning. We know him today by the name of Satan, or the Devil. He was an angel of light, but he rebelled and said in his heart, ". . . I will exalt my throne above the stars of God. . . . I will be like the most High" (Isa. 14:13–14). God

does not intend him or any angel to rule; but He has created man to rule.

Man, however, as we see him today is not capable of ruling. He is demonstrating this in all the capitals of the world—so much so that it makes me bow my head in shame. Man cannot rule, but he thinks he can—he has adopted Satan's viewpoint. He is attempting to rule without God. God could bless our nation today, as He blessed it in the past when men recognized their dependence upon God. But man in and of himself is not capable of ruling.

Because of making trips to England, I have studied a great deal of English history. I wanted to look at the abbeys, the castles, and the cathedrals with some degree of intelligence as to their background. I did not realize just how bloody the kings of England had been. The minute a man became king, he killed all his relatives so no one could take the throne away from him. If you were a brother or a cousin of a king, you were in trouble. He was apt to take you to the Tower of London—many a man lost his head there. Man, regardless of his race, is not capable of ruling this earth as God intended.

However, by redemption, God is going to bring man back to the place where he can rule. In Psalm 8 is the statement: "thou . . . hast crowned him with glory and honour. Thou madest him to have dominion over the works of thy hands." Man lost that dominion in the Garden of Eden when he disobeyed God, but Christ has recovered it.

Thou hast put all things in subjection under his feet. For in that he put all in subjection under him, he left nothing that is not put under him. But now we see not yet all things put under him [Heb. 2:8].

"Thou hast put all things in subjection under his feet"—whose feet? Christ's—not man's. "But now we see not yet all things put under him." Although our earth has not slipped out from under His control, He is not ruling today. When the Lord Jesus does rule on this earth, there will be no need of a hospital or a jail. There will be no crime or poverty. When He rules this earth it will be a millennial paradise. As the writer quotes Psalm 8, he makes it abundantly clear that the psalmist spoke of Christ, and the prediction is not fulfilled up to the present moment.

Now we have the very heart of this chapter—

But we see Jesus, who was made a little lower than the angels for the suffering of death, crowned with glory and honour; that he by the grace of God should taste death for every man [Heb. 2:9].

"But we *see* Jesus." Because of what the Lord Jesus has done, we behold Him. We see Jesus. This word *see* does not mean a casual look. The word means that we look upon Him with understanding. We recognize that in Him is something that our little minds do not grasp. We look upon Him in faith, in trust, in wonder, in awe, and in worship. All of this is wrapped up in the phrase, "We see Jesus." Do *you* "see" Him today? Has the Spirit of God taken the veil from your eyes so that you can *see* Him?

"We see *Jesus*." Notice that Jesus is His human name. At His conception the angel announced, ". . . thou shalt call his name JESUS: for he shall save his people from their sins" (Matt. 1:21).

"Who was made a little lower than the angels." The emphasis is not on being made lower than the angels, but upon the word *little*, and in that word the emphasis is upon time. We could say, "Who was made, for a little time, lower than the angels." For that brief time that He was upon earth (thirty-three years) He was made lower than the angels.

"For the suffering of death"—rather, *because* of the suffering of death. Christ alone could redeem man, and He could do it only by dying upon the cross. It was the *only* way.

"Crowned with glory and honour." He wasn't crowned with glory and honor by His death but because He came to this earth and died on the cross for you and for me. Let me emphasize again and again that there is a man in the glory. He wasn't there some twenty-five hundred years ago. Instead He was the second person of the Godhead—let's call Him Jehovah, for Jesus is Jehovah. And He was and is God, very God of very God. But today He is also very man of very man. He took upon Himself humanity, and because He did this, He was given glory and honor in heaven that wasn't there before.

"Should taste death for every man" means that He not only experienced the pangs of death, but He had the experience of what death really is—the very fullest depth of it. He drank the cup of death. That bitter cup was pressed to His lips, and He drank every bit of it. He did this for you and me.

"By the grace of God." He did this by the grace of God—that God could be gracious to you and to me today and save us.

For it became him, for whom are all things, and by whom are all things, in bringing many sons unto glory, to make the captain of their salvation perfect through sufferings [Heb. 2:10].

Jesus was not a man in whom God did something. The humanity of Jesus doesn't mean that He was a religious genius. It doesn't mean that He was a martyr to a cause. It doesn't mean that He was setting a good example. Christ's humiliation accomplished two things: (1) It brought glory and honor to the person of Christ; and (2) it procured man's salvation by making man's salvation possible. Christ took humanity to heaven, and there is not only a Man in glory, but there is a glory in that Man which was not there before.

"It became" simply means that it was fitting for Him—it was harmonious and consistent with His Person and purpose to bring many sons unto glory in this way.

"It became *him* [the Lord Jesus] *for* whom are all things, and by whom are all things." He made all things, and they were for *Him*. If you want to know why this universe exists, it is because *Jesus* wanted it; it was *His* will. That is the origin of this universe—it began in the mind of Christ.

"In bringing many sons unto glory" is God's present purpose. God also has a future purpose of putting His King on His holy hill of Zion (see Ps. 2). God is moving forward with that program, but right now He is calling out a people for His name; He is bringing many sons home to glory. I read a letter a few moments ago from a young man who had sunk as low as one can go on dope and had spent time in prison. Now the Lord Jesus has saved him. We are seeing this happening all over the world. God is still calling out people for His name, bringing many sons unto glory.

"To make the captain of their salvation perfect through sufferings." The word *captain*, translated "author," appears again in chapter 12, verse 2. The same word is translated "prince" in Acts 3:15. It means "originator or leader." A captain is one who initiates and carries through. In other words, the Lord Jesus is the Alpha and Omega of everything. He is the beginning and the ending. He starts it, and He completes it. He is the Captain. He originated our salvation, and He consummated it. How did He do it? He did it by coming down to this earth and taking upon Himself our humanity. What did He do when He came to earth? He tasted death for every man. He came to redeem mankind and to procure man's salvation. He revealed God on earth, and today He represents man in heaven. We will see that when we get to the subject of His priesthood.

"Perfect through sufferings." He was made perfect in the sense of being made complete. "Perfect" is from the Greek word *teleioō*, meaning "to carry to the goal; consummate; complete."

He was made perfect through suffering. Although He was the Son of God, and though He was God Himself, His perfect life does not save us. His virgin birth does not save us. Actually, His teaching does not save us. His miracles do not save us, nor does His example save us. But it is His death upon the cross that saves us. He was made complete; He reached completeness by dying on the cross. If you could convince me that God has decided to remain aloof from man, and all He did for this lost world was to pitch the Bible down here, and as He sits in heaven, He looks down on man and says, "It's too bad you are in such a mess; here is a Book, and I hope you can work your way out," then I am prepared to turn my back upon Him. But that is not what God did. He came down to earth and took upon *Himself* our humanity. Because He suffered and died upon the cross, I am prepared to trust in Him. I am prepared to love Him because of what He has done for me and all lost mankind.

For both he that sanctifieth and they who are sanctified are all of one: for which cause he is not ashamed to call them brethren [Heb. 2:11].

"He that sanctifieth"—to be sanctified doesn't mean what the average person thinks it means. For many years I thought it meant to be a nice, sweet, little boy. Well, sanctification when it is used in connection with the Holy Spirit has to do with the work of God in us, to make us the kind of representative He wants down here on this earth. It is the work of the Spirit of God in the heart of the redeemed. However, sanctification when it is used in connection with the person of Christ (as in this epistle to the Hebrews) is not purification. It is not a *condition* but a *position* that we have in Christ. He was the Just One who took the place of the unjust that He might bring us to God. And He has brought us now into the family of God.

"For which cause he is not ashamed to call them brethren." In the family of God, He is not ashamed to call us brothers. Now, of course, I would not dare call Him brother, but *He* has brought us into the family of God. He is the firstborn among many brethren; He is the *head* of the family, and He calls us brethren because we all become sons of God through faith in the Lord Jesus Christ.

My friend, this makes it very clear that the heresy about the universal fatherhood of God and the universal brotherhood of man is entirely false. It is probably the most damnable doctrine that is abroad today.

Saying, I will declare thy name unto my brethren, in the midst of the church will I sing praise unto thee [Heb. 2:12].

This verse is a quotation from Psalm 22, the great psalm of the cross. The first part of Psalm 22 denotes the humiliation of Christ, and you actually are given the seven last words of Christ on the cross. Beginning with verse 22 of the psalm you have the exaltation of Christ: "I will declare thy name unto my brethren: in the midst of the congregation will I praise thee" (Ps. 22:22). I am of the opinion that we could restrict this verse to the Hebrew brethren because it was written to the Jews.

"In the midst of the church will I sing praise unto thee." The word *church* is "congregation" rather than the technical meaning of the word *church*.

Now here is another quotation from the Old Testament, Isaiah 8:17–18.

And again, I will put my trust in him. And again, Behold I and the children which God hath given me [Heb. 2:13].

This verse reveals how the Holy Spirit interprets Scripture. There are those today who try to give an interpretation of the prophets that eliminates any reference to Jesus Christ at all. In fact, when I read Isaiah 8:17–18, it seems that the writer is talking about the sons of Isaiah, at least that is the way I understand it. But here in verse 13 the Holy Spirit of God interprets that reference in Isaiah in such a way that it refers to the Lord Jesus Christ. Anyone today who attempts to eliminate the Lord Jesus from the prophets, therefore, is contradicting the interpretation that the Holy Spirit has given in the New Testament.

You will remember that when the Lord Jesus came back from the dead He said, ". . . go to my brethren, and say unto them, I ascend unto my Father, and your Father; and to my God, and your God" (John 20:17). When Jesus said, "Go to my brethren," He was referring to His apostles at that particular time, and they were, of course, all Jewish. I emphasize this because I think it is very important to keep before us the ones to whom this epistle was written. It will enable me to give a correct *interpretation* that, I trust, might lead to an *application* to your heart and to my heart.

Forasmuch then as the children are partakers of flesh and blood, he also himself likewise took part of the same; that through death he might destroy him that had the power of death, that is, the devil [Heb. 2:14].

This statement emphasizes the Lord's incarnation.

"As the children are partakers of flesh and blood, he also himself likewise took part of the same." Christ came in a way they were not expecting Him to come. However, they should have known, because the prophets had made clear the way He would come to earth the first time. As George Macdonald put it:

They were looking for a King
  To slay their foes and lift them high;
Thou cam'st, a little baby thing
  That made a woman cry.

Because we were made of flesh and blood, He took upon Himself flesh and blood. And He came into this world by human birth just like you and I came into the world.

"That through death he might destroy him." Christ Jesus came not only through birth— His birth didn't save anyone—but through death. It is by His death He saves us, not by His birth or by His life. His death brought to us salvation and deliverance from spiritual and eternal death.

And deliver them who through fear of death were all their lifetime subject to bondage [Heb.2:15].

In my opinion, E. Schuyler English (*Studies in the Epistle to the Hebrews*, p. 82) has the correct interpretation of this verse:

The Law of God demanded and does demand death for sin. "The soul that sinneth, it shall die." "The wages of sin is death." Satan was the cause of man's sin in the first place and, even though he is a usurper, he can claim, justly so in a sense, that the sinner must die. He had the power, the authority to demand that every sinner should pay sin's penalty. And on account of this all men, because all are sinners, were fearful of death and subject

to bondage, because of sin, to serve it and thus serve Satan.

For verily he took not on him the nature of angels; but he took on him the seed of Abraham [Heb. 2:16].

In the Old Testament Christ took on the nature of angels. He did that when He appeared as the Angel of the Lord, and these Hebrews understood that. When Christ left heaven and came to earth, He came past the angels and came to fallen man. He took on Him the seed of Abraham. He came in the line of Abraham. God began the preparation at the very beginning with Adam and Eve. At that time God said that there would come the seed of the woman (see Gen. 3:15). Then God said He would come in the line of Abraham, and a little farther along we learn that He would be born in the tribe of Judah, of the family of David, of the nation Israel. He was to be born of a virgin. The Lord put up enough highway markers so that everybody—not only wise men, but everybody—should have found their way to Bethlehem when Jesus was born.

Wherefore in all things it behoved him to be made like unto his brethren, that he might be a merciful and faithful high priest in things pertaining to God, to make reconciliation for the sins of the people [Heb. 2:17].

The Lord Jesus came down to earth in the likeness of men. In Philippians 2:7 we read, "But made himself of no reputation, and took upon him the form of a servant, and was made in the likeness of men." It was a real likeness to men. This likeness, Vincent tells us, is "closest where the traces of the curse of sin were more apparent—in poverty, temptation, and violent and unmerited death." Christ could have been born in the palace of Caesar, but He was born in real poverty, in a stable behind an inn. Why? So that He could know something of the effect of sin on humanity. Where do you see it? You see it in poverty. You see it in temptation. You see it in violent and unmerited death. That is where you see sin manifested.

I think it is tragic when innocent people suffer. Some time ago in Pasadena a dear, talented, Christian woman, an outstanding artist up in her 80s, was followed home by a teenager who cruelly and brutally murdered her. How terrible it was! And nothing was done about it. Thank God, He is going to make things right some day.

When Christ came to earth, He knew what

real poverty was. During World War II, I went through El Paso, Texas, on the train. Before the train pulled into the station, the conductor came by and said, "Don't get off the train because there are people in this station who have been there for a week and cannot get out. They are desperate. If you leave your seat, one of them will take it and you will never get it back. Stay right where you are." We did what he said, but once the train started its journey again, I searched out the conductor and asked him what it was all about. He told me that many of those people were camping in the station, waiting for a seat on a train. Remember, this was during the war, and many men were being shipped overseas. One young woman told the conductor that her husband had been shipped out and she was stranded. She couldn't get back to her people; so she was just waiting in the station. He also told me that a little boy had been born in that station the other night. Imagine being born in a station! The little fellow is a great big fellow now, and I sure hope someone has told him about Jesus, because He also was born in a crush like that when there was a great movement of humanity. You recall that it was Caesar who made a tax bill requiring that every person under the domain of Rome be enrolled in their hometown for taxing. Mary *had* to go to Bethlehem although it was near the time for her baby to be born. When she got to Bethlehem, there was no room in the inn, and so the Lord Jesus Christ was born in a stable. He could sympathize with that baby born in El Paso's Union Station, couldn't He?

The Lord Jesus came to earth and took on a human body. He is able to sympathize with you and me. I don't care who you are or where you are, He knows *you* and He understands you—not just because He is God, but because He became a man. He knows exactly what you and I are going through today.

At the time this book is being written there is a great deal of poverty in the Middle East, especially among the Arabs. My heart goes out to the refugees there. We cannot condone their rash acts and murder which they have committed, but do you know that some of them have been living in those wretched camps since 1948? Their living conditions are absolutely horrible. Even their own brethren, the other Arabs, have not permitted them to integrate among their people. They have been confined to these camps. Well, there was wretched poverty in the Middle East when Jesus lived there. And "it behoved him to be made like unto his brethren." He came in pov-

erty. The poverty of Jesus' family is almost unspeakable. He was born into a race that was under the heel of Rome; they were in subjection to Rome. He wasn't born in a palace; He was born in a stable. He was in all points made like unto His brethren. He became one of them. If you had seen that little boy playing in Bethlehem, wearing a little ragged garment, you would not have known who He was. When the artist paints Him, He stands out like a bright cameo, but He was probably just a dirty-faced little boy, not any different in appearance from His playmates. He was made like unto His brethren.

In emphasizing the deity of Christ there is a danger of underestimating His humanity. I am happy that I was not born in Bethlehem. I am delighted that I was not raised in Nazareth. I want to tell you that even today the children in those towns don't have much of a chance. Just think of what it was like in Jesus' day! Jesus Christ became a real human being, and He came out of that background. He was a root out of a dry ground. You have never had a thought nor have you ever suffered anything that He doesn't already know about. For this reason He can be a merciful and faithful High Priest.

"That he might be a merciful and faithful high priest in things pertaining to God, to make reconciliation for the sins of the people." It is more accurate to say "to make *propitiation*," rather than "reconciliation." Christ made a mercy seat for you and me to come to. And, my friend, what we need is *mercy*. God has a great deal of it available to us because Jesus made a mercy seat, and you can go there and get all you need. I don't know about you, but I need a whole lot of it, and after I have used up a great deal of it, there is still plenty of it for you today. Christ made a mercy seat for the *sins of the people*, and that is the only place you can get God's mercy.

For in that he himself hath suffered being tempted, he is able to succour them that are tempted [Heb. 2:18].

"For in that he himself hath suffered being tempted"—the word should be *tested*. The Lord Jesus was tested, not only for forty days (that was a testing in a particular way), but during His entire life He was tested.

I want to look closely at this verse because some of you are going to disagree with what I am going to say about it. The question is asked concerning the testing of Jesus, "Could He have succumbed to the temptation? Could He have fallen?" The answer is *no*. When we speak of being tempted to do something wrong, what we actually mean is that we have the *opportunity* to do wrong, and we want to do it. Now the opportunity was the testing, but the desire to do wrong was sin, and a sinful *desire* is itself sin. The Lord Jesus never had that sinful desire. He was not a sinner, but He certainly had the opportunity. Knowing how hungry and weak He was from going without food for forty days, Satan began his temptation by saying, "Why don't you make these rocks into bread?" If you have been to that land, you know that there are a whole lot of rocks there! That was the temptation. He *could* have made stones into bread, but He didn't. His test was greater than mine. I want you to know that if I could make stones into bread I'd be in the bakery business! He could have, but He didn't. He had the opportunity to do it, and that is the test. He did not yield to it. He did not desire to yield to the test; and he could not so desire because of the very fact that He was God.

Again I ask the question: Could Jesus have sinned? The answer is no, He could not have sinned. What then was the purpose of the testing? I feel that I can answer that best with an illustration.

When I was a boy, I lived in West Texas on the east fork of the Brazos River. In the summertime there wasn't enough water in the river to rust a shingle nail, but in the wintertime you could have floated a battleship down there. The little town has disappeared now, but when I lived there, the Santa Fe Railroad went through it and across the Brazos River. One winter we had a flood that washed out the railroad bridge—it was a wooden bridge. So the railroad company came in and replaced it with a steel bridge. When it was completed, they brought two engines to our town, stopped them on top of the new bridge, and tied down their whistles. Well, nobody in our little town had ever heard two whistles at one time, so we all rushed down to the bridge—all twenty-seven of us. We stood there watching, and one of the extroverts of our town asked the engineer, "What are you doing?" He said, "We are testing the bridge." So he asked, "Do you think it will fall down?" With a sneer, the engineer said, "Of course it won't fall down!" "Then why are you doing this?" This was the engineer's answer: "We are putting these two engines there to *prove* that it won't fall down."

Jesus, you see, was tested to *prove* that He was who He claimed to be. That is very important. Actually, if Jesus of Nazareth had sinned, it would not have proven that God in the flesh could sin. Rather, it would have proven that Jesus of Nazareth was not God in the flesh. The testing proved that He was God in the flesh. Because of who He is, He cannot sin. And the writer of the Hebrew epistle adds that He was tested in all points like we are, yet was without sin (see Heb. 4:15).

"For in that he himself hath suffered being tempted, he is able to succour them that are tempted." The word *succour* means, of course, "to come to the aid of, help, assist." Because He suffered being tempted, He is able to help others who are tested. As we get further along in this epistle, we will be studying the priesthood of God. We will see that the Lord Jesus Christ is able to help those who are tested. If there is one thing I hope this study in the Book of Hebrews will achieve, it is to make you and me very conscious that we have an High Priest. He is alive at this moment. He is at God's right hand, and, best of all, He is available to us. When I wake up in the dark watches of the night and toss and turn, as I sometimes do, with some burden on my heart, I can look up. My High Priest is up there. He knows me, He understands, and I can take my burden to Him. When that dark moment comes, and you and I go down into the valley of the shadow of death, we have a great High Priest up yonder who will help us. No matter what happens, no matter what the test, He is able to help us. I am afraid that we do not use His services as we should. We forget about Him and try to fight our battles alone. My friend, He is available. He wants you to come to Him.

CHAPTER 3

THEME: *Christ is superior to Moses*

We have already seen that Christ is superior to the prophets, and we have just concluded the section which proves Him to be superior to the angels. Now we will see that He is superior to Moses.

Wherefore, holy brethren, partakers of the heavenly calling, consider the Apostle and High Priest of our profession, Christ Jesus [Heb. 3:1].

This chapter begins with the word *Wherefore,* and this is another reason I feel that Paul is the author of this epistle. Paul used the words *wherefore* and *therefore* as sort of a hinge or cement to present that which is logical. Now in the verse before us, *wherefore* is even more than that. It is like a swinging door which goes back and forth both ways. Or it can be looked at as a marker when you come in on a freeway or come in on a main thoroughfare. The warning is, "Look both ways." The word *wherefore* looks back at what the writer has already said, and it looks forward to what he will say.

"Wherefore, holy brethren." The word *brethren* means those who were Hebrews like Paul was. Paul after the flesh was a Hebrew. He called the Jews his brethren after the flesh. They are called "holy" brethren in this verse, not because of the things they did, but because the word *holy* means "separated"— they were separated unto God. They belonged to Him.

"Partakers of the heavenly calling." The nation Israel had an earthly calling. All the promises of the Old Testament given to Israel had to do with this earth. He promised them rain from heaven; He promised them fertility of the soil and bountiful crops. These are physical blessings, although He promised them spiritual blessings as well. Today the idea that anything physical cannot be used in a spiritual way is wrong. That is one reason people don't like to have money mentioned in church. What is wrong with money? It can be used in a spiritual way; it is not very impressive to hear somebody pray for something and then not back it up with his pocketbook. For example, if you are going to pray for missions, I would suggest you give to missions if you want to make your prayer effective. Otherwise your prayer is just like a lot of wind escaping— that's all. It is spiritual to give; that is one of the ministries a priest performs. He offers up spiritual sacrifices. Giving is one of them, and the praise of our lips is another.

The brethren who are partakers of the heavenly calling previously had an earthly calling, but now they have come up to date and they belong to the "now" generation of those of Israel who have turned to Christ. The writer to the Hebrews will be making it very clear that they have moved into a different age. In the past they offered animal sacrifices according to the Mosaic system, and it was right to do so. But now it is wrong because the sacrificial system has all been fulfilled in Christ, and they have a heavenly calling. The earthly calling hasn't disappeared, but it has been changed for the heavenly calling—so that they are partakers of the heavenly calling.

Several missionaries in Israel try to make this clear to us in our day. When witnessing to a Jew we tend to give the impression that he will have to cease being a Jew. I don't know why we do this. A man can still be a Jew and be a Christian. If we are German, English, or French, we are still that when we become a child of God. Nobody asks us to give up our nationality. And the Jew is still a Jew after he has come to Christ. He has moved along with the revelation of God, and he is a partaker now of the heavenly calling. This is important to see. The Epistle to the Hebrews becomes almost meaningless if you don't consider to whom it was written—and also when it was written.

Someone sent me John Wycliffe's *Golden Rule of Interpretation.* John Wycliffe lived from 1324 to 1380, and although that was a long time ago, I think his Golden Rule is still gold; it is not tarnished at all. Listen to his Golden Rule:

It shall greatly help thee to understand Scripture if thou mark not only what is spoken or written, but of whom and to whom, with what words, at what time, where, and to what intent, under what circumstances, considering what goeth before and what followeth.

My friend, you can't improve on that. If we just take that rule of John Wycliffe's and apply it to Hebrews, I don't think we will have trouble understanding this epistle. The phrase "partakers of the heavenly calling" would be perfectly meaningless apart from applying it to these Hebrew Christians.

"Consider the Apostle and High Priest of our profession, Christ Jesus." I would like to change the word *profession* to *confession*. And the word for "Christ" is not in the better manuscripts. Some of the newer translations have made that clear, and for that reason I would like to change the verse as follows: "Wherefore, holy brethren, partakers of the heavenly calling, consider the Apostle and High Priest of our confession [that which we confess], Jesus."

"Consider" Him. The Greek word translated by our English word *consider* conveys the fact of faithful attention, giving of time, and perceiving thoroughly with the mind. It is a very significant word, and we need to recognize that it means we are to give careful and serious and prolonged thought to this One.

"Consider the Apostle." What does the writer mean? The Lord Jesus was an apostle in the very basic meaning of the word. I don't think we need to read anything into this word. After all, what is an apostle? An apostle is one who is sent. Jesus was sent from God to this earth. "Consider the Apostle," because He was sent from God to this world. He is a messenger; He is God's messenger. He is the revelation of God. *Consider* Him. He comes from God as an Apostle, but notice also—

"Consider the Apostle and High Priest." His priestly function will be the subject of this epistle. (The writer just mentions it at this point, but when he comes back to it, that is all he is going to talk about. We will have to wait until we get to chapter 5 to see that.) An high priest is going in the opposite direction from an apostle. An apostle, like a prophet, came from God to man with a message; he spoke for God to man. However, an high priest was going on the other side of the freeway in the opposite direction. He was going from man to God; he represented man before God.

Now Jesus is our High Priest. Who is He? He is *Jesus*—the emphasis is upon His humanity. Again let me remind you that there is a Man in the glory today, and He represents us up there. My, I'm very happy that He is up there, because we are told that He is an Advocate for us; He defends us; He is on our side.

There are times when I feel that I am not quite making myself clear when I am talking to somebody. For example, some time ago I tried to explain to an audience the feeling I had when I was told that I had cancer. I felt that I wasn't getting through, that they really didn't understand. But I have the comfort of knowing that there is somebody who understands—Jesus understands exactly how I felt.

The Lord Jesus Christ understands how *you* feel today. My friend, we need to consider this—give serious thought to it and our careful attention. We have an Apostle who came from God, and He is our High Priest who has gone back into God's presence and is there for you and for me today.

This is quite a wonderful verse, as you can see!

CHRIST IS SUPERIOR TO MOSES

Now the writer is going to show that Christ is superior to Moses. You see, having shown the superiority of Christ over the prophets who spoke for God in the Old Testament, and having shown His superiority over the angels, now he must show that He is superior to Moses because Moses is very important to the Hebrews. Several years ago a group of rabbis held a debate in Denver, Colorado. The subject of the debate was: "Who was greater, Abraham or Moses?" It is my understanding that it was decided that Moses was greater than Abraham. If that is true, if Jesus is to be considered, He has to be superior to Moses. The writer to the Hebrews is going to show this.

Who was faithful to him that appointed him, as also Moses was faithful in all his house [Heb. 3:2].

The Lord Jesus "was faithful to him that appointed him." He was faithful as He came down to this earth to represent God to man, and He is faithful as He represents us to God.

"Also Moses was faithful in all his house." Whose house are we talking about here? The word *house* occurs seven times in the next few verses. It is very important to determine whose house this is. Is it Moses' house? I don't think so. It is God's house. Moses was faithful in God's house. He was called to do a certain thing, and he did it. He was found faithful.

It is true that Moses made some mistakes— in fact, he recorded them. He wrote the Pentateuch, but the mistakes are not in what he wrote, because God told him what to write. The mistakes were in his actions. He had a temper, and one time when God told him to speak to the rock, he hit it instead. It was wrong because that rock pictured Christ, and Christ's work for us. Many years earlier God had instructed Moses to smite the rock (see Exod. 17:6), and once smitten it need not be smitten again. Christ was smitten once for us; it was not necessary for Him to be smitten again. But Moses lost his temper. He did not know the implication of what he was doing when he smote the rock the second time. Although he made some mistakes, now that his life is past, it is wonderful indeed to note that the thing God remembers is his faithfulness. Faithfulness is the thing for which the Lord Jesus will commend His own—". . . Well done, thou good and faithful servant . . ." (Matt. 25:21). Regardless of who we are or what work the Lord has given us to do, we are to be faithful.

I once held meetings for a wonderful preacher. He did not play golf, but since his assistant did, his assistant took me out to play golf. While we were playing, he took the opportunity to let me know he was unfaithful to the pastor. He made little dirty digs about the man and said things he would not have said had he been faithful to the pastor for whom he was working. He was disloyal to him. The following day he said to me, "I have made arrangements for us to play at a certain golf course." I said, "I'm sorry, but I won't be able to go out today," and I never played golf with that man again.

The next time I went back to that church the assistant pastor was gone, and I asked the pastor about it. He told me, "That man got us in a lot of trouble. We found out he was very disloyal." I wondered at the time if I should have told the pastor about his assistant. I have no use for a man who is not faithful to the man he is to serve. If you cannot be faithful to the man you are working under, you ought to leave your position. If you are not faithful to him, you are not faithful to God. If you are like that, and I am especially thinking of pastors, then you are a man that cannot be trusted. I would never trust that man as an assistant pastor under any circumstances. That assistant pastor wrote to me later and wanted me to recommend him to a church. I did not recommend him. How can you recommend a man as a pastor when he was not faithful as an assistant?

God says that Moses was faithful. Wouldn't it be wonderful to hear God say of *you*, "He was faithful"?

Now notice that the verse began by saying that Christ was faithful—"who was faithful to him that appointed him." How, then, was He superior to Moses?

For this man was counted worthy of more glory than Moses, inasmuch as he who hath builded the house hath more honour than the house [Heb. 3:3].

Moses was faithful in God's house, but the Lord Jesus is the one who built the house. He is the Creator; Moses is a creature. There is the difference, my friend.

For every house is builded by some man; but he that built all things is God [Heb. 3:4].

"Every house is builded by some man [someone]." You can't have a house without a builder—it can't just grow! Every house is built by someone.

"But he that built all things is God." The Lord Jesus is God, and He is the Creator. Moses never made that claim for himself.

And Moses verily was faithful in all his house, as a servant, for a testimony of those things which were to be spoken after;

But Christ as a son over his own house; whose house are we, if we hold fast the confidence and the rejoicing of the hope firm unto the end [Heb. 3:5-6].

Not only is Christ superior to Moses in that He is the Creator and Moses is a creature, but also the best thing that could be said of Moses is that he was a *servant* of God—never was he called a son of God. Christ is *the* Son of God. There is quite a difference between the son in the house and a servant in a house. So Christ is superior to Moses on two counts: Christ is the Creator and He is the Son. This is very important to see.

"If we hold fast the confidence and the rejoicing of the hope firm unto the end." Paul had a way of using "ifs," not as a condition but as a method of argument and of logic. We would understand him better if he had said, "*Since* we hold fast the confidence." In other words, if we are sons of God and if we are partakers of the heavenly calling, we *will* be faithful and we will hold fast. This is the proof that we are of God's house.

For example, 1 John 2:19 puts it this way, "They went out *from* us, but they were not *of* us; for if they had been *of* us, they would no doubt have continued with us: but they went out, that they might be made manifest that they were not all *of* us" (italics mine). I have always believed that God has permitted the cults to come along to draw out of the churches those who are not really believers. The cults serve as God's strainer. The proof that you are a child of God is that you hold to the faith. That doesn't *make* you a child of

God, but it does prove that you *are* a child of God. If you are a believer, you will hold on, not because you are able but because *He* is able to make you stand.

So the writer of this Hebrew epistle (who I believe to be the apostle Paul) is using the "if" of argument. "If we hold fast the confidence and the rejoicing of the hope firm unto the end" means that you are a partaker of the heavenly calling; you are among the brethren.

I have always used the Bible as a means of testing. If a person really is a child of God, he will hold to the Word of God, and he is going to love the Word of God because he wants to hear his Father talking to him.

Now let's pursue a little further the contrast between Moses and the Lord Jesus Christ. Both Moses and the Lord Jesus enunciated an ethical system. It is generally agreed, even among those outside the fold of Christ, that Moses gave the greatest legal system which ever has been given and that Jesus in His Sermon on the Mount enunciated a tremendous system of laws. However, there is a vast difference between the two. You see, the laws which came from God through Moses had to do with *conduct*. However, when the Lord Jesus gave what we call the Sermon on the Mount (beginning with those marvelous beatitudes: "Blessed are the pure in heart, for they shall see God"), we see that instead of dealing with conduct, they deal with *character*. The ethical demands of Christ, apart from the saving grace of the Lord Jesus Christ in His death and resurrection, present a hopelessly high system. The Sermon on the Mount, apart from the redemption we have in Christ, has made more hypocrites in the church than anything else. Folk today teach the ethic and say we are to keep the commandments of the Sermon on the Mount! My friend, only through the redemption in Christ can we even *approach* that standard. When God spoke through Moses yonder on top of Mount Sinai, there was thunder and lightning and earthquake and terror. God warned the people to stand afar off and not to let even the cattle touch the mount. But in this age of grace God has not spoken in that manner; He has spoken from the top of a hill called Calvary. On that hill there was a cross and on that cross there was a broken, bruised, dying man—who was more than a man. He was God. And by His death upon that cross has flowed down to this world the *grace* of God.

How I thank God that He does not save by law! If He did, Vernon McGee would have to admit that he had failed and would have to look for another route. Thank God, there is another route—the *grace* of God.

"If [since] we hold fast the confidence and the rejoicing of the hope firm unto the end." Since you are a child of God you will be *rejoicing* in the hope firm unto the end. This is another reason it is difficult to tell if folk in our churches are really saved. Some of them look and act as if they had been weaned on a dill pickle! They are not rejoicing in Christ.

Oh, my friend, Jesus is superior to the prophets, He is superior to angels, and He is superior to Moses. How wonderful He is! No wonder we are told to consider Him. In Hebrews 3:1 we are told to consider the Apostle and High Priest of our profession [confession], Christ. In Hebrews 12:3 we are going to be admonished again: "For consider him that endured such contradiction of sinners against himself, lest ye be wearied and faint in your minds." A person would be very discouraged if all he had was the Sermon on the Mount. I feel sorry for you if you are attempting to make the Sermon on the Mount your religion. If you don't have redemption in Christ, you are flying under false colors.

We are to consider Him—consider Him in His person, consider Him in His performance, His work upon the cross. Someone has put it poetically:

When the storm is raging high,
When the tempest rends the sky,
When my eyes with tears are dim,
Then, my soul, consider Him.

When my plans are in the dust,
When my dearest hopes are crushed,
When is passed each foolish whim,
Then, my soul, consider Him.

When with dearest friends I part,
When deep sorrow fills my heart,
When pain racks each weary limb,
Then, my soul, consider Him.

When I track my weary way,
When fresh trials come each day,
When my faith and hope are dim,
Then, my soul, consider Him.

Clouds or sunshine, dark or bright,
Evening shades or morning light,
When my cup flows o'er the brim,
Then, my soul, consider Him.

"Consider Him"
—Author unknown

My friend, we are to consider Him in this epistle, and we will need the Spirit of God to make Him real to us.

THE PERIL OF DOUBTING

Wherefore (as the Holy Ghost saith, To-day if ye will hear his voice [Heb. 3:7].

Notice that we have another *wherefore* which opens this section. We had a *wherefore* in verse 1, a *wherefore* here in verse 7, and we are going to have *wherefore* again in verse 10. It is a very important word. As I said, it is a swinging door that swings back into the past and swings out into the future. Also it is a danger signal as you come down the great highway that leads to heaven. In effect, it warns: Look both ways before you pull out—some crazy driver may be coming down the wrong side of the highway.

Wherefore, that is, in view of what has already been said, since the word spoken by the prophets and the word spoken by angels and the word spoken by Moses was so important, what about the importance of the word spoken by Jesus? We need to be very careful about doubting Him.

"To-day if ye will hear his voice" begins the quotation from Psalm 95:7–11.

Harden not your hearts, as in the provocation, in the day of temptation in the wilderness:

When your fathers tempted me, proved me, and saw my works forty years.

Wherefore I was grieved with that generation, and said, They do alway err in their heart; and they have not known my ways.

So I sware in my wrath, They shall not enter into my rest.) [Heb. 3:8–11].

I believe that Christ is in every psalm, although I admit that I am not able to find Him in every psalm. However, here He is in Psalm 95: "For he is our God; and we are the people of his pasture, and the sheep of his hand. To-day if ye will hear his voice, Harden not your heart, as in the provocation, and as in the day of temptation [testing] in the wilderness: When your fathers tempted [tested] me, proved me, and saw my work. Forty years long was I grieved with this generation, and said, It is a people that do err in their heart, and they have not known my ways: Unto whom I sware in my wrath that they should not enter into my rest" (Ps. 95:7–11).

Hebrews 3:7–11 interprets this portion of Psalm 95, and Israel is given to us as an example. Let's consider this for a moment. The generation of Israel that came out of Egypt doubted God, and because of their doubt they never entered the land of Canaan.

"They shall not enter into my rest." I have marked in my Bible that final word *rest*. There are at least a dozen references in this chapter and the next chapter to the word *rest*, but it does not always mean the same kind of rest.

There is the rest of salvation. The Lord Jesus referred to this in Matthew 11:28 when He said in effect, "Come unto me, all ye that labour and are heavy laden, and I will rest you; that is, I'll lift the burden of sin from you." Because He bore it for us upon the cross, our sins are forgiven, and we have redemption through His blood, even the forgiveness of sins. Therefore, you don't have to do anything so that God will forgive you; Christ has already done it when He died for you. All you have to do is believe and receive Christ.

The people of Israel now know the rest of redemption. They are no longer slaves in Egypt. They came out by blood—blood on the doorposts. They came out by power—God brought them across the Red Sea. God had delivered them. But then the Lord Jesus went on to say, "Take my yoke upon you, and learn of me; for I am meek and lowly in heart: and ye shall find rest unto your souls" (Matt. 11:29). That is a different kind of rest. It is not the rest of redemption; I would call it the rest of obedience, the rest of enjoying the Christian life.

When the children of Israel came out of the land of Egypt, as they crossed over the Red Sea, they sang the song of Moses—". . . I will sing unto the LORD, for he hath triumphed gloriously: the horse and his rider hath he thrown into the sea!" (Exod. 15:1). "God has delivered us—how great He is!" After they left Sinai, an eleven-day journey could have gotten them into the Promised Land. But no, they had to send spies in to search out the land. It wasn't necessary—God said He would take care of them, but they didn't believe God. So God yielded to their wishes and let them send in spies. Although the spies did see the wonderful land, they were most impressed by the giants, and they saw themselves as grasshoppers. They didn't see God. They returned to the people with a false report—except Caleb and Joshua who insisted that God could handle the giants if they trusted Him. But the people accepted the majority report (this is my reason for believing that committees are not satisfactory for doing the Lord's work), and they spent forty years on a journey that should have taken a few days. What was the reason? Unbelief.

You see, they didn't believe God enough to enter into the land. They believed Him enough to come out of Egypt, but not enough to enter Canaan. God said that that generation of unbelievers would die in the wilderness and He would bring their children into the Land of Promise. And we find later that Joshua did bring the next generation into the land. They had to cross another body of water, the river Jordan. How did they do it? Well, God sent the ark of the covenant (symbolic of God's presence) ahead on the shoulders of the priests. When their feet touched the brink of the river, the waters of Jordan were cut off. "And the priests that bare the ark of the covenant of the LORD stood firm on dry ground in the midst of Jordan, and all the Israelites passed over on dry ground, until all the people were passed clean over Jordan" (Josh. 3:17). Then they took twelve stones out of the middle of the river, where the priests still stood with the ark, and placed them as a memorial on the shore. Then they replaced them with twelve stones from the Land of Promise. When the waters of Jordan returned and covered those twelve stones, it was symbolic of the death of Christ. The twelve stones which were taken out of the river and placed as a monument on the other side speak of the resurrection of Christ.

Paul talks about this in Romans 6:4, where he says, "Therefore we are buried with him by baptism into death: that like as Christ was raised up from the dead by the glory of the Father, even so we also should walk in newness of life." We are now joined to a living Christ, and that is the only way we will enjoy Canaan. Canaan is *not* heaven. We are going to find out that there is an *eternal* rest, and Jesus gives that rest, but the question today is, "Have you entered into the rest that believers are to have as they sojourn on earth?" Are you a rejoicing Christian today? You will find out that the only way to do it is to study and believe the Word of God. How many Christians today, how many church members really study the Word of God? The Book of Hebrews is going to tell us that the Word of God is quick and powerful. Now that refers to the Lord Jesus Christ, but it also refers to the written Word. Therefore, the only way you and I can stay close to Him is to stay close to the Word of God. And the only way you and I can enjoy the grapes and fruits of the land, and the beauty and enjoyment of it, is by studying God's Word. Without a personal acquaintance with the Word of God, being a church member is like wearing a yoke, being browbeaten to give money, and having to *do* certain things. Everything is a duty instead of a drawing to the wonderful person of Christ.

The writer of this Hebrew epistle is speaking to those who are already saved but have not entered into the blessings of the Christian life. They doubt God, and as a result they are having a wilderness experience.

"Wherefore I was grieved with that generation, and said, They do alway err in their heart; and they have not known my ways." Notice where they erred. In their minds? No, in their hearts. Now hold that thought in your mind for a moment. The generation of Israel who came out of Egypt were cited to the Hebrew believers in the apostolic days as a warning not to repeat their sin. There was a danger of their doing that. And, my friend, we have the same danger, the danger of erring in our hearts.

"So I sware in my wrath"—it was not necessary for God to take an oath, but He did.

"They shall not enter into my rest." God said that, because of unbelief, the generation of Israelites would not enter into the land of promise. And, my friend, until you not only accept the Lord Jesus Christ as your Savior, but walk with Him by faith, committing your life to Him, you are not going to know anything about the joys of Canaan. Unfortunately, we have a great many wilderness Christians in our churches. The wilderness is a place of death; it is a place of unrest; it is a place of aimlessness; and it is a place of dissatisfaction. To those Israelites out there in the wilderness God said, "You are not going to know what rest is." And there are many believers today who just don't know what rest really means. They have never entered into it because they must enter by faith.

Take heed, brethren, lest there be in any of you an evil heart of unbelief, in departing from the living God [Heb. 3:12].

You may ask, "Could that be true of a believer?" It certainly could. It is very important to realize that God was angry with their *sin*. What was their sin? It was not murder; it was not stealing; it was not lying. What was it? My friend, they didn't *believe* God. That was their great sin.

But exhort one another daily, while it is called To-day; lest any of you be hard-

ened through the deceitfulness of sin [Heb. 3:13].

"Exhort one another"—we ought to do this, my friend, exhort and encourage one another.

"Lest any of you be hardened through the deceitfulness of sin." Although this is primarily a warning to believers not to miss their blessings because of the deceitfulness of sin, it has application to the unsaved person also. Unbelief in the heart is what is robbing folk of salvation. When someone tells me that he has an intellectual problem that hinders him from receiving Christ, I simply do not believe it.

Let me illustrate this from an experience I had when teaching a weekly Bible class in downtown Los Angeles. One evening a broker noticed the great crowd going into the church. They all had Bibles, and they looked as if they were interested in where they were going, so he was curious as to what could attract so many people to church in the middle of the week. Now this broker was a fine man in many ways. If you had met him, you would have said he was a fine man. Well, he followed the crowd into church and stayed through the service. Later he came up to me and said, "All you did was teach the Bible! Is that what brings people in?" I told him that I thought it was since that's all we did on Thursday nights. Well, the man continued to come on Thursday nights, and then he started coming on Sundays, and soon he was under conviction.

One day he came to my study and said, "I thought I was a Christian. Now I know I am not. I am only a member of a church. But, I have a few intellectual problems with some of the things you have said. One of them is the story of Jonah. It is impossible for me to believe that a man could live inside a fish for three days and nights."

I asked him, "Who told you that Jonah lived three days and three nights inside a fish?"

"I have heard preachers say it. Isn't it in the Bible?"

"Not in my Bible." So I turned to the Book of Jonah and showed him what it did say, then turned to the New Testament and read what Jesus had said about it: "For as Jonas was three days and three nights in the whale's belly; so shall the Son of man be three days and three nights in the heart of the earth" (Matt. 12:40). I said to this broker, "If you are going to have trouble with the resurrection of Jonah, then you will have trouble with the resurrection of Jesus."

"Well," he said, "I didn't know it was that way. That is no problem for me at all now."

"Do you have another intellectual problem?"

"Maybe I don't."

I looked him straight in the eye and asked, "What *sin* do you have in your life that is keeping you from Christ?"

He turned red and asked, "Has somebody been telling you about me?"

"No, I just know that your intellectual problem is really a heart problem. There is something in your life that is keeping you from Christ."

He broke down. In fact, he wept and confessed that he had been paying the rent for his secretary's apartment and was spending a great deal of time there. I asked if his wife knew about it. He said that he had kept it a secret. Then I asked him, "Then that's your trouble, isn't it—you wouldn't want to give up your secretary for Christ?"

He looked at me and said, "Yes." Then he said, "I'll stop the rent and I'll talk to her tomorrow."

Well, he not only talked to her, but he fired her. She threatened to expose him, but she didn't. He got down on his knees that very day in my office and accepted Christ as his Savior.

My friend, I have been a preacher for a long time, and I have learned that people don't really have intellectual problems which keep them from Christ, but they sure do have sin problems.

There is another passage of Scripture (in 2 Corinthians 3, beginning with verse 6) that deals with Moses, which I would like to call to your attention. "Who also hath made us able ministers of the new testament [covenant]; not of the letter, but of the spirit: for the letter killeth, but the spirit giveth life." The Law condemns us, you know, but only the Holy Spirit can give us life. "But if the ministration of death, written and engraven in stones [this is the Ten Commandments], was glorious, so that the children of Israel could not stedfastly behold the face of Moses for the glory of his countenance; which glory was to be done away." Paul is not saying that the Law wasn't glorious; it *was*, but that glory was to disappear. Now let's drop down to verse 11: "For if that which is done away was glorious, much more that which remaineth is glorious." He is making a contrast between the glory of the Law, which actually made Moses' face shine, and the greater glory that we have in Christ. "Seeing then that we have such hope, we use great plainness of speech: And not as Moses, which put a veil over his face, that the children of Israel could not stedfastly look to the end of that which is abolished" (2 Cor. 3:12–13). You see, Moses didn't put a veil over his face as a dimmer, to dim the glory (which is the general interpretation) but the glory was disappearing and he put a veil over his face so that folk wouldn't know about its disappearance. But there is another glory now, the glory which is in Christ. "But their minds were blinded: for until this day remaineth the same veil untaken away in the reading of the old testament; which veil is done away in Christ. But even unto this day, when Moses is read, the veil is upon their heart" (2 Cor. 3:14–15). You see, unbelief is not an intellectual problem; it is a heart problem. Perhaps you, my friend, are one who has not come to Christ because there is sin in your life and you do not want to give it up. The minute your heart is ready to give it up, at that moment your "intellectual" problems will dissolve. He will take the veil away from your mind, and you can come to Christ and be saved. Now notice verse 16: "Nevertheless when it [the heart] shall turn to the Lord, the veil shall be taken away." The veil will be removed from your mind when your heart turns to Christ. And the next verse: "Now the Lord is that Spirit: and where the Spirit of the Lord is, there is liberty." The Holy Spirit will move into your life and make Christ real to you, as He is doing for multitudes of folk in our day. Then when we come to Him—". . . we all, with open face beholding as in a glass the glory of the Lord, are changed into the same image from glory to glory, even as by the Spirit of the Lord" (2 Cor. 3:17–18). If you turn to Him—oh, my friend, the future that will await you as you grow in grace and in the knowledge of Him!

Now let's return to verse 13 where we are reminded, "But exhort one another daily, while it is called To-day; lest any of you be hardened through the deceitfulness of sin." We as believers need to beware of the deceitfulness of sin. We can actually come to the place where we feel our lives are *satisfactory* to God although we are leading a wilderness life. For example, a believer can be dishonest and yet say that his conscience does not condemn him! Then he should condemn his conscience, because it has become hardened through continuance in sin. I know men in the ministry who have been totally dishonest; they have been found to be liars, yet they can get down on their knees and pray the most pious prayers I've ever heard. And their conscience does not condemn them. Of course it doesn't condemn them, because it has become hardened; they are permitting sin in their lives.

This writer of the Hebrew epistle goes back to the wilderness experience of Israel, applies it to the Hebrew believers of the first century, and steps on our toes also. It is the Holy Spirit who applies these truths to our own hearts.

For we are made partakers of Christ, if we hold the beginning of our confidence stedfast unto the end [Heb. 3:14].

"We are made partakers of Christ." Just think of that! We are *in* Christ. He *belongs* to us.

"If we hold the beginning of our confidence stedfast unto the end" is the same argument he used in verse 6. We prove that we are members of Christ's house, that we belong to Him, "if we hold fast the confidence and the rejoicing of the hope firm unto the end."

Now in this section the emphasis is upon the *rest* which is ours if we trust Christ. Scripture presents a fivefold rest: (1) creation rest; (2) entrance into Canaan; (3) the rest of salvation; (4) the rest of consecration; and (5) heaven. Here the writer is talking about the rest of fully trusting God, not only for salvation but for daily living.

While it is said, To-day if ye will hear his voice, harden not your hearts, as in the provocation [Heb. 3:15].

The quotation concludes with a quotation from Psalm 95, which we have already seen in verses 7 and 8. Obviously he repeats it to remind the reader that these truths are not for yesterday only, but for us today.

If you would ask me, "Preacher, what is the great sin in your life, what is it that has held you back more than anything else?", I would have to admit that it is *unbelief.* As I look back upon my years of ministry, I realize that I did not believe God as I should have. And today there is one thing I want above everything else, and that is to *believe* God. I want to commit my life to Him completely, turn everything over to Him.

Flying from London to Los Angeles not long ago, we had a cloud cover until we got over Greenland. Then I could see the icebergs. They may be pretty in pictures, but when I looked at them from a height of thirty-eight thousand feet, they didn't look so pretty. They looked cold and foreboding. I saw a glacier coming down between two mountains to the water's edge. I prayed right there. I said, "Lord, You know I trust You when I am on the ground, but I have difficulty trusting You when I am flying. I am in a place right now where I need to trust You. Help me to put all of my weight down in Your arms and rest in

You." For the first time in my life I went to *sleep* on an airplane! I have never done that before. I always had to stay awake so I could help the captain of the ship. But this time I went to sleep and left it all to the Captain of my salvation. When the plane landed in Los Angeles, I said, "Thank You, Lord, for the little victories. Maybe it wasn't much for You, but it was a whole lot for me."

My friend, this is the "rest" the writer of this Hebrew epistle is talking about, the rest of fully trusting God—not only for salvation but for daily living, for the help and the wisdom and the strength we need to live the Christian life.

The people of Israel wandered in the wilderness because they did not have faith to enter the Promised Land. As we have seen, Canaan does not represent heaven; it represents the place of spiritual blessing and victory. The apostle Paul was, I believe, speaking of his own experience when he cried, "O wretched man that I am! who shall deliver me from the body of this death?" (Rom. 7:24). That is not the cry of an unsaved man, it is the cry of a saved man who is a defeated Christian, who finds no satisfaction in Christ because he is not trusting. The problem was lack of faith.

For some, when they had heard, did provoke: howbeit not all that came out of Egypt by Moses [Heb. 3:16].

In the word *provoke* is the thought of God's being highly displeased with them because they had heard but did not believe. They had had faith enough to come out of Egypt, but that was as far as it went.

But with whom was he grieved forty years? was it not with them that had sinned, whose carcases fell in the wilderness? [Heb. 3:17].

Again, what was their sin that so grieved God? It was unbelief. We do not recognize—and I am sure they did not recognize—that doubting God's Word is such a serious sin. It is one of the worst because it leads to other sins. For these Israelites in the wilderness it led to calf worship; it led to fornication, and it led to an absolute denial and rejection of God, as they turned their backs upon Him and even wanted to go back to Egypt. They decided that slavery in Egypt was better than walking by faith into the Promised Land!

Unfortunately, there are many Christians who still walk after the world. They do not know what it is to really trust Christ and walk in complete faith and trust in Him.

Now notice the question: "With whom was he grieved forty years?" He was grieved with that crowd that came out of Egypt. They had sinned, and their carcases fell in the wilderness. Only two men out of that crowd had faith to believe God, and they were Joshua and Caleb. They were the only two who made it into the land. Even Moses did not make it into the Promised Land, although his problem was not so much a lack of faith, as it was actual disobedience when he struck the rock in anger rather than speaking to it as God had commanded.

And to whom sware he that they should not enter into his rest, but to them that believed not? [Heb. 3:18].

"And to whom sware he that they should not enter into his rest"—that is, the rest of Canaan; he is not speaking of heaven. Because of their unbelief they knew nothing about walking in Canaan, enjoying its fruits, and finding satisfaction in simply trusting God. God said that they would not enter into His rest. And He took an oath on that. Believe me, God doesn't have to take an oath, but when He does, you know He really means business.

Again, about whom is He talking? Those who did not believe. Their worship of the calf and their fornication were not the sins that kept them from God's blessing. It was the sin of *unbelief.* Oh, my friend, unbelief not only robs us of blessing, but it leads to other sins as well. The other day a man said to me, "Here I am a Christian and I did this stupid thing." Well, the thing that he did was actually dishonest. But the point is that he was deeply concerned about his dishonesty but was ignoring the root of it—he hadn't believed God. That did not disturb him at all.

So we see that they could not enter in because of unbelief [Heb. 3:19].

I suggest that you underline this verse in your Bible. This is what is robbing you and me of many blessings—*unbelief.*

CHAPTER 4

THEME: *Christ is superior to Joshua; Christ is superior to the Levitical priesthood*

In the first two verses of chapter 4 we have a continuation of the warning concerning doubting which was given in chapter 3.

Let us therefore fear, lest, a promise being left us of entering into his rest, any of you should seem to come short of it [Heb. 4:1].

We have come to the first "Let us" in this Epistle to the Hebrews. Constantly Paul urges the Hebrew believers to go on with the Lord; he is constantly challenging them. This is the first "Let us," but there is a whole lot of "Let us" in this epistle.

"Let us therefore fear." There are always those folk who are eager to find fault even with the Word of God, and they will say that this statement is a contradiction of other statements in the Bible. We are told in Romans 8:15, "For ye have not received the spirit of bondage again to fear. . . ." And in 2 Timothy 1:7 Paul wrote, "For God hath not given us the spirit of fear; but of power, and of love, and of a sound mind." Well, I have an answer for those folk in a message I have called, "When It Is Not Wrong to Fear." I hope that you are afraid of a rattlesnake. If I see one coming down the road, I don't simply move to the righthand side, I give him the whole road! There are certain things that you and I would do well to fear—"Let us therefore *fear*." I wish there were more concern among believers today about ignorance of the Word of God. In a church I pastored, a man was on our church board who was on about every board in town because he had a lot of money. He actually boasted of how many boards he was on. Then one day he boasted to me of how ignorant he was of the Word of God! The writer to the Hebrews said, "Let us therefore *fear*." That man should have said to me with great concern, "Oh, my ignorance of the Word of God! I am afraid of it." There are very few believers who are afraid of their ignorance of the Scriptures.

When Paul says, "Let us therefore fear," he is speaking of a good fear. When I take my grandsons for a walk, I warn them not to go out into the street. I want them to be afraid to go out into the street—that is a good fear. The Word of God says, "The fear of the LORD is the beginning of knowledge . . ." (Prov. 1:7). That is the kind of fear you and I are to have.

The fear he is talking about is for a purpose: "Lest, a promise being left us of entering into his rest, any of you should seem to come short of it." He is going to talk a great deal about rest in this chapter. The word *rest* occurs eight times here. There are several different kinds of rest, including Sabbath day or creation rest, and Canaan rest. Here he is speaking of Canaan rest. He is saying to believers, "Be afraid, because you do not want to miss it." How many believers are missing that rest today? Have *you* entered into rest? Do you know, Christian friend, what it is to really trust Christ and rest in Him?

For unto us was the gospel preached, as well as unto them: but the word preached did not profit them, not being mixed with faith in them that heard it [Heb. 4:2].

Here is the "rest" of salvation, the rest of trusting Christ as Savior. They heard the gospel but did not believe it.

CHRIST IS SUPERIOR TO JOSHUA

Moses led the children of Israel out of the land of Egypt, but he could not lead them into Canaan. Joshua led them into the land, but we will see here that he couldn't give them rest. Many of them never found rest—they never really laid hold of their possessions in the land. The world, the flesh, and the Devil rob many of the blessing God has for them. You and I live in a mean, wicked world. This world is not a friend of grace; it is not the friend of believers. Many of us have not discovered that yet.

For we which have believed do enter into rest, as he said, As I have sworn in my wrath, if they shall enter into my rest: although the works were finished from the foundation of the world [Heb. 4:3].

He is discussing here salvation rest, the rest of trusting Christ. Let me ask you a question: If you knew a man who professed to be a Christian and whom you really believed was a born-again believer, and he suddenly stopped living the Christian life and began acting like the world, if he stopped going to church, stopped giving to the Lord's work, and stopped all his participation in Christian activity, would you think that he had lost his salvation? If *you* were that person, would you feel that you had lost your salvation? If you think that this would cause you to lose your salvation, may I say to you that way back in your mind and deep down in the recesses of your heart, you are not really trusting *Christ*. You are believing that those *activities* add to your salvation, but they do not. You are to completely trust Christ. Don't misunderstand me. I believe that if you are trusting Christ you are going to be doing those things, but doing those things have nothing in the world to do with your salvation. My friend, have you really entered into rest?

For he spake in a certain place of the seventh day on this wise, And God did rest the seventh day from all his works [Heb. 4:4].

This is the Sabbath. God rested on the seventh day, and that was the Sabbath day. However, the Sabbath today is not a *day* you keep or observe. Have you entered into the *real* Sabbath today? Do you know what it is to trust Christ and Christ alone for your salvation? Are you trusting anything else? Is *He* it? Have you entered into rest?

I had a good friend who was a doctor and who observed Saturday as the Sabbath. We used to play tennis together, and we got pretty well acquainted with one another. One day after we had played three sets of tennis, we sat down on the bench, and we began to have what you would call a religious argument. He looked at me and said, "McGee, do you keep the Sabbath day?"

"Yes, I keep the Sabbath."

He looked at me real hard and said, "*What* day?"

I said to him, "Saturday, Sunday, Monday, Tuesday, Wednesday, Thursday, Friday, and then I start all over again on Saturday."

He said to me, "What in the world do you mean?"

"Well, the way I understand the Epistle to the Hebrews, the Sabbath day is now this day of grace in which we live, and Christ, after He died on the cross and came back to life, went back to the right hand of the Father and sat down. He sat down, not because He was tired, but because He had finished your redemption and mine. So now He tells me, 'You rest in Me.' I have a Sabbath day everyday—I rest in Christ."

That doctor friend looked at me in amazement. "Well," he said, "that's better than having just one day, isn't it?"

I said, "It sure is. Seven days a week is a sabbath of resting in Christ."

And in this place again, If they shall enter into my rest.

Seeing therefore it remaineth that some must enter therein, and they to whom it was first preached entered not in because of unbelief [Heb. 4:5–6].

It is unbelief that robs you of the rest of salvation, that robs you of the rest of satisfaction and blessing which God can give to you. Oh, the wonderful rest that He wants to give to us!

Again, he limiteth a certain day, saying in David, To-day, after so long a time; as it is said, To-day if ye will hear his voice, harden not your hearts [Heb. 4:7].

He is not saying tomorrow, but today. *Today* is the day for you and me. Today, right now, wherever you are, look at your watch or clock. What time is it? Well, this is the time of salvation. *Now*, right now you can trust Christ to save you. "To-day if ye will hear his voice, harden not your hearts."

For if Jesus had given them rest, then would he not afterward have spoken of another day [Heb. 4:8].

Joshua is the Old Testament or Hebrew word for "savior"; *Jesus* is the Greek or New Testament word, meaning "savior." In the verse before us—Joshua: "For if Joshua had given them rest, then would he not afterward have spoken of another day." When Joshua was old and stricken in years, there was yet very much land to conquer. The people of Israel had not entered into all the blessing God had in store for them. Joshua wasn't able to secure it for them. But, my friend, if you trust Christ, Christ can let you enter into the Canaan of the present day, in which there will be fruit and blessing and joy in your life. Oh, how we need this today! What robs us of it? Unbelief.

There remaineth therefore a rest to the people of God [Heb. 4:9].

Here the writer is projecting into the future when all the people of God are going to find a heavenly rest. Heaven will be a place of deep satisfaction, of real joy, and real blessing. "There remaineth therefore a rest to the people of God."

For he that is entered into his rest, he also hath ceased from his own works, as God did from his [Heb. 4:10].

We shouldn't get the impression that when God rested on the seventh day He sat down and said, "My, I'm tired. I've been working for six days, eight hours a day, from sunup to sundown, and I'm weary! I'll pull up the rocking chair and rest." That is not the thought behind "rest" at all. The thought here is the rest of *completeness*. Creation is finished. God has never been in the business of creating since then. There were just so many atoms which He needed for His universe, and He just made them all at once. He hasn't made any more since then. Now there have been quite a few changes taking place in the universe, but it is just those original little atoms rearranging themselves.

You and I live in a universe where creation is over with—except in the new creation. That new creation began yonder at Calvary and the Day of Pentecost. "Therefore if any man be in Christ, he is a new creature: old things are passed away; behold, all things are become new" (2 Cor. 5:17). Sons of God are the only things God is creating today—through faith in Christ. And there is a rest that He has promised to them. God has promised a heavenly rest, but, my friend, He wants us to enjoy ourselves even *now*. As someone has said, "All the way to heaven is heaven." We ought to enjoy this life. That is what the writer is talking about here: God rested, He ceased from His labors, and He is finished. Therefore, you do not have to lift your little finger to do something toward your salvation. Isn't it really a matter of conceit on our part to think that you and I as sinners could do anything that would cause God to say, "Oh my, what a nice little fellow you are! I'm so happy to have you in heaven because you are going to add a great deal to it."? Well, my friend, that is not the picture at all. He did it *all* for us. Even our righteousness is filthy rags in His sight. He cannot accept our righteousness, because we really do not have any. "There is none righteous, no, not one" (Rom. 3:10). Therefore He offers a *finished* salvation to us, and when we trust Christ we become new creations in Him.

Let us labour therefore to enter into that rest, lest any man fall after the same example of unbelief [Heb. 4:11].

I think the supreme satisfaction that can come to a child of God is that he is in the will of God, doing the work of God, and trusting and just resting in Him. That is the glorious place to which God wants you and me to come. Mary came to that place. She sat at Jesus' feet while Martha was back yonder in the kitchen with those pots and pans. Martha wanted to serve Christ, but she just didn't know what real rest was. She probably decided she was going to bake something and reached for a pan. It was not big enough and she was going to put it back and get a bigger one, but she dropped it on the floor. What a time she had with those pots and pans! She was really worn to a frazzle and finally lost her temper. But Mary was just sitting at Jesus' feet, doing nothing—she had already done her work. We need to learn to find our satisfaction sitting at Jesus' feet.

"Let us labour therefore to enter into that rest." Someone will say, "Do I have to *labor* to enter into rest?" Yes, my friend. This is sort of like the Irishman who said he intended to have peace in his home even if he had to fight for it. Fighting for peace? Yes! I wish America had learned that lesson. May I say to you, you must win a war before you can have peace. You have to have a victory before you can have peace. He says here, "Let us labor in order to rest." After all, when you have worked at something and come to the end of the day and sit down, isn't there a satisfaction in what you have done? Oh, today, we need to lay hold of God! To lay hold of God in prayer, and in faith, and to be used of Him. Oh, my Christian friend, let us *labor* toward that end.

"Lest any man fall after the same example of unbelief." The only thing in the world that can rob you of that rest is unbelief. Ever since I retired from the pastorate my prayer has been, "Oh, God, help me to trust You." I was a pastor for forty years, and very frankly, I look back and have to say that I wish I had trusted Him more. Many times I was so fearful and unbelieving. So today I want to simply lean back and trust Him. How wonderful He is! He is worthy of our trust.

For the word of God is quick, and powerful, and sharper than any two-edged sword, piercing even to the dividing asunder of soul and spirit, and of the joints and marrow, and is a discerner of the thoughts and intents of the heart [Heb. 4:12].

"For"—Paul used the words *wherefore*, *therefore*, and *for* as cement to hold together his argument. Someone has said, "Regardless of what you want to say about Paul, one thing you have to say is that Paul is logical." Paul was a marvelous logician, and I believe he wrote this epistle. *For* is a little word, but it is a big word. Someone has said, "God swings big doors on little hinges." Here is one of those little hinges, but there is a big door hanging on it.

"The word of God." There are some expositors who consider the "word" here not to be the written Word, but the living Word who is the Lord Jesus Christ. However, in Scripture the written Word is called the living Word. I believe the reference here is primarily to the written Word of God. As the written Word reveals Christ—it is a frame that reveals the living Christ—the reference here could be to both the written and living Word.

Quick is "living." The Word of God is living.

"Powerful"—the Greek word is *energes*, meaning "energizing." The Word of God is living, and it energizes.

"Sharper than any two-edged sword." I had a professor in seminary who said to a group of us young preachers: "Remember when you preach the Word of God that it is quick and sharp, but it is a *two-edged* sword. It will cut toward the congregation, but the other side is going to cut toward you. Therefore, don't preach anything that you are not preaching to yourself." I have found many times in my ministry that I am preaching to myself. The sermon might not have been for anybody else, but it *was* for me.

I have a friend who likes to kid me about my recording of tapes for our radio Bible study broadcasts. He says, "There you are, sitting in your study, just talking to yourself!" Very candidly, that is the way it works out many times as I sit there teaching the Bible. I'm speaking to myself. It may not apply to anyone in the radio audience, but it applies to me. The Word of God is two-edged. It will cut toward the other fellow, but it will also cut toward you and me. The Word of God is a two-edged sword, and it will penetrate.

Paul wrote to the Thessalonians, "For this cause also thank we God without ceasing, because when ye received the word of God which ye heard of us, ye received it not as the word of men, but as it is in truth, the word of God, which effectually worketh also in you that believe" (1 Thess. 2:13). The Thessalonians received the Word not just as an ordinary word, but they received it as the very Word of God. Paul said that when he gave out the Word of God ". . . my speech and my preaching was not with enticing words of man's wisdom, but in demonstration of the Spirit and of power" (1 Cor. 2:4). We receive many letters from those who listen to our radio Bible study broadcasts, from folk who through the Word have been brought to a saving knowledge of Christ, brought to a place where they enjoy their Christian faith, and brought to a place where they enjoy prayer. That is the purpose of the Word of God—it will have an effect upon you and your life.

It has been said, "The Word of God will keep you from sin, or sin will keep you from the Word of God." A great many believers do not spend enough time in the Word of God. A great many preachers do not spend enough time in the Word of God. The greatest discipline a preacher can have is to go through the Bible book by book with his congregation. That is a discipline which even if it does not help the congregation, it will surely help the preacher. In every church which I have served as a pastor, I have gone through the Bible with the congregation. It surely helped me—it was good for me. The Word of God is sharp; it is living and powerful and sharp.

"Piercing even to the dividing asunder of soul and spirit." There are many people who try to make a distinction between soul and spirit, devising some ingenious psychological division between the two. Do you know that only the Word of God can divide the soul and spirit? You and I cannot do that. When I talk about the soulish part of man and how God has given us the Holy Spirit, I suddenly find that I am no longer making a distinction between the soul and spirit—only the Word of God can do that. There are times in the Scriptures when "soul" and "spirit" are used synonymously. There are other passages where it is clear that the soul and spirit are separate and are not the same thing. Only the Word of God can divide soul and spirit.

"Of the joints and marrow." The Word can get right down even in this flesh of ours and make a distinction (see Ps. 32:3).

"A *discerner* of the thoughts and intents of the heart." The Greek word for "discerner" actually means "critic." We have today many critics of the Word of God. However, the Word of God is *the* critic. It criticizes you. It criticizes me. No man is in a position to sit in judgment on the Word of God. There are many reasons for that, and one reason is that there is no other book like it. The Word of God was written over a period of fifteen hundred years, by about forty-five different authors, some of whom had never heard of the others. Yet they are all in agreement. They all present the same great story. They all present a glorious salvation. May I say to you, no man is in a position to sit in judgment on such a remarkable book.

I had an opportunity one time to listen to a very fine, brilliant, Shakespearean scholar.

Many scholars are not humble, but this man was a very humble man. When he had finished his lecture he said, "Today I have attempted to give to you a critique of Shakespeare, but now I would like to say to you that I am in no position to sit in judgment on Shakespeare." It took a humble man to say that. Nor can any man sit in judgment on the Bible, my friend. You really don't know enough to sit in judgment on this Book. This Book surely sits in judgment on us. It is sin that keeps men from Christ today. It is not intellectual problems of the head, but it is problems in the heart which keep men from God.

"A discerner [critic] of the *thoughts* and *intents* of the heart." You see, the Bible does not deal with *acts* primarily. What the hand does is because of what the heart thought. The heart had the action of the hand in hand before the hand got hold of it. Therefore the Word of God goes down and deals with the heart. The Lord Jesus said, "For out of the heart proceed evil thoughts, murders, adulteries, fornications, thefts, false witness, blasphemies" (Matt. 15:19). My, that's a filthy list, but that is what is in your heart and mine. "The heart is deceitful above all things, and desperately wicked: who can know it?" (Jer. 17:9). No man can, but God does. The Word of God gets down and deals with the nitty-gritty of our hearts. It gets down and meets us right where the rubber meets the road, right down where you and I live and move and have our being.

Neither is there any creature that is not manifest in his sight: but all things are naked and opened unto the eyes of him with whom we have to do [Heb. 4:13].

You cannot conceal anything from God. I labored under the delusion as a young Christian that I would not let God in on everything in my life, even my plans. I prayed that He would give me certain things and do certain things for me, but I never let Him know my motives. I thought the prayer would sound better that way. To tell the truth, I didn't need to let Him know my motive because He knew it all the time. He is the one who knows the thoughts of the heart, and everything is open to Him. My friend, your life is an open book to Him. People ask me, "Do you think we ought to confess everything to Him?" Well, why not? He already knows—you might just as well tell Him all about it.

CHRIST IS SUPERIOR TO THE LEVITICAL PRIESTHOOD

Beginning with verse 14 of this chapter through verse 28 of chapter 7, the writer of this epistle is going to show that Christ is superior to the Levitical priesthood. This was very important for Hebrew believers to see because they were accustomed to approaching God through their high priest of the Levitical order, the priests who served first in the tabernacle and then in the temple. It was through them that they made their commitment to God and brought their sacrifices.

OUR GREAT HIGH PRIEST

The Lord Jesus Christ himself is our Great High Priest. Paul was so concerned and enthusiastic about the priesthood of Christ that way back in chapter 3 he said, "Wherefore, holy brethren, partakers of the heavenly calling, consider the Apostle and High Priest of our profession, Christ Jesus" (Heb. 3:1). He wanted to get the folk who were reading the epistle to immediately consider our High Priest. This is going to be the subject of much of the rest of the epistle, and, of course, there will be application of this great truth also.

Seeing then that we have a great high priest, that is passed into the heavens, Jesus the Son of God, let us hold fast our profession [Heb. 4:14].

Christ is our High Priest. The pagan notion of priesthood colors our thinking in reference to a priest. A pagan priest actually barred the approach to God, claiming possession of some mystical power essential to bringing an individual to God. A person had to go through this priest who claimed to have this particular access. That type of thing denies the finished work of Christ and the priesthood of all believers. The priesthood of all believers was one of the great truths which John Calvin emphasized. All of us need a priest—we have a lack; we need help, and we all have our hang-ups. Job's heart-cry was, "Neither is there any daysman betwixt us, that might lay his hand upon us both" (Job 9:33). Job longed for a mediator or priest who would stand between him and God, who would put one hand in Job's hand and his other hand in God's hand, and thus bring them together. Christ is that mediator, that priest, through whom every believer has personal access to God.

"We have a great high priest, that is passed into the heavens." Let me say right away that the Lord Jesus Christ was not a priest while here on the earth. The only mention in Scripture of His ever making any kind of sacrifice (He never needed to make a sacrifice for Himself, of course) was the time He told Simon Peter to catch a fish and take the gold piece out of its mouth that He might pay a necessary temple tax from which the priests were exempt. He did that, I think, to make it very clear that He was not a priest here on earth. To be a priest you had to be born in the line of Aaron, of the tribe of Levi. The Lord Jesus was a member of the tribe of Judah. He was not in the priestly line. He was in the kingly line. When He was here on earth He came as a prophet speaking for God. He went back to heaven a priest to represent us to God. He became a priest when He ascended into heaven. He died down here to save us, and He lives up there to keep us saved. It is true that when He was here He offered Himself upon the cross, and that is the function of a priest, but to be a priest to represent you and me He had to wait until He returned to heaven.

Christ occupies a threefold office: (1) He was a prophet when He came over nineteen hundred years ago—that is the past; (2) He is a priest today—that is for the present; and (3) He is coming someday to rule as a king—that is for the future. He occupies all three of these offices, and He is the great subject of this Epistle to the Hebrews.

"Let us hold fast our profession"—"profession" should be *confession*. Paul says, "Let us," to challenge us, to call us to do it, actually, to command us to do it. Let us hold fast our confession.

Notice that he does not say, "Let us hold fast our salvation." He is not talking about our salvation, but about our testimony, our witness down here. He is talking about our living for Christ. Christ died down here to save us, and He lives up yonder to keep us saved and to enable us to give a good witness. Some people say, "I can't live the Christian life." Well, I have news for you. It is true that you cannot live the Christian life, and God never asked you to live the Christian life. I have been thankful that He has not asked that of me, because I have tried it and it didn't work. We cannot do it in our own strength, but He asks that *He* might live it through us. He lives up yonder in order that you and I might hold fast to our confession, our testimony down here.

When we come to chapter 11 we will find a regular roll call of the heroes of the faith which shows what faith has done in the lives of men and women in all ages. All of those listed there had a good witness, a good report. Theirs was a good witness through faith—they lived by faith.

For we have not an high priest which cannot be touched with the feeling of our infirmities; but was in all points tempted like as we are, yet without sin [Heb. 4:15].

You will notice in your Bible that the word *yet* is in italics, meaning that it has been added by the translators. Christ was tempted without sin—*tested* without sin. In the testing of Jesus in the wilderness, He could not have fallen because He is the God-man. However, the pressure of testing was actually greater upon Him than it would be upon us. He could say, ". . . the prince of this world cometh, and hath nothing in me" (John 14:30). Satan finds something in me and in you also, but he could find nothing in the Lord Jesus. Let me illustrate this for you: A boat standing in water can only tolerate so much pressure. If the pressure becomes too great, there will be a rip in the hull of the boat and water will come in, and thus the pressure is removed. That is the way you and I are—we give in to the pressure, we yield, and then the pressure is gone. Jesus never did yield, and therefore there was a building up of pressure that you and I never experience. In the same way, the cars of a freight train all have a weight limit which they can carry. If that limit is exceeded, you will have a swaybacked car, one that is bowed down in the middle. It gives in—it can only carry so heavy a load. That is true of all of us. We can carry just so much and not any more. May I say to you, the weight of temptation Jesus Christ could carry was infinite—He was tested without sin. But He *was* tested, and for that reason He knows how we feel. We have a High Priest who understands us.

I have always felt that for the nation Israel the death of Aaron was in one sense of greater significance than the death of Moses. Aaron was their great high priest. Many Israelites had been brought up with Aaron, had played with him as a boy, and had gone through the wilderness with him. They could go to Aaron and say, "Look, Aaron, I did this, and I should not have done it. I have brought my sacrifice." And Aaron could sympathize with them. He knew exactly how they felt. But when Aaron died I imagine they wondered whether that new priest, the son of Aaron, would understand. Would he be able to sympathize and to help? We have a Great High Priest who is always available, and He does understand. He does not understand us theoretically, but down here He was tested, and He was "touched with the feeling of our infirmities." He knew what it was to hunger. He knew what it was to be touched with sorrow—Jesus wept!

He was "touched with the feeling of our infirmities . . . yet without sin."

Let us therefore come boldly unto the throne of grace, that we may obtain mercy, and find grace to help in time of need [Heb. 4:16].

"Let us therefore come boldly unto the throne of grace." I must confess that I have never really liked our translation of "boldly," but neither do I know how to change it. The word *boldly* has the thought of being brazen—there is sort of a flippancy suggested by it—or of being cocksure. That is really not the idea. It is a very interesting word in the Greek—*parrhesia*. It denotes the freedom of speech which the Athenians prized so highly. They were perhaps the first to feel that the average citizen should have freedom to speak.

"Let us therefore come [with great freedom] unto the throne of grace." We can speak freely to the Lord Jesus Christ. I can tell Him things that I cannot tell you. He understands me. He knows my weaknesses, and I might just as well tell Him. I have learned to be very frank with Him. I have not attempted to become buddy-buddy with Him—I despise that approach. He is *God*, and I come to Him in worship and with reverence. But I am free to speak, because He is also a man. He is God, but He is a man, and I can come to Him with great freedom. I can tell Him what is on my heart. I can open my heart to Him. I suspect, therefore, that all these very pious and flowery prayers we make are not impressive to Him—especially when we are attempting to cover up what is in our hearts and lives. I wonder if the Lord doesn't tune us out when we do not come to Him with freedom and open our hearts to Him. That is one of the reasons our prayer meetings are not more effective. We come to Him rather restrained, without being open and sincere.

"Unto the throne of grace." God's throne is a throne of grace. Formerly a throne of judgment, it is now a mercy seat, a throne of grace.

"That we may obtain mercy." We need a lot of mercy. Mercy is something that is in one sense negative—it speaks of the past. We are redeemed by the mercy of God. "Not by works of righteousness which we have done, but according to his mercy he saved us . . ." (Titus 3:5). He has been merciful to me.

"And find grace to help in time of need." Help is a very positive thing—it speaks of the future. We may obtain mercy and find grace to help in time of need. David wrote, "The LORD is my shepherd; I shall not want (Ps. 23:1). I have noticed that one of the newer translations reads, "The LORD is my shepherd; I *have not* wanted." How ridiculous! Of course, he had not wanted in the past, but the beauty of it is that David could say, "I *shall* not want." Why? Because the Lord is my Shepherd. I have an High Priest up yonder, and I can go to Him as my shepherd.

By the way, have you been to Him yet today? What did you tell Him? Did you tell Him that you love Him? Did you confess your sins to Him? Well, why don't you? He already knows it, but why don't you tell Him? Don't put up a front to Him. He already knows that you can come to Him only on His merit. Go to Him with freedom and *talk* to Him—there is mercy and grace to help in time of need.

CHAPTER 5

THEME: *Definition of a priest*

This chapter continues the great theme of Christ as our High Priest, showing that He is superior to the Levitical priesthood, with which the Hebrews were so familiar.

In the first ten verses we have the definition of a priest. Christ, as we have already said, has the threefold office of prophet, priest, and king. He is God's final word to man. In Christ God has said all He intends to say. As a prophet, He spoke over nineteen hundred years ago. Now He is the Word of God. He is the priest for the now generation. Some day in the future He is going to come as king. Right now He is our Great High Priest. We have access to Him. He is a Great High Priest, just as Aaron was a great high priest.

And every believer is a priest, just as all the tribe of Levi were priests. We can offer sacrifices to God as priests. Praise is a sacrifice that we can offer. Have you praised Him today? We can also offer our substance, the fruit of our hands, the fruit of our minds, or our time. Believers can make all of these things an offering to Him. And prayer is the work of a priest. To recognize our position and privilege eliminates all of the mechanics we have today. It puts aside all of the methods that we use. We see two extreme approaches to God through worship today. One is a very emotional approach, and the other is a very ritualistic approach. Both of them are soulish and not spiritual worship at all. We simply need to come to Him and get rid of all the mechanics and the methods.

Someone sent me a story about the astronaut who was in his capsule just ready to close the door in preparation for the launching, when a reporter asked him a question. Reporters, I have observed, sometimes ask some rather asinine questions. This reporter asked, "How do you feel when you are an astronaut ready to take off?" The astronaut replied, "How would you feel if you were sitting on top of fifty thousand parts, each supplied by the lowest bidder?" That is the way many people worship today. They are ritualistic or they are emotional; they go by their feelings rather than by the Word of God.

The concluding verse of chapter 4 urges us to come in freedom to the throne of grace. We need mercy and we need help. He is in the position to supply these because He is our Great High Priest.

DEFINITION OF A PRIEST

For every high priest taken from among men is ordained for men in things pertaining to God, that he may offer both gifts and sacrifices for sins [Heb. 5:1].

This verse gives us the definition of a priest. He must be taken from among men, which means he must be a *man*. He must be a representative, you see. He represents man, but he represents man to God. He is ordained *for* man in things pertaining to God. Because he goes before God, he must be acceptable to God. That is the suggestion in "is ordained for men in things . . . to God." In verse 4 we are told specifically that no man takes this honor unto himself, but he that is called of God, as was Aaron. He must be ordained of God. Therefore a priest is: (1) taken from among men; (2) ordained for men (on behalf of men); and (3) goes to God for men.

We can now draw a distinction between a priest and a prophet. A priest goes from man to God; he represents man before God. A prophet comes from God to man with a message from God. Therefore the Old Testament priest did not tell men what God had to say— that was the ministry of the prophet. The priest's ministry was to represent man before God. Now in the present age our Lord Jesus Christ is the only priest. It is He who represents us before God.

The priesthood functions, not for lost sinners, but for saved sinners. You will recall that John said, "My little children [my little born ones], these things write I unto you, that ye sin not . . ." (1 John 2:1). Well, I'm sorry, John, but you are talking to a boy who has sinned. Even as a child of God I have sinned. I am thankful that he covered me when he added, "And if any man sin, we have an advocate with the Father, Jesus Christ the righteous." Christ represents me up there. When my enemy, Satan, accuses me before the Father, the Lord Jesus Christ represents me. He is my High Priest. That is one reason why I would never be satisfied just to have a priest on earth. I want to make this very clear, and I am not attempting to be critical. If someone is going to represent me before God, I want to be sure that he is acceptable to God. Is he one who has accreditation? Has he passed his bar examination so he can represent me in heaven? We can *pray* for one another, but we cannot represent one another in heaven. But because I need somebody to represent me, I am very happy that I have my Great High Priest who represents me before the Father.

"That he may offer both gifts and sacrifices." Notice that the priest may offer both gifts and sacrifices. The writer is going to make it abundantly clear that He had something to offer: He offered Himself. Compared to the precious blood of Christ which has redeemed us, silver and gold would be like lead or dirt.

"That he may offer both gifts and sacrifices for *sins*"—notice that it is sins, not sin; it is plural. It speaks of the life of the believer. For example, when you lost your temper, did you go to God and confess that sin? You have a representative who is there to make intercession for you. He represents you before God.

Who can have compassion on the ignorant, and on them that are out of the way; for that he himself also is compassed with infirmity [Heb. 5:2].

We have a Great High Priest who could say, when He came to the end of His ministry on earth, "Which of you convinceth [convicts] me of sin? . . ." (John 8:46). The Lord's disciples had been with Him for three years, and if there had been anything wrong, they would have known. He was impeccable; He did not commit any sin. Yet because He lived on this earth as a man, He understands us.

He "can have compassion on the ignorant." What does that mean? "Compassion on the ignorant" refers to sins of ignorance. Leviticus 4:1–2 deals with these sins. If you don't think you have committed a sin in the past few days, and you feel like you have really been living in the heights, I have news for you. You commit sins that you are not even aware of, and He, our Great High Priest, takes care of that for us. He can have compassion on the ignorant. You see, "There is a way which *seemeth* right unto a man, but the end thereof are the ways of death" (Prov. 14:12, italics mine). "All we like sheep have gone astray . . ." (Isa. 53:6). God compares us to sheep, because all sheep go astray.

"He himself also is compassed with infirmity." Aaron was touched with infirmity or weakness, but Christ was touched with a *feeling* of our infirmity or weakness. He knows how we feel about things. He is the perfect mediator, you see. When we fall, He doesn't get down in the dirt with us; He is there to lift us out of it.

The trouble with Aaron was that he might condone the sins that he also had committed. Or he might condemn the sins that he had not committed himself. That would always be a danger. But Christ is able to show mercy, and He neither condones nor condemns. When we come to Him to make confession of our sins, He doesn't give us a little lecture about doing better next time. He just extends mercy to us. "If we confess our sins, he is faithful and just [as our High Priest] to forgive us our sins, and to cleanse us from all unrighteousness" (1 John 1:9). It is wonderful to have a High Priest like He is!

Now we see a contrast between Aaron and Christ because there is no counterpart of this requirement of the Aaronic priesthood in our Lord Jesus Christ.

And by reason hereof he ought, as for the people, so also for himself, to offer for sins [Heb. 5:3].

You will recall that on the great Day of Atonement Aaron first brought a sacrifice and took the blood into the Holy of Holies for his own sins. He had to have his own sin question settled first before he could represent the people. There is no counterpart of this in Christ.

Christ did not have to make an offering for Himself. He made an offering for you and me.

And no man taketh this honour unto himself, but he that is called of God, as was Aaron [Heb. 5:4].

As we saw earlier, Christ was a priest because He was acceptable to God.

So also Christ glorified not himself to be made an high priest; but he that said unto him, Thou art my Son, to-day have I begotten thee [Heb. 5:5].

I want to make it abundantly clear that the "begotten" here has nothing to do with the birth of Christ in Bethlehem. It has everything to do with the garden near Calvary where He was buried after His crucifixion because that is where His resurrection took place. He was begotten from the dead. His priesthood began when he went back to heaven, and that speaks of His resurrection.

As he saith also in another place, Thou art a priest for ever after the order of Melchisedec [Heb. 5:6].

The order of Aaron is not adequate to set before us the priesthood of Christ. So our Lord is not an High Priest in the order of Aaron, although Aaron is the type, and Christ the antitype. Christ is the Son, and Aaron is just a servant.

"Thou art a priest for ever after the order of Melchisedec." Who is Melchisedec (spelled Melchizedek in the Old Testament)? The only historical record that we have of him is in Genesis 14 where he is described as a "priest of the most high God." He went out to congratulate Abraham on his victory over Chedorlaomer and his allies in which Abraham recovered all of the citizens of Sodom and Gomorrah, including his nephew Lot, and also brought back all the booty. The king of Sodom met Abraham and offered him all of the booty. Abraham was under some temptation, but he turned down the offer. In Genesis 14:18 we read, "And Melchizedek king of Salem brought forth bread and wine: and he was the priest of the most high God." The account continues in Genesis 14:19–20, "And he blessed him, and said, Blessed be Abram of the most high God, possessor of heaven and earth: And blessed be the most high God, which hath delivered thine enemies into thy hand. And he gave him tithes of all." We are told that Melchizedek was the king of Salem (*Salem* means "peace") and he was also king of righteousness. He walks out onto the pages of Scripture out of nowhere—

we have no inkling where he came from—and he walks off the page of Scripture the same way. There is no other historical mention of him.

In Psalm 110 we see the *prophecy* of Melchizedek—that there is coming one who is to be a priest after the order of Melchizedek. Hebrews now gives us the interpretation of Melchizedek.

Let me say at this point that there are some very fine expositors who think that Melchizedek is the preincarnate Christ. Well, I cannot accept that interpretation because Melchizedek is a *type,* of the Lord Jesus. Obviously, the antitype cannot be the type—or you wouldn't have a type. Therefore, I interpret Melchizedek as a human being who was the literal king of Salem. Two excellent expositors, G. Campbell Morgan and Lewis Sperry Chafer, hold that he was the preincarnate Christ; so you will be in good company if you take that position.

However, I believe Melchizedek was a type given to us by Moses and guarded by God. He just walks out of nowhere and walks back into nowhere. He had no beginning or ending of days. The Lord Jesus Christ is the beginning and the end. He is Alpha and Omega (see Rev. 1:8). He started it all, and He will end it all. He is the AMEN. He is the One who is the *eternal* God and as such has no beginning or ending. The writer is telling us that we have a priest like that—He is after the order of Melchizedek. We will see an interpretation of this in chapter 7.

This brings us to a verse that I feel totally inadequate to deal with. I feel that I am just standing on the fringe in my understanding of it.

Speaking of the Lord Jesus—

Who in the days of his flesh, when he had offered up prayers and supplications with strong crying and tears unto him that was able to save him from death, and was heard in that he feared [Heb. 5:7].

Scripture tells us that on three occasions Jesus wept. I am of the opinion there were other occasions, but the record gives us only three. One was at the tomb of Lazarus. At that time, although He knew He would restore Lazarus to life, His heart went out in sympathy to the two sisters who were so deeply grieved. Because He wept for *them,* I know how He feels when *you* and *I* stand at the graveside of a loved one.

At another time He wept over the city of Jerusalem. Since He wept over Jerusalem at that time, I am sure He has wept many times over the cities in which you and I live. They certainly provide Him with reasons for weeping!

Then the third time He wept was in the Garden of Gethsemane. Why did He weep there? A cynic and unbeliever made the statement that he wished he had been present so he could have killed the Lord Jesus in some way other than by crucifixion. In saying this, it is evident that he perceived something that some believers do not firmly grasp. He would have liked to have kept Jesus from the Cross, which is exactly what the Devil wanted to do. I believe that Satan attempted to slay the Lord Jesus in the Garden of Gethsemane. When He prayed in the garden, "Let this cup pass from me" (see Luke 22:42), the "cup" was death. He did not want to die in the Garden of Gethsemane.

"And was heard in that he feared." If our Lord Jesus prayed in the garden to let the cup pass because He didn't want to die on the cross, then He wasn't heard—because He *did* die on the cross. My friend, He was heard; He did not die in the Garden of Gethsemane.

You see, prophecy had made it abundantly clear that He was to die on a cross. We do not have a better picture of crucifixion than in Psalm 22. The cross was an altar on which the Son of God shed His blood, paying the penalty for your sin and my sin. "The life of the flesh is in the blood," God said, "and I have given it to you upon the altar to make an atonement for your souls . . ." (Lev. 17:11). In the Old Testament the blood of animal sacrifices only covered over the sin, but the blood of Christ was given "to make atonement for your souls." Christ shed His blood on the cross, which was an altar. He told Nicodemus, "And as Moses lifted up the serpent in the wilderness, even so must the Son of man be lifted up" (John 3:14). He did not want to die in the garden. That, I think, was His prayer, His human prayer, as He wept and sweat great drops of blood. Our Lord was near death as He approached the cross, and He prayed to be delivered from death so that He could reach the cross. And we are told that He "was heard in that he feared."

"In that he feared"—fear is not something that is always wrong, as we have seen elsewhere in this epistle. It would be abnormal not to fear some things. And I think we need a little more fear in our churches; we need the fear of the Lord, which is the beginning of wisdom. The Lord Jesus *feared.*

Though he were a Son, yet learned he obedience by the things which he suffered;

And being made perfect, he became the author of eternal salvation unto all them that obey him [Heb. 5:8–9].

"And being made perfect"—that is, made complete, made full.

"Eternal salvation"—the only kind of salvation He offers is eternal. If you can lose it tomorrow, then, my friend, it is not eternal. It is some other kind of salvation. But He offers only *eternal* salvation.

"Unto all them that obey him." What is obedience? A crowd of people asked Jesus, ". . . What shall we do, that we might work the works of God?" (John 6:28). Jesus replied, ". . . This is the work of God, that ye believe on him whom he hath sent" (John 6:29). Do you want to obey God? Then *trust* Christ. That is what He is saying.

But there is something here that I do not understand—I am frank to admit it. "Though he were a Son, yet learned he obedience by the things which he suffered." Why did the Son of God need to learn obedience by suffering? And why did He need to be made perfect when He already was perfect? I stand here in the presence of a mystery, a mystery that I cannot fathom. I know only that God got something out of the death of Christ that has made heaven more wonderful and has added something to heaven where everything is perfection and that the Son of God has learned something!

Now I am well acquainted with the explanations that men give, but none of them satisfy me. I just recognize that it is a great mystery. Christ took upon Himself our humanity, and in that humanity He obeyed God. He said, "I have come to do my Father's will" (see John 6:39). Paul said of Him, ". . . [He] took upon him the form of a servant, and was made in the likeness of men: And being found in fashion as a man, he humbled himself, and became *obedient* unto death, even the death of the cross" (Phil. 2:7–8, italics mine). My friend, I want you to know that when I die (if the Lord tarries) I won't do it obediently. I don't want to die. I think it is morbid when folk always talk about wanting to die. I want to live on earth as long as I can. When I had cancer, many people wrote to me and said, "We are praying for you. We are asking that the Lord spare your life." I am thankful because the Lord heard those prayers. But one dear lady in Southern California wrote to me and said,

"I am not praying that the Lord will leave you here. I know you are ready to go, so I am praying that He will take you home." I wrote back to her in a hurry and said, "Listen, you let the Lord alone in this matter. It is just between Him and me. I don't want you to tell the Lord when you think He ought to take me home. I want to stay here, and I'll appreciate it if you don't pray that prayer any more. At least, change it. Tell the Lord that you made a mistake, and that McGee wants to stay."

When the writer to the Hebrews says that Christ learned *obedience* by the things which he suffered, I don't understand it. I simply recognize that I am in the presence of a mystery—that even my Lord *learned* something!

Called of God an high priest after the order of Melchisedec [Heb. 5:10].

Called means "saluted" and refers to Melchizedek.

Now the writer will discuss this matter of the priesthood of Christ, that Melchizedek was given to us in the Old Testament as a type of the high priesthood of our Lord Jesus Christ.

THE PERIL OF DULL HEARING

The writer puts up the third danger signal; it is like a red light flashing. He is getting ready to bring us out on the highway, but before he does, we've got to look both ways. There is the danger of being dull of hearing. He devotes the remainder of the chapter to this, because in the next chapter (after still another danger signal) he will deal with the great subject of Christ our High Priest after the order of Melchizedek.

Of whom we have many things to say, and hard to be uttered, seeing ye are dull of hearing [Heb. 5:11].

"Of whom we have many things to say." The writer says, "I still have a lot of things to say."

"And hard to be uttered." Why is it hard to be uttered?

"Seeing ye are dull of hearing." The writer, who I think was Paul, could state it all right, but they couldn't grasp it.

Have you ever said to your husband or wife after a Bible-teaching sermon, "I don't think the pastor was quite up to it today. I didn't feel his message was equal to what he is capable of giving."? Did you ever stop to think that the problem that day may have been with you? Are you dull of hearing? The problem may not be in the speaking, but the problem may be in the hearing.

Ear trouble, today, is the big problem of believers. Christ as a priest after the order of Melchizedek is a difficult subject, and the writer is going to deal with it forthrightly. To understand the subject requires sharp spiritual perception. It requires folk to be spiritually alert and to have a knowledge of the Word of God and to be *close* to it. The Hebrew believers who are being addressed here had a low SQ, not an IQ, but an SQ—spiritual quotient. It was hard to teach them because it was difficult to make them understand. They were babies, as many of the saints are today, and they want baby talk even from the preacher. They don't want to hear anything that is difficult to understand. This is the reason some preachers are getting by with murder in the pulpit—they murder the Word of God. They absolutely kill it and substitute something from their own viewpoint, and the congregations like that kind of baby talk.

For when for the time ye ought to be teachers, ye have need that one teach you again which be the first principles of the oracles of God; and are become such as have need of milk, and not of strong meat [Heb. 5:12].

"Ye have need that one teach you again which be the first principles of the oracles of God." Some of them want a D.D. degree, but they don't even know their ABCs. "First principles" is from the Greek word *stoicheion* (from which we get our English word *atom*, by the way), meaning "primary elements"—the ABCs of the Christian life. They ought to be teachers and mature saints, but instead they are still little babies needing someone to burp them.

For example, one Sunday after the morning service a church member stopped to talk to me while I was shaking hands with folk who were leaving. He said, "Dr. McGee, do you have anything against me?" I said, "No. Why do you say that?" "Well, you passed me yesterday on the street, and you didn't speak to me." That is baby talk. I didn't even see that person, and it is perfect nonsense to talk like that. Someone else said, "Why didn't the soloist sing this morning? We wanted to hear the soloist sing." Oh, my gracious, what little babies, wanting their rattles, and wanting the bottle with the nipple on it!

To these Hebrew believers the writer says, "You are such as have need of milk, and not of strong meat. You are not of age; you are not full grown; you haven't reached maturation." Now a baby cannot eat meat, but an adult can enjoy milk. I will admit that a lot of saints today sit and listen to baby talk from the pulpit. It is tragic indeed that they have to endure this, but they do.

For every one that useth milk is unskilful in the word of righteousness: for he is a babe [Heb. 5:13].

He doesn't know the Word of God.

I don't want to step on your toes, my friend, but I'd love to be helpful to you. You cannot grow apart from the Word of God. I don't care how active you are in the church. You may be an officer. You may be on every committee in the church. You may be a leading deacon or elder. I don't care who you are, or what you are; if you are not studying the Word of God, and if you don't know how to handle it, you are a little baby. It is tragic to occupy a church office when you are just a little baby. You ought to come on and grow up. It is tragic that there are people who have been members of the church and have been saved for years, and they are still going around saying, "Goo, goo, goo." They have nothing to contribute but little baby talk. All they want is to be burped periodically.

But strong meat belongeth to them that are of full age, even those who by reason of use have their senses exercised to discern both good and evil [Heb. 5:14].

In 1 Corinthians 3:1–2, Paul says, "And I, brethren, could not speak unto you as unto spiritual, but as unto carnal, even as unto babes in Christ. I have fed you with milk, and not with meat: for hitherto ye were not able to bear it, neither yet now are ye able." In 1 Peter 2:1–2, Peter says, "Wherefore laying aside all malice, and all guile, and hypocrisies, and envies, and all evil speakings, As newborn babes, desire the sincere milk of the word, that ye may grow thereby."

CHAPTER 6

This chapter, by all odds, contains the most difficult passage in the Bible for an interpreter to handle, regardless of his theological position. Dr. R. W. Dale, one of the great minds in the earlier field of conservative scholarship, wrote:

> I know how this passage has made the heart of many a good man tremble. It rises up in the New Testament with a gloomy grandeur, stern, portentous, awful, sublime as Mount Sinai when the Lord descended upon it in fire, and threatening storm clouds were around Him, and thunderings and lightnings and unearthly voices told that He was there.

Every reverent person has come to this section with awe and wonder. And every sincere expositor has come to this passage with a sense of inadequacy, and certainly that is the way I approach it.

DANGER SIGNAL: PERIL OF DEPARTING

In the previous chapter the danger signal was the peril of dull hearing. Now as the Hebrew Christians can already see persecution coming, there is a danger of their turning from their confession of Christ and going back to Judaism. He mentions the baby things of Judaism which had to do with ritual. He encourages them to grow up, to go on to maturity.

Therefore leaving the principles of the doctrine of Christ, let us go on unto perfection; not laying again the foundation of repentance from dead works, and of faith toward God [Heb. 6:1].

"Leaving the principles of the doctrine of Christ" is literally "leaving the word of the beginning concerning Christ." For a builder it means to leave the foundation and go up with the scaffolding, or for a child in school to go on from his ABCs to work on his B.A. or Ph.D. It is preparing believers for a trip up to the throne of God.

"Let us go on" is horizontal, not perpendicular.

"Unto perfection" is maturity, full age.

There are six foundational facts in the Old Testament which prefigure Christ in ritual, symbol, and ceremony: (1) repentance from dead works; (2) faith toward God; (3) doctrine of baptisms; (4) laying on of hands; (5) resurrection of the dead; and (6) eternal judgment.

"Repentance from dead works." The works were the works of the Mosaic Law. They were continually trying to keep the Law, then breaking it, then repenting. That is baby stuff, the writer tells them.

"And of faith toward God." The Old Testament taught faith toward God; so just to say you believe in God doesn't mean you have come very far. The Old Testament ritual presented a faith in God by approaching Him through the temple sacrifices, not through Christ as High Priest.

Of the doctrine of baptisms, and of laying on of hands, and of resurrection of the dead, and of eternal judgment [Heb. 6:2].

"Doctrine of baptisms [washings]" has nothing to do with New Testament baptism. They refer to the washings of the Old Testament ritual, and there were many of them. The Hebrew believers were wanting to return to these things which were only shadows; they were the negatives from which the spiritual pictures were developed. They prefigured Christ, the reality.

"Laying on of hands." This was also an Old Testament ritual. When a man brought an animal offering, he laid his hands on its head to signify his identification with it. The animal was taking his place on the altar of sacrifice.

"Resurrection of the dead" was taught in the Old Testament, but now they needed to come up to the resurrection of Christ and to the living Christ.

"Eternal judgment" was taught in the Old Testament.

And this will we do, if God permit [Heb. 6:3].

This brings us to that passage which has caused as many difficulties as any in the Scriptures. Some consider it the most difficult passage to interpret.

For it is impossible for those who were once enlightened, and have tasted of the heavenly gift, and were made partakers of the Holy Ghost,

And have tasted the good word of God, and the powers of the world to come,

If they shall fall away, to renew them again unto repentance; seeing they crucify to themselves the Son of God afresh, and put him to an open shame.

For the earth which drinketh in the rain that cometh oft upon it, and bringeth forth herbs meet for them by whom it is dressed, receiveth blessing from God:

But that which beareth thorns and briers is rejected, and is nigh unto cursing; whose end is to be burned.

But, beloved, we are persuaded better things of you, and things that accompany salvation, though we thus speak [Heb. 6:4–9].

Verse 9 is the key to the passage, but we need the context to understand what is being said.

As we study this section, we are immediately confronted with the amazing fact that generally commentators have *avoided* this chapter. Even such a man as Dr. G. Campbell Morgan, the prince of expositors, has completely bypassed it in his book on Hebrews. However, when we do come upon the interpretations available and summarize each, we can well understand why men have chosen to remain clear of this scene of confusion because we can get many interpretations.

In the interest of an honest search after the evident meaning of these verses, let us examine some of the interpretations.

The most unsatisfactory to me of all interpretations is that the Christians mentioned here are Christians who have lost their salvation. That is, they were once saved but have lost their salvation. There are many folk who hold this position, and for the most part they are real born again Christians themselves. However, this belief makes them as uncomfortable as I am when I am making a trip by plane. I know that I am just as safe on that plane as anyone there, but I do not enjoy it as some of them do. There are many folk today who are not sure about their salvation and therefore are not enjoying it. Nevertheless they are saved if they have fixed their trust in Christ as their Savior. The essential thing is not the amount of faith they have but the one to whom it is directed. They turn to this passage of Scripture more than any other since they deny that we have a sure salvation which cannot be lost and that the believer is safe in Christ.

I want to make it abundantly clear that I believe we have a sure salvation because Scripture is very emphatic on this point. Paul says in Romans 8:1: "There is therefore now no condemnation to them that are in Christ Jesus . . ." and, my friend, he expands that great truth to the triumphant climax of such a bold statement as, "Who shall lay any thing to the charge of God's elect? It is God that justifieth" (Rom. 8:33). The throne of God is back of the weakest, humblest man who has come to trust Christ, and today there is not a created intelligence in God's universe that can bring a charge against one of these who is justified through faith in His blood. Paul continues in Romans 8:34–39: "Who is he that condemneth? [1] It is Christ that died, [2] yea rather, that is risen again, [3] who is even at the right hand of God, [4] who also maketh intercession for us." My friend, if you drink in those words you will have a great foundation of assurance. "Who shall separate us from the love of Christ? shall tribulation, or distress, or persecution, or famine, or nakedness, or peril, or sword? As it is written, For thy sake we are killed all the day long; we are accounted as sheep for the slaughter. Nay, in all these things we are more than conquerors through him that loved us." Does that satisfy you? Well, let's keep going. Paul is not through yet. "For I am persuaded, that neither death, nor life, nor angels, nor principalities, nor powers, nor things present, nor things to come, nor height, nor depth, nor any other creature, shall be able to separate us from the love of God, which is in Christ Jesus our Lord." Can you mention anything that Paul didn't mention in this passage? Can you find anything that could separate you from the love of Christ? May I say to you, this list takes in the whole kit and caboodle. Here we have a guarantee that *nothing* can separate us from the love of God—nothing that is seen, nothing that is unseen, nothing that is natural, nothing that is supernatural can separate us from the love of God which is in Christ Jesus our Lord.

The Lord Jesus Christ also makes some tremendous statements about our absolute security. Listen to Him, trust in Him, and believe Him. The Word of God is living and powerful, my friend. Jesus said, "My sheep hear my voice, and I know them, and they follow me: And I give unto them eternal life" (John 10:27–28). What kind of life? *Eternal* life. If you can lose it, it is not eternal! "And they shall never perish, neither shall any man pluck them out of my hand. My Father, which gave them me, is greater than all; and no man is able to pluck them out of my Father's hand" (John 10:28–29). It is not a question of your ability to hold on to Him; it is His ability to hold on to you. He says here with the infinite wisdom and full authority of the Godhead that He *can* hold us and that they who trust Him shall never perish. The question is: Is your hope fixed in God who is all-powerful, or in a god who may suffer defeat?

I have cited only some of the passages of Scripture that make it abundantly clear that you and I cannot be lost after we have been born again into the family of God. We become children of God through faith in Christ. Once a person has become a child of God through faith in Christ he has *eternal* life. I cannot accept the interpretation that the people in Hebrews 6:4–9 were once saved and had lost their salvation.

There is a second interpretation that has some merit in it. There are those who contend that this is a hypothetical case. "*If* they shall fall away." There is only a possibility that this might happen. The writer does not say that it happens, only that it might be possible. Those who contend that this is the correct interpretation say that it is the biggest "IF" in the Bible, and I would agree with them. If I did not take another position on the interpretation of this passage in Hebrews, I would accept this one.

The third interpretation points out that in verse 6 there really is no "if" in the Greek. It is a participle and should be translated "having fallen away." Therefore these folk have another interpretation, which is that the passage speaks of mere professors, that they are not genuine believers. They only profess to be Christians. Well, I cannot accept this view, although such scholars as Matthew Henry, F. W. Grant, and J. N. Darby hold this thinking, as does C. I. Scofield in his excellent reference Bible—a Bible which I feel every Christian should own, although in some cases I do not concur with the interpretations given in the notes, as in the instance before us.

I do not accept the view that these folk are professors rather than genuine believers. The Bible does speak of those who merely profess Christ. There are apostates in the church. For instance Peter in his second epistle wrote: "It has happened unto them according to the true proverb, The dog is turned to his own vomit again; and the sow that was washed to her wallowing in the mire" (2 Pet. 2:22, ASV). Those folk were professors, not genuine believers. But in chapter 6 we find genuine believers, because they are identified as such in many ways. If you will move back into chapter 4 to get the entire passage, you will notice

that it is said of these people that they are dull of hearing (see Heb. 5:11)—it does not say that they are dead in trespasses and sins (see Eph. 2:1). And in Hebrews 5:12 it says that "when for the time ye ought to be teachers, ye have need that one teach you . . . and are become such as have need of milk. . . ." They need to have milk because they are babes. An unsaved person doesn't need milk; he needs *life*. He needs to be born again. He is dead in trespasses and sins. After he is born again, a little milk will help him. Therefore I believe the writer to the Hebrews is addressing baby Christians, and he is urging them to go on to maturity.

There are other expositors who take the position that since the ones spoken of here are Jewish believers of the first century, the warning can apply only to them. At the time Hebrews was written, the temple was still standing, and the writer is warning Jewish Christians about returning to the sacrificial system, because in so doing they would be admitting that Jesus did not die for their sins. Therefore, those who hold this reasoning say that verses 4–6 apply only to the Jewish Christians of that day and have no reference to anyone in our day.

There is still another group which stresses the word *impossible* in Hebrews 6:4. It is impossible to renew them—the thought being that it is impossible for man, but it is not impossible with God. They remind us that the Lord Jesus said that ". . . It is easier for a camel to go through the eye of a needle, than for a rich man to enter into the kingdom of God" (Matt. 19:24). Of course it is impossible for any of us to enter heaven on our own; we must have a Savior, a Redeemer. Therefore, this again is an interpretation that I cannot accept.

You can see that there are many interpretations of this passage—and, of course, there are others which I have not mentioned.

Now there is one interpretation that has been a real blessing to my heart, and I trust you will follow me patiently, thoughtfully, and without bias as we look at it. Because I was dissatisfied with all the interpretations I had heard, I actually felt sad about it. Then several years ago I picked up a copy of *Bibliotheca Sacra*, a publication of the Dallas Theological Seminary, and read an article on the sixth chapter of Hebrews written by Dr. J. B. Rowell, who was then pastor of the Central Baptist Church in Victoria, British Columbia. His interpretation was the best that I had heard. I give him full credit for it. This is not something that I thought of, although I have developed it to fit my own understanding, of course.

First of all, let me call to your attention that the writer is not discussing the question of salvation at all in this passage. I believe he is describing saved people—they have been enlightened, they have tasted of the heavenly gift, they have been made partakers of the Holy Spirit, and they have tasted the good Word of God and the powers of the world to come.

The whole tenor of the text reveals that he is speaking of *rewards* which are the result of salvation. In verse 6 he says, "If they shall fall away, to renew them again unto repentance"—not to salvation, but to *repentance*. Repentance is something that God has asked *believers* to do. For example, read the seven letters to the seven churches in Asia, as recorded in Revelation 2 and 3. He says to every one of the churches to repent. That is His message for believers.

So the writer of Hebrews is talking about the *fruit* of salvation, not about the *root* of salvation. Notice verse 9 again: "But, beloved, we are persuaded better things of you, and things that *accompany* salvation [he hasn't been discussing salvation but the things that accompany salvation], though we thus speak." He is speaking of the fruit of the Christian's life and the reward that comes to him as the result. The whole tenor of this passage is that he is warning them of the possibility of losing their reward. There is danger, Paul said, of our entire works being burned up so that we will have nothing for which we could be rewarded. "For other foundation can no man lay than that is laid, which is Jesus Christ. Now if any man build upon this foundation gold, silver, precious stones, wood, hay, stubble; Every man's work shall be made manifest: for the day shall declare it, because it shall be revealed by fire; and the fire shall try every man's work of what sort it is. If any man's work abide which he hath built thereupon, he shall receive a reward. If any man's work shall be burned, he shall suffer loss: but he himself shall be saved; yet so as by fire" (1 Cor. 3:11–15). The work of every believer, my friend, is going to be tested by fire, and fire *burns*! The work you are doing today for Christ is going to be tested by fire. For example, when all of those reports that some of us preachers have handed in about how many converts we have made are tried by fire, they will make a roaring fire—if our work has been done in the flesh rather than in the power of the Spirit. We will have nothing but wood, hay, and stubble that will all go up in smoke.

Someday every believer is going to stand before the judgment seat of Christ. I wish I could lay upon the heart of believers that it is not going to be a sweet little experience where the Lord Jesus is going to pat us on the back and say, "You nice little Sunday school boy, you didn't miss a Sunday for ten years. You are so wonderful." The Lord is going to go deeper than that. He is going to test you and see if you really had any fruit in your life. Have you grown in grace and knowledge of Him? Have you been a witness for Him? Has your life counted for Him? Have you been a blessing to others? My Christian friend, I am not sure that I am looking forward to the judgment seat of Christ, because He is going to take Vernon McGee apart there. I will not be judged for salvation, but because I am saved, He is going to find out whether or not I am to receive a reward.

Now notice that he is illustrating the fruit of the Christian's life: "For the earth which drinketh in the rain that cometh oft upon it, and bringeth forth herbs meet for them by whom it is dressed, receiveth blessing from God: But that which beareth thorns and briers is rejected, and is nigh unto cursing; whose end is to be burned" (vv. 7–8). If the believer's life brings forth fruit, it receives blessing from God; if it brings forth thorns and briers, it is rejected.

When the apostle Paul wrote to Titus, a young preacher, he dealt with the matter of works: "Not by works done in righteousness, which we did ourselves, but according to his mercy he saved us . . ." (Titus 3:5, ASV). From this, one might be inclined to think that Paul is not going to have much regard for good works, but move down in that same chapter to verse 8: ". . . I desire that thou affirm confidently, to the end that they who have believed God may be careful to maintain good works. . . ." Good works do not enter into the matter of salvation, but when one becomes a child of God through faith in Christ, works assume supreme importance. My friend, if you are a Christian, it is *important* that you live the Christian life.

When I was a university student the psychologists were discussing a matter which they have moved away from now. It was: Which is more important, heredity or environment? Well, my psychology professor had a stimulating answer. He said that before you are born, heredity is more important, but after you are born, environment is the major consideration! Now let's carry that line of thought over to our present study. Before you are born again, works do not enter in, because you cannot bring them to God—He won't accept them. Scripture says that the righteousness of man is filthy rags in His sight (see Isa. 64:6). You don't expect God to accept a pile of dirty laundry, do you? He is accepting sinners, but He accepts us on the basis of the redemption that we have in Christ. When we receive Christ as Savior, we are born anew and become a child of God. When that happens, we are, as Peter put it, ". . . an elect race, a royal priesthood, a holy nation, a people for God's own possession, that ye may show forth the excellencies of him who called you out of darkness into his marvellous light" (1 Pet. 2:9, ASV). Now after you have been saved, you are to show forth by your good works before the world that you are redeemed to God. Therefore the Christian has *something* to show forth, and that is the thing which is to be judged. If he is going to continue as a baby and be nothing but a troublemaker, turning people from Christ instead of to Christ, there will certainly be no reward. In fact, there will be shame at His appearing.

"For as touching those who were once enlightened and tasted of the heavenly gift, and were made partakers of the Holy Spirit, and tasted the good word of God, and the powers of the age to come, and then fell away, it is impossible to renew them again unto repentance; seeing they crucify to themselves the Son of God afresh, and put him to an open shame" (vv. 4–6, ASV). These verses bring us to the very center of this study.

"And then fell away"—*fell away* is an interesting word in the Greek. It is *parapitō* and means simply "to stumble, to fall down." It would be impossible to give it the meaning of "apostatize." It is the same word used of our Lord when He went into the Garden of Gethsemane, *fell* on His face, and prayed.

There are many examples in Scripture of men who "fell away." The apostle Peter fell, but he was not lost. The Lord Jesus said to him, "I have prayed that your faith might not fail" (see Luke 22:32). Peter suffered loss, but he was not lost. John Mark is another example. He failed so miserably on the first missionary journey that when his uncle Barnabas suggested that he go on the second journey, Paul turned him down. He as much as said, "Never. This boy has failed, and as far as I am concerned, I am through with him" (see Acts 15:37–39). Well, thank God, although he stumbled and fell, *God* was not through with him.

Even the apostle Paul, before he died, acknowledged that he had made a misjudgment of John Mark. In his last epistle he wrote, ". . . Take Mark and bring him with thee; for he is useful to me for ministering" (2 Tim. 4:11). Now, neither Peter nor John Mark lost their salvation, but they certainly failed and they suffered loss for it.

Read again verse 1 and notice that the writer is talking to folk about repentance from dead works—not salvation, but *repentance*. You will recall that John the Baptist also preached this to the people: "Bring forth therefore fruits worthy of repentance . . ." (Luke 3:8). He was referring to that which is the *evidence* of repentance. Repentance in our day does not mean the shedding of a few tears; it means turning right-about-face toward Jesus Christ, which means a change of direction in your life, in your way of living.

Many of the Jewish believers were returning to the temple sacrifice at that time, and the writer to the Hebrews was warning them of the danger of that. Before Christ came, every sacrifice was a picture of Him and pointed to His coming, but after Christ came and died on the cross, that which God had commanded in the Old Testament actually became *sin*.

You see, those folk were at a strategic point in history. The day before the crucifixion of Jesus they had gone to the temple with sacrifices in obedience to God's command, but now it was wrong for them to do it. Why? Because Jesus had become that sacrifice—once and for all. Today if you were to offer a bloody sacrifice, you would be sacrificing afresh the Lord Jesus because you would be inferring that when He died nineteen hundred years ago it was of no avail—that you still need a sacrifice to take care of your sin. It would mean that you would not have faith in His atonement, in His death, in His redemption. As someone has said, we either crucify or crown the Lord Jesus by our lives. Today we either exhibit a life of faith or a life by which we crucify Him afresh—especially when we feel that we have to get back under the Mosaic system and keep the Law in order to be saved. It is a serious matter to go back to a legal system.

Notice again verse 6 as the Authorized Version translates it: "If they shall fall away, to renew them again unto repentance." Actually the *if* is not in the text at all. It is "having fallen away," or "then fell away"—a genitive absolute. It is all right to use the "if," providing you use it as an argument rather than in the sense of a condition.

Why would it be impossible to renew them again unto repentance? Remember we are talking about the fruit of salvation. It is a serious thing to have accepted Christ as Savior and then to live in sin, to nullify what you do by being a spiritual baby, never growing up, doing nothing in the world but building a big pile of wood, hay, and stubble. Paul said the same thing in different language in 1 Corinthians 3:11 which says, "For other foundation can no man lay than that is laid, which is Jesus Christ." Your salvation is a foundation. You rest upon it, but you also build upon it. You can build with six different kinds of materials—wood, hay, stubble, gold, silver, and precious stones. What kind of building materials are you using today? Are you building up a lot of wood, hay, and stubble? There is a lot of church work today that is nothing but that. We are great on organizations and committees, but do our lives really count for God? Are there going to be people in heaven who will be able to point to you and say, "I am here because of your life and testimony," or, "I am here because you gave me the Word of God." Oh, let's guard against building with wood, hay, or stubble!

By the way, there is a difference between a straw stack and a diamond ring. And you can lose a diamond ring in a hay stack because the ring is so small. I am afraid that a great many folk are building a straw stack to make an impression. One pastor told me, "I'm killing myself. I have to turn in a better report this year than the report last year. We have to increase church membership and converts and giving to missions." Oh, if this pastor would only dig into the Scriptures and spend much time in God's presence. Then he would be teaching his people the Word and many would be turning to Christ and would be growing in their relationship with Him. Every man's works are going to be tested by fire. What will fire do to wood, hay, and stubble? Poof! It will go up in smoke. There will be nothing left. That is what the writer is saying.

In John 15 the Lord Jesus talks about the fact that He is the vine, the genuine vine, and we are the branches. We are to bear fruit. "If ye abide in me, and my words abide in you, ye shall ask what ye will, and it shall be done unto you. Herein is my Father glorified, that ye bear much fruit . . ." (John 15:7–8). He wants us to bear *much* fruit. When there is a branch that won't bear fruit, what does He do? "If a man abide not in me, he is cast forth as a branch, and is withered; and men gather them, and cast them into the fire, and they are burned" (John 15:6). He will take it away; He will remove it from the place of fruitbearing and that is what the Lord Jesus is saying.

I see God doing this very thing today. And as I look back over the years, I have seen many men work with wood, hay, or stubble. And I have seen others work with gold. I know a layman who was a very prominent Christian when I came to the Los Angeles area almost forty years ago. Then he became involved in a dishonest transaction. He has lost his testimony, and yet he was a very gifted and likeable man. I still consider him my friend, but I wouldn't want to go into the presence of Christ as this man will have to go when his life is over.

Also I recall a minister who was very attractive—a little too attractive. He was unfaithful to his wife, had an affair with another woman, and finally divorced his wife. And all the while he tried to keep on teaching! But his teaching didn't amount to anything—he was just putting up a whole lot of straw. He was not even baling hay; he was just making a big old haystack. Finally the match was put to it, I guess, because he certainly didn't leave anything down here.

Oh, how careful we should be about our Christian lives. And we cannot live the Christian life in our own strength. We need to recognize that Christ is the vine. If we have any life, it has come from Him, and if there is any fruit in our lives, it comes from Him. We are sort of connecting rods, as branches connect into the vine and then bear fruit. Christ said that, "Abide in me, and I in you. As the branch cannot bear fruit of itself, except it abide in the vine; no more can ye, except ye abide in me" (John 15:4).

"If they shall fall away" or "having fallen away," it is impossible to renew them to repentance. They can shed tears all they want to, but they have lost their testimony. For example, a preacher came and talked to me about his situation. He moved away from this area and attempted to establish a ministry. But he failed. He had had an affair with a woman, and he had lost his testimony. He was through. "It is impossible to renew them again unto repentance." I don't question his salvation; he is a gifted man who could be mightily used by God but is not. "Seeing they crucify to themselves the Son of God afresh, and put him to an open shame." My friend, any time you as a born again child of God live like one of the Devil's children, you are crucifying the Son of God—because He came to give you a perfect redemption and to enable you by the indwelling of the Holy Spirit to be filled with the Spirit and live for Him.

"For the land which hath drunk the rain that cometh oft upon it, and bringeth forth herbs meet for them for whose sake it is also tilled, receiveth blessing from God" (v. 7, ASV). The garden produce is a blessing to man—my, it is delicious! "But if it beareth thorns and thistles, it is rejected and nigh unto a curse; whose end is to be burned" (v. 8, ASV). "Rejected" is *adokimos*, the same word Paul used when writing to the Corinthian believers, "But I keep under my body, and bring it into subjection: lest that by any means, when I have preached to others, I myself should be a castaway" (1 Cor. 9:27). "Castaway" is the same word *adokimos*, meaning "not approved." In effect, Paul is saying, "When I come into His presence I don't want to be disapproved. I don't want the Lord Jesus to say to me, 'You have failed. Your life should have been a testimony but it was not.'" Oh, my friend, *you* are going to hear that if you are not living for Him! I know we don't want to hear these things, but we need to face the facts.

Now notice the key to this chapter: "But, beloved, we are persuaded better things of you, and things that accompany salvation, though we thus speak" (v. 9). The writer to the Hebrew believers is saying, "I am persuaded that you are going to live for God, that you are not going to remain babes in Christ but will grow up."

For God is not unrighteous to forget your work and labour of love, which ye have shewed toward his name, in that ye have ministered to the saints, and do minister [Heb. 6:10].

"Work and labour of love" won't save you, but if you are saved, this is why you are rewarded. This is where good works come in. Although they have nothing to do with your salvation, they certainly do have a very important part in a believer's life.

And we desire that every one of you do shew the same diligence to the full assurance of hope unto the end [Heb. 6:11].

We *need* that "full assurance of hope unto the end."

That ye be not slothful, but followers of them who through faith and patience inherit the promises [Heb. 6:12].

God has made a lot of promises to us if we are faithful to Him.

For when God made promise to Abraham, because he could swear by no greater, he sware by himself [Heb. 6:13].

As you know, when you take an oath, you take it on something greater than you are. Since there is nothing greater than God, He swore by Himself.

Saying, Surely blessing I will bless thee, and multiplying I will multiply thee [Heb. 6:14].

God promised that to Abraham (see Gen. 22:15–18; Heb. 11:19).

And so, after he had patiently endured, he obtained the promise [Heb. 6:15].

There is something here that is quite wonderful. Abraham patiently endured, and a new assurance came by trusting God. When you *trust* God, you walk with Him. You grow in grace and in the knowledge of Him through the study of His Word. This brings you to a place of assurance that cannot be gainsaid.

For men verily swear by the greater: and an oath for confirmation is to them an end of all strife [Heb. 6:16].

When men confirm a statement with an oath, it is an end of every dispute.

Wherein God, willing more abundantly to shew unto the heirs of promise the immutability of his counsel, confirmed it by an oath [Heb. 6:17].

When God does a thing like this, He doesn't need to take an oath, but He does take one to make it very clear how all-important it is.

That by two immutable things, in which it was impossible for God to lie, we might have a strong consolation, who have fled for refuge to lay hold upon the hope set before us [Heb. 6:18].

"That by two immutable things"—what are the two immutable (or unchangeable) things? The Lord promised Abram descendants as innumerable as the stars of heaven (see Gen. 15:4–5), then later He confirmed His promise with an oath (see Gen. 22:16–18). God confirmed His unchangeable Word of promise by a second unchangeable thing, His oath. These two immutable things gave Abraham encouragement and assurance.

Now what are the two immutable things for us today? Not only do we have the promise made to Abraham for our encouragement, but we have a far richer revelation of God's love—the gift of His Son. The (1) death and resurrection of Christ and (2) His ascension and intercession for us are the two immutable things.

These four great facts give us an assurance and provide a refuge that we can lay hold upon.

"Who have fled for refuge to lay hold upon the hope set before us." This reminds us of the cities of refuge which God provided for the children of Israel (see Num. 35; Deut. 19; Josh. 20–21). Those cities of refuge serve as types of Christ sheltering the sinner from death. It was a very marvelous provision for a man who accidentally killed someone. Maybe the one whom he killed had a hotheaded brother who wanted vengeance. So the fugitive could escape to a city of refuge where he would be protected and his case tried. If he was acquitted of intentional killing he must remain within the city until the death of the high priest.

What a picture this is for us today! This reveals that Christ is our refuge. My friend, I have already been carried into court, and at the trial I was found guilty. I was a sinner. The penalty which was leveled against me was death—and it has already been executed. *Christ* bore the penalty for me, you see. Because He died in my place, I am free. I have been delivered from the penalty of sin; never do I have to answer for it again. I am free now to go out and serve Him. I now have a High Priest, a resurrected Savior, to whom I can go. What a wonderful picture of my Savior this gives! The apostle Paul wrote to the Corinthians: "Now all these things happened unto them for ensamples: and they are written for our admonition, upon whom the ends of the world are come" (1 Cor. 10:11). "Ensamples" are *types*, and Melchizedek is a type of Christ. Millions of things could have been recorded, but God chose to record only these things because they enable us to grow in our understanding of Him and our relationship to Him.

Which hope we have as an anchor of the soul, both sure and stedfast, and which entereth into that within the veil;

Whither the forerunner is for us entered, even Jesus, made an high priest for ever after the order of Melchisedec [Heb. 6:19–20].

When Christ ascended back to heaven, He assumed the office of High Priest.

"Entereth into that within the veil." Christ as High Priest entered into the temple in heaven (after which the earthly tabernacle was patterned, Hebrews 8:5). He passed through the veil into the Holy of Holies, into the presence of God, and presented His blood there. Then He "sat down at the right hand of the Majesty on high."

Now one difference between Aaron and the Lord Jesus is (and I say this reverently) that poor old Aaron never did sit down. There were no seats in the tabernacle—there was the mercy seat, but that typified God's throne. Aaron only hurried in and hurried out. But you and I have a superior High Priest. He has gone in. He has sat down. He has a *finished* redemption.

Jesus Christ is the "forerunner," which implies that others are to follow.

"As an anchor of the soul." We have an even stronger encouragement than Abraham had in his time, because our High Priest has entered in advance into the presence of God for us, and He is there today interceding for us.

CHAPTER 7

THEME: *Christ our High Priest after the order of Melchizedek*

The rest of the Epistle to the Hebrews deals with the subject of the living Christ who is at this moment at God's right hand. It is a subject that is really neglected in the church today. We talk a great deal about the death and resurrection of Christ—and that is wonderful—but my friend, we need to go on to a *living* Christ who is at God's right hand and who has a ministry there for us. Now the reality of that ministry to us is what is going to test our spiritual life. Here is a barometer or Geiger counter which you can put down on your life: how is the truth of this chapter of Hebrews going to affect your spiritual life?

The writer to the Hebrews is going to make a comparison and contrast of the priesthood of Melchizedek and the priesthood of Aaron.

CHRIST IS PERPETUAL PRIEST

For this Melchisedec, king of Salem, priest of the most high God, who met Abraham returning from the slaughter of the kings, and blessed him [Heb. 7:1].

The little word *for* is used by the writer to the Hebrews as cement to hold together what has been said previously and what he is now going to say. It refers us back to verse 20 of chapter 6. Melchizedek is a type of Christ. In the historical record Melchizedek is called "king of Salem" and "priest of the most high God" (see Genesis 14:17–24). Not much is said about Melchizedek in Genesis 14—frankly, I would have forgotten about him, but the Spirit of God didn't forget about him. When we come to Psalm 110 there is this prophecy concerning the Messiah, the Lord Jesus Christ: ". . . Thou art a priest for ever after the order of Melchizedek" (Ps. 110:4).

You and I are living in the day of Christ's priesthood. There are many critics today who do not like the term *dispensations*. Many preachers won't mention the word. I mention it because the Bible uses the term. Dispensations are the different ages or time-periods showing the progressive order of God's dealing with the human family. This is an example: Back in the Old Testament Aaron was the high priest and there was a literal tabernacle down here. Today we have an High Priest, but He is not ministering in any building down here. He is up yonder at God's right hand, and He is there right now.

While there are not many references to Melchizedek in the Old Testament, there are quite a few references to him right here in the Epistle to the Hebrews. In Hebrews 5:10 we read, "Called of God an high priest after the order of Melchisedec." Then again in Hebrews 6:20, "Whither the forerunner is for us entered, even Jesus, made an high priest for ever after the order of Melchisedec." Now here in verse 1 the writer says, "For this Melchisedec, king of Salem, priest of the most high God, who met Abraham returning from the slaughter of the kings, and blessed him." He is going to talk a great deal about Melchizedek in this chapter. The very key to this chapter is found in verse 17: "For he testifieth, Thou art a priest for ever after the order of Melchisedec."

Since we are going to look at Christ as a priest after the order of Melchizedek, we need to know all we can about Melchizedek, and we need to go back to the account in Genesis 14. The events of Genesis 14 took place after Abraham's nephew Lot had moved down to Sodom, and we have in this chapter the first account of a war. The kings of the east formed a confederacy and came against the kings of the west, that is, those who lived around the Dead Sea. The kings of the east won and lugged off the people as slaves and the wealth of the cities as booty.

Word was brought to Abraham that Lot was being carried away into captivity. Abraham immediately armed about 318 men out of his own household, which means he had quite a household. Each man that he could arm must have had at least one woman and a child. Therefore Abraham must have had about a thousand people who served under him! He took these 318 men, and by a surprise attack he was able to get a victory over the kings of the east. All he was concerned about was rescuing Lot, but in so doing he was able to rescue the king of Sodom and all the others.

In Genesis 14:17 we are told: "And the king of Sodom went out to meet him after his return from the slaughter of Chedorlaomer, and of the kings that were with him, at the valley of Shaveh, which is the king's dale." The king of Sodom made Abraham an offer which he refused, then out of nowhere we read: "And Melchizedek king of Salem brought forth bread and wine: and he was the priest of the most high God" (Gen. 14:18).

To whom also Abraham gave a tenth part of all; first being by interpretation

King of righteousness, and after that also King of Salem, which is, King of peace [Heb. 7:2].

It has been supposed by some that Salem was Jerusalem. I do not think that is true at all. Salem is not a place—the word *salem* means "peace." He does not say that Melchizedek was king of Jerusalem. He was king of peace; he was a man who could make peace in that day. I am sure he was king of a literal city somewhere, but it doesn't mean he was king of Jerusalem—it could have been any place. He was king of peace.

Melchizedek was also the "King of righteousness." That is what the name Melchizedek means: *melek* is a Hebrew word meaning "king," and *tsedeq* means "righteousness." Jeremiah speaks of *Jehovah-tsidkenu*, meaning "Jehovah our righteousness."

Melchizedek is a type of Christ—he represents Him in several different ways. He is king of peace and king of righteousness. The Lord Jesus Christ is a King. He is righteous—He was made unto us righteousness.

Melchizedek was "priest of the most high God." The Lord Jesus is our Great High Priest.

Now the very interesting thing is that when Melchizedek came out to meet Abraham, he brought bread and wine. I believe that these two Old Testament worthies, these patriarchs, celebrated the Lord's Supper together! They were looking forward to the coming of Christ two thousand years before He came. Today you and I meet and partake of bread and wine, looking back to the coming of Christ two thousand years ago. They celebrated the Lord's Supper together. Don't ask me to explain it—I can't explain it; I can just call your attention to it. This is something before which we stand in profound awe and wonder and worship. This is where faith treads on the high places.

Without father, without mother, without descent, having neither beginning of days, nor end of life; but made like unto the Son of God; abideth a priest continually [Heb. 7:3].

Here Melchizedek is a picture of Christ and a type of Christ in another way. The Lord Jesus comes out of eternity, and He moves into eternity. He has no beginning and no end. He *is* the beginning. He *is* the end. You can't go beyond Him in the past, and you can't get ahead of Him in the future. He encompasses all of time and all of eternity. Now how can you find a man who pictures that? Melchizedek is in the Book of Genesis, a book that gives pedigrees—it tells us that Adam begat so-and-so, and so-and-so begat so-and-so, Abraham begat Isaac, Isaac begat Jacob and Esau, and you follow the genealogies on down—it is a book of the families. Yet in this book that gives the genealogies, Melchizedek just walks out onto the pages of Scripture, out of nowhere, then he walks off the pages of Scripture, and we do not see him anymore. Why did God leave out the genealogy of Melchizedek? Because Melchizedek was to be a type of the Lord Jesus in His priesthood. From the prophecy given in Psalm 110 we see that Melchizedek is a picture of Christ in that the Lord Jesus is the *eternal* God, and He is a priest because He is the Son of God, and He is a priest continually. That is, He just keeps on being a priest—there will be no change in His priesthood because He is eternal.

In the Genesis account we see that Melchizedek came to Abraham at just the right moment. Abraham was about to be tested, and he needed someone to encourage him and to strengthen him. Melchizedek came with bread and wine, and he was the priest of "the most high God." (This is the first time in Scripture that God is called "the most high God.") He came just as the king of Sodom was making a proposition to Abraham: "Now Abraham, it was nice of you to recover Lot and the rest of the people, and we appreciate that. I know you don't want to make the people slaves; so give us the people, and you keep the booty. You keep it, Abraham, it's yours." Now according to the Code of Hammurabi of that day, the booty did belong to Abraham, but Abraham said, "Why, I wouldn't do that at all. I won't take even a shoestring from you—not even a thread. I refuse to receive anything from you" (see Gen. 14:23).

Then God appeared to Abraham and said, "I am thy shield, and thy exceeding great reward" (Gen. 15:1).

Melchizedek came and ministered to Abraham. The Lord Jesus Christ is the Great High Priest, and He ministers to us today. I will be very frank with you, if He doesn't minister to you and bless your heart and life, it is because you are still a little babe and you haven't grown up. You have not entered into the great truth presented here. My Christian friend, have you gone through trials and deep waters, and has Jesus ministered to you and helped you? Are you conscious of the fact that He blesses you every day?

On one tour that I conducted to Bible lands

I left half-sick and would not have gone if my wife had not urged me to do so. I just didn't feel up to the trip. On the trip I was sick several times and had to drop out of the tour a couple of days. But God was so *good* to us. We had good weather; we never had a bad flight, and the Lord was just good to me in so many ways. I was conscious of the fact that my High Priest was on the job; He was doing His job, my friend, and He was blessing. I'm talking to you about reality. I'm not talking to you about a theory, about a religion, or about a ritual that you go through. I'm talking to you about a Man in the glory who is alive, and He is the living God. Is He the living God to you?

Notice what it says in Genesis 14:19—"And he [Melchizedek] blessed him, and said, Blessed be Abram of the most high God, possessor of heaven and earth." You and I live in a universe that belongs to Him; He owns it, and He has said that all things are ours today. Do you enjoy a sunrise? Just this morning I went by myself out to a nearby golf course, and I saw the sun come up over the Sierra Madre mountains. He did that just for me this morning. What a performance He put on. He is wonderful! What a glorious day it is! He is the living Christ. I just thanked Him again for bringing me to another day, and I thanked Him for being so good to me, and I told Him that I love Him. The living Christ is yonder at God's right hand. How real is He to you?

CHRIST IS PERFECT PRIEST

Now consider how great this man was, unto whom even the patriarch Abraham gave the tenth of the spoils [Heb. 7:4].

Abraham paid tithes to Melchizedek. He recognized that Melchizedek was above him and that he was the priest of the most high God.

And verily they that are of the sons of Levi, who receive the office of the priesthood, have a commandment to take tithes of the people according to the law, that is, of their brethren, though they come out of the loins of Abraham [Heb. 7:5].

In Abraham the sons of Levi, who were descended from Abraham, paid tithes to Melchizedek. This shows that Melchizedek was superior to Aaron and his family.

My friend, one of the ways in which you recognize the lordship of Jesus Christ is by coming and making a gift to Him. Every gift ought to be more than just to a church or to some other ministry; it should be a gift to the Lord Jesus Christ. You recognize His lordship, and you are a priest worshiping when you bring a gift to Him.

But he whose descent is not counted from them received tithes of Abraham, and blessed him that had the promises [Heb. 7:6].

You would think that Abraham would be superior to Melchizedek, but he was not. Melchizedek was a Gentile who was the priest of the most high God. I do not know where he got his information about God, nor do I know the background of this man. If anyone tries to tell you more about him, he is guessing. Also there are a whole lot of things I can't explain about the Lord Jesus because He is *God.* I do know that He is my Great High Priest today—and that's all I need to know.

And without all contradiction the less is blessed of the better [Heb. 7:7].

Abraham was blessed by Melchizedek who was better than he was. When you and I worship the Lord Jesus and bow before Him, we recognize His superiority.

And here men that die receive tithes; but there he receiveth them, of whom it is witnessed that he liveth [Heb. 7:8].

"Here men that die" refers to the Levitical priests; "but there he" refers to Melchizedek. You can offer yourself to Him, and He will receive you. When I offer myself to Him, He doesn't get much, but I have offered myself to Him and am thankful that he will accept me.

And as I may so say, Levi also, who receiveth tithes, payed tithes in Abraham.

For he was yet in the loins of his father, when Melchisedec met him [Heb. 7:9–10].

"Levi also, who receiveth tithes, payed tithes in Abraham." The priestly tribe of Levi was in the loins of Abraham when he paid tithes to Melchizedek, and thus Levi also paid tithes to Melchizedek. In the same way, back yonder when Adam sinned, I also sinned. In Adam all died. The reason you and I are going to die, if the Lord tarries His coming, is that we are in Adam and we sinned in Adam. However, today I am perfect, because I am in Christ. Do you realize that? God sees me in Christ, and I am perfect in Him. I am accepted in the Beloved. My friend, this is great scriptural truth, and it is stated in simple language.

If therefore perfection were by the Levitical priesthood, (for under it the people received the law,) what further need was there that another priest should rise after the order of Melchisedec, and not be called after the order of Aaron? [Heb. 7:11].

In other words, the thing which characterized the Aaronic priesthood is that it was incomplete. It never brought perfection, complete communion with God. It *never* gave redemption and acceptance before God to the people. It never achieved its goal. Therefore we need Christ.

For the priesthood being changed, there is made of necessity a change also of the law [Heb. 7:12].

We are not under the Mosaic Law. The Mosaic Law belonged to the Aaronic priesthood where they offered bloody sacrifices. The Mosaic Law and the Aaronic priesthood go together.

For he of whom these things are spoken pertaineth to another tribe, of which no man gave attendance at the altar.

For it is evident that our Lord sprang out of Juda; of which tribe Moses spake nothing concerning priesthood [Heb. 7:13–14].

The Lord Jesus came in the tribe of Judah and therefore could never be a priest here on earth. The priestly tribe was the tribe of Levi. The priesthood had to be changed since Christ did not come from Levi.

And it is yet far more evident: for that after the similitude of Melchisedec there ariseth another priest [Heb. 7:15].

This is what the prophecy in Psalm 110 said concerning the Messiah who was to come.

Who is made, not after the law of a carnal commandment, but after the power of an endless life.

For he testifieth, Thou art a priest for ever after the order of Melchisedec [Heb. 7:16–17].

Christ became a priest by His resurrection from the dead; He has an endless life.

For there is verily a disannulling of the commandment going before for the weakness and unprofitableness thereof [Heb. 7:18].

The Mosaic system went out of style—it wore out. It never gave what man must have: perfection.

For the law made nothing perfect, but the bringing in of a better hope did; by the which we draw nigh unto God [Heb. 7:19].

We come to God through Christ. We have seen that the Lord Jesus Christ is a perpetual priest and He is a perfect priest. The Aaronic priesthood could not fill the bill. Now we have a perfect priest, and that one is the Lord Jesus Christ. He has provided salvation for you and me. God has taken us out of Adam and put us in Christ. "Therefore if any man be in Christ, he is a new creature: old things are passed away; behold, all things are become new" (2 Cor. 5:17). We are no longer joined to Adam but are now joined to the living Christ.

We will summarize the contrast between the priesthood of Aaron and the priesthood of Melchizedek as follows:

Law vs. Power
(law restrains—power enables)
Commandment *(external)* vs. Life *(internal)*
Carnal *(flesh)* vs. Endless *(eternal life)*
Changing vs. Unchanging
Weakness and unprofitableness vs. Nigh to God
Nothing perfect vs. Better hope

And inasmuch as not without an oath he was made priest:

(For those priests were made without an oath; but this with an oath by him that said unto him, The Lord sware and will not repent, Thou art a priest for ever after the order of Melchisedec:) [Heb. 7:20–21].

In Psalm 110 is a prophecy of the fact that the Messiah, the Lord Jesus Christ, would be in the line of Melchizedek as priest. "The LORD hath sworn, and will not repent, Thou art a priest for ever after the order of Melchizedek" (Ps. 110:4). One thing that makes the priesthood of Christ superior is the very simple fact that it rests not only upon the Word of God but upon the *oath* of God. All the Old Testament tells us of the tribe of Levi is that they were set aside for that particular function—no oath was given concerning them.

By so much was Jesus made a surety of a better testament [Heb. 7:22].

The word *testament* should be "covenant." We have not only a better priesthood in Jesus Christ, but it is also by a better covenant. Christ is our High Priest. He ministers in a superior sanctuary, by a better covenant, and built upon better promises—we will see this subject expanded in chapters 8 through 10. The Lord Jesus' priesthood is superior in every department.

CHRIST IN HIS PERSON IS PERPETUAL AND PERFECT PRIEST

And they truly were many priests, because they were not suffered to continue by reason of death [Heb. 7:23].

In other words, the Aaronic priesthood of the Old Testament always ended by death. Aaron died, just as Moses did. I have always felt that the death of Aaron—if it wasn't greater—was just as great a loss to Israel as the death of Moses. In his death they lost their high priest, the one who had gone with them through the wilderness, the one who knew them and understood them. Now they would have to have a new priest. You and I don't have a changing priesthood—Christ will always live to make intercession for us.

But this man, because he continueth ever, hath an unchangeable priesthood [Heb. 7:24].

The Lord Jesus won't be dying anymore. He died once for our sins, but never again will He die. He is there all the time for you.

I received a letter once from a man in Puerto Rico who comes home late at night from his work in an oil refinery. He listens every night at 11:30 to our radio Bible study program. The Spirit of God ministers the Word of God to him down there late at night. The Lord Jesus knew all about that man long before I got his letter and learned of him. I didn't know him, and I didn't know he was listening to the radio broadcast. The Lord Jesus knew all about him, because He has an unchangeable priesthood. He is on duty twenty-four hours a day. That means that at 11:30 at night He knows this man, understands him, and ministers the Word of God to him. I rejoice in being able to give out the Word of God today because I am assured that the Spirit of God will be ministering it to folk. The Lord Jesus is the Great High Priest. While that fellow was listening, I was asleep in bed on the other side of the continent. But while I am sleeping there is a High Priest up yonder who will make the Word effective. How wonderful this is! Let's give Him all the praise and glory.

The following verse is perhaps the key verse to this entire section, and it is the very heart of the gospel.

Wherefore he is able also to save them to the uttermost that come unto God by him, seeing he ever liveth to make intercession for them [Heb. 7:25].

"Wherefore"—again we have this little hinge on which a big door swings. It swings back into what has been said before and swings on into what is ahead.

"He ever liveth." It says, first of all, that Christ is not dead, but He is living. Right at this very moment He is alive. We emphasize the death and resurrection of Christ, but we ought to go beyond that. We have to do with a *living* Christ. We know Him no longer after the flesh. We know Him today as our Great High Priest at God's right hand. My friend, that is what we need to go on today—that is where we need to put the emphasis. He died down here to save us, but He *lives* up there to keep us saved.

"He is able also to save them to the uttermost that come unto God by him." He is able to keep on saving you. "To the uttermost" means all the way through. He is able to save us completely and perfectly. He is the Great Shepherd who up to this very moment has never lost a sheep. Do you want to know something? He *never will* lose one. If you are one of His sheep, you may feel like you are going to be lost, but He is up there for you and He is watching over you.

"He ever liveth to make intercession." *Intercession* actually means "intervention." He intervenes for us. ". . . We shall be saved by his life" (Rom. 5:10). John wrote, "My little children [born ones], these things write I unto you, that ye sin not." Well John, you are not talking to *me* because I do lots of things that are wrong. Now, John, do you have a word for me? John went on to say, "And if any man sin"— now we are getting somewhere!—"we have an advocate with the Father, Jesus Christ the righteous" (1 John 2:1). An advocate is a *paraclete*, a comforter, someone to stand at our side. He is Jesus Christ the righteous. Everything He does is right. Everything He does is righteous. We shall be saved by His life.

How wonderful to know we have a living Christ! You are not alone, my friend. It is just baby stuff to sit down and cry, "Oh, I'm having this problem, and I'm so alone. There's nobody to help me. To whom shall I go?" My friend, what do you think He is doing up there? Aren't you conscious of Him? Why don't you turn to Him?

I remember talking to the mother of a man who was leaving his wife and running away with another woman. I took the mother with me when I went to talk with the other woman. She would not change her mind and was determined to go with this man. This poor mother, as I took her home, just got down on the floor of the car and began to cry out, "Oh, God, why have you forsaken me?" But by the time I got her home, she was more composed and apologized, "I'm sorry I said that God has forsaken me. I don't believe that He has." I assured her that we can be sure of the fact that He ever lives to make intercession for us. Though we are faithless, He is always faithful to us. It is wonderful to know He is up there, my friend.

For such an high priest became us, who is holy, harmless, undefiled, separate from sinners, and made higher than the heavens [Heb. 7:26].

He "became us" means Christ is just what we need. He is the one who fills the bill. He is just right for us—we couldn't have anyone better than He is.

"Holy"—that is, in relationship to God. He is the holy one.

"Harmless" means that He is free from any malice, craftiness, or cleverness. When He gets you off when you sin, it is not because He is a clever lawyer. It is because He is the one who paid the penalty for you, and the penalty absolutely has been paid.

"Undefiled"—He is free from any moral impurity. My friend, this is God's answer to the blasphemous films, songs, and literature of our day. The Bible makes it clear that the Lord Jesus was free from moral impurity.

He is also "separate from sinners." He is like us, yet unlike us. He could mix and mingle with sinners, and they didn't feel uncomfortable in His presence, but He was not one of them. His enemies accused Him of associating with publicans and sinners. He sure did, yet He wasn't one of them. He was separate from sinners.

Who needeth not daily, as those high priests, to offer up sacrifice, first for his own sins, and then for the people's: for this he did once, when he offered up himself [Heb. 7:27].

Notice that the Lord Jesus did not need to offer any sacrifice for His own sin—He had none.

If it were necessary for the Lord Jesus to come back and die for you again, He'd be back, my friend. He would be back today. But He won't be back to die for you—He died *once*.

The continual sacrificing in the Old Testament must have gotten pretty old and pretty tiresome. I am sure that many times when the priests would meet there at the laver to wash their hands and feet, one of them would turn to the other and say, "How many times have you been here today?"

"Well, I don't know. I'm sure I have been here at least a dozen times."

The other would reply, "Well, I have been here fifteen times. I've washed my hands here so many times that I've got dishpan hands! And look at my feet—they look like I've been standing in water all day. I'm so tired of going to that altar and offering sacrifices again and again and again."

I want to tell you, it must have been pretty wearisome, and if Aaron had overheard them talking, I think he would have said, "I agree with you that this ritual gets tiresome, but do you know what God is trying to tell us? He is trying to tell us that sin is an awful thing and that it requires the shedding of blood. But He has One who is coming someday who is going to die on a cross for us. When He does, there is going to be no more shedding of blood. He will have paid the penalty."

For the law maketh men high priests which have infirmity; but the word of the oath, which was since the law, maketh the Son, who is consecrated for evermore [Heb. 7:28].

The high priest in the Old Testament had to offer a sacrifice for himself—the Lord Jesus never did.

We have a High Priest who can be touched, who can be reached today. He is there to help and He understands, but He is holy, harmless, undefiled, and separate from sinners.

CHAPTER 8

THEME: *The true tabernacle; the New Covenant is better than the old*

The high watermark of this magnificent epistle is before us in this chapter—actually it began in the previous chapter at verse 25: "Wherefore he is able also to save them to the uttermost that come unto God by him, seeing he ever liveth to make intercession for them." This verse is the key to this section. You see, the emphasis is upon the fact that the Lord Jesus Christ is living. He is not dead—He is not on a cross; He is not lying in a grave. He arose from the dead, and the emphasis is upon our living Christ. Then verse 26: "For such an high priest became us [He is what we need], who is holy [in His relation to God], harmless [He never does anything to harm—He is never moved by anger], undefiled [free from any moral impurity], separate from sinners [in His life and character, although He is right down here among us and wants us to come to Him], and made higher than the heavens [He is in the presence of God]." The value of His sacrifice is stated in verse 27: "Who needeth not daily, as those high priests, to offer up sacrifice, first for his own sins, and then for the people's: for this he did once, when he offered up himself." His sacrifice was not of silver or gold or bulls or goats; He offered up *Himself!* There is nothing of greater value than He. Verse 28: "For the law maketh men high priests which have infirmity; but the word of the oath, which was since the law, maketh the Son, who is consecrated for evermore." You do not place your confidence in a mere man when you place your confidence in Jesus; you place your confidence in the God-man. Because He is a man, He can sympathize with you and is able to meet your need. He is a royal priest. He is a righteous priest. He is a peace-promoting priest. He is a personal priest—He is *for* you personally. He didn't inherit the office; that is, He didn't come in the line of Aaron. He is an eternal priest.

Now here in chapter 8 we are told that He ministers in a superior sanctuary by a much better covenant, which is built upon better promises.

THE TRUE TABERNACLE

Now of the things which we have spoken this is the sum: We have such an high priest, who is set on the right hand of the throne of the Majesty in the heavens [Heb. 8:1].

"This is the sum." He is not actually summing this up, although that thought is included. He is doing more than that. Let me give you a literal translation: "In consideration of the things which are spoken, this is the focal (chief) point. We have such an high priest, who sat down in the heavens on the right hand of the Majesty." As we have said, this is the high watermark of Hebrews.

"Who is set on the right hand of the throne." Christ did something which no priest in the Old Testament ever did. There is not a priest in the line of Aaron who ever had a chair in the tabernacle where he sat down. He was on the run all the time. Why? Because he had work to do. All of these things are shadows that point to a finished sacrifice. Now that Christ has died, all has been fulfilled, and we do not need to wonder if we are *doing* enough to merit salvation. All we need to do is turn to Jesus Christ and trust Him as our Savior. He sat down because He had finished our redemption. He asks only that we accept it.

A minister of the sanctuary, and of the true tabernacle, which the Lord pitched, and not man [Heb. 8:2].

Bezaleel was the master craftsman who made the beautiful articles of furniture for the tabernacle. The mercy seat and the golden lampstand were of gold and highly ornate. It was all man-made, although the Holy Spirit directed him. In contrast, the Lord Jesus ministers in a tabernacle that He Himself has made in heaven.

Now we are going to see something that I feel totally inadequate to present.

For every high priest is ordained to offer gifts and sacrifices: wherefore it is of necessity that this man have somewhat also to offer.

For if he were on earth, he should not be a priest, seeing that there are priests that offer gifts according to the law [Heb. 8:3–4].

This verse makes it clear that at the time the Epistle to the Hebrews was written the temple in Jerusalem was still in existence and that in it priests were still going about their duties.

Who serve unto the example and shadow of heavenly things, as Moses

was admonished of God when he was about to make the tabernacle: for, See, saith he, that thou make all things according to the pattern shewed to thee in the mount [Heb. 8:5].

It is my belief that when God instructed Moses to build the tabernacle in the wilderness, God gave him a pattern of the original in heaven, the *true* tabernacle (v. 2), meaning genuine.

The tabernacle in its beautiful simplicity furnishes a type of Jesus Christ (which is almost lost in the complicated detail of the temple). The tabernacle was called a tent, the sides of which were upright boards, covered on both sides with gold. It measured thirty cubits long and ten cubits wide and was divided into two compartments. The first compartment was called the Holy Place. In it were three articles of furniture: the golden lampstand; the golden table of showbread; and the golden altar where incense was offered—no sacrifice other than incense. The lampstand was a type of Christ, the Light of the World. The table of showbread symbolized Him as the Bread of Life. The golden altar at which the high priest offered prayer, spoke of Christ, our Great Intercessor. Then on the great Day of Atonement the high priest passed through the separating veil to the inner compartment, the Holy of Holies, in which were two articles of furniture. (1) The ark of the covenant was a box made of wood, covered with gold inside and outside, in which were the Ten Commandments written on tables of stone, a pot of manna, and Aaron's rod that budded. The Ten Commandments speak of the fact that the Lord Jesus Christ came to fulfill the Law, and He is the only one who ever kept it in all of its detail. Then the pot of manna speaks of the fact that He is the Bread of Life even today. Aaron's rod that budded speaks of Christ's resurrection. (2) The ark of the covenant was covered with a highly ornamented top called the mercy seat. Crowning it were two cherubim of beaten gold. Once a year the high priest placed blood on the mercy seat, and that is what made it a mercy seat. That was God's dwelling place; that is, the place where God met with the children of Israel.

Around the tabernacle was a court, surrounded by a linen fence one hundred cubits long and fifty cubits wide. In that outer court were two articles of furniture. The first was the brazen altar where all sacrifices were made. The sin question was settled there, but since saints still sin, there was also a laver where the priests could wash, signifying the cleansing from sin.

Now, the Holy Place is where the priests served and where they worshiped. We worship God when we pray, feed upon His Word, and walk in the light of His presence, that is, in obedience to Him.

No one but the high priest (and he only once a year) entered into the next compartment, the Holy of Holies. But when the Lord Jesus died, the separating veil was rent in twain—torn in two—signifying that He had forever opened the way into the Holy of Holies and the presence of God. We might say that the Lord Jesus Christ took the tabernacle, which was horizontal, and made it perpendicular to the earth so that the Holy of Holies is now in heaven—because that is where *He* is. And we are going to find in the following chapter that the golden altar of incense, together with the ark of the covenant, are now in heaven. They are there because Christ Himself is there.

If you had been in the wilderness with Israel, you would have seen the tabernacle in the heart of the encampment, with the tents of the tribes camped all around it. You would have seen the pillar of cloud over the tabernacle by day and the pillar of fire by night. You would have seen the priests busily running to and fro carrying on their ministry of offering sacrifices and observing all of the ritual which God had commanded.

Now all of that was a shadow of a reality. The *reality* itself was in heaven. And today Jesus is there in the heavenly tabernacle functioning in behalf of you and me.

Now perhaps you are saying, "You said that when we got to this section that the writer of this epistle would start serving porterhouse steaks. Well, it seems that we are still drinking milk, because what we have been studying so far seems very simple. When are we going to get something deep?" Well, the beefsteak is ready now, and I'd like to put it right down before you.

I'll put it in the form of a personal question. My friend, is Christ *real* to you right now? If you still like to run around in a ritual and have a nice beautiful church service (there is nothing wrong with that—don't misunderstand me), but if you think that is worship, and if you think that you are serving God by just teaching a Sunday school class or singing in the choir, I have news for you. He is trying to tell us, friend, that *Jesus* is up yonder in heaven for *you* right at this very moment. What does that really mean to you? Come now, don't choke on this steak. Don't ask for a glass of milk. Don't start running around doing little things. Let the pots and pans alone, Martha; you don't need to be handling them right now. Let's sit at Jesus' feet. Let Him be a reality in our lives. When you left the house this morning, did you take Him with you? Were you conscious of His presence? He is in heaven *serving* you, friend! Christ is your intercessor. You are to go to Him to make confession of your sin. Why is it that you are worrying your pastor to death with your problems? Why do you keep going to him for counseling? Isn't Jesus real to you today? Quit being a little baby that has to be burped all the time. Grow up! Come into the presence of the living Savior. That is what the writer is talking about. Oh, may God take the veil from our eyes, and may He make Jesus Christ—in all of His power, and in all of His salvation, and in all of His love, and in all of His care for you—a true reality!

I have been asked, "Why don't you run up the American flag? Why don't you fight corruption and lawlessness?" The reason I don't preach about those things is because I teach the Word of God, and I am trying to get folk into the presence of the living Christ. When that is accomplished, all of those other things will drop into their right places. If you walk in the light of His presence, you are going to walk with Him down the street. If you go into a barroom, Christ is going to have to go in with you. I don't know whether you would want to take Him into a bar or not. When Christ is with you, there are many things you are going to have to stop and consider. You will watch your conduct when you are conscious of the presence of Jesus Christ with you all of the time. He is the living intercessor today. He is alive.

Again let me say that the Lord Jesus ministers in a better tabernacle, the genuine tabernacle in heaven. He has made the throne of God a throne of grace, and we have been bidden to come there with great confidence and assurance that He is there. The thing you and I need to pray above everything else is: "Lord, I believe. Help Thou mine unbelief." I don't know about you, but my unbelief is bigger than my belief. We need to come to Him by *faith*. "Without faith it is impossible to please him; for he that cometh to God must believe that he is, and that he is a rewarder of them that diligently seek him" (Heb. 11:6). So you and I need to have the reality of Jesus Christ in our lives. You will not see Him with your physical eye nor hear Him with your physical ear, but you will behold Him with that inner eye and hear Him with that inner ear which only faith can open.

Oh, how wonderful this is! Perhaps you think we have bogged down in this section. No, we are in His presence. We are at the high watermark. We are walking in the tall corn now. This is a wonderful section of God's Word.

THE NEW COVENANT IS BETTER THAN THE OLD

But now hath he obtained a more excellent ministry, by how much also he is the mediator of a better covenant, which was established upon better promises [Heb. 8:6].

"He obtained a more excellent ministry." The tabernacle down here was a shadow of the real tabernacle up yonder in heaven. Christ lives up there and He can keep us saved. Somebody asks me, "Do you think you can lose your salvation?" Well, I'll make a confession to you. I would lose my salvation before the sun goes down if Christ were not up there right now. He is having a problem with me—and maybe He is having a problem with you—but, thank God, He is there. My, how we need Him!

"He is the mediator of a better covenant." We have what is known as a New *Covenant* today; we call it a new *testament*. The New Testament is actually a New Covenant which God has made, and it is in contrast to the old covenant of the Old Testament. God gave to Moses the Law, then He gave to him instructions for the tabernacle with its service. It was there that sin was dealt with. No one was ever saved by keeping the Law. No one ever came to God and said, "I have kept all Your commandments, therefore receive me." No, instead they were continually bringing sacrifices because they had transgressed God's law. The Law revealed to them that they had come short of the glory of God. The sacrificial system was all shadow. Although the tabernacle God gave to them was a literal tabernacle, it was a shadow of the real tabernacle in which Christ ministers today. In other words, so far we have seen that we have a better priest; we have a better sacrifice; we have a better tabernacle. All of this converges yonder at the brazen altar because Christ is all three: He is the better *priest* who ministers there. He is the better *sacrifice*—He offered Himself. And He ministers in a better *tabernacle*, for He offered His own blood for your sin and my sin.

At this point I would like to refer you to my book, *The Tabernacle, God's Portrait of*

Christ. In it I go into much more detail, and I take the position that Christ offered His literal blood in heaven. It is my opinion that He was on His way to do this when He appeared to Mary. "Jesus saith unto her, Touch me not; for I am not yet ascended to my Father: but go to my brethren, and say unto them, I ascend unto my Father, and your Father; and to my God, and your God" (John 20:17). I think He was at that moment our High Priest on His way to offer His literal blood in heaven. And I believe it will be there throughout eternity to remind us of the price that He paid for our redemption. When my book was first published, it was reviewed by a Christian magazine. The critic recommended it but warned that I took this literal view. The critic called it a crude concept. Well, I don't think that the blood of Christ is crude—either when it was shed on earth or offered in heaven. Simon Peter, who was not what one might call a cultured individual, called it *precious* blood. A society dowager approached a great preacher in the East years ago. Looking at him through her lorgnette (a lorgnette, you know, is a sneer on the end of a stick), she said, "I hope you will not be like our last preacher. He was rather old-fashioned and put great emphasis on the blood. The blood offends my aesthetic nature. Don't you think it is crude?" His reply to her was, "Madam, I see nothing crude about the blood of Christ except my sin and your sin." I agree with him wholeheartedly. I say to you very definitely and dogmatically that I believe His blood is even now in heaven, and throughout the endless ages it will be there to remind us of the awful price Christ paid to redeem us.

"Which was established upon better promises." Back in the Old Testament God had given the Mosaic Law, and when the people of Israel broke it, they brought the sacrifices. *Before* God gave the Mosaic Law and the instructions for approaching Him through the tabernacle ritual, they came to God by faith like Abraham did. Then when we move back of the time of Abraham, we find that Noah was on a different basis altogether. I don't feel that you can read the Bible intelligently without seeing that God dealt with men differently in different ages. If you don't want to call them dispensations, then you use your own word, but if you accept the inerrancy of Scripture and believe it is the Word of God, you are faced with the dispensational system—if you read it aright.

The writer of this epistle says that now we have a "better covenant" and that it is based upon "better promises." Although you and I as Christians have been made a part of it, God is not through with the nation Israel, and these "better promises" are going to be fulfilled for them in the future Millennium.

When you read the Old Testament prophets, you just cannot get away from the fact that God is going to return the children of Israel back to their land. (As far as I can see, the present return of the Jews to Israel is not the fulfillment of prophecy.) For example, notice this prophecy in Jeremiah: "Thus saith the LORD; Behold, I will bring again the captivity of Jacob's tents, and have mercy on his dwellingplaces; and the city shall be builded upon her own heap, and the palace shall remain after the manner thereof" (Jer. 30:18). Then in Jeremiah 31:8 we read, "Behold, I will bring them from the north country, and gather them from the coasts of the earth, and with them the blind and the lame, the woman with child and her that travaileth with child together: a great company shall return thither." This verse mentions the north country, which is Russia. The Jews are having a hard time getting out of Russia today, but when God steps in, there will be no trouble getting out of Russia and going to Palestine. Continuing on in the Book of Jeremiah we are told, "Hear the word of the LORD, O ye nations, and declare it in the isles afar off, and say, He that scattered Israel will gather him, and keep him, as a shepherd doth his flock. For the LORD hath *redeemed* Jacob, and ransomed him from the hand of him that was stronger than he" (Jer. 31:10–11, italics mine). The Jews are not in Israel under God's redemption today— they are far from Him. But when that day comes, there will be a fulfillment of what the writer to the Hebrews is talking about when he says that there are going to be better promises on a better covenant that God will make with these people. "Behold, the days come, saith the LORD, that I will make a new covenant with the house of Israel, and with the house of Judah: Not according to the covenant that I made with their fathers in the day that I took them by the hand to bring them out of the land of Egypt; which my covenant they brake, although I was an husband unto them, saith the LORD: But this shall be the covenant that I will make with the house of Israel; After those days, saith the LORD, I will put my law in their *inward parts*, and write it in their *hearts;* and will be their God, and they shall be my people" (Jer. 31:31–33, italics mine). In effect, God says, "I gave it to them before and wrote it on a cold hard stone—and they couldn't keep it, but now I am going to write it on the fleshly tablets of the heart." He has not done this up to the present moment. As I write this, I have just returned from the land of Israel and I saw no turning to God at all. One of the tour guides whom I had the privilege of meeting was a very attractive and likeable fellow. After I had witnessed to him, I told him, "You ought to be telling me about Jesus. You are a Jew, and you are living here in this land where He lived. He died for the sins of the world. I'm a poor Gentile who has come from afar. You ought to be telling me about Him—and here I am telling you!" He just laughed. May I say to you, friend, the Jews are not back in their land according to this promise. But someday Jeremiah's prophecy is going to be fulfilled. Listen to him: "And they shall teach no more every man his neighbour, and every man his brother, saying, Know the LORD: for they shall all know me [they don't know Him today], from the least of them unto the greatest of them, saith the LORD: for I will forgive their iniquity, and I will remember their sin no more" (Jer. 31:34). This is what the writer to the Hebrews is talking about. The New Covenant is established upon better promises. Christ is the mediator of the better covenant because it contains better promises.

For if that first covenant had been faultless, then should no place have been sought for the second [Heb. 8:7].

"For if that first covenant had been faultless"—the first covenant was not adequate, which created a necessity for a better covenant. Somebody says, "Then the old covenant was wrong." Now, that is not the case. Listen to the next verse:

For finding fault with them, he saith, Behold, the days come, saith the Lord, when I will make a new covenant with the house of Israel and with the house of Judah [Heb. 8:8].

"For finding fault with *them*"—not with *it*. The problem never was with God's covenant. There is nothing wrong with God's law, but there is a whole lot wrong with you and me. You and I are not able to keep the Law; we are not able to measure up to its requirements.

"Behold, the days come, saith the Lord, when I will make a new covenant with the house of Israel and with the house of Judah." We have just read about that in Jeremiah's prophecy, and you can read about it in the rest of the prophets.

Not according to the covenant that I made with their fathers in the day when I took them by the hand to lead them out of the land of Egypt; because they continued not in my covenant, and I regarded them not, saith the Lord [Heb. 8:9].

The people broke the first covenant. It did not enable them to perform what it demanded.

For this is the covenant that I will make with the house of Israel after those days, saith the Lord; I will put my laws into their mind, and write them in their hearts: and I will be to them a God, and they shall be to me a people [Heb. 8:10].

The New Covenant will be written upon their hearts—not upon tables of stone—so that they will be able to obey it.

And they shall not teach every man his neighbour, and every man his brother, saying, Know the Lord: for all shall know me, from the least to the greatest.

For I will be merciful to their unrighteousness, and their sins and their iniquities will I remember no more [Heb. 8:11–12].

There will be full forgiveness of sin. There will be complete pardon.

In that he saith, A new covenant, he hath made the first old. Now that which decayeth and waxeth old is ready to vanish away [Heb. 8:13].

So, my friend, we are not under the Mosaic system. God says that it is an old model and He has brought in a new model. That New Covenant He has made through the Lord Jesus Christ who is our Savior. Let me repeat, He did it, not because there was something wrong with the old covenant, but because there is something wrong with us. I feel sorry for folk today who have come back to the old covenant. They try to keep the Sabbath day and they try to keep the Mosaic Law. Oh, my friend, if they will really study it and are honest, they *know* they are not keeping the Mosaic system. They come short. All of us need to come to God for *mercy,* and accept in His New Covenant the provision of a Savior.

The Law was totally incapable of producing any good thing in man. Paul could say, "For I know that in me (that is, in my flesh,) dwelleth no good thing . . . ." (Rom. 7:18). And, friend, that is Scripture, and that is accurate. Man is totally depraved. That doesn't mean only the man across the street or down in the next block from you, nor does it mean only some person who is living in overt sin; it means *you* and it means *me*. The Holy Spirit is now able to do the impossible. The Holy Spirit can produce a holy life in weak and sinful flesh.

Let me illustrate this truth by using a very homely incident. Suppose a housewife puts a roast in the oven right after breakfast because she is going to serve it for the noon meal. Time goes by and the telephone rings. It is Mrs. Joe Dokes on the phone. Mrs. Dokes begins with "Have you heard?" Well, the housewife hasn't heard, but she would like to; so she pulls up a chair. Someone has defined a woman as one who draws up a chair when answering a telephone. Mrs. Dokes has a lot to tell, and about an hour goes by. Finally our good housewife says, "Oh, Mrs. Dokes, you'll have to excuse me. I smell the roast—it's burning!" She hangs up the phone, rushes to the kitchen, and opens the oven. Then she gets a fork and puts it down in the roast to lift it up, but it won't hold. She can't lift it out. She tries again, closer to the bone, but still it won't hold. So she gets a spatula. She puts the spatula under the roast and lifts it out. You see, what the fork could not do, in that it was weak through the flesh, the spatula is able to do. Now, there is nothing wrong with the fork—it was a good fork. But it couldn't hold the flesh because something was wrong with the flesh—it was overcooked. The spatula does what the fork could not do.

The Law is like the fork in that it was weak through the flesh. It just won't lift us up; it *can't* lift us up. But a new principle is introduced: the Holy Spirit. What the Law could not do, the Holy Spirit is able to do. Therefore, you and I are to be saved and are to live the Christian life on this new principle. We have a New Covenant based upon better promises; God has given to us the Holy Spirit and Christ, our intercessor, is up yonder to help us today.

This is a very wonderful passage of Scripture. If you want to get off the milk diet (although milk is good for you, and there is milk in the Word), learn to eat some meat along with it. The meat is to put the emphasis upon the living Christ, His ascension, and His intercession yonder in heaven for you and for me. My friend, when we lay hold on the living Christ, we have gone to the heights. We cannot go any higher than that in this age in which we live.

CHAPTER 9

THEME: *New sanctuary better than old; the superior sacrifice*

NEW SANCTUARY BETTER THAN THE OLD

Our subject is the priesthood of the Lord Jesus Christ who is a priest after the order of Melchizedek. Presented to us are two ministries which are in sharp contrast. The Levitical service, the ministry of the Aaronic priesthood, was carried out in an earthly tabernacle down here. That sanctuary on earth was merely a type of the one which is in heaven, the sanctuary in which the Lord Jesus is serving today. This sanctuary in heaven provides for better worship. A great many people consider the Law from the standpoint of the Ten Commandments, but the Epistle to the Hebrews approaches the Law from the viewpoint of its place of worship and its priesthood. That approach puts the emphasis on the settling of sins, and, as the writer will point out, the Law never really settled the sin question.

"For it is not possible that the blood of bulls and of goats should take away sins" (Heb. 10:4).

Then verily the first covenant had also ordinances of divine service, and a worldly sanctuary [Heb. 9:1].

The word for "service" here would be better translated as "worship."

"A worldly sanctuary" does not mean worldly as we usually think of it, but it means a sanctuary of this world; that is, it was made of materials of this world. It was made so long, so wide, and so high, and there was a ritual that the people went through in the sanctuary down here. In that sense it was of the world. The writer is going to further contrast it with the sanctuary that is in heaven.

For there was a tabernacle made; the first, wherein was the candlestick, and

the table, and the shewbread; which is called the sanctuary [Heb. 9:2].

"For there was a *tabernacle* made"—notice that we are not taken back to the temple. There is no reference made to Herod's temple for the sake of this illustration. Although the third temple was then in existence, when the type is given, the writer goes beyond them all to that very simple structure that God gave to Moses in the wilderness. "There was a tabernacle made," and it was made of the things of this world. It was patterned after the one in heaven, but it was much inferior in many different ways, as we shall see.

"Which is called the sanctuary"—that is, it was the Holy Place. The tabernacle proper was just a big gold box thirty cubits (about forty-five feet) long, ten cubits (about fifteen feet) wide, and ten cubits high. It was divided into two sections. The first was the Holy Place in which there were certain articles of furniture: the table of the showbread and the golden lampstand. Then, in the background was the golden altar, the altar of incense, which speaks of prayer—no sacrifices were ever made there.

And after the second veil, the tabernacle which is called the Holiest of all;

Which had the golden censer, and the ark of the covenant overlaid round about with gold, wherein was the golden pot that had manna, and Aaron's rod that budded, and the tables of the covenant;

And over it the cherubims of glory shadowing the mercyseat; of which we cannot now speak particularly [Heb. 9:3–5].

In the Holy of Holies (which was separated from the Holy Place by a veil and into which only the high priest entered), there were two articles of furniture. There was the ark, which was just a box made out of gopher wood and overlaid inside and outside with gold, and on top of the ark was a highly ornamented top called the mercy seat. It was fashioned with cherubim, made of pure gold, looking down upon the top of the box. That was where the blood was placed, and that was what made it a mercy seat—for "without shedding of blood is no remission" of sins.

"Which had the golden censer," that is, the golden altar. Notice that a change has been made—we are told that the golden altar is inside the Holy of Holies rather than inside the Holy Place. Why has it been moved to the inside? The veil between the Holy Place and the Holy of Holies was made of fine twine Egyptian byssus linen with the cherubim woven into it, and it spoke of the humanity of the Lord Jesus. When He died on the cross, He gave His life, His human life, and at that time the veil was rent in twain. So the veil which was torn in two has been removed, signifying that the way to God is wide open, because Christ has made a way. He said, "No man cometh to the Father, but by me" (see John 14:6). The veil has been rent in twain, and we can come right into God's presence today. But what happened to the golden censer or the golden altar? It has been moved inside the Holy of Holies. Aaron on the great Day of Atonement came with the blood to sprinkle upon the mercy seat, taking a censer filled with coals and with incense in it, and he went inside the Holy of Holies. He was actually transferring, as it were, the altar of incense to the inside. He took the censer of burning coals from off the altar with sweet incense on it, and took it into the Holy of Holies, but he brought it back out again. And he had to do that again the next year and then again the next.

However, we have a Great High Priest who is our great intercessor always at the golden altar making intercession for us. His prayers are heard, by the way. Therefore, the golden altar is on the inside, but it is also on the outside, because you and I can come through Him by prayer. That is what Paul meant when he said, "Being justified by faith, we have peace with God through our Lord Jesus Christ: by whom also we have *access* . . ." (Rom. 5:1–2).

The writer mentions also the things which were in the ark. "Wherein was the golden pot that had manna"—this speaks of the present ministry of Christ. He feeds those who are His own. He feeds them with His Word. He is the Bread of Life. The Bible is God's bakery, and if you want bread, that is where you will go to get it.

"And Aaron's rod that budded." This speaks of the death and resurrection of Christ, because it was a dead rod and life came into it.

"And the tables of the covenant" speaks of the fact that the Lord Jesus Christ fulfilled all the law.

"Of which we cannot now speak particularly." The writer means he doesn't have time to dwell upon the tabernacle, because the things that he is emphasizing are the priesthood and worship. He is concerned about what real worship is and how we are to worship.

Now when these things were thus ordained, the priests went always into the first tabernacle, accomplishing the service of God [Heb. 9:6].

"The priests went *always* into the first tabernacle." The priests went continually—they never finished the job. If they went today, they would be going again tomorrow, and the next day, and on and on and on. I am of the opinion that it must have become very monotonous over the years for a priest to continually go through this ritual. The very repetition of it meant that it was not sufficient, that is, that one time would not do. However, we are going to see that Christ went *once* into the Holy Place—it was necessary for Him to go just one time.

"Accomplishing the service of God" should be "accomplishing the *worship* of God." This was the ultimate goal of it all, that God's people might worship Him. This is speaking of real worship, not just a church service where an order of service is followed. When real worship takes place it is a worship that draws us into the presence of Christ where we can adore Him.

The word *worship* comes from the same Anglo-Saxon root word as *worth*. To worship is to give someone something of which they are worthy. The Lord Jesus Christ is worthy to receive our praise and our adoration. That is worship, and from that follows service. Real worship will always lead to service. In the midst of His temptation in the wilderness, the Lord Jesus answered Satan, ". . . For it is written, Thou shalt *worship* the Lord thy God, and him only shalt thou *serve*" (Matt. 4:10, italics mine). You will not have to beg and coax and goad people into doing something, if they are participating in real worship of Christ—because real worship leads to service. Many ministers spend a great deal of time urging people to do something—urging them to give, urging them to do visitation, urging them to teach, or urging them to sing. Real worship will lead to service. Such worship is possible only through Jesus Christ.

The ritual of the tabernacle never brought the people into the presence of God. The high priest alone went into the Holy of Holies.

But into the second went the high priest alone once every year, not without blood, which he offered for himself, and for the errors of the people [Heb. 9:7].

He is speaking now of the great Day of Atonement. This was Yom Kippur, in one sense the high day in the life of the nation Israel. This is the day that the great high priest went into the Holy of Holies on behalf of the nation. And on the basis of his having done this, the nation was accepted for another year.

Our Great High Priest has gone into the Holy of Holies, into the very presence of God. He has gone in, and He has not come out. He is going to be there as long as we are in the world. When He does come out, He is coming out after His own—we are a part of Him; we are the "body" of Christ.

The purpose of all of this is to make real to your heart and mine the presence of the Lord Jesus. Did you start out the day with Him? This is a hurly-burly world you and I are in, and it has no time for Him. As you have rushed through this day, has He been with you? Have you worshiped Him? To worship Him we do not have to go to church and sing the doxology (although the writer of this epistle is going to urge us to do that, because we need to be with God's people and participate in concerted, corporate worship; it is essential for our growth) but we can worship Him anywhere. You can worship Him at the end of a cotton row or a corn row. You can worship Him on the freeway. You can worship Him in the office. You can worship Him in the classroom. My friend, I don't care where you are, you can worship Him. You and I need to pour out our hearts in adoration and praise unto His holy name.

Now our High Priest has gone into the Holy of Holies on our behalf this very day. And you can see how superior this is to the past when the high priest went in on just one day each year—and didn't stay; in fact, he hurried out. Tradition tells us that he actually had a chain around his foot, because if he did anything wrong, he would have been struck dead and they would have had to pull him out and get a new high priest.

Oh, the wonder and the glory of it all! Our High Priest has gone into the very presence of God for you and me, and He is there today. Someone has given a little different translation of Hebrews 9:24, and I want to give it to you at this point: "For Christ entered not into a holy place made with hands, like in pattern to the true, but into heaven itself, now to appear before the face of God for us." Moses asked to see God's face but was told that no man could see God. However, you and I have a High Priest who has gone into the very presence of God.

We do not worship Him by going through a ritual. We do not worship Him by burning candles or incense, or by having a nice little altar fixed up. Some Protestant churches have really gotten involved in such things.

The last time I was in the church of a minister friend I asked him why he had a cross set up on the table used for the Lord's Supper. He said, "Oh, not only that, but did you notice the candles?" I hadn't noticed them, but he also had a candle at each end of the table. He said, "That's to help the people with their worship." My friend, if you need that kind of help, you are not worshiping Him. The woman at the well asked the Lord Jesus where the people should worship God, and the Lord replied, "The hour cometh, and now is, when the true worshippers shall worship the Father in spirit and in truth: for the Father seeketh such to worship him" (John 4:23). I have another minister friend who is very concerned with Jewish evangelism, and he has a menorah with seven candles on it in his church. He told me that it was to keep their minds centered on the fact that they have an obligation to the Jewish people. If we need that sort of thing in our churches, we are not really worshiping God.

Oh, that you and I could get into His presence and smell the sweet incense of His presence—not with our noses but with our hearts and our souls and our minds. I pray that I might be conscious of the sweetness of His presence, that I might walk in the light of His Word, and that there might be reality in my life every day. I covet that for you too. We need to put away our bottle of milk with its little nipple, and we need to feed on the meat of the Word. We need to get into the presence of the living Christ who is our Great High Priest ministering yonder at a better tabernacle than the one that was on this earth. We can worship the living Christ today.

The Holy Ghost this signifying, that the way into the holiest of all was not yet made manifest, while as the first tabernacle was yet standing [Heb. 9:8].

In other words, all of this was a picture and a type that the way into the very presence of God (actually, right into the very *face* of God) had not yet been opened.

Which was a figure for the time then present, in which were offered both gifts and sacrifices, that could not make him that did the service perfect, as pertaining to the conscience;

Which stood only in meats and drinks, and divers washings, and carnal ordi-

nances, imposed on them until the time of reformation [Heb. 9:9–10].

"That could not make him that did the *service* perfect," could read "that could not make the *worshiper* perfect."

The way to God in the tabernacle was actually blocked by the three entrances and compartments. In other words, the people could come only to that outer entrance and bring their sacrifice. If a man brought a little lamb, he would put his hand on it in an act of identification since it would die in his place, and then the priest would take it from there. It would be slain and offered upon the brazen altar. The individual who brought the lamb could go no farther than the entrance. Then, as far as the Holy Place was concerned, only the priest could go in there. And into the Holy of Holies neither the priest nor the people could go. Only the high priest could enter in there. Therefore, the tabernacle was a temporary, makeshift arrangement. The service of ritual and ordinances, was given for just a brief time.

Now Christ can bring us to God, but only He can bring us there. ". . . No man cometh unto the Father," He said, "but by me" (John 14:6). Such is real worship, and real worship will lead to service. Once we get into the presence of God, there will be no problem about serving.

Worship is something that the liberal today condemns. Years ago the late Dr. Harry Emerson Fosdick said that the world tried to get rid of Jesus in two ways—one was by crucifying Him and the other was by worshiping Him! My friend, it is blasphemy to say that if you worship Him you are no better than those who crucified Him! We approach a holy God today on the basis of a crucified Savior. He alone can cause us to worship.

That is the reason for Paul's writing to the Ephesians: "And be not drunk with wine, wherein is excess; but be filled with the Spirit." Now notice the first thing Paul speaks of after being filled with the Spirit: "Speaking to yourselves in psalms and hymns and spiritual songs, singing and making melody in your heart to the Lord" (Eph. 5:18–19). That is worship. My friend, the greatest thrill in the world for a child of God is to be filled with the Spirit of God and to have the Spirit of God take the things of Christ and make them real to us. What joy that brings to our hearts! If you have been in the presence of God to worship, you will have joy in your heart and you will have a song in your heart. Some of us have difficulty getting that song to our lips—I always have!—but it is certainly down in my heart. It is wonderful to worship Him.

I want to recapitulate what we have said concerning the sanctuary here on earth which is inferior to the one in heaven. To do so, I will share from an outline put out by a good friend of mine, Dr. Warren W. Wiersbe (*Be Confident*). This is what we have seen concerning the sanctuary here on earth:

1. *It was on earth*. It was a worldly sanctuary, that is, it was made of earthly things, material things. It was erected on this earth down here.

2. *It was but a shadow of things to come*. It never was the reality. So many of us have things mixed up. We go back and study about the tabernacle, and we can really get our interest centered in that earthly tabernacle. But, at best it was just a shadow, a picture of the real one that is in heaven.

3. *It was inaccessible to the people*. You just couldn't get in there. If you had been an Israelite in that day, you couldn't go rushing into the presence of God. You would have been stopped at that first entrance. You would have needed a sacrifice there, and you couldn't have gone any further—the priest served for you. However, today we are a priesthood of believers, and each one of us has access to God. That is one of the great privileges we have because Christ has rent the veil in twain. He has gone into the presence of God, into the *face* of God. He is right there, my friend, and He is there for us. The Israelites didn't have that privilege under the old covenant.

4. *It was temporary*. But the Lord Jesus Christ is going to keep the way open for eternity. I have a notion that Vernon McGee is going to need someone who will keep it open for him throughout eternity. The earthly tabernacle was only a temporary arrangement.

5. *It was ineffective to change the hearts of the people*. This is the thing I want to emphasize above everything else. The earthly sanctuary had nothing in the world to do with changing people's lives. But today you can come to Christ, and He can change your life. He alone can enable you to worship God in spirit and in truth and make Him a reality in your life. Many folk today just play church—like we played house by the hours when we were kids. I know a lot of Christians who are grown up and have gray hair, and they're still playing church. They go to committee meetings, they're on the board, some sing in the choir, some teach a Sunday school class—they are as busy as termites and just about as effective. They think they are serving God. My friend, you can never serve Him until you have worshiped Him.

THE SUPERIOR SACRIFICE

But Christ being come an high priest of good things to come, by a greater and more perfect tabernacle, not made with hands, that is to say, not of this building [Heb. 9:11].

"Of good things to come" really means good things *that have come to pass*. Oh, the good things that have come through Him!

"A greater and more perfect tabernacle, not made with hands." This tabernacle is nothing that man has built down here. The better tabernacle does not belong to this natural creation as to materials or builders.

Let me say this very kindly. All of this business today of trying to sweeten up the worship service with pictures and stained glass windows and candles and crosses ministers to the *flesh*. It is fleshly—it ministers to the physical side of man. It doesn't minister to his spiritual needs at all. We need to recognize that there is a real tabernacle in heaven; there is a real High Priest there, and there is *spiritual* worship. You can worship Him anywhere, and it is wonderful when people can come together in a church and really worship God. I'm sure many of you have been in a service like that, and it is a wonderful thing.

Neither by the blood of goats and calves, but by his own blood he entered in once into the holy place, having obtained eternal redemption for us [Heb. 9:12].

I believe this verse proves that Christ took His literal blood to heaven. If that is not what the writer is talking about here, I do not know what he is saying. "Neither by the blood of goats and calves"—that is literal blood. "But by his own blood," this is the literal blood which He shed on the cross. "He entered in." How? By His own blood. His was a superior sacrifice and the only one worthy of the genuine tabernacle.

"Having obtained eternal redemption *for us*." Notice that in your Bible the words *for us* are in italics, indicating that they are not in the original manuscript. They were added to smooth out the translation, which is all right, but they are not the emphasis of the verse. The emphasis is upon the contrast that Christ entered *once* into the Holy Place and obtained *eternal* redemption. The Israelite priests went in *continually,* and they got a *temporary* sort of thing. Only Christ went in once and obtained eternal redemption. This now puts the authority and the importance upon the sacrifice of Christ, and it reminds us that the *life* of Christ never saved anyone. You can follow His teachings and think you are saved, but, my friend, His teaching never saved anyone. It is the *death* of Christ, it is His redemption that saves.

For if the blood of bulls and of goats, and the ashes of an heifer sprinkling the unclean, sanctifieth to the purifying of the flesh [Heb. 9:13].

"And the ashes of an heifer" is a reference to the ordinance of the red heifer in Numbers 19. The heifer was burned completely and its ashes kept in a clean place. When a man became ceremonially defiled (primarily by touching a dead body), the priest would take the ashes, mingle them with water, and sprinkle the offender. This served to ceremonially purify him so that he could be restored to fellowship. I would like to have you notice that here the heifer has a particular symbolism. A female, instead of a bull, is used. We are told in 1 Peter 3:7 that the female is the weaker vessel. Our defilement actually comes through our weakness. We are weak, and Christ came down and experienced physically, in the flesh, our weakness.

We are told also that a *red* heifer was used. The red, I think, speaks of the fact that Christ became sin for us—not in some academic way, but He actually *became* sin for us. How do we know that red is the color of sin? Isaiah said, "Come now, and let us reason together, saith the LORD: though your sins be as *scarlet,* they shall be as white as snow; though they be *red* like crimson, they shall be as wool" (Isa. 1:18, italics mine). So it must be a *red* heifer, speaking of the fact that He became sin for us.

The animal must also be without blemish. It certainly could not represent Christ unless it was perfect. He was holy, harmless, undefiled, and separate from sinners.

The red heifer must be an animal upon which a yoke had never been put. This symbolizes the fact that although Christ was made sin for us, He was never under the bondage of sin.

The heifer was to be led outside the camp and there slain before the high priest. In this we have pictured that the Lord Jesus is both the offering and the High Priest—He offered Himself.

The blood of the offering was to be sprinkled by the high priest before the tabernacle seven times. Many people think that seven is the number of perfection in Scripture. That is only indirectly true; the primary meaning is completeness. It speaks here of the fact that Christ's sacrifice is a *finished* transaction—one sacrifice takes care of the sin of the believer.

The carcass of the heifer was to be burned—again in the sight of the high priest. You see, God so loved the world that He *gave* His only begotten Son. Jesus freely gave Himself, but we probably have never thought of the sorrow that was in heaven the day He died.

Numbers also tells us that cedar and hyssop were to be put with the sacrifice. This is rather suggestive to me. First Kings 4:33 says, "And he [Solomon] spake of trees, from the cedar tree that is in Lebanon even unto the hyssop that springeth out of the wall. . . ." Solomon ran the gamut of trees and plant life; he was a dendrologist and knew the entire field. I think this is what Isaac Watts meant by "the whole realm of nature." Therefore I believe this speaks of the fact that the Lord Jesus Christ not only redeemed mankind, but He has redeemed this world. We live in a world that is cursed by sin; it is now groaning and travailing in pain, but it is to be delivered. Someday it is to be redeemed, and sin is to be removed.

A little later in this chapter we are told that even heaven itself had to be cleansed (see v. 23). Someone says, "My gracious, is it dirty in heaven?" Yes, that is where sin originated, where Lucifer led his rebellion. Therefore, Christ's sacrifice was adequate and it was complete. It was a finished transaction that covered all of God's creation which has been touched by sin.

Were the whole realm of nature mine,
That were a present far too small;
Love so amazing, so divine,
Demands my soul, my life, my all.

"When I Survey the Wondrous Cross"
—Isaac Watts

The ashes of the heifer were to be kept in a clean place and then mixed with water when they were used. I think that the water speaks of the Word of God. It is the Word of God which reveals sin in the life of the believer.

The sacrifice of Christ provided redemption for the future—for your redemption and my redemption. It also provided redemption for the sins of those in the Old Testament. The

Old Testament saints were saved by faith—Abraham was saved by faith. How? He believed God and brought a lamb. Was that lamb adequate? No; it prefigured Christ. The sacrifice of Christ looks forward and it looks backward.

How much more shall the blood of Christ, who through the eternal Spirit offered himself without spot to God, purge your conscience from dead works to serve the living God? [Heb. 9:14].

If the blood of animals could remove ceremonial defilement, surely the blood of Christ can take away the guilt of sin. After all, if the blood of bulls and goats had been adequate, Christ never would have shed His blood to do the adequate job.

"Purge your conscience." The ordinance of the red heifer in Numbers 19 speaks of the life of the believer and the fact that as believers you and I need constant cleansing. "But if we walk in the light, as he is in the light, we have fellowship one with another, and the blood of Jesus Christ his Son cleanseth [keeps on cleansing] us from all sin. . . . If we confess our sins, he is faithful and just to forgive us our sins, and to cleanse us from all unrighteousness" (1 John 1:7, 9). You see, the blood of Christ cleanses, not the flesh, but the conscience.

It is the conscience of man that needs to be cleansed. You and I have not really arrived until we enter into this marvelous sacrifice of Christ, recognizing His authority to absolutely forgive and cleanse us from sin. It is the conscience that has been made alert by the Word of God, but it can also rest in a finished salvation. We can pillow our heads at night knowing that our sins are entirely, totally, fully forgiven. We can know that we are right with God because Christ has made it right.

I heard a story of a man who had a little boy who did something wrong and went to his father to ask him to forgive him. The father told the little boy he would, and said, "Because you have come and confessed it, I will forgive you." But the little boy came again and asked forgiveness. The father said, "Sure. I've already forgiven you." The little boy kept coming back and coming back and coming back. Finally, the father said, "Son, I'm going to paddle you, if you don't quit coming to me! I told you I'd forgiven you."

How many times do we find believers who say, "Oh, I'm not sure I'm saved. I'm not sure I'm saved." And they keep going to the Lord. My friend, I think He would say, "I've already forgiven you. If you trust in My Son, your sins are forgiven." We need to enter into that and rest upon His Word.

"Purge your conscience *from dead works.*" Dead works have to do with works that you do thinking they will save you. You see, we are dead in trespasses and sins, and all that a dead person can do is dead works. I have never heard of a dead person doing live work—it just can't be done. Anything that you do to try to earn your salvation is a dead work.

Because good works are never a cause of salvation but are a result of salvation, the writer goes on to say, "purge your conscience from dead works *to serve the living God.*" The word *serve* is actually *worship*—"to worship the living God." Worship and service go together. You can't serve God without worshiping Him; neither can you worship Him without serving Him. When I see a lazy saint doing nothing for God, I don't question his salvation, but I do question his worship. Does he really worship God? Oh, if you fall down before Him in adoration and praise, then you are going to get up on your feet to start doing something for Him, my friend.

I had this bit of verse written in the first Bible I ever owned, which my mother had given to me:

> I do not work my soul to save—
> That work my Lord has done.
> But I will work like any slave
> For love of God's dear Son.
> —Author unknown

And for this cause he is the mediator of the new testament, that by means of death, for the redemption of the transgressions that were under the first testament, they which are called might receive the promise of eternal inheritance [Heb. 9:15].

"And for this cause he is the mediator of the new testament [or, covenant]." The emphasis is upon the fact that He is the mediator of the New Covenant. Those who came under the old covenant, the Old Testament saints, were saved because they were looking forward to His coming when they brought their sacrifices. I do not know how much they understood, and yet the Lord Jesus said, "Your father Abraham rejoiced to see my day: and he saw it, and was glad" (John 8:56). Genesis doesn't tell us that; the Lord Jesus did. I believe that all of the Old Testament worthies looked forward to the coming of Christ. In other words, God saved on credit. The blood of bulls and goats never took away their sins. They brought the sacrifices by faith, and when Christ came, He died ". . . for the remission of sins that are past . . ." (Rom. 3:25); that is, He died for the sins of all from Adam right down to the time of the cross. And since then, you and I also come to Him by faith.

For where a testament is, there must also of necessity be the death of the testator.

For a testament is of force after men are dead: otherwise it is of no strength at all while the testator liveth [Heb. 9:16–17].

"Testament" could be translated *will*. If you have made a will and you are still alive, your will does nothing for anyone. It doesn't operate until you die. Now the reference here is to a will that was made by a man who died. He couldn't save anyone as long as He lived. Don't misunderstand me—what I am saying is that the *life* of Christ could never save you. It is the *death* of Christ which saves you.

Whereupon neither the first testament was dedicated without blood.

For when Moses had spoken every precept to all the people according to the law, he took the blood of calves and of goats, with water, and scarlet wool, and hyssop, and sprinkled both the book, and all the people,

Saying, This is the blood of the testament which God hath enjoined unto you.

Moreover he sprinkled with blood both the tabernacle, and all the vessels of the ministry.

And almost all things are by the law purged with blood; and without shedding of blood is no remission [Heb. 9:18–22].

The word *blood* occurs in this section six times, revealing the place and the power of the blood in the Old Testament ritual. "Without shedding of blood is no remission" is the axiom of the Old Testament. Also the blood is very important in the New Testament. As the hymn writer put it, "there is power in the blood of the Lamb." In Revelation we find that the victory was won through the blood of the Lamb, not through some individual's ingenuity, or physical strength, or even spiritual strength.

It was therefore necessary that the patterns of things in the heavens should be purified with these; but the heavenly things themselves with better sacrifices than these [Heb. 9:23].

These heavenly things needed cleansing because sin originated in heaven (see v. 11). The blood of bulls and goats has never been shed in heaven—there is no denying that that would be crude. However, the blood of Christ, we believe, is in heaven and that is not crude at all.

For Christ is not entered into the holy places made with hands, which are the figures of the true; but into heaven itself, now to appear in the presence of God for us [Heb. 9:24].

The tabernacle on earth was just a figure—the reality is in heaven. "Now to appear in the *presence* of God for us" means before the very face of God. Christ has not entered into a man-made sanctuary. It is spiritual but real. He died on earth to save us. He lives in heaven to keep us saved. He is there for us.

Nor yet that he should offer himself often, as the high priest entereth into the holy place every year with blood of others [Heb. 9:25].

The high priest entered the earthly tabernacle with blood not his own, and he entered often.

For then must he often have suffered since the foundation of the world: but now once in the end of the world hath he appeared to put away sin by the sacrifice of himself [Heb. 9:26].

"But now once in the end of the world" should read "the end of the *age*." This has no reference to what some people call the end of the world. Actually, the Bible does not teach the end of the world; it does teach the end of the age.

"Hath he appeared to put away sin by the sacrifice of himself." Christ came, made under the Law. He appeared at the end of the Law age, and He instituted a new age, the age of grace.

And as it is appointed unto men once to die, but after this the judgment [Heb. 9:27].

Death is in the natural sequence of events for man. For the unsaved man, after death there is nothing but judgment. If the death of Christ does not save you, there is nothing ahead of you but judgment.

Death is not appointed unto *all* men—thank God for that. It is appointed unto men once to die, but some are not going to die. I hear people talk today about old age and, oh, how they want to die and get into the presence of the Lord. I don't know about you, but I don't mind waiting. I'm in no hurry to die! I hope I can live until He comes. I don't know whether I will, but that is the way I would like it.

Oh, joy! oh, delight! should we go without
    dying,
No sickness, no sadness, no dread and no
    crying,
Caught up through the clouds with our
    Lord into glory,
When Jesus receives "His own."
O Lord Jesus, how long, how long
Ere we shout the glad song, Christ
    returneth!
Hallelujah! hallelujah! Amen, Hallelujah!
    Amen.

"Christ Returneth"
—H.L. Turner

These words by H. L. Turner in "Christ Returneth" express the thoughts we cherish about His coming.

So Christ was once offered to bear the sins of many; and unto them that look for him shall he appear the second time without sin unto salvation [Heb. 9:28].

This is not speaking of the Rapture, but of His coming as sovereign to judge the earth. (However, believers will not come into judgment.) When He appears the second time it will not be to settle the sin question. He is not going to come the next time to walk around the Sea of Galilee or through the streets of Jerusalem to see what men will do with His sacrifice. He is coming in judgment.

Therefore today we can put it very simply: there is just one of two places for your sin—either your sin is on you, or it is on Christ. If you have not accepted the sacrifice of Christ, if you are not trusting Him as your redeemer, if He is no authority to you, then there is nothing ahead of you but the judgment of the Great White Throne. No one who appears there is going to be saved, but everyone will be given a fair chance to present their works and discover that God was right all along. And I have news for you: God is always right. So today if your sin is on you, there is nothing that can remove it but the death of Christ.

When Christ comes the next time it will be "without sin unto salvation"—that is, He will *complete* salvation at that time. Our salvation is in three tenses: I have been saved; I am being saved; I shall be saved. "Beloved, now are we the sons of God, and it doth not yet appear what we shall be: but we know that, when he shall appear, we shall be like him; for we shall see him as he is" (1 John 3:2). Now that is going to be a great day. It is going to be a great day for Vernon McGee, so don't you be dissatisfied with me, will you not? God is not through with me.

Down in Mississippi a dear little lady wearing a sunbonnet got up in a testimony meeting under the brush arbor and said, "Most Christians ought to have written on their backs, 'This is not the best that the grace of God can do.'" Well, that should be written on the backs of *all* Christians. God is not through with any of us. Thank God for that! He is going to appear the second time without sin unto *salvation*—He is going to deliver us. But, my friend, He will not come to settle the sin question for anyone who has not accepted Him—to them He is coming as judge.

Without a chapter break, the writer of this epistle continues with the subject of the superior sacrifice.

For the law having a shadow of good things to come, and not the very image of the things, can never with those sacrifices which they offered year by year continually make the comers thereunto perfect [Heb. 10:1].

As he concluded chapter 9 the writer said that if Christ had failed to save in His death at His first coming, there would be nothing afterward but *judgment*. My friend, if you reject Jesus Christ as Savior, you will have the saddest funeral possible. I have conducted many funerals, and some of them were for unsaved people. There is no sorrow like that of a funeral in a family of unsaved people—and that's the way it should be. I recall one instance in which a wife, who was almost an alcoholic, had lost her husband. She had leaned on him a great deal. I tried to give a message, not of comfort, but of good news, presenting the gospel. Afterward she came to me, looked into my face and asked, "Is there any hope at all?" I said, "Well, there is a hope for *you*." There was no hope for him whatsoever. He was a blasphemer, and he had told me that he had no use for the church; he had no use for Jesus Christ; he had no use for anything Christian. There was nothing ahead for him but judgment.

Beginning with this word *for* the writer continues the theme of Christ's sacrifice for sin.

"For the law having a shadow of good things to come, and not the very image of the things." The Mosaic Law served a good purpose in that it was a picture which *taught* Israel. Because God had taught Israel so thoroughly, He judged the nation severely. When the Lord Jesus was there in the flesh He said, ". . . how often would I have gathered thy children together, as a hen doth gather her brood under her wings, and ye would not!" (Luke 13:34). My friend, if you don't believe that God's judgment was really a severe one, go to Jerusalem and walk around the streets of old Jerusalem. Walk in the area where we know Jesus moved. All of it is covered over with debris today. Why? Because the city has been judged. Oh, how often the Lord had attempted to gather His chosen people to Himself! He had given them the Old Testament with the clear teaching of the tabernacle ritual.

Contrast the light that they had to the darkness in which my ancestors lived way up there in Germany. Boy, were they pagan and heathen in those days! And my ancestors over in Scotland were dirty and filthy. Then the gospel came to them, and, thank God, some of them trusted Christ. I had a grandfather on my father's side who apparently was a godly man. I am thankful for the men who carried the gospel to Europe. That gave the Gentiles a break, you see.

But the nation of Israel had the Old Testament, which was (and still is) a picture book, a book of ABCs. That is the reason so many folk miss its meaning. When theologians come to it, they have to find something profound in it. But it is a simple picture book in which God is trying to tell all of us little children down here that He died for us. It is just as simple as that, my friend.

Now let me call your attention to another thing that is very important. Notice that the Law had to do with the tabernacle and the sacrifices. This idea that you can separate God's commandments from His ceremonial law is entirely wrong. If you want to return to the legal system and put yourself under the Ten Commandments, you had better build a little tabernacle for yourself and start raising goats and sheep, because you are going to need them. But, my friend, Christ finished all of that. We now are on a different basis, a higher plane altogether. For instance, God wants to bring *joy* into your life. The Law never promised joy. There was thunder and lightning, and people were smitten dead at the giving of the Law. But when Jesus came, it was *He* who died that we might have life.

For then would they not have ceased to be offered? because that the worshippers once purged should have had no more conscience of sins [Heb. 10:2].

"For then would they not have ceased to be offered?" If the sacrifice they offered could have taken away their guilt, one sacrifice would have been enough.

It is very interesting to note that after the Lord Jesus died, it was only a few years until the temple was destroyed. And Israel has not been able to put up another temple. Oh, they have a little miniature temple for display over on the new side of Jerusalem at the Holy City Hotel, but they don't have a temple today. It doesn't look as if they will get one soon either. You see, when Christ became the sacrifice, that ended the need for the tabernacle and temple.

Today Israel is not offering sacrifices. I spoke to a very delightful Jewish guide in Jerusalem. His hair was as gray as it could be. He said that it had turned gray when he was only nineteen years of age after he had heard that his father and mother, sisters and brothers had been killed in Russia. He was a delightful fellow, and he took me around to show me the model of the temple at the hotel I mentioned. As we were looking at it, I asked him (although perhaps I should not have), "Where is the brazen altar?" He looked at me with surprise and said, "Oh, we have come past that. Today we have an *ethical* religion." Well, a lot of folk have an ethical religion, but, my friend, that bloody sacrifice was necessary that the human family might have forgiveness of sins.

"For then would they not have ceased to be offered? because that the worshippers once purged should have had no more conscience of sins." They would no longer have any feelings of guilt or consciousness of sin.

But in those sacrifices there is a remembrance again made of sins every year [Heb. 10:3].

So, actually, what those sacrifices did was to remind the Israelite that the sacrificial system was not complete—or they wouldn't have to come back and repeat it every day. The sacrifices were only a shadow, *skian* in the Greek, meaning "a hazy outline." The old sacrifices were shadow, never substance. And, my friend, shadows are not enough. You can't live in the shadow of a house; you need a house.

Again, the sacrifices would not have had to be repeated if they had been complete. For instance, when a man says that he is cured of disease and yet he is still taking medicine every hour, that man is not cured. And when a man keeps bringing sacrifices every year, that man is not cured of sin. It is Christ who made the one sacrifice once and for all. In those sacrifices there was a reminder of sins year by year. Here they go through the great Day of Atonement every year. What did it mean? The answer had not arrived until yonder on Golgotha when Jesus cried out, *"Tetelestai!"* Finished! My friend, then it was finished. And the next year there was no need for a Day of Atonement. In fact, he will tell us that to go

through a sacrifice today is to trod underfoot the blood of Jesus.

For it is not possible that the blood of bulls and of goats should take away sins [Heb. 10:4].

The blood of the animal sacrifices only covered over the sins until the Lamb of God would come to take away the sin of the world (see John 1:29).

Now here is a tremendous passage—

Wherefore when he cometh into the world, he saith, Sacrifice and offering thou wouldest not, but a body hast thou prepared me:

In burnt offerings and sacrifices for sin thou hast had no pleasure.

Then said I, Lo, I come (in the volume of the book it is written of me,) to do thy will, O God.

Above when he said, Sacrifice and offering and burnt offerings and offering for sin thou wouldest not, neither hadst pleasure therein; which are offered by the law;

Then said he, Lo, I come to do thy will, O God. He taketh away the first, that he may establish the second.

By the which will we are sanctified through the offering of the body of Jesus Christ once for all [Heb. 10:5–10].

I want to insert a cross reference here to make this section of the Word of God very meaningful to you. Going back to the Book of Exodus, we find in chapter 19 the preparation for the giving of the Mosaic Law, and in chapter 20 the giving of the Ten Commandments. After that, God makes a gracious provision by the sacrificial system. You see, the altar goes right along with the Law. Then in chapter 21 we come upon something that seems very much out of place. It is one of the most beautiful references in the Bible. The Law has been given, and now God says to Moses: "Now these are the judgments which thou shalt set before them. If thou buy an Hebrew servant, six years he shall serve: and in the seventh he shall go out free for nothing. [They couldn't have a slave of their own people more than six years.] If he came in by himself, he shall go out by himself: if he were married, then his wife shall go out with him. If his master have given him a wife, and she have born him sons or daughters; the wife and her children shall be her master's, and he shall go out by himself. And if the servant shall plainly say, I love my master, my wife, and my children; I will not go out free: Then his master shall bring him unto the judges; he shall also bring him to the door, or unto the door post; and his master shall bore his ear through with an awl [the lobe of the ear would be pierced]; and he shall serve him for ever." (Exod. 21:1–6).

In that day if you saw a man walking along with a hole in his ear, you would know that he had been given a wife, and that he had paid the price of permanent servitude for her. It was a tremendous law and certainly a lovely thing, but what is the meaning of it?

Well, let's follow the meaning of it. In Psalm 40:6–7 we read, "Sacrifice and offering thou didst not desire; mine ears hast thou opened [that is, pierced with an awl]: burnt offering and sin offering hast thou not required. Then said I, Lo, I come: in the volume of the book it is written of me." This is quoted in the Book of Hebrews and applied to the Lord Jesus Christ. Here is one of the most beautiful pictures in Scripture. The Lord Jesus came to this earth, grew to manhood, and at thirty years of age He began His earthly ministry. When He came to the end of that ministry, He could say, "Which of you convicteth me of sin?" (see John 8:46). He was holy, harmless, undefiled, and separate from sinners. He could have stepped off this earth any day that He wanted to, gone back to heaven and left this earth in sin—left you and me in the slavery of sin. But He loved us, and God so loved the world that He gave His only begotten Son. So instead of His ear being pierced with an awl, He was given a body. A body for what? For death—to die on the cross. "By the which will we are sanctified through the offering of the body of Jesus Christ once for all" (Heb. 10:10). Referring back to that law in Exodus, if a master gave his slave a woman to marry, and he loved her, he could choose to stay in slavery with her. In like manner the Lord Jesus Christ has been given the body of believers which we call the church as His bride. In His prayer in John 17:9 the Lord said to His Father concerning them, "They are mine. You gave them to Me." The Lord loves us; He paid the price for us. But the interesting thing is that He didn't stay in slavery; He went back to the right hand of the Majesty on high, and some day He is going to take us out of the slavery of sin to be with Him. He alone could do that. How wonderful this is!

There is a green hill, far away,
Without a city wall.
Where the dear Lord was crucified,
Who died to save us all.

There was no other good enough,
To pay the price of sin.
He only could unlock the gate
Of heaven to let us in.

"There is a Green Hill Far Away"
—Mrs. Cecil F. Alexander

What a beautiful picture of Christ this section of Scripture gives us!

And every priest standeth daily ministering and offering oftentimes the same sacrifices, which can never take away sins [Heb. 10:11].

The offerings could only cover the sin; they were an atonement, but they could never take away sins. The offerings were just a reminder that men were sinners and that the sin question had not yet been settled.

But this man, after he had offered one sacrifice for sins for ever, sat down on the right hand of God [Heb. 10:12].

Why did He sit down? Was He tired? No. Did He sit down because He did not want to do anything? No. Jesus sat down because His work was finished—"*one* sacrifice for sins *for ever*."

From henceforth expecting till his enemies be made his footstool [Heb. 10:13].

Our Lord is just waiting. There are a few more people to be saved. We pray, "O come now, Lord Jesus," but He says, "No, not yet. We are going to wait, because I want to save some more." He is giving you an opportunity, friend, if you are not saved. Psalm 110:1 says, "The LORD said unto my Lord, Sit thou at my right hand, until I make thine enemies thy footstool," referring to the second coming of Christ to the earth. But in the meantime He is waiting for more of the human family to come to Him.

For by one offering he hath perfected for ever them that are sanctified [Heb. 10:14].

One offering does what many offerings could not do. If *Christ* cannot save you and keep you, then God has no other way to save you and keep you.

Whereof the Holy Ghost also is a witness to us: for after that he had said before,

This is the covenant that I will make with them after those days, saith the Lord, I will put my laws into their hearts, and in their minds will I write them;

And their sins and iniquities will I remember no more [Heb. 10:15–17].

This is the essential part of the quotation from Jeremiah 31. God says, "I'm going to make a new covenant with Israel." God is not through with them. If you will read your Bible you will see that.

Now let me remind you that in this section of Hebrews we are seeing the greatest division in the Word of God. It is like a Grand Canyon which is placed between the old covenant and the New Covenant, the Old Testament and the New Testament. And let's remember that God gave both of them. Referring back to verse 9, notice that it says, "He taketh away the first, that he may establish the second." He taketh away the first (that is, the first covenant), that He may establish the second covenant. When the Lord Jesus died upon the cross, something very important happened: the veil was rent in twain. No longer are men to come to God through the sacrifice of the blood of bulls and goats; now the Lord Jesus has made a way for us through His own body— a way for you and me. Notice again verse 10: "By the which will we are sanctified through the offering of the body of Jesus Christ once." In the Authorized Version the two words *for all* that conclude this verse are in italics, meaning they were supplied by the translators. The verse is more accurate without them, because the emphasis is on the fact that Christ did it one time so that sacrifices are to end. It is interesting that ever since the destruction of the temple in A.D. 70 by Titus the Roman, there has been no bloody sacrifice offered in Jerusalem. There are no blood sacrifices being offered there today, and the prospects for them being offered in the near future are very dim. Christ took away the first that He might establish the second.

The importance of this cannot be overemphasized. You see, in the first covenant were many rules and regulations. The old covenant was a law, a law that had a great many details. There was the ceremonial law with many details in regard to the sacrifices; there were the Ten Commandments and other commandments or rules. Actually rules and regu-

lations appeal to human nature. Men feel that it is easy to obey rules, which is the reason so many folk today will tell you that the Sermon on the Mount is their religion. They may not know exactly what it says or what it means, but they like it because it has rules, which they kid themselves into believing they can follow. The whole history of mankind and the multitude of cults and "isms" springing up in our day demonstrate that this is true. Man likes to live by certain rules and follow certain rituals.

Now in the New Covenant we are under an altogether different system. Paul had mentioned to the Corinthian believers: "Who also hath made us able ministers of the new testament [the New Covenant]; not of the letter, but of the spirit: for the letter killeth, but the spirit giveth life" (2 Cor. 3:6). Some strange individuals have come up with the novel interpretation that this verse means they should not study the Bible! They say that "the letter" means the Bible and it is the Spirit that gives life. Well, of course that is not what Paul is saying, as the following verse makes clear. "But if the ministration of death, written and engraven in stones, was glorious. . . ." Obviously, this refers to the Ten Commandments, so now we know that the "letter" is the commandments. The Ten Commandments were the ministration of death. My friend, the Law *kills*. The Law never saved anyone. It will kill you because it brings you under the judgment of God. It is the Spirit who gives life, and you and I are living in this day when the Holy Spirit is the one who regenerates us, who leads us, and who shows us the will of God.

Now where remission of these is, there is no more offering for sin [Heb. 10:18].

"Now"—the sacrificial system began with Abel and ended with the death of Christ. This verse concludes the doctrinal section.

ENCOURAGEMENT

Hebrews 10:19–25 is the practical section of this chapter, and it speaks of privilege and responsibility.

Having therefore, brethren, boldness to enter into the holiest by the blood of Jesus [Heb. 10:19].

"Boldness" is boldness of speech; it has no thought of arrogance. Now notice this carefully—how do we get into the holiest, that is, into God's presence? By the blood of Jesus.

By a new and living way, which he hath consecrated for us, through the veil, that is to say, his flesh [Heb. 10:20].

That veil was torn in two when Christ was crucified on the cross, which indicated that the way to God was open.

"Through the veil, that is to say, his flesh"— *flesh* is the same word we find in the prologue of John's gospel where he said that "the Word became flesh." John didn't say that it was a new and living way open to God, because the Incarnation, the *life* of Christ saves no one. We enter into the holiest by the *blood* of Jesus. Our right of entrance is not through His incarnation but through the rending of the veil; that is, through His death. You and I have the privilege of worshiping God, not because of the *life* of Jesus, but because of His *death* for us upon the cross. Oh, my friend, this distinction is so important!

"By a new and living way." The word *new* is from the Greek word *prosphatos,* meaning "newly slain." It speaks of the fact that the Lord Jesus Christ has opened up for you and me a new and living way to God through His crucifixion, through His death upon the cross. The old sacrifices won't help you anymore, friend.

And having an high priest over the house of God [Heb. 10:21].

What a wonderful privilege to have an advocate with the Father, Jesus Christ, the righteous, who always lives to make intercession for us.

"Through the veil"—when Christ dismissed His spirit as He hung there upon the cross, the veil of the temple was torn in two, which opened the way into the very presence of the Father.

Now we have an invitation. Some expositors believe it is directed to the unsaved. I believe it is both to the unsaved and to the saved. Since we have an High Priest at the right hand of God—

Let us draw near with a true heart in full assurance of faith, having our hearts sprinkled from an evil conscience, and our bodies washed with pure water [Heb. 10:22].

This has to do with the dedication of priests in the Aaronic priesthood. Moses sprinkled them with the water of dedication. And they had to be washed, denoting that they were set aside for the service of God. In like manner our dedication to God enables us to draw near with a true heart.

"In full assurance of faith," or in fullness of faith, has nothing to do with the amount of our faith; it has everything to do with the *object* of

our faith. Real faith always depends on the object of faith. You see, faith can be misplaced—you can put your faith in some individual on earth and be disappointed. Faith is not just believing that there is a God—all that means is that you are not an atheist. Not only should you have a knowledge of God and know the way of righteousness, but you should act upon your faith. Real faith means that you have really received the Lord Jesus Christ as your personal Savior. That has been made very clear to us. In John 1:11–12 we read, "He came unto his own, and his own received him not. But as many as received him, to them gave he power [the authority] to become the sons of God, even to them that [do no more or less than] believe on his name." Faith in Christ means to *receive* Christ as Savior. Faith is action based on knowledge. God never asks us to take a leap in the dark. I disagree with the theologian who said, "Faith is to leap in the dark." If this is true, don't leap, because you may find yourself going off a ten-story building! You don't need to leap in the dark, because God has given us knowledge. "So then faith cometh by hearing, and hearing by the word of God" (Rom. 10:17). God has put down a foundation for our faith. "For other foundation can no man lay than that is laid, which is Jesus Christ" (1 Cor. 3:11). You get on the foundation, friend. That's knowledge, but it is faith that puts you there. Faith is action that is based on knowledge, which means to trust Christ personally as your Savior.

"Let us draw near with a true heart in full assurance of faith, having our hearts sprinkled from an evil conscience, and our bodies washed with pure water." This means that you and I as believers are members of a priesthood. One of the great truths that John Calvin recovered was the priesthood of all believers. Every believer is a priest, and as such, you can come to God with boldness of speech. So many people ask the preacher to pray for them, which is all right, but we need to remember that *all* believers have access to God. You have as much right in God's presence as I have, or as anyone else has, because we come by this "newly sacrificed" way that Christ has made for us. It is on that basis that we come to God.

Let us hold fast the profession of our faith without wavering; (for he is faithful that promised;) [Heb. 10:23].

"Let us hold fast the profession of our faith." Actually, "faith" has in it the thought of hope. Let us draw near to God, but let us hold fast our confession of faith. Why? Because we have a hope, and hope is for the future, you see. How wonderful it is that we can come near to God in the full assurance of faith, and also that we can hold fast the confession of our faith because we have a hope. As the hymn writer has put it,

So near, so very near to God,
  We cannot nearer be;
For in the Person of His Son,
  We are as near as He.

So dear, so very dear to God,
  We cannot dearer be,
For in the Person of His Son,
  We are as dear as He.

—Author unknown

We are to draw near (v. 22). We are to hold fast (v. 23). And now a third thing:

And let us consider one another to provoke unto love and to good works [Heb. 10:24].

"Let us consider one another to provoke"— "provoke" is from the Greek word *paroxusmos*, from which we get our English word *paroxysm*, which literally means "with a view to excitement." Let us consider one another to provoke unto love and to good works.

Do I annoy you? Some Christians tell me that I have troubled their conscience. Well, I hope I have troubled your conscience so that you will love one another and so that you will do some good works for God.

Not forsaking the assembling of ourselves together, as the manner of some is; but exhorting one another: and so much the more, as ye see the day approaching [Heb. 10:25].

If there ever was a time when believers needed to come together, it is today. Instead of chopping down each other, we need to draw together in love around the person of Christ.

"Exhorting one another." We need to study the Word of God together. God has something for a group that He will not give to any *one* individual. One of the reasons I like to teach the Word of God is selfish. It is because God won't let *me* grow in the knowledge of His Word unless I share it. We are not to forsake the assembling of ourselves together. If you have a Bible study at your church, be sure to go because there is a blessing for you there that you can't get when you study the Bible by yourself.

So these are the three "let us" verses:

Draw near in faith (toward God)
Draw near in hope (for ourselves)
Draw near in love (for others)

This presents again the three graces: faith, hope, and love. How practical this epistle is!

"As ye see the day approaching." To the Jewish people who are being addressed in this epistle, "the day approaching" probably meant the day when their temple would be destroyed, which it was in A.D. 70. Remember that the believers were meeting together in the temple. That is where they were on the Day of Pentecost when the Holy Spirit came. Peter and John were going into the temple when they met the lame man at the beautiful gate. But where will they gather together after the temple is destroyed? The writer is urging them, "As you see the day approaching when you won't have a meeting place, just keep meeting together." And the church started by meeting in private homes, by the way.

DANGER SIGNAL: THE PERIL OF DESPISING

This is the most solemn warning of all. In fact, it makes your hair stand on end!

For if we sin wilfully after that we have received the knowledge of the truth, there remaineth no more sacrifice for sins [Heb. 10:26].

It is a fearful thing to fall into the hands of the living God! Simon Peter said, "For it had been better for them not to have known the way of righteousness, than, after they have known it, to turn from the holy commandment delivered unto them" (2 Pet. 2:21). The warning is to the Hebrew believers because many of them were continuing to go to the temple and some were actually offering sacrifices there. They were keeping up a front, pretending that they were still under the Mosaic Law. In so doing they also were making it clear that the sacrifice of Christ was meaningless to them. Since the animal sacrifices prefigured Christ's sacrifice, now that Christ had died on the cross, all of that was fulfilled. Therefore, what before had been done in obedience to God's command, now has become willful sin. To continue to offer blood sacrifices which had been fulfilled by Christ was a frightful, terrible thing. They were acting as if the temple sacrifices were going on forever. The writer to the Hebrews is telling them that they cannot look to the temple any more, because there is no longer a sacrifice for sin. If a person rejects the truth of Christ's death for sin, there is no other sacrifice for sin available, and there is no other way to come to God. They are to look to Christ now rather than to the temple. If they refuse to do this, there is nothing left for them but judgment. The Word of God is very expressive in this connection.

"If we sin wilfully after that we have received the knowledge of the truth." This means to *go on* sinning willfully by offering the sacrifices. It is an attitude toward the Word of God which God calls willful rebellion. There is no more sacrifice in the Old Testament or the New Testament for presumptuous sins.

But a certain fearful looking for of judgment and fiery indignation, which shall devour the adversaries [Heb. 10:27].

If the death of Christ over nineteen hundred years ago was not adequate, then *nothing* is adequate. God is not going to do something else to redeem us. Christ is not going to die again—and, of course, it is not necessary for Him to do so. It becomes willful disobedience on the part of those who "have received the knowledge of the truth" to continue with the temple ritual and offering of sacrifices.

Now he will make a comparison.

He that despised Moses' law died without mercy under two or three witnesses [Heb. 10:28].

Now note the comparison—

Of how much sorer punishment, suppose ye, shall he be thought worthy, who hath trodden under foot the Son of God, and hath counted the blood of the covenant, wherewith he was sanctified, an unholy thing, and hath done despite unto the Spirit of grace? [Heb. 10:29].

This is probably the most solemn statement in the Word of God.

"Wherewith he was sanctified" refers to Christ, the Son of God. They crucified "to themselves the Son of God afresh" (Heb. 6:6). To act as if the death of Christ is inadequate to settle the sin question, and to go on as if He had not died, is to treat the blood of Christ as something you despise. Knowledge creates responsibility. If, after you have heard the gospel, you turn your back on Jesus Christ—my friend, someone ought to tell you that you are going to *hell*! This is not what *I* say; it is what *God* says.

For we know him that hath said, Vengeance belongeth unto me, I will recompense, saith the Lord. And again, The Lord shall judge his people [Heb. 10:30].

Friend, God is going to judge. He is the sovereign ruler of this universe. We are all going to have to appear before Him. God has a sovereign right to judge, which He has not surrendered. "For the time is come that judgment must begin at the house of God: and if it first begin at us, what shall the end be of them that obey not the gospel of God? And if the righteous scarcely be saved, where shall the ungodly and the sinner appear?" (1 Pet. 4:17–18).

It is a fearful thing to fall into the hands of the living God [Heb. 10:31].

This is a very interesting verse, and it will be profitable to spend a little time with it. This verse is for Christians and unbelievers also. It *is* a fearful thing to fall into the hands of the living God! In Ezra 7:9 we read, "For upon the first day of the first month began he [Ezra] to go up from Babylon, and on the first day of the fifth month came he to Jerusalem, according to the good hand of his God upon him." In this verse the hand of God is upon this man for *good*. And God wants to put His hand upon you for good, but sometimes He puts a very *heavy* hand upon His children. He chastens them—or, as we say, He takes them to the woodshed. I have been to the woodshed. Maybe you have been there, too. David had been there, and in Psalm 32:4 he says, "For day and night thy hand was heavy upon me: my moisture is turned into the drought of summer. Selah." What was God doing? He was chastening David. He had taken him to the woodshed. David tried to cover up his sin, but God forced him to confess it and deal with it. For a similar reason sometimes God's heavy hand is upon us who are His children.

However, God's hand of chastening is altogether different from His hand of judgment. He says, "Vengeance belongeth unto me, I will recompense." God does not take vengeance in a spiteful or vindictive manner. But God is going to *judge* sin, and that is something that needs to be emphasized in our day. Listen again to the psalmist: "For in the hand of the LORD there is a cup, and the wine is red; it is full of mixture; and he poureth out of the same: but the dregs thereof, all the wicked of the earth shall wring them out, and drink them" (Ps. 75:8). You see, the psalmist as well as the prophet spoke of judgment as a time coming when the cup of wrath will be filled up. And it is filling up today. God is in no hurry to move; He is longsuffering, not willing that any should perish, but that cup of judgment is filling up. And, my friend, it is a bitter cup.

This cup of God's judgment is ahead of everyone "who hath trodden under foot the Son of God, and hath counted the blood of the covenant, wherewith he was sanctified, an unholy thing, and hath done despite unto the Spirit of grace." My friend, if you despise what Christ has done for you on the cross, there is nothing ahead of you but judgment. You have no hope whatsoever.

This is the same point the writer is making to these Hebrew believers. Under the Mosaic Law they could bring a sacrifice every year— or any day if they wanted to. But they cannot do that any longer; that is over. Now they have to turn (even as we do) to the Lord Jesus Christ.

Now the writer gives a personal word to these Jewish folk to whom he is writing:

But call to remembrance the former days, in which, after ye were illuminated, ye endured a great fight of afflictions [Heb. 10:32].

I assume that the Hebrews to whom this epistle was written were saved. There seems to be no question in the writer's mind about their being believers.

Partly, whilst ye were made a gazingstock both by reproaches and afflictions; and partly, whilst ye became companions of them that were so used.

For ye had compassion of me in my bonds, and took joyfully the spoiling of your goods, knowing in yourselves that ye have in heaven a better and an enduring substance [Heb. 10:33–34].

"Partly, whilst ye were made a gazingstock." The Christians were made a public spectacle.

"And took joyfully the spoiling of your goods." Apparently some of the believers had been imprisoned for their faith while others had experienced the seizure of their possessions. The writer is reminding them of their faith and patience during this trying time.

Cast not away therefore your confidence, which hath great recompense of reward [Heb. 10:35].

"Cast not away therefore your confidence" is another way of saying "let us hold fast the confession of our faith without wavering."

For ye have need of patience, that, after ye have done the will of God, ye might receive the promise [Heb. 10:36].

Patience and faith are wedded in Scripture. After exercising faith in the midst of trials, then they are to display patience with the future hope of the fulfillment of faith.

For yet a little while, and he that shall come will come, and will not tarry [Heb. 10:37].

I hear the expression many times, "I'll see you next time, Dr. McGee, if the Lord tarry." I've got news for people who say that. The Lord is not going to tarry. Some folks act as though He keeps putting off His coming, that He is tarrying. He is not going to tarry. It is on His calendar to come. Somebody asks, "When is He coming?" Well, the Lord won't let me see His calendar; so I don't know. I hear some folk talk as if they have seen His calendar, but I think they have been looking at man's calendar, because nobody has seen God's calendar. However, we can be sure that Christ will come on the day appointed; it is as certain as His first coming to this earth.

Now the just shall live by faith: but if any man draw back, my soul shall have no pleasure in him [Heb. 10:38].

This verse is a quotation from Habakkuk 2:3–4, quoted also in Romans and in Galatians. It is an important verse. Each epistle that quotes this verse puts a different emphasis on it. In the Epistle to the Romans the emphasis is upon "the *just* shall live by faith"—how God justifies the sinner. Here in the Epistle to the Hebrews, the emphasis is upon "the just shall *live* by faith." There have been several references to the *living* God, and this epistle tells of a *living* intercessor. He is the same one who died on the cross for us and came back from the dead. The emphasis is upon His resurrection and His being the living Christ at God's right hand. Therefore since we who are His own have a living God and a living Savior at God's right hand, we shall *live* by faith. As I have said before, our faith is not a leap in the dark. It rests upon the Word of God. The just shall *live* by faith. Now in the Epistle to the Galatians Paul emphasizes faith; the just shall live by *faith*.

"If any man draw back, my soul shall have

no pleasure in him." *Draw back* means "to take in sail."

But we are not of them who draw back unto perdition; but of them that believe to the saving of the soul [Heb. 10:39].

The writer to the Hebrews did not consider that they had drawn back, but he is speaking of the *danger* of doing so, and he is giving them this warning. Since *draw back* means to "take in sail," the believer is like a sailor who should let out all the sail. That is what the writer has been telling these folk—"Let us go on!" His thought is that a believer could reef his sails—become stranded because of discouragement, because of persecution, because of hardship, because of depression. But since we have a living Savior, let's go on. Let's open up all the sails. Let's move out for God.

You remember the story of the French Huguenots. They were persecuted, and they were betrayed. When France destroyed them, it destroyed the best of French manhood and womanhood. The French Huguenots went into battle, knowing they were facing certain death, and their motto was: "If God be for us, who can be against us?" The nation of France has never since been the nation it was before it destroyed these people.

We believers today need a motto like the Huguenots. There is a lot of boo-hooing today among Christians. There is a lot of complaining and criticizing. There are a bunch of crybabies and babies that need to be burped.

Oh, my Christian friend, the whole tenor of this marvelous epistle is "Let us go on." So let *us* go on for God!

CHAPTER 11

THEME: *Faith*

CHRIST BRINGS BETTER BENEFITS AND DUTIES

Chapters 11–13 constitute the second major division of the Epistle to the Hebrews. Up to this point the epistle has largely dealt with that which is doctrinal, but we are now coming to that which is very practical. We begin with the chapter that is often called "the faith chapter," and that is very interesting because the average person does not think that faith is a very practical sort of thing—we will find that it is.

Chapter 11 is also called by many "the catalog of the heroes of faith." I want to look at this chapter from the viewpoint of faith—what faith has done in the lives of men and women in all ages, under all circumstances, from the very gate of the Garden of Eden down to the present moment. This chapter illustrates this for you and me, and these people are witnesses who encourage us to live by faith.

It is so easy to make the Christian life a series of rules. One of the reasons that so many people like to get under the Sermon on the Mount or the Ten Commandments is because men love rules and regulations. It seems so simple and easy to obey rules. Whenever I drive to a new location, I always ask the individual to tell me how to get there. They generally write it out for me: "Turn left here, go so many blocks, and then turn right." I like it that way because it is easy to follow. Life is like that for a great many folk—they want to follow a neat set of rules. But in this chapter we are going to find people who went an altogether different route. They walked by faith, and that is the way God wants us to walk today.

We will also see in this chapter that unbelief is the worst sin anyone can commit. God has a remedy for every sin but the *state* of unbelief. This does not mean that there is an unpardonable sin. There is no *act* which you could commit today that God would not forgive tomorrow. But if you continue in a state of unbelief, God has no remedy for that at all.

DEFINITION OF FAITH

The first statement in this chapter is a scriptural definition of faith:

Now faith is the substance of things hoped for, the evidence of things not seen [Heb. 11:1].

God has two ways in which men can come to Him today. The first is that you can come to

Him by works. Yes, if you can present perfection in your works, God will accept you—but so far nobody has been able to make it. Adam didn't, and no one since has ever been able to do it. Abraham didn't, and David didn't, and Daniel didn't. None of them made it by being perfect. Therefore this is not a satisfactory way to come to God, but many people are hobbling along that futile route.

The only other way to come to God is to come by faith. Many folk don't find faith a very satisfactory way either and feel like the little girl who was asked to define faith. She said, "Well, faith is believing what you know ain't so." That is what faith means to many. They think it is a leap in the dark, an uncertainty, or some sort of a gamble. If that is what it means to you, then you do not have faith, because "faith is the substance of things hoped for, the evidence of things not seen," which means that faith rests on a foundation.

To other folk faith is a great mystery. It is a sort of sixth sense, some intuition into the spiritual realm, or an open sesame to a new world. Faith to some of these people is like belonging to a secret order into which you are initiated, and there are some mystical works which God will accept in lieu of good works if you just believe hard enough. My friend, the demons do a pretty good job of believing, and they are not saved. There are a lot of cults and "isms" today which are demonic and are run by demons. Faith for these people is like a fetish or some good luck charm which you hang around your neck or carry with you. But that is not faith.

Charles Haddon Spurgeon said: "It is not thy hold on Christ that saves thee; it is Christ. It is not thy joy in Christ that saves thee; it is Christ. It is not even thy faith in Christ that saves thee, though that be the instrument. It is Christ's blood and merit." That is what saves you, my friend. Faith just lays hold of it—that is all. Faith, therefore, is not something mysterious at all—it is that which looks to the Lord Jesus Christ.

Faith is not something which is added to good works. Some folk in our churches today treat faith like it is the dressing which is added to the salad of good works. You have a salad and you put French dressing on it, or bleu cheese dressing, or Italian dressing. Many people just add their faith as a dressing on top of their good works. My friend, that is not faith at all.

Let's look at the scriptural definition of faith that is given to us here: "Faith is the substance of things hoped for, the evidence of things not seen." I like very much what Dr. J. Oswald Sanders (of the China Inland Mission which is now called the Overseas Missionary Fellowship) said: "Faith enables the believing soul to treat the future as present and the invisible as seen." That is good.

"Faith is the *substance* of things hoped for." The Greek word for "substance" is *hupostasis*. It is a scientific term, the opposite of hypothesis or theory. It is that which rests upon facts. In chemistry it would be the chemical which settles at the bottom of the test tube after you have made an experiment.

In my college chemistry class the teacher would give each one of us students a test tube and ask us to find out what was in it. I would take some of whatever was in the tube and add another chemical or two to it and heat it on the Bunsen burner to discover what was in the tube. One day I nearly blew up the laboratory with my experiment because something had been put in the test tube which should not have been put there. Five years later the janitor who swept out the laboratory told me he was still sweeping up little pieces of the big glass Florentine receiver which I had used in my experiment! Fortunately, the glass flew only onto my vest and not into my eyes. I experimented with one test tube for two weeks before I went to the professor to tell him what I thought was in it. I said it was a certain kind of powder and he told me I was right. I had a substance in the bottom of the test tube, and the professor, because he knew his chemistry, was sure of what it was (I'll be honest with you, I wasn't too sure!). But that substance in the bottom of the test tube was what I was looking for. That is the reality. And that is what faith is—faith is a substance.

Dr. A. T. Robertson translates *substance* as "title deed." What is the title deed? What is the substance? It is the Word of God, my friend. If your faith does not rest upon the Word of God, it is not biblical faith at all. It has to rest upon what God says. Actually, it means *to believe God.*

The question is whether you believe God or not. Don't come up with the "I've got intellectual problems" excuse, because that won't work. The thing that keeps men from the Word of God is *sin.* It is sin in your life that keeps you from coming to God. It is the heart that needs to believe—it is "the heart that believeth unto righteousness." When you are ready to give up your sin, the Holy Spirit will make real to you the Word of God.

A very fine man who heads up a wonderful Christian organization in this country sent me (and other ministers) a book he had written and requested my evaluation of it. It is a very fine book, but it is in the realm of apologetics, proving that the Bible is the Word of God. It is one of the best books on the subject I've seen, and I told him so. But I also told him very candidly that I have come to the place in my ministry where a book like that is of no value to me. I already believe the Bible to be the Word of God. I've already been through all those little experiments. I have proven what it is. I *know* the Bible is the Word of God. I've put it *all* in the test tube. I've made the experiment. "Faith is the *substance* of things hoped for." I know it is the Word of God. The Spirit of God has made it real to me.

Paul wrote to the Colossian believers, "For this cause we also, since the day we heard it, do not cease to pray for you, and to desire that ye might be filled with the knowledge of his will in all wisdom and spiritual understanding" (Col. 1:9). To know the will of God is to know the Word of God. He prayed that they might know the Word of God. The Greek word for "knowledge" which Paul used is *epignōsis*. There were Gnostics in that day who professed to have super knowledge. Paul told the Colossians that he wanted them to have super knowledge which was genuine by *knowing* that the Bible is the Word of God, and he believed that the Holy Spirit would make it real to them.

Don't misunderstand me: I did go through a period in college when I almost gave up the ministry. I had an unbelieving professor who was an ordained Presbyterian preacher. I admired the man because he was an intellectual, but he was taking the rug out from under me and taking it out fast. The things he was teaching were about to rob me of my faith, and I had to go to God in prayer. Then I met a man who had two degrees for every degree the first professor had, and this man put me back on the track. He showed me that there were answers for the questions the other man had raised. So I have the answers for myself. I've got a substance in my test tube, and I don't need to make any more experiments today. I *know* the Bible is the Word of God.

Therefore faith rests upon the Word of God. Our dogmatism comes from this Book. That is the reason the writer to the Hebrews said in Hebrews 10:39, "But we are not of them who draw back unto perdition; but of them that believe to the saving of the soul." There are only two ways to go. Either you are going backwards, or you are going to go forwards. Anything that is alive cannot stand still. Out yonder in the forest there is regression and deterioration taking place, but there is also growth and development. Nothing alive out there is standing still—it *cannot*.

"The *evidence* of things not seen." We have seen that faith is the substance of things hoped for—that is scientific. The second word used here is "evidence." In the Greek the word is *elegchos*. It is a legal term meaning "evidence that is accepted for conviction." When I was studying classical Greek in college, I observed that this word is used about twenty-three times in Plato's account of the trial of Socrates. Evidence is something you take into court to prove your case. It is that which the entire business world rests upon. Business is transacted by faith. I have a credit card, and when I drive into the gasoline station I hand it to the attendant. When he takes the card, he believes the oil company will pay him; he believes that I am the owner of the card and that I am the one who will pay for the gasoline in the long run. I say that man has a lot of faith. The oil company also believes that I'm going to pay. (Actually, they *know* I am going to pay, because they will take away my card if I don't!) But the whole transaction takes place by faith. Any man who accepts a check written to him by another is moving by faith. This is *elegchos*, evidence which is accepted in a court of law.

Faith is not a leap in the dark. Faith is not a hope-so. Faith is *substance* and *evidence*—substance for a scientific mind, and evidence for a legal mind. If you really want to believe, you can believe. You can believe a whole lot of foolish things, but God doesn't want you to do that. He wants your faith to rest upon the Word of God.

For by it the elders obtained a good report [Heb. 11:2].

Who are "the elders"? The elders could be one of three different groups. It could be just a group of old people, or it could refer to the office of elder in the New Testament church. Remember that Paul told young Titus that he was to appoint elders in the churches. Or, finally, "elders" could refer to Old Testament saints. These saints were referred to in Hebrews 1:1, "God, who at sundry times and in divers manners spake in time past unto *the fathers.* . . ." The fathers are the elders. This verse could be rendered, "By such faith as this the fathers received witness." These Old Testament worthies believed God, and for them it was not a leap in the dark and it was not a hope-so. Their faith rested upon evidence.

Noah built an ark, and he did it by faith. What kind of faith? Was it just some dream he had? No. God gave him an abundance of evidence because Noah *walked* with God for many years.

The problem with many of us today is that when a crisis comes to us and we ought to be able to rest in God and lay hold of Him, we are not able to do so. When we haven't been doing it all along, it is such a new experience for us that it is very difficult to do. However, if you learn to trust God when the sun is shining, it is easier to trust Him on the day when there are dark and lowering clouds in the sky and you are in one of life's storms.

"The elders obtained a good report." Because they were wonderful people? No, because they *believed* God. I think Abraham was a wonderful man. He probably had more going for him than the best Christian today. Even the world would have counted him an outstanding individual. But we are told that it was by faith that Abraham believed God. "Abraham believed God and it was counted to him for righteousness" (see Gen. 15:6). God put righteousness to his account, not because of his good works, but because he *believed God.* "The elders obtained a good report," and they did it by faith.

God wants us today not only to be saved by faith, but to *walk* by faith. Christ died down here to save us—we look back in faith to Him. Now we walk daily by faith—we look up to Him, the living Christ. That gets right down where the rubber meets the road. That's for right now. Are you going shopping today? Are you going to work? Are you going to school or to some social engagement? Well, then go by faith in the Lord Jesus Christ. We walk by faith, not by sight. That is how God wants us to live this life.

Through faith we understand that the worlds were framed by the word of God, so that things which are seen were not made of things which do appear [Heb. 11:3].

There are two explanations for the origin of this universe. One is speculation, and the other is revelation. By faith we accept revelation, and, my friend, by faith you will accept speculation. Speculation has many theories, and many of them have been abandoned. Right now the theory is evolution, but even evolution, I am told, is going out of style today. It is the best the unbeliever can hold on to, but it is mere speculation, and they have to have a whole lot of faith to go along with it!

"Through faith we understand that the worlds were framed by the word of God." Actually, this could read, "the ages were set up by the Word of God." The Word of God, we have already been told, is quick and powerful and sharper than any two-edged sword. The Word of God is more powerful than an atom or hydrogen bomb. Someone has said that atom bombs come in three sizes: "big," "bigger," and "where is everybody?" Well, the Word of God is even more potent than that, because the Word of God has the power to transform lives. And when you and I come to the Word of God, we either accept or reject God's statement concerning the origin of the universe: "In the beginning God created the heaven and the earth" (Gen. 1:1). That is revelation. Either you believe God, or you go by speculation. Don't tell me that evolution is scientific. It is not. If it were, then all the scientists would be in agreement—and they certainly are *not* in agreement. Today many outstanding scientists are beginning to let go of their worship of evolution. They see so many fallacies in it that they are moving away from it. You either believe God (that's revelation), or you believe speculation. Faith must be anchored in something.

I heard this whimsical story about a guide in a museum who was taking a group of people through the museum and they came to a reconstructed dinosaur. You know how they find one bone and make up the rest of it so that they have a great big dinosaur! Well, the guide said, "This dinosaur is two million and six years old!"

Of course, the crowd looked at him in amazement, and one extrovert said, "What do you meant two million and six years old? Where did you get the *six*?"

"Well," the guide said, "when I came to work here six years ago, it was two million years old. Now it is two million and six years old!" My friend, that shows how utterly ridiculous all this dating—which goes back millions of years—can really become.

Faith means that you have a solid basis for the origin of the universe. I won't have to change my theory as scientific knowledge grows; it has been in operation a long time: "God created the heaven and the earth."

We come now to consider the faith of individuals. I want to give you a quotation from *The Triumphs of Faith* by Dr. G. Campbell Morgan which is fitting at this point. He said, "Life is to be mastered by faith, and not by doubt; it is to be forevermore illuminated by hope, and not darkened by despair; and in its activity love is to be practised in fellowship." We are going to see this illustrated as we consider the lives of these people. Faith is not some jewel like a diamond which you put in a case and look at. That is the reason I do not want to call this chapter a catalog of the heroes of faith. These are men and women who got right down to the nitty-gritty of life—faith was operative in their lives. Faith is not something which you put on display in a showcase. Faith rests upon the Word of God.

We are given here the experience of three individuals who lived before the Flood—antediluvians we call them (one of them even lived through the Flood and after it). Abel is the first, and in him you have the *way* of faith. Then in Enoch we have the *walk* of faith. And in Noah we have the *witness* of faith. These men lived before the Flood, and faith was in operation at that time. These men walked by faith, lived by faith, and were saved by faith.

THE FAITH OF ABEL

Now with Abel God put down the principle once and for all that men must approach Him on only one basis: by faith, and that salvation will be by faith in Christ. Not only did Abraham see Christ's day and rejoice, but so did Abel.

By faith Abel offered unto God a more excellent sacrifice than Cain, by which he obtained witness that he was righteous, God testifying of his gifts: and by it he being dead yet speaketh [Heb. 11:4].

I want to go back to the Book of Genesis and the story of these two boys, Cain and Abel. I want us to see just what it was that Abel had and Cain didn't have. What was the difference between these two boys?

In Genesis 4:1 we read, "And Adam knew Eve his wife; and she conceived, and bare Cain, and said, I have gotten a man from the LORD." What she really said was, "I have gotten *the* man from the Lord." What man is she talking about? Well, God had made it clear to Eve that there would be coming one in her line, "the seed of the woman." Speaking to Satan, God said, "And I will put enmity between thee and the woman, and between thy seed and her seed; it shall bruise thy head, and thou shalt bruise his heel" (Gen. 3:15). But, you see, Adam and Eve did not know that the struggle with sin was going to last so long. They thought their first son would be the man who was coming to defeat Satan, but Cain was not the Savior; he was a murderer.

We read further in Genesis 4:2, "And she again bare his brother Abel. And Abel was a keeper of the sheep, but Cain was a tiller of the ground." We ought to stop here and make a comparison between the boys, because they were actually antipodes apart, although they were brothers, the sons of Adam and Eve. The late Dr. Henry Rimmer thought they were twins. I don't think they were twins, but I do think they were more alike than twins today could possibly be. For instance, in a family today you can have two boys, and the first boy might be a fine, upstanding boy. He goes through school, makes straight A's, goes to college, and then becomes a professional man, perhaps a doctor. But the other boy doesn't do well in school at all, and he drops out. He begins to drink and to smoke marijuana and get into trouble. Now what is the explanation? The psychologist will come along and say that according to the Mendelian theory the upstanding young man has taken after an ancestor on the mother's side of the family, but the other boy takes after an ancestor on the father's side. That is the explanation that is often given, but you cannot use that method with Cain and Abel. Who were the ancestors of Cain and Abel? They didn't even have grandparents. You cannot use the explanation of heredity for the difference in these two boys. I think they were as alike as two peas in a pod—they looked alike and acted alike in many ways, but they were different.

Neither can you use the explanation of environment as making the difference between Cain and Abel. A great many people today think that environment is what makes the real difference between men. They say that if we could just make the environment all right, every person would be all right. If we could just get rid of the slums and put people into nice homes, then the people would be nice also. But it doesn't always work that way. These two boys had the same environment. I cannot think of a home that was as much the same for two boys as was the home of Cain and Abel.

Genesis 4:3 goes on to say, "And in process of time it came to pass, that Cain brought of the fruit of the ground an offering unto the LORD." "In the process of time" means at the end of days. I think it was the Sabbath day, for these boys belonged to the first creation, the old creation. They came at a specified time.

"That Cain brought"—the word *brought* has in it the thought that it was brought to an appointed place.

"And Abel, he also brought of the firstlings

of his flock and of the fat thereof. And the LORD had respect unto Abel and to his offering: But unto Cain and to his offering he had not respect. And Cain was very wroth, and his countenance fell" (Gen. 4:4–5). Now what was the difference between the two offerings? Didn't both of them come in obedience to God? No, they did not. You see, God had revealed to them that they were to bring a sacrifice, a lamb, and that little lamb pointed to Christ. Someone will argue that Genesis does not say that. No, it doesn't say that, but Hebrews 11 does say it: "By faith Abel offered unto God a more excellent sacrifice than Cain." How could he? He came by faith.

What is faith? Let's look at it again: "Faith cometh by hearing, and hearing by the Word of God" (see Rom. 10:17). Abel had a revelation from God. So did Cain. They were both in the same family. But Cain ignored it, and he brought what he wanted to bring, the fruit of the ground—that which *he* had produced. In other words, here is the first man who brought *his works* to God. A lot of people are still coming to God the same way—they come by works. They have done this and that. Cain brought that which he had raised.

But Abel brought a lamb and slew it. If you had been there, you might have asked, "Brother Abel, why are you bringing a lamb?"

He would have said, "God commanded it."

"Do you think the little lamb takes away your sin?"

"Of course not," he would have said. "I just told you that God commanded us to bring it. He said to my mother that there is One coming in her line who is going to be a Savior, and that Person is the One to whom this little lamb points. I am coming by faith, looking to the time when a deliverer and a Savior will come."

There at the very beginning God made clear the way to Himself: "Without shedding of blood, there is no remission of sins." We come to God on the one basis that we are sinners and that the penalty for our sins must be paid. That is the reason a little lamb had to be slain. That little lamb couldn't take away sin, but it foreshadowed the coming of Christ who is "the Lamb of God that taketh away the sin of the world." And it was offered in faith.

Abel's offering pointed to Christ, and he came by faith—that is the way of salvation. God made the way very clear at the beginning, my friend. Today, though a man be a stranger and a wayfaring man and a fool, he need not err therein. God has made it very clear to us: Christ is the way to Himself; God gave Him to die for our sins. Abel, therefore, illustrates to us the *way* of faith—it is the blood-sprinkled way, the way that is Christ.

THE FAITH OF ENOCH

We come now to Enoch, and in him we see the *walk* of faith. If you come to God through Christ, then you are to walk with Him. It is then the walk of the believer that becomes important.

By faith Enoch was translated that he should not see death; and was not found, because God had translated him: for before his translation he had this testimony, that he pleased God [Heb. 11:5].

Genesis 5 is where we find Enoch mentioned for the first time, and it is a very sad chapter. "This is the book of the generations of Adam. In the day that God created man, in the likeness of God made he him" (Gen. 5:1). We are told that Adam lived an hundred and thirty years and begat a son, Seth. Then Adam died, and Seth lived and begat a son. Then Seth died. "In Adam all die"—that is the way that it's been going on for a long, long time. The fifth chapter of Genesis is just like walking through a cemetery and reading what is engraved on the tombstones. It really becomes monotonous, but it is still the rather sad story of mankind even today. It is the same picture as the present hour in which we live. Things haven't changed much—man still dies. Oh, I know we have extended man's life span, but what are a few years when you put them down next to a thousand years, or even eternity?

But in Genesis we read of Enoch: "And Jared lived after he begat Enoch eight hundred years, and begat sons and daughters: And all the days of Jared were nine hundred sixty and two years: and he died. And Enoch lived sixty and five years, and begat Methuselah: and Enoch walked with God after he begat Methuselah three hundred years, and begat sons and daughters: and all the days of Enoch were three hundred sixty and five years: and Enoch walked with God: and he was not; for God took him" (Gen. 5:19–24). That is the story of Enoch. Genesis 5 gives us a certain genealogy; it follows a very definite line. We are told that all these begat sons and daughters, but we are not told anything about them. Just one particular son is lifted out—Enoch, the son of Jared.

We are told that Enoch lived sixty-five years and begat a son by the name of Methuselah. Enoch had other children, but apparently his firstborn was Methuselah. "And Enoch walked with God after he begat Methuselah." I do not know what he did before he begat Methuselah, but I'm sure he did not walk with God. It might have been a careless life. It could have been a life that was lived in indifference, or perhaps in open sin. The record does not say. It simply says that he walked with God *after* he begat Methuselah. One day he went into the nursery and looked down into the crib at that little fellow who was kicking and gooing— his name was Methuselah. We always think of Methuselah as being an old man who had such a long beard that it got in his way and he walked on it. But at this time he was just a little baby, and when this man Enoch looked down at that little baby, he recognized his responsibility, and it changed his life. He started to walk with God.

My friend, if the presence of a baby in the home won't change your life-style, nothing else ill. Even the preacher won't be able to say much that will affect you, but these little ones have a way of speaking for God, even though they don't say a word. They come out of the everywhere into the here, and they seem so fresh, and somehow or other they bring a message from God. Certainly Methuselah did for this man Enoch, and it changed his life-style.

The record tells us that after Methuselah, Enoch had other children, but it does not tell us that he died. Notice: "And Enoch walked with God: and he was not; for God took him." In Enoch we see the *walk* of faith. The writer to the Hebrews says, "By faith Enoch was translated that he should not see death . . . for before his translation he had this testimony, that he pleased God." His walk pleased God because he walked by faith, not by rules and regulations. He believed in God, and he walked in a manner that pleased Him. Then God took him. He didn't die—he was translated. This is the first rapture of a man recorded in the Bible. He was removed from this earth's scene and was taken away.

We have quite a picture here, by the way, which I think has a spiritual message for us. There are those who believe the church will go through the Great Tribulation Period, and they have used Noah as an example. But Noah represents, not the church, but those in the world who are going to be saved during the Great Tribulation. God is going to keep them. Who are they? They are the 144,000 of Israel and also a great company of Gentiles. They are not part of the body of believers that we designate as the church. We are told in the Book of Revelation that before the winds of the Great Tribulation begin to blow across the earth and the four horsemen of the apocalypse begin to

ride, 144,000 out of the nation Israel will be sealed and also a great company of Gentiles. *These* are represented by Noah. My friend, God *can* keep you in the Great Tribulation, but it is not a question of whether or not God can keep you, the question is what God *says*, and He says He is going to *remove* the believers. He told the church in Philadelphia, "Because thou hast kept the word of my patience, I also will keep thee from the hour of temptation, which shall come upon all the world, to try them that dwell upon the earth" (Rev. 3:10). What hour is going to try the earth? The only one mentioned in Scripture is the Great Tribulation Period. This great company of both Jews and Gentiles are to be kept—and Noah represents them. Enoch is the man who represents the church. Enoch didn't go through the Flood. He had been translated. He was not in the ark. God could have put him in the ark, but He didn't. He could have kept Enoch in safety during the Flood, but instead He removed him, and that is what He is going to do with the church— Enoch represents the church.

"By faith Enoch was translated." *Translated* is a good translation, because it means to take something out of one language and put it into another. I have enjoyed listening to the tapes of our radio Bible study broadcasts in Spanish although I can't understand a word that is being said. The man who is giving my message in Spanish is reading it, but you would never know it. He's doing an excellent job. The manager of the station in South America says they have everything in that broadcast except my Texas accent! Well, I like the way the man does it, and it is a translation. It was taken out of the English language and put into the Spanish language for South America.

Enoch was translated out of one sphere of life and translated into another. The best way I know to describe it is the way it was told by a little girl who came home from Sunday school, and her mother asked, "What did your teacher tell you about today?"

The little girl said, "She told us all about this man Enoch." You can see that this was a good Bible teaching Sunday school.

And the mother said, "Well, what about Enoch?"

So the little girl told her mama this story: "Enoch lived a long time ago, and God would come by every afternoon and say to him, 'Enoch, would you like to take a walk with Me?' Enoch would say, 'Yes, I'd like to take a walk with You, God.' And so every day God would come by Enoch's house, and Enoch would go walking with God. One day God came by and said, 'Enoch, let's take a long walk today. I want to talk to you.' So they started out. Enoch got his coat—even took his lunch, and they started walking. They walked and they walked and they walked, and finally it got late. Enoch said, 'My, it's getting late, and I am a long way from home. Maybe we'd better start back.' But God said, 'Enoch, you are closer to My home than you are to your home, so you come on and go home with Me.' And so Enoch went home with God." I don't know how to tell the story any better than that. And that is what will happen one day with the church. The church, that is, the body of true believers, walking with God like Enoch was, will one day go home with Him. The Lord Jesus is coming: "For the Lord himself shall descend from heaven with a shout, with the voice of the archangel, and with the trump of God: and the dead in Christ shall rise first: Then we which are alive and remain shall be caught up together with them in the clouds, to meet the Lord in the air: and so shall we ever be with the Lord" (1 Thess. 4:16–17).

But without faith it is impossible to please him; for he that cometh to God must believe that he is, and that he is a rewarder of them that diligently seek him [Heb. 11:6].

"But without faith it is impossible to please him." Enoch pleased God. How did he do it? By faith. My friend, unless you are willing to come God's way and believe Him, you cannot possibly please God.

"For he that cometh to God must believe that he is, and that he is a rewarder of them that diligently seek him." In this Hebrew epistle there is a great deal said about rewards, and the reason is that the emphasis is on the Christian life. In light of the fact that we have a living Savior up there who is for us, there is a reward for living the Christian life. But salvation is *not* a reward—it is a free gift. You work for your reward, but not for salvation. Salvation comes by faith, and the walk of the Christian is also by faith. Enoch walked with God by faith.

THE FAITH OF NOAH

By faith Noah, being warned of God of things not seen as yet, moved with fear, prepared an ark to the saving of his house; by the which he condemned the world, and became heir of the righteousness which is by faith [Heb. 11:7].

Abel showed the way of faith; Enoch illustrated the walk of faith; and now Noah is the *witness* of faith.

"By faith Noah . . . to the saving of his house." Many of us are accustomed to saying that Noah preached 120 years and never made a convert. Actually, that is not quite accurate. It is true that he didn't win any of the Babylonians living there in Babel, but he surely won his family. He led every member of his family to the Lord, and that was really something.

Again, we need to go back to Genesis and look closely at this man Noah. We are told in Genesis 6:5, "And God saw that the wickedness of man was great in the earth, and that every imagination of the thoughts of his heart was only evil continually." That is a sad commentary on mankind. Man surely got away from God in a hurry after he left the Garden of Eden. However, we are told that there was one godly man left: "These are the generations of Noah: Noah was a just man and perfect in his generations, and Noah walked with God" (Gen. 6:9). Does this mean he was only a nice man who paid his debts and did many helpful things for people? No, he did more than that: "Noah walked with God." How did he walk with God? The writer to the Hebrews tells us: *"By faith* Noah, being warned of God of things not seen as yet, moved with fear, prepared an ark to the saving of his house."

This man Noah believed God when God told him He was going to destroy the earth by a flood. There are some people who suggest that up to this point it had never even rained on the earth—and that is probably true. But way up on dry ground, probably near Mount Ararat, away from even the Euphrates River, this man Noah began to build a boat because God said there was going to be a flood.

God gave Noah the instructions for the boat. It wasn't that clumsy-looking thing that you see pictured in Sunday school papers. When I was a little boy, my thought was, *I'd sure hate to be in that boat!* Probably it was very modern-looking equipment, and the size and construction of it would conform to modern ship building. We are told that the length of it was 300 cubits, the breadth of it was 50 cubits, and the height of it was 30 cubits. And it didn't have just one little window in the side. God said to Noah, "A window shalt thou make to the ark, and in a cubit shalt thou finish it above; and the door of the ark shalt thou set in the side thereof; with lower, second, and third stories shalt thou make it" (Gen. 6:16). The window went all the way around the top, and the roof came down over it. The ark was 300 cubits, or about 450 feet, long, and it had three decks. The men in that day were good builders and they were familiar with this type of construction. Therefore Noah began to do what I'm sure the population in his day considered to be a very foolish thing. I'm of the opinion that the sightseeing buses ran a tour out to where he was building the boat—and I'm sure it was a popular tour.

I have often wondered what it was that brought Noah's three sons, Ham, Shem, and Japheth, back home. These boys, I'm sure, had moved away and started their own businesses. Perhaps Ham was a contractor, a successful builder himself, down in Babel. Maybe one day he was meeting with a contractors' convention where he heard a man telling about a trip he'd made to the north country. There he had heard of a man who was building a boat on dry ground. He felt it was really ridiculous, and everybody agreed, including Ham. But then Ham, knowing his dad lived up there and having heard some things about his dad, asked the man if he had seen the boat builder. The man said he had seen the builder and the builder's name was Noah. Ham probably turned white when he heard that. He stood up and said, "Listen, that's my father who is building that boat. I agree with you—it sounds foolish. I laughed as you laughed, but you don't know my dad. My dad walks in the fear of the living God. I've gotten away from that, but if my dad says a flood is coming, it's because God has caused him to give out a message of warning. You can just put it down that God has spoken to him and a flood is coming. I was brought up in that home, and I know that I might cut corners but my dad wouldn't. My dad never told a lie. My dad lived for God. If you don't mind, I'm going to get my hammer and saw, and I'm going up there to help him build that boat!" I think Shem and Japheth had similar experiences and went back home to help their dad. Why? Because this man Noah had a witness for God.

My friend, I say this very candidly, the most important thing you can do is to witness to your own family—not by everlastingly giving them the gospel, but by living it before them and letting them see that you have a reality in your life. This reminds me of an encounter that Gypsy Smith had when he was holding meetings in Dallas, Texas. A lady came up and told him that God had called her to preach. He felt the same way about women preachers as I do, and so he asked her if she was married. She was. He said, "How many children do you have?" She had five children. "Isn't that won-

derful," Gypsy told her, "God has called you to preach, and He's already given you a congregation!" May I say to you, whether you are a preacher or not, if you are a child of God and you have a family, that is your congregation. God gave you that congregation. Noah won his family. No one outside his family believed, but his family believed because they knew his witness. Noah "prepared an ark to the saving of his house." What a wonderful thing that he was able to do that!

THE FAITH OF ABRAHAM AND SARAH

We come now to Abraham, the man who is known as the man of faith. That is the way he is identified in the Word of God. Abraham is the supreme illustration of faith in the Epistle to the Romans and also in the Epistle to the Galatians. The writers of the Gospels refer to him, and even the Lord Jesus said, "Your father Abraham rejoiced to see my day: and he saw it, and was glad" (John 8:56). In Abraham we will see the *worship* of faith.

By faith Abraham, when he was called to go out into a place which he should after receive for an inheritance, obeyed; and he went out, not knowing whither he went [Heb. 11:8].

We have seen in this epistle that the worship of God leads to obedience to God. It leads to work for God. It leads to doing the thing God wants you to do. We do not need to spend time browbeating people, telling them they should get busy for God—that is not the proper motivation. But if they can truly worship God and catch something of the glory of the person of Christ, then you can depend on them to work for God and to obey Him. The most important word in this verse and in this entire section is *obeyed*, and worship leads to obedience.

In Genesis 12 where the story of Abraham begins, we read that he came out of Ur of the Chaldees and went to Haran. He delayed in Haran and lost a great deal of time, but finally he went to the land of Canaan. When he appeared in the land, God appeared to him. "And the LORD appeared unto Abram, and said, Unto thy seed will I give this land: and there builded he an altar unto the LORD, who appeared unto him" (Gen. 12:7). Everywhere this man went he built an altar. When he came into the land of Shechem he built an altar. When he went down to the plains of Moreh he built an altar unto the Lord. Everywhere Abraham went he built an altar to God. I have been impressed on my trips to the Holy Land with the number of buildings that Herod put up. He not only built the temple, which was never really completed, but he also built palaces and forts and cities all over that land. But there was no actual worship of God on his part. All Abraham did was put up an altar, but he worshiped God, and that led to obedience of God. He worshiped God by faith; then he obeyed God by faith.

By faith he sojourned in the land of promise, as in a strange country, dwelling in tabernacles with Isaac and Jacob, the heirs with him of the same promise:

For he looked for a city which hath foundations, whose builder and maker is God.

Through faith also Sara herself received strength to conceive seed, and was delivered of a child when she was past age, because she judged him faithful who had promised [Heb. 11:9–11].

When God told Sarah at ninety years of age that she was to have a child, she laughed because it was ridiculous—it seemed utterly preposterous. She couldn't accept it, but God gave her the strength and power to believe Him. Many of us need such strength. Do you remember the man who brought the demon-possessed boy to the Lord Jesus? The Lord Jesus told the man that He could help him if he would believe. The man said, "I believe. Help thou mine unbelief." The man recognized that he had a weak faith, but the Lord Jesus must have given him the faith because He healed the boy (see Mark 9:17–27). Sarah had a little boy named Isaac. Why? She "received strength to conceive seed, and was delivered of a child when she was past age, because she judged him faithful who had promised." Sarah represents the *power* (or strength) of faith.

Therefore sprang there even of one, and him as good as dead, so many as the stars of the sky in multitude, and as the sand which is by the sea shore innumerable [Heb. 11:12].

This is what happened, and it all took place by faith. But notice that Abraham and Sarah never saw the fulfillment of God's promise to them:

These all died in faith, not having received the promises, but having seen them afar off, and were persuaded of them, and embraced them, and confessed that they were strangers and pilgrims on the earth [Heb. 11:13].

Walking by faith will cause all of us to recognize that as children of God we are just pilgrims and strangers down here on this earth.

For they that say such things declare plainly that they seek a country [Heb. 11:14].

Faith looks out yonder to the future. And the child of God today is looking to the future.

I am not in the employ of the local chamber of commerce, but I very frankly love Southern California. I have lived here longer than I've lived any place in my life—since 1940—and I love it, in spite of the smog and the traffic and all these people who followed us out here. I wish we could have put a wall around California (after *we* got here, of course!), and then we could have had this wonderful place to ourselves. All of us who have come out here certainly haven't helped the place, but I still prefer it to any other. I have a "ranch" out here in California. It's not what you call a big ranch—it's about 72 feet wide and about 128 feet deep. But I have my house right in the middle of it, and I have it well stocked. I have orange trees, avocado trees, tangerine trees, nectarine trees, apricots, plums, and lemons. You see, I'm really a rancher. The other day I just looked up and thanked the Lord that He gave me that place. It is the first place I have ever owned and paid for, but *He* gave it to me, and I thank Him for it. However, I told Him, "Don't let me get in love with this place, or I won't want to leave it to go to a better place." We are strangers and pilgrims down here, because we are walking by faith, looking to a better place. "For they that say such things declare plainly that they seek a country."

And truly, if they had been mindful of that country from whence they came out, they might have had opportunity to have returned.

But now they desire a better country, that is, an heavenly: wherefore God is not ashamed to be called their God: for he hath prepared for them a city [Heb. 11:15–16].

Anyone can turn around and go back to the world if he is satisfied with the things of the world. However, a child of God, by faith, is going ever onward.

By faith Abraham, when he was tried, offered up Isaac; and he that had received the promises offered up his only begotten son [Heb. 11:17].

Now we come to the end of Abraham's life, and the supreme sacrifice he made in offering up Isaac, the boy that God had given to him.

Of whom it was said, That in Isaac shall thy seed be called [Heb. 11:18].

Abraham had other children, but Isaac is the one called "his only begotten." (The word *son* in verse 17 is not in the original text.) Isaac was the only begotten because God gave the promise concerning him.

Accounting that God was able to raise him up, even from the dead; from whence also he received him in a figure [Heb. 11:19].

God did not ask Abraham to offer up Isaac until he had come to the end of his life. The reason is that Abraham would not have had the faith to do it. God will never test you "above that ye are able" (see 1 Cor. 10:13). Therefore God never asked Abraham to give up Ishmael, that is, to sacrifice him on an altar. Do you know why? Well, to begin with, Ishmael wasn't the promised son. And the second thing is that Abraham would not have done it, you can be sure. Abraham even begged God not to send Ishmael away but to let him keep the boy and make him the son of promise. You see, Abraham wasn't ready at that time to do such a thing. And certainly at the beginning of Isaac's life when he was just a baby, Abraham never would have offered him. When Isaac was about thirty-three years of age, Abraham was ready to obey God and trust Him. Therefore, we have here the testing of faith.

I want to look at Abraham a little bit differently from the way we ordinarily see him. We usually think in terms of the great promises which God made to him concerning the land to be given to him and the multitudes which would come from him. But what was it that Abraham actually *received* during his lifetime? What was it that he actually saw? He did not see the fulfillment of those great promises, but what God did give to him was a home. When he was a young man living in Ur of the Chaldees, he one day said to a beautiful young girl, "I love you. I want to marry you." And so Abraham and Sarah got married.

Then one day Abraham came home—it was a home of idolatry—and he said to Sarah, "The living God has called me. He wants me to leave this place."

I can just hear Sarah say, "But you have a

good business. All your relatives live here. Your friends live here. And, by the way, *where* are you going?"

Abraham would have to say, "I don't know."

"What do you mean that God called you and you don't know where?"

He said, "God will lead me, and I'm going out."

And Sarah said, "I'll go with you." And so this young couple went out. They didn't have too much faith. They took papa with them and some of the relatives, and they came to Haran. They hung around Haran until Papa Terah died and they buried him.

Then Abraham moved into the land and God appeared to him. God said to him, "Abraham, I am going to do all these things I promised, but I am also going to give you a son." Now that is what is going to *make* the home—Abraham and Sarah are going to have a son.

Abraham and Sarah had the basis for a godly home in that day. It was the kind of home God wants young people to have today—we call it a Christian home. To establish this godly home God did not give them a course or send them to a preacher for counseling. Frankly, we preachers have done too much counseling, telling young people how they ought to do it. We have become too idealistic, but God was very practical. He said, "Abraham, if you are going to have the kind of home I want you to have, you are going to have to get away from papa and mama." That is what God meant at the very beginning when He said to Adam and Eve, "Therefore shall a man leave his father and his mother, and shall cleave unto his wife: and they shall be one flesh" (Gen. 2:24). Although Adam and Eve didn't even have a mother and father, God set down this great principle at the very beginning.

I never thought that I would be a grandfather who would tell the parents how to raise a child. I didn't do so well myself as a parent, but I have learned that it is the easiest thing in the world to tell them how to do it. Well, they *will* make mistakes, but it is none of my business. We made our mistakes, and they will make theirs. Papa and mama are not to interfere with the home of the children. God got Abraham as far away as possible where relatives were not going to be able to interfere. I think this is primary to building a godly home.

God had Abraham leave his home. It was a godless home he left, a home of idolatry. Joshua made that clear (see Josh. 24:2).

A great many rules and regulations concerning marriage are being given to young couples in our day. I don't want to sound revolutionary, but I do want to say what the Word of God says to do. You can forget the rules and regulations until you are walking by faith. If you are a child of God, you are to walk by faith in that home. The father is to walk by faith, and the mother is to walk by faith. And do you want to know something? The home will never be an ideal home. I am weary of hearing folk tell how they went to a counseling session and now they have the most glorious home you have ever heard of. Well, may I say to you, I have been married to my wife for a long time and we disagree on many things. The fact of the matter is, she has a right to be wrong! But we've always been able to come to the place where I could put my arm around her and tell her I love her in spite of the fact that she is wrong. My young Christian friend, if you think you are going to start an ideal Christian home, I think you are mistaken. You will find that you will be tested just as Abraham was tested when he ran off to Egypt. I am of the opinion that all the way to Egypt, Sarah said, "Abraham, I don't want to go down to Egypt." But they went to Egypt. He almost lost Sarah to someone else down there because he lied and said she was not his wife. That certainly is not an ideal home, is it?

When Abraham returned to the Promised Land from Egypt, we find that he had trouble there with his nephew. Maybe Abraham should have left him in Ur of the Chaldees, but finally Lot moved down to Sodom, leaving Abraham alone up in the hill country. Here again, we see that neither Abraham nor Sarah were what we would call ideal. Abraham doubted God. He didn't believe that God ought to destroy Sodom and Gomorrah. God had to make it clear to him that what He was doing was a righteous and just thing. And He had to make it clear to Sarah that He could give her power to have a son. He gave them that little child to raise in their home.

Abraham and Sarah's home was the kind of home God wants you to have. If you think that following a few little rules is going to avoid all the rough places and hardships in life, you are wrong. You will find out that one day you will argue with your wife. You are going to find out that one day you are going to have a problem with the child God gives you. Your home will not be ideal by any means. How are you going to handle all these problems? By faith, my friend, by faith. When you and I have reached the place where we are willing to put our child upon the altar for God, then you and I have arrived. Abraham and Sarah's home was just

about as near to what God wants down here as any of us will be able to attain.

Christian friend, if it is going hard with you and you are having problems, then God is trying to teach you something. Let God be your teacher. Don't run to your pastor or think you can take a course that will solve all your problems. You and I are going to have problems, but if we walk by faith, He will see us through.

Abraham's *worship* of faith led to obedience in his life, so that it could be said of him, ". . . Abraham believed God, and it was counted unto him for righteousness" (Rom. 4:3).

THE FAITH OF ISAAC

By faith Isaac blessed Jacob and Esau concerning things to come [Heb. 11:20].

Notice that very little is said concerning Isaac, especially when it is in contrast to his father Abraham. What can we say concerning Isaac? He represents the *willingness* of faith. Isaac was a grown man, probably around thirty-three years of age, when his father Abraham offered him on the altar. That certainly demonstrates his willingness!

"By faith Isaac blessed Jacob and Esau concerning things to come." The one thing that is pinpointed in Isaac's life is his faith in blessing his sons. Now that seems a very strange thing. Isaac was a well digger. He would dig a well in a certain place, and the enemy would take it away from him. He would then dig another well, and again it would be taken away from him. In many ways he was a rather colorless individual, but the thing that characterized him was willingness. He was willing to bless Jacob and Esau concerning things to come, but there was nothing in the immediate present that would cause him to bless them.

THE FAITH OF JACOB

We come now to a very colorful individual—

By faith Jacob, when he was a-dying, blessed both the sons of Joseph; and worshipped, leaning upon the top of his staff [Heb. 11:21].

This man Jacob lived a life of faith in relationship to his father, and to his son Joseph, and to his grandsons. But the one thing that was selected out of his life happened when he was dying. You must wait until the end of this man's life before you can say that he was a man of faith. At the time of his death he blessed both of the sons of Joseph, his grandsons, and he worshiped "leaning upon the top of his staff."

There are several things which we can observe from the life of Jacob. He is an illustration of human nature and of the fact that it is by grace that we are saved. If it had not been for the grace of God, Jacob would have been lost. He had no human merit—none whatsoever. I'm not sure but what that is a picture of all of us.

> Nothing in my hand I bring,
> Simply to Thy cross I cling.
>> "Rock of Ages"
>> —Augustus M. Toplady

Dr. J. Hudson Taylor, founder of the China Inland Mission, had a way of emphasizing the fact that before God we are nothing, and that God is the only one who can take nothing and do something with it. He told the story of a young, self-confident missionary who arrived on the field with his wife. Finally one day the young fellow came to Dr. Taylor and told him that it was difficult for him to think he was nothing. "Young man," Dr. Taylor said, "you *are* nothing, whether you believe it or not. You can just take God's word for it!"

This man Jacob is a picture of our human nature. We hear a great deal today in psychology about prenatal care, natal care, and postnatal care, and how important these are in shaping the life of the individual. The gynecologist and the psychologist give a lot of emphasis to the care of a baby before birth, at birth, and immediately after birth. What can be said of Jacob's life in these respects? The Bible tells us that Jacob and Esau struggled within their mother. Even before birth, Jacob was wrestling and trying to get the upper hand! He struggled even at birth. He came out last, but he came out holding on to the heel of his brother. He was a heel-grabber, and he was that all of his life. Also Jacob was a deceiver and he was a rascal. God, however, *did* transform his life.

First of all, in the life of this man, we find that he was a deceiver in relationship to his father. God had promised Jacob the blessing, but he couldn't wait for it. He took it from his brother Esau by a very deceptive method, which forced him to leave home, and he spent the night in Beth-el. He was very homesick, but no change had taken place in his life. Even when he went down to live with his Uncle Laban he was still relying on his wits. Then God had to stop him when he was finally re-

turning to the land. The Lord wrestled with him that night at the brook Jabbok. That night God crippled him—He had to get Jacob.

Later in the life of Jacob we see that the very sin he committed came home to him in the life of his son Joseph. One day his sons brought that very bloody coat of many colors which belonged to Joseph, and they said to Jacob, "Is this the coat of your son? Do you recognize it?" And Jacob began to weep. In the same way in which he had deceived, he was deceived by his sons into thinking that Joseph had been killed. The sins of the fathers are visited upon the children—this is certainly an example of that.

However, at the end of this man's life, the writer to the Hebrews shows us Jacob's faith in relationship to his grandsons, Ephraim and Manasseh. "By faith Jacob, when he was a-dying . . . ." He is on his deathbed, and this is the first thing in his life you can lift out and say, "By faith Jacob. . . ."

He "blessed both the sons of Joseph; and worshipped." For the first time there will be obedience in his life. It has always interested me that he worshiped "leaning upon the top of his staff." What staff? Remember that he had been crippled, and he had a staff that enabled him to walk. Even when death came, this man did not want to lie down and die. There was no blessing in the *life* of Jacob. It was a life of sin and deception, chicanery and crookedness—and no blessing ever eventuates from sin.

The important thing for you and me to see is that God can take any life and straighten it out. Where there is confusion and deception, if there is faith anchored in the Lord Jesus Christ, we can lay hold of Him. Faith was operative in the life of Jacob, but we have to come to the end of his life to see it.

THE FAITH OF JOSEPH

By faith Joseph, when he died, made mention of the departing of the children of Israel; and gave commandment concerning his bones [Heb. 11:22].

I am confident that the writer to the Hebrews and the Holy Spirit of God could have chosen many incidents from the life of Joseph which would illustrate faith. We could cite the time when this man was down there in Egypt and put into prison. You would think that this was going to be the end for him, and many of us would have cried out in complaint at that time. But that incident was not recorded here. And there are so many other illustrations of faith in the life of this man

Joseph. What a contrast he is to his father Jacob! There are no faults or flaws in his life.

There is probably no one in the entire Old Testament who is more closely a type of the Lord Jesus Christ than is Joseph; however, he is never spoken of as a type in Scripture. The analogy between the two is striking. Joseph was the best beloved son as was the Lord Jesus. Joseph had a coat of many colors which set him apart from his brethren and gave him lordship over them; he had a vision and his brethren thought he was a dreamer. The Lord Jesus, too, came with a message, and they thought he was a dreamer. Joseph obeyed his father, and the Lord Jesus said He had come to do the Father's will. Joseph's brethren hated him; it is said of the Lord Jesus, "He came unto his own, and his own received him not" (John 1:11). Joseph was sent by his father to seek his brethren, and the Lord Jesus came to this earth seeking the lost. Joseph found his brothers who were shepherds in a field; shepherds came by night when the Lord Jesus was born. His brethren mocked Joseph, refused him, and plotted to kill him; the same happened to the Lord Jesus. Joseph was sold into slavery, and the Lord was sold for thirty pieces of silver. Joseph's coat was dipped in blood; the soldiers gambled for the vesture of the Lord Jesus Christ, with His blood upon it. Joseph was sold into Egypt where God raised him up to save (in a material way) the world; the Lord Jesus went down into death—after having been tempted by the world, the flesh, and the Devil—to become the Savior of the world—both Jew and Gentile. While on the throne, Joseph gave bread to the people; Christ is the Bread of Life. While in Egypt, Joseph got a gentile bride; the Lord Jesus is calling out of this world a people to His name. Joseph made himself known to his brethren when they came to Egypt; someday the Lord Jesus will make Himself known to His own brethren.

The interesting thing about Joseph is that he had faith in the dream which was given to him, faith while in the pit into which he was placed, faith all the while he was in Egypt, and faith was what buoyed him up through all the adverse circumstances. You would think that at the end of his life he would be satisfied with Egypt—but not this man. He said, "When the day comes that the children of Israel leave this land, be sure and take my bones with you" (see Gen. 50:25). Why didn't they take his body right then and bury it yonder in the land of Ephraim? The reason is quite obvious: this man was a national hero at the time. But there came a day when there rose a pharaoh who knew not Joseph, and when the children of Israel left, they took up his bones and buried them at Shechem in the Samaritan country.

THE FAITH OF MOSES

Now we move down quite a few years to the time when the children of Israel are in slavery in the land of Egypt. Moses represents the *sacrifices* of faith.

By faith Moses, when he was born, was hid three months of his parents, because they saw he was a proper child; and they were not afraid of the king's commandment [Heb. 11:23].

Moses had godly parents who were willing to take a real stand for God. Faith was involved in the very birth of Moses.

By faith Moses, when he was come to years, refused to be called the son of Pharaoh's daughter;

Choosing rather to suffer affliction with the people of God, than to enjoy the pleasures of sin for a season [Heb. 11:24–25].

We see faith at work in the life of Moses. He was brought up in the palace and would have been the next pharaoh, but Moses had faith to choose the right.

Esteeming the reproach of Christ greater riches than the treasures in Egypt: for he had respect unto the recompence of the reward [Heb. 11:26].

Someone else other than Abraham saw Christ's day and rejoiced—Moses did.

By faith he forsook Egypt, not fearing the wrath of the king: for he endured, as seeing him who is invisible [Heb. 11:27].

Moses had faith to act—faith will lead to action. Many folk today are saying, "I believe, I believe," but do nothing. May I say, faith reveals itself in action. God saves us without our works, but the faith that saves produces works. Therefore Moses "forsook Egypt, not fearing the wrath of the king: for he endured, as seeing him who is invisible."

Through faith he kept the passover, and the sprinkling of blood, lest he that destroyed the firstborn should touch them [Heb. 11:28].

Moses had faith to obey God. God said to do this, and Moses did it. This is exemplified in the life of this man. He forsook the pleasures of Egypt, went out into the desert, and came back to deliver his people. This is faith to obey God.

By faith they passed through the Red sea as by dry land: which the Egyptians assaying to do were drowned [Heb. 11:29].

Whose faith do we see here? Is this the faith of the children of Israel? No. They had none. When they saw Pharaoh and his chariots coming, they said in effect to Moses, "Let's get back to Egypt as quick as we can! We made a mistake in leaving." It was Moses who had faith. *He* went down to the water's edge and smote it with that rod; and it was by *his* faith that the waters opened up and they were able to march over to the other side. Then they sang the song of Moses. The people are identified with Moses, but this was Moses' faith.

THE FAITH OF JOSHUA

By faith the walls of Jericho fell down, after they were compassed about seven days [Heb. 11:30].

We have in the life of Joshua the *watch* of faith. If you had met Joshua about the fifth day they were marching around the city of Jericho, you might have said to him, "It doesn't look like you are getting very far. Why are you doing such a foolish thing? You are a general with a whole lot of intelligence, but you are not using your intelligence."

He would have said to you, "You have forgotten that I saw the captain of the hosts of the Lord, and He told me that headquarters is not in my tent, but in heaven. I found out that I am not the general. I happen to be a buck private in the rear ranks, and I am to take my orders from Him. He said to march around the city, and I am marching around. You just watch—these walls will come down. I'm following the strategy of Someone who knows."

In Joshua we see the watch of faith. Faith to believe God—General Joshua had learned that.

THE FAITH OF RAHAB

By faith the harlot Rahab perished not with them that believed not, when she had received the spies with peace [Heb. 11:31].

I want to call Rahab's story the *wonder* of faith.

Her story is in connection with the story of the walls of Jericho. She was living inside the city, and I am sure that after seven days those on the inside were wondering what was going to happen.

"By faith the harlot Rahab perished not with them that believed not." Many years ago a book was published with the title *Religion in Unlikely Places*. I do not know if Rahab was included in that book—I never read it—but she certainly should have been. Jericho was the last place in the world you would have looked for faith. Rahab lived in a very wicked, pagan, and heathen city—*and* she practiced the oldest profession there. Those who practice that profession have usually been considered to be sinners—until recently, of course, when the "new morality" came along. This woman was a sinner, and yet we are told here, "by faith the harlot Rahab perished not with them that believed not." I'm sure that the mayor of the city and others who were in high position felt that they were good enough to have been saved, but they were not saved. We are told they perished in the city because of just one reason: they did not believe God.

We will see that God was very generous in the way He dealt with the city of Jericho. I know the critic finds a great deal of fault with God for destroying the people of Jericho. I had a professor in college who could weep crocodile tears because of what happened to the people in the city of Jericho. The thing that always disturbed me about this man was that he showed very little interest in other people—including his students, by the way—but he could really work up a lather when it came to the people of Jericho.

We want to look closely at this woman Rahab, because she expressed her faith in a very definite way. When the people of Israel had crossed over the Red Sea, that word got to Jericho, and the inhabitants of Jericho lost their courage. But they never dreamed that during flood season the great host of Israel could be brought across the Jordan River. There was no bridge on which they could cross, and the river was on a rampage at that time. How in the world could the people get over? The people of Jericho had felt that they had time to plan a defense and didn't have to worry until the flood season was over.

Then Joshua sent spies into the city of Jericho, and they came into contact with the harlot Rahab. I have a notion she made a business proposition to them, but I do not know whether they accepted or not. I do know they made it very clear that they were on a mission, that they needed protection, and that God was going to give the city of Jericho into their hands. They at least gave her that much information. She took them in and hid them on the roof of her house and no doubt risked her own life in doing that. She asked one favor from these men, "When you take this city, I want you to remember me and my family. I want you to save us." And they promised to do that. They told her to put out a scarlet line in the window to identify her house, and that when Joshua took the city he would be very careful to save her and her household.

Rahab's testimony is found in the Book of Joshua: "And she said unto the men, I know that the LORD hath given you the land, and that your terror is fallen upon us, and that all the inhabitants of the land faint because of you. For we have heard how the LORD dried up the water of the Red sea for you, when ye came out of Egypt; and what ye did unto the two kings of the Amorites, that were on the other side Jordan, Sihon and Og, whom ye utterly destroyed. And as soon as we had heard these things, our hearts did melt, neither did there remain any more courage in any man, because of you: for the LORD your God, he is God in heaven above, and in earth beneath" (Josh. 2:9–11).

This is a strange statement that comes from this woman, but it is a tremendous revelation of the fact that God did not arbitrarily destroy the city of Jericho. You see, for *forty* years word had been filtering into Jericho about a people who crossed the Red Sea. In other words, Rahab said, "It was forty years ago when we heard about that. And I for one believed. Others believed the facts, but they did not believe in God. They never trusted the living God." Later on, they heard how God was leading Israel and that He had given them victory on the other side of the Jordan against the Amorites. Jericho should have profited from that information. Finally Israel miraculously crossed the Jordan River and parked right outside the door of Jericho. What had God been doing? He had been giving the city an opportunity to believe in Him, to trust Him, and to turn to Him.

I think it should be obvious to anyone that if God saved this harlot who believed in Him, He would have saved the mayor of Jericho and He would have saved anyone in the city if he had trusted Him as this woman trusted Him. He saw all of them on one basis—He saw them all as sinners. "All have sinned and come short of the glory of God." Rahab probably was a more open sinner than the mayor was. I am of the opinion that the mayor's private life would not have stood inspection, and I am sure that that was true of many others in that city, but they had ample opportunity to trust God. They had forty years to decide whether they would believe God, and they did not.

If that college professor of mine were still alive, there is a question I would love to ask him. God gave them forty years to make up their minds whether they would trust Him or not. Only one woman made up her mind to trust God, and God saved her. It is obvious that since she was saved, anyone else would have been saved if they had trusted God. Now if you think forty years was not quite long enough, do you feel that God probably should have given them forty-*one* or forty-*two* years? My friend, if after forty years they are not going to believe God, they are not ever going to believe God. God is longsuffering. He is patient. He is not willing that any should perish. Even a harlot who will trust Him, God will save. The people of Jericho believed the facts which they heard, but they didn't trust God. If they had, they would have been saved.

Now when this woman evidenced that she believed God by asking the spies to save her when they took the city, she took a step of faith, and in that step of faith she risked her life. Her faith began to move. Faith goes into action—it does not sit on the sidelines. So this woman Rahab "perished not with them that believed not, when she had received the spies with peace." Faith cometh by hearing, and hearing by the word of God. "We have heard what God has done through you, and we believe it," she said. "I trust Him. I trust Him to the extent that I am willing to risk my life." She evidenced the faith that she had.

We see in this woman Rahab the wonder of faith. We see that in this lost world God doesn't view one group of people as so much better than another group of people. God sees us all as sinners, and when anyone will turn to Him, God will save him. How wonderful He is!

THE FAITH OF "OTHERS"

And what shall I more say? for the time would fail me to tell of Gedeon, and of Barak, and of Samson, and of Jephthae; of David also, and Samuel, and of the prophets [Heb. 11:32].

The writer of this epistle has come to a point in the history of the Old Testament at which he says, "What more can I say now?" He could go in any direction and could list heroes of faith, if you want to call them that.

He could demonstrate how faith has worked in the lives of many men and women. So he gives us a list and makes it clear that he is not able to discuss them in detail, but that all should be included in this marvelous chapter.

We see the *war* of faith in the lives of these men he mentions. Not one of them is dealt with in detail, but all have something in common: everyone mentioned here was a ruler. Gideon, Barak, Samson, Jephthah, and Samuel were all judges; David was a king. They were all rulers, and they were all engaged in a war for God. Each one of them won that battle by faith.

I will not be able to go into detail with each of these men, but I would like to take note of this man Gideon. Many people say that all they have in their church is a "little Gideon's band." What they mean is that they have a small number of people. But, my friend, it was not the small number that was significant about Gideon's band—it was the faith these men had. Yet Gideon was a man who actually had very little faith at the time when the Lord called him.

Gideon was a judge at the time the Midianites had taken the land of Israel. The Hebrews couldn't even harvest their crops—the Midianites would take it from them. This young man Gideon was down by the winepress harvesting grain. That is not where he should have been. The grain was usually taken up to the top of the hill, pitched up in the air where the wind could drive the chaff away. In that land the wind blows in the afternoon. But Gideon was a coward. He took the grain down there by the winepress—way down in the valley, where no one could see him. Talk about an operation of frustration! You can just see Gideon down there pitching up the grain. When there is no wind to blow the chaff away, do you know what is happening? The straw comes falling down around his neck. I can't think of anything more uncomfortable and discouraging than to pitch up the grain and have all the straw down your back!

Well, that was Gideon, and it was at that time the angel of the Lord appeared unto him and said, ". . . thou mighty man of valour" (Jud. 6:12).

That really wasn't the proper address for Gideon, and he didn't think the angel was talking to him. I think he looked up and said, "Who me?" He was the biggest coward of all, and he was willing to admit it. "Why," he said, "I belong to the smallest tribe. My family is the small family in the tribe. And I'm the smallest potato in the family. You picked the smallest pebble on the beach—I'm a nobody."

And God said to him, "That's the reason I picked you—because you are a nobody. I want you to believe Me." We will find that God began to strengthen the faith of that man until the day came when with only three hundred men he was able to get a victory over the Midianites. Faith operated in the life of this man Gideon.

How many Christians today feel like there must be some great big show, some big demonstration, some big meeting if the ministry is going to be of the Lord? May I say to you, God doesn't move quite like that. I'm of the opinion that the greatest work for God is being done by individuals and by little groups throughout this country and around the world. I was amazed to meet a man in Lebanon who, by the way, is a member of the Gideons International. He is an active Christian layman and a real witness for Christ. You don't hear about him—he's not one who is getting publicity. And then, in the land of Israel, there is a very wonderful Hebrew Christian who has been persecuted a great deal, but he is a real witness to God. There are a great many "Gideons" around today, and they move by faith. God will use a nobody if he will trust Him. God is moving in mysterious ways His wonders to perform.

The writer to the Hebrews mentions Gideon, Barak, and Samson. I don't know whether I would have put Samson in the list or not. Samson was a real failure as far as his service was concerned, but He did believe God. There was a time when the Spirit of God came upon him and he began to deliver Israel; he never completed the job, however. The writer goes on to mention Jephthah and David (oh, we could stop and talk a long time about David!) and Samuel and the prophets. But the writer makes it clear that time would fail him to mention them all.

Now notice what all these men did—theirs was the war of faith:

Who through faith subdued kingdoms, wrought righteousness, obtained promises, stopped the mouths of lions [Heb. 11:33].

"Stopped the mouths of lions"—we know this refers to Daniel, although he isn't mentioned by name here.

Quenched the violence of fire, escaped the edge of the sword, out of weakness were made strong, waxed valiant in fight, turned to flight the armies of the aliens [Heb. 11:34].

This is the war of faith, and these are the victors.

We see now the *wideness* of faith—faith has moved into every area of life:

Women received their dead raised to life again: and others were tortured, not accepting deliverance; that they might obtain a better resurrection [Heb. 11:35].

"Women received their dead raised to life again"—remember the widow of Zarephath whose son Elijah raised back to life (see 1 Kings 17:17–24).

"And others were tortured, not accepting deliverance; that they might obtain a better resurrection." In other words, he is now talking about martyrs.

And others had trial of cruel mockings and scourgings, yea, moreover of bonds and imprisonment:

They were stoned, they were sawn asunder, were tempted, were slain with the sword: they wandered about in sheepskins and goatskins; being destitute, afflicted, tormented;

(Of whom the world was not worthy:) they wandered in deserts, and in mountains, and in dens and caves of the earth [Heb. 11:36–38].

Here is another group of people. They didn't gain great victories out on the battlefield. They didn't enter the arena of life before large audiences and perform great feats for God. These are the "others," and they are the ones who, if you want heroes, are really God's heroes. They had trials and mockings and scourgings and bonds and imprisonment. They were stoned and they were "sawn asunder." Jerome insists that it was Isaiah who was sawn asunder, but of course that is only tradition. We don't know who suffered that cruel, horrible death. And others were tested, tempted, and slain by the sword.

I want you to notice a contrast here. Back in verses 33 and 34 when we were talking about the victories which were won, it spoke of how they "subdued kingdoms, wrought righteousness, obtained promises, stopped the mouths of lions, quenched the violence of fire, escaped the edge of the sword." They *escaped* the edge of the sword, but here in verse 37 the others were "*slain* with the sword." How do you explain this? One group by faith escaped the edge of the sword, and another group by faith were slain with the sword. We have come to a question which is still to me a very difficult subject: Why do the righteous suffer?

I know that if you are in good health today it is easy for you to toss it off and say of others, "Well, God is testing them." However, these people went through all these things *by faith*. They didn't look upon it as if they were being tested. They endured because they did it by faith. They could trust God when the day was dark, when the night was long, the suffering was intense, and when there was no deliverance for them at all.

Others were tortured; others were slain by the sword. It is wonderful to be able to get up and quote Scriptures such as Psalm 34 which says, "The angel of the LORD encampeth round about them that fear him, and delivereth them. . . . The righteous cry, and the LORD heareth, and delivereth them out of all their troubles" (Ps. 34:7, 17). That is wonderful, and God does that. But what about the "others," the others who didn't escape the edge of the sword? What about those who suffered? Stephen could look at the religious rulers of his day and say, "Which of the prophets have not your fathers persecuted?" Prophets never had it easy, my friend. Stephen himself was the first martyr to the Christian faith. Before they stoned him to death, Stephen told them, ". . . they have slain them which shewed before of the coming of the Just One; of whom ye have been now the betrayers and murderers" (Acts 7:52). And when the Lord Jesus called Saul of Tarsus, that brilliant young Pharisee, He said, "For I will shew him how great things he must suffer for my name's sake" (Acts 9:16). The Lord Jesus has also made it very clear to us, ". . . In the world ye shall have tribulation [trouble]: but be of good cheer; I have overcome the world" (John 16:33). Finally, it says of Paul and Barnabas as they went out on one of their missionary journeys that they went "confirming the souls of the disciples, and exhorting them to continue in the faith, and that we must through much tribulation [trouble] enter into the kingdom of God" (Acts 14:22).

My friend, there are a great many people who have demonstrated their faith by winning battles and by being delivered, but there are others, multitudes of them, who have suffered for the faith. Down through the long history of the church there have been the Waldensians, the Albigenses, the Huguenots, the Scottish Covenanters, and many others.

The poetess Martha Snell Nickelson was a member of my church when I was pastor in downtown Los Angeles, and I had the privilege of baptizing her. She suffered a great deal—so much so that we had to baptize her in the bathtub in her own home. She screamed with pain whenever she was touched. This woman went through untold suffering before she passed on into the presence of the Lord. And right now there are literally thousands of heroes of faith lying on beds of pain. It is nice to read about walking out onto the stage of life and gaining a great victory. It is wonderful to be able to report that you have been healed. But what about those who are suffering? What about that unknown missionary out yonder on the field who is suffering for Jesus' sake? What about the minister who suffers?

Let me pass on to you something which I learned recently that deals with this question. The apostle Peter wrote, "Beloved, think it not strange concerning the fiery trial which is to try you, as though some strange thing happened unto you: But rejoice, inasmuch as ye are partakers of Christ's sufferings; that, when his glory shall be revealed, ye may be glad also with exceeding joy" (1 Pet. 4:12–13). Paul made this statement to the Colossians: "Who now rejoice in my sufferings for you, and fill up that which is behind of the afflictions of Christ in my flesh for his body's sake, which is the church" (Col. 1:24). How could Paul fill up the sufferings of Christ? Wasn't Christ's redemption for us complete and perfect? It certainly was, but there are certain sufferings that the Lord Jesus experienced in His life down here which were not redemptive sufferings. His redemptive sufferings took place on the cross—none of us can add anything to that. But you and I, if we are going to stand for Him, are going to have to pay a price for it. Some of us may have to suffer just a little.

Will you forgive me for being personal here? When I had my first bout with cancer, the Lord healed me. I rejoice in His goodness and grace and mercy to me. I have gloried in that, and I promised Him that I would give Him all the glory if He would heal me. I guess I have talked pretty loud about what God has done for me. Then I began to receive hundreds of letters from people—people who have terminal cancer and ask for prayer. I try to be faithful in remembering them in prayer. But frequently I get a letter from a loved one saying that one of these suffering saints has gone to be with the Lord. I especially remember a letter from a woman whose husband had suffered a great deal with cancer and then died. I had to take a second look at this thing. God doesn't always raise up a person from a bed of sickness. While some are healed, there are thousands today who are in the hospitals, thousands lying on beds of pain.

Do you know what the Lord did after healing me of cancer? He gave me gallstone trouble. It took a while for the doctors to even diagnose the problem, and I suffered a great deal. I think the Lord was saying to me, "I'm going to give you a thorn in the flesh so you will keep your mouth shut. You boast too much about the way I moved in your behalf. I want you to remember that I do not always heal everyone. The ones who really suffer are the greatest saints. They are the ones who know what real faith is. You don't know what it is to trust Me in a time like that." The Lord put me flat on my back, and I have never suffered as I suffered at that time. Then the Lord sent me through a battle with hepatitis, and I want to tell you, I thought He was against me. I went to Him and talked this thing over. It was at that time that He spoke to me from this chapter about the "others"— the others who were slain by the sword, the others who suffered—and who did it *by faith*.

My friend, if you can walk up and give your testimony and tell how God has healed you— and I could join you in that—or if you can get up and say how successful you have been in business, I want to remind you that there are multitudes of God's saints today who are *suffering*. They are paying a tremendous price. Do you know how they are doing it? They are doing it *by faith*. They have lots more faith than I have, and I think they are choicer saints than I am. I have been humbled by many a letter from some wonderful saints who are doing a work for God, tucked away in out-of-the-way places and suffering for their faith.

The writer to the Hebrews is speaking of a company of people who lived by faith. He simply calls them "others"—I love that! I don't want you to forget the "others" who are today living by faith and dying by faith. The suffering has ended for many of them, and they have already gone into the presence of the Lord and will never have to die again. This passage means something to me that it didn't before, and I hope it means something new to you also.

And these all, having obtained a good report through faith, received not the promise [Heb. 11:39].

What promise is it that they did not receive? God made many promises, and many of them received the promises that He made to them. But *the* promise is His promise that He will raise them up and that there will be a kingdom established here on this earth. They have not received that promise yet, because God is still today calling out a people to His name, and, as it says here in Hebrews, "bringing many sons home to glory." "And these all, having obtained a good report through faith, received not the promise." We are told here the reason for that—

God having provided some better thing for us, that they without us should not be made perfect [Heb. 11:40].

God has *us* in mind! Wasn't that gracious of Him? "That they without us should not be made perfect." God is very patiently calling people out of this world to His name—and that is the church. And until that church is completed, He is just going to keep calling them out.

We have seen in this chapter the world and the work of faith. I want to say something, and I hope I will not be misunderstood. I do not want to hear the testimony of a person who has been saved a week or a month or three months, although I *do* rejoice in their salvation. But let me illustrate my point: I got a letter the other day which told me about a man who had accepted the Lord Jesus under my ministry in 1943. He had just died, and I understand that a marvelous testimony was given at his funeral as to the wonderful man of faith he was. When I am told by young people how many have accepted Christ through their witnessing, I want to say to them, "Well, it will be wonderful if three years from today or thirty years from today you can come back to me and say that these all lived and died by faith."

Some people feel that faith is something untried, something you really can't be sure of, something that doesn't really rest upon a foundation. My friend, we have had here a company of witnesses. Many of them lived long lives—they lived by faith. They found out that it works.

Again may I say that I no longer give apologetic messages, proving that the Bible is the Word of God. I just give messages from the Bible. I let the Holy Spirit minister the Word to folk. I just preach the Word of God to them and, when I do that, I receive many letters telling how their faith has been strengthened. You do not have to tell me how wonderful faith is. I am an old man now. I've been at this a long time, and you don't have to tell me this thing works. I know it works.

You see, when they made the first airplane and even when the thing flew off in the air, there were those present who said they didn't believe it and they couldn't believe their eyes. Well, there are a lot of folk today who are just as blind as a bat spiritually. They say, "I want it proven to me." My friend, if you are honest and are willing to put away the sin in your life and turn to Jesus Christ and trust Him as your Savior, then I would like to talk to you three years from today, because nobody would need to *prove* anything to you. You would *know* faith works.

There are multitudes around us right now who can say "Amen" to all of this. They already know that faith works. It's operative. It's real. It is something genuine. My friend, have you come out of the realm of make-believe and into the realm of reality? Have you found out what Jesus Christ really can do for you?

CHAPTER 12

THEME: Hope

We are in the practical section of the Epistle to the Hebrews where we see that Christ brings better benefits and duties. Chapter 11 is the *faith* chapter; chapter 12 is the *hope* chapter; and chapter 13 is the *love* chapter.

THE CHRISTIAN RACE

Wherefore seeing we also are compassed about with so great a cloud of witnesses, let us lay aside every weight, and the sin which doth so easily beset us, and let us run with patience the race that is set before us,

Looking unto Jesus the author and finisher of our faith; who for the joy that was set before him endured the cross, despising the shame, and is set down at the right hand of the throne of God [Heb. 12:1-2].

We read in the first part of this epistle of the peril of drifting; that is, of just being hearers, drifting along, and doing nothing at all about God's salvation. Now in the last part of the epistle the writer is speaking to believers of the peril of remaining stationary. He is saying, "Let's get into the race. Let's get moving and not just drift along. We are racers." I would say that one of the greatest dangers in the Christian life is the peril of just remaining stationary, of doing nothing.

When someone becomes lost in the extreme cold of the far north there is grave danger of freezing to death. The first step in that process is to fall asleep. You have to fight sleep, and you must keep moving or you will freeze to death. In a spiritual sense, the danger is the same for us as believers. We have to force ourselves to stay awake and keep moving forward in our relationship with Christ. Otherwise we will just fall asleep.

I like to tell the story about the old cowboy at one of the great camp meetings they used to have years ago in West Texas. A little lady got up and gave her testimony. She said, "The Lord filled up my cup twenty years ago. Nothing has run in, and nothing has run out." The old cowboy sitting in the back spoke out and said, "I bet it's filled with wiggletails by now!" I think that is the condition of a lot of believers today. They can say the Lord has filled their cup, but there's no running over. They've just remained that way. I agree with the cowboy, there are a whole lot of wiggletails in the cups that people are boasting of today.

"Wherefore," we are told, we are to move out, and we are to live by faith. Why? *Wherefore* is another one of these little words that cement the chapter that goes before with the chapter that is coming up—and that is what it does here. "Wherefore seeing we also are compassed about with so great a cloud of witnesses."

For many years I took the position that the "witnesses" are the Old Testament saints, many of whom are listed in chapter 11, and that they are sitting in the grandstand watching us run the race of life today. I personally couldn't think of anything more boring for them than to watch us run the Christian race down here the way some of us are running it! And I no longer believe that that is what this verse means.

When my understanding of this verse changed, it cost me the use of a marvelous illustration, but I will pass it on to you because it is a very sentimental story which does make a point. Years ago a friend invited me to the kickoff luncheon for the Rose Bowl game in Pasadena where I heard a newscaster tell this story. He told of a famous football coach in the East. The coach had a player who was known for two things. The first thing he was noted for was his faithfulness at football practice. He was the first one out and the last one to leave, but he never could make the team—he just wasn't quite good enough. The second thing he was famous for was that his father often visited him on campus and they would be seen walking arm in arm across campus, very much engrossed in conversation. Everyone noticed that and thought it was wonderful. Well, one day the coach got a telegram saying that the boy's father had died. The coach was the one chosen to tell the sad news to the boy, and so he called him in and told him. The boy was greatly shaken, of course, and had to go home for the funeral. But he was present at the next game, sitting there on the bench. Then he came over to the coach and said, "Coach, this is my fourth and last year, and I've never played in a game. I'm wondering if today you could put me in for just a few minutes and let me play." And so the coach put him in because the boy's father had just died. To his amazement, the boy turned out to be a star! The coach had never seen anyone play a better, a more brilliant game, than this boy played—so he never took him out of the game. When the game was over, the coach called the boy off to the side and said to him, "Listen, I've never seen anyone play like you played today, but up to today you were the lousiest football player I've ever seen. I want an explanation." And the boy said, "Well, coach, you see, my dad was blind, and this is the first day that he ever saw me play football."

If this Scripture means that the Old Testament saints who have gone before are sitting in the grandstand watching us run the race, then that story would be a good illustration. However, that interpretation is not accurate at all. The witnesses are not sitting in the grandstand; they are the ones who have already run the race down here. They are the ones who were down on the racetrack as you and I sat in the grandstand watching them run the race of life in chapter 11. And they ran it by faith. Those who would be called a howling success by the world ran the race by faith. And those who suffered what the world would call miserable defeat, also ran the race by faith. Although they suffered and were slain by the sword, they were just as great heroes. They all witnessed to us. We watched them as we went through chapter 11, and there were many more in the Old Testament, as the writer told us that time would fail him to tell of all of them. They witnessed to us, and encouraged us to run by faith and to live by faith.

Therefore the Christian life is here likened to a Greek race. Christ is the way to God, and along the way the Christian as a soldier is to stand firm, as a believer is to walk, but as an athlete, he is to run the race. And one day we are going to *fly*, my friend—that will be at the Rapture. We are going to do a little space travel to the New Jerusalem.

"Wherefore seeing we also are compassed about with so great a cloud of witnesses, let us lay aside every weight, and the sin which doth so easily beset us, and let us run with patience the race that is set before us." We have here another "let us" salad. Now this is not a danger signal that is put up here at all, but it is a challenge to us. Let us now get out of the grandstand; let us get down on the racecourse of life, and let us do whatever God has called us to do wherever He has called us to live and move and have our being. Let us run the Christian race, and let us move out for God. That is the whole thought here.

We are challenged to run with patience, having laid aside every weight and the sin which doth so easily beset us. God has saved us from sin. He has brought us into the heavens, actually, into the holy place, and He has made us to sit in heavenly places. He's given to us His Holy Spirit. But in spite of all that He has provided, the average Christian falls down and stumbles and wanders like a man lost in the dark. What is wrong with the Christian life as it is being lived at the present time? I will come back to the same string which I play on all the time, because I think this is the answer: the problem is that Christians do not go on with God. They get saved, give a testimony of their salvation, and that's all they ever have. They never maintain a serious study of the Word of God, which is essential to growth. They are like the little girl who fell out of bed one night. When the little girl began to cry, her mother rushed in and said, "Honey, how come you fell out of bed?" The little girl replied, "I think I stayed too close to the place where I got in." That is the problem of the Christian today. We stumble and falter and fail because we are staying too close to the place where we got in. We need to go on—this is a race, you see.

The Christian life is a race—win or lose—and it is the only race where everybody can win. Paul wrote, "Know ye not that they which run in a race run all . . ."—they *all* run to receive a prize. He went on to say, "I therefore so run, not as uncertainly . . ." (1 Cor. 9:24, 26). And again, he rebuked some of his followers saying, "Ye did run well; who did hinder you . . .?" (Gal. 5:7).

We are encouraged by these witnesses. They are not spectators; they are testifying to us. They are in the cheering section, encouraging us to run the Christian life. Abraham is saying to you and me, "Move out by faith." Moses is saying to you and me, "Move out by faith." Daniel is saying to you and me, "Move out by faith."

Now there are two conditions to be met: "Lay aside every weight, and the sin which doth so easily beset us." What does he mean by "lay aside every weight"? Weights are highly unnecessary in a race; in fact, they are a hindrance. We ought not to be using weights.

I remember years ago when Gil Dodds, a very fine Christian, was a famous runner in this country. Some of us went out to the track at the University of Southern California, to watch him run. He ran around the track a couple of times with tennis shoes on. Then he stopped and changed into some other shoes. One of the fellows there asked why he needed to change shoes. He took one of the tennis shoes and one of the lighter pair of shoes and tossed them both to the man who had asked the question. Believe me, there was not much difference in the weight of the shoes, but just enough, he said, to cause him to lose the race.

In the Christian life there are a lot of things that are not wrong in and of themselves, but Christians should not be carrying those weights around. Why? Because you won't *win* the race. I'm going to use an illustration, but please don't think I am picking on this one particular thing, because I am not. You must determine for yourself what you can do as a child of God, and I must determine that for myself. But one young lady went to her pastor and asked, "Is it all right to dance?" Her pastor replied, "Sure it is, if you don't want to win." The point is that it is not a question of right and wrong for a Christian in his conduct—it is taken for granted that you are going to do what is right. The question is: Will it hurt my testimony? Will this keep me from winning the race? Will this be a weight in my life? There are many Christians today who are carrying around a weight they ought not to be carrying around. Don't ask me to argue with you about whether dancing is wrong. I won't argue about any of those things which separationists say you cannot do if you are a Christian. I don't say you can't do it. All I'm saying is: Are you in a race? Do you want to win? Are you looking to Jesus? That becomes the important thing.

"And the sin which doth so easily beset us." What is *the* sin"? This is not just sin in general; it is *the* sin. Again, we are cast back into the previous chapter by the *wherefore* which opened this chapter. What was the great sin in the last chapter? It was unbelief. Unbelief is *the* sin, and there is nothing which will hold you back as unbelief will. It is just like trying to run a race with the weight of a sack of wheat on your shoulder and your feet stuck inside an empty sack! You'll never be able to do it, and you cannot do it in the Christian life either. Unbelief is what holds many of us back, and if I may make a personal confession, I am confident that it has held me back more than anything else in my Christian life.

BELIEVERS ARE NOW IN CONTEST AND CONFLICT

For consider him that endured such contradiction of sinners against himself, lest ye be wearied and faint in your minds [Heb. 12:3].

The words *patience* (in v. 1) and *endured* (in v. 2) are from the same root. Trouble generally produces patience and endurance.

These Hebrew believers had come out of a religion that had a tremendous ritual and a great temple. The temple of Herod, although it was not completed even at the time it was destroyed in A.D. 70, was a thing of beauty and actually awe inspiring. Also there was a great ritual that went with it. It had been a God-given religion at the beginning, but it had been debauched and prostituted by the time this Hebrew epistle was written. Nevertheless, as far as religion was concerned, they had it. Now these believers had given up all of that; they no longer were going through all that religious ritual. They had now come to consider Him, that is, Christ, and He was everything. He was the temple. He was the ritual. He was Christianity. He was all of it. There was this simplicity in Christ, and the writer now calls them to consider Him.

They are to know what He endured when He was down here and how He learned patience. We are told in the beginning of this epistle, in the section which presented His humanity, that He learned a great many things down here although He was and is God. In the flesh He learned something which God had to experience by taking on our humanity and suffering for us. He endured and He learned patience.

"Lest ye be wearied and faint in your minds." May I say this to you very candidly: unless you stay close to the Word of God where the Holy Spirit can take the things of Christ and make them real to you, you are going to get weary of the Christian life, and you are going to faint in your minds. This is the reason there are so many discouraged Christians around today. My friend, if you come to the Word of God and get close to Jesus Christ, you are going to be encouraged. You will not grow weary of this life down here. Oh, my friend, *we* are living in the greatest days that have ever been!

Ye have not yet resisted unto blood, striving against sin [Heb. 12:4].

This simply indicates that at this time the temple was not yet destroyed. The persecution from the Gentiles of the Roman Empire which was going to come had not yet broken upon these believers. "Ye have not yet resisted unto blood."

He is saying to them, "Although you are having a very difficult time and you are having your problems and troubles, the only cure for your weakness, your weariness, your faltering, your failing, your stumbling, and your discouragement is to consider Him. Consider Christ."

Turn your eyes upon Jesus,
Look full in His wonderful face;
And the things of earth will grow strangely dim
In the light of His glory and grace.
　　　" Turn Your Eyes Upon Jesus"
　　　　—Helen H. Lemmel

And ye have forgotten the exhortation which speaketh unto you as unto children, My son, despise not thou the chastening of the Lord, nor faint when thou art rebuked of him [Heb. 12:5].

The writer is quoting here from Proverbs 3:11–12—"My son, despise not the chastening of the LORD; neither be weary of his correction: For whom the LORD loveth he correcteth; even as a father the son in whom he delighteth."

Their only resource was Christ—not a temple, or a ritual, or a religion. They were almost outcasts at this time, and the writer is telling them not to forget this exhortation from God to His children.

The word *children* is used in the Authorized Version, but in the Greek *son* and *sons* are used six times in verse 5–8. The Greek word for "son" is *huios*, and it means "full-grown son." Now there are a great many saints today who do not think they need to be disciplined, but discipline is for mature saints, people who have been walking with the Lord for a long time. There was a time when I had come to the place where I thought I didn't need to be disciplined anymore. I thought I had come a long ways. But the Lord put me flat on my back physically to let me know that there was some more disciplining to be done.

The word *chastening* means something a little different from what we think today. We think that chastening is punishment. The Greek word is *paideuō*, and it means "child training or discipline." You see, the Lord disciplines His own children.

For whom the Lord loveth he chasteneth, and scourgeth every son whom he receiveth.

If ye endure chastening, God dealeth with you as with sons; for what son is he whom the father chasteneth not?

But if ye be without chastisement, whereof all are partakers, then are ye bastards, and not sons [Heb. 12:6–8].

The question is sometimes asked, and it is a very pertinent question: Why do the righteous suffer? When illness confined me to my home and I spent most of my time flat on my back for about a month, I had a great deal of time to study, and I want to pass on to you what the Lord has shown me through my own experience.

Let's put this down as an axiom of Scripture: God's children *do* suffer. The Bible doesn't argue about that—the Bible just says that it is true. "Many are the afflictions of the righteous: but the LORD delivereth him out of them all" (Ps. 34:19). In the Book of Job we read, "Yet man is born unto trouble, as the sparks fly upward" (Job 5:7). The Lord Jesus said, ". . . In the world ye shall have tribulation: but be of good cheer; I have overcome the world" (John 16:33). And even Paul said, "Yea, and all that will live godly in Christ Jesus shall suffer persecution" (2 Tim. 3:12).

Why do God's people suffer? There is no pat answer to that. No one little verse of Scripture answers it. I have gone through the Scriptures and listed seven reasons why God's children suffer. I would like to share them with you:

1. The first reason that we suffer as God's children (and even as His mature sons) is because of our own *stupidity* and our own sin.

First Peter 2:20 reads, "For what glory is it, if, when ye be buffeted for your faults, ye shall take it patiently. . . ." The word *faults* refers to a sin where you missed the mark—you just didn't quite make it. "For what glory is it, if . . . ye shall take it patiently?" Peter says there is no value in the suffering which was caused by our own foolishness.

How many of you years ago invested some of your savings in a wildcat oil well in Texas? I was a pastor in Texas for many years, and I can tell you about a whole lot of folk who own dry oil wells. I know of one man in particular whose family is practically in poverty today because of such an investment. He has suffered because he played the fool.

I know another man who came to me in Los Angeles, and said, "Dr. McGee, I have certainly played the fool. My wife and I haven't been getting along too well recently. I had to work late one evening and called my wife and told her so. There is a very attractive woman in my office who has been very sympathetic toward me, and she had to work late also. All of a sudden it occurred to me that it would be nice to have dinner together. We didn't do anything but go out to dinner, and it was a friendly sort of dinner. But the wrong person was in that restaurant and saw us. He called my wife and told her. It never went any further than that, but it could have turned into a really bad thing. I played the fool." You know, a lot of saints suffer because of stupidity.

2. The second reason we suffer is for *taking a stand* for truth and righteousness. I can guarantee that if you take a stand for truth and righteousness, you are going to suffer. How many men and women could testify to that? Peter says, "But and if ye suffer for righteousness' sake, happy are ye: and be not afraid of their terror, neither be troubled" (1 Pet. 3:14). Many people deliberately take a stand for God, and they have suffered for it.

However, we can be foolish and misguided in our thinking concerning this. One man came to me and told me that where he worked everybody was his enemy because he had stood up for God. Well, another Christian man who was an official in that same concern told me that this man was trying to lecture everybody—even during work hours! He was making an absolute nuisance of himself by attempting to witness to people while they were busy on their jobs. You see, he wasn't really suffering because he took a stand for truth and righteousness.

3. We suffer for *sin* in our lives. Paul says, "For if we would judge ourselves, we should

not be judged" (1 Cor. 11:31). However, if we are God's children and refuse to deal with the sin in our lives, *God* will deal with it. He will judge us.

4. The fourth reason we suffer is for our *past sins.* "Be not deceived; God is not mocked: for whatsoever a man soweth, that shall he also reap" (Gal. 6:7). One time when I was a pastor in Nashville, Tennessee, we had Mel Trotter, the great evangelist and converted drunkard, for a series of meetings. One night after the service we all went to a place called Candyland. The rest of us got big sodas or malts, but he got a little glass of soda water. The others began to kid him about it, and he made this statement, "When the Lord gave me a new heart, He didn't give me a new stomach." Liquor had ruined his stomach, and he was still suffering because of that.

5. The fifth reason God's children suffer is for some lofty *purpose of God* which He does not always reveal to the believer. We see this in the Book of Job. Job suffered because he was demonstrating to Satan and the demon world and to the angels of heaven that he was not a timeserver, that every man does not have his price and that he loved God for Himself alone. I hope I never have to suffer as Job did.

6. The sixth reason Christians suffer is for their *faith,* as we saw in chapter 11 of this epistle. Some demonstrated their faith, and great victories were won. Some were delivered by the sword; some were slain by the sword. I think of the French Huguenots who went into battle, knowing they would all be slain. Yet they went into battle saying, "If God be for us, who can be against us?" You see, they suffered for their faith.

7. The seventh and last reason God's children suffer is for *discipline.* That is what we have here in verse 6: "For whom the Lord loveth he chasteneth, and scourgeth every son whom he receiveth." This means child training or discipline, not punishment. Punishment is to uphold the law. A judge punishes, but a father chastens and he does it in love. God uses chastening to demonstrate His love for us. And the writer makes it very clear that you are an illegitimate child if you are not chastened by the Lord, my friend. Many people say, "Oh, why did God let this happen to me? I must not be a Christian." The fact is that your suffering is the proof that you are a child of God.

I think that if you are an intelligent Christian, when you are in trouble and do not know why, you will go to the Lord and talk to Him about it. I am sure that He will get the message to you and let you know why you are in trouble. The reason may not be that He is judging you. God does judge us, and that is punishment, but He is also our loving, heavenly Father who disciplines His children.

When I was a boy I, with several other boys at school, got into trouble. My dad came down to the school where there were several hundred children, but when he walked across that schoolyard, do you know who he was after? He was after *his* son, and he took *his* son home and disciplined him. He didn't discipline those hundreds of other children—because they weren't his. He disciplined only his boy, the boy whom he loved. My dad died when I was fourteen, and now I have a heavenly Father who does the same thing— He disciplines me in love.

Furthermore we have had fathers of our flesh which corrected us, and we gave them reverence: shall we not much rather be in subjection unto the Father of spirits, and live? [Heb. 12:9].

Believe me, I listened to my dad. I hadn't heard about the new psychology in which you don't pay any attention to your parents, and your parents aren't supposed to discipline you. My dad disciplined, and I listened to him. The writer says that if we listen to our earthly parents, "shall we not much rather be in subjection unto the Father of spirits, and live?" Whether or not you listen to your earthly father, you had better listen to your heavenly Father.

The writer to the Hebrews goes on to make a suggestion. He says, "Be in subjection to the father of spirits, *and live.*" Does he mean live it up? I think he means to live a Christian life in all its fullness—that's the positive side. But I think there is also a negative aspect, which is that the heavenly Father disciplines in very severe ways sometimes, and there is a sin unto death. The sin unto death is a sin that a child of God can commit, and sometimes the heavenly Father will take a disobedient child out of this world because he is disgracing Him. The writer is saying that you had better listen to your heavenly Father because He is disciplining you in love, but if you persist in going on in sin, He may take you home.

For they verily for a few days chastened us after their own pleasure; but he for our profit, that we might be partakers of his holiness [Heb. 12:10].

Sometimes I think my earthly dad got a little angry with me and vented his anger on me—

but even then he did it for my profit, I'm sure. My heavenly Father disciplines me for my profit also—there is no doubt about that!

"That we might be partakers of his holiness." I believe that there is no way you can become a full-grown child of God living in fellowship with Him (that is the main thought behind "holiness") *except* through the discipline of God.

> **Now no chastening for the present seemeth to be joyous, but grievous: nevertheless afterward it yieldeth the peaceable fruit of righteousness unto them which are exercised thereby [Heb. 12:11].**

This is like the boy whose father said to him before he whipped him, "Son, this is going to hurt me more than it hurts you." The boy said, "Yes, Dad, but not in the same place." God chastens His children. He does not get any particular joy out of it, but He does it because you and I need it. Not only does chastening not *seem* to be joyous, it *isn't* joyous, but grievous—that is our experience.

Although no chastening at the time is fun, "afterward it yieldeth the peaceable fruit of righteousness unto them which are exercised thereby." God does not discipline you without purpose.

I am reminded of the story of the man who lived in a home for the mentally ill. There was a visitor one day who saw the man beating himself on the head with a baseball bat. The visitor went up to him and said, "Why in the world are you hitting yourself on the head with the baseball bat?" The man replied, "It feels so *good* when I quit!" God does not discipline you just to make you feel good when it is over. He doesn't give you ill health just so you will appreciate good health when it returns. There is always a purpose in the discipline of God for you.

Now what is your reaction when God disciplines you? There are four reactions we can have to God's discipline that are mentioned in this chapter. I want us to take a look at each of them:

1. "And ye have forgotten the exhortation which speaketh unto you as unto children, My son, *despise* not thou the chastening of the Lord . . ." (v. 5). The first reaction is that you can despise the chastening. You can treat it lightly and accept no message from it at all. You simply become a fatalist and say, "Well, I'm having trouble. Everybody has trouble." You do not recognize the fact that your heavenly Father is disciplining you, and you do not get His message in it at all.

2. ". . . nor *faint* when thou art rebuked of him" (v. 5). There are those who respond in this way (I would call it the crybaby reaction): They begin to cry and say, "Why did this happen to me? It is not worth living a Christian life. I have served the Lord, and now He's letting this happen to me." In other words, they just faint away. Many saints take that attitude. However, when I was going through a serious illness several years ago, I received several thousand letters from people all over this country and throughout the world. Many of those people were suffering much more than I, and their attitude made me feel ashamed of myself. They had been on beds of pain for months—several of them for *years*— and they wrote the sweetest letters I have ever read. Those letters came from folk who had real victory. We hear of meetings where people are healed and where they talk of great victories. Well, to be very frank with you, if you want to know where the great victories are being won today, go to the hospitals or visit some dear shut-in saints who have been in bed for months, and listen to them talk. You can faint, but these saints don't faint because the Lord is strengthening them.

3. "If ye *endure* chastening . . ." (v. 7). This is a dangerous response to have because it is so close to that which is true, but this is the response of the super-duper pious saints. To me they are like the Indian fakir who crawls up on a board filled with nails and lies down. He doesn't have to lie down there, but he does it. There are a lot of saints who accept the discipline of the Lord in a passive way: "Oh, this is of the Lord, and I will endure it." God never asks you to take that pessimistic, super pious attitude. If you are in trouble, why don't you go and ask Him, "Lord, why did You send this to me? There is a lesson here, and I want to learn it." Don't accept it in a passive manner, simply enduring it but complaining all the time.

4. "Now no chastening for the present seemeth to be joyous, but grievous: nevertheless afterward it yieldeth the peaceable fruit of righteousness unto them which are *exercised* thereby" (v. 11). Have you ever done sitting-up exercises? Once I became acquainted with a man who jogged around the golf course where I played golf. He was inclined to be a little chubby, so he exercised in order to lose weight. Are you exercised when you get into trouble? When you have to suffer? When an enemy comes across your pathway? Stop and

ask God, "Why in the world did You let that fellow come across my pathway?" You know, God does it for a purpose. God does all these things for a purpose, and we need to be exercised by them. The apostle Paul said, "But I keep under my body, and bring it into subjection: lest that by any means, when I have preached to others, I myself should be a castaway" (1 Cor. 9:27). Paul exercised himself—that is, he didn't give in to the desires of his body—because he did not want to come before God's presence some day and be disapproved. My friend, whoever you are or wherever you are, it is time to take your sitting-up exercises.

I would like to give this word of personal testimony. A number of years ago when I had cancer, my first question to the Lord was, "Why?" It didn't take me long to discover that it was my heavenly Father punishing me—I understood that. I was a hardheaded child of God, but I got things squared away with Him. He healed me of the cancer and richly blessed the growth of our radio broadcast ministry. Then suddenly I was knocked down with another illness. The doctor told me to stay on my back, and I did so for three weeks or more. I learned something during that time which I would like to pass on to you. God wasn't judging me this time, because I've learned to keep my account short with Him. I get things straightened out with Him about every day. I do fail Him—I guess I'm still as hardheaded as I ever was—but I go to Him and confess my sin. I believe I am in the will of God. So I went to Him that second time and cried, "Lord, why in the world did You let this happen to me? I want to go on with the radio ministry." He put me flat on my back, and He said, "You are My son, and I am your Father. There are a lot of things you haven't learned yet. You may have the notion that your radio ministry is essential and that I can't get along without you, but how did I get along without you before you got here? You are going to lie here and learn something. I am your Father, and you need to learn to endure for Me. You do not know how to rest, and you do not know how to wait on Me." It took me a while, but I finally said to Him, "All right, Father, if You want me to lie here, I'll lie here. I want to learn the lesson You have for me."

We need to be exercised by the Lord's discipline, and then we will not find ourselves in the position described in the following verse—

Wherefore lift up the hands which hang down, and the feeble knees [Heb. 12:12].

Don't go through life as a Christian, complaining all the time. I used to have a friend who, when I asked how he felt, always told me how he felt—he took fifteen minutes to tell me how he felt, and he never felt good. Therefore I quit asking how he felt. He was going around all the time with his hands hanging down and with feeble knees. May I say to you, someone is watching you. How do you endure the trouble that comes from God? Do you endure it by being exercised by it? Do you say to yourself, *It is my Father, and He is chastening me. There is a purpose in it and a lesson I want to learn.* We should start our sitting-up exercises: "One, two, three. One, two, three. Lord, I'd like to know why I am suffering this way."

And make straight paths for your feet, lest that which is lame be turned out of the way; but let it rather be healed [Heb. 12:13].

I'll be very honest with you and admit that I have never clearly understood what the writer meant when he said, "Make straight paths for your feet." Are we to walk the straight path so that the weak saints might follow in our footsteps? Or, are we to walk the straight path so that we don't get in the habit of limping through life? There are a lot of lamebrained Christians today who complain and criticize and are not witnesses for God at all—and yet they appear very super pious.

Follow peace with all men, and holiness, without which no man shall see the Lord [Heb. 12:14].

Be encouraged and be at peace with all men; that is, with all who will let you be at peace with them. There are some people who just won't be at peace. Follow peace with all men—with all Christian men. We should make this one big cross-country race where there are a lot of us running the Christian life together.

"And holiness, without which no man shall see the Lord." If that means that I have to produce holiness, then I am going to give up, because I haven't any holiness. But, oh, the peace that I have which came through the blood of Christ! "Being justified by faith, we have peace with God through our Lord Jesus Christ" (Rom. 5:1). If I have any holiness, it is because Christ has been made unto me righteousness—*He* is my righteousness. If I get into the presence of God it will be because Christ died for me. That is encouraging, my friend. It makes me want to get out and run the Christian race.

DANGER SIGNAL:
THE PERIL OF DENYING

Looking diligently lest any man fail of the grace of God; lest any root of bitterness springing up trouble you, and thereby many be defiled [Heb. 12:15].

"Looking diligently" has in it the thought of *direction*. And what is that direction? "Looking unto Jesus the author and finisher of our faith . . ." (Heb. 12:2).

"Lest any man fail of the grace of God." The word here for "fail" is not apostasy—this is not speaking of the danger of apostatizing. It means simply to fall back. In other words, a believer must keep his eyes on the Lord Jesus, not on men. If he doesn't keep his eyes on Him, he is apt to get to the place where he does not avail himself of the grace of God.

Now God has a tremendous reservoir of grace, and He wants to lavish it upon His children. He is prepared to do that, and He is able to do that. Christ paid the penalty for our sins, and God is rich in mercy, rich in grace, and He wants to expend it upon us. The problem is that many of us do not avail ourselves of His grace. But you see, we are talking here about reality—something that you can go to God for and lay hold of it. That is the glory of it all, and that is the message of this epistle. Have you gone to Him today, my Christian friend? Have you talked to Him—yes, reverently, but really talked to Him like He is your Father? Tell Him about yourself. Tell Him you need grace. We all need grace and it is available, but we've got to apply for it. We need to ask Him for it. Do not fail of the grace of God.

"Lest any root of bitterness springing up trouble you, and thereby many be defiled." One critical, ugly saint in a church can stir up more trouble than you can possibly imagine, just like one rotten apple in a barrel spoils all the others. We need to ask God for grace to endure whatever we are going through, and not become bitter toward any one or toward any circumstances.

Lest there be any fornicator, or profane person, as Esau, who for one morsel of meat sold his birthright [Heb. 12:16].

Fornication here is spiritual fornication. There is the danger of turning from God to the things of the flesh, and it could be most anything of the flesh. As far as Esau was concerned, it was the selling of his birthright, a spiritual birthright that entailed so much. It meant that Esau would be in the line that led to the Messiah, and it meant that he should be the priest of the family of Abraham. But he didn't care for it; he was not interested in spiritual blessings.

"Profane person" does not mean that Esau cursed a great deal. It has no reference to that at all. The word *profane* comes from two Latin words: *pro*, meaning either "before" or "against," and *fanum*, meaning "temple." Therefore, it means against the temple or against God. It means that Esau was just a godless fellow. He saw no need of any recognition of God, or of any relationship to Him, or of any responsibility toward Him. So he despised his birthright and counted it as something of no value. He was even willing to trade it in for a bowl of food! There is many a man who has sold his soul. Some have sold it for liquor, some for drugs, some for sex, and some for dishonesty. There is a danger for the child of God to turn from God to the things of the flesh. We will either go forward in our relationship with Christ or fall back—we won't stay in the same place.

For ye know how that afterward, when he would have inherited the blessing, he was rejected: for he found no place of repentance, though he sought it carefully with tears [Heb. 12:17].

Few passages have been as misunderstood as has this passage of Scripture. It gives the impression that poor Esau wanted to repent and God wouldn't accept his repentance. However, the writer is saying something altogether different from that. Esau despised his birthright and then found out later that there was also an inheritance attached to it—he would inherit twice as much as any other son of Isaac. The point is that Esau was interested in that which was physical. When it says, "he sought it carefully with tears," it means that he did a great deal of boohooing. He was like the thief who began to weep when he was caught and to say he was sorry. But he wasn't sorry he was a thief; he was sorry that he'd been caught. Likewise, Esau was not repenting because he wanted to turn to God and receive His spiritual blessing. He repented because he had missed out on something material. He was actually against God.

For ye are not come unto the mount that might be touched, and that burned with fire, nor unto blackness, and darkness, and tempest,

And the sound of a trumpet, and the voice of words; which voice they that

heard entreated that the word should not be spoken to them any more:

(For they could not endure that which was commanded, And if so much as a beast touch the mountain, it shall be stoned, or thrust through with a dart:

And so terrible was the sight, that Moses said, I exceedingly fear and quake:) [Heb. 12:18–21].

The writer is speaking here of the giving of the Law to Moses on top of Mount Sinai, and he is speaking of the old covenant. The people to whom he was writing were Hebrews who had turned to Christ. We need to keep that in mind all the time in this epistle. We must remember that the early church—the three thousand who were saved on the Day of Pentecost—were not Gentiles but were Jews. Until Paul and Barnabas and the other missionaries began to move out, the early church for those first few years was 100 percent Jewish.

Now these Jews in Jerusalem who had turned to Christ find themselves at a great loss. They had been accustomed to going to the temple. They had been accustomed to hearing the Mosaic Law read. But now they are shut away from the Law, and now they are shut out from the temple. They are no longer a part of the system at all, and they feel very much on the outside. Therefore, I think the writer is saying to them, "You come now to a mount that is different from Mount Sinai, and you do not want to go back to that." Mount Sinai was the place where the Law was given and three thousand people were slain (see Exod. 32), but three thousand people were *saved* on the Day of Pentecost. There was death at the giving of the Law; there was new life when the gospel was preached on the Day of Pentecost. The giving of the Law was by no means a delightful experience. There was thunder and lightning, earthquake and storm, blazing fire and the blast of a trumpet that grew louder and louder and louder. It was a terrifying experience—so much so that the people said to Moses, "Speak thou with us, and we will hear: but let not God speak with us, lest we die" (Exod. 20:19). Now the writer to the Hebrews says, "You don't want to go back to that system. We have left all that behind us."

When I was a pastor in Nashville, Tennessee, there was a lady in my church who was a very lovely person, but I always felt that she was one of those Paul spoke of when he said, ". . . Silly women laden with sins, led away with divers lusts, Ever learning, and never able to come to the knowledge of the truth" (2 Tim. 3:6–7). She was a woman who was sort of a social hanger-on. She belonged to a very wealthy family, went to their cocktail parties, and engaged in their sins, but she still wanted to go to the Bible classes. She attended my church but never became a member. And she pretended to be quite a Bible student. She said to me one day after I had preached a sermon about the Law, "Dr. McGee, the giving of the Law is so beautiful, isn't it?" I had to say to that dear lady, "The giving of the Law is *not* beautiful. I think it is one of the most frightening scenes in the Bible! And it was a law that these people were told would never be able to save them. God gave them a sacrificial system whereby they could bring a sacrifice. A little animal had to die because the Law couldn't save them. The Law actually condemned them."

These Hebrew Christians had been accustomed to going to the temple and going through that ritual. Now there was nothing for them to go to, no ceremony, and no sacrifice to bring. So the writer tells them that they really do have something—

But ye are come unto mount Sion, and unto the city of the living God, the heavenly Jerusalem, and to an innumerable company of angels [Heb. 12:22].

Remember that he is speaking to Hebrews. Mount Zion was David's place in Jerusalem. His palace was located there, and he was buried up there. Zion was David's favorite spot. Many of the Jewish believers had still been going up to the feast in Jerusalem, but the persecution had broken out, and Christians had been driven out of Jerusalem. So he assures them they have a Jerusalem in heaven. Mount Zion is the heavenly city, the eternal city of the living God. The Book of Revelation calls it the New Jerusalem. I cannot give you the number or the street name, but my future address is in the New Jerusalem. This is what we have come to by God's grace. We have something far better in Christ than the Jews ever had under the Law.

"And to an innumerable company of angels." I have made the statement—and I will stick to it—that angel ministry is not connected with the church. But we are going into the New Jerusalem some day, and the Book of Revelation shows us a huge worship scene there, a great scene which John saw and tells us about. John said in effect, "There is a company of created intelligences there, ten thousand times ten thousand of them." And then he looked around and said, "My, I didn't see that other crowd out there—there are more than any man can number." They are God's created intelligences called angels.

I have never seen an angel, but I've often wondered about them. I am going to come some day to the New Jerusalem and join with you in that great worship of the Lamb, and all these created intelligences will be there. One thing I want to do is just to talk to some of them. Wouldn't you like to talk to them? I've never had the privilege. Whenever I meet someone who tells me they have had a dream or a vision and an angel spoke to them, I tell them they ought to think back to what they had for supper the night before—that may explain the presence of an angel! You haven't seen an angel my friend; you may think you have, but you haven't. Yet the time will come when we will go to the place where they are.

To the general assembly and church of the firstborn, which are written in heaven, and to God the Judge of all, and to the spirits of just men made perfect [Heb. 12:23].

"The firstborn" does not refer to Christ here, although He is called that elsewhere in Scripture. The writer is speaking of the ones who have been born again. They are the only ones who are going to be there. This is the church of firstborn ones, those who at the Rapture will be caught up to this place.

Their names "which are written in heaven, and to God the Judge of all." I thank God that when I get into the presence of "the Judge of all," there is one who will already have paid the penalty for my sins, and my record will be clear.

"And to the spirits of just men made perfect." "Perfect" does not mean complete or perfect as you and I think of it. It refers to Old Testament saints whose salvation has been made complete now that Christ has died as the Lamb of God who took away the sin of the world.

And to Jesus the mediator of the new covenant, and to the blood of sprinkling, that speaketh better things than that of Abel [Heb. 12:24].

"And to Jesus"—then we are going to be brought into the presence of Jesus.

"The mediator of the new covenant." He is the mediator of the *New* Covenant—He is not going to thunder from Mount Sinai. Even when He was here, He sat down on a mountain and gave the law for His kingdom. I think it is going to be lots sweeter when we come into His presence some day and see Him as the mediator of the New Covenant.

"And to the blood of sprinkling, that speaketh better things than that of Abel." Abel's blood cried for vengeance, but the blood of Christ speaks of salvation. This is wonderful.

Back in verse 3 we read, "Consider him that endured such contradiction of sinners against himself. . . ." The writer is trying to get these Hebrew Christians to take their eyes off the temple, off a bloody sacrifice, off a ritual, and on to the person of Christ. Today we need to get our eyes off a church, off religion, off an organization, and off a man. No man down here should be the one to whom we are looking. Look to Jesus—look only to Him. The temple with all its splendor and ritual was passing away and was to be destroyed—now they are under a new economy.

Consider Him. Look to Jesus. Someone has said that this is the simplicity of our faith, and I agree with that, but there is a danger of oversimplification under the evangelistic methods which are being used today. I have a little book which I have entitled *Faith Plus Nothing Equals Salvation* because I believe this is true. Faith alone can save. However, today we have an epidemic of easy believism. Many folk have made salvation a simple mathematical equation: If you can say yes to this, yes to that, and yes to a half-dozen questions, then you are a Christian. This type of approach leaves no room for the work of the Holy Spirit and for the conviction of sin. It just means a nodding assent, a passing acquaintance with Jesus. It does not mean that you are born again.

There is a word that is being overworked today: *commit* your life to Christ. What kind of life do you have to commit to Christ? If you are coming to Christ as a sinner, you don't have any *life*—you are dead in trespasses and sins. The Lord Jesus is the one who said, "I have come that you might have life." *You* do not commit a life, but He committed *His life* for you and He died for you. You are dead in trespasses and sins, and He has life to offer to you: "I am come that they might have life, and that they might have it more abundantly" (John 10:10).

We also hear people say, "Give your heart to Jesus." Well, my friend, what do you think He wants with that dirty, old heart? Read the list of things He said come out of the heart (see Matt. 15:19). They are the dirtiest things that

I know. He didn't ask you to give your heart to Him. He says, "I want to give you a *new* heart and a new life." We need today the conviction of sin, to know that we are sinners. We have made salvation a very jolly affair. An evangelistic crusade today is just too ducky; it's so sweet, and it's so lovely. I don't see people come weeping under conviction of sin.

See that ye refuse not him that speaketh. For if they escaped not who refused him that spake on earth, much more shall not we escape, if we turn away from him that speaketh from heaven [Heb. 12:25].

"See that ye refuse not him that speaketh." Since the Lord Jesus Christ is so wonderful and since His words are very important, it pays you to give attention to Him—it will be very profitable to you.

"For if they escaped not who refused him that spake on earth, much more shall not we escape, if we turn away from him that speaketh from heaven." If you want to see what happened to a people under the Law, go to the nation of Israel even today. They are not dwelling in peace. Theirs has been a really sad story for over nineteen hundred years. Why? Because they refused to hear Him. They also refused to hear the Law, and for that God judged them. It is a serious business not to listen to this warning. Jesus said, "If any man will do his will, he shall know of the doctrine, whether it be of God, or whether I speak of myself" (John 7:17). If you do His will you will find out whether it is true or not, but if you refuse—how will you escape if you neglect so great a salvation?

Whose voice then shook the earth: but now he hath promised, saying, Yet once more I shake not the earth only, but also heaven [Heb. 12:26].

At the giving of the Law there was an earthquake, and at the crucifixion of Christ there was an earthquake. Now God is saying that the day is coming when He is going to shake everything. When I look at the tall buildings in downtown Los Angeles, I am tempted to say to them, "I want to get a good look at you today because you may not be here tomorrow." God says He is going to shake the earth and heaven itself. Do you know why He is going to do that? God is going to shake everything to let all His created universe know that there are some things which are unshakeable, and one of those things is living faith in Jesus Christ. He is the Rock that we rest upon, and

He cannot be shaken. Do you want a secure place today? He is the place to go. He is the air raid shelter that is safe today. Men want to make the world safe, but no man can make this world safe, nor can any world organization such as the United Nations make it safe. It is not even safe for me to walk at night down the street on which I live. However, God is going to make it safe some day, and in order to do that, He is first going to shake everything.

And this word, Yet once more, signifieth the removing of those things that are shaken, as of things that are made, that those things which cannot be shaken may remain [Heb. 12:27].

In other words, we had better be very careful that we build our lives on the right foundation. Are we building on sinking sand? Or are we building upon the Rock which is Christ?

"That those things which cannot be shaken may remain." God will remain. His word will remain, and the eternal kingdom to which believers belong will remain.

Wherefore we receiving a kingdom which cannot be moved, let us have grace, whereby we may serve God acceptably with reverence and godly fear [Heb. 12:28].

As believers we are moving toward a heavenly kingdom, but as we move toward the heavenly kingdom we need to recognize that we should be serving God down here. But how are we to serve Him? Well, we are to serve Him "acceptably." How do we serve Him acceptably? "With reverence and godly fear." My friend, Christianity is not playing church, and it is not assuming a pious attitude. It is a living, vital, and real relationship with Jesus Christ that transforms your life and anchors you in the Word of God.

For our God is a consuming fire [Heb. 12:29].

You can take that or leave it, but it just happens to be in the Word of God. This is a solemn reminder that grace is available for you to serve God, but don't trifle with God, my friend. Don't think you can play fast and loose with God and get by with it.

I remember that when I first came to Pasadena as a pastor in 1940 I was asked by a lady to go see her husband. They were a lovely couple, but the husband was sick and in bed at home. In fact, he never got out of that bed; he died there. When I went to see him, I presented the gospel to him. He heard me courteously and then said this, "Dr. McGee, I would like to tell you right now that I accept Christ as my Savior, and I will do that, but I have trifled and played with God so often down through the years that I don't even know myself when I'm sincere and when I'm not sincere."

My friend, don't trifle with God. That day may come when you won't even know where you stand with Him at all. I tell you, our God is a consuming fire, but he is also a gracious, glorious, wonderful Savior.

CHAPTER 13

THEME: *Love*

As we have said, chapter 11 is the faith chapter of the Epistle to the Hebrews; chapter 12 is the hope chapter; and chapter 13 is the love chapter. Another outline that has been suggested for this section is as follows: chapter 10 the Christian's privilege; chapter 11 the Christian's power; chapter 12 the Christian's progess; and chapter 13 the Christian's practice. That is not the best outline, but it is good for Chapter 13—in chapter 13 we will see the Christian's practice.

SECRET LIFE OF THE BELIEVER

Let brotherly love continue [Heb. 13:1].

"Brotherly love" should be translated as brother love. The writer of this epistle is writing primarily to Hebrews, but what he has to say has application to us. Both Jew and Gentile have been brought into one body, the body of believers. The cement, the Elmer's glue, that holds us together is brother love— not brotherly love, but brother love. We are not to love *like* brothers, but we are to love because we *are* brothers.

Now if you are a child of God you are my brother. I get many letters that say, "I am a black person. But I listen to your program and I want you to know that I am a believer and I love you." I appreciate that so much. What difference does the color of the skin make when we are children of God? When He has given us new hearts and washed us white as snow, we are brothers, we are in the family of God, and we are to love one another.

I like to illustrate the Christian life as a triangle:

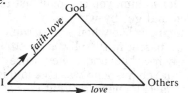

The Christian life is a life of faith and of love toward God and of love toward others. "Let *brother* love continue."

Now here is *stranger* love—

Be not forgetful to entertain strangers: for thereby some have entertained angels unawares [Heb. 13:2].

"Some have entertained angels unawares." The word *angel* may refer to superhuman beings or it may refer to human beings who are messengers from God. The same word is used to address the leaders of the seven churches of Asia Minor in chapters 2 and 3 of the Book of Revelation, in which I take the position that the "angels" are human messengers; that is, they are the teachers or leaders of the churches being addressed.

The writer mentions that there are those in the Old Testament who "entertained angels unawares." Abraham was one of them, and Jacob was another (although he didn't do much entertaining that night as he was too busy wrestling!); Joshua also entertained an angel.

The basic thought of this verse in the Hebrew epistle is that we are to extend love to strangers by showing hospitality to them. We ought to be careful that our love is exercised with judgment, but we need to recognize that there are folk around us to whom we could be very helpful. We should extend our love to them, and in doing this we might meet some very wonderful people.

Remember them that are in bonds, as bound with them; and them which suffer adversity, as being yourselves also in the body [Heb. 13:3].

Paul himself was in bonds. He knew a great deal about that, and so he says, "Remember the needy and those in trouble. Show love to those who are in need." You see, the church is a body—when one member suffers, all of us suffer. When I was seriously ill sometime ago I had the opportunity to experience this myself. A letter from one dear lady caused me to shed tears: "Dr. McGee, I'm inactive now, and I'm not able to do anything. I prayed to God that I would be able to take your disease upon myself so that you could go on with your ministry." May I say to you, we don't find that kind of spirit in every church or every group of believers, but we need it and I thank God there is a lot of it around.

We talk a great deal about the Christian fellowship which we have in our little group meetings or around the banquet table. But what about the poor saint who is off yonder lying on a bed and whom no one has visited? Many of you could have a wonderful ministry visiting the sick and lonely. This is the brother love that he is talking about here. Brother love is not something that takes place only in the church or in little groups that meet together. There has been a new phrase coined in our day: "body truth." Gracious, that truth has been in Scripture all these years; it is not something new. And you exercise that body truth by going out there to that individual who is in need. We do not hear that aspect emphasized very much today.

Marriage is honourable in all, and the bed undefiled: but whoremongers and adulterers God will judge [Heb. 13:4].

"Marriage is honourable in all." The writer is condemning asceticism here. Young man, if you find a Christian girl who will have you, get married. Young lady, if you find a Christian fellow who will have you, get married. I believe that God will lead you to the right one, if you are willing to be led in that way.

Marriage is honorable in all, and sex is to be exercised within the framework of marriage. God gave marriage to mankind for the *welfare* of mankind. I know I sound like a square, because this idea of living together without being married has become very commonplace, but I must tell you, young person, that you will surely pay for it if you attempt to live together outside the bonds of marriage. The home is the very center of the whole social structure, and it is the very center of the church.

"And the bed undefiled." There is nothing wrong with sex—except that it is being taught too much in our schools today. When I was in London sometime ago, I learned that they were going to cut down on teaching sex. They found that it led to more rapes in the schools than ever before, and they felt it to be responsible for an epidemic of venereal disease.

"But whoremongers and adulterers God will judge." "Be not deceived; God is not mocked: for whatsoever a man soweth, that shall he also reap" (Gal. 6:7). This is very severe, but after years in the ministry, I have watched many Christians who have tried to get by with sexual sins, and I do not know of any who have been able to do it. Maybe they have not been detected, but they have not gotten by with it; God has judged them.

Let your conversation be without covetousness; and be content with such things as ye have: for he hath said, I will never leave thee, nor forsake thee [Heb. 13:5].

"Your conversation" means your manner of life. Don't be known as a moneygrabber, as one who puts the almighty dollar above almighty God. He may not make you a millionaire, but He will never leave you or forsake you. Isn't it wonderful to have Him say that to you? It does not matter who you are or what you do, if you have responded in faith to the Word of God, you have been brought to the place where you can know that He will never leave you or forsake you. I have a notion that I have friends today who *would* forsake me, and I may have relatives who would forsake me. But the Lord Jesus will never forsake me. I hope you have Him on your side.

So that we may boldly say, The Lord is my helper, and I will not fear what man shall do unto me [Heb. 13:6].

The Hebrew Christians in Jerusalem, Judea, and Samaria were going to face punishment and trials in the next few years. They needed to remember that God was not going to forsake them, and that they could say in spite of what happened, "The Lord is my helper, and I will not fear what man shall do unto me."

It is interesting to note what happened when some of the prisoners of war finally were able to return home after the war in Vietnam. During the war, many radicals in the United States were concerned over the fate of the POWs, and they made trips to Vietnam and led protest rallies on their behalf. But when the POWs were released, very few of the radicals showed any interest in them. When the prisoners of war came back to this country many of them testified that they had turned to Jesus, and it was Jesus who helped them. Of course, the news media didn't like that or want to talk about that. But Jesus never forsook them—He stayed with them and saw them through. He is the one who will see you through, too. I don't think the radicals or the politicians will help you much. I am tired of listening to them. I want to listen to Jesus, because He will never leave me nor forsake me.

SOCIAL LIFE OF THE BELIEVER

Remember them which have the rule over you, who have spoken unto you the word of God: whose faith follow, considering the end of their conversation [Heb. 13:7].

There are some ministers who use this verse and say that the members of their church are to obey them. However, it seems rather that the thought here is of *leadership.* He is speaking of spiritual leaders, and spiritual leaders are to lead folk to Christ. If a man is presenting Christ and is attempting to bring people into the presence of Christ, then that is a man to whom you should be loyal. But to be loyal to a man simply because he is the pastor of a church is not what Paul is talking about at all.

Jesus Christ the same yesterday, and today, and for ever [Heb. 13:8].

"Jesus Christ." There is no accident in the Word of God; that is, no word is ever used carelessly. *Jesus* is His human name; *Christ* is His title, that which speaks of His deity.

Jesus is the name which links Him with mankind. It identifies Him as the most wonderful person in this world.

> Jesus, Name of sweetness,
> Jesus, sound of love;
> Cheering exiles onward
> To their rest above.
>
> Jesus, oh the magic
> Of the soft love sound;
> How it thrills and trembles
> To creation's bound.
> —Author unknown

How wonderful Jesus was as a person when He was down here. People crowded around Him because He was so human. The mobs followed Him and they loved Him. It was the *teaching* of Jesus they hated—it was not Jesus the man. *He* was wonderful, my friend.

Christ is a title which speaks of His messianic mission to this earth—He is God manifest in the flesh. "Jesus Christ"—how marvelously these two are meshed together here. He is Jesus Christ, and He is the same.

I feel inadequate to deal with this very marvelous verse, but I do want to say that it has probably been misapplied as much as any verse in the Word of God. There are many who use this verse and say, "When Jesus was here nineteeen hundred years ago, He performed miracles; therefore we ought to perform them today. He healed nineteen hundred years ago, and so we ought to be healing today. He is still in that same business."

Jesus Christ *is* the same, but we need to understand *how* He is the same. He is the same in His character, in His person, and in His attributes, but He is not the same in place or in performance. When I was in the land of Israel I didn't see Him over there. I saw very little evidence at all of Him in that land. Over nineteen hundred years ago He was in Bethlehem as a little baby, but He is no longer a baby and He is not in Bethlehem. Later He was a little boy playing in the streets of Nazareth. I walked down the streets of Nazareth, but I didn't see Him. I saw a lot of little boys, but He was not one of them. A few years later as a man He walked through that land, and He *did* heal. I was in Jerusalem and I saw Golgotha, but there is not a cross there and He is not on a cross today. The whole thought of this epistle is that He is now at the right hand of God: ". . .We have such an high priest, who is set on the right hand of the throne of the Majesty in the heavens" (Heb. 8:1); and we are to look "unto Jesus the author and finisher of our faith . . ." (Heb. 12:2). He accomplished our redemption nineteen hundred years ago, and He sat down at the right hand of God. Right now He is up yonder, but some day He will come as the King to the earth to establish His kingdom. He has not yet called His church out of the world, but some day He will do that. You see, Jesus is not the same in place and performance, but He is the same in His attributes.

When He was here nineteen hundred years ago, He was God who came down to our level. When I have been in the land of Israel and have considered that fact, I have truly marveled at it. He came to a place where there was no great wealth or pomp or ceremony. He did not come to Rome, the center of power and government. He did not come to Athens, the great cultural center. He did come to an insignificant outpost of the Roman Empire, and He came to the level of the common man.

Because we are often afraid that we will be misunderstood when we speak of Christ's humanity, we do not emphasize it as we should. Rather, we emphasize His deity, and we need to do that because the liberal speaks of nothing but His humanity, and even that he does not truly understand. But in His humanity, I think that Jesus was the most attractive person who ever walked this earth—not because He was God, but because He was a man, a real man.

Have you ever wondered why the crowds were attracted to Him and followed Him? He was strong but gentle—so gentle that little children came to Him. However, He could drive the money-changers out of the temple and they ran for cover, because He was *man* enough to put them out. Also He was attractive. He had what we call today charisma. People followed Him because they loved Him, and they knew they were in the presence of a man who *was* a man. In Capernaum He healed a leper and then had to leave because the crowds pressed around Him so that He couldn't even continue His ministry. Even publicans and sinners came to Him, which was the thing that so angered the religious crowd. If He came to your town today—I hate to say this—I don't think He would come to your church. I have a notion you would find Him where the crowd is; He would be mixing with people and probably holding a child or two. When He went to Jericho at the end of His ministry, again we find that the crowds lined the way so that little Zacchaeus had to climb up a tree in order to see Him, but even there our Lord stopped and brought him down out of the tree. How sensitive the Lord Jesus was to human need, and how wonderful He was in His person!

I want to say something very carefully: it was the *person* of Christ that appealed; it was not His *teachings*. His great declaration that He was going to die to redeem men was not popular. At the very beginning of His ministry, it was His teaching that offended. He taught that He was the Bread of Life and that He had come to give His life that men might have spiritual food, and added, "Therefore said I unto you, that no man can come unto me, except it were given unto him of my Father." And John's record tells us, "From that time many of his disciples went back, and walked no more with him. Then said Jesus unto the twelve, Will ye also go away? Then Simon Peter answered him, Lord, to whom shall we go? thou hast the words of eternal life" (John 6:65–68). The crowd narrowed down, and only twelve stayed with Him. Why? Because of His teaching. And actually Simon Peter rebuked Him when He spoke of His impending death, ". . . Be it far from thee, Lord: this shall not be unto thee" (Matt. 16:22). Even His loyal disciples didn't like that kind of teaching. When men came into contact with the Lord Jesus Christ, they found grace and truth; they found sweetness and strength; they found meekness and majesty; they found light and love. He appealed to men, but when he died on a cross that cross became an offense. The cross is still an offense, but Jesus is still attractive.

It is said that when Savonarola in the city of Florence went before the great populace and said, "Be free," they applauded him. But when he said to them, "Be pure," they ran him out of town. They refused his teaching when it did not appeal to them. The Lord Jesus said to men, "You have to turn from sin. You cannot live in sin. I have come to make you free, but I will have to give My life for you and you will have to come as sinners to Me." And sinners came—when men were desperate, they would come to Him. I believe that is the only way men will come to Him even today.

I wish that I could present Him as He really was nineteen hundred years ago when He came to this earth. How wonderful He was! Today, your sorrow is His sorrow, and your joy is His joy. He will be the same in the future— "the same yesterday, and to-day, and for ever." He is never going to change. Some day we will be in His presence. How wonderful that will be!

Before we leave this subject, let me share with you an excerpt from a booklet written by Dr. C. I. Scofield, entitled *The Loveliness of Christ:*

First of all, as it seems to me, this loveliness of Christ consists in His perfect humanity. Am I understood? I do not now mean that He was a perfect human, but that He was perfectly human.

In everything but our sins, and our evil natures, He is one with us. He grew in stature and in grace. He labored, and wept, and prayed, and loved. He was tempted in all points as we are—sin apart. With Thomas, we confess Him Lord and God; we adore and revere Him, but beloved, there is no other who establishes with us such intimacy, who comes so close to these human hearts of ours; no one in the universe of whom we are so little afraid. He enters as simply and naturally into our twentieth century lives as if He had been reared in the same street.

He is wonderful, my friend, and you ought to know Him. Paul, who came to know Him, found that even at the end of his life he wanted to know Him better. He said, "That I may know him, and the power of his resurrection . . ." (Phil. 3:10). Today my one ambition is to know Him and to get out His Word—I cannot think of anything better to do.

Be not carried about with divers and strange doctrines. For it is a good thing that the heart be established with grace; not with meats, which have not profited them that have been occupied therein [Heb. 13:9].

It is amazing that most of the cults today go in for special diets. I believe that food is important as far as the health of the body is concerned, but it has nothing to do with your relationship to God. Paul wrote, "But meat commendeth us not to God: for neither, if we eat, are we the better; neither, if we eat not, are we the worse" (1 Cor. 8:8). He is saying the same thing here. Do not go off into these strange cults and teachings in which diet and ceremonies and rituals and little study groups are supposed to make you a super-duper saint. Nothing in the world is going to build you up but the Word of God. The Word of God will build you up if it brings you to the person of Christ, and only the Holy Spirit can take the things of Christ and make them real unto you.

We have an altar, whereof they have no right to eat which serve the tabernacle [Heb. 13:10].

A comparison is being made here between what Israel had under the old covenant in contrast to the better things of the New Covenant. Believers today have an altar, but this altar is not the Lord's Supper as some people have mistakenly interpreted it to mean. We do not have a material altar with a local address, but we have an altar which is in heaven. It is the throne of grace up yonder. It was a throne of judgment—He condemned us there—but now that the blood has been placed there, we can come and find grace and salvation.

I would like to say at this point that Christian fellowship is not a church banquet. For years while I was in the ministry I heard it said: "Come to the banquet. We are going to have some marvelous Christian fellowship." No, you're not, my friend. You are just going there for a good time and to fill your little tummy. The only place you can have real Christian fellowship (koinōnia) is around the Word of God. It is the Word of God which brings you to the person of Christ and enables you to see Him in all His glory. It is then that you will have fellowship and a good time with other believers. Our Lord is wonderful, my friend—it is terrible to pass Him by.

For the bodies of those beasts, whose blood is brought into the sanctuary by the high priest for sin, are burned without the camp [Heb. 13:11].

The writer is referring to the sin offering. When Christ died it was for the fact that you and I are sinners. Not only do we commit sin, we are sinners by nature, and He took our sins on Himself that He might give us a new nature.

Wherefore Jesus also, that he might sanctify the people with his own blood, suffered without the gate [Heb. 13:12].

Jesus died outside the city. Why? Because He was the sin offering. The sin offering was taken away from the temple and "burned without the camp." Jesus was our sin offering, and He paid the penalty for our sin.

Let us go forth therefore unto him without the camp, bearing his reproach [Heb. 13:13].

The writer is saying to these Hebrew Christians, "Don't mind leaving the temple. Don't mind leaving the rituals. Those things are not helpful. Go to Him—Go to Christ."

My friend, we, too, are to go to Him. We are on our way to a heavenly Jerusalem. This is real separation he is talking about here. Today we put the emphasis on separation *from;* we are separated from something—that is, "I don't do this and I don't do that." Real separation is not *from;* it is *unto.* Paul said he was separated *unto* the gospel, separated *unto* Christ, separated *unto* the Word of God. In fact the word *Hebrew* means the "one who crossed over." Abraham was called a Hebrew because he had come from the other side of the Euphrates River, signifying that his old life was gone. The children of Israel crossed the Red Sea, and they were delivered from slavery; they were redeemed, and a new life was then possible. Then they had to cross the Jordan River to live in the Promised Land, the land of Canaan, the kind of life that we also should live down here.

We are to go "without the camp, bearing his reproach." The Hebrew Christians hated to leave the temple and their religion. Many people today are wrapped up in "churchianity," thinking that because they are members of a church they are saved. They need to get away from ritual and religion and come to Christ. Come to Him—that is real separation, and that is real salvation.

For here have we no continuing city, but we seek one to come [Heb. 13:14].

Again the writer makes it clear that we have nothing permanent down here.

SPIRITUAL LIFE OF THE BELIEVER

By him therefore let us offer the sacrifice of praise to God continually, that is, the fruit of our lips giving thanks to his name [Heb. 13:15].

A child of God is a priest today and can bring sacrifices to God. There are four sacrifices of a believer. (1) You can sacrifice your *person* (see Rom. 12:1). Someone has said, "When one truly gives himself to the Lord, all other giving becomes easy." (2) You can sacrifice your *purse* (see 2 Cor. 8:1–5). If He doesn't have your purse, He doesn't have you. (3) You can offer the sacrifice of *praise,* which we find in this verse: "By him therefore let us offer the sacrifice of praise to God continually, that is, the fruit of our lips giving thanks to his name." (4) Finally, you can offer the sacrifice of *performance* or doing good, which we find in the following verse—

But to do good and to communicate forget not: for with such sacrifices God is well pleased [Heb. 13:16].

When you took that basket of fruit over to that dear, lonely, and sick child of God whom everyone has forgotten about, you were a priest offering a sacrifice to God. It was well pleasing to Him—He took delight in your doing that. Again I must refer to the time when I was seriously ill and flat on my back. At that time I received many letters from folk who were lots worse off physically than I was. They wrote lovely letters, and every one of them was a sacrifice. And many folk helped me in a tangible way, and that too was a sacrifice well pleasing to God. My friend, if Christianity does not walk in shoe leather it is no good at all. The Lord Jesus is up yonder at the right hand of God—that is where He is as Head of the church—but His feet are down here right where the rubber meets the road. He wants Christianity to be in shoe leather, and He would like to walk in *your* shoes.

Obey them that have the rule over you, and submit yourselves: for they watch for your souls, as they that must give account, that they may do it with joy, and not with grief: for that is unprofitable for you [Heb. 13:17].

We had this same thought in verse 7. If your pastor is a man of God who is teaching the Word of God then you are to obey the Word of God as he has given it to you. It would be better to not hear the Word of God, than to hear it and not obey it.

Pray for us: for we trust we have a good conscience, in all things willing to live honestly [Heb. 13:18].

"Pray for us." Evidently the readers of this epistle knew the writer, and I believe the writer was Paul.

"For we trust we have a good conscience, in all things willing to live honestly." It is wonderful to pillow your head at night with a good conscience, a conscience enlightened by the Word of God. A great many people are not walking in the light. "If we say that we have fellowship with him, and walk in darkness, we lie, and do not the truth: But if we walk in the light, as he is in the light, we have fellowship one with another, and the blood of Jesus Christ his Son cleanseth us from all sin" (1 John 1:6–7).

But I beseech you the rather to do this, that I may be restored to you the sooner [Heb. 13:19].

This statement also makes me believe that Paul wrote this epistle. Apparently he was in prison at this time, and he is saying to these Hebrew Christians, "I want to come back and be among you again"—after all, he was a Hebrew himself.

BENEDICTION

Now we come to the benediction, a benediction which I have used thousands of times in my ministry.

Now the God of peace, that brought again from the dead our Lord Jesus, that great shepherd of the sheep, through the blood of the everlasting covenant,

Make you perfect in every good work to do his will, working in you that which is well-pleasing in his sight, through Jesus Christ; to whom be glory for ever and ever. Amen [Heb. 13:20–21].

"That great shepherd of the sheep." The Lord Jesus is here called the Great Shepherd. In Psalm 22 He is presented as the Good Shepherd, and in John 10:11 He calls Himself the Good Shepherd. As the Good Shepherd He gave His life for the sheep. As the Great Shepherd He is the one who perfects the sheep and builds them up. We see that here and also in Psalm 23. He leads us beside the still waters and leads us to the place where the grass is good and green and very tender, that is, to the Word of God. Then in Psalm 24 He is presented as the Chief Shepherd. "And when the chief Shepherd shall appear, ye shall receive a crown of glory that fadeth not away" (1 Pet. 5:4). He died in the past as the Good Shepherd; He is the Great Shepherd today; and He is coming some day as the Chief Shepherd for His sheep. He started out with one hundred sheep, and do you know how many sheep He is going to have with Him in heaven? Ninety-nine? No. He is going to have all one hundred sheep with him there.

"Through the blood of the everlasting covenant." Christ's blood is the basis of every covenant God has ever made.

"Make you perfect"—this has been the purpose of the Epistle to the Hebrews. We have been told, "Let us go on to perfection." He means for us to go on to maturation, to being full-grown children of God. It is marvelous to admire a little baby lying in the crib, but if you come back in twenty years and he is still lying there, saying, "Da-da-da," something is radically wrong. There are a lot of such saints who need to come to maturation, to grow up, and the Epistle to the Hebrews will help them to do that.

"In every good work to do his will." What is the important thing for a child of God? To do His will—to allow Him to work His will in your life, "working in you that which is well-pleasing in his sight, through Jesus Christ; to whom be glory for ever and ever. Amen."

And I beseech you, brethren, suffer the word of exhortation: for I have written a letter unto you in few words [Heb. 13:22].

Notice how personal this is. I have to smile when he says he wrote this "in few words." To my judgment this is a long letter, but he calls it "few words."

Know ye that our brother Timothy is set at liberty; with whom, if he come shortly, I will see you [Heb. 13:23].

Again, this sounds like Paul. Apparently Timothy had been in prison. A note in my Bible at the bottom of this chapter says, "Written to the Hebrews from Italy by Timothy." That is not part of the text, but it is some man's interpretation. This man could be wrong, and I could be wrong in saying that Paul wrote this epistle. The important thing is that the Holy Spirit wrote it and that He takes the things of Christ and shows them unto us.

Salute all them that have the rule over you, and all the saints. They of Italy salute you [Heb. 13:24].

The writer was in Italy, and so was Paul.

He closes this epistle with a wonderful benediction, and I will close with it also. I cannot improve on it because it interprets itself—

Grace be with you all. Amen [Heb. 13:25].

APPENDIX

THEME: The authorship of Hebrews or did Paul write Hebrews?; internal evidences on authorship; date and destination; arguments available on authorship; a defense of the Pauline authorship

THE AUTHORSHIP OF HEBREWS OR DID PAUL WRITE HEBREWS?

The Epistle to the Hebrews presents many moot problems. Some of them are in conjunction with the question of authorship, which we shall consider under the following divisions:

1. Internal evidence on authorship
   (Is Hebrews an epistle or treatise?)
2. Date and Destination
3. Arguments available on authorship
4. A defense of the Pauline authorship

It is evident that we are contending for the Pauline authorship of Hebrews. First we shall present all arguments against it, as indicated by the headings. Then we shall present the evidence that establishes the Pauline authorship in our own thinking.

INTERNAL EVIDENCES ON AUTHORSHIP

The deciding factor in determining the authorship, according to one writer, is that tradition and history shed no light upon the question of the authorship of Hebrews. This probably is being considered first because we do not agree with the writer on this statement. Rather, we believe that both history and tradition lend a deciding voice to this question.

We are therefore thrown back, in our search for the author, on such evidence as the epistle itself affords, and that is wholly inferential. It seems probable that the author was a Hellenist, a Greek-speaking Jew. He was familiar with the Scriptures of the OT and with the religious ideas and worship of the Jews. He claims the inheritance of their sacred history, traditions and institutions (1:1), and dwells on them with an intimate knowledge and enthusiasm that would be improbable, though not impossible, in a proselyte, and still more in a Christian convert from heathenism. But he knew the OT only in the LXX [Septuagint] translation, which he follows even where it deviates from the Hebrew. He writes Greek with a purity of style and vocabulary to which the writings of Luke alone in the NT can be compared. His mind is imbued with that combination of Hebrew and Greek thought which is best known in the writings of Philo. His general typological mode of thinking, his use of the allegorical method, as well as the adoption of many terms that are most familiar in Alexandrian thought, all reveal the Hellenistic mind. Yet his fundamental conceptions are in full accord with the teaching of Paul and of the Johannine writings.

The central position assigned to Christ, the high estimate of His person, the saving significance of His death, the general trend of the ethical teaching, the writer's opposition to asceticism and his esteem for the rulers and teachers of the church, all bear out the inference that he belonged to a Christian circle dominated by Pauline ideas. The author and his readers alike were not personal disciples of Jesus, but had received the gospel from those who had heard the Lord (2:3) and who were no longer living (13:7). . . . The letter [Paul] quotes the OT from the Hebrew and LXX but Hebrews only from LXX. . . . For Paul the OT is law, and stands in antithesis to the NT, but in Hebrews the OT is covenant, and is the "shadow" of the New Covenant. (*The International Standard Bible Encyclopedia*, vol. II, p. 1357.)

We have quoted voluminously from this writer because his main thesis is to show that Paul could not have been the author. His sole proof is based on the internal evidence from the epistle.

In considering the internal nature of the epistle, a word must be said relative to the question: Is it really an epistle? There is no word of salutation or greeting in this Epistle to the Hebrews, such as marks the other New Testament books, with the possible exception of 1 John. It is in the form of a treatise rather than a letter. In it are long, philosophical sentences written in purest idiomatic Greek. It bears no mark of a translation from the Hebrew, as Clement of Alexandria suggests.

This is an inference on his part because it was written to Hebrew-speaking Jews. The length of the epistle is another thing that might suggest a treatise, yet note the author's own words in this respect, ". . . for I have written a letter unto you in few words" (Heb. 13:22). Delitzsch has this enlightening comment to make on this epistle:

> We seem at first to have a treatise before us, but the special hortatory reference interwoven with the most discursive and dogmatic portions of the work soon show us that it is really a kind of sermon addressed to some particular and well known auditory; while at the close the homiletic form changes into that of an epistle.

According to Deissmann's definition of an epistle as distinct from a letter, we feel sure that this would allow it to fall under the category of an epistle. Its conclusion is that of an epistle. Later in our discussion we shall present a reason for the omission of a greeting. These problems are intimately tied up with the question of authorship, especially when one attempts to maintain the Pauline authorship. We agree with Plumer that this is an epistle.

As we conclude this section on the internal nature of the Epistle to the Hebrews, we should note that this epistle is in composition and lofty concept the masterpiece of the New Testament, although there is no conclusive evidence for the authorship. Only suggestions and intimations shed light on this problem. In our defense for the Pauline authorship we shall undertake to show that the suggestions and intimations point to Paul as the author, yet we are not dogmatic in stating that the proof is positive.

DATE AND DESTINATION

The latest date for the composition of Hebrews is A.D. 96. The earliest date cannot be determined so easily. It must have been written after A.D. 50 if it is made dependent on Paul's epistles. All critics fix the dating between these two terminal points. Moffatt shows that Clement, Justin Martyr, Hermas, and Tertullian knew of it and quoted from it. Clement quoted from it at length. By the second century it was widely circulated and read. Rees places the date around A.D. 80, Moffatt around A.D. 85. Here is a list of the probable datings: Basnage—A.D. 61; L'Enfant and Beausobre—A.D. 62; Horne and Bagster—A.D.

62 or 63; Pearson, Lardner, Tomlin, Mill, Wetstein, and Tillemont—A.D. 63; Authorized Version and Lloyd—A.D. 64; Michaelis—A.D. 64–65; Scott—A.D. 65; Ebrard before A.D. 58. The number of dates given suggests that the means used to arrive at a date was by way of the lottery, not by process of scholarship. However, Hebrews must have been written before the destruction of Jerusalem in A.D. 70. Because there is constant reference to the Old Testament ritual being in progress at that time, certainly there would have been reference to the destruction of the temple. Having examined the arguments carefully, we are fully persuaded that those who place the dating of it after the destruction of Jerusalem do not sufficiently answer the question of why the writer omitted reference to this catastrophe.

E. Schuyler English gives us this word:

> It is also obvious that the epistle was written before the destruction of Jerusalem in A.D. 70. For at the time of its composition Mosaic institutions were still being observed—priests were offering gifts according to the Law (8:3–5) and the temple was still standing (13:11–12). The temple was in Jerusalem.

Godet has a fitting comment:

> This epistle, without introduction or subscription, is like the great High Priest of whom it treats, who was without beginning of days or end of years, abiding an High Priest continually. It is entirely fitting that it should remain anonymous.

The epistle was first accepted by the Eastern church. Athanasius accepted it, and the council of Carthage confirmed it in A.D. 397. Paul's name was on the epistle about the time it began to circulate.

The consensus is that Hebrews was written to Jewish Christians. But where were the Jewish Christians located? It was not written for the whole body of Jewish believers everywhere. It was written to a particular church located in a particular place. The epistle bears testimony to this: The church had for some time obeyed the gospel (Heb. 5:12); past conduct inspired confidence in their sincerity (Heb. 6:9); they had been kind to God's people (Heb. 6:10); note other personal references in Hebrews 10:32–34; 13:19, 23. Was this church in Palestine or out of Palestine? It is around this question that the argument on destination is based.

First of all, there is evidence that the first readers were Jews. The epistle assumes an intimate knowledge with the Old Testament. The readers were of the same lineage as Jews in the Old Testament (Heb. 1:1; 3:9). Zahn has this comment to make:

> Hebrews does not contain a single sentence in which it is so much as intimated that the readers became members of God's people who descended from Abraham, and heirs of the promise given to them and their forefathers, and how they became such. 13:13 shows that both the readers and author were members of the Jewish race.

Now we shall try to determine to whom or rather what particular church the author was addressing. This epistle is addressed to the Hebrews, which word in the New Testament does not apply to all Jews. It was used for those who were more thoroughly of Jewish origins and habits and who spoke the vernacular of Palestine. The other Jews outside of Palestine were designated Hellenists. Lindsay says that Acts 6:1 makes this distinction clear. DeWette says that Eusebius, speaking of the Jews of Asia Minor, styles them not Hebrews but *ex Hebraion ontes*. Chrysostom says that this epistle was sent to Jerusalem. The fact that the epistle was written in Greek does not negate the evidence that it was sent to Palestine, for it is natural for a writer out of Palestine to write in the universal language of his day. The Palestinian Jews were well acquainted with Greek, as Deissmann has clearly demonstrated. In fact, it was the language of communication. DeWette held to the opinion that this epistle was destined to parts other than Palestine; yet he acknowledges that the Jewish character of the epistle—the persecutions which they were enduring, the consequent risk of apostasy, and the ancient opinion—reveal Palestine as the more probable destination. Ebrard wrote, "We are at liberty to seek these Jewish Christians only in Jerusalem."

ARGUMENTS AVAILABLE ON AUTHORSHIP

We can say with Shakespeare that we have now come to the very heart of the matter. There is less evidence for the authorship of this epistle than of any other book of the New Testament. Others have problems of authorship, but there is some definite evidence available and some general agreement, at least, regarding the author. For example, nearly all critics say that some John wrote the fourth Gospel. But there is no such agreement regarding Hebrews. Moffatt rightly says that few characters in the New Testament have escaped the attention of those in late days who have sought to identify them as the author of Hebrews. Apollos, Peter, Philip, Silvanus, Prisca, Barnabas, and Paul have all been suggested as the possible author. To Moffatt's list we might add the names of Luke, Silas, Clement of Rome, Ariston, and Titus, all of whom have been suggested as the possible author. Out of this dozen, one is privileged to take his choice—or refrain from doing so, as Moffatt does. Moffatt concludes that the author was one of those unknown personalities in whom the early church was more rich than we realize. There is absolutely no basis, other than conjecture, for asserting that most of these were the author, although several have a plausible claim.

As we examine their claim to authorship, Luke and Clement are easily eliminated because a comparison of their writings to the Epistle to the Hebrews reveals a difference in style, composition, and influence. Clement quotes from Hebrews, and his own writings show marked differences. (See introduction of Moffatt's commentary on Hebrews.) So little is known of the others, with the exception of Barnabas, that it is impossible to establish a case for or against them. Barnabas will be considered in the three theories that are presented.

In the early church were three traditions regarding the authorship of Hebrews: The Alexandrian tradition supported the Pauline authorship; the African tradition supported the authorship of Barnabas; Rome and the West supported the idea that it was anonymous.

1. *Alexandrian tradition:* Clement says that his teacher, probably Pantaenus, explained why Paul did not address his readers under his name. He further states that Paul wrote it in Hebrew and Luke translated it into Greek. Origen follows Clement, but knowing that the view of Alexandria was criticized, he concludes that the author is "known only to God." By the fourth century the tradition of the Pauline authorship was well established in Alexandria, Syria, and Greece. This tradition prevailed until the revival of learning. Eusebius favored the Pauline tradition, as did Dionysius of Alexandria, Alexander of Alexandria, Athanasius, Cyril of Jerusalem, Epiphanius, the Council of Laodicea of A.D. 363, and Erasmus. Among those who denied the

Pauline tradition were Irenaeus, Cyprian of Carthage, Tertullian, Caius and Novatus, presbyters of the church at Rome. Calvin did not accept the tradition, for he says, "I, indeed, can adduce no reason to show that Paul was its author." Luther and Moll defend the authorship of Apollos against the Pauline tradition. Thus we see that tradition was probably equally divided.

2. *African tradition:* This view supported Barnabas as the author of Hebrews. Tertullian was the leading exponent, for he attributed the epistle, without question, to Barnabas. This is the most tempting suggestion, as Wickham remarks. It suits the character of Barnabas. Barnabas was a "Levite of the country of Cyprus," a Hellenist by birthplace, but a Hebrew by race, interested in the sacrificial system, companion of Paul (yet one who entertained views of his own), the "son of consolation," the mediator and peacemaker between old and new. Zahn infers that this tradition arose in Montanist churches and originated in Asia. However, this tradition was superseded by the Alexandrian tradition, for in A.D. 393 the council of Hippo reckons thirteen epistles to Paul, but in A.D. 419 the council of Carthage reckons fourteen to Paul, which would include Hebrews.

3. *Roman tradition:* This view said the author was anonymous. No tradition of authorship appears before A.D. 400, according to Rees. Stephen Gobarus, writing in A.D. 600, says that both Irenaeus and Hippolytus denied the Pauline authorship. The epistle was known to Clement of Rome, and he mentions no one as author. Another suggestion as to the authorship of Hebrews is mentioned by Plumer. It is that of Zenas, the lawyer. This makes thirteen guesses as to the author of Hebrews.

A DEFENSE OF THE PAULINE AUTHORSHIP

We are not holding dogmatically or tenaciously to an obsolete view. Rather, we have examined the evidence and find no reason to reject the Pauline authorship. It is not our purpose in this section to affirm that Paul wrote Hebrews, but to set forth our reasons for tentatively accepting the Pauline authorship, or the authority, that this epistle rests upon, for the canonicity of this epistle depends largely upon the view of authorship. It was accepted into the canon on Pauline authority; and with that removed, it is possible to reject this great epistle.

Under the first heading (Internal Evidences on Authorship) we attempted to show that all the light from the epistle itself reveals only the fact that the author is anonymous. His name is nowhere mentioned in the epistle. Now, using the internal evidence, we want to show how Paul *could be* the author.

So far we have tried to show two things: (1) there is no evidence, external or internal, to support any claim as to the authorship, except it be Paul; (2) there is nothing incompatible with thinking that Paul wrote it.

Now we shall take our third burden of proof and attempt to show that internal and external evidence support the Pauline authorship.

1. *Internal Evidence:* Origen remarked that the thoughts (*noemata*) of this epistle all bore the stamp of Paul's mind, but the language was *Hellenikotera*, purer Greek than his. Following is Lindsay's list of representations and images which are found in Hebrews and in Paul's other epistles, which are not found in the works of other New Testament writers.

Compare Heb. 1:1, 3 with 2 Cor. 4:4; Col. 1:15–16.

Compare Heb. 1:4, 2:9 with Phil. 2:8–9.

Compare Heb. 2:14 with 1 Cor. 15:54, 57.

Compare Heb. 7:16, 18–19 with Rom. 2:29; Gal. 3:3, 24.

Compare Heb. 7:26 with Eph. 4:10.

Compare Heb. 8:5; 10:1 with Col. 2:17.

Compare Heb. 10:12–13 with 1 Cor. 15:25.

DeWette and Bleek have concluded that since Hebrews reads more like Paul's writing than any other New Testament writings, it was written by a disciple of Paul. The opponents of the Pauline authorship are quoted to show that this book is not unlike Paul's writings and could have been written by Paul. Paul obviously meets this requirement.

Some have claimed that Hebrews 2:3 excludes Paul as the author because he says in Galatians 1:11–12 that he received his gospel not from men but from God. However, this is not incongruous with Paul's statement in Galatians. Paul is evidently using the editorial "we" that is used so effectually in the New Testament. If Paul places himself in the same category with the other Christians at Jerusalem, he could not say that *we* received it from God on the road to Damascus about midday on a mule. Paul's conversion was peculiar to himself. Then the Galatians passage does not exclude the fact that Paul did not have it confirmed unto him by the ones who heard the Lord. In Galatians he is defending his apostleship and is therefore showing from whence he received his authority.

As to the statement that Hebrews 13:7 reveals that the apostles were no longer living at the time Hebrews was written, we can hardly see where this verse establishes any such view.

Regarding the fact that the Epistle to the Hebrews quotes the Old Testament from the Septuagint Version, it is possible for Paul to have quoted only from the Septuagint in Hebrews and from both the Septuagint and the Hebrew in his other epistles. The fact that there are more quotations in this book than in any other New Testament book shows that the author is placing a great deal of stress on these quotations. Instead of quoting from memory, he would have a copy of the Old Testament at hand. Paul did quote from the Septuagint frequently, and he could easily have used it exclusively in the Epistle to the Hebrews.

Rees says that Paul's Christology turns about the death, resurrection, and living presence of Christ in the church. In contrast, the Epistle to the Hebrews centers about the high priestly nature of Christ's work. He evidently is thinking of Ephesians, Colossians, 1 Corinthians, and Romans, for the rest of Paul's epistles deal no more with these subjects than does Hebrews. This method of trying to distinguish different authors by difference of style is not conclusive, to say the least. Certainly it is not a valid argument in this epistle.

We come now to the problem of the absence of the author's name in the Epistle to the Hebrews. Why did the author conceal his name? The theory has been advanced that had Paul been the author he would have subscribed his name, and the fact that his name does not appear shows he did not write it. We submit Plumer's answer to this sort of reasoning:

Moreover, if Paul is proven not to be its author because it lacks his name, the same reasoning would prove it had no author at all, for it bears no name whatever.

Now let us examine the reasons why Paul might have concealed his name. Dr. Biesenthal, writing on Hebrews, advances a new and interesting theory for the reason the writer concealed his name. He shows that Christianity's teaching that animal sacrifices were no longer needed was being felt in heathendom. Consequently, sacrifices at births, marriages, and other occasions, were being neglected. The priestly class, which lived by these sacrifices, and the large cattle industry, were being threatened by utter ruin. This created a great antagonism against Christianity. Dr. Biesenthal, a Hebrew by race, concludes that for this reason the writer withheld his name from this epistle which so bitterly denounces animal sacrifices.

Also Paul himself was a man who was hated by the Jewish nation. To them he was no less than a traitor. This brilliant young Pharisee, who was well versed in the ritual of Moses, as he himself claims, was anathema to his brethren in the flesh. In writing to them this learned work, composed in the best Greek, he withheld the name that would prevent its circulation among those to whom it was originally destined.

There is another reason we think to be more valid, which was presented even by the Alexandrian tradition. It is that Paul left off his salutation, "Paul, an apostle of Jesus Christ," because he was not the apostle to the Jews but to the Gentiles. Another more recent suggestion on this line comes from a consideration of Hebrews 3:1: ". . . Consider the Apostle and High Priest of our profession, Christ Jesus." Christ is the great Apostle in this epistle and the writer would not subscribe his name beside the one of Christ. Certainly the fact that the writer did not mention his name does not eliminate Paul from the list of possible authors.

There are a few suggestions in the epistle that point to Paul as author. The writer was a Jew acquainted with the details of Mosaic ritualism (Heb. 13:13). He was acquainted with Greek philosophy, or rather, Alexandrian thought. The author of this epistle had been in prison in the locality where the ones addressed resided (Heb. 10:34). He was at that time in prison in Italy (Heb. 13:19, 24). Timothy was his companion and messenger (Heb. 13:23). When Paul was in Rome in prison he used Timothy to carry messages, and he sent him on a trip from the west to the east (Phil. 2:19). The writer hoped to be liberated (Heb. 13:19). This is the same thought that is expressed in Philippians 1:25 and Philemon 22. While these suggestions are not conclusive, who better fits this description than Paul? An appropriate supposition from Lightfoot concludes this section on internal evidence: "The very style of it may argue the scholar of Gamaliel."

The dating of the Epistle to the Hebrews does not conflict with the Pauline authorship. If it were written before the destruction of Jerusalem, which we believe to be correct, it coincides nicely with Paul's imprisonment at

Rome. Paul's last visit to Jerusalem helps explain the epistle. The Book of Acts tells us that Paul went up to Jerusalem in spite of the warning of the Spirit. His arrest was the result of having gone into the temple to purify himself with the four men who had a vow. This he was asked to do and to make apparent that he walked orderly and kept the Law. Did he do wrong? This is not a question for us to answer. The point is that he—knowing that he was dead to the Law—acted through zeal and love for his brethren. The believers at Jerusalem still clung to the Law and to the temple. When Paul was in Rome, he wrote this epistle to show these Jews the better things of the New Covenant and to warn them not to be drawn back into Judaism. This throws a great deal of light on Hebrews 13:13: "Let us go forth therefore unto him without the camp [Judaism], bearing his reproach."

The Spirit of God could have used this epistle for the comfort of Jewish Christians right before the destruction of the temple. We suggest this to show that the dating and destination are not incompatible with the Pauline authorship.

2. *External Evidence:* Several of the early church fathers who favored the Pauline authorship have been mentioned, but we have reserved for this section other evidence that confirms us in our view that Paul wrote Hebrews. This is Origen's statement in full regarding the author of Hebrews.

> The thoughts are Paul's, but the phraseology and composition are by someone else. *Not without reason have the ancient men handed down the Epistle as Paul's,* but who wrote the Epistle is known only to God.

We especially note that clause which is italicized. Evidently there was already in Origen's day a tradition that Paul wrote this epistle. Quite evidently it was the opinion of the earliest church in the East that Hebrews was Paul's epistle. It was not until a later day, and by a church more remote from Palestine, that the tradition arose of another author. Jerome, the greatest of the Latin fathers, considered Paul the author. It was during the third and fourth centuries that the Pauline authorship was denied in Rome. It is also interesting to note that during this same period the epistle was held in disrepute. After it regained its place as canonical Scripture, it was also considered as Pauline. Lindsay makes this valuable comment on the Western tradition.

Jerome suggests that at first it was received in Rome as Scripture and received also as Pauline. It is significant that both go together.

Others could be mentioned, but they would add nothing decisive either way.

We now turn to a bit of evidence that is enlightening. Peter wrote to those of the circumcision, to believing Jews everywhere. In 2 Peter 3:15 he mentions the fact that Paul had written to them. He separated this epistle from the others of Paul (v. 16). No epistle of Paul other than Hebrews answers to this statement. If Hebrews is not the epistle, then the epistle to which he refers has been lost.

To conclude our remarks, we quote a statement from Weymouth that illustrates how easy it is to defend a theory and support it with misinformation:

> The only fact clear as to the author is that he was not the Apostle Paul. The early Fathers did not attribute the book to Paul, nor was it until the seventh century that the tendency to do this, derived from Jerome, swelled into an ecclesiastical practice. From the book itself we see that the author must have been a Jew and a Hellenist, familiar with Philo as well as with the Old Testament, a friend of Timothy and well known to many of those whom he addressed, and not an Apostle but decidedly acquainted with Apostolic thoughts; and that he not only wrote before the destruction of Jerusalem but apparently himself was never in Palestine. The name of Barnabas, and also that of Priscilla, has been suggested, but in reality all these distinctive marks appear to be found only in Apollos. So that with Luther, and not a few modern scholars, we must either attribute it to him or give up the quest.

This statement is very sweeping, incorrect, and superficial. He does not even present the facts.

While we do not dogmatically assert our thesis of the Pauline authorship with any such note of certainty, we do not see fit to change our view without sufficient evidence. We still believe it to be reasonable to accept the Pauline tradition.

We deplore the fact that the King James Version carries the heading, *The Epistle of Paul the Apostle to the Hebrews.* It should read, *The Epistle to the Hebrews.* Such is the tenet that we affirm in this paper.

BIBLIOGRAPHY FOR APPENDIX

Calvin, John. *Commentary of Paul the Apostle on Hebrews*. 1567 Reprint. Grand Rapids, Michigan: Baker Book House, n.d.

Edwards, T. C. "The Epistle to the Hebrews," *Expositor's Bible*. Grand Rapids, Michigan: Baker Book House, n.d.

Gaebelein, Arno C. "The Epistle to the Hebrews," *The Annotated Bible*. Neptune, New Jersey: Loizeaux Brothers, n.d.

International Standard Bible Encyclopedia, article on the Epistle to the Hebrews. Grand Rapids, Michigan: Wm.B. Eerdmans Publishing Co., 1925.

Lindsay, W. *Lectures on The Epistle to the Hebrews*. *International Critical Commentary*. Edinburgh, Scotland: T. & T. Clark, 1867.

Moffatt, James. "The Epistle to the Hebrews," *International Critical Commentary*. Edinburgh, Scotland: T. & T. Clark, 1924.

Plumer, William. *Commentary on Paul's Epistle to the Hebrews*. Carlisle, Pennsylvania: The Banner of Truth, n.d.

Wickham, E. C. *Epistle to the Hebrews*. London, 1910.

BIBLIOGRAPHY

(Recommended for Further Study)

Bruce, F. F. *The Epistle to the Hebrews*. Grand Rapids, Michigan: Wm. B. Eerdmans Publishing Co., 1964.

DeHaan, M. R. *Hebrews*. Grand Rapids, Michigan: Zondervan Publishing House, 1959. (Message given on the Radio Bible Class.)

English, E. Schuyler. *Studies in the Epistle to the Hebrews*. Neptune, New Jersey: Loizeaux Brothers, 1955.

Hoyt, Herman A. *The Epistle to the Hebrews*. Winona Lake, Indiana: Brethren Missionary Herald Co., n.d.

Hughes, Philip Edgecumbe. *A Commentary on the Epistle to the Hebrews*. Grand Rapids, Michigan: Wm. B. Eerdmans Publishing Co., 1977.

Ironside, H. A. *The Epistle to the Hebrews*. Neptune, New Jersey: Loizeaux Brothers.

Kelly, William. *An Exposition of the Epistle to the Hebrews*. Addison, Illinois: Bible Truth Publishers, 1905.

Kent, Homer A., Jr. *The Epistle to the Hebrews*. Grand Rapids, Michigan: Baker Book House, 1972. (Excellent.)

MacDonald, William. *The Epistle to the Hebrews*. Neptune, New Jersey: Loizeaux Brothers, 1971.

Meyer, F. B. *The Way into the Holiest*. Fort Washington, Pennsylvania: Christian Literature Crusade, 1893. (A rich devotional study.)

Murray, Andrew. *The Holiest of All*. Old Tappan, New Jersey: Fleming H. Revell Co., 1894. (Excellent devotional treatment.)

Newell, William R. *Hebrews, Verse by Verse*. Chicago, Illinois: Moody Press, 1947. (Excellent.)

Pfeiffer, Charles F. *The Epistle to the Hebrews*. Chicago, Illinois: Moody Press, 1962. (Good, brief survey.)

Phillips, John. *Exploring Hebrews*. Chicago, Illinois: Moody Press, 1977.

Thomas, W. H. Griffith. *Hebrews: A Devotional Commentary*. Grand Rapids, Michigan: Wm. B. Eerdmans Publishing Co., 1962. (Excellent.)

Vine, W. E. *The Epistle to the Hebrews*. London: Oliphant, 1957.

Wiersbe, Warren W. *Be Confident*. Chicago, Illinois: Moody Press, 1977.

Wuest, Kenneth S. *Hebrews in the Greek New Testament for English Readers*. Grand Rapids, Michigan: Wm. B. Eerdmans Publishing Co., 1947.

The General Epistle of

JAMES

INTRODUCTION

The Epistle of James is the first in a group of epistles customarily called General Epistles, which includes James, 1 and 2 Peter, 1, 2, and 3 John, and Jude. They are designated as general or "catholic" epistles in the sense that they are universal, not being addressed to any particular individual or church, but to the church as a whole.

The problem of authorship is a major one. There is no question that James wrote the Epistle of James, but *which* James was the author? Some find at least four men by the name of James in the New Testament. I believe that you can find three who are clearly identified:

1. James, the brother of John and one of the sons of Zebedee. These two men were called "sons of thunder" by our Lord (see Mark 3:17). He was slain by Herod who at the same time put Simon Peter into prison (see Acts 12:1–2).

2. James, the son of Alphaeus, called "James the less" (see Mark 15:40). He is mentioned in the list of apostles, but very little is known concerning him. I automatically dismiss him as the author of this epistle.

3. James, the Lord's brother. He was a son of Mary and of Joseph, which made him a half brother of the Lord Jesus. In Matthew 13:55 we read: "Is not this the carpenter's son? is not his mother called Mary? and his brethren, James, and Joses, and Simon, and Judas?" In the beginning, the Lord's brethren did not believe in Him at all, but the time came when James became head of the church at Jerusalem. In Acts 15 James seems to have presided over that great council in Jerusalem. At least he made the summation and brought the council to a decision under the leading of the Holy Spirit. I believe it was this James whom Paul referred to in Galatians 2:9, "And when James, Cephas, and John, who seemed to be pillars, perceived the grace that was given unto me, they gave to me and Barnabas the right hands of fellowship; that we should go unto the heathen, and they unto the circumcision." This James is the man whom we believe to be the author of this epistle.

This epistle was written about A.D. 45–50. There have been those who have said that James wrote his epistle to combat the teachings of Paul; they argue that James empha-sizes works while Paul emphasizes faith. However, the earliest of Paul's epistles, 1 Thessalonians, was written about A.D. 52–56. Therefore, even Paul's first epistle was not written until after the Epistle of James, which was the first book of the New Testament to be written.

It is clear that James' theme is not works, but faith—the same as Paul's theme, but James emphasizes what faith produces. Both James and Paul speak a great deal of faith *and* works. They give us the two aspects of justification by faith, both of which are clear in the writings of Paul:

1. *Faith*—we are not justified *by* works. Paul wrote, "For by grace are ye saved through faith; and that not of yourselves: it is the gift of God: Not of works, lest any man should boast" (Eph. 2:8–9). And he also wrote, "Not by works of righteousness which we have done, but according to his mercy he saved us . . ." (Titus 3:5).

2. *Works*—we are justified *for* works. In Titus 3:8 Paul says, "This is a faithful saying, and these things I will that thou affirm constantly, that they which have believed in God might be careful to maintain good works. . . ." In Ephesians 2:10 he tells us, "For we are his workmanship, created in Christ Jesus unto good works, which God hath before ordained that we should walk in them."

Faith is the *root* of salvation—Paul emphasizes that; works are the *fruit* of salvation—that is the thing James emphasizes. Or, we can express it this way: Faith is the *cause* of salvation, and works are the *result* of salvation.

When Paul says that works will not save you, he is talking about the works of the Law. When James emphasizes that works are essential, he is talking about works of faith, not works of the Law. He said, "Yea, a man may say, Thou hast faith, and I have works: shew me thy faith without thy works, and I will shew thee my faith by my works" (James 2:18). God looks down and sees your heart, and He knows whether you believe or not—that is justification by faith. But your neighbor next door doesn't see your heart; he can only judge by your works, the *fruit* of your faith.

The following are what I consider to be the two key verses of this epistle. "But be ye doers of the word, and not hearers only, deceiving your own selves" (James 1:22). "But wilt thou know, O vain man, that faith without works is dead?" (James 2:20).

The Epistle of James deals with the ethics of Christianity, not doctrine. He is really going to bear down on the practical, but he will not get away from the subject of faith. James was evidently a very practical individual. Tradition says that he was given the name "Old Camel Knees" because he spent so much time in prayer.

Due to its practical nature, this epistle has been compared to the Book of Proverbs as well as to the Sermon on the Mount. James argues that justification by faith is demonstrated by works; it must be poured into the test tube of works (ch. 1–2), of words (ch. 3), of worldliness (ch. 4), and of a warning to the rich (ch. 5).

OUTLINE

I. **Verification of Genuine Faith, Chapters 1–3**
   A. God Tests Faith by Trials, Chapter 1:1–12
   (Twofold result: development of patience here, v. 3; reward hereafter, v. 12.)
   B. God Does Not Test Faith with Evil, Chapter 1:13–21
   (Evil comes from within—the flesh, v. 14.)
   C. God Tests Faith by THE WORD, Not by Man's Words, Chapter 1:22–27
   (Doing, not doctrine, is the final test of faith; knowing is not enough.)
   D. God Tests Faith by Attitude and Action in Respect of Persons, Chapter 2:1–13
   E. God Tests Faith by Good Works, Chapter 2:14–26
   (Abraham is an illustration of works, v. 21.)
   F. God Tests Faith by the Tongue, Chapter 3
   ("What is in the well of the heart will come up through the bucket of the mouth.")

II. **Vacuity and Vapidness of Worldliness, Chapter 4**
   (Worldliness is identified with fighting and the spirit of dissension, vv. 1–2.)

III. **Vexation of the Rich; Value of the Imminent Coming of Christ, Chapter 5**
   (The soon coming of Christ produces patience, vv. 7–8, and prayer, vv. 13–18.)
   A. Riches Are a Care (Rich Warned), Chapter 5:1–6
   B. The Coming of Christ Is a Comfort, Chapter 5:7–12
   C. The Prayer of the Righteous Is a Power, Chapter 5:13–20

CHAPTER 1

THEME: God tests faith by trials; God does not test with evil; God tests faith by the Word, not by man's words

The Epistle of James is a very practical book which deals with the ethics of Christianity rather than with doctrine. James will really bear down on some practical issues, but the theme of faith is also seen throughout his entire epistle. The emphasis in James is on the works which are produced by faith. In the first three chapters he is going to speak of the verification of genuine faith and give us some of the ways God tests faith.

GOD TESTS FAITH BY TRIALS

James, a servant of God and of the Lord Jesus Christ, to the twelve tribes which are scattered abroad, greeting [James 1:1].

"James, a servant of God and of the Lord Jesus Christ." "Servant" is literally a bond slave. Now I do not know about you, but I am confident that if I had been the Lord's half brother on the human side, somewhere in this epistle I would have let you know that. I would have brought in that fact in a very pious and humble way, but I surely would have let you know. However, James does not do that. Instead, he calls himself a bond slave of God and of the Lord Jesus Christ.

At first the Lord Jesus' human brethren did not believe He was the Son of God. They had been brought up with Him and had played with Him. They had seen Him grow. They noticed that He was unusual, but they did not believe that He was the Savior of the world. Our Lord Jesus was so human when He was here on this earth that even His own brethren did not believe at the first. Of course, your family members are always the hardest people to reach, yet they are the ones we should reach. James came to know the Lord Jesus not only as his blood brother but as his own Savior, and then he became His bond slave. Notice what James calls Him—he uses His full name, the Lord Jesus Christ. James says, "He is my Lord." Jesus was His human name, and James knew Him as Jesus, his half brother; but he also knew Him as Christ, the Messiah who had come and had died for the sins of the world. *Jesus* was not just a name, but He was called Jesus because He would save His people from their sins.

"To the twelve tribes which are scattered abroad, greeting." It is obvious that James is referring to the believers in Israel. He is writing to the Christian Jews of that day. After all, the early church was 100 percent Jewish for quite a period of time. A few Gentiles became believers, and then a great revival broke out in the heart of the Roman Empire in the area of what is Turkey today. That is where the seven churches of Asia Minor were located. But James, evidently writing before this took place, is addressing the Jewish believers.

"To the twelve tribes which are scattered abroad." Today people speak of the "ten lost tribes of Israel," but no tribes really got lost. God scattered them throughout the world. They did not settle in England or the United States, although there are many Jews in both places. They are on every continent of the world. There is a tremendous Jewish population in Russia. There are some in China, some in Japan—they are "scattered abroad." James wrote this epistle to believing Jews of that day who were scattered abroad.

"Greeting"—that translation is a little stilted, for the word in the Greek literally means "rejoice." He writes to them and says, "Rejoice." James was not sour-tempered. James was a man with a lot of life in him.

Now James is going to speak of rejoicing under unusual circumstances—

My brethren, count it all joy when ye fall into divers temptations [James 1:2].

"Divers temptations" means various trials. In other words, when you are having trouble, don't start crying as if something terrible has happened to you. You are to *rejoice* and count it all joy that God is testing you in this way!

The question is often asked whether the Christian is to experience joy in depth in all the trials and tensions of life. Very frankly, the answer is no—that is not what James is saying here. It leads to unreality to say that you are reconciled to the will of God when troubles come to you when you really are not reconciled. People piously say they have accepted God's will yet go around with a long face and weep half the time. My friend, you are not reconciled to the will of God until you can rejoice.

James goes on to make it clear that God does not give us trouble for trouble's sake; it is not an end in itself.

Knowing this, that the trying of your faith worketh patience [James 1:3].

God has a goal in mind—you can count on that. James is speaking here about the attitude of your heart toward your trouble. The Greek aorist tense used here suggests that the joy is the result of the trial. In Hebrews 12 we see that one method God uses in the life of the believer is chastening, which literally means "child training." Trials are meaningless, suffering is senseless, and testing is irrational unless there is some good purpose for them. God says there is a reason for them, and it is a *good* reason. "And we know that all things work together for good to them that love God, to them who are the called according to his purpose" (Rom. 8:28). When the external pressures of testing are upon us and we are placed in the fires of adversity and tragedy and suffering, the attitude of faith should be that God has permitted it for a purpose and He has a high and lofty goal in view. We can know that God is working something out in our lives.

I must hasten to add that this does not necessarily mean that we will *understand* what purpose God has in it. This is the test of *faith*. We walk by faith and not by sight. Someone in the Middle Ages said, "God nothing does, nor suffers to be done, but what we would ourselves, if we could see through all events of things as well as He."

What are some of the purposes served in the testing of faith? In this epistle, James says that testing is the proof positive of genuine faith. Let me use a rather homely illustration. Some years ago I had the privilege of leading to the Lord a secretary to one of the officers in a large airplane plant here in Southern California. On a number of occasions she asked me to speak to a Bible study class in that plant. While I was there I learned something of how airplanes are built. They start out by designing a new plane on the drawing board. Then blueprints are drawn up and models are made. The models are tested, and then construction begins. After about two years the first plane will roll off the assembly line. The question remains: Will it fly? Will it perform? Will it stand the test? So a test pilot must then put the plane through the paces up in the air. When the plane has proven to be all that the maker has said it is, there is confidence in the plane and the airlines will buy it. It is then brought to the airport where passengers will board it, and the plane thus becomes serviceable and useful. In the same sense, ore is brought to an assayer to prove that it is gold or

that it is silver. He will put a fire under it and pour acid on it, and then he declares whether or not it is genuine. Likewise God puts faith to the test to prove that it is genuine. Someone has expressed it like this: "The acid of grief tests the coin of belief." There is a lot of truth in that.

God tests our faith for a purpose: "Knowing this, that the trying of your faith worketh patience." He tests us in order that He might produce patience in our lives.

But let patience have her perfect work, that ye may be perfect and entire, wanting nothing [James 1:4].

It is patience which will make you a full-grown Christian, but how does God produce patience in you? The very interesting thing is that patience is the fruit of the Holy Spirit. You will never become patient by trying to be patient, but neither will the Holy Spirit place it on a silver platter and offer it to you as a gift. Patience comes through suffering and testing.

"But let patience have her perfect work, that ye may be perfect and entire, wanting nothing." You will never be a "perfect"—that is, a complete, fully mature—Christian without patience. Some Christians therefore have never really grown up but have remained babes. I made the statement as a pastor one Sunday morning that there were more babes in the church service than there were in the nursery downstairs. I tell you, I didn't get too many laughs from that comment. The difference, however, is that the babies in the nursery were beautiful, but the ones sitting in the church service were not very pretty. There is much clamoring and criticizing, turmoil and tension in our churches today. The reason is that many Christians have not grown up; they are still babes.

David wrote in Psalm 131, "LORD, my heart is not haughty, nor mine eyes lofty: neither do I exercise myself in great matters, or in things too high for me. Surely I have behaved and quieted myself, as a child that is weaned of his mother: my soul is even as a weaned child" (Ps. 131:1–2). In other words, David said, "I found out I had to grow up. I needed to get off milk and start eating porterhouse steak. I needed to eat of the Bread of Life." God tested David, and that testing enabled him to grow up.

Paul wrote in the Book of Romans that patience is one of the results of being justified by faith: "And not only so, but we glory in tribulations also: knowing that tribulation worketh patience; And patience, experience; and experience, hope" (Rom. 5:3–4). There is a purpose in it all, you see.

There are many shallow and superficial saints today. There are many who are insecure as Christians. There are believers who try to be intellectual and who question the Word of God. And there are those who feel that as Christians we should try the "new morality." My friend, the problem with such believers is that they have never grown up—they are still little babes. God gives testing and trials to produce patience in our lives and that we might become full-grown children of God. How we need that today.

God must send us trouble so that we learn patience, which will also produce hope and love in the lives of men and women. Over the years of my ministry I have seen the Holy Spirit work this out in the lives of many folk. I recall one man who, when I first knew him, was always finding fault; as a pastor I had never had such a critic before. Then he began to attend the midweek Bible study at the church. I noticed that he brought his Bible and took notes. Over a period of ten years God sent that man a great deal of trouble, but he grew up and became one of the sweetest Christians I have ever known in my life. This is the type of testing which God gives to those who are His own.

If any of you lack wisdom, let him ask of God, that giveth to all men liberally, and upbraideth not; and it shall be given him [James 1:5].

"Wisdom" here is related to the trials which James has been talking about. You and I have troubles and trials and problems. How are you going to solve this problem? How are you going to meet this issue? How are you going to deal with this person? If you lack wisdom in regard to a problem, you need to go to God in prayer.

Wisdom is the exercise and practical use of knowledge. Many people have knowledge, but they do not have any practical sense whatsoever. Even to this day I get a good laugh just thinking about the man with a Ph.D. with whom I used to play golf. One day out on the golf course it began to rain, and he looked at me in utter amazement and asked, "What shall we do now?" Well, you don't need a Ph.D. to know that you need to get in out of the rain! I said to him, "I think we'd better seek shelter." Wisdom is to know how to act under certain circumstances of testing, of trial, or when problems or questions arise. Life is filled with these, and you and I need wisdom from God.

"That giveth to all men liberally, and upbraideth not." God is in the business of giving out wisdom "liberally," that is, simply. He will just simply help you out in times like that. He "upbraideth not" means, according to Marvin R. Vincent in his *Word Studies in the New Testament*, it is the "pure, simple giving of good without admixture of evil or bitterness." If we lack wisdom, let's go to God who will hear and answer our prayer.

But let him ask in faith, nothing wavering. For he that wavereth is like a wave of the sea driven with the wind and tossed [James 1:6].

Maybe it is not your problem, but it has been my problem over a great deal of my Christian life that I simply have not believed God. Don't misunderstand me—I have trusted Christ as my Savior, and I believe with all my soul that He saved me and is going to save me for heaven. I believe that with all my heart, but down here in this life, where the rubber meets the road, is where I have had my problems. For example, I went through college in almost total unbelief—I didn't believe God could put me through college. I was a poor boy who had to borrow money and work at a full-time job. It was difficult. Every year I would finish, thinking I would not be able to come back the next year. Lo and behold, God always opened up a door, and I was able to continue. I was actually a miserable fellow as I went through college; when I look back, I realize I could have had a lot more fun if I had only believed God.

"But let him ask in faith, nothing wavering." Why don't you believe God, my friend? Do you as a Christian have a long face today? Are you wondering how your problems are going to work out? I know exactly how you feel—I've been there. Why don't you believe God? Why don't you trust Him and turn them over to Him? I know I do not have the brains to meet the problems of life; I know I am not capable of living in this complex civilization, but I have a heavenly Father who can supply the wisdom that I need.

"For he that wavereth is like a wave of the sea driven with the wind and tossed." We say, "I believe God is going to work this out," but then we jump at it ourselves and make our own decision. So often I turn a problem over to the Lord and believe Him, but then the next day I do not believe Him. I decide that nothing has shown up by way of solution, so I will solve it myself. That's where I make my mistake.

Such a man is "like a wave of the sea driven with the wind and tossed."

For let not that man think that he shall receive anything of the Lord [James 1:7].

If you are going to work out your problem for yourself, then God cannot work it out for you. Instead of going like a bull into a china closet and trying to work something out, why not turn it over to God?

Now James gives a proverb, and it is a good one—

A double-minded man is unstable in all his ways [James 1:8].

This was Israel's big problem. Hosea said Israel was like a silly dove. She first flew off to Egypt seeking help, and then she flew to Assyria. She turned first to one and then to the other, but she did not turn to God. Many times when a problem comes up we go here and there trying to solve it, until it occurs to us that we have never taken it to God. When you started out today did you turn the issues of the day over to God? I used to do a great deal of counseling as a pastor, and I would meet many new people during the day. One of the prayers I always prayed was, "Lord, I'm going to meet some new people today, and I don't know how to treat them. This man may prove to be a wonderful friend who wants to help me get out the Word of God. This other man may be seeking to hurt my ministry. Lord, help me to know the difference. Help me to be able to know which man I can put my arm around and help, and make me wary of the man who does not want my help at all. Lord, give me wisdom today." We need wisdom to meet the issues of life.

Let the brother of low degree rejoice in that he is exalted [James 1:9].

You may say, "I'm just a poor individual. I don't have very much. I don't have any wealth." My friend, if you are a child of God you have a lot of wealth. You have treasure in heaven. And have you ever stopped to think what you have down here, what you have in Christ? We have everything in Him. Paul wrote, "Therefore let no man glory in men. For all things are yours; Whether Paul, or Apollos, or Cephas, or the world, or life, or death, or things present, or things to come; all are yours; And ye are Christ's; and Christ is God's" (1 Cor 3:21–23). I belong to Christ, and everything He has He will make over to me. I have life. I have blessings. Even death is coming to me someday, if Christ doesn't come in the meantime. All of that is from Him, and all of these things we can rejoice in. It does not matter if you are the humblest saint or the poorest person on earth, you are rich in Christ, my friend, and you have something to rejoice over.

But the rich, in that he is made low: because as the flower of the grass he shall pass away [James 1:10].

I always think of this verse when I walk across the campus of my alma mater. Every building there is named for some rich man. Do you know where those rich men are today? They are like the flowers which bloomed yesterday but are gone today. I think of how powerful they were, the riches and the influence they had, but today they are pushing up daisies somewhere and they have faded away. Don't rejoice in the fact that you are a rich man, because you will not have your money very long. You may have invested in gilt-edged bonds, and you may have stocks which you do not think you will lose. My friend, you may not lose them, but those stocks and bonds are going to lose *you* one of these days. In death you will not be able to hold on to them. The old adage says, "There's no pocket in a shroud." You won't be able to take it with you. The rich man is like the flower of the grass—he shall pass away.

For the sun is no sooner risen with a burning heat, but it withereth the grass, and the flower thereof falleth, and the grace of the fashion of it perisheth: so also shall the rich man fade away in his ways [James 1:11].

I had the privilege years ago of speaking occasionally to a group of Christians in Hollywood, California. Among those who attended was a movie star who had become a Christian later on in life. She was getting old at that time, and when I looked at her I thought of how that beauty, which had brought her fame and fortune at one time, was now passing away. God says that the rich man shall "fade away in his ways."

My friend, rejoice today that you have a Savior who is not only going to save you for heaven—that's good enough for me—but He is going to help you this very day.

When I teach the Book of Proverbs I liken it to a young man who is considering the catalogs he has received from different universities—among which is the University of Wisdom. Here in the Epistle of James we find a different school—the School of Hard Knocks. That is the school most of us are in today. God wants to bring all those who are His own to full maturity as Christians, and He has many tests for doing that. He tests all of His children to see whether or not they are genuine, to weed out the phonies and the pseudosaints. He also wants to give assurance to His children. We should not regard our trials as evidence that we are not His children but rather as proof positive of our faith. My friend, if you are not having a little trouble today, you should question your salvation; if you are having trouble, that is a good sign that you belong to Him. While God has many goals in His testing, the one James has emphasized here is patience. God not only wants to give you proof that you are a genuine child of His, he also wants to produce patience in your life.

Much has been written about testing and God's purposes in it. William Penn, the man from whom the state of Pennsylvania got its name, made this statement: "No pain, no balm. No thorn, no throne. No gall, no glory. No cross, no crown."

Someone else has expressed it like this: "If I must carry a burden, Christ will carry me. Sometimes we must be laid low before we look high. In ourselves we are weak, even where we are strong. In Christ we are strong, even where we are weak. It's not how long you'll live, but how you are going to live." This perspective is important to have.

Many people wonder why in the world they must endure a particular experience. A number of years ago I received a letter from a Christian man who wrote: "I have a wife who has been sick for the past twenty years and has been paralyzed for the last ten years with Parkinson's disease. There is no hope of her ever leaving the hospital. How can a loving Father make a person suffer and linger as she has? And I know she loves the Lord." This man was genuinely concerned. He didn't have an answer for his problem, and neither did I. I couldn't tell him why it was happening, but I could tell him there was a purpose in it and that God was working out something in her life.

Blessed is the man that endureth temptation: for when he is tried, he shall receive the crown of life, which the Lord hath promised to them that love him [James 1:12].

"Temptation" is the same word as we have had before, which is sometimes translated as "testing" or "trying." "Temptation" is a good translation if you understand it in a good sense, as we will see later in this chapter.

"Blessed is the man that endureth temptation: for when he is tried, he shall receive the crown of life, which the Lord hath promised to them that love him." Testing is one of God's methods of developing us in the Christian faith. This is the way He is going to enable us to grow and develop patience in our lives down here, but He also has something in mind for the future—"the crown of life."

Testing of any kind, but especially if it is a severe calamity or tragedy, has a tendency to produce a miasma of pessimism and hopelessness. I do not blame the man whose wife was ill with Parkinson's disease for feeling like he did. I do not blame him for asking, "Why?" But the child of God can have the confidence that God is doing it for a very definite reason and that He has a purpose in it all.

However, the man of the world will sink beneath the waves of adversity. Life, even at its best, makes him pessimistic. How many pessimists are there today? How many cynics? How many are there who are filled with bitterness, although they have everything? We are seeing an epidemic of suicides among teenagers, and thousands of other young people are dropping out of society today. Why? It is because they have no goal in life. One of the more sensible news commentators made this remark: "Back during the depression people had a will to live and there were very few suicides, but today when everything has been given to them they want to die."

When faith is tested and surrounded by darkness, when the waves are rolling high and all seems lost, the child of God knows that this is not the end. It may be gloom now, but it will be glory later on. As the psalmist said, ". . . weeping may endure for a night, but joy cometh in the morning" (Ps. 30:5). James says here, "He shall receive the crown of life, which the Lord hath promised to them that love him."

I have noticed that people who have suffered a great deal have been brought into a closer loving relationship with the Lord Jesus Christ. Someone has expressed it like this:

Is there no other way open, God,
Except through sorrow, pain, and loss,
To stamp Christ's likeness on my soul—
No other way except the cross?

And then a voice stills all my soul
As stilled the waves of Galilee,
"Can'st thou not bear the furnace heat
If midst the flames I walk with thee?

"I bore the cross. I know its weight.
I drank the cup I hold for thee.
Can'st thou not follow where I lead?
I'll give thee strength. Lean hard on Me."

—Author unknown

You see, suffering brings an individual into a loving relationship with Christ. And it causes him to look forward to that day when he will be brought into the presence of the Lord Jesus who will give him the crown of life.

What is "the crown of life"? There are many crowns mentioned in Scripture which are given as *rewards* to believers. A crown is not salvation, but it represents a reward. It is something that is given to an individual as a reward. For example, there was an unknown boy from California who went to the Olympic Games and won six gold medals. Suddenly his face was seen on every billboard, on television, and even in commercials. I am told he also signed a movie contract. He won six medals— he received his rewards. My Christian friend, the Lord Jesus has a reward for those who will endure down here. James says, "He shall receive the crown of life, which the Lord hath promised to them that love him."

Testing will either drive you to the Lord or it will drive you away from Him. So many Christians become bitter. My friend, it is not going to be a pleasant experience to come someday into the presence of Christ if you have let the very thing your heavenly Father was using to develop your character and to bring you into a loving relationship with the Lord Jesus Christ make you bitter. We will have testings, but there is going to be a crown of life for those who persevere under trial.

I have done a great deal of reading about the crowns which are mentioned in Scripture, and I sometimes wonder where some of the interpreters get all their information. Let me give you my very simple interpretation of what I think a crown of life is. We find in Scripture that there are different kinds of punishment for the lost. Some will receive so many stripes, others will receive more stripes. There are *degrees of punishment* for the lost. Likewise there are *degrees of rewards* for believers. I do not expect to receive the reward that a man like Paul the apostle or Martin Luther or John Wesley will receive. Although I don't expect to receive a reward as they will, I do hope that I can come in for something—I am very much interested in that. I think that a "crown of life" is that which can bring you into a closer relationship with the

Lord Jesus more than anything else possibly could.

In the Book of Revelation it speaks about the Lord giving to each of His own a stone with a name written on it (see Rev. 2:17). We have assumed that that means He will give each of us a new name. There's an old favorite gospel song that says, "There's a new name written down in glory. . . ." Well, it is not the new name spoken of in Revelation, but it is *your* name that is written down in glory if you are a child of God. As best as I can determine, the new name spoken of in Revelation means that God is going to give each of us a stone on which there is written a name of Christ which applies to our experience with Him. To you He means something a little special other than what He might mean to someone else. In other words, the Lord Jesus means something to you that He does not mean to me. He means something to me that He does not mean to you.

I can remember a time in my life as a young fellow that I stood at the crossroads at a Bible conference, trying to decide if I would go into the ministry or continue to follow a life of sin. There was a girl there at that conference in whom I was very much interested, but she was not really what you would call Bible conference material. I never shall forget that night yonder in Middle Tennessee. I crawled in under a water maple tree which was thick with leaves. In the shade—for the moon was shining brightly—I got down on my face and told the Lord Jesus that I needed His help and strength to make a decision. As a result of that night He means something to me that I'm sure He does not mean to you. You probably have a precious moment in your life which I have not experienced. I believe that the new name written on a stone is going to reflect what Christ means specially to you.

It is my conclusion that the crown of life means that you are going to have a degree of life in heaven which someone else will not have. There are a lot of folk who have gone through this world without doing anything for God. I thank God there was one thief on a cross who turned to Christ, but I cannot imagine that he will get very much of a reward, especially when I compare him to a man like Paul the apostle. Imagine what it is going to be like someday when Paul receives the crown of life!

Paul was very much interested in the crown of life, and James was interested in it too. There will be a crown of life, but you cannot receive that crown of life until you have been out on the racecourse of life, until you have gotten right down where the rubber meets the road and where life is being lived out. If you can live for God down here, my friend, He has a crown of life for you someday. That is something to which we can look forward.

When I think of the testings of this life, I am reminded of the deacon who got up in a testimony meeting in which the people were being asked to give their favorite verses of Scripture. This deacon got up and said, "My favorite verse is 'It came to pass.'" The minister looked up in amazement, and all the people were puzzled. Finally, the pastor asked, "Brother, what do you mean your favorite verse is 'It came to pass'?" The man replied, "When I have trouble and trials, I just go to the Lord and praise Him and say, 'I thank You, Lord, that it came to pass—it didn't come to stay!'" Thank God for that, my friend. I don't know a better way of putting it: The trouble hasn't come to stay.

James uses the same argument to warn the rich when he says, "You are like the grass and the flower of the grass." It may look pretty for you today. Life may be beautiful, my friend, but the flower is withering and your riches will not deliver you. Someday you will stand before Jesus Christ. Every human being is to stand before Him—the unbelievers will stand before God at the Great White Throne judgment. Also all believers, called the church, will go beforehand to the *bema* seat of Christ to see whether or not they will receive a crown of life. I don't know about you, but I'd like to have that crown, the crown which He offers to those who, after they have endured the testings of this life, *love* Him.

GOD DOES NOT TEST WITH EVIL

"Temptation" is used in two senses: testing under trial, as we have seen in verse 12, and now solicitation to evil, verses 13–14. James is now going to talk about that temptation, which is temptation to do evil. People often say that the Lord tested them when it wasn't the Lord at all. God cannot be tempted with evil, and He does not tempt with evil. James deals with something here which is very important for God's children to understand, because we often blame God for a great many things in our lives for which He is not responsible.

Let no man say when he is tempted, I am tempted of God: for God cannot be tempted with evil, neither tempteth he any man [James 1:13].

We have seen in the preceding verses that God tests His own children, but now James makes it very clear that God never tests men with evil and with sin. "Let no man say when he is tempted, I am tempted of God"—a more literal translation is this: "Let not one man being tempted say, I am tempted of God." Notice that James is no longer using the noun *temptation* as he was previously. He is now using the verb; he is speaking of the action.

The natural propensity of mankind is to blame God for his own fumbles, all of his foibles, all of his faults and failures and filth. From the very beginning, since the time of the fall of man, this has been true. Adam said, ". . . The woman whom thou gavest to be with me, she gave me of the tree, and I did eat" (Gen. 3:12)—he really passed the buck! The woman did the same thing; she said, ". . . The serpent beguiled me . . ." (Gen. 3:13). Actually, all three of them were responsible.

We often hear questions like this: Why does God send floods and earthquakes and allow the killing of babies? We blame God today for the result of the greed and avarice and selfishness of mankind—that is what is really responsible for floods and earthquakes. Man builds too close to a river and, when in the natural course of events the river rises, he calls it a flood and an act of God. But man thinks it is more pleasant to build by the river, or it's nearer transportation, or that is where the business is. It is actually the greed and avarice of man that causes him to build where it is really dangerous to build.

If you are going to live in Southern California, for example, you are going to take a chance on having an earthquake—you can be sure of that. We had a small one just the other evening as my wife and I were sitting in our den. The seismologists predict that we are in for a big earthquake here, yet people are still streaming into Southern California and putting up high-rise buildings. We ought not to blame God if a slab of concrete falls off one of those high-rise buildings and kills one of our loved ones. It would be much safer in the wide open spaces of Texas. I'm a Texan, but who wants to go back there? I know it's nicer there than when I was just a boy growing up, but I want to stay here in California. However, I'm not going to blame God when the earthquake comes. We have already been warned that it is coming.

Men also blame God in their philosophies today. Pantheism, for instance, says that everything is God, but good is God's right hand and evil is His left hand. Fatalism says that everything is running like blind necessity. If there is a God, they say, He has wound up this universe like an eight-day clock and has gone off and left it. Materialism's explanation of the problem with the human race is that the loftiest aspirations and the vilest passions are the natural metabolism of a physical organism.

God has answered these philosophies in His Word. There is no evil in God. In Him all is goodness and all is light and all is right. John wrote in his first epistle, "This then is the message which we have heard of him, and declare unto you, that God is light [that is, He is holy], and in him is no darkness at all" (1 John 1:5). The Lord Jesus made this very interesting statement: ". . . for the prince of this world cometh, and hath nothing in me" (John 14:30). That means there is no evil or sin in Him. But every time Satan gets around me, he is able to find something in me.

Let me introduce something which is theological at this point: *Jesus could not sin.* Someone will immediately ask, "Why, then, was He tempted?" In Matthew 4:7 our Lord said to Satan, ". . . It is written again, Thou shalt not tempt the Lord thy God." God wants to *save* from sin, and He does not tempt men to sin—He wants to *deliver* men. He never uses sin as a test, but He will permit it, as we shall see. The Lord Jesus had no sin in Him— "The prince of this world cometh, and hath nothing in me." The reason He was tempted was to *prove* that there was nothing in Him. After He had lived a life down here for thirty-three years, Satan came with this temptation, a temptation that appealed to man's total personality—the physical side, the mental side, and the spiritual side of man. The Lord Jesus could not fall, and the testing was given to demonstrate that He could not fall. If He could have fallen, then any moment your salvation and mine is in doubt. The minute He yielded to sin, we would have no Savior. His temptation was to prove that He could not sin.

Let me illustrate this with a very homely illustration from my boyhood in west Texas. My dad built cotton gins for the Murray Gin Company, and we lived in a little town that was near a branch of the Brazos River. In the summertime there wasn't enough water in that river to rust a shingle nail, but when it began to rain in wintertime, you could almost float a battleship on it. One year a flood washed out the wooden bridge on which the Santa Fe railroad crossed the river. They replaced it with a steel bridge, and when they completed it, they brought in two locomotives, stopped them on top of the bridge, and tied down both of the whistles. All of us who lived in that little town knew for sure that something was happening. We ran down to see what it was—all twenty-three of us! When we got there, one of the braver citizens asked the engineer, "What are you doing?" The engineer replied, "Well, we built this bridge, and we are testing it." The man asked, "Why? Do you think it's going to fall down?" That engineer drew himself up to his full height and said, "Of course it will not fall down! We are *proving* it won't fall down." For the same reason, Jesus was tested to prove that you and I have a Savior who could not sin. God cannot be tempted with sin, and God will not tempt you with sin.

However, God does *permit* us to be tempted with sin. In 2 Samuel 24:1 we read, "And again the anger of the Lord was kindled against Israel, and he moved David against them to say, Go, number Israel and Judah." Frankly, that was sinful. Then, *did* God tempt David with evil? My friend, to understand the Bible you always need to get the full story. In 2 Samuel you have man's viewpoint of the events recorded. From man's viewpoint it looked as if God was angry with Israel and He simply had David do this. However, in 1 Chronicles we are told God's viewpoint of it: "And Satan stood up against Israel, and provoked David to number Israel" (1 Chr. 21:1). Who provoked David to sin? It was Satan, not God. God merely permitted Satan to do that because He was angry with Israel and their sin. God never tempts men with evil.

Who is responsible for our propensity to evil? What causes us to sin? Someone will say, "Well, you have just shown that it is Satan." Let's look at what James has to say in verse 14—

But every man is tempted, when he is drawn away of his own lust, and enticed [James 1:14].

We are talking here about the sins of the flesh. Who is responsible when you are drawn away to do evil? When you yield to evil temptation? God is not responsible. The Devil is not responsible. *You* are responsible.

A man got lost in the hills of Arkansas back in the days of the Model T Ford. He had lost his way, and there were no highway markings. He came into a small town and saw some little boys playing there. He asked one of them, "Where am I?" The little fellow looked at him puzzled for just a moment. Finally he pointed at the man with his finger and said, "*There* you are!" My friend, when you ask, "Who tempted me to do this?" God says, *"There* you are. It's in your own skin—that is where the problem is."

"Every man is tempted." *Every* man—this is the declaration of the individuality of the personality in the race of mankind. Just as each one of us has a different fingerprint, each one of us has a different moral nature. We have our own idiosyncrasies, our own eccentricities. All of us have something a little different.

One man was talking to another and said, "You know, everybody has some peculiarity." "I disagree with you," said the other. "I don't think I have a peculiarity." "Well, then, let me ask you a question. Do you stir your coffee with your right hand or with your left hand?" asked the first man. "I stir it with my right hand," the other man replied. "Well, that's your peculiarity. Most people stir their coffee with a spoon!" May I say to you, all of us have our peculiarities. One person may be tempted to drink. Another may be tempted to overeat. Another may be tempted in the realm of sex. The problem is always within the individual. No outside thing or influence can make us sin. The trouble is here, within us, with that old nature that we have.

I think of the little boy who was playing around one evening in the pantry. He had gotten down the cookie jar. His mother called to him and said, "Willie, what are you doing in the pantry?" He said, "I'm fighting temptation!" He was in the wrong place to fight temptation, but that is the same place a lot of grown-up people are today. Many things are not bad within themselves, but it is the use we make of them that is wrong. Food is good, but you can become a glutton. Alcohol is medicine, but you can become an alcoholic if you abuse it. Sex is good if it is exercised within marriage. When it is exercised outside of marriage, you are going to experience several kinds of damage. Our society has an epidemic of venereal disease because of the looseness of the "new morality" today.

Many psychologists are trying to help us get rid of our guilt complexes. A Christian psychologist who taught in one of our universities here in Southern California told me one time, "You need to emphasize in your teaching that guilt complex more than you do. A guilt complex is as much a part of you as your right arm. You just cannot get rid of it."

However, the godless psychologist may attempt to remove the guilt complex in the wrong way. For example, a Christian lady called me one time and said, "Dr. McGee, a most frightful thing has happened to me. I've been having a real problem and have been on the verge of a nervous breakdown due to certain trials I've been going through. I went to a psychologist whom my doctor recommended. When he found out that I was a Christian, he said, 'What you need to do is to go downstairs to the barroom and pick up the first man you find there. Then you'll get rid of your guilt complex.'" I agree with the woman that such counsel is frightful indeed!

Then there are other psychologists who say, "What about your background? Did your mother love you? Did anything unusual happen while you were in the womb?" If you said, "Well, my mother was caught in a rainstorm while she was carrying me," the psychologist would say, "That's the reason you're a drip!" Well, he *practically* says that when he blames his patient's problems on the mother.

My friend, you could solve a great deal of your problems for which you are blaming someone else if you would say to the living Lord Jesus who is right now at God's right hand, "I'm a sinner. *I'm* guilty." Then He will remove your guilt complex—He is the only One who can do that.

Proverbs says, "For as he [man] thinketh in his heart, so is he . . ." (Prov. 23:7). The solicitation to sin must have a corresponding response from within. James says that it is of your own lust (lust is an overweening desire and uncontrolled longing) that you are drawn away into sin. The Lord Jesus said, "I will draw all men unto Me" (see John 12:32), but the scoffer says, "He'll *not* draw me!" My friend, He will not force you. Hosea tells us that He will only use bands of love to draw us to Himself. He wants to woo and win you by His grace and love. Frankly, evil is attractive today; it is winsome. We are told that Moses was caught up at first in the pleasures of sin. Man can be enticed; the hook can be baited. If he yields, before long a person will become an alcoholic or a dope addict.

Then when lust hath conceived, it bringeth forth sin: and sin, when it is finished, bringeth forth death [James 1:15].

In other words, when the desire of the soul, having conceived, gives birth to sin, the sin, having been completed, brings forth death. James uses a very interesting word here: "when lust hath *conceived.*" The word actually means "to become pregnant." Conception is the joining or union of two. The desire of this old nature of ours joins with the outward temptation that faces us and thus becomes sin. The Lord Jesus said, "If you are angry with your brother, you are guilty of murder"—because it begins in the heart and moves out into action. He also said, "If you look upon a woman to lust after her, you have already committed adultery with her"—because it begins in your heart. That is where sin always begins.

The natural question at this point is: Is temptation sin? Of course it's not sin; the answer is definitely no. It is when the conception takes place—when the thought in the heart is carried out in action—that temptation becomes sin. Martin Luther expressed it in this novel way: "You cannot keep birds from flying over your head, but you can keep them from nesting in your hair." Sin is the consummation of the act inwardly and outwardly.

Temptation in and of itself is not sin. We all have an evil nature—there is no use trying to kid ourselves concerning that. We all have been tempted to do evil; everyone has a weakness in the flesh. One person may be a glutton and another may be a gossip. Both sins are absolutely of the flesh; both come from within. It is only the Lord Jesus who could say, ". . . for the prince of this world cometh, and hath nothing in me" (John 14:30).

"Then when lust hath conceived, it bringeth forth sin." There cannot be a stillbirth. Lust is going to bring forth something. When that evil thought in the heart is joined to the outward temptation, there is a birth—a birth of the act, a birth of *sin*.

Now we rationalize sin today. We rationalize our bad tempers. We rationalize our gossip. We rationalize a lot of polite sins, and we even rationalize gross immorality; but the Bible calls them *sins*.

"And sin, when it is finished, bringeth forth death." There are three kinds of death spoken of in Scripture. There is (1) *physical* death, and that comes to every man, you can be sure of that. Then there is (2) *spiritual* death, which is the condition of the lost man—he is "dead in trespasses and sins" (see Eph. 2:1). Finally, there is (3) *eternal* death, which is the fate of the man who dies an unbeliever. The word *death* here primarily means "separation." Therefore, for a believer it means that when sin is born in his life, when it becomes an action, his fellowship with God is broken. There is a separation. In 1 John 1:6 we read, "If we say that we have fellowship with him, and walk in darkness, we lie, and do not the truth." You cannot have fellowship with Him and permit sin continually to happen in your life.

The great sin today, I suppose, is adultery. It is something that nearly every person has been faced with—and it is not something new. I think that the emphasis that is given to sex in our society and the present-day mode of dress have led to the committing of adultery probably more than it ever has been committed in American history. Certainly, adultery along with the free use of alcohol have pulled down the great nations of the past. Wine, women, and song have brought down the great nations of the world. Rome did not fall to some outside conqueror; Rome fell from within because it was honeycombed with sin.

I recall a fine-looking young man who came to me and said, "I've fallen in love with a very beautiful girl. I want her to be mine." I asked him, "Have you asked her to marry you?" "Well, not exactly," he said. "She's married." I said, "You had better give up this notion right now." The young man went on to say, "But I want to ask you if it would be wrong for her to get a divorce and for us then to get married?" I told him, "Certainly it would be. You've been tempted, and I mean tempted a great deal, but as a child of God you would never be able to get by with such sin." I went on to tell him of several instances of couples who thought they could get by with it but were never happy.

It is tragic today when people think they can get by with sin. When lust conceives, it brings forth sin. The only kind of little brat that lust can bring into the world is sin, and sin will bring forth death. Sin will bring forth separation of fellowship with God if you are His child, and He will judge you for it unless you judge yourself.

That young man left my office after I had tried to put the fear of God in him. He was a wonderful Christian, and he surely had been tempted. He came back a few weeks later and said, "Dr. McGee, we have made our decision." I was certainly afraid they had made the wrong one, but he went on, "We recognize that in this life we never could be joined together. That's entirely out of the question for us. I'm simply asking God to let us be together someday in heaven." He worked with a very large company, and he told me that he had asked for a transfer to another city. I don't think a month went by before he came to me after the morning church service, shook my hand, and told me good-bye.

Temptation—there is a lot of it today. Many Christians say, "Oh, the Devil tempted me." My friend, temptation cannot conceive until it is joined with the desire of your evil nature.

The important thing is that when it is joined, it will bring forth sin, and sin eventually brings forth death. If you are a child of God, it immediately breaks your fellowship with Him—and that is a death, by the way.

Do not err, my beloved brethren [James 1:16].

"Do not *err*"—the word here means to wander, to roam about, or to stray. It is like the little lost sheep the Lord Jesus told about which the shepherd went out after. James is saying, "Don't wander. Don't think that somehow you can get by with sin." The habitual and perpetual sinner definitely does not have a line of communication with God; he never has been born again. If you can live in sin and enjoy it, you are not a child of God—it's just that simple.

The story is told of the Calvinist and the Arminian who were having an argument. The Calvinist believes that once you are saved you can never be lost; the Arminian believes you can lose your salvation. The Arminian said, "If I believed your doctrine and were sure I was converted, I would take my fill of sin." To which the Calvinist replied, "How much sin do you think it would take to fill a genuine Christian to his own satisfaction?" May I say to you, that is a tremendous answer. If you can be satisfied with sin, you need to examine yourself to see whether or not you are in the faith. "He that falls into sin is a man," someone has said. "He that grieves at sin is a saint. He that boasts of sin is a devil." My friend, all of us are subject to temptation, but let's make sure that we do not give birth to sin. There can be no abortion here if you go through with temptation. Sin and death *will* be the end result.

Every good gift and every perfect gift is from above, and cometh down from the Father of lights, with whom is no variableness, neither shadow of turning [James 1:17].

One side of the moon is dark, and the other side is light. But in God there is no dark side. In all of us there is a shadow; you and I cast a shadow. The story is told that when Alexander the Great had conquered the world and returned to Greece, he looked up his old teacher, Aristotle, to tell him all that had happened. When he found Aristotle, he was taking a bath. Alexander stood in the doorway and told Aristotle what had happened. Then he said, "Now I am prepared to give you anything in the world that you want. What do you want?" Aristotle looked up and replied, "I want you to

get out of my light!" May I say to you, that's all any of us do—we cast a shadow. But there is no shadow in God at all.

"With whom is no variableness." God doesn't vary, He doesn't change, as the laws of creation reveal. God is not on a yo-yo like a lot of Christians are today—up today and down tomorrow, and round and round they go.

"Every good gift and every perfect gift is from above." I have a friend who is an insurance agent, and I like to kid him about the wording in his house insurance policy. It says that the policy does not include certain things which might happen to your house, including "any act of God." I said to him, "What in the world do you think God is going to do to my house?" "Well," he said, "there could be a cyclone or something like that." I asked, "Do you think God is to be blamed for that?" I realize that it is just an expression which is used, but it has been the custom down through the centuries to blame God for such things. My friend, if you have a *good* gift, it came from Him. Count your many blessings today: the sunshine, the rain, the cloudy day, the bright day, the green grass, the water you drink, and the air you breathe. God gave us clean air and pure water. It is man who has polluted it. God gives *good* gifts, my friend. God is *good*! You and I don't really understand how good He is.

Of his own will begat he us with the word of truth, that we should be a kind of firstfruits of his creatures [James 1:18].

This is definitely a reference to the new birth. How does He beget us? "With the word of truth, that we should be a kind of firstfruits of his creatures." *Beget* means "to bring forth." There are those who say, "Well, if I am predestined to be lost, there is nothing I can do about it. And if I am to be saved, I'll be saved." There are two wills involved here—"Of his own will begat he us." Again, you have in conception *two* coming together—there is no other way for a conception to take place. Therefore, when *His* will is joined with *your* will, you will be born again. Don't tell me that you are not responsible. It is not His will that any should perish. You are begotten by the Word of God. When you are willing to come, when you believe the Word of God and accept Jesus Christ as your Savior, you will be born again. "Being born again, not of corruptible seed, but of incorruptible, by the word of God, which liveth and abideth for ever" (1 Pet. 1:23).

Wherefore, my beloved brethren, let every man be swift to hear, slow to speak, slow to wrath [James 1:19].

"Wherefore, my beloved brethren"—James is talking to the child of God.

"Let every man be swift to hear." Swift to hear what? To hear the Word of God, of course. After you have been begotten by the Word of God, you are not through with it. You are going to *grow* by the Word of God. You have something that is living, powerful and sharper than any two-edged sword (see Heb. 4:12). "But the natural man receiveth not the things of the Spirit of God: for they are foolishness unto him: neither can he know them, because they are spiritually discerned" (1 Cor. 2:14). However, as a child of God you are indwelt by the Spirit of God who wants to teach you the Word of God. The Creator of this universe and the Redeemer of lost sinners wants to talk to you, my friend. James says, "Be swift to hear. Be alert." As I stand before a church congregation, I sometimes feel like crying out to them, "Wake up!" or, "The place is on fire!" because I would like to get them alert and moving. Oh, how we need to be alert and quick to hear the Word of God.

"Slow to speak." God gave us *two* ears and *one* mouth—there must be a very definite reason for that. There is a real danger of our talking too much. There are those who argue that the minute someone is saved they should begin to witness. I do not think a newborn Christian is quite ready to witness. If he got saved last night, we want to hear his testimony today—especially if he is a prominent person, if he is a rich man, if he has been a gangster, if he is in the entertainment business, or if he happens to be an outstanding politician. Those are the ones whose testimonies we are eager to hear. I often regret it when singers give a little talk before they begin their song. Many times I have just bowed my head in embarrassment at some of the things they have said. One sweet little girl had a lovely voice, but when she got up and said, "I've just been saved two months," I cringed, and I had a right to, because what she went on to say was as contrary to the Word of God as anything possibly could be. I also think it is a tragedy that some of these Hollywood entertainers have been encouraged to testify shortly after their salvation experience simply because they are well-known persons. Their theology is sometimes as rank as it can be. They need to study and know the Word of God before they are pushed up front to speak. God says we are to be quick to hear but slow to speak.

Someone will ask, "But aren't we to witness?" Yes, but be very careful how you witness and make sure about your own life first. The story is told about Socrates and a young man who was brought to him to enter his school. Socrates was a school teacher as well as a philosopher. The young man came in and was introduced to Socrates. Before he could say a word, the young man started talking, and he talked for about ten minutes. Finally, when the young man finished, Socrates said, "I'll take you as a student, but I'm going to charge you twice as much." The young man asked, "Why are you going to charge me double?" Socrates' reply was this: "First I am going to have to teach you how to hold your tongue and then how to use it." James says, "Quick to hear but slow to speak." Christians need to be very careful not to reveal their ignorance of the Word of God. *Listen* to Him. Yes, the Bible says, "Let the redeemed of the Lord say so," but we need to be very careful what we say.

"Slow to wrath"—that is, slow to anger. Don't argue about religion and lose your temper. It is good to be a fundamentalist, but don't start fighting about every little jot and tittle of theology with everybody in sight who disagrees with you. After all, you don't have *all* the truth.

Be "slow to wrath." Don't get angry. Jonathan Edwards was the third president of Princeton and probably one of America's greatest thinkers and preachers, but he had a daughter who had an uncontrollable temper. One day a fine young man at the school, who had fallen in love with her, came to Jonathan Edwards and asked for her hand in marriage. (That was the custom in that day, but it seems to have fallen by the wayside now.) Jonathan Edwards said, "You can't have her." The young man said, "But I love her." Edwards said, "You can't have her." The young man said, "But she loves me." Again Edwards said, "You can't have her." "Why can't I have her?" he protested. "Because she is not worthy of you," replied Jonathan Edwards. "Yes, she *is* a Christian, but the grace of God can live with some people with whom no one else could ever live." May I say to you, there are a lot of unworthy Christians today with uncontrollable tempers that spoil their testimonies as much as anything in this life can spoil them.

For the wrath of man worketh not the righteousness of God [James 1:20].

The anger of man is contrary to the will and work of God. This is the reason we shouldn't argue about religion. I have never yet found anybody who agrees with me 100 percent or with whom I agree 100 percent, but that is no reason for me to fall out with him. Someone came to my office the other day while I was listening to our broadcast as it came over the radio. He said to me, "What are you doing?" And I said to him, "You know, I am listening to the only man with whom I agree 100 percent!"

James says, "The wrath of man worketh not the righteousness of God." You may feel that you are angry because you are a defender of the faith, but, my friend, the wrath of man simply does not work the righteousness of God. Don't kid yourself that you are angry for His sake, because He's not angry—He's in the saving business.

Wherefore lay apart all filthiness and superfluity of naughtiness, and receive with meekness the engrafted word, which is able to save your souls [James 1:21].

"Wherefore lay apart all filthiness"—that is, put away all filthiness of the flesh. "And super-fluity of naughtiness" is better translated as "abundance of wickedness."

"And receive with meekness the engrafted word." The word *engrafted* should be "implanted"—the implanted Word of God. In other words, you are to receive the Word of God. I believe the Word of God is the greatest preventative against the sins of the flesh. The old Scottish preacher said, "Sin will keep you from the Bible, or the Bible will keep you from sin." He was certainly accurate in that.

"Which is able to save your souls." James is speaking to those who have been saved. You have received the implanted Word—it has been planted in your hearts. The Word has already brought salvation to you, but you have a life to live as a Christian. Salvation is in three tenses: I have been saved; I am being saved; I shall be saved. James is speaking here of salvation in the present tense.

GOD TESTS FAITH BY THE WORD, NOT BY MAN'S WORDS

The child of God can never get away from the Word of God. Every child wants to hear the voice of his father, especially if it is a voice of comfort as well as a voice of correction. One who isn't interested in the Word of God or doesn't stay near it—if he *is* a child of God—is going to get into trouble.

For a great many people this is the most familiar verse in the Epistle of James—

But be ye doers of the word, and not hearers only, deceiving your own selves [James 1:22].

You and I live in a day when we have many translations of the Bible. They are multiplying—every year, two or three new translations are published. Personally, I have not found a new translation that I feel is really adequate to take the place of the Authorized Version. I think the Authorized Version needs improving in certain places, but I still use it, as you well know. However, we do need a new translation! It should be different from Tyndale's and from the Authorized Version and from the American Standard and from all of these new translations. Any Christian could make this new translation. *You* could make a new translation of the Bible. You might say, "You don't know me. I'm not capable—I'm not familiar with the original languages, and I know nothing about the handling of manuscripts." My friend, in spite of your limitations—which may be many—it is still possible for you to make the best translation of Scripture that has ever been made. Do you know what the name of that translation is? It is known as the Doer's Translation. "Be ye *doers* of the word." That's a good translation— a Doer's Translation.

Paul put the same thought in just a little different phraseology: "Ye are our epistle written in our hearts, known and read of all men: Forasmuch as ye are manifestly declared to be the epistle of Christ ministered by us, written not with ink, but with the Spirit of the living God; not in tables of stone, but in fleshy tables of the heart" (2 Cor. 3:2–3). The world today is not reading the Bible, but they are reading you and me. Someone has expressed it poetically:

The Gospel is written a chapter a day
By deeds that you do and by words that
    you say.
Men read what you say, whether faithless
    or true.
Say, what is the Gospel according to you?

In verses 22 through 25 we have come to the real pragmatism of James. I like to outline these verses like this: (1) Verse 22—the *demands* of the Word; (2) verses 23–24—the *danger* of the Word; and (3) verse 25—the *design* of the Word. We have in this section that which is substantive, that which really gets down to where we live.

Here in verse 22 we have the *demands*, or the imperatives, of the Word: "But be ye doers of the word, and not hearers only, deceiving your own selves." There is an element about the Word of God which makes it different from any other book. There are many books which you can read to gain information, knowledge, intellectual stimulation, spiritual inspiration, amusement, or entertainment. But the Word of God is different, and this is probably the reason it is not as popular as other books: it *demands action.* "Be ye *doers* of the word, and not hearers only." It requires attention. The Lord Jesus said, "If any man will *do* his will, he shall know of the doctrine, whether it be of God, or whether I speak of myself" (John 7:17, italics mine). The Word of God demands action: "O *taste* and see that the LORD is good . . ." (Ps. 34:8, italics mine).

You can read history, but it asks nothing of you. You can read literature, but there are no imperatives, no declarations, and no explanations, although it may have a lesson to teach which may or may not have been in the mind of the author. You can read science, but it makes no demands on you whatsoever. You can read a cookbook and it gives you a recipe, but it does not say you have to cook. There is no demand that you mix up a batch of biscuits or that you make a chocolate cake. However, the Word of God is a command. It is a trumpet. It is an appeal for action. "He that believeth on the Son hath everlasting life: and he that believeth not the Son shall not see life; but the wrath of God abideth on him" (John 3:36). The message of the Lord Jesus Christ is (1) "repent"; (2) "come unto Me"; and (3) "believe" (see Matt. 11:28; Mark 1:15). The Word of God demands belief.

All advertising today is high-pressured. It is being used on radio, television, billboards, and in newspapers and magazines. They all use the hard sell. We are not only being brainwashed by the news on television and radio, we are also being brainwashed by advertising. Madison Avenue is throwing everything at the consumer. You are to buy a certain make of car, and you are told how wonderful it is over last year's model—when about all they did was to make the steering wheel a little smaller than last year's. And you are told if you don't use a certain deodorant you will lose your job. But the Word of God says that you are going to *die* in your sins if you don't turn to Christ! Talk about high pressure—that is high pressure! The Word of God says, ". . . behold, *now*

is the accepted time . . ." (2 Cor. 6:2, italics mine), and, ". . . *To-day* if ye will hear his voice" (Ps. 95:7, italics mine).

I believe that the greatest failure of the Christian church in recent years has been at this point. After World War II the Western world came out of the bomb shelters and went to church—prompted by fear of the bombs but not by fear of God. Church membership and attendance soared to new heights. I am very thankful I had a ministry during that period. I had a full church, and it was to me a glorious, wonderful time for ministry. But at that same time, lawlessness and immorality increased dramatically. Drunkenness, divorce, and juvenile delinquency escalated. And in the lives of Christians there was a total breakdown in separation from the things of the world. What had happened? The church had been getting out the Word of God in the passive voice; it had been giving it out in the subjunctive mood, but God had originally given it in the *imperative* mood. We had forgotten that a leather-bound Bible needs some shoe leather to go with it. Memorizing Scripture is good, but it also demands action.

"But *be ye* doers of the word." James does not use the ordinary Greek verb for "be," which is *eimi;* the word here is *ginesthe* which literally means "to become, to be born, to come into existence." The imperative given here is for the born-again child of God. God is not asking the unsaved person to do anything, except one thing—and that is actually not *doing*, but believing. When the people came to the Lord Jesus and asked, "What shall we *do* that we might inherit eternal life?" He replied, "Do? Why, this is the will of God that ye *believe* on Him whom He has sent" (see John 6:28–29). *Doing*, as far as God's will is concerned, for the unsaved is *believing* on Christ. God is not asking the unsaved to do anything at all; He wants to tell them that *He* has done something.

As a boy I played baseball on the school lot on Saturdays. I played first base, and it was a wonderful thing to which I really looked forward. We played the teams of other high schools around us, and it generally ended up in a fight no matter who we played. One Saturday as I was playing ball, I saw my dad coming up, and I knew he wasn't coming to see the game. He had come to tell me he had some work for me to do. The truth is, I had neglected taking care of my chores before I had left home. My dad didn't ask any of the other boys to do a single thing—he just asked me. Why? Those other boys weren't his sons; I was.

My friend, God isn't asking anything of you until you become His child. But to those of us who have become children of God, He says, "Be ye doers of the word, and not hearers only, deceiving your own selves."

It is sometimes difficult for us preachers to see that we also need to be doers of the Word. I remember one time playing golf with a medical doctor friend who is also a wonderful Christian. Another friend of this doctor wanted to join us, so the doctor introduced me to his friend, saying, "This is Dr. McGee." The man said, "Oh, we have two doctors." I wanted to make it clear to him what kind of doctor I was, so I said, "I'm a doctor who *preaches*, and he's a doctor who practices." May I say, we need more Th.D.'s who practice as well as preach!

Someone expressed it in a little poem like this:

It's easier to preach than to practice;
It's easier to say than to do.
Most sermons are heard by the many,
But taken to heart by the few.

—Author unknown

Hearing the Word of God will lead to doing by those who are His children. It will not lead to rote and ritual and habitual action; it will not lead to the drab, the monotonous, or the routine. The intent of the Word is to produce creative action and to make for productive performance, exciting living, and a thrilling experience. If we are motivated by an inner desire and are enjoying Spirit-filled living, you and I can go out on the golf course and enjoy playing golf and then enjoy Bible study equally as well—in fact, it will be thrilling to us.

Hearing the Word will lead to doing for God that which is motivated by an inner desire. As we began our radio broadcast ministry, we also began to build up our office staff. I know that it is the finest staff I have ever had in all my years of ministry. God has sent each individual to us, and each has made a marvelous contribution. They are creative and dedicated workers. It is my feeling that in God's work we need that which is creative, that which is dynamic, that which produces.

"And not hearers only." There is a difference between being a student in a class and being an auditor. I used to have quite a few folk who would audit my classes when I was teaching at the Bible Institute in downtown Los Angeles many years ago. I had more trouble with the auditors than I ever did with the students. They were constantly telling me I was too hard on the students. They didn't realize I needed to be hard-boiled, but the students understood that I was kidding them half the time. Those auditors never had to take exams; they never had to make preparation; they never wrote any papers; they never got a diploma. They didn't do anything. They just sat there. Faith leads to *action*, my friend—it will make you more than an auditor.

The story is told of a man who was always talking about his faith—he never did anything for anybody, he just talked about his faith. One day a friend came along and saw him stuck in the mud with his wagon. The friend said, "Well, you sure are well established in the faith!" May I say to you, what we need to do today is to keep moving. After we get established, we need to keep moving in the faith and not get stuck in the mud.

"Deceiving your own selves." Self-deception is a terrible thing. The apostle John says that those who say they don't have any sin in their lives do not deceive anyone but themselves (see 1 John 1:8). It is very easy to fall into the trap of rationalizing our sin and rationalizing our inaction.

In verses 23 and 24 we have the *danger* of the Word—

For if any be a hearer of the word, and not a doer, he is like unto a man beholding his natural face in a glass [James 1:23].

"A man beholding his natural face in a glass." A very highly polished piece of brass was used as a mirror in that day. A mirror is a very interesting thing, and it is used here as a picture of the Word of God. When you look into a mirror, you see a reflection of yourself—you see yourself as you really are.

You may have noticed that on some pictures of Abraham Lincoln there is a wart on his cheek but that on others it is not there. As one artist was preparing to paint his portrait, he began to have Lincoln move around. He said, "President Lincoln, will you sit here?" Then this man would move his easel and have Lincoln shift around again. President Lincoln began to smile because he saw what the artist was doing. He was trying to get Lincoln in a position where the wart would not show. Finally the artist was satisfied, and he asked, "President Lincoln, how do you want me to paint you?" Lincoln replied, "Paint me just as I am—wart and all." That's what a mirror would tell you; if you have a wart, it will show up. That is one reason many of us don't like to spend too much time in the presence of a mirror. My friend, the Word of God will tell you what you are.

"For if any be a hearer of the word, and not a doer, he is like unto a *man* beholding his natural face in a glass." Someone will say, "It ought to say *woman*." A woman usually carries a little mirror around with her to be sure her hair and makeup are all right. But what about men? Do they look in mirrors? They are just as vain, my friend. A man likes to be sure his tie is straight and his hair is combed. We are living in a day when our appearance seems to be very important. A mirror reveals our flaws.

There is a danger, though, of looking into the mirror, seeing the flaw but doing nothing about it.

For he beholdeth himself, and goeth his way, and straightway forgetteth what manner of man he was [James 1:24].

James is answering what he has said in verse 19 where he wrote, "Be swift to hear, slow to speak." Here his emphasis is, "Don't be so quick or hasty as you look into the mirror." The thought in being "swift to hear" is to give it all your attention, to be alert to the Word of God. What James is saying here is, "Don't treat it casually. Don't go over it hurriedly like that." Any man who is just a hearer of the Word and not a doer—his knowledge of the Bible doesn't lead to action—is like a man beholding his natural face in a mirror, "for he beholdeth himself, and goeth his way, and straightway forgetteth what manner of man he was."

Folk who do not like to read in the Bible the fact that they are sinners simply pass over those sections. That is the reason, I think, that textual preaching is outmoded. I feel that we need to go through the entire Word of God and not pull out nice, sweet verses here and there. God did not give His Word in verses; verses are man-made. We need to take the Word of God as it is. The Word is a mirror that reveals what is wrong with you. A man who goes to the doctor and has an X-ray taken which reveals a cancer in his body can respond by saying, "Now, look, doctor, I don't put much confidence in X-rays. I think I'll just ignore it and forget it." I've known some people who have said that, and they have died. When the doctor told me that I had cancer, I wanted treatment just as quickly as I could get it. My friend, you cannot afford to read the Word of God and not respond to it. It demands your response; and if you don't respond, *you* are responsible. If the doctor tells you you

have cancer and you don't do anything about it, is the doctor responsible? He absolutely is not responsible at all. God has given you His Word, and you are responsible for your response to it. To a man who has been born again, the Word will say, "Look, you are no longer growing. You are actually leaving your first love." God uses His Word to remind us of Himself and to call us back.

One time I heard a song leader down in Chattanooga, Tennessee, say, "Let's stand and sing 'Standing on the Promises,' but the trouble is that we sing 'Standing on the Promises' when we are really sitting on the premises." That is what James is telling us not to do. The Word of God is a mirror which reveals our shortcomings, and we are not to forget what it says. "For the word of God is quick, and powerful, and sharper than any two-edged sword, piercing even to the dividing asunder of soul and spirit, and of the joints and marrow, and is a discerner of the thoughts and intents of the heart" (Heb. 4:12). The Word reveals us as we are, penetrating below the surface of our beings.

The Bible is not a popular book today. It is the best seller but the worst read. It is not popular because it shows us who we are. Many years ago in eastern Tennessee the story went around about a mountaineer's contact with some tourists who had camped in the hills around his area. Because the mountain folk didn't see many tourists in those days, when the tourists left, this particular mountaineer went to look around the area where they had camped. He found several things they had left behind, including a mirror. He had never seen a mirror before. He looked into it longingly and said, "I never knew my pappy had his picture took!" He was very sentimental about it, of course, and took it home. He slipped into the house, climbed up into the loft and hid the mirror. His wife saw him do that but didn't say anything. After he went out of the house, she went up to see what he had hidden. She found the mirror, and when she looked into it, she said, "So that's the old hag he's been running around with!" May I say to you, it is so easy to read the Word of God and to think it is a picture of someone else. It is a picture of you, and it is a picture of me.

In verse 25 we see the *design* of the Word—

But whoso looketh into the perfect law of liberty, and continueth therein, he being not a forgetful hearer, but a doer of the work, this man shall be blessed in his deed [James 1:25].

Looketh means "to look attentively, penetratingly."

"The perfect law of liberty." This is not the Mosaic Law; it is the law of grace. James does not talk about law here in the same sense that Paul does. When Paul talks about law, he is talking about the Mosaic Law. When James talks about law, it is the law of faith. There is love in law in the Old Testament, and there is law in love in the New Testament. "If the Son therefore shall make you free, ye shall be free indeed" (John 8:36). However, the Lord also said, "If ye love me, keep my commandments" (John 14:15), and Paul said, "Bear ye one another's burdens, and so fulfil the law of Christ" (Gal. 6:2). What law? Christ's law. John says in his first epistle, "For this is the love of God, that we keep his commandments . . ." (1 John 5:3).

When you are driving down a freeway, you will see that it is loaded with traffic, and it is also loaded with laws. If you want to have freedom to drive down that freeway, you had better obey the laws. There is liberty in Christ, and it is the only true freedom. However, you can be sure that if you are in Christ, you are going to obey Him—and His laws are not hard; they are not rigorous. Because you are a child of God, your freedom does not entitle you to break the Ten Commandments. Those laws are for the weak, for the natural man. Laws are for lawbreakers: what to do, where to go, and how, with a punishment prescribed for those who break over. Honest citizens do not need the law. I do not know one half of the laws of this state in which I live, but every shyster lawyer knows them, because he is seeking loopholes to break those laws.

Today God has called His children to a higher level. A child of God has a spiritual spontaneity, a high and lofty motive, an inspiration of God. The believer has no desire to murder. He lives above the law. He is now motivated by the love of the Savior, and he desires to obey Him. The more we read and study the Word, the more we will learn, we will love, and we will live. Joy fills and floods the soul. We are not like galley slaves, whipped and chained to a bench and doing that which we do not want to do.

You and I may not need to know all the laws of our state or of our country, but we certainly need to know the Word of God if we are to live for Him. I do not agree with the popular song today which says, "You don't need to understand, you just need to hold His hand." My friend, you *do* need to understand. You're not apt to be holding His hand unless you do understand. There are too many folk today who are ignorant of the Word of God. It is no disgrace to be ignorant. I don't know about you, but I was born ignorant. I didn't know A from B when I was born. I couldn't even walk or talk. I was in bad shape, but I didn't stay in that shape and neither did you. It's no disgrace to be ignorant, but it's a disgrace to stay ignorant if you are a child of God.

> **If any man among you seem to be religious, and bridleth not his tongue, but deceiveth his own heart, this man's religion is vain [James 1:26].**

Religious and *religion* are not actually Bible words—that is, they occur only about half a dozen times in the New Testament. James uses them more than any other New Testament writer. The word *religion* comes from a Latin word which means "to bind back." Although Herodotus used the word, it was not a word used commonly in the Greek language. He spoke of the *religion* of the Egyptian priests. The word has to do with going through a ritual, a form, or a ceremony.

There are many religions today, and they can demonstrate that they have faithful, zealous followers. But you cannot call a religion Christian simply because it conforms to certain outward forms of ritual. Christianity is not a religion; it is a person, and that person is Jesus Christ—you either have Him or you don't have Him.

James is saying here that if a religious man does not control his speech, his religion—regardless of what it is—is vain. What about the Christian and his tongue? James is going to have a great deal to say in chapter 3 about the child of God and this matter of bridling the tongue. Someone has said, "You can't believe half of what you hear, but you can repeat it." That is a real problem in the church today. We have too many people who have unbridled tongues.

> **Pure religion and undefiled before God and the Father is this, To visit the fatherless and widows in their affliction, and to keep himself unspotted from the world [James 1:27].**

This is a tremendous statement. "Pure" is the positive side, and "undefiled" is the negative side. You need to have both if you are to have the right kind of religion—and Christianity certainly ought to produce this.

"To visit the fatherless and widows in their affliction." This is the positive side. A child of

God ought to be in personal contact with the sorrow of the world and the problems of the people of the world. This is where the politicians are very clever. They go out and meet the people and shake their hands. They make a personal contact. In the same way, Christians should be getting out where the people are. I feel there is a grave danger in our having a religion of the sanctuary but not a religion of the street. We need a religion of the street also. We should be in contact with the world in a personal way, with tenderness and kindness and helpfulness.

"And to keep himself unspotted from the world." This now is the negative side. Contact with the world does not mean that we should become implicated in the things of the world. As believers we are *in* this world but we are not *of* this world.

I think of the story of the little boy whose mother had died. His father was a poor man, but he worked and tried to raise the little

fellow. There was a wealthy couple, relatives, who became interested in the boy. They said to the father, "You are not able to give the boy everything in life. We are wealthy; we can give him everything." So the father went to the little boy to talk to him about going to live with these folks. He said to the little fellow, "They'll give you a bicycle, give you toys, and give you wonderful gifts at Christmas. And they will take you on trips. They will do things for you that I can't do for you." The little boy said, "I don't want to go." And the father said, "Why?" The boy said, "They can't give me *you*." That's what the little fellow wanted. There are a lot of people out yonder today who want that personal contact. My friend, you can bring a Christian contact to these people with sweetness and love and consideration and kindness. But let us remember to keep ourselves unspotted from the world. We can get so implicated in the things of the world that it becomes a dangerous thing.

CHAPTER 2

THEME: *God tests faith by attitude and action in respect of persons; God tests faith by good works*

GOD TESTS FAITH BY ATTITUDE AND ACTION IN RESPECT OF PERSONS

In the first thirteen verses of this chapter, James is going to deal with how we are to treat people in the different strata of society. How do you treat the rich man? How do you treat the poor man? How do you treat the average man whom you meet today? This section deals with God's war on poverty and, interestingly enough, also God's war on riches. This is God's war on poverty *and* riches. His war on poverty is a little different from that of our government; no matter which political party has been in office, neither the federal nor the state governments have been able to deal successfully with this problem.

Both poverty and riches can be a curse. Part of the curse on the human race is poverty and riches. The writer in the Book of Proverbs says, ". . . give me neither poverty nor riches . . ." (Prov. 30:8). The most difficult people to reach are those who are the most poverty-stricken and those who are the richest; it seems to be almost impossible to reach either class with the Word of God.

The real problem is actually the imbalance of wealth in the world. The problem today is not between political parties, and it is not even between the races. The problem in the world is the imbalance of wealth. Take for example the nation of India where it is estimated there will soon be a population of one billion. There is great famine and starvation in that land; they starve by the thousands over there. Contrast that with the luxury and abundance which the wealthy have today. God goes after this problem in this epistle. He is on the side of the poor—I'm very delighted to say that. After all, when the Lord Jesus came into the world, He wasn't a rich man's boy; He wasn't born with a silver spoon in His mouth. He was born in poverty. He was born in a borrowed stable. He had to borrow loaves and fishes from a little lad to feed the crowd. He spoke from a borrowed boat. He said, "The foxes have holes, and the birds of the air have nests; but the Son of man hath not where to lay his head" (see Matt. 8:20). He had to borrow a coin to illustrate a truth. He borrowed a donkey to ride into Jerusalem. He borrowed a room to celebrate the Passover. He died on a borrowed cross—it belonged to Barabbas, not to Him. They put Him in a borrowed tomb—it belonged to Joseph of Arimathaea.

When I was in college, we had a preacher who came and talked about "the blessings of poverty." Now I was a poor boy, and I mean *poor*, my friend. I was going to school on borrowed money and was working full time. That man spoke every morning in chapel, and I was told that he got $15,000 a year (that was back in the days when a dollar was worth a dollar). It was a lot of money for a preacher in that day. You know, what he had to say just ran off my mind like water off a duck's back—he had no message for me. The blessings of poverty? I just happen to know, since I was born that way and haven't gotten too far from it yet, that there are no blessings in poverty. Poverty is a curse, and part of the curse which Christ bore was poverty.

Riches can also be a curse, as James will show in this epistle. Paul said, "For the love of money is the root of all evil . . ." (1 Tim. 6:10). Paul and James certainly agree here. You can spend your money for the wrong items. You can deposit your money in the wrong bank. "Lay not up for yourselves treasures upon earth, where moth and rust doth corrupt, and where thieves break through and steal" (Matt. 6:19). All the banks are telling us where to put our money, but God says, in effect, "I've got a bank, and I will keep investments up there for you." James will be harsh with the rich, as we will see in chapter 5. Proverbs 30:8 should be the philosophy of every Christian: "Give me neither poverty nor riches."

What is God's solution to the problem of poverty? It is not to rob the rich in order to take care of the indigent, the lazy, the indolent, the drones, the loafers, the sluggards, and the laggards. On the other hand, God would never destroy the dignity and the self-respect and the integrity and the honor of the poor by placing them on charity. God's war on poverty and riches does not march under the banner of the dollar where millions are appropriated for relief. And it is not aimed primarily at the head or at the stomach, but at the heart. It is a war against class. James is talking about distinctions and divisions among believers which have been brought about by money.

My brethren, have not the faith of our Lord Jesus Christ, the Lord of glory, with respect of persons [James 2:1].

"*Have* not the faith of our Lord Jesus Christ" should be "*Hold* not the faith of our Lord Jesus Christ." Notice that James is His half brother according to the flesh, but he gives Him here the full name, "our Lord Jesus Christ." And he calls Him "the Lord of glory." Here is a strong assertion of the deity of Christ. I know of no one who was in a better position to determine the deity of Christ than a younger brother of the Lord Jesus who was brought up in the same home with Him. Frankly, I think James is in a better position to speak on the deity of Christ than some theologian sitting in a swivel chair in a musty library in New York City, removed from the reality of even his own day. Such a man is really far removed from the reality of the first century and the home in which Jesus was raised. Therefore, I go along with James, if you don't mind. He is the "Lord Jesus Christ, the Lord of glory."

What James is telling us here is not to profess faith in Christ and at the same time be a spiritual snob. Don't join some little clique in the church. *All* believers are brethren in the body of Christ, whatever their denomination. There is a fellowship of believers; friendship should be over them as a banner. James is addressing the total community of believers—the rich, the poor, the common people, the high, the low, the bond and free, the Jew and the Gentile, the Greek and the barbarian, male and female. They are all *one* when they are in the body of Christ. There is a brotherhood within the body of believers, and the Lord Jesus Christ is the common denominator. Friendship and fellowship are the legal tender among believers.

James says, "Don't hold your faith with respect of persons." If you belong to the Lord Jesus Christ and another person belongs to the Lord Jesus Christ, he is your brother. Furthermore, if a sinner comes into your assembly or you otherwise come into contact with him, remember that he is a human being for whom Christ died. He stands at the foot of the cross, just as you stand at the foot of the cross.

The Old Testament taught Israel not to regard the person of the rich or of the poor. God, in the Mosaic system, cautioned: "Ye shall do no unrighteousness in judgment: thou shalt not respect the person of the poor, nor honour the person of the mighty: but in righteousness shalt thou judge thy neighbour" (Lev. 19:15). Simon Peter learned this lesson at Joppa when God let down from heaven the sheet full of unclean animals and commanded him to eat of them. Peter concluded from that experience,

". . . Of a truth I perceive that God is no respecter of persons" (Acts 10:34).

James uses a stinging illustration to make his point:

For if there come unto your assembly a man with a gold ring, in goodly apparel, and there come in also a poor man in vile raiment [James 2:2].

The word *assembly* here means synagogue. Evidently the Jewish Christians were calling the place where they met a synagogue. They had erected no buildings and frequently met in private homes, but the chances are that in many places they rented a synagogue. They met on Sunday rather than on Saturday and therefore did not conflict with the meeting of the Jews.

"A man with a gold ring" doesn't mean he wore a single ring, but that he had his fingers loaded down with gold rings, which was an evidence of wealth. "Goodly apparel" means that he had on fine clothes, bright clothes. He was ostentatious, if you please. His clothing is contrasted with that of the poor man.

Someone has said, "Some go to church to close their eyes, and others go to eye the clothes." We have made Sunday a time when we Christians put on our Sunday-go-to-meeting clothes. A great many people come to church overdressed. There is a dash and a splash and a flash about them. There is a pomp and pomposity. It's glitter and gaudy, and vulgar and vain, also.

This rich man makes his entrance into church with flags flying and a fanfare of trumpets. There is parade and pageant. It is as if he drives up in his gold Cadillac, getting out as his chauffeur opens the door for him. He walks in, strutting like a peacock. He is like the rich man the Lord Jesus spoke of in the true story of the rich man and Lazarus: "There was a certain rich man, which was clothed in purple and fine linen, and fared sumptuously every day" (Luke 16:19). He "fared sumptuously" means that life was one continual party for him.

In contrast, the poor man, whom James mentions here, comes in with tattered and torn clothing. It may be clean, but there is evidence of patches and poverty. He may even be shabby and shoddy. He may be dilapidated and deteriorated. He may have seen better days, but he doesn't have any Sunday clothes. James places these two men in contrast—each is at an extreme end of the social ladder.

In our affluent society we use other occasions as an excuse to dress up, but certainly many people use church as an occasion to do that. Easter Sunday is a good example of this. In Southern California, ladies usually don't wear hats to church, but on Easter Sunday we always have a parade of new hats in church. When I was a pastor I would sometimes look out over the congregation and say, "Well, they are as wild as ever!" and everybody knew I was talking about the hats. My wife told me the ladies didn't like my wisecracks, so I had to quit doing that. Another example is that when I began in the ministry I wanted to look like a preacher, and I think I really overdid it. I wore a Prince Albert coat and striped trousers. I had a wing collar and a black bow tie. I even wore a derby hat. You would have thought I was a barker in a circus or the maitre d' at the Waldorf Astoria in New York City. Then one day I looked down into the congregation at a couple who were people of means; in fact, they were very wealthy. I noticed how unostentatiously this man was dressed. He had on a highpriced suit, but it was very modest. And his wife was well dressed, but not overdressed. I thought, *My, here I am up here dressed as a person ought not to be dressed who is coming in to worship God.* So the next Sunday I came to church in everyday clothes, and I have been wearing them ever since, just like the man who is sitting in the pew. My friend, there is a danger of putting an emphasis upon clothes.

And ye have respect to him that weareth the gay clothing, and say unto him, Sit thou here in a good place; and say to the poor, Stand thou there, or sit here under my footstool [James 2:3].

In our day this would be like putting the poor man way back where the ushers sit or telling him to stand up in the rear. In that day there were a few seats down front where only the prominent people were allowed to sit. In the United States there was a day when we had paid pews in our churches. They had a little door to them, and only the family which paid for that pew could sit there on Sunday. You couldn't sit with whomever you wanted to sit. Today we have our little cliques who take a certain section in a church, and woe to the stranger (especially if he is not well dressed) who comes in and sits next to that crowd! I can assure you he will get a cold shoulder.

Are ye not then partial in yourselves, and are become judges of evil thoughts? [James 2:4].

After James has put these two men in contrast, he asks, "Aren't you actually being partial in yourselves or aren't you making distinctions among yourselves and becoming judges with evil motives?"

Hearken, my beloved brethren, Hath not God chosen the poor of this world rich in faith, and heirs of the kingdom which he hath promised to them that love him? [James 2:5].

"Hearken, my beloved brethren"—James is talking to believers, and he calls them "brethren."

A poor believer certainly is looked down upon in certain churches, and yet he may be the richest man spiritually in that church.

The Word of God says a great deal about the poor. God has made it very clear from Genesis to Revelation that He has a concern and consideration for the poor. It is as true in Moscow, Russia, as it is in the cities of New York, Washington, or Los Angeles that the poor never get a fair deal, and they never have. As long as men are natural men who are not born-again Christians, the poor will never get a fair deal in this world. Their only hope is in Jesus Christ.

Listen to the Word of God: "But he saveth the poor from the sword, from their mouth, and from the hand of the mighty" (Job 5:15). And in Job 36:15 we read, "He delivereth the poor in his affliction, and openeth their ears in oppression." Psalm 9:18 says, "For the needy shall not alway be forgotten: the expectation of the poor shall not perish for ever." Again in Psalms we read, "Thy congregation hath dwelt therein: thou, O God, hast prepared of thy goodness for the poor" (Ps. 68:10). "For the LORD heareth the poor . . ." says Psalm 69:33. "For he shall deliver the needy when he crieth; the poor also, and him that hath no helper. He shall spare the poor and needy, and shall save the souls of the needy" (Ps. 72:12–13). Then in Psalm 102:17 we read, "He will regard the prayer of the destitute, and not despise their prayer." There is Scripture after Scripture that speaks of the poor and of God's concern for them. In marvelous Psalm 45 we read of the One who is coming who will reign on this earth in righteousness, and in Isaiah 11 we read, "But with righteousness shall he judge the poor . . ." (Isa. 11:4).

God has a great deal to say about the mistreatment of the poor on this earth by the rich and by those who are in power. Someday they will have to answer to Him for it. But the poor can be rich in spiritual things, and that is the important thing for the poor man to see.

But ye have despised the poor. Do not rich men oppress you, and draw you before the judgment seats? [James 2:6].

Whether it is at the hands of a rich corporation or of a rich labor union, the powerful are not giving the poor an honest deal. Every year the politicians come out to us when they are running for office and say that they are going to work for and help all of us poor people. It does not make any difference what political party is in power, they wind up exploiting us. If I sound rather cynical, my friend, it is because I was born a poor boy and I have not gotten very far from that even to this day. From that viewpoint I am cynical because I have seen the way the poor are treated on this earth. Their only hope is in Jesus Christ. They have been despised by the world. The rich and powerful want their vote, but that ends their interest in them.

Do not they blaspheme that worthy name by the which ye are called? [James 2:7].

Worthy is better translated as "honorable." My friend, when you mistreat the poor, you are blaspheming the name of Christ.

If ye fulfil the royal law according to the scripture, Thou shalt love thy neighbour as thyself, ye do well [James 2:8].

If you want to please God, to obey Him, and to discharge your responsibility, James makes it very clear what you are to do: "Thou shalt love thy neighbour as thyself." That is the summation of the whole manward aspect of the Mosaic Law.

But if ye have respect to persons, ye commit sin, and are convinced of the law as transgressors [James 2:9].

The Law condemns discriminating between the rich and poor. Someone will say, "Well, I didn't commit murder, and I haven't committed adultery." You haven't? Listen to what James says—

For whosoever shall keep the whole law, and yet offend in one point, he is guilty of all [James 2:10].

James is not saying that if you break one commandment, you have broken them all. He is saying you are guilty of breaking the commandments no matter which one it is that you broke. A man may be in prison as a murderer, look across the aisle and say to another fellow, "I'm not a rapist. I never broke *that* law"— yes, but he is behind bars; he is a murderer. It is ironic when a prisoner actually murders another prisoner because he considers *his* crime a terrible thing! But, my friend, you do not have to go to the penitentiary to find that attitude; you will find people outside of prison who are looking down upon others in the same way.

We all stand before God as lawbreakers.

For he that said, Do not commit adultery, said also, Do not kill. Now if thou commit no adultery, yet if thou kill, thou art become a transgressor of the law [James 2:11].

To break one law makes a lawbreaker.

So speak ye, and so do, as they that shall be judged by the law of liberty [James 2:12].

The "law of liberty" is the law of Christ. The Lord Jesus said, "If ye love me, keep my commandments" (John 14:15). What is His commandment? "This is my commandment, That ye love one another, as I have loved you" (John 15:12).

For he shall have judgment without mercy, that hath shewed no mercy; and mercy rejoiceth against judgment [James 2:13].

Many years ago in New York City there lived a wealthy couple by the name of Mr. and Mrs. Whitemore. They were entertaining guests one night and, in order to do something different, they went down to the Bowery to the mission of Jerry McAuley. These people went in and sat down in the back to take in the service that night. This wealthy couple belonged to a very fashionable church, but they had no more heard the gospel than a person living in the darkest heathenism in the world. As they heard Jerry McAuley preach, their hearts were touched, and they saw themselves as sinners. They went forward, and that night the mink knelt with the rags as they accepted Christ. Mr. and Mrs. Whitemore became workers in that area, and she established a home for wayward girls. She became known as the Rose of Mulberry Bend and was instrumental in beginning the movement for a ministry to such troubled girls.

How we need to recognize today that it is *sinful* to think that we are better than someone else and to look down upon others. It does not matter who the man is, before God that man is on the same plane as you are. We are sinners and need to come as that rich couple came—we need to come to the Cross and accept Christ as our Savior.

Another story is told that took place in London when a great preacher, a very fine young man, by the name of Caesar Milan was invited one evening to a very large and prominent home where a choice musical was to be presented. On the program was a young lady who thrilled the audience with her singing and playing. When she finished, this young preacher threaded his way through the crowd which was gathered around her. When he finally came to her and had her attention, he said, "Young lady, when you were singing, I sat there and thought how tremendously the cause of Christ would be benefited if you would dedicate yourself and your talents to the Lord." "But," he added, "you are just as much a sinner as the worst drunkard in the street, or any harlot on Scarlet Street. But I am glad to tell you that the blood of Jesus Christ, God's Son, will cleanse you from all sin if you will come to Him." In a very haughty manner, she turned her head aside and said to him, "You are very insulting, sir." And she started to walk away. He said, "Lady, I did not mean any offense, but I pray that the Spirit of God will convict you."

Well, they all went home, and that night this young woman could not sleep. At two o'clock in the morning she knelt at the side of her bed and took Christ as her Savior. And then she, Charlotte Elliott, sat down and, while sitting there, wrote the words of a favorite hymn "Just As I Am":

Just as I am, without one plea,
But that Thy blood was shed for me,
And that Thou bidd'st me come to Thee,
O Lamb of God, I come!

Just as I am, and waiting not
To rid my soul of one dark blot,
To Thee whose blood can cleanse each spot,
O Lamb of God, I come!

And then the final stanza:

Just as I am—Thou wilt receive,
Wilt welcome, pardon, cleanse, relieve;
Because Thy promise I believe,
O Lamb of God, I come!

My friend, may I say to you, that this is the basis on which all of us must come to Christ.

GOD TESTS FAITH BY GOOD WORKS

In verses 14–26 James shows that God tests faith by good works. There are those who say that we have in this section a contradiction to the writings of Paul, because Paul made it abundantly clear that faith *alone* could save you. We have his clear statement in Galatians 2:16—"Knowing that a man is *not* justified by the works of the law, but by the *faith* of Jesus Christ, even we have believed in Jesus Christ, that we might be justified by the faith of Christ, and not by the works of the law: for by the works of the law shall no flesh be justified" (italics mine).

I have divided this section up as follows: (1) The interpretation of faith (v. 14); (2) the identification of faith (vv. 15–20); and (3) the illustration of faith (vv. 21–26).

First we have *the interpretation of faith.* When we understand the definition of faith as it is used by Paul and James in the context of their writings, we can see that Paul and James are in perfect agreement, that they are discussing the same subject from different viewpoints.

Paul says that a man is not saved by the works or the deeds of the Law. In Romans 3:28 he writes, "Therefore we conclude that a man is justified by faith without the deeds of the law." In Galatians, as we have noted, Paul says that a man is justified not by works but by faith in Christ Jesus. How then are we going to reconcile Paul and James? As someone has said, "Paul and James do not stand face to face, fighting against each other, but they stand back to back, fighting opposite foes." In that day there were those who were saying that you had to perform the works of the Law (the Mosaic Law), that you had to come by the Law, in order to be saved. Paul answered that by saying that the works of the Law will not save you and that only faith in Christ can save you. Both Paul and James, therefore, are defending the citadel of *faith.* To see that, we need to understand the use of their terminology. Paul says that *saving faith*—a faith which is genuine and real—will transform a person's life. Paul said of himself, "But what things were gain to me, those I counted loss for Christ" (Phil. 3:7). A real revolution took place in his life when he came to Christ. In 1 Corinthians 15:1–2 Paul wrote, "Moreover, brethren, I declare unto you the gospel which I preached unto you, which also ye have received, and wherein ye stand; By which also ye are *saved,* if ye keep in memory what I preached unto you, unless ye have be-

lieved in vain;" that is, unless it was just an empty faith (italics mine).

Now let us look at what James has to say—

What doth it profit, my brethren, though a man say he hath faith, and have not works? can faith save him? [James 2:14].

James is not talking about the works of the Law. He simply says that the faith which saves you *will* produce works, works of faith. The faith that James is talking about here is *professing faith,* that which is phony and counterfeit. Paul refers to the same idea when he says in 1 Corinthians 15:2, ". . . unless ye have believed in vain." Paul also wrote, "Examine yourselves, whether ye be in the faith . . ." (2 Cor. 13:5).

One of the greatest dangers for us preachers of the gospel is that we like to see people converted, and we are willing to accept a brazen and flippant yes from some individual who says, "Yes, I'll trust Jesus." However, it might be just an impertinent, impudent, and insolent nod of the head; it is so easy today to be as phony as a three-dollar bill.

The story is told that the Devil had a meeting with his demons to decide how to persuade men that God was nonexistent. Since they themselves believed in His existence, they wondered just how to do it. One demon suggested that they tell people Jesus Christ never really existed and that men should not believe such fiction. Another demon suggested that they persuade men that death ends all and there is no need to worry about life after death. Finally, the most intelligent demon suggested that they tell everyone that there is a God, that there is Jesus Christ, and that believing in Him saves, but all you have to do is profess faith in Christ and then go on living in sin as you used to. They decided to use this tactic, and it is the tactic the Devil uses even today.

Paul and James are in perfect harmony in their teaching. When Paul speaks of works, it is *works of the Law.* He says in Romans 3:20, "Therefore by the deeds of the law there shall no flesh be justified in his sight: for by the law is the knowledge of sin." He is saying in effect, "Yes, the Law is a mirror—it reveals you are a sinner—but it cannot save you; the works of the Law cannot save you at all." James also says that you have to have something more than just the works of the Law. He wrote, "For whosoever shall keep the whole law, and yet offend in one point, he is guilty of all" (v. 10). As someone has put it, "Man cannot be saved by perfect obedience, for he cannot render it. He cannot be saved by imperfect obedience because God will not accept it." The only solution to this dilemma is the redemption that is in Christ Jesus, and both James and Paul emphasize that.

In Galatians 2:16 Paul made it clear that men are not saved by the Law, but later in that epistle he wrote, "And let us not be weary in well-doing . . ." (Gal. 6:9). There is a lot of *doing* that goes with *believing*. "Let him that is taught in the word communicate unto him that teacheth in all good things. Be not deceived; God is not mocked: for whatsoever a man soweth, that shall he also reap" (Gal. 6:6–7). In this section of his epistle when James speaks of works, he is speaking of the *works of faith*. Paul also wrote about works of faith: "For in Jesus Christ neither circumcision availeth any thing, nor uncircumcision; but faith which worketh by love" (Gal. 5:6). Both of these men taught that faith must be a working faith. As John Calvin put it, "Faith alone saves, but the faith that saves is not alone."

Saving faith, therefore, is alive; professing faith is dead. We have a lot of so-called professing Christians today who are members of churches. They are nothing in the world but zombies. They are walking around as if they are alive, but they are dead.

A girl once asked her Sunday school teacher, "How can I be a Christian and still have my own way?" The teacher gave to her Romans 8:5 which says, "For they that are after the flesh do mind the things of the flesh; but they that are after the Spirit the things of the Spirit." If you are a child of God, you cannot have your own way. You are going to do His way. "Because the carnal mind is enmity against God: for it is not subject to the law of God, neither indeed can be. . . . But ye are not in the flesh, but in the Spirit, if so be that the Spirit of God dwell in you . . ." (Romans 8:7, 9). Paul says that now that you are indwelt by the Spirit of God, you can produce the fruit of the Spirit in your life; if you don't, there is something radically wrong. A Christian doesn't do as he pleases; he does as Christ pleases.

During the depression there lived in Pittsburgh a tycoon who was having all kinds of problems in his life. He went to his pastor and, after talking over his problems, he said, "I love my Savior. I love my family. I love my church. I love my business. But there are times I feel like walking out on all four of them." The pastor looked him straight in the

eye and said, "Well, why don't you?" The man replied, "The reason I don't is that I am a Christian." May I say to you, saving faith which makes one a Christian will lead to good works. However, we are so anxious to get church members that we accept them on the slightest profession. As a result, many churches are filled with professing Christians who are really unbelievers.

When we understand how Paul and James use the words *faith* and *works*, we can see that they are in total agreement in their teaching.

Now James deals with the *identification of faith*. Saving faith can be recognized and identified by certain spiritual fingerprints. There is a verification of genuine faith. James gives us this practical illustration—

If a brother or sister be naked, and destitute of daily food,

And one of you say unto them, Depart in peace, be ye warmed and filled; notwithstanding ye give them not those things which are needful to the body; what doth it profit? [James 2:15–16].

Pious clichés and Christian verbiage are not the evidence of saving faith. There must be a vocation to go along with the vocabulary. You can be very pious and say to an individual, "Brother, I will pray for you, and I know the Lord will provide." My friend, the Lord put *you* there as a child of God to do the providing. I get a little weary sometimes when wealthy Christian laymen pat me on the back and say, "Dr. McGee, you are doing a fine thing. You are doing the right thing in giving out the Word of God," but they do not have a part in supporting this ministry financially. I have a hard time believing they are sincere. You may piously say to someone, "Oh, brother, I'm for you." *Are* you for him? Are you back of him? My friend, a living faith *produces* something—you can *identify* it.

The Lord Jesus said, "By this shall all men know that ye are my disciples, if ye have love one to another" (John 13:35). Then in Romans 13:8, Paul says, "Owe no man any thing, but to love one another: for he that loveth another hath fulfilled the law." The point is that you cannot say you are a child of God and live like a lawless individual. I do not mean that whenever a bum asks you for twenty-five cents in order to buy wine you should give it to him. And I do not think that you should believe every individual who professes to be a Christian. We need to test them out to see whether they are or not. My heart is warmed when I think of a certain man I know who is rendering financial assistance to someone in need and of a lady of means who is supporting a missionary abroad and telling no one about it. May I say to you, you are telling by your life whether your faith is genuine or not.

Even so faith, if it hath not works, is dead, being alone.

Yea, a man may say, Thou hast faith, and I have works: shew me thy faith without thy works, and I will shew thee my faith by my works [James 2:17–18].

"Faith, if it hath not works, is dead." The faith is dead? Why? Because living faith, saving faith, produces works. You have to draw that conclusion from James' illustration. He is talking about the fruit of faith. Paul talks about the root of faith. Those are the separate emphases of each man, but both Paul and James say that faith alone saves. Paul also says that faith is going to produce fruit—"But the fruit of the Spirit is love, joy, peace . . ." (Gal. 5:22). The Lord Jesus said, "I am the vine, ye are the branches: He that abideth in me, and I in him, the same bringeth forth much fruit . . ." (John 15:5).

A minister once talked to a man who professed conversion, and he asked, "Have you united with the church?" "No, I haven't," the man replied. "The dying thief never united with the church, and he went to heaven." The minister asked, "Have you ever sat at the Lord's table?" "No, the dying thief never did, and he was accepted" was the answer. The minister asked, "Have you been baptized?" "No," he said, "the dying thief was never baptized, and he went to heaven." "Have you given to missions?" "No, the dying thief did not give to missions, and he was not judged for it" was the reply. Then this disgusted minister said to the man, "Well, my friend, the difference between you two seems to be that he was a dying thief and you are a living thief."

My friend, we often sing, "O for a thousand tongues to sing my great Redeemer's praise," but we do not even use the one tongue we have. And we sing, "Were the whole realm of nature mine, that were a present far too small," and then we give nothing at all to Him. James says it is faith that saves, but saving faith produces something.

Thou believest that there is one God; thou doest well: the devils also believe, and tremble [James 2:19].

Lip service is not the evidence of saving faith—even the demons believe.

But wilt thou know, O vain man, that faith without works is dead? [James 2:20].

Faith without the fruit of faith is empty and futile as far as the world is concerned.

Now James will give us the *illustration of faith*—in fact, there will be two illustrations.

Was not Abraham our father justified by works, when he had offered Isaac his son upon the altar?

Seest thou how faith wrought with his works, and by works was faith made perfect?

And the scripture was fulfilled which saith, Abraham believed God, and it was imputed unto him for righteousness: and he was called the Friend of God.

Ye see then how that by works a man is justified, and not by faith only [James 2:21–24].

Paul said that Abraham was justified by *faith* (see Rom. 4:3), and Genesis tells us that he was justified by *faith* (see Gen. 15:6; 22:1–14). Was Abraham justified when he offered his son Isaac? The question is: *Did* he offer his son Isaac? And the answer is: No, he didn't. Then what was Abraham's work of faith? How did works save him? His faith caused him to lift that knife to do a thing which he did not believe God would ever ask him to do. But since God had asked him, he was willing to do it. He believed that God would raise Isaac from the dead. Abraham never actually offered Isaac, because God provided a substitute, but he would have done it if God had not stopped him.

This is a choice illustration of the fact that you demonstrate your faith by your actions. The action of this man was that *he believed God.*

James uses a second illustration—

Likewise also was not Rahab the harlot justified by works, when she had received the messengers, and had sent them out another way? [James 2:25].

How was Rahab justified by works? She received the Israelite spies, concealed them from her own people, then told them how to escape without being detected (see Josh. 2). That woman living there in the city of Jericho jeopardized her life by turning her back on her old life and on her own people. What was gain to her became loss. She did not say to the Israelite spies, "I'll just stand on the sidelines when you enter the city and sing, 'Praise God from whom all blessings flow.'" She did not just say, "Jesus saves and keeps and satisfies." She did not say, "Hallelujah! Praise the Lord!" She said to them, "I'm going to *do* something. I will hide you because I believe God is going to give the people of Israel this land. We have been hearing about you for forty years, and I believe God." My friend, she believed God, and she became involved. She was justified before God by her faith: "By faith the harlot Rahab perished not with them that believed not, when she had received the spies with peace" (Heb. 11:31). However, before her own people and before the Israelites, she was justified by works.

Many years ago I went to a nursery and bought a bare root which was labeled "Santa Rosa plum." It wasn't even as big as a broom handle, and it looked no more alive than a broom handle. I was told to put it in the ground in a certain way, and I did that. I watched it, and the next spring it began to shoot out leaves. In three years there were blossoms on it, and then there was fruit. Do you know what kind of fruit was on that tree? Plums. The root of that tree was a plum root.

Faith is the root, and the root produces the kind of fruit that the root itself is. If you have a living faith, there is going to be fruit in your life. Paul says, "Examine yourselves, whether ye be in the faith; prove your own selves . . ." (2 Cor. 13:5).

And James continues—

For as the body without the spirit is dead, so faith without works is dead also [James 2:26].

Faith without works is like a dead body in a morgue. James said that; Paul said that, and Vernon McGee believes both of them because they are giving us God's Word for it.

CHAPTER 3

THEME: God tests faith by the tongue

GOD TESTS FAITH BY THE TONGUE

I have written a booklet on the third chapter of James, and it has a sensational title; but my sensationalism is no greater than that of the Bible, for my title is a Bible title: *Hell on Fire*. We will see that that is the expression James uses here in talking about the tongue.

We have heard a great deal in recent years about freedom of speech and freedom of the press, and it has become sort of a sacred cow. However, freedom of the press in our day means that they can brainwash you according to the liberal viewpoint, and freedom of speech means that you can use vile language. I would like for someone to grant us freedom of hearing. I have only one mouth, but I have two ears, and I think my ears ought to be protected as well as my mouth. We need freedom of hearing today as well as freedom of speech.

This chapter deals with "Freedom of Speech in God's University," which is another way I have labeled this particular chapter. I also like the title, "God Bugs Your Conversation." There is no question that God has the right to bug, or to listen in on, our conversations. He has had that right for a long time, and He has heard everything that you and I have said. It is estimated that the average person says about thirty thousand words every day. (I know two or three people who exceed that number!) That is enough to make a good-sized book. In a lifetime, you or I could fill a library with the words we have said. God has that recorded, by the way, because He bugs your conversation.

I suppose that the present-day movement for freedom of speech began at the Berkeley campus of the University of California some years ago. It was given coverage by the news media out of all proportion to its importance; that news coverage itself was another attempt at brainwashing. A great many taxpayers and prominent citizens were concerned that this great university, which is supported by their tax money, could be shut down and made a ridiculous spectacle by a few radicals, while the majority of the students were intimidated and their good intentions of getting an education were reflected upon.

Now the problem of freedom of speech is not only out yonder in the university and in the news media, but it is in the church also. The problem in the church is the problem of gossip.

Each one of us who is a Christian needs to be concerned about our freedom of speech.

Just as I do with the Book of Proverbs, I liken the Epistle of James to a course in God's university. James is the dean of God's university as we consider this controversial subject, and he has quite a bit to say concerning the use and abuse of the tongue. We have seen in this epistle that God tests faith in many different ways. Here God tests our faith by our tongue. We want to reach up on the shelf of the laboratory of life and take down an acid to test our faith. Actually, this acid is more potent than hydrochloric or sulfuric or any other acid. The label on the bottle is "Tongue."

However, we are not talking about the chemistry of the tongue but about the theology of the tongue. James has already indicated that he was going to come to this subject. He said back in chapter 1, verse 26, "If any man among you seem to be religious, and bridleth not his tongue, but deceiveth his own heart, this man's religion is vain." He also said, "let every man be swift to hear, slow to speak" (James 1:19). You have two ears, and God gave them to you so that you can hear twice as much as you can say.

The tongue is the most dangerous weapon in the world. It is more deadly than the atom bomb, but no careful inspection is made of it. Some wag made the statement that it was a miracle in Balaam's day for an ass to speak, but today it is a miracle when he keeps quiet. Someone else pointed out that it takes a baby two years to learn to talk and fifty years to learn to keep his mouth shut.

The story is told of a man who had been fishing out on a pier for several hours and had not caught anything. As two women walked out on the pier, he finally pulled in a fish. It wasn't a very large fish, and one of these two women took it upon herself to rebuke this man: "Aren't you ashamed of yourself for so cruelly catching this poor little fish?" And the man, without even looking up, because he was a little discouraged anyway, said, "Maybe you are right, lady, but if the fish had kept his mouth shut he wouldn't have been caught."

Another has expressed it this way:

If your lips would keep from slips,
Five things to observe with care:
To whom you speak, of whom you speak,
And how, and when, and where.

—Author unknown

The importance of the tongue has been expressed in many different ways, and practically every nation has had something to say about it. I read this in Spurgeon's "Salt Cellars" years ago:

"The boneless tongue, so small and weak,
Can crush and kill," declared the Greek.
"The tongue destroys a greater hoard,"
The Turk asserts, "than does the sword."

A Persian proverb wisely saith,
"A lengthy tongue—an early death";
Or sometimes takes this form instead,
"Don't let your tongue cut off your head."

"The tongue can speak a word whose speed,"
The Chinese say, "outstrips the steed";
While Arab sages this impart,
"The tongue's great storehouse is the heart."

From Hebrew wit this maxim sprung,
"Though feet should slip, ne'er let the tongue."
The sacred writer crowns the whole,
"Who keeps his tongue doth keep his soul!"

All of these sayings are very wise. I believe fervently that the most dangerous thing in the world is the tongue. I think the church is more harmed by the termites within than by the woodpeckers on the outside. Someone has put it like this: "Thou art master of the unspoken word, but the spoken word is master of you." In other words, my friend, once you have said it, it is beyond your control.

All of that is preliminary. Let us look now at what James has to say concerning the tongue—

My brethren, be not many masters, knowing that we shall receive the greater condemnation [James 3:1].

Masters means "teachers." James is saying that a teacher has a greater responsibility, and the reason for that is the grave danger of teaching the wrong thing. I am absolutely amazed and overwhelmed at the way so many Christian folk fall for all kinds of teaching, particularly that which has to do with prophecy. All a teacher needs today is a glib tongue. People are accepting all kinds of methods and cults and "isms"; yet many of these teachers, as far as the total Word of God is concerned, are absolutely ignorant. I rejoice in home Bible classes, and I think they have filled a real vacuum that existed, but I find that some of the leaders are teaching all kinds of vagaries, giving the wrong interpretation of Scripture. They need to know more of the Word of God than they do.

The ease with which people fall for their teachings has ministered to a great deal of conceit and pride on the part of many teachers. One young fellow that I had the privilege of leading to Christ has gone off on a tangent in his teaching. I tried to get him to study the Word, but he did not. He has now started a class, and he is very glib of tongue. Someone in his class went to him and said, "Do you know that what you have taught is contrary to most Bible teachers and especially to the man who led you to the Lord?" The young man replied, "Oh, Dr. McGee? Well, maybe he needs to correct *his* theology." Well, frankly, maybe I do. I am amazed the more I study the Word of God. The thing that discourages me is that it reveals my ignorance, not my knowledge. I realize I have a long way to go, but the young man who made that statement has even farther to go. However, he does not recognize his own ignorance.

I am reminded of what a preacher said of another young man who had just started out in the ministry. When someone pointed out his prideful attitude, the preacher said of the young man, "Yes, he thinks he is the fourth person of the Trinity." It is so easy for a preacher or teacher to become proud.

The tongue is very dangerous. James is saying here, "My brethren, be not many teachers." Don't think that the minute you become a child of God you can start a Bible class and teach the Book of Revelation.

"Knowing that we shall receive the greater condemnation." Frankly, it is frightening to realize that God will judge us for the way in which we teach His Word, and we will be under His condemnation if our teaching is wrong. My friend, the more opportunity you have to give out the Word of God, the greater is your responsibility to God Himself.

For in many things we offend all. If any man offend not in word, the same is a perfect man, and able also to bridle the whole body [James 3:2].

"For in many things we offend all" means that in many ways we all stumble. All of us do—there is no exception to that.

"If any man offend not in word, the same is a perfect man." The word *perfect* means he is a full-grown Christian as he should be—just as a baby grows up, becomes a little child and matures to full adulthood.

James says the perfect man is "able also to bridle the whole body." In other words, if he can control his speech, he can control his entire body, in fact, his whole life. The tongue lifts man from the animal world. It keeps him from being a gibbering ape or an aping parrot. Man is not an inarticulate animal or a mockingbird. Man can put thought into words; he can express himself; he can be understood; he can communicate on the highest level. The tongue is a badge which you and I wear—it identifies us. It is the greatest index to life. It is the table of contents of our lives.

Our tongues give us away; they tell who we are. Quite a few years ago I was rushing with my wife and little girl from a conference at Salt Lake City to a conference in the San Francisco Bay area. As we came over the High Sierras and Donner Pass, we stopped at a little town—I don't even know the name of it—and pulled into a filling station. I stepped out of the car and said to the young man there, "Fill 'er up!" That's all I said, but as I was looking out at those mountains and the lovely scenery, I became conscious that he was eyeing me. Finally, I turned to him and smiled. He said to me, "Are you Dr. McGee?" I said, "I sure am. Do I know you?" He said, "No." I said, "Do you know me?" He said, "No. I've never seen you before, but up here, especially during the wintertime when we are all snowed in, we listen to you every Sunday night on the radio. We've been doing it for years. I'd know your voice anywhere." I've had that same experience a number of times. You see, my tongue gives me away.

Remember the maid who said to Simon Peter, ". . . thy speech betrayeth thee" (Matt. 26:73)—he could not deny that he was from Galilee. Your speech tells who you are; your tongue gives you away. It tells where you came from. It tells whether you are ignorant or educated, cultured or crude, whether you are clean or unclean, whether you are vulgar or refined, whether you are a believer or a blasphemer, whether you are a Christian or a non-Christian, whether you are guilty or not guilty. My friend, I am of the opinion that if you had a tape-recorded message of everything you have said this past month, you would not want the world to hear it.

Now let's put the acid down on your tongue and mine. James will first deal with the unbridled and unrestrained tongue—

Behold, we put bits in the horses' mouths, that they may obey us; and we turn about their whole body [James 3:3].

The illustration James uses here is the horse. It was David who said, "I said, I will take heed to my ways, that I sin not with my tongue: I will keep my mouth with a bridle, while the wicked is before me" (Ps. 39:1). In other words, David said that because he wanted to give the right kind of testimony, he would put a bridle on his mouth. My friend, there are a lot of Christians today who ought to have a bridle put on their mouths.

The bridle bits are not impressive in size, but they can hold a high-spirited horse in check and keep him from running away. If you are old enough, you may have recollections of the horse-and-buggy days. I can recall seeing a horse run away, turn over a buggy, and bring death and destruction to a family. In the same way, the tongue can run away. Someone said of another individual, "His mind starts his tongue to wagging, and then goes off and leaves it." We should not go through life like that—there needs to be a bridle for the tongue.

Now James is going to use a different illustration—✓

Behold also the ships, which though they be so great, and are driven of fierce winds, yet are they turned about with a very small helm, whithersoever the governor listeth [James 3:4].

Large ships can be controlled by a little rudder which few people even see. A fierce storm may drive a ship, but a little rudder can control it. The tongue can also change the course of our lives. Men have been ruined by the tongue; many the fair name of a woman has been wrecked by some gossipy tongue.

James says that the tongue is more dangerous than a runaway horse or a storm at sea. I believe that liquor is eating at the vitals of our nation today, but did you know that the tongue is condemned more in Scripture than alcoholism is condemned? Liquor and alcoholism may bring our nation down, yet the tongue is even more dangerous than that. Proverbs 6:16–17 says, "These six things doth the LORD hate: yea, seven are an abomination unto him: A proud look, a lying tongue, and hands that shed innocent blood." A lying tongue is one of the seven things God hates.

The tongue can really get us into trouble—there is no question about that. Again, someone has put it in words like this:

A careless word may kindle strife;
A cruel word may wreck a life.
A bitter word may hate instill;
A brutal word may smite and kill.

A gracious word may smooth the way;
A joyous word may light the day.
A timely word may lessen stress;
A loving word may heal and bless.
—Author unknown

I was very impressed when I read General Montgomery's farewell words addressed to the Eighth Army in Italy following World War II. He said to them, "Command must be personal and it must be verbal; otherwise it will have no success, because it is wrapped up in the human factor." Continuing, he said this: "I often have at the back of my mind a passage from the New Testament, 'Except ye utter by the tongue words easy to be understood, how shall it be known what is spoken?'" (see 1 Cor. 14:9). That is the kind of tongue I want to have as I teach the Word of God—the tongue that both a little child and the older folk can understand. Someone asked me one time, "How in the world can the same message bring a nine-year-old child and a university professor to the Lord?" I must confess, I do not know the answer to that question. But I do believe that God blesses His Word and that it must be taught simply. We must put the cookies on the bottom shelf where the kiddies can get them. God did not say, "Feed My giraffes"; He said, "Feed My lambs" (see John 21:15).

Even so the tongue is a little member, and boasteth great things. Behold, how great a matter a little fire kindleth!

And the tongue is a fire, a world of iniquity: so is the tongue among our members, that it defileth the whole body, and setteth on fire the course of nature; and it is set on fire of hell [James 3:5–6].

This is where I got the title for my little book on this third chapter of James, *Hell on Fire*. That is what the tongue can be and is in many cases. There are those who have questioned my use of the word *hell*, arguing that it is not properly translated in this verse. The Greek word used here is *gehenna;* it is not *sheol*. It refers to the valley of Hinnom where the fire never went out. This word is used only twelve times in the New Testament; the Lord Jesus used it eleven times, and James used it once. This is a correct translation: the tongue is "set on fire of *hell*."

It is quite impressive that James compares the tongue to a fire. I do not know whether you have ever seen a forest fire, but each summer out here in California we have an epidemic of them. They are very devastating, and many times absolutely uncontrollable; they have to burn themselves out in many instances.

Fire has been, of course, one of the greatest friends of man and nature. Some historians say that civilization began when man discovered fire. When it is under control, it warms our bodies, it cooks our food, and it generates power to turn the wheels of industry. It is dangerous, though, when it is out of control. It is a tragedy when a house is on fire. You hear a siren in the night, and you know that a group of men is rushing to put out a fire. Even in our present civilization we are not able to control fires. The London fire of 1666 destroyed London. Mrs. O'Leary's cow kicked over a lantern in Chicago in 1871 and started that great and historic fire. And still today we see great devastations caused by fire.

The tongue is like a fire; when it is under control, it is a blessing; when it is out of control, it is devastating. It can be a cure, or it can be a curse. In Proverbs 12:18 we read, "There is that speaketh like the piercings of a sword: but the tongue of the wise is health." The tongue can be like a sword that kills, but it also can be health itself. What a picture this is of the tongue! Again in Proverbs we read, "The heart of him that hath understanding seeketh knowledge: but the mouth of fools feedeth on foolishness" (Prov. 15:14).

Let me repeat the proverb I quoted a little earlier: "Thou art master of the unspoken word, but the spoken word is master of you." If you haven't said it, you cannot be held responsible, but once you've said it, it can condemn you. I have learned through personal experience that a slip of the tongue (especially if it's made on a radio broadcast which is heard by many) can have great repercussions. You remember that Simon Peter's tongue betrayed him, and he denied that he knew his Lord. But on the Day of Pentecost, what was it that the Lord used? It was the tongue of that blundering, stumbling, bumbling fellow, Simon Peter. The tongue can be either a curse or a cure.

Brush and forest fires scorch and blacken and are a plague. Like a fire, the tongue can burn through a church, burn through a community, burn through a town, and even burn through a nation.

For every kind of beasts, and of birds, and of serpents, and of things in the sea, is tamed, and hath been tamed of mankind:

But the tongue can no man tame; it is an unruly evil, full of deadly poison [James 3:7–8].

In my younger days, when the circus was coming to town, a group of us young folk would gather at some home, have a time of fellowship and a late dinner, then go down to the railroad yards to watch the circus come in and unload. As the parade of moving it out to the circus grounds was in progress, we would go along with it and then watch the tent being put up. One time we were even invited to have breakfast with them in the cook tent. My, what a thrill that was! Clyde Beatty was then with the Ringling Brothers, Barnum and Bailey Circus, and he had charge of the wild animals. He was the one who went into the cages and put them through their paces. We were in that tent, not as paid customers, but just watching them put up everything. Clyde Beatty went to a cage in which there were some little lion cubs; I think there were three or four of them. He took them out and began to play with them. He rolled them, and they bit at him; he grabbed them and turned them over, just having a big time with them. We went over and asked him why he did that. He said this: "I would never go into a cage with a lion that I had not brought up from the time it was a cub. You cannot train an old lion. I begin with these little ones, and when they grow up into fine, fierce-looking young lions, I will take them into the cage with me. But they know me, and I know them." May I say to you, you can tame a lion; you can tame an elephant, but you cannot tame the little tongue. As someone has said, "The most untamable thing in the world has its den just behind the teeth." That's one little animal which no zoo has in captivity, no circus can make it perform, no man can tame it. Only a regenerate tongue in a redeemed body, a tongue that God has tamed, can be used for Him.

It is interesting to note that Paul said, "That if thou shalt *confess with thy mouth* the Lord Jesus, and shalt *believe in thine heart* that God hath raised him from the dead, thou shalt be saved" (Rom. 10:9, italics mine). In other words, we are to sing a duet, the tongue and the heart are to be in tune. The Lord Jesus said, ". . . for out of the abundance of the heart the mouth speaketh" (Matt. 12:34)—what is in the heart will come out. Someone has said, "What is in the well of the heart will come out through the bucket of the mouth." If it is in your heart, you are going to say it sooner or later. It is interesting that when our Lord came to that dumb man, the gospel writer is very careful to say, "He touched his mouth!" My friend, if He has touched you, He has touched your mouth also.

Therewith bless we God, even the Father; and therewith curse we men, which are made after the similitude of God.

Out of the same mouth proceedeth blessing and cursing. My brethren, these things ought not so to be [James 3:9–10].

The tongues which you and I have are capable of praising God or blaspheming God. As we have said before, the tongue is that which lifts man above the animal world. Man is not a gibbering ape or a mockingbird. Man can communicate with man, and he can communicate with God. When a man can sing like an angel on Sunday and then talk like a demon during the week—you label him as you want to—the Bible calls that man a hypocrite.

When I announced in the bank where I worked as a young man that I was going to study for the ministry, one of the vice-presidents of the bank called me into his office. He had been a good friend of mine, and he knew something of my life and how I had lived. He said to me, "Vernon, I hope you are going to be a genuine preacher and a genuine servant of God." He said, "The reason I am not a Christian today is because of an experience had during the war." (He was referring to World War I.) He went on to tell me how the bank had set up a branch bank at the powder plant at Old Hickory outside of Nashville, Tennessee. One of the tellers there was also a soloist in a church in downtown Nashville. One Sunday as that teller came out of church, the bank vice-president overheard one of the ladies say, "You know, that man is one of the most wonderful men in the world. He sings just like an angel!" This vice-president made no comment at the time. But that woman owned property, and she had business at the bank out at Old Hickory. She came in one day and was talking to him when suddenly they heard the vilest language imaginable. It came from the teller who had attempted to balance and he hadn't balanced. (I was a teller for several years, and I know that this is one of the most discouraging things that can happen.) Well, when this man didn't balance, he began to explode with blasphemies, and the lady said, "Who in the world is that?" The bank vice-president said, "That's your soloist who sings like an angel on Sunday!" A man can bless God with his mouth, and he can blaspheme God. You can do both with the mouth you have. The Lord Jesus said that what is in the heart will come up through the mouth; you can be sure your tongue is going to say it.

Doth a fountain send forth at the same place sweet water and bitter?

Can the fig tree, my brethren, bear olive berries? either a vine, figs? so can no fountain both yield salt water and fresh [James 3:11–12].

In other words, a man can be a two-faced, double-minded, and forked-tongued individual—he can say both good and bad. But no fountain down here on this earth is going to give forth both sweet and bitter water, nor will a tree bear both figs and olives.

Now the tongue reveals genuine faith, because it is with the mouth that confession is made of that which is in the heart—

Who is a wise man and endued with knowledge among you? let him shew out of a good conversation his works with meekness of wisdom [James 3:13].

The tongue can reveal genuine faith. It can give a testimony for God. It can speak wisdom.

But if ye have bitter envying and strife in your hearts, glory not, and lie not against the truth [James 3:14].

Strife and bitterness are certainly not the fruits of faith, but the tongue can stir up that kind of thing. James is making a contrast between the tongue of the foolish believer and the tongue of the wise believer. In fact, an uncontrolled tongue raises the question in the minds of others whether a man is a child of God or not. You cannot make me believe that a genuine believer can curse six days a week and then sing in a choir on Sunday. He cannot tell dirty jokes and then teach a Sunday school class, telling about the love of Jesus. That tongue which you have can do either one, but if it does both, it is that which stirs up strife. We are told here, "Lie not against the truth." A lying tongue is one that denies the Lord during the week by its conversation.

This wisdom descendeth not from above, but is earthly, sensual, devilish [James 3:15].

James makes it very clear that strife and envying do not originate with God. They do not come from Him at all—it is "earthly, sensual, devilish."

> Knowledge is proud that she has learned so much; Wisdom is humble that she knows no more.
>
> —Author unknown

For where envying and strife is, there is confusion and every evil work [James 3:16].

An uncontrolled tongue produces envying and strife which lead to "confusion and every evil work." Scripture makes it very clear that God is not the author of confusion. The confusion we find in the world today is a confusion brought about by the work of the Devil using that little thing, the tongue, which causes so much trouble. This verse will tie in very closely with what James has to say in the next chapter where he will define what worldliness really is.

But the wisdom that is from above is first pure, then peaceable, gentle, and easy to be entreated, full of mercy and good fruits, without partiality, and without hypocrisy [James 3:17].

"But the wisdom that is from above is first *pure*"—that is, it's not mingled or mixed; it's undiluted; it's the original. It is that wisdom which comes down from God, and James clearly identifies it: it is "then peaceable, gentle, and easy to be entreated, full of mercy and good fruits, without partiality, and without hypocrisy."

Dr. Samuel Zwemer mentions the fact that false teaching always produces strife and envy and trouble. He says, "You cannot explain the wickedness of the world as merely human. It is human plus something, and that is why non-Christian religions are successful. They are supernatural, but from beneath." Anything that causes divisions and strife—it matters not which church it is in—is not of the Lord, you may be sure of that. You may boast of your fundamentalism, but if you are causing strife, you are sailing under false colors.

And the fruit of righteousness is sown in peace of them that make peace [James 3:18].

These are the fruits of faith. There must be righteousness before there can be peace. I wish this idea would reach the United Nations. I wish it would reach Washington, D.C., and Moscow and Peking and all the other capitals of the world. You cannot have peace without righteousness. There is a day coming, the psalmist says, when peace and righteousness will have kissed each other (see Ps. 85:10). Today they don't even know each other; they wouldn't even recognize each other.

Chapter 3 concludes the first major division of the Epistle of James in which James has dealt with the verification of genuine faith. There is a difference in faith: you can believe the wrong thing, or you can just nod your head and call that faith, but *saving faith* is that which produces good works.

In these three chapters James has shown various ways in which God tests our faith to prove that it is genuine. First of all, God tests faith by trials. Dr. Richard H. Seume is an outstanding Bible teacher who has suffered with kidney trouble for a number of years. I would like to share with you something which he said (as quoted by Dr. Lehman Strauss in his book, *James Your Brother*), because I know that it comes from a preacher who is not giving us his theory or his ideas but who knows what it means to suffer. Dr. Seume wrote:

> Life on earth would not be worth much if every source of irritation were removed. Yet most of us rebel against the things that irritate us, and count as heavy loss what ought to be rich gain. We are told that the oyster is wiser; that when an irritating object, like a bit of sand, gets under the mantle of his shell, he simply covers it with the most precious part of his being and makes of it a pearl. The irritation that it was causing is stopped by encrusting it with the pearly formation. A true pearl is therefore simply a VICTORY over irritation. Every irritation that gets into our lives today is an opportunity for pearl culture. The more irritations the devil flings at us, the more pearls we may have. We need only to welcome them and cover them completely with love, that most precious part of us, and the irritation will be smothered out as the pearl comes into being. What a store of pearls we may have, if we will!

We saw, therefore, that (1) God tests faith by trials; (2) God does not test faith with evil; (3) God tests faith by the Word; (4) God tests faith by attitude and action in respect of persons; (5) God tests faith by good works; and (6) God tests faith by the tongue. James has made it very clear that genuine faith will be evident in the life of the believer.

CHAPTER 4

THEME: Vacuity and vapidness of worldliness

VACUITY AND VAPIDNESS OF WORLDLINESS

James will deal with several very important questions in this chapter: What is worldliness? How does a Christian fight the Devil? What is your life? All of these will anchor back into the subject of worldliness.

James will first answer the question: What is worldliness? I believe the average Christian in our so-called fundamental churches would give one of several answers. Some would say that worldliness is a matter of the kind of amusements you attend or indulge in: What kind of movies do you go to? Do you dance? And, do you drink? That is what they would call worldliness. May I say to you, James would not agree with them.

Others would say that it is the kind of crowd you run with, the gang you hang around with. After all, birds of a feather flock together, and if you are with a worldly crowd that engages in these things, then you are worldly. I am sorry to have to tell you, if you gave that answer in James' college, you would fail; you wouldn't pass the course.

Still others would say that worldliness is a matter of the conversation you engage in. You must learn to say "Praise the Lord" and "Hallelujah" at the right times. Worldliness is when you engage in worldly conversation. Again, that is not the answer; you have failed the course.

Someone else will answer that worldliness is the way that you dress. I have news for you: you have not passed the course.

Others may say it is a person who engages in business and the making of money to the exclusion of all else and who neglects the church; that person, they say, is a worldly individual. You still have not passed the course in James' college.

Yet another may answer that it is the person who does not go to church, but spends time on the golf course, fishing, boating, or watching his favorite team play baseball.

My friend, I do not approve of any of the things which I have mentioned here, but they just don't happen to be worldliness. Most of those sins are sins of the flesh—not of the world. If you put down any one of those as your answer to James' question, you have flunked the exam; you've failed the subject, and you've busted the course. None of those answers is correct. They may be symptoms of the disease, but nobody ever died of symptoms—they die of the disease. These are simply evidences of the real problem, which is deeper.

A brother of Henry Ward Beecher, a pastor in upper New York state, had a clock in his church that never would keep accurate time. So this man put a sign under that clock which read: "Don't blame the hands. The trouble lies deeper." This is what we need to recognize in ourselves. What we call worldliness is just the hands of the clock; the real trouble lies deeper.

William Thackeray, who was a Christian, dealt with this subject in his novel, *Vanity Fair*, in a way that probably no one else has dealt with it. His novel is about the world, and he wrote it on the background of the wars of Napoleon. He presents characters who are all filled with weaknesses and littleness, pettiness and jealousy, envy, discord and strife—all of that is there. Someone once asked Thackeray, "Why don't you have some wonderful heroes in your novels? You always present *little* people." Thackeray replied, "I hold a mirror up to nature, and I do not find heroes among mankind. They are filled with littleness and pettiness and strife and sin." When you get to the end of *Vanity Fair*, Thackeray does a masterly thing. He says, "Come, children, let us shut up the box and the puppets, for our play is played out." That is man. As Shakespeare said, he "struts and frets his hour upon the stage." Man is filled with worldliness.

Dr. Griffith Thomas pinned it down a little closer when a person who was very much distressed came to him one day and asked, "Don't you think that the world is becoming Christian today?" Dr. Thomas said, "No, I do not think that is true. I think the world is becoming a little churchy, but I think the church is becoming immensely worldly."

Since World War II there has been a breakdown of the wall of separation between the church and the world. The separation that many had practiced was legalistic and, I think, unscriptural. The church was like the little Dutch boy who was keeping his thumb in the dike. Then, in the aftermath of the war, along came television, lawlessness, immorality, and juvenile delinquency; first the beatniks, then the hippies, then dope and marijuana, and the philosophy of existentialism. A tidal wave swept over the dikes of separation, and even the little Dutch boy was washed away.

There is no simple answer to the question: What is worldliness? But I am going to let James give what I think is his very definitive answer. What is worldliness? James says that worldliness is strife and envy. We need to go back to chapter 3 to pick up his thoughts. In James 3:13 we read, "Who is a wise man and endued with knowledge among you? Let him shew out of a good conversation his works with meekness of wisdom." Faith is the major in James' university, and all elective courses are related to faith. Works of faith bring meekness. Then we read, "But the wisdom that is from above is first pure, then peaceable, gentle" (James 3:17). There is meekness or humility, and humility means submission.

In James 3:16 we read, "For where envying and strife is, there is confusion and every evil work." That is worldliness. And worldliness in the church has produced all the cults, denominations, factions, divisions, and cliques which have arisen and abound in the church today. There is a spirit of rivalry and jealousy in the church. In the previous verse, James describes this as "earthly"—that is, it is confined to the earth. It is "sensual"—that is, psychological. And then it's "devilish" or demonic, which is something quite terrible, my friend.

What do envy and strife produce in this world? They produce "confusion and every evil work." With this as background, we can recognize what James is saying now in chapter 4—

From whence come wars and fightings among you? come they not hence, even of your lusts that war in your members? [James 4:1].

"Wars" have to do with the wars of nations. "Fightings" have to do with little skirmishes—that little fight you had in the church—you remember?

"Come they not hence, even of your lusts that war in your members?" You wanted to have your own way. "Lusts that war in your members" are actually sensual pleasures. Strife and turmoil are created by conflicts and the overweening demands of the members of the body for satisfaction.

Ye lust, and have not: ye kill, and desire to have, and cannot obtain: ye fight and war, yet ye have not, because ye ask not [James 4:2].

Selfish desires, James makes it very clear,

lead to war. This spirit of strife is worldliness; it is not Christian, and it is not the Christian approach. These are the things which represent the old nature. A man must be regenerated by faith in Christ and be indwelt by the Holy Spirit.

What James describes here is the spirit of the world. When the spirit of the world gets into the church, you have a worldly church. My friend, do you think it is bad out on the battlefield? Did you think it was bad in Vietnam? Well, it was, but inside some churches and inside the hearts of some individuals it is just as bad. In the business world there is dog-eat-dog competition—that is worldliness. Political parties split, and one group becomes pitted against another. As capital and labor meet around the conference table, there is a battle going on. In the social world there are climbers on the social ladder who are stepping on the hands of others as they go up. In your neighborhood and mine one family does not speak to another family. Within families there are quarrels, brother against brother. Then that spirit gets into the church. *That*, my friend, is worldliness.

"Yet ye have not, because ye ask not." Our desires should be taken to the Lord in prayer—to have them satisfied or denied or refined—and then we need to accept the answer from Him. What is the cure for worldliness? It is prayer. It is, therefore, faith in God. The apostle John put it like this, "For whatsoever is born of God overcometh the world: and this is the victory that overcometh the world, even our faith" (1 John 5:4). The answer is to trust in God absolutely, to go to Him in prayer and commit to Him that which is in your heart. When you find that there is strife and envy in your heart, talk to Him about it. Many of us go to the Lord to tell Him how good we are. And because we have been good little boys and girls who have gone to Sunday school, we think He ought to give us a lollipop or a Brownie button or something of that sort. My friend, we need to get right down to the nitty-gritty where we live. Consider these words which were written by a great saint, a mystic of the Middle Ages, Fénelon:

Tell God all that is in your heart, as one unloads one's heart, its pleasures and its pains, to a dear friend. Tell Him your troubles, that He may comfort you; tell Him your joys, that He may sober them; tell Him your longings, that He may purify them; tell Him your dislikes, that He may help you to conquer them; talk to

Him of your temptations, that He may shield you from them; show Him the wounds of your heart, that He may heal them; lay bare your indifference to good, your depraved tastes for evil, your instability. Tell Him how self-love makes you unjust to others, how vanity tempts you to be insincere, how pride disguises you to yourself as to others.

If you thus pour out all your weaknesses, needs, troubles, there will be no lack of what to say. You will never exhaust the subject. It is continually being renewed. People who have no secrets from each other never want subjects of conversation. They do not weigh their words, for there is nothing to be held back; neither do they seek for something to say. They talk out of the abundance of the heart, without consideration, just what they think. Blessed are they who attain to such familiar, unreserved intercourse with God.

When I was laid aside for some time with an illness, I found that all things do work together for good. My wife and I were able to sit at home for a longer period of time than we ever had since we were married. Even on our honeymoon I candidated at a church. From that day to this we have been on the go. We found that there were some things we really needed to talk over that otherwise might have been misunderstood. We had wonderful talks, and we just laid bare our hearts to each other. It was the most joyous experience. I said to her, "Honey, this is more wonderful than our honeymoon was!" That is the kind of relationship we ought to have with God.

Having studied the Word of God and having read these words by Fénelon, I came to the conclusion that I was going to tell the Lord Jesus everything. I have talked to Him about everything in my life that was sinful and questionable. He knows, He understands, and He's forgiven me.

The only way to take away that envy and jealousy and strife which is in your heart is to go to the Lord Jesus. You don't need to go to the psychiatrist; he'll just move your problem from one area to another. You need to get rid of that hang-up by going to the Lord Jesus, getting on *His* couch, and telling Him everything.

James says that the solution is for you and me to pray, but we often pray for selfish ends—

Ye ask, and receive not, because ye ask amiss, that ye may consume it upon your lusts [James 4:3].

Even when we do ask God for something, we ask in order that we might spend it in a very selfish way.

Ye adulterers and adulteresses, know ye not that the friendship of the world is enmity with God? whosoever therefore will be a friend of the world is the enemy of God [James 4:4].

Because we are willing to compromise with the world in order to attain our goals, James calls us "adulterers and adulteresses." This is the way of the world: take by force what you want; by hook or by crook lay hold of it; be envious and jealous of other folk, and cause strife. That is worldliness.

"Know ye not that the friendship of the world is enmity with God?" I have never joined any of the clubs or lodges such as the Lions, the Moose, the Elks, or the Rotary Club. I have been asked to join, but I do not join them. I'll tell you the reason. I have enough trouble with worldliness in the church; I do not need to join a worldly organization.

Do ye think that the scripture saith in vain, The spirit that dwelleth in us lusteth to envy? [James 4:5].

Are we trying to kid ourselves that we are nice, sweet, little folk who have no envy and jealousy in our hearts? I heard a woman say one time, "I have a very wonderful husband. He is not jealous of me." I want you to know that something is wrong if a husband is not jealous of his wife. If he loves her, he will be jealous of her. God says that He is jealous of His children. But what about jealousy in the wrong sense—jealousy when we do not get elected to a committee or do not receive recognition in the church that we feel we deserve? And what about the strife we cause with these tongues of ours? James says that the solution to the problem is to go to the Lord Jesus and tell Him about our problem, tell Him everything.

But he giveth more grace. Wherefore he saith, God resisteth the proud, but giveth grace unto the humble [James 4:6].

I have said this again and again: God is overloaded with grace. You and I just don't know how gracious He is. He has an abundance of grace. *Grace* has been defined as unmerited favor, but I call it love in action. God didn't save us by love. He gave His Son, and it is by His grace that we are saved. He has so much of it. You may say, "Oh, I am so wrong on the inside, so sinful." Go to Him and tell Him you are wrong on the inside, and ask Him for grace to overcome it. He will give you grace. He is the living Christ, interceding at God's right hand for you.

Now some may doubt the surplus of His grace. May I say to you, all the medicine in the world cannot cure the sick; the remedy *must be taken*. Likewise, God has the grace, my friend; lay hold of it! It is possible for a man to die of thirst with a pure spring of water right before him. He has to drink of it; he has to appropriate it before it can save his life. You don't blame soap and water for the fact that there are dirty people in the world, do you? There is plenty of soap and water to clean you up, my friend.

"God resisteth the proud, but giveth grace unto the humble." This is the kind of container that the grace of God must be carried in; it must be carried in an humble individual.

Submit yourselves therefore to God. Resist the devil, and he will flee from you [James 4:7].

When you go to a doctor for medical care, you submit yourself to him. One time when I was sick, the doctor gave me half a dozen prescriptions. The man might have been trying to poison me, but I had faith in him and took his pills. They helped me because I submitted to him. "Submit yourselves therefore to God."

"Resist the devil, and he will flee from you." You may ask, "How am I going to resist the Devil?" James is going to be very practical. He has just said that we need a little more grace—He "giveth grace unto the humble." In other words, you are not going to be able to resist the Devil in your own strength. You and I are surrounded by evil influences. Temptation, as we have seen, is on every hand. God supplies His grace as needed, and His supply never runs out. "This is yours," God says. "You are to lay hold of it."

Draw nigh to God, and he will draw nigh to you. Cleanse your hands, ye sinners; and purify your hearts, ye double-minded [James 4:8].

God comes to the door of your heart; He will not come any farther. He knocks, and you have to let Him in. That is the only way He is going to get in, my friend.

It is said that one time Martin Luther threw

an inkwell at the Devil. Somebody might say that was a crazy thing to do, but it is not if you are resisting the Devil. James tells us that the way to resist the Devil is to draw near to God. The Devil will flee from you, because he doesn't like God as company. The Devil will not get to you unless you get too far away from God. A wolf never attacks a sheep as long as it is with the rest of the sheep and with the shepherd. And the closer the sheep is to the shepherd, the safer it is. Our problem is that we get too far from God.

Be afflicted, and mourn, and weep: let your laughter be turned to mourning, and your joy to heaviness [James 4:9].

There are certain conditions which call for mourning and not for joy. Sin is never to be treated lightly. When I hear a Christian make light of sin, I have a sneaking notion that, on the side, when nobody is looking, he is indulging in sin. You are not to treat sin lightly, my friend; you are to *mourn* over your sins. The problem today is that Christians are not mourning over their sins.

We have several outstanding evangelists and some great evangelistic meetings in our day, but why is it that there is no revival in the church? I think James is giving us something to think about in what he says here. I remember asking this same question of Dr. John Brown, who was one of the great evangelists in the past. As we sat on his front porch in Siloam Springs, Arkansas, I asked him why, even in that day, evangelism was not reviving the church as it had when he was active in the ministry. He told me about the meetings which he had held in my present hometown of Pasadena, California, where he had a tent set up on a big vacant lot at the corner of Washington and Holliston. He said this to me, "Dr. McGee, I preached six weeks to the Christians before I ever attempted to give an altar call for the unsaved—and revival came to the churches." When I came as pastor to a church in Pasadena, I could still see the effects of Dr. Brown's meetings in that church. Why? For the very simple reason that sin had been dealt with in the lives of believers. Too often we refuse to deal with it. We need to mourn over our sins.

Humble yourselves in the sight of the Lord, and he shall lift you up [James 4:10].

"*He* shall lift you up." This is our problem today: We think *we* are smart. We think *we* are strong. We think *we* have ability. We think *we* are good. God says that there is no good within us. There is nothing in us that attracts Him, that is, in the way of goodness; it is just our great need that draws Him to us. If we are willing to humble ourselves and get down where He can lift us up, He will lift us up.

I observed a lifeguard once as he hit a drowning fellow with his fist and knocked him out. The lifeguard explained that the drowning man was struggling and that he could not help him until he gave up. I think sometimes God gives us the fist so that we just give up and let Him take over.

Speak not evil one of another, brethren. He that speaketh evil of his brother, and judgeth his brother, speaketh evil of the law, and judgeth the law: but if thou judge the law, thou art not a doer of the law, but a judge.

There is one lawgiver, who is able to save and to destroy: who art thou that judgest another? [James 4:11–12].

If you judge your brother, you disobey the law, which is putting yourself above the law and treating it with contempt. In other words, who do you think you are? When you begin to talk like that, you are moving into the position of God. There are two types of people today who seek to take the position of God. One is the sinner who says, "I'm good enough to be saved. Lord, I don't need your salvation. You just move over, and I am going to move up and sit beside you. I am my own savior." But, my friend, God says in His Word that He is the only Savior. Then there is the other fellow who sits in judgment on everyone else. He doesn't judge himself, but he judges everyone else. James is saying that judgment is God's business. Jesus said, "For the Father judgeth no man, but hath committed all judgment unto the Son" (John 5:22). There are many Christians who, in effect, say to the Lord Jesus, "You move over. I'm going to help You. We are going to have a Supreme Court, and I am going to be one of the judges." We have a lot of believers like that today; boy, what a Supreme Court the church could furnish Him! James says that we are to judge ourselves and to go to Him in humility.

Go to now, ye that say, To-day or to-morrow we will go into such a city, and continue there a year, and buy and sell, and get gain [James 4:13].

Here is something else Christians do—we like to make big plans for the future. It has taken me a long time in life to learn just to play it by

ear. Normally I accept speaking engagements quite some time ahead of schedule, but in periods of serious illness I have been forced to cancel some engagements. I have hated to cancel them, but the Lord has brought this passage of Scripture to my mind: "Come now, ye that say, Today or tomorrow we will go into such a city and hold a Bible conference. We will have a wonderful time there, and we believe it is the Lord's will." That is not exactly what James said, but that is how the Lord has said it to me.

Whereas ye know not what shall be on the morrow. For what is your life? It is even a vapour, that appeareth for a little time, and then vanisheth away [James 4:14].

James says that we do not know what tomorrow holds. "For what is your life?" He says it is just a vapor, a fog. "It is even a vapour, that appeareth for a little time, and then vanisheth away." We have a lot of fog here on the West Coast. You can be driving along the coast on a marvelous day when the ocean is as blue as indigo and the sky almost as blue as the ocean, but if you stop at a motel for the night, you may find in the morning that everything is shrouded by fog. Life is like a mist on a mountainside—uncertain, transient, and temporary.

Human life lived apart from and without God is the most colossal failure in God's universe. Everything else serves a long and useful purpose. The sun in the sky is prodigal of its energy—we use very little of it. The moon also serves a purpose; many of you fellows got married because of that moon up there. It is the poet who said, "Only man is vile." Human life apart from God is out of joint, dislocated, a colossal failure. One of the reasons is the brevity of this life. We are allotted only three score and ten years; if we get any more, they are filled with aches and pains. Oh, the brevity of human life! Many of us never learn to really live down here upon this earth.

For that ye ought to say, If the Lord will, we shall live, and do this, or that [James 4:15].

Our lives are in the hand of God.

But now ye rejoice in your boastings: all such rejoicing is evil [James 4:16].

Man cannot boast; if he does, it is sin.

Therefore to him that knoweth to do good, and doeth it not, to him it is sin [James 4:17].

There are a great many people today who are sinning and don't know it. If you know to do good in certain cases—if you know that you should do a certain thing or help a certain cause—and you do not do it, *that* is sin.

Our lives are brief, and we should not spend our time in strife and envy and jealousy. It spoils a life. We need to come to Christ, put our lives down before Him, and really start living. He has said, ". . . I am come that they might have life, and that they might have it more abundantly" (John 10:10). He wants to give you a life that is a life indeed. Are you living that life today?

CHAPTER 5

THEME: *Riches are a care; the coming of Christ is a comfort; the prayer of the righteous is a power*

RICHES ARE A CARE

We have come to a remarkable section of the Epistle of James which may seem out of place in this epistle. A cursory reading of these first six verses might give the impression that James is teaching a socialistic doctrine of "soak the rich" or "let's divide the wealth." But on the contrary, a careful reading of these verses reveals that James is not teaching any such thing. He was instructing believers as to their attitude and action in a world that was going to the bowwows, a world filled with injustice, where freedom was only a dream. The Roman world of James' day was not like the modern world in which we live. The life-styles were entirely different. There was no middle class in the days of James. There were the very rich, the filthy rich, and the very poor, the filthy poor. The majority of the Christians of that day came from the very poor and slave classes. They had no great cathedrals on boulevards, and they were not building kingdoms as are many of these great churches which are spending millions of dollars these days. The early church just wasn't that kind of church.

As we approach this passage of Scripture, we should understand that James is not condemning riches. Riches in themselves are not immoral; they are not moral, either. They are just unmoral or amoral. The Bible actually does not condemn money. A great many people have the viewpoint that there is something dirty about money; they call it "filthy lucre." Scripture doesn't say that. What Scripture does say is that ". . . the love of money is the root of all evil . . ." (1 Tim. 6:10). The problem is not in the coin; the problem is in the hearts of men and women. It is the *love* of money that is the root of all evil. James was not condemning people just because they were rich but because of their wrong relationship to their riches. He was concerned with how they got their money and what they were doing with it after they got it.

The Lord Jesus Christ had a great deal to say about money and about riches. He gave three parables which I think will help us to understand what James is saying. In Luke 16:19–31 we have the story (which I think is a true story) of the poor man, Lazarus the beggar, and the rich man. This parable has to do with the way the rich man spent his money. He was really living it up. It is interesting that this beggar, Lazarus, was placed at his gate. Who put him there? I don't know, but in some way the rich man was responsible for him. And the rich man let the beggar have the crumbs from his table. May I say to you, I would wager that the rich man deducted those crumbs from his income tax! Nevertheless, we are told that the dogs licked the beggar's sores while the rich man "fared sumptuously." It was the way this man became rich that in some way made him responsible for the beggar's condition. Someone will ask, "What makes you think that?" Well, where did the two men go after death? Lazarus went to Abraham's Bosom, and the rich man went to hell. That shows us how God judged the lives of these two men, my friend.

In Luke 12 the Lord Jesus gave a second parable about a rich man. This man is the one who built bigger barns—at least he had plans to build them. However, he never did build the barns because he died. The Lord Jesus Christ never condemned that man for being rich; when He stated it, He just stated it as a fact. To all outward appearances, this man was a good man and an honest citizen. But he hoarded his money. He wanted to live it up in his old age, and he gave no thought to eternity. The Lord Jesus called him a fool. Actually, he was more than covetous; he was selfish. He was hoarding his money for himself, and that, may I say, is a form of idolatry. We are told in the Word of God that covetousness is idolatry; it is the worship of things. But selfishness is when you worship yourself. There is a lot of that going on today; in fact, it is even being taught as a Christian virtue. We are told that we are to have great respect for ourselves and great confidence in ourselves. But the Lord Jesus said, ". . . without me ye can do nothing" (John 15:5).

There is a third parable concerning riches which the Lord Jesus gave. It is the parable of the unjust steward by which we are taught the wise use of money by Christians. God holds man responsible not only for how he makes his money but also for how he spends it.

There is another question we should consider before we examine the text: Are the rich whom James is condemning here Christians or non-Christians? Are they the godly rich or the godless rich? There is some controversy and difference of opinion among commentators on this question. I personally believe that they are the godless rich, and in that I follow the opinion of one whom I respect a great deal, John Calvin. Thomas Manton writes that it was Calvin's judgment that "these six verses are not so much an admonition as a denunciation, wherein the apostle doth not so much direct them what to do, as foretell what should be done to them, that the godly might be encouraged to the more patience under their oppressions; for that the apostle inferreth plainly."

Why does James turn from talking to the godly and begin talking to the ungodly? The fact of the matter is that he doesn't change. He is still speaking to the godly. How can that be, when he is so obviously speaking to the rich? As he speaks to the ungodly, he is at the same time telling the godly that they live in a godless world, where the godless rich will impose certain hardships upon them and take advantage of them and where they will be at the mercy of these wicked, rich men. The Lord Jesus Christ had already made a general reference to this when He said, ". . . In the world ye shall have tribulation [trouble]: but be of good cheer; I have overcome the world" (John 16:33).

The godly are to be patient in these circumstances, knowing that God will deal with the godless rich in eternity if not here. This is made very clear in verse 6 of this chapter: "Ye have condemned and killed the just"—God condemns these actions of the rich; "and he doth not resist you"—but God permits them, so it seems, to get by with it. However, He will judge them in the end. May I make this rather startling statement. I would rather go to hell a poor man than a rich man. But I thank God that I am not going there, and that is because Christ died for me and I have accepted His gift of eternal life.

David was troubled by the prosperity of the wicked; it bothered him no end. In Psalm 37:35–36 we read, "I have seen the wicked in great power, and spreading himself like a green bay tree. Yet he passed away, and, lo, he was not: yea, I sought him, but he could not be found." Earlier in this psalm, David gives the same advice that James gives: "Rest in the LORD, and wait patiently for him: fret not thyself because of him who prospereth in his way, because of the man who bringeth wicked devices to pass" (Ps. 37:7). That is a tremendous statement, and he is speaking of the godless rich. David was troubled by this until he went into the temple and saw that, in time, God would deal with these people.

Let us come now to the text—

Go to now, ye rich men, weep and howl for your miseries that shall come upon you [James 5:1].

Is James speaking to the godless rich of his day or of some future day? He is giving a warning to the rich in his day, and it has an application for *any* day and certainly for our day. James wrote this epistle, we believe, somewhere between A.D. 45 and 50. Many others now give the date as AD. 60. Regardless of the date, the destruction of Jerusalem was in the near future, for in A.D. 70 Titus the Roman came and destroyed Jerusalem as it had never been destroyed before. He plowed it under. He hated Christians and he hated Jews, and they both were in that city. Believe me, when he got through, there were no rich Jews left. They had either been killed or had been put in slavery, and all the riches had been destroyed or lost or confiscated. James can make these strong statements in view of what was coming, for the Lord Jesus had predicted this before He ascended back to heaven. He told His disciples, "And when ye shall see Jerusalem compassed with armies, then know that the desolation thereof is nigh" (Luke 21:20). That was fulfilled in A.D. 70.

Your riches are corrupted, and your garments are motheaten [James 5:2].

In light of the coming of Christ, they are warned that all the riches of the world will come to naught. This obviously would not impress a godless rich person in that day any more than it would today; however, the rich man knew that the future was uncertain for him, just as many realize that today. There is always a danger of a panic, a crash, a drought, or a depression. That has been the order of the day since men started to mint money.

There will always be good years, and there will always be bad years. Some of us can remember the depression of the early 1930s when millionaires by the score leaped out of the windows of skyscrapers, and many rich found that they became paupers overnight. Some former millionaires sold apples at street corners, and gilt-edged stocks and bonds in safety deposit boxes were not worth the paper they were written on.

Your gold and silver is cankered; and the rust of them shall be a witness against you, and shall eat your flesh as it were fire. Ye have heaped treasure together for the last days [James 5:3].

James says, "Do you know how your silver and gold are going to rust? It is because *you* are going to decay." This is the judgment that comes upon the godless rich like the men in two of the parables which Christ gave. Death came to both of them, and death certainly separates a rich man from his money. It is said that when one of the Vanderbilts was dying, the family was waiting in an outer room. When the lawyer and the doctor came out, one of the more outspoken members of the family stepped up to the lawyer and asked, "How much did he leave?" The lawyer replied, "He left it all. He didn't take any of it with him." May I say to you, that is the way that it rusts, my friend. A gentleman was being shown through the magnificent grounds of a rich nobleman's estate, and he said to the owner, "Well, my lord, all this and heaven would be noble; but this and hell would be terrible."

James is condemning the godless rich for hoarding their money. Gold and silver *do* rust. It's boom today and bust tomorrow. When a man makes a million, he is not satisfied with that. He wants to make *two* million. It's like drinking sea water—the more you drink, the thirstier you get. The rich keep on making millions, but it doesn't make them any happier.

We had here in America two men who were billionaires whose lives are an example of the futility of riches. Both of them were remarkable men who built great financial empires. Howard Hughes was one of them, but in his last days, from all we can learn, he was a recluse and a sick man. He could not have been happy in those years. All that money just didn't seem to do him very much good. The other man, J. Paul Getty, was reported in the press to have made this statement: "I'd give all my wealth for just one happy marriage." How tragic!

God gave wealth not to be hoarded but to be dispensed. The rich man in Christ's parable planned to build bigger barns in which to store his goods and his fruits. But you can eat only so much; you can drink only so much, and you can wear only one suit at a time. After the first million dollars, when you start gathering more millions, they are just like a pile of rocks. You cannot eat them; there is nothing you can do with them. That is the reason our Lord called that man a fool. Instead of filling his own barn, he should have gone and filled someone else's barn.

I know a Christian farmer who lives in the fruit belt of California. He told me that the organization of farmers to which he belonged asked him to dump some of his fruit crop in order to keep the prices up. He said that tons of fruit had been destroyed. There were a lot of folk who could have used and enjoyed that fruit. James says that wealth is to be dispensed and not hoarded.

Let me pass on to you two little stories which have come my way. A certain young person very impatiently said, "I'm living now, and I mean to have a good time. The hereafter isn't here yet!" A very wise companion replied, "No—only the first part of it; but I shouldn't wonder if the 'here' had a good deal to do with shaping the 'after.'"

There was an irreligious farmer who gloried in the fact that he was an agnostic. He wrote a letter to a local newspaper, saying, "Sir, I have been trying an experiment with a field of mine. I plowed it on Sunday. I planted it on Sunday. I cultivated it on Sunday. I reaped it on Sunday. I hauled it into my barn on Sunday. And now, Mr. Editor, what is the result? I have more bushels to the acre in that field than any of my neighbors have had this October." The editor wasn't a religious man himself, but he published the letter and then wrote below it: "God does not always settle His accounts in October." God has eternity ahead of Him, my friend.

Behold, the hire of the labourers who have reaped down your fields, which is

of you kept back by fraud, crieth: and the cries of them which have reaped are entered into the ears of the Lord of sabaoth [James 5:4].

James condemns the godless rich not only for hoarding money but for making it in a dishonest way. They have robbed the poor to get rich. In the parable, the rich man let fall some crumbs for the beggar. What a message is in that! That beggar had been placed at the rich man's gate because the rich man was responsible for him.

In Proverbs 22:7 it says, "The rich ruleth over the poor, and the borrower is servant to the lender." God condemns the godless man who makes his money in a dishonest way, especially when it is by putting down the children of God. God may do nothing now, but He is going to judge in the future. If men are making their riches by stepping on the hands of those beneath them, then God will judge that. This should serve as a word of warning to the rich man, to great corporations and labor unions, and also to great church organizations. God will judge the way men make their money and the way they spend it.

Ye have lived in pleasure on the earth, and been wanton; ye have nourished your hearts, as in a day of slaughter [James 5:5].

The rich were spending their money in a sinful manner. The miser says, "Dollars are flat to stack them," but the spendthrift says, "They are round to roll them." Either way, God says that you are wrong, my friend.

Again, let me quote a proverb: "The rich man's wealth is his strong city, and as an high wall in his own conceit" (Prov. 18:11). Then in Proverbs 28:11 we read, "The rich man is wise in his own conceit; but the poor that hath understanding searcheth him out." This is the picture of the two godless rich men whom the Lord Jesus told about; both wanted to live it up. One wanted to store it up now and then live it up in his old age. The other rich man was living it up at the time while the beggar lay outside his gate. If you have decided to live for this life only, be sure to live it up, but God says you are a fool, my friend.

Ye have condemned and killed the just; and he doth not resist you [James 5:6].

"Ye have condemned and killed the just." When we look about us at our own government and the other governments of the world, it would seem that there is a power structure which manipulates government and which ma-

nipulates the economy. We hear a great deal about the freedom of the press, but that freedom is a freedom to brainwash people to their way of thinking. Although we are supposed to have freedom of speech and of religion, on the most powerful radio stations in any city in this country, you cannot buy time on weekdays for the teaching of the Word of God. That is true no matter how much money you might have to pay for it.

"And he doth not resist you." The rich seem to be getting by with it today, and the sinner is getting by with it. That disturbed David at first. He said, "They spread themselves like a green bay tree and do not cease from flourishing." If I do something wrong, I get punished for it. God takes me to the woodshed, but the king of Babylon just keeps on going and nothing stops him. Actually, that is God's judgment on the wicked. He is not judging them now, but the end to which they come is very terrible. Riches have never brought happiness to mankind at all.

There is a lesson here for the rich man who is a Christian. How big is your bank account? If Jesus should come right now, would you be willing to let Him look into your safety deposit box? He is going to do that someday. How are you making use of your riches?

Proverbs 30:8 says, ". . . give me neither poverty nor riches; feed me with food convenient for me." I am thankful that I am neither rich nor poor, because if I were rich, I would forget God, and if I were poor, I might steal. I thank God that I can go down the middle of the road today in the middle class.

THE COMING OF CHRIST IS A COMFORT

James had made it very clear what kind of world we live in. It's a big, bad world with a dog-eat-dog philosophy. Those who are climbing up the ladder of riches are stepping on the fingers of others as they go up. Should Christians join some organization and go all out for good government? Certainly we ought to be interested in trying to elect the best men. However, we cannot change this world, my friend. What, then, *can* we do? Listen to God; He is speaking now to His own children—

Be patient therefore, brethren, unto the coming of the Lord. Behold, the husbandman waiteth for the precious fruit of the earth, and hath long patience for it, until he receive the early and latter rain [James 5:7].

The Word of God has a great deal to say about the fact that when Christ comes and sets up His kingdom, the poor are going to get a good deal, a right and honest deal, for the first time in the history of the world. This is something that all of the prophets mentioned and which they emphasized. In Isaiah 11:4 we read, "But with righteousness shall he judge the poor. . . ." Believe me, the poor have not had a good deal yet. If you think that by changing a political party you will somehow get a good deal for the poor, you are wrong. I don't mean to be a pessimist, my friend, but you simply cannot look to mankind, to men who are grasping for power and money, and expect them to act righteously. It does not matter what they promise, they are *not* going to take care of the poor. Our only hope is in Jesus Christ. If there is any group of people who ought to be interested in the Lord Jesus Christ, it is the poor people of this world, because He is going to give them the right kind of deal when He establishes His kingdom here upon earth.

"Be patient therefore, brethren, unto the coming of the Lord." This is a tremendous statement. The coming of Christ will correct the wrongs of the world. We can read this again and again in Scripture. Not only do the prophets mention it, but Christ Himself made it clear in the Sermon on the Mount (which will be the law of His kingdom) that He intends to give the poor a square deal under His reign (see Matt. 6:19–24).

"Behold, the husbandman waiteth for the precious fruit of the earth, and hath long patience for it, until he receive the early and latter rain." In other words, when the farmer plants his grain, he doesn't go out the next morning to see if it is time to harvest it. James says, "Be patient. The harvest is coming."

We often hear it said that Christians are *harvesting* when they go out in evangelism to give out the Word of God. I disagree with that. The Lord Jesus was at the end of an age when He said to His disciples (He was sending them out to the lost sheep of the house of Israel, not worldwide), ". . . The harvest truly is great, but the labourers are few . . ." (Luke 10:2). They were at the end of the age of law. Every age has ended in judgment; the present age will end in a judgment from God. *That* will be the harvest. In Matthew 13 the Lord Jesus said that He will send His angels to do the gathering in for the harvest. Believers do not harvest. *He* is the one who separates the wheat from the tares. Therefore, what are we doing when we give out the Word of God? The

Lord Jesus is also a sower, and today He is sowing seed. I consider that to be my business. I teach the Word of God, and there is nothing in the world I can do but simply give it out. I'm just sowing seed. Some falls on good ground. Maybe not too much of it, but some falls on good ground. Hallelujah for that! Our business is growing seed.

Be ye also patient; stablish your hearts: for the coming of the Lord draweth nigh [James 5:8].

All the way through Scripture we are taught that we should live in the light of the coming of Christ.

Grudge not one against another, brethren, lest ye be condemned: behold, the judge standeth before the door [James 5:9].

It would be very embarrassing if the Lord should come while you are sitting in judgment on someone else. You would suddenly find yourself in His presence with Him judging you. What James is really saying here is, "Set your house in order. Get your affairs straightened out before He comes, because He is going to straighten them out if you don't." This is very important for believers to realize.

Take, my brethren, the prophets, who have spoken in the name of the Lord, for an example of suffering affliction, and of patience [James 5:10].

The prophets are an example to us. They suffered, and they were patient.

Behold, we count them happy which endure. Ye have heard of the patience of Job, and have seen the end of the Lord; that the Lord is very pitiful, and of tender mercy [James 5:11].

"Ye have heard of the patience of Job." That is about all I know about Job's patience—I've *heard* of it. As I read the Book of Job, I feel Job was very impatient. Actually, he *learned* patience. He was an impatient man, but he learned patience.

"And have seen the end of the Lord; that the Lord is very pitiful, and of tender mercy." In other words, the Lord is full of pity or compassion and is merciful. You have to go to the end of Job's trial to see that he learned a great lesson and that the Lord was indeed compassionate and generous with him.

But above all things, my brethren, swear not, neither by heaven, neither by

the earth, neither by any other oath:
but let your yea be yea; and your nay,
nay; lest ye fall into condemnation
[James 5:12].

In other words, my friend, when you say you
are going to promise something, it ought to be
as if you were in a courtroom and had taken an
oath to tell the truth. All your *conversation*
ought to be like that. I can remember when
my dad went to the bank one year to borrow
money to get his cotton gin started. The
banker was busy and said to my dad, "Go
ahead and take the money." My dad said, "But
I haven't signed the note." I never shall forget
what the banker said, "If you *say* you will
repay it, that is just as good as if you have
signed a note. So come in later and sign up."
May I say to you, a man's word ought to be
just that good. Some people, even if they take
an oath on a stack of Bibles, do not honor their
word.

THE PRAYER OF THE RIGHTEOUS
IS A POWER

**Is any among you afflicted? let him
pray. Is any merry? let him sing psalms
[James 5:13].**

James says that the afflicted are to pray and
the merry are to sing psalms. Sometimes a
song leader will get up in a service and say,
"Now everybody sit up and smile." I used to
have a song leader like that in a church I
pastored years ago. I told him, "Don't you
know that in this congregation there are people who are really burdened? As I look out
there, I see one man who is a doctor and who
has been busy all week taking care of patients.
I also see a lady who is a buyer in a department store. She is weary and tired. And you
ask them to sit up and smile!" No, you don't
have to sit up and smile. The afflicted are to
pray. The merry are to sing psalms. Some
people go to church and then try to work up
some enthusiasm. We ought to have the great
passion and enthusiasm in our hearts even
before we go to church, but we do not need to
put on a false front.

**Is any sick among you? let him call for
the elders of the church; and let them
pray over him, anointing him with oil
in the name of the Lord [James 5:14].**

A few years ago there was a tragic incident
which occurred in a little town near Los Angeles where a man threw away the insulin that
his little son was supposed to take because he
said God was going to heal his son. The little
fellow died, and then the man, who must be
very fanatic, said, "The Lord is going to raise
him up from the dead because he has been
anointed." The leaders of the denomination to
which the man belonged said that he had
never been taught anything like that. I believe
that is true because I have had the privilege of
meeting on several occasions with the man
who taught theology in one of the outstanding
Pentecostal schools. He said this to me, "Dr.
McGee, I want you to know that I agree with
you that not everyone can be healed. It must
be the will of God in order for someone to be
healed." That is my position, and I agree with
what he said.

If you say that it is God's will for every
Christian who gets sick to be healed, you must
agree that the logical conclusion of that line of
thinking is that the Christian will never die.
He will be healed of every disease which
causes death. May I say, that is ridiculous. I
have been healed of cancer, but I expect to die,
if the Lord does not come in the meantime. It
is a cruel hoax perpetrated upon simple believers that it is God's will for *all* to be healed.

James is not actually asking a question here.
He is saying, "Someone is sick among you."
What are you to do? "Let him call for the
elders of the church; and let them pray over
him"—that's the first thing. The second thing
is—"anointing him with oil in the name of the
Lord."

There are two Greek words which are translated "anoint" in the New Testament. One of
them is used in a religious sense; that word is
chriō in the Greek. From that we get the word
Christos; Christ was the Anointed One. It
means to anoint with some scented unguent or
oil. It is used only five times in the New Testament, and it refers to the anointing of Christ
by God the Father with the Holy Spirit.

The second word translated "anoint" is *aleiphō*. It is used a number of times in the New
Testament. In Matthew 6:17 we read, "But
thou, when thou fastest, anoint thine head,
and wash thy face." That simply means to put
oil on your hair so that you will look all right.
Trench comments that *aleiphō* is "the mun-
dane and profane word." The other, *chriō*, is
"the sacred and religious word." The word
used in this verse in James is *aleiphō*, and all it
means is to rub with oil. You remember that
when Hezekiah was sick, they put something
medicinal on that boil he had. James is saying
something very practical here. He says, "Call
for the elders to pray, and go to the best
doctor you can get." You *are* to use medicine,

my friend. It is a mistaken idea to say that this refers to some religious ceremony of putting a little oil from a bottle on someone's head, as if that would have some healing merit in it. It has no merit whatsoever. James is too practical for that.

James is also a man of prayer. He says, "Call for the elders to pray." This is the reason that when I get sick I ask others to pray. I believe in the priesthood of believers. James makes this very clear in the following verses—

And the prayer of faith shall save the sick, and the Lord shall raise him up; and if he have committed sins, they shall be forgiven him.

Confess your faults one to another, and pray one for another, that ye may be healed. The effectual fervent prayer of a righteous man availeth much [James 5:15–16].

"And the prayer of faith shall save the sick." I believe you are to call on God's people to pray for you when you are sick.

"Confess your faults one to another, and pray one for another, that ye may be healed." We are to confess our *sins* to God but our faults one to another. If I have injured you, then I ought to confess that to you. But I will not confess my sins to you, and I do not want you confessing your sins to me. You are to confess that to the Lord. "If we confess our sins, he is faithful and just to forgive us our sins, and to cleanse us from all unrighteousness" (1 John 1:9). I cannot forgive sins; neither can any clergyman forgive sins—only God can do that.

"The effectual fervent prayer of a righteous man availeth much." James was a great man of prayer. He was called "Old Camel Knees" because, having spent so much time on his knees in prayer, his knees were calloused. He speaks now of another great man of prayer, Elijah (*Elias* is the Greek form of *Elijah*)—

Elias was a man subject to like passions as we are, and he prayed earnestly that it might not rain: and it rained not on the earth by the space of three years and six months.

And he prayed again, and the heaven gave rain, and the earth brought forth her fruit [James 5:17–18].

Can you imagine that? Elijah was a weatherman for three and a half years, and for three and a half years he held back the rain! It did not come until he prayed. You are the same kind of person Elijah was. Elijah wasn't a superman; he was "a man subject to like passions as we are." But he was a man who prayed with passion, and that is the kind of praying we need today.

Brethren, if any of you do err from the truth, and one convert him;

Let him know, that he which converteth the sinner from the error of his way, shall save a soul from death, and shall hide a multitude of sins [James 5:19–20].

"Converteth the sinner from the error of his way." Some expositors believe that this refers to a child of God who has gone astray. However, I believe it refers to an unsaved person who has not yet come to the truth.

"Shall hide a multitude of sins." When he comes to a saving knowledge of Christ, his sins—though they be multitudinous—will be covered by the blood of Christ. The wonder of justification by faith is that once God has pardoned our sins, they are gone forever—removed from us as far as the east is from the west.

This is a wonderful conclusion for this very practical Epistle of James.

BIBLIOGRAPHY

(Recommended for Further Study)

Adamson, James. *The Epistle of James*. Grand Rapids, Michigan: Wm. B. Eerdmans Publishing Co., 1976. (For advanced students.)

Brown, Charles. *The Epistle of James*. London: The Religious Tract Society, 1907. (Devotional.)

Criswell, W. A. *Expository Sermons on the Epistle of James*. Grand Rapids, Michigan: Zondervan Publishing House, 1975.

Gaebelein, Frank E. *The Practical Epistle of James*. Great Neck, New York: Doniger & Raughley, 1955.

Gwinn, Ralph A. *The Epistle of James*. Grand Rapids, Michigan: Baker Book House, 1967. (Shield Bible Study Series.)

Hiebert, D. Edmond. *The Epistle of James*. Chicago, Illinois: Moody Press, 1979. (Highly recommended.)

Ironside, H. A. *Notes on James and Peter*. Neptune, New Jersey: Loizeaux Brothers, n.d.

Johnstone, Robert. *Lectures on the Epistle of James*. Grand Rapids, Michigan: Baker Book House, 1871. (Comprehensive.)

Kelly, William. *The Epistle of James*. London: G. Morrish, n.d.

King, Guy H. *A Belief That Behaves*. Fort Washington, Pennsylvania: Christian Literature Crusade, 1945. (Excellent.)

Knowling, R. J. *The Epistle of St. James*. London: Methusen, 1904.

Luck, G. Coleman. *James, Faith in Action*. Chicago, Illinois: Moody Press, 1954. (A fine, inexpensive survey.)

Neibor, J. *Practical Exposition of James*. Erie, Pennsylvania: Our Daily Walk Publishers, 1950.

Plummer, Alfred. *The General Epistles of St. James and St. Jude*. Grand Rapids, Michigan: Wm. B. Eerdmans Publishing Co., n.d. (Expositor's Bible.)

Robertson, A. T. *Studies in the Epistle of James*. Nashville, Tennessee: Broadman Press, 1915. (Excellent.)

Strauss, Lehman. *James, Your Brother*. Neptune, New Jersey: Loizeaux Brothers, 1956. (Very practical.)

Tasker, R. V. G. *The General Epistle of James*. Grand Rapids, Michigan: Wm. B. Eerdmans Publishing Co., 1957. (Tyndale Commentary series.)

Vaughan, Curtis. *James, A Study Guide*. Grand Rapids, Michigan: Zondervan Publishing House, 1969.

Zodhiates, Spiro. *The Behavior of Belief*. Grand Rapids, Michigan: Wm. B. Eerdmans Publishing Co., 1970. (Comprehensive.)

The First Epistle of
PETER
INTRODUCTION

Simon Peter—"Peter, an apostle of Jesus Christ, to the strangers" (1 Pet. 1:1).

Peter has been called the ignorant fisherman, but no man who had spent three years in the school of Jesus could be called ignorant. The Epistles of Peter confirm this. Peter deals with doctrine and handles weighty subjects. In the first few verses he deals with the great doctrines of election, foreknowledge, sanctification, obedience, the blood of Christ, the Trinity, the grace of God, salvation, revelation, glory, faith, and hope. My friend, you just couldn't have any more doctrine crowded into a few verses! The way in which he handles these great themes of the Bible reveals that he was by no means an ignorant fisherman.

A great change is seen in the life of Peter from these epistles. He had been impetuous, but now he is patient. He was bungling, fumbling, and stumbling when he first met Jesus. Our Lord told him in effect, "You are a pretty weak man now, but I am going to make you a *Petros*, a rock-man. And you will be built upon the foundation of Jesus Christ who is the Rock." Peter made it very clear that the Lord Jesus is the Rock on which the church is built. It is very interesting that although his name means "rock," he says that all believers are little rocks also: "Ye also, as lively stones, are built up a spiritual house" (1 Pet. 2:5). In other words, he is saying that every believer is a Peter. Simon Peter never takes an exalted position, as we shall see in his epistles. As he opens his epistle, he calls himself an apostle— he is just one of them. Although whenever the names of the apostles were enumerated, his was always first on the list, and although the Lord chose him to preach the first sermon on the Day of Pentecost, he did not feel that he was exalted above the others.

Peter wrote his epistles after Paul had written his epistles, somewhere between A.D. 64 and 67, after bloody Nero had come to the throne and persecution was already breaking out. According to tradition, Peter himself suffered martyrdom.

"The church that is at Babylon, elected together with you, saluteth you; and so doth Marcus my son" (1 Pet. 5:13). There are those who think that Babylon is used here in a symbolic manner or in a metaphorical sense and that Peter really meant Rome. However, there is no reason for him to use it in a metaphorical sense. Peter was an apostle who did not write in a symbolic manner such as we find used by John in the Book of Revelation. Peter writes very literally and practically. He gets down to where the rubber meets the road, right down on the asphalt of life. I believe that if he had meant Rome, he would have said Rome.

My own opinion is that Simon Peter never did go to Rome. I think he was in Asia Minor, the great heart of the Roman Empire, but he was not the apostle who opened up that territory. I think he followed Paul. Paul would not have gone to Rome if Peter had already been in Rome preaching the gospel there, because Paul made it very clear that he went into places where the gospel had not been preached before. Since Rome was on Paul's itinerary, it seems obvious that Paul, not Peter, founded the church at Rome.

Another very valid argument to indicate that Peter was in Babylon rather than Rome is based on the list of places which he addresses: "To the strangers scattered throughout Pontus, Galatia, Cappadocia, Asia, and Bithynia" (1 Pet. 1:1). All those places are in Asia Minor (the area which is called Turkey today). In listing them, he moves from east to west. This suggests that the writer was in the east at the time of writing. The natural and ordinary way to list geographical places is beginning from the point where you are. When I am in California and talk about going east, I would say that I am going through Arizona, Texas, and finally New York. It is normal to begin where I am and to name the places in sequence. Since Peter lists the places form east to west, it would seem logical that he was in literal Babylon.

After the Babylonian captivity, only a very small group of Jews returned to their land— actually there were fewer than sixty thousand. There was still a great colony of Jews in Babylon. Additional Jews had fled to Babylon when severe persecution began under Claudius in Rome. We know, for example, that Priscilla and Aquila fled to Corinth from Rome. Many others fled to Babylon. There was persecution both of Christians and of Jews. Since we know that the ministry of Peter was primarily to the Jews, it seems most logical that he ministered to Jewish colonies in Asia Minor, and particularly in Babylon. Babylon was still a great city there on the Euphrates River, and many of the Jews had remained there after the end of the Captivity.

In spite of the fact that Papias mentions the death of Peter as occurring in Rome, there is no substantial historical basis for this supposition. I see no reason to discount the fact that Simon Peter was the apostle to those of the nation of Israel who were scattered abroad. I believe Peter went east while the apostle Paul went west.

The great theme of this epistle of Peter is Christian hope in the time of trial. Although Peter deals with great doctrines and handles weighty subjects, he doesn't write in a cold manner. Peter has been called the apostle of hope while Paul has been called the apostle of faith and John has been called the apostle of love. This epistle puts a great emphasis upon hope, but I believe that the word which conveys the theme of this epistle is *suffering*. Peter also emphasizes the grace of God, and some expositors feel it is his main emphasis. However, the word *suffering* or some cognate words that go with it occur in this epistle sixteen times. *Hope* is always tied with the suffering. Therefore, I think it is fair to say that the theme is the Christian hope in the time of trial.

Peter will have a great deal to say about the suffering of Christ. The suffering of Christ has been dealt with by the writer of the Hebrew epistle and by James in his epistle. Also the prophets certainly mentioned it. However, Peter will handle the subject a little differently.

Peter speaks out of a rich experience. Dr. Robert Leighton, in his book, *A Practical Commentary on First Peter*, makes a very timely comment that applies to Simon Peter. Let me share this with you because it is worth noting:

> . . . it is a cold and lifeless thing to speak of spiritual things on mere report; but when men can speak of them as their own—as having share and interest in them, and some experience of their sweetness—their discourse of them is enlivened with firm belief and ardent affection; they cannot mention them, but straight their hearts are taken with such gladness as they are forced to vent in praises.

For this reason, Simon Peter, while writing of suffering, emphasizes *joy!*

This leads me to say something very important regarding young preachers. In this day we have about us some very wonderful young expositors of the Word. I thank God for them. However, as I have listened to two or three of them, I feel very much as Dr. G. Campbell Morgan felt in his day. He and his wife went to hear a young preacher in whom they were particularly interested. He was eloquent, fine-looking, and he delivered a great sermon. Afterward, on the way home, Mrs. Morgan was profuse in her praise and was surprised that Dr. Morgan made no response. Finally she asked, "Don't you think he is a great preacher?" He answered, "He will be after he suffers." Well, time went by, and this young man found out by experience what it cost to stand for Christ. He went through persecution; he experienced problems in his church; and one day he stood at an open grave as he buried one of his little children. Dr. Morgan and his wife went to hear him again because they loved this young man. After the service Mrs. Morgan asked, "Well, what do you think of him now?" Dr. Morgan answered, "He is a great preacher." You see, suffering had made the difference.

This has been my personal experience also. As a young preacher, I spoke a great deal about standing for the Lord and about suffering. I used to go to hospitals and pat people on the hand and pray with them. I would tell them that the Lord would be with them. At that time I was a professional preacher, saying what I did not know to be true from my own experience, although I believed it. But the day came when I went into the hospital myself. Another preacher came in and prayed with me. When he started to go, I said to him, "I've done the same thing you have done. I've been here, and I have told people that God would be with them. Now you are going to walk out of here, but I am staying, and I will find out if it is a theory or if what I have been telling people is true." Friend, I found out it is *true*. Now it is no longer a mere theory. I know it by the fact that the Word of God says it and by the fact that I have experienced it. I don't argue with people about these things any more because there are certain things I *know*. I would never argue with you about whether honey is sweet or not. If you don't think it is sweet, that is your business. I had some this morning for breakfast, and I know it is sweet. That is the knowledge that comes from experience.

Simon Peter is not going to give us his theory of suffering. Simon Peter is going to speak to us out of his own tremendous experience, and it will become very wonderful to us as it becomes your experience and my experience.

OUTLINE

CHAPTER 1

THEME: *Suffering and security produce joy; suffering and the Scriptures produce holiness*

SUFFERING AND THE SECURITY OF BELIEVERS

A great many folk have never had the feeling of assurance in their salvation. The security of the believer is a doctrine which I believed, although it took me a long time to come to the place of assurance in my own salvation. And there are many folk who do not have the assurance of their salvation. Why? Because suffering and the security of the believer go together. And do you know what this produces? It produces *joy!* Can you imagine that?

Now this first verse is just loaded with meaning.

Peter, an apostle of Jesus Christ, to the strangers scattered throughout Pontus, Galatia, Cappadocia, Asia, and Bithynia [1 Pet. 1:1].

First of all, note his name: Peter, *Petros*, a stone. He is now the rock-man. The Day of Pentecost is behind him, and he knows what it is to take a stand for Christ. He has been arrested and put in jail. He has been threatened, and he realizes that there is crucifixion on a cross ahead of him. Peter is a man who knows what he is talking about.

My friend, I must confess that I am not impressed by professors in theological seminaries, with little if any experience as pastors, who get up and spin off some little theory to prepare young men for the ministry. They don't really know the problems of a pastorate because they haven't had the experience. They don't know what it is really to suffer for Christ. After hearing them, I feel like turning back to Peter's first letter and reading it again, because I *believe* Peter—he knew what he was talking about. I'm sorry, but I don't trust these young professors. I want to hear from the man who has gone through the experiences.

"Peter, an apostle of Jesus Christ." Peter is an apostle of Jesus Christ—that is all he claimed to be. Although he always heads my list of apostles—I love him—he is not to be placed above the other apostles. When Paul went to Jerusalem to confer with the apostles, he talked with Peter, James, and John. He said that they seemed to be pillars of the church, but he did not learn the gospel from them. Paul makes it very clear that he received the gospel directly from Jesus Christ by revelation. Nowhere does Peter claim superiority. He was an apostle—that's all.

"To the strangers scattered throughout Pontus, Galatia, Cappadocia, Asia, and Bithynia." He is writing to the strangers, or aliens, who were scattered throughout the Roman Empire. They were Jews, called the *Diaspora* because they were no longer in the land of Palestine. Due to persecution and other reasons, they had settled throughout the empire. If you will check a map, you will find these places are all in Asia Minor, the area we know as Turkey today. You may recall that Paul on his second missionary journey tried to go into Bithynia, but the Spirit of God would not allow him to go there. It is my conviction that Simon Peter had already preached the gospel there and that the Holy Spirit wanted Paul to go to people who had not heard the gospel. Paul was the Apostle to the Gentiles, and Simon Peter was the apostle to Israelites who had turned to Christ.

Elect according to the foreknowledge of God the Father, through sanctification of the Spirit, unto obedience and sprinkling of the blood of Jesus Christ: Grace unto you, and peace, be multiplied [1 Pet. 1:2].

The apostle Peter immediately plunges us into deep doctrinal waters. For instance, he presents the doctrine of the Trinity: the foreknowledge of *God the Father*, sanctification of the *Spirit*, and sprinkling of the blood of *Jesus Christ*. My friend, don't let anyone tell you that the Bible does not teach the Trinity—the Bible is full of it! We certainly cannot consider Peter to be an ignorant fisherman, by the way, because he is talking about things that most of us do not know much about.

Theologians try to help us understand the tremendous doctrines of election and foreknowledge. For example, here is a statement from Lewis Sperry Chafer's *Systematic Theology:*

Having recognized the sovereign right of God over His creation and having assigned to Him a rational purpose in all His plan, the truth contained in the doctrine of election follows in natural sequence as the necessary function of one who is divine (Vol. VII).

We must recognize that our God is a sovereign God and that this little universe is *His*. He created it. I don't know why He created it as He did, but since He is absolutely omniscient (knowing everything), and since He is omnipotent (having all power), and since He is sovereign, I conclude that He can do anything He wants to do that is consistent with His character.

He has a right to plan for the future. Apparently He did some planning. We call those plans the decrees that God had in His mind in the very beginning. That is to say, He had a plan that He was going to follow. He decreed to create the universe, and He did it. He never asked you or me about it. In fact, He has never asked me whether I wanted to be in existence. He could have left me out altogether. And He could have left you out, but He didn't! Thank God, He thought of you and me.

Also there was the decree to permit the fall of man. This, I think, took a great deal of planning on God's part, knowing that when He created the free moral agent called man, he would fall when given a free choice. Mankind chose to disobey God, but God had made arrangements for it. He had the decree to elect some to salvation, and He had the decree that He would send a Savior into the world. He certainly did that. He made a decree that He would save those who came to Him, the elect. You can call them anything you wish, but the people who turned to Christ for salvation are the elect. You may say, "Well, He didn't choose everybody." I don't find that in Scripture. The Lord Jesus said, "All that the Father giveth me shall come to me; and him that cometh to me I will in no wise cast out" (John 6:37). His invitation to "whosoever will" is, "Come unto me" (see Matt. 11:28). It is a legitimate invitation to everyone, but there must be a response, and the response is your responsibility and my responsibility.

Peter really gets us into deep water when he says, "Elect according to the foreknowledge of God." You see, God is moving according to His plan. There must have been an infinite number of plans before Him, but He chose this one. Why? Because He knew it was the best possible plan, and little man is in no position to challenge His choice. He is the Creator and we are only creatures. You and I didn't even determine the time we would be born, or the family into which we would come, or our height, or the color of our eyes, or our IQ. Whatever we are today is by the grace of God. He is the one who determined all of those

things for us. They are all a part of His great plan.

I don't know why we find fault with God for having a plan. Perhaps some folk imagine that He is up to some dirty tricks—but He is not. Oh, my friend, God is good and gracious and long-suffering. He wants to save us, and He wants us to have happy lives. God is the one we can trust. How strange it is that some folk object to God's having a plan when they are perfectly happy to have men follow a plan.

For example, when my wife and I were to leave London, we boarded a plane that would bring us home to Los Angeles. When we were airborne, the captain talked to us on the intercom. I was happy to note that his voice sounded mature and that he spoke with assurance. I was sure he had flown that plane before. He outlined our flight plan, "We are going to fly over Scotland and over northern Ireland, and then we will cross the Atlantic. We will be going over Iceland, but we won't be able to see it because there are clouds over it. When we get to Greenland, I hope you will be able to see it. We may hit a little choppy weather there, but it's not bad. The cloud cover that is there now is breaking up. We will cross Hudson Bay and Labrador and will fly across those ice fields there. It looks like a very pleasant flight and a very smooth trip." You talk about foreknowledge and election! That whole trip was decided for us. And no one ran up to the cabin to protest, "You have no right to plan our trip!" We were delighted that he was following a plan.

My friend, I am sure glad that the God of this universe has a plan and that He knows what He is doing and where He is going and that He is doing the very best for us. I say hallelujah for election which is according to the foreknowledge of God. God is able to carry out His plan exactly because He knows everything. The pilot of the plane had gotten word about weather conditions, and his flight was plotted for him to follow—but it could have been upset. Not so with God's plan. Our God knows everything. He knows every condition; He knows everything that is foreseeable and unforeseeable. So you and I can trust Him implicitly. When Peter says, "Elect according to the foreknowledge of God," he is telling us what God the Father did.

Now he tells us about the work of the Holy Spirit: "through sanctification of the Spirit."

Let me remind you that when the word *sanctification* is identified with Christ, it means that *He* is our sanctification; we will never be any better, as far as our position is concerned, than we are at this moment because we are complete in Him, and we are accepted in the beloved. We cannot add to that; it is our position in Christ.

However, when the word *sanctification* is identified with the Holy Spirit, it means something else. When Peter says, "Through sanctification of the Spirit," he is talking about the ministry of the Holy Spirit in the world who not only converts us—is responsible for our New Birth—but He also begins to work in our lives to bring us up to the place of maturation where we become full, mature Christians. Unfortunately, there are many Christians who have been saved for fifty years or more and yet will be going into heaven as babes in Christ. They haven't matured at all. It will be embarrassing to go into the presence of God as still a burping baby! The work of the Holy Spirit is to sanctify us down here on this earth. How I wish there were more emphasis on that!

There are abroad in our land, at the time of this writing, at least twenty-five organizations or ministries which have become expert in telling you how to become an adequate Christian, a fulfilled Christian, and how you can be comfortable as a Christian. My friend, I hope you never get to the place where you do not feel your inadequacy and your dependence upon Jesus Christ as your Savior. I am tired of these "adequate" Christians. And some of them I meet convince me that I don't want to be "adequate," if that is adequateness! Now, please don't feel that I am being critical of one particular person or organization. I am simply insisting that the Word of God tells us that sanctification is by the Holy Spirit of God—not by some method of man's design.

Let me repeat that all of the Trinity is mentioned in this verse: "Elect according to the foreknowledge of God the Father"—He planned it; "through sanctification of the Spirit"—He protects us today; and it is through the "sprinkling of the blood of Jesus Christ"—personal application of the sacrifice of Christ on the cross, obedience.

Perhaps you are wondering how you can know if you are elect. Henry Ward Beecher divided folk into two categories: the "whosoever wills" and the "whosoever won'ts." You can know which one you are by making this simple test: Have you become obedient to Him? Is Christ really your *Lord?* If He is, you will love Him. The Lord Jesus said, "If you love me, keep my commandments." Do you do what *you* want to do and call that the will of God for your life? Or do you do what He wants

you to do? If you are His, you will be obedient to Him.

"And sprinkling of the blood of Jesus Christ." There is often a silence about the blood of Christ, even in fundamental circles. As long as the blood of our Lord coursed through His veins, it had no saving value for us; but when that precious blood was shed, Christ Jesus gave His life. The life of the flesh is in the blood. He shed that blood that you and I might have life.

Remember that Peter is writing to Jews who had been brought up in Judaism. They were the *Diaspora*, believing Jews living in Asia Minor. They knew the Old Testament, and they understood that the high priest on the Day of Atonement took blood with him when he went into the Holy of Holies, and that he sprinkled the blood seven times on the mercy seat. Now the Lord Jesus Christ has taken His own blood to the throne of God (the throne at which we are judged as guilty sinners), and He sprinkled His blood there. He gave His life and paid the penalty for us. Now that throne of judgment is the throne of grace where you and I can come and receive salvation.

My friend, the gospel has not been preached until the meaning of the blood of Christ has been explained. It may offend you aesthetically—the offense of the cross is that He shed His blood. Of course it is not pretty, but your sin and my sin are not pretty either. Our ugly sin is what made it necessary for Christ to die for us.

This reminds me of a story about a terrible accident which occurred at a railroad crossing. Several people were killed when the train hit a car. There was a court trial, and the watchman who had been at the crossing at the time of the accident was questioned.

"Where were you at the time of the accident?"

"I was at the crossing."

"Did you have a lantern?"

"Yes."

"Did you wave that lantern to warn them of the danger?"

"I certainly did."

The court thought that was enough evidence. When the watchman walked out of the court he was heard to mumble to himself, "I'm sure glad they didn't ask me about the light in the lantern because the light had gone out."

My friend, there can be a lot of lanterns waved in the circles of fundamentalism and evangelicalism and conservatism. However, unless there is the message of the blood of

Jesus Christ and the sprinkling of the blood which cleanses us from all sin, there is no light in the lantern.

Now we come to one of the key words: "*Grace* unto you." Because of the work of the Trinity—*God* had you in mind, *Christ* died for you, and the *Holy Spirit* has come to indwell you to make you a better person—now God can save you by grace.

"Grace unto you, and peace." Without the grace of God, you will never know the peace of God. I received a letter from a man in a cult which revealed that he didn't have peace. I can tell you right now that if you do not believe that Christ shed His blood for your sins, you will not have peace in your heart. You don't even need to tell me that you don't have peace. Peace and assurance and joy come when you know that your sins have been forgiven.

Simon Peter is not waving a lantern that has no light. He is not talking about something that is purely theoretical. This rugged fisherman knows grace and peace through the blood of Christ because Jesus Himself told him about it. He knows it because he had seen Jesus die; he saw where He had been buried, and he saw the resurrected Christ. The old wishy-washy, mollycoddling, shilly-shally man has now become a rock-man. He could stand at the Day of Pentecost and preach about Christ's death and resurrection. He could go to jail, be persecuted, write an epistle like this, and finally be crucified for the gospel.

Now, after spending some time considering the second verse of Peter's epistle, I am sure you will agree with me that Peter was not an ignorant fisherman, by any means. He has been dealing with the tremendous doctrines of election, foreknowledge, foreordination, and predestination. All of these great concepts are on God's side of the fence, and none of us can come up with a final explanation. We are dealing with an infinite God who knows everything. His foreknowledge means that He knows every plan that is imaginable, and He knows exactly what He is going to do. We call that foreordination. At this point, let me give you another statement, which is a good one, from Dr. Lewis Sperry Chafer's *Systematic Theology:*

. . . foreknowledge in God is that which He Himself purposes to bring to pass. In this way, then, the whole order of events from the least detail unto the greatest operates under the determining decree of God so as to take place according to His sovereign purpose. By so much, divine

foreknowledge is closely related to foreordination. Likewise, foreknowledge in God should be distinguished from omniscience in that the latter is extended sufficiently to embrace all things past, present, and future, while foreknowledge anticipates only the future events (Vol. VII).

My friend, let me repeat that we are dealing with an infinite God. You and I have a little, finite mind. I am told that if a brain weighs eight ounces, it is pretty heavy. But I don't believe that an eight-ounce brain can comprehend the infinite God of the universe. Since He is omniscient, knowing everything that is possible to know—everything that is happening and everything that could happen—I am trusting Him and I intend to continue in that direction.

Now in the next verse Peter looks back to the past.

Blessed be the God and Father of our Lord Jesus Christ, which according to his abundant mercy hath begotten us again unto a lively hope by the resurrection of Jesus Christ from the dead [1 Pet. 1:3].

The word *blessed*, which is used here, is a different word from the *blessed* that is used in the Sermon on the Mount. The word used here is the Greek word from which we derive our word *eulogy*. It means "to praise." In the New Testament this word is never used in reference to man. God does not praise man, but man is to praise God, and He is the Father.

In our culture today we hear the fathers praising their sons. It isn't very often that we find a son praising his father. But we are to praise God the Father.

"The God and Father of our Lord Jesus Christ." He is the Father of our Lord Jesus Christ in a unique way. Remember that the Lord Jesus made this distinction when He spoke to Mary Magdalene on the morning of His resurrection: ". . . I ascend unto my Father, and your Father; and to my God, and your God" (John 20:17). He is the Father of the Lord Jesus Christ because of His position in the Trinity. They are equal. But you and I do not call Him Father, except on the basis that Peter mentions here: He has begotten us. The word *begotten* has to do with the regenerating work of the Holy Spirit.

"Hath begotten us again unto a living hope." (I have substituted the word *living* for the Old English word *lively*.) You and I have a *living* hope, a hope that rests upon the fact of the resurrection of Jesus Christ from the dead. And since Christ was raised from the dead by the Spirit of God, this is a further reference to the Holy Spirit.

This is a paean of praise to the Trinity. This is our song because we have been begotten, born again, as we shall see in verse 23, "not of corruptible seed, but of incorruptible, by the word of God, which liveth and abideth for ever."

Notice that the *living* hope we have rests upon the blood of Christ. A body without blood is a dead body—it has to be. If it is a living body, it will have blood coursing through it. You and I today have a living hope because of the blood of Christ shed for us. He died that you and I might live—because He paid our penalty. It is "a living hope by the resurrection of Jesus Christ from the dead."

Peter emphasizes the resurrection of Christ. The Resurrection was his great theme on the Day of Pentecost and in all of his messages. He said in effect, "All that you have seen here today is because Jesus whom you crucified has come back from the dead." And when he writes his epistles, he anchors them in the resurrection of Christ.

Paul does the same thing. He tells us that Jesus Christ was delivered for our offenses; He died for our sins. But He was raised for our justification, that we might be in Christ, accepted in the beloved, able to stand before God. He doesn't simply subtract sin from us; He makes over to us His righteousness. We stand before God in the righteousness of Jesus Christ.

Peter has described to us what God has done for us in the past. Now he moves into the future.

To an inheritance incorruptible, and undefiled, and that fadeth not away, reserved in heaven for you [1 Pet. 1:4].

"An inheritance incorruptible," meaning that it is nondestructible. It cannot be damaged in any way—no rust, no moth, no germ, no fire can touch it.

"Undefiled" indicates that it is not stained or defiled by anything. We will not get this inheritance illegally.

"That fadeth not away." We won't inherit it and then find it to be worthless, like some stock that once had value and then became completely valueless.

"Reserved in heaven for you." The word *reserved* means it is guarded. God the Father, God the Son, and God the Holy Spirit are taking care of it for us. We couldn't have it in a better safety deposit box than that!

I heard of a man who was willed a beautiful Southern home in Louisiana, but the very night the original owner died, the house caught on fire and burned down—and there was no insurance. The wonderful home that he was to inherit went up in smoke.

My friend, as believers, we have an inheritance that is incorruptible. This is a wonderful thing to look forward to!

It will help us to appreciate this verse if we remember that Peter had in mind Jewish Christians who were suffering trial and persecution for their faith. They had been forced to leave their homelands and whatever inheritance would have been theirs. Their ancestors had been delivered out of Egypt, and all through the wilderness wanderings they had the hope of the Promised Land before them. They praised God as the Creator of the world and as their Redeemer from Egypt. However, the believers to whom Peter was writing (and you and I as well) praise God as the Father of the incarnate Son, the Lord Jesus, the author of the new creation and of a spiritual redemption. Also, He gives a living hope, a hope that will never die. He has begotten us and made us His sons through the regenerating work of the Holy Spirit. And in addition He has reserved for us an inheritance—not on earth but an inheritance in heaven. That inheritance is imperishable, indestructible, and no enemy can take it away from us. Someone has expressed it poetically:

It will always be new; it will never decay.
No night ever comes; it will always be day.

How it gladdens my heart with joy that's untold
To think of that land where nothing grows old.

Unfortunately, in our day our attention has been taken away from that which is future because so much emphasis is placed on the present.

Who are kept by the power of God through faith unto salvation ready to be revealed in the last time [1 Pet. 1:5].

"Kept by the power of God" emphasizes the keeping power of God. *Kept* is probably one of the most wonderful words we have here— "kept by the power of God through faith."

The story is told of a Scotsman, who was typically economical, leaving instructions that only one word should be engraved upon his tombstone. But that one word, taken from this verse, is one of the greatest I know. It was the single word *KEPT*. He was "kept by the power of God through faith unto salvation ready to be revealed in the last time."

The apostle Paul said the same thing: "Being confident of this very thing, that he which hath begun a good work in you will perform it until the day of Jesus Christ" (Phil. 1:6). My friend, do you think He can keep you? Oh, I am weary of the emphasis being put on the work of the flesh. We are being told that if we follow some little set of rules, we can become "adequate Christians." I wonder if the fellows who are giving all these messages have reached some celestial level which the rest of us have not been able to attain. They ask, "Are you sufficient, are you satisfied?" My answer is, "No—I am pressing on the upward way, I am pressing toward the mark for the prize of the high calling of God in Christ Jesus. I am not satisfied. I have not found life sufficient." My friend, let me add a strong statement that may startle you: *You cannot live the Christian life!* Perhaps you are asking, "Do you really mean that?" Yes, I do. I would challenge you to show me a verse or any Scripture where God has asked you to live the Christian life. He has never done that. I have an old nature, and that old nature will be with me as long as I am on this earth. Sometimes that old nature really shows. I have a bad temper that flares at times. I say things even to my wonderful wife so that I must go later and make up with her. I take her in my arms and tell her I'm sorry for what I said. She forgives me, and it is always wonderful to make up, you know. However I still have an old nature—and *you* do, too. And neither of us can change our old natures by trying to follow a little set of rules. We can no more change that old nature than we can take a gallon of perfume out to the barnyard, pour it on a pile of manure, and make it as fragrant as a bed of roses. My friend, you have that old nature, and you cannot change it.

The only way in the world that you can live the Christian life is by the power of the Holy Spirit and by the fact that you are kept by the power of God—right on through until the day when you will be delivered to Him in heaven. As we are going to see, it all has to do with a personal relationship with Jesus Christ.

We come now to the key verse of this epistle—

Wherein ye greatly rejoice, though now for a season, if need be, ye are in heaviness through manifold temptations [1 Pet. 1:6].

The suffering and the security of the believer produce—of all things—joy! They can do that because of the work of the Triune God. God our Father, according to His mercy—oh, He has been so merciful!—has begotten us, given us a new nature and a living *hope* by the resurrection of Jesus Christ from the dead. And out yonder in the future He has a marvelous inheritance waiting for us.

"Wherein ye greatly rejoice." Rejoice in what? In something good? No, "in heaviness through manifold trials." This places in contrast two words that are worlds apart: *rejoice* and *trials*.

Peter gives us reasons for enduring trials down here in this life. "Now for a season"—the trials will not be long, compared to eternity. In our day there is too much emphasis on the present life. Psychology and materialism have slipped into the church. We are told that we must develop ourselves into a full-orbed individual. If we are having trouble, something is wrong with our Christianity. Oh, my friend, it doesn't mean that at all!

Instead of so much introspection, we ought to be looking outward to the great God we have and to the marvelous inheritance which He has ready for us to receive some day. We should stop this attempt to improve our old nature through the power of the flesh. God is the one who is in the business of improving us. He is the one who is trying to bring us to a maturity in our Christian life. God's way of improving us is through manifold trials.

We have been told this in previous books— in fact, it is almost like a stuck recording. Jesus told us not to be dismayed. He said that in the world we would have troubles. In the Epistle to the Hebrews we learned that God tests us by trials and troubles. James wrote about the testings that come from God. And Paul had a great deal to say about suffering. Now Peter comes along and says the same thing.

I know it is not at all popular to teach that God will prove us and lead us on to maturity through suffering. People would rather be encouraged to think that they are somebody important and that they can do great things on their own. My friend, we are nothing until the Spirit of God begins to move in our hearts and lives. We have nothing to offer to God. He has everything to offer to us.

We need always to remember that our trials are only temporary. Paul says the same thing: "For our light affliction, which is but for a moment, worketh for us a far more exceeding and eternal weight of glory; while we look not at the things which are seen, but at the things which are not seen: for the things which are seen are temporal; but the things which are not seen are eternal" (2 Cor. 4:17–18).

The things at our fingertips which we consider so valuable are not really of value. They are simply passing things when measured in the perspective of eternity. All these things are destructible. They are corruptible, and they can be defiled. The things of this world do fade away. The things we cannot see are the eternal things. They are of real value.

That the trial of your faith, being much more precious than of gold that perisheth, though it be tried with fire, might be found unto praise and honour and glory at the appearing of Jesus Christ [1 Pet. 1:7].

Peter uses here a very apt illustration, and he uses a wonderful word: *precious*. A dear lady of my acquaintance, a real saint of God up in her seventies, really overworks this word *precious*. Everything is precious to her. She has told me that I am precious and my radio program is precious. She told me that something I had said was precious. People had given her a gift and that was precious, and she says she had a precious time visiting with her friends, and they had a precious meal together. Well, *precious* is a woman's word, but notice who uses it here—Simon Peter, that great, big, rugged fisherman. He speaks of the trial of our faith being precious. And he uses the word *precious* seven times, as we shall see.

"The trial of your faith, being much more precious than of gold." After gold is mined, it is put into a smelter, a red-hot furnace. The purpose is not to destroy the gold; it is to purify the gold. When the gold is melted, the dross is drawn off to get the pure gold. Later on, Peter will also make an application of this regarding the suffering of our Lord. He says that we have been redeemed, not with gold or silver, but with something infinitely more precious than that—the blood of Christ.

When God tests us today, He puts us into the furnace. He doesn't do that to destroy us or to hurt or harm us. But He wants pure gold, and that is the way He will get it. Friend, that is what develops Christian character. At the time of *testing*, the dross is drawn off and the precious gold appears. That is God's method. That is God's school.

We don't hear that teaching very much in our day. Rather, we are being taught to become sufficient within ourselves. Oh, my friend, you and I are not adequate; we are not sufficient, and we never will be. We simply come to God as sinners, and He saves us by His grace through the blood of Christ. Then He wants to live His life through us. He tries to teach us this through our trials. He is drawing us closer to Him.

There are no shortcuts to maturity. All the gimmickry and new methods will lead to a dead-end street. The only thing that will bring us into a true maturation is the trial of our faith which God sends to us.

"At the appearing of Jesus Christ." I believe that at the appearing of Jesus Christ, we will thank God for our trials—in fact, we may wish we had experienced more of them because, when we are in His presence, we will see the value of them. Just think of the trials the apostles went through! Simon Peter, when he wrote this epistle, knew that crucifixion was ahead of him. He says that the trials are going to bring out the gold when we appear in Christ's presence. That's the thing toward which we are to look forward.

Now Simon Peter will say something very precious—

Whom having not seen, ye love; in whom, though now ye see him not, yet believing, ye rejoice with joy unspeakable and full of glory [1 Pet. 1:8].

This verse ought to mean a great deal to us. Remember that Peter had seen the Lord Jesus personally and had traveled with Him for three years. He had failed miserably during that period. Then one morning on the shore of the Sea of Galilee, the Lord prepared breakfast for the men who had been fishing all night, and I guess He was waiting for Peter. I would have expected Him to say, "Peter, I can't trust you. Why did you deny Me? I'm going to have to put you on the sidelines. I cannot use you." But no, He didn't say that. Rather, He said, "Simon, son of Jonas, lovest thou me?" (see John 21:17). That was His question: Do you love Me? The man who had been a braggadocio before was no longer bragging. He finally just cried out, "Lord, You know all things; You know that I love You." And the Lord Jesus said, "I'm going to let you feed My sheep" (see John 21:16–17). And it was Peter who preached the first sermon on the Day of Pentecost. Now Peter says to you and me,

"Whom having not seen, ye love." The Holy Spirit is the one who can make Him real to you and me. My friend, this is the secret of the Christian life. When we *love* Him, everything else falls into place. If you do not love Him, no course in the world is going to help you. And neither will He commission you to feed His sheep.

"Though now ye see him not, yet believing, ye rejoice with joy unspeakable and full of glory." Does this set your heart to beating faster? Are you really in love with Him, or do you have a dead religion that is quite meaningless? Oh, my friend, Christ is so wonderful! Simon Peter loved Him. Paul loved Him, and all of those who have genuinely served Him have loved Him. I hope you love Him today. If you do, it will solve a lot of your problems. It will help the husband-wife relationship. It is wonderful how the love of Christ draws our hearts together. Not only will it help you in your home, it will help you in your church. Loving Christ draws believers together. It will help you in all your relationships if you love Him.

"Ye rejoice with joy unspeakable and full of glory." Loving Christ brings rejoicing to your heart. Are you a rejoicing Christian, my friend? You should be. You are a child of the King, and you have an inheritance coming to you some day. How wonderful it is to be His child!

Receiving the end of your faith, even the salvation of your souls [1 Pet. 1:9].

Salvation was a subject of prophecy in the Old Testament. Both the prophets and apostles bore witness to the truth of it. What an encouragement that was to the *Diaspora*, those who were suffering for their faith.

SUFFERING AND THE SCRIPTURES

Of which salvation the prophets have inquired and searched diligently, who prophesied of the grace that should come unto you [1 Pet. 1:10].

All the prophets prophesied diligently concerning it.

Searching what, or what manner of time the Spirit of Christ which was in them did signify, when it testified beforehand the sufferings of Christ, and the glory that should follow [1 Pet. 1:11].

The prophets spoke of "the sufferings of Christ" and the grace of God. We find this in Isaiah 53 and in Psalm 22 as well as in many other Scriptures.

"And the glory that should follow" is found, for example, in Isaiah 11 and Psalm 45. The prophets all spoke of Christ's suffering and of the sovereignty and of the glory that is to come when Christ comes as King to the earth to establish His kingdom.

"The Spirit of Christ which was in them did signify." This tells us specifically that the prophets of the Old Testament wrote by the Spirit of Christ. This is one of the many statements contained in the Word of God declaring that the Old Testament was inspired of God. These men wrote by the "Spirit of Christ."

The prophets wrote some things which they themselves did not grasp. They searched for the meaning diligently, "searching what, or what manner of time the Spirit of Christ which was in them did signify, when it testified beforehand the sufferings of Christ, and the glory that should follow." There are many places in the Old Testament that speak of the suffering of Christ, and there are many other places that speak of the sovereignty of Christ, of the kingdom age. Grace and glory are combined, and it was difficult for them to understand this. For example, Isaiah wrote in the fifty-third chapter of the sufferings of Christ; then in the eleventh chapter he wrote of the Messiah coming in power and glory to the earth to establish His kingdom. This seeming contradiction was very puzzling to the prophets, and they tried to find out how both could be true. As the prophets looked down the corridors of time, they saw these two events as two great mountain peaks, but they could not see the valley of time between them.

You and I are in the unique position of living in that interval of time between the suffering of Christ, which is in the past, and the glory of Christ, which is yet in the future.

It will help you to understand the prophecies of the suffering and sovereignty of Christ if you picture the two events as two great mountain peaks. Here in Pasadena we have a backdrop of the Sierra Madre mountains. As the crow flies, they are about five miles away, but driving the winding road to get there makes them about twenty-five miles away. Mount Wilson is in the foreground and is approximately six thousand feet high. Behind that peak we can see another peak, Mount Waterman, which looks as if it is the same height as Mount Wilson. Actually, Mount Waterman is over eight thousand feet high. However, it looks as if they are the same height and that they are right together. In actual fact, they are not together at all. A tremendous valley separates them—between twenty-five and thirty-five miles across—and I estimate that it is probably fifty miles from one mountain peak to the other. Yet, seeing them from a distance, you would think they were right together.

In just such a way, the prophets looking into the future saw the suffering of Christ and the glory of Christ as two mountain peaks, which appeared to be right together. I am of the opinion that there were sceptics and higher critics in those days who argued, "This is a conflict; the Scriptures are in contradiction. You cannot have it both ways. Either He comes in suffering or He comes to reign." Of course we know now that both are true. And the valley between is the church age, which already is approaching two thousand years in length.

Unto whom it was revealed, that not unto themselves, but unto us they did minister the things, which are now reported unto you by them that have preached the gospel unto you with the Holy Ghost sent down from heaven; which things the angels desire to look into [1 Pet. 1:12].

Now the apostles are saying, "We are preaching the same thing that the prophets did." The only difference was that the prophets could not make the distinction between Christ's suffering and glory while the apostles were in the position of being able to understand the distinction.

"Which things the angels desire to look into." It is my opinion that the angels, God's created intelligences, are standing up yonder looking at you and me wondering why we don't get busy and give out this tremendous message today. They desire to do it themselves. They would love to come and proclaim it to the world. You recall that the angel Gabriel came and made the announcement to Mary and later to Joseph that Jesus was to be born. Also, he came to tell Zacharias that he was going to have a son, named John, who would be the forerunner of the Messiah. I am sure that Gabriel would love to come down

again and say to me as I make my radio broadcast, "Move over, McGee, you are not putting enough into it. This thing is lots more wonderful than you are making it!" Although he would like to come down, God won't let him. He says to Gabriel, "No, I've got to use that poor instrument, McGee." Today he is using *human* instruments to get out His Word, because we are not living in the day of the ministry of angels. We are living in the day of the ministry of the Holy Spirit. As children of God we are indwelt by the Holy Spirit—". . . if any man have not the Spirit of Christ, he is none of his" (Rom. 8:9). If you are Christ's, you are indwelt by the Spirit of God.

Now, do you think that an angel could do something for you that the Spirit of God could not do? No. We are living in the day of the ministry of the Holy Spirit, the day of grace, when the Spirit of God takes the things of Christ and reveals them unto us. What are we to do in light of this?

Wherefore gird up the loins of your mind, be sober, and hope to the end for the grace that is to be brought unto you at the revelation of Jesus Christ [1 Pet. 1:13].

"Gird up the loins of your mind." This is a figure of speech based on the gathering and fastening up of the long Eastern garments so that they would not interfere with the wearer's vigorous movements. It was an expression that was understood in Peter's day, but I would like to bring it down to good old Americana. I think we would say, "Get with it!" Or maybe we would say, "Get turned on!"

"Be sober." You won't need drugs; you won't need alcohol. Let the Word of God turn you on. However, "be sober" means more than this. It means to be sober minded, to adopt a serious attitude in the study of the Word of God.

"And hope to the end." This is the great epistle of hope. Why (as we have already seen) should the child of God be willing to endure trials? Because we have a hope, and that hope rests upon the resurrection of Jesus Christ.

"The grace that is to be brought unto you at the revelation of Jesus Christ." At the time

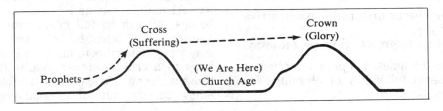

when the Lord Jesus comes to take the church out of the world, He will bring plenty of grace with Him. By His grace, He will take out *every* believer. And each believer's works are to be judged at Christ's judgment seat (*Bēma Seat*). At that time we will either suffer loss or receive a reward—and that certainly will be by His grace!

The fact that we will be judged someday is another incentive to endure the trials of this world. How we live down here upon this earth is very important. Today believers are confronted with the demand to lead transformed lives which only the Word of God can produce in us. One of the reasons God lets us go through trials and troubles is because He wants to fashion us according to His plan. We are to yield to Him in all our tribulations.

As obedient children, not fashioning yourselves according to the former lusts in your ignorance [1 Pet. 1:14].

"As obedient children." The Scriptures will lead us to obedience. You may recall that James said, "Be ye doers of the word, and not hearers only . . ." (James 1:22). The Word of God not only brings us hope, but it also leads to our obedience. The Word of God is to be obeyed; we are to yield to its instruction.

While I was ill, several folk sent copies of this poem by Alice Hansche Mortenson, which was a great comfort to me:

I NEEDED THE QUIET

I needed the quiet so He drew me aside,
Into the shadows where we could confide.

Away from the bustle where all the day
    long
I hurried and worried when active and
    strong.

I needed the quiet though at first
    I rebelled
But gently, so gently, my cross He up-
    held,

And whispered so sweetly of spiritual
    things
Though weakened in body, my spirit took
    wings

To heights never dreamed of when active
    and gay.
He loved me so greatly He drew me away.

I needed the quiet. No prison my bed,
But a beautiful valley of blessings in-
    stead—

A place to grow richer in Jesus to hide.
I needed the quiet so He drew me aside.

Why did He draw me aside? So that I might spend time in the Word of God. Oh, how important it is in the lives of believers!

"Not fashioning yourselves according to the former lusts in your ignorance"—that is, not conforming your behavior to what it used to be before you knew better. We are to live lives which reveal that we have been transformed from the inside. We are not to walk around with an artificial smile on our face like a floor-walker at Macy's who acts as if he is delighted to serve you when in reality his corns are killing him and he wishes you would go home and stay home. We are not to be artificial. We are to so yield to God that we will be genuinely transformed.

But as he which hath called you is holy, so be ye holy in all manner of conversation [1 Pet. 1:15].

Holiness is something that is really misunderstood. To the average person, holiness means to assume a very pious attitude, to become almost abnormal in everyday life. It is thought to be a superficial thing.

My friend, the Lord wants you to be a fully integrated personality. He wants you to enjoy life and have fun—I don't mean the sinful kind of fun, but real delight and enjoyment in the life He has given to you. Holiness is to the spiritual life what health is to the physical life. You like to see a person who is physically fine, robust, and healthy. Well, holiness is to be healthy and robust spiritually. Oh, how we need folk like this today!

Because it is written, Be ye holy; for I am holy [1 Pet. 1:16].

Is our holiness to be an attribute like God's holiness? No. Our God is absolutely perfect, and we will never, while we are in this life, reach that state. Oh, I have met several folk who thought they had reached that state, but I could not find anyone who would agree with them that they had reached that exalted level. Then what does it mean to be holy as God is holy?

Our God is a complete, wonderful personality. Although you and I are mere human beings, we can be full grown; we can reach maturation. A beautiful little baby in a crib may win a blue ribbon, but if he is still a little baby in a crib seventeen years later, something is wrong. He should be a healthy young fellow turning out for football practice. As

Christians, we should be growing spiritually like that. What can produce this kind of growth? The Word of God.

And if ye call on the Father, who without respect of persons judgeth according to every man's work, pass the time of your sojourning here in fear [1 Pet. 1:17].

"Without respect of persons" means without partiality. God judges every man's work impartially. God doesn't have little pets. God is going to judge the work of every Christian fairly. This has nothing to do with your salvation; it has everything to do with the kind of life you are living down here on this earth. The fact that God is going to judge us ought to cause us to become very sober minded and to give a little more attention to the life that we are living. My friend, let's make sure that we are not superficial. Are you trying to keep a smile on your face and radiate happiness and sunshine everywhere you go? The gospel does not sprinkle rosewater on a bunch of dead weeds. The gospel *transforms* lives and brings with it a living hope which rests upon the resurrection of Christ. Believers have *life* from the living Savior who is up yonder at God's right hand.

Forasmuch as ye know that ye were not redeemed with corruptible things, as silver and gold, from your vain conversation received by tradition from your fathers;

But with the precious blood of Christ, as of a lamb without blemish and without spot [1 Pet. 1:18–19].

"Forasmuch as ye know"—and I hope *you* know that you have been redeemed.

In these verses Peter is speaking of the objective work of God for your salvation, which is redemption. My friend, He had to pay a price for you. You and I stood under the judgment of God, for the Scripture says ". . . the soul that sinneth, it shall die" (Ezek. 18:4). God has never revoked that decree. God never changes. He is the same yesterday, today, and forever. The immutability of God is the terror of the wicked—if they give any thought to it at all. We hear it said that we are living in a new age with new thoughts and new values, but *God* has not changed. There would be no reason for Him to change because He knew the end from the beginning. Neither did He learn anything when He looked at the morning newspaper or heard the television newscaster this morning. It didn't give Him any information because He knows all things—past, present, and future. And God has not changed His decree that "the soul that sinneth, it shall die."

"Ye were not redeemed with corruptible things, as silver and gold." Although silver and gold can be purified by being put into a crucible—heated red-hot so the dross can be drawn off—even they will corrupt in time. If you have table service of silver which you use only for guests, you know that whenever you bring it out, it is tarnished and looks like pewter. It is corrupting. Silver and gold are perishable. We are not redeemed with corruptible things.

"From your vain conversation received by tradition from your fathers." Life is vain; that is, it is empty without the redemption of Christ. There is nothing quite so meaningless as human life apart from the redemption of Christ. Everything else in this world serves a purpose. Every animal and every plant on this earth serves a purpose. The sun, the moon, and every star in the sky serves a purpose. But man without God is meaningless. Someone has said that mankind is just a rash on the epidermis of a minor planet! Well, that's about all man is apart from God. We have not been redeemed by corruptible things—not anything from this empty life. Man has nothing to offer to God for his own redemption. My friend, what do you have that God needs?

God taught me how unimportant I was one summer when He put me flat on my back. I was scheduled to conduct Bible conferences in the Northwest, and I thought they were important. God said to me something like this, "Listen, I got along without you before you got here, and I'm going to get along without you after you leave. You think that speaking at those conferences is important, but I want you to learn what *is* important. I want you to lie here flat on your back and look up to Me to find out that your relationship with Me is the most important thing there is. I have some things to teach you. Sometimes when you teach My Word, you teach way out ahead of where you are living. I want you to find out that what I say in My Word is true, and a little suffering isn't going to hurt you at all. It is going to mold you and shape you the way I want you to be." My friend, I learned that I have nothing that God needs.

What can you or I *do* today to redeem ourselves? *Nothing!* Then how can we be redeemed?

"With the precious blood of Christ." Here

again Simon Peter, that rugged fisherman, says that the blood of Christ is *precious*. As I have said before the blood of Christ is not mentioned in some religious circles. The words are omitted from the hymnals of many liberal churches. Their reasoning is that the blood is crude. Well, I don't think it is crude, and certainly Simon Peter didn't think it was crude. He said it was *precious*.

"With the precious blood of Christ, as of a lamb without blemish and without spot." Simon Peter, who lived with Jesus Christ for three years, said that He was without blemish and without spot. He was absolutely sinless. I will take Peter's word for it—certainly he is in a better position to judge than modern authors who depict Jesus as just another sinful man. The modern authors write for money, but Simon Peter wasn't in the moneymaking business. All he got for his witness of Christ was suffering and finally crucifixion. He said that we were not redeemed with corruptible things, as silver and gold, "but with the precious blood of Christ, as of a lamb without blemish and without spot." This is an objective statement of our redemption. This is what God did for you and me.

Who verily was foreordained before the foundation of the world, but was manifest in these last times for you [1 Pet. 1:20].

"Who verily was foreordained"—a better word is *foreknown*. Christ was foreknown before the foundation of the world.

Now let me give you a tremendous statement from *The Scofield Reference Bible* (p. 1333):

The sovereign choice of God in foreordination, election, and predestination logically originated in the divine decision based on His eternal omniscience of all possible plans of action. The order logically, not chronologically, is omniscience, divine decision (foreordination, election, predestination), and foreknowledge. As God's decision is eternal, however, so also His foreknowledge is eternal. As foreknowledge extends to all events, it includes all that is embraced in election, foreordination, and predestination. Election is, therefore, according to foreknowledge, and foreknowledge is according to election, meaning that both are in perfect agreement.

When we begin to deal with words like *foreordination, election, predestination, foreknowl-*

edge, etc., I feel that we, with our finite minds, treat God as if He were a great big computer. He isn't that at all. He has a heart bigger than the whole universe. When I was in seminary studying theology, it seemed pretty important to know whether or not foreknowledge comes before foreordination; but, frankly, since that time I have not been concerned with which comes first. I realize now that the important thing is that Christ was "foreknown before the foundation of the world, but was manifest in these last times for you." To put it very simply, the cross of Christ was not an ambulance sent to a wreck. Christ was the Lamb who was slain before the foundation of the world because God knew all the time that Vernon McGee would need a Savior, and He loved him enough to provide that Savior. I don't need a computer to go over this. I only need a God with a great big heart of love who provided redemption by His grace.

Who by him do believe in God, that raised him up from the dead, and gave him glory; that your faith and hope might be in God [1 Pet. 1:21].

"That raised him up from the dead"—Simon Peter keeps reminding us of the resurrection of Christ.

"That your faith and hope might be in God." Previously he put together the words *grace* and *hope;* now it is faith and hope. Peter is the great apostle of hope, and hope rests upon the resurrection of Christ and upon the fact that we have a living Savior who will be returning some day.

Seeing ye have purified your souls in obeying the truth through the Spirit unto unfeigned love of the brethren, see that ye love one another with a pure heart fervently [1 Pet. 1:22].

"Seeing ye have purified your souls in obeying the truth through the Spirit." The Word of God is a miracle cleansing agent. On television today advertisers make great claims for their soaps and other cleansing agents. They tell us how superior their product is over the products of their competitors. All of them are trying to sell a "miracle" product. My friend, the only true miracle cleanser in this world is the Word of God. It is the best bar of soap that you can get. The Word of God will really take spots out, and many of us need to get closer to it.

"Unto unfeigned love of the brethren, see that ye love one another with a pure heart fervently." Your relationship to the Word of

God will lead you to a right relationship with other believers.

Being born again, not of corruptible seed, but of incorruptible, by the word of God, which liveth and abideth for ever [1 Pet. 1:23].

Peter brings us back to the Word of God again. He is talking now about the subjective work of God in salvation. We have seen that the objective work of God was that Christ died—that's our redemption. It happened over nineteen hundred years ago, and we can't add anything to it. However, if you are to become a child of God, you must be born again, born from above. This, you recall, is what the Lord Jesus said to Nicodemus, as recorded in John 3:3. Nicodemus was a man who was religious to his fingertips, yet the Lord Jesus told him that he must be born *anothen*, meaning "from above," by the Spirit of God.

"Not of corruptible seed, but of incorruptible, by the word of God, which liveth and abideth for ever." You cannot be saved, you cannot be born again apart from the Word of God. This Book is the miracle that is in the world today. Although I believe this, I never cease to marvel at the letters I receive from folk who tell me that they have been born again and their lives have been transformed from listening to my Bible-teaching radio broadcast. It is wonderful, but I don't understand how it happens; I only know that it is the result of the Word of God which liveth and abideth for ever.

We are living in a day when a great deal is said about virility. Men want to be vigorous and virile; women want to be sexy. Much emphasis is put upon that today. I hope you won't misunderstand when I say to you that if you want something that is virile and vigorous and sexy in a proper sense, turn to the Word of God. It is full of life, and it is life-giving. Put your arms around the Savior by putting your trust in Him, and a new birth will take place. There will be a miraculous birth because the Word of God is virile and vigorous and it can penetrate your heart and make you a child of God. Oh, my friend, how important this is! Yet people are so preoccupied with sex and virility that they miss it. They are running around after emptiness. Sometimes I think that the whole human race is becoming obsessed with it. You would think that this generation had discovered sex! If they would only realize that the thing that really brings a birth within us is the Word of God as it reveals Christ to us. Then something tremendous takes place within us, and we are *born again!*

For all flesh is as grass, and all the glory of man as the flower of grass. The grass withereth, and the flower thereof falleth away [1 Pet. 1:24].

Don't ever think that there is something of value in us that we can offer to God. All the glory of mankind is like the fragile flower of grass. In other words, mankind is like the grass which I can see from my window. It is nice and green in the summertime, but it is brown and dead in the wintertime.

But the word of the Lord endureth for ever. And this is the word which by the gospel is preached unto you [1 Pet. 1:25].

My friend, we need the preaching and the teaching of the Word of God above everything else. I do not mean to minimize the place of music, the place of methods, and the place of organization, but there is absolutely no substitute for the Word of God today. "The word of the Lord endureth for ever."

CHAPTER 2

THEME: *The suffering of the saints and the suffering of Christ; suffering produces separation*

THE SUFFERING OF THE SAINTS AND THE SUFFERING OF CHRIST

In chapters 2–4 Peter deals with the suffering of God's children and the suffering of the Lord Jesus Christ. And in these three chapters we will see what suffering accomplishes in the lives of believers: Suffering produces separation (ch. 2); suffering produces Christian conduct (ch. 3); and suffering produces obedience to the will of God (ch. 4).

SUFFERING PRODUCES SEPARATION

In speaking of separation, or living for the Lord, there is the danger of adopting one of two extreme viewpoints, both of which I consider very much out of line with Scripture. One of them is thinking that human nature is such that all it needs is merely new direction, it needs to be given a purpose and a little reformation. The folk who take this position believe that since there is nothing wrong with human nature, they need only to awaken the individual to his marvelous energy and intellect and moral nature so that he will be able to live for the Lord. That is one view of what it means to live the Christian life.

The second extreme viewpoint is that when one is born again, he receives something that is supernatural (which he does receive), but then he merely sits on the sidelines while God accomplishes in his life all that needs to be done. Folk in this class become very pious. To me they are like a puffed up frog. They never seem to grow and develop into loving, full-orbed, normal Christians.

Now this second chapter will make it very clear that you and I, through the New Birth (born again of incorruptible seed, the Word of God), have a new nature, and we are to live in that new nature by the power of the Holy Spirit. We have been brought into a loving relationship with the one whom, having not seen, we love. Simon Peter saw Him and loved Him, and although you and I have not seen Him, the Holy Spirit can make Him real to us so that we love Him in that way also.

My friend, when you were first born again, do you remember how sweet and wonderful it was? Paul wrote to the Corinthian believers: "For I am jealous over you with godly jealousy: for I have espoused you to one husband, that I may present you as a chaste virgin to Christ" (2 Cor. 11:2). The Corinthian Christians had become very carnal. Their first love, that honeymoon love for Christ, was gone. God spoke of this same thing to His people Israel just before they went into the Babylonian captivity: ". . . Thus saith the LORD; I remember thee, the kindness of thy youth, the love of thine espousals, when thou wentest after me in the wilderness, in a land that was not sown" (Jer. 2:2). The children of Israel demonstrated that love when they first came out of Egypt and crossed the Red Sea. They sang a song of praises to Jehovah: ". . . I will sing unto the LORD, for he hath triumphed gloriously: the horse and his rider hath he thrown into the sea" (Exod. 15:1). Yet it wasn't too long before they became complainers before God. God remembers that.

My friend, today real separation rests upon the fact that you have been born again, you now have a new nature, and you are now in love with Christ. Your love for Him makes you want to please Him.

The great object in the purposes of God is to have folk saved, not only from judgment and the lake of fire, but saved from the present world. He wants them saved, not only for heaven by and by, but for the heart of Christ now. The work of Christ on the cross settled every question that sin has raised between God and our souls. The future is bright with the glory of God, and we have been brought into the value of that work of redemption. We have been born again, and no one—not even Satan—can change that.

However, my friend, how are we doing today in our Christian lives down here on the earth? How is our relationship with our fellowmen and with the Lord Jesus Christ?

Wherefore laying aside all malice, and all guile, and hypocrisies, and envies, and all evil speakings,

As newborn babes, desire the sincere milk of the word, that ye may grow thereby [1 Pet. 2:1–2].

You see, we cannot expect God to do everything for us; He has certain things for us to do for ourselves. First, there are certain things that we are to lay aside. Paul, in his letter to the Ephesian believers, likens it to the taking off of a garment: "That ye put off concerning the former conversation the old man, which is corrupt according to the deceitful lusts. . . . Wherefore putting away lying, speak every man truth with his neighbour: for we are members one of another" (Eph. 4:22, 25).

Paul uses a different figure to describe this to the Corinthians. "Purge out therefore the old leaven, that ye may be a new lump, as ye are unleavened. For even Christ our passover is sacrificed for us: Therefore let us keep the feast, not with old leaven, neither with the leaven of malice and wickedness; but with the unleavened bread of sincerity and truth" (1 Cor. 5:7–8). When the Israelite observed the Passover and the Feast of Unleavened Bread, he didn't eat leavened bread; that is, he didn't go on living the same kind of life he had lived before. He was feeding in a different place on a different kind of bread. And it was a means of growth for him. Likewise, Paul is saying to the Corinthian believers that when they come to Christ, they are to get rid of the old leaven, which is symbolic of malice and wickedness in their lives. You see, we will never become perfect in this life, because we will always have that old nature.

"Laying aside all malice." What is malice? The best definition I have found is *congealed anger.* It means to have an unforgiving spirit. My friend, are you carrying bitterness in your heart and a chip on your shoulder? Although you witness about being born again and about loving Jesus, nobody around you will be able to distinguish that if you are carrying malice, congealed anger, in your heart.

"And all guile." Guile is using cleverness to get even or to try to make a good impression upon someone. Ananias and Sapphira used guile when they tried to represent themselves as being very generous givers to the church. That old nature which you and I have is good at that sort of thing. J. B. Lightfoot calls it "the vicious nature which is bent on doing harm to others."

"And hypocrisies, and envies, and all evil speakings." Hypocrisy is, of course, attempting to be what you are not. And evil speaking means slander.

"As newborn babes, desire the sincere milk of the word." Instead of "sincere" milk, I translate it *pure* milk or *spiritual* milk. Just as a hungry baby reaches for the bottle, a believer is to desire the Word of God.

I remember when our little grandson was born. Because his father was over in Turkey at the time, his mother brought him into our home. We had him with us those first few months, and every now and then it was my task to give him his bottle. I want to tell you, that little fellow went into high gear when he saw that bottle of milk. He started moving his hands, his mouth, his feet—he was reaching out for it with every part of his body. At that time I was still the pastor of a congregation, and I thought, *I wish I had a congregation that would reach out after the Word of God like that!*

My friend, without a hunger for the Word of God you will not grow in grace and in the knowledge of Christ. You will not develop as a Christian—you will always be in your baby-hood. We must remember that a little baby and a full-grown man are both human beings, but they are in different stages of growth and development. The little one needs milk so he can grow up to become a man. Now, how does a Christian grow? He grows by studying the Word of God. There is no growth apart from the Word of God.

I receive letters from many pastors who tell me that they are wet nurses for a lot of little babes. As one pastor said, "I spend my time burping spiritual babies!" Those babies should grow up so they wouldn't need a pastor to pat them and burp them all the time. And they would grow if they desired the pure milk of the Word.

It is my conviction that the "pure milk of the word" means the *total* Word of God. We don't grow spiritually by lifting out a verse for comfort here and there. We need the total Word of God to grow. We need a full, well-balanced diet. Of course, we start out with milk, but the day comes when we want a porterhouse steak, a good baked potato, a green salad, and maybe some black-eyed peas on the side. And you get all the spiritual nutrition you need in the total Word of God.

If so be ye have tasted that the Lord is gracious [1 Pet. 2:3].

"If so be" should be translated "since"—since ye have tasted that the Lord is gracious. You see, at the moment of salvation, a child is born with an appetite for the Word of God, just as a newborn infant immediately starts to eat. When my little grandson came home from the hospital at only two or three days old, all we had to do was stick a nipple in his mouth. He knew what to do. I didn't give him a lecture on how to drink milk; he seemed to know all about it. In the same way, I don't think we need programs to teach the spiritual babes in Christ how to get into the Word of God. Instead of *programs*, we need to give them the *Word* so they can feed on it.

What, then, is real separation? Real separation (we need to note this carefully) is a separation from the *works* of the flesh. Too many Christians feel that they must be separated from the world. No, we are *in* the world, and we must live in the world even though we are not *of* the world.

Let me give you an illustration about the wrong idea concerning separation. I drove an evangelist around Nashville, Tennessee, almost half of one night, trying to find a restaurant that didn't serve beer. This was his idea of separation from the world. We finally found one, and he got ptomaine poisoning from eating in that place! I wouldn't have eaten in it. I told him, "If I were you, after this I would go into a restaurant that serves good food and simply disregard the beer." You don't need to drink the beer just because you eat the food. Separation from the world does not mean that you cannot go into a restaurant that serves liquor.

Malice, hypocrisy, envy, evil speaking—these are the things from which we should be separated. Only the Spirit of God working within us will produce that kind of separation. And until you and I are willing to give up malice, hypocrisy, envy, and evil speaking, we will never grow to Christian maturity.

To whom coming, as unto a living stone, disallowed indeed of men, but chosen of God, and precious [1 Pet. 2:4].

"To whom coming, as unto a living stone." We don't come to a little Babe in Bethlehem; *we* come as little babes to a *living stone*. The living stone is Christ. After the confession of Simon Peter, the Lord Jesus said, ". . . upon this rock I will build my church . . ." (Matt. 16:18). Simon Peter makes it very clear here that the living stone is not himself but that the living stone is Jesus Christ.

Jesus again refers to Himself as a stone in Matthew 21:42, 44: "Jesus saith unto them, Did ye never read in the scriptures, The stone which the builders rejected, the same is become the head of the corner: this is the Lord's doing, and it is marvellous in our eyes?" This is a quotation from Psalm 118. Now, speaking of Himself He says, "And whosoever shall fall on this stone shall be broken: but on whomsoever it shall fall, it will grind him to powder."

Christ Jesus is that foundation stone of the church. He is that stone today. Paul writes, "For other foundation can no man lay than that is laid, which is Jesus Christ" (1 Cor. 3:11). When you come as a sinner and fall on that stone, you are broken. However, in your brokenness that stone becomes a foundation for you, and that is your salvation. However, if you reject that stone, you are not through with the stone. Daniel, in his vision, saw a "stone was cut out without hands, which smote the image upon his feet" (see Dan. 2:34). That is the stone of judgment which will come to smite the earth. This stone symbolizes Christ. He also will be the stone of judgment to this earth. What a picture of the Lord Jesus is given to us here!

Here is something else that is wonderful—

Ye also, as lively stones, are built up a spiritual house, an holy priesthood, to offer up spiritual sacrifices, acceptable to God by Jesus Christ [1 Pet. 2:5].

"Ye also, as lively stones." *Lively* is an old English word for *living*. "Ye also, as living stones." How are we living stones? We have been "*born* again, not of corruptible seed, but of incorruptible, by the word of God, which liveth and abideth for ever" (v. 23, italics mine).

"Ye also, as living stones, are built up a spiritual house." You will recall that after Peter's confession, "Thou art the Christ, the Son of the living God," the Lord Jesus said to him, "Thou art Peter, and upon this rock I will build my church" (see Matt. 16:16, 18). The name *Peter* means "rock," and the Lord Jesus was saying to him in effect, "You are going to be a little stone, a pebble, but on this foundation stone [Christ] I am going to build My church." The Lord Jesus is the foundation stone, and we know that Peter understood it that way, because he said, "Ye also, as living stones, are built up a spiritual house." Just as Simon Peter was one of the little stones, you are one of the little stones and I am one of the little stones which are built into this spiritual house. When we are born again, become children of God, we are put into this building of God.

If we turn back to the Epistle to the Ephesians, we will find that Paul also uses this illustration of a building. "Now therefore ye are no more strangers and foreigners, but fellow-citizens with the saints, and of the household of God; And are built upon the foundation of the apostles and prophets, Jesus Christ himself being the chief corner stone; In whom all the building fitly framed together groweth unto an holy temple in the Lord: In whom ye also are builded together for an habitation of God through the Spirit" (Eph. 2:19–22). Today God is building a temple, a living temple. Those of us who come to Him as the sinners we are, who fall upon Him, cast ourselves upon Him for mercy, are saved. And he makes us a part of the living temple He is building upon the foundation stone, which is Christ Himself.

"An holy priesthood, to offer up spiritual sacrifices, acceptable to God by Jesus Christ." Another picture which this epistle gives to us is that of a holy priesthood. All believers are living stones. All believers are priests. We are a holy priesthood, and later Peter calls it a royal priesthood. As priests we are to offer up spiritual sacrifices, acceptable to God in Jesus Christ. Praise to God is such a spiritual sacrifice. Your monetary offering to the Lord is such a spiritual sacrifice. I don't know why people think that money cannot be spiritual. It all depends on the way money is used. And then, you can offer yourself to God. That is a spiritual sacrifice.

Wherefore also it is contained in the scripture, Behold, I lay in Sion a chief corner stone, elect, precious: and he that believeth on him shall not be confounded [1 Pet. 2:6].

This is a quotation from Isaiah 28:16: "Therefore thus saith the Lord GOD, Behold, I lay in Zion for a foundation a stone, a tried stone, a precious corner stone, a sure foundation: he that believeth shall not make haste." This stone is symbolic of Christ. Scripture makes this fact very clear.

Unto you therefore which believe he is precious: but unto them which be disobedient, the stone which the builders disallowed, the same is made the head of the corner [1 Pet. 2:7].

"Unto you therefore which believe he is precious." A better translation would be, "For you therefore which believe is the preciousness." For you who believe there is the preciousness of Christ. I think it is so interesting that Simon Peter, the big, rugged fisherman, uses the word *precious*. We think of it as a word used in the vocabulary of women, but whenever Peter speaks of Christ or of His blood or any part about Him, he uses the word *precious*.

"But unto them which be disobedient, the stone which the builders disallowed [rejected], the same is made the head of the corner."

And a stone of stumbling, and a rock of offence, even to them which stumble at the word, being disobedient: whereunto also they were appointed [1 Pet. 2:8].

This is a very important passage of Scripture. You will recall that it is a quotation from Psalm 118:22. There is a tradition that takes us back to the time of the building of Solomon's temple in Jerusalem. In 1 Kings 6:7 we read this about the actual construction of the temple: "And the house, when it was in building, was built of stone made ready before it was brought thither: so that there was neither hammer nor axe nor any tool of iron heard in the house, while it was in building." The stones, you see, were hewn to exact measurement in the quarry; and when they reached the building site, there was no sound of a hammer—they were just fitted into place.

Well, the tradition is that at the beginning of the project a very large, fine-looking stone came up from the quarry, but the builders couldn't fit it in any place; so they moved it to one side. Because it was in the way, eventually they just pushed it over the brow of the hill to make room for the other stones that they were receiving and forgot about it. Finally, when all the stones had been fitted into place, they sent down word to the quarry, "Send up the cornerstone." The building was finished except for the cornerstone. Word came back, "We sent the cornerstone to you at the very beginning." Then they remembered, "That's the stone we pushed off the hill!" So with a great deal of effort, they had to haul that stone back to the top of the hill, and they found that it did fit right into place. If this tradition is accurate, it certainly explains the verses before us.

The stone, which the builders rejected, has become the head of the corner. The stone is, of course, a picture of the Lord Jesus Christ. When He came into the world He was rejected by His own people—"He came unto his own, and his own received him not" (John 1:11). Not only then was He rejected, but you and I live today in a Christ-rejecting world. At the time this is being written, we are in the Christmas season. I don't know about your town, but in my town Christmas is being celebrated, but Jesus Christ is being rejected. About the most hypocritical thing in the world is to reject the one whose birthday you are celebrating! My friend, the Lord Jesus Christ is to you today either a stepping stone or a stumbling stone.

This brings us to a very wonderful passage of Scripture which reveals that a Christian's life is to be commensurate with his position in Christ. And until we live that life, we are not experiencing normal Christian living.

But ye are a chosen generation, a royal priesthood, an holy nation, a peculiar

people; that ye should shew forth the praises of him who hath called you out of darkness into his marvellous light [1 Pet. 2:9].

He is saying several very wonderful things about us here. We are a chosen generation, a royal priesthood, a holy nation, and a people of His own—not a "peculiar people." God's people are not supposed to be oddballs or crackpots or ready for the funny farm. Some folk seem to think that is what "peculiar" means. It is more meaningful to use the translation: *a people of His own.*

1. We are a "chosen generation," that is, an elect race. Back in the Old Testament God chose Israel as His people, and in the Scriptures there are two elect groups of people: the nation Israel, called an elect nation, and the church, called an elect nation and an elect people.

Now keep in mind that Peter is writing to his own people, the *Diaspora,* Jewish Christians who were scattered throughout the Roman Empire and even beyond it. In effect he is saying, "Although right now you certainly do not look like a chosen generation, an elect race, you are. Because you have come to Christ, you are a chosen generation, you are an elect nation, just as the children of Israel were elect. The keys of the kingdom have been given to the church, and we today are to give out the gospel because the church is the chosen instrument. This honor has been conferred upon believers. It is as if God had stamped out for you and me a wonderful medal on which is inscribed: You are an elect race; you are a chosen generation.

Many vain attempts are being made in our day to identify certain people of this earth with the ten "lost" tribes of Israel. They are said to be the gypsies, the Mormons, the Adventists, or the British-Israel group—which is probably the most vocal. Well, if they could prove that England and America were settled by the ten "lost" tribes of Israel, what have they proven? God has set aside the nation Israel temporarily, and today God is doing a new thing. He is calling out an elect race, a chosen generation, from every tongue and nation and people—both Jew and Gentile—and they are brought into a new relationship to God in the church.

Although you and I say that we have come to Christ, *He* says that He has chosen us. I like that. It reminds me of the story of two little urchins from the slums of New York who got to Macy's department store and were look-ing in the window at the merchandise on display. They saw things which they could never have, but they played a game with each other.

One said, "I choose this."

The other said, "I choose that."

The boy said, "I choose the ball."

The girl said, "I choose the doll."

You and I are just like poverty-stricken little urchins in this world, but when we say, "I choose Jesus," we find that He has already chosen us. How wonderful that is! The Lord Jesus said of His own apostles, "Ye have not chosen me, but I have chosen you . . ." (John 15:16). It is wonderful to know this. I am not being irreverent when I say that, since He has chosen me, He is responsible for me. The responsibility is His because I belong to Him. How wonderful it is that He has chosen us!

2. We are "a royal priesthood." Back in the Old Testament God first of all chose the entire nation of Israel to be His priests. (I believe that in the Millennium the whole nation of Israel will be priests here on this earth.) However, they sinned, and so God chose one tribe out of that nation. The priests came from this one tribe. Today there is no priesthood on earth which God recognizes—except one. Today every *believer* in the Lord Jesus Christ is a priest. Israel *had* a priesthood; today the church *is* a priesthood.

When I was a pastor, I preached a message entitled, "You Are a Catholic Priest." The word *catholic* means "general," of course. In that sense every believer is a catholic priest, and all have access to God. Since we belong to Christ, we can come into His presence, into the very holy of holies. Simon Peter tells us here that we as believers are members of a *royal* priesthood. We are children of the *King.* A little later on in this epistle we will read that the eyes of the Lord are over the righteous and that He *hears their prayers.* Oh, how wonderful this is!

3. We are "an holy nation." The nation Israel was never holy in conduct, and the same can be said of the church. Israel's failure is glaring; the church's failure is appalling. Yet we are holy in our relationship with Him because *Christ* is our righteousness. If you have any standing before God, it is not in yourself; it is in Christ. I can't think of anything more wonderful than that today I stand complete in Him. What a joy it is to be a member of a holy nation, which is a new nation in the world today.

4. We are "a peculiar people"—a people of His own. We are a people for acquisition, a people for God's own possession. We belong to

Him. Therefore, there is in the world not only a new nation but also a people that belong to Him. I don't know why some Christians are afraid of this concept. It doesn't mean that we are to be peculiar in conduct and act strangely but that we belong to Him. We are His very own people. We can compare it to a boy who goes out and gets a job and makes his own money for the first time. His dad has been giving him an allowance, but now the money belongs to him. It is something that he worked for, and it is his very own. Well, Christ's work, His work of redemption, required the shedding of His blood, as we have seen in this epistle, and now He has a people for His very own.

In the high priestly prayer of the Lord Jesus, He says, "I have manifested thy name unto the men which thou gavest me out of the world: thine they were, and thou gavest them me . . ." (John 17:6). Also He said, "All that the Father giveth me shall come to me; and him that cometh to me I will in no wise cast out" (John 6:37). How wonderful it is that the Father has given us to Christ!

And God calls His own. He calls *you* today, my friend. It doesn't matter who you are or to which race you belong. Jesus Christ is calling to you to be His own. He wants you to join a chosen generation and a royal priesthood. He is not inviting you to wear robes or to recite rituals but to join a priesthood that has access to God. He is asking you to belong to a new nation. He does not mean Germany or England or Japan or even the United States. He asks you to belong to that great company of believers out of every nation. ". . . happy is that people, whose God is the LORD" (Ps. 144:15). "So we [are] thy people and sheep of thy pasture . . ." (Ps. 79:13). Through the prophet Isaiah God says, ". . . for the transgression of my people was he stricken" (Isa. 53:8). And in the New Testament, "Wherefore Jesus also, that he might sanctify the people with his own blood, suffered without the gate" (Heb. 13:12). Oh, what a wonderful position we have in Christ!

Which in time past were not a people, but are now the people of God: which had not obtained mercy, but now have obtained mercy [1 Pet. 2:10].

"Which in time past were not a people." We didn't belong to God but were far from Him.

"Which had not obtained mercy, but now have obtained mercy." My friend, there is one gift that you won't want to miss, and the name written on the box is "mercy." It is a big box

because God is *rich* in mercy. If you need any today, you can go to Him for it.

Again, remember that Peter is writing specifically to the *Diaspora*, his people who were scattered abroad. "Which in time past were not a people"—they had rejected Christ as their Messiah and God had rejected them. "But are now the people of God." God was (and *is*) doing a new thing in calling out a people and extending His mercy to them.

Dearly beloved, I beseech you as strangers and pilgrims, abstain from fleshly lusts, which war against the soul [1 Pet. 2:11].

The child of God is to publish His praises. In what way? By singing hymns? Well, it is all right to do it that way, but you can better show forth His praises by not manifesting the works of the flesh. Earlier Peter has told us that the works of the flesh are malice, guile, hypocrisies, envies, and slander. We publish His praises by displaying our attitudes which have been shaped by the Word of God.

Having your conversation honest among the Gentiles: that, whereas they speak against you as evildoers, they may by your good works, which they shall behold, glorify God in the day of visitation [1 Pet. 2:12].

"Having your conversation [behavior] honest among the Gentiles." You see that true Christian separation is not some pious position that is to be assumed. It is not simply refraining from doing worldly things. It is very positive action. It includes honesty and good works. All believers in any kind of business dealing show forth the praises of God by their honesty. That is a witness to the world.

Submit yourselves to every ordinance of man for the Lord's sake: whether it be to the king, as supreme;

Or unto governors, as unto them that are sent by him for the punishment of evildoers, and for the praise of them that do well [1 Pet. 2:13–14].

Mad Nero was just coming to the throne in Rome as the new emperor. The Roman Empire boasted itself that it gave justice to man. However, it was like every other government, including our own. The poor man has never had a fair chance. The rich man has always been able to buy lawyers who were smart enough to evade the law. The poor man is the one who has the problems with the law.

Then what should be the believer's relationship to the law? He is to obey the law. That is what Peter is saying here—"submit yourselves to every ordinance of man for the Lord's sake." Since they were under Roman law, they were to obey it. Although Rome intended that their laws should be just, they were not. Remember that Roman law crucified Christ and persecuted the early Christians; yet Rome boasted loudly about justice. It sounds like modern America where religion—that is, the preaching of the Word of God—is very politely being suppressed. Are we to rebel against the government? No. We are to obey the laws of the land.

For so is the will of God, that with well-doing ye may put to silence the ignorance of foolish men [1 Pet. 2:15].

When the Christian submits to government and to those who are in authority over his life, he is again revealing the praises of God through his life. I have never accepted joyfully a traffic ticket, but I pay my fine and try to be more careful to obey the laws. We are to be obedient to the law because we are giving a testimony.

As free, and not using your liberty for a cloak of maliciousness, but as the servants of God [1 Pet. 2:16].

The relationship of the believer to other people is a testimony which speaks louder than the message from the pulpit. You see, the believer in Christ has a liberty which the man outside of Christ does not have. Believers have a marvelous liberty in Christ Jesus. I personally believe that I could go places and see things which the average Christian could not. Although I don't think I would be hurt by them, I avoid them because of my testimony. I don't want to use my liberty as a cloak of maliciousness; that is, I don't want my weaker brother to be hurt by what I do. We must remember that although we are *free*, we are the *servants* of God.

Honour all men. Love the brotherhood. Fear God. Honour the king [1 Pet. 2:17].

"Honour all men." A Christian should respect other human beings. He doesn't say to *love* all men—believe me, some of them are very unlovely!

"Love the brotherhood." While we respect all men, we are to love the brotherhood, meaning other believers.

"Fear God." Certainly we as believers are to reveal by our lives that we are God-fearing people.

"Honour the king." We owe an honor to the office of the man who rules over us. I have never voted for a president whom I really wanted. I have always voted *against* the other candidate. I have never known a president who I felt was really capable. However, regardless of who is president and regardless of his inability, he should be honored because of his office. I am not impressed by some Scripture-spouting, pious individuals who attack the president of the United States. The office is to be honored.

Servants, be subject to your masters with all fear; not only to the good and gentle, but also to the froward [1 Pet. 2:18].

"Servants, be subject to your masters." In our contemporary culture we would say, "Employees, be subject to your bosses." Many folk tell me how wonderful it is to work for a Christian boss. But what if you are working for a godless fellow?

"Not only to the good and gentle, but also to the froward [perverse or unreasonable]." You are to be subject to him also, as long as he is not asking you to do that which is illegitimate or dishonest.

"Be subject" has in it the idea of freedom of choice. It is subjecting yourself, something you do voluntarily—not because you feel that your boss is a great person but because of your testimony for Christ. Christians also reveal the praise of God by their attitudes and actions in labor relationships.

For this is thankworthy, if a man for conscience toward God endure grief, suffering wrongfully.

For what glory is it, if, when ye be buffeted for your faults, ye shall take it patiently? but if, when ye do well, and suffer for it, ye take it patiently, this is acceptable with God [1 Pet. 2:19–20].

"For what glory is it, if, when ye be buffeted for your faults, ye shall take it patiently?" "Glory" could be translated "fame or praise." *Buffeted* means "to be struck with the fists." This was often the treatment of slaves in Peter's day. If a slave would steal or lie or become rebellious and refuse to work, his master might take him and give him a real going over with his fists. Peter is saying that if you have been beaten for any such fault, and you take it patiently, you have nothing to brag about. The beating was your own fault. God is not going to commend you for your patience in a case like that.

My friend, it may be possible that you are having problems and difficulties because you played the fool. A businessman said to me recently, "I have played the fool!" He had played the stock market and lost all his capital. He went bankrupt. When I was talking to him, he was suffering for his own foolishness. To recognize his fault and take the subsequent suffering patiently did not commend him to God.

"But if, when ye do well, and suffer for it, ye take it patiently, this is acceptable with God." Of course, the natural reaction in all of us is to strike back when we have been unjustly treated. I confess that this is my first reaction, but I am learning to let God take care of it. God says in Romans 12:19, "Vengeance is mine; I will repay," and He does a much better job of it than I could. The Lord Jesus Himself said, "Blessed are ye, when men shall revile you, and persecute you, and shall say all manner of evil against you falsely, for my sake. Rejoice, and be exceeding glad: for great is your reward in heaven . . ." (Matt. 5:11–12). And Peter says, "This is acceptable with God."

Peter doesn't get very far without telling us about the Lord Jesus again, and here he reminds us of the sufferings of Christ, which are an example to us as believers.

For even hereunto were ye called: because Christ also suffered for us, leaving us an example, that ye should follow his steps:

Who did no sin, neither was guile found in his mouth [1 Pet. 2:21–22].

When our Lord Jesus Christ was here on earth, He suffered two kinds of suffering: He suffered as a human being down here when He became a man, suffering for righteousness' sake. Also, He suffered for the sins of the world.

Now, His suffering for the sins of the world is not an example for us—it is our *redemption*. It is something we believe and accept, but we can by no means imitate it. However, in His life down here He did leave us an example. In Nazareth during His first thirty years He suffered ridicule and misunderstanding, as Psalm 69 makes clear. Then, when He moved out in a public ministry, the gospel records tell us how He suffered for righteousness' sake. When you and I suffer for our faith, we remember the example He left for us in that connection.

Who, when he was reviled, reviled not again; when he suffered, he threatened not; but committed himself to him that judgeth righteously [1 Pet. 2:23].

He let His Father settle the account. Again let me remind you of Romans 12:19: "Dearly beloved, avenge not yourselves, but rather give place unto wrath: for it is written, Vengeance is mine; I will repay, saith the Lord." Let's allow God to handle those accounts for us also. And He *will* handle them, by the way.

Jesus is suffering for the sins of the world in the next verse—

Who his own self bare our sins in his own body on the tree, that we, being dead to sins, should live unto righteousness: by whose stripes ye were healed [1 Pet. 2:24].

This is not an *example* that is set for us. You and I cannot suffer to wash away our own sins, much less suffer for the sins of the world. Peter is talking here about redemption. "That we being dead to sins"—that was our condition.

"By whose stripes ye were healed." Healed of what? I notice that when so-called faith healers use the words, "by whose stripes ye were healed," they refer to Isaiah 53:5 rather than to this verse in 1 Peter, because Peter makes it evident that the healing is of *sins*. I certainly agree that the Lord Jesus came to be the Great Healer—but the Great Healer heals of sins. No human physician can handle that problem. And Peter's use of these words from Isaiah 53:5 reveals that the prophet Isaiah was not speaking primarily of physical healing but of that which is more important and more profound, healing from sin.

For ye were as sheep going astray; but are now returned unto the Shepherd and Bishop of your souls [1 Pet. 2:25].

Humanity, both lost and saved, are called sheep. "Ye were as sheep going astray." This, too, is a quotation from Isaiah 53: "All we like sheep have gone astray; we have turned every one to his own way; and the LORD hath laid on him the iniquity of us all" (Isa. 53:6).

As you can see, the suffering of Christ is actually the theme of the last part of this chapter. Christ suffered to set us an example, and He suffered a vicarious, substitutionary death for our sins.

"But are now returned [the same word is often translated *converted*] unto the Shepherd and Bishop [overseer] of your souls."

CHAPTER 3

THEME: Suffering produces Christian conduct in the home—in the church; Christ's suffering preached by the Spirit in Noah's day

In chapter 3 Peter teaches that suffering will also produce Christian conduct in the life of the believer. This conduct will be manifested in two different places, in the home and in the church.

CONDUCT IN THE HOME

Likewise, ye wives, be in subjection to your own husbands; that, if any obey not the word, they also may without the word be won by the conversation of the wives [1 Pet. 3:1].

"Likewise" means "in the same manner"; thus verse 1 ties right back into chapter 2 which discussed separation. "Conversation" would be better translated as "behavior." Separation and conduct are blended and molded together here.

In Ephesians 5 we find this same theme of the position of the wife in the home. However, Peter is presenting an altogether different situation from that which Paul discussed in Ephesians. Paul dealt with the relationship between a Christian wife and a Christian husband who were both *Spirit-filled* believers. That entire section in Ephesians begins with ". . . be filled with the Spirit" (Eph. 5:18). When you are filled with the Spirit, what are you to do? Paul says, "Wives, submit yourselves unto your own husbands, as unto the Lord" (Eph. 5:22), and "Husbands, love your wives, even as Christ also loved the church, and gave himself for it" (Eph. 5:25). He is speaking of a Christian home in which both the husband and wife are Spirit-filled believers, and the relationship is one in which the man loves his wife and is willing to die for her.

Now for the sake of order in any situation, there must be headship. In marriage, that headship has been given to the husband. When the wife is told to submit, however, it is not like the obedience of a child. Many men when they marry think of their wife as being a sort of first child and that she is to obey them like a child is to obey. That is not true at all. As we have suggested before, submission has to do with that which is voluntary. Paul is saying to the wife, "Submit yourself. This man loves you, and you are to submit to him." The better word, because it means more, is *respond*. Re-

spond to this man. If he comes to you as your Christian husband and puts his arms around you and says, "I love you more than anything else," then certainly you should respond, "I love you."

Down through the years I have counseled a great many young people who have asked me to unite them in marriage. I never majored in trying to marry as many as I could; very frankly, I always did it with fear and trembling. I would like to mention very briefly some things I have told them.

Marriage is made on three different planes. The first is the physical plane, and that is important. It is the thing which the world talks about a great deal, the sexual relationship. It is a wonderful thing to have a wife whom you can put your arms around and love. Between two believers, sex can become the most precious, most beautiful, most wonderful thing there is in this world. It is my conviction that believers are the only ones who can really enjoy the physical relationship to the fullest. There is no question that the physical relationship is a wonderful thing.

When I got married, my wife felt she was not cut out to be a preacher's wife. She had been brought up in a little town in Texas and had seen how the preacher's wife was expected to do so much work in the church. I took her over to talk with Dr. Lewis Sperry Chafer one day, and I explained her fears to him. Neither of us will ever forget what Dr. Chafer said. He told my wife, "I am out speaking in Bible conferences a great deal. When I come home, I am not looking for an assistant pastor, I'm not looking for an organist, I'm not looking for a soloist, and I'm not looking for the president of the missionary society. I want a woman there to meet me who is my wife and whom I can put my arms around and love." The physical relationship is an important relationship.

The second plane in a marriage is the mental or psychological relationship, which is also very important. It is nice when the husband and wife enjoy doing the same things. On one of our tours to Bible lands, there was a very wonderful couple who were in their fifties. They would get up early in the morning and take a hike, and again at night they would walk together. They would visit certain places which were not included in the tour. They enjoyed doing things together, and it is wonderful to have that kind of relationship. The thing that makes the comic strip "Maggie and Jiggs" so funny is that Jiggs wants to go to Dinty Moore's where they have corned beef, cabbage, and beer, and Maggie wants to go to the opera where they have champagne. Their interests and their appetites are altogether different. That, of course, does not make for a healthy relationship. Because so many husbands and wives do not share the same interests, there are many clubs and lodges today where each can get away from the other and do what they want to do. How tragic that is!

The third plane in a marriage is the spiritual relationship, and this applies to a marriage between two believers. When problems and trouble and sorrow and suffering come, a husband and wife should be able to kneel down, come to God in prayer, and meet around the Word of God together. You can break the other two ties, but ". . . a threefold cord is not quickly broken" (Eccl. 4:12). When you have all three, you have a wonderful marriage. The first two cords can break, but if the third one will hold, the marriage will hold. However, when the third one is broken with the others, the marriage has gone down the tube, my friend. I have to admit it, there is very little hope for a marriage like that.

We have been discussing marriage between two believers. Suppose, however, that the wife is married to a man who is not a Christian. To begin with, she should not have married him, if that was the situation before they married. Any man or woman who marries a non-Christian is in trouble. Scripture forbids marriage between a believer and an unbeliever. In Deuteronomy we read, "Thou shalt not plow with an ox and an ass together" (Deut. 22:10). There are a lot of them yoked together today, and it is a big mistake.

One young lady came to me and said, "Dr. McGee, my fiancé is not a believer, but I am going to win him for the Lord." I said to her, "Have you won him yet?" "No," she said, "he won't even come to church with me yet." So I told her this: "Your greatest influence with that young man is right now. The day you get married, your influence to win him for the Lord will greatly diminish. You'll never be able to preach to him again. You are going to be living with him, and he's going to be watching you very carefully from now on. If you can't get him to church now, you're in trouble." She didn't like what I said. In fact, she went and got another preacher to perform the ceremony because I would not perform it. I do not

marry—and have never knowingly married—a saved and an unsaved person; I believe that is entirely wrong. She got someone else to marry them, but she came back in two years weeping and wanting to talk to me because she had gotten a divorce from him. That marriage was headed in that direction even before it started, my friend.

In this passage here in 1 Peter, we have that unfortunate relationship in which there is a saved wife and an unsaved husband; apparently, the wife became a Christian after they had married. Is she to change after her conversion and become a sort of female preacher in the home in order to lecture her husband and to present the gospel to him? No, she is to continue on in the same position of being in subjection to him. To be in subjection means to submit yourself. This is a voluntary step; it is not a command. The wife is to continue on in this relationship of voluntarily being in subjection, letting her husband—though unsaved—continue to be the head of the house.

Suppose, however, that her husband wants her to go with him to the nightclub and drink cocktails? Is she to do that? I would hope that even these most rabid folk who say that she should obey her husband would agree that she should not do such things. However, there are those who are giving that kind of counsel today.

A lady who attended my church when I was a pastor in downtown Los Angeles had an unsaved husband who wanted her to go to a nightclub, which apparently was a sort of burlesque. Some evangelist had counseled her that she was to obey her husband even in this, and so she went. It offended her sensibilities, and she was under great conviction about it. She actually came to the place where a doctor told her that she would have to enter an institution for psychopathic treatment because she could not go on under that type of pressure. Well, she heard me speaking on the radio, and it was evident that I had a little different idea about it. When she came to talk to me, I told her that I did not believe that Simon Peter intended for her to do these things. I said that after her conversion she was to try to win her husband and to be subject to him. But I went on to ask her what she would do if her husband wanted her to go out and commit a robbery. Would she have to join him in that and drive the car for him? She said she was sure that the evangelist would not want her to go that far.

May I say to you, her submission was to be voluntary. God certainly did not command her to engage in sinful or questionable activities which would spoil her testimony. A Christian wife must live very carefully before an unsaved husband. Her preaching is not going to do a bit of good. "That, if any obey not the word, they also may without the word be won by the behavior of the wives." In other words, she is to preach a wordless sermon by her pure life which she lives before him. And that has nothing in the world to do with submission to him.

While they behold your chaste conversation coupled with fear [1 Pet. 3:2].

Peter says that your husband will recognize that you have now changed and want to live a pure life for God and that you no longer want to indulge in the things of the world. Therefore, that is the testimony which you can give to him.

Another lady came to me when I was a pastor and said, "Dr. McGee, I bring my husband to church every Sunday." (She was the kind of woman who *could* bring her husband; she was a dominant personality.) She continued, "He is not saved, and every Sunday I think he will make a decision for Christ but he doesn't. On Monday morning I sit at the breakfast table just weeping and telling him how I wish he would accept Christ. When he comes home from work in the evening, again I just sit there at dinner and weep and beg him to accept Christ." I got to thinking about what she had said. How would you like to have dinner every evening and breakfast every morning with a weeping woman? I wouldn't care for it myself, and I'm sure you wouldn't want that either. So I called her up and said, "Suppose that for a year's moratorium you simply do not talk to your husband about the Lord at all?" She said, "Oh, you mean that I'm not to witness?" I said, "No, I didn't say that. Peter says that if you cannot win your husband with the Word, then start preaching a wordless sermon. How about your life? What kind of life are you living before him?" I want to tell you, that put her back on her heels because she wasn't living as she knew she should live. But she agreed to my suggestion because she *did* want to win him, and she was a wonderful woman in many ways. I was amazed myself when, in six months' time, her husband made a decision for Christ one Sunday morning. The wordless sermon had won, my friend.

Whose adorning let it not be that outward adorning of plaiting the hair, and of wearing of gold, or of putting on of apparel [1 Pet. 3:3].

Obviously, this verse does not prohibit all adorning—if it did, it also would prohibit all apparel!

In the Roman Empire a great emphasis was put upon the way women arranged their hair. If you have seen any pictures of that period, you know that the women loaded their heads down with all kinds of hair, not their own hair but someone else's. They really built their hair up, and they wore jewelry in it. Today we have very much the same kind of emphasis upon hair and dress. If the unsaved man you are going to marry cannot be won to Christ by your sex appeal before you marry, you will never win him to Christ by sex appeal afterward. A wife can apply a gallon of perfume and wear the thinnest negligee there is, but I tell you, she will not win him for the Lord that way.

I do believe, though, that a Christian woman should dress in style. At the Bible institute where I used to teach, someone had given the girls the notion that they should never use any make-up and need not give any care to the way they dressed. I used to tell those girls that we all ought to look the best we can with what we've got to work with, although some of us don't have much to work with! I said, "Some of you would look a little bit better if you would put on just a little make-up, because you look like you came out of the morgue. That is simply not attractive, and it does not commend you to God."

Peter's point here is that you cannot win an unsaved man by sex appeal.

But let it be the hidden man of the heart, in that which is not corruptible, even the ornament of a meek and quiet spirit, which is in the sight of God of great price [1 Pet. 3:4].

A woman is to wear an ornament, but it is to be an ornament on the inside, the ornament of a gentle and quiet spirit. In the little Book of Ruth, we read that when Boaz went into the field and saw that beautiful maid of Moab, Ruth, he fell in love with her. But have you noticed something else? Boaz had heard of her character. He had heard that she had a marvelous, wonderful character, and he fell in love with her total person.

We have many very helpful cosmetic products today, and I see nothing wrong in using anything that will make you look better. All of us want to look the best we possibly can. Alexander Pope has well advised:

Be not the first by whom the new are
    tried,
Nor yet the last to lay the old aside.

Be in style. Dress up in a way that is becoming, but don't try to use that as the means of winning someone to the Lord. We need more *inward* adornment today—that is the thing which is important.

For after this manner in the old time the holy women also, who trusted in God, adorned themselves, being in subjection unto their own husbands [1 Pet. 3:5].

There are a number of fine examples of such women in the Old Testament. I have already mentioned Ruth who was in the genealogical line that led to Christ. We are also told that Rachel was a beautiful woman, and Jacob fell in love with her. She was the one bright spot in that man's life, which was a pretty dark life, by the way.

Even as Sara obeyed Abraham, calling him lord: whose daughters ye are, as long as ye do well, and are not afraid with any amazement [1 Pet. 3:6].

Sarah was such a beautiful woman that several kings wanted her as a wife, and Abraham had a great problem in that connection. But she called Abraham "lord." She looked up to Abraham. It is wonderful when a wife can look up to her husband.

Now Peter speaks to the husbands—

Likewise, ye husbands, dwell with them according to knowledge, giving honour unto the wife, as unto the weaker vessel, and as being heirs together of the grace of life; that your prayers be not hindered [1 Pet. 3:7].

Although this seems to imply that both the husband and wife are Christians, I believe that these instructions to husbands would be applicable either way.

A husband is to treat his wife as the weaker vessel, and he is to give her honor because of that. I do not think the current women's liberation movement is going to last very long. I think a woman wants to be a woman, just as a man wants to be a man. Because she is the weaker vessel, she is to be treated with honor. The man is to give first place to her. She gets into the car first as he holds the door for her. When they enter a room, she goes first. As they walk down the sidewalk, he walks on the outside for her protection. He is to treat her

with honor. When a woman loses her place, she doesn't go up; she goes down. When she takes her place, she can be treated with honor and given her rightful position. I think every husband ought to treat his wife as someone special.

"That your prayers be not hindered." Peter says that if you are not getting along as husband and wife, it will ruin your family altar, and there is no use praying together. If you are fighting like cats and dogs, well, God just doesn't hear cats and dogs. But when you are in agreement, you can pray together and your prayers will not be hindered.

Before we leave this particular section of Scripture, I would like to add one further word. Marriage is something which God has given to the entire human family, not only to Christians or to the nation Israel. In the Book of Genesis we are told that God made man, and at that time man was alone. I think the Lord let Adam be alone for a long time to let him know he was missing something. Then Scripture says that God took man and from man He made woman. Using the Hebrew words, Genesis 2:23 reads, "She shall be called *Isha*, because she was taken out of *Ish*." She is called ". . . an help *meet* for him" (Gen. 2:18, italics mine); that is, a help that was *fit* for him. In other words, she was to be the other half of him. He was only half a man, and she was to be the other part of him. With that in mind, you can see that the marriage relationship is not to be one of a man insisting on treating his wife like a little child who has to jump every time he says so. She is there to *help* him. She is there to be a *part* of him. She is there to *love* him. And he is there to *love* and *protect* her. That is the ideal relationship in marriage.

CONDUCT IN THE CHURCH

Finally, be ye all of one mind, having compassion one of another, love as brethren, be pitiful, be courteous [1 Pet. 3:8].

Believers are to be like-minded, sympathetic, tenderhearted, and courteous, which means they are to be humble-minded, not trying to lord it over one another. This is to be the attitude and action of a believer among other believers.

Not rendering evil for evil, or railing for railing: but contrariwise blessing; knowing that ye are thereunto called, that ye should inherit a blessing [1 Pet. 3:9].

This is turning the other cheek. If another believer says something evil about you, something that is not true, are you to strike back? No. Commit him to the Lord—the Lord will take care of him. If we take this position it will break down all the little cliques and stop all the fighting within the church. Remember that we are representing the Lord.

For he that will love life, and see good days, let him refrain his tongue from evil, and his lips that they speak no guile [1 Pet. 3:10].

All of us want to live, but unfortunately there are a lot of believers today who are not enjoying life. They are not living life to its fullest, not getting all they should out of life. When I was a pastor in Nashville, Tennessee, many years ago, a young medical student—who was the president of the young people's group in the church and not much younger than I was—said one day, "Vernon, I want life to be like an orange to me, an orange out of which I can squeeze every drop. I want to live for God!" "For he that will love life"—if you want to really live, here is a good formula, and here is the key to it. Peter says that we are to refrain from constantly speaking evil of others. And we are to refrain from speaking "guile," from being deceptive and not telling the truth.

Let him eschew evil, and do good; let him seek peace, and ensue it [1 Pet. 3:11].

A child of God is not to sit back and act piously. Let's live it up, my friend, but let's not live it up by indulging in gossip and evil. Let's live it up by turning away from evil and pursuing that which ministers to peace. Let's live for God today. How important this is!

For the eyes of the Lord are over the righteous, and his ears are open unto their prayers: but the face of the Lord is against them that do evil [1 Pet. 3:12].

This is an amazing passage of Scripture. Peter is quoting here from Psalm 34: "The eyes of the LORD are upon the righteous, and his ears are open unto their cry. The face of the LORD is against them that do evil, to cut off the remembrance of them from the earth" (Ps. 34:15–16). This is a strong statement as it is given here in this psalm. It is something the Word of God has emphasized a great deal. God has guaranteed to hear the prayers of those who are His own. He has *not* guaranteed to hear the prayers of those who are not His own.

The only prayer that a sinner can pray is, "Lord, I admit that I am a sinner, and accept Jesus Christ as my Savior, and ask that You accept me in Him." That is a prayer that God will hear and that God will answer. Many people today have the idea that an old reprobate can live any kind of life he wants and then come to God in prayer when he is in trouble and expect God to hear and answer him. As the movies and the novels tell it, the old reprobate comes home to find his little girl sick in the hospital, and so he gets down on his knees and calls upon God to raise her up. How sentimental that is! May I say this very plainly: it is nonsense, and it is absolutely unscriptural. Let that old reprobate get right with God, and then God will hear and answer his prayer. It is a false idea today to think that you can call on God under any circumstances whether or not you are His child. My friend, He has not promised to hear the prayers of those who are not His own.

In Ecclesiastes 2:17 we read the statement of a man who has tried everything in life. He has lived like a reprobate, and he says, "Therefore I hated life; because the work that is wrought under the sun is grievous unto me: for all is vanity and vexation of spirit." How many men and women today who are involved in living for the things of this world suddenly wake up and find that it's not worth it? Life is monotonous, and life is not worth it. No wonder they put a gun to their heads and blow their brains out. No wonder some of them jump off bridges. No wonder some take an overdose of sleeping pills. My friend, it is not until you come into a right relationship with God that you can live life to its fullest.

Does that mean that a child of God is living on a pretty high plane above the problems of this world? Listen to Peter—

And who is he that will harm you, if ye be followers of that which is good? [1 Pet. 3:13].

Does that mean that God gives you an armor so that nobody can touch you at all?

But and if ye suffer for righteousness' sake, happy are ye: and be not afraid of their terror, neither be troubled [1 Pet. 3:14].

Suffering for the right should bring joy to the child of God. Some Christians actually make themselves obnoxious in their witness to others, thinking they are taking a stand for the Lord. But if we have simply taken a quiet stand for the right and for God, we ought to rejoice if we suffer for that. I must repeat this again: you are not going to escape suffering in this world if you are a child of God. Someone has said, "Jesus often spoke of Christianity as a banquet but never as a picnic." How true that is! He never said that we are going to have it easy down here.

I truly wish that I could elucidate this next verse in such a way that it would bless your heart. I will do my best.

But sanctify the Lord God in your hearts: and be ready always to give an answer to every man that asketh you a reason of the hope that is in you with meekness and fear [1 Pet. 3:15].

This means you ought to know more than a little about the Bible. The tragedy of the hour is that there are so many folk who say they are Christians, but the sceptic is able to tie them up into fourteen different knots like a little kitty caught up in a ball of yarn—they cannot extricate themselves at all. Why? Because of the fact that they do not know the Word of God.

"Sanctify the Lord God in your hearts." Oh, today, do you have a little sanctuary, a little chapel in your own heart? When you are riding along in the car or walking down the street or are in the shop or office or classroom, is there a little chapel in your heart where you can withdraw and sanctify the Lord God in your heart? If there is, folk outside will know that you belong to God, and you will not have to mouth it all the time or make yourself obnoxious by making some pious statement. Oh, if in our lives today we would sanctify the Lord God in our hearts. How we need to do that!

Habakkuk wrote, "But the LORD is in his holy temple: let all the earth keep silence before him" (Hab. 2:20). On Sunday you may go to your church, but the world is passing you by, headed for the beach, headed for the mountains, headed for the desert, headed for places of amusement. The whole world is not keeping silence before Him. Why? Because we as individuals need to sanctify the Lord God in our hearts.

Having a good conscience; that, whereas they speak evil of you, as of evildoers, they may be ashamed that falsely accuse your good conversation in Christ [1 Pet. 3:16].

In other words, make sure that those who speak evil of you are in error. Shortly after I had come to downtown Los Angeles as pastor of a church there, I met Dr. Jim McGinley in Chicago at the Moody Founder's Week conference, and he asked me, "How do you like being pastor of that great church?" I said, "It's wonderful, but I find myself in a place where I cannot really defend myself. I don't intend to get up in the pulpit every Sunday morning to explain all the things that have been said about me. My business is teaching the Word of God. Yet none of the things that have been said are true." Dr. McGinley said to me, "Just thank the Lord that what they say is not true." In this verse Peter is saying, "Have a good conscience so that when you hear these rumors about yourself, it will not bother you because you know they are not true."

For it is better, if the will of God be so, that ye suffer for well-doing, than for evil-doing [1 Pet. 3:17].

If you suffer for Christ's sake, you can rejoice in that; but if you are suffering because you have played the fool, because you have gotten into trouble and into sin, then that is a different story altogether.

CHRIST'S SUFFERING PREACHED BY THE SPIRIT IN NOAH'S DAY

For Christ also hath once suffered for sins, the just for the unjust, that he might bring us to God, being put to death in the flesh, but quickened by the Spirit [1 Pet. 3:18].

It is important for us to see that Jesus Christ became a human being, and it was in His humanity that He died on the cross. He *died* on the cross, and it was the Holy Spirit who raised Him from the dead.

By which also he went and preached unto the spirits in prison [1 Pet. 3:19].

This has been a most misunderstood passage of Scripture. The key word to this entire passage is in verse 20; it is the little word *when*—

Which sometime were disobedient, when once the longsuffering of God waited in the days of Noah, while the ark was a-preparing, wherein few, that is, eight souls were saved by water [1 Pet. 3:20].

When did Christ preach to the spirits in prison? "When once the longsuffering of God waited in the days of Noah." In Christ's day, the spirits of those men to whom Noah had preached were in prison, for they had rejected the message of Noah. They had gone into *sheol*. They were waiting for judgment; they were lost. But Christ did not go down and preach to them after He died on the cross. He preached through Noah "when once the long-suffering of God waited in the days of Noah." For 120 years Noah had preached the Word of God. He saved his family but no one else. It was the Spirit of Christ who spoke through Noah in Noah's day. In Christ's day, those who rejected Noah's message were in prison. The thought is that Christ's death meant nothing to them just as it means nothing to a great many people today who, as a result, will also come into judgment.

The like figure whereunto even baptism doth also now save us (not the putting away of the filth of the flesh, but the answer of a good conscience toward God,) by the resurrection of Jesus Christ [1 Pet. 3:21].

"The like figure whereunto even baptism doth also now save us." To what baptism does this refer? It is not water baptism but the baptism of the Holy Spirit. The baptism of the Holy Spirit is real baptism, and water baptism is ritual baptism. Now I believe in water baptism, and I believe immersion is the proper mode. However, the important thing here is to see that it is the baptism of the Holy Spirit which puts you into the body of believers.

"Not the putting away of the filth of the flesh"—it is not just by water, for that will not put away the filth of the flesh. "But the answer of a good conscience toward God, by the resurrection of Jesus Christ"—that is, a faith in the resurrection of Jesus Christ which brought the work of the Holy Spirit into your life and regenerated you.

Who is gone into heaven, and is on the right hand of God; angels and authorities and powers being made subject unto him [1 Pet. 3:22].

This verse is speaking of the Lord Jesus Christ. You and I are little sinners down here, but we can come to Him, receive Him, and thus join the great company of the redeemed. We are baptized by the Holy Spirit into the body of Christ because He is raised from the dead and is today at God's right hand.

CHAPTER 4

THEME: *Suffering produces obedience to the will of God*

SUFFERING PRODUCES OBEDIENCE TO THE WILL OF GOD

In this passage of Scripture Peter makes it very clear that when life is easy there is danger of drifting into a state of mind which accepts every blessing in life as if it were owed to us. We come to the place where we do not prize or value life as we should. As a Christian, what value do you put upon life? God permits His children to suffer in order to keep us from sin and to give us a proper value of life. I hear so many young people today say that they did this or that in order to find a new direction for their life. May I say to you, suffering will give a new direction to life. David discovered this and wrote in Psalm 66:10, "For thou, O God, hast proved us: thou hast tried us, as silver is tried." God puts us through the test that it might draw us to Himself and give us a new direction and drive for life. Such is the purpose of suffering.

Forasmuch then as Christ hath suffered for us in the flesh, arm yourselves like-wise with the same mind: for he that hath suffered in the flesh hath ceased from sin [1 Pet. 4:1].

I must confess that I have recently been given new insights into this verse. Over the years it is a verse that has disturbed me a great deal, and I have never gone into a great deal of detail in my teaching on it. I have been rather amazed to discover that other commentators have likewise more or less bypassed it rather than dealing with it in detail. I trust that the Spirit of God will give us an understanding that will make this verse helpful to us.

"Forasmuch" refers us back, I believe, to 1 Peter 3:18, "For Christ also hath once suffered for sins, the just for the unjust, that he might bring us to God, being put to death in the flesh, but quickened by the Spirit." These two verses go together, and this is again a reminder that in His human body Christ not only endured pain but He was actually put to death in the flesh.

In recent years there was a very popular

book, *When God Died*, as well as a popular theology which said, "God is dead." Well, God never died, my friend, and He is not dead today—He hasn't even been sick. Christ died in His human body, which He took yonder at Bethlehem. As the writer to the Hebrews put it, He was "in all points tempted like as we are." He knew what it was to suffer. He knew what it was to bleed. He knew what it was to shed tears. He knew what it was to be brokenhearted. He was perfectly human, and He *died* in that human body.

Christ brought an end to His relation to the sins of man when He died on the cross because He bore the penalty for sin in His own body. We are told back in 1 Peter 2:24, "Who his own self bare our sins in his own body on the tree, that we, being dead to sins, should live unto righteousness: by whose stripes ye were healed." Three times (1 Pet. 2:24; 3:18; 4:1) Peter says that it was in His flesh and in His body that Christ paid the penalty for man's sin. That leads me to say this: Christ did not die *in* sin, nor did He die *under* sin, but He died *to* sin. He took my place, He took your place, and He paid the penalty for our sin. From that point on, Christ will not come back to die for sin. He will no longer have any relationship to sin Himself because of the fact that He arose from the dead. When He came back from the dead, He came in a glorified body. He was "quickened by the Spirit," or "made alive by the Spirit" is the better translation (see 1 Pet. 3:18). He has a life that now lives in a body. He is up yonder in a body that is completely devoted to the service of God, for He is God and He is in the enjoyment of full and free access to God and to all creation.

Now Christ is able to make over this benefit to us. Peter tells us, "Arm yourselves likewise with the same mind." "The same *mind*" actually means "the same *thought*." Some people have said that it means *resolution*, but that is not quite the idea. This refers to the *thought* which leads to a resolution. This is what Paul spoke of when he said, "Let this mind be in you, which was also in Christ Jesus" (Phil. 2:5).

"Christ hath suffered for us in the flesh," Peter says, and those of us who have suffered in the flesh have "ceased from sin." The translation of the word *ceased* is a very unsatisfactory one, and this is what had disturbed me about this verse. The Greek word translated as "ceased" is *pauō*. In the active voice, *pauō* means "to stop or to cease." It is used like that in 1 Corinthians 13:8, "Whether there be tongues, they shall *cease*"; that is, tongues are

going to stop, and that is something I have emphasized in my teaching. When I was in Athens, Greece, I took a walk from the Hilton Hotel down to Constitution Square. As I would come to a corner, I would see a sign like our "Stop" sign, only there it said, *Pauō*. *Pauō* means "to stop" when it is used in the active voice. An active verb means that the subject does something; a passive verb (or the middle voice in the Greek) means that the subject is acted upon and the subject itself doesn't do anything. In this verse which we are studying, *pauō* is in the middle voice or the passive. Therefore Dr. Joseph Thayer, in his lexicon of the New Testament, translates this literally as "hath got release." In other words, if you have suffered in the flesh, you've got release from sin.

Just what does Peter mean by this? First of all, I would say that God will use suffering to keep you from sin. I am confident that many of us have experienced that personally. Suffering will keep us from sin, but Peter is saying more than that here. Peter says we have got *release* from sin. That means that God has made an adequate provision for you and me to live the Christian life. Dr. Griffith Thomas has said that in this verse Peter puts Paul's Romans 6 into a nutshell of just one verse. Romans 6 is that chapter which speaks of the provision God has made for you and me to live the Christian life.

Peter has made it very clear that we have been born again by the Word of God. The Spirit of God using the Word of God will produce a son of God. And that son of God now has a new nature, a new nature that is *not* going to live in sin.

The Bible's illustration of this truth, which I use a great deal, is the story of the Prodigal Son (see Luke 15:11–32). The Prodigal Son got down in the pigpen, but, you see, he wasn't a pig. He had the nature of his father who lived down the road in that wonderful mansion. Because that boy had the nature of his father, he didn't like eating out of a trough. He didn't like eating the swill that the swine ate. He enjoyed sitting down at a table covered with a white linen tablecloth and eating with a knife and fork. He liked having a nice steak or prime rib before him, with all the other delicacies, topped off with ice cream. That boy didn't care for the pigpen for he had the nature of his father.

Peter says you are now identified with Christ. When you came to the Lord Jesus and were born again, the Spirit of God baptized you, that is, He identified you with Christ.

Now let that mind, that thought, be in you which is in Christ. Christ is up yonder at God's right hand in a body totally devoted to the service of God for you and me. Do you think, my friend, if you have really been born again, if you are really a child of God with a new nature, that you can go on living in sin? Now I am a Calvinist and I emphasize the security of the believer. However, I think that there is such an overemphasis on that point that many of our Arminian friends also need to be heard today. This is one reason I feel as kindly as I do toward the Pentecostals; they are preaching a doctrine that has been largely forgotten, the doctrine of holiness. They emphasize that believers should live a holy life for God today. My friend, you *cannot* be a child of God and go out and live in the pigpen. Let's face it—if you do, you are a pig. Pigs live in pigpens and they love it, but sons do not love the pigpen.

Peter says that God has made every provision for you: you are born again, indwelt by the Spirit, baptized by the Spirit, identified with Christ, and you can now live life by the power of the Spirit of God. In Romans 7 Paul shows how the Christian is defeated when he lives in the flesh, but in Romans 8 he tells how God has provided the Holy Spirit that we might live by the power of the Spirit. Again I come back to this word *pauō*. It is not used in the active voice; what we have here is a word that does not mean "cease," but means "hath got release." God has made every arrangement for you and me not to live in sin today. It would be impossible for us to live in sin. Oh, the son might go to the pigpen, but you can put this down for sure, he will not *stay* in the pigpen. One day he has to say, "I will arise and go to my father . . ." (Luke 15:18).

If you are living in sin today and you are comfortable in it, I would surely question your salvation. Someone may ask, "Can a Christian do this or do that?" He might do it one time, my friend, but if he lives in sin there is something radically wrong. A child of God with a new nature longs to please Christ in all things. This is the reason that I believe the study of the entire Word of God is essential today. I know that I will be accused of playing on an instrument of only one string. Well, since I'm no musician, I have an instrument with only one string on it, and it is this: You need the *total* Word of God—not just a few little verses to draw out some little legalistic system by which to live the Christian life. You *cannot* live the Christian life by following rules. You can live the Christian life only by having the mind of Christ, by having the Spirit of God moving in you to please God and to refrain from those things which bring disgrace to Him.

That he no longer should live the rest of his time in the flesh to the lusts of men, but to the will of God [1 Pet. 4:2].

Paul speaks very strongly in this connection in Romans 8: "For they that are after the flesh do mind the things of the flesh; but they that are after the Spirit the things of the Spirit. For to be carnally minded is death; but to be spiritually minded is life and peace" (Rom. 8:5–6). What does Paul mean when he says "to be carnally minded is death"? Do you lose your salvation? No, it means you are dead to any fellowship with God. "If we say that we have fellowship with him, and walk in darkness, we lie, and do not the truth" (1 John 1:6). My friend, you *cannot* live in sin and have fellowship with God. Sin is what is keeping people away from the Word of God today. I have to confess that Christians are a minority, and in teaching through the entire Bible as I do, I appeal only to the minority of the minority. A great many folk are trying to find a shortcut to living the Christian life, and there is no shortcut. God says that He will use suffering in your life in order to keep you from sin.

"That he no longer should live the rest of his time in the flesh to the lusts of men, but to the will of God." We no longer take life for granted, for we have suffered, and God will use that suffering to keep us from sin.

As he continues, Peter begins to look ahead. Life is short—

For the time past of our life may suffice us to have wrought the will of the Gentiles, when we walked in lasciviousness, lusts, excess of wine, revellings, banquetings, and abominable idolatries [1 Pet. 4:3].

After we have been converted, we would be very foolish to spend our lives in the things which we did before. In fact, we cannot do that. We are now joined to Christ; we are united to Him, and we cannot run with the world to sinning. We must live today for God. What a tremendous truth this is! Life is short; time is fleeting, and we must recognize that we are going to come before Him for judgment before long.

"When we walked in lasciviousness, lusts, excess of wine, revellings, banquetings, and abominable idolatries." Simon Peter spells out the sins here. Homer Rodeheaver was a personal friend of mine, and I loved him in the

Lord. Years ago as we were having lunch together, I said to him, "Homer, you were with Billy Sunday for so many years. What do you say was the secret of his ministry?" He replied, "He preached on sin, and he always was specific when he spoke about sin. He spelled it out." Simon Peter spells it out here.

"Lasciviousness"—that's living in sexual sin. "Lusts"—that includes a great many things, lusting after the things of the flesh. "Excess of wine" is drunkenness. "Revellings, banquetings, and abominable idolatries." "Banquetings" should be translated "carousing." "Abominable idolatries"—the Scriptures tell us that the love of money is the root of all evil; covetousness is idolatry in our day. These are the things which will take you away from God, and Peter clearly spells them out.

I am afraid that today we have a great many preachers who are pretty indefinite about sin. Some wag wrote: "If you've got religion, you don't know it. If you know it, you haven't got it. And if you've got it, you can't lose it. And if you lose it, you didn't have it. And if you never had it, you can't get it." Some of the talk I hear today sounds as vague as that. My friend, sin is spelled out here. It is written in bold letters; it's in neon lights in the Word of God, and there is no way of missing it.

Wherein they think it strange that ye run not with them to the same excess of riot, speaking evil of you [1 Pet. 4:4].

Either you are going to please God or you'll please men. And if you are pleasing men, you will not please God. The Lord Jesus said, "If the world hate you, ye know that it hated me before it hated you" (John 15:18). If the world does not hate you, then there is something radically wrong.

When I was sixteen years old, I began to work in a bank. They put me on the teller's cage when I was seventeen and promised me that the next year I would be made a junior officer. I felt that I was well liked and popular in that bank. Then I went to a young people's conference where I made my decision for Christ and to study for the ministry. I came back to the bank and resigned, yet they let me have a part-time job—they were good to me in that way. But I found out that I was no longer the popular boy in that place. As a Christian I became very unpopular. In fact, the fellows with whom I had run ridiculed me, and they did a good job of it because they knew what my life had been before. That was a very difficult decision I made at that particular time.

I hope that I am not misunderstood when I tell this little story. In those days I went to dances; in fact, I was chairman of a dance committee. After I made my decision for Christ, I thought I would break off my old ties gradually. I went to the next dance with the idea that I would not dance but I would just stand around in the stag line. As I was standing there, I felt very much out of place. There was a fellow there from the bank above whom I had been promoted. He didn't care much for me, especially when I announced that I was studying for the ministry—yet he was an officer in a church himself. He came over to me at that dance and said, "This is a h—— of a place for a preacher to be!" Do you know, that was the first time he had ever told me the truth. I agreed with him. I found out that you cannot break off gradually. The world is not going to appreciate you very much when as a Christian you try to continue on with them. I walked out of that place, never to walk back in again.

My friend, I do not believe that you can go on in sin if you are a child of God. You have the nature of Christ; you are joined to Him. He suffered down here once; He is suffering no more, but He can help you. He sent the Holy Spirit down to indwell those who are His own. We have been baptized into the body of believers, as Peter has pointed out to us, and now, being filled with the Holy Spirit, we can live for God. We cannot do it in our own strength but in His strength.

Who shall give account to him that is ready to judge the quick and the dead [1 Pet. 4:5].

"Ready to judge the quick [the living] and the dead." The whole world, the living and the dead, are going to be judged by the Lord Jesus someday. Will He judge believers, too? He sure will! Not for salvation, which was assured when they became children of God, but He will not let a believer get by with sin since He is judging the world for sin. Because God does judge Christians in the world—He chastens His children—the unbeliever had better beware. He is warned that he will come up someday for judgment.

For for this cause was the gospel preached also to them that are dead, that they might be judged according to men in the flesh, but live according to God in the spirit [1 Pet. 4:6].

"For this cause"—that is, because of coming judgment, the gospel was preached. God wants the gospel preached to all men. And if they don't hear the gospel or respond to the gospel, He makes it very clear that they are already dead in trespasses and sins, and they will be judged as men in the flesh. But if they accept Christ, they can live according to God in the Spirit. The Lord Jesus said in John 5:24, "Verily, verily, I say unto you, He that heareth my word, and believeth on him that sent me, hath everlasting life, and shall not come into condemnation; but is passed from *death* unto life"—he was in a state of death. He further amplified this thought at the time of the death of Lazarus: "Jesus said unto her [Martha], I am the resurrection, and the life: he that believeth in me, though he were *dead*, yet shall he live: And whosoever liveth and believeth in me shall never die. Believest thou this?" (John 11:25–26, italics mine). In other words, you and I were *dead* in trespasses and sins. Paul meant the same thing when he wrote to the Ephesians, "And you hath he quickened, who were dead in trespasses and sins" (Eph. 2:1). We were spiritually dead. Paul went on to say, "Wherein in time past ye walked according to the course of this world. . . . fulfilling the desires of the flesh . . ." (Eph. 2:2–3). Peter is saying the same thing here in this verse. The gospel is being preached, and when the gospel is being preached, two things happen. Some accept it, and if they accept it, they are going to live for God and live throughout eternity. Others reject it, and those who reject the gospel are the men who are dead in sins and are dead to God throughout eternity; that is, they have no relation to Him whatsoever.

But the end of all things is at hand: be ye therefore sober, and watch unto prayer [1 Pet. 4:7].

"But the end of all things is at hand." That has been true since the day the Lord Jesus went back to heaven. Paul could say that the coming of Christ was imminent: "Looking for that blessed hope, and the glorious appearing of the great God and our Saviour Jesus Christ" (Titus 2:13). Peter says, "The end of all things is at hand." God is going to bring this world to a standstill one of these days while He judges it. He will take His own out of the world, and there will be a lot of things to straighten up in the lives of believers. They will go before the judgment seat of Christ, not regarding salvation but regarding rewards, regarding the life which they have lived for God. This is another reason we should live for God—we are coming up for judgment.

"Be ye therefore sober, and watch unto prayer." "Sober" should be translated "sober-minded." Peter uses this expression a great deal. He actually means, "Be ye therefore *intelligent*." Be an intelligent Christian. An intelligent Christian is one who knows the Bible; that is, he will know it the best he can. (I often make the confession that I marvel at my ignorance of the Word of God. The more I study it, the more I see how little I really know about the Word of God.) But, my friend, an intelligent, sober-minded Christian is going to know all he can about the Word of God.

The Christian is also to be intelligent in this evil world. The Lord Jesus said to His disciples, "Be ye therefore wise as serpents, and harmless as doves" (Matt. 10:16). You need to have the wisdom of a serpent today; if you don't, another snake around the corner is going to bite you, I can assure you of that!

"Watch unto prayer." In other words, prayer should have in it that anticipation, that expectation of the coming of Christ. Our prayer meetings are dead today because we are not looking for Him. He is the *living* Christ. We ought to talk to Him now for we are going to talk to Him hereafter. And at the judgment He is going to talk to us—that is the thing I'm not so sure I'm looking forward to!

And above all things have fervent charity among yourselves: for charity shall cover the multitude of sins [1 Pet. 4:8].

"Have fervent love among yourselves: for charity [love] shall cover the multitude of sins." Peter is talking about our relations as believers today. The writer of the Proverbs said, "Hatred stirreth up strifes: but love covereth all sins" (Prov. 10:12). Hatred in a church will stir up strife. This little clique will be against that little clique, and these folk will be against somebody else, and all that type of thing. But love covers up all that. Maybe you don't like the way your pastor combs his hair. I knew a pastor in Texas who told me that he had a lock of hair right on top of his head which would always stand up no matter how he combed it. He said that the choir threatened to quit because of it. They sat behind him and could always see that hair come up sometime during his sermon. They actually became angry with him because of that lock of hair. Every time he went for a haircut he had the barber cut it off because he did not want to offend his choir. Imagine that type of thing! If they had had love in their hearts, that lock of hair wouldn't have bothered them one bit.

Use hospitality one to another without grudging [1 Pet. 4:9].

I think hospitality can also be expressed in ways other than entertaining in your home. The minister who is traveling and speaking in conferences needs to be alone. He and his wife need to have a room in a motel where he can study and pray rather than be in a home where he has to carry on conversation all the time. May I say, if you want to extend hospitality to your visiting speaker, take care of his motel bill. Maybe you could also invite him out for dinner.

"Without grudging." However we extend our hospitality, it should be done with real warmth.

As every man hath received the gift, even so minister the same one to another, as good stewards of the manifold grace of God [1 Pet. 4:10].

"As every man hath received the gift"—"the gift" means a particular spiritual gift, and there are many gifts. Paul tells us in 1 Corinthians 12 that there is one body and many members and that the church is a body in which there are many members and many gifts. I don't know who you are, and I don't know what your gift is; I do know that if you are a child of God, you have some gift and you are to be using it in serving one another.

If any man speak, let him speak as the oracles of God; if any man minister, let him do it as of the ability which God giveth: that God in all things may be glorified through Jesus Christ, to whom be praise and dominion for ever and ever. Amen [1 Pet. 4:11].

If a man is not speaking the Word of God, he has no business standing in the pulpit. We have no business saying we are teaching the Bible when we are not really teaching it.

"If any man minister, let him do it as of the ability which God giveth." In other words, here is one man who teaches the Bible one way and another who teaches it another way, and you say, "I like this one, and I don't like the other." Well, the other man's method may appeal to someone to whom your man doesn't appeal. We should let each one minister "as of the ability which God giveth."

"That God in all things may be glorified through Jesus Christ, to whom be praise and dominion for ever and ever. Amen." Peter says that we are to teach the Word of God in such a way that God may get glory through Jesus Christ.

Peter is now going to talk about a different type of suffering. The people to whom he was writing were now moving into the orbit of the hurricane of persecution which broke out during the reign of Nero. Nero had already begun the persecution of the Christians in Rome, and it was spreading out through the empire. Peter warns his people that they are moving into that orbit of suffering. Many of them would become martyrs. You and I may not become martyrs—I trust we won't—but we are going to suffer in this world, my friend.

Beloved, think it not strange concerning the fiery trial which is to try you, as though some strange thing happened unto you [1 Pet. 4:12].

"Think it not *strange* concerning the fiery trial which is to try [test] you." When suffering comes most of us react as if it were something strange—we feel that nobody else has ever suffered like we have suffered. When I was a pastor in Cleburne, Texas, I went one day to a home on one side of the railroad tracks to visit a family in which there had just been a suicide. I went there to minister the Word to them. They said to me, "Dr. McGee, why in the world did this happen to us? No one has ever been called upon to suffer as we are suffering." When I left their home I crossed over to the "wrong side of the railroad tracks" to visit another family. They too had just had a suicide in the family. Do you know what they said to me? "Dr. McGee, why should this happen to us? No one has ever been called upon to go through anything like this." We all tend to think that our suffering is strange, that it is unlike anything that has been suffered before.

My friend, I do not know what your problem is, but I assure you that it is not something strange. Others have gone through the same thing, and you will never be the one who will suffer more than anyone else. When Paul was chosen as an apostle, the Lord said, ". . . I will shew him how great things he must suffer for my name's sake" (Acts 9:16). Paul has gone the limit of suffering; therefore you will not be going the limit, and you should not consider your suffering a strange thing. All of us fall into this fallacy in our thinking. I know that I could not believe it when the doctor told me that I had cancer. I thought *you* could have cancer, but I never thought *I* could have cancer. I thought that cancer was something for somebody else but not for me.

"The fiery trial which is to try [test] you" should be "which *is testing* you"—that is, it was going on right then—"as though some strange thing *was happening* unto you." These believers were already being tested by suffering. Suffering is not something which is accidental; it is the normal Christian experience. Peter says, "Don't think it's strange, because this is the normal experience of believers."

"Fiery trial" is literally *smelted in a furnace*. David spoke of the fact that God's testing of him was like putting silver into a furnace to purify it. We find this thought throughout all of Scripture. Peter has now mentioned this fiery trial several times. He had personally endured suffering, and he was yet to die a martyr's death by crucifixion.

This little poem expresses it the best—

Out from the mine and the darkness,
  Out from the damp and the mold,
Out from the fiery furnace,
  Cometh each grain of gold.
Crushed into atoms and leveled
  Down to the humblest dust
With never a heart to pity,
  With never a hand to trust.

Molten and hammered and beaten
  Seemeth it ne'er to be done.
Oh, for such fiery trial,
  What hath the poor gold done?
Oh, 'twere a mercy to leave it
  Down in the damp and the mold.
If this is the glory of living,
  Then better to be dross than gold.

Under the press and the roller,
  Into the jaws of the mint,
Stamped with the emblem of freedom,
  With never a flaw or a dint.
Oh, what a joy, the refining,
  Out of the damp and the mold.
And stamped with the glorious image,
  Oh, beautiful coin of gold!

"In the Crucible"
—Author unknown

God has a purpose in our suffering, my friend.

But rejoice, inasmuch as ye are partakers of Christ's sufferings; that, when his glory shall be revealed, ye may be glad also with exceeding joy [1 Pet. 4:13].

Why are we to rejoice in trials? Because suffering prepares us for the coming of Christ. Paul wrote in Romans 8:17, "And if children, then heirs; heirs of God, and joint-heirs with Christ; if so be that we suffer with him, that we may be also glorified together." I think we need to face up to the fact that there is no shortcut to living the Christian life. There is

no easy way. Let me repeat, the Christian life is a banquet—because He has invited us to the table of salvation—but it is not a picnic. We are to suffer for Him and with Him. And we will know the reason for each testing when we stand in His presence someday. I tell you, I would be embarrassed to sit down with Paul in glory and be on the same level with him, because he suffered so much. And today some folk criticize Simon Peter, but we are also going to look up to him when we get to heaven. The Word of God makes it very clear that suffering is a part of the Christian life. Suffering is what develops you. We hear so much talk about how everything is supposed to be smooth and lovely in the Christian marriage and in the Christian home. My friend, I do not agree with that at all—sorrow and suffering will come to the Christian home. I know of nothing that drew my wife and me together like the death of our first little one. And believe me, we wanted that little one. We sat in that hospital room and simply wept and prayed together. That is still a sacred memory in our lives—it *did* something for us.

If ye be reproached for the name of Christ, happy are ye; for the spirit of glory and of God resteth upon you: on their part he is evil spoken of, but on your part he is glorified [1 Pet. 4:14].

This is strange language, whether it is in the Greek or in the English. "If you are reproached for the name of Christ, you ought to rejoice in it," Peter says.

"For the spirit of glory and of God resteth upon you." Again may I say, suffering is a token that you are a child of God. The greatest proof that you are a child of God is that you can endure suffering. If you are being carried around on a silver platter with a silver spoon in your mouth, you must not be God's child because that is not the way He does things.

"On their part he is evil spoken of, but on your part he is glorified." You can glorify God whatever comes. It is said that during the devastating San Francisco earthquake of 1906 there was a dear, wonderful Christian lady who came out and was singing praises to God. Everybody else was crying, and some were praying for the first time in their lives. Someone asked her, "What do you mean by singing praises to God at a time like this?" She replied, "I thank God that I have a God who is strong enough to shake this little earth!" I say "amen" to that. However, there are very few people who could praise God during the time of an earthquake.

But let none of you suffer as a murderer, or as a thief, or as an evildoer, or as a busybody in other men's matters [1 Pet. 4:15].

Peter puts murder right down with gossiping and criticizing others; he makes no distinction between them at all. Paul did the same thing. Actually, Paul and Peter and James agree on everything. They are all preaching the same gospel that produces the same kind of a life.

Peter says that we ought not to be suffering for our own sins. God never tests you with sin, my friend; He never tests you with evil, as James makes clear to us in his epistle. Peter says, "Let none of you suffer as a murderer."

Yet if any man suffer as a Christian, let him not be ashamed; but let him glorify God on this behalf [1 Pet. 4:16].

My heart goes out to the Christian who is in prison today because he is truly suffering punishment. However, if he is suffering because of his own sin, he cannot glorify God for the fact that he is in prison, but he can glorify the Lord and witness for Him in the midst of it.

For the time is come that judgment must begin at the house of God: and if it first begin at us, what shall the end be of them that obey not the gospel of God? [1 Pet. 4:17].

"For the time is come that judgment must begin at the house of God." Believers are going to appear before the judgment seat of Christ. Paul wrote, "For we must all appear before the judgment seat of Christ; that every one may receive the things done in his body, according to that he hath done, whether it be good or bad" (2 Cor. 5:10). "We"—Paul is talking about Christians. "That every one may receive the things done in his body"—that is, the things done while you were living down here. "According to that he hath done, whether it be good or bad"—we all must come before Christ's judgment seat.

Peter continues, "If it first begin at us, what shall the end be of them that obey not the gospel of God?" Christ has paid the penalty for our sins, but suppose that we have lived a life that has not brought glory to Him? My friend, we are to be judged. And if God is going to judge His own, what about the lost world which would not hear or obey the gospel of God?

And if the righteous scarcely be saved, where shall the ungodly and the sinner appear? [1 Pet. 4:18].

In other words, we as believers just barely made it. The righteous are saved only by the death of Christ and their faith in Christ. That is the only way we ever got saved, and we just barely made it, my friend. During a recent period of physical recuperation, my wife and I reminisced about our past lives. We really got acquainted in new ways, and I kidded her, "My, I'm just now coming to know you. I think maybe we ought to get married now that I know you!" But I also said to her, "When I look back at my life, how I started out on the wrong track, the wrong foot, it is nothing but a miracle that God ever saved me. I just marvel at it. I just barely made it."

John Wesley spoke of himself as "a brand plucked from the burning," and that is true of most of us. When John Wesley came to America, he was not saved, he was not a Christian. He made this statement, "I came to America to convert Indians, but who is going to convert John Wesley?" His biographer tells us that at the governor's court in Georgia he met one of the noblemen of Great Britain who had been sent over to administer that area. He was a very wealthy man with a name, and he had married a beautiful, young wife. That young woman and John Wesley began to eye each other, and evidently John Wesley fell in love with her. He asked her to leave and go with him to live among the Indians. And he thought he was a Christian and a missionary! But she sent him back to England, saying, "John, this won't work. I love you, and I'll always love you, but God has called you to do something for Him." She evidently was a Christian, and so she sent him back to England. It is said that three times he started up the gangplank, and three times he started to walk back. But she motioned him to go, and he went back to England. One night walking down Aldersgate, he went upstairs and heard a man speaking on Galatians. Later, he could write in his journal, "I felt my heart strangely warmed. I felt that I did trust Christ, Christ alone, for my salvation, and there was given to me an assurance that He had forgiven me of my sins."

Now if the righteous scarcely be saved, if they be but brands plucked from the burning, "where shall the ungodly and the sinner appear?" Peter asks. My friend, if you are not a Christian, and if Vernon McGee just barely made it and made it only by trusting Christ, how do you think you are going to make it? There is not but one hope—there is only one way of salvation. The Lord Jesus said, "I am the way" (see John 14:6).

Wherefore let them that suffer according to the will of God commit the keeping of their souls to him in well-doing, as unto a faithful Creator [1 Pet. 4:19].

Those who have really suffered know what it is to commit themselves to God. Paul spoke of this when he said, ". . . I know whom I have believed, and am persuaded that he is able to keep that which I have committed unto him against that day" (2 Tim. 1:12). What had Paul committed unto Him? Some people believe this refers to the gospel which God committed to Paul. I'll agree with that, but I think the deeper meaning is that Paul is saying, "I came to Christ and simply committed everything to Him. I made a deposit. What things were gain to me I counted loss, and what was loss became gain to me, in order that I might win Christ." Paul listed about eight different things that he formerly trusted for his salvation (see Phil. 3:1–6). Then he said, "But what things were gain to me, those I counted loss for Christ. Yea doubtless, and I count all things but loss for the excellency of the knowledge of Christ Jesus my Lord: for whom I have suffered the loss of all things, and do count them but dung, that I may win Christ" (Phil. 3:7–8). In effect, he was saying, "I flushed all that down; I trusted that no longer. I only trusted Christ."

Peter says, "Let them that suffer . . . commit the keeping of their souls to him." Have you really trusted Him? You probably have a safety deposit box in which you keep your valuables. When you go to sleep at night, you don't worry about them at all. My friend, I went to sleep last night, and I didn't worry about Vernon McGee's soul. Do you know why? I went to sleep last night in peace because Christ has taken care of all that. I've made my deposit with Him, and I trust Him today. Have you made a deposit with Him? Have you committed your soul to Him? May I say, if you have done that, even when trouble comes to you, even when the dark day comes, even when you are called to go down through the valley, you can do it knowing that He will take care of you.

God hath not promised skies always blue,
  Flower-strewn pathways all our lives
    through;
God hath not promised sun without rain,
  Joy without sorrow, peace without
    pain.

God hath not promised we shall not know
  Toil and temptation, trouble and woe;
He hath not told us we shall not bear
  Many a burden, many a care.

God hath not promised smooth roads and
    wide,
  Swift, easy travel, needing no guide;
Never a mountain, rocky and steep,
  Never a river, turbid and deep.

But God hath promised strength for the
    day,
  Rest for the laborer, light for the way,
Grace for the trials, help from above,
  Unfailing sympathy, undying love.

"God Hath Not Promised"
—Annie Johnson Flint

Have you made your deposit, my friend? Have you committed your soul unto Him?

CHAPTER 5

THEME: Suffering and the second coming of Christ produce service and hope, humility and patience

SUFFERING AND THE SECOND COMING OF CHRIST

In this final chapter of 1 Peter, suffering and the second coming of Christ are brought together. What is the relation of our suffering to the second coming of Christ? The Christian life began for each of us with the suffering of the Lord Jesus Christ on the cross where He bore the penalty of our sins. There is also suffering in the life of the child of God today because God uses suffering in our lives to sharpen us and to make us the kind of Christians that He wants and that He can use. I have divided this chapter into two sections: Verses 1–4 teach that suffering produces service and hope; verses 5–14 teach that suffering produces humility and patience.

We have, therefore, the suffering of Christ in the past and the present suffering of the saints, and then we have the second coming of Christ. Every Christian ought to have the second coming of Christ in his plan and his program for the future. We are often told that we need to have a life plan. Is the second coming of Christ—when He comes to take you out of the world and then returns with you to reign on the earth—a part of your program? Or is it some ethereal, ephemeral thing which hangs out there in space like a will-o'-the-wisp that really has no meaning in your life at all? His second coming is not just a doctrine; it is something which enters into our lives. There is nothing which will buoy you up in time of trouble and suffering like the *reality* of the second coming of Christ. I am going to see Him some day; I am going to come into His presence! What a time of real blessing that will be, and Peter tells us that our present suffering is related to that.

SUFFERING PRODUCES SERVICE AND HOPE

The elders which are among you I exhort, who am also an elder, and a witness of the sufferings of Christ, and also a partaker of the glory that shall be revealed [1 Pet. 5:1].

Peter begins by asserting his position; however, he doesn't call himself even an apostle here. He is speaking of the fact that he is an elder—"who am also an elder." That means there were other men who were elders.

The Greek word used here, *presbuteros*, is a word which is sometimes used in speaking of a person being an elder or older person. The Greek word which is translated "bishop" is *episkopos*, and it speaks of the office of the man, not the person of the man. It is the spiritual office of shepherding; the same word is used for "shepherd." This is all that Simon Peter ever claimed to be—he calls himself a fellow elder. He never claimed a superior place above his brethren, but as a fellow elder he exhorts them.

"And a witness of the sufferings of Christ." Peter was in a unique position because he was a witness of the sufferings of Christ.

"And also a partaker of the glory that shall be revealed." In the past Peter saw that glory. In his second epistle, Peter identifies this as taking place on the Mount of Transfiguration. Peter saw Him die yonder on Mount Calvary, and he saw Him transfigured yonder on the Mount of Transfiguration. That mount was probably in the north, and I have always felt that Mount Hermon could have been the place, although the geographical location is not important. What took place there is important, and Peter says that he was a witness of it. However, there is a glory that is coming in the future which will be greater than that— "the glory that shall be revealed."

Feed the flock of God which is among you, taking the oversight thereof, not by constraint, but willingly; not for filthy lucre, but of a ready mind [1 Pet. 5:2].

Peter is emphasizing the fact that an elder, occupying the office of a bishop (elders are never spoken of in the singular, there was never to be only one), is to be the shepherd of a flock. Shepherding suggests provision and protection, supervision and discipline, instruction and direction. The ministry of an elder is to be performed in a very positive way, but Peter also gives a negative injunction.

First of all, Peter says that elders are to minister for the right reason, in the right spirit, not because they *must* do it but because they freely choose to do so. Will you notice what he says: "Feed the flock of God which is among you, taking the oversight thereof, not by constraint, but *willingly*." Do it willingly. God doesn't want you to take an office in the church in this pouting spirit: "Well, if you can't get anybody else to do it, I'll do it." My friend, don't you do it, because that is not the reason to serve Him. There is no value in serving Him if you are doing it under constraint.

"Not for filthy lucre, but of a ready mind." Peter makes it clear that there must not only be the right reason—the right spirit, because they freely choose to serve—but there must also be the right motive for service. It is not to be for material gain but for the sheer delight of doing it. An elder is to find satisfaction in the job itself rather than in what he gets out of it.

A number of years ago my daughter and I were driving the freeway into Los Angeles together since she also had a job with the church that I was then serving as pastor. As usual, we got stuck in the traffic on the freeway. I said to her, "Look around at these people. Do you see anybody who looks happy? There they sit, under tension and pressure, trying to get to a job which they despise. Most people today are doing a job they do not like to do at all. It's wonderful to be in the Lord's service where you can do your job because you love to do it and you want to do it." That has made the ministry of teaching the Word of God a sheer joy to me. Simon Peter says that there must be a right motive in Christian service.

Neither as being lords over God's heritage, but being ensamples to the flock [1 Pet. 5:3].

In other words, an elder should exercise his ministry in the right manner, not driving but leading, not domineering but setting an example. It is a work, therefore, in which he ought to be an example to the flock. I do not think that a preacher should get into the pulpit and browbeat his congregation to do something that he actually is not doing himself. I made it a practice never to ask my congregation to give to any cause to which I didn't also give. I do not think we have a right to make a demand of other folk that we are not doing ourselves.

And when the chief Shepherd shall appear, ye shall receive a crown of glory that fadeth not away [1 Pet. 5:4].

An elder's ministry should be done with the proper awareness that he serves the Chief Shepherd to whom he is answerable and who will Himself reward his service with rewards which are eternal. Don't get the impression that we are working for nothing. We are not.

Paul made it clear that a Christian is not to work for nothing. You are to work for Him and look to Him for a reward some day. That is the way we are to serve Him.

"Ye shall receive a crown of glory that fadeth not away." There are many crowns mentioned in Scripture, including the crown of life and the crown of righteousness. What is a crown of glory? I believe that it means we are going to share some day in His glory.

In a study I made many years ago, I found about a dozen different words in the Old Testament which were translated by the word *glory. Glory* is a word that is often used today. What do you understand by the word *glory?* How big is glory? What shape is it? What color it is? What is glory? I suspect that the average Christian would have nothing but the foggiest notion about the meaning of *glory.*

I have found that glory does have shape and size. Listen to the Word of God: "The heavens declare the glory of God; and the firmament sheweth his handiwork" (Ps. 19:1). The size of the universe, as determined by our scientific measurements, is staggering yet is probably only the front yard of God's great universe. That is glory—the greatness of our God.

What about the color of glory? Look up at this vast universe at night; look up at the sky. And look at the earth. In the fall, especially if you live in New England, take a good look at the leaves on the trees. It is wonderful to be in that part of the country and to see all the color. That's glory—the glory of God. I know a retired man who lives here in Southern California, and he raises some of the most beautiful roses and zinnias I have ever seen. Oh, are they colorful! One time while I was visiting him in his garden, he reached down and lifted up the head of one of those zinnias, and he said, "In the springtime I simply put a little seed in the ground. Look at what has come up! And then they try to tell me there is no God!" Glory has color, my friend.

May I say to you, God's glory is something that is quite wonderful, and we are going to share in that some day. He calls it a *crown* of glory.

Peter calls Him "the chief Shepherd" here. The *Good* Shepherd gives His life for the sheep—that is seen in Psalm 22. The *Great* Shepherd watches over the sheep—that is seen in Psalm 23. In Psalm 24 He is the *Chief* Shepherd who is coming again. Some day our Chief Shepherd is going to appear, and He will still have with Him His flock, and we will be members of that flock. How wonderful this is!

SUFFERING PRODUCES HUMILITY
AND PATIENCE

**Likewise, ye younger, submit your-
selves unto the elder. Yea, all of you be
subject one to another, and be clothed
with humility: for God resisteth the
proud, and giveth grace to the humble.**

**Humble yourselves therefore under the
mighty hand of God, that he may exalt
you in due time [1 Pet. 5:5–6].**

"**L**ikewise, ye younger, submit yourselves
unto the elder." This has been reversed
in our day—today the elder is supposed to
submit to the younger. Young people are the
ones who are protesting, and they are the ones
who want to discard the establishment.
However, the Christian young person needs to
realize that the Word of God says, "Ye
younger, submit yourselves unto the elder."
After all, your father, if you have a good or a
godly father, has a lot of sense and maybe
more sense than you have.

A friend of mine told me, "I was ashamed of
my dad at the time when I went away to
college. Although he had made good money,
and he was an executive, I was ashamed of
him. He had such old-fashioned ideas; he was a
real square. When I finished college and got
out in the business world, I didn't see him for
a couple of years. When I did see him again, I
was absolutely amazed to see how much he'd
learned in just six years!" A lot of young people find out, after they themselves have been
out in the school of hard knocks for awhile,
that their dads have learned a great deal.

"Yea, all of you be subject one to another."
In other words, believers should not insist on
having their way over others.

"And be *clothed* with humility." Actually, we
are to be armed with it; that is the picture that
is given here.

"For God resisteth the proud, and giveth
grace to the humble." Peter has talked a great
deal about humility and about grace. A proud
person will not be able to experience the grace
of God. It is only when you and I come in
humility that we will be able to know the grace
of God.

"Humble yourselves therefore under the
mighty hand of God, that he may exalt you in
due time." In view of the coming of Christ,
humility should be the attitude of the child of
God. Christ is the one who will establish justice and make things right when He comes.
You cannot straighten out this world, although you may think you can.

**Casting all your care upon him; for he
careth for you [1 Pet. 5:7].**

"He careth for you" literally means that it
matters to Him concerning you. Peter is talking about anxiety. The Lord Jesus said,
"Come unto Me all ye that labor and are heavy
laden, and I will rest you" (see Matt. 11:28).
Bring your burden of sins to Him, and He will
save you. Then come to Him later on, and He
will meet you and help you with your problems. Cast your care upon Him. Paul told the
Philippian believers, "Worry about nothing;
pray about everything." That is, take it to the
Lord in prayer, and leave it there—don't pick
it up again.

**Be sober, be vigilant; because your ad-
versary the devil, as a roaring lion,
walketh about, seeking whom he may
devour [1 Pet. 5:8].**

The word *sober* is from a different Greek word
than that used in 1 Peter 4:7. Here the word
means "to be watchful."

"Be sober, be vigilant; because your adversary the devil, as a roaring lion, walketh
about, seeking whom he may devour." We are
told to resist Satan; the Devil is loose in the
world today.

**Whom resist stedfast in the faith, know-
ing that the same afflictions are accomplished in your brethren that are in the
world [1 Pet. 5:9].**

"Whom resist stedfast in the faith." The picture here is of an army standing against an
enemy. We should stand with other believers.
I do not think you can resist the Devil by
yourself. You not only need the armor of God,
but you will also need other believers to stand
with you. That is the reason that whenever I
have need, I let all the listeners to my radio
broadcast know about it. I want them to stand
with me in prayer—we need to do that.
"Whom resist stedfast in the faith, knowing
that the same afflictions are accomplished in
your brethren that are in the world."

**But the God of all grace, who hath
called us unto his eternal glory by
Christ Jesus, after that ye have suffered
a while, make you perfect, stablish,
strengthen, settle you [1 Pet. 5:10].**

"But the God of all grace, who hath called us
unto his eternal glory by Christ Jesus"—that
is, "*in* Christ Jesus." We will have no glory in
ourselves. The church is sort of like the moon
which simply reflects the light of the sun. Our

glory will be only reflected glory, but we in Christ are going to share in that glory. Actually, the word *Jesus* is not in the better manuscripts; rather, this is that phrase which we often find in the New Testament—"*in* Christ."

"After that ye have suffered a while, make you perfect"—that is, bring you to perfection. "Stablish, strengthen"—the Lord Jesus told Simon Peter to strengthen the brethren (see Luke 22:32). "Settle you"—that means to restore you.

To him be glory and dominion for ever and ever. Amen [1 Pet. 5:11].

This is the benediction. And then Peter adds a little P.S.—

By Silvanus, a faithful brother unto you, as I suppose, I have written briefly, exhorting, and testifying that this is the true grace of God wherein ye stand [1 Pet. 5:12].

Peter is the author, but Silvanus wrote this for him. If you don't like the quality of the Greek here, blame Silvanus.

The church that is at Babylon, elected together with you, saluteth you; and so doth Marcus my son [1 Pet. 5:13].

"The church that is at Babylon, elected together with you, saluteth you." I think "Babylon" here means Babylon, although some think it is a figurative name for Rome. Simon Peter is too practical to have used a figurative term.

"And so doth Marcus my son." Marcus is John Mark, the writer of the Gospel of Mark, who was not Peter's natural son but his son in the faith. Although at one time Paul would not take him along on a missionary journey, Mark made good.

Greet ye one another with a kiss of charity. Peace be with you all that are in Christ Jesus. Amen [1 Pet. 5:14].

"Greet ye one another with a kiss of charity." Someone has said, "A kiss to a young girl is hope, to a married woman is faith, but to an old maid is charity." In our country and culture, I think we had better just use the handshake as the means of Christian greeting.

This is Peter's final benediction: "Peace be with you all that are in Christ Jesus. Amen."

BIBLIOGRAPHY

(Recommended for Further Study)

Barbieri, Louis A. *First and Second Peter.* Chicago, Illinois: Moody Press, 1977. (Fine, inexpensive survey.)

English, E. Schuyler. *The Life and Letters of St. Peter.* New York, New York: Our Hope, 1941. (Excellent.)

Hiebert, D. Edmond. *The Epistle of I Peter.* Chicago, Illinois: Moody Press, 1983. (Excellent, comprehensive treatment.)

Ironside, H. A. *Notes on James and Peter.* Neptune, New Jersey: Loizeaux Brothers, n.d.

Kelly, William. *The Epistles of Peter.* Addison, Illinois: Bible Truth Publishers, n.d.

Leighton, Robert. *A Practical Commentary on First Peter.* Grand Rapids, Michigan: Kregel Publications, 1845.

Lumby, J. Rawson. *The Epistles of Peter.* (Expositor's Bible.) Grand Rapids, Michigan: Wm. B. Eerdmans Publishing Company, 1943.

Meyer, F. B. *Tried by Fire* (1 Peter). Fort Washington, Pennsylvania: Christian Literature Crusade, n.d. (Rich, devotional study.)

Robertson, A. T. *Epochs in the Life of Simon Peter.* Grand Rapids, Michigan: Baker Book House, n.d.

Stibbs, Alan. *The First Epistle General of Peter.* Grand Rapids, Michigan: Wm. B. Eerdmans Publishing Company, 1959.

Thomas, W. H. Griffith. *The Apostle Peter.* Grand Rapids, Michigan: Wm. B. Eerdmans Publishing Company, 1956. (Excellent.)

Wolston, W. T. P. *Simon Peter—His Life and Letters.* London, England: James Nisbet and Company, 1896. (Excellent.)

Wuest, Kenneth S. *Wuest's Word Studies from the Greek New Testament for English Readers.* Grand Rapids, Michigan: Wm. B. Eerdmans Publishing Co., 1942. (1 Peter.)

The Second Epistle of

PETER

INTRODUCTION

Simon Peter is the author of this epistle (see 2 Pet. 1:1). However, the Petrine authorship of this epistle has been challenged more than the authorship of any other book in the New Testament. Dr. W. G. Moorehead wrote years ago, "The Second Epistle of Peter comes to us with less historical support of its genuineness than any other book of the New Testament." Nevertheless, this challenge caused conservative scholars to give adequate attention to this epistle so that today it is well established that Peter wrote this letter.

In my teaching I spend very little time on issues of introduction, that is, on the authorship and other critical issues that have been raised concerning the different books of the Bible. I would ordinarily just pass over this because, to me, 2 Peter is a part of the Word of God and I think there is an abundance of evidence both internal and external. However, since I would not want to be accused of not even being familiar with the questions that have been raised concerning its authorship, we will face the facts on this issue.

The Second Epistle of Peter was a long time in being accepted by the church into the canon of Scripture. It was accepted at the council that met at Laodicea in A.D. 372 and then again at Carthage in A.D. 397, which was really the first time that the church had taken that kind of stand. Jerome accepted 2 Peter for the Vulgate version of the Scriptures, but it was not included in the Peshitta Syriac version. However, that version is not an acceptable one at all—there are other things about it that I am sure we would all reject—and, therefore, it is perfectly meaningless that 2 Peter was not included in it. Eusebius, one of the early church fathers, placed 2 Peter among the disputed books. Origen accepted it. Clement of Alexandria accepted it, and he wrote a commentary on it. Second Peter is quoted in the Apocalypse of Peter, which, of course, is not accepted as canonical. The Epistle of Jude apparently draws from 2 Peter and demonstrates that Jude was well acquainted with it. There are allusions and quotations from 2 Peter by some of the early church writers, including Aristides, Justin Martyr, Irenaeus, Ignatius, and Clement of Rome. You will also find that Martin Luther accepted it as genuine. Calvin actually doubted it but did not reject it. Erasmus did reject it.

That gives you some of the history of the background of this epistle, but the reasons that this epistle has been rejected by some cannot be substantiated. There is a great deal of internal evidence, especially certain autobiographical sections (see 2 Pet. 1:13–14; 1:16–18; and 3:1), which are to me absolutely conclusive that Simon Peter wrote this epistle.

Peter's second epistle was written about A.D. 66, shortly after his first epistle (see 2 Pet. 3:1) and a short while before his martyrdom (see 2 Pet. 1:13–14).

Second Peter is the swan song of Peter, just as 2 Timothy is the swan song of Paul. There are striking similarities between the two books. Both epistles put up a warning sign along the pilgrim pathway the church is traveling to identify the awful apostasy that was on the way at that time and which in our time has now arrived. What was then like a cloud the size of a man's hand today envelops the sky and produces a storm of hurricane proportions. Peter warns of heresy among teachers; Paul warns of heresy among the laity.

Both Peter and Paul speak in a joyful manner of their approaching deaths (see 2 Pet. 1:13–14; 2 Tim. 4:6–8). Paul said that he knew that the time of his departure had come. He had finished his course. He had been on the racetrack of life, and now he was leaving it. He had fought a good fight, and he had kept the faith. A crown of righteousness was laid up for him. You will find that same triumphant note here in 2 Peter as Peter also faced the prospect of death.

Both apostles anchor the church on the Scriptures, on the Word of God, as the only defense against the coming storm of apostasy. It is no wonder that the enemy has attacked 2 Peter, because this is one of the finest shields that has been given to us to ward off the darts that the Wicked One is shooting at us today.

The similarities between 2 Peter and Paul's last epistle, 2 Timothy, also explain the sharp contrast between Peter's first and second letters. The subject of the second epistle has changed from that of the first; and the difference is, therefore, as great as that which exists between Paul's letters to the Romans and to Timothy.

In 2 Peter we see that apostasy is approaching, the storm is coming. How are we to prepare to meet it? There is only one way, Peter says, and that is through knowledge. Not only through faith in Christ, not only by believing in Him, but also to *know* Christ. "And this is life eternal," the Lord Jesus said, "that they might know thee the only true God, and Jesus Christ, whom thou hast sent" (John 17:3). We are to know *Him* and not only know *about* Him. I read the other day of an American preacher in Europe who is trying to start what he calls a Christian church without using the names of God and Christ. That is the most ridiculous thing that any man could possibly do. If he wants to start some kind of organization, let him go ahead and do it, but he cannot start anything that is Christian without Christ! To attempt to do that would be just like trying to make a peach pie without peaches or like trying to drive a car without any gasoline in the tank. If you are a Christian, you must know Christ. That means not to know about Him but to know Him—there is a great difference there.

The great subject of this epistle is going to be not only the apostasy but also that which will be our defense—knowledge. Where is this knowledge, and how does it come to us? Peter will say that the only way is through the Word of God, "a more sure word of prophecy," which he will talk about (2 Pet. 1:19).

You see, my friend, the Christian life is more than just a birth. It is a growth, and it is a development. The key to this entire epistle is the last verse: "But grow in grace, and in the knowledge of our Lord and Saviour Jesus Christ. To him be glory both now and for ever. Amen" (2 Pet. 3:18). Throughout the years of my ministry, I have often made the statement that I am not an obstetrician, I am a pediatrician. An obstetrician brings the little baby into the world. I thank the Lord that hundreds of people have been converted through listening to the Word of God, but actually I began my radio ministry of teaching the Word of God with the intention of helping believers to grow up in the faith. I am not an obstetrician bringing babies to birth, but a pediatrician whose job it is to give believers the milk of the Word and then to try to give them a porterhouse steak now and then. My friend, you will not be able to live for God in these days of apostasy unless you have a knowledge of the Word of God—and that is Peter's theme.

The theme of this second epistle is explained on the basis of the words which Peter uses here as contrasted to his first epistle. He does use certain words in both epistles. One word is *precious* which occurs twice in the first chapter. Peter, a great, big, rugged fisherman talked about things that are precious— that's a woman's word. The word *faith* is used again in this epistle and occurs twice in the first chapter. But the word that is especially characteristic of this second epistle is *knowledge*. It occurs sixteen times with cognate words. The epitome of the epistle is expressed in the injunction given in the final verse. This man Simon Peter went off the air saying, "But grow in grace, and in the knowledge of our Lord and Saviour Jesus Christ. To him be glory both now and for ever. Amen." This is what true Gnosticism is all about. The Gnostic heresy was that they had some little esoteric knowledge that no one else had. They had a form or formula, a rite or ritual, a secret order or password that you had to get on the inside in order to find out. Peter says that real knowledge is to know Jesus Christ.

OUTLINE

CHAPTER 1

THEME: *Addition of Christian graces gives assurance; author-ity of the Scriptures attested by fulfilled prophecy*

As I mentioned in the Introduction, this marvelous little epistle is the "swan song" of the apostle Peter; that is, it is his final word to believers before his death by crucifixion. He warns them of the apostasy which is coming, particularly of the heresy among teachers, and he seeks to anchor their faith on the Scriptures as the only defense against the coming storm.

In the first fourteen verses of this chapter, we shall see that the full "knowledge of God, and of Jesus our Lord" is the foundation on which Christian character is built.

ADDITION OF CHRISTIAN GRACES GIVES ASSURANCE

Simon Peter, a servant and an apostle of Jesus Christ, to them that have obtained like precious faith with us through the righteousness of God and our Saviour Jesus Christ [2 Pet. 1:1].

When we run across that little word *precious* in this very first verse, we recognize it as Peter's word—he uses it several times in his first epistle, and he is the only writer of Scripture who uses it in this sense. It is like being able to recognize the handwriting on a letter. It *is* like seeing Simon Peter's signature when we see the word *precious* here.

"Simon Peter" is the way he begins this second letter. In his first epistle he simply used the name *Peter.* Simon was the name given to him at his birth, but *Peter,* meaning "rock," is the name our Lord Jesus gave to him. He uses both names in this epistle. Simon, the man of weakness, and Peter, the man of strength, the wishy-washy man and the rock-man—he has been both. But as he writes this epistle, we may be sure of one thing: he is the rock-man now, the man who is to be crucified for Christ.

"Simon Peter, a servant and an apostle." The word *servant* actually means "bond slave." He doesn't take an exalted position in the church. He refers to himself as a bond slave—also an apostle (that is his authority), but notice that he does not say *the* apostle, but *an* apostle; he was only one of them.

"To them that have obtained like precious faith with us." What he is saying here is quite wonderful. When he uses the word *faith,* I think he means the body of truth which we call the gospel. He is saying, "You have received it, and it is up to you what you do with it."

Those who hold what I call a hyper-Calvinistic viewpoint say that you have to be chosen before you can be saved and that God has to give you the faith to believe. Well, I'll go along with part of that, but I also insist that the reason some folk don't come to Christ is made clear for us in the Word of God. Notice 2 Corinthians 3:15–16: "But even unto this day, when Moses is read, the veil is upon their heart. Nevertheless when it shall turn to the Lord, the veil shall be taken away." When it says that "it" shall turn to the Lord, what is "it"? Well, since the antecedent is the word *heart,* it is saying that when the heart shall turn to the Lord, the veil shall be taken away. My friend, if you are not a believer today, don't say it is because you have some *mental* reservations. The fact is that you have some *sinful* reservations. When the *heart* will turn to the Lord, then He will lift the veil. Anytime you are ready God is ready, and He will save you. It is not God's will that any should perish. Today it is "whosoever will may come" and ". . . God so loved the world, that he gave his only begotten Son, that *whosoever* believeth in him should not perish, but have everlasting life" (John 3:16, italics mine). All He asks you to do is believe. He doesn't even ask you to clean up before you come to Him—but *He* will clean you up if you really mean business with Him.

They "have obtained like precious faith"—how? "Through the righteousness of God and our Saviour Jesus Christ." This is the righteousness which is made over to us when we trust Christ as Savior. You see, He not only subtracts our sin, He also adds to us His own righteousness. We are not like criminals who have been pardoned and turned loose; we have been given a standing before God, and that standing is in Christ—accepted in the beloved!

Grace and peace be multiplied unto you through the knowledge of God, and of Jesus our Lord [2 Pet. 1:2].

"Grace and peace be multiplied." Grace and peace are always in this order. We must first know the grace of God—that God has saved us, not through our merit, our character, or anything in us, but He has saved us because of our faith in Christ. Because He loved us enough to die for us on the cross to pay the penalty of our sins, it is possible for Him to reach down and save us. Therefore, my friend, God saves you by grace. He saves you when you simply trust Christ, with no merit on your part. Once we experience God's grace, we can experience the peace of God also. This is what Paul is saying in his epistle to the Romans: "Therefore being justified by faith, we have peace with God through our Lord Jesus Christ" (Rom. 5:1).

Again let me say that we cannot consider Simon Peter an ignorant fisherman. As we see in his first epistle, he deals with more doctrine in a brief letter than any other New Testament writer. He takes up all controversial matters and handles them in a masterful way.

And he is a New Testament writer who uses arithmetic. He says, "Grace and peace be multiplied"—he is talking about multiplication. Paul didn't go into mathematics. He said that God is rich in grace and that the peace of God passes all understanding, but Simon Peter gets down to where the rubber meets the road. He takes out the multiplication table and says, "I hope grace and peace will be *multiplied* unto you." How wonderful this is.

He doesn't just leave it there. *How* will "grace and peace be multiplied unto you"? Will it be through some vision you have? Oh, no— "through the knowledge of God, and of Jesus our Lord."

Now we are back to this word *knowledge*. We will be seeing it again and again in this epistle because of its importance. Paul also emphasizes this. Writing to the Philippians, he said, "That I may know him, and the power of his resurrection, and the fellowship of his sufferings . . ." (Phil. 3:10)—oh, to *know* Him! Christianity is a Person. We are not only to believe Him but also to *know* Him, my friend. He is the living Savior who right at this moment is at God's right hand.

It was the prophet Daniel who wrote, ". . . but the people that do know their God shall be strong, and do exploits" (Dan. 11:32). My friend, you are not going to do anything for God in the way of service until you *know* Jesus Christ.

How does this knowledge come to you? Well, Peter won't leave you in doubt; he won't let you hang in midair. When he gets through with this epistle, you will know that the knowledge of Jesus Christ comes through a knowledge of the Word of God, the *sure* Word of God.

To illustrate what Peter is meaning by the knowledge of God, let me use the example of a well-known man who is no longer living. Suppose someone were to ask me, "Do you know the late President Eisenhower?" I would answer, "No, I never knew him."

"But you certainly heard about him."

"Yes."

"And you have seen him."

"Yes, I even saw him play golf once. I watched him hit the ball one time, but then the Secret Service men glared at me; so I had to get out of the territory. I did see him hit the ball, and the interesting thing is that he didn't do much better than I do. But I cannot really say that I knew him."

"If he were living today and were to walk right into your study, do you think you would know him?"

"I think I would recognize him, but I can't say that I would know him. I never knew how he felt about things. I suppose that Mrs. Eisenhower and his other loved ones knew him, but I never knew him."

When Peter writes, "Grace and peace be multiplied unto you through the *knowledge* of God, and of Jesus our Lord," he uses the Greek word *epignōsis*, meaning "super knowledge." It is a knowledge which comes by the Holy Spirit's taking the things of Christ and making them *real* to us. My friend, I believe that you can know Jesus Christ better than you can know your closest loved one. And you can tell Him things that you would not dare tell your closest loved one. The important thing is that to *know* Him is life eternal.

To know Him in this way, we first have to be born again, as Peter says, ". . . not of corruptible seed, but of incorruptible, by the word of God, which liveth and abideth for ever" (1 Pet. 1:23).

I remember hearing the late Dr. Herbert Bieber make the statement that after he was saved, he went to seminary to find out what had happened to him. That's good, and it reveals that you can *trust* Him and still not really *know* His Word.

According as his divine power hath given unto us all things that pertain unto life and godliness, through the knowledge of him that hath called us to glory and virtue [2 Pet. 1:3].

"His divine power" has given to us all of the things which you and I need to live life to the full. I don't know about you, but I have always wanted to live it up. I don't mean that I have wanted to go out and paint the town red—you run out of paint when you attempt that sort of thing. But "his divine power hath given unto us all things that pertain unto *life* and *godliness*." Don't say that God has not made an arrangement for you to live for Him. He has made *every* arrangement for our life in Christ and our godliness of life for Him.

"Through the knowledge of him that hath called us to glory and virtue." Again we see this word *knowledge*. It is only through the knowledge of Christ that you can really learn to live down here and grow to be a more godly person. The only way in the world that you can become the kind of person with a fully developed personality is through knowing Jesus Christ. The knowledge of Him that "hath called us to glory" means to be like Christ.

"And virtue"—*virtue* means something more than we commonly think it means. I have spent a great deal of time with some of the words Peter uses because of their importance. The word *virtue* is not confined to chastity. We use it today when we refer to a woman being virtuous or morally chaste. Actually, *virtue* as Peter uses it has to do with excellence and courage. It means that you have the courage to excel in life. You don't have to live a little, mousy Mr. Milquetoast life and be a yes-man to everything that comes along. You can stand on your own two feet, state your position, and be counted for God. We certainly need that kind of "virtue" in this hour in which we are living, and the only way we can get it is through the knowledge of Christ. This is the formula Peter is giving to us here: "through the *knowledge* of him that hath called us to glory and virtue."

Whereby are given unto us exceeding great and precious promises: that by these ye might be partakers of the divine nature, having escaped the corruption that is in the world through lust [2 Pet. 1:4].

Now why would Simon Peter call promises "precious"? In the first verse he talks about the precious faith that we have; now he talks about the precious promises that have been given to us. My friend, there have been given to you and me some glorious, wonderful promises here in the New Testament. Peter calls them "exceeding great and precious promises." For example: ". . . him that cometh to me I will in no wise cast out" (John 6:37); and "Come unto me, all ye that labour and are heavy laden, and I will give you rest" (Matt. 11:28)—the rest of redemption. "Take my yoke upon you, and learn of me; for I am meek and lowly in heart: and ye shall find rest unto

your souls" (Matt. 11:29)—that's the rest of commitment of your heart and life to Christ. And another promise: "Jesus saith unto him, I am the way, the truth, and the life: no man cometh unto the Father, but by me" (John 14:6). Another wonderful promise is that of eternal life: "He that hath the Son hath life . . ." (1 John 5:12). "Being born again, not of corruptible seed, but of incorruptible, by the word of God, which liveth and abideth for ever" (1 Pet. 1:23). All these wonderful promises come through a knowledge of Jesus Christ and by faith in Him.

"That by these ye might be partakers of the *divine nature*," that is, that you might be a child of God! What a tremendous truth this is. This is overwhelming! When you are born again, you are given the nature of *God*, my friend. Don't let anybody deceive you into thinking that the Christian life is a little series of dos and don'ts—that if you do this and don't do that, you are living the Christian life. Oh, my friend, you are a partaker of the divine nature, the nature of God, and you *want* the things of God.

"Having escaped the corruption that is in the world through lust." This in itself is a tremendous statement. A little later Peter will speak of the make-believers who have escaped the pollutions of the world. What a difference there is between escaping the pollutions of the world and escaping the corruption of the world. The corruption of the world is that which is within us. The pollution of the world is that which is on the outside. At the time I am writing this, a great deal is being said about the antipollution programs. The feeling is that if we clean up the environment, it will produce nicer people. Well, it won't do a thing for the old nature, my friend.

Religious people go through an antipollution program on Sundays. They participate in a little ritual, a little washing, a little of this and a little of that. My friend, you can be religious to your fingertips and still be as corrupt as anyone can possibly be. Some folk that you see on Sunday don't look like the same folk when you see them on Monday. Why? Well, they only have been through an antipollution program on Sunday.

If you are going to escape the corruption of the world, you will have to have a new nature. You will need to be a partaker of the divine nature, having escaped the corruption that is in the world through lust.

However, although you have the nature of God through being born again, that doesn't mean that you have lost your old nature. There is a continuing conflict in the life of a believer between his new nature and his old nature. The best illustration of this in Scripture is that which our Lord gave us when He told the parable of the Prodigal Son (see Luke 15:11–32). Notice that the son *could* go to the far country because he still had an old nature. He *could* spend his money in riotous living, and he *could* even get down in the pigpen. But, you see, he was a partaker of the nature of his father, and his father didn't live in a pigpen. His father lived up there in a wonderful mansion. His father believed in godliness and cleanliness, and there was nourishing food on his table.

Now, that boy wouldn't have been his son if eventually he hadn't said, "I will arise and go to my father . . ." (Luke 15:18). He *had* to say it. You couldn't find a pig in the pigpen that would say that. Not one of those pigs went with him to the father's house. I read an article the other day by a man who raises pigs, and he claimed that they are clean little fellows. Well, he evidently has a breed of pigs which I know nothing about. However, we will see in 2 Peter 2:22 that a pig can get washed and cleaned up. Although he may become a tidy little fellow, even join a church, and become a deacon or a minister in the pulpit, he is still a pig and will eventually return to that pigpen. But the son is a partaker of the nature of his father, and he will eventually return to his father's house.

My friend, when you and I are children of God, we have the nature of God. Isn't that wonderful! We can understand God when He speaks through His Word and the Spirit of God makes it real to us.

But Peter doesn't stop with this, he goes on to say, "And beside this. . . ." I feel like saying to Simon Peter, "What in the world can you add to the promises of the Lord Jesus Christ and the fact of our being partakers of the divine nature?" I think that Simon Peter would answer, "Well, when you get that far, you have only started. There is a great deal beyond salvation."

Perhaps it will surprise you to know that there is something beyond salvation. You may recall that Paul said to Timothy that the Scriptures ". . . are able to make thee wise unto salvation . . ." (2 Tim. 3:15). Since Timothy was already saved, what does Paul mean by that? Well, salvation is in three tenses. Salvation is in the past tense: "I have been saved." It is also in the present tense: "I am being saved." And it is in the future tense: "I shall be saved"—"Beloved, now are we the sons of God, and it doth not yet appear what we shall be: but we know that, when he shall appear, we shall be like him; for we shall see him as he is" (1 John 3:2). I am not like the Lord Jesus now—I have not yet arrived—but I am in the process.

Now Peter is going to talk to us about Christians maturing. After a person is born again, he should not stay in the crib saying, "Da-da-da," the rest of his life. Nor should he need to be burped every so often. He should get to the place where he begins to grow up.

And beside this, giving all diligence, add to your faith virtue; and to virtue knowledge;

And to knowledge temperance; and to temperance patience; and to patience godliness;

And to godliness brotherly kindness; and to brotherly kindness charity [2 Pet. 1:5–7].

"And beside this, giving all diligence." The Christian life is a very serious business. However, we have made it sort of an extracurricular activity. The present-day thinking is that it is not something to be taken into the business world or the schoolroom or into social life. Rather, it is something sort of like your Sunday-go-to-meeting clothes which you wear only at certain times. However, Peter said that it is something to which we are to give "all *diligence*."

When Peter lists these graces which are to be added to our faith, they are not like a series of beads that you count off. Nor are they like a stack of dominoes which you stand on end in a long line, then when you push the first domino down, all the others fall down in a line. It is not like that at all. Neither is it like placing one brick upon another in building a structure. I know that Peter, in his first epistle, uses the figure of living stones being built up into a "spiritual house," but remember that all the stones were *living* stones.

Rather, the Christian life is a growth. This is the way Peter explains it in this epistle which closes with the tremendous statement, "Grow in grace, and in the knowledge of our Lord and Saviour Jesus Christ" (2 Pet. 3:18). A familiar illustration is that of a growing tree. You know the old proverb that great oaks from little acorns grow. (Sometimes we turn it around and say, "Great aches from little toe-corns grow," but that is a different matter!) I am sure that you have watched a tree grow. I have a little redwood tree which was given to me by a dear lady who had previously lived in Oregon. It was just a little, bitty fellow in a can when she brought it to me. I didn't have a place for it at the time; so I just put it down in front of our living room window, intending to move it sometime. Well, the years went by, and that little six-inch tree is now almost as tall as I am and probably too big to move successfully. Likewise, the Christian life is to be a growth and a development.

Out in the woods two things are happening, things which are actually transfigurations. The vegetation that is living is growing, and the vegetation that is dead is decaying. Those are the two processes which are taking place out there. And one of those processes is taking place in your Christian life and mine.

If you are a child of God, you are to *grow.* And Peter lists the different attributes which are to characterize our growth. At the beginning, my little tree had very delicate needles, but they are different now—they are sturdy looking. And there should be growth and development like that in the Christian life.

Peter begins by saying, "Add to your faith virtue." The "faith" is saving faith, that which gave you your divine nature, that which gave you forgiveness of sins and made over to you the righteousness of Christ. Now you are to add to that, first of all, "virtue." Down through the centuries, some English words have changed their meaning, and *virtue* is one of them. *Virtus* to the Roman of the first century meant a great deal more than chastity. It characterized the very finest of Roman manhood: strength, valor, courage, and excellence. My friend, these same qualities should also characterize your life and mine. How the world needs believers who have the courage to stand for that which is right and to stand up and be counted for God in this day! Therefore Peter is saying, "Add to your faith courage."

"Add . . . to virtue [courage] knowledge." Here the Greek word for "knowledge" is *gnosis*, meaning "to know God in His salvation." It indicates growth. In verse 2 the word *knowledge* was the Greek word *epignōsis*, meaning "super knowledge." Paul, writing to the Colossian believers, said that he prayed that they might have this *epignōsis*, the super knowledge. The Gnostic heresy, which was abroad in that day, claimed to impart super knowledge by their secret rituals. However, "knowledge" for both Peter and Paul meant growth and development in the Christian life, and super knowledge was the goal as the Holy Spirit confirmed the Word of God to the heart.

Let me give you a personal example. When I was in college, I had doubts; in fact, I was very much of a skeptic and rather cynical at that time. Although I believed the Word of God, my faith was being torn to shreds in the liberal college I was attending. In fact, I said to one of the ministers who helped me a great deal that if I could not be convinced that the Bible was the Word of God, I would get out of the ministry. At that time I had faith, but it was a very weak faith. However, I can say dogmatically today that I not only believe the Bible is the Word of God, I *know* it is the Word of God. The Holy Spirit has confirmed it to me, and, friend, you cannot have a higher confirmation than when the Holy Spirit confirms the Word of God to your heart and life and makes it very real to you.

When young people ask me about a book which will show that the Bible is the Word of God, I have several in my library to suggest, but I haven't read one of those books in years. When I was their age, all I did read was books on apologetics. Well, I have long since passed that stage. My faith doesn't need that kind of propping up now. Some folk accuse me of being too dogmatic. No, I'm not too dogmatic; I am just sure and positive, that's all. If I didn't believe the Bible to be the Word of God, I wouldn't be teaching it. As I told that minister when I was in college, I would not go into the ministry unless I could stand in the pulpit with complete confidence in the Book which I was presenting.

Can you imagine a pilot taking two or three hundred people across the country in one of those great planes and saying, "Throw out the logbook and the maps and the charts. I don't have any confidence in them"? May I say to you, if you are sitting on such a plane, you are in trouble. But, of course, a man who is a commerical pilot believes in his logbook and his maps and charts. There is no need for you to get out of your seat and go to the cockpit and argue with him about them. He knows. He has information which has been confirmed to him—he has flown that route hundreds of times.

My friend, you can be sure of the Word of God, and as you study it and share it with others, the Spirit of God will confirm it to your heart, and you will experience growth in your spiritual life. This is what Peter had in mind when he said to add to your courage knowledge. You need courage to declare the Word of God. You are not apt to give out the knowledge that you have of Christ unless you have the courage to do it.

"Add . . . to knowledge temperance." That

word *temperance* in our day refers to only one thing. A better word is *self-control*. As believers, we are to be self-controlled in every area of our lives.

"Add . . . to temperance [self-control] patience." Many folk have the wrong concept of what patience really is. They think it means sitting in a traffic jam on the freeway in the morning without worrying about getting to work. Well, that is not patience. It just gives you an excuse for being late to work. Patience is being able to endure when trials come. Patience is endurance. It is built upon knowledge and courage. Like a growing tree, a Christian should be developing courage, then knowledge, then self-control, and then endurance.

"Add . . . to patience godliness." *Godliness* is another word which has been lost in the shuffle. It means exactly what it says—to be like God. After you have been born into the family of God, you want to be like your Father—Godlike. It doesn't mean that you will *be* like God, but it does mean that you have that desire and aim in your life. I think of the words of a song we sing, "Oh, to be like Him. . . ." Well, it should be more than a song; it should be the desire of every individual who is a partaker of the divine nature. I believe there is a time in every boy's life when his dad is his hero and sometimes his idol. It is a terrible day when that idol falls from its pedestal, but it happens, and often the boy grows bitter. Well, we are children of God, and because of this, we want to be like our Father. And, my friend, He will never disappoint us. He is not only our hero, He is our God, the one we worship and praise. The word *godliness* has in it that very thought of praise and worship of God. It speaks of a dependence upon God and a life that is devoted to Him.

"Add . . . to godliness brotherly kindness." We can make that a stronger expression by translating it "love of the brethren." We are to love other believers. I receive many letters from those who listen to my Bible teaching on radio in which they say that they *love* me. And I can respond, "And I *love* you." If I met these folk personally, I am sure we would be more restrained, but certainly we should love the brethren. I have the opportunity of meeting with some very wonderful Christians—both laymen and preachers. Sometimes we eat lunch together; sometimes we play golf together; and sometimes we have a service together. It is a joy to have a sweet and loving relationship with the brethren.

"Add . . . to brotherly kindness charity." Again, the word *charity* means something entirely different in modern America from what it meant in 1611 when the King James Version was written. Since "brotherly kindness" is specifically for other believers, it is obvious that "charity" is to be directed to outsiders. I interpret it as meaning that we are to love the sinner as God loves him. God loved him enough to redeem him, but He hates his sin and will judge it unless he does turn to Christ. I take the position that loving a sinner does not mean getting down on his level and participating in his sin. Rather, we are to love him by bringing the gospel to him. My friend, the way we reveal our love to those outside the faith is to care enough to attempt to win them to Christ.

For if these things be in you, and abound, they make you that ye shall neither be barren nor unfruitful in the knowledge of our Lord Jesus Christ [2 Pet. 1:8].

"If these things be in you." You see, Peter is not talking about the externalities of religion. He is not speaking of rituals or religion or liturgy. He is speaking of that which is inside the Christian. The reason he said that we have escaped the corruption of the world is because we are partakers of the divine nature. Corruption is inside the human heart. Later on he will say that the unsaved, that is, the apostates, escape the pollutions of the world (by going through a ceremony or acting religious), yet their hearts are not changed.

When he says, "If these *things* be in you"— what things? The things he has mentioned in the preceding verses: faith and courage and knowledge and self-control and patience and godliness and love of the brethren and love for the outsider. All of these things are to be within us.

"If these things be in you, and *abound*." Here he starts multiplying again. Peter is great with mathematics.

"They make you that ye shall neither be barren nor unfruitful." The word *barren* actually means "idle." This has to do with what we call the fruit of the Spirit. We cannot produce the fruit of the Spirit by sitting on the sidelines. While it is true that the fruit of the Spirit is the work of the Holy Spirit—that is, we cannot produce it by ourselves—we are to yield ourselves to Him, present our bodies definitely to Him, and draw from the Vine, the Lord Jesus Christ, the fruit of the Spirit. Again, the fruit is: faith, courage, knowledge, self-control, patience, godliness, love of the brethren, and love for the unsaved. He doesn't want us to be barren.

"Nor unfruitful" has to do with that which is, I believe, objective. Being barren has to do with that which is subjective, that which is internal. You have had, I am sure, the experience of meeting Christians who sound like sounding brass or a tinkling cymbal or an empty barrel. They are barren as far as the fruit of the Spirit is concerned. In contrast to this, we as believers are not to be unfruitful. Our lives are to be characterized by the fruit of the Spirit that Peter has been telling us about. My friend, does your life influence other people? Are you helping to get the Word of God out to folk who need it?

But he that lacketh these things is blind, and cannot see afar off, and hath forgotten that he was purged from his old sins [2 Pet. 1:9].

Now Peter is touching on something which is very important to us; that is, sterility in the lives of many church members in our day. Their lack of enthusiasm will eventuate in their not being sure that they were ever really saved. Paul gives this admonition: "Watch ye, stand fast in the faith, quit you like men, be strong. Let all your things be done with charity" (1 Cor. 16:13–14). Then when he concluded his second letter to the Corinthians, he said, "Examine yourselves, whether ye be in the faith; prove your own selves. Know ye not your own selves, how that Jesus Christ is in you, except ye be reprobates?" (2 Cor. 13:5). This is a very strong statement. You are to *examine* yourself to make sure you are in the faith. If you have the idea that you can live a careless life and still be a Christian and *know* it, you are wrong. It is impossible. You may be a Christian, but you sure won't know it. Many years ago a young preacher in Cannon Beach, Oregon, said to me one evening, "There are many Christians who believe in the security of the believer, but they do not have the assurance of their salvation." You see, the security of the believer is objective; the assurance of salvation is subjective. Peter has well stated it: "He that lacketh these things is blind, and cannot see afar off, and hath forgotten that he was purged from his old sins." He has forgotten that he has been saved.

Wherefore the rather, brethren, give diligence to make your calling and election sure: for if ye do these things, ye shall never fall [2 Pet. 1:10].

"Give diligence to make your calling and election sure"—he means, of course, *more* sure. In other words, the security of the believer is objective; it is something that cannot be disturbed. However, your assurance can certainly be disturbed by the life you live. If your life is not lived in sincerity and truth, you are bound to lie on your bed at night and wonder if you really have been born again. While it is true that Christ has done everything necessary to save you and keep you saved, your Christian life to be meaningful is something that you have to work at.

I have been married for a long time, and I never have to lie awake at night and wonder whether or not I am married; but to make my marriage meaningful, I have to work at it, and I have been working at it for a long, long time.

Likewise in your Christian life, "make your calling and election *more* sure." That is, let it become subjective in your own heart—to know that you are a child of God.

"For if ye do these things, ye shall never fall." I have talked with many Christians who have gotten into sin. It is very interesting to me that I have never yet talked to one who had the assurance of his salvation before he got into sin. You see, the person who lacks assurance lacks a solid foundation under him.

For so an entrance shall be ministered unto you abundantly into the everlasting kingdom of our Lord and Saviour Jesus Christ [2 Pet. 1:11].

Notice that Peter will put an emphasis not upon the Rapture but upon the coming of Christ to establish His kingdom upon this earth. Why? We find out in verse 14: "Knowing that shortly I must put off this my tabernacle, even as our Lord Jesus Christ hath shewed me." You see, Peter is one apostle who did not look forward to the Rapture. He knew he would never live to see the Rapture because the Lord Jesus had told him that he was to die a martyr's death. Therefore, he knew that shortly he must put off his tabernacle, that is, his body. This is a wonderful way to speak of death. Since Simon Peter knew that shortly he would move out of his body and into God's presence, he spoke of the everlasting kingdom of our Lord and Savior Jesus Christ, knowing that there would be no Rapture ahead for him.

Wherefore I will not be negligent to put you always in remembrance of these things, though ye know them, and be established in the present truth [2 Pet. 1:12].

Knowing that he would not be with them very much longer, he felt called upon to stir up these saints to grow in grace, lest spiritual senility set in. There are Christians today—and I am sure you have met some of them—who are actually spiritually *senile*. They are tottering around, not seeming to have all of their faculties.

Yea, I think it meet, as long as I am in this tabernacle, to stir you up by putting you in remembrance [2 Pet. 1:13].

"I think it meet"—that is, I think it *fitting*—"as long as I am in this tabernacle." Again he is speaking of his body as his tabernacle. As long as he had life, he was going to remind them of these important things.

Knowing that shortly I must put off this my tabernacle, even as our Lord Jesus Christ hath shewed me [2 Pet. 1:14].

Here Peter is referring to what Jesus had told him that morning when He had prepared breakfast for them on the shore of the Sea of Galilee after His resurrection. He had said, "Verily, verily, I say unto thee, When thou wast young, thou girdest thyself, and walkedst whither thou wouldest: but when thou shalt be old, thou shalt stretch forth thy hands, and another shall gird thee, and carry thee whither thou wouldest not." Then John comments, "This spake he, signifying by what death he should glorify God . . ." (John 21:18–19).

This passage in 2 Peter has been one of the most important sections in the entire Word of God. I have gone over it rather carefully so that you might know and understand what Peter is saying here.

You can see now why I have been calling this epistle Peter's swan song. It is, as it were, his deathbed statement. When a man is on his deathbed, he is apt to say something of importance even though he has not said anything of importance up to that time. If he has been a liar all of his life, the chances are that on his deathbed he will tell the truth.

It is interesting that the Word of God attaches some importance to deathbed statements. Let me illustrate this from the Old Testament.

Genesis 49 gives us a scene that is sad and rather dramatic. Jacob called his twelve sons to stand around his deathbed as he makes a prophecy concerning each one of those boys. Those prophecies have been literally fulfilled.

When Moses knew that he would not enter the Promised Land but would die on Mount Nebo in the land of Moab, he gathered the twelve tribes about him and blessed each of them before his death—very much as Jacob had done before him. It was a very important discourse that he gave to them at that time.

When Joshua was old and ready to depart from this life, he also gathered the tribes of Israel together and delivered to them his final charge. Then he challenged them to follow God and gave the testimony of his own life: ". . . as for me and my house, we will serve the LORD" (Josh. 24:15).

When David was about to die, he called Solomon to him. I don't believe that David would have chosen Solomon for his successor; he would have preferred Absalom, but Absalom had been slain. David said to Solomon, "I go the way of all the earth." (What a picture that is of death! I don't know who you are or where you are, but I can tell you the road on which you are traveling. You are going the way of all the earth, and that is to the cemetery. I realize that this doesn't sound very good, but all of us are on that route.) Then David charged Solomon with the responsibility of building the temple of God, and he exhorted all Israel to help him, for ". . . Solomon my son, whom alone God hath chosen, is yet young and tender, and the work is great: for the palace is not for man, but for the LORD God" (1 Chron. 29:1).

Then, in the New Testament when the Lord Jesus came into Jerusalem for that last Passover, He made it very clear to His own in His Upper Room Discourse that it was His last time with them while He was here in the flesh—before He would die and rise again in a glorified body. Oh, what tremendous truths He gave to them on that last evening!

The apostle Paul, as we have seen, gave his final epitaph in 2 Timothy. This is his swan song: "For I am now ready to be offered, and the time of my departure is at hand. I have fought a good fight, I have finished my course, I have kept the faith: Henceforth there is laid up for me a crown of righteousness, which the Lord, the righteous judge, shall give me at that day: and not to me only, but unto all them also that love his appearing" (2 Tim. 4:6–8).

Now Simon Peter says, "Knowing that shortly I must put off this my tabernacle." He knows that he has come to the end of his earthly life. Tradition tells us that he was crucified with his head down, and some folk have interpreted that to mean upside down. I personally don't think it means that. Rather, I believe the implication is that our Lord held his head up as He looked into the heavens, but

Simon Peter felt himself to be unworthy to die in the same manner his Lord had died; so he died with his head down.

When Simon Peter said, "I must put off this my tabernacle," he was referring, of course, to his body. The word Peter used for "tabernacle" is the Greek *skēnōma*, which means "a tent or a dwelling place." Both Peter and Paul used that expression when referring to the body. Paul wrote, "For we know that if our earthly house of this tabernacle were dissolved, we have a building of God, an house not made with hands, eternal in the heavens" (2 Cor. 5:1). A tent is a pretty flimsy sort of thing, and if you don't believe that your little tent is flimsy, you step out on one of the freeways across this country, and you will find that your little tent will fold and you will silently slip away.

When we die, it is this little body that you and I live in that is put to sleep. The body sleeps in the dust of the earth. When God created Adam, He took his body out of the dirt. Man was created out of the earth. Our bodies contain fifteen or sixteen elements which can be found in the average soil today—that is the composition of the body. The body is put to sleep and returns to the dust of the earth. The Greek word that the Bible uses for "sleep" means "to lie down." In classical Greek it means "to go to bed."

A man who believes in "soul sleep" discussed this with me. I told him that "to sleep" means to go to bed and facetiously asked him to tell me which end of the soul he would stick under the cover and which end would go on the pillow. He hasn't been able to enlighten me yet, of course, because it is the *body* that sleeps, not the soul. It is the body that is like a tent. It is very feeble, and one of these days we are going to put it aside.

Paul also says, "We are confident, I say, and willing rather to be absent from the body, and to be present with the Lord" (2 Cor. 5:8). That is the way both Peter and Paul speak of death. This little tent we live in is put down into the grave. It goes to sleep, but the soul never dies. And, of course, the soul is never raised from the dead since it never dies. The word *resurrection* refers to the body. In the Greek it is *anastasis*, which means "to stand up," and obviously that refers to the body.

AUTHORITY OF THE SCRIPTURES ATTESTED BY FULFILLED PROPHECY

Moreover I will endeavour that ye may be able after my decease to have these things always in remembrance [2 Pet. 1:15].

"After my decease"—the word he uses means "exodus." He will just be moving out of his house, his tabernacle, down here; he will be putting it off as if it were a garment, and he will be making his exodus. Now the word *exodus* implies that death doesn't end it all. When the children of Israel went out of Egypt, the Egyptians said, "We are through with them. This ends it." But it didn't end it. Israel continued on in the wilderness and finally entered into the Promised Land, and Egypt doesn't seem to be through with them even to this good day! And for this man Peter, death was merely an exodus; it wasn't an end to it all.

"To have these things always in remembrance." Peter is saying that, in the light of his approaching death, he wants to bring before us certain things to keep in remembrance. And the thing he will really emphasize is the validity of the Word of God.

Now, there is a way of looking at the remainder of Peter's epistle that may be a little difficult to understand, but there are two forces in the world today. There is centrifugal force and centripetal force. A centrifugal force impels outward from a center. If you tie a ball on a string and swing it around your head, the ball will pull on the string, trying to get away from you. The centripetal force is just the opposite—it pulls toward a center or axis. Peter will deal with these two conflicting forces in relationship to the Word of God. There is a centrifugal force that impels outward from the world in which you and I live today, and there is centripetal force that pulls us into the world and away from the Word of God. My friend, the centrifugal force is the Word of God. It is the only thing that can pull us away from the world system. A letter from an alcoholic who began listening to our Bible teaching program by radio tells how the Word of God pulled him away from the bottle and from a worldly life and pulled him toward God.

Peter has already told us that we are to make our calling and election more sure, and he wants us to know that we have an authority on which we can depend. Somebody is going to raise the question, "How do you know that the Bible is really the Word of God?"

For we have not followed cunningly devised fables, when we made known unto you the power and coming of our Lord Jesus Christ, but were eyewitnesses of his majesty [2 Pet. 1:16].

This is something that is very important for us to see.

"We have not followed cunningly devised fables." The Bible is not a pack of lies. The Bible is not a fairy story. The Bible is not a myth. The Bible is historical and factual. If you are sincere and want to give up your sins, God will make it real to you. If there is a veil over your eyes, it is not because you are mentally blind; it is because you do not want to give up your sins. When you and I are willing to do that, God will make the Bible real to us.

"But were eyewitnesses of his majesty." Now, I tell you, *that* is just a little disconcerting. When did Simon Peter see the power and coming of Jesus Christ?

He will make it clear that he is referring to the transfiguration of Jesus Christ.

For he received from God the Father honour and glory, when there came such a voice to him from the excellent glory, This is my beloved Son, in whom I am well pleased.

And this voice which came from heaven we heard, when we were with him in the holy mount [2 Pet. 1:17–18].

Obviously, Peter is referring to the Transfiguration. We need to understand the significance of this event. What did Jesus mean in Matthew 16:28? "Verily I say unto you, There be some standing here, which shall not taste of death, till they see the Son of man coming in his kingdom." This has led some people to claim that the kingdom was well established at this point. (It is unfortunate that we have a chapter break at this point in Matthew's account— remember that in the original manuscripts there are no chapters.) The account continues: "And after six days Jesus taketh Peter, James, and John his brother, and bringeth them up into an high mountain apart, And was transfigured before them: and his face did shine as the sun, and his raiment was white as the light" (Matt. 17:1–2).

The transfiguration of Jesus Christ was a miniature picture of the kingdom. Moses and Elijah appeared there with Christ. Moses represents the Law in the Old Testament. Elijah represents the prophets in the Old Testament. What were they discussing? They were discussing Christ's decease, His exodus, His passing from the room of this world into the presence of the Father. That is what they had written about in the Old Testament, and that is what they were talking about at the Transfiguration. Then there were the three disciples present to observe the Transfiguration. They represent the living saints. Moses and Elijah represent the dead saints of the Old Testament. The church was not yet in existence, but the three disciples who were there would constitute the beginning of that body of believers which is the church. They would be the apostles. So the Transfiguration gives us a miniature picture of the kingdom.

Immediately after the Transfiguration, Jesus Christ and the disciples came down from the mount, and there they found a man with a demonized son. The other disciples could do nothing to help the boy. The observing people were jeering and ridiculing the disciples. That is a picture of the present day. The kingdom is in abeyance. Jesus Christ is at the right hand of God, and all the Old and New Testament saints who have gone before are with Him. While down here on this earth we are living in a demonized world. If you doubt this, all you have to do to be convinced is to read your newspaper or watch your television newscast. The world is in a terrible mess. The church, which ought to have a message of hope and power for the world, is not helping this demonized world. As a result, the church is being ridiculed—and in one sense, rightly so—because the church is not about the Father's business as it should be.

Now Simon Peter has said that he was with the Lord Jesus on the Mount of Transfiguration. He was one of the eyewitnesses. Then he says this strange thing:

We have also a more sure word of prophecy; whereunto ye do well that ye take heed, as unto a light that shineth in a dark place, until the day dawn, and the day star arise in your hearts [2 Pet. 1:19].

"We have also a more sure word of prophecy"—when he uses the word *prophecy* he doesn't necessarily mean the prediction of the future, although he includes that. He means the entire Word of God, because he speaks of the Scriptures as having been spoken by God. And the prophets, as he will make it clear in the next verse, were more than amanuenses who took dictation from God; rather, they expressed their own feelings and thoughts. Nevertheless, God was able to transmit His complete will and word through the men who wrote Scripture. This is the thing that makes it a miraculous Book. You see, the Word of God is not only deity, it is human, very human. It is like the Lord Jesus who was both God and man. The Bible is a God-book and a man-book. It deals with human life, right down where you and I live and move and have our being, yet it is *God* speaking to man in a language that is understandable to him.

A great many people think, "Oh, if only I could have been with Peter. If only I could have seen those things." Friend, you have something even better. You have the Word of God. It will speak directly to you if you will open your heart and allow it to speak. The Word of God is better than seeing and hearing.

"We have also a more sure word of prophecy"—rather, "the word of prophecy is made more sure."

"A light that shineth in a dark place." The Word of God is a light, a lamp, a source of light, like the sun in the sky. It is a centrifugal force. As the sun gives out its light, throwing it out to the universe, so the Word of God sends out a light, a force, and a power. It is the only tangible supernatural thing that we have in this world today. The Word of God is the only physical miracle that we have from God in this hour in which we live.

It will be that until Jesus comes—"until the day dawn, and the day star arise in your hearts." Jesus is called the Bright and Morning Star in Revelation 22:16. Until He comes, His Word is the centrifugal force going throughout the world and drawing men away from the world system and putting them into the arms of God. What a picture we have here!

Knowing this first, that no prophecy of the scripture is of any private interpretation [2 Pet. 1:20].

"Knowing this first." Simon Peter says that this is the first thing we are to know. The word *knowing* is a knowledge that comes, not only from the Word of God, not only from facts that can be ascertained—if you have an honest heart, you can find out whether the facts in the Bible are accurate or not—but these are things which you can know by the Holy Spirit's making them real to you. As I have said before, I have long since passed the stage when I wanted the Bible proved to me. When I was in college, I did want the Bible proved to me; and if I found that archaeology had dug up a spadeful of dirt somewhere that proved a fact in the Bible, I would clap my hands like a little child and shout, "Wonderful!" I don't do that anymore. I don't need a spadeful of turned-up dirt to prove the Bible to me. The Spirit of God Himself has made the Word of God real to my heart. I know there is a transforming power in God's Word. I get letters from all over the world which testify to that fact. There is

power in the Word of God. This is something that we can *know*, and the facts, confirmed by the Holy Spirit, make it real to us.

"No prophecy of the scripture is of any private interpretation." What Peter is saying here is that no portion of the Scripture is to be interpreted apart from other references to the same subject. That is the reason I put up such an objection to this idea of pulling out one little verse of Scripture and building a doctrine on that one verse. If you cannot get the whole body of Scripture to confirm your doctrine, then you had better get a new doctrine, my friend.

I think a good illustration is the difference between riding in a good, solid, four-wheeled wagon and on a unicycle. If you have ever seen a person ride on that one wheel of a unicycle, you have noted that he does a lot of twisting and turning and maneuvering around to stay balanced on that one wheel. In the circus I once saw a man riding way up high on a unicycle, and all of a sudden it went out from under him, and he fell backwards. Believe me, he had a bad fall. And I thought, *Oh, how many Christians are like that today. They base what they believe on a single verse.* While it is wonderful to have one marvelous verse of Scripture, if it tells a great truth, there will be at least two or three verses and usually a whole chapter on it somewhere in the Bible. Simon Peter is telling us that no passage of Scripture should be interpreted by itself. We need to confirm it with other Scriptures.

For the prophecy came not in old time by the will of man: but holy men of God spake as they were moved by the Holy Ghost [2 Pet. 1:21].

"For the prophecy came not in old time by the will of man." Obviously he is referring to Old Testament prophecy. It didn't come by the will of man. That is, Isaiah, for example, did not sit down saying, "I think I'll write a book because I need some money. I'll send it to the publisher, and he will send me an advance check, and then I'll get royalties for it." That is the reason some men write in our day, but that is not the way Isaiah did it. Listen to Peter: "For the prophecy came not in old time by the will of man." The prophecy of Isaiah was not something that Isaiah thought up.

"But holy men of God spake as they were moved by the Holy Ghost." "Holy men" does not mean that the writers were some super-duper saints. It means holy in the sense of being set apart for this particular office. If you are a holy Christian, it means that you are set apart for Jesus Christ. *Holy* means "to be set apart."

"As they were moved by the Holy Ghost [Spirit]" is a delightful figure of speech. The Greek actually portrays the idea of a sailing vessel. The wind gets into those great sails, bellies them out, and moves the ship along. That is the way the Holy Spirit moved these men.

Here in California we have a yacht regatta each year. The yachts line up and start for Honolulu, Hawaii, to sail in around Diamond Head. (A man must be rich enough to own such a sailing yacht and to have the time to enter such a regatta.) Some time ago a doctor performed an operation on me one day, and the next day he was off sailing to Honolulu! When he got back, I was asking him about it. He told me that they have an extra sail which they put out when they get a good wind and that moves the boat right along. Well, this is exactly what Peter is saying in this verse of Scripture. These men who were set apart for the writing of the Scriptures were moved along by the Spirit of God.

Now let me remind you that this is Peter's swan song, and, like Paul in his swan song, he emphasizes the importance of the Word of God for the days of apostasy. Paul said, "All scripture is given by inspiration of God . . ." (2 Tim. 3:16), and Peter is saying that the writers of Scripture were moved along by the Holy Spirit. The thought is the same. It is wonderful to see how God could take each man and use him, without changing his style or interfering with his personality, to write His Word so that His message comes across. While Paul the apostle wrote eloquent Greek, Peter the apostle—since he was a fisherman and Greek was his second language—wrote Greek that was not quite as good. Yet God used both of these men to write exactly what He wanted to say—so much so that, if God spoke out of heaven today, He would have to repeat Himself, because He already has said all that He has to say to mankind. God has gotten His Word to us through men of different personalities and different skills. For this reason I call it a man-book and a God-book.

The written Word, like the Lord Jesus, the living Word, is both human and divine. The Lord Jesus could weep at a grave, but He could also raise the dead. He could sit down at a well because He was tired and thirsty, but He could also give the water of life to a poor sinner. He could go to sleep in a boat, but He could also still the storm. He was a man, but He was God also. And the Bible is both human and divine.

Simon Peter is telling us that we have "a more sure word of prophecy." He puts a sure rock under our feet. The Scriptures are something that we can have confidence in. No wonder the Word of God has been attacked more than anything else. If the enemy can get rid of the foundation, he knows that the building will come crashing down.

It is sheer nonsense for a preacher to stand at a pulpit and preach a sermon showing that he does not believe that the Bible is the Word of God. That, to my judgment, is as silly as the poor fellow in the insane asylum whom a visitor saw using a pickax on the foundation at the corner of the dormitory in an attempt to destroy the foundation. The visitor, wanting to be sympathetic, asked the man with the pick, "What are you doing?"

"I'm digging away the foundation. Can't you see?"

"Yes, but don't you live in this building?"

"Of course I do, but I live upstairs."

For a preacher to discredit the Word of God is equally as insane. My friend, the Scriptures as we have them are a solid foundation on which to rest our faith.

The last time I was in Greece, I went again to the Acropolis in Athens and examined the Parthenon. I have examined it several times to make sure I am accurate in this statement: there are not two parallel lines in the place, nor is there a straight line. If you go to one end and look down, you will see that it comes up to a hump in the middle and then goes back down. The Greeks had learned that the human eye never sees anything straight which is straight. This, I believe, is the reason God says that we are to walk by faith and not by sight. We can't trust our own eyes nor our own ears, but we can rest upon the Word of God.

One of the greatest proofs that the Bible is indeed the Word is fulfilled prophecy. Over one-third of the Scripture was prophetic at the time it was first written. It is not to be treated as speculation or superstition because of the fact that a great deal of it has already been literally fulfilled. As someone has well said, "Prophecy is the mold into which history is poured." Fulfilled prophecy is, to me, one of the great proofs of the accuracy of Scripture. Peter has said, "We have also a more sure word of prophecy." Since one-fourth of prophecy has been fulfilled, this means that one-fourth of one-third of the Bible is fulfilled prophecy. Man cannot guess that accurately!

There were three hundred thirty prophecies in the Old Testament concerning the first coming of Christ, and all of them were literally fulfilled. No human being can guess like that.

Let me give you an example. Suppose that right now I should make a prophecy that it is going to rain tomorrow. I'd have a 50 percent chance of being right, because it either will or it won't. But suppose I add to that the prediction that it would start raining tomorrow morning at nine o'clock. That would be another uncertain element. I am no mathematician, but it seems to me that this would reduce my chance of being right by another 50 per-cent. Now suppose that I not only say it is going to start raining at nine o'clock but also that it will stop raining at two o'clock. According to my figuring, that would bring down my chance of being correct to 12½ percent. And it would be a lot less than that if you figure it according to a twenty-four hour day. But suppose I add three hundred uncertain elements. I would not have a ghost of a chance of being accurate. Yet the Word of God hit it, my friend. It is accurate. The Bible has moved into the area of absolute impossibility, and that to me is absolute proof that it is the Word of God.

CHAPTER 2

THEME: Apostasy brought in by false teachers

APOSTASY BROUGHT IN BY FALSE TEACHERS

We have seen in the previous chapter the centrifugal force of the light of Jesus Christ that draws men away from the world and toward God. Now let's talk about the centripetal force; that is, the force that impels folk toward the world. It is a gravitational force, the pull of the world away from the Word of God.

The days that Peter is talking about in this chapter have now come upon us in our day.

But there were false prophets also among the people, even as there shall be false teachers among you, who privily shall bring in damnable heresies, even denying the Lord that bought them, and bring upon themselves swift destruction [2 Pet. 2:1].

"But there were false prophets also among the people." Peter is writing to Jewish Christians, and "the people" he is talking about is Israel. There were false prophets among the people of Israel, Peter says, "even as there shall be false teachers among you," that is, among believers, the church. There were false *prophets* in the Old Testament, but there are false *teachers* today. My friend, we do not need to beware of false prophets at all—that is not our problem. Any man who attempts to prophesy today will soon be proven a liar—there is no question about that.

During World War II, there was here in Pasadena, California, a man who predicted that the end of the world would come (if I remember correctly) on September 15, 1943. When that day came, newspaper reporters filled his yard and waited. Eventually he had to come out and say that he had misfigured it. He said that instead it would be September 15, 1944. The ministers in Pasadena who were meeting together in a prayer fellowship at that time were concerned about this man's prophecies and wanted to get a statement into the newspaper. I said to them, "Forget it. As far as I am concerned, on September 15, 1944, the man will be proven a liar." You know, the world didn't come to an end the next year either. What happened was that the newspaper reporters laughed at and ridiculed that man. Of course, it hurts the cause of Christ when anyone does that sort of thing. The man disappeared from this area, and I do not know where he is today.

We do not need to pay any attention to false prophets, but let me say this to you: You do need to check false *teachers*. You need to check all teachers, including the one whose book you are reading right now. I urge you to check what I say by the Word of God. Don't believe it because Vernon McGee says it. One man told me, "I teach a Sunday school class, and if anyone questions what I say, I tell them, 'Well, *McGee* says that.'" That is the wrong approach, my friend. The Word of God is what you are to rest upon.

I am amazed today how easily people are

deceived by all kinds of teaching. People will fall for anything, and if you do not believe that, you ought to see the elaborate operations and headquarters of some of the cults which are located here in Southern California. You would be amazed, for it reveals that there are a great many people who have not heeded Peter's warning that false teachers are abroad. Instead, they listen to them and give them financial backing.

Some wag has put it like this:

> Little drops of water,
> Little grains of sand
> Make the mighty oceans
> And the beauteous land.
>
> So the daily pressures,
> Subtle though they be,
> Serve to shape the oddballs
> We call you and me.
>
> "Little Drops of Water"
> —Author unknown

We oddballs down here can really be taken in. Peter says, "Beware of false teachers."

In chapter 1 we saw that there were prophets of God in the Old Testament, and they prophesied 100 percent accurately. Peter now says, "But there were false prophets also among the people." There were not only true prophets but also false prophets among the people of Israel. One example of this is the time that Ahab and Jehoshaphat went out against the Syrians (see 1 Kings 22). They called in a bunch of the false prophets of Baal who urged Ahab and Jehoshaphat to go to battle. Jehoshaphat saw immediately that they were not getting a word from God, and he said, "Don't you have a true prophet of God here?" Ahab said, "Yes, but I keep him in prison because he never says anything good about me." Today a great many people don't like a preacher unless he says something nice about them all the time. Ahab was like that. This prophet of God, Micaiah, told him the truth, and Ahab didn't like that. But they brought Micaiah in, and he told Ahab, "If you go to battle, you will be slain." Ahab turned to Jehoshaphat and said, "See, he never says anything good about me!" It's too bad that Ahab didn't listen to him, because he *was* slain just as Micaiah said he would be. Micaiah was a true prophet of God, but there were also several hundred false prophets at that time.

"Even as there shall be false teachers among you." Dr. Marvin R. Vincent, in his very fine *Word Studies in the New Testament*, says that this Greek word for "false teachers," *pseudo-didaskalos*, occurs only here in the New Testament. As we have said before, false teachers are the danger for the church today, and believe me, they are dangerous. What is a false teacher? A false teacher is one who knows the truth but deliberately lies for some purpose. It is either for some selfish reason, or he wants to please people, or he does it for money. There are many teachers like that today. They preach and say what people want them to say, although they know what the truth is—*that* is a false teacher.

There are other men who teach error *ignorantly*. Some of the great reformers of the past and some of the great post-apostolic church fathers believed and taught some things which we do not hold to today. We believe they were entirely in error on certain things. Those men were not false teachers. They believed they were teaching the truth, and that does not put them in the category of a false teacher. A false teacher knows what he is doing, and he does it deliberately.

"Even as there shall be"—Peter puts this period of apostasy out yonder in the future because it would be beyond his death. Jude also discusses this same subject of apostasy. The very fact that 2 Peter and Jude are so much alike has caused some of the critics to say that one copied from the other. Let me state it a little differently: When God wants to emphasize something, He says it twice. That is the reason that the Lord Jesus said, "*Verily, verily,* I say unto you." One "verily" is enough for Him, but when He says it twice, you had better sit up and listen. Therefore, this is something that God considers rather important. However, when Jude wrote, he said that there were *already* false teachers in the church. They came in quite early, by the way, and they have been in the church ever since.

I think we have in this first verse a good definition of false teachers: "Who privily shall bring in damnable heresies, even denying the Lord that bought them, and bring upon themselves swift destruction." "Damnable heresies" actually means *destructive* heresies. That which identifies these false teachers is that they deny Christ's work of redemption for them. They will appear in the church as members of the church; they will claim to be Christians, and they will work secretly under cover of hypocrisy.

Years ago I preached in a church which was a very fine, fundamental church where the people loved the Word of God. They called a pastor to that church whom they had questioned concerning whether he believed the Scriptures and whether he believed in their plenary, verbal inspiration. He had answered affirmatively to every question they asked. About two years later, I was in that city and found that the members of the church had scattered and were attending other churches. They told me that this man had absolutely misrepresented himself—that's what the kinder people said. Some said, "He *lied* to us." That's exactly what he had done. He had come into that church and actually been a hypocrite. He said one thing when he actually believed another.

Now false teachers have some true doctrine. There is not a cult that I know of which does not have some truth in it. That is the one thing that makes them very dangerous, ten thousand times more dangerous than if they were 100 percent in error. These teachers generally believe some things that are true. Our Lord said, "Beware of false prophets, which come to you in sheep's clothing, but inwardly they are ravening wolves" (Matt. 7:15). Paul warned the church at Ephesus, "For I know this, that after my departing shall grievous wolves enter in among you, not sparing the flock" (Acts 20:29). These wolves in sheep's clothing will absolutely destroy the flock and scatter them.

Our Lord made this clear when He gave us a picture of the condition of the kingdom after His rejection, crucifixion, and resurrection. He would not establish His kingdom on earth at that time, but He said that the kingdom of heaven would be like a sower sowing seed, like a mustard tree, and like leaven. Leaven has gotten into the bread today. The bread is the Word of God, and there is a lot of false teaching that goes out under the guise of being the Word of God.

And many shall follow their pernicious ways; by reason of whom the way of truth shall be evil spoken of [2 Pet. 2:2].

"And many shall follow their pernicious ways." False followers will go after false teachers. I do not believe that God's elect can be permanently deceived. I believe that God permits a lot of the cults and "isms" in order to draw away from the true church that which is false, because those who are phony will go after that sort of thing. This is exactly what Paul said would take place: "For there must be also heresies among you, that they which are approved may be made manifest among you" (1 Cor. 11:19). In other words, the genuine child of God will not go in that direction. The Lord Jesus said, "My sheep hear My voice, and they will not follow a false shepherd" (see John 10:27). When you see people take out after one of these false teachers, they are either ignorantly deceived or they are deliberately deceived because that is what they believe and what they wanted to hear all the time.

And through covetousness shall they with feigned words make merchandise of you: whose judgment now of a long time lingereth not, and their damnation slumbereth not [2 Pet. 2:3].

"Feigned words"—the Greek word for "feigned" is *plastos.* Dr. Joseph H. Thayer, in his lexicon of the New Testament, says that *plastos* means "moulded, formed, as from clay, wax, stone." *Plastos*—does that sound like another word you've heard? We have a new word, a word that wasn't even in existence in Peter's day, yet in a way it was. *Plastic*—that's the word Peter uses here. I love that, because today you can buy a plastic pitcher, you can buy a plastic bucket, you can buy plastic dishes, you can buy plastic toys. You can buy almost anything in plastic because plastic can be molded into every possible shape.

May I say this, and I do want to say it kindly. There are also plastic preachers who can be molded and shaped by the people that they serve. They say what their congregations want to hear. They use plastic words. This is the reason that neo-orthodoxy, when it first appeared, deceived so many people. When I came to Pasadena many years ago to pastor a church here, another pastor came about the same time. He was an outstanding liberal who is pretty much known all over the world today. A member of his church attended my Bible class, and she said, "Oh, he is sound in the faith because he uses the same language that you do." I said, "Fine, but does he mean what I mean by it?" She was sure that he did. On Easter Sunday she called me and said, "Dr. McGee, you have been wrong in criticizing this man. He spoke of the *resurrection* of Jesus today." I asked her, "But did you go up afterward and ask him whether he believed that Jesus was raised *bodily* from the tomb?" She replied, "I'm sure that that is what he meant." I told her, "I'm sure that he didn't, but you ask him." The next day she called me, weeping, and said, "You know, he just ridiculed the idea of the bodily resurrection!" So I explained to her, "These fellows use our vocabulary, but they don't have our dictionary." In other words, they may say something, but the important thing is what they *mean* by what they say.

Peter tells us that false teachers will speak with feigned words, plastic words, words that are just molded words. They will fit their words to the people to whom they are speaking. They speak one thing to one crowd and then talk differently to another crowd. I know a man who can bring a fundamental message if he is in a fundamental group, but when he gets with a liberal group, he is just about as liberal as they are. He is a plastic preacher—you can pour him into any mold, and he will accommodate himself to it.

What is the motivation for these false teachers? I tell you, Simon Peter puts it right out in the open here: "And through covetousness." They do it because they are covetous. Covetousness is actually a form of idolatry. Sometimes it may be that they are covetous for a position, for a name, for popularity. Many of them are covetous of money.

I am not talking through my hat, my friend. I could give you example after example of the fact that there are many false teachers abroad today, but I will give you just one. I read a report in a very fine Christian publication which tells about a service held by a well-known evangelist. They reported that the preacher introduced the evangelist, saying, "He is a man after my heart because he loves money just like I love it." As the evangelist spoke, he was forceful, he was dynamic, and he put on quite a show. For forty-five minutes he did not read one Scripture verse, not even his text. He partially quoted only three or four verses. He used the personal pronoun *I* 175 times. He referred to Jesus Christ only eleven times. There was laughter every two minutes during his message—he was quite a comedian. When the invitation was given, some twenty young people responded to the urgings of the evangelist and went forward. For what? They had not heard the gospel! This is something that is so prevalent in our country today. The average church member doesn't know the gospel when he hears it and does not recognize when he doesn't hear it. This is the tragedy of the hour in which we live. There are many false teachers abroad today.

I urge you to check on all Bible teachers and radio preachers that you listen to. Check on me. Am I teaching the Word of God? Examine the Word of God and *see* whether I am or not. And check yourself. Every child of God should examine himself to see whether or not he is in the faith.

"And through covetousness shall they with feigned words *make merchandise of you.*" In other words, these false teachers are doing it for money. I personally resent all forms of promotion today. When I return from a trip and sort through my accumulated mail, I will sometimes pitch letters into my wastebasket without even opening them. The name of the organization is on the envelope, so I know who they come from. I've been getting their letters for years, although I've never contributed to those organizations. I don't know why they keep sending out all that propaganda, but I do know this: they want to make merchandise of me. It is my conviction that an organization ought to appeal only to folk who are interested in their certain work. There are many fine mission organizations, and there are many fine Christian radio programs, but there are some that are nothing in the world but promotion. One of the marks of a false teacher is that he is a promoter. He is not interested in giving you the Word of God; he is not attempting to help you. He is attempting to get something from you, to make merchandise of you. You are sort of a food trading stamp for him or a luxury car for him.

"Whose judgment now of a long time lingereth not, and their damnation slumbereth not." This is something that has disturbed a great many folk, including some in the Bible. For example, the psalmist was disturbed that the wicked were getting by with their sin—or so he thought. But then he said, "I went into the temple of the Lord." What did he learn in the temple? All he learned in the temple was that God is in charge and He will take care of the wicked (see Ps. 73).

The apostle Paul was mistreated again and again, and he resented it. He would not let the authorities at Philippi release him from jail and urge him to leave town secretly. He was a Roman citizen, and he forced them to do it the right way. But Paul told us not to take vengeance. We are to turn our case over to God. The minute that we try to get revenge we are taking God's place, because ". . . Vengeance is mine; I will repay, saith the Lord" (Rom. 12:19). And if you try to get revenge, you depart from your walk of faith. However, walking by faith does not mean that you are a Mr. Milquetoast whom everyone can push around and treat any way they please. Rather, it means that you can say, "All right, brother, you have mistreated me, you have done this to me, but I'm going to turn you over to the Lord." Paul wrote, "Alexander the coppersmith did me much evil: the Lord reward him according to his works" (2 Tim. 4:14). "The

Lord will take care of him. I've turned him over to the Lord," Paul said concerning another brother who had mistreated him.

Peter assures us that God will also take care of these false teachers someday. When I heard of the death of a certain liberal not long ago, a man said to me, "Well, he's better off today than he was when he was in this life." Frankly, I'm not so sure about that because he must give account to God for his life. I would not want to have to go into the presence of God someday and have the Lord say to me, "Look, McGee, you came to a passage of Scripture that time, and you soft-pedaled it because you were afraid of criticism. You didn't teach it like it is written." God would hold me accountable for that. I will have to turn in a report to Him for my Bible-teaching ministry. May I say to you, *you* are going to have to turn in an account to God also.

It may look like God is slumbering; it may look like God is taking a nap. He may not seem to be doing very much about these false teachers, but He is, my friend. Habakkuk wondered whether God would do anything about the enemies of Israel, but he found out that in reality God was moving much too fast for him—He was not slumbering at all.

Now Peter will give us three examples of apostates in the past. His first example is of the angels who sinned (v. 4), and it is an example of how the *Devil* works. His second example is that of the world of Noah's day (v. 5), and it is the example of the *world*. The third example (v. 6) is the turning of the cities of Sodom and Gomorrah into ashes, and that is the example of the *flesh*. We have here the world, the flesh, and the Devil, but Peter puts the Devil first—the Devil, the world, and the flesh. These are the three enemies that you and I need to be aware of. John, the apostle of love, says, "*Love not* the world, neither the things that are in the world . . ." (1 John 2:15, italics mine). "The world" does not mean the beautiful flowers, the mountains, the trees, and the sea. It means the world system down here that is against God—*that* is what we are not to love.

Peter will talk first about the Devil and about the fact that God in the past has judged angels. The subject of angels and demons is highly debatable and very popular today. In fact, there is too much attention being given to it. Many books are being written about Satan and about demons and all that sort of thing. I suppose they have their place, but my feeling is that the positive side needs to be emphasized more. I have a message that I give,

"Who is Antichrist?" and I always conclude that message by saying that I don't know much about Antichrist and I don't *want* to know much about him. The One I want to know is the Lord Jesus Christ. I cannot find anywhere where Paul or any other of the writers in Scripture say, "That I might know the Antichrist. . . ." But Paul does say, "That I may know him [the Lord Jesus], and the power of his resurrection, and the fellowship of his sufferings . . ." (Phil. 3:10). It is life eternal to know God, the Father, and the Son, the Lord Jesus, whom He has sent (see John 17:3). Scripture does not instruct us to know Antichrist or to know all about Satan. It is true that we are not to be ignorant of his devices. We need to beware of him, but we can pay too much attention to him.

For if God spared not the angels that sinned, but cast them down to hell, and delivered them into chains of darkness, to be reserved unto judgment [2 Pet. 2:4].

"For if God spared not the angels that sinned." Many commentators feel that this refers to the events of Genesis 6. I do not agree, because I do not believe that the "sons of God" mentioned there were angels. Genesis talks about the genealogy of *man*. It concerns that family which was leading to the coming of Christ, which would bring Him into the world. That line intermarried with the world, with the line of Cain, and brought about a generation who were so sinful that God finally brought the Flood upon them. That is what Genesis 6 is all about, and I do not think this verse here in 2 Peter has any reference to that at all.

Then what does this verse have reference to? I will have to do just a little bit of speculating, yet Scripture does give us some hazy glimpses of this. We find that Jude refers to these things also; the Book of Revelation gives us some inkling of it; and several of the prophets open this area to us just a little.

Man was sort of a Johnny-come-lately on this earth—we haven't been here too long. Before man was here on earth, apparently there was another creation. God had a program going long before man appeared on the scene, and there were many created intelligences. From among those angels, who were God's creation and who were His messengers, some rebelled against Him and apparently followed Satan. We are told in Revelation 12:7, "And there was war in heaven: Michael and his angels fought against the dragon; and the dragon fought and his angels." Back in the past there was a rebellion against God led by the creature we know today as Satan or the Devil. He has many names—he is the great deceiver; he is a liar from the beginning. This creature rebelled against God, and there followed with him a great company of angels.

Peter tells us that some of the angels who rebelled are already in chains, they are already incarcerated, but some of them have not yet been brought into that place of being inoperative. They are very active in the world today, and I believe they are the demons that we read about in the Word of God. I think we are seeing today a reappearance of the supernatural. I have considered giving a message on this subject of demons because so much that is false is being taught today. There is a reality in the supernatural world, and because a so-called miracle takes place does not mean that God did it. After all, Satan has a certain degree of power.

Therefore, this verse is a reference to that which took place before man was put on this earth, when there was a rebellion against God led by Satan.

"Cast them down to hell." The word for "hell" here is an unusual word which does not occur in very many places in Scripture. The Greek word is *tartarus*. The Greeks spoke of the lost being in *tartarus*. It is not hell as we think of it. Hell has not really been opened up to do business yet and will not be opened up until much later. The Devil is not in hell; he is abroad in God's creation. He goes into the presence of God, according to the Book of Job; and he is like a roaring lion, going up and down this earth, seeking whom he may devour, Peter told us in his first epistle. Although Satan is not in hell, certain of his angels have already been incarcerated.

"And delivered them into chains of darkness." The Greek word for "chains" is *seira*. Many believe it should be *seirōs*, for that is the word used in many of the better texts. *Seirōs* means "pits or caverns." The two words are very similar. Apparently these angels are in pits of darkness. People think of hell as being a place of fire, but I think it is a place of darkness. Darkness and fire just don't go together, because a fire makes light. Can you imagine being in darkness for eternity?

"To be reserved unto judgment." They have not yet been judged. The indictment has been made against them. God has declared them guilty, and they are waiting for the judgment to come.

And spared not the old world, but saved Noah the eighth person, a preacher of righteousness, bringing in the flood upon the world of the ungodly [2 Pet. 2:5].

"And spared not the old world." In chapter 3 Peter will talk about three worlds—the world that was, the world that is, and the world that is to come. God "spared not the old world," that is, the world before Noah.

"But saved Noah the eighth person, a preacher of righteousness." There were seven others with Noah. Noah, his three sons, their wives, and Noah's wife are the eight persons who came through the Flood.

"Bringing in the flood upon the world of the ungodly." The people were religious; they simply left the living and true God out of their religion. They were living as if God didn't exist at all. They were living in the flesh. It is a false idea today that you and I, in the flesh, have some good in us. Paul says, "I have discovered that in my flesh dwelleth no good thing" (see Rom. 7:18).

I read a report by Dr. Turnbull in his book, *Mountain People*. He made a study of a people called the Ik who have been discovered in Africa and who are absolutely living lower than animals. Dr. Turnbull reports that the children are cast off by the mother at the age of three and must provide for themselves or die. They find berries and bark and insects, and they scavenge around for what is left by wild animals. The stronger ones literally take food from the mouths of the elderly. The author said that it would be an insult to animals to call these people's behavior bestiality. Dr. Turnbull (who is a humanist and not a Christian) said that the Ik teach us that our much-vaunted human values are not inherent in humanity at all, but are associated only with a particular form of survival called society, and that all, even society itself, are luxuries that can be dispensed with. In other words, man apart from God is nothing in the world but an animal, and it is an insult to an animal to say that. You see, it is *God* who gives values; it is *God* who gives moral standards, and none of them are inherent in us.

Noah lived in a day when there was rebellion against God, a day when the world had become lawless. Genesis tells us, "And God saw that the wickedness of man was great in the earth, and that every imagination of the thoughts of his heart was only evil continually" (Gen. 6:5). Violence was abroad in the earth in that day. God moved in with the judgment of the Flood and brought an end to that pre-Noachic world. It was a world that had become, with the exception of one man and his family, a totally godless world. God did well in bringing judgment at that particular time. You can well see that it would not have been long until the entire world would have been in such a condition that God would have had to judge it and there would have been salvation for no one after that. In His judgment God had in mind the future that was coming, and His judgment reveals His care and respect for the human life He had created.

Immediately after the Flood, in order to curtail lawlessness and crime, God gave to man this edict: "Whoso sheddeth man's blood, by man shall his blood be shed: for in the image of God made he man" (Gen. 9:6). It is nonsense today to argue against capital punishment by saying that the Bible says, "Thou shalt not murder." "Thou shalt not murder" has reference to an individual who harbors hatred in his heart and, expressing his own fleshly feelings in anger or hatred, he slays another human being. My friend, *that's* murder. But God has given to governments the authority to execute any man who takes another man's life. Why? Listen to me for just a moment: You do not show respect for human life by letting off a murderer who has destroyed another human being. You show respect and value for human life when you take the life of a murderer who fails to respect another human being but despises him by killing him for some selfish or sinful reason.

Today the pendulum of the clock of public opinion is over on the side of the criminal. The sympathy goes to him: "Oh, he's a human being. We don't want to take his life." But he took someone else's life! We have had many softhearted and softheaded judges in this land, and we are far from God and His Word. Lawlessness has become so bad that the people of California have voted to reinstate capital punishment. Yet it is almost impossible to enforce it because of the godless leaders we have today. They know not God. They know not God's plan and program. Instead of being put in prison, the criminals are running the streets today, and the honest citizens are in prison in their own homes. I was in a home recently in the East where there were half a dozen locks on one door because that lovely home had been broken into. Criminals and thieves are abroad today. Dignity and respect for human life are shown when they are locked up, my friend.

Our nation has more than three strikes against it. Not only are we a nation of alcoholics, but also of murderers and thieves. The situation is alarming. Why have we come to this point? When I was in college, they didn't teach morals because they said that was not the purpose of education. "After all," they said, "if you just educate little Willy, he will come out all right." Little Willy is sort of a cross between a piece of Dresden china and a hothouse orchid. You don't want to apply the board of education to the seat of knowledge for fear you might ruin his little "umph" and he won't be able to express himself like the little flower that he is! Well, little Willy is expressing himself today: he is a thief, he's a murderer, he's a homosexual. My friend, may I say to you, the Lord Jesus said that out of the human heart proceed the ugliest, nastiest things that are imaginable. We need discipline. The unsaved world must have discipline from a government. If it does not, that nation will be destroyed. God laid down this principle for governments following His judgment upon the world of Noah's day.

And turning the cities of Sodom and Gomorrha into ashes condemned them with an overthrow, making them an ensample unto those that after should live ungodly [2 Pet. 2:6].

You can read the record of this in Genesis, chapter 19. It was the flesh that God judged at Sodom and Gomorrah. The inhabitants were given over to sodomy. Homosexuality was approved of in Sodom, and it is approved of in the United States.

The flesh is an ugly thing. You and I have that old nature, and it is a nature which expresses itself in that which is ugly, that which is wicked, that which is nasty. You cannot make me believe that by making homosexuality lawful somehow or other you have added dignity to it. God has said that when men go down that low, He gives them up. You can take it or leave it, but that's what the Word of God says (see Rom. 1:18–32). The very fact that we have been lenient and have smiled on this type of thing has caused it to increase and grow within our land.

And delivered just Lot, vexed with the filthy conversation of the wicked:

(For that righteous man dwelling among them, in seeing and hearing, vexed his righteous soul from day to day with their unlawful deeds;) [2 Pet. 2:7–8].

"And delivered just Lot, vexed with the filthy conversation of the wicked." This word *vexed* doesn't seem to me to convey what Peter is really saying. Many people say that Peter does not use good Greek, and yet I have had to look up the meaning of more words that Peter uses than even the apostle Paul uses. The Greek word he uses here is *kataponeō*, which means, according to Trench, "to tire down with toil, to exhaust with labor." It means "to afflict, to oppress with evil," actually, "to torment." One of the methods that communism has used and which apparently is used now in many places is to break down an individual by constantly putting him under a bright light, constantly plaguing him with questions, by pulling out his fingernails, and by doing all manner of torture to him. This word has that idea in it. Lot vexed his soul in the city of Sodom. He was never happy there. He was tormented on the inside. It was torture for him to live in Sodom.

I never got that impression of Lot while reading the Book of Genesis, by the way. I'm glad for Peter's comment—otherwise I would be apt to say that Lot was not saved. By reading the story back in Genesis of when Lot went down to the city of Sodom, got into politics there, and lost most of his family, I would come to the conclusion that he was not saved. Even when you read what happened with the two single daughters who escaped with him, you might wish that they too had stayed back in Sodom. The point Peter is making is that God got Lot out of that city; He knows "how to deliver the godly."

We are told in verse 6 that all of this is given to us as an example. An example of what? I think that you and I are going to get two big surprises when we get to heaven. The number one surprise will be that there are not going to be some people in heaven who we were sure were going to make it. They really weren't genuine, although we thought they were. The second and bigger shock will be this: There are going to be some people in heaven who we never even suspected were real born-again children of God. They didn't have very much of a testimony down here. Lot is an example of this—I don't think this man had any testimony for God at all. When the angels came and said that the cities of Sodom and Gomorrah would be destroyed, Lot went around to his sons-in-law and said, "I've got word from God that He is going to destroy this city. He's going to judge it. Let's leave!" The record says, "But he seemed as one that mocked." I suppose that they said, "We don't believe you,

old man. The kind of life you've been living down here doesn't reveal to us that you have had very much faith and confidence in God." If I had only Genesis to read, I would have come to the conclusion that Lot didn't make it to heaven, that he was not a saved man. But Peter says, "He delivered *just* Lot"—and that does not mean *only* Lot, because his two daughters went with him, and his wife, although she didn't get too far away. Lot was called "just" because he was justified in God's sight.

"And delivered just Lot, vexed with the filthy conversation [manner of life] of the wicked." He didn't go for the way they lived; he hated it. He was a just man, which means that he was justified before God because he trusted God as Abraham did, although he didn't lead a life like Abraham, one that was a testimony to the world. Lot stands on the page of Scripture as a saint of God who was justified because of his faith, but his life denied everything he believed and he never had a moment's peace down here.

"For that righteous man dwelling among them, in seeing and hearing." Just think of the filth that that man had to listen to! Very candidly, I do not believe that a child of God can continually engage in filthy conversation. Filthy conversation will lead to filthy action.

God said to this man, "Lot, you will have to get out of the city. I cannot destroy it with you in it." You see, in the meantime there was a man named Abraham who was not criticizing Lot but was praying for him. That is a good lesson for many of us. There is a preacher, a friend of mine, who criticizes everything and everybody. One day he was criticizing an outstanding Bible teacher whom I respect and know that God has mightily used. I said to my friend, looking him right straight in the eye, "Have you ever prayed for him?" He turned red and said he hadn't. I said, "Instead of criticizing him, why don't you pray for him? If you think he is wrong, pray for him."

Abraham prayed for the city of Sodom. He wanted his nephew Lot to be spared. Abraham asked God to spare the city for the sake of fifty righteous people. He finally got it down to ten righteous people, and then he stopped praying because he was afraid that Lot was not really a child of God. But Lot was, and God got him out. God said, "I cannot destroy the city until you get out."

Mrs. Lot left with him, but she looked back and was turned into a pillar of salt. That may sound strange. Why should she be turned into a pillar of salt just because she looked back?

My friend, it's what turning and looking back means. Why did she look back? It is obvious that, although she walked out of Sodom, she had left her heart back there. She was intertwined in everything that took place in that town—she belonged to the country club, the Shakespeare club, and every other kind of club. Perhaps the bridge club was having a meeting that afternoon and she really wanted to go. I think she plagued Lot, saying, "Why do we have to leave like this?" Another reason she turned and looked back was because she didn't believe God would destroy the city. Well, He did destroy the city, and He turned her into a pillar of salt.

The greatest lesson for us in these verses is that God's rescue of Lot from Sodom prefigures the rapture of the church. May I say to you, the rapture of the church will take place before the Great Tribulation Period, before the judgment comes, because God will not let any of His saints go through it. Even those who are like Lot, the weakest saints, will be taken out. Lot made it, and if you have trusted Christ as your Savior, you can be sure that you will be going out too. This is a marvelous example of the fact that the church will not go through the Great Tribulation Period. They have been justified by faith in Christ, and this man Lot was justified also.

The Lord knoweth how to deliver the godly out of temptations, and to reserve the unjust unto the day of judgment to be punished [2 Pet. 2:9].

To those who believe that the church is going through the Great Tribulation Period, I would like to say that God knows how to deliver His own. *You* may not know how, but *God* knows how. He also knows how "to reserve the unjust unto the day of judgment to be punished." God knows the difference between the godly and the unjust—I don't. The wheat and tares are growing together today, and He said, "Let them alone. Let them both grow together." I'm not worried about the tares today, although I must confess that I wish there weren't so many of them. But wheat and tares are growing—the Word of God is getting out in this glorious day in which we live. One of these days He will make the separation, when He takes His own out of the world and when the lost will be brought before the Great White Throne for judgment.

But chiefly them that walk after the flesh in the lust of uncleanness, and despise government. Presumptuous are

they, self-willed, they are not afraid to speak evil of dignities [2 Pet. 2:10].

"But chiefly them that walk after the flesh in the lust of uncleanness." This is a strong statement that Peter makes here. It actually means in the *defilements*—the defilements of uncleanness. This is a picture of those who are really lower than animals. They are those who delight in that which is vulgar, vile, and vicious. They relish that type of thing.

"And despise government." Many commentators say that this refers to government here on earth. I have reason to believe, since this word occurs so few times in the Word of God, that it really means "dominion." The same word *kuriotēs* is translated "dominion" in verse 8 of Jude and "lordship" in the first chapter of Ephesians. In Ephesians it has to do with spiritual governments. In other words, they despise that which is spiritual, that which God has ordained above us: the angels and the way God is running His universe. They are the ones who ask God to damn everything under the sun. They are not pleased with anything.

Not only that, Peter says, "Presumptuous are they." That means they are daring. They are daredevils. They don't mind blaspheming. It makes them feel expansive and big to use such language.

"Self-willed"—that is, they are going to do their own thing.

"They are not afraid to speak evil of dignities." The word for "dignities" is actually *glories*. They speak evil of that which is sacred, that which is holy. Isn't it interesting that men take *God's* name in vain? They don't take the city's name in vain or their boss's name in vain or the name of some person they hate. But they take God's name in vain. They are not afraid to speak evil of dignities, of glories, of this order that God has established in His universe.

Whereas angels, which are greater in power and might, bring not railing accusation against them before the Lord [2 Pet. 2:11].

The false teachers are lifted up with pride, and they do something that angels don't dare to do. In the little Epistle of Jude, we find that Jude gives a specific instance of this when Michael the archangel was disputing with Satan about the body of Moses. You see, the Devil didn't want Moses to appear later in the Promised Land (at the transfiguration of Jesus), and so there was some dispute. God buried the body of Moses. And Jude tells us that Michael would not bring a railing accusation against the Devil, but he simply said, ". . . The Lord rebuke thee" (Jude 9). This is a spirit that we need to manifest today, a spirit of humility, in the sense that we turn all of this over to God. It is pride that causes us to speak as we do. When I hear someone, sometimes even a Christian, talking about the Devil, ridiculing him and calling him names, I have to say that Michael the archangel wouldn't do that, and if Michael, exalted as he is, wouldn't do it, a little man down here on earth needs to be very careful.

But these, as natural brute beasts, made to be taken and destroyed, speak evil of the things that they understand not; and shall utterly perish in their own corruption [2 Pet. 2:12].

"But these, as natural brute beasts." These apostates are like wild animals. We hear a great deal today about man descending from an animal, but both the Old and New Testaments make it very clear that man is capable of living *lower* than the animals. He's not descended from anything. He's right down with them, if you please, and lives like an animal. Peter will give an illustration of this a little later on in this chapter.

They are natural wild animals, "made to be taken and destroyed" just like an animal is taken. They've descended to that low plane and have reached the place where they are hopeless and helpless.

They "speak evil of the things that they understand not." This that Peter says of false teachers can also be applied to many others. Something that has amazed me ever since I became a Christian is how smart some men who are not Christians can be and yet they do not at all understand the Word of God. There have been many brilliant men in the past who had no knowledge of what the Word of God is about. Let me give you an example.

William Wilberforce, a member of the British Parliament, was an alcoholic and lived a very fast life until he was converted. He wanted his friend, Edmund Burke, to hear one of the great preachers of Scotland, and when they were up in Scotland, he took Burke to hear this preacher. Afterward, he was interested to get Burke's reaction to the sermon. His reaction was very simple, and it revealed something. Burke said, "That man is a brilliant orator, but *what* was he talking about?" Edmund Burke, one of the great English statesmen, when he heard a gospel message, said, "I don't even know what he is talking about!"

Also I was very much interested to read recently something about a great denomination in this country, a church that down through the years has preached justification by faith. They made a survey and found that 40 percent of their members believe they are saved by their own works. How tragic it is to see that people do not understand the gospel! Many who have been hearing it year in and year out do not understand it at all.

"And shall utterly perish in their own corruption." Earlier Peter talked about the fact that the child of God has escaped the corruption of the world—but these have not escaped the corruption. Some of them have escaped the pollutions of the world. In other words, there are many lost sinners who say, "I wouldn't do the things that this low-down individual is doing"—and he wouldn't. He has escaped the *pollutions*, but he has not escaped the *corruptions*. On the outside he is religious; he goes through forms; he does certain works, but his heart is not right with God at all. He has a corrupt heart, and he has done nothing whatsoever about that.

And shall receive the reward of unrighteousness, as they that count it pleasure to riot in the day time. Spots they are and blemishes, sporting themselves with their own deceivings while they feast with you [2 Pet. 2:13].

In verses 13–14 we see in the description of apostates the utter corruption of the human heart. When a man thinks wrong, he is going to act wrong—you just cannot escape that fact. There are a great many people who say, "This is my life. I can live it as I please." It is well known that we have men today in government who are definitely immoral. They have affairs with women who are not their wives. We know that most of them drink, and many of them drink to excess. They say, "This is *my* business. My private life is my business." My friend, their private lives are not their business if they are representing this government and representing my country. If they want to lead that kind of life, they ought to get out of government, because they are hurting their country and they are hurting us. We want men in government who are sober, men who are honest, men who are moral men. This is what is desperately needed today.

Having eyes full of adultery, and that cannot cease from sin; beguiling unsta-

ble souls: an heart they have exercised with covetous practices; cursed children [2 Pet. 2:14].

My, this is harsh language that Peter uses in speaking of false teachers! They are guilty of all of these immoral excesses, and don't kid yourself that God does not intend to judge them someday.

Which have forsaken the right way, and are gone astray, following the way of Balaam the son of Bosor, who loved the wages of unrighteousness [2 Pet. 2:15].

Balaam is mentioned three times in the closing books of the New Testament. In 2 Peter it is the *way* of Balaam. In Jude it is the *error* of Balaam. And it is the *doctrine* of Balaam in the Book of Revelation. Each one is different. What is "the way of Balaam"? Peter says he is "the son of Bosor, who loved the wages of unrighteousness." Balaam knew that he should not go and prophesy against Israel, but he loved the price that was being offered to him. Therefore, "the way of Balaam" is the covetousness of one who does religious work for personal profit.

But was rebuked for his iniquity: the dumb ass speaking with man's voice forbad the madness of the prophet [2 Pet. 2:16].

Peter says that Balaam was mad to go and that the jackass he was riding spoke to him. Some wag has said that in the old days it was a miracle when a jackass spoke and now in our day it is a miracle when one of them keeps quiet! This jackass spoke to Balaam and rebuked him because of his covetousness.

My friend, I believe that you can judge the religious racketeer by his standard of living. A friend of mine heard me make the statement that people should check up on radio broadcasters and see what kind of homes they live in and what cars they drive. He thought I was wrong to have made a statement like that, but he decided to check up on one man. He found that man living in a very costly home with two Cadillacs parked in front and an expensive swimming pool behind it. My friend had also heard about certain other excesses in that man's life, and so he decided that he was supporting the wrong broadcaster. "The way of Balaam"—covetousness. This is one of the ways a false religious teacher can be identified, and God will judge him for it.

These are wells without water, clouds that are carried with a tempest; to

whom the mist of darkness is reserved for ever [2 Pet. 2:17].

As a boy I lived in West Texas. We left there in the third year of a three-year drought. I can remember when we would go into the fields and chop cotton—believe me, in those days cotton didn't grow well in that country even if there was rain. But sometimes late in the afternoon big thunderheads, big clouds, would gather overhead, and there would be lightning. We'd think, *My, we are going to have rain*—but we didn't have rain. How dry it was! Many people are following false teachers who are like that. They are "wells without water." They are like clouds, beautiful clouds. Oh, how tremendous it is to see and hear these folks. They are very impressive, but there is no water in the well, and there is no rain in the clouds. People are thirsting today for the Word of God, and yet it is not being given to them.

For when they speak great swelling words of vanity, they allure through the lusts of the flesh, through much wantonness, those that were clean escaped from them who live in error [2 Pet. 2:18].

"For when they speak great swelling words of vanity." These false teachers use beautiful, flowery language. They soar to the heights oratorically, speaking in basso profundo voice.

"They allure through the lusts of the flesh, through much wantonness." It is a religion that appeals to the eye, a religion that appeals to the ear, a religion that appeals even to the nose. One preacher said to me, "I always have my church sprayed on Sunday morning." He wants it to smell good. Don't misunderstand me—I think the place ought to look nice; the music ought to be good music, and I don't mind a fragrant smell, but those things are not to be depended upon. They are the lusts, the desires, of the flesh. But Peter is accusing the false teachers of more than this. "Through much wantonness" refers to lewdness, sexual excesses.

This man Simon Peter is really being sarcastic now—

While they promise them liberty, they themselves are the servants of corruption: for of whom a man is overcome, of the same is he brought in bondage [2 Pet. 2:19].

"While they promise them liberty, they themselves are the servants of corruption." Some habit has these false teachers enslaved, and yet they are promising liberty to others!

"For of whom a man is overcome, of the same is he brought in bondage." This is the picture that we have before us: they promise liberty, but they don't really know what it is themselves.

For if after they have escaped the pollutions of the world through the knowledge of the Lord and Saviour Jesus Christ, they are again entangled therein, and overcome, the latter end is worse with them than the beginning [2 Pet. 2:20].

These apostates have a head knowledge of Christ. They know the truth but have no love of the truth. They reject what they once professed and become enslaved in some sort of corruption.

And, my friend, I hear many folk say, "Oh, I am very religious. I belong to a certain church. We don't believe the Bible is really the Word of God, but we talk a lot about love and brotherhood. We have a beautiful church and a lovely service that makes us feel good." Such people have escaped the pollutions of the world. They are horrified when they read of crime and violence in the newspaper. You see, they have escaped the pollutions of the world but not the corruptions.

"Through the knowledge of the Lord and Saviour Jesus Christ." It is not that they haven't heard the gospel. They *have* heard the gospel. One man told me, "I listen to your Bible broadcast nearly every day." But he had to admit that he didn't believe anything; he even doubted that there was a God. That man knows the gospel. When someone asked me, "Why don't you present the gospel to him sometime when you're playing golf?" I told him, "He's heard me present the gospel over a hundred times. There is no need of saying any more." Peter says, "They are again entangled therein, and overcome, the latter end is worse with them than the beginning."

In this chapter Peter has dealt very definitely with the apostasy that was coming into the church through false teachers who were creeping in and teaching false doctrines, teaching that which is contrary to the Word of God. Peter says that they pervert the truth of God, and they do it for their own advantage. These false teachers exalt themselves instead of exalting Christ. They do not use the Word of God except for a few little proof texts that more or less clothe their teaching with a pious halo. They use big words which are counterfeit

words. They try to impress people that they are very intellectual, and they are interested in making money. They claim that they can change people. I know that I will get into trouble by saying this, but I think you ought to examine very carefully anyone who claims to have a supernatural power to heal or to perform miracles. Another thing that sometimes identifies a false teacher is that he is living secretly in lust and sin. You and I cannot fight these false teachers; I'm not attempting to fight them; I'm just trying to expose them. But one day *God* is going to expose them, and He is going to judge them.

For it had been better for them not to have known the way of righteousness, than, after they have known it, to turn from the holy commandment delivered unto them [2 Pet. 2:21].

Now Peter concludes all this by saying that it actually would have been better for them not to have known the way of righteousness than, having known it, to then turn from the gospel.

I have done something in my ministry which has not been original with me at all. I heard the late Dr. A.C. Gaebelein say this, and it was so effective and so true that I have used it on many occasions. I will sometimes conclude a message by saying, "Friends, if you came in here today unsaved and you walk out of here unsaved, I am the worst enemy that you have ever had, because you have heard the gospel and you can never go into the presence of God and tell Him that you have never heard the gospel. You have heard it, and it will be worse for you when God pronounces judgment than for any heathen in the darkest part of the earth today."

But it is happened unto them according to the true proverb, The dog is turned to his own vomit again; and the sow that was washed to her wallowing in the mire [2 Pet. 2:22].

Peter speaks of these false teachers, using the term *dog*. To the Jewish mind there was nothing lower than a dog, by the way. "The dog is turned to his own vomit again." Peter draws from Proverbs 26:11 to show that they will return to their true, natural, unchanged condition.

"And the sow that was washed to her wallowing in the mire." It is Simon Peter who gives us the parable of the prodigal pig. You may never have heard the parable of the prodigal pig, but here it is. It is, of course, based on the parable of the Prodigal Son, which is one of the greatest parables the Lord Jesus ever gave (see Luke 15:11–32).

There are those who say that you cannot preach the gospel from the parable of the Prodigal Son. However, the first time that I ever went forward in a meeting was under a brush arbor in southern Oklahoma in a little place called Springer. It's not much of a place today, I'm told, and it certainly wasn't in that day. I went forward and knelt down, and all I can remember of that night is that the preacher preached on the Prodigal Son. I can remember the figures of speech that he used. He took the Prodigal Son through all the nightclubs and places of sin. That night all the saints sinned vicariously through the preacher's message. Believe me, it was a very effective message. I'm confident that others got saved that night, but nobody took the time to explain to me about the gospel. I didn't really understand it, and my life afterward revealed that I wasn't saved, but my heart was certainly open for it.

Actually, the story of the Prodigal Son is not how a sinner becomes a son but how a son becomes a sinner. The account, as recorded in Luke 15, is a familiar story. You remember that there was a father who had two boys. One of the boys, the younger one, wanted to take off for the far country. Dr. Streeter calls this the sin of propinquity. That is a big word, but it simply means that the things near at hand are not so attractive but that the faraway places have an allurement, an enchantment. I think the chief allurement of sin is its mystery. The old bromide that grass is greener on the other side of the fence is the story of this boy.

So the boy ran away and soon was living it up. When he had plenty of money, the fair-weather friends were with him, but they soon faded away. He ended up having to go out and get a job working for a man who raised pigs. When the Lord Jesus mentioned that, both the publicans and Pharisees winced, because a Jewish boy could have sunk no lower than that. He hit bottom. In effect, he was on drugs, involved in sexual immorality, and all that type of thing. This boy was down in the pigpen.

Again, let's understand what the parable is primarily teaching. It is not showing how a sinner gets saved, but it reveals the heart of the Father who will not only save a sinner but will take back a son who sins. Someone asked the late Dr. Harry Rimmer, "Suppose the boy had died in the pigpen? What then?" Dr. Rimmer said, "Well, if he had died in the pigpen, there is one thing for sure, he would not have

been a dead pig. He was a son." He was a son when he left home; he was a son when he got to the far country; he was a son while he was living in sin; and he was a son in the pigpen. And because he was a son, he made a statement one day, a statement that no pig could ever have made. He said, "My father lives up yonder in that great big home. He has servants who are better off than I am. I am his son, but I'm living down here with the pigs. I will arise, and I will go to my father." No pig could say that, unless he was going in the opposite direction, heading back toward the pigpen.

Now what is the father going to do with his boy when he returns home? According to the Mosaic Law, that boy was to have been stoned to death (see Deut. 21:18–21)—but he wasn't stoned to death. The son went back and made his confession, "Father, I have sinned against heaven and against you." But his father wouldn't let him finish. You would expect the father to have said to one of his servants, "Go down and cut off some hickory limbs and bring them back to me. I'm going to whip this boy within an inch of his life. He has disgraced my name; he's spent my substance; he's wasted his time. He has been in sin, and I'm going to teach him." But that's not what happened at all. The boy, you see, had gotten his whipping in the far country. All prodigals get their whipping when they are away from home. When they come back to the heavenly Father, there is always a banquet, a robe, and a ring. And "they began to be merry." The fun was up at the father's house and never in the pigpen.

The interesting thing now is that Peter says, "And the sow that was washed [returned] to her wallowing in the mire." Now we can add something to the parable of the Prodigal Son. One of those little pigs in the pigpen said to the Prodigal Son, "You say you want to leave this lovely pigpen with all of this nice mud and goo, and you want to go up to your father's house? That sounds good; in fact, you've sold me. I think maybe I'd like to go up there with you and try it myself."

So the Prodigal Son told him, "If you go up there, things are sure going to be different! You are going to have to clean up."

When they got to the father's house, the father put his arms around the boy and said, "Bring forth the robe." Actually, he could smell those clothes his son had been wearing in the pigpen, and what he really meant was, "Give him a good bath and then put a new robe on him. He can't smell like that or live like that in my house."

The little pig went with the Prodigal Son, and he had to get all cleaned up too. They washed this little pig up nicely and tied a pink ribbon around his neck. They brushed his teeth with Pepsodent, and the little pig went squealing through the house. But it was only a couple of days until the little pig came to the Prodigal Son with a downcast look and said, "Prodigal Son, I don't like it here."

And the son said, "Why, I am having the best time I've ever had in my life since I came home, and you say you don't like it here! What's wrong?"

The little pig replied, "I don't like this idea of having white sheets on the bed. If we could just get to a place where there is plenty of good, sloppy mud, I could sleep better there."

"We just don't do that here in the father's house," said the Prodigal Son. "You just can't live in a pigpen here."

"Another thing I don't like is sitting at a table, using a knife and fork, and having a white tablecloth, and eating out of a plate. Why couldn't we have a trough down on the floor and put everything in there? We could all jump in and have the biggest time of our lives."

"We don't do that here!" said the son.

And the little pig said, "Well, I think I'll arise and go to my father." His old man wasn't in that house, and so he started back to his home. He had been all cleaned up, but he went back to the pigpen and found his old man right down in the middle of the biggest loblolly you've ever seen—mud all around him, dirty, filthy, and smelly. That little old pig began to squeal and made a leap for it. He jumped in right beside his father, saying, "Old man, I sure am glad to get back home!" You know why? Because he was a pig.

I had the privilege of being pastor in a downtown Los Angeles church beginning in 1949. Those were the years when subdivisions were beginning to be built in Southern California. That's the period when the population doubled again and again. People came from everywhere, and we saw a tremendous ingathering in the church I pastored during that period. I have always thanked the Lord that He gave me the privilege of being in that unique position at just the right time.

Although it was a great time because so many folk turned to the Lord, there was always the problem of how to tell the pigs from the sons—that is, professing Christians from real born-again believers. It was difficult and confusing, but I learned something. I found that at one end of the road was the Father's house, at the other end of the road was a pigpen, and there were always prodigal sons who were going back to the Father's house.

I talked to a preacher's son one time when he came in to see me. He was a handsome young man who had come out to Hollywood to make it big, but he was one of those who didn't have the charisma and didn't quite make it. He got in with the wrong crowd and began to drink. He saw that he was going down and down. He was a prodigal son—he wasn't a pig. He hated the life he had been living. When he came to see me, he said "My dad is a wonderful man. I've let him down so, and I just don't know how he would receive me. I don't know whether I can go home or not."

I said, "Let me call him, and if he doesn't want to talk to you, we'll just hang up," and the boy agreed. So I called this man who is a very fine minister, and after we had exchanged a few pleasantries about the weather and such, I knew that he was wondering why I was calling him. I said, "I have somebody here in my study who would like to talk to you."

He knew who it was. He knew that his boy wasn't a pig but a son. That father broke down and said, "Is it my boy?"

I said, "Yes."

"Let me talk to him." The boy began to weep, and I'm sure the father was weeping too.

I just walked out of my study to let them talk. I came back in after the young man had hung up, and he said to me, "I'm going home."

However, the transition is always confusing because sometimes the prodigal sons are on the other side of the road going down to the pigpen. To add to the confusion, sometimes a pig will get out of the pigpen and go up to the Father's house. But he is a pig—he won't like it there. He may get all washed and cleaned up and become very religious. Sometimes he may even be made a deacon in the church. You just can't tell because he's all cleaned up on the outside; but inside he has the heart of a pig, and a pig loves the mire.

One time a lady came to me and said, "I used to know this man back East when he was a superintendent of a Sunday school and a deacon in the church. He's here on the West Coast now. He's drinking, he's divorced his wife, and he's running around. Is he saved or not?" I told her I didn't know, and she said, "You mean that you are a preacher, and you don't know whether that man is saved or not?"

I said, "No, I really don't know. I couldn't tell you, because all I can see is the outside. But I'll tell you what we'll do. We are in this great metropolitan area where there is a road with a pigpen at one end of it and the Father's house at the other end. I've learned that, if you wait long enough, all the pigs will go down to the pigpen and all the prodigal sons will go home to the Father's house. Just wait and see. If that man continues to live in the pigpen, we can know that he is a pig—because Peter says that the pig that was washed has now returned to her wallowing in the mire."

This is the mark of the apostate, and it is a frightful picture. I know of no more frightful picture in the Word of God other than chapter 18 of the Book of Revelation.

I will conclude with a poem written by a friend who heard me preach on this subject of the prodigal pig.

A Pig is a Pig

"Come home with me," said the prodigal
     son.
"We'll sing and dance and have lots of fun.

"We'll wine and dine with women and
     song.
You'll forget you're a pig before very
     long."

So the pig slipped out while the momma
     was asleep,
Shook off the mud from the mire so deep.

Around his neck was a bow so big,
He's gonna show the world, a pig's not a
     pig!

With his snout in the air he trotted along,
With the prodigal son who was singin' a
     song.

It must be great to be a rich man's son,
He would surely find out 'fore the day was
     done!

It didn't take him long to realize his mis-
     take—
He'd been scrubbed and rubbed till his
     muscles ached!

He squealed when they put a gold ring in
     his nose
And winced with pain when they
     trimmed his toes.

He sat at the table on a stool so high,
A bib around his neck and a fork to try,

While the prodigal son, in his lovely robe,
Kept feeding his face, so glad to be home!

When the meat came around, the pig gave
     a moan—
It looked too much like a kind of his own.

He jumped from his chair with a grunt
     and a groan,
Darted through the door and headed for
     home.

His four little feet made the dust ride
     high
For he didn't stop till he reached that sty!

It's what's on the inside that counts, my
     friend,
For a pig is a pig to the very end!

                —Evelyn C. Sanders

CHAPTER 3

THEME: Attitude toward return of the Lord, a test of apostates; agenda of God for the world—past world, present world, future world; admonition to believers

There are three major divisions in this chapter: (1) The attitude toward the return to the Lord as a test of apostates; (2) the agenda of God for the world; and (3) the admonition to believers.

This is another remarkable chapter which Peter has written.

ATTITUDE TOWARD RETURN OF THE LORD— A TEST OF APOSTATES

This second epistle, beloved, I now write unto you; in both which I stir up your pure minds by way of remembrance [2 Pet. 3:1].

Simon Peter makes it clear that he is the writer of both epistles.

"I stir up your pure minds"—"pure" is not the best translation. A better translation would be "sincere." I don't think that the saints back in Peter's day had minds which were any more pure than our minds are today—and I haven't found anyone yet who I thought had a pure mind. If you feel that you have a pure mind, I just haven't met you yet.

There is a certain cult which began in Chicago and majored in contemplation. Instead of having a big temple, as many of the cults do, this cult prepared little booths where a person may go and contemplate and think beautiful thoughts. These booths have beautiful pictures in them; the furnishings are rather plush, and everything is there for comfort to make the person *feel* good. Everything about the surroundings is lovely. The person is to sit in that booth and think pure thoughts.

I read about that when I was in Chicago many years ago and thought I would try it out. I didn't want to go to the cult's booths; so I sat in my hotel room. There were pictures on the wall—they weren't masterpieces, to be sure, but the room was attractive. I sat there and said to myself, "Now I am going to think some beautiful thoughts." Do you want to know something? I could think of the meanest, dirtiest things I have ever thought of in my whole life!

My friend, our minds are not *pure* minds, and the word Peter uses means "sincere" rather than pure. He is addressing genuine believers.

He is saying, "I want to stir up your sincere minds *by way of remembrance*." This is not something *new* he is going to talk to them about; he just wants to stir up their memories.

A man said to me, "I have a good memory. My problem is that my forgettery is even better." Well, many of us have that same problem, and Simon Peter could tell you about it from his own experience. On that night when he denied our Lord while he was warming his hands by the enemy's fire, he forgot all about the fact that the Lord Jesus had said that he would deny Him. The record tells us, "And the Lord turned, and looked upon Peter. And Peter remembered the word of the Lord, how he had said unto him, Before the cock crow, thou shalt deny me thrice" (Luke 22:61). Peter had forgotten all about it, you see. He had the same frailties that we have, and so he wants to stir up their (and our) sincere minds by way of remembrance.

Now what is it that he wants them to remember?

That ye may be mindful of the words which were spoken before by the holy prophets, and of the commandment of us the apostles of the Lord and Saviour [2 Pet. 3:2].

"The holy prophets" are the Old Testament writers. "And of the commandment of us the apostles." Notice that Simon Peter doesn't put himself in a position of being above the other apostles; he is just one of the boys. Before he finishes this epistle, he will refer to something Paul had written, which means he includes Paul as an apostle also. He is saying that the things he is going to remind them of had been written about by the other apostles and also had been the subject of the Old Testament prophets.

Now notice the subject—

Knowing this first, that there shall come in the last days scoffers, walking after their own lusts [2 Pet. 3:3].

"Knowing this first"—this was something they were to know first of all.

"There shall come in the last days"—these are the days in which you and I live, and they will continue on into the Great Tribulation

Period after the church is gone from the earth.

"Scoffers" will be the apostates whom he described so vividly back in chapter 2. These scoffers evidently will be members of churches, and many of them pastors, who will be "walking after their own lusts," their own desires, not attempting to follow the Word of God. You see, it is this type of person who attacks the truths of the Bible. If a man is willing to forsake his sins and is willing to receive Christ, God will make His Word real to him. Paul, writing in 2 Corinthians 3, said that a veil is over their minds; but if their hearts will turn to God, the veil will be removed. Their problem is not intellectual; their problem is heart trouble. And so they put forward a false argument:

And saying, Where is the promise of his coming? for since the fathers fell asleep, all things continue as they were from the beginning of the creation [2 Pet. 3:4].

"Where is the promise of his coming?" In other words, they will say something like this, "Some of you premillennial folk have been saying for years that the Lord Jesus is going to come back and take the church out of the world, and then after a seven-year period of tribulation, He will come to the earth to establish His kingdom. Well, where is He? Why hasn't He come?" They are going to scoff at it. The second coming of Christ will be denied— not only by the atheist or Communist standing out yonder on a soap box, but it will also be denied by those who stand in the pulpit and profess to be believers.

Now what did the Old Testament prophets write about? They wrote about the coming of Christ to the earth to establish His kingdom. What did the New Testament apostles write about? They wrote about Christ's coming to take the church out of the world and then, after the Great Tribulation, about His coming to the earth to establish His kingdom. Notice that the Old Testament prophets did not write about the church—not one of them did. They wrote only about His coming to earth to establish His kingdom.

It was the Lord Jesus Himself who first revealed that He would be coming for His own. He said, as recorded in John, ". . . I go to prepare a place for you. And if I go and prepare a place for you, I will come again, and receive you unto myself . . ." (John 14:2–3). The place He was going to prepare was not down here. It was not on the other side of the

Mount of Olives—if you doubt that, go look at it; it is a desolate place. Our Lord went back to heaven, and that is where He is preparing a place for us. And He promised to come back for us. In 1 Thessalonians 4:17, we are told that we will meet Him in the air.

Let me repeat: The prophecy in the Old Testament of Christ's coming was to establish His kingdom upon the earth; the prophecy in the New Testament of His coming was first to take His church out of the world and *then* to come to establish His kingdom upon the earth.

"For since the fathers fell asleep, all things continue as they were from the beginning of the creation." This is the "proof" which the scoffers will offer, and, by the way, it is the most prevalent argument given in our day. "The fathers" would refer all the way back to father Adam.

The scoffers adopt the doctrine of *laissez faire* or let's continue with the status quo. Nothing unusual has happened in the past. Things have just progressed along. Man has evolved, and things have come along gently and nicely in the past. Peter is going to say, "That's where you are absolutely wrong. If you think nothing has happened in the past, let me tell you about it!"

AGENDA OF GOD FOR THE WORLD

Now Peter is going to talk about three worlds in one. That is not something strange to us. Older folks will remember using two-in-one shoe polish. Then there was a sewing machine company that put out three-in-one oil. Well, you and I live in a three-in-one world.

We have been hearing a great deal about one world, and certainly the world is moving toward the day when a world dictator will take over. I don't think there is any question about that in the minds of thoughtful men. Great thinkers of this century have taken the position that we have come to a crisis and to the end of man on the earth.

PAST WORLD

Peter presents a three-in-one world. Let's first look at world number one, the world that *was*.

For this they willingly are ignorant of, that by the word of God the heavens were of old, and the earth standing out of the water and in the water:

Whereby the world that then was, being overflowed with water, perished [2 Pet. 3:5–6].

"For this they *willingly* are ignorant of." My, this puts a great many scientists and Ph.D.'s in a pretty bad light!

"The world that then was, being overflowed with water, perished." That is, the world of people and of animals disappeared. This could refer to the world before Adam was put here, or it could refer to the Flood in Noah's day. I have vacillated between these two viewpoints, but I lean toward the latter now.

Regarding the first viewpoint, let me say that many of us believe that there is a hiatus between Genesis 1:1 and Genesis 1:2 and that a great catastrophe took place at that time. Today this view is largely rejected by the majority of Christians who are scientists. However, scientists change their theories over the years, and I am not prepared to go along with them yet.

There was a judgment in the pre-Adamic world, before man was put here. We have a suggestion of what took place in Isaiah 14:12–14: "How art thou fallen from heaven, O Lucifer, son of the morning! how art thou cut down to the ground, which didst weaken the nations! For thou hast said in thine heart, I will ascend into heaven, I will exalt my throne above the stars of God: I will sit also upon the mount of the congregation, in the sides of the north: I will ascend above the heights of the clouds; I will be like the most High." Satan's desire was never to be *unlike* God. He wanted to take God's place. And there are a great many human beings who want to be little gods down here. Any man who is working on his own salvation, whose theory is that he is good enough for heaven, ignores the fact that he is dealing with the holy God. He does not seem to realize that man is a sinner, that man is lost, and that God has provided a way of redemption for him. The Lord Jesus said, ". . . no man cometh unto the Father, but by me" (John 14:6). Remember that it was the God-man who said that! Now, if you think you can go to the Father on your own, what you are saying is this: "Move over, God. I'm coming up to sit beside you because I am a god also." That, you see, was Satan's desire, and it occasioned a judgment which evidently took out of heaven a great company of angels who had joined forces with Satan, Lucifer, son of the morning.

The other possibility is that Peter is speaking about the water judgment that took place in Noah's day. I have asked several outstanding Bible teachers what judgment they thought Peter had in mind, and there was some disagreement although most of them thought it referred to the Flood of Noah's day. Surely that seems to be the suggestion here.

The antediluvian civilization was destroyed with a flood, and there is abundant evidence for this. The great shaft which was put down at the site of ancient Ur of the Chaldees shows that there were several civilizations destroyed. In the excavation, the archaeologists came to a great deal of sand and silt with quite a bit of sediment which was deposited there by a flood. Then beneath all this, they found the remains of a very high civilization. Personally, I believe that Peter refers directly to the Flood of Noah's day, and surely this earth bears abundant evidence of such a flood.

Now, whether Peter was referring to the pre-Adamic judgment or to the judgment in Noah's day is a matter of conjecture. It makes no difference at all which view you hold as to *when* the world was "overflowed with water, [and] perished." The important thing is that it did occur at some point in the past. There is abundant evidence that some great cataclysm did take place and that all things have *not* continued as they were from the beginning of the creation.

PRESENT WORLD

Now Peter presents world number two, the world that *is*. You and I live in world number two.

But the heavens and the earth, which are now, by the same word are kept in store, reserved unto fire against the day of judgment and perdition of ungodly men [2 Pet. 3:7].

This says that this earth has been stored up for fire. This is a very interesting expression, by the way, and it not only means stored up *for* fire but also stored up *with* fire (that could easily be the translation of it). The suggestion is that there are resident forces present in the world which could destroy it. It is not that God is going to rain fire down from heaven but that this earth carries its own judgment. How well we know this today! You and I are living on a powder keg—or, more literally, on an atom bomb. There will never be another flood to destroy the world. That judgment is past; water destroyed the world that *was*. Now the world that *is* is reserved for another judgment, the judgment of fire. In other words, this present order of things in this world is temporary. It is moving toward another judgment, and Peter will give us more details in verse 10.

"Kept in store" is the same Greek word that the Lord Jesus used when He told of the man who was laying up treasure. Well, God had been laying up this secret of how He made this universe, and it seems that man has broken into God's secret treasure house. It seems that man has opened a veritable Pandora's box, and today thoughtful men are frightened.

Dr. Urey from the University of Chicago, who worked on the atomic bomb, began an article several years ago in *Collier's* magazine by saying, "I am a frightened man, and I want to frighten you."

Winston Churchill said, "Time is short."

Mr. Luce, the owner of *Life, Time,* and *Fortune* magazines, addressed a group of missionaries who were the first to return to their fields after World War II. Speaking in San Francisco, he made the statement that when he was a boy, the son of a Presbyterian missionary in China, he and his father often discussed the premillennial coming of Christ, and he thought that all missionaries who believed in that teaching were inclined to be fanatical. And then Mr. Luce said, "I wonder if there wasn't something to that position after all."

Dr. Charles Beard, the American historian, says, "All over the world the thinkers and searchers who scan the horizon of the future are attempting to assess the values of civilization and speculating about its destiny."

Dr. William Yogt, in the *Road to Civilization*, said, "The handwriting on the wall of five continents now tells us that the Day of Judgment is at hand."

Dr. Raymond B. Fosdick, president of the Rockefeller Foundation, said, "To many ears comes the sound of the tramp of doom. Time is short."

H. G. Wells declared before he died, "This world is at the end of its tether. The end of everything we call life is close at hand."

General Douglas MacArthur said, "We have had our last chance."

Former President Dwight Eisenhower said, "Without a moral regeneration throughout the world there is no hope for us as we are going to disappear one day in the dust of an Atomic Explosion."

And Dr. Nicholas Murray Butler, ex-president of Columbia University, said, "The end cannot be far distant."

If men from all walks of life are speaking in this manner, certainly you and I, who have believed the Bible and who have had through all these years such a clear statement concerning the judgment that is coming upon this world and the way in which it is to be destroyed, should be alert. Do not misunderstand me, I am not saying that the atomic bomb will be God's method for the destruction of this world. I am merely saying that man at last has found out that this passage in 2 Peter makes good sense. This is a way that is not only logical but is scientific by which God can destroy this universe.

But, beloved, be not ignorant of this one thing, that one day is with the Lord as a thousand years, and a thousand years as one day [2 Pet. 3:8].

Now it is obvious that the destruction of the earth and heavens will take place during the Day of the Lord, which is an extended period of time including the seven years of tribulation and the one thousand years of the millennial kingdom. When the Lord Jesus returns to the earth at the end of the Great Tribulation Period and establishes His kingdom here, He is going to renovate this earth—but that will not be a permanent renovation. Not until after the Tribulation and after the Millennium will the dissolution of the earth and the heavens (of which Peter speaks) occur. So you see, my friend, even if the Rapture should take place tomorrow, it still would be a thousand and seven years before this destruction.

The Lord is not slack concerning his promise, as some men count slackness; but is longsuffering to us-ward, not willing that any should perish, but that all should come to repentance [2 Pet. 3:9].

God is longsuffering; He is patient; He is not rushing things. After all, He has eternity behind Him and eternity ahead of Him. He doesn't need to worry about *time!* To Him a thousand years is as one day and one day is as a thousand years. But the point is that the final judgment, the dissolution of the earth and the heavens, *is* coming. In the meantime, He is giving men everywhere a further opportunity to repent and turn to Himself. This is the reason you and I need to get the Word of God out. It is the only thing that can change hearts and lives. It is by the Word of God that folk are born again—as Peter said in his first epistle, "Being born again, not of corruptible seed, but of incorruptible, by the word of God, which liveth and abideth for ever" (1 Pet. 1:23).

"Not willing that any should perish, but that all should come to repentance." It is not God's will that you should perish. One of the reasons that you have been reading this book is simply because God does not want you to come into judgment; He wants you to pass from death unto life. And you can do that—you can turn to Him and receive the wonderful salvation that He has for you.

Do you know that you cannot keep God from loving you? You can reject His love, but you cannot keep Him from loving you. Neither can you keep it from raining, but you can raise an umbrella to keep the rain from falling on you. Also, you can raise the umbrella of indifference or the umbrella of sin or the umbrella of rebellion so that you won't experience God's love, but you cannot keep Him from loving you.

A story comes out of Greek mythology which illustrates my point: A young man had a very wonderful mother, but he fell in love with a very ungodly girl. The ungodly girl hated the boy's mother and could not bear to be in her presence. It was not because the mother rebuked her, but her very character and her very presence were a rebuke to this girl. Nevertheless, this boy was desperately in love with her, for she was beautiful. And finally he pleaded with her to marry him, and she said, "Only on one condition: you must cut out your mother's heart and bring it to me." Well, this boy was so madly in love and so desperate that he descended to the low plane of committing this diabolical deed. He killed his mother, cut out her heart and was taking it to the girl when, on the way, he stumbled and fell. The heart spoke out, "My son, did you hurt yourself?"

My friend, you can slap God in the face; you can turn your back on Him; you can blaspheme Him, but you cannot keep Him from wanting to save you. You cannot keep Him from loving you, for He provided a Savior, His own Son, to die in your place. The Lord Jesus will save you if you will receive the salvation He offers. My friend, things are not going to continue as they are now. Oh, I know the monotony of life today, the ennui of it all. Well, it is coming to an end, and judgment *will* come. You and I are living in a world which is moving toward judgment.

But the day of the Lord will come as a thief in the night; in the which the heavens shall pass away with a great noise, and the elements shall melt with fervent heat, the earth also and the works that are therein shall be burned up [2 Pet. 3:10].

"But the day of the Lord will come as a thief in the night." There is some argument as to whether this takes place at the coming of Christ to establish His kingdom or at the end of the millennial kingdom. I am convinced that the Day of the Lord is an extended period of time which opens with the Tribulation, followed by the thousand-year reign of Christ, the brief rebellion led by Satan, and the judgment of the Great White Throne. Then, as we find in the Book of Revelation, the new heavens and the new earth come into view.

"As a thief in the night," the same expression which Paul uses in 1 Thessalonians 5:2, indicates that it will begin unexpectedly.

"In the which the heavens shall pass away with a great noise." The Greek word used here for "noise" is *rhoizēdon*. It is the word used for the swish of an arrow, the rush of wings, the splash of water, the hiss of a serpent. Have you ever listened to an atom bomb go off? Do you remember a number of years ago when they were experimenting with the bombs and we could see and hear them on television? This is the very word and the only word I know that could describe such a noise.

"And the elements shall melt with fervent heat." You see, matter is not eternal as was once believed; you *can* get rid of matter—that is, it can be converted into energy. Peter speaks here of "the elements," the little building blocks of the universe, the *stoicheia* as it is in the Greek. *Stoicheion* is a better word than our word *atom* which comes from a Greek word meaning something you cannot cut, because we have found that an atom can be cut and it can be taken apart.

"Melt" employs one of the simplest Greek words, the verb *luō*, which simply means "to untie or to unloose." By untying the atom, man has been able to produce a little bomb that can do tremendous wonders. Today men are trying to release that energy because you and I live in a world that is running out of resources. When God stocked this earth, He put plenty of oil in it, and He put plenty of groceries here. It was like a great supermarket. Men came and prostituted this earth. They have polluted the earth and are beginning to use up all that God had put in the pantry and all that He had put in the filling station. But there is a tremendous potential of energy in the little atom, and I tell you, when God destroys this earth someday, it is going to be a tremendous thing. I think that it will be just like a great atomic explosion, and the earth will go into nothing. I have always felt that the Lord will probably turn the little atoms wrong side out and use the other side of them for a while. When He does that, man will never be able to untie them again.

"The earth also and the works that are therein shall be burned up." This will certainly include the tremendous amount of water that is on the earth—it will be burned up. We know today that water is made up of two elements, hydrogen and oxygen, and both of them are gases that are inflammable and can be very explosive. Firemen tell us that there are certain kinds of fire which, when water is put on them, are only helped along by it. Firefighters have to use certain kinds of chemicals to put out such fires. "The works that are therein shall be burned up."

Peter is saying that God will judge in the future just as He has in the past. At the beginning of this chapter, Peter says that the scoffers will say, "All things continue as they were from the beginning of the creation" (v. 4). The scoffer's great fallacy is in not knowing the past, yet it is the evolutionist who makes so much of the fact that there was a great catastrophe in the past. The great mountains out here in the West, the High Sierras, were thrown up at that time by some great convulsion of nature. That happened sometime in the past, and it was a judgment of God, if you please.

The Day of the Lord will include judgment also. The "day of the Lord" is a familiar term in Scripture. The prophets used it, the Lord Jesus used it, and many of the New Testament writers used it. It is a technical term. The Day of the Lord begins in darkness, as the Old Testament prophets said—it begins with tribulation. It ends with this great atomic explosion, this great judgment of the earth by its being dissolved by fire. Between these two great events is the period of the seven years of tribulation, the coming of Christ to the earth to establish His kingdom, the millennial kingdom, the brief release of Satan and the rebellion of those who rally to him, Satan's final confinement, and the Great White Throne judgment of the lost. Then after the judgment of the earth, which Peter is describing, the new heaven and the new earth come into view.

Seeing then that all these things shall be dissolved, what manner of persons ought ye to be in all holy conversation and godliness [2 Pet. 3:11].

Now Peter says that, in view of the fact of what has happened and what God is going to do in the future, you and I ought not to be standing on the sidelines, twiddling our thumbs, and indulging in criticism. Christians find it so easy to criticize others, but specifically, what are *you* doing today to get out the Word of God? That is the important question in this hour for every Christian, every church, every pastor. Every person sitting in the pew needs to say to himself: "I am not here to sit in judgment on the preacher; I'm not here to judge other Christians; I am here to get out the Word of God, to do something positive. The question is: What am I doing to that end?"

Looking for and hasting unto the coming of the day of God, wherein the heavens being on fire shall be dissolved, and the elements shall melt with fervent heat? [2 Pet. 3:12].

"Looking for and hasting unto the coming of the day of God." Peter is writing to the *Diaspora*, the Jews scattered abroad, and he says that the day of God is coming.

"Wherein the heavens being on fire shall be dissolved." After the dissolution of the present heavens, the day of God, which is eternity, as we see in Revelation 21:1, will come.

"Wherein the heavens being on fire shall be dissolved, and the elements shall melt with fervent heat?" This is one of the most remarkable statements you could possibly have coming from a fisherman on the Sea of Galilee. I don't imagine that Peter figured out how the water, that sea where he fished, would *burn*. He didn't know how all this could be dissolved and melted. But the elements, that which we call atoms, the building blocks of the universe, are to be absolutely melted. However, this time Peter uses a different Greek word for "melt" than he used in verse 10. It is *tēkomai*, a word that means actually "wasting away, the wasting away of nature." This could possibly suggest the effects of radioactivity when an atomic bomb goes off.

FUTURE WORLD

Now Peter comes to that which is ahead— the world that *shall* be. Just because the earth will be dissolved does not mean that God is through with the earth. As the earth was judged in the past, it will be judged in the future, but the earth will go on.

Nevertheless we, according to his promise, look for new heavens and a new

earth, wherein dwelleth righteousness [2 Pet. 3:13].

Righteousness does not *dwell* in this earth today. It is not at home in this earth. It's not at home in Washington, D.C. It's not at home in any of the capitals of the world. It's not at home in your hometown, and it's not at home where you live today. But righteousness will dwell in the new earth and in the new heavens.

In *Hamlet* Shakespeare described his day by saying, "The times are out of joint." He was right—the times *are* out of joint. Some other poets have waxed rather eloquent, have soared to the heights and, I think, have misrepresented things. For instance, Browning, in "Pippa Passes," wrote:

> The lark's on the wing;
> The snail's on the thorn:
> God's in his heaven—
> All's right with the world!

The lark is on the wing, the snail is on the thorn (in fact, he's in my backyard), God *is* in His heaven, but things are *not* right in the world today. I'm glad there is another world, a new heaven and a new earth, that is coming on. It is going to be wonderful. I have always enjoyed trading in my old car and getting a new model. God has a new model of the earth coming on, and I'll be glad when it arrives. It will be a wonderful earth because it will be characterized by righteousness, and it will be an earth in which righteousness will actually *dwell*.

ADMONITION TO BELIEVERS

Wherefore, beloved, seeing that ye look for such things, be diligent that ye may be found of him in peace, without spot, and blameless [2 Pet. 3:14].

"Wherefore, beloved, seeing that ye look for such things"—that is, since we know that the earth and all its works will be burned up, we realize how important a life of godliness is here and now. We are to live a holy life down here, a life separated unto God. Friend, after all, what is really worthwhile in this earth today? What are your goals? Are you a productive Christian moving toward a worthwhile goal? Somebody says, "I want to raise my family." That's worthwhile. Somebody else says, "I want to make a good living for my family and to educate my children." That's worthwhile. Although these things are worthwhile, what is really the object of your life? Is it to live for God? If you live for God, all

of these secondary issues, I believe, will take care of themselves.

And account that the longsuffering of our Lord is salvation; even as our beloved brother Paul also according to the wisdom given unto him hath written unto you [2 Pet. 3:15].

"The longsuffering of our Lord is salvation." That is, His patience in delaying His return in judgment is providing an opportunity for men to be saved. *Our* patient waiting is a mental adjustment to the present world situation. We do not need to be alarmed today. God *is* in His heaven. Things are not right in the world, but He is going to make them right someday. This is the message of the New Testament, and Peter reminds us that Paul also wrote of this.

As also in all his epistles, speaking in them of these things; in which are some things hard to be understood, which they that are unlearned and unstable wrest, as they do also the other scriptures, unto their own destruction [2 Pet. 3:16].

Peter says that what Paul wrote was Scripture. And he says that Paul wrote of truth in depth. He certainly did that, and in my opinion Peter did that pretty well himself here in this epistle.

Ye therefore, beloved, seeing ye know these things before, beware lest ye also, being led away with the error of the wicked, fall from your own stedfastness [2 Pet. 3:17].

There is something that we are to *know*, my friend. Oh, don't be a lazy Christian not learning the Word of God. There is no little gimmick, there is no little course you can take in a week, there is no little program that you can go through that will change and revolutionize your life—there is no easy way. We are to seriously study the entire Word of God, not just a few little verses of Scripture that we throw about and kick around like a football. Peter says, "Ye know these things before, beware lest ye also, being led away with the error of the wicked, fall from your own stedfastness." My friend, if you have a comprehensive knowledge of Scripture and apply it to your own life, you will be a steadfast Christian.

As we saw at the beginning of this epistle, Peter's characteristic word is *knowledge*. The epitome of his entire epistle is expressed in the injunction of this final verse:

But grow in grace, and in the knowledge of our Lord and Saviour Jesus Christ. To him be glory both now and for ever. Amen [2 Pet. 3:18].

"Grow in grace, and in the knowledge of our Lord and Saviour Jesus Christ." True knowledge is not some esoteric information concerning a form or formula, a rite or ritual; nor is it some secret order or password, as the Gnostics claimed. It is to know Jesus Christ as He is revealed to man in the Word of God. This is the secret of life and of Christian living (see John 17:3).

Notice how Peter uses the name—"our Lord and Saviour Jesus Christ." How precious the Lord Jesus had become to this rough, old fisherman! As J. Niebor has well said, "He obeyed Him as Lord, he loved Him as Saviour, he adored Him as the greatest human, Jesus, he worshipped Him as the mighty anointed Son of God, Christ."

Peter concludes his swan song with this paean of praise: "To him be glory both now and for ever. Amen."

Oh, my friend, that you and I might *know* Jesus Christ! Someone has put it like this:

We mutter and sputter;
We fume and we spurt;
We mumble and grumble;
Our feelings get hurt.

We can't understand things;
Our vision grows dim,
When all that we need
Is a moment with Him.

—Author unknown

Only as we spend time with Him, as He is revealed in His Word, can we grow in our knowledge of Him.

BIBLIOGRAPHY

(Recommended for Further Study)

Barbieri, Louis A. *First and Second Peter.* Chicago, Illinois: Moody Press, 1977. (A fine, inexpensive survey.)

Criswell, W. A. *Expository Sermons on the Epistles of Peter.* Grand Rapids, Michigan: Zondervan Publishing House, 1976.

English, E. Schuyler. *The Life and Letters of St. Peter.* New York, New York: Our Hope, 1941. (Excellent.)

Ironside, H. A. *Notes on James and Peter.* Neptune, New Jersey: Loizeaux Brothers, n.d.

Kelly, William. *The Epistles of Peter.* Addison, Illinois: Bible Truth Publishers, n.d.

Robertson, A. T. *Epochs in the Life of Simon Peter.* Grand Rapids, Michigan: Baker Book House, 1933.

Thomas, W. H. Griffith. *The Apostle Peter.* Grand Rapids, Michigan: Wm. B. Eerdmans Publishing Co., 1956. (Excellent.)

Wolston, W. T. P. *Simon Peter—His Life and Letters.* 1896 Reprint. Addison, Illinois: Bible Truth Publishers, n.d. (Excellent.)

Wuest, Kenneth S. *In These Last Days.* Grand Rapids, Michigan: Wm. B. Eerdmans Publishing Co., 1954. (Deals with the epistles of 2 Peter, John, and Jude.)

The First Epistle of

JOHN

INTRODUCTION

Some expositors consider the epistles of John to be the final books written in the Bible. Certainly John's epistles are the last which he wrote.

The three epistles are called letters; yet the first epistle is not in the form or style of a letter. It has no salutation at its beginning nor greeting at its conclusion. Its style is more that of a sermon. It bears all the marks of a message from a devoted pastor who had a love and concern for a definite group of believers.

John served as pastor of the church in Ephesus, which was founded by Paul. It has been the belief of the church down through the years that John wrote his gospel first, his epistles second, and finally the Revelation just before his death. However, in recent years some of us have come to the position that John wrote his epistles last. Therefore, he wrote his first epistle after his imprisonment on the Island of Patmos. This places the date about A.D. 100. John died in Ephesus and was buried there. The Basilica of St. John was built over the grave of John by Justinian in the fifth century.

To understand the First Epistle of John we must know something about the city of Ephesus at the beginning of the second century. It was very much like your city or hometown today. There were four important factors which prevailed in Ephesus and throughout the Roman world:

1. There was an easy familiarity with Christianity. Many of the believers were children and grandchildren of the first Christians. The new and bright sheen of the Christian faith had become tarnished. The newness had worn off. The thrill and glory of the first days had faded. My, how exciting it had been to be a believer on that day when Paul had come to town and challenged Diana of the Ephesians! The whole town had been in an uproar. In Acts 19 we read of the effect Paul's teaching had upon the synagogue at Ephesus and also the impact of his daily sessions in the school of Tyrannus for two years. How fervent their love and zeal for Christ had been in those days. But many years later, when the Lord Jesus sent a letter to the Ephesian believers through John while he was in exile on the Island of Patmos, He said, "Nevertheless I have somewhat against thee, because thou hast left thy first love" (Rev. 2:4). It was as Jesus had long before warned, ". . . because iniquity shall abound, the love of many shall wax cold" (Matt. 24:12). The Ephesians' devotion and dedication to Christ was at a low ebb.

2. The high standards of Christianity made the Christians different, and the children and grandchildren of the first Christians did not want to be different. The believers were called saints—from the Greek word *hagios*. The primary intent of the word is "set aside for the sole use of God—that which belongs to God." The pots and pans in the temple were said to be holy because they were for the use of God. The temple was *hagios;* the Sabbath was *hagios.* Now the Christians were to be *hagios*—different, set aside for the use of God.

But the Ephesians had become assembly-line Christians, programmed by the computer of compromise. They had become plastic Christians. They were cast in a different mold from the disciples to whom Jesus had said, "If ye were of the world, the world would love his own: but because ye are not of the world, but I have chosen you out of the world, therefore the world hateth you" (John 15:19). And also in His high priestly prayer to His Father are these words: "I have given them thy word; and the world hath hated them, because they are not of the world, even as I am not of the world" (John 17:14). There was a breakdown of the Judeo–Christian ethics and a disregard of Bible standards.

3. Persecution was not the enemy of Christianity. The danger to the Ephesian church was not persecution from the outside but seduction from the inside. The Lord Jesus Himself had warned of this: "For there shall arise false Christs, and false prophets, and shall shew great signs and wonders; insomuch that, if it were possible, they shall deceive the very elect" (Matt. 24:24). And the apostle Paul had said to the Ephesian elders: "For I know this, that after my departing shall grievous wolves enter in among you, not sparing the flock. Also of your own selves shall men arise, speaking perverse things, to draw away disciples after them" (Acts 20:29–30).

Christianity was not in danger of being destroyed; it was in danger of being changed.

The attempt was being made to *improve* it, give it intellectual respectability, and let it speak in the terms of the popular philosophy.

4. Gnosticism was the real enemy of Christianity, and, my friend, it still is. Gnosticism was the basic philosophy of the Roman Empire.

Gnosticism took many forms. However, one primary principle ran through this philosophy: matter or material was essentially evil; only the spirit was good. All the material world was considered evil. Therefore Gnosticism despised the body. They held that in the body was a spirit, like a seed in the dirty soil. The same principle is in modern liberalism which maintains that there is a spark of good in everyone and that each person is to develop that spark of good. The Gnostics sought to cause the "seed," the spirit within them, to grow and tried to get rid of the evil in the body.

There were two extreme methods of accomplishing this goal as practiced by the Stoics and the Epicureans. The apostle Paul's encounter with these two sects is recorded in Acts 17:18: "Then certain philosophers of the Epicureans, and of the Stoics, encountered him. And some said, What will this babbler say? other some, He seemeth to be a setter forth of strange gods: because he preached unto them Jesus and the resurrection."

The Stoics were disciples of Zeno, and their name came from the Painted Portico at Athens where Zeno lectured. They were pantheists who held that the wise man should be free from passion, unmoved by joy or grief, and submissive to natural law. They observed rigid rules and self-discipline.

The Epicureans took their name from Epicurus who taught in Athens. They accepted the Greek gods on Mount Olympus. They considered pleasure rather than truth the pursuit of life. Originally they sought to satisfy intellectual, not sensual, gratification; but later they taught their followers to satisfy the body's desires so it wouldn't bother them any more.

There were all shades and differences between the two extremes of Stoicism and Epicureanism, but all of them denied the messiahship of Jesus. I believe John had them in mind when he wrote: "Who is a liar but he that denieth that Jesus is the Christ? He is antichrist, that denieth the Father and the Son" (1 John 2:22). They denied the Incarnation, reasoning that God could not have taken a human body because all flesh is evil. Therefore John distinctly declared, "And the Word was made [born] flesh, and dwelt among us, (and we beheld his glory, the glory as of the only begotten of the Father,) full of *grace* and truth" (John 1:14). And in his epistle he wrote: "Hereby know ye the Spirit of God: Every spirit that confesseth that Jesus Christ is come in the flesh is of God: And every spirit that confesseth not that Jesus Christ is come in the flesh is not of God: and this is that spirit of antichrist, whereof ye have heard that it should come; and even now already is it in the world" (1 John 4:2–3).

Docetic Gnosticism, considering the Incarnation impossible since God could not unite Himself with anything evil such as a body, taught that Jesus only *seemed* to have a body, but actually He did not. For example, when He walked He left no footprints.

Cerinthus was more subtle in his teaching. He declared that there was both a human Jesus and a divine Christ, that divinity came upon Him at His baptism and left Him at the cross. In fact, the Gospel of Peter, which is a spurious book, translates the words of Jesus on the cross like this: "My power, my power, why hast thou forsaken me?"

The early church fathers fought this heresy and maintained that "He became what we are to make us what He is." It is my firm opinion that John wrote his first epistle to answer the errors of Gnosticism. Actually there is a fivefold purpose expressed in 1 John: (1) 1:3, "That ye also may have fellowship with us [other believers]: and . . . with the Father, and with his Son Jesus Christ;" (2) 1:4, "That your joy may be full"; (3) 2:1, "That ye sin not"; (4) 5:13, "That ye may know that ye have eternal life"; and (5) 5:13, "That ye may believe on the name of the Son of God."

First John has been called the *sanctum sanctorum* of the New Testament. It takes the child of God across the threshold into the fellowship of the Father's home. It is the *family* epistle. Paul's epistles and all the other epistles are church epistles, but this is a family epistle and should be treated that way. The church is a body of believers in the position where we are blessed ". . . with all spiritual blessings in the heavenlies in Christ" (Eph. 1:3, Translation mine). We are given that position when we believe on the Lord Jesus Christ. Believing on the Lord Jesus brings us into the family of God. In the family we have a relationship which can be broken but is restored when "we confess our sins." Then "he is faithful and just to forgive us our sins, and to cleanse us from all unrighteousness" (1 John 1:9).

First John is the book which I used when I began my ministry in a new church. (I didn't at the first church I served because I was a seminary student and didn't know enough to begin in the right place.) But in the four churches I served during my forty years of pastoring, I began the midweek service with a study in 1 John. I am convinced that this epistle is more important for believers in the church than the church epistles. When we moved into this wonderful book, I saw the midweek service attendance increase. We saw a phenomenal increase in attendance in the last two churches I served. During the time we studied this little epistle the attendance doubled, doubled again, and then doubled again, so that we had as many people in attendance at the midweek service as we had in the Sunday evening service. Sometimes the midweek service would surpass the Sunday night service. My friend, it is *very* important to understand this little book.

OUTLINE

In 1 John there are three definitions of God: God is *light*, God is *love*, and God is *life*, which I have used to form the three major divisions of this epistle.

I. God Is Light (1:5), Chapters 1:1–2:2
    A. Prologue, Chapter 1:1–2
    B. How the Little Children May Have Fellowship with God, Chapters 1:3–2:2
        1. By Walking in Light, Chapter 1:3–7
        2. By Confessing Sin, Chapter 1:8–10
        3. By the Advocacy of Christ, Chapter 2:1–2

II. God Is Love (4:8), Chapters 2:3–4:21
    A. How the Dear Children May Have Fellowship with Each Other, Chapter 2:3–14
       (By Walking in Love)
    B. The Dear Children Must Not Love the World, Chapter 2:15–28
    C. How the Dear Children May Know Each Other and Live Together, Chapters 2:29–4:21
        1. The Father's Love for His Children, Chapters 2:29–3:3
        2. The Two Natures of the Believer in Action, Chapter 3:4–24
        3. Warning Against False Teachers, Chapter 4:1–6
        4. God is Love: Little Children Will Love Each Other, Chapter 4:7–21

III. God Is Life (5:12), Chapter 5
    A. Victory Over the World, Chapter 5:1–5
    B. Assurance of Salvation, Chapter 5:6–21

CHAPTER 1

THEME: God is light; how the little children may have fellowship with God

Under the broad heading, God is Light, we see first the prologue of this epistle, then we shall see how the "little children," as John calls believers, may have fellowship with God.

As I mentioned in the Introduction, John has written to meet the first heresy which entered the church, Gnosticism. The Gnostics boasted of a superknowledge. They accepted the deity of Jesus but denied His humanity. Notice how John will give the true gnosticism—that is, the true knowledge of God.

GOD IS LIGHT: PROLOGUE

That which was from the beginning, which we have heard, which we have seen with our eyes, which we have looked upon, and our hands have handled, of the Word of life [1 John 1:1].

"That which was from the beginning." What beginning is John talking about? In the Scriptures are three beginnings, two of which we are very familiar with. The first is found in Genesis 1:1: "In the beginning God created the heaven and the earth." That is an undated beginning. We do not know *when* God created the heaven and the earth. I have read book after book, volume after volume, on the questions raised by the first chapter of Genesis. If I stacked up all those books, I am confident that they would reach the ceiling of my study. And after reading all of them, I am convinced that not one scientist or one theologian has the foggiest notion when Genesis 1:1 really happened.

I am told that today there are some Christian scientists who are taking what they call the "new earth view." They are claiming that the earth on which we live is not as old as the science of the past claimed it to be.

When I started school it was estimated that the earth was three to seven hundred thousand years old. Then science began to speak in terms of millions of years. By the time I finished school it was estimated that the earth was about 2½ million years old, and then, I understand, they reached the billion mark.

Now some scientists are moving away from the older dating of the earth and are setting a more recent date. Well, Genesis 1:1 would fit into either theory, a new earth or an old earth, since it is not dated. All that the first verse in Genesis declares is that God created the heaven and the earth. Until you are ready to accept that fact, you are not prepared to read very much further in the Word of God, because the remainder of the Bible rests upon that first verse. Did God create this universe or is it a happenstance? It is ridiculous to think that the universe just happened. As Edwin Conklin put it, "The probability of life originating by accident is comparable to the probability of the unabridged dictionary originating from an explosion in a print shop." My friend, there is intelligence behind this universe in which you and I live. As to the date of the beginning, we do not know; but if you need a few billion years to fit into your scheme of interpretation, it is here because we are dealing with the God of eternity. God has eternity behind Him. Although I don't know what He was doing before He created the heaven and the earth, I know He was doing something. Then God created the heaven and the earth, and He did it for a purpose. He is working out a plan in His universe today which is bigger than any human mind can comprehend. When God recorded His act of creation, He wasn't trying to give us a study in geology. However, He put a lot of rocks around for you to look at if you are interested in trying to figure out a date.

There is a second beginning which we find in the Word of God. It is the first verse in John's gospel: "In the beginning was the Word, and the Word was with God, and the Word was God." He adds, "The same was in the beginning with God." Then he comes to the act of creation: "All things were made by him; and without him was not any thing made that was made" (John 1:1–3). My friend, go back as far as you can think, beyond creation, back billions and trillions of years, and out of eternity comes the Lord Jesus Christ. Way back there He is already past tense; He is the Ancient of Days. Notice that John has written, "In the beginning *was* [not *is*] the Word." In other words, this is a beginning that doesn't even have a beginning because He had no beginning. "In the beginning *was* the Word" means that you can go back in the past as far as you want to, put down your peg anywhere, and Christ comes out of eternity to meet you. That is big stuff; it is bigger than my little mind can comprehend. I am unable to grasp the immensity of it until I come to John 1:14: "And the

Word was made [born] flesh. . . ." That takes me back to Bethlehem where He was born, and I begin to catch on at that time.

The third beginning is the one we began with in 1 John 1:1—"That which was from the beginning," which refers to the time Christ came into this world at Bethlehem. When He was about thirty years old, John became acquainted with Him. John and his brother James met Him in Jerusalem. Later they were with their father, mending nets, when Jesus came by and called them to follow Him. They left their father (probably a well-to-do fisherman) with the hired men and followed Jesus. Now John says, I want to tell you about Him, and he asserts the reality of the total personality of Jesus: (1) "We have heard" (through the ear-gate); (2) "we have seen" (through the eye-gate); (3) "we have looked upon" (lit., *gazed intently upon*); and (4) "our hands have handled."

John, of course, is speaking of the incarnation of Jesus and of his own association with Him when He was here upon this earth.

"Which we have heard." John is not prattling about his opinions and his speculations. He is talking about the fact that he *heard* the Lord Jesus, heard His voice, and when he listened to Him, he listened to God.

"Which we have seen with our eyes." Not only had the apostles heard Him speak, but they also had seen Him with their own eyes. In our day we cannot see Him with our physical eyes, but we can see Him with the eye of faith. Peter told us, "Whom having not seen, ye love; in whom, though now ye see him not, yet believing, ye rejoice with joy unspeakable and full of glory" (1 Pet. 1:8). And the Lord Jesus said to Thomas, who would not believe He had been resurrected until he could see and handle Him, ". . . Thomas, because thou hast seen me, thou hast believed: blessed are they that have not seen, and yet have believed" (John 20:29). We today are walking by faith, and the Lord Jesus Christ can be made as real to us as He was to Thomas. As the hymn writer expressed it—

> But warm, sweet, tender, even yet
> A present help is He;
> And faith has still its Olivet,
> And love its Galilee.
> "We May Not Climb"
> —John G. Whittier

"Which we have looked upon." The word *looked* is from the Greek word *theaomai* from which we get our English word *theatre*, meaning "to gaze intently upon." The theatre is a place where you sit and look, not just with a passing glance but with a gaze—a steady gaze for a couple of hours. John is saying that for three years they gazed upon Jesus. It was John who wrote, "And as Moses lifted up the serpent in the wilderness, even so must the Son of man be lifted up" (John 3:14). During the wilderness march, the people who had been bitten by the serpents were to look for healing to that brass serpent which had been lifted up on a pole. John is applying that to the Lord Jesus and saying that now we are to look to Him in faith for salvation. After we have done that, we are to gaze upon Him—and we will do that in this epistle. To look, saves; to gaze, sanctifies. John wrote in his gospel, "And the Word was made flesh, and dwelt among us, (and we beheld his glory, the glory as of the only begotten of the Father,) full of grace and truth" (John 1:14). Many of us need to do more than simply look to Him for salvation. We need to spend time gazing upon Him with the eye of faith.

"Our hands have handled." John says that they did more than merely gaze upon Him from a distance; they handled Him. John himself reclined upon His bosom in the Upper Room. Speaking to His own after His resurrection, He said, "Behold my hands and my feet, that it is I myself: handle me, and see; for a spirit hath not flesh and bones, as ye see me have. And when he had thus spoken, he shewed them his hands and his feet" (Luke 24:39–40).

Dr. G. Campbell Morgan takes the position that when the Lord Jesus held out His hands to Thomas and to the other disciples, they were so overwhelmed that they did not handle Him. Instead, they bowed down in reverence to Him. That would be the normal thing to do, but John makes it clear that they handled the Lord. This is one place where I disagree with Dr. Morgan, (and I disagree with him in a few other places, too,) but I dare not disagree with a man of his caliber unless there is a reason for it. But when John says that they handled Him, I think he means they *felt* His hands and fingered the nailprints which convinced them that He was indeed man, the Word made flesh, God manifest in the flesh.

After the death of Paul, about A.D. 67, a heresy arose in the church called Gnosticism. Gnosticism is the opposite of agnosticism. Agnosticism holds that the reality of God is unknown and probably unknowable. There are many agnostics in our colleges and universities, as you know. Charles Spurgeon used to say that *agnostic* is but the Greek word for the Latin *ignoramus*. So one might say, "I don't believe the Bible, because I am an ignoramus!" The agnostic says, "I do not know." The Gnostic says, "I *do* know." The Gnostics were a group which came into the church claiming to have a superior knowledge which simple Christians did not have. They considered themselves super-duper saints, knowing more than anyone else knew.

The Gnostics came up with quite a few novel ideas, which I have dealt with in more detail in the Introduction. One of their heretical teachings was that Jesus was merely a man when He was born. He was just like any other human being at the time of His birth, but at His baptism, the Christ came upon Him, and when He was hanging on the cross, the Christ left Him. John refutes this teaching in no uncertain terms when he said in his gospel record, "The Word was *born* flesh." And here in his first epistle, he emphatically declares that after Jesus came back from the dead, He was still a human being. In essence John says, "We *handled* Him—He was still flesh and bones." You see, John is not talking about a theory. He is talking about Someone he heard, he saw, and he handled.

(For the life was manifested, and we have seen it, and bear witness, and shew unto you that eternal life, which was with the Father, and was manifested unto us;) [1 John 1:2].

"For the life was manifested." That is, the life was brought out into the open where men could see it. John is talking about the Word of Life, the Lord Jesus Christ, as we shall see in the next verse.

On one occasion after I had given a message, a man whom I would call a smart aleck came to me with this question: "You talked about eternal life. What is eternal life? I would like to know what eternal life is." So I gave him this verse: "The life was manifested, and we have seen it, and bear witness, and shew unto you that eternal life, which was with the Father, and was manifested unto us." Then I said to him, "The eternal life that John is talking about is none other than Jesus Christ. If you want a definition, eternal life is a Person, and that Person is Christ. It is so simple that even you can grasp it. You either have Christ, or you don't have Christ. You either trust Christ, or you don't trust Christ. If you do trust Christ, you have *eternal life*. If you don't trust Christ, you don't have eternal life. Now, since that's eternal life, do *you* have eternal

life?" He turned and walked away without answering, which was an evidence that he did not have eternal life, and he did not want to pursue the matter any further.

• HOW TO HAVE FELLOWSHIP WITH GOD

Now John is going to say something which is quite wonderful. He is going to tell us that we can have fellowship with *God!* One of the most glorious prospects before us today is that you and I can have fellowship with God.

That which we have seen and heard declare we unto you, that ye also may have fellowship with us: and truly our fellowship is with the Father, and with his Son Jesus Christ [1 John 1:3].

"That which we have seen and heard"—this is the third time he has said this, and it should be penetrating our consciousnesses by now.

Why, John, are you repeating this? "That ye also may have fellowship with *us*." He is saying that believers can have fellowship one with another.

"And truly our fellowship is with the Father, and with his Son Jesus Christ." How are we going to have fellowship with God? It does present a dilemma. God is holy. Man is unholy. How can this gulf be bridged? How can you bring God and man together, or as Amos put it, "Can two walk together, except they be agreed?" (Amos 3:3). How are we ever going to have fellowship? To get over this seemingly impossible hurdle, John is going to present three methods. Two of them are man-made methods and won't work. The other one is God's method, and it is the only one that will work.

Before we get into that, let me say a word about the word *fellowship*. *Fellowship* is the Greek word *koinōnia*, and it means "having in common or sharing with." Christian fellowship means sharing the things of Christ. And to do this, we must know the Lord Jesus—not only know about Him, but know Him as our personal Savior.

In our day we have lost the true meaning of the word *fellowship*. Let me give you an example of what I mean. Several years ago I used to go to Huntington Beach in Southern California and speak to a Rotary Club. A wonderful doctor who was the program chairman told me that they could probably take me once a year; so he invited me for either Christmas or Easter and told me to give them both barrels. (I tried to give them both barrels, and since he is no longer program chairman, they haven't invited me back!) One of the things I noticed in the place where the Rotary Club met was a large banner over the elevated speaker's table with the words, "Fun, Food, Fellowship." Well, the food was nothing to brag about— embalmed chicken and peas as big as bullets. The fun was corny jokes. The fellowship consisted of one man patting another on the back and saying, "Hi, Bill, how's business?" or, "How's the wife?" Then they sang a little song together. That was their idea of fellowship.

Well, the Christian idea of fellowship is not much different. When you hear an announcement of a church banquet, it is almost certain that you will be urged to come for food and fellowship. What do they mean by fellowship? They mean meeting around the table and talking to each other about everything under the sun except the one thing that would give them true fellowship, the person of Christ.

Now let me give you an illustration of one place where the word *fellowship* is used correctly. I had the privilege of being at Oxford University as a tourist and seeing the Great Quad, the Wren Tower, and the different schools that comprise Oxford University. I visited one school which specialized in Shakespeare. Now suppose you wanted to know all about Shakespeare because you wanted to teach that particular subject. You would go to Oxford University and attend the particular school specializing in that subject. When you ate, you would sit down at the board, and there you would meet the other men who were studying Shakespeare, and you would meet the professors who did the teaching. You would hear them all talking about Shakespeare in a way you never had heard before. For instance, in the play *Romeo and Juliet* most of us think that Juliet was the only girl Romeo courted. It is shocking to find that when he said,

"One fairer than my love! the all-seeing
   sun
Ne'er saw her match since first the world
   begun,"

that fickle fellow Romeo was talking about another girl! You would hear many things that would alert you to the fact that you had a lot to learn about Shakespeare. So you would begin to study and pull books off the shelf in the library and go to the lectures. After you had been at the school for two or three years, they would make you a fellow. *Then* when you would go in and sit at the board with the other students and professors, you would join right

in with them as they talked about the sonnets of Shakespeare. You would have *fellowship* with them, sharing the things of Shakespeare.

Now fellowship for the believer means that we meet and share the things of *Christ*. We talk together about the Lord Jesus Christ and His Word. That is the kind of fellowship that John is speaking of when he says, "That ye also may have fellowship with us: and truly our fellowship is with the Father, and with his Son Jesus Christ."

WALK IN LIGHT

And these things write we unto you, that your joy may be full [1 John 1:4].

Now this is the second reason he mentions for writing his epistle: "That your joy may be full." How wonderful to have joy—not just a little joy but a whole lot of joy because we are experiencing fellowship. *Koinōnia* sometimes refers to the *act* of fellowship—the communion service in a church is an *act* of fellowship; giving is an *act* of fellowship, and praying is an *act* of fellowship. But in this chapter John is talking about the *experience* of fellowship, such as Paul had in mind when he wrote, "That I may know him, and the power of his resurrection, and the fellowship of his sufferings . . ." (Phil. 3:10).

My friend, the ultimate aim in preaching is that, through conviction and repentance, men and women might come to salvation and that it might bring great joy to their hearts, like the Ethiopian eunuch who came to know Christ with the help of Philip. He didn't continue his trip bragging about what a great preacher Philip was; he went on his way rejoicing. Why? Because he had come to know Christ. The purpose of John's epistle is that you and I might share together these wonderful things of Christ, that the Spirit of God might make the Lord Jesus and the Father real to us in such a way that our fellowship might be sweet.

Now we return to the problem which I mentioned earlier. John has said that he has written these things so that we can have fellowship and so that our joy might be full, and our joy would naturally be full if we could have fellowship with God. However, there is a hurdle to get over. John faces up to a real dilemma which every child of God recognizes. The very possibility of man having fellowship with God is one of the most glorious prospects that comes to us, but immediately our hopes are dashed when we face up to this dilemma:

This then is the message which we have heard of him, and declare unto you,

that God is light, and in him is no darkness at all [1 John 1:5].

"God is light, and in him is no darkness at all" means that God is holy, and we know that man is unholy. How can the gulf be bridged between a wonderful Savior and Vernon McGee? What a difference there is! The canyon between us is steep and deep. How can God and man be brought together? The cry of Job was for a "daysman" who might lay his hand upon Job and upon God and bring them together (see Job 9:33). Through Isaiah God says, "For my thoughts are not your thoughts, neither are your ways my ways . . ." (Isa. 55:8). How is a sinful man going to walk with God?

John tells us that God is light. This is, in fact, a definition of God. I have divided this epistle into three parts and each part is a definition of God: (1) God is light; (2) God is love; and (3) God is life. But how in the world are we going to have fellowship with God? It looks as if we are going to have to do one of two things. We either have to bring God down to our level, or we will have to take man up to God's level. Neither one of these things can be done, and yet men have tried it. John shows the impossibility of the first one and then gives us a great definition of God: *God is light.*

Modern science, I am told, is not quite sure what light is. Is it energy or is it matter? What is light? Oh, the source of light is one thing, but when you turn on the light in your room, the darkness lurking in the corner becomes light. What has happened? What was it that went over there in the corner and drove out the darkness? Or *did* it drive out the darkness? Because when the source of light up in the ceiling goes off, darkness returns to the corner. What is light?

Well, when John says that God is light, he is revealing many facets about the person of God. Although it doesn't cover the whole spectrum of the attributes of God, it says a great deal about Him.

First of all, light speaks of the glory, the radiance, the beauty, and the wonders of God. Have you seen the eastern sky when the sun comes up like a blaze of glory? A friend and I once camped on the edge of Monument Valley in Arizona. It was a beautiful spot. We spent the night in sleeping bags. When I awoke the next morning, my friend was standing there, watching as the dawn was breaking. I asked him what he was doing up so early, and he made this statement: "I am watching God create a new day." Oh, what a thrill it was to be there and watch God create a new day! All of a sudden the sun peeped over the horizon, then it came marching over in a blaze of glory. I must confess that it became pretty hot later in the day, but what a sunrise it was! God is light. Oh, the beauty and radiance and glory of God!

Another characteristic of light is that it is self-revealing. Light can be seen, but it diffuses itself. It illuminates the darkness. It is revealing. It lets me see my hands—I've been handling books, and I see that one of my hands has dirt on it, and I'm going to have to take it out and wash it. If it hadn't been for the light, I would not have seen the soil. Light reveals flaws and impurity. Whittier put it like this:

Our thoughts lie open to Thy sight;
    And naked to Thy glance;
Our secret sins are in the light
    Of Thy pure countenance.

And Dr. Chafer used to say it this way: "Secret sin down here is open scandal in heaven." Our sins are right there before Him, because God is light.

Also light speaks of the white purity of God and the stainless holiness of God. God moves without making a shadow because He is light. He is pure. The light of the sun is actually the catharsis of the earth. It not only gives light, it is also a great cleanser. Many of you ladies put a garment out in the sun to clean it or to get an odor out of it. The sun is a great cleansing agent. Light speaks of the purity of God.

Light also guides men. It points out the path. Light on the horizon leads men on to take courage. It gives them courage to keep moving on. God is light. Let me go to the other extreme. Darkness is actually more than a negation of light. It is not just the opposite of light. It is actually hostile to light. The light and holiness of God are in direct conflict with the evil darkness and chaos of the world.

Now we are presented with this dilemma. I am a little creature down here on earth, filled with sin. If you want to know the truth, I am totally depraved. Without the grace of God for salvation, I would be nothing in the world but a creature in rebellion against God, with no good within me at all. God has made it very clear that He finds no good within man. Paul says, "For I know that in me (that is, in my flesh,) dwelleth no good thing . . ." (Rom. 7:18). Paul also says, ". . . There is none righteous, no, not one" (Rom. 3:10). Not only have they no innate goodness, but they are in *rebellion* against God.

Paul goes on to tell us about the rebellion that is in the human heart. He says, ". . . the carnal mind is enmity against God: for it is not subject to the law of God, neither indeed can be" (Rom. 8:7). We are living in a world today that is in rebellion against almighty God. God is holy. I am a sinner. I am saved by grace, yes, but how am I going to have fellowship with Him? How am I going to walk with Him? Men have attempted to do this in three different ways which are presented here, and two of those ways are wrong.

REDUCE GOD TO MAN'S LEVEL?

The first method is to bring God down to the level of man.

If we say that we have fellowship with him, and walk in darkness, we lie, and do not the truth [1 John 1:6].

"If we say that we have fellowship with him"—there are a lot of folk claiming to have fellowship with Him when they do not in reality at all.

"We lie, and do not the truth." Do you understand what John says in this verse? He is rather blunt, don't you think so? He says that we lie. It is not a nice thing to call another man a liar. John says that if you say that you have fellowship with God and you walk in darkness—that is, in sin—you are *lying*. I didn't say that. I am too polite to say that, but John said it. We always think of John as being that little ladylike apostle who carried a handkerchief in his sleeve. I don't know how the rumor got started that John was that kind of a man, unless it began during the Middle Ages when an artist painted him with *curls!* I suppose the artist got the idea of curls from the fact that John is called the apostle of *love*. But our Lord never called him that—He called him a son of thunder! If John and that artist meet on the corner of Glory Avenue and Hallelujah Boulevard in heaven, I tell you, that artist is going to know what thunder and lightning both are, because I think John is going to level with him, "What is the big idea of giving the world the impression that I was a sissy-type individual?" John was a great, big two-fisted, rugged fisherman, and he is the one who says, "If you say you are having fellowship with God, and you walk in darkness, you *lie*, because God is light; God is holy."

We hear so much about sin among Christians today. One of the headlines in a newspaper here in Southern California told of some members of a cult committing adultery. (I don't know if that report was accurate or not,

but I don't think the paper would have risked a lawsuit by printing it if it had no basis of truth.) Yet this cult brags about keeping the Mosaic Law and having reached a wonderful level of life. Of course, one of the Ten Commandments is "Thou shalt not commit adultery" (Exod. 20:14), but they would attempt to explain that away in some manner. My friend, if you are going to walk with God, you are going to walk in *light*. And if there is sin in your life, you are *not* walking with Him. You cannot bring Him down to your level.

But if we walk in the light, as he is in the light, we have fellowship one with another, and the blood of Jesus Christ his Son cleanseth us from all sin [1 John 1:7].

"If we walk in the light," that is, if we walk in the light of the Word of God. Dr. Harry Ironside tells of his own confusion of mind relative to this verse. Noticing that the cleansing of the blood depends upon our walking in the light, he read it as though it said, "If we walk *according to* the light, the blood of Jesus Christ His Son cleanseth us from all sin." He thought it meant that if he was very punctilious about obeying every command of God, God would cleanse him. Then he noticed that it does not say if we walk *according to* light, but if we walk *in* the light. The important thing is *where* we walk, not *how* we walk. Have we come into the presence of God and allowed the Word of God to shine upon our sinful hearts? You see, it is possible to walk in darkness, thinking you are all right.

Let me illustrate this. I went squirrel hunting several years ago when I was holding meetings in my first pastorate in Middle Tennessee in a place called Woodbury. After the morning service a doctor came to me and asked me if I would like to go squirrel hunting, and I told him there was nothing I would rather do. After lunch he brought me a shotgun, and we drove out to his farm and parked in the barnyard. We walked along by the creek there and had some good hunting. Finally we came to a fork in the creek, and he said to me, "I'll take the right fork, and you take the left fork. It will lead you around the hill and back to the barnyard. We will meet there." In the meantime it looked like it was going to rain. It had drizzled once or twice and stopped. When I started out by myself, it started drizzling again. I kept going, and I made the turn around the hill. I noticed quite a few caves in the hill, and when it started to really rain, I knew I was going to get wet; so I crawled into one of those caves. I went into the largest one I could find and sat in that dark cave for about thirty minutes. I began to get cold and decided I needed a fire; so I gathered together a bunch of leaves scattered on the floor of the cave and put a match to them. I soon had a small fire going, and when I looked around the cave, I found out that I wasn't alone. I have never been a place in which there were so many spiders and lizards as there were in that cave! Over in one corner was a little snake all coiled up, just looking at me. My friend, I got out of there in a hurry, working on the assumption that possession is nine-tenths of the law, and since those creatures had the cave ahead of me, it belonged to them. I proceeded down to the barn and really got soaking wet, but I wasn't going to stay in that cave!

Now let me make an application. I had been sitting in comfort for about thirty minutes while I was in darkness, but when the light of the fire revealed what was in the cave, I could no longer be comfortable there. My friend, across this land today are multitudes of folk who are sitting in churches every Sunday morning but are not hearing the Word of God. As a result, they are sitting there in darkness, hearing some dissertation on economics or politics or the "good life" or an exhortation on doing the best they can. And they are comfortable. Of course, they are comfortable! But if they would get into the light of the Word of God, they would see that they are *sinners* and that they cannot bring God down to their level. John has said that if a person says he is having fellowship with God but is living in sin, he is *lying*.

During my many years as a pastor I have encountered a great deal of this. I think of a layman who was a good speaker and went about giving his testimony to different groups. Then it was discovered that he was living in adultery—for several years he had been keeping a woman on the side. When it was discovered, my, the damage it did to the cause of Christ. And that man still insists that he is having fellowship with God! I recognize that we are living in a day when moral standards are changing drastically and folk rationalize their sinning and try to explain it away, but they *cannot* bring God down to their level. If you are living in sin, God will not have fellowship with you. If you think otherwise, you are fooling yourself or using a psychological ploy to put up a good front. And many of our psychological hang-ups today center around this very point. As someone commented, after hearing me speak on this subject, "What you mean, Dr. McGee, is that there are hypocrites in the church." And when you come right down to the nitty-gritty, that's what we are talking about. Hypocrites. They profess one thing, "I'm having fellowship with God," and all the while they are walking in darkness. John says that they are lying.

Now, suppose you are a child of God, and you are living in sin—but you see it now in the light of the Word of God. Have you lost your salvation? When the light in my study revealed that spot of dirt on my hand, I went and washed it off. And John says, "And the blood of Jesus Christ his Son cleanseth us from all sin." That word *cleanseth* is in the present tense—Christ's blood just keeps on cleansing us from all sin. You haven't lost your salvation, but you have lost your fellowship, and you cannot regain your fellowship with God until you are cleansed.

You see, John is talking about *family* truth. At the time I am writing this, there is abroad a great emphasis on what is known as *body* truth. Some folk have stumbled onto it for the first time and have gone off the deep end in their overemphasis of it. *Body* truth is great and it is an important part of New Testament teaching, but *family* truth is also important. If you are in the family of God and have sin in your life, God is not going to treat you like the sinner outside of Christ. He is going to treat you like a disobedient child. He will take you to the woodshed for punishment. Remember that He took David to the woodshed, and certainly Ananias and Sapphira didn't get off easily. My friend, our attempt to bring God down to our level simply will not work. However, that is one method which is often used in an attempt to bridge the gap between a holy God and sinful man.

CONFESS SIN

Another method which is often used is an attempt to bring man up to God's level. They say that man has reached sinless perfection and that he is living on that very high plateau. Well, John deals with that approach. Listen to him—

If we say that we have no sin, we deceive ourselves, and the truth is not in us [1 John 1:8].

This is even worse than being a liar. When you get to the place where you say you have no sin in your life, there is no truth in you at all. This doesn't mean you are simply a liar; it means you don't even have the truth. You are deceiving yourself. You don't deceive anyone else. You deceive only yourself.

I ran into this problem very early in my training for the ministry. When I went to college as a freshman, my first roommate was a young man who was also studying for the ministry. He was a sweet boy in many ways. The only trouble with him was that he was *perfect.* When I found the room which had been assigned to me, my roommate was not at home, but when he came in, he introduced himself and informed me that he had not committed a sin in so many years—I have forgotten if he said one, two, or three years. It shocked me to meet a fellow who didn't sin. I had hoped he would be my buddy, but he wasn't a buddy. You see, in every room where I have lived, things go wrong once in awhile. And there I was living in a room in which there were only two of us and one of us couldn't do anything wrong. So when something went wrong, guess who was to blame? Now I admit that *usually* it was my fault—but not *always.* Although he was a nice fellow, he hadn't reached the level of perfection which he claimed; he wasn't perfect. After the first semester, a freshman was permitted to move wherever he wished, so I told him, "I'm moving out." He was greatly distressed and said, "Oh, no! Where are you going?" I told him, "I have met a fellow down the hall who is just as mean as I am, and I'm going to move in with him." So I did move out, and I understand he didn't get a roommate after that. My new roommate and I got along wonderfully well. In fact, I still visit him down in the state of Florida. We are old men now and we still have wonderful times together. Neither of us is perfect although we have mellowed a bit down through the years.

My friend, if you feel that you have reached the state of perfection, I really feel sorry for your spouse because it is hard to live with someone who thinks he is perfect. John says, "If we say that we have no sin, we deceive ourselves, and the truth is not in us." We cannot bring ourselves up to God's level. It is impossible to reach perfection in this life.

Let me give you another instance of this because I think it is important. When I first came to Pasadena, I knew a man who served for a while as chaplain at the jail. He was a wonderful, enthusiastic Christian. I certainly had no criticism of him. But one day he met me on the street and said, "Brother Vernon, I got sanctified last night." I said, "You did! What really happened to you?" He told me that he had reached the place where he could no longer sin.

Well, I didn't see him for a while after that, but one of the officers of the church I served at the time lived next door to him. The son of the man who had reached perfection came to visit and parked his trailer in the back yard with part of it on the property of the man who was an officer in my church. He said nothing for a while, but the time came when he had to build a shed on that spot. The neighbor knew he was intending to do this, but he made no mention of it. Finally, when it looked as if the son was going to stay and he felt that he could wait no longer to build, he went to his neighbor and asked him to move the trailer. Well, the fellow lost his temper and really told him what kind of a neighbor he thought he was. The man who was the officer in my church casually mentioned the incident to me one day; so I couldn't wait to meet that fellow and finally I looked him up. I said to him, "Didn't you tell me that you got sanctified?"

"Yes."

"And when you got sanctified, you reached the plane of sinless perfection?"

"Yes, I think I have reached it."

"Well, your neighbor is a member of my church, and he tells me that you really lost your temper the other day and told him off in a very unkind, un-Christianlike manner."

He began to hem and haw. "I guess I did lose my temper. But that is not sin."

"Oh, if it's not sin, what is it?"

"I just made a mistake. I recognize that I shouldn't have done it—so that's not a sin."

"Well, I want you to shake hands with me now, because I've reached that plane, too. I don't sin; I just make mistakes—and I make a lot of them. But, brother, the Word of God will make it very clear to you that losing your temper and bawling out your neighbor as you did *is sin.*"

My friend, whom do you think you deceive when you say that you have no sin? You deceive *yourself,* and you are the only person whom you do deceive. You don't deceive God. You don't deceive your neighbors. You don't deceive your friends. But you sure do deceive yourself. And John says that the truth is not in a man like that because he can't *see* that he is a sinner and that he has not reached the place of perfection. Yet a great many folk are trying that route in their effort to bridge the gap between themselves and a holy God.

Since you cannot bring God down to your level and you cannot bring yourself up to His level, what are you going to do? John gives us the alternative here—

If we confess our sins, he is faithful and just to forgive us our sins, and to cleanse us from all unrighteousness [1 John 1:9].

"If we confess our sins." Here is another one of our "ifs." We have seen several of them: "If we say that we have fellowship" (v. 6); "If we walk in the light" (v. 7); and "If we say that we have no sin" (v. 8). Now here is the right method for bringing together a sinful man and a holy God: *confession* of sins.

What does it mean to confess our sins? The word *confess* is from the Greek verb *homologeō*, meaning "to say the same thing." *Logeō* means "to say" and *homo* means "the same." You are to say the same thing that God says. When God in His Word says that the thing you did is sin, you are to get over on God's side and look at it. And you are to say, "You are right, Lord, I say the same thing that You say. It is *sin*." That is what it means to confess your sins. That, my friend, is one of the greatest needs in the church. This is God's way for a Christian to deal with sin in his own life.

The other day I talked to a man who got into deep trouble. He divorced his wife—he found out that she had been unfaithful. He lost his home and lost his job. He was a very discouraged man. He said to me, "I want to serve God, and I have failed. I am a total failure." I very frankly said to him, "Don't cry on *my* shoulder. Go and tell *God* about it. He wants you to come to Him. Tell Him you have failed. Tell Him you have been wrong. Tell Him that you want to say the same thing about your sin that He says about it. Seek His help. He is

your Father. You are in the family. You have lost your fellowship with Him, but you can have your fellowship restored. If you confess your sins, He is faithful and just to forgive you your sins."

After we confess our sins, what does God do? He *cleanses* us. In the parable, the Prodigal Son came home from the far country smelling like a pigpen. You don't think the father would have put a new robe on that ragged, dirty boy, smelling like that, do you? No, he gave him a good bath. The Roman world majored in cleanliness, and I am confident that the boy was bathed before that new robe was put on him. The next week he didn't say, "Dad, I think I will be going to the far country and end up in the pigpen again." Not that boy.

When you have confessed your sin, it means that you have turned from that sin. It means that you have said the same thing which God has said. Sin is a terrible thing. God hates it and now you hate it. But confession restores you to your Father.

John concludes this by saying—

If we say that we have not sinned, we make him a liar, and his word is not in us [1 John 1:10].

Now don't make God a liar. Why don't you go to the Lord, my friend, and just open your heart and talk to him as you talk to no one else. Tell Him your problems. Tell Him your sins. Tell Him your weakness. Confess it all to Him. And say to your Father that you want to have fellowship with Him and you want to serve Him. My, He has made a marvelous, wonderful way back to Himself!

CHAPTER 2

THEME: The advocacy of Christ; how the dear children may have fellowship with each other; the "dear children" must not love the world

This chapter is a continuation of the thought begun in the previous chapter regarding the manner in which "little children" may have fellowship with God. We have seen that we can have fellowship with God by walking in the light, that is, in God's presence. The second thing we must do in order to maintain that fellowship is to confess our sins to Him. When we walk in the light, we know that the blood of Jesus Christ keeps on cleansing us

from all sin, but we also know that there is imperfection in our lives and that we must go to Him in confession.

In chapter 2 we come to the matter of the advocacy of Christ. We will now see the conclusion of that which began with 1 John 1:5, where John said, "This then is the message." What is the message? It is the message of the gospel of the grace of God that takes the hell-doomed sinner and by simple faith in Christ brings him into the family of God where he becomes an heir and joint-heir with Jesus Christ. It is the relationship with the Father that is all important.

FELLOWSHIP WITH GOD BY THE ADVOCACY OF CHRIST

My little children, these things write I unto you, that ye sin not. And if any man sin, we have an advocate with the Father, Jesus Christ the righteous [1 John 2:1].

"**M**y little children, these things write I unto you, that ye sin not." John is writing these things to us because God does not want His children to sin. Although God has made ample and adequate provision for us not to sin, our entrance into His provision is imperfect—because of our imperfection. Notice that this verse does not say that we *cannot* sin, but John is writing to us that we *may* not sin. God wants us to walk in a manner that is well pleasing to Him; that is, He wants us to walk in obedience to His Word.

Let me remind you that 1 John is a *family* epistle; it emphasizes the relationship of the family of God. I mention this again because there is so much emphasis in the contemporary church on "body" truth; that is, that all believers are part of a body. "Body" truth is the message of Ephesians, and it is wonderful, but now we need to move out a little farther into "family" truth. We need to recognize that we are in God's family and that our relationship is all important. We need to have *fellowship* with our heavenly Father.

"My little children" is an interesting expression. It comes from the Greek word *teknia* and probably should be translated "my little born ones" or "my little born-again ones." I like the Scottish term best, "my little bairns."

"These things write I unto you, that ye sin not." None of us has reached that exalted plane, although there are those who claim sinless perfection. I am reminded of an occasion when a speaker was emphasizing the fact that nobody is perfect. Finally he became very dramatic and oratorical and asked, "Is there anybody here who has ever seen a perfect man?" No one responded until one little fellow in the back of the auditorium, sort of a Mr. Milquetoast, put up his hand.

The speaker asked, "Have *you* seen a perfect man?"

The little fellow stood to his feet and said, "Well, I have never *seen* him, but I have *heard* about him."

"Who is he?"

"He is my wife's first husband."

Well, I imagine he had heard about him a great deal! But the truth is that none of us has reached that exalted position of perfection.

Several years ago a speaker was telling a story about a family that was going to take a trip for a couple of days. They did not want to take their little girl along, so they left her with neighbors, who had four boys. When they returned, the little girl said to her daddy, "There are four boys in that house where I have been staying. They have family worship there every night. Each night their father prays for his four little boys."

Her father replied, "That certainly is good to hear."

"Daddy, he prays that God will make them good boys, and he prays that they won't do anything wrong."

Her father said, "Well, that's very fine."

The little girl was silent for a moment, and then she added, "But, Daddy, He hasn't done it yet."

If we are honest with ourselves, we too will have to say that God hasn't made us perfect yet either. We have not reached that exalted plane of sinless perfection. John says, "My little born ones, my little bairns, I write these things unto you that you may not be sinning." God doesn't want you to live in sin. We are going to find later that John is going to say, "Whosoever is born of God sinneth not" (1 John 5:18). This means that whosoever is born of God does not *practice* sin; that is, *live* in sin. The Prodigal Son got up out of the pigpen and went home to his father. He did not stay in the pigpen. Why not? Because he was a son and not a pig. Also we need to realize, as it is stated in Ecclesiastes 7:20, "For there is not a just man upon earth, that doeth good, and sinneth not."

Today you and I may be able to say, "I don't think I have done anything real bad." But how about doing good? James says, "Therefore to him that knoweth to do good, and doeth it not, to him it is sin" (James 4:17). There are sins of commission and sins of omission. You and I are to walk in the light. When we walk in the light, we will see just how far we have fallen short of what God wants. Every sincere child of God wants to have fellowship with Him, and yet he knows within himself that he has fallen far short of the kind of life he should have. There is sin in his life, and sin, be it ever so small, breaks communion with the Father.

It is said of Spurgeon that when he was crossing a street one day, he suddenly stopped. It looked like he was praying, and he was. One of his deacons waited for him on the other side of the street and said to him, "You could have been run down by a carriage [this was before the day of the automobile]. What were you doing? It looked like you were praying."

Spurgeon replied, "I was praying."

The deacon then asked, "Was it so important?"

"Indeed it was. A cloud came between me and my Savior, and I wanted to remove it even before I got across the street."

Many Christians are living lives in which they are constantly disobeying God, yet they wonder why they aren't having fellowship with Him. They need to recognize that sin causes a break in fellowship.

They need to know that they have not lost their salvation, because in the next breath John adds, "If any man sin, we have an advocate with the Father, Jesus Christ the righteous." Notice that John says, "We have an advocate with the Father"—John doesn't call Him by the impersonal name *God* because He is still our *Father* even though we have sinned. Therefore we need to recognize that our salvation rests upon what Christ has done for us, and that is a finished work. Someone has expressed it like this:

> Upon a life I did not live,
>   Upon a death I did not die,
> Another's life, Another's death,
>   I stake my whole eternity.
>
> It is finished, yes, indeed;
>   Finished, every jot!
> Sinner, this is all you need!
>   Tell me, is it not?
>
> —Author unknown

We cannot add anything to a finished work. What Christ has done is all we need for salvation.

However, if you and I are going to have fellowship with Him, we need to recognize something else.

"And if any man sin, we have an advocate with the Father." Who is He? He is "Jesus Christ the righteous." The word *advocate* is from the Greek *paraklētos*, the same word which is translated "comforter" in John's gospel. The Holy Spirit is our Comforter down here, and Christ is our Comforter up there.

Advocate—a paraclete, a helper—is a legal term. It means "one who will come to your side to help in every time of need." We have a wonderful heavenly Father, and we don't lose our salvation when we sin, but there is somebody up there who wants us to lose it, and that is Satan. Satan is the accuser of the brethren. In Revelation 12:10 we are told that he accuses us before our God day and night. Satan is there at the throne of God accusing you and accusing me. Remember how he accused Job. In effect, he said to God, "If you will let me get to him, I'll show You that he will curse you." When that happens in our case, the Lord Jesus is able to step in as our Advocate. He died *for* us! Yet the accuser is there, and some folk are very disturbed by that. But the Advocate is far greater than the accuser. Someone has expressed this in beautiful poetic language:

> I hear the accuser roar
>   Of ills that I have done;
> I know them well, and thousands more,
>   Jehovah findeth none.
>
> Though the restless foe accuses—
>   Sins recounting like a flood,
> Ev'ry charge our God refuses;
>   Christ has answered with His blood.
>
> —Author unknown

And he is the propitiation for our sins: and not for ours only, but also for the sins of the whole world [1 John 2:2].

"And he is the propitiation for our sins." The word *propitiation,* as it is used here in John's epistle, is a different word from that used in the Epistle to the Romans. In Romans the meaning is "mercy seat"—Christ is the propitiation, the mercy seat, the meeting place between God and man. However, here in 1 John *propitiation* means "an atonement or an expiation." It means that sins have been paid for by the suffering of Another. Christ is my Advocate, interceding for me, and He Himself is the propitiation.

Notice that John does not say that if anyone *repents,* he has an Advocate nor if anyone confesses his sins, he has an Advocate. Neither does he say that if anyone goes through a ceremony to get rid of his sins, he has an Advocate. What he does say is that if any man *sin,* we have an Advocate with the Father. Before we even repent of that cruel or brutal word we said, the very moment we had that evil thought, and the moment we did that wrong act, Jesus Christ was there at the throne of God to represent us as Satan was there accusing us.

Then, because of the faithful advocacy of Christ, the Holy Spirit brings conviction to us, and we confess our sin to the Father. As we said before, to confess means that we get on God's side and we see our sin from His viewpoint and confess that it *is* sin.

The sincere child of God wants to please the Father, and he walks along with that in mind. The psalmist expressed it this way: "Search me, O God, and know my heart: try me, and know my thoughts: And see if there be any wicked way in me, and lead me in the way everlasting" (Ps. 139:23–24).

Dr. Harry Ironside has illustrated the confession that God requires with an incident in his own home. He had trouble one evening with one of his boys, so he sent the boy upstairs and told him not to come down to supper until he confessed the thing he had done wrong. The boy would not admit anything at all. Finally the boy called for Dr. Ironside to come upstairs and asked if he could go down to supper. His father said, "It depends upon you." The boy said, "If you think I have done something wrong, I am sorry." His father said, "That won't do." Later the boy called him upstairs again, and this time he changed his story a little. He said, "Well, since you and mother both think I have done something wrong, I guess I have. I want to come down to supper." Once again his father told him that that wasn't good enough. Dr. Ironside went downstairs, and later on he heard the boy almost weeping. He said, "Dad, please forgive me. I know I have done wrong. Please forgive me." Then the lad came downstairs, and the family had a wonderful supper together because fellowship had been restored.

My friend, if you are a child of God, you are in the *family* of God, and He wants to have *fellowship* with you. I don't care about these little rules you are following. You think that some way you are going to be able to live the Christian life by following rules. My friend, God doesn't want you to be a programmed computer. He is not trying to do that to you. You are a human being with your own free will, but you are a member of His family, and He wants to have fellowship with you. We can talk to Him like we can talk to no one else.

Up to this point, John's subject has been that God is light and how God's dear children may have fellowship with Him. Now in this second section, the subject is that God is love and how God's dear children may have fellowship with each other. Before, he was talking about walking in *light;* now he will be talking about walking in *love.* Love is the very heart of this epistle. The word occurs thirty-three times, and there is a great emphasis upon it.

HOW TO HAVE FELLOWSHIP WITH EACH OTHER

And hereby we do know that we know him, if we keep his commandments [1 John 2:3].

First of all, let me point out that this verse has nothing to do with the security of the believer. John is talking about assurance. As God's children, we are in a family. But how can we have the assurance that we are in God's family? He is telling us that assurance comes by keeping His commandments.

"If we keep his commandments" does not refer to the Ten Commandments. John is not dealing with any legal aspects; he is dealing with family matters. The Ten Commandments were given to a nation, and on these commandments every civilized nation has based its laws. The Ten Commandments are for the unsaved. Now God has something for His own family, and they are commandments for His children. For example, in Galatians 6:2 the family is told, "Bear ye one another's burdens, and so fulfil the law of Christ." In 1 Thessalonians 4:2 Paul tells the family of Christ, "For ye know what commandments we gave you by the Lord Jesus." Some of those commandments are mentioned in the last chapter of 1 Thessalonians. I have counted twenty-two commandments in that chapter, and here are a few of them. "Rejoice evermore"—God wants you to be a joyful Christian. "Pray without ceasing" refers to an *attitude* of prayer. That is, when you get off your knees, you still are to walk in a prayerful attitude. "Quench not the Spirit"—don't say no to Him. These are some of the commandments which the Lord Jesus has given to believers, and if we are to have fellowship with the Father and enjoy it by having assurance in our own hearts, we must keep His commandments. We do not feel that we are free to do as we please. The Christian doesn't do as *he* pleases; he does as *Christ* pleases.

"And hereby we do know that we know him." Remember that throughout this epistle John is answering the Gnostics who claimed to have a superior knowledge that no one else had—and generally it was heresy. The apostle John is saying that the important thing is to know Jesus Christ. And how can we have the assurance that we know Him? My friend, although a great many folk believe in the security of the believer, they don't have the assurance of salvation, and the reason is obvious. We cannot know that we are children of God if we are disobedient to Him. Obedience to Christ is essential and is the very basis of assurance. You cannot have that assurance (oh, you can bluff your way through, but you cannot have that deep, down-in-your-heart assurance) unless you keep His commandments.

He that saith, I know him, and keepeth not his commandments, is a liar, and the truth is not in him [1 John 2:4].

I would call this very plain talk! In the previous verse John has said that we *know* that we *know* Him—this is the positive side. We know by experience in contrast to the esoteric knowledge of the Gnostics. Now he presents the negative side: disobedience to Christ is a proof that we do not know Him. This is plain and direct language. Disobedience to Christ on the part of a professing Christian is tantamount to being a liar. In other words, his life is a lie.

There are a great many people who say they are children of God, but are they? It is one thing to *say* you are a child of God, and it is another thing to be a possessor of eternal life, to have a new nature that cries out to the Father for fellowship and wants to obey Him. You cannot make me believe that all of these church members who have no love for the Word of God and are disobedient to Christ are really His children. I do not believe they have had the experience of regeneration. John is making it very clear that we know that we know Him because we keep His commandments.

Let me repeat that John is *not* talking about the Ten Commandments that were given to the nation Israel in the Old Testament. John is talking about the commandments that Christ gave to the church. If a child of God does not have a love for these commandments, he is in the very gall of bitterness and in the bond of iniquity, as the Scripture says (see Acts 8:23). The Lord Jesus, when He was here in the flesh, said of the Father, ". . . I do always those things that please him" (John 8:29). I can't say that, but I can say that I *want* to please Him, and I have dedicated my life to that end. Although I sometimes stumble and fall, I *want* to please Him. While it is true that "he that believeth on the Son hath everlasting life . . ." (John 3:36), it corroborates his faith when in his heart he knows that he wants to do God's will. The natural man never did want to do God's will. Oh, boy, this is a strong statement which John makes! "He that saith, I

know him, and keepeth not his commandments, is a liar, and the truth is not in him." And John will tell us that the Holy Spirit is the one who prompted him to say it. The truth is not in a man who claims to be a child of God but does not keep His commandments.

But whoso keepeth his word, in him verily is the love of God perfected: hereby know we that we are in him [1 John 2:5].

I want to make a distinction that I find very few expositors make. Even *The Scofield Reference Bible* does not make this distinction. I feel there is a difference between the *Word* of God and the *commandments* of God. Somebody is going to call my attention to the fact that the commandments are the Word of God. Well, commandments are the Word of God, but the Word of God is not all commandments. It is more than that. I hope you see the distinction. There are commandments in the Word of God, but the Word of God is not only commandments. The Word is the expression of the will of God, either by commandment or otherwise. In the Word of God you have His complete revelation to us about His will for our lives.

In John 14:15 the Lord made this statement: "If ye love me, keep my commandments." In John 14:23 He said, ". . . If a man love me, he will keep my words. . . ." What is the distinction here? Let me illustrate this. Suppose the home of a young boy is in the country. His father is a farmer. One day, when the boy is on his way to school, his father says, "Son, I'll milk the cow when I come in from the field each day, but when you get home from school, I want you to chop wood, put it on the back porch, and tell your mama so she can make a fire in the cook stove and in the fireplace." When the boy comes home, he obeys his father's commandment that he chop wood. He spends about an hour and a half chopping wood after school, and he stacks it on the back porch. Then one morning at the breakfast table, the father says, "I don't feel well today. I feel so bad that I don't think I can go out and work in the field today." But he goes out anyway. Now when the boy comes home from school, although his only commandment is to chop wood, he knows that his father is sick and doesn't feel like milking the cow, so he not only chops the wood but he milks the cow also. He chops the wood because he was commanded to do so, but he milks the cow because he loves his father.

In just this way a child of God not only

wants to obey the commandments of God but he also wants to obey the *Word* of God. He wants to please his Father in everything that he does. I get the impression from many folk that they want to live as much like the unsaved as possible and still be Christians. I would never give an answer to a young person who asked me if a Christian could do this or that and still be a Christian—because they were asking the wrong questions. The right question to ask is this: "What can I do to please my heavenly Father?" You see, a genuine child of God wants to *please* Him; he does not try to live right on the margin of the Christian life.

There are many Christians in our day who feel that they need to be broad-minded. They are against whiskey, but they use beer and they use wine, which gives them the feeling of being broad-minded. And, of course, they feel that I am very narrow-minded. Well, it is not a question of a thing being right or wrong—I hope you are above that plane, my Christian friend—the question is: does it please my heavenly Father? I want to do the thing that will please Him, bring joy to His heart and fellowship and joy to my own life. All of this, you see, is on the basis of love: "If you love me, keep my commandments," and "If a man love me, he will keep my words." If you love Him, you will do more than keep His commandments; you will do something extra for Him.

I feel that a great many folk have in their thinking only the sins of commission and forget about the sins of omission. James said, ". . . to him that knoweth to do good, and doeth it not, to him it is sin" (James 4:17). There are many things I know I should do, but I neglect to do them. These are sins of omission. The Bible makes no distinction between the gravity of sins of commission and sins of omission. They are equally bad.

My friend, verse 5 is very important. Let me repeat it: "But whoso keepeth his word, in him verily is the love of God perfected [that is, realized in practice]: hereby [by this] know we that we are in him." When the love of God is perfected in you, it means that you have passed the commandments and you just want to please God.

I suggest that you take an inventory of yourself. What is your attitude toward sin? Does it trouble you? Does it break your fellowship with the Father? Does it cause you to cry out in the night, "Oh, God, I'm wrong, and I want to confess the wrong I have done. I want fellowship with You." On that basis God will restore fellowship with us, and the assurance of salvation comes to our hearts.

He that saith he abideth in him ought himself also so to walk, even as he walked [1 John 2:6].

We cannot do or be all that the Lord Jesus Christ did or was, but if we set our hearts on doing our Father's will, which was the thing that the Lord Jesus put uppermost in His life, then we are walking as (in the same manner as) He walked.

I hear the word *commitment* a great deal these days. When an invitation is given after a message, the question is asked, "Do you want to commit your life to Christ?" What do they mean by that? Well, let me tell you what John means by full commitment. It is to love Christ. And if you love Christ, you are going to keep His Word—you can't help it. You *want* to please the person you love. You don't want to offend; you want to please. This is the reason I send a dozen American Beauty roses to my wife occasionally. You see, the question is not "Are you committed to Christ?" The question is, "Do you *love* Christ?"

Brethren, I write no new commandment unto you, but an old commandment which ye had from the beginning. The old commandment is the word which ye have heard from the beginning [1 John 2:7].

"An old commandment which ye had from the beginning." From what beginning? Well, the "beginning" in 1 John is the incarnation of Christ. It began in Bethlehem, then worked itself out in a carpenter shop and three years of public ministry. The "commandment which ye had from the beginning" was what the Lord Jesus gave to His apostles when He was with them on earth—which He repeated many times. For example, in John 13:34–35 we read, "A new commandment I give unto you, That ye love one another; as I have loved you, that ye also love one another. By this shall all men know that ye are my disciples, if ye have love one to another." And in John 15:10, 12, "If ye keep my commandments, ye shall abide in my love; even as I have kept my Father's commandments, and abide in his love. . . . This is my commandment, That ye love one another, as I have loved you."

John is saying, "This old commandment is what I am giving to you. It is what the Lord Jesus said when He taught here upon this earth." Then John continues—

Again, a new commandment I write unto you, which thing is true in him and in you: because the darkness is

past, and the true light now shineth [1 John 2:8].

Now, why is it a new commandment for believers who are regenerated and indwelt by the Holy Spirit? Because it was given on the other side of the cross, before the coming of the Holy Spirit. On this side it is *new*.

Believers are to do the will of God; and the will of God, first of all, is to love Him. This identifies a believer. A believer is one who delights to do the will of God. Because "the darkness is past, and the true light now shineth," the believer ought to be able to say that he is getting to know the Lord God better and that he is understanding His will more perfectly. Schiller, the great German poet, said, "I see everything clearer and clearer." And that should be the experience of every child of God. Every day we should be growing, and it is impossible to grow apart from a study of the Word of God. The written Word reveals the living Word, the Lord Jesus Christ, and He is the Bread of Life and the Water of Life. We will famish if we don't feed upon Him.

Let me repeat that the great problem in the world today is that the majority of believers are trying to follow a few little rules and regulations; they are programmed like a computer. They feel that they are living the Christian life if they do all those little things. Oh, my friend, you are not a computer; you are a human being. If you are a child of God, you have a new nature—although you still have your old nature in which ". . . dwelleth no good thing . . ." (Rom. 7:18). But your new nature wants to do God's will; it wants to please Him.

"The darkness is past, and the true light now shineth" would be better translated, "the darkness is passing." As you look around you today, you will see that the darkness has not passed yet. Ignorance of the Word of God is still much in evidence. The "true light," who is the Lord Jesus Christ, is breaking upon this world. He still is the most controversial person who has ever lived on the earth.

He that saith he is in the light, and hateth his brother, is in darkness even until now [1 John 2:9].

It is impossible for you as a child of God to walk in the light and hate your brother. If you do hate another Christian, it means there is something radically wrong with your confession of faith. This doesn't mean that there are not some people whose manners and habits will be objectionable to you. This doesn't mean that there won't be some believers who have

certain habits that you don't approve of—that is understandable. But to *hate* them reveals that you are in darkness. Hatred of a fellow believer is evidence that a person is not in the light. This is something we need to keep in mind. There is the natural darkness in which all men are born. Paul talks about it in Ephesians 4:18, where he says, "Having the understanding darkened, being alienated from the life of God through the ignorance that is in them, because of the blindness of their heart." That is the condition of mankind by nature. But our condemnation is not because of what we are by nature. "And this is the condemnation, that light is come into the world, and men loved darkness rather than light, because their deeds were evil" (John 3:19). This is important. Don't let it slip by you. We are not responsible because we are sinners by nature; we are responsible if we reject the Savior. We are not responsible because we were born in darkness and because our understanding is darkened; we are responsible if we reject the light that comes to us through the Word of God.

If you walk in the light, it will chase away all darkness. Instead of turning from its searching rays, let it search your heart. If a man keeps on rejecting this light, there will come a day when God will withdraw the light altogether. Or that man will become sunburned. Esau was that kind of man. He was red. He was sunburned. He was not only sunburned physically, he was also sunburned spiritually. What is sunburn? It means the skin will absorb all the rays of the light except one particular ray, and that is what burns. The soul that will not accept the Lord Jesus Christ as Savior, the Light of the World, will become sunburned, just as Esau was.

John gives us a test to see if we are in darkness. This is the test—

He that loveth his brother abideth in the light, and there is none occasion of stumbling in him.

But he that hateth his brother is in darkness, and walketh in darkness, and knoweth not whither he goeth, because that darkness hath blinded his eyes [1 John 2:10–11].

When the Lord Jesus was here on earth, He said, ". . . I am the light of the world: he that followeth me shall not walk in darkness, but shall have the light of life" (John 8:12). My friend, we need to apply John's test to our own lives. Have you really trusted Christ? Is He your light? Is He the one who is so guiding you that you are not hating your brother?

Here is a bit of poetry which sets this truth before us—

> I heard the voice of Jesus say,
> "I am this dark world's light.
> Look unto Me, thy morn shall rise,
> And all thy days be bright."
>
> I looked to Jesus, and I found
> In Him my star, my sun,
> And in that light of life I'll walk,
> Till traveling days are done.
>
> "I Heard the Voice of Jesus Say"
> —Horatius Bonar

Now, of course, there are other believers whose habits you dislike. You may have a distaste for some of their expressions. You may even have a personality that clashes with that of another brother. But that doesn't mean you hate him.

When I was attending seminary, I roomed with a fellow who had some of the meanest habits I have ever seen in a Christian. He would start singing at night after I went to bed and was asleep. He wouldn't sing all day long, but at eleven o'clock at night, he was ready to tune up. He had a lot of mean habits like that. So one day I told him, "You know, you are the greatest proof to me that I am a child of God." He asked, "What do you mean?" I replied, "You are the most nauseating, the most sickening Christian that I have ever met, but I do want you to know something—I love you." He looked right at me and said, "I want you to know that you are the most abominable Christian I have ever met, and I also want you to know you are the hardest person in the world to love, but I love you." Years later that fellow got into some trouble. I made a trip to see him, to see if there was anything I could do to help him. When I met him, I found that he wasn't any more lovable than he had been when I roomed with him. He was even more objectionable, and I think he found me the same, but I didn't hate him. That man was a child of God, and God marvelously used him in the ministry. In many ways he was a great fellow. I don't know why it is that when a Christian finds he doesn't like somebody, he thinks the only alternative is to hate him. You don't have to hate him at all; you are to love him as a child of God.

My friend, John has given here a tremendous statement: "He that hateth his brother is in darkness, and walketh in darkness, and knoweth not whither he goeth, because that darkness hath blinded his eyes." If you want to know for sure that you are a child of God, apply this test to your own life. If you are hating your brother, you are dwelling in darkness. If you are loving your brother, you are dwelling in light.

The Christian life is like a triangle. Let me diagram it for you (see below). God is at the top of the triangle, and the light of God comes down into your heart and life. Your love for God goes up, for you love Him because He first loved you. If you are walking in the light down here, it means you are going to love your brother also. You cannot say you love God and hate your brother. That is absolutely impossible, and John will make this very clear later on.

At this point it seems to me that we have a departure from the theme which John has been following. He begins to talk about the three different degrees of believers.

I write unto you, little children, because your sins are forgiven you for his name's sake [1 John 2:12].

These whom he calls "little children," the Greek *teknia*, little born ones, I think refer to all believers, regardless of their age or their

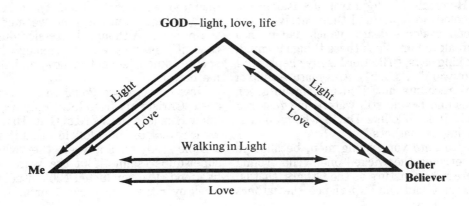

maturity as believers. The basis on which all Christians rest is the forgiveness of sins because of the shed blood of Christ. "Your sins are forgiven you for his name's sake."

Some Christians stay in that position of little children and never move out of that area.

Now John moves to another group—

I write unto you, fathers, because ye have known him that is from the beginning. I write unto you, young men, because ye have overcome the wicked one. I write unto you, little children, because ye have known the Father [1 John 2:13].

"Fathers" are the saints who have known the Lord Jesus for many years and have grown and matured. Personally, I think that David wrote Psalm 23 when he was an old man. He could never have written that psalm as a young shepherd, because it is a psalm which had grown out of life's vicissitudes. David had faced all sorts of problems and dangers, and he had lived in fellowship with God. He was a matured child of God and would certainly fall under John's classification of "fathers." I have called Psalm 23 the psalm of an old king. I believe David wrote it as he was seated upon his throne, looking back over his life. He remembers that shepherd boy who would take the flocks out to pasture on the hills of Bethlehem, how he would protect them from the bears and lions. Then he remembers when he was made king and became the shepherd of a people. As he looks back over his checkered career, he recalls his wonderful friendship with Jonathan, his flight from King Saul, then his reign in Hebron, and finally when God made him king over all twelve tribes. Then he remembers his awful sin and God's gracious forgiveness when he confessed it to Him. He recalls the trouble in his home (because God had taken him to the woodshed), especially the rebellion of Absalom, the son whom he most loved. He recalls his flight from Jerusalem and being holed up again and then receiving the news of Absalom's death, which had been a heartbreak to him. With these things in mind, the old king says, "The Lord is my shepherd; I shall not want" (Ps. 23:1). As a mature child of God, he recounts how God led him in green pastures and beside still waters and restored his soul. It is folk like David whom John is addressing as "fathers."

"I write unto you, young men, because ye have overcome the wicked one." The "young men" are not as mature as the fathers, that is, they haven't had the experience the fathers have had, but they have learned the secret of overcoming the enemy by the blood of Christ. They have learned how to live for God. Don't tell me that a young person cannot live for God in this day.

"I write unto you, little children, because ye have known the Father." The "little children" in this case is the Greek *paidia*, immature little folk. They are the ones who know they are the children of God, but that is about all they know—and some of them feel that is all they want to know. Oh, how many children of God fall into this classification! In some churches you feel as if you are in a spiritual nursery! Although the folk are physically full-grown, some of them with gray hair, they are still spiritually immature. They never did grow up.

Now John has something more to add; so he goes over each of these degrees of believers again.

I have written unto you, fathers, because ye have known him that is from the beginning. I have written unto you, young men, because ye are strong, and the word of God abideth in you, and ye have overcome the wicked one [1 John 2:14].

"I have written unto you, fathers, because ye have known him that is from the beginning." John doesn't add anything to that because you can't go beyond that. As Paul expressed it, knowing ". . . him, and the power of his resurrection, and the fellowship of his sufferings, being made conformable unto his death" (Phil. 3:10) is what makes one a father in Christ.

My friend, how do you get to know somebody? By living with him day by day. I have discovered that my wife knows me. She has been living with me for over forty years so she knows me very well. And the summer I was forced to stay home because of illness, she and I sat on our back patio and really got acquainted with each other. We talked about many things from the time we met down to the present. Although I was sick during that time, it was the greatest summer I have ever spent. I know her better now, and she knows me better.

Now how are we going to know the Lord Jesus Christ? My friend, the only way you can know Him is in the Word of God. That is where He is revealed. Many folk feel that if they go to a Bible study once a week, they will become super-duper saints. But the Word of God is like food. I've conducted Bible studies once a week over the years, and I certainly approve of them, but imagine going in and eating a good meal and then saying, "I'll be back for another meal in a week." Well, if you don't get any food in the meantime, you will be in bad shape. This is the reason I have maintained a *daily* Bible-teaching program by radio. The Word of God is the Bread of Life. If we are to know Christ, we must live with Him in His Word as we go through the joys and sorrows of this life.

Now John addresses the second group—"I have written unto you, young men, because ye are strong, and the word of God abideth in you, and ye have overcome the wicked one." In the previous verse John said that the young men were strong and they were able to overcome the wicked one. But now he gives the secret: "the word of God abideth in you." My friend, how can you and I overcome the wicked one? With the Word of God. In Ephesians 6 the Christian's armor is listed, piece by piece, and the weapon of offense is the ". . . sword of the Spirit, which is the word of God" (Eph. 6:17). If you are going to be able to defend yourself against the Devil, you will have to have a good knowledge of the Word of God. The reason so many believers are succumbing to the sins of the world is that they are not studying the Word of God. You eat three times a day—you need physical food to be strong—and, believe me, you need spiritual food to be strong also.

DEAR CHILDREN MUST NOT LOVE THE WORLD

This is a section which a great many would separate from what has gone before, but I feel that it is very much a part of what John has been talking about. John has been telling us how we as God's children can know that we *are* His children. He has said that the way we can know is by the fact that we love Him and keep His commandments. Later on, John is going to say that His commandments are not grievous. We are not talking about the Ten Commandments here but about the commandments which the Lord Jesus gave, for we have been brought into the Holy of Holies in a very personal relationship with the Lord Jesus Christ. Someone has made this division which I like: The Epistle to the Romans deals with how we come out of the house of bondage; Ephesians is how we enter the banqueting house; Hebrews is how we approach the throne of grace, but 1 John is how we approach the divine presence.

The way in which we can have assurance and be a proof not only to our neighbor but also to ourselves that we are genuine children of God is by our obedience to Him and our desire to please Him in all we do. I feel that there are some folk today who more or less grit their teeth and say, "Yes, I'll obey Him." But their motive is not love, and love should be the motive for obedience to Him. The Lord Jesus said, "If ye love me, keep my commandments" (John 14:15).

My friend, when you obey the commandments of Christ because you love Him, a great many of the family problems will be solved and a great deal of the uncertainty in your own heart will disappear. If someone is offering a little course to follow in living the Christian life, people come running. A great many folk like to lean on something—even if it is a poor, broken reed which won't hold them up.

Christianity is based on a love relationship. Salvation is a love affair. John is going to tell us more about this later when he says, "We love him, because he first loved us" (1 John 4:19).

Love not the world, neither the things that are in the world. If any man love the world, the love of the Father is not in him [1 John 2:15].

"Love not the world, neither the things that are in the world." What "world" is John talking about? He does not mean the world of creation, that is, the system and order found in the physical creation. In spring the flowers bloom and the trees put out leaves. In the fall the leaves begin to turn all kinds of beautiful colors, like yellow and gold and red. Then the leaves fall off, and winter soon comes. This is not the world we are warned against loving. This is the world God created for our enjoyment.

It is just as the poet says in "The Vision of Sir Launfal"—

And what is so rare as a day in June?
    Then, if ever, come perfect days;
Then Heaven tries earth if it be in tune,
    And over it softly her warm ear lays;
Whether we look, or whether we listen,
    We hear life murmur, or see it glisten.

—James Russell Lowell

I learned that poem when I was in grammar school, and it has always stayed with me. My birthday is in June, and in June I always think of how wonderful nature is.

The hymn writer has put it like this—

Heav'n above is softer blue,
   Earth around is sweeter green!
Something lives in every hue
   Christless eyes have never seen:

Birds with gladder songs o'erflow,
   Flow'rs with deeper beauties shine,
Since I know, as now I know,
   I am His, and He is mine.

       "I Am His, and He Is Mine"
         —Wade Robinson

Isn't that lovely? John is not talking about the physical earth where beautiful roses and tall trees grow. The wonderful mountains and the falls and the running streams are not what we are to hate. Rather, they are something we can admire and relish and enjoy.

Nor is the world about which John speaks the world of humanity or mankind. We are told that "God so *loved* the world." What world? The world of people, of human beings. ". . . God so loved the world, that he gave his only begotten Son . . ." (John 3:16).

Then what world does John mean? The Greek word for "world" here is *kosmos*. It means the world system, the organized system headed by Satan which leaves God out and is actually in opposition to Him. The thing which we need to hate today is this thing in the world which is organized against God.

Believe me, there is a world system in operation today, and it is satanic. John mentions this in his gospel where the Lord Jesus says, "Hereafter I will not talk much with you: for the prince of this world cometh, and hath nothing in me" (John 14:30). "The prince of this world"—the prince of the world system, which is included in the civilization that you and I are in today. The world system belongs to Satan. He offered the kingdoms of this world to the Lord Jesus, and I don't think he left out the United States when he made the offer—it all belongs to him, and we are not to love this world. We read in John 16:11, "Of judgment, because the prince of this world is judged." Again, the Lord Jesus is referring to the satanic system that is in this world today. In Ephesians 1:4, when Paul speaks of ". . . the foundation of the world . . .", he is talking about the material creation, but when we come to Ephesians 2:2, he says, "Wherein in time past ye walked according to the course of this world. . . ." What is "the course of this world"? This is a world that is filled with greed, with selfish ambition, with fleshly pleasures, with deceit, and lying and danger. That

is the world we live in, and John says that we are not to love the world. We are living in a godless world that is in rebellion against God. Our contemporary culture and civilization is anti-God, and the child of God ought not to love it. We are *in* the world, but we are not *of* the world. Many of us must move in the business world, many of us must move even in the social realm, but we do not have to be a part of it.

We need to recognize that we are going to be obedient to one world or the other. You are either going to obey the world system and live in it and enjoy it, or you are going to obey God. Listen to Paul in Galatians 6:14: "But God forbid that I should glory, save in the cross of our Lord Jesus Christ, by whom the world is crucified unto me, and I unto the world." In effect Paul is saying, "There stands between me and this satanic world system, a cross. Both are bidding for me and, as a child of God, I am obedient unto Him, and I glory in the cross of Christ." You can be sure that the world today is not glorying in the cross of Christ!

Peter also speaks of this: "For if after they have escaped the *pollutions* of the world . . ." (2 Pet. 2:20, italics mine). He spoke earlier of the *corruption* of the world. We live in a world that is corrupted and polluted. We are hearing so much today about air pollution and water pollution, but what about the minds which are being polluted by all the pornography and vile language? What about the spirit of man that is being dulled by all these things?

"If any man love the world, the love of the Father is not in him." You may run with the Devil's crowd all week long and then run with the Lord's crowd on Sunday, but it is obvious that the love of the Father is not in you.

In Romans 7 Paul describes his own struggle as a Christian. He says in effect, "I have discovered that in my flesh dwelleth no good thing. I have found that there is no power in the new nature. What I would not do, I'm doing. What the new nature wants to do, the old nature balks at—the old nature backslides and will not do that thing." So there is a real conflict which goes on in the heart of the Christian as long as he is in the world with that old nature. For the old nature is geared to this world in which we live; it's meshed into the program of the world.

For all that is in the world, the lust of the flesh, and the lust of the eyes, and the pride of life, is not of the Father, but is of the world [1 John 2:16].

John lists these three things that are in the world. These are not only the temptations which face us, they are also the temptations which Satan brought to Eve (see Gen. 3:6) and to the Lord Jesus Christ (see Matt. 4:1–11).

1. *"The lust of the flesh."* Eve saw that the tree was good for food—if you were hungry, it was a good place to eat. Scripture condemns gluttony and the many other sins of the flesh. So many things appeal to the flesh. There is an overemphasis on sex today both in the church and out of the church—it is all of the flesh. Satan brought this same temptation to the Lord Jesus: "And when he had fasted forty days and forty nights, he was afterward an hungered. And when the tempter came to him, he said, If thou be the Son of God, command that these stones be made bread" (Matt. 4:2–3). The Lord Jesus could have done that. The difference between the Lord Jesus Christ and myself is that if I could turn stones into bread, I suspect that I would be doing it, but He didn't. He was being tested in that same area in which you and I are being tested—the desires of the flesh. We *are* being tested, and there is no sin in being tested. The sin is in yielding to the temptation. This same principle applies to sex or to any other realm of the desires of the flesh.

2. *"The lust of the eyes."* Eve saw that the tree was pleasant to the eyes. Remember also that Satan showed the Lord Jesus Christ all the kingdoms of this world. Let me tell you, they are very attractive, and they *are* in the hands of Satan. There is a godless philosophy which is trying to get control of the world today. There will come a day when Antichrist will arise—he is coming to rule this world for Satan. This is an attractive world that we live in, with all of its display, all of its pageantry, all of its human glory.

3. *"The pride of life."* Eve saw that the tree was to be desired to make one wise. Many people like to pride themselves on their family. They pride themselves on the fact that they come from a very old family and upon the fact that they belong to a certain race. There are a number of races which are very proud of that. That was the appeal which Hitler made to the German people, and it is an appeal to *any* race. That is a pride of life. It is that which makes us feel superior to someone else. It is found even in religion today. I meet saints who feel they are super-duper saints. As one man said to me, "I heartily approve of your Bible study program on radio." In fact, he has given financially to our program to help keep it going. He said, "I know a lot of people who listen to it, and they need it," but he very frankly told me, "I don't listen to it." He felt that he didn't need it, that he had arrived, that he was a very mature saint. Of course, it proves that he is a very immature saint when he even talks like that. Satan took the Lord Jesus to the pinnacle of the temple and said, "Cast yourself down. A great many people will witness it, and You will demonstrate to them Your superiority." It was probably at a feast time when many would have seen Him, but the Lord Jesus never performed a miracle in order to demonstrate His superiority.

These are the three appeals that the world makes to you and me today. But when we make our tummy our goal in life, when we attempt to make beauty our goal, or even when we attempt to make that which is religious our goal, it leads to the most distorted view of life that is possible. These things are of the world, and they become deadly. We are told that we are not to love these things because God does not love them—He intends to destroy this world system someday. What is our enemy? The world, the flesh, and the Devil. This is the same temptation which Satan brought to Eve and to the Lord Jesus. He has not changed his tactics. He brings this same temptation to you and to me, and we fall for it.

Now John gives us the reason we are not to love this world—

And the world passeth away, and the lust thereof: but he that doeth the will of God abideth for ever [1 John 2:17].

I have always enjoyed going to England and visiting such places as the Tower of London, Tewkesbury Castle, Warwick Castle, Hampton Court, Windsor Castle, and Canterbury. Many of us have ancestors who came from over there, but those folk were a bloody, cruel, vain, and worldly people. Just recall the way Henry VIII took Hampton Court away from Cardinal Wolsey who was the one who had built it. Poor old Cardinal Wolsey before he died said something like this, "If I had only served my God like I served my king, I wouldn't be here today."

My, how Henry VIII could eat! And when he got tired of a wife—he had several—he just sent her to the Tower to be beheaded. Go and look at all of that today—"the world passeth away." What a story of bloodshed is told at the Tower of London, of the pride of life and of the lust of the flesh. The lust of the eyes also—how beautiful Windsor and Hampton Court are! Even the arrangement of the flowers was made by Sir Christopher Wren, the wonderful architect who also built St. Paul's Cathedral. There is a glory that belongs to all of that, but it has already passed away. England is just a third-rate power in the world today and maybe not even a third-rate power. All of that has passed away and the lust of it. Where is the lust of Henry VIII today? It is in one of those tombs over there. Just think of all the glory which is buried in Westminster—all of that has passed away.

When I look back to when I was a young man, I wish that somehow I could reach back there and reclaim some of those days and some of the strength which I had then. I wish I could use for God what I squandered when I was young. "The world is passing away."

"But he that doeth the will of God abideth for ever." Why don't you work at something which is permanent, something which has stability, something which is going to last for eternity?

Little children, it is the last time: and as ye have heard that antichrist shall come, even now are there many antichrists; whereby we know that it is the last time [1 John 2:18].

The word translated "little children" here is slightly different from the word that is translated in the same way back in verse 12. There it is a term of affection and implies all who are born into God's family, God's little born ones, little *bairns* as the Scottish term is. These little children here indicate the first degree of spiritual experience which we have seen in verses 12–14: the fathers at the top, then the young men, and then the little babies. Here John is talking to the little babies again. The little babies haven't grown up yet. They are passing through this world, and the chances are that they have been tripped up by one of these three things which John has just mentioned.

"It is the last time." We are living in the last day here upon the earth. It has been the last time for a long time. This is the age when God is calling out a people for His name. You can say at any time during this period, "*Now* is the acceptable time. *Today* if you will hear His voice." Why the urgency about salvation? Because, my friend, you might not be here tomorrow. Tomorrow I might no longer be heard preaching on the radio. It just might be that we will not be around, so it is important that I give out the Word, and it is important that you hear the Word.

"As ye have heard that antichrist shall come, even now are there many antichrists; whereby we know that it is the last time." Many antichrists had already appeared in John's day, but there is coming the Antichrist. What do we mean by *antichrist?* I think that this word has been misunderstood and, as a result, the person who is coming has been misunderstood. *Antichrist* is made up of two words: the title *Christ* and the preposition *anti*. It is important to see that *anti* has two meanings. It can mean "against." If I am anti-something, that means I am against that thing. *Anti* can also mean "instead of, an imitation of." Therefore, it can be a substitute. It can be either a very good substitute or just a subterfuge for something.

The question arises, therefore: Is the Antichrist to be a false Christ or is he an enemy of Christ? Where does Scripture place the emphasis? There are several references to Antichrist in 1 John, but the only things we can derive from this verse is that there is going to be the Antichrist and that there were already many antichrists in John's day. What was the thing which identified an antichrist? He was one who denied the deity of Christ. That is the primary definition of an antichrist which we are given in 1 John, as we shall see when we come to verse 22. This is the emphasis in 1 John, but you will recall that the Lord Jesus said, ". . . many shall come in my name, saying, I am Christ; and shall deceive many" (Matt. 24:5). That is antichrist—instead of Christ, claiming to be Christ.

I personally believe that there are going to be two persons at the end of the age who will fulfill both of these types—being against Christ and claiming to be Christ. Scripture presents it that way in Revelation 13. There we have presented a "wild beast" who comes out of the sea, and Satan is the one who calls him forth. That is the political ruler, and he is definitely *against* Christ. There is a second beast who comes out of the land. He appears to be a lamb, but he is a wolf in sheep's clothing. He *pretends to be* Christ who is ". . . the Lamb of God, which taketh away the sin of the world" (John 1:29). He will be a religious ruler. The political ruler will come out of the gentile world, the former Roman Empire. The religious ruler will come out of the nation Israel—they would not accept him as their Messiah unless he did. So that you have actually two persons who will together fulfill this term *antichrist*. They are coming at the end of the age, and both of them can be called Antichrist—one against Christ and the other instead of Christ.

They went out from us, but they were not of us; for if they had been of us, they would no doubt have continued with us: but they went out, that they might be made manifest that they were not all of us [1 John 2:19].

This is very solemn. John says that some who had made a profession of being Christians in that day had all the outward trappings of being Christians. They bore the Christian name, and they identified themselves with some local assembly, some church. They were baptized, immersed, in the name of the Father, the Son, and the Holy Spirit. They took the bread and the cup at the communion service. But John says that the way you can tell whether or not one is really a child of God is that eventually a man will show his true colors and will leave the assembly of God if he is not a child of God. He will withdraw from the Christians, the body of believers, and he will go right back into the world.

We see in 2 Peter what I call "the parable of the prodigal pig." Peter speaks in that epistle of ". . . the sow that was washed . . ." (2 Pet. 2:22). Not only did a son get down in the pigpen, but also a little pig got washed. A little girl pig went up to the Father's house, became very religious, got all cleaned up with a pink bow around her neck and her teeth washed with Pepsodent, but she found she didn't like the Father's house because she was a pig. So one day she said, "I'm going to arise and go to my father, my old man." Her old man was down in a big loblolly of mud. The little pig went home, and when she saw her old man, she squealed, made a leap, and landed in the mud right by the side of him. Why? Because she was a pig. "They went out from us, but they were not of us." That's a harsh, cruel statement, but it happens to be a true statement. There are many who make professions of being Christians, but they are not really Christians.

Remember that the Lord said of Judas, "But, behold, the hand of him that betrayeth me is with me on the table" (Luke 22:21). Right there, at the first communion service, there was a traitor, Judas Iscariot, and he was one who was identified with the group of faithful disciples. We read in John 6:70, "Jesus answered them, Have not I chosen you twelve, and one of you is a demon?" Judas was never anything else although he looked like an apostle, he acted like an apostle, and he had power, I believe, to perform miracles. He went out with the others, and they were not able to identify him as being a phony, but he was.

John makes a very solemn and serious statement here, and he makes this statement to us today. The Lord Jesus said to a very religious man, Nicodemus, that he must be born again. He said to him that night, "Except a man be born again, he cannot see the kingdom of God" (John 3:3). John says here, "They went out from us, but they were not of us." They looked as if they were true children of God, but they actually were not, and the real test, of course, was the Word of God. This ought to cause every Christian, including this poor preacher who writes this, to ask himself the question: Have I really faced up to my sins in the light of the cross of the Lord Jesus Christ? Have I come to God in repentance, owning my guilt and acknowledging my iniquity? Have I cast myself upon Him and Him only for my salvation? Have I evidence in my life of being a regenerate soul of God? Do I *love* the Word of God? Do I want the Word of God? Is it bread to me? Is it meat to me? Is it drink to me? Do I *love* the brethren? And do I *love* the Lord Jesus Christ? These are the things which we need to consider, my friends, and the Word of God enjoins us in this particular connection.

After presenting justification by faith in no uncertain terms, Paul goes on to make it clear in Galatians 6:15, "For in Christ Jesus neither circumcision availeth any thing, nor uncircumcision, but a new creation." You cannot even boast of the grace of God and say, "Oh, I don't trust in church membership. I don't trust in baptism." Well, whether or not you believe they are necessary for your salvation, the essential question is: Have you really been born again? Or, perhaps you *are* one who is trusting in these things. Again the important question is: Are you a new creation in Christ Jesus?

Paul spoke to the Corinthians, some of whom had reason to believe they might not be children of God: "Examine yourselves, whether ye be in the faith; prove your own selves. Know ye not your own selves, how that Jesus Christ is in you, except ye be reprobates?" (2 Cor. 13:5). My friend, it is very important that you really know that you are a child of God. Paul also wrote earlier to the believers in Corinth, "Watch ye, stand fast in the faith, quit you like men, be strong" (1 Cor. 16:13). Friend, how are you doing with the Christian life? Are you really a child of God today? Is there evidence in your life that you are a child of God? I'm not talking about whether you have committed a sin or not, but what did you do after you committed the sin? Did you continue on in sin? The Prodigal Son got into a pigpen, but he did not continue there—that was not his permanent address. If you had mailed him a letter after he had been there a few weeks or months, unless the pigs had forwarded it, he wouldn't have gotten your letter. That was no longer his address; he had gone home. The child of God, after he has sinned, is going to go to God with hot tears coursing down his cheeks and crying out to Him in confession. If he doesn't do that, he's not God's child.

God's child must hate sin. This light view of sin which we have today is simply something that is not quite scriptural. I am afraid that there are many church members who are just taking it for granted that they are children of God because they are as active as termites in the church—and they have just about the same effect as termites.

Let me pass this little story on to you. I have heard it told several different ways, and I don't know which way is accurate. Years ago in London, living down in the slums, there was a woman of the underworld, a prostitute. She had a little son, and she became terribly sick. She was frightened because she knew she was dying, and she sent her little son to get a minister, as she put it, "to get me in." She told the little fellow, "You go get a minister to get me in."

The little fellow went out looking for a church. He had to go a long way before he found a very imposing looking church. He went around to the rectory, and the minister came to the door when he rang the bell. The minister looked at this little urchin and said, "What do you want?" The little boy replied, "My old lady is dying. She wants you to come and get her in." At first the minister thought the boy meant that his mother was out drunk somewhere, so he said, "Get a policeman. It's raining tonight, and I don't want to go out. Get a policeman to get her home." The little fellow said, "She's already home. She's not drunk. She is home in bed, and she is dying. She wants somebody to get her in, and she wants me to get a minister. Would you come?" That liberal minister was stunned for a moment. He knew that he should go, that he couldn't turn down a request like that, so he got his coat and umbrella, and he went with the little fellow. They walked and walked and came finally to a very poor section of London and found the creaky stairs which led to an upstairs bedroom.

All the way over, the minister had thought, *What will I say to her? I can't say to her what I have always preached to my people.* He had always told his congregation that they were people of culture and refinement, that they were to keep that up and continue to be very cultured and refined. He thought, *What in the world can I say to her? I can't even tell her to reform. She ought to be reformed, but it is too late now. What can I tell her?* Then he remembered that as a boy his mother had always quoted John 3:16, and in desperation he turned to that verse when he sat down beside this woman. It actually wasn't too familiar to him, but he read it to her: ". . . God so loved the world, that he gave his only begotten Son, that whosoever believeth in him should not perish, but have everlasting life." The dear woman wanted to go over the verse with him. She said, "Do you mean that in spite of the type of person I am, all I have to do is just trust in Jesus?" He said, "Well, that is what it says here. It says that God gave His Son to die on a cross. It says, 'As Moses lifted up the serpent in the wilderness, even so must the Son of man be lifted up' (see John 3:14). That is what I read here, and so that is what you are to do." This dear woman, before she died, right there accepted Christ as her Savior. The preacher himself told the story afterwards, and he said, "That night I not only got *her* in, but I got *myself* in." My friend, are you sure that *you* are in? Are you sure that you have trusted Him and that He is your Savior?

Some people will write me and say, "You have no right to ask questions like that because we have been members of the church for thirty years." Well, I think you ought to examine yourselves and see whether you are in the faith or not. It is wonderful to make an inventory and find out where you are. There was a time in the Thru the Bible radio ministry when we didn't know where we were financially because our accountant became too ill to help us. When we got an accountant, we found that, although we had thought we were sailing along on nice, blue seas, we really weren't. Thank the Lord, we found it out in time—but it was only because we *examined* our condition. A great many church members need to *examine* themselves. Are you really in the faith? Do you really trust Christ? Someone will say, "You are robbing me of my assurance of salvation." My friend, I believe in the security of believers, but I also believe in the insecurity of make-believers. We need to examine ourselves to see what kind of believer we really are.

At the beginning of this chapter, John made it very clear that we can know that we are God's children and that we can have fellowship with Him. In spite of the fact that we are His feeble, frail, faltering, falling little children, we can still have fellowship with Him because the blood of Jesus Christ, God's Son, just keeps on cleansing us from all sin. We have an Advocate up there with the Father, and He's for us—He is on our side.

Then beginning at verse 3 we saw that God is love. This is the very heart of this epistle. Love is mentioned about thirty-three times. John said that the dear children may have fellowship with each other by walking in love. In other words, the little children must recognize that they are called to live a different kind of life. They now have been given a new nature. They now can live for God. Obedience is the test of life. We can know whether we really have life or not if we keep His commandments—and not only His commandments but His Word. Obeying His Word means we are willing to go even farther than anything he had commanded.

The difference between law and grace is brought out by what John has said. The law said: If a man do, he shall live. But grace says the opposite: If a man live, he will do. That is, a man must have a life from God before he can live for God. He cannot by the old nature live for God. This is the radical difference between law and grace. The law says, "Do," but grace says, "Believe." It is a different approach to the same goal. The only problem is that law never did work for man because it is impossible for the old nature to please God. We all have come short of the glory of God. John showed that the real test is: Do I delight in the will of God? Do I love His commandments? If you are a child of God, you have a new nature, and now you want to please Him. It has been expressed like this in a little jingle:

My old companions, fare you well.
I cannot go with you to hell.

I mean with Jesus Christ to dwell.
I will go with Him, and tell.
                                    —Author unknown

That may be a very poor piece of poetry, but it certainly expresses it as it really is. You cannot be having fellowship with God and other believers if you are living in sin.

Proverbs 28:13 says, "He that covereth his sins shall not prosper: but whoso confesseth and forsaketh them shall have mercy." Though we know that the blood of Christ does indeed cover us from all sin, we cannot walk and live in sin and at the same time have fellowship with God and with other believers. If you and I have a life which commends the gospel, it is another assurance that is given to us. I personally do not think you can have real assurance down deep in your heart unless you are obedient unto God. I believe that you can know beyond the peradventure of a doubt that you are a child of God. Such assurance is not presumptuous, it is not audacious, it is not being arrogant, it is not effrontery, it is not a gratuitous assumption, it is not overconfidence, it is not self-deception, it is not wild boasting, it is not self-assertion. In fact, it is true humility. Knowing that you are saved and the eternal security of the believer are not the same; they are not synonymous, although they are related. The Lord Jesus said, "My sheep hear my voice, and I know them, and they follow me: And I give unto them eternal life; and they shall never perish, neither shall any man pluck them out of my hand" (John 10:27–28). If you are His sheep, you will hear His voice. You are not boasting when you say that you know you are saved. You are saying that you have a wonderful Shepherd. You are not saying that *you* are wonderful but that your *Shepherd* is wonderful. What a tremendous truth this is!

But ye have an unction from the Holy One, and ye know all things [1 John 2:20].

What John means here by "unction" is anointing. We have an anointing, and that is the anointing of the Holy Spirit. We are going to see this later in verse 27 where John says, "But the anointing which ye have received of him abideth in you."

"But ye have an unction from the Holy One, and ye know all things." The Holy Spirit indwells every real believer and is able to reveal to him all things. ". . . Eye hath not seen, nor ear heard, neither have entered into the heart of man, the things which God hath prepared for them that love him. But God hath revealed them unto us by his Spirit . . ." (1 Cor. 2:9–10) so that we have someone dwelling in us who can reveal to us these things which are in the Word of God. We have an anointing, and every person can have the assurance of his salvation. If you really want to do business with God, if you really want to get right down to the nitty-gritty with Him, come to Him, ask for light, ask for guidance, and ask for His assurance.

"And ye know all things." John means that all the things that you should know as a child of God are potentially yours to know. This does not mean that you have suddenly been given a Ph.D. degree in spiritual things. It does mean that by the Holy Spirit you can study the Word of God, and then through the experiences which God sends to you, you have the possibility of growing in these matters.

Many a child of God grows in grace and in the knowledge of Christ. I have been amazed at the number of lay people whom I have met in my ministry who have done so. The first time I discovered this was when I was a student in my first year in seminary during the depression, way back in the late 1920s. I was asked to go to a little Baptist church in the cotton mill section of Sherman, Texas. I went up there and preached four times that Sunday. I never will forget that! Because the cotton mill hadn't been operating for over a year, they gave me thirty cents for an honorarium! A friend of mine, a fellow student, went with me, and on the way home he asked, "Why are you so quiet?" I told him, "The offering I got was thirty cents!" He said, "Well, this is a real event for you. This is probably the only time that you will ever be paid exactly what you are worth." Thirty cents—but, gracious, that had to be spread over the four sermons which I had given!

We had had dinner, that is, the noon meal, that day in a home where there was an elderly woman whom everybody called "Grandma." (There were about twenty people there, but I don't think she was a grandmother to everybody!) She told me that she had come in a covered wagon in the early days and that she had loaded the rifle for her husband as he had shot at attacking Indians. She had been a real pioneer. But she had never learned to read nor write, and she wasn't able to go to church. The people asked me, "Would you read something to Grandma?" Being a first-year seminary student, I thought I would give her the benefit of my vast knowledge of Scripture (which, by the way, wasn't so vast). I thought I would take something easy and familiar so I began to read John 14. As I went along, I wanted to explain it to Grandma—after all, she couldn't read nor write, and I thought I should help her. I made a comment or two as she sat there, and I thought she looked a little bored. After a few minutes she said, "Young man, had you ever noticed this?" Frankly, she made comments to bring out some things in that passage which I had never heard before. In fact, there was no professor in school who had ever mentioned what she mentioned about that passage of Scripture. Before we got through the chapter, she was telling *me* and *I* was listening.

This friend of mine who had come with me was sitting over in the corner, and I knew he was really going to get me for this. On the way home that night, he made another comment. He said, "My, you sure were helpful to Grandma today!" I said, "Where in the world do you suppose that woman learned so much about John 14?" He replied, "Did it ever occur to you that maybe the Holy Spirit is her Teacher? Maybe you and I have been listening to the wrong teachers!" John is saying here that we need to let the Holy Spirit be our Teacher. "Ye have an unction from the Holy One, and ye know all things." That's potential—it is up to you whether you are going to learn or not.

I have not written unto you because ye know not the truth, but because ye know it, and that no lie is of the truth [1 John 2:21].

"I have not written unto you because ye know not the truth"—they had the gospel; they had the truth. John is not writing something new to these folk. He is writing to them for what I think is a twofold purpose. One is to encourage them, and the other is to warn them because there was false teaching going out in that day.

"But because ye know it, and that no lie is of the truth." John is saying that they had the truth, but now lies were coming in. Gnosticism was coming in, and there were many antichrists who were appearing.

Who is an antichrist? We have already said just a few words about this, but now John will say a little bit more—

Who is a liar but he that denieth that Jesus is the Christ? He is antichrist, that denieth the Father and the Son [1 John 2:22].

The language is much stronger here; it is, "Who is *the* liar?" In other words, all lies are summed up in the one who is the prince of liars, the Devil. There is coming a man who is Satan's man, and he is *the* liar. And a liar is one who does not tell the truth.

"Who is a liar, but he that denieth that Jesus is the Christ? He is antichrist, that denieth the Father and the Son." John gives us now the definition of antichrist. This will be the embodiment of *the* Antichrist, but there are many antichrists. There were some in John's day; there have been some down to our day, and there are many today. Who are they? They are easy to recognize—they are those who deny the *deity* of the Lord Jesus Christ, those who deny that Jesus the man is the Christ, the Messiah, the one who is God, the one whose name is Wonderful, Counselor, the Mighty God, the one who is pictured in the Old Testament. To deny that is being antichrist.

We have many systems in the world today which deny Him. They are against Christ, and they also imitate Him and try to take His place. In the early church it was Gnosticism. Irenaeus made this statement, "They [that is, the Gnostics] say that Jesus was the son of Joseph and born after the manner of other men." That is the way Irenaeus identified the Gnostics in his day.

Liberalism and all of the cults and "isms" today have also denied His deity. Very candidly, I do not mind saying that the rock opera, "Jesus Christ Superstar," is antichrist. It does not by any means present the Jesus of the Bible who is the Savior of the world. Many years ago Dr. William E. Hocking, who was professor of philosophy at Harvard University, wrote *Living Religions and a World Faith*. He made this statement, "God is in His world, but Buddha, Jesus, Mohammed are in their little private closets, and we shall thank them, but never return to them." You can see that that is simply a direct, rank denial of the deity of Christ. The one "that denieth the Father and the Son"—that will be the sure mark of the Antichrist, and there are many antichrists even today, of course.

John has identified antichrist for us as the one who denies the Father and the Son. Now he will make it clear in verse 23 that you cannot deny the Son without denying the Father. You see, the deity of Christ is essential to your salvation because if He is not God, the man who died on the cross over nineteen hundred years ago cannot be your Savior—in fact, He could not even be His own Savior. None of us as human beings can die for the other. It was necessary for God to become a man in order that you and I might have redemption. Therefore, John says—

Whosoever denieth the Son, the same hath not the Father: [but] he that acknowledgeth the Son hath the Father also [1 John 2:23].

When you say that you believe in God and deny the deity of Christ, you really do not believe in God, certainly not the God of the Bible. The God of the Bible is the one who sent His Son into the world to die for our sins. And since the Son is God, He alone is the one who could make a satisfactory sacrifice to God for our sins. Had he been anyone else other than God, He Himself would have been a sinner.

In the great Riverside Church in New York City when Dr. Harry Emerson Fosdick was the pastor, the cover page of a bulletin at that time said, "Whoever you are that worship here, in whatever household of faith you were born, whatever creed you profess, if you come to this sanctuary to seek the God in whom you believe or to rededicate yourself to the God in whom you do believe, you are welcome." It goes on to say a lot about peace and the Fatherhood of God, but I'm nauseated reading that far so I will not quote any more of it. It sounds sweet and flowery; it appeals to the natural man, but John's whole point is that we need to beware of this, for this is antichrist. We need to emphasize this very important verse.

Let that therefore abide in you, which ye have heard from the beginning. If that which ye have heard from the beginning shall remain in you, ye also shall continue in the Son, and in the Father [1 John 2:24].

"Let that therefore abide in you, which ye have heard from the beginning." "The beginning" in 1 John goes back to the incarnation of Christ. That "which ye have heard from the beginning," that which you heard concerning His incarnation, that which you heard concerning His life, that which you heard concerning His death and resurrection—in other words, that which they had heard from the beginning when the apostles began to preach the gospel.

"If that which ye have heard from the beginning shall remain in you, ye also shall continue in the Son, and in the Father." I know a man who heard our Bible-teaching radio program more than twenty years ago in San Diego. I'm not going to tell you about his life before then, but when he heard the broadcast, right there and then he accepted Christ as his Savior. God put him at the head of the Christian Servicemen's Center in San Diego, and it is one of the finest in the world. Down through the years, he has been responsible for leading literally thousands of sailor boys and soldier boys to the Lord. I thank God for the testimony of this man's life because John says that if you abide in Him, that is the evidence that you are a child of God.

It is essential, therefore, to have a living faith which rests in the One who came to this earth more than nineteen hundred years ago. In his gospel John wrote, ". . . the Word was made [became] flesh, and dwelt among us . . ." (John 1:14). How tremendous that is! "No man hath seen God at any time; the only begotten Son, which is in the bosom of the Father, he hath declared him" (John 1:18). He has "declared"—*exēgeomai*, exegeted God. He has led God out to where we can know about Him because God became a man. That is the only way you and I could know about Him. We *can* now know about God. The important thing in this whole section of Scripture is communion with the Father and with the Son. The emphasis here is not so much upon having life in Christ through faith in Him, but the emphasis is upon having communion and enjoying that fellowship with Him which is so essential.

And this is the promise that he hath promised us, even eternal life [1 John 2:25].

The only kind of life that God offers is eternal life. If you lose it tomorrow or next week or next year, it isn't eternal life that you have. It is some other kind of life, but not eternal life.

These things have I written unto you concerning them that seduce you [1 John 2:26].

Seduce means "to lead astray, to lead from the truth." I think that *seduce* is a good word here because it applies in exactly the same way in both the physical and spiritual realms. In other words, you lead a person to commit spiritual adultery when you lead him away from the truth.

Even in John's day there were those coming along who were beginning to deny the Father and the Son, beginning to deny that the Lord Jesus Christ was who He claimed to be. They were seducing some of those who were professing Christians. John says that the thing which you must hold onto is that God has promised you eternal life if you put your faith in Christ, and you do not need to add anything to that.

John was telling the people of his day that they did not need what the Gnostics were teaching. The Gnostics pretended to have super-duper knowledge, that they knew a little bit more than anyone else. I am afraid that in our own day there is a real danger when a great many people are going to so many Bible classes. There is the danger of their becoming super-duper saints. A lady said something to me the other day which I didn't appreciate very much because I know her husband so well and he is a wonderful Christian. She's been going to Bible classes, and they have been fine classes. Don't misunderstand me, I'm not criticizing the Bible classes. However, she was adopting a very superior attitude toward her husband, that she knew more than he knew, and that she was really the one who could teach him. Very frankly, I don't think she could. He is a very intelligent man, and although he is not able to be in as many Bible classes as she is, what he does hear has an effect upon his life. So there is a real danger of present-day Gnosticism, of professing to have a superknowledge and maybe even a superexperience, of becoming a super-duper saint where there is just no one else at your level.

Such a position is a dangerous one to come to because if you come into a knowledge of Christ and you begin to grow in grace and knowledge of Him, you will have the same experience that John the Baptist had, which he expressed this way, "He [Christ] must increase, but I must decrease" (John 3:30).

I'm going to make a confession to you, and I hope you won't let it out but will just keep it in the family. In one sense it is a little disturbing to me that my study of the Word of God does not reveal how much I know, but rather it reveals how much I *don't* know and how woefully ignorant I am. I am studying the Bible now as I never have in my entire life, but when I graduated from seminary, I practically knew it all; there was very little that I thought I needed to learn after that. There were certain things I thought I knew at that time, but very frankly, I'm coming now to find that I didn't know them at all. I thought I did, but I didn't know them at all. There is a vast field of knowledge today for the child of God. It behooves us to make this matter of coming to know Christ through His Word a serious business and to give it top priority in our lives. That is the thing that is all important, and all that John is really saying is, "I don't want you to become a super-duper saint. I want you to rest upon the promise of God."

Now John is going to say to them, "You know Him as your Savior—hold on to that—but now you also want to have communion with Him and the Father, and to have fellowship with Him and the Father and with other believers."

But the anointing which ye have received of him abideth in you, and ye need not that any man teach you: but as the same anointing teacheth you of all things, and is truth, and is no lie, and even as it hath taught you, ye shall abide in him [1 John 2:27].

"Anointing" is the Greek word *charisma*. We speak of a certain speaker or preacher as having charisma. If he doesn't have charisma, he doesn't get very far today, you'll have to admit that. When I went to my classical dictionary, I must say I was shocked and disappointed. This word means "to smear on"; it means to take an ointment and smear it on. It is like when you take a medicated petrolatum and put it on your chest at night—you are anointing yourself, you are smearing it on. That is literally what *charisma* means. I checked with Dr. R.C. Trench and Dr. Marvin Vincent, two outstanding Greek scholars, and they also have come up with the same meaning. *Charisma* means "to smear on."

But what does this mean for us today as believers? Back in the Old Testament, by the command of God, the Israelite priests were anointed with oil. That anointing indicated in a physical way that they were specially endued by the Holy Spirit to perform a certain function. That is what the anointing here means for us today. "But the anointing which ye have received of him"—that is, you and I have received an anointing of God. When you are saved, one of the things which the Spirit of God does for you is that He anoints you. He anoints you to understand divine truth which you could not understand before.

"But the anointing which ye have received of him abideth in you, and ye need not that any man teach you." The important thing to note here is that John is not saying that we do not need teachers. We *do* need teachers, or else Paul was certainly wrong in Ephesians when he made the statement that God has given to the church certain men who are gifted—some who are teachers, some who are evangelists, and some who are shepherds to minister to and counsel folk. Paul said that God has given these men to the church to build up the body of believers. I think it is important that we all sit under good teachers.

As I think back over my life, I thank God for the godly men who have crossed my pathway. They are the ones who are responsible for my being in the ministry. I have the pictures of four men hanging on the wall of my office at the headquarters of our radio ministry. The combined influence of these four men is the reason that I entered the ministry. These men affected my life. You may not know these men, but I am going to give you their names. The first man is a man by the name of Joe Boyd who was a layman in Nashville, Tennessee. When no one else seemed interested in a young fellow who wanted to study for the ministry, Joe Boyd got interested. He is actually the man who did the footwork of making it possible for me to get a job so that I could go

to college and for me to get a loan so that I could go to college and seminary. He followed my ministry, and I was his pastor for three years. He was a wonderful man, and I thank God for him. Next to his picture is the picture of the pastor whom I followed in that church in Nashville, Dr. A.S. Allen. He is one of those unsung preachers whom you never hear about today, but he is one of the greatest preachers I ever listened to. Next to his picture is that of Dr. Lewis Sperry Chafer, the founder and first president of Dallas Theological Seminary. My, when I heard him preach, that's what turned me on. I thought, *This is the thing that I want to do.* Next to Dr. Chafer is the picture of probably the brainiest man whom I have ever met, Dr. Albert Dudley. He is a man who had great influence upon the turn which I took in the ministry to become an expository preacher rather than a preacherette giving little sermonettes to Christianettes. I thank God for him and for all these men.

Therefore, John is not saying that teachers are not essential, but he is saying something that is important for God's children today. "But the anointing which ye have received of him"—this has been referred to before when he spoke of "the unction of the Holy One," the anointing of the Holy Spirit. One of the Holy Spirit's ministries is to teach us. He is able to guide us into all truth. The Lord Jesus, the great Teacher, said, "But the Comforter, which is the Holy Ghost, whom the Father will send in my name, he shall teach you all things, and bring all things to your remembrance, whatsoever I have said unto you" (John 14:26). The Holy Spirit will teach us all things, that is, all that you and I are able to contain.

"But as the same anointing teacheth you of all things, and is truth, and is no lie, and even as it hath taught you, ye shall abide in him." There has been given to you an anointing whereby you are *enabled* to understand all truth because ". . . the natural man receiveth not the things of the Spirit of God: for they are foolishness unto him: neither can he know them, because they are spiritually discerned" (1 Cor. 2:14). Paul also wrote earlier, ". . . Eye hath not seen, nor ear heard, neither have entered into the heart of man, the things which God hath prepared for them that love him. But God hath revealed them unto us by his Spirit . . ." (1 Cor. 2:9–10). This is the anointing of the Holy Spirit for a believer.

This is one reason we encourage folk to get into the Word of God and to study it. I received a letter from a dear lady who makes a tape recording of our radio program and then listens to it again and again. She also reads repeatedly the passage of Scripture being taught. All of a sudden her eyes are opened, and she sees the Lord Jesus in a new way. What has happened? She has had an anointing. I believe in that kind of anointing, but I don't believe in a lot of the silly stuff that is going on today which is purely emotional and which doesn't enlighten you to understand and love the Word of God and to love the Lord Jesus. It does not matter how much whoopee you put into your religion, you can just whoop it up and have all kinds of emotion, but all that is of no value. It is *enlightenment* that we need today.

The whole point is that there ought to come a day when you and I can stand on our two feet as far as the Word of God is concerned and, as Peter says, ". . . be ready always to give an answer to every man that asketh you a reason of the hope that is in you with meekness and fear" (1 Pet. 3:15). We ought to be able to do that. But there is also a grave danger in this which I want to very carefully point out. I know people who have been going to Bible classes and have been studying the Bible for years, but they never get anywhere. They are the ones who bring Bible teaching into disrepute. I see people at Bible conferences in the summertime—I've seen them there every summer for thirty years—and they are today right where they were thirty years ago. They are like ". . . silly women laden with sins, led away with divers lusts, Ever learning, and never able to come to the knowledge of the truth" (2 Tim. 3:6–7). They don't seem quite to arrive, but they always have their Bibles and are always writing a few little notes down. At a summer conference where I was speaking sometime ago, a woman came to me with the same question that I am confident she had asked me twenty-five years ago at another summer conference! She had a notebook, and she was still taking it down—"ever learning, and never able to come to the knowledge of the truth."

In other words, we ought to get to the place where the Spirit of God is our Teacher. As you study the Word of God, do you ask the Spirit of God to teach you and to lead you? If you don't understand something the first time, get down on your knees and say, "Lord, I miss the point. I don't understand this. Make it real to me. I want this to be real to me." This is important, and this is what John is saying here. "The anointing which ye have received of him abideth in you, and ye need not that any man teach you." There are certain things which the Spirit of God can make very real to you.

"But as the same anointing teacheth you of all things, and is truth, and is no lie." The Lord Jesus said, "For there shall arise false Christs, and false prophets, and shall shew great signs and wonders; insomuch that, if it were possible, they shall deceive the very elect" (Matt. 24:24). But it will not be possible to deceive the elect. The Antichrist will not deceive the elect who are left on the earth when he comes. And today no antichrist will deceive them. I knew a couple who had recently been saved, and they got into a liberal church. I met them when I was a pastor in downtown Los Angeles. They told me, "We worked our way down Wilshire Boulevard, going from church to church until we got to your church. We knew we were not hearing the truth of God at the churches we visited, but we couldn't put our finger on it. We knew the teaching was wrong, but we didn't know *how* it was wrong"—they were just new converts. God's little children are going to follow the pattern the Lord Jesus spoke of when He said, "My sheep hear my voice . . ." (John 10:27). God's children are not going to follow a false shepherd. They hear His voice, and the Spirit of God can be their Teacher. This should be a great comfort to us. We need to test every teacher we hear—it would be well if you tested me. Ask the Holy Spirit, "Is this that McGee is teaching the truth of God? Make it real to my heart, too. I want to know for myself whether it is true or not."

And now, little children, abide in him; that, when he shall appear, we may have confidence, and not be ashamed before him at his coming [1 John 2:28].

"And now, little children"—dear little bairns, little born ones, meaning all God's children, irrespective of maturity.

"Abide in him." This is not really the imperative here but the indicative. In other words, John is saying, "You *are* abiding in Him." I want to repeat that John is speaking here of fellowship. To abide in the Lord Jesus is to live in fellowship with Him. To abide in Him means to have communion with Him.

"That, *when* he shall appear." This is actually, "*If* he appear," but the *if* is not one of doubt. The *if* hasn't anything in the world to do with a doubt of the fact of His coming, but it has to do with the uncertainty as to the circumstances. Although we may have an anointing, we *do not* know when Jesus is coming. That is one thing which He has reserved for Himself to know.

Why has He not revealed to us the time of His coming? "That, when he shall appear, we may have confidence, and not be ashamed before him at his coming." A Christian ought to live in the light of the *imminent* coming of Christ. If you tell me today that He is not coming for another ten years (I may not live that long!), then I do not need to worry about today, and I can be a little careless in my living. But if He might come today, if He came right at this moment, He would catch me preparing this Bible study and that would be fine. I hope He will come at a time like that, but I don't know when He will come. There are times when I get behind a driver who won't let me around to pass him, and I tell him what I think of him. If the Lord were to come at that moment, I might be ashamed at His appearing. So you and I need to be living all the time in the light of His imminent return.

"When he shall appear, we may have confidence, and not be ashamed before him at his coming." A great many people are talking about the coming of Christ, and they get very excited about it; but it certainly is going to be embarrassing for them because they will not have any confidence and they are going to be ashamed before Him at His coming. Why? Because of their lives. The Lord Jesus says, "And, behold, I come quickly; and my reward is with me, to give every man according as his work shall be" (Rev. 22:12). Many people will look around for their reward, and they will find that they haven't got any. Paul wrote, "If any man's work shall be burned, he shall suffer loss: but he himself shall be saved; yet so as by fire" (1 Cor. 3:15). It is very important to have a life that commends the gospel.

John is saying here the same thing that Peter said: False doctrine and false living go together; true doctrine and true living go together. Every now and then you hear of a cult leader who is in trouble because he is guilty either of adultery, or of taking money which doesn't belong to him, or of beating some person out of money. Why? False doctrine leads to false living. True doctrine leads to true living. There is nothing that will affect your life as much as the knowledge that you are going to stand in the presence of Christ and give an account of your works. Every believer will stand before the judgment seat of Christ. Paul writes, "For we must all appear before the judgment seat of Christ; that every one may receive the things done in his body, according to that he hath done, whether it be good or bad" (2 Cor. 5:10). The issue of salvation has already been settled because we are His children and in His presence. It is not a question of whether you are saved or lost; it is a question of whether or not you are going to get any reward or recognition. There will be some folk who will not get any recognition. Paul writes further, "Knowing therefore the terror of the Lord, we persuade men . . ." (2 Cor. 5:11). The Rapture is not going to be such a thrilling event for a great many believers because of the lives they lived down here.

If ye know that he is righteous, ye know that every one that doeth righteousness is born of him [1 John 2:29].

This is the final proof, this is the litmus paper which is put into the solution to tell whether it is acid or base. It surely will tell every time. The Word of God is the real test. In effect John is saying that God's children look like the Father—they take after their Father. If they don't take after the Father, they must not be the Father's children. It is just as simple as that, my friend.

CHAPTER 3

THEME: How the dear children may know each other and live together; the Father's love for his children; the two natures of the believer in action

HOW THE DEAR CHILDREN MAY KNOW EACH OTHER AND LIVE TOGETHER

The last verse of chapter 2 belongs here with the first three verses of chapter 3. First John 2:29 reads: "If ye know that he is righteous, ye know that every one that doeth righteousness is born of him." It is one thing to testify that we know Christ and are in Him; it is quite another to have a life that reveals that He is our righteousness. It is wonderful to know positionally that we are in Christ and that we are accepted in the Beloved, but it is altogether different to have a life down here that is commensurate with that. John is telling us that the way we recognize other believers is by their lives and not by their lips. Righteousness is a family characteristic of the Father and His children. God's children take after their Father—they have *His* characteristics.

THE FATHER'S LOVE FOR HIS CHILDREN

Behold, what manner of love the Father hath bestowed upon us, that we should be called the sons of God: therefore the world knoweth us not, because it knew him not [1 John 3:1].

This is a very wonderful statement that John makes here. Let me give you my very literal translation of this verse: "Behold ye, of what sort of love the Father hath bestowed upon (given to) us, that we should be named children of God, and we are: and because of this the world does not know (begin to understand) us, because it did not know (begin to understand) Him."

John is saying that we do not *expect to be* the sons of God, we *are* the sons of God. A better translation includes the words *"and we are."* The child of God can say emphatically, "I am a child of God through faith in Jesus Christ." We don't hope to be, we don't expect to be, but the thrilling fact is that every believer can exult and rejoice and constantly thank Him that he is God's child. We are boasters not in ourselves, but we are boasting of the wonderful Shepherd that we have. John makes it perfectly clear that if you are a born again child of God, you are going to exhibit a life that conforms to the Father. A child of God need not be

in the false position of saying as an old hymn says:

'Tis a point I long to know,
Oft it causes anxious thought,
Do I love my Lord or no?
Am I His, or am I not?
—Author unknown

John says, "Now we are the children of God"—*right now* we are the children of God.

"Behold, what manner of love the Father hath bestowed upon us, that we should be called the sons of God." The kind of love that John is talking about is a strange kind of love, an unusual kind of love, a kind of love to which we are not accustomed. God loves us. What manner of love the Father has for us! The love of God—that is, His love for us—is shed abroad in our hearts by the Holy Spirit. John will go on to show that God has demonstrated His love by giving His Son to die for us. How many of us have someone who would die for us? How many folk would you be willing to die for? God loves you, and He has proven His love—He gave His Son to die for you.

The greatest motivating force in the world is God's love. Love is the greatest drive in the human family. A man falls in love with a woman, a woman falls in love with a man, and some make such tremendous sacrifices for each other. When human love is genuine love, it is a beautiful thing, it is a noble thing, it is a wonderful thing, and it is a tremendous drive. But God's love for His children far exceeds anything we can experience on the human plane.

The true child of God is going to prove his spiritual birth by being obedient to God's Word. God's wonderful love for us should motivate us. It is that which is going to cause us to want to live for God. Behold, what an unusual kind, what a different kind of love the Father hath bestowed upon us that we should be called the children of God.

John has emphasized that we are God's children *right now.* This brings me to say that our salvation is in three tenses: I have been saved; I am being saved; and I shall be saved.

1. *I have been saved.* The Lord Jesus said, "Verily, verily, I say unto you, He that heareth my word, and believeth on him that sent me,

hath everlasting life, and shall not come into condemnation; but is passed from death unto life" (John 5:24). The moment you trust Christ you receive everlasting life, and you will never be any more saved than you are the moment you trust Him. You are born again, born into the family of God. John is addressing "little children"—these are God's children. He says, "What manner of love the Father hath bestowed upon *us*." Why? Because we are His children. He has bestowed His love upon His children, and they respond to that love by obedience unto Him and by living a life that is well pleasing to Him.

2. *I am being saved.* Paul said, ". . . work out your own salvation with fear and trembling. For it is God which worketh in you both to will and to do of his good pleasure" (Phil. 2:12–13). Peter said, "But grow in grace, and in the knowledge of our Lord and Saviour Jesus Christ . . ." (2 Pet. 3:18). John is talking to us along the same lines here. If we are the children of God, we are going to be obedient unto Him, we are going to grow, we are going to develop, and we are going to go on in the Christian faith. Therefore, we can say that we are being saved.

3. *I will be saved.* When the Lord Jesus comes again for His own, we will experience the final stage of our salvation. Sin no longer will have power over us, and we will be with the Lord forever.

Beloved, now are we the sons of God, and it doth not yet appear what we shall be: but we know that, when he shall appear, we shall be like him; for we shall see him as he is [1 John 3:2].

"Beloved, now are we the sons of God"—not tomorrow, but *right now*—that is the wonderful part of it. The world won't understand us, that's for sure, because it didn't understand Him. It takes a *spiritual* insight, and that comes through the anointing which we have talked about that He has given to us. The Spirit of God is the one who can make this real to us, and only the Spirit of God can do that, my friend. Until He confirms it to your heart, of course, you must say, "I don't know whether I am saved." But the Spirit of God can confirm this to your heart.

John says, "Beloved, now are we the sons of God." But someone says to me, "McGee, I'm a little discouraged with you. I think you ought to be a little farther along." I would agree with you on that. I wish I were a better man, and I wish I knew more about the Word of God. Yes, I'd be willing to go along with that—I ought to be farther along than I am. But don't you be discouraged with me, and then I won't be discouraged with you because of the fact that "it doth not yet appear what we *shall* be."

"But we know that, when he shall appear, we shall be like him." This is a wonderful prospect! He sees in you and in me what He will make out of us. I'm thankful that God is not through with me. If I thought He was through with me now, I would be very much discouraged, but He is yet to perform a work.

The story is told that when a great big piece of marble was brought in to him, Michelangelo walked around it, looking at it, and then said, "My, isn't it beautiful!" One of his helpers who was standing there said, "Well, all I see is a great big piece of marble—that's all." Michelangelo exclaimed, "Oh, I forgot. You don't see what I see. I see a statue of David there." The helper looked again and replied, "Well, I don't see it." Michelangelo said, "That is because it is now in my own mind, but I am going to translate it into this piece of marble." And that is what he did. God says, "It doth not yet appear what you shall be." He sees what He is going to make out of us someday. We are discouraged when we look at each other as we are now, but God sees us as we shall be when He shall appear and we shall be like Him. What a glorious prospect this is for us!

"We shall be like him; for we shall see him as he is." We are going to see the glorified Christ. We are not going to be equal to Him, but we are going to be like Him in our own way. This does not mean that all of us are going to be little robots or simply little duplicates—it is not that at all. We will be like Him but with our own personalities, our own individualities, our own selves. He will never destroy the person of Vernon McGee. He'll not destroy the person that you are, but He is going to bring you up to the full measure, the stature where you will be like Him—not identical to Him, but like Him.

It is going to be wonderful in heaven that we will love everybody—I'm excited about that. But the most wonderful thing about heaven to me is that everybody is going to love me! That's going to be quite a change, and I'm looking forward to it. "Beloved, now are we the sons of God, and it doth not yet appear what we shall be: but we know that, when he shall appear, we shall be like him; for we shall see him as he is." This is another great incentive to Christian living. I do not think there is anything else quite like it.

And every man that hath this hope in him purifieth himself, even as he is pure [1 John 3:3].

If you believe that Jesus is coming and that someday you are going to be like Him, that will cause you to live a pure life down here. I know of nothing that is such a great incentive for holy living. We are not wonderful now, but we shall be wonderful someday.

There is nothing that should encourage holy living like the study of Bible prophecy. Today we see a lot of careless, slipshod living, but also a great emphasis on prophecy. I hear people say, "Oh, I'm waiting for the Lord to come!" Brother, my question is not whether you are looking for the Lord to come, but how are you living down here? How you live down here determines whether or not you are really looking for the Lord to come.

We are going to accomplish our goal someday. The New Jerusalem where we will live is going to be a place where He will wipe away all tears. There'll be no sorrow, there'll be no suffering. All of that is wonderful, but the most wonderful thing that strikes me in Revelation 21 is that He says, ". . . Behold, I make all things *new* . . ." (Rev. 21:5, italics mine). That is what I like. I do not know about you, I can speak only for myself, but I very frankly make this confession: I have never really been the man that I've wanted to be. I am at the age now where I guess a man begins to dream a little. And as I look back over my life, I realize I've never been the man that I have wanted to be, and I've never been the preacher I have wanted to be. I've never really preached the sermon that I wanted to preach. People have been kind to me and have said nice things, and I appreciate that, but I know in my own heart that I wish I could do better.

I've never been the husband that I've wanted to be. Previously I mentioned an illness I had several years ago which necessitated a three-month rest. My wife and I sat out on our patio and did a great deal of reminiscing. As I reviewed my life, I thought, *My, I wish I had been a better husband than I was. I should have been.* And I've never been the father that I wanted to be. Some people think I'm a little too much for my grandsons. Well, I'm trying to make up for them what I left out for my own child.

I've never really attained my goal. I thank God for the way He has led me. He's been good to me in my life, and I rejoice in the fact that He's given to me a Bible-teaching radio ministry. I never thought He'd do that, but He

has. I have not attained my goal, but He says, "Behold, I make all things new." He is saying, "Vernon McGee"—and He is saying this to *you*, too—"We are going to be able to start all over again. You are really going to live an eternal life, and you are going to attain your goal." Won't that be wonderful to grow in grace and the knowledge of Him, not only in this life, but for all eternity? What a prospect lies before us!

John is telling us here of the wonderful love the Father has for His children. I have been saved, I am being saved, and I am going to be saved. It's going to be wonderful someday. So you don't be discouraged with me, and I won't be discouraged with you.

THE TWO NATURES OF THE BELIEVER IN ACTION

Whosoever committeth sin transgresseth also the law: for sin is the transgression of the law [1 John 3:4].

Again let me give you my very literal translation of this verse: "Everyone that doeth sin, doeth also lawlessness, and sin is lawlessness." I have before me two very fine Greek commentaries, and they make it clear that the word translated "committeth" sin is literally "doeth" sin, meaning one who lives continually and habitually in sin. You know folk like that. I used to live that way, and the fellows working around me in the bank lived that way. Frankly, working in the bank was secondary. Our interest was in women, in liquor, and in having a good time. That was what we thought life was all about in those days, and that was what we called living. We lived in it continually, and we talked about it continually. That is what John means here: "Whosoever committeth sin"—whoever goes on committing sin, whoever simply *lives* in sin.

"Transgresseth also the law." God *has* made certain laws. God *did* say, "Thou shalt not commit adultery" (Exod. 20:14), and He means that today also. All of this free, new way of looking at things is not a new way at all. It is as old as the hills. The fact of the matter is that it goes back to the jungle, it goes back to paganism.

"For sin is the transgression of the law." God has put up the Law so that we can know that we are sinners, so that we can know what He requires. That is the purpose of the Law. The Law was never given to save, it was given to *reveal* to man that he is a sinner.

Sin is basically and fundamentally that which is contrary to the will of God. In other words, a sinner is one who is insubordinate to the will of God. A little girl was asked in Sunday school to give her definition of what sin is. She said, "I think it is anything that you like to do." You know, she wasn't far from the truth, because this old nature that you and I have is absolutely contrary to the will of God. Paul emphasizes that in Romans 8:5, "For they that are after the flesh [the old nature] do mind [obey] the things of the flesh; but they that are after the Spirit the things of the Spirit." How are you living? In the flesh or in the Spirit?

Paul goes on to say, "For to be carnally minded is death. . . ." Death is separation from God, and that is the thing which John is talking about. You cannot have fellowship with Him and be a carnal Christian. It is impossible to do that. I am afraid that there is too much talk today about, "Oh, how I love God, how I am serving Him, and How wonderful He is." How pious some folk are! But, my friend, they are not in fellowship with Him because ". . . to be carnally minded is death; but to be spiritually minded is life and peace. Because the carnal mind is enmity against God [that is, disobedient to God]: for it is not subject to the law of God, neither indeed can be" (Rom. 8:6–7).

Paul makes it clear that before the Law was given there was sin, but it wasn't transgression. The statement here in 1 John, "Whosoever committeth sin transgresseth also the law," does not give a complete definition and is not really a good translation. That is why in my translation I have put it like this: "Everyone that doeth sin, doeth also *lawlessness.*" Paul wrote earlier in Romans, ". . . for where no law is, there is no transgression" (Rom. 4:15); but there is *sin* because he says, "Wherefore, as by one man sin entered into the world, and death by sin; and so death passed upon all men, for that all have sinned" (Rom. 5:12). That is, we sinned in Adam—his sin was ours. "For until the law sin was in the world: but sin is not imputed when there is no law" (Rom. 5:13). Man was still a sinner and was insubordinate to God; nevertheless, it was not transgression of the Law—because the Law hadn't been given yet.

We read further in Romans: "Nevertheless death reigned from Adam to Moses, even over them that had not sinned after the similitude of Adam's transgression, who is the figure of him that was to come" (Rom. 5:14). They sinned—why? Because they were sinners. In Isaiah 53:6 we have a true picture of every unsaved man: "All we like sheep have gone astray; we have turned every one to his own way; and the LORD hath laid on him the iniquity of us all." Everyone has turned to his own way. Those three words tell our story: *his own way.* What's *your* problem? What's *my* problem? We want to have our way. The little baby in the crib is squealing at the top of his voice—what's the matter with the little fellow? He wants his own way! We are born with that nature, a nature which is in rebellion against God.

This is the way the hymn "I Was a Wandering Sheep" by Horatius Bonar puts it:

> I was a wandering sheep,
>   I did not love the fold,
> I did not love my Shepherd's voice,
>   I would not be controlled:
>
> I was a wayward child,
>   I did not love my home,
> I did not love my Father's voice,
>   I loved afar to roam.

But the child of God has now come to God, and he has been born again.

And ye know that he was manifested to take away our sins; and in him is no sin [1 John 3:5].

Only the Lord Jesus can take away sin. He came for that purpose.

Two things are important for us to see here. In John's gospel he wrote, ". . . Behold the Lamb of God, which taketh away the sin of the world" (John 1:29). He bore the *penalty* of sin. "For God so loved the world, that he gave his only begotten Son, that whosoever believeth in him should not perish, but have everlasting life" (John 3:16). Christ died for the sin of the world. Now here in John's epistle he shows that Christ takes away the *practice* of sin in the life of the believer. Christ is the "propitiation for our sins: and not for ours only, but also for the sins of the whole world" (1 John 2:2). What is the difference? Well, He died a redemptive death to pay the *penalty* of our sin, but He also died that He might deliver us from the *power* of sin right here and now.

"And in him is no sin." The literal translation of this is: "in Him sin is not." He died a redemptive death—He was our sin offering. He was without sin; He was without spot or blemish as was the Levitical sin offering. Therefore He is able to remove the guilt of sin and to provide the power to deliver us from the habit of sinning. He has given to us a new nature that we might live for Him today.

Whosoever abideth in him sinneth not: whosoever sinneth hath not seen him, neither known him [1 John 3:6].

"Whosoever abideth in him sinneth not"—that is, that new nature of yours will not sin; it never sins. Dr. H. A. Ironside puts it this way: "[Christ], this absolutely sinless One, who in grace became sin for us that we might be reconciled to God, dwells by the Spirit in the believer, and our new nature is really His very life imparted to us." If you are God's child, that new nature will not go along with the old nature and commit sin. The believer who abides in Christ does not practice sin—he doesn't live in it. The sinner lives in it all the time, but the child of God has a new nature, and he cannot live a sinful life. This is pictured for us in the story of the Prodigal Son (see Luke 15:11–24). Only pigs live in pigpens; sons do not. Somebody will say, "But the son got into the pigpen." He surely did, my friend, but he got *out* of the pigpen, too—let's remember that. The child of God can get into it, but he will get out. Why? Because he is a son of the Father, and he takes after his Father. His Father is righteous, and the son wants to live that kind of life.

God provides the power to deliver from the habit of sinning, and that is all that John is saying here—"Whosoever abideth in him sinneth not." Now if you go off to the pigpen, that's the old nature, and if you stay in that pigpen, you never were God's child. If you can be happy in sin, my friend, then you are not God's child because God's children have the nature of their Father. Sometime ago I received a letter from a young man which may help to illustrate my point here:

> I come to you with a very critical problem and hope that you will help me for I am desperate and have nothing left to try or anybody to turn to . . . . I know that I am a new born again Christian, although many times I had doubts. But I know that I have been saved. Brother, I don't know what you are going to think when you find that I am a homosexual. Perhaps you'd think that I am living in false assurance of eternal life, but, believe me, this is not the case. I *know* I'm saved, but I lost the joy of my salvation for awhile. And I try to live a Christian life, and I never was so miserable . . . .

This young man's letter is actually encouraging because he says that he is a homosexual but that he is *miserable* in it. He has no joy; he has

no peace. Of course, he doesn't. I will not question whether or not he is a child of God, but I do want to say something to him and to the many others who are just like him: My friend, God can give you deliverance from it. You need to claim that from Him. Ask Him to bring you to the place of peace and joy in your life. If you are God's child, you will never be content in a sinful state. The people are wrong who maintain that homosexuality is merely another life-style. God calls it sin, and God says there is a deliverance. Now there may be an abnormality involved. I am confident that consulting a Christian psychologist would help, but make sure you go to a true Christian psychologist. The other crowd would probably push you farther into your problem, and you would never be delivered out of it. God *can* and *will* deliver you because you are His child. That is what the Word of God says here, and if you believe it, God can deliver you.

Little children, let no man deceive you: he that doeth righteousness is righteous, even as he is righteous [1 John 3:7].

"Little children"—John is talking to those who are God's children; he is not talking to the world.

"Little children, let no man deceive you: he that doeth righteousness is righteous, even as he is righteous." This is the thing which reveals the child of God. To abide in Him does not mean just positionally. It is true that you have a position in Christ that can never be disturbed, but there is also a practical consideration down here. If you abide in Him in fellowship and service, sin must be given up.

I talked to a young man in Phoenix, Arizona, one time who said to me, "Dr. McGee, I've been listening to you on the radio. I think you can help me. I'm an alcoholic. I accepted Christ several years ago, and I can go for a long time without drinking, but then I will again find myself drunk. I hate myself." This fine looking young fellow who was an executive began to weep as he talked. He said, "I know eventually it will affect my job if I keep this thing up. I don't want to drink, because I *am* a child of God. And don't tell me I'm not because I have accepted Christ. I've driven fifty miles to get here this morning so that I might ask you this question: Is there deliverance for me?" I told him there was. If he has the nature of his Father, there is one thing that is sure—God will not let him be content and happy in his sin. That was an unhappy young man, the most unhappy young man I had seen in a long time. I told him, "Every time you fall down, brother, go back to your heavenly Father and tell Him what you did. Tell Him that you don't want to disgrace Him again. The day will come when He will deliver you." That has been the story of other men, and it is the story of any sinner who professes Christ and finds himself bound down by a habit. God can and will deliver him.

I happen to be a fellow who knows something about that of which I am speaking here. When I was young, God in a very marvelous way intervened in my life. My mother's side of my family were German, and I want to tell you, they were heavy drinkers—the whole outfit. My father was not an alcoholic, but he was also a heavy drinker. I grew up in that atmosphere, and I started out that way. I thank God for a deliverance from it when I was still just a boy. My friend, I know He can deliver you, and He will deliver you from your sin. This epistle deals with living, right where we are. You cannot simply take some little course and get the deliverance. You are going to have to call upon God for it and have real contact with Him.

> **He that committeth sin is of the devil; for the devil sinneth from the beginning. For this purpose the Son of God was manifested, that he might destroy the works of the devil [1 John 3:8].**

"He that committeth sin is of the devil." We need to recognize that the Devil is the source of all sin. He is the one who is responsible for sin being brought into the world. He is the one who led our first parents into sin. And the reason that you and I have a sinful nature today is because of the Devil. "He that committeth sin is of the devil." Remember that the Lord Jesus said to the religious rulers of His day, "Ye are of your father the devil, and the lusts of your father ye will do . . ." (John 8:44). The interesting thing is that we will take after our father. If your father is the Devil, then you are going to act like him. If your father is our heavenly Father, then you have His nature, and you are going to act like Him.

"For the devil sinneth from the beginning"—that is, he started out sinning, and he has been at it ever since. He is in rebellion against God.

"For this purpose the Son of God was manifested, that he might destroy the works of the devil." Only Jesus Christ can deliver you, my friend. Go to Him. Don't come to me because I cannot help, and no one else can either. But He can, He is the Great Physician, and I urge you to go to Him with your problem.

The Lord Jesus Christ died for the sin of the world. John the Baptist said, ". . . Behold the Lamb of God, which taketh away the sin of the world" (John 1:29). He took away the penalty of sin. Since you've trusted Christ, your sins are behind you, and you are saved in Him. Your sins will never again be brought up as far as your salvation is concerned because you have trusted Him. But John tells us here that the Lord Jesus not only takes away our sin, but He also was manifested to take away our *sins*—plural. He was without sin—He had no sin nature. "For such an high priest became us, who is holy, harmless, undefiled, separate from sinners . . ." (Heb. 7:26). But He was a human being, and He died as our sin offering, paying the penalty for our sin. But John also says back in verse 5 of this chapter that He was "manifested to take away our sins." The word *our* is not in the better manuscripts; it is literally "manifested to take away sins"—that is, to take away the sins of all believers. In other words, He died to make it possible for you and me to live the Christian life.

This brings us right to the subject of this section from verse 4 to verse 24: every believer has two natures. This is what Paul talks about at length in Romans 7. He says there, "For the good that I would [the desire of this new nature that I have] I do not [that is, the old nature which has been in control so long takes over]: but the evil which I would not, that I do" (Rom. 7:19). The new nature desires to do good, but the old nature drags its feet. The old nature will not serve God; it is in rebellion against God. Paul writes further, "Because the carnal mind is enmity against God: for it is not subject to the law of God, neither indeed can be. So then they that are in the flesh cannot please God" (Rom. 8:7–8). You cannot please God until you are born again. "But ye are not in the flesh, but in the Spirit, if so be that the Spirit of God dwell in you"—there is no idea of a condition here, but rather Paul is saying, *since* "that the Spirit of God dwell in you. Now if any man have not the Spirit of Christ, he is none of his" (Rom. 8:9). Let me be very clear that we are talking about *born-again believers.* We are not talking about professing Christians; we are not talking about church members; we are not talking about those that have simply been baptized without ever having been saved; we are not talking about those that go through a ritual or belong to some system. We are talking about those that have been born again. The Lord

Jesus was manifested "that he might destroy the works of the devil," to make it possible for you and me to live for God.

Whosoever is born of God doth not commit sin; for his seed remaineth in him: and he cannot sin, because he is born of God [1 John 3:9].

"Whosoever is born of God"—this is the new birth we have been talking about. This is what the Lord Jesus spoke of when He said to a religious ruler, "Marvel not that I said unto thee, Ye must be born again" (John 3:7).

"Whosoever is born of God doth not commit sin." A child of God is given a new nature, and that new nature does not and will not commit sin. The reason that the Prodigal Son could not stay in the pigpen is that he was not a pig. He was a son of the Father, and he longed for the Father's house. If you are a child of God, you will want to be in the Father's house, and you will *long* for it.

"Whosoever is born of God doth not *commit* sin"—unfortunately, this gives a wrong impression here. The idea is not just one act of sin; the idea is that he does not *live* in sin. John has said earlier in chapter 2, "If any man [any *Christian* man] sin, we have an advocate with the Father"—the believer will sin. However, John makes it very clear that it is God's will that we live without sin: "My little children, these things write I unto you, that ye sin not" (1 John 2:1). Sin is anything contrary to the will of God, but when sin comes into our lives, John says that we have an advocate with the Father, and "If we confess our sins, he is faithful and just to forgive us our sins, and to cleanse us from all unrighteousness" (1 John 1:9). Again, John is talking to believers, and he is saying that believers will sin. Therefore, when John says, "Whosoever is born of God doth not commit sin," he is saying that that new nature will not continue to *live* in a pigpen—never, under any circumstances will it do that.

"For his seed remaineth in him." If you are a child of God, you have a divine nature.

"And he cannot sin." Why? Because he "is born of God." John is talking about something that is real and genuine. He is not talking about some little profession which you made when you went down to the front of a church and shed a few tears. The question is: Have you been *born of God?* I believe in the security of the believers, but I also believe in the insecurity of make-believers. It is well for us to take an inventory and to look at our lives. We must examine ourselves and see whether we are in the faith or not. Are you really a child of God? Do you long after the things of God? That is the important thing.

Someone might say of this young man who is a homosexual, "He cannot be a child of God." I say that he can be; but if he is a child of God, he is going to give up that sin. A prodigal son ought not to be in a pigpen, and he will not live there. He is going to get out. The day will come when he will say, "I will arise and go to my Father." And his Father is not anywhere near that pigpen—He is as far from it as He possibly can be.

Whosoever is born of God does not *practice* sin. He does not go on in sin. When we received a new nature, we did not lose our old nature—that is the problem. No wonder Paul cried out, "O wretched man that I am! who shall deliver me from the body of this death?" (Rom. 7:24). Only the Spirit of God can deliver you, my friend. If you recognize that you are helpless and hopeless, if some sin binds you down, spoils your life, robs you of your joy, and you are miserable, then may I say to you that He can and He will deliver you—if you *want* to be delivered. If you want to get rid of that sin, if you really want to serve Him, if you mean business with Him, He means business with you. "For his seed remaineth in him: and he cannot sin, because he is born of God."

In this the children of God are manifest, and the children of the devil: whosoever doeth not righteousness is not of God, neither he that loveth not his brother [1 John 3:10].

"In this the children of God are manifest, and the children of the devil." I think we need a little more manifesting today because many of the children of God look like they belong to someone else, or at least they look as if they are orphans. There are two families in the world. The teaching of the universal Fatherhood of God and the universal brotherhood of man I consider to be a damnable heresy. The Bible doesn't teach that God looks upon all people as His children. The Lord Jesus said to the religious rulers, "Ye are of your father the devil . . ." (John 8:44). Someone has said that the reason a Christian ought not to marry a non-Christian is that if you marry in the family of the Devil, you are going to have trouble with your father-in-law! How true that is. There are the children of God and the children of the Devil—there are two families in the world.

John is going to show that there are two things which manifest the child of God. Now

God knows our hearts and knows whether or not we have really been born again and are His children. But our neighbor next door doesn't know that. The only way for him to know is for the life of God to be manifested in us. It is not necessarily manifested by lip and language, but it is manifested by our living.

I want to use a very homely illustration which I trust will demonstrate the fact that the believer has two natures. I live on a ranch here in California. Now before I go any further, I must tell you about a lady who asked her neighbor, "Did you know that Dr. McGee owns a *ranch* in California? I'm amazed that a poor preacher can own a ranch!" The neighbor laughed and said, "Why didn't you listen to him carefully? He told you how big his ranch is." So I will tell you that my "ranch" is 72 feet wide and 123 feet deep. In the middle of that ranch is my home. But I do have a lot of fruit trees. I have three orange trees, a tangerine tree, a lemon tree, and a plum tree. I have an apricot tree, a fig tree, and quite a few guava bushes. So that is quite a ranch! I love fruit, and I enjoy getting out in my ranch and looking around. Very seldom, when I am at home, does a day pass without my going all the way around my yard, looking at every tree.

Also, I have four avocado trees which had grown wild out here in this dry land, but grafted into them are several very fine varieties of avocados. You can see where the bud is—it is just about as high as my head on one particular tree.

Below that graft, every now and then a branch will come out from the wild or the old nature of that old avocado, and I have to trim it off. Sometimes I am busy in our conference ministry, and I don't get to tend to things like that. The limb will then come out below the bud, and it will bloom and bear fruit. But it's the poorest fruit you can imagine—it's just no good at all. Above the bud, oh, it bears luscious fruit. My problem is to keep those limbs cut off below the bud so that it will not bear fruit down there. I want it to bear fruit up above where it has a new nature. This avocado tree can bear either kind of fruit—it's just up to me which I want.

My friend, I'm just like that avocado tree. I have two natures. I can be mean and live on a pretty low plane. I have a nature that is that way. All of us have that old nature. We never get rid of it in this life, and we all come short of the glory of God. But above that, in my new nature, is where I can bear the fruit of love, joy, peace, longsuffering, etc. I feel good today, and I have the joy of the Lord in my heart, but tomorrow you may find me down in the dumps. Now I ought not to be there, but that is something that happens, and when it does, I'm living in the old nature.

In Galatians Paul tells the believers to learn to walk in the Spirit. You cannot do it yourself. In Romans 7 Paul discovered two things: there is no good in the old nature, and there is no power in the new nature. You must have help. It does not matter who you are, you cannot live the Christian life yourself. It is only by the Spirit of God working in you that you can produce that good fruit, and He *wants* us to produce fruit.

The Lord Jesus said, "I am the true [genuine] vine, and my Father is the husbandman. Every branch in me that beareth not fruit he taketh away: and every branch that beareth fruit, he purgeth it, that it may bring forth more fruit" (John 15:1–2). He wants us to produce fruit, but He also tells us that He will prune us. When I prune that avocado tree up above the graft, it bears better fruit. God prunes *us* to get good fruit. Sometimes down there in that old nature, we will also bear fruit. That is called the works of the flesh, and they are not very attractive, they are not anything to brag about.

"In this the children of God are manifest, and the children of the devil." You can tell them apart by their fruit. "Wherefore by their fruits ye shall know them" (Matt. 7:20), the Lord Jesus said. As the late Dr. James McGinley used to say, "I'm not to judge you, but I am a fruit inspector." We ought to be able to find a little fruit on our fellow believers, and in 1 John 3:10 John gives us two clear marks of identification of a true child of God.

"Whosoever doeth not righteousness is not of God." It does not matter who he is or what profession he makes, if a person is not trying to live for God, he is not a child of God. It does not matter how active you are—you may be a deacon in the church, you may be as busy as a termite—but John says that the important mark of identification is: "whosoever doeth not righteousness is not of God." That is a strong statement, but John said it, and the Spirit of God said it through him.

"Neither he that loveth not his brother." Here is the second mark of identification. Do you love other Christians? If you are a child of God, you are going to love other Christians.

The word *love* is going to occur again and again in this epistle. We need to get our understanding of it straight right here at the beginning. There are actually three Greek words that are translated by our one English word *love*. The first Greek word is *eros*, and it is never used in the New Testament. It refers to erotic love, having to do with sex. The Greeks talked a great deal about sex, and they had the god Eros and the goddess Aphrodite, the worship of whom involved sex. Again may I say, the word *eros* is never used in the New Testament. The second word, *phileō*, means "friendship." It means a love of the brethren; it is a brother sort of love. The third word, the highest word, is *agapaō*. That is God's love: "For God so *loved* the world . . ." (John 3:16, italics mine). *Agapaō* is the word John uses here as he tells us that we are to love our brother. We hear a great deal of talk today about love, love, love, and many times it is articulated in the context of sex; but in the Bible, love has no relationship to that whatsoever.

"Neither he that loveth not his brother" means that we are to have a concern for our Christian brother; we are to be helpful to him. It does not mean that you necessarily care for his ways, his conversation, or the things that interest him. It does not mean you have to run up and put your arms around him. It means that you are to be concerned for him. You cannot harbor hatred in your heart against another believer. We will see in the next chapter that this love is not something that is sloppy and slippery by any means. It does not mean that you are to help, that is, to be taken in by every Tom, Dick, and Harry who comes along. We are warned to be very careful indeed and to keep our eyes open, but we are to have a love in our hearts for our brethren in the Lord. This love is to be a concerned love, a love that acts, a love that does something beneficial.

For this is the message that ye heard from the beginning, that we should love one another [1 John 3:11].

John often speaks in this epistle about "the beginning." The beginning he is talking about is the incarnation of Christ.

"For this is the message that ye heard from the beginning, that we should love one another." John is merely reaffirming here what the Lord Jesus had taught: "By this shall all men know that ye are my disciples, if ye have love one to another" (John 13:35). This love is to be the mark of Christ's disciples. John says, "What I am telling you is not new. You have heard this from the beginning. The Lord Jesus taught it to us, and all the apostles have taught this. We have heard from the beginning that we should love one another." Love of other believers is something that is woefully lacking today in many places.

Not as Cain, who was of that wicked one, and slew his brother. And wherefore slew he him? Because his own works were evil, and his brother's righteous [1 John 3:12].

"Not as Cain, who was of that wicked one, and slew his brother." Cain and Abel were blood brothers and were very much alike in many ways. But Cain killed his brother. Why? "Wherefore slew he him? Because his own works were evil, and his brother's righteous." What was Cain's problem? His problem was jealousy or envy—that was Cain's sin.

Jealousy is perhaps not the best word to describe Cain's problem. Jealousy has in it the note of suspicion; for example, a man may be jealous of his wife, meaning that he probably loves her but suspects that she may not be faithful to him. Therefore, I think the better word to use here would be *envy*. Envy and jealousy are given in the dictionary as synonyms, but there is a distinction between them without there really being a difference.

Envy is the thing which characterized Cain. He was envious of his brother, and it led to murder. Envy is that which is in the human heart. As someone has said, "The most destructive force in the world is jealousy and envy."

Let me give you a definition of *envy*: "discontent or uneasiness at the sight of another's excellence or good fortune, accompanied with some degree of hatred and a desire to possess equal advantages." That exactly describes Cain. A definition of *envious* would be: "actuated or directed by or proceeding from envy; jealously pained by the excellence or good fortune of another." This kind of distinction should be noted: a woman is not envious or jealous of a man's courage, and it is also true that a man is not jealous of a woman's beauty; rather, we are envious of that which we would desire to have.

Envy and jealousy among believers in the church hurt the cause of Christ today probably more than anything else. It is that old secret sin that many believers cover up. How many soloists are jealous of another soloist? How many preachers are jealous of another preacher? A great deal of backbiting that goes on in the church has its root in one thing: jealousy. Boy, that is a mean one! And jealousy is the reason that Cain killed Abel—God had accepted his brother's works and not his own.

Marvel not, my brethren, if the world hate you [1 John 3:13].

John says, "Don't act as if some strange or weird thing has happened to you if the world doesn't accept you, because the world is *not* going to accept you." John makes it very clear all the way through this epistle that he is merely passing along the teachings which the Lord Jesus Christ Himself gave. In John 15:18–19 the Lord Jesus said, "If the world hate you, ye know that it hated me before it hated you. If ye were of the world, the world would love his own: but because ye are not of the world, but I have chosen you out of the world, therefore the world hateth you."

This has always been a problem for many of us in the ministry. I have never really appreciated it when anyone would say, "When you were a pastor in such-and-such a place, you were a popular minister." I'm not sure that I care for that because there is a certain crowd I would deeply regret to be popular with. If I ever was popular with them, I should not have been, and I don't want to be popular with them because the Lord Jesus is not popular with that crowd. I watched a minister on television the other night as he had a marvelous opportunity to witness for Christ. But instead he played up to that unbelieving crowd, and he said some nice, flowery, complimentary things, and he was applauded for it. I wondered if there was not sorrow in heaven because he was in a crowd where Jesus was not popular but he was popular with them.

The child of God needs to recognize that the world will hate him. There is an offense of the Cross, but we should guard against magnifying the offense by making ourselves objectionable and obnoxious. Many Christians do that, and they are rejected, not because they are Christians, but because they are simply obnoxious—they would be obnoxious whether they were Christians or not. Let's make sure that Christ's rejection and our rejection are for the same reason.

We know that we have passed from death unto life, because we love the brethren. He that loveth not his brother abideth in death [1 John 3:14].

"We know that we have passed from death unto life." You can *know* whether you are a child of God or not. The idea that we cannot know is a big mistake because the Word of God says that we *can* know that we have passed

from death unto life. How do we know it? "Because we love the brethren." Do you have a love in your heart for the brethren?

One of the greatest experiences that I have had in my ministry is to travel throughout this country, speaking at conferences in many places and meeting many wonderful believers. We have had several rather interesting experiences as we have gone on our way. I recall one time when I was in a city in the East, and I felt very much alone. My wife was not with me at the time, and I felt very, very lonesome. I had gone into a restaurant and had just given my order to the waitress when a man sitting at the next table got up and came over to me. He said, "Dr. McGee, I didn't expect to see you here!" I said, "Well, to whom do I have the pleasure of speaking?" He said, "I have never met you before. To tell the truth, I've never seen you before, but I listen to you on the radio. May I sit down?" So he sat down, and he and I had one of the most wonderful times of fellowship. How did we have it? Well, he was a child of God, and I am a child of God. He hadn't even known that I was to be speaking in that area, but he came with his wife to the meetings after I told him about them. We went out after the service for refreshments, and I probably ought to say that he picked up the tab—which to me was a proof that he was a real brother! It is quite wonderful to be in the ministry today and to meet wonderful Christians all around the country.

Another time I was on a golf course in Florida, and there was a couple ahead of us who were slowing us down. I even yelled at them one time because of it. Finally, when we came right up to where they were playing, the man looked at me and said, "Dr. McGee, I didn't know you were here playing golf. In fact, I didn't even know you were in this part of the country. Were you the fellow who was trying to hurry us along?" When I admitted that I was, he said, "I'll be very frank with you. I've been to the doctor, and I'm not too well yet so I must play slowly." So I had to apologize to the man for my being very rude and abrupt and trying to get him to hurry. Then we just had a wonderful time of fellowship. Our twosome joined his twosome, and we played along together. We got so involved talking that the foursome behind us yelled at us for not moving along! Again, that was someone I had never seen before, and yet I found him to be my brother, and we enjoyed fellowship together. This is what John is talking about. Do you love the brethren? When you can meet around the person of Christ, when you can talk about

Christ with other folk, you have a brother or sister, my friend.

"He that loveth not his brother abideth in death." There are those who do not seem to have any concern for the children of God, but you and I are to have a concern. I always look forward to our Bible conference tours because a lot of the folk will be people whom I have never met before. Yet we will have about two weeks of the most wonderful fellowship that you have ever heard of. Why? Because we love the brethren, and that's a proof of our salvation, friend. There is no greater proof than that as far as your heart is concerned.

Whosoever hateth his brother is a murderer: and ye know that no murderer hath eternal life abiding in him [1 John 3:15].

"Whosoever hateth his brother is a murderer." I didn't say that; John said that, and again he is quoting the Lord Jesus. In Matthew 5:21–22 we read, "Ye have heard that it was said by them of old time, Thou shalt not kill; and whosoever shall kill shall be in danger of the judgment: But I say unto you, That whosoever is angry with his brother without a cause shall be in danger of the judgment: and whosoever shall say to his brother, Raca, shall be in danger of the council: but whosoever shall say, Thou fool, shall be in danger of hell fire." May I say to you, these are strong words. The Lord Jesus said that if you have hatred in your heart toward your brother, it means that you are a murderer. Envy and jealousy lead to hatred, and hatred is murder. How many murderers are there around today? By this standard that God has put before us, there are more murderers out of jail than there are in jail.

I am sure you realize that this passage does not teach that an actual murderer cannot be saved. Christ paid the penalty for *all* sins— even taking the life of another. However, when a man is saved, he will no longer live in hatred.

May I remind you that John's emphasis in this section is the two natures of the believer. When you become a child of God, you do not get rid of your old nature. Rather, you have two natures—an old nature and a new nature. We have seen that the new nature is the only nature that can please God. Man in his natural state is unable to please God; the carnal mind is enmity against God. Therefore, as believers, there are times when we feel like praying, and there are times when we do not feel like praying. There is a hymn ("Come Thou Fount" by Robert Robinson) that says:

Prone to wander, Lord, I feel it
Prone to leave the God I love.

Someone read that and said that it didn't express his feelings; so he changed the wording. You will find one version in some songbooks, the other version in other songbooks. The other wording is:

Prone to worship, Lord, I feel it,
Prone to serve the God I love.

Which is true of a believer? Is he prone to *wander*, or is he prone to *worship?* I would say that both are true. I have a nature that I've discovered is prone to wander. I have another nature that's prone to worship. God says, "If you are My child, then you will manifest My nature. You will manifest that new nature which I have given to you."

Hereby perceive we the love of God, because he laid down his life for us: and we ought to lay down our lives for the brethren [1 John 3:16].

"Hereby perceive we the love of God." You will note that in your Bible *of God* is in italics which means that those words are not in the better manuscripts or not in the manuscripts at all. They were added for clarification, but I don't think they are necessary. It literally says, "Hereby perceive we the love." This is to be our example—the way God loves. How does God love? "Because he laid down his life for us." This is the standard that is put before us.

"And we ought to lay down our lives for the brethren." Now I don't know about you, but I have not come up to that level in my life. Do you know many people who would put their lives on the line for you? And how many of us would be willing to put our lives on the line for someone else? Today we do not see this spirit manifested as it should be. And yet I was greatly touched when I was ill with cancer the first time because several people wrote to me and said that they would be willing to take my cancerous disease to themselves. They wanted me to be able to finish making the tape recordings for our five-year "Thru the Bible" radio program. I had never known anyone who would be willing to go that far. I recognized, of course, that those folk couldn't do that for me. When one has a disease, that is a case where every man bears his own burden. Although they couldn't take my disease, their willingness to do so was the thing that made such a tremendous impression upon my heart and life.

This is the real proof that God loves us: He gave His Son to die for us. That is the standard—He is our example—and John says therefore that we should be willing to lay down our lives for the brethren. Until you and I have come up to that high level, we are not exhibiting the love that we should have for the brethren.

Now how does this love in action work itself out?—

But whoso hath this world's good, and seeth his brother have need, and shutteth up his bowels of compassion from him, how dwelleth the love of God in him? [1 John 3:17].

John is saying that love is not a sentiment; it is that which expresses itself in action. James also had a great deal to say about this in his epistle. There he wrote, "If a brother or sister be naked, and destitute of daily food, And one of you say unto them, Depart in peace, be ye warmed and filled; notwithstanding ye give them not those things which are needful to the body; what doth it profit?" (James 2:15–16). When a brother in need comes to some folk, they simply say, "I'll pray for you, brother." But the important thing is whether or not our love is manifested in what we are doing. One of the most tragic things in the world will be when many believers come into the presence of Christ, having had this world's goods down here and not having used them for the cause of Christ.

In a family situation you may talk about loving, but love is not made in the parlor or in the bedroom; love is made in the kitchen. A man may leave his home at five o'clock in the morning and explain it by saying, "I'm going to work. I have a wife and two children to feed." You might say to him, "I wouldn't worry about them. You are not going to make a fool of yourself by going out and killing yourself working for them, are you?" He will tell you, "I sure am. I love them, and they are mine." If you went up into the kitchen of his home, you would likely find his wife up early in the morning, having burned her fingers taking the biscuits out of the hot oven. The poor girl is tired and weary in the evening when he gets home, and yet she continues to work and to care for the children. You say to her, "I wouldn't be bothered if I were you," but she says, "This man is my husband, and I love him."

Real love gets into action. We see it in a home where there is love between a man and a woman, but what about love among believers?

It ought to get into action; it ought to start doing something one for another. Until it does, my friend, it is the worst kind of hypocrisy. You express your love of the brethren by what you *do* for them, not by what you say. Our tongue is very good at running way ahead of our feet, but true Christianity, the real article, is a matter of the heart and not of the head or the tongue. John tells us very definitely here that if we are children of God, we will manifest this love.

My little children, let us not love in word, neither in tongue; but in deed and in truth [1 John 3:18].

Self-sacrificing love is required of us as believers. It may not be necessary to give our lives, but certainly it is necessary to give of our substance. Christianity is a love relationship.

And hereby we know that we are of the truth, and shall assure our hearts before him [1 John 3:19].

If our lives manifest these things that John has talked about, we will have an assurance when we come before God in prayer. John has made it very clear that it is possible to be ashamed at the appearing of Christ. A great many folk talk about the coming of Christ, but they don't seem to be *doing* anything. When you and I come into His presence, it is going to be a very awesome experience because He is going to demand some fruit. What have you been doing? He said, "If ye love me, keep my commandments" (John 14:15). One of His commandments is to get the Word of God out, to take it to the ends of the earth. Are you involved in that in any way? Are you involved in anything that reveals that you are a child of God?

When I was a boy living out in the country, how wonderfully love was expressed among those people. Whenever anybody got sick, the neighbors would come in and help. I know that there are all kinds of new methods of doing things, but frankly, I'd sure like to get back to that day when the neighbors did come in to help and to take an interest. Today we expect some bureau of the government to take care of an individual and to take him to the hospital which we think is the best place for him. A great many Christians are not getting involved in the very thing that the Lord is interested in, but, my friend, we are going to have to give an account before Him someday.

"My little children, let us not love in word, neither in tongue; but in deed and in truth.

And hereby we know that we are of the truth, and shall assure our hearts before him." If you are a child of God and are using your substance—whether you are rich or poor—to get the Word of God out, God give you an assurance in your heart that you are in His will and that you are doing the thing He wants done. Then you have an assurance when you go before Him in prayer, and you will have an assurance when you stand before Him someday. Paul had this assurance when he said, "Henceforth there is laid up for me a crown of righteousness . . ." (2 Tim. 4:8)—Paul *knew* that; he had that assurance.

For if our heart condemn us, God is greater than our heart, and knoweth all things [1 John 3:20].

The child of God can have an assurance, but suppose we are not doing what we should be doing? Does that mean that we have lost our salvation or that we did not have it to begin with? John says, "For if our heart condemn us, God is greater than our heart, and knoweth all things." We don't lose our salvation. If our hearts condemn us, God is greater than our hearts, greater than our lack of assurance. He is going to hear our prayer. Isn't He a wonderful God? When we fail Him, He won't fail us. You may not have any assurance when you go before Him. A great many Christians come to Him really empty-handed: "I have done nothing for You, Lord. I have done nothing at all, and yet I am coming to You in prayer." God is greater than your heart; He will hear your prayer. He is going to deal with you. He will hear and answer according to His will. "For if our heart condemn us, God is greater than our heart, and knoweth all things." You can depend on Him. Even if you don't have assurance, friend, just keep going to Him.

That young man who was struggling with alcoholism said to me, "I've prayed about this," and I said, "Pray some more." He said, "Well, I just don't feel like I have any assurance at all. I've failed Him so." I told him, "God knows your heart. The way you're talking to me, I believe you're sincere, and I believe you mean business. I know that God is going to give you deliverance from this. Of course you don't have any assurance because you've failed Him. But He is greater than your heart, and He knows you, and He knows you are sincere. He is going to deal with you—you can depend on it."

Beloved, if our heart condemn us not, then have we confidence toward God [1 John 3:21].

If our heart does not condemn us, it gives us a confidence, an assurance in prayer. There was a certain minister who meant a great deal to me when I was a young preacher. I always loved to hear him pray because he prayed with assurance. He did not pray to God willy-nilly, shilly-shally, mollycoddle—he went to God with great assurance. I always wanted to be on that man's prayer list. I had a feeling that whenever he began to pray, whatever the Lord was doing, He would say, "Wait a minute. I'm going to listen to My child down there. He's praying, and he knows what he is talking about." I wanted to be on that man's prayer list. I even prayed that he would put me on his prayer list, but I didn't ask him to because I felt that it wouldn't be as effective as if he volunteered it. He knew I was a pastor of a church and had a great opportunity, and one day he said to me, "Vernon, I'm praying for you." Oh boy, that was a great day! May I say to you, it is wonderful to have assurance when we pray. "If our heart condemn us not, then have we confidence toward God."

And whatsoever we ask, we receive of him, because we keep his commandments, and do those things that are pleasing in his sight [1 John 3:22].

Love in action gives assurance in prayer. When your life is pleasing to God, you can expect Him to hear and answer your prayer. That is something that is desperately needed today. Remember the early church when persecution first broke out and the apostles were warned to stop preaching the name of Jesus. They went back and reported this to the other Christians, and the group went to God in prayer. They didn't pray that the persecution would stop—they didn't pray anything like that. They began their prayer by saying, "Lord, thou art God" (see Acts 4:24). This is the thing which seems to be absent in so many churches today. Folk are not sure that our heavenly Father is God, that He *does* run this universe, and that He *is* in charge. John says, "Whatsoever we ask, we receive of him, because we keep his commandments, and do those things that are pleasing in his sight."

And this is his commandment, That we should believe on the name of his Son Jesus Christ, and love one another, as he gave us commandment [1 John 3:23].

In other words, John says, "Don't say you believe on Him and then not love one another." With one breath you praise the Lord and say you trust the Lord Jesus, but then you say how much you dislike So-and-so. John is not talking about a love in which you just go up and put your arms around someone; he's not talking about a love that you just talk about. His love is not in your lip or your language but in your life. It will be expressed in genuine concern for the individual. You will not be gossiping about him. You will not be hurting him in any way. But you will be concerned about him. This is so desperately needed today. This is the Christian life in a nutshell: "That we should believe on the name of his Son Jesus Christ, and love one another, as he gave us commandment."

And he that keepeth his commandments dwelleth in him, and he in him. And hereby we know that he abideth in us, by the Spirit which he hath given us [1 John 3:24].

The Holy Spirit verifies these things to our hearts if we have not grieved Him. We grieve the Holy Spirit when we do not do His will. Jesus said, "If ye love me, keep my commandments" (John 14:15). If we do not do that, we grieve the Holy Spirit. The Holy Spirit is given to every believer, as Paul makes clear in Romans 8:9, "But ye are not in the flesh, but in the Spirit, if [lit., *since*] so be that the Spirit of God dwell in you. Now if any man have not the Spirit of Christ, he is none of his." The mark that you are a child of God is that you are indwelt by the Spirit of God, and it is the Holy Spirit who will verify these things and make them real to your heart.

CHAPTER 4

THEME: Warning against false teachers; God is love—little children will love each other

WARNING AGAINST FALSE TEACHERS

We have come to a very difficult section of Scripture here in the fourth chapter of 1 John. One of the reasons is that we are dealing with the spirit world which none of us knows too much about. The second reason is that we are in the Devil's territory. As a pastor I found that whenever I would preach about the Devil, he always managed to cause some interruption in the church service. Generally, he would pinch some baby, or someone would cause some kind of disturbance in the service. It is amazing how he works.

This is a very important passage, but there is a danger of going off the deep end here and becoming rather fanatical. I believe that there is an abnormal preoccupation with the occult on the part of many Christians today which is a most dangerous thing, but we do need to know what the Bible teaches about it.

In the first six verses of this chapter, John gives a warning against false teachers, false prophets. He gives us this warning, having just established the fact that we have been given the Spirit of God and that we have been given an anointing to understand the things of God.

Beloved, believe not every spirit, but try the spirits whether they are of God: because many false prophets are gone out into the world [1 John 4:1].

We are dealing here with the spirit world, and the Bible has a great deal to say about it. For instance, we read in Psalm 104:4, "Who maketh his angels spirits; his ministers a flaming fire." That is quoted in Hebrews 1:7, "And of the angels he saith, Who maketh his angels spirits, and his ministers a flame of fire." Down a little farther in the first chapter of Hebrews, we read, "Are they not all ministering spirits, sent forth to minister for them who shall be heirs of salvation?" (Heb. 1:14). I have never seen an angel, and I have never had a visit from one of them. I personally do not feel that they have a ministry to the church today. My belief is that since we are indwelt by the Holy Spirit, no improvement can be made on that arrangement. I would much rather have the uncreated Holy Spirit than a created angel following me around and ministering to me. I think that we need to put the emphasis upon the ministry of the Holy Spirit in our hearts and in our lives.

Not only are there good angels who serve God, but there are also fallen angels. They too are called spirits in the Scriptures. The Gospels speak a great deal of the fact that in Christ's day there were "unclean spirits." That is what is known as demonism; we call them demons because the Scriptures use that term.

As believers we are warned to put on the whole armor of God because we are in a gigantic battle which is beyond the flesh, a battle that is a spiritual battle. Paul writes in Ephesians 6:12, "For we wrestle not against flesh and blood, but against principalities, against powers, against the rulers of the darkness of this world, against spiritual wickedness in high places." As this verse suggests, the Devil has his demons pretty well organized. In his army of demons he has the generals at the top, the lieutenant colonels, and then on down to the sergeants, the corporals, and the plain, ordinary infantrymen or soldiers. I think that God has His angels organized in pretty much the same way.

"Beloved, believe not every spirit, but try [prove] the spirits whether they are of God." A few years ago that sounded rather spooky, but we have moved from the time when the supernatural was ridiculed, especially among the intelligentsia, to a day when Satan has become an obvious reality and is now worshiped openly. Much of this is taking place on or near our college campuses. I know of a couple of satanic churches here in Los Angeles, and there may be many more. What a few years ago was considered to be way out in left field today exists out in the open. The report came from Florida that a young boy of only seventeen years of age was murdered, and they found that it was done to appease Satan. The satanic priestess down there, just a young woman of twenty-two, had said that this boy should be killed!

Quite a few things which have happened in our day are really spooky. We had, for instance, the appearance of the book, *Jonathan Livingston Seagull*. The author, Richard Bach, said that a voice dictated the book to him and that it was not his own style of writing. I understand that many churches recommended the reading of this book and that several good men were taken in by it. It is the story about a theological concept of a young sea gull which has human attributes. He soared off toward unlimited perfection and found that each of us is just an idea of the Great Gull. This book teaches that birth and sin and sickness and death are not realities but only illusions, that what the biblical writers call sins really are virtues, and that freedom is freedom to do what one pleases. All of that is not new but is actually out of the very pit of hell itself—it is satanic.

We are seeing a manifestation of demonism today, and it is all around us. It is strange that this has happened in this materialistic age that once would have nothing in the world to do with the supernatural. When I was in college any concept of the supernatural was frowned upon and looked down upon. It did not make any difference what IQ you had or what grades you made in school, if you believed in the supernatural, you were considerably less than intelligent and you were radically wrong—and they didn't hesitate to tell you so. Today that has all changed. Many young people have gone off the deep end into this because they never have had any Bible training at all.

John has been speaking here to God's children. He has told us how we are to love each other and to help each other, but we must be careful. Paul wrote to the Philippians whom he loved a great deal, "And this I pray, that your love may abound yet more and more in knowledge and in all judgment" (Phil. 1:9). It is a wonderful thing to love, but you and I are in a big, mean, wicked world, and this world we live in will take us in; it will deceive us. We need to be careful. This lovey-dovey idea the liberals have—love slopping over on every side—is not what the Word of God teaches. Paul prayed that the Philippians' love might abound in *knowledge* and *judgment*. Don't be taken in by everyone who comes along and says that he is a Christian, because many of them are not.

When I was first a pastor in downtown Los Angeles, I had to discover through experience that all of the bums—and that's the best word I know for them—will take advantage of you. One Sunday morning after the service, those who had come forward in response to the invitation were being dealt with, when one of them said that he wanted only me to talk to him. I was quite flattered when the personal worker came and said, "This man wants *you* to talk with him." So I went over to him and gave him the plan of salvation. He seemed very interested. In fact, when I would read a verse, he would then take the Bible and read it for himself. (He knew what he should do!) Then he said that he wanted to accept Christ; so we got down on our knees; he shed tears and professed to receive Christ. When we got up, I made the mistake of asking him how he was getting along. He said, "I hate to say this, but my suitcase is down yonder in a hotel." It was one of the cheap hotels in the downtown area. "They won't let me have my suitcase because I can't pay my bill. I'm greatly embarrassed by it." He told me that his bill was seven dollars. Well, what are you going to do for a man who has apparently just accepted the Lord and has lost his suitcase? I gave him seven dollars. I went out and got into our car where my wife was waiting for me. I became very expansive as I told her what I had done and how wonderful it was.

Time went by, and about six weeks later I saw the man's picture in the newspaper. He had been arrested. He said, "I've been living in Los Angeles for six months, and I've lived off the preachers. They are the biggest saps in the world." Well, I happened to have been one of them! I called up a good friend of mine, the late Dr. Bob Shuler, who was then pastor of Trinity Methodist Church. I asked him, "Did he come to see you?" He said, "Yes." "Well, did he get to you?" I asked, and he said that he hadn't. When I told Dr. Shuler that he *had* gotten to me, he said, "Well, Vernon, I have been in downtown Los Angeles longer than you have, and I've had a little more experience. Don't let them take you in. Remember that the Bible says to *try* the spirits to see whether they are of God or not. A lot of these men are phonies." Yes, the bum was a phony, and he had taken me for seven dollars, but I had learned my lesson. Paul prayed that the Philippians might not only grow in their love, but in judgment and knowledge. You need to use love wisely. You need to be very careful.

John says here, "Believe not every spirit, but try the spirits." When I hear of some person who seems to have supernatural power, to heal, or to impart a gift, I don't get excited. Someone asks me, "Why don't you go hear So-and-so?" Well, I don't want to waste my time. I am told to test, to prove the spirits. There is a lot of hocus-pocus going on today which I can assure you has nothing supernatural in it at all. It is just camouflaged Christianity.

"Because many false prophets are gone out into the world." The "false prophets" are false *teachers*. Paul used the word that way in 1 Corinthians 14:3, "But he that prophesieth speaketh unto men to edification, and exhortation, and comfort." *Prophesy* here means "to teach, to exhort, to instruct."

There are many teachers abroad today of whom we need to beware. Right now prophecy is becoming an interesting subject and rightly so. But again, the thing which needs to be said was said very well by Sir Robert Anderson: "Beware of the wild utterances of prophecymongers." There are many today who are saying more than the Scriptures say so that we need to be very careful. Just because a man comes along saying, "Lord, Lord," does not mean that we should love him. That may be the man who is more dangerous than a rattlesnake because he may be teaching a false doctrine. He may not really be teaching the Word of God, although he carries a big Bible under his arm.

Hereby know ye the Spirit of God: Every spirit that confesseth that Jesus Christ is come in the flesh is of God [1 John 4:2].

"Hereby know ye the Spirit of God." How are we to distinguish? John tells us the way: "Every spirit that confesseth that Jesus Christ is come in the flesh is of God." This is where it all begins—in Bethlehem. Jesus Christ was born in Bethlehem, and it begins there with His incarnation. Calvary and the Garden Tomb are meaningless unless He is who He claimed to be, unless He is the God-man. The way that you can determine the false teachers is that they will deny the deity of the Lord Jesus Christ. That does not mean that they do not talk nicely about Him. They talk about what a remarkable youth He was and that He was a superior child who was born into the world. They say that He was a religious genius and that He was intoxicated with God. They say that He probably had a greater knowledge of God than any other man. He was a "superstar," you know. They can say a lot of nice things about Him, but ask them if He was *God manifested in the flesh?*

John speaks of "the Word" in his gospel. Who was the Word? He was God, and He created all things, and He became flesh. Where? Yonder at Bethlehem, at the Incarnation. Jesus came there. When you deny the Incarnation, the deity of Christ, then you deny His work upon the cross because it all rests upon who He is. The false teachers attempt to tear Him down by complimenting Him. That is the way the Lord Jesus is being treated today in many circles. But He is who He claimed to be—*God* of very God.

John is meeting head-on the early heresy of Gnosticism, one of the branches of which said that Christ came upon Jesus at His baptism and left Him at Calvary. That is not what the Word of God teaches. The Word of God says that that Babe in Bethlehem was more than a remarkable baby, that His death upon the cross was not an ordinary death, and that when He rose from the dead, He rose bodily from the dead. He ". . . was delivered for our offences, and was raised again for our justification" (Rom. 4:25). Isaiah wrote, "For unto us a child is born, unto us a son is given . . ."

(Isa. 9:6). The child is *born*, but the Son is *given*. The Son came out of eternity, the Ancient of Days, but the child, His humanity, was conceived in the virgin's womb. He came forth yonder in Bethlehem where a few shepherds and wise men came to worship Him. He was more than just a precocious child. He was the precious Prince of Peace who made peace by the blood of His cross and some day shall bring peace to this war-weary world that we are living in. The important thing for us to note is that this is the mark of whether a man is a false prophet or not—"*Hereby* know ye the Spirit of God." Let's find out what a person believes about Jesus Christ. That's important, very important.

And every spirit that confesseth not that Jesus Christ is come in the flesh is not of God: and this is that spirit of antichrist, whereof ye have heard that it should come; and even now already is it in the world [1 John 4:3].

This is the third time John has mentioned Antichrist. John is the only writer who mentions him and he does so only in his epistles. In the second chapter of this epistle, John says, "Little children, it is the last time: and as ye have heard that antichrist shall come, even now are there many antichrists; whereby we know that it is the last time" (1 John 2:18). And then again we read, "Who is a liar but he that denieth that Jesus is the Christ? He is antichrist, that denieth the Father and the Son" (1 John 2:22).

As we saw in chapter 2, *anti* can mean two different things. It can mean either "against" or "instead of," that is, an imitation. We have that idea presented in Scripture. The Lord Jesus said, "For many shall come in my name, saying, I am Christ; and shall deceive many" (Matt. 24:5)—in other words, they imitate Him. Antichrist is used, therefore, in the sense of pretending to be Christ. The other meaning is to be against Christ.

Revelation 13 presents to us the two beasts of the end time. The first beast is the great political ruler who is coming—Antichrist to rule the world, a world dictator. Then there is a religious ruler who is coming, and he is called the false prophet. He will cause the world to worship the first beast. He will come like a lamb, but underneath he is a wolf—he will imitate Christ. I believe that there will be two men and that it will take both of them to fulfill all that is said in Scripture about Antichrist. There will be a great *political* ruler at the end of time, and there will be a great *religious* ruler at the end of time.

All our contemporary civilization is building up to the coming of Antichrist. There is coming a great religious ruler, and all the religions of the world will amalgamate under his leadership. The movement is in that direction even today. We also have that same kind of movement politically. There is a moving today toward one ruler for this world. He will bring peace into the world temporarily, but it is going to be the most frightful time the world has ever seen.

In chapter 2 John says, "Even now are there many antichrists" (1 John 2:18), and there are quite a few of them about in our day, but they are not *the* Antichrist. They are false teachers who are moving the world closer and closer to that day, preparing the world for the one finally to appear.

In these first six verses of chapter 4, we have what some have called a parenthesis. Maybe they are not quite that, but this is certainly a red light that John puts up here, a caution sign, a stop-look-and-listen sign. He says that love must be exercised with judgment and knowledge. We are to love believers, but we need to be sure that the so-called believers are not false teachers. We are to prove the spirits, for there are false prophets around who are teaching false things. In John's own day there were the Docetic and Cerinthian Gnostics who denied the humanity of Christ, and in so doing, they also denied the deity of Christ; they made Him out to be a very strange and weird individual.

For some reason, God's people have always been credulous and gullible. There are many believers who fall victim to what Dr. A. T. Robertson called "the latest fads and spiritualistic humbuggery." There is a lot of that going around in our day. Therefore, John spends the time to give us this warning to beware that false teachers will deny the incarnation of Christ. Don't tell me that the Virgin Birth is not important. Some people ask, "Can you be a Christian and deny the Virgin Birth?" You cannot—that is impossible because the mark of a false teacher is at that very point. When you destroy the Virgin Birth, you destroy His death upon the cross for the sins of the world and His bodily resurrection—in other words, you wreck the Christian faith. This is the reason that the Virgin Birth is the place where there has been so much denial in our day, and that denial, of course, is that which reveals a false teacher immediately.

John is saying that God's children ought not

to be deceived by false teachers. The objective way to identify them is that they deny the incarnation of Christ. Now John gives us the internal, the subjective evidence in verse 4—

Ye are of God, little children, and have overcome them: because greater is he that is in you, than he that is in the world [1 John 4:4].

There is no reason for you to be taken in by satanic teaching or the denial of the deity of Christ. A man said to me once, "I used to be in a certain church, and I was a high officer in the church. Then I got saved, and my eyes were opened. I knew then I was in the wrong place because they were denying the deity of Christ. So I got out." Why did he get out? Well, he was indwelt by the Spirit of God who had revealed the truth to him. "Greater is he that is in you, than he that is in the world"—so that there is no excuse for you to be taken in today by a false teacher, a false prophet, or a false teaching. The thing to do is to go to God and ask that the Holy Spirit lead you and teach you. If you are in fellowship with Him, the Spirit of God is going to make the issue clear to you.

I knew a dear lady right here in Southern California who told me that when she first began to listen to my radio broadcasts, she was very critical of them. She was in a cult, and she felt that what I said contradicted what she was being taught—it sure did! But she began to test it by the Word of God. She was really a born-again Christian but had gotten caught up in this cult. Her eyes were opened because the Spirit of God was there to teach her. "Greater is he that is in you, than he that is in the world." *You* can overcome all the false teaching you hear because of the indwelling Spirit of God.

Every Christian is indwelt by the Spirit of God. Listen to what Paul has to say: "But ye are not in the flesh, but in the Spirit, if so be that the Spirit of God dwell in you. Now if any man have not the Spirit of Christ, he is *none of his*" (Rom. 8:9, italics mine). Back in the fifth chapter of Romans, Paul tells us of one of the present results of being justified by faith: ". . . the love of God is shed abroad in our hearts by the Holy Ghost which is given unto us" (Rom. 5:5). Again, we read in 1 Corinthians 6:19, "What? know ye not that your body is the temple of the Holy Ghost which is in you, which ye have of God, and ye are not your own?" Was Paul talking to some super-duper saints, some who had really arrived, some very spiritually-minded saints who were living

on a high plane? No. He was writing to the Corinthians, and he called them carnal and babes in Christ. The Corinthian Christians were just about everything they should not have been, and yet they were indwelt by the Holy Spirit. *Every* child of God is indwelt by the Spirit of God.

This is the reason that you do not need an angel to appear to you tonight to tell you what you need to know. Rather, you need to have the Holy Spirit teach you, and the Holy Spirit teaches through His Word. You cannot stay away from the Bible, be ignorant of it, ignore it, and yet expect to have the Spirit of God lead you and guide you. I try to get people into the Word of God because I have seen that the Spirit of God opens people's hearts, and He protects them from this world in which we live. We are living in a big, bad world, and we need to be warned concerning the false teaching that is around us.

John tells us that we can test the teachings of men. This test is just like putting litmus paper into a solution to tell whether it is an acid or a base. This is a test which will work: Does the teaching deny the incarnation of Christ? That is the spirit of antichrist, my friend. You do not want to follow that. It is contrary to Christ, although it may imitate Him. Generally, these false teachers are very attractive persons. Many of them have charisma, and they make a fleshly appeal to folk. But they can be tested by the Word of God for the Holy Spirit is there to be our teacher and guide.

They are of the world: therefore speak they of the world, and the world heareth them [1 John 4:5].

False teachers do get a following. The occult and the cults are growing much faster today than is Christianity. They have the advantage of appealing to the flesh which we do not. I think it is tragic to have Christians using fleshly means to draw in a crowd. We need to be very careful of the methods which we use. If they are fleshly methods, God cannot bless them at all. We need to be sure that the Word of God is being given out. I do not care whether several thousand people come to your church—that is not the important thing. I am interested in the message. Is the Word of God being given out? Is it given out in the power of the Spirit so that the Spirit of God can take it and use it? The message should not be a great deal of pious promotion for some sentimental appeal that causes you to give. The question is: Is the Word of God going out from your church? Are folk coming to know Christ? You would not want to invest money in a company simply because they have a nice, beautiful building and the president is a very handsome fellow with a warm personality and charisma. If you are going to invest in that company, you will want to know whether it is making money or not. Is it getting results? Is something happening there? God intends us to use a little consecrated common sense when we are dealing in the area of religion.

"They are of the world: therefore speak they of the world, and the world heareth them." When John used Cain and Abel as an illustration in chapter 3, he said that Cain was not righteous and was not God's child. He did not say that Cain wasn't *religious*. Cain did bring an offering; in fact, I have a notion his offering was much more attractive than Abel's offering. Cain's was beautiful; it was the fruit of the field, but Abel's was bloody and would have been sickening, nauseating to some people. However, Abel's offering is the one which God accepted because it recognized the sin of man and his need of a Savior. Cain did not recognize that at all. The flesh depends on itself; it does not depend upon God.

John has made very clear to us that the important thing is that Jesus Christ is who he claimed to be, and that is the thing that we need to be very clear on in order to determine whether a teaching is true or not.

We are of God: he that knoweth God heareth us; he that is not of God heareth not us. Hereby know we the spirit of truth, and the spirit of error [1 John 4:6].

I used to tell the people of my church that I use the Bible as a Geiger counter. A Geiger counter tells you whether or not there is uranium there in the rocks and in the soil. So I just run the Geiger counter over the congregation, and the Bible is what I use—it's my Geiger counter. I want to tell you, God's children will always respond to it. That was my confidence as a pastor, and that is my confidence as I write this book: God's people are going to hear. And, my friend, I do not expect the other crowd to hear. If they don't want to hear it, all they have to do is close this book. The Christian ministry does not depend upon them for support; God's people are to support God's work. After all, the ark of the covenant was carried on the shoulders of the priests of Israel. The ark speaks of Christ, and if we are to take Him to the world, we must carry Him on our shoulders. The supreme encourage-

ment of the ministry is to know that God's children will hear you. The elect cannot permanently be deceived. Christ said it is not possible to deceive the elect.

John was sure of who the Lord Jesus was. He could say, "And the Word was made [became] flesh, and dwelt [pitched His tent] among us, (and we beheld his glory, the glory as of the only begotten of the Father,) full of grace and truth" (John 1:14). Then John gave us the purpose of his gospel: "And many other signs truly did Jesus in the presence of his disciples, which are not written in this book: But these are written, that ye might believe that Jesus is the Christ, the Son of God; and that believing ye might have life through his name" (John 20:30–31). John had indubitable, indestructible, inevitable evidence that Jesus was who He claimed to be. John *knew* that, and that is something we need to be a little more sure of today.

GOD IS LOVE: LITTLE CHILDREN WILL LOVE EACH OTHER

Beloved, let us love one another: for love is of God; and every one that loveth is born of God, and knoweth God [1 John 4:7].

"**B**eloved, let us love one another." Why? "For love is of God." Let's be very careful here as to what John is talking about. He has just given a warning against false teachers who are *not* to be loved—let's be clear on that. I don't pray for them. I do not give any pious platitude, saying, "Oh, I'll pray for them." I'm not praying for them. They are the children of the Devil. I'm praying for God's people, and I'm praying for the lost sinner who will turn to Christ if I can just get the Word to him. Having given a warning against these false teachers, John returns now to the theme of this section: believers are to love one another.

Again, may I say that the word for love here is not *eros;* John is not talking about sex. All through this section, the word for love is *agape* love. It is not sentimental, it is not sexual, and it is not social love. It is supernatural love. It is that which the Holy Spirit can put in our hearts, and only the Spirit of God can make it real to us. It is the love of God, and only the Spirit of God can enable us to extend this love to others.

This is not the kind of love you have for friends whom you delight in being with. I am afraid this verse has been misused by many. When I was a student in college, I used this verse in courting a girl: "Beloved, let us love one another: for love is of God." But the kind of love I was talking about was not the kind John was talking about, I can assure you of that! I surely did misinterpret this, and I must confess that I did not have a very lofty purpose at that particular time. "Beloved, let us love one another"—that is, love other believers.

"Every one that loveth is born of God, and knoweth God." This is approaching it from the human viewpoint. When you meet a person who says he is a believer, and you find that he loves you and loves other brethren, you can know that he is a born-again child of God. I think people write things in letters to me that they probably would not say to me in person. Many people write, "Dr. McGee, I love you," and then they go on to tell me why. One family, for instance, wrote, "You brought our two children to the Lord." Their love for me is an evidence that they are real born-again children of God.

He that loveth not knoweth not God; for God is love [1 John 4:8].

"He that loveth not knoweth not God." This is another test of whether or not you are a child of God. I'm not asking you if you love your papa and your mama. I'm not asking you whether you love your wife or your husband or your children or your kissin' cousins—I'm not asking you that. But I am asking you this: Do you love other believers?

Maybe someone will say, "Well, I can love *some* of them." That is helpful—you are moving in the right direction. There are some believers who are very unlovely, but I think that we can love them in the sense that we can have a concern for them. I do not think it is essential to put our arms around them. The way you can show your love is by your concern for others which is going to result in helping them.

John gives us now another definition of God: "God is love." We have three great definitions of God in this wonderful little book: (1) "God is light" (1 John 1:5), and that was the theme from chapters 1:1 to 2:2; (2) "God is love" (1 John 4:8–16), the very heart of this epistle is the theme from chapters 2:3 to 4:21; and (3) "God is life" is the theme of chapter 5. These are the three great definitions of God which John gives to us, and they constitute the major divisions of this very marvelous epistle.

John says here and again in verse 16, "God is love." Dr. Harry Ironside has a very remarkable story relative to this which I am going to pass on to you because I think it demonstrates in a wonderful way the truth that only Chris-tianity reveals the God of love. In *The Epistles of John* Dr. H. A. Ironside writes:

> Years ago a lady who prided herself on belonging to the intelligentsia said to me, "I have no use for the Bible, for Christian superstition, and religious dogma. It is enough for me to know that God is love." "Well," I said, "do you know it?" "Why, of course I do," she said; "we all know that, and that is religion enough for me. I do not need the dogmas of the Bible." "How did you find out that God is love?" I asked. "Why," she said, "everybody knows that." "Do they know it yonder in India?" I asked. "That poor mother in her distress throwing her little babe into the holy Ganges to be eaten by filthy and repulsive crocodiles as a sacrifice for her sins—does she know that God is love?" "Oh, well, she is ignorant and superstitious," she replied. "Those poor wretched negroes in the jungles of Africa, bowing down to gods of wood and stone, and in constant fear of their fetishes, the poor heathen in other countries, do they know that God is love?" "Perhaps not," she said, "but in a civilized land we all know it." "But how is it that we know it? Who told us so? Where did we find it out?" "I do not understand what you mean," she said, "for I've always known it." "Let me tell you this," I answered; "no one in the world ever knew it until it was revealed from heaven and recorded in the Word of God. It is here and nowhere else. It is not found in all the literature of the ancients."

In this was manifested the love of God toward us, because that God sent his only begotten Son into the world, that we might live through him [1 John 4:9].

How does God love you? Well, you won't find that love in nature, but you *will* find a bloody tooth and a sharp claw—that is what nature reveals to us. You will find the love of God at Calvary. There is where you find the love of God manifested. "In this was manifested the love of God toward us, because that God sent his only begotten Son into the world, that we might live through him." God has proven His love. He laid down His life for us, and that is the proof of His love. Paul wrote, "For scarcely for a righteous man will one die: yet peradventure for a good man some would even dare to die" (Rom. 5:7). I don't know whether or not you could get anyone to lay down his life for you; I think I'd have a little problem finding someone myself. But God has proven His love by giving His Son to die for you! He gave Him to die for you, not after you won a Sunday school attendance bar for not missing a Sunday in five years, but God loved you when you were yet a *sinner.* "For when we were yet without strength [while we were lost, while we were absolutely unlovely], in due time Christ died for the ungodly (Rom. 5:6). God loved us! "But God commendeth his love toward us, in that, while we were yet sinners, Christ died for us" (Rom. 5:8). The explanation of this love is found in Him and not in us— because we are not lovely, and some of us do not ever seem to become very lovely.

"God sent his only begotten Son into the world." Here is another verse to which those who would like to rob us of the deity of Christ turn. When Jesus Christ is called "the only begotten Son," it means that He has a unique relationship with the Father. He was not created. God called the created angels His *sons,* and He says that those who trust Christ are *sons* of God, but yet He says that the Lord Jesus is "the only begotten Son." It is interesting that the same thing is said of Isaac: "By faith Abraham, when he was tried, offered up Isaac; and he that had received the promises offered up *his only begotten son*" (Heb. 11:17, italics mine). At that time Abraham already had his son Ishmael, and later on he had other sons. Ishmael was Abraham's son, just as much his son as Isaac was. In fact, Ishmael probably looked as much like Abraham as Isaac ever did. But Isaac is called "his only begotten." Why? Because he was unique, his birth was miraculous, and he stood in a unique relationship which was not shared by Abraham's other sons. The position of the Lord Jesus Christ in the Godhead is that of the eternal Son of the eternal Father. We cannot have an eternal Father without an eternal Son. God is not a father in the sense that a human being is a father. "God is a Spirit" (see John 4:24), the Lord Jesus said. The "only begotten Son" is the Father's unique son. Others are sons by creation, as Adam and the angels, or by new birth, as believers are, but Jesus Christ alone is the unique Son.

"That we might live through him." How are we going to live through Him? We are going to live through Him because He died. His death gives us life.

Herein is love, not that we loved God, but that he loved us, and sent his Son to

be the propitiation for our sins [1 John 4:10].

John has used the word *propitiation* previously: "And he is the propitiation for our sins: and not for ours only, but also for the sins of the whole world" (1 John 2:2). This word is quite remarkable. I recognize that there are two different Greek words translated as "propitiation" in the New Testament; actually, it is the same word, but two different forms of it. Dr. A. T. Robertson, whom I consider to be the greatest Greek scholar of them all, writes that here the word *propitiation* is a predicate accusative in apposition with *huion,* that is, the Son.

Propitiation means "mercy seat"; it is the same as the Old Testament word *atonement,* meaning "to cover." Let me make this as clear as I possibly can. In the tabernacle in the Holy of Holies there was the ark of the covenant. On top of that ark there was a highly ornamented lid crowned with two cherubim of solid gold, facing each other and looking down upon the lid of the box. The ark was a very beautiful thing, for it was all made of acacia wood, and covered inside and outside with gold. The lid was called the mercy seat. It was here that the nation of Israel met God in the person of the high priest. Once a year and only once a year, the high priest came into the Holy of Holies, bringing blood to be sprinkled on the mercy seat. That is what made it a mercy seat because they could meet God only in that way. God loved them, but He didn't simply slop over with love and say, "You can come to Me any way you want." This was the way they were to come to God: On that great Day of Atonement, the high priest went in and sprinkled the blood on the mercy seat. That meant that the nation was accepted by God for another year, and then they would need to go through it again the next year.

Now here in the verse before us, the Lord Jesus Christ is called "the propitiation for our sins" which means that He is the mercy seat for our sins. Jesus is Himself the mercy seat because He died down here for us—"Who was delivered for our offences, and was raised again for our justification" (Rom. 4:25). He has made expiation for our sins so that you and I can come with boldness to God's throne of grace. That throne is now a throne of grace because there is *mercy* there for us. That is what Christ did, and that is the way God demonstrated His love for us.

Twice in this chapter John gives us the definition, "God is love"—in verse 8 and again in verse 16. This is a very wonderful thing, but I would have you notice something about it. You cannot say God is mercy. You cannot say God is grace. You cannot even say God is justice. You can say God is holy because that is what "God is light" means. But you can also say God is love. However, I must add that God does not save us by love. He loves us, and we don't want to lose sight of that, but God just *cannot* open the back door of heaven and slip us in under cover of darkness because He loves us. And God cannot let down the bars of heaven and bring us in the front door. God cannot do that, and God will not do that because He is a holy and righteous God.

We have seen so many shenanigans go on in the execution of justice in this nation of ours, and as a result, the judges and others who are in authority have wanted to get rid of capital punishment. Why? Because they know that if a man has money or influence, his life will not be taken. It is the poor fellow who cannot escape his due punishment. The tragic thing today is that we believe that justice can be bought. My friend, even though God loves you, He does not save you by love, and He *cannot* save you by love. God had to do something about the fact of sin because He is holy and righteous, and what He does is right. So God gave His Son to die on the cross for you and me, to pay the penalty for our sin so that a holy God can now reach down and save us. It is only on that basis that a holy God can save us. Christ is the mercy seat, and that is where God reveals His love. "For God so loved the world, that he gave his only begotten Son, that whosoever believeth in him should not perish, but have everlasting life" (John 3:16).

"Herein is love, not that we loved God"—we didn't love Him first. God didn't give His Son for us because we were attractive, or because we were good, or because we promised to do something. God loved us "while we were yet sinners." We need to recognize that you and I today are sinners and that ". . . God commendeth his love toward us, in that, while we were yet sinners, Christ died for us" (Rom. 5:8). God did it at that time, and God loved us at that time. He has made a way for us, if we will accept it. Jesus said, ". . . I am the way, the truth, and the life: no man cometh unto the Father, but by me" (John 14:6). You either come His way, or you don't come, my friend. It is nonsense to think that because God is love, everything will work out all right and everyone will ultimately go to heaven. It *is* going to work out all right because the lost are going to a lost eternity, and the saved are going to a saved eternity—that's the reason things are going to work out all right. Are they going to work out all right for you? They will, if you come God's way—this is tremendously important.

Beloved, if God so loved us, we ought also to love one another [1 John 4:11].

God has demonstrated His love for us; therefore, you and I ought to love on that plane. John says, "Beloved, if God *so* loved us." This carries our minds back to verse 10: "Herein is love . . . that he loved us, and sent his Son." He loved us enough to give His Son as a propitiation for our sins.

If we love those who love us, or if there is a selfish motive in our loving them, there is no value in that. The Lord Jesus said, "For if ye love them which love you, what reward have ye? do not even the publicans the same?" (Matt. 5:46).

"We ought also to love one another." I like that—when John says *ought*, he means it. He is not talking about the cheap sentiment which a great many people entertain today. Jesus said, "If ye love me, keep my commandments" (John 14:15). If you really love Him, keep His commandments. "This is my commandment, That ye love one another, as I have loved you" (John 15:12). How about it, my friend? Do you mean to tell me that you can hate Christians down here and still love God? I want to say to you very frankly that if you cannot demonstrate in your life that you have love for other believers, there is a serious question whether you are a child of God or not. There is a lot of nonsense going on today. We are not talking about backslapping, calling somebody "brother," or behaving so nicely in the church. But do you have a concern for believers? Do you have a concern to get out His Word? Do you have a concern to serve Him?

The Lord Jesus could say even on the cross, ". . . Father, forgive them; for they know not what they do . . ." (Luke 23:34). The first martyr of the church, Stephen, said the same thing. Can *you* forgive like that today? Are you able to forgive those who have hurt you and harmed you and yet profess to be children of God? And if they cannot return your love, there is some question whether they are children of God or not. This is the real test, the acid test, and it hurts—does it not? We do not hear this type of teaching in these little seminars which talk about how to live the Christian life and how to get along with your spouse. John gives us the bedrock of it all: Do you love God? And do you love other believers?

No man hath seen God at any time. If we love one another, God dwelleth in us, and his love is perfected in us [1 John 4:12].

"No man hath seen God at any time." Some folk challenge this statement by pointing out scriptural illustration of those who have seen God. Of course, there was Adam, and then Moses who talked with God face to face and was hidden in the cleft of the rock as He went by. And Isaiah says, "In the year that king Uzziah died I saw also the Lord sitting upon a throne, high and lifted up, and his train filled the temple" (Isa. 6:1). We find that Ezekiel had visions of God, and the Lord appeared to Daniel and to others. And yet John said in his gospel, "No man hath seen God at any time." But John does not conclude his statement with that; he goes on to say, ". . . the only begotten Son, which is in the bosom of the Father, he hath declared him" (John 1:18)—that is, He has *exegeted* Him. When God appeared to men in the Old Testament, they did not see God, for God is a Spirit and that is the way we worship Him. Those men saw what is known as a *theophany*. That is, God manifested Himself in some form to these men, but He did not reveal Himself in all of His fullness. So that John says in his epistle, even after the Lord Jesus had gone back to heaven, "No man hath seen God at any time." The Lord Jesus said to Philip, ". . . he that hath seen me hath seen the Father . . ." (John 14:9). But how did they see Him? He was veiled in human flesh, so much so that multitudes who saw Him did not recognize Him. He grew to manhood yonder in Nazareth, veiled in human flesh—they did not know that He was the Son of God. No man has seen God in all of His fullness. That is still true today.

The point that John is making here is that no man has seen God at any time, but God today can manifest Himself through believers loving each other. Since the world in general is not seeing Jesus as He is presented in the Word of God, the only way it will know of God's love is through the lives of believers who represent Him. None of us knew about God's love until God showed it to us on the cross when Christ died, and He makes it real to us by the Holy Spirit. "And . . . the love of God is shed abroad in our hearts by the Holy Ghost which is given unto us" (Rom. 5:5). And ". . . God commendeth his love toward us, in that, while we were yet sinners [while we were dead in trespasses, while we were ungodly], Christ died for us" (Rom. 5:8). It is still true that there is none

that seeketh after God, so God has come down seeking man. He came down nineteen hundred years ago, manifesting Himself in the Lord Jesus Christ, and all I know about God is what I know in the person of Christ. I do not know how God feels about certain things; I do not know what He thinks about certain things. But when I follow the Lord Jesus and listen to Him, I know what God is thinking, I can feel the heartbeat of God. I know how He feels at a funeral, for the Scriptures tells us that "Jesus wept" (John 11:35). I know how He feels about little children because He took them up in His arms and blessed them. I know these things because the Lord came and manifested God.

How is this wicked world in which you and I live to know God? Unfortunately, too many believers are trying to *please* the world instead of trying to *preach* to the world. We are concerned about what the world thinks of us, but the important thing is: What do they think of Jesus? What do they think of us as we represent Him? Someone has put it like this: "At the age of twenty, we do not care what the world thinks of us. At thirty we worry about what the world is thinking of us. At forty we discover that it wasn't thinking of us at all!" That is about true. We today are to witness to the world. How are we going to witness? By giving out the Word? Yes, that is all important. But the world is hungry for love; they do not know what love is. Their definition of love would be a three-letter word spelled s-e-x. That is the love the world knows about, but they don't know anything about the love of God. They do not know how wonderful He is, but He can be manifested in us.

"And his love is perfected in us." His love is developed in us. It is a growth in us. The world is not seeing enough of this love, and yet it has seen it in the lives of a great many believers.

Hereby know we that we dwell in him, and he in us, because he hath given us of his Spirit [1 John 4:13].

You see, it is only by the Holy Spirit within us. This is not a human love. You and I cannot work it up. "But the fruit of the Spirit is love, joy, peace, longsuffering, gentleness, goodness, faith, meekness, temperance: against such there is no law" (Gal. 5:22–23). *Love* heads the list. Many believe that love is *the* fruit and that the others stem from love. If you read 1 Corinthians 13, you will come to the conclusion that joy comes out of love and peace comes out of love. In *The Epistles of John* Dr. Ironside records this incident concerning

Chiang Kai-shek at the time he was ruling mainland China.

We all noticed a short time ago the account of the professed conversion of the President of China. We hope there has been a real work in his soul, but time will tell. I was reading how he came to his Christian wife who was saved long before he made a profession, and said, "I can't understand these Christians; why, they have been treated most abominably here, they have been robbed, beaten, many of them killed, they have been persecuted fearfully, and yet I never find one of them retaliating, and any time they can do anything for China, for our people, they are ready to do it; I do not understand them." "Well," said his wife, "that, you see, is the very essence of Christianity. They do that because they are Christians."

There is a need for a great many more pagans to be able to see this love in the lives of believers. This is a teaching that is surely neglected today. How often do you hear this taught in the church, on radio, or in these little seminars which are held? Is this the teaching which is given as being basic and all important?

When the love of God is in a home you don't need to worry about the wife's place and whether she is to obey her husband or whether the husband is to be the head of the house, and all of that argument. Paul writes, "Husbands, love your wives, even as Christ also loved the church, and gave himself for it" (Eph. 5:25). If he loves her, if she is a woman for whom he would lay down his life, if the wife can say that she loves him with all her heart and would do anything for him, then I don't think you need a lot of little rules to go by. There is a monument which I have seen, a statue of a pioneer woman, a fine looking young woman with a sunbonnet on. She has about five children around her holding on to those long skirts which they wore back in those days. She's holding a gun, and out ahead of her is her husband. She is loading one gun, while he shoots another. He is out there protecting her. Do you know, friend, I don't think that woman needed any lectures on sex. If she had five children, I think she could have given you some lectures on it! And I don't think she needed to have a lecture on how to keep her husband. She had no trouble keeping him. They loved each other, and they were bound together. How wonderful love is! If the child of

God could only manifest the love of God to others round about him!

"Hereby know we that we dwell in him, and he in us, because he hath given us of his Spirit." Back in verse 4 John says, "Greater is he that is in you, than he that is in the world." You are indwelt by the Spirit of God, and the Spirit of God *can* produce this love in your heart. You cannot produce it; I cannot produce it. I cannot love like this. My natural bent is that when somebody hits me, I hit back. But if we are filled by the Spirit of God who indwells us, we are going to manifest this kind of love to the world.

And we have seen and do testify that the Father sent the Son to be the Saviour of the world [1 John 4:14].

This is the gospel witness. This is the message which we have to give. This is the purpose of our love. Again I must come back and repeat: Christian love is not sloppy or sentimental; it is not sexual; it is not social. It is not something that you have at the church banquet. It is something which reveals itself when we take Christ to a lost world of sinners. That is the way we manifest our love.

This kind of love is hard to understand. I have been with missionaries in many places— in Israel, in Africa, in Lebanon, in Turkey. I have been with them in France and in Italy, and I have been with them in Mexico, in Venezuela, and in the Caribbean. The thing which I have noted about these missionaries is that they love people, and a lot of the people they love are very hard to love. But they have a love for them, and it is wonderful to see it. What are they doing? They are taking the gospel out to these people, and that is the thing that God has commanded them to do. When they first got there, maybe they didn't love the people. But after you have ministered to people, my friend, you will love them, or you just couldn't be God's child.

Whosoever shall confess that Jesus is the Son of God, God dwelleth in him, and he in God [1 John 4:15].

This is where you begin with Him—don't tell me that the Virgin Birth is not important. This is the gospel: ". . . how that Christ died for our sins according to the scriptures; And that he was buried, and that he rose again the third day according to the scriptures" (1 Cor. 15:3–4). My friend, if He is not who He said He was, His death and resurrection are absolutely meaningless; in fact, He was not raised from the dead if He is not who He said He was. But the evidence is all on the side that He did arise from the dead, and the proof of it is that He was virgin born; He was who He claimed to be.

"Jesus is the Son of God, God dwelleth in him, and he in God." This is the reason that the Lord Jesus could say, "Whatever God does, I do." He made this tremendous claim: "Verily, verily, I say unto you, He that heareth my word, and believeth on him that sent me, hath everlasting life, and shall not come into condemnation; but is passed from death unto life" (John 5:24). How is that possible? He had just said in John 5:19, ". . . The Son can do nothing of himself, but what he seeth the Father do: for what things soever he doeth, these also doeth the Son likewise." He is going to raise the dead, and He is going to judge all of the dead. Therefore, He can say to you today that because of who He is, if you will hear His voice and if you will believe on Him, you will be saved.

And we have known and believed the love that God hath to us. God is love; and he that dwelleth in love dwelleth in God, and God in him [1 John 4:16].

These are inextricably intertwined and interwoven together. You simply cannot say that you love God and that you are a child of God when you hate the brethren down here.

This is the second time in this chapter that we have had the definition, "God is love." An easy way to remember where in chapter 4 it occurs is this: multiply four by two and you get eight—it occurs in verse 8 the first time; then multiply eight by two and you get sixteen—it occurs in verse 16 the second time. First John 4:8 and 16 give the definition, "God is love."

Herein is our love made perfect, that we may have boldness in the day of judgment: because as he is, so are we in this world [1 John 4:17].

Our love is made "perfect," and that means *complete.*

"That we may have boldness in the day of judgment." If you and I love God, love the Lord Jesus, and love one another as brothers and sisters in the faith, then that will give us boldness, and we will not have any fear of the day of judgment.

"Because as he is, so are we in this world."

In other words, we are just like the Lord Jesus. He was raised from the dead, we are told here, and He has life. Well, we have that life too, and He is up yonder at God's right hand for us. We are in Christ, and we are accepted in the Beloved.

Therefore, John can go on to say—

There is no fear in love; but perfect love casteth out fear: because fear hath torment. He that feareth is not made perfect in love [1 John 4:18].

There is nothing like fear in the human heart, but the child of God does not need to fear any judgment which is coming. It was all settled when Christ died for you.

"He that feareth is not made perfect in love." If you are fearful, you cannot enjoy your salvation. Joy stems from love, and if you have love for the Lord Jesus, for God, and for your brethren, then fear has been cast out.

We love him, because he first loved us [1 John 4:19].

He loved us when we were unlovely. He is worth loving. He is worthy. The Lamb is worthy of all of our love, all of our devotion, all of our service.

If a man say, I love God, and hateth his brother, he is a liar: for he that loveth not his brother whom he hath seen, how can he love God whom he hath not seen? [1 John 4:20].

I didn't say this; John said it. John says that if you say you love God and hate your brother, you are a liar.

"For he that loveth not his brother whom he hath seen, how can he love God whom he hath not seen?" There is a great deal of nonsense and pious hypocrisy going on today even in our fundamental churches. If we do not love our brother, then we do not love God either.

And this commandment have we from him, That he who loveth God love his brother also [1 John 4:21].

This is a commandment. God does not ask you if you feel like it or if you want to. He says, "This is what I *command* you. Because I love, you are to love." I get a little weary hearing the talk of "dedicated" and "consecrated" Christians who are lazy on the job. You are not dedicated to the Lord unless you demonstrate it in your life and in your service.

CHAPTER 5

THEME: God is life; victory over the world; assurance of salvation

GOD IS LIFE

In this chapter we have come to the last major division of this very wonderful little book. In the first part of this epistle, we saw that God is light. In the very extensive center section, we saw that God is love. The subject of this final chapter is God is life.

VICTORY OVER THE WORLD

In these first five verses, John talks about victory for the believer over the world. The "world" here is the *cosmos*, that is, the world with all of its organizations, all of its governments, all of its selfishness, its greed, its sorrow, its sickness, and its awful sin. John is going to say that it is possible for the child of God to have a victory right down here over this world.

Whosoever believeth that Jesus is the Christ is born of God: and every one that loveth him that begat loveth him also that is begotten of him [1 John 5:1].

God is life, and that life comes through being born of God. "Whosoever believeth that Jesus is the Christ is born of God"—this is the method, this is how one is born again. John makes it very clear here and in the opening of his gospel that you become a child of God through simple faith in the Lord Jesus Christ. "But as many as received him, to them gave he power [the *exousian* power, the right, the authority] to become the sons of God, even to them that [don't do any more nor less than simply] believe on his name" (John 1:12). This means that when you trust Christ, you trust who He is as well as what He did. What He did has no value if He is not who He said He was. Again I must say that the Virgin Birth is very essential. Who is this that died for the sins of the world? It was not an ordinary man who did that because an ordinary man is sinful himself and could not even die to obtain his own salvation. He could die only a judgment death, being eternally separated from God. "Whosoever believeth that Jesus is the Christ is born of God." It is faith which produces the New Birth.

Once you have been born again, how do you know that you have been born again? Do you have some great, overwhelming experience? Do you enter some ecstatic state? Not necessarily; some people do I am told, but that is not the usual procedure. "Whosoever believeth that Jesus is the Christ is born of God: and every one that loveth him that begat loveth him also that is begotten of him." When you trust the Lord Jesus Christ, you are born again, and God becomes your heavenly Father. He is God the Father, and He becomes your heavenly Father. If He is your heavenly Father and you are begotten of Him, then you will love Him. But it doesn't stop there—you are also going to love the one who is begotten of Him. In other words, you are going to love other of God's little children. John has said this before, and he has said that it is not something new with him. In 1 John 3:11 we read, "For this is the message that ye heard from the beginning, that we should love one another." And the Lord Jesus said, "By this shall all men know that ye are my disciples, if you have love one to another" (John 13:35).

This expression, "born of God," is very, very important. Being born of God hasn't anything to do with the fact that you have joined a church or gone through a ceremony. If you are born of God, I hope you have joined a church and that you take part in the ordinances of your church, but following certain rituals does not make you a child of God. The important thing is: Are you born of God? Have you been born again? You *are* born again when you trust the Lord Jesus Christ as your Savior, and the proof of it is that you love God. You love your Father—He begot you—and you are going to love His other children because they are your brothers and sisters. This cannot be confined to a certain denomination, church, race, clique, or group. The one who is born again will love others who are born again.

This is the epistle on how you can have the assurance of your salvation, and all along John has been giving to you some of the evidences that you are a child of God:

1. "If you know that he is righteous, ye know that every one that doeth righteousness is born of him" (1 John 2:29). A child of God will *practice righteousness* in his life. This does not mean that righteousness is the unusual thing, the abnormal thing, or that once in awhile you practice it. It is to be the practice of your life. You will slip and fall sometimes, but righteousness will be the practice of your life if you are His child.

2. "Whosoever is born of God doth not com-

mit sin; for his seed remaineth in him: and he cannot sin, because he is born of God" (1 John 3:9). A child of God will *not practice sin*. He will not live in it, revel in it, or make it his life. The life-style of a sinner is sin; he lives in sin all the time, and you don't expect him to do differently. We all lived in sin until we came to Christ.

3. "Beloved, let us love one another: for love is of God; and every one that loveth is born of God, and knoweth God" (1 John 4:7). A child of God will *love other Christians*. This is another test that will give assurance to you that you are born of God: Do you love other Christians?

4. "For whatsoever is born of God overcometh the world: and this is the victory that overcometh the world, even our faith" (v. 4). A child of God will *overcome the world*.

5. "We know that whosoever is born of God sinneth not; but he that is begotten of God keepeth himself, and that wicked one toucheth him not" (v. 18). A child of God *keeps himself from Satan*.

Two of the evidences, two of the birthmarks of a child of God are given right here in this chapter. We will discuss these last two in more detail as we come to them. John is going to emphasize certain tests of true sonship—love, obedience, and truth. No one can quarrel with these words. Love, obedience, and truth are marks of the child of God.

By this we know that we love the children of God, when we love God, and keep his commandments [1 John 5:2].

What does John mean here by "his commandments"? The commandments, as I understand it here, are not referring to the Old Testament law at all, but they are the commandments which the Lord Jesus gave when He was here. For example, we find not ten commandments but about twenty-two in the fifth chapter of 1 Thessalonians: "Rejoice evermore" (v. 16); "Pray without ceasing" (v. 17); and "Quench not the Spirit" (v. 19), etc. These are the commandments for believers today. Every child of God wants to keep these commandments as the practice of his life. This is something that he desires to do, something that he longs to do.

For this is the love of God, that we keep his commandments: and his commandments are not grievous [1 John 5:3].

The New Scofield Reference Bible has changed "grievous" to *burdensome*. I'm not going to quarrel with that because it is a good transla-

tion, but the literal is really, *heavy*. His commandments are not heavy. This does not mean that they are difficult to keep but rather that they do not impose a burden when they are kept. John is saying that the child of God *wants* to keep His commandments. It is something that he wants to practice; it is not difficult for him to do these things at all. The little girl who was carrying a big, heavy baby was asked by a concerned woman, "Little girl, isn't that baby too heavy for you?" The child replied, "He's not heavy. He's my brother." It makes all the difference in the world, you see, when he's your brother. "For this is the love of God, that we keep his commandments: and his commandments are not grievous." The point is that they impose no burden on us because we are keeping them through love.

The story is told about a man and his family who years ago drove into a little town in Oklahoma in a covered wagon. They stopped at the town store to talk to the owner as he sat on an apple box out in front of the store. "What kind of town is this here?" they asked him. The storekeeper said, "Well, what kind of town did you come from?" "Oh," the man said, "we came from a wonderful town. Everybody there seemed to know each other, seemed to care about each other, and had a concern for each other. They were very wonderful people. We really hated to leave, but we wanted to move west. We're not sure where to settle down. What kind of town is this?" The storekeeper said, "This is just the same kind of town which you left. It's that kind of town." The man said, "Well, then, I think maybe we'll settle here," and they drove on down the street.

In a little while another covered wagon drove up in front of the little store. The man asked the storekeeper, "What kind of town is this?" So the storekeeper again said, "What kind of town did you leave?" "We were glad to get away from it," the man said. "They were some of the meanest people that I have ever met. They were never very neighborly or very helpful. We never had any friends there, and that's the reason we left." The storekeeper told him. "Well, I think you are going to find this is the same kind of town. We are the same kind of people." And the second man decided to drive on.

Another citizen of the town who had been sitting there with the storekeeper said, "Wait a minute! What do you mean by giving those two men two different viewpoints of this town?" And the storekeeper replied, "I've learned that any town will be the same kind of town that you have left—because you will be the same kind of person."

May I say to you, the child of God ought to recognize that he is not to be looking for someone to do something for him, but he is to be expressing love in real action and in real concern for others. "By this shall all men know that ye are my disciples, if ye have love one to another" (John 13:35). If you love the Lord Jesus, if you love your heavenly Father, you are going to love other believers. You will know that you are keeping His commandments, and they will not be a burden to you at all. The Lord Jesus said, "For my yoke is easy, and my burden is light" (Matt. 11:30). It will be heavy unless you have the real love for the Lord and you truly want to serve Him. Then church work and other ministries will never become difficult.

Dr. Ironside taught this epistle of John while I was in seminary, and he told us this story:

Some time ago I read of a man who spent a few months in India. When he came back, he was discussing India at the home of some of his friends, and the talk drifted to missions, and this man, out of his wide experience, about five months in India, said, "I have no use for missions and missionaries. I spent months there, and didn't see that they were doing anything; in fact, in all that time I never met a missionary. I think the church is wasting its money on missions." A quiet old gentleman sat near. He had not said anything, but now spoke up and said, "Pardon me; how long did you say you were in India?"

"Five months."

"What took you there?"

"I went out to hunt tigers."

"And did you see any tigers?"

"Scores of them."

"It is rather peculiar," said the old gentleman, "but I have spent thirty years in India, and in those years I never saw a tiger but I have seen hundreds of missionaries. You went to India to hunt tigers and you found them. I went to India to do missionary work and found many other missionaries."

It's owing to what you are looking for, my friend. Are you concerned about God's work today? Are you concerned about getting out God's Word? Some folk say, "Well, I don't see that much progress is being made." You just don't happen to be where the action is, for the Word of God *is* going out, and it is having its effect in hearts and lives.

For whatsoever is born of God overcometh the world: and this is the victory that overcometh the world, even our faith [1 John 5:4].

Since we hear so much about "victory" in the Christian life today, it may seem strange to you that it occurs so rarely in the New Testament.

What is it that overcomes the world? It is our faith. It is faith that saves us, and it is faith that keeps us. We are saved by faith; we walk by faith. We are born children of God by faith in Jesus Christ, and faith is the only way in which you and I will be able to overcome this world around us.

Now we have an enemy, and John has talked about this enemy before: "Love not the world, neither the things that are in the world" (1 John 2:15). There is in the world that which is of the flesh, that which is of the world, and that which is of the Devil. As Wordsworth put it, "The world is too much with us." As believers we are in the world, but we are not to be of it. This world that you and I are in is a big, mean, bad world. We can be caught up in it very easily—we can be trapped by it.

There is an illustration of this in the Old Testament which I think might be helpful to us at this point. It is the story of Joshua and the children of Israel entering the Promised Land. First, I must say that the Promised Land is not a figure of heaven. Our songs which talk about Canaan being heaven and the place to which believers are going simply do not fit what God teaches us in His Word. Actually, Canaan represents a condition in which believers ought to be living down here. We can live out in the wilderness, and there are a great many wilderness believers today. They do not have any fun at all, although they think they do at times. There's no fun out in the wilderness. The wilderness march was not easy. But the land of Canaan is where we are blessed with all spiritual blessings.

When Joshua entered the land, it was not handed to him on a silver platter. If you and I today are to enjoy the spiritual blessings which are ours, we need to recognize that we have a battle to fight; the enemy holds the territory, and he is not going to let us have any kind of deliverance or victory without a battle. When Joshua entered the Promised Land, therefore, there were three enemies that stood before him. Until he overcame them, he was not able to take the land.

The first enemy was Jericho, and Jericho represents the world. That was the first place Joshua struck. It was obvious that what he was trying to do was to split the land into two divisions and then take one at a time. Then the second enemy was little Ai which represents the flesh. Joshua sent a small contingent up there, thinking it would be easy to take, but that is the one place where he received a telling defeat. Many Christians overcome the world, but they are always overcome by the flesh. In other words, there are many saints who don't engage in worldly practices, but they go to church and gossip—they indulge the flesh. They can blow the trumpet around Jericho, but they don't blow the trumpet around Ai. Then finally there were the Gibeonites who represent the Devil. They deceived Joshua. The Devil was a liar from the beginning. He still deceives and works wilily.

Let's come back to verse 4 and look at it in reference to Jericho. "For whatsoever is born of God overcometh the world." If you are a child of God, you are going to overcome the world. How will you gain that victory? "And this is the victory that overcometh the world, even our faith." It is not by fighting but by faith. How did this man Joshua overcome Jericho? Jericho was the enemy which was out in front of him, and he had to take that city. How was he going to take the city? By fighting it? He did not fight it at all, but God told him what to do. God said, "I don't want you to make an assault upon the city. I don't want you to use a battering ram to try to get through the gate. The thing which I want you to do is to march around the city. Instead of putting only your elite army up in front—the Marines or the special guards—I want you to also put the priests up there with the ark of the covenant. And the priests shall carry horns, and the trumpets are to be blown as they go around the city. But you are not to make an attack upon the city." It was a most unusual method which God gave to Joshua!

I am confident that the city of Jericho had braced itself for the onslaught of these people who had crossed the Jordan River at flood stage—which must have seemed to Jericho to be an impossibility and a foreboding of things to come. So they shut up their city, ready to defend themselves against Israel. I think that their guard up on the gate gave the signal, "Here they come—the whole army of Israel!" As Israel marched up to the gate, you must remember that there was an army on the in-

side ready and waiting for them. But when the children of Israel came up to the gate, they made a right face and kept on marching. They marched once around the walls of the city, and then they went back into camp!

You can be sure that there was a meeting of the general's staff in the city of Jericho that night to try to figure out the strategy that Israel was using against them. As best they could, they prepared themselves for the next day when the guard on the gate again yelled down and said, "Here they come!" They braced themselves for the battle in case Israel tried to break through the gates. Probably there were soldiers up on top ready to pour boiling oil or water down upon them and to shoot arrows, but Israel didn't attempt to come through. They simply marched around the city again, and they repeated that for six days. By that time, the army staff inside the city of Jericho had just about gone crazy. They didn't know what in the world was taking place.

On the seventh day, when Israel had gone around one time, the general's staff heaved a sigh of relief and said, "It sure looks like they're not going to take the city. They are just doing something very crazy." From the world's viewpoint, it was *very* crazy—you must admit that this was an unusual strategy. But this time the guard said, "Wait a minute! They are not returning to camp. They are marching around again!" And Israel proceeded to march around the city *seven* times. Then what happened? The priests of Israel blew the trumpets, the people shouted, and the walls of Jericho fell down! The children of Israel probably completely encircled the city, and when the walls of Jericho fell down, the army on the inside was certainly taken by surprise.

How did the children of Israel take the city of Jericho? By fighting? They did not fight at all. They were marching around according to the order given not by Joshua but by that unseen Captain of the host of the Lord. Frankly, I used to have a problem with this incident in Scripture. My problem was not with the walls of Jericho falling down—that fact has been pretty well established by archaeological excavations—but the thing that disturbed me was why a man of Joshua's proven ability as a military leader would use tactics like this. It is true that God commanded it, but I still think that Joshua might have disagreed with the tactics.

The answer lies in that earlier incident when Joshua saw the man with the drawn sword standing at the edge of the Israelite camp (see Josh. 5:13–15). Joshua went out and said to the man—if you want it in good old Americana—"What's the big idea? Who told you to draw a sword?" Joshua's question was, ". . . Art thou for us, or for our adversaries?" (Josh. 5:13). That's the way our translation gives it, and it is a good translation, but probably Joshua really meant, "What's the big idea? Who gave you an order to draw a sword?" Joshua thought *he* was in charge. But when the man turned and answered, Joshua realized that He was a supernatural person. I personally believe that He was none other than the preincarnate Christ. Then Joshua fell at His feet and worshiped Him. So you see, before the battle of Jericho, this man Joshua learned that he was not really in charge. General Headquarters was not in his tent but in heaven with the Captain of the host of the Lord, for that is how the Stranger identified Himself, ". . . Nay; but as captain of the host of the LORD am I now come . . ." (Josh. 5:14). In other words, the Lord was telling Joshua, "This battle you are fighting is a spiritual battle as well as a physical one, and I'm the Captain." So General Joshua was now going to take his orders from the "captain of the host of the LORD," and the Captain said, "March around the city." With this incident in mind, I don't have any trouble understanding Joshua. If you had met him and asked him why in the world he was using such a crazy maneuver, I think he would have agreed with you, "Say, this is crazy, isn't it? But after all, I'm just taking orders."

If you have ever had any army experience, you know that a buck private never talks back to a captain. That is, when the captain says, "Go, do this," the private doesn't stop and say, "I've been thinking this over myself, and I think there is a better way of doing it." Did you ever hear of a buck private saying that to a captain? No! He says, "Yes, sir! I'll go do it." And he goes and does whatever the captain has commanded. When I was in the National Guard, some fellows got into trouble by slipping out during the night. The next day, the captain gave them an order to dig a hole. He said, "I want this hole six feet long, I want it three feet wide, and I want it five feet deep." The fellows dug the hole and then went in and reported to the captain. The captain came out, looked at the hole, and he said, "Now I want you to fill it back up with the dirt." They had to fill it back up! That sounds sort of crazy, but they had to obey orders.

Joshua was obeying orders. He was being obedient. He *believed* the Captain. Hebrews 11 tells us, "By faith the walls of Jericho fell down . . ." (Heb. 11:30). It wasn't by fighting or military skills but by faith that the walls of Jericho fell down.

What is the lesson for us today? You and I cannot overcome the world by fighting it. This is one reason that as a pastor I never engaged in any reform movement, no matter how worthwhile it was—and I agreed that many of them were good. I would never serve on the committee, nor would I have part in it as pastor of a church because I do not think I was called to get into that at all. You don't overcome the world by fighting it. I knew a former movie star many years ago who called me when I was a pastor in downtown Los Angeles and asked if I would serve on a committee to help reform downtown Los Angeles. Downtown Los Angeles needed reforming then, and it still does, but I never felt I was called to do that. I refused to serve on the committee, and she couldn't believe it. She said, "Do you mean to tell me that you won't serve on the committee? As a preacher you are not interested in that?" I said, "I didn't say that. I just won't serve on the committee." And I told her why. I said, "The Lord called me to fish in the fishpond, but He never told me to clean up the fishpond. So my business is fishing, giving out the Word of God. I let the Spirit of God do any cleaning up that's to be done. That is the department He is in, and I'm not in that department." She didn't like it, but she had to accept it, of course. I don't fight the world today. I'm not in any great reformation movement. I'm not trying to straighten up our government, although I think it needs straightening up. I think that both the Democratic and the Republican parties are in a shambles today. We are without leadership as a nation. Although I recognize all of this, it is not my business to try to change it. My business is to give out the Word of God.

Although he had the army, Joshua's business was not to fight. His business was to believe God. He believed God, and the walls fell down. My friend, today we are saved by faith, and if we are going to overcome this world, we'll not overcome it by fighting it. We are going to overcome it by faith. That is the only way you and I can deal with this world in which we live, and that is the great message which is here for us.

Who is he that overcometh the world, but he that believeth that Jesus is the Son of God? [1 John 5:5].

When you really trust Christ, it is not a question of your own power, but you are kept by the power of God through faith. We have faith in Christ for salvation in the future and faith in Christ for salvation from the world here and now.

ASSURANCE OF SALVATION

This is he that came by water and blood, even Jesus Christ; not by water only, but by water and blood. And it is the Spirit that beareth witness, because the Spirit is truth [1 John 5:6].

You will recall that at the crucifixion of Jesus His bones were not broken in fulfillment of Scripture. In order to hasten death, the Romans would sometimes break the legs of those who were hanging on the crosses, but John tells us in his gospel: "But when they came to Jesus, and saw that he was dead already, they brake not his legs: But one of the soldiers with a spear pierced his side, and forthwith came there out blood and water. And he that saw it bare record, and his record is true: and he knoweth that he saith true, that ye might believe" (John 19:33–35). John was present at the crucifixion of Christ, and he noted something that no one else noted. Chances are that he was closer to the cross than any of the other apostles. He noted that when that soldier pushed the spear into the side of Christ, there came out blood and water—not just one element, but both elements.

Here in his epistle John makes application of this. He emphasized it in his gospel, and now he comes back to it here and says, "He that came by water." "Water" speaks of what? It speaks of the Word of God. The Lord Jesus said to Nicodemus, ". . . Verily, verily, I say unto thee, Except a man be born of water and of the Spirit, he cannot enter into the kingdom of God" (John 3:5). The water is the living Word applied by the Spirit of God. "He that came by water"—the Word of God that the Spirit of God uses. "And blood" refers to the death of Christ. "Even Jesus Christ; not by water only, but by water and blood."

"And it is the Spirit that beareth witness, because the Spirit is truth." It is the Spirit who can make these truths live. May I make this rather startling statement: The Lord Jesus told the disciples that between His death and resurrection and the Day of Pentecost they were to tarry in Jerusalem and to do nothing—they were *not* to witness. Why? They could not witness effectually without the Holy Spirit. Therefore, if anyone is to be saved, not only is Christ's redemptive death essential, but also that the Spirit of God work in hearts and lives. I am encouraged by letters from listeners to our Bible-teaching radio broadcasts because they demonstrate that the Word of God taken by the Spirit of God can apply the blood of Christ to hearts and lives. Christ died for our sins, but the Spirit of God must make that real to us. Only the Spirit of God can make the death of Christ real to you, and only the Spirit of God can make the resurrection of Christ real to you.

In verse 7 it looks as if there are added three more witnesses which are in heaven—

For there are three that bear record in heaven, the Father, the Word, and the Holy Ghost: and these three are one [1 John 5:7].

In a very scholarly presentation, Dr. A. T. Robertson states that this verse is not in the better manuscripts. I heard Dr. Robertson lecture when I was a student in seminary, and he probably knew more Greek than anybody who has lived in our generation. I remember that when he got up the first day to lecture on the Epistle to the Romans, he had a great big sheaf of notes. He didn't even look up at the class because he was busy just straightening out those notes. Then he looked up and said, "I don't see how the apostle Paul ever wrote the Epistle to the Romans without my notes!" Of course, everybody roared at that. Well, Dr. Robertson was a great Greek scholar, and he makes the statement that verse 7 is not in the better manuscripts but was probably written in the margin by some scribe. You must remember that the Bible at first was handwritten. The first book printed was the Bible, but that was not until Gutenberg invented the printing press which was a long time after John and his day. Evidently some scribe put what we have as verse 7 in the margin, and then later on another scribe came along and thought it was to be included in the text. There is nothing wrong with the verse, but we do need to recognize that it is not in the better manuscripts. If we want to be scholarly and accurate and to be able to defend the verbal, plenary inspiration of the Bible, we need to know these things.

In other words, there are not six witnesses presented here. The three in heaven given in verse 7 would do us very little good down here on earth, but it is the three witnesses on earth which we are concerned about and which have a direct bearing on us. That is what needs to be emphasized.

And there are three that bear witness in earth, the Spirit, and the water, and the blood: and these three agree in one [1 John 5:8].

What is the agreement which these three witnesses have? Well, they agree in one purpose, that is, the purpose of presenting Jesus Christ as the Savior of the world who shed His blood upon Calvary and paid the penalty for our sins.

"There are three that bear witness in earth," and these three are right here right now. The Holy Spirit will take the Word of God and apply it to your heart. You are reading this book long after the time I actually wrote it. I believe that the Holy Spirit is here, leading right now as I write. When you read this, the Holy Spirit will be there to take His Word and apply it to your heart. He bears record, if you please, and He is a witness. His witness is that you might come to a saving knowledge of Jesus Christ.

How are you going to come to that knowledge? Through the Word of God. You see, the blood of Christ delivers us from the penalty of sin. The Word of God delivers us from the defilement of sin in the world today. This is my reason for being a fellow with a one-track mind. All I have ever emphasized in my ministry is the Word of God. I just have one tune that I play—I just have one message that I give. I hope it doesn't get too monotonous but, my friend, the Word of God is the only thing which can clean up your life even as a believer, and it is the only thing which will keep it clean. This is something very important to know.

We are living in a day when a great deal of attention is given to cleanliness, in fact, too much attention. You are led to believe that if you don't use a certain miracle bar of soap, you will be out of it, you may even lose your job, and certainly all of your friends are going to desert you. But if you use a certain brand—it's a "miracle" substance—it will clean you up, and even clean your clothes up. It will clean up everything but what is on the inside of you; it won't clean up that. Only the Word of God can do that.

The only true miracle cleansing agent in the world today is the Word of God. It can clean you up; it can save you: "Being born again, not of corruptible seed, but of incorruptible, by the word of God, which liveth and abideth for ever" (1 Pet. 1:23). For the Word of God presents Christ who shed His blood for your sins and my sins. He died for our sins; He was raised for our justification. Not only can it save you, but the Word of God can also keep you clean while you are down here. You can use every kind of spray deodorant there is, you can rub it on, you can pour it on, you can buy it in the giant economy size, put it in your swimming pool, and swim in it, my friend, but it won't clean you on the inside. Only the Word of God can keep you clean today. That is the thing which John is emphasizing here. These three bear witness on earth—the Spirit uses the water of the Word and applies the blood for our salvation. These three all agree in one—that is, they want to get you saved and keep you saved.

If we receive the witness of men, the witness of God is greater: for this is the witness of God which he hath testified of his Son [1 John 5:9].

I don't know about you, but many folk whom I have talked to have reached a credibility gap between themselves and the news media, the politicians, and all who are on television today. I'll be very candid with you that there are certain news commentators whom I won't listen to any longer. I know that they are doing nothing in the world but giving out propaganda. They are not giving facts. Everything they give is biased and distorted and twisted for a liberal position. Apparently, they are willing even to misinform you, and they are willing to withhold facts to gain their objective. I have come to the place where it does not matter who they are or to what party they belong, I have no confidence in politicians. Therefore, we are in a place today where it is difficult to receive the witness of men, but the interesting thing is that John Q. Public swallows it hook, line, and sinker. You can tell by the different polls which are taken that a man's influence or his popularity is determined by what the news media say about him. The biggest frauds in the world can be built up by the media—Hollywood, of course, has done this for years. Most people *do* receive the witness of men; they are taken in by it. If it is said over television or if it is put into print, they will believe it. There are many people who believe whatever they read or hear, but they will not receive the witness of God! Oh, my friend, the witness of God is *greater!*

"For this is the witness of God which he hath testified of his Son." God today is not giving out news on every subject. His news is good news, and it is about His Son who died for us on the cross. That is His message.

He that believeth on the Son of God hath the witness in himself: he that believeth not God hath made him a liar; because he believeth not the record that God gave of his Son [1 John 5:10].

"He that believeth on the Son of God hath the witness in himself." If you have trusted Christ as your Savior, the Holy Spirit indwells you, and He testifies that these things are true. This is one of the great encouragements in teaching the Word of God by radio. Many people who listen have never seen me (I guess that may be a good thing!), but they have the Holy Spirit indwelling them, and when they hear the Word of God, they accept it because the Spirit bears witness that they are hearing the Word of God. This is quite wonderful, and it is the greatest encouragement in preaching and teaching the Word of God, whether it be from the pulpit, over radio, or through the printed page.

"He that believeth not God hath made him a liar." When you don't believe God, you add to your other sins by implying that He is a liar. God says, "Trust Christ, and I'll save you." If you say, "I don't need Christ to be saved," then you are calling God a liar. I receive many letters like the one from a woman who thought that since she was a member of the church and did a lot of good things, she was all right. She had to listen to the teaching of the Word of God for a long time before she realized that she was a sinner and that she needed Christ as her Savior.

"Because he believeth not the record that God gave of his Son." What is "the record"? John is going to tell us—

And this is the record, that God hath given to us eternal life, and this life is in his Son [1 John 5:11].

What is the record? "This is the record, that God hath given to us eternal life, and this life is in his Son." Eternal life is to have Christ. It boils down to this one point. This is the gospel in a nutshell. This is the simplest test that can be made—

He that hath the Son hath life; and he that hath not the Son of God hath not life [1 John 5:12].

"He that hath the Son hath life." He didn't say, "He that belongs to the church has life." You might say, "I'm a Baptist" or "I'm a Methodist" or "I'm a Presbyterian" or "I'm a Nazarene" or "I belong to the Church of God." It does not matter what church you belong to—

your church membership does not mean you are saved. Then *what* does it mean to be saved? "He that hath the Son hath life." The question is: Do you have Christ? Is He your Savior? Are you trusting Him in such a way that no one on earth or in heaven can shake your confidence in Him? My friend, if you haven't come to that point, you haven't come anywhere at all. To be saved means you trust Christ, and it means you have Christ as your Savior. "He that hath the Son hath life." He's our lifeboat. He's our lifeline. He's our only hope. We are lost without Him, but if we have Him, we have life.

"And he that hath not the Son of God hath not life." My friend, can it be made any clearer than that? Let's forget about religion. Let's forget about all this churchianity. Let's forget about all this gimmickry that is going on today—taking little courses, going through little rituals, all that sort of thing. Forget about it, my friend! The important thing is: *Do you have Christ? Is He your Savior?*

This is the reason John has emphasized that Jesus is the Son of God. I want to say to you, He is wonderful. He is God manifest in the flesh. He is the only one who can save us. He is absolutely unique. There is no one else like Him. He's the only begotten Son of God. He died upon the cross because He alone could pay the penalty for our sins. He rose again, and He is living right this moment at God's right hand for us. He is the living Christ. Do you have Him today as your Savior? That is the only question you need to answer. If you have Him, you have life—you are saved. That is the record. Do you believe God, or don't you believe God? If you don't believe Him, you make Him a liar.

My friend, John has this down right where you can get it. You cannot miss this. The only thing right now that will keep you from coming to Christ is the sin in your life that you don't want to give up. That is the only thing in the world which will stop you. That is the decision you make.

These things have I written unto you that believe on the name of the Son of God; that ye may know that ye have eternal life, and that ye may believe on the name of the Son of God [1 John 5:13].

John has a twofold purpose in writing this epistle: (1) "that ye may *believe* on the name of the Son of God"—that's salvation, and (2) "that ye may *know* that ye have eternal life"—if you have Christ, if you have believed Him, you have life. A great many people say, "I just want to believe that I have eternal life." The question is: Whom do you believe? Not *what* do you believe, but *whom* do you believe? Do you believe God? Do you believe the record that He gave? He says that if you have the Son, you have life. Now do you believe that? John didn't say if you feel like it or if you have joined something, but if you believe in the Lord Jesus Christ as your Savior. And if you have Him, then you have life.

This is the reason John has written this epistle—"that ye may know that ye have eternal life." This was also the purpose of the gospel which John wrote: "And many other signs truly did Jesus in the presence of his disciples, which are not written in this book: But these are written [John didn't write everything, just certain things], that ye might believe that Jesus is the Christ, the Son of God [that's who He is]; and that believing ye might have life through his name" (John 20:30–31).

If you have the Son, you have life—John wants you to know that, and you honor God when you know it. That simply means that you are not making God a liar, but you're trusting Him. It is not a matter of how much faith you have or how you feel about it, it is whether or not you trust Christ. That's all important.

Having this assurance of eternal life will do something for our Christian life here and now—

And this is the confidence that we have in him, that, if we ask any thing according to his will, he heareth us [1 John 5:14].

Our assurance will give us confidence in prayer, and believe me, we need confidence in prayer. This word *confidence* actually means "boldness." "This is the *boldness* that we have in him." This assurance will give boldness in prayer to the child of God.

"If we ask any thing according to his will"—our prayer must be according to the will of God. If you and I are in fellowship with Him, walking with Him, then our prayer would be for God's will in every circumstance. George Müller put it like this: "Prayer is not overcoming God's reluctance. It is laying hold of His willingness." It is not trying to get God to do something which He is reluctant to do, but prayer is to be our thinking His thoughts after Him. This is the thing which gives us confidence when we turn to God in prayer.

"He heareth us." You can be sure that He not only hears our prayer, but He also answers our prayer. God will hear the prayers of His children, but He will not always answer them by giving us what we ask. John is saying here that we can have the confidence that He will answer our request according to the way we pray—when we pray in His will.

And if we know that he hear us, whatsoever we ask, we know that we have the petitions that we desired of him [1 John 5:15].

It is wonderful to know that you and I have a heavenly Father. If we are in fellowship with Him, if we are not regarding sin in our lives, and if there are no other hindrances to prayer in our lives, we are not going to pray selfishly. When we are walking in fellowship with Him, when we are following Him, we can have the confidence that He will hear what we ask and answer our prayer. We are not to come to Him with mistrust or in a begging attitude, but we are to come with boldness to ask that God's will be done.

If any man see his brother sin a sin which is not unto death, he shall ask, and he shall give him life for them that sin not unto death. There is a sin unto death: I do not say that he shall pray for it [1 John 5:16].

"Death" refers here to *physical* death. It has no reference at all to spiritual death because the child of God has eternal life. John is saying that believers can commit a sin for which their heavenly Father will call them home; that is, He will remove them from this life physically, perhaps because they are disgracing Him.

Let us look at some people in Scripture who have committed a sin unto death. Moses and Aaron committed a sin unto death. You will recall that Moses got angry when the children of Israel kept begging for water and, instead of speaking to the rock as God commanded him, he smote the rock twice. He shouldn't even have touched that rock. It had already been smitten once before, and he should have rested upon that. The rock was to be an example and a type of Christ. Paul wrote, "And [the children of Israel] did all drink the same spiritual drink: for they drank of that spiritual Rock that followed them: and that Rock was Christ" (1 Cor. 10:4). Christ died only once, and Moses spoiled the type by striking the rock twice. "And the LORD spake unto Moses and Aaron, Because ye believed me not, to sanctify me in the eyes of the children of Israel, therefore ye shall not bring this congregation into the land which I have given them" (Num. 20:12). There was for this man

Moses a restoration in that he could continue leading. However, he began to plead with God to forgive him and to permit him to enter the land, but the Lord told him in effect, "Although I have restored you to your place of leadership, you are not going to enter the land." When Moses kept after the Lord, the Lord said to him, ". . . speak no more unto me of this matter" (Deut. 3:26). Moses and Aaron both had sinned a sin unto death—physical death.

In the New Testament we have another example of this in Ananias and Sapphira. They were a part of the early church, and they were guilty of a lie (see Acts 5:1–11). They had been willing to give a false impression to the early church; they were willing to live a lie. Because of that, God removed them from this earthly scene.

There is another incident of this mentioned in 1 Corinthians. Some of the people there had actually been getting drunk at the Lord's Supper, and they were missing the meaning of it altogether. Paul wrote to them, "For this cause many are weak and sickly among you, and *many sleep*" (1 Cor. 11:30, italics mine)— that is, they were dead. Paul is saying that they had committed a sin unto death.

Someone might ask at this point, "What is a sin unto death?" First, let me be clear that John was not speaking of an unpardonable sin. We are talking about a sin unto physical death, not spiritual death. These people were God's children. He would never have taken them home if they had not been His children. The Lord doesn't whip the Devil's children—He whips only His own. When His children sin unto death, He will take them home.

What is this sin? What is it specifically? Well, for Moses and Aaron it was one thing— they lost their tempers, and they destroyed a type of the Lord Jesus. Ananias and Sapphira were living like hypocrites. And in the city of Corinth, there were believers who were getting drunk and were disorderly at the Lord's Table. So a sin unto death is no one thing specifically. I have a notion that for you it would be different from what it would be for me, but I am of the opinion that every believer is capable of committing the sin unto death— whatever it is for him. You can go on in sin until God will remove you from the scene. This does not mean that every Christian who dies has committed the sin unto death, but it is possible to do that.

Absalom also committed a sin unto death. I believe that Absalom was really a child of God, but he led a rebellion against his father, King David. I have observed something over a period of years. I have watched how God has dealt with troublemakers in the church. I've not only seen Him remove them by death, but I've also seen Him set them aside so that they were of no more use in the service of God at all. It is possible to commit the sin unto death. Let me repeat that it is physical death not spiritual death.

Let me illustrate this. There is a mother who has a boy, Willie—her little angel child, of course. Next door, though, there lives a little brat about the age of her little angel, and they play together out in the backyard. One day as she is working in the kitchen, she hears that little brat yelling at the top of his voice. She rushes to the door, looks out, and there is her precious little angel on top of the little brat next door, just beating the stuffing out of him! She says, "Willie, you are going to have to come into the house if you are not nice to the little boy next door." He says, "Yes, Mama. I'll be better." She says, "Well, if you are not, I'm going to have to bring you into the house." So she goes back in, and about thirty minutes go by, but again she hears that familiar cry of the little brat next door. She goes to the door, and the same sight greets her. Her precious little angel is on top of the brat next door, just beating the stuffing out of him. She says, "Willie, come into the house." He says, "I don't want to come into the house." She says, "I said that if you did that again, you would have to come into the house." He balks, "I don't want to come into the house!" So what does she do? She goes out and gets him by the hand, and she takes her precious little angel, yelling at the top of his voice, into the house. He had to come in. He may not be her precious little angel anymore, but he still is her son— that fact never was disturbed, but he can no longer play outside. I think that if a child of God goes on disgracing the Lord down here, the Lord will either set him aside or take him home by death. God doesn't mind doing that. I think He does it in many instances.

All unrighteousness is sin: and there is a sin not unto death [1 John 5:17].

Believers who are alive today have all sinned, but we haven't sinned a sin unto death. We did something that was wrong, it was unrighteousness, but God didn't take us home. If He were taking home every believer who sinned, I would have been taken home a long time ago.

We know that whosoever is born of God sinneth not; but he that is begotten of

God keepeth himself, and that wicked one toucheth him not [1 John 5:18].

"We know that whosoever is born of God sinneth not." As we have seen in this epistle, you and I have two natures: an old nature and a new nature. That new nature will not sin. It never sins but has a desire for God and for the things of God. That old nature *will* sin, and it is because of it that a believer does sin.

"But he that is begotten of God keepeth himself, and that wicked one toucheth him not." This is another verse which makes me believe that the child of God can never be demon possessed. I believe that Christians can get to the place where they are oppressed by demons, but if they are actually demon— possessed, I would question their salvation— even though they may think that they are born again. Why? Because "greater is he that is in you, than he that is in the world" (1 John 4:4). The Holy Spirit would not be dwelling where a demon was.

And we know that we are of God, and the whole world lieth in wickedness [1 John 5:19].

This is the text of a sermon which I have preached on several occasions entitled "When the Devil Puts the Baby to Sleep." "And we know that we are of God, and the whole world lieth [actually, lies asleep] in wickedness [or, in the arms of the wicked one]." In other words, the Devil has the world asleep. The Devil is saying to Vernon McGee, "Sh-h-h. Hush! You're waking people up, and we don't want to do that! They are very comfortable. Many people in churches are dead in trespasses and sins, and we don't want to wake them up. Let's leave them alone." The Devil is concerned when people are awakened. You and I are living in a world that is asleep in the arms of the wicked one—if you look around today, you must agree with that statement.

And we know that the Son of God is come, and hath given us an understanding, that we may know him that is true, and we are in him that is true, even in his Son Jesus Christ. This is the true God, and eternal life [1 John 5:20].

My friend, Christianity is not a religion. It is a Person, and that Person is Christ. If you have Him, you have salvation—and it is not a religion.

John concludes his epistle by saying—

Little children, keep yourselves from idols. Amen [1 John 5:21].

Anything that stands between Christ and the believer is an idol. John says that you are to keep yourself from the things of the world which occupy your mind and your attention. Covetousness is idolatry; other things are idolatry. Many people are worshiping many things in this wicked world today. These things are nothing in the world but idols. God's first statement to us is: "In the beginning God created . . ." (Gen. 1:1). Among His last words to us are these: "Little children, keep yourselves from idols."

(For Bibliography to 1 John, see Bibliography at the end of 3 John.)

The Second Epistle of
JOHN
INTRODUCTION

A man whom I knew years ago in the South had the best way to divide the three epistles of John that I have ever heard. He called them "one-eyed John," "two-eyed John," and "three-eyed John." I do not think you will forget the three epistles of John if you remember them like this. That man, by the way, was one of the three conservative ministers in the community in which I served in Nashville, Tennessee, at that time. He was a real brother in Christ. Any Christian, regardless of his race, nationality, or station in life, if he is right on the inside, if he has been born again, is my brother. That is the great truth taught in 1 John which will be continued in 2 and 3 John with a different emphasis.

We are considering here, then, "two-eyed John." Your first impression, I am sure, is the brevity of these two last epistles. It is something that is almost startling. You might wonder why just thirteen verses in the second epistle and fourteen verses in the third epistle should be included in the Scriptures. Both of the epistles are very brief indeed. Someone will say, "Doesn't their brevity discount their message? Obviously, John didn't have too much to say." Not at all. Their brevity does not in any way take away from the importance of these epistles. In fact, it actually enhances them. Although they are very brief, these epistles are very important, and they are essential for getting a proper perspective of the first epistle and avoiding a perverted viewpoint. Let me illustrate it like this. My doctor at one time gave me two kinds of medication that I was to take whenever I suffered certain symptoms. One was a pill so small that I had trouble locating it in the bottle. The other was a capsule which looked like it was too big to swallow. I needed almost a gallon of water to get it down—I had to float it first! But I discovered in using both of them that the smaller one, the teeny-weeny one, was the more potent of the two. In fact, I found out it was the more important one: if the big one didn't work, then I used the little one. So it is with 2 and 3 John. Their brevity does not make them less potent.

The writer of this epistle is the apostle John. We call him the apostle of love. The Lord Jesus called him a "son of thunder" (see Mark 3:17). I think you can add to the thunder a little lightning, for in his epistles he makes it very clear that you must exhibit love to the brethren or you are not a child of God. John wrote this epistle around A.D. 90–100.

This epistle is like the Book of Philemon in that it is a personal letter. It is written by John to "the elect lady." The question is often asked whether the Greek word *electa* is a title or whether it refers to a Christian lady in the early church by the name of Electa. You must recall that John is the apostle who writes of the family of God. Paul writes of the church of God, while Peter writes of the government of God. If you will keep that in the background of your thinking as you come to these epistles written by these different men, it will help you to understand many things they are saying. Regardless of whether it is addressed to an individual or to a church, John is thinking of it in the context of the family of God. Apparently, there was some Christian lady or a local church which was extending hospitality to all those who claimed to be Christian, although some were heretics who denied the deity of Christ and the other great truths of the Christian faith. John warns here in this epistle against entertaining such folk. This is actually the purpose of this little epistle.

The theme of this epistle is: "For truth's sake." When truth and love come into conflict, truth is the one that is to predominate; it is the one that has top priority. Have you noticed that in 1 Corinthians 13:13 Paul didn't say, "Now abideth faith, hope, truth, and love"? He just said, "And now abideth faith, hope, charity [love], these three; but the greatest of these is charity [love]." But when truth is brought in, then truth comes first.

In other words, truth is worth contending for, and it is wrong to receive false teachers. This is the position that I take very definitely. I believe that the truth in the Word of God is worth contending for. When I say truth, I mean, first, that which is basic to the fact that the Bible is the Word of God—there is no question in my mind about it. The second thing of essential importance is the deity of Christ and His work upon the cross for us. When I meet a man who is true on these essentials, then he and I can disagree on nonessentials. I have a very good friend who is a Pentecostal preacher. When we play golf, he and I naturally get into a friendly argument. I always end up by saying to him, "Brother, you and I agree on so many things. I love to hear you talk about the Lord Jesus and about His death on the cross. You thrill my heart when I hear you talk about those things. But I want you to know that we disagree on a few points, and I'm going to pray for you because I think you are wrong." Well, you know, he turns around and says the same thing to me, and we leave each other laughing. As far as I know, that man has never said an unkind word to me or about me. He is my brother. I wish he could see some things as I do, but it will just have to be that way until he gets a little more light— and I want to be patient with him! But he stands true on the inspiration of the Scriptures, he stands true on the deity of Christ, and he stands true on the fact that Christ died for us. When a man does that, he's my brother, and I cannot escape that fact.

The key word in John's first epistle is *love*, but it is a love that is confined to the family of God. The little children are to love each other in the family of God. This is the mark of a child of God: he loves Christ, and he loves the brethren. How God's little children are to love each other is the entire sum and substance of that epistle.

It would be helpful to go back to the first epistle and pick up this thought again: "In this the children of God are manifest, and the children of the devil: whosoever doeth not righteousness is not of God, neither he that loveth not his brother" (1 John 3:10). John purposely cast this truth in the negative so that there would be no way in the world that any individual who claims to be a Christian and does not measure up could wiggle out of it. You cannot wiggle out of this: if you do not practice righteousness in your life, you are not of God. This is the outward badge of a child of God. You are to know the Lord Jesus as your Savior, and the proof to others is that you practice righteousness in your life. And if you do not love your brother (your *Christian* brother— this is not the universal brotherhood of man, for the Bible does not teach that), then you are not a child of God. *I* didn't say this—*John* said it. If you don't like it, then you take it up with him. John said that you can tell if someone is a genuine believer by his righteous life and his love for other Christians.

But what about the lost sinner who is not in the family of God? Are we to love him? Well, we are told in the Gospel of John: "For God so loved the world, that he gave his only begotten Son, that whosoever believeth in him should not perish, but have everlasting life" (John 3:16). Follow me carefully now. We are to love people to the extent of taking the gospel to them. We see in the Book of Jonah that Jonah did not love the Ninevites, but God sent him there because God loved them and God said, "Since I love them and they have turned to Me, Jonah, I want you to love them also." This is the relationship the child of God is to have to the lost world. You cannot love the sinners and their sin—we are not asked to do that. We *are* asked to love them enough to take the gospel to them. That is the important thing. We are to love them in that sense because God loves them. And then, when they turn to Christ, we will love them also.

Now another question arises: What is to be our relationship to false teachers, to those who deny the deity of Christ? John is going to make it very clear in this second epistle that this is something we need to beware of. He says in verse 7, "For many deceivers are entered into the world, who confess not that Jesus Christ is come in the flesh. This is a deceiver and an antichrist." What should be our relationship to false teachers? Follow me very carefully because this is going to be the nub of this epistle, and if you and I don't get this correctly, we are going to go haywire in our interpretation and come up with a pseudoliberal viewpoint. All of this "love, love, love" stuff today actually is not biblical at all. We are told to love everybody, but there are some whom the Scriptures tell us not to love but to be very careful of. John writes, "Love not the world, neither the things that are in the world . . ." (1 John 2:15). The things that are in the world are identified with the people who are in the world and who have made it as it is. Our love is to take the gospel to them, to give them the Word of God.

John's emphasis in his first epistle is upon love, but the key word in this second epistle is *truth*. Now when truth and love are in contrast and conflict, which one should prevail? If we get the answer to that, then that will determine our relationship to the false teacher, to the one who denies the deity of Christ. The so-called apostle of love is going to shock you and me out of our sentimental complacency and our sloppy notion of love. Which one should prevail—truth or love? His startling reply is that *truth* comes first. Christ said, "I am the way, the truth, and the life." He didn't say, "I am love," but He said, ". . . I am the way, the truth, and the life: no man cometh unto the Father, but by me" (John 14:6). You have to come to the Father through Jesus Christ. There is no other way. Why? Because He's not only the Way, but He is the Truth. It was John who wrote later on that "God is love." After the Lord Jesus was here and had said that He was the Truth, then John said, "God is love" (see 1 John 4:16). My friend, love can be expressed only within the bounds and context of truth. Love can be expressed only within the limitation and boundary that Scripture sets. Therefore, what about the false teacher? May I say to you, you are not to love the false teacher. John is going to make that abundantly clear. In fact, he is going to say something quite amazing. He says, "You are not even to entertain him in your home. You are not in any way to receive him or to have fellowship with him." That is just about as strong as it possibly can be.

We need to notice another important word in order to get a proper perspective of what John will be talking about in this second epistle as well as in the third epistle. In the first epistle John said that we are to ". . . walk in the light, as he is in the light . . ." (1 John 1:7). Truth and light are the same; they are the Word of God. As we have already seen, love and truth are inseparable. Christ is the epitome of both; He is the incarnation of both. He is *the* Truth, and He is love. God is love, and He is God. In addition to *truth*, there is a second word which is featured in this brief epistle—it is the word *walk*. In 2 John 1:4 you will notice that John says, "I rejoiced greatly that I found of thy children *walking* in truth, as we have received a commandment from the Father" (italics mine). And then in 2 John 1:6, we read, "And this is love, that we *walk* after his commandments. This is the commandment, That, as ye have heard from the beginning, ye should *walk* in it" (italics mine). Back in the first epistle, John wrote, "In this the children of God are manifest, and the children of the devil: whosoever doeth not righteousness is not of God, neither he that loveth

not his brother" (1 John 3:10). That righteousness is Christ, and to deny the deity of Christ is certainly not to do righteousness—the truth is essential. "Neither he that loveth not his brother"—this is the second thing that is very important, the walk. With this second word, we go to the opposite end of the spectrum of the Christian life. Not only is truth essential, but the walk is essential, and therefore we are told to love the brethren.

This epistle, therefore, will not give us a balanced viewpoint of the first epistle. Our contemporary idea of "love, love, love," that we are to love everyone who comes along, I do not find in the Word of God. When John is speaking of love here, he makes it clear that it is love within the family of God. We need to be very careful about this because a great many are interpreting *agape* love as nothing in the world but sex. One morning I received a phone call from a lady who had come to know the Lord through our radio ministry. She said to me, "Dr. McGee, I just want you to know that I love you." She sort of caught herself and then said, "I hope you understand that I'm not talking about man and woman love. I'm saying that I love you as a brother in the Lord who led me to Christ." Well, I understand that, and I believe that is the kind of love which John is talking about here.

This love in the family of God needs to be exhibited today in the church. I think it is time for many of the churches that have built up a reputation for being fundamental in the faith to now exhibit love among the brethren. I would say that I need that in my own life; I am sure you need more love in your life also.

However, this love is not to slop over. We need to recognize that it has a boundary within the family of God. Along comes one of these heretics, as they did in John's day. He is apostate; he is actually an antichrist; that is, he denies the deity of Christ. John says, "When one of these fellows comes along, you are not to extend love to him. You are not even to entertain him."

OUTLINE

The message of John's second epistle is essential to having a proper perspective of what he has said in his first epistle. He deals here with the polarity of the Christian life—truth and love. He answers the question: When truth and love come into conflict, which is to predominate, which is to have top priority?

LOVE EXPRESSED IN THE BOUNDARY OF TRUTH

The elder unto the elect lady and her children, whom I love in the truth; and not I only, but also all they that have known the truth [2 John 1].

The Second Epistle of John is a personal letter from "the elder unto the elect lady and her children." The Greek word for "elder" is *presbuteros* (presbyter), and it has a twofold meaning. It can mean a senior citizen, referring to age, or it can be a title, referring to an office in the church, a minister or a teacher. I am sure that John is primarily calling himself an elder, speaking of his office in the church. I think he also infers the fact that he is now an old man. He is actually up in his nineties, approaching one hundred, as he writes this epistle. Notice that John does not call upon his office as an apostle. I think the reason is quite obvious: the one to whom he is writing accepts his authority. All he calls himself here is "the elder."

"Unto the elect lady and her children." The word *electa* could be the name of a prominent woman in the church, or it could be the local church itself that John has in mind. "Her children" could be either the physical children of the woman or the spiritual children of the church. These could be interpreted either way. I emphasize the church rather than the individual, applying it to the church at large and the church today. When I say the church, I am not thinking of any local church or any denomination, but the total body of believers in the Lord Jesus Christ. This epistle has been relevant for the church down through the centuries, and what is written here has been very productive in the life of the church. I believe that since our contemporary church has such an emphasis on love, we need this little epistle to cause us to shape up and to get a correct perspective of what love is.

"Whom I love in the truth." The word *truth* is emphasized in this epistle, and as I have said in the Introduction, it is the key word to the epistle. Christian love can only be expressed in the bounds of the family of God, those who have the truth. "The truth" here is the Word of God and also the one who is revealed in the Word, the Lord Jesus Christ Himself. "Whom I love in truth" is the correct, literal translation. John is saying two things here: (1) That the object of his love must be another believer in Christ, a genuine believer; and also (2) that he is genuine in asserting this, that expressing his love is not just a pious platitude he is uttering here.

"And not I only, but also all they that have known the truth." John embraces the rest of the body of believers here. They also love either this church or this particular woman in the church because of her outstanding testimony.

For the truth's sake, which dwelleth in us, and shall be with us for ever [2 John 2].

"For the truth's sake" means a defense of the truth. We need to recognize that the truth needs to be defended. We need to stand for the truth of God and for the Word of God. Many of our so-called conservative men have adopted a very sophisticated and blasé method in an attempt to be clever in what they teach and preach. They will not come out flat-footed and say it just as it is, but they toy around with it and build up some clever alliteration. I'm for alliteration, as you well know, but the point is that the truth needs to be stated clearly.

I had an interesting encounter with a certain teacher several years ago. I was told by a student of his that he didn't believe a certain doctrine, and I quoted him on it. The man became very much irritated with me, which he had a right to be if I were wrong. I told him, "I'd like for you to clarify this. If you will just write me a letter and state clearly what you believe, I'll be very happy to read it and to make my apology." Instead of writing that kind of letter, he wrote a letter in which he made it clear he was highly incensed at me for even suggesting he didn't believe such and such a doctrine. So I wrote to him again and said, "All you have to do to clear this up is just to state clearly what you do believe." At the bottom of the page I wrote, "I believe——" and "I do not believe——" and I left him space for his answer, making it very easy for him to reply. That really irritated him, and I was blasted with another letter. So I dropped the matter and found out later that the reason he didn't answer was because he actually did not believe the doctrine I had questioned him about. But he had attempted to cover up his disbelief. My feeling is that I would respect him for what he believes. Although it is different from what I believe, I would never consider a man to be a heretic or an apostate who believes what he believes. But I cannot respect the fact that his method was and is today never to be clear on exactly what he does believe.

"For the truth's sake, which dwelleth in us, and shall be with us for ever." Thank God, we will have the truth forever. In this day when you can't believe politicians, you can't believe college professors, you can't believe the scientists, and you can't believe the military leadership, it's nice to have someone in whom you can believe—the Lord Jesus Christ. "For the truth's sake, which dwelleth in us"—the indwelling Spirit of God makes these things real to us. "And shall be with us for ever"—the truth will not change; it is unchangeable. Someone has put it like this: "What is true is not new, and what is new is not true." Like a great many generalizations, that has some exceptions to it, of course, but usually it is true.

In verse 3 John adopts a greeting that is a little different from that of Paul and Peter and James and even himself.

Grace be with you, mercy, and peace, from God the Father, and from the Lord Jesus Christ, the Son of the Father, in truth and love [2 John 3].

There are three words here that we need to be clear on in our thinking. They differ without there really being a great difference in the sense that they all apply to the same thing. The words are *love, mercy,* and *grace.* John introduces the word *mercy* here in his greeting.

What is the difference between the love, the mercy, and the grace of God? We read in Ephesians 2:4–5, "But God, who is rich in mercy, for his great love wherewith he loved us, Even when we were dead in sins, hath quickened us together with Christ, (by grace ye are saved;)." This is such a wonderful Scripture because it combines all three: Paul says that God is rich in *mercy,* and because of His great *love* for us, He saves us by *grace.* What is the love of God? Well, God is love. Before anything was created, God was love. Somebody says, "Whom did He love?" Well, the Trinity existed, and we know the love which existed between God the Father and God the Son. Dr. Lewis Sperry Chafer writes, "Love is that in God which existed before He would

care to exercise mercy or grace." Love is the nature of God; it is what is called an attribute of God. God is love, but the interesting thing is that the love of God never saved a sinner. The love of God caused God to move in the direction of mercy and grace; it caused Him to exercise mercy and grace.

Now the question arises: What is the difference between mercy and grace? Dr. Chafer very exactly expresses it: "Mercy, on the other hand, is that in God which duly provided for the need of sinful man." God is rich in mercy. Why is He rich in mercy? Because He is love. And because God is love, He, by mercy, provided for the need of sinful man. But mercy didn't save man. Again, I quote Dr. Chafer: "Grace is that in Him which acts freely to save because all the demands of holiness have been satisfied." God today is free to act in grace. You are a sinner who cannot provide anything for God. You haven't anything to offer to Him. But now grace means that God can come to you, a lost sinner, and say, "I am love, and I am rich in mercy. I love you, and I have provided by My mercy a Savior for you." Now if you will trust Him, "By grace are ye saved through faith; and that not of yourselves: it is the gift of God" (Eph. 2:8).

There is a fine distinction here between these words, and someone will say, "It looks like a distinction without a difference." Well, there is a difference in that which doesn't differ. Salvation all stems from the love of God, but God does not save by His love or His mercy. After all, our God is a holy God, and the Bible says, "For God so loved the world, that he gave his only begotten Son . . ." (John 3:16): You see, God did not so love the world that He saved the world—He didn't do that. God so loved the world that by His mercy He provided a Savior for the world, and He can now save by grace.

There is something else here that is important to see. Salvation is not only the expression of the love of God, but it is also an expression of the justice and righteousness of God. We not only need John 3:16, but we also need Romans 3:26: "To declare, I say, at this time his righteousness: that he might be just, and the justifier of him which believeth in Jesus." In order to justify you when you trust Christ, God has to be righteous and holy and just. He cannot simply open the back door of heaven and slip you in under cover of darkness. You and I are not fit for heaven. We are alienated from Him. We have no fellowship with Him. Communication broke down in the Garden of Eden, and He is the one who renewed it. Because He must be just and righteous, His mercy provided a Savior, and it was because He loves you. He can be righteous and do this—"that he might be just, and the justifier of him which believeth in Jesus."

Therefore, John can now write, "Grace be with you"—that is the way God saves you. "Mercy"—mercy provided a Savior. "And peace"—when you have all this, then the peace of God that passeth all understanding is going to keep your heart. As John said, "For the truth's sake, which dwelleth in us, and shall be with us forever." You will know that these great truths are not something which God is going to change. He is not going to change His mind tomorrow and say, "Well, I'm going to act differently. I think public opinion is going in another direction, so I'll change and go with public opinion." God doesn't change; He is not a weather vane. I am reminded of the farmer who had on his barn a weather vane which said on it, "God is love." A preacher drove up to the farm and said to this man, "Do you mean that God's love is as variable as that weather vane?" The farmer said, "No, I don't mean that. I mean that it does not matter which way the wind is blowing, God is still love." My friend, that is true. Our God is love, and because He is love, He has provided salvation for you. He will never change.

"Grace be with you, mercy, and peace, from God the Father, and from the Lord Jesus Christ." The Lord Jesus Christ is the one who died for you. He is "the Son of the Father"—that is His position in the Trinity.

"In truth and love." Remember that love must be exercised in the context of truth. There are folk who write to me and say, "You are very dogmatic in your teaching." I always appreciate those letters because I am not always sure that I give that impression. I *want* to give that impression when I am teaching the Word of God. I am very dogmatic about it. Now if you ask me what I think I'll be doing this afternoon, I must say that I don't know because my wife hasn't decided yet! I'm not dogmatic about what I am going to do this afternoon. But right now I am writing about 2 John, and I am very dogmatic about what he says here.

I rejoiced greatly that I found of thy children walking in truth, as we have received a commandment from the Father [2 John 4].

"Thy children" are either the physical children of this woman or the members of the local church. I think it could be either, and it probably refers to both. "I rejoiced greatly that I found of thy children walking in truth." "Walking in truth" refers to the manner of life, meaning walking in obedience to the commandments from the Father. It is wonderful to have children who are walking in truth.

"As we have received a commandment from the Father." The commandment is that we walk in the light as He is in the light, that we order our lives by the Word of God.

And now I beseech thee, lady, not as though I wrote a new commandment unto thee, but that which we had from the beginning, that we love one another [2 John 5].

"The beginning" refers to the beginning of the ministry of Christ in His incarnation.

The teaching that the Lord Jesus gave was: "If ye love me, keep my commandments" (John 14:15). He said, "By this shall all men know that ye are my disciples"—not because you are fundamentalists but "if ye have *love* one to another" (John 13:35, italics mine). John says that this is the commandment that we have had from the beginning, that we are to love one another.

Here we have it: walking in truth and loving one another (again, we are talking about loving fellow believers). This is the balance that is needed today in the church, or else any church will become lopsided. We can become oversentimental in the church. There is a lot of sentimental tommyrot going on, and it is as sloppy as can be: "Oh, we love each other. We have the *agape* love"—and all that sort of thing. But are you walking in the truth? Are you really walking in the knowledge of the Word of God? All the apostles emphasized that we are to walk in love. My friend, this is very important in these days in which we live. It's wonderful if you are a fundamentalist—I hope you are— but I hope you are walking in love because you really are not a fundamentalist unless you are.

The objective polarity of the Christian faith and the Christian life is truth and love. John emphasized love in his first epistle, but he also said that that love is for the brethren, it is for believers, it is for those who are in Christ. He said, "My little children, I want you to love one another"—that is, other believers. I do not quite understand this idea of watering down the Christian faith and saying that we are to love everybody, because I know that when you make a statement like that, you *don't* love everybody. It is just impossible to do that. There are too many in this world who are unlovely. A lot of us are unlovely, and, as a result, we are not loved. But God loves the world. We are not worth loving, but God loves us all. The important thing is that He tells believers to take the gospel to the world. *That* is the way that you and I can show our concern and love, if you want to call it that. We are to take the gospel to the lost because God loves them, and then if we take it to them, a love will be begotten in our hearts for those who are actually our enemies. The important thing to see is that God is love—it is His attribute—and His love has provided a Savior for us. But truth is also very important, and you cannot put love above truth, because when you do, then you sacrifice truth. This is John's emphasis in this second epistle.

And this is love, that we walk after his commandments. This is the commandment, That, as ye have heard from the beginning, ye should walk in it [2 John 6].

What is love? It is to walk after His commandments. The Lord said, "If ye love me, keep my commandments" (John 14:15). This is another way of saying the same thing. The Lord's commandments are more than the Ten Commandments. The Ten Commandments are basic to government and basic to civilization, but the Christian is called to a higher plane where he is to produce in his life, by the Spirit (it is the fruit of the Spirit), love, joy, peace, longsuffering, etc. If these things are in us and abide in us, you and I are walking after His commandments. If they are not in us, we are not walking after His commandments.

"And this is love." Let me say it again: Love is not made in the parlor—it is made in the kitchen. Love is not made in the bedroom—it is made out there in the laundry room. Does she wash his clothes? Does he bring home his paycheck? Does he support his family? That is the way you express love in the family, and that is the way you express love in the church—in your concern and in your help for others. You cannot say that you are loving someone unless you have a concern for him, especially a concern for his spiritual welfare.

"And this is love, that we walk after his commandments." Now this is getting right down into shoe leather. This is getting right down where the rubber meets the road. This is sidewalk salvation. It is that which can walk down the street. You must recall that men like John and Paul were writing to people who lived in the Roman world. In Paul's day the emperor was bloody Nero. John saw one emperor after another rise who persecuted the

Christians. Beginning with Titus, the Roman general who destroyed Jerusalem in A.D. 70, the persecution was severe. The Roman world was a brutal world, a cruel world, a world that was pagan to the core. And yet here were men and women who were walking down Roman roads, living in pagan cities, and they were walking after His commandments. They were translating the gospel into life. This is the thing that is desperately needed in our day.

"This is the commandment, That, as ye have heard from the beginning, ye should walk in it." In other words, John is saying, "This thing is not to be put on ice. It is not something to be stored on the shelf. You have heard it from the beginning. The Lord Jesus taught this. Now let's get busy and walk in it. Let's manifest love to those outside."

LIFE IS AN EXPRESSION OF THE DOCTRINE OF CHRIST

Again there arises before us the other end of this polarization: love is on one side, and the truth is on the other. John now issues his warning—

For many deceivers are entered into the world, who confess not that Jesus Christ is come in the flesh. This is a deceiver and an antichrist [2 John 7].

"An antichrist" should read *the* antichrist. John said in his first epistle that already there were many antichrists and that there was the spirit of antichrist. How do we identify the spirit of antichrist? John gives us the answer: "Who confess not that Jesus Christ is come in the flesh." The spirit of antichrist is to deny the deity of Christ. It is to deny everything that is said about Him, everything that He said, and everything that He did for us in redemption by dying on the cross and by being raised bodily from the dead. That is antichrist, and that is the spirit of antichrist.

The spirit of antichrist eventually will be headed up, I believe, not by one man but by two men, because two men are described in Revelation 13. One of these is a great political ruler, an enemy of Christ—he is *against* Christ. The other is a religious ruler who will *imitate* Christ and cause the world to worship the first beast, that is, to worship the political ruler. This is coming in the future, and everything this side of it is preparing the way for the coming of this one; so much so that when the political ruler and the religious ruler finally appear, the world will be ready for them. And it looks to me like the world is almost ready for them right now. To begin with, the political ruler will promise peace in the world, and for three and one-half years, he will do a pretty good job of it—but it is not permanent. It will build up to a mighty catastrophe that is ushered in by the war of Armageddon which will last for approximately three and one-half years until the coming of Christ to the earth to establish His kingdom.

At that time also, there will be one religion, and certainly we are moving in that direction even now. It will be a world religion where they will all pool their thinking. It will be a religion that doesn't really believe anything. There will be nothing to hold them together. We are so often urged today to get rid of that which separates us. My friend, if we get rid of all that separates us, there will not be anything left to hold us together. This is the problem with that type of thing. I am reminded of the story of the little boy who was walking down a jungle trail in Africa, carrying a polka-dot umbrella. He met an elephant who said to him, "Where are you going, little boy?" The little boy said, "I'm not going anywhere," to which the elephant replied, "Well, I'm not either. Let me go with you." That is the kind of church union that is coming about today. They are going nowhere, they believe nothing, and therefore, they can all get together. This is the deceiver who is finally going to come, one to head up religion and one to head up the politics of this world. This is the Antichrist who is to come.

"For many deceivers are entered into the world." Gnosticism was running riot in John's day. Everywhere the gospel has gone, the cults have always followed. The "isms" always follow the preaching of the gospel—they never go before. There were coming along at that time quite a few of what was known as the Gnostic sect which was actually divided into many groups. There were the Cerinthian Gnostics who followed a teacher in Ephesus whose name was Cerinthus. There is a tradition that John, who was the pastor of the Ephesian church, went down to the public bath and saw old Cerinthus taking a bath also. So John got out of the pool, grabbed up his clothes, and didn't put them on until he got outside, because he wouldn't have anything to do with that heretic. Well, that is a tradition and may or may not be true, but it certainly expresses the viewpoint of John in his letter here. The Cerinthian Gnostics correspond to several of the cults today in that they taught that Jesus and Christ were two different entities altogether and that the divine came upon Jesus at His baptism and left Him at the cross. There were also the Docetic Gnostics who denied the reality of the physical body of Christ. They said that the apostles *thought* they saw Jesus, but He actually was not a real person; He was just an appearance. We have a few cults which have picked up that heresy also. This is the reason John said in his first epistle, "We have seen Him. We have heard Him. We've gazed upon Him. We've handled Him. We know what we are talking about, and He was a real man."

Then there were certain Jewish sects in that day, and when Christianity came along, they picked up a great deal of the Christian teachings. Evidently, there was a group of Essenes down at Qumran where they found the Dead Sea Scrolls. And at Masada, which fell in A.D. 73, three years after the fall of Jerusalem, there were about 967 zealots who had also picked up some of the teachings of Christ. Both groups had twisted, distorted, and warped conceptions of the person of Christ.

The thing that John is saying here and which is all-important today is that there are many deceivers who have entered into the world. They seem to have sort of centered right here in Southern California. This is a great incubation center for all kinds of false teachings. I used to say, as I spoke across this country, "I come from a land of flowers, fruits, and nuts—mostly religious nuts. I trust that you folk don't think that I am one of them!" The important thing is that the way you tell one who is true is by his viewpoint, his teaching, his beliefs concerning the person of the Lord Jesus Christ. Unless he thinks rightly of Him, everything else goes down the tube, and that person is a false teacher.

This does not mean that a person cannot hold a different view from what you and I would hold, for example, on election. Election has been a debatable point. John Wesley taught one thing, and John Calvin taught another viewpoint on it. But both of those men believed in the deity of Christ, and when you believe in the deity of Christ, it means you believe in the Virgin Birth, it means you believe the record that we have in the Word of God, and it means you believe in the apostles' doctrine which they taught in their epistles. There was a difference of opinion about election between these two men, but neither of them was a false teacher because both of them agreed on the essentials of the faith.

Let me use just one other illustration in this connection. I graduated and received my B.D. degree from my denominational seminary, as well as having done graduate work at Dallas

Theological Seminary where I received my master's and doctor's degrees. That denominational school was amillennial, and they were dead set against the premillennial position. One of the professors and I became very good friends, and I admired him a great deal. That man could exalt the person of Christ. He could defend the virgin birth, the blood redemption, and the bodily resurrection of Christ in a way that I have heard no other person do. I actually sat in his classroom in tears as I heard him exalt the Lord Jesus. But he simply hated premillennialism. He didn't hate me—he and I were good friends. Because of the fact that he exalted Christ, I never felt we ought to separate or that I ought to break fellowship with him. He was no antichrist. He was a believer. He was an intellectual, and even they are wrong in some things, so I just took it for granted that he was wrong in that particular sphere. I am sure that someday, when he and I get to heaven, we will be in agreement. It may be that both of us will have to change a little relative to our beliefs concerning these secondary matters. I do consider them secondary when you put them down beside the person of Christ. It is what you think of Him that is all-important.

John has emphasized that you are to walk according to the commandments of Christ, and the proof that you are a child of God is that you walk in love for the brethren. Now John has uttered a warning that many deceivers have come into the world. The believer today walks a very dangerous pathway through the world. To the left side of the pathway is the jungle of liberalism and apostasy. It is a beautiful but dangerous jungle because in it are beautiful but dangerous animals which are ready to devour us. I heard recently of a young man who had been in the armed forces and had had a real witness for Christ. But he apparently was lured to a seminary that destroyed his faith. This boy now has gone out into social service work, and his testimony is null and void. He is doing nothing but treading water. My heart goes out to a young fellow like that.

Then, on the opposite side of the pathway, there is a wilderness filled with rattlesnakes. It is the wilderness of extreme fundamentalism which is totally devoid of love. The only thing they think is important is to have the right doctrine. A brother may pat you on the back one day, but the next day, because you do not cross your t's or dot your i's as he does, he will attempt to destroy you by circulating a report in order to nullify your influence. Be-cause of an overweening ambition, he will trample you underfoot. Your reputation is not safe in his hands, and he will exhibit hatred and bitterness rather than love toward you.

I have been in active Christian service since 1930, and I've met some of the great men of this century, giants of the faith who preached the truth. None of these men ever attempted to separate brethren or to dull the effectiveness of another's ministry by some slurring gossip. May I say to you, these men were great men, not only in doctrine but also in their lives. I have learned over the years that God's men who stand for the truth and who preach the Word of God, by and large, are men upon whom you can depend and who are very gracious in every manner.

I remember hearing this story of the late Dr. Harry Ironside when he was holding a conference at one of the prominent conference centers across this country. Some people go to these summer conferences for just one purpose, and that is to compare one speaker to another speaker and to try to set up some sort of conflict between them. I was told that a man came to Dr. Ironside at this conference and said to him, "Dr. Ironside, Dr. So-and-so was here last week and said such and such. But today you said the very opposite thing. Now which is correct?" The man was mentioning a minor point of doctrine. It was nothing vital but was simply a difference of opinion. All of us have differences of opinion, but we can differ without being disagreeable. So Dr. Ironside said to the man, "Well, I didn't know that Brother So-and-so taught that. That's quite interesting. Maybe I should look into it. I could be wrong." And then he walked away. The man stood there with his mouth open, because he surely couldn't get an argument there! May I say to you, I am confident that Dr. Ironside didn't feel that he was wrong, but he at least shut up that brother and kept him from trying to drive a wedge between brethren. This is the thing that, in my judgment, is actually more dangerous than liberalism.

I can spot a liberal, and I can say truthfully that I do not associate or fellowship with them. I have nothing in common with them. At one time, I was accused falsely by extreme fundamentalists of fellowshiping with a certain bishop during an evangelistic campaign here in Southern California. The truth is that I never even met the man. I had no reason to. He and I were in two different spheres of activity altogether, and I had no fellowship with him. But I have found that the most dangerous ones for me are the extreme fundamentalists. I would say that I am more afraid of them. They prattle pious platitudes and claim that they have the truth. But woe unto the man who disagrees with them on minor matters, especially the matter of separation, as if that were the all-important issue. Their priorities are not doctrine but assassination of character and name-calling on the lowest level. I have met both ministers and members of churches who frighten me more than a rattlesnake. The venom of bitterness and jealousy and hatred was dripping from their mouths as they feigned their love and devotion to Christ and to the truth. The great message of 2 John is that truth walks in shoe leather, and if it does not, it is dangerous. My friend, we need to be very careful of both extremes of the spectrum of faith today.

John says that the way you are going to tell if one is not a child of God is: "Whosoever doeth not righteousness is not of God, neither he that loveth not his brother" (1 John 3:10). Love and righteousness are the two manifestations of a child of God. We are to be aware of those who are not believers, the deceivers who deny the deity of Christ. John is saying that if you deny the deity of Christ, you are not a Christian. You may be religious, but you are not a Christian—let's understand that. After all, *Christian* means one who is a follower of Christ, one who believes in Him. You cannot be a follower of Christ unless you believe in His virgin birth, unless you believe in His deity, His miraculous life, and His work of redemption upon the cross.

Look to yourselves, that we lose not those things which we have wrought, but that we receive a full reward [2 John 8].

You do not lose your salvation when you have fellowship with the wrong folk—we need to understand that very clearly—but you do put yourself in a dangerous position. It does mean that the minute you and I identify ourselves with a cult or go off into this type of thing which denies the deity of Christ, we have lost our reward. There will be no reward for a believer who has done this.

Every believer ought to be working for a reward, to be able to hear Him say someday, "Well done, thou good and faithful servant" (see Matt. 25:21). At the end of his life, Paul was able to say, "I have fought a good fight, I have finished my course, I have kept the faith: Henceforth there is laid up for me a crown of righteousness, which the Lord, the righteous judge, shall give me at that day . . ." (2 Tim.

4:7–8). During his life, he wasn't sure of it, for he said that he didn't want to be disapproved when he came into the presence of Christ. Therefore, it will behoove us to be very careful not to be taken in by deceivers.

Whosoever transgresseth, and abideth not in the doctrine of Christ, hath not God. He that abideth in the doctrine of Christ, he hath both the Father and the Son [2 John 9].

The word *transgresseth* is a very interesting word. In the Greek it is *proagō*. *Agō* means "to go"; *pro* means "before." *Proagō* means "to go before or to go ahead." Therefore, the meaning here is not so much to transgress as to go farther than is right. This is the meaning that Thayer gives in his Greek lexicon of the New Testament—to go farther than is right. "Whosoever goes farther than is right, that is, goes to some extreme." This is what the Gnostics claimed for themselves. The word *gnosis* means "knowledge." The Gnostics claimed to have a little more knowledge than anyone else, something that made them super-duper saints. There are a few saints in that category today; they feel that they have something the rest of us don't have. Every now and then, I get a letter from some person who tells me I'm lacking somehow. I recognize that I am, but I don't feel they are the ones to tell me because they tell it from the viewpoint that *they* have it and I don't. They feel like they are super-duper, and they manifest no love for the brethren, which means they are not abiding in the doctrine of Christ. This is the thing that characterizes them.

In my Southland there were a group of people when I was a boy who were known as Holy Rollers. I attended several of their meetings when I was a young fellow just for the entertainment of watching them roll, and they actually rolled. Yet they preached the gospel, and many of them were real believers. Bishop Moore of the old Southern Methodist church was at a conference of Methodist preachers where he was approached by a young country preacher who asked, "Bishop Moore, do you think the Holy Rollers will go to heaven?" The bishop replied, "They will if they don't run past the place!" It seems to me that that is the condition of which John is speaking here: Whosoever goes farther than is right, whoever becomes an extremist "and abideth not in the doctrine of Christ, hath not God."

I was reading sometime ago about several theologians in the East who met with a group of preachers. Together they came to the conclusion that they no longer needed to answer the fundamentalists on the question of the virgin birth of Christ or the deity of Christ or whether Christ died for our sins. They feel like they have graduated from that. They have become highly intellectual, totally sanctified, and have reached the *summum bonum* of life. They are now up at the apex, looking down on all the rest of us poor folk who believe in the deity of Christ and His death for our sins. To my judgment they have transgressed, abide not in the doctrine of Christ, and have not God. No wonder they came to the conclusion that God was dead! But He wasn't dead. They were dead—"dead in trespasses and sins" (see Eph. 2:1). "Whosoever transgresseth, and abideth not in the doctrine of Christ, hath not God."

"He that abideth in the doctrine of Christ, he hath both the Father and the Son." If you are abiding in the doctrine of Christ, you have God the Father, and you have God the Son, and you have access to the Father through the Son. We have access to God through Christ, by His marvelous, infinite grace if we abide in the doctrine of Christ.

The word *abide* means "to remain"—this is a permanent arrangement. Someone told me that he had asked a liberal preacher in Los Angeles years ago what he thought about me. This liberal preacher is an outstanding man, a very fine man in many ways. I have always respected him because he is one of the few honest liberals I have met. He just came out and said that he believed practically nothing, and he stuck by his guns. I simply feel he should not be in the ministry. He is sort of like a man selling Fuller brushes who doesn't have any brushes to sell. This liberal preacher said, "Well, I respect McGee and his viewpoint. The thing is that it's old-fashioned, and he hasn't changed it in years. He apparently hasn't grown a bit." May I say to you, that is about the nicest compliment the man could have returned to me because I haven't changed and I intend for it to be that way. John is saying here that he who abides in the doctrine of Christ, who remains in it and doesn't change, has both the Father and the Son.

If there come any unto you, and bring not this doctrine, receive him not into your house, neither bid him God speed [2 John 10].

I cannot think of a stronger statement than this. We need to recall the background of this letter again. John is writing to "the elect lady," who may have been an outstanding woman in the church, noted for her hospitality. Apparently, she is a woman of means who can entertain guests lavishly. She is very generous. Evidently, some of these Gnostics came by, and she entertained them. Then she was under conviction about it, and she wrote to John. What should she do in a case like that? Should she entertain them? She would feel badly if she turned them away. What really should be her attitude toward an apostate, toward a heretic, toward one who denies the deity of Christ but pretends to be a follower of Christ? Should she entertain him in her home?

We need to understand also that there were no Howard Johnson motels or Holiday Inns or Hilton Hotels or Ramada Inns in the Roman Empire. The little inns that they had were pretty bare places to stay. An inn was not even a place where you got a bed. You had to bring your own bed with you. All you did was rent a space to put down your little mat or pad on which you would sleep. Maybe there were people sleeping on both sides of you, at your head, and down at your feet—all around you. That was the method for travelers in that day. So the homes of believers were always open to traveling evangelists and Bible teachers in the days of the early church. When these men would arrive in a town, there would always be some home where they would be entertained. Remember how Paul stayed in the home of Aquila and Priscilla when he was in Corinth? That was the method in the early church and the general practice of the day.

I can remember when I was a boy in our little town in west Texas that my mother would invite a visiting preacher to come for dinner and sometimes to spend the night. My dad never liked that, I can tell you. He was not a believer, and he didn't care to have a preacher for dinner or to have him spend the night. We were poor folk, and so the preacher didn't get lavish entertainment. But he would usually get fried chicken, and my mother really knew how to fry chicken. That was the practice in our little town. Even up to this day, the Holiday Inn hasn't gotten there; in fact, there isn't a motel of any kind or description there. In that day the preacher was entertained in the home, but today my recommendation to you is to entertain him in a motel or hotel. That would be the proper way to do it today. The average minister needs a great deal of privacy for study and prayer, and he cannot get it when he is entertained in a home. However, I must say that there are a few homes across this country that I have always enjoyed going into, because I can make myself at home and I feel at home there. They just let me do what I need and want to do, and it is a joy to be there.

This woman to whom John is writing is a woman of hospitality, and she has this question about entertaining false teachers. John lays it on the line here: "If there come any unto you, and bring not this doctrine, receive him not into your house, neither bid him God speed."

Now John says something else that ought to alert everyone of us today—

For he that biddeth him God speed is partaker of his evil deeds [2 John 11].

If you entertain a false teacher, if you support him, you are a partner with him in his deeds. This is the reason that you ought to investigate everything that you give to as a Christian, because if you are giving to the wrong thing, God considers you a partner in it.

The Lord Jesus gave a parable in this connection in which he told about a man who was working for another man and was about to be fired (see Luke 16:1–13). The man called in all his employer's creditors and offered them a discount if they would pay their bills, which they, of course, were glad to accept. He did this so that after he was fired he would be able to appeal to them for help since he had helped them. That was crooked—our Lord did not say it was right; He made it clear that it was wrong. He said, "The children of this world are in their generation wiser than the children of light." They are clever out yonder in the business world. There's many a man trying to make a fast buck today. It is a case of dog-eat-dog. Therefore, if the man in the world is wise about the way he invests his money and the way he uses his money, what about you, Christian friend? Are you moved by some sentimental story, and do you give because of that? Are you moved by a picture of a few orphans, of little children in foreign countries? Do you *know* that your money is getting to them? Are you motivated today by sentiment? If you are a partner in that which denies the deity of the

Lord Jesus Christ and all that He is and stands for and all that He did for us, if you are supporting that sort of thing, God will hold you responsible for it. He said that the children of the world are wiser than we are. We ought to get smart. We ought to wise up to this and not be taken in by it. Charity has become a big racket today. Collecting money under false pretenses is one of the biggest rackets there is. This is the reason I sometimes mention that I haven't yet started an orphans' home for stray cats in the Aleutian Islands! In fact, I don't know whether there are any cats up there or not. My business is giving out the Word of God, and I hope this is your business, too.

PERSONAL GREETING

Having many things to write unto you, I would not write with paper and ink: but I trust to come unto you, and speak face to face, that our joy may be full.

The children of thy elect sister greet thee. Amen [2 John 12–13].

In other words, John says, "I can tell it better than I can write it." David said the same thing, ". . . my tongue is the pen of a ready writer" (Ps. 45:1). When David began to write that wonderful forty-fifth psalm, a psalm of praise to Christ, he simply said, "I wish I could *tell* it to you. I can *say* it better than I can write it." This is the reason I love the radio ministry. I can say it lots better than I can write it.

"The children of thy elect sister greet thee. Amen." Apparently, they were children of a sister of this elect lady, or it was a sister church sending greetings to this lady and to the local church there.

This is a tremendous little letter, and its message ought to alert every believer today.

(For Bibliography to 2 John, see Bibliography at the end of 3 John.)

The Third Epistle of
JOHN
INTRODUCTION

The writer of this little epistle is John the apostle. I rather facetiously call this epistle "three-eyed John" because a very fine black preacher whom I knew years ago in the South called John's epistles "one-eyed John," "two-eyed John," and "three-eyed John." I don't know of a better way of remembering these epistles than this. This epistle, therefore, is "three-eyed John."

It is now the belief of some expositors that John wrote these epistles last—after he wrote the Book of Revelation. I'm rather inclined to agree with that viewpoint. This means that these epistles were written close to the end of the first century, somewhere between A.D. 90–100, but it would be very difficult to date them exactly. John probably wrote all three epistles very close together. I don't think there would be much difference in time from one epistle to the other.

In his first epistle, John emphasizes the fact that the family of God is held together by love and that the little children are to love one another. He makes it very clear that if they don't love one another, they are not God's children. Children have a love for those who are in their family—that is the normal thing even in natural relationships down here on this earth.

In the second epistle, however, John puts up a tremendous warning that there are apostates, there are many antichrists, and there are many deceivers in the world. He says that a child of God is not to love them. We are not to be concerned with their welfare in the sense of entertaining them in our homes. The child of God is to keep a very close account and to make sure that those he entertains, those he supports, are true to the Word of God; that is, that they believe in the deity of Christ, that they believe that He is God manifest in the flesh. John wrote, "And the Word was made flesh . . ." (John 1:14). He had already said that the Word was God. Therefore, Jesus Christ is God manifest in the flesh. He is God dwelling, tabernacling in human flesh. Until a

person believes that, he doesn't have a Savior. If Jesus Christ is just a man and that is all that He is, we do not have a Savior. There is no reason to remember His birth and no reason to remember His death or resurrection if He is just a man. It is all-important to recognize that He is God manifest in the flesh and that His work on the cross was a work that has power to save us. There is power in the blood because of who He is and because He died and rose again bodily. Those who deny these truths are not to be extended the fellowship or the support of the church. John goes so far in the second epistle as to say that believers are not to even bid such a person Godspeed. John said not to help him on his way or give him support. If you do, you are a partaker of his evil deeds, and you are a partner with him. Therefore, it behooves a child of God to know whom he supports.

As we come now to the third epistle, there is a similarity to John's second letter in some ways. It is very personal in character, and it carries the same theme of truth. Truth again is presented as all-important. When truth and love come into conflict, truth must survive. This means that you are not to love the false teacher. Walking in truth is all-important.

However, this third letter differs from the second in other ways. As you will note from the Outline which follows, this epistle deals with personalities. Also, in the second epistle, John says that the truth is worth standing for, but in this third epistle, John's emphasis is that the truth is worth working for. Someone has put it like this: "My life in God—that's salvation. My life with God—that's communion and fellowship. But my life for God—that's service." This epistle deals with my life for God, and it has to do with walking and working in the truth. Love can become very sloppy; it can become misdirected, and it certainly can be misunderstood if it is not expressed within the boundary of truth.

OUTLINE

Years ago I preached a sermon on the subject, "You Will Find Them in the Yellow Pages," in which I dealt with two men from this little epistle of 3 John—Diotrephes and Demetrius—and with Demas whom Paul spoke of in 2 Timothy 4:10 (see also Col. 4:14; Philem. 23–24). Demas had been a fellow laborer with Paul but had deserted the work; he loved the world and departed from Paul. My sermon was about Demas, Diotrephes, and Demetrius—each of their names begins with a *D*. I probably should have included Gaius who is also mentioned in this epistle—and if his name had been *Daius*, I'm sure I would have!

Modern advertising tells us that we can always find it in the Yellow Pages. It does not matter whether you want to purchase an aardvark or a zebra, an atom splitter or a zymometer, an abacus or a zygote, you will find it in the Yellow Pages. If we could get ahold of the Yellow Pages of the Roman Empire in the first century, we would probably find these men listed there. However, we do find them in the Word of God, and they give us the answer to some very interesting questions: How did the believers of the first century make out? How were they holding out at the close of the first century? Did they all become martyrs? Were they all paragons of virtue? Were they all worthy followers of Christ? Were they worthy examples of the faith? Among the millions who turned to Christ in the first three centuries, how did the average believer turn out? Well, here in this epistle we find two who were outstanding men of God—Gaius and Demetrius. These men really stood for the faith of God. We also find one who was not outstanding. Diotrephes was not standing at all; he was doing anything but standing for the truth.

GAIUS—A DELIGHTFUL BROTHER

The elder unto the well-beloved Gaius, whom I love in the truth [3 John 1].

"The elder." As he did in the second epistle, John adopts the term *elder*. It could refer to his age. He is in his nineties, and certainly he is a presbyter, an elder, in the sense of age. He is a senior citizen at this time. Also, *elder* speaks of an officer in the early church, and certainly John could claim that. In fact, he could have claimed more. He could have said, "I am an apostle," but he doesn't do that. Gaius is a friend, and you don't write that way to your friend. At least, I don't write that way to very personal friends. I write to several fellows with whom I was in school and who are old men now—I'm the only one who has managed to stay young, but they've gotten old! I call each one of them by his first name, and when I sign my name, I don't mention the title *Doctor* at all—those fellows would laugh at me. I simply write my name, Vernon or Mac. I was called Mac when I was in college and seminary. I go by that appellation, and so I just sign that way. John is writing to a personal friend, and he simply says, "The elder unto the well-beloved Gaius."

"Unto the well-beloved Gaius"—I love that. John's letter is addressed to a believer in the early church by the name of Gaius. Gaius was a beloved brother in the church. Four times John calls him "beloved" (vv. 1, 2, 5, 11). John knows and loves him in the Lord, and he now writes a letter to this brother who apparently is in some local church.

"Whom I love in the truth." Immediately we are told that Gaius is sound in doctrine. He accepted the deity of Christ. Gaius is a man who stood for the truth, and he not only stood for the truth but he also worked for the truth. Here is a man who walked and worked in love. He manifested love. You have to think right if you are going to act right—that is true in any sphere of life today.

Beloved, I wish above all things that thou mayest prosper and be in health, even as thy soul prospereth [3 John 2].

"Beloved"—John evidently thought a great deal of Gaius and was very close to him since, again, he calls him "beloved."

"I wish above all things that thou mayest prosper and be in health." Very frankly, John makes it clear that he wants Gaius to prosper not only financially (he apparently was a man of means), but John also says, "I want you to prosper in your health." Evidently, Gaius was not a well man.

"Even as thy soul prospereth." And John wanted him to prosper also in his soul, to grow spiritually. There are a lot of Christians today who are sick spiritually. They have good health physically, but they have pretty bad health spiritually. It is certainly well for a child of God to have both. Good health physically is wonderful to have—many of us didn't appreciate it until we lost it. And it is important to have good health spiritually. What physical health is to the body, holiness is to the spiritual life of the believer. To be healthy spiritually is holiness; it is to be growing in grace and in the knowledge of Christ.

There were traveling around in that day many men who were teaching the Word of God and doing missionary work. Gaius would open his home to them and entertain them. He was not only a largehearted man, he not only walked in love, but he also walked in truth, and he tested these teachers. And in spite of his poor health, he was able to be very active in hospitality.

For I rejoiced greatly, when the brethren came and testified of the truth that is in thee, even as thou walkest in the truth [3 John 3].

Many of these traveling evangelists and missionaries reported to John the graciousness of Gaius and his walk in the truth. They said, "When you go to the church where Gaius is one of the leaders, you will find he is a very wonderful man. He is not only a man of means but also a very generous man. I was entertained in his home." In that day they didn't put the traveling preacher in a Howard Johnson's or a Ramada Inn because there weren't any. If there had been, I believe they would have put him there. But generally, the little inns in the Roman Empire were flea-bitten places, dirty, and sometimes very sinful; so the custom of that day was to entertain these men in homes.

"For I rejoiced greatly, when the brethren came and testified of the truth that is in thee, even as thou walkest in the truth." This is the testimony that other brethren gave concerning Gaius. This was their judgment of him. "The truth" is actually the doctrine and the teaching of the apostles. The article should be omitted: "walkest in truth." This refers not only to doctrine but also to his conduct. The mark of the believer is to walk in truth. Truth is that which is dominant. The *summum bonum* for the Christian is whether or not he is walking in the truth and walking in the light. It isn't how you walk but where you walk that is important. Are you walking in the truth? Walking in the truth also means walking in the right conduct or walking in love of the brethren.

Those who were out in a teaching ministry in the early church would come to Gaius' town and to his church, and they would find that his home was wide open to true brethren. Gaius had a spiritual discernment. He could tell who were the genuine believers and who were not. After all, all you need to do is to make sure about a man's relationship to the person of Jesus Christ.

What think ye of Christ? is the test
To try both your state and your scheme.
You cannot be right in the rest
Unless you think rightly of Him.
　　　　　　　　—Author unknown

You must think rightly of Him in order to be right in everything else. These brethren testified, "Brother Gaius tested us out. He found out whether we believed in the deity of Christ. He found out whether we believed in the Virgin Birth and whether we believed that Christ died a redemptive death upon the cross and was raised bodily from the grave. When he found out that we did believe these things, he opened his home and received us and discovered that we also had a love for the brethren. And then his heart was open to us." What a marvelous testimony Gaius had!

I have no greater joy than to hear that my children walk in truth [3 John 4].

This is a great comfort. This is wonderful encouragement. "I have no greater joy than to hear that my children walk in truth." John had been the pastor of the church in Ephesus and had led many to the Lord. It is a great joy to him, now that he is an old man, to hear that his converts, scattered out over the area of Asia, are still walking in truth. Here again "walking in truth" means walking in right doctrine and in love for the brethren—his children manifested these things.

It is a great joy to me today to get letters from those who were led to the Lord over the years of my ministry. They say, "We are still walking in the truth," and perhaps they tell about how they are in a Bible church and are attempting to serve the Lord. That brings joy to my heart. When I hear of young ministers who used to be in my classes and who are now standing for the truth, that brings joy to the heart. My daughter is like a great many other young people today. She thinks her dad is just a little old fogy, more or less a back number. The other day she went out to hear a young man whom I had the privilege of teaching. After she and her husband had gone to hear him, she came back to tell me how wonderful he was and what a glorious message he brought. She told me what the message was as if it was something I had never heard before. It did sound strangely familiar, but I never said anything to my daughter—I just listened as she told me how wonderful it was. Then she said, "You know, Dad, you may not be able to speak to young people today, but he is able to speak to young people, and they listen to him. His church is filled with young people." Well, I couldn't help but smile. I didn't really want to tell her that that fellow's message just happened to be one of my messages. I was glad that he gave it. I am sure that my daughter has heard me give it, but it didn't mean anything when Dad gave it because I'm an old fogy. But this young, sharp boy put in a lot of new words that young people use today that aren't a part of my vocabulary, and of all things, it is just a brand-new message! Do you think I feel badly over that? You do not know what great joy that brought to me in my heart. I know exactly how John felt. John says, "I have no greater joy than to hear that my children walk in truth." Isn't that wonderful? You cannot help but rejoice in that, especially when you have come to the sundown period of life and you know that your future is no longer ahead of you. My future is behind me, and I rejoice in these young preachers who are coming along. And to feel that maybe I had a little part in their training and to know that young people are crowding in to hear them is a wonderful thing.

Beloved, thou doest faithfully whatsoever thou doest to the brethren, and to strangers [3 John 5].

Gaius was evidently one of the children of John, one of John's converts. His conduct conforms to his doctrine, and it is marvelous when that takes place.

From verse 5 to 8, John commends Gaius for having received and entertained the true teachers of the Word. Let me draw the contrast: In 2 John the apostle warns against receiving false teachers, but in 3 John he encourages the believers to receive the true brethren. Just because you have been deceived and stung for awhile ought not to keep you from receiving the true brethren. I know a lady who supports our radio ministry in a very wonderful way. She is down on the church, and I recently found out why. She happens to be a widow and a very attractive person. She went to a couple of churches where the pastors made a pass at her. Believe me, that turned her off, and she now has nothing to do with the church. Frankly, I have urged her to get into a good Bible church where there are real men of God who will not be doing that sort of thing. Many of us have been disappointed and deceived by false brethren, but we should not let that deter us

from supporting that which we believe is of the Lord. This woman gives support only to radio ministries today. Very frankly, I think she's wrong. I don't think she is wrong to support radio—don't misunderstand me—but I do feel that one or two sour experiences ought not to sour you against the church.

John tells us in his second epistle that many deceivers have gone out into the world. Why not be like Gaius and have a little discernment? Don't support anything—including a church or a radio ministry—until you are sure that it is of God. Be sure that the Word of God is being given out. Be sure that they love the brethren (and that they don't love the "sistern" too much!). John is talking about things that are very practical today. He is really getting down to the nitty-gritty, right down where the rubber meets the road, right down where the ball hits the bat. He is encouraging Gaius to support the true brethren in the Lord.

Which have borne witness of thy charity before the church: whom if thou bring forward on their journey after a godly sort, thou shalt do well [3 John 6].

These brethren would return from a trip to John's church. I have a notion that when they came together for the purpose of worship, John would say, "Well, I see Brother So-and-so. He's been out evangelizing, and we'd like to have a word from him. We'd like to have a report as to how the Lord led him and how the Lord blessed him." Brother So-and-so would get up and give his report, and he would say, "When I came to this place, there was a brother there by the name of Gaius, and he is a choice servant of God. He opened his home to me, but he doesn't do that for everybody because he certainly examined me. He made an inspection of me to make sure I was teaching the Word of God. He wanted to know whether or not I believed the Word of God and whether or not I was walking in love. He tested me and found that I was, and then he just opened up his heart and home to me, and we had wonderful fellowship." Now John is writing to Gaius, and he says, "I have heard this now from several, and I want you to know how much it delights my heart."

"Whom if thou bring forward on their journey after a godly sort, thou shalt do well." In the second epistle, John says that if you bid Godspeed to false teachers, you are a partaker with them, you are guilty of their deeds. But now he says that if you help those who are giving out the Word of God and who are walking in love, you do well. This is actually something you *should* be doing. Why?—

Because that for his name's sake they went forth, taking nothing of the Gentiles [3 John 7].

John writes to Gaius, "These brethren went forth, trusting the Lord, and you opened up your home to them. They are genuine, they are real, and you received them." These men went out at great sacrifice. They didn't receive a salary; they didn't receive any remuneration. They went out trusting the Lord, and homes were opened to them. In some places they were given support; in other places they were not.

"Taking nothing of the Gentiles." This, my friend, is another way of testing that which is genuine or not. Are you supporting something that is simply a religious racket for money, something that is trying to get every Tom, Dick, and Harry to donate to the cause? Or is it a work of the Lord that depends on the Lord's people? John says that these true men would take nothing of the Gentiles, that is, from unbelievers.

I always try to make it clear on our radio broadcast that we are just asking believers to support the program. If an unbeliever is listening, we'd rather he not give. We hope he listens; we hope he sends for the literature, but very frankly, I do not really believe God can bless what an unbeliever gives. We believe the scriptural method is to ask only believers to give. These men went forth, taking nothing from the Gentiles. They would not appeal to unbelievers to give to the Lord's work. I know there are many who disagree, but I do not believe that unbelievers should be asked to support the Lord's work. As the ark went through the wilderness, it was carried on the shoulders of the Israelite priests. They could not even put it on a cart. God said that the priests were to carry it. And God's priests today are His believers. Every believer is a priest, and you and I are to carry the Lord Jesus Christ into this world today. Therefore, we do not ask unbelievers to give, but we do ask believers to give—especially those who not only believe in Christ but who also believe that we are giving out the Word of God today. And we do not apologize for asking believers to give because we believe that the Lord's work is to be carried forward in this method.

We therefore ought to receive such, that we might be fellow-helpers to the truth [3 John 8].

In other words, you would be a partner with these men if you opened your home to them, if you supported them and helped them on their way. In the second epistle, John warns "the elect lady" not to receive apostates into her home because if she does, she is a partner with them in their evil deeds. Now that warning might cause someone just to shut his home and not receive true brethren either; that is, some might shut up their homes to all who might come in order to make sure that they did not entertain false teachers. But John says, "Wait just a minute. If they are men walking in the light, if they are men walking in love, and if they are men who have the life of God within them, you should receive them." I think you can tell when a man is speaking by the Holy Spirit. I am sure there was better discernment in the early church than there is in the church today. I am confident that, although we may know more Bible than they did, we certainly do not have the spiritual discernment that they did. But when a man is distinguished as being a man of God who is doing God's work, he should be supported. "That we might be fellow-helpers to the truth." When Gaius helped them along, he became a partner with them in getting out the Word of God.

DIOTREPHES—A DICTATOR

Gaius was such a wonderful fellow, one of those choice saints in the early church. You could wish that all of the men in the early church were like that, but I am sorry to have to report that they were not. We come now to another man, Diotrephes, and this is what John has to say of him—

I wrote unto the church: but Diotrephes, who loveth to have the preeminence among them, receiveth us not [3 John 9].

John wrote a pentateuch of the New Testament (just as Moses wrote the Pentateuch of the Old Testament); John wrote a gospel, the Revelation, and three epistles. That makes five books—he wrote a pentateuch. If it is true that John wrote his epistles after the Book of the Revelation, this epistle is his swan song. It was written toward the close of the first century, and by that time, many wonderful believers had been brought into the truth and into the church. We might wonder how they got along. Were they all paragons of virtue? Were they all outstanding men of God? Were they worthy followers of Christ? Well, there were some like Gaius, real men of God, men of courage, outstanding men who stood for the things of God. However, there were also men like this man Diotrephes. He is a very different type of individual from Gaius. The thing that marks Diotrephes is that he loved to have the preeminence. Gaius is the delightful brother, but Diotrephes is the dictator. It is said that he even opposed the apostle John. John had written to this church to receive certain men, among whom was an outstanding preacher of the gospel, one of those unknown saints of God, whose name was Demetrius, but this man Diotrephes would not receive him. As I have mentioned previously, the early Christians practiced hospitality. Peter mentions it in 1 Peter 4:9, "Use hospitality one to another without grudging." Paul also talks about it in 1 Timothy 5:9–10; Romans 12:13; and Titus 1:8. I do not know whether Diotrephes was a preacher or a layman in his church, but he would not even open his home to any of these men whom John had recommended. The reason is that he loved to have the preeminence. His motto was "to rule or ruin." He was going to have his own way, and it did not make any difference what the result might be.

In verse 8 John urged, "We therefore ought to receive such, that we might be fellow-helpers to the truth." May I say to you, there is a real compulsion today upon the child of God to support those who are giving out the Word of God. If you have a preacher who is doing that, you should support him. That was the practice in the early church.

Diotrephes is a man who puts on airs. He is pretentious. He is vainglorious. He struts around as a peacock. He has an overweening ambition. He is puffed up, inflated like a balloon. He is one whom you have to receive with a flourish of trumpets. He comes in in a blaze of glory. That's Diotrephes. John will bring five charges against him: (1) He must occupy the leading place in the church; (2) he actually refused to receive John; (3) he made malicious statements against the apostles; (4) he refused to entertain the missionaries, the ones who were traveling through the country (and the reason obviously is that he wanted to do the speaking and teaching himself); and (5) he excommunicated those who did entertain the missionaries. In other words, Diotrephes wanted to be the first exalted ruler of the church. Woe unto you if you attempted to oppose him. If he was a layman, I sure feel sorry for his pastor. I am of the opinion he tried to keep his pastor under his thumb in order that he could preside. He wanted to be the one to

be heard. Diotrephes was a man who was self-opinionated. He was self-exalting instead of self-effacing. I am sure that he would have claimed to have been a self-made man instead of having let the Holy Spirit make him over. He was self-sufficient, and I think he was guilty of self-admiration also. He was self-willed, self-satisfied, and self-confident. He felt that he could do all the teaching and preaching and that he did not need these other men to come and minister.

As I am saying all of this, I wonder if you recognize this fellow. In many churches today, there are men like Diotrephes, men who want to run the church. I am no longer a pastor of a church, and I can say frankly what I think and what I know to be true. I'm not speaking of any theory whatsoever but of what I know from experience over the years. I have met men who, although they put up a very pious front, have tried to run the church. I have known men like that in churches I have served but, thank the Lord, I never had much trouble with them. Sometimes it is a little clique which will do anything in order to rule. I have watched such people wreck church after church—a little group or an individual like Diotrephes who loves to have the preeminence.

I am going to say something now that may be very harsh. There are many men who may mean well but who enjoy leading in the church. They enjoy being up before a group of people. For the most part, the ones I have met are almost Bible ignoramuses—they know very little about the Word of God. But they love to talk, and their talk has actually sometimes caused me to bow my head in shame as I was sitting there on the platform. Some of the things they say are totally unscriptural, totally beside the point, and dead as a doornail. Then they wonder why their church is losing members. They wonder why people are not coming. It is very evident why. There are many who ought to keep quiet in the church. Remember that Paul said, "Study to be quiet" (see 1 Thess. 4:11). Instead of trying to teach young people to talk, we ought to teach them to keep quiet because we have many older ones today who talk too much. My friend, we ought not to talk in church unless we have something to say, unless we have something *from God* to say.

Many folk want to be up front in church. Not only have I met Diotrephes, but I have also met Mrs. Diotrephes in the church today. May I say that there are certain people who ought not to sing solos in the church. They do not bring glory to God, and sometimes they select songs which absolutely hurt the service rather than help it. My friend, you ought to search your heart before God before you stand up in the church and begin to sing or talk. Some soloists like to make a little talk before they sing a song. Many times the message they bring is just about as phony as anything can be. They want to tell you why they are going to sing that particular song. Why not just sing the song? If the song has a message, that is all the message a soloist needs to give.

I say all this because I am deeply concerned. I once had the opportunity to observe the moviemakers out here in Hollywood as they worked on the filming of a scene. When I got tired of watching and left, they had already shot that one scene *fifteen* times, and they were still working on it! I thought as I left, *Oh, if only God's people would work as hard to do everything in the church service to bring glory to the name of Christ!* It all deserves the best we've got, my friend.

All of us need to search our hearts—even the ministers. Why are you presiding? Why are you leading? Why do you sing? Do you love to have the preeminence? Are you doing this for the glory of God? Certainly we need somebody to preside. We need somebody to sing a solo. We need somebody to teach the Word. Many are needed, but search your heart before you do anything because you can wreck a church if you are one like Diotrephes who loves to have the preeminence.

Mrs. McGee and I were ministering in a certain church where they did not have a pastor at the time. When we left after the service, she said to me concerning the man who presided, "He certainly did enjoy presiding, didn't he?" I replied, "Yes, he loved it, and I'm wondering whether they *really* are seeking for a pastor with that man presiding." He was not only presiding, he was killing the church. The attendance was way down. I felt very sorry for the pastor who would come to the church because he certainly was going to have trouble with that individual.

John now says that he is going to deal with this problem—

Wherefore, if I come, I will remember his deeds which he doeth, prating against us with malicious words: and not content therewith, neither doth he himself receive the brethren, and forbiddeth them that would, and casteth them out of the church [3 John 10].

"Wherefore, if I come"—I do not think this is the *if* of doubt. We shall see at the end of the epistle that John intends to come and he is coming. But we never know what a day will bring forth. John says, "If I come," in the sense of, "If something should come up, if something should happen, I might be unable to make the trip." But his intentions are to come. There is no doubt in his mind about that.

"I will remember his deeds which he doeth." In Christianity, the important word is *truth*, and truth manifests itself in love—it is just as simple as that and as important as that. Diotrephes loved to have the preeminence which, by the way, is a characteristic of the flesh. The fruit of the Spirit is meekness, but Diotrephes was a dictator. Meekness does not necessarily mean weakness or cowardice. Someone has said, "Silence is golden, but sometimes it is yellow." It is too bad there weren't those in the church who spoke out against Diotrephes. Moses was considered a meek man, but when he got up and talked to the children of Israel, he didn't sound like a meek man according to our notion of meekness. He spoke with the authority God had given him. The Lord Jesus was meek and lowly, but He went in and cleansed the temple. This is the reason I feel I should speak out on this because nobody else speaks along these lines as far as I know. When this thing is hurting our churches, somebody should say, "Look, brother, sit down. You are spoiling things. You ought not to be loving the preeminence all the time. You should learn to be meek and let others speak." John says, "Wherefore, if I come, I will remember his deeds which he doeth." Diotrephes exhibits that which is not the mark of a believer, by any means. He apparently did not have the truth.

"Prating against us with malicious words." Diotrephes was attempting to completely destroy the effectiveness of the apostles and especially of John. John says, "When I get there, I'm going to deal with him. I'm going to speak out against him. I'm going to let it be known that this man is using malicious words."

A man called me sometime ago who was a member of a church that I served at one time. He wept as he said, "I want you to forgive me for saying the things I said about you." He had gone so far as to say that I had left the church in debt. I have never left in debt any church that I have served. The fact of the matter is that I left that church with a tremendous reserve fund, but he, along with a few others, simply did not mention that. As a result, a false report went out. I told him, "You don't have to ask me to forgive you. You need to ask the Lord's forgiveness." He said, "I've already repented and talked to Him." I told him, "It would be nice if you would now give the true report to those you gave the false report." He had been a Diotrephes. He enjoyed presiding. He enjoyed having his way. Apparently, a change has come over him now. He is in another church, and I understand that he is doing a good job. I rejoice in that. But he was a Diotrephes. I feel that I should have dealt with him more severely than I did when I was there because John says, "I intend to deal with Diotrephes."

"And not content therewith, neither doth he himself receive the brethren, and forbiddeth them that would, and casteth them out of the church." Imagine this fellow! He is excommunicating anybody who would entertain these men John had recommended. What a horrible picture this is! If you want to wreck a church, just have a man like this or a little group like this and, my friend, you will wreck the church. The sad situation is that there are too many men like this today in Christian circles.

You can call John an apostle of love if you want to, but the Lord Jesus called him a son of thunder. I think they had a regular thunderstorm when John arrived at this church because he said he was going to deal with Diotrephes. It is too bad other churches don't deal with Diotrephes, because he will wreck a church if he is permitted to go on.

Beloved, follow not that which is evil, but that which is good. He that doeth good is of God: but he that doeth evil hath not seen God [3 John 11].

John encourages Gaius to continue doing that which is good. Again, he emphasizes that the one who practices righteousness is a child of God but the one who does not practice righteousness is not born of God.

DEMETRIUS—A DEPENDABLE BROTHER

We come now to the third man, Demetrius. He is a lovely fellow. You just cannot help but rejoice in him. Gaius is a delightful brother, Diotrephes is a dictator, and now we will find Demetrius to be a dependable brother.

Demetrius hath good report of all men, and of the truth itself: yea, and we also bear record; and ye know that our record is true [3 John 12].

"Demetrius hath good report of all men, and of the truth itself." Here is a man sound in the faith. "Yea, and we also bear record." In the mouth of two witnesses, a thing is established. Demetrius has a good report of all men; the truth bears witness to him, and John says, "I bear witness also." "And ye know that our record is true." This church knows that John bears a true witness.

Demetrius is obviously one of these wonderful saints of God whom Diotrephes had shut out of the church. We have only one verse about Demetrius—this is all we know. He is never mentioned again in Scripture. However, this one verse of Scripture gives us an insight into the Christian character of this noble saint of God. We cannot identify him with any other of the same name. His name means "belonging to Demeter," that is, Ceres, the goddess of agriculture. This identifies him as a convert from paganism. He evidently was brought up in a pagan home and worshiped the gods of the Greeks and Romans. This man, converted, now goes around teaching the Word of God. He adorned the doctrine of Christ. Others testified to his character, and he was true to the doctrine of Scripture.

Demetrius is evidently among the group of men whom John mentions that Diotrephes was not receiving. He is one of the itinerant preachers who went about in the first century—humble, unknown, and unsung. He is a member of that great army which carried the gospel throughout the Roman Empire so that it could be said that the whole world had heard the gospel. The whole Roman world of that day, the whole civilized world, was entirely evangelized. They were pushing out beyond its borders when the apostasy began to set in, when there came in men like Diotrephes.

Demetrius is one of the shining lights of the New Testament, a humble saint of God. Around us today, there are multitudes of people like him. They are not a Diotrephes. And they are not even a Gaius—they are not outstanding Christians. They are just humble saints of God, doing the thing God has called them to do. In a humble way, they are maybe just teaching a little Sunday school class. I heard the other day about one who teaches the handicapped. How wonderful that is, but nobody knows about her. Nobody has ever given her a loving cup. They ought to, but they never have. She doesn't want it, and she would be embarrassed if you gave her one. There are many saints of God like that today. God is using them in a small way. They are not trying to be the chief soloist; they are just singing in the choir. They don't try to be the main speaker. They don't want to preside. They don't want to be the chairman of every board in the church. They are willing just to fade into the woodwork of the church. But they are pillars of the church. They are supporting the work, and they are encouraging the preacher.

One of the most wonderful church members I ever knew was a dear little lady who came in every Sunday morning on a cane. She never missed a Sunday morning, and she always had something nice to say. She was always encouraging the preacher. She told me one time, "I think that's my job. It's all I can do." Well, she did other things, too. The church is filled with wonderful saints of God. Don't get the impression that I think that everybody in the church is a Diotrephes. Thank God that there are very few of them. In this epistle here, it is two good men to one bad. I think the average is better than that today in the church—I think maybe it is one hundred to one. Thank God for the Demetrius folk in our churches today.

The tense that John uses here indicates that Demetrius had a good reputation in the past and that he still has a good reputation. Over a long period, Demetrius has demonstrated a time-tested faith. He is Demetrius, the dependable brother. The church knows him as a man of God. Now you might deceive the church, but Demetrius was tested by the truth. He measures up to the definition of a believer. John knows him and agrees. There are three witnesses to the fact that Demetrius adorns the doctrine of Christ.

The real test of the Christian life is not in the arena backed by applause. It was not before the crowd in the Colosseum. There were five million martyrs who bore testimony to the truth of the gospel in the first three centuries and who laid down their lives for Christ. Did you know that there were many more millions who bore witness by the faithful lives they lived each day? Nothing spectacular, nothing sensational, nothing outstanding—they just lived for God. They had a purpose, they had a direction, and they had a thrilling experience. (Our contemporary civilization is experiencing a decadence that characterized Rome in the first century. After World War II, an Englishman wrote the play, *Look Back in Anger*. It revealed a bottomless pessimism without any hope for the future. This attitude produced the Beatle-brained mob of youth we

have today who are without direction. Three young people I met in Athens told me they simply wanted to drop out of society.) Into the decadent first century, with its low morals and erosion of character, there came the message from God that He had given His Son. There were multitudes who came into contact with Him, and they got involved. May I say to you, you may not find their names in the Yellow Pages, but you will find them in the Lamb's Book of Life. They lived for God unknown to the world, and they died unknown to the world. But they are known to God, and their names are inscribed on high.

I had many things to write, but I will not with ink and pen write unto thee [3 John 13].

Though he wrote the Gospel of John and the Book of Revelation, two of the longest books of the New Testament, John very frankly says he would much rather tell it to you than write it to you.

But I trust I shall shortly see thee, and we shall speak face to face. Peace be to thee. Our friends salute thee. Greet the friends by name [3 John 14].

Someday this will be true for you and me: we will be able to speak face to face with John. I want to talk with him about these little books he wrote. There are a lot of questions I want to ask him. But, of course, he is referring to the fact that he will come and speak face to face with these men of the first century. He will speak face to face with Diotrephes. I feel sorry for old Diotrephes—I'm sure he really got it in that day. And John will speak to Gaius and Demetrius, those wonderful men of God. He says, "We shall speak face to face."

"Peace be to thee. Our friends salute thee. Greet the friends by name." Isn't that a lovely way to end this letter? John says, "I want you to know that our friends who are here with me greet you. And will you greet the friends by name? Go and say to Demetrius, 'Demetrius, I have a message from John. He wanted to greet you and to tell you he will be coming our way before long.'"

Gaius, Diotrephes, and Demetrius—these are the three men who pass before us in this little epistle. Christianity was on trial in the first century. Two of these men who are mentioned in this epistle are genuine. They are real and wonderful children of God. One is a delightful brother; another is a dependable brother. But the third is a dictator and a phony. May I say to you, the gospel walked in shoe leather in the first century in the Roman Empire. And it needs to get down where the rubber meets the road in our day. In spite of any energy shortage, we need to get the gospel onto the highways and byways of life.

BIBLIOGRAPHY

(Recommended for Further Study)

Boice, James Montgomery. *The Epistles of John*. Grand Rapids, Michigan: Zondervan Publishing House, n.d.

Burdick, Donald W. *The Epistles of John*. Chicago, Illinois: Moody Press, 1970.

Ironside, H. A. *The Epistles of John*. Neptune, New Jersey: Loizeaux Brothers, 1931.

Kelly, William. *An Exposition of the Epistles of John*. Addison, Illinois: Bible Truth Publishers, 1905.

Mitchell, John G. *Fellowship: Three Letters From John*. Portland, Oregon: Multnomah Press, 1974.

Robertson, A. T. *Epochs in the Life of the Apostle John*. Grand Rapids, Michigan: Baker Book House, 1933.

Stott, J. R. W. *The Epistles of John*. Grand Rapids, Michigan: Wm. B. Eerdmans Publishing Co., 1964.

Strauss, Lehman. *The Epistles of John*. Neptune, New Jersey: Loizeaux Brothers, n.d.

Thomas, W. H. Griffith. *The Apostle John*. Grand Rapids, Michigan: Wm. B. Eerdmans Publishing Co., 1956.

Vaughan, Curtis, *1,2,3 John*. Grand Rapids, Michigan: Zondervan Publishing House, 1970.

Vine, W. E. *The Epistles of John*. Grand Rapids, Michigan: Zondervan Publishing House, n.d.

Wuest, Kenneth S. *In These Last Days*. Grand Rapids, Michigan: Wm. B. Eerdmans Publishing Co., 1954. (Deals with the epistles of 2 Peter, John, and Jude.)

The General Epistle of
JUDE
INTRODUCTION

Studying the little Epistle of Jude is like working a gold mine because of all the rich nuggets which are here just for the mining.

The writer is Jude, which is the English form of the name *Judas*. Jude, he tells us here, is the brother of James. Now, in the gospel records there are three or four men by the name of James, and there are three men by the name of Judas. We are helped in our identification of the writer of this epistle by the record in Matthew: "Is not this the carpenter's son? is not his mother called Mary? and his brethren, James, and Joses, and Simon, and Judas?" (Matt. 13:55). So two of these brothers, James, the writer of the Epistle of James, and Judas, the writer of the Epistle of Jude, are half brothers of the Lord Jesus Christ. There are two other men by the name of Judas, and they both were among the twelve apostles of our Lord. The best known, of course, is Judas Iscariot, the apostle who betrayed the Lord. The other apostle by the name of Judas is distinguished in this way: "Judas saith unto him, *not Iscariot*, Lord, how is it that thou wilt manifest thyself unto us, and not unto the world?" (John 14:22, italics mine). The way he is identified is just that he is not Judas Iscariot. Therefore we believe that the writer of this epistle is the third Judas which Scripture mentions, Judas, the half brother of the Lord Jesus Christ.

Notice that neither James nor Jude identify themselves as brothers of the Lord Jesus. James introduces himself as ". . . a servant of God and of the Lord Jesus Christ . . ." (James 1:1). And Jude introduces himself as "the servant of Jesus Christ, and brother of James." Jude calls himself the servant, meaning "bond slave," of Jesus Christ. Why didn't James and Jude capitalize on their blood relationship with Jesus? I think the reason is obvious. Neither James nor Jude believed in the messianic claims of Jesus until *after* His resurrection. It was the Resurrection that convicted them and confirmed to them that Jesus was who He claimed to be. Up until that time they thought He had just gone "off" on religion, that He was, as the Scripture puts it, *beside* Himself. But after His resurrection they became believers. You see, it was possible to grow up in a home with Jesus in the days of His flesh and not recognize Him. I believe we see in Psalm 69 that He suffered loneliness and misunderstanding during those growing up years in Nazareth. Therefore His brothers felt that, although they had been reared with Him, they hadn't really *known* Him at that time. As Paul expressed it later, "Wherefore henceforth know we no man after the flesh: yea, though we have known Christ after the flesh, yet now henceforth know we him no more" (2 Cor. 5:16). Jude, though a half brother, recognizes that Jesus is the glorified Christ and that human relationship is not meaningful to him in any way. He had to come to Christ as a sinner, accepting Him as Savior just as anyone else did.

By the way, this is the marvelous answer of both James and Jude to an attitude which arose after the era of the apostles. There was a brief period when the family of Jesus was revered in a rather superstitious and sacred way as if they were something special. Actually, they were not superior; they were simply human beings who had to come to Christ just as you and I must come to Christ.

I have always felt that Protestantism has ignored Mary. She was a wonderful person. It was no accident that she was chosen of God to bear the Son of God, but that does not mean she is to be lifted up above all other people. She takes her own rightful place. Elizabeth called her blessed among women, not blessed *above* women, and Mary herself confessed her need of a Savior (see Luke 1:47). Therefore the brief period through which the church went when the family of the Lord Jesus was elevated to a very high position would certainly have been opposed by James and Jude. They themselves took the position of being merely bond slaves of Jesus Christ.

This book was written around A.D. 66–69.

The theme of the book is assurance in days of apostasy. Jude picked up the pen of inspiration to write on some theme or truth concerning the gospel and our salvation. He could have chosen the subject of justification by faith, but Paul had written on that in Romans. He could have chosen the resurrection of Christ, but Paul had written on that in 1 Corinthians. Or he could have chosen the doctrine of reconciliation, but Paul had written on that in 2 Corinthians. Probably Jude could have written on the great subject of faith, but Paul had written on that in Galatians. Or he could have selected the church as the body of Christ, but Paul had written on that in Ephesians. Or he could have selected the person of Christ, but Paul had written on that in Colossians. Jude could have written about our Great High Priest, but the writer to the Hebrews had already written on that. Or he could have chosen the subject of fellowship, but John was going to write on that later on. So the Spirit of God caused him to develop another subject rather than to develop one of the great doctrines. The Spirit of God arrested his purpose before he could even put down his subject and directed him into another channel. Jude's subject is the coming apostasy. He gives us the most vivid account that we have of the apostasy, and he presents it in a very dramatic manner. Jude hangs out a red lantern on the most dangerous curve along the highway the church of Christ is traveling. Jude describes in vivid terms and with awe-inspiring language the frightful conditions that were coming in the future. This little epistle is like a burglar alarm. Apostates have broken into the church. They came in the side door while nobody was watching. And this little epistle is like an atom bomb. The first bomb did not fall on Hiroshima or Nagasaki; it fell when Jude wrote this little epistle. It's an atom bomb, and it exploded in the early church as a warning.

Jude gives the only record in Scripture regarding the contention of Satan with Michael the archangel over the body of Moses. It is a very remarkable passage of Scripture.

Also, Jude records the prophecy of Enoch, which is found nowhere else in Scripture. He sees the Lord coming with ten thousands of His saints.

The little prophecy of Jude affords a fitting introduction to the Book of Revelation.

OUTLINE

I. Occasion of the Epistle, Verses 1–3
 A. Assurance for Believers, Verses 1–2
  (Sanctified, kept, called)
 B. Change of Theme to Apostasy, Verse 3

II. Occurrences of Apostasy, Verses 4–16
 A. Inception of Apostasy, Verse 4
 B. Israel in Unbelief Destroyed in Wilderness, Verse 5
 C. Angels Rebelled; Kept in Chains, Verse 6
 D. Sodom and Gomorrah Sinned in Sexuality; Destroyed by Fire, Verse 7
 E. Modern Apostate Teachers Identified, Verses 8–10
  (Despise authority)
 F. Cain, Balaam, Korah—Examples of Apostates, Verse 11
 G. Modern Apostate Teachers Defined and Described, Verses 12–16

III. Occupation of Believers in Days of Apostasy, Verses 17–25
 A. Believers Warned by Apostles That These Apostates Would Come, Verses 17–19
 B. What Believers Must Do in Days of Apostasy, Verses 20–25
  1. Build Up
  2. Pray In
  3. Keep Themselves
  4. Look For
  5. Have Compassion
  6. Save Others
  7. Hate Evil

OCCASION OF THE EPISTLE

In the first three verses, Jude gives the occasion for his writing this epistle. Jude will tell us that he intended to write on some theme of our salvation, but the Spirit of God put up a red warning sign and instructed him to call attention to the days of apostasy which would be coming upon the church.

ASSURANCE FOR BELIEVERS

Jude, the servant of Jesus Christ, and brother of James, to them that are sanctified by God the Father, and preserved in Jesus Christ, and called [Jude 1].

"Jude," as I pointed out in the Introduction, is the English form of the name *Judas*. In the New Testament, there are three men who bear the name *Judas*, but we have very good evidence which identifies the writer of this epistle as the half brother of the Lord Jesus Christ.

"The servant of Jesus Christ." The word *servant* is literally "bond slave." He claims no blood relationship with the Lord Jesus as if that would give him a superior position. This ought to lay to rest the notion which arose in the early church, in the post-apostolic period, that the family of Jesus was to be held in reverence because they were super-duper folk. Dr. Marvin R. Vincent, the outstanding Greek scholar, comments in *Word Studies in the New Testament*:

That Jude does not allude to his relationship to the Lord may be explained by the fact that the natural relationship in his mind would be subordinate to the spiritual (see Luke xi. 27, 28), and that such a designation would, as Dean Alford remarks, "have been in harmony with those later and superstitious feelings with which the next and following ages regarded the Lord's earthly relatives."

"The brother of James," as we have said in the Introduction, is the way Jude identifies himself. Both James and Jude were half brothers of the Lord Jesus, and James was the writer of the epistle which bears his name. He was mentioned by the apostle Paul as one of the pillars in the church at Jerusalem.

"To them that are sanctified by God the father." The Greek text of Nestle and that of Westcott and Hort, which are the best Greek texts that we have, use the verb *agapaō*, meaning "to love," instead of *hagiazō*, meaning "to sanctify." Most scholars agree that "to love" is more accurate than "to sanctify," and it makes it a little bit more precious to our hearts to know that we are loved or beloved by God the Father.

I would like to share with you the translation of Kenneth S. Wuest, the late Greek scholar at the Moody Bible Institute. His translation *(Word Studies from the Greek New Testament)*, though a bit involved, in many places brings out the original meaning:

Jude, a bondslave of Jesus Christ and brother of James, to those who by God the Father have been loved and are in a state of being the permanent objects of His love, and who for Jesus Christ have been guarded and are in a permanent state of being carefully watched, to those who are called ones.

This is a wonderful passage of Scripture. We are beloved by God the Father and preserved for Jesus Christ.

There are several words I must deal with in this text because of their importance. The first word is *preserved*. It is this word that gives us the key to the Book of Jude which presents the apostasy as it is presented nowhere else in Scripture. How frightful it is! But Jude doesn't write just to frighten the daylights out of us. Nor does he write just to draw a vivid picture for our information; he gives us this background in order that he might give *assurance* in days of apostasy. He uses the word *keep* four times, which is what the word *preserve* means. They are kept in Jesus Christ—God is the one who keeps them. Notice verse 21 says "*keep* yourselves in the love of God"; and verse 24 says "now unto him that is able to *keep* you from falling." You may call it anything you want to, but it gives assurance of salvation to the believer even in the dark days of apostasy.

As we shall see, you and I are presently living in the apostasy. How much farther we will go into it before the Rapture, I do not know—nor does anyone else know. But we definitely are in times of apostasy.

Now looking again at the word *preserved*, it is interesting to note that in the physical world there are two ways of preserving food. One is with vinegar, and the other is with sugar. There are many saints in our day who I think are preserved all right, but they are preserved in vinegar—that is, they act that way. They have a vinegar disposition. Also, there are saints who are preserved in sugar. They are sugar and spice and everything nice—and these are not all women either. But even those who seem to be preserved in vinegar are preserved by God's grace, which preserves or keeps them. The apostle John will tell us in Revelation 12:11 that ". . . they overcame him [Satan] by the blood of the Lamb . . .", and that is the only way believers are going to make it through the Great Tribulation. And that is the only way *we* are going to overcome—by the blood of the Lamb. There is no merit or power in us to overcome the Evil One.

I must resort back to the illustration which the Lord Jesus Himself gave when He said, "I am the good shepherd: the good shepherd giveth his life for the sheep" (John 10:11). Then He goes on to talk about His sheep, "My sheep hear my voice, and I know them, and they follow me: And I give unto them eternal life; and they shall never perish, neither shall any man pluck them out of my hand. My Father, which gave them me, is greater than all; and no man is able to pluck them out of my Father's hand" (John 10:27–29).

Now if a sheep is kept in safety, it is no credit to the sheep. A sheep cannot defend itself. It doesn't have sharp fangs and claws to fight its enemy. Neither can it run. A jackrabbit can't defend itself either, but a jackrabbit can get away from trouble. A sheep can't even do that. A sheep is helpless. When one of God's sheep says that he knows he is saved, he is not boasting of his own merit; he is boasting of his Shepherd. He has a wonderful Shepherd. My friend, if you are saying that you are not sure of your salvation, you really are reflecting upon your Shepherd, because He says that He can keep you. He says that no created thing is able to take you out of His Father's hand. It is not a question of whether or not you can hold on to Him. It is a question of His holding on to you. He says that He can, and it is a matter of your trusting Him.

You see, salvation rests upon the Word of God. It is up to you whether you will believe Him or not. Your assurance of salvation rests upon that because He has made it very clear that you have a sure salvation. Here in Jude we are presented with the dark days of apostasy, and God still says that He is able to keep His own.

"And called." Not only are we preserved in Jesus Christ, safe in Him, but we are also called. The word *called*, as it is used in Scripture, is not only an invitation that is sent out, but it is an invitation that is sent out and accepted and made real because of the Spirit of God. Let me give you Paul's statement as found in 1 Corinthians 1:22–24: "For the Jews require a sign, and the Greeks seek after wisdom: But we preach Christ crucified, unto the Jews a stumblingblock, and unto the Greeks foolishness; But unto them which are *called*, both Jews and Greeks, Christ the power of God, and the wisdom of God" (italics mine). My friend, if you have found in Christ the wisdom and power of God and you have trusted Him, you are one of "the called." The invitation is sent out, and when it is accepted and believed, then you are the called. That is exactly what Jude means here, and Paul spelled it out for us as well.

Mercy unto you, and peace and love, be multiplied [Jude 2].

We need to recognize the difference between these three words: *mercy, peace*, and *love;* then we need to see the strong relationship between them.

Love is an attribute of God. Because God is love, He is merciful and has provided grace. The love of God encompasses all mankind—"God so loved the *world*" (see John 3:16). It is not His will that any should perish. Today He loves every human being on this earth. He has no favorites. Way back in the Book of Exodus, God made it clear to even a man like Moses that He did not answer his prayer because he was Moses; "And he said, I . . . will be gracious to whom I will be gracious, and will shew mercy on whom I will shew mercy" (Exod. 33:19). God answered Moses' prayer because He found the explanation in Himself; He treats all His creatures alike in that sense. My friend, God loves *you* today. If you knew how much He loves you, it would break your heart—you would be in tears.

Now you can keep from experiencing God's love, but you cannot keep Him from loving you. You can't keep the sun from shining, but you can put up an umbrella to keep the sun from shining on *you*. And there are certain umbrellas you can put up to keep from experiencing the love of God: the umbrella of resistance to His will, the umbrella of sin in your life, etc.

Although God loved you, He did not save you by love. You see, God has other attributes. He is holy. He is righteous. He is just. He simply cannot let down the bars of heaven and, by lowering His standards, bring you in. He cannot do that any more than a human judge can uphold the laws of the land and yet accept a bribe under the table for letting a criminal off. If he does that, he is a crooked judge. And if God is going to do that with human beings, He is no better than a crooked judge. I do not mean to be irreverent because God is not a crooked judge. God has to maintain His holiness and His righteousness and His justice.

"God so loved the world," and He loved the world with a merciful love, a love that had a concern and care for human beings. And because of it, He gave His only begotten Son— He provided His Son as the substitute. Now God, on a righteous basis, can save a sinner if he will come to Him and accept His salvation. This is called the *grace* of God. "For by grace are ye saved through faith; and that not of yourselves: it is the gift of God: Not of works, lest any man should boast" (Eph. 2:8–9).

In *Synonyms of the New Testament* Dr. R. C. Trench, who was a great Greek scholar, made a clear distinction between these words:

> While *charis* [grace] has thus reference to the *sins* of men, and is that glorious attribute of God which these sins call out and display, His *free gift* in their forgiveness, *eleos* [mercy], has special and immediate regard to the *misery* which is the consequence of these sins.

Now you can see that the *grace* of God, not the love of God, has to do with the sins of men. God has provided a Savior who has paid the penalty for sins. On that basis, God saves sinners. That is the grace of God.

However, sin has brought tragedy to the human family. We often hear the question: Why does a God of love permit cancer? Well, disease and death came to the human family as consequences of sin. God sees the misery that sin has caused, and the mercy of God goes out to man. God is rich in mercy. If you come to Him as a sinner and accept His salvation, He will save you by grace. Then, because He is rich in mercy, He will extend His mercy to you. He will bring comfort to you at that time. He will help you and comfort your heart. You can trust Him in your time of need.

The fellow who is writing these words has had two major operations for cancer, and the doctors tell me the cancer is still in my body and can break out anytime. To be frank with you, from where I sit right now I have a great big question: Why? And I am asking the Lord why. But my only refuge is in my heavenly Father. I *know* He has the answer, although

He hasn't told me what it is. What I'm asking from Him is mercy. He has already saved me by His grace, but now I want His mercy. Mercy is that love of His which goes out to us in our misery here upon this earth.

A sinner needs the grace of God, and he sure needs a whole lot of mercy—I've been using a great deal of it these past few years.

Let me share with you from Dr. Trench again. I will repeat what I have already quoted and then go on:

> While *charis* has thus reference to the *sins* of men, and is that glorious attribute of God which these sins call out and display, His *free gift* in their forgiveness, *eleos*, has special and immediate regard to the *misery* which is the consequence of these sins, being the tender sense of this misery displaying itself in the effort, which only the continued perverseness of man can hinder or defeat, to assuage and entirely remove it. . . . In the divine mind, and in the order of our salvation as conceived therein, the *eleos* (mercy) precedes the *charis* (grace). God so loved the world with a pitying love (herein was the *eleos*), that He *gave* His only begotten Son (herein the *charis*), that the world through Him might be saved (compare Eph. 2:4; Luke 1:78–79). But in the order of the manifestation of God's purposes of salvation the grace must go before the mercy, the *charis* must go before and make way for the *eleos*. It is true that the same persons are the subjects of both, being at once the guilty and the miserable; yet the righteousness of God, which it is quite necessary should be maintained as His love, demands that the guilt should be done away before the misery can be assuaged; only the forgiven can be blessed.

God must pardon before He can heal. Men must be justified before they can be sanctified. In the order of the manifestation of God's purposes of salvation, the grace of God must go before the mercy of God. The grace must go before and take away and make way for the mercy of God.

The "peace" of God is that experience which comes to the heart that is trusting Christ. Paul says, "Therefore being justified by faith, we have *peace* with God through our Lord Jesus Christ" (Rom. 5:1, italics mine). Peace with God is to know that God is not difficult to get along with. He is not making it hard for me; He is not making it hard for you. He wants us to know that He hasn't anything against us now that we know that we are sinners and have trusted Christ as our Savior. The world may point its finger at you and reject you, but God has accepted you. He loves you, and He wants to give you that peace so that at night you can pillow your head on God's promises. "And we know that all things work together for good to them that love God, to them who are the called according to his purpose" (Rom. 8:28). Dr. R. A. Torrey used to call this verse a soft pillow for a tired heart. What a wonderful promise it is!

CHANGE OF THEME TO APOSTASY

Beloved, when I gave all diligence to write unto you of the common salvation, it was needful for me to write unto you, and exhort you that ye should earnestly contend for the faith which was once delivered unto the saints [Jude 3].

"**B**eloved." When Jude uses that term, it really means folk who are loved of God, God's beloved children.

"Common salvation." Let's understand that the word *common* is the English translation of the Greek word *koinēs*. The New Testament was not written in classical Greek but in *koinē* Greek or common Greek, meaning that it was understood by everyone, educated and uneducated, all over the Roman Empire in the days of the apostles. When Jude said that he had intended to write of the "common salvation," he must have been referring to something that people throughout the Roman Empire would understand.

Now Jude says here that he was planning on writing on some facet of our salvation. It could have been on redemption, on the person of Christ, on sanctification, or any number of themes, but he didn't write on any of those themes because "it was needful for me to write unto you, and exhort you that ye should earnestly contend for the faith which was once delivered unto the saints." The thought here is that the Holy Spirit detoured Jude from writing on some theme of the faith in order that he might sound a warning concerning the impending apostasy.

The apostasy is a departure from *the* faith, that is, from the apostles' doctrine. Apostasy was just a little cloud the size of a man's hand in Jude's day, but now it is a storm of hurricane force that fills the land. As Jude writes about the apostasy that was coming on the earth, we can see that many of the things he mentions are already taking place in the world in our day. My friend, the apostasy is not something *we* are looking forward to; the apostasy is *here*. It is all about us today.

"Needful." There was a compulsion, a necessity, a constraint upon Jude. He said, "When I was about to write to you about some great doctrine which the apostles gave us, a necessity was laid upon me instead to exhort you that you should earnestly contend for the faith."

"Contend." There are expositors who suggest that this means to contend on your knees. Well, I have never been able to find any authority for that view, but the thought here is to contend without being contentious. I wish we fundamentalists could contend for the fundamentals of the faith without being fiery and contentious. As Paul put it, "And the servant of the Lord must not strive; but be gentle unto all men, apt [ready] to teach, patient, In meekness instructing those that oppose themselves; if God peradventure will give them repentance to the acknowledging of the truth; And that they may recover themselves out of the snare of the devil, who are taken captive by him at his will" (2 Tim. 2:24–26). The word *contend*, as Jude uses it, has in it the idea of agony. The Greek word is *epagōnizesthai*, and we get our English word *agony* from the noun of this word. Instead of writing on some great doctrine, Jude is saying that we are to contend or defend the great doctrines of Christianity.

"Contend for the faith which was once delivered unto the saints." "The faith" was the body of truth given once for all. In the Book of Acts it is called the apostles' doctrine: "And they continued stedfastly in the apostles' doctrine and fellowship, and in breaking of bread, and in prayers" (Acts 2:42). Notice that the apostles' doctrine is the first thing mentioned. Since that is number one on God's church parade, our church is not a church unless it is doing just that.

We are told in Ephesians 4:15 to speak the truth in love or, as someone has translated it, "truthing in love." My friend, if you are going to give out the truth, give it out in love. If you do not give it out in love, there is some question about whether or not you are actually giving out the truth. And we are to be ready to give an answer to anyone who asks us—in meekness and fear. A believer should not have a short fuse and become angry when someone differs with him.

Dr. Kenneth S. Wuest has one of the finest books available which gives the literal translation of Jude. Notice his translation in *Word Studies from the Greek New Testament*:

> Divinely-loved ones, when giving all diligence to be writing to you concerning the salvation possessed in common by all of us, I had constraint laid upon me to write to you, beseeching (you) to contend with intensity and determination for the Faith once for all entrusted into the safekeeping of the saints.

OCCURRENCES OF APOSTASY

Now Jude will set before us the reason we should contend for the faith. Something is happening to the church, and Jude sounds an alarm.

INCEPTION OF APOSTASY

For there are certain men crept in unawares, who were before of old ordained to this condemnation, ungodly men, turning the grace of our God into lasciviousness, and denying the only Lord God, and our Lord Jesus Christ [Jude 4].

"Who were before of old ordained to this condemnation" should be made clear first of all. It actually means that they were written of beforehand. The word *ordained* is *prographō*, meaning "to write beforehand." It simply means that other writers had sounded the warning about apostates.

"There are certain men crept in unawares"—they are creeps! *Crept in* is one of the most interesting phrases in the Greek language. It is *pareisdunō. Dunō* means "to enter;" the preposition *eis* means "into;" and *para* means "beside." It means "to enter alongside" or, as Dr. Vincent puts it in his commentary: "To get in by the side, to slip in a side door." This is the way the apostates have come into the church.

I have been in the church for many years. I have been and am still an ordained Presbyterian preacher—although I am in *no* denomination today and have no denominational connections at all. As a young person I remember that the church was by and large sound in the faith. When I went to the denominational college, I began to discover that there were ministers who denied practically every tenet of the faith. That opened up a new world to me. Then when I went to the denominational seminary, I found that the liberal element was still growing. The day came when I left that denomination and came to California.

Here I entered another denomination, and when I saw it going into liberalism, I got out. I wasn't put out; I just stepped out voluntarily. During that long period I saw how these men were able to take over a church. They came in the side door. They came in by professing one thing and believing another. They did not come in the front door—that is, they did not declare their doctrinal position. Many of our good laymen have been deceived by ministers like that. Scripture has warned about them. For instance, Paul wrote to the Corinthians: "For such are false apostles, deceitful workers, transforming themselves into the apostles of Christ. And no marvel; for Satan himself is transformed into an angel of light. Therefore it is no great thing if his ministers also be transformed as the ministers of righteousness; whose end shall be according to their works" (2 Cor. 11:13–15). The expression "transforming themselves" in this verse is very interesting. It is in the Greek *metaschēmatixontai*, meaning "the act of an individual who is changing his outward expression by *assuming* an expression put on from the outside." It is a method of Satan.

Over the years I have seen as many as a dozen strong, outstanding churches across America fall into the hands of liberalism by this method. It is the most deceitful method in the world. Let me give you an instance of one church. I won't give the location, because the chances are that you know one like it in the area in which you live. It was at one time a church in which the Word of God was preached, people were being saved, and hearts were being blessed. Then the pastor retired or resigned, and a new man appeared on the scene. When he met with the pulpit committee and met with the elders, they asked him about his doctrinal beliefs. He assured them that he believed in all the great doctrines of the faith. You see, he came in the side door because he really did not believe them. He only pretended to believe them and pretended to be sound in the faith. And the interesting thing is that his trial sermon sounded as though he were sound in the faith. He had probably read Spurgeon or Warfield or G. Campbell Morgan and had borrowed enough of their material to preach a good sermon. Hearing him, the congregation thought, *This young man is just fine;* so they called him as their pastor. But remember that he came in by the side door; he did not believe the doctrine that he preached. Before long they discovered that they had a liberal on their hands. Generally, fundamental churches consider ousting the preacher to be a bad method; so they tolerate him. However, my feeling is that since he came in by the side door, he should be booted out the back door. But they don't do that. Right at this moment I know of two or three churches which are being ruined by men who pretended to be what they were not.

Remember that Jude said that they "were before of old ordained to this condemnation"— that is, they were written of beforehand. Jude is saying, "I'm not telling you something new—others have written of this also and have warned you of that which is coming."

Paul is one who repeatedly warned of the apostate. The last time he went by Ephesus, at his last visit with the Ephesian elders, he gave this warning: "For I know this, that after my departing shall grievous wolves enter in among you, not sparing the flock. Also of your own selves shall men arise, speaking perverse things, to draw away disciples after them. Therefore watch, and remember, that by the space of three years I ceased not to warn every one night and day with tears" (Acts 20:29–31). Although Paul warned them of apostates, the day came when the Ephesian church yielded to them.

Paul also warned the young preacher Timothy: "Having a form of godliness, but denying the power thereof: from such turn away. For of this sort are they which creep into houses, and lead captive silly women laden with sins, led away with divers lusts" (2 Tim. 3:5–6). One of the greatest movements we have seen in our day is the formation of women's Bible study classes all across this country. I thank God for them. However, it needs to be watched very carefully because, since it is a success, you will find that somebody is going to try the side door and slip in. In the history of the church there has never been a woman theologian, and that is very strange indeed. Also, it is true that women have played a prominent part in many of the cults and heresies that have come into the church. While I don't claim to be an authority in this field, it seems to me that a woman is built finer than a man. She has finer sensibilities and a closer perception than a man has. For this reason she needs to be treated with more care. I have to be more particular with my watch than I have to be with the motor in my car. There is a grave danger (and I have heard this voiced by several ministers across the country) of these women's movements operating totally outside the church and not cooperating with the church at all. This is also true of the youth

movement which is taking place. Also, I have found in my radio ministry that I move largely outside the local church. However, I do try to work with the local church, and I believe that all of these movements should work with the local church if it is a Bible-believing church. Paul is warning about false teachers coming in the side door, and I believe that any movement today which the Spirit of God seems to be blessing needs to be watched very carefully because of the fact that the Devil is going to come in the side door if he can. And if you think he is coming in as the *Devil*, you are wrong. His ministers pretend to be ministers of light.

The final test, the acid test, of any movement is the teaching regarding the person of Jesus Christ. If it denies the deity of Christ, you can rule it out immediately, but you have to be very careful about this matter of the deity of Christ. There are many facets by which they can deny the deity of Christ and yet give the impression that they actually believe in Him as the Savior of the world. Simon Peter warns of this: "But there were false prophets also among the people, even as there shall be false teachers among you, who privily shall bring in damnable heresies, even denying the Lord that bought them, and bring upon themselves swift destruction" (2 Pet. 2:1).

And Paul, writing to the Galatians, warns: "And that because of false brethren unawares brought in, who came in privily to spy out our liberty which we have in Christ Jesus, that they might bring us into bondage" (Gal. 2:4). My friend, we need to guard every movement today which God is blessing. These organizations which are outside the church may go off on tangents because the ministers of Satan are waiting to come in the side door.

"Ungodly men, turning the grace of our God into lasciviousness, and denying the only Lord God, and our Lord Jesus Christ." They are by nature ungodly men, and they do two things: (1) They distort and deny the grace of God— "turning the grace of our God into lasciviousness"; and (2) they deny the deity of the Lord Jesus Christ—"denying the only Lord God, and our Lord Jesus Christ."

"Ungodly" means that they simply leave God out of their lives.

It is important to evaluate whether or not a man who teaches and preaches the Word of God is a godly man. I was amazed to hear from a couple who, I thought, had good spiritual discernment. They attended the classes of a Bible teacher and were greatly impressed by him. In fact, they considered him outstanding. They were willing to tolerate the fact that this Bible teacher was having an open affair with a woman who was not his wife! A man may be an interesting Bible teacher and still be an ungodly man. We need to look at their lives. Are they leaving God out of their lives?

Lasciviousness is a very important word. I suppose the best synonym is *wantonness* because wantonness has in it the thought of lawlessness and arrogance—doing as you please even if you offend the sensibilities of others. Jude says that the ungodly turn the grace of our God into lasciviousness—into immorality. The apostle Paul warned the Galatian believers about the danger of turning the grace of God into license—permitting them to live any way they pleased. "For, brethren, ye have been called unto liberty; only use not liberty for an occasion to the flesh, but by love serve one another" (Gal. 5:13).

Gross immorality characterizes the apostasy of our day. They have thrown overboard all of the great precepts of Scripture concerning morality, and they call it the new morality. There is a growing danger in this country of the church actually espousing and condoning gross immorality. One writer has said that "one of the troubles with the world is that people mistake sex for love, money for brains, and transistor radios for civilization." The creed of the present day, according to the late Dr. Wallace Petty, can be stated in the following six articles: "God is a creation of wishful thinking; religion is a mechanism of escape from reality; man is a glorified gorilla who asks too many questions and represses too many desires; morals are a matter of taste; love is an art; and life is a racket." That is the viewpoint of some folk in our day.

The wantonness that we are seeing is marked by an arrogant recklessness of justice. Another definition is "willfully malicious." Marriage is flouted and considered unessential. You may live with whomever you wish to live with in total disregard of the morality which builds homes and thereby builds a nation. As far back as 1959 Vice Admiral Robert Goldthwaite, Chief of Naval Air Training, told a large group of leading educators, businessmen, law enforcement officials, and others that there is "a surge of immorality in civilian and military life." He said that "moral decay" is an acute national problem, and there is urgent need to improve "moral leadership" among youth. During the years since then, the moral decay has reached such proportions that we should be alarmed. We ought to be very careful about the folk who are teaching in our churches. Are they teaching a loose morality? Jude warns us to be on our guard against that.

The other thing that characterizes an apostate is that he denies the Lord God and our Lord Jesus Christ. He will talk about God and the Lord Jesus, but he denies who and what they actually are.

In Jude's day the apostasy was Gnosticism. Gnosticism taught that the body was essentially evil, that all matter was evil, and that the spirit alone was good. The conclusion drawn from this was that it didn't matter what a man did with his body. He was free to satisfy the lusts of the body. He was free to practice blatant immorality, shameless sin, and arrogantly and proudly to flout that sin publicly. That was a perversion of grace.

The same ideas have sprung up again today. The new morality is no newer than the old Gnosticism, the first heresy. The other facet of Gnosticism was a denial of the true God and true Man, our Lord Jesus Christ. That is the mark of an antichrist. John calls such people antichrists in his epistle. It is always the spirit of antichrist which denies the Lord Jesus Christ.

I have spent a long time on this verse because of the importance of the matters it sets before us.

ISRAEL IN UNBELIEF DESTROYED IN THE WILDERNESS

Now Jude is going to give us six examples of apostasy in the past.

Before we look at this section, let me remind you of what the apostasy is. Thayer gives this meaning for the Greek word *aphistēmi:* "to remove, to withdraw, to go away, to depart." When the word is used in 2 Thessalonians, I take the position that it has a twofold meaning. It means the removal of the church since in Paul's first epistle to the Thessalonians he spoke of the rapture of the church. The Rapture must come first—the *aphistēmi*, the departure, the removal of the church. The removal of believers from the earth will lead to the total apostasy—that is, the departure from the faith. Our Lord Jesus asked the question, ". . . when the Son of man cometh [to the earth], shall he find [the] faith . . . ?" (Luke 18:8). The way the question is couched in the Greek demands a negative answer. Therefore, the answer is no, He will not find the faith on the earth when He returns. There will be a total departure, a total apostasy. Now that cannot come about until the true believers are removed from the earth—and, of course, this can occur at any moment.

Jude is now going to give us six examples of apostasy in the past; that is, departures from the faith. There will be three groups and then three individuals. First, the three groups—

I will therefore put you in remembrance, though ye once knew this, how that the Lord, having saved the people out of the land of Egypt, afterward destroyed them that believed not [Jude 5].

In the wilderness Israel in unbelief was destroyed, and it is an example that God does judge apostates. When Israel came to Kadesh-Barnea, they refused to enter the Promised Land.

Now the spies had brought back a report to Kadesh-Barnea that everything God had told them about the land was accurate. But the spies (with the exception of two) didn't believe that God could bring them into the land, and they persuaded the people to believe that. At first they didn't want to believe that it was a good land. After they were convinced it was a good land, they wouldn't believe that God could bring them into the land. They preferred to stay in the wilderness rather than believe God. That is an example of apostasy, a departure from the faith. They departed from the whole basis on which they had left Egypt. God had given them a promise with two parts to it: "I will take you out of Egypt, and I will bring you into the land." But Israel's unbelief pushed them back into the wilderness, and God left them there for thirty-eight more years until all of the adult generation had died— with the exception of Caleb and Joshua. Israel had used their children as an excuse for not going into the land; so God said, "But your little ones, which ye said should be a prey, them will I bring in, and they shall know the land which ye have despised" (Num. 14:31).

My friend, in our own lives we sometimes use our children's welfare as an excuse for not serving the Lord. While that sounds very noble, it infers that *God* isn't thinking of our children. God will take care of them and us when we obey Him.

The new generation of Israel did cross the Jordan River and enter the Promised Land, even as God had promised. However, the generation that had apostatized, that had departed from the faith, were destroyed in the wilderness, and they are the first example that Jude gives.

ANGELS IN REBELLION KEPT IN CHAINS

And the angels which kept not their first estate, but left their own habitation, he hath reserved in everlasting chains under darkness unto the judgment of the great day [Jude 6].

This opens up to us a truth that we don't get with such clarity in any other section of the Word of God, although we are told that there will be a judgment of angels. Sometime in the past they didn't keep "their first estate." God created angels with a free will. Angels do not reproduce as human beings do; therefore, they do not inherit a sinful nature as humans do. Each angel is created by God with a free will. Now, some of these spiritual creatures were caught up in a rebellion, and now they are reserved in chains.

Apparently, the fallen angels are divided into two groups. The group whose rebellion was so great is evidently locked up, incarcerated, and has no freedom of movement any longer. The other group of fallen angels apparently has freedom of movement and is under the leadership of Satan. It seems evident that these are the demons mentioned in Scripture and that are coming into prominence in our day.

For many years the liberal wing of the church has denied the supernatural and denied that there were any such creatures as angels. We are living in a materialistic age, and the viewpoint was that God and the idea of angels were superstitions that we no longer needed. I believe it was Huxley who said that the belief in God was like the fading smile of a Cheshire cat, that it was disappearing in this scientific age.

Back in 1963 Ben Hecht wrote an article under the title, "New God for the Space Age." Let me quote the first few paragraphs:

The most amazing event to enter modern history has been generally snubbed by our chroniclers. It is the petering out of Christianity. Not only are the Bible stories going by the board, but a deeper side of religion seems also to be exiting. This is the mystic concept of the human soul and its survival after death.

Parsons are still preaching away on this topic and congregations are still listening. But congregation and parson both seem to have moved from church to museum.

Fifty years ago religion was an exuberant part of our world. Its sermons, bazaars, tag days, taboos and exhortations filled the press. Its rituals brought a glow to our citizenry. At their supper tables a large part of the voting population bowed its head and said grace.

Religion today is a touchy subject, not because people believe deeply and are ready to defend such belief with emotion, but because they do not want to hear it discussed. They do not know quite what they feel and they do not know what to say about God, His angels and the record of His miracles. Not wanting to sound anti-Christian (or antisocial or anti-anything not under general condemnation) they settle for silence. In this silence, more than in all the previous agnostic hullabaloos, religion seems swiftly disappearing.

Remember that Ben Hecht wrote that in 1963. Since that time there has been a tremendous revival.

For many years liberalism has been predicting the death knell of the church and of all that is supernatural. Around 1963 Gibson Winter, a professor of ethics at the University of Chicago Divinity School, wrote a book entitled *The Suburban Captivity of the Churches* in which he made this statement:

U.S. Protestantism—once famous for its diversity—is homogenizing into what is almost a new faith, and if it continues in its present direction, it will be stone-cold dead in a couple of dozen years.

I could give you quotations *ad nauseam* of what liberals said a few years ago. For instance, a man at the Chicago Theological Seminary made the statement that Protestantism has gotten so prosperous statistically that it has lost all internal discipline whatsoever. "It looks frightfully confining from the outside, but on the inside it has no discipline, no integrity."

These quotations give a picture of the contemporary liberal church.

However, more recently there has been a revival of interest in that which is supernatural. It is quite interesting that the revival did not come from within the church, not even from within the fundamental church. It came on the campuses of the colleges, especially the campuses of some colleges which a few years ago were totally materialistic and denied everything of the supernatural. Today they are talking about demonism, about Satan, and actually about God and the Bible. All of a sudden an interest in the supernatural has appeared again, and angels seem to make sense even in the space age.

Men and women are concerned as they look about at a world of materialism that has gone crazy. We know how to get to the moon, but we do not know how to control human nature here on this earth. A great problem is arising right here in Southern California. A reputable paper has come out with the fact that Los Angeles is becoming an armed city with gangs who roam the streets. They are free to roam the streets while law-abiding people are imprisoned in their homes, afraid to venture out. Los Angeles has become an armed camp.

A few years ago this materialistic generation was saying that human nature was getting better, and since it has been improved, we don't need all of our laws; so the lid was taken off. My friend, we found out that instead of its being a bucket of rosewater, it was a bucket of stinking garbage! Vile and unspeakable crimes have been committed; unbelievable immorality has taken place. The question is being asked, "Where does all this vileness and evil come from?" As someone has expressed it, "If there were not the Devil, men would have to invent a devil to explain all the evil which is in this world today."

It really is not possible to deny that humanity is depraved. None of us seems to realize fully that we belong to a race that is totally depraved and that we live in a world that is under the control of Satan. It was thought that the removal of laws and restrictions would produce a wonderful, free society. However, the developments of recent years have caused men to return to the supernatural. Unfortunately, the emphasis has been on the evil spirits. Men have found they must believe in the evil spirits to explain the wickedness they find in the world.

Well, the Bible has something to say about it. My friend, the Bible is very much up to date. It is the Bible that tells us about the angels which rebelled against God and about those whom "he hath reserved in everlasting chains under darkness unto the judgment of the great day."

The Word of God has a great deal to say about the judgments that are coming. Folk without a knowledge of the Bible speak of one great judgment day which is coming. Well, the Great White Throne judgment is coming in the future for the unsaved (see Rev. 20:11–15), but actually there are eight judgments mentioned in the Word of God. One of those eight judgments is the judgment of angels, which will take place during the last days.

In 1 Corinthians we are told the order of the resurrections—". . . Christ the firstfruits; afterward they that are Christ's at his coming. Then cometh the end, when he shall have delivered up the kingdom to God, even the Father; when he shall have put down all rule and all authority and power. [The power is obviously evil power, the demonic forces which are in the world.] For he must reign, till he hath put all enemies under his feet" (1 Cor. 15:23–25). So during the Millennium these demonic powers will be judged.

The Scriptures have a great deal to say about the judgment of angels. Let me cite another passage: "Know ye not that we shall judge angels? how much more things that pertain to this life?" (1 Cor. 6:3). This is something that we would not have known if Paul hadn't mentioned it. We will be with our Lord during the Millennium. (We'll probably commute back and forth from earth to the New Jerusalem which is the eternal home of the church.) And at some period, probably during that thousand-year reign of Christ on the earth, there will be the judgment of angels. Although we were created lower than the angels, someday we will have part in their judgment.

Peter gives another reference to the judgment of angels which corresponds to that of Jude: "For if God spared not the angels that sinned, but cast them down to hell [hades, the place of the unsaved dead], and delivered them into chains of darkness, to be reserved unto judgment" (2 Pet. 2:4). "Chains of darkness" could not refer to our conception of chains as a series of connected metal links, because angels are spiritual creatures and it would be pretty difficult to put a physical chain on them! The word *chains* is "bonds," indicating that they are heavily guarded in a certain place. Again I turn to Dr. Wuest's translation:

And angels who did not carefully guard their original position of preeminent dignity, but abandoned once for all their own private dwelling-place, with a view to the judgment of the great day, in everlasting bonds under darkness, He has put under careful guard.

As we have seen, this company of angels is awaiting the judgment which apparently will come during the last days.

The other group of fallen angels are the demons which are abroad in the world today. Demonic power, of course, is a reality, although I personally feel that it is being overplayed at the time I am writing this. There is probably a good percentage of so-called demon activity that is phony, but certainly some of it is impossible to explain as natural phenomena. This is the reason the movie, *The Exorcist*, got under the skin of so many people. Although some of it was fictional, it was based on a factual case. It is an example of the forces of evil that are in the world. It actually took place, and there are other cases like it.

The Book of Revelation has several references to the judgment of fallen angels. "And the devil that deceived them was cast into the lake of fire and brimstone, where the beast and the false prophet are, and shall be tormented day and night for ever and ever" (Rev. 20:10). This is a reference to hell, which is the lake of fire. If you want to argue about its being literal fire, that is all right. It is even more literal than fire and worse than fire. Fire is a very weak symbol of how terrible it is going to be. After all, these are spiritual beings which are mentioned here, and fire as we know it would have no effect upon a spiritual being. Also, we learn from this verse that the Devil is not in hell today. A great many folk think he is there now, but instead he is very busy in your town and mine. Also, he has quite an army of helpers, both supernatural and natural—many folk are helping him, perhaps without realizing it.

Also, the Devil will be responsible for the terrible persecution of believers and especially of Israel during the Great Tribulation of the last days. He will be cast out of heaven: "And the great dragon was cast out, that old serpent, called the Devil, and Satan, which deceiveth the whole world: he was cast out into the earth, and his angels were cast out with him" (Rev. 12:9). Satan will be bound during the kingdom age: "And I saw an angel come down from heaven, having the key of the bottomless pit and a great chain in his hand. And he laid hold on the dragon, that old serpent, which is the Devil, and Satan, and bound him a thousand years, And cast him into the bottomless pit, and shut him up, and set a seal upon him, that he should deceive the nations no more, till the thousand years should be fulfilled: and after that he must be loosed a little season" (Rev. 20:1–3). And finally he will be consigned to the lake of fire, which we have seen in Revelation 20:10.

SODOM AND GOMORRAH SINNED IN SEXUALITY

Even as Sodom and Gomorrha, and the cities about them in like manner, giving themselves over to fornication, and going after strange flesh, are set forth for an example, suffering the vengeance of eternal fire [Jude 7].

This is Jude's third example of apostasy in the past. He has mentioned Israel in their unbelief, the angels which kept not their first estate, and now the people of Sodom and Gomorrah and the cities about them. These cities were so completely judged that they probably are buried beneath the Dead Sea today. Some people believe that they have located them. I am not sure whether or not this is true, and the exact location is unimportant. The important thing to know is that God destroyed these cities because the people defiled their flesh. They were given over to homosexuality or sodomy.

It is interesting that in the parlance of our day sodomy is called homosexuality, adultery is called free love, the drunkard is a respected alcoholic, and the murderer is temporarily insane. Satan is doing a good job of indoctrinating the world with a new vocabulary. Nevertheless, sodomy in God's sight is gross immorality and the vilest sin of all. The fact that God has judged men in the past for sins of sensuality ought to be a warning to our generation. God will judge any civilization that moves too far in this direction, and I wonder if we haven't done just that.

MODERN APOSTATE TEACHERS IDENTIFIED

Likewise also these filthy dreamers defile the flesh, despise dominion, and speak evil of dignities [Jude 8].

These apostate teachers are the ones that we are to beware of. As Jude puts it back in verse 4, they "crept in unawares"; that is, they came in sideways, they came in the side door, they slipped into the church under false colors. Their credentials and their creeds were not the same. They pretended to be something they were not.

There are four points of identification of apostate teachers that Jude gives to us in this verse:

1. They are "filthy dreamers." You will notice that the word *filthy* is in italics in the Authorized Version, which indicates that it is not in the better manuscripts, and we can

actually leave it out. They are dreamers—they live in an unreal world, a world that does not exist. My feeling is that the theological liberal has never dealt with reality. Liberalism is rather romantic. It sounds good on paper. It is nice to be able to solve all your problems by positive thinking, but there is a lot of power in negative thinking also. We need today to learn how to say no as well as to say yes. Liberals are dreamers in the sense that they will not face up to reality.

Many years ago I read an editorial in *Woman's Home Companion* which refers to a group of liberals who have since disappeared from the scene (however, there is a new crop of them abroad in the land today). The editorial reads:

A pledge "to have no part in any war" has been taken by a large body of leading Protestant clergymen in the east. Among them are some of the wisest and most influential ministers we have—men such as Fosdick, Holmes and Sockman in New York for example. This Covenant of Peace Group declares that war settles no issues, is futile and suicidal and is a denial of God and the teachings of Christ. It asserts that the "chain of evil" which holds us to war can and must be broken now. This is noble doctrine. However much events may lead us to differ with it, when these bold and sincere men stand in their pulpits and preach this rejection of all war, let us remember that these clergymen by their record have earned the right to their belief. In a great democracy suppression of the clergy in war or in peace can never justly become an instrument of policy, as it has under the dictators.

Such antiwar philosophy was carried over recently into the years of the war in Vietnam. It got us into a great deal of trouble and difficulty. The protest meetings that it inspired in this country actually prolonged the war and led to the killing of a great many more American boys who would not have been killed otherwise. Such thinking is to not realize that we live in a big, bad world and that reality is something you have to rub your nose into. It is something that you simply cannot ignore. Even steel-belted tires have to get down and go over the rough places, and some of them go flat, by the way. These men are dreamers. They are dealing with that which is not real at all. As long as we have a big navy and as long as we have atom bombs, it is nice to sit back in the cloister of the church and to make brave statements like this, but it just doesn't work out.

I have a notion that these men stay out of the ghettos and other such places at night, although they may talk very bravely in the daytime. In a denomination which has boasted of how they want to work among the minority groups, they have closed one of their churches which was located in a minority community. I think they have made a big mistake in doing that.

These men are dreamers, and they have gotten into the church and have used the church of the Lord Jesus Christ. Imagine making the statement that war is a denial of the teachings of Christ! The Lord Jesus made the statement, "When a strong man armed keepeth his palace, his goods are in peace" (Luke 11:21). The way you are going to protect your own is by being armed. He also said that the king who is going to war is going to sit down and figure it out (see Luke 14:31). He didn't say it was wrong to figure it out. He said the king had better figure it out, and if he is smart, he will figure out how he is going to carry on that war. May I say to you, these men have failed to face up to what the Lord Jesus Christ really said. He told His disciples, when He first sent them out, that they were to take nothing with them, not even a pocketbook (see Mark 6:7–9). However, when they had returned and He was sending them out to the ends of the earth, He said, "Be sure and take your pocketbook. And you had better take your American Express and Diner's Club cards and your gasoline credit cards. Also, it might be well to have a sword. You will need it to protect yourselves" (see Luke 22:35–36). May I say to you, what nonsense this is— these are dreamers who talk like this. It sounds good to say you don't want to have a part in war. All of us can agree with that. That's sort of like Mother, apple pie, and the American flag—we all are for it. It's great to have no part in war, but we have to face up to reality also. This is a deceptive message that they bring. It's nice to preach it to a well-heeled crowd on Sunday morning when there is no war and everything seems peaceable.

2. The second thing that Jude says about the apostate teachers is that they "defile the flesh." The thought that Jude has in mind here is that they engage in base and abnormal immorality. This is the same as the "strange flesh" in the cities of Sodom and Gomorrah that he talked about earlier. Many churches today have gone on record that they approve of homosexuality. My friend, God judged the cities of Sodom and Gomorrah. The angels are also a warning to us because they are going to be judged—they are being held for a judgment. And God would not let even His own people whom He had brought out of Egypt enter the Promised Land because of their unbelief. All these are examples to us today, and we had better recognize the fact that God will judge our "new morality." It is neither new morality nor new immorality; there is really nothing new about it. It goes back to Sodom and Gomorrah, and it goes back even to the days of Noah.

3. These apostate teachers "despise dominion," which means they reject authority. They are the crowd that wants to get rid of the death penalty. They are the crowd that wants to turn everybody loose to do his thing in his own way. We are seeing what is taking place as a result. Society has broken out today like a cancer in the body politic. We thought we were a civilized people, but we are nothing in the world but a group of savages. And it is because of this matter of despising dominion, of rejecting authority. We want certain laws repealed. For example, we don't want divorce. The argument given is that there is no reason to have divorce laws, that we ought to just let people stop living together. This breaks right across the morality of any nation, my friend, for the home is the bedrock of any society. During the war in Vietnam, it was tragic to see men with their collars buttoned in the back leading in the protest marches. I felt that the collar buttoned in the back was a real token that they were going in the wrong direction.

4. False teachers "speak evil of dignities." This means that they disrespect dignities. They protest against rules and those in authority. In other words, they take it out on the police because they represent authority, or they take it out upon men in high places. The president, the governors, and the mayors are made responsible for anything that happens in the nation or the state or the city, regardless of whether they are responsible or not. Why? Because there has been a loss of respect for authority. Now I will grant you that some men in authority have not been worthy of respect, but the office certainly demands respect. Jude will give us an example of this in the next verse.

Let's notice again the characteristics of these apostates who have come into the church. They came in the side door. They are ungodly. They turn the grace of God into lasciviousness. They deny the Lord Jesus Christ. They are dreamers, they defile the flesh, they despise dominion, and they have disrespect for dignities. These are the things that characterize them, and they are dangerous because of the way they have come into the church.

For ten long and weary years, the Greeks laid siege to the city of Troy, but they did not make a dent in the fortifications. It seemed impregnable, and they could not get an entrance into the city. Then there came forth a suggestion. The suggestion was to build a wooden horse with soldiers concealed inside, to leave it outside the gate, and then to pretend to sail away. So they made the wooden horse, the soldiers were put inside, and it was put by the gate of the city of Troy. Well, curiosity got the best of the Trojans. When they saw the Greeks sailing away, they thought the war was over. They went out, saw the horse, and decided to pull it inside the city. It certainly was a novelty, something to have. That night, the soldiers who were on the inside climbed out, and they were able to unlock the gates of the city from the inside. In the meantime, under cover of darkness, the fleet of Greek ships returned. They had only pretended to sail away. What an entire army of mighty men could not do from the outside in ten years, a few soldiers did from the inside. In the same way, the church has been harmed today from the inside and has been taken over by liberalism. Actually, the church has never been harmed from the outside. Persecution caused it to grow by leaps and bounds. Today we are witnessing the destruction of the church from the inside—it's an inside job. Christ was betrayed from the inside, not from the outside. One of His own betrayed Him over to His nation; His nation betrayed Him over to the Romans, and the Romans brought Him to the cross. The church is being betrayed today by the ones who have gotten in by the side door.

The apostasy that was a little cloud the size of a man's hand is now a raging storm that is lashing across the church, casting up foam and fury. We need to hang out this epistle as a storm warning because the apostasy is here in our midst today. I do not say this with any joy or bitterness, but I make it as a statement of fact. All the great denominations of the past are largely gone; that is, they have departed from the faith, probably never to return. They've gone into never-never land. As far as I know, there is no record of a church or any organization or an institution, having once departed from the faith, ever returning. I am told there have been some individuals who have, but I do not know any of them.

The Wesley movement which began in England, for example, was a come-out movement. It was begun when the church became cold and indifferent in that day, and the church of Wesley became a warm incubator in which to reproduce life. But I am sorry to say that today in many places it is a deep freeze that preserves the outward form of Wesley but does not have the warmth and the life that was once there.

I must be very frank to say that I do not think that fundamentalism as it is today is the answer. I perceive a real weakness which I think will ultimately undermine even fundamentalism. That weakness is this: Fundamentalism has been exact and precise in doctrine, but in many places it has been devoid of ethics and morals. There are no high principles and practices. There has been a moral breakdown outside in contemporary society, and, unfortunately, it is mirrored in our conservative churches. I was with a group sometime ago which is a fine group, but they are an illustration of what I mean. They are insistent and even belligerent about doctrine and about separation. But when it was called to their attention that one in their midst was guilty of immorality, they actually defended him! The ethical practices of another individual smelled to high heaven although he called himself a fundamentalist. May I say to you, this group took a ho-hum attitude. This hurts the cause of Christ a great deal because it comes from the inside.

We are living in days of apostasy. It may be that there are some who would say to me, "Preacher, you are really being sensational. Aren't you exaggerating just a little bit?" I don't think I am, my friend; in fact, I am not sure but what I am giving this in low key to you. I would like to pass on to you the results of a study that was made and some statements made by liberal preachers some years ago now. The situation today is even more alarming than this:

Out of a poll of 700 preachers, the following results were given: 48% denied the complete inspiration of the Bible; 24% rejected the atonement; 12% rejected the resurrection of the body; 27% did not believe that Christ will return to judge the quick and the dead. A Washington, D.C., minister said, "We liberal clergymen are no longer interested in the fundamentalist-modernist controversy. We do not believe we should even waste our time engaging in it. So far as we are concerned, it makes no difference whether Christ was born of a virgin or not. We don't even bother to form an opinion on the subject." An Arlington, Va., minister said, "We have closed our minds to such trivial consideration as the question of the resurrection of Christ. If you fundamentalists wish to believe that nonsense we have no objection, but we have more important things to preach than the presence or absence of an empty tomb 20 centuries ago." A leading minister in Washington, D.C., said flatly, "In our denomination what you call the 'faith of our Fathers' is approaching total extinction. Of course a few of the older ministers still cling to the Bible. But among the younger men, the real leaders of our denomination today, I do not know of a single one who believes in Christ, or any of the things that you classify as fundamentals."

My friend, have I exaggerated? Have I overstated the case of whether we are in the apostasy or not?

Yet Michael the archangel, when contending with the devil he disputed about the body of Moses, durst not bring against him a railing accusation, but said, The Lord rebuke thee [Jude 9].

This is a most remarkable verse of Scripture. Here is Wuest's very fine translation of it: "Yet Michael, the archangel, when disputing with the devil, arguing concerning the body of Moses, dared not bring a sentence that would impugn his dignity, but said, May the Lord rebuke you."

Satan is a fallen creature and an avowed enemy of God, yet Michael, when contending about the body of Moses, would not bring a sentence that would inpugn the dignity of Satan. Michael even respected the position of Satan. Clement, one of the early church fathers, quotes from an apocryphal writing dealing with the funeral of Moses. When Michael was commissioned to bury Moses, Satan opposed it on the grounds that, since he was the master of the material and matter, the body belonged to him. Michael's only answer was, "The Lord (that is, the Creator) rebuke thee." Satan also brought the charge of murder against Moses. Also it is suggested

that Satan wanted to hinder the later appearance of Moses at the Mount of Transfiguration.

Lucifer was a creature of God and apparently the highest creature that God created. And then evil was found in him. Don't think that evil means that he went out and stole something. The evil that was in him was that he put his will against the will of God. He was lifted up by pride, and he wanted to become independent of God. He actually thought he could dethrone God—at least from part of His universe. As far as this world is concerned, God has permitted him to carry on this rebellion, and God has a high and holy purpose in it. But this creature still believes he will be able to take a segment of God's created universe and be the ruler over it. I'm sure that Satan wants this earth as his.

"Yet Michael . . . durst not bring against him a railing accusation, but said, The Lord rebuke thee." Michael didn't curse Satan. He didn't call him a long list of names. I'm sure that many of us would have been perfectly willing to have done that. We really would have read the riot act to him, but Michael didn't. Do you know why? Michael is an archangel, and all he did was to say, "The Lord rebuke you." He didn't go into a long tirade of epithets or of condemnation, although he could have. Why? Michael had respect unto his office, his position—Lucifer had been created the highest creature.

This is a lesson that you and I need to learn. A great many believers have not learned to bow even to God. My friend, you and I are creatures; He is the Creator. What right have you and I to question anything that He does? Don't misunderstand me. If you think that I piously accept everything that comes my way, you are wrong. I talk back to Him many times, and I want to know why He lets certain things happen to me. Maybe you do that also. But we need to recognize that God is the Creator; He is also our Redeemer. He is the One who loves us. But our God is high, holy, and lifted up. He is a just and righteous God. He never makes any mistakes. He never does anything wrong. Everything He does is right and, therefore, you and I can trust Him. But do we do that? Do we respect His authority? Do we respect His person? In that day when men must give an account, the Lord Jesus Christ is going to say, "You said, 'Lord, Lord,' but you didn't do the things I commanded. Each one went his own way and did that which was right in his own eyes." This is the picture of mankind. How about you? How about me today? What a lesson Michael the archangel is to us!

But these speak evil of those things which they know not: but what they know naturally, as brute beasts, in those things they corrupt themselves [Jude 10].

I would like, as best I can, to make this verse understandable to you because it is another very important verse in this epistle. When Jude says, "But these speak evil," the Greek word is *blasphemeō* which by transliteration is our English word *blaspheme*. The apostates actually blaspheme.

"These speak evil of [blaspheme] those things which they know not: but what they know naturally." Jude uses two different words here which are both translated "know." May I say, without recognizing that, it is difficult to determine exactly what Jude means here. The first "know" is *eidō* which speaks of "mental comprehension and knowledge . . . referring to the whole range of invisible things," as Vincent defines it. Knowledge is *not* confined to what you can pour into a test tube or look at under a microscope, although a great many people think that it is. The finer things of life are things you cannot put under the microscope; you cannot pour them into a test tube. For example, what about a wonderful piece of music? What happens if you try to stick it down a test tube or look at it under a microscope? Music needs to be translated into sound, and the ear needs to hear it—you cannot see it at all; it is actually invisible. Love is also invisible—you couldn't put love under the microscope. How about faith?—you can't put it under the microscope. My friend, there are a great many things I know, and I know them without any proof from the laboratory. I know them because I have experienced them. The Holy Spirit has made them real to my own heart. "But these speak evil of those things which they know not." That Washington, D.C., preacher thought he was very brilliant to say that he no longer believed in the Resurrection. May I say to you, there are many things he doesn't know.

The second word for "know" which Jude uses here is *epistamai*, which means "to understand." Vincent says that it was used "originally of *skill in handicraft*" and that it "refers to palpable things; objects of sense; the circumstances of sensual enjoyment." These are things you can pour into the test tube. All that these folk know is what they can handle and what they can see. They are like brute beasts

because, after all, a brute only knows about the hay or the grass or the corn or another animal that it can eat. This refers to that which they know by instinct. For example, in the fall of the year, the ducks are in Canada, having had a nice summer up there, but all of a sudden they take off. Somebody says, "Boy, are they smart! Those ducks know that before long it will be winter, that snow will be on the ground, and that the lake is going to freeze over. So they take off for the south, and they go all the way down to Mexico and into Central America. They are really very smart!" No, they are not. They move just like a beast, just like a bird moves—by instinct. There is no comprehension, no understanding.

This generation that thinks it is so smart because it only believes what it can pour into a test tube is a poor generation. They do not understand anything that a brute beast couldn't understand. They have not reached the higher plane of knowledge, what Paul called *epignōsis*. Paul says, "You *can* know that the Bible is the Word of God. You *can* know that Jesus is the Savior of the world." These men, knowing just physical things, think they know everything that can be known, and they corrupt themselves in these things. This is the picture of the apostates that Jude gives to us.

CAIN, BALAAM, AND KORAH—EXAMPLES OF APOSTATES

Woe unto them! for they have gone in the way of Cain, and ran greedily after the error of Balaam for reward, and perished in the gainsaying of Core [Jude 11].

Jude has already given three examples of apostate groups: the children of Israel, the angels who rebelled, and the cities of Sodom and Gomorrah. Now we are given another three by way of illustration, and these three are individuals.

"Woe unto them!" The word for "woe" is the Greek word *ouai*. The very pronunciation of this word is a wail—"*Ouai, ouai!*" It denotes a wail of grief or of denunciation. Here it is more a wail of denunciation, but it is both. Of these apostates whom Jude has just identified, he now says, "Woe unto them!"

"For they have gone in the way of Cain." Cain was a religious man but a natural man. He believed in God and believed in religion, but he did it after his own will. He denied that he was a sinner, rejected redemption by blood, and thought that he could come his own way to

God. Hebrews 11:4 certainly tells the story: "By faith Abel offered unto God a more excellent sacrifice than Cain, by which he obtained witness that he was righteous, God testifying of his gifts: and by it he being dead yet speaketh." Cain is dead also, yet he speaks. The way of Cain is the way of a man who refused to bring a little lamb which pointed to Christ. In other words, Cain did not come to God by faith. He did not believe God when He said that man was to bring a little lamb for a sacrifice, that without shedding of blood there is no forgiveness of sins, and that the penalty must be paid. Cain thought that he could come to God his own way, and that is the picture of the apostate today. The apostate calls himself a liberal and a modernist; but, my friend, this is as old as the Garden of Eden. Right outside the Garden of Eden, Cain was a modernist and a liberal. He believed in religion and God, but he did it his own way, not God's way.

"And ran greedily after the error of Balaam for reward." Here we have the *error* of Balaam; in 2 Peter 2:15 it is the *way* of Balaam; and in Revelation 2:14 it is the *doctrine* of Balaam.

In 2 Peter we see the thing that was the undermining of the man; that is, Balaam was guilty of covetousness which is idolatry. He was a hired preacher. He wanted to make a buck with the gift he had, a gift that was apparently God-given. This was the way of Balaam, and it was his undoing. A man can seek for something other than money, however. He can seek for prominence, for popularity, for fame, for applause, or for position. There are many different things which would put a man in the way of Balaam. Jude says that this marks the apostate.

In the Book of Revelation, you have the doctrine of Balaam. Numbers 22–25 tells us that this man could not bring a curse against the nation Israel, and so he told Balak that by sending the Moabite women into the camp of Israel, he would be able to bring fornication and idolatry into their homes through mixed marriages. You can be sure of one thing: from Genesis to Revelation, God warns against the intermarriage of believers and unbelievers. You cannot condone such marriages on any basis whatsoever. It is unfortunate that too many young people are not warned of this because it has resulted in a great deal of unhappiness.

The error of Balaam here in Jude is that he thought God would have to punish Israel for their sins. He did not recognize that there is a morality that is above natural morality. He thought that a righteous God *had* to curse Israel. He was totally unaware of the morality of the Cross. It is taught in the Old Testament that God can maintain and does enforce His authority, but He can be just and the justifier of a believing sinner. Balaam did not understand that God would forgive the nation Israel when they turned to Him. It is sometimes difficult for someone to understand how a man can be converted. When I worked in a bank, was led to Christ, and wanted to study for the ministry, my fellow workers, most of whom were church members, could not understand how *I* could study for the ministry. And they had ample reason to wonder about that, by the way. They couldn't understand that God had forgiven me and that I had a new life now. They just didn't believe that. They didn't believe it because they couldn't understand it. This is the same problem that Balaam had.

"And perished in the gainsaying of Core [Korah]." You will perhaps recall that Korah led a rebellion against Moses (see Num. 16). He came to the conclusion that Moses was not the only one around who had access to God. Korah rebelled against God's constituted authority, who was Moses. He wanted to intrude into that which was sacred. In effect he asked, "Has God only spoken to Moses? Who does Moses think he is?" Actually, Moses didn't think too much of himself or that he had any undue qualifications; in fact, Moses wanted to disqualify himself as the leader of the people out of Egypt. But God had called Moses, and this man Korah rebelled against him. He contradicted the authority of Moses; he intruded into the office of the priests, and he died. In other words, he was a rebellious man, rebelling against God. Jude says that such rebellion characterizes the apostate.

Notice that the things which are true of these three individuals from the Old Testament are also the things which are true of apostates. Cain did not believe that you need to come to God by faith and that you need a bloody sacrifice because man is a sinner. He believed that if you have a religion, that is all you need. The apostate goes along with that. The error of Balaam is to think that a holy God must punish sin and that sinners cannot be forgiven. The apostate makes the same mistake. He says, "How in the world can the sacrifice of Christ save anyone? A man has to do this for himself." And the apostate rebels against God as Korah did. They assume an authority that is not theirs. They stand in the pulpit and give out politics instead of giving out the Word of God. Instead of telling what

God says, they tell people what they say and what they think. A man said to me sometime ago, "I have dropped out of my church. I am tired of listening to a preacher who gives political economics and attempts to stand in the position of being an authority on government. He assumes that he has all knowledge, and he never uses the Word of God. He never tells what God says or what God thinks, and I'm tired of listening to him." I know nothing about that man's church, but I assume that that preacher is an apostate because he has the mark of the apostate. These three men from the Old Testament illustrate this to us today.

MODERN APOSTATE TEACHERS DESCRIBED

In the next few verses the modern apostate teachers are defined and described. You will not find anywhere language more vivid, more graphic, more dramatic, more frightening than the description of the apostate in the last days.

> These are spots in your feasts of charity, when they feast with you, feeding themselves without fear: clouds they are without water, carried about of winds; trees whose fruit withereth, without fruit, twice dead, plucked up by the roots [Jude 12].

Again let me share with you Dr. Wuest's translation, which makes the description of the apostate teachers even more vivid:

> These are the hidden rocks in your love feasts, sumptuously feasting with you without fear, as shepherds leading themselves to pasture, waterless clouds carried past by winds, autumn trees without fruit, having died twice, rooted up.

What a picture we have here!

"These are spots in your feasts of charity." The word *spots* is better translated "hidden rocks" by Dr. Wuest. The picture is of hidden rocks which wreck a ship. They make what Paul calls "shipwreck" of the faith, and Paul names two men who evidently ran into an apostate, a hidden rock, and made shipwreck of the faith (see 1 Tim. 1:19–20). An apostate may be compared to the tip of an iceberg. Very little of it is visible, but if a ship runs into it, the ship will go to the bottom of the sea. Oh, how many people there are, especially young people, whose faith has not only been shaken but wrecked by a person who is an apostate!

"These are spots in your feasts of charity." The "feasts of charity" were love feasts which were held in the early church before the communion service. It was a time of fellowship when believers brought food and shared a meal together. The poor could bring very little, but it was a time of sharing what they had. Well, the apostates came in with ravenous appetites. They could eat more than anyone else—"feeding themselves without fear." They were shepherds who were feeding themselves instead of their flock. Not only in the matter of food but also in their failure to teach the Word of God to their flock, it was evident that they were concerned only about themselves.

Milton describes this kind of situation when he writes of his friend, Lycidas. In his poem, he expresses his grief for the young man who had been a great preacher and expositor of the Word but was drowned in the Irish Channel. Milton describes the situation in England as it prevailed in his day: "The hungry sheep look up and are not fed." What a picture of an apostate in the pulpit!

"Clouds they are without water." They may look as if they are filled with the Word of God, but they are empty and dry. They may wear robes and speak in pompous, pontifical voices with great authority. They have had courses in public speaking and homiletics, and they know how to spiritualize a text of Scripture and make it mean something entirely different from what God intended. They are like beautiful clouds that drift across the sky without giving any refreshment to the earth.

In my boyhood days I can remember chopping cotton in the summertime and watching the clouds pass over. Oh, how I prayed for rain so I could quit chopping cotton, but there was no rain in those clouds. They were nothing but snowy white puffs. There was no water in them at all. Well, that is Jude's picture of apostates. They do not have the water of life. They actually know nothing about the Word of God.

"Trees whose fruit withereth, without fruit, twice dead, plucked up by the roots." When the Lord Jesus gave the warning against false teachers, He said, ". . . by their fruits ye shall know them" (Matt. 7:20). Jude says that the apostate has withered fruit, he is "twice dead, plucked up by the roots." It was Dwight L. Moody who said that when a man is born once, he will have to die twice and that when a man is born twice, he will have to die only once. Well, Jude says that the apostates are spiritually dead, dead in trespasses and sins—and yet trying to lead others! Also the apostate's body will have to die; so he is twice dead. What a picture of the apostate—and Jude is not through with him.

Raging waves of the sea, foaming out their own shame; wandering stars, to whom is reserved the blackness of darkness for ever [Jude 13].

In the previous verse he said they were like clouds carried about by the wind. These men generally speak on current events every Sunday. They pick up something out of the newspaper or something they have seen on television, and that becomes their subject for the coming Lord's Day. They do not really give the interpretation of the Word of God which would be applicable for the day.

Now here Jude says that they are "raging waves of the sea." They just stand in the pulpit and rant. Dr. Thayer says that these false teachers are "impelled by their restless passions. They unblushingly exhibit in word and deed, their base and abandoned spirit."

"Wandering stars." Wandering stars just wander through space. They are lawless in that they follow no course whatsoever.

"To whom is reserved the blackness of darkness for ever." This refers to hell. One symbol of hell is fire, and the other is blackness of darkness. The great emphasis has been placed upon the symbol of fire. Hell is literal, of course, but to say it is literal fire isn't quite adequate for this reason: there will be spiritual creatures there as well as man—and the worst sins of man are spiritual sins such as unbelief. Therefore, physical punishment wouldn't be quite adequate. My feeling is that man will wish it were literal fire because it will be so much worse than fire. The other symbol, "blackness of darkness," is to me far more frightening. And I believe that a lost man carries his darkness with him—not only physical darkness but spiritual darkness. John Milton, who had an insight into many spiritual truths, penned these lines:

He that has light within his own clear
  breast,
May sit in the centre, and enjoy bright
  day;
But he that hides a dark soul, and foul
  thoughts
Benighted walks under the midday sun;
Himself is his own dungeon.

That is tremendous! My feeling is that the horrors of hell will be increased by those who go there. For instance, there is a place on earth called Hell's Kitchen. Is the difference in the kind of real estate that is there? No, the difference is in the *people* who are there. This, together with the concept of physical darkness, is to me frightful beyond words. If you have ever been down in Carlsbad Caverns when the lights are turned out, you know what real darkness is. I'd hate to be down there forever, my friend!

We come now to another remarkable passage of Scripture, and the only place it occurs in the Word of God is here in Jude.

And Enoch also, the seventh from Adam, prophesied of these, saying, Behold, the Lord cometh with ten thousands of his saints,

To execute judgment upon all, and to convince all that are ungodly among them of all their ungodly deeds which they have ungodly committed, and of all their hard speeches which ungodly sinners have spoken against him [Jude 14–15].

This prophecy of Enoch is not found in the Old Testament. In Genesis 5 we have the *record* of Enoch, but we are told nothing about his prophecy. Enoch is not a common name; so we may be sure that the man Jude mentions is Enoch of the antediluvian period, the man who walked with God and God took him.

Now let me quote what Dr. Wuest has written about this Book of Enoch:

The quotation is from the apocryphal Book of Enoch. This book, known to the Church Fathers of the second century, lost for some centuries with the exception of a few fragments, was found in its entirety in a copy of the Ethiopic Bible in 1773 by Bruce. It consists of revelations purporting to have been given to Enoch and Noah. Its object is to vindicate the ways of divine providence, to set forth the retribution reserved for sinners, and so show that the world is under the immediate government of God.

Enoch prophesied regarding the false teachers of the last days, and that is a remarkable thing! God apparently did not want the Book of Enoch in the canon of Scripture or it would be there—you may be sure of that. Godly men recognized that it was an apocryphal book, but here is one prophecy that God wanted put into His holy Word. It is a prophecy concerning the coming of Christ with His saints.

We know from the record in Genesis that Enoch was translated, that is, he was removed from the earth without dying. And sometime in the future the church, meaning true believers, are to be removed from the earth without dying. Of course, through the centuries since the time of Christ, believers have been dying so that at the present time most of the church has already passed through the doorway of death. And at the time of the Rapture they are to be caught up together with the living believers to meet the Lord in the air. This teaching is not in the Old Testament at all, yet Enoch is a type or a representative of the believers who will take part in the Rapture. Enoch was removed from the earthly scene before the judgment of the Flood came upon the earth. And the believers who compose the true church will be removed from this earth, will be caught up to meet the Lord in the air, before the judgment of the Great Tribulation breaks upon the earth.

Now, after the Great Tribulation, the Lord Jesus will return to the earth. However, at the time of the Rapture He does not come to the earth, but the believers are caught up to meet Him in the air. When we say that the Rapture is the second coming of Christ, we are not quite accurate if we mean that Christ is coming to earth at that time. No, the Rapture is the removal of the church. Then the visible church which is left on the earth, composed of folk who are not true believers, will totally depart from the faith and will enter the Great Tribulation Period. And at the end of the Tribulation, the Lord Jesus will actually come to the earth "to execute judgment upon all, and to convince all that are ungodly among them of all their ungodly deeds which they have ungodly committed," as Jude has prophesied. This is a remarkable passage of Scripture.

Now notice the penetrating truth brought out in Dr. Wuest's translation of Jude 14–15:

And there prophesied also with respect to these, the seventh from Adam, Enoch, saying, Behold, there comes the Lord with His holy myriads, to execute judgment against all and to convict all those who are destitute of a reverential awe towards God, concerning all their works of impiety which they impiously performed and concerning all the harsh things which impious sinners spoke against Him.

It is quite interesting that "holy myriads," which has to do with the numbers of the saints, can be supernatural or natural creatures, which probably means that the church will come back with Christ when He returns to the earth. If the church does come back with Him to reign on the earth, obviously it had to leave the earth sometime before. You simply have to believe in the Rapture if you believe that Christ is coming back to earth with His saints.

"To execute judgment upon all." When Christ returns to the earth, He is going to execute judgment. Jesus Himself said this in His Olivet Discourse. It is mentioned again and again in the Word of God, and we have seen it in the Old Testament.

"To convince all that are ungodly among them" or, as Dr. Wuest has translated it, "to convict all those who are destitute of a reverential awe towards God." They are ungodly in the sense that they leave God out. And that is something that is quite popular today.

"Of all their ungodly deeds which they have ungodly committed." Dr. Wuest translates it: "concerning all their works of impiety which they impiously performed." Their works are actually anti-God.

"And of all their hard speeches [harsh things] which ungodly sinners have spoken against him."

Now this prophecy of Enoch, and it is a great prophecy, deals with the judgment upon the organized church which will be in total apostasy after the Rapture. You see, the Rapture will rupture the church—the true believers will leave the earth, and the make-believers will remain and will be here when Christ comes to judge men in that day.

These are murmurers, complainers, walking after their own lusts; and their mouth speaketh great swelling words, having men's persons in admiration because of advantage [Jude 16].

Here are five additional identifications of apostates. (1) They are murmurers. Murmuring means to mutter complaints. This is not loud, outspoken dissatisfaction but muttering against God in an undertone. (2) They are complainers, complaining about their lot in life, discontented, never satisfied. If they recognize God at all, they blame Him for everything that has happened to them. I have received hundreds of letters from folk who tell me how discontented, dissatisfied, and unhappy they were with their lot. Then when they came to Christ, all of that changed. And another characteristic of apostates is that (3) they walk after their own lusts or desires.

Those desires could be good or bad—not necessarily desires which are base like immorality. It could be anything that leaves God out. It could be a sailing boat, good music, or literature, or even religion in which they find a certain amount of satisfaction, but in their hearts they are discontented. (4) Their mouth speaks great swelling words; that is, they are immoderate and arrogant; they use extravagant language, which is fizz and foam but has no content. I was rather amused by listening to a politician being interviewed. He used a great many modern expressions which are being overworked today. When he had finished, I analyzed what he had said and realized that he hadn't said anything—he had been just talking. He had not committed himself to anything whatsoever. Well, there are a great many men in the ministry who talk like that also. (5) They have men's persons in admiration because of advantage. This is literally "admiring countenances." They are great at applauding others—and they say a lot of things which are not true—because they are looking to men for their promotion, their advantage. You may recall that the Epistle of James has something to say about this: "My brethren, have not the faith of our Lord Jesus Christ, the Lord of glory, with respect of persons. For if there come unto your assembly a man with a gold ring, in goodly apparel, and there come in also a poor man in vile raiment; And ye have respect to him that weareth the gay clothing, and say unto him, Sit thou here in a good place; and say to the poor, Stand thou there, or sit here under my footstool: Are ye not then partial in yourselves, and are become judges of evil thoughts?" (James 2:1–4).

We see this kind of thing going on in our churches all the time. I went into a church sometime ago where I was to preach. The folk didn't know me very well—certainly the ushers did not. Since I arrived early, I thought I would just go in without identifying myself. When I entered the sanctuary, two ushers were busy talking to each other and paid no attention to me; so I just waited. Finally one of them said, "Want a bulletin?"

"Yes, thank you."

"Where do you want to sit?"

"Well, I don't know. Where would you want to seat me?"

"How about taking that seat right there?" He wasn't about to take me down to the front section although there were plenty of seats available. He was not in a friendly mood at all. So, instead of sitting down, I just walked on back. Later when I came out on the platform, I looked back at that usher. Believe me, he was white. After the service he came to me very apologetically. He said, "I didn't know you were going to be our speaker today. I didn't realize that you were Dr. McGee."

"Well," I said, "it really wasn't very important for you to recognize me because, very frankly, I was going to preach here today regardless of whether the ushers let me in or not. But I really think it is important that you usher strangers and visitors to a seat and be very friendly with them."

My friend, as believers we certainly should not have "men's persons in admiration because of advantage." Yet I notice this attitude both in churches and in certain Christian schools. One school will give a man from another school an honorary doctor's degree—something he didn't work for. Then that brother will arrange to have his school confer a doctor's degree on the brother who gave him his degree.

Also, this same type of thing is sometimes practiced by preachers. We speak in a certain church, and the pastor introduces us as some great person, which we certainly are not. Then when he comes over to our church to speak, we introduce him as some great person—whether he is or not. Frankly, we should not use that method because it is less than honest. And that is the method of apostates. They do not look to God. They are not concerned whether or not the Lord Jesus will say to them, "Well done, thou good and faithful servant." They are more concerned to have the applause of the crowd.

When I was in a certain conference, a very timid preacher came to me with a question. He asked, "Do you preach in your church the way you are speaking here?"

"Certainly. Why not?"

"Well, if I preached that way in my church, I am confident that I would have to resign."

I said to him very frankly, "I certainly feel sorry for *you*, and I think that your church is in a bad way. The message you heard me give was given in my church before I came here—I practiced on them!"

Having men's persons in admiration because of some advantage they will get from it, looking to men for promotion instead of looking to God for promotion, is certainly a condemnation and the mark of an apostate.

OCCUPATION OF BELIEVERS IN DAYS OF APOSTASY

In verses 17–19, believers are warned by the apostles that these apostates would come.

Then in verses 20–25, we will see what believers must do in these days of apostasy.

BELIEVERS WARNED THAT APOSTATES WOULD COME

Jude reminds believers that the apostles warned that these apostates would come. In other words, he is saying that this ought not to disturb us. The apostasy is something God has permitted, and He has permitted it for a purpose.

But, beloved, remember ye the words which were spoken before of the apostles of our Lord Jesus Christ [Jude 17].

Jude is turning away from describing the apostates, and he says, "But, beloved." He is turning the page as it were, and now he is talking to the beloved. The beloved are not those beloved of Jude. (However, I do think Jude loved them because he would not have written such a strong epistle if he had not loved them and desired to tell them the truth.) The word he uses here means that they are beloved of God. These are the ones who are experiencing the love of God in their lives, and for that reason they are called "beloved."

"Remember ye the words which were spoken before of the apostles of our Lord Jesus Christ." All the way through the Word of God, you will find that we are told to remember. In other words, we are to remember the Word of God. You and I should know the Word of God so that our memories can call it up when we need to have these great truths brought to our attention.

"But, beloved, remember ye the words which were spoken before of the apostles of our Lord Jesus Christ." This is evidence that Jude was not the apostle by that name. He is, as we have indicated, Jude, the half brother of the Lord Jesus. In spite of his blood relationship to Jesus, he takes a very humble attitude. He will use the apostles to corroborate what he is going to say, as he has done before in this epistle. He said earlier, "What I am going to write to you about the apostasy is not new with me. I'm not the only one who has written on it. Others have written of it beforehand." Now he says here, "You are to remember the words that were spoken to you by the apostles of the Lord Jesus Christ." We will see before we finish this epistle that it is all-essential to know what the Word of God has to say. I do not believe that you can stand for God in this world without tripping up unless you have a knowledge of the Word of God—it is essential. I have seen individual after individual, both

men and women, trip up and fall in their Christian walk. I can attribute every such instance that I know of to a lack of knowledge of the Word of God. How important it is for us to know what the Word of God has to say.

We come now to a very important passage of Scripture where I feel that I need a special anointing of the Holy Spirit as I write because it deals with a distinction that is not always made today.

How that they told you there should be mockers in the last time, who should walk after their own ungodly lusts.

These be they who separate themselves, sensual, having not the Spirit [Jude 18–19].

I will begin by giving you Dr. Wuest's translation of verses 17–19:

But, as for you, divinely-loved ones, remember the words which were spoken previously by the apostles of our Lord Jesus Christ, that they were saying to you, In the last time there shall be mockers ordering their course of conduct in accordance with their own passionate cravings which are destitute of reverential awe towards God. These are those who cause divisions, egocentric, not holding the spirit.

In verses 17–18, Jude says in effect, "Remember what the apostles said to you. They told you that there would come mockers in the last time and that they would walk after their own ungodly lusts." That is, the desires of the apostates are totally apart from God and from the will of God.

In verse 19 Jude defines the apostates: "These be they who separate themselves, sensual, having not the Spirit." He has given us so many descriptions of the apostate that there is no reason for us to miss him at all. I believe that you can test an unregenerate person, even an unregenerate minister, by the Word of God. I like to say that I use the Word of God as a Geiger counter. When I give out the Word of God, the Geiger counter registers, and I get a response from the folk who have heard it. Many tell us how the Word of God has actually revolutionized their lives and their homes. It has made everything different, even for those who are believers. But there is another group of people who think that I am a loony bird, that I'm way out in left field, and that teaching the Word of God is a very foolish sort of thing. So you can see that the Geiger counter of the Word of God works, and by it you can test the unregenerate person.

"These be they who separate themselves." First of all, Jude says that the apostates cause divisions in the church. Vincent says that Jude is speaking of those who "cause divisions in the church. . . . Of those who draw a *line through* the church and set *off* one part from another." Liberalism was responsible for splitting the great denominations of the church. The liberals took over the church and then said that the fundamentalists were the ones dividing it. Of course, it was not the fundamentalists who divided the church. They were the ones who were holding to the great doctrines upon which the denominations were founded. The original creeds of all the denominations are sound creeds. Although they differ a little at some points, there are no differences at all on the great basics.

The liberals were first called modernists because they wanted to change things. They never liked that name, but they like the name of liberal today. However, the liberal, instead of being broad-minded, whether he is in theology or politics, is to my judgment the most narrow-minded person in the world. Frankly, he is a dangerous man to deal with, because he will deal with you in a vitriolic manner, with bitterness and hatred, and he will not mind hurting you.

"Sensual"—the word is *psuchikos* from which we get our English word *psychology*. It means a life that centers about the individual; that is, the "I." It is an egotistical way of living in which the individual becomes all important: "I come first." It is selfish; it is natural. It is the life of the unrenewed man, the man who is not born again.

This is Alford's statement:

The *psuchē* [that is, the soul] is the centre of the personal being, the "I" of each individual. It is in each man bound to the spirit, man's higher part, and to the body, man's lower part; drawn upwards by the one, downward by the other. He who gives himself up to the lower appetites, is *sarkikos* (fleshly): he who by communion of his *pneuma* (spirit) with God's Spirit is employed in the higher aims of his being, is *pneumatikos* (spiritual). He who rests midway, thinking only of self and self's interests, whether animal or intellectual, is the *psuchikos* (sensual), the selfish man, the man in whom the spirit is sunk and degraded into subordination to the subordinate *psuchē* (soul).

The natural man, the sensual man, is a selfish man who lives like an animal. He wants to get all he can. He wants to eat all he can. He wants to get all the money and favor he can. He lives entirely for himself. All this has to do with a man in his natural makeup today.

"Having not the Spirit." The apostates do not have the Holy Spirit of God; they are not indwelt by the Spirit of God. You will remember that when Paul got to Ephesus, this was the question he directed to those people who were passing as believers but who were not believers. They had heard only of the baptism of John, and Paul asked them, "Did you receive the Holy Spirit when you first believed?" They knew nothing about it. They had heard about the ministry of John but had not been taught about the Lord Jesus' death and resurrection. When Paul explained these things to them, they accepted Christ and received the Holy Spirit (see Acts 19:1–7).

We need to understand that man is a tripartite being; that is, he has a threefold nature. In 1 Thessalonians 5:23 we read: "And the very God of peace sanctify you wholly; and I pray God your whole spirit and soul and body be preserved blameless unto the coming of our Lord Jesus Christ." Man has a body, a soul, and a spirit.

If you read very carefully the account of the creation of man in the Book of Genesis, you will find that physically, man was taken from the ground. There are about fifteen elements in the dirt which are made into our bodies. When we get through with our bodies, at the time of death, we will be moving out of them, and these bodies will return back to the earth. At the resurrection of the believer, the body will be raised a spiritual body. It is sown in corruption, and it is going to be raised in incorruption.

What happened to this physical man that God created? He was given what we would call a soul—but that word is often misunderstood. He was given the psychological part of himself; that is, that part which directs him in his approach to the physical universe. He gets hungry; so he goes and eats. He desires entertainment, and he provides that for himself. He may be a very generous individual, very amiable, very attractive, and he may have what we call charisma. Many unsaved people are like that. They are likable folk, and I sometimes wish that all believers were as gracious as some unsaved people whom I meet. Although unsaved folk can be very attractive on the surface, they are very different underneath, of course. This is man's psychological nature.

But God also breathed into man's breathing places the breath of life, or the wind, the *pneuma*, the spirit. This is man's human spirit, and it is above the psychological. It is that which looks to God, that which longs for God, that which wants to worship.

Man, therefore, has a tripartite nature. He is a trinity: the body or the physical side, the soul or the psychological side, and the spirit or the pneumatic side. The psychological side is what Jude calls "sensual" here in verse 19.

Now what really happened at the fall of man? I like to think of man in his tripartite nature as a house with three floors. On the first floor is the dining room and the kitchen—that is the physical. On the second floor is the library and the music room—that is the psychological. On the top floor is a chapel, a place to worship—that is the spiritual. On the top floor is also the Word of God, because man will not understand it without the Spirit of God leading him; the natural man would not even want it. The spiritual was on the top floor, but at the Fall, man actually died spiritually, and the house turned upside down. The physical side got up on top. Man today in his natural state is primarily physical. Meat and potatoes are top priority. Self-preservation is the first law of life. Man is like the animal world in that he is physical, but man is also psychological. He is self-conscious. He enjoys music. He loves beauty. And he also indulges in immorality. This is the area, the sensual part of man, that Jude refers to here. At the Fall, therefore, the spiritual part of man died. Man no longer had a capacity for God; in fact, he was now an enemy of God.

However, when you and I came to Christ and trusted Him as Savior, we were given a new nature, and that new nature can now respond to the Holy Spirit of God. But we still have that old nature. We are still fleshly, and we can live in the flesh. Paul had a great deal to say about this in the eighth chapter of Romans. He writes in verse 5: "For they that are after the flesh [this is the natural man, the apostate] do mind the things of the flesh [that is all they are interested in]; but they that are after the Spirit the things of the Spirit [these folk seek to please God]." Paul goes on in verse 6 to say, "For to be carnally minded is death; but to be spiritually minded is life and peace." When you live in the lower nature—the psychological, the sensual—you are dead to God and have no fellowship with Him. That fellow-ship is broken. John says, "If we say that we have fellowship with him, and walk in darkness, we lie, and do not the truth" [1 John 1:6]. But he who lives in the Spirit and attempts to please God is truly living it up. The spirit of such a man, instead of going downward and doing the things the flesh wants to do, does the things God wants done. Now Paul says in Romans 8:7, "Because the carnal mind is enmity against God [this is the reason Adam ran away from God]: for it is not subject to the law of God, neither indeed can be." You cannot bring that old nature into obedience to God. You cannot reform man. Romans 8:8–9 tells us: "So then they that are in the flesh cannot please God. But ye are not in the flesh, but in the Spirit, if so be that [lit., *since*] the Spirit of God dwell in you. . . ." You cannot please God in the flesh. You can only please Him when you yield to Him and come to the place where He can use you.

This brings me to consider what happens when a man is converted. Before our conversions, you and I were dead in trespasses and sins. We could walk around, we were physically alive, but we were spiritually dead. When a man hears the gospel, the Spirit of God applies it to his heart, and he trusts Christ. We say that he is born again. The spiritual nature is reborn, and he now has a capacity for God. There is no power in that new nature; so the Holy Spirit comes to dwell within him. This is what Paul meant when he wrote, "But ye are not in the flesh, but in the Spirit, if so be that the Spirit of God dwell in you . . ." (Rom. 8:9). In other words, the indwelling Spirit is the mark that you are a child of God. The Holy Spirit is not something that you get ten days or so after you are converted. If you don't get Him at the moment you are converted, you are not converted because it is the Holy Spirit who regenerates—we are "born of the Spirit" (see John 3:8). The Holy Spirit is there not only to help you but also to interpret to you the Word of God. And the Word of God is no longer foolishness to you, because a new world and a new life have been opened to you.

However, there is the struggle that goes on which Paul talks about in Galatians 5:17: "For the flesh lusteth [warreth] against the Spirit, and the Spirit against the flesh: and these are contrary the one to the other: so that ye cannot do the things that ye would." There are these two natures within a believer. The old nature, this lower nature, this psychological part of man, wants to turn away from God. This spiritual part now wants to turn to God.

If you are a child of God, you know about that conflict. There are times when you want to turn away from Him, and there are times when you want to turn to Him. This is the reason most of us are like a roller coaster in our Christian lives. We go up today, and it is great, but then we go down tomorrow. What a trip it is—up and down! It ought not to be that way, but, unfortunately, most of us would have to testify that that is true of us.

In 1 Corinthians 15:45 Paul talks about the Resurrection, and he has this to say: ". . . The first man Adam was made a living soul [that is, the psychological]; the last Adam was made a quickening spirit [that is, a life-giving spirit]." This is the difference between Adam No. 1 and Adam No. 2, between Adam in the Garden of Eden and the Lord Jesus Christ on the cross. The Lord Jesus came to give His life that He might be a life-giving Spirit. Paul goes on to say in verses 46–47: "Howbeit that was not first which is spiritual, but that which is natural [Adam was a psychological being]; and afterward that which is spiritual. The first man is of the earth, earthy: the second man is the Lord from heaven." This, I believe, is the big difference between Adam before his fall and the man today who is regenerated. We are today made sons of God and are given a spiritual nature with a capacity for God. Man's highest nature at the beginning was that God breathed into his breathing places, but that was a spirit that could fall. We have a nature today that is a sinful nature, and we will have it as long as we are in this body because it actually controls this body—this is the psychological part of man. But at the moment of regeneration we were given a new nature which responds to God and cannot fall.

When I first studied psychology (it was one of my major areas of study at one time), they said that psychology was the study of the soul of man. Then they got away from that, and they said it was the study of the mind of man. Behaviorism came along and then Freudianism later on, and they took their theory of man farther and farther away from anything psychological or even mental. Man became nothing in the world but a sort of robot or IBM computer. You can press a certain button and always get a certain reaction from him. As a result, the saying went around that psychology first lost its soul, and then it lost its mind. I do not know whether it has recovered it or not!

The thing that I want to emphasize here is that the flesh pulls man down and the Spirit pulls man up. Jude says that these apostates never get into the realm of the Spirit—"having not the Spirit." They are "sensual"; they never get above the psychological state. Therefore, it is very easy to tell whether or not you are a child of God, my friend. Paul lists the works of the flesh in Galatians 5:19–21, and if you are producing those in your life, you are living in the flesh. He then lists the fruit of the Spirit in verses 22–23. If you have those things in your life, you are a child of God. But the apostate does not have those things in his life. He cannot have them because he does not have the Spirit of God.

I have spent a little time with this because I feel it is very important that you and I understand ourselves and why we have all the conflicts and frustrations that we Christians have. We have two natures. The psalmist says that we are "fearfully and wonderfully made" (see Ps. 139:14). Man is a very complicated creature. A man walks this earth today with a body that is taken out of the dirt, but he also has a capacity for God. A man who wants to worship and serve God can become a son of God through faith in Jesus Christ—what a glorious prospect this is!

WHAT BELIEVERS MUST DO IN DAYS OF APOSTASY

Now having described the apostasy that was coming and the apostates who would come into the church, Jude mentions seven things which believers can do in days like these in which you and I are living.

But ye, beloved, building up yourselves on your most holy faith, praying in the Holy Ghost [Jude 20].

"But ye, beloved"—he is talking to believers, those beloved of God. What can we do today?

1. "Building up yourselves on your most holy faith." What does he mean by that? Well, building up yourselves on your most holy faith means that you *study* the Word of God. It is my conviction that since God gave to us sixty-six books, He meant that we are to study all sixty-six of them—not just John 3 or John 14 and other favorite passages. Oh, how many Bible classes go over and over the same books: John, Romans, maybe Ephesians, and they don't miss Revelation. Do not misunderstand me, all those books are very important, but what about the other sixty-two books? Why don't we study *all* of them? My friend, if you are going to build up yourself on your most holy faith, you must have the total Word of

God. You cannot build a house without a foundation; then you will need to put up some timbers that will hold the roof; then you are going to need a roof on it and siding and plaster on the inside. And this is what the total Word of God will do for you. This is what we are to do in days of apostasy.

Both Peter and Paul urged believers to study the Word of God in days like these. Paul wrote in his swan song: "Study to shew thyself approved unto God, a workman that needeth not to be ashamed . . ." (2 Tim. 2:15). Then in the next chapter Paul said that *all* Scripture is given by inspiration of God. My friend, the recourse that you and I have as children of God in these days is the Word of God.

The reason many folk fall by the wayside is because the seed (which is the Word of God) fell among stones. It didn't get deeply rooted. Unless you study all of the Word of God, get down in the good, rich soil, you are not going to become a sturdy, healthy plant. It won't be long until you will be stepped on and the sun will burn you out. You will not be able to stand in days like these.

Peter in his second epistle, writing of the apostasy, says, "We have also a more sure word of prophecy; whereunto ye do well that ye take heed, as unto a light that shineth in a dark place, until the day dawn, and the day star arise in your hearts: Knowing this first, that no prophecy of the scripture is of any private interpretation" (2 Pet. 1:19–20). You cannot just pull out one or two little verses and think you have a good knowledge of the Bible. It is a tragedy to build a system of doctrine based on a few isolated verses drawn out of the Scriptures.

This reminds me of the story of President Lincoln having his portrait painted. The artist kept shifting Lincoln around trying to get him at an angle so the wart on his face wouldn't show. Finally, after he had him adjusted to his satisfaction, he said, "Mr. Lincoln, how do you want me to paint you?" Lincoln said, "Paint me just as I am—wart and all."

My friend, certainly there are parts of the Word of God that you will not enjoy reading. There are sections that will step on your toes, and you would like to avoid that. But today it is necessary to build up ourselves on our most holy faith because these *are* days of apostasy.

"Your most holy faith" does not refer to your own personal faith. Rather, it is *the* faith, the body of truth which has been given to us in the Word of God. When the church first came into existence, this was called the apostles' doctrine. Of this Mayor says:

The faith here is called 'most holy' because it comes to us from God, and reveals God to us, and because it is by its means that man is made righteous, and enabled to overcome the world.

2. "Praying in the Holy Ghost." Jude mentions the second thing we are to do in days of apostasy. The word *Ghost* is the Greek *pneuma*, more frequently translated "Spirit." "Praying in the Holy Spirit" is an unusual phrase, occurring at only one other place in the Scriptures. In the Epistle to the Ephesians, Paul mentions putting on the whole armor of God, and each piece of armor is for defense with the exception of two items. One offensive weapon is "Praying always with all prayer and supplication in the Spirit, and watching thereunto with all perseverance and supplication for all saints" (Eph. 6:18). The second offensive weapon was mentioned in verse 17, "the sword of the Spirit, which is the word of God." This is precisely what Jude writes. First, we are to build up ourselves on our most holy faith; then we need to pray in the Spirit.

Many years ago in Dallas, Texas, there was a very fine man, Mr. Will Hawkins, who had a radio program which he called The Radio Revival. I do not know of any program during the depression and afterwards that influenced people more than his program did. One of the features of his radio broadcast was what he called a sword drill, a test of the knowledge of the Word of God, and I thought it was about the best way it could be used. My friend, you and I need a sword drill; that is, we need to listen to *God* first before He has to listen to us, because we could say a lot of foolish things. We are to take the sword of the Spirit, because we need to build up *ourselves* in the faith—we should learn to *use* that sword.

Praying in the Holy Spirit is a little different from handing God a grocery list of "Gimme, gimme, gimme." Don't misunderstand me, petition, as it is called in theology, is a part of prayer. But how about praise and how about worship? Our prayer should include adoration and praise to almighty God. Dr. Earl Radmacher once told me about directing a prayer meeting in a church he pastored. The prayer meetings had been pretty dead, as most church prayer meetings are, unfortunately. They should be the real powerhouse of the church body, but they usually are not. One night Dr. Radmacher announced that they were not going to have any requests but only praise and thanksgiving to God for what He had done for them. Dr. Radmacher said that it turned out to be the briefest prayer meeting they had ever had! It is amazing how few things we thank God for and how little praise goes up to Him. However, petition is certainly important, and prayer that includes that is a real ministry. When Paul asked the Christians in Rome to pray for him, he wrote: "Now I beseech you, brethren, for the Lord Jesus Christ's sake, and for the love of the Spirit, that ye strive together with me in your prayers to God for me" (Rom. 15:30). The word for "strive" is *agonize*. We are to pray like that.

Praying in the Holy Spirit means that we pray by means of the Holy Spirit; we are dependent upon Him. Paul wrote in Romans 8:26, "Likewise the Spirit also helpeth our infirmities: for we know not what we should pray for as we ought: but the Spirit itself maketh intercession for us with groanings which cannot be uttered." You and I actually do not know what to pray for. We are like little children. When I take my little grandson to the store, he wants everything he sees. He asks for things that he shouldn't even have because they would not be good for him. Then I think, *That's just the way we pray*. We are like little children: "Lord, I want this—Lord, give me that." God doesn't always give us what we want. Why doesn't He? Because when we pray like that, we are not praying in the Spirit. We need to learn to let the Holy Spirit make intercession for us.

Years ago a missionary in Venezuela sent me a little cross on which was printed a definition of prayer: "Prayer is the Holy Spirit speaking in the believer, through Christ, to the Father." That is a very good definition of prayer.

My friend, we need to learn to pray. No wonder the disciples, having heard the Lord Jesus pray and thinking of their own little paltry prayers, said, "Lord, teach us to pray" (see Luke 11:1). Many of us need that, but there is very little instruction today about learning to pray. Yet we need to learn to really *pray* in these days of apostasy.

Keep yourselves in the love of God, looking for the mercy of our Lord Jesus Christ unto eternal life [Jude 21].

This verse gives us two more things we as believers are to do in days of apostasy.

3. "Keep yourselves in the love of God." We need to recognize that God *loves* the believer. We have seen that Jude addresses the believers as "beloved." Let me repeat—this does not imply that *he* loves them or that they love him but that they are beloved of *God*. Again, let me say that you cannot keep God from loving you, although you can put up an umbrella or a roof so that you will not feel the warmth of God's love. Jude is saying, "Keep yourselves out there in the sunshine of God's love." Let His love flood your heart and life. This is needed in days of apostasy.

4. "Looking for the mercy of our Lord Jesus Christ unto eternal life." There was a man here in Southern California, a professor in a seminary, whom I had asked to preach in the church I served, and someone questioned that he really believed in the rapture of the church. So I had lunch with him and asked him this specific question: "Do you believe in the imminent coming of Christ?"

"I do."

"On what basis do you believe that He will take the church out? That is, on what grounds do you and I expect to be taken out at the time of the Rapture?"

He said very definitely, "I was saved because God extended *mercy* to me, and when He takes me out of the world at the time of the Rapture, it still will be by the *mercy* of God."

That is a good answer, and it cleared up all doubts of his position on the rapture of the church.

My friend, as we have seen, the mercy of God is the fact that God has a concern and care for you today. And He has an abundance—He is *rich* in mercy. He was so concerned about you that He extended His mercy to you and saved you by His grace.

Notice that Jude says, "Looking for the mercy." The word *looking* is the Greek word *prosdechomai*, meaning "to expect, to wait for." The Lord Jesus wants us to live in an attitude of expectation for His return. At the time of the Rapture, I am expecting to leave this world, and I hope it will happen during my lifetime. But I will be going out because of His mercy, not because of who I am. If it depended upon who I am, I wouldn't make it.

When I first went to Nashville, Tennessee, there was a very fine Bible class there that had been taught the theory of a partial rapture; that is, that only the super-duper saints would go out at the Rapture. They were a wonderful group of folk, and they supported my ministry in Nashville. I even had the privilege of teaching the class several times. However, in talking with some of them, especially the leaders, they made it clear that they expected to go out at the time of the Rapture because they were the super-duper saints, but

I had the feeling that they weren't sure about me. Well, I want them and everyone else to know that when the Lord takes the church out, I'm going along—whether you like it or not—because I am *looking* for that mercy of the Lord Jesus Christ.

Now notice Dr. Wuest's translation of verse 21:

With watchful care keep yourselves within the sphere of God's love, expectantly looking for the mercy of our Lord Jesus Christ resulting in life eternal.

And of some have compassion, making a difference [Jude 22].

5. "Of some have compassion." There is some question among Greek scholars as to the correct translation of this verse. Instead of "making a difference," I prefer the rendering "who are in doubt." There are a great many good, sincere folk today who are in doubt. They do have honest doubts, and we need to be patient with them. Being in the ministry I have had some difficulty in being patient with some folk. I remember a woman who came to our midweek Bible study in a church I served many years ago. *Every* week for six weeks she came to me with some question. I had the feeling that she was trying to trap me or trick me with her questions, and one night I answered her so sharply that she turned and walked out. The woman who always came with her was a member of my church, and she came to me afterward and said, "Dr. McGee, be patient with her. She is a very brilliant woman. In fact, she is listed in *Who's Who*. But she has been in practically every cult here in Southern California, and she is really mixed up. Now she is trying to find her way out. Will you be patient with her?" Well, knowing her background, of course, I was patient after that and answered her questions the best I could. About three months later she accepted Christ as her Savior. I had a wonderful letter after she had returned to Ohio in which she told how the Lord was leading her.

My friend, we are living in days when there is so much doubt cast upon the Word of God that those who really want to believe it have problems in doing so. We do well to be patient with them—they are honest doubters.

And others save with fear, pulling them out of the fire; hating even the garment spotted by the flesh [Jude 23].

6. "And others save with fear, pulling them out of the fire" refers to sinners whom we consider hopeless. It seems impossible that they will ever be saved. And yet I have seen some of these folk come to know Christ by hearing God's Word by radio. Jude admonishes us not to give them up—"others save with fear, pulling them out of the fire." What a tremendous statement!

In Zechariah 3:2 we read this: "And the LORD said unto Satan, The LORD rebuke thee, O Satan; even the LORD that hath chosen Jerusalem rebuke thee: is not this a brand plucked out of the fire?" When God intended to save Jerusalem, He said, "I am just taking a brand out of the fire." Apparently there is no one who is beyond redemption, if they want to be saved.

7. "Hating even the garment spotted by the flesh." The word *flesh* refers to the psychological part of man, the part of man that can go only so far. It can, for example, appreciate good music, but it cannot be acceptable to God. There have been attempts to come up with the right word for this psychological part of man. The word *soul* is not adequate because it doesn't express what it should. Some call it the *selfish* part of man. That is not a good definition because some psychological people are very generous although they are not Christian. Others speak of it as the *animal*, which is even worse. Although these people generally attempt to satisfy the lower nature, *animal* is not the proper word. Still others call them *intellectual*, which is the worst one of all. Lange, in his *Commentary on the Holy Scriptures*, attempts to adequately describe these folk:

He is becoming flesh, wholly carnal or animal. If allowed to continue he will become utterly dehumanized, or that worst of all creatures, *an animal with a reason*, but wholly fleshly in its ends and exercises, or with a reason which is but the servant of the flesh, making him worse than the most ferocious wild beast—a very demon—a brutal nature with a fiend's subtlety only employed to gratify such brutality. Man has the supernatural, and this makes the awful peril of his state. By losing it, or rather by its becoming degraded to be a servant instead of a lord, he falls wholly into nature, where he cannot remain stationary, like the animal who does not "leave the habitation to which God first appointed him." The higher being, thus utterly fallen, must sink into the demonic, where evil becomes his god, if not, as Milton says, his good.

The fact is that the child of God should hate "even the garment spotted by the *flesh*." God cannot use anything that the flesh produces. Everything that Vernon McGee does in the flesh is repulsive to God; He *hates* it. And *we* should learn to hate it.

This little Epistle of Jude closes with a glorious benediction.

Now unto him that is able to keep you from falling, and to present you faultless before the presence of his glory with exceeding joy,

To the only wise God our Saviour, be glory and majesty, dominion and power, both now and ever. Amen [Jude 24–25].

Let me give you a literal translation:

Now unto him who is able to keep you from stumbling, and to present you (make you stand) before the presence of his glory blameless with great rejoicing, to the only wise God our Savior, through Jesus Christ our Lord, be glory and majesty and might and authority, before all time both now and forever. Amen.

If you want to know the place that Jesus Christ should have in your life, especially in these days of apostasy, here it is in this marvelous benediction.

"Through Jesus Christ our Lord"—He is God. And He is our Lord; He should be the Lord of our lives. Glory should be given to Him. We should glorify Him, tell how great He is, how wonderful He is, how mighty He is and mighty to save. He is majestic, the King of Kings and Lord of Lords. He is mighty—all power is given unto Him in heaven and in earth. This universe has not slipped from under His control. All authority belongs to Him, and whether you like it or not, you are going to bow the knee to Him someday.

In these days of apostasy, God's children need to bring glory to the name of Jesus Christ and to try to hold Him up before a gainsaying world.

BIBLIOGRAPHY

(Recommended for Further Study)

Coder, S. Maxwell. *Jude: The Acts of the Apostates*. Chicago, Illinois: Moody Press, 1958.

Ironside, H. A. *Exposition of the Epistle of Jude*. Neptune, New Jersey: Loizeaux Brothers, n.d.

Kelly, William. *Lectures on the Epistle of Jude*. Denver, Colorado: Wilson Foundation, 1970.

Wolff, Richard. *A Commentary on the Epistle of Jude*. Grand Rapids, Michigan: Zondervan Publishing House, 1960.

Wuest, Kenneth S. *In These Last Days: II Peter, I, II, III John, and Jude in the Greek New Testament for the English Reader*. Grand Rapids, Michigan: Wm. B. Eerdmans Publishing Co., 1954.

REVELATION
INTRODUCTION

As we begin this book of Revelation, I have mingled feelings. I am actually running scared as we come to this, one of the great books in the Word of God. Candidly, I must also say that it is with great joy that I begin it. Let me explain why I say this.

It has long been my practice, when I need a time of relaxation, to read a mystery story, a detective story. I confess that mystery stories have been more or less a hobby of mine over the years.

I do not read much of Agatha Christie anymore for the very simple reason that I have read so many of hers that I can usually figure out who the killer is, who committed the murder. Now I read Dorothy Sayers. By the way, she is a Christian, and she gets a great deal of Scripture into her books. The unsaved are reading the Bible without realizing it. Anyway, I have always enjoyed mystery stories.

When I began my ministry, I was a single man, and on Sunday nights after the evening service, I would get into bed and read one of the mystery stories.

Well, about one o'clock in the morning I would get to the place where the heroine has been tied down to the railroad tracks by the villain, and old Number 77 is going to be coming along in about twenty minutes. She is in a desperate situation. I think that the hero is going to be able to get there and rescue her, but I find out that he is in that old warehouse down by the pier, tied to a chair under which is a stick of dynamite with the fuse already lighted! Well, I can't leave the hero and heroine at one o'clock in the morning in that kind of position. But, since it is time for me to turn over and go to sleep, I slip over to the final page. A different scene greets me there. I see the hero and the heroine sitting out in a yard. I see a lovely cottage encircled by a white picket fence. They are married now and have a little baby who is playing there on the lawn. What a wonderful, comfortable scene that is!

So I would just turn back to the place where I stopped reading, and I would say to the hero and heroine, "I don't know how you are going to get out of it, but I tell you this: It's going to work out all right."

My friend, I have a book in the Bible called the Book of the Revelation, and it tells me how this world scene is going to end. I will be frank to say that I get a little disturbed today when I see what is happening in the world. It is a dark picture as I look out at it, and I wonder how it is going to work out. Well, all I do is turn to the last book of the Bible, and when I begin to read there, I find that it's going to work out all right. Do you know that? Emerson said that *things* are in the saddle, and they ride mankind. It does look that way. In fact, it looks as if the Devil is having a high holiday in the world, and I think he is, but God is going to work it out. God Himself will gain control—in fact, He has never lost control—and He is moving to the time when He is going to place His Son, the Lord Jesus Christ, upon the throne of His universe down here. It does look dark now. I think that any person today who looks at the world situation and takes an optimistic view of it has something wrong with his thinking. The world is in a desperate condition. However, I'm no pessimist because I have the Book of Revelation, and I can say to every person who has trusted Christ, "Don't you worry. It's going to work out all right." My friend, the thing is going to come out with God on top. Therefore, I want to be with *Him*. As Calvin put it, "I would rather lose now and win later than to win now and lose later." I want to say to you, friend, that I am on the side that appears to be losing now, but we are going to win later. The reason I know this is because I have been reading the Book of Revelation. And I hope that you are going to read it with me.

As I have said, I approach the Book of Revelation with fear and trembling, not primarily because of a lack of competence on my part (although that may be self-evident), but many other factors enter into this feeling. First of all, there may be a lack of knowledge on the part of the readers. You see, the Book of Revelation is the sixty-sixth book of the Bible, and it comes last. This means that we need to know sixty-five other books before we get to this place. You need to have the background of a working knowledge of all the Bible that precedes it. You need to have a feel of the Scriptures as well as have the facts of the Scriptures in your mind.

There is a second factor that gives me a feeling of alarm as I enter this book. It is the contemporary climate into which we are giving these studies in Revelation. It is not primarily because of a skeptical and doubting age—although it is certainly that—but it is because of these dark and difficult and desperate days in which we live. We see the failure of leadership in every field—government, politics, science, education, military, and entertainment. Since the educators cannot control even their own campuses, how are they going to supply leadership for the world? Business is managed by tycoons. And the actors can be heard on the media talk programs. Listening to them for only a brief time reveals that they have nothing to say. They do a lot of talking, but they say nothing that is worthwhile. None of these groups or segments of our society have any solutions. They are failures in the realm of leadership. There is a glaring lack of leadership. There is no one to lead us out of this moral morass or out of the difficult and Laocoön-like problems which have us all tangled up. We are living in a very difficult time, my friend. In fact, I think that it is one of the worst in the history of the church.

Knowledgeable men have been saying some very interesting things about this present hour. Please note that I am not quoting from any preachers but from outstanding men in other walks of life.

Dr. Urey, from the University of Chicago, who worked on the atomic bomb, began an article several years ago in *Collier's* magazine by saying, "I am a frightened man, and I want to frighten you."

Dr. John R. Mott returned from a trip around the world and made the statement that this was "the most dangerous era the world has ever known." And he raised the question of where we are heading. Then he made this further statement, "When I think of human tragedy, as I saw it and felt it, of the Christian ideals sacrificed as they have been, the thought comes to me that *God is preparing the way for some immense direct action.*"

Chancellor Robert M. Hutchins, of the University of Chicago, gave many people a shock several years ago when he made the statement that "devoting our educational efforts to infants between six and twenty-one seems futile." And he added, "The world may not last long enough." He contended that for this reason we should begin adult education.

Winston Churchill said, "Time may be short."

Mr. Luce, the owner of *Life, Time,* and *Fortune* magazines, addressed a group of missionaries who were the first to return to their fields after the war. Speaking in San Francisco, he made the statement that when he was a boy, the son of a Presbyterian missionary in China, he and his father often discussed the premillennial coming of Christ, and he thought that all missionaries who believed in that teaching were inclined to be fanatical. And then Mr. Luce said, "I wonder if there wasn't something to that position after all."

It is very interesting to note that *The Christian Century* carried an article by Wesner Fallaw which said, "A function of the Christian is to make preparation for world's end."

Dr. Charles Beard, the American historian, said, "All over the world the thinkers and searchers who scan the horizon of the future are attempting to assess the values of civilization and speculating about its destiny."

Dr. William Yogt, in the *Road to Civilization*, wrote: "The handwriting on the wall of five continents now tells us that the Day of Judgment is at hand."

Dr. Raymond B. Fosdick, president of the Rockefeller Foundation, said, "To many ears comes the sound of the tramp of doom. Time is short."

H. G. Wells declared before he died, "This world is at the end of its tether. The end of everything we call life is close at hand."

General Douglas MacArthur said, "We have had our last chance."

Former president Dwight Eisenhower said, "Without a moral regeneration throughout the world there is no hope for us as we are going to disappear one day in the dust of an atomic explosion."

Dr. Nicholas Murray Butler, ex-president of Columbia University, said, "The end cannot be far distant."

To make the picture even more bleak, the modern church has no solutions for the problems of this hour in which we are living. There was a phenomenal growth in church membership, especially after World War II, but that took place for only a few years. The growth went from 20 percent of the population in 1884 to 35 percent of the population in 1959. That was the high point of Protestant church membership. And it would indicate the possibility of a church on fire for God. Then it had wealth and was building tremendous programs, but recently the church has begun to lose, and it certainly is not affecting the contemporary culture of the present hour.

As far back as 1958 the late David Lawrence wrote an editorial which he entitled "The 'Mess' in the World." He described it very accurately, but even he did not have a solution for it. As we look out at the world in this present hour, we see that it is really in a *mess*.

For a long time now men in high positions have looked into the future and have said that there is a great crisis coming. (I wonder what they would say if they lived in our day!) As a result of this foreboding, there has been a growing interest in the Book of Revelation.

Although good expositors differ on the details of the Book of Revelation, when it comes to the broad interpretation, there are four major systems. (Broadus lists seven theories of interpretation and Tregelles lists three.)

1. The *preterist* interpretation is that all of Revelation has been fulfilled in the past. It had to do with local references in John's day and with the days of either Nero or Domitian. This view was held by Renan and by most German scholars, also by Elliott. The purpose of the Book of Revelation was to bring comfort to the persecuted church and was written in symbols that the Christians of that period would understand.

Now let me say that it was for the comfort of God's people, and it has been that for all ages, but to hold the preterist interpretation means that you might as well take the Book of Revelation out of the Bible, as it has no meaning at all for the present hour. This viewpoint has been answered and, I think, relegated to the limbo of lost things.

2. The *historical* interpretation is that the fulfillment of Revelation is going on continuously in the history of the church, from John's day to the present time. Well, I believe that there is a certain amount of truth in this as far as the seven churches are concerned, as we shall see, but beyond that, it is obvious that the Book of Revelation is prophetic.

3. The *historical-spiritualist* interpretation is a refinement of the historical theory and was advanced first by Sir William Ramsay. This theory states that the two beasts are imperial and provincial Rome and that the point of the book is to encourage Christians. According to this theory, Revelation has been largely fulfilled and contains only spiritual lessons for the church today.

The system we know today as amillennialism has, for the most part, adopted this view. It dissipates and defeats the purpose of the book. In the seminary of my denomination, I studied Revelation in both Greek and English from the standpoint of the amillennialist. It was amazing to see how the facts of the Revelation could be dissipated into thin air by just saying, "Well, these are symbols." But they never were able to tell us exactly what they were symbols *of.* That was their problem. The fact of the matter is that some very unusual interpretations arise from this viewpoint. One interpreter sees Luther and the Reformation in a symbol that to another student pictures the invention of the printing press! In my opinion, interpretations of this type have hurt and defeated the purpose of the Book of Revelation.

4. The *futurist* interpretation is the view which is held by all premillennialists and is the one which I accept and present to you. It sees the Book of Revelation as primarily prophetic. Most premillennialists follow a certain form of interpretation that conforms to the Book of Revelation. (We will see this in the outline of the book.) It begins with the revelation of the glorified Christ. Then the church is brought before us, and the whole history of the church is given. Then, at the end of chapter 3, the church goes to heaven and we see it, not as the church anymore, but as the bride which will come to the earth with Christ when He comes to establish His kingdom—that thousand-year reign that John will tell us about. It will be a time of testing, for at the end of that period Satan will be released for a brief season. Then the final rebellion is put down and eternity begins. This is the viewpoint of Revelation which is generally accepted.

In our day there are many critics of this interpretation who not only attempt to discount it but say rather harsh things about it. One recent book of criticism, written by a layman, quotes me as being unable to answer his argument. Well, the fact of the matter is that he called me at home one morning as I was getting ready to go to my office. I wasn't well at the time, and I didn't want to get involved in an argument with a man who obviously was very fanatical in his position. In his book he makes the statement that I was *unable* to answer his question. If he misquotes the other Bible expositors as he misquotes me, I would have no confidence in his book whatsoever.

In his book he maintains that the premillennial futurist viewpoint is something that is brand new. I'll admit that it has been fully developed, as have all these other interpretations, during the past few years. When I was a young man and a new Christian, I was introduced to the theory known as postmillennialism. The postmillennialists believed that the world would get better and better, that the church would convert the whole world, and then Christ would come and reign. Well, that viewpoint is almost dead today. After two world wars, a worldwide depression, and the crises through which the world is passing, there are very few who still hold that viewpoint. By the time I enrolled in the seminary of my denomination, every professor was an amillennialist, that is, they didn't believe in a millennium. It was to that view that most of the postmillennialists ran for cover. There was one professor in the seminary who was still a postmillennialist. He was very old and hard of hearing. In fact, when they told him that the war was over, he thought they meant the Civil War. He was really a back number, and he was still a postmillennialist.

At the risk of being a little tedious, I am going to give you the viewpoints of many men in the past to demonstrate that they were looking for Christ to return. They were not looking for the Great Tribulation, they were not even looking for the Millennium, but they were looking for *Him* to come. This expectation is the very heart of the premillennial viewpoint as we hold it today.

Barnabas, who was a co-worker with the apostle Paul, has been quoted as saying, "The true Sabbath is the one thousand years . . . when Christ comes back to reign."

Clement (A.D. 96), Bishop of Rome, said, "Let us every hour expect the kingdom of God . . . we know not the day."

Polycarp (A.D. 108), Bishop of Smyrna and finally burned at the stake there, said, "He will raise us from the dead . . . we shall . . . reign with Him."

Ignatius, Bishop of Antioch, who the historian Eusebius says was the apostle Peter's successor, commented, "Consider the times and expect Him."

Papias (A.D. 116), Bishop of Hierapolis, who—according to Irenaeus—saw and heard the apostle John, said, "There will be one thousand years . . . when the reign of Christ personally will be established on earth."

Justin Martyr (A.D. 150) said, "I and all others who are orthodox Christians, on all points, know there will be a thousand years in Jerusalem . . . as Isaiah and Ezekiel declared."

Irenaeus (A.D. 175), Bishop of Lyons, commenting on Jesus' promise to drink again of the fruit of the vine in His Father's kingdom, argues: "That this . . . can only be fulfilled upon our Lord's personal return to earth."

Tertullian (A.D. 200) said, "We do indeed confess that a kingdom is promised on earth."

Martin Luther said, "Let us not think that the coming of Christ is far off."

John Calvin, in his third book of *Institutes,* wrote: "Scripture uniformly enjoins us to look with expectation for the advent of Christ."

Canon A. R. Fausset said this: "The early Christian fathers, Clement, Ignatius, Justin Martyr, and Irenaeus, looked for the Lord's speedy return as the necessary precursor of the millennial kingdom. Not until the professing Church lost her first love, and became the harlot resting on the world power, did she cease to be the Bride going forth to meet the Bridegroom, and seek to reign already on earth without waiting for His Advent."

Dr. Elliott wrote: "All primitive expositors, except Origen and the few who rejected Revelation, were premillennial."

Gussler's work on church history says of this blessed hope that "it was so distinctly and prominently mentioned that we do not hesitate in regarding it as the general belief of that age."

Chillingworth declared: "It was the doctrine believed and taught by the most eminent fathers of the age next to the apostles and by none of that age condemned."

Dr. Adolf von Harnack wrote: "The earlier fathers—Irenaeus, Hippolytus, Tertullian, etc.—believed it because it was part of the tradition of the early church. It is the same all through the third and fourth centuries with those Latin theologians who escaped the influence of Greek speculation."

My friend, I have quoted these many men of the past as proof of the fact that from the days of the apostles and through the church of the first centuries the interpretation of the Scriptures was premillennial. When someone makes the statement that premillennialism is something that originated one hundred years ago with an old witch in England, he doesn't know what he is talking about. It is interesting to note that premillennialism was the belief of these very outstanding men of the early church.

There are six striking and singular features about the Book of Revelation.

1. It is the only prophetic book in the New Testament. There are seventeen prophetic books in the Old Testament and only this one in the New Testament.

2. John, the writer, reaches farther back into eternity past than does any other writer in Scripture. He does this in his gospel which opens with this: "In the beginning was the Word, and the Word was with God, and the Word was God" (John 1:1). Then he moves up to the time of creation: "All things were made by him; and without him was not any thing made that was made" (John 1:3). Then, when John writes the Book of Revelation, he reaches farther on into eternity future and the eternal

kingdom of our Lord and Savior Jesus Christ.

3. There is a special blessing which is promised to the readers of this book: "Blessed is he that readeth, and they that hear the words of this prophecy, and keep those things which are written therein: for the time is at hand" (Rev. 1:3). It is a blessing *promise*. Also, there is a warning given at the end of the book issued to those who tamper with its contents: "For I testify unto every man that heareth the words of the prophecy of this book, If any man shall add unto these things, God shall add unto him the plagues that are written in this book: And if any man shall take away from the words of the book of this prophecy, God shall take away his part out of the book of life, and out of the holy city, and from the things which are written in this book" (Rev. 22:18–19). That warning ought to make these wild and weird interpreters of prophecy stop, look, and listen. It is dangerous to say just *anything* relative to the Book of Revelation because people today realize that we have come to a great crisis in history. To say something that is entirely out of line is to mislead them. Unfortunately, the most popular prophetic teachers in our day are those who have gone out on a limb. This has raised a very serious problem, and later on we will have repercussions from it.

4. It is not a *sealed* book. Daniel was told to seal the book until the time of the end (see Dan. 12:9), but John is told: "Seal not the sayings of the prophecy of this book: for the time is at hand" (Rev. 22:10). To say that the Book of Revelation is a jumble and impossible to make heads or tails out of and cannot be understood is to contradict this. It is not a sealed book. In fact, it is probably the best organized book in the Bible.

5. It is a series of visions expressed in symbols which deal with *reality*. The literal interpretation is always preferred unless John makes it clear that it is otherwise.

6. It is like a great union station where the great trunk lines of prophecy have come in from other portions of Scripture. Revelation does not originate or begin anything. Rather it consummates and concludes that which has been begun somewhere else in Scripture. It is imperative to a right understanding of the book to be able to trace each great subject of prophecy from the first reference to the terminal. There are at least ten great subjects of prophecy which find their consummation here. This is the reason that a knowledge of the rest of the Bible is imperative to an understanding of the Book of Revelation. It is calculated that there are over five hundred references or allu-

sions to the Old Testament in Revelation and that, of its 404 verses, 278 contain references to the Old Testament. In other words, over half of this book depends upon your understanding of the Old Testament.

Let's look at the Book of Revelation as an airport with ten great airlines coming into it. We need to understand where each began and how it was developed as it comes into the Book of Revelation. The ten great subjects of prophecy which find their consummation here are these:

1. The Lord Jesus Christ. He is the subject of the book. The subject is not the beasts nor the bowls of wrath but the Sin-bearer. The first mention of Him is way back in Genesis 3:15, as the Seed of the woman.

2. The church does not begin in the Old Testament. It is first mentioned by the Lord Jesus in Matthew 16:18: "And I say also unto thee, That thou art Peter, and upon this rock I will build my church; and the gates of hell shall not prevail against it."

3. The resurrection and the translation of the saints (see John 14; 1 Thess. 4:13–18; 1 Cor. 15:51–52).

4. The Great Tribulation, spoken of back in Deuteronomy 4 where God says that His people would be in tribulation.

5. Satan and evil (see Ezek. 28:11–18).

6. The "man of sin" (see Ezek. 28:1–10).

7. The course and end of apostate Christendom (see Dan. 2:31–45; Matt. 13).

8. The beginning, course, and end of the "times of the Gentiles" (see Dan. 2:37–45; Luke 21:24). The Lord Jesus said that Jerusalem will be trodden down of the Gentiles until the Times of the Gentiles are fulfilled.

9. The second coming of Christ. According to Jude 14–15, Enoch spoke of that, which takes us back to the time of the Genesis record.

10. Israel's covenants, beginning with the covenant which God made with Abraham in Genesis 12:1–3. God promised Israel five things, and God says in Revelation that He will fulfill them all.

Now I want to make a positive statement: The Book of Revelation is *not* a difficult book. The liberal theologian has tried to make it a difficult book, and the amillennialist considers it a symbolic and hard-to-understand book. Even some of our premillennialists are trying to demonstrate that it is weird and wild.

Actually, it is the most *orderly* book in the Bible. And there is no reason to misunderstand it. This is what I mean: It divides itself. John puts down the instructions given to him by Christ: "Write the things which thou hast seen, and the things which are, and the things which shall be hereafter"(Rev. 1:19)—past, present, and future. Then we will find that the book further divides itself in series of sevens, and each division is as orderly as it possibly can be. You will find no other book in the Bible that divides itself like that.

To those who claim that it is all symbolic and beyond our understanding, I say that the Book of Revelation is to be taken literally. And when a symbol is used, it will be so stated. Also it will be symbolic of *reality*, and the reality will be more real than the symbol for the simple reason that John uses symbols to describe reality. In our study of the book, that is an all-important principle to follow. Let's allow the Revelation to say what it wants to say.

Therefore, we have no right to reach into the book and draw out of it some of the wonderful pictures that John describes for us and interpret them as taking place in our day. Some of them are symbolic, symbolic of reality, but not of a reality which is currently taking place.

The church is set before us in the figure of seven churches which were real churches in existence in John's day. I have visited the ruins of all seven of them and have spent many hours there. In fact, I have visited some of them on four occasions, and I would love to go back tomorrow. To examine the ruins and study the locality is a very wonderful experience. It has made these churches live for me, and I can see how John was speaking into local situations but also giving the history of the church as a whole.

Then after chapter 3, the church is not mentioned anymore. The church is not the subject again in the entire Book of the Revelation. You may ask, "Do you mean that the church goes out of business?" Well, it leaves the earth and goes to heaven, and there it appears as the bride of Christ. When we see her in the last part of Revelation, she is not the church but the bride.

Then beginning with chapter 4, everything is definitely in the future from our vantage point at the present time. So when anyone reaches in and pulls out a revelation—some vision about famine or wars or anything of that sort—it just does not fit into the picture of our day. We need to let John tell it like it is. In fact, we need to let the whole Bible speak to us like that—just let it say what it wants to say. The idea of making wild and weird in-

terpretations is one of the reasons I enter this book with a feeling of fear.

It is interesting to note that the subject of prophecy is being developed in our day. The great doctrines of the church have been developed in certain historical periods. At first, it was the doctrine of the Scripture being the Word of God. This was followed by the doctrine of the person of Christ, known as Christology. Then the doctrine of soteriology, or salvation, was developed. And so it has been down through the years. Now you and I are living in a day when prophecy is really being developed, and we need to exercise care as to what and to whom we listen.

When the Pilgrims sailed for America, their pastor at Leyden reminded them, "The Lord has more truth yet to break forth from His Holy Word. . . . Luther and Calvin were great shining lights in their times, yet they penetrated not the whole counsel of God. . . . Be ready to receive whatever truth shall be made known to you from the written word of God." That, my friend, is very good advice because God is not revealing His truth by giving you a vision or a dream or a new religion. Therefore, we need to be very sure that all new truth comes from a correct interpretation of the *Word of God*.

As I have indicated, the twentieth century has witnessed a renewed interest in eschatology (the doctrine of last things) which we call prophecy. Especially since World War I, great strides have been made in this field. New light has fallen upon this phase of Scripture. All of this attention has focused the light of deeper study on the Book of Revelation.

In the notes which I have made on this book, I have attempted to avoid the pitfall of presenting something new and novel just for the sake of being different. Likewise, I have steered clear of repeating threadbare clichés. Many works on Revelation are merely carbon copies of other works. In my own library I have more commentaries on the Revelation than on any other book of the Bible, and most of them are almost *copies* of those that have preceded them.

Another danger we need to avoid is that of thinking that the Book of Revelation can be put on a chart. Although I myself have a chart and have used it in teaching, I will not be using it in this study. The reason is that if it includes all it should, it is so complicated that nobody will understand it. On the other hand, if it is so brief that it can be understood, it doesn't give enough information. I have several charts sent to me by different men in whom I have great confidence. One of them is so complicated that I need a chart to understand his chart! So, although I won't be using a chart, I will use the brief sketch below to attempt to simplify the different stages of the Revelation and also give the overall picture.

Here in Revelation you see Him in glory. You see Him in charge of everything that takes place. He is in full command. This is the *unveiling* of Jesus Christ.

Snell has put it so well that I would like to quote him:

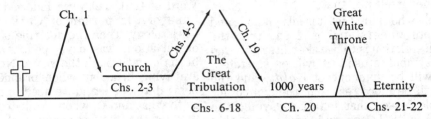

As you can see, it begins with the cross of Christ and His ascension. In chapter 1, we see the glorified Christ. In chapters 2–3 we see the church. In chapters 4–5 we see that the church is in heaven. Then on earth the Great Tribulation takes place, chapters 6–18. In chapter 19 we see that Christ returns to the earth and establishes His kingdom, and chapter 20 gives us the thousand-year reign of Christ. Then the Great White Throne is set up, the place where the lost are judged, and in chapters 21–22 eternity begins. That is the Book of Revelation.

Stauffer has made an important observation:

Domitian was also the first emperor to wage a proper campaign against Christ, and the church answered the attack under the leadership of Christ's last apostle, John of the Apocalypse. Nero had Paul and Peter destroyed, but he looked upon them as seditious Jews. Domitian was the first emperor to understand that behind the Christian movement there stood an enigmatic figure who threatened the glory of the emperors. He was the first to declare war on this figure, and the first also to lose the war—a foretaste of things to come.

The subject of this book is very important to see. To emphasize and reemphasize it, let me direct your attention to chapter 1, verse 1—"The Revelation of *Jesus Christ*, which God gave unto him, to shew unto his servants things which must shortly come to pass" (italics mine). Let's keep in mind that this book is a revelation of Jesus Christ. In the Gospels you see Him in the days of His flesh, but they do not give the full revelation of Jesus Christ. There you see Him in humiliation.

In the Revelation the Lamb is the center around which all else is clustered, the foundation upon which everything lasting is built, the nail on which all hangs, the object to which all points, and the spring from which all blessing proceeds. The Lamb is the light, the glory, the life, the Lord of heaven and earth, from whose face all defilement must flee away, and in whose presence fullness of joy is known. Hence we cannot go far in the study of the Revelation without seeing the Lamb. Like direction posts along the road to remind us that He, who did by Himself purge our sins, is now highly exalted and that to Him every knee must bow and every tongue confess.

To that grand statement I say hallelujah! For the Lamb is going to reign upon this earth. That is God's intention, and that is God's purpose.

As I have said, the Book of Revelation is not really a difficult book. It divides itself very easily. This is one book that doesn't require our labor in making divisions in it. John does it all for us according to the instructions given to him. In verse 18 of the first chapter the Lord Jesus speaks as the glorified Christ: "I am he that liveth, and was dead; and, behold, I am alive for evermore, Amen; and have the keys of hell and of death." Notice the four grand statements He makes concerning Himself: "I am alive. I was dead. I am alive for evermore. And I have the keys of hell [the grave] and of death." Then He tells John to write, and He gives him his outline in chapter 1, verse 19: "Write the things which thou hast seen, and the things which are, and the things which shall be hereafter." My friend, this is a wonderful, grand division that He is giving. In fact, there is nothing quite like it.

He first says, "I am he that liveth." And He instructs John, "Write the things which thou hast seen." That is past tense, referring to the vision of the Son of Man in heaven, the glorified Christ in chapter 1.

Then He says, "I was dead, and, behold, I am alive." And His instruction is, "Write the things which are." This is present tense, referring to Christ's present ministry. We are going to see that the living Christ is very busy *doing* things today. Do you realize that He is the Head of the church? Do you know the reason the contemporary church is in such a mess? The reason is that the church is like a body that has been decapitated. It is no longer in touch with the Head of the church. We will see Christ's ministry to the church in chapters 2–3.

Thirdly, Christ said, "I have the keys of hell and of death." And when we get to chapter 5, we will see that no one could be found to open the book but one—the Lord Jesus Christ. So chapters 4–22 deal with the future, and Christ said to John, "Write the things that you are about to see after these things." It is very important to see that "after these things" is the Greek *meta tauta*. After what things? After the church things. So in chapters 4–22 he is dealing with things that are going to take place after the church leaves the earth. The fallacy of the hour is reaching into this third section and trying to pull those events up to the present. This gives rise to the wild and weird interpretations we hear in our day. Why don't we follow what John tells us? He gives us the past, present, and future of the Book of Revelation. He will let us know when he gets to the *meta tauta*, the "after these things." You can't miss it—unless you follow a system of interpretation that doesn't fit into the Book of Revelation.

As you will see by the outline that follows, I have used the divisions which John has given to us:

I. The *Person* of Jesus Christ—Christ in glory, chapter 1.

II. The *Possession* of Jesus Christ—the church in the world is His, chapters 2–3.

III. The *Program* of Jesus Christ—as seen in heaven, chapters 4–22.

The last section deals with the consummation of all things on this earth. This is what makes Revelation such a glorious and wonderful book.

In the first division of the Book of Revelation we will see the person of Christ in His position and glory as the Great High Priest who is in charge of His church. We will see that He is in absolute control. In the Gospels we find Him to be meek, lowly, and humble. He made Himself subject to His enemies on earth and died upon a cross! We find a completely different picture of Him in the Book of the Revelation. Here He is in absolute control. Although He is still the *Lamb* of God, it is His wrath that is revealed, the wrath of the Lamb, and it terrifies the earth. When He speaks in wrath, His judgment begins upon the earth.

The person of Jesus Christ is the theme of this book. When the scene moves to heaven, we see Him there, too, controlling everything. Not only in Revelation but in the entire Bible Jesus Christ is the major theme. The Scriptures are both theocentric and Christocentric, God-centered and Christ-centered. Since Christ is God, He is the One who fills the horizon of the total Word of God. This needs to be kept in mind in a special way as we study the Book of Revelation—even more than in the Gospels. The Bible as a whole tells us what He has done, what He is doing, and what He will do. The Book of Revelation emphasizes both what He *is doing* and what He *will do*.

The last book of the Old Testament, Malachi, closes with the mention of the Sun of Righteousness which is yet to rise. It holds

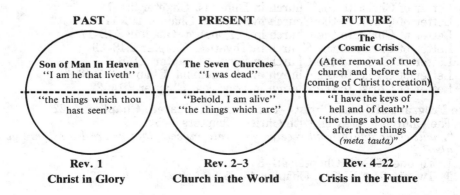

PAST	PRESENT	FUTURE
Son of Man In Heaven "I am he that liveth"	**The Seven Churches** "I was dead"	**The Cosmic Crisis** (After removal of true church and before the coming of Christ to creation)
"the things which thou hast seen"	"Behold, I am alive" "the things which are"	"I have the keys of hell and of death" "the things about to be after these things (*meta tauta*)"
Rev. 1	**Rev. 2–3**	**Rev. 4–22**
Christ in Glory	**Church in the World**	**Crisis in the Future**

out a hope for a cursed earth, and that hope is the coming again of the Lord Jesus Christ. The Book of Revelation closes with the Bright and Morning Star, which is a figure of Christ at His coming to take the church out of the world. The Rapture is the hope of the New Testament, just as the revelation of Christ was the hope of the Old Testament. And the Book of Revelation will complete the revelation of Christ.

Notice also that there is a tie between Genesis and Revelation, the first and last books of the Bible. Genesis presents the beginning, and Revelation presents the end. Note the contrasts between the two books:

In Genesis the earth was created; in Revelation the earth passes away.

In Genesis was Satan's first rebellion; in Revelation is Satan's last rebellion.

In Genesis the sun, moon, and stars were for earth's government; in Revelation these same heavenly bodies are for earth's judgment. In Genesis the sun was to govern the day; in Revelation there is no need of the sun.

In Genesis darkness was called night; in Revelation there is "no night there" (see Rev. 21:25; 22:5).

In Genesis the waters were called seas; in Revelation there is no more sea.

In Genesis was the entrance of sin; in Revelation is the exodus of sin.

In Genesis the curse was pronounced; in Revelation the curse is removed.

In Genesis death entered; in Revelation there is no more death.

In Genesis was the beginning of sorrow and suffering; in Revelation there will be no more sorrow and no more tears.

In Genesis was the marriage of the first Adam; in Revelation is the marriage of the Last Adam.

In Genesis we saw man's city, Babylon, being built; in Revelation we see man's city, Babylon, destroyed and God's city, the New Jerusalem, brought into view.

In Genesis Satan's doom was pronounced; in Revelation Satan's doom is executed.

It is interesting that Genesis opens the Bible not only with a global view but with a universal view—"In the beginning God created the heaven and the earth" (Gen. 1:1). And the Bible closes with another global and universal book. The Revelation shows what God is going to do with His universe and with His creatures. There is no other book quite like this.

OUTLINE

I. The Person of Jesus Christ—Christ in Glory, Chapter 1
   A. Title of the Book, Chapter 1:1
   B. Method of Revelation, Chapter 1:2
   C. Beatitude of Bible Study, Chapter 1:3
   D. Greetings from John the Writer and from Jesus Christ in Heaven, Chapter 1:4–8
   E. The Post-Incarnate Christ in a Glorified Body, Judging His Church (the Great High Priest in the Holy of Holies), Chapter 1:9–18
     "we know him no longer after the flesh"
   F. Time Division of the Contents of Apocalypse, Chapter 1:19
   G. Interpretation of the Seven Stars and Seven Lampstands, Chapter 1:20

II. The Possession of Jesus Christ—The Church in the World, Chapters 2–3
   A. Letter of Christ to the Church in Ephesus, Chapter 2:1–7
   B. Letter of Christ to the Church in Smyrna, Chapter 2:8–11
   C. Letter of Christ to the Church in Pergamum, Chapter 2:12–17
   D. Letter of Christ to the Church in Thyatira, Chapter 2:18–29
   E. Letter of Christ to the Church in Sardis, Chapter 3:1–6
   F. Letter of Christ to the Church in Philadelphia, Chapter 3:7–13
   G. Letter of Christ to the Church in Laodicea, Chapter 3:14–22

III. The Program of Jesus Christ—The Scene in Heaven, Chapters 4–22
   A. The Church in Heaven with Christ, Chapters 4–5
     "I will come again, and receive you unto myself; that where I am there ye may be also"
     1. Throne of God, Chapter 4:1–3
     2. Twenty-four Elders, Chapter 4:4–5

(4) Wild Beast, Designation, Chapter 13:18
4. Looking to the End of the Great Tribulation, Chapter 14
   a. Picture of the Lamb with the 144,000, Chapter 14:1–5
   b. Proclamation of the Everlasting Gospel, Chapter 14:6–7
   c. Pronouncement of Judgment on Babylon, Chapter 14:8
   d. Pronouncement of Judgment on Those Who Received the Mark of the Beast, Chapter 14:9–12
   e. Praise for Those Who Die in the Lord, Chapter 14:13
   f. Preview of Armageddon, Chapter 14:14–20
5. Pouring Out of the Seven Mixing Bowls of Wrath, Chapters 15–16
   a. Preparation for Final Judgment of the Great Tribulation, Chapters 15:1–16:1
     (1) Tribulation Saints in Heaven Worship God Because He Is Holy and Just, Chapter 15:1–4
     (2) Temple of the Tabernacle Opened in Heaven that Seven Angels, Having Seven Golden Bowls, Might Proceed Forth, Chapters 15:5–16:1
   b. Pouring Out of the First Bowl, Chapter 16:2
   c. Pouring Out of the Second Bowl, Chapter 16:3
   d. Pouring Out of the Third Bowl, Chapter 16:4–7
   e. Pouring Out of the Fourth Bowl, Chapter 16:8–9
   f. Pouring Out of the Fifth Bowl, Chapter 16:10–11
   g. Pouring Out of the Sixth Bowl, Chapter 16:12
   h. Interlude: Kings of Inhabited Earth Proceed to Har-Mageddon, Chapter 16:13–16
   i. Pouring Out of the Seventh Bowl, Chapter 16:17–21
6. The Two Babylons Judged, Chapters 17–18
   a. The Apostate Church in the Great Tribulation, Chapter 17
     (1) Great Harlot Riding the Wild Beast, Chapter 17:1–7
     (2) Wild Beast Destroys the Great Harlot, Chapter 17:8–18
   b. Political and Commercial Babylon Judged, Chapter 18
     (1) Announcement of Fall of Commercial and Political Babylon, Chapter 18:1–8
     (2) Anguish in the World Because of Judgment on Babylon, Chapter 18:9–19
     (3) Anticipation of Joy in Heaven Because of Judgment on Babylon, Chapter 18:20–24
C. Marriage of the Lamb and Return of Christ in Judgment, Chapter 19
   1. Four Hallelujahs, Chapter 19:1–6
   2. Bride of the Lamb and Marriage Supper, Chapter 19:7–10
   3. Return of Christ as King of Kings and Lord of Lords, Chapter 19:11–16
   4. Battle of Armageddon, Chapter 19:17–18
   5. Hell Opened, Chapter 19:19–21
D. Millennium, Chapter 20
   1. Satan Bound 1000 Years, Chapter 20:1–3
   2. Saints of the Great Tribulation Reign with Christ 1000 Years, Chapter 20:4–6
   3. Satan Loosed After 1000 Years, Chapter 20:7–9
   4. Satan Cast into Lake of Fire and Brimstone, Chapter 20:10
   5. Setting of Great White Throne Where Lost Are Judged and Follow Satan into Lake of Fire and Brimstone, Chapter 20:11–15
E. Entrance Into Eternity; Eternity Unveiled, Chapters 21–22
   1. New Heaven, New Earth, New Jerusalem, Chapter 21:1–2
   2. New Era, Chapter 21:3–8
   3. New Jerusalem, Description of the Eternal Abode of the Bride, Chapter 21:9–21
   4. New Relationship—God Dwelling with Man, Chapter 21:22–23
   5. New Center of the New Creation, Chapter 21:24–27
   6. River of Water of Life and Tree of Life, Chapter 22:1–5
   7. Promise of Return of Christ, Chapter 22:6–16
   8. Final Invitation and Warning, Chapter 22:17–19
   9. Final Promise and Prayer, Chapter 22:20–21

CHAPTER 1

THEME: *The person of Jesus Christ*

In the first division of this book we see the person of Christ. We see Christ in His glory and position as the Great High Priest who is in charge of His church. We see Him in absolute control. In the Gospels we find Him meek, lowly, humble, and dying upon a cross. He made Himself subject to His enemies on earth. He is not like that in the Book of Revelation. He is in control. He is still the Lamb of God, but we see the wrath of the Lamb that terrifies the earth.

The major theme of the entire Bible is the Lord Jesus Christ. The Scriptures are both theocentric and Christocentric. Since Christ is God, He is the One who fills the horizon of the total Word of God. This needs to be kept in mind in the Book of Revelation more than in any other book of the Bible, even more than in the Gospels. The Bible tells what He has done, is doing, and will do. Revelation emphasizes what He is doing and what He will do. We need to keep that in mind.

THE TITLE OF THE BOOK

The Revelation of Jesus Christ, which God gave unto him, to shew unto his servants things which must shortly come to pass; and he sent and signified it by his angel unto his servant John [Rev. 1:1].

In my book *Reveling Through Revelation* I have included my own literal translation of each verse of the Book of Revelation, and in this book I will use some of it also. I don't use it because it is better. For many years I have called my translation the McGee-icus Ad Absurdum translation. I would not defend it if anyone made an attack upon it. It is merely an attempt to lift out of the Greek what John is actually saying and to try to couch it in language that may be a little more literal and understandable to us in our day. It will appear in italicized type after the King James version:

The unveiling of Jesus Christ which God gave Him to show unto His bond servants things which must shortly come to pass completely, and He sent and signified it (gave a sign) by His angel (messenger) to His servant John.

First of all, please note that the title of this book is Revelation—singular, not plural. A re-

tired preacher came to me when I was a pastor in downtown Los Angeles to make an attack upon my interpretation of the Book of Revelation. He said, "You just don't know anything about Revelations," using the plural. I replied, "Brother, you are absolutely accurate in that I know nothing about the Book of Revelations. I have never even seen that book." He was astounded and later embarrassed by his own ignorance when he realized that the Book of Revelation is *the* Revelation. It is the *apokalupsis*, that is, "the uncovering, unveiling, or revelation" of Jesus Christ.

"To shew unto his servants things which must shortly come to pass." In the last chapter of Revelation, John is instructed, "Seal not the sayings of the prophecy of this book: for the time is at hand" (Rev. 22:10). It is not a sealed book; it is open and to be understood in our day. This is in contrast to the prophecy in the Book of Daniel which Daniel was instructed to seal. Our Lord Jesus gave what are known as the "mystery" parables. Very frankly, to the majority of the church today they are still a mystery. But our Lord put it like this: "And he said unto them, Unto you it is given to know the mystery of the kingdom of God: but unto them that are without, all these things are done in parables: That seeing they may see, and not perceive; and hearing they may hear, and not understand; lest at any time they should be converted, and their sins should be forgiven them" (Mark 4:11–12). You see, my friend, in the Gospels we have only the half-story. We need the Book of Revelation because it is the consummation of it. Of course, it can be understood only if the Spirit of God is our teacher. But the Book of Revelation takes off the veil so we can see Christ in His unveiled beauty and power and glory. This book is the opposite of a secret or a mystery. It is a disclosure of secrets, and it is called *prophecy* in the next verse, as we shall see.

When a so-called Christian says that he does not understand the Book of Revelation, it makes me wonder, because this book was given to us in order that we might understand these mysteries of the kingdom of God.

"To show" means by word pictures, by symbols, by direct and indirect representations.

"And he sent and signified it." That is, he used symbols. And keep in mind that the symbols are symbolic of reality. Peter gave us a great rule for the interpretation of prophecy in

2 Peter 1:20: "Knowing this first, that no prophecy of the scripture is of any private interpretation." You don't interpret a single text by itself; you interpret it in the light of the entire Word of God. Ottman said, "The figurative language of Revelation is figurative of facts."

"To shew . . . things" assures us that what John tells us is not ethereal and ephemeral

There will be no waiting around for it. That implies that the Lord is not coming soon, but that when He does return, the things He is talking about will happen shortly and with great speed. His vengeance will take place in a brief period of time.

John tells us that it is the revelation of Jesus Christ which *God* gave to Him. Notice the steps of revelation:

THE STEPS OF REVELATION

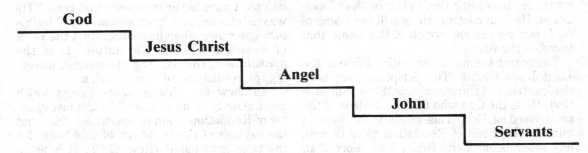

dream stuff. There is a hard core of real facts in this book. What are "things"? One night Mrs. McGee and I took care of our little grandson. We let him play in the den where we keep a bunch of toys for him to play with when he stays with us. He went into the den and got out all of those *things*. In fact, he calls them his *things*. He spread them all over the floor of the den. We indulge the little fellow, and we didn't make him pick up all of his toys after he was through playing. We didn't pick them up either. So later that night, when I walked through the den, I stepped on some of his *things*. In fact, I stumbled over them and took a tumble. You can *say* that "things" are symbols, but you don't take a tumble over symbols. And in the Book of Revelation, the "things" are made out of hard stuff. These "things" are reality. Any time John uses a symbol, he will make it clear to us that he is using a symbol. And we can be sure that he is using a symbol because the reality is far greater than the symbol. In fact, the symbol is a poor representation of the reality.

"Must"—He says that they *must* shortly come to pass. The word *must* has in it an urgent necessity and an absolute certainty.

"Shortly" has a connotation that is very important for us to note. The word occurs quite a few times in the Scriptures. For instance, we have it in Luke 18:8 where our Lord says, "I tell you that he will avenge them [His elect] speedily. . . ." The word *speedily* is the same word as *shortly*. It means that when the vengeance begins, it will take place in a hurry.

It originated with God, it was given to Jesus Christ, He gave it to His angel, His angel gave it to John, and from John it goes to His servants that they might know what is coming to pass. And that is the way it has come to you and me today.

By the way, this raises a question that I sometimes hear. Someone says, "Well, preacher, you painted yourself into a corner, because you said that angels are not connected with the church age." Yes, and I still say that. The angel mentioned here is a heavenly messenger, but notice that John is writing primarily about future things; that is, what Jesus is going to do in the future. And beginning with chapter 4, everything is future and will take place after the church has left the earth. Therefore, we see angels coming back into prominence. This is true to the way the book moves.

THE METHOD OF REVELATION

Who bare record of the word of God, and of the testimony of Jesus Christ, and of all things that he saw [Rev. 1:2].

Who bore witness of the Word of God, and of the testimony (witness) of Jesus Christ, even as many things as he saw.

"Who bare record" or, as I have translated it, "who bore witness" is in the Greek an epistolary aorist. It means that John projects himself up to where his readers are, where you and I are in this day, and he looks back at what he is writing.

"Of the word of God." The "word of God" refers, I believe, to both Christ and the contents of this book. He is the living Word, and when the written Word reveals Him to us, He is the living Word, you may be sure of that.

"And of the testimony [witness] of Jesus Christ." I prefer the word *witness* rather than *testimony*. It occurs ninety times in the writings of John—fifty times in his gospel record.

"And of all things that he saw." He was an eyewitness of the visions. What John saw, he made pictures of, and the Book of Revelation is television, friend. It was the first television program ever presented, and it is one you would do well to watch. It came from heaven from God the Father, through His Son, Jesus Christ, and it was given to an angel who gave it to John, who wrote about what he saw. Not only did John hear, he also saw, and these are the two avenues through which we get most of our information. I sometimes wonder if John didn't smell things just a little bit, too, because there are parts of this book where you catch the odor also.

THE BEATITUDE OF BIBLE STUDY

Blessed is he that readeth, and they that hear the words of this prophecy, and keep those things which are written therein: for the time is at hand [Rev. 1:3].

This verse gives us the beatitude of Bible study. This is the first of *seven beatitudes* found in the Book of Revelation. This verse says, "Blessed is he that readeth," and that means the reader, or in the church, the teacher. Both those who read this book and those who hear it will be blessed. And both the reader and the hearer are to keep those things which are written in the book. The threefold blessing comes from reading, hearing, and keeping. I believe those who go through the Book of Revelation will receive a special blessing. I really believe it because that is what John says.

"For the time is at hand" does not mean that the things which are mentioned at the end of the book are happening in our day, but it does mean that the beginning of the church on the Day of Pentecost began this movement of the Lord Jesus' ministry in heaven. We are going to see a vision of Him in this chapter, a vision of the glorified Christ. Then we will see what His ministry is, and that will move us right on into the future.

GREETINGS FROM JOHN, THE WRITER, AND FROM CHRIST IN HEAVEN

John to the seven churches which are in Asia: Grace be unto you, and peace, from him which is, and which was, and which is to come; and from the seven Spirits which are before his throne [Rev. 1:4].

This is a very wonderful greeting! "John to the seven churches which are in Asia." "Asia" encompassed a great deal of what we generally call Asia Minor or modern Turkey. Notice that John connects no title with his name. I have a notion that John was well known in these seven churches. We know that he had been pastor of the church at Ephesus, and apparently he had oversight of all the churches in that area.

Before we go further, let me call your attention to the number *seven*. In this verse there is the mention of seven churches and seven Spirits. The number seven has a religious meaning in the Word of God, which was apparent to the people in John's day but is totally foreign to us in our day. The gambling sector of our society is very conscious of numbers, as are folk who are superstitious, but we are not accustomed to attaching any religious significance to numbers. However, in the Word of God the number seven is prominent. It does not denote perfection, but it does denote completeness. Sometimes completeness is perfection, but not always.

Seven speaks of that which is complete and that which is representative. In a particular way, *seven* has to do with God's covenant and dealings with Israel. For instance, the Sabbath, circumcision, and worship are all hinged around the seventh day. As you go through the Word of God, you notice that Jericho was compassed about seven times, Naaman was instructed to dip in the Jordan River seven times, there were seven years of plenty and seven years of famine in Joseph's time in Egypt, Nebuchadnezzar was insane for seven years, there are seven beatitudes in the New Testament, there are seven petitions in the Lord's Prayer, there are seven parables in Matthew 13, seven loaves fed the multitude, Jesus spoke seven times from the cross, and in the Book of Revelation the number seven cannot be ignored or considered accidental. Seven is the key number of this book.

Here in the fourth verse, John writes to the "seven churches." Weren't there other churches in Asia? We know there were churches at Colosse, Miletus, Hierapolis, Troas, and at many other places. I have stayed at Hierapolis. It is still a place, and it is about ten miles from Laodicea, which is now in ruins. There are three motels at Laodicea and a store or two. The ruins of Hierapolis are absolutely magnificent and quite significant, because they reveal what a tremendous place it was at one time. In contrast, the ruins of Laodicea are, for the most part, under a wild oat field. They have not been excavated. John was directed to write to seven churches, and Hierapolis was not one of the seven, although it was an important center of Christian influence and the ruins of four early Christian churches have been found there. John was directed to write to only seven certain churches because he was giving the complete history of the church and they were representative churches, as we shall see.

"Asia" refers to the provinces which include Lydia, Mysia, Caria, and parts of Phrygia. It does not mean the continent of Asia nor does it include all of Asia Minor (Asia Minor is a term which was not used until the fourth century A.D.), but it covers a great area of Asia Minor, especially along the coast.

"Grace be unto you, and peace." The word *grace* is *charis*, the Greek form of greeting, and *peace* is *shalom*, the Hebrew form of greeting. Peace flows from grace, and grace is the source of all our blessings today. The Book of Revelation reveals the grace of God and also peace. We don't need to be frightened as we study this book; we can have the peace of God in our hearts.

It is "from him . . . and from the seven Spirits," which brings the Trinity before us. The "seven Spirits" refer to the Holy Spirit and probably have reference to the seven branches of the lampstand, as we shall see later on.

"Which is, and which was, and which is to come" emphasizes the eternity and immutability of God. Notice now the mention of each member of the Trinity: "Jesus Christ" (in the next verse) refers to God the Son, the "seven Spirits" refer to the Holy Spirit, and "him which is, and which was, and which is to come" refers to God the Father.

And from Jesus Christ, who is the faithful witness, and the first begotten of the dead, and the prince of the kings of the earth. Unto him that loved us, and washed us from our sins in his own blood,

And hath made us kings and priests unto God and his Father; to him be glory and dominion for ever and ever. Amen [Rev. 1:5–6].

In these two verses we have the titles which are given to the Lord Jesus Christ, and the interesting thing is that there are seven titles:

1. "Faithful witness"—Jesus Christ is the only trustworthy witness to the facts of this book. The facts are about Him. He testifies of Himself. It is difficult to believe other people, but we can believe the Lord Jesus.

2. "First begotten of the dead" is firstborn from the dead. *Firstborn* is the Greek *prototokos*, which has to do with resurrection. He is the first to rise from the dead, never to die again. This is a marvelous picture! Death was a womb which bore Him. He came out of death into life. The tomb was a womb, as far as He was concerned. He is the only One back from the dead in a glorified body. No one else has come that route yet, but His own are going to follow Him in resurrection, and the Rapture will be next (see 1 Thess. 4:14). Then will come the revelation when He will come to the earth.

3. "The prince [ruler] of the kings of the earth" speaks of His ultimate position during the Millennium. "Wherefore God also hath highly exalted him, and given him a name which is above every name: That at the name of Jesus every knee should bow, of things in heaven, and things in earth, and things under the earth; And that every tongue should confess that Jesus Christ is Lord, to the glory of God the Father" (Phil. 2:9–11).

4. "Unto him that loved us" is actually in the present tense and emphasizes His constant attitude toward His own. The Book of Revelation should not frighten us too much because of the fact that it is from the One who *loves* us. Jesus Christ didn't love us only when He died on the cross, although He loved us at that time, but He also loves us today. Right at this very minute, Jesus loves you.

5. "Washed [loosed] us from our sins in his own blood." The blood of Christ is very important. It is not just a symbol. In the Old Testament, God taught His people that the ". . . life of the flesh is in the blood . . ." (Lev. 17:11). In this verse God goes on to say, "I have given it to you upon the altar to make an atonement for your souls. . . ." When Christ shed His blood, I think every drop came out of His body. He gave *that* for you and for me. He gave His *life*, if you please. He died, and I am not inclined to belittle the blood of Christ as

some men are doing today. I still like the song with these words:

> There is a fountain filled with blood
>   Drawn from Immanuel's veins;
> And sinners, plunged beneath that flood,
>   Lose all their guilty stains.
>
>   "There Is a Fountain"
>   —William Cowper

Peter wrote, "Forasmuch as ye know that ye were not redeemed with corruptible things, as silver and gold, from your vain conversation received by tradition from your fathers; But with the precious blood of Christ, as of a lamb without blemish and without spot" (1 Pet. 1:18–19). Because of that shed blood, Paul could write to the young preacher Timothy, "For there is one God, and one mediator between God and men, the man Christ Jesus" (1 Tim. 2:5). He loosed us from our sins in His own blood. What a wonderful, glorious thing!

6. "And hath made us kings and priests [a kingdom of priests] unto God and his Father"—believers are never called kings. They are a kingdom of priests and are going to rule with the Lord Jesus. Quite frankly, I don't get wrought up over the popular song, "The King Is Coming." The King is coming, all right, but when He comes as King, He will come to the *earth*, and at that time He is going to put down all unrighteousness. But before He comes to earth as King, He will come in the air, an event we call the Rapture. At that time He will come as my Savior. He comes as the Bridegroom for His bride, the church, whom He loves and gave Himself for. He comes as the lover of my soul. For this reason I am not thrilled with "The King Is Coming." My relationship to Him is much closer. He is my Lord. He has not made us "kings and priests," He has made us a kingdom of priests, and we are going to reign with Him.

It is interesting to note that it reads, "unto God and *his* Father." Why doesn't it read, "unto God and *our* Father"? Because He is the Father of Jesus in a sense that He is not our Father. You see, we become sons of God through regeneration, being born from above, by accepting Him as Savior. But Christ's *eternal* position in the Trinity is that of the Son.

7. "To Him the glory and the dominion unto the ages of the ages" (my own translation). This is emphasizing eternity. "Amen." Christ is the amen, as we saw in Isaiah. That is a title for Him. Jesus Christ is both the subject and the object of this book. He is the mover of all events, and all events move toward Him. He is

the far-off eternal purpose in everything. All things were not only made *by* Him, but all things were made *for* Him. This universe exists for Him.

Behold, he cometh with clouds; and every eye shall see him, and they also which pierced him: and all kindreds of the earth shall wail because of him. Even so, Amen [Rev. 1:7].

"Behold, he cometh with clouds" denotes the personal and physical coming of Christ.

"And every eye shall see him" reveals that His coming will be a physical and bodily appearance, an appeal to the eye-gate. As far as we know, when Christ takes the church out of the world at the Rapture, He doesn't appear to everyone. I don't believe in a secret rapture as some folk have attempted to describe it, but at the time of the Rapture He does not come to the earth. Believers are to be caught up to meet the Lord in the air. If Christ will be coming to the earth at that time, there is no point in being caught up in the air. Therefore, this is not the Rapture which is being described in this verse. This is His return to the earth as King.

"Every eye shall see him." The emphasis in the Book of Revelation is upon His coming to this earth to establish His kingdom.

"All kindreds of the earth shall wail because of him." Probably a better translation is this: "All the tribes of the earth shall beat their breasts because of him." This is going to be the reaction of all Christ-rejectors. The world will not want to see Him.

"Even so, Amen" means "Yea, faithful." He is going to do it, my friend. He is not going to change His mind about it. He is faithful.

I am Alpha and Omega, the beginning and the ending, saith the Lord, which is, and which was, and which is to come, the Almighty [Rev. 1:8].

"I am Alpha and Omega." This is quite a remarkable statement in the Greek language. The alpha and omega are the first and last letters of the Greek alphabet. From an alphabet you make words, and Jesus Christ is called the "Word of God"—the full revelation and intelligent communication of God. He is the only alphabet you can use to reach God, my friend. The only language God speaks and understands is the language where Jesus is the Alpha and the Omega and all the letters in between. He is the "A" and the "Z," and He is the "ABC." If you are going to get through to God the Father, you will have to go through the Son, Jesus Christ. Here the emphasis is upon the beginning and the end. Here in the original Greek the Omega is not spelled out as is the Alpha. Why? Because Christ is the beginning, and the beginning is already completed. But the end is yet to be; so He didn't spell out the Omega in this instance. One day He will complete God's program. This is a very interesting detail in the Greek text.

"The beginning and the ending" refers to the eternity of the Son and His immutability. Concerning this, Hebrews 13:8 says, "Jesus Christ the same yesterday, and to-day, and for ever." When it says that He is the same, it does not mean that He is walking over yonder by the Sea of Galilee today. He is not. But it means that in His attributes He is the same. He has not changed. He is immutable. Since He is the beginning and the ending, He encompasses all time and eternity.

"Saith the Lord" is an affirmation of the deity of the Lord Jesus Christ.

"Which is," that is, at the present time, He is the glorified Christ.

"Which was"—past time, the first coming of Christ as Savior.

"Which is to come"—future time, the second coming of Christ as the Sovereign over this earth.

Verses 4–8 have comprised this very remarkable section of greetings from John, the writer, and from the Lord Jesus Christ. Remember that He says He loves us; so let's not be afraid of anything that is to follow.

THE POST-INCARNATE CHRIST IN A GLORIFIED BODY JUDGING HIS CHURCH

I John, who also am your brother, and companion in tribulation, and in the kingdom and patience of Jesus Christ, was in the isle that is called Patmos, for the word of God, and for the testimony of Jesus Christ [Rev. 1:9].

I, John, who am your brother, and partaker with you in the persecution (for Christ's sake), and kingdom and patience in Jesus; I was (found myself) in the isle called Patmos because of [Gr.: dia, on account of] the Word of God and the witness of Jesus.

"I John" is used three times in this Book of Revelation—the other two are at the end of the book.

"Your brother, and companion in tribulation" does not refer to the Great Tribulation.

John was in *trouble*. Domitian (A.D. 96), the Roman emperor, had put him in prison on the Isle of Patmos. John had been active in the church at Ephesus, and he had supervision over all the other churches, and he had been teaching the Word of God. You get into trouble when you teach all of the Word of God. John knew all about trouble, and so did the early church. So if it comes to you and me, it is nothing new at all.

Again let me say that John is not referring to the Great Tribulation but to the persecution that was already befalling believers. And "the kingdom" refers to the present state of the kingdom. By virtue of the new birth, which places a sinner in Christ, he is likewise in the kingdom of God. This is not the millennial kingdom—that has not been established yet. Christ will institute it at His coming.

Someone has said that we are living today in the kingdom and patience—patience is where the emphasis is.

John explains the reason he was on the Isle of Patmos. He was exiled there from about A.D. 86 to 96. It is a rugged, volcanic island off the coast of Asia Minor. It is about ten miles long and six miles wide.

"Jesus," you will notice, is the name used by John in both his gospel and in the Apocalypse. When he wants to bring glory to Him, he calls Him *Jesus*, and then he lifts Him to the skies. I hope that we can do that, also.

Before we look at the next verses, let me remind you that John was given this great vision on the lonely Isle of Patmos. It is a vision of the post-incarnate Christ in His glorified body as He is judging His church. In other words, we shall see the Great High Priest in the holy of holies.

I was in the Spirit on the Lord's day, and heard behind me a great voice, as of a trumpet,

Saying, I am Alpha and Omega, the first and the last: and, What thou seest, write in a book, and send it unto the seven churches which are in Asia; unto Ephesus, and unto Smyrna, and unto Pergamos, and unto Thyatira, and unto Sardis, and unto Philadelphia, and unto Laodicea [Rev. 1:10–11].

I was (found myself) in (the) Spirit in the Lord's Day, and heard behind me a great sound, as of a (war) trumpet, saying, What you are seeing, write (promptly) into a book, and send (promptly) to the seven churches, unto Ephesus, and unto

Smyrna, and unto Pergamos, and unto Thyatira, and unto Sardis, and unto Philadelphia, and unto Laodicea.

My own translation is not a finished translation by any means, and I do not recommend it, but it is an attempt to get from the original Greek what is actually being said.

The Holy Spirit is here performing His office work. That is why I pray that the Spirit of God might take the things of Christ and show them unto us. That is exactly what the Lord Jesus Christ said the Holy Spirit would do when He came. The Lord's exact words were, "Howbeit when he, the Spirit of truth, is come, he will guide you into all truth: for he shall not speak of himself; but whatsoever he shall hear, that shall he speak: and he will shew you things to come. He shall glorify me: for he shall receive of mine, and shall shew it unto you" (John 16:13–14).

We are beginning to get a vision of the glorified Christ. We are considering Him in His office as the Great High Priest today.

I fully recognize that in myself I am totally incompetent to try to explain these tremendous verses. Only the Spirit of God can make them real to us. However, Hebrews 3:1 tells us, "Wherefore, holy brethren, partakers of the heavenly calling, consider the Apostle and High Priest of our profession, Christ Jesus." So we are *considering* Him in His present office of Great High Priest.

"I was in the Spirit," John says. The Holy Spirit was moving upon John and giving him a panoramic picture. This is cinerama. It is sight and sound. It is an appeal to both the eye-gate and the ear-gate.

"On the Lord's day." The meaning of this is controversial. Some outstanding Bible scholars interpret this as being a reference to the Day of the Lord. While I certainly respect them and their viewpoint, I cannot accept this view, although the great theme of Revelation will deal with the Day of the Lord, which is the Tribulation Period and the millennial kingdom. But John says that he was in the Spirit on the Lord's Day and, in my judgment, the Day of the Lord and the Lord's Day are two different things. We recognize that anti-fat and fat auntie are two different things and that a chestnut horse and a horse chestnut are two different things. And I would say that the Day of the Lord and the Lord's Day are two different things also, and that the Lord's Day refers to what we call Sunday.

"I . . . heard behind me a great voice, as of a trumpet." Who was it? He will tell us—

And I turned to see the voice that spake with me. And being turned, I saw seven golden candlesticks;

And in the midst of the seven candlesticks one like unto the Son of man, clothed with a garment down to the foot, and girt about the paps with a golden girdle [Rev. 1:12–13].

And I turned to see the voice which was speaking with me, and when I turned, I saw seven golden lampstands, and in the midst of the lampstands One like to a Son of Man, clothed with a garment, reaching to the foot, and girt about the breasts with a golden girdle.

John heard a voice like a war trumpet, and it spoke to him. When the Lord Jesus descends from heaven to remove His church from the earth, He will come with a shout. First Thessalonians 4:16 tells us about it: "For the Lord himself shall descend from heaven with a shout, with the voice of the archangel, and with the trump of God: and the dead in Christ shall rise first." His voice will be *like* the voice of an archangel, and His voice will be *like* a trumpet, because it is identified here as just that. But it will be Christ's own voice. He is not going to need any archangel to help Him raise His own from the dead.

What a thrill it is to see this picture of the Lord Jesus Christ! It is a vision of One like the Son of Man. He is "clothed with a garment down to the foot, and girt about the breast with a golden girdle." The seven golden lampstands remind us of the tabernacle. There it was one lampstand with seven branches. Here it is seven separate lampstands. Since these lampstands represent seven separate churches (v. 20), the difference is explained. The function of all is the same. The Lord Jesus said, "I am the light of the world, and when I leave, *you* are to be the light in the world" (see John 8:12).

We see the Lord Jesus Christ pictured here as our Great High Priest. His garments are those of the high priest—check Exodus 28:2–4. The garments represent the inherent righteousness of Christ. In Him is no sin, and He knew no sin.

Concerning the *girdle*, Josephus states that the priests were girded about the breasts. The ordinary custom was to be girded about the loins. But the emphasis here is not on service but on *strength*. It speaks of His *judgment* in truth.

We are asked to consider our Great High

Priest as He stands in the midst of the churches. He is *judging* the churches; He is judging believers that the light might continue to shine. My friend, it is important to see what Christ's present ministry is.

This is a subject about which I have wanted to write. I haven't gotten around to it yet and may never write it, but I have a title for it: The Contemporary Christ. I hear so many foolish things that are being said about what Jesus is doing in our day. My friend, the Scripture does not leave us in the dark regarding what He is doing today. It mentions three very definite ministries.

First, there is the *intercession* of Christ. He is our Great High Priest. He is standing at the golden altar in heaven today, where He ever lives to make intercession for us (see Heb. 7:25). We love that part of His ministry. It is a wonderful thing.

Secondly, we have the *intervention* of Christ. He steps outside of the Holy Place to the laver. There He washes the feet of those who are His own. He washes those who have confessed their sins. Christians have sin, and those sins must be confessed in order to have fellowship with Him. "If we confess our sins, he is faithful and just to forgive us our sins, and to cleanse us from all unrighteousness" (1 John 1:9). He is girded today with the towel, and He carries the basin; He intervenes on our behalf.

John also says in his first epistle: "My little children, these things write I unto you, that ye sin not." He has made every provision that we sin not. I don't know about you, but I haven't reached that state yet. And, frankly, I have never met anyone who has. But John says, "And if any man sin, we have an advocate with the Father . . ." (1 John 2:1). Christ is our advocate. That is, He is on our side defending us when we are accused, and Satan is the accuser of the brethren.

There is yet another ministry of Christ that is not very popular. It is the ministry mentioned in the first chapter of Revelation, and I think that is one reason this section of Revelation is so little known. Here we see His ministry of *inspection*. What Christ is doing today is clearly outlined in the Scriptures. He ascended to heaven and sat down at the right hand of God, but He did not start twiddling His thumbs. When we are told that He "sat down," it means that He finished His work of redemption for man. He died on earth to save us, and He lives in heaven to keep us saved. I think He is busier today trying to keep us saved than He was when He was on earth.

We have the three ministries of Christ; we have His *intercession*, His *intervention*, and His *inspection*. The inspection of Christ is what we are going to look at now. Where is He now? We see Him walking in the midst of the lampstands. In the Book of Exodus we see the golden lampstand. It was the most beautiful article of furniture in the tabernacle. It was made of solid gold, and there were three branches on each side of the main stem. The top of each stem was fashioned like an open almond blossom, and the lamps were set there. The lamps represent the Holy Spirit; the golden lampstand itself represents Christ—His glory and His deity. Christ sent the Holy Spirit into the world. The golden lampstand holds up the lamps, and the lamps, in turn, reveal the beauty and glory of the lampstand. That is the picture we have in Revelation. I trust that even now the Holy Spirit will make Christ, in all of His glory, wonder, and beauty, *real* to you that you may see yourself in the light of His presence as He inspects you. That is not a popular teaching today. We don't like to be inspected, but in Revelation we see Him walking in the midst of the lampstands, performing His ministry of inspection.

In the tabernacle the high priest had the sole oversight of the lampstand. The other priests had other duties to perform, but the high priest took care of the lampstand. He was the one who lighted the lamps. He poured in the oil and trimmed the wicks. If one of the lamps began to smoke and did not give a good clear light, he was the one who snuffed it out. The Lord Jesus is walking in the midst of the lampstands today. He is in the midst of His church, made up of individual believers. He is doing several things: He trims the wicks. In John 15 we are told that He prunes the branches of believers so that they might bring forth fruit. One of the reasons He lets us go through certain trials on earth is so that He might get some fruit off our branches or that He might make our light burn more brightly. He is the One who pours in the oil, which represents the Holy Spirit. I get so tired today of hearing people say, "The Holy Ghost this, and the Holy Ghost that." My friend, Jesus Christ is the Head of the church. He is the One who sent the Holy Spirit into the world. He said that when the Holy Spirit came He would do certain things, not just any old thing you want Him to do. The Holy Spirit is doing what the Lord Jesus sent Him into the world to do. Christ is the Head of the church. The Lord wants light, and He is the One who pours in the Holy Spirit to get that light. If there is any light coming from my ministry, it comes from the Holy Spirit. He is the source. No light originates in Vernon McGee. I found that out a long time ago.

Christ does something else, and it makes me shiver. He sometimes uses a snuffer. If a lamp won't give good light and it keeps smoking up the place, the Lord Jesus snuffs it out. This is what John meant when he said that there is a sin unto death (see 1 John 5:16). You and I can be set aside. Oh, the number of people whom I have known to be set aside—preachers and elders and deacons and Sunday school teachers! Christ put them aside. He is walking in the midst of the lampstands, and He wants them to produce light.

His head and his hairs were white like wool, as white as snow; and his eyes were as a flame of fire;

And his feet like unto fine brass, as if they burned in a furnace; and his voice as the sound of many waters [Rev. 1:14–15].

"His head and his hairs were white like wool, as white as snow" speaks of His eternal existence. He is the Ancient of Days (see Dan. 7:9).

"His eyes were as a flame of fire" speaks of His penetrating insight and eyewitness knowledge of the total life of the church. He knows all about you. He knows all about me. He sat over the treasury and watched how the people gave. Last Sunday He watched you when you put your offering in the plate. You didn't think anybody knew what you gave, did you? Also, His eyes met those of Simon Peter after he had denied Him. After that happened, Peter went out and wept. If you could only see the eyes of your Savior today! My friend, He is looking at us.

"His feet like unto fine brass" or *burnished* brass is symbolic of judgment. That brass or brazen altar outside the tabernacle proper represents Christ's work down here on earth when He died on the cross. It was there that He bore your judgment and my judgment for sin. And now He is judging those of us who are His own.

General Nathan Twining was the man who gave the command to drop the first atom bombs on Hiroshima and Nagasaki. He later became the chairman of the U.S. Joint Chiefs of Staff, and he dropped another "atom bomb" on December 10, 1959, and it had just about as great a repercussion as the literal bomb did. He dropped the latter bomb when he told the French in particular, and the other European

countries in general, that they were not carrying their share of the defense of NATO and that they were falling down on their responsibility in defending Europe. He told them that NATO was coming unglued. The repercussions from his announcement are still reverberating through Europe today. Although General Twining was accurate in his charges, the reaction was bitter, and there were counter charges made, and denials and excuses were offered. About that time, when President Eisenhower went to Europe, he received the coolest reception he had ever experienced. Why? The human heart resents criticism.

Human nature rebels against judgment being passed upon it. Man likes to be handed a passel of little rules and regulations which he can keep. That is the reason so many study courses are popular with Christians—they want to be legalistic. They don't want to live by grace. Give Christians a few little rules they can go by, and they are very happy. The result, however, is a group of Band-Aid believers. They put on a little Band-Aid here and another one there, and they think that is all that is necessary to heal a broken leg. Why? The human nature that man has will purr like a pussycat when flattered, but it will bristle like a porcupine when failure to do a job is noted. That is the reason that the present position of Christ and His contemporary work of inspection are largely ignored by the church. He occupies the position of Judge of the church, and He does not flatter; He does not ignore what He sees; He does not shut His eyes to sin and wrongdoing. His constant charge and command to His own is "Repent!" We are going to see this as we move along in the Book of Revelation. He says to His church, "Change or I will come to you and I will remove your lampstand" (see Rev. 2:5). The church has smarted and squirmed under this indictment down through the ages and still does. This is the result of the natural resentment that is in the heart of lukewarm believers. And the "Laodicean" church pays scant attention to what Christ has to say. As someone has said, "There is a Man in glory, but the church has lost sight of Him."

"His voice as the sound of many waters" is the voice of authority—the voice that called this universe into existence, the voice that will raise His own from the grave, the voice that will take His own out of the world to be with Him.

All these figures add to the picture of Christ as our Great High Priest, inspecting and judging His church. Consider your Great High

Priest. The Spirit of God will help you see Him in all of His beauty and glory. How wonderful He is!

And he had in his right hand seven stars: and out of his mouth went a sharp two-edged sword: and his countenance was as the sun shineth in his strength [Rev. 1:16].

"He had in his right hand seven stars" means that He controls this universe.

"Out of his mouth went a sharp two-edged sword." One man asked me, "Do you think that a literal sword goes out of His mouth?" Of course not! Scripture tells us that the sword represents His Word. In Hebrews 4:12 we read, "For the word of God is quick, and powerful, and sharper than any two-edged sword, piercing even to the dividing asunder of soul and spirit, and of the joints and marrow, and is a discerner of the thoughts and intents of the heart." God judges by His Word. He judges by it today. When He speaks the Word, my friend, you had better sit up and take note because He means business.

"His countenance was as the sun shineth in his strength." You can't even look at the sun. Do you think you will be able to look at the Creator who made the sun, the One who is the glorified Christ? How wonderful He is!

And when I saw him, I fell at his feet as dead. And he laid his right hand upon me, saying unto me, Fear not; I am the first and the last [Rev. 1:17].

John is the disciple who had an easy familiarity with Christ on earth. He is the man who reclined upon His bosom in the Upper Room. John was very close to the Lord Jesus—in fact, he didn't mind rebuking Him on an occasion. But when he saw the glorified Christ on the Isle of Patmos, he did not go up to Him and pat Him on the back or shake hands with Him. He didn't even try to begin a conversation. He fell at His feet as dead! The effect of the vision upon John was nothing short of paralyzing.

My friend, since John reacted like that, we can be sure that when you and I get into the presence of the Lord Jesus, we are not going to approach Him in a familiar way. We will fall at His feet as dead. He is the glorified Christ today. And let me say that I do not like the irreverence of the "Jesus culture" that we see today, speaking of Him or to Him as if He were a buddy. Nor do I like to hear someone sing or say that Jesus is a friend of theirs. Now, you may think I am hard to please. You are right; I am. But Jesus said, "Ye are my friends, if ye do whatsoever I command you" (John 15:14). If you say that Jesus is a friend of yours, you must be implying that you are *obeying* Him. Oh, my friend, if we could see Him in all of His glory and His beauty, we would not get familiar with Him.

But the marvelous thing is that He says, "Fear not." This is the greeting of Deity addressing humanity. And He gives four reasons why we should not fear.

1. "I am the first and the last." This speaks of His deity. He came out of eternity, and He moves into eternity. The psalmist says, "Before the mountains were brought forth, or ever thou hadst formed the earth and the world, even from everlasting to everlasting, thou art God" (Ps. 90:2). The word *everlasting* means from the vanishing point in the past to the vanishing point in the future He is God. He is first because there were none before Him, and He is last for there are none to follow Him.

I am he that liveth, and was dead; and, behold, I am alive for evermore, Amen; and have the keys of hell and of death [Rev. 1:18].

2. "I am he that liveth, and was dead"—or, the living One who became dead. This speaks of His redemptive death and resurrection. Most of us have a guilt complex. We are afraid somebody will point a finger at us and say, "You are guilty." We are, of course, but Paul deals with this question in Romans 8:34, where he says, "Who is he that condemneth? It is Christ that died, yea rather, that is risen again, who is even at the right hand of God, who also maketh intercession for us." Where is the fellow who is going to condemn you? Paul says, "Who is he that condemneth? It is Christ who died." Do you find fault with me? Do you say I am a great sinner? I want you to know that Christ died for me, and He is risen from the dead. He rose for my justification to show that I am forgiven and that I am going to heaven someday. And He is even at the right hand of God—how wonderful—and He makes intercession, that is, He prays for me. We see this in His next reason:

3. "And, behold, I am alive for evermore." This refers to His present state. He is not only judging, but He is making intercession for us. How we need that!

4. "And have the keys of death and of hades." The keys speak of authority and power. Jesus has power over death and the grave right now—because of His own death and resurrection. *Hades* is the Greek word for the unseen world. It can refer to the grave where the body is laid or to the place where the spirit goes.

My friend, you and I can take comfort in the fact that Jesus has the keys of death. He is the One who can relieve us of the terrible fear of death.

TIME DIVISION OF THE APOCALYPSE'S CONTENTS

The following verses give us the chronological order and division of this Book of Revelation in three time series: past, present, and future. Right now I am making this division arbitrarily, and then as we progress through the book I can demonstrate that it is accurate.

Write the things which thou hast seen, and the things which are, and the things which shall be hereafter [Rev. 1:19].

1. "Write the things which thou hast seen." Up to this point what had John seen? He had seen the glorified Christ. Let me remind you that this is a Christocentric book. The glorified Christ is the subject. Don't get your eyes on the horsemen or on the bowls of wrath or on the beasts—they are just passing through. Fix your eyes on the Lord Jesus Christ. He is the One who *was*, who *is*, and who *will be*. He is the same yesterday, today, and forever. And John is to write the vision he has had of Him.

2. "The things which are." What are the things that *are*? They are the things that pertain to the church, church things. And we are still here after nineteen hundred years. The matters concerning the church are recorded in chapters 2–3.

3. "The things which shall be hereafter." Or, as my own translation reads: *the things which you are about to see after these things [meta tauta].* This is the program of Jesus Christ, and we shall see that the church goes to heaven, and then we shall see the things that take place on the earth after the church leaves it. This program of Christ is covered by chapters 4–22.

INTERPRETATION OF SEVEN STARS AND SEVEN LAMPSTANDS

The mystery of the seven stars which thou sawest in my right hand, and the seven golden candlesticks. The seven stars are the angels of the seven churches: and the seven candlesticks which thou sawest are the seven churches [Rev. 1:20].

You see, John will make it clear when he is using symbols, and he will help us understand what the symbols mean. Otherwise, he is not using symbolic language but is talking about *literal* things.

"The mystery of the seven stars . . . and the seven . . . candlesticks." A mystery in Scripture means a sacred secret, that which has not been revealed before. And this had not been revealed before it was given to John. It pertains specifically to that which John has seen. He is the only one who has looked upon the glorified Christ. You may ask, "Hadn't Paul seen the glorified Christ?" Well, what did Paul see? He said that he saw ". . . a light from heaven, above the brightness of the sun . . ." (Acts 26:13). I can't even look at the sun, and I don't think Paul could have *seen* Christ in all of His glory, but he knew that He was there. The brightness even blinded Paul for a few days. Therefore, John was the first to see the glorified Christ.

The "seven stars" are identified as the "seven angels." The stars represent authority. In Jude, verse 13, apostates are called wandering stars. The word *angel* literally means "messenger" and may be either human or angelic beings. It could refer to a messenger of the angelic hosts of heaven or to a ruler or a teacher of a congregation on earth. I like to think that it refers to the local pastors of the seven churches which we are going to look at in the next two chapters. I like to hear a pastor called an angel because sometimes they are called other things. So, if you don't mind, I'll hold to that interpretation.

"The seven candlesticks which thou sawest are the seven churches." The English word *candlestick* should be *lampstand* since it holds lamps rather than candles. It represents the seven churches of Asia, as we shall see. Then, in turn, these represent the church as a whole, the church as the body of Christ.

INTRODUCTION TO CHAPTERS 2 AND 3

This brings us to the section on the "church," which is also called the body of Christ. He loved the church and gave Himself for it. The church is the body of believers which the Father has given Him and for whom He prayed in John 17.

After chapter 3, the church is conspicuous by its absence. Up to chapter 4, the church is mentioned nineteen times. From chapter 4 through chapter 20 (the Great White Throne Judgment), the church is not mentioned one time. The normal reaction is to inquire as to the destination and location of the church during this period. It certainly is not in the world. It has been removed from the earth.

These seven letters have a threefold interpretation and application:

1. Contemporary—they had a direct message to the local churches of John's day. I intend to take you to the location of these seven churches in these next two chapters. I have visited the sites of these churches several times, and I want to visit them again and again, because it is such a thrill and because it brings me closer to the Bible. You can get closer to the Bible by visiting these seven churches than you can by walking through the land of Israel. The ruins have an obvious message. John was writing to churches that he knew all about. In *The Letters to the Seven Churches of Asia* Sir William Ramsay said, "The man who wrote these seven letters to the seven churches had been there, and he knew the local conditions."

2. Composite—each one is a composite picture of the church. There is something that is applicable to all churches in all ages in each message to each individual church. In other words, when you read the message to the church in Pergamum, there is a message for your church and a message for you personally.

3. Chronological—the panoramic history of the church is given in these seven letters, from Pentecost to the *Parousia*, from the Upper Room to the upper air. There are seven distinct periods of church history. Ephesus represents the apostolic church; Laodicea represents the apostate church. This prophetic picture is largely fulfilled and is now church history, which makes these chapters extremely remarkable.

Now let me call your attention to the well-defined and definite format which the Lord Jesus used in each one of the letters to the seven churches:

1. There was some feature of the glorified Christ (whom John saw in chapter 1) that was emphasized in addressing each church. A particular thing was emphasized for a particular purpose, of course.

2. The letters are addressed to the angel of each church. As I have said, it is my understanding that the angel is just a human messenger whom we would designate as the pastor of the church.

3. He begins by stating to each, "I know thy works," although there has been some question about that in regard to a couple of the letters.

4. He first gives a word of commendation, and then He gives a word of condemnation. That is His method, but the exceptions should be noted. There is no word of condemnation to Smyrna or Philadelphia. Smyrna was the martyr church, and He is not about to condemn that church. Philadelphia was the missionary church that was getting out His Word, and He didn't condemn it. He has no word of commendation for Laodicea, the apostate church.

5. Each letter concludes with the warning, "He that hath an ear, let him hear what the Spirit saith."

In this second major division of the book, we see the things that *are*, that is, church-related things. Each of the seven letters is a message which the Lord Jesus sent to a particular church.

We today may not be conversant with the fact that in the first and second centuries letter-writing and travel were commonplace in the Roman Empire. There was extensive communication throughout the Roman Empire during that period. Therefore, the seven letters of the Apocalypse are very remarkable for other reasons, the most important of which is that they are direct letters from Christ to the churches. (This means that we have two epistles to the Ephesians—one that Paul wrote and one that the Lord Jesus gave through John.) Dr. Deissmann, in his book, *Light from the Ancient East*, made a distinction between letters and epistles which has been proven to be artificial and entirely false. The fact that these are called *letters* to the seven churches rather than *epistles* does not lessen their importance. They had an extensive outlet, and they reached multitudes of people. There were many outstanding churches in the Roman Empire, but these seven outstanding churches were chosen for several reasons, one of which was that they were located in probably the most important area of the Roman Empire during the first, second, and even third centuries. The area was important because it was where East and West met. By 2000 B.C. there was a civilization along the coast of Asia Minor (the modern west coast of Turkey). It is a very beautiful area. It reminds me of Southern California—but without smog, of course. Not only is it beautiful, but some of the richest land is there. In ancient times the heart of the great Hittite nation was located there. Ephesus was founded about 2000 B.C. by the Hittites, as was Smyrna (modern Izmir). Pergamum obviously was founded later, and then Thyatira and Sardis even later, and they were made great during the time of Alexander the Great. The Anatolian civilization met the Greek civilization there. You can always tell the difference because the gods of the Anatolians (a more primitive people) were beasts, whereas the gods of the Greeks were projections and enlargements of human beings.

Ephesus was a city of about two hundred thousand people. It was a great city and had a huge outdoor theater which could seat about twenty thousand people. It was a place of re-sorts, and the Roman emperors came there. It was a city constructed of white marble, a beautiful place, and Paul commented on that. If we think that the impact of the gospel was not great in that area, we are entirely mistaken. Such was the impact of the gospel on Ephesus that four great pillars or towers were placed at the entrance to the harbor, and upon them was the emblem of the cross. One monument was dedicated to Matthew, one to Mark, one to Luke, and one to John. Only one pillar stands there today, but it still bears the symbol of the cross. And there are other evidences of the tremendous impact of the gospel where pagan temples were later turned into churches.

After the ministry of Paul and John, there was a tremendous Christian population in that area. It seems that Paul had his greatest ministry in the city of Ephesus, and Luke writes, ". . . all they which dwelt in Asia heard the word of the Lord Jesus, both Jews and Greeks" (Acts 19:10). Not all turned to Christ, but everyone heard. That was probably the greatest movement that has ever taken place in the history of the church.

CHAPTER 2

THEME: *The church in the world*

Ephesus was not only a beautiful city, it was the chief city of the province of Asia. It was called "the Vanity Fair of Asia." Pliny called it "the Light of Asia." It was both the religious and commercial center of that entire area which influenced both East and West— Asia and Europe. When Paul landed at the harbor in Ephesus, he looked down Harbor Boulevard, all in white marble. As he moved toward the center of the city, he saw all sorts of lovely buildings, temples, and gift shops. There was a large market on his right as he went up the boulevard, and ahead of him on the side of a mountain was a theater that seated twenty thousand people. Off to his left was the great amphitheater that seated over one hundred thousand people. At times there were as many as one to two million people gathered in Ephesus. It was here that Paul had his greatest ministry, and it was here that John later became pastor.

This city was first formed around the temple of Diana by the Anatolians who worshiped Diana. The first temple was a wooden structure, built in a low place very near the ocean— in fact, the waters lapped at the very base. In time, the Cayster and the little Maeander River brought down so much silt that, by the time of Alexander the Great, it had filled in around the temple. I have never seen any country that washes as much as that valley washes. The river itself is as thick as soup because it is carrying so much soil deposit. When Alexander took the city (by the way, the temple burned on the night Alexander was born), he turned it over to one of his generals, Lysimachus. Because the silt was coming and the harbor was filling up, Lysimachus moved the people to a higher location, and that is where the ruins of the city can be seen today. It is the city which was there when Paul came.

At the site of the old temple, a foundation of charcoal and skins was laid over this low, marshy place, and Alexander the Great led in the construction of a new temple of Diana which became one of the wonders of the ancient world. It was the largest Greek temple ever constructed. In it were over one hundred external columns about fifty-six feet in height, of which thirty-six were hand carved. The doors were of cypress wood; columns and walls were of Parian marble; the staircase was carved out of one vine from Cyprus.

The temple served as the bank of Asia and was the depository of vast sums of money. It was an art gallery displaying the masterpieces of Praxiteles, Phidias, Scopas, and Polycletus. Apelles' famous painting of Alexander was there. Behind a purple curtain was the lewd and crude image of Diana, the goddess of fertility. She was many-breasted, carried a club in one hand and a trident in the other. *Horrible* is Diana of the Ephesians could be accurately substituted for "Great is Diana of the Ephesians." Diana was the most sacred idol of heathenism. Her temple was four times larger than the Parthenon at Athens, and it was finally destroyed by the Goths in A.D. 256. Of course, it was standing in Paul's day. If you want to see something of the magnificence of the place, go to Istanbul, to the Hagia Sophia. Those beautiful green columns that are there were taken out of the temple of Diana by Justinian when he built Hagia Sophia. Seeing only these columns gives us some conception of the beauty of the temple of Diana.

Around the temple of Diana were performed the grossest forms of immorality. She was worshiped by probably more people than was any other idol. The worshipers indulged in the basest religious rites of sensuality and the wildest bacchanalian orgies that were excessive and vicious. And farther inland, the worship of Diana became nothing more than sex orgies, and her name was changed from Diana to Cybele.

Paul came to Ephesus on his third missionary journey to begin a ministry. For two years the Word of God went out from the school of Tyrannus. Of this experience Paul wrote, "For a great door and effectual is opened unto me, and there are many adversaries" (1 Cor. 16:9). Later John, the "apostle of love" and the "son of thunder," came to Ephesus as a pastor. He was exiled to Patmos, then after about ten years of being exiled and imprisoned, he returned to Ephesus. The Basilica of Saint John, which is located on the highest point there, is built over the traditional burial spot of the apostle John.

CHRIST'S LETTER TO THE CHURCH IN EPHESUS

The Lord Jesus Christ speaks to this church in the midst of crass materialism, degraded animalism, base paganism, and dark heathenism. Note this carefully, because I consider this message to be one of the most important of all.

Unto the angel of the church of Ephesus write; These things saith he that holdeth the seven stars in his right hand, who walketh in the midst of the seven golden candlesticks [Rev. 2:1].

This is my translation:

Unto the messenger of the church in Ephesus write; These things saith the One holding the seven stars in His right hand, the One walking (up and down) in the midst of the seven golden lampstands.

Notice that He holds in His hand the church. It is under His control. He doesn't have that control now, but He did then. "He walketh" literally means that He is walking up and down. I believe that He is still walking up and down in our day and that He is still judging the church.

He has seven words of commendation for this church:

I know thy works, and thy labour, and thy patience, and how thou canst not bear them which are evil: and thou hast tried them which say they are apostles, and are not, and hast found them liars:

And hast borne, and hast patience, and for my name's sake hast laboured, and hast not fainted [Rev. 2:2–3].

1. "I know thy works." We need to understand that He is speaking to believers. The Lord Jesus does not ask the lost world for good works. For example, "Not by works of righteousness which we have done, but according to his mercy he saved us, by the washing of regeneration, and renewing of the Holy Ghost" (Titus 3:5). In Romans 4:5 Paul says, "But to him that worketh not, but believeth on him that justifieth the ungodly, his faith is counted for righteousness." Christ is talking to His own. After you are saved, He wants to talk to you about good works. He has a lot to say about this subject. In Ephesians 2:8–10 we read, "For by grace are ye saved through faith; and that not of yourselves: it is the gift of God: Not of works, lest any man should boast. For we are his workmanship, created in Christ Jesus unto good works, which God hath before ordained that we should walk in them." Paul could write to Titus, "They profess that they know God; but in works they deny him, being abominable, and disobedient, and unto every good work reprobate" (Titus 1:16). Someone has said, "The Christian ought to be like a good watch—all gold, open-faced, well-regulated, dependable, and filled with good works." The Lord Jesus is saying to the church in Ephesus, as Paul had said, ". . . be filled with the [Holy] Spirit" (Eph. 5:18). And Paul went on to tell them what they could do as Spirit-filled believers. And now the Lord Jesus commends them for their good works.

2. "I know . . . thy labour." What is the difference between work and labor? The word *labor* carries a meaning of weariness. In the gospel record it says that Jesus became wearied with His journey. That was the weariness which Ephesian believers experienced. They suffered weariness in their labor for Him.

3. "I know . . . thy patience." Patience is a fruit of the Holy Spirit.

4. "How thou canst not bear them which are evil." They would not endure evil men.

5. "Thou hast tried them which say they are apostles, and are not, and hast found them liars." They tested everyone who came to Ephesus claiming to be an apostle. They would ask them if they had seen the resurrected Christ, and they soon found out whether or not they were really apostles. If they were not, they asked them to leave town. The Lord Jesus commended them for testing men, and I feel this is more needed today than it was even then.

6. "Hast borne . . . for my name's sake hast laboured." For His name's sake they were bearing the Cross. They preached Christ. They believed in the virgin birth of Christ; they believed in His deity; they believed in His sacrificial death and resurrection. And they paid a price for their belief.

7. "And hast not fainted." More accurately, it is "hast not grown weary." What does He mean by this? Earlier He said that they had grown weary, and now He says they have not grown weary. Well, this is one of the great paradoxes of the Christian faith. I can illustrate it by what Dwight L. Moody once said when he came home exhausted after a campaign and his family begged him not to go to the next campaign. He said to them, "I grow weary *in* the work but not *of* the work." There is a lot of difference. You can get weary *in* the work of Christ, but it is tragic if you get weary *of* the work of Christ.

These seven words of commendation, which the Lord Jesus gave to the local church at Ephesus, also apply to the period of church history between Pentecost and A.D. 100, which the Ephesian church represents.

Now He has one word of condemnation:

Nevertheless I have somewhat against thee, because thou hast left thy first love [Rev. 2:4].

Nevertheless I have against thee that thou art leaving thy best love.

They had lost that intense and enthusiastic devotion to the person of Christ. It is difficult for us to sense the state to which the Holy Spirit had brought this church. He had brought the believers in Ephesus into an intimate and personal relationship to Jesus Christ. He had brought them to the place where they could say to the Lord, "We *love* you." This may seem like a very unimportant thing to us today, but their love for the Lord was very important to Christ. He was saying to the Ephesians, "You are leaving your best love." They hadn't quite departed from that love, but they were on the way. It is difficult for us in this cold, skeptical, cynical, and indifferent day in which we live to understand this. The world has intruded into the church to such an extent that it is hard for us to conceive of the intense, enthusiastic devotion the early church gave to the person of Christ. The early church first went off the track not in their doctrine but in their personal relationship to Jesus Christ.

Ephesus was a great city, and it had many attractions that were beginning to draw believers away from their first love for Jesus Christ. This was the church that became so potent in its evangelism in that area of about twenty-five million people that even the Roman emperors and the nobility of that day had an opportunity to hear the gospel. In that area there was such a mighty moving of the Spirit of God that it has probably never been duplicated since.

Every now and then we meet someone or read about someone who has had that close personal relationship with Christ. David Brainard, the missionary to Indians in this country, was such a man. He suffered from what was then called consumption (we know it as tuberculosis). He would travel to the Indians by horseback, and sometimes he would have a convulsion, vomit blood, become unconscious, and fall off his horse. He would lie in the snow, and when that happened, his horse learned to stay right there. When he regained consciousness, he would crawl back onto his horse and be on his way to preach to the Indians. As he went, he would cry out, "Lord Jesus, I've failed You, but You know that I love You." He had that close, intimate relationship with Christ.

My friend, that personal relationship is all-important in our day, also. We are so involved in methods—I am rather amused at some of the Band-Aid courses which are being offered—and they are making Band-Aid believers. Generally, the course is some little legal system that gives you certain rules to follow and certain psychological patterns to observe which will enable you to solve all your problems. They try to teach you how to get along with yourself (that's a pretty big order!), with your neighbors, and especially with your wife. All of those relationships are very important, and a great many people think that if they can follow a few rules, they will have the key to a successful Christian life. My friend, let me put it in a nutshell by asking one question: Do you love Jesus Christ? I don't care what your system is, what your denomination is, what your program is, what little set of rules you follow, they will all come to naught if you don't love Him. Although some systems are better than others, almost any system will work if you *love* Christ. An intimate relationship with Christ will make all of your relationships and all of your Christian service a joy.

The story is told in New England about two girls who worked in a cotton mill. They were friends, but when one of them quit working there, they lost touch with each other. Finally, they met one day on the street. The working girl asked her friend,

"Are you still working?"

"No," she said, "I got married!"

When that girl worked in the mill, she watched the clock, and every evening when five o'clock came, she had her coat on and was on her way out. It was hard work, and she didn't like it. Now she is married and she says that she has quit working.

Well, if you could look at her life, you wouldn't think she had quit working. She gets up earlier than ever before to prepare breakfast for her husband and to pack his lunch. Then she throws her arms around him as she tells him good-bye. All day long she is busy cleaning house and washing clothes and caring for two little brats who are two little angels to her because they are hers. Then when five o'clock comes, she doesn't put on her coat and leave; she starts cooking dinner. About six o'clock here comes her husband. She is right there at the door to throw her arms around him and tell him how much she has missed him that day. When a man comes home in the evening, opens the door, and hears a voice from upstairs or from the rear of the house calling, "Is that you?", he knows the honeymoon is over. But this girl is in love. Her husband's workday is over, but hers has only just gotten started. She serves dinner to her husband and feeds the children. Then she washes the dishes, puts the children to bed—and that's not easy—and works around getting things ready for her husband for the next day. I tell you, she is weary when she finally gets into bed—but she's not working anymore, she says! Why? Because she is in love. That's the difference.

My friend, when your home life and your church life become a burden, there is something wrong with your relationship with Christ. When you get that straightened out, other things will straighten out also.

This is the reason the Lord Jesus said to the Ephesian believers, "You are getting away from your first love, your best love." What is the solution for them?

Remember therefore from whence thou art fallen, and repent, and do the first works; or else I will come unto thee quickly, and will remove thy candlestick out of his place, except thou repent [Rev. 2:5].

"Remember." That is the first thing they were to do. Memory is a marvelous thing. Someone has said that God has given us memories so we can have roses in December. Well, here in California we have short memories so we have roses all year-round. But memory is a wonderful thing. Someone else has said that memory is a luxury that only a *good* man can enjoy. My friend, do you remember when you were converted? Do you remember what a thrill it was and what the Lord Jesus meant to you? Have you become cold and indifferent to Him? Are you in a backslidden condition? Remember. Remember where you once were. You can get back to that same place.

"And repent." Believe me, Christians need to repent. We need to break the shell of self-sufficiency, the crust of conceit, the shield of sophistication, the veneer of vanity, get rid of the false face of "piosity," and stop this business of everlastingly polishing our halo as if we were some great saint. Repent! Repentance means to turn back to Him, and it is the message for *believers*. How dare the church tell an unsaved man to repent. What he needs to do is to turn to Christ for salvation. When he turns to Christ, he will turn from his sin—as the Thessalonians ". . . turned to God from idols to serve the living and true God; And to wait for his Son from heaven. . ." (1 Thess. 1:9–10). But the church needs to repent, and that is the message they do not want to hear today. Remember, repent, and return unto Him.

"Or else I will come unto thee quickly, and will remove the candlestick out of his place, except thou repent." Christ says that He will remove your lampstand. Oh, how many churches in our day have been practically closed. Once the crowds came, but they don't come anymore because the Word of God is no longer being taught. My friend, Christ is still watching the lamps, and He doesn't mind trimming the wicks or even using the snuffer when they refuse to give light.

But this thou hast, that thou hatest the deeds of the Nicolaitans, which I also hate [Rev. 2:6].

Nicolaitans is a compound word. *Nikao* means "to conquer," and *laos* means "the people." We get our word *laity* from that. It is difficult to identify who the Nicolaitans were. Some scholars think that they were a priestly order which was beginning to take shape and attempt to rule over the people. Another theory is that there is no way to identify this group in any of the early or late churches. The third explanation is that there was a man by the name of Nicolaus of Antioch, who apostatized from the truth and formed an Antinomian Gnostic cult which taught (among other doctrines) that one must indulge in sin in order to understand it. They gave themselves over to sensuality with the explanation that such sins did not touch the spirit. That "Nicolaitans" refers to this cult is probably the best explanation. The church in Ephesus hated it. A little later on we will see that the church in Pergamos [Pergamum] tolerated it.

He that hath an ear, let him hear what the Spirit saith unto the churches; To him that overcometh will I give to eat of the tree of life, which is in the midst of the paradise of God [Rev. 2:7].

"He that hath an ear." This is what I call a "blood-tipped ear," which was the requirement for the Old Testament priests. Not everyone can hear the Word of God. Oh, I know they can hear the audible sound, but they miss the message. The Lord Jesus uses the phrase to alert dull ears. We learn from the gospel records that He often used that expression. He said that they have ears to hear but they hear not. Now He speaks to those with spiritual perception.

"Let him hear what the Spirit saith unto the

churches." "The Spirit" is the Holy Spirit, the Teacher of the church.

"To him that overcometh" refers to genuine believers, and we can overcome only through the blood of the Lamb.

"Will I give to eat of the tree of life." You will recall that man was forbidden to eat of the Tree of Life after the Fall, as recorded in Genesis 3:22–24. But in heaven the "no trespassing" sign will be taken down, and all of us will be given the privilege of eating of the Tree of Life. I don't know what kind of fruit it has, but I believe it will enable us really to live it up. Most of us don't know much about living yet. We have sort of a vegetable existence down here, but we will have a good fruit existence up there—we'll eat of the Tree of Life. We are going to live as we have never lived before.

"The paradise of God" means the *garden* of God. Heaven is a garden of green primarily and is not just a place with streets of gold.

The church of Ephesus represents the church at its best, the apostolic church.

CHRIST'S LETTER TO THE CHURCH IN SMYRNA

Smyrna is the martyr church, the church that suffered martyrdom for Christ. The word *Smyrna* means "myrrh" and carries the meaning of suffering.

The city of Smyrna is still in existence in our day. It has a Turkish name, Izmir, which may lead you astray, but it is the same city. It has been continuously inhabited from the time it was founded. I have been there; in fact, we stay in Izmir when we visit the sites of the early churches in that area. It is a commercial city. There are those who have told us that Izmir will soon be larger than Istanbul. It will certainly be a larger commercial center. There is a tremendous population there. The modern city covers so much of the ruins of ancient Smyrna that you are apt to miss the beauty which was there.

I have taken some pictures of it and use them as slides in an illustrated message. I try to point out the beauty of that harbor. It is very large and one of the most beautiful harbors that I have seen. In fact, Smyrna was one of the loveliest cities of Asia. It was called a flower, an ornament, and it has been called the crown of all Asia. The acropolis is located on Mount Pagos. In fact, the early city that goes back to about 2000 B.C., a Hittite city at that time, was built around the slope of Mount Pagos. Later Alexander the Great had a great deal to do with building it into the beautiful

city that it became. There were wide boulevards along the slopes of Mount Pagos. Smyrna was called the crown city because the acropolis was encircled with flowers, a hedge, and myrtle trees. The city was adorned with noble buildings and beautiful temples—a temple of Zeus, a temple of Cybele (Diana), a temple of Aphrodite, a temple of Apollo, and a temple of Asclepius. Smyrna had a theater and an odeum, that is, a music center—it was the home of music. Also it had a stadium, and it was at that stadium that Polycarp, bishop of Smyrna and student of the apostle John, was martyred, burned alive in A.D. 155.

In Christian literature, *Smyrna* means "suffering." The Lord Jesus, in His letter addressed to the church there, said that He knew their sufferings and their poverty. He had no word of condemnation for them or for the church at Philadelphia. They were the churches that heard no word of condemnation from Him, and it is interesting that these two cities, Smyrna and Philadelphia, are the only two which have had a continuous existence. Their lampstand has really been moved, but there are a few Christians in Izmir. Although they are under cover, they have made indirect contact with us when we have been there. They do not come out in the open because Christians are persecuted even today in modern Turkey.

As Ephesus represents the apostolic church, so Smyrna represents the martyr church which covers the period from about A.D. 100 to approximately A.D. 314, from the death of the apostle John to the Edict of Toleration by Constantine, which was given in A.D. 313 and ended the persecution of Christians—not only in Smyrna but all over the Roman Empire.

Now here we have the Lord Jesus addressing the church at Smyrna. It is His briefest message, and it is all commendatory—everything He has to say to them is praise.

And unto the angel of the church in Smyrna write; These things saith the first and the last, which was dead, and is alive [Rev. 2:8].

And to the messenger of the church in Smyrna, write, These things saith the first and the last, who became dead, and lived.

This verse is a reference to chapter 1, verses 17–18, which says, "And when I saw him, I fell at his feet as dead. And he laid his right hand upon me, saying unto me, Fear not; I am the first and the last: I am he that liveth, and was dead; and, behold, I am alive for evermore, Amen; and have the keys of hell and of death." The Lord chose from the vision of Himself that particular figure which was fitting for each church. To the church in Smyrna the Lord describes Himself as "the first and the last, which was dead, and is alive."

"The first and the last" means that there was nothing before Him and there will be nothing to follow Him. He has the final disposition of all things. The persecuted believers needed to know that He was the One in charge and that the persecution was in the planning and purpose of God.

"Who became dead, and lived" has a real message for martyrs. His experience with death identified Him with the five million who were martyred during this period. (According to *Fox's Book of Martyrs*, five million believers died for Christ during this period.) Christ was triumphant over death and can save to the uttermost those who are enduring persecution and martyrdom.

He has something further to say to them—

I know thy works, and tribulation, and poverty, (but thou art rich) and I know the blasphemy of them which say they are Jews, and are not, but are the synagogue of Satan.

Fear none of those things which thou shalt suffer: behold, the devil shall cast some of you into prison, that ye may be tried; and ye shall have tribulation ten days: be thou faithful unto death, and I will give thee a crown of life [Rev. 2:9–10].

There are *seven* things in this church which the Lord commended:

1. "Tribulation" is mentioned first. The word *works* is not in the best manuscripts. I prefer to leave it out, but if you want to include it, fine. Remember, this is *not* the Great Tribulation; it means simply *trouble*. Since the awful persecution of the church by the Roman emperors is not called the Great Tribulation, surely our small sufferings are not the Great Tribulation. But the church in Smyrna endured much tribulation, and they suffered for the Lord Jesus Christ.

2. "Poverty" denotes the lack of material possessions. The early church was made up largely of the poorer classes. When the wealthy believed in Christ, their property was confiscated because of their faith. "But thou art rich" denotes the spiritual wealth of the church—they were blessed with all spiritual blessings. Notice the contrast to the rich church in Laodicea. To that church He said, "You think you are rich, but you are really poor and don't know it."

When I am a visiting conference speaker in churches across the land, pastors like to tell me about the millionaire or persons of prominence whom they have in their congregation. Well, the martyr church couldn't brag about that. They had in their congregation slaves, ex-slaves, runaway slaves, freed slaves, poor people, and those who had lost whatever money they had when they became Christians.

3. "The blasphemy of them which say they are Jews . . . but are the synagogue of Satan." The implication is that the Jews in Smyrna who had come to Christ were Jews inwardly as well as outwardly. In Romans 9:6 Paul says that not all Israel is Israel. It is his religion that makes a Jew a real Jew. His religion is the thing that identifies him. Speaking of them nationally, the Lord said that their father was ". . . a Syrian ready to perish . . ." (Deut. 26:5). But Smyrna was a city of culture in which many Jews had discarded their belief in the Old Testament. Although they said they were Jews, when a Jew gives up his religion, there is a question whether or not he is a Jew. In Germany many tried to do that, by the way. Down through the years there has been only a remnant of these people who have truly been God's people.

4. "Fear none of those things" is the encouragement of the Lord to His own in the midst of persecutions. This is the second time in this book that the Lord has offered this encouragement. History tells us that multitudes went to their death singing praises to God.

5. "The devil [Satan] shall cast some of you into prison." We are going to look at this fearful creature later on, but Christ labels him as being responsible for the suffering of the saints in Smyrna. You and I tend to blame the immediate person or circumstance which serves as Satan's tool, but the Lord Jesus goes back to the root trouble.

I would like to insert a personal word at this point. I could classify and pigeonhole everything that has come into my life as God's judgment or God's chastisement, but when I began experiencing so many physical problems, I was puzzled. Then quite a few people began writing to say, "I believe Satan is responsible for the things that are happening to you." And I decided this must be the explanation for the many physical problems that afflicted me.

6. "Ye shall have tribulation ten days."

There were ten intense periods of persecution by ten Roman emperors (these dates are approximate):

Nero—64–68 (Paul was beheaded under his reign)

Domitian—95–96 (John was exiled during that period)

Trajan—104–117 (Ignatius was burned at the stake)

Marcus Aurelius—161–180 (Polycarp was martyred)

Severus—200–211

Maximinius—235–237

Decius—250–253

Valerian—257–260

Aurelian—270–275

Diocletian—303–313 (the worst emperor of all).

7. "Be thou faithful unto death"—and they were. They were martyrs for Him. He promises them "a crown of life." Remember that He is addressing the believers who lived in Smyrna, the crown city. It is interesting that to *them* He is saying that He will give crowns—not crowns of flowers—or of anything else perishable—but crowns that will be eternal.

The Lord has special crowns for those who suffer. I know many wonderful saints who are going to get that crown some day. My friend, if you are suffering at this moment and you have wondered if He cares, He has something good for you in eternity. You will get something that no one else will be getting, except others in your condition. God's Word says, "Blessed is the man that endureth temptation: for when he is tried, he shall receive the crown of life, which the Lord hath promised to them that love him" (James 1:12). That crown of life means that you are really going to live it up someday. What a glorious prospect that is for invalids and those on beds of pain today.

He that hath an ear, let him hear what the Spirit saith unto the churches; He that overcometh shall not be hurt of the second death [Rev. 2:11].

"He that hath an ear, let him hear what the Spirit saith unto the churches." Have *you* heard Him today? Is He speaking to you?

"The second death." Dwight L. Moody put it like this: "He who is born once will die twice; he who is born twice will die once." And if the Rapture occurs during his lifetime, he won't even have to die that one time. The "second death" is the death which no believer will experience. The first death concerns the body. The second death concerns the soul and the spirit; it is eternal separation from God. No believer will have to undergo that.

CHRIST'S LETTER TO THE CHURCH IN PERGAMUM

In our King James text this city is called Pergamos, but in Turkey it is called Pergamum, and I assume that is the correct spelling.

The church in Pergamum is representative of church history during the period of approximately A.D. 314 to A.D. 590. I call it *paganism unlimited* because during this time the world entered into the church and it began to move away from the person of Christ. This letter was Christ's message to the local church at Pergamum, of course, but it also has this historical significance.

First, let me give you the location of Pergamum. Izmir is the great city where tourists go because the airport and the hotels are there. You go about sixty-five miles south to reach Ephesus and about seventy miles north to reach Pergamum. These three were the royal cities, and they vied one with another. Smyrna (Izmir) was the great commercial center, Ephesus was the great political center, and Pergamum was the great religious center.

Pergamum was the capital of the kingdom of Pergamum. The acropolis still stands there, and the ruins of the great temples and the city are on top of it. It was a city in Mysia, labeled by Pliny "by far the most illustrious of Asia." It is one of the most beautiful spots in Asia Minor. Sir William Ramsay says that it was the one city that deserved to be called a royal city. In it was a temple built to Caesar Augustus, which made it a royal city. Augustus came to this beautiful area when the climate got cold in Rome. There was a healing spa there. It was not the commercial city that Smyrna was because it was not a seacoast town and it was off the great trade routes which came out of the Orient. But it was a fortified, stronghold city, built to withstand the enemy. It was built on a mountain, and the acropolis dominated the whole region of the broad plain of the Caicus. The original city was built between the two rivers which flowed into the Caicus and entirely surrounded this huge rocky hill, this promontory that stood out there alone. To visit it makes quite an impression. First you see that great mountain standing there, and you see the ruins on top.

Not only did Pergamum boast great temples, but it also had the greatest library of the pagan world. It was a library of over two hundred thousand volumes. In fact, the city got its name from the parchment (pergamena) which was used. This great library was the one which Mark Antony gave to his girl friend, Cleopatra. She lugged it off to Alexandria in Egypt, and that library was considered the greatest library the world has ever seen—and it originally came from Pergamum.

If you are ever in Istanbul and go into Hagia Sophia, you will see there a great alabaster vase, taller than I am and a thing of beauty, which was brought there from Pergamum. Of course, the city of Pergamum was rifled and denuded by the enemy when they finally took the city and destroyed it.

And to the angel of the church in Pergamos write; These things saith he which hath the sharp sword with two edges [Rev. 2:12].

"To the angel of the church in Pergamos." This letter was addressed, as were other letters, to the angel or messenger of the church, which was probably the one we would call the pastor.

"These things saith he which hath the sharp sword with two edges" means the Word of God. The Word of God has the answer to man's need and man's sin, which in Pergamum was false religion. It was a city that emphasized religion, and the only way it could be reached would be by the Word of God.

I know thy works and where thou dwellest, even where Satan's seat is: and thou holdest fast my name, and hast not denied my faith, even in those days wherein Antipas was my faithful martyr, who was slain among you, where Satan dwelleth [Rev. 2:13].

"Where thou dwellest." The Lord commends this church for three very definite things. First, He takes note of their circumstances. He knew that these believers were living in a very difficult place. And, my friend, the Lord takes note of *our* circumstances. Sometimes we are inclined to condemn someone who is caught in a certain set of circumstances, but if we were in the same position, we might act in an even worse way than he is acting.

"Even where Satan's seat [throne] is" reveals that religion was big business in Pergamum and that Satan's headquarters were there. This ought to settle the question for those who think that Satan is in hell at the present time. He has never yet been in hell because hell hasn't opened up for business yet. Satan will not be in hell until much later, as we

shall see in chapter 20. At the present, Satan is loose and is the prince of this world, controlling kingdoms and going up and down the earth as a roaring lion, hunting for whom he may devour (see 1 Pet. 5:8). But he *does* have headquarters, and Christ said they were in Pergamum at that time. Since those days, I think that he has moved his headquarters around to different places. I used to get the impression that he had moved them to Los Angeles, and he may have done so because that is another great religious center of every kind of cult and "ism" and schism.

The reason our Lord said that Satan's throne was in Pergamum was because of the heathen temples there. Of course, all of this is in ruins today. There are markers and some reconstruction going on there now. But in John's day it was Satan's throne. As you enter the gate of the city, you see that the first temple to your right is the imposing temple of Athena. Directly above it is the great library. You would see the great temple of Caesar Augustus and Hadrian's great temple, which covers quite a bit of territory. There are other things that are quite interesting. There is the great altar to Zeus with an idol on it near the palace of the king. It is a very impressive spot, and some folk believe that it was the throne of Satan. Well, I think that it is included but that Satan's throne is a combination of all of these.

There are two other areas which are especially outstanding. One of them is the temple of Dionysius. I crawled down the side of that mountain to get pictures of the ruins of the temple of Dionysius, which is beside the ruins of the theater there. Some folk asked me why I did that. Well, Dionysius is the same as Bacchus, the god of wine, the goat-god. He is depicted with horns, but with his upper part as a man and his lower part as a goat, with cloven feet and a tail. In our day that is the modern idea of Satan, but the notion that Satan has horns, cloven feet, and a forked tail did not come from the Bible. Where did it come from? Well, it came from the temple of Dionysius, the god Bacchus, the god of wine or alcohol. My friend, we ought to be proud that we are Americans, but we also need to bow our heads in shame. Do you know how we got this country in which we live? We got it from the Indians (and I guess they got it from someone else), but the way we got it was not by bullets but by alcohol. Also Hawaii was taken away from the Hawaiians by giving them liquor. Alcohol has taken more territory than anything else. Satan is the god of liquor all right!

Then the other outstanding temple was of the god Asklepios. Down from that great promontory was the greatest hospital of the ancient world. It was the Mayo Clinic of that day. It was, first of all, a *temple* to Asklepios. If you are looking at the Greek god Asklepios, it is a man, but when you see the Anatolian or Oriental Asklepios, it is a serpent. There in Pergamum it was a serpent. I have pictures which I took of that great marble pillar which stands like an obelisk now but apparently was a pillar in the temple of Asklepios. The construction of the temple was unusual in that it was round. There they used every means of healing imaginable. They used both medicine and psychology—and about everything else.

Put yourself in this situation: you go down long tunnels, and above are holes that look like airholes for ventilation but are not. As you walk along these tunnels, sexy voices come down through the holes, saying to you, "You are going to get well. You are going to feel better. You are going to be healed." (Does that have a modern ring?) You go down to the hot baths where you are given a massage. There is a little theater there where they give plays of healing. If they haven't healed you by now, as a last resort they put you in that temple at night and turn loose the nonpoisonous snakes which crawl over you. (That is known as the shock treatment in our day!) If they don't heal you, they will drive you crazy, that's for sure. They have a back door where they take out the dead. They don't mention the ones they don't heal; they speak only of those who recover.

Caesar Augustus loved to go there. He wasn't exactly sick; he was an alcoholic. They just dried him out every year when he would come over. This was a great place, and for seven hundred years it was a hospital that people came to from all over the world. May I say to you, healing was *satanic* in those days. There is no question about the fact that there were good men there who used medicine, but basically, it was satanic. It was where Satan's throne was. That is important to see.

Now here is another word of commendation to the believers at Pergamum, "thou holdest fast my name." They were faithful in their defense of the deity of Christ.

As we have noted, the church at Pergamum is representative of the church in general during the years of A.D. 314 to approximately A.D. 590. Actually, it was an age that produced great giants of the faith. When the Arian heresy (which denied the deity of Christ) arose, Athanasius from North Africa was the great defender of the faith, and because of him

the Council of Nicea in A.D. 325 condemned Arianism. And another man was Augustine, who answered the Pelagian heresy which denied original sin and the total corruption of human nature and also denied irresistible grace. These are two giants during this period who stood unshakably for the great doctrines of the faith.

"And hast not denied my faith" refers to the body of true doctrine which is believed by Christians.

"Even in those days wherein Antipas was my faithful martyr." Antipas was a martyr about whom we know nothing at all. He apparently was the first one at Pergamum, and there was a great company of martyrs who followed him.

So far Christ has had only words of commendation for the church at Pergamum, but now He condemns two things which were in that church—

But I have a few things against thee, because thou hast there them that hold the doctrine of Balaam, who taught Balac to cast a stumblingblock before the children of Israel, to eat things sacrificed unto idols, and to commit fornication.

So hast thou also them that hold the doctrine of the Nicolaitans, which thing I hate [Rev. 2:14–15].

The two items for condemnation were the doctrine of Balaam and the doctrine of the Nicolaitans. "The *doctrine* of Balaam" is different from the *error* of Balaam (see Jude 11), which revealed that Balaam thought that God would curse Israel because they were sinners. It is also different from the *way* of Balaam (see 2 Pet. 2:15), which was covetousness. But here in the verse before us, it is the *doctrine* or teaching of Balaam. He taught Balac the way to corrupt Israel by intermarriage with the Moabite women. This introduced into the nation of Israel both idolatry and fornication. And during the historical period which the church at Pergamum represents, the unconverted world came into the church.

"The doctrine of the Nicolaitans." We have seen that the church in Ephesus hated it, but here in Pergamum there were some who were holding that doctrine. Although we do not know exactly what the doctrine was, it probably was a gnostic cult developed by Nicolaus which advocated license in matters of Christians' conduct and apparently a return to religious rituals by clergy, ignoring the priesthood of all believers. Christ says that He *hates* it! You see, Christ hates as well as loves. We had better be careful that we are not indulging in the things that He hates.

> **Repent; or else I will come unto thee quickly, and will fight against them with the sword of my mouth [Rev. 2:16].**

"Repent." In other words, the only cure was repentance (*metanoēson*, "a change of mind"). God's Word says, "If we confess our sins, he is faithful and just to forgive us our sins, and to cleanse us from all unrighteousness" (1 John 1:9). If they would not repent, the Lord said He would fight against them with the sword of His mouth, which is the Word of God. What a mistake we make if we think that the church has the authority to decide what is right and what is wrong. The true church is made up of believers in Jesus Christ, and they form what Scripture calls the body of Christ. They are to be lights in the world. And if we are going to be lights in this dark world, we need to be careful to identify with the person of Jesus Christ and to recognize, not the church, but the Word of God as our authority.

> **He that hath an ear, let him hear what the Spirit saith unto the churches; To him that overcometh will I give to eat of the hidden manna, and will give him a white stone, and in the stone a new name written, which no man knoweth saving he that receiveth it [Rev. 2:17].**

"He that hath an ear, let him hear what the Spirit saith unto the churches." This is to you and me today.

"To him that overcometh" is the definition of a genuine Christian. We overcome by the blood of the Lamb. Never are *we* overcomers, but we overcome by His shed blood. We know that the victory was won by Christ and not by ourselves.

"Hidden manna" speaks of the person and the death of Christ as He is revealed in the Word of God. In fact, Jesus said that He Himself was the Bread: "Then Jesus said unto them, Verily, verily, I say unto you, Moses gave you not that bread from heaven; but my Father giveth you the true bread from heaven. For the bread of God is he which cometh down from heaven, and giveth life unto the world. Then said they unto him, Lord, evermore give us this bread. And Jesus said unto them, I am the bread of life: he that cometh to me shall never hunger; and he that believeth on me shall never thirst" (John 6:32–35). The believer needs to feed on Christ—this is a *must* for spiritual growth. And, actually, Christ is hidden from view; He is not known or understood in our day. My, how folk misrepresent Him and abuse Him!

"I . . . will give him a white stone, and in the stone a new name written, which no man knoweth saving he that receiveth it." A *white* stone suggests that believers are not blackballed in heaven. Trench said, "White is everywhere the color and livery of heaven." Frankly, this is rather a difficult figure to interpret. But it is helpful to learn that the people of Asia Minor to whom John was writing had a custom of giving to intimate friends a *tessera*, a cube or rectangular block of stone or ivory, with words or symbols engraved on it. It was a secret, private possession of the one who received it. Well, Christ says that He is going to give to each of His own a stone with a new name engraved upon it. I do not believe that it will be a new name for you and me but that it will be a new name for *Him*. I believe that each name will be different because He means something different to each one of us. It will be His personal and intimate name to each of us.

CHRIST'S LETTER TO THE CHURCH IN THYATIRA

The church at Thyatira is representative of Romanism, which takes us into the Dark Ages from A.D. 590 to approximately A.D. 1000. It was a dark period.

When you leave Pergamum, you begin to move inland. Thyatira and the remaining three churches are inland. Thyatira was situated in a very beautiful location. Sir William Ramsay has written this about it:

Thyatira was situated in the mouth of a long vale which extends north and south connecting the Hermus and Caicos Valleys. Down the vale a stream flows south to join the Lycus (near whose left bank Thyatira was situated), one of the chief tributaries of the Hermus, while its northern end is divided by only a ridge of small elevation from the Caicos Valley. The valleys of the two rivers, Hermus and Caicos, stretch east and west, opening down from the edge of the great central plateau of Anatolia towards the Ægean Sea. Nature has marked out this road, a very easy path, for the tide of communication which in all civilised times must have been large between the one valley and the other. The railway traverses its whole length now: in ancient times one of the chief routes of Asia Minor traversed it.

Thyatira was located in this long vale or pass. Thyatira was a city built for defense. However, most cities built for defense were situated upon an acropolis or a promontory and walls were put around them. But Thyatira was different. It stood in the middle of that vale on a very slight rising ground. Its strength lay in the fact that Rome stationed the elite guard there.

Thyatira was built by Lysimachus and again by Seleucus I, the founder of the Seleucid dynasty, whose vast realm extended from the Hermus Valley to the Himalayas. It finally fell to the enemy. No city in that area was so completely destroyed and rebuilt as was this city. For this reason, it is very disappointing to visit the ruins of Thyatira in our day. They cover only one very small block.

This city became prosperous under the sponsorship of Vespasian, the Roman emperor. It was the headquarters for many ancient guilds: the potters', tanners', weavers', robe makers', and dyers' guilds. It was the center of the dyeing industry. This is where the labor unions must have originated! Lydia, the seller of purple, who in Philippi became Paul's first convert in Europe, came from here (see Acts 16:14). That purple color spoken of is what we know today as "Turkey red"—and I mean that color is *red*. The dye was taken from a plant that grows in that area. Apollo, the sun god, was worshiped here as Tyrimnos.

And unto the angel of the church in Thyatira write; These things saith the Son of God, who hath his eyes like unto a flame of fire, and his feet are like fine brass [Rev. 2:18].

This pictures the Son of God in judgment. His eyes are like a flame of fire, searching them out, and His feet are like burnished brass, which represents judgment. Christ is judging this church.

However, He has words of commendation for this church. If you think that the Roman church during the Dark Ages is to be condemned wholeheartedly, you need to check up on the history of it. The Lord Jesus says,

I know thy works, and charity, and service, and faith, and thy patience, and thy works; and the last to be more than the first [Rev. 2:19].

Christ has six words of commendation for the church of the Dark Ages in which were many true believers who had a personal love of Christ which was manifested in works. Works are actually credentials of true believers. James says, "Yea, a man may say, Thou hast faith, and I have works: shew me thy faith without thy works, and I will shew thee my faith by my works" (James 2:18).

The six words of commendation are:

1. "Works" were the credentials of real believers. There were many who lived spotless lives and by their good works "adorned the doctrine."

2. "Love." It was a church in which there was love, in spite of the fact that it had gone in for ritualism. There were some wonderful saints of God during that period: Bernard of Clairvaux, Peter Waldo, John Wycliffe, John Huss, Savonarola, and Anselm were all men in the Roman church.

3. "Faith." Though it is placed after works and love in this instance, it is the mainspring that turns the hands of works and love.

4. "Ministry" is service.

5. "Patience" is endurance in those days of darkness.

6. "Thy last works are more than the first." In this church, works increased rather than diminished.

All *six virtues* are produced within the believer by the Holy Spirit.

There is one frightful charge of condemnation:

Notwithstanding I have a few things against thee, because thou sufferest that woman Jezebel, which calleth herself a prophetess, to teach and to seduce my servants to commit fornication, and to eat things sacrificed unto idols [Rev. 2:20].

But I have against you that you tolerate the woman (wife) Jezebel, who calls herself the prophetess, and she teaches and seduces my servants to commit fornication and to eat things sacrificed to idols.

Jezebel had brought paganism into the northern kingdom of Israel. And evidently there was in the local church at Thyatira a woman who had a reputation as a teacher and prophetess who was the counterpart of Jezebel, the consort of Ahab.

And concerning the historical period of the Dark Ages which the church at Thyatira represents, pagan practices and idolatry were mingled with Christian works and worship. The papacy was elevated to a place of secular power under Gregory I (A.D. 590), and later by Gregory VII, better known as Hildebrand, (A.D. 1073–1085). The introduction of rituals and church doctrine supplanted personal faith in Jesus Christ. Worship of the Virgin and Child and the Mass were made a definite part of the church service. Purgatory became a positive doctrine, and Mass was said for the dead. The spurious documents labeled Donation of Constantine and Decretals of Isidore were circulated to give power and rulership to the pope.

As Jezebel killed Naboth and persecuted God's prophets, so the Roman church instituted the Inquisition during this period.

"Seduce" means a fundamental departure from the truth, according to Vincent. Jezebel stands in sharp contrast to Lydia, who came from Thyatira. Jezebel is merely a forerunner of the apostate church, as we shall see in chapter 17.

And I gave her space to repent of her fornication; and she repented not [Rev. 2:21].

"Space" is time. The Lord Jesus Christ has patiently dealt with this false system for over a thousand years, and there has been no real change down through the centuries in this system. In fact, Rome boasts that she never changes—*semper idem*, always the same.

Behold, I will cast her into a bed, and them that commit adultery with her into great tribulation, except they repent of their deeds [Rev. 2:22].

"Great tribulation" could refer to the persecution which Rome is enduring under communism. Or it may mean the Great Tribulation into which the apostate church will go.

"Their deeds" should be translated *her* deeds.

And I will kill her children with death; and all the churches shall know that I am he which searcheth the reins and hearts: and I will give unto every one of you according to your works [Rev. 2:23].

"Children" are those who were brought up under this system.

"And I will kill her children with death" is translated by Vincent: "Let them be put to death with death," referring to the second death.

"All the churches" refers to the church of all the ages.

"The reins" means literally the kidneys and refers to the total psychological makeup—the thoughts, the feelings, the purposes. When He searches the reins and the hearts, it means that He searches our entire beings.

But unto you I say, and unto the rest in Thyatira, as many as have not this doctrine, and which have not known the depths of Satan, as they speak; I will put upon you none other burden [Rev. 2:24].

But I say to you, to the rest in Thyatira, who do not hold this doctrine, which are of those who have not known the depths of Satan, as they say, I will put upon you none other burden (weight).

The church in Thyatira, we know from history, had a very brief existence because it went down with the city when it was captured by the enemy.

"The depths of Satan" perhaps refers to a gnostic sect known as the Ophites who worshiped the serpent. They made a parody of Paul's words. All heresy boasts of superior spiritual perception, and that is what this group did.

But that which ye have already hold fast till I come [Rev. 2:25].

Obviously, Christ is beginning to say to His church, "I am coming to take you out, and because of this, you should stand fast for Me."

And he that overcometh, and keepeth my works unto the end, to him will I give power over the nations [Rev. 2:26].

The works of Christ are in contrast to the works of Jezebel. The works of Christ are wrought by the Holy Spirit. We overcome by faith and not by effort.

"I give power over the nations" was explained by Paul when he wrote to the Corinthian believers: "Do ye not know that the saints shall judge the world? . . . (1 Cor. 6:2).

And he shall rule them with a rod of iron; as the vessels of a potter shall they be broken to shivers: even as I received of my Father [Rev. 2:27].

This is a reference to the millennial reign of Christ in which believers are to share.

And I will give him the morning star [Rev. 2:28].

Christ is the Bright and Morning Star (see Rev. 22:16). Christ's coming for His own at the Rapture is the hope of the church. "Looking for that blessed hope, and the glorious appear-ing of the great God and our Saviour Jesus Christ" (Titus 2:13).

He that hath an ear, let him hear what the Spirit saith unto the churches [Rev. 2:29].

The children of Jezebel will not hear, but the true children of the Lord Jesus will hear, for the Holy Spirit opens the "blood-tipped ear."

CHAPTER 3

THEME: *The church in the world—continued*

CHRIST'S LETTER TO THE CHURCH IN SARDIS

In the panorama of church history, Sardis represents the Protestant church during the period between A.D. 1517 and approximately A.D. 1800. It began, I believe, when Martin Luther nailed his *Ninety-Five Theses* onto the chapel door of the church at Wittenburg, Germany. It is an era which started with the Reformation and takes us into the beginning of the great missionary movement in the history of the church.

Sardis was the capital of the great kingdom of Lydia and one of the oldest and most important cities of Asia Minor. It was located inland and built on a small, elevated plateau which rises sharply above the Hermus Valley. On all sides but one the rock walls are smooth, nearly perpendicular and absolutely unscalable. The only access is on the southern side by a very steep and difficult path. One time when I was there, another preacher and I tried to make the climb. He went farther than I did, but we both gave up long before we reached the top.

As the civilization and the commerce grew more complex, the high plateau became too small, and a lower city was built chiefly on the west side of the original city. The old city was used as an acropolis. Actually this made it a double city, and it was called by the plural noun *Sardeis* or *Sardis*. The plain was well watered by the Pactolus River. It became the center of the carpet industry and was noted for its wealth. Coins were first minted there. Its last prince was the wealthy Croesus who was captured by Cyrus. He was considered the wealthiest man in the world, and everything he touched seemed to turn to gold. Sardis was ruled by the Persians, by Alexander, by Antiochus the Great, and finally by the Romans. It was destroyed by an earthquake during the reign of Tiberius.

In our day the ruins of the temple of Cybele and also of the temple of Apollo can still be seen. It is one of the few double temples that you will find in the world. Cybele was known as Diana in Ephesus, but when you get inland, she becomes a nature goddess. She was the goddess of the moon, and Apollo was the god of the sun—they were brother and sister. This was a very corrupt worship, much like the worship of Diana at Ephesus.

Extensive excavations have taken place at Sardis. They are rebuilding the gymnasium and also the synagogue. And they have dug up the Roman road that is there. The thing that thrilled me when I looked at that road was that I knew the apostle Paul had walked up and down it.

And unto the angel of the church in Sardis write; These things saith he that hath the seven Spirits of God, and the seven stars; I know thy works, that thou hast a name that thou livest, and art dead [Rev. 3:1].

"These things saith he that hath the seven Spirits of God, and the seven stars." He presents Himself to the church at Sardis as the One having the seven Spirits of God; that is, *He* is the One who sent the Holy Spirit into the world.

As we have seen, Sardis represents the

Protestant church. My friend, the church today needs the Spirit of God working in it. We think we need methods, and we have all kinds of Band-Aid courses for believers in which you put on a little Band-Aid, and it will solve all your problems. What we really need to do is to get to the person of Christ whom only the Holy Spirit can make real and living to us. This is the thing Protestantism needs today.

Following the dark night of the Dark Ages, the Holy Spirit was still in the world doing His work. He moved in the hearts of men like Martin Luther, John Calvin, John Knox, and many, many others.

"I know thy works." This is the word of commendation. Remember that the Reformation recovered the doctrine of justification by faith, and this faith produced works.

"That thou hast a name that thou livest, and art dead." Protestantism today, as a whole, has a name that it lives, but it is dead. Many Protestant churches today are just going through the form. They are building all the time, and people are coming, especially on Sunday mornings. But there are not many at the midweek service, when they really ought to come to hear the Word of God. "Thou hast a name that thou livest, and art dead." This is a frightful condemnation and is a picture of Protestantism today.

We need to recognize that all of the truth was not recovered by the Reformation. For example, I believe that the doctrine of eschatology, prophecy, is just now being developed in our own day.

Be watchful, and strengthen the things which remain, that are ready to die: for I have not found thy works perfect before God [Rev. 3:2].

Let me give you my translation of this verse:

Wake up and watch out and establish the things that remain which were about to die, for I have found no works of thine fulfilled (perfected) before my God.

This is the second word of condemnation, and it is a word of warning which had particular meaning in Sardis. As I have said, Sardis was located on the top of a mountain. It had one entrance on the southern side which was the only way you could get into the city in the old days. Therefore, all that Sardis had to do was to put a detail at that one place to watch the city. But on two occasions in their history they had been invaded by their enemies because they had felt secure, believing that the

hill was impregnable, and the guard went to sleep on the job. In 549 B.C. the Median soldiers of Cyrus scaled the parapet, and then again in 218 B.C. Antiochus the Great captured Sardis because a Cretan slipped over the walls while the sentries were careless. What the Lord says to this church at Sardis is this: "You wake up and watch out!" This was embarrassing because of the two occasions in their history when they had been caught napping. He says to the church, "Don't *you* go to sleep!"

Protestantism, as a whole, has turned away from looking for the coming of Jesus Christ, and they have built up these systems that certain things must be fulfilled before He can come. My friend, it is *tissue-thin* from where we are right now to the coming of Christ for His church. He could come the next moment or tomorrow. Don't say that I said He is coming tomorrow because I don't know. It may be a hundred years, but, my friend, His imminent return is what we are to look for. Sardis didn't know when the enemy was coming, and *we* don't know when Christ is coming—we have no way of knowing at all.

In view of the fact that the Rapture could take place at any moment, the church is to be alert. The date is not set, nor even the period in which He will come, and the reason for that is that the church is to be constantly on the alert for His coming—"Looking for that blessed hope . . ." (Titus 2:13). You see, anyone can make ready for a fixed hour, but you must *always* be ready for an unexpected hour. The Lord Jesus is saying to Protestantism that they are constantly to be on the alert.

"For I have not found thy works perfect before God." Protestantism did recover the authority of the Word of God, the total depravity of man, and justification by faith, but there are many other things that they did not recover. The Reformation was not a return to the apostolic church.

Remember therefore how thou hast received and heard, and hold fast, and repent. If therefore thou shalt not watch, I will come on thee as a thief, and thou shalt not know what hour I will come upon thee [Rev. 3:3].

"Remember therefore how thou hast received and heard, and hold fast, and repent." The idea is that they were to hold fast to these things because they were about to die. The great truths which were recovered in the Reformation are being lost. For instance, the Protestant church, by and large, has lost the authority of the Word of God. Rather than holding to the doctrine of the total depravity of man, many of our conservative churches are improving and using cosmetics on the carnal nature, thinking that somehow or another you can get up a few little rules and regulations which are going to enable you to live the Christian life. Also, the great doctrine of justification by faith has been pretty much abandoned, and a legalistic message is given that you have to *do* something in order to be saved. These are the things which characterize Protestantism today; it is very far from its original position.

"If therefore thou shalt not watch, I will come on thee as a thief, and thou shalt not know what hour I will come upon thee." As we have seen, Sardis was built high upon a mountaintop which was impossible to scale except at one point. There is so much erosion of the soil in Turkey that two thousand years ago—in the days of Paul and John—the mountain was much higher and even more inaccessible than it is today. In spite of that, there were these two occasions when enemy soldiers gained entrance to the city. This was very embarrassing to this city—two times it was captured because the guard went to sleep. The Lord says to the church at Sardis, "Don't *you* go to sleep. Wake up and watch out." He could come at any moment. The people of Sardis did not know when the enemy was coming, and we do not know when the Lord Jesus is coming.

Thou hast a few names even in Sardis which have not defiled their garments; and they shall walk with me in white: for they are worthy [Rev. 3:4].

But thou hast a few names (persons) in Sardis that did not besmirch (defile) their Christian life (garments); and they shall walk with me in white (garments); for they are worthy.

In Israel it was never the corporate body of the total national life but always a remnant that was true to God. Here the church is told, "You have a few." In Luke 12:32 the Lord called His church "little flock." Protestantism today has its saints who love the Word, who are faithful to Him even in these days, and who stand by the Word of God. They do not engage in sin-defiling activities, nor are they engaged in fleshly activity.

Protestantism has produced some great men, and I will mention some, although I am going to leave out a great many. I think of the Reformation leaders: Martin Luther and John Calvin stand out, head and shoulders, above

all others. Of course, there was John Knox, a great man of God who did so much for Scotland. Later on, there was John Bunyan, the great Baptist who wrote *Pilgrim's Progress*, which tells of his own life and how God marvelously saved him. John Wesley was the founder of the Methodist church. God marvelously saved that man and used him in such a way that he is given credit by historians for saving England from the revolution which destroyed France and prevented it from ever becoming a first-rate nation again. Wesley has been called the greatest Englishman of all. He certainly did more for that country than any other Englishman who has ever lived. Then there was a man like John Moffat, the Scotchman who went to Africa, and David Livingstone who first opened up that continent. William Carey went to India and later was followed by a sickly young man by the name of Henry Martyn. Finally, I always like to include Titus Coan, who led the greatest revival since Pentecost out in the Hawaiian Islands.

Protestantism has had some names who didn't defile themselves and were true to the Word of God. There are quite a few such men living today, but I wouldn't dare to begin to name them because of the fact that I would be apt to leave some out who ought to be included.

Protestantism has certainly produced some great men of God. Romanism did the same thing, even during the Dark Ages, but that does not mean to commend the system. The system of Romanism and the system of Protestantism, as they are revealed in the great denominations which have departed from the faith, to me are the organizations which will eventually bring in the apostate church because they have departed from the great tenets and doctrines of the Christian faith.

Verse 5 is a difficult passage of Scripture—

He that overcometh, the same shall be clothed in white raiment; and I will not blot out his name out of the book of life, but I will confess his name before my Father, and before his angels [Rev. 3:5].

"He that overcometh." The one who overcomes by the blood of Christ, of course, never does it because of his own strength, cleverness, or ability.

Now He makes this statement which has caused the difficulty in understanding: "I will not blot out his name out of the book of life, but I will confess his name before my Father, and before his angels." It is interesting to note that in the genealogies there are only two books which are identified: (1) "the book of the generations of Adam" (see Gen. 5:1)—we are all in that book, but it is a book of death—and (2) "the book of the generation of Jesus Christ" (see Matt. 1:1). The phrase, "the book of the generation," is an unusual expression. It occurs only in connection with Adam and then in connection with Christ.

The book of the generation of Jesus Christ is the Book of Life. I believe that you get into that book by faith in Christ. This, then, raises the question here: Is it possible for you to be in the Book of Life and then have your name blotted out? Can you lose your salvation? If that is true, then the Lord Jesus should not have said, "And I give unto them eternal life; and they shall never perish, neither shall any man pluck them out of my hand" (John 10:28). Again and again throughout Scripture we have the assurance given to us of our salvation.

I would like to give you now an excerpt from Dr. John Walvoord's book *The Revelation of Jesus Christ*, which is a very good explanation of what is meant in this verse:

> Some have indicated that there is no explicit statement here that anybody will have his name blotted out, but rather the promise that his name will not be blotted out because of his faith in Christ. The implication, however, is that such is a possibility. On the basis of this some have considered the book of life not as the roll of those who are saved but rather a list of those for whom Christ died, that is, all humanity who have possessed physical life. As they come to maturity and are faced with the responsibility of accepting or rejecting Christ, their names are blotted out if they fail to receive Jesus Christ as Saviour; whereas those who do accept Christ as Saviour are confirmed in their position in the book of life, and their names are confessed before the Father and the heavenly angels.

I think that that is a good, sound interpretation.

In Revelation there is a great importance placed on this book (see Rev. 13:8; 17:8; 20:12, 15; 21:27; 22:19). In these references the thought is that there are those whose names are recorded and those whose names are not recorded in the Book of Life. We will talk about it again, especially when we get to the last reference in the twenty-second chapter.

Some have identified the two books in chapter 20, verse 12, as the book of profession and the book of reality. They hold that names are erased from the book of profession but not from the book of reality. Others have suggested that all names are placed in the Book of Life at the beginning, but some are removed. A person's lack of decision for or rejection of Christ causes his name to be removed at the time of death. Both of these views propose serious objections as well as having good points to commend them.

I am confident that the whole thought is simply that it was amazing that anyone in Sardis would be saved but that there were some whose names He said would not be blotted out of the Book of Life. He didn't say that anybody had been blotted out; He just said that even in Sardis there would be some saved. May I say to you, the important thing is whether or not your name is written in the Lamb's Book of Life. I do not believe that after you are saved you would ever be able to lose that salvation.

He that hath an ear, let him hear what the Spirit saith unto the churches [Rev. 3:6].

This, again, is the blood-tipped ear that needs to hear the voice of the Spirit speaking through the Word of God the message of Christ to His church today.

CHRIST'S LETTER TO THE CHURCH IN PHILADELPHIA

The church in Philadelphia represents what I call the revived church, dating from approximately the beginning of the nineteenth century to the Rapture. This is the church that has turned back to the Word of God. Today in Protestantism and also in the Roman Catholic Church, there are multitudes of people who are turning to the Word of God. Mail which I receive from all over the world indicates that there are people wanting to hear the Word of God and who are hungry for it. This period is pictured in the church of Philadelphia.

I have visited the city of Philadelphia, and it is today a rather prosperous little Turkish town. It is located in a very beautiful valley that is inland a great distance, about 125–150 miles from the coast. The valley is a very wide one which runs north and south, and the Cogamis River of that valley is a tributary of the Hermus River. The city was built on four or five hills in a picturesque setting. Today it is spread out a great deal, and it is a typical Turkish town.

Philadelphia is in an area that is subject to earthquakes. The great population that was in that area left primarily because of earthquakes and, of course, because of warfare. When Tamerlane and the other great pagan leaders came out of the East, it was a time when all those who were left were slaughtered. Therefore, today no descendants of the original population are there. However, this city has had continuous habitation from its very beginning.

This city was like a Greek island out in Lydia, out in the Anatolian country, an area which the Greeks considered to be heathen and pagan—the Greek word for it was *barbarian*. In fact, anyone who was not a Greek was considered a barbarian in those days. The Lydian language was spoken there at first, but by the time of the apostles, the Greek language had taken over, and it was a typical Greek colony. This was the outpost of Greek culture in a truly Asiatic and Anatolian atmosphere. It was called a "little Athens" because of the fact that it was in this area and yet was truly Greek.

It was a fortress city used to waylay the enemy who would come in to destroy the greater cities like Ephesus and Smyrna and Pergamum—those were the three great cities. These other cities were largely fortress cities where garrisons were stationed either to stop the enemy or delay him as he marched toward the western coast.

Philadelphia is in a country where erosion is at work; the soil is quite alluvial, but it is very fertile soil. Beautiful laurel trees, many flowers—I noticed that they are growing just about everything that is imaginable. It was particularly celebrated for its excellent wine. Great vineyards covered the surrounding hills, and the head of Bacchus was imprinted on their coins.

The city did not get its name, as so many seem to think, from the Bible. Actually, the city got its name because of the love that Attalus II had for his brother Eumenes who was king of Pergamum. Attalus had a great love and loyalty for his brother, and because of that it is called "the city of brotherly love."

In A.D. 17 a great earthquake struck this city and totally destroyed it. The same earthquake totally destroyed Sardis and many other Lydian cities throughout that area. Tiberius, the emperor at that time, allocated a vast sum of money for the rebuilding of these cities, and they were then restored.

This is the one church besides Smyrna for which our Lord had no word of condemnation. Why? Because it had turned to the Word of God. It is interesting concerning the two churches which He did not condemn that the places are still in existence, although the churches have disappeared. However, in Philadelphia there is something quite interesting about which I would like to tell you. First of all, there are the remains of a Byzantine church, which reveals that Christianity was active there up until the twelfth or thirteenth century. The people who are caretakers of that area today must be Christians. Although I could not converse with them, they very graciously brought me a pitcher of water and a dipper on the very warm day I was there. The man and his wife who brought it were all smiles. I couldn't talk to them, and they couldn't talk to me, but I felt that we did communicate something of Christian love.

The remains of that Byzantine church are still there, but that is not the pillar that is mentioned in verse 12, although many believe that it is, and that is where the guides take the tours. However, before my first trip there, I had seen a picture of a big amphitheater in Adam's *Biblical Backgrounds;* so I told my guide that I wanted to go up there on the side of the hill. The amphitheater was no longer there, but there was a Turkish coffee shop where my guide talked to a man. He said that there had been an amphitheater but it was totally destroyed except for one pillar. I have a picture of that pillar which is hidden away under the trees. Why did the Turkish government get rid of that amphitheater? I'll tell you why: The Seljuk Turks brutally killed the Christians in Philadelphia, and they wanted to get rid of every vestige of that old civilization. Today they would rather that you and I forget about it.

Philadelphia is the place where Christian and Saracen fought during the Crusades, and in 1922 Turkey and Greece fought in Philadelphia. There are apparently a few Christians there today, as I have suggested, but they are under cover because they would be severely persecuted.

The church of Philadelphia continued into the thirteenth century. This church was in a very strategic area to be a missionary church, and that is actually what it was. I have labeled it the revived church because it returned to the Word of God and began to teach the Word of God.

This represents something that I think we see in Protestantism today. It began back in the last century and has gained since then, so that Bible teaching is not something that is new, by any means, but it has certainly become rather popular today. We feel very definitely that our Bible-teaching radio program has come in on the crest of a wave of interest in the Word of God.

And to the angel of the church in Philadelphia write; These things saith he that is holy, he that is true, he that hath the key of David, he that openeth, and no man shutteth; and shutteth, and no man openeth [Rev. 3:7].

"And to the angel of the church in Philadelphia write." The angel is the human messenger, the pastor, of the church. This is the Lord's method in all of these churches.

"These things saith he that is holy, he that is true, he that hath the key of David, he that openeth, and no man shutteth; and shutteth, and no man openeth." In each of these messages, the Lord always draws something from that vision of Himself as the glorified Christ, our Great High Priest, in chapter 1. Here He reminds them that He is holy. He was holy at His birth, He was holy at His death, and He is holy today in His present priestly office. He was so called at His birth when the angel said to Mary, ". . . therefore also that *holy* thing which shall be born of thee shall be called the Son of God" (Luke 1:35, italics mine). And in His death He was holy. We are told in Acts 2:27: "Because thou wilt not leave my soul in hell, neither wilt thou suffer thine *Holy One* to see corruption" (italics mine). He was holy in His death and in His resurrection. What a marvelous thing this is! He is also holy today in His high priestly office. "For such an high priest became us, who is *holy*, harmless, undefiled, separate from sinners, and made higher than the heavens" (Heb. 7:26, italics mine).

"He that is true." John 14:6 tells us, ". . . I am the way, the truth, and the life. . . ." *True* means "genuine" with an added note of perfection and completeness. Moses did not give the true bread; Christ is the true Bread (see John 6:32–35).

"He that hath the key of David." This is different from the keys of hades and death which we saw in chapter 1, verse 18. This speaks of His regal claims as the Ruler of this universe. "He shall be great, and shall be called the Son of the Highest: and the Lord God shall give unto him the throne of his father David: And he shall reign over the house of Jacob for ever; and of his kingdom there

shall be no end" (Luke 1:32–33). He will sit on the throne of David in the Millennium, but today He is sovereign, sitting at His Father's right hand, waiting for His enemies to be made His footstool.

"He that openeth, and no man shutteth; and shutteth, and no man openeth." He is the One today who is able to open and to close, and because of that He is a comfort to us (see Matt. 28:18–20).

I know thy works: behold, I have set before thee an open door, and no man can shut it: for thou hast a little strength, and hast kept my word, and hast not denied my name [Rev. 3:8].

I know thy works: behold, I have given thee a door opened, which none can shut, for thou hast a little strength [Gr.: dunamin], and didst keep my word, and didst not deny my name.

This is the verse that we have taken as the maxim for our "Thru the Bible" radio program. We began with it at the first, and it means a great deal to us.

The church at Philadelphia was the one which was true to the Word of God. In our day the church which it represents could not be called the Protestant church or the Roman Catholic church or any other church. Actually, it represents all churches the world over—regardless of their labels—which still remain true to the Word of God.

The Lord commends the Philadelphian church on seven counts:

1. "I know thy works." The Lord Jesus is looking for fruit; He is looking for works in the lives of believers. "For by grace are ye saved through faith; and that not of yourselves: it is the gift of God: Not of works, lest any man should boast. For we are his workmanship, created in Christ Jesus unto good works, which God hath before ordained that we should walk in them" (Eph. 2:8–10).

My friend, there is something wrong with your faith if it doesn't produce works. Good, old, practical, camel-kneed James was a great man of prayer who said, ". . . shew me thy faith without thy works, and I will shew thee my faith by my works" (James 2:18). "Works" are not works of law but works of faith. Calvin said, "Faith alone saves, but faith that saves is not alone." Saving faith produces works.

2. "Behold, I have set before thee an open door, and no man can shut it." This could be a door to the joy of the Lord or to a knowledge of the Scriptures. I personally believe that it is

a door to the knowledge of the Scriptures, which means that if He opens the door, He intends for you to move in because He will open a door of opportunity for witnessing and for proclaiming the Word of God. I believe that both go together.

3. "For thou hast a little strength [*dunamin*]." *Dunamin* is the Greek word from which we get our English word *dyna-mite*. He says, "You have a *little* power." This was a humble group of believers which did not have impressive numbers, buildings, or pro-grams. I get a little weary today hearing every Christian group making reports. Even here at "Thru the Bible" we like to tell you how many radio stations our broadcast is heard on. My, how we like to talk about those things! My friend, that type of thing is not worth anything. We like to talk about the hundreds of letters we receive from those who have accepted Christ—that's nothing. The im-portant thing is whether or not we are getting out the Word of God. *He* will do the counting. God has His own computer which is register-ing all this, and He tells us that we had better not. The apostle Paul said, "I don't even judge myself" (see 1 Cor. 4:3). Why not? In effect he is saying, "I may report too many converts. I may speak 'evangelistically' and give you a wrong figure. I may look at this a little differ-ently than God does. I need to wait until I get into His presence for the accurate rendering of it."

4. "And hast kept my word." In a day when there was a denial of the inspiration of the Scriptures, this church believed the Bible to be the authoritative, inspired Word of God. A twentieth-century theologian, of course of the liberal ranks, stated that no intelligent person could believe in the verbal inspiration of the Bible. Well, that sure puts me in a bad light! I am, therefore, not an intelligent person be-cause I *do* believe in the inspiration of the Bible—that is, *if* his definition is right, but I do not think he is right even about that.

5. "And hast not denied my name." In a day when the deity of Christ is blatantly denied by seminary and pulpit, here is a group of be-lievers who have remained true to Him by proclaiming the God-man and His substitu-tionary death for sinners.

This church in Philadelphia has been labeled many things. Some have called it the mission-ary church; some have called it the serving church; some have called it a live church—all of these are accurate. I personally like to call it the revived church or the Bible-believing church; it is the Bible church. The thing that

the Lord Jesus emphasizes is this: "Thou . . . hast kept my word, and hast not denied my name." In that day of unbelief and skepticism, the Lord Jesus is commending this church because it has kept His Word. This is the church that got out the Word of God and, as far as we know, this church lasted longer than any other of the seven churches mentioned here. Until the thirteenth century, it had a continuous existence. It was destroyed by the Seljuk Turks when they came in and brutally murdered all the believers who were left in this church. It was also a missionary church. It is the belief now that the fact that Chris-tianity penetrated into India as early as it did was because this church had sent out mission-aries.

Behold, I will make them of the syna-gogue of Satan, which say they are Jews, and are not, but do lie; behold, I will make them to come and worship before thy feet, and to know that I have loved thee [Rev. 3:9].

Let me give you my translation:

Behold I give of the synagogue of Satan, of them that say they are Jews, and are not, but lie. Behold, I will make them that they shall come and worship before your feet, and to know that I have loved you.

The remnant of Israel which was being saved had left the synagogue by this time. They had given up the Law as a means of salvation and sanctification. Those who continued in the synagogue were now in a false religion. As Paul makes it clear, ". . . For they are not all Israel, which are of Israel" (Rom. 9:6)—they were no longer true Jews. He considered the true Israelite to be the one who had turned to Christ.

Ignatius, according to Trench and reported by Vincent, refers to a logical situation where converts from Judaism preached the faith they once despised. By the way, the Roman Empire used Jews for the purpose of colonizing. They would send a regular colony of them into a foreign area, as they did into this section, and this is the reason there were so many Jews there.

6. "Behold, I will make them to come and worship before thy feet, and to know that I have loved thee." The Lord Jesus says here that He will make the enemies of the Phila-delphian church to know that He loves this church. This is His sixth point of commenda-tion.

Because thou hast kept the word of my patience, I also will keep thee from the hour of temptation, which shall come upon all the world, to try them that dwell upon the earth [Rev. 3:10].

Because thou didst keep the word of my patience, I, also, will keep you out of (from) the hour of the trial, which is (about) to come upon the whole inhabited world to test (try) them that dwell upon the earth.

7. This last commendation is that this church kept the Word of Christ in patience. This is evidently the patient waiting for the coming of Christ for His own (see 2 Thess. 3:5). It has been in the present century that the doctrines of eschatology have been developed more than in all previous centuries combined. During the past forty years, there has been a revival of interest, both in Europe and in America, in fact, all over the world, relative to the second coming of Christ. Even the liberals talk about it now and then.

"Because thou hast kept the word of my patience." I believe that God today is still patient with a world that has rejected His Word. It is not like it was back in the days of Noah. They didn't have the written Word of God, yet God judged them; they did have a man bringing the message to them. But today we *do* have the Word of God. There is a Gideon Bible in practically every hotel and motel room throughout the world. In the different countries of Europe, Asia, and Africa, I find that the Word of God has penetrated all of these areas. The Philadelphian church is the church that believed in the Word of God.

"I also will keep thee from the hour of temptation, which shall come upon all the world, to try them that dwell upon the earth." Christ's final word of encouragement to His church is that it will not pass through the Great Tribulation. The church is to be removed from the world (see 1 Thess. 4:13–18), which is its comfort and hope (see Titus 2:13). Such is the patient waiting of the church ". . . who through faith and patience inherit the promises" (Heb. 6:12). The church is not anticipating the Great Tribulation with all of its judgment (see John 5:24; Rev. 13:1–8,11–17), but rather it is looking for *Him* to come.

"The hour of temptation" is definitely a reference to the Great Tribulation—it's worldwide. After the preliminaries are put down in chapters 4–5, in chapters 6–19 you have presented the Great Tribulation Period. This is

the period that He says is coming upon all the world to test those that are upon the earth.

"I also will keep thee from the hour of temptation." He says that He will keep them not only from that awful holocaust that is coming on this earth, that period of judgment, but also from the *hour* of temptation. Therefore, this is to my judgment a complete deliverance. When He says, "keep thee from the hour," I have translated it, "keep thee *out of* the hour of trial." By any stretch of the imagination, you could not say that this church is going through the Great Tribulation Period. I believe that the period of the Philadelphian church continues right on through to the rapture of the church. This is the church which will go out at the time of the Rapture.

The church of Laodicea, as we shall see, is an organization which will continue on in the world, although the Lord gives a marvelous invitation to it, and many even in that Laodicean church will turn to Christ and be taken out at the time of the Rapture. But there is a church that goes through the Great Tribulation Period, and that is the apostate church, the church of Laodicea.

What we have here, therefore, is the coming of Christ to take His own out of the world and His promise to the church of Philadelphia that it will not go through that particular period that is coming on the earth.

I would like to give here another quotation from Dr. John Walvoord's book, *The Revelation of Jesus Christ:*

If the rapture had occurred in the first century preceding the tribulation which the book of Revelation describes, they were assured of deliverance. By contrast, those sealed out of the twelve tribes of Israel in 7:4 clearly go through the time of trouble. This implies the rapture of the church before the time of trouble referred to as the great tribulation. Such a promise of deliverance to them would seemingly have been impossible if the rapture of the church were delayed until the end of the tribulation prior to the second coming of Christ and the establishment of the kingdom.

Christ says to the church—

Behold, I come quickly: hold that fast which thou hast, that no man take thy crown [Rev. 3:11].

"Behold, I come quickly." "Quickly" does not mean soon. Rather, it has the idea of suddenness and an air of expectation; that is, He will come at a time they know not. It does not mean He is coming immediately, but His coming will be sudden. This is the promise that is the hope of the church. Actually, the church is not looking for the Great Tribulation Period. Nowhere are you told that you are to gird up your loins, grit your teeth, and clench your fists because the Great Tribulation is coming and you are certainly going through it! He never said that, but "Looking for that blessed hope, and the glorious appearing of the great God and our Saviour Jesus Christ" (Titus 2:13).

Let me say again that the Philadelphian church represents the revived church, the church that has returned to the Word of God. It is this church that is to be raptured, His true church, and I do not think you can put them in any denomination or any local church. They are scattered throughout the world today, and you will find some of them belonging to some very funny organizations. I don't understand that, but that is apparently none of my business; that is something they will have to straighten out with the Lord.

Him that overcometh will I make a pillar in the temple of my God, and he shall go no more out: and I will write upon him the name of my God, and the name of the city of my God, which is new Jerusalem, which cometh down out of heaven from my God: and I will write upon him my new name [Rev. 3:12].

There are two pillars in Philadelphia today. One is that of the Byzantine church, which I do not think is the reference here. But there is also a pillar on the side of the hill, hidden among those cedar and laurel trees. That pillar is all that remains of the city of John's day. "Him that overcometh will I make a pillar in the temple of my God." The church down here was destroyed, but the permanent pillar is up yonder.

"And I will write upon him the name of my God, and the name of the city of my God, which is new Jerusalem, which cometh down out of heaven from my God: and I will write upon him my new name." This is the passport and visa of the believer which will enable him, as a citizen of heaven, to pass freely upon this earth or anywhere in God's universe. He is a pillar to "go no more out," but with God's passport he is to go everywhere. Although this is paradoxical, it is all wonderfully and blessedly true.

"I will write upon him my new name." This is *His* name. We do not have a new name; rather, He is saying that He has a new name for Himself that He will give to us. This new name is a personal relationship we will have with Him.

He that hath an ear, let him hear what the Spirit saith unto the churches [Rev. 3:13].

The Lord has a message that He gives to each one of these churches. It applied to that local church, but it also applies to us today.

CHRIST'S LETTER TO THE CHURCH IN LAODICEA

The letter of Christ to the church in Laodicea is the last of these seven letters. Sir William Ramsay calls Laodicea "the city of compromise." This city was founded by Antiochus II (261–246 B.C.). It had a Seleucid foundation. Seleucus was one of the generals of Alexander who took Syria. Lysimachus took Asia Minor, but apparently Seleucus moved over into his territory and took some of his ground, including this city.

Laodicea was about forty miles east and inland from Ephesus on the Lycus River, which flows into the Maeander River. It is located at what is known as the "Gate of Phrygia." Out of the Oriental East, the great camel caravans came down through the Gate of Phrygia and through Laodicea. This road came out of the East and went to Ephesus, to Miletus, and also up to what is called Izmir today but was Smyrna in that day. Laodicea was in a spectacular place, a great valley. Today its ruins are largely covered up with the growth of what looks like wild oats. Its name means "justice of the people." It was named for Laodice, the wife of Antiochus. Although there were several cities which bore this name, this was the most famous one of all.

Between Laodicea and going on up to the Phrygian mountains, there was in this valley a great Anatolian temple of the Phrygian god, Men Karou. This was the primitive god of that area. The temple was the very center of all society, administration, trade, and religion. There was a great market there, and strangers came from everywhere to trade. I suppose that the large market in Istanbul today is very similar to it.

Laodicea was a place of great wealth, of commerce, and of Greek culture. It was a place of science and of literature. It boasted an excellent medical school which, again, was very primitive and actually very heathen. Here is where they developed what was known in the Roman world as Phrygian powder, a salve for the ears and the eyes. Laodicea was also a center of industry with extensive banking operations. Cicero held court here. It is said that he brought notes here to be cashed in this city. Jupiter, or Zeus, was the object of worship in Laodicea.

The city was finally abandoned because of earthquakes. The very impressive ruins of two Roman theaters, a large stadium, and three early Christian churches are still there. The city itself has not been excavated. In other words, these ruins which I have mentioned protrude through all the debris and wild growth that is there. I have heard that there is an American foundation which has set aside two to three million dollars to excavate Laodicea. I would love to join that excavation for it would be very worthwhile.

Laodicea was a place of great commerce where they made clothing. As you stand on the ruins of Laodicea, you can look around at the nearby hills and see where Colosse is located and also Hierapolis, where there are springs. The greatest ruins are not in Colosse or Laodicea but in Hierapolis. The hills have a very funny color. The people took the clay from those hills, put it with a spikenard, and made it into a salve for the eyes and ears. This salve was shipped all over the Roman Empire. Today the chemical analysis reveals that there is nothing healing in that clay at all, but somebody made good money at it in that day. We like to think we are civilized today, but there is a lot of medicine on the market that won't do you a bit of good; yet we are buying it just as fast as we can because of high-pressure advertising. We had better not criticize these people too much—but the Lord Jesus did. He is going to tell them that they had better get the *real* eye salve that will open their eyes.

And unto the angel of the church of the Laodiceans write; These things saith the Amen, the faithful and true witness, the beginning of the creation of God [Rev. 3:14].

And to the messenger of the church in Laodicea write; These things saith the Amen, the faithful and true witness, the beginning of the creation of God.

This is the only place in Scripture where *Amen* is a proper name, and it is the name of Christ. In Isaiah 65:16 it should read, "the God of the amen." In Isaiah 7:9 the word *believe* is *amen*. In 2 Corinthians 1:20 we read, "For all the promises of God in him are yea,

and in him Amen, unto the glory of God by us." The Lord Jesus is the Amen. He has the last word. He is the Alpha and the Omega. He is the One who is going to fulfill all the promises of God, and He lets the Laodiceans know this because this is the church that has rejected the deity of Christ. The word *Amen* is the only thing that He draws out of the vision of Himself that we had in the first chapter.

"The faithful and true witness." This reveals that the Lord Jesus Christ alone is the One who will reveal all and tell all. This is the day when it is very difficult to hear the truth. We certainly don't get it through the news media or from the government. Both our educational institutions and the military are great brainwashing institutions. Whom can you believe? Well, there is One who is the faithful and true witness even in the days of apostasy. You cannot believe the church in many instances today; the liberal church has no message for this hour.

"The beginning of the creation of God" means that He is the Creator. We live in a day when the myth of evolution, the evolutionary hypothesis, is that which is accepted. A college professor, a friend of mine, who has accepted the evolutionary hypothesis, said to me, "I want facts. I want science." I said, "Wait a minute. There are not but two explanations for the origin of this universe in which you and I live. One is *speculation*, because nobody was there to see it and nobody is able to come up with the answer. The other is *revelation*—what the Word of God has to say. Very frankly, the difference between you and me is that you accept speculation and I accept revelation. As far as I am concerned, I feel that I am on more solid ground because I have the testimony of the One who did the creating, and He ought to know something about it." The Lord Jesus is "the beginning of the creation of God."

I know thy works, that thou art neither cold nor hot: I would thou wert cold or hot.

So then because thou art lukewarm, and neither cold nor hot, I will spue thee out of my mouth [Rev. 3:15–16].

With the other churches, when the Lord Jesus said, "I know thy works," He meant good works; He was commending them for good works. But the Lord Jesus has no word of commendation for this church. All is condemnation here. Even the "works" here are not good works; they are evil works.

"That thou art neither cold nor hot: I would thou wert cold or hot." This had a background and a local meaning for the people in that day. Being down in the valley, they had difficulty getting water in Laodicea. As I stood there in the ruins, I looked south toward the Phrygian mountains, some of which are very high. I was there around the first of June, and there was still an abundance of snow on top of those mountains. The Laodiceans built an aqueduct to bring that cold water down from the mountains. When it left the mountains, it was ice cold, but by the time it made that trip all the way down the mountains to Laodicea, it was lukewarm. And lukewarm water is not very good.

Down in the valley where the Lycus River joins the Maeander River, there are hot springs. The springs are so hot that steam is produced. The Turkish government has capped it and is using it today, and I understand they intend to develop its use even more because it is there in abundance. It is the hottest water you can imagine; a lot of it is just steam. However, when they would take this hot water up to Laodicea, by the time it got there, it was no longer hot—it had become lukewarm water.

When the Lord Jesus said to the Laodicean church, "You are neither cold nor hot," they knew exactly what He was talking about. They had been drinking lukewarm water for years. Water left the mountains ice cold, and it left the springs steaming hot, but when they got it, both were lukewarm, and it was sickening. We like to put a little ice in our water, and many folk drink hot water, but lukewarm water is just not good, my friend. The Lord Jesus said that this church was neither cold nor hot and He would spew it out of His mouth.

A *cold* church actually means a church that has denied every cardinal doctrine of the faith. It is given over to formality and is carrying on in active opposition to the Word of God and the gospel of Christ. You find today in liberalism that they are in active opposition to the gospel of Jesus Christ. *Hot* speaks of those with real spiritual fervor and passion like the Christians in Ephesus, although they were even then getting away from their best love. Oh, the Spirit of God had brought them to a high pitch in their personal relationship to Christ!

But the Laodicean church was neither hot nor cold—just lukewarm. Between those positions of hot and cold, you have this lukewarm state. I would say that this is a picture of many, many churches today in the great de-

nominations that have departed from the faith. Many churches—both in and out of these denominations—attempt to maintain a middle-of-the-road position. They do not want to come out flatfootedly for the Word of God and for the great doctrines of the Christian faith. And at the same time, they do not want to be known as a liberal church. So they play footsie with both groups. I have broken fellowship with quite a few men who are extremists in both directions, some extreme fundamentalists and some extreme liberals. And many of these men attempt to play both sides of the street. That is a condition that is impossible. This is the thing that makes the Lord Jesus sick. He very frankly says that He will spew them out of His mouth.

To my judgment this middle-of-the-road position is the worst kind of hypocrisy there is. "Thou hast a name that thou livest, and art dead" (v. 1). "Having a form of godliness, but denying the power thereof: from such turn away" (2 Tim. 3:5).

In its beginning Protestantism assumed the position of believing all the great doctrines of the Christian faith. The creeds of all the great historic denominations are wonderful creeds. The Westminster Confession of Faith is unparalleled in my estimation, but it is now largely repudiated by the church that owned it for years. The Heidelberg Catechism is a marvelous confession, but who is following it? Who believes these wonderful creeds in our day? The churches have a form of godliness but are denying the power thereof. They have a name that they live, but they are dead. They are neither hot nor cold—they are lukewarm.

This is the condition of the church today, and unfortunately, it is the condition of a great many so-called fundamental, conservative churches. Thank God that there are many who do not come under this classification. But the thing that is absolutely startling and frightening and fearful is that He says, "I will spue thee out of my mouth." In other words, "I will *vomit* you out of my mouth." Does that sound to you like the church which He's going to rapture, to whom He says, "I go to prepare a place for you. And if I go and prepare a place for you, I will come again, and receive you unto myself; that where I am, there ye may be also" (John 14:2–3)? I don't think so. That is the church He draws to Himself, but here is a church He just vomits out because it is lukewarm. Lukewarm water makes you sick at your stomach. I am of the opinion that if He spoke to a lot of churches today, He would say, "You make Me sick at My stomach. You're *professed* Christians. You say you love Me. You *say* it, but you don't mean it."

This is a heart-searching message for this hour because we are living in the time of the Laodicean church and of the Philadelphian church. Both of them are side by side, and there is a great bifurcation in Christianity today. It is not in denominations, and it is not Romanism and Protestantism. The great bifurcation consists of those who believe the Word of God and follow it, love it, obey it, and those who reject it. That is the line of division today.

Because thou sayest, I am rich, and increased with goods, and have need of nothing; and knowest not that thou art wretched, and miserable, and poor, and blind, and naked [Rev. 3:17].

Thou sayest, I am rich, and have gotten riches, and have need of nothing; and thou dost not know that thou art the wretched one and miserable (the object of pity) and poor and blind and naked.

"Because thou sayest, I am rich." The city of Laodicea was a rich city. I suppose that Laodicea and Sardis were probably two of the richest cities in that entire area at that particular time.

"Because thou sayest, I am rich, and increased with goods, and have need of nothing." They believed that the dollar was the answer to every problem of life. After World War II that was the assumption that the American government was run on. All we did was dole out dollars all over the world, thinking that we would buy friends, make peace, and settle the problems of the world. Very frankly, I believe that our nation has probably complicated the world more than anything else. We thought that all we had to do was to allocate money and we would solve the problems of the world. My friend, riches never solved any problem. This church in Laodicea tried it: "I am rich, and increased with goods, and have need of nothing; and knowest not that thou art wretched, and miserable, and poor, and blind, and naked."

The Laodicean church made its boast of material possessions. Conversely, the church in Smyrna was poor in material things. It was the church of slaves and poor folk. There were not many rich and not many noble in the early church. Paul writes in 1 Corinthians 1:26, "For ye see your calling, brethren, how that not many wise men after the flesh, not many mighty, not many noble, are called."

The present-day church boasts of large membership, prominent people, huge attendance, generous giving, and ornate buildings. A phenomenal growth in Protestant congregations, 242,000 in 1970 to 78,900,152 in 1980 (according to the *World Christian Encyclopedia*) would indicate the possibility of a church on fire for God. And there are other indications: Wealth beyond the wildest dreams of our forefathers; mass evangelistic meetings attended by tens of thousands; and use of other mass media such as radio and literature increasing constantly.

Worldly wealth is the measuring rod for the modern church. Spiritual values have been lost sight of or are entirely ignored. The church as a whole is not only rich in earthly goods, but it actually is in the business of accumulating wealth. People are urged to make their wills in favor of so-called Christian organizations. Some radio and television programs and other professed Christian works are operated as promotional schemes to raise money to provide luxurious care for the promoters. My friend, you ought to check how the money you give to Christian work is being spent. When you write your will, I hope you will leave money for Christian work, but you ought to make sure that after you are gone, it is going to be spent for that which you intended.

On the spiritual side of the ledger, the Laodicean church is "the wretched one." It is worse off than any of the seven churches. It is to be pitied because it is spiritually poverty-stricken. In it is no study of the Word, no love of Christ, and no witnessing of His saving grace; yet it is blind to its own true condition. It lacks the covering of the robe of righteousness.

A pastor in Arlington, Virginia, put this in his church bulletin some years ago. It is an "Open Letter to Jane Ordinary"—

Dear Jane:
I am writing to help you shake this feeling of uselessness that has overtaken you. Several times you've said that you don't see how Christ can possibly use you. The church must bear part of the responsibility for making you feel as you do. I have in mind the success-story mentality of the church. Our church periodicals tell the story of John J. Moneybags who uses his influential position to witness for Christ. At the church youth banquet, we have a testimony from All-American football star, Ox Kickoffsky, who commands the respect of his teammates when he wit-

nesses for Christ. We are led to think that if you don't have the leverage of stardom or a big position in the business world, you might as well keep your mouth shut. Nobody cares what Christ has done for *you.*

We've forgotten an elementary fact about Christian witness, something that should encourage you: God has chosen what the world calls foolish to shame the wise. He has chosen what the world calls weak to shame the strong. He has chosen things of little strength and of small repute, yes, and even things which have no real existence to explode the pretensions of the things that are, that no man may boast in the presence of God.

When Jesus Christ chose His disciples, He didn't choose Olympic champs or Roman senators. He chose simple people like you. Some were fishermen, one was a political extremist, another was a publican, a nobody in that society. But these men turned the Roman world upside down for Christ. How did they do it? Through their popularity? They had none. Their position? They had none. Their power was the power of Christ through the Holy Spirit.

Jane, don't forget that we still need the ordinary in the hands of Christ to turn the world upside down.

In the church today we sing:

> The Church's one foundation is Jesus
> Christ her Lord;
> She is His new creation by water and the
> word:
> From heaven He came and sought her to
> be His holy bride;
> With His own blood He bought her, and
> for her life He died.
> "The Church's One Foundation"
> —Samuel J. Stone

Yet the inscription on the cathedral in Lübeck, Germany, is still true:
Thus speaketh Christ our Lord to us:

Ye call Me Master and obey Me not.
Ye call Me Light and see Me not.
Ye call Me Way and walk Me not.
Ye call Me Life and choose Me not.
Ye call Me Wise and follow Me not.
Ye call Me Fair and love Me not.
Ye call Me Rich and ask Me not.
Ye call Me Eternal and seek Me not.

Ye call Me Noble and serve Me not.
Ye call Me Gracious and trust Me not.
Ye call Me Might and honor Me not.
Ye call Me Just and fear Me not.
If I condemn you, blame Me not.

This is the church in Laodicea. This is the church that Stanley High spoke of when he said:

> The church has failed to tell me that I am a sinner. The church has failed to deal with me as a lost individual. The church has failed to offer me salvation in Jesus Christ alone. The church has failed to tell me of the horrible consequences of sin, the certainty of hell, and the fact that Jesus Christ alone can save. We need more of the last judgment and less of the Golden Rule, more of the living God and the living devil as well, more of a heaven to gain and a hell to shun. The church must bring me not a message of cultivation but of rebirth. I might fail that kind of church, but that kind of church will not fail me.

My friend, we are living in the Laodicean period today, and the church is failing to witness to the saving grace of God.

I counsel thee to buy of me gold tried in the fire, that thou mayest be rich; and white raiment, that thou mayest be clothed, and that the shame of thy nakedness do not appear; and anoint thine eyes with eye-salve, that thou mayest see [Rev. 3:18].

"I counsel thee to buy of me gold tried in the fire, that thou mayest be rich"—this is the precious blood of Christ.

"And white raiment, that thou mayest be clothed, and that the shame of thy nakedness do not appear"—this speaks of the righteousness of Christ.

"And anoint thine eyes with eye-salve, that thou mayest see"—this speaks of the Holy Spirit who opens the eyes of believers today.

This admonition was very meaningful to the church at Laodicea. Sir William Ramsay has this very helpful comment in his excellent book, *The Letters to the Seven Churches of Asia:*

> The Laodicean Church must also learn that it is blind, but yet not incurably blind. It is suffering from disease, and needs medical treatment. But the physi-

cians of its famous medical school can do nothing for it. The tabloids which they prescribe, and which are now used all over the civilized world, to reduce to powder and smear on the eyes, will be useless for this kind of ophthalmia. The Laodiceans must buy the tabloid from the Author himself, at the price of suffering and steadfastness.

As many as I love, I rebuke and chasten: be zealous therefore, and repent [Rev. 3:19].

This word *zealous* means "to be hot." This is His last message to the church. He says, "Be zealous." Be hot. Get on fire for God. He is ordering this church to forsake its lukewarm state, and He says, "Repent." This church needs repentance more than all the others. And the message of repentance is for the contemporary church, but you will not be popular if you preach that, I can assure you. It is not too late even for those in this church to turn to Christ: "As many as I love, I rebuke and chasten: be zealous therefore, and repent."

Beginning at verse 20 is a general invitation which goes out from the Lord Jesus at any time—

Behold, I stand at the door, and knock: if any man hear my voice, and open the door, I will come in to him, and will sup with him, and he with me [Rev. 3:20].

This is a picture of the Lord Jesus at the heart's door of the sinner. It is a glorious picture. The English artist, Holman Hunt, attempted to put this concept on canvas. He pictured Christ standing at a door. When he first painted the picture, he invited his artist friends to criticize. One of them said to him, "Holman, you have left off a very important part of the door. You left off the handle of the door." Hunt replied, "This door is a picture of the human heart, and the handle of the door is on the *inside*." This is the picture of Christ we have in Revelation. He stands at the door and knocks. He will not crash the door. Regardless of what some extremists say on this matter of election, the Lord Jesus has moved heaven and hell to get to the door of your heart, but when He gets there, He will stop and knock. You will have to open the door to let Him in.

"I will come in to him, and will sup with him, and he with me." This speaks of fellowship, of feeding on the Word of God, and of coming to know Jesus Christ better.

To him that overcometh will I grant to sit with me in my throne, even as I also overcame, and am set down with my Father in his throne [Rev. 3:21].

Again, I call attention to the fact that when the Lord Jesus speaks of His relationship with the Father, He always makes it unique. He says, "My Father." He said, ". . . I ascend unto *my* Father . . ." (John 20:17, italics mine)—not *our* Father—because the relationship is always different with Him.

The Lord Jesus is preparing us for the next scene that will be coming up when He says, "and am set down with my Father in his throne." This is the picture that we are going to see in the chapters which follow.

He that hath an ear, let him hear what the Spirit saith unto the churches [Rev. 3:22].

This is a special message from the Lord Jesus to all the churches for which you need the blood-tipped ear to hear. This is the reason that you and I must be very careful in our study of the Word of God, that we not run ahead of the Spirit of God, but that we let Him be our teacher. If you have a blood-tipped ear, He wants you to hear what He has to say. Only the Spirit of God can make the Word of God real to you.

This concludes the messages to these seven churches. These are "the things which are," and they have been very important. I have spent a lot of time with these seven churches because they relate to the period in which we live and to our crowd. If we are a member of His church, we are also a member of His body, a part of that great company, beginning with the Day of Pentecost and coming down to the present hour, who have trusted the Lord Jesus as their Savior.

We have seen these seven churches blocked off into very definite periods of time, and they are largely fulfilled. I believe that we are in the period of the last two churches. As we have said before, there is a bifurcation in the organized, visible church today. There is that church, represented by the Laodicean church, which is moving farther and farther into the apostasy, and there is also that church which is staying by the Word of God, the church represented by the Philadelphian church. This is the church which will be raptured. The other church has a tremendous organization, including all the denominations, all those which profess to be Christian churches but which have long since departed from the Word of God and from the person of Christ. This is the division that exists in the church. One church will be raptured; the other will go into the Great Tribulation Period.

There has been a message for each of these churches. Personally, I enjoy going through these messages since I have now made several trips to the churches in Turkey, that is, Asia Minor. I have visited the ruins of all seven of these churches at least twice and some of them as many as four or five times. As we have come to each church, I can see the ruins before my eyes, and I can visualize the local situation. The Lord Jesus spoke to that local situation, and He was also blocking off all of church history because these are seven representative churches which cover the complete period of the church while it is here on the earth. And there is also a message in each of these for you and for me today.

To the church at Ephesus, there was a warning given that is also for us today. It was a warning of the danger of getting away from the best love, that is, getting away from a personal and loving relationship with Jesus Christ. The real test of any believer, especially those who are attempting to serve Him, is not your little method or mode or system or your dedication or any of the things that are so often emphasized today. The one question is: Do you love Him? Do you love the Lord Jesus? When you love Him, you will be in a right relationship with Him, but when you begin to depart from the person of Christ, it will finally lead to lukewarmness. The apostate church was guilty of lukewarmness. It may not *seem* to be too bad, but it is the worst condition that anyone can be in. A great preacher in upper New York state said: "Twenty lukewarm Christians hurt the cause of Christ more than one blatant atheist." A lukewarm church is a disgrace to Christ.

The Lord Jesus told the church in Smyrna not to fear suffering. Believe me, that is one thing that we in the church are frightened of today. We do not want to pay a price for serving the Lord Jesus, and yet that is His method.

To the church in Pergamum He said, "But I have a few things against thee, because thou hast there them that hold the doctrine of Balaam . . . . So hast thou also them that hold the doctrine of the Nicolaitans, which thing I hate" (Rev. 2:14–15). There is a grave danger in wrong doctrine today, and that was the thing that was wrong in the church in Pergamum.

To the church in Thyatira He said, "Notwithstanding I have a few things against thee, because thou sufferest that woman Jezebel, which calleth herself a prophetess, to teach and to seduce my servants to commit fornication, and to eat things sacrificed unto idols" (Rev. 2:20). The "new morality" is a grave danger for many today. Some folk think they can accept Christ and then live on a low plane. You will not get by with it, my friend, if you are His child.

In the church in Sardis, the Protestant church, there was the danger of spiritual deadness. He said, "I know thy works, that thou hast a name that thou livest, and art dead" (v. 1). What about your church, brother? Is it alive? Are you alive? Or are you dead in a dead church today? Many folk are in that condition, and yet they talk about holding the historic doctrines of the faith. But, my friend, the glaring defect in Protestantism today is deadness. And that is the worst thing of all.

The church in Philadelphia was not in any grave danger. The Lord Jesus does not condemn that church at all, but He does say, "Behold, I come quickly: hold that fast which thou hast, that no man take thy crown" (v. 11). What was it they had? He had commended them because they had kept His Word. We, too, need to be careful about this. As I look back now over the years of my ministry, I see men who started out true to the faith, many of them much stronger men than I was, men who defended the Word of God in a way that I did not in those early days, but they have now departed from the faith. I am amazed at that, but that is a grave danger even in the church in Philadelphia today. Nothing should deter us at all from keeping His Word.

To the church in Laodicea the Lord Jesus said, "So then because thou art lukewarm, and neither cold nor hot, I will spue thee out of my mouth" (v. 16). This is the apostate church which professes to be Christian but lacks reality. But even to this church He issues a final call to repentance and an invitation to come to Himself.

CHAPTER 4

THEME: *The church in heaven with Christ*

We have seen the history of the church in the seven churches of chapters 2–3, but as we come to chapter 4, the question naturally arises: What has happened to the church? From chapter 4 through the rest of the Book of Revelation, there is no mention of the church except when you get to the invitation at the end, which is a general invitation and hasn't anything to do with the chronology of the book. From here on you will not find the word *church* mentioned. Up to this point, the word *church* has occurred again and again, in fact nineteen times. But now the church goes off the air—there is no mention of it. It has gone off the air because it went up in the air; it was caught up in the air to meet the Lord in the air. The church has gone to heaven—that is what has happened to it. The Rapture takes place during the Philadelphian period, and the so-called church which continues on the earth is just an organization. It will go through the Great Tribulation Period, and we are finally going to hear it called a great harlot—what a frightful designation! Actually, the most frightful picture in the Bible is the seventeenth chapter of Revelation. Are we going to see the church again? Yes, but she is no longer a church; she is a bride—a bride adorned for her Husband.

Chapters 4–22 comprise the final major division of this very wonderful book. John was given the division of this book, and he passed it on to us. We ought not to miss it, for He said in chapter 1, verse 19, "Write the things which thou hast seen, and the things which are, and the things which shall be hereafter"—that is, *meta tauta*, meaning "after these things." "Things which must be hereafter" of verse 1 corresponds to "the things which shall be hereafter" of chapter 1, verse 19. Both are *meta tauta* in the Greek, indicating a change from this to an entirely different scene and subject.

Several striking facts make it self-evident that we advance to a new division beginning with chapter 4. The climate and conditions change radically:

1. The church is no longer seen in the world, although up to chapter 4, there have been nineteen references to the church in the world. In fact, the subject of chapters 2–3 has been entirely devoted to the church in the world. However, from chapter 4 to the end of the Revelation the church is never mentioned in connection with the world. The final and lone reference is a concluding testimony after the world's little day has ended (see Rev. 22:16). Christ said of His own, "They are not of the world, even as I am not of the world" (John 17:16). He also said to His own men, ". . . I will come again, and receive you unto myself; that where I am, there ye may be also" (John 14:3).

2. The scene definitely shifts to heaven in chapter 4. Since the church is still the subject, we follow it now to its new home—heaven. How did the church get to heaven? This is a good question, and Paul gives the answer: "Then we which are alive and remain shall be caught up together with them in the clouds, to meet the Lord in the air: and so shall we ever be with the Lord" (1 Thess. 4:17). He defines the operation in 1 Corinthians 15:51–52: "Behold, I shew you a mystery; We shall not all sleep, but we shall all be changed, In a moment, in the twinkling of an eye, at the last trump: for the trumpet shall sound, and the dead shall be raised incorruptible, and we shall be changed."

Faith places the sinner on the launching pad, in the guided missile of the church, from whence he shall go to meet the Lord in the air. The saints enter the opened door to heaven. The church is with Christ, and Christ is in heaven, directing the events of the Great Tribulation Period that we are going to see when we get to chapter 6.

3. The church is not a name but a definition of those who have trusted Christ in this age. This is something which we need to get fixed in our minds because our thinking on this today is often muddled. The word *church* is *ekklesia* in the Greek; *kaleō* means "to call," and *ek* means "out of." Therefore, *ekklesia* means "a group of people called out of the world."

When the church arrives at its destination in heaven, it loses the name by which it was known in the world and other terms are used to describe it. We are going to see it in chapter 4 as twenty-four elders, representatives of the church in heaven. We are also going to see the church in heaven as a bride, coming down to her new home, the New Jerusalem.

The apostate organization, which bears the ecclesiastical terminology and continues on in the world, is not hereafter given the title of "church" either, but the frightful label of "the harlot." The late Dr. George Gill said years ago in a seminary class, "There are going to be some churches which will meet the next Sunday after the Rapture, and they won't be missing a member—they will all be there." Why? Because it is the church of Laodicea—that is, it professes to be Christian but lacks reality.

4. The judgments beginning at chapter 6 would not be in harmony with the gracious provision and promise that God has made to the church. If the church remained in the world, it would frustrate the grace of God because He has promised to deliver us from judgment.

5. Finally, to continue from chapter 3 to chapter 4 without recognizing the break is to ignore the normal and natural division in the book as stated in chapter 1, verse 19.

As we enter this last division of the book with all of its judgment and wrath, it is well to keep in our perspective that Jesus Christ is central. He is directing all events as He brings them to a successful but determined conclusion. There is "in the midst of the throne . . . a Lamb" (Rev. 7:17). He is a Lamb because He died for the sins of the world. And He is the One who is going to judge.

After these things, after the church things have concluded, the scene shifts from earth to heaven. It is a radical change. However, the Word of God describes personages and activities in heaven as normally as it described them on earth. There is no strain or involvement in superstition or mystery. The bridge over the great gulf is passed with ease and a reverent restraint. Only the Holy Spirit could describe things in heaven with as much ease as He describes things on the earth. What would have happened if a man had written this book? You know that the minute he got to the heavenly scene, he would have the wildest sort of things to say. How do I know that? Well, read the books that are out today which try to describe the overworld and the underworld and the unseen world. They are always rather startling and amazing. In fact, the use of this approach is one way that we can know a book is false. There is an awful obsession today, even among some Christians, with the subject of demons and of the Devil. I have no truck with that outfit at all. I have often been asked why I haven't written a book on this subject. Frankly, at first I thought I would, but when so many books started coming out, all as wild as a March Hare and all dealing with the sensational, I changed my mind. You don't have the sensational here in Revelation. We simply move to heaven, and the scene is awe inspiring, but it lacks that which man would put in.

The church is not seen under the familiar name it had in the world, but is now the priesthood of believers with the Great High Priest. Heavenly scenes and creatures greet us in this section (chs. 4–5) before our attention is drawn to the earth where, at the opening of the Great Tribulation, the four horsemen are to ride.

THE THRONE OF GOD

Christ is viewed here in His threefold office of Prophet, Priest, and King. He is worshiped as God because He is God.

After this I looked, and, behold, a door was opened in heaven: and the first voice which I heard was as it were of a trumpet talking with me; which said, Come up hither, and I will shew thee things which must be hereafter [Rev. 4:1].

Here is my translation of this first verse:

After these things [Gr.: meta tauta] I saw, and behold a door set open in heaven; and the first voice which I heard, a voice as of a trumpet speaking with me and saying, Come up hither, and I will show thee the things which must come to pass after these things [meta tauta].

"After these things" *(meta tauta)* is used twice here; it both opens and closes the verse. This repetition certainly lends great emphasis and importance to the phrase. Apparently, John was afraid the amillennialists would miss it; so he used it twice in this particular place.

"I saw"—that is the eye-gate. "I heard"—that is the ear-gate. This is like a television program which we are looking at. This is the first great television program. We have had a wonderful treat in our day to view a television program from the moon, but that is nothing in comparison—here is a television program from heaven! This ought to interest believers a great deal and not cause us to take off like a skyrocket into some wild sort of dreamy stuff. Heaven is a real place. There is a lot of reality there, and we ought not to get uptight over this scene that is now before us. We need to handle it in a normal way, but I admit that I cannot help but get excited about it all.

"I saw, and behold a door set open in heaven." This is one of the four open doors in the Book of Revelation:

1. In chapter 3, verse 8, speaking to the church in Philadelphia, the Lord Jesus says, "I have set before thee an open door." It seems

that this refers to a door of opportunity for giving out the Word of God.

2. The open door of invitation and identification with Christ is in chapter 3, verse 20: "Behold, I stand at the door, and knock: if any man hear my voice, and open the door, I will come in to him, and will sup with him, and he with me." That door is the door to your heart.

3. We have an open door here in verse 1, which is the way to God through Christ, as we shall see.

4. In chapter 19, verse 11, we see a door opened in heaven again. That is the open door through which Christ will come at His second coming. He comes out at the end of the Great Tribulation to put down all of the unrighteousness and rebellion against God and to establish His kingdom.

John did not see this door opening as the Authorized Version of verse 1 suggests. This door was open all the time. It is the door through which believers have come to God for over nineteen hundred years. "Jesus saith unto him, I am the way, the truth, and the life: no man cometh unto the Father, but by me" (John 14:6). He also said, "I am the door: by me if any man enter in, he shall be saved, and shall go in and out, and find pasture" (John 10:9). The open door to heaven is the Lord Jesus Christ. He also is the One who will come to the door of your heart—that is the wonder and glory of it all.

We enter by faith. In modern terminology, we might express it thus: faith puts us on the launching pad of the church, which is Christ, and at the Rapture we go through this door like a guided missile. It is not just shot out into space going nowhere, but if man can hit the target of the moon, I do not think the Lord Jesus will have any trouble getting His church into heaven.

"Come up hither" is heaven's invitation to John, and it is an invitation to all of the fellowship that know Christ as Savior. John wrote in 1 John 1:3: "That which we have seen and heard declare we unto you, that ye also may have fellowship with us: and truly our fellowship is with the Father, and with his Son Jesus Christ."

John is saying in effect, "We heard it, we saw it, and we declare it unto you. I am letting you know this so that you can have fellowship also, and one of these days you will be going up through that open door."

"And the first voice which I heard, a voice as of a trumpet speaking with me." This is the sound which calls the church to meet Christ in the air. And whose voice is it? It is the voice of Christ. This introduces us to one of the simple symbols which occurs frequently from here on in the Revelation. That it is a symbol is evident—a trumpet does not speak. Jazz devotees describe the trumpet playing of certain musicians by saying that their trumpets "talk." When jazz addicts say that, they are just using a symbol. A trumpet never talks. The *voice* of Christ is like a trumpet, and this is the voice that Paul wrote of in 1 Thessalonians 4:16–17: "For the Lord himself shall descend from heaven with a shout, with the voice of the archangel, and with the trump of God: and the dead in Christ shall rise first: Then we which are alive and remain shall be caught up together with them in the clouds, to meet the Lord in the air: and so shall we ever be with the Lord."

This is a definite statement concerning the Rapture. When anyone tells you that the word *rapture* is not in the Bible, remember that the Greek word for "caught up" is *harpazō;* it means "caught up, raptured, or snatched up." Hal Lindsey calls the Rapture "the great snatch." I guess that is good vocabulary for young people today, but I prefer the term "caught up," and it means rapture. If you don't like the word *rapture,* then call it *harpazō.* That's what Paul called it. We are to be caught up, and His voice will be like a trumpet. It pulled John up, and someday it will pull you and me up.

"Come up hither, and I will shew thee the things which must come to pass after these things." After what things? After the church has completed its earthly run and is caught up.

And immediately I was in the spirit; and, behold, a throne was set in heaven, and one sat on the throne [Rev. 4:2].

At once (straightway) I found myself in the Spirit: and behold, a throne set in heaven, and one sitting on the throne.

"At once (straightway)" denotes the brevity of time, which is one of the characteristics of the Rapture. Paul said that we are to be caught up "in a moment, in the twinkling of an eye" (see 1 Cor. 15:51–52). A twinkling of an eye is pretty brief. Some psychologist has measured it. He considered the twinkling of an eye to be, not the going down of the eyelid, but the going up of the eyelid—that is reducing it to a fine point! But he determined that it is 1/1000 of a second. That is how quick the Rapture is going to be—immediately, straightway, at once.

"I found myself in the Spirit." In other

words, the Holy Spirit is still guiding John into new truth and is showing him things to come (see John 16:13).

"And, behold, a throne set in heaven, and one sitting on the throne." The throne was already there, but John now sees it for the first time. Our attention is now directed to the center of attraction. The throne represents the universal sovereignty and rulership of God. It means that He is in control. The general headquarters of this universe is in heaven, not in Washington, D.C., or London or Moscow or any other place down here. This is the picture that we are given in the Word of God. We read in Psalm 11:4, "The LORD is in his holy temple, the LORD's throne is in heaven: his eyes behold, his eyelids try, the children of men" (see also Ps. 47:8; 97:2; 103:19; Ezek. 1:26–28). It is the throne of God the Father, and Jesus sits at His right hand. Psalm 110:1 tells us, "The LORD said unto my Lord, Sit thou at my right hand, until I make thine enemies thy footstool" (see also Heb. 1:3; 12:2). The Lord Jesus is in charge of all events here.

The throne of grace now becomes a throne of judgment. This is another reason that I say very definitely that the church is gone from the world when this takes place. If the church were still on the earth when Christ has left the place of intercession and has come to the place of judgment, He is in the wrong place for the church.

And he that sat was to look upon like a jasper and a sardine stone: and there was a rainbow round about the throne, in sight like unto an emerald [Rev. 4:3].

All that we see here is color, beautiful color like precious stones. We do not get a picture of God at all—He never has been photographed. Our attention is directed to the One who is seated on the throne. Although He is God the Father, we should understand this to be the throne of the triune God. Nevertheless, the three persons of the Trinity are distinguished: (1) God the Holy Spirit in verses 2 and 5; (2) God the Father here in verse 3; and (3) God the Son in verse 5 of chapter 5. What we have before us here is the Trinity upon the throne.

John could distinguish no form of a person on the throne, only the brilliance and brightness of precious stones.

"And he that sat was to look upon like a jasper." The jasper stone was the last stone identified in the breastplate of the high priest (see Exod. 28:20). It was first in the foundation of the New Jerusalem and also the first

seen in the wall of the New Jerusalem (see Rev. 21:18–19). It was a many-colored stone with purple predominating. Some identify it with a diamond. It was in the breastplate of the high priest of Israel, representing little Benjamin whom Jacob called "the son of my right hand." Perhaps this speaks of Christ as He ascended and took His place at the right hand of the Father.

The "sardine stone" is the sixth stone in the foundation of the New Jerusalem (see Rev. 21:20). Pliny says it was discovered in Sardis from which it derived its name. In color it was a fiery red. The sardine stone was the first stone in the breastplate of the high priest, representing the tribe of Reuben, the first-born of Jacob. And Christ is the Son of God, the firstborn from the dead.

"Rainbow" is the Greek word *iris*, which can also mean "halo." While the rainbow is polychrome, here it is emerald, which is green (see Ezek. 1:28). After the judgment of the Flood, the rainbow appeared as a reminder of God's covenant not to destroy the earth again with a flood (see Gen. 9:13–15). It appears here before the judgment of the Great Tribulation as a reminder that a flood will not be used in judgment. Green is the color of the earth. The suggestion here is that of the prophet Habakkuk: ". . . in wrath remember mercy" (Hab. 3:2)—and God will do that.

THE TWENTY-FOUR ELDERS

And round about the throne were four and twenty seats: and upon the seats I saw four and twenty elders sitting, clothed in white raiment; and they had on their heads crowns of gold [Rev. 4:4].

There has been a great deal of speculation as to who these elders are. The Greek word for "elders" is *presbuteros*. By the way, the word *presbyterian* comes from that, and I am reminded of the story about the little girl who came home from her Presbyterian Sunday school, and her mother asked her what they had talked about. "We talked about heaven," the little girl replied. "Well, what did they say about it?" her mother asked. "The teacher said that there were only twenty-four Presbyterians there!"

Seriously, elders were representatives. We know that Israel had elders and that elders were appointed in the early churches to rule and to represent the entire church (see Titus 1:5). Their role was clearly understood by the people in John's day. These twenty-four elders stand for the total church from Pentecost to the Rapture. Therefore, I can say categorically and dogmatically that here is the church in heaven.

"White raiment" is the righteousness of Christ (see 2 Cor. 5:21).

"Crowns of gold" indicates that the church will rule with Christ (see 1 Cor. 6:3). Crowns are also given as rewards (see 2 Tim. 4:8; James 1:12; 1 Pet. 5:4) when the *bema* judgment, the judgment seat of Christ, takes place.

And out of the throne proceeded lightnings and thunderings and voices: and there were seven lamps of fire burning before the throne, which are the seven Spirits of God [Rev. 4:5].

The tense here is the present tense; it should be *proceed*, not *proceeded*. It is taking place right there and then.

"Lightnings and thunderings" always precede a storm in the Midwest and generally indicate the intensity of the storm. I think that the meaning here is that judgment is coming.

"And voices" indicates that it is not a haphazard judgment, but it is directed by the One on the throne.

"The seven Spirits of God" is a clear reference to the Holy Spirit.

THE FOUR LIVING CREATURES

And before the throne there was a sea of glass like unto crystal: and in the midst of the throne, and round about the throne, were four beasts full of eyes before and behind [Rev. 4:6].

"A sea of glass" denotes its appearance and not the material of which it is made. This sea is before the throne of God and is another indication that the emphasis is not on mercy but on judgment. This sea represents the holiness and righteousness of God (see Matt. 5:8; Heb. 12:14).

We are told in 1 Thessalonians 3:13, "To the end he may stablish your hearts unblameable in holiness before God, even our Father, at the coming of our Lord Jesus Christ with all his saints." This placid sea indicates the position of rest to which the church has come. No longer is she the victim of the storms of life. No longer is she out there on the tossing sea.

"Four beasts" are literally "four living creatures." The Greek word is *zōa*, from which we get our English word *zoo*. It doesn't mean a wild beast as we might think. We will have a wild beast when we get to chapter 13, but that is a different word and a different type of beast. This is just a living creature. The emphasis is not upon the bestial, but upon the vital, upon the fact that they are living.

"Four beasts full of eyes before and behind." This speaks of their alertness and awareness. They resemble both the cherubim of Ezekiel 1:5–10; 10:20; and the seraphim of Isaiah 6:2–3.

And the first beast was like a lion, and the second beast like a calf, and the third beast had a face as a man, and the fourth beast was like a flying eagle [Rev. 4:7].

I agree with those who identify each of these living creatures with the gospel which it represents, and I believe this is accurate, although such an application is questioned a great deal.

"The first living creature was like a lion," and the first Gospel represents the Lord Jesus as the King. He was born a King, He lived a King, He died a King, He was raised a King, and He is coming again as a King. Everything He does in the Gospel of Matthew He does as the King. Remember that God said that the tribe of Judah was like a lion, that the King, the Ruler, would come from that tribe, and that the scepter would not depart from Judah until Shiloh came (see Gen. 49:9–10; Rev. 5:5).

"The second living creature like a calf [ox]." This is the beast of burden, the servant animal domesticated. In the Gospel of Mark, Christ is presented as the Servant. There is no genealogy given in this gospel. If you hire someone to mow your lawn or to wash your dishes, you do not ask him who his papa and mama are. What difference does it make? You want to know whether or not he can do the job. The Gospel of Mark presents Christ as the Servant.

"The third living creature had a face as a man." The third Gospel, the Gospel of Luke, presents the Lord Jesus as the Son of Man. It is His humanity that is emphasized.

"The fourth living creature was like a flying eagle." He communicates the deity of Christ as seen in the Gospel of John.

These living creatures also represent the animal world, as suggested by Godet. The lion represents wild beasts, the calf represents domesticated beasts, the eagle represents birds, and man is the head of all creation. Note that there is no mention of fish. In the new heaven and the new earth, there will be no more sea, and since there is no sea, you will not need any fish. Nor will there be reptiles. The serpent will not be there to introduce sin as he did at the beginning.

And the four beasts had each of them six wings about him; and they were full of eyes within: and they rest not day and night, saying, Holy, holy, holy, Lord God Almighty, which was, and is, and is to come [Rev. 4:8].

These six wings correspond to the seraphim of Isaiah 6:2.

Instead of *had*, it should be *having*—this is the present tense. This is where the action is, and this is taking place.

That which they say repeatedly is, "Holy, holy, holy, Lord God Almighty." This is the same refrain as that of the seraphim in Isaiah 6:3.

"Which was, and is, and is to come" refers to Christ. He identified Himself at the very beginning of this book in just that way: "I am Alpha and Omega, the beginning and the ending, saith the Lord, which is, and which was, and which is to come, the Almighty" (Rev. 1:8). He is identified for us, and therefore we do not need to speculate in places like this.

And when those beasts give glory and honour and thanks to him that sat on the throne, who liveth for ever and ever,

The four and twenty elders fall down before him that sat on the throne, and worship him that liveth for ever and ever, and cast their crowns before the throne, saying,

Thou art worthy, O Lord, to receive glory and honour and power: for thou hast created all things, and for thy pleasure they are and were created [Rev. 4:9–11].

This is the first great worship scene which we see in heaven.

When should be *whensoever*, indicating that this is a continual act of worship. In other words, praise and adoration are the eternal activity of God's creatures in heaven. The creature worships the Creator as the triune God: "Holy, holy, holy." Worship is the activity of heaven.

I have a sermon which I have not preached in quite some while, which is entitled, "Why Do You Want to Go to Heaven?" Many people say that not everybody who is talking about heaven is going to heaven. The better question is, Why do you want to go to heaven? Is the idea to miss hell? I myself do not think that to be an unworthy motive, but may I say to you that if you go to heaven, you are going to find yourself either getting down on your face or getting up, worshiping the triune God and especially the Lord Jesus Christ. If you find worship boring down here and you are not interested in worshiping the Lord Jesus and expressing your heart's desire to Him, why in the world do you want to go to heaven? We are going to spend a lot of time up there worshiping Him.

"And cast their crowns before the throne." The crowns of the church are laid at Jesus' feet as an act of submission and worship. Many people talk of there being a crown for them over there. Frankly, if we get a crown at all, I think that after we wear it for awhile and the newness wears off, we are going to feel embarrassed. What in the world are *we* doing wearing a crown? The only One worthy up there is the Lord Jesus. Therefore, we are going to lay our crown at His feet.

"For thou hast created all things." Dr. Walvoord, in his very excellent book, *The Revelation of Jesus Christ*, calls attention to something here that I think is important. The living creatures give glory and honor and thanks to Him who sits on the throne. They worship Him for His attributes, because He is who He is. However, the four and twenty elders who represent the church worship Him not only because of His attributes but also because of what He has done. Here they worship Him as Creator—"thou hast created all things, and for thy pleasure they are and were created." In other words, the church comes out of this little earth which is God's creation, and they join in the worship because He created this earth down here. Genesis 1:1 is accurate, and the church believes it.

"And for thy pleasure they are and were created." "For thy pleasure" is more accurately translated "because of thy will." The reason that God created this earth and that things are as they are is because it was in His plan and purpose. I do not understand a great deal of what He is doing, and I do not understand a great deal about this universe in which I live, but I do know that it is created this way because this is the way He wanted it. He is in charge, and we are to worship Him because He created this little earth. I am glad that He did, and I am glad that He created me. He could have forgotten all about me, but I am glad that I was in the plan and purpose of God. We worship Him because of that.

CHAPTER 5

THEME: *The church in heaven with Christ—continued*

Chapter 5 continues this scene of the church in heaven with Christ. I think it is well for us to spend a little time here to get acquainted with where we are going. I am sure that you would not buy real estate in Florida without seeing it first, although I had an uncle who did just that. After he went down and saw it, he reported that he had some of the finest alligators that he had ever seen—all of his property was under water! He had bought it sight unseen. We have a lot of uninhabitable desert here in California, and even in the Hawaiian Islands there are great areas of nothing but a lava bed. You had better know what you are buying. Therefore, if you are going to heaven, you will want to know something about where you are going, and that is the reason this chapter ought to be interesting to you.

In chapters 4–5 we find that the church (the body of believers) is in heaven with Christ. The Lord Jesus said to his disciples, ". . . I go to prepare a place for you. . . . that where I am, there ye may be also" (John 14:2–3). We are going to be with Him.

The scene of chapter 5 is set in heaven, preparatory to the events of the Great Tribulation. Since the church is in heaven with Him, it surely could not go through the Great Tribulation down here on the earth. The throne was the center of chapter 4. The Lion and the Lamb, both of whom represent Christ, are the center of chapter 5. Christ is the Lamb on the throne. He is both Sovereign and Savior. He is in full charge of all the events which follow in this book. Let us not lose sight of Him.

THE BOOK WITH SEVEN SEALS

This chapter opens with *and*, a connective, a little conjunction, which indicates that something went before. It is the string that ties us back to chapter 4. Actually, we don't need a chapter division here because it is all the same subject.

> **And I saw in the right hand of him that sat on the throne a book written within and on the backside, sealed with seven seals [Rev. 5:1].**

Here is my translation of this verse:

> *And I saw on the right hand of Him that sat on the throne a book written within and on the back, close sealed (sealed tightly) with seven seals.*

"I saw"—John is the witness of these events; this is something that he sees. Someone pointed out to me in a letter sometime ago that I have the habit of saying, "Isn't this a wonderful picture?" or, "Isn't that a picture for you?" I wasn't aware that I use that expression as I teach, but I guess I do. I think that we ought to bring all our senses to bear upon the Word of God and especially in studying Revelation. John is *seeing*, and he is *hearing*. This is the reason that I frequently use slides to illustrate my sermons. I receive some criticism for that, but may I say to you, we need to see and to hear a lot of things to aid our understanding of the Scriptures. The Word of God should grasp and lay hold of all of our senses, even of our taste and smell. For example, there are certain scenes in Revelation where you can smell the fire and brimstone.

God the Father holds here in His hand a scroll which is rolled tightly and sealed closely with seven seals. Stauffer is the one who calls our attention to the fact that the Roman law required that a will be sealed seven times, as illustrated in the wills left by Augustus and Vespasian. While it is interesting that this method was used, we know that in the Book of Revelation the number seven is not just an accidental number and that it wasn't used only because they used it in the Roman Empire.

Godet considers this scroll to be "the book of the new covenant." Others label it "the book of judgment." Walter Scott considered it "the revelation of God's purpose and counsel concerning the world." It perhaps should bear no title because it is, as Dr. Harry Ironside has suggested, the title deed to this world. You will remember that when the children of Israel were going into captivity, Jeremiah was instructed to have his servant go and buy some property and to get the title deed to it, because God promised that Israel was going to be returned to the land (see Jer. 32:6–15).

Who holds the title deed to this earth down here? It is none other than the Lord Jesus; He alone has it. In Daniel 7:13–14 we read: "I saw in the night visions, and, behold, one like the Son of man came with the clouds of heaven, and came to the Ancient of days, and they brought him near before him. And there was given him dominion, and glory, and a kingdom, that all people, nations, and languages, should serve him: his dominion is an everlasting dominion, which shall not pass away, and his kingdom that which shall not be destroyed."

This suggests, I believe, that what is being handed over to the Lord Jesus (we will see it handed over to Him) is the title deed to this world in which you and I live. He created it, He redeemed it, and it belongs to Him.

In Zechariah, which is a book that you need to know in order to know Revelation, we read: "Then I turned, and lifted up mine eyes, and looked, and behold a flying roll. And he said unto me, What seest thou? And I answered, I see a flying roll; the length thereof is twenty cubits, and the breadth thereof is ten cubits. Then said he unto me, This is the curse that goeth forth over the face of the whole earth: for every one that stealeth shall be cut off as on this side according to it; and every one that sweareth shall be cut off as on that side according to it" (Zech. 5:1–3).

This flying roll is the same thing as the scroll here in Revelation. Some think that the Ten Commandments are on this roll and that the world is to be judged by those commandments. I am not sure that that is it. Many suggestions have been made in an attempt to identify this book, but this is one place where we cannot be dogmatic.

The suggestion, which I consider to be more in line than any other, is that this book represents God's new covenant with Israel. God talks about this covenant a great deal. In Jeremiah we read, "Behold, the days come, saith the LORD, that I will make a new covenant with the house of Israel, and with the house of Judah. . . . I will put my law in their inward parts, and write it in their hearts; and will be their God, and they shall be my people" (Jer. 31:31, 33). Paul writes in Romans: "And so all Israel shall be saved: as it is written, There shall come out of Sion the Deliverer, and shall turn away ungodliness from Jacob: For this is my covenant unto them, when I shall take away their sins" (Rom. 11:26–27).

In Hebrews we find these words: "This is the covenant that I will make with them after those days, saith the Lord, I will put my laws into their hearts, and in their minds will I write them" (Heb. 10:16). This is what Jeremiah had spoken of. The writer to the Hebrews continues: "And their sins and iniquities will I remember no more. Now where remission of these is, there is no more offering for sin" (Heb. 10:17–18).

The old covenant which God had made with Israel depended upon man. The Ten Commandments said, "Don't, don't, don't." It depended upon the weak arm of the flesh, and as a result, it failed. This was not because there was anything wrong with the Ten Commandments or with the Law that God gave. The problem was with man. The same thing occurred in the Garden of Eden. Many people think that there was something wrong with the forbidden fruit or that the tree was something unusual. I think it was good fruit and just like any other. The problem was not the fruit on the tree but the pear (pair) on the ground! This New Covenant depends upon the power of the throne of God; it depends upon the Lord Jesus Christ.

And I saw a strong angel proclaiming with a loud voice, Who is worthy to open the book, and to loose the seals thereof? [Rev. 5:2].

Who has the right and title to this world? Who can rule it? Who can establish justice and righteousness? Do you think that maybe the Democrats can do it? Do you think that the Republicans can do it? Do you think that any administration can do it? Do you think the United Nations can do it? I trust that you are not so deluded at this late time in the history of the world that you believe that man can solve his own problems. The Word of God makes it very clear that he cannot.

"A strong angel" means a powerful angel. He has "a loud voice." This is speaking now of power, that which is needed to make this covenant effective.

And no man in heaven, nor in earth, neither under the earth, was able to open the book, neither to look thereon [Rev. 5:3].

No man of Adam's line has a right to open the book and to take charge of this earth. There have been a great many who have tried to do it. Adam lost dominion through sin. Moses was the lawgiver, but he was also a lawbreaker. David and his line failed. None of Adam's line qualifies. There is none today. The Ruler must be a Redeemer, the Sovereign must be a Savior of mankind, and Jesus Christ is the only One. Stand aside, Adam, you cannot do it, and neither can any of your children. Satan is working at it, but he cannot do it either. The question is: Who is going to be able to do it?

And I wept much, because no man was found worthy to open and to read the book, neither to look thereon [Rev. 5:4].

John is disturbed by this a great deal. This man had a real passion for prophecy. He had a holy affection and a pious curiosity. He wanted to look into the things that even angels cannot look into. John enters into the drama because he has come from earth. The Revelation was written in tears. Is the earth to continue in sin and sorrow? Is there no future for the earth? Listen to what Paul has to say: "And not only they, but ourselves also, which have the first-fruits of the Spirit, even we ourselves groan within ourselves, waiting for the adoption, to wit, the redemption of our body" (Rom. 8:23).

Is no one competent to rule this earth? John is overwhelmed by the possibility that there may be no one. Again Paul writes: "For we know that the whole creation groaneth and travaileth in pain together until now" (Rom. 8:22).

Personally, I believe that evolution is the most pessimistic philosophy and theory that anyone can entertain today. No wonder it has led to so many suicides among the intelligentsia. What hope is there for the future if it took millions of years to get to where we are today? Isn't there someone who can straighten out this problem? It is so petty and little and narrow-minded for politicians to say that they are going to make peace in our time. It is even more tragic to hear the church say that they can straighten out the affairs of the world or even that they can evangelize the world. My brother, may I say to you, there are just not any around who can qualify to open this book and to take charge of this earth that we are on. And John weeps a great deal because of this.

It is a good thing that this book was not opened here in Southern California because we have a whole passel of preachers who say that they can tell you what is on the inside of this book, on the outside, and all around it. They can even tell you what's on the cover! They have all the answers. If John had just been in California, instead of being on the island of Patmos, they could have given him the answers! Well, John didn't have the answer, but there will be One who can open the book, as we shall see.

CHRIST, THE LION AND THE LAMB

And one of the elders saith unto me, Weep not: behold, the Lion of the tribe of Juda, the Root of David, hath prevailed to open the book, and to loose the seven seals thereof [Rev. 5:5].

And one from among the elders saith unto me, Weep not: behold, the Lion of the tribe of Juda, the Root of David, hath

overcome to open the book, and the seven seals thereof.

Evidently, any one of the elders could have answered. They had spiritual illumination. I think that this further identifies them as the church because the Lord Jesus had said to His own: "Henceforth I call you not servants; for the servant knoweth not what his lord doeth: but I have called you friends; for all things that I have heard of my Father I have made known unto you" (John 15:15).

The Lord Jesus Christ is the only One who has the right and title to this earth. He not only redeemed you and me, but He also redeemed the earth. He is identified in this section in all His ministries that relate to the earth.

"The Lion of the tribe of Juda" identifies Him, of course, with the tribe of Judah of the people of Israel. When old Jacob was dying, he called his twelve sons around him, and this is the prophecy he gave concerning Judah: "Judah is a lion's whelp: from the prey, my son, thou art gone up: he stooped down, he couched as a lion, and as an old lion; who shall rouse him up? The sceptre shall not depart from Judah, nor a lawgiver from between his feet, until Shiloh come; and unto him shall the gathering of the people be" (Gen. 49:9–10). The Lord Jesus is the Lion of the tribe of Judah. He is also "the Root of David." In 2 Samuel 7, that great chapter of God's covenant with David, He says, "I am going to bring One in your line who shall rule, not only over these people, but over the whole earth." The Lord Jesus Christ has the right to rule, as He is the fulfillment of the prophecies made in the Old Testament relative to the future of the world. All of those prophecies will be fulfilled at His second coming to the earth to establish His kingdom.

And I beheld, and, lo, in the midst of the throne and of the four beasts, and in the midst of the elders, stood a Lamb as it had been slain, having seven horns and seven eyes, which are the seven Spirits of God sent forth into all the earth [Rev. 5:6].

John is still a spectator to this scene. He says, "I beheld, I saw this."

"A Lamb"—the word there is in the diminutive; literally, it means a little lamb. This denotes its gentleness and its willingness to be sacrificed. Christ was led as a lamb to the slaughter, and He did not open His mouth at all (see Isa. 53:7). He was the Lamb of God who taketh away the sin of the world (see John 1:29).

"As it had been slain" indicates the redemptive and vicarious, substitutionary death of Christ. The emphasis is upon the fact that He was slain with violence.

"Stood" should rather be "standing." This speaks of His resurrection. He is no longer seated at the right hand of God. He is moving now, and He is moving to power. He is coming to this earth. The judgment of the Tribulation is about to strike the earth. The winds are already blowing on the earth.

"In the midst of the throne" is indicative of the fact that He is before the throne and ready to act as the righteous Judge.

"Seven horns" denotes complete power. A horn speaks of power (see Dan. 7–8). He is omnipotent. "Seven eyes" denotes complete knowledge. Christ is omniscient. He is the omnipotent and omniscient God. He moves in the fullness of the Spirit, who is the Spirit of wisdom and understanding.

The Lord Jesus Christ is a Lion and a Lamb. The lion character refers to His second coming; the lamb character refers to His first coming. The lion is symbolic of His majesty; the lamb is symbolic of His meekness. As a lion He is a Sovereign; as a lamb He is a Savior. As a lion He is a Judge; as a lamb He is judged. The lion represents the government of God; the lamb represents the grace of God.

And he came and took the book out of the right hand of him that sat upon the throne [Rev. 5:7].

"Took" is correctly "hath taken." The Lord Jesus moves to the throne through the Tribulation Period. He *judges* the world in righteousness before He *reigns* in righteousness. He is no longer the intercessor of the church, for the church is now with Him. He is beginning to act as Judge. The movement here is important.

And when he had taken the book, the four beasts and four and twenty elders fell down before the Lamb, having every one of them harps, and golden vials full of odours, which are the prayers of saints [Rev. 5:8].

"When he had taken [took] the book" is in the aorist tense, meaning completed action. This is the great movement of all creation, and the Lord Jesus takes over now.

Notice the worship of the Lamb by the four living creatures and the twenty-four elders. "Harps" denote praise. The elders do not play on the harps; they are just a token of praise to God. I am so glad to have found out that I am not going to be an angel playing on a harp in heaven—that just doesn't appeal to me! You may want a harp, and if you want one, I guess in heaven they will get one for you, but I am thankful that I don't have to have one.

The twenty-four elders act as priests. Only the church is a priesthood of believers in heaven. Dr. Carl Armerding gives the arresting thought that the prayer of Christ for believers in John 17 is answered in the elders: our Lord's prayer that they might know Him, that they might be with Him, and that they might behold His glory is all answered in this scene of the elders in heaven.

The "vials full of odours" is more accurately "bowls full of incense." These are identified as "the prayers of saints." Obviously, the elders represent the body of Christ, which is called the church and they are the priesthood.

And they sung a new song, saying, Thou art worthy to take the book, and to open the seals thereof: for thou wast slain, and hast redeemed us to God by thy blood out of every kindred, and tongue, and people, and nation;

And hast made us unto our God kings and priests: and we shall reign on the earth [Rev. 5:9–10].

And they sing a new song, saying, Worthy art thou to take the book and to open the seals of it: for thou wast slain and didst purchase unto God in thy blood [men] of every tribe, tongue, people, and nation, and madest them unto our God a kingdom and priests, and they shall reign on the earth.

"They" indicates that both the living creatures and the elders sing this song. The angelic hosts join the church in praise.

"Sing" (present tense) denotes the continuation of praise. Praise is directed to the Lamb with the book. He is praised now as the Redeemer of men in all ages and races. In heaven is going to be the first time that I will sing. I have never been able to sing, but I am going to be in that chorus, and I am going to sing praises unto Him.

The "new song" is the song of redemption. The old song is the song of creation. In the Book of Job we are told that the sons of God sang. They were singing because God was the Creator; they didn't really know anything about the love of God then. Now we can sing about our Savior who loves us and who gave Himself for us. What a picture we have here!

"Worthy" reveals that He now fills the entire horizon of praise and worship. Actually, worship is returning to *worth*, that which belongs to Him; and He is the only One worthy of praise.

"And hast redeemed us to God by thy blood." They sing of His shed blood in heaven. Down here many denominational churches are taking out of their hymn books all references to His blood, but in heaven they will be put back in the hymn book. I guess that may be the reason the Lord isn't going to embarrass some of those folk by taking them into heaven, because they would have to sing about the blood there.

The change of the pronoun from "us" to "them" is important. They are praising the Lamb for those yet to be saved on the earth—the tribulation saints.

"A kingdom and priests" refers to the tribulation saints. The church will not reign *on* the earth, but *over* the earth.

MYRIADS OF ANGELS JOIN THE SONG

And I beheld, and I heard the voice of many angels round about the throne and the beasts and the elders: and the number of them was ten thousand times ten thousand, and thousands of thousands;

Saying with a loud voice, Worthy is the Lamb that was slain to receive power, and riches, and wisdom, and strength, and honour, and glory, and blessing [Rev. 5:11–12].

And I saw, and I heard a voice of many angels round about the throne and the living creatures and the elders, and the number of them was ten thousands of ten thousands (myriads), and thousands of thousands, saying with a great voice, Worthy is the Lamb that hath been slain

to take the power, and riches, and wisdom, and might, and honor, and glory, and blessing.

When John says, "ten thousand times ten thousand, and thousands of thousands," I think that he means they were innumerable. In effect John says, "At first I looked and I saw a company of angels around the elders, and they were singing—and I thought that was great. But all of a sudden I looked out yonder and, boy, there was a crowd which I could not count!" Nobody could have counted them. A computer couldn't count them. God's created intelligences were praising Him. My friend, I do not know why you want to go to heaven if you do not want to worship and praise Him down here.

UNIVERSAL WORSHIP OF THE SAVIOR AND SOVEREIGN

And every creature which is in heaven, and on the earth, and under the earth, and such as are in the sea, and all that are in them, heard I saying, Blessing, and honour, and glory, and power, be unto him that sitteth upon the throne, and unto the Lamb for ever and ever.

And the four beasts said, Amen. And the four and twenty elders fell down and worshipped him that liveth for ever and ever [Rev. 5:13–14].

Every animate creature of God joins in this universal act of worship, both in heaven and earth. Evidently, the animals in the earth and the fish in the sea join in this volume of praise! The living creatures add their amen to it, and the church falls down in silent adoration and praise.

If I could, I would sing the Hallelujah chorus, for as we come to the end of this very remarkable scene in heaven, we see that all praise and honor and worship must go to the Lord Jesus Christ. If you are not in the habit of praising and worshiping Him, why don't you start right now?

CHAPTER 6

THEME: Opening of the first six seals

The sixth chapter of Revelation is the great watershed, the great divide, of the Book of Revelation. Here is a division that is all-important. Traveling on Highway 66 across northern New Mexico, you go through Albuquerque, then Gallup, to Winslow, Arizona, and up to Flagstaff. Somewhere in that area there is a place called the Continental Divide. I am told that you could drop a chip in a stream which is flowing on the west side of the divide, and it would end up in the Pacific Ocean, or you could put a chip in a stream on the east side of the divide, and it would eventually end up in the Atlantic Ocean by way of the Gulf of Mexico. This is a very important division which separates those two chips so that they find themselves worlds apart. We have such a great divide at chapter 6 of the Book of Revelation.

The third and final major division of Revelation began with chapter 4 where we found ourselves transferred to heaven. John was caught up to heaven, and we went right up with him and began to see things in heaven. However, we did not see anything labeled the church, because the church was the name given to it down here on the earth. But we did see the twenty-four elders. The elders had to get there some way—they were caught up, and they represent the church which will be at this time in heaven with Christ. From here on in the Book of Revelation, the church is no longer mentioned on the earth at all. There is an invitation at the end of the book which comes from the church, but that refers to this day in which we live.

You can see an orderly process in the Book of Revelation, and we need to follow Peter's rule for prophecy: "Knowing this first, that no prophecy of the scripture is of any private interpretation" (2 Pet. 1:20)—that is, you do not interpret any prophecy by itself. Each prophecy must be looked at as a part of a system and a program, and it must fit in with the others. By the time we get to the sixth chapter, a great many forget that John gave to us an orderly division of the Book of Revelation. John was told in Revelation 1:19, "Write [1] the things which thou hast seen"—that was that glorious vision of the glorified Christ as the Great High Priest amidst the lampstands, where He is keeping the light burning here upon the earth. [2] ". . . And the things which are"—that was the seven churches which represent the total earthly experience of the church from the Day of Pentecost to the *parousia*, from the Upper Room to the upper air, the total history of the church on earth. [3] ". . . And the things which shall be hereafter [*meta tauta*]." The earthly career of the church was ended in chapter 3. John said *meta tauta*, after these things, twice at the opening of chapter 4. He did that for the benefit of those who hold the historic viewpoint of Revelation, the amillennialists. Beginning, therefore, with chapter 4, John is showing us "the things which must be hereafter."

In chapters 4–5, we were in heaven with John. The first thing that we saw was a throne, and the Lord Jesus was there. He is the Lion of the tribe of Judah who is sitting at God's right hand, waiting until His enemies are to be made His footstool down here. He is also the Lamb, and we saw the emphasis upon His first coming. The Lamb, because He is the Redeemer, is the One who is able to take the seven-sealed book, which is the title deed of this earth.

Do you know that the Lord Jesus is the only One who is able to judge this earth? He is the One who is able to judge, not only because of who He is—He is God manifest in the flesh—but also because of what He has done. He created this earth, and that gives Him a right. He is worshiped in chapter 4 as the Creator. But then He also redeemed this earth, and in chapter 5 He is worshiped as the Redeemer. Since He is the Creator and the Redeemer, He is the only One worthy to judge this earth. He is the only One who is able to rule this earth. What a reflection upon the consummate conceit of little men down here who want to be judges! What right has the Supreme Court to judge anyone? What right has the Senate or the House of Representatives or the president to judge anyone? Who do they think they are? May I say to you, the Lord Jesus Christ alone is worthy to sit in judgment. Until one of these men can measure up to Him, he is not really in a position to judge in his own ability and strength. Any human judge who does not look to God is not worthy to sit on any bench and judge anyone. The injustice that is upon this earth today is brought about by little man sitting in judgment upon others. Jesus Christ is worthy. That is the picture that is given to us at the close of chapter 5.

OPENING OF THE SEVEN-SEALED BOOK

As we come to chapter 6, the scene shifts to the earth, and the question naturally is: What happens on the earth when the church leaves? The Great Tribulation takes place, and that is the subject of chapters 6–18. The opening of the seven-sealed book is the subject specifically of chapter 6 through verse 1 of chapter 8. These seven seals open up the Great Tribulation Period. The Lord Jesus breaks the seals, and the four horses ride forth. We will see the martyred dead during that period and the coming of the day of wrath. In a very orderly way, the seventh seal introduces the blowing of seven trumpets (see Rev. 8:2–11:19). The blowing of the seventh trumpet introduces seven startling persons (see Rev. 12–13). The beast out of the sea introduces the seven bowls of wrath (see Rev. 15–16). The last bowl of wrath brings to us the burden, or the judgment, of Babylon, and that brings to an end the Great Tribulation Period (see Rev. 17–18), and then Christ comes to the earth.

It is interesting to note that upon Babylon are the first and the last judgments. Babylon, at the Tower of Babel, represents the first organized rebellion against God (see Gen. 11:1–9). Babylon also represents the last rebellion against God, both religiously (see Rev. 17) and politically (see Rev. 18). This brings to an end man's little day on this earth.

The important thing for us to keep before us is the One who is worthy to open this book. He is directing everything now. As we were told at the beginning, this is the Revelation, the unveiling, of Jesus Christ. He is no longer walking among the lampstands, for they have all been removed from this earth. He is no longer the High Priest, standing as intercessor, but He is now the executor of God's will upon the earth as He opens the seals of the book. All the judgments of the Great Tribulation usher forth from the seals out of which come the trumpets, the persons, and the bowls.

The Great Tribulation is triggered from heaven. Jesus Christ directs the entire operation. This is the reason that Psalm 2:9 says, "Thou shalt break them with a rod of iron. . . ." Many will say that they don't like all this. Do you have a better suggestion as to how He should put down the rebellion on this earth? If you do, would you pass it on to the Lord Jesus? How do you think He should put it down? Suppose He came like He did more

than nineteen hundred years ago. Do you think they are ready in Moscow, in the Kremlin, to turn authority over to Him? How about in any other country? How about in our country? I'm telling you, they are not about to turn it over to Him in Washington, D.C. Neither of our political parties is interested in putting Jesus Christ on the throne. They have some very unworthy men on both sides who would like to be on the throne. My friend, may I say to you that He *alone* is the One who is worthy. And how is He going to come to power? Exactly as the second psalm says: "Thou shalt break them with a rod of iron." We are going to see that taking place from now on in the Book of Revelation—this is judgment on the earth.

The church will be delivered from this period of judgment. Why? Is it because they are such nice, sweet, Sunday school children? Oh, no. They are sinners, but they are saved by the grace of God. Only those who reject the grace of God go into the Great Tribulation Period. This is my reason for believing that God has raised up the medium of radio in our day to get the Word of God out to the ends of the earth. He is going to let them all hear the gospel, and when they make their decision, that will decide whether or not they are going into the Great Tribulation.

Chapters 4–5 were but the preparation for that which was to follow—the judgment of the earth. In chapter 4 we saw the throne and the triune God; in chapter 5 we saw the book and the Lord Jesus Christ.

There are certain factors that are brought into focus which increase the intensity and the ferocity of the Great Tribulation:

1. The Holy Spirit will restrain evil no longer. Do I mean that He will leave the world? No, He won't leave. He was in the world before the Day of Pentecost, but on the Day of Pentecost He assumed a new ministry of baptizing believers into the body of Christ, a ministry of indwelling them, of filling them, and of leading and guiding them in this world. He will take the church out of this world, but that does not mean that *He* is going to leave. He will still be here, but He will not restrain evil any longer. In other words, man is going to have his little day during that period, and so is Satan. This is the reason I don't want to be here.

2. The true church, as light and salt, will be gone from the earth. Although the church has very little influence in the world today, it still has a little, but when it leaves the earth, there will be none left.

3. The Devil knows that he has but a short time. He is going to make hay while the sun shines. He is going to take advantage of it during this period, and God is going to give him free rein.

4. Evil men will be free to carry out their nefarious plans. In other words, Antichrist will be able to take over this earth for a brief period of time.

5. There will be direct judgment from God. We see that here in v. 17, which says, "For the great day of his wrath is come; and who shall be able to stand?"

I do not think that the Great Tribulation breaks suddenly like a great tornado. The opening of the seals is gradual, logical, chronological. They are opened one at a time. The Book of Revelation makes sense, my friend.

As we come to the text of this chapter, may I make the statement very carefully that, from chapter 4 on, this is speaking of the future. Now if it is future and if we today are in the time of "the things which are," the period of the church, we cannot drag any of the seals, the trumpets, the bowls, or the persons up into our own day. I do believe we are seeing the setting of the stage, but I do not think that any of these things are taking place today. Yet we find that a great many persons are interpreting this section in just that way. It is sensationalism, of course, and I guess it gets listeners and sells books, but it surely isn't according to the way John put it down here. I simply want to lay it down as an axiom that from chapter 6 on it has reference to the future, and none of these things has come to pass as yet.

The section of Revelation which deals with the seven churches could be fitted into history, but you cannot fit any of this which follows into history. The differences between the two great systems of interpreting prophecy—the futurist and the historic viewpoints—really become manifest at this point in Revelation. The historical theory takes the position that all of this is history and can be fitted into history. It is quite interesting to me that many who hold the historical viewpoint assume that this is future from here on, or a little farther down they make it future—in other words, they just can't fit it into history. The amillennialist tends to fit everything from here on into history. As a result, there are about fifty different systems of interpretation, according to Dr. Walvoord, that have come out of the historical viewpoint. My friend, forty-nine of those are bound to be wrong, and personally, I think the other one is also wrong!

I went to a seminary that was amillennial, where they attempted to fit the rest of Revelation into the historical, or the amillennial, viewpoint. It became ridiculous and even comical at times. For example, when we reached the place where Scripture says that Satan was put into the bottomless pit, we were taught that that has already taken place. I asked the professor, "How do you explain the satanic activity that is taking place today?" He replied, "Satan is chained, but he has a long chain on him. It is like when you take a cow out into a vacant lot and tether her out on a long rope and let her graze." That was his explanation! And my comment was, "Doctor, I think Satan's got a pretty long chain on him then, because he is able to graze all over the world today!" It really makes some Scriptures seem rather ridiculous when you follow the historical viewpoint.

May I say very definitely that John has made it clear that we have now come to *future* things, and anything from here on through chapter 20 is still future. We are following a chronological order here, and it is very logical. You simply cannot say that these events are taking place today, and you cannot fit them into history.

OPENING OF THE FIRST SEAL— RIDER ON A WHITE HORSE

The Lord Jesus Christ takes the seven-sealed book, and He breaks the first seal.

And I saw when the Lamb opened one of the seals, and I heard, as it were the noise of thunder, one of the four beasts saying, Come and see.

And I saw, and behold a white horse: and he that sat on him had a bow; and a crown was given unto him: and he went forth conquering, and to conquer [Rev. 6:1–2].

Here is my own translation of these verses:

And I saw when the Lamb opened one of the seven seals, and I heard one of the four living creatures saying as a sound of thunder, Go. And I saw, and behold a white horse, and one sitting on him having a bow, and a crown was given to him, and he went out conquering, and to conquer.

Christ is going to break all the seals, *ad seriatum*, right in order. He is in full charge, and every creature in heaven is moving at His command. So the four horsemen are now going to ride forth. He breaks the seal, and says, "Go." Although the King James Version gives the impression that an invitation is given to John to "Come and see," the phrase "and see" should be omitted, and since the order issues from heaven, the proper translation is "Go."

It is restated by John that he "saw" and he "heard." This is television that we are looking at.

Attempts to determine the symbolism of the rider on the white horse have given rise to many differences of opinion. The preponderate interpretation among commentators is that he represents Christ. They use Psalm 45 and Revelation 19 in support of their position. But most of the contemporary Bible expositors of the premillennial school say that the white horse and the rider is Antichrist. That is the position of Scott, Ironside, Chafer, Walvoord, Woodbridge, and Pentecost. And it happens to be my position also. It would be pretty difficult for the Lord Jesus, who is the One opening the seals, now to make a quick change, mount a horse, and come riding forth.

To me that would be a rather inconsistent and unbelievable position. I personally take the viewpoint that this is Antichrist, this is an *imitation* of Christ, this is one who *pretends* to be Christ, who comes forth.

We are moving today in the direction of a world dictator. More and more is this true. All the nations of the world are disturbed. Lawlessness abounds, and governments are not able to control as they should. This is all preparing the way for the coming of one who is going to rule.

Antichrist does not appear as a villain. After all, Satan's angels are angels of light. He is not going to have horns or cloven feet. Rather, he is going to be the most attractive man the world has ever seen. They will elect him, and the world will acclaim him because he has come in his own name. But when he takes over, it sure is going to be bad for the world.

This is not just the ravings of a preacher here in California. This is something that other men in other walks of life, who apparently make no great claims to being Christians, have said. Professor A. J. Toynbee, Director of Studies in the Royal Institute of International Affairs, said:

By forcing on mankind more and more lethal weapons and at the same time making the whole world more and more interdependent economically, technology has brought mankind to such a degree of distress that we are ripe for deifying any new Caesar who might succeed in giving the world unity and peace.

That will be the platform that Antichrist will come in on—world unity and peace. I think that if anybody appeared on the scene now and offered the world that, the world wouldn't ask whether he came from heaven or hell. I don't think they would care, because they want peace at any price, and we have spent billions of dollars trying to attain it.

G. K. Chesterton observed in his day: "One of the paradoxes of this age is that it is the age of Pacifism, but not the age of Peace." There is a great deal of *talking* about peace.

In a news item sometime ago, we read of a woman in Fayetteville, Arkansas, who named the United Nations as the beneficiary to her $700,000 estate "in the fervent hope that this relatively small contribution may be of some effect in bringing about universal peace on earth and good will among men." I want to say that she poured that money down a rat hole, because you are not going to buy peace with $700,000 or even millions of dollars. We have given away *billions* of dollars throughout the world, and we do not have peace.

The Ford Foundation, one of the world's wealthiest private organizations, has announced that their money eventually will be used to work for world peace and better government, living and education conditions—yet the world gets worse all the time.

When Antichrist comes to power, he is going to talk peace, and the world will think that it is entering the Millennium when it is actually entering the Great Tribulation. The Great Tribulation comes in like a lamb, but it goes out like a lion. A promise of peace is the big lie the world is going to believe.

This rider could not be Christ, therefore, in view of the fact that Christ is the Lamb in the midst of the throne who, as the Lion of the tribe of Judah, the Root of David, is directing these events from heaven and is giving the orders to the four horsemen to ride. Christ is *clearly* identified in Revelation 19, while here the identity is certainly obscure, which suggests that it is not Christ but an imitation of Him.

OPENING OF THE SECOND SEAL— RIDER ON A RED HORSE

And when he had opened the second seal, I heard the second beast say, Come and see.

And there went out another horse that was red: and power was given to him that sat thereon to take peace from the earth, and that they should kill one another: and there was given unto him a great sword [Rev. 6:3–4].

And when He opened the second seal, I heard the second living creature saying, Go. And another horse, fiery red (flame colored) went out. And there was given to the one sitting on him to take peace from the earth, and that they should kill (violently) one another, and there was given to him a great sword.

The first horseman could not be Christ, because when *He* brings peace to this earth, it is going to be permanent. This is a short-lived peace. Immediately after the white horse went forth, here comes the red horse of war on the earth. The peace which the rider on the white horse brought to the earth was temporary and counterfeit. The Antichrist presents himself as a ruler who brings peace to the world, but he cannot guarantee it, for God says, "There is no peace, saith my God, to the wicked" (Isa. 57:21). And that passage of Scripture certainly has been fulfilled.

Isn't peace exactly what every candidate for office in our country has promised? Certainly that has been true in my lifetime. I never shall forget the candidate who said that our boys would never again go across the ocean to fight. What baloney that was! We were promised peace, and every candidate since then has promised peace. One of them dropped two atom bombs, and immediately afterward we began to talk about peace. Every candidate since then—no exception and regardless of party—has said he was going to bring peace. My friend, we are as far from peace today as we have ever been. Already the clouds are gathering for World War III.

Antichrist will be a phony. He won't bring peace because here goes the fiery red horse of war riding throughout the earth again. And this is going to be a *real* world war. Don't say that this has been fulfilled—it hasn't been. It is future.

OPENING OF THE THIRD SEAL—RIDER ON A BLACK HORSE

And when he had opened the third seal, I heard the third beast say, Come and see. And I beheld, and lo a black horse;

and he that sat on him had a pair of balances in his hand.

And I heard a voice in the midst of the four beasts say, A measure of wheat for a penny, and three measures of barley for a penny; and see thou hurt not the oil and the wine [Rev. 6:5–6].

And when He had opened the third seal, I heard the third living creature saying, Go. And I saw, and behold a black horse, and the one sitting on him having a balance (scales) in his hand. And I heard a voice in the midst of the four living creatures say, a choenix (a quart) of wheat for a denarius, and three choenix (quarts) of barley for a denarius; and do not hurt the oil and the wine.

John again says, "I heard" and "I saw." He just wants to make sure that we know that.

The color of the black horse indicates mourning (see Jer. 4:28; Mal. 3:14, "mournfully in black"), and it also speaks of famine. In Lamentations 4:8–9 we read: "Their visage is blacker than a coal; they are not known in the streets: their skin cleaveth to their bones; it is withered, it is become like a stick. They that be slain with the sword are better than they that be slain with hunger: for these pine away, stricken through for want of the fruits of the field."

The black horse represents the worldwide famine that is to come on the earth. Always after a war there is a shortage of foodstuff.

The Greek historian Herodotus says that a choenix (quart) of corn was a soldier's daily supply of food. A denarius was a day's wage (see Matt. 20:2). Therefore, a working man will be unable to support his family in that day.

The oil and the wine are luxuries that are enjoyed by the rich. Oil would correspond to our toiletries, the beauty aids and the body conditioners that we use today; that is, the luxuries of life. The wine corresponds to the liquor that will be in abundance. Isn't it interesting that there will not be enough foodstuff, not enough barley for food, but there will be enough barley to make liquor! They will make it in that day, and the rich are the ones who will get it.

Let me be very frank. During World War II the rich, for the most part, were able to get meat. They were able to get the luxuries of life. A very wealthy man told me that he never missed getting a big T-bone steak anytime that he wanted it. But I can remember getting very tired of eating tongue, which was one thing we didn't have to have blue chips to get and was something that was not rationed. In this day that is coming, things won't change. The rich are going to get theirs, but the poor won't be able to get theirs. That is the way it has always been. I feel like saying, "Ho hum," when I hear these sincere egg-headed boys talking about how they are going to work out the poverty problem. All that it has accomplished is that it has given a good job to a lot of *them*, but so far it hasn't filtered down and been a blessing to the poor. It has never helped the poor to lift themselves up with any degree of pride. Why? Because the only Man who can lift up the poor is Jesus Christ. None of these egg-headed boys is able to do it. I am sorry to have to say that, but somebody needs to speak out against all of this tomfoolery that our government is going through. All that this wasteful spending of money does is to create more bureaucracy and to sap our tax dollars. This is the sort of thing that is abroad today, but just think what it is going to be like in that future day. This which we are talking about in the Revelation is future. The only reason that I make application to today is to show that this is not unreasonable; it *is* going to take place.

Way back in 1798, the Rev. Thomas Malthus concluded that "the power of population is infinitely greater than the power of the earth to produce subsistence for man." His prediction had little weight in his day. In 1959 the United Nations' seventy-seven-nation Food and Agriculture Organization met in Rome to talk about "the fight against hunger and malnutrition." At this meeting Toynbee declared: "Sooner or later food production will reach its limit. And then, if population is still increasing, famine will do the execution that was done in the past by famine, pestilence and war combined." Sir John Boyd Orr, at one time the Director-General of the UN Food and Agriculture Organization, warned, "I shall finish my office by giving a last warning to the world. If it is not solved there will be world chaos in the next fifty years. The nations of the world are insane." Someone has reported, "There are today 750 million people getting hungrier in countries bordering the Communist sphere." This thing is growing, my friend. Famine always follows war.

OPENING OF THE FOURTH SEAL— RIDER ON A PALE HORSE

And when he had opened the fourth seal, I heard the voice of the fourth beast say, Come and see.

And I looked, and behold a pale horse: and his name that sat on him was Death, and Hell followed with him. And power was given unto them over the fourth part of the earth, to kill with sword, and with hunger, and with death, and with the beasts of the earth [Rev. 6:7–8].

And when He had opened the fourth seal, I heard the voice of the fourth living creature saying, Go. And I looked and behold a pale (greenish-yellow) horse; and the one sitting upon him, Death was his name; and Hades followed with him. And there was given unto them authority over the fourth part of the earth, to kill with the sword, and with famine, and with death (pestilence), and by the (wild) beasts of the earth.

Here is a pestilence that is going to take out one-fourth of the population of the earth. There will not be enough antibiotics and penicillin to go around in that day to stop it.

"Death was his name." Death is no more personalized here than is war—although the rider is given the name of death. There is more involved in physical death than meets the eye, for the human being is more than physical, and death is more than cessation of physical activity. While death takes the body, hades is the place where the spirit of a lost man goes (see Luke 16:23, ASV).

A literal translation of Romans 5:14 reads thus: "And nevertheless death became king from Adam down to Moses, even over them who did not sin after the fashion of Adam's sin [transgression] who is the type of Him [The Adam] who was to come [The Coming One]."

"Death was his name; and Hades followed with him." The word for *hades* is sometimes unfortunately translated by the word *hell* as in Luke 16:23 where, speaking of the rich man and Lazarus, we read: "And in hell he lift up his eyes, being in torments, and seeth Abraham afar off, and Lazarus in his bosom." *Hell* is a very unfortunate translation there; it is this same word *hades*, and, actually, it does not refer to hell at all. It speaks of physical death—either where the spirit goes or of the grave where the body is placed. In other words, while death takes the body, hades is the place where the spirit of a lost man goes. The Lord Jesus spoke of it in that way.

Paul personifies death in Romans 5:14, as he does sin in that same section, and he does it for emphasis. Sin and death entered the world at the same time. Death is the result of sin. During the interval from Adam to Moses, men did not commit the same sin as did Adam, nor was their sinning a transgression of a law, as was Adam's, because the Ten Commandments had not been given. Yet it was a period when men sinned and died. Adam's sin became their sin, for they died as Adam died. Even babies died in the Flood.

Death evidently has an all-inclusive, three-fold meaning that we do not ordinarily attach to it. We think of death as referring only to the body. (1) This is *physical* death, and it refers only to the body. It comes to a man because of Adam's sin. (2) Then there is what is known as *spiritual* death, which is separation from, and rebellion against, God. We inherit a dead nature from Adam; that is, we have no capacity for God and no desire for Him at all. (3) Finally, there is *eternal* death, which is eternal separation from God. Unless a man is redeemed, this inevitably follows. This is the second death that we will find later on in chapter 20, verse 14.

Before Adam sinned, God said to him, ". . . for in the day that thou eatest thereof thou shalt surely die" (Gen. 2:17). Well, Adam lived *physically* for more than nine hundred years after that, but he was dead *spiritually* to God. He ran from God. He no longer had a desire for fellowship with God. He died spiritually, and physical death followed and has come into the human family. More and more it deteriorates mankind. Most of us are being propped up today by modern medicine and the marvelous developments of science in order to stay alive. Actually, the human race is deteriorating all the time. Human life would be much shorter than it is if it were not for all the modern gadgets which keep us alive down here.

Adam is definitely declared here to be a type of Christ. Death must be laid at Adam's door as his total responsibility. You see, God did not create man to die. It was a penalty imposed because Adam transgressed God's command. Because Adam is the federal head of our race, his transgression is our transgression, and his death is our death. Now Christ is the head of a new creation, and this new creation has life only in Christ. He alone can give life. He is totally responsible for the life and eternal bliss of those who are His own.

Dr. Lewis Sperry Chafer put it like this, and this is a theological statement:

Thus spiritual death comes mediately through an unbroken line of posterity. Over against this, physical death is received from Adam immediately, as each person dies in body because of his own personal share in Adam's first sin.

During the Great Tribulation, death will ride unbridled. The Lord Jesus put it like this: "And except those days should be shortened, there should no flesh be saved: but for the elect's sake those days shall be shortened" (Matt. 24:22).

At the Great White Throne judgment, death will be finally destroyed (see Rev. 20:14). This is confirmed by Paul who writes, "The last enemy that shall be destroyed is death" (1 Cor. 15:26). And John reasserts it in Revelation 21:4: "And God shall wipe away all tears from their eyes; and there shall be no more death, neither sorrow, nor crying, neither shall there be any more pain: for the former things are passed away."

The sword, famine, pestilence, and wild beasts will decimate this earth's population by one-fourth. This is something that, through His prophet Ezekiel, God had said would come: "For thus saith the Lord GOD; How much more when I send my four sore judgments upon Jerusalem, the sword, and the famine, and the noisome beast, and the pestilence, to cut off from it man and beast?" (Ezek. 14:21).

The pale horse represents plague and pestilence that will stalk the earth. It also encompasses the possibility of germ warfare. Dr. Frank Holtman, head of the University of Tennessee's bacteriological department, said, "While the greater part of a city's population could be destroyed by an atomic bomb, the bacteria method might easily wipe out the entire population within a week."

We have seen the riding of the four horsemen, and this follows exactly the pattern that the Lord Jesus gave while He was on the earth. In Matthew 24:5–8, in the Olivet Discourse, He said: "For many shall come in my name, saying, I am Christ; and shall deceive many [the white horse]. And ye shall hear of wars and rumours of wars [the red horse]: see that ye be not troubled: for all these must come to pass, but the end is not yet. For nation shall rise against nation, and kingdom against kingdom: and there shall be famines [the black horse], and pestilences [the pale horse], and earthquakes, in divers places. All these are the beginning of sorrows." This is the opening of the Great Tribulation.

OPENING OF THE FIFTH SEAL— PRAYER OF THE MARTYRED REMNANT

And when he had opened the fifth seal, I saw under the altar the souls of them that were slain for the word of God, and for the testimony which they held:

And they cried with a loud voice, saying, How long, O Lord, holy and true, dost thou not judge and avenge our blood on them that dwell on the earth? [Rev. 6:9–10].

And when He opened the fifth seal, I saw under the altar of burnt sacrifice the souls [Gr.: psuchas] of those slain on account of the Word of God, and on account of the witness which they had; and they cried with a great voice, saying, How long (until when) O Master, the Holy and True, dost Thou not judge and avenge our blood on them that dwell on the earth (earth dwellers)?

This altar is in heaven and is evidently where Christ offered His blood for the sins of the world. I take the position that His literal blood is in heaven. Let me confirm that with Hebrews 9:23–24 which says: "It was therefore necessary that the patterns of things in the heavens should be purified with these; but the heavenly things themselves with better sacrifices than these. For Christ is not entered into the holy places made with hands, which are the figures of the true; but into heaven itself, now to appear in the presence of God for us."

The souls mentioned here are the Old Testament saints. As the Lord Jesus put it: "That the blood of all the prophets, which was shed from the foundation of the world, may be required of this generation; From the blood of Abel unto the blood of Zacharias, which perished between the altar and the temple: verily I say unto you, It shall be required of this generation" (Luke 11:50–51).

Included with these are those who will be slain in the Great Tribulation Period, as we have already found that one-fourth of the population will be wiped out. They are resting on solid Old Testament ground as they plead for justice on the basis of God's holy law.

And white robes were given unto every one of them; and it was said unto them, that they should rest yet for a little season, until their fellow-servants also and their brethren, that should be killed as

they were, should be fulfilled [Rev. 6:11].

My translation of this verse is:

And there was given to them to each one a white robe; and it was said to them, that they should rest (in peace) yet for a little time until their fellow servants also, and their brethren who should be killed even as they were, should be fulfilled.

In other words, the tribulation saints are to be included with the Old Testament saints in the second resurrection.

OPENING OF THE SIXTH SEAL—THE DAY OF WRATH HAS COME

And I beheld when he had opened the sixth seal, and, lo, there was a great earthquake; and the sun became black as sackcloth of hair, and the moon became as blood;

And the stars of heaven fell unto the earth, even as a fig tree casteth her untimely figs, when she is shaken of a mighty wind [Rev. 6:12–13].

And I saw when He opened the sixth seal, and there was a great earthquake; and the sun became black as sackcloth of hair, and the whole moon became as blood; and the stars of heaven fell into the earth, as a fig tree casteth her unripe figs when she is shaken of a great wind.

This is evidently the beginning of the last half of the Great Tribulation Period. The great day of His wrath is before us. The Great Tribulation opens and closes with these upheavals in the natural universe: (1) The beginning of the Tribulation (compare Joel 2:30–31 with Acts 2:20) and (2) the end of the Tribulation (see Joel 3:9–17; Isa. 13:9–13; 34:1–4; Matt. 24:29).

The fact that we are having an increase in earthquakes today is no fulfillment of this at all. This is to take place in the Great Tribulation Period. But the interesting thing is that in the past earthquakes have really destroyed a great deal of the population of this earth. Professor R. A. Daley, in his book *Our Mobile Earth*, has written this:

In the last 4,000 years earthquakes have caused the loss of 13,000,000 lives, and far the most awful earthshock is yet to come. "And there was a great earthquake, such as there was not since there were men upon the earth, so great an earthquake, so mighty; and the cities of the nations fell" (Rev. 16:18).

What a picture we have here! The earthquakes today are not a fulfillment. They merely show that it could happen as God's Word says it will.

And the heaven departed as a scroll when it is rolled together; and every mountain and island were moved out of their places [Rev. 6:14].

Here is my translation:

And the heaven was removed as a scroll when it is rolled up, and every mountain and island were moved out of their places.

I think that this verse is to be taken quite literally. We see the same thing in Nahum 1:5 and again in chapter 20, verse 11.

And the kings of the earth, and the great men, and the rich men, and the chief captains, and the mighty men, and every bondman, and every free man, hid themselves in the dens and in the rocks of the mountains;

And said to the mountains and rocks, Fall on us, and hide us from the face of him that sitteth on the throne, and from the wrath of the Lamb:

For the great day of his wrath is come; and who shall be able to stand? [Rev. 6:15–17].

And the kings of the earth and the princes, and the chief captains, and the rich, and the strong, and every bondman and free man hid themselves in the caves and rocks of the mountains. And they say to the mountains and to the rocks, Fall on us and hide us from the face of the One sitting on the throne, and from the wrath of the Lamb, for the Great Day of their wrath came, and who is able to stand?

There are those on the earth who are praying to the rocks and to the mountains to fall upon them, because they want to be hidden. Hidden from whom? From the wrath of the Lamb. This is the great day of the wrath of God.

"The wrath of the Lamb" is a paradoxical phrase. The wrath of God is the Day of the Lord, that day that is spoken of all the way through the Old Testament prophets, a day

that is coming upon the earth and is yet future. It is called here "the wrath of the Lamb"—that is a strange statement.

The Bible is filled with paradoxes, and I am sure that you have discovered that. A paradox is a proposition which is contrary to received opinion; that is, it is that which is seemingly contradictory. On the surface the assertion seems contradictory, but closer examination reveals it is factual. For example, here are several paradoxes. The farther an object goes from you, the larger it gets. That is not true, but it is true. When a balloon goes up, it gets smaller to the eye, but the balloon is getting larger all the time as the atmosphere gets thinner. Another paradox is that water flows uphill in Sequoia National Park. You may not believe that, but there are tons of water flowing uphill there. The Sequoia National Park is filled with giant redwood trees, and those redwoods are pulling up tons of water all the time. They call it osmosis, which is a scientific word which means they don't really know what is happening. A third paradox is that the closer you get to the sun, the hotter it is. But out in the Hawaiian Islands, a tropical climate, if you look up on the top of Mauna Kea, there is snow up there although it is closer to the sun than you are. May I say to you, there are a lot of paradoxes that are true.

Here we have "the wrath of the Lamb." The lamb is a familiar figure of Christ. Suppose a little lamb, which is noted for gentleness and meekness, did get angry? What then? It is like a tempest in a teapot. From the days of Abel to those of John the Baptist, the Lord Jesus is depicted as a lamb. The apostle John calls Him "the Lamb slain from the foundation of the world" (Rev. 13:8). In other words, God did not choose the lamb because it possessed characteristics of Christ, neither did He choose it for the sacrificial aspect. God *created* such an animal to represent Christ. Christ is the Lamb slain before the foundation of the world, before any lamb was ever created.

The Lord Jesus Christ has the qualities of a lamb. He was meek—"Come unto me, all ye that labour and are heavy laden, and I will give you rest. Take my yoke upon you, and learn of me; for I am meek and lowly in heart: and ye shall find rest unto your souls" (Matt. 11:28–29). He was gentle—". . . Suffer the little children to come unto me, and forbid them not: for of such is the kingdom of God" (Mark 10:14). He was harmless—You never see a sign saying, "Beware of the lamb." You see "Beware of the dog," but not of the lamb. He was humble—Christ washed the feet of His disciples. This is a tremendous thing. He is One whose life was marked by winsomeness. His life was like the perfume of a lovely and fragile flower. His coming was a doxology. His stay was a blessing. His departure was a benediction. Even the unbelieving world has been fascinated by His life. The lamb sets forth His sacrifice. Abraham said, ". . . God will provide himself a lamb . . ." (Gen. 22:8), and God *did* provide Himself a Lamb.

But what about "the wrath"? Wrath is strange and foreign even to the person of God, is it not? God loves the good. God hates the evil. He does not hate as you and I hate. He is not vindictive. God is righteous, God is holy, and He hates that which is contrary to Himself. He says that Jehovah is a man of war. He is strong and mighty. He is mighty in battle. The gospel reveals the wrath of God. Paul said, "For the wrath of God is revealed from heaven against all ungodliness and unrighteousness of men, who hold the truth in unrighteousness" (Rom. 1:18). Look at this world we are in, my friend. It already reveals the wrath of God, the judgment of God.

It is like mixing fire and water to bring wrath and the Lamb together, but all the fury of the wrath of God is revealed in the Lamb. When the Lord Jesus was on earth, He made a scourge of small cords, and He drove the moneychangers out of the temple. Was He bluffing? He was not. He called the religious rulers a generation of vipers, whited sepulchres. He cursed the fig tree. He said, "Woe unto thee, Chorazin and Bethsaida" (see Matt. 11:21). Christ rejected Jerusalem, but He had tears in His eyes when He did so. He still controls the forces of nature, and He uses them in judgment. God has declared war against sin. I say, Blessed be His name. He will not compromise with that which has brought such havoc to the human family! There is a day coming when the wrath of the Lamb will be revealed. Somebody says, "I thought He was gentle and would not punish sin." My friend, God said, "Be wise now therefore, O ye kings: be instructed, ye judges of the earth. Serve the LORD with fear, and rejoice with trembling. Kiss the Son, lest he be angry, and ye perish from the way, when his wrath is kindled but a little. Blessed are all they that put their trust in him" (Ps. 2:10–12).

CHAPTER 7

THEME: *God seals a remnant of Israel and saves a redeemed company of Gentiles*

The Book of Revelation has been labeled a book difficult to understand. Some folk say that it is just a mumbo jumbo of a great many visions which are out of this world and which no one can understand. It is my conviction that this book is very logical and is divided in a very simple manner which no one can miss. If we get bogged down in some passage and try to take symbols and juggle them to fit into any system that we might choose, then we are going to be in real trouble. Rather, we should just let John tell us where we are as we go along. We are now in a section that the Lord Jesus labeled the Great Tribulation. This period takes place after the church leaves the earth, after the church concludes its mission and is taken to be with the Lord. I think that this is not only a reasonable conclusion, but I personally feel it is very clear, not only here, but elsewhere in Scripture.

Peter said that ". . . no prophecy of the scripture is of any private interpretation" (2 Pet. 1:20). In other words, you cannot lift out just one verse here or there or even consider only the Book of Revelation and expect to interpret accurately the whole of prophecy. It is essential to recognize that the Book of Revelation happens to be the last book of the Bible. When you are studying arithmetic in school, you begin with "two plus two equals four." You do not start the little ones in first grade with atomic physics or with higher mathematics. Since this book is the last book of the Bible, the only requirement is to have a working knowledge of the sixty-five books which go before. Then you will find that this book makes a great deal of sense and is quite logical.

John is going into detail now concerning the Great Tribulation Period, a period that has not been elaborated upon in any other place in Scripture except in the Olivet Discourse which the Lord Jesus gave (see Matt. 24–25). John is merely widening that out and giving us additional information. What he says is based on what the Lord Jesus had to say.

In chapter 6 we saw the opening of the seven seals; actually, we have had the opening of only six seals so far. These six seals revealed the four great tragedies that are coming upon the earth, the beginning of the judgments. The fifth seal let us look at a martyred company of people, a great throng. In the sixth seal we were introduced to some of the signs of the doom that is to come upon a godless world in the Great Tribulation Period.

In this period the church is never mentioned by name. The reason it is never mentioned by name is because John is recording things on earth, and at this particular time the church is not on earth. John was told to write the things he had seen, and he saw the vision of the glorified Christ. Then he was to write about "the things which are." He was in the church period, and we are still in it today. Since the church is still in the world, we are in the period of "the things which are." The church was the theme of chapters 2–3: the church in Ephesus, the church in Smyrna, the church in Pergamum, the church in Thyatira, etc. But in the chapter before us there is no talking to the church because the church is not here on earth. We saw in chapters 4–5 that the church was in heaven—that is where the church will go at the time of the Rapture. I will deal later with the reason why the church cannot go through the Great Tribulation Period. There is actually a moral and a theological problem if the church were to enter even one phase of the Tribulation Period.

The subject, therefore, has changed, and we are now talking about things other than the church. We have been introduced to a book with seven seals, and the seals are being removed. Six seals have been removed in the previous chapter. The four horsemen introduce the Great Tribulation Period, and the seven seals give an overall picture of that seven-year period. The last of the seals bears down on the last three and one-half years of the Great Tribulation Period. At this point, one-fourth of the population of the earth has been destroyed in judgment, destroyed in death. I am sure that anyone reading Revelation senses the fact that it is going to be very difficult to make it through this period—especially for those who turn to God, accept Christ, and stand for Him. The question is: Will believers be able to stand for Him during this period?

John is now going to put down another principle which he will follow because he knows that you and I are going to have trouble with the Revelation. Therefore he has made it very simple for us. He introduces series of sevens, but the way that he deals with them is the important thing for us to see. A format is followed from the breaking of the seals to the bowls of wrath. Between the sixth and seventh of each, there is an interlude of seemingly extraneous matter, but it is explanatory matter—it explains the action and answers certain questions. This is what chapter 7 will do for us. This principle of an explanatory interval will be true of the seven trumpets, of the seven performers and of the seven bowls of wrath. You will find John following this principle all the way through this particular section of Revelation, so that we do not lose our way.

We need now to deal with the question that any reasonable person would raise at this point: What about people turning to God and getting saved during this period? Second Thessalonians makes it clear that the Holy Spirit, the Restrainer, is removed from the earth (see 2 Thess. 2:7). He has taken the church to present it to Christ. Since you cannot have any turning to God without the work of the Holy Spirit, will anybody get saved without the Holy Spirit being present on the earth?

My friend, the Holy Spirit will be present. I did not say that the Holy Spirit will have left the world but that He no longer will restrain evil. The Holy Spirit came on the Day of Pentecost to perform a specific ministry of calling out a body of believers in the church which is referred to as the body of Christ. When the church is removed from the earth, that peculiar ministry of the Holy Spirit will end. One of His ministries in this particular era has been that of restraining evil. It was absolutely essential that He be a restrainer in order for the gospel to penetrate a Satan-controlled and Satan-blinded world. How could the Word go out unless the Spirit of God held back evil? Just think of the forces of evil that are working against the getting out of the Word of God today. In my own experience with our Bible-teaching radio ministry, we just sailed along like a breeze for a year or two. Then problems came along. I became ill, and all sorts of things took place. When we finally regained our equilibrium and began to look around, we saw what was happening: the enemy was busy. Believe me, if the Restrainer had not been at work, I am sure that we would have been removed from the scene.

How are people going to get saved during the period of the Great Tribulation if the Holy Spirit will not be restraining evil? The Great Tribulation is the Devil's holiday. That is the day when he is going to have freedom to do as he pleases. We will see why God is going to grant that: it is a period of the judgment of God upon a Christ-rejecting world. Then, does anybody get saved in the Great Tribulation Period? My friend, I believe that there will be a greater company saved in that period than in any other seven-year period in the history of the world. Chapter 7 is going to tell us how that will take place. The Holy Spirit is in the world after the church is removed just as He was in the world before Pentecost. In reading the Old Testament, you will find the Spirit of God working in the hearts and lives of men and women. Many multitudes were brought to God, but He was not restraining evil in the world, and He was not baptizing believers into the body of the church in the Old Testament. That is what He is doing today, but that ministry will cease. However, He will still be in the business of getting men and women to Christ. He will continue His ministry which has always been one of taking God's creation and renovating it. We are told in the beginning, ". . . the spirit of God moved [brooded] upon the face of the waters" (Gen. 1:2). The Spirit of God broods over this earth today and has from the very beginning and will continue doing so after the church is removed from the earth. He will have to have an unusual, special program during this period, and John is now going to tell us what that program is going to be.

REASON FOR THE INTERLUDE

The reason for the interlude between the sixth and seventh seals is given to us in the first three verses of this chapter.

And after these things I saw four angels standing on the four corners of the earth, holding the four winds of the earth, that the wind should not blow on the earth, nor on the sea, nor on any tree [Rev. 7:1].

I give my own translation simply in an attempt to give the literal words and try to say what John was saying:

After this I saw four angels standing on the four corners of the earth, holding firmly the four winds of the earth, that no wind might blow on the earth nor on the sea, nor on any tree.

"After this" refers to the tremendous judgment of the previous chapter, the riding of the four horsemen. In the riding of the four horsemen I believe we have been given a bird's-eye view of the Great Tribulation Period, an overall picture, and now the details are going to be given to us.

"After this I saw four angels standing on the four corners of the earth." A smart-alecky young fellow got up at a meeting years ago where Dr. Harry Ironside was speaking and said: "I told you the Bible was unscientific! The Bible teaches that the earth is flat because it says 'the four corners of the earth.'" Dr. Ironside replied, "Young man, I am amazed that you didn't know that the earth has four corners. They are North, East, South, and West." Those are the four corners, and that is the direction of the four angels. There is one in the North, the East, the South, and the West.

"Holding firmly the four winds of the earth, that no wind might blow on the earth, nor on the sea, nor on any tree." These would be the winds of judgment. God uses wind in judgment, and He controls the wind. Psalm 148:8 says, "Fire, and hail; snow, and vapours; stormy wind fulfilling his word."

The winds of judgment are now to be held back. Nothing can move until God accomplishes His purpose. What is His purpose going to be? I do not think that God would permit any period to continue on this earth in which there were not some of the human family turning to God, because that is His purpose. I do not think He would continue to keep this world running; I think He would shut it down, turn it off, and speak it out of existence if there were not folk turning to Him. Therefore, this will be a period when multitudes will turn to Him.

A great company is going to be saved, and this reveals that these judgments will accomplish a purpose for God. It will cause multitudes to turn to Him in this period, and it will cause another multitude to turn against Him. It is just like the effect of the sun shining down on a piece of soft clay. What will the sun do to the clay? It will harden it. What would be the effect of that same sunlight upon wax? It would melt it. The sun has the opposite effect upon clay and wax. The judgments of God are the same. In our lives as believers, when trouble comes to us—I've discovered this in my own life—it will either draw us to

God or drive us from Him. We need to be drawn to Him, and that is the reason the Lord lets some of us have sicknesses. He wants to draw us closer to Himself, and this is His way of doing it.

We cannot explain every little detail here in this chapter—at least, *I* cannot. I get a little irritated and provoked that I do not know as much as some of these so-called prophetic teachers claim to know today. They seem to have a private line in to the Lord. They now know the date when the Lord is coming again, and not only that, they can actually interpret some of these passages in the most amazing fashion. Where the Scriptures say that the blood during the war of Armageddon will be up to the bridle bits, some of these fellows can tell you the type of blood it is! They irritate me because I don't seem to be able to get that kind of information—and then I wonder what the value of it is when you get it. To begin with, the church ought to understand clearly that we have been delivered from going through this period. The Lord Jesus said, "Verily, verily, I say unto you, He that heareth my word, and believeth on him that sent me, hath [right now] everlasting [eternal] life, and shall not come into condemnation [judgment]; but is passed from death unto life" (John 5:24). The Great Tribulation is a judgment, and the church is not coming into it. He made it clear to the church of Philadelphia that He was going to deliver them from that hour. What hour? The hour that John is talking about right now. We need to let Scripture speak for itself.

And I saw another angel ascending from the east, having the seal of the living God: and he cried with a loud voice to the four angels, to whom it was given to hurt the earth and the sea,

Saying, Hurt not the earth, neither the sea, nor the trees, till we have sealed the servants of our God in their foreheads [Rev. 7:2–3].

Again, this is my translation:

And I saw another angel ascending from (the) sunrising, having (the) seal of (the) Living God, and he cried with a great voice to the four angels, to whom it had been given to hurt the earth and the sea, saying, Hurt not the earth, nor the sea, nor the trees, until we shall have sealed the servants (bond slaves) of our God, in their foreheads.

"Another angel" means this is a fifth angel. He is apparently of a higher rank than the other four because he gives them orders. As we see in the Book of Daniel and also in the Epistle to the Ephesians, there are gradations of orders of angels, both good and bad. Satan has the demon world well organized; he probably has generals, lieutenant colonels, majors, lieutenants, sergeants, and then a great many privates. On the other side, God also has His angels arranged. This angel gives orders to the other four.

"He cried with a great voice." In the Greek this is *phōne megale*. If you turn *phōne megale* around, you can see where we get our English word *megaphone*. *Megale* means "great"; *phōne* means "noise or voice."

This is an indication that frightful and fearful judgment is getting ready to break upon the earth, and it is therefore necessary to secure the servants of God. If He does not seal them, they are not going to make it through. However, they are going to be preserved in this day of wrath that is coming on the earth. The Lord Jesus Himself mentioned this in Matthew 24:21–22: "For then shall be great tribulation, such as was not since the beginning of the world to this time, no, nor ever shall be. And except those days should be shortened, there should no flesh be saved: but for the elect's sake those days shall be shortened." For the sake of these who have been sealed, this terrible time will be shortened.

What is the mark that is put upon their foreheads? Now here is a place where I must confess (I sure hope you won't let this get out) that I do not know the answer, and I can only make suggestions. There are many who know what the mark is, but the interesting thing is that you cannot get any two of them to agree as to what it is. I have come to the conclusion that they are all wrong. We are not told what it is, and I do not think it is important for the church to know what the mark is. We are simply told that they are going to be marked. We do know that there are those who will not be able to trade during this period when the Antichrist comes to power unless they have the mark of the Beast. This mark of God's is in contrast to the mark of the Beast. My feeling is that it is a spiritual mark that will be in their lives: ". . . by their fruits ye shall know them" (Matt. 7:20)—by their lives. I believe that is going to be the mark of God's own during this period because the godless are really going to be godless in this period. I personally don't see how they can be any more godless than the godless in the world today, but the Word of

God says they can go much farther than they have gone even in our day.

We now have this interlude before the seventh seal is opened. This angel is apparently more than a sergeant; he is probably a lieutenant colonel or a general. He says, "Hold everything! Hold back the winds of judgment, the winds of the Great Tribulation Period, because we have to seal these folk so they can make it through." There will be two great companies sealed, one out of the nation Israel and the other out of the Gentiles.

Where is the church? The church is not here; they are with Christ in, I believe, the New Jerusalem. He said that He was going to prepare a place for those who were His, and now that He has taken them off the earth, they are with Him. That city will come down from God a little later on in the Revelation, and we will get a look at it.

The reason, therefore, for the interlude between the sixth and seventh seals is to make sure that these sealed ones are going to make it through the Great Tribulation Period. The Lord Jesus made it very clear that they *are* going to make it through.

REMNANT OF ISRAEL SEALED

When God deals with Israel, I have always noticed that He deals with dates and He deals with numbers. When He is dealing with the church, He does not deal with either dates or numbers. Paul never turned in a report to anybody as to how many were saved. Even when we get to the great company of Gentiles who are saved in the Great Tribulation Period, the number is not given. When God deals with Israel, however, He deals with numbers and He deals with dates. The insistence of some Bible teachers to set dates for these prophetic events has hurt the study of prophecy and has brought it down to a low level, whereas this aspect ought to be kept on as high a level as any other subject of prophecy.

And I heard the number of them which were sealed: and there were sealed an hundred and forty and four thousand of all the tribes of the children of Israel [Rev. 7:4].

And I heard the number of those sealed, a hundred and forty and four thousand, sealed out of every tribe of the children of Israel.

One hundred forty-four thousand is the number sealed from the nation Israel, but we will see that out of the earth there will be a multi-

tude of Gentiles saved—too numerous to count. I notice that all the evangelists and preachers today are able to give you a count of the number saved in their meetings. In fact, some may give you a count that is a little bit larger than it really is. But here is one company of saved that they couldn't count.

Apparently, in the Great Tribulation there is going to be a great company who are to be saved. How are they going to be saved? They are going to be sealed. The Holy Spirit is going to be here, not only to regenerate them, but He will also have a special ministry of sealing in this period. The seal guarantees that they are going to be delivered. When you go down to the post office to register a letter, a postal clerk puts a stamp on it and puts a seal on it, and you pay a little extra for that. That seal means that the entire postal department is going to get behind that letter and see that it is delivered. They may be a little late in delivering it, but they guarantee that they are going to deliver it. That is what "sealed" means here. The Holy Spirit guarantees that they will make it through the Great Tribulation. If it weren't for the seal, they wouldn't make it through.

If you really want to know the truth, Vernon McGee would not make it through today if it weren't for the Holy Spirit. I wonder if you and I really realize how weak we are? I would deny Him before the sun went down if it wasn't for His work in me by the Spirit of God. We all have that nature which is in rebellion against God.

This company of the 144,000 can be identified without any speculation whatsoever. To me it is almost nonsense for any group to claim that they are the 144,000. Two cults did that in their beginnings, but then they passed 144,000 in membership. Apparently, they were not very optimistic when they started out. They say they take it literally, but they have a problem, now that they have passed that number. They should have gone out of business when they got to 144,000, but they didn't.

This number does not refer to any group in existence today, nor does it refer to the church. During the Great Tribulation, 144,000 are going to be saved "out of every tribe of the children of *Israel*." If you think that you are in the 144,000, you are not only saying that you belong to Israel, but you also had better know your tribe because the tribes are going to be identified.

It is very clear that God will have a remnant of His people who are going to be saved. This may seem to you like a big number, but actually, it is very small. There are over fourteen million Jews today in the world, and in comparison to that number, you can see that the remnant of the children of Israel is really going to be very small.

There is no use speculating here or trying to draw on symbols. Some even say that the number—144,000—is a symbol of another number. Cannot God say what He wants to say? Cannot He count? Certainly He can. If He says 144,000, I do not think He means 145,000. I think He means exactly 144,000.

"Out of every tribe of the children of Israel." From the day God called Abraham, there has always been a remnant that is true to God. There is a remnant today. I know many wonderful Christian Jews. I don't know why I say "Christian Jews" since I don't say Christian Americans or Christian Germans. But we do say this of Israel because of the fact that there is the remnant that trusts Christ in our day. It is not a large remnant, but there is not a very large remnant of Gentiles either. I suppose that the great minority group is that of real believers in Christ.

Paul says in Romans 9:8: "That is, They which are the children of the flesh, these are not the children of God: but the children of the promise are counted for the seed."

That is true today. Again Paul writes in Romans 11:4–5: "But what saith the answer of God unto him? I have reserved to myself seven thousand men, who have not bowed the knee to the image of Baal. Even so then at this present time also there is a remnant according to the election of grace." Paul said that in his day there was a remnant in the church. There is a remnant in our day in the church. During the Great Tribulation there will be a remnant, and the number is 144,000.

These are the ones who are going to witness of Christ in the Great Tribulation Period. In Matthew 24:14, speaking of this period, the Lord Jesus said: "And this gospel of the kingdom shall be preached in all the world for a witness unto all nations; and then shall the end come."

Some will say that the gospel of the kingdom is a different gospel. Of course, it is not. God has never had but one way to save sinners, and that is through the death of Christ. If you had asked Abel when he brought that little lamb to God, "Abel, do you think that little lamb will save you?" he would have said, "No, this little lamb is representing the One who God told my mother was coming from a woman to be the Savior of the world. This little lamb typifies Him." John the Baptist al-

most stepped out of character when he said, ". . . Behold the Lamb of God, which taketh away the sin of the world" (John 1:29). The gospel of the kingdom is the gospel of the death and burial and resurrection of Christ, which is going to alert the nation Israel, and many will turn to Christ. These will preach the gospel, but they will have something to add that we have no right to say today. They will say, "And then shall the end come." In other words, it is not going to be long until He will be back. We have no right to say that Christ will be returning soon, because we know neither the day nor the hour when He shall come.

Of the tribe of Juda were sealed twelve thousand. Of the tribe of Reuben were sealed twelve thousand. Of the tribe of Gad were sealed twelve thousand.

Of the tribe of Aser were sealed twelve thousand. Of the tribe of Nepthalim were sealed twelve thousand. Of the tribe of Manasses were sealed twelve thousand.

Of the tribe of Simeon were sealed twelve thousand. Of the tribe of Levi were sealed twelve thousand. Of the tribe of Issachar were sealed twelve thousand.

Of the tribe of Zabulon were sealed twelve thousand. Of the tribe of Joseph were sealed twelve thousand. Of the tribe of Benjamin were sealed twelve thousand [Rev. 7:5–8].

Here is my translation:

Of the tribe of Judah were sealed twelve thousand; of the tribe of Reuben twelve thousand; of the tribe of Gad twelve thousand, of the tribe of Asher twelve thousand; of the tribe of Naphtali twelve thousand; of the tribe of Manasseh twelve thousand; of the tribe of Simeon twelve thousand; of the tribe of Levi twelve thousand; of the tribe of Issachar twelve thousand; of the tribe of Zebulun twelve thousand; of the tribe of Joseph twelve thousand; of the tribe of Benjamin were sealed twelve thousand.

Twelve thousand are sealed out of each tribe. The 144,000 are divided by twelve, and one-twelfth is in each tribe, so that we know that John is talking about the children of Israel. I do not see how anyone can spiritualize this and attempt to appropriate it either to themselves or to some group other than the children of Israel. God promised, as we see again and again in the Old Testament, that He would come and establish His kingdom, which we will see is first a thousand-year kingdom, a time of testing, and then moves right into eternity.

We are given here the twelve tribes of Israel. One writer says that there are thirteen times in the Bible that the twelve tribes are listed, and another writer says that they are given eighteen times. I do not know which is accurate, but in every case where the twelve tribes are named, it is always *twelve* tribes. Sometimes changes are made, and I cannot always determine the reason for the changes, but I know that God had something in mind when He did it.

There are certain peculiarities in this list which I will call to your attention, but I don't think it is essential to go into detail concerning these twelve tribes. First of all, you will notice that Judah heads the list. The tribe of Reuben should come first, for Reuben was the oldest, but because of his very gross immorality, he lost the first place—but he is still included. The question often arises: When a Christian sins, does he lose his salvation? No, but he may lose his reward. Very frankly, there will be many Christians who are saved but who indulged in sin and will lose their reward. Reuben is a very good example of how God deals, and this principle is set down here. Reuben lost first place, he lost the place of honor, but he did not lose out altogether. He is mentioned here, but he is number two; he should have been number one. Judah was the tribe given preeminence (see Gen. 49:8–10) and was the tribe from which the Lord Jesus came.

We also find that the tribes of Dan and Ephraim are omitted from this list. Both of these tribes were guilty of leading the nation into idolatry.

In history you will find that Dan was the first tribe that fell into idolatry (see Jud. 18:30). The tribe of Dan later on became the headquarters for calf worship whereby "Jeroboam made Israel to sin" (see 1 Kings 12:28–30). That Dan is given top priority in the Millennium (see Ezek. 48) reveals that the grace of God can reach down and meet the needs of any sinner. The tribe of Dan is in the Millennium, but they are not sealed for the purpose of witnessing during the time of the Great Tribulation. I think that this tribe lost out a great deal.

Ephraim was also guilty of idolatry. In Hosea 4:17 we read, "Ephraim is joined to idols: let him alone." That has reference to the entire northern kingdom of Israel, but remember that Ephraim was the leader there. Also, Ephraim was the tribe which led in the division of the kingdom (see 1 Kings 11:26).

In the list of the 144,000 who will be sealed, Joseph takes the place of Ephraim, and to take the place of Dan is Levi. Levi was the priestly tribe, and they are going to be witnesses in the Great Tribulation Period, which is quite proper.

I trust that we can understand and see that God has now turned again to the nation of Israel. He has not given them up. He said, "How shall I give thee up, Ephraim? . . ." (Hos. 11:8). In other words God said, "I can't do it," and God didn't give them up. They are going to make it through the Great Tribulation Period even though they will lose out as witnesses for God during that period.

The Old Testament is filled with prophecy that God has given to these people that they are to be a nation forever and that they are to be in the land of Israel forever. If you come to the New Testament and write Israel off as having disappeared and that God is through with them, you have to contradict the whole tenor and tone of the Old Testament. I have said that the Book of Revelation is like a great union station or an airport where trains or planes come in from everywhere: all the major themes of prophecy come in to Revelation. Therefore, you would certainly expect Israel to be here in the Book of Revelation—and, lo and behold, here it is.

"Israel" means Israel. If God had wanted to call Israel the church, I think He would have just said "church" because He was able to say "church" when the time came. But now the church is not mentioned anymore, and He is talking about Israel and the 144,000 who are sealed to witness for Him.

The 144,000 are sealed, especially because they are going to witness during this period, and it is going to cost them a great deal. If they were not sealed, they sure wouldn't be able to make it through. God never leaves Himself without a witness upon this earth.

REDEEMED MULTITUDE OF GENTILES

After this I beheld, and, lo, a great multitude, which no man could number, of all nations, and kindreds, and people, and tongues, stood before the throne, and before the Lamb, clothed with white robes, and palms in their hands;

And cried with a loud voice, saying, Salvation to our God which sitteth upon the throne, and unto the Lamb [Rev. 7:9–10].

After these things I saw, and behold, a great multitude which no man could number, out of every nation and out of tribes, and peoples, and tongues, standing before the throne and before the Lamb arrayed (clothed) in white robes and palm branches in their hands; and they cry with a great voice saying, The salvation to our God, who sitteth on the throne and to the Lamb.

"**A**fter these things I saw." John is seeing as well as hearing these things.

"And behold, a great multitude which no man could number." Someone will say, "You mean to tell me that men couldn't count that crowd?" What it says is that no *one* man could number these—and it doesn't say anything about a computer. It says that no one man could number this crowd because it is such a large crowd. I wouldn't dare to venture any guess whatsoever, but the size of this multitude is obviously stupendous. It is not a one-man job to number them.

"Out of every nation and out of tribes, and peoples, and tongues." These are Gentiles, people from every tribe and nation under the sun. This means that in the Great Tribulation the gospel of the kingdom will be preached throughout the world. I want to repeat this: the 144,000 witnesses in the Great Tribulation Period are going to do in seven years what the church up to the present has not done in over nineteen hundred years. Do not boast about your missionary program. None of us are reaching very many. But, during the Great Tribulation, there will be a great company of people who will be saved.

It is my own private judgment—I don't think that Scripture says this anywhere, because nothing has yet to be fulfilled before the Lord removes the church—but it looks to me now as if He is going to let the world hear the gospel before the Rapture of the church. I believe that radio is one of the media that will be used. I think there are other media that will be used: the tape ministry, the printed page, and evangelism. Many evangelists are reaching multitudes of people today. Other radio programs are doing a much bigger job than we are doing, but if you put us all together, we are making quite an impact on this world in which we live.

"Standing before the throne and before the Lamb." Here is a great company who have come out of the Great Tribulation Period and are rejoicing in their salvation. They are redeemed and have made it through the Great Tribulation Period. Again may I say, the greatest days of God's salvation are in the future.

It is possible that most of this company were martyred during the Great Tribulation Period, but they were faithful to the end. The Lord Jesus said in the Olivet Discourse, speaking of this same period, "But he that shall endure unto the end, the same shall be saved" (Matt. 24:13). Did they endure to the end because they gritted their teeth, clenched their fists, and pulled themselves up by their bootstraps? No, they didn't do that at all—they were sealed by the Holy Spirit.

The "white robes" set before us the righteousness of Christ in which they are clothed. We cannot stand before God in our own righteousness because our own righteousness is as filthy rags, and I do not think you are going to wear filthy rags in the presence of God.

"Palm branches" is literally in the Greek "palm trees." They are the sign of victory, victory in Christ. This multitude is part of the great triumphal entry that will occur when Christ returns to the earth. The triumphal entry has really never taken place yet. That was actually more like a triumphal exit when He rode into Jerusalem on that little donkey, for He was getting ready to leave the earth, and He was on the way to the cross at that time. Since then, there has been a great company who have come to Him, and in the Great Tribulation there will be another great company. When He returns to the earth, the great company, martyred for Him in the Great Tribulation, will be included in the first resurrection, and they are going to be there. This is a wonderful, glorious picture that is given to us.

And all the angels stood round about the throne, and about the elders and the four beasts, and fell before the throne on their faces, and worshipped God,

Saying, Amen: Blessing, and glory, and wisdom, and thanksgiving, and honour, and power, and might, be unto our God for ever and ever. Amen [Rev. 7:11–12].

And all the angels were standing around the throne, and about the elders and the four living creatures; and they fell before the throne on their faces, and worshipped God, saying, Amen, blessing, and glory, and wisdom, and thanksgiving, and

*honor, and power, and might, be unto our
God for ever and ever. Amen.*

This is a fabulous, fantastic scene of universal worship of God by His creatures. The church is here, the Old Testament saints are here, and the tribulation saints are here. And now the angels join in on it.

There are just one or two things I would like to say about the angels. I do not want to labor the point, and I would not contend with anyone about it, but nowhere in Scripture does it say that angels sing. They are *saying* this here. However, the important thing to note is that the other companies thank God for their redemption, "Salvation to our God," but the angels do not mention it. They praise God for His attributes and goodness, but not for salvation. Why? They are sinless creatures, not redeemed sinners. I do not think the angels will be able to sing, but I do believe that Vernon McGee will be able to sing in that day. I cannot do it now, but I sure will be able to sing with that great company.

I hope that this will begin to broaden your vision and your comprehension as to what heaven is going to be. A great many people think that the only ones to be in heaven are their little group, their little church, or their little denomination. Well, my friend, there will be other redeemed people there besides even the church. I think that it will surprise a lot of the saints to discover this when they get to heaven. I wish that we could discover it down here because it would give us a greater love for God and lead us to worship Him more in a very real way, to worship Him in spirit and truth.

One of the elders now wants to bring John up to date on what is taking place:

And one of the elders answered, saying unto me, What are these which are arrayed in white robes? and whence came they?

And I said unto him, Sir, thou knowest. And he said to me, These are they which came out of great tribulation, and have washed their robes, and made them white in the blood of the Lamb [Rev. 7:13–14].

And one of the elders answered, saying unto me, These which are arrayed in the white robes, who are they, and whence came they? And I say unto him, My lord, thou knowest. And he said to me, These are they which came out of the great tribulation, and they washed their robes, and

made them white in the blood of the Lamb.

This is a very enlightening passage of Scripture. One of the elders went over to John and said, "John, who are these believers here arrayed in the white robes?" And John said, "My lord, thou knowest." This is an idiomatic expression, and I think we have one like it in our day. When someone asks us a question and we don't know the answer, we just sort of lift up our hands and say, "Search me!" which means, "I don't know!" This is exactly what John is saying here: "You know that I don't know. You tell me because I don't know."

"And he said to me, These are they which came out of great tribulation." If these people gathered here were the church, John would have known it. John wrote to the believers in his day. He knew about the church, he knew about the body of believers, and he wrote to them about love, that great unifying cement that holds them together. But John doesn't know who this company is. The elder, who is a representative of the church now in heaven, knows that this company is not the church. It is an altogether different company. It is those who came out of *the* Great Tribulation. Doesn't that tell you that the church is not going through the Great Tribulation? This is a special company, out of all tribes and tongues and nations, who have come out of the Great Tribulation.

We live in a day when God makes a division in the human family. One division is between the saved and the lost, of course—that is the great bifurcation of the human family. But if you want a racial division or a group division of the human family, the Word of God has something to say about it: "Give none offence, neither to the Jews, nor to the Gentiles, nor to the church of God" (1 Cor. 10:32). Paul says to the Corinthians that there are three groups— the Jews, the Gentiles, and the church of God—and they are not to give offense to any one of these groups. This is one of the divisions that the Scripture makes of the human family. The Jews, Gentiles, and the church of God comprise the division that runs right down through the human family today. In the Great Tribulation, we come to a period when there are but two groups: Jews and Gentiles. Where is the church of God? It went to be with Him. The Lord Jesus said, ". . . I go to prepare a place for you. And if I go and prepare a place for you, I will come again, and receive you unto myself . . ." (John 14:2–3). The church is with Him in heaven as we move through the Revelation. In 1 Corinthians 12:13 Paul says: "For by one Spirit are we all baptized into one body, whether we be Jews or Gentiles, whether we be bond or free; and have been all made to drink into one Spirit." God today is calling out of the two divisions, both Jews and Gentiles, a people for His name that are different—the church—and that church will be taken out of the world.

I do not like the impression given today by some—it is a pessimistic viewpoint—that somehow or another God is failing. My friend, God is doing exactly what He said He was going to do: that in this age He would call a people out of this world to Himself. He is doing a much better job at that than you and I think He is. When I was a pastor of a church, I did not think He was doing very much, but I have discovered as our radio ministry has reached out across this land and around the world that there are multitudes who are turning to Christ everywhere. And others are reporting the same thing. God is calling a people out of this world to Himself.

John makes it clear that this group he sees in heaven is different from the church. They came through *the* Great Tribulation. Let me remind you that it was the Lord Jesus Christ Himself who gave us the term, "great tribulation." Some may think that some rank, wild-haired fundamentalist thought of this term, but the Lord Jesus Christ is the One who thought of it and designated this period as the Great Tribulation. In Matthew 24:21 He says: "For then shall be great tribulation, such as was not since the beginning of the world to this time, no, nor ever shall be." Both in Matthew and in Revelation, it is expressed in the Greek in a way we cannot express in English. There is an article with the adjective *great* and an article with *tribulation;* it is "the tribulation, the great one." It is given to us like that for emphasis. In other words, this is something that is different; this is something that is indeed unique.

Let me repeat that when John is quizzed by one of the elders, he is unable to identify this great company. John would have known them if this were the church; or if they were Old Testament saints or Israelites, I think John would have known it. This company he does not recognize at all. They are identified as redeemed Gentiles who have come out of the Great Tribulation.

Their robes were white, which speaks of the righteousness of Christ. How did they get that righteousness? It is because Christ shed His blood. The only reason that you and I will be able to stand before God is because Christ paid the penalty for our sins. He died that you and I might live, and that is true of this group here also. It has always been true that God has only one way of saving mankind, and it is by faith in the death and resurrection of Jesus Christ. Paul wrote: "Moreover, brethren, I declare unto you the gospel which I preached unto you, which also ye have received, and wherein ye stand; By which also ye are saved, if ye keep in memory what I preached unto you, unless ye have believed in vain. For I delivered unto you first of all that which I also received, how that Christ died for our sins according to the scriptures; And that he was buried, and that he rose again the third day according to the scriptures" (1 Cor. 15:1–4). "For I delivered unto you first of all that which I also received." Paul says that this is not new with him. He did not originate it. It was given to him when the Lord Jesus taught him for two years out yonder in the Arabian desert.

Now this is the gospel: "How that Christ died for our sins according to the scriptures [according to the Old Testament]; And that he was buried, and that he rose again the third day according to the scriptures." The gospel is not God asking you to do something; it is God telling you that He has done something for you. The gospel is not your giving something to God; the gospel is God's giving something to you. The gift of God is eternal life in Christ Jesus. How do you get it? By faith. That is the only way you can receive a gift. Suppose it is Christmastime and you come to me and say, "Dr. McGee, here is a gift for you." Now what do I have to do to receive it? I could say to you, "I'll come and mow your lawn for you." But you would say, "I don't want you to mow my lawn. This is a *gift*." I would insult you if I tried to pay you for your gift. Suppose I offered you the few cents in my pocket in exchange for your gift—that would be an insult. My friend, the thing has gotten all mixed up today. The gospel is what God has done for us. It is His gift.

Again Paul writes in Ephesians 1:7: "In whom we have redemption through his blood, the forgiveness of sins, according to the riches of his grace." God has plenty of grace. It does not matter who you are, He can save you. You may think you are a dirty, mean sinner. Well, that is the only kind He saves—we are all that.

We have therefore this great company of Gentiles who are not part of the church. We need to enlarge our conception of the redeemed to the extent that it goes beyond the borders of the church and certainly beyond the borders of your little group or denomination or my little group.

Therefore are they before the throne of God, and serve him day and night in his temple: and he that sitteth on the throne shall dwell among them.

They shall hunger no more, neither thirst any more; neither shall the sun light on them, nor any heat.

For the Lamb which is in the midst of the throne shall feed them, and shall lead them unto living fountains of waters: and God shall wipe away all tears from their eyes [Rev. 7:15-17].

Therefore are they before the throne of God, and serve Him day and night in His temple (sanctuary); and He that sitteth on the throne shall spread His tabernacle (tent) over them. They shall hunger no more, neither thirst any more; neither shall the sun strike upon them, nor any heat (scorching wind): for the Lamb in the midst of the throne shall be their shepherd, and shall guide them into fountains of waters of life; and God shall wipe away every tear from their eyes.

"Therefore are they before the throne of God, and serve him day and night in his temple." We now know for sure that this is not the church, for the church is never identified with the temple. At the end of this book, when the church is in the New Jerusalem, there is no temple there. The church will never have a temple. There is going to be one here on the earth, but there is not one in heaven where the church is. Therefore, this could not be the church.

"And He that sitteth on the throne shall spread His tabernacle (tent) over them." This is for their protection, you see.

This company has had it; they have been through the Great Tribulation. Most of them, I believe, were martyrs and laid down their lives for Christ. Although we are not specifically told that, they are presented to us as being before the throne of God in heaven. The things that are mentioned now are things they have endured. They are not going to hunger or thirst—they apparently did. They have been out in the burning heat of the sun. They have also been thirsty for spiritual things which they did not have. And they wept, but now God will wipe away every tear from their eyes. They made it through the Great Tribulation because of the blood of the Lamb. This is a wonderful company of folk that is presented to us here.

My friend, the Lord Jesus has other sheep. He told His disciples, and it was hard for them to understand: "And other sheep I have, which are not of this fold" . . . (John 10:16). He could say the same thing to the church today, "I have other sheep that you do not know anything about." This company of Gentiles are some of the other sheep who will be redeemed but are not a part of the church.

CHAPTER 8

THEME: *Opening the seventh seal*

In chapter 8 we have the opening of the seventh seal which introduces the seven angels blowing seven trumpets. Four of the trumpets will be dealt with in this chapter. After the parenthetical matter of chapter 7, the sealing of two companies, we now have the opening of the seals resumed. Only the seventh seal remains to be opened. This is the pattern that John sets for the remainder of the Book of Revelation so that we cannot be led astray. There will be series of sevens and, in fact, there are four such series which relate to the Great Tribulation Period. John will give the first six of whatever the series is. Then he will present parenthetical material that contributes to the understanding of that particular series. Finally, the opening of the seventh of the series will introduce the next series of seven, which means that these series are interrelated, tied together, and actually belong to the same period.

There is no reason to get bogged down or to be sensational at this point. To begin with, we have said that everything from chapter 4 on is future—"the things that shall be after these things" (see Rev. 1:19). We are living in the things that are present, the church age, and in one sense these things do not concern us. Many people say, "Oh, it frightens me to study the Book of Revelation!" I will admit that, beginning with the riding of the four horsemen of the Apocalypse, these are terrible, terrific judgments that are coming on this earth. They are so tremendous that they boggle the mind just to read about them. But we can at least know where we are: these are things that will take place after the church has left the earth. If you are a child of God, you have been sealed by the Holy Spirit to be delivered to Christ when the church goes out of the world before the Great Tribulation Period. This is what is called "the blessed hope" of the church.

These seven trumpets will bring us to the full intensity of the Great Tribulation. The seven seals bring judgments which are the natural results of the activities of sinful man apart from God. The sixth seal brings the judgment of nature. The seven trumpets reveal that God is directly and supernaturally judging a rebellious race.

The seven seals, the seven trumpets, the seven personalities, and the seven vials or bowls of wrath all concern the same period, but from a little different angle. (1) In the seven seals we see the judgment which is the result of man's willful activity. The judgment of God will be coming upon sinful man. In the first seal we saw the riding of the white horse—a false peace; "For when they shall say, Peace and safety; then sudden destruction cometh upon them . . ." (1 Thess. 5:3). The second seal was the riding of the red horse of war. War comes because it is in the heart of man. A great many people think that if we took all the guns away from people, if there were no arms and no atom bombs, then we would have peace on the earth. My friend, war is in the heart of man, and you have to change the heart of man before you can get rid of war. Frankly, I would have more confidence in a real, born-again Christian who has a gun than an unsaved man who does not have a gun, because if he is unarmed, he can still choke his victim to death. We are seeing that murder is in the human heart. (2) In the seven trumpets, to which we are coming in this chapter, we see the judgment which is the direct activity of God. (3) When we come to the seven personalities, we will see the judgment which is the result of Satan's fight against God. Satan will be brought out in the open at that time. (4) In the seven bowls of wrath, we will see the final judgment of the Great Tribulation, which is the direct activity of God because of man's and Satan's rebellion—God will judge both, by the way.

As we come to this section in which symbols will be used, let us remember that a symbol is a symbol of a fact. We will find that there is a strange and strong similarity between the plagues of Egypt in Moses' day and the trumpet judgments. It is quite reasonable and logical to conclude that if the plagues of Moses were literal, then the plagues that are coming in the Great Tribulation Period are going to be literal. The symbols that are used are symbols of the reality which is coming. Plain language could not make it clear to our minds how terrible and tragic the Great Tribulation will be. It beggars description, and so God exhausts language and brings in symbols. It is well to keep in mind that this book is a revelation of Jesus Christ. We see Him now in a new role of Judge. The symbols that are used are not hazy and shadowy symbols which can be dissipated into thin air by some specious system of hermeneutics. When symbols are used—and they are used in this book—the key to their meaning is supplied. Scripture will furnish the explanation, and you do not need to draw upon your imagination.

The Book of Revelation is the last book in the Bible because a working knowledge of the sixty-five books preceding it is the basic requirement for an understanding of its vivid language. I get a little irritated when I see a new Christian immediately start teaching a class in the Book of Revelation. Why doesn't he go back to the beginning and start with Genesis? Take some other book, but do not *begin* with Revelation. I come to the teaching of Revelation only after having taken nearly five years to go through the rest of the Scriptures. I believe that gives us the right to teach the Book of Revelation; I would not want it otherwise. It was Peter who said, "Knowing this first, that no prophecy of the scripture is of any private interpretation" (2 Pet. 1:20). You do not interpret Revelation by itself; there are sixty-five books before it. The symbols are going to be given to us, but we need to remember that the symbols stand for awful realities.

The opening of the seventh seal introduces the seven trumpets, and that is the way this entire book is built. If the structure of the book is followed, it will prevent you from going off into fanaticism and sensationalism and, as a Christian, it certainly ought to keep you from saying, "The Book of Revelation is so frightful! It terrifies me!" It ought not to terrify you.

Actually, it ought to be a comfort to you. I thank God that He is going to judge this world that is running wild today. The way that mankind has blundered and gotten this world into a mess makes it look like it is filled with madmen. I thank God He is going to judge it, and He is going to judge it *rightly*. It is very comforting to recognize that.

People often urge me to speak out on my radio broadcast against certain things that are taking place. It is not my business to get on radio and denounce every wrong. My business is to give out just the Word of God, and that is what I am going to do. *He* is going to straighten this world out someday. I wouldn't have that job for anything in the world. I am glad it is His job. He is going to straighten out this world, and He is going to move in judgment.

Maybe you don't like the fact that the gentle Jesus is going to judge. We have already seen that the wrath of the Lamb will be terrifying to those on earth. My friend, when you talk about the gentle Jesus, you had better get acquainted with Him. He died for you, He loves you, and He wants to save you, but if you will not have Him, I tell you, there is waiting ahead of you a terrifying judgment. Someone will say to me, "You are trying to frighten people." I would like to scare you into heaven if I could, but I know you are too sophisticated and cynical for that. But, my beloved, *judgment is coming on this earth.* I say, Hallelujah! I am glad that it is coming and that God is not going to let the world go on like it is now. It has gone on long enough.

OPENING OF THE SEVENTH SEAL— INTRODUCTION OF SEVEN TRUMPETS

The first verse of this chapter describes what takes place as the seventh seal is opened.

And when he had opened the seventh seal, there was silence in heaven about the space of half an hour [Rev. 8:1].

Here is my translation of this verse:

And when (ever) He opened the seventh seal there came to pass a silence in heaven of about a half hour.

"There was silence in heaven about the space of half an hour." Many years ago I was speaking at a conference to about three or four hundred young people here in Southern California. I was out on the grounds of the camp, and coming toward me was a group of girls, and in the middle of them there was one boy.

It looked like the girls were going to take him apart, and they were making a great deal of noise about it. Finally, they came up to me, and the girls wanted me to hear what this fellow had said. He said to me, "Dr. McGee, did you know that there are not going to be any women in heaven?"

I said, "No, I didn't know that. Do you have Scripture for it?"

He said, "Yes. The Bible says that there is going to be silence in heaven for the space of half an hour. If there are any women there, there couldn't be any silence for that long!"

That young man was surrounded by a bunch of girls who were attempting to correct him on that particular interpretation, and frankly I agreed with the girls that that is not the meaning here at all. This verse does not mean that there are not going to be any women in heaven!

I probably did wrong to open this passage on that very light note, because here is a passage that has to do with great solemnity and great seriousness. The Lord Jesus Christ is still in command. He opens the seventh seal, and there is introduced a fanfare of seven trumpets. He directs the action now from heaven. We need to keep that before us through the entire book. Do not lose sight of the fact that Revelation presents Him in His glory as the Judge of all the earth.

It may deceive you to have Him presented as the gentle Jesus who went about doing good—which He did, but we are also going to see the *wrath* of the Lamb some day. The Lamb is the One of whom John the Baptist said, ". . . Behold the Lamb of God, which taketh away the sin of the world" (John 1:29). Men are not lost because they are sinners; they are lost because they have rejected Jesus who died for them. Even if you go into a lost eternity and have not accepted Christ, He died for you, and you simply made His sacrifice for you of no avail. You have trodden underfoot the blood of Christ when you take that kind of attitude and position toward Him.

This is a very solemn scene. The Lord Jesus Christ orders a halt on all fronts: heaven, hell, and earth. Nothing can move without His permission. He had already ordered the cessation of natural forces on the earth when He ordered the sealing and saving of two definite groups. Now, for a brief moment, there is a lull in judgment activity; there is a heavenly hush. Godet defined it: "This silence is a pause of action." It is the lull before the storm.

Why is there this strange silence? God's patience is not exhausted. When the sixth seal was opened and nature responded with a mighty convulsion, brave men weakened for a moment. Christ gave them opportunity to repent. But like the Pharaoh of old who, when the heat was taken off, let his willful heart return to its original intention, many men will go back to their blasphemous conduct when there is a calm. They probably will even rebuke themselves for showing a yellow streak. They will say, "It was only nature reacting. It wasn't God, after all. Everything can be explained by natural causes." This, my friend, is the lull before the storm. As someone has said, "The steps of God from mercy to judgment are always slow, reluctant, and measured." God is reluctant to judge for He is slow to anger. Judgment is His strange work. Isaiah writes: "For the LORD shall rise up as in mount Perazim, he shall be wroth as in the valley of Gibeon, that he may do his work, his strange work; and bring to pass his act, his strange act" (Isa. 28:21).

What is strange about God? That He judges, that He is a God of love, judging His creatures. "For I have no pleasure in the death of him that dieth, saith the Lord GOD . . ." (Ezek. 18:32). This silence marks the transition from grace to judgment. God is waiting. By the way, He is waiting for you today if you have not come to Him. You *can* come to Him, for He is a gracious Savior.

BLOWING OF THE SEVEN TRUMPETS

Judgment is getting ready to come upon the earth. This is the lull before the storm of judgment which is coming on the earth during this particular period. When I was a boy, my dad built a storm cellar wherever we moved. I spent half of my boyhood, during the spring and early summer, sleeping in the storm cellar. Late one evening my dad and I were standing in the storm cellar doorway. He was watching a storm come up, and he saw that it was not going to hit our little town in southern Oklahoma. It hit one just about ten miles away. We could see the funnel as it let down near that little town. But before that storm hit, there was a certain stillness. The wind had been blowing, the rain had been coming down, there had been a great deal of thunder and lightning, but suddenly all of that stopped, and for a few moments there was a deathlike silence. Then the wind began to blow like I've never seen it blow. It was not a funnel-shaped hurricane or a tornado, but just a straight wind. It was all my dad could do to get that storm cellar door down, and I helped him hold onto the chain. The storm broke in all

its fury. This is the way the Great Tribulation will break upon the earth, and it is presented to us in this way in the blowing of the trumpets, which is the subject of chapter 8, verse 2, through chapter 11.

ANGEL AT THE ALTAR WITH CENSER OF INCENSE

And I saw the seven angels which stood before God; and to them were given seven trumpets [Rev. 8:2].

And I saw the seven angels who stand before God, and there was given to them seven (war) trumpets.

These "seven angels" are introduced to us as a special group. I believe that Gabriel is in this group because we are told that he stood before God. When he announced the birth of John the Baptist to Zacharias, he said, ". . . I am Gabriel, that stand in the presence of God . . ." (Luke 1:19). The seraphim are also identified as beings who stand before God (see Isa. 6:1–2). However, these seven angels are seemingly a different order from the seraphim as their mission and service are altogether different.

"Seven trumpets" have a special meaning for Israel. I don't want you to miss this; I consider this all important. Here is where it is essential to have a knowledge of the Old Testament. In the Book of Numbers, Moses was given instructions by God for the making of two silver trumpets. Two was the number of witnesses. The Lord has said on several occasions that in the mouth of two witnesses a matter would be established. These two trumpets were used on the wilderness march in a twofold way. They were used for the calling of the assembly, and they were used to start the procession moving on the wilderness march. "Make thee two trumpets of silver; of a whole piece shalt thou make them: that thou mayest use them for the calling of the assembly, and for the journeying of the camps" (Num. 10:2).

When Israel entered the land, the trumpets were used for two other purposes: "And if ye go to war in your land against the enemy that oppresseth you, then ye shall blow an alarm with the trumpets; and ye shall be remembered before the LORD your God, and ye shall be saved from your enemies. Also in the day of your gladness, and in your solemn days, and in the beginnings of your months, ye shall blow with the trumpets over your burnt offerings, and over the sacrifices of your peace offerings; that they may be to you for a memorial before your God: I am the LORD your God" (Num. 10:9–10).

A single trumpet was blown on the wilderness march to assemble the princes: "And if they blow but with one trumpet, then the princes, which are heads of the thousands of Israel, shall gather themselves unto thee" (Num. 10:4).

This single trumpet is, to my judgment, that which corresponds to "the last trump" which Paul mentions in 1 Corinthians 15. This trumpet was for the bringing together of a certain group out of Israel. Paul writes: "Behold, I shew you a mystery; We shall not all sleep, but we shall all be changed, In a moment, in the twinkling of an eye, at the last trump: for the trumpet shall sound, and the dead shall be raised incorruptible, and we shall be changed" (1 Cor. 15:51–52).

Unfortunately, there are some who assume that "the last trump" of 1 Corinthians 15 is the seventh trumpet of Revelation—there is no relation at all. Listen again to Paul: "For the Lord himself shall descend from heaven with a shout, with the voice of the archangel, and with the trump of God: and the dead in Christ shall rise first" (1 Thess. 4:16).

The "shout" is the voice of the Lord Jesus. "The voice of the archangel" means that His voice is *like* that of an archangel. "The trump of God" is still His voice—His voice will sound like a trumpet. We see that from chapter 1, verse 10, where John says that he heard a voice like the sound of a trumpet, and he turned to see the glorified Christ. The glorified Christ is going to call His own out of the earth. When Paul speaks of "the last trump"— "the trumpet shall sound, and the dead shall be raised"—he means the call of the Lord Jesus. It is the last call that He makes to the church, and it is therefore called "the last trump." But the Old Testament type of it is the calling of the princes from out of the children of Israel. One trumpet is blown, and it has no relation to the movement of the children of Israel on the wilderness march.

However, the trumpets did sound an alarm which moved Israel on the wilderness march, and an alarm was sounded to move each division. The tribes were divided into four groups of three tribes each which camped on the four sides of the tabernacle. In addition there were three separate families of Levi who carried the articles of furniture of the tabernacle: Kohath, Gershon, and Merari. Four and three make *seven*. There were seven blowings of the trumpets to move Israel out. When the first trumpet was blown, the ark moved out with the Kohathites carrying it. Then the tribe of Judah moved out with the two other tribes under the banner of Judah, and so on until they were all on the march. Every man knew his place and stayed in his station. There was no disorder in the camp of Israel whatsoever. (The apostle Paul says that everything is to be done decently and in order in the church. I wish the church were as orderly as Israel was on the wilderness march.) But note particularly that it took *seven trumpets* to move them out.

The seven trumpets of Revelation will likewise have the positive effect of moving Israel into the land of Palestine. I believe that it will take these seven trumpets to get all of Israel back into that land. This is another reason I do not believe their present return to the land is a fulfillment of prophecy. Rather, it will be fulfilled in the Great Tribulation with the blowing of the seven trumpets as they were on the wilderness march. After the seventh trumpet, Israel is identified for us in chapter 12 as the special object of God's protection. An understanding of the trumpets, therefore, will prevent us from identifying "the last trump" of the church with the seven trumpets of Revelation.

As the trumpets of Israel were used at the battle of Jericho, so the walls of this world's opposition to God will crumble and fall during the Great Tribulation. When the Lord Jesus comes, He will put down the last vestige of rebellion against Himself and against God and establish His kingdom here upon this earth. This is a book of triumph and of victory for our God. At the end it has the Hallelujah chorus, and maybe you and I can sing it when we get there!

And another angel came and stood at the altar, having a golden censer; and there was given unto him much incense, that he should offer it with the prayers of all saints upon the golden altar which was before the throne [Rev. 8:3].

And another angel came and stood over [Gr.: epi] the altar, having a golden censer (bowl); and there was given unto him much incense, that he should add it unto (give it unto) the prayers of all the saints upon the golden altar which was before the throne.

"Another angel" is positively not Christ. The Lord Jesus Christ is no longer in the position of intercessor for the church. We saw in chapters 4–5 that He moved away from that position and was given the seven-sealed book. He is in charge of everything that happens from there on in Revelation. He is not moving as one of the actors down on earth's stage; He is in heaven with the church, and He is not the intercessor. He is now in the place of judgment. He holds the book of the seven seals, and He directs all the activities from the throne. This angel is, as it is stated here, just "another angel." I do not think the Lord Jesus would be identified as that. Although it is true that in the Old Testament the preincarnate Christ appeared as an angel, I do not believe He will ever appear again as an angel. He will be as He is in the glorified body, and we will see Him as He is someday.

The "golden altar" is the place where prayer is offered. Christ is not in the place of intercession before the golden altar. He is now upon the throne. Incense is likened unto prayer and is a type of prayer. David said in Psalm 141:2, "Let my prayer be set forth before thee as incense. . . ."

Incense speaks of the value of Christ's name and work in prayer. "If you ask in My name" is His injunction. Many today who really believe the Word of God are falling into the habit of ending their prayer by just saying "Amen." Someone said to me, "It is redundant to say, 'In Jesus' name,' because in your heart you are praying in Jesus' name." I agree that to pray in Jesus' name means more than simply putting on a tag end, "in Jesus' name." But I want to say that if you are making a prayer in Jesus' name, and especially a public prayer, be sure to say that it is in Jesus' name. I believe that is very important. Here they are offering incense, a sweet smelling incense. You and I are not heard for our much speaking or for our flowery prayer. We are heard when our prayer is made in Jesus' name.

It is interesting that the incense was given to this angel. Christ didn't need anything given to Him when He prayed. The prayers of saints which were offered under the fifth seal (see Rev. 6:9–11) are now being answered because of the person and sacrifice of Christ.

And the smoke of the incense, which came with the prayers of the saints, ascended up before God out of the angel's hand [Rev. 8:4].

And the smoke of the incense, with the prayers of the saints, went up before God out of the angel's hand.

Prayer is going to be answered because of Christ.

And the angel took the censer, and filled it with fire of the altar, and cast it into the earth: and there were voices, and thunderings, and lightnings, and an earthquake [Rev. 8:5].

And the angel hath taken (takes) the censer, and filled it with the fire of the altar, and he throws (casts) it upon (into) the earth: and there were (came to pass) thunders, and voices, and lightnings, and an earthquake.

The high priest of Israel took a censer with him as he carried the blood into the Holy of Holies. Here the ritual is reversed, because out of heaven the censer is hurled upon the earth. In other words, the prayers ascended as incense, and now we have the answer coming down. The tribulation saints had prayed, "Oh, God, avenge us!" The people of the earth, having rejected the death of Christ for the judgment of their sins, must now bear the judgment for their own sins. The Great Tribulation is going to get under way.

"Thunders" denotes the approach of the coming storm of God's judgment.

"Voices" reveals that this is the intelligent direction of God and not the purposeless working of natural forces. God is in charge.

"Lightnings" follow the thunder. This is not a reversal of the natural order. We see the lightning before we hear the thunder due to the fact that light waves move faster than sound waves. Actually, the thunder comes first, but we do not hear it until after we have already seen the lightning.

The "earthquake" is the earth's response to the severe pressure which will be placed upon it during the judgment of the Great Tribulation Period.

And the seven angels which had the seven trumpets prepared themselves to sound [Rev. 8:6].

And the seven angels having the seven trumpets prepared themselves that they should blow the trumpets.

This is a solemn moment. The half hour of silence is over. The prayers of the saints have been heard. The order is issued to prepare to blow. The angels come to attention, and at the blowing of the trumpets, divine wrath is visited upon rebellious men. The blowing of the trumpets does not introduce *symbols* or *secrets*. The plagues here are *literal* plagues. This method today of evaporating the meaning of Scripture by calling it symbolic is just as bad as denying the inspiration of the Word of God. In other words, it is saying that God doesn't mean what He says but that He means something else altogether.

FIRST TRUMPET—TREES BURN

The first angel sounded, and there followed hail and fire mingled with blood, and they were cast upon the earth: and the third part of trees was burnt up, and all green grass was burnt up [Rev. 8:7].

And the first angel blew the trumpet, and there followed hail and fire, mingled in blood, and they were cast into the earth and the third part of the earth was burnt up, and the third part of the trees was burnt up, and all the green grass was burnt up.

This is a direct judgment from God. Judgment falls upon plant life, from the grass to the great trees. Every form of botanical life is affected first. Notice, however, that it is only one-third, but it makes a tremendous impact upon the earth. Fire, the great enemy, is the instrument God uses. The Flood was used in the first global judgment; now it is going to be fire. This earth is to be purified by fire. The forests and the prairies covered with grass are partially destroyed by fire. One-third of the earth denotes the wide extent of the damage. "One-third" means not one-fourth or one-half; it means one-third. Plant life was the first to be created, and it is the first to be destroyed. In the record given in Genesis 1:11, God began with the creation of plant life after order had been brought into the physical globe.

This is a *literal* judgment upon plant life in the same way that the seventh plague of Egypt was literal (see Exod. 9:18–26). I called attention before to the fact that there is a striking similarity between the plagues in Egypt and the trumpet judgments—this is no accident. If you go back to the Book of Exodus, you will see that the plagues are literal—every believer in the Bible has to grant that; then you must also grant that these plagues in Revelation should be taken in the same fashion. I do not know by what flip-flop method of hermeneutics you could interpret one way in one passage and another way in another passage—unless the Scripture makes it clear that you can do such a thing. When hail came down on Egypt, we are told that ". . . the hail smote every herb of the field, and brake every tree of the field" (Exod. 9:25)—it was 100 percent

destruction in Egypt; it will be one-third of the earth.

SECOND TRUMPET—SEAS BECOME BLOOD

And the second angel sounded, and as it were a great mountain burning with fire was cast into the sea: and the third part of the sea became blood;

And the third part of the creatures which were in the sea, and had life, died; and the third part of the ships were destroyed [Rev. 8:8–9].

And the second angel sounded (blew the trumpet), and as it were a great mountain burning with fire was thrown (cast) into the sea, and the third of the sea became blood; and there died the third of the creatures which were in the sea, (even) they that have life. And the third of the ships was destroyed.

The sea, which occupies most of the earth's surface, is next affected by this direct judgment of God. The separation of the land and the sea occurred on the same day in which plant life appeared (see Gen. 1:9–10).

I want you to notice the exact language used here. John does not say that a burning mountain was cast into the sea but rather he indicates that a great mass or force "as it were a great mountain burning with fire was [*thrown*] cast into the sea"—*as it were* a great mountain. This careful distinction in the use of language should be noted, especially since it is the common practice to lump together everything in Revelation and call it symbolic. You might think that it gets you out of a lot of trouble, but it gets you out of the frying pan into the fire, by the way.

The mountain represents something as literal and tangible as that which we have in Jeremiah 51:25 where the Lord is talking about Babylon: "Behold, I am against thee, O destroying mountain, saith the LORD, which destroyest all the earth: and I will stretch out mine hand upon thee, and roll thee down from the rocks, and will make thee a burnt mountain."

This literal mass falls into the literal sea, one-third becomes literal blood, and one-third of all the literal living creatures in the literal sea die a literal death. Nothing could be plainer than this. Also, one-third of the literal ships of all literal nations are literally destroyed. If we just let John say what he wants to, he makes it very clear.

There is no use to try to find some symbol. John doesn't say that this is symbolic. He makes it very clear that a great mass, a force, is put into the ocean. I do not know what this could possibly be, and there are two reasons for that. First of all, John didn't tell me; he didn't tell anybody, and therefore, I do not think that anyone has the answer. The second reason is that I don't expect to be here at that time to be reading the evening papers. The bad news that we get in the papers and on television today will continue, only more so, during the Great Tribulation. I won't be here to see it. Therefore, this does not concern me too much, other than it is an awful tragedy that is coming on a Christ-rejecting world which actually ridicules the Word of God today. This is something that certainly makes the believer sorrowful in his heart—but it ought to do more than that. It not only ought to affect our hearts; it ought also to affect our wills and our feet to start us moving to get the Word of God out to the world. That is our responsibility, and I believe it is a very solemn responsibility. We cannot keep this judgment from coming on the earth, but we *can* get the Word of God out and reduce the population that will be left on the earth so that fewer people will go through that terrible time.

THIRD TRUMPET—FRESH WATERS BECOME BITTER

And the third angel sounded, and there fell a great star from heaven, burning as it were a lamp, and it fell upon the third part of the rivers, and upon the fountains of waters;

And the name of the star is called Wormwood: and the third part of the waters became wormwood; and many men died of the waters, because they were made bitter [Rev. 8:10–11].

And the third angel blew the trumpet (sounded), and a great star burning as a torch fell from (out of) heaven, and it fell upon the third part of the rivers, and upon the fountains of the waters; and the name of the star is called Wormwood [Gr.: Apsinthos]; and the third part of the waters became wormwood; and many men died of the waters, because they were made bitter.

We are living in a world today where a great deal is being said about pollution, and it is a real problem. Man seems to have gotten a head start on the star in polluting all the waters. Personally, I think that man is going to be forced to clean up the water of the world if he is going to be able to exist at all. Self-preservation is considered to be the first law of nature, and man wants to hang on to this little earth; so he's going to do something about it. In the Great Tribulation, the fresh water is polluted, and the drinking water for mankind is contaminated, that is, one-third of it is.

Those of us who live in Southern California know something of the scarcity of fresh water for drinking and domestic use. I am told that in Los Angeles it costs somewhere around $100 million just to turn on the spigot to get the water here to us. Fresh water is something that is essential for man and beast. I remember the drought of the '50s in Dallas, Texas. The city's water supply came from man-made lakes; the lakes dried up, and the supply was exhausted. It was necessary to get water from the Red River, but the oil companies had allowed salt water from their deep wells to drain into the river. Nobody worried about it until they needed the water for drinking. It was so salty, it was barely possible to drink it. Many people traveled to surrounding little towns to get a bottle of water to bring home. These experiences teach man how dependent he is upon fresh water.

When the children of Israel crossed over the Red Sea, they came to Marah where the waters were bitter. Moses was directed to take a tree and cast it into the waters to make them sweet. Here in Revelation, the sweet waters are made bitter by a meteor, a star out of heaven. The tree that Moses put into the water speaks of the cross of Christ.

"Wormwood" is a name used metaphorically in the Old Testament, according to Vincent (*Word Studies in the New Testament*, vol. 2, p. 506), in the following ways: (1) idolatry of Israel (see Deut. 29:18); (2) calamity and sorrow (see Jer. 9:15; 23:15; Lam. 3:15, 19); and (3) false judgment (see Amos 5:7).

This star is literal and is a meteor containing poison which contaminates one-third of the earth's fresh water supply. The star's name suggests that this is a judgment upon man for idolatry and injustice. Calamity and sorrow are the natural compensations that are coming upon man because of this judgment.

FOURTH TRUMPET—SUN, MOON, AND STARS SMITTEN

And the fourth angel sounded, and the third part of the sun was smitten, and the third part of the moon, and the

third part of the stars; so as the third part of them was darkened, and the day shone not for a third part of it, and the night likewise [Rev. 8:12].

And the fourth angel blew the trumpet (sounded), and the third part of the sun was smitten, and the third of the moon, and the third of the stars; in order that a third part of them might be darkened, and the day not shine for the third part of it, and the night in like manner.

Another phase of creation upon which mankind on this earth is solely dependent for light and life is the sun. To a lesser degree, man is dependent on the moon and stars. It was on the fourth day of re-creation that these heavenly bodies appeared. They had been created before, but the light broke through on the fourth day. Now the light is put out, as it were, over a third part of the earth. God let these lights break through, the greater light to rule the day, the lesser light to rule the night, and they were to be for signs and seasons. The Lord Jesus indicated that in the Great Tribulation there would be special signs in these heavenly bodies: "Immediately after the tribulation of those days shall the sun be darkened, and the moon shall not give her light, and the stars shall fall from heaven, and the powers of the heavens shall be shaken" (Matt. 24:29).

The laws of nature are radically altered by these disturbances. There is a definite limitation—only a third part of the light and of the day is affected. The intensity of the light has the wattage reduced by one-third. Talk about an energy shortage! Believe me, my friend, one is coming to this earth someday.

I saw an arresting billboard in Seattle, Washington, when Boeing had shut down many of its plants, laid off several thousand men, and people were beginning to leave town. On this billboard on Highway 5, some wag put this sign: "The last one leaving town, please turn out the lights." Well, God is getting ready to turn out the lights here on this earth. However, the Lord has made it clear, "While the earth remaineth, seedtime and harvest, cold and heat, and summer and winter, and day and night shall not cease" (Gen. 8:22).

A statement from Robert Govett (*The Apocalypse Expounded by Scripture*, p. 180) is intensely interesting in this connection, in view of present-day efforts to eliminate the death penalty:

Hence day continues still, though its brightness is diminished. God shows His right to call in question man's right to the covenant. He has not kept the terms. Blood for blood is not shed by the nations. By this time the command to put the murderer to death is, through a false philanthropy, refused by the world.

This is another angle to the question of capital punishment. These judges with soft heads as well as soft hearts eliminate capital punishment and turn the criminals loose on us in this world today. Man continues to move in that direction, but God says, "I gave you a covenant that you were to protect human life, and you are protecting human life when you execute murderers." Capital punishment is a deterrent to crime, and any person who says it is not a deterrent to crime must be like an ostrich with his head in the sand. I think that capital punishment will be abolished by Antichrist if it is not done so before.

And I beheld, and heard an angel flying through the midst of heaven, saying with a loud voice, Woe, woe, woe, to the inhabiters of the earth by reason of the other voices of the trumpet of the three angels, which are yet to sound! [Rev. 8:13].

And I saw and heard one eagle, flying in mid-heaven (the meridian), saying with a great voice [Gr.: phonē megale], Woe, woe, woe to them dwelling upon the earth, by reason of the remaining voices of the trumpet of the three angels who are about to blow the trumpet (sound).

When the fourth trumpet is blown, the announcement is made of a peculiar intensity of woe and judgment that is coming on the earth. The last three trumpets are separated from the other four; they are "woe" trumpets.

"And I saw and heard one eagle." Somebody says, "This eagle is *talking*! Is it a literal eagle?" My friend, if God can make a parrot and a few other birds talk, I do not think He will have any problem at all with an eagle.

It is interesting to note that our Lord used the eagle to speak of His coming: "For wheresoever the carcase is, there will the eagles be gathered together" (Matt. 24:28)—that is after the great Battle of Armageddon.

CHAPTER 9

THEME: The fifth and sixth trumpets

The last three trumpets are separated from the other four by the fact that they are three woe trumpets. My translation of chapter 8, verse 13, reads, "And I saw and heard one eagle, flying in midheaven, saying with a great voice, Woe, woe, woe to them dwelling upon the earth, by reason of the remaining voices of the trumpet of the three angels who are about to blow the trumpet." We are coming to a section that is weird and wild; it boggles the mind as we read through this chapter. All kinds of interpretations have been given of this section. But let us get our feet back on the ground, and we will find that the things mentioned here ought not to frighten us. If you are a child of God, you are not going through these things. It is not the "blessed hope" of the church to endure these things. The church will have been taken out of the world by this time, and these are the things which will happen in the Great Tribulation Period to a Christ-rejecting world.

These woes mark the deepest darkness and the most painful intensity of the Great Tribulation Period. They are generally associated with the last three and one-half years of the Seventieth Week of Daniel, which is the Great Tribulation Period. These will be the blackest days in human history.

The language used in this section is admittedly the most difficult of interpretation, but this does not preclude our policy of following the literal line, even when the figures adopted are the most vivid and wild. If another interpretation is proper, John will furnish us the key.

FIFTH TRUMPET—FALLEN STAR AND PLAGUE OF LOCUSTS

Here in verse 1 we have a description of the scene as the fifth angel sounds a trumpet and a star falls from heaven.

And the fifth angel sounded, and I saw a star fall from heaven unto the earth: and to him was given the key of the bottomless pit [Rev 9:1].

And the fifth angel sounded (blew the trumpet), and I saw a star out of heaven fallen into the earth, and there was given to him a key of the long shaft (pit, well) of the abyss.

Notice the proper meaning of "the bottomless pit" is the long shaft (or pit or well) of the abyss.

"I saw a star fall from heaven unto the earth." We have already seen two stars, and we said that they were literal stars, meteors, that fall to the earth. I recall several years ago sitting with my wife on a lanai of a hotel on Waikiki Beach and watching a shower of meteors or shooting stars. Meteors are the shooting stars which we see on a summer night. But here we have a different kind of star because it is called "him" and acts with intelligence. We are talking now about an unusual person. This star is different, therefore, from the stars mentioned at the sounding of the fourth trumpet. This star not only acts with intelligence, but he is given a key which he uses—no inanimate star could do this.

We believe that this star is Satan. Some have identified this star as Antichrist; if this is so, it lends support to the view that Antichrist is Satan incarnate, but I do not accept that. My point is that Antichrist is exactly that: he is everything Christ is not, and he is motivated by Satan. The reasons for interpreting this star as Satan are abundant. The prophet Isaiah writes: "How art thou fallen from heaven, O Lucifer, son of the morning! how art thou cut down to the ground, which didst weaken the nations!" (Isa. 14:12).

In Luke's Gospel we read: "And he [Jesus] said unto them, I beheld Satan as lightning fall from heaven" (Luke 10:18).

That would be like a fallen star, you see. Also, Paul writes: "And no marvel; for Satan himself is transformed into an angel of light" (2 Cor. 11:14). These Scriptures confirm the position that Satan is in view here. John will state later that Satan was put out of heaven and cast to the earth (see Rev. 12:7–9). If we have established the fact that the "star" is Satan being cast out of heaven, then what does he do? He goes down and takes the key to the abyss, which apparently means that God is permitting him to do so. A key denotes authority and power, and this is given to him of God; it is the permissive will of God.

"The long shaft of the abyss" means the long shaft leading to the abyss. The abyss is the bottomless pit which will be seen in chapter 20, verse 3. The abyss and hades may be synonymous terms, but the abyss and hell are not the same. Our Lord probably referred to the abyss in Matthew 12:40: "For as Jonas was three days and three nights in the whale's belly; so shall the Son of man be three days and three nights in the heart of the earth."

The Lord speaks here of His descent into the "heart of the earth." The body of Jesus was not actually buried in the earth—it was put in a new tomb—and it certainly was not in the *heart* of the earth. Rather, what we have in this language of Matthew is that He went to the abyss, which apparently is hades or sheol. When the Lord Jesus told about the deaths of the rich man and Lazarus (see Luke 16:19–31), He made it quite obvious that hades is in two compartments. The rich man died and went to the place of torment. The poor man died and went into Abraham's Bosom, or paradise as our Lord called it. The Lord went down there in His death to announce to the saved His victory and that He would be leading them into the presence of God. That is, I believe, what Paul meant when he said that the Lord Jesus ". . . led captivity captive . . ." (Eph. 4:8). He went to the abyss to announce that His redemption had been wrought.

It behooves us not to be dogmatic where the Scriptures are silent, but there is the thought that a shaft leads from the surface of the earth to the heart of the earth. I know that may sound very much like I am being superstitious. I do accept this idea, but I would not be dogmatic about it. If you have some advance information and can prove to me that it means something else, I would certainly be glad to accept it.

The Lord now holds the key to the abyss (see Rev. 1:18). Peter tells us the demons are imprisoned there (see 2 Pet. 2:4). In Luke 8:30–31 we read: "And Jesus asked him, saying, What is thy name? And he said, Legion: because many devils were entered into him. And they besought him that he would not command them to go out into the deep [abyss]."

The abyss is a very literal place. The idea that heaven and hell are mythological and that heaven is a beautiful isle of somewhere, a Shangri-la hanging out in space, is not the teaching of the Word of God. The teaching of the Word of God is that heaven is as literal as the place where you live today and that hell is equally as real as the place where you now live.

During the last part of the Great Tribulation, the key to the abyss is given to Satan, and he is given a freedom that he never has had before. I believe this explains why men cannot die during this period. Satan wants to

keep them alive; he does not want his army decimated at all.

And he opened the bottomless pit; and there arose a smoke out of the pit, as the smoke of a great furnace; and the sun and the air were darkened by reason of the smoke of the pit [Rev. 9:2].

And he opened the long shaft (pit, well) of the abyss, and there came smoke out of the long shaft of the abyss as the smoke of a great furnace; and the sun and the air were darkened from the smoke of the shaft of the abyss.

Out of the shaft, like a great erupting volcano, will come smoke to cover the entire earth. This is smog of the most vicious type. The literal interpretation of this verse is the correct and most satisfying one.

And there came out of the smoke locusts upon the earth: and unto them was given power, as the scorpions of the earth have power.

And it was commanded them that they should not hurt the grass of the earth, neither any green thing, neither any tree; but only those men which have not the seal of God in their foreheads [Rev. 9:3–4].

And out of the smoke came forth locusts upon the earth, and power was given to them as the scorpions of the earth have power. And it was said to them in order that they should not hurt the grass of the earth nor any green things, nor any tree, but only (except) the men who do not have the seal of God on their foreheads.

To me this beggars description. John uses symbolic language which describes creatures so frightful that this is the only way he could speak of them.

These are locusts, but they are of a very unusual character. As Govett remarks (*The Apocalypse Expounded by Scripture*, pp. 185–186), they are "no common locusts," and he gives the following reasons:

(1) for they eat no vegetable productions;
(2) the locusts of the earth have no king (Prov. 30:27); these have;
(3) in the plague of Egypt the inspired recorder had said, "Before them there were no such locusts as they, neither after them shall be such" (Exod. 10:14);
(4) yet they are literal creatures resem-

bling the literal animals named: the lion, the horse, the scorpion, the man.

This is a plague of locusts which is as literal as the plague of locusts in Egypt. Joel prophesied of a coming plague of locusts (see Joel 1). Again, a working knowledge of the Old Testament is essential to the understanding of Revelation. The difference between the locusts here and the locusts in Joel is the character of the locusts and the object of their destruction. They sting as scorpions, and their objects are evil men.

And to them it was given that they should not kill them, but that they should be tormented five months: and their torment was as the torment of a scorpion, when he striketh a man [Rev. 9:5].

And it was given to them in order that they should not kill them, but in order that they should be tormented five months; and their torment was as the torment of a scorpion, when it striketh a man.

The scorpion is shaped like a lobster and lives in damp places. His sting is in his tail; though it is not fatal, it is very painful indeed. This is the picture we are given here. These were mentioned by Joshua when he spoke of the hornet, "And I sent the hornet before you, which drave them out from before you . . ." (Josh. 24:12). Therefore you can see that believers, living during the Great Tribulation who will be acquainted with the Old Testament, will understand what John is talking about regarding these scorpions.

And in those days shall men seek death, and shall not find it; and shall desire to die, and death shall flee from them [Rev. 9:6].

And in those days shall the men seek death, and shall not find it; and they shall earnestly desire to die, and death fleeth from them.

Satan is given the key to this long shaft (which evidently is what is called sheol in the Old Testament and hell [hades] in the New Testament). The shaft leads to the abyss where the spirits of the dead of the ages past have gone. This is where the Lord Jesus went to announce the redemption that He had wrought on the cross. Satan does not want his crowd to die, and it is only his crowd that are attacked by these locusts. Men during this period try to

commit suicide and are unable to do it—this reveals something of the awfulness of that day. Satan wants them here because there is a battle between light and darkness that is being waged. There are others who think that maybe it is God who will not let these men die because sinful man must face the consequences of his rebellion—there is no escape. It is not a laughing matter to reject Jesus Christ; it is not a simple thing to ignore Him. People say there are so many important things in this life—and I am willing to grant that many things take second, third, and fourth place— but the most important thing is your decision concerning Jesus Christ.

And the shapes of the locusts were like unto horses prepared unto battle; and on their heads were as it were crowns like gold, and their faces were as the faces of men.

And they had hair as the hair of women, and their teeth were as the teeth of lions.

And they had breastplates, as it were breastplates of iron; and the sound of their wings was as the sound of chariots of many horses running to battle.

And they had tails like unto scorpions, and there were stings in their tails: and their power was to hurt men five months [Rev. 9:7–10].

And the likenesses of the locusts were like unto horses prepared for war; and on their heads were as it were crowns like gold, and their faces were as the faces of men. And they had hair as the hair of women, and their teeth were as the teeth of lions. And they had breastplates, as it were breastplates of iron; and the sound of their wings was as of chariots of many horses rushing into battle. And they had tails like scorpions, and stings; and in their tails was their power to hurt men five months.

I am sure you will agree that this is a frightful, weird, and unnatural description. A little closer examination, however, will reveal a striking similarity to the locusts of Palestine, which I think we need to note. Dr. Vincent makes this comment in his Book on Revelation:

The likeness of a locust to a horse, especially to a horse equipped with armor, is so striking that the insect is named in

German *Heupferd hay-horse*, and in Italian *cavaletta little horse*.

The faces of locusts resemble the faces of men, and the antennae of the locust are compared to a girl's hair. Joel compares the teeth of the locust with those of a lion (see Joel 1:6). Many have commented on the weird sound that the locust makes. In his *Word Studies in the New Testament*, Dr. Vincent quotes Olivier, a French writer:

It is difficult to express the effect produced on us by the sight of the whole atmosphere filled on all sides and to a great height by an innumerable quantity of these insects, whose flight was slow and uniform, and whose noise resembled that of rain.

There are those today who have attempted to liken this description of the locust to the airplane. I remember as a young fellow hearing a preacher who said that since the sting of the locust is in the tail, it compares to the rear gunner on a bomber! Well, that all sounds very good, but we have now passed from the propeller plane to the jet plane and into the missile age. Maybe you would want to compare these locusts to the missile. Seriously, I do not want to compare it to anything that is known today, because this is not the weapon that is used today but the weapon that is going to be used in the Great Tribulation Period—whatever that is going to be. Our weapons today are so frightful that even Russia and the United States (although they are at opposite poles) are willing to sit down and talk, as long as one thinks the other is as strong or stronger than he is.

"Their power was to hurt men five months." It will be five months of unspeakable agony for those who have been attacked by these unnatural locusts.

And they had a king over them, which is the angel of the bottomless pit, whose name in the Hebrew tongue is Abaddon, but in the Greek tongue hath his name Apollyon [Rev. 9:11].

They have over them (as) king, the angel of the abyss: his name in Hebrew is Abaddon, and in the Greek tongue he hath the name Apollyon.

These locusts are further differentiated from ordinary locusts in that they have a king over them. Proverbs 30:27 says of natural locusts

that they have no king. The king or leader of these locusts is probably one of the fallen angels, the chief henchman of Satan, and he is permitted to lead an invasion of earth for the first time. This is something that is going to be rather frightening. His name in Hebrew means "destruction," and in Greek it means "the destroyer." This confirms what Daniel told us, that the demon world of the fallen angels is divided into gradations. I think there are generals, majors, lieutenants, sergeants, and buck privates. In Ephesians we find that the angels of God are divided in the same way.

One woe is past; and, behold, there come two woes more hereafter [Rev. 9:12].

The one woe is past; behold there come yet two woes after these things.

The first woe introduced to us the last half of the Great Tribulation Period, and it had a duration of five months. Apparently, the last two woes will cover the remainder of that period. The warning here indicates that worse things are to follow, and the next trumpet reveals that this was not just an idle warning.

SIXTH TRUMPET—ANGELS LOOSED AT RIVER EUPHRATES

And the sixth angel sounded, and I heard a voice from the four horns of the golden altar which is before God,

Saying to the sixth angel which had the trumpet, Loose the four angels which are bound in the great river Euphrates [Rev. 9:13–14].

And the sixth angel blew (sounded) the trumpet. And I heard one (a single) voice out of the horns of the golden altar which is before God, saying to the sixth angel having the trumpet, loose the four angels which have been bound at the great river Euphrates.

When the sixth angel blew the trumpet, a command came from the horns of the golden altar. That golden altar speaks of prayer; that is what it spoke of in the tabernacle here on earth. This is where the angel offered prayer at the beginning of the blowing of the trumpets (see Rev. 8:3). The sixth angel not only blows the trumpet but is also given a command to loose the four angels bound at the river Euphrates. This angel receives in turn his orders from a voice that was there at the horns of the golden altar. It is the voice of

Christ. He has now ripped off the seventh seal which led into the trumpets and which will lead into the seven personalities and the seven bowls of wrath.

The angels who are bound are evidently evil. Why would they be bound if they were not evil? Releasing them turns loose a flood tide of destruction on the earth. They were bound away from the others, I believe, because of the enormity of their crime.

Why were they bound at this particular location at the Euphrates River? Though this is rather difficult to explain, the prominence of this area in Scripture cannot be overlooked. The Garden of Eden was somewhere in this section. The sin of man began here. The first murder was committed here. The first war was fought here. Here was where the Flood began and spread over the earth. Here is where the Tower of Babel was erected. To this area were brought the Israelites of the Babylonian captivity. Babylon was the fountainhead of idolatry. And here is the final surge of sin on the earth during the Great Tribulation Period.

The Euphrates actually marks the division between East and West. It was Kipling who said that East is East and West is West, and never the twain shall meet. That is true to a certain extent. Perhaps there has been a restraining influence in the past which has kept the hordes of the East from spilling over into the West, but it is going to be broken down. It was Napoleon who made the statement: "China is a sleeping giant, and God pity the generation that wakes her up." Well, we woke her up, and she is very much alive today. China represents one-fourth of the world's population. If you take the peoples of the East, of the Orient, beyond the Euphrates River, you have most of the population of the world. Suppose they start moving? My friend, they are going to move someday. From the time of Alexander the Great, the white man has had his day. Colonialism, as far as the white man is concerned, is over now, but communism's colonialism is still on the march. The dark races are awakening. They have been held back, and apparently these four angels had something to do with holding them back.

Zechariah locates Babylon as the last stand of false religion (see Zech. 5). This is where Satan's last stand will take place.

And the four angels were loosed, which were prepared for an hour, and a day, and a month, and a year, for to slay the third part of men.

And the number of the army of the horsemen were two hundred thousand thousand: and I heard the number of them [Rev. 9:15-16].

And the four angels were loosed, who had been prepared for the hour, and day, and month, and year, that they might kill the third of men. And the number of the armies of the cavalry was two ten thousands (myriads) of ten thousands (myriads).

"And the four angels were loosed, who had been prepared for the hour, and day, and month, and year." You will have to take that literally, my friend, because I do not know how else you would take it. The very hour is marked out.

"That they might kill the third of men." At the blowing of the sixth trumpet, one-third of the population of mankind will be removed. We have already seen a fourth removed, and now a third is removed. Over one-half of the population of the earth will be destroyed in the Great Tribulation Period. No wonder that the Lord Jesus said, "And except those days should be shortened, there should no flesh be saved . . ." (Matt. 24:22).

The size of the army is stupendous. It is numbered at 200 million. China and India and Japan could easily put that many in the field tomorrow. The great population is in the East today. God help the white man, my friend, when these angels are removed—he will not stand a chance.

What is spoken of here in this passage is the wholesale invasion of the earth by the demon world represented in the locusts. Now they are motivated to a world war. Actually, we have never yet had a real world war in which every nation was involved, but that will take place in the Great Tribulation Period. Are these 200 million human beings? I have so far indicated that they could be, but frankly, I believe that what we have here is the invasion by the demon world, which is a further result of Satan's opening the door of the shaft of the bottomless pit. The following description of these horsemen further confirms this fact.

And thus I saw the horses in the vision, and them that sat on them, having breastplates of fire, and of jacinth, and brimstone: and the heads of the horses were as the heads of lions; and out of their mouths issued fire and smoke and brimstone.

By these three was the third part of men killed, by the fire, and by the smoke, and by the brimstone, which issued out of their mouths [Rev. 9:17–18].

And, thus (after this manner) I saw the horses in the (my) vision, and those that sat on them, have breastplates as of fire (fiery red), and hyacinth, and brimstone; and the heads of the horses were as the heads of lions; and out of their mouths proceed fire, and smoke, and brimstone. By these three plagues was the third of men killed, by the fire, and the smoke, and the brimstone that proceeded out of their mouths.

Many suppose these to be tanks. How do they know that tanks will be used in the Great Tribulation Period? We are talking about a period that is in the future. Modern tanks reveal that this may well be, but I have a notion that they are going to have something more refined and sophisticated in that period.

Notice that the colors are as striking as the horsemen are unnatural. "Fire" is fiery red; "hyacinth" is the same color as the flower—dull, dark blue; "brimstone" is light yellow.

The horse is the animal of war (see Job 39:19–25). The underworld is now making war on mankind. These creatures from the underworld are unnatural. They are probably demons or demon-controlled. We are given a literal description of them. In his book on Revelation, William R. Newell makes this very timely observation, "Believe, and you scarcely need any comment." The problem with men who come to Revelation and say that it is difficult to understand and impossible to interpret is that they do not believe it. If you simply believe it and read it, it is very clear. Hellish forces will be at work during this period.

These three plagues mentioned here are literal plagues. The fire is literal, the smoke is literal, and the brimstone is literal. The same thing took place at the destruction of Sodom and Gomorrah. I believe this world during the Great Tribulation Period will actually be worse than Sodom and Gomorrah. People talk about homosexuality attaining respectability in our day. Well, it was the accepted life-style in Sodom and Gomorrah, but homosexuals went out of business—God put them out of business. If you think God is going to permit mankind to go into eternity an unnatural creature, you are wrong.

At this point one-third of the population is killed. One-third of nature had already been affected, but mankind had not been touched with a judgment of this magnitude. If the population of the world were 1.5 billion, this would mean that 500 million would be slain. Remember that a fourth part had been slain under the fourth seal. This terrible decimation of the earth's population seemed incongruous with all of history until the atomic bomb fell upon Hiroshima. Since then men have been using more frightening language than that of Revelation. They now talk of the total decimation of earth's inhabitants. But the Lord Jesus said that He will not permit it: ". . . except those days should be shortened, there should no flesh be saved . . ." (Matt. 24:22)—and the human race would commit suicide if it could.

For their power is in their mouth, and in their tails: for their tails were like unto serpents, and had heads, and with them they do hurt [Rev. 9:19].

For the power of the horses is in their mouths, and in their tails; for their tails are like serpents, having heads, and by them they hurt.

These are unnatural horses which are able to kill with their mouths. The weirdest feat of all is that, instead of horses' hair for tails, they have serpents which are also used in destroying mankind.

And the rest of the men which were not killed by these plagues yet repented not of the works of their hands, that they should not worship devils, and idols of gold, and silver, and brass, and stone, and of wood: which neither can see, nor hear, nor walk:

Neither repented they of their murders, nor of their sorceries, nor of their fornication, nor of their thefts [Rev. 9: 20–21].

And the rest of men who were not killed by these plagues, repented not of the works of their hands, that they should not worship demons, and idols of gold and silver and copper and stone and wood, which can neither see, nor hear, nor walk. Neither repented they of their murders, nor of their sorceries, nor of their fornication, nor of their thefts.

"Sorceries" is the Greek word *pharmakeion*, from which we get our English word *pharmacy. Pharmacy* means "drugs." What were called drugstores when I was a boy are today called pharmacies. The Great Tribulation will be a period when the use of drugs will not be controlled. Drugs will play a large part in the lives of the unsaved and will serve several purposes. Drugs will enable them to bear the judgments of the Great Tribulation Period. I am sure that many a person will turn to drugs when he is stung or bitten by these unnatural creatures. Although they will not die, they will feel like they are going to die, and as a result, they will take drugs to overcome the pain and help them endure the Great Tribulation.

Drugs will also figure largely in the religion of that day. There will be a regular drug culture and drug religion in the days of the Great Tribulation Period. What we are seeing today is very small in comparison to what it will be then. People will resort to everything that will deaden the pain or lift them out of the trouble of that time. Liquor will certainly be very prominent as it is even now. I want to share with you a statement by Dr. J. A. Seiss from his book (*The Apocalypse*, p. 106) published about 1906. The reason I mention the date is that it seems like he wrote it yesterday or that maybe he was preparing it for tomorrow's edition of your local paper. This is his comment on the word *sorceries:*

> We have only to think of the use of alcoholic stimulants, of opium, of tobacco, of the range of cosmetics and medicaments to increase love attractions, of resorts to the pharmacopoeia in connection with sensuality—of the magical agents and treatments alleged to come from the spirit-world for the benefit of people in this—of the thousand impositions in the way of medicines and remedial agents, encouraging mankind to reckless transgression with the hope of easily repairing the damages of nature's penalties—of the growing prevalence of crime induced by these things, setting loose and stimulating to activity the vilest passions, which are eating out the moral sense of society—for the beginnings of that moral degeneracy to which the seer here alludes as characteristic of the period when the sixth trumpet is sounded.

You would think that he had written that for today, but in his day there was no great drug culture nor were drugs and alcohol as big a problem as they are today. Drugs are used today in practically every modern cult which uses sex as a drawing card.

We are told here that they were guilty not only of sorceries, of indulging in drunkenness and in drugs, but also of fornications which lead to thefts. It is alarming the way that adultery is being practiced in the United States. It is promoted as an evidence of our liberty and of the tremendous advancement of civilization! It is interesting that, instead of playing the requiem, this crowd wants to sing and dance and say that the race is improving.

Sorceries and fornication and robbery are going to be increased and a greater emphasis placed upon them. I believe that the Antichrist will use all three of these to bring mankind into subjection to himself. Mankind will be easily lured in that day. Under the influence of drugs, he will accept anything. One of the reasons that our contemporary nightclubs push liquor is not only for the money that is in it, but it also makes their entertainers acceptable. A very inferior singer or comedian goes over well if you've had two cocktails; and if you've had three, then he is a star. Drugs and liquor will put Antichrist over. Paul wrote: "Even him, whose coming is after the working of Satan with all power and signs and lying wonders, And with all deceivableness of unrighteousness in them that perish; because they received not the love of the truth, that they might be saved" (2 Thess. 2:9–10).

I believe that the gospel will go out to every creature before the Rapture, and certainly each one is going to hear it during the Great Tribulation Period. What Paul describes here will only happen to those who have rejected the Word of God. "And for this cause God shall send them strong delusion, that they should believe a lie: That they all might be damned who believed not the truth, but had pleasure in unrighteousness" (2 Thess. 2:11–12).

The moment that you reject the gospel and shut your heart to God, you are wide open for the big lie when it comes. This is the reason so many today fall for everything that comes along. Someone has said that those who stand for nothing will fall for anything. This is it exactly: those today who are not standing for the Word of God are easy prey for the cults.

CHAPTER 10

THEME: Interlude between the sixth and seventh trumpets

Chapter 10 is the hiatus, the interlude between the sixth and seventh trumpets. This chapter begins the second of a series of interludes. Between the sixth and seventh seals, there was an interlude as two groups were redeemed and sealed during the Great Tribulation. Here, between the sixth and seventh trumpets, we have an interlude as three personalities are introduced. In this chapter the mighty angel is described, and in the first fourteen verses of chapter 11, the two witnesses are introduced, though not identified.

THE STRONG ANGEL WITH THE LITTLE BOOK

In verse 1 the mighty angel comes from heaven and is introduced.

And I saw another mighty angel come down from heaven, clothed with a cloud: and a rainbow was upon his head, and his face was as it were the sun, and his feet as pillars of fire [Rev. 10:1].

Let me give you my own translation:

And I saw another strong (powerful) angel coming down out of heaven clothed with a cloud, and the rainbow was upon his head, and his face was as the sun, and his feet as pillars of fire.

There has been definite disagreement among outstanding and fundamental Bible expositors as to the identity of the mighty angel. Godet, Vincent, Pettingill, DeHaan, Ironside, Walter Scott, and William Kelly all identify the strong angel as Christ. Newell and others consider him to be just an angel of great power and authority, but not Christ. Dr. John Walvoord takes this viewpoint, and Vernon McGee takes it also. If you go with either crowd, you will be in good company. In the first group are some men I have great respect for and whom I love in the Lord. I have personally known three of those men, and they were my dear friends. If you follow them, it will be all right, and you will be in good company; but if you want to be right, you want to come along with me on this! There is ample evidence to show that this angel is only a mighty angel. Christ does not appear in Revelation as an angel. It is true that in the Old Testament the preincarnate

Christ was seen as *the* Angel of the Lord. But after He took upon Himself our humanity, after He died and rose again and received a glorified body, we now see Him in the place of great power and glory yonder at God's right hand. We never see Him as an angel again. When He was here in His humanity, He was not an angel—He was a man. Therefore, He is revealed in the Book of Revelation as the glorified Christ, as the postincarnate Christ. He is exalted to the nth degree. It is well to keep before us constantly that this book is the unveiling of Jesus Christ. New glories of His person and of His power and performance are unfolded in each chapter. He is now the One judging a Christ-rejecting earth.

"And I saw another strong angel." *Another* means that it is another of the same kind. The other strong angel to whom we were introduced was back in Revelation 5:2. There was no argument there; it was not Christ. It is the livery of this angel (that is, the way in which he is garbed) which has led some to identify him as Christ. Though all angels are the servants of Christ, in this final book of the Bible, this is evidently the special envoy of Christ, bearing all the credentials of his exalted position. He comes down out of heaven from the presence of Christ, the One who is in the midst of the throne.

He is "clothed with a cloud." This is his uniform as a special envoy from Christ. The clouds of glory are associated with the second coming of Christ, but the angel described here is not coming in clouds of glory, but he is clothed with a cloud. Furthermore, this is not the second coming of Christ to the earth to establish His kingdom; rather, this angel makes the announcement that He is coming soon. Angels, you recall, announced His first coming, and they will announce His second coming to the earth.

"And the rainbow was upon his head." This is the cap for his uniform and is a reminder of God's covenant with man. Although the judgments have come, thick and fast, weird and wild—it beggars language to describe them— this rainbow indicates that God will not send a flood to destroy man again.

"And his face was as the sun." This is his badge of identification. This is the signature of the glorified Christ (see Rev. 1:16). It does not follow that this one must therefore be the Son of God. Moses' face shone after he had been in the presence of God (see Exod. 34:29). This angel's face is shining because he has come out from the presence of Christ. You will recall that the raiment of the angels at the resurrection of Christ also shone (see Luke 24:4). The angel of Revelation 18:1 is a light giver, as the sun and moon, yet no one asserts that he is Christ. Also, I take it that this angel in chapter 10 is not Christ, but he is what it says: an angel, another great, mighty angel.

"And his feet as pillars of fire." This is still part of his uniform. He has come to make a special and solemn announcement of coming judgment. All of these features of identification are his credentials and connect him to the person of Christ as His special envoy. The Lord Jesus is running everything at this particular point. He is the Judge of all the earth.

And he had in his hand a little book open: and he set his right foot upon the sea, and his left foot on the earth,

And cried with a loud voice, as when a lion roareth: and when he had cried, seven thunders uttered their voices [Rev. 10:2–3].

And he had in his hand a little book opened; and he set his right foot upon the sea, and his left foot upon the earth; and he cried with a great voice as (when) a lion roareth: and when he cried the seven thunders spoke their own voices.

There are several reasons that I believe that this little book or scroll is the seven-sealed book which we have seen before. One reason is simply because it is the only book that has been before us, and it is not identified in any other way than it is called "a little book." Frankly, a different word is used here for this book instead of the Greek word *biblion* which is used for the seven-sealed book. But that would not preclude the possibility of its being the same book.

This little book, if it is the same as the seven-sealed book, was originally in the hands of the Father in heaven (see Rev. 5:1). It should be noted how it is first transferred to the nail-pierced hands of God the Son. It was given to the Lord Jesus who was the only One who could open it. The breaking of the seven seals opened the book; and the seven trumpets, six of which have already been blown, are still part of what is in the book. After He removes the seals, the Lord Jesus Christ in turn transfers the book to the angel, who gives it finally to John to eat.

This is the book of the title deed of the earth, and it contains the judgments of the Great Tribulation by which the Lord Jesus is coming to power. The book is now open, and the judgments are on display. This book is the angel's authority for claiming both the sea and the earth for Christ. He puts one foot on the sea and the other foot upon the earth, and he is claiming both for God. In Leviticus 25:23 the Lord gave instructions to Israel concerning the land He had given them: "The land shall not be sold for ever: for the land is mine; for ye are strangers and sojourners with me."

It may be that you think you own a pretty good piece of the real estate of this earth. You hold the title deed. The title has been transferred down through the years to you, and you paid good money for it. You feel it is yours. I say that you are wrong because your title doesn't go back far enough. Sometime in the past, somebody stole it from the Indians. The Indians got it from somebody else—or maybe they just walked in and occupied vacant property. But to whom does it belong? My friend, your property belongs to God, and no matter who you are, you haven't paid Him for it. The earth is His and the fulness thereof (see Ps. 24:1).

God not only claims the land, but He claims the sea as well as the land. "Thou madest him to have dominion over the works of thy hands; thou hast put all things under his feet: All sheep and oxen, yea, and the beasts of the field; The fowl of the air, and the fish of the sea, and whatsoever passeth through the paths of the seas" (Ps. 8:6–8).

God says, "I own the seas also, as well as the land, and I have given this to you. I put man on the earth." Man is a tenant on the earth—some of us haven't paid our rent lately—but we are in a little world that God created. It belongs to Him, and man hasn't been able to pay Him for it yet.

This angel now claims the earth and the sea for the Lord Jesus Christ. When Columbus landed on an island here in the Western Hemisphere, he got off the ship and went to the shore and planted the flag of Spain, claiming the island in the name of the king and queen of the country that had sent him out. That method has been used from time to time. When men came to unoccupied territory, they claimed it. With the title deed of the earth in his hand, and by placing his right foot on the sea and his left foot upon the earth, in a great voice this angel claims all for Christ. The kingdoms of this world *will* become the kingdoms of the Lord Jesus Christ through judgment.

As Creator and Redeemer, the world belongs to Him.

The book is described here as "a little book" because the time of the Great Tribulation is not going to be long. We have come here to sort of the halfway mark, and we are going to be told that there is not much more time left. There is not much more to write down, and it has to be a little book. We are told in Romans 9:28: "For he will finish the work, and cut it short in righteousness: because a short work will the Lord make upon the earth."

The Great Tribulation is really a short time. The Lord Jesus said it was a brief time. Daniel labeled it as seven years, which certainly is not long.

The "seven thunders" is God's amen to the angel's claim. Psalm 29:3 says: "The voice of the LORD is upon the waters: the God of glory thundereth: the LORD is upon many waters."

And in Job 37:5 we read: "God thundereth marvellously with his voice; great things doeth he, which we cannot comprehend."

Dr. Vincent makes this very enlightening comment, "The Jews were accustomed to speak of thunder as 'the seven voices.'" In Psalm 29, although it is a brief psalm, "the voice of the LORD" occurs seven times. Israel spoke of thunder as being the voice of the Lord, the seven voices of God.

We need to take time to study these things to find out what they mean instead of trying to cut off the corners, trim them down, and make them fit into some system of prophecy. I am reminded of the lady who went into a shoe store, and when the clerk asked her what size she wore, she replied, "I can get a four on, but really five is my size, but since six feels so good on my foot, I always buy a six!" That is just like some systems of biblical interpretation: they trim Scripture down to fit into the system. Let John mean what he is saying. These seven thunders here are the voice of God. I think it is the voice of the Lord Jesus now in heaven, confirming what this angel has claimed because He *is* going to come to power on this earth.

And when the seven thunders had uttered their voices, I was about to write: and I heard a voice from heaven saying unto me, Seal up those things which the seven thunders uttered, and write them not [Rev. 10:4].

And when the seven thunders spoke, I was about to write; and I heard a voice from heaven saying, Seal up the things which the seven thunders spoke and write them not.

The seven thunders therefore were intelligible. This confirmation was also a statement. John was a scribe, and he was taking down the visions as they were given to him (see Rev. 1:11). He was about to write what the seven thunders had spoken—he heard it, and they were audible words—but he was forbidden to do so. Since this is a book of *revelation*, why is there something concealed? This is the only place in the Book of Revelation where anything is sealed—nothing else is. God makes it very clear at the end of the book that He has told everything. He is not holding back anything from man today. At the end, John writes: "And he saith unto me, Seal not the sayings of the prophecy of this book: for the time is at hand" (Rev. 22:10).

Yet this particular message of the seven thunders John is not permitted to write down. This is quite interesting.

If this angel were Christ, John probably would have fallen down and worshiped him. He did so when he saw the glorified Christ in the first chapter of Revelation. Evidently, the reason John did not fall down and worship him was because this is only an angel.

It is a mere assumption to presume to know what the thunders spoke. There are wild speculators who have made ridiculous guesses. Vitringa interpreted the seven thunders as the seven Crusades. Danbuz made them the seven nations which received the Reformation. Elliott believed them to be the pope's bull against Luther. Several of the cults have presumed to reveal the things which were uttered. The Lord Jesus Christ said to John, "Seal them up. Don't write this down." They remain to this day a secret which you don't know, I don't know, and no man knows. If we attempt to say what was spoken, in a few years we will find ourselves to be ridiculous. Why not leave it as it is and draw the lesson from it? Although Jesus Christ is being revealed in this Book, there are a great many things that God is not telling us.

And the angel which I saw stand upon the sea and upon the earth lifted up his hand to heaven,

And sware by him that liveth for ever and ever, who created heaven, and the things that therein are, and the earth, and the things that therein are, and the sea, and the things which are therein, that there should be time no longer [Rev. 10:5–6].

And the angel whom I saw standing upon the sea and upon the earth lifted up his right hand to heaven, and sware by (in) Him that liveth for ever and ever (into the ages of the ages), who created heaven and the things in it, and the sea and the things in it, that there shall be no longer delay.

This angel makes it clear that he could not be Christ, since he takes an oath by the eternal Creator. He "lifted up his right hand to heaven, and sware"—he took an oath by the eternal Creator—"by Him that liveth for ever and ever." If he were Christ, he would swear by himself. The writer to the Hebrews says: "For when God made promise to Abraham, because he could swear by no greater, he sware by himself" (Heb. 6:13). God could not swear by anything else because there is none greater than God. The angel swore by another, not by himself, because he is not God, and therefore he is not the Lord Jesus. The Lord Jesus Christ is the eternal God. "In the beginning was the Word, and the Word was with God, and the Word was God. The same was in the beginning with God" (John 1:1–2). We have this statement from the Lord Jesus Himself: "Jesus said unto them, Verily, verily, I say unto you, Before Abraham was, I am" (John 8:58). Christ is the Creator. Listen to John 1:3: "All things were made by him; and without him was not any thing made that was made." In Colossians 1:16 we read: "For by him were all things created, that are in heaven, and that are in earth, visible and invisible, whether they be thrones, or dominions, or principalities, or powers: all things were created by him, and for him." The angel takes an oath in the name of Christ who is in heaven; and as Christ's representative, he claims it all for Christ.

Notice that in my translation I have changed the last part of verse 6 from "that there should be time no longer" to "that there shall be no longer delay." Actually, it does not mean that there shall be time no longer. Rather, this is the glad announcement from heaven to God's saints on earth who are in the midst of all this trouble and who wonder how long it will last. The meaning is that now it will be a very brief time until Christ returns. It is a confirmation of the words of Christ in His Olivet Discourse: "And except those days should be shortened, there should no flesh be saved: but for the elect's sake those days shall be shortened" (Matt. 24:22). The angel is telling the elect that it is not going to be long. He is saying to them, "Don't worry. He that en-

dures to the end, the same shall be saved." Why? Because they are sealed, and they are going to make it through the Great Tribulation Period.

This is likewise in answer to the prayers of the martyrs in Revelation 6:10, and also it is the fulfillment of what we call the Lord's Prayer, "Thy kingdom come" (see Matt. 6:10). The kingdom is coming at this point in time in the Book of Revelation but it does not refer to the time I am writing this. I do not know, and no one on earth knows, whether or not Christ is coming soon.

But in the days of the voice of the seventh angel, when he shall begin to sound, the mystery of God should be finished, as he hath declared to his servants the prophets [Rev. 10:7].

But in the days of the sound of the seventh angel, when he is about to blow (sound the trumpet), and the mystery of God is finished, as He gave the glad tidings to His servants, the prophets.

This all takes place when the seventh angel is preparing to blow the trumpet. This would indicate that the seventh trumpet brings us to the conclusion of the Great Tribulation. It is at this time that the mystery of God is finally made clear. Many single facets of this mystery have been given as the total answer, yet it seems that this is greater than any one and is the sum total of all.

There is a mystery concerning the nation Israel, judgment, suffering, injustice, the silence of God, and the coming kingdom. The basic problem is this: Why did God permit evil, and why has He tolerated it for so long? Do you want to know something? I have studied theology for many years, and I know the answers that men give, but God has not handed in *His* answer yet. He is going to do so someday. There are many things I cannot answer, and I am disturbed that we have some brethren who seem to have all the answers. Candidly, no one has all the answers. As this passage of Scripture indicates, the fact that there is something that we don't know about because it has been sealed means that God has a whole lot to tell us yet. When we get into His presence, we will find out.

May I say this to you: although I do not know the answer to your problem, I know the One who does. I don't have the answer to all my questions either, but I put my hand in His, and He says to me, "My child, walk with Me through the dark. It is going to be all right.

We are going to come out into the light, and then you will understand." I suggest that you put your hand into the hand of the One who is your Creator and your Redeemer, very man of very man and very God of very God.

JOHN EATS THE LITTLE BOOK

And the voice which I heard from heaven spake unto me again, and said, Go and take the little book which is open in the hand of the angel which standeth upon the sea and upon the earth [Rev. 10:8].

And the voice which I heard out of heaven, (I heard) it again speaking with me, and saying, Go, take the book which is open in the hand of the angel who standeth upon the sea and upon the earth.

This order comes from Christ in heaven as He is directing every operation recorded in the Book of Revelation. He is in full charge. Revelation is the book that glorifies our wonderful Savior. He is the Judge of all the earth here, and we see Him as God has highly exalted Him and given Him a name above every name. If the voice here is not Christ's, then He has given the order to the angel to speak from heaven.

John has apparently returned to the earth in spirit, because the little book which was formerly in the hand of God the Father is now transferred to John.

And I went unto the angel, and said unto him, Give me the little book. And he said unto me, Take it, and eat it up; and it shall make thy belly bitter, but it shall be in thy mouth sweet as honey.

And I took the little book out of the angel's hand, and ate it up; and it was in my mouth sweet as honey: and as soon as I had eaten it, my belly was bitter [Rev. 10:9–10].

And I went away to the angel, saying to him, Give to me the little book, and he said to me, Take, and eat it up; and it shall make thy belly bitter, but in thy mouth it shall be as sweet as honey. And I took the little book out of the hand of the angel, and ate it up. And it was in my mouth as sweet as honey. And when I had eaten it, my belly was made bitter.

John becomes a participant in the great drama which is unfolding before us. He is required to do a very strange thing, one that has a very typical meaning. He eats the little book at the instructions of the angel, and the results are bittersweet. Eating the little book means to receive the Word of God with faith. This is the teaching of the Word of God, for in Jeremiah 15:16 we read: "Thy words were found, and I did eat them; and thy word was unto me the joy and rejoicing of mine heart: for I am called by thy name, O LORD God of hosts." Jeremiah likens the appropriation of the Word to eating it.

Ezekiel does the same thing: "Moreover he said unto me, Son of man, eat that thou findest; eat this roll, and go speak unto the house of Israel. So I opened my mouth, and he caused me to eat that roll. And he said unto me, Son of man, cause thy belly to eat, and fill thy bowels with this roll that I give thee. Then did I eat it; and it was in my mouth as honey for sweetness" (Ezek. 3:1–3). The "roll" here is not a bread roll, but the scroll of that day. Ezekiel said that he ate it, and it was just like cake. That is what the Word of God is to the believer. In Proverbs 16:24 we are told: "Pleasant words are as an honeycomb, sweet to the soul, and health to the bones." In Psalm 119, the psalm which glorifies the Word of God, we find: "How sweet are thy words unto my taste! yea, sweeter than honey to my mouth" (Ps. 119:103).

The part of the Word of God taken by John was judgment. It was sweet because the future is sweet. In Genesis 18:17 we read, "And the LORD said, Shall I hide from Abraham that thing which I do . . . ?" In effect He was saying to Abraham, "We are friends, and I would like to tell you what I am going to do." It is sweet to know what God is going to do, but when you find out that judgment is coming, it is bitter. John eagerly received the Word of God, but when he saw that more judgment was to follow, it brought travail of soul and sorrow of heart. It was sweet in his mouth and bitter in his digestive system. If you and I can take delight in reading this section of the Word of God and the judgments that are to fall upon the earth, then we need to do a great deal of praying to get the mind of God. It is sweet to know the Book of Revelation and what God intends to do, but when we find out that judgment is coming to the Christ-rejecting world around us, we cannot rejoice in that. The prophecy becomes bitter.

There is another very real application of this. Many folk begin the study of prophecy with enthusiasm, but when they find that it is applicable to their life and that it makes demands on them personally, they lose interest, and it becomes a bitter thing. Many people say, "I don't want to hear about the Book of Revelation. I don't like prophecy. It frightens me!" May I say to you that it is supposed to do that, but it should be in your mouth sweet as honey. Unfortunately, there are a lot of people who like to study prophecy because of the natural curiosity to know the future, but they will discover that there is nothing in the Word of God that ministers more to a holy life than the thoughtful study of prophecy. "And every man that hath this hope in him purifieth himself . . ." (1 John 3:3). To be a student of prophecy and live a dirty life will only lead to abnormality. The reason we hear so much abnormality in the interpretation of prophecy in our day is that the Word of God is not having its way in the hearts and lives of the folk who study it. It is unfortunate that people will get interested in prophecy but not in Christian living.

Years ago after I had recently come to California, I went to see Dr. Gaebelein who was visiting here. He said to me, "How do you like your church in California?" I told him, "It's wonderful. I enjoy it, but there is something strange out here. [I have since learned that this is true everywhere, but I had not detected it before.] I can teach the Book of Revelation in my church, and it will fill up on Wednesday nights. But if I teach the Epistle to the Romans, I empty the church." I never shall forget what Dr. Gaebelein said in his broken Prussian accent, "Brother McGee, you are going to find that a great many of the saints are more interested in Antichrist than they are in Christ." I have discovered that he was accurate.

And he said unto me, Thou must prophesy again before many peoples, and nations, and tongues, and kings [Rev. 10:11].

And they say to me, It is necessary for you to prophesy again against peoples and nations and tongues and kings.

You can be sure of one thing, that John was properly integrated. He believed that all nations, all peoples, all tongues, and all colors ought to hear the Word of God. They need to hear it because they need to be warned that judgment is coming. If they go through the Great Tribulation, they will soon recognize that it is not the Millennium—in fact, they will feel as if they have entered hell itself. This is the part that made John sad. This is the reason this little book became bitter to John: he must prophesy against many before Christ comes to His kingdom. Much prophecy is to follow. We are not quite halfway through the Book of Revelation. Prophecy about the nations and peoples is necessarily *against* them; it is of judgment to come. This new series of prophecies will begin in chapter 12, and it will reveal the fact that there was a great deal more to say.

My friend, the study of prophecy will have a definite effect upon your life: it will either bring you closer to Christ, or it will take you farther from Him.

CHAPTER 11

THEME: *Interlude between sixth and seventh trumpets; the seventh trumpet blown*

In the first fourteen verses, chapter 11 continues with the interlude between the sixth and seventh trumpets, and in the concluding verses, we have the blowing of the seventh trumpet. In this chapter we learn that forty-two months remain of the Times of the Gentiles and that there are two witnesses who will prophesy for forty-two months. We also have the second woe and then the blowing of the seventh trumpet.

This chapter brings us back to Old Testament ground. The temple, the dealing with time periods, and the distinction which is made between Jews and Gentiles all indicate that we are again under the Old Testament economy. Chronologically, the seventh trumpet brings us to the return of Christ at the end of the Great Tribulation Period.

DATE FOR THE ENDING OF "THE TIMES OF THE GENTILES"

Here we deal with an indication of projected time periods for the close of the Great Tribulation.

And there was given me a reed like unto a rod: and the angel stood, saying, Rise, and measure the temple of God, and the altar, and them that worship therein.

But the court which is without the temple leave out, and measure it not; for it is given unto the Gentiles: and the holy city shall they tread under foot forty and two months [Rev. 11:1–2].

Let me give you my own translation:

And there was given me a reed like a rod, saying, Rise and measure the temple (holy place) of God, and the altar, and them that worship therein. And the court which is without the temple cast out [Gr.: ekbale, throw out] and measure it not; for it is given to the nations, and the holy city shall they tread under foot forty and two months.

We are dealing here with that period that the Lord Jesus spoke of in Luke 21:24, ". . . and Jerusalem shall be trodden down of the Gentiles, until the times of the Gentiles be fulfilled." A great many people thought that when Israel captured Jerusalem, that was the end of the Time of the Gentiles. My friend, Jerusalem is still trodden down of the Gentiles. All you need to do is to walk down the streets of the old city, and if you see a Jew, you let me know because I did not see any there myself. All other races are there. Non-Jewish religious groups are all over the place; they have built holy places everywhere in the old city of Jerusalem. Jerusalem is still trodden down of the Gentiles. But when you get into the Great Tribulation Period and come to the last half of it, the Time of the Gentiles will run out in forty-two months. Forty-two months is one-half of the Great Tribulation Period.

"And there was given me a reed like a rod." Every time you see the beginning of measurements, in either the Old or New Testament, it indicates that God is beginning to deal with the nation Israel (see Jer. 31:38–39; Zech. 2). This reed is like a rod; a rod is used by a shepherd. In Psalm 2:9 we see that a rod is used for chastisement and judgment: "Thou shalt break them with a rod of iron; thou shalt dash them in pieces like a potter's vessel." What we are dealing with here is a measurement of time given for the Time of the Gentiles, after which judgment will come upon them. The rod is also for comfort: "Yea, though I walk through the valley of the shadow of death, I will fear no evil: for thou art with me; thy rod and thy staff they com-

fort me" (Ps. 23:4). Therefore, we have both judgment and solace in this chapter.

"The temple of God" is limited to the Holy Place (notice that "holy place" is the literal rendering) and the Holy of Holies. The temple of God places us back on Old Testament ground, for there is no temple given to the church. The church *is* a temple of the Holy Spirit today; that is, believers (not a building) are the temple of the Holy Spirit: "In whom all the building fitly framed together groweth unto an holy temple in the Lord: In whom ye also are builded together for an habitation of God through the Spirit" (Eph. 2:21–22).

"The altar" refers to the golden altar of prayer since the altar for burnt offering was not in the temple proper but in the outer court.

Even the worshipers are to be measured. John is told to rise and measure, not only the Holy Place and the altar, but also "them that worship therein." God does count the number of those who worship Him.

"And the court which is without the temple cast out [Gr.: ekbale, throw out] and measure it not." This excludes all that does not belong to the temple proper. The altar of burnt offering (and also the brazen laver) would be outside the temple. Since this altar was a picture of the cross of Christ, it would seem that the implication is that the gospel of the cross of Christ will still be available to all mankind during the intensity of this brief crisis. It is not to be measured, and it will still be available.

"For it is given to the nations [that is, the Gentiles]" declares that although this period still belongs to the Gentiles, their dominion is limited to forty-two months. As we have said, this confirms the words of the Lord Jesus in Luke 21:24.

"Forty and two months" is the three and one-half year period identified with the last half of the Great Tribulation Period. We find this repeated in Revelation 13:5: "And there was given unto him a mouth speaking great things and blasphemies; and power was given unto him to continue forty and two months." This is the last half of the reign of Antichrist here upon this earth. This period is mentioned again in chapter 12, verse 14: "And to the woman were given two wings of a great eagle, that she might fly into the wilderness, into her place, where she is nourished for a time, and times, and half a time, from the face of the serpent." "A time, times [dual], and half a time" means three and one-half years. Daniel adopts this unit of measurement for this period: "And he shall speak great words against the most High, and shall wear out the saints of the most High, and think to change times and laws: and they shall be given into his hand until a time and times and the dividing of time" (Dan. 7:25). "A time and times and the dividing of time"—again, this means three and one-half years. "And from the time that the daily sacrifice shall be taken away, and the abomination that maketh desolate set up, there shall be a thousand two hundred and ninety days" (Dan. 12:11). Twelve hundred and ninety days is three and one-half years. We have yet another reference in Daniel which says: "And he shall confirm the covenant with many for one week: and in the midst of the week he shall cause the sacrifice and the oblation to cease, and for the overspreading of abominations he shall make it desolate, even until the consummation, and that determined shall be poured upon the desolate" (Dan. 9:27). Here the Great Tribulation is divided into two equal parts. This "week" of Daniel is seven years, and this seven-year period is the Seventieth Week of Daniel, or the Great Tribulation Period.

DURATION OF THE PROPHESYING OF THE TWO WITNESSES

And I will give power unto my two witnesses, and they shall prophesy a thousand two hundred and threescore days, clothed in sackcloth [Rev. 11:3].

And I will give to my two witnesses, and they shall prophesy a thousand, two hundred and three score [60] days, clothed in sackcloth.

There is a great deal of difference of opinion as to the identity of the two witnesses. They are introduced to us without any suggestion as to who they are. Godet makes this comment: "They are one of the most startling features of the book." If the identity of these two was essential for the understanding of this book, I think there would have been some indication given about their persons. It is always in these areas that the sensational preachers concentrate. They can tell you what the seven thunders said (John was told not to write it down, and he didn't), and they can tell you the names of these two witnesses. Those who have espoused the historical view of Revelation have named such men as John Huss, Pope Sylvester, Waldenson, and the two Testaments. You can see that you could come up with almost anything from that viewpoint. Men who hold the futurist view—which is the

view I hold—are not in complete agreement as to who they are. Seiss and Govett say that they are Enoch and Elijah. Govett (*The Apocalypse Expounded by Scripture*, p. 225) says that *The Gospel of Nicodemus* contains the following statement:

I am Enoch who pleased God, and was translated by him. And this is Elijah the Tishbite. We are also to live to the end of the age: but then we are about to be sent by God to resist Antichrist, and be slain by him, and to rise after three days, and to be caught up in the clouds to meet the Lord.

Dean Alford, Walter Scott, and Donald Grey Barnhouse state that they are Moses and Elijah. William Newell does a very smart thing— he does not even attempt to identify them. There is also the possibility that they are two unknown witnesses—that is, they have had no previous existence, and they have not yet appeared on the scene.

That they are human witnesses seems certain from the description given of them. Two is the required number of witnesses according to the Law: "At the mouth of two witnesses, or three witnesses, shall he that is worthy of death be put to death; but at the mouth of one witness he shall not be put to death" (Deut. 17:6).

The Lord Jesus said the same thing relative to the church: "But if he will not hear thee, then take with thee one or two more, that in the mouth of two or three witnesses every word may be established" (Matt. 18:16). Scripture has always required two witnesses to bear testimony to anything before it was to be heard. Therefore, we can definitely say that these witnesses are human beings and that there are two of them. These are the two things we know for sure.

It seems to me to be almost certain that Elijah is one of them, since it was predicted that he would return: "Behold, I will send you Elijah the prophet before the coming of the great and dreadful day of the LORD" (Mal. 4:5). It is also recorded in Matthew's Gospel: "And Jesus answered and said unto them, Elias truly shall first come, and restore all things" (Matt. 17:11). It would seem that we can say with a certain degree of assurance that Elijah is one of the witnesses. It is said in verse 4 that these two witnesses are two lampstands standing before "the God of the earth." This was a favorite expression of Elijah who walked out onto the pages of Scripture, saying, ". . .

As the LORD God of Israel liveth, before whom I stand . . ." (1 Kings 17:1). These witnesses are two lampstands; they are lights in the world. The presence of Elijah on the Mount of Transfiguration further suggests this, but it would necessitate the second witness being Moses, which is more difficult to sustain, and after all, the Mount of Transfiguration is not the only point of similarity.

I would like to make a suggestion about which I will not be dogmatic nor will I argue. My suggestion is that John the Baptist is the second witness. He was the forerunner of Christ at His first coming. He was similar to Elijah in manner and message. I am sure that those two fellows would get along with each other. Both knew what it was to oppose the forces of darkness and to stand alone for God against impossible odds. They surely have had good training in the past. John the Baptist would be the witness of the New Testament, as Elijah would be the witness of the Old Testament. John the Baptist actually was not part of the church, the bride of Christ. He very candidly said that he was a friend of the bridegroom. He wasn't a bride; he was a friend of the bridegroom.

It seems unlikely that Enoch would be one of the witnesses since he was a Gentile. The very fact that he did not die does not qualify him for the office for, by the time you come to the Great Tribulation Period, the church has already been translated, and some of them were translated without dying.

Let us say with some assurance that Elijah is one of the witnesses. As to who the other one is, your guess is as good as mine.

"And they shall prophesy a thousand, two hundred and three score days." The significant feature about the two witnesses is not their identity but the time they appear. Is this during the first half or the last half of the Great Tribulation? The first half seems to fit the text more accurately because they testify until the Beast appears, and then they are martyred.

"Clothed in sackcloth" is the garb better suited to the period of the Law than of grace. It is becoming both to Elijah and to John the Baptist.

These are the two olive trees, and the two candlesticks standing before the God of the earth.

And if any man will hurt them, fire proceedeth out of their mouth, and devoureth their enemies: and if any man will hurt them, he must in this manner be killed [Rev. 11:4–5].

These are the two olive trees and the two lampstands standing before the Lord of the earth. And if anyone wishes to hurt them, fire proceedeth out of their mouth and devoureth their enemies; and if anyone wishes to hurt them, thus must he be killed.

Everything here is associated with the Old Testament. The two olive trees immediately suggest the vision in Zechariah 4. There the lampstands are two individuals, Joshua and Zerubbabel, who were enabled by the Holy Spirit to stand against insurmountable difficulties. The explanation is found in the words, ". . . Not by might, nor by power [or, not by brain, nor by brawn], but by my spirit, saith the LORD of hosts" (Zech. 4:6). The Holy Spirit will be present during the Great Tribulation Period.

These two witnesses are lights before the powers of darkness. These men are accorded miraculous power to bring fire down from heaven—they are filled with the Holy Spirit. Here again, the suggestion is strongly in favor of Elijah (see 1 Kings 18:38; 2 Kings 1:10). Also, John made an announcement about One baptizing with fire (see Matt. 3:11).

These two witnesses are immortal and immune to all attacks until their mission is completed. My friend, it is encouraging to know that all of God's men are immortal until He has accomplished His purpose through them. This is one reason that I have had a weak and feeble faith through several cancer surgeries and other physical problems. I will be honest with you, there were times when I wondered if I would make it through or not. But I prayed to God and asked other people to pray that I might be enabled to finish the taping of our five-year "Thru the Bible" radio broadcasts—and He has answered that prayer. That all of God's men are immortal until God is through with them is a wonderful, comforting thought for today. And when He is through with you, He will remove you from the earth.

These have power to shut heaven, that it rain not in the days of their prophecy: and have power over waters to turn them to blood, and to smite the earth with all plagues, as often as they will [Rev. 11:6].

These have the authority [Gr.: exousian— power] to shut up the heaven, that the rain may not wet during the days of their prophecy; and they have power over the waters to turn them into blood, and to smite the earth with every plague, as often as they wish.

These two witnesses are granted unlimited authority. They control rainfall on the earth, and they are able to turn the water into blood. This certainly reminds us of both Elijah and Moses. This is the verse that has caused certain outstanding men to decide that Elijah, who was the man that stopped the rain, and Moses, who was the one who brought the plagues upon Egypt, will be the two. They may have good ground for that, but anything you say about these two witnesses is speculation.

"And to smite the earth"—they are given the same power Christ will have when He returns (see Rev. 19:15).

"With every plague" suggests the plagues Moses imposed on Egypt, but the plagues here are greater in number as the territory is more vast.

"As often as they wish" reveals the confidence God places in these faithful servants. God cannot trust you and me like this. He cannot trust some of us with money; certainly He wasn't able to trust me with very much. He does not trust us with power, and this is the reason that He removes men from office after a period of time—time is always on His side—because He cannot trust men with power. It is a good thing that many of us do not have it.

And when they shall have finished their testimony, the beast that ascendeth out of the bottomless pit shall make war against them, and shall overcome them, and kill them [Rev. 11:7].

And when they shall have finished their testimony, the wild beast that cometh up out of the abyss, shall make war with them, and overcome them, and kill them.

The witnesses will finish their testimony. In the midst of the week, the Antichrist, who is the Beast, the Man of Sin who is moving to power, will bring back first the Roman Empire. Then, when he gets the whole world under his control, he will not hesitate to overcome and destroy these two witnesses. At that time he will be permitted to do so. This is the temporary victory of darkness over light, evil over righteousness, hell over heaven, and Satan over God, because God is going to let Satan loose during this period.

These witnesses live up to their name. *Martus* is the Greek word for "witness"; we get our English word *martyr* from that.

And their dead bodies shall lie in the street of the great city, which spiritually is called Sodom and Egypt, where also our Lord was crucified [Rev. 11:8].

And their dead bodies (carcasses) shall lie upon the street of the great city, which spiritually is called Sodom and Egypt, where also their Lord was crucified.

These men are not given even a decent burial. This reveals the crude, cold barbarism of the last days which will be covered with but a thin veneer of culture. There is a strange resemblance to the sadistic curiosity which placed two dead men, Lenin and Stalin, on display in Red Square in Moscow. They have removed Stalin, but at this writing Lenin is still there, and I understand that that body is beginning to deteriorate.

The word used for *bodies* (carcasses) denotes the contempt and hatred the world will have for the two witnesses. They are treated as dead animals.

"The great city" is Jerusalem. It is likened unto Sodom by Isaiah (see Isa. 1:10). It is called Egypt because the world has entered into every fiber of its life—social and political. It is conclusively identified as Jerusalem by the sad designation, "where also their Lord was crucified."

And they of the people and kindreds and tongues and nations shall see their dead bodies three days and an half, and shall not suffer their dead bodies to be put in graves [Rev. 11:9].

And out of the peoples, and tribes, and tongues, and nations do some gaze upon their dead bodies (carcasses) three days and one half and shall not permit their dead bodies (carcasses) to be put in a tomb.

After Christ was crucified, even Pilate permitted His friends to take down the body and give it a respectable burial, but not so with the two witnesses. The world will be startled to hear they are dead. Some will be skeptical. Apparently, this future generation will have something that corresponds to a television camera, and a satellite will carry the picture all over the world, so that people everywhere will be able to look upon the features of these men for three and one-half days. The morbid curiosity of a godless society will relish the opportunity of gazing with awe upon these dead bodies. This is the worst indignity that a depraved world could vent upon the men who denounced them and their wicked ways. Perhaps the witnesses had predicted their resurrection. We are not told that, but they might have. To prevent the possibility of another empty tomb, there was no burial. They will decide to just leave the bodies out there and keep the camera on them. I think all the television networks will have their cameras trained on these dead men. Three and one-half days they are lying there.

And they that dwell upon the earth shall rejoice over them, and make merry, and shall send gifts one to another; because these two prophets tormented them that dwelt on the earth [Rev. 11:10].

And the dwellers upon the earth rejoice over them, and make merry, and shall send gifts one to another; because these two prophets tormented (vexed) the dwellers on the earth.

The death of the two witnesses is an occasion for high carnival on the earth. The world engages in a modern Christmas and Mardi Gras, both rolled into one. The world has adopted the philosophy, "Let us eat, drink, and be merry, for tomorrow we die." Dr. Newell describes it like this: "Now comes the real revelation of the heart of man: glee, horrid, insane, inhuman, hellish, ghoulish glee!"

"And shall send gifts one to another" indicates a lovely occasion on the surface, but this is the Devil's Christmas. The modern celebration of Christmas gets farther and farther from the birth of Christ and closer and closer to paganism. The day will come when it will be anti-Christian—it is almost that now. Here is the celebration of what Antichrist has done instead of the celebration of the coming of Christ to Bethlehem.

Then something happens—

And after three days and an half the Spirit of life from God entered into them, and they stood upon their feet; and great fear fell upon them which saw them [Rev. 11:11].

And after the three days and a half the breath (spirit) of life from God entered into them, and they stood upon their feet; and great fear fell upon them that beheld them.

While the world is celebrating in jubilation the death of these witnesses and while the television cameras are focused upon them, the witnesses will stand on their feet. And all of the

networks will regret that they had their cameras pointed to them, because they will not really want to give the news as it is. The scriptural word for resurrection is used here—the Greek word *histeme*—"they stood upon their feet." These witnesses are among the tribulation saints who have part in the first resurrection (see Rev. 20:4–6). Any news like this would be a scoop, but I am sure that all of the networks will have their cameras on it. By that time they may well have some new gadget which will make television, as we know it, look very much antiquated and out of place.

And they heard a great voice from heaven saying unto them, Come up hither. And they ascended up to heaven in a cloud; and their enemies beheld them [Rev. 11:12].

And they heard a great voice out of heaven saying to them, Come up here, and they went up into heaven in the cloud, and their enemies beheld them.

They are caught up into heaven. We have the *resurrection* of the two witnesses in verse 11; we have the *ascension* of the two witnesses in verse 12. The cloud of glory is associated with the ascension and the coming of Christ also.

DOOM OF THE SECOND WOE—GREAT EARTHQUAKE

We have had the blowing of the sixth trumpet, and we are in that interval or lull between the sixth and seventh trumpets. These are woe trumpets, and the second woe is connected with the sixth trumpet—it is a great earthquake.

And the same hour was there a great earthquake, and the tenth part of the city fell, and in the earthquake were slain of men seven thousand: and the remnant were affrighted, and gave glory to the God of heaven [Rev. 11:13].

And in that hour there came to pass a great earthquake, and a tenth of the city fell, and 7000 names of men were killed in the earthquake, and the rest were afraid, and gave glory to the God of heaven.

This number of the slain was to be added to those already slain. A fourth of the population of the world was slain at first, and then a third of the population of the world—totaling over one-half—and now seven thousand more are killed. It is little wonder that the Lord Jesus said, "And except those days should be short-

ened, there should no flesh be saved . . ."
(Matt. 24:22).

The earthquake seems to be limited to the
city of Jerusalem, just as it was when Christ
rose from the dead (see Matt. 28:2), and also at
His crucifixion (see Matt. 27:51–52).

"Seven thousand names of men were killed
in the earthquake." This is an idiom to indicate
that they were men of prominence. They were
the ones who had gone along with Antichrist,
men whose names got into the headlines when
Antichrist came to power.

**The second woe is past; and, behold, the
third woe cometh quickly [Rev. 11:14].**

This ends the second woe. The third woe begins shortly, though not immediately. The
third woe is not the blowing of the seventh
trumpet which will come next, as that leads us
beyond the Great Tribulation into the Millennium. The seventh trumpet likewise opens up
to us the seven personalities of chapters 12
and 13. The third woe begins when Satan, one
of the personalities, is cast down to earth, and
we will come to that in chapter 12, verse 12.

SEVENTH TRUMPET—END OF GREAT TRIBULATION AND OPENING OF TEMPLE IN HEAVEN

In the middle of all the woes and judgments
of the Great Tribulation Period, this is inserted for the encouragement of the believers
who will be left on the earth, those who were
sealed. They are apt to get very much discouraged after several years, although the
total length of the Great Tribulation is but
seven years and the intensity of it breaks in
the last half of that period. The Great Tribulation does not seem long to read about, but I
have found seven *days* in the hospital to be the
most trying experience of life. I thought those
days would never end; so you do need a little
encouragement as you go along.

**And the seventh angel sounded; and
there were great voices in heaven, saying, The kingdoms of this world are become the kingdoms of our Lord, and of
his Christ; and he shall reign for ever
and ever.**

**And the four and twenty elders, which
sat before God on their seats, fell upon
their faces, and worshipped God,**

**Saying, We give thee thanks, O Lord
God Almighty, which art, and wast, and
art to come; because thou hast taken to
thee thy great power, and hast reigned.**

**And the nations were angry, and thy
wrath is come, and the time of the dead,
that they should be judged, and that
thou shouldest give reward unto thy
servants the prophets, and to the saints,
and them that fear thy name, small and
great; and shouldest destroy them
which destroy the earth [Rev. 11:15–18].**

*And the seventh angel blew the trumpet;
and there followed (came to pass) great
voices in heaven, saying, The kingdom of
the world (cosmos) is become (the kingdom) of our Lord, and of His Christ; and
He shall reign unto the ages of the ages
(for ever and ever). And the twenty-four
elders, sitting before God on their
thrones, fell upon their faces, and worshipped God, saying, We give thanks to
you, O Lord God the Almighty, who art
and who wast; because thou hast taken
thy great power and didst reign. And the
nations were angry (wroth), and thy
wrath came, and the time (period) of the
dead to be judged, and to give the reward
to your servants the prophets and to the
saints and to them that fear thy name, the
small and great; and to destroy those who
destroy (corrupt, the destroyers of) the
earth.*

The blowing of the seventh trumpet is of
utmost significance, and it is of special rele-
vance in the understanding of the remainder of
this book. In the program of God, it brings us
chronologically to the breathtaking entrance
of eternity where the mystery of God is finally
unraveled. It brings us in God's program as far
as chapter 21 where eternity begins. The
broad outline of events which are significant to
God is given to us here by the Holy Spirit.
This section is a summary, a syllabus, or a
capsule synopsis of events up to the door of
eternity. The following list will help focus
these events in our minds:

1. "Great voices in heaven" follow the blowing of the seventh trumpet. At the opening of
the seventh seal, there was silence in heaven.
The contrast should be noted, because here
the blowing of the seventh trumpet reveals
God's program and clears up the mystery of
God. All of God's created intelligences can see
the end now and are jubilant in anticipation of
the termination of evil being so close at hand.
It is a time of joy for them.

2. "The kingdom of the world (cosmos) is
become (the kingdom) of our Lord, and of His
Christ; and He shall reign unto the ages of the
ages (for ever and ever)." It is not kingdoms

(plural) but kingdom (singular) which denotes the fact that the kingdoms of this world are at present under Satan, to whom there is no distinction of nations, no East or West, no Iron Curtain—all are his; both sides are included in his domain. A great many people think that Satan is controlling Russia but that the Lord is controlling the United States and angels are hovering over the capitol at Washington, D. C. May I say that those angels may not be God's angels who are hovering over Washington today—it certainly doesn't look like they are. Actually, *all* of the kingdoms of this world are Satan's. It is therefore called the kingdom—not kingdoms—of the world. It is the totality of a civilization and society of which men boast of self-improvement but which becomes more godless and wicked each day. It is a condemned civilization that is moving toward judgment.

It is going to become the kingdom "of our Lord, and of His Christ." Satan's kingdom is going to be subdued someday, but not by some little saccharine-sweet talk on brotherhood and love. It is going to be delivered to the Lord Jesus Christ, and He is going to rule. We are told in Scripture: "The kings of the earth set themselves, and the rulers take counsel together, against the LORD, and against his anointed, saying, Let us break their bands asunder, and cast away their cords from us" (Ps. 2:2–3). Rebellion broke out against the Lord and His Christ (Messiah, Anointed) at the arrest of Jesus. The early church understood that this was the condition of the world, for they quoted Psalm 2 when persecution broke out in the early church (see Acts 4:23–26). We read in Psalm 2:9: "Thou shalt break them with a rod of iron; thou shalt dash them in pieces like a potter's vessel." In Revelation 19 we are going to see the details of what is given here in this section. The Lord Jesus is coming to put down rebellion. The seventh trumpet is moving along, step by step, toward eternity.

3. "And the twenty-four elders, sitting before God on their thrones, fell upon their faces, and worshipped God, saying, We give thanks to you, O Lord God the Almighty, who art and who wast; because thou hast taken thy great power and didst reign." This revelation causes the church in heaven to worship and celebrate the coming of Christ to the earth. This will be the answer to our prayer, "Thy kingdom come. Thy will be done in earth, as it is in heaven" (Matt. 6:10).

4. "The nations were angry (wroth)" reveals the fact that the stubborn rebellion of man will continue right down to the very end. Right down to the wire, the stubborn heart of man is in rebellion against God. This old nature, this carnal nature that you and I have, is not obedient to God. My friend, you cannot make this old nature obey God. This is exactly what Paul says: "Because the carnal mind is enmity against God: for it is not subject to the law of God, neither indeed can be" (Rom. 8:7). The human family could not bring this old nature under control; that is the reason God is going to get rid of it someday.

5. The nations were angry because "thy wrath came." They had been fed all this putrid pabulum we hear today about the fact that God never intends to punish sin and that man is getting better and better every day—while, actually, all the time he is getting worse and worse.

6. "And the time (period) of the dead to be judged" brings us to the Great White Throne judgment of the lost dead (see Rev. 20:11–15).

7. "And to give the reward to your servants the prophets and to the saints and to them that fear thy name, the small and great." The church has already gone into His presence, and the believers there have already been rewarded as indicated by the crowns we have seen on the heads of the elders. This refers now to Old Testament saints and tribulation saints, who are included in the first resurrection, but at a different time. They are now going to be rewarded as the kingdom begins.

8. "And to destroy those who destroy (corrupt, the destroyers of) the earth." We believe that this refers to both man and Satan. Man is a destroyer as well as Satan. Peter warns us of Satan: "Be sober, be vigilant; because your adversary the devil, as a roaring lion, walketh about, seeking whom he may devour" (1 Pet. 5:8).

The next verse brings us to the glad gate of eternity:

And the temple of God was opened in heaven, and there was seen in his temple the ark of his testament: and there were lightnings, and voices, and thunderings, and an earthquake, and great hail [Rev. 11:19].

And the sanctuary (temple) of God in heaven was opened, and the ark of His covenant was seen in His sanctuary (temple), and there followed lightnings, and voices, and thunders, and an earthquake, and great hail.

When we see the church again, it will be in the New Jerusalem, and we are told definitely that there is no temple there. Here there is a temple in heaven. The temple which Moses made was made after the pattern in heaven. "And the sanctuary (temple) of God in heaven was opened" means that God is dealing now with Israel.

"Was opened" indicates worship and access to God. All of this points to the nation Israel, for the church has no temple. The measuring of the temple on earth and the opening of the temple in heaven declare the prominence of Israel in this section. The next chapter will substantiate this.

"And the ark of His covenant was seen in His sanctuary (temple)" reminds us that we are dealing with a covenant-making and covenant-keeping God. He is going to keep the covenant He has made with Israel, and He will make a New Covenant with them at this time—that is, the Law will be written in their hearts instead of on cold tablets of stone (see Jer. 31:31–34; Heb. 8:8–13).

"Lightnings, and voices, and thunders, and an earthquake, and great hail" speak of judgment yet to come.

CHAPTER 12

THEME: Seven performers during the Great Tribulation

The theme of this chapter is the final conflict between Israel and Satan after he is cast out of heaven. Seven performers are introduced to us (see chs. 12–13) by the blowing of this seventh trumpet during the Great Tribulation Period. Although the seventh trumpet brings us through the Great Tribulation and the Millennium to the very threshold of eternity, a great deal of detail was omitted. Beginning with chapter 12, this will be compensated for in the presentation of seven prominent personages who play a dominant part in the Great Tribulation Period. After that, we will have the pouring out of the seven bowls of wrath and then the final destruction of commercial Babylon and religious Babylon.

The prominence of the nation Israel is brought before us. It was suggested in the previous chapter with the measuring of the temple on earth and the opening of the temple in heaven. The last verse of chapter 11 is actually the opening to this chapter.

These seven personages are representatives of persons, both natural and supernatural, physical and spiritual, rulers and nations. The identification and clarification of these are essential for a proper understanding of the Revelation.

THE WOMAN—ISRAEL

As we take up the very first one of these personalities, it will illustrate this point. We come now to the crux of the interpretation of the entire Book of Revelation which revolves about this first personality. An outstanding and very intellectual minister years ago made the statement: "If you tell me your interpretation of the woman in the twelfth chapter of Revelation, then I'll tell you your interpretation of prophecy." At the time, I thought he was foolish, but I have come to agree with him. I believe that the identification of this woman is the key to the understanding of the Book of Revelation.

And there appeared a great wonder in heaven; a woman clothed with the sun, and the moon under her feet, and upon her head a crown of twelve stars:

And she being with child cried, travailing in birth, and pained to be delivered [Rev. 12:1–2].

Let me give you my translation:

And a great sign was seen in heaven: a woman arrayed with the sun, and the moon under her feet, and upon her head a crown of twelve stars; and she was with child, and travailing in birth, and being tormented to be delivered.

The important thing here is: "Who is the woman?" You are acquainted with the interpretation of the Roman church that she represents the Virgin Mary. There are Protestant interpreters who have been as far wrong as that. Today most of them follow the method of Rome and interpret the woman as the church of all ages. Practically all denominational literature follows this line.

There have been several female founders of cults who could not resist the temptation of seeing themselves pictured in this woman. Joanna Southcott said that she herself was the woman in chapter 12 and that in October, 1814, she would have the man child. She never did, but she had 200,000 followers. We have had in the United States several founders of cults and religions who thought they were this woman. In Southern California, we even had a few female preachers who got the idea they might be the woman, but they weren't. We can dismiss all these claims, unless we want to forsake all intelligent approach to the interpretation of Scripture.

The identifying marks of the woman are the sun, moon, and stars. These belong to Israel as seen in Joseph's dream: "And he dreamed yet another dream, and told it his brethren, and said, Behold, I have dreamed a dream more; and, behold, the sun and the moon and the eleven stars made obeisance to me. And he told it to his father, and to his brethren: and his father rebuked him, and said unto him, What is this dream that thou hast dreamed? Shall I and thy mother and thy brethren indeed come to bow down ourselves to thee to the earth?" (Gen. 37:9–10). Old Jacob interpreted the sun, moon, and stars to mean himself, Rachel, and Joseph's brothers. And they did bow down before Joseph before things were over with (although Rachel had died by that time).

The woman is a sign in heaven, although her career is here on earth. She is not a literal woman; she is a symbol. The career of the woman corresponds to that of Israel, for it is Israel that gave birth to Christ, who is the Child.

At Christmastime we all use Isaiah 9:6 and other verses concerning the birth of Christ. This verse does concern the birth of Christ, but it does not concern us at all; rather, it concerns the nation Israel. "For unto us a child is born, unto us a son is given: and the government shall be upon his shoulder: and his name shall be called Wonderful, Counsellor, The mighty God, The everlasting Father, The Prince of Peace" (Isa. 9:6). Who is referred to here when Isaiah says, "Unto us"? The church? No; it's the nation Israel. It is quite obvious that Isaiah is speaking to the nation Israel, and he is speaking not relative to a Savior but to a Governor, a Ruler, a King, One who was to come and rule over them. "For unto us a child is born, unto us a son is given." It is interesting that as a child He was *born* in His humanity; but as a Son from eternity, He

was *given*. "And the government shall be upon his shoulder"—we are not talking now about the Savior but about the One who is coming as King. We will see that happen in the Book of Revelation. "And his name shall be called Wonderful, Counsellor, The mighty God, The everlasting Father, The Prince of Peace." There will not be any peace until He comes. When the rulers of this world say, ". . . Peace and safety; then sudden destruction cometh upon them . . ." (1 Thess. 5:3). They were having a big peace conference in Holland when World War I broke out, and most of the delegates almost got fired upon before they got home! When men say, "Peace and safety," it is idle talk, because man is working at peace from the wrong end. It is the human heart that is wrong, and only Jesus will bring peace. He is the Prince of Peace. Isaiah is talking to Israel when he says, "Unto us a child is born," and that is the figure that John picks up here in Revelation.

The writer to the Hebrews says, "For it is evident that our Lord sprang out of Juda . . ." (Heb. 7:14). Paul writes in Romans: "Who are Israelites; to whom pertaineth the adoption, and the glory, and the covenants, and the giving of the law, and the service of God, and the promises; Whose are the fathers, and of whom as concerning the flesh Christ came, who is over all, God blessed for ever. Amen" (Rom. 9:4–5). Paul is talking about Israel. He begins by asking the question: "Who are Israelites?" The answer just happens to be: "And of whom as concerning the flesh Christ came." The woman at the well was accurate when she identified the Lord Jesus as a Jew: ". . . How is it that thou, being a *Jew*, askest drink of me, which am a woman of Samaria? . . ." (John 4:9, italics mine). We read in Micah 5:2–3: "But thou, Bethlehem Ephratah, though thou be little among the thousands of Judah, yet out of thee shall he come forth unto me that is to be ruler in Israel; whose goings forth have been from of old, from everlasting. Therefore will he give them up, until the time that she which travaileth hath brought forth: then the remnant of his brethren shall return unto the children of Israel." Notice that He will be born in Bethlehem, but He comes out of eternity.

"Travailing in birth" is a figure associated with Israel: "Before she travailed, she brought forth; before her pain came, she was delivered of a man child. Who hath heard such a thing? who hath seen such things? Shall the earth be made to bring forth in one day? or shall a nation be born at once? for as soon as Zion travailed, she brought forth her children" (Isa.

66:7–8). Israel will go through the Great Tribulation after Christ was born in Bethlehem—"before her pain came, she was delivered of a man child," meaning Christ.

Therefore, we identify the woman as the nation Israel. No one woman who has ever lived, including the Virgin Mary, fits into this. It is the nation Israel and certainly not the church of all ages. If we just keep our bearings here and not lose our heads, we know that this is the Great Tribulation Period and that the church has already gone to heaven. This woman is not the church of all ages.

"Being tormented." Certainly Israel has suffered satanic anti-Semitism from the time of the birth of Christ to the present, in fact, even since before that day, because Satan knew that Christ would come from this nation.

THE RED DRAGON—SATAN

We now have introduced to us another character, and this character is really not a delightful one at all. This is the red dragon. This is not a comic-strip characterization, for there is nothing funny about him. This is very solemn and serious.

And there appeared another wonder in heaven; and behold a great red dragon, having seven heads and ten horns, and seven crowns upon his heads.

And his tail drew the third part of the stars of heaven, and did cast them to the earth: and the dragon stood before the woman which was ready to be delivered, for to devour her child as soon as it was born [Rev. 12:3–4].

And there was seen another sign in heaven, and behold, a great red dragon having seven heads and ten horns and on his head seven diadems (kingly crowns). And his tail draweth the third of the stars of heaven, and he did cast [aorist tense] them into the earth. And the dragon stood before the woman about to be delivered, that when she was delivered he might devour her child.

"And there was seen another sign in heaven." Notice that these are *signs* that are given to us; they are not literal. I told you that if John is giving you a symbol, he will make it clear that it is a symbol.

The red dragon is clearly identified as Satan in verse 9: "And the great dragon was cast out, that old serpent, called the Devil, and Satan, which deceiveth the whole world: he was cast out into the earth, and his angels were cast out with him." We can identify this character without speculating at all.

In this second sign, the true character of Satan is revealed with all the wrappings removed:

1. He is called "great" because of his vast power. He controls the nations of the world and offered them to the Lord Jesus if He would worship him (see Matt. 4:8–9). Worship of himself is Satan's ultimate goal. The kingdoms of this world are his, and he controls them today. In that day it was Rome, but he has controlled every nation.

2. He is called "red" because of the fact that he was a murderer from the beginning (see John 8:44). He has no regard for human life. I do not understand why so many serve him. Why is it that alcohol finally kills its victims? It is the worst killer there is today. It is because Satan is back of it, my friend, and he has no regard for human life at all.

3. He is called a "dragon" because of the viciousness of his character. He was originally created Lucifer, son of the morning (see Ezek. 28:12–19), but he is now the epitome of evil and the depth of degradation. He is the most dangerous being in all of God's creation. He is my enemy, and he is your enemy if you are a child of God.

The reason that the Beast in chapter 13 is similar to the dragon is because both the restored Roman Empire and Antichrist are empowered and controlled by Satan. Rome, through the instrumentality of both Herod and Pilate, sought to destroy the child of the woman.

"Seven heads" suggests the perfection of wisdom which characterized the creation of Satan who was originally the "covering cherub." Ezekiel 28:12 speaks of how he was at his origin: ". . . full of wisdom, and perfect in beauty." This reveals two of the fallacies that the world has concerning Satan. This world thinks he is ugly, but may I say to you, he was created "perfect in beauty." If you could see him, you would not see the foul creature that is often pictured for us by the world. Sometimes he is pictured as having horns, cloven feet, and a forked tail. That is the "great god" Pan that the Greeks and Romans worshiped. That is not Satan, although Satan is back of that worship, also. I have seen the ruins of the temple at Pergamum and of other temples to Pan in at least a dozen cities. It is not strange that men are worshiping him; when they will not have God, they certainly will take him. But Satan is smart, he's clever, and he's wise. You and I are no match for him at all. We will be overcome if we try to stand in our own strength against him. He is not only beautiful, he is also full of wisdom. This is the way he is presented in Scripture.

"Ten horns" suggests the final division of the Roman Empire, which is dominated by Satan and which is his final effort to rule the world. The crowns are on the horns, not on the heads, since it is delegated power from Satan. The crowns represent kingly authority and rulership.

"The third of the stars of heaven" indicates the vast extent of the rebellion in heaven when one third of the angelic host followed Satan to their own destruction. Daniel makes reference to this in an admittedly difficult passage (see Dan. 8:10; Jude 6).

The dragon hates the Man Child because it was predicted from the beginning that the child would be the undoing of Satan. "And I will put enmity between thee and the woman, and between thy seed and her seed; it shalt bruise thy head, and thou shalt bruise his heel" (Gen. 3:15).

THE CHILD OF THE WOMAN— JESUS CHRIST

And she brought forth a man child, who was to rule all nations with a rod of iron: and her child was caught up unto God, and to his throne.

And the woman fled into the wilderness, where she hath a place prepared of God, that they should feed her there a thousand two hundred and threescore days [Rev. 12:5–6].

And she was delivered of a son, a man child, who is to shepherd (rule) all the nations with a rod of iron, and her child was caught up unto God and His throne. And the woman fled into the wilderness, where she hath a place prepared of (from) God, that there they may nourish her a thousand two hundred and sixty (1260) days.

The "man child" is Christ. He is easily identified here. I hope that you will not fall into the error of equating the Child with the church, although many have done that.

"Who is to shepherd (rule) all the nations with a rod of iron" is a clear-cut reference to Christ. "Thou shalt break them with a rod of iron; thou shalt dash them in pieces like a potter's vessel" (Ps. 2:9). In Acts 4 the persecuted Christians quoted Psalm 2, identifying the One to rule with a rod of iron as the Lord Jesus Christ.

Christ will come to put down all enmity, all opposition, all rebellion on the earth. How will He do it? He will break them with a rod of iron and dash them in pieces like a potter's vessel. If this peace crowd would only come up with a program that would work, it would not be necessary to put down rebellion with a bit of violence. But there is no other way to put it down. How do you think Jesus Christ is going to come to power in a rebellious world? Suppose He was suddenly to appear at the capital of any nation in the world. Do you think they are prepared to surrender to Him and turn their authority over to Him? This includes my own country. Is the United States prepared to yield to Jesus Christ? If you say, "Yes," I will have to ask, "Why don't they?" They *could* yield to Him today. My friend, the world is in rebellion against Him. Maybe you are one of the peace crowd. You don't like the shedding of blood, you just hate violence and war— don't we all?—but this is the only way that rebellion can be put down. The Lord Jesus Christ is going to rule.

"And her child was caught up unto God and His throne." This is a reference to the ascension of Christ. In the Gospels the emphasis is on the death of Christ. In the Epistles the emphasis is upon the resurrection of Christ. In the Book of Revelation the emphasis is upon the ascension of Christ. Protestantism, and even fundamentalism, has ignored the ascension of Christ, and this is one reason we have not had a great enough emphasis upon the present ministry of Christ. "And when he had spoken these things, while they beheld, he was taken up; and a cloud received him out of their sight. And while they looked stedfastly toward heaven as he went up, behold, two men stood by them in white apparel; Which also said, Ye men of Galilee, why stand ye gazing up into heaven? this same Jesus, which is taken up from you into heaven, shall so come in like manner as ye have seen him go into heaven" (Acts 1:9–11).

The Book of Revelation is the unveiling of the ascended Christ, the glorified Christ, the Christ who is coming in glory. The Book of the Revelation rests upon the fact of the Ascension. He is the One who has been opening the seals which have brought to pass everything that has happened since then. We are told in Hebrews 12:2: "Looking unto Jesus the author and finisher of our faith; who for the joy that was set before him endured the cross, despising the shame, and is set down at the right hand of the throne of God." A great many have the impression that this means He is twiddling His thumbs, but that is because they do not know Revelation. He is not sitting up there doing nothing. He is going to do a great deal because of His ascension into heaven, and He has a present ministry today with the church.

"And she was delivered of a son, a man child." I believe this settles the identity of the woman. Israel is clearly the one from whom Christ came. While the church came from Jesus Christ, He, according to the flesh, came from Israel. Again let me quote Paul: "Who are Israelites. . . . of whom as concerning the flesh Christ came . . ." (Rom. 9:4–5). We are told in Galatians 4:4–5: "But when the fulness of the time was come, God sent forth his Son, made of a woman, made under the law, To redeem them that were under the law, that we might receive the adoption of sons." "Made under the law"—what law? It is the Mosaic Law which was given to Israel. He came "made [or, born] under the law" because He was an Israelite. Again in Galatians we read: "Now to Abraham and his seed were the promises made. He saith not, And to seeds, as of many; but as of one, And to thy seed, which is Christ" (Gal. 3:16). Before the nation came into existence, God said to Abraham, "I am going to make you a great nation, and through that nation I am sending a seed"—not many, but one, and that One is Christ. We have already looked at Isaiah 9:6 which says, "For unto us a child is born, unto us a son is given. . . ." "Us" does not mean the United States, although some seem to think so! "Unto us" means Israel. Isaiah was an Israelite and was speaking to that nation. He was not speaking either to the church or to the Gentiles, but to Israel.

"And the woman fled into the wilderness, where she hath a place prepared of (from) God." During the intense part of the Great Tribulation Period, this remnant of Israel will be protected by God. There are those who dogmatically say that Israel will go to the rock-hewn city of Petra and will be preserved there because no enemy can get in. But in our day an enemy now comes from above and drops down bombs. The last place I would want to be when bombs start falling is within that rock-hewn city of Petra. To make that dogmatic statement alongside clear-cut prophecies is certainly to deceive people. This is not a clear-cut prophecy, and I do not know where the place will be. It does not hurt us preachers to say we don't know something when we don't know. To my judgment it is tragic to be so dogmatic about that which is not revealed. If you want to make such a statement about a speculative Scripture, I will not object if you will say, "This is my judgment," or, "I think this is the way it will be."

MICHAEL, THE ARCHANGEL, WARS WITH THE DRAGON

And there was war in heaven: Michael and his angels fought against the dragon; and the dragon fought and his angels,

And prevailed not; neither was their place found any more in heaven.

And the great dragon was cast out, that old serpent, called the Devil, and Satan, which deceiveth the whole world: he was cast out into the earth, and his angels were cast out with him [Rev. 12:7–9].

And there arose war in heaven, Michael and his angels going forth to war with the dragon. And the dragon warred and his angels, and they prevailed not, neither was their place found any more in heaven. And the great dragon was cast down, the old serpent, the one called (the) Devil, and the Satan, he that deceiveth the whole (inhabited) world; he was cast down to the earth, and his angels with him were cast down.

We have here a startling revelation: "And there arose war in heaven." The United Nations could not do anything about this war any more than they could about any other war that has taken place since they came into existence. It is difficult to imagine that there is war in heaven, but Satan still has access to heaven and, as long as he does, there will be this problem.

We are told in the Book of Job that Satan came with the sons of God to appear before God (see Job 1–2). He apparently had as much right there as they did. He had been created the highest creation. We also read in Zechariah 3:1–2: "And he shewed me Joshua the high priest standing before the angel of the LORD, and Satan standing at his right hand to resist him. And the LORD said unto Satan, the LORD rebuke thee, O Satan; even the LORD that hath chosen Jerusalem rebuke thee: is not this a brand plucked out of the fire?" Satan has access to God, and he is able to carry on a communication with God. Luke 22:31 tells us: "And the Lord said, Simon, Simon, behold,

Satan hath desired to have you, that he may sift you as wheat." I do not think that Satan sent a Western Union telegram to God or that he telephoned Him. He was able to come into the presence of God, and he requested that he might test this man Simon Peter—and he was granted that permission.

"Michael" is the archangel. We are told this in the Book of Jude: "Yet Michael the archangel, when contending with the devil he disputed about the body of Moses, durst not bring against him a railing accusation, but said, The Lord rebuke thee" (Jude 9). Evidently there are other archangels, but Michael has a peculiar ministry with the nation Israel. Daniel 10:13 tells us: "But the prince of the kingdom of Persia withstood me one and twenty days: but, lo, Michael, one of the chief princes, came to help me; and I remained there with the kings of Persia." Michael is "one of the chief princes." Although there are probably other archangels, Michael and Gabriel are the only ones whose names are given in Scripture. Again in Daniel we read: "But I will shew thee that which is noted in the scripture of truth: and there is none that holdeth with me in these things, but Michael your prince" (Dan. 10:21).

"Michael your prince"—since the Lord is talking to Daniel, this refers to Daniel's people, the nation Israel. This is made clear in Daniel 12:1: "And at that time shall Michael stand up, the great prince which standeth for the children of thy people: and there shall be a time of trouble, such as never was since there was a nation even to that same time: and at that time thy people shall be delivered, every one that shall be found written in the book." At that time, we are told, there will be a time of trouble, the Great Tribulation. Michael will again step out and drive Satan out of heaven, because he happens to be the prince who watches over the nation Israel. This is a tremendous thing, and it beggars description.

There will be a fierce struggle, a war. Satan is not going to retire easily, but Michael and his angels will prevail, and Satan and his angels will be thrown out of heaven. The Lord Jesus referred to this in Luke 10:18, "And he said unto them, I beheld Satan as lightning fall from heaven."

There is no mistaking this creature who is called the great dragon, for he is marked out with great detail. His fingerprints are put down here in the Revelation. Because God knew that a great percentage of the preachers of this century would teach that Satan does not exist, He makes it so you cannot miss him.

If your enemy can get you to think he does not exist, he will have a tremendous advantage over you, and he will be able to get a crack at you that will sweep you off your feet. Satan moved in afresh and anew during my generation simply because my generation did not believe in him. Now we are getting an overdose of him, and he has been made a weird and wild thing. But, actually, he is not an ugly creature, by any means; he is an angel of light.

Notice how he is identified here:

1. He is called "the old serpent." This takes us back to the Garden of Eden. Our Lord said, ". . . He was a murderer from the beginning . . ." (John 8:44). The words *old* and *beginning* are akin, according to Vincent. Satan is that old serpent, the one who was at the beginning in the Garden of Eden.

2. He is called "Devil," a name which comes from the Greek *diabolos*, meaning "slanderer or accuser." He is so labeled in verse 10: "the accuser of our brethren." This is the reason believers need an Advocate with the Father. You and I have an enemy today who is not only causing us problems down here, but you would be surprised what he says about you and me in heaven! There is nothing that you do or say or think which he does not turn in against you up yonder. But God already knows about it, and I like to beat Satan to the draw and confess it before he gets up there to bring the accusation against me. The Lord Jesus is our Advocate. "My little children, these things write I unto you, that ye sin not. And if any man sin, we have an advocate with the Father, Jesus Christ the righteous" (1 John 2:1).

It would be wonderful if I did not sin, but I do. Thank God that we have an Advocate with the Father. Jesus Christ the righteous is up there to defend us. He has been kept busy ever since I have been in this world, and I have a notion He's been pretty busy defending you, too. Don't think He is up there sitting idly by. He is our Defender, our Advocate. The Devil is a slanderer; he is a liar from the beginning. He is the origin of all lies today. Where does the gossip that goes on in some of our churches originate? It originates in the pit of hell, my friend. That is the last place from which anything ought to be shipped into the church!

3. He is also called "Satan," which means "adversary." He is the awful adversary of God and of every one of God's children. We are told: "Be sober, be vigilant; because your adversary the devil, as a roaring lion, walketh about, seeking whom he may devour" (1 Pet. 5:8). I have received a great many letters from people who have been delivered out of cults and

"isms" through the study of the Word of God. One man wrote: "I was in a cult. I wrote you the letter I did [and it was a mean one!] to try to trap you, to try to trick you. I thought I was right and you were wrong. When I began to study the Word of God, I came to realize how Satan had me trapped." Satan has a lot of folk trapped today, even church members. We need to recognize that he is our enemy. That does not mean we ought to go overboard and just dwell on Satan and demons. It certainly is true that there is a new and fresh manifestation of him today that was not here a generation ago. But keep your eye on Jesus Christ, for He is your place of deliverance, and He is up yonder to help you.

4. Finally, he is called "he that deceiveth the whole (inhabited) world." During the Great Tribulation, Satan will be able to *totally* deceive men—today he deceives only partially. Satan deceives men relative to God and the Word of God. He caused Eve to distrust God: "Has God said you should not eat of that tree? You just can't trust Him, can you?"(see Gen. 3:1–4). Satan deceives man relative to man. Satan makes out mankind better than he is, yet he despises us. He builds us up and tells us we could become gods—how wonderful that would be (see Gen. 3:5). Satan deceives man relative to the world, the flesh, and the Devil. You and I think we are big enough to overcome the world, the flesh, and the Devil, but we are not big enough to overcome any *one* of them. The world is too big for us, and it will certainly draw us away from the Lord. Satan deceives man relative to the gospel. He does not mind a man going to church or even joining a dozen churches, but he does not want that man to be saved. "In whom the god of this world hath blinded the minds of them which believe not, lest the light of the glorious gospel of Christ, who is the image of God, should shine unto them" (2 Cor. 4:4).

Someone has said, "Satan is to be dreaded as a lion; more to be dreaded as a serpent; and most to be dreaded as an angel." That is where he traps multitudes today.

And I heard a loud voice saying in heaven, Now is come salvation, and strength, and the kingdom of our God, and the power of his Christ: for the accuser of our brethren is cast down, which accused them before our God day and night.

And they overcame him by the blood of the Lamb, and by the word of their tes-timony; and they loved not their lives unto the death.

Therefore rejoice, ye heavens, and ye that dwell in them. Woe to the inhabiters of the earth and of the sea! for the devil is come down unto you, having great wrath, because he knoweth that he hath but a short time [Rev. 12: 10–12].

And I heard a great voice in heaven, saying, Now is come the salvation, and the power, and the kingdom of our God, and the authority [Gr.: exousia] of His Christ; for the accuser of our brethren is cast down, the one accusing them before our God day and night. And they overcame him because of the blood of the Lamb, and because of the word of their testimony; and they loved not their life even unto death. Therefore, rejoice, O heavens, and ye that dwell in them. Woe for the earth and for the sea; because the devil is gone down unto you, having great wrath, knowing that he has but a short time.

"And I heard." This reminds us that John is still the spectator and auditor of these events. He does not want us to forget that, because it is very important.

When Satan has been cast out of heaven, it will cause great rejoicing among the redeemed who are in heaven. "A great voice in heaven" seems to refer to the Old Testament saints or to the tribulation saints who have been martyred up to this point (see Rev. 6:9–10), for they mention their brethren on the earth: "for the accuser of our brethren is cast down."

The first great demonstration of power to be exerted against evil after the death and resurrection of Christ is the casting out of Satan from heaven. That is the beginning of the movement that will lead to the Lord Jesus taking over the reins of government down here. When Christ died on the cross, He paved the way for Satan's being cast out of heaven. Listen to the language in Colossians: "Blotting out the handwriting of ordinances that was against us, which was contrary to us, and took it out of the way, nailing it to his cross" (Col. 2:14). The Lord Jesus made it possible for man to be saved by His death. God canceled our debt of sin by nailing it to the cross of Christ. Christ made full payment. Paul goes on to say: "And having spoiled principalities and powers, he made a shew of them openly, triumphing over them in it" (Col. 2:15). I personally believe that this began when He ascended into heaven and took that great company of saints with Him. He led captivity captive and took them into the presence of God. Those were the Old Testament saints, and I think they are in this group who are now saying that salvation is come.

This opens the way for the coming of four great, blood-bought, heavenly freedoms. We talk about four freedoms down here which have not yet come to pass, but here are four freedoms that are going to come to pass when Christ comes.

1. "The salvation"—its consummation is in the person of Christ. Our salvation will not be consummated until we are in His presence: "Beloved, now are we the sons of God, and it doth not yet appear what we shall be: but we know that, when he shall appear, we shall be like him; for we shall see him as he is" (1 John 3:2). This will be true when He comes to the earth. I believe this verse speaks of His visible return to the earth.

2. "The power." The way nations have handled power has been tragic. This has been true of every great nation. Some nations have been able to make war and, like a great prairie fire, they have spread across another nation, destroying cities and killing people. The nations have abused power, but it will be wonderful when Christ takes the power and controls this earth.

3. "And the kingdom of our God" is going to be established on the earth. Not until then will there be peace and righteousness and freedom on this earth. In this land of the free and home of the brave, there are not many brave left, and I don't know that there are many free who are left either. It will be wonderful when His kingdom comes on this earth. This very statement reveals that the kingdom was not established at the first coming of Christ.

4. "And the authority (Gr.: *exousia*) of His Christ" shows that Christ has not yet taken over the governmental authority of this world. He is not building a kingdom; He is not establishing His kingdom today. Wait until He starts moving. All of these judgments are in preparation for His return to this earth, giving men a warning and an opportunity to turn to Him—and multitudes will do so. There is always a note of grace in the judgment of God.

"The one accusing them before our God day and night" reveals that this is part of the present strategy of Satan which attempts to thwart Christ's purpose with His church today and with the tribulation saints tomorrow. This necessitates Christ's present ministry as Advocate for us.

Victory for the accused saints comes through three avenues which are mentioned to us in this section:

1. "The blood of the Lamb." There is wonder-working power in the blood of the Lamb. Don't you forget that. Let us not minimize that. The many references to the blood of the Lamb necessitate its being on display in heaven. This is not a crude conception; rather, the crudity is in our sins which made it necessary for Him to shed His blood. If you and I get any victory, it will be because He shed His blood for us. We will never, never be able to lead "the victorious life." The most defeated people I have ever met have been people who are supposedly living "the victorious life." All of them look anemic to me. They look to me like they are fugitives from a blood bank. They are shallow and sallow looking, and they need a blood transfusion. *They* don't live a victorious life—*Christ* does! If any of us overcome, it will be through the blood of the Lamb.

2. "The word of their testimony" reveals that they were true martyrs. Those who are Christ's cannot deny Him. "But whosoever shall deny me before men, him will I also deny before my Father which is in heaven" (Matt. 10:33). There is something that is strengthening in giving a testimony. Don't misunderstand me—some of the testimonies given today are pretty shallow. Some of them are given by those who ought not to be giving a testimony, because the people close to them know their shoddy living, and it makes them rather cynical and skeptical. The place to give a testimony is not at a nice, well-fed church banquet where all the saints say amen to everything you say. If you have a life to back it up, the place to give your testimony is out yonder in the world, when you are up against that godless, blaspheming crowd. Let them know that you belong to Christ and that you are in Christ. There is something strengthening in that. There is something that makes a man stand tall when he can give a testimony like that. I know of a man in business who is a big, double-fisted fellow. He is an executive in a very hard-hitting concern, and there are a lot of blaspheming folk around him. When he hears someone blaspheming, in a very quiet manner, he will say to that person, "I'd like to tell you what Jesus Christ means to me." The Lord Jesus says, "If you deny Me before men, I'll deny you before My Father in heaven" (see Matt. 10:33). These are the true martyrs. The

Greek word *martus* means "witness." These are the ones who witness for Him.

3. "They loved not their life even unto death." This is an exalted plane to come to, where you and I make the Lord Jesus the first love in our life and put love of self down in second, third, fourth, or some other place. Surely we ought to have respect for ourselves, and there ought to be a dignity about us, but let's put Him first. When we put Him first, we will not have any problem living for Him down here. The great problem today is not the set of rules you may be living by; it is what is behind the rules. Here is what you need behind them: the blood of the Lamb, the word of your testimony, and love for Him above everything else. Love is the very basis of service. The Lord said to Simon Peter, "Do you love me?" When Simon Peter finally could say that he did, although on a weak plane, the Lord Jesus said, "I am going to use you. You are going to feed My sheep" (see John 21:15–17). Peter preached the first sermon in the church and probably saw more people saved per capita of those then living than any other time in the history of the world.

There are two radical reactions to the casting out of Satan from heaven. There is rejoicing in heaven, for this awesome, treacherous, dangerous, and deadly serpent is out forever. Then there is woe on the earth. This is the third woe that extends through the pouring out of the seven bowls of wrath. The only consolation for the earth is that Satan's sojourn on earth is brief—forty-two months. There is an intensification of tribulation during this period.

THE DRAGON PERSECUTES THE WOMAN

And when the dragon saw that he was cast unto the earth, he persecuted the woman which brought forth the man child.

And to the woman were given two wings of a great eagle, that she might fly into the wilderness, into her place, where she is nourished for a time, and times, and half a time, from the face of the serpent [Rev. 12:13–14].

This is the last wave of anti-Semitism that will roll over the world, and it is the worst, because Satan is cast down to the earth and knows that his time is short. He hates Israel because Christ came from this nation according to the flesh. This is the Time of Jacob's Trouble, and this is the reason I cannot rejoice

in the present return of Israel to that land. Some people seem to think they are going back for the Millennium. They are not—they are going back for the Great Tribulation Period if they are going back for any purpose at all, according to the Word of God.

"Two wings of a great eagle" are given to her that she might fly into the wilderness. There are those who see in this the airplane that will take Israel to their hiding place, and they always pick the rock-hewn city of Petra as being that place. I do not know how an airplane would land in that place, but that is the problem of those who give that explanation.

"Two wings of a great eagle" is not something that is unusual or peculiar to the people of Israel, but it is reminiscent of the grace of God in His past deliverance of Israel from Egypt. He said to them: "Ye have seen what I did unto the Egyptians, and how I bare you on eagles' wings, and brought you unto myself" (Exod. 19:4). They had not come out of Egypt by their own effort or their own ability. They came out because God brought them out, and eagles' wings became a symbol to them. Here again in the Great Tribulation, the Israelites cannot deliver themselves, and no one is interested in delivering them. But God will get them out on eagles' wings by His grace.

"Into the wilderness, into her place." Scripture does not say that the rock-hewn city of Petra will be that place. It could be, but we just simply do not know. This "wilderness" has been variously identified—Petra is not the only place. Some say that it is the wilderness of the peoples of the world; that is, that there will be another worldwide scattering of Israel. Since Christ said, ". . . flee into the mountains" (Matt. 24:16), we believe it to be a literal wilderness, possibly that same one in which Israel spent forty years under Moses. This time it will be forty-two months, for that is the meaning of "a time, and times, and half a time." The important thing is not the place but the fact that God will protect them by His grace.

"Where she is nourished" reminds us that in the past God sustained them with manna from heaven and water from the rock. He will nourish them again in possibly the same way.

And the serpent cast out of his mouth water as a flood after the woman, that he might cause her to be carried away of the flood.

And the earth helped the woman, and the earth opened her mouth, and swal-

lowed up the flood which the dragon cast out of his mouth [Rev. 12:15–16].

And the serpent cast out of his mouth after the woman water as a river, that he might cause her to be carried away by the stream. And the earth helped the woman, and the earth opened her mouth and swallowed up the river which the dragon cast out of his mouth.

In view of the fact that the wilderness is literal, the water also could be literal. God had delivered Israel out of the water, both at the beginning of the wilderness march at the Red Sea and then again at the end of the wilderness march at the Jordan River. However, the floods of water could be armies flowing like a river upon them. This figure of speech has been used by Isaiah (see Isa. 8:7–8).

In Ezekiel's picture of the last days, the king of the north is seen marching on Israel. Satan will use every means to destroy the people. How will he be stopped? No nation is there to stop him. But God is there, and He will destroy him with natural forces when he invades Palestine: "And I will plead against him with pestilence and with blood; and I will rain upon him, and upon his bands, and upon the many people that are with him, an overflowing rain, and great hailstones, fire, and brimstone" (Ezek. 38:22). This gives us an indication of what John is talking about here in Revelation.

THE REMNANT OF ISRAEL

And the dragon was wroth with the woman, and went to make war with the remnant of her seed, which keep the commandments of God, and have the testimony of Jesus Christ [Rev. 12:17].

And the dragon was wroth with the woman, and he went away to make war with the rest of her seed, that keep the commandments of God and hold the testimony of Jesus.

"The rest of her seed" may refer to the remnant who is God's witness in this period—the 144,000 who have been sealed. They are evidently witnessing throughout the world. These "keep the commandments of God," which places them back under the Law. This precludes the possibility of the witnesses being the church.

All anti-Semitism is Satan inspired and will finally culminate in Satan's making a supreme effort to destroy the nation of Israel. From the brickyards of Pharaoh's Egypt, Haman's gallows, Herod's cruel edict, through Hitler's purge, and to the world of the Great Tribulation, Satan has led the attack against these people because of the man child—Jesus Christ.

CHAPTER 13

THEME: *Wild beast out of the sea and earth*

Seven personages are introduced to us by the seventh trumpet, five of whom we met in chapter 12: the woman, or Israel; the red dragon, Satan; the child of the woman, Christ; Michael, the archangel; and the remnant of Israel, that is, the 144,000 who were sealed of God and who are going to make it through the Great Tribulation. In chapter 13 the final two personages are brought before us. One is the wild Beast out of the sea; he is both a political power and a person. The other is the wild Beast out of the earth; he is a religious leader. Here is where the action is when we come to these personages. Here is revealed to us the great warfare that is going on between light and darkness, between God and Satan. It is manifested now as we draw to the end of the age during the Great Tribulation Period.

These two Beasts are presented to us as *wild* beasts—that is the literal translation. It is bad enough to be a beast, but to be a wild beast compounds the injury. There is much disagreement among reputable Bible expositors as to the identity of the Beasts. Some consider the first Beast to be a person, while others treat him as the last form of the Roman Empire. Some treat the second Beast as the Man of Sin, while others consider him merely as the prophet, or the John-the-Baptist type, for the first Beast. These difficulties arise because it is impossible to separate a king from his kingdom. A dictator must have a realm over which he rules, or he is no dictator. Though it is difficult to distinguish the two, it seems that the first Beast is the Antichrist, the ruler over the restored Roman Empire. In

Revelation 16:10 it speaks of "the throne of the wild beast." I would judge from this that there is somebody to sit on that throne, and that is the Beast who is presented here—but he would not be the Beast if he did not have the empire. After determining the identity of the first Beast, it is not really difficult to identify the second. He is a man, the false prophet, the religious leader, who leads in the worship of the first Beast—and he is Antichrist also.

There is another view being held today that Antichrist is the denial of the person of Christ rather than an actual person. In other words, Antichrist is false doctrine rather than a person yet to be revealed. The explanation, I believe, is found in the meaning of the preposition *anti*, which has two usages. The first meaning of *anti* is "over against." Its second meaning is "instead of" or "in place of." It has both meanings in Scripture. In both his first and second epistles, John mentions the Antichrist. He is the only one who uses that designation. We can see both of these characteristics in Antichrist; he is the one who is *against* Christ and the one who *imitates* Christ—Antichrist is both.

In his first epistle John writes: "Little children, it is the last time: and as ye have heard that antichrist shall come, even now are there many antichrists; whereby we know that it is the last time" (1 John 2:18). "Little children, it is the last time." John said that nineteen hundred years ago. We have been in the last time a long time! Note here that John not only says there is going to be an Antichrist, but that already in his day there were *many* antichrists. What was the thing which identified an antichrist? "Who is a liar but he that denieth that Jesus is the Christ? He is antichrist, that denieth the Father and the Son" (1 John 2:22). Antichrist denies the deity of Christ. He is against Christ. He is *the* enemy of Christ on the earth.

In the fourth chapter of his first epistle, John tells us some additional facts concerning Antichrist. "Beloved, believe not every spirit, but try the spirits whether they are of God: because many false prophets are gone out into the world. . . . And every spirit that confesseth not that Jesus Christ is come in the flesh is not of God: and this is that spirit of antichrist, whereof ye have heard that it should come; and even now already is it in the world" (1 John 4:1, 3). In other words, any person or any group or any book that denies the deity of Christ is antichrist. I consider the rock opera, *Jesus Christ Superstar*, to be antichrist. It is against the Jesus Christ of the Bible. Also, any minister who denies the deity of Christ is antichrist—he is *against* Christ.

In John's second epistle we read: "For many deceivers are entered into the world, who confess not that Jesus Christ is come in the flesh. This is a deceiver and an antichrist" (2 John 7). Antichrist is a deceiver—he *pretends* to be Christ, and he is not. The Lord Jesus Christ said, "There are going to be many who will come in My name, saying, 'I am Christ.' You are to test them because not every spirit is of God." We need to test the spirits today. My friend, you need to start by testing your little group or the cult in which you are interested. Instead of being super-duper saints, they may actually be following an antichrist. Our Lord warned of such in the Olivet Discourse: "For there shall arise false Christs, and false prophets, and shall shew great signs and wonders; insomuch that, if it were possible, they shall deceive the very elect" (Matt. 24:24). There will arise false Christs who will be able to perform miracles; this second Beast is really a miracle worker—he is an antichrist.

Therefore, the first Beast is political Antichrist, and the second Beast is religious Antichrist. Even the Devil cannot put it all together in one person. I believe there are two persons, these two Beasts, who are Antichrist.

WILD BEAST OUT OF THE SEA— DESCRIPTION, A POLITICAL POWER AND A PERSON

The first verse of this chapter introduces the Beast from the sea.

And I stood upon the sand of the sea, and saw a beast rise up out of the sea, having seven heads and ten horns, and upon his horns ten crowns, and upon his heads the name of blasphemy [Rev. 13:1].

Let me give you my translation:

And he stood on the sand of the sea; and I saw a (wild) beast coming up out of the sea, having ten horns and seven heads, and on his horns ten diadems, and upon his heads names of blasphemy.

My translation reads, "And *he* stood on the sand of the sea," but the Authorized Version reads, "And *I* stood upon the sand of the sea," as if it were John. The better manuscripts today show the subject of the sentence to be *he*. Who is he? Whom were we last talking about in the previous chapter? He is the same person, and that, of course, is Satan.

"And I saw a (wild) beast coming up out of the sea." Who brings him out of the sea? Satan brings him out of the sea. In Scripture the sea is a picture of the nations of the world, of mankind, like the restless sea.

"Having ten horns and seven heads, and on his horns ten diadems, and upon his heads names of blasphemy." This Beast really boggles the mind. If I were to meet him in the dark, I know for sure that he and I would be going in the same direction, only I would be *lots* farther down the road than he would be!

The dragon (Satan) stands on the sands of the sea, and it is he who brings the wild Beast out of the sea and dominates him. This is Satan's masterpiece. The first Beast is a person who heads up the old Roman Empire. Rome simply fell apart, and this is the only one who will ever be able to put it together again.

God is apparently taking His hands off this earth for awhile and turning it over to Satan. I believe this is poetic justice. God must let Satan demonstrate that, when he is given full sway, he will not be able to produce. Otherwise, Satan would always be able to say to God from the lake of fire, "You never gave me a chance. If You would have taken Your hands off and let me alone, I would have been able to accomplish my purpose and establish a second kingdom." But God is going to let Satan have his way so that he will not be able to say that.

An understanding of the prophecy of Daniel is very important to the understanding of the Revelation. This wild Beast is similar in description to the fourth beast, that nondescript beast, in the seventh chapter of Daniel. There it represents the prophetic history of the Roman Empire, down to "the little horn" and his destruction. That fourth beast looked like it became dormant for a little while, and then out of one of its seven heads there came up ten horns, out of which came a little horn. The little horn put together three of the horns and was able to take the other seven.

At the time of the writing of John, much of the prophecy of Daniel had been fulfilled. The first three beasts—Babylon, the lion; Media-Persia, the bear; and Graeco-Macedonia, the panther—had all been fulfilled. When Daniel gave it, it was prophecy, but it was fulfilled by John's time. Therefore, John centers on the fourth beast and upon the little horn because the fourth beast, the Roman Empire, had appeared. John was living in the time of the Roman Empire, having been exiled to the Isle of Patmos by the Roman emperor, Domitian. Already, signs of weakness and decay were visible in the empire, and John was spectator to that which was still future in Daniel's day. However, in the Book of Revelation the emphasis is upon the rule of the little horn of Daniel 7, and the little horn is set before us as a wild Beast, for he is now ruling and controlling the restored Roman Empire in John's prophecy. The little horn of Daniel 7 and the wild Beast of Revelation 13 are identical. You can see that an understanding of Daniel 7 would be basic to understanding this passage.

The wild Beast is the Man of Sin and Antichrist, the final world dictator. The last verse of this chapter confirms this view. "Here is wisdom. Let him that hath understanding count the number of the beast: for it is the number of a man; and his number is Six hundred threescore and six" (v. 18). We are dealing with the man who is the world dictator at the end.

There has been a great deal of excitement in our day (and I am included in the group that is excited) about the current existence of the Common Market in Europe. Throughout history, there have been many who have attempted to put Europe back together again. Charlemagne attempted it and failed. I think that the Roman Catholic church attempted it in the Holy Roman Empire and certainly did not succeed. The Holy Roman Empire was centered in Vienna, Austria, which makes it a very interesting place to visit today. Franz Josef was the last of the emperors of the Holy Roman Empire who tried to put Europe together, but he was the worst flop of all. His son apparently either was murdered or committed suicide, and that ended the Holy Roman Empire. Napoleon, Kaiser Wilhelm, Hitler, and Mussolini all attempted it. But God has not been ready yet, and He will not let that one appear until the time of the Great Tribulation. To me the Common Market is interesting, not because we are seeing prophecy fulfilled, but because we are seeing the stage set which reveals that prophecy *can* be fulfilled. Down through the centuries, many have said that it is impossible to get Europe together. It *is* impossible until God is ready— and Satan is going to supply the man. The Common Market is just an interesting instrument—that's all.

The ten horns with ten diadems speak of the tenfold division of the Roman Empire in the time of the Great Tribulation. The horns are the ten kings who rule over this tenfold division. This interpretation is confirmed by Revelation 17:12.

The little horn comes to power by first putting down three of these rulers, and afterward he dominates the other seven and thus becomes the world dictator.

The seven heads are not so easily identified. They are interpreted in Revelation 17:9–10 as seven kings. These do not reign contemporaneously as the ten horns do, but they appear in chronological order. Some have interpreted them as representing certain Roman emperors, such as Domitian who was then ruling. Others interpret these seven heads as the forms of government through which the Roman Empire passed. They had kings, councils, dictators, decemvirs, military tribunes, and emperors. The third view is that the seven heads could represent seven great nations of antiquity which blasphemed God: Rome, Greece, Media-Persia, Chaldea, Egypt, and Assyria. The kingdom of the Beast which is yet to come would be the seventh. Another likely view is that the seven heads correspond to the seven heads of the dragon which denote exceptional wisdom. Satan energizes the Man of Sin, the last dictator. I cannot be dogmatic about any one of these views and do not feel that it is crucial to do so.

All seven heads are guilty of blasphemy. Blasphemy manifests itself in two ways according to Govett: (1) making oneself equal with God, that is, usurping His place, and (2) slandering and taking God's name in vain. The emperors of Rome were guilty of the first form. They made themselves equal with God; there was emperor worship in the Roman Empire. The Pharisees were guilty of the latter when they blasphemed the Holy Spirit. The Beast here is guilty of both forms.

And the beast which I saw was like unto a leopard, and his feet were as the feet of a bear, and his mouth as the mouth of a lion: and the dragon gave him his power, and his seat, and great authority [Rev. 13:2].

And the wild beast which I saw was like unto a panther, and his feet were as the feet of a bear, and his mouth as the mouth of a lion: and the dragon gave him his power, and his throne, and great authority.

This is really a weird-looking creature! He has never been seen on land or sea or in the air. Without doubt, this is a real spectacle.

John notes that he is a composite Beast. We can begin now to formulate some very definite facts concerning Antichrist. He combines the characteristics of the other beasts representing kingdoms which Daniel saw in his vision of Daniel 7. Consulting that passage and my commentary on the Book of Daniel might be helpful to you at this point.

(a) "And the wild beast which I saw was like unto a panther." The outward appearance of the Beast was like a panther: "After this I beheld, and lo another, like a leopard, which had upon the back of it four wings of a fowl; the beast had also four heads; and dominion was given to it" (Dan. 7:6). *Panther* and *leopard* are the same Greek word; I prefer the word *panther*. This was the Graeco-Macedonian Empire. Greece was noted for its brilliance and its advancement in the arts and sciences. It was noted for its philosophy, its architecture, and its marvelous literature. The Greek language itself is a wonderful language. The empire of the Beast will have all the outward culture which was the glory of Greece.

(b) "And his feet were as the feet of a bear" reminds us of the second beast of Daniel: "And behold another beast, a second, like to a bear, and it raised up itself on one side, and it had three ribs in the mouth of it between the teeth of it: and they said thus unto it, Arise, devour much flesh" (Dan. 7:5). This was Media-Persia, noted for its pagan splendor as it paddled and waddled over the earth like a Gargantua. The empire of the Beast will have all the pagan splendor and wealth that Media-Persia had.

(c) "And his mouth as the mouth of a lion" reminds us of the first beast of Daniel: "The first was like a lion, and had eagle's wings: I beheld till the wings thereof were plucked, and it was lifted up from the earth, and made stand upon the feet as a man, and a man's heart was given to it" (Dan. 7:4). This was Babylonian autocracy. When Nebuchadnezzar ordered the death of his wise men and then later on the fiery furnace for the three Hebrew children, there was none to question his authority. He was the head of gold; he was an autocrat. Though the Man of Sin will be one of the toes of the image that Daniel saw, composed partly of clay and partly of iron, he will rule with the autocracy and dictatorial authority of Nebuchadnezzar.

This final world dictator comes to his zenith under the domination of Satan. The source of his power is found in Satan who raises him up, empowers and energizes him for the dastardly dictatorial job he will do. He is the closest to an incarnation of Satan that appears in Scripture. Luke said that Satan had entered into Judas Iscariot (see Luke 22:3). Christ used similar language when He spoke to Simon Peter in Matthew 16:23. Is the Man of Sin the incarnation of Satan? I think we can say that he is. Certainly Satan has entered into him. Paul wrote: "Even him, whose coming is after the working of Satan with all power and signs and lying wonders, And with all deceivableness of unrighteousness in them that perish; because they received not the love of the truth, that they might be saved" (2 Thess. 2:9–10).

WILD BEAST, DEATH-DEALING STROKE

And I saw one of his heads as it were wounded to death; and his deadly wound was healed: and all the world wondered after the beast [Rev. 13:3].

And I saw one of his heads as though it had been slain unto death; and his stroke of death was healed; and the whole (inhabited) earth wondered after the beast.

This verse, together with chapter 17, verse 8, has led many to the view that Satan actually raises the Beast from the dead. "The beast that thou sawest was, and is not; and shall ascend out of the bottomless pit, and go into perdition: and they that dwell on the earth shall wonder, whose names were not written in the book of life from the foundation of the world, when they behold the beast that was, and is not, and yet is" (Rev. 17:8).

Because of these two Scriptures, there are many who have taken the position that the Beast is actually raised from the dead by Satan. This cannot be because Satan does not have power to raise the dead; that power has not been given to him at all. The Lord Jesus Christ is the only One who can raise the dead. The Gospel of John records these words spoken by our Lord: "For as the Father raiseth up the dead, and quickeneth them; even so the Son quickeneth whom he will. . . . Verily, verily, I say unto you, The hour is coming, and now is, when the dead shall hear the voice of the Son of God: and they that hear shall live. . . . Marvel not at this: for the hour is coming, in the which all that are in the graves shall hear his voice, And shall come forth; they that have done good, unto the resurrection of life; and they that have done evil, unto the resurrection of damnation" (John 5:21, 25, 28–29). Only the Lord Jesus can raise the dead—Satan cannot. Therefore, I take it that the restoration is a false, a fake resurrection.

Those who take the view that Satan raises the Beast from the dead interpret the Beast as a man only. That the early church, for the most part, held to this view is indisputable. They disagreed as to the identity of the Beast. Some thought he was Judas Iscariot. Others identified him as Nero. Even Augustine, in his day, wrote:

What means the declaration, that the mystery of iniquity doth already work? Some suppose it to be spoken of the Roman Emperor, and therefore Paul did not speak in plain words, although he always expected that what he said would be understood as applying to Nero, whose doings already appeared like those of Antichrist. Hence it was that some suspected that he would rise from the dead as Antichrist [J. A. Seiss, *The Apocalypse, Lectures on the Book of Revelation,* p. 398, footnote].

There are others who take the view that the Beast here refers to the Roman Empire and that the imperial form of government, under which Rome fell, will be restored in a startling manner. I believe this will happen, but I do not think it is a resurrection, for Rome never died; Rome fell apart. Rome is like Humpty-Dumpty:

Humpty-Dumpty sat on a wall;
Humpty-Dumpty had a great fall;
All the King's horses, and all the King's men
Could not put Humpty-Dumpty together again.

But Antichrist can and will put Humpty-Dumpty together again, and it will be a marvelous thing. The Roman Empire has not truly died; it lives on in the nations of Europe today.

I think that both of these views do have something to commend them, while both views have serious objections. There can be no real resurrection of an evil man before the Great White Throne judgment. And, at that time, only Christ can raise the dead. Christ will raise the dead who stand before the Great White Throne (see Rev. 20:11–15). We have already considered John 5:28–29: "Marvel not at this: for the hour is coming, in the which all that are in the graves shall hear his voice, And shall come forth; they that have done good, unto the resurrection of life; and they that have done evil, unto the resurrection of damnation." Only Christ can raise the dead—both saved and lost. Satan has no power to raise the dead. He is not a life-giver. He is a devil, a destroyer, a death-dealer.

The Roman Empire is to be revitalized and made to cohere in a miraculous manner under the world dictator, the Beast, yet verse 3 seems to demand a more adequate explanation than this.

I believe the Beast is a man who will exhibit a counterfeit and imitation resurrection. This will be the great delusion, the big lie of the Great Tribulation Period. We are told that God will give them over to believe the big lie (see 2 Thess. 2:11), and this is part of the big lie. They will not accept the resurrection of Christ, but they sure are going to fake the resurrection of Antichrist.

"And his stroke of death was healed" shows the blasphemous imitation of the death and resurrection of Christ. The challenge in that day will be: "What has Christ done that Antichrist has not done?" Nobody can duplicate the resurrection of Christ; they might imitate it, but they cannot duplicate it. Yet Antichrist is going to imitate it in a way that will fool the world—it is the big lie. Believers say, "Christ is risen!" The boast of unbelievers in that day will be: "So is Antichrist!" The Roman Empire will spring back into existence under the cruel hand of a man who faked a resurrection, and a gullible world who rejected Christ will finally be taken in by this forgery.

We begin now to get a composite picture of the Antichrist. The rider on the white horse (see Rev. 6) brought a false peace to the world. In the recorded history of man, he has engaged in fifteen hundred wars and has signed some eight thousand peace treaties. Yet in his entire history, he has enjoyed only between two and three hundred years of true peace. Certainly G. K. Chesterton was accurate when he said, "One of the paradoxes of this age is that this is the age of Pacifism, but not the age of Peace." The Antichrist comes in on a false platform of bringing peace to the world. How many times in the United States have we elected a president on the platform that he would bring peace, only to find that he took us right into a war? We have been a warlike nation. We are not very peaceful.

Arnold Toynbee, an English historian, said this in 1953:

By forcing on mankind more and more lethal weapons, and at the same time making the world more and more interdependent economically, technology has brought mankind to such a degree of distress that we are ripe for deifying any new caesar who might succeed in bringing the world unity and peace.

That is all Antichrist will need to offer the world when he comes. He will say, "I am going to give you peace," and the people will say "Hallelujah!" and put him into office. That is the way we do it in the United States where we are supposed to be a very cultured, educated, sophisticated, and civilized nation. The world will put Antichrist into power.

Bishop Fulton J. Sheen made this remarkable statement:

The Antichrist will come disguised as the great humanitarian. He will talk peace, prosperity, and plenty, not as a means to lead us to God, but as ends in themselves. He will explain guilt away psychologically, make men shrink in shame if their fellowmen say they are not broad-minded and liberal. He will spread the lie that men will never be better until they make society better.

This is one statement made by Bishop Sheen which I'll agree with one hundred percent.

WILD BEAST, DEITY ASSUMED

And they worshipped the dragon which gave power unto the beast: and they worshipped the beast, saying, Who is like unto the beast? who is able to make war with him? [Rev. 13:4].

And they worshipped the dragon, because he gave his authority unto the beast; and they worshipped the beast, saying, Who is like unto the beast? and who is able to make war with him?

This is the supreme moment for Satan. He wants to be worshiped, and the whole world is going to worship him during this period. My friend, if the Spirit of God took His hand off this world today and off you and me, I am afraid that many of us would be in the position of backsliders; and if Antichrist appeared, we would follow him like a little faithful dog follows his master.

"And they worshipped the beast, saying, Who is like unto the beast?" What a parody on the worship of the true God. They say, "Look, we are worshiping something more wonderful than the God of the Bible!"

And there was given unto him a mouth speaking great things and blasphemies; and power was given unto him to continue forty and two months [Rev. 13:5].

And there was given to him a mouth speaking great things and blasphemies;

and there was given to him authority to continue (to work) forty and two months.

The only good news here is that Antichrist will be reigning like this for only forty-two months, or three and one-half years.

"A mouth speaking great things" means he is a big-mouthed fellow. Daniel also mentions this concerning him. He is really going to be a big talker; he will promise anything. This is one reason you ought to be careful listening to anyone on radio or television today, including this poor preacher or any politician or educator or newsman. We need to test everything that we hear. Antichrist is going to have charisma. He is going to be able to talk himself into the good graces of this Christ-rejecting world.

WILD BEAST, DEFYING GOD

And he opened his mouth in blasphemy against God, to blaspheme his name, and his tabernacle, and them that dwell in heaven [Rev. 13:6].

And he opened his mouth for blasphemies against God, to blaspheme His name and His tabernacle and those which dwell (tabernacle) in heaven.

This is the dreadful limit to which the Beast goes in blasphemy. He is against Christ and His church which are in heaven. Thank God that the church is no longer on the earth! I do not see how anyone who studies Revelation can believe that the church is going to go through this period of the Great Tribulation.

And it was given unto him to make war with the saints, and to overcome them: and power was given him over all kindreds, and tongues, and nations.

And all that dwell upon the earth shall worship him, whose names are not written in the book of life of the Lamb slain from the foundation of the world [Rev. 13:7–8].

And it was given unto him to make war with the saints and to overcome them: and there was given to him authority over every tribe and people and tongue and nation. And all that dwell on the earth shall worship him, every one whose name hath not been written from the foundation of the world in the book of life of the Lamb that hath been slain.

"And it was given unto him to make war with the saints." The saints (there will be saints during the Tribulation Period, although they are not, of course, the church) will be overcome by the brutal Beast. In the will of God many believers, both Jew and Gentile, will suffer martyrdom.

"And all that dwell on the earth shall worship him, every one whose name hath not been written from the foundation of the world in the book of life of the Lamb that hath been slain." Spurgeon used to say something like this: "I am glad that my name was written in the Lamb's Book of Life before I got here, because if God had waited until I got here, He never would have chosen me." That is true of all the saints, both in the church age and in the Great Tribulation Period.

This will be the darkest hour in the history of the world; and the church, thank God, will not be here. I am thankful I am not going through the Great Tribulation Period. I will not be under Antichrist; I am under Christ. I am not looking for Antichrist; I am looking for Christ to come.

WILD BEAST, DEFIANCE DENIED TO ANYONE

If any man have an ear, let him hear.

He that leadeth into captivity shall go into captivity: he that killeth with the sword must be killed with the sword. Here is the patience and the faith of the saints [Rev. 13:9–10].

If any man hath an ear, let him hear. If any one is for captivity (bring together captives) into captivity he goeth (away): if any man shall kill with the sword, with the sword must he be killed. Here is the patience and the faith of the saints.

This is without doubt one of the most awe-inspiring statements in the Word of God. "If any man" is a thrice-repeated invitation to the ear of anyone to hear the Word of God at any time, in any age. "So then faith cometh by hearing, and hearing by the word of God" (Rom. 10:17). "If any man hath an ear, let him hear." Here again is the wedding of free will and election. "If any man"—any man means *any* man. "If any man hath an ear"—does not everybody have ears? Yes, but there are some people who do not hear although they have ears. There are people who simply do not listen at all—they do not hear.

I had a neighbor who was retired, and his wife was a very wonderful person, but she talked a great deal. When he would go outside to work, he would remove his hearing aid from his ear. He did it, I discovered, for a purpose. He was pruning a tree one day when his wife came out of the house and talked a blue streak to him for about five minutes. All of a sudden she noticed that he did not have his hearing aid on. She said, "You haven't heard a word I've said!" He just kept on sawing, and she turned around and went back into the house. That was exactly what he wanted! He was out there to prune the tree and not to carry on a conversation.

There are a great many people who do not have a hearing aid to hear the Word of God—they don't want to hear it. I would like to make it possible for every person in this country to study the Word of God with us through our radio Bible studies. But I do not have the wildest dream that *everybody* in the country is going to be studying the Word of God. I know that it will be only those who have an ear, an ear to hear the Word of God. "Any man"—that's free will; that "hath an ear" is election; and this is the way God weds these two truths together.

"He that leadeth into captivity shall go into captivity: he that killeth with the sword must be killed with the sword." What John is saying here is not for you and me—at least, I hope it is not for you; I know it is not for me—because, beginning with chapter 4, Revelation is dealing with future things which are beyond the church. The church (meaning all born-again believers in this age) will no longer be on earth. John is speaking to God's saints who will be in the world at that time. Remember that during the Tribulation the Antichrist will be the world dictator. Men are not going to buy or sell without his permission. They will not be able to travel without his permission. He will rule the world as no one has ever ruled in the past. God is saying to those who are His own, "Don't resist him." To begin with, it would not do you any good. The second thing is that this is "the patience and the faith of the saints" of that time. If you are in the world during the Great Tribulation, then you are going to have to bear with patience and faith the awful trials that will be coming even upon God's children.

God will apparently withdraw from the world, and He will turn it over to Satan. Today the Holy Spirit is in the world, and He curtails, He smothers, resistance. He is holding back evil, although it may not look that way. Just think what it will be like when He is removed from that office and when evil men are permitted to have their day. Satan will have full sway. As we have said before, this actually is poetic justice. The Devil and his minions of evil and lost mankind will never be able to say to God, "You never gave us a chance. If You had just given us a chance, we would have been able to work things out." God is going to give them a chance for a brief period. If it was not for just a brief period, there would be no flesh left on the earth, as the Lord Jesus said (see Matt. 24:22).

THE WILD BEAST OUT OF THE EARTH—DESCRIPTION, A RELIGIOUS LEADER

The first Beast is a political leader, a political power and a person, and his power will become worldwide. We come now to the second wild Beast, the one who comes out of the earth and is a religious leader.

And I beheld another beast coming up out of the earth; and he had two horns like a lamb, and he spake as a dragon [Rev. 13:11].

And I saw another wild beast coming up out of the earth and he had two horns like a lamb, and he was speaking as a dragon.

This wild Beast is easier to identify than was the first. After you establish who the first Beast is it is not too much trouble to identify the second. The first Beast comes out of the sea, and the second one comes out of the earth. What is the difference? The sea represents the peoples of the world. The great mob of mankind today is like the surging and restless sea—that has always been true. The earth from which this second Beast arises is symbolic of Palestine, and it is naturally assumed that the second Beast comes from Israel. He is a messiah, and Israel would not accept him unless he had come from their land and was one of them.

"And he had two horns like a lamb." This suggests his imitation of Christ. The first Beast is *opposed* to Christ—he is *Anti*christ. The second Beast *imitates* Christ. He also is Antichrist (considering *anti*, meaning "instead of"); he poses as Christ. He has two horns like a lamb, but he is a wolf in sheep's clothing. He imitates the ". . . Lamb of God, which taketh away the sin of the world" (John 1:29), only this pseudolamb does not subtract sin; he adds and multiplies it in the world. He does not come to do his own will, but the will of the first Beast. He is a counterfeit Christ. He will do a lot of talking about loving everyone, but underneath he is a dangerous Beast, just as the first one was, deceiving the whole world.

The Lord Jesus said in Matthew 7:15: "Beware of false prophets, which come to you in sheep's clothing, but inwardly they are ravening wolves." This second Beast is the epitome of all false prophets, and he is an Antichrist. It takes two men to fulfill the position that Christ fulfills—and of course, they do *not* fulfill it. But Satan needs two men to attempt even an imitation of Him.

Again, the Lord Jesus said in Matthew 24:24: "For there shall arise false Christs, and false prophets, and shall shew great signs and wonders; insomuch that, if it were possible, they shall deceive the very elect." The false prophet is sort of a "John the Baptist" to the first Beast. Some have identified him as King Saul or Judas, which is mere assumption and cannot be proved.

WILD BEAST, DELEGATED AUTHORITY

And he exerciseth all the power of the first beast before him, and causeth the earth and them which dwell therein to worship the first beast, whose deadly wound was healed [Rev. 13:12].

And he exerciseth all the authority of the first wild beast in his presence. And he maketh the earth and the dwellers therein to worship the first wild beast, whose wound of death was healed.

The second wild Beast has a delegated authority from the first wild Beast, which actually makes him subservient to him, but he is also on a par with him—he has the same power.

This second wild Beast leads in a movement to exterminate the harlot of Revelation 17, which is the false church that will go into the Great Tribulation Period. John does not even dignify that church by calling it a church; it is called a harlot. The true church, which has now left the earth, is called the bride of Christ. But here you have the last vestige of an apostate church with all of its humanism. The false prophet will offer the world something new to worship—the first wild Beast, the willful king, the Man of Sin, the last world dictator (see Dan. 11:36–39; Matt. 24:24; 2 Thess. 2:3–10). Here is presented to us this terrible second Beast who will exalt the first Beast to the place of worship.

"Whose wound of death was healed" reveals that both the first and the second Beasts are

healers and miracle workers. This is the big lie, the "strong delusion" that is going to come to the world.

And he doeth great wonders, so that he maketh fire come down from heaven on the earth in the sight of men,

And deceiveth them that dwell on the earth by the means of those miracles which he had power to do in the sight of the beast; saying to them that dwell on the earth, that they should make an image to the beast, which had the wound by a sword, and did live [Rev. 13:13–14].

And he doeth great signs, that he should even make fire to come down out of heaven into the earth in the sight of men. And he deceiveth the dwellers on the earth through [Gr.: dia] the signs which it was given him to do in the presence of the wild beast; saying to the dwellers on the earth that they should make an image [Gr.: eikon] to the beast who hath the stroke of the sword and lived.

This false prophet is a worker of signs and miracles (see Matt. 24:24). Our Lord warned against this false prophet. His deception is that he apes Elijah in bringing down fire from heaven. He is a combination of Jannes and Jambres: "Then Pharaoh also called the wise men and the sorcerers: now the magicians of Egypt, they also did in like manner with their enchantments. For they cast down every man his rod, and they became serpents: but Aaron's rod swallowed up their rods" (Exod. 7:11–12). In other words, they were clever magicians, and I believe they had satanic power. This Beast in the end time will also have satanic power.

We read in Matthew 3:11: "I indeed baptize you with water unto repentance: but he that cometh after me is mightier than I, whose shoes I am not worthy to bear: he shall baptize you with the Holy Ghost, and with fire." John the Baptist specifically said he had nothing to do with fire, but this false prophet is going to imitate Elijah.

The false prophet plays with fire until he is cast into the lake of fire (see Rev. 19:20). The world is taken in by this deception, with the exception of God's elect, those who are His—they *cannot* be deceived.

The false prophet shows his hand by causing to be made an image of the man of sin. The Greek word for image is *eikon*, which means "likeness." The big production is a likeness of the first Beast that emphasizes the wound of death that was healed. It is interesting to note that the Lord Jesus did not permit anything connected with His physical appearance to survive. But the likeness of the Antichrist will evidently be placed in the temple at Jerusalem, and I believe it is the abomination of desolation to which our Lord referred: "When ye therefore shall see the abomination of desolation, spoken of by Daniel the prophet, stand in the holy place, (whoso readeth, let him understand:)" (Matt. 24:15). This is the abomination of desolation that is to appear, and although we cannot be dogmatic, we believe it will be this image of Antichrist, the first wild Beast.

WILD BEAST, DELUSION PERPETRATED ON THE WORLD

And he had power to give life unto the image of the beast, that the image of the beast should both speak, and cause that as many as would not worship the image of the beast should be killed.

And he causeth all, both small and great, rich and poor, free and bond, to receive a mark in their right hand, or in their foreheads:

And that no man might buy or sell, save he that had the mark, or the name of the beast, or the number of his name [Rev. 13:15–17].

And it was given to him to give breath [Gr.: pneuma] to the image of the wild beast, that the image of the wild beast should both speak, and cause that as many as should not worship the image of the beast should be killed. And he causeth all, the small and the great, and the rich and the poor, and the free and the slave, that there be given them a mark on their right hand or upon their forehead; and that no one should be able to buy or to sell, except the one having the mark, even the name of the beast or the number of his name.

"**A**nd it was given to him to give breath (the Greek word is *pneuma*) to the image of the wild beast." This is going to be a different kind of idol. Isaiah and all the prophets mention the fact that idols cannot speak. Paul also mentions it. But here is an idol that will speak. I think they will call all the scientists of the world to look at this im-

age. The scientists will give a report that they cannot understand it, they cannot explain it, and that it is a miracle. This is something that will cause the whole world to turn and worship the Beast.

He is now wedding religion and business, for you will have to have the mark of the Beast to do business. In John's day soldiers were branded by their commanders, slaves were branded by their masters, and those attached to certain pagan temples were branded by the mark of the god or goddess whom they served. Ptolemy Philopater had all Jews in Alexandria marked with the ivy leaf, which was the symbol of Dionysus. In our day a newspaper columnist who wrote an article entitled, "Living by the Numbers," deplored the fact that we have to carry so many different cards in our wallets and concluded with this paragraph:

It would simplify matters if the government would assign each of us a single all-purpose number, which we could have tattooed across the forehead to spare us the trouble of carrying all these cards.

Don't misunderstand me. This is *not* the fulfillment of prophecy, but it sure shows how prophecy *can* come to pass. What is the mark of the Beast? It is not given us to know. We are not told, but that has not kept many expositors from telling us what it is!

WILD BEAST, DESIGNATION

Here is wisdom. Let him that hath understanding count the number of the beast: for it is the number of a man; and his number is Six hundred threescore and six [Rev. 13:18].

Here is wisdom. He that hath understanding, let him count the number of the beast; for it is the number of man; and his number is six hundred and sixty and six.

"**H**ere is wisdom" seems to be a rather ironical declaration when we consider the maze of speculation that has been accumulated through the centuries on this verse.

In the Greek there is a very beautiful arrangement of this number.

hexakosioi — 600
hexekonta —   60
hex   —   6

A numerical value is attached to each letter to be sure, but we must let it stand there, for the visible number of the Beast and its meaning await the day of his manifestation. And I do not believe he has yet been manifested. This number has made a nice little jigsaw puzzle for a lot of people to play at, but, my friend, you will not know who he is until you get to the Great Tribulation Period.

I would suggest that we not waste our time trying to identify a person by this number. Instead, we need to present Jesus Christ that we might reduce the population of those who have to go through the Great Tribulation Period and who will therefore know what the number of the Beast is.

I am not anxious to know the number of the Beast, and I am thankful I will not have to live in that period. I am very thankful today that I know Jesus Christ as my Savior. Instead of spending time with Antichrist, I want to know Christ. I can say with Paul: "That I may know him, and the power of his resurrection, and the fellowship of his sufferings, being made conformable unto his death" (Phil. 3:10).

The only positive and important item for us today is that the first Beast is a man. This teaches me not to trust man. "Thus saith the LORD; Cursed be the man that trusteth in man, and maketh flesh his arm, and whose heart departeth from the LORD. For he shall be like the heath in the desert, and shall not see when good cometh; but shall inhabit the parched places in the wilderness, in a salt land and not inhabited. Blessed is the man that trusteth in the LORD, and whose hope the LORD is. For he shall be as a tree planted by the waters, and that spreadeth out her roots by the river, and shall not see when heat cometh, but her leaf shall be green; and shall not be careful in the year of drought, neither shall cease from yielding fruit" (Jer. 17:5–8).

The passage in Revelation does not interest me a bit as to what the number of the Beast is or who he is or anything about him, but it makes me want to know Jesus Christ more, because my plan is to be with Him—not because of who I am or what I have done, but because Jesus Christ died for me on the cross, and by His grace I will go into His presence.

CHAPTER 14

THEME: *Looking to the end of the Great Tribulation*

This chapter contains several events. It is an interlude in which we see the Lamb on Mount Zion, hear the proclamation of the everlasting gospel, the pronouncement of judgment upon Babylon and on those who receive the mark of the Beast, then the praise for those who die in the Lord, and the preview of Armageddon.

The chapter before us constitutes an hiatus in the series of seven performers. It is obvious that this interlude could not be fitted in between the sixth and seventh performers who are the two wild Beasts. Of course, they had to be considered together, as they are like Siamese twins, and the continuity between them could not be broken. Therefore, this interlude follows the seventh performer in recognition of the logical sequence of this book, which is not a hodgepodge of visions but unfolds in a logical, chronological, and mathematical order.

There are certain performers called to our attention in this chapter (others beside the seven whom we have seen previously) in order to give us a full-orbed view of the spectacular events of the previous two chapters. As we have seen, this is the darkest day and the most horrible hour in the history of the world. It is truly hell's holiday. Every thoughtful mind must inevitably ask the question, "How did God's people fare during this period? Could they remain faithful to the Lord through to the end with the overwhelming odds against them?" The answer is found in this chapter before us.

The Shepherd who began with 144,000 sheep is now identified with them as the Lamb. And notice that He doesn't have 143,000 sheep; He has 144,000 sheep—He did not lose one! He redeemed them, He sealed them, and He kept them, for He is the Great Shepherd of the sheep. These sheep are of a different fold from the one we are in today, and the Good Shepherd brought them through the Great Tribulation. That is the picture before us as we open this chapter. It is encouraging to know that the Lamb—not the two Beasts— is going to have the last word. And He is not a lamb that speaks like a dragon; He is the Lord Jesus Himself. And since He is going to have the final word, Babylon will fall—the great political capital, the great commercial capital, and the great religious capital of the world during the Great Tribulation Period. And the followers of the Beast will be judged.

Although many of Christ's own will become martyrs during the Tribulation, they will not lose; they will win! Again I say with Calvin that I would rather be on the side that seems to be losing today but will win finally than to be on the side that seems to be winning today but is going to lose eternally. I'm glad to be on the winning side. Christ will reward those who will be martyred for Him.

In chapter 19 we will see the Lamb returning to the earth. The morning is coming. The darkness will fade away, and the Sun of Righteousness will arise with healing in His wings.

PICTURE OF THE LAMB WITH 144,000

And I looked, and, lo, a Lamb stood on the mount Sion, and with him an hundred forty and four thousand, having his Father's name written in their foreheads [Rev. 14:1].

"I saw" indicates that John is still the spectator to these events. The reel continues to roll, and the story continues to unfold.

The "Lamb" is the Lord Jesus Christ, as we have seen in chapters 5–7 and 12–13.

"Mount Sion" is at Jerusalem. There is no use trying to locate this at any other place than at Jerusalem in the land of Israel.

This verse pictures a placid, pastoral scene which opens the millennial kingdom here upon this earth. The Lord Jesus is going to reign from Jerusalem. God Himself called it the city of the great King. And in Psalm 2:6 He says this: "Yet have I set my king upon my holy hill of Zion." It is the Father's intention to place the Lord Jesus upon the throne of David in Jerusalem, and specifically at Mount Sion.

"An hundred forty and four thousand" I believe to be the ones who were sealed back in chapter 7, although I recognize that there are some problems connected with this view. They came through the Great Tribulation like the three Hebrew children came through the fiery furnace.

Notice that the Lamb is standing with them on Mount Sion. Although He is in His person the Lamb, He is also the Shepherd. Remember that He started out with 144,000 and that He came through the Great Tribulation with 144,000. He didn't lose one.

My friend, in our day when the pressures of Satan bear us down, the living, victorious Christ is available to us. Oh, that you and I might come to know Him better and that He might occupy a greater place in our lives day by day. I am convinced in my own experience that the Lord Jesus Christ in person is the answer. When I see plaques with the motto: "Jesus is the Answer," I always say that it depends on what the question is. But certainly He is the answer to problems for which men are trying to work out solutions by some little method. They will tell you that if you follow their little legal system, you can solve the problems of your personal life, your home, your work, and your church. I doubt that there ever was a day in which there was so much teaching in all of these areas, and yet there is less victorious living in the daily experience of believers. What is the real problem today? We don't need a method; we need Christ. We need to know Him in a meaningful way. We need to draw closer to Him. By the way, when was the last time that you told Him that you loved Him? He has said that He loves you, and you ought to tell Him that in return.

And I heard a voice from heaven, as the voice of many waters, and as the voice of a great thunder: and I heard the voice of harpers harping with their harps:

And they sung as it were a new song before the throne, and before the four beasts, and the elders: and no man could learn that song but the hundred and forty and four thousand, which were redeemed from the earth [Rev. 14:2–3].

"I heard." John is not only a spectator but is also an auditor to this scene.

The 144,000 join the heavenly chorus in the Millennium. My friend, have you ever heard a choir of 144,000 voices? Well, up to this time earth has been out of tune with heaven, but here the rule of Satan is over, and the earth and heaven are in tune. What Browning said about God's being in His heaven and all's right with the world is going to be true when we get to the Millennium. All's wrong with the world right now, but in that day all will be right. The 144,000 learn the new song and join the harmony of heaven.

"I heard the voice of harpers harping with their harps." God has put His harpers in heaven while the 144,000 are on earth, on Mount Sion (that is a long way from the instruments). Having been a pastor for many years, I have heard many harpers—harping about this or that, but these are a different kind of harper. The harpers I have listened to were not musical, I can assure you. But these heavenly harpers are going to make beautiful music.

"The hundred and forty and four thousand, which were redeemed from the earth" means that they have been purchased to enter the Millennium on earth. They are not taken to heaven. Remember that this is a picture of the Millennium on earth, and these will live on the earth. The unsaved are not going to live on the earth.

"And no man could learn that song but the hundred and forty and four thousand, which were redeemed from the earth." No one can sing praises to God but the redeemed. I wish that truth could be gotten over to a great many song leaders in this day in which we live. I understand their desire to hear everybody in the congregation sing, but when they have a mixed audience of saved and unsaved people, they should not ask the unsaved to sing the songs of redemption. Don't ask them to sing:

Amazing grace! how sweet the sound,
    That saved a wretch like me!
I once was lost, but now am found,
    Was blind, but now I see.

               "Amazing Grace"
               —John Newton

If an unsaved person sings that, you have made him a liar. Just let the redeemed sing. The psalmist wrote: "O give thanks unto the Lord, for he is good: for his mercy endureth for ever. Let the redeemed of the Lord say so, whom he hath redeemed from the hand of the enemy" (Ps. 107:1–2). My friend, no one but the redeemed are going to say God is good. This is the reason we need a say-so Christianity in our day. We need to *say* that God is good.

But in this millennial scene, heaven and earth are brought into marvelous harmony. What a contrast this is to chapter 13 where earth is in rebellion against heaven under the Beasts. Here all is tranquility under the Lamb.

These are they which were not defiled with women; for they are virgins. These are they which follow the Lamb whithersoever he goeth. These were redeemed from among men, being the firstfruits unto God and to the Lamb.

And in their mouth was found no guile: for they are without fault before the throne of God [Rev. 14:4–5].

These are they that were not defiled (besmirched) with women; for they are virgins [Gr.: parthenoi]. These are they that follow the Lamb whithersoever He goeth. These were purchased from among men, to be the firstfruits unto God and unto the Lamb. And in their mouth was found no lie: they are without blemish.

"Were not defiled with women; for they are virgins." What does that mean? To be frank with you, it used to puzzle me. It can have a literal or spiritual meaning, and I think it includes both. The Great Tribulation is a period of unparalleled suffering. The 144,000 have been through that period. The abnormal times demanded an abnormal state. That was the reason they were unmarried. When I was a boy, I remember a young fellow who went to war during World War I. He was engaged to a girl, but he never came home. I know other boys who married right before they left, and they fathered children that they never saw. That was wartime. And many girls said that they wished they had not married during that time. Well, during the Tribulation Period the times are going to be so frightful that it will be wise not to get married. You may remember that the prophet Jeremiah also lived in a critical period, the time of the Babylonian captivity. Because of the dark days, God forbade him to marry: "The word of the Lord came also unto me, saying, Thou shalt not take thee a wife, neither shalt thou have sons or daughters in this place. For thus saith the Lord concerning the sons and concerning the daughters that are born in this place, and concerning their mothers that bare them, and concerning their fathers that begat them in this land; They shall die of grievous deaths; they shall not be lamented; neither shall they be buried; but they shall be as dung upon the face of the earth: and they shall be consumed by the sword, and by famine; and their carcasses shall be meat for the fowls of heaven, and for the beasts of the earth" (Jer. 16:1–4).

Our Lord Jesus mentioned those who would be mothers during the Great Tribulation: "And woe unto them that are with child, and to them that give suck in those days!" (Matt. 24:19).

You and I are living in a day when marriage is honorable and even encouraged. However, God's injunction to Noah to multiply and replenish the earth is hardly the Scripture to apply to a world faced with a population explosion and at a time when believers can see the approach of the end of the age.

During the Great Tribulation there will be an exaggerated emphasis upon sex, and obviously immorality will prevail. The 144,000 will have kept themselves aloof from the sins of the Great Tribulation.

Now, considering adultery in the spiritual sense, in the Old Testament idolatry was classified as spiritual fornication. The classic example is in Ezekiel 16 where we find God's severe indictment against Israel for fornication and adultery—which was idolatry. The 144,000 will also have kept themselves from the worship of the Beast and his image during the Great Tribulation.

Therefore, the comment, "These are they which were not defiled with women; for they are virgins," is probably referring to chastity in both the literal sense and the spiritual sense. And this makes good sense, by the way.

"Firstfruits unto God and to the Lamb" has definite reference to the nation Israel. "For if the casting away of them be the reconciling of the world, what shall the receiving of them be, but life from the dead? For if the firstfruits be holy, the lump is also holy: and if the root be holy, so are the branches" (Rom. 11:15–16). So Israel is described as the firstfruits, especially the 144,000. I believe that they will occupy a unique place in the millennial kingdom. They evidently will be the vanguard with the Lamb when He returns to set up the kingdom, as we will see in chapter 19.

"In their mouth was found no lie" means that they did not participate in the big lie of the Beast when he used lying wonders. They didn't fall for his lie. Remember that the Lord Jesus said that if it were possible to deceive the very elect, they would be deceived. But they will not be deceived.

"They are without blemish." Are they without blemish because they have been purified by the Great Tribulation? No. They are without blemish because they are clothed in the righteousness of Christ. And, friend, that's the way I am going to heaven, also. I'm not going to heaven because I think I am good, because I know that I am not good. And don't look down your nose at me, because *you* are not good either. Both of us are sinners saved by the grace of God.

PROCLAMATION OF THE EVERLASTING GOSPEL

And I saw another angel fly in the midst of heaven, having the everlasting gospel to preach unto them that dwell on the earth, and to every nation, and kindred, and tongue, and people,

Saying with a loud voice, Fear God, and give glory to him; for the hour of his judgment is come: and worship him that made heaven, and earth, and the sea, and the fountains of waters [Rev. 14:6–7].

And I saw another angel flying in mid heaven, having an eternal gospel (good tidings) to proclaim unto (over) them that dwell (sit) on the earth, and unto (over) every nation and tribe and tongue and people; and he saith with a great voice, Fear God and give Him glory, for the hour of His judgment is come: and worship Him that made the heaven and the earth and sea and fountains of water.

"Another angel" denotes another radical change in protocol of God's communication with the earth. This angel is the first in a parade of six "another" angels mentioned in verses 8–9, 15, and 17–18.

During our age the gospel has been committed to men, and they alone are the messengers of it. Angels would like to give the message of the gospel, but they have not been permitted to do so. At the beginning of the Great Tribulation men are the messengers of God, as the 144,000 reveal. Even the two witnesses with supernatural power could not stand up against Satan, but were removed from the satanic scene of earth. Angels as well as men were the messengers of the Old Testament—". . . the word spoken by angels was stedfast . . ." (Heb. 2:2). The times are so intense in the Great Tribulation Period that only angels can get the messages of God through to the world. Angels are indestructible.

"Flying in mid heaven" was a ridiculous statement a few years ago, and some of the critics of the Bible laughed at such a thing. It is no longer a ridiculous statement to a generation that has been treated to television via satellite. Worldwide television is a practical reality so that we don't have to wait for the evening news to learn what is happening in Israel or England or Japan, we can *see* it just as it is happening. And the angel whom John mentions "flying in mid heaven" will serve as a broadcasting station to the entire world.

"An eternal gospel." The question naturally arises, How is this the gospel, since the word *gospel* means "good news"? Is this angel bringing good news? Yes, it is good news to those who are God's children, but it is bad news for the unbelievers.

"Fear God" is the message of this "eternal gospel." That is the message. The writer of the Proverbs said that the fear of the Lord is the beginning of wisdom. In effect, the angel is saying to God's people, "Get wise, get smart, because you need to *fear God*. God saved you by His grace, but He is going to judge this earth." This is God's final call before the return of Christ in judgment.

PRONOUNCEMENT OF JUDGMENT ON BABYLON

In this chapter God is bringing before us those who will appear again in the Book of Revelation, but He is giving us now more or less of a program which He is going to follow.

And there followed another angel, saying, Babylon is fallen, is fallen, that great city, because she made all nations drink of the wine of the wrath of her fornication [Rev. 14:8].

And another angel, a second, followed saying, Fell, fell is Babylon the great, that hath made all the nations to drink of the wine of the wrath of her fornication.

There is a book entitled *The Two Babylons*, by Alexander Hislop, which you ought to read. It is especially pertinent in these days in which you and I live. It reveals that Babylon has been Satan's headquarters from the very beginning. Babylon is the place where idolatry began. Semiramis was the wife of Nimrod; some scholars think that she was his mother and that she married her own son. She was queen of Babel, which later became Babylon, and she devised a nice little story (beginning a whole system of idolatry) in which she came out of an egg in the Euphrates River—she cracked the shell and stepped out fully grown. The worship of Semiramis introduced the female principle in the deity. This reveals that Babylon was the fountainhead of false religions.

"Fell, fell is Babylon." This second angel runs ahead and announces that which is yet to come as though it had already taken place. In the original Greek, "fell" is in the prophetic aorist tense. In other words, God's prophetic word is so sure that He speaks as though the event had already taken place. It is just as sure as if it were history already.

The city of Babylon will evidently be rebuilt during the Great Tribulation Period. If you have my book on Isaiah, you will see that I deal with the probability in chapter 13. I believe that ancient Babylon will be rebuilt,

though not at the same location, and that judgment upon it, which is predicted in the Book of Isaiah, is yet to come.

The idolatry of Babylon is a divine intoxication which will fascinate the entire world. This is the reason we are seeing so much experimentation in our day with Satan worship, exorcism, and all the cults which are definitely satanic. Notice what the Old Testament prophets have said about it: "Babylon hath been a golden cup in the LORD's hand, that made all the earth drunken: the nations have drunken of her wine; therefore the nations are mad" (Jer. 51:7). If you could get away far enough and look back at this earth, I am of the opinion that you would be disappointed in mankind and in the nations of the world. Then in the prophecy of Isaiah we read: "And I will punish the world for their evil, and the wicked for their iniquity; and I will cause the arrogancy of the proud to cease, and will lay low the haughtiness of the terrible" (Isa. 13:11). This brings down the wrath of God upon the world (see Jer. 25:15–26). "And Babylon, the glory of kingdoms, the beauty of the Chaldees' excellency, shall be as when God overthrew Sodom and Gomorrah" (Isa. 13:19).

This is a judgment on Babylon that we are going to see: judgment upon religious Babylon in chapter 17 of Revelation and upon commercial Babylon in chapter 18.

PRONOUNCEMENT OF JUDGMENT ON THOSE WHO RECEIVE THE MARK OF THE BEAST

It is probably true that those who live through all or most of the Great Tribulation do so because they had received the mark of the Beast. However, part of the Great Tribulation is not caused by Satan's being released but by Christ's judgment upon this earth. He will move personally and directly in putting down the rebellion against Him here on this earth.

And the third angel followed them, saying with a loud voice, If any man worship the beast and his image, and receive his mark in his forehead, or in his hand,

The same shall drink of the wine of the wrath of God, which is poured out without mixture into the cup of his indignation; and he shall be tormented with fire and brimstone in the presence of the holy angels, and in the presence of the Lamb:

And the smoke of their torment ascendeth up for ever and ever: and they have no rest day nor night, who worship the beast and his image, and whosoever receiveth the mark of his name.

Here is the patience of the saints: here are they that keep the commandments of God, and the faith of Jesus [Rev. 14:9–12].

And another angel, a third, followed them, saying with a great voice, If any man worshippeth the beast and his image, and receiveth a mark on his forehead, or upon his hand, he also shall drink of the wine of the wrath of God, which is mingled unmixed in the cup of His anger; and he shall be tormented with fire and brimstone in the presence of the holy angels, and in the presence of the Lamb; and the smoke of their torment goeth up for ever and ever (unto the ages of the ages); and they have no rest day and night, they that worship the wild beast and his image, and whoso receiveth the mark of his name. Here is the patience of the saints, who keep the commandments of God and the faith of Jesus.

He is speaking to a group of people who "keep the commandments of God," the Old Testament law. Scripture tells us that sacrifices will be brought during the Great Tribulation and even into the Millennium.

This section makes it crystal clear that no one can assume a neutral position during this intense period under the Beast. Even today we see Christian businessmen who are capitulating to the ethics of the hour. In chapter 13 we saw that the awful alternative for refusing to receive the mark of the Beast was starvation. On the other hand, the person who receives the mark brings down upon his head the wrath of God.

"He also shall drink of the wine of the wrath of God." If you believe that the church is going through the Great Tribulation, you also believe that the Lord Jesus Christ is going to subject His own to the mingled, unmixed cup of His anger. I simply cannot believe that Christ would do this to the church which He has redeemed.

"The wine of the wrath of God" is a figure adopted from the Old Testament. In Psalm 75:8 we read: "For in the hand of the LORD there is a cup, and the wine is red; it is full of mixture; and he poureth out of the same: but the dregs thereof, all the wicked of the earth shall wring them out, and drink them." The Old Testament prophets picked up that theme. They saw the cup of wrath filling up to the brim. God was patient and let man go on and on in his sin, but when the cup of wrath was filled, then God would press it to the lips of a godless society. Rebellious men kept building this thing up until judgment had to break.

"Tormented with fire and brimstone." Now let me say that if this is not literal fire and brimstone, whatever it is must be worse than fire and brimstone. If it is a symbol, remember that a symbol is used to give a faint representation of the real. It is rather like the essence of something. There is the essence of pepper and the essence of perfume. Essence is the faint odor that is left in the bottle after the substance is gone. A symbol is an essence or just a faint copy of the real thing, and the reality can be much worse than the symbol indicates. But remember, the brimstone of Sodom was quite literal. That is a fact you should mull over in your mind if you want to reject a literal hell.

You will notice in this passage that hell is visible to Christ and the holy angels. It does not say that hell is visible to the twenty-four elders. Are we to assume from that that the church does not know what is taking place on the earth? I am inclined to believe that the church will not see what is taking place on the earth during the Great Tribulation Period, but certainly Christ and the holy angels will see it.

All that God's own can do during this period is to be patient and wait for the coming of Christ. Our Lord said: "But he that shall endure unto the end, the same shall be saved" (Matt. 24:13). Why will he endure? He will endure because he has been sealed by the Spirit of God, and he is clothed in the righteousness of Christ. He is able to overcome by the blood of the Lamb. Our Lord said, "In your patience possess ye your souls" (Luke 21:19). All they can do is wait out the storm, and that is what they will do during the Great Tribulation.

PRAISE FOR THOSE WHO DIE IN THE LORD

Here again is a verse that is taken to a funeral in our day, and certainly to use it at a funeral completely robs it of its application. This verse refers only to the Great Tribulation Period:

And I heard a voice from heaven saying unto me, Write, Blessed are the dead

which die in the Lord from henceforth: Yea, saith the Spirit, that they may rest from their labours; and their works do follow them [Rev. 14:13].

And I heard a voice from heaven saying, Write, Blessed are the dead who die in the Lord from henceforth: yea, said the Spirit, that they may rest from their labors (sorrows), for their works follow with them.

Apparently many of God's tribulation saints, both of the 144,000 and of the untold number of Gentiles that will be saved during that time, are going to lay down their lives for Christ. They will be martyred. During the time of the Great Tribulation, it will be better to die than to live. At that time this verse will give comfort and assurance. They will have rest from their sorrows, and their works will follow them, and the Lord will reward them.

As I have said, this is not a verse for God's saints in comfortable, affluent America, as I see it. For most of us it is unnatural to want to die. I feel as Paul expressed it: "For I am in a strait betwixt two, having a desire to depart, and to be with Christ; which is far better: Nevertheless to abide in the flesh is more needful for you. And having this confidence, I know that I shall abide and continue with you all for your furtherance and joy of faith; That your rejoicing may be more abundant in Jesus Christ for me by my coming to you again" (Phil. 1:23–26).

Personally, I would like to stay down here for quite a few more years and teach the Word of God. I am in no hurry to get to heaven. This old story illustrates my viewpoint: A black boy in my southland years ago went to church on a Sunday night. The preacher asked, "How many of you want to go to heaven?" Everybody but this boy put up his hand. The preacher looked at him and asked, "Son, don't you want to go to heaven?" "Sure," the boy answered, "but I thought you were getting up a load for tonight!"

Well, I don't want to be on that load leaving tonight either. I'm going there ultimately, but I would like to live and serve as long as possible. For me it would be unnatural to want to die, but in the Great Tribulation it will be a different story. They will just be waiting in patience and in sorrow. If they are martyred, it will be a wonderful thing. "Blessed are the dead which die in the Lord." He is going to reward them for their faithfulness to Himself.

You can see that this verse is not appropriate for a funeral, especially for a wealthy man who has been living in clover all of his life. In Texas I heard it used at a rich man's funeral, a man who had been brought up in a home of wealth. He had never known what it was to lift his little finger in actual work. He just toyed around with a ranch and lost money on it—he had so much money, he had to get rid of it some way. Yet the preacher applied this verse to him! That is a terrible abuse of the Word of God. Death is going to be precious to the people in the Great Tribulation but not for the saints of our society in which everything is geared to comfort.

"For their works follow with them" reveals that they will be rewarded for their faithfulness, patience, and works in this period. God does not save anyone for his works, but He does reward us for our works. Our works (good or bad) are like tin cans tied to a dog's tail; we cannot get away from them. They will follow us to the *bema* seat of Christ.

PREVIEW OF ARMAGEDDON

And I looked, and behold a white cloud, and upon the cloud one sat like unto the Son of man, having on his head a golden crown, and in his hand a sharp sickle [Rev. 14:14].

"I looked, and behold" emphasizes the fact that John is not only a hearer but a spectator.

"A white cloud, and upon the cloud one sat like unto the Son of man" is evidently the Lord Jesus Christ. The cloud is a mark of identification: "And then shall appear the sign of the Son of man in heaven: and then shall all the tribes of the earth mourn, and they shall see the Son of man coming in the clouds of heaven with power and great glory" (Matt. 24:30). I think that the "clouds" are the *shekinah* cloud, which is "the sign" in heaven.

"On his head a golden crown" further confirms this One as the Lord Jesus Christ. He is the hero of the Book of Revelation, my friend, and you need this book to get a true picture of Him. He is seen as King—not as Prophet or Priest. His office as King is always connected with His return to the earth.

"A sharp sickle" establishes this and speaks of the judgment of the wicked. Dr. Newell calls attention to something that is quite interesting: he notes that the word *sickle* occurs only twelve times in the Scriptures, of which seven are in the verses of this section. Also, the word *sharp* occurs seven times in the Revelation, and four times in this chapter.

And another angel came out of the temple, crying with a loud voice to him that sat on the cloud, Thrust in thy sickle, and reap: for the time is come for thee to reap; for the harvest of the earth is ripe.

And he that sat on the cloud thrust in his sickle on the earth; and the earth was reaped [Rev. 14:15–16].

And another angel came out of the temple, crying in a great voice to the One seated on the cloud. Send forth thy sickle, and reap; for the hour is come to reap; for the harvest of the earth was dried. And He that sat on the cloud cast his sickle upon the earth; and the earth was reaped.

"Send forth thy sickle, and reap" refers to the judgment of men on the earth. "As therefore the tares are gathered and burned in the fire; so shall it be in the end of this world. The Son of man shall send forth his angels, and they shall gather out of his kingdom all things that offend, and them which do iniquity; And shall cast them into a furnace of fire: there shall be wailing and gnashing of teeth" (Matt. 13:40–42). In Matthew the "harvest" has so long been identified with Christian witnessing, and believers have been urged to pray for laborers for the harvest, that it is difficult for the average Christian to fit this scene into the true context of Scripture. Actually, believers are *not* urged to harvest today; they are urged to sow, to sow the Word of God.

". . . a sower went forth to sow" (Matt. 13:3) is a picture of Christendom today. The Lord Jesus Christ is the Son of Man. He is the sower and the seed is the Word of God and the field is the world. He is flinging out the seed into the world. There is going to be a harvest someday, but that will come at the end of the age. You and I are not in the harvesting business today. Our business is to sow the seed. That is the reason I do not worry about results. I worry a great deal about the source. I want to do my best in giving out the Word of God. Why? Because sowing seed is my business. I am not really concerned about the number of folk who claim to have been converted through my ministry. I just sow the seed. Christ is the One who is going to have the harvest, and the harvest is the judgment at the end of the age. This is the picture given to us here in the Revelation.

Note God's instructions to His Son in the Old Testament: "I will declare the decree: the LORD hath said unto me, Thou art my Son; this day have I begotten thee. Ask of me, and I shall give thee the heathen for thine inheritance, and the uttermost parts of the earth for thy possession. Thou shalt break them with a rod of iron; thou shalt dash them in pieces like a potter's vessel" (Ps. 2:7–9). Did this take place at the Lord's first coming? No. This is no missionary text. When, then, will it take place? It will take place at Christ's second coming to earth. At that time He will come in judgment.

"For the hour is come to reap" is in conformity to the words of Jesus, ". . . the harvest is the end of the world . . ." (Matt. 13:39). The time will come to reap, so let's sow the seed today, and let's not be so everlastingly busy trying to get somebody's hand up and have that one come forward to receive Christ as Savior. Let's make sure that we give out the Word of God, and the Spirit of God will take care of the results.

The time of harvest is set before us in the Old Testament: "Put ye in the sickle, for the harvest is ripe: come, get you down; for the press is full, the vats overflow; for their wickedness is great. Multitudes, multitudes in the valley of decision: for the day of the LORD is near in the valley of decision" (Joel 3:13–14).

And another angel came out of the temple which is in heaven, he also having a sharp sickle.

And another angel came out from the altar, which had power over fire; and cried with a loud cry to him that had the sharp sickle, saying, Thrust in thy sharp sickle, and gather the clusters of the vine of the earth; for her grapes are fully ripe [Rev. 14:17–18].

And another angel came out from the sanctuary which is in heaven, he also having a sharp sickle. And another angel came out from the altar, he that hath (having) power over the fire, and he called with a great voice to him that had the sharp sickle, saying, Send forth thy sharp sickle, and gather the clusters of the vine of the earth; for her grapes are fully ripe.

"The sanctuary which is in heaven" identifies this with the Old Testament, not with the church.

The "sharp sickle" indicates judgment. "Her grapes are fully ripe" conveys the thought of their being dry like raisins. This is a change of metaphor for the war of Armageddon, and this is the picture Isaiah gives: "Who is this that cometh from Edom, with dyed garments from Bozrah? this that is glorious in his apparel, traveling in the greatness of his strength? I that speak in righteousness, mighty to save. Wherefore art thou red in thine apparel, and thy garments like him that treadeth in the winevat? I have trodden the winepress alone; and of the people there was none with me: for I will tread them in mine anger, and trample them in my fury; and their blood shall be sprinkled upon my garments, and I will stain all my raiment. For the day of vengeance is in mine heart, and the year of my redeemed is come. And I looked, and there was none to help; and I wondered that there was none to uphold: therefore mine own arm brought salvation unto me; and my fury, it upheld me. And I will tread down the people in mine anger, and make them drunk in my fury, and I will bring down their strength to the earth" (Isa. 63:1–6).

This vivid picture is not of Christ at His first coming but of Christ when He returns in judgment. In Isaiah's day men would get into the winepress barefooted to tread out the grapes. The red juice would spurt out of the ripe grapes and stain their garments. The picture in this verse is of spectators seeing that there is blood on our Lord's beautiful garments as though He had trodden the winepress. When Christ came the first time, He shed His blood for them, but they have rejected it. Now He is trodding down the wicked, and it is their blood that is shed. He will gather them, as we will see in Revelation 16:16, "into a place called in the Hebrew tongue Armageddon." It is not a single battle but a war—the war of Armageddon (Heb.: *Har-Megiddon*).

Notice in this passage from Isaiah's prophecy that He is seen treading the winepress alone. It is positively terrifying. Little wonder that the men of this earth will cry to the rocks to fall upon them and hide them from the wrath of the Lamb. This will be the sad end of that civilization which at the Tower of Babel demonstrated an active rebellion against God, a rebellion which has been mounting like a mighty crescendo ever since and will break in all of its fury during the Great Tribulation Period. As we will see when we come to chapter 19, when Christ comes He will put down that rebellion against God in order to establish His kingdom here upon the earth. He will (in the language of Psalm 2) "break them with a rod of iron" and "dash them in pieces like a potter's vessel."

You see, the "gentle Jesus" who wouldn't swat a fly, whom we have heard so much about, is just not the Jesus of the Word of God. The Lord Jesus Christ is the *Savior* of the world, but He is also the *Judge* of all the world. If you do not accept His blood shed for you, then if the Great Tribulation Period comes during your lifetime, *your* blood will be shed.

My feeling is that no careful study of the Word of God would lead any person of reasonable intelligence to believe that the church is going through this awful period. Folk who want to push the church into the Great Tribulation seem to think that it will be no more unpleasant than a trip to the dentist to get a tooth pulled. Such a trip is not pleasant; no one enjoys having a tooth pulled, but it can be endured. My friend, if that is in your thinking, you just haven't seen what the Tribulation really will be. Isaiah gives us another picture of it: "Come near, ye nations, to hear; and hearken, ye people: let the earth hear, and all that is therein; the world, and all things that come forth of it. For the indignation of the Lord is upon all nations, and his fury upon all their armies: he hath utterly destroyed them, he hath delivered them to the slaughter. Their slain also shall be cast out, and their stink shall come up out of their carcases, and the mountains shall be melted with their blood. . . . The sword of the Lord is filled with blood, it is made fat with fatness, and with the blood of lambs and goats, with the fat of the kidneys of rams: for the Lord hath a sacrifice in Bozrah, and a great slaughter in the land of Idumea" (Isa. 34:1–3, 6).

What a picture this is! The *precious blood* of the Lamb having been rejected, the blood of those who defied God and followed and worshiped the Beast bathes the earth. It is frightful. As a ripe grape is mashed and the juice flies in every direction, so will little man fall into the vat of God's judgment. This is Armageddon—the mount of slaughter.

And the angel thrust in his sickle into the earth, and gathered the vine of the earth, and cast it into the great winepress of the wrath of God.

And the winepress was trodden without the city, and blood came out of the winepress, even unto the horse bridles, by the space of a thousand and six hundred furlongs [Rev. 14:19–20].

And the angel cast his sickle into the earth, and gathered the vine of the earth, and cast it into the winepress, the great winepress of the wrath of God. And the winepress was trodden without the city, and there came out blood from the winepress, even unto the bridles of the horses, as far as a thousand and six hundred furlongs.

"Without the city" means outside of Jerusalem.

"Unto the bridles of the horses" means about four feet deep.

"A thousand and six hundred furlongs" is about 185 miles, and that is the distance from Dan to Beer-sheba. All of Palestine is the scene of this final war which ends in what is called Armageddon. It is a campaign beginning about the middle of the Great Tribulation and is concluded by the personal return of Christ to the earth. Psalm 45:3–7 is an Old Testament prediction of this: "Gird thy sword upon thy thigh, O most mighty, with thy glory and thy majesty. And in thy majesty ride prosperously because of truth and meekness and righteousness; and thy right hand shall teach thee terrible things. Thine arrows are sharp in the heart of the king's enemies; whereby the people fall under thee. Thy throne, O God, is for ever and ever: the sceptre of thy kingdom is a right sceptre. Thou lovest righteousness, and hatest wickedness: therefore God, thy God, hath anointed thee with the oil of gladness above thy fellows." Psalm 45 is a messianic psalm.

Let me make it clear that I make no apology for these scenes of judgment. God has not asked me to apologize for His Word. He has told me to give it out. We need to face up to the facts:

1. Sin is an awful thing.
2. Sin is in the world.
3. You and I are sinners. The only remedy for sin is the redemption Christ offered when He shed His blood on the cross and paid the penalty for our sins.
4. You and I merit the judgment of God. Our only escape is to accept the work of Christ for us on Calvary's cross. The Bible asks a question that even God cannot answer: "How shall we escape, if we neglect so great salvation? . . ." (Heb. 2:3). Escape what? Escape judgment—The Tribulation is *judgment*. The way out is to accept Christ. Call it an escape mechanism if you want to; but, my friend, when the house is on fire, I'll go out a window or any other way that is an escape. This judgment must inevitably come on Christ-rejecters. Mankind has rejected Him, trodden under foot the Son of God, and counted the blood of the covenant as an unholy thing. If

God is just (and He is) there will be *judgment*. The generation of today needs to hear this. Instead of being given this, they are offered endless little methods of living the Christian life. My friend, there is nothing that will straighten out your life like knowing that our God is a holy God, that the Lord Jesus Christ is righteous, and that He is *not* going to tolerate sin in your life.

And this same concept should be taught to our children. I am heartened to see that some psychologists are returning to this position. My friend, the problem with your little Willie is that he is a mean little brat and should be turned across your knee and spanked instead of being treated as a cross between a piece of Dresden china and an orchid. As someone has well said, the board of education should be applied to the seat of learning.

Before we leave this chapter, I would like to draw your attention again to the viewpoint which is abroad concerning the church's going through the Great Tribulation Period. I have an article from a magazine that presents this viewpoint. The author of the article is a layman, and yet he has the audacity to write the following:

There is a shallow Christianity moving across our land. Those who do not have deep roots in Christ shrink from the idea that God would test His people with the Tribulation, or that He would use suffering to help the church make herself ready as a Bride for Christ. Very clearly, though, suffering is the pathway to glory. We are called to it. Why? "Because Christ also suffered, leaving us an example that we should follow in His steps." As a result of this thinking, I no longer teach Christians they will not have to go through the Tribulation. Maybe they won't, but I can do more for them by preparing them to face testing in His name than by teaching them that the Lord is going to rapture them out of the hour of trial.

In his article this layman also says, "There is a tremendous growth in that person who puts on the whole armor of God, that he may be able to withstand in the evil day." My friend, I want you to know that the Great Tribulation is not called the "evil day." It is called the great day of God's wrath. That is how the Tribulation is described in the Bible. I don't know how anyone could read and study the Book of Revelation and believe that going through the Great Tribulation would *purify* the church or that the bride has to make herself ready! What do you think Christ did when He died on the cross? *He* made us ready there. We can never become *worthy* to enter into the presence of God. We are going to enter His presence "in Christ," and you can't add anything to that. You can't equate the hour of trial with the great day of the wrath of God that is going to come on this earth. The church will be delivered from that. The Book of Revelation has made that clear. The 144,000 have already been identified for us as Israelites, and even the tribes are identified for us, so there is no way in the world of saying that this group is the church; nor is that great company "which no man could number" the church, the bride of Christ (see Rev. 7:9).

We have seen that God was able to keep the 144,000 during the Great Tribulation. So it is not a question of whether God *can* keep the church in the Great Tribulation Period. Of course, He can keep the church if that is His will and plan. But, according to the Word of God, this is *not* His will and plan. The Lord Jesus said, "I am going to keep you *from* that hour that is coming on this earth," from that *terrible* time of testing that is coming. I would like to put it like this: The church is not going through the *Great* Tribulation Period, but we are going through the *little* tribulation. All of us have troubles and trials, and I don't know of a Christian who doesn't have problems and difficulties. It seems like the more spiritually mature the saint of God is, the more he suffers. This is the method God uses to develop His children. We never become wonderful saints of God. We are just His little children, immature and undeveloped. When we come into His presence, we will be accepted because of what *Christ* has done for us, not because we have endured the Great Tribulation.

Another point to consider is that *most* of the church has already missed the Great Tribulation. For over nineteen hundred years believers have been going into the presence of Christ through the doorway of death. I hope you don't believe that God is going to send them back to earth so they can go through the Great Tribulation Period! At best there will be only a small percentage of believers who are still alive when the time of tribulation comes upon the earth. The great majority of the church has already missed the Great Tribulation.

I have always had the impression that the folk who believe that the church will go through the Great Tribulation feel that our crowd needs it, and specifically that *I* need it, that I deserve to go through it. Well, I agree that I do deserve it, and I also deserve hell. But I'm not going to hell because Christ bore it for me, and I have trusted in Him. Neither am I going through the Great Tribulation. Why? Because Christ died for me, and He saves me by His grace. Isn't the One who says that He is rich in grace able to deliver me out of the Great Tribulation?

It is true that God allows us to go through the little tribulation of this life. After having cancer and several major operations, I feel as if I have been through the little tribulation period. And it is by this method that God refines us and purifies us. A preacher friend said to me recently, "I can tell a difference in your ministry since you have gone through those illnesses." I trust that he is correct in that. I know God allowed it for a purpose.

When I read the article by the brother who thinks the church should go through the Great Tribulation, I wondered if he had ever really suffered for Christ. A preacher friend of mine who holds this view was discussing it as we were having lunch together one day. As he was eating a T-bone steak, he talked as nonchalantly about the Great Tribulation as if it would not be any worse than the church wading through a river or enduring a very hot summer or experiencing an energy shortage. He apparently did not think of it as being the terrible time which is depicted in the Book of Revelation. Is God misrepresenting the facts to us? Is He just trying to scare us?

Well, my friend, there are places in this book where God uses symbols. Do you know why He uses symbols? He doesn't do it in order to evaporate the facts so that we can dismiss them, but because the reality which the symbol represents is lots worse than the symbol. Many of the things which John tries to describe to us beggar description. Even God cannot communicate some of them to us—not because He is not able, but because we are dull of hearing, as He has told us. We don't always understand. I am afraid that a great many folk just do not realize that the Great Tribulation is a *terrible* thing, and it is *miraculous* that the 144,000 will come through it. He won't lose one of them. Why? Because they will be big, strong, robust fellows? No. They will overcome by the blood of the Lamb. That's how they will do it.

CHAPTER 15

THEME: Preparation for final judgment of the Great Tribulation

In this chapter we have another sign in heaven, seven angels with the seven last plagues. Chapters 15 and 16 belong together because in them we have the pouring out of the seven mixing bowls of wrath. I imagine that you thought the worst was over, but the worst is yet to come. We have already seen the seven seals, the seven trumpets, and the seven personalities. Now the coming seven bowls of wrath are the worst of all. Chapter 15, besides being the shortest chapter in Revelation, is the preface to the final series of judgments which come on the earth during the Great Tribulation. These judgments are the most intense and devastating of any that have preceded them.

The purpose of the Great Tribulation is judgment. It is *not* for the purifying of the church! It is to give Satan his final opportunity. God is going to remove the church before this time of tribulation because of His marvelous, infinite grace. If you are willing to accept His grace, then you can escape the Great Tribulation. Believe me, the bowls of wrath are not the "blessed hope" for which believers are looking. No, we are "Looking for that blessed hope, and the glorious appearing of the great God and our Saviour Jesus Christ" (Titus 2:13). If we will grow in love with Him, we will not consider the judgments of the Great Tribulation terrifying. You don't have to stick your head in the sand like the proverbial ostrich and refuse to read the Book of Revelation. My friend, if you are trusting Christ, you won't be going through it. But you need to know what the unsaved will have to go through, and that might make you a zealous witness for Christ in these difficult days.

Someone said of Dwight L. Moody that in his day he looked into the faces of more people than any man who ever lived and that he reduced the population of hell by two million. We hear a lot of talk about reducing the population explosion of this earth. Well, hell has had a population explosion for many years, and I would like to help reduce that.

Before these angels begin to pour out their bowls of wrath, there may be the question still in the minds of some if any believers were able to stand up against the Antichrist. If that question has not been answered to the satisfaction of the reader, it is answered here. There will be those who will be enabled to stand.

First of all, we will see the preparation for the final judgment of the Great Tribulation.

TRIBULATION SAINTS IN HEAVEN WORSHIP GOD

In the first four verses we see that the tribulation saints in heaven worship God because He is holy and just. This is another interlude.

And I saw another sign in heaven, great and marvellous, seven angels having the seven last plagues; for in them is filled up the wrath of God [Rev. 15:1].

And I saw another sign in (the) heaven, great and wonderful, seven angels having seven plagues, which are the last, for in them (was) finished the wrath of God.

This will bring us to the end of the Great Tribulation Period. I don't know about you, but I will be glad to get to the end of it. And then we will see the coming of Christ to the earth.

"And I saw" assures us that John is still a spectator to these events. He is attending the dress rehearsal of the last act of man's little day upon the earth.

"Another sign" connects this chapter with Revelation 12:1, the first sign, which, in the opening of chapter 12, was Israel. These seven angels of wrath are connected with the judgments to follow until Christ comes (see ch. 19). From chapter 12 to the return of Christ is a series of events which are mutually related. This does not mean that there is a chronological order but rather a logical order of retracing the same events with added detail. This method is the personal signature of the Holy Spirit, seen first in Genesis 1–2. In Genesis 1 we are given the account of the Creation, the seven days describing God's handiwork. In chapter 2 the Holy Spirit lifted out the account of the creation of man and went over it again, adding details. It is known as the law of recapitulation, and it runs all the way through the Scriptures. For another example, we have the giving of the Mosaic Law in Exodus and then in Deuteronomy the interpretation of the Law with forty years of experience in the wilderness and a great deal of detail added. Also, when we come to the New Testament, we find not one, not two, but four gospel records because it takes four to give the many sides of the glorious person of Christ who came to earth over nineteen hundred years ago.

Satan, having been cast into the earth, brings down *his* wrath upon the remnant of Israel. Also, he makes a final thrust for world domination through the two Beasts. Then God makes a final display of His wrath and concludes earth's sordid tragedy of sin. "The LORD said unto my Lord, Sit thou at my right hand, until I make thine enemies thy footstool" (Ps. 110:1).

"Was finished" in the Greek language is in the prophetic aorist tense, which considers an event in the future as already accomplished.

"The wrath of God" marks the final judgment of the Great Tribulation. God has been slow to anger, but here ends His longsuffering. Judgment in the final stages of the Day of Wrath proceeds from God, not from Satan or the wild Beast. It comes directly from the throne of God. *God will judge.*

And I saw as it were a sea of glass mingled with fire: and them that had gotten the victory over the beast, and over his image, and over his mark, and over the number of his name, stand on the sea of glass, having the harps of God [Rev. 15:2].

And I saw as it were a glassy sea mingled with fire, and them that came off victorious from the wild beast, and from his image, and from the number of his name, standing by (on the shore of) the glassy sea, having harps of God.

"A glassy sea mingled with fire" represents the frightful persecution by the Beast during the Great Tribulation Period. This is the period of time, as we have seen, where no man could buy or sell unless he had the mark of the Beast. It is going to be very difficult to get things to eat in that day. That is the reason the Lord Jesus, speaking of this period in His Olivet Discourse, said that whoever would give a cup of cold water in His name would not lose his reward. You see, anyone in that day who would give even a cup of cold water to one of the 144,000 would put his life in jeopardy because the Beast would put him to death for harboring what he would classify as a criminal.

Those will be very difficult days. Again I ask the question: Will anyone make it through the Great Tribulation? No, they won't unless they are sealed. Although multitudes will be martyred during this period—and I think that a great many of the 144,000 will lay down their lives for Jesus—they will be faithful to Him

until death. As we have seen, *all* of the 144,000 will be with the Lamb on Mount Zion.

"And them that came off victorious"—here are the tribulation saints who have come through the fires of persecution on the earth and yet have not lost their *song*. They have the harps of God, and in the next couple of verses we will see that they are able to sing, and they do sing.

How about us today, Christian friend? We are not in the Great Tribulation now and never will be, but even in these days are you having trouble keeping from your heart just a little root of bitterness? We are warned against this in Hebrews 12:15 because it is so easy for it to happen. Maybe this has no application to you, but it does have application to me. When I was in my teens, I came to know the Lord and at seventeen or eighteen made my decision to study for the ministry. I expected the Christians to support me in my decision. One wealthy family in Nashville actually turned against me. I was dating their daughter at the time, and they didn't want a poor preacher in the family. A teenage boy feels these things most keenly, I guess, but even to this day I have to fight that little root of bitterness against that class of people who treated me so badly at that time. Now that wasn't tribulation at all. It was a heartbreak, but it was not a Great Tribulation by any means.

What about that little root of bitterness? Are you having a problem with it? I meet people, Christian people, who have let that little root of bitterness spoil their lives to the point that it actually causes them to deteriorate in their Christian life and testimony. I know of a lovely Christian family back East. Something happened that caused them to become very bitter towards another family, and they refused to let it go. That root of bitterness has entered into their lives. I have seen the family sitting in church on Sunday without a smile on one of the faces. Bitterness can ruin your Christian life. We need to pray, in the face of life's circumstances, that there will be no root of bitterness within us.

It is remarkable to see that these tribulation saints who have lived through the horror of the Great Tribulation have kept their song!

Let me share a poem on prayer with you. It was sent to me by one of our radio listeners.

Unanswered yet? Faith cannot be unanswered.
Her feet were firmly planted on the rock.
Amid the wildest storm she stands undaunted

Nor quails before the loudest thunder
   shock.

She knows Omnipotence has heard her
   prayer
And cries, It shall be done sometime,
   somewhere.
Unanswered yet? Nay, do not say un-
   granted.
Perhaps your part is not yet wholly done.

The work began when your first prayer
   was uttered,
And God will finish what He has begun.
If you will keep the incense burning
   there,
His glory you will see, sometime, somewhere.

          "Sometime, Somewhere"
          —Ophelia Guyon Browning

My friend, in this life which you and I are
living down here, a little bitterness will come
in. What will we do about it? We need to pray.
In fact, we need to pray about this more than
anything else. If these saints can come
through the Great Tribulation and still sing,
you and I certainly ought to have a song in our
hearts regardless of our circumstances.

The psalmist wrote, "For his anger endureth but a moment; in his favour is life:
weeping may endure for a night, but joy
cometh in the morning" (Ps. 30:5). I have
learned over the years that God will never let
anyone cross your pathway, not even an enemy, unless it will teach you a lesson. He
permits it for a purpose, for the development
of your character. We need to be in prayer that
we not fall into the trap of Satan and lose the
joy of our salvation.

**And they sing the song of Moses the
servant of God, and the song of the
Lamb, saying, Great and marvellous
are thy works, Lord God Almighty; just
and true are thy ways, thou King of
saints.**

**Who shall not fear thee, O Lord, and
glorify thy name? for thou only art
holy: for all nations shall come and
worship before thee; for thy judgments
are made manifest [Rev. 15:3–4].**

*And they sing the song of Moses the ser-
vant of God, and the song of the Lamb,
saying, Great and wonderful are thy
works, Lord God, the Almighty; righteous and true are thy ways, thou King of
the ages (nations). Who shall not fear,
Lord, and glorify thy name? For thou
only art holy; for all the nations shall
come and worship before thee; for thy
righteous acts were made manifest.*

If you want to learn "the song of Moses," you
will find it in Exodus 15:1–21 and Deuteronomy 32:1–43. Both songs speak of God's deliverance, salvation, and faithfulness. "The song
of the Lamb" is the ascription of praise to
Christ as the Redeemer. We have seen that in
Revelation 5:9–12.

Again let me call your attention to the fact
that the Book of Revelation is Christocentric,
that is, Christ-centered. Don't let the four
horsemen carry you away, or don't be dis-
tracted by the blowing of the trumpets or by
the seven performers. And don't let your interest center on these bowls of wrath. Let's
keep our eyes centered on Christ. He is in
charge; He is the Lord. In this book we have
the unveiling of Jesus Christ in His holiness,
in His power, and in His glory. The Man Christ
Jesus is wonderful! He is the One who can put
His hand in the hand of God and who can put
His other hand in the hand of man and bring
them together. He can do this because He is
God.

"King of the ages" has two other renderings,
King of saints and *King of the nations.* Any
rendering indicates that Christ will be the object of universal worship and acknowledgment. There will be no place where He will not
be worshiped.

"Who shall not fear, Lord, and glorify thy
name?" In our day there is very little reverential fear of God, even among believers. We
have been caught up in this love attitude, and I
don't think we should lose sight of the fact that
God is love. But God is also light, which means
He is holy. God is moving in on churches and
dealing with Christians as I have never seen
Him do before. I am one Christian who can
testify to that. If you are God's child, you had
better not do as you please. If you think God
would mind sending you a little trouble, you
are wrong. God is to be *feared.* Our God is a
holy God.

"Nations shall come and worship before
thee." The day will come when nations will
come and worship before the Lord Jesus
Christ. This is not true of nations today. That
little prayer breakfast in Washington is a
pretty sorry substitute for universal worship
of God. One man used that prayer breakfast as
an argument that we are living in a Christian
nation. What nonsense! We are not living in a

Christian nation, but there will come a day when every nation will worship Him. This knowledge should cause us to take heart as we see our own nation moving in the wrong direction. The day will come when God will remove the rebellious men and leave only those who will worship Him.

In Psalm 2:8 we read, "Ask of me, and I shall give thee the heathen [nations] for thine inheritance, and the uttermost parts of the earth for thy possession." The nations are going to be His. And in Isaiah 11:9: "They shall not hurt nor destroy in all my holy mountain: for the earth shall be full of the knowledge of the LORD, as the waters cover the sea." In that day there will be no need for our Thru the Bible study because all men are going to have a knowledge of God. In Jeremiah 23:5 we are told, "Behold, the days come, saith the LORD, that I will raise unto David a righteous Branch, and a King shall reign and prosper, and shall execute judgment and justice in the earth."

It is true that our country has been through awful travail, but we have been so engrossed in our own problems that our hearts have grown weary from all the scandal. Other nations, however, have had this same problem. Today it is nauseating to see the immorality, the godlessness, and the injustice in the world. If I weren't a Christian, I would be one of the most radical persons you have ever met. As a child of God, I can see what is happening in the world, but I know I cannot remedy one thing. But Christ is going to reign someday, and He is going to execute judgment and justice in the earth. Thank God for that! I get so tired of politicians telling me that they represent me in Washington and that they are going to do what I want them to do—when all the time they are doing everything they can for their own interests. With rare exceptions, this is equally true of each political party. In the face of gross immorality and gross injustice, what can we do? Well, all of us who are God's children need to *pray* for our country and rejoice that there is coming One who will execute justice and judgment upon the earth.

In Philippians 2:9–11 we read this: "Wherefore God also hath highly exalted him, and given him a name which is above every name: That at the name of Jesus every knee should bow, of things in heaven, and things in earth, and things under the earth; And that every tongue should confess that Jesus Christ is Lord, to the glory of God the Father." Those who are in hell will not acknowledge Him as their Redeemer, but they are going to ac-

knowledge that He is the boss, He is running the universe, and it belongs to Him. And they are going to acknowledge the glory of God—they will *have* to do that.

"For thy righteous acts were made manifest." This testimony, coming from witnesses of this period, is inexpressibly impressive and should settle in the minds of believers the fact that God is *right* in all that He does. What God is doing may not look right to you, but if you don't think God is doing the right thing, *you* are wrong, not God. We need to adjust our attitudes and our thinking. Notice the testimony of the Psalms: "Oh let the wickedness of the wicked come to an end; but establish the just: for the righteous God trieth the hearts and reins" (Ps. 7:9). "For the righteous LORD loveth righteousness; his countenance doth behold the upright" (Ps. 11:7). "O give thanks unto the LORD, for he is good: for his mercy endureth for ever. . . . He poureth contempt upon princes, and causeth them to wander in the wilderness, where there is no way. . . . The righteous shall see it, and rejoice: and all iniquity shall stop her mouth" (Ps. 107:1, 40, 42). This will happen when God takes charge.

TABERNACLE OPENED IN HEAVEN FOR ANGELS WITH SEVEN BOWLS

At this point the temple of the tabernacle is opened in heaven in order that seven angels, having seven golden bowls, might proceed forth.

And after that I looked, and, behold, the temple of the tabernacle of the testimony in heaven was opened:

And the seven angels came out of the temple, having the seven plagues, clothed in pure and white linen, and having their breasts girded with golden girdles [Rev. 15:5–6].

And after these things I saw, and the sanctuary (temple) of the tabernacle [Gr.: skenes] of the testimony (witness) in (the) heaven was opened; and there came out from the temple (the) seven angels, having the seven plagues, clothed in linen (precious stone) pure and white, and girt about the breast with golden girdles.

The "temple" is referred to fifteen times in the Book of Revelation. Its prominence cannot be ignored. In the first part of Revelation, through chapter 3, the church is the subject and there is no mention of a temple. Beginning with chapter 4 the scene shifts to heaven, and we see the temple in heaven; also there is a temple on earth patterned after the one in heaven. There is no temple in the New Jerusalem where the church is going. Why? Because the church is not identified with a temple. This fact makes it abundantly clear that, beginning with chapter 4, God is dealing with people who have had a temple, and only to Israel had God given a temple, patterned after the one in heaven. In this instance, the reference is specifically to the tabernacle *(skenes)* and the Holy of Holies in which the ark of the testimony was kept. In the ark were the tables of stone. Both the tabernacle and the tables of stone were duplicates of originals in heaven. "And look that thou make them after their pattern, which was shewed thee in the mount" (Exod. 25:40). "It was therefore necessary that the patterns of things in the heavens should be purified with these; but the heavenly things themselves with better sacrifices than these" (Heb. 9:23).

The originals are referred to in Revelation 11:19: "And the temple of God was opened in heaven, and there was seen in his temple the ark of his testament: and there were lightnings, and voices, and thunderings, and an earthquake, and great hail." The action of God here is based on the violation of His covenant with Israel—the broken Law. God is righteous in what He is about to do. He will judge, then He will carry out His covenant with Israel.

The prominence of angels in this book is again called to our attention by the appearance of angels at this point. Previously, seven angels blew on seven trumpets. Here is the new series of seven angels who have the seven plagues of the seven bowls of wrath. The departure of the angels from the temple demonstrates that they depart from the throne of mercy, and now God acts in justice instead of in mercy.

"Clothed in linen." The angels are clothed in linen—another meaning is clothed with precious stones. It is an enigmatic expression due to a variant reading in the text. Were they clothed in linen or a stone? The intention, it seems, is to describe their garments as studded and set with precious stones. Though their garments identify them in a priestly activity, they forsake that work of mercy for plagues of judgment.

The "golden girdles" reveal the angels in the livery of Christ, who no longer is exercising a priestly function but is seen here judging the world.

And one of the four beasts gave unto the seven angels seven golden vials full of the wrath of God, who liveth for ever and ever.

And the temple was filled with smoke from the glory of God, and from his power; and no man was able to enter into the temple, till the seven plagues of the seven angels were fulfilled [Rev. 15:7–8].

And one of the four living creatures gave to the seven angels seven golden bowls, full of the wrath of God, who liveth for ever and ever. And the sanctuary (temple) was filled with smoke from the glory of God, and from his power; and no one was able to enter into the sanctuary (temple), till the seven plagues of the seven angels should be finished.

"Seven angels seven golden vials." Again let me call your attention to the repetition of the number seven. I sometimes hear it said that seven is the number of perfection, which is not exactly accurate. It is the number of completeness, and sometimes completeness is perfection. For example, in six days God created heaven and earth and rested on the seventh day—not only because it was complete, but because it was perfect. But here in the Revelation the series of sevens denote a completion. My feeling is that we have a complete history of the church in the seven churches, and that we have a complete Great Tribulation Period in each one of the series of sevens; in other words, each covers it all. First, in the seven seals we see a broad outline, then, as we read along in the prophecy, we see that God zeroes in and focuses on the last three and a half years.

"Bowls (vials), full of the wrath of God." Notice, they are not filled with the *love* of God but with God's *wrath*.

"The sanctuary (temple) was filled with smoke from the glory of God." The very fact that this section continues to deal with the temple ought to indicate to anyone who is knowledgeable that the church is not involved. Neither the temple nor the tabernacle had anything to do with the church. They present marvelous pictures of Christ which have spiritual applications for us today, but that does not mean that the church should build a temple or a tabernacle. Rather, this section refers to Israel, a people who had a tabernacle and a temple. A great many are reluctant to admit this fact because they dismiss Israel from the plan and purpose of God at the beginning of the New Testament. As you can see, the New Testament by no means dismisses Israel!

The "seven golden bowls" represent the final part of the Great Tribulation Period. I think that "bowls" better describes the container than "vials"—a vial makes me think of a little test tube that is used in a laboratory. Bowls were used in the service of the temple. For example, a bowl of blood was taken by the high priest one day each year into the Holy of Holies. And that bowl of blood spoke of redemption for sin.

These seven angels with priestly garments, having departed from the temple proper, are no longer engaged in a service of mercy but are beginning a strange ministry of pouring out bowls of wrath on a Christ-rejecting world. A world that has rejected the blood of Christ must bear the judgment for sin. This judgment is not the result of man's or Satan's

enmity. It is the direct action of the Lord Jesus Christ. We have seen the gentle Jesus, and now we see the wrath of the Lamb. You never think of a little lamb as being angry. A lion can roar, but not a little lamb. The wrath of the Lamb is going to startle the world someday.

The prophets of the Old Testament used the figure of the cup of iniquity and wrath filling up and spoke of God's patience in waiting for it to fill. Then, when it is full, God moves in judgment.

These seven angels with seven golden bowls make it clear that the judgments of the bowls proceed from God and are not the result of man's mistakes or of Satan's enmity. These judgments are the direct action of God.

CHAPTER 16

THEME: *Pouring out the seven bowls*

The seven angels pouring out the seven bowls of God's wrath upon the earth is the theme of this chapter. Also, it includes the interlude between the sixth and seventh bowls. Chapter 15 was the prelude to this chapter and is organically connected with it.

It is worth repeating that the bowls of wrath contain the direct judgment of God upon the world; they do not proceed from either man's misdoings or Satan's machinations. They are poured out during the reign of the Beast. They cover a very brief period of time, comparatively speaking.

There is a definite similarity between the judgments in this chapter and God's judgments upon Egypt through Moses.

PREPARATION FOR FINAL JUDGMENT OF THE GREAT TRIBULATION

The first verse of this chapter speaks of the message the great voice gives the seven angels.

And I heard a great voice out of the temple saying to the seven angels, Go your ways, and pour out the vials of the wrath of God upon the earth [Rev. 16:1].

As usual, I'll give the literal translation of the Greek text throughout this chapter.

And I heard a great voice out of the sanctuary (temple) saying to the seven angels, Go and pour out the seven bowls of the wrath of God into the earth.

Let me remind you that the Lord Jesus Christ is still in full charge. Remember that way back in chapter 5 the Lord Jesus was the only One found worthy to open the seven-sealed book, and His opening of the seals ushered in this entire series of sevens. He is in command to the end of this book. He is the One who is marching to victory. The power and the glory and the majesty belong to Him. This is His judgment upon a Christ-rejecting world. The Father has committed all judgment unto Him. Christ is the One who gives the command that sends out these seven angels with the final judgments. There is no longer a delay, no longer an interval or intermission. The hour has come. The order is given, and the seven angels execute the command.

It is difficult for man, even Christians, to believe that God is going to pour out His wrath on a rebellious and God-hating world and destroy this civilization. But, my friend, everything you see today is under the judgment of God.

When Mrs. McGee and I first came to Southern California, we almost thought that we had entered the Millennium. Those were the good old days before the great population came, before we had smog and heavy traffic. I still love California, but it is not like it was then. Every Monday we would take the day off and go to see some of the sights. We would drive to the beach, to the mountains, or to the desert. One evening as we were driving down Wilshire Boulevard, a very attractive street, all around us we could see liquor signs and the world of glamour designed to satiate the demands of the flesh. I was reminded of what the Lord Jesus said to the apostles when they came to Him to show Him the buildings of the temple, how beautiful they were. He said to them, "See ye not all these things? verily I say unto you, There shall not be left here one stone upon another, that shall not be thrown down" (Matt. 24:2). They were amazed that He would make a statement like that. And I said to my wife, "All of this beauty and glamour that we are seeing is going to pass away. It is under the judgment of God. It all is going up in smoke someday." Believe me, we need to make our investments in heaven where neither moth nor rust doth corrupt, and where thieves do not break through nor steal. Perhaps you are saying, "But I have gilt-edged investments and bonds in a safety deposit box." Yes, but you are still going to lose them because you are going to leave them. You are going to release your hand in death. You are going to turn them loose and move out.

This world in which we are living is under the judgment of God. It is hard for even believers to accept that fact. After almost a century of insipid preaching from America's pulpits, the average man believes that God is all sweetness and light and would not discipline or punish anyone. Well, this Book of Revelation tells a different story!

POURING OUT OF THE FIRST BOWL

And the first went, and poured out his vial upon the earth; and there fell a noisome and grievous sore upon the men which had the mark of the beast, and upon them which worshipped his image [Rev. 16:2].

And the first went and poured out his bowl into the earth; and it became (there broke out) a noisome and grievous sore upon the men that had the mark of the wild beast, and that worshipped his image.

Vincent writes in his *Word Studies in the New Testament,* "Each angel, as his turn comes, withdraws from the heavenly scene." In other words, the angel leaves the place of the mercy seat in heaven and executes judgment. He leaves heaven and pours a judgment bowl of wrath upon the earth.

The first bowl of judgment is quite interesting. It looks as though God is engaged in germ warfare upon the followers of Antichrist. Scripture states that the life of the flesh is in the blood, and also *death* is in the blood. These putrifying sores are worse than leprosy or cancer. As man discovers a remedy for one disease, another that is more frightful appears. These are judgments of God by which He reveals physically what man is morally— utterly corrupt.

The first bowl of wrath compares to the sixth plague in Egypt and is the same type of sore or "boil" (see Exod. 9:8–12). It is interesting to note that Moses predicted coming judgment upon Israel similar to this. It has not as yet been fulfilled. This prediction is found in the Book of Deuteronomy: "But it shall come to pass, if thou wilt not hearken unto the voice of the LORD thy God, to observe to do all his commandments and his statutes which I command thee this day; that all these curses shall come upon thee, and overtake thee" (Deut. 28:15). Now here is a list of them: "The LORD will smite thee with the botch of Egypt, and with the emerods, and with the scab, and with the itch, whereof thou canst not be healed" (Deut. 28:27). These diseases are incurable, according to Deuteronomy 28:35: "The LORD shall smite thee in the knees, and in the legs, with a sore botch that cannot be healed, from the sole of thy foot unto the top of thy head." These are predictions of Moses.

Now here in the Book of Revelation, the "noisome and grievous sore" is for those who received the mark of the Beast. As we have already seen, those who did not receive the mark have been in a bad way also. They have not been able to buy or sell. If a man has a starving family, I'm not going to blame him for breaking into a market to get food for them. It has been a desperate time for those who have refused the mark. But now, at the end of the Great Tribulation, those who have the mark and have enjoyed all the privileges it brought are going to be judged by God.

May I add a personal comment here: I have always felt that my first bout with cancer was a judgment from God. I still feel the same way today. The fact that God healed me is a sign that He forgave me, and He has given me my greatest ministry since then. I am rejoicing in that. But during the Great Tribulation, God's judgment of this terrible sore—which is probably worse than cancer—does not cause men to turn to God.

POURING OUT OF THE SECOND BOWL

And the second angel poured out his vial upon the sea; and it became as the blood of a dead man; and every living soul died in the sea [Rev. 16:3].

This plague is more severe than that of the second trumpet, where only one-third of the sea became blood. Here it is the *total* sea, and the blood is that of a dead man!

Blood is the token of life. "For the life of the flesh is in the blood . . ." (Lev. 17:11). The sea is a great reservoir of life. It is teeming with life, and the salty water is a cathartic for the filth of the earth. However, in this plague, blood is the token of death; the sea becomes a grave of death instead of a womb of life. The cool sea breezes become a stench from the carcasses floating on the surface of the bloody water and lining the shore. Commerce is paralyzed. Human beings died like flies. The first plague in Egypt was the turning of the waters of the Nile River into blood (see Exod. 7:20–25). There is a striking similarity here.

I wonder if we realize how much we are dependent upon God today? The light company, the gas company, the water company send us bills, but where did they get the light, the gas, and the water? It is obvious that these companies have something to do with getting these things to us, but God was the One who created the light and the gas and the water. Has God ever sent you a bill for the sunshine, for the water you drink, and the air you breathe? Have you paid Him? He has not sent His bill, and you would not be able to pay it if He did. God, who has been so gracious to a Christ-rejecting world, will at last judge all the earth. The angels pour out the bowls in the day of God's wrath.

POURING OUT OF THE THIRD BOWL

And the third angel poured out his vial upon the rivers and fountains of waters; and they became blood.

And I heard the angel of the waters say, Thou art righteous, O Lord, which art, and wast, and shalt be, because thou hast judged thus.

For they have shed the blood of saints and prophets, and thou hast given them blood to drink; for they are worthy.

And I heard another out of the altar say, Even so, Lord God Almighty, true and righteous are thy judgments [Rev. 16:4–7].

And the third angel poured out his bowl into the rivers and the fountains of the waters and it became (there came) blood. And I heard the angel of the waters saying, Righteous art thou, who art and who wast, The Holy One, because thou didst judge these things. For they shed the blood of saints and prophets, and blood didst thou give them to drink; they are worthy. And I heard the altar saying, Yea, the Lord God, the Almighty, true and righteous are thy judgments.

This plague, similar to that of the third trumpet, again is more severe. There, only one-third of the fresh water was affected, and here the *total* water supply of the earth will be cut off. This means destruction of human life on an unparalleled plane.

"The angel of the waters" is the superintendent of God's water department here on earth. This reveals another ministry of angels as it affects creation. They are in charge of the different physical departments of the universe. We have seen four angels who control the winds. This angel, who knows the whole story, now declares that God is right and holy in this act of judgment.

My friend, whatever God does is righteous and holy. If you don't agree with Him, it is too bad. You are wrong, not God. Imagine a little man standing up and saying, concerning the Creator, "I don't think He is doing right." I have a question for the person who would make a statement like that: "What are you going to do about it? In fact, what *can* you do about it?" If you are not in agreement with God, you had better get in agreement with Him. God is righteous in everything He does.

"They shed the blood of saints and prophets, and blood didst thou give them to drink." This is poetic justice with a vengeance. Those who take the sword will perish by the sword, and the shedding of blood leads to the shedding of blood. These who are being judged had made martyrs of God's people, and now God is forcing them to drink blood for the righteous blood they spilled.

"The altar saying" evidently refers back to the saints under the altar who had been praying for justice to be done: "And when he had opened the fifth seal, I saw under the altar the souls of them that were slain for the word of God, and for the testimony which they held:

And they cried with a loud voice, saying, How long, O Lord, holy and true, dost thou not judge and avenge our blood on them that dwell on the earth? And white robes were given unto every one of them; and it was said unto them, that they should rest yet for a little season, until their fellow-servants also and their brethren, that should be killed as they were, should be fulfilled" (Rev. 6:9–11). Here their prayer is answered. God was a long time getting to it, but now the time is come for answering their prayer.

POURING OUT OF THE FOURTH BOWL

And the fourth angel poured out his vial upon the sun; and power was given unto him to scorch men with fire.

And men were scorched with great heat, and blasphemed the name of God, which hath power over these plagues: and they repented not to give him glory [Rev. 16:8–9].

Our Lord predicted signs in the sun during the Great Tribulation: "And there shall be signs in the sun, and in the moon, and in the stars; and upon the earth distress of nations, with perplexity; the sea and the waves roaring" (Luke 21:25).

The Old Testament had a great deal to say about judgment during the Great Tribulation Period due to the excessive heat of the sun: "They shall be burnt with hunger, and devoured with burning heat, and with bitter destruction: I will also send the teeth of beasts upon them, with the poison of serpents of the dust" (Deut. 32:24).

Also the prophet Isaiah speaks of this: "Therefore hath the curse devoured the earth, and they that dwell therein are desolate: therefore the inhabitants of the earth are burned, and few men left" (Isa. 24:6). Also— "Therefore he hath poured upon him the fury of his anger, and the strength of battle: and it hath set him on fire round about, yet he knew not; and it burned him, yet he laid it not to heart" (Isa. 42:25).

Back in the prophecy of Malachi we are told: "For, behold, the day cometh, that shall burn as an oven; and all the proud, yea, and all that do wickedly, shall be stubble: and the day that cometh shall burn them up, saith the LORD of hosts, that it shall leave them neither root nor branch" (Mal. 4:1).

To accomplish this, all that the Lord would have to do is to remove one or two blankets of atmosphere. Or He would need only to pull the earth a little closer to the sun—not

much—and we would not be able to survive. It is this frightful period that Isaiah had in view when he wrote that the earth would be decimated. And our Lord said, ". . . Except those days should be shortened, there should no flesh be saved . . ." (Matt. 24:22).

Nevertheless, His own are preserved; "The sun shall not smite thee by day, nor the moon by night" (Ps. 121:6). Though this promise is quite meaningless to us today, it will be a great comfort to the believer during the Great Tribulation.

"And men were scorched with great heat, and blasphemed the name of God." In spite of all of this, instead of turning to God for mercy, they blaspheme His name. This reveals that the human heart is incurably wicked. No amount of punishment will purify it and change it. By the same token, the Great Tribulation is not for the purification of the church. Nowhere is it stated that the saints are being purified by the Great Tribulation. Rather, it is a *judgment* upon the earth.

POURING OUT OF THE FIFTH BOWL

And the fifth angel poured out his vial upon the seat of the beast; and his kingdom was full of darkness; and they gnawed their tongues for pain,

And blasphemed the God of heaven because of their pains and their sores, and repented not of their deeds [Rev. 16:10–11].

And the fifth poured out his bowl upon the throne of the wild beast; and his kingdom was darkened, and they chewed their tongues from their pain, and they blasphemed the God of heaven because of their pains and their sores; and they repented not of their works.

"The throne of the wild beast" makes it clear that the first Beast of chapter 13 is a man. He also represents a kingdom, as you cannot have a king without a kingdom.

"His kingdom was darkened" indicates a strange darkness which might be called black light. We are familiar with that in our day. It will be a frightening thing. As the sun's wattage is increased, it grows darker instead of lighter. The heat will be greater, but the light will be less. Note the similarity to the darkness of Egypt during the ninth plague (Exod. 10:21–22).

The Old Testament prophets had a great deal to say about this coming darkness: "For, behold, the darkness shall cover the earth, and gross darkness the people: but the LORD shall arise upon thee, and his glory shall be seen upon thee" (Isa. 60:2). "Blow ye the trumpet in Zion, and sound an alarm in my holy mountain: let all the inhabitants of the land tremble: for the day of the LORD cometh, for it is nigh at hand; A day of darkness and of gloominess, a day of clouds and of thick darkness, as the morning spread upon the mountains: a great people and a strong; there hath not been ever the like, neither shall be any more after it, even to the years of many generations. . . . The sun shall be turned into darkness, and the moon into blood, before the great and the terrible day of the LORD come" (Joel 2:1-2, 31).

In addition to these two prophets, Nahum mentions it, Amos mentions it, and Zephaniah mentions it. Now the apostle John is merely saying, "This Great Tribulation Period is where these prophecies fit into the program of God." And our Lord Himself confirmed it when He said, "But in those days, after that tribulation, the sun shall be darkened, and the moon shall not give her light" (Mark 13:24).

"They chewed their tongues from their pain." Just think of the intensity of the suffering that is caused by these bowl judgments! But they don't turn men from their wickedness.

There are two self-evident facts at this point: (1) God is righteous in pouring out the bowls of wrath. Let's remember that. Jesus is the judge. He is in charge of handing out the punishment. (2) Yet mankind is not led to repentance through this suffering. The apostle Paul predicted this: "Or despisest thou the riches of his goodness and forbearance and longsuffering; not knowing that the goodness of God leadeth thee to repentance? But after thy hardness and impenitent heart treasurest up unto thyself wrath against the day of wrath and revelation of the righteous judgment of God" (Rom. 2:4-5). And here it is—the righteous judgment of God. And man continues to harden his heart and refuses to repent.

POURING OUT OF THE SIXTH BOWL

And the sixth angel poured out his vial upon the great river Euphrates; and the water thereof was dried up, that the way of the kings of the east might be prepared [Rev. 16:12].

And the sixth poured out his bowl upon the great river, the river Euphrates; and the water was dried up, that the way

might be made ready for the kings that come from the sunrising.

The Euphrates is called "the great river" in the Bible just as the Mediterranean Sea is called "the great sea." The prominence of the Euphrates River in the Word of God should not be overlooked. First mentioned in Genesis 2, it is designated over twenty-five times in the Bible. In the verse before us it is seen in connection with the sixth plague. As it was prominent in the first state of man on the earth, so it is featured in his last state—that of the Great Tribulation. It was the *cradle* of man's civilization and obviously will be the *grave* of man's civilization. It was a border between east and west, eighteen hundred miles long, over half of it navigable. It was wide and deep, which made it difficult for an army to pass over it.

Abraham was called a Hebrew, and some interpret that as meaning he came from the other side of the Euphrates. The Euphrates was the eastern border of the land God promised to Abraham. "In the same day the LORD made a covenant with Abram, saying, Unto thy seed have I given this land, from the river of Egypt unto the great river, the river Euphrates" (Gen. 15:18). It also became the eastern border of the Roman Empire.

The Euphrates River will be miraculously dried up, thus erasing the border between East and West, so that the kings of the sunrising might come to the Battle of Armageddon. In the past Tamerlane came out of the East and swept across those plains with a tremendous horde, and Genghis Khan did the same thing. Those were just little previews of what is going to happen in the last days. After the Euphrates River is gone, the great hordes in the East that have never moved west will come in a great crusade to Palestine. The bulk of the world population is in the East, and having only a smattering of the gospel, they will choose Antichrist. The picture is frightful. Can anyone doubt, with the hundreds of millions pouring into Palestine, that the blood will be as deep as the horses' bridles?

INTERLUDE: KINGS OF INHABITED EARTH PROCEED TO HAR-MAGEDON

Now between the sixth and seventh bowls of wrath is this interlude. (As I have pointed out, there is interlude, an hiatus, between the sixth and seventh features of each series of seven—with the exception of the seven performers.) It is a break for the filling in of details.

And I saw three unclean spirits like frogs come out of the mouth of the dragon, and out of the mouth of the beast, and out of the mouth of the false prophet.

For they are the spirits of devils, working miracles, which go forth unto the kings of the earth and of the whole world, to gather them to the battle of that great day of God Almighty [Rev. 16:13–14].

And I saw (coming) out of the mouth of the dragon, and out of the mouth of the wild beast, and out of the mouth of the false prophet, as it were frogs. For they are spirits of demons, working signs; which go forth upon the kings of the whole inhabited earth, to gather them together to the war of the great day of the God, the Almighty.

This is Armageddon (more correctly spelled Har-Magedon). It is not to be a single battle but a war, the war of Armageddon.

It will be triggered, I believe, by the coming down of Russia from the north sometime around the middle of the Tribulation Period. The campaign extends the length of Palestine to the Valley of Jehoshaphat and the mountains of Edom. It will continue for approximately three and one half years. It will be concluded by the coming of the Lord Jesus Christ from heaven to establish His kingdom. The Sun of Righteousness will arise with healing in His wings.

Here we are introduced to the trinity of hell—Satan, Antichrist, and the False Prophet. They act in unison in forcing the nations of the world to march against Israel in an attempt to destroy God's purposes on earth. God gave certain promises to Abraham and to those who would come after him. He made certain covenants with the Hebrew people, and those covenants are going to stand, just like John 3:16 stands for believers today.

I want to say carefully and kindly that there is a system of theology abroad today that passes as conservative, but it takes the position that God is through with the nation Israel, that all of God's covenants with Israel are negated, that God does not intend to make good any of His promises to Israel—yet there are literally hundreds of them in the Old Testament. This theological system simply spiritualizes these promises, and the proponents do so with no scriptural grounds whatsoever. Origen, one of the early church fathers who came from North Africa, started this method of spiritualizing instead of literalizing the Scriptures. We need to remember that the Bible is a literal book. It is the purpose of Satan to destroy God's covenants with Israel, and that is the reason Satan moves in and brings the whole world against this little nation. This will happen during the Great Tribulation.

As the study of prophecy develops, it is my conviction that this spiritualization of prophecy, although presently accepted by a great many expositors, will become a heresy in the church. I may not be around to see it, but just remember that McGee said it would happen.

Now let's look at the tremendous scene before us.

"As it were frogs." The question is: Will they be literal frogs? Well, they were literal in Egypt, and they could be literal in this case, but I am willing to accept them as a symbol. Perhaps you are saying, "Wait a minute, McGee, I thought you didn't accept a symbol unless it was clearly a symbol." Yes, that is right, and notice that John says, "as it were frogs"; he doesn't say they were frogs. It seems to me that John is always very careful to give us an accurate picture of what he sees.

J. A. Seiss, in his book, *The Apocalypse, Lectures on the Book of Revelation*, comments on the frogs in a vivid manner:

They are spirits; they are "unclean spirits;" they are "demon spirits;" they are sent forth into activity by the Dragon Trinity; they are the elect agents to awaken the world to the attempt to abolish God from the earth; and they are froglike in that they come forth out of the pestiferous quagmires of the universe, do their work amid the world's evening shadows, and creep, and croak, and fill the ears of the nations with their noisy demonstrations, till they set all the kings and armies of the whole earth in enthusiastic commotion for the final crushing out of the Lamb and all His powers. As in chapter 9, the seven Spirits of God and of Christ went forth into all the earth to make up and gather together into one holy fellowship the great congregation of the sanctified: so these spirits of hell go forth upon the kings and potentates of the world, to make up and gather together the grand army of the Devil's worshippers.

In our own day we have seen that the news media can become a propaganda agent to carry out the purposes of men who are in the background. The news media can brainwash the public. This is exactly what the trinity of evil will do. They will brainwash the nations of the world into marching against Israel.

The Lord Jesus is the only One who can stop this. Israel's help does not come from the north or the south or the east or the west—that's where their *trouble* is coming from. Their help comes from the Lord, the Maker of heaven and earth.

Behold, I come as a thief. Blessed is he that watcheth, and keepeth his garments, lest he walk naked, and they see his shame [Rev. 16:15].

"Behold, I come as a thief." Christ will never come as a thief to the church: "But ye, brethren, are not in darkness, that that day should overtake *you* as a thief" (1 Thess. 5:4, italics mine). A thief is someone you shut out; you don't welcome him. You don't put a note on the door when you leave your house which says, "Mr. Thief, I left the back door open for you. The silver is on the third shelf; help yourself." You never welcome a thief. You lock him out. Christ does not come as a thief to His church which is looking for Him. "Looking for that blessed hope, and the glorious appearing of the great God and our Saviour Jesus Christ" (Titus 2:13).

The Lord Jesus Christ *does* come as a thief to the world at the end of the Great Tribulation, as the verse before us indicates. As we saw at the beginning of the Revelation, the whole earth will *mourn* because of Him. They don't want Him to come. They would like to shut Him out from ever returning to the earth.

"Blessed is he that . . . keepeth his garments." What garments are these? Edersheim sheds light on this phrase by explaining that the captain of the temple made his rounds during the night to see if the guards were awake and alert. If one was found asleep, he was either beaten or his garments set on fire. I suppose it could be paraphrased, "Don't lose your shirt. Be sure that you are clothed with the righteousness of Christ."

And he gathered them together into a place called in the Hebrew tongue Armageddon [Rev. 16:16].

This is the only occurrence of the word *Armageddon* in Scripture, although there are many references to it. It means "Mount of Megiddo." It is a compound word made up of the Hebrew words *Har*, meaning "mountain," and *Me-*giddo, which is a mount in the plain Esdraelon. I have been there several times. I. is one of the most fertile valleys I have ever seen. I guess it is the most fertile valley in the world today. It is a place where many battles have been fought in the past. Vincent cites *Clarke's Travels* regarding Megiddo in the plain of Esdraelon:

. . . Which has been a chosen place for encampment in every contest carried on in Palestine from the days of Nabuchodonozor king of Assyria, unto the disastrous march of Napoleon Bonaparte from Egypt into Syria. Jews, Gentiles, Saracens, Christian crusaders, and anti-Christian Frenchmen; Egyptians, Persians, Druses, Turks, and Arabs, warriors of every nation that is under heaven, have pitched their tents on the plain of Esdraelon, and have beheld the banners of their nation wet with the dews of Tabor and Hermon.

"He gathered them together." The "he" is possibly God Himself. Although Satan, Antichrist, and the False Prophet act in unison to force the nations of the world to march against Israel, they nevertheless fulfill the Word of God.

POURING OUT OF THE SEVENTH BOWL

And the seventh angel poured out his vial into the air; and there came a great voice out of the temple of heaven, from the throne, saying, It is done.

And there were voices, and thunders, and lightnings; and there was a great earthquake, such as was not since men were upon the earth, so mighty an earthquake, and so great [Rev. 16:17–18].

And the seventh poured out his bowl upon the air; and a great voice came out of the temple, from the throne, saying, It is done. And there were lightnings, and voices and thunders; and there was a great earthquake, such as was not since there were men upon the earth, so great an earthquake, so mighty.

"The seventh poured out his bowl upon the air." This is the last series of seven judgments before the coming of Christ, and this is the seventh and last of the last seven. In other words, we are right at the end of the

Great Tribulation here. At this point the only One who could deliver these people and set up a righteous kingdom on earth and bring peace to the world is the Lord Jesus Christ. Let us keep our eyes on Christ through this. He is the judge now.

"Upon the air" means in space, with no specific geographical location. The Lord Jesus Christ controls space. He is getting ready to come through space.

"The temple" has been mentioned again and again and again. It has been mentioned with the bowls of wrath, the trumpets, and the seals; in fact, it has been mentioned with each series of judgments. However, the temple has been mentioned with the bowls of wrath six times—more than with all the other judgments combined—and this is the last reference to it. There is no temple in the New Jerusalem, so this obviously has no reference to the church. Whether we like it or not, Israel will go through the Great Tribulation Period. We know that the remnant, all 144,000 of them, will make it through; that is, they will be faithful until death. And I do not know how many more there will be. We do know that a great company of Gentiles were sealed and that they are going to make it through the Great Tribulation also.

Again let me repeat that the church is not a part of this scene. The church is not going through the Time of Jacob's Trouble. God has two ways of saving people in the Great Tribulation Period: first, saving them *out* of it by taking them out of the world, as He took Enoch before the judgment of the Flood; second, by saving them *in* it, as He preserved the life of Noah during the Flood. God will definitely save people during the days of the Great Tribulation, but the church will not be a part of that, for it will have been taken from the earth before the Tribulation begins.

"A great voice came out of the temple, from the throne." That voice is not identified for us, but I personally believe that it is the voice of none other than the Son of God. His message is recorded: "It is done." This is the second time we have heard Him say this. When He was hanging upon the cross, He said, "It is finished"—in Greek it is one word: *Tetelestia*, "It is done." At that point in history redemption was wrought and salvation was finished for man. There is nothing man can contribute to his salvation; he must simply receive it by faith. You can have a finished redemption; but if you won't accept it, there will be a judgment. For those who have refused God's salvation, there is nothing they can do to escape the

judgment of God. It is done. No wonder the writer to the Hebrews wrote: "How shall we escape, if we neglect so great salvation; which at the first began to be spoken by the Lord, and was confirmed unto us by them that heard him" (Heb. 2:3). Christ is the judge, and the judgment of the Great Tribulation is now concluded. "It is done" is His announcement, and there is nothing ahead but judgment, the Great White Throne judgment.

Lightnings, voices, and thunders were the solemn announcement in the beginning of the Great Tribulation that judgment was impending. "And out of the throne proceeded lightnings and thunderings and voices: and there were seven lamps of fire burning before the throne, which are the seven Spirits of God" (Rev. 4:5). Now again at the conclusion of the Tribulation are voices and thunders and lightnings.

"There was a great earthquake, such as was not since men were upon the earth." The Word of God makes it very clear that here at the end of the Great Tribulation Period there is to be a horrendous earthquake which probably will shake the entire world.

And the great city was divided into three parts, and the cities of the nations fell: and great Babylon came in remembrance before God, to give unto her the cup of the wine of the fierceness of his wrath.

And every island fled away, and the mountains were not found.

And there fell upon men a great hail out of heaven, every stone about the weight of a talent: and men blasphemed God because of the plague of the hail; for the plague thereof was exceeding great [Rev. 16:19–21].

And the great city became (divided) into three parts, and the cities of the nations fell: and Babylon the great was remembered before God, to give to her the cup of the wine of the indignation of His wrath. And every island fled away, and mountains were not found. And great hail, as it were a talent weight, comes down out of heaven upon men: and men blasphemed God because of the plague of the hail; for the plague thereof is exceeding great.

This concludes the Great Tribulation Period. There is a great earthquake, and it divides the "great city," which is Jerusalem. The earthquake divides this city into three parts. Although the center of the earthquake is in Jerusalem, it is not confined to Jerusalem, because we are told that "the cities of the nations fell." This tells us something of the extent and the vast destruction of the earthquake.

"Babylon" is mentioned specifically again. It was mentioned in chapter 14, verse 8, which says, "And there followed another angel, saying, Babylon is fallen, is fallen, that great city, because she made all nations drink of the wine of the wrath of her fornication." The next two chapters give us the details concerning Babylon.

"Every island fled away" reveals that even the islands are shifted from one place to another by the earthquake.

The final act of judgment is the hailstorm. The size of the hailstones is enormous—"a talent weight." The Greek talent was fifty-six pounds, and the Jewish talent was one hundred fourteen pounds. In Texas I can remember seeing hailstones as big as baseballs, but this beats the Texas story altogether. A very interesting hailstorm is recorded during the time of Joshua: "And it came to pass, as they fled from before Israel, and were in the going down to Beth-horon, that the LORD cast down great stones from heaven upon them unto Azekah, and they died: they were more which died with hailstones than they whom the children of Israel slew with the sword" (Josh. 10:11).

According to the historian Josephus, the Roman catapults threw stones the weight of a talent, into Jerusalem in A.D. 70 when Titus leveled the city.

The miraculous hailstorm ends the Great Tribulation Period.

CHAPTER 17

THEME: *The apostate church in the Great Tribulation*

In chapters 17–18 we see the judgment of the two Babylons. We will first see the apostate church in the Great Tribulation in chapter 17, and then we will see not only religious Babylon but also commercial Babylon in chapter 18.

So many great issues are brought to a crisis in the Great Tribulation that it is difficult to keep them separated, and many fine expositors disagree on details. We have already noted this as we have gone through this Book of Revelation. Although we agree with the *system* of interpretation, we do disagree on details.

This fact should not be disturbing to believers, as many details will not be clarified until the world enters the Great Tribulation Period and actually faces the climax to each crisis.

This is especially evident relative to the two Babylons in chapters 17–18. The questions are: "Are there two Babylons, and are they in two different geographical locations? Are they representative of two systems? Are they two literal cities, or are they the same?" The answers to these questions will become more apparent as our redemption draws near. It appears at the present time, in my judgment, that two distinct cities are in view.

Here in chapter 17 it is mystery Babylon, the cosmic church, the apostate church. The church of Thyatira, described in chapter 2, verses 18–29, which permitted Jezebel to teach, will become the apostate church of the Great Tribulation. It will attain the goal of the present-day apostates of all the great systems of the world: Romanism, Protestantism, pagan religions, cults and "isms." Even in our so-called independent Bible churches there will be those who are not believers, and during the Tribulation they will join this great organization that may call itself a church but is not. The Bible calls it a harlot. There couldn't be a worse label than that! This is ecumenical ecclesiasticism of the one-world church. The location of this system could be in Rome. Rome, the city built on seven hills, is probably the city in mind here. However, Geneva, where the World Council of Churches has its headquarters, is also included, and other places, such as Los Angeles—if I know Los Angeles, and I think I do—can also make a healthy contribution to it!

It is called *mystery* Babylon because of its origin. At the Tower of Babel man attempted to rally against God. Under Nimrod, Babylon became the origin of all false religion. Now the dream of Nimrod will be realized in the first half of the Great Tribulation Period, for the cosmic church dominates the wild Beast. The church that should have been the bride of Christ is a harlot here. This church is guilty of spiritual fornication, selling herself to the world for hire. This is the church that says, "I am rich and increased with goods, and I have need of nothing."

Looking back at the study of the seven churches, in chapters 3–4 of the Book of Revelation, I pointed out that the church in Philadelphia represented the church that would be raptured before the time of the Tribulation Period. He said to that church, "I also will keep thee from the hour of temptation" (Rev. 3:10). That "hour" is the Great Tribulation, and we have been in that "hour" a long time in our study of this Book of Revelation.

The true church will not go through the Great Tribulation; it will be raptured before the Tribulation begins. Let's be specific: who will be raptured? Not certain denominations and not just individual churches, but *His* church, a collective term meaning all true believers, those who are *in Christ*. That is the group that will be taken out at the Rapture, and the rest of the church members will be left here on this earth to go through the Great Tribulation. As Dr. George Gill used to say, some churches will meet the Sunday after the Rapture and will not miss a member. But let's clearly understand that they are not true believers. They are not part of the church of the Lord Jesus Christ. He never calls them His church; He calls it a *harlot!* It is a pseudo-religious system, which controls the wild Beast during the first half of the Great Tribulation, yet it is hated by him. During the last half of the Tribulation, the Beast destroys the harlot in order to set up his own religion. J. Dwight Pentecost in his book, *Things To Come,* (p. 368) gives this comment concerning the harlot system:

> The Beast, who was dominated by the harlot system (Rev. 17:3), rises against her and destroys her and her system completely. Without doubt the harlot system was in competition with the religious worship of the Beast, promoted by the False Prophet, and her destruction is brought about so that the Beast may be the sole object of false worship as he claims to be God.

Babylon is to be rebuilt, as we have seen in Isaiah and Jeremiah, and here in chapters 17–18 we see it destroyed. Ecclesiastical Babylon will be destroyed by the wild Beast.

Ecclesiastical Babylon is destroyed by the wild Beast.

Commercial Babylon is destroyed by the return of Christ.

Ecclesiastical Babylon is hated by the Beast.

Commercial Babylon is loved by the world.

Ecclesiastical Babylon is destroyed at the *beginning* of the last three and one-half years of the Great Tribulation.

Commercial Babylon is destroyed at the *end* of the last three and one-half years of the Great Tribulation—that is, at the very end. Zechariah 5:5–11 also has something interesting to say in this connection.

GREAT HARLOT RIDING THE WILD BEAST

I do not have words to describe how frightful this picture is. The harlot is the false church, as we have said. And the wild Beast is the restored Roman Empire, which will be brought back together by Antichrist with the assistance, I believe, of the false church.

And there came one of the seven angels which had the seven vials, and talked with me, saying unto me, Come hither; I will shew unto thee the judgment of the great whore that sitteth upon many waters:

With whom the kings of the earth have committed fornication, and the inhabitants of the earth have been made drunk with the wine of her fornication [Rev. 17:1–2].

As usual, I'll give my own literal translation of the Greek text throughout the chapter.

And there came one of the (7) seven angels that had the (7) seven bowls, and spake with me, saying, Come hither, I will show thee the judgment of the great harlot that sitteth upon many waters; with whom the kings of the earth committed fornication, and they that dwell in the earth were made drunken with the wine of her fornication.

"The great harlot" is that part of the church that will remain after the true church has been raptured. It will be composed of those who have never trusted Christ as Savior; they have never been in the body of Christ. This is the group that enters the Great Tribulation.

We are told certain things about her. She "sitteth upon many waters." According to verse 15, which we will see later, the "waters" refer to great masses of people and nations. The harlot will pretty much control the world.

"The kings of the earth committed fornication" show that there is an unholy alliance between church and state during that period.

My friend, the movement in our day of bringing all religions together certainly falls into the pattern of this false church which is to appear—and Scripture doesn't even dignify it by the name of church, although I am sure it will call itself that. I believe that this movement is more dangerous to our own country than is any foreign political system and that it is more dangerous than the so-called new morality. I believe that it is more dangerous than any other movement. It will become a power-bloc that will dazzle the unthinking mob. It will bring the world under the influence of the wild Beast out of the sea and the wild Beast out of the earth. They will use the apostate church to control the masses, and the church will yield to this arrangement for political preferment and power.

You see, when you reject the genuine, you are wide open for the spurious. Paul wrote to the Thessalonians that when someone rejects the love of the truth that they might be saved, they will believe the big lie.

"The judgment of the great harlot." God's cup of judgment will be pressed to the lips of the harlot. And who is going to destroy her? The Beast himself will destroy her. You see, the Antichrist and the False Prophet will not want her around after she has served their purpose. Antichrist wants to be worshiped, and he doesn't want any competition from the church.

So he carried me away in the spirit into the wilderness: and I saw a woman sit upon a scarlet coloured beast, full of names of blasphemy, having seven heads and ten horns [Rev. 17:3].

And he carried me away in the Spirit into a wilderness; and I saw a woman sitting upon a scarlet-colored wild beast, full of names of blasphemy, having seven heads and ten horns.

"He carried me away in the Spirit into a wilderness." Remember that John was on the Isle of Patmos in the Spirit for the vision of the glorified Christ and His message to the churches. At that time John was caught up to heaven. From then on the scene shifts from heaven to earth. However, here we are told again that John was in the Spirit. Did he need a fresh anointing of the Spirit for this vision? I

rather think so. Is the wilderness literal? Remember that this chapter is a vision where symbols are used. Around both Babylon and Rome there is a literal wilderness. This is a matter of recorded history. Babylon was to become a wilderness, and in this connection read Isaiah 47–48 and Jeremiah 50–51. Outside of Rome the wilderness is called the *campagna*. I believe that the wilderness mentioned in this verse is literal but also that it is a sign of the chaotic condition of the world brought about by the religious confusion of Babylon.

John saw a woman "sitting upon a scarlet-colored wild beast." This is a frightful and frightening scene. The wild Beast has previously been identified as the Antichrist ruling over the restored Roman Empire. The woman is identified for us in verse 18: "And the woman which thou sawest is that great city, which reigneth over the kings of the earth." The woman is a city, and the city is Rome, the religious capital of the world. She is religious Rome, which at that time will have inherited all the religions of the world. You see, all true believers will have left the world scene at the time of the Rapture. This includes *all* true believers, and I have discovered that there are many true believers in Romanism and in liberal churches and even in some very weird religious systems. All genuine believers, regardless of where they have gone to church, will be raptured. This will leave a church on earth that is totally apostate. Rather than being "the bride of Christ," God calls it a harlot.

The city is further identified in verse 9: "And here is the mind which hath wisdom. The seven heads are seven mountains, on which the woman sitteth." Rome was the city set on seven hills and was known as such to both pagan and Christian writers. Horace wrote, "The gods, who look with favour on the seven hills. . . ." Ovid added, "But Rome looks around on the whole globe from her seven mountains, the seat of empire and abode of the gods." Augustine wrote, "Babylon is a former Rome, and Rome is a later Babylon." In these verses the city of Rome is assuredly in view. The woman, the harlot represents a religious system that will be revealed during the first part of the Great Tribulation Period after the true church has been removed from the earth. And this religious system, as the symbol given to us indicates, dominates and rides the Roman Empire at the beginning of the Great Tribulation Period.

"Full of names of blasphemy" reveals how

far religion will have departed from the living Christ.

And the woman was arrayed in purple and scarlet colour, and decked with gold and precious stones and pearls, having a golden cup in her hand full of abominations and filthiness of her fornication:

And upon her forehead was a name written, MYSTERY, BABYLON THE GREAT, THE MOTHER OF HARLOTS AND ABOMINATIONS OF THE EARTH [Rev. 17:4–5].

And the woman was clothed in purple and scarlet, and gilded with gold, and precious stone and pearls, having in her hand a golden cup full of abominations, even the unclean things of her fornication, and upon her forehead a name written MYSTERY, BABYLON THE GREAT, THE MOTHER OF THE HARLOTS AND OF THE ABOMINATIONS OF THE EARTH.

"Clothed in purple and scarlet." Purple was the predominant color of Roman imperialism. Every senator and consul wore a purple stripe as a badge of his position, and the emperor's robes were purple. Scarlet is the color adopted by Roman Catholicism.

"Gilded with gold" shows the beauty of the outward display, but, like the Pharisees, it is within "full of dead men's bones and of all uncleanness."

"Precious stone and pearls" are pretty cold, though they may be genuine, and are a sordid imitation of genuine heartfelt religion. The Lord Jesus said, "Woe unto you, scribes and Pharisees, hypocrites! for ye make clean the outside of the cup and of the platter, but within they are full of extortion and excess" (Matt. 23:25).

"A golden cup full of abominations" is the religious intoxication of the anti-church (not Antichrist) and a pseudoreligion, counterfeit Christianity, a fake and false gospel, and a sham and spurious system. This is the cup which makes the world drunk. "Babylon hath been a golden cup in the LORD'S hand, that made all the earth drunken: the nations have drunken of her wine; therefore the nations are mad" (Jer. 51:7).

"Upon her forehead a name written" is a startling revelation of the character of this woman. She does not wear a crown but rather the mark of her profession. It is of interest to see that Seneca, in addressing a wanton priestess, said, "Thy name hung from thy forehead." "MYSTERY, BABYLON THE GREAT, THE MOTHER OF THE HARLOTS AND OF THE ABOMINATIONS OF THE EARTH" is the disgraceful title for the "church" which should belong to Christ as a bride.

Now I know that we live in a day of changing morality, but I am a little old-fashioned, and I still think that the Word of God is right in its values. I think that the finest thing in the world is a woman and that God has made her that way. When she marries, she is brought into a relationship in which she can give to a man that which puts him in orbit. It is my firm conviction that the thing our civilization has done for a woman has not been to liberate her but to enslave her so that she has become more of a sex symbol than ever before. Instead of taking her rightful place where she can lift a man to the heights, she is characterized as the one who pulls him down to the depths. And the lowest picture you can have is that of a harlot. You may not like it, but that is how the Word of God sees it.

"MYSTERY BABYLON." The true church is a mystery in that it was not revealed in the Old Testament (see Eph. 3:1–9). The anti-church, designated here as a harlot, is a mystery in that it was not revealed until John wrote Revelation 17. Let me say again that when the true church left the earth at the time of the Rapture, the phonies, those who were only church members, entered the Great Tribulation Period, and the system continued—not now a church, but a harlot. Paul had written of the mystery of iniquity: "For the mystery of iniquity doth already work: only he who now hinders will hinder until he be taken out of the way" (2 Thess. 2:7). The anti-church is the antithesis of the true church, which is the virgin bride of Christ, and it is the consummation of the working of "the mystery of iniquity." It is "MYSTERY BABYLON" because it is given this designation just as Jerusalem is called Sodom.

Babylon is the fountainhead for all false religion; therefore she is "THE MOTHER OF THE HARLOTS AND OF THE ABOMINATIONS OF THE EARTH." This is, by far, Scripture's more expressive and vivid picture of awful and abominable sin. Sex and false religions are related, you may be sure of that. I believe that many young people are really missing it in marriage when they do not stand at the marriage altar in the presence of God presenting themselves to each other, having kept their bodies for the marriage. That was God's ideal and still is.

Have you noticed that this "MYSTERY BABYLON" is called the "MOTHER OF THE HARLOTS"? The mother of harlots— not singular but plural. In our day the ecumenical church has faced a lot of problems. It seems that they have recognized psychological differences in people and that it is impossible to water down theologies and practices to suit everyone. So each group will come into this great world ecumenical system but retain some of its peculiarities. For example, those who want to immerse will immerse. Those who want to sprinkle will sprinkle. Those who want elaborate ritual will have it, and those who want no ritual will have that. You see, there is going to be more than the mother harlot—there will be a whole lot of harlots, a regular brothel.

And I saw the woman drunken with the blood of the saints, and with the blood of the martyrs of Jesus: and when I saw her, I wondered with great admiration.

And the angel said unto me, Wherefore didst thou marvel? I will tell thee the mystery of the woman, and of the beast that carrieth her, which hath the seven heads and ten horns [Rev. 17:6-7].

And I saw the woman drunken with the blood of the saints, and with the blood of the martyrs of Jesus. And when I saw her, I wondered with a great wonder. And the angel said unto me, Wherefore didst thou wonder? I will tell thee the mystery of the woman, and of the wild beast that is carrying her, which hath the seven heads and ten horns.

"Drunken with the blood of the saints." The harlot not only makes others drunk, but she is intoxicated by her acts of persecution. While it is true that the church will not go through the Great Tribulation, as we near the end of this age of grace, believers can expect some tribulation. It is my experience and that of other Christian leaders that today it is becoming increasingly difficult to stand for the Word of God and for the things of Christ.

"The saints" probably refer to Old Testament saints, and "the martyrs of Jesus" refer to New Testament saints. This indicates that "BABYLON" is more than just Romanism. Rather, it is an amalgam of all religions. All true believers were caught up at the Rapture, and Babylon is the residue of what is left.

Babylon is a composite religious system which includes Protestantism, Romanism, cults—the whole lot which was not raptured, you see. It is confusion compounded and is the fountainhead of all religious error and idolatry. Babylon in the Old Testament persecuted God's people and was the enemy of God. It was Babylon that put the three Hebrew boys in the fiery furnace because they would not worship an image.

When John saw the vision of the woman, he says that he "wondered with a great wonder." This is the first time that John has had his mind boggled. We have had our minds boggled before, but this really throws John. The angel asks why he should wonder when he (the angel) was present to explain the mystery of the woman.

The emphasis here is on the Roman Empire aspect of the wild Beast rather than on the Antichrist aspect. We should note that.

The beast that thou sawest was, and is not; and shall ascend out of the bottomless pit, and go into perdition: and they that dwell on the earth shall wonder, whose names were not written in the book of life from the foundation of the world, when they behold the beast that was, and is not, and yet is.

And here is the mind which hath wisdom. The seven heads are seven mountains, on which the woman sitteth.

And there are seven kings: five are fallen, and one is, and the other is not yet come; and when he cometh, he must continue a short space [Rev. 17:8-10].

The wild beast which thou sawest was and is not; and is about to come up out of the abyss, and to go (goeth) into perdition. And those dwelling on the earth shall wonder, whose names are not written upon the book of life from the foundation of the world (cosmos), when they behold the wild beast because it was, and is not, and shall come (be present). Here is the mind having wisdom. The seven heads are seven mountains on which the woman sitteth. And there are seven kings; the five have fallen (fell), the one is, the other is not yet come; and when he cometh, he must continue a little while.

The wild Beast "was" speaks of the past history of the Roman Empire. "Is not" refers to the present condition of the fragmented Empire. The Roman Empire is not dead. It has fallen apart into the nations of Europe today. "Is about to come up out of the abyss" speaks of the reactivation of the Roman Empire by Satan.

As I have indicated before, many have attempted to put the Roman Empire back together again but have never been successful. Charlemagne tried it, Napoleon tried it, Hitler tried it, Mussolini tried it, and at the time I am writing this, the United Nations is trying it, but they, too, are failing. The wild Beast, who is the Antichrist, will be the one who puts the Roman Empire back together again.

"Shall . . . go into perdition" speaks of the destruction of the Roman Empire by the coming of Christ. The reappearance of the Roman Empire in its great power will win the admiration of the peoples of the world who are not redeemed. They will respect and worship the Antichrist for his brilliant *coup d'etat.* God's saints will have the mind of the Spirit and will understand and not be spiritually stupid: "But ye have an unction from the Holy One, and ye know all things. . . . But the anointing which ye have received of him abideth in you, and ye need not that any man teach you: but as the same anointing teacheth you of all things, and is truth, and is no lie, and even as it hath taught you, ye shall abide in him" (1 John 2:20, 27).

"And there are seven kings" is taken by some (including Newell and Govett, who are excellent commentators on Revelation) to mean individual rulers. Govett gives the following list:

1. Julius Caesar—assassinated
2. Tiberius—poisoned or smothered
3. Caligula—assassinated
4. Claudius—poisoned
5. Nero—committed suicide

"The one is" refers to Domitian who was living in John's day, who was also assassinated.

"The other is not yet come" refers to the Antichrist. Other expositors (as Scofield and Walter Scott) consider these seven as the different forms of government through which Rome passed. These are listed as kings, consuls, dictators, decemvirs, and military tribunes. "The one is" refers to the sixth or imperial form of government set up by Julius Caesar and under which John was banished by Domitian. The seventh and last, though it has not yet appeared, will be satanic in form.

Regardless of the interpretation adopted, the end in view is the same—the Antichrist rules over the reactivated Roman Empire.

And the beast that was, and is not, even he is the eighth, and is of the seven, and goeth into perdition.

And the ten horns which thou sawest are ten kings, which have received no kingdom as yet; but receive power as kings one hour with the beast.

These have one mind, and shall give their power and strength unto the beast.

These shall make war with the Lamb, and the Lamb shall overcome them: for he is Lord of lords, and King of kings: and they that are with him are called, and chosen, and faithful [Rev. 17:11–14].

And the beast that was, and is not, is himself also an eighth, and is of the seven, and is going into perdition. And the ten horns that thou sawest are ten kings, who (of the kind which) have received no kingdom as yet; but they receive authority as kings, with the wild beast, for one hour. These have one mind, and they give (over) their power and authority unto the beast. These shall war with the Lamb, and the Lamb shall overcome them, for He is Lord of lords, and King of kings; and those with Him (shall overcome), called and chosen and faithful.

At times the wild Beast signifies, generally, the Roman Empire, but also it signifies the last or eighth head; that is, the individual emperor who is Antichrist. Now here the Antichrist is designated. He is the "little horn" in the vision that God gave to the prophet Daniel. The "little horn" puts down three other horns—that is, three kings—when he comes to power. "I considered the horns, and, behold, there came up among them another little horn, before whom there were three of the first horns plucked up by the roots: and, behold, in this horn were eyes like the eyes of man, and a mouth speaking great things. . . . And the ten horns out of this kingdom are ten kings that shall arise: and another shall rise after them; and he shall be diverse from the first, and he shall subdue three kings" (Dan. 7:8, 24). In my book, *Delving Through Daniel,* I go into detail on this "little horn."

"The beast that was" refers to the past history of the Roman Empire under the emperors.

"And is not" refers to the end of Imperial Rome with its global empire, which came to an end sometime between the third and fifth centuries.

"Is himself also an eighth, and is of the seven" identifies the Antichrist with the return to the imperial form of the restored Roman Empire. He is the "little horn" of Daniel, chapter 7. He is not one of the ten horns, but he is separate from them. He is an eighth head in this seven, yet he is one of the seven since he restores the last form of government to Rome. Now that will confuse you, I know, but that is exactly what is being said here in Revelation.

"The ten horns" are the same as the ten horns of Daniel 7:7. These ten kings will reign with the Antichrist but will be subservient to him. They willingly or unwillingly give over their authority to the Antichrist and become his puppets.

And he saith unto me, The waters which thou sawest, where the whore sitteth, are peoples, and multitudes, and nations, and tongues.

And the ten horns which thou sawest upon the beast, these shall hate the whore, and shall make her desolate and naked, and shall eat her flesh, and burn her with fire.

For God hath put in their hearts to fulfil his will, and to agree, and give their kingdom unto the beast, until the words of God shall be fulfilled.

And the woman which thou sawest is that great city, which reigneth over the kings of the earth [Rev. 17:15–18].

And he saith to me, The waters which thou sawest where the harlot sitteth, are peoples, and multitudes (mobs), and nations, and tongues. And the ten horns which thou sawest, and the beast, these shall hate the harlot, and shall make her desolated and naked, and shall eat her flesh, and shall burn her (down) with fire. For God did put into their hearts to do His mind, and to come to one mind, and to give their kingdom unto the beast, until the words of God shall be fulfilled. And the woman whom thou sawest is the great city, which hath a kingdom over the kings of the earth.

"The waters" are explained to be the many ethnological groups as well as the nations of the world. This figure is in harmony with that used in the Old Testament. You can check that out with Isaiah 8:7 and Psalm 18. The position of the harlot reveals that she is ruling over them for only a brief time.

"The ten horns" are ten kings (as told us in verse 12) who rule over the different divisions of the Roman Empire. They in turn give over to the Beast their kingdoms. This solidifies the Roman Empire and enables the Beast to lift himself up as a world dictator.

For a time the Beast (Antichrist) is willing to share his place of exaltation with the harlot, since she has also sought to advance his cause while dividing his glory. This he hates, and the ten kings are one with him in this. The Antichrist not only breaks his covenant with Israel, but he also breaks his relationship with the apostate church. This hatred against the apostate church is so violent that the reaction is described as the cannibalistic picking of her bones, then burning them with fire! This great hatred destroys the false church. This is what happens to the false church. It has no victory. It never comes into the presence of Christ. It is not raptured. Finally it is destroyed by the Antichrist.

In doing this the Antichrist and his ten allies are fulfilling the Word of God and carrying out His will as did the Assyrian (as predicted in Isaiah 10:5–19) and just as surely as Caesar Augustus did when he signed the tax bill that moved Mary and Joseph down to Bethlehem so Scripture could be fulfilled.

By eliminating the apostate church, the way is cleared for the worship of Antichrist, as advocated by the False Prophet.

"The woman" is a religious system, as we have seen. Also, I believe she is further identified as a city, the city of Rome.

This is the frightful but just end of the apostate church. However, it does not improve the situation. Rather it introduces the darkest period for religion in the history of the world. The reign and religion of Antichrist is the darkest hour earth will know, and yet it is the inevitable end of the distrust which began in the Garden of Eden when man failed to believe God. It was given new impetus at the Tower of Babel, which was a rallying place for those against God. And finally it climaxed in the crucifixion of Jesus Christ when man rejected the One who is the Way, the Truth, and the Life. Having rejected the truth, the only alternative left for man is to believe the big lie, the strong delusion. History will culminate in the catastrophic coming of Christ to this earth, as we shall see in chapter 19. This is the just retribution of error and evil.

My friend, you as a Christian should have thankfulness in your heart, knowing you will be spared from the Great Tribulation, but also you should have a real concern for your loved ones who may be facing this frightful period that lies ahead.

CHAPTER 18

THEME: *Political and commercial Babylon judged*

In the chapter before us we see the judgment of commercial Babylon and the reaction of both earth and heaven to it.

In chapters 17–18 two Babylons are brought before us. The Babylon of chapter 17 is ecclesiastical. The Babylon of chapter 18 is economic. The first is religious—the apostate church which entered the Great Tribulation Period. The second is political and commercial. The commercial center is *loved* by the kings of the earth; and the apostate church is *hated* by the kings of the earth, as we saw in chapter 17. The apostate church is destroyed by the kings of the earth. When Christ returns, political Babylon will be destroyed by the judgment of God. Obviously, mystery Babylon, the apostate church, is destroyed first in the midst of the Great Tribulation, while commercial Babylon will be destroyed at the second coming of Christ. These two Babylons are not one and the same city. I personally believe that mystery Babylon is Rome and that, when it goes down in the midst of the Great Tribulation, the religious center shifts to Jerusalem because it is at Jerusalem that the False Prophet will put up his image of the Antichrist to be worshiped. Commercial Babylon is ancient Babylon, rebuilt as the commercial capital of the world. This city is the final capital of the political power of the Beast.

A few years ago it seemed rather farfetched that the power could reach back into the Mideast, but since then we have experienced a shortage of energy, and when they cut off the oil supply, the whole world feels it. They wield tremendous power. The wealth of the world is moving into that particular area because of the price of oil. It could well become the great commercial capital of the world. And this great commercial center, which will be Babylon rebuilt, will be destroyed at the second coming of Christ.

Sometime ago a Jew challenged the Israeli minister of tourism by saying, "How does it come about that all the countries surrounding Israel have oil, but Israel doesn't?" His reply was this: "God gave the Arabs oil and the Jews the Bible. Do you want to exchange with them? God forbid. The oil will run out quick enough, but the Bible will last forever."

There had been some disagreement among conservative expositors about whether or not ancient Babylon will be rebuilt. Candidly, for many years I took the position that it would not be rebuilt. However, I believe now that it will be rebuilt. Isaiah 13:19–22 speaks of the fact that ancient Babylon is to be rebuilt and destroyed, and this destruction is what is mentioned in chapter 18 of Revelation, which is before us. Actually, I don't think it could be rebuilt on the same spot because the Euphrates River has moved about fourteen miles from the ancient city.

There are views of the destruction of Babylon which are diametrically opposed to each other. The viewpoint and perspective are highly important. (1) The reaction of men of business and politics is one of great anguish. To them it is the depth of tragedy. It means the total bankruptcy of big business. (2) The second reaction is that of heaven. It is one of joy that the holiness and justice of God is vindicated. It means the end of man's sinful career on earth. This will bring to an end the Great Tribulation Period.

ANNOUNCEMENT AND FALL OF COMMERCIAL AND POLITICAL BABYLON

Chapter 18 begins with "another angel" who comes down from heaven with a message.

And after these things I saw another angel come down from heaven, having great power; and the earth was lightened with his glory [Rev. 18:1].

As usual, I'll give my literal translation of the Greek text throughout this chapter.

After these things I saw another angel coming down out of heaven, having great authority; and the earth was lightened with his glory.

Again we have this very interesting statement, "after these things" (Gr.: *meta tauta*). After what things? After the series of sevens and after the judgment of religious Babylon come these things. Progress has definitely been made—through the seven seals, the seven trumpets, the seven personages, and the seven bowls of wrath—and we are advancing to the end of the Great Tribulation. In fact, this brings us to the end of the Great Tribulation.

John says, "I saw." He is still a spectator. He saw "another angel," which takes us back to chapter 14 where a series of six angels is mentioned, each with the sole identification of "another angel." This angel is a divine, supernatural messenger of God, but faceless and nameless. He has *great authority* (power), which indicates that he has a superior rank to the other "another angel," and he is bringing an important message.

"The earth was lightened with his glory" seems to further signify the prestige of this angel (cf. Ezek. 43:2).

And he cried mightily with a strong voice, saying, Babylon the great is fallen, is fallen, and is become the habitation of devils, and the hold of every foul spirit, and a cage of every unclean and hateful bird [Rev. 18:2].

And he shouted with a mighty voice, saying, Fell, fell is Babylon the great, and became a habitation of demons, and a prison (hold, cage) of every unclean spirit, and a prison (hold, cage) of every unclean and hated bird.

The preliminary announcement of the fall of Babylon was made in Revelation 14:8: "And there followed another angel, saying, Babylon is fallen, is fallen, that great city, because she made all nations drink of the wine of the wrath of her fornication." The angel here is greater in authority than the one who made that first announcement.

In the words, "Fell, fell is Babylon . . . and became," the tense in the Greek is prophetic aorist which speaks of coming events as if they have already transpired. When God says something is going to happen, you can speak about it as though it had already happened, because it is going to happen. It is just that sure. In God's plan and program it is just as

though it had already taken place because He knows the end from the beginning. Babylon, this great commercial center of the world, is going to be destroyed.

"A habitation of demons, and a cage of every unclean spirit, and a cage of every unclean and hated bird." This indicates that Babylon is where demons of the spirit world and unclean birds of the physical world will be incarcerated during the Millennium. The prophets Isaiah and Jeremiah confirm this (see Isa. 13:19–22; Jer. 50:38–40). These prophecies find a final fulfillment in the destruction of literal Babylon here in Revelation 18. If this is true, there is no prophecy which forbids Babylon from being rebuilt. Babylon is the headquarters of demons and has been the place of rebellion down through the years.

For all nations have drunk of the wine of the wrath of her fornication, and the kings of the earth have committed fornication with her, and the merchants of the earth are waxed rich through the abundance of her delicacies [Rev. 18:3].

For by the wine of the wrath of her fornication all the nations have drunk (or are fallen); and the kings of the earth committed fornication with her, and the merchants of the earth waxed rich by the power of her wantonnesss.

"Have drunk" (or are fallen) are the two permitted renderings—both have good manuscript authority. Both are true. The normal rendering is "have drunk." This is God's judgment on big business which denies God's authority. This is the unholy alliance of government and business. We have seen some of this in our day and, frankly, it smells to high heaven.

The word for merchants means "those who travel." It is not those who produce goods or manufacture goods, but those who are brokers, engaging in business for a big profit. Business is a sacred cow that nothing must harm or hinder. This is true today, of course. Man uses business as the biggest excuse for having no time for God, yet these same men must finally stand before God. God will judge godless commercialism. Big business is in for it, I can assure you of that. In fact, it has had a rough time in our day.

And I heard another voice from heaven, saying, Come out of her, my people, that ye be not partakers of her sins, and that ye receive not of her plagues [Rev. 18:4].

And I heard another voice out of heaven, saying, Come forth out of her, my people, that ye have no fellowship with her sins, and that ye receive not of her plagues.

This verse reveals that God's people are going to be in the world to the very end (it is not speaking of the church which has already been removed before the Great Tribulation began), but God will have His people on earth during the Tribulation. The question has always been: Will they be able to make it through? That is, will they remain faithful to Christ? Yes, they do make it through. Remember that God started with 144,000, and the number that will make it through the Tribulation is 144,000. This is like the parable the Lord Jesus told about the shepherd who started out with one hundred sheep and one of them got away. But he didn't end up with ninety-nine; he ended up with one hundred, because he went out and got that little sheep that was lost.

The One who is speaking in this verse is none other than the Son of God, and He is calling His people out of Babylon before the judgment comes. It is a physical separation with a corollary in the experience of Lot in Sodom. As Lot was warned to get out of Sodom to escape the deluge of fire (see Gen. 19), so these people of God are warned. God's Word tells us, "When thou art in tribulation, and all these things are come upon thee, even in the latter days, if thou turn to the LORD thy God, and shalt be obedient unto his voice; (For the LORD thy God is a merciful God;) he will not forsake thee, neither destroy thee, nor forget the covenant of thy fathers which he sware unto them" (Deut. 4:30–31).

Such was also God's warning to Israel in Jeremiah 51:5–6, 45 and in Isaiah 48:20. The warning is twofold: (1) They are to have no fellowship with the sins of Babylon and (2) they are to flee before judgment falls.

I think this has a pertinent application for us today. It should be a warning to us, not that God will fail to save His own from this hour, but that He wants us to be separate, not indulging the old nature, but walking by the Spirit. If we will not deal with sin in our own lives here and now by confessing and forsaking it, He will deal with it. Either He will judge sin now, or it will meet us at the judgment seat of Christ. God gives us the opportunity of judging our sin today: "For if we would judge ourselves, we should not be judged. But when we are judged, we are chastened of the Lord, that we should not be condemned with the world" (1 Cor. 11:31–32).

How can we judge our own sin? First John 1:9 has the answer: "If we confess our sins, he is faithful and just to forgive us our sins, and to cleanse us from all unrighteousness." To "confess" means to say the same thing that God says about it. It means to take God's viewpoint and say, "God, I agree with You. What I did was *sin*." It is so easy to make excuses for our own sin. We say that ours is not really sin—of course, if our neighbors do it, it is sin. But until you and I are willing to call our sin *sin*, we haven't confessed it at all. If we refuse to judge ourselves, we will be judged at the judgment seat of Christ. The sins of some folk will not be settled until they stand before the judgment seat of Christ. I hope to get all of my accounts straightened out down here. Just because God may not take us to the woodshed immediately does not mean that He is letting us get by without punishment. He doesn't spank the Devil's children, but if you are His child, judgment will come to you.

For her sins have reached unto heaven, and God hath remembered her iniquities [Rev. 18:5].

Babylon has a long history of accumulated sins, and God has the record. It is one of the oldest cities in the history of mankind and is probably mentioned more than any other city in the Bible, with the exception of Jerusalem. Finally judgment breaks like a flood upon this city and its system. The judgment of God may be delayed, but it is sure. It may seem to us that the unbeliever is getting by with sin, but God's judgment is coming.

Reward her even as she rewarded you, and double unto her double according to her works: in the cup which she hath filled fill to her double [Rev. 18:6].

Render unto her even as she also rendered, and double unto her the double according to her works; in the cup which she mingled, mingle unto her double.

This is poetic justice (see Obad. 15). The cup of iniquity is being filled to the brim; when the last drop is poured in, it is pressed to the lips of those who committed iniquity. My friend, this is *just*—read Psalm 137. God is right and just in what He does.

How much she hath glorified herself, and lived deliciously, so much torment and sorrow give her: for she saith in her heart, I sit a queen, and am no widow, and shall see no sorrow [Rev. 18:7].

How much soever she glorified herself,
and waxed wanton (lived in luxury), so
much give her of torment and mourning;
for she saith in her heart, I sit a queen,
and am no widow, and shall in no wise
see mourning.

You see, the prosperity of Babylon blinded her
to the judgment of God. Trading was active on
the stock market, and everyone bought blue
chip issues right up to the moment of judgment. Luxury, arrogance, pride, sin, and self-deception characterized the spirit of this godless city. World peace was in sight, and optimism was the spirit of the day. Only the
prophets of gloom issued a warning, and they
were classified as "squares," as was Noah (and
as Vernon McGee is today).

**Therefore shall her plagues come in one
day, death, and mourning, and famine;
and she shall be utterly burned with
fire: for strong is the Lord God who
judgeth her [Rev. 18:8].**

This calls to our attention the suddennesss of
destruction and that it will be by "fire." So
great is her grief that "mourning" is counted a
plague along with "death" and "famine."
Death, mourning, and famine are the three
horsemen who ride roughshod over Babylon.
The destruction is total and final. In the Scriptures this is the first city of prominence, but
its long, eventful and sinful history ends with
the judgment of God upon her.

"For strong is the Lord God who judgeth
her." It is God who destroys this city because
He alone is able to do it. He does this, we
believe, at the return of Christ. Notice this as
Isaiah predicts it: "Who is this that cometh
from Edom, with dyed garments from
Bozrah? this that is glorious in his apparel,
travelling in the greatness of his strength? I
that speak in righteousness, mighty to save.
Wherefore art thou red in thine apparel, and
thy garments like him that treadeth in the
winevat? I have trodden the winepress alone;
and of the people there was none with me: for
I will tread them in mine anger, and trample
them in my fury; and their blood shall be
sprinkled upon my garments, and I will stain
all my raiment. For the day of vengeance is in
mine heart, and the year of my redeemed is
come" (Isa. 63:1–4).

In His second coming Christ is seen coming
from Edom with blood-sprinkled garments. It
is my belief that He has come by way of
Babylon, and He has executed judgment upon
that wicked city. We will see Christ's second
coming in the following chapter.

Next we will see the reaction to the destruction of this great center. There will be anguish
in the world, and we will see who attends her
funeral. Also there will be the anticipation of
joy in heaven because of the judgment of Babylon. These are the two diametrically opposite
viewpoints. It will be bad for one crowd and
good for the other crowd.

ANGUISH IN THE WORLD BECAUSE OF BABYLON'S JUDGMENT

**And the kings of the earth, who have
committed fornication and lived deliciously with her, shall bewail her, and
lament for her, when they shall see the
smoke of her burning,**

**Standing afar off for the fear of her
torment, saying, Alas, alas that great
city Babylon, that mighty city! for in
one hour is thy judgment come [Rev.
18:9–10].**

*And the kings of the earth, who committed fornication and lived deliciously (in
luxury) with her, shall weep and wail
over her, when they look upon the smoke
of her burning, standing afar off for the
fear of her torment, saying, Woe, woe, the
great city, Babylon, the strong city! for in
one hour is thy judgment come.*

In that day Babylon will dominate and rule
the world. The capital of Antichrist will be
Babylon, and he will have the first total dictatorship. The world will become an awful
place. In that day everything will center in
Babylon. The stock market will be read from
Babylon—not New York. Babylon instead of
Paris will set the styles for the world. A play,
to be successful, will have to be a success in
Babylon, not London. Everything in that city
will be in rebellion against almighty God, and
it centers in Antichrist.

No one dreamed that this great city would
be judged. Yet by the time the sun goes down,
Babylon is nothing but smoldering ruins.
When the news goes out, the world is
stunned, and then begins the wail. The whole
world will howl when Babylon goes down. I
imagine that, if you were on the moon, you
would have to tune down your earphones because the howl would be so loud!

In chapter 17 we saw that the kings of the
earth hated religious Babylon and that Antichrist got rid of it in order that he might be
worshiped without any competition in the area
of religion. And the kings of the earth joined
in her destruction.

In contrast to this, here in chapter 18 we see that the kings of the earth love commercial Babylon because of the revenue she brought to their coffers. In fact, it is called here fornication—you can't find a better word for it than that! All the lobbyists were in Babylon, not Washington, D.C. They were representing all the great corporations in the world. But the kings desert Babylon like rats leaving a sinking ship; their mourning is both pathetic and contemptible. They eulogize her with panegyrics of praise, but there is a hopelessness in their anguish. They marvel at the sudden destruction of that which they thought was gilt-edged security. The judgment came in the space of one hour, reminding us of the sudden devastation caused by atomic explosions. This is a frightful picture presented to us, and it is the final conflagration and catastrophic judgment that will bring Christ to the earth to set up His kingdom.

And the merchants of the earth shall weep and mourn over her; for no man buyeth their merchandise any more:

The merchandise of gold, and silver, and precious stones, and of pearls, and fine linen, and purple, and silk, and scarlet, and all thyine wood, and all manner vessels of ivory, and all manner vessels of most precious wood, and of brass, and iron, and marble,

And cinnamon, and odours, and ointments, and frankincense, and wine, and oil, and fine flour, and wheat, and beasts, and sheep, and horses, and chariots, and slaves, and souls of men.

And the fruits that thy soul lusted after are departed from thee, and all things which were dainty and goodly are departed from thee, and thou shalt find them no more at all.

The merchants of these things, which were made rich by her, shall stand afar off for the fear of her torment, weeping and wailing,

And saying, Alas, alas, that great city, that was clothed in fine linen, and purple, and scarlet, and decked with gold, and precious stones, and pearls!

For in one hour so great riches is come to nought [Rev. 18:11–17a].

As you read these verses, did you feel as if you might be window-shopping down the main street of some of our great cities? In our store windows we see all these things in our day. These are the products of an affluent society, and these things were available to the Roman Empire in John's day. Babylon will make these luxury items necessities, just as we think these items are necessities today. You will not find a cotton dress or a pair of overalls anywhere in this list.

I remember when glazed bitreous terra cotta bathtubs first were introduced in this country. (Incidentally, it was opposed by the doctors in our land. They said that if you took a bath every day, it would shorten your life. They felt a bath once a week or once a month was enough.) In those days the bathtub was a luxury that many folk couldn't afford. But now, when we go to a hotel or motel, my wife looks to see if there is a tub and I look to see if there is a shower, and generally both are present. We live in a luxury age. Most of what we call necessities are actually luxuries.

Let's look at these items, using my literal translation. We will take them up separately: "And the merchants of the earth weep and mourn over her, for no man buyeth their merchandise (cargo) any more: merchandise (cargo) of gold, and silver, and precious stones, and pearls." Talk about a depression—they are having one! No one buys their merchandise or cargo anymore. In Babylon there is merchandise of gold and silver, precious stones and pearls. You see, we are in the jewelry department here.

Then we move from the jewelry department to the ladies' ready-to-wear: ". . . and fine linen, and purple, and silk, and scarlet."

Then to the luxury gift department: ". . . and all thyine (citron) wood, and every vessel of ivory, and every vessel made of most precious wood, and of brass, and iron, and marble."

We move on to the spice and cosmetic department: ". . . and cinnamon, and spice (amomum), and odours, and ointment, and frankincense." They have a great deal of spray deodorant, you see—probably the kind that works twenty-four hours a day.

Now we go to the liquor department and the pastry center: "and wine, and oil, and fine flour, and wheat." This is the food of the rich; barley is the food of the poor. The wealthy were eating gourmet food and enjoying luxury until Babylon went down.

We move on to the meat department where you can get porterhouse steaks, lamb chops and filet mignon—"and cattle, and sheep."

The merchandise covers every phase of business. The articles are for a society accustomed to the better things of the material universe. Even *men* were bought and sold, including their souls. I think this is becoming more and more true today where great corporations have men on the payroll who are bound there almost like slaves. Right now there is many a woman selling her soul. "And merchandise of horses, and chariots, and slaves (bodies), and souls of men."

"The merchants of these things who grew rich by her, shall stand afar off because of the fear of her torment, saying, Alas, alas." The Greek word for "alas" doesn't need to be translated to get its meaning. It is *ouai, ouai!* The very sound of the word is a form of wail. The merchants of the earth sit before their TV screens and cry, "Ouai, ouai!" for in one hour wealth so great is laid desolate.

We always have been able to find a parallel in the Old Testament. Do we have anything that corresponds to this in the past? Yes, Ezekiel predicted the judgment of Tyre, the capital of the Phoenicians. Tyre was to the ancient world what New York City is to us today and what Babylon will be to the future (see Ezek. 26–27).

And every shipmaster, and all the company in ships, and sailors, and as many as trade by sea, stood afar off,

And cried when they saw the smoke of her burning, saying, What city is like unto this great city!

And they cast dust on their heads, and cried, weeping and wailing, saying, Alas, alas, that great city, wherein were made rich all that had ships in the sea by reason of her costliness! for in one hour is she made desolate [Rev. 18:17b–19].

And every shipmaster and every one that sails anywhere (traveler) and sailors, and those who live by seafaring stood afar off. And cried out when they looked upon the smoke of her burning, saying, What city is like the great city? And they cast dust upon their heads, and cried, weeping and mourning, saying, Woe, woe [Gr.: ouai, ouai], the great city wherein all that had their ships in the sea were made rich by reason of her costly expenditure! for in one hour is she made desolate.

The third delegation of mourners is composed of those who are engaged in transportation, the great public carriers. They had become rich by transporting the merchandise of Baby-

lon, just as the Phoenicians had done in the ancient world. Now there is no more business. They mourn because of the depression. All went up in smoke in a moment. They, like the others, marvel at the sudden destruction.

All of this has an application for us. How do *we* see the luxury of this world? Do we see it as it really is? Can we use it without getting it into our hearts? How would you feel if the luxuries in your life which you have come to consider necessities suddenly went up in smoke?

Today we speak about spirituality and spiritual things. Even in our Christian organizations there is almost an overweening zeal to get people to give, especially the wealthy people. Recently some wealthy persons threatened to withdraw their support from my radio ministry if I did not do a certain thing. I did not listen to their threats. It seems to me that we have paid too much attention to this world today. The world is passing away, and the things you see at your fingertips are also passing away.

The great cities of the world are passing away. Los Angeles is a wonderful city, and I have enjoyed this city because I have lived in Southern California for many years, but it is passing away. God is going to judge Los Angeles. But the question is: Would it break your heart if you saw the things of this world go up in smoke? Or is your heart in heaven, fixed on Christ? It does make a lot of difference.

ANTICIPATION OF JOY IN HEAVEN BECAUSE OF BABYLON'S JUDGMENT

Rejoice over her, thou heaven, and ye holy apostles and prophets; for God hath avenged you on her [Rev. 18:20].

Rejoice over her, thou heaven, and ye saints, and ye apostles, and ye prophets; for God hath judged your judgment on her.

The viewpoint of heaven is entirely different. It is no funeral procession there. Rather, it is the celebration of an anticipated event. The saints prayed for it; the prophets of the Old Testament and the apostles of the New Testament predicted it. Now all is fulfilled and there is joy because God has exonerated His name. Judgment has come upon these things. Just what is your heart fixed on today? It will make a lot of difference in that day because you will either be with the mourners or you will be with the rejoicers.

And a mighty angel took up a stone like a great millstone, and cast it into the

sea, saying, **Thus with violence shall that great city Babylon be thrown down, and shall be found no more at all** [Rev. 18:21].

And one strong angel took up a stone like a great millstone, and cast it into the sea, saying, Thus with a mighty rush (fall) shall Babylon, the mighty city, be cast down, and shall be found no more at all.

Even heaven calls our attention to the violence, the suddenness, and the complete annihilation of Babylon. Like a stone that makes a big splash and then disappears beneath the waves will Babylon come to an end.

And the voice of harpers, and musicians, and of pipers, and trumpeters, shall be heard no more at all in thee; and no craftsman, of whatsoever craft he be, shall be found any more in thee; and the sound of a millstone shall be heard no more at all in thee;

And the light of a candle shall shine no more at all in thee; and the voice of the bridegroom and of the bride shall be heard no more at all in thee: for thy merchants were the great men of the earth; for by thy sorceries were all nations deceived [Rev. 18:22–23].

Again, using my translation: "And the voice of harpers and minstrels and flute-players and trumpeters shall be heard no more at all in thee." You see, rock music will go out of style then—and I thank God for that!

"And no craftsman, of whatsoever craft shall be found any more at all in thee." All the factories will close down.

"And the light of a lamp shall shine no more at all in thee." All the neon lights on Broadway will go out.

"And the voice of the bridegroom and the bride shall be heard no more at all in thee." It's all over—no more marrying and giving in marriage here.

"For thy merchants were the princes of the earth; for with thy sorcery were all the nations deceived." I believe that more and more we are going to see sorcery, magic, and demonism. Satanism will increase more and more as we draw near the end of the age. It will be Satan who is going to deceive and blind people, just as he blinds many in our day.

Popular music comes to an end in Babylon. Jazz and rock 'n' roll cease in the destruction. Classical music will be stilled, also.

The crafts that have been prostituted to the service of the Antichrist will end. The wheels of the factories will never turn again. The bright lights of the cities will go out forever. It is interesting to note the beginning of all these things as recorded in Genesis 4:16–22. Also, social life and family life shall end. The great tycoons of big business will disappear. This city deceived the world with the worship of Antichrist—this is the strong delusion.

And in her was found the blood of prophets, and of saints, and of all that were slain upon the earth [Rev. 18:24].

God's people got rough treatment in this city and God judged it. This is Satan's city, and he was a murderer from the beginning. Babylon was a city that murdered; its final crime was the slaying of God's people.

As we contemplate the destruction of Babylon, we think of other great cities and civilizations of the past which have fallen. One of the most widely read books of all time is *The Decline and Fall of the Roman Empire* written by Edward Gibbon in 1788. In it he gives five basic reasons why that great civilization withered and died:

1. The undermining of the dignity and sanctity of the home, which is the basis for human society.

2. Higher and higher taxes; the spending of public money for free bread and circuses for the populace.

3. The mad craze for pleasure; sports becoming every year more exciting, more brutal, more immoral.

4. The building of great armaments when the real enemy was within—the decay of individual responsibility.

5. The decay of religion; faith fading into mere form, losing touch with life, losing power to guide the people.

The oft-heard warning that history repeats itself has an ominous meaning in the light of the above. We can already see these five things at work in our contemporary culture in this country. The same things will bring Babylon down at the end. They destroy the nation and the home and the individual.

Thank God, the sad story of man's sin will come to an end.

This chapter brings to a conclusion the frightful period which was labeled by the Lord Jesus Christ the Great Tribulation. In the next chapter we will see Him coming to the earth to bring to an end this dark, doleful, and disastrous period.

This is the negative aspect to His coming.

The positive side is the dawning of the Day of the Lord, called the Millennium or thousand years in chapter 20.

Now let's take a final look at the Great Tribulation Period with its catastrophic and cataclysmic events taking place in rapid succession like a machine gun firing.

The total period is seven years. It is the "seventieth week" of Daniel's prophecy. In the Old Testament Daniel divided it, and in the New Testament John divided it into two separate and equal periods of three and one half years each.

However, after the church leaves this earth, the Antichrist comes to power as world dictator on a platform of peace, prosperity, and fame. During the first part of the Tribulation he will bring about radical changes that seem to benefit mankind. He will bring in a false peace. All government and religion are to be controlled by him. When that time comes, there will be one world, one religion, and one everything. The world will believe that they are entering the Millennium and that the world will become a Utopia. This is part of the big lie of that period. The true church, the body of Christ, will be removed from the earth before the Tribulation begins. It will become the bride of Christ, and we will see this bride shortly—near the end of this book.

Israel will once again become God's witness on earth—144,000 strong, sealed by the Spirit of God. And they will witness here upon the earth. Also, there will be a great company of Gentiles that will be sealed.

Somewhere near the middle of the seven-year period the king of the north, and I believe it will be Russia, will move against Israel. God will judge Russia just as He judged Sodom and Gomorrah. If you want to see that picture, you will find it in Ezekiel 38. This opens the floodgates of war. The Antichrist now begins to move, and the deception, I think, will become apparent to a great many folk. Restless mankind, under the control of Satan, begins to march. The world begins to fall apart, like a pear that is too ripe. The Man of Sin, the Antichrist, breaks his covenant with the nation Israel.

The Mideast will become the center of world activity during this period. Babylon will be the political and economic capital of the world, and Jerusalem (also called Babylon) will be the religious capital. The Antichrist will begin in Rome, and the False Prophet will begin in Jerusalem. Antichrist, when he comes to power, will rebuild Babylon. The apostate church will be destroyed by Antichrist and by the kings of the earth who will be subservient to him.

Ancient Babylon on the Euphrates River will become the political and economic center of the world. If a small nation in the Mideast can turn off the spigot to stop the flow of oil and thereby bring the world to its knees, what will it be when ancient Babylon in that very area becomes again the world center?

New York City will then be a whistle stop on the Toonerville Trolley or not even worth the legendary string of glass beads. Los Angeles will return to an adobe village and no longer will be the city of angels but a dwelling place of demons—it appears as if they are already beginning to move in. London and other great cities of the world will become mere villages with muddy streets. Judgments from God will fall swiftly and suddenly on a God-rejecting and blaspheming world. At one fell swoop one-fourth of the population of the world will be destroyed, and at another time one-third will be blotted out. Nature will be afflicted—the grass and trees of the earth, the sun, moon, and stars in the heavens. One disaster after another will fall on the earth, but the heart of man will still be unrepentant. In fact, he will defy and blaspheme the God of heaven.

Then armies will march toward Israel. For three and one-half years the war will rage. It is not the *Battle* of Armageddon but the *war* of Armageddon. Millions of men will march at that time in that land. They will be engaged in a conflict there, but they will be destroyed. There will be blood up to the bridles of the horses—about three feet deep! That is no exaggeration.

Into this horrible arena of chaos—the chaos of man's making and of Satan's scheming—comes the King of Kings and the Lord of Lords. Yes, the King is coming to the earth but, before all of this can take place, His church must be removed from the earth and go to be with Him. Then the church will return to the earth with Him when He comes to establish His kingdom. The church is not looking for the fulfillment of any of these things which we have looked at from chapter 4 through chapter 18. The church is looking for the blessed hope and the glorious appearing of our great God and Savior, Jesus Christ.

We do not know the day when Christ will return. We do not even know the period in which He will return. It may be soon. It could be today. On the other hand, He may not return for a hundred years or even several hundred years. No one can say with certainty when the Lord will return for His church. Anyone who sets a date for the Lord's appearing is entirely out of order. Anyone who claims to know when the Lord will return has information that is not in the Word of God.

The best that can be said today is that everything that is happening is significant. We live in a great period in the history of the world, but all we can say for sure is that our salvation is nearer than when we first believed.

The late Dr. Bill Anderson of Dallas, Texas, used to say, "God is getting the stage all set. It looks like He is coming soon. But if He is not planning to come now, and since it would take a lot of *doing* to get the world in this position again, if I were the Lord, I would just come on now and take the church out of the world."

Well, we hope He will come now, but all we know is that the terrors of the Tribulation will take place after the church has been removed at the Rapture. We have been given no signs by which to gauge the time of His return, but we do see the setting of the stage. And we see some very significant things happening in our day. Obviously, Western Europe is looking for a man strong enough to put the Roman Empire back together. And Antichrist is coming. They may not know it, but they are waiting for him. Also, we see a great power in the north—Russia. Egypt is alive again. China was a sleeping giant that we woke up, and from that great population center they are going to come marching out one of these days. Then the crowning scene of the setting of the stage is Israel, which is back in her land. Everything is in position, the church could be raptured at any moment, and the Tribulation could begin. But it may not. We do not know the day or the hour.

CHAPTER 19

THEME: *Marriage of the Lamb and return of Christ in judgment*

Now we come to the thrilling events that concern *us*. In chapter 19 we turn the page to that which marks a drastic change in the tone of Revelation. The destruction of Babylon, the capital of the Beast's kingdom, marked the end of the Great Tribulation. The somber gives way to the song. The transfer is from darkness to light, from the inky blackness of night to a white light, from dreary days of judgment to bright days of blessing. This chapter makes a definite bifurcation in the Book of Revelation and ushers in the greatest event for this earth—the second coming of Christ to the earth to establish His kingdom. It is the bridge between the Great Tribulation and the millennial kingdom that He will establish upon this earth. Great and significant events are recorded here. The two central features are the marriage supper of the Lamb and the return of Christ to the earth. One follows the other.

The hallelujahs open this chapter and the opening of hell concludes it. Two great suppers are recorded in this chapter: the marriage supper of the Lamb and the cannibalistic feast of carrion after the last part of the war of Armageddon.

FOUR HALLELUJAHS

As chapter 19 opens, the voices of heaven become one chorus.

And after these things I heard a great voice of much people in heaven, saying, Alleluia; Salvation, and glory, and honour, and power, unto the Lord our God [Rev. 19:1].

As usual, I will give my translation of the literal Greek text throughout this chapter.

After these things I heard as it were a great voice of a great multitude in heaven, saying, Hallelujah; Salvation, and glory, and honour, and power, unto the Lord our God.

"After these things" (Gr.: *meta tauta*) is an expression we first bumped into when John gave the division of the Book of Revelation in chapter 1, verse 19—literally, "the things that shall be after these things." After what things? After the church things. Chapter 4 opened with *meta tauta*, and we have been *meta tauta*ing ever since. There is a chronological progression, a sequence of events. Now we will see what will take place after the Great Tribulation. It is recorded in this chapter: the coming of Christ to the earth. He is the only One who can end the Tribulation. And so this is the last occurrence of the expression *meta tauta*.

"A great voice of a great multitude." In the worship scenes of chapters 5–7 we saw the elders, the church, and the uncounted numbers of angels and created intelligences all worshiping God. Now a great number of tribulation saints has been added to the chorus, and they are going to sing. This is something quite marvelous. This is the first time they have been able to utter the great note of praise of the Old Testament—*Hallelujah!* This word occurs four times in the first six verses. This is its only occurrence in the New Testament. It is reserved for the final victory. It is interesting to note that *hallelujah* occurs frequently in the Book of Psalms. It means "praise the Lord." It appears in frequent succession in Psalms 146–150. In fact, Psalm 150 is a mighty crescendo of praise. *Hallelujah* is a fitting note of praise at this juncture in the Book of Revelation. The Great Tribulation is over. Jesus is coming. The church is to be united with Christ in marriage. Hallelujah! Let's sing it, my friend! Every year I love to hear Handel's *Messiah* being sung, but regardless of what choir sings it, they don't even touch the rim of the great *Hallelujah* of this future day. Psalm 104:35 puts it this way: "Let the sinners be consumed out of the earth, and let the wicked be no more. Bless thou the Lord, O my soul. Praise . . . the Lord"—that is, Hallelujah! Hallelujah because God is coming to judge, and the wicked are going to be removed from the earth. Hallelujah is an expletive of praise as the final phase of salvation is coming to pass. This is something that Paul talked about in Romans 8:18–23: "For I reckon that the sufferings of this present time are not worthy to be compared with the glory which shall be revealed in us. For the earnest expectation of the creature waiteth for the manifestation of the sons of God. For the creature was made subject to vanity, not willingly, but by reason of him who hath subjected the same in hope, Because the creature itself also shall be delivered from the bondage of corruption into the glorious liberty of the children of God. For we know that the whole creation groaneth and travaileth in pain together until now. And not only they, but ourselves also, which have the firstfruits of the Spirit, even we ourselves groan within ourselves, waiting for the adoption, to wit, the redemption of our body."

My friend, this is that great day which is coming. The earth will be released from the bondage of sin. In the meantime it groans. Go down to the seashore and listen to the waves. One summer I slept by the Atlantic Ocean in a place at Virginia Beach. Every night I was put to sleep by the breaking of the waves on the shore. But the waves were sobbing, as it were, sobbing out their sorrow. Go up in the mountains and listen at night to the wind going through the pine trees. There is not a soprano in all of those pine trees, nor is there a redwood that can sing soprano. Their sounds are all subdued, quiet groans as they await the coming of that great day upon the earth.

And *we* groan. I don't know about you, but I groan. When I was a young man and built my home in Southern California, I used to come bounding down the stairs. Now when I come down the stairs, I groan with every step. My wife says, "You ought not to groan." I tell her that groaning is scriptural. We groan within these bodies, as the Scripture says. I'm all for groaning while we are here. But one day the groaning will be changed to hallelujahs, and that is what John is talking about here.

For true and righteous are his judgments: for he hath judged the great whore, which did corrupt the earth with her fornication, and hath avenged the blood of his servants at her hand.

And again they said, Alleluia. And her smoke rose up for ever and ever.

And the four and twenty elders and the four beasts fell down and worshipped God that sat on the throne, saying, Amen; Alleluia [Rev. 19:2–4].

For true and righteous are his judgments; for he hath judged the great harlot who (formerly) corrupted the earth with her fornication, and he hath avenged the blood of his servants at her hand. And the second time they said, Hallelujah. And her smoke goeth up for ever and ever. And the four and twenty elders and the four living creatures fell down and worshipped God that sitteth on the throne, saying, Amen; Hallelujah.

It is interesting to note that at the conclusion of all these judgments, those in heaven, who have more perfect knowledge than you and I have, are able to say that God's judgments are true and right. If you don't think what God is doing is right, it is because *you*, not God, are wrong. Your thinking is incomplete, of course, as mine is. God will be righteous in judging the great harlot. This is interesting because when we read about the judgment of the great harlot, representing the apostate church which went into the Tribulation, it says that the kings of the earth and the Antichrist destroyed the harlot. Yet here we are told that it was God who judged it. You see, God uses different instruments, and He will even use the Devil to accomplish His purpose. Those in heaven are saying, "True and righteous are his judgments," because the apostate church deserved to be destroyed; it had made martyrs of many of God's children.

In these verses we find a picture of the church in heaven saying, "Hallelujah." They say it twice. Why? As long as the imposter of the true church, the great harlot, is on the earth, the marriage of the Lamb will not take place in heaven. The anti-church is disposed of first, which makes way for the marriage of the Lamb. I assume that the marriage of the Lamb takes place in heaven sometime during the midst of the Tribulation which is going on upon the earth.

"He hath avenged the blood of his servants at her hand." You see, believers are forbidden to avenge themselves. It is true that some of us try to do it, but the moment we do so, we forsake the walk of faith. In Romans 12:19 God says to us: "Dearly beloved, avenge not yourselves, but rather give place unto wrath: for it is written, Vengeance is mine; I will repay, saith the Lord." God will take care of vengeance for you. If we have been injured, and many of us have been, we want to hit back. That is natural; it is the old nature striking out. However, we are to turn that department over to God. He doesn't intend to let anyone get away with wrong. Vengeance is His. And He will bring judgment on this apostate system.

The twenty-four elders for the first time sing *Hallelujah*. The elders we believe to be the church (see Rev. 4). This is the last time the elders appear as such, for the figure changes now, and the church is to become the bride of Christ. The word *church* means "called out." Here on the earth we are the church, the called-out ones, but after we leave the earth we are the bride.

And a voice came out of the throne, saying, Praise our God, all ye his servants, and ye that fear him, both small and great.

And I heard as it were the voice of a great multitude, and as the voice of many waters, and as the voice of mighty thunderings, saying, Alleluia: for the Lord God omnipotent reigneth [Rev. 19:5–6].

And a voice came forth from the throne, saying, Give praise to our God, all ye his servants, ye that fear him, the small and the great. And I heard as it were the voice of a great multitude, and as it were the voice of many waters, and as it were the voice of mighty thunders, saying, Hallelujah; for the Lord our God, the Almighty reigneth.

"A voice came out of the throne, saying, Praise our God." Notice that the call to praise comes directly from the throne of God, because the Lord Jesus Christ is preparing to take control of this world. This is truly the Hallelujah chorus and the most profound paean of praise in the entire Word of God. It takes us all the way back to that covenant which God made with David in which He promised that He would raise One upon David's throne who would rule the world. In 2 Samuel 7:16 we read: "And thine house and thy kingdom shall be established for ever before thee: thy throne shall be established for ever."

But before Christ returns to the earth, there is going to be a wedding, and you and I, as believers, will be part of it.

BRIDE OF THE LAMB AND MARRIAGE SUPPER

Let us be glad and rejoice, and give honour to him: for the marriage of the Lamb is come, and his wife hath made herself ready.

And to her was granted that she should be arrayed in fine linen, clean and white: for the fine linen is the righteousness of saints [Rev. 19:7–8].

Let us rejoice and be exceeding glad, and let us give the glory unto him; for the marriage of the Lamb is come, and his wife hath made herself ready. And it was given unto her that she should array herself in fine linen, bright and pure; for the fine linen is the righteous acts of the saints.

This will be the most thrilling experience that believers will ever have. The church—that is, the body of believers all the way from Pentecost to the Rapture—will be presented now to Christ as a bride for a marriage. The marriage takes place in heaven, and this is a heavenly scene throughout.

In Ephesians 5 the apostle Paul speaks about the husband and wife relationship when both are believers. By the way, he is speaking of those who are filled with the Spirit and of the relationships that flow from it. You cannot have a Christian home without a Spirit-filled husband and a Spirit-filled wife. In fact, I do not believe you can know what real love is until both marriage partners are believers. Notice Paul's instructions: "Husbands, love your wives, even as Christ also loved the church, and gave himself for it; That he might sanctify and cleanse it with the washing of water by the word, That he might present it to himself a glorious church, not having spot, or wrinkle, or any such thing; but that it should be holy and without blemish" (Eph. 5:25–27). This is the picture of the relationship of Christ and the church.

We are living in a day of "new" morality. Our contemporary society is drenched with sex. This generation knows a great deal about sex. I watched a young couple in Palm Springs one day, and I felt sorry for the boy and the girl. They were necking like nobody's business, right in public. I thought to myself, *What do they really know about love? Why, they know nothing about what it means for a man to love a woman and a woman to love a man.* I am afraid there are many Christians who don't know much about love either. Husbands, do you remember the first time you looked at your wife? Do you remember when you were joined in marriage and she became yours? Wasn't that a thrilling moment for you? Wives, do you remember when you first looked at that ugly old boy you married and thought he was so handsome? When he put his arms around you, wasn't that a thrilling moment? Well, Ephesians 5:25–27 is a picture of that day when Christ is going to draw us to Himself, cleansed and purified. Young lady and young man, that is the reason in this day of "new" morality that you should bring purity to your marriage. God have mercy on some of you fellows who are married to second-hand girls. Don't get them at the second-hand store; get them brand new. It is much better that way.

"The marriage of the Lamb is come." Marriage is a marvelous picture of the joining together of Christ and the church. Notice that the Old Testament saints are not included—only the believers during the church age are included. Even John the Baptist designated himself as only a friend of the Bridegroom. He said, "He that hath the bride is the bridegroom . . ." (John 3:29). The bride occupies a unique relationship with Christ. You see, Christ loved the church and gave Himself for it. Remember what He said in His High Priestly Prayer: "I in them, and thou in me, that they may be made perfect in one; and that the world may know that thou hast sent me, and hast loved them, as thou hast loved me. Father, I will that they also, whom thou hast given me, be with me where I am; that they may behold my glory, which thou hast given me: for thou lovedst me before the foundation of the world. O righteous Father, the world hath not known thee: but I have known thee, and these have known that thou hast sent me. And I have declared unto them thy name, and will declare it: that the love wherewith thou hast loved me may be in them, and I in them" (John 17:23–26).

The thing that is so wonderful is that we are going to *know* Christ—really know Him—for the first time.

"The fine linen is the righteous acts of the saints." The wedding gown of the church is the righteous *acts* of the saints. This is a difficult concept to accept, because it is impossible for us to stand before Christ in our own righteousness. Paul wrote of this: "And be found in him, not having mine own righteousness, which is of the law, but that which is through the faith of Christ, the righteousness which is of God by faith" (Phil. 3:9). You see, by faith we can trust Christ—not only for the forgiveness of sins but for the impartation to us of His own righteousness. Then why does John say that the wedding garment is the righteous *acts* of the saints? Well, the wedding gown will be used only once, but we will be clothed in the righteousness of Christ throughout eternity. We as believers will appear before the judgment seat of Christ, not to be judged for our sins in reference to salvation, but for rewards. Through the ages believers have been performing righteous acts which have been accumulating to adorn the wedding gown. By the way, what are *you* doing to adorn that wedding gown? What are you doing for the Lord today?

Again let me quote Paul: "Now if any man build upon this foundation [which is Christ] gold, silver, precious stones, wood, hay, stubble; Every man's work shall be made manifest: for the day shall declare it, because it shall be revealed by fire; and the fire shall try every man's work of what sort it is. If any man's work abide which he hath built thereupon, he shall receive a reward" (1 Cor. 3:12–14). Gold, silver, and precious stones will survive the fire; wood, hay, and stubble will go up in smoke. Therefore the good works are the wedding garment of the church. "For we are his workmanship, created in Christ Jesus unto good works, which God hath before ordained that we should walk in them" (Eph. 2:10).

After the wedding, the wedding dress is laid aside. We have already seen that the elders placed their crowns at the feet of the Lamb, proclaiming that He alone is worthy. The church will reveal His glory: "That in the ages to come he might shew the exceeding riches of his grace in his kindness toward us through Christ Jesus" (Eph. 2:7). We will be on display—sinners saved from hell, if you please, in heaven now. We have no right to heaven and would not go there except for the righteousness of Christ and the fact that we belong to Him. The relationship of Christ and the church is intimate, it is different, and it is delightful. No other creatures will enjoy such sweetness.

And he saith unto me, Write, Blessed are they which are called unto the marriage supper of the Lamb. And he saith unto me, These are the true sayings of God.

And I fell at his feet to worship him. And he said unto me, See thou do it not: I am thy fellow-servant, and of thy brethren that have the testimony of Jesus: worship God: for the testimony of Jesus is the spirit of prophecy [Rev. 19:9–10].

And he saith unto me, Write, Blessed are they that are bidden (invited) to the marriage supper of the Lamb. And he saith unto me, These are the true words of God. And I fell down before his feet to worship him. And he saith unto me, See thou do it not; I am a fellow servant with thee and with thy brethren that hold the testimony of Jesus; worship God: for the testimony of Jesus is the spirit of prophecy.

Hear me carefully now: the marriage of the Lamb will take place in heaven, but the marriage *supper* will take place upon the earth. The picture of this is in Matthew 25:1–13, which is the parable of the ten virgins. You see, the virgins were not the bride. Christ has only one bride, and that is the church. The Bridegroom will return to the earth for the marriage supper. He will return not only to judge the earth but to have the marriage sup-

per, which the ten virgins are expecting to attend.

Another picture of this same scene is given in Psalm 45. In this psalm Christ is seen coming as king. We are not told who she is, but the queen is there: "Kings' daughters were among thy honourable women: upon thy right hand did stand the queen in gold of Ophir" (Ps. 45:9). I believe this is a symbol or a type of the church.

Guests are present: "And the daughter of Tyre shall be there with a gift; even the rich among the people shall entreat thy favour" (Ps. 45:12). The marriage supper will take place on earth. Both Israelites and Gentiles who enter the Millennium are the invited guests. The marriage supper is evidently the Millennium. You talk about a long supper—*this* is going to be a long one! At the end of the Millennium the church is still seen as the *bride.* Imagine a honeymoon which lasts one thousand years! Yet that is only the beginning. What joy! What ecstasy! The angel puts God's seal on this scene: "These are the true words of God."

After acting as a scribe for this scene, John feels compelled to worship the angelic messenger. However, he is restrained from doing so. The angel is but a creature. Only God is to be worshiped. What a rebuke to Satan, the Antichrist, and the False Prophet who wanted to be worshiped. And there are many folk in our day who have that same desire.

After the marriage of the Lamb in heaven, the next great event is the return of Christ to the earth. My friend, the King is coming! But He will not come until after the church has been raptured and after the earth has undergone the Great Tribulation. Now when He comes to the earth, His bride will be with Him, and their marriage supper will be here upon the earth, as we have seen. Oh, my friend, what a glorious day is ahead of us! If we could only get our eyes off the muck and mire of this earth and onto that which is eternal!

RETURN OF CHRIST AS KING OF KINGS AND LORD OF LORDS

And I saw heaven opened, and behold a white horse; and he that sat upon him was called Faithful and True, and in righteousness he doth judge and make war.

His eyes were as a flame of fire, and on his head were many crowns; and he had

a name written, that no man knew, but he himself [Rev. 19:11–12].

And I saw the heaven opened, and behold, a white horse, and he that sat on him was called Faithful and True, and in righteousness doth he judge and make war. Now his eyes a flame of fire, and upon his head many diadems; having a name written which none knew but himself.

What a thrilling scene this is! Just to read it makes goose pimples come out all over me. This is the great climactic event toward which all things in this world are moving today. It is the coming of Christ to the earth.

Let me take a moment to remind you where this fits into the picture. From chapters 4–18 we were in the midst of the Great Tribulation Period, a frightful period. It ends by the coming of Christ to this earth to establish His kingdom.

In the past there has been a very naïve notion relative to the future, which is still held by some folk who are not students of the Bible. It is this: One of these days Jesus is going to come, and all the dead will be raised. The good guys will be on one side and the bad guys on the other. Christ will make the division so that one will enter heaven, the other hell, and eternity begins. May I say again that this is a very naïve notion.

You cannot read the Word of God without being conscious of the fact that He has a plan and program for this earth and that He is following it very carefully. The program, as we have outlined it, reveals that Christ's return to the earth takes place at the end of the Great Tribulation Period, right before the establishment of His kingdom.

The contrast to His first coming is stupendous. It is absolutely remarkable.

At the time of Christ's first coming, as George Macdonald put it:

> They all were looking for a King
> To slay their foes and lift them high;
> Thou cam'st, a little baby thing
> That made a woman cry.

That is the way He entered the world the first time. He was meek and lowly. He was the Savior who died for sinners. Now in the verses before us we see Him coming in His great glory. His coming will be the final manifestation of the wrath of God upon a sinful world. The rebellion of Satan, demons, and men is contained, put down, and judged. He puts down all unrighteousness before He establishes His kingdom in righteousness.

Heaven is opened in chapter 4, verse 1, to let John, as a representative of the church, enter heaven where he sees the elders, that is, the church, already there. And here in chapter 19 heaven opens to let Christ exit. The white horse on which He rides is the animal of warfare. When Jesus was on earth, He rode into Jerusalem upon a little donkey which, though an animal of kings, denoted peace, not war.

He is called "Faithful" because He has come to execute the long-time program of God. Remember that the scoffer said, "Where is the sign of His coming?" There is no sign at this point—He is here. He has made good. He is Faithful. He is the *only* One you and I can trust and rest upon.

He is called "True" for He is inherently true. He is not one who just tells the truth, although He does that; He is the bureau of standards of truth. He is the yardstick of truth. He *is* the Truth. How wonderful it is to have Someone in whom to trust in this day when everything we hear is slanted and used as propaganda.

He has come to "judge and make war"—not to die on a cross again.

"Now his eyes a flame of fire." Back in chapter 1, verse 14, His eyes were *as* a flame, as He walked among the churches, judging them. But now there is a difference—"his eyes a flame of fire" because He has come to judge the earth and put down its unrighteousness.

"Upon his head many diadems" indicates that He will be the sole ruler of this earth. And His rulership is going to be a dictatorship, I can assure you of that. My friend, if you don't love Jesus Christ—if He is not your Savior—and you live to enter this period of His return to the earth, it is going to be a most uncomfortable period for you because Christ is going to be a dictator. A chicken won't peep, a rooster won't crow, and a man will not move without His permission. He is the King of Kings and He is the Lord of Lords.

"And he had a name written, that no man knew." What is this name that no one knew but Himself? He is given four names here which correspond to the Gospels:

1. "King of kings" corresponds to the Gospel of Matthew, since Matthew presents Christ as the King.

2. "Faithful and True" corresponds to the Gospel of Mark where He is presented as the Servant of God. The important thing about a servant is not his genealogy but his trust-

worthiness. Is he faithful and truthful? Those are the qualities that are important.

3. "Word of God" repeats what He is called in the Gospel of John: "In the beginning was the Word. . . . and the Word was made flesh . . ." (John 1:1, 14).

4. What is the name that no one knows? Well, I have a suggestion. Perhaps it corresponds to Luke's gospel in which He is presented as Jesus, the Son of Man. In our day there is a great familiarity with that name, both in swearing and in blaspheming and in being overly free and presumptuous with Him. But, my friend, that is a name which you and I are going to probe throughout eternity. He is Jesus, the Son of Man. Do you really know Jesus? Well, no man knoweth the Son but the Father, and here we learn that when He comes, He has a name that no man really knows but Himself.

The apostle Paul, not at the beginning but at the end of his ministry, before his execution, said, "That I may know *him*, and the power of his resurrection, and the fellowship of his sufferings, being made conformable unto his death" (Phil. 3:10, italics mine). No one knows the Son but the Father. My friend, learning to know Him is one of the things that is going to make heaven *heaven*. He is so wonderful that it is going to take the rest of eternity to really know Him. The folk we meet down here are not very exciting folk when we get to know them, are they? But the more we know Jesus, the more exciting He will be.

In John 14:7, 9, we read: "If ye had known me, ye should have known my Father also: and from henceforth ye know him, and have seen him [that is, in the Person of the Son]. . . . Jesus saith unto him, Have I been so long time with you, and yet hast thou not known me, Philip? he that hath seen me hath seen the Father; and how sayest thou then, Shew us the Father?"

Then again in that High Priestly Prayer that Christ prayed: "And this is life eternal, that they might know thee the only true God, and Jesus Christ, whom thou hast sent" (John 17:3). When we come to Christ and receive Him as our Savior from sin, we have started to school. When we begin to know Him, we are in kindergarten. Let me make more or less of a confession; since I have retired from the pastorate, I have set before me a goal: I want to know Jesus better than I do now. I get up every morning and look out the window—I did *this* morning and in Southern California it is foggy—but I say, "Lord, thank You for bringing me to another day. I love You. I love You,

Lord Jesus, but, oh, You seem to be so far away at times. I want to know You. May the Spirit of God make You real to me." The name Jesus—oh, what it means, and what a person He is!

One more thing I would like to say about this subject: not only will we come to know the Lord better throughout eternity, we are also going to get to know one another better. I really don't think we know each other as we should. I find, at times, that I am greatly misunderstood. I make certain statements on the radio, and then I receive letters that almost shock me. It is difficult to understand how I could have been that misunderstood. But in heaven we are going to know as we are known. I think that will be good. Also, we will know ourselves. And we are going to know our loved ones. One summer when I tried to recuperate from an illness by resting, it enabled me to sit on my patio with my wife and get acquainted with her. It was quite wonderful. I discovered the sacrifices that she has made and her faithfulness down through the years. And I think I am *really* going to get acquainted with her in heaven. My friend, how glorious heaven is going to be! Even in this earthly life down here we find that when we grow in our love for Christ, we also grow in our love for each other.

Now notice the further description of Christ at His coming:

And he was clothed with a vesture dipped in blood: and his name is called The Word of God.

And the armies which were in heaven followed him upon white horses, clothed in fine linen, white and clean.

And out of his mouth goeth a sharp sword, that with it he should smite the nations: and he shall rule them with a rod of iron: and he treadeth the winepress of the fierceness and wrath of Almighty God.

And he hath on his vesture and on his thigh a name written, KING OF KINGS, AND LORD OF LORDS [Rev. 19:13–16].

And he is arrayed in a garment sprinkled with blood: and his name is called the Word of God. And the armies which are in heaven followed him upon white horses, clothed in fine linen, white and pure. And out of his mouth proceedeth a sharp sword, that with it he should smite

the nations; and he shall rule them with a rod of iron: and he treadeth the winepress of the fierceness of the wrath of God the All-ruler. And he hath on his garment and on his thigh a name written, KING OF KINGS, AND LORD OF LORDS.

Notice that His garment is sprinkled with blood and that He is treading the winepress of the fierceness and wrath of God. This picture takes us back to Isaiah 63: 1–6, which we have quoted previously.

Obviously, this refers not to Christ's first coming but to His second coming as described here in chapter 19.

"And he shall rule them with a rod of iron" takes us back to Psalm 2: "Yet have I set my king upon my holy hill of Zion. I will declare the decree: the LORD hath said unto me, Thou art my Son; this day have I begotten thee [from the dead]. Ask of me, and I shall give thee the heathen for thine inheritance, and the uttermost parts of the earth for thy possession. [He didn't get them at His first coming; how will He get them now?] Thou shalt break them with a rod of iron; thou shalt dash them in pieces like a potter's vessel" (Ps. 2:6–9).

The fury of His wrath at His second coming is in sharp contrast to His gentleness at His first coming. However, in both is revealed the "wrath of the Lamb."

"The armies . . . in heaven" are evidently the legions of angels that do His bidding.

THE WAR OF ARMAGEDDON

Now we come to the end of the war of Armageddon, and this concludes the final battle:

And I saw an angel standing in the sun; and he cried with a loud voice, saying to all the fowls that fly in the midst of heaven, Come and gather yourselves together unto the supper of the great God;

That ye may eat the flesh of kings, and the flesh of captains, and the flesh of mighty men, and the flesh of horses, and of them that sit on them, and the flesh of all men, both free and bond, both small and great [Rev. 19:17–18].

If there is one passage of Scripture which is revolting to read, this is it. You will notice that God included it at the end of His Word to remind us how revolting and nauseating to Him are the deeds of the flesh. Men who live in the flesh will have their flesh destroyed. This is an invitation at the end of the Battle of Armageddon to the carrion-eating fowl to a

banquet on earth where they will have A-1, blue-ribbon flesh to eat—kings and the mighty men of the earth. My friend, it is frightful to rebel against God because He is going to judge you someday. This scene reveals the heart of man and how dreadful that heart really is.

HELL OPENED

Now for the very first time hell is completely opened up:

And I saw the beast, and the kings of the earth, and their armies, gathered together to make war against him that sat on the horse, and against his army.

And the beast was taken, and with him the false prophet that wrought miracles before him, with which he deceived them that had received the mark of the beast, and them that worshipped his image. These both were cast alive into a lake of fire burning with brimstone.

And the remnant were slain with the sword of him that sat upon the horse, which sword proceeded out of his mouth: and all the fowls were filled with their flesh [Rev. 19:19–21].

And I saw the beast, and the kings of the earth, and their armies gathered together to make war against him that sat upon the horse and against his army. And the beast [Antichrist] was taken, and with him the false prophet that wrought the signs in his sight, wherewith he deceived them that had received the mark of the beast and them that worshipped his image: they two were cast alive into the lake of fire that burneth with brimstone; and the rest were killed with the sword of him that sat upon the horse, even the sword which came forth out of his mouth; and all the birds were filled with their flesh.

What a frightful picture this is. The Beast and the False Prophet defy God right up to the very last. They dare to make war with the Son of God! Surely "He that sitteth in the heavens shall laugh" at the utter futility of their efforts. It is preposterous that there is such a rebellion of man against God. The outcome is inevitable. The two arch-rebels and tyrants, the Antichrist and the False Prophet, have the questionable distinction of being the first two who are cast into hell. Even the Devil hasn't been put there yet.

The question arises: Is the "lake of fire"

literal? Well, let me give you something to think about because I am going to come back to this subject when we get to chapter 20. If hell is not literal, it depicts that which is *worse* than a literal fire of brimstone.

"The sword which came forth out of his mouth." What is that sword? An amillennial friend of mine asked me laughingly, "You don't believe that there is going to be a literal sword coming out of the mouth of Jesus, do you?" I told him that I would consider it to be literal if the Word of God had not made it clear that His Word is like a sword: "For the word of God is quick, and powerful, and sharper than any two-edged sword, piercing even to the dividing asunder of soul and spirit, and of the joints and marrow, and is a discerner of the thoughts and intents of the heart" (Heb. 4:12). "And take the helmet of salvation, and the sword of the Spirit, which is the word of God" (Eph. 6:17). "But with righteousness shall he judge the poor, and reprove with equity for the meek of the earth: and he shall smite the earth with the rod of his mouth, and with the breath of his lips shall he slay the wicked" (Isa. 11:4). Do you notice how clearly this symbol is explained by Scripture? The "sword" that comes from the mouth of Jesus is His Word. It was His Word that created this universe. It is the Word of God which will save you. And it will be the Word of God that will destroy the wicked at the end of this age.

CHAPTER 20

THEME: *The Millennium*

In the twentieth chapter we are dealing with the Millennium in relationship to Christ, Satan, man, the tribulation saints, the resurrections, the earth, and the Great White Throne. Unfortunately, a great many men in the past have thought that chapter 20 is not very important because the Millennium, the thousand-year period, is mentioned only here in Scripture, and therefore, they have practically dismissed this chapter altogether. It is true that the Millennium is mentioned only in this chapter, and it is mentioned as "a thousand years." Let's not argue about semantics. *Millennium* comes from the Latin word that means "one thousand." Millennium means a thousand years any way you slice it. You can call a person who believes in the Millennium a chiliast, and chiliasm is the way the early church spoke of it, because in the Greek *chiliasm* means "a thousand" also. I hope we understand that millennialism, chiliasm, and the thousand-year reign of Christ all refer to the same thing.

Chapter 20 is the division point for the three main schools of eschatology:

Postmillennialism assumed that Christ would come at the conclusion of the one thousand years. Man would bring in the kingdom by the preaching of the gospel. This was an optimistic view which prevailed at the turn of the century. At that time it looked like there might be a great worldwide turning to Christ and the world would be converted. This viewpoint has become obsolete as it could not weather the first half of the twentieth century, which produced two world wars, a global depression, the rise of communism, and the atom bomb with which worldwide destruction is imminent.

Amillennialism has become popular only in recent years and has largely supplanted postmillennialism. The addition of the prefix *a-* simply negates the belief in the Millennium. Amillennialism holds out no false optimism and has, for the most part, emphasized the coming of Christ. Its chief weakness is that it spiritualizes the thousand years, as it does all the Book of Revelation. It fits the Millennium into the present age. Dr. B. B. Warfield's interpretation is that the Millennium is going on in heaven while the Tribulation is going on down here on the earth. My belief is that in heaven they have a millennium, not just for a thousand years, but from eternity to eternity. Most amillennialists fit the Millennium into the present age, and all the events recorded in Revelation are somehow fitted into the facts of history like pieces are fitted into a crazy quilt. Frankly, I think that the results of this viewpoint are about the same: you come up with a crazy quilt.

Premillennialism, on the contrary, takes chapter 20 at face value, as it does all of the Book of Revelation, applying the literalist interpretation unless the context instructs otherwise. Let me cite the example we gave from chapter 19 where it says that, when the Lord Jesus comes, out of His mouth goes a sharp two-edged sword (see Rev. 19:15). Does this mean that a literal sword goes out of His mouth? I believe that Scripture makes it very clear that the sword is the Word of God. Paul writes, "And take . . . the sword of the Spirit, which is the word of God" (Eph. 6:17). With that kind of instruction, I do not see how we can misunderstand what John is talking about, but you must have a scriptural reason for your interpretation. You cannot spiritualize Scripture on any basis you choose, although that is the present custom and the popular method today. In the premillennialist interpretation, the one thousand years are treated as one thousand years, and Christ comes at the beginning of the Millennium. Chapter 20 makes it clear that there can be no Millennium until Christ comes.

In the first nine verses of this chapter, we have the word for a thousand years repeated six times. It must be pretty important to put that kind of emphasis on it. The early church believed in what was known as chiliasm, the belief in the literal thousand-year reign of Christ. Those who rejected that position were considered to be in a state of heresy. Later on there came in the teaching that the thousand years would be established by the church. The church would produce a perfect world, and then Jesus would come and find everything in apple-pie order. But that is not the way this section of Scripture presents it. He is coming in judgment, and if everything were in apple-pie order, there would be no need to put down rebellion and to judge and make war.

It has not been too long ago that men actually believed that the church was going to build the kingdom down here on this earth. Back in 1883 a commentator, Justin A. Smith, made this statement:

But upon the other hand, what a tremendous force is the Christianity of today when all is said. Is it conceivable that this auspicious power, which is so rapidly taking possession of the wide earth, can dwindle into the imbecility which some millennarians appear to predict for it?

Those of us who are premillennialists would be called a bunch of pessimists back in 1883 because we are predicting that the world is going to get worse and that there will be apostasy in the church. This man did not believe that, for he goes on to say:

It has been said that in twenty-five years more, if the present rate of progress continues, India will become as thoroughly Christian as Great Britain is today. There will be thirty millions of Christians in China, and Japan will be as fully Christianized as America is now. The old systems, they tell us, are honey-combed through and through by Christian influence. It looks as if a day may soon come when these systems, struck by vigorous blows, will fall in a tremendous collapse. Meantime, every weapon formed against Christianity breaks in the hand that holds it. Already, the Lord's right hand hath gotten Him victory.

But look at Great Britain today, for example— it is as bad off as India is. They talked bravely in those days, but they do not talk that way today.

In the book *The Problem of Evil*, the author made this statement:

The civilization of Europe, or to call it by its true name which derives from its origin, the Christian civilization, is visibly making the conquest of the world. Its triumph is only a matter of time. No one doubts it.

There are quite a few who doubt it today. In fact, the so-called European civilization, or Christian civilization, is going down the drink and has largely disappeared already.

These men belittle the twentieth chapter of Revelation. I consider Dr. B. B. Warfield to be the greatest scholar that this century has produced, and I was educated under his system, but he says that there is no reference to such an age as a millennium here on this earth "save in so obscure a portion as Revelation 20." He pays no attention to all of the Old Testament where God made a covenant that He would establish this kingdom on the earth through One in David's line.

Dr. Rothe many years ago said:

Our key does not open. The right key is lost. Until we are put in possession of it again, our exposition will never succeed. The system of biblical ideas is not that of our school at all.

In speaking with a student who had read a premillennial book and was enthusiastically telling him about it, Dr. R. L. Dabney, an honored theologian of the South in the past, said, "Probably you are right. I never looked into the subject." He was a great scholar but was honestly admitting that he had never studied prophecy!

The late Dr. Charles Hodge, who wrote two ponderous tomes on theology (and that was the theology I studied when I was in school), very frankly said that eschatology wasn't his bag—only he didn't use that expression:

The subject cannot be adequately discussed without taking a survey of all the prophetic teaching of the Scriptures, both of the Old Testament and the New. This task cannot be satisfactorily accomplished by anyone who has not made the study of the prophecies a specialty. The author, knowing that he has no such qualifications for the work, proposes to confine himself in a great measure to a historical survey of the different schemes of interpreting the scriptural prophecies relating to the subject.

Today all that has changed. There is a lively interest in prophecy, but I wish there were more who were as honest as Dr. Hodge was and would say, "I really haven't studied the subject as I should have." Unfortunately, a great many men are speaking on the subject of prophecy who have not actually studied it. This is a very important and vital subject. I do not claim to have any special qualifications for it at all, although I have studied it for forty years and have given a great deal of attention to it, even in the years past when it was largely ignored. But I think it is dangerous today that many are edging up to this matter of setting dates for the rapture of the church. I believe that the Rapture is absolutely a dateless event. It *may* be tomorrow, but it may *not* be tomorrow. We need to recognize that we are living in a period in which we are not given dates, but we are seeing the setting of a stage. I do not know what God has in mind for the future, but I do know that He sure has things in position.

I think it is obvious that I am premillennial and also pretribulational, and the reason is that I believe this is what John is teaching here. If you disagree with me and accept one of these other positions, you are in good company. Some of the finest men I have known hold a different viewpoint from mine, but if you want to be right, you will want to go along with me, of course!

First of all, there can be no Millennium until Satan is removed from the earthly scene. You could not have an ideal state down here as long as Satan is running loose.

In the second place, the curse of sin must be removed from the physical earth before a Millennium can be established. Scripture prophesies that the desert will blossom like a rose. If you live along the coast in California, the desert blossoms like a rose, but in eastern California, the desert is not blossoming like a rose. The curse of sin has not yet been removed from this earth.

In the third place, the resurrection of the Old Testament saints must take place at the beginning of the thousand years. If they were raised before the Great Tribulation, they would have to stand around and wait for the Millennium. There is no need for them to do that, and the Lord is not going to raise them until the Tribulation is over. Daniel makes this very clear: "And at that time shall Michael stand up, the great prince which standeth for the children of thy people: and there shall be a time of trouble, such as never was since there was a nation even to that same time: and at that time thy people shall be delivered, every one that shall be found written in the book. And many of them that sleep in the dust of the earth shall awake, some to everlasting life, and some to shame and everlasting contempt" (Dan. 12:1–2). This is talking about Israel. Following the Great Tribulation Period will be the resurrection of the Old Testament saints (see Isa. 25:8–9). Only Christ will raise the dead (see John 5:21, 25, 28–29), so He must come for that purpose.

In the fourth place, the tribulation saints are included in the resurrection of the Old Testament saints, and they reign with Christ during the Millennium.

Finally, the Millennium is the final testing of man under ideal conditions. This is the answer to those who say there is nothing wrong in man which circumstances and conditions cannot change. Man is an incurable, an incorrigible sinner. Even at the end of the Millennium, he is still in rebellion against God. The rebellion in the human heart and the depraved nature of man are impossible for any man to comprehend. If you and I could see ourselves as God sees us, we could not stand ourselves. But we think we are pretty good and that we are very nice people—do we not? The Millennium is the final testing of mankind before the beginning of the eternal state.

The Millennium is God's answer to the prayer, "Thy kingdom come." When we pray the prayer which we mistakenly call the Lord's Prayer, we say, "Thy kingdom come . . . in earth, as it is in heaven" (Matt. 6:10). That is the kingdom which He is going to establish here on earth, and it is called the Millennium. This is the kingdom which was promised to David (see 2 Sam. 7:12–17; 23:5). God took an oath relative to its establishment (see Ps. 89:34–37). This is the kingdom predicted in the psalms and in the prophets (see Ps. 2; 45; 110; Isa. 2:1–5; 11:1–9; 60; 61:3–62; 66; Jer. 23:3–8; 32:37–44; Ezek. 40–48; Dan. 2:44–45; 7:13–14; 12:2–3; Mic. 4:1–8; Zech. 12:10–14:21). All of the prophets spoke of this kingdom, the minor prophets as well as the major prophets—not one of them missed it. These are but a few of the manifold Scriptures that speak of the theocratic kingdom which was the great theme of all the prophets in the Old Testament. This is the kingdom, the theocratic kingdom, that is coming here upon this earth.

SATAN BOUND ONE THOUSAND YEARS

The opening verses of chapter 20 describe what is to precede the Millennium.

And I saw an angel come down from heaven, having the key of the bottomless pit and a great chain in his hand.

And he laid hold on the dragon, that old serpent, which is the Devil, and Satan, and bound him a thousand years,

And cast him into the bottomless pit, and shut him up, and set a seal upon him, that he should deceive the nations no more, till the thousand years should be fulfilled: and after that he must be loosed a little season [Rev. 20:1–3].

Let me give you my translation of these verses:

And I saw an angel coming down out of the heaven, having the key of the abyss and a great chain in his hand. And he laid hold on the dragon, the old serpent who is the Devil and Satan, and bound him for a thousand years, and cast him into the abyss, and locked and sealed (it) over, that he should deceive the nations no longer, until the thousand years should be finished: after that he must be loosed for a little time.

You will notice that the thousand years are mentioned two times in verses 1–3; they are mentioned a total of six times in the twentieth chapter. It is true that the Millennium is mentioned only in one chapter, but God mentions it six times. How many times does He have to

say a thing before it becomes true? He mentions it more than He mentions some other things that people emphasize and think are important just because they occur once or twice in Scripture. Six times the thousand years are mentioned, and here it is in relationship to Satan.

There are some expositors who separate this section from the Millennium, classifying it as the closing scene of the Day of Wrath. This view takes the edge from the sharp distinction that there will be on earth at the removal of Satan. His incarceration and total absence from the earth change conditions from darkness to light. He is the god of this age; he is the prince of the power of the air, and his power and influence in the world are enormous—beyond the calculations of any computer. His withdrawal makes way for the Millennium, for with him loose, there can be no Millennium. Therefore, we see that Satan's relationship to the Millennium is this: he must be removed from the earth's scene before it can take place. Men talk about bringing peace on this earth, about producing prosperity, and all that sort of thing. The world system will finally be headed up in the Antichrist, and he will not be able to accomplish peace and prosperity, although for a while it will look as if he will. But as long as Satan is abroad in this world, you cannot have a Utopia down here. You cannot have an ideal situation with him loose.

"An angel. . . . laid hold on the dragon"— Satan's great power is reduced, for an ordinary angel becomes his jailor and leads him away captive (see Jude 9; Rev. 12:7–9).

"The abyss" is a better description of the prison than is "the bottomless pit." In either case, it is not the lake of fire, which we shall see in verse 10.

"After that he must be loosed for a little time" is one of the imponderable statements of Scripture. Why is Satan loosed after God once had him put in the abyss in chains? Dr. Lewis Sperry Chafer's answer to this question is significant: "If you will tell me why God let him loose in the first place, I'll tell you why God let him loose in the second place." Why did God let him loose? God has a great purpose in it. This is the great problem of evil: Why has God permitted it? Well, I believe that God is working out a tremendous program which is the mystery of God that is yet to be revealed to us. It is going to be revealed someday, and all He is asking us to do is to walk with Him by faith. We need to trust God and know that whatever He is doing is right.

I remember one time when my dad took me with him on a trip in his horse and buggy. A storm came up out there in west Texas and, being just a boy, I was frightened. The wind was blowing up a real storm, and we were getting wet. I never shall forget that my dad put his arm around me and said, "Son, you can trust me." I just snuggled right up to him and trusted him, and we got through the storm. My earthly father is gone—he died when I was fourteen. I didn't have my earthly father very long, but I have had a heavenly Father now for a great many years whom I trust through the storms of this life. In all these problems that come up, I wish I had the answers to give you, but I don't—so let's both trust Him.

I once read a book on the problem of evil. When I finished the book, we still had the problem of evil—the author did not solve it. It took him about two hundred pages to say what I can say in one sentence: I do not know the answer to the problem of evil. But, my friend, we will get the answer someday if we walk by faith.

God had Satan incarcerated for one thousand years because there could not be a Millennium without that.

SAINTS OF THE GREAT TRIBULATION REIGN WITH CHRIST ONE THOUSAND YEARS

And I saw thrones, and they sat upon them, and judgment was given unto them: and I saw the souls of them that were beheaded for the witness of Jesus, and for the word of God, and which had not worshipped the beast, neither his image, neither had received his mark upon their foreheads, or in their hands; and they lived and reigned with Christ a thousand years.

But the rest of the dead lived not again until the thousand years were finished. This is the first resurrection.

Blessed and holy is he that hath part in the first resurrection: on such the second death hath no power, but they shall be priests of God and of Christ, and shall reign with him a thousand years [Rev. 20:4–6].

And I saw thrones and they sat upon them, and judgment was given unto them; and (I saw) the souls of them that had been beheaded for the testimony of Jesus, and for the Word of God; and who-soever worshipped not the wild beast neither his image, and received not the mark upon their forehead, or upon their hand. And they lived again and reigned with Christ one thousand years. This is the first resurrection. Blessed and holy is he that hath part in the first resurrection; over these the second death hath no authority [Gr.: exousian], but they shall be priests of God and of the Christ, and shall reign with him a thousand years.

Many are going to die for Christ in the Great Tribulation Period, but they will live again and reign with Christ one thousand years. The tribulation saints are going to trade in three and one-half years for one thousand years. I would say they are getting a pretty good deal. Those three and one-half years will be rugged and terrible, but the thousand years are going to be wonderful—imagine living and reigning with Christ upon this earth!

This prophecy is like any other prophecy in Scripture: "Knowing this first, that no prophecy of the scripture is of any private interpretation" (2 Pet. 1:20). That is, you cannot just lift out a verse of Scripture and base doctrine on it; you need to have the corroboration of other Scriptures. When this passage here is treated as a dignified statement of literal facts, it becomes reasonable, and it fits into the entire program of prophecy which we have been following. Any attempt to reduce it to the lowest common denominator of fanciful and figurative symbols makes the passage an absurdity. To spiritualize this passage is to disembowel all Scripture of vital meaning, making the interpretation of Scripture a *reductio ad absurdum*.

The thrones are literal; the martyrs are literal; Jesus is literal; the Word of God is literal; the Beast is literal; the image is literal; the mark of the Beast is literal; their foreheads and their hands are literal; and the thousand years are literal. It is all literal. A thousand years means a thousand years. If God meant that it was eternal, I think He would have said so. If He meant it was five hundred years, He would have said so. Cannot God say what He means? Of course He can, and when He says a thousand years, He means a thousand years.

The Greek word for "resurrection" is *anastasei*, which means "to stand up, a bodily resurrection." It is rather difficult for a spirit to stand up, and those who spiritualize this section are at a loss to explain just how a spirit stands up! This is the same word used by Paul

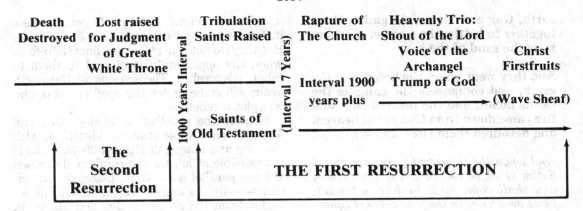

in 1 Corinthians 15 for the resurrection of Christ and believers.

"And I saw thrones and they sat upon them" is the one statement that is not entirely clear. Who are "they"? It is my judgment that they must be the total number of those who have part in the first resurrection, which includes the saved of all ages.

The first resurrection began with the resurrection of Christ. Then it is followed by the resurrection (at the Rapture) of His church sometime more than nineteen hundred years later—but before the Great Tribulation (see Rev. 4). At the end of the Great Tribulation is the resurrection of both the tribulation saints ("the souls of them that had been beheaded for the testimony of Jesus, and for the Word of God; and whosoever worshipped not the wild beast") and the Old Testament saints (see Dan. 12:1–2). The diagram above gives the resurrection as a parade. Christ, the firstfruits of resurrection, leads the parade.

It is a rather simple and naïve notion to think that somehow or another the world is going to end, Jesus will come, the dead will be raised, He will put the good guys on one side and the bad guys on the other, they will move into eternity, and that is it. My friend, God follows a very definite program; He always has, and He moves intelligently.

The tribulation saints and the Old Testament saints will evidently reign on this earth with Christ. I believe that David will be His vicegerent. The church, which is the bride of Christ, will reside in the New Jerusalem where she reigns with Him from that exalted place and, I believe, over a great deal of God's creation. Christ will commute from the New Jerusalem to the old Jerusalem on this earth. And I suppose that the church also will travel back and forth between its heavenly home and the earth.

Multitudes of both Israel and the Gentiles will enter the kingdom in natural bodies, not having died. These are the ones, together with those who are born during the Millennium, who are tested during this millennial period. As Christ in a glorified body mingled with His apostles and followers, so the church in glorified bodies will mingle with the multitudes in their natural bodies here on the earth. In glorified bodies, the church will be able to move out into space. That will be the first time I will do any space traveling, I can assure you of that. Gravitation will not be able to grab me by the seat of my pants and pull me back to the earth in that day.

"They shall be priests of God" refers to the entire nation of Israel. This was God's original purpose for Israel: "And ye shall be unto me a kingdom of priests, and an holy nation. These are the words which thou shalt speak unto the children of Israel" (Exod. 19:6). Abraham was a priest in his family. Levi was the priestly tribe, with the family of Aaron serving as high priest. In the theocratic kingdom here on this earth, the entire nation of Israel will be priests.

In Scripture there is more prophecy concerning the Millennium than of any other period. The kingdom was the theme of the Old Testament prophets. I do not know how else you would interpret it. In our day we hear very little about the minor prophets. There is a great silence, a great vacuum and void, when it comes to the teaching of the minor prophets, yet all of them look forward to the Millennium, that kingdom which is coming on the earth.

SATAN LOOSED AFTER ONE THOUSAND YEARS

And when the thousand years are expired, Satan shall be loosed out of his prison,

And shall go out to deceive the nations which are in the four quarters of the

earth, Gog and Magog, to gather them together to battle: the number of whom is as the sand of the sea.

And they went up on the breadth of the earth, and compassed the camp of the saints about, and the beloved city: and fire came down from God out of heaven, and devoured them [Rev. 20:7–9].

And when the thousand years are ended Satan shall be loosed out of his prison, and shall come forth to deceive the nations which are in the four corners (quarters) of the earth, Gog and Magog, to gather them together to the war; the number of whom is as the sand of the sea. And they went up over the breadth of the earth, and compassed the camp of the saints about, and the beloved city: and fire came down out of heaven, and devoured them.

Although the entire Book of Revelation deals with last things, especially do these last few chapters. Here is the last rebellion of Satan and man against God. The Millennium is a time of testing of man under ideal conditions, as this passage demonstrates. As soon as Satan is released, a great company, who have been under the personal reign of Christ under ideal circumstances, goes over to Satan. From where did such a company come is a worthy question. The answer lies in the fact that not only do multitudes enter the Millennium, but multitudes also are born during the Millennium (see Isa. 11:6; 65:20). This will be the time of the earth's greatest population explosion. Disease will be eliminated. Since the curse of sin will be removed from the physical earth, it will produce enough foodstuffs to feed its greatest population. The human heart alone remains unchanged under these circumstances, and many will turn their backs on God and will go after Satan. This seems unbelievable, but what about today? Satan is doing pretty well in our day.

This rebellion following the Millennium reveals how terrible the heart of man is. Jeremiah said, "The heart is deceitful above all things, and desperately wicked: who can know it?" (Jer. 17:9). You and I do not know how vile we really are. We just cannot bring our old nature into subjection to God. "Because the carnal mind is enmity against God: for it is not subject to the law of God, neither indeed can be" (Rom. 8:7). These folk will live under ideal conditions during Christ's thousand-year reign, and I think they will get a little tired of

it. When He reigns, He is really going to be a dictator—you had better stay in line or else. But they do not like staying in line; therefore, when the opportunity is offered to them to rebel, they rebel. The nations of the earth again will come under the spell of Satan and will plot a rebellion.

Because the rebellion is labeled "Gog and Magog," many Bible students identify it with the Gog and Magog of Ezekiel 38–39. This is not possible at all, for the conflicts described are not parallel as to time, place, or participants—only the names are the same. The invasion from the north by Gog and Magog in Ezekiel 38–39 breaks the false peace of the Antichrist and causes him to show his hand in the midst of the Great Tribulation. That rebellion of the godless forces from the north will have made such an impression on mankind that after one thousand years, that last rebellion of man bears the same label—Gog and Magog.

We have passed through a similar situation in this century. World War I was so devastating that when war again broke out in Europe, involving many of the same nations and even more, it was also labeled a World War, but it was differentiated by the number two. We have World War I, World War II, and people today are predicting World War III.

I can use a further illustration from my personal life. In my family there were so many Johns on both sides of the family that my mother decided I should be J. Vernon McGee. My "J" stands for John, but I have never been called John. An uncle, two grandfathers, and my dad were all named John. So you will understand why I bear the name of J. Vernon—I had to be separated from that crowd. Just because we had a similarity of names does not mean that we were all the same person.

The war in Ezekiel 38–39 relates to Gog and Magog I, and the reference here in Revelation 20:8 is to Gog and Magog II. Although the names are the same, this is a different war, the last rebellion of Satan. Just because the two events involve the same names does not mean they are the same.

In verse 9 there is the dropping of the last "atomic bomb." The phrase, "from God," is actually not in the best texts. It simply means that natural forces which destroyed Gog and Magog I will destroy Gog and Magog II.

This last resistance and rebellion against God was as foolish and futile as man's first rebellion in the Garden of Eden. Here it is not the beginning but the ending of man's disobedience to God. It is the finality of man's rebellion. Nothing remains now but the final judgment.

SATAN CAST INTO THE LAKE OF FIRE AND BRIMSTONE

And the devil that deceived them was cast into the lake of fire and brimstone, where the beast and the false prophet are, and shall be tormented day and night for ever and ever [Rev. 20:10].

And the devil that deceived them was cast into the lake of fire and brimstone, where are also the wild beast and the false prophet; and they shall be tormented day and night for ever and ever.

This is a most solemn statement, and it is rejected by this lovey-dovey age in which we live. However, it is a relief to God's child to know that the enemy—both his and God's—will at last be brought to permanent justice. There is nothing here to satisfy the curiosity or the sadistic taste. The fact is stated in a reverent reticence which is awe-inspiring. If man had written this, having said this much, he could not have restrained himself from saying more. In what Sir Robert Anderson calls "the wild utterances of prophecy mongers," we see that men do not hesitate to go farther than does the Word of God. The Word of God is very restrained—very little is said about this subject of hell, or even of heaven.

There are several facts here that contradict popular notions. First of all, the Devil is not in hell today. He is the prince of the power of the air. He is the one who controls this world to a large extent. God has limited him in our day, of course, but in the Great Tribulation Period, he will have full rein for a while.

In the second place, the Devil is not the first to be cast into hell. The wild Beast and the False Prophet will precede him by one thousand years.

Finally, hell is described as a lake of fire and brimstone. The Lord Jesus is the One who gave the most solemn description of hell. Consider these Scriptures: "Then shall he say also unto them on the left hand, Depart from me, ye cursed, into everlasting fire, prepared for the devil and his angels" (Matt. 25:41). "But the children of the kingdom shall be cast out into outer darkness: there shall be weeping and gnashing of teeth" (Matt. 8:12).

This ought to make anyone stop and think: How can hell be outer darkness and also a literal fire? Jesus Christ also said: "And shall cast them into a furnace of fire: there shall be wailing and gnashing of teeth" (Matt. 13:42). "Where their worm dieth not, and the fire is not quenched" (Mark 9:44). In my thinking, fire is the best symbol that could be used of the reality that hell is. For instance, how are sins that men have committed in the spirit to be punished in the body? I believe that to be in outer darkness and the abyss is to be separated from God and to look back upon a life which has been misspent in this world. Can you think of any fire that would be hotter than for a man in hell to hear the voice of his son saying, "Dad, I followed you down here"? This is a solemn thing. A man asked Dr. Bill Anderson, "Suppose we get over there and find out that what you preach about hell is not true at all?" Dr. Anderson replied, "Then I will just have to apologize and say that I must have misunderstood the Lord. But suppose we get over there and find that it is true? What then?" My friend, it *is* true; this is the Word of God that we are looking at. We love John 3:16, but what do we think about this?

Fire is a very weak symbol of the reality of what it means to be lost, to be separated from God for eternity. You cannot reduce these descriptions to something less than the reality, because a symbol is always a poor representative of the real thing. Nor can you dissolve this into the thin air of make-believe. The reality far exceeds the description, and human language is beggarly in trying to depict the awful reality. Hell is a place; it is also a state. It is a place of conscious torment. This is the language of the Word of God—you cannot escape it.

SETTING OF GREAT WHITE THRONE WHERE LOST ARE JUDGED

And I saw a great white throne, and him that sat on it, from whose face the earth and the heaven fled away; and there was found no place for them [Rev. 20:11].

The Great White Throne is what men mistakenly call the general judgment. It is general only in the sense that all the *lost* of all ages are raised to be judged here. All who are saved have been raised in the first resurrection. Even the tribulation saints had part in the first resurrection. This is the second resurrection in which the lost are raised to be given an equitable, fair, and just evaluation of their works in respect to their salvation.

A man on his deathbed said to me, "Preacher, you just don't need to talk to me about the future. I'll take my chances. I believe God is going to be just and righteous and let me present my works."

I told him, "You are right. He is just and righteous, and He will let you present your works. That is what He says He is going to do. But I have news for you: At that judgment nobody is saved, because you cannot be saved by your works. When you stand in the white light of the righteous presence of God, your little works will seem so puny that they won't amount to anything at all."

The other day our little grandson brought to his grandmother some flowers that he had picked. I want to tell you, they were a sad looking bunch of flowers. With great pride he gave them to his grandmother, and his grandmother patted him on the head and thanked him for the lovely flowers. As I looked at that scene, I could not help but smile, but I also immediately recognized how solemn it is going to be when a lot of these goody-goody boys stand with their little, bitty bouquets in the presence of a Christ whom they have rejected. They expect that He will be like a grandmother who will pat them on the head and say, "What a smart boy you were!" My friend, this is solemn, and this is serious. You need Him as Savior in order to stand in His presence; you need to be clothed with the righteousness of Christ. Don't you know that without this we are sinners and we are *lost?*

We like to compare ourselves with other people: "I'm as good as the Joneses down the street." Sure you are, but you ought to know about the Joneses! It was Samuel Johnson who said, "Every man knows that of himself which he dares not tell his dearest friend." You know yourself, don't you? You know things that you have covered up and smothered that you would not reveal for anything in the world. The Lord Jesus is going to bring them out at this judgment; while you are presenting your little bouquet, He is going to tell you about yourself. My friend, you need a Savior today.

This is the Great White Throne, and the holiness of this throne is revealed in the reaction of heaven and earth to it: "from whose face the earth and the heaven fled away." Of this, John F. Walvoord, in his book *The Revelation of Jesus Christ,* comments:

The most natural interpretation of the fact that earth and heaven flee away is that the present earth and heaven are destroyed and will be replaced by the new heaven and new earth. This is also confirmed by the additional statement in 21:1 where John sees a new heaven and a new earth replacing the first heaven and the first earth which have passed away.

The One seated on the throne is the Lord Jesus Christ: "For the Father judgeth no man, but hath committed all judgment unto the Son. . . . For as the Father hath life in himself; so hath he given to the Son to have life in himself; And hath given him authority to execute judgment also, because he is the Son of man. Marvel not at this: for the hour is coming, in the which all that are in the graves shall hear his voice, And shall come forth; they that have done good, unto the resurrection of life; and they that have done evil, unto the resurrection of damnation" (John 5:22, 26–29).

What is the work of God? It is to ". . . believe on him whom he hath sent" (John 6:29). Those who have done good are they who have accepted Christ, and they come forth unto the resurrection of life—that is the first resurrection. They who have done evil come forth unto the resurrection of damnation and condemnation—that is the Great White Throne judgment.

And I saw the dead, small and great, stand before God; and the books were opened: and another book was opened, which is the book of life: and the dead were judged out of those things which were written in the books, according to their works.

And the sea gave up the dead which were in it; and death and hell delivered up the dead which were in them: and they were judged every man according to their works [Rev. 20:12–13].

And I saw the dead, great and small, standing before the throne; and books were opened; and another book was opened, which is the book of life; and the dead were judged out of the things which were written in the books, according to their works. And the sea gave up the dead that were in it; and death and Hades gave up the dead that were in them; and they were judged every one according to their works.

Yes, my friend, you will be able to get a fair trial there. Your life is on tape, and Christ happens to have the tape. When He plays it back, you will be able to listen to it, and it is not going to sound good to you, by any means. Are you willing to stand before God and have Him play the tape of your life? I think He will have it on a television screen so that you can watch it, too. Do you think your life can stand the test? I do not know about you, but I could not make it. Thank God for His grace—"For by grace are ye saved through faith; and that not of yourselves: it is the gift of God" (Eph. 2:8).

The dead are classified as the small and the great. They are all lost, for evidently none have their names written in the Book of Life. They had never turned to God for salvation. The Lord Jesus said that in His generation ". . . ye will not come to me, that ye might have life" (John 5:40). These folk standing before His throne had not come.

These are books which record the works of all individuals. God keeps the tapes, and He will play them at the right time. There will be a lot of politicians who will have their tapes played in that day, and there will be a lot of public figures—even preachers—who will have their tapes played in that day, and they are not going to be happy about it. If you are saved, you are not going to stand before this judgment. Your works are to be judged as a child of God at the judgment seat of Christ, which will be for the purpose of rewards (see 2 Cor. 5:10). The Great White Throne judgment is the judgment of the lost. Multitudes want to be judged according to their works. This is their opportunity. The judgment is just, but no one is saved by works.

"And the sea gave up the dead that were in it." Multitudes who have gone to a watery grave in which the chemicals of their bodies have been dissolved in the waters of the sea will be raised. God will have no problem with this. After all, they are only atoms. He just has to put them together again. He did it once; He can do it again. The graves on earth will give up their bodies; and hades, the place where the spirits of the lost go, will disgorge for this judgment.

And death and hell were cast into the lake of fire. This is the second death.

And whosoever was not found written in the book of life was cast into the lake of fire [Rev. 20:14–15].

And death and Hades were cast into the lake of fire. This is the second death even the lake of fire. And if any were not found written in the book of life, he was cast into the lake of fire.

You will notice that in my translation I have changed "death and hell were cast into the lake of fire" to "death and *Hades* were cast into the lake of fire." *Sheol* or *hades* (translated *hell* in the New Testament) is the place of the unseen dead and is divided into two compartments: paradise and the place of torment (see Luke 16:19–31). Paradise was emptied when Christ took the Old Testament believers with Him at His ascension. "Wherefore he saith, When he ascended up on high, he led captivity captive, and gave gifts unto men. (Now that he ascended, what is it but that he also descended first into the lower parts of the earth? He that descended is the same also that ascended up far above all heavens, that he might fill all things)" (Eph. 4:8–10). Christ did two things: He gave gifts to men down here, but He also took with Him to heaven those Old Testament saints who had died and were in the place called paradise. But the place of torment will deliver up the lost at the judgment at the Great White Throne. All who stand at this judgment are lost, and we are told that they are cast into the lake of fire, which is the second death. The Lord also called it "outer darkness." We believe that this is symbolic of something worse than literal fire or outer darkness. It is eternal separation from God, for death means separation.

"Death," the great final enemy of man, is finally removed from the scene. No longer will it be said, "In Adam all die" (see 1 Cor. 15:22). Death is personified in this case, for it is man's great enemy. In the Old Testament we read: "I

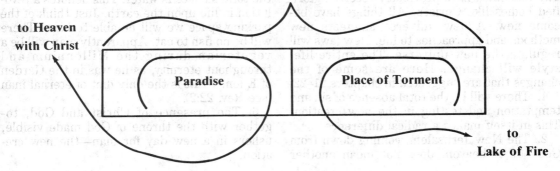

Sheol or *Hades* **(translated** *Hell* **in the New Testament)**

to Heaven with Christ

Paradise   Place of Torment

to Lake of Fire

will ransom them from the power of the grave; I will redeem them from death: O death, I will be thy plagues; O grave, I will be thy destruction: repentance shall be hid from mine eyes" (Hos. 13:14).

And Paul writes: "The last enemy that shall be destroyed is death. . . .O death, where is thy sting? O grave, where is thy victory?" (1 Cor. 15:26, 55).

"Hades," the prison of lost souls, is likewise cast into the lake of fire. The lost are no longer in hades but in the lake of fire. This is where Satan, the wild Beast, the False Prophet, and their minions were consigned. If man will not accept the life of God, he must accept the only other alternative: eternal association with Satan. God never created man to be put in this place, but there is no other place for him. Hell was created for the Devil and his angels. I take it that it is a place where God never goes. The second death means eternal and absolute separation from God.

CHAPTER 21

THEME: *Entrance into eternity; eternity unveiled*

Eternity is unveiled in chapter 21—a new heaven, a new earth, a New Jerusalem, a new era, and the eternal abode of the Lamb's bride where we will be new creations in Christ Jesus without the old nature that manifests itself so much today. Adopting a popular aphorism of the day, it can truly be said that this chapter is "out of this world." This chapter hasn't anything to do with the earth (except for the first few verses). In it we see the eternal abode of the church. What really is heaven? There is a lot of sticky, sentimental stuff said about heaven, and we get quite weepy when we talk about heaven. However, heaven is a place, a very definite place. You will have an address there. Your name will be put on you so that in eternity, when you wander around into outer space and get lost, some angel will bring you home—and you will have a home.

As the long vista of eternity is before us in this chapter, we move not only from time to eternity, but to a new creation. A new heaven, a new earth, and a New Jerusalem greet us. The redeemed have previously received glorified bodies like Christ's. All things have become new. A new universe suggests new methods and approaches to life. New laws will regulate the new universe. The entire lifestyle will change. Here are some of the changes that are suggested in chapters 21–22:

1. There will be the total absence of sin and temptation and testing in the new creation. This in itself makes a radical difference.

2. The New Jerusalem, coming down from God out of heaven, does not mean another satellite for the earth, but rather the earth and all of the new creation with all of the galactic systems will revolve about the New Jerusalem, because it is the dwelling place of God and of Christ.

3. The law of gravity, as we know it, will be radically revised. There will be traffic between the New Jerusalem and the earth. The church will have already left the earth, and its dwelling place is the New Jerusalem. I believe that we will have entirely different bodies, and the law of gravity will not affect us; that is, the law of gravity of this earth or of any other planet.

4. There will be no sun to give light, for God Himself will supply it directly to the universe. There will be the absence, therefore, of night. There is no night there because we just do not need that time to rest since we will have new bodies. I am looking forward to that, by the way.

5. There will no longer be any sea on the earth. The sea occupies most of the earth's surface today; approximately three-fourths of the total surface is water. This denotes a revolution in life upon the earth. Just think of the parking space we will be able to have! There will be no fish to eat. Apparently man will be a vegetarian during the Millennium and throughout eternity, as he was in the Garden of Eden. Fruit is the only diet of eternal man (see Rev. 22:2).

6. The presence of Christ and God, together with the throne of God made visible, ushers in a new day for man—the new creation.

NEW HEAVEN, NEW EARTH,
NEW JERUSALEM

John describes the passing of the heaven and earth we know in the opening verse of chapter 21.

And I saw a new heaven and a new earth: for the first heaven and the first earth were passed away; and there was no more sea [Rev. 21:1].

As usual, I'll follow the Authorized Version with my own literal translation of the Greek text.

And I saw a new heaven and a new earth: for the first heaven and the first earth passed away: and the sea is no more.

"And I saw" is the oft repeated statement of John to remind us that he was a spectator to all of these scenes. He was a witness to the panoramic final scene which ushers in eternity.

The Scripture clearly teaches that this present order of creation is to pass away in order to make room for a new heaven and a new earth. The Lord Jesus Christ Himself said, "Heaven and earth shall pass away . . ." (Matt. 24:35). The old creation was made for the first Adam. Christ, the Last Adam, has a new creation for His new creatures. "For, behold, I create new heavens and a new earth: and the former shall not be remembered, nor come into mind" (Isa. 65:17). "For as the new heavens and the new earth, which I will make, shall remain before me, saith the LORD, so shall your seed and your name remain" (Isa. 66:22).

God had promised Abraham a land forever and David a throne forever. Daniel prophesied of ". . . a kingdom, which shall never be destroyed . . ." (Dan. 2:44). The new earth will see the total fulfillment of these prophecies. Consider the faith of the Old Testament worthies: "These all died in faith, not having received the promises, but having seen them afar off, and were persuaded of them, and embraced them, and confessed that they were strangers and pilgrims on the earth. For they that say such things declare plainly that they seek a country. And truly, if they had been mindful of that country from whence they came out, they might have had opportunity to have returned. But now they desire a better country, that is, an heavenly: wherefore God is not ashamed to be called their God: for he hath prepared for them a city" (Heb. 11:13–16). "Heavenly" does not mean they are going to heaven, but that heaven is coming to this earth. This is what we mean when we pray the so-called Lord's Prayer, "Thy kingdom come . . . in earth, as it is in heaven" (Matt. 6:10).

"Nevertheless we, according to his promise, look for new heavens and a new earth, wherein dwelleth righteousness" (2 Pet. 3:13). In his second epistle Peter declares plainly that the present earth on which we live will be destroyed by fire: "But the heavens and the earth, which are now, by the same word are kept in store, reserved unto fire against the day of judgment and perdition of ungodly men. . . . But the day of the Lord will come as a thief in the night; in the which the heavens shall pass away with a great noise, and the elements shall melt with fervent heat, the earth also and the works that are therein shall be burned up. Seeing then that all these things shall be dissolved, what manner of persons ought ye to be in all holy conversation and godliness" (2 Pet. 3:7, 10–11).

The chief characteristic of the new earth, as we have suggested, is the absence of the sea. This would automatically change the climate, the atmosphere, and the living conditions. It is impossible for the human mind to comprehend the great transformations which will take place in a new creation. The sea in the past has been a barrier and also a border for mankind, which in some cases has been good and in others bad. Also, the sea was an instrument of judgment at the time of the Flood. However, by the disappearance of the sea, the population on the earth can be doubled again and again because of the increase of the land surface.

And I John saw the holy city, new Jerusalem, coming down from God out of heaven, prepared as a bride adorned for her husband [Rev. 21:2].

And I saw the holy city, new Jerusalem, coming down out of heaven from God, made ready as a bride adorned for her husband.

This is the part which should interest us. I believe that the New Jerusalem is where those of us who are children of God are going to live. When you talk about going to heaven, what do you think about it? To most people it is just "a beautiful isle of somewhere." However, it is a definite place. It is a city called the New Jerusalem. It is a planet within itself. Very candidly, very little is said in Scripture about heaven—but here it is, and that is the reason this ought to be important to us.

"I saw the holy city, new Jerusalem, coming

down out of heaven from God, made ready as a bride adorned for her husband." This New Jerusalem should not be identified with the old Jerusalem, the earthly Jerusalem down here.

I cannot think of a lovelier description than this: "made ready as a bride adorned for her husband." It has been my privilege in my many years in the pastorate to have married several hundred couples. I have *never* seen an ugly bride—they are always lovely. At the wedding ceremony, after the solos have been sung, the preacher walks in followed by the bridegroom and the best man. Nobody pays any attention to the bridegroom except his mama. She smiles at him and thinks he's wonderful, but nobody else looks at him. In a minute here comes the bride-to-be and, I tell you, everybody stands up and looks at her. I have never yet seen an ugly bride. On occasion when I would return from a wedding which my wife did not attend, she would always ask me, "Was the bride beautiful?" And I would always answer, "Yes. I've never seen an ugly one." Don't think I am just a doting old man when I say that. I have seen some brides *before* they got married or *after* the wedding, and I have wondered if she were the same girl who had come down the aisle. God gives to them at that time a radiance and a beauty. That is a thrilling moment for the bridegroom to look down the aisle and see the one whom he is going to make his own—she will belong to him. It seems that for that moment God transforms every girl into a lovely bride. I think the reason He does it is that the New Jerusalem where we are going to live is like the bride adorned for her husband. What a picture we have here!

The New Jerusalem is the habitation, the eternal home that is prepared for the church. The Lord Jesus said: "I go to prepare a place for you. And if I go and prepare a place for you, I will come again, and receive you unto myself; that where I am, there ye may be also" (John 14:2–3). You could not have a more lovely or more appropriate picture given. We have seen in Revelation 19:7–8 that ushering in the millennial period, actually before Christ returned to the earth, was the marriage of the Lamb, and the bride was the church.

This passage is the fulfillment of what Paul wrote to the Ephesians: "Husbands, love your wives, even as Christ also loved the church, and gave himself for it; That he might sanctify and cleanse it with the washing of water by the word" (Eph. 5:25–26).

At the judgment seat of Christ, there will be the straightening out and the judging of believers. Everything that is wrong will have to be corrected. All sin will be dealt with there. Rewards will be given out. And He is going to do something else—He is going to cleanse the church with the Word. The Word of God is a mighty cleansing agent. "That he might present it to himself a glorious church, not having spot, or wrinkle, or any such thing; but that it should be holy and without blemish" (Eph. 5:27).

This is the picture we are getting here in chapter 21. The holy city, the New Jerusalem, is coming down from God out of heaven, adorned as a bride for her husband. The marriage took place before the Millennium, and the Millennium is now over. This has sure been a long honeymoon, hasn't it? I think it is one that will go on into eternity.

Paul continues to talk about this marvelous relationship between Christ and the church, comparing it to human marriage down here. "So ought men to love their wives as their own bodies. He that loveth his wife loveth himself. For no man ever yet hated his own flesh; but nourisheth and cherisheth it, even as the Lord the church: For we are members of his body, of his flesh, and of his bones. For this cause shall a man leave his father and mother, and shall be joined unto his wife, and they two shall be one flesh. This is a great mystery: but I speak concerning Christ and the church" (Eph. 5:28–32). This idea is a mystery that is now being opened to us. The marriage relationship is the most beautiful and wonderful relationship. It is the oldest ceremony that God has instituted for man. It goes right back into the Garden of Eden, to the very beginning, and it is all-important. It is such a profound mystery that, even with all these marriage counselors and all the books they have written, I do not really think they have touched the fringe of how wonderful marriage *could be* for believers.

By the way, Paul is talking here to believers who are filled with the Spirit. All of these instructions are for Spirit-filled believers. They are not given to the lost world at all, and they are not given to the average believer. At the beginning of this section, Paul says, ". . . be filled with the [Holy] Spirit" (Eph. 5:18). That is the only commandment in Scripture in which you are required to do something about the Holy Spirit.

We find here something that is difficult to understand, but it gives us another insight into marriage. The wife is the same flesh as the man. How can that be? Have you ever seen a beautiful child that looked like the mother and had a mean disposition like the father? That is where they come together; that is where they are one flesh. But it is deeper than that. When a man loves his wife, he actually loves himself. This is true of the wife also. When she loves her husband, she is actually loving herself. You cannot have it any more intimate than that.

When I injure my foot, I do not ignore it. I do all I can to care for it. I go to the doctor and if necessary have it put into a cast. It may not be very pretty, and I might like to leave my foot at home, but it is part of me. Likewise, my wife is part of me. She is my flesh. We are the same flesh. This is difficult to understand, but that is how intimate it is. This takes us back to the time of creation: "And Adam said, This is now bone of my bones, and flesh of my flesh: she shall be called Woman, because she was taken out of Man. Therefore shall a man leave his father and his mother, and shall cleave unto his wife: and they shall be one flesh. And they were both naked, the man and his wife, and were not ashamed" (Gen. 2:23–25). They were naked, and they knew each other. It was an *intimate* and a *very personal* relationship. After a couple gets married, when they have their first fight, the wife often turns over in bed, and he is in a huff and maybe goes to the sofa and lies there. Then they wonder why there is disintegration in their marriage relationship. When your foot gets sick, you don't ignore it. You don't get angry with it. You don't kick with it. If you do, you are in deeper trouble. The thing that you are to do with the flesh is to do everything to doctor it and try to get it well again. This is the reason that young couples ought never to have a squabble without sitting down and talking things over. I think the wife ought to be very frank with her husband and tell him everything—how she feels, how he offends her, and what she thinks is wrong. And he ought to do the same thing. You see, they are the same flesh; they are one. They have been brought together in this very intimate, this very wonderful relationship in which a man leaves his family—his father, his mother, and his brothers and sisters. He has now been joined to a woman, and they are one flesh. They have started a new creation, if you please, and that is what the marriage relation should be. How wonderful it is to see a family where the man and his wife have no barrier between them. She knows him like a book, and he knows her like a book. They simply know each other, and they love each other. Until that kind of rela-

tionship is established, my friend, you are going to have trouble in the marriage, because God made us that way. Marriage is more than an arrangement to live together and to sleep together. When a man chooses a wife and a wife accepts her husband, they must understand that they are one flesh—and you would not hurt yourself, your own flesh, intentionally for anything in the world.

"This is a great mystery," Paul says, ". . . but I speak concerning Christ and the church" (Eph. 5:32). In heaven we are going to be like Him. John writes, ". . . it doth not yet appear what we shall be: but we know that, when he shall appear, we shall be like him . . ." (1 John 3:2). We are going to have glorified flesh like He has. We are going to be one with Him. We are part of His body, and we are going to be joined to Him. He said, ". . . I go to prepare a place for you. . . . that where I am, there ye may be also" (John 14:2–3). How glorious that we can be with Him throughout eternity! As far as I know, no other creatures, including the angels of heaven, are going to have this personal and intimate relationship with the Lord Jesus Christ. That is going to be the most glorious day! We are going to celebrate throughout eternity the very fact that we are *with* Him and that we have been joined to Him.

NEW ERA

And I heard a great voice out of heaven saying, Behold, the tabernacle of God is with men, and he will dwell with them, and they shall be his people, and God himself shall be with them, and be their God.

And God shall wipe away all tears from their eyes; and there shall be no more death, neither sorrow, nor crying, neither shall there be any more pain: for the former things are passed away [Rev. 21:3–4].

And I heard a great voice out of the throne saying, Behold the tabernacle [Gr.: skene, tent] of God (is) with men, and He shall tabernacle with them, and they shall be His peoples, and God Himself shall be with them, and be their God; and God shall wipe away every tear from their eyes; and death shall be no more, neither shall there be mourning, nor crying nor pain, any more; the first things are passed away.

"**B**ehold the tabernacle [tent] of God is with men." What is the tent? We are told by John in John 1:14, "And the Word was made flesh, and dwelt [pitched His tent] among us. . . ." That flesh was crucified on the cross, and He was raised in a glorified body. We, too, are going to have glorified bodies, and we are going to live with Him in the New Jerusalem. The golden street is not really important. What difference does it make what kind of asphalt you walk on? It *is* important to know the psychological and spiritual values that will be there.

"They shall be His peoples, and God Himself shall be with them, and be their God." Certain things that definitely are prominent today are going to be removed: "God shall wipe away every tear from their eyes." A columnist years ago wrote: "For every light that burns on Broadway, there is a broken heart." Several times my wife and I have driven up into the Hollywood hills and have looked down on that blanket of light which is Hollywood. I have said to my wife, "For every light down there, there is a broken heart." There is many a sad and lonely person in this world, but in the New Jerusalem there are not going to be any more tears.

"And death shall be no more"—that is going to be a very marvelous improvement. Since you began reading this chapter, a number of funeral processions have taken place. People are dying all the time. There is a continual march to the cemetery. This earth is nothing in the world but a cemetery. I once knew an engineer who in the early days had a great deal to do with the planning and plotting of the great freeways which crisscross this country today. I asked him, "Is it going over the mountains or down through the valleys or crossing the rivers that is the biggest problem for you?" He replied, "The big problem is missing the cemeteries." This earth is a great cemetery today, but all of that is going to end. There will be no burying ground in the New Jerusalem. The undertaker will be out of business. Even the doctors are going to be out of business, because there is not going to be any crying, "neither shall there be any more pain: for the former things are passed away."

And he that sat upon the throne said, Behold, I make all things new. And he said unto me, Write: for these words are true and faithful [Rev. 21:5].

And He that sitteth on the throne said, Behold, I make all things new. And He

saith, Write, for these words are faithful and true.

He is going to make all things new! This is more meaningful to me than anything else. I do not know about you, but I have never really been satisfied with this life. I have found myself frustrated, I have found myself hemmed in, and I have never been able to accomplish all that I have wanted to accomplish. I've never been the man I've wanted to be. I've never been the husband I've wanted to be. I've never been the father I've wanted to be. And I've never preached the sermon I've wanted to preach. I just do not seem to have arrived. All accomplishments seem to have a blot on them.

But He says to me, as He says to you, "I am going to make all things new. You are going to be able to start over again." I am waiting for that day when all things are going to be new and I can start over. Have you ever stopped to think about the potential of starting out all new again, of learning all over again, and never ceasing but going on into eternity? Oh, the potential and capability of man! Yonder at the Tower of Babel, God said, "I had better go down there, or nothing will be withheld from man" (see Gen. 11:5–7). It was very foolish for some scientists and preachers to say that man could not go to the moon; I think he is going farther than that. Man is a clever being which God has made. Death ends his potential down here, but with eternity ahead of him, oh, the prospects a saved man has!

We see here the glorious prospect of all things made new. We can start over, and there will never be an end to our growth. Remember that of Christ it is said, "Of the increase of His government and peace there shall be no end" (see Isa. 9:7). There is constant growth and development. Just think of the prospect of that for the future. Someday I am going to know something; today I don't, but I will then.

And he said unto me, It is done. I am Alpha and Omega, the beginning and the end. I will give unto him that is athirst of the fountain of the water of life freely.

He that overcometh shall inherit all things; and I will be his God, and he shall be my son [Rev. 21:6–7].

And He said unto me, They are come to pass. I am the Alpha and the Omega, the beginning and the end. I will give unto him that is athirst of the fountain of the water of life freely. He that overcometh

*shall inherit these things; and I will be
God unto him, and he shall be the son to
Me.*

"I am the Alpha and the Omega, the beginning and the end." This identifies the speaker
as the Lord Jesus Christ, as He was identified
like this in the first chapter of this book.

Believers in their new bodies will thirst
after God and the things of God, and they will
be satisfied: "I will give unto him that is
athirst of the fountain of the water of life
freely." In Matthew 5:6 the Lord Jesus said:
"Blessed are they which do hunger and thirst
after righteousness: for they shall be filled."

All believers are overcomers because of
faith: "He that overcometh shall inherit these
things." "For whatsoever is born of God overcometh the world: and this is the victory that
overcometh the world, even our faith" (1 John
5:4).

"I will be God unto him, and he shall be the
son to Me." All the sons of God became sons
through faith in Christ: "But as many as received him, to them gave he power to become
the sons of God, even to them that believe on
his name" (John 1:12).

They "inherit all things" because this was
promised to the sons of God: "The Spirit itself
beareth witness with our spirit, that we are
the children of God: And if children, then
heirs; heirs of God, and joint-heirs with
Christ; if so be that we suffer with him, that
we may be also glorified together" (Rom.
8:16–17).

"The son to Me" is in the Greek *moi ho
huios.* This is a very unusual expression. Vincent calls attention to the fact that this is the
only place in John's writings where a believer
is said to be a son *(huios)* in relationship with
God. (In other passages another Greek word
is used rather than *huios.*) God is the One who
says "my son," and He says it here. Believers
in the church are one of the peoples of God,
but they are more. They are the sons of God in
a unique and glorious fashion. "Beloved, now
are we the sons of God, and it doth not yet
appear what we shall be: but we know that,
when he shall appear, we shall be like him; for
we shall see him as he is" (1 John 3:2).

**But the fearful, and unbelieving, and
the abominable, and murderers, and
whoremongers, and sorcerers, and idolaters, and all liars, shall have their part
in the lake which burneth with fire and
brimstone: which is the second death
[Rev. 21:8].**

*But for the fearful, and unbelieving, and
defiled with abominations, and murderers, and fornicators, and sorcerers,
and idolaters, and all liars, their part
(shall be) in the lake that burneth with
fire and brimstone: which is the second
death.*

There are several amazing features about this
verse. First of all, the creation of the new
heavens and a new earth did not affect the
status of the lake of fire and of the lost. They
are going into eternity just that way.

In the second place, there is no possibility of
sin, which made man become fearful, unbelieving, liars, murderers, and all the rest,
ever breaking over the barriers into the new
heavens and the new earth. Sin and its potential are forever shut out of the new creation.

Finally, the lake of fire is eternal, for it is
the second death, and there is no third resurrection. It is eternal separation from God, and
there is nothing as fearful and frightful as
that.

NEW JERUSALEM, DESCRIPTION OF
THE ETERNAL ABODE OF THE BRIDE

The appearance of this city is the quintes-
sence of beauty, refined loveliness, and uncontrolled joy. Lofty language describes her
merits, and descriptive vocabulary is exhausted in painting her portrait. The contemplation of her coming glory is a spiritual
tonic for those who grow weary on the pilgrim
journey down here.

The New Jerusalem is really a postmillen-
nial city, for she does not come into view until
the end of the Millennium and the beginning of
eternity. This city was evidently in the mind of
Christ when He said, "I go to prepare a place
for you" (see John 14:2), but the curtain does
not rise upon the scene of the heavenly city
until earth's drama has reached a satisfactory
conclusion. Earth's sorrow is not hushed until
the endless ages begin.

The New Jerusalem will be to eternity what
the earthly Jerusalem is to the Millennium.
The earthly Jerusalem does not pass away, but
it takes second place in eternity. Righteousness *reigns* in Jerusalem; it will *dwell* in the
New Jerusalem. Imperfection and rebellion
exist even in the earthly Jerusalem during the
Millennium; perfection and the absence of sin
will identify the heavenly city. Just as a king's
queen is of more importance than the place of
his government, thus the New Jerusalem
transcends the city of earth. This will cast no
reflection on the earthly city, nor will it cause

her inward pain. She can say in the spirit of John the Baptist, "She that hath the bridegroom is the bride" (see John 3:29).

The New Jerusalem is the eternal abode of the church. The New Jerusalem is the home of the church, the hometown of the church. This is a city toward which the church is journeying as she pitches her tent in that direction. We are now to look at this new home by reading the architect's blueprint in this twenty-first chapter.

And there came unto me one of the seven angels which had the seven vials full of the seven last plagues, and talked with me, saying, Come hither, I will shew thee the bride, the Lamb's wife [Rev. 21:9].

And there came one of the seven angels who had the seven bowls, who were laden with the seven last plagues; and he spoke with me, saying, Come hither, I will show thee the bride, the wife of the Lamb.

What follows in verses 9–21 is a description of the city. We have seen the psychological or spiritual aspects of it that are wonderful, but this physical description is also worth contemplating.

We must pause here to consider the relationship of the city to the citizens—the city proper to the church. Certainly we are not to infer that the empty city without the citizens is the bride. The citizens are identified with the city in chapter 22, verses 3, 6, 19. Those outside are identified here in verse 8 as disfranchised. Although a distinction between the bride and the city needs to be maintained, it is the intent of the writer to consider them together.

This passage is a description of the adornments which reveal something of the love and worth that the Bridegroom has conferred upon His bride.

And he carried me away in the spirit to a great and high mountain, and shewed me that great city, the holy Jerusalem, descending out of heaven from God [Rev. 21:10].

And he carried me away in the Spirit to a mountain great and high, and showed me the holy city Jerusalem, coming down out of heaven from God.

Certainly this city has no counterpart among earth's cities which are built upon an earthly foundation and are built *up* from that base. This city comes *down* out of heaven. She origi-

nates in heaven, and the Lord Jesus is the builder. Although the city comes down out of heaven, there is no suggestion that she comes down to the earth. The earthly city never goes to heaven, and the heavenly city never comes to earth. Just how far down the city descends is a matter of speculation.

This has led to extreme views in interpreting the New Jerusalem. At the very beginning, Ebionism, one of the first heresies, went to the extreme of applying this whole passage concerning the New Jerusalem to the earthly Jerusalem. The Gnostics, another early heresy, went to the other extremity in spiritualizing the passage to make it refer to heaven. Many modern "isms" apply the New Jerusalem to themselves and set it up on earth at the geographical location of their choice. Liberal theologians and amillennarians have left the city in heaven, in spite of the scriptural statement that it comes down "out of heaven." Two facts are evident from this passage: (1) It comes down out of heaven, and (2) it is not stated that it comes to the earth. This passage of Scripture leaves the city hanging in midair. This is the dilemma that many seek to avoid, but why not leave the city in midair? Is anything incongruous about a civilization out yonder in space on a new planet? The New Jerusalem will either become another satellite to the earth or, what is more probable and what I think is true, the earth will become a satellite to the New Jerusalem as well as the rest of the new creation. This chapter indicates that the city will be the center of all things. All activity and glory will revolve about this city. God will be there, it will be His headquarters, and His universe is theocentric (God-centered). The New Jerusalem is therefore worthy to merit such a preeminent position for eternity.

Having the glory of God: and her light was like unto a stone most precious, even like a jasper stone, clear as crystal [Rev. 21:11].

Having the glory of God: her light was like unto a stone most precious, as it were a jasper stone, shining like crystal.

Paul instructs the believers to ". . . rejoice in hope of the glory of God" (Rom. 5:2). This hope will be realized in the holy city. Man in sin has never witnessed the revelation of the glory of God. The experience of Israel in the wilderness taught them that each time there was a rebellion in the camp, the glory of God appeared in judgment. The manifestation of

God's glory strikes terror to a sinful heart, but what glorious anticipation to be able to behold His glory when standing clothed in the righteousness of Christ!

Two wonderful facts make this city the manifestation of the fullness of God's glory. (1) The presence of God makes the city the source of glory for the universe. Every blessing radiates from the city. (2) The presence of the saints does not forbid the manifestation of the glory of God. Sin caused God to remove His glory from man's presence, but in this city all that is past. Redeemed man dwelling with God in a city "having the glory of God" is the grand goal which is worthy of God. This city reveals the high purpose of God in the church, which is to bring "many sons unto glory" (see Heb. 2:10).

The word translated "light" *(phoster)* is the Greek word for source of light. The city is a light giver. It does not reflect light as does the moon, nor does it generate light by physical combustion like the sun, but it originates light and is the source of light. The presence of God and Christ gives explanation to this, as He declared, ". . . I am the light of the world" (John 9:5). God is light.

The whole city is like a precious gem. This gem is likened unto a jasper stone. The modern jasper is a multicolored quartz stone. The stone referred to here cannot be that, for this stone is not opaque. "Jasper" is a transliteration of the word *iaspis*, which is of Semitic origin. Moffatt suggests that *iaspis* could mean the modern opal, diamond, or topaz.

The stone is transparent and gleaming, which suggests one of these stones, most likely the diamond. The diamond seems to fit the description better than any other stone known to man. The similarity of the Hebrew word for crystal in Ezekiel 1:22 to the Hebrew word for "ice" helps to strengthen this view. The New Jerusalem is a diamond in a gold mounting. This city is the engagement ring of the bride; in fact, it is the wedding ring. It is the symbol of the betrothal and wedding of the church to Christ.

THE GATES OF THE CITY

And had a wall great and high, and had twelve gates, and at the gates twelve angels, and names written thereon, which are the names of the twelve tribes of the children of Israel:

On the east three gates; on the north three gates; on the south three gates;

and on the west three gates [Rev. 21:12–13].

Having a wall great and high; having twelve (large) gates, and at the gates twelve angels; and names written thereon, which are the names of the twelve tribes of the children of Israel: on the east (day spring) were three gates; and on the north three gates; and on the south three gates; and on the west three gates.

There are twelve gates to the city, three gates on each side. On each gate is the name of one of the tribes of Israel. This is very striking and suggests immediately the order in which the children of Israel camped about the tabernacle in the wilderness wanderings. The tribe of Levi was the priesthood and served in the tabernacle proper. The New Jerusalem is a temple or tabernacle in one sense, for God is there dwelling with man. The bride constitutes the priesthood who serve Him constantly. They serve as such in the city and dwell there as Levi did about the tabernacle.

Everything in eternity will face in toward this city, for God is there. The children of Israel on earth will enjoy the same relationship to the city that they did toward the wilderness tabernacle and later the city temple. This city will be a tabernacle to Israel. The children of Israel will be among the multitudes who come into this city to worship in eternity. They will come from the earth to bring their worship and glory. They will not dwell in the city anymore than they dwelt in the tabernacle of old. Those who actually dwell there will be the priests, who are the bride. The bride occupies the closer place to God in eternity, and the bride, like John in the Upper Room, reclines upon His breast. "Who is this that cometh up from the wilderness, leaning upon her beloved? . . ." (Song 8:5). She is the bride, and she has come up from the wilderness which is this present world. But the twelve tribes of Israel will come up to the celestial city to worship, three tribes coming up on each of the four sides. They will then return back to the earth after a period of worship, but the bride will dwell in the New Jerusalem.

THE FOUNDATIONS OF THE CITY

And the wall of the city had twelve foundations, and in them the names of the twelve apostles of the Lamb [Rev. 21:14].

This city has twelve foundations, and the names of the twelve apostles are upon them. The church today is ". . . built upon the foundation of the apostles and prophets, Jesus Christ himself being the chief corner stone" (Eph. 2:20). When Christ returned to heaven, He committed the keys into the keeping of the apostles. On the human level, the church was in the hands of these twelve men. The Book of Acts gives the order: "The former treatise have I made, O Theophilus, of all that Jesus began both to do and teach, Until the day in which he was taken up, after that he through the Holy Ghost had given commandments unto the apostles whom he had chosen" (Acts 1:1–2). I do not believe that Matthias is the apostle who succeeded Judas. I personally believe it was Paul. Simon Peter held that meeting to elect Matthias before the Holy Spirit came, and I do not think he was in the will of God when he did so. You never hear Matthias mentioned again, but you surely hear of Paul the apostle, and I think he is the one whom God chose to succeed Judas, making Paul the twelfth apostle.

To these twelve apostles were committed all the writings of the church. These men preached the first sermons, they organized the first churches, and they were among the first martyrs. It is not honoring to Scripture to attempt to minimize the importance of the twelve apostles. In a real sense they were the foundation of the church. To them the church shall eternally be grateful. This is not to rob Christ of His place, for He is "the chief corner stone," but the church is built upon the foundation which the apostles laid.

THE SIZE AND SHAPE OF THE CITY

And he that talked with me had a golden reed to measure the city, and the gates thereof, and the wall thereof.

And the city lieth foursquare, and the length is as large as the breadth: and he measured the city with the reed, twelve thousand furlongs. The length and the breadth and the height of it are equal [Rev. 21:15–16].

The shape of this city is really difficult to describe, due largely to our inability to translate our concepts from a universe of time to the new creation of eternity. The measurements of the city have given rise to all sorts of conceptions as to the size and shape of the city. First of all, let us examine the size of the city. Twelve thousand furlongs is given as the mea-

surement of each side and the height of it. It is twelve thousand *stadia* in the text, which means about fifteen hundred miles. This figure is corroborated by Dr. Seiss, Dr. Walter Scott, and others. The amplitude of the city is astounding when first considered but is commensurate with the importance of the city. Certainly God as Creator can never be accused of stinting, economizing, or doing things that reveal littleness. When you go down to the beach, you notice that He has put plenty of sand there and plenty of water in the ocean. He has made many mountains and He has put rocks everywhere. With a lavish hand, He has garnished the heavens with stellar bodies. When He does something, He certainly does it in abundance. This city bears the trademark of its Maker. The Lord Jesus, the Carpenter of Nazareth, is the One who built this city.

Now consider with me the shape of the city. "The city lieth foursquare" is the simple declaration of Scripture. That would seem to indicate that the city is a cube with fifteen hundred miles on a side. Dr. Seiss sees it as a cube. Dr. Harry Ironside sees it as a pyramid. Still others interpret these measurements in as many geometric figures as can be conceived. However, it is difficult for us to conceive of either a cube or a pyramid projected out in space. We are accustomed to thinking of a sphere (that is a ball-shaped object) hanging in space, because that is the general shape of the heavenly bodies. As far as we know, there are none out there that are square like a cube or like a pyramid. Cubes and pyramids are appropriate for earth's buildings, but they are as impractical for space as spheres are impractical for earthly buildings. Yet it is definitely stated that the city is foursquare.

The difficulty resolves when we think of the city as a cube within a crystal-clear sphere. What we are given are the *inside* measurements. I think of it as a big plastic ball with a cube inside, having all eight of its corners touching the sphere. As this involves mathematics, which I could not figure out, I asked both a mathematician and an engineer involved in the space program to determine what the circumference of the sphere would be. They both came up with the same answer. To enclose a cube measuring 1,500 miles on each side, the circumference of the sphere would be about 8,164 miles. The diameter of the moon is about 2,160 miles, and that of the New Jerusalem sphere is about 2,600 miles. Thus, the New Jerusalem will be somewhat larger than the moon, and it will be a sphere like the other heavenly bodies. I personally believe that this is the picture that is given to us here.

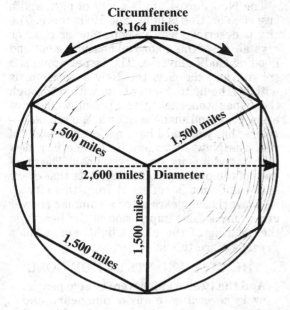

Circumference
8,164 miles

1,500 miles

1,500 miles

2,600 miles Diameter

1,500 miles

1,500 miles

My thinking is that we will live *inside* this sphere, not on the outside. Here on earth, we live on the outside, and that presents a few difficulties. The Lord had to make the law of gravity to hold us on the earth, or we would be flying out into space. We walk on the outside here, but I think that we will walk on the inside of the New Jerusalem.

THE WALL OF THE CITY

And he measured the wall thereof, an hundred and forty and four cubits, according to the measure of a man, that is, of the angel.

And the building of the wall of it was of jasper: and the city was pure gold, like unto clear glass [Rev. 21:17–18].

The wall of the city is for protection. A walled city is a safe city. The New Jerusalem is safe, and those who dwell therein dwell in safety. The heavenly Salem will enjoy the fruits of safety and peace. Made up of those who found peace with God on earth, she will experience the fullness of peace throughout eternity. The walls are a sign that this city has achieved the full meaning of her name—peace.

The walls are 144 cubits in height or about 216 feet. Herodotus gives the estimation for the walls of ancient Babylon as 50 cubits thick and 200 cubits high. Those walls were built to make the city impregnable. The great height of the walls of the New Jerusalem are but commensurate with the great size of the city.

Beauty, rather than protection, is the motive in design. It is a wall with jasper built into it and is generally designated as a jasper wall. The hardest of substances and the most beautiful gem constitute the exterior of the city.

THE STONES OF FIRE
IN THE FOUNDATION

And the foundations of the wall of the city were garnished with all manner of precious stones. The first foundation was jasper; the second, sapphire; the third, a chalcedony; the fourth, an emerald;

The fifth, sardonyx; the sixth, sardius; the seventh, chrysolyte; the eighth, beryl; the ninth, a topaz; the tenth, a chrysoprasus; the eleventh, a jacinth; the twelfth, an amethyst [Rev. 21: 19–20].

The twelve foundations of the city not only have the names of the twelve apostles, but they are twelve different precious stones. The most beautiful and costly articles known to man are precious stones. These stones express in human terms the magnificence of the city. The superlative degree of gems is used to convey something of the glory of the city to those who now ". . . see through a glass, darkly . . ." (1 Cor. 12:11). We are going to see through it clearly someday.

A close examination of these twelve stones in the foundation reveals a polychromed paragon of beauty; varied hues and tints form a galaxy of rainbow colors. The stones are enumerated as follows:

1. Jasper (Gr: *iaspis*)—its color is clear. As mentioned before, this is probably the diamond. It is crystal clear, a reflector of light and color. Dr. Seiss, in speaking of the New Jerusalem, describes it "as clean, and pure, and bright as a transparent icicle in the sunshine."

2. Sapphire (Gr.: *sappheiros*)—its color is blue. This stone occurs in Exodus 24:10 as the foundation of God, ". . . and there was under his feet as it were a paved work of a sapphire stone, and as it were the body of heaven in his clearness." Moffatt describes it as a blue stone. Pliny describes it as opaque with gold specks, to which Petrie agrees.

3. Chalcedony (Gr.: *chalkedon*)—its color is greenish. It is an agate. Pliny describes it as "a variety of emerald gathered on a mountain in Chalcedon." Robertson says, "Possibly a green silicate of copper."

4. Emerald (Gr: *smaragdos*)—its color is

green. Robertson describes it as a green stone.

5. Sardonyx (Gr.: *sardonux*)—its color is red. Robertson describes it as white with layers of red.

6. Sardius (Gr.: *sardios*)—its color is fiery red. Pliny says that it is the red stone from Sardis. Swete says that it is fiery red.

7. Chrysolyte (Gr.: *chrusolithos*)—its color is golden yellow. Moffatt assigns it a golden hue. Robertson says it is a golden color like our topaz.

8. Beryl (Gr.: *berullos*)—its color is green. It is like the emerald, says Robertson. Pliny says it is sea green.

9. Topaz (Gr.: *topazion*)—its color is greenish yellow. Robertson calls it a golden greenish stone.

10. Chrysoprasus (Gr.: *chrusoprasos*)—its color is gold-green. A golden leek, "a leek colored gem," says Robertson. The International Standard Bible Encyclopedia describes it as sea green.

11. Jacinth (Gr.: *huakinthi*)—its color is violet. It is the color of the hyacinth. Pliny gives the color as violet.

12. Amethyst (Gr.: *amethustos*)—its color is purple. Although the *International Standard Bible Encyclopedia* lists it as a ruby, Robertson gives the color as purple.

The foundations of the New Jerusalem are constructed of the flashing brilliance of rich and costly gems. On the inside is Jesus who, when He was here, was the Light of the World. There He will be the Light of the Universe. Astronauts tell us that in space the colors almost entirely are gray and black—but wait until you see the New Jerusalem. It is going to light up God's new heavens and new earth as they have never been lighted before. I think it is going to be the most breathtaking sight that you have ever seen. This New Jerusalem is a planet which comes down right out of heaven. Everything is going to revolve around it, and the light will come from there. It truly will be the Jesus Christ Light and Power Company then. The light will shine out in all these brilliant and beautiful colors.

Color is described to us today as dissected light. If you pass a ray of light through a prism, it is broken up into three primary colors: red, blue, and yellow. From these three primary colors come all colors and shades of colors. Light is a requirement for color. Where there is no light, there is no color. Objects of color reveal color to the eye because of their ability to absorb or to reject light rays. A red stone absorbs all the color rays except red; it rejects or throws back to the eye the red ray, which gives it the color of red.

The New Jerusalem is a city of light and a city of color. God is light, and He is there. The city is described as a jasper stone as clear as crystal. All of this color will be coming out and flooding God's universe. The jasper stone is a sphere, and the city, the New Jerusalem, is within. The light shining from within through the jasper stone, acting as a prism, would give every color and shade of color in the rainbow—colors that you and I have not even thought of yet. The New Jerusalem is, I believe, a new planet, and it is inside a crystal ball. The presence of the primary colors suggests that every shade and tint is reflected from this city. A rainbow that appears after a summer shower gives only a faint impression of the beauty in the coloring of the city of light. Oh, what a glorious place this is!

THE CITY AND STREET OF GOLD

And the twelve gates were twelve pearls: every several gate was of one pearl: and the street of the city was pure gold, as it were transparent glass [Rev. 21:21].

Notice that verse 18 also says, "and the city was pure gold, like unto clear glass." We were told at the beginning of this description that this city is transparent. This is the thing that gave me the lead and the key to believe that we will live on the inside and that everything is transparent. This would mean that the light shines from the inside out and goes through these many different-colored stones. Many colors which our natural eyes cannot see today we will be able to see with the new body that we shall have at that time.

We are also told here that the street is pure gold. Personally, I do not care about the asphalt of the place, but there are two things here that impress me. (1) It is not streets (plural) but street (singular)—this is not a city with many streets. (2) And it is "transparent"—even the street is transparent; it is gold, but transparent gold.

This leads me again to insist that what we are looking at is the inside of a globe. You could not have cities like we have today without having streets. You would certainly have a traffic jam with just one street. The New Jerusalem has just one street, which would begin at the four gates; it would start around the circle of the globe, go all the way to the top, and then circle and come back down. One would be the entrance and the other the exit. There is just one street, and my viewpoint lends itself to the idea that there is one street.

The fact that it is transparent gold means that the light can shine out. There will be nothing to hinder the light, not even the street.

NEW RELATIONSHIP—GOD DWELLING WITH MAN

And I saw no temple therein: for the Lord God Almighty and the Lamb are the temple of it.

And the city had no need of the sun, neither of the moon, to shine in it: for the glory of God did lighten it, and the Lamb is the light thereof [Rev. 21:22–23].

God lights the new creation directly by His presence. After the entrance of sin into the old creation, God withdrew His presence, and "darkness covered the face of the deep" (see Gen 1:2). Then God made use of the physical lights in His universe. He put them up like we put up street lights or lights in our homes. However, in the new creation sin is removed, and He again becomes the source of light. Today the Lord Jesus Christ is the Light of the World in a spiritual sense: "Then spake Jesus again unto them, saying, I am the light of the world: he that followeth me shall not walk in darkness, but shall have the light of life" (John 8:12).

In the new creation He is the direct physical as well as the spiritual light. In the tabernacle there was the golden lampstand, which is one of the finest pictures of Christ. In the New Jerusalem He *is* the golden lampstand. The nations of the world will enter the Holy City as the priests entered the Holy Place in the tabernacle for the purpose of worship. The nations of the earth, as well as Israel, will come to the New Jerusalem as the high priest of old entered the Holy of Holies. Instead of the blood being brought, the Lamb is there in person. What a picture we have here!

The temple, which supplanted the tabernacle back in the nation Israel, was an earthly enclosure for the *shekinah* glory. It was a testimony to the presence of God and the presence of sin. Where sin existed, God could be approached only by the ritual of the temple. However, in the New Jerusalem sin is no longer a reality but is like a hideous nightmare, even locked out of the closet of memory. The actual presence of God with the redeemed eliminates the necessity for a temple, although the whole city may be thought of as a temple. Some have called attention to the fact that the New Jerusalem is the same shape as the Holy of Holies in the tabernacle and temple where God dwelt: a perfect cube. That is no accident, by the way. In the city of light God is present, and sin is absent; therefore, an edifice of a material substance is no longer necessary. The physical temple was a poor substitute for the presence of God. The New Jerusalem possesses the genuine article—God in person. It is probably the first place where God will make a personal appearance before man. What a glorious prospect this is!

The New Jerusalem will be independent of the sun and moon for light and life. What a contrast to the earth, which is utterly dependent upon the sun and the moon. It may be that the sun and moon will even be dependent upon the celestial city for power to transmit light, since the One who is the source of light and life will dwell within the city. Neither will light be furnished by the New Jerusalem Light and Power Company. The One who is light will be there, and the effulgence of His glory will be manifested in the New Jerusalem unhindered.

NEW CENTER OF THE NEW CREATION

And the nations of them which are saved shall walk in the light of it: and the kings of the earth do bring their glory and honour into it [Rev. 21:24].

And the nations shall walk amidst the light thereof: and the kings of the earth bring their glory into it.

"And the nations shall walk amidst the light thereof." It does not say they will live there, but that they will walk in the light of it. In other words, the New Jerusalem (instead of the sun and the moon) will give light unto the earth.

"And the kings of the earth bring their glory into it." This is my reason for saying that there will be a great deal of traffic commuting back and forth between the New Jerusalem and this earth down here. Not only will Israel come up there to worship, but the nations of the world which have entered eternity will also come up. It will not be their permanent abode, but they will come up there to worship. I believe that the church will be the priests at that time. We are told that we are a priesthood of believers.

And the gates of it shall not be shut at all by day: for there shall be no night there [Rev. 21:25].

And the gates thereof shall in no wise be shut by day (for there shall be no night there).

It is nonsense to say that the gates will not be shut at night because there is no night. Therefore, he says that they will not be shut by day. In other words, they are going to throw away the key because there will be no danger. In John's day, a walled city had gates for the purpose of protection. When the gate of a city was closed, it meant that an enemy was on the outside and that they were trying to keep him there.

And they shall bring the glory and honour of the nations into it.

And there shall in no wise enter into it any thing that defileth, neither whatsoever worketh abomination, or maketh a lie: but they which are written in the Lamb's book of life [Rev. 21:26–27].

And they shall bring the glory and the honor of the nations into it: and there shall in no wise enter into it anything unclean, or he that maketh an abomination and a lie: but only they that are written in the Lamb's book of life.

God has apparently accomplished His original purpose with man—fellowship. He now has a creature who is a free moral agent and who chooses to worship and serve Him eternally.

There can be no night, since the Lamb is the light, and He is eternally present.

The gates are not for protection, and they are never closed. Rather, they are the badge or coat of arms of the bride. Notice that these gates are of pearl. The pearl of great price has been purchased at a great price. In the parable (see Matt. 13:45–46) that the Lord Jesus gave, the pearl is not Christ whom the sinner buys. What is a sinner to pay for Christ?—he hasn't anything that he can pay. It is the other way around. The merchant man who bought that pearl was the Lord Jesus Christ, and the pearl is the bride. It is interesting that a pearl is formed by a grain of sand that gets into the body of a little oyster or mollusk of some kind, and that little marine creature begins to put around that grain a secretion that before long makes the pearl. The pearl of great price is *margarites* in the Greek, and if the church has a name, it is Margaret. The Lord Jesus Christ paid a great price to buy this pearl. This pearl was formed from His side. Someone has said, "I got into the heart of Christ through a spear wound." He was wounded for our transgressions; He was bruised for our iniquities. The church will be for the display of His grace throughout eternity to the absolute myriads of God's created intelligences. "That in the ages to come he might shew the exceeding riches of his grace in his kindness toward us through Christ Jesus" (Eph. 2:7).

In other words, in eternity you and I will be there on display. They will look at Vernon McGee and say: "Do you see that fellow? He deserved hell, and the Lord Jesus Christ died for him and paid a tremendous price. He trusted Christ; that is all he had to offer. Now look what the Lord Jesus has done for him. He has made him fit for heaven and made him acceptable in the beloved."

The church will be the fairest jewel of all when He makes up His jewels (see Mal. 3:17–18). When He makes up His jewels, the church is going to be on display. This is the reason that the New Jerusalem will be the center of the new heavens and the new earth.

The Lamb's Book of Life contains the names of the redeemed of all ages. No one who was not redeemed by the blood of Christ will ever be permitted to enter the portals of the New Jerusalem. There is a great gulf fixed between the saved and the lost.

The greatest joy that will capture the heart of the redeemed will be that of abiding in the presence of Christ for eternity. "That where I am, there ye may be also" is what He said in John 14:3. This is heaven, my friend, to be with Him. Revelation is all about Jesus Christ—He is the centerpiece of God's universe.

Our attention has already been directed to the fact that a redeemed remnant of Israel makes regular visits to the city of God. In verse 24 another group is identified who come into the city to bring their glory and honor. These are the redeemed gentile nations which will occupy the earth together with Israel for eternity. These nations, like Israel, do not belong to the church, for they are redeemed after the church is removed from the earth (or before the church came into existence). They come as visitors to the city. They come as worshipers. In Hebrews 12:22 we are told there is also present an innumerable company of angels who evidently constitute the servant class. The city is cosmopolitan in character. All nationalities meet there, and the created intelligences of God walk the street of the New Jerusalem.

Among the multitudes, there is not one who will bring defilement or sin. How superior is this city to even the Garden of Eden where the lie of Satan made an entrance for sin. No lie or liar will ever enter the portals of the heavenly Jerusalem. All dwellers and all tourists are not only redeemed from sin but have also lost their taste for sin. They come through the gates which are never closed. The enjoyment of this glorious city is not restricted to the church, although they are the only ones who dwell there.

Jerusalem, the golden, with milk and
    honey blest!
  Beneath thy contemplation sink heart
    and voice oppressed;

I know not, O I know not what joys await
    me there;
  What radiancy of glory, what bliss be-
    yond compare.
                  "Jerusalem the Golden"
                  —Bernard of Cluny

What a picture and how inadequately I have dealt with it. Oh, if only you and I both could be lifted up so that we might get a glimpse of the glory of that city and of the glory of the One who is its chief adornment, even the Lord Jesus Christ, and of the glorious prospect and privilege of being with Him throughout eternity. There is nothing to compare to it!

CHAPTER 22

THEME: *River of the Water of Life, the Tree of Life; the promise of Christ's return; the final invitation*

This chapter brings us to the final scenes of this great book of scenic wonders. It likewise brings us to the end of the Word of God. God gives us His final words here, and because they are last words, they have a greater significance. We are brought to the end of man's journey. The path has been rugged. Many questions remain unanswered, many problems remain unsolved, but man enters into eternity in fellowship again with God, and there all will be answered.

The Bible opens with God on the scene: "In the beginning God created the heaven and the earth" (Gen. 1:1). It concludes with Him on the scene and in full control of His own. He suffered, He paid a price, and He died—but the victory and the glory are His, and He is satisfied. Isaiah 53:11 puts it like this: "He shall see of the travail of his soul, and shall be satisfied: by his knowledge shall my righteous servant justify many; for he shall bear their iniquities."

RIVER OF THE WATER OF LIFE AND THE TREE OF LIFE

Chapter 22 opens with a beautiful description of the New Jerusalem.

And he shewed me a pure river of water of life, clear as crystal, proceeding out of the throne of God and of the Lamb.

In the midst of the street of it, and on either side of the river, was there the tree of life, which bare twelve manner of fruits, and yielded her fruit every month: and the leaves of the tree were for the healing of the nations [Rev. 22:1–2].

As usual I'll give my own literal translation of the Greek text throughout this chapter.

And he showed me a river of water of life, bright as crystal, proceeding out of the throne of God and of the Lamb. In the midst of the street thereof. And on this side of the river and on that was the tree of life, bearing twelve fruits, yielding its fruit every month: and the leaves of the tree were for the healing of the nations.

Up to this chapter, the New Jerusalem seems to be all mineral and no vegetable. Its appearance is as the dazzling display of a fabulous jewelry store; we wonder if there is no soft grass to sit upon, no green trees to enjoy, and no water to drink or food to eat. However, here are introduced the elements which add a rich softness to this city of elaborate beauty.

There was a river in the first Eden which branched into four rivers. Although there was abundance of water, it is not called the water of life. Eden was a garden of trees among which was the Tree of Life. God kept the way open for man by the shedding of blood (see Gen. 3:24). In the New Jerusalem there is a river of the Water of Life, and the throne of God is its living fountain supplying an abundance of water.

"The tree of life" is a fruit tree, bearing twelve kinds of fruits each month. There is a continuous supply in abundance and variety. In eternity man *will* eat and drink. That is a great relief to many of us, I am sure. The menu is varied but is restricted to fruits, as it was in the Garden of Eden: "And God said, Behold, I have given you every herb bearing seed, which is upon the face of all the earth, and every tree, in the which is the fruit of a tree yielding seed; to you it shall be for meat. And to every beast of the earth, and to every fowl of the air, and to every thing that creepeth upon the earth, wherein there is life, I have given every green herb for meat: and it was so" (Gen. 1:29–30).

There is a tendency to spiritualize this passage in Revelation and compare it to the fruit of the Spirit. I have no objection to that and would rather take that viewpoint myself, provided we hold to the literal interpretation, which I think you can do through this section. Although it does seem highly symbolic, I think we are dealing with that which is quite literal, for we are still talking about heaven.

Even the leaves of the tree are beneficial— they have a medicinal value. Why healing is needed in a perfect universe is a very good question and a difficult problem to solve. Perhaps it is a sort of first-aid kit which demonstrates the old adage, "An ounce of prevention is worth a pound of cure." I personally believe that the bodies of the earth dwellers in eternity will be different from the bodies of the believers in the church who are to be like Christ (that is, their bodies will be like His). The bodies of the earth dwellers may need renewing from time to time. This may be the reason that they come up to the New Jerusalem—not only to worship, but also to be renewed physically and spiritually. At least the prevention is there.

However, the possibility of sin entering simply is not there.

And there shall be no more curse: but the throne of God and of the Lamb shall be in it; and his servants shall serve him:

And they shall see his face; and his name shall be in their foreheads.

And there shall be no night there; and they need no candle, neither light of the sun; for the Lord God giveth them light: and they shall reign for ever and ever [Rev. 22:3–5].

And there shall be no curse anymore: and the throne of God and of the Lamb shall be therein: and His servants shall do Him service: and they shall see His face; and His name shall be on their foreheads. And there shall be night no more; and they need no light of lamp, neither light of sun; for the Lord God shall give them light: and they shall reign for ever and ever.

The first creation was blighted by the curse of sin, and this old earth on which you and I live today bears many scar marks of the curse of sin. The new creation will never be marred by sin. Sin will never be permitted to enter even potentially. It was potentially in the Garden of Eden in the tree of the knowledge of good and evil. The very presence of God and the Lamb will be adequate to prevent it. It was during the absence of God in the Garden of Eden that the tempter came to our first parents.

The throne of God and the Lamb are in the New Jerusalem. It is general headquarters for God the Father and God the Son. The notable absence of any reference to the Holy Spirit does need some explanation. You see, in the first creation the Holy Spirit came to renovate and renew the blighted earth: "The Spirit of God brooded over the face of the waters" (see Gen. 1:2). He is the instrument today of regeneration in the hearts and lives of sinners. There will be no need of His work in the new creation in this connection; therefore the silence of God at this point is eloquent.

"His servants shall do Him service" reveals that heaven is not a place of unoccupied idleness but a place of ceaseless activity. It will not be necessary to rest in order to give the body an opportunity to recuperate. The word for "service" is a peculiar one. In his *Word Studies in the New Testament* Dr. Vincent says, "It came to be used by the Jews in a very special sense, to denote the service rendered to Jehovah by the Israelites as His peculiar people." We read this in the Epistle to the Hebrews: "Then verily the first covenant had also ordinances of divine service, and a worldly sanctuary. . . . Now when these things were thus ordained, the priests went always into the first tabernacle, accomplishing the service of God" (Heb. 9:1, 6). It will be a peculiar service to God that you and I will perform in eternity. What it is, I do not know. He may give us charge of universes. There will be ceaseless activity since there is no night. Man will at last fulfill his destiny and satisfy the desires of his heart.

Man will at last see His face. This was the supreme desire voiced by Moses in the Old Testament and Philip in the New Testament. It is the highest objective for living. What divine satisfaction!

"His name shall be in their foreheads." Each person will bear the name of Christ. Each will be like Him, yet without disturbing his own peculiar personality. I have always said this facetiously, but it could be true: If He will, I want God to let me teach the Bible in heaven. I want to attend the classes which Paul teaches, and then I would like to teach those people who were members of the churches I served on the earth but who would not attend the midweek Bible studies. I have asked to teach them for one million years and, I tell you, they won't think it is heaven for that first million years! I am really going to work them and make them catch up. Whether that will be true or not, I don't know, but I do say that we are all going to be busy there.

Our attention in this section is called to the direct lighting of the new creation. There will be no light holders such as the sun or light reflectors such as the moon. God lights the universe by His presence, for God is light.

It is in eternity that the bride will reign with Christ. Who knows but what He will give to each saint a world or a solar system or a galactic system to operate. Remember that Adam was given dominion over the old creation on this earth.

PROMISE OF THE RETURN OF CHRIST

And he said unto me, These sayings are faithful and true: and the Lord God of the holy prophets sent his angel to shew unto his servants the things which must shortly be done.

Behold, I come quickly: blessed is he that keepeth the sayings of the prophecy of this book [Rev. 22:6–7].

And he said unto me, These words are faithful and true: and the Lord, the God of the spirits of the prophets, sent His angel to show unto His servants the things which must shortly come to pass. And behold, I come quickly. Blessed is he that keepeth the words of the prophecy of this book.

The important thing to note is that when He says, "And behold, I come quickly," He means *rapidly*. This is repeated again in verse 12 and verse 20. It is repeated three times

here at the end: "Behold, I come quickly"—not *shortly* or *immediately* or even *soon*. These events that we have been looking at in Revelation, beginning with chapter 4, take place in a period of not more than seven years, and most of them are confined to the last three and one-half years. The encouragement here is that the Lord Jesus says that it will not be a long period: "I am coming shortly. I will soon be there." But that means *when* we get to this period. We are not exactly accurate when we speak of "the soon coming of Christ." I have said that many times myself, but I do not think it is an accurate term, and it gives the wrong impression.

The Lord Jesus puts His own seal upon this book: "These words are faithful and true" means that no man is to trifle with them by spiritualizing them or reducing them to meaningless symbols. Our Lord is talking about reality. At the beginning of this book, there was a blessing pronounced upon those who read and hear and keep these words. In conclusion, the Lord Jesus repeats the blessing upon those who keep these words. This is a book not to merely satisfy the curiosity of the natural man but to live and act upon.

And I John saw these things, and heard them. And when I had heard and seen, I fell down to worship before the feet of the angel which shewed me these things.

Then saith he unto me, See thou do it not: for I am thy fellow-servant, and of thy brethren the prophets, and of them which keep the sayings of this book: worship God.

And he saith unto me, Seal not the sayings of the prophecy of this book: for the time is at hand.

He that is unjust, let him be unjust still: and he which is filthy, let him be filthy still: and he that is righteous, let him be righteous still: and he that is holy, let him be holy still [Rev. 22:8–11].

And I John am he that heard and saw these things. And when I heard and saw, I fell down to worship before the feet of the angel that showed me these things. And he saith unto me, See (thou do it) not: I am a fellow servant with thee and with thy brethren the prophets, and with them that keep the words of this book: worship God. And he saith unto me, Seal not up the words of the prophecy of this book; for the time is at hand. He that is unrigh-

teous, let him do unrighteousness still;
and he that is filthy, let him be made
filthy still: and he that is righteous, let
him do righteousness still: and he that is
holy let him be made holy still.

Notice John's final and oft-repeated statement that he was both auditor and spectator to the scenes in this book. This is the method that was put down at the very opening of the book. It is the first television program, for John both saw and heard.

John was so impressed that his natural reaction was to fall down and worship the angel. The simplicity and meekness of the angel are impressive. Though the angels were created above man, this angel identifies himself as a fellow servant with John and the other prophets. He was merely a messenger to communicate God's Word to man, and he directs all worship to God. Christ is the centerpiece of the Book of Revelation—don't lose sight of Him.

"Seal not up the words of the prophecy of this book." Daniel was told to seal up the words of his prophecy because of the long interval before the fulfillment of it (see Dan. 12:4). In fact, we in the twentieth century have not come to the Seventieth Week of Daniel yet. In contrast, the prophecy given to John was even then in process of being fulfilled. For nineteen hundred years, the church has been passing through the time periods of the seven churches given in chapters 2–3.

"He that is unrighteous . . . he that is filthy"—probably the most frightful condition of the lost is revealed here, even more so than at the Great White Throne judgment of chapter 20. The sinful condition of the lost is a permanent and eternal thing, although it is not static, for the suggestion is that the unrighteous will increasingly become more unrighteous: "he that is filthy, let him be made filthy still." The condition of the lost gets worse until each becomes a monster of sin. This thought is frightful!

On the other hand, neither is the condition of the servant of God static. They will continue to grow in righteousness and holiness. Heaven is not static. Even in the Millennium "of the increase of His kingdom there shall be no end." What a glorious and engaging prospect this should be for the child of God! We shall have all eternity to grow in knowledge.

And, behold, I come quickly; and my reward is with me, to give every man according as his work shall be.

I am Alpha and Omega, the beginning and the end, the first and the last.

Blessed are they that do his commandments, that they may have right to the tree of life, and may enter in through the gates into the city.

For without are dogs, and sorcerers, and whoremongers, and murderers, and idolaters, and whosoever loveth and maketh a lie.

I Jesus have sent mine angel to testify unto you these things in the churches. I am the root and the offspring of David, and the bright and morning star [Rev. 22:12–16].

Behold, I come quickly; and my reward is with me, to render to each man according as his work is. I am the Alpha and the Omega, the first and the last, the beginning and the end. Blessed are they that wash their robes, in order that theirs shall be authority over the tree of life, and may enter by the gates into the city. Without are the dogs, and the sorcerers, and the fornicators, and the murderers, and the idolaters, and every one that loveth and maketh a lie. I Jesus have sent mine angel to testify unto you these things for the churches. I am the root and the offspring of David, the bright, the morning star.

The church should know this program of God. Either the angel is bearing a very personal word from Jesus, or else the Lord is breaking through and saying it personally. Our Lord promises that He is coming again. That is His personal declaration. No believer can doubt or deny this all-important and personal promise of the Lord Jesus.

He will personally reward each believer individually—those in the church at the Rapture as well as those of Israel and the Gentiles at His return to set up His kingdom at the Millennium.

It is little wonder that Paul could write: "That I may know him, and the power of his resurrection, and the fellowship of his sufferings, being made conformable unto his death; If by any means I might attain unto the resurrection of the dead. Not as though I had already attained, either were already perfect: but I follow after, if that I may apprehend that for which also I am apprehended of Christ Jesus. Brethren, I count not myself to have apprehended: but this one thing I do, forgetting those things which are behind, and reaching forth unto those things which are before, I press toward the mark for the prize of the high calling of God in Christ Jesus" (Phil. 3:10–14).

Again the Lord Jesus asserts His deity: "I am the Alpha and the Omega, the first and the last, the beginning and the end." He said this at the beginning of Revelation, and He concludes with it.

Only blood-washed believers have authority over the Tree of Life and access to the Holy City (see Eph. 1:7–12).

"Dogs" come off rather badly in Scripture. This perhaps does not mean that there will be no dogs in heaven, but because dogs were scavengers in the ancient world they were considered unclean and impure. Also, "dogs" was the designation for Gentiles (see Matt. 15:21–28) and Paul's label for Judaizers (see Phil. 3:2).

Apparently the Lord Jesus had sent His angel with this very personal message. "I Jesus"—He takes the name of His saviorhood, the name He received when He took upon Himself humanity, and the name that no man knows but He Himself. You and I are going to spend eternity just centering on Him and His person. My friend, if you are not interested in Jesus today, I do not know why you would want to go to heaven. That is all we are going to talk about up there; we are going to talk about Him.

He is called "the root and the offspring of David," which connects Him with the Old Testament. But He is "the bright and morning star" to the church. Have you noticed that the bright and morning star always appears at the darkest time of the night? Its appearance indicates that the sun will be coming up shortly. The Old Testament ended with the promise that "the Sun of righteousness will arise with healing in his wings"—that is the Old Testament hope (see Mal. 4:2). But to us, He is the Bright and Morning Star who will come at a very dark moment.

FINAL INVITATION AND WARNING

And the Spirit and the bride say, Come. And let him that heareth say, Come. And let him that is athirst come. And whosoever will, let him take the water of life freely.

For I testify unto every man that heareth the words of the prophecy of this book, If any man shall add unto these things, God shall add unto him

the plagues that are written in this book:

And if any man shall take away from the words of the book of this prophecy, God shall take away his part out of the book of life, and out of the holy city, and from the things which are written in this book [Rev. 22:17–19].

And the Spirit and the bride say, Come. And he that heareth, let him say, Come. And he that is athirst, let him come: he that will, let him take the water of life freely. I testify unto every man that heareth the words of the prophecy of this book, If any man shall add unto them, God shall add the plagues which are written in this book: and if any man shall take away from the words of the book of this prophecy, God shall take away his part from the tree of life, and out of the holy city, which are written in this book.

The bride is the church. This is a twofold invitation—an invitation to Christ to come and an invitation to sinners to come to Christ before He returns. The Holy Spirit is in the world today, and He joins in the prayer of the church which says, "Lord Jesus, come, come."

The Holy Spirit is performing His work in the world today in converting and convicting men. He works through the Word and through the church which proclaims His Word. The invitation to men is to come and to take the Water of Life: "Ho, every one that thirsteth, come ye to the waters . . . without money and without price" (Isa. 55:1). The Lord Jesus stood and said, ". . . If any man thirst, let him come unto me, and drink" (John 7:37). That is the invitation that goes out today. If you are tired of drinking at the cesspools of this world, He invites you to come. What an invitation this is to come to Him!

FINAL PROMISE AND PRAYER

He which testifieth these things saith, Surely I come quickly. Amen. Even so, come, Lord Jesus.

The grace of our Lord Jesus Christ be with you all. Amen [Rev. 22:20–21].

He who testifieth these things saith, Yea: I come quickly. Amen: Come, Lord Jesus. The grace of the Lord Jesus be with all the saints. Amen.

"Yea: I come quickly"—not *soon*, but when these things begin to come to pass, He is even then at the door.

"Come, Lord Jesus" is the heart cry of every true believer.

"The grace of our Lord Jesus Christ be with you all. Amen." The Old Testament ends with a curse; the New Testament ends with a benediction of grace upon the believers. Grace is offered to all, but if any man (regardless of his merit) refuses the offer which is extended, he must bear the judgment pronounced in this book.

Grace is still offered to man. It is God's method of saving sinners.

> Amazing grace! how sweet the sound,
> That saved a wretch like me!
> I once was lost, but now am found,
> Was blind, but now I see.
>
> —John Newton

BIBLIOGRAPHY

(Recommended for Further Study)

Barnhouse, Donald Grey. *Revelation, an Expository Commentary*. Grand Rapids, Michigan: Zondervan Publishing House, 1971.

Criswell, W. A. *Expository Sermons on Revelation*. Grand Rapids, Michigan: Zondervan Publishing House, 1966.

Epp, Theodore H. *Practical Studies in Revelation*. Lincoln, Nebraska: Back to the Bible Broadcast, 1969.

Gaebelein, Arno C. *The Revelation*. Neptune, New Jersey: Loizeaux Brothers, 1915.

Hoyt, Herman A. *The Revelation of the Lord Jesus Christ*. Winona Lake, Indiana: Brethren Missionary Herald, 1966.

Ironside, H. A. *Lectures on the Book of Revelation*. Neptune, New Jersey: Loizeaux Brothers, 1960. (Especially good for young converts.)

Larkin, Clarence. *The Book of Revelation*. Philadelphia, Pennsylvania: Published by the Author, 1919. (Includes fine charts.)

Lindsey, Hal. *There's a New World Coming*. Santa Ana, California: Vision House Publishers, 1973.

McGee, J. Vernon. *Reveling Through Revelation*. 2 vols. Pasadena, California: Thru the Bible Books, 1962.

Newell, William R. *The Book of Revelation*. Chicago, Illinois: Moody Press, 1935.

Phillips, John. *Exploring Revelation*. Chicago, Illinois: Moody Press, 1974.

Ryrie, Charles C. *Revelation*. Chicago, Illinois: Moody Press, 1968. (A fine, inexpensive survey.)

Scott, Walter. *Exposition of the Revelation of Jesus Christ*. London: Pickering and Inglis, n.d.

Seiss, J. A. *The Apocalypse, Lectures on the Book of Revelation*. Grand Rapids, Michigan: Zondervan Publishing House, 1957.

Smith, J. B. *A Revelation of Jesus Christ*. Scottsdale, Pennsylvania: Herald Press, 1961.

Strauss, Lehman. *The Book of Revelation*. Neptune, New Jersey: Loizeaux Brothers, 1964.

Walvoord, John F. *The Revelation of Jesus Christ*. Chicago, Illinois: Moody Press, 1966. (Excellent comprehensive treatment.)